The Complete Guide to Human Resources and the Law

2015 Edition

by Dana Shilling

The Complete Guide to Human Resources and the Law is an invaluable tool for the HR professional who needs to place legal principles and developments in the context of the practical problems he or she faces every day. The law as it relates to human resources issues is an ever-growing, ever-changing body of information that involves not just court cases but also statutes and the regulations of administrative agencies. *The Complete Guide to Human Resources and the Law* brings you the most up-to-date information as well as practical tips and checklists in a well-organized, easy-to-use resource.

Highlights of the 2015 Edition

The 2015 Edition provides new and expanded coverage of issues such as:

- Despite serious difficulties with online enrollment, the first cycle of health insurance enrollment under PPACA was completed. See § 18.19[H] for delays in enforcement of the employer mandate, a/k/a the "shared responsibility payment" or "pay or play" requirement. See § 18.19[M] for a guide to the revised schedule for implementation, reflecting the postponements. See § 24.01[D] for record-keeping requirements. Many suits challenge the PPACA requirement that group plans cover contraception, an issue with implications about whether corporations can exercise religious freedom—part of the ongoing national debate about corporate rights. [§ 18.03[D]]
- An IRS final rule was published in February 2014, dealing with the responsibilities of mid-sized employers (50–100 full-time employees in 2014) under the Code § 4980H shared responsibility requirement. These employers will not be subject to penalties until 2016 for failure to provide minimum required levels of coverage—unless they cut their workforce or reduce employees' hours to avoid coverage, or unless they eliminate or materially reduce the health coverage already available to employees. T.D. 9655, *Shared Responsibility for Employers Regarding Health Coverage*, 79 Fed. Reg. 8544 (Feb. 12, 2014). [§ 18.19[H]]

Wolters Kluwer

- The Supreme Court reversed the Sixth Circuit and held that the severance payments constituted FICA wages. The court held that "service" is defined broadly as the entire relationship between employer and employee, so severance payments are made to employees because of service to employers. The list of exemptions says that Supplemental Unemployment Benefit (SUB) payments are treated as if they were wages; the Supreme Court said that this provision was added to relieve terminated workers from the burden of year-end tax liability when they receive SUB payments: *United States v. Quality Stores Inc.*, 134 S. Ct. 1395 (2014). [§§ 1.01, 2.03[A], 3.03[C], 32.01]
- The SEC voted 3–2 in September 2013 to propose a new rule under Dodd-Frank § 953(b), requiring public companies to disclose the ratio of CEO compensation to the median compensation of all the company's employees. The new requirement does not apply to emerging growth companies covered by the JOBS Act, smaller reporting companies, or foreign private issuers SEC press release 2013-186, *SEC Proposes Rules for Pay Ratio Disclosure*, <http://www.sec.gov/News/PressRelease/Detail/PressRelease/1370539817895> (Sept. 18, 2013). [§ 1.01[A]]
- In September 2013, the Department of Labor adopted a final rule that extended minimum wage and overtime protection to close to two million home health care and personal care workers, although the rule does not take effect until January 1, 2015. The rule change applies to workers such as home health aides, personal care aides, and certified nursing assistants who work for home health agencies, but home care workers who are employed directly by the patient or patient's family are not covered: WHD News Release No. 13-1922-NAT, *Minimum Wage, Overtime Protections Extended To Direct Care Workers By US Labor Department*, <http://www.dol.gov/opa/media/press/whd/WHD20131922.htm> (Sept. 17, 2013). [§ 1.07]
- On March 13, 2014, President Obama signed a memorandum critiquing the current FLSA regulations, which provide that administrative workers are exempt from overtime if they earn over $455 a week. The president ordered the DOL to issue new regulations with a higher minimum, so that low-paid workers such as "managers" of fast food restaurants and convenience stores, would be eligible for overtime unless their earnings more accurately reflected current wage norms: *Presidential Memorandum-Updating and Modernizing Overtime Regulations*, <http://www.whitehouse.gov/the-press-office/2014/03/13/presidential-memorandum-updating-and-modernizing-overtime-regulations> (Mar. 13, 2014). [§ 1.15[B]]
- President Obama announced that he would apply his executive powers unilaterally to require federal contractors to pay a minimum wage of $10.10 on all new federal contracts: *Executive Order—Minimum Wage for*

Contractors, <http://www.whitehouse.gov/the-press-office/2014/02/12/executive-order-minimum-wage-contractors> (Feb. 12, 2014). [§ 1.07]

- The Supreme Court held in early 2014 that, in a unionized operation, the CBA controls whether employees will be paid for donning/doffing time. The Supreme Court characterized putting on and taking off required safety gear as "changing clothes," which is not compensable, because of FLSA § 203(o): *Sandifer v. U.S. Steel*, 134 S. Ct. 870 (2014). [§ 1.15[F]]
- Several additional states granted recognition of same-sex marriage (SSM), although it is difficult to list them because the various statutes and court cases (many of them holding that a state's refusal to issue licenses for SSM violates Equal Protection) are under appeal at various levels. [§ 18.06[A]]
- As a result of the Supreme Court's 2013 decision in *United States v. Windsor*, 133 S. Ct. 2675, the IRS has adopted the position that a same-sex couple are considered married for federal tax purposes if their marriage was legal at the place it was celebrated, whether or not same-sex marriage is legal in the state where they reside or the state where they work: IR-2013-72. [§§ 2.01[B], 18.06[B]]
- Changes were made to the PBGC premium under the Bipartisan Budget Act of 2013 (Pub. L. No. 113-67). The 2014 flat-rate premium is $49/participant for single-employer plans and $12/employee for multi-employer plans. The 2014 variable premium for single-employer plans is $14/$1,000 in unfunded vested benefits, subject to a cap of $412/participant. Starting in 2015, PBGC premiums will be due at the same time, irrespective of the size of the plan. The previous rules set the due date depending on the number of participants in the plan: 79 Fed. Reg. 13547 (Mar. 11, 2014). [§§ 4.01[A], 5.08[B]]
- President Obama signed a presidential memorandum directing the Department of the Treasury to set up a new retirement savings program, the myRA account for people who do not have access to employment-based retirement savings plans. [§§ 4.05, 6.04]
- The Supreme Court permitted enforcement of an ERISA plan's three-year contractual statute of limitations, even though it ended before the plaintiff could have filed suit about her disability claim. The suit was brought within three years of the final claim denial, but more than five years after her first assertion of the claim. The Supreme Court found that the three-year statute of limitations was reasonable and did not violate ERISA, but left the door open for equitable remedies such as tolling, waiver, and estoppels in rare cases where the claim process is so lengthy that the plaintiff cannot file a timely claim: *Heimeshoff v. Hartford Life*, 134 S. Ct. 604 (2013). [§§ 13.05[D], 15.18[D], 20.08, 25.01, 42.05[A]]
- The Supreme Court upheld enforcement of another kind of contract provision that can be used to work around legislative requirements, finding that

contractual forum selection clauses will be enforced except in the most egregious cases. This ruling is favorable for drafters of employment and noncompete agreements who want to avoid involvement of states that forbid noncompete agreements or place limits on their enforcement: *Atlantic Marine Construction Co., Inc. v. U.S. District Court for the Western District of Texas*, 134 S. Ct. 568 (2013). [§ 25.01]

- The 2013 final rules under the Rehab Act and the Vietnam Era Veterans' Readjustment Assistance Act of 1974 (VEVRAA) were issued by the Office of Federal Contract Compliance Programs (OFCCP) calling for affirmative action by federal contractors in hiring of persons with disabilities and veterans. There is no penalty for failure to meet the goals set out in the regulations, but federal contracts can be revoked if the contractor cannot demonstrate a legitimate effort to meet the target. [§§ 23.12, 24.03, 29.01[A], 34.05[D], 36.10]
- In 2014, the Supreme Court extended the definition of "whistleblower" under Sarbanes-Oxley to include employees of companies that are not publicly traded, but that are contractors for publicly traded companies. The whistleblower provisions of the Dodd-Frank Act are not restricted to public companies but could not be used in this case because it arose before Dodd-Frank's effective date: *Lawson v. FMR Inc.*, 134 S. Ct. 1158 (2014). [§§ 15.11[B], 39.04[B]]
- Joint EEOC and FTC guidance about background checks, published in March 2014, warns employers that whenever background information (from any source) is used to make employment decisions, compliance with anti-discrimination laws (including Title VII, GINA, the ADEA, and the FCRA) is mandatory. The EEOC said that seeking genetic information from applicants or employees is only permissible in rare circumstances. The FTC interprets the Fair Credit Reporting Act to require safeguards, such as notice to the applicant or employee, whenever an employer obtains a credit or criminal background report from a company that compiles background information: EEOC/FTC, *Background Checks: What Employers Need to Know*, <http://www.eeoc.gov/eeoc/publications/background_checks_employers.cfm> (March 2014). [§§ 23.08, 24.08, 26.04, 41.01[C]]
- *American Express Co. v. Italian Colors*, 133 S. Ct. 2304 (2013) is an antitrust rather than an employment case, but it has been immensely significant to employment-related arbitration cases because it holds that the FAA does not permit a court to invalidate a contract's waiver of class arbitration on the grounds that the cost of arbitrating small individual claims would outweigh the potential recovery that could be obtained. Employees are usually unsuccessful in seeking to have claims against employers arbitrated on a class rather than on an individual basis. [§ 40.07[C]]
- The Supreme Court reversed the California Court of Appeal, granting certiorari and remanding a putative class action charging violation of California labor

laws. After the case had been stayed for two years, the defendant moved under plaintiffs' employment agreement to compel individual arbitration as prescribed by the employment agreement. The Supreme Court held that the relevant state rule is preempted by Supreme Court precedent: *CarMax Auto Superstores California, LLC v. Fowler*, 134 S. Ct. 1277 (2014). [§ 40.07[D]]

- In June 2014, the Supreme Court ruled that it violates the RFRA to require closely held corporations to abide by contraception mandate, because corporations are "persons" as defined by the RFRA, and free exercise of religion is not restricted to non-profit organizations. The Supreme Court held that the RFRA was enacted to protect business owners from having to choose between their religious convictions and complying with the law: *Burwell v. Hobby Lobby*, No. 13-354/*Conestoga Wood Specialties v. Burwell*, 134 S. Ct. 2751 (2014). [§ 18.03[D]]
- The Supreme Court ruled that the NLRB lacked a quorum, because the appointments of several members were invalid. The appointments were characterized as recess appointments, but the Supreme Court held that they were made at a time when the Senate was not actually in recess, because it re-convened for pro forma sessions every three days. The NLRB announced that, after there was a full board of Senate-approved members, the NLRB ratified all of the decisions cast into doubt by the Supreme Court ruling: *NLRB v. Noel Canning*, 705 F.3d 490 (D.C. Cir. 2013), *aff'd*, 134 S. Ct. 2550 (2014). [§ 30.01[A]]
- The Court ruled that workers who provided home care to Medicaid recipients in Illinois were partial public employees who had the right to refuse to pay fair share fees (agency fees paid to unions by non-members). The Supreme Court held that the home care aides primarily worked for the elderly and disabled people who received the care, not for the clients, and requiring them to pay agency fees violated their First Amendment rights. However, the Supreme Court did not expand this holding to a more general rule that conventional public employees are exempt from paying agency fees: *Harris v. Quinn*. 134 S. Ct. 2618 (2014) [§ 30.06[A]]
- The Highway Transportation Funding Act of 2014, Pub. L. No. 113-159 extends the MAP-21 pension plan funding stabilization provisions, allowing employers to use "rate smoothing" to reduce the amount that they have to contribute to satisfy their minimum funding obligations. [§§ 4.01[B], 5.01[A], 5.05[I], 7.07[A], 11.03]
- In a mid-2014 Supreme Court case, the Court rejected the presumption of prudence that had generally been applied in "stock drop" cases. The Supreme Court held that ESOP fiduciaries have the same duties as other fiduciaries, although they are relieved of the obligation of diversifying the plan's portfolio. To assert a breach of the duty of prudence, a complaint must plausibly allege a lawful alternative course of conduct that would have yielded better results.

Fiduciaries never have an obligation to violate securities laws by using inside information: *Fifth Third Bancorp et al. v. Dudenhoeffer*, 134 S. Ct. 2459 (2014). [§§ 4.25, 6.01, 6.09[B], 15.03[C]]

10/14

For questions concerning this shipment, billing, or other customer service matters, call our Customer Service Department at 1-800-234-1660.

For toll-free ordering, please call 1-800-638-8437.

THE COMPLETE GUIDE TO HUMAN RESOURCES AND THE LAW

2015 Edition

Dana Shilling

Wolters Kluwer

Published by Wolters Kluwer in New York.

Wolters Kluwer serves customers worldwide with CCH, Aspen Publishers and Kluwer Law International products.

Printed in the United States of America

ISBN 978-1-4548-4288-0

1 2 3 4 5 6 7 8 9 0

SFI Certified Chain of Custody
Product Line Contains At Least 20% Certified Forest Content
www.sfiprogram.org
SFI-00756

About Wolters Kluwer Law & Business

Wolters Kluwer Law & Business is a leading global provider of intelligent information and digital solutions for legal and business professionals in key specialty areas, and respected educational resources for professors and law students. Wolters Kluwer Law & Business connects legal and business professionals as well as those in the education market with timely, specialized authoritative content and information-enabled solutions to support success through productivity, accuracy and mobility.

Serving customers worldwide, Wolters Kluwer Law & Business products include those under the Aspen Publishers, CCH, Kluwer Law International, Loislaw, ftwilliam.com and MediRegs family of products.

CCH products have been a trusted resource since 1913, and are highly regarded resources for legal, securities, antitrust and trade regulation, government contracting, banking, pension, payroll, employment and labor, and healthcare reimbursement and compliance professionals.

Aspen Publishers products provide essential information to attorneys, business professionals and law students. Written by preeminent authorities, the product line offers analytical and practical information in a range of specialty practice areas from securities law and intellectual property to mergers and acquisitions and pension/benefits. Aspen's trusted legal education resources provide professors and students with high-quality, up-to-date and effective resources for successful instruction and study in all areas of the law.

Kluwer Law International products provide the global business community with reliable international legal information in English. Legal practitioners, corporate counsel and business executives around the world rely on Kluwer Law journals, looseleafs, books, and electronic products for comprehensive information in many areas of international legal practice.

Loislaw is a comprehensive online legal research product providing legal content to law firm practitioners of various specializations. Loislaw provides attorneys with the ability to quickly and efficiently find the necessary legal information they need, when and where they need it, by facilitating access to primary law as well as state-specific law, records, forms and treatises.

ftwilliam.com offers employee benefits professionals the highest quality plan documents (retirement, welfare and non-qualified) and government forms (5500/PBGC, 1099 and IRS) software at highly competitive prices.

MediRegs products provide integrated health care compliance content and software solutions for professionals in healthcare, higher education and life sciences, including professionals in accounting, law and consulting.

Wolters Kluwer Law & Business, a division of Wolters Kluwer, is headquartered in New York. Wolters Kluwer is a market-leading global information services company focused on professionals.

WOLTERS KLUWER SUPPLEMENT NOTICE

This product is updated on a periodic basis with supplements and/or new editions to reflect important changes in the subject matter.

If you would like information about enrolling this product in the update service, or wish to receive updates billed separately with a 30-day examination review, please contact our Customer Service Department at 1-800-234-1660 or e-mail us at: *customer.service@wolterskluwer.com*. You can also contact us at:

Wolters Kluwer
Distribution Center
7201 McKinney Circle
Frederick, MD 21704

Important Contact Information

- To order any title, go to *www.wklawbusiness.com* or call 1-800-638-8437.
- To reinstate your manual update service, call 1-800-638-8437.
- To contact Customer Service, e-mail *customer.service@wolterskluwer.com*, call 1-800-234-1660, fax 1-800-901-9075, or mail correspondence to: Order Department—Wolters Kluwer, PO Box 990, Frederick, MD 21705.
- To review your account history or pay an invoice online, visit *www.aspenpublishers.com/payinvoices.*

Wolters Kluwer

CONTENTS

A complete table of contents for each chapter appears at the beginning of the chapter.

Chapter 12
PLAN DISTRIBUTIONS

Chapter 13
PROCESSING AND REVIEWING CLAIMS AND APPEALS

Chapter 14
AMENDING A PLAN

Chapter 15
ENFORCEMENT AND COMPLIANCE ISSUES FOR QUALIFIED PLANS

PART IV
BENEFIT PLANS

Chapter 18
EMPLOYEE GROUP HEALTH PLANS (EGHPs)

Chapter 19
HEALTH INSURANCE CONTINUATION AND PORTABILITY (COBRA AND HIPAA)

Chapter 20
DISABILITY PLANS

Chapter 21
INSURANCE FRINGE BENEFITS

Chapter 22
OTHER FRINGE BENEFITS

PART V
THE HR FUNCTION

Chapter 23
HIRING AND RECRUITMENT

PART VII
SUBSTANTIVE LAWS AGAINST DISCRIMINATION

Chapter 34
TITLE VII

Chapter 35
SEXUAL HARASSMENT

Chapter 36
AMERICANS WITH DISABILITIES ACT (ADA)

Chapter 37
AGE DISCRIMINATION IN EMPLOYMENT ACT

Chapter 38
THE FAMILY AND MEDICAL LEAVE ACT (FMLA)

PART VIII
PROCEDURE FOR HANDLING DISCRIMINATION CHARGES

Chapter 39
WRONGFUL TERMINATION AND AT-WILL EMPLOYMENT

Chapter 40
ARBITRATION AND ADR

PREFACE

This book, originally published in 1998, is reissued each year, in revised form, to deal with the cases, statutes, and administrative rulings affecting HR issues. This 2015 edition went to press in August 2014, so it reflects events from mid-2013 to mid-2014.

In this time period, there were few dramatic legal changes but, as usual, changes were made in areas such as tax law and ERISA compliance (including updates to correction programs).

Economic problems continued, affecting business in many ways including hiring and compensation. The process of PPACA implementation began, with the first cohort of sign-ups for health coverage (despite delays and challenges to the legality of the statute as a whole), and employers faced questions of how to provide health benefits affordably while still complying with PPACA obligations.

The Supreme Court's June 2013 decision that part of the federal Defense of Marriage Act was unconstitutional requires employers to treat legally married same-sex couples as spouses for various tax and benefit-related purposes. In 2013–2014, same-sex marriage was recognized in several additional states, with the status of other states awaiting resolution of court challenges, and the IRS espoused the principle of recognizing same-sex marriages for tax purposes if they were celebrated in a state in which same-sex marriage is legal. The new 2015 edition is divided into 43 chapters, in eight parts:

1. Part I: Pay Planning, including compensation planning, bonuses, severance pay, and tax issues.
2. Part II: Pension Law, comprising basic pension concepts, defined benefit plans, and the transition from the predominance of defined benefit plans to the rise of defined contribution and 401(k) plans; cash balance plans; nonqualified plans; and plans for early retirement and retiree health benefits.
3. Part III: Pension Plan Administration, going from the adoption of a plan to disclosures to plan participants, handling claims and appeals, amending the plan, complying with ERISA and tax rules, handling plans in the context of corporate transitions, such as mergers and acquisitions, and terminating a plan.

4. Part IV: Benefit Plans, such as health plans, continuation coverage and portability requirements for health insurance, plans that provide insurance coverage and disability plans.
5. Part V: The HR Function, including hiring and recruitment, HR computing, recordkeeping, corporate communications, employee privacy rights, diversity issues, and work-family issues.
6. Part VI: Employee Relations, not only the major topic of labor law but also occupational safety and health, unemployment insurance, and workers' compensation.
7. Part VII: Substantive Laws Against Discrimination, focusing on Title VII (and sexual harassment, which is considered a form of sex discrimination), age discrimination, disability discrimination, the Family and Medical Leave Act, and wrongful termination suits.
8. Part VIII: Procedure for Handling Discrimination Charges, not only in the context of lawsuits brought by the EEOC, by state regulators, or by private individuals, but by using arbitration and other alternative dispute resolution methods to resolve problems without going to court.

NOTE ON WEB SOURCES: Several Websites that are frequently cited, such as benefitslink.com, plansponsor.com, and Lexology.com, use very long URLs that are hard to cite. Therefore, for convenience, citations to cases and articles appearing there are simply cited; do a search for the name of the article if you'd like to retrieve it. I cite to online editions rather than print editions of the New York Times and Wall Street Journal.

For older online references, wherever possible I include the latest update of the resource, and the date I accessed it—a date on which the resource was available online. Unfortunately, the URL may change, or the item may no longer be available online, or may be behind a paywall when you attempt to access it.

Part I
PAY PLANNING

CHAPTER 1
PAY PLANNING

§ 1.01 INTRODUCTION

Since 2008, employers have been facing problems of managing HR functions in a recession. It has often been necessary to lay off workers, let positions go unfilled by attrition, or cut back on benefits.

One of the most significant pay planning issues is the determination of which workers are properly classified as independent contractors, and which ones are common-law employees. For common-law employees, one of the most significant issues is which of them are entitled to receive overtime, and which ones are exempt from overtime requirements because, for example, they are administrative workers or managers. But to escape the need to pay overtime, it isn't enough merely to give a worker an inflated title if his or her work is not really professional, administrative, or supervisory. There have also been a number of cases charging Wal-Mart and other large merchandisers with failure to provide employees with the break time required by law, as well as allegations that employees have been required to "work off the clock" (be paid for less time than actually worked).

Early in 2010, in a suit alleging unpaid overtime and benefits, the Supreme Court ruled that a corporation's principal place of business is its executive office, not where its products are sold. The effect is that fewer cases can be filed in state court—and state courts are less hostile to class actions than federal courts.

Previously, federal courts used various tests. Before 1958, a corporation was only a citizen of its state of incorporation. Congress did not want local businesses to be able to escape state court suits by incorporating out of state, so the federal rules of civil procedure were amended to make a corporation a citizen both of its state of incorporation and where it had its principal place of business. However, the statute did not define the company's principal place of business, and the Courts of Appeals had different standards. [*Hertz v. Friend*, 559 U.S. 77 (2010)]

In March 2010, as part of the economic recovery effort, the Hiring Incentives to Restore Employment (HIRE) Act was enacted, with a 6.2% payroll tax incentive (the employer's share of FICA tax was waived for the period February 3, 2010–January 1, 2011). Employers could also receive a general business tax credit of up to $1,000 per worker if the worker remained on the payroll for at least a year. [Rebecca Moore, *New Law Offers Tax Incentives for Hiring*, plansponsor .com (Mar. 18, 2010). See <http://www.plansponsor.com/New_Law_Offers_Tax_Incentives_for_Hiring.aspx>, discussed in McGuireWood LLP, *IRS Issues Additional FAQs for HIRE Act* (May 6, 2010) (benefitslink.com), for the IRS's three FAQ postings about payroll tax issues in May 2010.]

In late 2010, Congress took another approach to using tax incentives to increase hiring: reducing the employee's, but not the employer's, FICA rate. The Tax Relief, Unemployment Insurance Reauthorization, and Job Creation Act of 2010, Pub. L. No. 111-312 set the employee FICA rate at 4.2%, with the employer rate reverting to 6.2%, plus Medicare tax at a rate of 1.45% each for employer and employee. The Making Work Pay credit expired December 31, 2010. The

Temporary Payroll Tax Cut Continuation Act retained the 4.2% FICA rate for employees through the end of February 2012. This statute imposed a 2% recapture tax (capping the amount of wages eligible for the payroll tax cut at $18,350). A subsequent statue, the Middle Class Tax Relief and Job Creation Act of 2012, enacted February 22, 2012, Pub. L. No. 112-96, retained the 4.2% employee rate—a payroll tax cut that was estimated to benefit 160 million workers—and repealed the $18,350 limitation. However, the payroll tax cut was permitted to expire. [<http://www.irs.gov/pub/irs-pdf/f941.pdf>; see Rebecca Moore, *Payroll Tax Cut Extended, IRS Issues Revised Form*, plansponsor.com (Feb. 24, 2012); Naftali Bendavid and Siobhan Hughes, *Congress Reaches Payroll-Tax Deal*, WSJ.com (Feb. 16, 2012)]

High-income employees ($250,000 income on a joint return, $200,000 for single, head of household, surviving spouse with a dependent child, $125,000 for married persons filing separately) are subject to additional Medicare tax; this portion of the tax is applied only to the employee, with no employer match. T.D. 9645, 2013-51 I.R.B. 738, provides final regulations on the additional Medicare tax imposed on high earners by PPACA. The T.D. explains how to withhold the additional tax and correct any underpayments or overpayments. The employer is required to withhold the additional tax from wages in excess of $200,000 paid to any person, irrespective of filing status or wages paid by other employers. The employer is not permitted to modify its withholding of additional Medicare tax, but a person who expects to owe more than the amount withheld by the employer (e.g., a joint return with income over $250,000, but where neither spouse earns more than $200,000) can direct additional withholding on Form W-4. [Carrie Elizabeth Byrnes and Timothy Zehnder, *IRS Issues "Additional Medicare Tax" Final Rules*, Bryan Cave LLP (Dec. 10, 2013), available at Lexology.com]

In March 2014, the Supreme Court reversed the Sixth Circuit and held that the severance payments constituted FICA wages. The Supreme Court held that severance payments are made only to employees, and they are made because of service to employers because "service" is defined broadly as the entire relationship between the employer and employee. The court noted that the FICA statute provides a list of exemptions from the general rule that all compensation constitutes FICA wages. One of the exemptions is for severance payments made for disability retirement. The Supreme Court said it would not be necessary to specify this exemption if severance pay in general did not constitute FICA wages. Code § 3401(a), dealing with income tax withholding, also has a broad definition of taxable wages, subject to a list of exemptions. The list says that Supplemental Unemployment Benefits are treated as if they were wages: see § 3402(o). The defendant interpreted this to mean that, although SUB payments are treated "as if" they were wages, they are not wages for this purpose or for FICA purposes. However, the Supreme Court traced this provision to the history of tax withholding, when Congress wanted to relieve terminated workers from the burden of year-end tax liability. [*United States v. Quality Stores Inc.*, 134 S. Ct. 1395 (2014)]

FICA does not apply to work done by "students" who work for their educational institution. A 2004 Treasury regulation says that a full-time employee is not considered a student, even if the work has a training aspect. The regulation uses medical residents as an example of trainees who are considered full-time workers subject to FICA rather than students. The Mayo Foundation for Medical Education and Research sued to challenge the application of this rule to medical residents who are scheduled to work more than 40 hours per week. The Supreme Court upheld the rule, treating it as a reasonable construction of the statute. [*Mayo Foundation for Med. Research v. United States,* 131 S. Ct. 704 (2011); see Buck Consultants FYI, *Supreme Court Upholds Treasury Rule That Medical Residents Are Employees for FICA Purposes* (Jan. 21, 2011) (benefitslink.com)]

Traditional methods of distributing pay—whether cash in a pay envelope or paychecks—are not necessarily practical in the twenty-first century and employers are using new modes of payment. Direct deposit is efficient and inexpensive for the employer—but does not work for employees who do not have bank accounts. Payroll cards, like direct deposit, reduce employers' payroll costs, and it is faster to make a final payment to a terminated employee by adding value to a card than by overnight mailing a check. The use of payroll cards rose from 3.1 million cards in 2010 to 5.8 million in 2013, with total card payments of $43 billion in 2013 and projected payments of $68.9 billion in 2017. Many low-wage employees do not have bank accounts, so they cannot deposit checks or receive direct deposits.

A class action was filed in mid-2013 by former McDonald's employees arguing that they were entitled to be paid by check. The Consumer Finance Protection Bureau (CFPB) has held that, because of concerns about high fees, employers cannot require workers to take their pay on debit cards and employees must be given options as to how they will be paid. Payroll cards also carry consumer protections, such as disclosure of fees, limitations on liability for unauthorized use, and a procedure for resolving errors.

Some states require employees to be given at least a minimum number of free ATM withdrawals with payroll cards; others merely require the employee to be able to access the full wage amount in one lump sum without a fee, perhaps by getting cash from a bank teller or getting a courtesy check. Some states forbid employers to derive benefit from payroll card fees; a commission or even reduction in payroll costs might be deemed to fall into this category. [CFPB Bulletin 2013-10; see Alan Zibel and Robin Sidel, *Regulator Bars Employers From Requiring Pay on Debit Cards*, WSJ.com (Sept. 13, 2013); Jennifer S. Rusie, *To Fee Or Not To Fee—The Pros And Cons Of Payroll Cards*, Ogletree Deakins (Aug. 27, 2013), available at Lexology.com; William Ozier, *Tips On Using Payroll Debit Cards*, Bass, Berry & Sims PLC (Oct. 14, 2013), available at Lexology.com]

The health care reform act, the PPACA, enacted some Fair Labor Standards Act provisions. FLSA § 18A requires employers with more than 200 full-time employees to automatically enroll new full-time employees in one of the health plans the employer offers. Employees must be given a chance to opt out. In February 2012, DOL announced that this requirement will not be enforced until regulations are published. The PPACA also added § 18B to the FLSA, requiring FLSA-covered employers to notify employees of their coverage offerings and the availability of securing alternative coverage through an Exchange (health care Marketplace). A DOL FAQ says that there is no penalty for failure to give notice. Section 18C forbids retaliation against employees who get a tax credit or subsidy, who object to a PPACA violation, or who assist in investigation of a violation. [Brett C. Bartlett et al., *Fair Labor Standards Of Care: Examining The Affordable Care Act's Changes To The FLSA*, Seyfarth Shaw LLP (Oct. 23, 2013), available at Lexology.com. See Chapter 18 for more discussion of PPACA.]

[A] SEC Regulation of Compensation

In 2006, the SEC required public corporations to disclose information about the compensation of top managers. The final rule requires publication of both tables of top management compensation and narrative disclosure of three years' worth of compensation. Public companies must use the Compensation Discussion and Analysis (which will be filed with the SEC, so the CEO and CFO must certify it) to disclose the compensation for top management. The value of equity-based awards such as stock options must be disclosed, and the SEC required disclosure of timing of option grants, as a way to deter back-dating. A similar disclosure format is required for compensation of directors. Public companies must disclose the extent to which directors are independent, and must reveal more about officers' and directors' holdings of the company's own stock. [SEC Press Release, *SEC Votes to Adopt Changes to Disclosure Requirements Concerning Executive Compensation and Related Matters*, <http://www.sec.gov/news/press/2006/2006-123.htm> (July 26, 2006), finalizing provisions proposed in Rel. Nos. 33-8655, 34-53185, and IC-27218 (2006).]

The SEC voted 3–2 in September 2013 to propose a new rule under Dodd-Frank § 953(b), requiring public companies to disclose the ratio of CEO compensation to the median compensation of all the company's employees. The proposal does not require any specific methodology for calculating the pay ratio. (Previous rules required extensive disclosure about compensation of named executive officers including the CEO, but comparison with rank-and-file workers was not required.) The information must be included in registration statements, proxy and information statements, and annual reports that already include executive compensation information—but does not have to be disclosed in reports that do not require executive compensation information, such as current and quarterly reports. Emerging growth companies covered by the JOBS Act are exempt, as are smaller reporting companies and foreign private issuers. [SEC press release 2013-186, *SEC Proposes Rules for Pay Ratio Disclosure*, <http://www.sec.gov/News/PressRelease/Detail/PressRelease/1370539817895> (Sept. 18, 2013)]

Early in 2011, the SEC published the shareholder Say on Pay rules required by the Dodd-Frank Act (Pub. L. No. 111-203). The shareholder vote is non-binding, but the intention is that corporations would be too embarrassed to continue a policy that was disapproved by its stockholders. The rules also allow shareholders to vote on certain golden parachutes in connection with mergers and acquisitions, and require the corporations to make more extensive disclosures about the compensation packages for top executives. [Rebecca Moore, *SEC Adopts Say on Pay Rules*, plansponsor.com (Jan. 25, 2011)] The compensation packages nearly always obtain shareholder approval.

In 2013, 3363 companies held say on pay votes. Seventy-three companies failed, with an average 60% "No" vote; 15 of those companies had already failed previous votes. Two more companies got less than 50% approval of pay, but deemed it a victory because there were many abstentions. Looksmart got a 100% vote opposing the pay proposal, but its board recommended voting against the policies of the previous administration. [S. Hall and Partners, *2013 Say on Pay Voting Results* (Dec. 31, 2013) (benefitslink.com)] In the 2014 proxy season, as of the beginning of April, out of 170 Say on Pay votes, 93% resulted in approval of the compensation packages; in 2013, the average was 90% approval. The only company to fail at that point in 2014 was Hologic, which also failed the year before. In 2013, Institutional Shareholder Services recommended that its clients vote against the compensation package at 14% of companies, but in 2014, it only recommended voting against the package at 4% of companies. The difference has been attributed to companies eliminating "red flags" by making executive compensation more closely linked to results. Because the stock market was doing well in 2014, investors tended to be more sanguine about executive compensation. [Emily Chasan, *Early Say-on-Pay Results Show Rising Support, Few Failures*, WSJ.com (Apr. 2, 2014)]

Clorox won a say on pay class action that was filed in a California state court about a month before the 2012 annual meeting. The suit asked to enjoin shareholder votes on some compensation-related proposals, based on allegations that the proxy statement omitted material compensation-related information dealing with the say on pay proposal and the proposal to amend the equity plan. A preliminary injunction was denied: the court said that permitting the meeting to take place did not cause irreparable harm, because any shareholder action taken at the meeting could later be declared void, and Clorox could make additional disclosures and solicit proxies for a second vote. The court said that the proxy statement included ample information about the proposals, the way the compensation committee worked, and the effect of the proposals on the company and its shareholders. The information that the plaintiffs sought was not required in the proxy statement, and much of it was available in SEC filings. The court said that Delaware law does not require companies to provide all information that anyone could consider helpful. [Lizanne Thomas et al., *Clorox Prevails In Key Say-On-Pay Litigation*, Jones Day (Sept. 30, 2013), available at Lexology.com]

The Conference Board's report, *Proxy Voting Analytics (2008–2012)* available on the organization's Website, shows that, since the say on pay rules took effect, there have been fewer shareholder proposals on executive compensation and shareholders are more engaged with their companies. The say on pay process can be a catalyst for better communications with investors. The specific say on pay mechanism means that it is no longer necessary to launch generic compensation proposals. In 2008, there were 193 shareholder proposals dealing with executive compensation, dropping to 65 in 2011 (the year say on pay took effect), rising again to 92 in 2012. [Catherine Dunn, *Analysis of Proxy Voting Data Looks at Say-on-Pay, Shareholder Engagement*, Corporate Counsel (Jan. 30, 2013) (law.com)]

Suits have also been filed against top management, directors, and outside compensation consultants for causes of action such as breach of fiduciary duty, aiding and abetting breach of contract, and unjust enrichment. Fiduciary duty claims may involve the duty of loyalty and perhaps candor, good faith, and independence. These cases usually do not mention the duty of care—perhaps because some state statutes, such as Delaware General Corporation Law § 102(b)(7), provide defenses or allow corporations to indemnify their managers.

Before the shareholder vote, the company should decide how it will disclose a negative shareholder vote, and what will be said in the Form 8-K that discloses the results of the vote. If the vote is negative, some or all independent directors could be directed to examine executive pay, and stock awards and options could be made contingent on performance.

It is not uncommon for companies close to bankruptcy to pay bonuses to management shortly before a bankruptcy filing. The Wall Street Journal's research showed that in, in more than 80 Chapter 11 bankruptcy cases 2007–2012, more than 1,600 insiders received compensation, including bonuses and fees, totaling more than $1.3 billion in the months before the filing. Retention bonuses after a filing are regulated by federal law; those before filing are not. After union protests, Hostess reversed salary increases given to top management five months before the company's bankruptcy filing. [Mike Spector, Tom McGinty and Rachel Feintzeig, *In Trouble and Paying Out*, WSJ.com (Dec. 3, 2012)]

In mid-2011, the D.C. Circuit vacated Rule 14a-11, the proxy access rule, which would have permitted some shareholders to write in their nominees for the board of directors. The D.C. Circuit found that the SEC exceeded its discretion in adopting this rule. [*Business Roundtable & Chamber of Commerce v. SEC,* 647 F.3d 1144 (D.C. Cir. 2011)]

[B] TARP Restrictions

Restrictions on executive pay were first imposed by the Emergency Economic Stabilization Act of 2008 (EESA) Pub. L. No. 110-343, which set up a program for the federal government to purchase troubled assets from financial institutions. Institutions that transferred "toxic" assets to the federal government under the Troubled Asset Relief Program (TARP) had to agree to limits on deductions for compensation and bonuses for their top managers. Companies participating in TARP could not use certain types of golden parachutes; had to restrict their severance arrangements for top managers; and had to seek "clawback" (repayment) of certain sums paid to top managers if the payments were based on incorrect financial figures. [See, e.g., Buck Research FYI, *Executive Compensation Under the Emergency Economic Stabilization Act of 2008* (Oct. 20, 2008) (benefitslink.com)]

Additional restrictions were imposed by the American Recovery and Reinvestment Act of 2009 (ARRA), Pub. L. No. 111-5. Limits were imposed on top management's bonuses, retention awards, golden parachutes, and incentive compensation. [See Interim Final Rule, 73 Fed. Reg. 62205 (Oct. 20, 2008), finalized at 74 Fed. Reg. 28393 (June 15, 2009)] The TARP program ended in October 2010.

Public companies are subject to the requirements of Code § 162(m). The general rule is that only $1 million in compensation is deductible for the company's CEO and each of its four other highest-compensated officers. The $1 million limit does not apply to qualified performance-based compensation, that is only paid if the payee meets at least one objective performance goal that was set in advance. The performance-based compensation must have been ordered either by the company's board or a compensation committee consisting of outside directors, and the terms of the plan are disclosed to, and approved by, the shareholders in advance. In mid-2012, the IRS issued guidance on whether dividends on restricted stock, and the equivalent on RSUs, must satisfy the § 162(m) requirements separately to be treated as fully deductible performance-based compensation: Rev. Rul. 2012-19, 2012-28 I.R.B. 16.

Restricted stock is company stock that is released based on a vesting schedule, whereas RSUs are a right to get vested stock in the future. Usually, restricted stock carries voting rights but RSUs do not. Some companies make "dividend equivalent" payments on RSUs: cash payments equivalent to the dividends on the restricted stock for the period between the grant and the vesting date. Rev. Rul. 2012-19 says that, to qualify for exemption from the $1 million exemption, the dividends or dividend equivalents can only be payable if the payee meets performance goals. However, the performance goals for this purpose do not have to be the same ones for granting the underlying restricted stock or RSUs. [Buck Consultants FYI, *IRS Clarifies Treatment of Performance-Based Restricted Stock and Restricted Stock Units* (Aug. 8, 2012) (benefitslink.com)]

The Sarbanes-Oxley Act, EESA, and AARA also call for "clawback": companies must recover from the payee any bonus or incentive compensation that was paid to a top executive on the basis of false financial reporting, and compensation plans must not encourage future false reporting that would lead to higher compensation. The Treasury has the authority to review bonuses, retention awards, etc., paid to top management. If the Treasury deems the payments to have been inconsistent with the purposes of the TARP program, it can negotiate with the company and the recipients of the compensation about appropriate reimbursement to the U.S. government.

§ 1.02 DECISION FACTORS IN SETTING COMPENSATION

A business's compensation policies reflect many factors:

- What the business can afford to pay;
- Competitive factors (other local companies competing for workers, prevailing wages, unemployment rates);
- Impact on cash flow (until recently, cash-poor companies with bright prospects often relied heavily on stock options and/or the potential for an IPO as elements of compensation);
- Effect on future financing (venture capitalists who expect one-third of the shares in a new business, or a business receiving later rounds of funding, will not want too many of the shares to be assigned to employees);
- The compensation package favored by the kind of workers the employer wants to attract. If the objective is to minimize turnover, for instance, workers with families will place a high value on health benefits, whereas more mobile younger workers will tend to favor higher cash compensation and pension portability;
- Tax factors for both employer and employee; the objective is for the employer to get the highest permissible deduction and for the employee to retain as much as possible after taxes.

The Wall Street Journal found that shareholder activism was "keeping a lid" on the growth in CEO pay. The newspaper commissioned a study by the Hay Group. The results of the study showed that corporate CEO pay increased only slightly between 2012 and 2013. At 50 public companies with revenue of $8 billion or more, CEO pay grew 4.1% between 2012 and 2013. Some CEOs took drastic pay cuts when their company's stock results were poor; 15 out of the 50 CEOs had reduced compensation in 2013. The median salary increase was 2.2%, and bonuses increased by only 0.5%, although performance-based stock awards rose 16%; by definition, this type of compensation reflects the company's stock price. Even if a company passes its say on pay vote, the compensation committee might reduce CEO pay to avoid controversy. Median 2013 CEO pay for surveyed companies was $9.8 million. [Theo Francis and Joann S. Lublin, *CEO Pay Rising but Not for All*, WSJ.com (Mar. 26, 2014)]

The Wall Street Journal found that the biggest rewards went to a handful of executives, but pay did not necessarily correlate with the corporation's size or financial results. The top 10% of CEOs earned 23% of CEO compensation. The DOL said that in 2013, wages and salaries for all private-sector workers rose an average of 1.8%, whereas CEO pay rose a median of 5.5% to $11.4 million, but almost two-thirds of CEO compensation was performance-linked. [Theo Francis and Joann S. Lublin, *CEO Pay Rises Moderately; A Few Reap Huge Rewards*, WSJ.com (May 27, 2014)]

Inequality continues to become more marked. In April 2013, the Department of Labor (DOL) reported that, after adjusting for inflation, low-paid workers' wages declined, but compensation of highly paid workers has increased faster than inflation. Using 2013 dollars, the national median wage in 2000 was $819; in 2013, it was $827. The median income of college graduates in 2013 was $1,189 a week—1% less than the median in 2000, using constant dollars. [Floyd Norris, *Wage Disparity Continues to Grow*, NYTimes.com (Apr. 26, 2013)]

The pay gap between men's and women's earnings for full-time workers remained in 2013, with women earning 76.5 cents to every dollar earned by men (in 1980, the pay gap was 60.2 cents; in 2011, women earned an average of 77 cents for every dollar earned by men; in 2012, it was 88 cents for women aged 15–24, 81 cents for women aged 25–44, and 74 cents for women aged 45–64). For male full-time workers the median average earnings for 2012 was $49,398, versus $37,791 for female workers. [Brenda Cronin, *Male-Female Pay Gap Hasn't Moved Much in Years*, WSJ.com (Sept. 17, 2013)] However, among people who usually work less than 35 hours per week, the median weekly earnings for women were higher than men's in 2012 (110%). [Catherine Rampell, *In Part-Time Jobs, Women Outearn Men*, NYTimes.com (Nov. 5, 2013)]

For discussion of the federal Equal Pay Act (29 U.S.C. § 206) see § 34.06[C].

[A] Coping with the Downturn

Buck Consultants predicted base pay increases for 2014 of 3% (the same as for 2013), about 1% lower than pre-recession levels. Both short- and long-term incentive compensation declined. Buck expected fewer and smaller awards in 2013 than in 2012. Not many employers expected to change pay practices because of PPACA: only 8% capped hours for part-timers, and a further 12% considered doing so in the future. Eight percent of respondents gave employees incentives to get benefits from a different source, and another 9% considered it. [Xerox Corporation press release, *Average 2014 US Salary Increases to Remain at 3 Percent, According to Buck Consultants Survey* (Oct. 3, 2013) (benefitslink.com)]

Since the stock market crash of 2008, many businesses looked for ways to cut the size of their workforce, and to reduce the number of hours worked (e.g., by implementing furloughs).

Non-exempt employees are paid only for actual hours worked. But some exempt employees might become non-exempt if the reduction in hours reduces their compensation below the $455/week federal test. Exempt employees must be paid their full salary for any week in which they work at all. But an exempt worker can trigger payment of a week's salary, even when the office is closed, for example, by checking work-related e-mails, so exempts should be instructed not to do any work during a furlough without advance written approval.

The federal government shutdown in 2013 stopped work orders to many government contractors causing furloughs. Non-exempt workers do not have to be paid during furlough periods because they are paid only for hours actually worked. But the FLSA provides that if an exempt employee does any work in any part of a week—including making phone calls and checking e-mails—then the employee must receive full salary for the week. There are exceptions for bona fide sick leave or voluntary absences (e.g., the employee is granted extra time off at the end of a vacation).

Exempt employees do not have to be paid for weeks in which they do not work at all, whether the absence is voluntary or involuntary, but partial-week furloughs create difficulties. An employee might cease to be exempt if the employer fails to pay full salary for the week when it is due—but the exemption will not be lost for an inadvertent, isolated violation that is corrected by reimbursing the employee for improper deductions. But exempt status can be lost for all employees in a job classification who have the same supervisor if there is a pattern showing intent to avoid appropriate payment. The employer might also be liable for civil penalties (including treble damages for willful violations) and/or class actions. The employer might also be liable for civil penalties, including treble damages for willful violation, and class actions.

During the shutdown, some government contractors required exempt employees to use accrued vacation time. This is permissible under federal law but might not be under state law. Problems could be caused if a contractor's stop work order is lifted mid-week. [Janie Schulman et al., *Wages For Furloughed Employees*, Morrison & Foerster LLP (Oct. 16, 2013), available at Lexology.com]

Even before 2012 federal legislation encouraged the development of work-sharing programs (where employees whose hours have been cut can receive partial unemployment insurance benefits), 22 states and the District of Columbia had such programs. [Justin LaHart, *Work Sharing Gains Traction in Rhode Island, Elsewhere*, WSJ.com (Nov. 21, 2011)]

The Middle Class Tax Relief and Job Creation Act of 2012 provided federal funding so states could expand their STC (short-time compensation) work sharing programs; 28 states now have programs. To receive funding, state programs must require employers to maintain benefits for workers whose hours are reduced, and participating workers' hours cannot be reduced by more than 60%. [Hunton

& Williams LLP, *DOL Launches Website Promoting Work Sharing Programs*, Lexology.com (Nov. 21, 2013)]

§ 1.03 BENEFITS AS AN ELEMENT OF COMPENSATION

The accepted rule of thumb is that the cost of benefits adds about one-third to the employee's stated salary.

The size of the benefit package is often directly related to the size of the company. Generally, for any particular benefit, the percentage of companies offering that benefit increases with the size of the workforce, and it is also often true that larger companies offer a more generous benefit package.

In general, unionized workers have access to more benefits than non-unionized workers, and pay and benefits tend to be lower in the South than in other regions.

In March 2014, employer costs for employee compensation in private industry averaged $29.99/hour. Costs for paid leave averaged $2.09/hour (7.0%); supplemental pay 85 cents (2.8%), insurance $2.50 (8.3%), retirement and savings $1.15 (3.8%), legally required benefits $2.44 (8.1%). The average private-industry cost of health benefits was $2.36 per hour worked, representing 7.9% of total compensation. A decade before, in March 2014, health benefits were an average of 6.6% of total compensation ($1.53/hour). [BLS News Release, *Employer Costs for Employee Compensation—March 2014*, <http://www.bls.gov/news.release/pdf/ecec.pdf>. For more information on health insurance benefits, see *National Compensation Survey: Employee Benefits in the United States, March 2013*, <http://www.bls.gov/ncs/ebs/benefits/2013/benefits.htm>]

San Francisco adopted the first paid sick leave requirement in 2007. Since then, it has been joined by the District of Columbia, the state of Connecticut, and the cities of Seattle, Portland (Oregon), New York City, Jersey City, and Newark. [Michael J. Soltis, *Jersey City Adds Another Patch To The Paid Sick Leave Patchwork*, Jackson Lewis LLP (Oct. 10, 2013), available at Lexology.com; Jackson Lewis LLP, *Portland, Oregon, Issues Rules On Paid Leave*, Lexology.com (Oct. 11, 2013); Ebonee Hamilton Lewis and Lauren Marcus, *Newark Follows Jersey City to Enact Paid Sick Time Law*, Littler Mendelson (Mar. 4, 2014) (benefitslink.com)]

Some states (Connecticut, Hawaii, Illinois, New York, Oregon, and Rhode Island) have laws protecting victims of domestic violence in the workplace: e.g., forbidding discrimination and/or requiring time off to make court appearances and otherwise deal with domestic violence. California requires reasonable accommodation, such as changing the employee's telephone number or office location to hinder stalking. [Susan Gross Sholinsky, *Take 5: Views You Can Use: Labor And Employment*, Epstein Becker Green (Nov. 12, 2013), available at Lexology.com]

§ 1.04 AVOIDING DISCRIMINATION

The Equal Employment Opportunity Commission (EEOC) Compliance Manual contains a section dealing with compensation issues in the context of various antidiscrimination statutes. The EEOC's position is that antidiscrimination laws apply to all aspects of compensation, including salary, overtime, bonuses, options, profit sharing, fringe benefits, and expense accounts. The agency says that employers are never justified in taking race, color, sex, national origin, religion, age, or disability into account in setting compensation.

The EEOC says that equal severance benefits are required for all similarly situated employees, regardless of age. Employers may not deny severance because the employee is eligible for a pension, although sometimes pension benefits can be offset against the severance pay. Denying recall rights to older workers operates as involuntary retirement. Because the cost of providing severance pay does not rise with the employees' ages, employers are not allowed to assert an equal cost defense.

However, retiree health benefits can legitimately be offset against severance if the retiree is eligible for an immediate pension; if he actually receives health benefit coverage; and the retiree benefits are at least comparable to Medicare in type and value. If the retiree is over 65, benefits must be at least comparable to one-fourth the value of Medicare benefits. The offset itself must be reduced by any percentage by which the pension is reduced for retirement before normal retirement age, and by any percentage of the premium that the retiree has to pay for retiree health coverage.

The Compliance Manual says that "if the employer provides additional pension benefits that are enough, or are higher than those necessary to bring an employee up to the level of an unreduced pension, the employer can offset the full amount of those benefits. On the other hand, if the employer offers benefits that are insufficient to raise the employee to an unreduced pension, the employer cannot claim any offset at all."

The Eleventh Circuit reversed the district court's refusal to certify a RICO (Racketeer Influenced and Corrupt Organizations Act) class action in a case alleging that Mohawk used temporary agencies to hire illegal aliens to keep down wages. The Eleventh Circuit found a common question of whether Mohawk acted in concert with others in a pattern of illegal activities to reduce wages. [*Williams v. Mohawk Indus.*, 568 F.3d 1350 (11th Cir. 2009), *cert. denied*, 130 S. Ct. 500 (Dec. 8, 2009); see Fred Schneyer, *Employer May Have to Face More Plaintiffs in Wage and Hour Dispute*, plansponsor.com (June 16, 2009)]

Employers that need to cut costs often use a Reduction in Force (RIF) for this purpose. However, RIFs must be handled carefully to avoid findings that they were used selectively to eliminate employees who were the victims of discrimination. In order to carry out a Reduction in Force that complies with applicable laws, employers must document the preliminary steps to cut costs that were taken before the RIF. Increasing the compensation and benefits of top management when jobs are being cut looks suspicious. Discretionary spending on items such as office parties and corporate jets should probably be reduced before a RIF is instituted.

There are also alternatives such as hiring freezes, shorter workweeks, and furloughs. Management should document the steps that were taken, and that alternatives were considered but were not adopted for reasons that are fully documented. Voluntary exit programs can be used as an alternative to layoffs—either company-wide, in a particular division or unit, or a voluntary early retirement program could be offered to employees with a certain amount of age and service. (The risk is that employees the company wants to retain might opt for early retirement.) The economic necessity for a RIF should be documented (e.g., industry conditions, loss of a major contract, so fewer workers are required).

The ADEA provides a safe harbor for early retirement programs that are truly voluntary, but suits might still be filed if a participant claims the program was not really voluntary or if it is not consistent with the purposes of the ADEA. It is important to train managers not to make statements that could be interpreted as threatening to employees who are reluctant to retire. The most common employee claims about layoffs involve age discrimination, so the employer must be prepared to prove what the criteria were for selecting employees for RIFs, and that the criteria were appropriate and job-related. The least problematic structure is work elimination (eliminating an entire department or function) because personal selections are not made. A number of cases say that it is impossible to prove a prima facie case of discrimination when a whole job or department is eliminated.

If individual selections for RIF are made, there must be well-defined selection criteria that are uniformly applied within a department or group. In unionized businesses, it may be necessary to observe seniority. Performance ratings seem to be objective, but employees can argue that the evaluators were biased in rating performance. It is wise to train line managers not to assume that employees close to retirement age intend to retire, and it is not good practice to ask them about their retirement plans (in case they think they are being forced out of the company). Line managers should document their selection criteria and how employees were chosen for RIF or retained.

Mass layoffs may require notice under the WARN Act or its state counterparts. In unionized businesses, it is an Unfair Labor Practice for management to act unilaterally about wages, hours, and other terms and conditions of employment; it is necessary at least to bargain to an impasse before making changes. The NLRB's position is that a layoff for economic reasons (rather than layoffs based on a fundamental change in the organization's business) require prior bargaining about the decision and its implementation. [Alison B. Marshall and Julie M. Broas, *Getting It Right in Reductions in Force: How to Minimize Legal Risks*, Employee Benefit Plan Review (May 2009) (benefitslink.com)]

Executive Order 13664 (April 8, 2014) was promulgated to forbid federal contractors to retaliate against employees for disclosing their compensation, or discussing compensation with co-workers. The order says that ordering employees not to talk about compensation prevents applicants and employees from negotiating knowledgeably, and makes it harder to detect and punish discrimination in compensation. The order took effect immediately. [*Non-Retaliation for Disclose of Compensation Information,* 79 Fed. Reg. 20749 (Apr. 8, 2014)]

§ 1.05 VARIABLE PAY

A variable pay system makes part of the compensation dependent on meeting goals or targets. Because these plans are supposed to create incentives for better work, communication is key. Formal annual review explaining how the award was calculated is useful to pinpoint areas in which employees succeeded and those in which more work is necessary. The most effective plans had "moderate stretch" (i.e., they asked employees to achieve targets that were not impossible, but were not comfortably in view either).

It is important to make it clear whether the variable compensation is a commission on sales or a bonus, and whether the employee is entitled to a specific amount or percentage, or whether the variable pay award is discretionary with management and whether it is contingent on anything (e.g., continued employment with the same company). In some states, sales commissions are considered vested and must be paid when the employee quits or is terminated. [Rebecca E. Ivey and Rebecca Williams Shanlever, Troutman Sanders LLP, *Easy Come, Easy Go: State Rules on Post-Termination Forfeitures of Bonuses and Commissions* (Apr. 12, 2010) (benefitslink.com)]

In mid-2010, the Connecticut Supreme Court ruled that an attorney's year-end bonus was not "wages" as defined by the Connecticut Wage Act, so statutory double damages and attorneys' fees were not available. An amount is treated as wages if entitlement is based on specific definable goals such as billing a certain number of client hours per year—but does not constitute wages if payment of the bonus is discretionary and based on something like the employer's determination that it has had a financially successful year. [*Ziotas v. Reardon Law Firm PC*, 296 Conn. 579 (2010); see Thomas B. Scheffey, *Employers May Benefit from Lawyers' Feud Over Bonus*, Connecticut Law Tribune (June 18, 2010) (law.com)]

In 2012, the New York Court of Appeals held that a job offer to a financial services executive included an oral promise of a guaranteed $175,000 bonus, so when he was fired, the bonus constituted "wages," and he could collect attorneys' fees under the New York statute that calls for an award of attorneys' fees when "wages" are not paid on time. [*Ryan v. Kellogg Partners Institutional Servs.*, 19 N.Y.3d 1 (N.Y. 2012)]

§ 1.06 WAGE AND HOUR ISSUES

The HR department's many and varied responsibilities probably include handling (or outsourcing and supervising) payroll matters, including paying employees subject to the appropriate deductions.

The Fair Labor Standards Act (FLSA) [29 U.S.C. §§ 201–219 and 251–262] regulates wages and hour matters. The FLSA forbids sex discrimination in compensation, sets a minimum wage, requires extra pay when a "non-exempt" worker puts in overtime hours, and sets standards for record keeping and record retention. The Department of Labor's Wage and Hour Division is responsible for administering the FLSA. See <http://www.dol.gov/elaws/otcalculator.htm> (accessed Apr. 1, 2014), the DOL Wage and Hour Division's Web tool for calculating overtime pay, based on various scenarios including bonuses, commissions, and shift differentials.

DOL's Wage and Hour Division (WHD) receives over 35,000 complaints a year, so even though the agency has added 350 new investigators, it cannot fully pursue all complaints. As of December 13, 2010, when the WHD decides not to pursue an FLSA or FMLA complaint, the complainants will be given a toll-free number for the LRIS (the ABA's Lawyer Referral and Information Service). The complainant will be notified of the WHD's determination about the violations at issue and back wages owed, so the complainant's lawyer can use the information. WHD says that it has a procedure to expedite sending relevant case information and documents to complainants and their lawyers. [Rebecca Moore, *DOL Started Attorney Referral System for FLSA Claims*, plansponsor.com (Feb. 7, 2011)] A DOL newsletter reported that, in FY 2013, the Wage and Hour Division recovered $249,954,412 back pay for over 269,250 workers. Since early 2009, WHD has closed 145,884 cases, providing over $1 billion in back wages for 1,238,589 workers. [Alexander J. Passantino, *Wage & Hour Division Obtains Nearly $250 Million In Back Wages*, Seyfarth Shaw LLP (Dec. 17, 2013), available at Lexology.com]

The DOL Wage and Hour Division and its state counterparts usually begin enforcement efforts by asking employers for payroll and other business records. Investigators are often sent to work sites. The DOL has the power to repeat investigations as often as it deems necessary. Employers charged with wage and hour violations may be subject to wage restitution, interest, and liquidated damages. Cooperation with the DOL investigator is vital; underpayment liability can be imposed by the DOL based on the claimants' allegations, taken at face value, if the employer does not cooperate. Lack of cooperation will also reduce DOL's willingness to negotiate. Involving a lawyer is worthwhile for negotiations and for improving payroll records. Because the employer has the burden of proof on compliance with wage and hour laws, the quality of the payroll records is key. [Eric Su, *"There's A DOL Investigator At My Place Of Business . . . What Do I Do?" Five Tips On How To Deal When The DOL Comes Knocking*, Ogletree Deakins (Nov. 14, 2013), available at Lexology.com]

Maryland joined the group of states enacting laws to help employees recover unpaid wages. Starting October 1, 2013, Maryland employees can use Lab. & Emp. §§ 3-1101–3-1109 to initiate a lien for unpaid wages. The employee serves a written notice on the employer; if the employer does not dispute the claim by filing a complaint within 30 days, or if a state circuit court imposes a lien after reviewing the case, the lien is established. If the employer files a complaint, either side can request an evidentiary hearing. The employee must prove, by a preponderance of the evidence, that there were unpaid wages. Employees who are granted a lien have 180 days to file it against the real or personal property of the employer; the lien is enforceable for 12 years. [Rebecca Landon Tzou, *Maryland's New Lien For Unpaid Wages Law - A Reasonable "Stick" Or An Inequitable Bludgeon?*, Kelley Drye & Warren LLP (Aug. 29, 2013), available at Lexology.com]

A late 2013 DOL press release says that a company, its owner, plant manager, and office manager were convicted on separate felony counts of repeated, willful FLSA violations. FLSA § 16(a) authorizes criminal prosecution for intentional violation of the FLSA, or willful disregard of its requirements. A corporation can be liable, as can be owners, partners, directors, officers, shareholders, managers, and supervisors. More than $165,000 in restitution was ordered for unpaid overtime and liquidated damages, plus $12,100 in civil money penalties and a $10,000 fine. The individual defendants were sentenced to time served plus probation. The DOL reported that not only did the defendants fail to pay the wages mandated by the FLSA, the defendants required employees to kick back part of their pay; the company kept double books, submitted false payment records, and withheld records from Wage and Hour Division investigators. [John E. Thompson, *FLSA Investigations Result In Criminal Convictions*, Fisher & Phillips LLP (Oct. 30, 2013), available at Lexology.com]

As of January 2014, the IRS classifies automatic gratuities (e.g., 18% service charge for party of 8 or more) as service charges, which are regular wages, subject to payroll withholding, rather than as tips, which employees must report as income. As a result, some chain restaurants stopped including automatic gratuities on the bills of large parties. Many employees opposed the IRS ruling, preferring to receive tips at the end of a shift to waiting two weeks for a paycheck. [Julie Jargon, *Tax Change Affects Restaurant Tips for Large Groups*, WSJ.com (Sept. 4, 2013)]

FLSA § 203(m) permits employers to take a tip credit against the minimum wage of tipped employees, as long as the employee is aware of the credit and is permitted to keep all the tips. The FLSA also allows pooling of tips among employees who customarily and regularly receive tips. The Ninth Circuit held in 2010 that an employee's property right to tips under the FLSA only attaches if the tip credit is taken by the employer. In 2011, the DOL updated the tip credit regulations to provide that tips belong to the employee whether or not the employer takes a tip credit, and that mandatory tip pools are limited to employees who customarily and regularly receive tips. However, a 2013 district court case finds this amendment invalid as inconsistent with the FLSA's text, which limits the use of tips only if a tip credit is taken. [*Cumbie v. Woody Woo, Inc.*, 596 F.3d 577 (9th Cir. 2010); *Oregon Rest & Lodging Ass'n v. Solis*, No. 12-cv-1261 (D. Or. June 7, 2013); see Baker & McKenzie, *Federal Court Strikes Down DOL Rule Classifying Tips As Property Of Employees*, Lexology.com (Jan. 3, 2014)]

The District Court for the District of Nevada held that the FLSA only creates a property right in gratuities that fall under § 203(m)—so casino dealers had no claim if no tip credit is taken and they receive the full non-tipped minimum wage. (The plaintiffs challenged the policy of requiring dealers to submit their tips for redistribution under a tip pool.) [*Cesarz v. Wynn Las Vegas*, LLC, No. 2:13-cv-00109-RCJ-CWJ, 2014 U.S. Dist. LEXIS 3094 (D. Nev. Jan. 10, 2014); see Noel P. Tripp, *Citing To Precedent, Nevada Federal Court Rejects FLSA Tip Claim Asserted By Workers Receiving Minimum Wage*, Jackson Lewis PC (Jan. 29, 2014), available at Lexology.com]

Tip pooling cases raise broader questions of who can be considered a "supervisor." In mid-2009, the California Court of Appeal held that shift supervisors should not be considered agents of the owner because they usually do the same work as the baristas and can keep individual tips, so they should be allowed to share in the tip pool. [*Chau v. Starbucks Corp.*, 174 Cal. App. 4th 688 (Cal. App. 2009); see Mike McKee, *Court Dumps Grounds for $86 Million Verdict Against Starbucks*, The Recorder (June 3, 2009) (law.com)]

The First Circuit affirmed class certification and an award of over $14 million in damages ($7.5 million in damages plus 12% prejudgment interest per year, plus $6.6 million treble damages with respect to tips collected by shift supervisors contrary to the July 12, 2008 amendments to the Massachusetts Tips Act) in a suit about Starbucks' policy on tip pooling. The Massachusetts Tips Act forbids having waitstaff share their tips with anyone who is not a member of the waitstaff. The Tips Act says that the waitstaff are workers who do not have any managerial responsibilities. Starbucks took the position that shift supervisors do not have managerial responsibility and spend 90% of their time doing the same work as other baristas, so they are entitled to share the tips. The First Circuit rejected this argument: shift supervisors have to open and close the store, account for cash, and supervise baristas' break schedule. [*Matamoros v. Starbucks*, 699 F.3d 129 (1st Cir. 2012); see Sheri Qualters, *First Circuit Affirms Win for Starbucks Baristas Over Tip-Sharing*, Nat'l LJ (Nov. 12, 2012) (law.com)]

Instead of settling the question of whether assistant store managers should share in the Starbucks tip pool, the Second Circuit certified the question to the New York Court of Appeals. [*Barenboim v. Starbucks/Winans v. Starbucks*, 698 F.3d 104 (2d Cir. 2012)]. The New York Court of Appeals' answer, in 2013, was that shift supervisors, as workers with some supervisory duties, but who primarily serve customers, might be entitled to share in the tip pool. However, assistant managers are not entitled to share tips, because they have too much managerial authority. [*Barenboim v. Starbucks Corp.*, No. 122 (N.Y. 2013); John W. Egan and Nadia S. Bandukda, *Update On The Battle "Grande": Second Circuit Upholds*

Starbucks' Tip Policy, Seyfarth Shaw LLP (Nov. 25, 2013), available at Lexology.com]

California's Labor Code § 351 makes tips the sole property of the employee or employees for whom the tip was left, and it is illegal for employers to take the gratuity. However, California has ruled that this prohibition does not extend to tip pooling required by the employer. A card dealer brought a class action against a casino challenging a mandatory tip pool. The California Supreme Court ruled that there is no private cause of action to sue under Labor Code § 351—enforcement can only be done by the Department of Industrial Relations charging the employer with a misdemeanor. [*Lu v. Hawaiian Gardens Casino, Inc.*, 50 Cal. 4th 592 (2010); see Mike McKee, *Calif. High Court Tips Hand on Suits Over Gratuities*, The Recorder (May 27, 2010) (law.com); Kate Moser, *Calif. Justices Find No Private Right to Sue for Tip-Pooling Violations*, The Recorder (Aug. 11, 2010) (law.com)]

A 2010 New York statute, the New York State Wage Theft Prevention Act (S. 8380), amending New York Labor Law § 195 with respect to wage notice requirements, took effect April 9, 2011. It requires employers to give employees written notice (when they are hired and each year thereafter) of matters such as their regular payday, regular pay rate, overtime rate, commissions, etc. Employees can sue if they do not receive the required notice, and the Commissioner of Labor can also enforce the statute; criminal penalties are possible. Furthermore, the Commissioner can impose a civil penalty of up to $10,000 for retaliation, and retaliation is a misdemeanor. [John P. Furfaro, *New State Laws Cover Wage Notices, Tips, Independent Contractor Status*, N.Y.L.J. (Feb. 4, 2010) (law.com)]

In a FLSA/New York Labor Law action, the Second Circuit affirmed certification of a class of waiter/captains who alleged that they were forced to share their tips with employees who were not eligible for tips and that they were not given the required extra hour's pay for working over 10 hours in a shift. (New York law limits the tip credit to $2.25; the FLSA allows the employer to take a credit of up to 50% of the minimum wage—but not more than tips actually received. The FLSA forbids use of the tipped credit if tipped employees must share tips with non-tipped employees.)

FLSA collective actions are opt-in, and New York class actions are opt-out, so the issue in this case was whether it was proper for the federal court to hear the New York claims at the same time. The Second Circuit held that the cases could be combined because they involved the same basic facts. The Third, Seventh, Ninth, and D.C. Circuits have allowed federal courts to combine state class actions with an FLSA collective action. [*Shahriar v. Smith Wollensky Rest. Group*, 659 F.3d 234 (2d Cir. 2011). See also *Knepper v. Rite Aid Corp.*, 675 F.3d 249 (3d Cir. 2012); *Ervin v. OS Rest. Servs. Inc.*, 632 F.3d 971 (7th Cir. 2011); *Wang v. Chinese Daily News*, 623 F.3d 743 (9th Cir. 2010), *vacated on other grounds*, 132 S. Ct. 74 (2011) and 709 F.3d 829 (9th Cir. Mar. 4, 2013). The March 2013 decision was replaced in September. The Ninth Circuit applied *Dukes* to reverse certification of a (b)(2) class, because monetary relief was requested, and remanded for the district court to reconsider whether there were class-wide issues. The Ninth Circuit said that first the district court must determine commonality under (a)(2); if it is found, the district court should consider whether (b)(2) certification for injunctive relief can be sustained. None of the named plaintiffs is a current employee of the defendant, so none has standing to pursue class-wide injunctive relief, but the Ninth Circuit held that certification for injunctive relief might survive if there are still-employed identifiable class members: *Wang v. Chinese Daily News Inc.*, 737 F.3d 538 (9th Cir. 2013).]

The FLSA says that suit may be maintained in either state or federal court. In mid-2003, the Supreme Court interpreted this to mean that an FLSA suit for unpaid wages, liquidated damages, interest, and attorney's fees can be removed by the defendant employer from state to federal court. Just because the suit may be maintained in either system doesn't prevent removal, or require a case to remain in the same system from beginning to end. [*Breuer v. Jim's Concrete of Brevard Inc.*, 538 U.S. 691 (2003)]

Employees have a private right of action (that is, they can sue their employers) for unpaid minimum wages and/or overtime, plus liquidated damages, attorneys' fees, and court costs. Courts have the power to order legal and equitable relief against employers who fire employees, or otherwise discriminate or retaliate against them for making an FLSA complaint or participating in a Wage and Hour Division proceeding. [29 U.S.C. § 216]

Not only can employees sue their employers, the Secretary of Labor has the power to sue for unpaid minimum wages and overtime. The funds go directly to the employees who should have received them, not to the Department of Labor (DOL). The court can enjoin the employer against committing any further violations. Willful violations of the FLSA are criminal rather than civil in nature, so prosecution by the federal Attorney General's office is possible, in addition to DOL actions or civil suits by the employees.

After nine years of litigation, the California Supreme Court ruled in April 2012 that employers must provide meal and rest breaks for employees but they are not obligated to make sure that employees actually take the breaks instead of continuing to work. However, this decision was not entirely an employer victory: the California Supreme Court held that workers are entitled to more frequent rest breaks than the employers contended. A concurring opinion points out that class actions remain viable for pressing wage and hour claims. [*Brinker Rest. v. Superior Court (Hohnbaum)*, 53 Cal. 4th 1004 (Cal. 2012). See Scott Graham, *'Brinker' a Win for Employers, but Plaintiffs Cheering, Too*, The Recorder (Apr. 12, 2012) (law.com); Laura Reathaford, *Brinker Round 2: Plaintiffs Secure Class Certification In Trial Court*, Proskauer Rose LLP (Oct. 1, 2013), available at Lexology.com. Note that the statute of limitations for claims of denial of meal breaks is three years: *Murphy v. Kenneth Cole Prods. Inc.*, 40 Cal. 4th 1094 (Cal. 2007).]

Certiorari was denied in a Sixth Circuit case dismissing a nurse's FLSA claim because she did not follow the employer's procedure for reporting work done during meal breaks for which pay was automatically deducted. Commentators said that this decision shows how employers can avoid FLSA liability by being proactive about paying employees for all time worked—and for avoiding payment when the employee alleges extra work that he or she is unable to document. [*White v. Baptist Mem'l Health Care Corp.*, 699 F.3d 869 (6th Cir. 2012), 162 Lab. Cas. (CCH) P36,066, *cert. denied*, 134 S. Ct. 296 (2013); see Noel P. Tripp, *Supreme Court Declines To Review Nurse's Claim Of Off-The-Clock Work In Contravention Of Policy*, Jackson Lewis LLP (Oct. 8, 2013), available at Lexology.com; Paul E. Prather, *Supreme Court Denies Review Of Decision Holding Plaintiff Responsible For Recording Time Worked*, Littler Mendelson (Oct. 24, 2013), available at Lexology.com]

The District Court for the Central District of California gave final approval to settlement of a wage and hour class action against Starbucks. A total of $3 million was approved for up to $900 each to 14,800 employees for denial of required meal breaks and failure of wage statements to list the applicable overtime rate. [*York v. Starbucks Corp.*, No. 08-7919 (C.D. Cal. Oct. 29, 2013); see Mark Anstoetter and Madeleine McDonough, *Wage-And-Hour Class Action Against Starbuck's Settled, Attorney's Fees Slashed*, Shook Hardy & Bacon LLP (Nov. 1, 2013), available at Lexology.com]

Since *Brinker*, California has continued to hear wage and hour cases. The California Court of Appeal held that it was not an abuse of discretion for a trial court to deny class certification in a case about meal breaks at the Chipotle Mexican Grill fast food chain. Despite the *Brinker* decision, the Court of Appeal held that class certification was inappropriate because Chipotle locations differ greatly in their staffing and shift patterns. Managers determine when employees can take breaks; employees are neither permitted to schedule their own breaks nor refrain from taking the scheduled meal and rest breaks. Without a uniform corporate policy, class certification was unavailable. [*Hernandez v. Chipotle Mexican Grill, Inc.*, 208 Cal. App. 4th 1487, 146 Cal. Rptr. 3d 424 (2012)]

Wal-Mart has frequently been accused of labor law violations, such as denying employees legally mandated breaks and forcing them to work off the clock. Such cases raise important issues of when employees' claims are sufficiently similar to justify a class action. [See, e.g., Amaris Elliott-Engel, *Judge Upholds $185 Million Award in Wal-Mart Class Action*, The Legal Intelligencer (Sept. 4, 2008) (law.com) Alison Frankel, *Wal-Mart Loses $6.5 Million Wage-and-Hour Class Action*, The American Lawyer (July 2, 2008) (law.com); *Salvas v. Wal-Mart Stores Inc.*, 452 Mass. 337 (Mass. 2008)]

In 2009 alone, Wal-Mart lost court cases in Minnesota, Pennsylvania, and California and settled 63 suits nationwide for a total of $640 million. [Rebecca Moore, *Wal-Mart Settles with WA Workers Over Pay for Breaks*, plansponsor.com (July 28, 2009).] A class action involving three million Wal-Mart employees, the largest wage and hour class action ever reported, was settled in 2009; the District Court for the District of Nevada's approval also resolved 39 class actions in several states. [Rebecca Moore, *Wal-Mart Wage-and-Hour Settlement Approved in*

NV, plansponsor.com (Nov. 4, 2009)] On May 1, 2012, Wal-Mart agreed to pay $4.8 million in back wages and damages to those who received between $30 and $10,800 each, plus $464,000 in civil penalties. The Department of Justice found that more than 4,500 workers were improperly denied overtime, and security guards and vision-department managers were misclassified as exempt between 2004 and 2007. [Shelly Banjo, *Wal-Mart to Pay $4.8 Million In Back Wages, Damages*, WSJ.com (May 1, 2012)]

Wal-Mart argued that the largest class action verdict in Pennsylvania history, the *Braun/Hummel v. Wal-Mart* litigation, should be overturned because the workers alleging underpayment showed only individualized and not class-wide proof. The Pennsylvania Court of Common Pleas affirmed the $185 million award last September, finding that over 186,000 current and former employees in Pennsylvania were denied rest breaks and compensation for off-the-clock work between March 1998 and May 2006. [Amaris Elliott-Engel, *Wal-Mart Seeks Dismissal of Hefty Class Action Award*, The Legal Intelligencer (Aug. 20, 2009) (law.com)] The District Court for the District of Massachusetts denied a defense motion to compel plaintiffs to respond to written discovery about their immigration status—and ordered a restaurant to answer written questions about potential class members. The plaintiffs claimed that they routinely worked 60–80 hours a week and were not paid for all the hours they worked, and in fact earned less than the minimum wage and did not receive overtime. The court ruled that *Hoffman* does not affect illegal immigrant workers' right to receive back pay, because they are still employees for FLSA purposes. The DOL position is that allowing illegal workers to recover is compatible with federal immigration policy. [*Lin v. Chinatown Rest. Corp.*, No. 1:09-cv-11510-GAO (D. Mass. Mar. 23, 2011); see Sheri Qualters, *Plaintiffs' Immigration Status 'Irrelevant' to Their Wage Claims, Mass. Judge Rules*, Nat'l L.J. (Mar. 28, 2011) (law.com). The Eighth Circuit held that the FLSA applies to hiring of illegal aliens; employers are not permitted to profit by knowingly hiring employees who are not authorized to work in the United States: *Lucas v. Jerusalem Cafe LLC*, 721 F.3d 927 (8th Cir. 2013).]

The Seventh Circuit interpreted the FLSA regulations to mean that employees are not doing compensable work merely because they are subject to callout (i.e., being summoned back to work with a phone or beeper to respond to emergencies)—their activities are not restricted as long as the employer has a way to reach them. The court also found that the class action brought by utility workers was inappropriate because the class was not homogenous enough. Either classes should be certified containing similarly situated employees, or the lunch break grievance should be handled through arbitration. [*Jonites v. Exelon Corp.*, 522 F.3d 721 (7th Cir. 2008)]

The prevalence of electronic devices, such as pagers and increasingly sophisticated cell phones, raises questions about the status of workers who are on call, or who can be contacted when they are not in the workplace.

In mid-2009, there were two district court suits dealing with the issue of when hourly workers are entitled to pay for time responding to work telephone calls or e-mails when the employees are "off the clock." In March 2009, an ex-maintenance worker at the C.B. Richard Ellis Group Inc. brought suit in the Eastern District of Wisconsin, charging that he was required to use a work-issued cell phone to take messages. In July 2009, three current and former employees sued T-Mobile USA Inc. in the Eastern District of New York, alleging that they should have been paid for using company-issued smart phones to take work messages after hours.

An appellate court in California reinstated a suit by employees of the medical technology company Lincare Inc. who wanted to be compensated for on-call time spent answering customer questions on the telephone. The DOL position is that workers do not have to be paid merely for carrying pagers—but if they are summoned so often that they cannot use their on-call time for personal pursuits, compensation is due. But as technology gets cheaper, more and more employees are required to be on call electronically; previously, the devices were so expensive that they were only worthwhile for managers. [Michael Sanserino, *Lawsuits Question After-Hours Demands of Email and Cellphones*, WSJ.com (Aug. 10, 2009)]

[A] FLSA Litigation

Employers face not only class actions from groups of dissatisfied employees (asserting claims of discrimination and/or violations of state wage and hour laws), but also a special kind of "collective action lawsuit" authorized by FLSA § 216. There are many technical legal differences between class actions and FLSA collective actions.

An FLSA § 216(b) collective action can be brought by one or more employees on behalf of themselves and similarly situated employees; to join, similarly situated employees must opt in. Commencing a collective action requires the plaintiff to show that there is a similarly situated group of employees, although the FLSA does not contain a statutory definition of how similar the group must be. If the court grants conditional certification, it determines whether other similarly situated employees should be notified. The more significant differences appear among the opt-in plaintiffs, the less likely it is that the employees in the group are truly similarly situated.

NERA Economic Consulting's 2013 Trends in Wage Hour Settlements shows that the number of wage and hour cases settled in 2013 was slightly lower than in 2012, but this is still an active litigation area. In the first three quarters of 2013, 51 cases were settled for a total of $215 million. Since January 2007, there have been 497 settlements, totaling $2.95 billion. The average 2013 settlement was $4.5 million, far lower than the 2007–2012 average of $7.5 million. However, the average settlement per claimant was higher in 2013 ($7,000) than in 2007–2012 ($5,800). Since 2007, the proportion of large class actions has declined each year; in 2013, most wage and hour cases had fewer than 1,000 plaintiffs. [Laura E. Reasons, *How Much Does It Cost To Make A Wage And Hour Case Go Away?*, Seyfarth Shaw LLP (Nov. 20, 2013), available at Lexology.com]

Seyfarth Shaw's Annual Workplace Class Action Litigation Report 2014 says there were 1,123 class action rulings under a variety of laws. Wage and hour class actions rose, and are expected to keep rising in 2014—but other categories stayed flat. There were 7,672 FLSA class actions filed in 2012; 7,882 in 2013, but ERISA class actions dropped: 7,908 in 2012, 7,279 in 2013. Dukes had less impact in wage and hour than in other areas. Class arbitration was a trend; so was the use of individual arbitration agreements to prevent class action suits. [Rebekah Mintzer, *Seyfarth Report Says Wage and Hour Class Actions Rising*, Corporate Counsel (Jan. 9, 2014) (benefitslink.com)]

In June 2012, the Supreme Court ruled that drug "detail" representatives are exempt from overtime because they fall under the exemption for "outside salespersons." [*Christopher v. SmithKline Beecham Corp.*, 132 S. Ct. 2156 (2012)]

Although *Dukes* and other recent cases make class certification more difficult, some district courts allow class certification when plaintiffs can show a class-wide employment policy and a damages model that applies to the whole class. *Leyva v. Medline Industries*, 716 F.3d 510 (9th Cir. 2013) allows class certification in some cases where damages have to be calculated individually as long as the plaintiffs can show that the employer damaged the proposed class the same way (e.g., failure to calculate overtime properly and provide wage statements). But other cases reject class certification when there is no common formula for damages: e.g., *Roach v. T.L. Cannon Corp.*, No. 3:10 Civ. 0591 (TJM), 2013 WL 1316452 (N.D.N.Y. Mar. 29, 2013); *Cowden v. Parker & Assocs.*, No. 5:09-323-KKC, 2013 U.S. Dist. LEXIS 72253 (E.D. Ky. May 22, 2013). Plaintiffs might be able to use Rule 23(c)(4) to certify a class as to liability only, with damages computed by an individualized showing by each plaintiff. [Baker & McKenzie Wage and Hour Quarterly, *Do Individualized Damages Really Doom Wage and Hour Class Actions? Lower Courts Apply Dukes and Comcast*, 3rd Quarter 2013 (benefitslink.com); see *Comcast v. Behrend*, 133 S. Ct. 1426 (2013), a non-employment case requiring that, in a (b)(3) case, damages must be capable of measurement on a class-wide basis.]

The District Court for the Northern District of California rejected approval of a nationwide FLSA class, finding that the commonality requirement was not satisfied by general questions that do not advance the litigation, and where class members did not suffer the same injury. The plaintiffs argued that people described as assistant managers were not exempt "executives" because they were required to do routine work. Although the plaintiffs did not move for conditional certification of a nationwide collective action, the district court denied certification on its own motion, holding that the potential class members had different experiences, and some had already released their claims. [*Till v. Saks Inc.*, No. C 11-00504 SBA (N.D. Cal. Sept. 30, 2013); see Laura J. Maechtlen and Nadia S. Bandukda, *Saks Puts Up Its "Dukes"? Judge Rules Class Members Too*

Dissimilar In Denying Class Certification, Seyfarth Shaw LLP (Oct. 16, 2013), available at Lexology.com]

When the putative class representative in an FLSA case makes a colorable showing that there is a class of similarly situated employees, conditional certification helps the court find them and then process the case based on a known class. Some courts do not require much evidence to conditionally certify a class, so employers may face extensive litigation even if the actual claims are weak. There is no equivalent under the FLSA of FRCP Rule 23(f), which allows interlocutory appeal of decisions on conditional certification. In a recent Third Circuit case, a class of employees said the University of Pittsburgh Medical Center denied them breaks and meal periods. After conditional certification, about 4,000 employees opted in. The defendant's motion to decertify the class was granted. The plaintiffs said that dismissal of their claims made the order to decertify the class a final, appealable order. However, the Third Circuit held that dismissal deprived the Third Circuit of jurisdiction over the case, because the dismissal terminated not only the plaintiffs' individual claims but their interest in representing co-workers. [*Camesi v. University of Pittsburgh Med. Ctr.*, 729 F.3d 239 (3d Cir. 2013); see Gregory V. Mersol, *Third Circuit Finds That Putative Class Representatives Could Not Challenge Decertification Of An FLSA Collective Action Once They Dismissed Their Own Claims*, Baker & Hostetler LLP (Sept. 6, 2013), available at Lexology.com]

The standard of proof is lenient, so it is usually difficult for employers to defeat conditional certification of an FLSA collective action. But employers can often get the court to limit the size or scope of the class. The District Court for the Western District of Texas held that workers charging denial of overtime for off-the-clock work met the standard for a regional class, but not a nationwide class, of fitness consultants and sales managers for Gold's Gym. The chain had an official policy requiring payment for all hours worked, mandating that employees record all hours and that they obtain approval before working overtime. The plaintiffs alleged that the company had a nationwide de facto policy of encouraging unpaid overtime—and it falsified time cards. The district court found evidence of only a regional, not a national, policy of encouraging work off the clock. FLSA collective actions are different from class actions; while it might be difficult to determine damages in this case, the plaintiffs showed that the alleged damages stemmed from a regional policy of requiring off-the-clock work. Some of the plaintiffs and class members were commissioned salespersons who are ineligible for overtime, but the district court found that this issue could be better addressed at the decertification stage. [*Lay et al. v. Gold's Gym Int'l, Inc. et al.*, No. 5A-12-CV-754 DAE, 2013 U.S. Dist. LEXIS 144264 (W.D. Tex. Oct. 4, 2013); see William J. Anthony, *Employer Defeats FLSA Conditional Certification Of Nationwide Class Of Former Gym Employees Limiting Class To Include Only Those Employees Who Worked In Gym's South Texas Region*, Jackson Lewis LLP (Oct. 14, 2013), available at Lexology.com]

Late in 2003, the Eleventh Circuit held that once a named plaintiff in an FLSA collective action settles his own claims, he will not be allowed to continue the action and notify other class members of a potential case. The Eleventh Circuit distinguished between the FLSA collective action form and the Rule 23 class action, where class members can opt out and the representative plaintiff has the status of a private Attorney General to pursue grievances. [*Cameron-Grant v. Maxim Healthcare Servs. Inc.*, 347 F.3d 1240 (11th Cir. 2003) Another Eleventh Circuit case, *Prickett v. DeKalb Cnty.*, 349 F.3d 1294 (11th Cir. 2003) rules that, if an additional claim is added to an FLSA collective action for overtime pay, workers who opted in initially are not required to opt in again, because it cannot be concluded that they agreed only to the specific claims initially asserted.]

The Supreme Court decided a case about FLSA collective actions. The plaintiff sued on behalf of herself and similarly situated employees. However, the defendant made a settlement offered; the plaintiff ignored it. The Supreme Court held that, since no other employees joined the suit, and the settlement offer would have fully resolved her complaint, the Federal Rules of Civil Procedure required dismissal of the case. There was no longer an active case, because the plaintiff had no personal interest in representing other employees. The Supreme Court drew a distinction between the procedural rules for FLSA collective actions and the rules for class actions. [*Genesis Healthcare Corp. v. Symczyk*, 133 S. Ct. 1523 (2013)]

In a Texas district court case about settlements, plaintiff Silva brought an FLSA suit for unpaid overtime, and also asserted a FLSA retaliation claim. On the day the suit was filed, another employee opted in. The employer made an offer of judgment (Federal Rules of Civil Procedure 68) to the two plaintiffs, which they rejected. Silva moved for conditional certification of an FLSA collective action. Four more plaintiffs opted in and received offers of judgment. The defendants moved to dismiss for lack of subject matter jurisdiction, arguing that the offers of judgment had expired so the claims were moot and the court did not have subject matter jurisdiction. In 2008, the Fifth Circuit allowed an employee who got a Rule 68 offer of judgment to pursue conditional FLSA certification even if no other plaintiffs joined the case. In 2013, the district court said that FLSA collective actions are fundamentally different from class actions—so unaccepted offers can render FLSA claims moot. In this case, however, the court held that Silva's claims were not moot because the offer of judgment did not include any damages for her FLSA retaliation claim—so the offer did not fully satisfy her complaint. [*Silva v. Tegrity Personnel Servs., Inc*, No. 4:13-cv-00860, Civ. Action No. 4:13-cv-00860, 164 Lab. Cas. (CCH) P36,191 (S.D. Tex. Dec. 5, 2013); see Esteban Shardonofsky, *To Moot Or Not To Moot—The First FLSA Case In Texas To Grapple With The Genesis Healthcare Ruling*, Seyfarth Shaw LLP (Dec. 17, 2013), available at Lexology.com; Todd A. Dawson, *Rule 68 Offer That Excludes Individual Claim Does Not Moot Putative FLSA Collective Action*, Baker & Hostetler LLP (Dec. 12, 2013), available at Lexology.com]

In the Fourth Circuit view, the FLSA's anti-retaliation provision protects only employees, not potential employees. Therefore, a plaintiff who said that her job offer was withdrawn after she disclosed her FLSA suit against another company could not sue her potential employer. [*Dellinger v. Science Applications Int'l Corp.*, 649 F.3d 226 (4th Cir. 2011); see Sheri Qualters, *4th Circuit: Anti-Retaliation Provision Of Wage Law Does Not Cover Job Applicants*, Nat'l L.J. (Aug. 15, 2011) (law.com)]

The Seventh Circuit ruled that there is no hard-and-fast rule against certifying a Rule 23(b)(3) class action involving state-law claims in a case that also includes an FLSA collective action, because the FLSA's legislative history does not show an intention to replace other legal procedures. The case was brought by tipped employees who said that Outback Steakhouses maintained policies that violated the FLSA and state wage and hour laws dealing with tips, and employees were not paid for all hours worked. The district court said that a (b)(3) class action, which includes class members unless they opt out, cannot be combined with an FLSA collective action (which required potential plaintiffs to opt in to the action), but the Seventh Circuit disagreed. [*Ervin v. OS Rest. Servs. Inc.*, 632 F.3d 971 (7th Cir. 2011)].

In addition to arbitration agreements and class action waivers, some employers use contracts to alter other legal issues. In recent years, employers have succeeded in some of these cases. FedEx's employment agreement required suits against the employer to be brought within six months. An employee sued under the FLSA and the Equal Pay Act (EPA) (which is part of the FLSA) charging that she was paid less than other employees. Her suit was timely under both statutes, but was brought more than six months after the events. The district court dismissed her suit; the Sixth Circuit reversed, holding that shortening the statute of limitations was an unlawful waiver of the plaintiff's statutory rights. The Sixth Circuit drew a distinction between Title VII rights, which can be waived, and FLSA rights to minimum wage, overtime, and liquidated damages, which cannot be waived because employers profit directly from such violations. The Sixth Circuit also distinguished this case from mandatory arbitration agreements, which permit the employee to bring the claim in an arbitral forum; this agreement tried to completely eliminate employees' legal rights. [*Boaz v. FedEx Customer Info. Servs., Inc.*, 725 F.3d 603 (6th Cir. 2013); see Matthew J. Thomas, *Employers Cannot Shorten Limitations Periods For FLSA Or Equal Pay Claims*, Jenner & Block (Oct. 31, 2013), available at Lexology.com; Manatt Phelps & Phillips LLP, *6th Circuit: FLSA Rights Cannot Be Waived By Contract*, Lexology.com (Aug. 28, 2013)]

Illegal immigrants who worked for Wal-Mart contractors and subcontractors to clean Wal-Mart stores sued Wal-Mart for unpaid overtime, RICO civil damages, and damages for false imprisonment. They sought certification of an FLSA collective action, charging Wal-Mart with knowingly doing business with contractors that hire illegal aliens. The plaintiffs identified Wal-Mart as their employer for FLSA purposes because of its power to hire and fire employees and close supervision of store cleaning. In mid-2012, the Third Circuit rejected class certification and dismissed the RICO and false imprisonment claims. The plaintiffs worked in other places, not exclusively for Wal-Mart, and Wal-Mart hired other contractors and also assigned store employees to cleaning jobs. The false imprisonment charges were dismissed based on Wal-Mart's representation that managers could unlock doors when necessary, and there were emergency exits. The Third Circuit held that an FLSA collective action requires that the plaintiffs be similarly situated, as determined on a case by case basis, using all the relevant factors (similar claims; working in the same corporate location, division, or department; similar compensation and circumstances of employment; whether they all seek similar relief). The Third Circuit did not find enough similarities to certify a collective action: the plaintiffs worked in 180 different stores in 33 states, and the 70 contractors and subcontractors, not Wal-Mart, set wages and hours. The Third Circuit held that bad working conditions and threats of deportation do not constitute involuntary servitude, and there was no evidence that Wal-Mart violated immigration laws. [*Zavala v. Wal-Mart*, 691 F.3d 527 (3d Cir. 2012)]

For about 30 years, it was assumed that, to be enforceable, FLSA settlements would have to be approved by the DOL or by a court—creating problems for employers that wanted the settlement to be kept confidential. However, some recent cases suggest that private settlements might be enforceable, although it is a risk to settle an FLSA claim without court or DOL approval when there is a chance that the plaintiff(s) will later try to invalidate the settlement. See, e.g., *Martin v. Spring Break '83 Productions, LLC*, 688 F.3d 247 (5th Cir. 2012); *Martinez v. Bohls Bearing Equip. Co.*, 361 F. Supp. 2d 608 (W.D. Tex. 2005). According to *Fernandez v. A-1 Duran Roofing, Inc.*, No. 12-CV-20757 (S.D. Fla. Feb. 25, 2013), court approval is not necessary, although courts can grant motions to approve an existing settlement. *Picerni v. Bilingual Seit & Preschool Inc.*, No. 12 Civ. 4938 (BMC), 2013 WL 646649 (E.D.N.Y. Feb. 22, 2013) allows a court to give legal effect to any reasonable settlement of an FLSA case. *Lliguichuzcha v. Cinema 60, LLC*, No. 11 Civ. 4486(GWG), 2013 WL 2436526, (S.D.N.Y. June 5, 2013) summarizes the case law. See Thomas W. Carroll and Mary L. Will, *FLSA Settlements: Is DOL Or Court Approval Required?*, Faegre Baker Daniels (Oct. 4, 2013), available at Lexology.com]

Even if there is no legal requirement of DOL or court involvement, attempts to settle without lawyers can create difficulties, as a recent Eleventh Circuit case shows. Nall was a motel desk clerk. The owner told her not to use a time clock, so she verbally reported hours to him, but there was no accurate written record. She said that she periodically worked over 40 hours a week without getting overtime, and she estimated she was owed at least $3,780. She quit her job and hired a lawyer who filed an FLSA suit; the owner did not hire an attorney. The business owner, still proceeding pro se, called Nall about settlement, and told her not to bring her attorney, they would work it out themselves. He offered her $2,000–$3,000 to withdraw the suit. She agreed, because she trusted him and needed the money because she was homeless. She signed a voluntary dismissal with prejudice (i.e., the suit could not be re-filed) and a letter to her lawyer telling him the case was settled. The Eleventh Circuit held that the district court erred by approving the settlement; it was not a "stipulated judgment" as defined by the Eleventh Circuit in Lynn's Food Stores. FLSA suits can only be settled under DOL supervision or under a court's stipulated judgment after both parties submit a proposed settlement. But in Nall's case, she obviously wasn't proposing the settlement. [*Nall v. Mal-Motels Inc.*, 723 F.3d 1304 (11th Cir. 2013); see Thomas M. Eden III and James N. Nolan, *Private FLSA Settlement A Train Wreck*, Constangy, Brooks & Smith, LLP (Aug. 2, 2013), available at Lexology.com. See *Lynn's Food Stores v. United States*, 679 F.2d 1350 (11th Cir. 1982)]

The Ninth Circuit made it clear in early 2004 that one thing you don't have to worry about is RICO. A plaintiff charged his former employer and its managers with racketeering offenses, charging them with mail fraud for underpaying him and misrepresenting his entitlement to overtime pay. (The alleged wire fraud came in because his paychecks and W-2 forms were mailed, and employees could arrange for direct deposit of their wages.) The Ninth Circuit refused to expand RICO to allow what were essentially basic state contract claims to be brought in federal court. Furthermore, there was no predicate (underlying) RICO offense, because misrepresenting legal consequences, such as entitlement to overtime, does not constitute fraud. [*Miller v. Yokohama Tire Corp.*, 358 F.3d 616 (9th Cir. 2004)]

Although the heading for this discussion is "FLSA litigation," arbitration is also a possible means of resolving wage and hour disputes. In 2004, the Fifth Circuit confirmed that FLSA claims can be the subject of a compulsory pre-dispute arbitration agreement: there is nothing in the FLSA that requires the court system rather than arbitration to resolve disputes. The limitations on discovery in arbitration do not deprive plaintiffs of substantive rights under the FLSA. [*Carter v. Countrywide Credit Indus. Inc.*, 362 F.3d 294 (5th Cir. 2004); see also *Adkins v. Labor Ready Inc.*, 303 F.3d 496 (4th Cir. 2002) (there is no inherent conflict between the FLSA and the Federal Arbitration Act, and FLSA claims can be subject to mandatory arbitration because the FLSA's statutory language is similar to that of the ADEA, and ADEA claims are subject to mandatory arbitration)]

The Eleventh Circuit held that the right to bring FLSA collective actions is not a substantive right that can never be waived. Therefore, it upheld an arbitration agreement forbidding FLSA class claims. The Eleventh Circuit did not find any Congressional intention under the FLSA to overrule the FAA's strong support of arbitration. [*Walthour v. Chipio Windshield Repair*, 745 F.3d 1326 (11th Cir. 2014); see Christina Forte Meddin and Louisa Johnson, *Eleventh Circuit Compels Individual Arbitration of FLSA Claims, Finding Plaintiffs Have No Substantive Right to Proceed Collectively*, Seyfarth Shaw LLP (Mar. 25, 2014), available at Lexology.com; Bennet Alsher, *Eleventh Circuit Upholds Enforceability of Class Action Waiver*, Ford & Harrison LLP (Mar. 25, 2014), available at Lexolo gy.com. The Second, Fourth, Fifth, and Eighth Circuits had already taken this position. The Eastern District of Pennsylvania enforced an arbitration clause that forbids class arbitration, despite the judge's admission that he believed that the clause was unfair. The suit was brought by a waiter who charged FLSA violations (paying waiters the lower wage applicable to tipped employees, but also requiring them to do work for which they could not earn tips): *Walton v. The Rose Group*, No. 13-1674 (E.D. Pa. Dec. 11, 2013); see Saranac Hale Spencer, *Applebee's Squelches Class Action Through Arbitration Clause*, The Legal Intelligencer (Dec. 17, 2013), available at law.com]

In 2013, the Second Circuit decided two decisions (one unpublished) stating that class action waivers may be enforceable in FLSA cases. In both cases, the plaintiffs signed documents requiring all claims against the employer to be handled by individual arbitration; both plaintiffs filed putative class actions charging wage and hour violations. The Second Circuit rejected arguments that the right to pursue an FLSA collective action cannot be waived, and that the waivers were unconscionable because of excessive costs to the employees. Sutherland said that it would cost over $200,000 in attorneys' fees, costs, and expert testimony to recover what she said was under $2,000 owed to her. Relying on the Supreme Court's *Italian Colors* decision (not an employment case), the Second Circuit held that imbalance between cost and potential recovery does not preclude enforcement of a class action waiver. [*Sutherland v. Ernst & Young LLP*, 826 F.3d 290 (2d Cir. 2013); *Raniere v. Citigroup Inc.*, 533 Fed. Appx. 11 (2d Cir. Aug. 2013); see Peter C. Godfrey, Joshua Feinstein and Emma Poricanin, *Second Circuit Enforces Class Action Waivers In Two Wage And Hour Cases*, Hodgson Russ LLP (Sept. 25, 2013), available at Lexology.com; Manatt Phelps & Phillips LLP, *Reversing Circuit Precedent, 2nd Circuit Upholds FLSA Collective Action Waiver*, Lexology.com (Aug. 28, 2013). See *American Express v. Italian Colors Rest.*, 133 S. Ct. 2304 (June 20, 2013)]

The Ninth Circuit permitted an employer to compel individual arbitration after a class had been certified and a wage and hour class action had been in progress for several years. The Ninth Circuit held that *Italian Colors* requires enforcement of arbitration agreements, even in cases charging violations of federal statutes, and found the waiver of class arbitration to be valid. [*Richards v. Ernst & Young, LLP*, 734 F.3d 871 (9th Cir. 2013); see Michael T. Brody, *Ninth Circuit Compels Arbitration Of Wage And Hour Claims*, Jenner & Block (Oct. 31, 2013), available at Lexology.com; Loren Gesinksy, *D.R. Horton Who? Ninth Circuit Sends Claims to Individual Arbitration After Class Certification Below*, Seyfarth Shaw LLP (Aug. 27, 2013), available at Lexology.com]

In 2013, the California Supreme Court reversed its earlier position (that arbitration agreements waiving employees' right to make wage claims at administrative hearings are void and unenforceable). The California Supreme Court ruled that changes in federal precedent meant that the FAA preempts any state rule that waivers of administrative hearings are invalid. [*Sonic-Calabasas v. Moreno II*, 57 Cal. 4th 1109, 163 Cal. Rptr. 2d 269, 311 P.3d 184 (Cal. 2013); see Aaron I. Agenbroad, Christopher Lovrien and Jason C. Wright, *California Supreme Court Recognizes Concepcion Requires Reversal of Sonic-Calabasas But Continues to*

Display Skepticism Toward Arbitration, Jones Day (Nov. 13, 2013), available at Lexology.com]

California's Private Attorney General Act (PAGA) allows employees to bring suits if they are unable to get the California labor regulators to investigate their allegations. Successful PAGA plaintiffs receive 25% of any civil penalties imposed on the employer; the balance goes to the state. Although several California cases found class action waivers unconscionable and therefore unenforceable, in mid-2014 the California Supreme Court ruled that an employment agreement that waives the right to arbitrate grievances on a class basis is valid. However, arbitration agreements cannot make employees waive the right to bring PAGA actions. [*Iskanian v. CLS Transportation Los Angeles LLC*, No. S204032 (Cal. June 23, 2014); see Mark A. Neubauer and Meredith M. Moss, *California Law on Arbitration Changes...Again*, Carlton Fields Jorden Burt (June 23, 2014), available at Lexology.com]

§ 1.07 MINIMUM WAGE

For 2014, the federal minimum wage is $7.25/hour for non-tipped and $2.13/hour for tipped employees. The New York minimum wage went from $7.25 to $8/hour on December 31, 2013, then goes to $8.75/hour on December 31, 2014 and $9 (or the federal minimum wage, if it is higher) on December 31, 2015. On January 1, 2014, the Arizona minimum wage increased to $7.90 non-tipped, $4.90 tipped employees; the Connecticut wage is $8.70 as of January 1, 2014, $9.00 as of January 1, 2015. The Florida minimum wage rose to $7.93 ($4.91 for tipped employees) on January 1, 2014. Montana raised its minimum wage to $7.90 as of the same date. In Ohio, for businesses with annual gross receipts in excess of $292,000 a year, the minimum wage rose to $7.95/hour ($3.98 for tipped employees). Also on January 1, 2014, the Oregon minimum wage rose to $9.10/hour; the Washington minimum is $9.32. On July 1, 2014, the California minimum wage rose to $9.00 an hour, and to $10.00/hour on January 1, 2016. On January 1, 2014, the Missouri minimum wage rose to $7.50/hour.

In November 2013, New Jersey voters approved a constitutional amendment raising the minimum wage to $8.25/hour on January 1, 2014, with an annual inflation adjustment in each subsequent year. (Florida, Colorado, Nevada, and Ohio also have state constitutional provisions about the minimum wage, and annual COLAs are provided in Arizona, Colorado, Florida, Missouri, Montana, Nevada, Ohio, Oregon, Vermont, and Washington.) [Sebastian Chilco, *State Minimum Wages In 2014*, Littler Mendelson (Oct. 23, 2013), available at Lexology.com; Lawrence R. Sandak et al., *New Jersey Raises Minimum Wage By Constitutional Amendment*, Proskauer Rose LLP (Nov. 8, 2013), available at Lexology.com; Littler Mendelson, *Increased 2014 Minimum Wage For Missouri*, Lexology.com (Nov. 11, 2013); Zusha Elinson, *California Set to Raise State Minimum Wage*, WSJ.com (Sept. 13, 2013)]

The Obama administration announced that the president's executive powers would be applied to unilaterally raise the minimum wage of employees working for federal contractors. For new federal contracts, the minimum wage will be $10.10/hour. [<http://www.whitehouse.gov/the-press-office/2014/02/12/executive-order-minimum-wage-contractors> (Feb. 12, 2014); see Carol E. Lee and Eric Morath, *President to Raise Minimum Wage for Federal Contractors*, WSJ.com (Jan. 28, 2014); Peter Bakerjan, *Obama to Raise Minimum Wage Under Federal Contractors*, NYTimes.com (Jan. 28, 2014).

The minimum wage rule was published as Executive Order 13658. The Department of Labor issued a Notice of Proposed Rulemaking under 29 CFR Part 10 to implement it. The minimum wage requirement applies to people doing support work (e.g., payroll clerks; janitors) as well as those doing production work on federal contracts. However, the rule does not apply to workers who are exempt from the FLSA minimum wage requirement. [Leslie Stout-Tabackman, *DOL Issues Notice of Proposed Rulemaking to Implement New $10.10 Minimum Wage for Federal Contractors*, Jackson Lewis PC (June 12, 2014), available at Lexology.com]

Connecticut became the first state to increase the state minimum wage to $10.10/hour by 2017, reflecting the president's proposal for a minimum wage increase: AP, *Minimum Wage Bill Passes in Connecticut*, WSJ.com (Mar. 26, 2014).]

Michigan adopted an increase from $7.40 to $9.25, phased in until 2018. Several states adopted $10.10 or higher minimum wage requirements after the Executive Order was issued. Vermont called for raising the wage from $8.73 (2014) to $9.60 in 2016, $10 in 2017, and $10.50 in 2018. Minnesota adopted a $9.50 minimum wage to be paid by large employers by 2016. Rhode Island called for an increase to $9.00 an hour as of January 1, 2014. Hawaii and Maryland adopted the $10.10 minimum called for by the Executive Order; West Virginia and Delaware enacted smaller increases. [See, e.g., Eric Morath, *Michigan Raises Minimum Wage*, WSJ.com (May 28, 2014); Kelly Petrocelli, *No, It's Not Groundhog Day-Another State Raises Its Minimum Wage*, Barnes & Thornburg LLP (May 28, 2014), available at Lexology.com; AP, *Vermont: Minimum Wage to Climb to $10.50 by 2018*, NYTimes.com (June 9, 2014)]

The Obama administration asserted that the increase in the minimum wage for employees of federal contractors would benefit two million people. However, many employees of contractors were already paid more than $10.10 per hour under the Service Contract Act or the Davis-Bacon Act, which require contractors to meet locally prevailing wages. The main practical effect is likely to be experienced by food service, cleaning, and maintenance workers. For example, Fort Bragg has workers in 393 occupations that have standard Service Contract Act wage determinations; only 26 paid less than $10.10 when the wage increase was announced. [Michael D. Thompson, *New Minimum Wage For Government Contractors May Have Minimal Impact*, Epstein Becker Green (Jan. 30, 2014), available at Lexology.com]

As a result of both wage growth and increase in the number of states with higher minimum levels (21 states had higher than federal minimum wages in January 2014), the percentage of U.S. workers earning the federal minimum wage or less fell in 2013 to the lowest level since 2008. The DOL reported that 3.3 million workers were paid $7.25 or less: 4.3% of all hourly workers. In 2008, the percentage was 3.0%; it was 4.7% in 2012. About half (50.4%) of workers earning at or below the federal minimum wage level were younger than age 25; 62.4% were women. Only 35.5% of minimum wage workers were employed full-time, whereas 72.9% of all hourly workers were full-time employees. [Eric Morath, *Fewest Americans Earning Minimum Wage Since 2008*, WSJ.com (Mar. 26, 2014)]

A DOL regulation, 27 C.F.R. § 552.109(a), held that home care workers who provide companionship services to the elderly and infirm are not covered by the FLSA's minimum wage or overtime provisions, whether they were officially employed by the person receiving the care, the person's family, or a third-party agency. The Supreme Court upheld this regulation in mid-2007. [*Long Island Care at Home v. Coke*, 551 U.S. 158 (2007)]

The decision was reversed administratively by a DOL final rule adopted in September 2013, granting almost two million home health and personal care workers minimum wage and overtime protection under the FLSA. (In 1974, although Congress extended the FLSA to cover domestic service workers, they were excluded from minimum wage and overtime protection.) The rule has a delayed effective date: January 1, 2015 (not 2014). The rule applies to most direct care home care workers (home health aides, CNAs, personal care aides), although home care workers who are employed directly by the patient or family are not covered. When the rule was adopted, 15 states already required minimum wage and overtime protection, and another six states plus the District of Columbia already required payment of the minimum wage. [Web tools: <http://www.dol.gov/whd/homecare/>. See WHD News Release No. 13-1922-NAT, *Minimum Wage, Overtime Protections Extended To Direct Care Workers By US Labor Department*, <http://www.dol.gov/whd/media/press/whdpressVB3.asp?pressdoc=national/20130917.xml (Sept. 17, 2013) (benefitslink.com); Melanie Trottman and Kris Maher, *Labor Department Adds Protections for Home-Health-Care Workers*, WSJ.com (Sept. 17, 2013). States already protecting home care workers included Nevada, Montana, Illinois, Minnesota, Pennsylvania, and New York.]

Internships, unpaid or with a small stipend, are replacing traditional entry-level jobs for many recent college graduates. In January 2014, BLS reported that the general unemployment rate was 6.6%, but 8% for college graduates aged 20–24. The number of internships for college graduates is not tracked, but there is anecdotal evidence of increases in recent years. [Alex Williams, *Millennials Feel Trapped in a Cycle of Internships With Little Pay and No Job Offers*, NYTimes.com (Feb. 14, 2014)]

The Department of Labor permits unpaid internships for trainees, so the trainees can acquire usable job skills. The DOL has set out criteria for acceptable internship programs: for example, the real benefit of the training is to the trainee, not the employer; the training is similar to the curriculum of a vocational school; and trainees do not replace regular employees. The DOL has stepped up investigations, as some companies try to take advantage of the recession by obtaining unpaid labor from "interns." [Steven Greenhouse, *Growth of Unpaid Internships May Be Illegal, Officials Say*, NYTimes.com (Apr. 2, 2010)]

Two men who worked on the film "Black Swan" prevailed in a suit against Fox Searchlight alleging internship abuses and seeking back pay and an injunction. The Southern District of New York held that they were, in effect, regular employees and should have been paid. The judge said that unpaid internships are appropriate only in very limited circumstances—for example, when the work is similar to vocational training; it does not provide immediate benefits to the employer; and interns do not displace paid employees. Whether or not the intern receives academic credit is not relevant to the legal analysis. [Steven Greenhouse, *Interns File Suit Against* "Black Swan" *Producer* NYTimes.com (Sept. 28, 2011); *Glatt v. Fox Searchlight Pictures*, No. 11 Civ. 6784 (WHP) (S.D.N.Y. June 11, 2013); the ruling grants class certification to Fox Entertainment Group interns. Charlie Rose's production company made back pay payments of $1,100 each to almost 200 interns: *Judge Rules for Interns Who Sued Fox Searchlight*, NYTimes.com (June 11, 2013)]

A federal judge in New York gave preliminary approval to the largest settlement to date in an unpaid internship case: $450,000 to be paid by Elite Model Management for deliberate misclassification of unpaid interns as non-employees. The settlement provides $150,000 for class counsel and $700–$1,500 to each of more than 100 interns who did regular work. [Adam J. Smiley, *Run[A]Way Recovery: Unpaid Modeling Agency Interns Set To Cash In,* Seyfarth Shaw LLP (Jan. 15, 2014), available at Lexology.com]

In June 2013, ex-interns Ballinger and Leib sued Conde Nast in the Southern District of New York for violations of federal and state labor law, and will seek class action status. They say they were paid less than $1 an hour. [Lauren Weber, *Conde Nast Ends Internship Program*, WSJ.com (Oct. 23, 2013)]

The District Court for the Southern District of New York held that unpaid interns are not employees and, therefore, cannot sue for employment discrimination or harassment under the New York City Human Rights Law; dictum in the opinion extends this principle to Title VII and New York State human rights law as well. [*Wang v. Phoenix Satellite Television*, No. 13 Civ. 218 (PKC), 2014 WL 116220 (S.D.N.Y. Oct. 3, 2013); see Mark S. Goldstein, *NY Federal Court: Unpaid Intern Not "Employee" And Cannot Pursue NYC Human Rights Law Harassment Claim*, Reed Smith LLP (Oct. 10, 2013), available at Lexology.com]

The state of New York, and the city of New York, adopted statutes extending the protection of anti-discrimination laws to unpaid interns. However, the Wisconsin Supreme Court found that unpaid interns cannot bring anti-discrimination suits, because they are not "employees" who are subject to disciplinary action. [*Masri v. State Labor & Indus. Review Commission*, 2014 WI 81

(Wis. 2014); see Sandra R. King et al., *Courts, Lawmakers Consider Employment Protections For Interns*, Manatt Phelps & Phillips LLP (Aug. 6, 2014), available at Lexology.com]

The Supreme Court denied review of the Eleventh Circuit decision that unpaid medical billing externs for two Florida health administration firms were not employees and, therefore, were not entitled to wages. (A person who works for his own advantage, such as completing degree requirements, is not an employee for FLSA purposes.) There is a circuit split as to whether the employer or the unpaid worker is the primary beneficiary of the work, or whether a totality of circumstances test should be applied. [*Kaplan v. Code Blue Billing & Coding, Inc.*, 504 Fed. Appx. 831 (11th Cir.), *cert. denied*, 134 S. Ct. 618 (Nov. 12, 2013); see M. Scott Young, *Supreme Court Refuses To Hear Unpaid Externs' Wage Suit*, Thompson Hine LLP (Dec. 19, 2013), available at Lexology.com; Noel P. Tripp, *Supreme Court Declines Review Of Intern Compensability Issue*, Jackson Lewis LLP (Nov. 12, 2013), available at Lexology.com]

§ 1.08 DETERMINING WHO IS AN "EMPLOYEE"

There are many reasons why it becomes necessary to determine if a particular person who performs services is an independent contractor or an employee of the company for which the services are performed. For example, employment status is involved in determining who is allowed to participate in pension and benefit plans; who is entitled to overtime; who is entitled to unemployment benefits and Worker's Compensation; and who can sue under antidiscrimination laws. Although similar factors are used in analyses for different purposes, it is possible that someone will be considered an employee for some purposes but not for others.

If the individual is an employee, the employer will be responsible for paying FUTA taxes and its own share of FICA, and will have to withhold income taxes. In contrast, independent contractors are responsible for their own tax compliance.

Clearly, the company saves money if it can characterize workers as independent contractors, because it saves on taxes and benefits (even if the cash compensation is the same). To prevent abuses, this is an area where the IRS and other regulators are active in determining whether the so-called independent contractor is really an employee.

The Internal Revenue Code specifically identifies some groups as statutory employees, and others as statutory non-employees. [I.R.C. §§ 3121, 3401, 3306, 3508]

The categories of statutory employees are:

- Agents or commission drivers who deliver food products, laundry, or dry cleaning;

- Full-time traveling salespersons who solicit orders for merchandise to be delivered later;
- Full-time life insurance salespersons;
- Corporate officers;
- People who work in their own homes, but under the supervision of someone who supplies the materials to be used in work (e.g., assembling clothing components).

The Ninth Circuit affirmed the NLRB's determination that cab drivers were employees and not independent contractors, because of the substantial evidence of control over their means and manner of performance, and the non-entrepreneurial nature of the job. [*NLRB v. Friendly Cab Co.*, 512 F.3d 1090 (9th Cir. 2008)]

The Southern District of New York held that a banking "consultant" was an independent contractor for wage/hour and anti-discrimination laws purposes. He provided extended services to a bank under a series of 90-day contracts with an LLC he owned. He said that he was an employee because most of the LLC's revenue came from the bank and he kept regular hours working for the bank. But, because of the terms of the LLC's contract with the bank, his freedom to work for others, and e-mails where he described himself as a consultant he was an independent contractor. [*Sellers v. Royal Bank of Canada*, No. 12-cv-1577, 2014 U.S. Dist. LEXIS 4563 (S.D.N.Y. Jan. 8, 2014); see Noel P. Tripp, *New York Federal Court Finds Bank Properly Classified Financial Services Consultant Properly Classified As Independent Contractor*, Jackson Lewis PC (Jan. 22, 2014), available at Lexology.com]

The Fifth Circuit focused on economic reality in deciding whether an insurance company's "sales leaders" were independent contractors: whether the worker is economically dependent on the company it calls an employer, based on the degree of control over the worker, the relative investment by the worker and the company, the degree to which the potential employer determines the worker's opportunity for profit or loss; the permanency of the relationship; and the skill and initiative needed to perform the job. In this case, the insurer controlled the meaningful economic aspects of the business by hiring, firing, and assigning the agents who worked for the sales leaders (most of the sales leaders' income came from a share of the agents' commissions), so not being able to make personnel decisions limited the sales leaders' control over their income. The insurer also assigned geographic territories and controlled sales leads. The Fifth Circuit discounted the fact that the plaintiffs had signed independent contractor agreements: their subjective beliefs about their status could not overcome economic reality. [*Hopkins v. Cornerstone America*, 545 F.3d 338 (5th Cir. 2008)]

Under I.R.C. § 414(n), a long-term leased employee may have to be counted in testing pension and benefit plans for discrimination. A safe harbor is permitted when a company gets less than 20% of its non-highly compensated employees through leasing services, and if those services provide adequate pension coverage for their employees.

Bronk v. Mountain States Tel. & Tel. Inc. [140 F.3d 1335 (10th Cir. 1998)] holds that, although the Employment Retirement Income Security Act (ERISA) [29 U.S.C. §§ 1001 *et seq.*] forbids excluding employees from the plan once they have satisfied minimum age and service requirements, it is permissible to draft the plan to deny participation to leased employees, even if they are common-law employees of the sponsor company. The Tenth Circuit position is that I.R.C. § 414(n)(1)(A) merely requires that leased employees be treated as employees; it doesn't require them to be offered plan participation.

Independent contractors can be considered "beneficiaries" under ERISA plans and therefore a suit by a commodities trader that made state insurance and tort law claims about the denial of disability benefits was preempted by ERISA. [*Shyman v. Unum Life Ins. Co.*, 427 F.3d 452 (7th Cir. 2005); see *Ruttenberg v. U.S. Life Ins. Co.*, 413 F.3d 652 (7th Cir. 2005) (another case involving floor traders, for the proposition that independent contractors can be beneficiaries of ERISA plans)]

In 2010, the Eighth Circuit ruled that firing an independent contractor marketing representative and replacing her with a younger common-law employee did not violate the ADEA. The Eighth Circuit held that all factors must be considered to determine if a person is an independent contractor or an employee; the Darden factors are non-exhaustive, and no one factor is decisive. [*Ernster v. Luxco, Inc.*, 596 F.3d 1000 (8th Cir. 2010)]

The District Court for the District of Texas ordered the Department of Labor to pay more than $565,000 to compensate an oil drilling company for attorneys' fees in a case alleging that certain guards were improperly categorized as independent contractors. The district court awarded attorneys' fees because it held that the Department of Labor case should not have been pursued; interviewing more guards would have shown that they actually were independent contractors. [*Gate Guard Servs. v. Perez*, No. V-10-91, 2014 U.S. Dist. LEXIS 48859 (S.D. Tex. Apr. 9, 2014); see Andrew Ramonas, *Judge Socks Labor Department With Costs of Failed Lawsuit*, Nat'l L.J. (Apr. 9, 2014), available at law.com]

§ 1.09 STAFFING ARRANGEMENTS

The U.S. workforce can no longer be divided simply into full-time and part-time workers, or permanent workers and "temps." Many other arrangements have evolved, although, as noted above, the employer's characterization of the arrangement is not always accepted for tax and other legal purposes. Some of the possibilities are:

- Workers who are actually employed by a temporary agency that recruits, trains, and sends workers to companies that are clients of the agency;

- Long-term temporary assignments—where the temporary worker stays at one location for weeks or months, instead of being hired on a daily basis;
- Payrolling—a company wants to hire a specific person, and therefore arranges for a temporary agency to hire that person and be responsible for payment, taxes, and other employment-related matters;
- Part-time workers;
- Independent contractors—who are genuinely self-directed; have clients rather than employers who control their work; and are responsible for their own tax compliance;
- Contract workers—an arrangement usually made with technical workers who are formally employed by a technical services firm. This arrangement is often used for long-range projects, including those that require the contract worker to relocate to the employer's site;
- Leased employees—who are paid by the leasing company, which also handles administrative tasks like tax and Worker's Compensation compliance;
- Outsourcing—delegating a function such as payroll processing, guarding a worksite, or operating an employee cafeteria to a company that specializes in that function.

§ 1.10 SIZE OF THE CONTINGENT WORKFORCE

Clearly, many ways to work have evolved. The BLS uses more than one definition for "contingent workers," the broadest of which is workers "who do not expect their current job to last." The BLS also collects information about "alternative" work arrangements (employment can be both contingent and alternative at the same time).

In March 2013, about 7.6 million workers were "involuntary part-time" workers—i.e., they would have preferred full-time jobs. This was about the same number as in 2012, but three million more than in 2007. Involuntary part-time workers are not counted in the unemployment rate, but it has been estimated that about one-seventh of the workforce is now unemployed, discouraged (i.e., no longer seeking work after extended joblessness), or working on an involuntary part-time basis. About 19% of workers in 2013 worked less than 35 hours a week; this was true of 16.9% of workers at the beginning of the recession. [Catherine Rampell, *Part-Time Work Becomes Full-Time Wait for Better Job*, NYTimes.com (Apr. 19, 2013)]

Some analysts of the labor market believe that short-term employment represents a lasting structural shift; the number of temporary jobs rose 10% between March 2013 and March 2014. In March 2013, more than 2.8 million workers, about 2.5% of the workforce, were employed on a temporary basis. People move in and out of the temporary workforce; the American Staffing Association estimated that about 11 million people held a temporary job at some point in 2013. Almost 40% of temporary jobs are in manufacturing; employers value the ability to cut the workforce when demand slacks off without affecting their core workforce. The BLS said that the average pay for temporary jobs was $554, or one-third less than the general average, and wages for temporary jobs have risen more slowly than wages for permanent jobs. [Damian Paletta, *Temp Jobs Surge as Firms Contain Expenses*, WSJ.com (Apr. 6, 2014)]

Since the passage of PPACA, some restaurants, hotels, and retailers have reduced the schedules of hourly workers below 30 hours a week to avoid the pay or play requirement. For example, CKE Restaurants, which owns the Carl's Jr. and Hardee's chains, replaces full-time workers who leave with part-time workers. The HHS said that this trend will peter out: increasing the part-time census means higher turnover and lower morale. The HHS also pointed out that Romneycare did not cause major changes in employment patterns within Massachusetts. [Julie Jargon, Louise Radnofsky, and Alexandra Berzon, *Health-Care Law Spurs a Shift to Part-Time Workers*, WSJ.com (Nov. 4, 2012)]

The Northern District of Illinois held it did not violate the minimum-participation rule (ERISA § 202(a)) to deny pension participation to part time workers. The plaintiffs argued that anyone who worked over 1,000 a year is entitled to pension participation, but the district court said that it is legitimate for an employer to limit participation to certain groups or categories of workers, as long as the classification is not based on age or length of service. (In this case, the defendant, a University, defined only certain groups of employees as benefit-eligible, and the plaintiffs were not hired in benefit-eligible categories.) [*Krok v. University of Chicago*, No. 11-cv-1-01092 (N.D. Ill. Apr. 3, 2012); see Rebecca Moore, *Court Rules on Eligibility of Benefits for University Employees*, plansponsor.com (Apr. 6, 2012)]

§ 1.11 CO-EMPLOYERS

It's not always possible to say that one company is the employer and the other has no responsibility. Sometimes two companies (such as a leasing company and the company where the individual actually performs services) will be jointly liable—e.g., if the individual is injured at the workplace or harms someone else. Plaintiffs' attorneys are raising new theories of employer liability for wage and hour class actions: for example, citing defendants as joint employers who are responsible for the actions of their contractors, subcontractors, and temporary employment agencies.

Wage liability in joint employer cases is potentially imposed on anyone who makes key decisions about the economic realities of the employment relationship: e.g., corporate entities, officers, perhaps even board members. Shared or leased employees can create wage and hour duties even if the sharing or leasing employer believes that proper payments have been made. Under DOL regulations, joint employment exists when two or more employers appear to share an employee, act in each other's interests with respect to the employee, or multiple employers have common control. In most circuits, a four-factor economic reality test is applied: (1) direct or indirect power to hire, fire, discipline, or change working conditions; (2) ability to set compensation and means of payment; (3) maintenance of employment records; and (4) direct or indirect supervision and control of work schedules or conditions of employment. The recent trend is for courts to consider additional factors, such as resource sharing by employers; whether an entire business is shifted between primary and secondary employers; and whether original and secondary employers share business purpose, management, and staff. [Natasha Dorsey, *FLSA Liability Issues And Influence Over The Employment Relationship*, Foley & Lardner LLP (Nov. 11, 2013), available at Lexology.com]

Domino's delivery alleged that they were paid for far fewer hours than actually worked so managers could get higher bonuses. After dozens of workers joined the suit, the New York Domino's franchise entered into a $1.28 million settlement paying $400–$61,300 each to 61 workers, depending on their length of tenure. The New York organization filed for bankruptcy. The district court included the national organization as a defendant as a joint employer that knew or should have known about wage violations by franchisees. [Steven Greenhouse, *Domino's Franchise Settles Delivery Workers' Lawsuit for $1.28 Million*, NYTimes.com (Jan. 31, 2014)]

In 2000, the NLRB ruled that temporary workers could be included in the same bargaining unit as permanent employees, provided that the characteristics of the jobs were similar. But in 2004, the NLRB overturned this decision and ruled that the consent of both the agency supplying the workers and the company where the services are performed is required before temporary workers can be made part of the bargaining unit. [*M.B. Sturgis Inc.*, 331 N.L.R.B. 173 (Aug. 25, 2000), overruled by *Oakwood Care Center*, 343 N.L.R.B. 76 (Nov. 19, 2004)]

The First Circuit remanded a liability insurance case to determine whether a worker referred by an agency was a "leased employee" or a "temporary employee." If he was a leased employee, his employer would not be entitled to defense or indemnification under its Comprehensive General Liability (CGL) insurance policy, which excluded claims of bodily injury to employees. But if he was a temporary employee, the employer would be covered. He had worked for the same employer many times before, and his assignment was for an indefinite duration, but it was possible that other factors would lead to classifying him as a temporary employee hired to cope with a short-term workforce condition. [*Scottsdale Ins. Co. v. Torres*, 561 F.3d 74 (1st Cir. 2009)]

In the IRS' latest compliance initiative, most companies with leased employees were found to be in compliance with the rules. The few exceptions often used Employee Plans Compliance Resolution System (EPCRS) to correct their failures, so there were few enforcement actions against non-compliant plans.

Leased employees must be treated as common-law employees under the minimum participation, minimum coverage, vesting, nondiscrimination, and other pension rules.

The IRS says that there are four requirements for being a leased employee:

1. An agreement between a recipient company and a leasing organization to use the person's service, with a fee to the leasing organization;
2. The worker provides substantially full-time services for at least one year for the recipient, at least 1,500 hours in any 12-month period;
3. The recipient company has primary direction or control over services performed, such as when, where, how, in what order, and by whom services will be performed;
4. Considering all facts and circumstances, the leasing company is the common-law employer of the worker. [Guest Article, Deloitte's Washington Bulletin, *IRS Compliance Initiative Finds Most Plan Sponsors Are Correctly Applying the Leased Employee Rules* (Jan. 17, 2012) (benefitslink.com)]

In a case involving a garment factory with six subcontractors, the Second Circuit applied six factors to determine whether a company that is alleged to be a joint employer "suffers or permits" work to be done on its behalf (those factors were not exclusive; the Second Circuit allowed District Courts to consider any other factors that it finds relevant to the determination):

- Whose premises and equipment were used to perform the work?
- Did garment contractors shift work among the potential joint employers?
- Did the plaintiffs engage in a separate job that was essential to the alleged employer's production process?
- Could contractual responsibility shift to another subcontractor without material changes?
- What was the degree of supervision of the work by the alleged employer or its agents?
- Did the plaintiffs work exclusively or predominantly for the defendant? [*Zheng v. Liberty Apparel Co.*, 355 F.3d 61 (2d Cir. 2003)]

The First Circuit dismissed a sexual harassment case against a parent corporation, on the grounds that the plaintiff was actually employed by a subsidiary corporation. The First Circuit held that the subsidiary, not the parent, issued the plaintiff's W-2 form and had its own accounts, records, and payroll. [*DeLia v. Verizon Commc'ns Inc.*, 656 F.3d 1 (1st Cir. 2011); see Tara Cantore, *Worker for a Subsidiary not Parent Company's Employee*, plansponsor.com (Aug. 29, 2011)]

§ 1.12 APPLICABLE TESTS

[A] The 20-Factor Test

Determining employee status is not a simple matter. The internal IRS documents used to train tax auditors set out 20 factors to be used to determine if income tax withholding is required:

1. If the employer gives instructions that the employee has to follow;
2. If the employer trains the employee;

   ■ **TIP:** Don't assign independent contractors to take training sessions with employees!

3. If the person renders services that are specific to him or her and can't be delegated to someone else;
4. If the employer provides whatever assistants are needed for the work (someone who provides his own assistants is more likely to be an independent contractor);
5. Whether the services are integrated into the employer's ordinary work, or are separate;
6. If the work relationship continues over time;

   ■ **TIP:** Independent contractors should not be asked to be on call.

7. If the worker is subject to a shift system or other established, structured work hours or work schedule;
8. If the employer demands the worker's full-time commitment;
9. If the worker works for other companies at the same time (if the answer is "yes," it tends to imply independent contractor status, although part-time common-law employees may hold more than one job);
10. If work is done on the employer's premises;
11. If the employer determines the order or sequence of tasks to be done to accomplish the overall task;
12. If the worker has to submit regular oral or written reports;
13. If payment is by time (hour, week, or month) rather than project;
14. If the employer supplies tools and materials;
15. If the worker has to make a significant financial investment to accomplish the tasks;

16. If the employer pays business and travel expenses;
17. If the worker has a profit-and-loss interest in the underlying business of the employer;
18. If the worker gets paid by the employer's customers;
19. The employer's right to fire the worker (as distinct from carrying out the termination provisions of a contract, or refusing to renew the contract) tends to imply employee status;
20. The possibility of the worker's becoming liable to the employer if he or she quits suggests independent contractor status, because this is consistent with remedies for breach of contract.

At a minimum, if the IRS examines records and determines that common-law employees were incorrectly treated as independent contractors, the employer will have to make up the employment taxes that should have been paid but were not. Additional penalties may also be imposed. If the employer filed the required information returns (W-2s and 1099s) and did not intentionally misclassify the worker, then the penalty will be limited to 1.5% of the employee's wages, plus 20% of the FICA taxes that went unpaid because of the incorrect classification.

Those penalties are doubled if the information returns were not filed (unless there was no willful neglect, and there was reasonable cause for failure to file). Even heavier penalties are assessed if the employer not merely was mistaken about filing responsibilities, but deliberately attempted to avoid taxation.

The IRS' Topic 762, Independent Contractor vs. Employee says that evidence for characterization falls into three categories: Behavioral Control (the right, via instructions, training, etc., to direct or control how the work is done); Financial Control (whether business expenses are reimbursed; worker's investment in facilities to do the work; how the worker is paid; extent to which the worker can gain profits or risk losses); and the relationship between the parties (e.g., written contract terms; worker's ability to work for others as well; presence or absence of employment-type benefits). [<http://www.irs.gov/taxtopics/tc762.html> (revised Mar. 20, 2014). See also IRS Publication 1779, *Independent Contractor or Employee*.]

Either the worker or the firm can file IRS Form SS-8, available from <http://www.irs.gov/pub/irs-pdf/fss8.pdf> (accessed Apr. 1, 2014) to obtain an IRS determination (for federal income tax and withholding purposes) whether an individual is an employee or an independent contractor. It calls for information such as the firm's business, what the worker does (and his or her job title), and if there is a written service agreement. Part II of the form assesses behavioral control, Part III financial control, and Part IV the relationship between company and worker. Part V assesses the working conditions of salespersons and those who provide services directly to customers.

Fifteen states, including California, Connecticut, Massachusetts, New York, and Washington worked with the DOL to detect misclassification of employees as independent contractors. DOL said that, since implementing Memorandums of Understanding with states, it collected 97% more back wages in two years—a total of over $18.2 million for close to 20,000 improperly classified workers. Since the recession, DOL's Wage and Hour Division has increased its size and the budget devoted to detecting misclassification. [S. Jeanine Conley and Amy J. Traub, *Employers Under Continued Fire From Government Agencies And Legislature For Workplace Misclassification*, Baker & Hostetler LLP (Dec. 6, 2013), available at Lexology.com]

In 2011, the IRS created a new program, the Voluntary Classification Settlement Program (VCSP), under which employers can voluntarily re-classify workers to resolve past issues instead of waiting to be audited.

The Voluntary Classification Settlement Program (VCSP) was expanded in 2012 so more businesses, especially large employers, can use an inexpensive option to re-classify workers. Even employers that are being audited by the IRS (other than employment tax audits) can use the VCSP. In general, employers will be ineligible for VCSP if they did not file the required 1099s for the past three years for the workers whom they wish to reclassify, but this requirement was waived until June 30, 2013. The employer must consistently have treated the workers in question as non-employees. The ordinary payroll tax statute of limitations applies, whereas participants used to be subject to a special six-year statute of limitations. Application is made on Form 8952 at least 60 days before the employer intends to treat the workers in question as employees. Employers in the program pay about 1% of the reclassified workers' wages for the previous year, without interest or penalties. [Announcement 2012-45, 2012-51 I.R.B. 724, Announcement 2012-46, 2012-51 I.R.B. 725, discussed in IR-2012-23 IRS.gov, keyword VCSP. See *IRS Expands Voluntary Worker Classification Settlement Program; Relief From Past Payroll Taxes Available to More Employers Who Reclassify Their Workers As Employees* (Feb. 27, 2013).]

[B] Safe Harbor Treatment

In 1979, Congress passed a safe harbor provision, Section 530 of the Revenue Act of 1978. Under this provision, if an employer treats someone as an independent contractor, the IRS will not be able to reclassify that person as an employee (and will not be able to assess back taxes and penalties) as long as the employer made the characterization reasonably and in good faith. Employers can also apply for a refund of penalties that they believe were improperly assessed.

There are three safe harbor tests for reasonableness:

1. The court system or the IRS has created published authority (e.g., decisions, IRS rulings, or IRS Technical Advice Memorandums) that justifies independent contractor treatment in similar situations;
2. The IRS has already audited the employer, and the audit did not uncover any problems of worker characterization;
3. There is an established practice, within a significant segment of the employer's industry, of treating people who do similar work as independent contractors.

To use the safe harbor, the employer must have treated the person consistently as an independent contractor, including filing Form 1099 as necessary. If the person was treated as a common-law employee at any time after December 31, 1977, the safe harbor will not be available.

[C] Other Tests of Employee Status

The fundamental test is ability to control work behavior, both as to methods and as to results. This is the test used to determine employee status for ERISA purposes.

State unemployment insurance coverage typically depends either on the common-law right of control, or supplying a worker with a workplace, tools, and materials in addition to control. Most states use an "ABC test": someone who performs services is an employee, and the employer must pay unemployment insurance premiums for that person, unless:

- the person is customarily engaged in an independent trade, business, profession, or occupation;
- no direction or control is given in performing the services;
- the services are not performed in the usual course of the employer's business, or are not performed within any regular business location of the employer.

The employer must pay unemployment insurance plus penalties and interest for misclassified workers.

The FLSA test is based on economic reality. In other words, someone who is not economically dependent on a company, and is not an integral part of its operations, would not be an employee. Factors in the decision include:

- The worker's investment in facilities or equipment;
- Presence or absence of opportunity to earn profits or suffer losses due to managerial or special skills;
- Degree of control others have over the person's work;

- Permanence of the work relationship;
- Skill required to perform the services.

In this case, misclassification can lead to a duty to pay any unpaid minimum wages and overtime, plus liquidated damages, attorneys' fees, and court costs.

Nightclub chain Rick's argued that strippers are independent contractors, but a class action in the Southern District of New York held that they are hourly workers entitled to receive the minimum wage. The dancers were required to work eight-hour shifts at least three days a week, cover their tattoos with makeup, wear 4″ or higher heels, and were told how to structure their sets, proving employee status. [Patrick McGeehan, *Strippers Are Protected by Labor Laws, Judge Says*, NYTimes.com (Sept. 10, 2013)]

§ 1.13 BENEFITS FOR CONTINGENT WORKERS

This issue came to prominence in connection with Microsoft "permatemps" who were characterized by the company as freelancers and independent contractors, paid through invoices submitted to the accounts payable department rather than through the payroll process. The IRS ruled that these people were really common-law employees. They sued to be held eligible to participate in Microsoft's savings and employee stock ownership plans.

The Ninth Circuit ruled that eligibility for participation depends on being a common-law employee; the form in which payment is rendered is not relevant. The court also rejected the agreement signed by the workers, characterizing them as ineligible for plan participation, on the grounds that an agreement of this type cannot alter employee status. [*Vizcaino v. Microsoft Corp.*, 97 F.3d 1187 (9th Cir. 1996), *aff'd*, 120 F.3d 1006 (9th Cir. 1997), *cert. denied*, 522 U.S. 1088 (1998)] In 1999, the Ninth Circuit held that temporary agency workers can participate in the stock plan if they satisfy the common-law control test.

In December 2000, Microsoft agreed to pay $96.9 million to settle the *Vizcaino* case and another pending case. [The settlement agreement can be found at <http://www.bss.com/vizcaino/mssettle.pdf>.]

In March 2003, the Third Circuit decided an important case, holding that to draft a benefits plan to exclude hourly employees does not violate ERISA. [*Bauer v. Summit Bancorp.*, 325 F.3d 155 (3d Cir. 2003)] In this analysis, ERISA allows the employer to deny participation for any reason, as long as ERISA's age and length of service requirements are respected. Of course, if the employer wishes to draft the plan to cover hourly as well as salaried workers, this is permissible.

The Tenth Circuit held that it was reasonable for a pension plan administrator to rely on the method of payment, the plan provisions, and payroll data to deny coverage to a contract worker who was not on the corporate payroll. [*Scruggs v. ExxonMobile Pension Plans*, 585 F.3d 1356 (10th Cir. 2009); see Mercer Select,

Contractor Isn't Eligible "Employee" *Under Pension Plan, Appeals Court Says* (Nov. 19, 2009) (benefitslink.com)]

§ 1.14 WORK SCHEDULING

[A] Overview

To an ever-increasing extent, new (and usually longer) schedules are replacing the conventional nine-to-five or eight-to-four workday.

Some employees will have to work overtime and weekend hours occasionally. Some will have to work unconventional hours as a long-range or permanent condition of employment. As business becomes more international, it becomes necessary to be able to deal with customers during their workweek—which may occur on a very different schedule from the traditions of the U.S. workplace.

The FLSA allows employers to define the workweek as seven days starting on any day and any time of day—but, once the schedule is established, non-exempt employees must be paid overtime for work in excess of 40 hours per week. The FLSA workweek is not necessarily the same as the calendar week or the business' scheduled or pay week. Workers who are assigned to work, and do work, four 10-hour days in the same workweek are not entitled to overtime under the FLSA. However, if the employee actually works 42 hours in that week, two hours of overtime pay is required even if the employee was not scheduled for the extra work. [John E. Thompson, *The Legal Implications of Nontraditional Workweeks*, Workforce Mgmt. Online (October 2008) (benefitslink.com)]

"Flextime" is a schedule under which employees commit to working at least a certain number of hours per day, week, or month, and also agree to be present at certain agreed-upon times (e.g., for the weekly staff meeting or when customer demand is highest), but otherwise set their own hours to complete their assignments. Flextime can be an Americans with Disabilities Act (ADA) "reasonable accommodation" and can also be used by employees taking FMLA leave. [BLR/HR Daily Advisor Employee Fringe Benefit Survey Series: *Telecommuting, Flextime and Dress Code Practices* (2010) (benefitslink.com)]

There is a basic division between hourly workers, who get more pay if they put in longer hours, and salaried workers, whose compensation does not vary with the number of hours worked.

It is customary, although not legally required, for hourly employees to clock out when they leave the workplace (e.g., for lunch breaks or to do personal errands). They are not normally paid for this nonwork time. Salaried employees are usually not charged for such nonwork time, although personal time is sometimes charged against their sick leave. In a unionized workplace, the Collective Bargaining Agreement (CBA) determines issues like scheduling of meal breaks and when employees have to punch in and punch out.

See § 1.06 above, for discussion of meal and rest breaks.

[B] Telecommuting

To an increasing extent, employees are working from home or from other remote locations by "telecommuting," working on a computer and dealing with other employees and clients or customers by telephone or e-mail. Although telecommuting was hailed as a way to save money, save gasoline, and improve productivity, 2013 saw something of a reversal, with a growing belief that employees are not just more productive but more innovative when they collaborate face-to-face with co-workers. [See, e.g., Victor Fleischer, *The Benefits of Working in the Office*, NYTimes.com (Mar. 6, 2013); Claire Cain Miller and Catherine Rampell, *Yahoo Orders Home Workers Back to the Office*, NYTimes.com (Feb. 25, 2013)]

In 1997, according to the Census Bureau, 9.2 million people (7% of the workforce) worked at home at least one day per week. In 2010, this proportion rose to 9.4% of the workforce. Telecommuting was especially common on Mondays and Fridays, probably to extend the weekend. One-quarter of home-based workers are in management, business, or finance. Nearly half of at-home workers are self-employed. The Census Bureau found that employees who sometimes work at the central location and sometimes work at home tend to earn more than those who only work at the central location. In 2011, more than 8% of non-home workers had a long commute (an hour or more each way) and close to 600,000 workers had a "mega-commute" of 50 miles/90 minutes daily. [Neil Shah, *Census Report Finds More Americans Working Remotely*, WSJ.com (Mar. 5, 2013)]

According to the Census Bureau's American Community Survey, the typical telecommuter is a 49-year-old college graduate, earning about $58,000 a year, working for a company with more than 100 workers. Telecommuting rates were similar for men and women. The Telework Research Network said that, in the winter of 2013–2014, federal employees who worked at home during four snow days saved the government about $32 million. If you define telecommuting as full-time work, with at least half of it done at home, then the American Community Survey shows that there are about 3.2 million telecommuters, or about 2.6% of the workforce—a 79% increase between 2005 and 2012. The percentage of telecommuters could be as high as 30% if you include self-employed people, people whose work does not involve offices, and people who work at home one day a week or less. [Alina Tugend, *It's Unclearly Defined, but Telecommuting Is Fast on the Rise*, NYTimes.com (Mar. 7, 2014)]

The 2010 Telework Enhancement Act, Pub. L. No. 111-292, requires federal agencies to establish telework policies (including policies dealing with disaster recovery) and determine which employees can telework. [Fred Schneyer, *President Signs Federal Telework Legislation*, plansponsor.com (Dec. 13, 2010)]

There are many practical steps that a company can take to make the arrangement smoother and more productive. The "teleworkers" should sign written agreements clarifying whether they are independent contractors or common-law employees; who they will report to; whether the telework assignment is expected to be temporary or permanent; how often they will be expected to go to the office;

how many hours they will work; their work schedule; and promotion possibilities. Telework is most suitable for clearly defined projects with easily measured milestones.

Telecommuting relies heavily on electronics, so it's important to safeguard hardware and data, with backup equipment and an efficient source of online or other data storage.

Make sure the telecommuter has homeowner's insurance (if necessary, in the form of a rider or a separate policy) that covers the computer equipment against theft and damage. This is especially important if the employer supplies the equipment. A "consequential damages" provision that covers lost data and business opportunities is hard to find, but a valuable addition to the policy.

New York ruled in 2003 that a former telecommuter who lived in Florida and submitted work to a Long Island company over telephone lines was not entitled to New York unemployment benefits when the arrangement ended and the employer was no longer willing to allow her to work from home. The "work" occurred at her Florida home. [*Allen v. Comm'r of Labor*, 100 N.Y.2d 282 (N.Y. App. 2003)]

Permitting out-of-state employees to telecommute could create unexpected income tax exposure. Thirty-five states responding to a Bloomberg survey said that their state would find income tax nexus with the out-of-state employer, although that would not be true in Indiana, Kentucky, Maryland, Mississippi, Oklahoma, or Virginia. Twenty-three states said that reimbursing an employee's home office expenses would make that employee subject to income tax, but 18 states said that it would not. [Bloomberg BNA Payroll Library, *Telecommuting Creates Nexus in Many States, Survey Shows* (Apr. 25, 2012) (benefitslink.com)]

New York found that 100% of the earnings of a computer programmer who lives in Tennessee and spends only a quarter of his time in New York were taxable in New York, because he worked at home for his own convenience and not that of his employer. [*Matter of Huckaby v. State Div. of Tax Appeals*, 4 N.Y.3d 427, *cert. denied*, 546 U.S. 976 (2005)]

See <http://www.eeoc.gov/facts/telework.html> (accessed Apr. 1, 2014) for the EEOC's fact sheet on using telework to promote full employment opportunity for people with disabilities; how to supervise telecommuters; and the extent to which offering telework options is a reasonable accommodation to disability. But it has generally been held that the ADA does not require employers to grant permission to work at home as an accommodation to disabled employees. [*Raffaele v. City of New York*, 2004 WL 1969869 (E.D.N.Y. Sept. 7, 2004); *Dicino v. Aetna U.S. Healthcare*, Civil No. 01-3206 (JBS), 2003 WL 21501818 (D.N.J. June 23, 2003)] However, terminating a telework arrangement could be problematic. According to the D.C. Circuit, permitting a worker disabled by injuries to work at home for up to two days a week could be a reasonable accommodation. Therefore, a new managers' revoking permission to telecommute was discrimination. [*Woodruff v. Peters*, 482 F.3d 521 (D.C. Cir. Apr. 6, 2007); see Fred Schneyer,

FAA Telecommuting Setup Could Be Disabled Worker's Accommodation, plansponsor.com (May 8, 2007)]

[C] Integrated Time Off

An integrated time-off system is an attendance policy that gives the worker the right to take a certain number of days off per year, no matter what the reason for being away from work. The value to the employer is that it keeps people at work because they no longer have an incentive to take sick days for every minor illness just because otherwise they would lose the time. A common system is to provide a certain amount of paid vacation (e.g., one to three weeks a year), six to eight paid holidays, and six sick days a year. Employers vary as to whether they allow unused sick days to be carried over from year to year, or impose a "use it or lose it" rule.

A PTO (Paid Time Off) program integrates vacation and sick days. An Integrated Disability Program (also known as "24-hour coverage") adds disability benefits to the mix. State law determines whether the employer must cash out unused PTO upon termination. If the employer has an established policy, it must be observed; changes in time-off policy must be posted, or employees must be given written notice. The plan must specify whether PTO accrues all at once at the beginning of the year or by the month, week, or pay period. Some state laws treat accrued PTO as vested, so forfeitures are illegal.

The policy should also explain the increments in which PTO can be taken—a full day only, or half days or less? For exempt employees, deductions for personal, vacation, and sick leave can be taken only as full days, and the employer is forbidden to make deductions that exceed the time actually taken. [Keisha-Ann G. Gray, *PTO Bank Questions Answered*, Human Resource Executive Online (Sept. 8, 2008) (benefitslink.com); Jennifer Blum Feldman, *Paid Time Off Perils*, special to law.com (June 19, 2008) See Rev. Rul. 2009-31, 2009-39 I.R.B. 35 and Rev. Rul. 2009-32, 2009-39 I.R.B. 398, discussed in SunGard Relius, *IRS Offers Retirement Plan Options for Paid Time Off*, <http://www.relius.net/news/TechnicalUpdates.aspx> (Oct. 4, 2009)]

[D] Coping with Absenteeism

Employers must cope both with absenteeism (employees calling in sick when they are not sick enough to stay home) and presenteeism (when genuinely sick—and perhaps infectious—employees insist on coming to work). Epidemiologists suggest that a person with a contagious illness stay home for at least 24 hours after the fever and symptoms abate, About half (51%) of respondents to SHRM's survey said that they maintain a paid time-off bank, giving employees access to a specified number of days off for all reasons, up from 42% in 2009.

When a flu or other epidemic occurs, some employers temporarily allow employees additional sick leave without reducing their vacation entitlement. [Sue Shellenbarger, *The Art of Calling In Sick—Or Toughing It Out*, WSJ.com (Oct. 23, 2012)]

EEOC technical guidance, "*Pandemic Preparedness in the Workplace and the Americans With Disabilities Act*," permits employers to ask employees if they have cold or flu symptoms such as fever, sore throat, or chills; this is not a disability-related inquiry. It is also permissible to send employees home if they have symptoms. It is permissible for employers to adopt workplace infection control practices such as those set out on the OSHA Web page, "Workplace Safety and the Flu." [Melanie Trottman, *Flu Season Amplifies Calls for Paid Sick Leave*, WSJ.com (Feb. 22, 2013)]

[E] Catastrophe Planning

Employers must be prepared for a variety of adverse events, including the man-made (terrorist attacks) and natural (weather events and epidemics). In addition to practical questions such as determining when the business will be able to open and assembling the necessary staff (when travel conditions may be difficult), the disaster will have employment tax consequences, and many other laws may be invoked as well.

IRS Notice 2006-59 permits creation of a disaster leave donation program: other employees donate leave time for the benefit of co-workers who miss work because of a presidentially declared disaster that causes severe hardship to the employee or family. The leave must be used in connection with the disaster, and the severity of the disaster determines the reasonable period of time during which leave can be taken. At the end of the specified post-disaster period, any unused leave must be returned to the donor. [Peter Alwardt, *Tax Considerations in Implementing Donated Leave Policies*, Eisner Amper (Jan. 14, 2013) (benefitslink .com)]

A natural disaster can require the employer to take steps under many different statutes. Under the FLSA, if the worksite is open but an exempt employee chooses to remain at home for weather-related reasons, the DOL considers this a personal absence. For full days when an exempt employee did not report to work, the employer can treat it as unpaid leave or subtract it from the employee's accrued vacation time. If an employee is absent for one or more full days for personal reasons, the employee is still deemed to be salaried (rather than paid by the hour) if salary deductions are made on account of the absence—but the employer must deduct full days, not partial days. The employer is permitted to deduct partial days from the employee's leave bank, but if the leave bank is exhausted, it is not permissible to make salary deductions. Once exempt employees return to work, they can be required to make up the lost time. Non-exempt workers can be required to "catch up" only if they are paid overtime for hours over 40 per week.

Employees who are on call and not free to leave (such as maintenance workers assigned to remain onsite during a disaster to perform emergency repairs) must be paid even if they are not given any work assignments. Employees must also be compensated if they are required to wait (e.g., stay in the workplace waiting for power to be restored).

There is a WARN Act exception for closings or layoffs caused by disasters, although the employer must still give as much notice as possible and must explain why less than 60 days' notice was given. USERRA forbids taking adverse employment action against a person (e.g., a National Guard member) who is called up for active duty during an emergency. The employer is entitled to timely notice of the call-up, although it can be given in writing or orally, and can come either from the service member or from an officer.

Employers must make decisions about benefit coverage. If coverage will continue during a plant closure, the employer should consult its benefits vendor. If the plan is subject to COBRA, the plan administrator must be notified if any employees lose coverage because they are not working. At that point, the administrator must provide COBRA notice; in practical terms, the notice may not be received if the employee has had to evacuate from the last known address on file with the employer. (The legal obligation is simply to send notice to the last known address.) Someone who is physically or emotionally injured by the disaster may also be entitled to ADA reasonable accommodation, as long the accommodation does not impose undue hardship on the employer.

OSHA obligates employers to protect employees from unreasonable dangers in the workplace, which could mean keeping them out of harm's way before, during, and after a disaster. Employees who are forced to work under unsafe conditions, or who suffer retaliation for refusing or reporting unsafe conditions, may be entitled to whistleblower protection. The National Labor Relations Act may require changes in a workplace that has become unsafe. Refusing to work under dangerous conditions might constitute protected concerted activity, even if only one employee is acting on behalf of others.

Unionized employers may be subject to force majeure clauses in the CBA that explain rights and duties in emergencies. If the disaster causes enough damage to force the employer to go out of business, the employer does not have an obligation to bargain with the union about the decision to go out of business—but effects bargaining will be required. A number of states provide that the employer's Unemployment Insurance experience account will not be charged for layoffs caused by a natural disaster. The Disaster Unemployment Assistance program helps people, including farm owners and the self-employed, who lost jobs as a direct result of a declared disaster. [Duane Morris LLP, *When Disasters Strike: Pay, Leave and Related Issues* (Oct. 31, 2012) (benefitslink.com)]

Under Code § 139 and IRS guidance, when a disaster occurs, the employer can provide cash or benefits to assist employees affected by it. These payments are exempt from federal income and employment tax, and are deductible by the employer. Code § 139(a) provides that qualified disaster relief payments are not included in the employee's gross income; § 139(b) defines a qualified disaster relief payment as one that pays or reimburses personal, family, living, or funeral expenses caused by a disaster. A disaster, in turn, is defined as a presidentially declared disaster, a disaster caused by a common carrier accident, terrorism, military action, or anything else determined by the Secretary of the Treasury to be a catastrophic event. Recipients will probably not be taxed on amounts paid by a federal, state, or local government agency. But amounts are excluded from income only to the extent that the same expense is not already covered, e.g., by insurance.

Also covered are the repair or rehabilitation of the employee's personal residence (whether owned or rented) and repair or replacement of the contents of the personal residence required by the disaster. See IRS Publication 3833. However, replacement of lost wages or other income is not considered a qualified disaster relief payment. [Mary Hughes, *Employers May Provide Tax-Free Relief To Employees Hit By Storm, Attorney Says*, Human Resources Report (Nov. 5, 2012) (benefitslink.com)]

IRS Announcement 2012-44, 2012-49 I.R.B. 663, provides relief from some verification procedures under retirement plans for plan loans, hardship distributions, and other pension distributions. [<www.irs.gov/uac/Newsroom/Help-for-Victims-of-Hurricane-Sandy> is the list of covered disaster areas entitled to an extension on filing Form 5500, plus other relief. See EBSA News, *US Department Of Labor Issues Compliance Guidance For Employee Benefit Plans In Wake Of Hurricane Sandy* (Nov. 20, 2012) (benefitslink.com).]

Severe weather conditions in recent winters highlighted the need for companies to maintain a policy about when employees are required to come to work despite weather problems; when they can work at home; and if they will be paid if it is impossible to get to work. (Another option is to give employees a choice between extra pay and comp time if they are able to come to work despite severe weather conditions.) When a storm is forecast for the next day or day after, advise employees to take work home with them, but let employees wait to come in until after the roads have been plowed. Sometimes it is worthwhile to make a deal with a local hotel near the workplace, where key employees can stay and avoid commuting problems. However, the workload is also likely to be low—if employees can't get to work, neither can customers. [Sarah E. Needleman, *It's Snowing. Do We Get the Day Off?*, WSJ.com (Feb. 4, 2011)]

NIOSH has a summary of cold stress conditions, with suggestions about protecting outdoor workers: scheduling maintenance and repair for the warmer months, or at least the warmer part of the day; provide extra or relief workers for long jobs; provide warm drinks in heated break areas; train employees about appropriate dress and how to recognize cold damage; provide extra socks and blankets; and keep a thermometer and chemical hot packs in the first aid kit. OSHA forbids retaliation against workers who reject unsafe work assignments. OSHA fall protection requirements are in effect if employees are ordered to the roof to remove snow. Also see OSHA's hazard alert about falls during snow removal. The NLRA also allows workers to refuse to work in unsafe conditions but, unless the employer agrees that driving is too dangerous, it is lawful to fire employees who refuse to drive to work in difficult conditions.

If the workplace does not open, or shuts down early for weather and sends non-exempt workers home in the middle of the shift, they are only entitled to pay for time actually worked. But some states, such as California, have report-in laws requiring payment when employees are scheduled to work but are sent home early.

If exempt employees work at all, they must be paid for the full week, because the regulations do not include weather closures in circumstances permitting pay deductions. But if the business was closed for the entire week, and exempt employees did not work at all, the employer is not obligated to pay them. Exempt employees can be required to use paid time off such as vacation or personal time. If an employee has used up all paid time off, the employer is not permitted to take a salary deduction. If the business is open and an exempt employee chooses to stay home, accrued leave can be deducted from the individual's leave bank. If paid leave has been exhausted, pay can be reduced for full days of absences (see 29 C.F.R. § 541.602(b)(1)). If the employer knows that employees are working from home, they should be compensated for work time. [Sara H. Jodka, *Oh The Weather Outside Is Frightful! How Employers Can Handle The Impact Of Inclement Weather (Polar Vortex Anyone?) And What NIOSH, OSHA, The NLRA And The FLSA Have To Say About It*, Porter Wright Morris & Arthur LLP (Jan. 6, 2014), available at Lexology.com; Michael T. Miller, *Weather-Related Closures And Absences Under The FLSA*, Briggs and Morgan (Dec. 17, 2013), available at Lexology.com]

§ 1.15 OVERTIME AND OVERTIME PLANNING

[A] Generally

One of the major functions of the FLSA is to require "time and a half for overtime" to be paid to all nonexempt hourly employees who work more than 40 hours in a work week. They must receive 150% of their normal pay rate for the additional hours.

The District Court for the Eastern District of New York held that the one worker employed by a building owner as janitor/general laborer could not bring a FLSA claim for overtime. The FLSA did not apply because there was only one employee engaged in commerce or the production of goods for commerce; and there is a New York wage order making janitors ineligible for overtime under the New York Labor Law. [*Myung Seob Lee v. Kim*, No. 12-cv-316 (RER), 2013 U.S. Dist. LEXIS 121952 (E.D.N.Y. Aug. 27, 2013); see Noel P. Tripp, *New York Judge Concludes That Employer With One Employee Not Covered By FLSA*, Jackson Lewis LLP (Sept. 3, 2013), available at Lexology.com]

According to the D.C. Circuit, the FLSA does not require employers to pay overtime when a worker puts in more than eight hours in a particular day, as long as his or her hours for the week as a whole do not exceed 40. The plaintiff alleged that her CBA required payment of overtime, but even if that is true, the court ruled that it did not have federal subject matter jurisdiction over a contract interpretation claim. [*Fernandez v. Centerplate/NBSE*, 441 F.3d 1006 (D.C. Cir. 2006)]

Certain categories of employees are exempt from the FLSA's minimum wage and overtime provisions. [29 U.S.C. § 213(a)(1)] The major exempt categories are executives, administrators, professionals, and outside salespersons. Whether a person is exempt depends on the actual duties of the job, not the job title. Exemption is based on "primary duties"—what the person does for 50% or more of the work time.

Exempt workers do not have to be paid for weeks in which they do not work at all, but otherwise 29 C.F.R. § 541.118(a) provides that their salary cannot be reduced based on the number of hours worked or the number of hours of absences. The employer cannot reduce the wages of exempt employees for absences that were caused by the employer or the operating requirements of its business. Nor can the employer take deductions to penalize an exempt worker for work place infractions, other than violations of major safety rules.

Specifically, docking a worker's pay for "variations in quantity or quality of work" is appropriate for hourly workers who are entitled to overtime, but not for exempt workers. The real test, however, is whether reductions are ever taken. In 1997, the Supreme Court ruled that police officers were exempt salaried employees, even though the employee manual said that pay could be docked for various disciplinary infractions: the mere possibility didn't make them nonexempt. [*Auer v. Robbins*, 519 U.S. 452 (1997)]

[B] Categories of Exempt Employees

The FLSA defines executives, professionals, and other categories of workers, based on their main responsibilities. However, the statute left many important questions unresolved, and furthermore the existing regulations expressed obsolete concepts about the workplace and the economy.

Until a final rule was promulgated in 2004, the minimum salary test for the white-collar exemption under the FLSA had remained pegged at $155 a week since 1976. The 2004 Final Rule nearly triples this, to $455 a week. DOL also believed that changes in work categories were necessary because of shifts in the composition of the workforce since 1949—the last time the categories were changed!

The final rule (effective August 23, 2004) provides for both a minimum salary (anyone who earns less than $23,660 a year is automatically entitled to overtime) and a maximum. Employees who earn a total of more than $23,660 in combined U.S. and foreign currency qualify for the white-collar exemption even if their U.S.-currency earnings are below that amount: FLSA 2006-17 (May 23, 2006).

Highly compensated white-collar workers earning $100,000 or more a year are automatically exempt from overtime as long as their salary is at least $455 a week, and as long as they regularly perform at least one duty as an exempt executive, professional, or administrative worker.

The Final Rule applies only to white-collar workers. Blue-collar workers "who perform work involving repetitive operations with their hands, physical skill and energy" (69 Fed. Reg. 22122) are entitled to overtime pay.

On March 13, 2014, President Obama signed a memorandum about the exempt status of low-salaried workers such as managers of fast food restaurants and convenience stores, who are currently exempt as long as they earn at least $455/week. The president said that the current FLSA exemptions are outdated. (The California threshold is $640; New York's is $600). The memo orders the DOL to issue new regulations, but the new salary level was not specified; it was believed that it might be as high as $984/week. It was expected that the DOL regulations, when issued, will either modify the primary duty test, or replace it with more stringent standards. [*Presidential Memorandum-Updating and Modernizing Overtime Regulations*, <http://www.whitehouse.gov/the-press-office/2014/03/13/presidential-memorandum-updating-and-modernizing-overtime-regulations> (Mar. 13, 2014); see Jonathan R. Secrest, *President Obama Orders Revisions To Rules On Overtime Pay*, Roetzel & Andress (Mar. 14, 2014), available at Lexology.com; Damian Paletta and Colleen McCain Nelson, *Obama Seeks to Expand Overtime Eligibility*, WSJ.com (Mar. 12, 2014); Michael D. Shear and Steven Greenhouse, *Obama Will Seek Broad Expansion of Overtime Pay*, NYTimes.com (Mar. 11, 2014)]

In response to criticisms of chain stores and other operations charged with giving low-level personnel "management" titles (to preclude them from overtime eligibility), the amended version of 29 C.F.R. § 541.2 provides that "a job title alone is insufficient to establish the exempt status of an employee. The exempt or nonexempt status of any particular employee must be determined on the basis of whether the employee's salary and duties meet the requirements of the regulations in this part."

The exemptions discussed here all require that the person be compensated on a salary rather than hourly basis, and that the person must earn at least $455 a week. A person is considered to be paid on a salary basis if the set compensation for the pay unit (e.g., week or month) is not subject to reductions based on variations in how much work the person does, or how well the work is performed.

The general rule is that as long as a salaried worker does any work in a pay period, he or she must be paid for the entire period, and deductions must not be taken for time when the employee is ready, willing, and able to work but there is no work for him or her to do. However, employers of salaried workers are permitted to make deductions for full days away from work that the employee takes as personal days; sick days taken under a bona fide plan; unpaid FMLA leave; or when the employee is suspended for violating a major safety rule or for other workplace infractions. Deductions can also be made if the last week a salaried employee works is a partial week.

An individual can also be paid on a fee basis for administrative, professional, or computer-oriented work while remaining exempt from overtime entitlement. The minimum salary test is applied to work done on a fee basis by comparing the compensation and the time spent to complete the assignment with the standard $455 weekly salary.

■ **TIP:** Even if they do not satisfy the salary test, outside salespersons, teachers, lawyers, and doctors are exempt from overtime. See <http://www.dol.gov/esa/regs/compliance/whd/fairpay/fs17g_salary.htm> for discussion of issues about salaried employees. See also Snell & Wilmer's Overtime Compliance Guide and Audit, <http://www.swlaw.com/publications/files/Overtime_Guide_and_Audit_Web.pdf> for flow charts for determining which employees are entitled to overtime.

A worker will be considered an executive—and therefore not entitled to overtime pay because of executive status—if:

- The person's primary duty is management either of the entire enterprise that employs him or her, or a recognized subdivision or department of the enterprise.
- He or she "customarily and regularly" directs the work of two or more fellow employees (or two full-time equivalents in an enterprise that has some part-time workers).
- He or she has hiring and firing authority, or can make suggestions that "are given particular weight" with respect to (29 C.F.R. §§ 541.100, 541.102).

The C.F.R. defines "management" as activities such as hiring and training employees, appraising their work performance, assigning tasks, budgeting, and complying with legal requirements. Section 541.106 explicates the concept of "concurrent duties" (the issue involved when there is controversy about whether a person is a manager or a rank-and-file worker). If a person otherwise qualifies as an executive, he or she remains exempt despite the performance of concurrent duties (nonexempt work such as waiting on customers, stocking shelves, or cleaning business premises, undertaken by a person whose primary duty is management). However, a person such as a factory supervisor whose main duties are nonexempt does not become an executive merely because he or she occasionally has to make discretionary decisions.

A "business owner" (29 C.F.R. § 541.101) owns a bona fide equity interest of 20% or more in the business that employs him or her, and who is actively employed in the management of the business. A business owner is considered a manager and therefore is not entitled to overtime, even if he or she earns less than $455 a week.

An exempt administrative worker is primarily engaged in "work directly related to the management or general business operations" of the employer company or its customers. See 29 C.F.R. § 541.201—work in "functional areas" such as purchasing, marketing, HR, public relations, etc. The employee must be required to exercise discretion and independent judgment on significant matters. 29 C.F.R. § 541.203 provides examples of the administrative worker exemption, e.g., insurance claims adjusters; financial services employees who collect and analyze information about customers' income, assets, and investments; and executive assistants and administrative assistants. There is a specific provision (§ 541.203(e)) clarifying that personnel clerks are typically not exempt from overtime, but human resources managers "who formulate, interpret or implement employment policies" are exempt. A number of cases have been decided on the administrative worker exemption.

Insurance claims adjusters are exempt because they exercise discretion and make independent judgment after, e.g., investigating and settling claims and making repair adjustments: *Robinson-Smith v. GEICO*, 590 F.3d 886 (D.C. Cir. 2010); *Roe-Midgett v. CC Services, Inc.*, 512 F.3d 865 (7th Cir. 2008); *Miller v. Farmer's Ins. Exchange*, 466 F.3d 853 (9th Cir. 2006), amended 481 F.3d 1119 (9th Cir. 2007); *Harris v. Superior Court (Liberty Mut. Ins. Co.)*, 53 Cal. 4th 170 (Cal. 2011).

The Seventh Circuit held that an insurance company employee who was the expert on particular insurance products and trained sales staff about them, was an exempt administrative employee. He characterized himself as a salesperson who did not use discretion or independent judgment, but the Seventh Circuit held that he used discretion and independent judgment to assist salespersons. [*Blanchar v. Std. Ins. Co.*, 736 F.3d 753 (7th Cir. 2013); Noel P. Tripp, *Seventh Circuit Finds Insurance Company's Internal "Answer Man" Proper Classified As Exempt Administrative Employee*, Jackson Lewis LLP (Dec. 3, 2013), available at Lexology.com. See also *Schaefer-LaRose v. Eli Lilly & Co.,* 679 F.3d 560 (7th Cir. 2012).]

Mortgage loan officers are exempt on the basis of discretion and judgment, even though they use software to help choose the best products for customers: FLSA 2006-31 (Sept. 27, 2006). In a major victory for the Mortgage Bankers Association, the D.C. Circuit denied en banc review to a panel decision rejecting DOL's 2010 reclassification of mortgage loan officers as non-exempt. To change the status of the loan officers, DOL would have to complete the rulemaking process. The en banc D.C. Circuit held that the Administrative Procedure Act requires an agency to post notice and get comments about regulations that are inconsistent with previous regulations. [Robert E. Sheeder, *D.C. Circuit Halts Department Of Labor's Reclassification Of Loan Officers*, Bracewell & Giuliana LLP (Oct. 7, 2013), available at Lexology.com]

But the Second Circuit held, in 2009 that loan approval underwriters were non-exempt production employees with respect to loans. They simply applied an existing credit policy. It was also relevant that they could earn bonuses for processing more loans per day. [*Davis v. J.P. Morgan Chase & Co.*, 587 F.3d 529 (2d Cir. 2009)]

The Second Circuit decided that someone who was paid a base salary and commissions, but not overtime, to sell advertising in a publication most of whose revenues came from advertising was a salesperson and not an administrative employee. An employee who makes specific sales to individual customers is considered a salesperson for FLSA purposes, whereas someone who generally encourages greater sales among all customers is an administrative employee. [*Reiseck v. Universal Commc'ns of Miami, Inc.*, 591 F.3d 101 (2d Cir. 2010)]

The Northern District of Illinois ruled that employees who are paid commissions on goods and services are generally exempt from overtime, but piece-rate employees are not. Commissions are not earned until the sale is actually made. The District Court for the Northern District of Illinois held in 2013 that window washers, who said they were paid piece rates based on the number of windows washed, were commissioned (and exempt) because their work was dependent on sales. [*Alvarado v. Corporate Cleaning Servs.*, No. 07 C 06361, 2013 U.S. Dist. LEXIS 163894, 164 Lab. Cas. (CCH) P36,181 (N.D. Ill. Nov. 18, 2013); see James F. Ehrenberg, *Commission Or Piece-Rate? The Distinction Is Significant For FLSA Purposes*, Barnes & Thornburg LLP (Nov. 22, 2013), available at Lexology.com]

Overtime is not required for employees who earn more than 150% of the minimum wage when over half of their compensation comes from commissions. The California Court of Appeal held that employment recruiters were commissioned employees. A commission is a percentage of the price paid for selling a product or service. Recruiting employees for others is a kind of sale, and the firm was paid only if a successful placement was made. [*Muldrow v. Surrex Solutions Corp.*, 208 Cal. App. 4th 1381, 146 Cal. Rptr. 3d 447 (2012)]

Yet another overtime exemption applies to those employed in "a bona fide professional capacity," defined by 29 C.F.R. § 541.300 either as work requiring advanced knowledge acquired by formal education, or "requiring invention, imagination, originality or talent in a recognized field of artistic or creative endeavor." In addition to the traditional "learned professions" (e.g., medicine, law, engineering, teaching, pharmacy), registered nurses, registered or certified medical technicians, and physician's assistants, and dental hygienists are considered to be professionals. 29 C.F.R. § 541.302 defines creative professionals as those whose primary work requires creativity and artistry, e.g., in music, writing, acting, or graphic arts—work that cannot be done by a person with only general "manual or intellectual ability and training."

The Second Circuit found that a pharmacist was exempt from overtime under the FLSA's highly compensated employee exemption. His base salary for a 44-hour week was $1,250, with additional compensation for voluntarily working another 16–36 hours a week; his total compensation exceeded $100,000 a year. Compensation for the extra shifts was determined by dividing his weekly base salary by 44, multiplying by the number of hours worked, and adding $6 per hour in premium pay. DOL regulations (§ 541.601) make a person with total annual compensation over $100,000 exempt if the person customarily and regularly performs one or more exempt duties of an executive, administrative, or professional employee. The plaintiff admitted that he satisfied this "duties" test but said that the regulation was superseded by § 541.604, dealing with exempt pay computed on an hourly, daily, or shift basis with a minimum guarantee plus extras. The Second Circuit found that the two regulations apply to different groups, and § 541.604 applies only to those who earn less than $100,000 a year, so there is an overtime safe harbor for persons who earn more than $100,000 a year. [*Anani v. CVS RX Servs., Inc.*, 730 F.3d 146 (2d Cir. 2013); see William F. Allen, *Second Circuit Clarifies Application Of The Highly Compensated Employee Exemption*, Littler Mendelson (Oct. 10, 2013), available at Lexology.com]

The Fifth Circuit agreed that nurse practitioners and physician's assistants are not exempt and are entitled to be paid overtime. Although 29 C.F.R. § 541.3(d) specifically calls physician's assistants, nurses, and technologists "learned professionals" who are exempt under the duty requirement, they are not listed as one of the professions that fall outside the "salary basis" exception. They are paid by the hour; they are not licensed to practice medicine; and their work is similar to the work of non-exempt registered nurses. [*Belt v. Emcare, Inc.*, 444 F.3d 403 (5th Cir. 2006); see 69 Fed. Reg. 22,122 (Apr. 23, 2004) for the § 541.3(e) Regulation] Respiratory therapists do not need specialized advanced education and therefore are not a learned profession: FLSA 2006-26 (Sept. 27, 2006).

Systems analysts, computer programmers, software engineers (or people doing the same kind of work, even if their title changes to respond to this fast-moving field) are exempt from overtime under 29 C.F.R. § 541.400. There is an alternative test for computer professionals: a person who earns either the ordinary $455/week salary test, or an hourly rate of $27.63/hour or more, is not entitled to overtime. The Final Rule exempts computer professionals from overtime, but the exemption refers to those who, e.g., design and develop hardware and software, not to people who assemble or repair computers.

According to the Sixth Circuit, a computer help desk employee who does troubleshooting, maintenance, and support is not a "computer professional" exempt under the FLSA, because the work is not analytical enough; programming, software engineering, and systems analysis were not involved, and his work was completely directed by others, not performed with individual initiative. [*Martin v. Ind. Mich. Power Co.*, 381 F.3d 574 (6th Cir. 2004)] The final white-collar exemption, for Outside Sales staff, is defined by § 541.500 as workers whose primary duty is making sales or getting orders or contracts. The mainstay of such an employee's work is performed outside the employer's place of business. This category does not include mail, telephone, or online sales unless these media are only used to set up a personal appointment. When it comes to "drivers who sell" (§ 541.504), the test is whether sales predominates over delivery (thus making the person exempt) or whether delivery predominates (making him or her eligible for overtime).

The Third Circuit refused to revive an FLSA suit brought by NutriSystem salespersons, even though the DOL agreed with their position and filed an amicus brief. The Third Circuit found that their compensation falls within the FLSA's "retail commission" exception because it was proportional to the cost of products sold. [*Parker v. NutriSystem Inc.*, 620 F.3d 274 (3d Cir. Sept. 7, 2010)]

The Supreme Court resolved a circuit split about the proper treatment of drug "detailers" in June 2012. The Supreme Court ruled that these pharmaceutical representatives are outside salespersons exempt from overtime. [*Christopher v. SmithKline Beecham*, 132 S. Ct. 2156 (2012); see Marcia Coyle, *A Big Win for Pharma Companies in Overtime Case*, Nat'l L.J. (June 18, 2012) (law.com)]

The final Rule does not affect the eligibility of blue-collar workers for overtime pay. Its examples of blue collar workers are construction workers, carpenters, electricians, plumbers, laborers, etc. (69 Fed. Reg. 22122; 29 C.F.R. § 541.3). As a general rule, public safety workers (e.g., police officers, firefighters, paramedics, Emergency Medical Technicians) are also entitled to overtime. Employers continue to be bound by whatever overtime arrangements they have entered into under Collective Bargaining Agreements, and state laws that are more protective of workers are not preempted by the Final Rule (29 C.F.R. § 541.4). However, the Sixth Circuit held that police officers on airport duty did not prove that they were entitled to overtime pay for times when they were required to wear pagers and stay within a set radius of the airport in order to report when summoned for an emergency. The Sixth Circuit said that the test of whether comp time has to be granted is whether off-duty time is so severely burdened that workers cannot control their use of the time (29 C.F.R. § 553.221(d)). [*Adair v. County of Wayne*, 452 F.3d 482 (6th Cir. 2006); see Fred Schneyer, *Detroit Cops Lose OT Court Fight*, plansponsor.com (July 11, 2006)]

[C] Payment of Overtime

Nonexempt hourly employees must be paid time-and-a-half (150% of their normal pay rate, including commissions) when they work more than 40 hours in any work week. Work time is all the time when the employer controls the employee's actions, including times the employee is required to be on duty or at a prescribed place. However, bona fide meal periods are not considered work time. Ordinary commuting to work is not work time, Work-related travel, such as an assignment to deliver something or go to a meeting at a client's office, is work time.

These are some items that may require compensation or overtime:

- Rest breaks under 20 minutes;
- Down time or on-call time that prevents the employee from carrying out personal business;
- Preparation before shift or clean-up after shift;
- Mandatory classes, meetings, or conventions;
- Travel time other than normal commuting.

The workweek doesn't have to be Monday–Friday, 9–5: it can be defined as any 168 consecutive hours, starting any time. It doesn't have to be the same as the payroll period. Different work groups or individuals can have different workweeks. Usually, once an employer sets a workweek, it has to abide by it—but a permanent change that is not a subterfuge to evade the FLSA's overtime requirements is permitted. [See 29 C.F.R. § 778.104, averaging a long and a short week to see if overtime is payable is not allowed]

Once it is determined that employees have been misclassified as exempt, the question arises whether they are entitled to time and a half for overtime hours or only to the half time premiums. The Supreme Court has held that the employer could use a fluctuating work week (FWW) calculation, becoming liable for only the half time premium. A 2012 Seventh Circuit case also upholds this methodology. For example, a misclassified employee who worked 50 hours a week would receive time and a half for 10 hours a week, at a rate of the weekly salary divided by 40, under the time-and-a-half methodology. The FWW calculation would entitle the employee to the weekly salary divided by 50, with the half-time premium paid on this lower rate. In 2013, the Fifth Circuit applied the FWW method for 16 store managers, holding that the correct formula was their weekly salary divided by the number of hours worked, plus half time for hours worked in excess of 40 a week. [*Ransom v. M. Patel Enters., Inc.*, 734 F.3d 377 (5th Cir. 2013); see Gregory V. Mersol, *Fifth Circuit Applies Fluctuating Work Week In FLSA Misclassification Case*, Baker & Hostetler LLP (Aug. 30, 2013), available at Lexology.com. See also *Overnight Motor Transp. v. Missel*, 316 U.S. 572 (1942); *Urnikis-Negro v. Am. Family Prop. Servs.*, 616 F.3d 665 (7th Cir. 2012)]

A non-exempt paralegal at a law firm was reclassified as exempt because she supervised a legal secretary. After she was fired in 2010, she filed a collective action for overtime for paralegals whom she described as non-exempt. The jury found for the plaintiff, holding that the firm willfully violated the FLSA by misclassifying her, and awarded 274 hours of overtime. The district court used the FWW method, setting actual damages at about $4,000. The plaintiff appealed and the Fifth Circuit agreed that FWW is only appropriate in a misclassification case if the employer and employee have agreed that the employee will receive a fixed salary for fluctuating hours. In this case, the plaintiff's salary was intended to cover only a standard workweek of 37.5 hours; the case was remanded to calculate the overtime. [*Black v. SettlePou P.C.*, 732 F.3d 492 (5th Cir. 2013); see

Christopher E. Moore and Lindsey M. Johnson, *How To Calculate Unpaid Overtime, The Sequel: Fifth Circuit Rejects FWW Method In Misclassification Cases*, Ogletree Deakins (Nov. 7, 2013), available at Lexology.com; see also *Ransom v. M. Patel Enters. Inc.*, 734 F.3d 377 (5th Cir. 2013)]

[D] Case Law on Overtime

In a shaky economy, FLSA litigation (and employment discrimination litigation) predictably increases, because many potential plaintiffs are no longer employed and do not fear that filing suit will lead to their discharge. Employers often take the position that the FLSA rules are outdated, and fail to represent the current realities of the workplace, because the statutory categories represent outmoded categories.

Issues often raised in litigation include misclassification of workers as exempt and demands that workers (especially in the retail and restaurant industries) work "off the clock."

Many important cases have reached a verdict or settlement.

The largest overtime pay class action ever to be tried was settled in September 2004 for over $200 million, resolving claims that Farmers Insurance Exchange wrongfully deprived approximately 2,400 Californian claims adjusters of overtime pay. A separate multidistrict case covering claims adjusters nationwide in the District Court for the District of Oregon resulted in a $53 million judgment for the plaintiffs. [*Bell v. Farmers Ins. Exchange*, No. 774013-0 (Alameda Cnty. Superior Court); *In re Farmers Insurance Exchange Claims Representatives' Overtime Pay Litig.*, MDL No. 1439 (D. Or. 2004)]

High Performance Ropes of America was convicted of one felony count of making false statements, and was ordered to pay $165,356 in back overtime and liquidated damages to 31 employees. In addition, a civil money penalty of $12,100 was imposed for repeat willful violations; the court ordered an additional $10,000 fine. The business owner, plant manager, and office manager were convicted on separate felony counts. The case was prosecuted by the U.S. Attorney for the Western District of Texas. Three officers were sentenced to time served and probation for felonies including making false statements and aiding and abetting illegal reentry into the United States. [*High Performance Ropes of America*, No. 6: 13-cr-00140-WSS-1 (DOL Wage and Hour Division 2013); see DOL Press Release No. 13-1770-DAL, *US Department Of Labor Recovers More Than $165,000 For Workers* (Oct. 17, 2013) <http://www.dol.gov/whd/media/press/whdpressVB3.asp?pressdoc=Southwest/20131017.xml> (benefitslink.com)]

It's important to note that not all employee overtime claims result in victory.

The Seventh Circuit ruled that time (including travel time) spent attending counseling sessions mandated by the employer pursuant to a fitness for duty examination was work time compensable under the FLSA. [*Sehie v. City of Aurora*, 432 F.3d 749 (7th Cir. 2005)]

In a suit for the recovery of unpaid overtime, the California Supreme Court ruled that individual officers, directors, and shareholders were not personally liable. Corporate directors can be jointly liable with the corporation if they personally direct or participate in tortious conduct, but the court declined to impose personal liability in *Reynolds v. Bement* because failure to comply with statutory overtime requirements is not tortious, and there was no allegation that the officers or directors retained the unpaid overtime compensation for their own benefit. [*Reynolds v. Bement*, 36 Cal. 4th 1075 (Cal. Sup. 2005)]

The Supreme Court denied certiorari in grocery CEO John Catsimatidis's petition for certiorari. The Second Circuit found Catsimatidis personally as well as jointly and severally liable for employees' wages because of his control over the company under the economic reality test. The Second Circuit found that he had power to hire and fire, set schedules and conditions of employment so he could be personally liable for the unpaid portion of an FLSA settlement agreement. However, the First, Seventh, Eighth, and Eleventh Circuits have found that personal liability is available only for acts of personal responsibility. [*Irizarry v. Catsimatidis*, 722 F.3d 99 (2d Cir. 2013), *cert. denied*, 134 S. Ct. 1516 (2014); see Kevin A. Fritz and Jeremy W. Stewart, *Checkout Closed: Supreme Court Declines Review Of Decision Holding CEO Individually Liable For Wages Owed To Grocery Store Employees*, Seyfarth Shaw LLP (Mar. 11, 2014), available at Lexology.com]

The Supreme Court ruled in March 2011, that it is unlawful to retaliate against an employee who complains about an FLSA violation—even if the complaint is made orally, not in writing, and is made to the employer rather than to a government agency. [*Kasten v. Saint-Gobain Performance Plastics Corp.*, 131 S. Ct. 1325 (2011); see Tony Mauro, *Court Rules for 'Little Guys' Over Corporations in Two Business Cases*, Nat'l L.J. (Mar. 22, 2011) (law.com)]

According to the Eleventh Circuit, punitive damages are not available for violation of the anti-retaliation provision. [*Snapp v. Unlimited Concepts, Inc.*, 208 F.3d 928 (11th Cir. 2000)]

In a 2014 Sixth Circuit case, the plaintiffs were mortgage loan officers who were not paid overtime because they were classified as independent contractors. They filed a class/collective action under the FLSA and the Ohio Minimum Fair Wage Standards Act. The Sixth Circuit held that the employer could compel individual arbitration, even after the expiration of the plaintiffs' employment contracts. The contracts contained an arbitration clause, but did not specify whether class arbitration was available, so the Sixth Circuit held that class-wide arbitration is available only if the agreement specifically permits it. [*Huffman v. The Hilltop Cos.*, 747 F.3d 391 (6th Cir. Mar. 27, 2014); see Gregory V. Mersol, *Sixth Circuit Holds That Duty to Arbitrate Survives Expiration of Employment Contract, Requires Individual Arbitration*, Baker & Hostetler LLP (Mar. 28, 2014), available at Lexology.com. It was already clear that CBA disputes must be arbitrated even after the expiration of the CBA: *Litton Financial Printing v. NLRB*,

501 U.S. 190 (1991). See also *Reed Elsevier, Inc. ex rel. LexisNexis Div. v. Crockett*, 734 F.3d 594 (6th Cir. 2013): when the contract is silent on the issue of class arbitration, class arbitration is not available.]

Recent cases stress that FLSA overtime plaintiffs must do more than merely state they worked unpaid overtime. See *Lundy v. Catholic Health System of Long Island,* 711 F.3d 106 (2d Cir. 2013): to survive a motion to dismiss, the plaintiff must at least allege 40 hours of work in a particular workweek plus uncompensated time. The plaintiff at least must make an approximation of the number of overtime hours; failure to do so will mean dismissal. Paraphrasing the statutory language is not sufficient. Merely alleging unpaid work during meal breaks, training sessions, and extra shift time does not demonstrate that the employee was scheduled for 40 hours of work and actually worked more than that. [*Nakahata v. New York-Presbyterian Healthcare Sys., Inc.*, 723 F.3d 192 (2d Cir. 2013); *Dejesus v. HF Mgmt. Servs., LLC*, 726 F.3d 85 (2d Cir. 2013); see Melissa J. Osipoff, *Second Circuit Continues To Apply Heightened Pleading Standard In Overtime Claims Under The FLSA*, Ogletree Deakins (Aug. 30, 2013), available at Lexology.com]

[E] Scheduling Workers for Overtime

Sometimes, the employer will have to provide additional incentives, such as meal vouchers or free meals in the employee cafeteria or transportation home, for overtime work. But it is more common for employees to compete to be able to put in extra hours at the higher overtime rate. It is legitimate to assign overtime in order of seniority: to let employees bid for overtime work, with priority to the most senior.

In a unionized workplace, the CBA determines how much notice the company must give when overtime will be required; the extent to which overtime is assigned and when it is voluntary; who gets to bid on it; maximum overtime hours; and meal and rest breaks during overtime. If the employer assigns overtime, the disciplinary procedure should be drafted to specify that refusal to work mandatory overtime is a legitimate subject for discipline.

The FLSA allows employers to maintain a policy under which overtime work must be authorized. (Otherwise, employees would have an incentive to goof off during the day and catch up during better-paid overtime hours). But overtime pay is required if the employer permits or even is aware that nonexempt employees are working more than 40 hours a week.

■ **TIP:** The amount of overtime can be reduced by

- Planning further in advance;
- Being more realistic about deadlines;
- Coordinating tasks better, so materials and intermediate products are available when the production cycle requires them;

- Coordinating vacation and leave schedules so there will be enough employees available and it won't be necessary for a few workers to put in extra hours to cover for those who are absent.

[F] Donning and Doffing; Preliminary and Postliminary Activities

The Portal-to-Portal Act makes the FLSA applicable to the employee's "workweek": the time when he or she is engaged in the principal activities of the job. Walking around within the workplace is not considered to be work time, and neither are "preliminary" and "postliminary" activities prior to and after the employee begins to work.

However, it is often necessary to determine whether "donning and doffing" (putting on and removing required uniforms, equipment, and safety gear) time constitutes work time.

In November 2005, the Supreme Court ruled that putting on and taking off gear that is integral to work is compensable as part of the work day, as is walking between the production area and the area where protective clothing is put on and removed. However, the time employees spend waiting to put on their protective gear is not compensable because it is not closely enough related to the principal activities of the job. [*IBP v. Alvarez*, 546 U.S. 21 (2005)]

According to the Supreme Court, principal work activity includes anything integral and indispensable to that activity. Donning and doffing can qualify if predominantly performed for the benefit of the employer. If changing clothes on the employer's premises is required by law, the employer's rules, or the nature of the work, it is integral. When time to change clothes is compensable, so is time going to and from the changing room. Under FLSA § 203(o), a CBA can be drafted to make changing time non-compensable, but some jurisdictions make walking/waiting time compensable even if changing time is not. The critical issue is employer control over the process, not whether changing clothes constitutes enough effort to be deemed "work": *De Asencio v. Tyson Foods*, 500 F.3d 361 (3d Cir. 2007). The employer must inform employees what equipment is mandatory and what is provided for the comfort and convenience of employees.

The Eastern District of Pennsylvania denied summary judgment for the employer in a dispute about whether personal protective equipment (PPE) benefits the employees or the employer: *Lugo v. Farmer's Pride*, 802 F. Supp. 2d (E.D. Pa. 2011). The District Court for the Middle District of Georgia rejected summary judgment for the employer when employees were required to change at the plant and were not allowed to wear protective gear to go home, or even in the restroom or breakroom. However, in this case the court found that changing at the plant was necessary to prevent contamination of the employer's products, which is not always the case: *In re Tyson Foods Inc FLSA Litig.*, 581 F. Supp. 2d 1374 (M.D. Ga. 2008). [Natalie F. Hrubos, *3 Employer Pitfalls In Donning And Doffing Policies*, Duane Morris LLP (Oct. 4, 2013), available at Lexology.com]

The Supreme Court held in early 2014 that, in a unionized operation, it is up to the collective bargaining agreement whether employees will be paid for donning and doffing time. The case, a class action, was brought by steelworkers who alleged that they were entitled to pay for time spent changing in and out of work clothes and walking from the locker room to their work stations. The Supreme Court held that changing into the required safety gear was defined as "changing clothes"—which is rendered not compensable by FLSA § 203(o). [*Sandifer v. U.S. Steel*, 134 S. Ct. 870 (2014)]

The Eighth Circuit held that the time unionized employees spent walking to and from the time clock after donning and doffing required sanitary gear was not a compensable principal activity. The CBA obligated the company to provide and launder the gear. The company was unionized in 1980; changing time and walk-to-clock time had never been compensated. The district court said that donning/doffing time was not compensable because the gear (hard hats, smocks, ear protectors, steel-toed boots, etc.) constituted clothing, and the CBA did not compensate clothing-changing times. However, the district court said that walking time was compensable because donning/doffing were principal activities that started the continuous work day because the clothing was indispensable to the principal work activity. The Eighth Circuit reversed, saying that changing clothes could not start the work day because it was not an activity the employee is employed to perform. The Eighth Circuit distinguished *Alvarez*, because it did not involve a CBA that made donning and doffing non-compensable. [*Adair v. ConAgra Foods*, 728 F.3d 849 (8th Cir. 2013); see William F. Allen, *Eighth Circuit: Donning And Doffing Not A "Principal Activity" That Triggers Compensation*, Littler Mendelson (Sept. 6, 2013), available at Lexology.com; Jessica Schauer Lieberman, *Dressing The Part Is Not Enough: 8th Circuit Decides That Changing Into Uniforms Does Not Start The "Continuous Workday,"* Seyfarth Shaw LLP (Sept. 4, 2013), available at Lexology.com]

The Seventh Circuit affirmed dismissal of a suit under the FLSA and Illinois wage law. The plaintiffs were unionized poultry plant workers who said they were entitled to pay for donning/doffing time at the beginning and end of their meal periods. They said that changing time before and after lunch was taken out of their unpaid meal breaks. They argued that FLSA § 3(o) says that changing time is uncompensated at the beginning or end of the work day—but they had to change clothes before and after meal breaks. The Seventh Circuit held that the plaintiffs worked two four-hour workdays, separated by a 30-minute meal period and, because the employer was unionized, the meal periods were set by collective bargaining, bringing the case within the rule of *Sandifer*. The plaintiffs said that changing clothes took 10–15 minutes; the employer said it took two to three minutes. One of the Seventh Circuit judges made a videotape showing that the employer's estimate was more valid; although this was not evidence, the Seventh Circuit said that it was information about whether donning and doffing represented a substantial portion of the meal period. Changing time was not compensable under Illinois state law either, because the amount of time was minimal.

[*Mitchell v. JCG Industries*, 745 F.3d 837 (7th Cir. 2014); William F. Allen, *Seventh Circuit Affirms Dismissal of Donning and Doffing Suit by Unionized Workers*, Littler Mendelson (Mar. 26, 2014), available at Lexology.com]

A mid-2007 Eleventh Circuit decision held that time spent by workers on an airport construction project in going through security screening, and riding buses provided by the employer from the off-site location where they were required to park for security reasons, was not compensable under the FLSA, because no work-related activity occurred during this time. [*Bonilla v. Baker Concrete Constr., Inc.*, 487 F.3d 1340 (11th Cir. 2007); similarly *Gorman v. Consolidated Edison Corp.*, 488 F.3d 586 (2d Cir. 2007), holds that 10–30 minutes before work going through security and suiting up is not integral; the security requirements are essential to plant operations but not to the principal work activity.

In a warehouse workers' case seeking unpaid wages for time spent passing through security screening, the district court dismissed FLSA and Nevada state law claims. The Ninth Circuit reversed dismissal of the state claims, because certification was subject to different rules than the federal claims. The Ninth Circuit held that an FLSA collective action is not inherently incompatible with a state-law class action, even though plaintiffs must opt in to a collective action but must opt out of a Rule 23 class action. The Ninth Circuit held that they stated an FLSA claim for the time in screening: security checks after the end of the shift were an integral and indispensable postliminary activity. The Ninth Circuit distinguished Second and Eleventh Circuit cases, in which the security measures were imposed on everyone entering the building, not just workers; or the measures were required by a third party or a government agency, not by the employer. [*Busk v. Integrity Staffing Solutions*, 713 F.3d 525 (9th Cir. 2013); see Baker & McKenzie, *Ninth Circuit Holds Time Employees Spend Passing Through A Security Check After Their Shift May Constitute Compensable Time Under The FLSA*, Lexology.com (Jan. 3, 2014). Certiorari was granted on March 3, 2014, as No. 13-433: see Hera S. Arsen, *Is An End-Of-Shift Security Clearance Compensable? The Supreme Court Will Decide Next Term*, Ogletree Deakins (Mar. 6, 2014), available at Lexology.com.]

The Seventh Circuit held that time spent changing clothes and showering to remove lime dust and other chemicals after the end of the shift at a paper mill is non-compensable postliminary activity. The C.F.R. defines washing up and changing clothes as non-compensable unless they are integral to employment (29 C.F.R. §§ 785.24(c), 790.7(g)), and the employer had a policy of compensating clean-up after non-routine exposure to hazardous chemicals. [*Musch v. Domtar Indus., Inc.*, 587 F.3d 857 (7th Cir. 2009)]

In an FLSA collective action brought by over 400 iron foundry employees who claimed overtime for time spent showering and changing at the end of the shift, the Seventh Circuit held that summary judgment for the employer was inappropriate. The employees said that they were exposed to chemicals at work, so showering and changing clothes protected their health. The district court held that, because there is no OSHA standard requiring foundry employees to shower or change on site, the activities were not necessary. The Seventh Circuit reversed, holding that the court should be able to rely on scientific testimony about the necessity of these activities. [*DeKeyser v. Thyssenkrupp Waupaca, Inc.*, 735 F.3d 568 (7th Cir. 2013); see Karla E. Sanchez, *The Court Can Tell What's "Necessary" For Your Health*, Sherman & Howard LLC (Nov. 4, 2013), available at Lexology.com; William F. Allen, *Divided Seventh Circuit Panel Reverses Summary Judgment In Showering And Clothes Changing FLSA Case*, Littler Mendelson (Nov. 8, 2013), available at Lexology.com]

The District Court for the Southern District of New York ruled that tradesmen working for the Fire Department's Building Maintenance Division were not entitled to a recovery under the FLSA for time spent commuting or inspecting vehicles, even if they transported work tools and materials. Using employer vehicles brought them within coverage of the Employer Commuter Flexibility Act of 1996, because Fire Department vehicles were used to travel within New York City, the normal commuting area for the job. Transporting work equipment was not a compensable principal activity, because the tradesmen were employed to fix equipment, not to drive trucks. Vehicle inspections, securing items that moved in transit, and discussing scheduling with supervisors were not compensable because they were part of commuting, and they happened infrequently enough to constitute de minimis activities. [*Colella v. City of New York*, No. 07 Civ. 6312 (LAP), 2013 U.S. Dist. LEXIS 171687 (S.D.N.Y. Dec. 5, 2013); see Noel P. Tripp, *District Court Rejects FDNY Employees' Bid To Be Paid for Commuting Time*, Jackson Lewis Wage & Hour Law Update (Dec. 12, 2013), available at law.com]

§ 1.16 VACATIONS AND VACATION PAY

On the average, U.S. workers get less vacation than European workers. Furthermore, U.S. workers may feel that if they take their scheduled vacation time, they will not be able to complete all the work that falls to them in a downsized workplace.

In 1992–93, 82% of American workers reported they got paid vacation days, now only 77% do (BLS figures), with the greatest decline among part-time workers and workers in companies with under 100 employees. In 1992–93, 92% of full-time workers got paid vacation days, 91% did in 2012. But access to other kinds of paid leave has increased. In 1992–93, 2% of workers had access to paid maternity benefits, 1% to paid paternity benefits; in 2012, 11% of private-sector workers were entitled to paid family leave, not necessarily related to childbirth, and 61% of private sector employees had paid sick leave (only 50% did in 1992–93). In 1992–93, the average full-time private-sector worker got eight days of vacation after one year of service, versus 10 days in 2012, rising to 18 days (1992–93) or 20 days (2012) after 20 years' service. [2012 data from BLS. See Catherine Rampell, *Paid Vacation's Decline*, NYTimes.com (Sept. 3, 2013).]

■ **TIP:** Audit requirements may actually require employees with access to the firm's cash and books to take at least two consecutive weeks of vacation. An employee who never uses his or her full allotment of vacation time could be a conscientious person who wants to cope with a backlog, a workaholic who really needs to "get a life" outside the office, a subpar employee who needs extra time to make up for incompetence, or an embezzler who has to hang around to prevent crooked schemes from unraveling!

The federal Davis-Bacon Act requires government contractors to pay for unused vacation days when an employee terminates but there is no general FLSA provision covering other situations. Most of the states impose a similar requirement for state government employees, but not in the private sector. Some states, however, have rules about this.

Federal law doesn't require celebration of holidays, and does not require holiday pay, although some states impose special requirements for employees who do work on a holiday. However, once a company adopts a holiday policy, it must continue to follow it; failure would constitute not paying all wages due. The policy must explain who is entitled to holiday pay and what happens if the holiday coincides with a day when the workplace is closed. Generally, payment is required only for hours actually worked plus any holiday supplement promised to the employees. Comp time is another possibility, but it must be spelled out. [John Donovan, Fisher & Phillips LLP, *Solutions at Work, Does Your Holiday Policy Need a Tune Up?* (February 2011) (benefitslink.com)]

§ 1.17 GARNISHMENTS AND DEDUCTIONS FOR SUPPORT ORDERS

[A] Assignments versus Garnishments

There may be instances in which the HR department is asked to apply some of an employee's wages to a debt, such as consumer debts, student loan debt, and the obligation to support children, and/or an ex-spouse.

An "assignment" is an action undertaken by an individual to direct some of his or her future compensation to creditors. A "garnishment" is a deduction from wages made pursuant to a court order. Federal law doesn't say anything about wage assignments, although many states limit the amount or percentage of each paycheck that can be assigned, permit assignments only for certain classes of debts, or require the spouse's consent to the assignment.

BAPCPA made it harder for many consumer debtors to file for bankruptcy protection. Although the lesser of 75% of wages, or 30 times the minimum wage, is exempt from garnishment, the minimum wage has not kept up with inflation, with the result that only $217.50/week is exempt from seizure under the federal rules. (Some states exempt larger amounts.) Losing 25% of income may make it impossible for the low-wage debtor to pay bills. [Sidney Jones, *More Struggling Borrowers Face Pay Garnishment*, NYTimes.com (Apr. 2, 2010)]

Pensions cannot be assigned before they are received (except through a Qualified Domestic Relations Order (QDRO) See § 12.08). Once a pension payment is made, the recipient can do whatever he or she wants with it, but the "anti-alienation" rules of ERISA prevent advance assignment.

The federal Consumer Credit Protection Act (CCPA) [15 U.S.C. §§ 1671 *et seq.*] puts limits on garnishment. Generally, the maximum permitted garnishment will be 25% of the employee's "disposable" earnings, with stricter limits on garnishments for very low-income workers. "Disposable earnings" is defined as approximately equal to gross income minus Social Security taxes and withheld income taxes. Health insurance premiums and spousal and child support are not deducted, even if the support is ordered by a court. Thus, serious problems can occur if the same individual is subject to garnishment both for consumer debt and support payments.

Garnishment for support rather than consumer debt can be higher [15 U.S.C. § 1673]:

- 50%, if the employee is supporting a spouse or child other than the subject of the order, and the garnishment order covers less than 12 weeks' worth of arrears;
- 55%, if conditions are the same but more than 12 weeks of arrears are involved;
- 60%, if the employee does not have a new family to support, and arrears are 12 weeks or less;
- 65%, if there is no second family and arrears exceed 12 weeks.

There is no limit on garnishments that respond to an order issued by a Chapter 11 or Chapter 13 bankruptcy court, or on a debt due for any state or federal tax. The general rule against alienation of plan benefits doesn't prevent the IRS from garnishing a taxpayer's (or rather, nontaxpayer's) vested interest in qualified benefits when the agency has a judgment for unpaid taxes.

The CCPA says that, if state law limits garnishment more than the federal law does, employees are entitled to the protection of the stricter state-law limits. In other words, the garnishment is limited to what is permitted by state law. Under the CCPA, it's illegal to fire an employee for having one garnishment, but it's lawful to fire if additional garnishments are imposed. [16 U.S.C. § 1674] Willful violation of this provision can be punished by a $1,000 fine and/or one year's imprisonment.

It should be noted that qualified plan benefits can be garnished to collect a criminal restitution order under the Mandatory Victims Restitution Act of 1996, which provides restitution for property losses. Restitution orders have the same status as tax liens, for which plan benefits can also be garnished. [*United States v. Novak*, 441 F.3d 819 (9th Cir. 2006)]

Employers should never ignore garnishments (which are court orders) even if the subject of the order is not an employee or does not appear to earn enough money to satisfy the judgment. A few states require disclosure at the end rather than the beginning of garnishment, and a garnishee who does not respond is liable for the amount that would have been withheld from wages. In Georgia and Wisconsin, a default is automatically entered against an employer that fails to answer a garnishment order, but has 15 days to re-open the default by paying costs. If the order is not reopened, default judgment can be entered for the full amount of the outstanding debt even if the debtor is not—or never was—an employee of that employer. [Martin C. Brook, *Tips For Garnishee Employers, Part One: The Perils Of Ignoring Garnishment Orders*, Ogletree Deakins (Jan. 10, 2014), available at Lexology.com]

The federal Fair Debt Collection Practices Act (FDCPA) [28 U.S.C. § 3001] lets the federal government collect its judgments by garnishing property held by a third party on the basis of the debtor's "substantial non-exempt interest" in the property. According to the Sixth Circuit, tax levies do not violate ERISA's anti-alienation provisions. [*United States v. Sawaf*, 74 F.3d 119 (6th Cir. 1996)]

In mid-2010, the PBGC revised its regulations on debt collection, to add salary offset and administrative wage garnishment to the acceptable methods of collecting non-tax debts owed to the PBGC. Administrative offset is the process of having amounts that are owed to a business (such as a government contractor) paid to the PBGC instead, to pay the business' debts to the PBGC. Salary offset is withholding of up to 15% of a federal employee's disposable pay to collect debts. Administrative wage garnishment is withholding of wages of a former federal employee who now works for a non-federal employer. The PBGC has to inform debtors of the amount and type of the debt (such as an employer's failure to pay PBGC premiums, or amounts that the PBGC overpaid to an employee), how the PBGC intends to collect the debt, what happens if the debt is not repaid, and how the debtor can make alternate arrangements if the business or individual objects to the PBGC's proposed collection efforts. Under limited circumstances, the PBGC can waive interest, penalties, and administrative costs—but federal law forbids certain types of waivers. [PBGC Proposed Rule, *Debt Collection*, 75 Fed. Reg. 42662 (July 22, 2010)]

[B] Student Loan Garnishments

There are separate federal rules at 20 U.S.C. § 1095a with respect to garnishment to repay student loans. Up to 10% of disposable earnings can be garnished to repay those loans. The employee can sign a document agreeing to a higher garnishment level. Before the garnishment order is submitted to the employer, the employee has the right to contest the garnishment and suggest a voluntary repayment schedule. If a person is fired or laid off from a job, and is rehired (by the original employer or someone else) within 12 months after termination, student loan garnishment is deferred until the person has been back in the workforce for 12 months.

The federal provisions do not require employers to change or depart from their normal payment mechanisms to comply with student loan garnishment orders, but if they fail to comply with the order entirely, employers can be penalized by the amount that should have been withheld to satisfy the garnishment, plus costs, fees, and punitive damages.

Federal law forbids an employer to discharge, refuse to hire, or discipline a person because he or she is subject to a student loan garnishment. Employers that violate this rule can be ordered to reinstate the affected employee with back pay, and can also be ordered to pay punitive damages and attorneys' fees.

[C] Child Support Collection

State governments are heavily involved in child support enforcement, to prevent children from becoming welfare recipients because their parents do not support them. The federal government also requires state governments to take this enforcement role. Under a federal statute, the Child Support Enforcement Amendments of 1984 [P.L. 98-378], states can lose federal funding if they do not enact laws requiring wage withholding for support arrears. States must also have a procedure for Qualified Medical Child Support Orders (QMCSOs) under which parents who are covered by an Employee Group Health Plan (EGHP) are required to take steps to enroll their children under the plan.

Federal law also requires state-court child support orders to contain a withholding provision, so a withholding order can be issued as soon as a parent falls behind on support, with no need for separate court proceedings. The state child support enforcement agency notifies the employer that a particular employee has child support arrears. The employer is obligated to impose withholding as of the first pay period after 14 days of the date the agency mailed its notice. Once withholding begins, the employer has an obligation to notify the child support agency promptly if the employee quits or gets fired. The notice should give the termination date, the employee's last known address, and the address of the new employer (if known).

The CCPA percentage limits discussed above apply to child support orders. Depending on circumstances, up to 65% of disposable income may be subject to withholding for support. The Child Support Enforcement Amendments allow states to impose a late payment fee of 3 to 6% of the overdue support. Support withholding takes priority over other legal processes (e.g., for consumer debts or student loans) applying to the same income.

Employers must also submit data about newly hired employees to the state unemployment insurance agency within 20 days of hiring. The information is aggregated into a National Directory of New Hires that is used to track down "deadbeat parents" who fail to pay child support.

The basic federal report (which can be made by mail or magnetic tape; state support enforcement agencies can accept telephoned, faxed, and e-mailed reports) consists of:

- Employer's name, address, and Taxpayer Identification Number;
- Employee's name;
- Employee's address;
- Employee's Social Security number.

States may impose additional requirements, such as telephone numbers, driver's license number, and information about the group health plan (to be used in conjunction with a QMCSO). The employer also has to make a quarterly report of wages paid, for use in instituting withholding orders. Failure to make a required report can be penalized by $25 per employee, or $500 for conspiracy with an employee to avoid the requirement.

§ 1.18 USERRA

Under the Uniformed Services Employment and Reemployment Rights Act [38 U.S.C. §§ 4301 *et seq.*] (USERRA), employers have obligations toward their employees who temporarily leave employment to fulfill a military commitment. After the armed service member, reservist or National Guard member returns to civilian life, the employer is obligated to re-employ the person. USERRA requires the employee to give the employer advance written or verbal notice of leave, unless this would be impossible, unreasonable, or precluded by military necessity. The statute requires the employer to reinstate the service member after discharge, in the job he or she would have achieved but for the period of military service, applying the "escalator principle" to seniority, status, compensation, and other seniority-related rights. Furthermore, the employer is not obligated to offer the returned service member a job at the same location, and federal law does not require the employer to pay the service member during military leave. The employee can elect to use accrued vacation or other paid leave while he or she is serving, but employers are not allowed to require the service member to use accrued paid leave.

The employer is obligated to make a reasonable effort to provide training to refresh or upgrade the returning service member's skills. Employees who cannot qualify for their former job must be placed in an alternative position. However, re-employment is not required if circumstances have changed so much that it would be impossible, unreasonable, or impose an undue hardship to do it. When active duty lasted 181 days or more, the re-employed person can be fired only for cause during the first year of reinstatement (and only for cause in the first six months after re-employment following service of 30 to 180 days).

If the service member was on active duty for 30 days or less, USERRA requires him or her to report back to work after active duty on the next regular workday. If the military commitment was 31 to 180 days, the general rule is that USERRA requires the employee to apply for re-employment within 14 days of finishing the military commitment. The period to re-apply stretches to 90 days if the service member was on active duty for over 180 days.

Under USERRA, the employer must treat a period of military duty as active service with the employer for eligibility, vesting, and benefit accrual purposes. However, once the service member returns to work, he or she is entitled to benefits attributable to employee contributions only to the extent that he or she actually made such contributions. The employer is not obligated to make contributions to a 401(k) plan while the employee is on active service, but when the service member is re-employed, the employer must make whatever employer contributions would have been made if the service member had continued at work.

Veterans with service-connected disabilities are covered both by USERRA (enforced by the Department of Labor) and the ADA (enforced by the EEOC). Both statutes impose an obligation of reasonable accommodation on employers; the USERRA obligation is broader, because it requires employers to make efforts to assist returning veterans to become qualified, e.g., by training or retraining. Some service-related disabilities qualify for accommodation under USERRA even though they are not ADA-level disabilities.

Employer Support of the Guard and Reserve (ESGR), <www.esgr.net>, is a Department of Defense unit, staffed by over 900 volunteers, to provide liaison between Reservists and their civilian workers on USERRA issues. The Website <http://www.AmericasHeroesAtWork.gov> (accessed Apr. 1, 2014), jointly managed by the DOL Office of Disability Employment Policy and the Veterans' Employment and Training Service, provides resources for employers when veterans with traumatic brain injury or PTSD return to work. The site covers, e.g., implementing accommodations at work and services for veterans.

Creditors are legally obligated under USERRA to reduce interest rates to 6% or less on debts owed by those entering military service. The statute allows plan fiduciaries to petition the relevant court to maintain a higher interest rate, based on a showing of the servicemember's ability to pay. USERRA also allows (but does not obligate) the plan to suspend the obligation to make regular payments of plan loans during the term of military service. [See DOL guidelines, <http://www.dol.gov/ebsa/faqs/faq_911_2.html> (accessed Apr. 1, 2014). See also the Service Members Civil Relief Act, Pub. L. No. 108-189 clarifying that the 6% interest rate ceiling only applies to obligations incurred prior to entering military service. Therefore, a plan loan made to a plan participant who is already on military duty can charge the plan's normal interest rate. But interest over and above the permitted 6% level must be forgiven, not merely postponed until the servicemember returns.]

Under federal law, USERRA leave does not have to be paid leave (although some state laws do impose a requirement of a period of paid leave). The federal statute allows employees, at their option, to use accrued vacation or other paid leave while they are on active duty, but the employer is not permitted to force them to do so if they prefer unpaid leave and preservation of their leave accrual.

There is no requirement that employers provide pay supplements to prevent servicemembers from suffering a loss of income when they lose their civilian paychecks and get military pay (often much lower). However, some employers elect to do so as a patriotic statement of support for the troops. The time periods vary from three months to several years. The GAO studied past military operations, and concluded that 41% of reservists lost income when called up for active duty, 30% experienced no change, and 29% actually had higher income post-call-up.

In addition to the federal requirements, a number of states (e.g., California, Illinois, Indiana, Maine, Minnesota, Nebraska, New York, Rhode Island, and Washington) have enacted statutory employment rights for servicemembers. [See George P. Kostakos and Stephen T. Melnick, *New Rhode Island Law Grants Military Families Unpaid Leave*, Littler Press Releases, Media Advisories, and Newsletters (July 2008) (benefitslink.com)]

Being called for active service is also a COBRA event, requiring notice and giving the service member and family the option of continuing coverage in the employer's plan for up to 24 months by making premium payments. After a service member is deactivated, he or she and family members can also do a kind of reverse-COBRA election by choosing to remain within the TRICARE system for a period of time. [GAO-03-549T, *Military Personnel: Preliminary Observations Related to Income, Benefits, and Employer Support for Reservists During Mobilizations* (Mar. 19, 2003), <http://www.gao.gov/cgi-bin/getrpt?GAO-03-549T>]

As of 2009, two Circuit Courts (the Fifth and Sixth Circuits) had ruled that USERRA cases fall under mandatory arbitration clauses, finding that statutes that provide for lawsuits do not thereby rule out mandatory arbitration of discrimination claims. However, two District Courts have held that USERRA claims are not subject to mandatory arbitration, because the USERRA provision that says the law preempts state laws that eliminate, reduce, or limit USERRA rights forbid mandatory arbitration because the arbitration requirement limits servicemembers' rights under USERRA. [Compare *Landis v. Pinnacle Eye Care*, 537 F.3d 559 (6th Cir. 2008) and *Garrett v. Circuit City Stores*, 449 F.3d 672 (5th Cir. 2006) with *Lopez v. Dillard's, Inc.*, 382 F. Supp. 2d 1245 (D. Kan. 2005) and *Breletic v. CACI Inc.*, 413 F. Supp. 2d 1329 (2006).]

Note, however, that the California Court of Appeal ruled in late 2007 that USERRA rights cannot be waived by contract. Therefore, a release of rights under a severance agreement could not be enforced to the extent it dealt with allegations that a Marine Reserve captain was terminated because of his military status. (He was fired the day after he returned to work from Reserve duty.) 38 U.S.C.

§ 4302(b) provides that USERRA supersedes any state law or contract that reduces, limits or eliminates any USERRA right; the court interpreted this to cover suits for wrongful termination and breach of an oral employment contract. [*Perez v. Uline*, 157 Cal. App. 4th 953 (Cal. App. 2007)] The Sixth Circuit reached a different conclusion in mid-2010, finding that a veteran of the war in Afghanistan could not sue his former employer, IBM, under USERRA, because he negotiated an Individual Separation Allowance Plan under which he received $6,000 for release of all of his employment-related claims. The Sixth Circuit enforced the release because it was knowing and voluntary; the release form was not ambiguous; and there was no evidence of fraud or overreaching. [*Wysocki v. IBM*, 607 F.3d 1102 (6th Cir. 2010)]

The Supreme Court denied certiorari in the Sixth Circuit case of a Nashville police officer who charged that imposing a three-week delay in reinstating him after his discharge from the Army Reserves violated USERRA. The Sixth Circuit ruled in his favor because he satisfied the conditions for reinstatement (discharge under honorable conditions; military service lasting less than five years; prompt request for re-employment), even though the Nashville police department said that its internal policies called for the delay, and the plaintiff was charged with violating Army regulations. The Sixth Circuit held that USERRA rules prevail over internal employment policies. [*Petty v. Metropolitan Gov't of Nashville*, 538 F.3d 431 (6th Cir. 2008), *cert. denied* as *Metropolitan Government of Nashville v. Petty*, 556 U.S. 1165 (2009)]

The Eighth Circuit held that the purchaser of a business did not meet its USERRA obligations when the plaintiff, who was deployed in Iraq, was not included in the list of active employees. The purchase agreement required reasonable efforts to offer employment to the list of employees furnished by the selling company. Everyone on the list was hired, but the plaintiff was not rehired when he returned from deployment in December 2008. (He was eventually hired in April 2009.) He sued his ex-employer, which said that it was not obligated to rehire him because going out of business constituted changed circumstances. The Ninth Circuit held that an employee on military leave is entitled to the same rights and benefits as comparable employees without military commitments. Employers have better records than employees, so it was up to the seller corporation to explain whether employees on long-term non-military leave were included on the hire list when the plaintiff was not. [*Dorris v. TXD Servs., LP*, No. 12-3096, 2014 U.S. App. LEXIS 3716, 97 Empl. Prac. Dec. (CCH) P45,028 (8th Cir. Feb. 27, 2014); see Jackson Lewis PC, *Employers Must Treat Employees on Military Leave like Those on Comparable Leaves, Appeals Court Rules*, Lexology.com (Mar. 3, 2014)]

The First Circuit adopted a standard of proof in USERRA cases that is more pro-plaintiff than the rules under Title VII (see § 42.04). In a Title VII case, the burden of proof is always on the employee who charges discrimination. In a USERRA case, the employee has to start the ball rolling by showing that military service was at least a motivating or substantial factor in the employment action that the servicemember complains of. Then the employer has to show, by a preponderance of the evidence that the same adverse action would have been taken even if the employee had not had a military commitment. [*Velazquez-Garcia v. Horizon Lines of P.R., Inc.*, 473 F.3d 11 (1st Cir. 2007)]

Retaliation claims are one of the largest portions of the employment discrimination caseload, and retaliation allegations are also raised in the USERRA context. A California jury awarded $275,000 to a police officer who charged USERRA retaliation. The District Court dismissed the jury award, but the Ninth Circuit reinstated it. [*Wallace v. City of San Diego*, 460 F.3d 1181 (9th Cir. 2006); see Rebecca Moore, *Appellate Court Reinstates Jury Award in USERRA Case*, plansponsor.com (Sept. 20, 2006); Wallace's petition for rehearing was denied by the Ninth Circuit on February 12, 2007 (479 F.3d 616)]

A "cat's paw" is a tool used by someone to accomplish his purpose. In the employment law context, this theory imputes one person's discriminatory animus to the decision-maker, if the decision-maker was influenced by the other person. The Supreme Court allowed "cat's paw" liability to apply in a USERRA case: the plaintiff alleged he was fired because of his military history. The plaintiff charged that the hospital scheduler exerted influence to get him fired. The employer is liable because its agent, pursuing discriminatory animus, intends to and does cause an adverse employment action. [*Staub v. Proctor Hosp.*, 560 F.3d 647 (7th Cir. 2009), *rev'd*, 131 S. Ct. 1186 (2011)]

[A] Regulations

Although USERRA is a 1994 statute, the first proposed regulations were not issued until September 20, 2004, by the Department of Labor's Veterans' Employment and Training Service (VETS). A few months later, on December 10, 2004, President Bush signed the Veterans Benefits Improvement Act of 2004, Pub. L. No. 108-454, amending USERRA Title 38 § 4317 to allow servicemembers to elect and pay for continuation coverage. Another statute, the Heroes Earned Retirement Opportunities Act, Pub. L. No. 109-227, allows active servicemembers to treat combat pay as compensation that can be contributed to an IRA.

The Heroes Earnings Assistance and Relief Tax Act (HEART Act, Pub. L. No. 110-245) provides financial flexibility for servicemembers, in the form of special options in health care FSAs and Qualified Reservist Distributions. Notice 2010-15, 2010-6 I.R.B. 390, explains that differential pay provided to employees on active service must be included in pension calculations. Funds can be withdrawn without an early withdrawal penalty from defined contribution plans by a person on active duty for at least six months. Survivors of deceased servicemembers can make tax-free rollovers of the military death benefit and life insurance to a Roth IRA or education savings account. Employers must provide any otherwise applicable death benefit to survivors of persons who die on active service. All employers must give notice of USERRA rights, either by displaying the official poster in the workplace, or by mailing, e-mailing, or hand delivering a copy to employees. Under USERRA, military service is not a break in service when it comes to participation, vesting, or benefit accruals. For either a defined benefit or a defined contribution plan, pension calculations must be based on the pay rate the employee would have received if he or she had not been deployed. If the pay rate is uncertain (for example, it depends on sales commissions) the employer must use the average rate of compensation during the 12-month period prior to military service.

Applying for military service (rather than just performance of military service) is a protected right, so employers are forbidden to discriminate or retaliate on this basis (20 C.F.R. §§ 1002.18–.20). Joint employers are covered by USERRA, and so are a company's successor in interest, even if unaware of the servicemember's re-employment claims (20 C.F.R. §§ 1002.35–.37). The proposals make it clear that USERRA does not just protect full-time permanent workers. Job applicants, temporary, part-time, probationary, and seasonal employees; employees who have been laid off; strikers; employees on leave of absence—but not independent contractors—are covered by USERRA (20 C.F.R. §§ 1002.40–.44). The employer must treat the employee on active service as if he or she were on furlough or leave of absence; if the employer offers more than one type of non-military leave, military leave must provide the same benefits as the most generous of those (20 C.F.R. § 1002.149). If employees request, they must be allowed to apply their accrued vacation, annual or similar paid leave (but not unpaid leave) to their period of active duty, but the employer can't force an employee to use up paid leave while on active duty (20 C.F.R. §§ 1002.151–.153).

The employer must be prompt about re-employing a returned servicemember. Unless there are unusual circumstances, re-employment should occur within two weeks of the application, and for weekend National Guard duty, it should occur on the next regularly scheduled work period (20 C.F.R. §§ 1002.180–.181).

One acceptable alternative is for the employer to use the "escalator principle" and grant the re-employed employee the raises and benefit increases that were reasonably certain to have occurred if he or she had not been called to duty. However, the regulations permit other alternatives, such as returning the employee to the position held before deployment; giving him or her a comparable position to the pre-service or elevator position; or making the nearest possible approximation to one of those. If the person would have been laid off if he or she had remained at work, re-employment to layoff status is permitted (20 C.F.R. § 1002.194).

The appropriate placement of the employee depends on factors such as length of service, the employee's qualifications, and any extent to which military service caused or aggravated an existing disability (20 C.F.R. §§ 1002.196–.197). Sections 225 and 226 require the employer to make reasonable efforts to accommodate disability of persons seeking re-employment and to help the applicant become qualified to perform the duties of the offered job. [Ballard Spahr Andrews

& Ingersoll, LLP, *Department of Labor Proposes New Regulations Under USERRA for Military Leave Rights* (Jan. 4, 2005)]

USERRA protects the employment rights of persons who take up to five years' cumulative military leave with the same employer. However, see 20 C.F.R. § 1002.1. Under some circumstances (e.g., service during war or national emergency) the job is protected for more than five years.

The military services have "personnel locators" that can be used to verify that a person actually is in active service.

Veterans Opportunity to Work (VOW) to Hire Heroes Act, Pub. L. No. 112-56, was signed on November 21, 2011. The legislation provides job training and transition assistance to help reduce the unemployment rate for veterans, including a tax credit for hiring veterans. The highest level of credit available for hiring unemployed and/or disabled veterans. The VOW Act amends USERRA to recognize hostile work environment claims based on military status (using the same standards as Title VII). Therefore, EEO policies should be updated to forbid discrimination based on military deployment and veteran status, supervisors should be trained in the new requirements, and the company should adopt a reporting procedure for USERRA complaints. [Laura Broughton Russell, *New Veterans Law Offers Tax Credits to Employers and Recognizes Hostile Work Environment Claims Under USERRA* (Dec. 19, 2011) (benefitslink.com) The IRS has provided guidance: Notice 2012-13, 2012-9 I.R.B. 421]

[B] Recent Cases

USERRA has generated a number of important cases.

The First Circuit ruled that USERRA protects servicemembers who have not actually been recalled to active duty, but who have expressed a definite intent to return to active service in the near future. [*Vega-Colon v. Wyeth Pharm.*, 625 F.3d 22 (1st Cir. 2010)]

The Eleventh Circuit held that the Alabama Department of Mental Health violated USERRA by failing to rehire servicemember Roy Hamilton on a timely basis after return from his 2003 deployment. While he was on active duty, the facility where he had worked was closed. The Eleventh Circuit said that Hamilton's rejection of a transfer to a different city, for family reasons, did not prevent him from being entitled to reemployment. The Eleventh Circuit upheld the jury's $25,000 award for lost pay and benefits. The court held that the department was not entitled to sovereign immunity, because the suit was brought by the Department of Justice rather than by a private individual. [*United States v. Alabama Dep't of Mental Health & Mental Retardation*, 673 F.3d 1320 (11th Cir. 2012)

Two Chicago police officers seeking promotion to sergeant sued under USERRA. The promotion exam was scheduled for March 25, 2006, when the plaintiffs were on active duty. They took the test outside the United States; passed; and were placed on the eligibility list. They sued when the person with the highest score was promoted. The plaintiffs alleged that they would have scored higher if they had not had to travel long distances to take the test, and they should have been given a chance to take the promotion exam at the bases where they were stationed. The Seventh Circuit ruled that USERRA § 4311 does not require accommodation, and the plaintiffs were not entitled to better treatment than employees who were in Chicago on the test date. [*Sandoval v. City of Chicago*, 560 F.3d 703 (7th Cir. 2009)]

The First Circuit held in 2013 that when an employee is reinstated after active service USERRA requires the employer to consider whatever non-automatic discretionary promotions the employee might have received in addition to the "escalator position" reflecting automatic promotions such as those based on seniority. The First Circuit read the regulations to require promoting the employee to the position that would have been held, with reasonable certainty, absent active military service. [*Rivera-Melendez v. Pfizer Pharm., LLC*, 730 F.3d 49 (1st Cir. 2013); see Brooke A. Colaizzi, *USERRA Reinstatement Requires Consideration Of Discretionary Promotions, Too*, Sherman & Howard LLC (Sept. 26, 2013), available at Lexology.com]

The Veterans' Benefit and Improvement Act of 2008, Pub. L. No. 110-389, eliminated that statute of limitations on USERRA claims. However, this law is not retroactive. For cases before it took effect, the statute of limitations is four years. Therefore, a plaintiff who did not file his case within four years was time-barred. Even if the running of the statute of limitations was tolled (suspended) while he was on active duty, he still missed the deadline. There was no evidence of wrongdoing by his employer that would justify equitable tolling. [*Baldwin v. City of Greensboro*, 714 F.3d 828 (4th Cir. 2013)]

CHAPTER 2

TAX ASPECTS OF PAY PLANNING

§ 2.01 INTRODUCTION

One reason why corporations adopt pension and benefit plans is that, under appropriate circumstances, the employer will get a tax deduction, and the employee will receive valuable benefits—but the employee will not have immediately taxable income as a result of the benefits (or only part of the benefit will generate taxable income).

Therefore, an important part of pay planning is determining what portion of each employee's compensation is taxable, and performing tax withholding, depositing taxes, issuing information returns, and maintaining tax records. In most years, at least one tax bill is enacted that affects employers' tax responsibilities; in some years, there are several bills. In recent years, changes in FICA rules have been especially notable. See § 2.01[A] for a narrative account of recent tax changes.

The pace of change can be fast enough to make it difficult to keep up with current tax rules—and, in fact, there may be several tax rules that apply in the same year, depending on the effective date of the statutes passed during that year.

The basic tax rule is that everything received is taxable income, unless there is a specific exclusion. Therefore, the tax definition of "wages" includes vacation pay, commissions, bonuses, and some fringe benefits, not just straight salary. Severance pay is considered taxable wages, but payments for cancellation of an employment contract are not wages.

These items have been granted exclusions from taxable income:

- Worker's Compensation benefits;
- The employer's contributions to qualified pension plans (but the employee's pretax deferrals placed into 401(k) plans are FUTA and FICA wages);
- Up to $50,000 in § 79 group-term life insurance coverage. Additional coverage is taxable income that must be reported on the W-2 form, but income tax withholding is not required. The excess coverage is not subject to FUTA, but is subject to both the employer and employee share of FICA;
- Certain fringe benefits, e.g., employee discounts, working condition and de minimis fringes, qualified transportation fringes, qualified dependent care assistance within limits, etc.

The IRS issues annual updates of its Publication 15-A, Employer's Supplemental Tax Guide and Publication 15-B, Employer's Tax Guide to Fringe Benefits. See <http://www.irs.gov/pub/irs-pdf/p15a.pdf> and <www.irs.gov/pub/irs-pdf/p15b.pdf> respectively.

When a new employee is hired the employer must use Form I-9 to verify immigration status and that the person can lawfully work within the United States. [See § 23.11 for more information about immigration issues in hiring]

Employer Group Health Plans (EGHPs) that fail to satisfy certain federal requirements must pay excise taxes, which are reported on IRS Form 8928. Self-reporting is required for compliance with the COBRA requirements (including the subsidy program); HIPAA rules; benefits for childbirth, mental health parity, and Michelle's law; and the Genetic Information Nondisclosure Act.

If the employer fails to make contributions to MSAs or HSAs that are comparable as between rank and file and highly compensated employees, the excise tax generally equals 35% of aggregate employer contributions to all employees' MSAs and HSAs for the year. In this situation, Form 8928 is due by the fifteenth day of the fourth month of the year after the year in which a non-comparable contribution was made.

The excise tax is $100 per beneficiary per day for failure to comply with a variety of requirements (dealing with, e.g., pre-existing condition limitations, nondiscrimination in enrollment, minimum hospital stay for childbirth, mental health parity). But the excise tax is waived if the responsible person did not know, and could not have known with due diligence, of the failure; or the failure was reasonable, not caused by willful neglect, and was corrected within 30 days. There are additional penalties for late returns and late payments. [74 Fed. Reg. 45994 (Sept. 8, 2009); IRS Instructions for Form 8928, <http://www.irs.gov/instructions/i8928/ch01.html> (accessed Apr. 6, 2014)]

When a plan complies with PPACA and covers participants' adult children until their 26th birthday that coverage is tax-free for federal purposes—but not necessarily under state law. If state law does not track the federal law, then it may be necessary to report the fair market value of the coverage for state tax purposes.

Only 22 of the states that have state income taxes (plus the District of Columbia) automatically amend their tax rules to conform to federal rules, and in 10 states, EGHPs may have to extend coverage to employees' children even after age 26, in which case the coverage will be taxable unless the child is a dependent or disabled. The 10 states are Connecticut, Florida, Illinois, Nebraska, New Jersey, New York, Ohio, Pennsylvania, and South Dakota. [Buck Research FYI, *States Address Tax Consequences of Health Coverage for Adult Children* (Sep. 16, 2011) (benefitslink.com); Cynthia Lee, Beyond Health Care Reform Blog, *Wisconsin Bill Passed to Conform State Tax Treatment of Coverage of Adult Children* (Oct. 28, 2011) (benefitslink.com)]

Employers will need to learn these rules—but not right away. The employer mandate under PPACA, also known as the "pay or play" rules, was supposed to take effect in January 2014, subjecting employers with 50 or more employees to excise tax penalties for failure to offer at least a basic package of health care benefits to employees, further subject to requirements of affordability. Companies with under 50 employees are not subject to these requirements, and there are computation rules for determining full-time equivalence. However, effectiveness of these rules has been postponed several times. For companies with 100 or more employees, it has been postponed until January 1, 2015. In 2015, companies with 100 or more employee will be penalized if they fail to offer affordable coverage to at least 70% of their full-time employees; as of January 1, 2016, they will be required to offer affordable coverage to 95% of their full-time employees. However, medium-sized companies (50–99 employees) have an additional year, until January 1, 2016, before they will be subject to the pay or play requirement. [Robert Pear, *Further Delays for Employers in Health Law*, NYTimes.com (Feb. 10, 2014)]

It used to be common for employers to maintain an "employer payment plan," under which employees were reimbursed for the premiums of health insurance policies they purchased individually. However, in 2013, the IRS took the position that these plans are group health plans for PPACA purposes. Therefore, they must satisfy PPACA requirements—for example, limits cannot be imposed on the amount of benefits an employee can access in a year. The IRS position is that the § 4980D penalty of up to $100/day/eligible employee can be imposed if the employer maintains an employer payment plan that does not satisfy the PPACA requirements. Additional ERISA penalties might also be imposed by the DOL. [Notice 2013-54, 2013-40 I.R.B. 287. See Lindsey Surratt, *IRS Highlights Stiff Penalties for Reimbursing Individual Premiums* (May 21, 2014), available at Lexology.com; Robert Pear, *I.R.S. Bars Employers From Dumping Workers Into Health Exchanges*, NYTimes.com (May 25, 2014)]

In addition to welfare benefit plans that provide health insurance, some employers include health insurance coverage as a part of their retirement plans. T.D. 9665 provides that, starting with the 2015 tax year, most payments by qualified retirement plans for accident or health insurance will be taxable to the plan participants. There are exceptions for retiree health benefits and amounts used to pay disability insurance premiums. If the disability insurance replaces plan distributions when the participant is disabled, the premiums will not be taxable income for the employee, as long as the aggregate contribution for benefits is not greater than 25% of total plan contributions. [T.D. 9665, 79 Fed. Reg. 26838 (May 12, 2014). See The Tax Adviser, *Final Rules Govern Tax Treatment of Distributions to Pay Accident or Health Insurance Premiums*, <http://www.aicpa.org/interestareas/tax/newsandpublications/taxnews/pages/20140509aspx?action=print> (May 9, 2014); Jane Meacham, *Premiums Paid by Retirement Plans Become Taxable in 2015*, Smart HR (May 9, 2014) (benefitslink.com)]

Medical flexible spending accounts, also known as FSAs and flex accounts, permit employees to save up to $2,500 a year pre-tax. Initially, sums were forfeited to the extent they were not used for medical expenses during the plan year. Recently, the IRS has permitted a grace period for reimbursement of expenses incurred in the two and a half months after the end of the plan year. In late 2013, the IRS allowed employers to choose between offering either this grace period or a $500 carryforward of unused funds at any time during the next plan year. The Treasury said that rule changes under PPACA, reducing the amount that can be contributed to an FSA (the 2013 limit is $2,500), there is less need to prevent excess sheltering of funds in FSA accounts. [Notice 2013-71, 2013-47 I.R.B. 532; see Alison M. Stemler, *IRS Allows $500 Carry Forward Of Medical Flexible Spending Accounts*, Frost Brown Todd LLC (Dec. 13, 2013), available at Lexology.com; AP, *Rollovers for Flexible Spending Accounts*, NYTimes.com (Oct. 31, 2013); John D. McKinnon, *U.S. Allows $500 Rollovers in FSA Health Savings Accounts*, WSJ.com (Oct. 31, 2013); Fisher & Phillips LLP, *IRS Publishes New Cafeteria Plan Rule* (Nov. 1, 2013), available at Lexology.com]

An IRS phone forum listed factors triggering IRS audit of a retirement plan: e.g., presence of many separated participants who are not 100% vested; a high percentage of plan assets are classified as "other": income statements show significant distributions. Once a plan is selected for audit, there are several examination methodologies that might apply, such as risk-based compliance, LESE projects (Learn, Education, Self-Correct, Enforce) for small projects, Employee Plan Team Audit, and review for abusive transactions. Some plans are selected randomly for audit; sometimes the IRS carries out a joint investigation with another agency such as the DOL. The investigation usually begins with a telephone call from the IRS, followed up with an appointment letter or pre-planning meeting. The IRS sends a letter listing the records and documents required. Consulting the 11 sections in the IRS Examination Process Guide can give insight into what the IRS is looking for. [Kevin McGuinness, *IRS Offers Tips for Audit Preparation*, plansponsor.com (Aug. 30, 2013)]

[A] Changes in Tax Statutes

Although the tax bills since 2005 have not made tremendous changes in the employment tax picture, nevertheless they have made some modifications that are worth noting. The various tax bills since have made changes—often subtle—in employment-related taxes.

Small and medium-sized businesses often forgo targeted tax incentive tax breaks, because they are too hard to understand, cost too much to implement, or risk pushback from the IRS. According to tax consultants, eligible businesses claim only about 5% of the tax breaks they are entitled to. [John D. McKinnon, *Firms Pass Up Tax Breaks, Citing Hassles, Complexity*, WSJ.com (July 22, 2012)]

Pub. L. No. 109-264 amends Code § 114(a), to clarify that states do not have the power to tax retirement income paid by certain nonqualified plans to retired partners for past service. This treatment is retroactive to 1996. To qualify, the payments must be substantially equal periodic payments extending over at least 10 years, although payments can be subject to caps or entitled to COLAs and still be considered substantially equal. The test is also satisfied if the payment comes from both a qualified and a nonqualified plan. [No by-line, *Bill Prohibiting States from Taxing Nonresidents Cleared for President*, CCH Pension and Benefits News Story (Aug. 9, 2006) (benefitslink.com)]

As of January 1, 2010, eligible rollover distributions paid directly to a non-spouse beneficiary are subject to 20% mandatory withholding (not 10% voluntary withholding for non-periodic payments) if the amount is not directly rolled over to an IRA. [Elizabeth Thomas Dodd, Groom Law Group Memorandum to Clients, *RE: IRS Pension Distribution Reporting Changes for 2010* (Mar. 3, 2010) (benefitslink.com)]

In accordance with the PPA, the IRS explained how active duty reservists can take withdrawals from their Roth or conventional IRAs without becoming subject to the 10% early withdrawal penalty. (However, in most cases, the withdrawal will be taxable income for the reservist.) The provision is retroactive, so a reservist who incurred a penalty for past withdrawals can file Form 1040X, writing "active duty reservist" on the form and giving the date of call-up, the amount of distribution, and the penalty paid in the Part II Explanation of Changes. The reservist can return part or all of the withdrawal to the IRA. Generally, this must be done within two years of the end of active service, but can be done until August 17, 2008 (i.e., two years from enactment of the PPA) for reservists whose active duty ended pre-PPA. [Fred Schneyer, *IRS Implements Lifting of 10% Early Withdrawal Penalty for Reservists*, plansponsor.com (Sept. 29, 2006)]

The Heroes Earnings Assistance and Relief Tax Act (HEART Act, Pub. L. No. 110-245) allows servicemembers to take qualified reservist distributions, cash distributions from their FSAs that are taxable income but do not trigger the 10% penalty, and provides financial flexibility for servicemembers. See Notice 2008-82, 2008-41 I.R.B. 853 [JP Morgan Compensation & Benefit Strategies, *IRS Releases Guidance on Health FSA Distributions Under the HEART Act* (Oct. 10, 2008) (benefitslink.com)]

The American Recovery and Reinvestment Act of 2009 (ARRA; Pub. L. No. 111-5) enacted a temporary premium subsidy for COBRA premiums, but it was permitted to expire.

The Patient Protection and Affordable Care Act, Pub. L. No. 111-148 (PPACA), the health care reform bill, includes a number of tax-related provisions to finance the expansion of health insurance coverage. Most of the provisions have a deferred effective date to give employers time to gear up for the program.

PPACA §§ 1421 and 10105 provide a tax credit for small employers. The credit can be claimed for tax years beginning after December 31, 2009 if the employer makes non-elective contributions that cover at least half the premium for covering participating employees. A small employer is defined as an employer that maintains a qualified health arrangement, and that has up to 25 full-time equivalent employees (FTEs), whose average wage is not more than twice the dollar amount prescribed for the tax year. The prescribed amount for 2010–2013, is $25,000. The credit is reduced based on the number of employees and their average compensation, and is eliminated at 25 FTEs.

For tax years 2010–2013, the credit is 35% of the employer's total non-elective contributions on behalf of employees to pay premiums for qualified health coverage. However, the credit is capped at the amount that HHS determines is the average small-group premium for the relevant market. That is, employers who pay above-average premiums cannot claim the credit on the full amount paid.

For tax years that begin in 2014 or later years, the maximum credit is 50% of the premiums that the small employer pays on behalf of employees who get their health coverage through the Small Business Health Options Program (SHOP) exchange. [IRS, *What You Need to Know About the Small Business Health Care Tax Credit*, <http://www.irs.gov/uac/Small-Business-Health-Care-Tax-Credit-for-Small-Employers> (updated June 26, 2014)] However, there is a practical problem: businesses were supposed to be able to purchase coverage in 2014, but, because of problems with the first year of Marketplace enrollment, availability of business policies was delayed. In late 2013, the Obama administration announced a one-year delay in the availability of the online marketplace (SHOP Exchange) for small businesses to buy coverage, although businesses could still apply for coverage through brokers. [Robert Pear, *Online Health Law Sign-Up Is Delayed for Small Business*, NYTimes.com (Nov. 27, 2013)]

The small business health care credit is claimed on Form 8941. Qualifying employers have fewer than 25 employees, average wages under $50,000 per employee, and the employer pays at least half the premium for health insurance for enrolled employees. The employer can claim the credit for only two consecutive years beginning in or after 2014. [EBIA Weekly, *IRS Releases 2013 Form 8941 and Instructions for Claiming Small Business Health Care Tax Credit* (Jan. 16, 2014) (benefitslink.com)]

As of March 1, 2013, when automatic budget cuts were imposed as a result of the Balanced Budget and Emergency Deficit Control Act of 1985 mandatory "sequester," the refundable portion of the Code § 45R tax credit was reduced by 8.7%. The reduction is imposed until the end of the fiscal year (Sept. 30, 2013). [Cynthia Stamer, *Sequester Will Cut ACA Small Businesses Health Care Tax Credits*, WSJ.com (Mar. 5, 2013)]

As a result of PPACA, not only does paying above-average premiums restrict the credit for small employers, but also starting in 2018 a 40% excise tax will be imposed on high-cost plans (insured EGHPs and self-funded plans), irrespective of the number of employees covered. The tax is imposed when the premium exceeds $10,200 for individuals, or $27,500 for family coverage; the limits are higher for retirees over age 55 who are not yet Medicare-eligible, and for employees with high-risk jobs. [Lauren Bikoff, Health Reform Talk (CCH) *Inclusion of Cost of Employer-Sponsored Health Coverage on W-2* (Mar. 31, 2010) (benefitslink.com)]

PPACA § 9002 requires that, employers must disclose the aggregate cost (employer share plus employee share) of employer-sponsored coverage on Form W-2 The costs of long-term care insurance, accident & health, disability income insurance, fixed indemnity insurance, and coverage limited to a specified disease are not included in this figure. [See IRS, *Form W-2 Reporting of Employer-Sponsored Health Coverage*, <http://www.irs.gov/uac/Form-W-2-Reporting-of-Employer-Sponsored-Health-Coverage> (last updated May 5, 2014)]

Code § 6056 requires employers to report both to employees and the IRS. The reporting requirement was supposed to start earlier, but now has been delayed until 2015: see Notice 2013-45, 2013-31 I.R.B. 116. The IRS needs the information to administer the health care reform program; employees need the information to determine if they are entitled to a federal subsidy to help them with their share of health insurance premiums. There is a new Form 1095-C to be furnished to employees; IRS reporting uses Form 1094-C. [Chadron J. Patton, *Final Regulations Streamline ACA Reporting Rules*, Spencer Fane Britt & Browne (Mar. 13, 2014), available at Lexology.com]

Starting January 1, 2013, PPACA imposes higher Medicare payroll taxes on high-income persons. Instead of 1.45%, the employee share of Medicare tax is 2.35% for those whose income is over $250,000 (married persons filing a joint return) or $200,000 (all other filing statuses). The employer's share of the Medicare tax does not increase. High-income persons also pay a Medicare surtax on their investment income other than tax-exempt bond interest and profits on sale of their principal residence. [CCH Pension and Benefits, *Increased Medicare Taxes Imposed Under Health Reform Law Will Not Be Assessed on Plan Distributions* (Apr. 8, 2010) (benefitslink.com)]

The 3.8% investment surtax applies to gains on nonqualified stock options when they are issued. The surtax also applies to restricted stock when it vests. For high-income taxpayers, tax treatment of dividends depends on whether or not a Code § 83(b) election to accelerate income tax has been made. If there has been an election, the dividends are subject to the 3.8% tax; if not, the dividends are subject to the 0.9% tax. Taxable fringe benefits are also subject to the 0.9% tax. [Laura Saunders, *Tax Report: The New Investment Taxes*, WSJ.com (July 7, 2012)] On a related issue, see T.D. 9659, clarifying what constitutes "substantial risk of forfeiture" when stock that constitutes employee compensation under § 83 is transferred. [TD 9659, 2014-12 I.R.B. 653; see Sally P. Schreiber, *Final Substantial-Risk-Of-Forfeiture Rules Are Released*, AICPA.com (Feb. 25, 2014) (benefitslink.com); see also *Austin v. Comm'r*, 141 T.C. No. 18 (2014), finding that the discharge-for-cause provision in the taxpayer's employment agreement created a substantial risk of forfeiture]

See T.D. 9645, 2013-51 I.R.B. 738 for final regulations on the additional Medicare tax enacted on high earners by PPACA. The regulations explain how to withhold the additional tax and correct overpayments and underpayments. The tax applies to persons whose wages, compensation, or self-employment income exceed $250,000 (joint returns), $125,000 (married persons filing separately), $200,000 (single persons, heads of household, and qualifying widow(er)s with one or more dependent children). The employer must withhold the additional tax from wages over $200,000 paid to anyone, irrespective of the recipient's filing status or wages paid by other employers. The employer cannot modify its withholding of additional Medicare tax. However, a person who expects to owe more than the amount withheld by the employer can increase withholding on the W-4 (e.g., a joint return where neither spouse earns over $200,000, but the total is over $250,000). [Carrie Elizabeth Byrnes and Timothy Zehnder, *IRS Issues "Additional Medicare Tax" Final Rules*, Bryan Cave LLP (Dec. 10, 2013), available at Lexology.com]

The 2013 FICA base is $113,700 and the 2014 base is $117,000.

The IRS view is that severance payments are subject to FICA but some Supplemental Insurance Benefits (SUB payments) are not. Termination benefits that are excluded from FICA probably will not affect the recipient employee's eligibility for state unemployment benefits. A SUB plan is a severance plan to help employees after their involuntary termination. SUB payments supplement state unemployment benefits. To receive SUB pay, the employee must apply for and be granted state unemployment benefits and must verify each week that he or she is still unemployed but is available for work. A traditional SUB plan terminates benefits when the employee gets another job or otherwise ceases to be eligible for state unemployment benefits. SUB benefits must be paid weekly or with each payroll; they cannot be distributed as a lump sum. Benefits recognized by the state as SUB pay are not subject to state unemployment tax. Some states require SUB plans to be structured as offset plans: the amount the employer pays is reduced by the state unemployment benefits. Unless state law forbids it, SUB pay can be paid from the employer's general assets. If state law does forbid it, the employer can create a trust for the SUB plan. The trust can be—but is not required to be—a tax-exempt 501(c)(17) trust or a VEBA. [Vicki M. Nielsen, *The Advantages Of Offering Supplemental Unemployment Benefits Instead Of Severance, Part I: FICA Taxes And More*, Ogletree Deakins (Aug. 26, 2013), available at Lexology.com]

FICA taxes are owed on the exercise of nonqualified options or SARS, or when restricted stock vests. For compensation deferred in 401(k) or nonqualified deferred compensation plans, FICA is owed at the time of deferral even though income tax is not owed until the funds are removed from the account. Nonqualified stock options can be exercised without FICA tax consequences on income recognized at exercise if the employee's compensation for the year exceeds the FICA base. Medicare tax and additional Medicare tax are due on all compensation, with no limit. Therefore, 2012 was a good year to exercise nonqualified stock options, because of the payroll tax cut and because the extra Medicare tax had not yet taken effect. [MyStockOptions Blog, *Social Security Yearly Income Cap Will Rise In 2013: Impact On Stock Comp And NQDC* (Oct. 17, 2012) (benefitslink.com)]

For an account balance non-qualified plan, FICA is due when benefits are credited to the account or when they vest, whichever is later. For a non-account balance plan, FICA is due at retirement on the present value of the entire benefit, because that is when the deferred amount is both reasonably ascertainable and vested. A SERP participant claimed that his retirement benefits were reduced improperly because of the employer's mishandling of FICA taxes, and he moved for full benefits unreduced by FICA, which would make the employer responsible for both the employee and employer share of FICA. The SERP deferred base pay and bonuses and provided supplemental monthly benefits at retirement. During a compliance review, the sponsor discovered that FICA had not been properly paid. When FICA is not paid properly, the employer must withhold FICA tax on all benefits subsequently paid under the plan unless the three-year statute of limitations has not yet run, and the employer can file an amended return for the year the payment should have been made. Participants prefer that FICA be paid while they are still working, when their compensation is higher—and the amount over the FICA limit will not be taxed—rather than post-retirement, when they are likely to have lower income. The District Court for the Eastern District of Michigan permitted the suit to proceed, because the issue was framed as improper reduction of benefits, so it was not subject to limits on suits about improper tax withholding. [*Davidson v. Henkel Corp.*, No. 12-cv-14103, 2013 U.S. Dist. LEXIS 103185 (E.D. Mich. July 23, 2013); see Stephen Douglas and Russ Hall, *Employer Liability for Mishandling FICA Tax Under Nonqualified Plan*, Towers Watson (Oct. 21, 2013) (benefitslink.com); Angela Bohmann, *This Time the Employer Is Responsible for the Withholding Error*, Benefits Notes (Aug. 21, 2013) (benefitslink.com)]

The PPACA also imposes a small fee on self-insured plans and issuers of health insurance policies, for plan years that end on or after October 1, 2012 and before October 1, 2019. (The fee will be used to fund research into which treatments are the most effective.) The sponsor of a self-insured plan, or the insurer of a policy covering an insured plan, must pay $1 per person covered under the plan for the first year, and $2 per person for the second year, with subsequent inflation adjustments. The fee is paid on IRS Form 720. [77 Fed. Reg. 22691 (Apr. 17, 2012), see DOL, *FAQs About Affordable Care Act Implementation Part XI* (Jan. 24, 2013) (benefitslink.com)]

PPACA retains the ability of corporations to receive federal subsidies tax-free if they provide prescription drug coverage for their retirees. The subsidy is 28% of the cost of coverage, subject to a cap of $1,330 per retiree. However, PPACA provides that the subsidy amount will no longer be deductible, starting in 2013. [Kris Maher, Ellen E. Schultz, and Bob Tita, *Deere, Caterpillar: Health-Care Law to Raise Expenses*, WSJ.com (Mar. 26, 2010)]

Stimulus efforts continued with the enactment of the Hiring Incentives to Restore Employment (HIRE) Act, Pub. L. No. 111-147, in March 2010; there was a temporary payroll tax incentive for hiring unemployed workers if hiring occurred between February 3, 2010 and January 1, 2011. [Rebecca Moore, *New Law Offers Tax Incentives for Hiring*, plansponsor.com (Mar. 18, 2010)]

This was replaced by another payroll tax incentive, a cut in employees' FICA rates. The Temporary Payroll Tax Cut Continuation Act, Pub. L. No. 112-78 (December 2011) reduced the employee FICA rate to 4.2% (or 10.4% for self-employed persons) but subject to a wage cap of $18,350. The Middle Class Tax Relief and Job Creation Act of 2012, Pub. L. No. 112-96, enacted February 2, 2012, extended the 4.2% FICA rate for workers until the end of 2012, and repealed the cap. [<http://www.irs.gov/pub/irs-pdf/f941.pdf] However, there were no further extensions of the FICA cut after the end of 2012.

The Small Business Jobs and Credit Act, Pub. L. No. 111-240, also includes some miscellaneous employment-related provisions:

- Employees are no longer required to log personal use of cell phones provided by their employers so they can treat the personal use as taxable income;
- Retirees who own annuities outside their retirement plans can access income from only part of the annuity while leaving the rest invested;
- Balances (known as "eligible rollover distributions") can be transferred from 401(k) to Roth 401(k) plans, beginning on September 27, 2010, but only if the plan includes a Roth 401(k) feature. The transfer is taxable, but income tax on 2010 conversions can be deferred until 2011 and 2012, with half of the taxable amount reported in each of the two years. [Laura Saunders, *Tax Report: Surprise New Tax Breaks*, WSJ.com (Sept. 25, 2010)]

Although the Small Business Jobs and Credit Act of 2010 (SBJCA), Pub. L. No. 111-240, increases tax cuts and credit for small businesses, it also increases the penalty for not providing or filing Form 1099-series forms on time. The penalties depend on whether a Form 1099-R was required from a small business or a large business; whether it was filed late but corrected; or whether the taxpayer intentionally disregarded the filing obligation. The penalties, which can be as high as $100 per form (2011) will be adjusted for inflation in 2012 and every five years after that. [McKay Hochman Company, Inc. E-Mail Alert 2010-16, *Form 1099 Series Penalties Increased* (Oct. 15, 2010) (benefitslink.com)]

The Tax Relief, Unemployment Insurance Reauthorization, and Job Creation Act of 2010 (TRUIRJCA), Pub. L. No. 111-312, was signed December 17, 2010. Major provisions include:

- A one-year cut in payroll tax.
- 100% bonus depreciation on business equipment for 2011, 50% bonus depreciation for 2012.
- Taxpayers can continue to exclude from income the gain from selling qualified small business stock that was held for more than five years.

- For 2011, the maximum adoption credit or adoption assistance amount was $13,170.
- The enhanced dependent care credit is extended through December 31, 2012. The 35% rate is applied to $3,000 of expenses (or $6,000 if there is more than one qualifying dependent), with the result that the maximum credit is $1,050 for one dependent, $2,100 for two or more. The credit is reduced, but not below 20%, based on the employee's AGI in excess of $15,000.
- Educational assistance (including graduate school tuition) of up to $5,250 can be provided tax-free until December 31, 2012. The Making Work Pay credit expired as scheduled on December 31, 2010, and was not renewed. Payroll tax forgiveness for employers under the HIRE Act also expired on December 31, 2010 and was not renewed.
- The maximum transit assistance/van pooling benefit was $230/month for 2011.
- The Work Opportunity Tax Credit was extended. [CCH Tax Briefing, *Tax Relief/Job Creation Act of 2010 Special Report*, <http://tax.cchgroup.com/downloads/files/pdfs/legislation/bush-taxcuts.pdf> (Dec. 17, 2010);]

In November 2011, the VOW to Hire Heroes Act (Pub. L. No. 112-56) was enacted, including a new tax credit for hiring veterans, up to a maximum of $9,600 per veteran. The credit is available for hiring a qualifying veteran between November 22, 2011 and January 1, 2013. The amount of the credit depends on factors such as the length of time veteran was out of work prior to being hired, the number of hours worked, and the wages paid in the first year post-hiring. The maximum credit is provided for hiring veterans with service-related disabilities.

[Notice 2012-13, 2012-9 I.R.B. 421; VOW to Hire Heroes Act FAQ, <http://www.irs.gov/businesses/small/article/0,,id=253950,00.html> (Feb. 9, 2012]

The "fiscal cliff" tax bill, the American Taxpayer Relief Act of 2012 (ATRA; Pub. L. No.112-240) provides that in 2013 the employer's share of FICA tax is 6.2% of income up to $113,700. Fifty percent bonus depreciation has been extended for one year. [Baker McKenzie Executive Compensation & Employee Benefits, *New Tax Rates in Effect for 2013* (Jan. 3, 2013); Laura Saunders, *High Earners Facing First Major Tax Increase in Years*, WSJ.com (Jan. 1, 2013)]

The ATRA permits in-plant Roth conversions of defined contribution accounts that would not otherwise be distributable, with no income limitations. Under prior law, only amounts that were immediately distributable (e.g., to a participant who had reached age 59½) could be converted to Roth status. The provision is effective January 1, 2013, and account balances in existence on that date can be converted. [Rebecca Moore, *Fiscal Cliff Deal Extends Roth Conversions*, plansponsor.com (Jan. 3, 2013)]

See Notice 2013-74, 2013-52 I.R.B. 819 for guidance on in-plan Roth rollovers (rollovers within a 401(k) plan to a designated Roth account within the same plan). Under Code § 402A, designated Roth contributions are elective deferrals to a retirement plan that the participant elects to include in gross income, although they would otherwise be excludable. Designated Roth contributions and their earnings must be maintained in a separate account within the plan. Distributions from an individual's account in a retirement plan other than a designated Roth account can be rolled over to the participant's designated Roth account in the same plan. When in-plan Roth rollovers were first permitted by the Small Business Jobs Act, rollovers were limited to amounts that were otherwise distributable (e.g., the participant had reached age 59½ or terminated employment).

The American Taxpayer Relief Act enacted Code § 402A(c)(4)(E), providing that, for in-plan rollovers after December 31, 2012, otherwise non-distributable amounts can be rolled over to the Roth account. Notice 2013-74 explains that elective deferrals, matching contributions, and non-elective contributions can be rolled over to the Roth account. But amounts rolled over to a designated Roth account remain subject to the distribution restrictions applicable to the amount before the rollover. For example, a current participant who has not reached age 59½ cannot withdraw funds from the account until a distribution event occurs. The deadline for adopting an amendment permitting in-plan Roth rollovers is the last day of the first plan year for which the amendment is effective, or December 31, 2014—whichever is later. [Lisa A. Berkowitz Herrnson, *IRS Provides New Guidance On In-Plan Roth Rollovers*, Proskauer Rose (Dec. 17, 2013), available at Lexology.com]

At the end of 2013, a number of business credits were allowed to expire, such as the credit for research and experimentation, the work opportunity tax credit, and certain corporate charitable donation provisions. The 100% exclusion of gain on sale of small business stock expired, but for 2014, 50% of gain is excludable from taxable income. In general, the 50% additional first-year depreciation rule has been eliminated (except for some transportation assets and some long-production-period property placed into service before January 1, 2015). The ability to expense assets under Code § 179 has greatly decreased. [Joint Committee on Taxation JCX-1-14, *List of Expiring Federal Tax Provisions 2013-2024*, <http://www.jct.gov> (Jan. 10, 2014); David S. Lionberger, *Numerous Federal Tax Provisions Will Lapse In 2014*, Hirschler Fleischer (Jan. 13, 2014), available at Lexology.com]

[B] Tax Implications of Same-Sex Marriage

As the number of states permitting same-sex marriage, civil union, or domestic partnership increases (see § 18.06), employers are often faced with the problem of handling tax issues for employees who indicate that they have a same-sex life partner.

In mid-2013, the Supreme Court struck down the federal Defense of Marriage Act (DOMA). DOMA defined marriage, for federal purposes, as a union of one man and one woman. Because the Supreme Court found this statute unconstitutional (on due process and equal protection grounds), same-sex married couples are entitled to file joint income tax returns. There are many other federal consequences, including military spousal benefits and estate tax status as a surviving spouse.

In states that either allow same-sex couples to marry, or that recognize same-sex marriages in other jurisdictions, tax withholding for employees who are married to same-sex partners should be based on: see § 18.06[A] for further discussion of employment consequences of same-sex marriage. [*United States v. Windsor*, 133 S. Ct. 2675 (2013); *Hollingsworth v. Perry*, 133 S. Ct. 2652 (2013)

There are also issues specific to California, Nevada, and Washington, because they are community property states; domestic partners may qualify for favorable tax treatment. [IRS Q&As for Registered Domestic Partners in Community Property States & Same-Sex Spouses in California, <http://www.irs.gov/newsroom/article/0,,id=245869,00.html>(Sept. 16, 2011); see EBIA Weekly, *IRS Clarifications Affect Employee Benefits for Domestic Partners and Same-Sex Spouses* (Nov. 3, 2011) (benefitslink.com)]

ADP Research notes that states vary in their taxing practices for same-sex couples. This is not an issue in Arkansas, Florida, Nevada, New Hampshire, South Dakota, Tennessee, Texas, Washington, and Wyoming, because these states do not have income tax withholding. In the other states, the question is whether the state authorizes same-sex marriages in the state; whether same-sex marriages cannot be performed there, but marriages from other jurisdictions will be recognized; or whether the state does not recognize same-sex marriage at all. [Plansponsor staff, *States Rule On Taxation For Same-Gender Couples*, plansponsor.com (Dec. 19, 2013)] Guidance from state taxing authorities in Nebraska, North Carolina, Ohio, and Wisconsin says that, as of April 2014, these states did not recognize same-sex marriage, so employers who provided health benefits for employees' same-sex spouses would have to withhold income tax on the value of the coverage from the employees. It is possible, however, that these states will recognize same-sex marriage subsequently. [Megan E. Hladilek and Atul Jain, *Same-Sex Spouse Health Coverage-Recent Developments in State Tax*, Faegre Baker Daniels (Apr. 16, 2014), available at Lexology.com]

The federal employment tax consequences of *Windsor* are clarified by Notice 2013-61, 2013-44 I.R.B. 432. For 2013, employers have two options for correcting over-collection of FICA and income tax from employees with same-sex spouses. The employer can use the Form 941 for the fourth quarter of 2013 to correct the first three quarters, reimbursing the employees for excess collections no later than December 31, 2013. The employer can also correct the first three quarters by filing Form 941-X for the fourth quarter, labeling the form

WINDSOR in large, bold letters on Page 1 of the form. For open pre-2013 years only, and for FICA only (not income tax), a single Form 941-X marked WINDSOR on page 1 can be filed for each year within the limitations period. (In other words, refunds are available only for 2010–2012, because of the three-year statute of limitations.) Affected employees must be reimbursed for overwithholding; the employer must obtain written statements from the employees that they are not seeking reimbursement and will not do so in the future. The employer must also file Form W-2C. [Infinisource Newsroom, *IRS Clarifies Same-sex Marriage Rules for Payroll* (Sept. 26, 2013) (benefitslink.com); Durward James Gehring, *IRS Announces Special Procedures For Correcting Overwithholding On Same-Gender Spouse Benefit*, Seyfarth Shaw LLP (Sept. 25, 2013), available at Lexology.com]

Notice 2014-1, 2014-2 I.R.B. 270 explains treatment of cafeteria plan elections, FSAs, HSAs, and dependent care assistance program limits for same-sex married couples. Because *Windsor* was decided on June 26, 2013 (the middle of the calendar year), elections can be changed to reflect same-sex marriage during the plan year that includes either June 26, 2013 (the date of the Supreme Court decision) or December 16, 2013 (the date of the IRS notice permitting recognition of same-sex marriage for employee benefit purposes). When an employer is notified that an employee has a same-sex spouse, it must allow the employee to pay on a pre-tax basis to cover the spouse, even if the employee previously paid with after-tax dollars. The employee can also continue paying for the spouse's coverage with after-tax dollars for the rest of the cafeteria plan year, then seek a tax refund. The notice says that Health FSAs can reimburse health expenses of an employee's same-sex spouse and dependents that were incurred during the plan year that includes June 26, 2013 (or the date of the marriage, if later). However, marriage does not always reduce the taxes of same-sex couples. Under previous law, each partner sometimes contributed the household maximum limit to an HSA or dependent care assistant plan. Now, they are a single household, so the limit applies to the couple, not to each individual. Notice 2014-1 explains how to deal with excess contributions to avoid § 4973 excise taxes. [Stephen A. Riga, *At Year End, IRS Issues Guidance On Cafeteria Plan Transitional Rules For Windsor*, Ogletree Deakins (Dec. 26, 2013), available at Lexology.com]

§ 2.02 THE COMPENSATION DEDUCTION

Internal Revenue Code § 162 allows a corporation to deduct its ordinary and necessary business expenses, including reasonable salaries in exchange for personal services rendered to the corporation. Salaries are only reasonable if the person hired is qualified to perform the services, and actually performs them. If vacation pay is treated as deferred compensation, it is not deductible until the year it is actually paid. [See I.R.C. § 404(a)(5)]

The Working Families Tax Relief Act of 2004 (WFTRA) amended § 152(c) to define a "qualifying child" as one who satisfies relationship, residency, and age tests, and who does not provide more than half of his or her own support. The qualifying child must be either under 19 as of the close of the calendar year, a student under 24 at the end of the calendar year, or be permanently and totally disabled at any time during the year. This statute required the value of health coverage provided to a domestic partner or same-sex spouse to be treated as taxable income to the employee. [Notice 2004-79, 2004-49 I.R.B. 898]

The ATRA of 2012, Pub. L. No. 112-240, makes the adoption credit/adoption assistance provisions permanent.

For 2013, the maximum adoption credit and tax exclusion amount is $12,970 per child, phasing down at income of $194,580 and out at $234,580. For 2014, the maximum is $13,190, and the phase-out range is $197,880–$237,880. Taxpayers can e-file Form 8839 to claim the credit or exclusion; previously, this form had to be filed on paper. The credit was refundable until 2012. In 2013–2014, it is non-refundable, but carrybacks and carryforwards are permitted. A married taxpayer filing a separate return can claim an adoption credit carryforward if he or she filed a joint return in the year the adoption expenses first became allowable. [EBIA Weekly Archives, *IRS Releases 2013 Form 8839 (Qualified Adoption Expenses) and Instructions* (Jan. 2, 2014) (benefitslink.com)]

For public corporations, § 162(m) does not allow a deduction for over $1 million in compensation paid to "covered employees"—certain senior executives. However, the cap does not apply to "performance-based compensation"—compensation payable solely because the payee has achieved an objective goal (or goals) set in advance. [See Rev. Rul. 2008-13, 2008-10 I.R.B. 518, tightening up the rules for performance-based compensation, with the result that some compensation lost its deductible status; this ruling is discussed in Douglas J. Ellis, *IRS Confirms Controversial New Position on Section 162(m) Performance-Based Compensation Deduction*, <http://www.klgates.com/newsstand/Detail.aspx?publication=4353>.

In mid-2012, the IRS issued guidance on whether dividends on restricted stock, and the equivalent on restricted stock units (RSUs), must satisfy the § 162(m) requirements separately to be treated as fully deductible performance-based compensation: Rev. Rul. 2012-19, 2012-28 I.R.B. 16. To qualify for exemption from the $1 million exemption, the dividends or dividend equivalents can only be payable if the payee meets performance goals. However, the performance goals for this purpose do not have to be the same ones for granting the underlying restricted stock or RSUs. [Buck Consultants FYI, *IRS Clarifies Treatment of Performance-Based Restricted Stock and Restricted Stock Units* (Aug. 8, 2012) (benefitslink.com)]

The Supreme Court refused to review the Eighth Circuit's decision that cash distribution dividends paid to redeem stock held in an ESOP are not deductible—Code § 162(k)(1) provides that there is no § 404(k) deduction available for amounts paid to an ESOP trust to redeem shares of the parent company's stock, and the facts in this case were fairly similar. [*Nestle Purina Petcare Co. v. Commissioner of Internal Revenue*, 594 F.3d 968 (8th Cir.), *cert. denied*, 131 S. Ct. 86 (Oct. 4, 2010); see Rebecca Moore, *Decision Stands that Nestle Purina Cannot Deduct Distribution Dividends*, plansponsor.com (Oct. 5, 2010). The comparable case is *General Mills, Inc. v. United States*, 554 F.3d 727 (8th Cir. 2009)]

§ 2.03 INCOME TAX WITHHOLDING

[A] Calculation

A September 2007 IRS press release explains how taxpayers can request Employer Identification Numbers (EINs) in real time: go to <http://www.irs.gov>, access the Internet EIN System, and enter the required fields. A permanent EIN is issued for immediate use if the data passes automated validity checks. Employers whose application is rejected can correct the information and then re-submit the application. Once the application is complete, the taxpayer can view, print, and save the confirmation notice rather than having it mailed. [Nevin E. Adams, *IRS Now Offers Real-Time EINs*, plansponsor.com (Sept. 25, 2007)]

At the time of hiring, the employer must also have the employee submit Form W-4 (Employee's Withholding Allowance Certificate) to indicate the filing status (married filing a joint return, married filing a separate return, single, head of household) and the number of withholding allowances that he or she claims. The more withholding allowances, the less that will be withheld from the employee's paycheck.

Although there are other methods, the amount of income tax to be withheld is usually calculated under either the percentage method or the wage bracket method. (The calculations will be done by the payroll preparation contractor, if the employer outsources this function.)

Under the percentage method, the IRS tables are used. The number of allowances claimed is multiplied by the amount from the allowance table; the result is subtracted from the employee's wages. The wage rate table gives the actual dollar amount to be withheld.

Under the wage bracket method, tables are used to compute withholding per weekly, semiweekly, or other pay period, based on wage level, marital status, and number of claimed exemptions.

There was a "Making Work Pay" credit of up to $400 for an individual, $800 on a joint return. It was enacted by ARRA (Pub. L. No. 111-5) but expired at the end of 2010. For income tax purposes, "supplemental wages" means compensation other than, or in addition to, ordinary cash compensation. Bonuses, commissions, overtime pay, severance pay, back pay, taxable fringe benefits, and payments for accumulated sick leave are all supplemental wages.

For payments made after 2004, once a person's supplemental wage income exceeds $1 million, the employer must withhold on the supplemental income at the highest income tax rate (currently, 35%). Employers have an obligation to keep a cumulative record of this income so that they will be aware when the $1 million threshold is crossed.

T.D. 9276 clarifies that compensation can be treated as "supplemental" even if the payee had no regular wages for the year. The category of supplemental wages also includes nonqualified deferred compensation that is included in wages, imputed income when a non-dependent (e.g., a same-sex partner) receives health coverage, and income due to lapse on restrictions on property transferred from employer to employee. Commissions, bonuses, and taxable noncash fringe benefits cannot be treated as regular wages. Under the proposed regulations, commissions could be treated as regular wages if the employee did not receive any other compensation, but T.D. 9276 eliminates this option. [T.D. 9276, 2006-37 I.R.B. 423)]

Rev. Rul. 2008-29, 2008-24 I.R.B. 1149, provides guidance under the supplemental wage regulations for signing bonuses and various kinds of commissions. For severance pay, the employer can either add supplemental wages to regular wages and use the tax tables, or can withhold at a 25% flat rate. [G.J. Stillson MacDonnell and William Hays Weissman (Littler Mendelson), *IRS Provides Guidance on Proper Income Tax Withholding for Nine Common Supplemental Wage Payment Scenarios* (June 2008) (benefitslink.com)]

Central to the tax treatment of settlements and damages employees obtain from suing the employer is whether the money replaces compensation that the employee would have earned absent the factors that led to the suit.

The Second Circuit held that back pay is defined as the wages the plaintiff would have earned from the date of discharge to the date of reinstatement, plus lost fringe benefits, whereas front pay is awarded for lost compensation either instead or reinstatement or running from the judgment to the time of reinstatement. A former New York State employee was awarded back and front pay by the jury. State and federal taxes were deducted. The Second Circuit held that, even without direction from a court to deduct the taxes, the New York State Office of Comptroller was correct to do so: Back pay and front pay are wages subject to FICA and income tax withholding. [*Noel v. New York State Office Of Mental Health Cent. New York Psychiatric Ctr.*, 697 F.3d 209 (2d Cir. 2012)]

The Second Circuit held that settlement proceeds in an ADEA suit were wages subject to FICA. The agreement expressly permitted the employer to deduct and withhold all sums subject to withholding under applicable laws and regulations, but did not state how the $250,000 settlement proceeds would be treated for tax purposes. A court analyzing a settlement payment looks first to the nature of the claim that was settled, then remedies under governing law, then to the parties' intention. In ADEA cases, the remedies are lost wages, liquidated damages, and equitable relief—but not pain and suffering or emotional distress damages (which would probably not be treated as wages). [*Gerstenbluth v. Credit Suisse*, 728 F.3d 139 (2d Cir. 2013)]

The Tax Court reaffirmed that emotional distress damages are taxable income for recipient. The plaintiff was a professor who charged that she was demoted to a secretarial position in retaliation for reporting missing equipment. After a leave of absence, she was reinstated as professor and then filed another missing equipment report, leading to a grievance dispute with another member of the faculty. Sharp claimed that, as a result of the stressful hostile environment, she developed severe clinical depression and related physical symptoms. The university settled her suit, agreeing to make three installment payments of $70,000 each for emotional distress. When she received the first installment in 2010, she did not report it as taxable income, treating it as damages for personal physical injuries exempted by Code § 104(a)(2). The IRS assessed tax; she filed a Tax Court petition. The Tax Court agreed with the IRS, and upheld the accuracy-related penalty, finding that she did not prove the money was paid for settling a Workers' Compensation claim. The Tax Court said that agreements are analyzed according to their express language, and the settlement agreement had only one reference to the agreement being conditioned on the plaintiff settling her Workers' Compensation claim. The settlement was described as covering emotional distress; even if emotional distress has physical manifestations, the settlement proceeds are still taxable income for the recipient. [*Sharp v. Commissioner*, T.C.M. 290 (2013), Docket No. 21332-12, 106 T.C.M. (CCH) 700 (T.C. Dec. 23, 2013); see William Hays Weissman, *U.S. Tax Court Decision Shows Importance Of Carefully Drafting Settlement Agreements*, Littler Mendelson (Jan. 6, 2014), available at Lexology.com]

A Recent Chief Counsel Memo (CCM) explains the four-step approach to taxation of settlements of employment discrimination claims. The first step is the origin of the claim. The IRS says that wage-based payments must be reported on Form W-2, not Form 1099-MISC. The second step is that severance payments generally constitute gross income for the recipient unless an exclusion is available. The most common exclusions are under Code § 104(a)(2), damages for physical illness or injury and reimbursement of medical costs. If any part of a severance payment is taxable to the recipient, the allocable part of the attorney's fee is also gross income. The third step is that severance pay, back pay, and front pay, unless excluded from gross income, are FICA and FUTA wages subject to withholding, even if they are paid post termination of employment. The CCM says that if the settlement does not allocate the amount of attorney's fees, or if the settlement does not involve a fee-shifting statute such as Title VII, the ADEA, or the ADA, the entire amount of attorney's fees awarded to the ex-employee will be treated as wages for employment tax purposes. But the sum does not constitute wages if an employment-related claim under a fee-shifting statute is settled out of court and the settlement agreement clearly allocates a reasonable portion of the proceeds as attorney's fees. Step 4 is reporting the entire payment to settle a wage-based claim on the ex-employee's Form W-2. But if the settlement agreement specifically makes a reasonable allocation for attorney's fees, the employer reports the fee payments on separate 1099-MISCs, one to the former employee and one to the attorney. Noncompliance makes the employer subject to a penalty of $ 100 per failure under Code §§ 6721(a) and 6722(a), or $250 for each intentional disobedience of the filing requirements. [IRS Chief Counsel Memo No. 20133501F (Aug. 20, 2013); see J. Mark Poerio, *Severance Pay And Employment Taxes: Addressed In IRS Chief Counsel Memo*, Paul Hastings LLP (Sept. 16, 2013), available at Lexology.com]

The withholding system must distinguish between compensation paid to the employee and reimbursement of legitimate business expenses that the employee incurred on the employer's behalf (reimbursement is not taxable income).

For tax purposes, expense accounts are either "accountable" or "nonaccountable" plans. Amounts paid under an accountable plan are not wages for the employee, and therefore are not subject to FICA or FUTA. Withholding is not required. Employees must meet two tests under an accountable plan:

- They paid or incurred deductible expenses in the course of employment;
- They are required to provide adequate accounts of the expenses within a reasonable time of incurring them.

If they receive any amount over and above the expenses, they have an obligation to return it within a reasonable time. The general tax rule is that it is reasonable for employees to be reimbursed within 30 days of spending money; to provide an expense account within 60 days of spending the money; and to return excess amounts within 120 days of the initial advance.

Accounting for a per diem or a fixed allowance (e.g., X cents per mile for business travel) is considered adequate as long as the payment is no higher than the government per diem rates for meals and lodging (see IRS Publication 1542) and the standard mileage rate for travel. [IRS Publication 553]

If these tests are not met, the money is treated as if it were paid under a nonaccountable plan (one which does not require documentation of expenses). Expenses reimbursed under a nonaccountable plan are considered wages, included in income and subject to withholding in the first payroll period after there has been a reasonable time to return any excess funds.

Form 2106 is used for employees to claim business expense deductions for work-related travel, transportation, meals, or entertainment if the employee was reimbursed for deductible work-related expenses. The simplified Form 2106-EZ can be used by employees who use the standard mileage rate for vehicle expenses and who do not receive any expense reimbursement that is not reported as taxable income. The "accountable plan" rules relieve employees from tax on business expense reimbursement if the expenses are business-related, adequately substantiated, and the employee returns any amount of reimbursement that exceeds the expenses. If the reimbursement is less than the actual expense, an employee who can substantiate the actual amount can take a deduction on Form 2106 for the difference. See Rev. Proc. 2011-47, 2011-42 I.R.B. 520 for rules about per diem reimbursement to traveling employees, and Notice 2012-53, 2012-35 I.R.B. 317 for 2012–2013 special per diem rates for ordinary and necessary business expenses.

Regulations were proposed in August 2012 under Code § 274(n) dealing with the 50% limit on deductions for food, beverages, and entertainment under a reimbursement arrangement. In a reimbursement agreement with employees, the 50% limit applies to the employer—unless the reimbursement constitutes taxable wages, in which case the limit applies to the employee. For expenses under an accountable plan, the limit applies only to the employer. [Prop. Regs. at 77 Fed. Reg. 45520 (Aug. 1, 2012); see Elizabeth T. Dold, *Proposed Regulations Clarify the 50% Entertainment Limit for Expense Reimbursement Arrangements*, Groom Law Group (Aug. 31, 2012) (benefitslink.com)]

The optional 2014 standard mileage rates for business use of car or moving expenses are: 56 cents/mile for business use of a vehicle and 23.5 cents/mile when an employee moves for business reasons. (In 2013, the corresponding figures were slightly higher: 56.5 cents a mile and 24 cents a mile.) For cars used for business purpose, the portion of the standard mileage rate treated as depreciation is 23 cents per mile (2010), 22 cents (2011), 23 cents (2012–2013), falling to 22 cents/mile in 2014. The standard vehicle cost for allowance under a FAVR (Fixed and Variable Rate) plan is limited to $28,200 for cars, $30,400 for trucks and vans. [Notice 2013-80, 2013-52 I.R.B. 821]

Publication 521 for 2013 returns has only one big change from 2012: the standard mileage rate for using one's own vehicle to move to a new home now reflects the 2013 rate of 24 cents per mile. [<http://www.irs.gov/pub/irs-prior/p521--2013.pdf>; see BIA Weekly Archives, *IRS Releases 2013 Version of Publication 521 on Moving Expenses* (Nov. 7, 2013) (benefitslink.com)]

The tax exemption for mass-transit fringe benefits is scheduled to drop to $130 in 2014, while the benefit for parking rises slightly, from $245 to $250. Originally, the transit benefit was lower than the parking benefit. It was temporarily equalized between 2009 and 2013, but equalization provision expired December 31, 2013. The parking benefit is indexed by statute. [Andrew Grossman, *Mass-Transit Commuters Face a Tax Hit*, WSJ.com (Dec. 29, 2013)]

IRS Information Letter 2013-0032 says that bicycle share programs are not qualified transportation fringe benefits as defined by Code § 132, so the employer cannot exclude expenses for the program from an employee's gross income. A bicycle share program is not a transit pass because it does not involve mass transit and it is not bicycle commuting reimbursement because that involves the employee's purchase and repair of a bicycle for travel between home and work. Although other qualified transportation benefits can be provided via salary reduction agreement, qualified bicycle commuting reimbursement cannot. [PLC, *IRS: Bike Share Expenses Do Not Qualify for Favorable Fringe Benefit Tax Treatment* (Oct. 2, 2013) (benefitslink.com)]

All of the employee's taxable income is subject to income tax withholding, except to the degree that a withholding exemption is available. FICA (Social

Security) taxes are imposed on the employee's taxable income, up to a certain amount (the amount is $97,500 for 2007, $102,000 for 2008, $106,800 for 2009–2011, $110,100 for 2012, $113,700 for 2013, and $117,000 for 2014; each year's wage base must be published in the Federal Register no later than November 1 of the preceding year). The employer and employee are each taxed at a rate of 6.2% on income up to the limit, and Medicare taxes are imposed on all compensation.

AJCA § 251, affecting I.R.C. § 13121(a), 421(b), 423(c), provides that for FICA and FUTA purposes, the definition of "wages" does not include remuneration from exercising an ISO or option to buy stock under an employee stock purchase plan.

Quality Stores went through Chapter 11 bankruptcy. Terminated employees received severance benefits that were not tied to the receipt of state unemployment benefits. The payments varied based on the employee's job duties and length of employment. At first, Quality Stores withheld FICA taxes on these amounts. Then the company decided that the payments were not FICA wages, so it sought a tax refund for itself and about 1,850 ex-employees who received payments. In March 2014, the Supreme Court held that the severance payments constituted FICA wages. The Supreme Court held that severance payments are made only to employees, and they are made because of service to employers because "service" is defined broadly as the entire relationship between the employer and employee. The court noted that the FICA statute provides a list of exemptions from the general rule that all compensation constitutes FICA wages. One of the exemptions is for severance payments made for disability retirement. The Supreme Court said it would not be necessary to specify this exemption if severance pay in general did not constitute FICA wages. Code § 3401(a), dealing with income tax withholding, also has a broad definition of taxable wages, subject to a list of exemptions. The list says that Supplemental Unemployment Benefits are treated as if they were wages: see § 3402(o). Quality Stores interpreted this to mean that, although SUB payments are treated "as if" they were wages, they are not wages for this purpose or for FICA purposes. However, the Supreme Court traced this provision to the history of tax withholding, when Congress wanted to relieve terminated workers from the burden of year-end tax liability. [*United States v. Quality Stores Inc.*, 134 S. Ct. 1395 (2014)]

In mid-2004, district courts in Michigan clashed as to whether early retirement incentive payments offered to teachers in exchange for tenure rights were wages. The Western District said that such payments are wages for FICA purposes; two weeks later, the Eastern District said that because the payments were not wages, the retired teachers could get a refund of FICA withheld on the payments. [Compare *Klender v. United States*, 328 F. Supp. 2d 754 (E.D. Mich. 2004) with *Appoloni v. United States, 219 F.R.D. 116* (W.D. Mich. 2004); but see *N.D. State Univ. v. United States*, 255 F.3d 599 (8th Cir. 2001)]

The Sixth Circuit resolved the split in mid-2006 by ruling that the payments were FICA wages because "compensation" should be defined broadly, and because eligibility for the payments depended on at least a minimum tenure with the employer, showing that payments were made for services, not for relinquishments of tenure rights. [*Appoloni v. United States/Klender v. United States*, 450 F.3d 185 (6th Cir. 2006); the Federal Circuit earlier ruled that severance payments to retiring employees, reflecting past work, are FICA wages; *Abrahamsen v. United States*, 228 F.3d 1360 (Fed. Cir. 2000). The Western District of Michigan held that severance payments to RIFed employees were not FICA wages. [*United States v. Quality Stores, Inc.*, 2010 U.S Dist. LEXIS 15825 (W.D. Mich. Feb. 23, 2010); see Thomas M. Cryan, Jr. and Marianna G. Dyson, Miller & Chevalier, *Quality Stores Decision Muddies the Waters on the FICA Tax Treatment of Severance Pay* (Mar. 3, 2010) (benefitslink.com)]

Although other courts disagree, the Third Circuit held that the University of Pittsburgh's early retired payments to tenured professors are taxable income, not buyout payments. The Third Circuit deemed tenure to be a form of compensation for past work at the university, so giving up tenure was the equivalent of severance pay and thus FICA wages. [Fred Schneyer, *Payments to Tenured Profs Ruled Taxable Wages*, plansponsor.com (Nov. 5, 2007)]

The Supreme Court held, early in 2011, that medical residents working over 40 hours a week are not "students" for FICA purposes. Therefore, their compensation is subject to FICA tax. [*Mayo Found. for Med. Educ. & Research v. United States*, 131 S. Ct. 704 (2011); see Buck Consultants FYI, *Supreme Court Upholds Treasury Rule That Medical Residents Are Employees for FICA Purposes* (Jan. 21, 2011) (benefitslink.com)]

[B] Withholding on Pensions

The general rule is that income tax withholding is required when a plan makes payments to retired employees. There are circumstances under which the retirees can elect to waive withholding, but there are other circumstances in which withholding is mandatory.

For ordinary pension payments in annuity form, the plan can use its regular withholding procedures, based on the number of withholding exemptions on the retiree's Form W-4P. If no W-4P is submitted, the plan should withhold as if the retiree were married and claimed three withholding allowances.

However, if the distribution is a lump sum or other nonperiodic payment and not an annuity, the question is whether it is an "eligible rollover distribution." If it is not, the basic requirement is to withhold at a 10% rate, although the person receiving the lump sum can use the W-4P to claim exemption from withholding. If the recipient of the lump sum expects to be in a high tax bracket, the person can ask for withholding at a rate higher than 10%.

An eligible rollover distribution is an amount that could be placed in the retiree's IRA, Roth IRA, or transferred to another qualified plan. Any such amount that is not rolled over is subject to withholding at a rate of at least 20%.

The recipient of the distribution can increase the withholding rate, but cannot lower it below 20% or claim a withholding exemption. See Code § 3405 and the instructions for Form 1099-R. The Pension Protection Act also permits a non-spouse beneficiary of a qualified plan account to roll over inherited funds to his or her own IRA.

Withholding from lump-sum pension distributions is not reported on Form 941. Instead, Form 945 (Annual Return of Withheld Federal Income Tax) is used. The pension withholding amounts should be combined with the other Form 945 amounts, but for nonpayroll withholding only, not payroll taxes. [See Form 945 instructions.] The recipient of the distribution receives a Form 1099-R (Distributions from Pensions, Annuities, Retirement or Profit-Sharing Plans). [See Chapter 12 for further information on distributions from qualified plans.]

§ 2.04 FUTA TAX

FUTA (Federal Unemployment Tax Act) taxes are paid entirely by the employer, on the first $7,000 of the employee's wages that are subject to FUTA. The FUTA tax form is Form 940. IRS discontinued the previous Form 940-EZ (short form) in 2007, but redesigned Form 940 to be more logical and easier to use.

State and federal employment tax is due if an employer pays wages to employees totaling $1,500 or more in any quarter of a calendar year or had at least one employee during any day of a week, 20 weeks in a calendar year, even if the weeks are not consecutive. The 0.2% FUTA surtax expired June 20, 2011, so two rates are used for 2011 taxes: 6.2% of wages through June 30, 6.0% afterwards, applied to a wage base of $7,000. Most employers get a 5.4% offset, making the rate for the first half of 2011, 0.8% of $7,000, or $56 per employee; for the second half, it is generally 0.6% of $7,000, or $42 per employee. [DOL, *Unemployment Insurance Tax Topic: Unemployment Insurance Taxes*, <http://workforcesecurity.doleta.gov/unemploy/uitaxtopic.asp> (Jan. 9, 2012)] The states have their own taxable wage bases: see § 32.06.

In general, the 2014 FUTA rate remains 0.6% of wages up to $7,000, or $42 per employee per year. However, in 2014 employers in 13 states will pay extra based on their taxable wages in 2013. States receive money from a federal loan account when state UI funds are depleted. If the loan is not repaid within two years, the 5.4% FUTA credit is reduced, raising the state's effective FUTA rate. Generally, the increase is 0.3%, $21/worker payable with Form 940 in January of the next calendar year. The states in question are Arkansas, California, Connecticut, Delaware, Georgia, Indiana, Kentucky, Missouri, New York, North Carolina, Ohio, Rhode Island, and Wisconsin. [<http://www.workforcesecurity.doleta.gov/unemploy/uitaxtopic.asp>; see ADP Research Institute, *Federal Unemployment Tax Act (FUTA) Increases for 2013* (Nov. 15, 2013) (benefitslink.com)]

There are four quarterly deposit dates for FUTA taxes (April 30, July 31, October 31, January 31) for the quarter ending the previous month. Employers are not required to make a deposit in a quarter in which their liability is $500 or less; they carry it forward until it does reach $500, at which point the deposit must be made either through electronic funds transfer or to an authorized financial institution. An employer with eight or fewer employees generally will not have to make quarterly FUTA deposits. All federal tax deposits must be made by electronic funds transfer. [IRS, *Depositing and Reporting Employment Taxes*, <http://www.irs.gov/Businesses/Small-Businesses-&-Self-Employed/Depositing-and-Reporting-Employment-Taxes> (Feb. 3, 2014)]

Form 940 is the annual FUTA tax return, which is due January 31 (or February 10, if all FUTA taxes were deposited when due).

The Supreme Court seldom tackles employment tax issues, but see its 2001 decision in *United States v. Cleveland Indians Baseball Co.* [532 U.S. 200 (2001)] If an employee settles an employment case and receives back pay, for FICA and FUTA purposes the money is taxed in the year in which the wages were actually paid and not the year in which they were earned—whether the tax rates in the year of payment were higher or lower than the rates for the year in which the money was earned.

§ 2.05 TRUST FUND TAX COMPLIANCE AND THE 100% PENALTY

The FICA tax withheld from employees' salary (both the OASDI and the Medicare components) is called a "trust fund tax." (Although the employer must pay its FICA share, and must pay FUTA, these are not trust fund taxes.)

Frequently, the employer will collect employee FICA tax from each payroll, but will not have to deposit the tax until the end of the quarter. A cash-strapped company's temptation to "borrow" that money for its own immediate needs is strong. To reduce the temptation, I.R.C. § 6672 imposes a 100% penalty that cannot be discharged in bankruptcy on "responsible persons" who willfully fail to submit the withheld trust fund taxes to the government. The 100% penalty means that the penalty is as large as the amount of taxes that were not properly paid. Furthermore, all of the personal assets of the responsible party can be attached to satisfy the debt.

Tax law creates a very large class of responsible persons, including the corporation's officers, shareholders, and directors, based on their level of responsibility within the corporation. The factors include authority to hire and fire; to decide which creditors will be paid and in what order, control over payroll, and power to deposit federal tax amounts. Top managers will probably be liable because of their degree of control over corporate financial managers. Lower-level managers probably will not be liable unless their duties include actually writing checks (and thus actual knowledge of amounts disbursed or not disbursed). Even parties outside the corporation, such as its bankers and its accountants, can be liable if they have the real control over corporate funds. In an appeal from a conviction for willful failure to pay over payroll taxes, the Ninth Circuit held that "willful" is defined as a voluntary, intentional violation of a known legal duty. [*United States v. Easterday*, 539 F.3d 1176 (9th Cir. 2008)]

In 2013, the employer and employee each must pay up to a maximum of $7,049 in FICA on wages. In the past, payroll service companies in the entertainment industry collected the full employer share from each production company that hired them. If an employee worked for several production companies during the year, the service company sent the IRS the maximum payment on capped wages, and kept the rest as profit. The Federal Circuit ruled in 2013 that Cencast and other payroll service companies could not apply the cap on the employer's share of FICA because it was not the common-law employer of the employees who earned the wages. The Federal Circuit ruled that although the payroll service company is the statutory employer for payroll tax purposes, the production companies are the common-law employers, so the cap is applied to wages paid on behalf of each common-law employer. For example, if the employee earned $100,000 each from three production companies, the payroll service company would be required to remit FICA taxes of $6,200 per company, for a total of $18,600. The producers are jointly and severally liable for the taxes. However, the employer share of FICA tax is not a trust fund tax, so the owners, officers, and employees of payroll services and production companies are not personally liable. [*Cencast Services L.P. v. United States*, 729 F.3d 1352 (Fed. Cir. 2013); see Robin C. Gilden *Entertainment Industry Payroll Companies Must Pay Up To FICA "Cap" On Behalf Of Each Producer For Whom An Individual Performs Services*, Mitchell Silberberg & Knupp LLP (Oct. 3, 2013), available at Lexology.com]

The co-owner of Overhead Door Co. of Denver, who managed the accounting department, was sentenced to 28 months in prison for failure to pay $4.67 million in employment taxes. She had to pay that amount in restitution, plus a $25,000 fine. She did not submit payroll taxes or FICA contributions between September 2003 and June 2008. [*United States v. Pettyjohn*, No. 1:13-cr-00020 (D. Colo., sentencing Sept. 11, 2013); see Jay R. Nanavati, *Colorado Accounting Department Head Sentenced To Federal Prison For Failing To Pay Over Employment Taxes*, Baker & Hostetler LLP (Sept. 13, 2013), available at Lexology.com]

When a penalty is due, the government can either collect all of it from one responsible person or divide it among several. To avoid liability, an individual has to prove that he or she was incorrectly characterized as a responsible person, or that the failure to pay over the money was not willful. In this context, "willfulness" only means knowledge that the taxes were not submitted, and a failure to correct the situation. If a responsible person finds out that, a payment was missed in one quarter that creates a duty to investigate to find out if other payments were missed as well.

The responsible person's duty is to use all of the corporations "unencumbered funds" to pay trust fund taxes. Unencumbered funds are those not already assigned to a debt that existed before the tax liability arose.

Thanks to the Taxpayer Bill of Rights 2 [Pub. L. No. 104-168] a responsible person is entitled to notice before the IRS imposes the 100% penalty. The notice must also give the names of other responsible persons, the IRS's collection efforts against them, and the success of those efforts. (The other responsible parties who actually pay the IRS can sue other responsible parties to make them pay their fair share.) The recipient of the notice can pay the penalty and sue for a refund, or contest the penalty in federal court. Collection efforts will be suspended until the case is resolved.

TD 9356, 2007-39 I.R.B. 675 took effect Jan. 1, 2009. From that date, Subchapter S corporation subsidiaries, Limited Liability Companies, and certain single-owner entities are required to file employment tax returns and make payments separate from the business owner's return. (Under prior law, the taxpayer could handle all the employment obligations for the employees of a disregarded entity as if the business owner was their employer.) Under the new procedure, taxes paid by the owner are treated as overpayments (although they are not always fully refundable), but the business entity remains liable for the unpaid taxes, penalties, and interest. If no tax return is filed, the statute of limitations never begins to run, so the potential liability extends indefinitely.

IRS policy is to avoid assessing the § 6672 penalty against a responsible person as long as a corporate debtor complies with the terms of its bankruptcy payment plan. However, the IRS might depart from this policy close to the end of the statute of limitations, when failure to enforce might make the debt uncollectable.

Underpaying taxes creates an obligation to catch up on the payments, plus interest. Penalties may also be assessed for, e.g., failure to file, late filing, or serious understatement of the amount of tax.

Code § 6690 imposes a penalty of $50 per failure to furnish a statement required under § 6057(e) to a participant, or for willfully furnishing a false or fraudulent statement. Section 6693 imposes the same penalty for improprieties in connection with statements relating to IRAs, MSAs, or HSAs. Failure to keep records necessary for § 6047(d) reporting is penalized by $50 per person, up to a maximum of $50,000 a year. The administrator of a defined benefit plan who fails to file the actuarial report required by § 6059 is subject, under § 6692, to a penalty of $1,000 per failure (unless reasonable cause for the failure can be shown).

Rev. Rul. 2006-38, 2006-29 I.R.B. 80 sets out the procedures employers can use to calculate their tax obligations under Code § 4975 for delay in submitting employee contributions to 401(k)s and other retirement plans. The "first-tier excise tax" is a 15% penalty on any employer that profits from a prohibited transaction. Employers subject to the tax can apply the 15% rate to any interest they owe on late payments; the interest rate charged is the § 6621(a) rate for underpayments. Rev. Rul. 2006-38 deals only with the first-tier tax, not the 100% "second-tier tax" for failure to correct a prohibited transaction. [Allison Bell, *IRS Explains Taxation of Late Plan Payments*, NU Online News Service (July 5, 2006)]

Furthermore, criminal liability can be imposed in five situations:

- Willful failure to collect or pay over federal tax;
- Willful failure to pay tax, make a return, keep records, or provide mandated information to the IRS is a misdemeanor (not a felony);
- Willful furnishing of a false or fraudulent tax statement, or willful refusal to furnish a required statement;
- Willful tax evasion;
- It is perjury to willfully sign a return or other tax document that the signer knows to be false or inaccurate.

Although these penalties are heavy, in practice the IRS often attempts to collect civil penalties instead of criminal ones, because it's easy to prove that taxes were not paid as required, but hard to prove the state of mind of the person or organization who was supposed to make the payment.

The Voluntary Classification Settlement Program (VCSP) has been expanded so more businesses can clarify the status of their workers as employees or independent contractors and, therefore, report and pay employment-related taxes correctly.

Even employers being audited by the IRS (except for employment tax audits) can use VCSP. An employer is eligible to use VCSP for a particular worker if the employer is currently treating the worker as a non-employee; has consistently treated the worker that way, including filing 1099s; if that worker's status is not the subject of a current IRS payroll tax audit, or a DOL, or state agency labor audit; and the worker's status is not currently being contested in court. Under prior law, a special six-year statute of limitations applied to classification cases, but VCSP participants are subject to the regular statute of limitations for payroll taxes. Application is made on Form 8952 and must be made at least 60 days before the employer wishes to treat the worker as an employee. Employers accepted into the program must pay about 1% of the wages paid to the reclassified worker. No interest or penalties are imposed. The employer will not be audited for payroll taxes for those workers for the past year. If the employer is also participating in the temporary relief program for employers who failed to file 1099s, they must issue the 1099s and pay slightly more to resolve their liability. [Announcement 2012-45, 2012-51 I.R.B. 724, Announcement 2012-46, 2012-51 I.R.B. 725 discussed in IR-2012-23, *IRS Expands Voluntary Worker Classification Settlement Program; Relief From Past Payroll Taxes Available to More Employers Who Reclassify Their Workers As Employees* (Feb. 27, 2013) See *Voluntary Classification Settlement Program (VCSP)*, <http://www.irs.gov/Businesses/Small-Businesses-&-Self-Employed/Voluntary-Classification-Settlement-Program> (updated July 17, 2014)]

§ 2.06 W-2s AND OTHER TAX FORMS

The W-2 form, used to report employee compensation, is a multipart form. Forms are sent to the IRS and to state tax authorities (and city authorities, in cities that impose their own income tax). The employer must also furnish the employee with copies that the employees can use to prepare their tax returns. Of course, the fact that the employer submits the same information to the taxing authorities makes it harder for employees to omit employment income from their tax returns.

For distributions in 2009 and later years, IRS Announcement 2008-56, 2008-26 I.R.B. 1192 requires employers to report the dividends on employer securities distributed from an ESOP on a Form 1099-R that does not report any other distributions. (If the plan makes distributions that are not 404(k) distributions, they must be reported on a separate Form 1099-R.) ESOP distributions that are 404(k) dividends are not subject to the 10% excise tax under Code § 72; not subject to withholding; and are not eligible for rollover. [Announcement 2008-56, Rebecca Moore, *IRS Changes Reporting Requirements for Dividends on ESOP Distributions*, plansponsor.com (June 10, 2008)]

In late 2010, the IRS released final versions of Forms 3921 and 3922 (reporting information about exercise of Incentive Stock Options and options under an Employee Stock Option Plan)—e.g., grant and exercise dates and fair market value of shares at relevant times.

Failure to file the Form 3921 or 3922 on time is penalized by up to $50 per form (capped at $250,000 per year). Failure to give employees the form is penalized by $50 per form, up to a maximum of $100,000. [Fred Schneyer, *Employee Stock Reporting Deadlines Approaching*, plansponsor.com (Nov. 19, 2010)]

Employers with 50 or more employees have obligations under PPACA to report the cost of health care coverage provided by the employer on Form W-2. Starting in 2015, they will also have to issue the new IRS Form 1095-C (to employees) and Form 1094-C (to the IRS) reporting information about whether the health coverage offered to employees satisfies the federal minimum requirements, and also meets the definition of affordability. See § 18.19 for more detailed discussion. [See IRS, *Form W-2 Reporting of Employer-Sponsored Health Coverage*, <http://www.irs.gov/uac/Form-W-2-Reporting-of-Employer-Sponsored-Health-Coverage> (last updated May 5, 2014); Chadron J. Patton, *Final Regulations Streamline ACA Reporting Rules*, Spencer Fane Britt & Browne (Mar. 13, 2014), available at Lexology.com]

PPACA § 9006 imposed a requirement, starting January 1, 2012 that companies would have to issue a Form 1099 to any individual or corporation from which they buy over $600 in goods or services in a tax year. [Neil deMause, *Health Care Law's Hidden Tax Change To Launch 1099 Avalanche*, CNN Money.com (May 5, 2010) (benefitslink.com)] However, Congress repealed this requirement in the first quarter of 2011, and President Obama signed Pub. L. No. 112-9, the Comprehensive 1099 Taxpayer and Repayment of Exchange Subsidy

Overpayments Act, the repeal legislation, on April 15, 2011. [BNA Tax & Accounting Daily Tax Report, *Obama Signs Measure Into Law Repealing Expanded Form 1099 Rules*, <http://www.bnatax.com/insightsdetail.aspx?id=2147486071> (Apr. 15, 2011)]

§ 2.07 TAX DEPOSITS

Employment taxes (withheld income taxes, FICA) are usually remitted by the employer either once a month or every other week. The schedule for reporting depends on the size of the employer's tax obligation for the previous year; the IRS notifies employers every November which category they will fall into for the next year. [See Treas. Reg. § 31.6302-1]

The basic reporting form is the quarterly Form 941, but income tax and back-up withholding on nonpayroll amounts are reported once a year on Form 945—Annual Return of Withheld Federal Income Tax. The IRS will notify small employers if they qualify to use Form 944, the annual federal tax return; qualifying employers can, nevertheless, elect to continue to file Form 941. See IRS Publication 15, Employer's Tax Guide for details on filing and reporting.

Penalties of between 2%–15% are imposed for late deposits (rising with the extent of the delay), with the highest penalty imposed on continuing failure to deposit after a demand from the IRS. A failure-to-deposit penalty of 10% is imposed on employers who had an obligation to use EFTPS and did not.

Employers whose annual employment tax liability does not exceed $1,000 do not have to file a quarterly Form 941, and most employers in this category will not have to make monthly or semi-monthly payments. However, the IRS estimates that employers will qualify only if their wage payments are less than $4,000 a year. The IRS created an invitation program under which it notifies very small employers that they can file Form 944 rather than 941. (If they prefer, qualifying employers can still file Form 941.). Employers can request to participate in the Form 944 Program, but they must get the IRS permission before moving to annual filing and once they enter the program, they must file a Form 944 each year until a request to return to filing Form 941 has been made and granted, or until they no longer qualify for the 944 program. Qualifying employers are those whose annual employment tax liability (including FICA, Medicare, and federal income tax withholding) is very small: less than $1,000 for the calendar year. However, agricultural employers and employers of household employees (e.g., nannies, housekeepers) do not qualify. [T.D. 9566, 76 Fed. Reg. 77672 (Dec. 14, 2011)]

Form 944 and associated tax payments are due January 31 of the year after the year for which the return is filed, but employers who have paid all employment taxes accrued to date get an extra 10 calendar days to file. Employers can find out if they qualify by calling (800) 829-0115. New employers who expect tax liability below $1,000 a year can apply to the IRS and indicate on their Form

SS-4 that they project a minimal tax liability. If their actual liability exceeds $1,000, they should file Form 944 and then file Form 941 in the future.

An accrual basis taxpayer that meets the "all events test" and the "recurring item exception" under § 461 can treat its payroll tax (FICA and FUTA) liability as incurred in a given year, even if, under § 404, the compensation to which that liability relates is deferred compensation that is not deductible until the following year. The new rule is available if the employer pays the payroll taxes either in the first year, or before September 15 of the second year or the due date of the company's federal income tax for the first year—whichever is earlier. However, companies that want to change their treatment of payroll taxes on deferred compensation must get permission from the IRS. [Rev. Rul. 2007-12, 2007-11 I.R.B. 685; see Fred Schneyer, *Deferred Comp Payroll Tax Scenario Clarified*, plansponsor.com (Feb. 15, 2007)]

§ 2.08 TRANSITION TO ELECTRONIC FILING

For many years, the IRS has been developing rules for electronic filing of tax forms. According to the agency, more than eight million business returns were electronically filed in 2005, with a 99% accuracy rate. By 2006, most business and employment tax returns (including information returns) could be filed electronically. (The TeleFile program, which allowed some forms to be filed over the telephone, was discontinued in mid-2005.)

Business taxpayers can pay all of their federal taxes online or by phone using the Electronic Federal Tax Payment System (EFTPS). EFTPS does not impose any fees. EFTPS is set up to facilitate transmission and processing of tax information submitted by corporations. EFTPS is a highly secure site, using the highest available level of encryption. Users have to enroll on Form 9779, and need a Taxpayer ID, a PIN, and an Internet password to log on. EFTPS users go online or make a phone call at least one calendar day before the due date of a return to input the tax information for their accounts; then the taxpayer directs movement of funds from an approved bank account to the U.S. Treasury account. (Payments can be scheduled in advance, and taxpayers can check the status of any payment made in the preceding 16 months.) [See Publication 4132 (explaining how to enroll in EFTPS and make payments online); Publication 966 (business and individual e-filing rules), Publication 4169, guide to EFTPS for tax professionals, and Publication 4275 (express enrollment for new businesses). Telephone customer service is available at all times, via (800) 316-6541.]

Mid-size and large corporations (with assets of $50 million or more and at least 250 returns—including income tax returns, employment tax returns, and information returns—filed per year) are required to file their Forms 1120 and 1120-S electronically for tax years ending on or after December 31, 2005. The following year, corporations filing 250 returns must file electronically if their assets are $10 million or more. The IRS has revamped its corporate electronic filing system, known as Modernized e-file (MeF). Large corporations must either register with the IRS as a "Large Taxpayer" that prepares their returns in-house or work with an e-file service provider approved by the IRS. [Form 1120/1120S/1120-F e-file, <http://www.irs.gov/Tax-Professionals/e-File-Providers-&-Partners/Form-1120-1120S-1120-F-e-file> (Jan. 29, 2013)]

See <http://www.irs.gov/uac/Employment-Taxes---Electronic-Filing-and-Payment-Options> (Sept. 30, 2013) for links to the Employment Tax e-file System, which is available to "Reporting Agents," IRS-authorized service providers who file Forms 940, 941, and/or 944 electronically for their clients. Business taxpayers can also file online with the 940, 941, and 944 online filing programs, and all federal tax payments can be made by electronic funds transfer or by credit card. W-2 forms can be submitted electronically, although the Social Security Administration rather than the IRS site is the proper place of filing. The Social Security Administration has online help for employers who file W-2 forms electronically. [*Specifications for Filing Forms W-2 Electronically (EFW2) For Tax year 2013*, SSA Publication No. 42-007, <http://www.socialsecurity.gov/employer/efw/13efw2.pdf#zoom=100>]

§ 2.09 BANKRUPTCY ISSUES

In April 2005 the Supreme Court decided that IRA balances are exempt from creditor claims in bankruptcy because the right to receive IRA funds is "on account of age." Although IRA funds can be withdrawn at any age, there is a substantial penalty on withdrawals prior to age 59½ unless another exemption is available. The Supreme Court resolved a circuit split under which the Second, Fifth, Sixth, and Ninth Circuits took the position eventually adopted by the Supreme Court, but the Eighth Circuit deemed IRA account holders to have unlimited access to their funds, so creditors should be able to reach the funds. (It is likely that the Supreme Court accepted the policy argument that IRAs often receive rollovers from qualified pension plans.) [*Rousey v. Jacoway*, 544 U.S. 320 (2005)]

However, a mid-2014 Supreme Court decision says that creditors can assert claims on IRAs that are inherited by a non-spouse beneficiary (in this case, the daughter of the deceased account owner). [*Clark v. Rameker*, No. 13-299 (June 12, 2014); see Katy Stech, *Supreme Court Allows Creditors to Tap Into Inherited IRA Money*, WSJ.com (June 12, 2014)]

The Sixth Circuit held that income available to Chapter 13 debtors after repaying a 401(k) loan is projected disposable income that must be paid to unsecured creditors. If the bankruptcy trustee objects, the debtors will not be permitted to use it to make voluntary contributions to the plan. The Bankruptcy Abuse Prevention and Consumer Protection Act of 2005 (BAPCPA) provides a limited exclusion for amounts withheld by an employer from an employee's wages for contributions to a qualified plan, so the Sixth Circuit held that plan loan payments are excluded from debtor's disposable income, but voluntary contributions to a 401(k) plan are not. The Sixth Circuit said that contributions are only excluded from the bankruptcy estate if they were made before the date of the petition. [*In re Seafort*, 669 F.3d 662 (6th Cir. 2012)]

A 2004 Ninth Circuit case involves a Chapter 11 bankruptcy case that was converted to Chapter 13, raising the question of what priority should be awarded to administrative expense claims arising after the petition but before the conversion. The Ninth Circuit read 11 U.S.C. § 348(d) to permit federal employment taxes to retain their administrative-expense priority. The Ninth Circuit treated post-petition tax debt as an administrative expense as long as it relates to taxes incurred by the estate. 11 U.S.C. § 1322(a)(2) requires the Chapter 13 plan to provide full payment of administrative expenses (including penalties and interest) as first-priority claims. Pre-petition, unsecured tax debt generally takes eighth priority, and is paid over the life of the plan without interest. The Ninth Circuit cited cases from other circuits preserving the administrative expense status of tax debt when Chapter 11 cases are converted to Chapter 7, and saw no reason to treat Chapter 11 to Chapter 13 conversions differently. [*In re Fowler*, 394 F.3d 1208 (9th Cir. 2005)]

Although the primary impact of BAPCPA (The Bankruptcy Abuse Prevention and Consumer Protection Act of 2005; Pub. L. No. 109-8) is on individual filings, this legislation has some provisions that affect employment tax planning:

- Clarification that a broad range of retirement savings vehicles will be excluded from the individual debtor's bankruptcy estate—not just government plans and private employer plans subject to ERISA Title I, but also tax-deferred annuities under 403(b) plans, health insurance plans regulated by state law, IRAs (including education IRAs), and funds placed in a § 529 (tuition savings program) a year or more before the bankruptcy filing. In general, the IRA exemption is limited to $1 million, but qualified rollovers into the IRA are not counted for this purpose. Furthermore, protection is granted to employee contributions even before they are deposited into the plan. This wide scope of protection applies even if the debtor is an insider of the employer corporation, and whether the debtor elects the state or federal exemption scheme.
- BAPCA alters the previous treatment of plan loans. It is not a violation of the automatic stay to withhold a debtor-employee's wages to repay a plan loan from a qualified plan.
- Pre-BAPCA, wages, salaries, and commissions for services rendered filing of the bankruptcy petition generally could be paid and claimed as administrative expenses. BAPCA strictly limits payments of retention bonuses and severance payments to corporate insiders.

BAPCA extends the avoidance period (i.e., makes it easier for the bankruptcy trustee to reverse payments) with respect to transfers made to insiders—including certain transfers made under employment contracts that are not in the ordinary course of business.

In 2004, the Sixth Circuit held that an officer of a bankrupt corporation was a responsible person. He was the CEO and majority shareholder and controlled the corporation's financial affairs. He was aware of the tax deficiencies, and nevertheless chose to pay other creditors rather than satisfying the tax obligation. The Sixth Circuit rejected the taxpayer's argument that he did not have control over the funds as a result of lock-box arrangements with lenders. The court ruled that corporate funds can only be considered encumbered by legal obligations imposed by statutes and regulations, not by contractual agreements voluntarily accepted. [*Bell v. United States*, 355 F.3d 387 (6th Cir. 2004)]

§ 2.10 THE INTERACTION BETWEEN §§ 409A AND 415

In May 2005 the IRS proposed new Regulations covering Code § 415 (the previous regulations were published in 1981!). See 70 Fed. Reg. 31214 (May 31, 2005). One of the areas covered by these regulations is the issue of post-separation payments.

The general tax rule is that payments made after an employee's separation from service are not compensation for § 415 purposes. The practical effect is that after an employee is terminated, he or she can no longer defer funds (e.g., severance benefits) paid by the ex-employer by depositing them in a 401(k) or 403(b) or 457 account. However, under the Proposed Regulations, a payment made within the 2½-month period after separation can be deferred in two situations. Either the payment would have been made anyway, even if employment had not terminated, or the payment relates to bona fide vacation, sick leave, or other leave the employee would have had access to if employment had continued.

Code § 409A provision governing nonqualified plans also has implications for the taxation of post-severance compensation (see § 8.02[D] for a more detailed discussion). "Separation pay" is the term used in § 409A for severance pay. It is regulated as defined compensation if there is a legally binding right to payment in a future year—even if there is a substantial risk of forfeiture. However, if the payment is entirely at the payor's discretion, there is no legally binding right to payment, so § 409A will not apply. The Proposed Regulations exempt certain severance payments from § 409A, such as expense reimbursement, payments for involuntary termination or RIF, severance agreements paying less than $5,000 in any tax year, and collectively bargained arrangements. If the payee is a key employee of a public company, payments will probably have to be delayed for six months. [Thomas M. Greene, BNA Tax Management, *Severance . . . It's Not What It Used to Be*, <http://www.bnatax.com/tm/insights/greene.htm>; see Notice 2005-1, 2005-2 I.R.B. 274 and Prop. Regs. at 70 Fed. Reg. 57930 (Oct. 4, 2005)]

The golden parachute rules of Code §§ 280G and 4999 impose a 20% excise tax on certain payments made to top executives based on corporate change of control. Payments subject to the golden parachute rules are not deductible by the payor corporation. These rules apply to officers; the highest-paid 250 employees within the employer's controlled group of corporations (or the highest-paid 1% if there are fewer than 25,000 employees in the controlled group) if their annual compensation is higher than the threshold amount for that year. The rules also apply to employee-shareholders who own more than 1% of the fair market value of the outstanding shares of all classes of the employer's stock. The excise tax applies if the executive receives payments and benefits due to the change in control that are at least three times the base amount. The base amount is three times the executive's average annual compensation for the past five years. Employment agreements can be drafted to avoid application of the golden parachute rules—e.g., by reducing payments to the maximum that does not trigger the excise tax. The Code § 409A rules about nonqualified deferred compensation must also be consulted. A gross-up provision calls for reimbursing the executive for the excise tax incurred. But the payor corporation cannot deduct gross-up payments, and shareholders may be angered about this use of corporate funds. [PLC Employee Benefits & Executive Compensation, *Addressing Sections 280G and 4999 in Executive Employment Agreements* (Apr. 16, 2013) (benefitslink.com)]

CHAPTER 3

BONUSES AND SEVERANCE PAY

§ 3.01 INTRODUCTION

Although regular compensation and benefits are the main focus of compensation planning, there are two important types of nonrecurring compensation that also play an important role: bonuses and severance pay.

The 2005 Bankruptcy Reform Act (Pub. L. No. 109-8) limits the ability of a company that is a Chapter 11 debtor to offer retention bonuses and/or severance pay and then claim these payments as an administrative expense in the bankruptcy case. A retention bonus or severance payment to a director, officer, partner, or control person is allowed only if the fact and amount of the payment are both reasonable.

A retention bonus to an insider is allowed only if the insider has, in fact, received a bona fide job offer elsewhere paying at least as much as the insider's job, preventing the insider from taking the offer is essential to the business's survival, and the amount of the bonus is limited to either 10 times the average retention payment made to rank-and-file employees or 25% of any similar payment made to or on behalf of the insider in the previous calendar year. Severance payments to insiders are allowed only as part of a program covering all full-time employees, and insiders must not receive severance that exceeds 10 times the average severance payment to the rank and file.

[A] Limitations on Executive Pay

After many years of assuming that the setting of pay was purely a discretionary act on the part of the paying corporation, limitations began to be imposed: such as § 162(m) limitations on the tax deduction for compensation (see § 3.03[G], below), and restrictions on "shutdown benefits."

Even outside the bankruptcy context, a plan that is "at risk" (i.e., significantly underfunded) may be barred by the Pension Protection Act of 2006, Pub. L. No. 109-280, from providing "shutdown benefits"—payments to employees who are losing their jobs when an operation is shut down. In some cases, the employer will be permitted to make the payments if the employer makes an additional contribution to shore up the plan.

Companies that received Troubled Asset Relief Program (TARP) bailout payments under the Emergency Economic Stabilization Act of 2008 (EESA), as amended by the American Recovery and Reinvestment Act of 2009 (ARRA), were subject to limits on bonuses, incentive compensation, and retention awards as long as they had any outstanding obligations to the federal government. (The TARP program ended in 2010.)

Companies receiving TARP assistance were also forbidden to make "golden parachute" payments to top executives leaving the company. See § 3.03[D] below. EESA and AARA also call for "clawback": companies must recover from the payee any bonus or incentive compensation that was paid to a top executive on the basis of false financial reporting, and compensation plans must not encourage future false reporting that would lead to higher compensation. [Joseph E. Bachelder III, *How Recovery Legislation Amends Executive Pay Limits*, N.Y.L.J. (Apr. 20, 2009) (law.com)]

The Dodd-Frank Act, Pub. L. No. 111-203, was passed to prevent future economic meltdowns. Dodd-Frank Act § 951 requires public companies to allow their shareholders a "say on pay": input into the compensation process for top executives. Shareholders have the right to cast advisory (i.e., non-binding) votes on executive compensation and golden parachutes. As of January 21, 2011, proxy statements must include say on pay resolutions—and a vote on how often say on pay votes will be conducted.

Exchange Act Rule 14a-21(b) requires public companies to hold a say on pay vote at least once every six years as to whether the actual vote will be held every two or every three years. Shareholders must be given a vote on golden parachutes, and parachute arrangements for top executive officers must be disclosed. A separate vote is not required if the golden parachute has already been the subject of a say on pay vote. [Text of rule: <http://www.sec.gov/rules/final/2011/33-9178.pdf>; SEC press release: <http://www.sec.gov/news/press/2011/2011-25.htm> (Jan. 25, 2011); see Rebecca Moore, *SEC Adopts Say on Pay Rules*, plansponsor.com (Jan. 25, 2011); Harpreet S. Bal, Alison M. Kadzik, Susan P. Serota, Brian M. Wong, *SEC Proposes Rules on Say-on-Pay and Golden Parachutes*, Pillsbury Law Advisory (Nov. 17, 2010) (benefitslink.com)]

In 2013, 3,363 companies held say on pay votes. Seventy-three companies failed, with an average 60% "No" vote; 15 of those companies had already failed previous votes. Two more companies got less than 50% approval of pay, but deemed it a victory because there were many abstentions. Looksmart got a 100% vote opposing the pay proposal, but its board recommended voting against the policies of the previous administration. [S. Hall and Partners, *2013 Say on Pay Voting Results* (Dec. 31, 2013) (benefitslink.com)]

In 2014, among companies in the Russell 3,000 stock index, there were 2,229 say on pay votes in the first six months of the year (compared to 1,948 votes in 2013). Nearly all of the votes cast (91.7%) supported management. As a result, only 51 of the say on pay proposals failed. [Stephen Miller, *Say-on-Pay Support Hits Record High in 2014*, SHRM (July 14, 2014) (benefitslink.com)]

In mid-2011, the D.C. Circuit vacated Rule 14a-11, the proxy access rule, which would have permitted some shareholders to write in their nominees for the board of directors. The D.C. Circuit found that the SEC exceeded its discretion in adopting this rule. [*Business Roundtable & Chamber of Commerce v. SEC*, 647 F.3d 1144 (D.C. Cir. 2011).]

§ 3.02 BONUSES

For many years, the compensation of executives and professionals was enhanced by bonus amounts—often much greater than their salaries. This was especially true in technology, Internet companies, and financial services firms. Bonus practices became controversial in a recessionary environment, with widespread layoffs and benefit cuts.

A 2012–2013 trend was to reduce the bonuses paid to top management and to increase the degree to which compensation is linked to corporate performance. According to the Wall Street Journal/Hay Group Survey of CEO Compensation, which uses data from 300 large public companies, for 51 CEOs at least half of their 2012 compensation was tied to specific targets based on the company's financial performance or its stock market results. In 2009, only about one-third of CEO compensation was subject to performance conditions; the rest came from salaries and stock and option grants that were not subject to performance criteria. Shareholder activists now have a new target: determining if the company's compensation structure creates the proper relationship between pay and performance. [Scott Thurm, *'Pay for Performance' No Longer a Punchline*, WSJ.com (Mar. 20, 2013)]

In early 2014, New York State comptroller Thomas DiNapoli estimated Wall Street bonuses would be 15% higher than previous year, including a great deal of deferred compensation. The estimate was that securities firms in New York would pay cash bonuses and deferred compensation of $26.7 billion for 2013 performance. The average bonus rose 15%, to $164,530. This was the largest amount since the 2008 financial crisis, and the third highest in history. The estimate does not include stock options or deferred compensation for which taxes were not withheld. [Julie Steinberg, *Wall Street Average Bonus Up 15% in 2013*, WSJ.com (Mar. 12, 2014)]

The Wall Street Journal reported in early 2014 that there is a trend to determine bonuses based on "unconventional" earnings measures, making it easier for a company that pays large bonuses to executives to report high profits. In 2009, 249 companies set bonuses using financial measurements that differ from U.S. accounting standards (e.g., removing costs like employee stock payments and asset write-downs that can depress profits). In 2013, 542 companies did so. The SEC studied nonstandard earnings measures, but did not forbid their use in executive pay decisions. Regulators allow non-GAAP adjusted measures, with proper disclosure, to set executive pay. [Michael Rapoport, *Some Companies Alter the Bonus Playbook*, WSJ.com (Feb. 26, 2014)]

Many compensation plans provide that a bonus is not earned if the employee is no longer employed on the schedule date of payment (e.g., December 31). However, some states forbid forfeiture provisions. Other states distinguish between commissions on sales already made (which cannot be forfeited) and bonuses (based on performance figures for the person or the company as a whole). As a general principle of contract interpretation, ambiguous provisions will be construed against the party that drafted the agreement (and could have made it clearer)—so it is vital to make sure that the contract clearly sets out the intended terms.

A group of former managers of Speedway SuperAmerica (one who quit, two who were fired) sued the former employer under the Indiana Wage Payment and

Wage Claims statutes when they did not receive bonuses. The Seventh Circuit held that the bonuses were not "wages" under Indiana law; they were deferred compensation that was forfeited because the plaintiffs did not satisfy the continued employment condition. The Wage Payment Statute, which guarantees timely payment of wages (within 10 days of being earned) applies only to current employees and those who quit voluntarily; the Wage Claims Statute requires payment of full wages due on the regular payday after an employee has been involuntarily terminated. In the Seventh Circuit view, a bonus is a wage only if it is compensation for time worked, not linked to a financial contingency and it is not reasonable to expect bonuses to be calculated within 10 days of the end of employment. [*Harney v. Speedway SuperAmerica LLC*, 526 F.3d 1099 (7th Cir. 2008)]

A 2010 Connecticut Supreme Court case draws a distinction between bonuses that are recoverable as wages under the Connecticut Wage Act (including statutory double damages and attorneys' fees) and discretionary bonuses that are not subject to the wage law. The court found that an attorney's year-end bonus was not "wages" because it was discretionary and not premised on specific, definable goals (such as number of hours billed). [*Ziotas v. Reardon Law Firm P.C.*, 296 Conn. 579 (2010)]

A few months before Weiss was due to receive a $60,000 bonus from DHL, he was terminated for failure to supervise an employee who took kickbacks, gave customers unauthorized low "rogue rates," and otherwise caused losses to the company. Weiss sued in state court to recover the bonus, alleging he was entitled to the bonus because he had been terminated without good cause. The case was removed to federal court (it was a diversity case). Only the breach of contract claim went to the jury, which ruled in Weiss's favor. On appeal, DHL argued that the bonus plan left it up to the management committee to determine if there was good cause. The First Circuit reversed the jury verdict, holding that the bonus plan left the decision up to the management committee to decide if there was cause for termination. [*Weiss v. DHL Express Inc.*, 718 F.3d 39 (1st Cir. 2013)]

Termination of a bonus plan, even if the employer reserved the right to terminate, could lead to liability for breach of contract if the employer violates the implied covenant of good faith and fair dealing. The Seventh Circuit held in mid-2013 that an employer carrying out an express contract provision can still breach the contract if it exercises discretion in a manner contrary to the reasonable expectations of the parties. The plaintiff, Wilson, was a recruiter who found students to enroll in CEC's culinary arts college. The bonus plan paid representatives a bonus for each student recruited over a threshold number, if the student graduated or completed at least a year of study. However, when representatives are terminated, they are only entitled to bonuses for students who have already completed a year or graduated, not those enrolled. In October 2010, the federal Department of Education issued regulations forbidding such bonus plans, effective July 2011; CEC said that bonuses would not be paid after February 2011. [*Wilson v. Career Educ. Corp.*, 729 F.3d 665 (7th Cir. 2013); see Doug Darch, *Seventh Circuit Calls*

Employer's Right to Terminate Bonus Plans Into Question, Baker & McKenzie (Nov. 2013) (benefitslink.com)]

A financial services executive was approached about changing jobs. He said that he wanted a $350,000 compensation package to move; he signed an employment application stating that he was an at-will employee. He said that he was offered a $175,000 salary plus a $175,000 guaranteed bonus. He started working in 2003, but did not receive the bonus in that year. The managing partner asked him to forego the bonus until the end of 2004 or early 2005; he accepted. On February 3, 2005, he was offered a $20,000 bonus for his work in 2004, which he rejected. He was fired five days later and was offered a separation agreement and a $20,000 payment in return for surrendering all claims. He refused to sign, and sued his ex-employer for failure to pay wages and breach of contract. The New York Court of Appeals held that the jury decided that he was guaranteed a non-discretionary $175,000 bonus, in exchange for quitting his previous high-paid job. The bonus therefore was due and vested and he was entitled to collect it and get an award of attorneys' fees under New York law, which provides for a fee award when wages are not paid on time. [*Ryan v. Kellogg Partners Institutional Servs.*, 19 N.Y. 3d 1 (N.Y. 2012)]

In 2006, the Third Circuit ruled that it does not violate the FMLA to cut an employee's bonus when he or she is on FMLA leave, provided that the reduction is based on specific criteria that are set out in the plan, such as production or number of hours worked. [*Sommer v. Vanguard Group*, 461 F.3d 397 (3d Cir. 2006)]

Rev. Rul. 2011-29, 2011-49 I.R.B. 824, provides criteria under which an accrual-basis taxpayer can deduct employee bonuses in the year the services were performed, even though the bonus is not paid until the beginning of the next year. A deduction can be taken in the year of the services even if it is impossible to identify the specific recipients of bonuses from the bonus pool or the amount payable to each. The regulations under Code § 461(a) say that an accrual-basis taxpayer incurs a liability in the tax year in which the "all events" test is satisfied: all events establishing the fact of liability have occurred, the amount of liability can be determined with reasonable accuracy; and economic performance has occurred, e.g., the obligation to pay a minimum amount of bonuses is fixed at the end of the year. [Mercer Select News, *IRS Rules Favorably On Timing Of Tax Deductions For Some Bonus Pool Arrangements* (Nov. 11, 2011) (benefitslink.com); see Miller Johnson, *New IRS Ruling Discusses Tax Deductions for Cash Bonus Payments* (Dec. 7, 2011) (benefitslink.com)]

IRS Field Attorney Advice Memorandum 20134301F says that an employer could not deduct a bonus in the year it was earned rather than the year it was paid. The plan document gave the employer unilateral discretion to reduce or eliminate the bonus at any time until it was paid. The "all events" test permits deduction in the year the bonus is earned if all events to establish the fact and amount of liability have occurred, and the bonus is paid within two and a half months of the end of the year. The IRS ruled that ability to change the amount of the bonus means that the amount or even the fact of liability cannot be determined until payment has occurred. So if the employer waits until 2014 to certify that 2013 performance goals have been met, or has discretion to change the amount of the bonus, the deduction must wait until 2014. This is also true if the bonus is partly conditioned on a subjective evaluation performed in 2014. If the bonus is subject to approval by the board of directors or by a committee, the all events test is not met until approval has been given. However, a bonus pool established by the end of the year can be deducted even if the employer has discretion to allocate bonuses among eligible employees. Note that GAAP requires the reflection of a deferred tax asset on the year-end balance sheet if a current book expense is reported for accrued bonuses that cannot be deducted until they are paid. [Haynes and Boone LLP, *Employer With Discretion To Reduce Or Eliminate Bonuses Prior To Payment Not Entitled To Deduction In Year Bonuses Accrued, Rather Than In Year Paid*, Lexology.com (Dec. 6, 2013); Greg Daugherty, *IRS Limits Ability To Deduct Annual Bonus Payments In The Year Of Accrual, Rather Than The Year Paid*, Porter Wright Morris & Arthur LLP (Nov. 26, 2013), available at Lexology.com]

§ 3.03 SEVERANCE PAY

[A] Generally

There is no federal law requiring that employees receive severance pay, but nevertheless it is very common for employers to provide this type of compensation (unless the employee was fired for misconduct). Severance pay is often defined as a certain number of days or weeks of pay for every year of service with the employer.

The most important characteristic of severance pay is that it is over and above the normal salary or wages earned for past services. Severance payments are by and large discretionary, unlike payment for past services, which must be made when employment terminates. If the employer enters into an express or implied contract to provide severance benefits that contract can be enforced. However, employers typically retain the right to alter their severance pay plans, and this is sometimes done just before a major layoff. Employers may also provide benefits to only certain persons affected by a mass layoff, claiming that the others were terminated for poor performance.

Employees of companies in bankruptcy are at especially high risk of losing severance. Severance payments by bankrupt companies require court approval (and 2005's bankruptcy reform legislation limits payments to insiders), and must compete with other creditor claims.

There are two basic kinds of severance plan: the traditional plan, funded through the employer's general assets or with a trust, and Supplemental Unemployment Benefit (SUB) plans. SUB plans provide additional payments to supplement state unemployment insurance benefits. To receive SUB payments, employees must be eligible for state unemployment benefits, and must verify each week that they continue to be eligible and to look for work. Design changes can save money. A SUB plan resembles unemployment benefits in many ways. Employees have to be eligible for state unemployment to get SUB and they have to verify each week that they're eligible and looking for work. The benefit is often defined as a multiplier of years of service: for example, one to two weeks of benefits for each year that the employee worked for the company. Setting the appropriate level of benefits available under the plan depends on what the company's objective is in adopting the plan: to help employees bridge an income gap until they get a new job? To improve the company's profile after a layoff? There is a potential for a windfall if the employee gets a new job before the severance period ends; SUB plans eliminate this problem because they coordinate with state unemployment benefits, which end when the claimant gets another job. [Philip Parker, *Severance Plans: The Promise and the Savings*, Benefits Quarterly (Second Quarter 2012) (benefitslink.com)]

If the employee turnover is caused by a corporate transition (see Chapter 16), severance-related benefits can be provided under three main structures: a change in control agreement; a severance plan; or a change in control protection plan. Generally, individual agreements will be offered if the intent is to protect only selected executives, whereas a formal plan should be adopted if there is a broader-based group that might receive severance. (A formal plan will almost certainly be subject to ERISA.) For a change in control provision or retention agreement, the most important questions are which executives are significant enough to be awarded protection, and what will trigger benefits (Termination without cause? Resignation for good cause? Resignation during a window period following a change in control?) The usual term is one to two years after the change in control occurs. For the employee, the most favorable provision is for the employer to reimburse the employee for golden parachute tax penalties imposed under Code § 4999; the intermediate position is for the company and the executive to divide the payment; and the least favorable is for the employee to forfeit severance benefits in any situation in which the employer would lose the deduction as a result of § 280G.

Departing executives often have access to special terms that are not offered to rank-and-file employees: for example, keeping them in active status in the EGHP while they are receiving severance or paying their COBRA premiums after termination. These special terms are usually set out in a severance agreement. However, if the employer maintains a self-funded group health plan, it is subject to the Code § 105(h) nondiscrimination requirements and it is forbidden to maintain eligibility provisions that discriminate against non-HCEs. Therefore, § 105(h)(7) will probably require the market value of continuation coverage for departing executives to be treated as taxable compensation. The Patient Protection and Affordable Care Act (PPACA) extends the nondiscrimination rules to insured plans, and so, although specific PPACA nondiscrimination rules have not been published, limiting extended coverage to executives or subsidizing COBRA premiums only for them, could be treated as a PPACA violation. [E is for ERISA Blog, *Special COBRA Coverage Terms for the Departing Executive: Pitfalls to Avoid* (Dec. 12, 2011) (benefitslink.com)]

If a self-insured plan violates the nondiscrimination rule, the penalties are imposed on the executive, but for non-grandfathered insured plans, the penalty is imposed on the employer. The penalty can be as high as $100 per day of noncompliance for each employee experiencing discrimination, capped at $500,000 or 10% of the employer's EGHPs costs for the previous year. The penalty is waived for employers with fewer than 50 employees, or for employers of any size who had reasonable cause for their position and did not willfully neglect the requirements. [Steven Friedman, Terri Solomon, and Stephanie Kastrinsky, *Employers with Insured Health Plans Must Take Care in Providing Healthcare Subsidies to Departing Executives*, Littler Mendelson (Oct. 29, 2012) (benefitslink.com)]

There are three basic methods for handling insurance continuation in a severance package. The "choice method" gives the exiting employee a choice between making a COBRA election and accepting the alternative in the severance package. The "consecutive coverage" method offers a certain number of months being covered as if he or she were still an active employee, followed by up to 18 months of COBRA coverage. The "concurrent coverage" model treats the alternative coverage as part of COBRA: for example, 12 months coverage at the active-employee rate, with the employee paying the full COBRA premium for the next six months. [*Ten Harmsel v. Pfizer Inc.*, File No. 1:08-CV-880, 2009 WL 1771377 (W.D. Mich. June 18, 2009); see Thompson Newsletter, *Alternative Coverage Case Involving Premium Hike Raises COBRA Issues* (July 29, 2009) (benefitslink.com)]

If there is a formal plan, the employer can protect itself by reserving the right to amend or terminate the plan. If there is a dispute about an informal arrangement, it will probably end up in state court, with the court having broad scope to review the plan administrator's decision. If there is an ERISA plan, then participants must exhaust their administrative remedies within the plan before bringing suit; the suit will have to be filed in federal court; and jury trial will not be available. If the plan document gives the administrators discretion to interpret the plan, the court will review the decision deferentially and is likely to uphold the administrator's decision unless it was arbitrary and capricious. It is permissible to have multiple benefit formulas, as long as the plan does not discriminate in favor of employees in protected classes. A formal plan can be a morale-building tool, because employees know in advance what to expect.

However, the disadvantage is that a formal plan results in loss of flexibility. Individual negotiations with employees are ruled out. The plan requires more administrative time than occasional individual negotiations. It is possible that different treatment of employees will result in discrimination allegations, so it is vital to be able to show a rational business reason for the distinctions. ERISA compliance can be time consuming and costly.

Furthermore, even if the intention is to avoid maintaining an ERISA plan, a de facto plan might be found based on oral representations made to employees; the employer's intention (as manifested by, for example, past practices or maintaining a fund or account to pay benefits). If the plan is deemed to be an ERISA plan even though this was not the employer's intention, penalties might be imposed for reporting and disclosure violations. [Sandra W. Cohen and Carol Buckmann, *ERISA Considerations for Severance Pay Policy Checklists* (February 2011) (benefitslink.com)]

When a termination event does occur, severance benefits can be conditioned on the departing employee signing a covenant not to compete, and not to solicit the ex-employer's customers. Some severance agreements are subject to Code § 409A and its standards for "separation pay arrangements." A plan that is limited to paying lump sums after there has been a termination without cause, with payments completed within two and a half months of termination, would probably be exempt from § 409A. There are § 409A exemptions for collectively bargained plans; plans that are not created under a CBA, and that pay less than twice the participant's annual compensation, with payments completed by the end of the second post-termination calendar year. Benefits that add up to less than $5,000 and are not a substitute for other § 409A benefits are also exempt, as are vacation and sick leave, disability pay, tax-free health benefits, benefits under a qualified retirement plan, and rights accrued and vested before January 1, 2007 and not substantially modified since October 3, 2004. However, it is unusual for separation pay benefits to vest, because they are generally subject to a substantial risk of forfeiture.

In general, an agreement for severance benefits can permit payment at any time within the 90-day period following the event, but only if the employee cannot make a direct or indirect election about when compensation will be paid within this period. The IRS says a release condition in an agreement violates § 409A if the condition operates as an indirect election by the employee about benefit timing. The ADEA requires 45 days' notice for an employee to consider a release and gives him or her seven days after signing to revoke a release, so severance payments are generally not made until after the revocation period has elapsed. Problems can arise if a release is offered late in a year—but not signed until the following year.

IRS Notice 2010-6, 2010-3 I.R.B. 275, says that § 409A is triggered by this "straddle," and it is a major issue in 409A audits. A mid-2011 article suggests drafting releases to provide that if benefits could be paid in two different tax years depending on when the release is signed, benefits will automatically be paid in the later year. [McGuireWoods LLP, *Employee Release Provisions Present Section 409A Trap for the Unwary* (Aug. 31, 2011) (benefitslink.com)]

A Final Rule, 72 Fed. Reg. 16878 (Apr. 5, 2007) addresses the treatment of certain severance benefits vis-à-vis the § 415 limitations on the amounts employers can contribute to qualified plans and the amounts that plan participants can receive under the plan. Under the final regulations, certain amounts paid within two and a half months after severance from employment are considered compensation under § 415 (which means that the employer may be able to deduct them). Payments also qualify if they represent sick leave, vacation days, or other leave that the employee would have been able to take if he or she had continued to be employed. An amount can still qualify as § 415 compensation if it is paid later than 2½ months post-termination, as long as it is paid by the end of the plan's limitation year that includes the date of termination. However, for the employer to take advantage of this rule, the plan must state explicitly that the post-termination payments are included in compensation.

"Terminal leave" can be used if the employer is willing to stretch out a termination date—for example, to allow further vesting of retirement benefits or stock awards, or to extend the period before COBRA starts, perhaps with the result that the terminating employee will be eligible for Medicare once COBRA ends. However, terminal leave can create problems with insurers if they insist that coverage is limited to current active employees—or with the IRS, which might say that § 409A has been triggered. On the other hand, the employer might want to accelerate the termination date so that there is no gap period after an employee's signing a release, and during which further claims might arise.

"Garden leave" is a term used for a transition period during which the employment relationship continues in some way, and the employee is not permitted to get another job; in effect, the employee is paid to stay home. Garden leave is common in, e.g., England and the European Union, where there is a legal requirement of continuing wages during the notice period, and is gaining popularity in the United States. The provision could be structured to provide a fixed number of days of continuing salary and benefits followed by severance pay subject to a release of claims and agreements to maintain confidentiality and not to compete, or to solicit the employer's other employees. Executive stock awards, incentive compensation, and supplemental retirement benefits could be restructured into a post-termination package contingent on loyalty agreements. [J. Mark Poerio, Eric Loi, and Peter Haller, *The Basics of Garden Leave—and Why Careful Tilling Is Needed,* BNA Pension & Benefits Daily (Aug. 24, 2011) (benefitslink.com)]

The SEC said that it had received reports about improper language in severance agreements that inhibits disclosure of improprieties (e.g., bans on reporting wrongdoing to federal agencies; stipulations that the company will receive any award given to an employee or ex-employee for disclosures; or requiring advance notice of intent to contact the SEC or other federal enforcement agency). Terminated employees are likely to sign these provisions because they need severance benefits and/or a good reference. The Dodd-Frank Act gives the SEC the power to prosecute employers for retaliation. [Ben DiPietro, *Companies Trying to Contain Potential Whistleblowers*, WSJ.com (May 14, 2013)]

A recent IRS Chief Counsel Memo (CCM) provides guidance on the taxation of employment discrimination settlements. Severance payments generally will be included in the recipient's gross income unless an exclusion is available. The most common exclusions are reimbursement of a former employee's medical costs, and damages for physical illness or injury (Code § 104(a)(2)). If any part of a severance payment is included in the employee's gross income, a comparable part of the corresponding attorney's fee award is also gross income. Unless there is an exclusion, severance pay constitutes FICA and FUTA wages. The CCM says that if the settlement was not obtained under a fee-shifting statute (e.g., Title VII, the ADEA, the ADA), or the settlement does not allocate an amount for attorneys' fees, the entire amount of attorneys' fees paid to the former employee will constitute wages for employment tax purposes. If a wage-based claim is settled, generally the entire payment will be reported on Form W-2. But if the settlement agreement specifically makes a reasonable allocation to attorneys' fees, the employer reports the fee payments on one 1099-MISC to the ex-employee, one to the attorney. Disobedience of the rules subjects the employer to the $100/ failure penalty under Code §§ 6721(a) and 6722(a) or the $250 penalty for each intentional disregard of filing requirements. [IRS Chief Counsel Memo No. 20133501F (Aug. 20, 2013); see J. Mark Poerio, *Severance Pay And Employment Taxes: Addressed In IRS Chief Counsel Memo*, Paul Hastings LLP (Sept. 16, 2013), available at Lexology.com]

In mid-2009, the EEOC updated its guidance document, "Understanding Waivers of Discrimination Claims in Employee Severance Agreements," covering ADEA and OWBPA (Older Workers' Benefit Protection Act) implications reflecting the prevalence of economically motivated layoffs and terminations. The EEOC says that an employer cannot cure a defective waiver by later providing the OWBPA information that was omitted from the original agreement, then restarting the 21- or 45-day period after the employee has signed the agreement. The Guidance says that an employee can file an EEOC discrimination charge, even if the employee signed a waiver, because the EEOC still has the power to investigate and pursue such claims. The EEOC's position is that the employee does not have to return severance pay before filing a discrimination charge with the EEOC—although employees can waive their right to recover damages from the employer in a subsequent private suit or EEOC suit, and eventual damages might be reduced to correspond to the severance received. It is settled law that severance does not have to be returned in ADEA cases, but less clear for other statutes. The Guidance says that if an employee challenges the validity of an age discrimination waiver in court, the employer must continue complying with its obligations under the severance agreement, including making any ongoing payments still due. [<http://www.eeoc.gov/policy/docs/qanda_severance-agreements.html> (July 15, 2009) Appendix B, dealing with releases in group layoffs of persons over 40, was revised in April 2010. See *EEOC v. Watkins Motor Lines, Inc.*, 553 F.3d 593 (7th Cir. 2009) on the EEOC's right to proceed after a waiver by the complainant]

A county employee, who was told that her job was eliminated in a reorganization, sued the former employer charging that she was offered a less favorable severance package than comparable male employees and that the county found jobs for male employees but not for her. The district court dismissed, holding that there had been no adverse employment action because severance benefits could only create adverse employment action if there was a contract violation. The district court also argued that the employment relationship has ended when severance is paid so there can be no "adverse employment action." The Fourth Circuit rejected these arguments: discriminatory severance is unlawful, and the plaintiff alleged that she was fired only after rejecting the discriminatory severance package so she was an employee at that time. [*Gerner v. County of Chesterfield*, 674 F.3d 264 (4th Cir. 2012). *Hishon v. King & Spalding*, 469 U.S. 69 (1984) stands for the proposition that discrimination must be avoided in all benefits in the employment relationship.]

[B] Severance Arrangements as ERISA "Plans"

ERISA is not involved in an employer's one-time decision to grant or enhance severance benefits. Nor is there an ERISA component to an employer's payroll practices or payments of extra money for active workers' overtime or holiday work. However, ERISA does come into play if severance payments are made in connection with a "plan," and even an unwritten or informal arrangement might constitute a plan.

Once the severance payment comes within the ambit of ERISA, the degree and nature of regulation depend on whether the plan is characterized as a pension plan or a welfare benefit plan. The arrangement will not be a pension plan (and therefore will not be subject to the stringent rules imposed on pension plans) if:

- Payments are not contingent on the recipient's retirement—i.e., the recipient can retain the payments even if he or she gets another job;
- The total payments do not exceed twice the recipient's compensation for the year just before the termination;
- The payments are completed within 24 months of the termination. If the termination is part of a "limited program of terminations" then payments can be completed within 24 months of the time the recipient reaches normal retirement age, if that is later.

[See DOL Reg. 29 C.F.R. §§ 2510.3-2(b) and 2510.3-1(a)]

A pediatrician was employed by Montefiore Medical Center and Einstein College of Medicine. Hospital policy denied severance payments to employees terminated for cause. Montefiore retained the right to amend or terminate the policy at any time. The pediatrician gave notice May 1, 2011, stating that he had taken another job and would leave in September 2011. On May 13, 2011 he was fired for a cause that he disputed, and did not receive severance. He sued for denial of benefits under an ERISA plan. The Southern District of New York agreed with Montefiore: there was no subject matter jurisdiction, because there was no ERISA plan. A one-time calculation using a severance formula is not a plan because no managerial discretion is required. The district court held that the employer only exercised discretion over initial eligibility for severance, not the amount or timing of payments. Because the program could be terminated at any time, a reasonable employee could not expect it to be permanent. [*Okun v. Montefiore Med. Ctr.*, No. 11 Civ. 9615 (PGG), 2013 U.S. Dist. LEXIS 129742 (S.D.N.Y. Sept. 10, 2013); see Mark S. Thomas and Robert W. Shaw, *Court Holds That Severance Policy is Not an ERISA Plan: Okun v. Montefiore Medical Center*, Williams Mullen (Sept. 24, 2013), available at Lexology.com]

The District Court for the District of Puerto Rico held that a severance package was not an ERISA plan: there was no discretion in the size or timing of the payments. Although benefits could be denied to persons terminated for cause, the district court held this is not the kind of ongoing administration that ERISA refers to. Without an ERISA plan, there was no federal jurisdiction, and the case should have been brought in Puerto Rico's commonwealth court. [*Aguirre-Santos v. Pfizer Pharmaceuticals LLC*, No. 12-1393 (JAF), 2013 U.S. Dist. LEXIS 151515 (D.P.R. Oct. 21, 2013)]

The Eighth Circuit ruled in mid-2011 that a one-person employment contract is not an ERISA plan. However, the case was remanded to the district court because the federal system might still have had jurisdiction over part of the complaint. The plaintiff, Schieffer, had an employment contract. Shortly before a merger obtained regulatory approval, Schieffer was terminated without cause, triggering the payment of a lump sum severance payment. Schieffer alleged that he did not receive all the benefits he was entitled to and moved for arbitration. His employer moved to enjoin arbitration, arguing that the employment agreement was an ERISA severance plan so ERISA preempted the demand for arbitration. The Eighth Circuit held that the employment contract was not an ERISA plan because it covered only one person, not a class of employees. However, the other benefits he sought might have been promised by ERISA plans, so the Eighth Circuit sent the case back to see if those demands were preempted by ERISA. [*Dakota, Minnesota & Eastern Railroad Corp. v. Schieffer*, 648 F.3d 935 (8th Cir. 2011)]

The case was remanded to determine whether the contract operated as an amendment to an ERISA plan, or a promise to pay ERISA plan benefits in the future. In 2013, The Eighth Circuit rejected both of these possibilities. The severance agreement only came into operation when the ex-CEO had ceased to be a plan participant. It was also a free-standing agreement; although the amount to be paid was determined by reference to an ERISA plan, the benefits came from the employer's general assets, not plan assets; and making the payments would not affect the administration of ERISA plans. The arbitration demand did not seek benefits due under an ERISA plan—which meant that the determination of underlying rights had to be done by an arbitrator, not the federal courts. When the case got to arbitration, the state law claims (including the double damage claim) could be heard because ERISA preemption did not occur. [*Dakota, Minn. & E. Railroad Corp. v. Schieffer*, 711 F. 3d 878 (8th Cir. 2013).]

The District Court for the Eastern District of Washington dismissed a state breach of contract claim about denial of severance, finding that it was preempted by ERISA. In 2011, Lockheed adopted a voluntary executive separation program (VESP) offering selected employees a one-time lump sum, calculated based on years of service, if they resigned within a specified time period. The plaintiff applied and was told that his benefit would be approximately $245,353. He resigned and signed a release of claims. Just after resigning, he put in a claim for reimbursement of $4,700 of travel expenses, triggering an audit. Lockheed said that he received more than $42,000 in expense reimbursements he was not entitled to, so the company ruled that he was terminated for cause and was ineligible for VESP benefits. The district court held that there was an ERISA plan, because ongoing administration and non-trivial amounts of discretion were required. The district court held that the plan was adopted to reduce the size of the company's upper management, requiring discretion in selecting employees who could participate. [*Edwards v. Lockheed Martin Corp.*, 954 F. Supp. 2d 1141 (E.D. Wash. 2013); see Peter K. Bradley et al., *State Breach Of Contract Claim For Severance Preempted By ERISA*, Hodgson Russ LLP (Aug. 29, 2013), available at Lexology.com]

[C] Case Law on Other Severance Pay Issues

In a highly anticipated March 2014 decision, the Supreme Court resolved a Circuit split. Reversing the Sixth Circuit, the Supreme Court held that the severance payments in question constituted FICA wages. The Supreme Court held that severance payments are made only to employees, and they are made because of service to employers because "service" is defined broadly as the entire relationship between the employer and employee.

The court noted that the FICA statute provides a list of exemptions from the general rule that all compensation constitutes FICA wages. One of the exemptions is for severance payments made for disability retirement. The Supreme Court said it would not be necessary to specify this exemption if severance pay in general did not constitute FICA wages. Code § 3401(a), dealing with income tax withholding, also has a broad definition of taxable wages, subject to a list of exemptions. The list says that Supplemental Unemployment Benefits are treated as if they were wages: see § 3402(o). Defendant Quality Stores interpreted this to mean that, although SUB payments are treated "as if" they were wages, they are not wages for this purpose or for FICA purposes. However, the Supreme Court traced this provision to the history of tax withholding, when Congress wanted to relieve terminated workers from the burden of year-end tax liability. If the Supreme Court had decided the other way, corporations would have been entitled to billions of dollars in tax refunds. [*United States v. Quality Stores Inc.*, 134 S. Ct. 1395 (Mar. 25, 2014)]

In Florida, policy documents such as employee handbooks are generally non-binding and do not create enforceable contract rights. A company that was being "run down" (terminating its operations other than collecting its portfolio of structured settlements) set up a plan in 2001 to create share incentives for employees to remain at work. The plaintiff quit in 2009 and asked for the value of her vested shares. When this was refused, she sued for breach of contract, arguing that she would have quit her "dead end job" in 2001 without the incentives. A Florida trial court granted summary judgment for the employer, holding that there was no plan language creating a binding contract, but the Court of Appeals reversed, holding that the plan compensated employees for remaining at work, and there were jury questions as to whether offer and acceptance had occurred. [*Turton v. Singer Asset Finance Co., LLC*, 120 So. 3d 635 (Fla. 4th DCA, 2013); see Richard D. Tuschman, *Continued Employment In Dead-End Job May Entitle Employee To Incentive Benefits*, Akerman Senterfitt (Sept. 24, 2013), available at Lexology.com]

For high income executives, FICA tax on severance has little impact if the layoff occurred after the executive had already earned the FICA maximum; the only practical effect is on Medicare tax. Laid-off workers should ask if their former employer is pursuing FICA refunds. The company does not have to inform them until the IRS accepts the claim. At that point, the employer will ask the former employees for consent to include their refund claim. When the IRS refunds the FICA amounts, the employer will distribute the employee share to the former employee. If the employee believes that a refund is due, but the employer did not file for one, the employee may be able to file Form 843 to seek a refund, but this must be done before the statute of limitations expires. Generally this will be three years after the due date for the tax return covering the year the severance was received. If the IRS does make a refund, it will not be taxable to the employee. [Laura Saunders, *Tax Report: When Severance Pay Is Subject to Payroll Tax*, WSJ.com (Oct. 26, 2012).]

Severance package negotiations in a Seventh Circuit case included information about defined benefit pension benefits. (A terminated employee withdrew a potential ADEA suit in light of the severance settlement.) The plan provided five options: a lump sum, a five-year term certain annuity, 50% and 100% joint and survivor annuities, and a straight life annuity. The plaintiff was given accurate information about the lump sum, but the other benefit forms were overstated by almost 64% because the calculations assumed that he was eligible for normal retirement when he was only eligible for reduced early retirement benefits. (He was terminated at age 57½). He signed a severance agreement November 14, 2006 and filled out an election form option for $1,156 a month as a 50% joint and survivor annuity; the correct amount should have been $706.74. The mistake was discovered in January, and an HR clerk filled out a corrected form with the lower figure. Pearson did not return the recalculated form, so the company did not pay his pension and he sued, arguing that the plan was estopped from paying him less than the pension he was promised. The Seventh Circuit held that, to demonstrate extreme circumstances that will justify a departure from the written terms of the plan, a plaintiff must show reasonable, detrimental reliance on a knowing misrepresentation made in writing by the plan. In this case, the Seventh Circuit said that there was no misrepresentation, just a simple error, and the plaintiff was entitled only to the correct pension amount. (However, he might have claims against the employer, but not against the plan.) The Seventh Circuit said that, although Pearson argued that he surrendered his demand for 78 months of health insurance post-termination, worth over $40,000, in return for a written representation that he would receive an $1,156.89 monthly pension, he did not show any realistic chance of bargaining for a better deal, so his claim of economic harm was too speculative to award. [*Pearson v. Voith Paper Rolls, Inc.*, 656 F.3d 504 (7th Cir. 2011)]

The Seventh Circuit had to decide whether DHL violated the WARN Act in connection with its November 10, 2009 announcement that five out of its six Chicago-area facilities were going to close. Although the CBA did not provide severance benefits, the Teamsters Union negotiated severance benefits. On December 5, 2008, each bargaining unit received a severance agreement. Receiving severance was conditioned on waiving all claims, including WARN Act claims. Approximately 500 employees took a severance package, receiving either four or ten weeks' pay. Workers who did not take a severance package retained seniority and recall rights—and the right to sue the former employer. Two laid-off workers sued. The Seventh Circuit held that there was no plant closing because employees who accepted severance should not be counted; without them, the number of layoffs did not reach 33% of the workforce. Under the WARN Act, a voluntary departure is not an employment loss requiring notification. Voluntariness is determined based on whether employees were forced out or coerced. The plaintiffs argued that employees resigned under extreme economic uncertainty and pressure from the employer. The Seventh Circuit said that, although the situation was not perfect, the severance agreements were still voluntary. The agreements and the release were negotiated by the union; were not ambiguous; and informed employees of their right to consult an attorney. [*Ellis v. DHL Express Inc USA*, 633 F.3d 522 (7th Cir. 2011)]

A 2010 Sixth Circuit case permits enforcement of a clearly written release of USERRA claims that was part of a severance package, finding that the release was knowing and voluntary and was not obtained by overreaching. The Sixth Circuit allowed USERRA to be released on the same terms as any other employment-related claim. [*Wysocki v. IBM*, 607 F.3d 1102 (6th Cir. 2010); but see *Perez v. Uline*, 157 Cal. App. 4th 953 (2007) holding that USERRA claims cannot be waived by a written release]

To get payments under Pactiv Corp.'s ERISA severance plan, employees had to sign a separation agreement and a release acceptable to the company. There was no noncompete provision in the severance plan. The plaintiff was offered a separation agreement that included a noncompete clause. He refused to sign, and won a court case for the severance payment, which was close to $100,000. The court held that, although employers have some discretion in drafting, the company could not demand a noncompete agreement without amending the severance plan. [Angela Bohmann, *Can I Add a No-Compete Provision to a Severance Agreement?*, Leonard, Street and Deinard Benefits Notes Blog (Nov. 20, 2012) (benefitslink.com)]

Questions often arise as to whether a person who receives severance pay qualifies for unemployment benefits. As a general rule, employees who are in the position of voluntarily quitting their jobs will not be eligible for unemployment; those who receive severance when they lose their jobs through no fault of their own probably will be eligible. West Virginia found unemployment insurance benefits to be available to someone who participates in a voluntary severance program initiated by the employer if the claimant's separation from service is the result of lack of work and termination occurred under a workforce reduction plan. [*Baldwin*, Unempl. Ins. Rep. (CCH) ¶ 8787 (W. Va. 2005)], and also granted benefits to an employee who took a voluntary separation package in the course of downsizing; leaving was attributed to the employer's fault. [*Boggs*, Unempl. Ins. Rep. (CCH) ¶ 8797 (W. Va. Cir. Ct. 2006)] Employees who took a voluntary separation plan were eligible for benefits, based on testimony from a company Vice President and e-mails from the HR department stating that the plan was implemented because of lack of work. [*Verizon North*, Unempl. Ins. Rep. (CCH) ¶ 10,203 (Ohio App. 2006)] The Massachusetts Court of Appeals ruled in 2006 that benefits should have been awarded to claimants who took a voluntary separation package because they had an objectively reasonable belief that they would have been fired if they had not taken the packages. The employer neither announced that employees would be chosen randomly for RIF nor announced criteria for selecting RIF candidates, thus giving employees good cause to cut their losses by taking the package and leaving. [*State Street Bank & Trust Co.*, Unempl. Ins. Rep. (CCH) ¶ 8487 (Mass. App. 2006)]

In contrast, benefits were denied to an office manager who was given the choice of staying at work while she looked for a new job, or leaving immediately with severance pay. When she opted to leave right away, however, she was ineligible for benefits, because she was the one who made the departure decision. [*Arrow Legal Solutions Group PXC*, Unempl. Ins. Rep. (CCH) ¶ 8354 (Utah App. 2006)] A teacher who accepted a $1,000 payment from her school system for early notice of intent to resign or retire was not separated for lack of work, and was not eligible for benefits. She voluntarily quit in order to move to Florida with her husband. Although it is presumed that separation is for lack of work, the school testified that there was work for the following year; the $1,000 payment was an incentive for employees to provide information about their plans so the school district could estimate its hiring needs, not a means to cut back jobs. [*Parma City Schools*, Unempl. Ins. Rep. (CCH) ¶ 10,204 (Ohio App. 2006)]

To avoid having to cover $200,000 in loan interest to fund the state's unemployment insurance trust fund, New York made major reforms to its unemployment insurance system. As of January 1, 2014, an offset is imposed: an employee who receives "dismissal pay" (severance pay, or payment other than pension, accrued leave, or SUB, made on account of separation) within 30 days of dismissal is not eligible for unemployment benefits for weeks during which severance exceeds the maximum weekly benefit ($405 until October 2014, when it rises to $420). For severance paid in a lump sum, New York State allocates it on a weekly basis. Once severance pay is exhausted, the individual can collect benefits for the remaining weeks of benefit eligibility. Disqualification applies only to benefit claims filed after January 1, 2014, not previously filed claims. However, an ex-employee can receive unemployment benefits immediately if the initial payment or lump sum severance payment is made more than 30 days after the last day of employment. [Barbara E. Hoey and Mark A. Konkel, *Severance Payments Offset NY Unemployment Insurance Benefits As Of January 1, 2014*, Kelley Drye & Warren LLP (Feb. 11, 2014), available at Lexology.com; Christopher J. Collins and Jonathan Sokolowski, *New York Unemployment Benefits No Longer Available To Former Employees Receiving Severance*, Sheppard Mullin Richter & Hampton LLP (Jan. 10, 2014), available at Lexology.com]

[D] Parachute Payment Law and Regulations

A specialized form of severance, the "parachute" payment comes into play in the course of a hostile takeover or takeover attempt. The best-known form is the "golden parachute" for executives—the counterpart of the "golden handcuff" compensation packages that are supposed to keep top managers from leaving companies that depend on their services. A golden parachute arrangement is supposed to deter unwanted takeover attempts, because so much cash severance (and other benefits, such as stock, enhanced pension benefits, and insurance) is owed to the top managers that the acquisition becomes even more expensive—perhaps prohibitively so. A few states mandate the payment of "tin parachutes" to rank-and-file employees when they lose their jobs during a corporate transition.

A "single-trigger" golden parachute agreement gives the executive the right to additional compensation whenever the employer company merges or is acquired. A "double-trigger" agreement doesn't become effective until there has not only been a corporate transition, but the executive has been demoted or terminated and therefore has a real economic injury.

Golden parachute rules under Code §§ 280G and 4999 were enacted to prevent large payments to top executives when a change in control occurs. Certain change in control payments are subject to a 20% excise tax, and are not deductible to the employer. Compensation subject to these rules can include bonuses, accelerated vesting or payment of equity awards, severance pay, and post-termination benefits.

The provisions generally apply to officers; the 250 highest-paid employees within the employer's controlled group (the highest—paid 1% if the controlled group has fewer than 24,900 employees), if their annual compensation exceeds the threshold amount, which is indexed annually. (The 2013–2014 level is $115,000.) Employee-shareholders who own more than 1% of the fair market value of all classes of employer stock are also included. The rules are triggered if the aggregate value of payments and benefits to the executive as a result of the change in control is equal to or greater than three times the base amount (the executive's average annual compensation for the past five years). The amount that exceeds the base amount is taxed and is not deductible by the employer.

There are many ways to draft employment agreements to escape these rules. A safe harbor cutback provides that payments and benefits will be reduced to the maximum amount that will not trigger the excise tax. Drafters must consider § 409A: the employer's or executive's ability to elect which payments to change may constitute a late deferral election or accelerated payment for § 409A purposes.

A valley provision, also known as a better-off cutback, reduces the payment to the maximum amount that will not trigger the excise tax—unless the executive would be better off on a post-tax basis by receiving the payments and paying tax on them. Such a provision benefits the employee, but the employer loses the tax deduction, and § 409A issues might arise.

A full gross-up reimburses the executive for excise tax incurred, but this can be costly for the employer, particularly since the gross-up is not deductible. Shareholder advocates tend to oppose gross-ups, which can be a problem for public companies. A modified gross-up gives the executive a full gross-up unless reducing payments by a specified amount would avoid the excise tax. [PLC Employee Benefits & Executive Compensation, *Addressing Sections 280G and 4999 in Executive Employment Agreements* (Apr. 16, 2013) (benefitslink.com)]

On August 4, 2003, the IRS issued final regulations dealing with golden parachutes. [68 Fed. Reg. 45745, August 4, 2003] A corporation is exempt from the rules about excess parachute payments if, just before control of the corporation changed, the corporation was not publicly traded and holders of at least 75% of the voting power of the corporation approved the payment. Furthermore, only one change in ownership or control will be deemed to have occurred with respect to any transaction, even if the language might make it appear that there were multiple changes.

The final rule takes the position that accelerating the vesting of a stock option creates value that counts toward determining whether there has been a parachute payment.

The excise tax on excess parachute payments can be prepaid either in the year of the change in control or any later year—as long as the amount, form, and commencement date of the payments is already known and is reasonably ascertainable under the Code § 3121(v) rules on FICA taxation of nonqualified deferred compensation. However, the excise tax cannot be prepaid on any part of an excess parachute payment that is attributable to continuing to provide health benefits to the recipient of the parachute payment.

[E] Parachute Payment Cases

Eligibility to participate in the plan providing parachute payments was the issue in *Habets v. Waste Mgmt., Inc.* [363 F.3d 378 (5th Cir. 2004)] The Fifth Circuit ruled that once the company's Board of Directors exercised its discretion to decide who was a participant in the parachute plan by removing the plaintiff from the list of eligible persons (after he lost his officer status in a corporate restructuring), the plaintiff was no longer entitled to receive parachute payments. Under the plain language of the agreement, only corporate officers were entitled to parachute payments, so termination of his officer status also terminated eligibility for the payments.

An Eighth Circuit case from late 2003 was brought by an executive who, mistakenly believing that she was entitled to severance under a golden parachute agreement, gave her employer a "notice of termination," and took a higher-paid job within the organization that she viewed as a demotion because it carried fewer responsibilities. She believed that the parachute was triggered by the offer of a lesser position, but the Eighth Circuit held that the parachute was never triggered because there was no change in control, and she resigned and was not entitled to severance benefits. [*Curby v. Solutia, Inc.*, 351 F.3d 868 (8th Cir. 2003); see also *Jones v. Reliant Energy-ARKLA*, 336 F.3d 689 (8th Cir. 2003): it is not an adverse employment action to offer a new job in lieu of severance pay.]

[F] "Separation Pay" Under § 409A

Under § 409A, which was designed to be a comprehensive regulation of deferred compensation, the IRS calls severance (which was not previously analyzed as deferred compensation) "separation pay." Separation pay is regulated as deferred compensation if there is a legally binding right to payment that arises in one tax year and is paid in a future year, even if there is a substantial risk of forfeiture. The exception is a payment entirely in the discretion of the payor (so there is no legally binding right to receive the funds). A binding contract between employer and employee could give rise to deferred compensation where the employer promises to pay a defined amount when the employee separates from service. But there is no deferred compensation if the employer offers to trade an immediate lump sum for a release, because the right to payment and taxation occur in the same year. The Proposed Regulations exempt certain severance payments from § 409A:

- Payments due to involuntary termination or to participation in a RIF window program where severance does not exceed the § 401(a)(17) limit or twice annual compensation; payments must be completed by the end of the second calendar year after the year of termination.

- Reimbursement of expenses that are either excludable from the employee's gross income or are deductible by the employee as § 162 or § 167 business expenses.
- Severance agreements under which no more than $5,000 is paid in any tax year.
- Collectively bargained severance arrangements covering involuntary termination or RIFs (including voluntarily accepted RIFs or incentives), as long as the program window does not exceed one year, and the program specifies the circumstances under which an employee can terminate and receive severance.

Severance benefits subject to "good reason" provisions are not considered subject to substantial risk of forfeiture, so § 409A probably applies, and neither the safe harbor for involuntary termination nor the one for payment within 2½ months of the end of the plan year will apply.

The Proposed Regulations define separation from service as an employee dying, retiring, or terminating employment. The employment relationship continues during a bona fide leave of absence of less than six months—or longer, if there is a statutory or contractual right to reemployment. Without such a right, the employment relationship is presumed to end on the first day after a six-month absence.

If there is an agreement to continue the relationship after it would normally end, employment is deemed to terminate when the employee provides only insignificant services—i.e., working, and getting paid, less than 20% of pay as compared to the previous three years. (If the employee had worked for the employer less than three years, the comparison is based on the full term of employment.) The "same desk" rule does not apply in the context of § 409A, so if a corporate transaction involves the sale of substantially all of the employer's assets, termination of employment will be deemed to occur even if the employee is rehired by the purchaser of the corporate assets.

Furthermore, severance payments to a key employee of a public company that do not qualify for an exemption must be delayed for six months. [Thomas M. Greene, BNA Tax Management, *Severance . . . It's Not What It Used to Be*, <http://www.bnatax.com/tm/insights/greene.htm>. See Notice 2005-1, 2005-2 I.R.B. 274 and Prop. Regs. at 70 Fed. Reg. 57930 (Oct. 4, 2005). The § 415 Final Regulations at 72 Fed. Reg. 16878 (Apr. 5, 2007) allow payments, made after termination, from a nonqualified unfunded deferred compensation plan, to be treated as compensation if the payments are gross income for the employee, and would have been paid at the same time if the employment relationship had continued.]

Separation pay can be provided without triggering § 409A, for example, by using the short-term deferral and safe harbor exceptions; "stacking"; and integrating the payments with release of claims. Separation pay, for this purpose, is defined as amounts payable only because of separation from service, such as negotiated departure agreements, severance plans, and individual severance plan agreements. Payments are not considered deferred compensation if they are made within 2½ months of the end of the year in which the right to payment vests. "Stacking" means arranging separation pay so that some fits under the short-term deferral rule, some qualifies for the safe harbor, and some is deferred compensation that complies with § 409A. However, amounts that are not deferred compensation cannot be substituted for amounts of deferred compensation.

The § 409A correction program was originally set up in Notice 2008-113. Notice 2010-6, 2010-3 I.R.B. 275 extends this program to correct document failures as well as operational failures. Correction is required based on certain arrangements that condition separation pay or other forms of severance on employment-related actions that make the separation pay subject to § 409A, such as releasing claims or signing a noncompete agreement. There are limited situations under which separation pay is exempt from § 409A. Even when there is no exemption, the employer can address an existing arrangement without violating § 409A. For example, if the agreement has either a 21- or 45-day period for the employee to complete the employment-related action, followed by a seven-day revocation period, the payment date could be set more than seven days after the end of the revocation period. If the agreement does not provide for payment subject to employee action, it must provide for payment only on a fixed date of either 60 or 90 days after the occurrence of the permissible payment event. [Jeff Minzel, Kurt Linsenmayer, Susan J. Daley, *In 2010 Employers Should Respond to New Developments for Existing and Future Separation Arrangements*, Perkins Coie News (Oct. 29, 2010) (benefitslink.com)]

[G] Section 162(m) Issues

Code § 162(m) limits (to $1 million) the compensation that a public company can deduct for any executive's compensation in any one year. This general rule is subject to some exceptions—for example, performance-based compensation can be deducted even if it exceeds $1 million. The statutory definition of performance-based compensation is money payable solely as a result of achieving established, objective performance goals set by the company's compensation committee. Compensation will also be considered performance-based if there is a potential for it to be paid on the basis of death, disability, or change in control, but if compensation is in fact paid on such a basis, it will not be considered performance-based. See 76 Fed. Reg. 37034 (June 24, 2011), IRS proposed regulations setting requirements for stock option and stock appreciation awards to qualify as performance-based compensation.

However, Notice 2007-49, 2007-25 I.R.B. 1429 provides that Chief Financial Officers (CFOs) are never subject to § 162(m), even if they are among the corporation's highest earners.

See Morgan Lewis Hot Topics, *Section 162(m) Pitfalls* (Mar. 9, 2010) for a checklist of common problems—e.g., adjusting bonus amounts in light of subsequent events, when the plan does not provide authority for the adjustment—that can cause public companies to forfeit the safe harbor for performance-based compensation. [<http://www.morganlewis.com/pubs/EBHotTopics_Section162mPitfalls_09mar10.pdf>]

Part II
PENSION LAW

CHAPTER 4

BASIC PENSION CONCEPTS

§ 4.01 INTRODUCTION

This chapter provides a summary and overview of the major ERISA and tax issues that help shape plan design. Many of these subjects are taken up in greater detail in the other chapters in this part of the volume.

In the private sector, employers make part of the employee's compensation available immediately in cash. The employee's total compensation package also includes benefits such as health insurance and fringe benefits, plus deferred compensation that will eventually provide a lump sum or income at the time of the employee's normal, disability, or early or late retirement.

The subject of pensions and benefits is an important one. The retirement market is a hugely significant sector of the economy. On December 31, 2013, total retirement assets in the United States were $23.0 trillion—5% higher than at the end of the third quarter, and 15.6% higher than the end of 2012. Defined contribution assets were $5.9 trillion at the end of 2013 ($4.2 trillion of that in 401(k) plans); IRA assets were $6.5 trillion; defined benefit plans had $3.0 billion in assets, plus $2.0 trillion in annuity reserves outside retirement accounts; government plan assets were $5.6 trillion. [ICI Release, *Retirement Assets Total $23.0 Trillion in Fourth Quarter 2013* (Mar. 26, 2014) (benefitslink.com)]

Because of the high risk of improprieties or mistakes in handling the funds that the employees rely on for future security, pension plans are administered by fiduciaries. A fiduciary is an individual or institution that takes care of the property of others, and therefore must be held to the highest standards of ethics and prudence. [See Chapter 15 for further discussion of the obligations of plan fiduciaries, and penalties that can be imposed for misconduct or failure.]

In 1974, Congress, concerned about potential abuses of pension plans, passed the Employee Retirement Income Security Act (ERISA). ERISA provides very detailed rules for how pension plans must be administered; how they must accumulate funds for later benefit payments; who qualifies for various kinds of benefits; how those benefits are to be distributed; and how the plan must keep records and communicate with its participants and beneficiaries. ERISA governs not only how ongoing plans operate, but how they can be created and how they can change form by merging with other plans or undergoing termination.

Furthermore, ERISA establishes pensions and benefits as an entirely and inherently federal area of jurisdiction. States are forbidden to legislate in this area, so the question of whether "ERISA preemption" has occurred is an important one.

The bulk of ERISA deals with pension plans, although the statute has less extensive provisions dealing with other types of plans including profit-sharing plans, stock bonus plans, and welfare benefit plans such as health plans, vacation plans, and cafeteria plans.

The legal definition of a pension plan describes it as a plan established and maintained primarily to pay definitely determinable benefits to participants—usually monthly for the rest of the retiree's life, although lump sum payouts and annuities for a term of years are also permissible. Unlike profit-sharing plans, pension plans normally make distributions only on the basis of retirement, death, disability, or term of employment; hardship distributions are usually not available.

The mid-2006 passage of the Pension Protection Act (PPA), Pub. L. No. 109-280, enacted immense changes. Although the legislation focuses on shoring up the soundness of defined benefit plans, the PPA also has significant provisions about defined contribution and cash balance plans. As it turned out, however, this statute was passed shortly before the economy soured, and the PPA was modified to relieve some of the burden on already hard-pressed employers in stimulus legislation such as EESA, WRERA, and the Preservation of Access to Care for Medicare Beneficiaries and Pension Relief Act of 2010. The Moving Ahead for Progress in the 21st Century Act (MAP-21; Pub. L. No. 112-141) gives the sponsors of defined benefit plans interest rate relief: by allowing them to assume higher interest rates, they can lawfully reduce their contributions to their plans. See § 4.01[B] below.

> ■ **TIP:** In March 2004, the Supreme Court ruled that for the purposes of ERISA Title I, the sole shareholder/president of a Professional Corporation is an employee. As long as there is at least one other plan participant other than the business owner and spouse, then ERISA's anti-alienation provision applies, and the shareholder's creditors cannot reach his or her interest in the pension plan. [*Raymond B. Yates, M.D., P.C. Profit Sharing Plan v. Hendon,* 541 U.S. 1 (2004)]

As a general rule, the employer's tax deduction is taken on a cash basis—for the year in which money was contributed to a qualified plan. Employers that maintain nonqualified plans instead of, or in addition to, qualified plans do not get a deduction until the employee receives benefits from the nonqualified plan and includes them in income.

One of the most important criteria for plan qualification is that the plan must not discriminate in favor of highly compensated employees (HCEs). For the years 2006–2007 HCEs earned $100,000 or more; for 2008, rising to $115,000 in 2012–2014. Yet many companies identify a need for additional benefits to stay competitive in the executive recruiting stakes. It is legal to maintain nonqualified plans limited to, or offering superior benefits for, HCEs (see Chapter 8 for more discussion), but the expenses associated with these plans will not be federally tax deductible.

The Financial Accounting Standards Board (FASB) sets the rules for accounting for pension and benefits. FASB created a new codification of GAAP, reorganizing the thousands of GAAP documents into approximately 90 topics. The previous seven FASB statements relating to retirement and health plans (Nos. 35, 87, 88, 106, 112, 132(R), 158) were reorganized into five topics:

- 712, post-employment compensation other than retirement;
- 715, retirement benefits;
- 960, accounting for defined benefit plans;
- 962, accounting for defined contribution plans;
- 965, accounting for health and welfare benefit plans.

[CCH Pension and Benefits, *FASB Announces New Codification Structure, Superseding All Existing Statements* (June 26, 2009) (benefitslink.com). See <http://www.fasb.org> for the full codification.]

One of the most important questions in plan administration is the standard of review that will be applied when a decision (e.g., denying benefits; altering the terms of the plan) is challenged. In April 2010, the Supreme Court ruled that as long as the plan gives its administrators the power to interpret the plan, then courts must review plan administrators' decisions deferentially—as long as the decisions are reasonable. [*Conkright v. Frommert*, 559 U.S. 506 (2010)]

The case continued to be remanded, appealed, and remanded again. In late 2013, the Second Circuit sent the case back to the District Court for the Western District of New York for the third time. The latest version of the suit holds that the district court erred by denying the plaintiffs discovery on the plan administrator's conflict of interest. The Second Circuit found that the suit was meritorious, and the proposed offset was unreasonable because it led to an absurd, contradictory result. The Second Circuit also found the SPD inaccurate, because it said that the lump sum "may" reduce the benefit, not that it would. However, the Second Circuit found that, this time, the district court properly applied the *Firestone* standards, and its refusal to re-open discovery was not an abuse of discretion. [*Frommert v. Conkright*, 738 F.3d 522 (2d Cir. Dec. 23, 2013); see Kevin McGuinness, *Appellate Court Remands Case on Offsetting Pension Benefits*, plansponsor.com (Dec. 30, 2013)]

[A] PPA Changes

The PPA is a wide-ranging statute, and is referenced many times in this book. The major provisions of the PPA (some of which have been amended in light of economic factors) include:

- "At-risk plans" (defined benefit plans that fail to meet the PPA's new standards for adequate funding) are restricted in their ability to make certain types of distributions. If the risk is especially severe, the plan will be required to cease further accruals unless the employer makes additional contributions. The at-risk rules do not apply to plans covering fewer than 500 employees.

- The concept of the "minimum funding standard account" has been replaced by the "basic minimum funding contribution," and a new Code § 430 has been enacted for the purpose; the basic minimum funding contribution is calculated by adjusting the "target normal cost."
- The employer's tax deduction for plan contributions is capped.
- For 2008 and later plan years, plans must set their interest rate assumptions based on corporate bond yields. This requirement has caused compliance problems since the 2008 recession began; it has been the subject of several federal laws providing relief for plan sponsors.
- For plan years beginning after 2007 (collectively bargained plans: 2008) married participants must be given the option of a joint and 75% survivor annuity as well as the well-established joint and 50% survivor annuity. This is referred to as a Qualified Optional Survivor Annuity (QOSA);
- A court order allocating employee benefits order can be a Qualified Domestic Relations Order even if it issued after or revises an earlier order.
- Phased retirement is permitted—a plan can start pension distributions for a person who has reached age 62, but has not reached the plan's Normal Retirement Age, and who works a reduced schedule.
- Congress has given its approval to cash balance plans, but has imposed compliance requirements for new cash balance plans and conversions after mid-2005. The PPA provisions do not retroactively authorize cash balance plans created or converted earlier, and some courts find them age-discriminatory.

- Pub. L. No. 112-141, MAP-21, requires ongoing increases in the PBGC premiums. Further changes were made by the Bipartisan Budget Act of 2013, signed December 26, 2013. For 2014, the flat-rate premium is $49/participant for single-employer plans, $7 more than the 2013 level. The multi-employer flat-rate premium remains unchanged at $12/employee. The 2014 variable premium for single-employer plans rises from $9 to $14 per $1,000 of UVB, as a result of indexing and the $4 increase imposed by MAP-21. The variable premium cap rose from $400 per participant in 2013 to $412 in 2014. The proposed rates for 2015 are flat rate of $57, variable rate of at least $24, cap of at least $412. For 2016, proposed rates are flat rate of $64, variable rate of at least $29, capped at $500, with these figures indexed for inflation in 2017. [pbgc.gov, Premium Rates, Sarah Roe Sise and Carrie Elizabeth Byrnes, *PBGC Premium Rates Increase In 2014 For Single-Employer Plans: Time To Cash-Out Some Deferred Vested Participants?*, Bryan Cave LLP (Nov. 15,

2013), available at Lexology.com; Buck Consultants FYI, *PBGC Premium Hikes in Final Budget Deal*, Vol. 36 Issue 105 (Dec. 27, 2013) (benefitslink.com)] Starting in 2015, PBGC premiums will be due at the same time, irrespective of the size of the plan; under prior law, the due date depended on plan size. [79 Fed. Reg. 13547 (Mar. 11, 2014); see Rebecca Moore, *PBGC Finalizes Premium Changes*, plansponsor.com (Mar. 10, 2014)]

- The obligations of communicating with plan participants have been increased, starting with the 2008 plan year: defined benefit plans must give their participants an annual funding notice no later than 120 days after the end of the plan year. At-risk plans have to give additional disclosures.
- Starting in 2010, companies with fewer than 500 employees can maintain "eligible combined plans," a new type of plan that combines defined benefit and 401(k) components.

As for defined contribution plans, under the PPA:

- Employers are encouraged to implement automatic enrollment in their 401(k) plans.
- The defined contribution plans of publicly traded companies must offer the opportunity for participants to diversify their 401(k) accounts (to avoid excessive concentration of employer stock), and must be notified of this right.
- It is easier for employers to maintain automatic-enrollment 401(k) plans, as long as the participants are fully vested within two years of enrollment. Immediate participation is not required.
- If the employer/plan sponsor is a public corporation, and the plan holds employer securities, participants must be given at least three other investment options, and must be notified of their right to diversify out of the employer's stock.
- It is not a prohibited transaction for fiduciaries of 401(k) plans to give investment advice to participants, subject to some conditions.

PPA § 303 amends Code § 415(b), so that plan distributions other than straight life annuities are adjusted actuarially to see if they satisfy the assumptions of § 415(b). Pre-PPA, the interest rate assumption for the adjustment could not be lower than the rate specified in the plan or the § 417(e)(3) rate—whichever was lower.

As of August 17, 2006, 401(k) plans can allow distributions for health, tuition, or funeral expenses relating to a "primary beneficiary": that is, a person who is named as a plan beneficiary and has an unconditional right to part or all of the account balance when the plan participant dies. The hardship distribution must be necessary to satisfy the financial need. A § 409A plan can treat a beneficiary on a par with a spouse or dependent to decide whether the participant has incurred an unforeseeable financial emergency.

For distributions after December 31, 2006, PPA § 820 amends Code § 402(c)(11) so that a direct trustee-to-trustee transfer to the IRA of a non-spouse beneficiary can be treated as an inherited IRA and a direct rollover of an eligible rollover distribution, and will not be gross income for the recipient in the year of the distribution. To qualify, the rollover must be made to an IRA established on behalf of the designated beneficiary. Plans are not obligated to offer direct rollovers of distributions to non-spouse beneficiaries, but if they are offered, it must be on a nondiscriminatory basis.

Under pre-PPA law, a defined contribution plan satisfied the § 411(a) minimum vesting rule for employer non-elective contributions as long as vesting occurred on a five-year cliff, or three-to-seven-year graded vesting schedule. PPA § 904, however, requires faster vesting: for plan years beginning after December 31, 2006, vesting must occur vis-à-vis employer non-elective contributions on a three-year cliff or two-to-six-year graded schedule. Plan amendments that change the vesting schedule accordingly must satisfy § 411(a)(10). The plan can maintain separate vesting schedules for employer non-elective contributions, depending on whether or not they are subject to § 411(a)(2)(B).

PPA § 1102 permits notices under §§ 402(f), 411(a)(11), and 417 to be given as much as 180 days before the annuity starting date. However, the plan must revise its 411 notice to take the PPA rules into account. The notice must describe the increase in benefits under a defined benefit plan if receipt is deferred; a defined contribution plan notice must explain the plan's investment options (including associated fees) if distributions are deferred. The notice for either type of plan must reproduce any part of the SPD that contains special rules that could have a material effect on the decision to take benefits right away or defer them.

In mid-2007, the IRS issued a procedure for using plan-specific substitute mortality tables to compute defined balance obligations under Code § 430(h)(3)(C) and ERISA 303(h)(3)(C). [Adrien Martin, *IRS Release Guidelines on Substitute Mortality Table Requests*, plansponsor.com (May 31, 2007)]

Final regulations on this topic were issued in August 2008. See Rev. Proc. 2008-62, 2008-42 I.R.B. 935. The tables, which have separate rates for males and females, and for annuitants and non-annuitants, must be used beginning with 2008 plan years. A small plan (one with under 500 participants) can use a single blended static table for all participants. The PPA also allows certain large employers with adequate experience (at least 1,000 deaths for each sex over a five-year period) to use individualized plan specific tables that accurately reflect the plan's experience. [See Notice 2013-49, 2013-32 I.R.B. 127, for updated mortality tables to be used in 2014 and 2015, and tables of minimum present value under § 417(e)(3) for annuity start dates in calendar years 2014 and 2015.]

The Society of Actuaries released an exposure draft of a new set of actuarial tables, reflecting increasing life expectancies. For women aged 25–85, the tables call for an increase in pension liabilities of 5.5–10.5%; for men in those age cohorts, liabilities will probably increase 2.5–17.4%. Companies that are large enough to adopt custom tables will probably have those tables revised. If the IRS adopts these mortality tables, defined benefit plans' funding ratios will drop, and sponsors will have to provide additional funding. Audit firms will probably call for adopting the new tables proactively for fiscal 2014 disclosures, to avoid unpleasant surprises in the future. [Meaghan Kilroy, *New Actuary Tables May Be "Nail In The Coffin" For DB Plans*, Pensions & Investments (July 24, 2014) (benefitslink.com)—that is, the increased liabilities may be the final factor leading some sponsors to terminate their defined benefit plans.]

The Wall Street Journal reported in 2014 that pension plans are facing a "double whammy": a significant increase in the cost of regulatory compliance (e.g., much higher PBGC premiums), and increasing life expectancies (requiring more years of pension payments). The article predicts a life expectancy of 87.9 years for male retirees and 90.1 years for female retirees by 2029. These factors help explain the shift away from defined benefit plans. In 1979, 38% of private sector workers were covered by a defined benefit plan; in 2011, only 14% were. Some employers that still have defined benefit plans are taking steps like freezing the plan, moving workers to defined contribution plans, or buying annuities to satisfy defined benefit obligations. [Vipal Monga, *Pension Plans Brace For a One-Two Punch*, WSJ.com (Mar. 24, 2014)]

[B] Changes Under Recovery Statutes

The PPA was drafted during what, in retrospect, was a robust economy, where employers would be able to shoulder short-term burdens in order to maintain the long-term stability of the pension system. Financial events soon made it necessary to trim the PPA's remedial scheme. The PPA called for plans to become 100% funded within seven years. Congress voted in December 2008 for plans with large investment losses to comply without reaching 100% funding within the seven-year time frame. [Mary Williams Walsh, *Pensions Get a Reprieve in Congress*, N.Y. Times, Dec. 12, 2008]

Congress responded to corporations' pleas for relief by enacting the Preservation of Access to Care for Medicare Beneficiaries and Pension Relief Act, Pub. L. No. 111-192, allowing employers to pick two years to pay only the interest on the funding shortfall, or to amortize the funding shortfalls for any two plan years between 2008 and 2011 over an extended (15-year) period. [See Rebecca Moore, *Obama Signs Pension Relief Bill*, plansponsor.com (June 25, 2010)] [Gina Chon, *Private-Firm Pensions Face Deadline for Funding Level*, WSJ.com (Apr. 1, 2010)]

The Pension Protection Technical Corrections Act of 2008 (part of the Worker, Retiree and Employer Recovery Act, or WRERA, Pub. L. No. 110-458 (Dec. 23, 2008) provides relief to hard-pressed pension plans in many ways:

- A one-year moratorium (for 2009 only, not 2008) is imposed on the requirement that participants in defined contribution plans and IRAs take minimum distributions from the plan; participants did not want to have to sell securities at a loss to take the distributions (which would have been calculated based on pre-Crash values of their accounts).
- The PPA called for a three-year phase-in of the funding target percentage. Plans falling below the target funding percentage for a year must fund up to the funding percentage for that year—but do not have to reach 100% funding as quickly as originally provided by the PPA.
- Some smoothing is allowed—plans can recognize unexpected gains or losses over 24 months rather than in the year of the event.
- Employers will not be required to comply with all of the PPA's restrictions on accrual of pension benefits.
- The phase-in of full funding is slowed down; the threshold stays at 92% for an additional year.
- An underfunded plan that is not allowed to distribute lump sums is nevertheless permitted to cash out balances that do not exceed $5,000.
- The effective date of the PPA's rules about vesting and interest crediting in collectively bargained plans is delayed.
- Rollovers from Roth 401(k) or 403(b) plans to Roth IRA are not subject to the AGI limit for making Roth IRA contributions. [Fred Schneyer, *Pension Relief Bill with RMD Moratorium Slides Through U.S. Senate*, plansponsor.com (Dec. 11, 2008); Mary Williams Walsh, *Pensions Get a Reprieve in Congress*, N.Y. Times, Dec. 12, 2008 (times.com)]

In addition to PPA technical corrections, WRERA includes relief provisions for employers. The Worker, Retiree and Employer Recovery Act, or WRERA, Pub. L. No. 110-458 includes both PPA technical corrections and relief provisions. The PPA introduced the concept of the "target normal cost." WRERA allows expenses paid directly by the plan to be included in calculating the target normal cost; this is elective for 2009 but mandatory for later years.

WRERA requires the same interest rate assumptions to be used to calculate the funding target and the target normal cost. WRERA gives the IRS expanded authority to issue guidance about determining funded status for years before 2008—which is important for seeing if a plan is at risk.

The PPA includes provisions about cash balance and other hybrid plans (age discrimination rules, conversions, and the whipsaw calculation). WRERA limits the applicability of the new vesting requirements for cash balance plans (such as

100% vesting after three years of service). [Deloitte's Washington Bulletin, *PPA Technical Corrections Affecting Defined Benefit Plans*, <http://benefitslink.com/articles/guests/washbull090112.html> (Jan. 12, 2009) (benefitslink.com)]

MAP-21, Pub. L. No. 112-141, signed in July 2012, extends the period for calculating interest rates to 25 years—making recent years, when rates were very low, less influential in the calculation. For 2012, the plan's interest rates must be within 10% of the average benchmark bond rates for the previous 25 years.

Notice 2013-11, 2013-11 I.R.B. 610 provides guidance on MAP-21 funding calculations, such as the 25-year average segment rates to be used to adjust the 24-month segment rates for computing minimum contribution requirements for single-employer defined benefit plans.

The Highway Transportation Funding Act of 2014, Pub. L. No. 113-159, which includes "rate smoothing" provisions, was passed by both the House and the Senate on July 31, 2014, just before Congress adjourned for the August recess. The legislation extends the MAP-21 pension plan funding stabilization provisions. For most employers with defined benefit plans, "smoothing" reduces the employer's obligations with respect to minimum funding by adjusting the interest rates used to calculate the minimum funding obligation. For calendar years 2012–2017, the "corridor" is a minimum percentage of 90%, a maximum percentage of 110%. For 2018, the corresponding figures are 85% and 115%; for 2019, 80% and 120%; for 2020, 75% and 125%; after 2020, 70% and 130%. However, these smoothing rules do not apply to bankrupt companies: see Code § 463(d)(2) for benefit restrictions. An actuary for the consulting firm Milliman estimated that, thanks to this legislation, the 100 largest corporate pensions could save as much as 30% in their 2015 funding obligation compared to the 2014 figure. Other commentators said that reducing corporate contributions would increase the strain on the PBGC. [Groom Law Group Benefits Brief, *Extension of Pension Interest Rate Smoothing Relief Clears Congress Before August Recess*, <http://www.groom.com/media/publication/1444_Extension_of_Pension_Interest_Rate.pdf> (Aug. 1, 2014); Vipal Monga, *Welcome to the World of "Pension Smoothing,"* WSJ.com (Aug. 11, 2014)]

§ 4.02 EXTENT OF COVERAGE

In the more than 30 years since ERISA took effect, the pension sector of the economy has grown mightily, but has changed its characteristics very significantly. There has been a tremendous shift from plans in which the employer makes the contributions, decides how contributions will be invested, and takes the investment risk to plans in which employees bear a far greater burden of making both contributions and decisions. One of the major objectives of the PPA is to improve the soundness of the surviving defined benefit plans by requiring more realistic funding and reporting, although some of the more stringent rules were relaxed by 2008–2009 federal legislation.

In March 2014, 74% of private-industry full-time workers had access to a retirement plan, whereas only 37% of part-time workers did. Access depended on the size of the employer: 50% of employees of small employers had retirement plan access, whereas 82% of workers in medium to large establishments did. Two-thirds of all private-sector workers (i.e., considering both part- and full-time workers) had access to retirement benefits, but only 48% of employees participated in retirement plans. [Bureau of Labor Statistics News Release, *Employee Benefits in the United States-March 2014*, <http://www.bls.gov/news.release/pdf/ebs2.pdf> (July 25, 2014)]

The BNY Mellon Investment Strategy and Solutions Group said that the funded status of the average corporate pension plan increased by 1.4 percentage points in June 2014, reaching 92.0%. Pension plans benefited by increased asset value, and the slight rise in interest rates reduced corporate liabilities somewhat. [PRNewswire, *Funded Status of U.S. Corporate Pensions Rises to 92 Percent* (July 2, 2014) (benefitslink.com)]

As a result of changing valuation methods for their pension plans, some large companies (e.g., AT&T, Verizon) had increased earnings for the fourth quarter of 2013. They adopted mark-to-market pension accounting, which moves gains and losses from the pension plan into earnings faster, rather than smoothing the impact over several years. Mark-to-market accounting increases the volatility of earnings, but gives a more current picture of the status of the pension plan. In 2011–2012 when interest rates were falling, mark-to-market accounting was bad for earnings, but in 2013, there were surging interest rates and a strong stock market. [Michael Rapoport, *Pensions Could Lift Earnings at Some Big Companies*, WSJ.com (Jan. 8, 2014)]

§ 4.03 EFFECT OF DEMOGRAPHICS ON PLANS

The Baby Boom, people born after World War II, are the largest age cohort in U.S. history. The oldest boomers are already eligible for reduced-level Social Security benefits. That means that soon, employers will not only face the challenge of paying pensions to a very large group of retirees—they will have a smaller group of active workers to generate corporate income and profits. Furthermore, retirees may take priceless and irreplaceable skills and work ethics with them when they leave the workforce.

The population is aging. In 2001, senior citizens made up 12.4% of the population. The fastest-growing demographic group was the "oldest old": people over 85. Senior citizens consume more health services than younger people, so retiree health benefits (see Chapter 9) and the Medicare system will be severely strained.

The aging of the population means that the share of people over 60 in the workforce is likely to grow. On the one hand, older workers may be less productive than younger ones for health reasons; but they may also have greater experience and more formal education. The more formal education a person has, the longer he or she is likely to spend in the workforce, which is intuitive because less-educated people often work in jobs calling for hard physical labor, which is more difficult at older ages. In 2000, 7.3% of all earnings by male workers went to men in the 60–74 age group; this percentage rose to 12.7% in 2010. Corresponding figures for women are 5.8% and 11.7%. [Gary Burtless, *The Impact of Population Aging and Delayed Retirement on Workforce Productivity*, Brookings Institution, <http://www.brookings.edu/research/papers/2013/05/impacting-aging-population-workforce-productivity> (May 2013)]

A Gallup poll found more older Americans in the workforce since the end of the recession: a three-point increase between 2012 and late 2013, versus a two-point decrease in the number of people aged 18–29 in the workforce. In 2010, 9% of people aged 65 and older worked full-time or were self-employed on a full-time basis; 12% were employed in 2013. [Kevin McGuinness, *More Older Americans in Work Force*, plansponsor.com (Oct. 21, 2013)]

The PPA provides approval for plans to make in-service distributions starting at age 62, i.e., a person who reduces work effort can continue to draw both a reduced salary and a pension. [*Retirees Continue Working but Not for the Reason You Think*, plansponsor.com (Feb. 24, 2006)] See T.D. 9235, 2007-24 I.R.B. 1386, for Final Regulations defining "Normal Retirement Age" in connection with in-service distributions and phased retirement; issues of early retirement, including phased retirement, are discussed in Chapter 9.

The tax rules for retirement plans have been modified, effective July 2, 2014, to permit employees to buy longevity insurance inside retirement plans. They can purchase a deferred income annuity by exchanging a lump sum for a stream of guaranteed lifetime income to begin later, possibly in their late 70s or in their 80s. Under prior law, these annuities were uncommon, because the RMD rules required withdrawals to begin no later than age 70½. The 2014 rules, however, permit the use of part of a retirement account to buy annuities that begin by age 85. The participant can invest up to 25% of the account balance, or $125,000 (whichever is less) to purchase the annuity. The New York Times said that deferring annuity payments means that those who survive long enough to collect will get larger payments than those who invested in immediate annuities. For example, a 68-year-old man would have to pay about $170,000 to purchase an immediate annuity paying $12,000 a year. But a 58-year-old man who purchased an annuity at age 58 and deferred benefits until age 78 would have to pay only $40,000 for the right to receive annual income of $12,000. [T.D. 9673, 2014-30 I.R.B. 212; see Tara Siegel Bernard, *Longevity Insurance Joins the Menu of Retirement Plan Options*, NYTimes.com (July 1, 2014)]

After the recession intensified in 2008, it was anticipated that many Baby Boomers would delay retirement for several years past their original intended retirement date, because of loss of value in their 401(k) accounts, their personal investments, cutbacks by employers, and loss of housing equity.

According to Swiss Re's Risk Perception Survey, 57% of American workers expect to retire either later than age 65 or not at all. In the United States, 19% of survey respondents—more than in any other country—expect to work at least until 70; 12% say they will never be able to retire, and 21% don't know when they will be able to retire. [Kevin McGuinness, *Americans Foresee a Working Retirement*, plansponsor.com (Oct. 21, 2013)]

Financial planner Brad Glickman says that he asks his Baby Boomer clients, "What's your job after retirement?" A poll carried out in late 2013 by the Associated Press-NORC Center for Public Affairs Research showed that 82% of workers aged 50 and over said it was at least somewhat likely they would hold paid jobs post-retirement; 47% said that their estimate of when they will be able to retire is at least three years later than it was when they were 40. Workers earning under $50,000, non-white workers, workers with minor children, and those without health insurance were more likely to expect to work longer, and men expected to work longer than women did. A common pattern is for a person to retire, discover that the pension and savings are inadequate (especially if they have health problems), and return to part- or full-time work. One-third of retirees in the survey said that they were forced out of the workforce rather than voluntarily retiring; 8 % said they experienced age discrimination. [Matt Sedensky, *Poll: Half of Older Workers Delay Retirement Plans*, <http://finance.yahoo.com/news/poll-half-older-workers-delay-retirement-plans-072807063.html> (Oct. 14, 2013)]

§ 4.04 INVESTMENT FACTORS

For many years, the strong investment climate allowed plans to reduce or even suspend their contributions to defined benefit plans, because the plans were ample to satisfy the obligation to make future payments.

In the 1990s, many companies found that their investment experience was so favorable that they were able to suspend contributions to their plans, because the plan was already fully funded. This trend later reversed. [John D. McKinnon, *Warning of Pension-Plan Shortfall Raises Pressure for Financial Fix*, Wall St. J., Sept. 5, 2003, at A1] Then, in 2000 and 2001, the dot-com bubble collapsed; the September 11 attack and the Enron scandal also damaged investment results. For the period 2005–2010, the typical average annual return achieved by defined contribution plan participants was 3.7%, for a cumulative return of just over 20%—even considering the recession. Almost all (95%) of participants had positive total return for the five years, but just broke even for 2007–2010. [<https://institutional.vanguard.com/VGApp/iip/site/institutional/researchcommentary/article/InvResDuringCrisis>; see Tara Cantore, *Vanguard Study Finds DC Plan Account Accumulation Positive Through Recession*, plansponsor.com (Dec. 14, 2011)]

The 2008–2009 declines in the real estate market and financial markets, in conjunction with business problems caused by lack of access to borrowing, placed pension plans under great stress, leading to many plan freezes, plan terminations, and reductions or elimination of employer matching contributions. [Alicia H. Munnell, Jean-Pierre Aubry and Dan Muldoon, *The Financial Crisis and Private Defined Benefit Plans*, No. IB#8-18, Center for Retirement Research at Boston College]

Freezing or terminating a defined benefit plan can have unforeseen consequences for the sponsor's profit sharing plan, especially if the plan is top-heavy or uses the cross-testing method (for example, a professional firm's cash balance plan). For top-heavy or cross-tested plans, minimum benefits must be provided to non-key, non-HCE employees. If the sponsor has both defined benefit and defined contribution plans, the minimum benefit often includes a 5% top-heavy minimum for all participants who were employed at the end of the year or who worked at least 1,000 hours during the year, with cross-testing based on a 7.5% defined benefit/defined contribution gateway allocation. (Separate defined benefit and defined contribution options are permissible instead of a single 5% figure.)

When accruals in the defined benefit plan stop, the top-heavy minimum benefit falls from 5% to 3% of pay, and allocation is only required for employees who continue to be employed throughout the year. But if the defined benefit plan is terminated and its assets distributed, the defined benefit amounts for active employees are still considered in the top-heavy determination for the remaining plans for up to five years. If there are no more defined benefit accruals to test, the only cross-testing that might be required is for the defined contribution plan itself, so the gateway minimum allocation drops from 7.5% to 5% of pay. Although the ability to reduce the minimum profit-sharing benefit is good for the employer, it will probably have a negative effect on employee motivation, so the employer might choose to keep the profit-sharing rates stable at first and decrease them over time. [Mark Schulte, *Employers Need to Understand Minimum Profit Sharing Benefits for Frozen/Terminated Defined Benefit Plans*, VIA Retirement Plan Blog (Nov. 9, 2011) (benefitslink.com)]

Many pension plans reacted to the financial downturn by freezing defined benefit plans or ceasing or reducing contributions to defined contribution plans—or both. Many employers maintain plans of both types.

Chrysler Group LLC announced in mid-2013 that it would freeze the pension plan for about 8,000 salaried active workers, transferring them to a defined contribution plan in 2014. The move did not affect hourly workers or any retirees. For retirement on or after January 1, 2014, retirees will be permitted to collect pension benefits at age 58 rather than 62. GM also reduced its pension liabilities, by giving 42,000 of its 118,000 retired salaried workers a chance to take a one-time payout instead of receiving monthly checks. Ford made a similar offer in 2012. General Motors moved 26,000 salaried workers to a 401(k)-type plan with contributions based on salary and benefits. [Christina Rogers, *Chrysler Revamps Pension Plan for Salaried Workers*, WSJ.com (June 14, 2013)]

§ 4.05 DEFINED BENEFIT/DEFINED CONTRIBUTION

The traditional kind of pension plan, the one usually in effect when ERISA was passed, is the defined benefit plan. In a plan of this type, the employer agrees to provide benefits according to a formula. A typical formula would set the pension level as x% times the number of years the employee worked before retirement times the employee's average pay for his or her last five years working for the employer—or perhaps the average of the three years in which he or she earned the most.

The employer's contributions for all employees go into a single account or trust for the entire plan. However, there must be a separate account balance for each participant who makes voluntary contributions. [I.R.C. § 411(b)(2)(A)]

In some ways, this arrangement is problematic both from the employer's and the employee's point of view. When employees retire, they receive a fixed pension that will probably not be inflation-indexed and will not offer cost of living adjustments. In a highly inflationary environment, they will find that their pension buys less and less over time. Nor will their pension increase if the investment climate is favorable.

From the employer's point of view, defined benefit plans carry heavy burdens, including uncertainty. The employer's commitment is to contribute enough to the plan each year to ensure that the participants will receive the promised level of benefits. Not only does this require elaborate (and expensive) actuarial calculations, it places the investment risk on the employer, who will have to make larger contributions in years in which the value of the plan's securities portfolio declines.

A defined contribution plan is a different, and much simpler, structure. The employer establishes a separate account for each employee who has satisfied the criteria for plan participation. If the plan requires or accepts employee contributions, there will usually be separate subaccounts for employer and employee contributions, but this is not a legal requirement.

The employer's commitment is to contribute the amount required by the plan formula—generally a simple percentage of compensation. ERISA § 404(c) permits the plan to give control over the assets to the participant. If this is done, the plan's fiduciaries will not be liable for losses that result from the control exercised by the participants.

There is no limit on the number of plans a particular employer can maintain, and it is not uncommon for an employer to maintain both defined benefit and defined contribution plans. Under prior law, § 415(e) imposed a limit on benefits from a combination of defined benefit and defined contribution plans, but that limitation was repealed for limitation years beginning on or after January 1, 2000.

ERISA § 404(c) also requires the plan to give participants adequate information about the investment options they have for their accounts. The plan must offer at least three diversified investment types, with materially different characteristics with respect to risk and return.

The PBGC published a proposal in April 2014 to facilitate rollovers from defined contribution to defined benefit plans. PBGC director Josh Gotbaum said that annuities offer greater retirement security, so participants who have rollover options would be allowed to transfer between plans. Rolled over benefits would not be subject to the PBGC limit on the amount of benefits guaranteed. [FR Doc 2014-07379, 79 Fed. Reg. 18737 (Apr. 3, 2014); see Rebecca Moore, *PBGC Proposes DC Rollovers Into Pensions*, plansponsor.com (Apr. 1, 2014)]

President Obama signed a presidential memorandum on January 29, 2014 directing the Department of the Treasury to create a new "myRA" savings program for people who lack access to an employer-sponsored plan. The new accounts would be similar to Roth IRAs: contributions can be withdrawn tax-free at any time, but withdrawals of earnings will be taxed. The only permitted investment would be a variable-rate fund that invests in Treasury bonds. Once the balance reaches $15,000, or after 30 years, the myRA balance must be rolled over to a regular IRA; the owner can roll it over at any time. [Tara Siegel Bernard, *Obama Orders Creation of 'MyRA' Savings Accounts*, NYTimes.com (Jan. 29, 2014); Anne Tergesen and Colleen McCain Nelson, *Obama Signs Order for New myRA Retirement Accounts*, WSJ.com (Jan. 29, 2014); Damian Paletta and Anne Tergesen, *Obama Announces New myRA Retirement Accounts*, WSJ.com (Jan. 29, 2014)]

In a sense, the Social Security system is a kind of pension plan. Both employers and employees pay FICA taxes to fund retirement benefits. Although all earned income is subject to Medicare taxes, the FICA tax phases out at a figure that changes every year. (For 2009–2011, only the first $106,800 of earned income is subject to FICA tax; for 2012, the applicable amount is $110,100, for 2013, it is $113,700, and for 2014 it is $117,000.) The employer makes FICA contributions on all or nearly all of rank-and-file workers' pay, but only on a smaller proportion of the compensation of top earners. The Tax Relief, Unemployment Insurance Reauthorization, and Job Creation Act of 2010, Pub. L. No. 111-312 reduced the employee's share of FICA taxes (but not the employer's share) for 2011, [Plansponsor staff, *Principal Says Tax Holiday an Opportunity to Save*, plansponsor.com (Dec. 17, 2010)] PPACA also imposes additional Medicare tax on high-income earners.

The Temporary Payroll Tax Cut Continuation Act, Pub. L. No. 112-78, extended the 4.2% FICA rate but subject to a cap of the first $18,350 of compensation. The Middle Class Tax Relief and Job Creation Act of 2012, Pub. L. No. 112-96, enacted February 2, 2012, extended the 4.2% rate until the end of 2012, and removed the cap.

The Internal Revenue Code contains "permitted disparity" rules for "integrating" a qualified plan with Social Security (disparities are not permitted in 401(k) plans). Within limits, the employer can reduce its plan contributions on behalf of rank-and-file employees to compensate for the employer's FICA contributions. As long as the permitted disparity rules are satisfied, the plan will remain qualified, and will not be considered discriminatory—even though the practical effect is to cut down on contributions and lower the pension the rank-and-file employees will eventually receive. The 2014 table of covered compensation with respect to permitted disparities appears at Rev. Rul. 2014-3, 2014-2 I.R.B. 259.

§ 4.06 OTHER PLAN TYPES

An Employee Stock Ownership Plan provides employees with shares in the employer company as a form of deferred compensation. Sometimes ESOPs purchase the company. Commentators noted that ESOPs can provide tax and financing advantages that surpass other takeover alternatives. The transaction involves large-scale loans; as the company repays the loans, the interest is tax-deductible and may be large enough to significantly reduce or even eliminate taxable income for the business. The business is also exempt from capital gains taxation on purchases of certain securities that are retained within the ESOP for three years or more—provided that the ESOP owns at least 30% of the employer stock.

Employers interested in succession planning may be interested in creating an ESOP, so the business can eventually be owned by employees—who have a personal interest in its prosperity. However, setting up an ESOP is complicated, and usually costs $150,000–$250,000, a large amount for a small company. To be practical, an ESOP conversion probably requires at least 40 employees and annual sales over $5 million. Lawyers, a valuation expert, and an ESOP trustee will be required. There are also ongoing compliance costs. There must be good succession management and a training program to develop managers for the long haul. Some successful ESOPs took years or even decades for full transition to employee ownership. The deal can be structured to give the ESOP an initial minority position, so the deal can be reversed if it is not successful. [Josh Patrick, *The Questions to Ask Before Adopting an ESOP*, NYTimes.com (July 11, 2013)]

Employees are at high risk if their individual pension accounts are heavily invested in employer stock—and the stock does poorly. Because of the ESOP's mission of investing in employer stock, participants have generally been unsuccessful in challenging ESOP fiduciaries when the value of the stock falls. (See § 15.03[C] for discussion of "stock drop" suits in general.)

On November 16, 2009, the IRS released updated ESOP regulations, increasing the flexibility for satisfying the requirements of § 423 (favorable tax treatment for stock acquired under an ESOP option). To qualify for favorable treatment, the employee must hold the stock for at least two years from the grant, and one year from exercise of the option. For nonqualified options, the employee has ordinary income at the time of exercise, equal any excess of fair market value over the exercise price. To be a § 423 plan, the ESOP plan, including the maximum number of shares available, must be approved by the company's stockholders within a period of 12 months before or after the date the plan was adopted. In general, all employees of the corporation must be granted options. Up to $25,000 worth of stock can be optioned for each year the option is outstanding, whether or not the option is exercisable. The exercise price must be at least 85% of the fair market value at the time of grant or exercise. [Sonnenschein Nath & Rosenthal LLP, *IRS Releases Final Regulations on Employee Stock Purchase Plans* (Nov. 17, 2009) (benefitslink.com)]

Hybrid plans are defined benefit plans whose benefits accrue under the formula set by the sponsor rather than as a monthly payment. The benefit is usually defined as a lump-sum account balance and not an annuity benefit payable at NRA. Employers who adopt hybrid plans often do so because funding is predictable and the plan design is easier for employees to understand than other types of defined benefit plans. Although the PPA provided new rules for administration of hybrid plans, sponsors have not received any further guidance since then.

Most hybrid plans are cash balance plans, with the benefit based on a percentage of pay credited annually each year with interest determined based on the plan's interest crediting rate. Another plan design, the Pension Equity Plan (PEP) posts percentage credits to the employee's account each year. The lump-sum balance at retirement is the total of the percentages times the employee's final average pay.

Typically, hybrid plans increase the rate of pay credits as age and/or service increase. To avoid back-loading, IRS rules mandate crediting a minimum interest rate. Employees generally must meet age and service requirements to participate in hybrid plans, such as one year of service plus reaching age 21. The pension can be computed based on salary alone, or salary plus overtime and commission, but most plans include all compensation including overtime, bonuses, and commissions. In late 2010, the IRS issued final and proposed regulations for hybrid retirement plans, including cash balance plans, and Pension Equity Plans (PEPs). The 2010 final regulations deal with subjects such as age discrimination, vesting, conversions from conventional defined benefit plans, and safe harbor rates for crediting interest.

Under the final regulations, a lump sum-based benefit formula is any formula that expresses the accrued benefit either as the current balance of the participant's hypothetical account, or the current value of the accumulated percentage of the participant's final average compensation. Each participant has a hypothetical account that is credited with the employer's hypothetical contributions based on compensation credits (the participant's eligible compensation) plus interest credits (the hypothetical earnings on the account). Usually, compensation credits are defined as a percentage of eligible pay, although the formula may factor in age and years of service. The interest credits can operate as a fixed rate or be based on an extrinsic interest. Compensation credits end when the participant stops working for the employer, but interest rates generally continue until the pension is distributed. The PEP benefit equals a percentage of the final average pay, with the percentage set based on points earned each year by participants.

Under the final regulations, the entire accrued benefit for a plan using a hybrid formula must vest no later than three years of service. Although three-year vesting is required even if only part of the benefit is calculated using the hybrid formula, the final regulations clarify that the three-year vesting requirement does not apply to the traditional defined benefit portion of a floor offset arrangement when a defined benefit plan is combined with a separate hybrid plan. Usually, the defined benefit will be reduced by the value of the hybrid plan account.

The final regulations provide an ADEA safe harbor: the accumulated benefit of any participant must not be less than the accumulated benefit of any similarly situated younger participant. Whether two participants are similarly situated depends on their period of service, their job, compensation, date of hire, and work history. A hybrid plan that does not qualify under the safe harbor must satisfy the general age discrimination rule of Code § 411(b)(1)(H)(i).

To prevent wearaway, the final regulations provide that if an amendment adopted and effective on or after June 29, 2005 eliminates or reduces future benefit accruals, and part or all of the benefit is determined based on the statutory hybrid formula, the benefit after the conversion amendment must at least equal the accrued benefit on the conversion date plus the accrued benefit after the conversion, with no offsets between the two. A plan is considered amended if it changes the conditions of employment, such as a transfer to a different part of the company that has a different plan.

The PPA requires hybrid plans to credit interest at a rate that does not exceed a market rate of return. The final regulations define a market rate as a rate that does not exceed the rate on long-term investment-grade corporate bonds, the rate on certain Treasury bonds; or the actual rate of return on plan assets, if the benefits are indexed; or the rate of return on annuities issued by an insurance company. The rate of benefit accrual can increase as participants earn more, but any year's accrual rate must not exceed one-third more than the previous year's rate. [75 Fed. Reg. 64123 (Oct. 19, 2010) [final regulations], 75 Fed. Reg. 64197 (Oct. 19, 2010)]

[A] Money Purchase Plan

A money purchase plan provides definitely determinable benefits, funded by fixed employer contributions made in accordance with a single allocation formula for all participants. Money purchase plans are subject to the I.R.C. § 412 minimum funding standard. The plan must offer QJSAs and QPSAs. [See §§ 12.05, 12.06] Money purchase plans can accept employee contributions and make plan loans to participants.

[B] Profit-Sharing Plan

A profit-sharing plan must have a definite formula, set in advance, for allocating the employer's total contribution among the various plan participants, and for distributing the account money to participants. Distributions can be made after the funds have been in the account for a certain length of time (ERISA requires this to be at least two years), attainment of a stated age (which does not have to be retirement age) or an event such as retirement, termination, illness, or disability. Profit-sharing plans have to have formulas for allocating and distributing employer contributions, but the corporation's Board of Directors can legitimately be given discretion to set the level of contributions each year. Since 1986, it has not been necessary for the contributions to be made from corporate profits, or only in a year in which there are profits. The maximum contribution that the employer can deduct is 15% of the participant's contribution for the year. Profit-sharing plans are allowed to make plan loans.

[C] Target-Benefit Plan

A target-benefit plan is a money purchase plan (and therefore subject to the defined contribution rules), but contributions are calculated to fund a specified level of retirement benefits at normal retirement age. The participant receives the aggregate of all contributions plus their earnings, although the actual benefit may be either higher or lower than the target, depending on investment results. The IRS treats these plans as defined contribution plans with respect to the Rev. Proc. 2007-44 filing deadlines. Therefore, opinion and advisory letters for PPA restatements of prototype or volume submitter plans had a January 31, 2012 deadline. Rev. Proc. 2011-49, 2011-44 I.R.B. 608 requires master or specimen plans to have at least 30 sponsors registered as adopting that plan word for word. The only exception is for money purchase plans (when only 10 adopters required). Target benefit plans do not qualify for this exemption. [Suzanne L. Wynn, *Target Benefit Plans: On the Edge of Extinction*, Pension Protection Act Blog (Dec. 13, 2011) (benefitslink.com)]

[D] Floor-Offset Plan

A floor-offset plan is a hybrid plan, where the defined benefit portion of the plan guarantees a minimum level of benefits, offset by the annuity the retiree could purchase at retirement with the balance in the defined contribution portion of the plan. *Lunn v. Montgomery Ward & Co. Ret. Sec. Plan* [166 F.3d 880 (7th Cir. 1999)] holds that an employee who retired four years after normal retirement age was not entitled to additional retirement benefits to make up for the reduced duration of benefits. The court upheld the idea of floor-offset plans, finding that this type of plan does not violate ERISA benefit accrual requirements or anti-forfeiture provisions.

[E] New Comparability Plan

A new comparability plan is a special type of defined contribution plan (or combination of defined contribution and defined benefit plan) that can increase the allocation for HCEs without violating the antidiscrimination rules. See § 4.22.

The plan document can define the classes used to group the employees in various ways, although a plan amendment is required to change the number or definition of classes, and this cannot be done retroactively. A class could be specified, for example, as all employees born before a certain date, those hired after a certain date, those with a certain number of years of service, those working in a particular department, those with a stated title or type of job, or those assigned to a named region. The IRS and DOL have not issued technical guidance, but if every employee is placed in a separate class, the agencies might rule that the plan has become a deemed 401(k). For example, a medical practice could have three classes: owners, managers, and other employees. To reward productivity, the plan could have different classes for offices depending on their revenue streams and productivity levels. [Mark Papalia, *Class-Based Pensions: A Cost-Saving Alternative for Companies of All Sizes*, Journal of Accountancy (January 2005) <https://www.aicpa.org/PUBS/JOFA/jan2005/papalia.html>]

[F] SEP

A SEP (Simplified Employer Pension) is an IRA sponsored by the employer, under a written plan whose contribution formula does not discriminate in favor of HCEs. For 2009–2014, the § 402(k)(2)(C) compensation amount is $550. For 2009–2011, the SEP annual compensation limit (§ 408(k)(3)(C)) is $245,000, rising to $250,000 in 2012, $255,000 in 2013, and $260,000 in 2014. [IR-2012-77, *IRS Announces 2013 Pension Plan Limitations*, <http://www.irs.gov/uac/2013-Pension-Plan-Limitations> (Oct. 18, 2012); IR-2013-86, *IRS Announces 2014 Pension Plan Limitations*, <http://www.irs.gov/uac/IRS-Announces-2014-Pension-Plan-Limitations;-Taxpayers-May-Contribute-up-to-$17,500-to-their-401(k)-plans-in-2014> (Oct. 31, 2013)]

[G] SIMPLE

A Savings Incentive Match Plan for Employees (SIMPLE) plan, available only to companies with 100 or fewer employees, involves employer contributions to employees' own IRAs. The SIMPLE IRA offers tax advantages for both employer and employees in small companies, and is easier and less expensive to administer than a 401(k) plan. As a general rule, the company cannot offer any other retirement plan, and all participants must have earned at least $5,000 per year from the company in any two previous years, and expect to earn $5,000 in the current year. The employer can elect two kinds of plan. The most common plan form requires the employer to match employee contributions up to 3% of compensation. The limits remained identical from 2009 to 2012, rising slightly in 2013. For 2013–2014, employee contributions are limited to $12,000; employees over 50 can make catch-up contributions of up to $2,500. (The $12,000 limit is subject to the aggregate dollar limit of $17,500 for all elective contributions made by a person to all employer-sponsored plans.) The general rule is that the employer can deduct its contributions to the SIMPLE IRA plan.

[H] Cafeteria Plans

The underlying purpose of all employee benefits is to motivate employees to do better work. Employees differ in their characteristics and priorities, and it is reasonable to assume that employees will be most strongly motivated by benefits that fit their individual needs. Hence, the Internal Revenue Code, at § 125, regulates "cafeteria plans," giving employees choices from a "menu" of taxable and non-taxable benefits. In the summer of 2007, the IRS withdrew a number of earlier proposals and offered new guidance about cafeteria plans (general rules about qualified and nonqualified benefits in these plans; rules for elections; FSA plan rules; nondiscrimination; substantiating expenses for qualified benefits).

A cafeteria plan must be set out in writing. The written plan document must explain:

- How to make elections
- The employer's contributions under the plan
- The maximum salary reduction permitted under the plan, either as a maximum percentage of contribution or a maximum dollar amount
- The plan year (unless there is a valid business purpose for a shorter plan year, it must be 12 consecutive months)
- If the plan covers paid time off, ordering of non-elective and elective paid time off
- Rules for any Flexible Spending Account included in the plan
- If there is a Health Savings Account, who is eligible to contribute
- Grace period (if any) for health FSA or dependent care assistance

The rules deal with benefits recently added to the roster that cafeteria plans can offer (adoption assistance, HSAs, HSA distributions from health FSAs). The IRS proposed a Regulation clarifying that § 125 is the only way for employers to give employees a choice between taxable and nontaxable benefits without the choice itself creating tax liability for the employees. The proposal adds COBRA premiums and HSA contributions as acceptable qualified nontaxable benefits. The proposed regulations forbid cafeteria plans to offer scholarships, employer-provided meals and lodging, educational assistance, fringe benefits, long-term care insurance, contributions to an Archer MSA, group-term life insurance covering non-employees; or elective deferrals to a 403(b) plan.

All reimbursements under the plan must be individually substantiated by someone other than the employee. If the cafeteria plan discriminates in favor of highly compensated employees, the HCEs have income for tax purposes equal to the highest value of the benefits they could have elected. The Proposed Regulations incorporate some of the safe harbor testing rules of Code § 410(b), with an objective test to determine when the actual election of benefits is discriminatory: when HCEs have higher benefits, measured as a percentage of compensation, than non-HCEs.

PPACA creates a new form of cafeteria plan available to small employers starting in 2011. Like the Simple 401(k) and Simple IRA plan, the Simple Cafeteria Plan insulates small employers from nondiscrimination problems that might otherwise occur. (With only a few employees in a plan, it's likely that most of the benefits will go to key employees.) For this purpose, a small employer is one that, in either of the prior two years, had an average of 100 or fewer employees. For an employer that has been in business for less than two years, eligibility is based on the number of employees it can reasonably be expected to have. If a company grows in size, it can keep its Simple Cafeteria Plan until the end of the plan year in which it reaches 200 employees.

All qualified employees must be eligible to participate if they had at least 1,000 hours of service in the previous plan year. Highly compensated and key employees can participate in the Simple Cafeteria Plan, but the plan must avoid discrimination in their favor in eligibility and benefits. Employees can be excluded if they have not reached age 21 (or a younger age as provided by the plan) by the end of the plan year; if they have not performed at least one year of service; if they are non-resident aliens; or if they are covered by a CBA. All eligible employees must be allowed to elect any benefit in the plan under the same terms and conditions as all other participants.

The employer maintaining the Simple Cafeteria Plan must make a minimum contribution that the participant can apply toward any benefit within the plan. The minimum contribution for non-HCEs must equal or exceed the lesser of a uniform 2% of compensation (whether or not the employee contributes); a match equal to double the employee's contribution; or 6% of compensation. This is the minimum: the employer is permitted to make additional contributions, but the match percentage for HCEs must not be higher than the match rate for non-HCEs. [McKenna Long & Aldridge LLP, *Is a Simple Cafeteria Plan Right for You?*, <http://www.mckennalong.com/publications-advisories-2976.html> (May 16, 2012)]

See Notice 2013-61, 2013-44 I.R.B. 432 and Notice 2014-1, 2014.2 I.R.B. 270, explaining the cafeteria plan rules and rules about Health Savings Accounts (HSAs) as they apply to same-sex married couples. Change in marital status is one reason why employees are permitted to change their cafeteria plan elections in the middle of a plan year. The IRS treats a couple as married if they were legally married in any jurisdiction, even if they do not live in a state that recognizes same-sex marriage. Employees who previously made a pre-tax salary reduction election under a cafeteria plan and also furnished after-tax health coverage for a same-sex spouse can treat the after-tax amounts as a pre-tax salary reduction.

[I] QLACs

The Department of Treasury noted the role of "longevity risk" in the need for retirement income. A 65-year-old woman has a 50-50 chance of living past 86; a 65 year-old man has an equal chance of living past 84. The replacement of defined benefit plans by defined contribution plans as the predominant form leaves many people at risk of outliving their funds. The Treasury and DOL published a package of proposed regulations and rulings in early 2012 to encourage development of lifetime income alternatives. The proposals were finalized in mid-2014 as T.D. 9673, 2014-30 I.R.B. 212. The proposals make it easier for employers to offer combination options (e.g., the employee takes part of the account as a lump sum, but receives an annuity with the rest).

The rules contemplate the possibility of "longevity annuities"—annuities that protect the very-long-lived by commencing annuity benefits at an advanced age, such as 80 or 85. A lump sum 401(k) distribution can split: part going to the participant, part deposited with the employer to purchase an annuity.

Under prior law, it was difficult to have a split distribution because the statutory interest rates and mortality tables had to be used for both the lump sum and the annuity, precluding the plan from using its own figures in the annuity calculation. The proposal allows the use of the statutory assumptions for the lump sum only, with the plan's regular conversion factors for the partial annuity.

Prior law also worked against longevity annuities, because the minimum distribution requirements impose penalties if the entire account is not distributed over the individual's predicted life expectancy—which means that people who outlive their predicted life expectancy will have exhausted their accounts. The new rules allows 401(k) (and IRA) plans relief from the minimum distribution requirements for annuities that cost less than the smaller of $100,000 or 25% of the account balance and that start by age 85. This type of distribution is referred to as a QLAC, or "qualified longevity annuity contract." The annuity will be disregarded for RMD purposes until its benefits begin. Longevity annuities must satisfy some requirements for death benefits and cash-out to ensure that they are used only to hedge against longevity risk, and full disclosure of the annuity terms is required.

The proposals give the employer another alternative: the sponsor of a defined benefit plan can permit employees who have 401(k) accounts to roll over all or part of the 401(k) distribution to the defined benefit plan (or a hybrid plan such as a cash balance plan) in exchange for an immediate annuity. The annuity must be at least actuarially equivalent to the sum received by the plan.

Rev. Rul. 2012-4, 2012-8 I.R.B. 386 explains how an employer that offers both defined contribution and defined benefit plans can permit 401(k) plan participants who are ready to retire to roll over part or all of the 401(k) account balance to the defined benefit plan (starting January 1, 2013), receiving an immediate annuity under the defined benefit plan. The plan must use the same actuarial assumptions (such as interest rates and mortality tables) for annuitized rollovers as for defined benefit distributions. Defined contribution plan participants who elect a rollover are entitled to disclosures about what will happen if the plan terminates without enough money to pay its liabilities. Married participants must furnish notified consent from their spouses. [McKay Hochman Company, Inc. *E-Mail Alert 2012-8, Lifetime Income Options* (Aug. 30, 2012) (benefitslink.com)]

§ 4.07 IRA/QUALIFIED PLAN INTERFACE

As the name suggests, an Individual Retirement Arrangement (IRA) is maintained by an individual on his or her own behalf, not by a corporation. However, the two types of plan interact when an IRA is used as a "conduit" for a transfer of funds between two qualified plans, or when distributions from a qualified plan are sheltered from immediate taxation by being rolled over to an IRA.

Employers can maintain a program under which employees authorize payroll deductions to be invested in either regular or Roth IRAs. Such arrangements do not constitute ERISA plans (and therefore do not subject the employer to regulation or potential supervision) if:

- The employer doesn't make any contributions;
- Employee participation in the arrangement is completely voluntary;
- The employer's sole involvement is letting employees participate (without endorsing participation), making the payroll deductions, and forwarding the amounts to the IRA sponsor.

The employer can collect reasonable reimbursement for its services in connection with the employees' IRAs, but no other compensation. The employer can provide educational materials about IRAs and the value of saving for retirement, but must make it clear that the employer's role is purely administrative and does not involve contributions to the plan. It's also permissible for the employer to distribute literature prepared by the IRA sponsor, and even to display its own logo on the materials.

Either the employer can choose a single IRA sponsor or inform employees of criteria for choosing a sponsor. However, it is not permitted for the employer to negotiate special terms for its own employees that are not available to everyone who buys IRAs through that sponsor. The employer should inform employees that there are other ways to fund IRAs; that IRAs are not a suitable investment for everybody; and that IRAs work the same way whether the employee authorizes a payroll deduction or submits the contribution directly to the IRA sponsor.

EGTRRA increases the maximum amount that can be contributed to an IRA (especially by persons over 50) and institutes a tax credit for low-income IRA investors, so IRA options will be more attractive than ever before. Active servicemembers can also base IRA contributions on combat pay.

EGTRRA also creates another option, the "deemed IRA," for plan years beginning after December 31, 2002. A qualified plan can permit employees to contribute to a separate account within a qualified plan. If the separate account meets the criteria for being either a conventional or a Roth IRA, it is treated as an IRA and not a qualified plan—and the employer's qualified plan won't lose its qualified status just because of the IRA subaccounts. The difference between a deemed IRA and the payroll deduction plan described above is that the employer, not the employee, sets up the account, although deemed IRAs can take payroll deductions.

Deemed IRAs are considered IRAs rather than qualified plans, so it is not necessary to satisfy ERISA's coverage and nondiscrimination rules. However, deemed IRAs are subject to ERISA's fiduciary and enforcement provisions, including the requirements for processing claims. Each deemed IRA must be held in a separate account or separate annuity under the plan, and the plan must provide separate accounting for the IRS contributions and earnings.

Under the final rule published in 2004, the deemed IRA account must satisfy the rules for either a traditional or Roth IRA. SEP and SIMPLE IRAs cannot be used as deemed IRAs. Because the employer's qualified plan and the deemed IRA are treated as separate entities, rules such as the minimum distribution requirements must be satisfied separately for each.

The applicable 2014 dollar amount of adjusted gross income for determining the IRA deduction for taxpayers who are active participants in a qualified plan is $92,000 (joint return or qualified widow or widower); for other taxpayers who are not married filing separate returns, the limit is $58,000. The dollar amount for a taxpayer who is not an active participant but who is married to an active participant is $173,000. The traditional IRA deduction phases out for singles and heads of household who participate in a qualified plan between $60,000 and $70,000. The phase-out range for married couples (where the IRA account holder participates in a qualified plan) is $96,000–$116,000. The phase-out range, when, not the account holder but his or her spouse is a plan participant, is $181,000–$191,000.

For Roth IRAs, entitlement to contribute phases out at adjusted gross income of $181,000 to $191,000 (joint returns) or $114,000 to $129,000 (single or head of household returns); the range for married persons filing separate returns is very limited, topping out at $10,000 (2014 figures). [IR-2013-86, *IRS Announces 2014 Pension Plan Limitations*, <http://www.irs.gov/uac/IRS-Announces-2014-Pension-Plan-Limitations;-Taxpayers-May-Contribute-up-to-$17,500-to-their-401(k)-plans-in-2014> (Oct. 31, 2013)]

The Saver's Credit, also known as the retirement savings contributions credit, applies to individuals and married persons filing separate returns with incomes up to $29,500 (for 2014), joint returns with income up to $59,000, and heads of household with income up to $44,250. The person claiming the credit must be over 18, not a full-time student, and not the dependent of another taxpayer. The credit is a percentage of the amount contributed, with the highest percentage at the lowest income level. The credit is reported on Form 8800, Credit for Qualified Retirement Savings Contributions. [IRS Tax Tip 2014-28, *Boost Your Retirement Savings With a Tax Credit*, <http://www.irs.gov/uac/Newsroom/Boost-Your-Retirement-Savings-with-a-Tax-Credit> (Mar. 7, 2014)]

The American Taxpayer Relief Act of 2012 authorizes in-plan Roth conversions of defined contribution accounts that are not otherwise distributable, with no income limitation. Under prior law, only amounts that were distributable (e.g., to a participant who had reached age 59½) could be converted to Roth form. Although the provision is effective January 1, 2013, prior account balances can be converted. [Rebecca Moore, *Fiscal Cliff Deal Extends Roth Conversions*, plansponsor.com (Jan. 3, 2013)]

Roth 401(k) plans (i.e., plans that do not give rise to tax benefits at the time funds are deferred, but from which funds can be withdrawn tax-free at retirement) are another option. [See § 6.04[E]] Roth 401(k) plans were first authorized in 2006. There is no income limit on who can contribute. Account-holders do not get a tax deduction for their contributions, but they can withdraw funds from the account tax-free after retirement. Therefore, these plans are best for people who expect to be in a higher tax bracket after retirement than before—although it is very difficult to predict tax trends. If a Roth 401(k) account contains pre-tax matching contributions from the employer, these contributions must be kept in a separate sub-account, and will be taxable when they are withdrawn. Sponsors of prototype Roth IRA plans who wish to accept rollovers from Roth 402A accounts are required to amend their IRA documents. See Final Regulations covering 401(k), 403(b), and Roth IRA plans. [Fred Schneyer, *IRS Puts Out Roth IRA Rollover Final Regs*, plansponsor.com (June 4, 2007)]

See IRS Notice 2008-30, 2008-12 I.R.B. 638 for guidance on applying the PPA to Roth IRAs. Distributions from an eligible retirement plan can be rolled over to a Roth IRA, as long as the amount is eligible for rollover (i.e., not a periodic payment, required minimum distribution, or hardship distribution); and the taxpayer includes in gross income any amount that would be includible absent the rollover. However, withholding is not required on the amounts included in gross income. The additional tax under Code § 72(m) does not apply as long as the amount rolled over remains in the account for at least five years. [See Notice 2013-74, 2013-52 I.R.B. 819, on the requirements for amending a plan to permit in-plan Roth rollovers.]

The PPA increases the extent to which non-spouse beneficiaries will be able to roll over inherited benefits to an IRA, subject to most of the same rules as other eligible rollover distributions. The plan must permit the non-spouse beneficiary to make a direct rollover (a trustee-to-trustee transfer) of the eligible rollover distribution to an inherited IRA. The plan administrator must provide the non-spouse beneficiary with a written notice explaining the direct rollover rules and mandatory 20% withholding if amounts eligible for rollover are not rolled over.

The non-spouse beneficiary cannot contribute to the inherited IRA, cannot roll other amounts into or out of the inherited IRA, but can perform a trustee-to-trustee transfer to another inherited IRA in the name of the decedent with the same beneficiary. [CCH Pensions & Benefits, *IRS Explains Requirements for Nonspousal Distributions* (Jan. 5, 2010) (benefitslink.com). Notice 2009-68, 2009-39 I.R.B. 423, includes sample notice forms]

For the year 2009 only, the obligation to take the Minimum Required Distribution from IRAs was suspended.

§ 4.08 INCIDENTAL BENEFITS

A qualified plan is permitted to offer incidental benefits such as disability, Social Security supplements for early retirees, lump-sum death benefits, incidental death benefits, or 401(h) retiree health benefits. Life insurance can be provided as an incidental benefit as long as the death benefit does not exceed 100 times the estimated monthly retirement benefit under the qualified plan it supplements. However, offering other benefits, such as other medical benefits or layoff benefits, is forbidden, and can lead to loss of plan qualification.

The Tenth Circuit ruled in 2009 that the anti-cutback rule does not apply to a death benefit, or a plan feature that pays a lump sum at retirement that is the actuarial equivalent of a death benefit, so it could lawfully be terminated. The Tenth Circuit ruled that the death benefit was not an accrued benefit, because the plan's definition of accrued benefit excluded death benefits. It could not be a retirement-type subsidy because that means only benefits that continue after retirement. [*Kerber v. Qwest Pension Plan*, 572 F.3d 1135 (10th Cir. 2009); see Stanley D. Baum, *Tenth Circuit Determines That Elimination of a Pension Plan's Death Benefit Does Not Violate ERISA's Anti-Cutback Rule*, ERISA Lawyer Blog (July 22, 2009) (benefitslink.com). See also *In re Lucent Death Benefits ERISA Litigation*, 541 F.3d 250 (3d Cir. 2008)]

T.D. 9665 sets out the rules, starting in 2015 tax years, for taxability of payments for accident and health insurance to participants of qualified retirement plans. Participants will not be taxed on retiree health benefits or costs of disability insurance coverage. [T.D. 9665, 79 Fed. Reg. 26838 (May 12, 2014). See The Tax Adviser, *Final Rules Govern Tax Treatment of Distributions to Pay Accident or Health Insurance Premiums*, <http://www.aicpa.org/interestareas/tax/newsandpublications/taxnews/pages/20140509.aspx> (May 9, 2014); Jane Meacham, *Premiums Paid by Retirement Plans Become Taxable in 2015*, Smart HR (May 9, 2014) (benefitslink.com)]

§ 4.09 STRUCTURE OF ERISA

ERISA is not an easy statute to understand. A vast variety of plan provisions can legally be embodied in qualified plans, and many of these provisions depend on complex mathematical formulas. Furthermore, ERISA is both a labor law and a comprehensive and difficult piece of tax legislation.

Title I of ERISA, also referred to as the labor title, covers issues such as plan structure, fiduciary conduct, and prohibited transactions. Title II is the tax title, covering the requirements for plan qualification and tax deductions. The Title II provisions are duplicated in the Internal Revenue Code. There is some overlap between the two titles. For instance, prohibited transactions are defined in Title I, but the excise tax penalty is imposed under Title II.

Many of the provisions that are most significant for plan administration are found in Title I, Subtitle B. This subtitle is divided into six parts:

- Part 1: Reporting and disclosure;
- Part 2: Participation and vesting standards;
- Part 3: Funding standards;
- Part 4: Fiduciary responsibility;
- Part 5: Administration and enforcement;
- Part 6: Continuation coverage for health insurance.

Although there are some exceptions, the safest way to operate is just to assume that all benefit plans will be subject to at least some ERISA requirements. For example, a welfare plan (one that provides nonpension benefits such as health insurance or severance pay) is subject to most of the rules on reporting and disclosure, and the fiduciary, administration, and enforcement rules of Parts 4 and 5, but does not have to satisfy the participation, vesting, or funding standards.

§ 4.10 REQUIRED PROVISIONS FOR ALL QUALIFIED PLANS

Although within these confines a tremendous number of variations can be created, ERISA and the I.R.C. impose certain obligations on all qualified pension plans:

- The plan must be in writing [ERISA § 402(a)(1)];
- The employer must intend the plan to be permanent (although mergers and terminations are permitted under appropriate circumstances) [Reg. § 1.401-1(b)(2). Annuity, profit-sharing, and stock bonus plans are also subject to this requirement];
- The plan must provide a procedure for amendments and must indicate who has the authority to amend the plan [ERISA § 402(a)(1)];
- Plan funds must be managed through use of a trust [ERISA § 403(a), I.R.C. § 401(a)], unless they are held in a custodial account that is invested and managed by someone other than the account custodian.

- The plan must be operated for the exclusive benefit of its participants and their beneficiaries. [I.R.C. § 401(a)(2)] If the employer attempts to violate this rule by obtaining reversions of plan assets, an excise tax will be imposed under I.R.C. § 4980 unless an exception to the general rule applies. Even on termination, defined contribution plans generally cannot return any assets to the employer. Independent contractors must not be allowed to participate, because they are not considered employees;
- The plan must have a published funding policy [ERISA § 402(b)(1)];
- Contributions made to the plan, or benefits received under the plan, are subject to the limitations of the I.R.C.;
- Benefits must not be decreased when Social Security benefits increase;
- Employees must be permitted to participate in the plan as soon as they satisfy the plan's minimum participation standards [I.R.C. §§ 401(a)(3), 410];
- The plan must satisfy minimum coverage requirements, and defined benefit plans must satisfy a minimum participation rule;
- Employee contributions and salary deferrals intended for 401(k) plans must be deposited into the plan as soon as possible, always within 90 days [DOL Reg. § 2510.3-102];
- The plan must not discriminate in favor of highly compensated employees (HCEs);
- The plan's vesting schedule must satisfy federal standards—and if the plan is top-heavy (concentrates its benefits on the highest-paid group) it must vest even faster than the basic rule [I.R.C. §§ 401(a)(7), 404(a)(2), 411(b)] EGTRRA, the 2001 tax law, also increased the speed with which employer matching contributions must vest, and the PPA sped up the vesting schedule for employer's non-elective contributions;
- Benefits must be distributed only to participants and their beneficiaries (including "alternate payees" under Qualified Domestic Relations Orders). This is known as the "anti-alienation" rule. In particular, creditors cannot reach pension benefits before they have been distributed;
- Pension benefits must start within 60 days of the end of the plan year in which the individual reaches the plan's normal retirement age (NRA), reaches age 65, terminates service or has 10 years of service—whichever occurs last;
- The plan must furnish Summary Plan Descriptions (SPDs), Summaries of Material Modifications (SMMs) and other disclosure documents [see Chapter 11];

- The plan must designate at least one fiduciary who is responsible for management. Named fiduciaries are allowed to delegate certain plan responsibilities to other people, such as investment managers—but only if the plan specifically permits such delegation;
- The plan must have a procedure for making claims and appealing denials of applications. The claims procedure must be disclosed in the Summary Plan Description [See §§ 10.05, 11.02] but need not be included in the plan document itself;
- Defined benefit plans must pay premiums to the Pension Benefits Guaranty Corporation (PBGC);
- Transfers of assets between plans, and mergers and terminations of plans, are also regulated. [See I.R.C. § 411(d)(3)]

In response to the low level of savings by plan participants, many industry figures recommended that pension plans be permitted to enroll employees automatically in 401(k) plans, so that employees who did not wish to have amounts deducted from their salaries to save for retirement would have to opt out, rather than employees needing to make an affirmative commitment to open 401(k) plan accounts. Automatic enrollment began in the 1990s, and was popularized by the PPA. In September 2006, the Department of Labor released a Proposed Rule implementing relief under the PPA for fiduciaries who invest participants' assets in "qualified default investment alternatives (QDIAs)." The proposal was made to make it easier to design and administer automatic-enrollment plans. [News Release No. 06-1676-NAT U.S., <http://www.dol.gov/ebsaSearch> (Sept. 26, 2006)]

Final rules were issued in 2009 covering Qualified Automatic Contribution Arrangements (QACAs; for single-employer plans) and Eligible Automatic Contribution Arrangements (EACAs; the counterpart for multi-employer plans). The final rules allow employers to increase the percentage rate for automatic contributions during the plan year, not just at the beginning of the plan year, to reflect salary increases or performance evaluations—as long as the increase applies uniformly to all employees.

In a QACA, the employer's safe harbor contribution must be 100% vested after two years of service. Either the contribution must be 3% of pay for all eligible employees (whether or not they contribute), or the employer must match 100% of the first 1% deferred plus 50% of the next 5% deferred, up to a maximum of 3.5% of compensation. Employees must receive notice of automatic enrollment in a plan not less than 30 and not more than 90 days before they become eligible, and before the beginning of each plan year. However, if it is not practicable to give notice on that schedule (e.g., participants are eligible under the plan as soon as they are hired) then the employer can simply give notice as soon as it is practicable. Safe-harbor non-elective and matching contributions under a QACA are not eligible for hardship withdrawals. The QACA rules apply to plan years that begin on or after January 1, 2008; the EACA rules apply to plan years beginning on or after January 1, 2010. [T.D. 9447, 2009-12 I.R.B. 694]

Contributions to a QACA or EACA are invested in the QDIA (Qualified Default Investment Alternative), selected not just to preserve the safety of the invested capital, but to provide appreciation for participants' long-term retirement needs. Employees must be given notice about the QDIA, and how they can change the investment of their funds.

After earlier proposals about investment advice to plan participants were withdrawn, DOL returned to the subject in 2010, proposing a revised rule limited to implementation of the PPA statutory exemption for certain limited forms of investment advice. Under the 2010 revision, advice can be given two ways: through the use of an unbiased computer model, or when the adviser's fees do not vary no matter what investments the participants choose. The computer model or level fee arrangement has to be chosen by the fiduciary, independent of adviser and its affiliates; qualifications set for the investment expert who certifies the model; investment advisers can't get compensation from affiliates on the basis of their recommendations; and advice arrangements have to be audited each year. Additional requirements, including fee disclosure, are imposed. [Proposed rule, 75 Fed. Reg. 9360 (Mar. 2, 2010); see Rebecca Moore, *DOL Proposes New Advice Rule*, plansponsor.com (Feb. 26, 2010); Davis & Harman, LLP, *Summary of Investment Advice Regulations* (Mar. 1, 2010) (benefitslink.com); for history of the rule, see Fred Schneyer, *EBSA Delays Advice Rule Again*, pla nsponsor.com (Nov. 16, 2009) and *EBSA Pulls Back Controversial Advice Mandate*, plansponsor.com (Nov. 19, 2009)]

As the value of pension accounts declined, there was increasing attention to the subject of fees. In good times, high fees often are not noticed—or are accepted as a fair exchange for the excellent investment results obtained. But fees are more noticeable when account balances drop—and it is harder to argue that the mutual fund or other investment vehicle was successful enough to be entitled to high fees.

In 2010, the Supreme Court held that, in a case charging that excessive fees were imposed, the correct legal standard is whether the fees were so excessive that they must have reflected manipulation—they could not have been the result of arm's length bargaining. [*Jones v. Harris*, 559 U.S. 335 (2010); see Fred Schneyer, *High Court Sides with Investors in Fee Case*, plansponsor.com] However, the Supreme Court refused to hear the appeal of dismissal of another Seventh Circuit case about excessive 401(k) fees. [*Hecker v. Deere & Co.*, 556 F.3d 575 (7th Cir. 2009); see Fred Schneyer, *U.S. Supremes Turn Away Hecker Fee Case Appeal*, plansponsor.com (Jan. 19, 2010)]

The Supreme Court vacated an Eighth Circuit decision about whether mutual fund fees violated Section 36(b) of the Investment Company Act. The Eighth Circuit had relied on the marketplace to prevent excessively high fees from being imposed. However, the Supreme Court remanded the case to comply with *Jones v. Harris*: *Ameriprise Fin. Inc. v. Gallus*, 130 S. Ct. 2340 (2010); see

Rebecca Moore, *Supreme Court Sends Investment Adviser Fee Case Back to 8th Circuit*, plansponsor.com (Apr. 6, 2010). On remand, the Eighth Circuit held that the plaintiffs did not show that the fees were so unreasonably high that they could not have been the product of arm's length bargaining. [*Gallus v. Ameriprise,* 675 F.3d 1173 (8th Cir. 2012); see Rebecca Moore, *Ameriprise Wins Excessive Fees Case*, plansponsor.com (Apr. 12, 2012)]

In mid-2008, the DOL proposed regulations requiring the fiduciaries of individual account plans to provide specific disclosures about the plan's investment options—and the fees for these plans: see 73 Fed. Reg. 43014 (July 23, 2008). It was the third set of regulations about defined contribution plan fees—the previous ones were published at 72 Fed. Reg. 64710 and 64731 (Nov. 16, 2007), dealing with Form 5500 reporting requirements, and 72 Fed. Reg. 70988 (Dec. 13, 2007), requiring fiduciaries to obtain specific information about fees, compensation, and conflicts of interest from their service providers.

In July, 2010, DOL issued an interim final rule on fee disclosure for pension plans, concentrating on the substance of disclosures that must be made and not on their form. "Covered service providers" must provide disclosures—a category that includes not just fiduciaries, brokers, and investment advisers, but also those who receive indirect compensation from a plan—including disclosure of compensation received from third parties. [EBSA Interim Final Rule RIN 1210-AB08, <http://www.ofr.gov/OFRUpload/OFRData/2010-16768-Pl.pdf>; Regulations were published governing disclosure of fees to plan participants: see 75 Fed. Reg. 64910 (Oct. 20, 2010). Originally, these regulations were scheduled to take effect July 16, 2011, but to give employers more time to update their systems, and to conform to regulations about cost disclosure to the plan itself, their effective date was delayed until April 1, 2012: see 76 Fed. Reg. 42539 (July 19, 2011).]

Another question is the extent to which an account is invested in the employer's securities—a matter that often becomes controversial if the stock price falls, and the value of the account falls with it. T.D. 9484 [2010-24 I.R.B. 748, 75 Fed. Reg. 27927 (May 19, 2010)], effective for plan years beginning on or after January 1, 2011, provides Final Regulations under Code § 401(a)(35), a diversification requirement enacted by PPA § 901. Defined contribution plans subject to these requirements must give each participant who has at least three years of service (and beneficiaries of such participants and of deceased participants) the right to divest employer securities in their accounts and re-invest these amounts. The plan must offer at least three diversified investment options other than employer stock. Divestment/reinvestment must be allowed at reasonable intervals, at least quarterly. "Stock drop" suits are discussed in more detail in, e.g., § 15.03[C] and 15.09[A].

§ 4.11 NORMAL RETIREMENT AGE

Many ERISA and tax rules depend on the concept of drawing a pension at, before, or after the plan's Normal Retirement Age (NRA). The standard NRA remains 65, although perhaps this will change not only as life expectancies increase, but as the Social Security system phases in a higher age for receiving unreduced benefits. (The basic Social Security retirement age is gradually being increased from 65 to 67.)

However, a plan can set the NRA either higher or lower than 65. The plan can choose an NRA lower than 65 if this is customary for the company or for its industry—as long as this choice is not a device to accelerate funding. If the NRA is very low—below 55—I.R.C. § 415(b) requires that maximum pension payable under the plan be reduced, in light of the large number of payments that will be made. However, a profit-sharing plan is allowed to have an NRA lower than 55, even if this is below the industry average.

■ **TIP:** If the plan does not specify an NRA, the NRA will be deemed to be the age at which accrued benefits no longer increase solely on account of age or service.

If the plan sets the NRA above 65, or if there is no definition in the plan, then each participant will have an individual NRA. It will be either his or her 65th birthday or the fifth anniversary of plan participation, whichever comes later.

See T.D. 9325, 2007-24 I.R.B. 386, for Final Regulations giving rules for determining whether a plan's NRA is valid if the plan makes in-service distributions under a phased retirement program. In general, the NRA must be set at least as high as the industry standard, although there is a safe harbor if the NRA is at least 62, or is between 55 and 62 and the employer makes a good-faith determination that the NRA is appropriate for the industry.

The Supreme Court declined to review the Seventh Circuit's *Fry v. Exelon* decision from 2009. The Seventh Circuit ruled that a plan sponsor could define NRA other than as a specific age. In that case, Fry took a lump sum in 2003 from a cash balance plan, and later challenged the plan's definition of NRA, saying that it violated ERISA because it was used to avoid the whipsaw calculation. (This was pre-PPA, so there had not yet been a definitive statement that whipsaw is not required.) [*Fry v. Exelon*, 571 F.3d 644 (7th Cir. 2009), *cert. denied*, 130 S. Ct. 1504 (Feb. 22, 2010); see Rebecca Moore, *Supreme Court Lets Stand Alternate Definitions for Retirement Age*, plansponsor.com (Feb. 23, 2010)]

However, in 2013, the District Court for the Southern District of New York held that PriceWaterhouseCooper's cash balance plan did not define NRA appropriately. The plan defined NRA as five "years of service." The district court said that this was not an age. Unlike *Fry,* this case did not use a definition based on the employee's anniversary; the court held that ERISA allows a definition based on the employee's anniversary, but that is not identical to a year of service. [*Laurent v. PriceWaterhouseCooper*, No. 06 Civ. 2280 (JPO) (S.D.N.Y. Aug. 8, 2013)]

In mid-2012, the Fourth Circuit held that increases in benefit accruals to participants who have reached NRA do not violate ERISA's prohibition against backloading in later years of service. (The plan defined NRA as the earlier of age 64 or 60 months of vesting service.) The 133 1/3% test forbids accrual of benefits more than one-third greater than the annual rate of accrual in the previous year. This rule was adopted to prevent employers from skimping on accrual rates in the early years of service, when turnover is highest. The Fourth Circuit held that anti-backloading rules no longer apply after the participant reaches NRA. [*McCorkle v. Bank of Am. Corp.*, 688 F.3d 164 (4th Cir. 2012)]

§ 4.12 NORMAL RETIREMENT BENEFIT

The NRB, or Normal Retirement Benefit, is a related concept. It is either the benefit commencing at the NRA or the early retirement benefit (if the plan provides one)—whichever is greater. The early retirement benefit is not adjusted actuarially for this purpose, even though it will be paid for more years than if benefits had commenced at the NRA. Early retirement subsidies are not counted if they continue only until the retiree becomes eligible for Social Security, and if they do not exceed the Social Security benefit.

Not everyone retires on the anniversary of plan participation. If benefits depend on average compensation for, e.g., three or five years, then Treas. Reg. § 1.411(a)-7(c)(5) mandates treatment of the last partial year of service as a full year.

Although there is growing interest in "phased retirement" (a diminishing work schedule creating a transition between full-time employment and full retirement), tax law still has little flexibility in this area. In mid-2004, the Supreme Court ruled that the "anti-cutback" rule of ERISA § 204(g) prohibits a plan from being amended in a way that suspends payments of early retirement benefits the individual has already accrued. In this case, the suit was brought by workers who took early retirement at a time that their pension plan called for suspension of pension payments if they took another job as construction workers. Instead, they worked as construction supervisors. Later, the plan was amended to suspend the benefit payments to anyone who worked in the construction industry at all. The Supreme Court found the amendment improper because workers are entitled to rely on the terms of their pension plan in making career-planning decisions. [*Central Laborers' Pension Fund v. Heinz*, 541 U.S. 739 (2004)]

§ 4.13 PARTICIPATION AND COVERAGE

Both defined benefit and defined contribution plans are subject to "minimum coverage" rules under I.R.C. § 410(b). Remember, one of the main motives in passing ERISA was to prevent plans from concentrating unduly on providing benefits to stockholders and managers. However, it can be difficult to satisfy the various tests in a small company (See § 4.14[A] for top-heavy plan rules) or in a company where there is a great disparity between managers' pay and rank-and-file pay, or where there is a stable group of HCEs but heavy turnover in rank-and-file employees.

To satisfy the minimum coverage rules, the plan must either cover a percentage of the rank and file that is at least 70% of the percentage of highly compensated employees covered by the plan; or the plan must cover a reasonable classification of employees that is not discriminatory. Furthermore, the contributions made on behalf of, or the benefits provided to, the rank-and-file must equal at least 70% of those made or provided to the highly compensated.

Defined benefit plans are subject to a minimum participation rule. On each day of the plan year, the plan must benefit either 40% of all the company's work force, or 50 people, whichever is less. However, plans that are not top-heavy and do not benefit any highly compensated employee or former employee are exempt from the minimum participation rule.

The I.R.C. does not require qualified plans to cover all employees from the time of hiring. It is permissible for a plan to require employees to be at least 21 years old and to have completed one year of service before being eligible for participation. Part-time employees must be covered if they can work 1,000 hours within a 12-month period. If plan benefits become 100% vested after only two years, a qualified plan (other than a 401(k) plan) can require two years of service for participation.

§ 4.14 VESTING

[A] Generally

Participation in a plan is only the first step toward eventually receiving a pension. Vesting is the process of the benefits becoming nonforfeitable. ERISA includes detailed vesting rules to prevent earlier abuses, under which plans were often drafted so that so many years of service were required to achieve a pension that many rank-and-file employees would end up forfeiting their pensions (with the forfeitures going to swell the accounts of highly compensated executives and stockholders).

The normal benefit must always be nonforfeitable at the normal retirement age. It is not required that employees immediately gain 100% ownership of their defined contribution accounts, or the amounts contributed on their behalf to a defined benefit plan. Vesting is the process of moving toward 100% ownership. The Code prescribes minimum funding schedules; employers are always permitted to give employees faster vesting. "Cliff vesting" means that, for a period of time, the employee is not vested at all—but at a certain point, the entire account becomes vesting at once. "Graded vesting" means that part of the account vests each year, until 100% vesting is attained.

There are only two basic vesting schedules allowed by I.R.C. § 411(a):

- Five-year cliff vesting: participants are not vested at all for the first five years of service, but then they are immediately 100% vested as to employer contributions;
- Three-to-seven graded vesting: no vesting at all for three years, but full vesting by seven years of service, increasing proportionately in years 4, 5, and 6.

Top-heavy plans must provide even faster vesting—three-year cliff or six-year graded—but plans with a lot of participants usually are not top-heavy.

The PPA required cash balance plans to provide 100% vesting after three years of service—but WRERA suspended this requirement.

For an example of how vesting works, if a participant leaves employment at a time when he or she is 60% vested, then a participant in a defined contribution plan will be entitled to $60 of every $100 in his or her individual account. A participant in a defined benefit plan will be entitled to an annuity of $60/month for every $100/month that would have been payable if he or she had remained at work until becoming 100% vested.

EGTRRA, the 2001 tax legislation, provides even faster vesting for employer matching contributions (as distinct from the employer's own contributions). Vesting for matching contributions must be either three-year cliff vesting or graded vesting over two to six years (20% in the second year of service, 40% in the third year, etc.). Under the PPA, employer non-elective contributions made for years beginning after December 31, 2006 must satisfy either three-year cliff or two-to-six-year graded vesting.

[B] Vesting on Termination

All qualified plans must provide that, if the plan is completely or partially terminated, all affected participants immediately become 100% vested. [I.R.C. § 411(d)(3)] For plans that are not subject to the minimum funding standard of I.R.C. § 412 (for instance, profit-sharing and stock bonus plans), 100% vesting must also occur when the employer completely ceases to make contributions to the plan. A profit-sharing or stock bonus plan is deemed terminated on the day when the plan administrator notifies the IRS of the cessation of contributions.

[C] Vesting and Service

For vesting purposes, a year of service is a period of 12 consecutive months during which the employee performs at least 1,000 hours of service. Plans are not required to provide fractional years of service credit—i.e., if someone works only 500 hours, the employer does not have to credit half a year of service.

For the purposes of vesting or participation for accrual purposes, a year of service can be any period of 12 consecutive months that the employer designates. But a year of service for plan eligibility purposes must start on the first day of employment. A plan can have more than one vesting year. If the plan selects a single vesting year for convenience, it doesn't have to be the same as the plan year.

§ 4.15 BREAK-IN-SERVICE RULES

For some pension-related purposes, it makes a big difference whether the individual has been continuously employed by the employer sponsoring the plan, or whether employment has been interrupted: whether the person has been laid off and then recalled, for instance. Interruption of continuous employment is called a "break in service"—a concept that has many implications.

A one-year break in service has occurred when a person renders 501 or fewer hours of service for the employer in a particular year. If someone works more than 501 but less than 1000 hours for the employer in a given year the employer does not have to credit a year of service, but cannot penalize the employee for the break in service.

After someone has had a one-year break, the employer can disregard service before the break for vesting purposes until the employee has come back to work and completed a year of service. After there have been five consecutive one-year breaks in service, a defined contribution plan, or some insured defined benefit plans, can treat the vested benefits as forfeited, and allocate them to other participants.

If the participant was 0% vested before the break in service, the "Rule of Parity" requires the plan to add up the number of years of service before the break. If the number of consecutive one-year breaks is at least five, or is greater than or equal to the aggregate number of pre-break years of service (whichever is greater), the rule allows the pre-break years to be disregarded for vesting purposes, even if the participant is later rehired.

However, under the Retirement Equity Act of 1984 [Pub. L. No. 98-397], a break in service that is caused by parenting leave probably cannot be counted against the employee. A reservist who is called to active military duty does not have a break in service during the active-duty period. [See § 1.18, *supra*, for more about the employment law implications of call-ups of reservists and members of the National Guard]

In its May 18, 2009 decision, *AT&T Corp. v. Hulteen*, 556 U.S. 701, the Supreme Court ruled that AT&T did not commit sex discrimination when it failed to amend its pre-PDA seniority system to equalize the treatment of pregnancy leave taken before the effective date of the PDA with other leave. AT&T was operating a bona fide seniority system and was entitled to avoid liability.

§ 4.16 PLAN LIMITS

One of the basic purposes of ERISA is to prevent plans from unduly favoring executives, managers, and other highly paid employees. One of the ways ERISA furthers this objective is by placing limits on the amount that can be contributed each year to a defined contribution plan, deferred in a 401(k) plan, or provided as a benefit under a defined benefit plan.

The underlying principle is that plan limits are adjusted annually. The adjustment reflects changes in the Consumer Price Index. Starting in 2003, the changes are to be rounded down in $5,000 increments; previously, changes were adjusted in $10,000 increments.

Before 2000, I.R.C. § 415(e) imposed a combined limitation on the allocations to defined contribution plans plus accrued benefits from defined benefit plans. However, as of 2000, plans are permitted to—but not obligated to—impose a combined limitation with respect to employees who participate in both types of plans. Defined benefit plans are allowed to increase benefits (for retirees as well as active employees) to reflect repeal of the combined limitation. See Notice 2007-28, 2007-14 I.R.B. 880, for post-PPA application of the combined limit, and its effect on the employer's maximum deduction.

The breakdown below contains the limitations applicable to various amounts applicable to pension administration for the years 2001–2014. As noted above, figures remained the same in 2009, 2010, and 2011, but were increased in 2012, 2013, and 2014.

1. Maximum annual benefit under a defined benefit plan (§ 415(b)(1)(A)): $140,000/$160,000/$160,000/$165,000/$170,000/$175,000/$180,000/$185,000/$195,000/$195,000/$200,000/$205,000/$210,000; the maximum amount is reduced for benefits that begin before age 62, but increased for benefits beginning after age 65.

2. Maximum contribution to a defined contribution plan (§ 415(c)(1)(a)): $35,000 and 25% of compensation/$40,000 and 100% of compensation/$40,000 and 100% of compensation/$41,000 and 100% of compensation/$42,000 and 100% of compensation/$44,000 and 100% of compensation/$45,000 and 100% of compensation/$46,000 and 100% of compensation/$49,000 and 100% of compensation/$49,000 and 100% of compensation/$50,000/$51,000 and 100% of compensation/$52,000 and 100% of compensation.

3. Definition of a "highly compensated employee" under § 414(q)(1)(B): $85,000 a year/$90,000 a year/$90,000 a year/$90,000 a year/$95,000/$100,000/$100,000/$105,000/$110,000/$110,000/$115,000/$115,000/$115,000.

4. Limit on annual compensation that can be taken into account in making calculations, as prescribed by §§ 401(a)(17), 404(l): $170,000/

$200,000/$200,000/$205,000/$210,000/$220,000/$225,000/$230,000/ $245,000/$245,000/$ $255,000/$260,000.

5. Maximum 401(k) deferral: $10,500/$11,000 plus catch-up contributions for persons over 50/$12,000 plus catch-up contributions/$13,000 plus catch-up contributions/$14,000 plus catch-up contributions/$15,000 plus catch-up contributions/$15,500 plus catch-up contributions/ $15,500 plus catch-up contributions/$16,500 plus catch-up contributions/$16,500 plus catch-up contributions/$17,000 plus catch-up contributions $17,500 plus catch-up contributions/$17,500 plus catch-up contributions; For 2009–2011, the catch-up contribution is $2,500 for purposes of Code §§ 401(k)(11) and 408(p), and $5,500 for other purposes. These amounts did not change in 2012, 2013, or 2014.

§ 4.17 EMPLOYEE CONTRIBUTIONS

Although 401(k) plans get their basic funding from employees' deferred salary (and may get matching contributions from the employer), pension plans work the other way around. They get their basic funding from the employer, but some plans require and other plans permit employees to make additional contributions to the plan. Internal Revenue Code § 411(c)(2) characterizes employee contributions as mandatory if making the contribution is a precondition of the employer match.

■ **TIP:** The Bankruptcy Abuse Prevention and Consumer Protection Act of 2005 (BAPCPA; Pub. L. No. 109-8) gives employees additional protection against their contributions being seized by their employer's creditors, when the employee has made the contribution but the employer has not yet deposited it into the plan.

Employee contributions are also important in determining whether or not a plan discriminates in favor of highly compensated employees. I.R.C. § 414(g) contains the formula for testing whether the employer's aggregate contributions to the plan on behalf of HCEs are too high. If the plan fails to satisfy the requirements of this section, it will be disqualified, unless the excess contributions made on behalf of the HCEs, plus the earnings on the excess contributions, are returned to the company's employees by the end of the plan year after the year of the excess contribution. A 10% excise also applies to excess employee contributions (e.g., made by HCEs) that are not distributed within two and a half months of the end of the plan year.

Benefits attributable to employer contributions cannot be assigned or anticipated before they are received, except in the form of a QDRO. But employees can withdraw some or all of their voluntary contributions while continuing to be employed and to participate in the plan. Employees must always have the right to withdraw their own voluntary contributions to the plan at any time, without the accrued benefits attributable to employer contributions becoming forfeitable. [I.R.C. § 401(a)(19)] However, if the plan mandates employee contributions, I.R.C. § 411(a)(3)(D) allows the plan to provide that employer contributions will be forfeited if a participant withdraws any mandatory employee contributions at a time when he or she is less than 50% vested. If the benefits are repaid within five years after the withdrawal, or two years after the employee returns to participation under the plan (whichever comes first), the benefits must be restored.

Employees are always 100% vested in their own voluntary contributions to a pension plan. When an employer matches these voluntary contributions, EGTRRA requires vesting in the employer's matching contributions to occur either on a three-year cliff schedule, or a six-year graded schedule, beginning with 20% vesting in the second year of the employee's service.

A 2010 DOL Final Rule allows a safe harbor when a "small plan" (fewer than 100 participants) performs wage withholding or receives contributions from participants and the contribution is deposited within seven business days after the employer received or withheld the money—even if it would have been possible to deposit it sooner. However, if contributions or loan repayments are not deposited in a timely fashion, then losses and interest on late contributions are calculated from the actual date on which they could have been deposited, not from the end of the safe harbor period. [Transamerica Center for Retirement Studies 2010-01, *Department of Labor Final Rule on Definition of Plan Assets: Participant Contributions* (Jan. 22, 2010) (benefitslink.com)]

§ 4.18 PLAN LOANS

Under the right circumstances, plans are permitted to make loans to participants. These loans can be a useful resource if, for instance, a plan participant wishes to buy a house or pay a child's tuition. Loans to rank-and-file participants are usually permitted. However, a direct or indirect loan to a "party in interest" or a "disqualified person" is a prohibited transaction, unless a prohibited transaction exemption is available to justify the loan.

EBRI and the Investment Company Institute (ICI) reported that, in 2012, most 401(k) participants had the right to take loans, but few of them did so. In that year, 87% of participants could get loans, but only 21% of those with access to loans had one outstanding at end of year. The average unpaid loan balance was $7,153, about 13% of the average balance. [EBRI Fast Facts No. 264, *Many Have Access to 401(k) Loans, Few Have Outstanding Balances* (Jan. 16, 2014) (benefitslink.com)]

Under I.R.C. § 72(p), the general rule is that plan loans are treated as distributions—in other words, taxable income to the recipient. But there are certain exceptions. A loan will not be treated as a distribution if it does not exceed $50,000 or half the present value of the employee's nonforfeitable accrued benefit under the plan (whichever is less). (The employee can borrow up to $10,000, even if this amount is more than half the value of the accrued benefit.) Where the participant's account balance is the only security, the loan is theoretically not permitted to exceed half the pledged amount. The DOL Regulations dealing with plan loans do not forbid participants from borrowing funds from their accounts, pledging 50% of the account, and then taking hardship withdrawals, even though these steps have the effect of reducing the security below 50% of the account. [See Reg. § 2550.408-1(f)(2)]

The agreement to take a loan from the plan must call for repayment within five years, in payments made at least quarterly, with level amortization. Plans are permitted to impose variable interest rates on plan loans.

> ■ **TIP:** BAPCA (Pub. L. No. 109-8), the 2005 bankruptcy reform statute, makes it clear that when an employee files for bankruptcy protection (even a Chapter 13 wage-earner plan), it is not a violation of the automatic stay for the employer to withhold from the employee's wages in order to repay a plan loan from a qualified plan. Plan loans do not qualify for the automatic discharge provision of Bankruptcy Code § 523, and bankruptcy plans are not permitted to materially alter the terms of a plan loan. However, amounts that an employee uses to repay plan loans are not considered "disposable income" and therefore cannot be reached by the employee's other creditors.

For reservists and National Guard members on active duty, federal law limits interest rates on all loans to the service member (including plan loans) to 6%. However, plan fiduciaries have the right to petition the relevant court to permit a higher interest rate. Under USERRA (See § 1.18, *supra*), a pension plan is allowed—but not obligated—to suspend the obligation to make regular repayments of plan loans during active military service.

Publicly traded companies must also be aware of the Sarbanes-Oxley Act [Pub. L. No. 107-204] ban on loans made by such companies to their directors and executive officers; this prohibition took effect on July 30, 2002, although loan arrangements already in effect on that date are exempt as long as their terms are not materially modified after July 30, 2002.

Plan loans made to parties in interest are likely also to constitute prohibited transactions for ERISA fiduciary purpose, subject to a 15% excise tax.

Early in 2009, amendments to Regulation Z were published, exempting most retirement plan loans from the Truth in Lending Act (TILA). To qualify for the exemption, which takes effect July 1, 2010, the loan must be made to a plan participant, from fully vested funds in the participant's account, and the loan must comply with Internal Revenue Code requirements, including Code § 72. [Federal Reserve Reg. § 226.3(g), Document E8-31185, 74 Fed. Reg. 5244 (Jan. 29, 2009)]

Under Federal Reserve Board regulations revised July 1, 2010, loans to plan participants made from fully vested funds in the participant's account in a qualified plan are exempt from TILA, but loans to beneficiaries and QDRO alternate payees require disclosures. The TILA exemption is also unavailable for loans that violate Code § 72(p)—e.g., those that have a term greater than five years, exceed the maximum loan amount, or are not repaid in equal installments. If the plan is subject to the ERISA disclosure requirements, the SPD must disclose the fees or charges that can be imposed on plan loans. [Deloitte's Washington Bulletin, *Most Plan Loans Now Exempt from Truth-in-Lending Act Disclosures* (Aug. 9, 2010) (benefitslink.com)]

The IRS announced relaxation of the verification requirements for plan loans (and hardship distributions) taken in connection with Superstorm Sandy. A plan will not be deemed to violate the Code merely because it made a loan or hardship distribution between October 26, 2012 and February 1, 2013, based on needs caused by Sandy to an employee whose workplace, principal residence, or principal residence of a close family member was in the identified disaster area and whose financial records were destroyed. The usual calculation of maximum permitted hardship distribution will apply. [Announcement 2012-44, 2012-49 I.R.B. 663. This relief is in addition to relief under Code § 7508A provided by IR-2012-83.]

§ 4.19 EMPLOYER'S DEDUCTION

An employer that maintains a qualified defined benefit plan is entitled to deduct the greatest of these three amounts:

- The minimum funding standard as provided by I.R.C. § 412;
- The amount necessary to fund the cost of covering all the employees for their projected future service;
- The amount necessary to fund present and future costs, which may include liabilities stemming from service performed before the plan was established.

In 2007, the IRS published Q&A on the PPA's rules for the employer's deduction for contributions to the retirement plan (Code § 404). If the plan year is not the same as the employer's tax year, the employer can choose to use the deduction limit for the plan year that begins in the tax year; the plan year that ends in the tax year; or a weighted average of the two. For calculating the combined limit when an employer sponsors both defined benefit and defined contribution plans, and the employer's contributions to the defined contribution plan exceed 6% of compensation, the employer contribution to the defined compensation plan minus 6% of compensation is applied to the combined limit. [Notice 2007-28, 2007-14 I.R.B. 880]

§ 4.20 REVERSIONS

If there were no statutory ban, unscrupulous employers might raid pension assets when they needed cash, or might terminate plans merely to recoup assets or excess assets. To prevent this, defined contribution plans (including profit-sharing and stock bonus plans) usually cannot return any assets to the employer under any circumstances. Even forfeitures (amounts contributed on behalf of employees whose employment terminates before they become vested) are to be allocated to other participants in the plan.

Under appropriate circumstances, employers can receive reversions from a defined benefit plan after satisfaction of all obligations under the plan to employees. Nor may the employer lawfully transfer assets from an overfunded plan to an underfunded plan.

Internal Revenue Code § 4980 imposes an excise tax on the amount of assets reverting to an employer from a qualified plan. The tax rate, for reversions occurring after September 30, 1990, is at least 20%. The rate rises to 50% unless the employer either transfers 25% of the assets in question to a qualified replacement plan, or increases the benefits under the terminating plan to the extent of 20% of the previous benefits to participants. A qualified replacement plan covers at least 95% of the active employees from the terminated plan who continue to be employed.

§ 4.21 FORFEITURES

Depending on the plan, at least some employees—and perhaps the vast majority of the rank-and-file workforce—will terminate employment before they become vested. The contributions made on account of such employees are known as forfeitures.

Under I.R.C. §§ 401(a)(8) and 404(a)(2), defined benefit plans are required to provide that forfeitures will not be applied to increase the benefits any employee would otherwise receive. Instead, favorable plan experience when it comes to forfeitures (or mortality or employee turnover) reduces the amount the employer has to contribute to the plan. In contrast, defined contribution plans are allowed to—and usually do—allocate forfeitures to the accounts of other participants.

If someone leaves employment, and is later rehired by the same company, the eventual retirement benefit must be adjusted actuarially to reflect both periods of employment (unless the break-in-service rules make this unnecessary). Another option is for the plan to give timely notice of its provisions for suspension of benefits, so there is no forfeiture. [Treas. Reg. § 2520.203-3(b)(4)]

When an employee dies, the plan can impose forfeiture of his or her unvested benefits, except if a Qualified Preretirement Survivor Annuity (QPSA) is required. [See § 12.06] Mishandling of forfeitures is a common target of IRS audits. The IRS requires forfeitures to be used or allocated for the plan year in which they arise—or, in appropriate circumstances, in the following plan year. Forfeitures can be used to pay reasonable administrative expenses of the plan; to reduce the employer's contribution; to restore previously forfeited participant accounts; or to provide additional contributions to participants. Placing the forfeited amounts into a suspense account is not permitted. For two years after the error, mistakes in handling forfeitures can be corrected with the IRS' Employee Plans Compliance Resolution System (EPCRS), a program that allows plans to return to compliance on easy terms. After the two-year period, voluntary correction program (VCP) must be used unless the failure is considered insignificant. VCP must be used if the terms of the plan are incorrect and a retroactive plan amendment is required to correct them. [Chadron J. Patton, *Common Plan Mistakes: Failure to Timely Allocate Forfeitures*, Spencer Fane (Nov. 16, 2012) (benefitslink.com)]

§ 4.22 DISCRIMINATION TESTING

One of the most basic plan concepts is that a plan must be operated for the exclusive benefit of its participants and beneficiaries. Furthermore, one of the main reasons for the creation of ERISA, and its elaborate structure of rules, is to prevent plans from being administered so that company owners, or major executives, get generous benefits while rank-and-file workers get little or nothing. A qualified plan must be "tested" for "discrimination." In this context, discrimination does not mean discrimination on the basis of sex, race, nationality, and so forth; it means allowing a disproportionate share of plan benefits to go to Highly Compensated Employees (HCEs).

A pension, annuity, profit-sharing, or stock bonus plan can lawfully favor HCEs in terms of contributions or benefits, but not both. [See I.R.C. §§ 401(a)(4), 404(a)(2)] Internal Revenue Code § 414(q) says that, for plan years after 1996, an HCE is defined as someone who owned 5% or more of the employer company's stock in either the current or the preceding year—or someone whose compensation for the preceding year was at least $80,000, as adjusted for inflation. For 2013–2014, the adjusted figure is $ $115,000. The employer has the right to choose to use an alternative definition, under which HCEs are those who not only earn more than the adjusted amount, but are also in the top 20% of earners in the company.

The Code used to contain rules called "family aggregation rules" (nicknamed "aggravation rules" because of their complexity) under which the compensation of several members of the family owning a family business had to be combined for purposes including discrimination testing. However, effective for plan years beginning on and after January 1, 1997, the family aggregation rules were abolished by the Small Business Job Protection Act (SBJPA) of 1996. [Pub. L. No. 104-188]

It does not violate the antidiscrimination rules for a plan to be "integrated" with Social Security within limits set by the "permitted disparity" rules of Code § 401(l). In effect, the employer can treat the employee's Social Security benefit (which was partially funded by the employer's FICA contributions) as part of the pension, or the employer can treat its FICA contributions as pension contributions.

The subject of discrimination testing is too complex to be fully laid out in this book. However, it should be noted that the Code includes "safe harbor" provisions for discrimination testing. Plans are not obligated to follow the safe harbor rules; they can set their own formulas. But if they do follow the safe harbor rules, they are sure not to be challenged by the IRS on this issue.

In a "soft freeze," a defined benefit plan is closed to new hires, but accruals continue for workers hired before the freeze. Often, the employer adopts a new defined contribution plan for new hires, or enhances benefits under an existing defined contribution plan. Notice 2014-5, 2014-2 I.R.B. 276 provides temporary relief for satisfying the § 401(a)(4) nondiscrimination requirements by defined benefit plans that have been closed to new hires. On its own, the frozen defined benefit plan might not pass § 410(b) coverage testing, because there is more turnover among non-HCE participants than HCEs. The frozen defined benefit plan will therefore have to be aggregated with the defined contribution plan for coverage testing; if the plans are aggregated for coverage testing, they must also be aggregated for nondiscrimination testing, which many defined contribution plans will fail because HCEs have a higher normal allocation rate. Notice 2014-5 provides temporary relief for plan years beginning before January 1, 2016 for defined benefit plans that were amended to exclude new hires before December 13, 2013. The defined benefit plan must be part of an aggregated plan that either is primarily defined benefit in character, or the defined benefit plan passed nondiscrimination testing on its own, without aggregation, for the plan year beginning in 2013. [Paul Hamburger and Lisa A. Berkowtz Herrnson, *IRS Issues Temporary Non-Discrimination Testing Relief for Closed Defined Benefit Plans and Request for Comments*, Proskauer's ERISA Practice Center Blog (Dec. 20, 2013) (benefitslink.com)]

§ 4.23 LEASED EMPLOYEES

Leased employees (hired by a company from an agency that supplies workers) play a significant role in the economy. However, it is often the case that the treatment of a particular individual varies depending on the context. It is simplistic to say that a person is just an employee or a non-employee. Internal Revenue Code § 414(n) requires some people to be treated as employees eligible for plan participation even though they are formally employed by a leasing company rather than by the company for whom they perform services each day.

Section 414(n) refers to "leased employees," who are nominally employed by a "leasing organization" (e.g., an organization that furnishes temporary and contingent workers) but who "perform services" for a "service recipient." Instead of paying the leased employees directly, the service recipient pays the employees' wages (and an agency commission) to the leasing organization, which handles payroll functions including tax withholding.

However, the leased employees will be treated as employees of the service recipient when it comes to determining whether the service recipient's pension plans discriminate in favor of highly compensated employees. If the leasing organization maintains a pension plan for the employees it leases out, its contributions or benefits are treated as if they came from the service recipient for the service recipient's discrimination tests. The leasing organization's plan must count all service by leased employees for the leasing organization (even when they're leased out to a service recipient) with respect to coverage, vesting, contributions, and benefits under its own plan.

Service recipients have to count leased employees when they test their plans under the minimum participation, age and service, vesting, and top-heavy rules. They must be taken into account when computing limits on compensation and benefits and whether contributions to the plan are deductible. Furthermore, the leased employee will be treated as an employee under the Code's rules for fringe benefits such as group term life insurance, accident and health insurance, cafeteria plans, and dependent care assistance. Leased employees also have COBRA rights (they can elect continuation of health coverage).

For I.R.C. § 414(n) purposes, leased employees are those who provide services that last more than a year to a service recipient in conformity with the service recipient's agreement with the leasing organization. As a result of amendments made by the Small Business Job Protection Act of 1996, the test for 1997 and later years is whether the service recipient provides the primary direction or control for the work. (Service for related companies, such as the service recipient's controlled group of corporations, is aggregated with service for the service recipient.)

These rules relate to "substantially full-time service," which is defined as 1,500 hours of service in a 12-month period, or a job that is equivalent to 75% of the hours that the service recipient's actual employees put in during a 12-month period. In other words, after a year of the recipient's full-time work, the leased employee is treated as the service recipient's employee for pension testing purposes. However, if the worker is a common-law employee for other purposes, this safe harbor cannot apply.

Even if leased employees have to be counted in determining whether the service recipient's pension plans are discriminatory, they do not have to be offered participation in the plan until they satisfy any conditions for plan participation lawfully imposed by the plan (e.g., if the employer imposes an age-21 minimum for participation, and a leased employee starts working for the employer at age

19, completing a year of service at age 20, participation can be delayed until the leased employee reaches 21).

To qualify for the safe harbor, the service recipient must get 20% or less of its rank-and-file workforce (that is, workers who are not HCEs) through leasing—and the leasing organization must have its own qualified pension plan that fits particularly stringent criteria. The leasing organization's plan must be a money purchase plan. It must not be integrated with Social Security. The leasing organization's employees must be able to participate as soon as they are hired by the organization. They must be fully vested immediately. Furthermore, the leasing organization must contribute at least 10% of compensation for each plan participant.

Although it is good practice to have individuals you believe to be independent contractors sign waivers agreeing that they are not entitled to participate in pension and benefit plans, these waivers are not sufficient if, under otherwise applicable legal principles, they really are common-law employees. The IRS will issue determination letters as to whether contingent employees are leased employees and, if so, how it affects the plan's qualification.

§ 4.24 COMMUNICATING WITH EMPLOYEES

The subject of communications and notification to employees rates a chapter of its own (see Chapter 11), so here it will merely be noted that the plan administrator is responsible for reporting and disclosure, and can be held liable if appropriate disclosures are not made.

ERISA permits three methods of communication:

- Giving each employee a copy of the plan itself;
- Giving each employee a booklet containing the Summary Plan Description (SPD), describing the features of the plan in understandable language;
- Posting a notice on the bulletin board to inform employees that the company has adopted a plan, and where copies of the plan documents can be consulted.

Nearly all plans adopt the second alternative. The actual plan document is a lengthy, highly technical legal document, and doesn't do much to inform the average employee about rights and obligations under the plan.

■ **TIP:** The very important case of *Amara v. Cigna*, 131 S. Ct. 1866 (2011), discussed in more detail in Chapter 7, holds that the SPD is merely a tool used by the plan to communicate about the plan. If the SPD contradicts the terms of the plan, the plan terms—and not the SPD that the participant actually received—must prevail. The Supreme Court also said that employees cannot sue under ERISA § 502(a)(1)(B) if there are errors in the SPD.

To an ever-increasing extent, employers are permitted to use e-mail and secure Websites to deliver information to employees.

Traditionally, plan communications for defined benefit plans included a Summary Annual Report (SAR). The PPA adopted a new disclosure document, the Annual Funding Notice, to replace the SAR. Defined benefit plans that are not insured by the PBGC (e.g., professional service companies and owner-only plans) are not required to provide an Annual Funding Notice. [Form 5500 Help.com, *Clarification—SARs for Defined Benefit Plans* (Feb. 2, 2009) (benefitslink.com)]

§ 4.25 FIDUCIARY DUTY

A fiduciary is anyone who has charge of someone else's property or finances. Fiduciaries have legal duties to act honestly, prudently, and in the best interests of the owner of the assets. Pension plan fiduciaries have a duty to invest intelligently, selecting a diversified portfolio of appropriate investments that do not involve an excessive degree of risk.

ERISA obligates fiduciaries to administer the plan exclusively in the interests of plan participants and their beneficiaries. Specifically, if there is a situation in which one strategy would be most beneficial to the participants and another strategy would be most beneficial to the corporation sponsoring the plan, the fiduciaries must choose the first course of action, not the second.

If the plan has more than one named fiduciary, they are jointly and severally liable. Someone who alleges fiduciary impropriety can sue any one fiduciary, all of them, or any combination, and can collect the entire amount of liability from each one or from any combination of fiduciaries—no matter which fiduciary was actually at fault. The harshness of this high standard is relieved somewhat by the fact that fiduciaries who are sued can bring fiduciaries who weren't sued into the lawsuit, and can make them pay their fair share.

In recent years, fiduciary liability has been one of the most active areas of employment-related litigation (see Chapter 15 for details). In particular, allegations of breach of fiduciary duty have often been made based on a theory that it was imprudent to retain employer stock as a plan investment, or to fail to warn employees of various factors contributing to decline in the value of the stock. However, these allegations are very seldom successful.

In a mid-2014 Supreme Court case, plaintiffs charged that fiduciaries of an ESOP plan, who invested primarily in employer stock, violated their duty of prudence. According to the plaintiffs, they should have known that investing in employer stock was too risky—not only because of their status as officers, but because of publicly available information. The Supreme Court rejected the presumption of prudence that had generally been applied in "stock drop" cases. The

Supreme Court held that ESOP fiduciaries have the same duties as other fiduciaries, although they are relieved of the obligation of diversifying the plan's portfolio. The Supreme Court held that, to make out a claim of breach of the duty of prudence, the complaint must plausibly allege a lawful alternative course of conduct that would have yielded better results. Fiduciaries never have an obligation to violate securities laws by using inside information. [*Fifth Third Bancorp et al. v. Dudenhoeffer*, No. 12-751 (U.S. June 25, 2014)]

§ 4.26 BANKRUPTCY EFFECTS

Confusion may arise because the Bankruptcy Code uses the term "plan" to refer to the reorganization plan resolving creditors' claims, and not to ERISA plans. A Chapter 11 filing, in which the debtor continues to do business while reorganizing, sometimes affects ERISA plans, and sometimes does not; it is common for employers to modify or terminate ERISA plans as part of the reorganization process. Employee benefit claims against a bankrupt employer may include unpaid wages, vacation pay, severance pay, Worker's Compensation, insurance, and retirement benefits. Claims against the bankruptcy estate for wages and pension or welfare benefits are unsecured claims, and are paid according to the Bankruptcy Code's system of priorities. First priority is given to administrative claims, including wages, salaries, and commissions for services performed after the bankruptcy filing.

Before the 2005 bankruptcy reform legislation was passed, each employee was entitled to a third priority claim of up to $4,925 for wages, salaries, commissions, vacation, sick leave, and severance pay relating to the period 90 days before the bankruptcy filing or 90 days before the cessation of the employer's business—whichever came first. The Bankruptcy Abuse Prevention and Consumer Protection Act of 2005 (BAPCPA), Pub. L. No. 109-8, increased the amount to $10,000 and the period to 180 days before the filing or cessation of business. This amount is inflation-indexed; the 2014 level is $10,950.

Defined benefit plans, including 401(k) plans, are treated the same way as other employee benefits when priorities are set, based on whether the contributions relate to pre- or post-petition services. However, to motivate employees, employers often petition the bankruptcy court for permission to make contributions that were pending at the time of filing such as deferrals withheld from paychecks but not yet deposited into the 401(k) plan trust.

Bankruptcy Code § 1114 provides special protection for retirees' non-pension benefits (health coverage, life insurance, disability insurance). In effect, they become super-priority administrative expenses and a court order is required for the debtor or bankruptcy trustee to modify them. [Kenni B. Merritt, *Employee Benefits in Bankruptcy: The Employer's Perspective and the Employee's Perspective*, Oklahoma Bar J. (January 2005) (benefitslink.com)]

The IRS finalized regulations under the Code § 411(d)(6) anti-cutback rules, effective for plan amendments adopted and effective after November 8, 2012. A single employer defined benefit plan subject to ERISA § 4021 can be amended to eliminate lump sum or other optional forms of benefit that accelerate payment after bankruptcy. The PBGC and the bankruptcy court must determine that the plan would go through a distress or involuntary termination without the elimination of the optional benefit. The PBGC must also determine that the plan isn't sufficient for guaranteed benefits. If the sponsor eliminates an optional form of benefit under these regulations, and the plan does not offer other options with substantial survivor benefits, the sponsor can add other options to provide those benefits as part of the amendment that eliminates the lump sum distribution option. The entire plan amendment is considered together in determining if the amendment can take effect in accordance with § 436(c). [Kristen Heinzinger, *IRS Finalizes Relief for Bankrupt DB Sponsors*, plansponsor.com (Nov. 8, 2012)]

In late 2012, the DOL proposed to extend its Abandoned Plan Program to permit Chapter 7 bankruptcy trustees to distribute assets from bankrupt companies' individual account retirement plans. The proposal sets out streamlined provisions for terminating such plans and distributing their benefits. The Abandoned Plan Program was created in 2006, but applied only to financial institutions holding the assets of abandoned plans. [DOL/EBSA, *Fact Sheet: Proposed Amendments to Abandoned Plan Program* (December 2012) (benefitslink.com)]

There are two kinds of bankruptcy that may have an effect on pension plans: the employer's or an employee's. If the employer is one who seeks bankruptcy protection, an argument could be made under Bankruptcy Code § 547 that the employer's contributions to a qualified plan during the 90 days before the bankruptcy filing are "preferential transfers," and therefore should be returned to the bankruptcy estate and preserved so that creditors can make claims on them.

When it comes to the employee's bankruptcy, a highly relevant case is *Patterson v. Shumate* [504 U.S. 753 (1992)], which provides that ERISA plan law constitutes "applicable non-bankruptcy law" that will permit amounts in the plan to be excluded from the bankruptcy estate. The Supreme Court also held, in its 2005 *Rousey v. Jacoway* decision (544 U.S. 320), that IRAs are more akin to qualified plans than bank accounts from which withdrawals may be freely made. Therefore, the Supreme Court extended the exemption of qualified plans from the bankruptcy estate to IRAs. But this is only true of the debtor's own IRA, or an IRA inherited from a spouse. IRAs inherited from someone other than the debtor's spouse (e.g., a parent or sibling) are subject to claims of the debtor's creditors. [*Clark v. Rameker*, No. 13-299 (June 12, 2014); see Katy Stech, *Supreme Court Allows Creditors to Tap Into Inherited IRA Money*, WSJ.com (June 12, 2014)]

BAPCA contains a number of provisions affecting both employer and employee bankruptcies:

- Makes the employee's interest in qualified plans and IRAs exempt from the bankruptcy estate. The IRA exemption (which includes both conventional and Roth IRAs) is limited to $1 million—but the $1 million figure does not include amounts rolled over into an IRA from a qualified plan;
- As noted above, limits severance and retention payments to corporate insiders and makes it easier for the business' bankruptcy trustee to set aside preferential payments made to insiders;
- Increases the employer's ability to continue to collect repayments of plan loans from employees who have sought bankruptcy protection;
- Gives the bankruptcy court the power to cancel the employer's modifications of its retiree health benefits made during 180 days before filing of a bankruptcy petition, although if the court is persuaded that the balance of equities favors leaving the modifications in place, they can be affirmed.

Internal Revenue Code § 401(a)(33) forbids certain plan amendments if the plan is covered by ERISA § 4021. Plan benefits may not be increased while the plan sponsor is a bankruptcy debtor. The plan cannot be amended to increase the plan's liabilities because of an increase in benefits, any change in the accrual of benefits, or any change in the rate at which benefits become nonforfeitable. The ban applies only if the amendments in question take effect before the effective date of the employer's plan of reorganization.

The restrictions do not apply if the plan would otherwise have a funded current liability percentage of at least 100%; if the IRS determines that the amendment is reasonable and increases benefits only slightly; or if the amendment is actually required to conform to changes in tax law. The PPA's limitations on activities of "at risk" plans will also affect many companies that are contemplating bankruptcy or have already filed for protection.

§ 4.27 FACTORS IN CHOOSING A PLAN FORM

In deciding which form of plan to adopt, or whether to convert a plan or terminate an old plan and adopt a new one, the employer must balance many considerations, including financial and tax factors and the expected effect of a plan in motivating employee behavior (including retiring at the time most convenient for the employer).

Participants in a defined benefit plan know what their eventual pension will be if they stay with the plan until normal retirement age. If they terminate employment earlier, the vesting rules also control the size of the pension that will be paid later on, when they reach retirement age. This degree of certainty is valuable, but retirees have the problems caused by having a fixed income that does not reflect investment results.

In contrast, defined contribution plan participants know how large their account is at any given time. They can make projections of how large it will grow, based on predictions about interest rates and stock market trends. Market risk shifts from the employer to the employee and future retiree. Defined contribution plans also offer more portability: the contents of the employee's account from Plan A can simply be rolled over to Plan B when the employee stops being a Company A employee and is hired by Company B.

Before the 2008 recession began, there had been a very large-scale shift from defined benefit to defined contribution plans. One effect of the recession, however, was to increase interest in defined benefit plans and in features such as automatic enrollment and investment advice to participants that make defined contribution plans work more like defined benefit plans.

Defined benefits, but not defined contribution plans, are covered by the Pension Benefit Guaranty Corporation (PBGC)'s insurance program. The PBGC insures that employees will receive their pension benefits, at least the part that does not exceed a maximum figure. In exchange, employers must pay insurance premiums to the PBGC. If an underfunded defined benefit plan is terminated, the PBGC takes over part of the obligation to pay benefits.

About 85% of retirees who receive their benefits from the PBGC receive the full amount of benefit they were promised. For 2014, the PBGC's maximum guaranteed benefit for a 65-year-old retiree is approximately $59,320, rising from 2013's $57,500. At age 75, the maximum single life annuity is $180,327; the monthly maximum single life annuity is $15,027; the monthly maximum joint plus 50% survivor annuity is $13,524. At age 75, the corresponding figures are $98,468, $8,205, and $7,385; at age 60, $38,556, $3,213, and $2,891; at age 55, $26,693, $2,224, and $2,002; at age 50, $20,761, $1,730, and $1,557; at age 45, $14,829, $1,235, and $1,112. [PBGC press release, *PBGC Maximum Insurance Benefit Increases for 2014* (Nov. 6, 2013) (benefitslink.com)]

Because of the PPA, the maximum benefit payable to employees of a bankrupt company is determined as of the date of the bankruptcy filing, not the (usually later) date that the plan actually terminates. The Preservation of Access to Care for Medicare Beneficiaries and Pension Relief Act of 2010 (PRA), passed June 24, 2010, Pub. L. No. 111-192, allowed plan sponsors to amortize large losses in any two plan years between 2008 and 2011, using a nine-year schedule rather than the normal seven-year schedule prescribed by the PPA. [Milliman Insight, *Six Ways to Reduce Pension Costs and Combat Volatility* (Sept. 26, 2011) (benefitslink.com)]

Before the PPA, a number of companies adopted cash balance plans (which combine some features of defined-benefit plans with some features more typical of a defined-contribution plan) even though the tax status of these plans was ambiguous, and it was uncertain whether they violated the Age Discrimination in Employment Act. The PPA makes it clear that cash balance plans (as long as they are operated in accordance with the rules!) are tax-compliant and do not discriminate against older workers. (See Chapter 7.) However, this favorable treatment is prospective only. Most courts have ruled in favor of cash balance plans established before the PPA took effect—but some have found ERISA and/or ADEA violations.

An early 2012 article suggests that a company that has maxed out its 401(k) plan but still has steady cash flow and discretionary income that could be used for benefits might consider implementing a cash balance plan. For plan participants in their fifties who got a late start on retirement planning, even if they make catch-up contributions, they could not save as much in a 401(k) plan as in a cash balance plan. A cash balance plan can also be used as a mechanism for a young partner to indirectly buy out an older partner who wants to retire. [Tom Sigmund, Kegler, Brown, *How To Determine If a Cash Balance Pension Plan Is Right for Your Company*, Hill & Ritter Smart Business (Jan. 3, 2012) (benefitslink.com)]

CHAPTER 5

DEFINED BENEFIT PLANS

§ 5.01 INTRODUCTION

This chapter deals, in detail, with issues that are specific to defined benefit plans. See Chapter 4 for background issues on pensions, Chapter 6 for defined contribution plans and 401(k) plans, and Chapter 7 for cash balance plans.

One of the most important changes in the employment/retirement landscape has been the transition from the defined benefit plan to the defined contribution plan. Major legislation, the Pension Protection Act (PPA; Pub. L. No. 109-280), has been passed to improve the stability of the remaining defined benefit plans. However, due to financial problems occurring after the passage of the legislation, it was deemed necessary to relax some of the more onerous requirements, by passing the Worker, Retiree, and Employer Recovery Act of 2008 (WRERA; Pub. L. No. 110-458); the Preservation of Access to Care for Medicare Beneficiaries and Pension Relief Act of 2010 (PRA; Pub. L. No. 111-192), and the Moving Ahead for Progress in the 21st Century Act, aka MAP-21 (Pub. L. No. 112-141).

The number of defined benefit plans continues to decline. The DOL reported that there were 103,346 defined benefit plans in 1975—and only 46,543 in 2010. Towers Watson said that, for 400 large companies that have defined benefit plans, the total estimated deficit reached an all-time high of $418 billion, 23% higher than 2011. Companies are responding by buying out pension recipients, transferring pension accounts to third parties such as insurance companies, and increasing their contributions. Some companies, including Boeing, are disclosing "core earnings" separately to exclude pension expenses, so the figures look healthier. [Mike Ramsey and Vipal Monga, *Low Interest Rates Force Companies to Pour Cash Into Pensions*, WSJ.com (Feb. 3, 2013)]

An EBRI fact sheet published in March 2013 shows that in 1979, only 7% of U.S. workers participated only in a defined contribution plan; in that year, 28% of workers had only a defined benefit plan, and a further 10% had both. The situation changed greatly by 2011, when 31% of workers participated only in a defined contribution plan, 11% participated in both, and a mere 3% of workers had a defined benefit plan only. The fact sheet includes a dramatic graph showing that the proportion of workers with both types of plans has stayed within the 10%–15% range—but defined benefit plan participation plummeted throughout the period as defined contribution plan participation soared.[EBRI Fast Facts #225, *Pension Plan Participation*, <http://www.ebri.org/pdf/FF.225.DB-DC.28Mar13.pdf> (Mar. 28, 2013)]

The Wall Street Journal reported in 2014 that pension plans are facing a "double whammy": a significant increase in the cost of regulatory compliance (e.g., much higher PBGC premiums), and increasing life expectancies (requiring more years of pension payments). The article predicts a life expectancy of 87.9 years for male retirees and 90.1 years for female retirees by 2029. These factors help explain the shift away from defined benefit plans. In 1979, 38% of private sector workers were covered by a defined benefit plan; in 2011, only 14% were.

Aon Hewitt estimated that increasing life expectancy will require the sponsors of defined benefit plans to increase the pension obligations on their balance sheets by some 7%. Some employers that still have defined benefit plans are taking steps like freezing the plan, moving workers to defined contribution plans, or buying annuities to satisfy defined benefit obligations. [Vipal Monga, *Pension Plans Brace For a One-Two Punch*, WSJ.com (Mar. 24, 2014)]

Starting with the 2008 plan year, the PPA requires defined benefit plans to distribute Annual Funding Notices instead of Summary Annual Reports (SARs). For large plans, the notice is due 120 days after the end of the plan year; for small plans, the due date is the same as the due date for the Form 5500. But plans that are not insured by the PBGC (such as professional service companies and owner-only plans) are not required to provide either an Annual Funding Notice or an SAR. [Form 5500 Help.com, *Clarification SARs for Defined Benefit Plans* (Feb. 2, 2009) (benefitslink.com)]

Hybrid plans are defined benefit plans that accrue benefits under a formula, but define the benefit as a lump sum (the account balance) and not as a monthly payment after retirement. Funding of hybrid plans is predictable for the employer, and some employees find them easier to understand than traditional defined benefit plans. Cash balance plans (see Chapter 7) are the most popular type of hybrid plans. The benefit is based on a percentage of pay credited each year, plus interest at the plan's interest crediting rate. A Pension Equity Plan (PEP) posts percentage credits to the employee's account each year, defining the lump sum balance at retirement as the total of the percentages multiplied by the employee's final average pay. Final regulations on hybrid plans were published in 2010: see 75 Fed. Reg. 64123 (Oct. 19, 2010).

As a result of PPA § 504, employers must post actuarial information about the funding status of defined benefit plans on their corporate intranet (if they have one; it is not necessary to create an intranet just for this purpose). The posting must include basic information about the plan, and the actuarial information about the plan. However, if the employer chooses to post the entire form rather than just the mandatory information, Form SSA should be removed, because it contains the Social Security numbers of plan participants. The DOL informally indicated that the requirement does not apply to defined contribution plans such as 401(k)s. [Timothy D.S. Goodman, Dorsey & Whitney LLP Resources, *New Law Requires Employers with Defined Benefit Plans to Post Information on Their Intranet* (Nov. 2, 2009) (benefitslink.com)]

Defined benefit plans, in response to investment volatility, changing rules, and longer-lived participants, are looking for "de-risking" strategies. Traditional de-risking strategies include liability-driven investing and annuitizing accrued benefits. Annuitizing is expensive, but has the advantage of placing liability risk on a third party. More modern strategies are annuity buy-ins, where the insurer and plan sponsor share the financial risks. A plan can also cash out retirees completely, placing all the investment risk on them. Two PLRS, Nos. 201228045 and 2012280511, say that this is not a violation of the minimum distribution rules.

[Elizabeth Thomas Dold and David N. Levine, *A Look at Retiree Cashouts as the New De-Risking Strategy*, Taxes: The Tax Magazine (November 2012) (benefitslink.com)]

[A] PPA and Later Changes

Although it contains other types of provisions, the Pension Protection Act (PPA; Pub. L. No. 109-280) takes defined benefit plan reform as its central mission. Major changes wrought by the PPA include:

- Changing the rules for the interest rate assumptions sponsors must use in plan funding and operations.
- Amending the funding rules, so that plans will have to be 100% funded (earlier law allowed funding at a 90% level). This change is being phased in gradually to give plan sponsors time to adjust.
- Sponsors must meet "funding targets" by making at least the "minimum required contribution" required for the plan, a calculation involving the plan's "target normal cost."
- Contributions over and above the minimum required contribution give rise to "credit balances" which can be applied toward the required minimum contribution for later years.
- Valuation of plan assets can either be at fair market value or "smoothed" over a 24-month period, but values must always fall within 90%–110% of FMV.
- Special rules are imposed on the activities of "at-risk" plans (i.e., those that are at risk of becoming unable to pay benefits as they come due). Plans with fewer than 500 participants are exempt from the at-risk plan rules.

President Bush signed WRERA, the Worker, Retiree, and Employer Recovery Act of 2008, Pub. L. No. 110-458, on December 23, 2008. WRERA provides PPA technical corrections and relief from some of the more onerous PPA requirements. The PPA required plans to become 100% funded within seven years. Businesses asked for temporary relief, but Congress made it permanent, allowing companies with major investment losses to come into compliance without reaching the 100% level within the seven-year time frame. [Mary Williams Walsh, *Pensions Get a Reprieve in Congress*, <http://www.times.com> (Dec. 12, 2008)]

The PPA replaced the concept of the funding standard account with a requirement that contributions each year must be at least as great as the target normal cost (the cost of the benefits that accrued during the year) plus the amount needed to amortize the funding shortfall, as it stood at the beginning of the year, over a period of approximately seven years. Tougher funding requirements were imposed on at-risk plans.

WRERA provides that expenses paid directly by the plan are included in the target normal cost. Under the PPA, the plan's contributions and distributions had to be included in the calculation; WRERA also allows consideration of expected earnings. WRERA requires the same interest rate assumptions to be used to calculate the funding target percentage and the target normal cost.

WRERA expands the IRS' authority to issue guidance about how to determine the plan's funded status for years before 2008, which is important for determining if plan is at risk.

As a result of WRERA, the restrictions on lump sum distributions do not apply to mandatory cash-out of de minimis amounts under $5,000. To determine whether benefit accruals must cease in 2009, the plan can use either its 2008 or 2009 AFTAP—whichever is greater.

Section 415(b) requires benefits that are not in the form of a life annuity beginning between age 62 and age 65 to be converted to that form using actuarial assumptions prescribed by the IRS. The PPA said that the § 415(b) mortality assumptions would be based on the standard table for group annuity contracts, but WRERA requires instead that the table for converting benefit accruals to lump sums under § 407(e) must be used. [Deloitte's Washington Bulletin, *PPA Technical Corrections Affecting Defined Benefit Plans*, <http://benefitslink.com/articles/guests/washbull090112.html> (Jan. 12, 2009). See also T.D. 9467, 2009-50 I.R.B. 760, dealing with post-PPA funding requirements for single-employer defined benefit plans.]

In mid-2010, with financial conditions still hazardous, Congress provided additional relief for defined benefit plans. The Preservation of Access to Care for Medicare Beneficiaries and Pension Relief Act, Pub. L. No. 111-192) (PRA), gives employers two choices. The employer could select two years in which to pay only interest on the plan's funding shortfall (rather than contributing enough to actually reduce the shortfall as required by the PPA), or amortize the shortfall for any two plan years between 2008 and 2011 over 15 years. [Rebecca Moore, *Obama Signs Pension Relief Bill*, plansponsor.com (June 25, 2010). See also Notice 2011-3, 2011-3 I.R.B. 324 (Dec. 22, 2010)]

Important defined benefit plan provisions were included in MAP-21, the Moving Ahead for Progress in the 21st Century Act. [Hazel Bradford, Pensions & Investments, *Congress Passes Pension Changes in Highway Package* (June 29, 2012) (benefitslink.com)]

MAP-21 extends the period used to calculate interest rates to 25 years, so the recent period, with extremely low interest rates, has a lesser impact on the calculations. The interest-rate change is expected to save the typical defined benefit plan 15%–25% of its contribution requirement. MAP-21 also increases the PBGC premiums and allows overfunded plans to transfer money to a 401(h) plan providing either health benefits or group-term life insurance for retirees. [Rebecca Moore, *Congress Passes Bill With Pension Funding Relief*, plansponsor.com

(June 29, 2012); Buck Consultants FYI, *2012 Pension Plan Funding Stabilization Finally a Reality* (July 6, 2012) (benefitslink.com)]

Mid-2014 legislation, the Highway Transportation Funding Act of 2014 (Pub. L. No. 113-159) continues the MAP-21 relief by continuing to permit "pension smoothing," a form of stabilization. Smoothing reduces the employer's obligations with respect to minimum funding by adjusting the interest rates used to calculate the minimum funding obligation. The practical effect is that sponsors' contributions can be calculated based on average interest rates for a longer period of time, not just the most recent years, when interest rates were very low. The lower the interest rates, the more the employer must contribute to satisfy its funding obligations.

Under the 2014 legislation, for calendar years 2012–2017, the "corridor" is a minimum percentage of 90%, a maximum percentage of 110%. For 2018, the corresponding figures are 85% and 115%; for 2019, 80% and 120%; for 2020, 75% and 125%; after 2020, 70% and 130%. However, these smoothing rules do not apply to bankrupt companies: see Code § 463(d)(2) for benefit restrictions. [Groom Law Group Benefits Brief, *Extension of Pension Interest Rate Smoothing Relief Clears Congress Before August Recess*, <http://www.groom.com/media/publication/1444_Extension_of_Pension_Interest_Rate.pdf> (Aug. 1, 2014); Vipal Monga, *Welcome to the World of "Pension Smoothing,"* WSJ.com (Aug. 11, 2014)]

§ 5.02 BENEFIT LIMITS

The limit on the maximum benefit that anyone can receive from a qualified defined benefit plan in a year is set by I.R.C. § 415(b)(1).

For 2013, the limit on the annual benefit is $205,000, the compensation limit is $255,000, and the HCE level is still $115,000. [IR-2012-77, *IRS Announces 2013 Pension Plan Limitations; Taxpayers May Contribute Up to $17,500 To Their 401(k) Plans in 2013*, <http://www.irs.gov/uac/2013-Pension-Plan Limitations> (Oct. 18, 2012)] For 2014, the limit on the annual benefit is $210,000; the compensation limit is $260,000; and the HCE level remains $115,000. [IR-2013-86, *IRS Announces 2014 Pension Plan Limitations; Taxpayers May Contribute up to $17,500 to Their 401(k) Plans in 2014*, <http://www.irs.gov/uac/IRS-Announces-2014-Pension-Plan-Limitations;-Taxpayers-May-Contribute-up-to-$17,500-to-their-401(k)-plans-in-2014> (Oct. 31, 2013)]

As a result of the PPA, underfunded plans are restricted in their benefit distribution options: see § 5.10.

§ 5.03 BENEFIT FORMS FOR DEFINED BENEFIT PLANS

All pension plans must provide the basic payment form: a life annuity for single participants, and a QJSA (qualified joint and survivor annuity) for married participants. The basic form of QJSA provides a certain level of benefits while both the former employee and spouse are still alive. When one of them dies, the payment is cut in half, because only one person remains to be supported. Although employers are allowed to offer 50% survivor annuities, they are also allowed to subsidize the survivor annuity so that it is more than 50% of the initial payment, or even so that the payment does not decline when one payee dies. As a result of the Pension Protection Act, employers must now offer married participants not only a choice between a joint and 50% survivor annuity and a single-life annuity, but a choice between a survivor annuity at the 50% level and at the 75% level (Qualified Optional Survivor Annuity, or QOSA).

Internal Revenue Code § 401(a)(25) says that a plan that provides for alternative benefit forms (annuity, installment, lump sum, early retirement) must specify, in a definite form that precludes employer discretion, what actuarial assumptions (such as interest rates and mortality assumptions) are used to calculate equivalencies among different benefit forms. This disclosure obligation does not, however, extend to the plan's funding assumptions.

In a flat benefit plan, the pension is defined as a certain number of dollars per month, or a percentage of average annual compensation or average compensation for the "high three" years. A unit benefit plan defines the pension as compensation times years of participation times a percentage rate. Some plans of this type increase the accrual rate in later years, or are calculated using a "high five" or "final average pay" (the average of the last three years of work, when presumably earnings will be at their peak).

The IRS has ruled frequently on when and how plans can eliminate benefit forms that are hard to administer and are rarely chosen by participants, but the theme of all these rules is that the core benefit forms must remain available to participants. Final Regulations were published under § 411(d)(6) on August 11, 2005, further explaining the benefits and redundant payment forms that can be eliminated from defined benefit plans. The IRS also published proposals in the same document, allowing elimination of benefits that fail a utilization test.

Any benefit outside the core options can be eliminated after four years. The core options are defined as the straight life annuity; the 75% joint and contingent annuity; the 50%/100% joint and contingent annuity; the 10-year certain and life annuity; and an option such as a lump sum or a survivor annuity that would be valuable for a participant with a short life expectancy. [T.D. 9219, 2005-38 I.R.B. 538; see also 71 Fed. Reg. 45379 (Aug. 9, 2006)].

IRS Regulations proposed at 70 Fed. Reg. 31214 (May 31, 2005), finalized at 72 Fed. Reg. 16878 (Apr. 5, 2007) unify and systematize the § 415 rules, explaining how to calculate the maximum permitted benefit when a retiree has multiple annuity start dates and how to calculate qualified joint and survivor annuities when the benefit is partly taken as a lump sum and partly in annuity form. The IRS proposed a rule to encourage partial annuity distribution options in defined benefit plans. Proposals published in February 2012 amend § 417(e)(3) to permit combinations of lump sum payments and income streams. Plans that wish to take advantage of this opinion could be amended to allow participants to take a partial lump sum calculated with the statutory actuarial assumptions, plus an annuity using the plan's regular conversion factors. The annuity form is referred to as a Qualified Longevity Annuity Contract, or QLAC. [IRS Proposed Rules, 77 Fed. Reg. 5443 and 5454 (Feb. 3, 2012); see Retirement Town Hall, *IRS Proposes Rule To Encourage Partial Annuity Distribution Options In Pension Plans* (Feb. 9, 2012) (benefitslink.com)]

Rev. Rul. 2012-3, 2012-8 I.R.B. 383 explains how the qualified joint and survivor annuity (QJSA) and qualified preretirement survivor annuity (QPSA) rules work when a deferred annuity contract is purchased under a profit-sharing plan. Rev. Rul. 2012-4, 2012-8 I.R.B. 386, explains how to satisfy §§ 411 and 415 when a qualified defined benefit plan accepts a direct rollover of an eligible rollover distribution from the same employer's qualified defined contribution plan and uses the rollover amount to provide an annuity. [*Treasury Fact Sheet: Helping American Families Achieve Retirement Security By Expanding Lifetime Income Choices*, 020212 Retirement Security Factsheet; Rebecca Moore, *IRS Issues Guidance About Annuities in Retirement Plans*, plansponsor.com (Feb. 2, 2012)]

The Northern District of Texas denied injunctive relief to 41,000 Verizon management retirees who were opposed to Verizon's plan to buy a single-premium group annuity from Prudential to satisfy the obligation to make pension payments, holding that there was no ERISA § 510 violation because the annuity payment was the same as the current pension benefit. The court dismissed the breach of fiduciary duty claim, holding that amending or terminating a pension plan is not a fiduciary act. The case as a whole was dismissed in June 2013, because the district court held that plaintiffs did not prove loss of any benefits or rights. [*Lee v. Verizon*, No. 3:12-cv-04834-D, 2012 U.S. Dist. LEXIS 173559 (N.D. Tex. Dec. 7, 2012). See Maria Wood, *Judge Disconnects Lawsuit Vs. Verizon Pension Transfer*, LifeHealthPro, <http://www.lifehealthpro.com/2013/06/26/judge-disconnects-lawsuit-vs-verizon-pension-trans> (June 26, 2013)]

In 2008, the Northern District of Illinois held that Verizon was bound by the language in its defined benefit plan document even though a drafting error had possible consequences of $1.67 billion. The cashout value of interests in the predecessor plan was incorrectly drafted, calling for multiplying the balance twice by a variable transition factor based on age and years of service. However, on reconsideration, the Northern District held that the error was an honest mistake, and other actions in administering the plan showed an intent to use the multiplication factor only once. Judge Denlow said that employers would be discouraged from adopting plans at all if they feared that mistakes could have catastrophic consequences that could not be corrected. The Seventh Circuit affirmed in mid-2010 and the Supreme Court denied certiorari. [*Young v. Verizon's Bell Atlantic Cash Balance Plan*, 615 F.3d 808 (7th Cir. 2010), *cert. denied*, 131 S. Ct. 2924 (May 23, 2011), *reh'g denied*, 132 S. Ct. 47 (July 25, 2011)]

§ 5.04 MORTALITY TABLES

Before 2002, the IRS required defined benefit plans to use the 1983 Group Annuity Mortality (83GAM) table for making the actuarial calculations for the value of accrued benefits. [I.R.C. § 417(e)] The mortality tables must be used to make sure that the value of a lump sum benefit is at least as great as the predicted value of an annuity.

Defined benefit plans also have to calculate adjustments of the plan limitations, as required by I.R.C. § 415(b), when the benefit under the plan is paid in any form other than a QJSA, or when the employee retires before age 62 or after age 65.

The PPA imposed additional § 412 funding requirements for defined benefit plans that have unfunded current liability (§ 412(l)(8)). Current liability is determined using the mortality table prescribed by the Secretary, who is required to update the table at least once every 10 years. Additional tables are prescribed for disability retirees whose disability satisfies Social Security Act Title II standards: a table for disability occurring before January 1, 1995 and a table for disabilities with later onset. Under § 412(l)(7)(C)(ii)(III), the tables have to be reviewed at least once every five years to reflect trends in mortality rates. The mortality tables have been updated for use in 2014 and 2015: see Notice 2013-49, 2013-32 I.R.B. 127. [T.D. 9310 RIN 1545-BE72 72 Fed. Reg. 4955 (Feb. 2, 2007); Rev. Proc. 2008-62, 2008-42 I.R.B. 935]

Under the PPA, a defined benefit plan must provide that the present value of an accrued benefit, and the amount of any distribution (lump sum or otherwise) must be at least the amount calculated using the Regulations Section 1.417(e)-1(d) appropriate interest rate for the month and the prescribed mortality table.

In May 2007, the IRS explained the procedure for qualifying to use a substitute (plan specific) mortality table to compute defined benefit plan obligations under Code § 430(h)(3)(C)/ERISA § 303(h)(3)(C). The IRS will consider a substitute mortality table adequate if the plan has enough participants; the plan has been maintained long enough to have credible mortality experience; and the chosen table reflects the plan's actual experience and its projected mortality trends for participants. [Adrien Martin, *IRS Release Guidelines on Substitute Mortality Table Requests*, plansponsor.com (May 31, 2007)]

In 2014, the Society of Actuaries released an exposure draft of a new set of actuarial tables, reflecting increasing life expectancies. For women aged 25–85, the tables call for an increase in pension liabilities of 5.5–10.5%; for men in those age cohorts, liabilities will probably increase 2.5–17.4%. If the IRS adopts these mortality tables, defined benefit plans' funding ratios will drop, and sponsors will have to provide additional funding. Although the IRS probably will not approve the tables for a year or so, corporations are likely to find that their auditors call for adoption of the new tables for 2014 disclosures; otherwise, a sudden need to increase funding could come as a surprise to investors. [Kevin McGuinness, *Planning for Mortality Tables' Effect on Liabilities*, plansponsor.com (Mar. 14, 2014); Meaghan Kilroy, *New Actuary Tables May Be "Nail In The Coffin" For DB*

Plans, Pensions & Investments (July 24, 2014) (benefitslink.com)—that is, the increased liabilities may be the final factor leading some sponsors to terminate their defined benefit plans.]

§ 5.05 FUNDING THE DEFINED BENEFIT PLAN

[A] Funding Requirements

The process of funding a defined contribution plan is quite simple. The employer simply determines a percentage of compensation, and as long as the contribution does not exceed the Code maximum, then there are no further problems. No discretion is involved.

In contrast, funding a defined benefit plan requires subtle decisions about long-range economic and employment trends in order to deposit enough money to yield the correct stream of future benefits to plan participants and their beneficiaries.

Defined benefit, money purchase, and target benefit plans (but not profit-sharing plans, stock bonus plans, or plans under I.R.C. § 412(i) that are exclusively funded by the purchase of individual insurance or annuity contracts) are subject to a "minimum funding" requirement under I.R.C. § 412. Before the PPA, the benchmark was the status of the plan's "minimum funding standard account," but the PPA enacts a new Code § 430, setting out the requirements for "basic minimum funding contributions."

An excise tax of 10% is imposed by I.R.C. § 4971 for failure to meet the minimum funding standard. The excise tax rises to 100% of any deficiency that remains uncorrected a reasonable time after the plan receives notice of deficiency from the IRS.

According to the Supreme Court case, *United States v. Reorganized CF&I Fabricators of Utah Inc.* [518 U.S. 213 (1996)], the 100% assessment is a penalty (and therefore an ordinary unsecured claim) and not an excise tax entitled to seventh priority, if the company subject to it files for bankruptcy protection.

In June 2014, according to the BNY Mellon Investment Strategy and Solutions Group, the funded status of the average corporate pension plan was 92.0%, 1.4 percentage points higher than the previous month. [PRNewswire, *Funded Status of U.S. Corporate Pensions Rises to 92 Percent* (July 2, 2014) (benefitslink-.com)]

Underfunding has other implications. The PPA imposes limitations on benefits. If the plan is covered by PBGC insurance, the PBGC must be notified whenever the minimum funding standard is not met. If the plan is terminated (see Chapter 17), then underfunding can make the plan liable to the PBGC for accumulated funding deficiencies.

However, complying with the minimum funding standard doesn't solve all of the employer's problems, because I.R.C. § 4972 also imposes an excise tax on excess contributions to a defined benefit plan.

Therefore, the employer should make sure that its contributions to the defined benefit plan fall within the acceptable range. Contributions should not be small enough to constitute underfunding—especially not small enough to trigger PBGC termination of the plan. But the employer will not want to contribute more than can be deducted, and will particularly want to avoid the excise tax on excess contributions.

[B] Deduction Limit

The funding standard serves another purpose: it sets an upper limit on the amount that the employer can deduct under I.R.C. § 404. If the employer overstates its pension liabilities by 200% or more, and therefore takes too large a deduction, with the result that its income taxes are underpaid by 20% or more, then a 20% accuracy-related underpayment penalty can be imposed under I.R.C. § 6662. The penalty will be suspended if the pension overstatement was less than $1,000, or if the plan relied on substantial authority such as Revenue Rulings or IRS Notices.

Pensions are a form of deferred compensation, and any form of compensation is deductible only if it is reasonable and constitutes an ordinary and necessary business expense. Part of the compensation of particularly highly paid employees may have to be disregarded for certain tax-related purposes.

For example, under I.R.C. § 401(a)(17) only $200,000 of compensation (adjusted for inflation in increments of $5,000) can be taken into account. EGTRRA increased this amount from $150,000 (adjusted for inflation; the 2014 level is $260,000). Even legitimate compensation may have to be deducted over a span of several years, not all at once.

[C] Calculating the Contribution

Before the PPA, defined benefit plan actuaries used two basic methods (each of which had variations): the accrued benefit method and the projected benefit cost method. Contributions were made for each participant based on "normal cost" (the actuarial value of benefit units for that year) plus "supplemental liability" (adjustments for service before adoption of a plan, or after a plan is amended). The PPA approach starts with the "target normal cost" and, as [D], below, shows, this is the point of departure for various adjustments.

[D] From the Minimum Funding Standard Account to the Minimum Required Contribution

Pre-PPA law required that a "minimum funding standard account" be maintained in all plan years until the end of the year in which the plan terminates. [See I.R.C. § 412(b) and ERISA § 302(b)] Under the pre-PPA rules, the minimum funding standard is met when there is no accumulated funding deficiency at the end of the year. There is no deficiency if, for all plan years, the credits to the funding standard account are at least equal to the total charges.

The minimum funding standard account consists of charges for normal costs, past service liabilities, experience losses in investments, and funding deficiencies. The general rule is that experience losses and funding deficiencies have to be amortized, not deducted currently. The charges to the account are offset by credits for, e.g., the employer's contributions to the plan, investment experience gains, and funding deficiencies that are waived by the IRS. WRERA provides (as an option for 2008, but mandatory for later years) that expenses paid directly by the plan are included in the target normal cost. Under the PPA, the plan's contributions and distributions had to be included in the calculation; WRERA also allows consideration of expected earnings. WRERA requires the same interest rate assumptions to be used to calculate the funding target percentage and the target normal cost.

Internal Revenue Code § 412(l) imposes additional obligations on single-employer plans with 100 or more participants whose "funded current liability" percentage falls below 80% for the current year when it was below 90% for the preceding year. The funded current liability percentage equals the value of the plan assets divided by current liabilities. The underfunded plans are obligated to notify their participants and beneficiaries of the funding deficiency, and must pay an additional PBGC premium. In egregious cases, the PBGC may be able to bring a civil suit against the plan.

The PPA introduced several new concepts and new requirements. The employer's obligation is now the "minimum required contribution," defined as the amount the employer must contribute each year to fund benefits that will be paid in that year, as well as phasing out any existing funding shortfall over seven years. If the plan's assets are lower than its funding target, the minimum required contribution for the year is the "target normal cost" plus the amount needed to amortize the funding shortfall over seven years. The "funding target" is the accrued liability to date: the sum needed to pay all of the claims of participants and beneficiaries, as of the valuation date. The target normal cost, in turn, is defined as the benefit liabilities accruing in the current year, including past service benefits that increased reflecting the employee's higher compensation in the current year. A funding shortfall is any difference between the funding target and the plan assets. The "shortfall amortization installment" is the payment due in each of the seven years to close the gap. However, if the employer contributes more than the required amount, a credit balance is created that can be applied toward the required contribution for later years.

The carried-over balance is also credited with interest, but at the rate used to calculate the plan's liabilities, not the actual interest rate that the plan earns on its investments.

A degree of relief from the requirements for amortizing the shortfall was provided by the Preservation of Access to Care for Medicare Beneficiaries and Pension Relief Act of 2010, which allowed employers to elect to pay only the interest on their shortfall for two years, or to amortize the shortfall in any two plan years between 2008–2011 over 15 rather than seven years.

[E] Full Funding Limitation

Before 2004, it was necessary to calculate a "full funding limitation" because excise taxes could be imposed if the employer's contribution fell below that amount. EGTRRA reduced the full funding limitation for 2002 and 2003 and provided that the percentage test would expire in 2004, when the FFL would be the difference between the plan's accrued liability and the value of its assets.

[F] Funding Procedures

Actual funding of the plan is done by the employer's contributing cash, non-cash property, or its own securities. The valuation of cash is simple; for property and securities, it can be difficult. The prohibited transaction rules (see § 8.03) must be consulted to make sure that contributions do not violate these rules. Wherever possible, transactions should be structured so that the plan trust will not have Unrelated Business Taxable Income (UBTI). In general, plan trusts are not subject to income tax—unless they have unrelated income.

Wherever possible, the employer should avoid contributing depreciated property to the plan. That's because I.R.C. § 267(b)(4) provides that the employer will have taxable gain (capital or ordinary, depending on the facts) if it contributes appreciated property to the plan. But losses on contributions of depreciated property are not recognized, because there is a transfer between the trust grantor and the trust's fiduciary.

■ **TIP:** An employer that wants to use depreciated property in funding can sell the property to a third party, recognize the tax loss, then contribute the cash proceeds of the sale.

The PPA provides that most plans must make their required contribution no later than 8½ months after the end of the plan year. Some plans, however (those with more than 100 participants, and that had a funding shortfall in the previous year) will have to make quarterly contributions (April 15, July 15, October 15,

January 15) instead of being permitted to make the whole year's contribution at once. The quarterly installment must equal 25% of the lesser of 90% of the minimum required contribution for the current plan year, or 100% of the minimum required contribution for the previous year.

[G] Liens Based on Funding Failures

Under I.R.C. § 412(n), a lien can be imposed against the employer, and in favor of the plan subject to PBGC jurisdiction, if the employer fails to make a required contribution to the plan when it is due.

> ■ **TIP:** The person responsible for making the payment that was missed has an obligation to inform the PBGC within 10 days of the due date that the payment was missed.

The lien covers all of the employer's real and personal property. The lien can be imposed if the plan's funded current liability percentage fell below 100% and the unpaid balance, plus interest, was more than $1 million. It starts on the date the payment should have been made, and runs to the end of the plan year in which the liabilities go over the $1 million mark.

The PBGC can sue in federal district court under ERISA § 4003(e)(1) to enforce the lien against the employer. This power can be exercised at any time until three years after the PBGC knew or should have known of the failure to make the necessary payment (extended to six years if the employer committed fraud or concealment), or for six years after the due date from the payment.

[H] Plan Valuation Issues

An actuarial valuation must be performed at least once a year to determine the assets, liabilities, and contribution level for plans subject to I.R.C. § 412. (EGTRRA gives the Treasury the power to adopt regulations that call for even more frequent valuations.) The information is also used to prepare the Schedule B for the 5500-series form.

The basic factors in setting assumptions include:

- Employee compensation;
- Early retirement rate;
- Employee turnover;
- Disability and mortality rates (both before and after retirement);
- (For QJSAs) Life expectancy of employees' spouses;

- Expected percentage return on the plan's investments (interest assumptions may have to be adjusted in the future to reflect the plan's investment record);
- Administrative expenses, defined either as dollars per participant or a reduction in the plan's rate of return.

Within the limits set by I.R.C. § 412 and other relevant provisions, the size of the contribution can be increased or decreased somewhat based on corporate needs. However, the plan's actuarial assumptions must always be reasonable—each individual assumption, not just the aggregate. Courts have the power to overturn a plan's actuarial assumptions, even if the assumptions are not unreasonable. This is especially likely to happen if the plan has applied its own assumptions inconsistently.

■ **TIP:** In general, the valuation date has to be within the plan year for which the assets are being valued, or within a month before the start of the plan year—but EGTRRA § 661(a) creates an exception under which the valuation date can sometimes be in the previous year. This exception can only be used if the plan assets, valued as of the prior plan year's date, is at least 125% of the plan's current liability.

Certain large companies, such as AT&T and Verizon saw an increase in their 2013 fourth quarter earnings as a result of changes in valuation method for their pension plans. They joined the trend of adopting mark-to-market pension accounting, which puts pension plan gains and losses into earnings faster than the old rules calling for smoothing over several years. Mark-to-market companies have more volatile earnings, but have a more current picture of the status of their plans. In 2011–2012, when rates were falling, mark-to-market depressed earnings, but 2013 was characterized by surging interest rates and strong stock market performance. Not all mark-to- market companies had 2013 gains; some recorded adjustments only when the pension plan's gain or loss exceeded a "corridor" amount. [Michael Rapoport, *Pensions Could Lift Earnings at Some Big Companies*, WSJ.com (Jan. 8, 2014)]

ERISA § 302(c) provides that a plan covered by PBGC termination insurance requires IRS approval to change its actuarial assumptions, if the aggregated unfunded vested benefits of all underfunded plans maintained by the employer, or members of the same controlled group, exceed $50 million. Approval for the change is also required if the change in the assumptions raises the unfunded cumulative liability for the current plan year by more than $50 million, or more than $5 million, if this is 5% or more of the current liability.

Before the PPA, plans could use "smoothing" to cope with changes in the valuation of plan assets over time. The PPA requires plans either to value their assets at fair market value (FMV) or to restrict "smoothing" to a 24-month period, during which values fall within the range of 90–110% of FMV.

[I] Interest Rates

Internal Revenue Code § 412(l)(7)(C)(i) sets the parameters for the interest rates used to determine the employer's contributions and the plan's current liability.

Under pre-PPA rules, the Department of the Treasury has the power to issue Regulations that lower the permissible range [see I.R.C. § 412(b)(5)] but it is not allowed to fall beneath 80% of the weighted 30-year average Treasury rate.

Factors in the interest rate assumption include:

- The economic components of interest rates;
- Current long-term interest rates;
- The plan's individual actuarial and investment factors;
- Long-range economic trends, especially in the money supply and interest rates throughout the economy.

The basic principle under the PPA—that the present value of a plan's current liabilities must be calculated with an interest rate based on corporate bonds, not Treasury bills—survives. However, the lower the interest rates applied to the calculation, the more the employer must contribute to fund the plan. Congress permitted some funding relief in 2012, under the MAP-21 (Pub. L. No. 112-141). Defined benefit plans consider interest rates stretching back 25 years, so the recent, very low rates, will have less impact on the calculation. For 2012, the interest rates used in the calculation must be within 10% of the average of benchmark bond rates for the previous 25 years.

Employers are allowed to use two approaches to calculate the present value of future pension benefits. The future expected payments can be discounted using a yield curve based on corporate bond data published by the Treasury. The other approach is to use segment rates based on averages from the most recent two years of yield curves. For each year, MAP-21 specifies the range of rates that can be used.

MAP-21 requires plan administrators to disclose additional information if the plan had 50 or more participants on any day of the preceding plan year; the stabilized funding target is less than 95% of the regular funding target; and the plan would have a funding shortfall of $500,000 or more absent stabilization. If all three of those factors are present, the plan's Annual Funding Notice must disclose that the law has changed reducing the employer's contribution. The notice must include a table showing the MAP-21's effect on funding requirements, plan's funding shortfall, and the minimum contribution for the current year and the two years before. [Rebecca Moore, *Congress Passes Bill With Pension Funding Relief*, plansponsor.com (June 29, 2012); Buck Consultants FYI, *2012 Pension Plan Funding Stabilization Finally a Reality* (July 6, 2012) (benefitslink.com)]

Pub. L. No. 113-159, the Highway Transportation Funding Act of 2014, extends the ability of pension plan sponsors to reduce their contributions, probably until 2020. The PPA required calculations to reflect the average corporate bond yield going back only 24 months; MAP-21 allowed a corridor within a 25-year average. MAP-21 provided for the corridor to expand each year, so that, as of 2016, MAP-21 relief would phase out and PPA principles would once again be in force. But the 2014 statute keeps the 2014 corridor figure in effect until 2017. For calendar years 2012–2017, the "corridor" is a minimum percentage of 90%, a maximum percentage of 110%. For 2018, the corresponding figures are 85% and 115%; for 2019, 80% and 120%; for 2020, 75% and 125%; after 2020, 70% and 130%. Note that bankrupt companies cannot take advantage of this relief. [John Dowell, *Pension Funding Relief: What's In It for My Plan?*, Nyhart Actuary & Employee Benefits (Aug. 15, 2014) (benefitslink.com); Groom Law Group Benefits Brief, *Extension of Pension Interest Rate Smoothing Relief Clears Congress Before August Recess*, <http://www.groom.com/media/publication/1444_Extension_of_Pension_Interest_Rate.pdf> (Aug. 1, 2014); Vipal Monga, *Welcome to the World of "Pension Smoothing,"* WSJ.com (Aug. 11, 2014)]

The higher the discount rate, the higher the growth rate over the annuity period, so the present value of a lump sum will be lower. A lower discount rate requires a higher lump sum. In a class action about the discount rates used by a pension plan to convert a straight life annuity to a lump sum, the Seventh Circuit ruled in 2013 that the pension plan's segment rate of approximately 5.4% was acceptable. Under the PPA, discount rates can be increased retroactively; this is not a cutback. The plan forbade reduction in accrued benefits (the value of the straight life annuity), it did not forbid a retroactive reduction in the benefits of participants who took a lump sum distribution. [*Dennison v. MONY Life Ret. Income Security Plan*, 710 F.3d 741 (7th Cir. 2013); see Brian Stolzenbach, Sam Schwartz-Fenwick and Chris Busey, *Seventh Circuit Reads Plan Language To Discount Plaintiffs' Rate Argument*, Seyfarth Shaw ERISA & Employee Benefits Litigation Blog (Mar. 20, 2013) (benefitslink.com)]

[J] Funding Changes

Rev. Procs. 2000-40 and -41, 2000-42 I.R.B. 357 and 371, provide the procedures under which the sponsor or administrator of a defined benefit plan subject to I.R.C. § 412 or ERISA § 302 can get the Secretary of the Treasury to approve a change in the plan's funding method under I.R.C. § 412(c)(5)(A)—e.g., changing the method of valuing assets, the plan year, or the valuation date.

The IRS has jurisdiction to review the appropriateness of any change that significantly affects the plan's minimum funding requirement or full funding limitation. The agency will approve a change in funding method only if the proposed new method and the form of the transition are both acceptable. The due date for a request is the end of the plan year in which the change will be effective. The

IRS has discretion to extend the due date by up to two and a half months if the plan submits a statement giving adequate reason for the delay.

[K] Minimum Funding Waivers

Waivers from the minimum funding standard are governed by Code § 412(c). The current (i.e., post-PPA) version allows a waiver of all or part of the minimum funding standard if the employer would not be able to satisfy the minimum funding standard without encountering temporary substantial business hardship—and the plan participants would be worse off if the plan were compelled to meet the standard. However, a plan cannot get waivers for more than three years in any 15-year period, and amounts attributable to a waived funding deficiency in one year cannot be waived in the next. For a single-employer plan, if a waiver is granted, the minimum required contribution under § 430 is reduced by the amount of funding deficiency that is waived; this amount is amortized under § 430(e).

Factors in determining whether the employer is undergoing temporary substantial business hardship include whether:

- The company is operating at a loss;
- The industry is experiencing substantial under- or unemployment;
- The industry's sales and profits are declining or already reduced;
- The waiver is the only way for the plan to continue.

The plan can be required to give security for the waiver, to be enforced by the PBGC. The waiver application must be made not later than the fifteenth day of the third month beginning after the end of the plan year. The company applying for the waiver must prove that it has notified affected parties (e.g., plan participants and beneficiaries) of the application. The notice must be given within 14 days before the date of the application for the waiver, and must disclose the sponsor's name; the year for which the waiver is requested; the FMV of plan assets; the present value of vested benefits under the plan; the present value of all benefits if the plan terminated; and the interest rate used in the calculations. Plan participants and beneficiaries must be informed that they can get a copy of the plan's latest annual report, and can submit comments about the waiver application. [IRS EP Examination Process Guide § 9, <http://www.irs.gov/retirement/article/0,,id= 135804,00.html>]

Plans that have obtained a waiver are not permitted to adopt amendments that increase benefits, change accrual of benefits, or change vesting schedules—unless the amendment is required for compliance, repeals another amendment that would be problematic, or is reasonable and has only a minimal effect on plan liabilities.

See 78 Fed. Reg. 20039 (Apr. 3, 2013) for PBGC proposals greatly reducing the number of situations in which "reportable events" must be reported to the PBGC, but application for a minimum funding waiver would continue to be a reportable event.

[L] Pension Freezes

As of mid-2012, 47% of corporate defined benefit plans were still active and open to new hires; a further 24% were closed to new entrants, but existing participants continued to accrue benefits. (Thus, according to SEI's Pension Lifecycle Meter, 71% of participants continued to accrue benefits.) One percent of plans were terminating; 28% of plans were frozen but had not commenced the process of termination. [Rebecca Moore, *Majority of DB Participants Still Accruing Benefits*, plansponsor.com (June 13, 2012)]

As research by The Center for Retirement Research at Boston College shows, since the mid-2000s, pension freezes have been common even in plans maintained by companies that are financially sound. Previously, it was very rare for defined benefit plans to be frozen, and then usually in association with bankruptcy or serious financial problems. The researchers attributed the increased acceptability of freezes to:

1. Reducing workers' compensation to be able to compete in the global market.
2. Cutting back pensions because health costs had soared.
3. Financial risks (such as stock market exposure) that made funding defined benefit plans unattractive.
4. Upper management's lack of interest in rank-and-file pensions because so much of their compensation came from nonqualified plans.

The researchers identified three forms of plan freezes:

1. Closing the plan to new hires;
2. A partial freeze that covers new hires and some current employees; or
3. A total freeze that affects all employees.

Towers Watson research shows that more than 70% of companies that still enroll new hires in their pension plan expect to continue doing so five years from now. However, among those that have frozen their plans, almost 40% expect to terminate the plan and settle its liabilities within five years. Fifty-eight percent have made or expect to make lump sum payouts to resolve pension obligations, and 87% of companies expecting to terminate the plan expect to use lump sum offers as part of the process. Half of survey respondents already had a plan in place to reduce pension risk by moving to fixed-income investments as the plan's funded status improves, and another quarter plan to do so in 2014 or perhaps 2015. Only about 30% of respondents still had open pension plans—73% of them said that it was important for recruiting, 87% for employee retention. [James Willhite, *Pension Terminations May Spike in the Near-Term*, WSJ.com (Nov. 12, 2013)]

Whether it is more cost effective to terminate or immunize a frozen defined benefit plan depends on factors such as how much it would cost to buy annuities for the participants and how much management time is needed to administer the plan. (Immunization means buying assets to secure benefit payments, such as long-term, high-rated bonds that generate income in amounts and at the time needed to pay benefits.) The PPA, by allowing plan sponsors to make lump-sum calculations based on higher interest rates, reduces the size of lump sum payments, and, therefore, makes it easier to terminate plans than under prior law.

The demographics of the plan's participants greatly affects the decision. In most plans, liability is fairly equal for active participants, ex-employees who terminated when they had vested benefits, and retirees. A young plan is one where liabilities are concentrated on funding future benefits for active employees; a mature plan already has a high volume of retirees receiving benefits. The authors of the article concluded that termination is probably less expensive than immunization in a young plan, but costs are fairly similar for termination and immunization in either a typical or a mature plan.

When a plan terminates, it is common for retirees to want to keep their annuities, but active participants and terminated vested participants often opt for lump sums. [Nathan Zahm and R. Evan Inglis, *Frozen Pension Plans: Is Immunization or Termination the Right Choice?* Vanguard, <https://www.vanguardfrance.fr/content/documents/Articles/Insights/frozen-pension-plans.pdf> (November 2012)]

Notice 2014-5, 2014-2 I.R.B. 276 provides temporary relief for meeting the § 401(a)(4) nondiscrimination requirements when a defined benefit plan has been closed to new hires. In a "soft freeze," new hires cannot join the plan, but accruals continue for those hired before the freeze. The employer might adopt a new defined contribution plan for new hires, or enhance an existing plan. Eventually, however, the defined benefit plan might fail § 410(b) coverage testing because there is more turnover among non-HCEs than among HCEs, so the frozen defined benefit plan has to be aggregated with the defined contribution plan to satisfy coverage requirements. If the plans are aggregated for coverage testing, they must also be aggregated for nondiscrimination testing on the basis of equivalent benefits. The aggregated plan must be primarily defined benefit in character, and must either consist of separate plans that are broadly available, or satisfy the minimum aggregate allocation gateway (comparing the minimum aggregated normal allocation rate for non-HCEs to the rate for HCEs). Many defined contribution plans cannot meet this test. Notice 2014-5 provides temporary relief for plan years beginning before January 1, 2016, as long as the defined benefit plan was amended to exclude new hires before December 13, 2013. The defined benefit plan must be part of an aggregated plan that either was primarily defined benefit in character, or passed nondiscrimination testing without aggregation, for the plan year that began in 2013. [Paul Hamburger and Lisa A. Berkowtz Herrnson, *IRS Issues Temporary Non-Discrimination Testing Relief for Closed Defined Benefit Plans and Request for Comments*, Proskauer's ERISA Practice Center Blog (Dec. 20, 2013) (benefitslink.com); Rebecca Moore, *IRS Provides Nondiscrimination Relief for Closed DBs*, plansponsor.com (Dec. 17, 2013)]

[M] The Annual Funding Notice

Most plans that are subject to PBGC jurisdiction must provide participants and beneficiaries with annual funding notices—the document that replaced the SAR. PPA § 501(a) amended ERISA § 101(f) to require all PBGC-insured defined benefit plans to provide an annual funding notice to each participant and beneficiary, any unions for the workplace, and to the PBGC. Defined benefit plans that are not subject to the PBGC's jurisdiction (e.g., government plans; church plans; plans of professional service employers with 25 or fewer employees) must still file the SAR.

The annual funding notice must be provided to each participant, beneficiary, union, and the PBGC. The DOL will not take action against single-employer plans with liabilities under $50 million for failure to give notice to the PBGC, as long as they respond to the PBGC's request for the information within 30 days. [See 74 Fed. Reg. 17 (Jan. 2, 2009) for the EBSA final rule imposing civil penalties of up to $1,000 per day for each violation of ERISA § 101 or 514(e)(3) committed by not furnishing the annual funding notice, and 75 Fed. Reg. 70625 (Nov. 18, 2010).]

The 2012 pension funding relief bill, MAP-21 (Pub. L. No. 112-141), requires some plans to provide additional information in their annual funding notices. The requirement applies to plans that had at least 50 participants at any time in the previous year; the stabilized funding target is less than 95% than the regular funding target; and, without the relief provided by MAP-21, the plan would have a funding shortfall of $500,000 or more. Plans subject to the requirement must disclose that the law has changed, reducing the employer's required contributions. The funding notice must include a table showing the effect of the law on required contributions and the funding shortfall.

Notice 2012-46, 2012-3 I.R.B. 86, effective November 1, 2012, gives the ERISA § 101(j) notice requirements for single-employer plans subject to benefit limitations under § 436. When the funding status of a single-employer plan falls below a certain level, the administrator has 30 days to provide notice to participants and beneficiaries. The DOL regulations provide that noncompliance can be penalized by up to $1,000 per day for each participant who should have been notified. Notice 2012-46 requires the notice to be understandable by the average participant, containing the plan name, EIN, plan number, and a general description of the payment limitation. The prohibited benefits must be described in detail. The notice must explain when the limitation will cease to apply (e.g., when the AFTAP rises to at least 80%). If the limit is no longer in effect and participants can access distributions that were formerly prohibited, then the plan administrator must send a § 101(j) notice to participants no later than 30 days after the limitations no longer apply. The § 101(j) notice must be in writing and can be given electronically if this is reasonably accessible to the notice recipients. [McGuireWoods LLP, *IRS Provides Guidance on Notices for Funding-Related Pension Plan Benefit Limitations* (Aug. 28, 2012) (benefitslink.com)]

§ 5.06 BENEFIT ACCRUALS

Another issue in plan administration and compliance is the schedule on which benefits are contributed on the individual's behalf, being added to the pension account so that eventually the participant will receive his or her defined benefit. Vesting is a separate but related concept. Vesting determines the extent to which employees will be entitled to receive the accrued benefit when they retire or employment otherwise terminates.

Defined benefit plans must accrue benefits using one of the three permitted mechanisms:

1. The 3% rule: at all times, the accrued benefit must be at least 3% of the maximum benefit calculated under the plan's formula, multiplied by the number of years of participation.
2. The 133.5% test: the accrued benefit payable at Normal Retirement Age equals the normal retirement benefit, and accrual in any plan year does not exceed 133.5% of the accrual for any prior year. In other words, benefits must accrue in a fairly level manner in each year.
3. The fractional rule: the annual benefit an employee has accrued at the time of separation from service must be proportionate to what he or she would have received by remaining employed until normal retirement age.

Under § 412(i), insured plans whose accrued benefit is always at least equal to the cash surrender value of the insurance are exempt from the minimum funding rules.

The Second Circuit ruled in early 2006 that Xerox unlawfully reduced the pension benefits of persons who left the company and were rehired. Xerox used a "phantom account offset" system under which the lump sum received when the individual left the company for the first time was used to cut the benefits at eventual retirement. The Second Circuit ruled that a plan amendment occurs not when the plan administrator changes the way the plan operates, but when the employees are properly informed of the change. The court ruled that proper information was not provided until 1998, so applying it to anyone who was rehired before that date would be a violation of the anti-cutback rule. [*Frommert v. Conkright*, 433 F.3d 254 (2d Cir. 2006); the same offset method was also disapproved in *Miller v. Xerox Corp.*, 464 F.3d 871 (9th Cir. 2006), *cert. denied*, Mar. 19, 2007]. In its April 21, 2010 decision in this case [559 U.S. 506], the Supreme Court strongly affirmed the powers of plan administrators. According to the Supreme Court, the basic principle comes from *Firestone Tire & Rubber v. Bruch* [489 U.S. 101]. As long as the plan documents give the administrators the power to interpret the plan, courts must uphold the plan administrator's interpretation of plan terms as long as it is not unreasonable. The Supreme Court said that this principle is necessary to carry out ERISA's intention of making plan administration uniform and predictable. The Supreme Court sent the case back to the Second Circuit, which sent it back to the District Court for the Western District of New York. In December 2013, the Second Circuit held that the suit was meritorious. The proposed offset method was unreasonable and the SPD was not accurate because it did not clearly disclose that the lump sum distribution would reduce benefits. [*Frommert v. Conkright*, 738 F.3d 522 (2d Cir. 2013); see Kevin McGuinness, *Appellate Court Remands Case on Offsetting Pension Benefits*, plansponsor.com (Dec. 31, 2013)]

A mid-2012 Fourth Circuit decision holds that increased benefit accruals to participants who have reached normal retirement age (NRA) do not violate the prohibition against backloading in later years. The 133 1/3% test forbids accrual of benefits more than 1/3 greater than the annual rate of accrual in the previous year. The rule was adopted to prevent employers from offering inadequate accrual rates in the early years of employment (when turnover is highest). In this case, the NRA was defined as the earlier of age 64 or 60 months of vesting service. The Fourth Circuit held that ERISA anti-backloading rules no longer apply once the participant reaches NRA. [*McCorkle v. Bank of Am. Corp.*, 688 F.3d 164 (4th Cir. 2012)]

§ 5.07 NOTICES OF REDUCTION OF BENEFIT ACCRUALS

Defined benefit plans (and other plans subject to the I.R.C. § 412 full funding rules) have an obligation under ERISA § 204(h) and I.R.C. § 4980F (a new provision added by EGTRRA) to provide notice of plan amendments that significantly reduce future benefit accruals. The notice must contain the text or a summary of the plan amendment, and the effective date of the amendment. Notice must be given at least 15 days before the effective date of the plan amendment. [See the JCWAA § 411(u) for technical corrections to this provision]

Not only is an excise tax imposed on the failure, but in "egregious" cases (where the employer intentionally refused to give notice, or failed very badly to disclose the needed information) the plan amendment will not be given effect.

Therefore, participants will be entitled to the unreduced benefit that was in effect before the plan was amended. See T.D. 9052, RIN-1545-BA08 2003-19 I.R.B. 879. The plan is required to provide notice to plan participants when the rate of future accrual is significantly reduced, or when an early retirement subsidy is modified in a way that operates as a reduction in the rate of future benefit accruals.

In general, the notice must be given at least 45 days before the effective date of the change, but the notice can be as short as 15 days before the effective date for certain merger and acquisition-related transactions of small plans. Also in connection with mergers and acquisitions, where there is a plan-to-plan transfer or merger that affects only the early retirement benefit or subsidy, notice can be given after the effective date of the amendment, but no more than 30 days later.

The notice must be given in a form that is understandable to the average plan participant, providing enough information to understand the effect of the amendment. Excise tax penalties are imposed under ERISA § 204(h)(6) for failure to provide the required notice. See also T.D. 9219, 2005-38 I.R.B. 538.

The Pension Funding Equity Act of 2004, Pub. L. No. 108-218, provides that certain employers who are required to make additional contributions under I.R.C. § 412(l) can elect instead to make lower "alternative deficit reduction contributions" for certain plan years. This relief is available to commercial passenger airlines, steel mills, and 501(c)(5) organizations.

It is not necessary to give participants a § 204(h) notice with respect to PPA amendments reflecting mandatory changes in interest rates or mortality assumptions. Nor is a 204(h) notice required for changes to benefits that are not protected benefits, or to protected benefits that can be altered in accordance with § 411(d)(6), or for adoption of a retroactive amendment to comply with PPA § 1107. [T.D. 9472, 2009-51 I.R.B. 850]

Code § 4980F(e)(3) requires notice to be provided within a reasonable time before the plan amendment takes effect. In general, that means 45 days before the effective date (15 days for small or multi-employer plans). However, for some amendments that took effect by December 31, 2008, notice is acceptable if given at least 30 days before the effective date. T.D. 9472 covers amendments required by the PPA's special funding rules for airlines, and for single-employer plans with certain funding shortfalls. Unpredictable contingent event benefits are limited if a plan's AFTAP is, or would be, under 60%, and amendments increasing the plan's liabilities because of a benefits increase are limited if the AFTAP would be under 80%. Certain payments are prohibited when AFTAP is in the 60–80% range; the sponsor is in Chapter 11; and the plan's actuary cannot certify that AFTAP is at least 100%. Benefit accruals cease when AFTAP falls below 60%. [Transamerica Center for Retirement Studies, TCRS 2009-15: *IRS Issues Final Guidance on Section 204(h) Notice Requirements Post PPA* (Dec. 9, 2009) (benefitslink.com)]

The First Circuit held that it was permissible for an employer to eliminate participants' option to move defined contribution plan assets to a defined benefit plan. Although an accrued benefit was diminished, the anti-cutback rule was not violated because ERISA permits this type of benefit to be eliminated. [*Tasker v. DHL Ret. Savings Plan*, 621 F.3d 34 (1st Cir. 2010); see Fred Schneyer, *Interplan Asset Transfer Elimination Upheld*, plansponsor.com (Oct. 7, 2010)]

The Eleventh Circuit, noting that Social Security integration (reducing the benefit to coordinate the Social Security benefits the participant receives) is permitted by 29 U.S.C. § 1056(b)), held that it did not violate the anti-cutback rule for a frozen plan to adopt amendments that changed the Social Security integration formula for people who had not yet reached the plan's early retirement age. The change could not affect future benefit accruals because the plan was frozen and there would be no more benefit accruals. The test of an accrued benefit is what a participant would receive by terminating employment at that point, and the plaintiff here was younger than 52, the earliest age at which benefits were available. The right to a future benefit accrual based on additional service is not an accrued benefit, so changing it does not violate the anti-cutback rule. [*Cinotto v. Delta Air Lines Inc.*, 674 F.3d 1285 (11th Cir. 2012)]

In late 2012, the IRS finalized regulations under the § 411(d)(6) anti-cutback rules effective for plan amendments adopted and effective after November 8, 2012. Single-employer defined benefit plans that are subject to ERISA § 4021 can be amended to eliminate lump sum or other optional forms of benefit that accelerate payment after bankruptcy. The PBGC and the Bankruptcy Court must agree that the plan would go through a distress or involuntary termination if the optional benefits are not eliminated. The PBGC must also determine that the plan is not sufficiently funded to provide the guaranteed benefits. If an optional benefit form is eliminated, and the plan does not have other options with substantial survivor benefits, the same amendment that eliminates the lump sum distribution option can also adopt other options to provide survivor benefits. The entire amendment is considered together in determining if the amendment can take effect in accordance with § 436(c). [T.D. 9601, 77 Fed. Reg. 66915 (Nov. 8, 2012), finalizing proposals at 77 Fed. Reg. 37349 (June 21, 2012); see Kristen Heinzinger, *IRS Finalizes Relief for Bankrupt DB Sponsors*, plansponsor.com (Nov. 8, 2012)]

For example, the bankruptcy court permitted American Airlines to eliminate optional lump sum and installment forms of benefit payments, on the grounds that so many pilots would retire if they could get a lump sum when the airline emerges from bankruptcy that it would be difficult to adequately staff the schedule. [Rebecca Moore, *American Allowed to Eliminate Lump Sums*, plansponsor.com (Dec. 14, 2012)]

§ 5.08 PBGC COMPLIANCE

[A] PBGC Organization

Formally speaking, the Pension Benefit Guarantee Corporation (PBGC) is organized as a corporation, but it's really a quasi-governmental agency that draws its powers from ERISA § 4002. The PBGC's Board of Directors consists of the Secretaries of Labor, Treasury, and Commerce. The federal court system gives the agency special deference, by giving its cases the earliest possible calendar dates. Employers sued by the PBGC in connection with a plan termination can be required to pay part or all of the agency's litigation costs.

The PBGC's deficit increased to $36 billion in fiscal 2013, largely as a result of the worsening financial condition of multi-employer plans. The deficit for the multi-employer program rose from $5.2 billion (2013) to $8.2 billion (2013). The deficit for the single-employer program, which insures almost 32 million workers and retirees in 23,000 private-sector plans, was reduced from $29.1 billion in 2012 to $27.4 billion in 2013. In fiscal 2013, the PBGC insured the pensions of almost 32 million workers and retirees in 23,000 plans. In 2013, major companies such as Eastman Kodak Co. and the Tribune Co. emerged from bankruptcy with intact plans, benefiting 161,000 people. [PBGC.gov press release, *PBGC's Deficit Increases to $36 Billion as Multiemployer Risks Grow* (Nov. 13, 2013); Plansponsor staff, *PBGC Deficit Grows to $36B*, plansponsor.com (Nov. 18, 2013)]

The main task of the PBGC is to guarantee that participants in defined benefit plans will receive a basic benefit even if their plan is insufficiently funded, or if it is terminated.

[B] PBGC Premiums

The PBGC stays afloat by charging premiums to employers who maintain defined benefit plans. There are three types of premium: the flat-rate premium; the variable-rate premium (VRP) imposed on insured single-employer plans that have unfunded vested benefits; and a one-time termination premium In recent years, premiums have increased significantly, not only administratively but under the Moving Ahead for Progress in the 21st Century Act (MAP-21; Pub. L. No. 112-141) and the Bipartisan Budget Act of 2013, Pub. L. No. 113-67.

An additional premium of $1,250 per participant is imposed when a single-employer plan is terminated under ERISA § 4041(c)(2)(B) or 4042. If the plan is terminated while the sponsor's Chapter 11 bankruptcy case is pending, the special premium is not due until the sponsor's bankruptcy discharge or until the bankruptcy case is dismissed.

The flat rate PBGC premium for 2014 is $49/participant for single-employer plans ($7 more than the 2013 level), $12/participant for multi-employer plans (no change). The variable rate premium for single-employer plans rises from $9 to $14 per $1,000 of unfunded vested benefit, reflecting both indexing and the $4 increase provided by MAP-21. The cap on the variable premium rises from $400 (2013) to $412 (2014), although the cap may be lower for plans with fewer than 25 participants. [Sarah Roe Sise and Carrie Elizabeth Byrnes, *PBGC Premium Rates Increase In 2014 For Single-Employer Plans Time To Cash-Out Some Deferred Vested Participants?*, Bryan Cave LLP (Nov. 15, 2013), available at Lexology.com]

Under the Bipartisan Budget Act of 2013 (signed December 26, 2013), the proposed flat rate premium is $57/participant, the variable rate is $14/$1,000 UVB, with a cap of at least $412. For 2016, the proposed flat rate is $64, the variable rate at least $29, and the proposed cap $500, with those figures to be indexed in 2017. [Buck Consultants FYI, *PBGC Premium Hikes in Final Budget Deal*, Vol. 36 Issue 105 (Dec. 27, 2013) (benefitslink.com)]

A PBGC final rule was adopted in 2008, explaining how to measure the unfunded vested benefits used to calculate the variable-rate premium. The PPA increased the number of plans subject to the VRP, because it eliminated the exemption for satisfying the full funding limitation if the plan fails to meet the funding target. The calculation of the Unfunded Vested Benefit (UVB) uses the fair market value of the plan assets on the valuation date, excluding the employer's current year contributions. However, assets are not reduced by the plan's credit balances. [PBGC Final Rule, 73 Fed. Reg. 15065 (Mar. 21, 2008) The PBGC premium is charged for each participant, terminated vested participant, and beneficiary already receiving benefits, other than "lost" beneficiaries (the plan knows they may be entitled to benefits, but can't find them) for whom an insurance company has an irrevocable commitment to pay all the benefits. All defined benefit plans that are subject to PBGC insurance must file Form PBGC-1 each year as a combined annual report and declaration of premium payments.

The premium is paid with Form 1-ES (if the plan has more than 500 participants) or with Form 10-SP (short form for smaller plans). The contributing sponsor and the plan administrator are both liable for the PBGC premium. If the premium is not paid on time, interest runs from the due date, plus a late charge of 5% per month (capped at 100% of the original unpaid premium). The PBGC is also empowered to collect unpaid premiums from what would otherwise be the employer's federal tax refund. If the employer is a federal contractor, the PBGC can seize federal contract payments.

■ **TIP:** The forms are available online as PDF files. [See <http://www.pbgc.gov/practitioners/premium-filings/content/page1142.html>]

The PBGC proposed a new procedure, to take effect in 2014, that would make it easier for employers to administer the payment process. Prior law set the premium due date based on the size of the plan (small—under 100 participants; medium, 100–499 participants, large, over 500 participants) as well as on the type of premium. The proposal calls for a single, uniform due date, 9½ months after the beginning of the premium payment year, no matter what kinds of premiums are being paid or what size of the organization; for 2014, that would be October 15, 2014 for all premiums. As a result, small plans would have to pay both the 2013 and the 2014 premium in 2014. There are special rules for new plans and terminating plans. The proposal also affects the calculation of the VRP for some small plans. [Buck Consultants FYI, *PBGC Proposes New Premium Rules for 2014*, <http://www.buckconsultants.com/portals/0/publications/fyi/2013/FYI-2013-0725-PBGC-proposes-new-premium-rules-2014.pdf> (July 25, 2013)] The rules were finalized in March 2014. The PBGC allows small plans until 2015 to conform to the new schedule. Small plans are also permitted to use either current-year or prior-year figures to compute the variable-rate premium. (Some small plans determine their funding levels late in the year, so they do not have current year figures available at the new due date.)

The final premium for a terminating plan is due no later than the filing of the post-distribution certificate. This rule was adopted because the final premium was sometimes forgotten in standard terminations, when the due date was months later than the plan closed its books. Furthermore, plans will generally be exempt from the variable rate premium for the year in which a standard termination is completed and small plans may be exempt from the variable rate premium for the first year of coverage.

The late premium payment penalty is 1% per month for plans that self-correct and 5% for month for those that do not self-correct; the PBGC's intention is to encourage self-correction. However, before the 2014 rules, both penalties were subject to a cap of 100% of the underpayment. To favor self-correction, the PBGC is changing the cap on the 1% penalty to 50% of the underpayment. The September 2011 policy (that payments made not more than seven days late will not be penalized) has been codified in regulations. [79 Fed. Reg. 13547 (Mar. 11, 2014); see Rebecca Moore, *PBGC Finalizes Premium Changes*, plansponsor.com (Mar. 10, 2014). See also RIN 1212-AB26, 79 Fed. Reg. 347 (Jan. 3, 2014); see Segal, *PBGC Eliminates Early Flat-Rate Premium Payment Requirement for Large Plans, Including Multiemployer Plans* (Feb. 3, 2014) (benefitslink.com); Kevin McGuinness, *PBGC Moves Premium Date for Large Plans*, plansponsor.com (Jan. 2, 2014)]

If a premium is paid after the due date, the PBGC sends the plan a bill, called a Statement of Account (SOA), covering interest and penalty charges. The SOA is an invoice. To prevent additional interest and penalties from accruing the SOA must be paid within 30 days. Even if the plan has an extension, interest and penalties are computed as of the original due date. The PBGC can also assess penalties for failure to submit premium-related information on a timely basis. Late payments are subject to interest at the rate set by ERISA; the IRS publishes the rates quarterly. Plans can request a waiver of the penalty for up to 60 days by applying to the PBGC within 60 days after the due date and demonstrating substantial hardship. The PBGC can reconsider penalties if there was a reasonable cause for failure to make a complete, timely payment—e.g., the failure was beyond the plan's control and could not have been avoided by ordinary care and prudence. But the PBGC cannot waive the premium itself or reduce the interest rate. [PBGC, *Late Payment Charges*, <http://www.pbgc.gov/prac/prem/late-payment-charges.html> (accessed Apr. 4, 2014)]

In September 2011, the PBGC relieved defined benefit plan sponsors from certain penalties when the required annual premium payments are not made on time. Under ERISA § 4007 and 29 C.F.R. Part 4007, interest and penalties are applied when the annual premium payments are not made on time. But for plan years beginning after 2010, the PBGC automatically waives payment penalties imposed solely because of lateness of up to seven calendar days. [76 Fed. Reg. 57082 (Sept. 15, 2011); see Rebecca Moore, *PBGC Offers Relief to DB Plan Sponsors*, plansponsor.com (Sept. 14, 2011)]

The IRS' Employee Plans Compliance Unit (EPCU) launched a Form 5500 non-filer project late in 2011, sending compliance check letters to plan sponsors for whom there is no record of a 5500 or 5500-SF filing with the DOL, or 5500-EZ with the IRS after six to nine months have elapsed since the due date of the return. EPCU asks the sponsor to either file the return or explain why it was not necessary. If a form was required, the IRS sends out a CP 403 Notice (delinquency notice) seeking a response within 30 days. EPCU does not analyze whether employers' explanations for nonfiling are reasonable, although the IRS or the DOL may waive or reduce penalties on a showing of mitigating circumstances that reduced the plan's ability to file the return. [IRS Employee Plans News, Issue 2011-7 (Oct. 12, 2011); see CCH Pension & Benefits, *EPCU Begins Form 5500 Non-Filer Project* (Nov. 15, 2011) (benefitslink.com)]

A plan's failure to make a timely Form 5500 annual report filing can be penalized under both the Code and ERISA. Previous IRS guidance said that correcting the late filing under the DOL's DFVC program could relieve the plan of both IRS and DOL penalties. However, the IRS announced in mid-2014 that avoiding IRS penalties requires a separate filing. This requirement applies retroactively to all DFVC filings made since 2009. Before 2009, plan administrators reported about terminated participants with vested benefits on Form 5500, Schedule SSA. The IRs's transition to electronic filing included replacing Schedule SSA with Form 8955-SSA, which is filed only with the IRS. In 2013, the DOL required e-filing of all DFVC reports using the EFAST2 program. At that point, DOL stopped accepting Form 8955-SSA, with the result that the information that the IRS requires no longer can be submitted under the DFVC program.

IRs's Notice 2014-32 creates a relief program for years in which the plan administrator satisfies the DFVC requirements, and also files a complete Form 8955-SSA for the year no later than December 1, 2014—or 30 days after the DFVC filing. However, the Form 8955-SSA filed for this purpose must be on paper, not electronic. [Notice 2014-35 , 2014- . . . . I.R.B. . . . ; see Lawrence Jenab, *Additional Action Required By Late Filers Of Form 5500 (Even Those That Have Already Filed*, Spencer Fane Britt & Browne (May 27, 2014), available at Lexology.com. Notice 2014-35 does not apply to Form 5500-EZ or 5500-SF filers, because those forms are filed by non-ERISA plans; but see Rev. Proc. 2014-32, 2014- . . . I.R.B. . . . for a one-year pilot project, running from June 2, 2014 to June 2, 2015, providing relief in those situations. See Thomas E. Funk et al., *IRS Issues New Relief From Form 5500 Series Late Filer Penalties For Certain Employee Benefit Plans*, Reinhart Boerner Van Deuren SC (June 16, 2014), available at Lexology.com.]

All premium information required by ERISA § 4007 must now be e-filed. The plan can file by entering data directly into MyPAA, by uploading data from proprietary software, or by importing data into the MyPAA data entry screens from approved software. MyPAA accepts credit cards, electronic checks, and Automated Clearing House transfers; payments can also be made outside MyPAA. [<http://edocket.access.gpo.gov/2006/pdf/E6-8433.pdf> (no www), 71 Fed. Reg. 31077 (June 1, 2006)]

Electronic filing of Form 5500 and Form 5500-SF (the small plan form), using the EFAST-2 system (the system maintained by the DOL, the IRS, and the PBGC for electronic filing of Form 5500 and Form 5500-SF) has been mandatory since January 1, 2010. To file electronically, the sponsor or the person designated by the sponsor must use either IFILE, a free web-based filing application available at <http://www.efast.dol.gov>, or third-party software that has been approved by the DOL. [Seyfarth.com, *Mandatory Electronic Filing of 5500s to Begin in 2010* (Sept. 30, 2009) (benefitslink.com); [EBSA, *Annual Return/Report 5500 Series Forms and Instructions*, <http://www.dol.gov/ebsa/5500main.html>]

Under proposed regulations effective for plan years beginning on or after January 1, 2014, administrators of plans such as 401(k)s would have to file Form 5500 and Form 8955-SSA electronically or on specified magnetic media if the employer files at least 240 returns of any type, including income tax returns, W-2 and 1099 forms, and employment tax returns. The proposals deal with the tax requirements, which are separate from the ERISA reporting requirements. Failure to file electronically when this is mandatory is considered a failure to file, so the penalty is $25/day up to a maximum of $15,000 for Form 5500. According to EBIA, the proposals do not impose significant changes, because DOL already requires Forms 5500 and 5500-SF to be e-filed and Form 8955-SSA could already be e-filed with IRS's FIRE system. But the e-filing obligation has been extended to the limited number of 5500-EZ filers who are required to file more than 250 returns a year. [*Employee Retirement Benefit Plan Returns Required on Magnetic Media*, 26 C.F.R. Part 301, 78 Fed. Reg. 53704 (Aug. 30, 2013); see EBIA Weekly, *IRS Proposed Regulations Would Require Electronic Filing for Certain Retirement Plan Reporting* (Sept. 5, 2013) (benefitslink.com)]

[C] Accounting Issues

On the fifteenth of every month, the PBGC updates its Website [<http://www.pbgc.gov/practitioners/interest-rates/content/index.html>] to give the interest rates that should be used in that month for:

- Valuation of lump-sum payments made by the plan;
- Variable rate premiums;
- Valuation of annuity benefits;
- PBGC charges imposed with respect to employer liability, unpaid contributions, and unpaid premiums.

PBGC staff can be reached by e-mail to answer compliance questions about:

- Premium calculations and payments: premiums@pbgc.gov;
- Coverage and standard terminations: standard@pbgc.gov;
- Distress terminations: distress.term@pbgc.gov;
- Early warning program: advance.report@pbgc.gov;
- ERISA § 4010 reporting: ERISA.4010@pbgc.gov;
- Reportable events: post-event.report@pbgc.gov;
- General legal questions: AskOGC@pbgc.gov;
- Problem resolution officer: practitioner.pro@pbgc.gov;
- Other: Ask.PBGC@pbgc.gov.

§ 5.09 REPORTABLE EVENTS

The PBGC doesn't want to be caught by surprise when a plan fails. To this end, plan administrators have a duty to report unusual events to the PBGC that might eventually require the agency to take over payment of pensions. Depending on the seriousness of the event, the PBGC might merely maintain a watchful attitude; or it might seek the appointment of a temporary trustee to manage the plan, or even go to the appropriate federal District Court to seek authority to terminate the plan.

The PBGC regulations identify 19 reportable events. Some of them must be reported 30 days before the event is scheduled to occur; others may be reported after the fact. The events include the following:

- The plan's bankruptcy or insolvency;
- The sponsoring employer's liquidation, bankruptcy or insolvency;
- Notice from the IRS that the plan has ceased to be a qualified retirement plan;
- IRS determination that the plan has terminated or partially terminated;
- Failure to meet the minimum funding standard;

- Receiving a minimum funding waiver from the IRS;
- Inability to pay benefits as they come due;
- DOL determination that the plan fails to comply with ERISA Title I;
- Adoption of a plan amendment that decreases any participant's retirement benefit (except for certain decreases relating to integration with Social Security);
- A reduction in the number of active participants in the plan, to the extent that the number is less than 80% of the census at the beginning of the year or 75% of the number of active participants at the beginning of the preceding plan year;
- Distributing $10,000 or more to a participant who is a "substantial owner" (a definition roughly equal to 10% shareholder in the employer corporation) if the plan has any unfunded, nonforfeitable benefits after the distribution. Distributions made on account of the death of the substantial owner are not counted for this purpose;
- Merger or consolidation of the plan, or transfer of its assets;
- DOL requirement of an alternative method of compliance under ERISA § 110;
- A change of plan sponsor (or the same plan sponsor leaving a controlled group of corporations), if the plan has $1 million or more in unfunded nonforfeitable benefits;
- The controlling sponsor, or a member of its controlled group, engages in a highly unusual transaction, such as declaring an extraordinary dividend or redeeming 10% or more of its stock;

At one time, the sponsoring employer had a duty to report the events to the plan administrator, but now it is only required that the events be reported to the PBGC. ERISA § 4043 requires advance notice of liquidating bankruptcy, extraordinary dividends, transfer of 3% of plan liabilities, or leaving a controlled group of corporations. However, in 2013, the PBGC published proposals to greatly reduce reporting obligations.

In addition to the required report to the PBGC, whenever a defined benefit plan fails to satisfy the minimum funding standard, and there has been no waiver of minimum funding granted, then participants must be notified. Form 200 must be filed with the PBGC within 10 days of the time a failure to meet the minimum funding standard involves $1 million or more.

In late 2009, the PBGC proposed regulations to conform the agency's rules on reportable events (ERISA § 4043) to the PPA, adding two new reportable events (funding-based benefit limits; transfers to retiree health benefit accounts). [74 Fed. Reg. 61248 (Nov. 23, 2009)] The PBGC published final regulations under ERISA § 4010 on March 16, 2009 (reporting high levels of unfunded vested benefits). The 4010 filing is required so the PBGC will be aware of its potential liabilities if a significantly underfunded plan terminates. The PPA amended § 4010 by requiring a company to file if it fails the "gateway" test: that is, if the funding target attainment percentage of the plan (or any plan maintained by any member of its controlled group) falls below 80%. Filing may also be required when a plan gets a funding waiver, or fails to make the minimum contribution it was required to make. Plans must report their funding target attainment percentages and their funding targets (calculated as if the plan had been at risk for at least five years). To avoid having to make a 4010 filing, a sponsor can make additional contributions, bringing funding above the triggering 80% level. Reporting under § 4010 is not required if the shortfall for the entire controlled group is less than $15 million. [74 Fed. Reg. 11022 (Mar. 16, 2009)]

The 2009 rules were highly controversial and the PBGC has proposed to relax them. Technical Update 13-1 offers some small pension plans permanent relief from the provisions of the proposed amendments dealing with reportable events. The ERISA § 4034.25 waiver of the requirement of reporting missed quarterly contributions is extended for all years in which the plan either has fewer than 25 participants, or has between 25–100 participants and files a simplified notice with the PBGC. However, relief is not available if the quarterly contribution was missed as a result of the plan's financial inability to pay. The calculations for the variable rate premium are used to determine reporting requirements for the following year. [Mark Schulte, *Déjà Vu All Over Again: PBGC Extends Reportable Event Relief for 2013 and Beyond*, VIA Retirement Plan Blog (Jan. 30, 2013) (benefitslink.com)]

In April 2013, the PBGC published a new proposal, effective January 1, 2014, under which reporting obligations would be reduced significantly, so that financially sound plans would not have to report most of what would otherwise be reportable events. The PBGC estimated that over 90% of plans and sponsors would no longer have to make most reports. The proposal retains the Technical Update 13-1 relief (i.e., reporting of missed contributions is waived or reduced for plans with under 100 participants as long as the reason for missing the contribution was not inability to pay).

The 2013 proposal relieves "financially sound" plans and plan sponsors of the obligation to report, specifying five criteria for determining soundness. The most important factor is having a good credit rating from a commercial credit reporting company (e.g., Dun & Bradstreet) based on the company's ability to make timely debt repayment. Financially sound plans would not have to make a post-event report for most of the events already covered by a funding-based waiver—for example, an extraordinary dividend or stock redemption; reduction in active participants; or transfer of benefit liabilities.

The other four criteria are safe use of secured debt; two years of positive net income; two years without defaulting on a major loans; and two years of keeping current on pension plan contributions (other than quarterly contributions for which the duty to report has been waived).

The April 2013 proposal includes another safe harbor: plans that were fully funded on a termination basis at the end of the previous year or 120% funded on a premium basis for the previous year would not have to report. Plans with fewer than 100 participants would be given an extra month to report events eligible for these safe harbors.

Small (fewer than 100 participants) plans would not have a reportable event based on the number of participants falling below 80% of the number at the end of the previous year or 75% of the number at the beginning of the previous year. Larger plans would only have to report if the reduction was caused by a single event such as reorganization or mass layoff; if the reduction occurred in a period of 30 days or less; or if the number of participants in the same year falls more than 20%. Large plans can use the financial soundness safe harbor to avoid reporting based on reduction in the number of participants.

The proposal says that there are other reporting obligations that let the PBGC know about a plan's liquidity levels, so reporting is waived for missed contributions that reflect inability to pay benefits when due—unless the plan is exempt from the liquidity shortfall provisions. But reporting is not waived for small plans or under the financial soundness safe harbor.

The requirement to report distributions to substantial owners made when the plan is not fully funded is triggered only when one substantial owner receives distributions that exceed 1% of plan assets or more than 5% of plan assets are distributed to multiple substantial owners.

Reporting is not required if there has been a reorganization within a controlled group of corporations leading to one member of the group ceasing to exist because it has been merged into another member of the group.

However, the proposal eliminates the funding-based waiver for reporting liquidation. Even small plans and plans that qualify for the financial soundness safe harbor must report if they are liquidated.

Prior law makes it a reportable event if 3% or more of a plan's benefit liabilities are transferred within a 12-month period. The proposed regulations make it clear that satisfying benefit liabilities by paying a lump sum or buying an annuity is not a transfer of benefit liabilities for this purpose.

Under the proposal, reporting continues to be required when the plan applies for a minimum funding waiver, and the small-plan and financial soundness safe harbors are not available.

Prior law made it a reportable event when there is a default in payment of over 30 days on a loan of $10 million or more—not only by the plan sponsor, but also by any member of a controlled group of corporations it belongs to. Written notice of default based on reduced cash reserves or a lender's acceleration of a loan is also a reportable event. The proposed regulations not only retain this requirement but also make it stronger: reporting is required when there is a loan acceleration or any kind of default, including a lender's waiver of its right to declare a default. Small plans and plans entitled to the financial soundness safe harbor must still report this event.

The proposed regulations eliminate the sponsor's bankruptcy as a reportable event, because there are many other reliable sources of bankruptcy information available to the PBGC. Reporting of insolvency is not waived for small plans or plans meeting the financial soundness safe harbor.

Only six reportable events remain: loan default; failure to make the required contributions; application for a funding waiver; inability to pay benefits as they come due; insolvency; and liquidation.

[78 Fed. Reg. 20039 (Apr. 3, 2013); see Rebecca Moore, *PBGC Proposed Reduced Reporting Obligations*, plansponsor.com (Apr. 2, 2013); Buck Consultants FYI, *PBGC Reproposes Reportable Event Rules* (Apr. 5, 2013) (benefitslink.com)]

The PBGC has proposed regulations [72 Fed. Reg. 68542 (Dec. 5, 2007)] about disclosures required for distress terminations and terminations initiated by the PBGC. Under ERISA §§ 4041 and 4042, participants and other affected parties are entitled to request information about a pending termination; the plan (or the PBGC, if the agency initiated the termination) must provide the information within 15 business days of the request. ERISA § 4071 imposes a penalty of up to $1,100 a day for failure to make timely disclosure. [Guest article, *PBGC Proposes Rules on New Termination Information Disclosure Requirements*, Deloitte's Washington Bulletin, <http://benefitslink.com/articles/washbull080122a.html> (Jan. 22, 2008)]

§ 5.10 SPECIAL RULES FOR AT-RISK PLANS

The PPA creates a new category, the "at-risk" plan. Plans with under 500 participants are exempt. The determination of risk assumes that all participants who are eligible for benefits in the current plan year or the following 10 years retire as soon as they can and opt for the subsidized early retirement benefit (the benefit with the highest present value of liabilities). A plan is at risk if, in the previous plan year, it was less than 80% funded using the general funding rules and less than 70% funded using the tougher actuarial assumptions for at-risk plans. The 80% requirement is phased in gradually between 2008 and 2011. Plans that were at risk for two of the previous four years must make their calculations subject to an added load factor of $700 per participant, 4% of the funding target and target normal cost.

For at-risk plans, the controls depend on the "adjusted funding target attainment percentage," the ratio of plan assets to the plan's funding target. The funding target is calculated as if the plan had purchased annuities for every participant who was not a Highly Compensated Employee for the two years before the year of the calculation.

At-risk plans are restricted vis-à-vis benefit increases, payments, accruals, and shutdown benefits. The plan cannot be amended to increase benefits if the adjusted funding target attainment percentage is lower than 80%, or if the amendment has the effect of reducing the percentage below 80%. An exemption is available if the plan sponsor makes additional contributions or provides security to bring the plan up to the 80% funding level. The rule is not applied during a plan's first five years in existence. Amendments that increase benefits under a formula that is not based on compensation, and where the increase is not more than the average wage increase for plan participants, are exempt. So are cost of living increases in flat-dollar plans.

If the plan's adjusted funding target attainment percentage is below 60%, or if it is below 100% and the sponsor is bankrupt, then benefits must be paid in life annuity rather than lump-sum form. (This restriction does not apply to plans that were frozen as of September 1, 2005, and continues frozen.) Plans whose adjusted funding target attainment percentage is somewhere between 60%–80% are allowed to make a one-time lump sum payment, limited to the present value of the maximum amount guaranteed by the PBGC to the participant, or 50% of what would otherwise be paid—whichever is smaller. When the adjusted funding target attainment percentage is below 60% (except in the first five years of a new plan's operations), all future benefit accruals must be frozen unless the sponsor makes contributions or gives security to bring the funding up to the 60% level. Shutdown benefits, and other benefits based on an unpredictable contingent event, are forbidden when the target attainment percentage—before or after payment of the benefit—is below 60%.

Plan participants must be notified if funding deficiencies result in restrictions on benefits.

The benefit restrictions do not apply if the plan is fully funded: that is, if they satisfy the percentage requirements of the PPA as modified by WRERA.

The PBGC publishes tables for defined benefit plans to use to administer the partial restrictions imposed on lump sums distributions from plans that fall in the range of 60%–80% funded. The PPA limits lump sums and other accelerated distributions to the lesser of 50% of the benefit otherwise payable or the present value of the participant's maximum guarantee from the PBGC.

For benefits with an annuity starting date in 2014, the present value of the PBGC's maximum guarantee ranges from $111,472 at age 24, to $137,179 at age 30, $161,327 at age 35, $209,553 at age 40, $337,939 at age 60, $414,485 at age 65, $1,090,293 at age 70, etc. [PBGC.gov, *Present Value of PBGC Maximum Guarantee*, <http://www.pbgc.gov/prac/mortality-retirement-and-pv-max-guarantee/present-guarantee.html>]

Notice 2012-70, 2012-51 I.R.B. 712 gives defined benefit plans additional time to comply with § 436. Previously, the deadline was the last day of the last plan year beginning on or after January 1, 2012. Under Notice 2012-70, the deadline for adopting the amendment is the latest of:

- The last day of the plan year for which the plan is first subject to § 436;
- The last day of the plan year beginning on or after January 1, 2013;
- The due date (including extensions) of the employer's tax return for the year that § 436 first applies to the plan.

Notice 2012-70 also extends the relief period for anti-cutback amendments. Sponsors submitting determination letter applications on or after February 1, 2013 for individually designed plans must adopt the § 436 amendment before submitting the application. Cycle B plans, whose filing is before February 1, 2013, are not subject to § 436. [McDermott Will & Emery, *IRS Extends Deadline for Defined Benefit Plans to Adopt Code Section 436 Amendments* (Dec. 13, 2012) (benefitslink.com)]

In March 2011, the PBGC proposed a rule under PPA § 403, making the phase-in period for guarantee of benefits that are contingent on an unpredictable contingent event begin no earlier than the date of the event. (The example used in the proposal is a plant shut-down.) The rule was necessary because PBGC's guarantee of new pension benefits and benefit increases phases in over a five-year period starting with the later of the date of adoption or the effective date of the change, so the PBGC wanted to protect itself against plans adding new benefits when they knew they were about to terminate. [ERISA § 4022(b)(8); see PBGC Proposed Rule RIN 1212-AB18, 76 Fed. Reg. 13304 (Mar. 11, 2011). See also PBGC Final Rule, 75 Fed. Reg. 33688 (June 15, 2010) providing that there is no guarantee of benefits earned between the time an employer files for bankruptcy and the date the PBGC takes over the plan; in a bankruptcy situation, benefits are guaranteed only if they were nonforfeitable as of the bankruptcy filing date.

The rule was finalized in May 2014. The final rule provides that an Unpredictable Contingent Event Benefit (UCEB) is a benefit payable solely because of an event like a plant shutdown, or a non-event occurrence (such as reaching an age or length of service) that triggers benefit eligibility. The PBGC determines the date of an Unpredictable Contingent Event by consideration of all facts and circumstances, including the plan provisions, the level of activity in the facility that is being shut down, and the permanence of the situation. The provisions of the plan determine whether the determination is made for the entire facility; on a participant-by-participant basis; or otherwise. Phasing in of a UCEB guarantee starts on the date the UCEB provision was adopted; the effective date of the provision; or the date of the event—whichever comes last. [79 Fed. Reg. 25667 (May 16, 2013); see Robert B. Wynne and James P. McElligott Jr., *Final Rule Issued on Phase-In of PBGC Guarantee for Shutdown Pensions*, McGuire Woods LLP (May 8, 2014), available at Lexology.com]

Some employers who downsized were pursued by the PBGC under ERISA § 4062(e), which gives the agency the power to require immediate escrow payments or posting of bond when cessation of operations results in separation from service of over 20% of participants in a defined benefit plan. Regulations were published in 2006, creating potential liability even on plans that did not terminate. The PBGC could demand that the plan purchase a bond or place funds in escrow to guarantee payments in case the plan later went through an involuntary or distress termination. Section 4062(e) had been on the books since 1974, but was seldom enforced until the 2006 regulations appeared. Additional regulations were proposed in 2010 expanding the definition of "substantial cessation of operations" and explaining the calculations involved. Under the 2010 proposal, the test of whether there has been cessation is whether the employer discontinues all significant activity in the furtherance of the purpose of the operation (maintenance and security are disregarded) and no longer conducts the operation at the facility on an ongoing basis. Section 4062(e) applies to cessation of operations at a facility even if the operation is continued or resumed by another employer at the same facility or another facility (e.g., when corporate assets are sold). [PBGC, *Liability for Termination of Single-Employer Plans; Treatment of Substantial Cessation of Operations*, FR Doc 2010-19695, RIN 1212-AB20, 75 Fed. Reg. 48283 (Aug. 10, 2010)]

In late 2012, the PBGC proposed to concentrate its enforcement efforts under § 4062(e) on the few plans that are at greatest risk. Under the new policy, the PBGC would not take action under § 4062(e) against small (fewer than100 participants) or credit-worthy companies. The PBGC responded to business criticism that the August 2010 proposals subjected companies to enforcement action even though there was little real risk of default. [R. Randall Tracht, Brian J. Dougherty, Lisa H. Barton, and Eric P. Sarabia, *PBGC Changes Enforcement Policy Under ERISA Section 4062(e)* Morgan, Lewis & Bockius (Nov. 13, 2012) (benefitslink.com)]

In mid-2014, the PBGC announced a moratorium on § 4062(e) enforcement, until the end of 2014. The PBGC said it would use the time to work with stakeholders to determine when pensions are genuinely at risk. The PBGC directed businesses to report new § 4062(e) events as they occur, but reassured them that no enforcement action would be taken on those events in 2014. [PBGC Press Release No. 14-09, *PBGC Issues Moratorium on 4062(e) Enforcement*, <http://www.pbgc.gov/news/press/releases/pr14-09.html?cid=CPAD01PRJUL0820141> (July 8, 2014)]

If the employer responsible for maintaining a defined benefit plan is part of a controlled group, all members of the group are jointly and severally liable for funding. If the sponsor is no longer able to pay benefits, the PBGC can terminate the plan and require the sponsor and the controlled group to submit the unfunded benefit liabilities. The Eleventh Circuit considered whether the trustee of a bankrupt sponsor can sue the ex-owner of the corporation as a former member of the controlled group to recover the liabilities on behalf of the bankruptcy estate and the unsecured creditors. The Eleventh Circuit ruled that the trustee cannot: a reorganizing corporation cannot sue the ex-owner on behalf of the estate for termination liabilities. ERISA provides that once a plan is terminated, all parties except the PBGC are limited in the relief they can obtain from either the current or former controlled group. The PBGC can get legal or equitable relief from the controlled group for failure to fund the plan—but anyone else is limited to equitable relief. The Eleventh Circuit held that whether the trustee's intended relief was legal or equitable, it did not have a cause of action to recover funds for the bankruptcy estate to satisfy the PBGC claim. The ERISA duty of controlled group members to pay unfunded benefit liabilities runs to the plan's beneficiaries, not the unsecured creditors of the bankrupt sponsor. A complicating factor in this case was that the statute of limitations had run, so the PBGC could not sue the controlled group for termination liability. [*Durango-Georgia Paper Co v. H.G. Estate LLC*, 739 F.3d 1263 (11th Cir. 2014)]

CHAPTER 6
DEFINED CONTRIBUTION AND 401(k) PLANS

§ 6.01 INTRODUCTION

As explored in Chapters 4 and 5, the defined benefit plan not only places the investment risk on the employer (because the employer must adjust its contributions to provide the promised level of benefits—and if the value of the plan's assets declines, and its investment return goes down, the employer must supply additional funds) but also subjects the employer to complex and expensive administrative requirements.

In the 1990s, therefore, the trend was to shift from defined benefit to defined contribution or 401(k) plans. The 401(k) plan form grew fast, because (although employer matches are permitted) the predominant form of funding for these plans is deferral of employee compensation.

In recent years, court cases and regulations have centered on economic factors. Many disappointed plan participants have charged that they were not given adequate investment alternatives, or that they lost potential appreciation because excessive fees were charged. In general, however, these suits have been unsuccessful—although in mid-2014, the Supreme Court held that, in "stock drop" case (where the value of plan participants' accounts falls) fiduciaries are not entitled to a presumption of prudence when they are accused of retaining employer stock as a plan investment for too long. [*Fifth Third Bancorp et al. v. Dudenhoeffer*, No. 12-751 (U.S. June 25, 2014)] .

Federal regulators have responded to these concerns by increasing the amount of disclosure required in connection with defined contribution plans. Service providers (e.g., investment advisors; recordkeepers) must give the plan detailed information about the services they render the plan—and the cost of those services. The plan, in turn, must disclose information about investment costs to plan participants. Under appropriate conditions, service providers can render not just advice to the plan as a whole, but individual advice to plan participants.

Aon's 2013 report [<http://www.aon.com/attachments/human-capital-consulting/2013_report_Trends-Experience-DC-Plans_Highlights.pdf>] shows that more than three-quarters of survey respondents permitted new hires to participate in their 401(k) plan immediately after hiring. The most common match was $1 for every dollar deferred by the employee, up to 6% of compensation—twice as much as the once most-common rate of 50 cents per $1 of employee deferral. Half of employers offered a Roth 401(k) option, versus only 11% six years earlier. More than half (59%) of plans offered automatic enrollment, but the default savings rate is usually lower than the threshold for receiving a matching contribution. This means that the plan will probably attract a high participation rate—but that employees will have lower overall savings levels than if they qualified for a full employer match. The role of employer stock in plan investment has diminished greatly, but still represented about 14% of defined contribution plan assets.

The Plan Sponsor Council of America (PSCA) 55th Annual Survey of Profit Sharing and 401(k) plans showed more companies and participants are contributing to 401(k) plans, and at higher rates than in earlier years. More than three-quarters of eligible participants made contributions in both 2010 (76.9%) and 2011 (79.5%). In both years, almost half of plans allowed Roth 401(k) contributions (45.5% in 2010, 49%) in 2011, and in both years, 17.4% of employees who had this option made Roth contributions. In 2010, 41.8% of plans used automatic enrollment, rising to 45.9% in 2011. 401(k) plans offered an average of 19 funds in 2011. The most popular funds were actively managed domestic equity funds, actively managed international equity funds, indexed domestic equity funds, and actively managed domestic bond funds. [Stephen Miller, *Changes in 401(k) Plans Spur Higher Participation*, SHRM (Oct. 15, 2012)]

On December 31, 2013, total retirement assets in the United States were $23.0 trillion—5% higher than at the end of the third quarter, and 15.6% higher than the end of 2012. Defined contribution assets were $5.9 trillion at the end of 2013 ($4.2 trillion of that in 401(k) plans); IRA assets were $6.5 trillion; defined benefit plans had $3.0 billion in assets, plus $2.0 trillion in annuity reserves outside retirement accounts; government plan assets were $5.6 trillion. [ICI Release, *Retirement Assets Total $23.0 Trillion in Fourth Quarter 2013* (Mar. 26, 2014) (benefitslink.com)]

An EBRI fact sheet published in March 2013 shows that in 1979, only 7% of U.S. workers participated only in a defined contribution plan; in that year, 28% of workers had only a defined benefit plan, and a further 10% had both. The situation changed greatly by 2011, when 31% of workers participated only in a defined contribution plan, 11% participated in both, and a mere 3% of workers had only a defined benefit plan. The fact sheet includes a dramatic graph, showing that the proportion of workers with both types of plans has stayed within the 10%–15% range—but defined benefit plan participation plummeted throughout the period as defined contribution plan participation soared. [EBRI Fast Facts #225, *Pension Plan Participation*, <http://www.ebri.org/pdf/FF.225.DB-DC.28Mar13.pdf> (Mar. 28, 2013). For more detailed statistics, see <http://bit.ly.WEiMfD>.]

Although the defined contribution plan is the primary mechanism for workplace savings in the United States, EBRI said that only about 40% of workers contribute to a workplace plan and the ones who do probably do not save enough. When they were first authorized, defined contribution plans had an opt-in structure, where employees decided whether to save and how much and which of the plan's investment alternatives should be deployed. This led to substantial growth in defined contribution plan assets, but most participants' portfolios were poorly constructed. The DOL permitted safe harbors such as QDIAs, leading to a new architecture featuring automatic enrollment. The majority (60%) of plans with more than $1 billion in assets feature automatic enrollment. Many large plans are approaching double-digit savings rates either by escalating the contribution rate each year or with each promotion, and by setting higher default rates (e.g., 5–6%

rather than 3%). [Charlie Ruffel, *The New Hybrid DC Plans in Corporate America*, aiCIO (Apr. 28, 2013) (benefitslink.com)]

According to Cogent Research, 63% of defined contribution plan sponsors use social media as a regular source of 401(k) information. Sponsors connect to service providers through Websites or blogs (39%), LinkedIn (24%), and Facebook (22%). More than three quarters (77%) of mid-sized plan sponsors (those with assets in the $20 million–$100 million range) use some kind of social media for 401(k) information; almost half (47%) use provider sites or blogs regularly, and 39% use LinkedIn. [Kevin McGuinness, *Plan Sponsors Embracing Social Media*, plansponsor.com (May 13, 2013)]

§ 6.02 DEFINED CONTRIBUTION PLANS

The 401(k) plan, also known as a CODA (Cash or Deferred Arrangement) is the most popular type of defined contribution plan, but a variety of defined compensation plan designs can be used, e.g., profit sharing; money purchase; target benefit; ESOP; leveraged ESOP; new comparability plans, as stand-alones or in conjunction with 401(k) plans.

The profit-sharing plan is the most basic defined contribution plan design. The employer does not have to have profits to make contributions, nor is it required that contributions be made whenever there are profits. Allocations can be made by a fixed formula such as a specified percentage of pay; as a flat dollar amount; a formula tied to age and/or years of service (such as X% of pay until the sum of age plus service reaches a certain amount, then a different percentage); a formula related to corporate profits; pro rata contributions by pay, or a completely discretionary amount. A profit-sharing plan can be integrated with Social Security benefits, so that the contribution percentage rises after the participant's income hits the FICA contribution base. In practice, most sponsors of profit-sharing plans do not actually make profit-sharing contributions; the plan is a vehicle for attaching 401(k) savings and matches.

Money purchase pension plans are defined contribution plans that are also pension plans. The formula must be fixed, not discretionary; ERISA rules apply; and the sponsor must meet a minimum funding standard. The contributions can be related to pay, be a flat amount, follow an age-plus-service formula, or other variations. Money purchase pension plans used to be fairly popular, especially among companies that wanted to offer very generous defined contribution plans—more than the 15% of eligible contribution that was once the limit for defined contribution plans. However, true money purchase plans are now obsolete, because a profit-sharing plan contribution can be as much as 25% of compensation.

A target benefit plan is a special money purchase pension plan that mirrors the accruals in a defined benefit plan, reflecting the underlying defined benefit plan formula—but each participant has an account balance which determines the eventual benefit. Target benefit plans were never very popular, and almost no new ones have been created since 1986, when that year's tax bill imposed anti-discrimination regulations that made it difficult to operate a target benefit plan.

An ESOP is a money purchase plan designed to invest primarily in employer securities. This was a popular plan design in the 1980s, but heavy investments in employer stock are now extremely controversial. A Leveraged ESOP (aka LESOP) is partially or wholly financed with loans that the plan sponsor obtains from banks or other lenders. Employees get shares allocated to their LESOP accounts (and can also diversify their investments), then receive shares or cash representing their vested balance when employment terminates. [JP Morgan Compensation & Benefit Strategies, *Rediscovering Defined Contribution Plans—Design Basics*, plansponsor.com (Nov. 13, 2008)]

The maximum employer contribution to a defined contribution plan is $50,000 for 2012, $51,000 for 2013, and $52,000 for 2014. The accrued benefit for a participant in a defined contribution plan equals the balance in the account. The balance, in turn, consists of employer contributions, any mandatory employee contributions that the plan requires, plus any voluntary contributions that the plan permits and the employee chooses to make. Defined contribution plans usually maintain separate subaccounts for the employer and employee component of each employee's account, but this is not a legal requirement.

The IRS issued final rules applying to loans made on or after January 1, 2004 from qualified defined contribution plans, including loans made to participants who are on military leave (see § 1.18), refinanced loans, and exceptions to the ban on new loans to participants whose earlier loans are in default. A participant who suspends loan repayment during military service and then returns to work must repay the entire loan and its interest in substantially level installments by the end of the original loan term plus the period of military service. If the loan was not a mortgage on the principal residence, repayment must occur within five years plus the period of service, if the original loan term was less than five years. A new loan can be made despite a default based on an enforceable agreement to repay by payroll withholding, or if the plan receives security for the loan in addition to the participant's account balance. [CIGNA's Pension Analyst, *IRS Issues Additional Loan Rules* (September 2003) <http://www.cigna.com/professional/pdf/loanCPA2003.pdf>]

Early in 2009, amendments to Regulation Z were published, exempting most retirement plan loans from the Truth in Lending Act. Effective July 1, 2010, qualifying loans are made to a plan participant, from fully vested funds in his or her account, complying with all tax requirements including the § 72 annuity rules. [Rebecca Moore, *Plan Loans Exempt from Truth-in-Lending Disclosure Requirements*, plansponsor.com (Mar. 13, 2009)]

EBRI and Investment Company Institute (ICI) report that, for almost two decades, most 401(k) participants have had the right to take loans, but few of them do. In 2012, 87% of participants could get loans, but only 21% of those with access to loans had one outstanding at end of year in 2012. At that time, the average unpaid balance was $7,153, which was about 13% of the average balance. [EBRI Fast Facts No. 264, *Many Have Access to 401(k) Loans, Few Have Outstanding Balances* (Jan. 16, 2014) (benefitslink.com)]

The Sixth Circuit held that income available to Chapter 13 debtors after repaying a 401(k) loan is projected disposable income that must be paid to unsecured creditors. The debtors will not be permitted to use it to make voluntary contributions to the plan. The 2005 bankruptcy reform law, Bankruptcy Abuse Prevention and Consumer Protection Act (BAPCPA), provides a limited exclusion for amounts withheld by an employer from an employee's wages for contributions to a qualified plan. The Sixth Circuit held that plan loan payments are excluded from debtor's disposable income, but voluntary contributions to a 401(k) plan are not. Contributions are only excluded from the bankruptcy estate if they were made before the date of the petition. [*In re Seafort*, 669 F.3d 662 (6th Cir. 2012); see CCH Pension & Benefits, *Debtors Could Not Begin Making Post-Petition Contributions To 401(k) Plans Following Repayment Of Plan Loans* (Mar. 23, 2012) (benefitslink.com)]

In early 2014, participants in the Penn Speciality Chemicals plan got access to their 401(k) accounts—but it took five years, two articles in the New York Times, assistance from the DOL and IRS, and severe comments by the bankruptcy judge to get them their money. When a company goes bankrupt, 401(k) funds are supposed to be transferred to the account owners, but this did not occur for the Penn employees. They were charged high fees for administrative and legal work and some of them faced tax penalties for failure to take required minimum distributions. DOL launched an investigation in 2012. The IRS issued a determination letter on January 24, 2013, but the plan denied receiving the letter so it did not distribute the account funds. A participant contacted the bankruptcy judge, who gave the trustees two months to resolve the problems—which they failed to do; funds were not actually released until January 2014. [Gretchen Morgenson, *A Long Fight to Get What Was Theirs, in a 401(k)*, NYTimes.com (Feb. 1, 2014)]

ERISA § 404(c) allows the participant to control the assets in a defined contribution account, including directing the investment of the account. If the participant assumes control, the plan's fiduciaries will not be liable for losses that result from participant control over the funds. Section 404(c) requires the plan to disclose adequate information about their investment alternatives. The plan must offer at least three diversified investment types, with materially different risk and return characteristics. Intent to use the § 404(c) safe harbor for part or all of a plan must be disclosed on Item 8a on the plan's Form 5500—and the form is signed under penalty of perjury. Participants must be allowed to change their portfolios at least once a quarter—more often if volatility requires. Participants must be given the mandatory disclosures (that the plan is a § 404(c) plan; that fiduciaries can be relieved of liability; what the plan's investment options are; and how to give investment instructions for the account). Participants can also request additional information, such as the annual operating expenses for each investment option, copies of financial statements and prospectuses, and the description and value of the assets in the portfolio. The Seventh Circuit agreed with the Fourth Circuit (and the Department of Labor): choosing investment options for the plan, and deciding to retain an investment within the plan, are fiduciary acts that are not entitled to § 404(c) immunity because § 404(c) protects fiduciaries from being blamed for decisions over which they did not have control. However, the Seventh Circuit found for the plan: the stock fund was not worthless, and was not so risky that retaining it in the plan was imprudent. The plan was diversified and offered many other options. [*Howell v. Motorola Inc.*, 633 F.3d 552 (7th Cir. 2011); see EBIA Weekly, *Seventh Circuit Concludes Employer's Selection of Investment Options Is Not Protected Under ERISA Section 404(c)* (Feb. 10, 2011) (benefitslink.com); see also *Lingis v. Dorazil*, 633 F.3d 552 (7th Cir. 2011); see Fred Schneyer, *7th Circuit Stock Drop Rulings Seen as Helping Employers*, plansponsor.com (Jan. 31, 2011)]

The Third Circuit, relying on decisions in the Seventh and Eighth Circuits, allowed dismissal of a breach of fiduciary duty claim alleging that funds with excessive fee profiles (e.g., retail mutual funds) were included in the plan—as long as the fiduciary selected a broad enough range of funds with varying fee characteristics. At the time the complaint against Unisys was filed, the 401(k) plan had 73 different investment options, including 67 individual retail mutual funds with varying characteristics. However, the Third Circuit did not consider whether the 404(c) safe harbor was available, on the grounds that the complaint was properly dismissed so it didn't matter if the safe harbor would have applied. The Third Circuit treated Fidelity as a directed trustee with no contractual authority to control investment options—therefore, it was not a fiduciary for this purpose. All claims against Fidelity were dismissed, because Fidelity did not have knowledge of Unisys' process for selecting investment options. [*Renfro v. Unisys Corp.*, 671 F.3d 314 (3d Cir. 2011); see Richard Black, *The Latest Word on 401(k) Fee Litigation: Third Circuit Narrows Plaintiffs' Ability to Bring ERISA Breach of Fiduciary Duty Claims*, Littler Mendelson ASAP (August 2011) (benefitslink.com); Rebecca Moore, *Court Upholds Decision for Fidelity Unisys in Excessive Fee Case*, plansponsor.com (Sept. 9, 2011)]

But if the § 404(c) safe harbor is not available, a fiduciary can be liable for allowing participants to invest in company stock when it was manifestly imprudent to let them. A Seventh Circuit case held that the plan made no effort to show § 404(c) compliance, and the plaintiff remained 98% invested in employer stock, while its profit margins declined 70–80% over five years. [*Peabody v. Davis*, 636 F.3d 368 (7th Cir. 2011); see Rebecca Moore, *Fiduciaries Showing No Compliance with 404c Breached Duties*, plansponsor.com (Apr. 21, 2011)]

DOL's FAB 2009-03 (September 2009) permits the SPD to be used to satisfy the requirements of ERISA § 404(c), the provision that relieves fiduciaries of liability for investment losses in self-determined accounts. To obtain relief under FAB 2009-03, the plan sponsor must provide a copy of its most recent prospectus either right before or right after a participant's or beneficiary's initial investment in a registered security. Prospectuses must also be provided on request. In January 2009, the SEC published a new summary prospectus option for satisfying the SEC's prospectus rule, and the DOL will accept the short-form summary prospectus under this rule for ERISA § 404(c) purposes if it is the most recent prospectus provided to the plan. The DOL published final regulations on the selection of annuity providers for individual account plans in late 2008, creating a safe harbor for fiduciary obligations. The fiduciary must perform an objective, thorough, and analytical search to select annuity providers; consider enough information to determine the provider's ability to make all future payments under the contract; the total cost of the annuity contract (including fees and commissions) compared to the benefits of the deal. However, once the provider is selected, the fiduciary does not have to review the appropriateness of the provider. The safe harbor covers only the fiduciary's decision to buy an annuity to distribute the balances of individual account plans—not the selection of a particular investment product. [DOL Reg. § 2550.404a-4, 73 Fed. Reg. 58447 (Oct. 7, 2008); Amendment to Interpretive Bulletin 95-1, 73 Fed. Reg. 58445 (Oct. 7, 2008); Amendments to DOL Reg. §§ 2550.404a-3 and 2578.1, 73 Fed. Reg. 58459 (Oct. 7, 2008); Amendment to PTE 2006-06, 73 Fed. Reg. 58629 (Oct. 7, 2008)]

[A] § 415 Regulations

In 2005, the IRS proposed regulations to update the § 415 regulations first published in 1981. The regulations were finalized in 2007. Plans can provide that payments in any limitation year will not exceed the § 415(b) limit as of the annuity starting date, and increased pursuant to § 415(d); if this is done, the plan does not require actuarial adjustments for automatic increases unless the benefit is subject to § 417(e)(3).

Under the PPA, compensation used to calculate the "high 3" years does not have to be earned while the employee is an active plan participant. In general, the "high 3" is calculated subject to the annual compensation limit of § 401(a)(17), but the Final Regulations allow grandfathering-in of some additional compensation based on plan provisions that were in effect before April 5, 2007.

In general, money received after severance from employment is not considered § 415 compensation, but the Final Regulations allows inclusion of certain payments under bona fide sick or vacation leave plans—even if the payments are made more than 20½ months after severance from employment or the end of the year.

The Final Regulations allow some payments from non-qualified plans to be treated as § 415 compensation, as well as certain payments to disabled participants. The IRS announced its intentions to revise the rules covering multiple annuity starting dates. Various technical changes are made in the way that defined benefit payouts are adjusted when payment begins between age 62 and age 65. [Final Rule, 72 Fed. Reg. 16878 (Apr. 5, 2007)]

[B] Pension Protection Act (PPA) Changes

As Chapter 5 shows, the PPA was intended in part to improve the stability of defined benefit plans. Nevertheless, there are important PPA provisions that will affect the operation of defined contribution plans.

One PPA focus is protecting plan participants against excessive risk from declines in the value of the employer's stock. If the employer corporation's stock is publicly traded, then defined contribution plan participants must be given at least three investment options other than employer stock, and participants must have a right to diversify out of their holdings in employer stock—and must be notified of this right. (Because ESOPs are intended to hold employer stock, they are exempt from these requirements.)

The fiduciaries of 401(k) plans are permitted to give investment advice to participants: a prohibited transaction exemption is available if banks, insurance companies, broker/dealers, or registered investment advisers give advice after December 31, 2006. To qualify for the exemption, the adviser either must use an independently verified computer model to make recommendations, or the adviser's compensation must not vary based on the participant's investment choices. The PPA doubles the size of the bond (from $500,000 to $1 million) that fiduciaries must post if the plan they administer holds employer securities.

The PPA also gives small employers (fewer than 500 employees) a new option: maintaining an eligible combined plan that has some features of a defined benefit and some features of a 401(k) plan. An eligible combined plan must comply with the rules for both plan types. The eligible combined plan rules are effective starting in 2010. The plan consists of a single trust, with its assets allocated between a defined contribution plan such as a 401(k) plan, and a defined benefit plan.

§ 6.03 NEW COMPARABILITY PLANS

On October 6, 2000, the IRS published Proposed Regulations at 65 Fed. Reg. 59774-59780 setting the nondiscrimination requirements for "new comparability plans." The regulations were finalized by T.D. 8954, 66 Fed. Reg. 3435 (June 29, 2001). These are defined contribution plans that are allowed to perform cross-testing and demonstrate nondiscrimination under Treas. Reg. § 1.401(a)(4)–(8) by reference to their benefits rather than the employer's contributions, although they must satisfy a "gateway" requirement preserving at least a minimum rate of accrual for non-HCEs. In practice, this is usually done by finding a defined benefit equivalent for the allocations and then arranging them in rate groups.

The plan document can specify the classes in many ways—by age, hiring date, length of service, type of job, or the location in which they work, for example. The number or definition of classes can only be changed via plan amendment, and the changes must be prospective only, not retroactive. [Mark

Papalia, *Class-Based Pensions: A Cost-Saving Alternative for Companies of All Sizes*, Journal of Accountancy (January 2005) (benefitslink.com)]

§ 6.04 401(k) PLANS

[A] Overview

The Cash or Deferred Arrangement (CODA), also known as the 401(k) plan, has achieved prominence as one of the leading forms of plans for providing post-retirement income. Such plans were authorized by a 1978 amendment to the Internal Revenue Code and first became available in 1981. About 75% of 401(k)-eligible employees participate, but less than 10% save the maximum permitted amount. For the typical plan, this is 6% of compensation, and 3% remains the most common employer match. [Jilian Mincer, *As the 401(k) Turns 25, Has It Improved With Age?*, Wall St. J., Nov. 14, 2006, at D2]

Although 401(k) plans are subject to the rules for defined contribution plans, strictly speaking 401(k)s are not conventional pension plans. In a 401(k) plan, the employee agrees to have part of his or her salary, up to the limitation provided by the plan (which, in turn, is subject to limitations under the Tax Code) deferred and placed into an individual account instead of being paid in cash as it is earned. The advantage to the employee (apart from the forced savings aspect) is that the appreciation in value of the account is not taxed until withdrawals begin.

Many 401(k) plans feature an "employer match" (the employer contributes a percentage of what the employee contributes) but this is not a mandatory feature of this type of plan.

In September 2004, the Department of Labor proposed regulations covering the rights of service members returning from active service (see § 1.18) that also affect 401(k) plans. Periods of uniformed service must be counted with respect to 401(k) plan vesting and benefit accrual. Returning service members must be permitted to catch up with voluntary contributions such as elective deferrals that could have been made if they had not been in the military. The employer's obligation to make matching contributions depends on the service member's making the contributions within specified time frames. The Regulations require the employer contributions to be made within 30 days after reemployment for profit-sharing and other contributions for which the employee is not required to participate. [EBIA Weekly, *Proposed USERRA Regulations Address Elective Deferrals, Timing of Employer Contributions* (law.com)]

President Obama signed a presidential memorandum January 29, 2014, directing the Department of the Treasury to create "myRA" accounts as a savings vehicle for the workers (approximately half the workforce) who do not have access to 401(k)s or other retirement accounts. Single filers with income up to $129,000 and joint return filers with income up to $191,000 can contribute.

According to the AARP, only 5% of eligible Americans make tax-advantaged Roth IRA contributions on a regular basis.

MyRAs are structured like Roth IRAs: money is contributed to the account on an after-tax basis, and investment gains and withdrawals are tax-free. The only investment option permitted for myRAs is a variable-rate Treasury bond carrying the same interest rate as the Thrift Savings Plan Governmental Securities Investment Fund for federal workers. When a myRA account reaches a balance of $15,000, it must be rolled over to a regular IRA. However, it will probably take a very long time to reach this level: a person who contributes $50 every two weeks, with an annual return of 1.5%, will need close to 11 years to reach the $15,000 level. There are no fees for the account, and participating employers can offer payroll deductions. However, the myRA is strictly an opt-in account, and employees cannot be automatically enrolled. [Anne Tergesen and Colleen McCain Nelson, *Obama Signs Order for New myRA Retirement Accounts*, WSJ.com (Jan. 29, 2014)]

[B] Deferral Limits

Thanks to EGTRRA, and as carried forward by the PPA, the amount that employees can defer will increase after 2001. EGTRRA also includes other novel 401(k) provisions. Participants in 401(k) plans who are over 50 are permitted to make additional "catch-up" contributions, and low-income plan participants are allowed to take a tax credit and not a mere deduction in connection with part of their 401(k) deferrals.

For 2013, the maximum annual contribution to a defined contribution account is $51,000, and persons over 50 can make a catch-up contribution of $5,500. For 2014, the maximum contribution rises to $52,000, but the catch-up contribution limit remains the same. Participants in 401(k) plans are always 100% vested in their deferrals at all times. Employees must be allowed to participate in the cash or deferred part of the plan starting with the first entry date after they have one year of service with the employer. Participants must be re-admitted to the plan immediately if they terminate their jobs but are re-employed at the same company before they have undergone a one-year break in service.

[C] Catch-Up Contributions

EGTRRA added a new I.R.C. § 414(v), which allows employees who are age 50 or older to order additional deferrals, over and above the normal limits. These additional amounts are referred to as catch-up contributions. The intent is to make sure that older employees will come closer to getting the same benefit from the enhanced opportunities for deferrals over the course of their careers as younger employees who can make the greater deferrals for a greater number of years. Catch-up contributions can be made for taxable years beginning after December 31, 2001.

The maximum catch-up contribution is $5,000 in 2006–8, $5,500 in 2009–2014. [IR-2012-77, <http://www.irs.gov/uac/2013-Pension-Plan-Limitations> (Oct. 18, 2012), IR-2013-86 <http://www.irs.gov/uac/IRS-Announces-2014-Pension-Plan-Limitations;-Taxpayers-May-Contribute-up-to-$17,500-to-their-401(k)-plans-in-2014> (Oct. 31, 2013)] EGTRRA § 631 provides that, if all employees who have reached age 50 are permitted to make catch-up contributions, the amount of the catch-up contributions will not be used in calculating the contribution limits. Nor will the catch-up amounts be used in nondiscrimination testing.

A plan participant is eligible to make catch-up contributions as of January 1 of the calendar year in which he or she reaches age 50—irrespective of the plan year.

[D] Other EGTRRA 401(k) Changes

Low-income 401(k) plan participants are entitled to a tax credit for their deferrals, for tax years beginning after December 31, 2001. This "saver's credit" was made permanent by the PPA. The 2013 saver's credit figures are $59,000 (joint return), $44,250 (head of household) and $29,500 (single/married filing separately). [IR-2012-77, <http://www.irs.gov/uac/2013-Pension-Plan-Limitations> (Oct. 18, 2012)] These figures remain unchanged for 2014. [IRS Tax Tip 2014-28, <http://www.irs.gov/uac/Newsroom/Boost-Your-Retirement-Savings-with-a-Tax-Credit> (Mar. 7, 2014)]

Under current law, a small (under $5,000) balance can be "cashed out"—i.e., even if the employee wants the money to remain within the plan, the employer has the right to close out the account and send such small, hard-to-administer sums to the account owner's last known address. (Tax should be withheld, and an early distribution penalty should be taken if the person is under age 59½.)

[E] Roth 401(k)s

Yet another EGTRRA legacy is I.R.C. § 402A, which authorizes "qualified plus contribution programs"—in effect, 401(k) accounts that operate like Roth IRAs. An employee can make an irrevocable designation of part or all of the employee's elective salary deferral as designated Roth contributions. Employees' elective salary deferrals are taxed when they are placed in the account, but can be withdrawn tax-free as long as they have remained in the account for five years and the person withdrawing is at least 59½ or disabled (or the withdrawal is made by the estate of a deceased account holder).

A person who cannot contribute to a Roth IRA because of excess income can nevertheless contribute to a Roth 401(k). Furthermore, the maximum contribution to a Roth 401(k) is the normal 401(k) maximum, which is much higher than the Roth IRA maximum contribution. Roth 401(k) plans are subject to the minimum distribution rules. [Rev. Proc. 2006-53, 2006-48 I.R.B. 997]

In 2006, the IRS issued final regulations, covering Roth 401(k) plans, under Code § 402A, applicable to plan years beginning on or after January 1, 2006. [T.D. 9237, RIN 1545-BE05, 4830-01-p, 2006-6 I.R.B. 394; see *Final Regulations on Roth 401(k)s Issued*, Watson Wyatt Insider (January 2006) (benefitslink.com)]

Employers are not permitted to offer a 401(k) plan that accepts only designated Roth contributions: contributing employees must be given a choice between making pre-tax elective contributions and designated Roth contributions.

Employer matches are not permitted, although employers can use automatic enrollment in a Roth 401(k) plan. Designated Roth contributions can be treated as catch-up contributions, and can be collateral for plan loans to participants. [T.D. 9237, RIN 1545-BE05, 4830-01-p, 2006-6 I.R.B. 394; see *Final Regulations on Roth 401(k)s Issued*, Watson Wyatt Insider (January 2006) (benefitslink.com). See also Announcement 2007-59, 2007-25 I.R.B. 1448, explaining how to make mid-year changes in a 401(k) safe harbor plan to implement a Roth program or take advantage of other PPA changes. Regulations were proposed at 71 Fed. Reg. 4320 (Jan. 26, 2006) on Roth 401(k) distribution issues, and T.D. 9324, 72 Fed. Reg. 21103 (Apr. 30, 2007) addresses designated Roth distributions.]

Designated Roth contributions are aggregated with all other 401(k) and 403(b) contributions, so for 2013, the annual contribution limitation is $17,500, plus $5,500 in catch-up contributions by persons aged 50 and over. [IR-2012-77, <http://www.irs.gov/uac/2013-Pension-Plan-Limitations> (Oct. 18, 2012)] For 2014, the figures remain unchanged: see IR-2013-87.

An in-plan Roth rollover is a rollover within a 401(k) plan to designated Roth account in the same plan. Designated Roth contributions and their earnings must be maintained in a separate account under the plan. Code § 402A defines designated Roth contributions as elective deferrals to a retirement plan that would otherwise be excludable from gross income, but the plan participant elects to include them in gross income.

The Small Business Jobs Act of 2010, Pub. L. No. 111-240, allows in-plan Roth conversions for 401(k)s, effective on signing of the bill (September 27, 2010). Employers can amend their plans to permit Eligible Rollover Distributions (ERDs) to be transferred to a designated Roth account in the plan. If the plan did not already offer Roth accounts, the plan must be amended, and the payroll system updated accordingly. This provision benefits sponsors who were concerned about large balances being taken out of the plan, but does not make a major change for participants, who already had the option of rolling over the funds to a Roth IRA. A participant who rolls over an ERD into a designated Roth account in 2010 can either include the rollover amount in income in 2010, or defer taxation by including half of the taxable amount in gross income for 2011 and half for 2012. [*New Law Allows In-Plan Rollovers to Designated Roth Accounts*, <http://www.irs.gov>]

The American Taxpayer Relief Act of 2012 (ATRA; Pub. L. No. 112-240) enacted Code § 402A(c)(4)(E), which permits in-plan Roth conversions of defined contribution accounts that would not otherwise be distributable, with no income limitations, as of December 31, 2012. Under prior law, only amounts that were immediately distributable (e.g., to a participant who had reached age 59½) could be converted to Roth status. The provision is effective January 1, 2013, but account balances in existence on that date can be converted. [Rebecca Moore, *Fiscal Cliff Deal Extends Roth Conversions*, plansponsor.com (Jan. 3, 2013)]

Notice 2013-74, 2013-52 I.R.B. 819 requires sponsors who want to permit in-plan Roth conversions to amend the plan by December 31, 2014, or the last day of the first plan year for which the amendment is effective—whichever comes later. The notice explains that elective deferrals, matching, and non-elective contributions qualify for in-plan rollovers, but the rolled-over amount continues to be subject to whatever distribution restrictions applied to the amount before the rollover. For example, the money cannot be taken out of the plan until a distribution event occurs. [Lisa A. Berkowitz Herrnson, *IRS Provides New Guidance On In-Plan Roth Rollovers*, Proskauer Rose (Dec. 17, 2013), available at Lexology.com; Rebecca Moore, *IRS Clarifies Roth In-Plan Rollover Rules*, plansponsor.com (Dec. 12, 2013)]

§ 6.05 401(k) ANTIDISCRIMINATION RULES

Understandably, highly compensated employees are in a better position to bypass immediate receipt of part of their salaries than rank-and-file employees. Therefore, the Internal Revenue Code includes detailed provisions for determining whether the plan is excessively unbalanced in favor of deferrals by HCEs.

The IRS Website includes a chart of 10 potential mistakes that 401(k) plans can fall into, but that can be retrieved by going through a correction program such as SCP, VCP, or Audit CAP.

1. Is the plan document updated to reflect changes in the law? (The IRS suggests establishing a tickler file to ensure annual review).
2. Is the plan operated in accordance with the plan document? (Due diligence to make sure plan terms are followed is suggested.)
3. Does the plan define compensation correctly for deferrals and allocations?
4. Did the employer make matching contributions for all eligible participants?
5. Does the plan satisfy the applicable nondiscrimination tests?

6. Were all eligible employees given a chance to opt for elective deferrals? (The plan sponsor must monitor employee census information and apply the participation requirements correctly.)
7. Are elective deferrals kept within the § 402(g) limit for the year, with any excess deferrals promptly distributed to resolve the problem?
8. Are employee elective deferrals promptly deposited?
9. For top-heavy plans, were required minimum contributions made? The IRS says plans should be tested each year to see if they are top-heavy.
10. Were hardship distributions made properly? [IRS chart of *401(k) Plan Potential Mistakes*, <http://www.irs.gov/pub/irs-tege/401k_mistakes.pdf> (Apr. 24, 2013, accessed Mar. 31, 2014)]

There are two antidiscrimination tests: the ADP test (Actual Deferral Percentage) and the ACP test (Aggregate Contribution Percentage). A full discussion is beyond the scope of this book; you should just be aware that the 401(k) plan will be scrutinized for compliance with at least one of these tests.

The employer can correct the situation in three ways:

- Distributing the excess contributions (and the income allocated to them) out of the plan before the end of the following plan year;
- Recharacterizing the excess contributions as after-tax contributions;
- Making qualified nonelective or qualified matching contributions.

Given the complexity of these rules, the IRS has recognized various safe harbor mechanisms that employers can use to simplify compliance. Companies that use the safe harbor are required to give plan participants notice that is accurate and comprehensive enough to inform them of their rights. The notice must be given a reasonable period (30–90 days) before the beginning of the plan year. Therefore, in a calendar year plan, notice is required on or before December 1 of the previous year.

Another option for employers who do not want to commit to using the safe harbor, but who want to make non-elective contributions, is to give notice, again by December 1 of the preceding year, that the plan may be amended in the next calendar year to provide for safe harbor non-elective contributions, and that the employees will receive a further notice explaining their rights if such an amendment is adopted.

The IRS will generally treat a plan as having lost its status as a 401(k) safe harbor plan if it fails to provide a timely annual safe harbor plan notice for a year. If this status is lost, the plan must satisfy the nondiscrimination requirements from which it was exempted. This could limit highly compensated employees' ability to defer compensation, or could require the plan sponsor to refund some amounts already deferred. Penalties could also be imposed for failure to provide the automatic enrollment or Qualified Automatic Contribution Arrangement (QACA) notice. Failure to give timely Qualified Default Investment Alternative (QDIA) notice forfeits fiduciary protection of the sponsor, plan administrator, or investment company for investment loss. Protection is only restored for amounts invested in the QDIA after compliance with the notice requirements. [McKenna Long & Aldridge LLP, *2011 Year-End Disclosure Reminders for Qualified Defined Contribution Plan Sponsors* (November 2011) (benefitslink.com)]

Current IRS audit policy calls for asking the employer for evidence that participants were given the 401(k) safe harbor notice. The IRS is requiring corrections, and perhaps a closing agreement sanction, from employers that cannot provide the evidence. To protect themselves, employers should keep copies of the notice (including the date it was sent) and the cover letter. If the notice was delivered electronically, the proper evidence would be a copy of the e-mail, the date it was sent, and the list of addressees. Failure to give the safe harbor notice is considered failure to comply with the terms of the plan, not merely a failure to satisfy the statutory requirements under § 401(k). The failure can be corrected under the IRS Self Correction Program, but not under the Employee Plans Compliance Resolution System (EPCRS) (although future versions of EPCRS are likely to include it). If the participant was actually aware of his or her eligibility to defer, the employer can correct the notice failure by giving the notice late, and improving its procedures for the future. But if the participant was not aware of the deferral opportunity, the employer must treat the employer as improperly excluded, and make a corrective contribution equal to 50% of the missed deferral plus any employer match required by the plan. [SunGard Relius, *Failure to Provide Safe Harbor Notice Correction* (Nov. 30, 2012) (benefitslink.com)]

§ 6.06 DISTRIBUTIONS FROM THE 401(k) PLAN

[A] General Rule

Pre-tax deferrals from a 401(k) plan cannot be distributed to the participant until:

- Retirement,
- Death,
- Disability,
- Separation from service (see below for the abolition of the "same desk" rule),
- Hardship,
- The participant reaches age 59½.

Although profit-sharing plans can make distributions purely because of the number of years the participant has worked for the employer, or the number of years the funds have remained in the account, these are not acceptable rationales for distributions from a 401(k) plan. [I.R.C. § 401(k)(2)(B)(ii)]

EGTRRA enacted § 411(d)(6)(E), providing that the accrued benefit is not reduced by elimination of a form of distribution—if the participant can receive a single-sum distribution at the same time as the eliminated form of distribution, and the single-sum distribution is based on at least as great a portion of the account as the form of distribution that was eliminated. A plan amendment under the Final Regulation can apply only to distributions whose annuity starting date occurs after the adoption of the amendment, not to distributions that have already commenced.

The Heroes Earnings Assistance and Relief Tax Act (HEART Act; Pub. L. No. 110-245) also revives an expired provision that allows reservists called for at least six months of active duty to take money out of their 401(k) and other defined contribution plans before age 59½ without having to pay the 10% penalty for early withdrawals. Employers must also recognize differential pay to called-up employees when they calculate pension benefits. The HEART Act includes the HEROES Act, which protects the (employment-related) survivor's benefits for survivors of servicemembers killed in the line of duty. [Rebecca Moore, *Reservist Benefits Bill Signed Into Law*, plansponsor.com (June 19, 2008)]

The Second Circuit required a profit-sharing plan to give a participant over $1.5 million in assets, earnings, and interest that were wrongly transferred to his ex-wife—even though the plan did not recoup the money from the ex-wife. (The Northern District of New York granted a judgment for the plan against the ex-wife, but the money was not recovered.) The Second Circuit found a legal duty to reimburse the plan participant, finding that undistributed funds held in trust are not considered benefits for purposes of the ban on alienating plan benefits. Furthermore, plan assets can be used to satisfy a judgment against the plan itself. [*Milgram v. Orthopedic Assocs. et al.*, 666 F.3d 68 (2d Cir. 2011); see Rebecca Moore, *Plan Must Restore Misplaced Assets Although not Recovered*, plansponsor.com (Jan. 17, 2012)]

Similarly, according to the Tenth Circuit, the ERISA ban on forfeitures does not make the plan liable for third-party wrongdoing. It was not a forfeiture when the plan incorrectly paid benefits to a participant's ex-wife instead of to him. It was the participant's fault that he did not give the plan his current address. His ex-wife learned how to access the benefits, got a user ID, changed the account password, filed a change of address form listing her P.O. box as an address, and withdrew all the money from the account. The participant did not sue his ex-wife; he sued the plan under ERISA § 1132(a)(1)(A) for refusing to distribute the plan funds to him. [*Foster v. PPG Indus. Inc.*, 693 F.3d 1226 (10th Cir. 2012); see Rebecca Moore, *DC Assets Withdrawn Fraudulently Not Forfeited*, plansponsor.com (Dec. 5, 2012)]

A couple who had been married to and divorced from each other twice before marrying for a third time signed a prenuptial agreement both before and after the third wedding. The wife waived rights to the husband's 401(k) plan. He named his parents as beneficiaries. The husband died after there had been a filing for a third divorce. Both his wife and his parents attempted to collect the 401(k) balance. The Eighth Circuit ruled for the wife: the prenuptial agreement was not an effective waiver of the wife's interest, because the agreement did not clearly disclose that spousal rights were being waived. The agreement seemed to contemplate execution of an additional waiver in the future, but that never occurred. [*MidAmerican Pension and Employee Benefits Plans Administrative Committee v. Cox*, 720 F.3d 715 (8th Cir. 2013); see Peter K. Bradley et al., *Prenuptial Agreement Not An Effective Waiver Of Spousal Rights,* Hodgson Russ LLP (Sept. 30, 2013), available at Lexology.com]

Although some employers have added annuities as defined contribution plan options, others are reluctant to do so because there has not been strong demand for them from participants. Young workers are often not interested in annuitizing. The current uncertainty in the market also deters some participants from accepting market risks by taking a lump sum that then has to be invested. There is also a concern about lack of portability: if a plan participant invests in a deferred annuity product, changes jobs, and rolls over the money, expenses already paid may be lost. If, instead of rolling over the amount, the employee leaves the funds in the original plan, he or she will have to manage and track multiple plans. There are also concerns about the size of the fees and charges associated with annuities. [Sharon F. Fountain, *"Annuitizing" a 401(k) – Options for Plan Sponsors and Participants*, Bloomberg BNA (Nov. 30, 2012) (benefitslink.com)]

On the tax front, the Treasury and Department of Labor are working to reduce the risk of employees outliving the balances in their defined contribution plans. Two Revenue Rulings and two Proposed Regulations from 2012 make it easier for plans to offer full and partial lifetime annuities. Rev. Rul. 2012-3, 2012-8 I.R.B. 383, allows defined contribution plans to offer deferred annuities as investments without forcing the entire plan to comply with the QJSA/QPSA (Qualified Joint and Survivor Annuities/Qualified Preretirement Survivor Annuities) rules—as long as the deferred annuity contract is accounted for separately. When the tax-deferred annuity reaches pay status, only that investment requires a QJSA. But if the plan permits the participant spouse to waive the QPSA the non-participant spouse must receive disclosures and must give notarized consent to the waiver.

Rev. Rul. 2012-4, 2012-8 I.R.B. 386 explains how an employer that offers both defined contribution and defined benefit plans can permit 401(k) plan participants who are ready to retire to roll over all or part of the 401(k) account balance to the defined benefit plan, receiving an immediate annuity under the defined benefit plan. The plan must use the same actuarial assumptions (such as interest rates and mortality tables) for annuitized rollovers that are used to calculate the retirement benefits of defined benefit plan participants. Participants in defined contribution plans who elect a rollover are entitled to disclosures about what will happen if the plan terminates without enough money to pay its liabilities. Married participants must furnish notified consent from their spouses. This ruling applies to rollovers made on or after January 1, 2013, but plan sponsors can rely on the ruling for earlier rollovers.

Regulations proposed in 2012, and finalized in mid-2014, add the possibility of using a QLAC (Qualifying Longevity Annuity Contract). As the name suggests, this tool provides lifetime income even if the plan participant survives to an advanced age. Plan participants in 401(k) plans and IRAs are not required to take RMDs on amounts used to purchase the QLAC between age 70 and the deferred start date of the annuity: for example, at age 80 or 85. The final rule, T.D. 9673, limits the amount of the account balance used to purchase the QLAC to $125,000 or 25% of the balance, whichever is less. Annuity payments must begin no later than when the annuitant reaches age 85 (but this age limit will be adjusted actuarially to reflect increasing lifespans). The annuity must not be variable or indexed, and cash surrender provisions are forbidden. [T.D. 9673, 2014-30 I.R.B. 212; see Tara Siegel Bernard, *Longevity Insurance Joins the Menu of Retirement Plan Options*, NYTimes.com (July 1, 2014). The proposed regulations appeared at 75 Fed. Reg. 5253 (Feb. 2, 2010) and were amended at 77 Fed. Reg. 5443 (Feb. 3, 2012).]

[B] Hardship Distributions

Treas. Reg. § 1.401(k)-1(d)(2)(i) defines hardship as an immediate and heavy financial need that cannot be satisfied by reasonable access to the participant's other assets. The hardship withdrawal from the plan must not exceed the amount of the need plus any taxes and penalties that the participant can reasonably expect to incur. Note that, post-PPA, hardship distributions can also be made based on the needs of plan beneficiaries as well as of plan participants.

Certain categories have been identified as automatically satisfying the financial needs test:

- Medical expenses of the employee, spouse, and dependent children;
- Purchase of a principal residence (but not routine mortgage payments);
- Staving off eviction or foreclosure of the mortgage on the principal residence;
- Tuition, room, board, and related expenses for the next 12 months for post-secondary education of the employee, spouse, or dependents.

Employees are expected to seek insurance reimbursement wherever it is available to cope with financial hardship; to liquidate their other assets to the extent this is reasonable; to cease further elective contributions to pension plans;

to seek other distributions and nontaxable loans from employer plans; and to engage in commercial borrowing on reasonable terms, before they take hardship distributions from their 401(k) plans.

Under the Final Regulations, 69 Fed. Reg. 78143 (Dec. 29, 2004), a hardship distribution must satisfy both the "events test" (the participant has an immediate and heavy financial need) and a "needs test" (the distribution must be necessary to satisfy the need). A hardship distribution for medical expenses is limited to expenses that would be deductible as medical care under I.R.C. § 213(d), although the 7.5% of AGI limit does not apply. The Final Regulations add two new grounds for distributions: funeral or burial expenses within the immediate family, and expenses for repairs to the principal residence. See also IR-2012-83 and Announcement 2012-44, 2012-49 I.R.B. 663, for tax relief for Superstorm Sandy hardships.

[C] Elimination of "Same Desk" Rule

One basis on which employees can get distributions from a 401(k) plan is separation from service—i.e., ceasing to be an employee. Before EGTRRA was passed, the "same desk" rule was applied. Under this rule, a person would not be considered separated from service if the original employer had gone through a merger, consolidation, or liquidation, but the employee continued to carry out the same job for the successor company, and thus would not be entitled to a distribution from the plan.

EGTRRA provides, for distributions made after December 31, 2001, that if a corporation sells "substantially all" (defined as 85% or more) of its business assets to an unrelated company, or sells a subsidiary to an unrelated person or company, the selling company's employees have separated from service even if, in practice, they carry out the same tasks for the new employer. [See also Rev. Proc. 2000-27, 2000-21 I.R.B. 1016.]

[D] "Orphan" Plans

In addition to plan freezes (see § 5.05[L]), problems arise because of "orphan" or "abandoned" plans—plans in which the sponsor went out of business, without making arrangements to terminate the plan and distribute benefits. The DOL estimates that roughly 1,650 401(k) plans are abandoned each year (about 2% of the total), affecting approximately 33,000 workers and balances of about $850 million. One advantage of a defined contribution plan over a defined benefit plan is that defined contribution plans are designed to be portable. But participants in these "orphan" plans, although they retain ownership of their accounts, often have difficulty in accessing them, because under previous law, if there was no representative of the sponsor company available, the financial institution could not release funds until DOL appoints an independent fiduciary to supervise the distribution. The DOL issued rules in April 2006, effective in late 2006, so that financial institutions holding assets from the defunct plans of bankrupt companies will be able to roll over the 401(k) balances with no requirement of court approval.

The April 2006 document comprises three rules: one describing the procedure to be used by a financial institution to terminate the plan and distribute benefits to the plan's participants; another creating a safe harbor for fiduciaries who make distributions to participants and beneficiaries of "orphaned" plans when there is no election on file covering the method of distribution; and the third creating a procedure for filing a simple terminal report for an abandoned plan. [71 Fed. Reg. 20820 (Apr. 21, 2006); see Rebecca Moore, *DOL Issues Final Rules Regarding Abandoned Plans*, plansponsor.com (Apr. 20, 2006); Robert Guy Matthews, *When Access Is Denied to Your 401(k)*, Wall St. J., Feb. 14, 2006, at D1]

EBSA's Abandoned Plan Program provides standards for determining if a plan is abandoned (e.g., no contributions or distributions for at least 12 consecutive months; the sponsor cannot be located by reasonable effort, no longer exists, or is unable to maintain the plan), with streamlined shut-down and distribution procedures. A Qualified Termination Administrator (QTA), qualified to serve as trustee and hold the assets, determines if the plan is abandoned. The QTA is not required to file Form 5500 on behalf of the abandoned plan, but is obligated to file a summary terminal report, as described on the "abandoned plan program" link at <http://www.dol.gov/ebsa>.

At the end of 2012, the DOL announced its intention to extend the Abandoned Plan Program to help trustees in Chapter 7 bankruptcy cases when they act as plan administrators for companies that have made Chapter 7 filings. Under this proposal, the bankruptcy trustee can terminate and wind up the plan or appoint an eligible financial institution to do so. If collecting the delinquent contributions costs less than the amount to be collected, the trustee must pursue it. [DOL/EBSA, *Fact Sheet: Proposed Amendments to Abandoned Plan Program* (December 2012) (benefitslink.com)]

§ 6.07 ADMINISTRATION OF THE 401(k) PLAN

There were a number of reasons why defined contribution plans, especially 401(k) plans, became the dominant form of retirement savings. The initial impetus included lower risk for the employer, and the greater simplicity of operating an individual account plan that does not require the complex actuarial calculations required for a defined benefit plan. However, since the 2008 stock market crash, there has been a trend for employers to attempt to take more control over 401(k) accounts, for example, by moving all participants into target date funds or suggesting automatic deposits of a percentage of their pay. [Eleanor Laise, *Employers Begin Driving Your 401(k)*, WSJ.com (Oct. 17, 2009)]

Defined contribution plans must give their participants a variety of notices:

- Safe harbor 401(k) plan's annual notice about the features of the plan, such as the safe harbor non-elective contribution or matching contribution of the plan; this must be given 30–90 days before the beginning of the plan year;
- Qualified Automatic Contribution Arrangement (QACA) safe harbor 401(k) plans must provide an annual notice on the same schedule;
- Qualified Default Investment Alternative (QDIA) notice of rights and obligations, such as the participant's right to transfer the account to other investments, and when funds will be invested in the QDIA; must be provided at least 30 days before the beginning of the plan year;
- 401(k) automatic enrollment notice, providing information such as deferrals made without an affirmative election, and how the plan invests contributions where there is no election; must be provided 30–90 days before the beginning of the plan year;
- Employer stock diversification notice: information about the right to transfer the participant's investment from employer stock into other investments (if the employer's stock is publicly traded). The notice must be given no later than 30 days before the first date that diversification rights can be exercised.

In general, two or more notices can be combined into a single document as long as the time requirements are satisfied. Electronic distribution is permissible if the electronic disclosure requirements are satisfied—but the defined contribution plan requirements cannot be satisfied in the SPD even if it is distributed annually. [McKenna Long & Aldridge LLP, *2011 Year-End Disclosure Reminders for Qualified Defined Contribution Plan Sponsors* (November 2011) (benefitslink.com)]

[A] Automatic Enrollment

Even prior to the recession beginning in 2008, there was concern that many employees would not have a secure retirement because many workers would refuse or neglect to take the affirmative steps necessary to open a 401(k) account, select investments, and have the necessary discipline to save part of their compensation. (It also became clear that even workers who faithfully saved their money were at the mercy of market forces that could greatly reduce the value of a 401(k) account.)

In 2000, the IRS gave its blessing for 401(k) plans to operate by automatically enrolling eligible workers rather than by permitting participation only by those workers who took steps to opt in: Rev. Rul. 2000-8, 2000-7 I.R.B. 617.

An automatic plan sets a default savings rate such as 2% to 3% of pay and establishes a default investment, such as a money market or stable value fund. Usually only about 4% of eligible opt out; Hewitt Associates estimates that in a plan where opting in is required, 30% of eligible workers never join. A step-up program gets the employee's advance consent to increasing his or her contributions as income increases.

The PPA makes it easier for employers to operate 401(k) plans that automatically enroll employees and then permit them to opt out, rather than requiring employees to choose to participate in the plan. Automatic-enrollment plans must have employer matches (and the PPA contains a schedule for calculating the required match). Participants in an automatic enrollment plan must be 100% vested after two years, although the employer is not required to offer immediate participation in the plan.

Final Regulations, effective December 24, 2007, were published at 72 Fed. Reg. 60452 covering investments in Qualified Default Investment Alternatives (QDIAs) for participants who do not direct the investment of their accounts. Under the Final Regulations, fiduciaries are not liable for losses on amounts invested in a QDIA, and the plan's fiduciaries are not liable for decisions made by the managers of the QDIA. A QDIA can mix equity and fixed income investments—for example, in a life cycle or targeted retirement date fund; it can also be a balanced fund or a professionally managed fund. However, a capital preservation fund or other stable value fund can be a QDIA only for the first 120 days after a participant's first elective contribution.

Two plaintiffs appealed the judgment for the defendant in an ERISA fiduciary breach case based on transfer of their investments from a stable value fund to a QDIA. The Sixth Circuit affirmed the district court. The plaintiffs allocated 100% of their investment in the stable value fund, which was also the default investment for 403(b) participants who did not make an election. The PPA created a safe harbor against fiduciary liability for directing automatic enrollment investments into QDIAs ("investments capable of meeting a worker's long-term retirement savings needs"); existing stable value funds were grandfathered in. The DOL's intention was to induce employers to select default investments that allow employees to keep up with inflation. In 2008, the employer changed its default and transferred investments from the old default fund to a new fund. The employer did not know which investments in the stable value fund were defaults and which were affirmatively elected, so it sent a notice to all participants who were 100% invested in the stable value fund telling them that the investments would be transferred if they did not give notice by a specific date. The plaintiffs allege that they never received the notice; the employer said that it was mailed to their correct addresses. They switched their investments when they received the quarterly notice reflecting the change. The plaintiffs argued that the safe harbor is limited to default investments, not investments selected by the participant, and they said they picked the stable value fund as an investment. However, the safe harbor regulations specifically state that they are not limited to default investments. The Sixth Circuit said it was "troubling" that they did not get the notice, but the employer's actions did not violate ERISA: a fiduciary is obligated to take measures reasonably calculated to ensure actual receipt, but it seems that the employer sent the correct number of letters, by first class mail, to the address they had on record. [*Bidwell v. University Med. Ctr.*, 685 F.3d 613 (6th Cir. 2012)]

The IRS Website includes a sample automatic enrollment notice for a hypothetical QACA: <http://www.irs.gov/pub/irs-tege/sample_notice.pdf> (accessed Apr. 7, 2014), and the DOL announced that using this notice also complies with ERISA. Employees are fully vested in employer matching contributions in two years. Participants can choose among the various investment funds available, but funds are invested in the QDIA if there is no direction, and absent an election, 3% of eligible pay will be deposited into the account. The employer match is dollar-for-dollar up to 1% of eligible pay and 50 cents per dollar for employee deferrals of 1%–6% of eligible pay. DOL says that using this notice also complies with ERISA.

Final IRS rules in T.D. 9447 (2009-12 I.R.B. 694) permit employers to add an automatic enrollment feature to 401(k) plans without performing nondiscrimination testing, but the plan must be a QACA or an EACA (Eligible Automatic Contribution Arrangement—the equivalent for multi-employer plans). T.D. 9447 reflects changes in the law under the Pension Protection Act of 2006 and The Worker, Retiree and Employer Recovery Act (WRERA; Pub. L. No. 110-458).

QACA plans must automatically enroll all employees, with contributions beginning at 3% of salary, rising 1% a year until they reach 6%. An employee who opts out can withdraw from the plan and have contributions end within 90 days. The distribution from the plan is taxable to the employee, but is not subject to the 10% penalty tax on premature withdrawals. The Final Regulations apply to plan years beginning on or after January 1, 2008. [Joanne Wojcik, *IRS Rules on 401(k) Will Help Some Employers*, Business Insurance (Feb. 25, 2009) (benefitslink.com); AICPA, *IRS Issues Final Regs on Automatic Contribution Agreements* (Feb. 25, 2009) (benefitslink.com)]

For QACAs and EACAs, the employer is permitted to increase the percentage of automatic contributions in the middle of the plan year, not just at its beginning, in order to reflect salary increases or performance evaluations, as long as the increases are uniformly applied. Employees must be notified of their automatic enrollment in the plan before they become eligible and at the beginning of each plan year. The QACA rules apply for plan years beginning on or after January 1, 2008; the EACA rules apply to plan years beginning on or after January 1, 2010. [Hodgson Russ LLP Employee Benefits Developments, IRS Publishes Final Automatic Enrollment Rules (May 2009) (benefitslink.com). See 74 Fed. Reg. 17 (Jan. 2, 2009): for plan years beginning on or after January 1, 2008, civil penalties of up to $1,000 per day can be imposed for failure to inform participants of their rights with respect to automatic contributions.

The safe harbor rules allow employers to avoid some of the most stringent non-discrimination standards, on condition that they make minimum contributions on behalf of all eligible employees. Final regulations were published in late 2013, dealing with permitted midyear reduction or suspension of safe harbor non-elective and matching contributions. The regulations took effect immediately for safe harbor non-elective contributions, and will be effective for plan years beginning on or after January 1, 2015 for safe harbor matching contributions. The regulations permit employers to suspend or reduce safe harbor contributions when running at a loss, or if the annual safe harbor notice discloses that the plan can be amended to reduce or suspend safe harbor contributions. The notice must be given 30 days in advance, telling employees the effective date of the amendment, how it works, and how they can change their elective deferrals. Contributions cannot be reduced or suspended before the effective date of the amendment or 30 days after notice is given. The plan must be amended to provide that the Actual Deferral Percentage (ADP) test (and the Actual Contribution Percentage test, if applicable) will be satisfied for the entire year of the suspension. For plan years beginning before January 1, 2015, the employer must satisfy the more stringent "substantial business hardship" test from the 2009 proposed regulations, which were adopted in the wake of the financial crisis caused by the 2008 collapse of the housing market. The new rules make it easier for financially troubled companies to reduce their contributions. The pre-2009 rules were believed to be limited to companies that were bankrupt or close to bankruptcy. The 2013 rule permits suspension or reduction if the company is running at a loss—or even if it is not running at a loss, but has retained the right to suspend or reduce its contributions. [T.D. 9641, 78 Fed. Reg. 68735 (Nov. 11, 2013); Marc D. Bussone et al., *IRS Issues Final Regulations On Suspending Or Reducing Safe Harbor 401(K) Contributions*, Bradley Arant Boult Cummins LLP (Nov. 20, 2013), available at Lexology.com; John Manganaro, *IRS Revises Safe Harbor Plan Rules*, pla nsponsor.com (Nov. 15, 2013)]

Notice 2009-65, 2009-39 I.R.B. 413, facilitates automatic enrollment in 401(k) plans by giving two sample plan amendments for adding automatic contribution features to the plan. One of the amendments adds automatic contributions to a 401(k) plan; the other adds an eligible automatic contribution arrangement pursuant to Code § 414(w) (90-day withdrawals).

[B] Fees

Plan participants disappointed in the returns of their accounts often charge the fiduciaries of the plan with breach of duty, and often the claims include a charge that the fiduciaries allowed the plan to pay excessively high fees, e.g., to brokers and mutual funds. See §§ 15.03[C], 15.15, and 15.17. Plaintiffs frequently allege that retail mutual funds are an unsuitable plan investment; the plaintiffs say that these funds charge fees that are inappropriate when there is little marketing or administration that must be done.

In 2013, costs stayed flat for larger plans, and actually went down slightly for small plans; the trend was attributed to greater requirements for fee disclosure and competitive pricing. According to the 401k Averages Book, the average total plan cost for small retirement plans (50 participants; $2.5 million in assets) dropped from 1.46% to 1.44%. For large plans (1000 participants, $50 million in assets) costs remained level at 1.03%. For micro-plans (10 participants, $500,000 in assets) the average plan expense was 1.90%. [Kevin McGuinness, *Most 401k Plan Fees Declining or Flat*, plansponsor.com (Feb. 18, 2014)]

A late 2013 settlement under which International Paper agreed to pay $30 million to 70,000 employees and former participants who challenged excessive fees and inappropriate investments was believed to the second-highest amount paid to resolve a fee dispute. (The largest settlement was $35 million paid by CIGNA Corp. in July 2013, for naming itself as administrator of the 401(k) plan and offering imprudent investment alternatives.) [Kelly Greene, *International Paper Pays $30 Million Over 401(k) Claims*, WSJ.com (Oct. 1, 2013). On June 21, 2013, the case of *Nolte v. CIGNA* was settled for $35 million: *Nolte, et al. v. Cigna Corp.*, No. 07-02046 (C.D. Ill., settled Oct. 16, 2013). The case was filed by CIGNA employees about their 401(k) plan. The plaintiffs alleged that the plan was not operated for the exclusive benefit of participants, as required by ERISA, but as a profit center for CIGNA because of unreasonable fees, failure to obtain competitive bids for plan services, and engaging in prohibited transactions with plan assets. CIGNA's retirement division was sold to Prudential Financial in 2004, but the plan participants did not share in the profits from the sale: FRA Plan Tools, *Breaking-Cigna and Prudential Settle Excessive Fee Lawsuit for $35 Million* (June 21, 2013) (benefitslink.com).]

The 12th edition of the 401k Averages Book, says that the average total plan cost for a small 401(k) plan (with 100 participants) is 1.3%, 1.24% of which represents average investment expense. For very large plans, with 1,000 or more participants, the average total plan cost is 1.08%, including 1.05% of investment expense. [Tara Cantore, *Book Reveals Wide Range of 401k Plan Fees*, plansponsor.com (Jan. 17, 2012)]

Fiduciaries must file notices with the DOL to get prohibited transaction relief under ERISA § 408(b)(2)'s fiduciary-level fee disclosure rules when they discover they have not received required notices. The fiduciaries must make a written request to the service provider to get the missing information. If the service provider does not comply within 90 days, the fiduciary must notify the DOL. The procedure was modified in mid-2012. Notice can be given either by mail at DOL, EBSA Office of Enforcement, P.O. Box 75296, Washington, D.C. 20013, or through the link at <www.dol.gov/ebsa/regs/feedisclosurefailurenotice.html>. The site will provide immediate electronic confirmation that notice is received. [Final Rule, DOL EBSA, *Amendment Relating to Reasonable Contract or*

Arrangement Under Section 408(b)(2)—Fee Disclosure, 77 Fed. Reg. 41678 (July 16, 2012)]

[1] Case Law

The Supreme Court held that the correct legal standard in an excessive fund fee case was whether the fees were so disproportionately large that they could not have been the product of arm's length bargaining (the standard used by most federal courts). [*Jones v. Harris*, 559 U.S. 335 (2010); see Fred Schneyer, *High Court Sides with Investors in Fee Case*, plansponsor.com (Mar. 30, 2010); Drinker, Biddle Investment Management Alert, *Supreme Court Rules in Jones v. Harris* (Mar. 30, 2010) (benefitslink.com).

However, the Supreme Court refused to hear the appeal of the dismissal of another Seventh Circuit case about excessive 401(k) fees: *Hecker v. Deere & Co.* 556 F.3d 575 (7th Cir 2009); [see Fred Schneyer, *U.S. Supremes Turn Away Hecker Fee Case Appeal*, plansponsor.com (Jan. 19, 2010)]

The Supreme Court vacated an Eighth Circuit decision about whether mutual fund fees violated Section 36(b) of the Investment Company Act. The Eighth Circuit had relied on the marketplace to prevent excessively high fees from being imposed. However, the Supreme Court remanded the case to comply with *Jones v. Harris*, where the standard is whether a fee is so unreasonably large that obviously there was no arm's length bargaining between the fund and its clients. [*Ameriprise Fin. Inc. v. Gallus*, 130 S. Ct. 2340 (2010) On remand, the Eighth Circuit found that the plaintiffs did not demonstrate a breach of fiduciary duty; the fees were not so high that they fell outside the range of reasonable fees that could have been negotiated at arm's length. [*Gallus v. Ameriprise*, 675 F.3d 1173 (8th Cir. 2012)]

Participants in a 401(k) plan sued under ERISA and the Investment Company Act, alleging that the fees on their annuity insurance contracts were excessive. The district court dismissed the Investment Company Act claims, requiring an ownership interest to bring a derivative suit—the plaintiffs were no longer investors in those funds. The district court also dismissed the ERISA claims because the plaintiffs did not make a pre-suit demand on the plan's trustees to make them correct the problem, nor were the trustees named as parties to the suit. The Third Circuit affirmed the Investment Company Act ruling, but reversed on the ERISA question, deciding that ERISA does not require a pre-suit demand, and trustees do not have to be named as parties. [*Santomenno v. John Hancock Life Ins. Co.,* 677 F.3d 178 (3d Cir. 2012)]

Exelon employees charged that their plan, offering 32 funds (24 retail mutual funds) generated excessive fees. The Seventh Circuit held that fiduciaries are not obliged to include only the lowest-cost funds, and noted that the fees were set competitively for the retail funds. The Seventh Circuit rejected the argument that institutional funds are always superior to retail funds; institutional funds might offer less liquidity or transparency than retail funds. [*Loomis v. Exelon*, 658 F.3d 667 (7th Cir. 2011)]

The Eighth Circuit upheld an award of $14.3 million against a 401(k) plan sponsor for breaching the fiduciary duty to control the costs of recordkeeping. The plaintiffs alleged that the sponsor breached its fiduciary duty by failing to monitor costs; paying above-market costs; and choosing investments that were more expensive than comparable investments. The Eighth Circuit found that it was acceptable to pay for recordkeeping through revenue sharing and bundled service agreements—but the fiduciaries failed to investigate adequately before incurring the costs. However, the Eighth Circuit remanded a separate award of $21.8 million in alleged financial losses that were calculated by comparing the investment results of one of the plan's investments in a mutual fund to the returns of a different mutual fund; the Eighth Circuit held that the hindsight calculation was too speculative. The Eighth Circuit also reversed $1.7 million against Fidelity; the district court found that Fidelity breached its fiduciary duty when it failed to pay "float" income (interest earned before plan assets were transferred from one account to another) to the 401(k) plan. The Eighth Circuit held that these amounts did not constitute plan assets. As a result, Fidelity could not be liable for attorneys' fees or costs in the litigation. [*Tussey et al. v. ABB*, 746 F.3d 327 (8th Cir. 2014) *reh'g denied* (May 20, 2014); see Goodwin Proctor ERISA Litigation Update, *In Tussey, Eighth Circuit Weighs in On Excessive Fee Claims* (Mar. 20, 2014) (benefitslink.com)]

The District Court for the Central District of California denied the plaintiffs' application for attorneys' fees in a suit about the selection of funds in their 401(k) plan. The court held that they had only minimal success because they won in only one of 10 claims against plan fiduciaries who included retail-class funds in the plan. [*Tibble v. Edison Int'l*, CV 07-5359 SVW (AGRx) (C.D. Cal. Aug. 22, 2011); see Rebecca Moore, *Court Denies Attorneys Fees in Institutional Versus Retail Shares Case*, plansponsor.com (Aug. 29, 2011). Fees were awarded in December 2010, but this decision reduces the fee award from $2.5 million to $410,000]

On appeal, the Ninth Circuit applied a six-year statute of limitations, beginning when the decision was made to include the allegedly improper investments in the plan. The Ninth Circuit held that the 404(c) safe harbor does not apply to designating investment options. The Ninth Circuit said that revenue sharing is not a prohibited transaction, in light of the prohibited transaction exemption stating that revenue sharing is not "consideration" given to fiduciaries. The Ninth Circuit held that, in general, including retail funds in the portfolio is not per se imprudent, and the portfolio can also include short-term funds—but, because the plan failed to do a proper analysis, it was imprudent to include two of the retail funds. The fiduciaries still had an obligation to consider all available share classes, even though they used a consultant. [*Tibble v. Edison*, 711 F. 3d 1061 (9th Cir. 2013)]

The Ninth Circuit denied rehearing in August 2013, but amended its opinion. The amended opinion reaffirms that the statute of limitations is six years for cases about the appropriateness of retaining employer stock in a 401(k) plan. The amended opinion limits the discretion that fiduciaries have with respect to employer stock. In some circumstances, the decision to keep the stock in the plan will not be entitled to deference—for example, if the decision furthers the interests of non-beneficiaries in the plan; fiduciary duty requires protecting the interests of beneficiaries. But the Ninth Circuit did not find those circumstances present in this case. [*Tibble v. Edison Int'l*, 729 F.3d 1110 (9th Cir. 2013); see Thomas E. Clark, Jr., *Breaking: 9th Circuit Amends Tibble v. Edison Opinion on Rehearing*, FRA Plan Tools (Aug. 2, 2013) (benefitslink.com)]

On the grounds that the change from a pension landscape where defined benefit plans predominated to one dominated by defined contribution plans calls for re-thinking ERISA remedies, the Seventh Circuit allowed a class of defined contribution plan participants to sue under ERISA § 502 in an excessive-fee case, building on the 2008 Supreme Court ruling that individual participants could seek ERISA relief. The Seventh Circuit held that a plan and individual participants can be injured at the same time if the plan's investment advisor charges excessive fees or makes imprudent investment choices. However, although the Seventh Circuit upheld the possibility of ERISA § 502 excessive-fee class actions, the court held that the district court did not certify properly defined classes: they did not have enough similarity of interest among class members because some class members were satisfied with the funds. Furthermore, some fees that were challenged were specific to particular funds, and others were imposed equally on all plan participants, so the classes as certified did not satisfy the "typicality" requirement for class action plaintiffs. [*Beesley v. International Paper Co.*, consolidated with *Spano v. Boeing*, 633 F.3d 574 (7th Cir. 2011); see Rebecca Moore, *Court OKs Class Actions for ERISA Cases*, plansponsor.com (Jan. 24, 2011)]

After the Seventh Circuit remanded the case, the District Court for the Southern District of Illinois certified a class of participants in Boeing's 401(k) plan. The district court approved the creation of sub-classes (for each mutual fund at issue). The district court accepted the defendant's argument that the class should be limited to people who participated in the plan at the time of the alleged breach because the original class of all past and future participants was excessively broad. [*Spano v. Boeing Co.*, No. 06-0743-DRH, 294 F.R.D. 114 (S.D. Ill. 2013); see Todd Mobley, *Seventh Circuit Again Grants Class Certification In Excessive Fee Case*, Proskauer Rose LLP (Oct. 17, 2013), available at Lexology.com]

[2] Regulations

In late 2010, EBSA published a final rule dealing with disclosure of investment options, including the fees imposed on employees in participant-directed individual account plans. The final rule says that investing plan assets is a fiduciary act subject to ERISA § 404(a)(1), requiring fiduciaries to be prudent and act solely in best interests of plan's participants and beneficiaries. Plan administrators are not liable if they rely, reasonably and in good faith, on information given by a service provider. The plan administrator must make sure that participants and beneficiaries who have investment responsibilities are informed of their rights and responsibilities in connection with their accounts. They must be given the fee and expense information they need to make informed decisions.

Participants must receive performance data, such as one, five, and 10-year historical returns. If the investment does not pay a fixed rate of return, the total annual operating expenses as a percentage of assets, and as a dollar amount per $1,000 invested, must be disclosed. For investments with a fixed rate of return, fees and any restrictions on ability to purchase or withdraw investments must be disclosed. The mandatory information must be given to participants on or before the first date they can direct their investments, then annually thereafter. They must receive general information about the structure and mechanics of the plan, how to give investment instructions, a list of the current investment choices, and fees and expenses for general plan services that can be charged to the account. Participants must receive statements, at least quarterly, showing the dollar amount of fees and expenses actually charged to their accounts, with a description of the services rendered.

This information must be provided in a chart or similar comparison format; DOL drafted a model chart. The final rule differs from previous law by entitling participants to disclosures no matter the size of the plan; previous law applied only to plans with 100 or more participants. Fee disclosure for individual plans extends beyond the fees charged for the plan's investment options, and includes general administrative services such as recordkeeping, accounting, and legal services. Participants must be advised whether the fees are charged pro rata or per capita, so they can determine if some participants pay more than their fair share. Benchmark returns must be compared with a broad-based market index that is not affiliated with the investment firm. [Final Rule, *Fiduciary Requirements for Disclosure in Participant-Directed Individual Account Plans*, <http://www.dol.gov/ebsa/pdf/frparticipantfeerule.pdf> and 75 Fed. Reg. 64910 (Oct. 20, 2010). See Fact sheet, *Final Rule to Improve Transparency of Fees and Expenses to Workers in 401(k)-Type Retirement Plans*, <http://www.dol.gov/ebsa/newsroom/fsparticipantfeerule.html> (Oct. 20, 2010). The model disclosure form is at <http://www.dol.gov/ebsa/participantfeerulemodelchart.doc>.]

DOL's FAB 2013-02 gives employers a one-time election to change the deadline for furnishing either the 2013 or 2014 comparison chart, as long as the plan fiduciary determines that the delay is in the best interests of participants and beneficiaries—and no more than 18 months elapses between charts. [FAB 2013-02, <http://www.dol.gov/ebsa/regs/fab2013-2.html>; see EBSA News, *Labor Department Permits 401(k) Plans to Reschedule Annual Disclosures to Employees*, <http://www.dol.gov/ebsa/newsroom/2013/ebsa072213.html> (July 22, 2013)]

In May 2013, EBSA published an advance NPRM about a more detailed benefit statement, giving not only the current account balance but also an estimate of the lifetime income stream it could yield, assuming that participant had reached NRA at the time of statement. For participants who have not reached NRA, the statement would provide the projected account balance and estimated lifetime income stream assuming retirement at NRA, expressed in current dollars. The income streams would be reported as estimated monthly payments reflecting the participant's projected mortality. For married participants, income streams would be based on the joint lives of both spouses. A calculator for lifetime income streams under these rules is available at <www.dol.gov/ebsa/regs/lifetimeincome calculator.html>. [RIN-1210-AB20, 78 Fed. Reg. 26727 (May 8, 2013); see EBSA.gov, *Fact Sheet On Lifetime Income Illustration*, <http://www.dol.gov/ebsa/newsroom/fsanprm.html> (May 7, 2013)]

A final rule requiring service providers to report the direct and indirect compensation paid by plan sponsors for account services was published in February 2012. The rule applies to service providers who are expected to receive $1,000 or more in compensation from defined benefit or defined contribution plans, for providing services or furnishing investment options in connection with brokerage or recordkeeping. The disclosures, on paper or electronic, must be given to the plan fiduciary. The final regulation is effective July 1, 2012, for both existing and new contracts. [77 Fed. Reg. 5632 (Feb. 3, 2012); DOL Fact Sheet, *Final Regulation Relating to Service Provider Disclosures Under Section 408(b)(2)* (February 2012) (benefitslink.com)]

An NPRM was published in the *Federal Register* for March 12, 2014, proposing to require a guide to be provided to disclosures by covered service providers that appear in multiple or lengthy documents. The guide assists plan fiduciaries in locating specific items of information that relate to their contracts with the service provider—e.g., the services that will be provided, if the provider has fiduciary status, how much the service provider will be paid, plus required investment disclosures for fiduciary, brokerage, and recordkeeping services (e.g., total annual operating expenses). [FR Doc 2014-04868, 79 Fed. Reg. 13949 (Mar. 12, 2014); see DOL Fact Sheet, *Proposed Regulation to Require a Guide to Assist Plan Fiduciaries in Reviewing 408(b)(2) Disclosures* (March 2014), <http://www.dol.gov/ebsa/newsroom/fs408(b)(2)disclosures.html>]

§ 6.08 INVESTMENT ADVICE FOR PARTICIPANTS

PWBA Advisory Opinion 2001-09A [(Dec. 14, 2001), <http://www.dol.gov/ebsa/programs/ori/advisory2001/2001-09A.htm>] says that it would not be a prohibited transaction for a company that provides financial services to retain an independent professional to use computer modeling and modern portfolio theory to offer discretionary asset allocation services and recommended asset allocation services in connection with individual account plans—i.e., 401(k) plans. Participants will be given advice about how to allocate assets within their accounts, but would be permitted to either accept or reject the advice.

In effect, this was the approach adopted by PPA Title XI (§§ 601–625). It is not a prohibited transaction for a plan to provide plan participants with investment advice as long as the plan fiduciaries' fees for providing the advice do not vary based on the actual recommendations. There is also a safe harbor for investment advice that is generated by a valid computer model.

In early 2008, the Supreme Court ruled that the purpose of ERISA is to safeguard benefits. Therefore, although the general rule is that ERISA § 502(a)(3) can only be used to provide remedies for the plan as a whole, in a defined contribution plan, a participant can bring suit charging that fiduciary misconduct reduced the value of his or her plan account. [*LaRue v. DeWolff, Boberg & Assocs., Inc.*, 552 U.S. 248 (2008)]

In 2010, the DOL withdrew an earlier, controversial rule and replaced it. Under the revised rule, advice can be given two ways: through the use of an unbiased computer model, or when the adviser's fees do not vary no matter what investments the participants choose. The computer model or level fee arrangement has to be chosen by the fiduciary, independent of adviser and its affiliates; qualifications set for the investment expert who certifies the model; investment advisers can't get compensation from affiliates on the basis of their recommendations; and advice arrangements have to be audited each year. Additional requirements, including fee disclosure, are imposed. [Proposed rule, 75 Fed. Reg. 9360 (Mar. 2, 2010). The earlier rule was RIN-1210-AB-13, *Investment Advice: Participants and Beneficiaries*, 74 Fed. Reg. 23951 (May 22, 2009).]

Late in 2011, the DOL finalized the ERISA § 408(g) regulations that say it is not a prohibited transaction for fiduciary advisors to give individualized investment advice to participants in individual account plans. Fiduciary advisors qualifying for this exemption include broker-dealers, registered investment advisors, banks, and insurance companies. The effective date is December 27, 2011. The DOL's Fact Sheet on the regulations estimates that about 134,000 defined contribution plans having 17 million participants and beneficiaries will contract with 16,000 investment advisory firms under these rules, and an estimated 3.5 million participants and beneficiaries will access the advice.

Advice must be based on generally accepted investment theories considering historic returns of different asset classes over time, plus information about the individual's age, life expectancy, current investments, assets and income, and investment preferences. The adviser's direct or indirect compensation must not vary based on which options the participant selects. Asset allocations in a computer model must be based on objective criteria, and must not be based on the size of the fee the advisor receives. Before a computer model is used, an eligible investment expert has to certify that it satisfies the requirements.

To use an eligible investment advice arrangement, the plan must have express authorization from a fiduciary. At least once a year, the arrangement must be audited by an independent auditor. The advisor must retain its records for at least six years after furnishing advice. [76 Fed. Reg. 66637 (Oct. 7, 2011); Prudential, *DOL Investment Advice Compliance Advisory* (December 2011) (benefitslink.com); Guest Article, Deloitte's Washington Bulletin, *Labor Department Finalizes* "Investment Education" *Regulation* (Oct. 31, 2011) (benefitslink.com)]

§ 6.09 401(k) PLANS RESPOND TO THE ECONOMY

[A] Market Effects

In the 1990s, 401(k) plans rose to prominence. Employers wanted plan participants to be able to benefit from the bull market—and employers were also concerned about the complexity and investment risk involved in operating a defined benefit plan.

The recession caused significant losses to 401(k) accounts, even those managed by reputable firms. A 2012 article [Steven Greenhouse, *Should the 401(k) Be Reformed or Replaced?* NYTimes.com (Sept. 11, 2012)] suggests what would once have been a ludicrous suggestion: for many years, 401(k)s were acclaimed as a solution for both employers' and employees' needs. Now some commentators are questioning whether the 401(k) form has failed or is so questionable that it requires major changes—if it can or should survive at all.

[B] Employer Stock and Diversification

During the bull market, publicly traded companies had very strong incentives to use their own stock to compensate employees. Not only could they save cash by offering stock or stock options, but distributing stock to employees reduces the risk of unfriendly takeovers, increases employees' stake in the company and therefore at least theoretically their loyalty, and gives employees the chance to benefit from increases in the value of the stock. The problem is that, in a bear market, employees suffer correspondingly as a result of decreases in the value of the stock. Diversification is a basic principle of investment theory. By law, defined benefit plans cannot be more than 10% invested in the employer's stock; however, employees, especially those who get employer matches in the form of the employer's stock, often have more than one-quarter of their account invested in employer stock. As Chapter 15 shows, many suits have tried (generally unsuccessfully) to penalize plan fiduciaries for retaining employer stock as an investment for an unduly long period.

PPA §§ 507 and 901 enacted a new Code § 401(a)(35) and a related ERISA provision at 204(j), explaining diversification rights for publicly traded employer securities held by a defined contribution plan. Participants (and some beneficiaries) are entitled to notice of the right to diversify their elective deferrals and after-tax contributions. Plans must offer at least three other investment options, with materially different risk and return characteristics. (Because ESOPs are designed to invest in employer stock, they are exempt from these rules.) Plan administrators must notify participants of their rights to divest at least 30 days before the first date the right to divest can be exercised. [IRS Notice 2006-107, 2006-5 I.R.B. 1114 (Nov. 30, 2006), <http://www.irs.gov/pub/irs-drop/n-06-107.pdf>] Failure to provide the statement is penalized by up to $110 per day elapsed without providing the required statement. All defined contribution plans must issue a statement at least annually, and quarterly statements are required for individual account plans (e.g., 401(k)s) whose participants can direct the investment of their account balances. The quarterly statement must disclose:

- The total account balance;
- The amount that is vested; if none is, the earliest vesting date for the participant;
- A breakdown of the value of each of the investments within the account;
- Whatever limitations or restrictions are placed on the right to direct investments by the terms of the plan;
- An explanation of why diversification is important;
- URL for the DOL Website containing investment information;
- (For profit-sharing plans integrated with Social Security) an explanation of plan integration.

The DOL also imposes Civil Money Penalties of up to $100/day for failure to provide notice of the right to sell company stock to diversify. [72 Fed. Reg. 44970 (Aug. 10, 2007); see DOL press release, *U.S. Labor Department Publishes Civil Penalty Rules Under Pension Protection Act* (Aug. 9, 2007)]

Employers can use the general DOL and IRS procedures for distributing statements in electronic rather than hard-copy form. The information can be provided on a secure Website as well as through individual e-mails. But if the sponsor chooses to use a Website to distribute the information, participants and beneficiaries must be given a written notice explaining how to access the information online—and that they can get a free paper copy if they prefer.

Individual account plans that do not permit individuals to direct the investment of their accounts must also furnish annual statements within 45 days of the end of the year. The statements are similar but need not include information about restrictions on investments or the explanation of the importance of diversification. The information can be furnished on a secure Website. [Gregory B. Kuhn, *New Benefit Statement Requirements for Retirement Plans*, <http://www.utzmiller/benefitstatement.pdf?> (Mar. 16, 2007). The DOL URL is <http://www.dol.gov/ebsa/investing.html>]

Regulations proposed in early 2008 were finalized in July 2010, explaining the diversification requirements imposed on plans that invest in publicly traded securities of the employer. Under the Final Rule, a participant who has at least three years of service (or the beneficiary of such a participant, or the beneficiary of a deceased participant) must be given a chance at least every quarter to diversify out of employer securities held in that person's account. The plan must offer at least three investment options other than employer stock, and those three must be diversified and must have materially different risk and return characteristics. [Proposed regulations: Prop. Reg. 136701-07, 2008-11 I.R.B. 616; final regulations, T.D. 9484, 75 Fed. Reg. 27927 (May 19, 2010); see Rebecca Moore, *IRS Issues Final Regs on Diversification Requirements for Company Stock*, plansponsor.com (May 18, 2010)]

As § 15.03[C] shows, a number of "stock drop" cases have been filed over the years. That is, plaintiffs whose account value has declined significantly because they invested in employer stock that declined in value frequently bring suits alleging that the plan's fiduciaries were imprudent to retain employer stock as a possible investment. Most of these cases have been dismissed. Many plans removed employer stock as an investment alternative, heading off suits. Improvement in the stock market climate also reduces the number of suits because there are fewer employer companies whose stock shows a sharp decline.

The *Wal-Mart v. Dukes* Supreme Court ruling (see § 42.06[A]) creates problems for class certification in stock drop cases, although *Dukes* is an employment discrimination case. *Dukes* increases the evidence requirement for certifying a class action. In the stock drop context, the problem is that the plan participants have different experiences based on investing for different periods of time. In mid-2013, the Seventh Circuit permitted 401(k) class actions for investment losses due to imprudent plan investment options, although in this case the plaintiffs said that the stable value fund's choices were imprudent not because they were too risky, but because too many money market funds were included, making it difficult to keep up with inflation. The plaintiff class was defined as 56,000 plan participants who invested in the stable value fund. [*Abbott v. Lockheed Martin Corp*, 725 F.3d 803 (7th Cir. 2013); see Carol Buckmann, *Can a Class of Participants Challenge 401(k) Plan Investments? An Appeals Court Says "Yes,"* Osler, Hoskin & Harcourt LLP Pensions & Benefits Law (Sept. 10, 2013) (benefitslink.com). But see *Palmason v. Weyerhaeuser Co.*, Case No. 2:11-cv-00695 (W.D. Wash).: defined benefit plan participants did not have standing to recover damages for plan losses caused by aggressive investments, because the plan had a duty to make up for their losses. However, participants were allowed to seek equitable relief for alleged fiduciary violations, possibly subjecting the fiduciaries to surcharges. Ian Morrison and Anne Harris, *Where Oh Where Did The Stock Drops Go*?, Seyfarth Shaw ERISA & Employee Benefits Litigation Blog (Dec. 2, 2013) (benefitslink.com)]

The *Moench* presumption is a legal theory that fiduciaries are presumed to be prudent when they keep employer stock as a plan investment. The nature of a presumption is that it can be rebutted if the plaintiffs produce enough evidence. The presumption stems from a 1995 Third Circuit case [*Moench v. Robertson*, 62 F.3d 553 (3d Cir. 1995)]; in the 1990s and 2000s, it was adopted by many other courts: the Second, Fifth, Sixth, Ninth, and Eleventh Circuits, although they differed on the technical legal rules for applying the presumption.

However, in 2014, the Supreme Court rejected the presumption in a case involving an ESOP that invested primarily in employer stock. According to the plaintiffs, the fiduciaries were imprudent to retain the stock in the plan, because their status as officers—and publicly available information—should have made them realize that the investment was too risky. The Supreme Court held that ESOP fiduciaries are subject to the same standard of prudence as other fiduciaries, except that ESOP fiduciaries do not have a duty to diversify the plan's investment portfolio; ESOPs are supposed to invest heavily in employer stock. The Supreme Court remanded the case to determine if the plaintiffs had pled their case adequately. The Supreme Court held that it is generally not enough for plaintiffs to charge that the market either over- or undervalued publicly traded stock. To assert a tenable claim for breach of the duty of prudence, the complaint must plausibly allege a superior alternative that the fiduciaries could have adopted—without breaking the law. It is never imprudent for fiduciaries to refuse to trade on non-public information. Furthermore, it might have violated fiduciary duty if the ESOP trustees had disposed of the employer stock, because it could have caused the stock's value to decline even further. [*Fifth Third Bancorp et al. v. Dudenhoeffer*, No. 12-751 (U.S. June 25, 2014)]

A former employee of SunTrust Banks, Inc. brought a putative class action alleging that adding SunTrust proprietary mutual funds as plan investments for the 401(k) plan breached the fiduciary duties of loyalty and prudence. The plaintiffs charged that these funds had inferior performance and higher fees than other available funds. The defendants said the complaint was untimely. The statute of limitations for an ERISA fiduciary breach claim is the earlier of three years after the plaintiff obtained actual knowledge of the breach or six years after the breach (date of last action that was part of the violation; or, for an omission, the last date on which the fiduciary could have cured the omission or breach). The Eleventh Circuit held that the motion to dismiss was premature, without evidence about when the plaintiff had actual knowledge. The Eleventh Circuit held that the accrual date was the date the funds were selected, making the complaint untimely. [*Fuller v. SunTrust Banks, Inc.*, 744 F.3d 685 (11th Cir. 2014); see Katherine Lange, *Southeastern ERISA Watch: Eleventh Circuit Joins Fourth Circuit In Rejecting Continuing Breach Approach To ERISA's Statute Of Limitation* (Mar. 11, 2014) (benefitslink.com)]

A $3 million preliminary settlement was announced in a 401(k) class action against Flagstar Bank. The money will be paid to the plan. The suit charged that retaining employer stock as a plan investment was a breach of fiduciary duty.

DOL's amicus brief said that Flagstar suffered huge losses from non-performing mortgages, and the value of its stock fell 95% between early 2007 and mid-2010. The settlement was approved by the District Court for the Eastern District of Michigan on December 12, 2013. [*Griffin v. Flagstar Bancorp.*, No. 2:10-cv-10610, settlement approved <http://milawyersweekly.com/files/2013/12/02-83901.pdf>; see Pete Daly, *Bank Settles Class Action Lawsuit Over 401(k) Investments For $3M*, Grand Rapids Business Journal (Sept. 4, 2013) (benefitslink.com)]

The Sixth Circuit held that an employee who sold most of her shares of employer stock at a time when she alleged the share price was artificially inflated by the company's financial misconduct did not have standing to maintain a stock-drop suit. She had no actual injury: if anything, the so-called misconduct benefited her by increasing the price she received for selling the stock. [*Taylor v. KeyCorp.*, 680 F.3d 609 (6th Cir. 2012)]

The Bank of America won a suit alleging that the bank violated ERISA by investing retirement plan assets in funds affiliated with the bank. The Fourth Circuit held that the plaintiffs did not have constitutional standing to bring the case. They did not plead any cognizable injury in fact that they were likely to prevail on at trial. They did not claim that they were deprived of benefits or likely to be deprived in the future. The plaintiffs alleged that there was a fiduciary breach each time the plan committee overseeing the 401(k) plan met but did not remove bank-affiliated funds from the investment portfolio, but the Fourth Circuit said that the claim was time-barred. The suit was brought in 2006, and the challenge would have to be raised within six years of the initial selection of funds, which occurred in 1999. [*David v. Alphin*, 704 F.3d 327 (4th Cir. 2013); see Plansponsor staff, *Bank of America Wins Suit Over Affiliated Fund Use*, plansponsor.com (Jan. 22, 2013)]

[C] Blackout Periods

In certain instances, often associated with corporate mergers and acquisitions, or with the release of corporate earnings and other financial statements, a "blackout period" is imposed, and ordinary activities in connection with plan accounts are suspended. Because of concerns that rank-and-file employees are at risk of losing money during blackouts, the Sarbanes-Oxley Act [Pub. L. No. No. 107-204] not only limits the trading activities of corporate insiders, but also obligates the corporation to provide notice of future blackout periods to the employees at large.

A blackout period, according to § 306(a)(4) of the Act, means a period that lasts more than three consecutive business days, during which at least 50% of the plan's participants or beneficiaries' ability to trade in the employer company's stock is affected. An "individual account plan" means a retirement plan that has more than one participant, and where each participant has his or her own separate account. For instance, a 401(k) plan is an individual account plan, but a defined benefit pension plan is not, because the whole plan has only one account from which benefits are paid.

Certain events that affect trading are not considered blackout periods, so the notice requirement doesn't apply. Under the legal definition, blackout periods are only temporary, so if rights are permanently amended or eliminated, this does not constitute a blackout period, and notice will not be required.

Furthermore, if the plan imposes regularly scheduled blackouts—for instance, every quarter at the time that earnings figures are released—and if the scheduled blackouts have been disclosed to participants and beneficiaries in the Summary Plan Description (SPD) or other plan communications, notice will not be required.

Finally, an event is not a blackout period if it is imposed just because someone becomes—or ceases to be—a participant or beneficiary in an individual account plan because of a corporate merger, acquisition, or divestiture. Limitations on just one person's account (relating to a divorce-related court order or a tax levy, for instance) are not considered blackout periods either, because a blackout period is a mass rather than an individual event.

[D] Changes in the Employer Match

Under prior law, the sponsor of a safe harbor 401(k) plan could eliminate or reduce matching contributions under certain circumstances, but could only suspend or cut non-elective contributions by terminating the plan. Proposed regulations published in mid-2009 [74 Fed. Reg. 23134 (May 18, 2009)] allow plan sponsors to reduce or suspend their safe harbor non-elective contributions during a plan year in which they encounter a substantial business hardship. The eligible employees must be notified of the reduction or suspension, and the plan must be amended to provide that anti-discrimination tests must be satisfied for the whole plan year. Substantial business hardship means that the sponsoring corporation is operating at a loss; unemployment or underemployment is common in the sponsor's industry; the industry as a whole is depressed or in a decline; and it is reasonable to predict that the plan cannot be continued without reducing or suspending non-elective contributions. The rules are complex, so sponsors must get legal advice before attempting to alter plan contributions. [See Towers Perrin Governance and Compliance Advisory Insight, *New IRS Regulations Allow Safe Harbor 401(k) Plans to Suspend Non-Elective Contributions* (May 2009) (benefitslink.com)]

The regulations were finalized in late 2013: 78 Fed. Reg. 68735 (Nov. 15, 2013). The final rules make it somewhat easier for the employer to show entitlement to suspend or reduce the contributions during a plan year. The final regulations generally apply to amendments adopted after May 18, 2009; they apply for plan years beginning on or after January 1, 2015 with respect to mid-year reductions or suspensions.

In response to economic difficulties, some plan sponsors reduced or eliminated their matching contributions—although some of those employers reinstated the match as conditions improved. [See, e.g., Stephen Miller, *Changes in 401(k) Plans Spur Higher Participation*, SHRM (Oct. 15, 2012) (benefitslink.com); Karen DeMasters, *401(k) Matching Funds Being Eliminated, Study Shows*, Financial Advisor Blogs (May 2, 2013) (benefitslink.com)]

Another possibility is that employers will impose additional conditions before employees can receive a match. International Foundation of Employee Benefit Plans (IFEBP)'s twelfth annual 401(k) Benchmarking Survey revealed more companies delaying eligibility. In 2011, two-thirds of employers with 401(k) plans made employees eligible for a match as soon as they were hired, but only 56% did so in 2012. This survey shows 21% of respondents stating that they are considering changing the plan design to make all employer contributions discretionary rather than automatic. [Joanne Sammer, *Are 401(k) Matches an Endangered Species?*, Business Finance (May 7, 2013) (benefitslink.com)]

CHAPTER 7

CASH BALANCE PLANS

§ 7.01 INTRODUCTION

A cash balance plan is a hybrid pension plan that shares features of a conventional defined benefit plan with characteristics more like a profit-sharing or 401(k) plan. Cash balance plans are subject to the defined benefit plan rules.

The IRS's definition of a cash balance plan, found at 64 Fed. Reg. 56579, is "a defined benefit pension plan that typically defines an employee's retirement benefit by reference to the amount of a hypothetical account balance." In a typical cash balance plan, this account is credited with hypothetical allocations and interest that are determined under a formula set out in the plan.

The plan is drafted so that the corporation's books reflect an individual account for each participant. The employer funds the plan each year, based on a percentage of pay, and subject to the I.R.C. § 415 limit on employer contributions. The pension the employee will eventually receive reflects two elements: an annual benefit credit (a percentage of pay) and annual interest credited at the rate specified by the plan. Because cash balance plans provide individual accounts, the plans are more portable than ordinary defined benefit plans.

At retirement, the employee's retirement annuity is based on the vested account balance. In practice, although in most defined benefit plans accrual is greatest in the later years of employment, in cash balance plans accrual is greatest in the early years. Defined benefit plans often provide early retirement subsidies; cash balance plans seldom do.

In 2001, cash balance plans represented only 2.9% of all defined benefit plans. The percentage rose steadily, until cash balance plans represented 20% of defined benefit plans in 2011; the projected 2012 percentage was 24%. Virtually all cash balance plans (5,244) now in existence were adopted between 2006-2011 (i.e., after the PPA made it clear that this plan form is legal). Only 1,684 cash balance plans were adopted between 2000 and 2005, 265 between 1990 and 1999, and 82 between 1985 and 1989. [<http://cashbalancedesign.com/articles/documents/NationalCashBalanceResearchReport2013.pdf>, discussed in Matthew Heimer, *Cash-Balance Plans Grow, 401(k)s Shrink*, WSJ.com (June 13, 2013) and Kevin McGuinness, *Cash Balance Plans Show Decade-Long Growth*, plansponsor.com (June 12, 2013)]

Hybrid plans accrue benefits under the fixed formula set by the employer. A hybrid defined benefit plan usually defines the benefit as a lump sum account balance rather than an annuity benefit payable at age 65. Cash balance plans are the most popular type of hybrid plans. The account balance is the sum of periodic pay credits (a percentage of pay) plus interest credits reflecting the interest rate chosen by the employer.

Pension equity plans (PEPs) post pay credits to participants' accounts, so the lump sum account balance at retirement is the sum of the percentages over the years times final average pay.

The legal status of cash balance plans was highly ambiguous until the Pension Protection Act of 2006 (PPA; Pub. L. No. 109-280) made it clear that a cash balance plan that satisfies the statutory criteria will not be considered discriminatory. (See § 7.07.) However, this relief is prospective only, and cash balance conversions that occurred before June 29, 2005 are not affected by the legislation. As § 7.04 shows, although most courts have ruled in favor of cash balance plans, a few cases have found the cash balance form in general, or specific plans and plan provisions, to violate ERISA or discriminate against older workers.

Although plan amendments cannot reduce benefits earned before the conversion, some conversions have the effect that employees who already earned benefits do not earn additional retirement benefits for varying periods of time after the conversion. This effect, often referred to as "wearaway" or "benefit plateau," continues until the employee's benefit under the ongoing cash balance formula catches up with the employee's protected benefit.

The ERISA Advisory Council defines wearaway as an effect of plan transitions. The employee can get either the frozen benefit under the old plan formula or the total benefit under the cash balance plan—whichever is greater. But for employees who are close to early retirement age, the frozen benefit may be so much larger than the accruals under the new cash balance formula that, in effect, little or nothing will be accrued for a long time, until the benefit under the old rules is "worn away."

Although it is a cash balance plan case, the Supreme Court's mid-2011 decision in *Amara v. Cigna* has much broader implications for ERISA enforcement, looking at the remedies plan participants can receive based on the traditional "equitable" suits that descend from medieval English church court practice. In this case, Cigna performed a cash balance conversion of its plan. Cigna distributed summaries and an SPD stating that the new plan provided an overall improvement in retirement benefits, and that the participants' opening account balance equaled the full value of their accrued benefits. These documents also said that the conversion did not save money for the employer. Plan participants filed a class action charging that many participants were subject to wearaway; that the opening account balance did not reflect the early retirement subsidy, so it offered less than full value; and that the employer saved $10 million a year as a result of the conversion. (Cigna eventually conceded the last point, but said that it spent the money on other benefit plans.) The district court ruled for the plaintiffs, and ordered reformation of the plan to conform to description in the employee communications. The district court ordered the plan to provide beneficiaries their pre-conversion frozen benefits, plus the cash balance benefits they earned after the conversion. The Second Circuit affirmed.

The case went to the Supreme Court, which held that the SPD merely communicates about the plan, and the terms of the SPD are not part of the plan itself. The settlor of the plan sets the terms of the plan; the plan administrator is responsible for communicating with participants. This decision wipes out a long line of cases that hold that, if the SPD conflicts with the plan terms, the SPD should be enforced because it is the document that the beneficiaries saw. The Supreme Court also said that plaintiffs cannot use ERISA § 502(a)(1)(B) to enforce a contract claim for benefits. Asserting a likelihood of harm to a class is not enough to support relief, and (a)(1)(B) does not give courts the authority to reform the terms of a plan.

However, with regard to what constitutes appropriate equitable relief under ERISA § 502(a)(3), the Supreme Court left open the possibility of getting the plan reformed, seeking equitable estoppel, or even getting the trustee to reimburse the plan ("surcharge"). In general, plaintiffs do not have to prove detrimental reliance in equitable proceedings for reformation or surcharge. To win, plaintiffs must show actual harm (e.g., that they lost money), and that the defendants' actions caused the harm. However, they do not have to prove that they actually relied on the provisions of the SPD.

The Supreme Court remanded the case for further proceedings. [*Amara v. Cigna*, 131 S. Ct. 1866 (May 16, 2011)]

When *Amara* was remanded, the District Court for the District of Connecticut reformed the plan terms and ordered additional benefits as appropriate equitable relief. The district court said that contract, rather than trust, standards justified reformation, based on fraud on one side and mistake on the other. The Supreme Court used a trust-law analysis, but the district court said that contract analysis conforms better to economic reality. The district court used the "likely harm" standard: once an initial showing of likely harm is made, it is presumed that the participants in the plan were prejudiced. According to the district court, the defective notice misled the employees about the contract, and CIGNA prevented the employees from getting accurate information about changes to the plan and misled them into believing their accrued benefits would be protected. The district court ruled that CIGNA could be required to pay surcharges based on two theories: make-whole relief or unjust enrichment. The make-whole argument would require plaintiffs to prove that they suffered a loss related to CIGNA's breach of fiduciary duty, but if they prove this, CIGNA can show that they would have had the loss even without the breach. Because the district court believed that the plaintiffs received less than their benefits under the cash balance plan plus the benefits under the predecessor plan, the court did not consider the unjust enrichment theory. The district court ordered that the plaintiffs receive full benefits under both plans. [*Amara v. CIGNA Corp.*, No 3:01-cv-2361, 2012 U.S. Dist. LEXIS 180355 (D. Conn. Dec. 20, 2012); see Mark Casciari and Sara Eber, *Amara—The Beat Goes On*, Seyfarth Shaw ERISA & Employee Benefits Litigation Blog (Jan. 10, 2013) (benefitslink.com); Rebecca Moore, *Court Makes Repeat Decision in Amara v. CIGNA Corp*, plansponsor.com (Jan. 23, 2013)]

In October 2011, the PBGC proposed a rule to implement PPA provisions for allocating assets and determining the amount of benefits when a cash balance or other statutory hybrid plan terminates. The PBGC's intention was to give participants more certainty about their benefits when a plan is terminated and trusteed by the PBGC. An applicable defined benefit plan must have provisions for plan termination. If the interest crediting rate is variable, the interest rate applied to accrued benefits at termination is the average of interest rates for the five-year period ending on the date of termination. The interest rates and mortality tables as of the termination date are used to compute plan benefits that are payable as annuities at normal retirement age. Any variable rate must be the average of the five-year period ending on the termination date.

For distress terminations, the proposed termination date determines the benefits. If the proposed termination date is delayed, benefits accrued between the proposed and actual termination dates are recalculated using the interest rate that would have applied before the actual date of termination.

The PPA provides that a defined benefit plan fails to meet accrual requirements related to age if the plan provides for an interest credit in any plan year that exceeds the market rate of return. A plan satisfies the present value requirements if the present value of any participant's accrued benefit equals either the balance in the participant's hypothetical account, or an accumulated percentage of final average compensation.

Under the PBGC's proposed rule, some benefits are calculated differently for valuation than for payment purposes. The PBGC determines if a benefit can be cashed out (*i.e.*, is small enough to be distributed in a lump sum). If, after August 17, 2006, the plan made lump sum payments based on the hypothetical account balance without regard to the present value rules, the PBGC makes a de minimis lump sum determination using the same method as the plan did. The proposed rule says that Category 3 benefits for participants who were eligible to retire three years before plan termination or the sponsor's bankruptcy, but did not retire, are determined based on the account balance and interest rate that would have applied if the person had retired before the applicable date.

For bankruptcy terminations in general, the PBGC determines the hypothetical account balance as of the bankruptcy filing date using the actual crediting interest rate for interest between the bankruptcy filing date and the date of termination. For credits after the plan's determination date and before NRA or the annuity start date, the rate in effect on the termination date is used. [76 Fed. Reg. 67105 (Oct. 31, 2011); see PLC, *PBGC Implements Rules Changing Method for Determining Benefits When Hybrid Plan Terminates* (Oct. 31, 2011) (benefitslink.com); Rebecca Moore, *PBGC Issues Proposed Rule on Hybrid Plan Terminations*, plansponsor.com (Oct. 29, 2011); Deloitte's Washington Bulletin, *PBGC Proposes Rules on Determining Benefits in Terminating Hybrid Plans* (Nov. 7, 2011) (benefitslink.com)]

§ 7.02 CASH BALANCE PLANS: PROS AND CONS

The PPA provision authorizing cash balance conversions was adopted because many employers had already converted their plans to cash balance form, or showed an interest in doing so. Employers wanted to keep the difference between the plan's actual investment return and the rate of return promised to employees. They hoped that the plan could become self-funding without additional employer contributions if the difference were large enough. Perhaps ironically, the development of a positive body of decisions and regulations supporting cash balance plans and cash balance conversions has occurred when financial conditions are not necessarily suitable for conversions.

Sibson Consulting published a report in Spring 2011 suggesting that the IRS final and proposed regulations cleared up some confusion and made cash balance plans more attractive for some employers. Sibson suggested that a simple cash balance plan can be much less expensive for the employer than a defined contribution plan because the discount rate for a cash balance plan is based on the rate of return on investment-grade corporate bonds—and, under conditions prevailing in the first quarter of 2011, the difference between corporate and Treasury bond rates could be as much as 2%, allowing the sponsor to save money. Cash balance plans tend to have less interest rate risk than defined benefit plans.

Cash balance plans, like defined benefit plans but unlike 401(k) plans, cover all employees—so employees will get some employer contributions in a cash balance plan even if they would not get an employer match in a 401(k) plan if they could not save enough money to fund a 401(k) account. Combining a cash balance plan with a defined contribution plan places some of the risk on each. [Plansponsor staff, *New Regs May Warrant Reconsidering Cash Balance*, plansponsor.com (Mar. 25, 2011)]

§ 7.03 "WHIPSAW" AND FINANCIAL FACTORS

The "whipsaw" issue arises because I.R.C. § 417 specifies the interest and mortality assumptions that must be used in converting from annuity to lump sum payment. When a worker covered by a defined benefit plan terminates employment, the sponsor must calculate the present value of any lump sum distribution.

This is done by projecting the account balance that would be available at normal retirement age, using PBGC-authorized interest rate assumptions. The next step is to find the value of the annuity that could be purchased with that sum. Finally, the PBGC interest rate assumptions are used again, to reconvert the annuity to a lump sum that represents the present value of the participant's account.

Applying this so-called whipsaw calculation to some cash balance plans increases the lump sum available to some plan participants. The participants who benefit naturally argue that the calculation has to be applied—and plan sponsors want to argue that they can bypass the whipsaw calculation. The higher the interest rates used, the less likely participants are to complain. Therefore, the whipsaw problem is most acute for disputes about plan actions taken before 1995, because in 1994 the PBGC raised its interest rate assumptions significantly.

The PPA avoids the whipsaw problem by requiring the lump sum distribution to equal the hypothetical account balance, and by specifying the range of interest rates. See § 7.07, below.

The Sixth Circuit held in April 2007 that although the whipsaw calculation is not required after the PPA took effect, it was required before that, and therefore upholds an award of $46 million in benefits and prejudgment interest to a class of 1,250 former employees who retired early and received lump sum distributions. [*West v. AK Steel Corp.*, 484 F.3d 395 (6th Cir. 2007), *cert. denied*, 129 S. Ct. 895 (Jan. 12, 2009)]

The Sixth Circuit held that 92 plan participants had the right to file a claim against the plan, charging that their payments were incorrect because the plan administrators did not use the whipsaw calculation. The Sixth Circuit upheld the district court's grant of about $3 million in unpaid benefits. The named plaintiff, Schumacher, brought suit in October 2009, asking for a whipsaw calculation of benefits for 92 participants excluded from the *West* case. The Sixth Circuit held that the *Schumacher* suit was timely because ERISA suits borrow the most analogous state statute of limitations, which in this case could be as much as 15 years. The Sixth Circuit held that the plaintiffs' severance agreements mentioned "claims" in general terms but did not specifically address ERISA or pension claims, so the agreements did not prevent the plaintiffs from maintaining their suit. [*Schumacher v. AK Steel Corp. Ret. Accumulation Pension Plan & AK Steel Corp. Benefit Plans Administrative Comm.*, 711 F.3d 675 (6th Cir. 2013); see Erin Adams, *The Whipsaw Effect*, plansponsor.com (Sept. 2013)]

The Seventh Circuit held, in late 2011 that, when a district court creates a remedy for participants who were subjected to impermissible whipsaw calculations that did not add future interest credits to their lump sum distributions, the court does not have to defer to the plan's preferred method for recalculating the lump sums. The plan conceded that unlawful whipsaw had occurred but said that the suit was time-barred or, as an alternative, that the plan's method of calculation should be used. The Seventh Circuit said that the unlawful calculations were part of the plan, so the plan's fiduciaries did not engage in any interpretive discretion to which the court could grant deference. [*Thompson v. Retirement Plan for Employees of S.C. Johnson & Son*, Inc., 651 F.3d 600 (7th Cir. 2011); see CCH Pensions & Benefits, *Deference to Plan's Method for Re-Calculating Distributions Not Required to Remedy Pre-PPA* "Whipsaw" *Violations* (Oct. 25, 2011) (benefitslink.com)]

For most of the 1990s and 2000s, the Treasury rate was below the guarantees offered by cash balance plans, giving employees an incentive to quit early and take lump sums. In a case interpreting plan language from 2003 (i.e., before the 2007 regulations that now limit the ability to establish a normal retirement age (NRA) lower than age 62), the Seventh Circuit permitted a cash balance plan to define NRA as the completion of five years of service to avoid the whipsaw calculation of lump sum benefits. Because the plan set NRA at five years of service—the vesting date—without reference to age, his virtual account balance was also the value of his lump sum. [*Fry v. Exelon*, 571 F.3d 644 (7th Cir. 2009); see Deloitte Washington Bulletin, *Five Years of Service Is a Permissible* "Normal Retirement Age" *for Cash Balance Plan* (July 20, 2009) (benefitslink.com).

Certiorari was denied on February 22, 2010 (559 U.S. 936); see Rebecca Moore, *Supreme Court Lets Stand Alternate Definitions for Retirement Age*, plansponsor.com (Feb. 23, 2010); for history of the case, see Fred Schneyer, *Appellate Judges Affirm Years-of-Service Definition for Retirement*, plansponsor.com (July 10, 2009)]

The Fourth Circuit rejected claims that the Bank of America violated the anti-backloading provision by defining the NRA as the earlier of the first day of the calendar month after the participant reached age 65 or having 60 months of vesting service. The court held that it was not necessary for every employee to have the same NRA and it was permissible to set the NRA on the basis of vesting service to prevent some participants from being entitled to whipsaw distributions. In the Fourth Circuit view, the backloading rules cease to apply once a plan participant reaches NRA. [*McCorkle v. Bank of Am.*, 688 F.3d 164 (4th Cir. 2012); see Rebecca Moore, *Plan Definition of NRA Did Not Lead to Backloading*, plansponsor.com (Aug. 27, 2012)]

The Sixth Circuit held that an ex-employee who challenged the calculation of her lump sum distribution from a cash balance plan was not required to exhaust her administrative remedies under the plan—an appeal would have been futile. According to the Sixth Circuit, participants can go straight to court when they challenge the legality of a plan's entire methodology. The plaintiff admitted that she received the proper amount under the plan's method of calculation—what she objected to was the method. [*Durand v. The Hanover Ins. Group*, 560 F.3d 436 (6th Cir. 2009); see CCH Pension & Benefits, *Legality of "Whipsaw" Lump Sum Calculation Under Cash Balance Plan Can Be Challenged in Court* (Apr. 3, 2009); *French v. BP Corp. North Am. Inc.*, No. 08-216-DLB, 2009 U.S. Dist. LEXIS 104408 (E.D. Ky. Nov. 15, 2009) reaches a similar conclusion.]

§ 7.04 CASE LAW ON CASH BALANCE PLANS

The fundamental age discrimination issue is how ERISA § 204(b)(1)(H)(i) and Code § 411(b)(1)(H), which forbid terminating benefit accrual or reducing the rate of accrual because of a plan participant's attainment of any age, define "rate of accrual." If the rate of accrual is the change, from year to year, in the annuity that the participant can expect at age 65, then cash balance plans are inherently age-discriminatory because of the greater number of years over which younger participants can accrue interest credits. However, if it is merely the pay and interest credits to the hypothetical account, then cash balance plans are not discriminatory, they merely reflect the basic economic concept of the time value of money. [See the chart prepared by the American Benefits Council, *Cash Balance Plan Litigation*, <http://www.americanbenefitscouncil.org/documents/cb_litigation_120706.pdf> (Dec. 7, 2006).]

By mid-2008, five of the courts of appeals (Second, Third, Sixth, Seventh, Ninth) had already ruled that cash balance plans are not inherently discriminatory against older workers. These courts generally held that the higher balance for younger workers was a simple effect of the time value of money. [*Hurlic v. Southern California Gas Co.*, 539 F.3d 1024 (9th Cir. Aug. 20, 2008) [allowing, however, maintenance of a claim that the plan violated ERISA's notice requirements by not providing notice of wear-away]; *Hirt v. Equitable Ret. Plan for Emps., Managers & Agents*, 533 F.3d 102 (2d Cir. 2008); *Register v. PNC Fin. Servs. Group, Inc.*, 477 F.3d 56 (3d Cir. 2007); *Drutis v. Rand McNally & Co.*, 499 F.3d 608 (6th Cir. 2007), *cert. denied*, 129 S. Ct. 68 (2008); *Cooper v. IBM Personal Pension Plan*, 457 F.3d 636 (7th Cir. 2006), *cert. denied*, 549 U.S. 1175 (2007); see Fred Schneyer, *A Fifth Federal Appellate Court Upholds Cash Balance Plan Designs*, plansponsor.com (Aug. 20, 2008) and *U.S. Supreme Court Denies Cash Balance Challenge Review*, plansponsor.com (Oct. 7, 2008)

In June 2010, the District Court for the District of New Jersey ended 12 years of litigation by ruling that AT&T's cash balance plan did not violate ERISA or the ADEA. Nor did the plan violate IRS regulations, requiring subsidized early retirement benefits to be the actuarial equivalent of the standard retirement benefit. The court held that the plan participants did not prove that the plan was "backloaded" (allowed accrual of benefits in any year in excess of 133% of benefits in any prior year): *Engers v. AT&T Inc.*, No. 98-3660 (SRC) (D.N.J. 2010). See Fred Schneyer, *AT&T Cleared in Cash Balance Suit*, plansponsor.com (June 9, 2010).]

Verizon Communications' cash balance plan document included a drafting error (a transition factor for calculating opening balances was used twice instead of once). According to the Northern District of Illinois, the plan's administrative committee should have gone to court to reform the plan documents to correct the mistake; it did not have the power to reform the plan. However, it was not an abuse of discretion to use 120% of the PBGC interest rate instead of 100% to calculate the opening account balance. [*Young v. Verizon's Bell Atlantic Cash Balance Plan*, No. 05 C 7314 (N.D. Ill. Aug. 28, 2008; see Fred Schneyer, *Verizon Hit for Cash Balance Conversion Error*, plansponsor.com (Sept. 2, 2008)] The Northern District re-heard the case in 2009 and ruled that Verizon could correct the error, holding this time that requiring the language to be applied literally would give participants a $1.67 billion windfall. Magistrate Judge Morton Denlow said that employers would be discouraged from adopting plans if they suffered unduly harsh penalties for mistakes. The Seventh Circuit affirmed in 2010. The Supreme Court refused to review the case. [*Young v. Verizon's Bell Atlantic Cash Balance Plan*, 615 F.3d 808 (7th Cir. 2010), *cert. denied*, 131 S. Ct. 2924 (May 23, 2011), *reh'g denied*, 132 S. Ct. 47 (July 25, 2011). See Fred Schneyer, *Verizon Escapes $1.6B Pension Liability*, plansponsor.com (Nov. 5, 2009).]

The Southern District ruled in 2009 that J.P. Morgan Chase and its predecessors did not violate ERISA when they converted the plan to a cash balance form, rejecting the argument that the plan did not provide "definitely determinable" benefits because it did not specify a method of projecting interest rates. Under ERISA § 402, employers have discretion to choose interest rates, as long as the plan has a written instrument that explains its funding and distribution mechanisms. [*Bilello v. J.P. Morgan Chase Ret. Plan*, No. 07 Civ. 7379 (DLC) (S.D.N.Y. Apr. 24, 2009); see Rebecca Moore, *Court Dismisses Claims Against JP Morgan Cash Balance Plan*, plansponsor.com (Apr. 28, 2009). Despite this ruling, the Southern District of New York approved settlement of two cash balance suits against J.P. Morgan Chase in mid-2010; both cases alleged failure to give adequate notice of conversion. [*In re J.P. Morgan Chase Cash Balance Litig.*, 255 F.R.D. 130, No. 06-cv-0732 (DLC) (THK) (S.D.N.Y. 2010); see Fred Schneyer, *Cash Balance Settlement Gets Court Approval*, plansponsor.com (July 20, 2010)]

The Seventh Circuit cleared Monsanto of class action age discrimination allegations, ruling that the rate of accrual did not decrease because of age. The class action dealt only with the Prior Plan Account (PPA), one of two accounts employees received after the conversion. The PPA accounts were supposed to preserve the accrued balances while also standardizing the disparate provisions of the earlier plans. The PPA's opening balance was calculated with a credit of the actuarial equivalent lump sum for the accrued benefit, discounted by an interest rate of 8½% per year, for each month between the participant's age at the time of conversion and age 55. Pay credits were credited each month, but interest credits ceased at age 55. The Seventh Circuit held that the plan was not an "eligible cash balance plan" as defined by IRS regulations (because it distributed lump sums), and in fact operated more like a defined benefit plan. The interest credits were not benefit accruals, because they did not increase the accrued benefit at retirement. If the credits were not benefit accruals, then stopping them could not violate the ban on age-based changes in accruals. [*Walker v. Monsanto Co. Pension Plan*, 614 F.3d 415 (7th Cir. 2010); see Fred Schneyer, *Monsanto Cash Balance Plan Cleared of Age Bias Wrongdoing*, plansponsor.com (Aug. 2, 2010). For background, see Fred Schneyer, *Employer Wins One, Loses One in Cash Balance Case*, plansponsor.com (June 15, 2009). Certiorari was denied, 131 S. Ct. 1678 (Mar. 21, 2011): see Rebecca Moore, *High Court Lets Stand Monsanto Cash Balance Ruling*, plansponsor.com (Mar. 22, 2011)]

The Eighth Circuit held in 2009 that a defined benefit plan that converted to cash balance form in 2000 (i.e., long before the PPA took effect) did not reduce accrued benefits when the discount rate it used to calculate the accrued benefit portion of the opening account balance was 8% at a time when the § 417(e)(3) rate was slightly over 6%. A lower discount rate would have yielded a higher opening balance, and therefore a larger lump sum. At the time of the cash balance conversion, ERISA did not include a definition of "opening account balance." The Eighth Circuit held that using the statutory discount rate to determine the opening balance would have given participants a windfall. However, since the PPA, § 411(b)(5)(B)(iii) has provided that the benefit under the converted plan must be at least as great as the accrued benefit under the old plan, plus the accrued benefit since the conversion. [*Sunder v. U.S. Bancorp Pension Plan*, 586 F.3d 593 (8th Cir. 2009)]

The Sixth Circuit held that the anti-cutback rules prevent a converted cash balance plan from reducing the early retirement subsidy that was available under the pre-conversion defined benefit plan—even though the participant did not become eligible for the subsidy until after the conversion. The case was remanded for the district court to decide whether the participant's benefit was actually reduced. Before the 1998 cash balance conversion, the plan provided early retirement benefits to participants with five years of service who had reached age 55. Nine participants retired after the conversion, electing lump sums. They all filed administrative claims protesting that the lump sum did not include the pre-conversion early retirement subsidy. Only one of the nine made the claim within five years after the distribution. The district court dismissed the eight claims as untimely, and dismissed the one claim it found timely on the merits. The Sixth Circuit agreed that eight claims were time-barred, applying the Kentucky five-year statute of limitations for claims brought under a statute that does not have an explicit statute of limitations. The Sixth Circuit held that it violated ERISA § 204(g) not to include the pre-retirement subsidy in the ninth plaintiff's benefit, because the age condition can be fulfilled either before or after the plan amendment. The case was remanded to decide the fact issue of how to characterize the benefit: whether it was an early retirement benefit or subsidy protected by § 204(g), or an optional benefit form that is only protected from elimination. [*Falllin v. Commonwealth Indus., Inc. Cash Balance Plan*, 695 F.3d 512 (6th Cir. 2012); see Wolters Kluwer Law & Business News Center, *Cash Balance Plan May Not Reduce Pre-Conversion Early Retirement Subsidy* (Oct. 22, 2012) (benefitslink.com)]

The Seventh Circuit affirmed certification of a Rule 23(b)(2) ERISA class action with more than 4,000 current and former participants in a cash balance plan. The plaintiffs made cutback, whipsaw, and wearaway claims covering a 23-year period. The district court certified 10 subclasses. The employer challenged class certification, arguing that *Dukes* (see § 42.06) rules out (b)(2) class actions for monetary, declaratory, or injunctive relief. The employer argued that certification of a (b)(2) class is appropriate only if a single injunction or declaratory judgment could provide relief to all the subclasses. The employer also argued that claims for monetary relief were inappropriate in (b)(2) cases, at least where they are not incidental to injunctive or declaratory relief. The Seventh Circuit rejected these arguments, reading *Dukes* to mean that the requirement of a single injunction or declaratory judgment does not apply where each member in a subclass has the same claim. The Seventh Circuit held that the plaintiffs were seeking a declaration of rights under the plan and reformation of the plan to follow the declaration—any monetary relief would be incidental. It was too early to determine if individualized proceedings would be required at a later stage, but the Seventh Circuit held that it might be possible to bifurcate the case, with subclasses that obtained Rule 23(b)(2) declaratory relief following up with an opt-out (b)(3) proceeding to set relief for the individual members of the class. [*Johnson v. Meriter Health Servs. Emp. Ret. Plan*, 702 F.3d 364 (7th Cir. 2012);

see Mark Casciari and Sara Eber, Seyfarth Shaw ERISA & Employee Benefits Litigation Blog, *Rule 23(B)(2) Certification—The Seventh Circuit Strikes Again, This Time In The ERISA Defined Benefit Context* (Dec. 5, 2012) (benefitslink.com).]

§ 7.05 THE CONVERSION PROCESS

At least 15 days' notice must be given in advance of adoption of a plan amendment that significantly reduces the rate of benefit accruals in the future. [See § 11.05 for a discussion of EGTRRA rules increasing the amount of disclosure that participants are entitled to in this situation] The plan may also have to issue a revised SPD and/or a Summary of Material Modification in connection with the conversion.

Based on requests to develop a pre-approved plan program for defined benefit plans with cash balance features, the IRS extended the deadline for submitting on-cycle applications for opinion and advisory letters for the second six-year remedial amendment cycle until February 2, 2015. Plans with some cash balance features can be submitted as part of defined benefit plan submissions. The extension gives the IRS more time to develop forms and tools for this situation. See Rev. Proc. 2014-8, 2014-1 I.R.B. 242 for user fees for applications submitted after January 31, 2014. [Announcement 2014-4, 2014-7 I.R.B. 52; modifies Rev. Proc. 2007-44 and Rev. Proc. 2011-49; see Rebecca Moore, *IRS Readies for Pre-Approved Cash Balance Plan Program*, plansponsor.com (Jan. 24, 2014)]

EBSA's cash balance plan FAQ [<http://www.dol.gov/ebsa/faqs/faq_consumer_cashbalanceplans.html>] Question 11 says that neither ERISA nor the Tax Code obligates employers who convert to a cash balance plan to give employees the option of remaining in the old plan. The employer can simply replace the old formula with the new formula for all participants, as long as the benefits already accrued as of the date of the conversion are not reduced. Or the employer can keep current employees under the old plan formula, applying the new formula only to those hired after the change. Another option is for some employees to be "grandfathered in," or allowed to receive their pensions under the old formula.

The first suit under the Lilly Ledbetter Fair Pay Act (Pub. L. No. 111-2) was filed eight days after the bill was signed. The case involved the El Paso pension plan's cash balance conversion. The plaintiff sought to reverse a January 21, 2009 decision that his age discrimination charge against the conversion was untimely. (The Ledbetter Act provides that an unlawful practice occurs when a violative plan is adopted, when the plaintiff became subject to the practice, or each time the plaintiff was affected by that practice. [Suzanne L. Wynn, Pension Protection Act Blog, *And the Lilly Ledbetter Litigation Begins* (Feb. 11, 2009) (benefitslink.com)]

In 2011, the Tenth Circuit held that the wearaway provision of Tomlinson's cash balance plan did not violate the ADEA § 4(i) accrual requirement, because credits were posted to the accounts of both young and older employees in a nondiscriminatory manner. Many employees were subject to wearaway because it took several years after the cash balance conversion for the minimum benefit to exceed the former benefit, especially for older employees. (The conversion occurred in 1997; wearaway was not forbidden until June 29, 2005.) The Tenth Circuit said that § 4(i) requires equality in inputs (benefit accruals) rather than outputs (accrued benefits), agreeing with the argument that the effect of the time value of money cannot be treated as age discrimination. The Tenth Circuit held that, absent deceit by the employer or failure to explain how the benefits are calculated, an SPD will not be invalidated for failure to inform employees about a wearaway period. [*Tomlinson v. El Paso*, 653 F.3d 1281 (10th Cir. 2011)]

[A] The 204(h) Notice Requirement

ERISA § 204(h), nicknamed the "anti-cutback rule," imposes notice requirements: plan participants and beneficiaries must be informed of plan changes that significantly reduce their entitlement to benefits. T.D. 9472, 74 Fed. Reg. 61270 (Nov. 24, 2009) is a final rule covering the 204(h) notice requirements for plan amendments that reduce accrued benefits. It provides that the effective date of an amendment that is adopted retroactively is the date the amendment goes into effect on an operational basis.

The Tenth Circuit upheld Solvay Chemicals' cash balance conversion, and said that the ERISA § 204(h) regulations did not mandate telling employees in either percentage or dollar terms that the conversion would reduce their future accrual rates. It was permissible to use tables of hypothetical benefit figures, because the data would allow employees to estimate their benefits, and it was clear from the tables that most employees were worse off after the conversion. The Tenth Circuit held that the cash balance plan did not violate the ADEA and satisfied ERISA requirements. However, the Tenth Circuit sent the case back to the district court to determine whether participants could use the information they were given to understand how the early retirement subsidy was calculated, or whether the company committed an egregious failure. [*Jensen v. Solvay Chems. Inc.*, 625 F.3d 641 (10th Cir. 2010)]

The district court found that there was no egregious failure under either standard. The plaintiffs appealed to the Tenth Circuit once again; the Tenth Circuit found no reason to disturb the district court's finding. [*Jensen v. Solvay Chems., Inc.*, 721 F.3d 1180 (10th Cir. 2013)]

§ 7.06 DECEMBER 2002 REGULATIONS: PROPOSAL AND WITHDRAWAL

In December 2002, the IRS published a set of Proposed Regulations, REG-209500-86, at 67 Fed. Reg. 76123 (Dec. 11, 2002), while the moratorium on cash-balance plan conversions was in effect. The proposal created the concept of an "eligible cash balance plan," for which the rate of benefit accrual includes additions to the participant's hypothetical account for the plan year, but not previously accrued interest credits. The Proposed Regulations stated that merely converting a defined benefit plan to an eligible cash balance form plan would not make the plan fail under Code § 411(b)(1)(H) as long as there was no wearaway. Under the proposal, plans could not stop or reduce accruals on the basis of age after NRA.

However, this proposal was politically controversial, and was withdrawn in mid-2004 by Announcement 2004-57, 2004-27 I.R.B. 15. Eventually, however, the PPA gave approval to the cash balance form.

§ 7.07 CASH BALANCE PLANS UNDER THE PPA AND WRERA

In 2006, Congress resolved legal uncertainties going forward, by providing rules under which cash balance plans can be created, or existing plans can be converted. However, the PPA specifically provides that it does not govern the validity or propriety of cash balance plans already in existence on June 29, 2005, so sponsors who "jumped the gun" by adopting cash balance plans, or making cash balance conversions, in the absence of guidance, could find themselves vulnerable in court. See § 7.04, above.

The statute uses the term "applicable defined pension plan" to refer to cash balance plans. Because other PPA provisions restrict the extent to which pension plans can "smooth" their investment results over several years, many sponsors will have to increase their contributions to defined benefit plans accordingly—a further incentive to convert to cash balance form.

A cash balance plan adopted or converted on or after June 29, 2005 will not be considered discriminatory if participants are 100% vested after three years of service. The plan must calculate interest credits with a rate of return that is not higher than market rates. The rate of return can be set as the greater of a fixed or a variable rate of return, and plans can implement a guaranteed minimum rate of return as long as it is reasonable.

No matter what their ages, all similarly situated employees must have equal accrued benefits. Participants are similarly situated if they have the same position, compensation, date of hire, and terms of service, and differ only in age. This provision adopts the argument that effects of the time value of money do not constitute age discrimination.

The PPA forbids the use of wearaway (adjusting plan formulas in a way that harms long-standing participants) under any plan amendment adopted after June 29, 2005. When a defined benefit plan is converted to a cash balance plan, each participant must receive the benefit accrued before the conversion, calculated under the pre-conversion formula, plus the benefit accrued after the conversion using the cash balance plan formula. Wearaway is also forbidden if a company freezes its defined benefit plan and adopts a cash balance plan. Qualifying participants must be permitted to receive early retirement subsidies.

The PPA eliminates whipsaw by mandating that the lump sum distribution from the plan must be equal to the hypothetical account balance. Cash balance plans are allowed to use a variable interest crediting rate, but the rate must not be higher than the market rate of return, and must be at least zero. Therefore, the account balance never falls below the cumulative total of pay credits. See proposed regulations about Code § 411 minimum vesting and accrual requirements, because cash balance plans are considered defined benefit plans. [NPRM REG-104946-07, 2008-11 I.R.B. 596]

WRERA, the relief bill for employers harmed by the economic downturn, signed December 23, 2008, eases the PPA's provisions dealing with such matters as age discrimination, conversions, and whipsaw, for cash balance and other hybrid plans. Although the PPA required 100% vesting in cash balance plans after three years of service, WRERA says this only applies if the participant has at least one hour of service after the effective date of the new rules. As a result of WRERA, the whipsaw rules are not applied in determining whether a participant is subject to mandatory cashout; it depends on the balance in the hypothetical cash account. [Deloitte's Washington Bulletin, *PPA Technical Corrections Affecting Defined Benefit Plans*, <http://benefitslink.com/articles/guests/washbull090112.html> (Jan. 12, 2009) (benefitslink.com)]

In mid-2008, The IRS proposed regulations allowing the same relief permitted by Rev. Rul. 2008-7, to clarify how defined benefit plans, especially hybrid plans that use a "greater of" benefit formula, can satisfy the anti-backloading test. In general, they can test each formula separately. This is useful for employers who want to convert defined benefit to cash balance plans, but still provide pensions for older employees that are more generous than the required transitional relief. [NPRM, *Accrual Rules for Defined Benefit Plans*; RIN 1545-BH50, 73 Fed. Reg. 34665 (June 18, 2008); see Buck Research FYI, *IRS Proposed Regulations Would Encourage Generosity in Cash Balance Conversion* (July 7, 2008) (benefitslink.com)]

[A] 2010 Final and Proposed Regulations

In late 2010, the IRS issued final and proposed regulations for hybrid retirement plans, a category that includes not only cash balance plans but Pension Equity Plans (PEPs). In the 1990s, hybrid plans grew in popularity, but also attracted a number of lawsuits, generally charging age discrimination, challenging the calculation of lump sums, or challenging wearaway within the plan. The IRS issued proposed regulations implementing the Pension Protection Act in December 2007. The 2010 regulations deal with age discrimination, vesting, conversion from defined benefit to cash balance form, and safe harbor interest crediting rates (final regulations) and alternative rates that constitute a "market rate of return" (proposed regulations).

In general, a hybrid plan can be described as one that calculates accumulated benefits with a hybrid formula. Each participant has a hypothetical account, which is credited with the employer's hypothetical contributions based on "compensation credits" (reflecting the participant's salary) plus "interest credits" (hypothetical earnings from investing the account). PEPs define the benefit as a percentage of final average pay, with participants earning points each year to set the percentage. Compensation credits are usually defined as a percentage of the employee's eligible pay, possibly adjusted based on age and years of service. When the participant stops working for the employer, compensation credits end. Interest credits usually continue until the benefits are distributed.

The 2010 final regulations require the entire accrued benefit of hybrid plans to vest in no more than three years of service (with an exception for the traditional defined benefit portion of a floor offset arrangement that combines a defined benefit plan and a separate hybrid plan). The 2010 final regulations include an ADEA safe harbor, as long as the accumulated benefit of any participant is not less than the accumulated benefit of any similarly situated younger participant (similar in terms of date of hire, work history, compensation, and job duties). A hybrid plan that does not satisfy the safe harbor must satisfy the general Code § 411(b)(1)(H)(i) age discrimination rule. The final regulations say that the safe harbor can be used if the plan gave the participant a choice between a traditional defined benefit plan and the hybrid plan at the time of conversion; the safe harbor is not limited to plans that used a sum-of or greater-of formula at conversion.

The final regulations protect benefits against wearaway if a defined benefit plan is converted to a hybrid plan by an amendment adopted and effective on or after June 29, 2005. If the amendment eliminates or reduces future benefit accruals, and part or all of the benefit is determined based on a statutory hybrid formula, then the post-amendment benefit must be at least as great as the accrued benefit as of the conversion date plus the accrued benefit after the conversion, with no integration of the two.

The PPA forbids crediting interest at a rate greater than a "market rate of return"; the 2010 regulations use the rate of return on investment-grade long-term corporate bonds, certain Treasury bonds, the actual rate of return on plan assets, and the rate of return on an annuity contract for an employee as benchmarks.

It is permissible for the rate of benefit accrual to increase as participants earn more, as long as any year's accrual rate is not more than one-third higher than the previous year's rate. [Final regulations: 75 Fed. Reg. 64123 (Oct. 19, 2010); proposed regulations, 75 Fed. Reg. 64197 (Oct. 19, 2010).]

The Moving Ahead for Progress in the 21st Century (MAP-21) Act, Pub. L. No. 112-140, allows plan sponsors some relief from interest crediting rules that can make defined benefit and cash balance plans unduly expensive. (See § 5.01[A].) Notice 2012-61, 2012-42 I.R.B. 479 says that final regulations on

[Mark L. Lofgren, *Cash Balance Plans IRS Further Delays Reasonable Interest Rate Rules and Provides Guidance for Plans with Rates Affected by Map-21*, Groom Law Group (Sept. 17, 2012) (benefitslink.com)]

Subsequent legislation, the Highway Transportation Funding Act of 2014, Pub. L. No. 113-159, allows employers to continue making use of smoothing to reduce the amount that they must contribute to their plans; the statute prescribes rates to be used until 2017. [Groom Law Group Benefits Brief, *Extension of Pension Interest Rate Smoothing Relief Clears Congress Before August Recess*, <http://www.groom.com/media/publication/1444_Extension_of_Pension_Interest_Rate.pdf> (Aug. 1, 2014); Vipal Monga, *Welcome to the World of "Pension Smoothing,"* WSJ.com (Aug. 11, 2014)]

CHAPTER 8
NONQUALIFIED PLANS

§ 8.01 INTRODUCTION

[A] Generally

One of the most important aspects of maintaining a qualified plan (and therefore obtaining a tax deduction for related costs) is satisfying the Internal Revenue Code's tests for nondiscrimination.

However, it is not illegal for an employer to set up a discriminatory plan, and in fact many types of nonqualified plans have evolved for companies that want to recruit, retain, or motivate senior management and/or persons who own significant amounts of stock in the corporation. Nonqualified plans are also used to provide post-retirement income higher than the levels that can be generated through a qualified plan. Unlike qualified plans, which are subject to detailed funding and operational requirements under ERISA, nonqualified plans need not be funded in advance. Payments to distribute benefits can be made as they come due, out of the employer's general assets instead of from a special trust. Insurance policies, and other investments that would not be permissible in an ERISA plan, can also be used to fund nonqualified plan benefits.

Since 2004, sponsors have faced a new set of tax challenges for nonqualified plans under the American Jobs Creation Act of 2010 (AJCA), Pub. L. No. 108-357, which enacted Code § 409A, and under the Pension Protection Act of 2006 (PPA), Pub. L. No. 109-280.

A deferred compensation plan is a plan or individual agreement to pay compensation to one or more employees in one or more later years for services rendered. Such plans can be taxable or tax-exempt. A nonqualified plan is exempt from most ERISA and IRS requirements, but at the cost of foregoing the tax deductions available to sponsors of qualified plans.

A 2012 article says that the five vital things to know about nonqualified deferred compensation (NQDC) plans are:

- Their role in providing incentives to a company's best-performing executives by permitting them to save more when they have maxed out contributions to the other plans—or, an NQDC can operate as a bonus plan, with contributions made only if goals are met. NQDC funds can be accessed while the executive is still working, for example, to pay children's college tuition or buy a second home;
- Eligibility criteria must be set when the plan is designed; if the standards are too broad, the plan might become subject to ERISA. As a rule of thumb, the plan might cover 10%–20% of the employees, based on their title and compensation level, or by their duties;
- Even if the plan is not subject to ERISA, it must satisfy § 409A, and penalties will be imposed on the participants if the plan violates its rules;

- Participants have less security than participants in qualified plans—even a rabbi trust is still subject to the claims of the corporation's creditors;
- NQDCs are good for providing incentives to best-performing executives, permitting them to save more for retirement after they have made maximum contributions to their other plans.

[Pathfinder, *5 Things You Need to Know About Nonqualified Deferred Compensation Plans* (Feb. 29, 2012) (benefitslink.com)]

Yong Lee, the COO of MullTBG, says that there are four main areas for sponsors of NQDC plans to consider:

- Do they understand the regulatory consequences of the plan?
- In light of what the regulations permit, how do they want to design the plan?
- How do they want to finance the plan?
- How can participants be educated about the plan? Older employees may prefer paper documents and face-to-face meetings; younger employees often prefer online delivery, but Webinars appeal to both groups.

According to Lee, plans are usually financed with taxable securities, such as mutual funds or Company-Owned Life Insurance. [Kevin McGuinness, *Ensuring Best Practices for NQDC Plans*, plansponsor.com (Feb. 13, 2014)]

Prudential reported in 2014 that the most common executive benefit was the nonqualified deferred compensation plan (NQDCP): 95% of respondents offered it to HCEs, versus 90% offering this benefit in 2012. About 42% of respondents said they could change their NQDCPs to enhance plan communications and education. About one-quarter of participants used title to decide who qualifies to participate in the NQDCP (23.5% did this); another 23% relied on job grade. More than half of respondents use informal funding measures (57.2%); 46.2% use company-owned life insurance, 44.7% use mutual funds. In 2012, 41.5% of respondents offered stock options as an executive benefit, a proportion that rose to 50% in 2013. Restricted stock units were utilized by 43.4% of responding companies in 2012, and 57.6% in 2012. Almost half (45%) of respondents said they offer financial planning advice to nonqualified plan participants, such as model or managed portfolios and retirement planning advice. Among companies using a security vehicle to protect NQDCP benefits, nearly all (97%) used a rabbi trust. About three-quarters of sponsors (70%) called their plan effective or extremely effective. [Prudential press release, *MullinTBG/PLANSPONSOR Survey: Higher Participation, Deferrals for 2014* (Mar. 31, 2014) <http://news.prudential.com/article_print.cfm?article_id=6815>]

Eastman Kodak's Executive Deferred Compensation Plan was established in 1982 so key employees could elect pre-tax deferrals of salary and annual incentives. At first, it was a very popular savings vehicle, with balances over $200 million in the mid-1990s. Then, the future of the company became dubious and there were many layoffs. Balances dropped because of accelerated distributions and a decline in the number of participants. The adoption of Code § 409A also made the plan less attractive to executives. Deferrals were discontinued in 2007.

In January 2012, Kodak filed for bankruptcy. Its reorganization plan provides that EDCP participants, whose total balances have fallen to $15 million, will get 4–5% of their earned but deferred salaries and incentive awards, paid in shares of common stock in the reorganized company after it exits Chapter 11. The $15 million in salary and bonuses owed to executives is treated as unsecured debt, on a par with unfunded pensions. [John Lawson, *Unfunded And Unsecured: Nonqualified Deferred Comp Lessons From Kodak's Chapter 11* (Sept. 3, 2013) (benefitslink.com)]

The general practice is for the payor corporation to record the expense on its books when the compensation is earned, even if the tax deduction is not available until a much later year. The general rule of § 409A is that elective participant deferrals are irrevocable, and the election must be made before the beginning of the calendar year in which the services commence. The election must identify the amount to be deferred; the length of the deferral period; and the form of payment. However, for performance-based compensation for services performed over a period of 12 months or more, the initial deferral election can be made at any time up through six months before the end of the performance period. Payments to key employees of public companies triggered by separation from service (other than in case of death, disability, or similar event) must be delayed at least six months after separation. The Code § 83 economic benefit doctrine makes income taxable upon grant if the executive receives tangible, quantifiable value, and there is no substantial risk of forfeiture.

To escape taxation under theories of constructive receipt and economic benefit, benefits under a nonqualified plan must be funded and must be subject to the claims of the corporation's general creditors. If the company becomes insolvent or bankrupt, the executive's right to payment cannot be greater than the right of any other general unsecured creditor.

Corporations with nonqualified deferred compensation plans usually engage in informal funding, e.g., by setting money aside in trusts such as rabbi trusts to cover future payments under the plan. The trusts are assets of the corporation and can be reached by its creditors. Section 409A accelerates income tax and imposes penalties if assets are transferred outside the United States, or if benefit payments are triggered by the corporation's financial problems (i.e., if executives are insulated against the consequences of the company's financial difficulties).

Penalties are also imposed on key executives if the employer sets aside assets to pay nonqualified deferred compensation when the corporation is bankrupt, within six months of termination of an underfunded plan, or if the plan is "at risk" as defined by the PPA and is funded below the 80% level. In many instances, registration exemptions will be available, but absent an exemption, an employee's interest in an elective deferred compensation arrangement is a security that will have to be registered. "Blue sky" compliance (with state securities laws) may also be required. [David Wang and Melissa Rasman, *Elective Nonqualified Deferred Compensation Plans—A Primer*, Hay Group's Executive Edition Newsletter (Feb. 1, 2008) (benefitslink.com)]

In a qualified plan, a "bad boy" clause (one that removes entitlement to benefits) is allowed only for fraud or abuse of fiduciary duty. In a nonqualified plan, benefits can be forfeited by an executive who leaves the company.

Under a qualified plan, the employer gets a current deduction each year as it makes contributions to the plan. The employer's deduction for nonqualified plan expenses is not available until the year in which the participant receives money from the plan and includes it in income. The corporation's general creditors are entitled to make claims against reserves set aside to pay nonqualified plan benefits, but the qualified plan trust is protected against creditors' claims.

[B] Structures for Nonqualified Plans

Various structures and funding mechanisms have evolved for providing nonqualified plan benefits to executives, managers, and other favored corporate employees. Objectives include providing incentives for managers by providing generous deferred compensation, and protecting entitlement to these sums against the corporation's creditors.

The most popular structures for nonqualified plans include SERPs, QSERPs, top hat plans, rabbi trusts, and secular trusts, as discussed below. Other structures used for non-qualified plans include:

- Excess benefit plans: plans that provide benefits higher than those permitted by Code § 415. Unfunded excess benefit plans are exempt from ERISA Title I, but that renders them vulnerable to state regulation;
- Integrated plans provide benefits over and above 401(k) plan benefits, using the same investment options and subject to the same employer match rules. The deferral percentage is set by the plan participant. Transfers of both elective deferrals and employer matches are made first to the qualified plan, then to the nonqualified plan;
- Tandem plans combine with qualified plans to accrue more savings for retirement-but usually offer features and investment choices that are different than those offered under the regular qualified plan;
- Wrap plans collect funds throughout the year on behalf of top executives. Once a year, the maximum amount that can be transferred for those

executives without violating the nondiscrimination rules is transferred to the qualified plan; the rest is placed in a non-qualified plan.

[See *New Options in Nonqualified Retirement Plans*, <http://institutional.vanguard.com>]

[1] SERP

A Supplemental Executive Retirement Plan (SERP), also known as an excess-benefit plan, can be used to defer amounts that exceed the qualified plan limits on behalf of executives. Hay Group says that the most popular formula aims to 60% of the executive's pre-retirement income, which would be impossible under most qualified plans. A performance-based SERP makes accrual of benefits dependent on achievement of one or more performance measures. The measures could be the ones used in the company's incentive programs (e.g., revenues, profitability, or earnings), or could be personalized (a sales target or profitability goal for a particular corporate unit) or depend on other goals or events (developing a product; successful bankruptcy reorganization).

The Sixth Circuit held that claims by executives of Metaldyne corporate executives' claims about cancellation of their SERP plan could be tried in state court. Metaldyne was once partially owned by Heartland Industrial Partners, LP, an investment firm. In mid-2006, Heartland agreed to sell its Metaldyne stake to another investment firm. The SERP included change in control provisions under which Metaldyne would owe the plaintiffs about $13 million. The Metaldyne board canceled the SERP to avoid this obligation. The SERP participants sued in state court for tortious interference with contractual relations. The Sixth Circuit found that these claims were not preempted by ERISA because the state court would not have to interpret the SERPs, just calculate damages if the plaintiffs proved that canceling them violated state law. [*Gardner v. Heartland Industrial Partners*, 713 F.3d 609 (6th Cir. 2013); see Stephen D. Rosenberg, *Cancelling a SERP and the Limits of Preemption*, Boston ERISA Law Blog (June 25, 2013) (benefitslink.com); Stanley D. Baum, *ERISA-Sixth Circuit Holds That State-Law Claim for Tortious Interference With a Contract Is Not Completely Preempted by ERISA*, <http://www.erisalawyerblog.com/2013/05/erisa-sixth-circuit-holds-that-2.html> (May 20, 2013)]

A late 2010 decision holds that the widow of a SERP participant was not entitled to benefits because she did not fit the plan's definition of "spouse," and the definition in the plan prevailed over the language of the SPD. The SERP's provisions required a marriage of at least one year's duration before the participant's death or retirement for the spouse to qualify as a surviving spouse. In this case, the marriage occurred after the participant's retirement. The Northern District of Ohio said that while the SPD's language may have created misrepresentations, it did not alter the terms of the plan, and it was not arbitrary or capricious to say that the survivor did not qualify for the benefits. [*Parr v. Diebold Inc.*, No. 5:09 CV 1041 (N.D. Ohio 2010)]

Because a SERP is a top-hat plan, it is not protected against the claims of the employer's creditors, even if the employer includes an anti-alienation provision in the SERP agreement. Therefore, at least 25% of a bank executive's SERP was subject to garnishment by a creditor of the bank. The state's garnishment law was not preempted by ERISA, because it was a law of general application not related to employee benefit plans. The state Consumer Credit Protection Law protects 75% of a pension or retirement benefit from garnishment, so the judge reserved decision on the fate of 75% of the executive's SERP. [*Sposato v. First Mariner Bank,* No. 1:2012-cv-01569, 2013 WL 1308582 (D. Md. Mar. 28, 2013); see Rebecca Moore, *"Top Hat" Plan Assets Not Protected by ERISA*, plansponsor.com (Apr. 19, 2013); Jane Meacham, *ERISA Does Not Protect Executive Benefits From Garnishment*, Smart HR (June 7, 2013) (benefitslink.com)]

In the Second Circuit view, early retirement benefits from a SERP are not severance payments that get "administrative expense" (i.e., high) priority in bankruptcy, because the benefits accrue over the entire course of employment—they are not a new benefit earned at termination, and only new benefits can be administrative expenses. [*In re Bethlehem Steel*, 479 F.3d 167 (2d Cir. 2007)]

[2] QSERP

A Qualified Supplemental Executive Retirement Plan (QSERP) is a qualified plan used to enhance retirement benefits for executives. The plan must satisfy nondiscrimination requirements and is subject to the I.R.C. § 415 limits. However, the employer's contributions can be integrated with Social Security, reducing the amount the employer has to contribute on behalf of lower-paid employees. To adopt a QSERP, the employer corporation can simply amend the plan documents to include an annual list of people or job titles entitled to additional benefits of $X/year. Usually, QSERP amounts are subtracted from the amounts that would otherwise be payable under nonqualified plans. Because the QSERP is a qualified plan, the employer gets a current deduction, and the employee is not taxed until benefits are actually paid (and the employee has some certainty that they will be paid because of prefunding). If the QSERP is a defined contribution plan, it is subject to the overall limitation on contributions to all defined contribution plans; if the employer is already making close to the maximum contribution under other qualified plans there is little leeway for the QSERP. [Pension Rights Center, *Q-SERPs: How Companies Manipulate the Law to Fund Executive Pay Packages with Workers' Pension Money*, <http://www.pensionrights.org/pubs/facts/Q-SERPS.html> (September 2008)]

For the executive, having a QSERP provides the advantage of securing the benefit (although PBGC limits will apply if the plan sponsor goes bankrupt). QSERPs are not subject to § 409A. Blogger John Lowell, pointed out advantages of QSERP. While the benefit remains in the plan, there has been no constructive receipt under § 83. Benefits payable in lump-sum form can be rolled over to an IRA, further deferring taxation. The executive can wait until just before the benefit commencement date to choose the time and form of benefit distribution. Shareholders benefit because the QSERP is income-neutral or income-positive, and it protects the company from cash flow demands of having to make large payments. [Michael S. Melbinger, *Another Blogger Sings the Praises of QSERPs*, Winston & Strawn LLP Executive Compensation Blog (Sept. 19, 2011) (benefitslink.com)]

[3] Rabbi Trust

A rabbi trust (so-called because the first one was created by a synagogue for its clergyman) sets aside assets in an irrevocable trust to pay the benefits, although the corporation's creditors can reach the assets. The assets in the trust cannot revert to the employer until all of the obligations to pay deferred compensation have been satisfied. Executives are not taxed until they receive benefits from the trust, because of the risk that creditor claims will prevent benefit payments. A "springing" rabbi trust is set up with only minimal funding. However, if the control of the corporation changes (for instance, because of a merger or acquisition), then the trust provides for funding for payment of benefits. The rabbi trust will not be considered "funded" for ERISA purposes just because it has a spring provision.

A rabbi trust furnishes the greatest permissible degree of protection for participants in deferred compensation plans. Many such trusts are set up with a directed trustee, who follows directions from the sponsor or a committee, and has no discretion over the trust or the plan. A few plans give the trustee full discretion, or discretion for some services. Another option is to increase the trustee's discretion over benefit decisions after a change in control, to relieve participants' anxieties about whether new management will pay the benefits promised by the predecessor. Depending on circumstances, the trustee may have to issue a W-2, Form 1099-R or Form 1099-Misc when the rabbi trust makes distribution. [No by-line, *Special Report: Deferred Compensation: Change Management*, plansponsor.com (magazine article, June 2006)]

One of the effects of the AJCA (see § 8.02[D]) is to ban offshore rabbi trusts.

[4] Secular Trust

A secular trust is an irrevocable trust whose assets cannot be reached by the employer's creditors, including its bankruptcy creditors. It offers more protection to the executive's right to receive deferred compensation than a rabbi trust, but has less favorable tax consequences. The price of increased protection for the employee is that the employee has taxable income (taxed using the I.R.C. § 72 annuity rules) equal to the employer contributions to the trust on the employee's behalf. The employer can deduct its contributions to the trust, to the extent they are ordinary and necessary business expenses, in the tax year in which the contributions become taxable income for the employee.

Secular trusts gained in popularity because of economic conditions and the difficulties of complying with § 409A. In general, nonqualified benefits offered through a secular trust are immediately taxable to the employees, but the trust assets are protected from the company's creditors. Rev. Rul. 2007-48, 2007-30 I.R.B. 129, tended to promote the use of secular trusts simply because it was clear what the rules are.

This ruling states that a participant in a secular trust does not have gross income on account of an interest in the trust until accrued benefits vest. The gross income for a given year is the fair market value of the vested part of the account as of the last day of the trust's tax year (whether or not this amount is distributed), plus the amount distributed to the participant during the participant's tax year, minus the participant's investment in the contract (the FMV of the vested portion of the account at the end of the trust's previous tax year), because the participant has already been taxed on the investment in the contract.

The secular trust must maintain separate accounts for each participant (although there can be multiple accounts in one trust). The sponsor corporation can deduct its contributions in the corporate tax year in which the recipients include the funds in the gross income. The income of a secular trust is taxed to the trust itself, not to the sponsor, and the trust can deduct trust income that vests in the participants during the tax year even if the income is not actually paid. [Michael Melbinger, Winston & Strawn LLP, *Protecting Non-Qualified Deferred Compensation—The Secular Trust* (June 9, 2009) (benefitslink.com)]

[5] Top Hat Plan

A top hat plan is an unfunded deferred compensation plan limited to managers and/or HCEs. Top hat plans that are pension plans must file a brief notice each year with the Department of Labor, although less disclosure is required than for a qualified plan. An unfunded top hat pension plan is not subject to the ERISA participation, vesting, funding, or fiduciary responsibility rules. The plan must have a claims procedure. Even the modest role that ERISA plays in regulating top hat plans is probably enough to preempt state law, so suits cannot be brought in state court involving claims against top hat plans.

Employers that contribute to NQDCs typically set a vesting schedule at least as strict as the schedule for the qualified plan. It may even be stricter—e.g., a "bad boy" clause that denies payments to persons who are terminated for cause or who breach a non-compete agreement. Courts will uphold these stricter requirements only if the NQDC plan is a top hat plan that is exempt from ERISA. Relevant factors are whether eligibility is limited to a select group of management or highly compensated employees; what percentage of employees are eligible; how the compensation of eligible employees compares to the workforce as a whole; the titles and duties of covered employees; and the extent to which covered employees have influence over management decisions. [Michael S. Melbinger, *Follow-Up on Top Hat Plan Testing/Review*, Winston & Strawn Executive Compensation Blog (Dec. 12, 2013) (benefitslink.com)]

In general, top hat plans are subject to ERISA Part I reporting and disclosure obligations, including annual Form 5500 filing. However, top hat plan sponsors can obtain exemption from annual reporting by filing a statement with the DOL. If the sponsor did not file a timely request for a filing exemption, it can use the DOL Delinquent Filer Voluntary Compliance Program (DFVC) to submit the statement instead of filing the past-due annual reports. The statement goes to DOL, EBSA, Apprenticeship and Training Plan Exemption, 200 Constitution Avenue NW, N-1513 Washington, DC, 20210. A single combined statement can be filed if the sponsor has more than one top hat plan seeking DFVC participation at the same time. There is a $750 penalty for each DVFC submission (for any number of plans filed at once, not per plan) and the penalty is a personal obligation of the plan administrator—plan assets may not be used to pay the penalty. [Prudential Pension Analyst, *DOL Updates Delinquent Filer Voluntary Compliance (DFVC) Program*, <http://www.retire.prudential.com/media/managed/EBSA_Updates_DFVC_Program-Final.pdf> (March 2013)]

In mid-2008, the Second Circuit ruled that it did not violate ERISA or the ADEA for a company (that had reserved the right to terminate) to terminate its top hat plan, even if the plaintiff relied on the representations made in his early retirement package. The plan had become financially untenable, so it was not arbitrary or capricious for the board of directors to terminate it.

The Second Circuit pointed out that many ERISA provisions, such as the fiduciary duty provisions, do not apply to top hat plans. However, the ERISA administration and enforcement provisions do apply to top hat plans, so state law claims such as breach of contract, bad faith, and negligent misrepresentation were preempted. [*Paneccasio v. Unisource Worldwide*, 532 F.3d 101 (2d Cir. 2008)]

The Seventh Circuit ruled in 2011 that the actions of plan administrators had to be reviewed deferentially, because the plan terms gave them discretion. The court held that it was not arbitrary and capricious to describe a discretionary stock-linked payment as a bonus that is not included in the benefit formula. The Seventh Circuit reviewed the decision with deference, even though top hat plan administrators are not ERISA fiduciaries—and even though in 2001, the Third Circuit refused to give deference to interpretations by top hat plan administrators. [*Comrie v. IPSCO, Inc.*, 636 F.3d 839 (7th Cir. 2011); see Mercer Select US, *7th Circuit Says Courts Owe Deference to Top-Hat Plan Administrator's Interpretation* (Mar. 3, 2011) (benefitslink.com)]

DOL has not provided any guidance about what constitutes a select group of management or highly compensated employees, although there are a few illustrative court cases. In 1989, the District Court for the Eastern District of North Carolina said that a plan offered to more than 18% of workers, whose compensation did not vary greatly from the overall corporate average, was not a top hat plan. In

2000, the Second Circuit said that a plan covering 15.34% qualified as a top hat plan, although it was at the upper range of acceptability. The plan was limited to managers, and their average compensation was more than double that of the workforce as a whole. In 2007, the Sixth Circuit promulgated an influential four-part test: the percentage of the workforce eligible to participate; the nature of their duties; their compensation as compared to non-eligible employees; and the actual language of the plan. [*Demery v. Extebank Deferred Comp. Plan*, 216 F.3d 283 (2d Cir. 2000); *Bakri v. Venture*, 473 F.3d 677 (6th Cir. 2007); see AALU/Greenberg Traurig Washington Report, *"Top-Hat Plan" Exemption Compliance for Deferred Compensation Arrangements* (Sept. 19, 2013) (benefitslink.com)]

In 2012, the Eastern District of Kentucky characterized a plan as a top hat plan because less than 1% of the total workforce was eligible and most of them were high-ranking managers. The district court rejected the argument that the plan also included a few participants who were not top managers, ruling that a top hat plan merely has to be primarily for such employees. [*Cramer v. Appalachian Reg'l Healthcare, Inc.*, No. 5:11-49-KKC, 2012 U.S. Dist. LEXIS 154624 (E.D. Ky, Oct. 29, 2012); see Angela Bohmann, *Do I Have A Top Hat Plan?*, Leonard, Street and Deinard Executive Compensation Blog (Nov. 21, 2012) (benefitslink.com)]

The Sixth Circuit reversed the district court's decision that a nonqualified plan was an ERISA plan but not a top-hat plan. Apparently, the plan was intended to be an unfunded top-hat plan; the author of the article said that an ERISA plan that was not a top-hat plan would create a "tax debacle." The Sixth Circuit ruled that the district court should have remanded the matter to the plan administrator to expand the administrative record. [*Daft v. Advest*, 658 F.3d 583 (6th Cir. 2011) see Ann Caresani, *The Top-Hat Plan Test for Your ERISA Executive Deferred Compensation Plan—Daft v. Advest, Inc.*, Porter Wright (Jan. 13, 2012) (benefitslink.com)]

In a class action about the discount rates used by a top hat plan and a pension plan to convert straight life annuities to lump sums, the Seventh Circuit upheld the lower court's grant of summary judgment for the plan. The top hat plan used a 7.5% discount rate (the pension plan used a rate of approximately 5.4%). As a non-qualified plan, the top hat plan was not subject to the PPA cap on discount rates. The plan terms permitted a 7.5% discount rate to be used by any non-qualified plan, and top hat plans are by definition non-qualified. [*Dennison v. MONY Life Ret. Income Sec. Plan*, No. 710 F.3d 741 (7th Cir., 2013); see Brian Stolzenbach, Sam Schwartz-Fenwick and Chris Busey, *Seventh Circuit Reads Plan Language To Discount Plaintiffs' Rate Argument*, Seyfarth Shaw ERISA & Employee Benefits Litigation Blog (Mar. 20, 2013) (benefitslink.com)]

Participants in a top hat plan could not recover under ERISA § 502 from the company that bought all of the assets of the bankrupt company that formerly maintained the plan. The buyer did not assume any of the sponsor's liabilities under the plan. At that point the seller was a shell company with no assets, so it was unable to pay benefits. The Seventh Circuit rejected the plaintiffs' arguments that the buyer was a de facto plan administrator, holding that the buyer did not connive with the seller to cheat plan participants, and that the buyer was not just a continuation of the seller. Therefore, the buyer did not have to acquire the liabilities of the unfunded top-hat plan, and the buyer did not violate ERISA § 510 either—it did not interfere with the attainment of ERISA benefits. In the Seventh Circuit view, § 510 refers to employment actions, and many of the plan beneficiaries were former employees or non-employees of the seller. [*Feinberg v. RM Acquisition, LLC*, 629 F.3d 671 (7th Cir. 2011)]

A commentator suggests that one way to make sure that nonqualified plan benefits are paid to the executives is to put the money in an irrevocable rabbi trust, separate from the corporation's general assets. Rabbi trust assets are subject to the claims of the corporation's general creditors if the company becomes insolvent, but are protected in other situations—including the case of a new or successor employer that does not want to pay the benefits. [Michael S. Melbinger, *How Can SERP and Non-Qualified Plan Participants Protect Themselves Against the Loss of Benefits?*, Winston & Strawn LLP Executive Compensation Blog (Mar. 20, 2011) (benefitslink.com)]

§ 8.02 TAXATION OF NONQUALIFIED PLANS

[A] General Considerations

Nonqualified plans can create some subtle tax problems for plan participants. The mere fact that the employer promises to pay benefits in the future doesn't create income for the plan participants, until plan benefits are either actually or constructively received. Constructive receipt is a tax concept roughly equivalent to deliberately turning down money that the taxpayer is entitled to.

Employees are taxed on benefits from nonqualified plans as they are distributed. To the extent that the employee already had to pay tax on amounts not yet distributed, employees are entitled to compute an exclusion ratio (percentage of a distribution that has already been taxed and will not be taxed again).

Nonqualified plan participants are taxed in the year in which rights to property become transferable, or the substantial risk of forfeiture ends, whichever comes first. Sometimes, property rights depend, directly or indirectly, on the plan participant continuing to perform services for the employer. If there is a covenant not to compete, however, property rights might depend on not performing services! Under the IRS Regulations, the facts of each case must be examined to determine whether there is a substantial risk of forfeiture because of a requirement of continued employment or noncompetition.

As for the trust income, there are complex factors (centering around the extent of the employer's contributions and degree of control) that determine ownership of the trust, and therefore whether the employer, the employee, or the trust itself should be taxed on income earned by a secular trust arrangement.

The 2014 FICA base is $ 117,000. When nonqualified options and Stock Appreciation Rights are exercised, or when restricted stock and restricted stock units vest, FICA taxes are owed. For compensation deferred in a nonqualified deferred compensation plan, FICA is owed at the time of deferral even though income tax is only owed when money is withdrawn from the account. If the employee's compensation for the year exceeds the FICA base, non-qualified stock options can be exercised without FICA tax on the income being recognized at exercise (because maximum FICA tax has already been paid). Medicare tax is due on all compensation, without limit. High-income individuals are also subject to additional Medicare tax. [MyStockOptions Blog, *Social Security Yearly Income Cap Will Rise In 2013: Impact On Stock Comp And NQDC* (Oct. 17, 2012) (benefitslink.com)]

See T.D. 9645, 2013-51 I.R.B. 738, for final regulations on the additional Medicare tax that PPACA imposed on high earners (persons whose wages, compensation, or self-employment income exceed $250,000 on a joint return, $125,000 for married persons filing separately, or $200,000 for single persons, heads of household, and surviving spouses with dependent children). The employer must withhold the additional tax from wages over $200,000 paid to anyone, irrespective of the recipient's filing status or wages paid by other employers. The employer cannot modify its withholding of additional Medicare tax. However, a person who expects to owe more than the amount withheld by the employer can increase withholding on the W-4 (e.g., a joint return where neither spouse earns over $200,000, but the total is over $250,000). [Carrie Elizabeth Byrnes and Timothy Zehnder, *IRS Issues "Additional Medicare Tax" Final Rules*, Bryan Cave LLP (Dec. 10, 2013), available at Lexology.com]

The rules for income tax and FICA treatment of nonqualified deferred compensation are different. Generally, income tax applies at the time the benefits are paid or made available to the individual—but FICA applies at the earlier of the time the amounts vest or are paid. If nonqualified deferred compensation vests at retirement age, FICA tax applies to the present value of the entire benefit. Thus, if the employee has already reached the FICA wage base, he or she will only have to pay the Medicare portion of the FICA tax (which is not capped). FICA regulations require the employer to withhold FICA from each deferred compensation payment as it is made.

To see how these rules play out, see *Henkel,* a case brought by a SERP participant who alleged that his retirement payments were improperly reduced because of the employer's mishandling of FICA taxes. The remedy he asked for was to receive the full benefit, unreduced by FICA, which would make the employer responsible for both the employer's and employee's FICA shares. The SERP allowed deferral of base pay and bonuses and offered supplemental monthly benefits at retirement. The sponsor discovered, during a compliance review, that FICA had not been properly paid, so it informed retirees that FICA should have been paid on the present value of the entire benefit at retirement—the point at which the amount deferred was reasonably ascertainable and vested.

(This is the rule for a non-account balance plan; for an account balance plan, FICA is paid when benefits are credited to the account or when they vest, whichever is later.) The employer paid the back taxes and withheld FICA going forward, and reduced several monthly benefit payments to recoup. If proper timing rules are not applied, the employer must withhold FICA tax on all benefits subsequently paid under the plan.

The plaintiff's theory was that the amount of FICA tax was higher than it would have been if paid at the time of retirement, violating ERISA. The employer asserted that the suit was an improper suit to terminate withholding. The district court allowed the suit to proceed, characterizing it as a suit for the full benefit payment the plaintiff would have received if withholding had been correct. [*Davidson v. Henkel Corp.*, No. 12-cv-14103, 2013 U.S. Dist. LEXIS 103185 (E.D. Mich. July 23, 2013); see Stephen Douglas and Russ Hall, *Employer Liability for Mishandling FICA Tax Under Nonqualified Plan*, Towers Watson (Oct. 21, 2013) (benefitslink.com); Angela Bohmann, *This Time the Employer Is Responsible For the Withholding Error*, Benefits Notes (Aug. 21, 2013) (benefitslink.com)]

Effective January 1, 2005, transfers of interests in nonqualified deferred compensation and nonstatutory stock options from employee spouse to non-employee spouse incident to a divorce are not "wages" for FICA/FUTA purposes. FICA and FUTA come into play, however, when the options are exercised or the deferred compensation is paid or made available. Nonstatutory options are subject to FICA and FUTA when exercised by the spouse who received them in the divorce. The employee spouse is liable for FICA taxes on the exercise, because the payments relate to the employee spouse's employment. The income the non-employee spouse realizes on exercise of options constitutes wages subject to withholding; the withheld taxes must be deducted from payments to the non-employee spouse. Because the non-employee spouse is by definition not an employee, W-2 reporting is not required. Instead, the employer's obligation is to issue a Form 1099-MISC to the non-employee spouse, and to report the wage withholding on Form 945. [Rev. Rul. 2004-60, 2004-24 I.R.B. 1051. (See § 22.02 and § 22.08 for further discussion of stock options.)]

Under Code § 415, "compensation" includes any nonqualified deferred compensation under § 409A that is includible in the employee's income. [Final Regulations, 72 Fed. Reg. 16878 (Apr. 5, 2007)]

[B] I.R.C. § 83 Issues

Tax planning for nonqualified plan participants also requires a look at I.R.C. § 83, which sometimes requires employees to include in income amounts that have not been distributed from the nonqualified plan. Section 83 provides that whenever property is transferred to anyone except the employer for the provision of services, the employee's taxable income includes the fair market value of the transferred property, minus any amount paid for the property.

Section 83 doesn't apply to transfers to qualified plan trusts, or to a deferred compensation arrangement that gives the employee a mere contractual right to receive compensation in the future. Many stock option transactions are also exempt from this section. However, § 83 does apply to assets set aside in trusts, escrows, or similar arrangements that are not subject to the claims of the corporation's general creditors.

Where § 83 applies, the employee's tax is based on the value of the employee's income on the plan trust at the time of taxation, and not on the fair market value of the employer's contributions from the trust.

In early 2014, the IRS finalized regulations to clarify when there is a "substantial risk of forfeiture" on transfer of stock that is treated as employee compensation under § 83. Substantial risk of forfeiture can be established only through a service condition or a condition related to the purpose of the transfer (e.g., achieving a performance goal). A service condition means that the employee's rights are contingent on performance or refraining from performance—such as under a non-compete agreement. In determining substantial risk based on a condition related to the purpose of the transfer, both the likelihood of the event occurring and the likelihood of the forfeiture being enforced must be considered. In general, transfer restrictions such as lock-ups, bans on insider trading, and blackout periods, do not create a substantial risk of forfeiture. But if the stock cannot be sold because of Securities Exchange Act § 16(b)'s short-swing profit rules, unless the taxpayer elects under § 83(b) to be taxed when the stock is issued, the stock is considered subject to a substantial risk of forfeiture. [T.D. 9659, 2014-12 I.R.B. 653; see Sally P. Schreiber, *Final Substantial-Risk-Of-Forfeiture Rules Are Released*, AICPA.com (Feb. 25, 2014) (benefitslink.com); Sharon L, Klingelsmith, Mona Ghude and Sharde Armstrong, *IRS Issues Final Regulations on Property Transferred for Services Under Section 83*, Drinker Biddle & Reath LLP (Mar. 27, 2014), available at Lexology.com. These regulations finalize the proposal at 77 Fed. Reg. 31783 (May 30, 2012).]

IRS's § 83 regulations provide that a provision calling for forfeiture of stock if the employee is discharged for cause or for committing a crime does not create a substantial risk of forfeiture. Nevertheless, in 2014 the Tax Court held that the discharge for cause provision in the taxpayer's employment agreement did create a substantial risk of forfeiture. The clause permitted termination for cause for several reasons, including failure to perform his duties diligently and adhere to the employment agreement. The Tax Court said that the regulations, as interpreted, focus on termination for committing a crime, which is unusual enough not to constitute a substantial risk. In this case, however, the Tax Court believed that the broader terms in the taxpayer's employment agreement did create a substantial risk of forfeiture. [*Austin v. Comm'r*, 141 T.C. No. 18 (2014); see Michael G. Falk, *Definition of "Substantial Risk of Forfeiture" Gets Murky?*, Winston & Strawn LLP (Apr. 4, 2014) (benefitslink.com)]

[C] Employer's Tax Deduction (Pre-AJCA)

Before the AJCA was enacted, the employer's deduction, as provided by the texts of Code sections 404(a)(5) and 404(d)(2) was not available if the plan provided deferred compensation for shareholders who were not employees of, or independent contractors to, the employer corporation. The employer's deduction for paying deferred compensation occurred in the year the employee received the compensation, not the year of the contribution. Each employee covered by funded, nonqualified deferred compensation arrangements had to have a separate account. Distributions from nonqualified plans were FICA and FUTA wages, but I.R.C. § 3121(v)(2) provided that amounts deferred under a nonqualified deferred compensation plan were taken into account only once—at the later of the time services were rendered, or when there ceased to be a substantial risk of forfeiture of the amounts.

[D] AJCA and § 409A

The American Jobs Creation Act of 2004 (AJCA), Pub. L. No. 108–357, adds new I.R.C. § 409A to the Internal Revenue Code. It is effective for amounts deferred after 2004. There is no requirement of common-law employment, so deferred payments to independent contractors and outside directors are also subject to these rules. The I.R.C. § 409A rules supplement those already in place governing economic benefit and constructive receipt of deferred compensation. In effect, amounts deferred under a nonqualified plan are included in the recipient's gross income unless they were previously included in his or her income, or unless they are subject to a substantial risk of forfeiture. Compensation is taxed when I.R.C. § 409A is triggered, or the previous rules apply—whichever comes first.

Compliance with I.R.C. § 409A is critical because the AJCA carries a big stick: unless its requirements are satisfied, all compensation deferred under the nonqualified plan for all taxable years is included in the participant's gross income for the current year, plus interest and a penalty of 20% of the compensation included in gross income. Penalties are also imposed if plan assets are placed into a trust outside of the United States, whether or not the assets are available to satisfy the claims of creditors. Another creditor protection measure applies the penalties if plan assets are placed in a domestic trust triggered by the employer's financial condition.

A plan is considered a nonqualified deferred compensation plan if it is not a qualified pension or welfare benefit (e.g., vacation, sick leave, disability pay, death benefit plan, HSA, HRA, medical reimbursement plan). Whether an option plan is subject to I.R.C. § 409A depends on the terms of the arrangement. If the exercise price for the option is at least as high as the underlying stock's fair market value on the date of the grant, then the option is not considered deferred compensation unless it includes some deferral feature over and above the ability to exercise the option in the future. There is a statutory exemption for ISOs and employee stock purchase plans. By and large, Stock Appreciation Rights (SARs) will be subject to I.R.C. § 409A, although a SAR, that has a fixed payment date, or a non-discounted publicly traded SAR, will be exempt.

I.R.C. § 409A requires elections to defer compensation to be made on or before the end of the taxable year before the year in which the compensation will be earned. For performance-based compensation (e.g., sales commissions) based on services rendered over a period of 12 months or more, the election can be made within the six months before the end of the service period.

Distributions to key employees cannot be made earlier than six months after separation from service, or upon the key employee's death. A key employee is one covered by I.R.C. § 416(I)(l)(c). The AJCA forbids acceleration of distributions. Distributions from a deferred compensation plan can be made only when the person earning the money is separated from service, dies, when a specified time is reached (or when a specified schedule begins), when the corporation changes control, the participant becomes disabled (unable to engage in substantial gainful activity as a result of a condition expected to result in death or last for at least 12 months; or receives income replacement benefits for at least three months under an Accident & Health plan on account of total disability), or there is an unforeseeable emergency (e.g., severe financial hardship to a participant because of illness or accident to the participant or close family member; casualty loss to the participant's property; or results of other events beyond the participant's control; otherwise, elective withdrawals are forbidden, even with a penalty). Even if an unforeseeable emergency has occurred, the amount of the distribution must not exceed the amount needed to cope with the emergency and pay the taxes on the premature distribution. Nor can distributions be made if the hardship could be handled through insurance reimbursement or liquidation of the participant's other assets.

Changes in the form of distribution that have the effect of accelerating payment of deferred compensation are forbidden to the same extent as acceleration of the distribution. However, I.R.C. § 409A is not violated merely because a plan provides a choice between cash and taxable property, if the same amount of income is included in income in the same year irrespective of the participant's election. Therefore, the plan can provide for a choice of a lump sum or a fully taxable annuity contract without falling afoul of I.R.C. § 409A.

The initial election to defer must specify the form of any payment that is supposed to be received at a specified time or on a specified schedule. Exceptions are made to this general rule for payments under a QDRO, payments made to comply with federal conflict of interest requirements, amounts needed to pay FICA taxes, and amounts withheld when there has been an I.R.C. § 457(f) vesting event. A lump sum payment of up to $10,000 is also permitted to a terminated employee.

To prevent an error in one participant's plan from affecting the other participants, the general rule is that all account balance plans for a given employee are considered a single plan, and all non-account-balance plans for him or her are considered a single plan, and any other plans are aggregated into another single plan. The plan aggregation rules are not applied in determining if a payment exceeds $10,000.

If an election is made to defer distribution past its original date, the election must be made 12 months before the scheduled distribution date, and must defer payment for an additional five years.

For an account balance plan, the amount that can be grandfathered is the earned and vested account balance as of December 31, 2004, plus subsequent earnings (as long as the right to the earnings was vested on that date). For a non-account-balance plan, the value of the grandfathered benefit is the present value of the earned and vested benefit that would have been paid at the earliest possible date if the plan participant had voluntarily separated from service on December 31, 2004. Therefore, early retirement subsidies are not grandfathered if they were not payable as of that date, but post-2004 benefits that accrued solely by passage of time are included when the present value of the grandfathered benefit is determined. The employer can use the plan's actuarial assumptions for valuation, as long as the assumptions are reasonable.

A payment (e.g., a bonus) is not subject to I.R.C. § 409A as long as the employer makes the payment no later than the next taxable year after the amount ceases to be subject to a substantial risk of forfeiture. The payment must be made within two and a half months after the end of the employer's tax year or the end of the employee's tax year in which the condition lapses—whichever is later.

I.R.C. § 409A does not apply to payments when all the taxpayers involved use the accrual method. Nor does it apply to payments made to someone who is actively engaged in providing non-employee or non-director services to two or more unrelated recipients. An entity is deemed related if the service provider owns at least a 20% interest in it. Property (such as restricted stock) that is subject to I.R.C. § 83 is not subject to I.R.C. § 409A, but a service provider's enforceable right to receive property in a later year (e.g., under a restricted stock unit plan) can be subject to I.R.C. § 409A.

It does not constitute prohibited acceleration for a company to waive or accelerate the satisfaction of a condition that is a substantial risk of forfeiture, as long as the other conditions of I.R.C. § 409A are satisfied. For example, if a plan will pay a lump sum upon separation from service after at least 10 years, changing the requirement to five years will not violate I.R.C. § 409A. Plans can be amended to allow cashout of up to $10,000. Plans can also be amended so that the entire interest under a future deferral will be distributed in a lump sum whenever the participant's interest in the plan falls below the *de minimis* amount specified by a plan when a distribution event occurs. It is also permissible to accelerate distributions to someone other than the participant to satisfy a QDRO; to the participant to pay FICA and income taxes under § 3121(v); or to a participant to the extent required to pay income taxes generated by a § 457(f) plan's vesting event.

Deferred compensation payments can be accelerated in connection with a change in control (change in ownership or effective control of the company); the change-in-control event must be objectively determinable.

The general rule is that employers cannot use the termination of a nonqualified plan as a means of accelerating distributions. A valuation method that would be acceptable for valuing property in a decedent's estate will be accepted as an I.R.C. § 409A valuation method. The exercise price or base value of non-grandfathered stock options or discounted SARs can be reformed, by means of an amendment adopted by December 31, 2005, to reset the price or value to the fair market value of the stock on the original grant date. (See Notice 2005-1, 2005-2 I.R.B. 274 for detailed discussion of the pre-PPA rules.) [These rules are discussed in, e.g., Haynes & Boone § 409A News Alert, *§ 409A Stock Valuation Guidance for Privately-Held Companies* (Jan. 23, 2006) (benefitslink.com)]

Under § 409A, disability can trigger deferred compensation; many plans provide for 100% vesting on disability. Even if the plan does not make disability a payment trigger, the onset of disability can affect vesting and the timing of payments made for separation from service. If disability leads to full vesting but does not affect the actual payment, then the plan can use any definition it wants and need not satisfy standards under § 409A. But sometimes accelerating vesting can make a plan subject to § 409A. If there is full vesting on disability but payments are not accelerated, and an employee becomes disabled during the first year of a three-year service vesting period, the payment will not be made during the short-term deferral period. Therefore, for that employee, the restricted stock unit is subject to § 409A, whereas if payment had occurred at the point of disability vesting, then the arrangement could be exempt from § 409A under the short-term deferral rule. [Randy L. Gegelman, The Law Firm of Faegre & Benson LLP, *Practical 409A: The Impact of Disability on Non-Qualified Deferred Compensation Under Code § 409A* (Mar. 23, 2009) (benefitslink.com)]

[E] The PPA, 2005 Proposals, and 2007 Final Rules

In 2005, the IRS issued a lengthy and detailed set of proposed regulations [70 Fed. Reg. 58930 (Oct. 4, 2005)] dealing with many aspects of nonqualified plans: valuation; severance pay plans; initial elections to defer compensation; performance-based compensation; commissions; and rules for distributing deferred compensation, including relief for certain delays in distribution.

The basic rule is that a nonqualified stock option is not subject to § 409A if it is granted for at least the FMV of the stock on the date of the grant; it is taxable under § 83; and the option does not have the effect of deferring compensation. Generally speaking, stock appreciation rights (SARs) are treated like stock options.

Severance pay plans are exempt from § 409A if they are collectively bargained; if they are broad-based (i.e., not limited to key employees); or if payments are made within two years after the year of termination of employment. There is a special exception for severance payments that would not otherwise be exempt, but are made within 2½ months of the end of the year of termination of an employee who was involuntarily terminated. An initial election to defer severance resulting from involuntary separation from service can be made at any time before the employee has a legally binding right to the payment, as long as the severance pay is the subject of bona fide arm's-length negotiations. For severance payments under a window program, the initial election to defer the payment can be made until participation in the program becomes irrevocable.

Distributions made to a key employee of a public corporation cannot be made because of separation from service until at least six months have elapsed since the separation.

The plan must have a schedule for making the distribution (e.g., three months after the participant becomes disabled). Employees must make their initial election to defer compensation under a nonqualified plan by the end of the year preceding the year in which the compensation subject to deferral is earned.

The Pension Protection Act of 2006 had a seismic impact on many aspects of the pension and tax world—and nonqualified plans did not escape this phenomenon. Section 116 of the Pension Protection Act (PPA; Pub. L. No. 109–280) amends § 409A to add new categories of compensation that are taxable to the recipient of deferred compensation. The provisions of § 116 apply to transactions after the PPA's enactment date (August 17, 2006).

When a defined benefit plan is "at risk," there will be a "restricted period" during which transfers of funds to a trust or other arrangement in order to pay nonqualified deferred compensation to a "covered employee" will result in the employee being taxed on the amounts transferred, and also on the value of plan assets that are restricted to providing nonqualified deferred compensation. Not only are the assets in question taxable to the employee, the employee will have to pay a 20% excise tax. In some instances, the employee will also have to pay interest on underpayments of tax resulting from this inclusion in income. Furthermore, if the transferred or restricted assets increase in value or accrue earnings, those additional amounts are simply treated as more property transfers taxable to the employee. For this purpose, it is irrelevant whether the assets used for deferred compensation are subject to the claims of the sponsor's general creditors—so rabbi trusts do not protect the employee against taxation.

The definition of covered employees comes from § 162(m)(3) and includes the CEO and the four highest paid executive officers other than the CEO plus officers, directors and 10% stockholders, because the definition incorporates the Securities Exchange Act § 16(a) definition as well. The restricted period means any time when the sponsor company is bankrupt, when its defined benefit plan has at-risk status (see § 4.01[A]) and a 12-month period measured as the six months before and the six months after an involuntary or distress termination of any defined benefit plan maintained by the sponsor. If the payor corporation is publicly traded, it may be subject to SEC rules about management compensation. If the company received federal "bail-out" funds, it may also be subject to limitations on executive compensation, including incentive and deferred compensation. See § 1.01[B].

A plan is considered at risk if its funding status falls below 70% (considering various factors set out in the PPA) and below 80% (when these factors are not considered).

If the employer provides a gross-up (i.e., indemnifies the employee for the extra tax burden), payments of this type will be treated as taxable income to the employee, plus a 20% penalty. The employer will not be permitted to deduct the gross-up payment on its own income tax return. [This issue is discussed, e.g., in Gardner Carton & Douglas Client Memorandum, *Pension Protection Act Restricts Funding of Certain Nonqualified Deferred Compensation Arrangements*, <http://www.gcd.com/PPARestrictsFunding.pdf> (September 2006)]

In April 2007, reflecting public comments as well as the PPA, the IRS published final regulations, defining the types of plans (e.g., short-term deferral of compensation; Stock Appreciation Rights; some health reimbursement arrangements) that are exempt under § 409A. Qualified plans, welfare benefit plans (e.g., disability plans, sick and vacation leave plans) are exempt from § 409A coverage, as are ISOs and other statutory stock options and ESOPs.

The documents for a § 409A plan must reflect the limitations on the amount that can be deferred under or distributed from a nonqualified plan. The plan must be in writing and must disclose the payment schedule, trigger events for payments, amount to be paid, and conditions imposed on making elections under the plan. Most of the time, participants will have to make elections about how much to defer and when and how the deferred compensation will be paid out before the taxable year in which the participant will do the work for which compensation is deferred. Some participants will find this requirement onerous, because they find it hard to estimate their future earnings, investment and other income, and future needs.

Nonqualified plans sponsored by public companies must explicitly provide that key employees wait at least six months after separation from service to receive benefits. Short-term deferrals are not covered by § 409A: amounts that are distributed as soon as they vest, or no later than 2½ months after the end of the year to which they refer. Under the final regulations, amounts are exempt from § 409A treatment as separation pay as long as they are completed by the end of the second calendar year after the year of separation, and they do not exceed twice the § 401(a)(17) limit. For larger amounts, only the portion that exceeds this amount is subject to § 409A. Sometimes when an employee leaves for "good reason" (as defined by the final regulations as a material negative change in the employment relationship), separation pay can be treated as involuntary separation pay. Payments can also be accelerated without tax penalty to comply with a QDRO or pay FICA taxes.

Separation from service is deemed to occur either when it is reasonably anticipated that the ex-employee or independent contractor will not work for the employer any more, or will permanently reduce services to a level of 20% or less of the service provided in the previous three years. Separation is presumed to occur if services actually drop below the 20% level—and is presumed not to occur if services remain at the 50% or greater level. To facilitate phased retirement (see § 1.06), a plan can define separation from service as a reduction in services in the range of 20%–50% of previous effort.

Section 409A also applies to substitution of compensation for § 409A deferred compensation—for example, when a say on pay vote leads to some compensation being returned to the employer. [Gary M. Ford, Bloomberg, *Be Ever Vigilant Regarding 409A and Include 409A Interpretive Provisions!*, Benefits Practice Blog (Feb. 3, 2012) (benefitslink.com)]

In general, when a nonqualified plan is terminated and benefits are distributed, there is deemed to have been an acceleration of payments, which results in taxation under § 409A. However, there is an exception if all plans of the same type are terminated, distributions occur over a period of 12 to 24 months—and the sponsor refrains from creating new plans of the same type for a period of three years.

The final regulations expand the kinds of stock that can be exempt from § 409A when used to fund stock options and stock appreciation rights plans; the valuation rules in the final regulations are quite similar to those in the proposed rules. They give participants in nonqualified plans even more choices of how they can receive their payments, including term-certain annuities, "pop-up" annuities (where the benefit increases when the plan participant dies and the benefit continues to be paid to a surviving spouse), and annuities with COLAs or cash refund features.

The final regulations explain how to treat gross-ups under § 409A, and create a safe harbor for treating certain voluntary terminations as involuntary for separation pay purposes. However, the IRS has left some questions unresolved, such as how to calculate amounts of deferred compensation to be included in income; withholding rules if there is taxable income; how to apply § 409A to partner compensation; and which leave programs rate as bona fide plans of sick leave or vacation leave. [T.D. 9321, RIN 1545-BE 79, 73 Fed. Reg. 19234 (Apr. 10, 2007) See also Notice 2007-34, 2007-17 I.R.B. 996 for a discussion of the § 409A consequences of split-dollar insurance plans, and corrections in FR Doc E7-14624, 72 Fed. Reg. 41620 (July 31, 2007).]

Two main ways of structuring separation pay to avoid falling under § 409A are the short-term deferral exception and the separation pay safe harbor.

Employees who are required to release their claims against the employer in order to receive severance should be given releases at or shortly after the termination date, so they will have time to consider the releases and still receive payments within two and a half months if they agree to sign the release. [Randy L. Gegelman and Kathlyn E. Noecker, *Practical 409A: Separation Pay Options Under Code Section 409A* (Mar. 23, 2009) (benefitslink.com)]

Generally, an agreement to provide severance benefits can permit payment at any time within 90 days after the triggering event but only if the employee does not have the capacity to directly or indirectly control when the compensation will be paid. Remember that ADEA releases require 45 days for employees to consider the release and employees have a further seven days after signing to revoke the release, so severance payments are usually delayed until the right to revoke has elapsed. Releases offered in the third quarter of the year, therefore, potentially straddle two years.

The IRS's position, as expressed in Notice 2010-6, 2010-3 I.R.B. 275, effective April 1, 2011, is that this is precisely what § 409A is designed to penalize. This is a common issue in § 409A audits. The way to avoid trouble is to draft releases to say that, if benefits could be paid in more than one tax year depending on when the release is signed, payment will be made in the later year no matter when the release was actually signed. Plans should also be amended by December 31, 2012: Notice 2010-80, 2010-51 I.R.B. 853 says that the transition period for eliminating the "straddle" problem will end then.

Some inadvertent errors can be corrected using IRS correction programs; for the year of a corrective plan amendment, the tax return should include a note that the amendment was adopted in reliance on the correction program.

The IRS will permit the company to drop its requirement that the departing employee sign a release—but that would leave the company vulnerable to suits for things such as discrimination or ERISA violations. The IRS will also permit the payment window to be shortened from 90 days to 30 or 45 days—which makes this tax problem less likely but increases the burden on the company's HR department or benefits administration vendor to process the payment on time. [McGuireWoods LLP, *Employee Release Provisions Present Section 409A Trap for the Unwary* (Aug. 31, 2011) (benefitslink.com); George L. Chimento, Davis Malm & D'Agostine, *Release Me: 4th Quarter Complications for 409A Plans* (Oct. 14, 2011) (benefitslink.com)]

See Rev. Rul. 2010-27, 2010-45 I.R.B. 620, for the types of expenses (illness; funeral expenses; uninsured casualty causing property loss) expenses that could qualify for an unforeseeable emergency distribution from a 409A plan.

The participant must show that the expenses could not otherwise be met by insurance, or by liquidating assets that could be liquidated without severe financial hardship. The distribution must not exceed the amount needed to cope with the emergency (plus taxes). [McGuireWoods LLP Legal Updates, *IRS Issues Guidance on Unforeseeable Emergency Distributions from 409A and 457(b) Plans* (Dec. 30, 2010) (benefitslink.com)]

Not only is § 409A an issue in the corporation's dealings with individual executives, but also it must be considered when there is a change in control of the corporation—for example, in a merger or takeover, when many employees are involved. Section 409A potentially applies to many compensation arrangements in change-of-control situations, such as severance arrangements, stock options, and incentives. Violating the rule leads to accelerated inclusion in income, and a 20% federal penalty. California imposes its own 20% penalty.

Alternative payment methods for a double-trigger severance plan (see § 3.03[A]) could violate § 409A. Some employers fail to realize this because the pre- and post-change severance provisions are found in different documents, such as a company-wide severance plan and an individual change-in-control agreement with a key executive. A double-trigger arrangement typically falls under § 409A if its "good reason" payment trigger is excessively broad—for example, if the executive can resign and collect severance based on a minor reduction in pay or duties, or if the installment payments exceed $490,000 (as indexed for inflation) or extend more than two years after separation from service. An installment or lump sum double trigger violates § 409A unless the definition of change in control complies with § 409A, and it often does not. To avoid this problem, the plan can be structured to make pre- and post-change in control payments in the same way.

Stock options can be assumed in corporate transactions without violating § 409A if the assumption satisfies the rules for assuming ISOs. In general, that means that the economics of the option must be preserved by valuing the consideration paid for the target company's stock, potentially including the earn-out. If the calculations are wrong, overvaluing the options violates § 409A and undervaluation causes economic detriment to the holders of the options. [Juliano P. Banuelos, *Recent Compensation Trends in Mergers and Acquisitions and Section 409A*, Orrick Perspectives (October 2011) (benefitslink.com)]

§ 8.03 PROHIBITED TRANSACTIONS AND CORRECTIONS

Section 409A requires nonqualified plans to provide for payment only on a permitted event, for example death, disability, or separation from service. They must specify that the date of the event is the payment date or specify a fixed schedule or a different payment date that is objectively determinable and not discretionary. A nonqualified plan can also provide that payment is determinable and non-discretionary when it is made, but only if the period begins and ends in the same tax year for the employee or the period is not more than 90 days and the employee does not have the right to designate the taxable year of the payment. (It is common for plans to call for payment within a period of time after an event, because it can be inconvenient to make the payment exactly on the day of the event.)

As a result of these requirements, a nonqualified plan may discover that it has created additional tax liability for the plan and for its beneficiaries.

Notice 2008-113, 2008-51 I.R.B. 1305 provides a correction program for inadvertent, unintentional operational errors in administering § 409A plans. Failures that can be corrected include failing to defer compensation or making incorrect payments of compensation. The correction program is effective for tax years beginning on or after January 1, 2009. [Snell & Wilmer Legal Alert, *IRS Announces Section 409A Correction Program*, <http://www.swlaw.com/Alert_CorrectionProgram_Apr2009.pdf> (April 2009); Fred Schneyer, *IRS Issues Final 409A(a) Relief Procedures*, plansponsor.com (Dec. 5, 2008)] This Notice explains how to correct operational failures; see Notice 2010-6, 2010-3 I.R.B. 275, for guidance on how to correct document failures.

Notice 2010-80, 2010-51 I.R.B. 853, offers additional relief for § 409A plans—more types of plans will be eligible for relief under Notice 2010-6; a new correction method is permitted when there is a failure of payment at separation of service subject to a requirement to release claims; and transition relief is available under Notice 2010-6 to correct plan documents. [Rebecca Moore, *IRS Offers Additional 409A Relief*, plansponsor.com (Nov. 30, 2010); Frank Palmieri, *Employers Should Review Severance Plans in Light of IRS Guidance*, Employee Benefit News (Feb. 1, 2011) (benefitslink.com)]

Nor are tax problems the only potential issues for nonqualified plans. ERISA § 502(i) gives the DOL power to assess a civil penalty against a "party in interest" who engages in a prohibited transaction with a nonqualified plan. The penalty, which is usually assessed in connection with top-hat plans, is 5% for every year or partial year in which the prohibited transaction continues in effect. There is an additional 100% penalty if the DOL issues a notice of violation, but the violation is not corrected within 90 days (or whatever extension of time the DOL grants).

CHAPTER 9

EARLY RETIREMENT AND RETIREE HEALTH BENEFITS

§ 9.01 INTRODUCTION

The timing of retirement is an individual choice, but employers can take steps to make early retirement either more or less attractive. Sometimes employers pursue early retirement incentives because they find it less expensive to encourage retirement than to maintain a large payroll. At other times, employers want to encourage older, skilled, and experienced employees to remain in the workforce—or they do not wish to devote funds to paying incentives to retire early!

Without careful planning and drafting, early retirement programs can also have a legal downside. The employer must make sure that incentives are available without unlawful discrimination. Furthermore, although it makes sense to ask early retirees to waive their claims against the employer, the waiver must be drafted with due attention to the Older Worker's Benefit Protection Act (OWBPA).

An early retirement program can create risks from two directions. Employees who are eligible may charge that the plan is a subterfuge for forcing them into involuntary retirement. On the other hand, employees who are not offered the incentives can charge that the unavailability of the program was the result of discrimination against them. Furthermore, if the early retirement program changes over time, employees who accepted a first offer may claim that the company should have informed them of the potential for getting a better offer by waiting longer. [This topic is discussed in more detail in Chapter 15, § 15.07, as an issue of fiduciary responsibility to make full disclosure to plan participants]

The questions of early retirement programs and retiree health benefits need to be examined in tandem, because one of the most important questions in deciding whether to retire early is the availability of health coverage. Medicare eligibility depends on age (65 or over) or disability, not employment status. Furthermore, the Medicare system does not provide spousal benefits: each spouse must qualify independently. Therefore, a potential early retiree who is younger than 65 will need retiree health coverage, COBRA coverage, or private insurance. HRAs and Health FSAs (see § 18.19[F]) are considered group health plans for PPACA purposes. A standalone HRA that covers only retirees is not subject to PPACA's market reforms, but constitutes minimum essential coverage. Hence, retirees cannot get a premium tax credit for the purchase of Exchange coverage. (See § 18.19[J][1].) [Notice 2013-54, 2013-40 I.R.B. 237 and DOL Technical Release 2013-03; see Taylor Wedge French, James P. McElligott Jr., and Larry R. Goldstein, *New Requirements Affect HRAs, FSAs And Employer Payment Plans Beginning In 2014*, McGuire Woods LLP (Oct. 13, 2013), available at Lexology.com]

A Gallup poll shows an increase in the proportion of older Americans in the workforce since the end of the recession: a three-point increase since 2010, when there was a two-point decrease in the percentage of persons aged 18–29 in the workforce. In 2010, 9% of people aged 65 and older were working full-time or in full-time self-employment, rising to 12% in 2013. [Kevin McGuinness, *More Older Americans in Work Force*, plansponsor.com (Oct. 21, 2013)]

Swiss Re's Risk Perception Survey says that 57% of American workers expect to retire either later than age 65 or not at all. Nineteen percent of U.S. respondents (more than in any other country) expect to work at least until 70; 12% say they will never be able to retire, and 21% don't know when they'll retire. [Kevin Mcguinness, *Americans Foresee A Working Retirement*, plansponsor.com (Oct. 21, 2013)]

PPA § 841 amends Code § 420: a plan whose assets are at least 120% of current liability is permitted to fund a 401(h) plan with at least two years' worth of estimated retiree health costs. However, a sponsor that chooses to do so must keep the plan funded at a level of at least 120%; if funding drops below this level, the sponsor must withdraw funds from the 401(h) plan until the plan's funding level returns to at least 120%. The PPA also permits transfers to fund the expected future costs of retiree health benefits under a CBA, as long as the employer used at least 5% of its 2005 gross receipts for the purpose of providing retiree health benefits. See § 9.13, below, for more discussion.

§ 9.02 ADEA ISSUES OF EARLY RETIREMENT INCENTIVES

At what point does an incentive provided to motivate early retirement turn into pressure that adds up to "constructive discharge" (the equivalent of firing the employee)? The relevant statute is the Older Worker's Benefit Protection Act, which allows voluntary early retirement incentives but only if they satisfy the objectives of the ADEA: promoting employment opportunities for qualified and willing older workers.

The OWBPA allows employers to subsidize early retirement via flat dollar benefits, extra benefits, or percentage increases. Employees who retire early can be offered a more favorable benefit formula (e.g., adding a certain number of years to the number of years actually worked). It does not violate the OWBPA to impose a "window" period that is the only time that the incentive is available. HHS published an Interim Final Rule, implementing the reinsurance program, on May 5, 2010: see 75 Fed. Reg. 24450 (May 5, 2010).

■ **TIP:** The mandates imposed by PPACA on plans that are not "grandfathered" plans (for example, the requirement of covering employees' children up to age 26) do not apply to plans that cover only retirees, and no active workers. [Seyfarth Shaw LLP, *Health Care Reform Mandates Do Not Apply to Retiree-Only Plans*, <http://www.seyfarth.com/e613f530-2fb9-48e0-8330-44fk5ab6d960_documentupload.pdf> (June 17, 2010)]

A defined benefit plan can pay a "Social Security supplement" starting at the date of early retirement, extending until the first date the retiree will be able to receive reduced Social Security benefits—or, if the employer prefers, until the retiree will be eligible for a full unreduced Social Security benefit.

> ■ **TIP:** The employer can amend the pension plan to raise the NRA from 65 to 67 (a change that the Social Security Administration is gradually implementing), as long as accrued early retirement benefits, including subsidies, are preserved.

A university offered early retirement incentives to both tenured professors and top-level administrators. The North Dakota district court said (and the Eighth Circuit agreed) that payments to the faculty members were not "wages" (and therefore not subject to Social Security taxes) because the payments were made in exchange for property rights in university tenure. The payments to administrators, although similar, were subject to FICA, because the administrators were at-will employees, whereas the tenured faculty could only be dismissed for grave cause. [*N.D. State Univ. v. United States*, 85 A.F.T.R.2d ¶ 2000-332 (D.N.D. Nov. 19, 1999), *aff'd*, 255 F.3d 599 (8th Cir. 2001)]

In 2000, the Federal Circuit ruled that severance payments made to retiring employees are "wages" subject to FICA because they reflect past work. In 2006, the Sixth Circuit held that early retirement incentives exchanging payments for tenure rights were subject to FICA, based on a broad definition of "compensation," and because the payments were made because of the recipients' past services for the employer, not in exchange for surrender of tenure rights. [*Appoloni v. United States/Klender v. U.S.*, 450 F.3d 185 (6th Cir. 2006); *Abrahamsen v. U.S.*, 228 F.3d 1360 (Fed. Cir. 2000). In late 2007, the Third Circuit held that the University of Pittsburgh's early retirement payments to tenured professors were taxable income, not buyout payments. The Third Circuit deemed tenure to be a form of compensation for past work at the university, so giving up tenure was the equivalent of severance pay and thus FICA wages. See Fred Schneyer, *Payments to Tenured Profs Ruled Taxable Wages*, plansponsor.com (Nov. 5, 2007).]

The District Court for the District of Minnesota ruled that the Minnesota Department of Corrections violated the ADEA by maintaining an early retirement incentive plan that had different health and dental plans depending on whether or not the retiree was under 55 at the time of retirement. Those who retired at 55 and under received employer contributions for health and dental coverage until age 65, whereas those who retired after 55 did not receive employer contributions. The district court ruled that this constituted facial discrimination, and ordered damages equal to the premiums that would have been paid from 2001 to 2010 if the plan had not discriminated. [*EEOC v. Minnesota Dep't of Corrs.*, No. Civ 098-05252 PAM/FLN (D. Minn. Apr. 12, 2010); see Rebecca Moore, *Court Finds Early Retirement Incentive Discriminatory*, plansponsor.com (Apr. 12, 2010)]

§ 9.03 DISCLOSURES TO EMPLOYEES

An employee can't make a meaningful decision about whether or not to retire without understanding the choices that will be available in the near future. If the terms of the early retirement program change, people who were not eligible for the improved terms, or who elected early retirement without knowing that they could have gotten a better deal by waiting longer, may charge the employer with fraud, and may charge various parties involved with the plan with violations of fiduciary duty.

The Third Circuit announced a rule in *Fischer v. Philadelphia Elec. Co.* [96 F.3d 1533 (3d Cir. 1996); see also *Bins v. Exxon Co.*, 189 F.3d 929 (9th Cir. 1999), on rehearing, 220 F.3d 1042 (9th Cir. 2000)] that a revised early retirement incentive has received "serious consideration," and therefore must be disclosed to potential early retirees, once senior managers discuss the proposal for purposes of implementation.

The First Circuit held that ERISA preempts state-law claims of negligence, equitable estoppel, and negligent misrepresentation made by an early retiree who blamed his employer's erroneous estimate of his benefits for inducing him to retire early. The plaintiff said that he was not suing over plan administration issues that would be preempted by ERISA, only about the employer's legal obligations to keep proper records. He also said that he sought damages for the employer's negligence, not plan benefits. The First Circuit did not accept this argument, holding that resolution of the claim would require determining whether the plan complied with the record requirements imposed by ERISA. [*Zipperer v. Raytheon Co.*, 493 F.3d 50 (1st Cir. 2007)]

It is a breach of fiduciary duty to inform potential early retirees that lump-sum payouts are available, without also disclosing the I.R.C. § 415 limitations on rollovers and explaining the tax consequences. [*Farr v. U.S. West Commc'ns, Inc.*, 58 F.3d 1361 (9th Cir. 1998)] Given that the fiduciaries' common-law duty of loyalty requires them to deal fairly and honestly with plan participants, it is a violation to give them incomplete information.

Gearlds alleged that his employer negligently induced him to take early retirement by promising health benefits. The district court dismissed the case, arguing that all he asked for was compensatory damages (past and future medical expenses, attorneys' fees, and costs), which are not an available equitable remedy. However, the Fifth Circuit said that *Amara* [*CIGNA Corp. v. Amara* 131 S. Ct. 1866 (2011)] allows relief that makes a plaintiff whole for losses caused by breach of fiduciary duty. [*Gearlds v. Entergy Servs. Inc.*, 709 F.3d 448 (5th Cir. 2013); see Rebecca Moore, *5th Circuit Revives Suit for Retiree Medical Benefits*, plansponsor.com (Mar. 8, 2013)]

To assist older employees in making decisions about Medicare Part D (the prescription drug program that took effect in 2006), employers are required to issue a notice to all Part D-eligible employees (with disclosure to the Center for Medicare and Medicaid services as well) informing them as to whether there is prescription drug coverage under the employer's plan, and whether that coverage is creditable or non-creditable. [See § 9.10[B]]

§ 9.04 EEOC MANUAL ON EARLY RETIREMENT INCENTIVES

Late in 2000, the EEOC updated Section 3 of its Compliance Manual to deal with benefits. [No. 915.003 (Oct. 3, 2000), <http://www.eeoc.gov/policy/docs/benefits.html>] As of press time in 2014, this section of the manual had not been updated. The agency's position is that an early retirement incentive (ERI) program is lawful as long as it's voluntary. The EEOC will not get involved if the employer chooses to:

- Set a minimum age or minimum number of years of service for employees who participate;
- Have a window (i.e., the incentive is only available for a limited time period);
- Limit the ERI to a manager, a department, a particular facility, etc.

However, ERI benefits can't be reduced or denied for older employees versus similarly situated younger employees unless the employer qualifies for one of five defenses:

- Equal cost;
- Subsidizing a portion of the early retirement benefit;
- Integrating the incentives with Social Security;
- (For a university) incentives for a tenured faculty member;
- The plan is consistent with the objectives of the ADEA.

The equal cost defense probably will not be available in connection with ERIs, because the cost of early retirement benefits generally does not increase with the employee's age.

The EEOC allows the employer to limit the ERI or pay higher ERI benefits to younger employees where the benefits are used to bring early retirees up to the level of the unreduced pension they would receive at the NRA from a defined benefit pension plan. But the subsidized pension can't be greater than the pension of a similarly situated older employee who has reached NRA.

It is also permissible to offer an ERI to bridge the gap to Social Security eligibility, for a person who has not yet reached the Social Security early retirement age (currently slightly over 62). The supplement can't exceed the Social Security benefit that the employee will eventually receive as an early or normal age retiree.

According to the EEOC, equal severance benefits are required for all similarly situated employees irrespective of their age. Employers may not deny severance on the grounds that the employee is eligible for a pension, although sometimes pension benefits can be offset against the severance pay. Denying recall rights to older workers operates as unlawful involuntary retirement. The cost of providing severance does not rise with the employees' age, so employers are not allowed to assert an equal cost defense in this context.

Retiree health benefits can legitimately be offset against severance if the retiree is eligible for an immediate pension; the retiree actually receives health benefits; and the retiree benefits are at least comparable to Medicare in type and value. If the retiree is over 65, the benefits must be at least comparable for one-fourth the value of Medicare benefits. The offset itself must be reduced by any percentage by which the pension is reduced for retirement before the NRA, and any percentage of the retiree health coverage premium that the retiree has to pay.

In the EEOC view, an ERI ignores age as a criterion (and therefore is consistent with the ADEA's objectives) as long as it gives all employees above a certain age:

- A flat dollar amount (e.g., $20,000);
- Additional service-based benefits, for instance, $1,000 for each year of service;
- A percentage of salary;
- A flat dollar increase in pension benefits, such as an extra $200 a month;
- A percentage increase (e.g., 10%) in pension benefits;
- Extra years of service and/or age used in pension computations.

§ 9.05 ERISA ISSUES

[A] Generally

Because one of the primary purposes of ERISA is to make sure that retirement benefits will be paid in accordance with the terms of the plan, ERISA issues often arise when early retirement plans must be construed. Sometimes, ERISA welfare benefit plans will also be involved.

[B] Preemption

It is very likely that ERISA will be held to preempt state-court cases about group health plans. In its June 2004 decision in the consolidated cases of *Aetna Health Inc. v. Davila*, and *Cigna Healthcare of Texas, Inc. v. Calad*, 542 U.S. 200 (2004), the Supreme Court found that ERISA § 502(a) completely preempts state-law claims alleging that managed care plans improperly denied care (in one case, it was claimed that the plaintiff was injured by taking a lower-cost drug rather than the safer, more expensive drug that was not covered by the plan; in the other case, alleged premature discharge from hospitalization). [See § 15.18] Preemption is much less likely to be found in the early retirement context. According to the Sixth Circuit, ERISA does not preempt age discrimination claims merely because the plaintiff had already retired and was collecting a pension as of the time of the suit. [*Warner v. Ford Motor Co.*, 46 F.3d 531 (6th Cir. 1995)]

The 1996 case of *Lockheed v. Spink* [517 U.S. 882 (1996)] found (among other issues) that it is not a prohibited transaction (as defined by ERISA § 406) to establish an early retirement program that is conditioned on waiving enforcement of employment claims. Under this analysis, paying benefits under any circumstances shouldn't be treated as a prohibited transaction.

[C] Fiduciary Duty

Persons dissatisfied with the terms of an early retirement plan, or the way those terms are applied, often bring suit for breach of fiduciary duty. Whether a breach will be found depends on factors such as whether potential retirees received materially misleading information—possibly whether or not intent to mislead, or even negligence, was present. It does not violate ERISA to deny early retirement to employees who are deemed especially valuable to the company, if the plan gives management discretion as to whether early retirement is in the company's best interests. [*McNab v. Gen. Motors*, 162 F.3d 959 (7th Cir. 1998)] Another General Motors case says that the LMRA and NLRA do not preempt an early retiree's state-law claims that the employer fraudulently induced acceptance of early retirement. [*Voilas v. Gen. Motors*, 170 F.3d 367 (3d Cir. 1999)]

In the fourth opinion in this case, rendered October 2009, the Third Circuit found that it was a breach of fiduciary duty to give employees the impression that their retiree health benefits would continue for life when, in fact, the employer had the power to terminate the benefits at any time. In this view, employees received "at best a half truth" when the company did not disclose the power to amend the plan. Although the SPD disclosed the right to amend, the Third Circuit said that this was irrelevant because it was not distributed until after the plaintiffs retired, so it could not have affected their knowledge of the plan. The Third Circuit upheld the injunction issued by the district court, because the injunction corrected a violation of fiduciary duty, and the specific provisions in ERISA dealing with equitable relief outweigh the general principle that ERISA does not regulate settlor activity. [*In re Unisys Corp. Retiree Medical Benefits ERISA Litigation*, 579 F.3d 220 (3d Cir. Oct. 19, 2009), *cert. denied*, 559 U.S. 940 sub nom. *Unisys Corp. v. Adair* (Feb. 22, 2010)]

[D] Anticutback Rule

ERISA § 204(g) forbids cutbacks in benefits. On June 7, 2004, the Supreme Court ruled that it is a violation of the anticutback rule to amend a plan to further restrict the type of work that retirees can do without forfeiting their pensions, if the result of the amendment is that early retirement benefits that were already accrued would be suspended. (The plan ruled out benefits for retirees who engaged in post-retirement work as "construction workers"; the plaintiffs were "construction supervisors." Then the plan was amended to rule out benefits for anyone who did any work at all in the construction industry.) [*Central Laborers' Pension Fund v. Heinz*, 541 U.S. 739 (2004)]

The Ninth Circuit ruled that plan trustees improperly suspended early retirement benefits. The trustees said that the retiree engaged in "employment as an electrical contractor," which was forbidden. But the Ninth Circuit held that installing HVAC equipment for an electrical contractor was not the same as being a contractor, and the plan provision only forbade setting up in business as an independent business. [*Brown v. Southern California IBEW NECA Trust Funds*, 588 F.3d 1000 (9th Cir. 2009)]

The Ninth Circuit held that it was an abuse of discretion for plan trustees to forbid participants to work certain post-retirement jobs if they wanted to collect pension benefits. The trustees identified post-retirement jobs as traffic flagger and snowplow driver as falling within the same classification as their pre-retirement union jobs as skilled mechanics. The plan allowed early retirement at age 52 with 10 or more years of credited service. Early and normal-age retirees can collect retirement income while working, as long as they do not have more than 51 hours of post-retirement service in any month in their former job classification and in the industry in which the employers are involved. The trustees called the post-retirement jobs similar in duties, skills, and general competencies to the pre-retirement jobs; the Ninth Circuit said the post-retirement jobs were unskilled roadwork. [*Tapley v. Locals 302 & 612 of the Int'l Union of Operating Eng'rs*, 728 F.3d 1134 (9th Cir. 2013)]

Participants must receive a "§ 204(h) notice" informing them in plain English if there has been a significant reduction in the rate of future benefit accrual, or whenever an early retirement benefit or early retirement subsidy has been eliminated. Although the basic rule is that notice must be given at least 45 days before the effective date of the amendment, small (under 100 participant) plans can comply by giving notice at least 15 days before the effective date. Amendments relating to mergers and acquisitions can also give only 15 days notice. If the amendment significantly reduces an early retirement benefit or subsidy, but does not significantly reduce the rate of future benefit accruals, the notice can even be given after the effective date of the amendment, as long as it is within 30 days after the effective date.

Before a cash balance conversion in 1998, Commonwealth Industries' defined benefit plan provided early retirement benefits to participants who had reached age 55 and had five years of service. Nine participants retired after the conversion, taking lump sums. They filed administrative claims protesting when they did not receive the pre-conversion early retirement subsidy. However, only one of the nine claimed within five years of receiving the lump sum. The district court held that the other eight claims were untimely and dismissed the one timely claim on the merits. The Sixth Circuit applied the five-year Kentucky statute of limitations for statutes that lack an explicit limitations period, upholding the district court's determination that eight of the claims were time-barred. However, for the ninth claim, the Sixth Circuit held that reducing the early retirement subsidy violated the anti-cutback rule, even though the participant did not become eligible for the subsidy until after the conversion: ERISA § 204(g) allows fulfillment of an age condition either before or after the plan is amended. The case was remanded to decide the fact issue of whether the subsidy was protected by § 204(g), or whether it was an optional form of benefit that the employer could eliminate. [*Falllin v. Commonwealth Indus., Inc. Cash Balance Plan*, 695 F.3d 512 (6th Cir. 2012); see Wolters Kluwer Law & Business News Center, *Cash Balance Plan May Not Reduce Pre-Conversion Early Retirement Subsidy* (Oct. 22, 2012) (benefitslink.com)]

The Tenth Circuit found that converting a defined benefit plan to cash balance form had the effect of depriving employees of early retirement subsidies. The Tenth Circuit remanded the case to the district court for consideration of remedies for the plaintiffs—bearing in mind that remedies for § 204(h) notice failures are available only if the employer's failure to give notice was egregious. An egregious failure means that the circumstances were within the employer's control, and the employer nevertheless intentionally failed to give notice after discovering an unintentional past failure to satisfy the § 204(h) requirements. In this case, the Tenth Circuit ruled that there were no egregious circumstances, only a forgivable omission in the course of drafting the complex notice required by ERISA. [*Jensen v. Solvay Chems.*, 721 F.3d 1180 (10th Cir. 2013)]

T.D. 9601, 77 Fed. Reg. 66915 (Nov. 8, 2012) permits a bankrupt sponsor to amend its plan to eliminate optional forms of benefits that accelerate payment after bankruptcy. Approval by the PBGC and the bankruptcy court is required. [Kristen Heinzinger, *IRS Finalizes Relief for Bankrupt DB Sponsors*, plansponsor.com (Nov. 8, 2012)]

[E] Other ERISA Issues

Whether a severance plan is an ERISA welfare benefit plan depends on the nature and extent of the employer's role. There is no plan without ongoing administrative responsibility for determining eligibility and calculating benefits. In *O'Connor v. Commonwealth Gas Co.* [251 F.3d 262 (1st Cir. 2001)] the employer wanted to reduce its census before a merger. The plaintiffs charge they were deceived into retiring early because the employer lied about future retirement incentives. The employer provided a one-time severance bonus calculated based on years of service. The First Circuit found that there was no ERISA "plan" because the program lasted only 15 weeks, covered only 300 workers, and involved only simple arithmetic, not discretionary judgment.

The Seventh Circuit ruled that it was not an abuse of discretion for the district court to approve a settlement of an ERISA class action that was less favorable to early retirees than to other members of the class. The Seventh Circuit had already ruled that a defined benefit plan with a cost-of-living adjustment (COLA) must provide the actuarial equivalent of the COLA to participants who receive lump sum benefits. The Seventh Circuit ordered the district court to draft a damage award. The plan argued that the early retirees were not entitled to damages. Then a settlement was reached, giving each early retiree 3.5% of the original lump sum amount. A group of early retirees objected to this amount. The Seventh Circuit held that the district court did not abuse its discretion, and the settlement award was fair to the early retirees because it balanced their risk of continuing to litigate a case where they might lose. [*Williams v. Rohm and Haas Pension Plan*, 658 F.3d 629 (7th Cir. 2011); see CCH Pension & Benefits, *District Court's Approval of Class Action Settlement Less Favorable to Early Retiree Class Members Not Abuse of Discretion* (Nov. 23, 2011) (benefitslink.com)]

The Pension Benefit Guaranty Corporation (PBGC) publishes a table every year in November or December, most recently Table I-14,78 Fed. Reg. 72018 (Dec. 2, 2013), for plans with valuation dates in 2014, which estimates the probability that a person will retire early from a plan that is being terminated by the PBGC, or in a distress termination initiated by the employer. The table is used to determine the total value of the benefits under the plan by computing the value of early retirement benefits. The likelihood of early retirement is considered low if the monthly benefit is below a certain amount, high if it exceeds a certain amount, and medium if it falls in between.

The table is based on the monthly benefit the worker will receive at "URA" (Unreduced Retirement Age)—either the plan's Normal Retirement Age or the age at which the worker could first receive a benefit that is not actuarially reduced to account for early retirement.

For example, if the participant reaches URA in 2015, the likelihood of early retirement is considered low if the benefit is under $614 a month; medium, if the benefit is between $614 and $2,594; and high if it exceeds $2,594. The table includes figures for retirement in or after 2024, at which time likelihood is considered low if the benefit is under $747 a month, high if it exceeds $3,156 a month, and moderate for amounts in between.

§ 9.06 PHASED RETIREMENT

In many instances, the needs of both employer and employee would be well served by the option of "phased retirement" (a gradual transition out of the workforce) rather than a bright-line test of being either fully active or retired. Employers would certainly save money if they could reduce the full-time payroll yet continue to receive part-time services from older workers, instead of offering them early retirement subsidies.

For many years, phased retirement was quite difficult to implement because of rules limiting "in-service" distributions, other than those made on account of hardship, from defined benefit or 401(k) plans. Many commentators have raised the question of how to structure phased retirement equitably, e.g., by determining that a person is 50% retired, and therefore paying him or her 50% of the salary for the position, and also 50% of the retirement benefits that would be available if the person had completely retired.

Many pension plans (perhaps deliberately to encourage early retirement or as an unintended result of other design features) in effect grant the most rapid accrual of pension benefits when workers are in their fifties; between their mid-fifties and retirement, workers may find that pension accrual is actually negative. That is, even though they will eventually qualify for a larger pension because they work longer, they also receive the pension for one year less for each additional year worked.

The Pension Protection Act of 2006, Pub. L. No. 109-280, includes two major provisions dealing with early retirement and retiree health issues. PPA § 905 amends ERISA § 3(2)(A) and the corresponding Code § 401(a)(36) to permit plans to retain qualification even if they make in-service distributions for the phased retirement of persons aged 62 or older who continue to work on a reduced schedule. This is true even if the recipient of the distributions has not reached the plan's Normal Retirement Age.

2007 final regulations concentrate not on whether the plan's NRA is a subterfuge to avoid qualified plan requirements, but whether it is at least as high as the typical age for the industry. If the NRA is set between 55 and 62, the employer's good-faith determination that the NRA falls within industry norms will be given deference if it is reasonable in light of the facts and circumstances. An NRA below 55 is presumed unreasonable, although not if the employer can prove the contrary. Note that an NRA of 50 will be considered reasonable for public safety employees like police or firefighters. [TD 9325, RIN 1545-BD23, 2007-24 I.R.B. 1386; see, e.g., Rebecca Moore, *IRS Releases Final Rules on In-service Distributions Past Retirement Age*, plansponsor.com (May 22, 2007)]

Phased retirement usually means a reduction of work schedule, for example, beginning at age 62 after at least 10 years of service. Management may impose other requirements, such as limiting phased retirement to specific job categories. The employee's concern is that phased retirement might mean outliving his or her retirement savings. If phased retirement begins before the age at which unreduced

Social Security benefits are available, then the retiree will lose Social Security benefits based on the earned income. If the plan allows part-timers to participate, but charges higher premiums, the arrangement might be financially unsustainable for a phased retiree. [Anne E. Moran, *Phased Retirement: Challenges for Employers*, 38 Employee Relations Law Journal 68 (Autumn 2012) (benefitslink.com)]

§ 9.07 RETIREE HEALTH BENEFITS: INTRODUCTION

At one time, it was very common for part of the incentive for early retirement to come in the form of health benefits to replace the employer's group health plan. Employers often promised "lifetime health benefits at no cost." However, health care costs rise significantly every year, and employees in poor health are more likely to be interested in health benefits than employees in good health. Therefore, a retiree health benefit program can become a major burden on the employer.

According to the Employee Benefits Research Institute (EBRI), the prevalence of retiree health benefits began to diminish seriously in December 1990. One of the precipitating factors was the Financial Accounting Standards Board (FASB)'s release of a standard called SFAS 106, requiring employers to record their unfunded retiree health benefit liabilities on their financial statements—with the result that corporate earnings decreased.

In response, some employers stopped providing retiree health benefits altogether; others put their plans on a defined contribution basis, added age and service requirements, or maintained the level of benefits for current retirees but reduced the benefits that would eventually be available to people retiring in the future.

The SHRM's survey, "2013 Employee Benefits: An Overview of Employee Benefits Offerings in the U.S.," <http://www.shrm.org/research/surveyfindings/articles/documents/13-0245%202013_empbenefits_fnl.pdf> (undated, last accessed Mar. 25, 2014) reports that only 23% of respondents offered retiree health benefits, and only 1% planned to add them in the next 12 months.

The Kaiser Family Foundation reported that, in 2013, 28% of companies with 200 or more employees provide retiree health benefits—slightly higher than the 2012 figure of 25%. Among these large employers that provide retiree health benefits, 90% offer health benefits to early retirees, 67% cover Medicare-age retirees, and 4% have a retiree plan that provides prescription drug coverage but no other benefits. [Kaiser Family Foundation, *2013 Employer Health Benefits Survey*, <http://kff.org/report-section/2013-summary-of-findings/> (Aug. 20, 2013)]

Some employers have contracts with private-sector exchanges such as Extend Health (which are not the same as the Exchanges required by PPACA: see § 18.19[L]) so that Medicare-eligible retirees can enroll in plans to replace their lost coverage under the company's EGHP. The plan employs counselors to explain financial programs like Medicare Advantage and Medigap insurance. Part or all of the coverage can be funded by the employer depositing amounts into HRAs for retirees. (See § 18.18 for more about HRAs). These exchanges are helpful to employers by making costs more predictable, setting a cap on them, and reducing the burden of administration. Retirees benefit by having access to more plans and rates. [Michelle Andrews, *Some Employers Offer Aid To Retirees After Cutting Their Health Insurance* Washington Post (Oct. 29, 2012) (benefitslink.com)]

FASB's SFAS No. 158 (generally effective for fiscal years ending after December 15, 2006) requires the funded status of all post-retirement plans—including retiree health plans—to be recorded on the company's balance sheet, not just included as a footnote to the financial statements. This FASB document does not require prefunding of retiree health liabilities, but the reporting obligation might provide an incentive to do so.

Among companies continuing to provide some kind of retiree health plans, there has been a strong trend to shift more and more of the costs to the retirees. To reduce the cost of the plan, many employers adopted caps, i.e., maximum amounts that they will devote to retiree health benefits; if costs increase past this point, the additional cost will be entirely passed along to the participants. Another tactic is to impose a combination of age and service requirements for participation in the retiree health plan, e.g., limiting it to persons over 55 with 10 years' service. Or, the amount of financial contribution an employee is expected to make to the retiree health plan could be made proportional to length of service. Or, retirees can be placed into a separate risk pool rather than a shared risk pool with active employees; premiums can be set higher for one group of retirees than another. [Ellen E. Schultz, *Conquering Retirement: When Retirees Face Health-Plan Cuts,* WSJ.com (Apr. 20, 2012)]

The Early Retirement Reimbursement Program (ERRP), created by PPACA, reimbursed employers for claims incurred by retirees over 55 who are not Medicare eligible, or incurred by their dependents of any age. Five billion dollars was appropriated to fund the program. It was scheduled to last until January 1, 2014 or when the money ran out.

As expected, the money ran out, and the termination of the ERRP program on January 1, 2014 was announced. [78 Fed. Reg. 23936 (Apr. 23, 2013); see Kevin McGuinness, *ERRP Will Sunset at Start of 2014*, plansponsor.com (May 17, 2013)]

One important factor in the financial problems of the U.S. auto industry is high retiree health costs. Voluntary Employee Benefit Arrangements (VEBAs; see § 22.07) have been used to remove post-retirement benefit obligation from the car manufacturers' balance sheets. VEBAs are operated through trusts, managed by an independent board of trustees, and funded with cash, cash plus promissory notes, or equity securities. [Haynes Boone newsletter, *Weathering the Storm: Options to Remove Liabilities for High Retiree Medical Costs from a Company's Balance Sheet: VEBAs* (June 19, 2009) (benefitslink.com); Fred Schneyer, *EBSA Proposes ERISA Exemption for Chrysler VEBA*, plansponsor.com (Oct. 2, 2009);

Fred Schneyer, *Chrysler VEBA Funded in Post-Bankruptcy Deal*, plansponsor.com (May 1, 2009); Tresa Baldas, *The Legal Minefield of Cutting Workers' Health Care Benefits*, Nat'l L.J (Feb. 25, 2009) (law.com)]

In 2011 and 2012, VEBAs were running out money and had to cut costs, reduce benefits, and seek additional contributions from sponsors and plan beneficiaries. The largest VEBA, the UAW trusts covering more than 820,000 people, had a shortfall of close to $20 billion, according to DOL filings made in October 2011. Because VEBAs are partially funded by employer stock, they are vulnerable to market volatility as well as responsive to increasing medical costs. In 2009, the UAW VEBA cut its ties to auto makers and became an independent trust—and also reduced prescription benefits and required retirees to make higher copayments. [Sharon Terlep and Matthew Dolan, *VEBA Retirement Trusts Face Funding Shortfalls*, WSJ.com (Nov. 7, 2011)]

§ 9.08 THE RIGHT TO ALTER OR TERMINATE RETIREE HEALTH BENEFITS

At one time, it was common for employers to promise their employees that, after the employees retired, they would receive lifetime health benefits without cost. Economic developments in the interim have led many employers to terminate their retiree health plans, or to impose premiums and copayment requirements, or increase retirees' financial responsibilities. It is also common for retirees to sue their ex-employer to roll back these changes.

The general rule is that, as long as the employer drafts the plan to provide that the employer retains the right to amend, modify, or terminate the health benefits, the employer can do so unilaterally. ERISA has rules about vesting of pension benefits (i.e., the circumstances under which the right to a pension becomes nonforfeitable) but ERISA does not provide for vesting of welfare benefits such as retiree health benefits. Furthermore, ERISA preempts state law on this subject, so the states do not have the power to impose vesting requirements. [See, e.g., *Gen. Dynamics Land Sys. Inc. v. Cline*, 540 U.S. 581 (2004) (terminating retiree health benefits did not violate the ADEA).]

Early in 2009 the Sixth Circuit held that the 1998 CBA did not provide a permanent right to retiree medical benefits at no cost, vesting as soon as a worker became eligible for retirement. A group of retirees sued under LMRA § 301 and ERISA, seeking an injunction and a declaratory judgment that they were entitled to health benefits fully paid by Caterpillar. The district court held that the retiree benefits vested when they became eligible to retire or receive a pension, even if they continued working after the CBA expired. However, the Sixth Circuit reversed, drawing a distinction between active workers who will retire in the future and those who have already retired: retirees are usually not represented by a union, but active workers are. [*Winnett v. Caterpillar, Inc.*, 553 F.3d 1000 (6th Cir. 2009). In later proceedings in this case, the Sixth Circuit had to "borrow" a six-year state statute of limitations, because there is no explicit statute of limitations under ERISA § 502 or LMRA § 301. The Sixth Circuit held that the statute of limitations begins when the breach of promise becomes unequivocally clear—in this case, in 1998, so a suit brought in 2006 was untimely under the six-year statute of limitations. *Winnett v. Caterpillar, Inc.*, 609 F.3d 404 (6th Cir. 2010)]

The Sixth Circuit ruled in 2013 that, although retiree health care is a welfare benefit, it is not entitled to the same ERISA protection as pension benefits; employers can surrender the power to alter welfare benefits—in this case, by offering vested healthcare coverage to retired employees and spouses, and by agreeing that the company's CBAs could only be modified with signed, mutual consent of the parties. The case was brought by retired unionized employees who were covered by collective bargaining agreements that addressed healthcare benefits. The parties contested whether the CBAs guaranteed employees and their spouses lifetime healthcare benefits after retirement. After retiring, the employees and spouses continued to receive healthcare insurance from the defendant. When the plaintiffs were between the ages 62 and 65, the defendant paid 80% of the premium costs. When the retirees turned 65, the defendant assumed 100% of premium costs. In 2006, the defendant informed the plaintiffs that the company was instituting a new health care plan that would no longer cover 100% of the premiums. The plaintiffs alleged violations of the Labor Management Relations Act, 29 U.S.C. § 185, and ERISA, 29 U.S.C. § 1132. The district court ruled in plaintiffs' favor as to employee coverage, but in favor of defendant as to spouses. The Sixth Circuit reversed in part, requiring coverage of spouses as well. [*Moore v. Menasha Corp.*, 690 F.3d 444 (6th Cir. 2013)]

The Sixth Circuit held in September 2012 that the right to vested health benefits for life did not prevent management from reducing or restricting the benefits, as long as the changes were reasonable. In this analysis, vesting does not fix the bundle of services for all time. The case was remanded once again for consideration of the reasonableness of the change: whether the new benefits were reasonably commensurate with the old ones, were appropriate in light of changes in health care since the promise was made, and whether the changed benefits were consistent with the benefits that current employees receive. On remand, the district court is required to assess out-of-pocket costs for retirees under the old and new plans, how much retirees must pay for coverage, and the quality of care. [*Reese v. CNH America*, Nos. 11-1359/11-1857, 2012 WL 4009695 (6th Cir. Sept. 13, 2012)]

In another case, the Sixth Circuit once again ruled in favor of employees claiming that a CBA entitled them to lifetime health benefits fully funded by the former employer. The pre-2005 CBA vested a right to lifetime non-contributory benefits, with "full contribution" by the employer. The question was whether side letters intended to cap the employer's payment of health care costs were part of the CBA. The Sixth Circuit held that the cap agreements did not apply; they were not ratified by the union. The Sixth Circuit held that there was a vested right to non-contributory health benefits that could not be bargained away without consent of the retirees. The Sixth Circuit reinstated the plaintiffs in the plan that was bargained for in 2007. The plaintiffs wanted to be reinstated to a more generous earlier plan, but the Sixth Circuit deemed the changes in copayments and deductibles to be reasonable in light of changes in health care costs. [*Tackett v. M&G Polymers USA*, 733 F.3d 589 (6th Cir. 2013); see Plansponsor Staff, *Court Finds Employer Owes Lifetime Health Benefits*, plansponsor.com (Aug. 21, 2013)] Certiorari was granted on May 5, 2014, as No. 13-1010, to resolve the Circuit split; most other circuits require specific durational language to find vesting of retiree health benefits, whereas the Sixth Circuit applies an inference of vesting. [McDermott Will & Emery, *Supreme Court Grants Certiorari to Review Sixth Circuit's Pro-Union Inference in Retiree Health Insurance Benefit Cases* (May 6, 2014) (benefitslink.com)]

However, there are circumstances under which an employer's promise of retiree health coverage will become an enforceable contract. Under the "promissory estoppel" theory, if the employer makes an unambiguous promise of lifetime benefits, it will no longer be permitted to change the plan.

A limitation on this theory is that the plaintiff might be required to prove that he or she would have obtained comparable medical insurance at his or her own expense if the plan had not been misleading about future health benefits. Employers might also be bound by a promise of lifetime no-cost retiree health benefits if employees actually traded cash compensation or some other benefit in exchange for the employer's promise.

The Ninth Circuit found that retirees were entitled to implied vested contractual rights to fully paid-up retirement and health benefits, so their rights were violated when the board of supervisors cut its benefit contribution to $500 a month. The retirees sued, bringing state-law breach of contract and promissory estoppel claims, and federal constitutional due process and Contract Clause claims. The Ninth Circuit held that retirees plausibly alleged that the county made an express contract with implied terms of lifetime health care coverage. The retirees were given another chance to amend their complaint to state a claim of an implied right to benefits based on an express contract—although the Ninth Circuit ruled that this is a heavy burden to sustain. [*Sonoma Cnty. Ass'n of Retired Emp. v. Sonoma Cnty.*, 708 F.3d 1109 (9th Cir. 2013); see Ronald Kramer, Justin T. Curley, and Barbara Borowski, *Ninth Circuit Breathes New Life Into Retirees' Claim for Lifetime Healthcare Benefits*, Seyfarth Shaw ERISA & Employee Benefits Litigation Blog (Mar. 5, 2013) (benefitslink.com). See also *Retired employees Ass'n of Orange Cnty., Inc. v. County of Orange* (Cal. 2011), holding that an express contract created by county ordinance or resolution can create a vested right to healthcare benefits for retirees.]

Another argument that employers can make to cut back or eliminate retiree health benefits is that the benefits were provided under a particular collective bargaining agreement and do not survive the expiration of that agreement unless the agreement specifically calls for their survival. Retirees are no longer employees, and therefore are not part of the bargaining unit. The bargaining agent does not have a duty to represent retirees—and there is a real potential for conflict of interest between current employees and retirees. Retiree benefits are not included among the mandatory subjects of bargaining. [See § 30.07[A]]

There is a circuit split on the issue of whether the promise to pay retiree health benefits ends when the CBA expires. The Sixth Circuit has decided a number of cases using evidence outside the CBA to show that the retiree benefits vested (but this court has allowed cuts in health benefits for active workers who will retire in the future). In contrast, the Seventh Circuit tends to assume that the promises expire when the CBA ends. The Third and Fourth Circuits will treat retiree health benefits as vested—if there is a clear and express statement in the CBA that they will vest. [See Rebecca Moore, *Early Retirees Non-vested in Health Benefits Lack ERISA Standing*, plansponsor.com (Sept. 23, 2008); Pamela A. MacLean, *Retiree Benefit Cutbacks Roil Courts*, Nat'l L.J. (Feb. 16, 2009) (law.com); but see *Dewhurst v. Century Aluminum Co.* 649 F.3d 287 (4th Cir. 2011), discussed in James P. McElligott Jr., McGuireWoods LLP, *Fourth Circuit Rules for Employer in Retiree Medical Lawsuit* (Sept. 20, 2011) (benefitslink.com): the benefits were not vested under either the plan document or the CBA so they did not show a duty to continue the retiree benefits when the CBA expired.]

The First Circuit ruled in mid-2006, in two related cases involving union and non-union retirees that collectively bargained retiree benefits are not presumed to vest. (The retirees were told that dental benefits were for life, and their surviving spouses could have dental benefits for 12 months after a retiree's death—but the plan documents reserved the usual right to amend, modify, or terminate the plan.) The First Circuit held that, for non-unionized retirees, welfare benefits (in this case dental benefits) do not vest unless the employer gives up the right to amend or terminate the benefits. In this case, far from surrendering such a right, the employer told participants that dental benefits would end at age 65. For unionized retirees, the fact that management did not negotiate about whether the employer intends to retain the right to modify benefits does not create an inference that benefits will remain at the same level for life [*Senior v. NStar Elec. & Gas Co.*, 449 F.3d 206 [unionized retirees] and *Balestracci v. NStar Elec. & Gas Corp.*, 449 F.3d 848 [non-union retirees] (both 1st Cir. 2006)]

The Sixth Circuit reversed a district court determination that a series of CBAs did not provide vested retiree health benefits. The Sixth Circuit's rationale was that an SPD, issued unilaterally and after the fact, cannot supersede a CBA's amendment provisions. The CBA was ambiguous as to whether retiree health benefits had to be maintained at the same level for life. The CBA obligated the company to give each employee an individual contract guaranteeing retiree health benefits until age 65, with reimbursement for Medicare Part B premiums after age 65. The SPD included a reservation of rights clause permitting amendment or modification at any time. The Sixth Circuit found that the CBA was at least ambiguous about supplemental insurance after age 65 and the extent of prescription drug coverage. Because the CBA's zipper clause forbade amendment without mutual signed consent, the CBA could not be unilaterally modified by SPDs. [*Prater v. Ohio Educ. Ass'n*, 505 F.3d 437 (6th Cir. 2007)]

In 2006, the Seventh Circuit permitted insurance benefits described as "lifetime" to be terminated, based on the employer's reservation of the right to alter the benefits, and under the principle that when a nonambiguous CBA expires, so does the obligation to provide any benefits that have not vested. In this reading, unless the contract provides for vesting, welfare benefits are presumed to terminate when the CBA ends, unless a party can show latent ambiguity in the contract. In the Seventh Circuit's view, contract language providing benefits for surviving spouses until their death or remarriage refers only to eligibility, not duration; the duration of the benefit is limited to the CBA term. Statements by company officials that benefits would continue for life were held not to be definitive because they could not supplant the CBA language. [*Cherry v. Auburn Gear Inc.*, 441 F.3d 476 (7th Cir. 2006). See also *UAW v. Rockford Powertrain, Inc.*, 350 F.3d 698 (7th Cir. 2003) for the proposition that benefit eligibility ends with the CBA unless the benefits are vested, and *Barnett v. Ameren Corp.*, 436 F.3d 830 (7th Cir. 2006) for the proposition that statements by company officials do not replace the contractual language.]

Another Sixth Circuit case required the restoration of lifetime health benefits for retirees—even though the corporation had reorganized in the interim and the employer retained the right to terminate or modify the benefits—because the benefits were vested under a labor contract. Management and union entered into a letter of agreement capping the employer's obligation, but stating that no covered person would have to pay any part of the excess over the cap before a stipulated date. After the merger, retirees were billed $56 a month for coverage. The employer and union set up a transition fund, but when it ran out, the premium rose to $290 and then $501 a month, leading the retirees to move for a declaratory judgment that they did not have to pay the increased premiums because of their vested right to lifetime coverage. The Sixth Circuit granted a preliminary injunction because of the risk of harm to the retirees and the likelihood that they would prevail, saying that although welfare benefit plans can expire or be changed at the end of a CBA, courts have the power to interpret ambiguous provisions that might be deemed to create vested benefit rights. (The retirees introduced substantial extrinsic evidence of intent that the benefits last for their lifetimes, including documents about lifetime coverage.) [*Yolton v. El Paso Tenn. Pipeline Co.*, 435 F.3d 571 (6th Cir. 2006). In mid 2011, the case was settled. El Paso continued to deny liability but, to resolve the long-lasting suit, agreed to provide a managed care plan for retirees not eligible for Medicare, to pay for Medicare Supplement coverage for Medicare-eligible retirees, and to continue dental, vision, hearing, and life insurance benefits for the life of all retirees. [*Yolton v. El Paso Tennessee Pipeline Co.*, No. 2:02-cv-75164-PJD-DAS (E.D. Mich. 2011); see Rebecca Moore, *Settlement Approved in Years Long Retiree Benefit Case*, plansponsor.com (Aug. 23, 2011)]

In another successorship case, the Seventh Circuit held that the plant closing agreement promised lifetime benefits. The Seventh Circuit drew a distinction between a plant shutdown agreement, creating an enduring relationship, and a CBA, which is a short-term agreement that is not presumed to create rights after the termination date: *Temme v. Bemis Co Inc.*, 622 F.3d 730 (7th Cir. 2010)]

The Ninth Circuit upheld summary judgment for plaintiffs who were employed by Hughes and then its successor corporation Raytheon, finding that the obligation to pay retirees' health premiums in full survived the three-year term of each CBA—although the obligation did not continue past the CBA's expiration for active employees. Raytheon could terminate medical benefits to the extent allowed by the plans, but could not terminate the agreement to continue paying premiums. However, the Ninth Circuit said that the plaintiffs did not introduce proof that would justify punitive damages for breach of the CBA. [*Alday v. Raytheon Co.*, 620 F.3d 1219 (9th Cir. 2010)]

This opinion was withdrawn in May, 2012. The substitute opinion said that Raytheon did not have authority to abrogate benefit obligations (to pay premiums for workers who contributed 3% of salary to the plan) that had been collectively bargained. Once again, the Sixth Circuit held that punitive damages were not available. [*Alday v. Raytheon Co.*, 693 F.3d 772 (9th Cir. 2012)]

In January 2013, Raytheon agreed to settle the long-running litigation by reimbursing the *Alday* plaintiffs 100% of the premiums they paid after Raytheon's 2004 policy change. Plaintiffs in a related 2009 case will receive a percentage of their out of pocket medical costs after waiving Raytheon coverage. [GoIAM.org, *IAM, Retirees at Raytheon Win Long Battle for Justice*, <http://www.goiam.org/index.php/imail/latest/10988-iam-retirees-at-raytheon-win-long-battle-for-justice-> (Jan. 29, 2013)]

A class of 277 plaintiffs worked for Westinghouse before Siemens purchased the unit where they worked in late 1997. The Westinghouse plan said that benefits would not be payable to employees who were hired by a purchaser or if their employment ended after 1998. Under ERISA § 208, plan participants cannot be denied benefits when their plan consolidates with another plan or transfers its assets and liabilities to another plan. In this case, however, liabilities were transferred, but ERISA does not provide an entitlement to benefits that did not exist under the original plan. ERISA § 204(g) does not protect the cutback of an early retirement benefit for someone who has not satisfied the conditions for receiving the benefit. These plaintiffs were offered employment by the successor, so they did not qualify. The Third Circuit said that, because Siemens did not establish or maintain the plan, it could not be liable for benefits. [*Shaver v. Siemens Corp.*, 670 F.3d 462 (3d Cir. 2012); see Amaris Elliott-Engel, *3rd Circuit Rejects ERISA Benefits for Siemens Plaintiffs*, The Legal Intelligencer (Mar. 1, 2012) (law.com)]

The Seventh Circuit held that it was a breach of fiduciary duty to increase the retiree health insurance premium without notice to the participants. When the plaintiff retired, the CBA required the plan to apply the value of his accrued but unused sick leave toward his 10% share of the health insurance premium. Without notice, the plan administrator increased the plaintiff's share of the premium to 100% and billed him for additional payments. The Seventh Circuit held that retirees are entitled to notice of changes in the plan; both unwritten and secret modifications are forbidden. Because of the plan's deceptive conduct, the Seventh Circuit upheld an award of restoration of accrued sick leave benefits, plus attorneys' fees. [*Orth v. Wisconsin State Employees Union*, 546 F.3d 868 (7th Cir. 2008)]

The Sixth Circuit ruled that, in arbitration about changes in a corporation's health plan, the union can represent retirees as well as active workers. However, although the union automatically has status to represent the actives, consent of the retirees is necessary. Although retirees are no longer part of the bargaining unit, management and union can still bargain on the subject of retiree health benefits and, once they do that, retirees can have enforceable rights to those benefits. In fact, retirees can have individual rights under LMRA § 301 that active workers do not have (because the union is their sole representative). So they must consent to being represented by the union because when the union represents them, their individual claims are waived. [*Cleveland Elec. Illuminating Co. v. Utility Workers Union of Am., Local 270*, 440 F.3d 809 (6th Cir. 2006)]

The IBEW sought to compel arbitration of a claim that reducing retiree benefits violated the CBA. The Ninth Circuit compelled arbitration, rejecting the employer's argument that the union required the consent of the retirees to pursue the grievance. The Ninth Circuit's rationale was that reductions in retiree benefits also affect the current employees who are represented by the union under an ongoing CBA. Active workers' compensation includes future retirement benefits. [*IBEW Local 1245 v. Citizens Telecommunications Co.*, 549 F.3d 781 (9th Cir. 2008)]

§ 9.09 TAX ISSUES FOR RETIREE HEALTH BENEFITS

Internal Revenue Code § 419A(c)(2) permits the employer to deduct the cost of retiree health benefits as part of a nondiscriminatory funded welfare plan. Key employees' retiree health benefits must be drawn from separate accounts, not the main account. Failure to maintain the separate accounts, or discrimination in furnishing retiree health benefits, is penalized by the 100% excise tax on disqualified benefits imposed by I.R.C. § 4976.

A funded welfare plan can maintain a reserve for future retiree health benefits, funded over the work lives of employees, without violating the account limit. The reserve must use a level-basis actuarial determination, making use of reasonable assumptions and current medical costs.

The Voluntary Employees' Beneficiary Association (VEBA) [I.R.C. § 501(c)(8)] is a possible funding vehicle for retiree health benefits. Caution must be exercised. The VEBA is a tax-exempt organization, so its investment income is subject to taxation. VEBAs are required to use current health costs to calculate the contributions to be made for future retirees. So if costs increase more than anticipated, or if retirees use more health care than expected, the VEBA may be exhausted.

One of the most important functions of ERISA is to make sure that pensions are properly funded in advance of the time that benefits must be paid. However, with respect to retiree health benefits, prefunding is allowed but not required. An argument can be made both for prefunding and for keeping the benefits unfunded.

Unfunded benefits are unsecured and can be changed at any time. They give rise to a large annual expense under the FASB rules. This expense generally increases over time, and can be higher than the pension expense precisely because of the mandate of prefunding pensions. There will also be a large accrued liability on the corporate books. The income received on sums that remain general assets of the corporation (because the money is not dedicated to prefunding retiree health benefits) is taxable. The employer's income tax deduction attributable to the retiree health plan is limited to the annual cost of benefits actually paid in that year.

In contrast, if the plan is funded, the money dedicated to this purpose is protected from diversion. Therefore, the plan is not very flexible. However, the corporation can accelerate its tax deduction, and there is more opportunity to manage the tax deduction. The corporation receives the investment income of a 401(h) account tax-free. Such income reduces the operating expenses of the plan and helps level out the future expenses. That makes the plan's accounting results look more favorable—and therefore the company will have less incentive to cut the benefits in the future.

Early in 2003, the Tax Court held in *Wells Fargo & Co. v. Comm'r* [120 TC 69 (2003)] that employers could deduct the cost of prefunding the present value of retiree medical benefit liabilities for current retirees. The employer deducted the entire amount under Code § 419(c)(2) as a retiree medical benefits reserve, funded over the working lives of the covered employees, actuarially determined on a level basis using assumptions that are reasonable when taken in the aggregate. The Tax Court treated this as a proper deduction, because if the year in which the allocation is first recognized occurs after the employee's retirement, there are no future years to which the benefit can be allocated. Therefore, there are no future normal costs, and the entire present value of the project benefit can appropriately be allocated to the first year.

§ 9.10 MPDIMA AND THE MEDICARE INTERFACE

[A] In General

There are two ways a person can qualify for Medicare: either being completely and permanently disabled for a period of at least two years—or reaching age 65. Income and assets are irrelevant—and so is employment status. In other words, people who are still working can be entitled to Medicare benefits (although the employer's group health plan will usually be the primary payor) but a person under 65 who is not disabled will not qualify for Medicare merely because he or she is retired. Nor does Medicare provide benefits for the under 65 spouses of retirees (or retirees' dependent children, if the unusual case but not impossible case that they have any).

The Medicare system includes "secondary payor" rules under which retirees can elect to make Medicare the primary payor for their medical care, with the employer group health plan merely the secondary payor. However, the employer does not have this option, and is not permitted to draft the health plan to make Medicare the primary payor.

Because of its role as secondary payor, Medicare is entitled to seek reimbursement from any entity (including Medicare beneficiaries, health care providers and suppliers, and attorneys) that has received payment from a primary payor. Rules published in 2006 clarify the statutory definitions, including the legal basis for recovery when Medicare paid first although it should have been secondary. If the primary payor is an EGHP or large group health plan, all of the employers that sponsor or contribute to the plan must reimburse Medicare, whether the plan is insured or self-insured. [71 Fed. Reg. 9466 (Feb. 24, 2006)]

If the EGHP fails to make primary payments for active employees of Medicare age, or the Medicare-age spouse of a plan participant, double damages under the Medicare Act or treble damages under the False Claims Act can be imposed. However, the EGHP is exempt from the secondary payor rule if it has fewer than 20 employees; if the participant receives treatment for End Stage Renal Disease; or if the participant is in a large group health plan is disabled. Effective January 1, 2009, the Medicare, Medicaid, and SCHIP Extension Act of 2007 (SCHIP Act; Pub. L. No. 110–173) imposes new Medicare Secondary Payor reporting requirements. EGHPs must find out which participants are Medicare-eligible, and report to CMS for use in the agency's enforcement efforts. Failure is subject to a CMP of $1,000 per day as well as the regular MSP penalties such as the excise tax.

[McDermott Newsletters, *Medicare Secondary Payor Reporting Requirements Will Affect Self-Insured Health Care Providers, Captive Insurers* (Jan. 6, 2009) (benefitslink.com)]

Medicare is only a secondary payor, and not a primary payor, with respect to Worker's Compensation, so employers and insurers must also report WC claims involving Medicare beneficiaries to CMS. If Medicare pays medical expenses for such a worker, it is entitled to be reimbursed if there is a recovery from an insurer or tort defendant. The claims that must be reported are those involving a Medicare beneficiary who has received a settlement, judgment, award, or other medical expense reimbursement on or after July 1, 2009. [Littler, Mendelson Press Releases, *New Medicare Secondary Payer Reporting Obligations for Workers' Compensation Plans*, <http://www.littler.com/PressPublications/Lists/ASAPs/DispAsaps.aspx?id=1359&asapType=National> (April 2009)]

[B] MPDIMA Statute and Regulations

The Medicare Prescription Drug, Improvement and Modernization Act of 2003 (abbreviated MPDIMA) [Pub. L. No. 108-173], in addition to creating the Health Savings Account plan type discussed in § 18.09, and including provisions for the Medicare Advantage managed-care system to replace the existing Medicare + Choice plans, also enacted the Medicare Part D prescription drug insurance program. Congress passed a subsidy program benefiting employers who provide prescription drug coverage that is "actuarially equivalent" to the Medicare coverage. Part D is voluntary: Medicare beneficiaries decide whether or not to enroll. They pay a monthly premium (e.g., $30 a month), then are responsible for an annual deductible and copayments for certain drug costs. Until 2020, there is a "doughnut hole": a level of drug spending after which Part D beneficiaries pay the full cost of their drugs. But if spending reaches a specified higher level, Part D will pay the full cost of drugs used by the Part D beneficiary. Employers can coordinate with Part D in several ways—by paying retirees' Part D premiums, or by providing supplementary coverage when retirees pay their own Part D premiums. [Segal Capital Checkup, *COBRA and the Medicare Part D Retiree Subsidy*, <http://www.segalco.com/publications/capitalcheckup/05606no2pf.zhtml> (May 16, 2006)].

Unlike most health costs, the benefit parameters for 2014 declined slightly from 2013 levels. For 2014, the cost threshold is $310, the initial coverage limit is $2,850, the out-of-pocket threshold is $4,550. The minimum copayment under the catastrophic portion of the benefit is $2.55 for generic or multi-source drugs and $6.35 for other drugs. [<http://www.cms.gov/Medicare/Health-Plans/MedicareAdvtgSpecRateStats/downloads/Announcement2014.pdf>] The 2015 parameters were higher than those for 2014. For 2015, the deductible is $320, the initial coverage limit is $2,960, the out-of-pocket threshold is $4,550. The minimum copayment for the catastrophic benefit is $2.65 for generic or multi-source drugs, $6.60 for other drugs. [Segal, *Medicare Part D Amounts Will Increase in 2015* (Apr. 24, 2014) (benefitslink.com); EBIA Weekly, *CMS Issues Medicare Part D Benefit Parameters for 2015* (Apr. 10, 2014) (benefitslink.com)]

MPDIMA requires the plan sponsor to attest to the Department of Health and Human Services at least once a year (more often if the agency requests it) that the actuarial value of the prescription drug coverage under the plan is at least equivalent to Plan D coverage. HIPAA disclosures must be made to both the qualified covered retirees and to HHS as to the extent to which the employer's plan offers creditable coverage (see § 19.05). Disclosure is made by e-filing at <http://www.cms.hhs.gov/CreditableCoverage> (accessed Apr. 5, 2013). Employers have several choices for handling retiree prescription drug coverage, e.g., include offering drug coverage that is at least the actuarial equivalent of Part D, and receiving the subsidy; creating a wrap-around plan to supplement Part D (foregoing the subsidy) and operating a private drug plan under contract with CMS. (This last option will probably be taken only by very large employers.)

Under the final regulations, to receive the subsidy, an employer must:

- Provide prescription drug coverage under a program that constitutes "creditable coverage" (the concept of creditable coverage is important because it determines whether someone who delays enrolling in Part D because of being covered by another plan will be able to avoid paying the late enrollment penalty);
- Notify eligible participants whether the program qualifies as creditable coverage;
- Satisfy the final regulation's definition of actuarial equivalence;
- Submit an application to CMS by September 30 of each year, disclosing data about plan participants and attesting that the plan is actuarially equivalent to Part D.
- [Final regulations, reflecting PPACA changes: 76 Fed. Reg. 21431 (Apr. 15, 2011)]

PPACA, the health care reform bill, maintains the subsidy for companies that provide retiree prescription drug benefits. However, it provides that, starting in 2013, the subsidy will no longer be tax-deductible. [Kris Maher, Ellen E. Schultz, and Bob Tita, *Deere, Caterpillar: Health-Care Law to Raise Expenses*, WSJ.com (Mar. 26, 2010)]

[C] Accounting Issues Under MPDIMA

As noted above, PPACA removes the corporate tax deduction, as of 2013, for the retiree health benefit prescription drug subsidy. David Zion, a Credit Suisse analyst, said that the S&P 500 companies will suffer a $4.5 billion loss in first quarter earnings. Large companies said that the loss of this deduction would have a severe negative impact on their earnings. Some of them took a charge against earnings in 2009 to reflect the unavailability of this tax deduction in the future. John Deere & Co. took a $150 million one time charge because of the loss of deduction; Caterpillar Inc. took a $100 million charge (about 40,000 retirees receive drug benefits from the company), and AK Steel took $31 million. The companies say they need the charge now to reflect future tax deductions that will not be available. [Kris Maher, Ellen E. Schultz, and Bob Tita, *Deere, Caterpillar: Health-Care Law to Raise Expenses*, WSJ.com (Mar. 26, 2010)]

[D] *Erie* Issues

The Third Circuit in *Erie County Retirees Ass'n v. County of Erie* [220 F.3d 193 (3d Cir. 2000)] ruled that the ADEA applies to retiree benefits, including health benefits. Therefore in this reading, an employer violates the ADEA by offering Medicare-eligible retirees health benefits that are inferior to those offered to employees who are not yet eligible for Medicare, unless the employer can demonstrate that it incurred equal costs or provided equal benefits for both retiree groups. On April 16, 2001, when the case was remanded to the lower court, the Western District of Pennsylvania decided that the plan did not satisfy the equal cost/equal benefit test. [*Erie Cnty.*, 140 F. Supp. 2d 466 (W.D. Pa. 2001)]

Although at first the EEOC adopted the Third Circuit's position, in July, 2003, the EEOC proposed "anti-Erie" regulations allowing employers to reduce or eliminate retiree health benefits when a retiree becomes eligible for Medicare. [68 Fed. Reg. 41542 (July 14, 2003), adding 29 C.F.R. § 1625.32]

The EEOC proposal soon became the subject of litigation. AARP sued the EEOC, and the Eastern District of Pennsylvania permanently enjoined implementation of the regulations in March 2005, holding that the EEOC's rule was not entitled to deference because the EEOC violated the plain language and Congressional intent of the ADEA.

Then Judge Brody reversed her earlier decision, in compliance with a Supreme Court ruling, in an unrelated case, that federal administrative agencies' regulations are entitled to a high degree of deference. In June 2007, the Third Circuit affirmed the District Court's change of policy, and ruled that the EEOC had the power to enact the regulation permitting reduction of retiree health benefits for Medicare-eligible retirees, under the section of the ADEA that allows the EEOC to grant exemptions from ADEA requirements. [*AARP v. EEOC*, 489 F.3d 558 (3d Cir. 2007)] In August 2007, the Third Circuit announced its refusal to review its ruling, [Jerry Geisel, *Review of Retiree Health Care Bias Ruling Denied*, Business Insurance (Aug. 22, 2007) (benefitslink.com)] and in March 2008, the Supreme Court refused to hear an appeal of the Third Circuit decision. [*AARP v. EEOC*, 128 S. Ct. 1733, *appeal dismissed* (Mar. 24, 2008)]

In December 2007, the EEOC issued a final rule, permitting coordination of retiree health benefits with Medicare. However, the rule affects only the ADEA, not other issues (such as the status of Medicare as secondary payor for Medicare beneficiaries who continue to be employed). [EEOC Final Rule, 72 Fed. Reg. 72938 (Dec. 26, 2007)]

§ 9.11 SOP 92-6 REPORTS

The American Institute of Certified Public Accountants (AICPA) requires health and welfare benefits to prepare SOP 92-6 reports. SOP stands for "Statement of Position." [See the online newsletter by the Segal Company, *Timing Is Everything: Anticipating and Preparing for Higher Retiree Health Expenditures* (June 2001), <http://www.segalco.com/publications/newsletters/june01.pdf>]

The cash flow projections for the 92-6 project the amount of money needed every year to pay health costs. Although prefunding of welfare benefits is not required, it is often a good idea to create an asset pool (e.g., using a VEBA) to generate tax-free investment income that can be used for future costs.

The 92-6 report deals with issues such as the number of active employees, retirees, spouses, and surviving spouses covered by the plan; the cost of plan benefits; and projections of the cost of providing benefits in the future.

§ 9.12 IMPLICATIONS OF THE EMPLOYER'S BANKRUPTCY

Retiree benefits are often central to bankruptcy cases, because the high cost of providing such benefits adds to the financial stress on the company.

The basic rule, as created by *In re White Farm Equipment Co.* [788 F.2d 1186 (6th Cir. 1986)] is that vesting of welfare benefits is not automatic. It is a subject of bargaining, to be contracted for. In that case, the bankrupt company maintained a no-contributory, non-collectively bargained plan that provided retiree benefits. The plaintiffs were retirees who wanted a declaratory judgment (an official statement) that their claims were both valid under ERISA and allowable as bankruptcy claims.

They also asked the court to order the employer to reinstate the plan retroactively and to resume funding it. But the court found that employee benefits regulation is strictly a federal concern. Furthermore, the employer had reserved the power to terminate the plan and could do so at that time.

Ironically, retirees of bankrupt companies may have more protection for their benefits than retirees of solvent companies. Conversely, bankruptcy may solve some of a company's problems while creating others.

Under 11 U.S.C. § 1113, a company that has filed for Chapter 11 status can ask the bankruptcy court for the right to reject an existing collective bargaining agreement, including provisions covering retiree health benefits. The company must disclose the relevant information to the union and bargain in good faith about the termination.

If the company in Chapter 11 was already paying retiree benefits, the Retiree Benefits Bankruptcy Protection Act of 1988 (RBBPA) [Pub. L. No. 100-334] requires medical and disability payments to retirees to continue, on their original terms, either until the parties agree to modify the benefits or the bankruptcy court orders a modification.

The Act includes standards for bankruptcy courts to use in deciding whether a modification is appropriate. Any modifications proposed by the bankruptcy trustee must be equitable, not just to current and former employees, but also to the company's creditors. The retirees must not have had good cause to reject the proposals. The proposed modifications must be necessary to permit the employer to reorganize in bankruptcy on fair terms.

The RBBPA also requires the employer to negotiate with retiree representatives and to disclose the best available information about the employer's financial condition. Generally speaking, the union will serve as the representative of the retirees, unless the union refuses to do so or unless the court rules that a different representative should be appointed. Any party can petition the court to appoint a committee of retirees to represent benefit recipients who are not covered by a collective bargaining agreement.

The court considering the trustee's proposal does not have the power to order benefits lower than the proposed schedule. Once the parties reach an agreement, or once the court orders changes in the benefits, the authorized representative of the retirees can petition the court for an increase, which will be granted if it appears clearly just to do so.

■ **TIP:** The RBBPA's protection does not apply to retirees, their spouses, or dependents if the retiree's gross income was $250,000 or more in the year before the employer's bankruptcy petition. The only exception is retirees who can prove they are unable to get comparable individual health care coverage. Nor does the RBBPA require bankrupt employers to maintain retiree health benefits that were provided by the union, not the employer, prior to the bankruptcy.

Congress returned to the subject of protection of retiree health benefits when the employer files for bankruptcy protection in the 2005 statute, the Bankruptcy Abuse Prevention and Consumer Protection Act (Pub. L. No. 109-8). § 1403 of this statute amends Bankruptcy Code § 1114. If the corporation, at a time it was insolvent, modified retiree benefits during the 180-day period before the bankruptcy filing, then any party in interest has the right to move for a court hearing. After the hearing, the bankruptcy court is required to order reinstatement of the provisions that were altered—unless the court finds that the balance of the equities clearly favors the modification. That is, if the modification is challenged, it is up to the employer to prove that the modification is fair; the opponents of the change don't have to prove its unfairness.

Under Bankruptcy Code § 1114, first the debtor must try to negotiate or get an agreement to modify the benefits from a union or a court-appointed committee representing the retirees. All affected parties must be treated fairly and equally. The debtor must propose only modifications that are necessary to permit its reorganization. The debtor must release relevant information to the representatives of the retirees, and must bargain with them in good faith.

According to the Seventh Circuit, Bankruptcy Code § 1114 was not intended to be the exclusive remedy for disputes between retirees and their bankruptcy representative. Therefore, state law claims (negligence, misrepresentation, promissory estoppel) by retirees who alleged that their union failed to protect benefits that the union promised would be safe are not completely preempted by the Bankruptcy Code. Because the union's duties in bankruptcy are not identical to the duty of fair representation, the claims also are not preempted by the Labor-Management Relations Act. [*Nelson v. Stewart*, 422 F.3d 463 (7th Cir. 2005)]

Retirees of bankrupt companies have access to the Health Coverage Tax Credit (HCTC), which pays 72.5% of health insurance premiums for retirees after a PBGC takeover of their pension plan. (The HCTC was originally scheduled to expire at the end of 2010 but in fact it was not only extended through 2013 but expanded to pay 72.5% of the premium. Eligible retirees are those aged 55–64 and enrolled in a qualified health plan for which they pay more than 50% of the cost. The program provides comprehensive major medical coverage; in some cases, prescription drugs and dental and vision care are also included. The retiree can either pay the other 27.5% of the premium to the HCTC program, which forwards it to the employer, or pay the health insurer directly each month and take a credit on their federal taxes for 72.5% of the premium. [Ellen E. Schultz, *Conquering Retirement Saving: Retiree Health Plans*, WSJ.com (Jan. 28, 2012)]

A mid-2010 decision of the Third Circuit required Visteon Corporation to comply strictly with § 1114 before terminating retiree health benefits—even though the plan documents reserved the right to modify the plan. Although Visteon argued that it had the right to change the benefit structure when there was no bankruptcy case pending, the Third Circuit said that the plain language of § 1114 forbade the modification. [*IUE-CWA v. Visteon Corp.*, 612 F.3d 210 (3d Cir. 2010) Visteon announced that it would terminate the benefits when it exits Chapter 11 and the benefits are no longer protected under bankruptcy law: see Rebecca Moore, *Visteon Ordered to Restore Retiree Benefits*, plansponsor.com (Aug. 18, 2010)]

In 2007, the Supreme Court ruled that a bankrupt company does not have a fiduciary duty to consider merging its pension plan into a multi-employer plan. It is not a violation of ERISA to shut down the plan using a standard termination and to purchase annuities to satisfy payment obligations. [*Beck v. PACE Int'l Union*, 551 U.S. 96 (2007)]

Some courts have refused to apply § 1114 if the retiree benefit plan specifically reserves the right to make unilateral changes. If § 1114 does not apply, then the debtor needs only to satisfy the less stringent "business judgment" standard under Bankruptcy Code § 363. [See, e.g., *In re Delphi Corp.,* No. 05-44481 (Bankr. S.D.N.Y. Mar. 10, 2009), discussed in Arthur Carter, Samuel Glass, Scott Night, Kenric Kattner, Lenard Parkins, Stephen Pezanosky, Sarah Foster, Eric Terry, Haynes and Boone, LLP, *Weathering the Storm: Retiree Benefits and Section 1114* (May 27, 2009) (benefitslink.com)]

A company purchased another company under an asset purchase agreement that included a promise of retiree health benefits for the employees of the acquired company. The benefit could not be reduced or premiums increased without the written consent of the seller—who refused to consent. The purchaser company reorganized in bankruptcy, leading to the rejection of the asset purchase agreement. The purchaser company said that the agreement was no longer in force, so retirees' health premiums could be increased substantially. The retirees sued alleging that the asset purchase agreement amended the retiree health plan and the amendment remained valid after the bankruptcy. The Fifth Circuit held that the asset purchase agreement amended the plan, because any writing that follows certain formalities can amend an ERISA plan. The plan survived bankruptcy, and its terms could only be changed with the consent of the seller company. [*Evans v. Sterling Chemicals, Inc.*, 660 F.3d 862 (5th Cir. 2011); see EBIA Weekly, *Provision in Asset Purchase Agreement Amends Plan and Survives Bankruptcy* (Oct. 20, 2011) (benefitslink.com)]

§ 9.13 401(h) PLANS

[A] Basic Principles

The basic principle is that assets must remain within a qualified pension plan until they are distributed to participants or beneficiaries. However, the Code permits transfers of certain assets of overfunded plans to special funds known as 401(h) plans that are segregated to provide retiree health benefits.

A 401(h) plan is a pension or annuity plan that also provides incidental health benefits for retirees: benefits for sickness, accident, hospitalization, or medical expenses. The health-type benefits must be subordinate to the plan's main business of offering retirement benefits. The incidental (insurance and health) benefits must not cost more than 25% of the employer's total contributions to a defined benefit plan.

An employer that maintains a 401(h) plan must maintain separate accounts for retiree health benefits and pension benefits. The transfers are not treated as reversions to the employer, so the § 4980 excise tax is not imposed. The employer must make reasonable and ascertainable contributions to fund the retiree health benefits. These contributions must be distinct from the contributions to fund pension benefits. At first, Code § 420(b)(5) allowed one transfer a year to a 401(h) account for tax years beginning between January 1, 1991–December 31, 2005; this was extended until December 31, 2013 by the Pension Funding Equity Act of 2004, Pub. L. No. 108-218.

Before making a transfer to a 401(h) plan, the plan administrator must give the DOL at least 60 days' notice, and must also notify participants, beneficiaries and any union representing the participants.

The American Jobs Creation Act of 2004 (AJCA) amends I.R.C. § 420, so that, for tax years after the date of the AJCA's enactment, the determination of whether a 401(h) plan satisfies the minimum cost requirements during the five years after a transfer of pension assets permits the employer to reduce costs only as much as they would have been reduced if the employer had used the maximum amount permitted under current Regulations. In effect, overall benefit costs for all retirees can be cut by the same amount that would have been saved by reducing the number of retirees. [Ellen E. Schultz, *More Retirees May See Health Cuts*, Wall St. J., Oct. 14, 2004, at A5]

The Pension Protection Act of 2006, Pub. L. No. 109-280, permits a plan whose assets are at least 120% of current liability to transfer at least two years' worth of estimated retiree health costs to the 401(h) plan. However, for the year of the transfer, the employer must either make plan contributions sufficient to keep the plan funded at the 120% level, or must recoup money from the 401(h) plan until the 120% level is reached. Transfers to fund the expected cost of retiree health benefits that must be paid in the future under Collective Bargaining Agreements are also permitted, as long the employer used at least 5% of its 2005 gross receipts to provide retiree health benefits.

[PBGC Proposed Rules, *Pension Protection Act of 2006; Conforming Amendments; Reportable Events and Certain Other Notification Requirements*, RIN 1212-AB06 74 Fed. Reg. 61248 (Nov. 23, 2009)]

The Moving Ahead for Progress in the 21st Century Act (MAP-21; Pub. L. No. 112-141) extends the authorization of 401(h) plans, which was supposed to expire in 2013, until December 31, 2021. Plans that achieve more than 125% of their funding target and target normal cost are allowed to transfer excess funds to a 401(h) plan covering either retiree health benefits or retiree group-term life insurance (generally limited to $50,000 per person). The provision for life insurance benefits is added by MAP-21. Life insurance assets must be kept in a separate account within the plan, separate both from the retiree medical account and from the defined benefit plan.

[B] Final Regulations

Effective June 19, 2001, the IRS issued final regulations on the I.R.C. § 420 minimum cost requirements. [T.D. 8948, R.I.N. 1545-AY43] An employer that significantly reduces its retiree health coverage during a cost maintenance period does not satisfy the I.R.C. § 420(c)(3) minimum cost requirement. The Uruguay Round Agreements Act of 1994 [Pub. L. No. 103-465] shifted the focus in regu lating 401(h) plans from health costs to health benefits, allowing the employer to take into account cost savings recognized in managing retiree health benefit plans, as long as the employer keeps up substantially the same level of coverage for the four years after the transfer as for the year of the transfer itself and the year before the year of the transfer.

PART III
PENSION PLAN ADMINISTRATION

CHAPTER 10

ADOPTING AND ADMINISTERING A PLAN

§ 10.01 INTRODUCTION

The process of creating a plan and getting it approved by the IRS and Department of Labor is exacting. Many alternatives are permitted, and choosing one of them requires projections about the future of the business, the future of the workforce, trends in the economy as a whole, and the laws, court decisions, and regulations that will come into effect in the future. For plans that are subject to ERISA Title I, the Department of Labor must be notified. The IRS does not have to be notified of the intention to adopt a qualified plan, unless and until a determination letter is sought. The employees must always be notified of the adoption of a plan.

Once the plan is in operation, its activities are subject to regulation both on the ERISA and on the tax front.

An ERISA employee benefit plan requires several elements. At a minimum, there must be an intended benefit, an intended beneficiary or group of beneficiaries, a source of financing, a procedure for claiming benefits, and an ongoing administrative scheme.

Plan administration is difficult, painstaking, and mistakes can incur heavy penalties. For these and other reasons, it is common for tasks to be delegated to service providers. Because the term "third-party administrator" (TPA) does not have a uniform definition, it is difficult to estimate how many TPAs there are. An estimate from early 2012 is that about half of all workers covered by private industry plans are covered by plans with some degree of TPA involvement in administration, although some TPAs carry out quite sophisticated tasks, whereas others just process clerical transactions. [Fred Hunt, *Numbers: How Many TPAs are There? Explanation and Legal Liability Factors*, Society of Professional Benefit Administrators (January 2012) (benefitslink.com)]

The PBGC proposed a rule in mid-2009, amending its benefit payment regulations to conform to USERRA amendments. The proposed rule says that as long as a servicemember is re-employed within the USERRA time limits, the servicemember is treated as qualified as of the plan's termination date—even if re-employment occurred after the termination date. The effect is that more servicemembers will be entitled to PBGC-guaranteed benefits. [F.R. Doc E9-17623, *USERRA Benefits Under Title IV of ERISA*, 74 Fed. Reg. 37666 (July 29, 2009)]

In 2012 and 2013, the PBGC made sweeping proposals reducing reporting obligations for the vast majority of plans under its jurisdiction.

[A] Plan Expenses

Running a qualified plan is a difficult business involving the input of many people, including professional advisors. Not all expenses of administration can be paid from the assets of an employee benefit plan. The decision to use plan assets to pay expenses if a fiduciary decision, subject to ERISA fiduciary enforcement.

As long as the plan document allows, or at least does not prohibit, the use of plan assets for this purpose, ERISA allows payment of reasonable administrative expenses. (If the plan document is silent, expenses can be paid by the plan unless the document requires the employer to pay the expenses.) If the employer has retained the right to amend the plan, a prospective amendment can be made to allow payment of expenses from plan assets.

Individual account plans can set out a method for allocating the expenses paid by the plan to participants' accounts. Any allocation method described by the plan is a settler decision, and plan fiduciaries must abide by it. If the plan is silent or unclear, the fiduciaries must select a reasonable method of allocation.

Because businesses are not required to have pension or benefit plans at all, ERISA permits (within limits) the plan to be established, amended, or terminated as the sponsor wishes. Such activities are settlor functions. However, if the employer administers the plan, it acts as a fiduciary. Although settlor decisions are not subject to fiduciary standards, expenses for settlor activities must be paid by the employer—and plan assets cannot be used for this purpose.

Settlor functions include setting up, amending, and terminating a plan, so it is improper for the plan to pay for, for instance, plan design studies, drafting of discretionary plan amendments, determining if the employer satisfies financial accounting standards, and negotiating with a union about proposed plan amendments.

If the plan pays legal expenses, the person who receives the advice will probably find it impossible to deny that the advice was received in a fiduciary capacity—which could make lawyer-client privilege unavailable.

Plan-wide basic administrative services can be paid from the assets of an ERISA plan, because they are fiduciary rather than settlor expenses. Expenses that probably can properly be paid from plan assets include:

- Providing required disclosures to participants, including SPDs, SARs, required benefit statements, and complying with disclosure requests from participants,
- Communicating with participants about issues such as benefit windows. (Allocation is required if the communication relates to more than one plan, or combines plan and non-plan information,
- Making calculations to implement a plan merger or spin-off,
- Maintaining tax-qualified status (applying for a determination letter; performing nondiscrimination testing; drafting plan amendments needed to comply with ERISA or Internal Revenue Code changes),
- TPA expenses,
- PBGC premiums,
- ERISA bond,

- Fiduciaries liability insurance for the fiduciaries of the plan—but only if the policy gives the insurer recourse against the fiduciary for losses due to breach of fiduciary obligations,
- Making legally required reports, such as Form 5500,
- Enrollment and claims processing,
- Management fees and sales charges for the plan's investments,
- Recordkeeping, including preparing audited financial statements,
- Investment management and advice.

The plan can pay the cost of drafting any legally required amendment, but the general rule is that the employer must pay for drafting discretionary amendments, including amendments that relieve the employer of the obligation to pay plan expenses.

Sanctions and penalties can be paid out of plan assets if they were imposed on the plan—but not if they were imposed on a plan administrator in his personal capacity. Sanctions for late payment of PBGC premiums can be paid from plan assets (as long as the plan is not involved in a distress or involuntary termination)—but correction costs under the Voluntary Fiduciary Correction Program cannot be. [Andree M. St. Martin and Jennifer E. Eller, *Paying Employee Benefit Plan Expenses Chart*, Practical Law Co. (undated) (benefitslink.com) (a chart giving the source for the treatment of various items)]

§ 10.02 DETERMINATION LETTERS

A determination letter is the IRS' determination that a proposed plan is qualified under I.R.C. § 401(a) or 403(a)—and, if the plan is operated through a plan trust, whether the plan trust is qualified under I.R.C. § 501(a). A qualified plan receives favorable tax treatment: employees are not taxed on contributions to the plan, or increase in the value of these contributions, until the benefits are distributed. From the employer's point of view, qualification is important because operation of qualified plans give rise to significant tax deductions. The determination letter process exists so employers can find out in advance if the IRS approves of the provisions of the plan and also approves of the way it is operated. Qualified plans are subject to a long list of requirements (e.g., about eligibility, vesting, and nondiscrimination). They must be drafted—and operated—in conformity with these rules. The rules change frequently, so the plan must be amended in response to tax code and ERISA changes. There are major negative consequences, including taxes owed and tax penalties, if a plan is ever disqualified.

Although employers do not have to get an IRS determination letter before setting up a qualified retirement plan, a plan that has a determination letter and that is amended on a timely basis to conform to changes in the law will probably be able to rebut the IRS' attempts at retroactive disqualification of the plan. [See IRS Publication 794, *Favorable Determination Letter*, < http://www.irs.gov/pub/irs-pdf/p794.pdf> (January 2013); IRS, *What Is a Favorable Determination Letter?*, <http://www.irs.gov/Retirement-Plans/Determination-Opinion-and-Advisory-Letter-for-Retirement-Plans-Scope-and-Benefit-of-a-Favorable-Determination-Opinion-or-Advisory-Letter> (Feb. 5, 2014)]

See Rev. Proc. 2014-6, 2014-1 I.R.B.198, effective February 1, 2014, for the procedures for issuing determination letters, reflecting the dates of the current submission cycle and payment rules for user fees paid through <http://www.pay.gov>. Further information about user fees is available in Rev. Proc. 2014-8, 2014-1 I.R.B.242, including updated fee amounts for requests for letter rulings and determination letters. [Rebecca Moore, *IRS Updates Procedures for Determination Letters User Fees*, plansponsor.com (Jan. 8, 2014)]

Interested parties (current employees who will be eligible to participate if the plan is implemented) are entitled to notification that an application has been made. If the plan is collectively bargained, all employees covered by the CBA are entitled to notice. Notice to unionized employees can be given in person (e.g., printed and handed to all employees; slips placed in all pay envelopes), by mailing, or by posting in the usual place for posting employer and/or union notices. The appropriate time for giving notice to employees is 7–21 days before the IRS gets the application. If the employees are notified by mail, the notices should be mailed 10–24 days before submission of the application.

Employees must be notified because interested parties have the right to comment directly to the IRS about the application. The PBGC or a group of interested parties can also invite the Department of Labor to comment on the application. The PBGC has standing to submit its own comments directly. The comment period runs for either 45 or 60 days after the IRS receives the request for a determination letter.

After 60 days have elapsed, the IRS does its own investigation of the qualification of the proposed plan, including consideration of any comments that have been submitted. A reviewing agent in the relevant IRS Key District Office issues the determination letter (or denies the application). If there are questions about the application, the agent tries to resolve them by telephoning or writing to the company that applied for the determination letter.

If the IRS refuses to issue the letter, there are several levels of review within the IRS, and then the employer has the right to appeal to the Tax Court.

Determination letters are requested on official IRS forms. The IRS charges user fees, depending on the nature of the application. Furthermore, a particular plan may have to apply several times. Nor is initial qualification the end of the process. Plans must continually be amended to keep up with changes in tax law and ERISA—as well as to respond to changes in business and the economic climate.

For an individually designed plan (i.e., one that is drafted to conform to a particular employer's needs), the employer applies for the determination letter. There is a five-year "remedial amendment cycle." The IRS spaces out its workload by having only one-fifth of all individually designed plans apply for determination letters each year. The plan's cycle depends on the last digit in its employer ID number (EIN). Cycle A (plans whose EINs end in 1 or 6) had a due date of January 31, 2012. For Cycle B (EINs ending in 2 or 7), the deadline is January 31, 2013. For Cycle C (EINs ending in 3 or 8), the deadline is January 31, 2014; the Cycle D deadline (EINs ending in 4 or 9) is January 31, 2015, and the Cycle E deadline (EINs ending in 5 or 10) is January 31, 2016.

Master & Prototype and volume submitter plans, which are drafted by a financial service provider, which is also responsible for getting and keeping the plan qualified, are generally reviewed on six-year cycle.

As of February 1, 2012 for plans with a five-year remedial amendment cycle, and May 1, 2012, for terminating plans and plans with a six-year remedial amendment cycle, plan sponsors are no longer permitted to submit Form 5300, Schedule Q, to receive an IRS determination that the plan satisfies the requirements of Code §§ 401(a)(4), 401(a)(26), or 410(b). But the IRS will still review whether the plan qualifies for the safe harbor from the anti-discrimination requirements of Code §§ 401(k) and 401(m).

If an employer adopts a pre-approved M&P or Volume Submitter plan, it can generally rely on the plan's opinion or advisory letter to prove that the plan satisfies most of the qualification requirements. Since May 1, 2012, the IRS has accepted determination letter applications on Form 5307 only from volume submitter plan adopters who modify the plan's terms—but not enough for it to be considered an individually designed plan.

Also as of May 1, 2012, employers are required to file Form 5300 (not form 5307, as was previously required) if they modify a pre-approved M&P plan to satisfy Code §§ 415 and 416, or the Normal Retirement Age for their pre-approved plan is earlier than age 62. [IRS.gov, *Retirement Plan FAQs-Changes Relating to Form 5307 and Demos*, <http://www.irs.gov/Retirement-Plans/Retirement-Plan-FAQs-regarding-Changes-to-the-Employee-Plans-Determination-Letter-Program> (Mar. 28, 2014)]

Announcement 2011-82, 2011-52 I.R.B. 1052 provides that IRS determination letters for qualified plans will no longer consider minimum coverage or most nondiscrimination testing issues. The changes take effect with Cycle B, for submissions made on or after February 1, 2012, with a later effective date for terminating plans. Nor will individual determination letter requests for preapproved plans consider these issues, effective May 1, 2012, when the IRS stopped accepting the Form 5307 Determination Letter application for prototype plans. Volume submitter plans can continue using Form 5307, but only for plans with only minor modifications of pre-approved document language. The coverage and nondiscrimination demonstrations previously filed on Schedule Q have been eliminated.

[Mercer Select, *Determination Letters Will No Longer Consider Coverage, Nondiscrimination Testing* (Dec. 19, 2011) (benefitslink.com); Ftwilliam.com, *IRS Eliminates Determination Letters for Pre-approved Plans Without Modifications* (Dec. 19, 2011) (benefitslink.com)]

Between early 2013 and January 31, 2014, Cycle C applications could be filed. Cycle C plans are individually designed plans maintained by an employer whose EIN ends with a 3 or an 8. The determination letter application requires complete restatement of the plan document, including all amendments adopted since the previous restatement. The restatement must also reflect the relevant changes listed in Notice 2012-76 (2012 Cumulative List of Changes in Plan Qualification Requirements), 2012-52 I.R.B. 775. A plan that misses the deadline for applying for a determination letter might be audited and found noncompliant, because its existing determination letter becomes obsolete. [Steve Flores, *Don't Drop The Ball On Your Determination Letter Applications*, Winston & Strawn LLP (Nov. 26, 2013), available at Lexology.com; Reinhart Boerner Van Deuren SC, *Cycle C Determination Letter Filings Due January 31, 2014*, Lexology.com (Nov. 14, 2013); Spencer Fane, *IRS Now Accepting "Cycle C" Determination Letter Applications* (Feb. 18, 2013) (benefitslink.com)]

§ 10.03 PROTOTYPE AND MASTER PLANS

The IRS publishes master and prototype plans for the guidance of employers who want to be sure that the plan they adopt satisfies the various requirements for qualification. The significance of the determination letter is that a plan that has one generally will not be disqualified if the IRS subsequently discovers defects in the plan documents. However, this immunity does not extend to operational defects, only to design defects. [Steptoe & Johnson LLP ERISA Advisory, *The 7th Circuit's Big ERISA Day* (Feb. 15, 2011) (benefitslink.com)] A prototype plan has a separate funding mechanism for each employer; a master plan has a single funding mechanism (such as a trust) that covers multiple employers.

It is frequently necessary to amend plans as the tax laws change. The IRS has launched a new cycle for approval of amendments. The IRS divides plans into two groups: the pre-approved and the individually designed. Most pre-approved plans fall into two categories: prototype plans (with very few choices) and volume submitter plans (allowing more options).

The IRS maintains a separate six-year submission cycle for pre-approved plans. For defined contribution plans, volume submitter document sponsors had to submit language for approval by January 31, 2006. The IRS processed all the submissions and issued approval letters for all the approved plans on March 31, 2008, with a filing deadline of April 30, 2010 for all plans using pre-approved documentation.

Form 4461-A, with its Attachment 1-A and Form 8717-A (user fee form), is used to seek IRS approval of a master or prototype or volume submitter defined benefit plan. Sponsors should consult the defined benefit Listing of Required Modifications (LRM) for language that sponsors and mass submitters can use to draft plans to comply with the Code and the Cumulative List of changes (Notice 2012-76). The IRS says that mass submitters of VS plans may also find this language useful. [IRS, *Pre-Approved Defined Benefit Plans-Revised Forms and LRM*, <http://www.irs.gov/Retirement-Plans/Preapproved-Defined-Benefit-Plans-Revised-Forms-and-LRM> (Mar. 25, 2014)]

As discussed above, a new series of filing cycles has begun: Cycle A (plans whose EINs end in 1 or 6) had a due date of January 31, 2012. For Cycle B (EINs ending in 2 or 7), the deadline is January 31, 2013. For Cycle C (EINs ending in 3 or 8), the deadline is January 31, 2014; the Cycle D deadline (EINs ending in 4 or 9) is January 31, 2015, and the Cycle E deadline (EINs ending in 5 or 10) is January 31, 2016.

The deadline to submit on-cycle applications for opinion and advisory letters for pre-approved defined benefit plans for the second six-year remedial amendment cycle has been extended to February 2, 2015. It applies to defined benefit mass submitter lead and specimen plans, word-for-word identical plans, master and prototype minor modifier placeholder applications, and non-mass-submitter defined benefit plans. The deadline was extended based on requests from plan sponsors that the IRS develop a pre-approved plan program for defined benefit plans with cash balance features to be available during the second cycle. The IRS agreed to expand the pre-approved program so plans with some cash balance features can be submitted as part of the defined benefit submission. The extension gives the IRS more time to develop forms and tools. The extension applies to all on-cycle pre-approved defined benefit plans, even if they do not have cash balance features. The IRS requested that sponsors not submit applications for opinion or advisory letters until guidance has been provided.

Sponsors of individually designed Cycle C plans that intend to adopt a pre-approved defined benefit plan document, and do not intend to file a determination letter as an individually designed plan had until March 31, 2014 to complete Form 8905.

Rev. Proc. 2013-8, 2013-1 I.R.B. 237 governs the user fees that apply to pre-approved defined benefit applications submitted before January 31, 2014 that do not have cash balance features. See Rev. Proc. 2014-8, 2014-1 I.R.B. 242 for user fees for applications submitted after January 31, 2014. [Announcement 2014-4, 2014-7 I.R.B. 523; modifies Rev. Proc. 2007-44 and Rev. Proc. 2011-49; see Rebecca Moore, *IRS Readies for Pre-Approved Cash Balance Plan Program*, plansponsor.com (Jan. 24, 2014)]

In March 2014, the IRS announced that it would issue opinion and advisory letters for pre-approved defined contribution plans that were restated for qualification requirements listed in the 2010 Cumulative List and were filed with the IRS during their second submission period under the Rev. Proc. 2007-44 remedial amendment cycle. In this context, pre-approved plans means master and prototype and volume submitter plans. The letters were expected to issue on March

31, 2014. The IRS will accept applications for individual determination letters under the second six-year remedial cycle between May 1, 2014 and April 30, 2016.

The remedial amendment cycle for pre-approved defined contribution plans for changes in the plan qualification requirements on the 2010 Cumulative List ends April 30, 2016. An employer whose defined contribution plan is eligible for the six-year remedial amendment cycle that adopts a Master & Prototype or Volume Submitter plan by April 30, 2016 is considered to have adopted the plan within the six-year remedial amendment cycle. An employer adopting a master & prototype plan, whether it is standardized or not, cannot use Form 5307 to apply for the plan's determination letter. An employer adopting a Volume Submitter plan can only use Form 5307 if the employer has modified the terms of the approved plan, but not enough for the plan to become an individually designed plan. Employers permitted to file Form 5307 to get a determination letter can do so between May 1, 2014 and April 30, 2016. [Announcement 2014-16, 2014-17 I.R.B. 983. The 2010 Cumulative List is found at Notice 2010-90, 2010-52 I.R.B. 909.]

§ 10.04 ROUTINE TAX COMPLIANCE

[A] Necessary Forms

Day-to-day administration of a plan involves creation of tax records and submission of many forms to the IRS and state taxing authorities.

One of the most important forms is Form W-2, disclosing compensation paid to each individual employee. The form must be submitted to the IRS and also to the employee. The normal due date for employee W-2s is January 31 following the end of the year of employment. However, employees who leave during the year have a right to demand that they get a W-2 form within 30 days of the last paycheck (or of the request, if made at a later date). The employer can use IRS Form 8809 to request additional time to file W-2s.

One of the requirements of the health care reform bill, PPACA, is that employers provide information reporting on Form W-2 of the cost of health coverage provided by the employer. This amount is not taxable, but it is relevant to the determination of whether the employer provides adequate coverage, whether it is subject to penalties, and whether the employee is entitled to a subsidy if he or she obtains health insurance through an Exchange. [See § 18.19[K] for more discussion of these issues.]

When PPACA was first enacted, it was intended that the cost of coverage would be reported on the 2011 W-2 forms (distributed in 2012). However, in Notice 2010-69, 2010-44 I.R.B. 576, the IRS recognized that employers need more time to update their payroll systems, so the information does not have to be provided until the 2012 W-2 forms issued in 2013, but can be done voluntarily before then.

Notice 2012-9, 2012-4 I.R.B 315 explains how employers must report the value of EGHP coverage on employees' W-2 forms. At present, this amount does not constitute taxable compensation, but employees must receive this information as part of their decision whether to seek insurance coverage from an Exchange. [Birgit Anne Waidmann, PricewaterhouseCooper HRS Insight, *IRS Provides Guidance on Mandatory Reporting of the Value of Health Coverage on 2012 Forms W-2* (Jan. 6, 2012) (benefitslink.com)]

IRS guidance from May 2014 explains how to report the cost of coverage on Box 12 of Form W-2. Reporting is required for major medical coverage, the value of a Health FSA that exceeds the employee's salary reductions, hospital indemnity or specified illness coverage paid via pre-tax salary reduction or by the employer, and domestic partner coverage included in the employee's gross income. However, the IRS says not to report the cost of Health FSA coverage funded entirely via salary reduction; employer or employee contributions to an HSA or Archer MSA; indemnity or specified illness coverage paid for on an after-tax basis; the cost of long-term care, accident or disability income, liability insurance, or Worker's Compensation. Reporting is optional for dental or vision coverage, HRA contributions, certain COBRA situations, and self-funded plans that are not subject to COBRA. [IRS, *Form W-2 Reporting of Employer-Sponsored Health Coverage*, <http://www.irs.gov/uac/Form-W-2-Reporting-of-Employer-Sponsored-Health-Coverage> (updated May 5, 2014)]

Employers will also have to report to the IRS about their compliance with the employer mandate ("pay or play" requirement; Code §§ 6055 and 6056), although the effective date of this requirement has been postponed. On July 24, 2014, the IRS published drafts of Forms 1095-B and 1095-C, which will be used for reporting. Sponsors of self-funded health plans and insurers use Form 1095-B. Employers of at least 50 full-time employees use Form 1095-C. The draft forms were issued to help employers and HR professionals get ready to submit the forms when they are required. [Roetz & Andress Alerts, *IRS Issues Draft Forms for 2015 ACA Reporting*, <http://www.ralaw.com/media-events.cfm?type=alert&id=1346> (Aug. 11, 2014)]

Other forms include:

- Form W-3: a transmittal form filed with the Social Security Administration consolidating all the W-2 and W-2P forms for the entire company. The regular due date for any year's W-3 is February 28 of the following year;
- Form W-4P: is used by employees to opt out of withholding or increase withholding on their pension and annuity payments. This form goes straight from employer to employee, no IRS filing is required;

- Forms 941/941E: these are the forms for quarterly returns of federal income tax. Form 941 is used if there are FICA taxes withheld or paid, 941E otherwise. The due date is the end of the month after the close of the calendar quarter being reported on. However, some employers can file an annual Form 944 in lieu of quarterly 941s, if their annual employment tax liability, including income tax withholding, FICA, and Medicare tax, is under $1,000 for the calendar year: [T.D. 9566, 76 Fed. Reg. 77672 (Dec. 14, 2011)]
- Form 945: the report on withheld taxes that are not payroll taxes (e.g., withholding on retirement plan distributions);
- Form 1041: trust income tax return, required if the plan's trust becomes disqualified (or otherwise does not operate as a tax-exempt organization) and if it also has income equal to or greater than $600. The due date is the fifteenth day of the fourth month after the end of the trust's tax year;
- Form 1099-R: 1099-series forms are used to report miscellaneous sums that might otherwise escape the attention of the taxing authorities. The 1099-R is used to report lump sums and periodic distributions. The entire group of a company's transmittal forms requires its own transmittal form, Form 1096. The filing is due by February 28 each year for the preceding year;

■ **TIP:** Within two weeks of making a distribution, the plan administrator must provide each recipient with a written explanation of the tax consequences of taking a lump sum, including how to elect lump-sum tax treatment and how to roll over the sum to another qualified plan or to an IRA.

- Form 5308: form filed in connection with a change in the tax year of a qualified plan or trust;
- Form 5330: excise tax form for failure to meet the minimum funding standard, or for receipt of an impermissible reversion of plan assets. Disqualified persons who engage in prohibited transactions are also required to file this form. There is no fixed due date: the timing depends on the nature of the transaction subject to excise tax. Form 5558 is used to request additional time to file this form;
- Form 8109: the quarterly estimated tax return when a plan trust has unrelated business taxable income (UBTI) [see I.R.C. § 512(a)(1)] from operation of an unrelated trade or business. UBTI is limited to business net income (after deducting the costs of generating the income). It does not include dividends, interest, annuities, loan fees, or royalties;

- Form 8928: used (starting with the 2010 plan year or taxable year) by employers to self-report and pay excise taxes for certain compliance failures of EGHPs—COBRA requirements (including the ARRA premium subsidy, HIPAA rules, mental health parity, the Genetic Information Nondiscrimination Act, and failure to make comparable contributions for all employees if there is an HSA or MSA plan. [74 Fed. Reg. 45994 (Sept. 8, 2009), discussed in Guest article, Deloitte's Washington Bulletin, *New for 2010: Employers Must Self-Report Excise Tax for Failure to Comply with Group Health Plan Requirements* (Dec. 14, 2009) (benefitslink.com)]
- Form 8955-SSA, replacing Form 5500 SSA to report information about participants who had deferred vested benefits when they separated from a plan. Unless an extension is granted, Form 8955-SSA must be filed by the last day of the seventh month after the last day of the plan year: July 31 for a calender year plan. Form 8955-SSA is filed only with the IRS (the predecessor form reported to both the IRS and DOL). Therefore, some plans attempting to correct failure to file timely Form 5500 annual reports will have to file both with the IRS and with DOL—including retroactive filings going back to 2009. [Notice 2014-35 , 2014- . . . I.R.B. . . . ; see Lawrence Jenab, *Additional Action Required By Late Filers Of Form 5500 (Even Those That Have Already Filed*, Spencer Fane Britt & Browne (May 27, 2014), available at Lexology.com. The requirements for non-ERISA plans that file Form 5500-EZ or 5500-SF are found in Notice 2014-34, 2014- . . . I.R.B. . . . See Thomas E. Funk et al., *IRS Issues New Relief From Form 5500 Series Late Filer Penalties For Certain Employee Benefit Plans*, Reinhart Boerner Van Deuren SC (June 16, 2014), available at Lexology.com.] [EBIA Weekly, *IRS Releases 2013 Form 8955-SSA and Instructions* (Jan. 23, 2014) (benefitslink.com)]

The IRS' project of moving all business tax form filing online is well underway. (The next important planned step is the integration of federal and state tax filings through a coordinated electronic system.) (The TeleFile program, allowing telephone filing of many forms, was discontinued in mid-2005.)

Business taxpayers file taxes via the Electronic Federal Tax Payment System (EFTPS), a highly secure encrypted Website. See <http://www.irs.gov/efile> and IRS Publications 4132, 966, 4169, 4321, 4130, 4276, and 4048. Rev. Proc. 2010-26, 2010-30 I.R.B. 91 provides updated specifications for electronic filing of Forms 1098, 1099, 5498, and W-2G information returns using the FIRE (Filing Information Returns Electronically) system. The new procedure has to be used for preparing tax year 2010 information returns, and information returns for earlier years filed as of January 1, 2011. [CCH Pensions and Benefits, *IRS Updates Specifications for Electronic Filing of Certain 2010 Information Returns, Including Forms 1099-R and 5498* (Aug. 11, 2010) (benefitslink.com)] Notice 1036,

<http://www.irs.gov/pub/irs-pdf/n1036.pdf> provides the percentage withholding tables required after February 15, 2013.

For tax years ending on or after December 31, 2005, corporations with assets of $50 million or more that file at least 250 returns a year, including income and employment tax and information returns, are required to file their 1120 and 1120-S forms electronically. The next year, the electronic filing requirement is extended to corporations with assets of more than $10 million who file 250 returns a year. To file electronically, large and mid-size corporations must use the IRS e-file system Modernized e-File (MeF). W-2 forms also can be submitted electronically, although those forms must be filed with the Social Security Administration rather than the IRS.

On the subject of routine compliance under non-routine circumstances, see Rev. Proc. 2005-27, 2005-20 I.R.B. 1050 for a list of 32 employee benefit issues that are affected automatically whenever the President declares a disaster.

A mid-2013 IRS phone forum described some factors triggering IRS audit of a retirement plan:

- A large number of separated participants who are not 100% vested;
- A high percentage of plan assets are classified as "other" rather than described in detail;
- The income statement shows significant distributions;
- A 401(k) plan or plan for a self-employed individual is top-heavy.

Selection of a plan for audit can be random, or part of a joint examination with another agency, such as the DOL. The IRS usually telephones the plan, then follows up with an appointment letter or pre-planning meeting. The IRS submits a list of records and documents that it seeks. The IRS Examination Process Guide, available online, offers clues to what the IRS expects. [Kevin McGuinness, *IRS Offers Tips for Audit Preparation*, plansponsor.com (Aug. 30, 2013)]

If the contributions to the plan reflect an incorrect amount of compensation, there will be an operational failure, because the operation of the plan will not conform to its terms. A plan is not required to use the same definition of compensation for all types of contributions. For example, discretionary contributions might be allocated based only on base salary, but salary deferral contributions could reflect all compensation, including bonuses and commissions. Compensation errors occur when a payroll processor or TPA does not know the plan's various definitions of compensation, or is not alerted to plan amendments, or if payroll systems are not updated. The Employee Plans Compliance Resolution System (EPCRS) can be used to fix the mistakes. Self-correction without IRS approval is permitted for insignificant errors, or for significant errors that are corrected within two years. However, a plan sponsor is only entitled to self-correct if it has implemented practices and procedures that promote overall tax-law compliance.

The Voluntary Correction Program (VCP) can be used to correct errors, with IRS approval. The VCP submission should explain the plan failure and the proposed correction, including the corrective contributions to be made, and the plan's proposal for improving administration to prevent future errors. The correction method should restore participants to the status they would have been in if there had been no error (for example, making larger contributions, or distributing excess amounts from the plan). If too much compensation was included in the calculations, the correction consists of distributing the excess elective deferrals and earnings to the affected participant, with excess discretionary contributions forfeited as required by the plan document. Forfeitures should either be reallocated to participants based on correct contributions, or transferred to an unallocated account that reduces future contributions.

Conversely, if the error was omitting some forms of compensation from elective deferrals, matches, or discretionary contributions, corrective contributions must be made for the affected participants. For missed salary deferrals, the amount of omitted compensation should be multiplied by the deferral percentage specified in the employee's salary reduction agreement. The missed deferral opportunity is equal to 50% of the omitted compensation. The missed deferral opportunity should be contributed to the employee's account, plus earnings up to the date of the corrective contribution. If discretionary contributions were made to participants for a plan year, the same percentage of omitted contribution should be contributed, plus earnings to the date of correction.

Rev. Proc. 2013-12, 2013-4 I.R.B. 313 updates EPCRS, superseding Rev. Proc. 2008-50 effective April 1, 2013. The VCP submission procedures have been revised to provide rules for plans subject to § 436 restrictions. The safe harbor correction methods and fee structures have been changed.

Rev. Proc. 2013-12 also includes a procedure for using Appendix C, Schedule 1 to correct a failure to adopt a mandatory interim amendment that was required to conform to the PPA or HEART Act. The fee for this program is $375. However, the procedure cannot be used to correct failure to adopt an interim amendment required by a pre-EGTRRA restatement—for example, the 401(k) final regulations. Those failures require correction under Appendix C, Schedule 2, which carries a higher fee. [Sungard Relius, *Correcting a Failure to Adopt an Interim Amendment Under the New EPCRS* (Mar. 19, 2013) (benefitslink.com)]

Rev. Proc. 2013-12 includes model VCP submission documents. These documents are for submissions under Rev. Proc. 2013-12 only, not for submissions made before April 1, 2013 pursuant to Rev. Proc. 2008-50. The documents must be used exactly as published, without modification. The available schedules are:

- Schedule 1, Interim and certain discretionary non-amender failures;
- Schedule 2 Non-amender failures (not covered by schedule 1);
- Schedule 3 SEPs and SARSEPs;

- Schedule 4 SIMPLE IRAS;
- Schedule 5 Plan loan failures;
- Schedule 6 Employer eligibility failure;
- Schedule 7 Failure to distribute excess elective deferrals;
- Schedule 8 Failure to make timely payment of required minimum distributions;
- Schedule 9 correction by plan amendment.

[IRS.gov, updated Jan. 23, 2013 *Correcting Plan Errors—Fill-in VCP Submission Documents*] Rev. Proc. 2013-12 streamlines the VCP process. The material previously found in Appendices D and F is combined in Appendix C. Form 8950 (including a checklist of procedures) and 8951 (compliance fee) can be completed online.

> ■ **TIP:** The IRS processes VCP and determination letter applications separately, so overlapping documents should be filed in duplicate with each application. [Elizabeth Thomas Dold, *Plan Corrections Take on a Slightly New Look with Revenue Procedure 2013-12,* Journal of Pension Benefits (December 2013) (benefitslink.com)]

Plans can submit voluntary closing agreement requests to VCP, for issues where the Rev. Proc. 2013-12 version of EPCRS is unavailable. The IRS decides whether a closing agreement is appropriate. The sponsor submits a detailed letter explaining the problem, how it occurred, the number of employees and the amount of money involved, how the sponsor will correct the problem, and how the tax, interest, or penalties were calculated. Issues that can be resolved under VCP should be resolved that way; if a case has mixed issues, the IRS may accept a closing agreement, but the VCP-eligible issues will be resolved under Rev. Proc. 2013-12.

The request for a closing agreement will not be considered if the plan or sponsor is under investigation by the IRS or has an appeals or Tax Court matters pending. The IRS may refuse to enter into a closing agreement if the plan, its sponsor, or any other party to the closing agreement was a party to an abusive tax avoidance transaction. A closing agreement generally is not appropriate if there was a willful or intentional plan to evade or avoid taxes.

Plans subject to ERISA Title I should use DOL's VFCP before requesting a closing agreement from the IRS, and all actions described in the agreement must be completed before signing the agreement. Closing agreements cannot be used to address future events or seek guidance about retirement plan issues or actions. For the agreement to be worthwhile for the IRS, the sponsor should be prepared to show that it will document its tax liabilities; that the agreement is in the best interests of the IRS and the federal government in general; and if there was any violation or tax deficiency, it was unintentional.

The request for a closing agreement must be made by an authorized employee of the plan or its sponsor, or a representative who is authorized to sign Form 2848. The request is submitted to Internal Revenue Service TE/GE:EP:VC Group 7554: Gina Jacquez. Request for Voluntary Closing Agreement. 9350 Flair Drive, 3rd Floor El Monte, CA 91731 [Plansponsor staff, IRS *Establishes System for Voluntary Closing Agreements*, plansponsor.com (Dec. 23, 2013); IRS, *Employee Plans Voluntary Closing Agreements*, <http://www.irs.gov/Retirement-Plans/Employee-Plans-Voluntary-Closing-Agreements> (Dec. 19, 2013)]

VCP fees rise with the size of the plan, ranging from $750 for a plan with fewer than 20 participants to $25,000 for plans with more than 10,000 participants. Various discounts are available for specific failures, or if the plan has had only one failure. [McKay Hochman Company, Inc., *E-mail Alert 2013-13* (Aug. 27, 2013) (benefitslink.com)]

Previously, sponsors often used the IRS letter forwarding service to find payees of benefits. For requests postmarked on or after August 31, 2012, however, Rev. Proc. 2012-35, 2012-37 I.R.B. 341 announces that the IRS no longer considers finding missing persons a "humane purpose." Employers must therefore devise other means of finding the payees. The DOL's suggestions are Internet searches, credit reports, and commercial locater services. The Social Security Administration's forwarding service is still available, but at a cost of $25 per letter, whereas the IRS service was free for up to 50 participants. If the plan is terminating, it can use the PBGC's missing participants program, which requires the employer to submit the amount of the benefit to the PBGC, which looks for participants in connection with the termination. The Pension Protection Act mandated that the PBGC extend the program to non-defined benefit plans (e.g., 401(k)s) that terminate, but the PBGC never issued implementing regulations. [McDermott Will & Emery, *IRS Eliminates Use of Letter Forwarding Service to Find Missing Participants and Beneficiaries* (Sept. 27, 2012) (benefitslink.com); Rebecca Moore, *IRS Updates Compliance Resolution System*, plansponsor.com (Jan. 3, 2013)]

An "operational error" is a failure to comply with the terms of the plan. Often this can be corrected without IRS involvement and without penalties to the plan. The sponsor must put the plan and its participants in the position they would have been in if there had been no error. However, if correction requires a plan amendment, then it will probably be necessary to use EPCRS, as set out most recently in Rev. Proc. 2013-12, and to file under the Voluntary Correction Program. However, there are five situations under which a sponsor can use the Self-Correction Program (SCP) to adopt a retroactive corrective amendment without making a VCP filing:

- A hardship distribution was made from a plan that did not have a hardship distribution option;

- Making a plan loan where, once again, this option was not included in the plan;
- Letting an employee participate in the plan prematurely—before he or she satisfied the eligibility requirements;
- Allocating a contribution to correct a violation of the § 401(e)(17) compensation limit;
- Correcting an ADP failure by making a Qualified Nonelective Contribution (QNEC) that would not otherwise be available under the plan.

The plan must comply with the requirements of Code §§ 401(a), 410(b), and 411(d)(6). If the correction is a retroactive amendment to allow hardship distributions or loans, the best practice is to make sure that enough non-highly compensated employees (NHCEs) had access to them to satisfy the nondiscrimination rules. Amendments to change eligibility dates should also predominantly benefit NHCEs. The general rule is that correcting operational errors in an individually designed plan by amendment will probably require the sponsor to make an application for a determination letter reflecting the amendment the next time the plan's cycle requires a determination letter. If the plan terminates before the next cycle, a determination letter including the amendment will have to be obtained in connection with the termination. But if the plan is an approved prototype or volume submitter plan, a determination letter is not only not required for the amendment, the IRS forbids applying for one. [Sungard Relius, *Self-Correction Program Retroactive Corrective Amendments* (Mar. 29, 2013) (benefitslink.com)]

A forfeiture generally occurs when a participant leaves the employer before becoming fully vested for matching or other employer contributions. The rules permit forfeiture of the non-vested portion, although in practice many plans do not call for forfeiture until there have been five consecutive one-year breaks in service. Mishandling of forfeitures is a common target of IRS audits. The IRS requires forfeitures to be used or allocated for the plan year in which they arise—or, in appropriate circumstances, in the following plan year. Forfeitures can be used to pay reasonable administrative expenses of the plan; to reduce the employer's contribution; to restore previously forfeited participant accounts; or to provide additional contributions to participants. The IRS' position is that forfeitures cannot be used to fund 401(k) safe harbor contributions, because these contributions have to be 100% vested when they are made. Placing the forfeited amounts into a suspense account is not permitted. The most common reasons for not allocating forfeitures on a timely basis are:

- Failure by the sponsor or TPA to monitor the forfeiture account to make sure the allocations are proper;
- Where the plan has both a sponsor and a TPA, each one thinks the other one is monitoring;

- When the plan sponsor incorrectly believes it has more discretion to apply forfeitures than the rules allow;
- When the plan terms do not explain how to handle forfeitures;
- When the sponsor elects not to make discretionary contributions for the plan year; with no contributions to be offset by the forfeited amount, the sponsor does not allocate them;
- When the sponsor does not think of using forfeitures to pay administrative expenses.

In the first two years, mistakes can be corrected with EPCRS. After two years, the VCP must be used unless the failure is considered insignificant. The VCP must be used if the terms of the plan are incorrect and a retroactive plan amendment is required to correct them. [Chadron J. Patton, *Common Plan Mistakes: Failure to Timely Allocate Forfeitures*, Spencer Fane (Nov. 16, 2012) (benefitslink.com)]

In recent years, IRS audits of 401(k) plans often ask the employer for evidence that participants were given the safe harbor notice. Plans that cannot produce this evidence are often asked for corrections and perhaps subjected to a closing agreement sanction. To avoid this problem, the plan should keep a dated copy of the notice and the cover letter sent with it. If the participants were given notice electronically, proper evidence would be a dated copy of the e-mail that was sent and the list of recipients. Failure to give the safe harbor notice is considered failure to comply with the terms of the plan, not just a failure to satisfy the statutory requirements of § 401(k). It is an operational failure that can be corrected under the VSCP, although it is not included in EPCRS. If the participant was aware of his or her eligibility to defer, the employer can correct the failure by giving the notice, even if it is late, and improving its procedures in the future. But if the participant was not aware of the option to defer, the employer must treat the employee as improperly excluded, and make a contribution equal to 50% of the missed deferral, plus any employer match required by the plan and an additional amount to compensate for lost earnings on the amount that should have been contributed. [SunGard Relius, *Failure to Provide Safe Harbor Notice Correction* (Nov. 30, 2012) (benefitslink.com)]

[B] Investment-Related Costs

The DOL undertook several measures in 2009–2011 to increase the transparency of defined contribution plan fees. The first step was the new Schedule C requirements that took effect in 2009, enhancing the disclosure that has to be made to the federal government about indirect compensation (revenue sharing) paid to service providers.

The second step was a rule released in July 2010, requiring providers to report to plan sponsors on direct and indirect compensation that the sponsors paid for account services. [EBSA press release, *U.S. Department of Labor Announces Intention to Extend Applicability Date of Section 408(b)(2) Fee Disclosure Regulation* (Feb. 11, 2011) (benefitslink.com); Plansponsor staff, *DoL Extends Applicability Dates for Fee Disclosure Rules*, plansponsor.com (July 13, 2011)] The rule was finalized in early 2012, effective July 1, 2012, requiring service providers to give the plan written disclosure of compensation and other information about the arrangement under which services are provided to a defined contribution plan. EBSA published a sample guide to disclosure. [77 Fed. Reg. 5632 (Feb. 3, 2012); DOL Fact Sheet, *Final Regulation Relating to Service Provider Disclosures Under Section 408(b)(2)* (February 2012) (benefitslink.com)]

The DOL requires fiduciaries to be prudent in choosing a fiduciary investment adviser, and must monitor their abilities and qualifications periodically (including whether the adviser continues to comply with securities laws, compliance with the terms of engagement), but the plan's fiduciaries are not obligated to oversee the provision of specific advice. The advisers should be chosen based on an objective process analyzing qualifications, quality of services offered, and the reasonableness of fees. The process must be free of self-dealing, conflict of interest, and improper influence. Advice should be based on generally accepted investment theories. The Pension Protection Act of 2006 (Pub. L. No. 109-280 § 601) adds a prohibited transaction exemption under Code § 4975(d)(17) and ERISA § 409(b)(14) for advice from a fiduciary adviser under an investment advice arrangement.

The DOL published Final Regulations on the selection of annuity providers for individual account plans in late 2008, pursuant to the PPA. Including the option of distributing an individual account plan by purchasing an annuity contract does not trigger the "safest available annuity" standard of Interpretive Bulletin 95-1, but other fiduciary standards apply. Fiduciaries qualify for a safe harbor when they adopt annuities as a distribution method if the provider is selected after an objective investigation. To qualify for the safe harbor, the fiduciary must also retain an appropriate expert to monitor compliance, although the fiduciary is not required to perform ongoing review of the appropriateness of the initial selection. [DOL Reg. § 2550.404a-4, 73 Fed. Reg. 58447 (Oct. 7, 2008); Amendment to Interpretive Bulletin 95-1, 73 Fed. Reg. 58445 (Oct. 7, 2008); Amendments to DOL Reg. §§ 2550.404a-3 and 2578.1, 73 Fed. Reg. 58459 (Oct. 7, 2008); Amendment to PTE 2006-06, 73 Fed. Reg. 58629 (Oct. 7, 2008)] See also §§ 6.07[B], 15.15, and 15.17 for discussion of cost issues in the plan context.

[C] Satisfying PPA Requirements

The Pension Protection Act (PPA), Pub. L. No. 109-280, although primarily focused on improving the stability of defined benefit plans, has had important effects on other types of plans as well.

Rev. Rul. 2007-67, 2007-48 I.R.B. 1047, held that it does not violate the anti-cutback rule to adopt a plan amendment that adopts the PPA amendments to § 417(e)(3) [actuarial assumptions used in calculating the minimum present value of the accrued benefit]. Accordingly, in the spring of 2008, the IRS proposed amendments to Code § 4980F and ERISA § 204(h), under which a 204(h) notice would not be required if the effect of complying with PPA changes in actuarial assumptions is to reduce a lump sum distribution from a defined benefit plan. [EB095625, REG-110136-07, RIN 1545-BG48, 73 Fed. Reg. 15101 (Mar. 21, 2008). See also Notice 2007-86, 2007-46. I.R.B 990.] However, some cash balance plans must issue 204(h) notices if an amendment to eliminate whipsaw also has the effect of reducing lump sum distributions, and T.D. 9472, 2009-51 I.R.B. 850.

Only about two-thirds of eligible workers participate in 401(k) plans; the PPA promotes automatic enrollment, on the theory that very few workers would actually opt out of a plan once enrolled in it. In September 2006, DOL proposed a regulation explaining the PPA safe harbor for default investments by fiduciaries who have not been instructed by plan participants.

Under the PPA, a plan participant or beneficiary is deemed to have exercised control over the account (thus exonerating the fiduciary) if the fiduciary invests in a "qualified default investment alternative" (QDIA) in a situation where the participant or beneficiary had the opportunity to give investment directions but did not. Notice must be given 30 days before the first investment, and 30 days before each subsequent plan year, explaining the circumstances under which assets will be invested in a QDIA. If the investment gives the plan any materials (e.g., prospectuses for securities), it must be passed along to the participants and beneficiaries.

The participant or beneficiary must be permitted to remove and redirect QDIA funds as often as other plan investments without incurring a penalty—at least quarterly. The plan must offer the broad range of investment alternatives in addition to the QDIA, as required by the ERISA § 404(c) regulations. The QDIA must be diversified, and must be managed by an investment manager or a registered investment company. The QDIA is forbidden to directly invest participant contributions in the employer's stock, and money market and stable value funds are not suitable because their rate of return is too low to provide reliable retirement security. However, life cycle funds, targeted retirement date funds, balanced funds, and professionally managed accounts are all permitted. [<http://www.dol.gov/ebsa>, Fact Sheet, *Proposed Regulation Relating to Default Investment Alternatives Under Participant Directed Individual Account Plans* (Sept. 26, 2006)] If all of these requirements are satisfied, the fiduciary then qualifies for safe harbor relief. However, the selection of the default investments remains a fiduciary decision—which, in turn, must be prudent, considering fees and expenses. Once selected, the default arrangement must be monitored for continued appropriateness. [EBSA FAB 2007-1, discussed in Fred Schneyer, *DOL Sets Out Fiduciary Adviser Selection/Monitoring Guidelines*, plansponsor.com (Feb. 2, 2007)]

Fiduciaries are not liable for losses on amounts invested in a QDIA, and the plan's fiduciaries are not liable for decisions made by the managers of the QDIA. A QDIA can mix equity and fixed income investments—for example, in a life cycle or targeted retirement date fund; it can also be a balanced fund or a professionally managed fund. However, a capital preservation fund or other stable value fund can be a QDIA only for the first 120 days after a participant's first elective contribution.

The DOL announced a final rule on improving access to financial advice for 401(k) and IRA accounts in January 2009, but this rule was withdrawn and replaced by a proposal published in March 2010. Under the March 2010 proposal, advice can be given two ways: through the use of an unbiased computer model chosen by the fiduciary, or when the adviser's fees do not vary no matter what investments the participants choose. Additional requirements, including fee disclosure, are imposed. [Proposed rule, 75 Fed. Reg. 9360 (Mar. 2, 2010) For history of the rule, see 74 Fed. Reg. 11847 (Mar. 20, 2009) and 74 Fed. Reg. 23951 (May 22, 2009), discussed in Fred Schneyer, *EBSA Delays Advice Rule Again*, plansponsor.com (Nov. 16, 2009) and *EBSA Pulls Back Controversial Advice Mandate*, plansponsor.com (Nov. 19, 2009)]

Final IRS rules in T.D. 9447 (2009-12 I.R.B. 694) permit employers to add an automatic enrollment feature to 401(k) plans without performing nondiscrimination testing, but the plan must be a QACA or an EACA (the equivalent for multi-employer plans). A QACA is a CODA that satisfies the 401(k)(13) rules about notice, automatic deferrals, and matching or nonelective contributions. A QACA must begin automatic contributions at 3% of salary, adding 1% a year until reaching 6%. Company matches and mandatory nonelective contributions vest in two years. If an employer offers a QACA, all employees must be automatically enrolled. If the employer withholds excess contributions from employees who opt out of coverage, the employer must make a corrective distribution by June 30. An employee who opts out can withdraw from the plan and have contributions end within 90 days. The distribution from the plan is taxable to the employee, but is not subject to the 10% penalty tax on premature withdrawals. The Final Regulations apply to plan years beginning on or after January 1, 2008. [Joanne Wojcik, *IRS Rules on 401(k) Will Help Some Employers*, Business Insurance (Feb. 25, 2009)]

Late in 2011, the DOL finalized the ERISA § 408(g) regulations, so it is not a prohibited transaction for fiduciary advisors to give individual account plan participants individualized investment advice—as long as the advice is based on generally accepted investment theories considering the individual's investment characteristics as well as the performance of various asset classes over time. Either the adviser's remuneration must be independent of the choices made by the individual, or the advice must be rendered based on a valid computer model. [76 Fed. Reg. 66637 (Oct. 7, 2011)]

A mid-2012 final rule revises the procedure for mailing or e-filing certain notices with DOL under the ERISA § 408(b)(2) rules about the fee disclosures that must be made to the plan's fiduciaries. The fiduciaries are required to file these notices to secure a prohibited transaction exemption. If fiduciaries find out that they have not been given the appropriate information, they must make a written request to the service provider to get the missing information. If the service provider fails to comply within 90 days, the fiduciary must either mail a written notice to DOL, EBSA Office of Enforcement, P.O. Box 75296, Washington, D.C. 20013, or use the link at <www.dol.gov/ebsa/regs/feedisclosurefailurenotice.html> The advantage of online filing is that the site gives immediate electronic confirmation that notice is received. [Final Rule, DOL EBSA, *Amendment Relating to Reasonable Contract or Arrangement Under Section 408(b)(2)—Fee Disclosure*, 77 Fed. Reg. 41678 (July 16, 2012)]

§ 10.05 ERISA COMPLIANCE ISSUES

Many compliance issues (e.g., payment of premiums; reporting events that may imperil a plan's future; terminating a plan) involve interaction between plan sponsors and the PBGC. PBGC.gov has been updated, to make the site run faster and make it easier to search. The links have been re-labeled for clarity, and there is a new Resources tab to find reference materials. Many of the guidance documents have been moved to the Resources tab, which includes fact sheets, databooks, and annual reports. [PBGC press release, *PBGC Website Gets New Look with Faster and Easier Navigation Tools* (Jan. 24, 2011) (benefitslink.com)]

The Summary Plan Description (SPD) for a newly created plan must be filed with the Department of Labor within 120 days of the plan's adoption. (If this is later than the date of establishment, filing must be made within 120 days of the first time the plan covers common-law employees and therefore becomes subject to ERISA Title I.) It is wise to include a disclaimer in the SPD, to the effect that the plan instrument and not the SPD will govern in case of conflict.

ERISA § 104(a)(4)(A) gives the DOL the power to reject an incomplete SPD filing. The plan administrator has 45 days to file again to answer the DOL comments. If the second filing is not made, DOL has the power to sue for legal or equitable relief, or any other remedy authorized by ERISA Title I.

According to EBSA, it is a violation of ERISA's "exclusive purpose" rule for fiduciaries to use plan assets to advance proxy resolutions for political or policy issues that are not connected to increasing the value of the plan assets. Fiduciaries are barred from accepting higher expenses, lower investment returns, or risks to the security of the plan's assets in order to advance any goals that are not directly related to the plan. [EBSA Advisory Opinion 2007-07A; see Rebecca Moore, *Use of Plan Assets for Non-Plan Related Political Issues Violates ERISA*, plansponsor.com (Jan. 3, 2008)]

DOL published a final rule on January 14, 2010, creating a safe harbor for small plan (under 100 participants). The safe harbor explains when funds received from participants or withheld from their wages for contribution to a pension or welfare benefit plan become plan assets under ERISA Title I. In 1988, DOL ruled that the contributions became plan assets on the earliest date they could reasonably be segregated from the employer's general assets, but in any case within 90 days of the employer's receipt of the funds. A 1996 rule reduced the period to the fifteenth business day of the month after receipt. The 2010 rule deems a contribution timely if it is placed into the plan no later than the seventh business day after the employer received it—even if it would have been possible to deposit it faster.

For a SIMPLE IRA, the maximum period for depositing participants' contributions continues to be 30 days after the end of the month in which the employee would otherwise have received the money in cash form. For a welfare benefit plan, the safe harbor period remains 90 days from the date the employer received or withheld the money. [Transamerica Center for Retirement Studies 2010-01, *Department of Labor Final Rule on Definition of Plan Assets—Participant Contributions* (Jan. 22, 2010) (benefitslink.com); the proposed rule was published at 73 Fed. Reg. 11072 (Feb. 29, 2008)]

Starting with the 2002 plan year, some small plans (usually those having fewer than 100 participants) will be required to get a report from an independent auditor to accompany their Form 5500-series filing, even though they were excused from the audit requirement in earlier years. [65 Fed. Reg. 62957 (Oct. 19, 2000); this issue is discussed in a Reminder from BenefitsLink, *Changed 5500 Rules Will Require 2002 Independent Audit for Some Small Plans*, <http://benefitslink.com/erisaregs/2520.104-41-final.shtml>]

See PBGC, *Late Payment Charges*, <http://www.pbgc.gov/prac/prem/late-payment-charges.html>, accessed April 4, 2014, for an explanation of how the PBGC bills interest and penalty charges for late payments of premiums. Penalties can be reconsidered if failure to make a full, timely payment was beyond the plan's control, but the PBGC does not have the authority to waive the premium itself or reduce the official interest rate.

The 2012 legislation, Pub. L. No. 112-141, the Moving Ahead for Progress in the 21st Century Act (MAP-21), schedules ongoing increases in the PBGC premium. Subsequent legislation, the Bipartisan Budget Act of 2013, signed on December 26, 2013, attempts to reduce the PBGC's deficit by increasing PBGC premiums by $8 billion. As a result, the 2013 flat rate premium is $42 per participant. The 2013 variable rate premium is $9 per $1,000 in underfunding, subject to a $400 cap. For 2014, the flat rate is $49 for single-employer and $12 for multi-employer plans, the variable rate is $14/$1,000 in underfunding, and the cap is $412. Rates have also been proposed for 2015–2017: for 2015, a $57 flat rate, variable rate of at least $24/$1,000 in underfunding, a cap of at least $412; for 2016, a flat rate of $64, a variable rate of at least $29/$1,000 in underfunding, and a cap of $500; and for 2017, a flat rate of $64 as indexed for inflation, a variable rate of at least $29/$1,000, and a cap of $500 as indexed. [Buck Consultants FYI, *PBGC Premium Hikes in Final Budget Deal*, Vol. 36 Issue 105 (Dec. 27, 2013) (benefitslink.com; Sarah Roe Sise and Carrie Elizabeth Byrnes, *PBGC Premium Rates Increase In 2014 For Single-Employer Plans: Time To Cash-Out Some Deferred Vested Participants?*, Bryan Cave LLP (Nov. 15, 2013), available at Lexology.com]

The PBGC also changed the payment procedure, making it simpler and more uniform. As a result of Executive Order 13563, "Improving Regulation and Regulatory Review," effective for plan years beginning on or after January 1, 2014, the PBGC has eliminated the requirement that plans with 500 or more participants pay their estimated flat-rate premiums early in the plan year (February 28). The new rule is that flat rate premiums are due on October 15 in a single payment, with no need to make estimated payments—and the flat-rate premium is due on the same date as the variable-rate premium. The same date applies to plans of all sizes, with the result that plans with fewer than 100 participants now must file earlier, on the date that already applied to mid-sized plans, whereas large plans get more time to file. [79 Fed. Reg. 13547 (Mar. 11, 2014); see Segal Co., *PBGC Eliminates Early Flat-Rate Premium Payment Requirement for Large Plans, Including Multiemployer Plans* (Feb. 3, 2014) (benefitslink.com); Kevin McGuinness, *PBGC Moves Premium Date for Large Plans*, plansponsor.com (Jan. 2, 2014); Buck Consultants FYI, *PBGC Finalizes Remaining New Premium Rules for 2014*, Volume 37 Issue 29 (Mar. 13, 2014) (benefitslink.com)]

Small plans are also permitted to use either current-year or prior-year figures to compute the variable-rate premium. (Some small plans determine their funding levels late in the year, so they do not have current year figures available at the new due date.) The final premium for a terminating plan is due no later than the filing of the post-distribution certificate. This rule was adopted because the final premium was sometimes forgotten in standard terminations when the due date was months later than the plan closed its books. Furthermore, plans will generally be exempt from the variable rate premium for the year in which a standard termination is completed and small plans may be exempt from the variable rate premium for the first year of coverage.

The late premium payment penalty is 1% per month for plans that self-correct and 5% for month for those that do not self-correct; the PBGC's intention is to encourage self-correction. However, before the 2014 rules, both penalties were subject to a cap of 100% of the underpayment. To favor self-correction, the PBGC is changing the cap on the 1% penalty to 50% of the underpayment. The September 2011 policy (that payments made not more than seven days late will not be penalized) has been codified in regulations. [79 Fed. Reg. 13547 (Mar. 11, 2014); see Rebecca Moore, *PBGC Finalizes Premium Changes*, plansponsor.com (Mar. 10, 2014)]

Starting with filings covering the 2009 plan year, the DOL requires electronic filing of Form 5500, using EFAST2. (Filings could be made using the original EFAST until June 30, 2010; October 15, 2010 was the last date when paper filings could be accepted, although all late and amended filings must use EFAST2). [Mercer Select US, *Oct. 15 Deadline Completes The Transition to Form 5500 E-filing* (July 28, 2010) (benefitslink.com)]

Under IRS proposed regulations published in mid-2013, the administrators of large (250 or more tax returns filed per year) 401(k) and other plans would have to file Form 5500 and Form 8955-SSA electronically or on specified magnetic media. The proposals do not deal with ERISA reporting requirements. For plan years beginning on or after January 1, 2014, failure to make a required electronic filing will be penalized as failure to file. Waivers are theoretically available for hardship cases, but the preamble to the proposal says that waivers will rarely be granted. In practical terms, the proposal does not greatly change the employers' obligations, because DOL already required e-filing of Form 5500 and 5500-SF, and IRS's FIRE system allows e-filing for Form 8955-SSA. However, the small number of companies that file Form 5500-EZ and also file at least 250 returns a year must e-file the Form 5500-EZ. [*Employee Retirement Benefit Plan Returns Required on Magnetic Media*, 26 C.F.R. Part 301, 78 Fed. Reg. 53704 (Aug. 30, 2013); see EBIA Weekly, *IRS Proposed Regulations Would Require Electronic Filing for Certain Retirement Plan Reporting* (Sept. 5, 2013) (benefitslink.com)]

Informational copies of the 2013 Form 5500 have been released. A section called Form M-1 compliance information was added to reflect the PPACA rules increasing DOL enforcement authority, and additional filing requirements, for multi-employer welfare plans. Any welfare plan required to file Form M-1 must file Form 5500 no matter the size of the plan or how it is funded. Schedule H has been updated to include a new question about whether defined benefit plans are PBGC-insured. The Schedule SB instructions have been updated to reflect MAP21 provisions. [Kevin McGuinness, *DOL Releases Updated Form 5500*, plansponsor.com (Dec. 5, 2013)]

EBSA announced in early 2013 that migration to the fully electronic EFAST2 system is complete for all filing years and paper filings will no longer be accepted. See the DOL Website for an explanation of which version of the Form 5500/5500SF is required for your plan, and which schedules to use. The announcement, which primarily deals with the Delinquent Filer Voluntary Compliance Program, says that although DFVCP does not offer relief from late filing penalties under the Code or ERISA Title IV, the PBGC has agreed to provide some ERISA § 4071 penalty relief for delinquent filings of annual reports if the conditions of the DFVCP are satisfied. The IRS announced that it would issue separate guidance on penalty relief for Form 5500/5500-SF delinquencies where both DFVCP and IRS requirements are met. [Notice: <http://www.dol.gov/find/20130128>, FAQs at <http://www.dol.gov/ebsa/faqs/faq_dfvc.html>. See Rebecca Moore, *EBSA Updates Delinquent Filer Correction Program*, plansponsor.com (Jan. 28, 2013)]

The EFAST2 FAQ explains how to make a DFVCP filing. The DFVCP allows plan administrators to pay reduced civil penalties if they make the required filings before the DOL gives the administrators written notice of their failure to file timely annual reports under ERISA Title I. (Form 5500-EZ filers and filers of Form 5500 for plans without employees are not eligible for DFVCP because they are not subject to ERISA Title I.) The plan administrator is personally liable for ERISA § 502(c)(2) civil penalties, which cannot be paid from plan assets.

For a small plan (i.e., fewer than 100 participants at the beginning of the plan year), the applicable penalty is $10 per day the annual report is filed after the due date, not counting extension, subject to a cap of $750. If the same plan is delinquent in filing more than one annual report, the maximum is $750 per annual report, up to a maximum of $1,500. For a large plan, the penalty is $10 per day of lateness up to a $2,000 cap; for multiple delinquent filings, the limit is $2,000 per report and $4,000 per plan. All filings for a plan should be submitted together so the submitter gets the benefit of the cap. Payment of the DFVCP penalty waives the right to receive notice of assessment from the DOL—as well as the right to contest the amount of the assessed penalty.

Penalties for plans that do not file a timely annual report and do not participate in DFVCP are $50 per day with no limit; failure to file the annual report is penalized by $300 per day up to $30,000 per year until a complete annual report is filed. If, during the period when the reports were not filed, the plan went from small to large, the large-plan penalties apply. A plan that has received an IRS late-filer penalty letter can participate in DFVCP, but a plan that has received a DOL Notice of Intent to Assess a penalty cannot. [DOL/EBSA, *FAQs about the Delinquent Filer Voluntary Compliance Program* (no date; benefitslink.com). More info about DFVCP: <www.efast.dol.gov.>]

Starting January 1, 2012, Forms 5500 and 5500-SF must be signed electronically by the employer, plan sponsor, or plan administrator. The signer must have a valid EFAST2 user ID and personal ID. If the electronic signature is rejected by the online filing system, it may be necessary to get new credentials. Forms that do not have an electronic signature will not be processed, and the plan might be penalized. Forms that have an invalid electronic signature will be characterized as "processing stopped." Forms can also be signed by an authorized plan service provider (APSP) who has specific written authorization from the plan administrator, including the plan administrator's manual signature on a paper copy of the form. A PDF of the first two pages of the manually signed form must be attached to the filing, so the DOL can add an image of the manual signature to its online database. [John Iekel, *Electronic Signatures for Forms 5500 and 5500-SF Mandatory Jan. 1*, Smart HR (Dec. 21, 2011) (benefitslink.com)]

For 401(k) plans and health and welfare plans, EFAST2 requires the plan administrator's electronic signature to Form 5500. For most single-employer plans that means the employer/plan sponsor. The 2012 instructions clarify that where the plan administrator is an entity, the electronic signature must belong to an individual who is authorized to sign on behalf of the entity. Form 5500 now includes optional information about paid preparers; although the information is optional, the IRS encourages providing it. Schedules H and I have been revised so that the plan can indicate the name and EIN of its trust. If the plan has more than one trust, the one with the highest dollar amount or the one holding the largest percentage of plan assets should be listed. The filing should not give a Social Security Number as identification. If the filer does not have the EIN for the plan trust, the EIN for the Form 1099-R should be used. Form 5500-SF, for certain small plans, has also been revised to include the paid preparer and trust information [<http://www.dol.gov/ebsa/5500main.html>; see EBIA Weekly, *Form 5500 for 2012 Plan Year Released* (Dec. 6, 2012) (benefitslink.com)]

The PBGC required MyPAA users to adopt new, stronger passwords no later than August 1, 2012: the new passwords must have between 10 and 24 characters, and must include at least one uppercase character, one lowercase character, one special character, and one numeral. [What's New For Practitioners, <http://www.pbgc.gov/prac/whatsnew.html> (June 18, 2012)]

Code § 6057(a) requires reporting of certain information about participants who separate from service with deferred vested benefits. Until 2009, this was done on Schedule SSA of the Form 5500. IRS and SSA developed Form 8955-SSA, which is filed directly with the IRS for plan years beginning on or after January 1, 2009.

The information reported on the new form is similar to the Schedule SSA information: participants separated from service when entitled to a deferred vested benefit. The Social Security Administration uses this information to tell retirees who are applying for Social Security what pension plan benefits are available to them. [Jeffrey Ashendorf, *Legal Alert: IRS Replaces Schedule SSA* (Mar. 4, 2011) (benefitslink.com)]

In mid-2010, the PBGC revised its debt collection rules, to add salary offset and administrative wage garnishment to the acceptable methods of collecting non-tax debts owed to the PBGC. The PBGC had previously adopted debt collection regulations in 1994 and 1995 to conform to the Federal Claims Collection Act, Debt Collection Act, and Debt Collection Improvement Act, and to implement the Department of the Treasury's program of offsetting federal debts against tax refunds. Administrative offset is the process of having amounts that are owed to a business (such as a government contractor) paid to the PBGC instead, to pay the business' debts to the PBGC. Salary offset is withholding of up to 15% of a federal employee's disposable pay to collect debts. Administrative wage garnishment is withholding of wages of a former federal employee who now works for a non-federal employer. The PBGC has to inform debtors of the amount and type of the debt (such as an employer's failure to pay PBGC premiums, or amounts that the PBGC overpaid to an employee), how the PBGC intends to collect the debt, what happens if the debt is not repaid, and how the debtor can make alternate arrangements if the business or individual objects to the PBGC's proposed collection efforts. Under limited circumstances, the PBGC can waive interest, penalties, and administrative costs—but federal law forbids certain types of waivers. [PBGC Proposed Rule, *Debt Collection*, 75 Fed. Reg. 42662 (July 22, 2010)]

ERISA § 412 requires all plan officials who handle the plan's money or property to carry a bond of at least 10% of the amount the manager handles, with a minimum of $1,000. The maximum bond required of a plan is $500,000 per plan official—rising to $1 million per official for plans that hold employer securities. EBSA's Field Assistance Bulletin (FAB) 2008-04 provides guidance about the bonding requirements, such as how to calculate the amount of a bond covering multiple plans; if the $1 million maximum for bonds applies; if the plan holds employer securities only because it invests in pooled investment funds; and when third-party service providers that handle plan funds must be bonded. [Rebecca Moore, *EBSA Provides Guidance on Plan Official Bonding Requirements*, plansponsor.com (Nov. 25, 2008)]

The PBGC published a final rule, effective August 4, 2008, amending 29 C.F.R. Part 4003, formalizing the existing practice of referring some routine appeals to the PBGC's Benefits Administration and Payment Department or the staff of the Appeals Board, not the Appeals Board itself. Referral is appropriate where the claimant says there was a mistake of fact, or asks for a more detailed explanation of benefits. [Rebecca Moore, *PBGC Amends Appeals Procedures*, plansponsor.com (July 3, 2008)]

[A] Reportable Events

The PBGC's model of operations requires the agency to be aware of events that could lead a plan to terminate, or be taken over by, the PBGC. Therefore, a number of business and financial events are designated as "reportable events" about which a plan sponsor must advise the PBGC. Some events are reportable in advance; others, promptly after they have occurred. However, in 2012-2013, the PBGC proposed significant reductions in reporting requirements.

In late 2009, the PBGC proposed regulations to conform the agency's rules on reportable events (ERISA § 4043) to the PPA, eliminating most of the automatic waivers and extensions in filing and adding two new reportable events (one dealing with funding-based benefit limits, the other with transfers to retiree health benefit accounts). This proposal called for advance reporting when aggregate unvested benefits exceed $50 million and the plan's funded vested benefit percentage is under 90%. Both advance and post-event notice would be required if the AFTAP fell below 60%. Under ERISA § 4043(c)(12), a report to the PBGC is required if, in any 12-month period, 3% or more of the plan's benefit liabilities are transferred outside the plan's controlled group. (But see below for proposed waivers of this requirement.) Reporting is required because the PBGC is concerned that transfers could reduce the plan's funded percentage—and the transferee might be in even worse financial condition than the transferor.

There are three PBGC forms for reportable events: Form 10 for post-event reporting under Subpart B of the regulation; Form 10—Advance for advance reporting (Subpart C) and Form 200 (subpart D). Previously, Subpart B and C reports did not require the use of official forms, but the proposal makes this mandatory. [PBGC Proposed Rules, *Pension Protection Act of 2006; Conforming Amendments; Reportable Events and Certain Other Notification Requirements*, RIN 1212-AB06 74 Fed. Reg. 61248 (Nov. 23, 2009); see CCH Pension & Benefits, *PBGC Issues Proposed Regs on Reportable Events and Other Notice Rules Reflecting PPA* (Dec. 10, 2009) (benefitslink.com)]

ERISA § 4071 allows the PBGC to impose a penalty of up to $1,100 per day for noncompliance, including failing to contact the PBGC about a reportable event within 30 days of the event, failing to report under ERISA § 4010, failure to give participants the required notices under ERISA § 101(f), and failing to give notification of missing contributions when the shortfall, including interest, is greater than $1 million. The rate for the penalty for late payment of premiums is specified by 29 C.F.R. § 4007.8, but the PBGC has discretion to determine the amount of any information penalty assessed.

Penalties can be waived if there is reasonable cause for the delay, e.g., circumstances beyond the business' control. A partial waiver is also a possibility—for example, if the business could have reconstructed its records after a fire within a month, but in fact took two months. Penalties can be waived if paying the premium would cause undue hardship to the business (although the difficulty or expense the PBGC would incur in collecting the penalty is not a factor). Penalties are also waived if the premium is paid within 30 days of the bill. [Harold J. Ashner, *PBGC Reportable Events: Traps for the Unwary*, Journal of Pension Planning & Compliance (Winter 2007) Volume 32, Number 4 (benefitslink.com); 71 Fed. Reg. 66867 (Nov. 17, 2006)]

Effective December 18, 2006, the PBGC's Final Rule on premium penalties defines "reasonable cause" that will justify waiving premium penalties pursuant to ERISA Section 4007. "Reasonable cause" means situations such as circumstances beyond the responsible party's control; failure to pay in full and/or on time could not have been avoided by using ordinary business care and prudent for an organization of that size; records were destroyed; or reasonable reliance on incorrect advice from a PBGC employee.

Notice 2012-46, 2012-30 I.R.B. 86, effective November 1, 2012, gives the ERISA § 101(j) notice requirements for single-employer plans subject to benefit limitations under § 436. When the funding status of a single-employer plan falls below a certain level, the administrator has 30 days to provide notice to participants and beneficiaries. The DOL can collect a penalty of up to $1,000 per day for each participant who should have been, but was not, notified. The notice must be in plain English and must include the plan name, its EIN and plan number, and a general description of the payment limitation. The prohibited benefits must be described in detail. The notice must explain when the limitation will cease to apply (e.g., when the AFTAP rises to at least 80%). Once the limitations cease to apply, participants will be entitled to additional forms of distributions, so the plan administrator must distribute a § 101(j) notice within 30 days of the date the limitations cease to apply. The notice must be written, but can be given electronically if it is reasonably accessible to the participants who are entitled to notice. [McGuireWoods LLP, *IRS Provides Guidance on Notices for Funding-Related Pension Plan Benefit Limitations* (Aug. 28, 2012) (benefitslink.com)]

The PBGC's, Technical Update 13-1, offers some small pension plans relief from the provisions of the proposed amendments dealing with reportable events. The relief is permanent, not just for 2013, but could be superseded if the PBGC issues final rules that are different. The ERISA § 4034.25 waiver of the requirement of reporting missed quarterly contributions is extended for all years in which the plan either has fewer than 25 participants, or has between 25–100 participants and files a simplified notice with the PBGC. However, relief is not available if the quarterly contribution was missed as a result of the plan's financial inability to pay. Technical Update 13-1 applies the assets and liabilities used to calculate the variable rate premium to determine the reporting requirements for events in the next plan year—including eligibility for reporting waivers, extensions, and mandatory advance reporting. [Mark Schulte, *Déjà Vu All Over Again: PBGC Extends Reportable Event Relief for 2013 and Beyond*, VIA Retirement Plan Blog (Jan. 30, 2013) (benefitslink.com)]

ERISA § 4062(e) requires reporting of certain substantial cessations of operations by employers who maintain single-employer plans. An employer that ceases operations at a facility in any location, causing more than 20% of the employees who are participants to be separated from employment will be treated as if it were a substantial employer under a multi-employer plan, and ERISA §§ 4063–4065 will apply. A rule proposed in mid-2010 creates a new Subpart B within 29 C.F.R. Part 4062 to give further details of the calculation.

Under these provisions, the PBGC must be notified within 60 days after withdrawal from the plan. The employer must maintain a specific amount in escrow or a corresponding bond for five years from the date of withdrawal. If the plan terminates during this five-year period, the bond or escrow is applied toward any underfunding. However, § 4063(e) authorizes the PBGC to waive this liability if the sponsors of the plan have an appropriate indemnity agreement, and the PBGC can make alternative arrangements to satisfy the obligation (see § 4067).

The proposal introduces a new term, "active participant base," to describe the baseline number of active participants to be used to determine if there has been a 20% reduction. Section 4062(e) applies to cessation of operations at a facility in any location, even if the employer continues or resumes the operations somewhere else. If the discontinuance is the result of employee action (e.g., a strike or sick-out), then the cessation date is delayed until after the employee action ends; the employer is given a week to resume work. For sudden and unanticipated events not caused by employee action (e.g., natural disasters), the cessation date is deferred for 30 days so work can resume.

The 60-day period for notice does not begin until both cessation and reduction in the number of employees have occurred. Only current employees are included in calculating the number of participants just before cessation. However, an employee does not have to accrue benefits to be considered a participant: the PBGC does not want employers to be able to benefit from plan freezes. [PBGC, *Liability for Termination of Single-Employer Plans; Treatment of Substantial Cessation of Operations*, FR Doc 2010-19695, RIN 1212-AB20, 75 Fed. Reg. 48283 (Aug. 10, 2010)]

However, in 2012, the PBGC launched a pilot program under which § 4062(e) would not be enforced against companies that are small (fewer than 100 participants) or credit-worthy, so that the PBGC can concentrate its enforcement efforts on the truly risky plans. [R. Randall Tracht, Brian J. Dougherty, Lisa H. Barton, and Eric P. Sarabia, *PBGC Changes Enforcement Policy Under ERISA Section 4062(e)* Morgan, Lewis & Bockius (Nov. 13, 2012) (benefitslink.com)]

In 2009, the PBGC made another controversial proposal, this time to reduce the availability of waivers of the reporting requirements. In April 2013, the PBGC published a new proposal, under which reporting obligations would be reduced significantly, so that financially sound plans would not have to report most of what would otherwise be reportable events. The PBGC estimated that over 90% of plans and sponsors would no longer have to make most reports.

The 2013 proposal relieves "financially sound" plans and plan sponsors of the obligation to report. Financial soundness means satisfying five criteria for meeting obligations in full and on time. The primary criterion is the "credit report test"—the company must have a credit rating from a commercial credit reporting company that indicates stability. Financially sound plans would not have to make a post-event report for most of the events already covered by a funding-based waiver—for example, an extraordinary dividend or stock redemption; reduction in active participants; transfer of benefit liabilities. Commercial credit reporting companies such as Dun & Bradstreet usually consider the business' ability to pay its debts as the main test of financial soundness, whereas credit rating agencies focus on the company's financial statements. The PBGC considers ability to pay debts to be a more accurate gauge.

The other four criteria are safe use of secured debt; two years of positive net income; two years without defaulting on a major loans; and two years of keeping current on pension plan contributions (other than quarterly contributions for which the duty to report has been waived).

The proposal also provides another safe harbor where reporting would be waived, if the plan either was fully funded on a termination basis at the end of the previous year, or was 120% funded on a premium basis for the previous year. Plans with fewer than 100 participants would be given an extra month to report events eligible for these safe harbors.

As a general rule, there is a reportable event when the number of participants falls below 80% of the number of participants at the end of the previous year or below 75% of the number at the beginning of the previous year, but the proposal waives reporting of this event for small (fewer than 100 participant) plans. Larger plans would only have to report if the reduction was caused by a single event such as reorganization or mass layoff; if the reduction occurred in a period of 30 days or less; or if the number of participants in the same year falls more than 20%. Large plans can use the financial soundness safe harbor to avoid reporting based on reduction in the number of participants.

The proposal retains the Technical Update 13-1 relief (i.e., reporting of missed contributions is waived or reduced for plans with under 100 participants as long as the reason for missing the contribution was not inability to pay).

The proposal says that there are other reporting obligations that let the PBGC know about a plan's liquidity levels, so reporting is waived for missed contributions that reflect inability to pay benefits when due—unless the plan is exempt from the liquidity shortfall provisions. But reporting is not waived for small plans or under the financial soundness safe harbor.

Prior law required reporting of distributions of more than $10,000 in any year to substantial owners of the sponsor company, unless the plan is fully funded. The proposal does not require reporting of this event unless one substantial owner receives distributions that exceed 1% of plan assets, or distributions to all substantial owners are greater than 5% of plan assets. If the distribution to substantial owner(s) takes the form of an annuity and reporting is required, it is only necessary to make one report, unless the annuity changes.

Reporting is not required if there has been a reorganization within a controlled group of corporations leading to one member of the group ceasing to exist because it has been merged into another member of the group.

However, the proposal eliminates the funding-based waiver for reporting liquidation, and reporting is not waived either for small plans or under the financial soundness safe harbor.

Prior law makes it a reportable event if 3% or more of a plan's benefit liabilities are transferred within a 12-month period. The proposed regulations make it clear that satisfying benefit liabilities by paying a lump sum or buying an annuity is not a transfer of benefit liabilities for this purpose.

Under the proposal, reporting continues to be required when the plan applies for a minimum funding waiver and the small-plan and financial soundness safe harbors are not available.

Prior law made it a reportable event when there is a default in payment of over 30 days on a loan of $10 million or more—not only by the plan sponsor, but also by any member of a controlled group of corporations it belongs to. Written notice of default based on reduced cash reserves or a lender's acceleration of a loan is also a reportable event. The proposed regulations not only retain this requirement but make it stronger: reporting is required when there is a loan acceleration or any kind of default, including a lender's waiver of its right to declare a default. Small plans and plans entitled to the financial soundness safe harbor must still report this event.

The proposed regulations eliminate the sponsor's bankruptcy as a reportable event because there are many other reliable sources of bankruptcy information available to the PBGC. Reporting of insolvency is not waived, however, for small plans or plans meeting the financial soundness safe harbor.

If this proposal is finalized, there would be for most situations, only six reportable events:

- Loan default;
- Failure to make required contributions;
- Applying for a funding waiver;
- Not being able to pay benefits as they fall due;
- Being insolvent;
- Liquidation.

For the second half of 2014, the PBGC suspended § 4062(e) enforcement. Businesses were told to report new § 4062(e) events as they occurred, but the PBGC said no action would be taken on the reports at least until the end of the year. The PBGC needed the extra time to work with stakeholders to determine which plans are genuinely at risk. [PBGC Press Release No. 14-09, *PBGC Issues Moratorium on 4062(e) Enforcement*, <http://www.pbgc.gov/news/press/releases/pr14-09.html?cid=CPAD01PRJUL0820141> (July 8, 2014)]

The PBGC retains the power to grant waivers of the reporting requirements in meritorious cases. The 2013 proposal takes the requirements for documentation of reportable events out of the regulations; only the instructions for the reporting form will provide the reporting requirements. However, the rule requires that whatever reportable event notifications are required must be done electronically rather than on paper. The PBGC asked for comments on the pros and cons of this plan.

The PBGC stipulated a January 1, 2014 effective date [78 Fed. Reg. 20039 (Apr. 3, 2013); see Rebecca Moore, *PBGC Proposes Reduced Reporting Obligations*, plansponsor.com (Apr. 2, 2013); Buck Consultants FYI, *PBGC Reproposes Reportable Event Rules* (Apr. 5, 2013) (benefitslink.com)]

The PBGC offered further guidance in May, 2013, defining a creditworthy company as one whose unsecured debt is rated at least Baa3 by Moody's or BBB- by Standard & Poor's. If the company's debt does not have a rating, it is considered creditworthy if its D&B Financial Stress Score is at least 1477 and its secured debt (other than debt to buy real estate or equipment) does not exceed 10% of asset value. However, a company will not be considered creditworthy if the Office of Negotiations and Restructuring finds signs of financial weakness such as lack of ongoing operations or engaging in transactions that will lead to a downgrade. If the PBGC enters into a § 4062(e) settlement, it will suspend obligations under the agreement if the company achieves financial soundness at any time during the five-year period of supervision, but the obligations will be reinstated if the company ceases to be financially sound. [PLC Employee Benefits & Employee Compensation, *PBGC Releases Enforcement Guidelines for ERISA Section 4062(e) Financial Assurance Program* (May 3, 2013) (benefitslink.com)]

CHAPTER 11

COMMUNICATIONS WITH EMPLOYEES AND REGULATORS

§ 11.01 INTRODUCTION

Although ERISA does not require corporations to have employee benefit plans at all, if they choose to implement plans, there are many rules that must be followed, including procedural rules. Plan participants must be given enough information from the plan itself to understand their benefits—especially benefits available in multiple forms—so that informed choices must be made.

The Summary Plan Description (SPD) is the main document for communications between the plan and its participants, although other documents may also be required, for example when the terms of the plan are altered. If the plan is materially modified, or if there are changes in the information given in the SPD, the plan administrator has a duty to give participants a Summary of Material Modifications (SMM).

For a calendar-year plan that has undergone a material modification, the SMM must be sent to participants and beneficiaries by July 27 of the following year. Fiscal-year plans have until the 210th day after the end of the plan year.

The due date for the Form 5500 is July 31 (calendar-year plans) and the last day of the seventh month of the plan year after the plan year being reported, for plans that have a fiscal year. This is also the reporting schedule for individual statements of deferred vested benefits, to be sent to plan participants whose employment terminated during the plan year and who were entitled to deferred vested benefits at the time of termination.

For defined benefit plans only, the PBGC Form 1 is due on September 15 (calendar year plans) or eight and a half months after the close of the plan fiscal year being reported on. For most defined benefit plans, the PPA has replaced the former requirement of issuing a Summary Annual Report with an Annual Funding Notice: see § 11.03, below.

The DOL's *Reporting and Disclosure Guide for Employee Benefit Plans* [<http://www.dol.gov/ebsa/pdf/rdguide.pdf> (Aug. 2013)>] is a 11-page chart that, for a variety of documents, lists in tabular form the kind of information covered; who receives it; and when it must be provided. Numerous documents are included, such as the SPD, SMM, various COBRA notices, and QDRO notices.

Magistrate Judge Denlow allowed Verizon relief from the consequences of a typographical error that led to a class claim of $1.6 billion. When Verizon acquired Bell Atlantic, the new plan was incorrectly drafted: the lawyer drafting the plan included a multiplier in the middle of a sentence, and forgot to delete it from the end of the sentence, so that plan participants argued that they were entitled to have the multiplier applied twice. The magistrate judge allowed correction of the "scrivener's error" because applying the multiplier twice would give plan participants a windfall. His decision was affirmed by the Seventh Circuit in mid-2010. [*Young v. Verizon's Bell Atl. Cash Balance Plan*, 615 F.3d 808 (7th Cir. 2010); Alison Frankel, *Verizon Defeats Billion-Dollar ERISA Class Action Over Lawyer's Typo*, The American Lawyer (Nov. 5, 2009) (law.com) and

In the Case of the Billion-Dollar ERISA Typo, 7th Circuit Upholds Win for Verizon, The American Lawyer (Aug. 13, 2010) (law.com). The Supreme Court refused to hear the case: *cert. denied,* No. 10-765 (May 23, 2011), *reh'g denied,* July 25, 2011.]

Previously, sponsors often used the IRS letter forwarding service to find payees of benefits. For requests postmarked on or after August 31, 2012, however, Rev. Proc. 2012-35, 2012-37 I.R.B. 341 announces that the IRS no longer considers finding missing persons a "humane purpose." Employers must therefore devise other means of finding the payees. The DOL's suggestions are Internet searches, credit reports, and commercial locater services. The Social Security Administration's forwarding service is still available, but at a cost of $25 per letter, whereas the IRS service was free for up to 50 participants. If the plan is terminating, it can use the PBGC's missing participants program, which requires the employer to submit the amount of the benefit to the PBGC, which looks for participants in connection with the termination. The Pension Protection Act mandated that the PBGC extend the program to non-defined benefit plans (e.g., 401(k)s) that terminate, but the PBGC never issued implementing regulations. [McDermott Will & Emery, *IRS Eliminates Use of Letter Forwarding Service to Find Missing Participants and Beneficiaries* (Sept. 27, 2012) (benefitslink.com)]

Plan documents should state whether it is permissible to pay plan expenses out of the plan's assets. If the document does not give this information, then it is allowable to use plan assets to pay plan expenses unless the plan document obligates the employer to pay the expenses. However, an employer that retained the right to amend the plan can adopt an amendment allowing payment of expenses in the future. An individual account plan can specify the way to allocate expenses paid by the plan to the participants' accounts. An allocation method described in the plan is a settlor decision, so the fiduciary must abide by it. If the plan does not specify, or if it is unclear, the fiduciaries must adopt a reasonable allocation method.

Assets of an ERISA plan can be used to pay expenses that are considered "fiduciary" expenses, but not those considered to be "settlor" expenses. For example, the plan can pay for recordkeeping, accounting, legal services dealing with fiduciary issues, trustee services, custodial services, annual or other periodic compliance audits, completion of legally mandated forms such as Form 5500, processing claims, and communicating with participants, including furnishing required disclosures such as SPDs and benefit statements and furnishing documents requested by plan participants and beneficiaries. Expenses for investment advice, educational seminars, and providing electronic access to plan information can also be paid out of plan assets. So can management fees and sales charges for plan investments.

However, settlor expenses that cannot be paid out of plan assets include, e.g., legal services for setting up a plan; costs of plan design; legal fees for plan termination; and most actuarial services used for planning.

If a communication relates to more than one plan, or includes non-plan information, allocation will be required. [Andree M. St. Martin and Jennifer E. Eller, *Paying Employee Benefit Plan Expenses Chart*, Practical Law Co. (benefitslink.com) (chart giving the source for the treatment of various items)]

[A] Communications Requirements Under PPACA

The health care reform act, the Patient Protection and Affordable Care Act of 2010 (PPACA) adds a number of communications and compliance requirements, covering both data that must be provided to plan participants and data to be submitted to regulators. Many of the provisions of PPACA require notices to be furnished, either to specific participants, or as a part of the plan's general benefits materials. Many plans include these notices in the annual enrollment package or the plan's SPD.

All plans, including grandfathered plans, must offer a one-time special enrollment period for adult children who were not covered because of age, or who aged out of the plan, and for persons who lost coverage because they reached the plan's maximum coverage, and notice must be given of the special enrollment period.

PPACA also requires notices of:

- Grandfathered status.
- Patient Protection Model Notice: If the plan requires participants to designate a primary care provider, how to choose one; notice that female enrollees can see an OB/GYN without prior authorization or referral. (Not required for grandfathered plans.)
- Explanation of the external review process; many plans include this in the SPD. (Not required for grandfathered plans.)
- Notice of internal adverse benefit determination.
- Advance notice that coverage will be cancelled or rescinded. [Christy Tinnes and Brigen Winters, *What Notices Are Required by PPACA?*, plansponsor.com (Sept. 21, 2010)]

Another PPACA requirement is notifying all eligible employees of their right to maintain EGHP enrollment of their children up to age 26. In order to remain grandfathered, a grandfathered plan must include an explanation of why the plan is grandfathered in all plan materials that are distributed to existing employees, new hires, and COBRA beneficiaries. The notice must be repeated for each year that the plan maintains grandfathered status, although it can be incorporated into the open enrollment materials furnished to employees and COBRA beneficiaries. [Ben Cohen, Kushner & Company, *Required Health Plan Annual*

Notices—2010 Edition, <http://www.kushnerco.com/article.php?fileName=Adult-Child>]

The PPACA requires the employer to give each employee a summary of benefits and coverage (SBC) that explains (in understandable form) the covered benefits, exclusions, cost sharing, and continuation coverage aspects of the plan. A penalty of $1,000 per violation is imposed for non-compliance with this disclosure requirement.

Final Regulations on the Code § 6055 requirements for minimum essential health coverage were published on March 10, 2014. The regulations explain the requirements imposed on companies with 50 or more full-time employees to report to the IRS and to employees about health care coverage available to employees. The requirements will be used by the IRS to enforce the pay-or-play mandate once it takes effect, and to administer the tax credit that certain individuals will receive for buying health care coverage on an Exchange under Code § 36B.

The penalty for not providing coverage will not be imposed on companies with 50-99 employees until 2016, but reporting under § 6056 is nonetheless required for 2015. Information is reported to employees on Form 1095-C, then transmitted to the IRS on Form 1094-C. E-filing is mandatory for employers who are required to file 250 or more tax returns. Notice to employees can be given electronically if the employees agree. Employers that sponsor self-funded plans can use Form 1094-C to combine reporting for §§ 6055 and 6056.

Failure to satisfy these reporting requirements can be penalized under § 6721 (failure to file required information returns) and § 6722 (failure to provide payees with reports). However, if there is reasonable cause, § 6724 may offer relief by waiving penalties. There is a special transition rule for returns and statements filed in 2016 dealing with 2015 coverage: penalties will not be imposed for incorrect or incomplete information, but relief will not be granted if employers fail to make required reports, or if they do not attempt in good faith to comply. [79 Fed. Reg. 13220 (Mar. 10, 2014); see Chadron J. Patton, *Final Regulations Streamline ACA Reporting Rules*, Spencer Fane Britt & Browne (Mar. 13, 2014), available at Lexology.com]

An information return is prepared for each employee, then the returns are transmitted to the IRS. For insured plans, the insurer prepares Form 1095-B (for individuals) and Form 1094-B (transmission form to the IRS). Self-insured small employers also use these forms, whereas applicable large employers with self-insured health plans use Form 1095-C to report to employees and Form 1094-C as a transmittal form.

An applicable large employer is one that had at least 50 full-time or full-time equivalent employees in the year before the year of the report. The Form 1095-C contains information that the IRS uses to determine whether the employer met the requirement of offering its employees adequate coverage (i.e., satisfying the standards not only for adequacy of benefits, but for affordability).

For the 2015 plan year, employers with more than 50 but fewer than 100 employees will not be subject to the employer mandate penalty—but must nevertheless file Forms 1095-C and 1094-C.

The due date for giving employees the appropriate 1095-series form is January 31. If the employee agrees, the statement can be sent electronically rather than in hard copy. In most cases, the employer will have to e-file the form with the IRS, with a due date of March 31; the rare cases of paper filing with the IRS are subject to a February 28 due date. [Bill O'Malley and Jill Harris, *New Information Reporting Requirements Under the Affordable Care Act*, McGladrey Tax Alert, (Aug. 7, 2014)]

The Summary of Benefits and Coverage can be distributed electronically to plan participants and beneficiaries who are already covered by an EGHP. DOL electronic disclosure requirements must be satisfied. For eligible people who are not yet enrolled (e.g., newly hired employees), the SBC can be distributed electronically in a readily accessible format, but the plan must make free hard copies available on request. If the electronic distribution occurs via a Website, then the employer must send written notice or e-mail to give the URL for the site and tell employees that they can request free hard copies. [Tracey Giddings and Birgit Anne Waidmann, *Administration Issues Final Rules on PPACA Summary of Benefits and Coverage*, PricewaterhouseCooper HRS Insight No. 12/06 (Feb. 14, 2012) (benefitslink.com)] Almost all (86%) of employers use electronic distribution for the Summary of Benefits and Coverage (SBC; the summary of the various health plan options offered by the employer), especially because many employers offer a large number of coverage alternatives, making paper distribution impractical. About half of employers had to produce more than 10 separate SBCs, and more than a quarter had to provide 25–100 different SBCs. Nearly half of the companies (41%) distributed both paper and electronic SBCs, and 14% used paper only. [Kevin McGuinness, *Many Using Electronic Distribution for SBCs*, plansponsor.com (Apr. 29, 2013)]

As of January 1, 2014, large employers that offer health insurance must automatically enroll employees in the EGHP, and employees must be given reasonable advance notice and the opportunity to choose different levels of coverage that are available, or to opt out. For plan years beginning on or after January 2, 2014, EGHPs may not impose waiting periods that exceed 90 days.

No later than January 1, 2011, administrators of self-insured plans (and health insurers) must report to the HHS on the "loss ratios"—the amount of premiums devoted to paying claims rather than administrative expenses. In the large group market, if the loss ratio falls below 85%, the plan must give each enrollee a pro rata rebate each year.

Another implication of PPACA is that employers have a duty to inform laid-off employees that they can purchase health insurance on the Exchange instead of making a COBRA election. Individuals can purchase Exchange coverage outside the open enrollment period if they undergo an event affecting their insured status, such as job loss. However, employees who want to keep the same doctors might prefer COBRA coverage to Exchange coverage. Another factor is that low- or moderate-income individuals may qualify for a federal subsidy if they purchase Exchange coverage. [Louise Radnofsky, *Employers Must Notify Laid-Off Workers of Health Care Options, New Rule Says*, WSJ.com (May 2, 2014)]

§ 11.02 SUMMARY PLAN DESCRIPTION (SPD)

[A] Basic Requirements

ERISA § 102 imposes a duty on the plan administrator to furnish a copy of the Summary Plan Description (SPD) to each participant and to each beneficiary receiving benefits under the plan. The SPD must be furnished within 90 days of the time a person becomes a participant or first receives benefits. (For a new plan, the SPD can be furnished within 120 days of the time the plan comes under Title I of ERISA, if this is later than the 90-day period.)

ERISA § 102 requires the SPD to be written in a way that can be understood by the average plan participant. The document must be accurate and comprehensive enough to inform them of their rights and obligations. ERISA requires the following items to be included in the SPD:

- The formal and common names of the plan;
- The name and address of the employer (or of the organization maintaining a collectively bargained plan);
- The employer's EIN and the plan's IRS identification number;
- What kind of plan it is;
- How the plan is administered—e.g., by contract or by an insurer;
- The name and address of the agent for service of process (the person designated to receive summonses, complaints, subpoenas, and related litigation documents);
- A statement that process can be served not only on this designated agent, but also on the plan's administrator or trustee;
- The name, address, and title of each trustee;
- Disclosure of whether the plan is a collectively bargained plan, and a statement that the participant can examine the collective bargaining agreement or get a copy of the agreement from the plan administrator;
- Rules of eligibility for participation;
- The plan's normal retirement age;

- Circumstances under which plan benefits can be altered or suspended;
- How to waive the normal payment mechanism (the Qualified Joint and Survivor Annuity) and elect a different payment form, such as a lump sum;
- Procedures for QDROs and QMCSOs, either through a description in the SPD itself or disclosure that a free copy of a separate document will be provided on request;
- A description of the circumstances under which the plan can be terminated, the rights of participants and beneficiaries after termination occurs, and the circumstances under which benefits can be denied or suspended; what will happen to the plan's assets upon termination. (All amendments must be made with the necessary corporate governance steps, such as adoption of a resolution by the Board of Directors);
- If the plan benefits are insured by the PBGC; if they are not, the reason why insurance is not required; if they are, a disclosure that PBGC insurance is in place, how it works, and where to get more information (from the plan administrator or the PBGC; the PBGC's address must be given in the SPD);
- An explanation of the plan's rules for determining service to calculate vesting and breaks in service;
- Do the contributions to the plan come exclusively from the employer, or are employee contributions accepted or mandated?
- Method of calculating the contribution. (A defined benefit plan is allowed to simply say that the amount is "actuarially determined");
- The funding medium and entity for the plan. Usually this will be a trust fund, but sometimes an insurance company is involved;
- The plan's fiscal year;
- How to present a claim for plan benefits;
- If the plan will use the "cutback" rule to change the vesting or accrual rules described in the SPD, participants must be informed which provisions of the plan are subject to modification; when modified, the nature of the modification must be explained;
- Remedies that are available if a claim is denied;
- A statement of the rights of participants and beneficiaries and what protections are available for those rights. A model statement that can be used for this purpose is published at 29 C.F.R. § 2520.102-3.

After reviewing public comments, EBSA decided that the current disclosure requirements give enough information about cash balance conversions and operations, so it was not necessary to impose any special requirements.

SPDs must be given to participants and beneficiaries within 90 days after they achieve that status. For a new plan, all participants must get an SPD 12 days after the plan becomes subject to ERISA reporting and disclosure requirements. If a company offers different benefits to different groups of SPDs, the company can issue a separate SPD for each group.

■ **TIP:** If a significant percentage of the participants in a plan are not literate in English, but are literate in the same non-English language, the SPD must include a notice in that language offering assistance in understanding the English SPD. In this context, a significant percentage means over 25% of the participants in a plan with fewer than 100 total participants, or the lesser of 10% of the participants or 500 people in a large plan.

The best distribution methods are handing the SPDs to the employees at the workplace, or mailing them to employees' homes. It isn't enough to put them out in the workplace, because there's no guarantee that employees will take them.

The Second Circuit held in late 2013 that an SPD was inaccurate because it did not state clearly that distribution of lump sums would reduce the benefit—only that it might. [*Frommert v. Conkright*, 738 F.3d 522 (2d Cir. 2013); see Kevin McGuinness, *Appellate Court Remands Case on Offsetting Pension Benefits*, plansponsor.com (Dec. 31, 2013)]

When Verizon purchased a single-premium group annuity contract from Prudential Insurance to settle about $7.4 billion in liabilities to 41,000 retirees, retirees brought an ERISA § 102(b) class action. The suit charged Verizon with failure to disclose in the SPD that the company retained the right to remove participants from the plan by transferring pension obligations to an insurance company. The District Court for the Northern District of Texas held that § 102(b) merely requires disclosure of the existing terms of the plan, not changes in the future. [*Lee v. Verizon Commc'ns Inc.*, No. 3:12-CV-4834-d (N.D. Tex. June 24, 2013); see Kevin McGuinness, *Court Dismisses Verizon Pension Buyout Suit*, plansponsor.com (June 25, 2013)]

The SPD can also be distributed as an insert in an employee periodical such as one published by the company or the union. If you choose this option, be sure to put a prominent notice on the front page of the periodical, stating that this issue contains an insert that has important legal consequences, and that it should be retained for reference and not discarded.

■ **TIP:** The statement of participant rights required by ERISA can be incorporated into the SPD.

If a plan is amended—and most are, sooner or later—the plan administrator must issue an updated SPD every five years (measured from the time the plan first became subject to ERISA) reflecting the changes of the past five years. Even if there are no changes at all, the administrator must provide an updated SPD to all participants every 10 years.

If there are any false statements in the SPD, ERISA disclosure regulations have been violated, and the employer could face penalties from the Department of Labor. Most plan participants never see the trust documents for the plan, so they get their information from the SPD.

Until mid-2011, there was a split in authority about which provisions should prevail if the SPD contradicted the plan terms. The Supreme Court settled the question in the very important mid-2011 *Amara v. Cigna* decision, holding that the terms of the plan prevail over the SPD, because the plan terms reflect the intentions of the settlor that adopted the plan. [*Amara v. Cigna*, 131 S. Ct. 1866 (May 23, 2011), *on remand*, No. 3:01cv 2361 (JBA) (D. Conn. Dec. 20, 2012). See, however, *Koehler v. Aetna Health Inc.*, 683 F.3d 182 (5th Cir. 2012) holding that even post-*Amara*, SPDs must be drafted so participants can understand them—so ambiguities in the plan and SPD must be resolved in favor of the plan participant.]

A 2012 Sixth Circuit plaintiff alleged that her survivor benefits were incorrectly calculated because of a conflict with the SPD. The SPD defines the survivor benefit was 50% of the participant's pension reduced by 50% of the surviving spouse's Social Security benefit, with a minimum benefit of $140 a month. However, the plan document says that 50% of the pension is reduced by 50% of the Social Security benefit, without regard to any offset imposed by law. The Social Security Administration pays only the higher of the old age or the widow's benefit to a person entitled to both. The plaintiff said that Social Security paid her only $458 as surviving spouse. The Sixth Circuit held that SPD language can control over conflicting plan terms—but omitting something from an SPD does not alter the terms of the plan. The Sixth Circuit found that the omission from the SPD was not misleading and the discrepancy between the two provisions was not severe enough to constitute a conflict. [*Lipker v. AK Steel*, 698 F.3d 923 (6th Cir. 2012); see Rebecca Moore, *SPD Omission Not a Conflict with Plan Terms*, plansponsor.com (Dec. 21, 2012)]

[B] Health Plan SPDs

ERISA § 104(b)(1)(B) requires that plan participants and beneficiaries be notified within 60 days of a material reduction in the services provided under an Employee Group Health Plan (EGHP). Or the plan sponsor can simply provide notices at regular intervals, not more than 90 days apart, of changes in the interim. The SPD for an EGHP must indicate if a health insurer is responsible for financing or administration (including claims payment). If an insurer is involved, the insurer's name and address must appear in the SPD.

Group health plans SPDs must include the following:

- Participants' responsibility for cost-sharing (premiums, deductibles, coinsurance, copayments);
- Lifetime or annual caps on plan benefits; any other benefit limits;
- Procedures for Qualified Medical Child Support Orders (QMCSOs);
- Coverage of preventive services;
- Coverage (if any) of established and new drugs;
- Coverage of medical tests, devices, and procedures;
- Which health care providers are part of the network, and how the network is created;
- Circumstances under which network providers must be used; coverage, if any, for out-of-network services;
- How primary care and specialty providers must be selected;
- Conditions for getting emergency care;
- Requirements for preauthorization of treatment and utilization review;
- Information about the required length of hospital stays for childbirth, including descriptions of the federal law and any additional protection furnished by state law;
- Either a description of claims procedures or a statement that a free copy of the claims procedure is available on request;
- The role of health insurance in the plan; the EBSA says "particularly in those cases where the plan is self-funded and an insurer is serving as contract administrator or claims payor, rather than as an insurer";
- Extent to which the sponsor has the right to eliminate benefits or terminate the plan;
- Participants' rights under ERISA.

The SPD can include only a general description of the provider network, as long as the SPD explains that a separate document, available without charge, lists all the network providers.

A health plan's SPD must describe employees' and their families' COBRA rights:

- What constitutes a qualifying event;
- Premiums ex-employees must pay for continuation coverage;
- Notice procedures;
- How to make a COBRA election;
- How long coverage will last.

The SPD for an EGHP must either describe the plan's procedures for validating Qualified Medical Child Support Orders (QMSCO), or must inform participants that a free copy of the plan's QMCSO procedures is available on request. The description should be complete enough to assist potential alternate payees in asserting their rights.

A welfare benefit plan must also have an SPD, containing information such as:

- Plan name;
- Employer's name and address;
- EIN and plan number for annual reporting purposes;
- Contact information for the plan administrator;
- Information about the trustees;
- Who is eligible to participate in the plan;
- Claims procedure;
- Statement of participants' rights under ERISA;
- Where to serve process;
- (For EGHPs) Information about COBRA coverage and HIPAA's rules about preexisting condition limitations.

Failure to provide a participant with a copy of the SPD within 30 days of a request is subject to a penalty of $110 a day.

However, welfare benefit plan participants are entitled to SPDs only if they are "covered by the plan," which happens on the earliest of these dates:

- The date the plan says participation begins;
- The date the person becomes eligible to receive a benefit subject to contingencies such as incurring medical expenses;
- The date of the initial voluntary or mandatory plan contribution.

Therefore, SPDs (and SMMs) must be furnished to employees; retirees covered under the plan; the parent or guardian of a minor child who is the "alternate recipient" under a QMCSO; and spouses or other dependents of deceased participants. Although ERISA doesn't say this, some court decisions require SPDs to be furnished to guardians or other representatives of incapacitated beneficiaries.

Health plans must inform the Centers for Medicare and Medicaid Services (CMS), which plan participants and beneficiaries are eligible for Medicare; and whether the plan offers prescription drug benefits that are at least actuarially equivalent to the coverage under Medicare Part D, the prescription drug program.

Actuarially equivalent benefits are referred to as "creditable coverage." (Employers that offer an actuarially equivalent plan may also be able to collect a federal subsidy; see Chapter 9.) The notice must be given at least once a year, before the start of the annual Medicare enrollment period, which is now October 15–December 7 of each year. (The period was extended and moved to earlier in the year by the PPACA.)

Notice must also be given when an employee who is eligible for Medicare enrolls in the health plan, although this can be included in the new-hire package; on request; and when the plan's coverage either becomes creditable or ceases to be creditable.

[See § 11.01[A] for discussion of disclosure requirements added by PPACA (the health care reform bill)]

§ 11.03 SUMMARY ANNUAL REPORT (SAR)/ANNUAL FUNDING NOTICE

One of the administrator's more complex tasks is preparing the plan's annual report, usually on Form 5500. This information is then used to draft the Summary Annual Reports (SARs) that must be distributed to defined contribution plan participants.

The administrator has nine months from the end of the plan year (or two months after the end of the extension, if an extension was granted for filing the underlying Form 5500). DOL regulations [29 C.F.R. § 2520.104b-10(d); see 68 Fed. Reg. 16400 (Apr. 3, 2003)] provide a simple "fill in the blanks" form that must be used for the SAR.

The SAR form consists of a basic financial statement about the plan and its expenses, the net value of plan assets, and whether the plan's assets appreciated or depreciated in value during the year. If the plan is subject to the minimum funding standard, the plan must disclose either that contributions were adequate to satisfy the requirement, or the amount of the deficit. Participants must also be informed of their right to receive additional information, including a copy of the full annual report, a statement of the plan's assets and liabilities, or a statement of the plan's income and expenses. Plans that have simplified reporting requirements can use alternative compliance methods to satisfy the SAR requirement.

Yet another feature of the PPA is that, for most defined benefit plans, the SAR has been replaced by the Annual Funding Notice [ERISA § 101(f) as amended by PPA § 501]. (More precisely, the annual funding notice is required from most defined benefit plans that are subject to PBGC jurisdiction; certain government and church plans and small professional service corporation plans are not insured by the PBGC and continue to issue the SAR.) Before the PPA, multi-employer plans had to issue annual funding notices, but single-employer plans did not.

Notice must be given within 120 days of the end of the plan year (for plans with 100 or more participants) or by the extended date for filing Form 5500 (for smaller plans), to each participant and beneficiary and union, and to the PBGC. However, the PBGC will not take enforcement action against a plan whose liabilities exceed its assets by $50 million or less, as long as the plan provides the mandatory information within 30 days of a request from the PBGC.

DOL issued proposed regulations, RIN 1210-AB 18, in November, 2010, about the annual funding notice. The rule applies to about 29,500 plans, with about 43.9 million participants. The notice must include:

- Plan's funding percentage;
- Funding target attainment percentage for past three years;
- Information about the value of the plan's assets and liabilities, determined as of the date for determining the funding percentage;
- The plan's investment policy and how the assets were invested on the last day of the plan year;
- Description of plan benefits eligible to be guaranteed by the PBGC (and limitations on the guarantee);
- Number of plan participants, divided into three groups: active workers, retired and separated employees already receiving benefits, retired and separated employees not yet receiving benefits;
- Information about material events during the year in which the notice is distributed (i.e., the year after the notice year)—events that are likely to increase or decrease the plan's assets or liabilities by 5% or more, or that are identified by the plan's actuary as having a material effect on the funded percentage;
- A summary of the plan termination rules;
- An explanation of how the participant or beneficiary can obtain a copy of the filed Form 5500 for the plan;
- Disclosure if the plan sponsor had to make a § 4010 filing with the PBGC.

The general requirement is that the notice is to be given within 120 days of the close of the plan year. However, if the plan has 100 or fewer participants, the notice can be given no later than the filing date for the plan's annual report (including any extensions). The proposal includes a model notice form. [75 Fed. Reg. 70625 (Nov. 18, 2010), effective January 18, 2011; EBSA Fact Sheet, *Annual Funding Notice for Defined Benefit Plans* (Nov. 18, 2010) (benefitslink.com),]

The Moving Ahead for Progress in the 21st Century Act (Pub. L. No. 112-141, aka MAP-21) helps the sponsors of defined benefit plans by allowing them to calculate their contributions using more favorable interest rate assumptions.

However, plans that take advantage of this assistance have additional disclosure obligations. MAP-21 requires plan administrators to disclose additional information if the plan had 50 or more participants on any day of the preceding plan year; the stabilized funding target is less than 95% of the regular funding target; and the plan would have a funding shortfall of $500,000 or more absent stabilization. If all three of those factors are present, the plan's Annual Funding Notice must disclose that the law has changed reducing the employer's contribution. The notice must include a table showing MAP-21's effect on funding requirements, plan's funding shortfall, and the minimum contribution for the current year and the two years before. [Rebecca Moore, *Congress Passes Bill With Pension Funding Relief*, plansponsor.com (June 29, 2012); Buck Consultants FYI, *2012 Pension Plan Funding Stabilization Finally a Reality* (July 6, 2012) (benefitslink.com) (The Highway & Transportation Funding Act of 2014, Pub. L. No. 113-159, extends the period for which defined benefit plan sponsors can get relief from the implications of low interest rates; this legislation does not alter the employer's disclosure obligations.)]

§ 11.04 INDIVIDUAL ACCOUNT PLAN DISCLOSURES

Defined contribution plans must give their participants a variety of notices:

- Safe harbor 401(k) plan's annual notice about the features of the plan, such as the safe harbor non-elective contribution or matching contribution of the plan; this must be given 30–90 days before the beginning of the plan year;
- Qualified Automatic Contribution Arrangement (QACA) safe harbor 401(k) plans must provide an annual notice on the same schedule;
- Qualified Default Investment Alternative (QDIA) notice of rights and obligations, such as the participant's right to transfer the account to other investments, and when funds will be invested in the QDIA; must be provided at least 30 days before the beginning of the plan year;
- 401(k) automatic enrollment notice, providing information such as deferrals made without an affirmative election, and how the plan invests contributions where there is no election; must be provided 30–90 days before the beginning of the plan year;
- Employer stock diversification notice: information about the right to transfer the participant's investment from employer stock into other investments (if the employer's stock is publicly traded). The notice must be given no later than 30 days before the first date that diversification rights can be issued.

In general, two or more notices can be combined into a single document as long as the time requirements are satisfied. Electronic distribution is permissible if the electronic disclosure requirements are satisfied—but the defined contribution plan requirements cannot be satisfied in the SPD even if it is distributed annually.

The IRS will generally treat a plan as having lost its status as a 401(k) safe harbor plan if it fails to provide a timely annual safe harbor plan notice for a year. If this status is lost, the plan must satisfy the nondiscrimination requirements from which it was exempted. This could limit highly compensated employees' ability to defer compensation, or could require the plan sponsor to refund some amounts already deferred. Penalties could also be imposed for failure to provide the automatic enrollment or QACA notice. Failure to give timely QCIA notice forfeits fiduciary protection of the sponsor, plan administrator, or investment company for investment loss. Protection is only restored for amounts invested in the QDIA after compliance with the notice requirements. [McKenna Long & Aldridge LLP, *2011 Year-End Disclosure Reminders for Qualified Defined Contribution Plan Sponsors* (November 2011) (benefitslink.com)]

Safe harbor accounts free the employer from having to satisfy the most stringent nondiscrimination standards—as long as minimum contributions are made on behalf of all eligible employees. In 2008–2009, during the financial crisis, interim regulations were adopted allowing employers to reduce or suspend non-elective contributions due to substantial business hardship. Before the interim regulations were adopted, the employer could not reduce or eliminate elective contributions to safe harbor plans in mid-year, although it was permissible to suspend or reduce matching contributions in mid-year on 30 days' notice to participants.

The final regulations published in late 2013 define substantial business hardship as operating at an economic loss; notice to employees is still required. Before these rules were published, many employers thought they could only use the safe harbor if they were bankrupt or close to bankruptcy. As of January 1, 2015, a company operating at a loss can suspend its matching contributions in mid-year. Such contributions can be reduced in mid-year even if the employer is not suffering economic hardship, as long as the right to reduce contributions is reserved in the annual safe harbor notices given to participants. Employers could suspend safe harbor non-elective contributions as soon as the final regulations took effect. The 30 days' notice to employees must inform employees of the effective date of the plan amendment, how the amendment works, and how they can change their elective deferrals. [John Manganaro, *IRS Revises Safe Harbor Plan Rules*, plansponsor.com (Nov. 15, 2013); Marc D. Bussone et al., *IRS Issues Final Regulations On Suspending Or Reducing Safe Harbor 401(k) Contributions*, Bradley Arant Boult Cummins LLP (Nov. 20, 2013), available at Lexology.com]

In recent years, many IRS audits have asked employers for evidence that the 401(k) safe harbor notice was given to participants. Failure to give the safe harbor notice is an operational failure that requires correction under the IRS Self Correction Program; the Employee Plans Compliance Resolution System is not available. Plans that cannot provide the evidence are required to engage in corrections and possibly pay closing agreement sanctions. Plans should protect themselves by keeping dated copies of the notice and cover letter (for electronic communications, the e-mail, the date it was sent, and a list of addressees). If the plan can't provide the evidence, the IRS is requiring corrections and perhaps a closing agreement sanction. [SunGard Relius, *Failure to Provide Safe Harbor Notice Correction* (Nov. 30, 2012) (benefitslink.com)]

The modern trend is for plans to provide participants with a greater degree of control over the way their pension plan accounts are invested. DOL Reg. § 2550.404c-1(b), dealing with "participant directed individual account plans" (profit-sharing, stock bonus, and money purchase plans) obligates plans to offer at least three diversified categories of investments, with materially different risk and return characteristics, so that overall the participant can choose the balance between risk and return that he or she prefers. Plan fiduciaries are not liable if the participant's own investment choices result in losses, unless obeying the participant's instructions violates the terms of the plan.

Participants are entitled to receive a great deal of information in connection with individual account plans. The burden is on the plan to supply the information, not on the individual participant to request it. The mandated disclosures include:

- A description of the available investment alternatives available under the plan; the general risk and return characteristics of each, including the composition of each portfolio and how they are diversified;
- The designated investment managers for each alternative;
- When and how participants can give investment instructions; any limitations imposed on those instructions (for instance, only four changes in investment per year);
- Fees and expenses that affect the participant's account balance;
- Contact information for a fiduciary (or designee of a fiduciary) who can provide additional information about plan investments on request;
- The fact that fiduciaries are not liable if they follow the participant's investment directions, even if losses result;
- (If participants can invest in securities of the employer) Procedures to maintain confidentiality about the participant's voting and tendering shares of employer stock, and contact information for the fiduciary who monitors the confidentiality provisions.

For most 401(k) plans, participants would have been entitled to receive a comparison chart (showing items such as fees and investment performance for the investment alternatives under the plan) by August 30, 2013. However, the Employee Benefits Security Administration (EBSA) announced one-time relief for plan sponsors. For either the 2013 or the 2014 comparison chart, delivery can be deferred so that this disclosure can be made at the same time as other plan disclosures required later in the year. Deferral requires a finding by the responsible plan fiduciary that the delay is in the best interests of participants and beneficiaries. Even if the plan elects to defer delivery, not more than 18 months can be permitted to elapse between charts. [EBSA News, *Labor Department Permits 401(k) Plans to Reschedule Annual Disclosures to Employees*, <http://www.dol.gov/ebsa/newsroom/2013/ebsa072213.html> (July 22, 2013)]

EBSA published an Advance Notice of Proposed Rulemaking (ANPRM) on May 5, 2013, dealing with lifetime income illustrations in defined contribution plans' periodic pension statements. EBSA sought comments on how to present accrued benefits as an estimated lifetime stream of benefits as well as an account balance. EBSA's position is that disclosing the lifetime income stream will help employees prepare for retirement. [EBSA.gov, *Fact Sheet On Lifetime Income Illustration* (May 7, 2013) (benefitslink.com). A calculator for lifetime income streams under these rules was published at <www.dol.gov/ebsa/regs/lifetimeincomecalculator.html>.]

When a participant invests in publicly traded securities and other assets subject to the Securities Act of 1933 [15 U.S.C. § 77a], the participant must be given a prospectus for the investment either before or right after making the investment. If the plan "passes through" to participants the rights to vote and/or tender the shares, the plan must provide the participant with the proxy materials and other relevant documents, and must provide instructions on how to exercise the rights.

The plan further has a duty to disclose, based on the latest information available to the plan, at least this much information (either to all participants, or on request by a participant):

- For each investment alternative, the fees and operating expenses as a percentage of the average net assets of the investment alternative;
- Whatever prospectuses, financial statements, and reports the plan has about the investment alternative;
- A description of the portfolio of each alternative;
- The value of shares in each alternative;
- The current and past performance of each alternative, net of expenses, calculated on a "reasonable and consistent basis";
- The value of the shares in the individual participant's account.

Since 2010, the DOL has been issuing regulations on two important topics: the information that service providers (such as brokers and investment advisers) must give qualified plans about their fees and services—and the way the plan must disseminate this information to plan participants and beneficiaries.

A 2010 EBSA final rule says that investing plan assets is a fiduciary act subject to ERISA § 404(a)(1), requiring fiduciaries to be prudent and act solely in best interests of plan's participants and beneficiaries. If the participants and beneficiaries have investment responsibility for their own accounts, the plan administrator has a duty to ensure that they are informed of their rights and responsibilities in connection with the investments in their accounts, including fee and expense information.

Participants must be given plan-related information before the first date on which they can direct investments, and then each year afterward. Participants must also receive a statement, at least quarterly, disclosing the dollar amount of plan-related fees and expenses actually charged to their accounts, and why. They must receive one-, five-, and ten-year performance data for their investments. Any fees or restrictions on their ability to purchase or withdraw from an investment must be disclosed. Information must be disclosed in a chart or similar format that facilitates comparisons; the final rule includes a model chart that can be used for this purpose. Participants must also be given whatever materials the plan receives with respect to voting, tender, or other rights with respect to the investment.

On request from a participant, the plan administrator must furnish prospectuses, financial reports, and statements of asset value for that particular investment option. The general disclosure rules at 29 C.F.R. § 2520.104b-1, including the electronic disclosure rules, also apply to material furnished under this final rule. [EBSA Fact Sheet, *Final Rule to Improve Transparency of Fees and Expenses to Workers in 401(k)-Type Retirement Plans* (Oct. 20, 2010); see Haynes & Boone, *Final Participant Fee Disclosure Regulations* (Feb. 8, 2011) (benefitslink.com)]

Under DOL's final regulations on disclosure of fees and expenses in participant-directed defined contribution plans, three types of plan information have to be disclosed:

- General plan information,
- Administrative expense information,
- Individual expense information.

As long as the timing requirements are satisfied, the information can be included on the plan's quarterly benefit statements. Certain investment-related information (about fees, expenses, and investment alternatives), in comparative format, must be provided no later than the first date on which participants can direct their investments, and at least once a year after that.

Plan-related information in a pension benefit statement can be given in the same manner as the other information in the statement—including online, if that is otherwise permitted. Investment-related information that is not contained in a pension benefit statement can be provided using the DOL's safe harbor for electronic disclosure or the DOL alternative e-mail method, but not under the IRS electronic disclosure rules. (The alternative e-mail method requires a notice to participants and beneficiaries informing them that they can volunteer to receive information by e-mail, allowing them to submit the e-mail address to be used for this purpose.) Participants must be informed that they can request a free paper copy of the information, and they can opt out of receiving e-mail notices at any time. Once the initial notice is given, it must be repeated annually.

The plan administrator must take reasonable steps to see that the information is received (for example, using a return receipt or notice of non-delivery; conducting reviews or surveys to confirm receipt). The administrator must also take reasonable steps to maintain the confidentiality of the information, and notices must be written in a way that is calculated to be understood. [Prudential Pension Analyst, *DOL Issues Interim Guidance on Electronic Disclosures to Participants* (December 2012) (benefitslink.com)]

Cogent Research reported that 65% of sponsors of defined contribution plans used social media as a regular source of 401(k) plan communications. More than a third (39%) connected to plan providers with Websites or blogs; 24% used LinkedIn, 22% used Facebook. More than three-quarters (77%) of sponsors of mid-sized plans, with assets in the $20 million to $100 million range, used some kind of social media for 401(k) information; 47% use provider sites or blogs regularly, and 39% use LinkedIn. [Kevin McGuinness, *Plan Sponsors Embracing Social Media*, plansponsor.com (May 13, 2013)]

In February 2012, EBSA published a final rule on disclosure obligations that plan service providers owe to fiduciaries. The definition of service providers includes registered investment advisors, certain broker-dealers, TPAs, and other providers who receive direct or indirect compensation from plan assets in the amount of $1,000 or more. There were some changes between the Interim Final Rule (IFR) and the final rules. The final rule applies to plans that are defined benefit or defined contribution plans as defined by ERISA, but not to SEPs, SIMPLE plans, 403(b) plans, IRA plans, or welfare benefit plans.

The information must be submitted, in writing, to the fiduciary responsible for the plan. Electronic means of disclosure are permitted as long as the disclosures are readily accessible to the fiduciary. EBSA strongly encourages service providers to furnish a summary or similar tool that helps fiduciaries locate all the required disclosures. Service providers can use Employee Benefits Security Administration (EBSA's) sample guide, published as an appendix to the final rule, as a model. Whenever the individual information changes, the service providers must disclose the change; in any event, disclosure is required within 60 days of the time the service provider learns of the change. Good-faith correction of errors is permitted within 30 days of discovery of an error or omission.

When a plan fiduciary or plan administrator requests, the service provider must divulge information (e.g., compensation) about the service arrangement. The final regulation is effective for both existing and new contracts as of July 1, 2012. Failure to comply with these requirements is a prohibited transaction for the fiduciary, whereas compliance secures a prohibited transaction exemption. The final rule requires plan fiduciaries to terminate service arrangements as soon as possible if a provider fails to respond to a fiduciary's request for information within 90 days. [DOL Fact Sheet, *Final Regulation Relating to Service Provider Disclosures Under Section 408(b)(2)* (February 2012) (benefitslink.com); E is for ERISA blog, *401(k) Fee Disclosure Deadlines Extended Three Months; Other Changes Made in Final Regulations Under ERISA 408(b)(2) Guidance Easing Access to Lifetime Payout Options* (Feb. 3, 2012) (benefitslink.com). See also 76 Fed. Reg. 66136 (Oct. 25, 2011) for previous final regulations on this topic.]

An NPRM was published in the *Federal Register* for March 12, 2014, proposing to require a guide to be provided to disclosures by covered service providers that appear in multiple or lengthy documents. The guide assists plan fiduciaries in locating specific items of information that relate to their contracts with the service provider—e.g., the services that will be provided, if the provider has fiduciary status, how much the service provider will be paid, plus required investment disclosures for fiduciary, brokerage, and recordkeeping services (e.g., total annual operating expenses). [FR Doc 2014-04868, 79 Fed. Reg. 13949 (Mar. 12, 2014); see DOL Fact Sheet, *Proposed Regulation to Require a Guide to Assist Plan Fiduciaries in Reviewing 408(b)(2) Disclosures* (March 2014), <http://www.dol.gov/ebsa/newsroom/fs408(b)(2)disclosures.html>]

A DOL final rule from mid-2012 revises the rules for mailing or e-filing certain DOL notices falling under the ERISA § 408(b)(2) rules for fiduciary-level fee disclosure. Fiduciaries must file these notices to get prohibited transaction relief when they find out that there has been a failure of fee disclosure. The fiduciary must first make a written request to the service provider to get the fee information. If the service provider has not complied within 90 days, the fiduciary must notify the DOL. Notification can be mailed to DOL, EBSA Office of Enforcement, P.O. Box 75296, Washington D.C. 20013, or submitted online at <http://www.dol.gov/ebsa/regs/feedisclosurefailurenotice.html>. The Website provides immediate electronic confirmation that notice is received. [EBSA Final Rule, *Amendment Relating to Reasonable Contract or Arrangement Under Section 408(b)(2): Fee Disclosure*, 77 Fed. Reg. 41678 (July 16, 2012)]

The general rule is that fiduciaries are forbidden to deal with plan assets in their own interest and, unless they qualify for a Prohibited Transaction Exemption, they cannot provide investment advice to participants if the advice results in higher fees for the fiduciaries or their affiliates. The PPA creates an exemption for advisers who receive fees for advice—under an eligible investment advice arrangement, with either level fees or advice generated by a certified, objective computer model. The DOL's 2011 final rule applies to banks, insurance companies, broker-dealers, registered investment advisers, and their affiliates, employees, representatives, and agents. A qualifying arrangement must be based on generally accepted investment theories and consider historical returns. Investments must be suitable for the individual investor, bearing in mind the fees and expenses of the investment. Computer models must also use generally accepted investment theories and analyze historic risks and returns. At least annually, the fiduciary advisor has to get an independent audit, and auditor has to issue a written report within 60 days of completing the audit. [76 Fed. Reg. 66637 (Oct. 27, 2011)

T.D. 9484, 75 Fed. Reg. 27927 (May 19, 2010) contains the Final Regulations under Code § 401(a)(35)'s diversification requirement. Defined contribution plans that invest in publicly traded employer securities must give certain plan participants and beneficiaries (e.g., those who have at least three years of service) the right to change their investments in the plan out of employer securities. At least three diversified investment options other than the employer's stock must be offered, and covered employees and beneficiaries must be allowed to change their investment choices at reasonable intervals—at least once every quarter.

EBSA published a Final Rule in August, 2007, effective October 9, 2007, amending the ERISA § 502(c)(7) civil penalty rules (29 C.F.R. § 2560.502c-7) in light of the PPA. Civil penalties of up to $100 per day can be assessed for violation of ERISA § 101(m), which obligates the administrators of individual account plans to notify participants and beneficiaries of their right to sell the employer stock in their accounts and reinvest, and to advise them of the importance of diversification. [EBSA Direct Final Rule, RIN 1210-AB23, 72 Fed. Reg. 44970 8/10/07. See <http://www.irs.gov/irb/2006-51_IRB/ar09.html> (accessed Apr. 7, 2014) and Notice 2006-107, 2006-51 I.R.B. 1114, for the content of the model notice.]

§ 11.05 NOTICES OF REDUCTION OF BENEFIT ACCRUALS

Under ERISA § 204(h), plan administrators are required to notify participants, alternate beneficiaries under QDROs, and any union representing the workers whenever a plan amendment significantly reduces future benefit accruals under any qualified plan that is subject to ERISA's minimum funding standards (e.g., defined benefit plans).

The Tenth Circuit has held that a wear-away period does not have to be explicitly disclosed as long as the notice provided by the employer provides sufficiently representative examples of the effects of a plan amendment. A wear-away period is a consequence of a change in the terms of a plan and does not have to be disclosed as a new eligibility requirement. The Tenth Circuit said that plaintiffs who were informed that their benefits would be frozen received adequate notice for § 204(h) purposes. The court said that it would not invalidate an SPD for failure to discuss a wear-away period unless the employer was guilty of deceit or failed to explain the benefit calculation. [*Tomlinson v. El Paso*, 653 F.3d 1281 (10th Cir. 2011); see CCH Pensions & Benefits, *El Paso Wins Cash Balance Case; No Age Discrimination or Backloading Provisions Were Violated* (Sept. 2, 2011) (benefitslink.com); see also *Jensen v. Solvay Chemicals*, 625 F.3d 641 (10th Cir 2010) The case was remanded; the district court held once again that the plaintiffs would only be entitled to recover lost benefits if the failure of notice was "egregious." The district court, affirmed by the Tenth Circuit in 2013, ruled that the employer's conduct was not egregious—there was no intention to violate employees' rights, only an unintentional error when drafting a complex notice: *Jensen v. Solvay Chems., Inc.*, 721 F.3d 1180 (10th Cir. 2013)]

If a plan "egregiously" fails to meet the notice requirement, then the affected participants and alternate payees will be entitled to receive whatever benefits they would have received if the plan had never been amended to cut back the benefits. An "egregious" failure is intentional refusal to provide notice, or simple failure to provide most of the affected individuals with most of the information they are entitled to receive.

An amendment reduces the rate of future benefit accrual if it can reasonably be expected that the annual benefit commencing at NRA (or at the later actual retirement age) will decline because of the amendment. For example, if the plan provides a normal retirement benefit of 50% of the average pay for the highest five years multiplied by the number of years of participation and divided by 20, a change in either the numerator or the denominator of this fraction could produce a substantial reduction.

The required notice must be given in plain English, with enough information for participants and beneficiaries to understand the assumptions that will be used in future calculations, and the effect of the amendment on their benefit entitlement. In general, notice must be given at least 45 days before the effective date of the amendment, but advance notice can be reduced to 15 days if the plan has fewer than 100 participants, or if the amendment was made pursuant to a corporate merger or acquisition. Notice can be given after the effective date (as long as it is no more than 30 days after the effective date) if the amendment reduces or eliminates an early retirement benefit or retirement-type subsidy but does not substantially reduce the rate of future benefit accruals.

If there is an egregious failure (circumstances within the plan sponsor's control that either are intentional or lead to deprivation of information for most of those entitled to receive it), the amendment cannot be used to reduce benefits—affected individuals will continue to be entitled to receive the unreduced benefit as if there had been no amendment.

When a merger or acquisition transaction affects the surviving company's pension and benefit plans, it will probably be necessary to communicate with employees about the effect of the transition on their benefits. Notice will be required if a plan is terminated. A § 204(h) notice will probably be required if there is a potential reduction in benefits under a defined benefit plan or an individual account plan subject to minimum funding standards. In general, the notice must be furnished 45 days before the plan is amended, but a shorter, 15-day notice period is permitted in the mergers and acquisitions context. If restrictions are imposed on participants' ability to access their accounts, a blackout notice is required at least 30 but not more than 60 days before the restrictions take effect. [Principal Financial Group ThoughtCapital, *The Impact of Mergers, Acquisitions and Dispositions on Your Retirement Plan* (July 2010) (benefitslink.com)]

The PPA amended § 417(e)(3) to change the actuarial assumptions to be used in calculating the minimum present value of the accrued benefit. Because Rev. Rul. 2007-67, 2007-48 I.R.B. 1047, held that amendments to conform to the new requirements do not violate the anti-cutback rule, it is not necessary to provide a 204(h) notice if a lump sum distribution from a defined benefit plan is reduced by conformity to the assumptions required by the PPA. See also IRS final regulations published November 24, 2009: A 204(h) notice is not required for amendments reflecting PPA requirements about interest rates and mortality assumptions. Nor is a 204(h) notice required to eliminate a benefit that is not a protected benefit or a protected benefit that can be eliminated or reduced in compliance with § 411(d)(6).

§ 11.06 OTHER NOTICES AND DISCLOSURES

There are many other circumstances under which the plan will be required to communicate with participants and beneficiaries, with the IRS, with the DOL, the PBGC—or all of them!

When an individual account plan is abandoned, 29 C.F.R. § 2578.1 explains how to terminate the plan and distribute benefits. [The Qualified Termination Administrator Special Terminal Report Instructions for Abandoned Plans U.S. Department of Labor <www.dol.gov/ebsa> (June 21, 2006); see also EBSA's Interim Final Rule, *Amendments to Safe Harbor for Distributions from Terminated Individual Account.* Plans for further rules about such distributions, reflecting PPA changes: 72 Fed. Reg. 7516 (Feb. 15, 2007)].

In late 2012, DOL announced its intention to extend the Abandoned Plan program, adding streamlined plan termination and distribution procedures to help bankruptcy trustees distribute the assets from individual account retirement plans maintained by companies in Chapter 7. The assets of such plans are held by custodians such as banks and mutual funds—but the custodians do not have the authority to terminate the plans or distribute their assets, even at the request of participants. Under the proposal, the trustee, as Qualified Termination Administrator (QTA) would be able to hold the assets, wind up the plan (or designate a suitable financial institution to do so), and then file a summary terminal report. The QTA has to determine abandonment; the QTA has to hold assets and be eligible as trustee. [DOL/EBSA, *Fact Sheet: Proposed Amendments to Abandoned Plan Program,* <http://www.dol.gov/ebsa/newsroom/fsAPPamendment.html> (Dec. 2012)]

The Tax Increase Prevention and Reconciliation Act of 2005 (TIPRA; Pub. L. No. 109–222) § 516 targets improper corporate tax shelters by enacting new excise taxes: a Code § 4965(a)(1) tax of $20,000 per approval or other act, on entities and entity managers who get the entity involved in the transaction. Parties to a prohibited tax shelter transaction are required, under § 6033, to disclose not only their own participation but the identity of the other parties to the transaction. There is a penalty of $100 per day of failure to disclose (subject to a limit of $50,000 for any one disclosure) (see § 6652(c)(3)(A)). The Treasury has the power to make a written demand to a plan or its manager, giving a reasonable date for return to compliance. Failure to return to compliance by that date makes the plan manager personally liable for the § 6652(c)(3)(B)(ii) penalty of $100/day, up to a limit of $10,000 per disclosure. [See Notice 2006-65, 2006-31 I.R.B. 102]

[A] Notice of Deferred Benefits

Frequently, an employee will leave for one reason or another ("separation from service") at a time when he or she is entitled to a deferred vested benefit, but is not yet entitled to a retirement pension. The person in that situation is entitled to a notice containing:

- The name and address of the plan administrator;
- The nature, form, and amount of the person's deferred vested benefit;
- An explanation of any benefits that are forfeitable if the employee dies before a certain date.

The notice must be given no later than the date Schedule SSA is to be filed with the IRS. [Schedule SSA is the annual report that I.R.C. § 6057 requires of pension plans and other plans that are subject to the vesting requirements of ERISA Title I, Part 3] The IRS has the power to impose a penalty of $50 per erroneous statement or willful failure to furnish a statement.

Not less than thirty, or more than ninety, days before the annuity start date of any benefit that is immediately distributable before the participant reaches 62 or normal retirement age, the participant must also be given notice of any right he or she has to defer distribution. [See Treas. Reg. § 1.411(a)–11(c)(2)]

[B] Rollovers; Withholding Certificate

Not more than 90, and not less than 30, days before making a distribution, the plan administrator must notify the participant of the potential consequences of receiving a distribution that could be made the subject of a rollover. The notice should inform participants of their right to have the distribution deposited into an IRA, or to another qualified plan that will accept it.

Participants must be warned about the 20% withholding that will be imposed on all taxable distributions that are neither rolled over nor transferred—and that the sums that are received are taxable in the year of receipt. Participants must also be told that they can roll over the distribution within 60 days of its receipt to an IRA or another qualified plan. The notice must also provide information about capital gains treatment of lump sums, and the limited circumstances under which five-year averaging will be permitted. IRS Form 1099-R is used to report the taxable component of a designated distribution.

There is also a corresponding notice obligation before a plan makes a distribution that is *not* an eligible rollover distribution; the plan must send the participant IRS Form W-4P, Withholding Certificate for Pension or Annuity Payments. The W-4P informs the participant of the options he or she has with respect to withholding:

- Direct the plan not to withhold;
- Direct withholding based on marital status or the number of allowances;
- Increase withholding on periodic payments (for instance, if the participant has high outside income and might otherwise owe a large balance at the end of the tax year).

[C] QJSA/QPSA Notice

Thirty to ninety days before receipt of benefits, a plan that permits payouts in annuity form must provide all participants with a plain English statement. [All participants—vested or otherwise—are entitled to the statement. See I.R.C. § 417(a)(3), Treas. Reg. §§ 1.401(a)(11), and 1.417(e)-1(b)(3)] The notice should contain:

- The terms and conditions of the joint and survivor annuity;
- The participant's right to waive the annuity, including a description of the consequences of the waiver;
- Rights of the participant's spouse;
- Description of the right to revoke the election, and consequences of the revocation.

A comparable explanation must be given about the Qualified Preretirement Survivor Annuity (QPSA), although the timing requirement is more complicated. The notice is due by the latest of:

- The period that begins on the first day of the plan year in which the participant reaches age 32, and ends at the end of the plan year before the participant reaches 35;
- A reasonable time (deemed to mean no more than a year) after a person becomes a plan participant;

- A reasonable time after the employer stops subsidizing the survivor benefit;
- A reasonable time after the I.R.C. § 401(a)(11) survivor benefit provisions become applicable to the participant. This might happen, for example, if a single or divorced person marries and acquires a spouse who could become entitled to a QPSA;
- A reasonable time after separation from service. If the employee leaves before he or she is 35, the period runs from one year before to one year after the separation.

■ **TIP:** The plan can accept waivers at earlier stages (as long as the spouse consents), but the plan must give the participant a written explanation of how QPSAs work. The waiver becomes void at the beginning of the plan year in which the participant reaches age 35. If a new waiver is not signed, and the participant dies before retirement age, then the spouse gets a QPSA despite the attempt to waive this form of benefit.

The plan can omit the notice of the right to waive the QPSA/QJSA if the benefit is fully subsidized by the plan, and the participant can neither waive the QPSA/QJSA nor name a nonspouse as beneficiary. The benefit is fully subsidized if not waiving neither lowers the benefit nor results in higher costs for the participant.

A retroactive annuity starting date is allowable only if the plan provides for it and the participant specifically asks for the retroactive starting date. Benefits must be determined in a way that puts the participant in the same position as if he or she had received benefit payments starting on the retroactive annuity starting date. The participant must get a make-up amount to reflect any missed payments (and interest on those missed payments). Furthermore, although commentators requested that this provision should be extended to defined contribution plans, the Final Rule continues to limit the availability of a retroactive start date to defined benefit plans.

If the participant is married, the spouse must consent to the election of the retroactive start date if the survivor payments under the retroactive annuity are less than the QJSA with a start date after the provision of the QJSA explanation. This is true even if the actual form of the benefit elected is a QJSA. But consent is required only if the survivor annuity is less than 50% of the annuity payable during the life of the participant under a QJSA that does not commence retroactively.

As for lump sums, electing a retroactive annuity starting date cannot reduce the size of the lump sum. The distribution must not be smaller than the distribution resulting from applying the applicable interest rate and mortality table to the annuity form that was used determine the benefit amount as of the retroactive start date.

For years beginning on or after January 1, 2007, the PPA increased the period for the notices required under §§ 402(f) [rollover notices], 411 [notice of right to defer] and 417 [notice and election period for annuity distributions from a 401(k) plan] from 90 to 180 days. The election period for waiving QJSA distributions is also extended from 90 to 180 days. [Prop. Treas. Regs. §§ 1.401(a)-13, 1.401(a)-20, 1.402(f)-1, 1.411(a)-11, 1.417(e)-1, 73 Fed. Reg. 59575 (Oct. 9, 2008); see EBIA Weekly, *IRS Proposes Regulations Addressing Notice of Participant's Right to Defer a Distribution and 180-Day Notice Period* (Oct. 9, 2008) (benefitslink.com)]

[D] QDRO Notices

The general rule is that no one can garnish or otherwise get hold of plan benefits before they are paid. The exception to the rule is that a plan administrator not only has the right, but has the obligation, to comply with valid court orders that direct part of the benefit to the participant's separated or divorced spouse. However, not every divorce-related order must be treated as a Qualified Domestic Relations Order (QDRO).

Once a plan receives a court order, I.R.C. § 414(p) obligates the administrator to review it to see if it is qualified. The plan participant and the alternate payee (nearly always the spouse) must be notified that the plan has received an order and what the plan will do to assess its qualification. Then the administrator carries out that procedure and sends another notice to the participant and alternate payee, if the order has been determined to be qualified and therefore must be obeyed by the plan. EBSA published a Final Rule reflecting PPA changes, clarifying that an order can be QDRO even if it is issued after another domestic relations order, if it revises another DRO, or even if it is issued after the employee spouse's death. [RIN 1210-AB15, 75 Fed. Reg. 32846 (June 10, 2010)]

[E] Break-in-Service Notice

ERISA's break-in-service rules are complex and difficult for participants to understand. Participants have the right to make a written request (although only once a year) when they are separated from service, or have a one-year break in service. The notice defines their accrued benefits under the plan, and the percentage of the accrued benefits that is nonforfeitable.

[F] "Saver's Credit"

One effect of EGTRRA was to increase substantially the amount that taxpayers can contribute to IRA accounts (or defer in 401(k) or 403(b) accounts). See the IRS Announcement 2001-106 [2001-44 I.R.B. 416] for a description of the "saver's credit," which is an income tax credit under I.R.C. § 25B for low-income taxpayers who contribute to an IRA or pension plan. The Announcement contains a sample notice that can be given to employees explaining the credit.

Although the Saver's Credit as originally enacted had a sunset date, it was made permanent by the PPA.

For 2014, the AGI limit for the saver's credit is $60,000 for joint returns, $45,000 for heads of household, and $30,000 for single persons and married persons filing separate returns. [IR-2013-86, *IRS Announced 2014 Pension Plan Limitations*, <http://www.irs.gov/uac/IRS-Announces-2014-Pension-Plan-Limitations;-Taxpayers-May-Contribute-up-to-$17,500-to-their-401(k)-plans-in-2014> (Oct. 31, 2013)]

[G] FASB Changes

The Financial Accounting Standards Board (FASB) requires employers to disseminate financial statements that accurately reflect their ongoing obligations relating to pension and retiree health plans. As of December 2008, FASB had a proposed staff position, FAS 132(R)-a, in two parts. One applies FAS 157 (Fair Value Measurements) to defined benefit plans; assets must be divided into three risk levels, and plans must disclose their valuation techniques. The other explains additional disclosures of asset categories (e.g., cash, equity securities, debt securities, structured debt, real estate, and derivatives).

The final staff position, FAS 132(R)-1, is effective for fiscal years ending after December 15, 2009. The objective of this rule is to show a plan's investment allocations are made, among what major categories of plan assets, how they are valued, and where risk is concentrated within the plan's asset structure. The plan sponsor must state its overall investment objectives and strategies, including the allocation percentage for each major category of plan assets, the investment goals, the plan's risk management practices, diversification, and which assets are permitted and which are forbidden as investments for the plan. Mutual and hedge fund investments must be disclosed. [JP Morgan Compensation and Benefits Strategies, *FASB Finalizes Rules for Financial Reporting of DB Plan Assets* (Feb. 10, 2009) (benefitslink.com) and *FAS 132 Update* (Dec. 11, 2008) (benefitslink.com)]

In 2009, FASB reorganized thousands of guidance documents into a new organization structure of approximately 90 topics. The previous seven FASB statements relating to retirement and health plans (Nos. 35, 87, 88, 106, 112, 132(R), 158 were reorganized into five topics:

- 712, post-employment compensation other than retirement;
- 715, retirement benefits;
- 960, accounting for defined benefit plans;
- 962, accounting for defined contribution plans;
- 965, accounting for health and welfare benefit plans.

[CCH Pension & Benefits *FASB Announces New Codification Structure, Superseding All Existing Statements* (June 26, 2009) (benefitslink.com). See <http://www.fasb.org> for the full codification.]

[H] Notices About Funding Problems

Before the enactment of the PPA, ERISA § 4011 required the administrator to notify participants and beneficiaries of the funding standards—and of the fact that the PBGC did not guarantee payment of all the benefits that might have been payable absent a PBGC takeover of the plan. Every year, the PBGC published a Model Participant Notice Form to be used for this purpose, and provided Technical Updates including a worksheet for determining whether notice was required. Technical Update 06-03 explains how to make interest rate calculations for the 2006 participant notice; in general, plans subject to the variable-rate PBGC premium for 2006 had to issue this notice.

For plan years beginning after 2006, PPA § 501 repeals ERISA § 4011. Disclosure is still required, but now it is under Department of Justice jurisdiction as prescribed by ERISA Title I. [FR Doc E7-761, 72 Fed. Reg. 2615 (Jan. 22, 2007). See also Technical Update 06-04 (Aug. 30, 2006, revised Sept. 28, 2006) for further interest rate discussion, and explaining how the PBGC will treat missed quarterly contributions now that the § 4011 notice is no longer required. The Technical Updates can be found at <http://www.pbgc.gov/practitioners/WhatsNew>.]

The PBGC published final regulations under ERISA § 4010 on March 16, 2009. Section 4010 requires notification to the PBGC if a plan fails the "gateway" test: that is, if its funding target attainment percentage drops below 80%. The notice alerts the PBGC to its potential liabilities if the plan terminates with substantial underfunding. Filing may also be required when a plan gets a funding waiver, or fails to make the minimum contribution it was required to make. Filers under § 4010 must also report on any restrictions imposed on benefit payments during the year because the plan was underfunded. If any required payments were missed, leading to imposition of a lien, this must be disclosed. The due date is 105 days after the plan's fiscal year—i.e., April 15 for a calendar year plan. The reporting requirement is waived if the shortfall for the plan's entire controlled group does not exceed $15 million. To avoid making the 4010 filing, a plan sponsor can make additional contributions to bring the funding level above the 80% threshold. [JP Morgan Compensation and Benefits Strategies, *PBGC Finalizes Rules for 4010 Reporting* (Apr. 10, 2009) (benefitslink.com). For basic rules, see <http://www.pbgc.gov/prac/reporting-and-disclosure/4010-reporting.html> (undated, accessed Apr. 7, 2014).]

Notice 2012-46, 2012-30 I.R.B. 86 (effective November 1, 2012) explains the ERISA § 101(j) notice requirements for single-employer plans subject to benefit limitations under § 436 because of deficient funding status. The administrator must give the notice to participants and beneficiaries within 30 days of the time the plan's funding status falls below the required level. DOL regulations state that noncompliance can be penalized by up to $1,000 a day per participant entitled to notification. The notice must be understandable to the average plan participant. Notice must be in writing, but can be electronic if it is reasonably accessible to the recipients. The notice must include:

- Plan name;
- Plan number;
- EIN;
- General description of the payment limitations.

For notice of unpredictable contingent event benefits, prohibited payment limitations, and cessation of benefit accruals, the notice must disclose that these measures are required by the plan's AFTAP (and an explanation of the concept of AFTAP) and what the effect is on the benefits, with the prohibited benefits described in detail. If the limitation is caused by the sponsor's bankruptcy, this must be disclosed. Prohibited benefits must be described in detail. The notice must explain that the limitations will end. The administrator must also notify participants and beneficiaries within 30 days of the date that limitations cease to apply because the plan's AFTAP has increased. [McGuireWoods LLP, *IRS Provides Guidance on Notices for Funding-Related Pension Plan Benefit Limitations* (Aug. 28, 2012) (benefitslink.com)]

[I] Notice of Termination

Before a standard or distress termination of a pension plan the administrator must give written notice to the parties affected, e.g., the amount and form of the benefit due of the proposed termination date. The notice must explain how the benefit was calculated (e.g., length of service, participant's age, interest rate and other assumptions, and other factors that the PBGC requires to be disclosed).

Defined benefit plans that undergo an involuntary termination (ERISA § 4042) or a distress termination (ERISA § 4041)—that is, that terminate when they are underfunded—must follow up their PBGC filings (Form 600) by notifying plan participants and beneficiaries of the same information that was filed with the PBGC. This notice is due within 15 days of filing the notice of intent to terminate or the involuntary termination disclosures with the PBGC.

Late in 2007, the PBGC published Proposed Regulations on the disclosure requirements for distress terminations and PBGC-initiated plan terminations beginning on or after the PPA's August 17, 2006 enactment date; final regulations were published in November 2008, requiring plan participants and other affected parties to be given certain information about terminations within 15 business days of the request. (The PBGC is responsible for providing in the information for terminations that it initiates; participants and beneficiaries are not entitled to request information about PBGC-initiated terminations until the plan administrator has received the PBGC's Notice of Determination that the plan should be terminated—presumed to be delivered three days after the PBGC issues it.) Plan sponsors and administrators are required to preserve the confidentiality of information that identifies individual participants or beneficiaries. A court order can be obtained to avoid disclosure of trade secrets or other information exempt from disclosure under FOIA. The penalty for violating these rules can be up to $1,100 a day: see ERISA § 4071. [72 Fed. Reg. 68542 (Dec. 5, 2007) [proposed] and 73 Fed. Reg. 68333 (Nov. 18, 2008) [final], discussed in Guest Article, *PBGC Proposes Rules on New Termination Information Disclosure Requirements*, CCH Pension & Benefits, *PBGC Final Regs Issued on Plan Termination Disclosure Requirements* (Dec. 1, 2008)]

[J] PPA Benefit Statement

The PPA obligates plan administrators to issue periodic benefit statements to participants and beneficiaries. The statement requirement took effect on January 1, 2007 for calendar-year plans. Failure to provide the statement is penalized by up to $110 per day elapsed without providing the required statement. All defined contribution plans must issue a statement at least annually, and quarterly statements are required for individual account plans (e.g., 401(k)s) whose participants can direct the investment of their account balances. The quarterly statement must disclose:

- The total account balance;
- The amount that is vested; if none is, the earliest vesting date for the participant;
- A breakdown of the value of each of the investments within the account;
- Whatever limitations or restrictions are placed on the right to direct investments by the terms of the plan;
- An explanation of why diversification is important;
- URL for the DOL Website containing investment information;
- (For profit-sharing plans integrated with Social Security) an explanation of plan integration.

Employers can use the general DOL and IRS procedures for distributing statements in electronic rather than hard-copy form. The information can be provided on a secure Website as well as through individual e-mails. But if the sponsor chooses to use a Website to distribute the information, participants and beneficiaries must be given a written notice explaining how to access the information online—and that they can get a free paper copy if they prefer.

Individual account plans that do not permit individuals to direct the investment of their accounts must furnish annual statements within 45 days of the end of the year, starting with January 14, 2008. The statements are similar but need not include information about restrictions on investments or the explanation of the importance of diversification. The information can be furnished on a secure Website.

The PPA's disclosure requirement for defined benefit accounts is a benefit statement furnished at least once every three years. The first statement is required for the 2009 plan year. Only current employees are automatically entitled to statements. The defined benefit account statement contains:

- The participant's total accrued benefit;
- The amount vested (or the date on which vesting will occur);
- (Integrated plans) The formula for integrating the plan with Social Security.

In the alternative, plans can give notice once a year that a statement is available and explain how to access it; in this case, the first notice must be given by December 31, 2007. Defined benefit plans can give notice electronically, but cannot rely on the availability of the information on a secure Website—individual notice must be given electronically or in hard copy.

[<http://www.dol.gov/ebsa/investing.html> (last accessed Mar. 22, 2014)]

[K] Health Plan Notices

When a female beneficiary enrolls in a plan, and each year thereafter, she must receive a notice about availability of benefits available for mastectomy and reconstruction under the WHCRA. [See <http://www.dol.gov/ebsa/publications/whcra.html>]

In plans that are subject to HIPAA's privacy policies, either because the plan receives PHI or because the employer sponsors an FSA or HRA, all participants must receive notice when the policies are adopted. An explanation of how to obtain notice of the plan's privacy practices must be provided at least once every three years.

The Children's Health Insurance Program Reauthorization Act of 2009 (CHIPRA), signed February 4, 2009, obligates employers to amend their plans to allow special enrollment of employees and dependents who lose eligibility for

Medicaid or SCHIP, or who became eligible for state subsidies of their health care premiums as part of a state Medicaid or SCHIP program. A state can either provide coverage to low-income families directly, or subsidize coverage provided by the employer. The subsidy, in turn, can be administered by the state making payments to either the employer or the employee, although employers have the right to opt out of receiving payments (for example, if they are concerned about the difficulties of administering the program).

The CHIPRA imposes notice requirements both on employees (they must inform the health plan within days of becoming eligible under CHIPRA) and on health plans. Plans must notify participants of the potential for premium assistance, and must notify the state of information from participants who disclose their eligibility for premium assistance. To obtain special enrollment, an employee must request coverage within 60 days of either the date of termination of Medicaid or SCHIP coverage or the date the qualifying child or parent is found eligible for assistance. Plan administrators must report to the state the information needed to determine employees' eligibility for premium assistance.

[Norbert F. Kugele, Warner Norcross & Judd LLP, *New Federal SCHIP Law Requires Cafeteria and Health Plan Amendments* (Feb. 10, 2009) (benefitslink.com)]

See § 18.19[K] for notice requirements under PPACA (health care reform).

§ 11.07 DISCLOSURE ON REQUEST

In addition to disclosures that must be made, and documents that must be furnished, automatically to all plan participants and beneficiaries, ERISA and the Internal Revenue Code require certain disclosures to be made only if a participant or beneficiary requests them.

Materials that can be requested include:

- A complete copy of the plan's latest Form 5500;
- The plan instrument (that is, the Collective Bargaining Agreement or trust that actually creates the plan);
- The latest updated SPD;
- A report on plan termination;
- Statement of accrued benefits (but the administrator only has to furnish this once in every 12-month period);
- Percentage of vesting; and, for participants who are not fully vested, the schedule on which full vesting will occur.

If a request is made, the information should be mailed within 30 days to the last known address of the requester. The plan is allowed to impose a reasonable charge for the information, based on the least expensive available means of reproducing the documents.

The plan documents, plan description, and latest annual report must be kept on file for participants who want to inspect them, at the plan administrator's principal office. If there is a request to make them available there, copies of the documents must also be kept at the employer's principal office and at each of the employer's locations where 50 or more employees work.

The Department of Labor can impose penalties of up to $110 a day, subject to a maximum of $1,100, for failure to furnish documents on request. The Secretary of Labor has the power to demand documents that were requested by, but not furnished to, plan participants and beneficiaries under 29 C.F.R. § 2520.104a-8. Although some Circuits (such as the Seventh) will impose liability on a "de facto" plan administrator, in the Sixth Circuit, only the official plan administrator can be liable under § 1132(c). The administrator, for penalty purposes, is either the party designated by the plan instrument; the person designated by the sponsor (if the plan instrument does not make a designation) or the party named as administrator in Department of Labor regulations. [*Gore v. El Paso Energy Corp.*, 477 F.3d 833 (6th Cir. 2007)]

§ 11.08 ELECTRONIC COMMUNICATIONS

The Taxpayer Relief Act of 1997 (TRA '97) [Pub. L. No. 105-34] ordered the IRS to create rules for integrating computer technology into plan administration and the disclosure process. Since that time, the IRS, DOL, PBGC, and other agencies have developed rules for using the Internet, e-mail, and other electronic means to communicate with plan participants and beneficiaries—and to file official documents. The basic principle is that the electronic communication must be at least as accessible and understandable as a paper copy, and in general, participants and beneficiaries must not only have the right to receive a hard copy without charge, but must be informed of this right.

Treasury Regulations provide that notices can be delivered electronically only if the consent requirement is met or if the plan qualifies for an exemption. Participants receiving an electronic notice must be informed, in a readily understandable manner, what the subject matter of the notice is and how to access it. The recipient must give explicit consent to electronic delivery and must be informed that he or she can request a paper copy at no charge and withdraw consent. Disclosure is also required about the scope of the consent, how to update contact information, and the hardware and software requirements for using the system. If the hardware/software requirements change, a new consent form is required. PINs or other security devices must be implemented to prevent unauthorized persons from accessing the system or inputting information into it. Electronic witness affidavits and notarizations are acceptable as long as a notary or plan representative physically witnesses the application of the signature.

Commentator Stephen M. Saxon described the DOL rules for electronic disclosure as "both completely antiquated and ridiculously complex," with the result that paper disclosures still continue to be made. The specific rules were promulgated without guidance, so they can be withdrawn. According to Saxon, electronic disclosure is not on the DOL's regulatory agenda, so comprehensive reform is unlikely in the short term. [Stephen M. Saxon, Saxon Angle, *The Electronic Age*, plansponsor.com (January 2013)]

In 2013, the GAO recommended that DOL and the Treasury clarify the regulatory requirements for delivering pension disclosures electronically. The GAO also recommended giving participants additional chances to opt out of electronic disclosures, including a chance to request all deliveries in hard copy rather than having to make the request on a document-by-document basis. Electronic delivery eliminates printing and mailing costs, and the notices are always available and can be archived—but there is a risk of loss of access if there is a computer malfunction or loss of Internet connection. Electronic delivery also makes the notices vulnerable to hacking and phishing. [GAO-13-594, *Private Pensions: Revised Electronic Disclosure Rules Could Clarify Use and Better Protect Participant Choice*, <http://www.gao.gov/assets/660/657868.pdf> (September 2013)]

EBSA made electronic filing available starting in 2005. [70 Fed. Reg. 51542 (Aug. 30, 2005)] Mandatory e-filing of PBGC documents was originally scheduled for 2006 (large plans) and 2007 (smaller plans) but was deferred based on industry comments. Payments can be made by paper check or by electronic check, credit card, wire transfer, or Automated Clearing House. [Leslie Ziober, *PBGC Says Mandatory E-Filing Begins July 1*, plansponsor.com (June 1, 2006); *Mandatory Electronic Filing of Form 5500 Delayed One Year, Pension and Benefits Alerts*, <http://www.thompson.com/public/printversion.jsp?id=1594&cat=BENEFITS> (July 16, 2007)]

The PBGC announced that both estimated flat-rate filings and comprehensive filings for plan years that begin in 2011 can be submitted electronically using MyPAA, the PBGC's online system. Only electronic, not paper, filing is acceptable. The actual payment of the premium can either be done electronically via MyPAA, by electronic funds transfer, or by check. [*Premium Payment Instructions and Addresses*, <http://www.pbgc.gov> (Dec. 16, 2010)]

T.D. 9294 is the IRS' Final Rule, including a new Reg. § 1.401(a)-21, explaining how, effective January 1, 2007, qualified plans should use electronic means to provide notices to participants and obtain their consent and elections. The rule also applies to notices provided under various welfare benefit plans (accident & health plans; cafeteria plans; educational assistance plans; qualified transportation fringe plans; Archer MSAs; and HSAs). However, T.D. 9294, as an IRS rule, does not apply to ERISA Title I or IV notices (dealing with, e.g., SPDs, COBRA notices, and notices of benefit suspension) because those documents are under DOL or PBGC jurisdiction.

T.D. 9294 applies to the § 402(f) notice of the right to roll over plan distributions; the § 411(a)(11) notice about rights with respect to commencement of benefits; § 417(a)(2) spousal consent elections about QJSAs; and the ERISA § 204(h) notice of significant reduction in the rate of future benefit accrual. [T.D. 9294, RIN 1545-BD68, 4830-01-p, 2006-48 I.R.B. 980]

DOL Technical Release 2011-03 allows information about fees in individual account plans to be distributed electronically, and Websites can be used subject to certain safeguards (e.g., those prescribed by the DOL's FAB 2006-03, which allows quarterly individual benefit statements to use the IRS electronic disclosure rules). As long as the plan follows the technical release, the DOL will not take enforcement action merely because fee disclosures were made electronically rather than on paper. There is a general safe harbor for making electronic disclosures, even if the participant has not affirmatively agreed to this, if using a computer or other electronic system is an integral part of the employee's duties.

Under this interim policy, investment information and disclosure of administrative and individual expenses can be included in quarterly benefit statements that are transmitted electronically using FAB 2006-03 standards. However, certain investment data (e.g., a comparative chart of performance data) can be sent under the DOL safe harbor or the alternative e-mail method, but not under FAB 2006-03.

Six conditions are required to justify the use of e-mail:

- The person entitled to the disclosures responds to an initial notice by voluntarily providing an e-mail address;
- The plan submits the request on a clear and conspicuous initial notice;
- The participant or beneficiary must receive an annual notice satisfying most of the initial content notice requirements;
- Electronic delivery uses a method that is reasonably calculated to actually be received;
- Personal information must be kept confidential;
- The notice must be drafted to be understandable to the average participant.
- The notice must explain the rights to receive a free paper copy and/or opt out of receiving notices electronically.[DOL Technical Release 2011-03, <http://www.dol.gov/EBSA/pdf/tr11-03.pdf> (Sept. 13, 2011)]

The DOL revised and restated Technical Release 2011-03 in Technical Release 2011-03R. EBSA received many inquiries about whether continuous access Websites can be used to make electronic disclosures, and said that they can be, if the conditions of Technical Release 2011-03 are satisfied. EBSA also said that investment information can either be furnished as part of, or along with, a paper or electronic pension benefit statement. [Technical Release 2011-03R, <http://www.dol.gov/ebsa/newsroom/tr11-03r.html> (Dec. 8, 2011); see Rebecca

Moore, *EBSA Revises Electronic Fee Disclosure Rules*, plansponsor.com (Dec. 8, 2011)]

§ 11.09 DISCLOSURE OF DOCUMENTS TO THE DOL and PBGC

ERISA required plan administrators to file all SPDs and SMMs with the Department of Labor (DOL) until it was amended by the Taxpayer Relief Act of 1997. The current version of ERISA § 104(a) requires plan administrators to respond to DOL requests by providing documents relating to an employee benefit plan—including the latest SPD, a summary of plan changes not reflected in the SPD, and the plan instrument.

However, the DOL sees its primary role in this arena as helping participants and beneficiaries get documents from the plan, so the DOL can ask for documents that participants or beneficiaries are entitled to, have requested, but have not received. But the DOL will not ask for documents that the participants and beneficiaries are not entitled to see.

If the plan administrator doesn't respond to the request within 30 days, the DOL has the power (under ERISA § 502(c)(6)) to impose civil penalties of up to $110 a day (but not more than $1,100 per request). Penalties will not be imposed if factors beyond the administrator's control prevent compliance.

The DOL's Final Rule about document disclosure and civil penalties is set out at 67 Fed. Reg. 777–789 (Jan. 7, 2002).

Effective March 3, 2009, the DOL can assess penalties, under ERISA § 502(c)(4) as amended by the PPA, against plan administrators who fail to provide the notices required under the PPA dealing with subjects such as limitations on distributions from underfunded plans; responsibilities of employers that participate in or withdraw from multi-employer plans; and participants' rights and obligations under defined contribution plans that automatically enroll employees as participants.

The amount of the penalty depends on the degree of willfulness. Failing to notify each person entitled to notice constitutes a separate violation. Plan administrators are personally liable for the penalties, and if there are multiple responsible parties, they can be held jointly and severally liable. [Final Regs, 74 Fed. Reg. 17 (Jan. 2, 2009); see EBSA Press release, *U.S. Department of Labor Finalizes Civil Penalty Rules Under the Pension Protection Act* (Dec. 31, 2008) (benefitslink.com); Deloitte's Washington Bulletin, *Procedures for Assessing Civil Penalties Under ERISA § 502(c)(4) Are Finalized*, <http://benefitslink.com/articles/guests/washbull090112a.html> (Jan. 12, 2009)]

Because reportable events occur sporadically, compliance with the reporting rules can be tricky; it's hard to set up a routine. Sometimes reporting is required because of events outside the corporation—for example, occurring in the corporation's controlled group. The penalty for failure to report can be as much as

$1,100 a day, although PBGC's penalty guidelines are much lower: $25/day for the first 90 days, followed by $50/day, with relief available for small plans.

A variety of negative financial results must be reported to the PBGC. Events are reportable because they signal plan problems that might lead to termination. When it gets a report, the PBGC can ask for additional information, and can either close the file, continue to monitor the plan, or take action.

In general, the reporting requirements call for post-event reporting; advance reporting is more or less limited to significantly underfunded plans of privately held controlled groups. The reporting obligation is imposed on the plan administrator and the plan sponsor; but a filing by any party is deemed filed for anyone else who is potentially liable. Post-event reports are due within 30 days of the time the reporter knew, or had reason to know that a reportable event had occurred. [Harold J. Ashner, *PGBC Reportable Events: Traps for the Unwary*, J. of Pension Planning & Compliance, Winter 2007, Volume 32, Number 4 (benefitslink.com)]

In late 2009, the PBGC proposed regulations updating § 4043 in light of the PPA, and adding two new reportable events (funding-based benefit limits; transfers to a 401(h) retiree health benefit account). Under the proposal, most waivers of liability and extensions of time are eliminated, because the PBGC believes that it requires notice of potentially troubled plans that may need PBGC intervention later on. [PBGC Proposed Rules, *Pension Protection Act of 2006; Conforming Amendments; Reportable Events and Certain Other Notification Requirements*, RIN 1212-AB06, 74 Fed. Reg. 61248 (Nov. 23, 2009)]

This proposal was extremely unpopular with business, however, and the PBGC has issued two statements greatly reducing the amount of required reporting. The PBGC's intention is to concentrate on the few plans that are genuinely at risk, relieving other, sounder plans of reporting responsibilities.

The PBGC's Technical Update 13-1 offers some small pension plans relief from the provisions of the proposed amendments dealing with reportable events. The relief is permanent, not just for 2013, but could be superseded if the PBGC issues Final Rules that are different. The ERISA § 4034.25 waiver of the requirement of reporting missed quarterly contributions is extended for all years in which the plan either has fewer than 25 participants, or has between 25–100 participants and files a simplified notice with the PBGC. However, relief is not available if the quarterly contribution was missed as a result of the plan's financial inability to pay. Technical Update 13-1 applies the assets and liabilities used to calculate the variable rate premium to determine the reporting requirements for events in the next plan year—including eligibility for reporting waivers, extensions, and mandatory advance reporting. [Mark Schulte, *Déjà Vu All Over Again: PBGC Extends Reportable Event Relief for 2013 and Beyond*, VIA Retirement Plan Blog (Jan. 30, 2013) (benefitslink.com)]

In April 2013, the PBGC published a new proposal, under which reporting obligations would be reduced significantly so that financially sound plans would not have to report most of what would otherwise be reportable events. The PBGC estimated that over 90% of plans and sponsors would no longer have to make most reports.

The 2013 proposal relieves plans that are "financially sound" (using five criteria, primarily having a commercial credit rating agency's report indicating fiscal stability) of the obligation to make most reports. Financially sound plans would not have to make a post-event report for most of the events already covered by a funding-based waiver. Reporting is also waived for fully funded plans.

Small plans would no longer have to report reductions in the number of participants. Larger plans would only have to report this if the reduction was caused by a single event such as a reorganization or mass layoff; if the reduction occurred in a period of 30 days or less; or if the number of participants in the same year falls more than 20%. Large plans can use the financial soundness safe harbor to avoid reporting based on reduction in the number of participants.

The proposal retains the Technical Update 13-1 relief (i.e., reporting of missed contributions is waived or reduced for plans with fewer than 100 participants as long as the reason for missing the contribution was not inability to pay). Reporting is waived for missed contributions that reflect inability to pay benefits when due—unless the plan is exempt from the liquidity shortfall provisions. But reporting is not waived for small plans or under the financial soundness safe harbor.

However, the proposal eliminates the funding-based waiver for reporting the sponsor's liquidation and reporting is not waived for small plans or under the financial soundness safe harbor. The proposed regulations eliminate the sponsor's bankruptcy as a reportable event because there are many other reliable sources of bankruptcy information available to the PBGC. But insolvency must be reported. As a result of the relief provided by this proposal, the only reportable events would be: (1) loan default; (2) failure to make required contributions; (3) application for a funding waiver; (4) inability to pay benefits as they come due; (5) insolvency; and (6) liquidation. [78 Fed. Reg. 20039 (Apr. 3, 2013); see Rebecca Moore, *PBGC Proposed Reduced Reporting Obligations*, plansponsor.com (Apr. 2, 2013); Buck Consultants FYI, *PBGC Reproposes Reportable Event Rules* (Apr. 5, 2013) (benefitslink.com) See PLC Employee Benefits & Employee Compensation, *PBGC Releases Enforcement Guidelines for ERISA Section 4062(e) Financial Assurance Program* (May 3, 2013) (benefitslink.com) for May, 2013 guidance from the PBGC about the definition of "creditworthy."]

In mid-2014, the PBGC announced that new § 4062(e) events should still be reported as they occur—but the PBGC would not take action based on the reports. The enforcement moratorium was announced until the end of 2014. [PBGC Press Release No. 14-09, *PBGC Issues Moratorium on 4062(e) Enforcement*, <http://www.pbgc.gov/news/press/releases/pr14-09.html?cid=CPAD01PRJUL0820141> (July 8, 2014)]

§ 11.10 FORM 5500

Qualified plans must report each year to the IRS, DOL, and PBGC so that these agencies can monitor plan operations and see if the plans remain qualified, are financially sound, and are operated in accordance with all applicable requirements. The basic Form 5500 covers plans with 100 or more participants; single-participant plans can use the less complex Form 5500-EZ. For 2007 and later plan years, the threshold for filing Form 5500-EZ rises from $100,000 to $250,000. Only one filing is necessary—the IRS transmits the information to the DOL and PBGC. [The toll-free telephone hot line for questions about plan coverage, premiums, or terminations is (800) 736-2444]

Form 5500, like the Form 1040, consists of a basic form and various schedules that provide additional information. Form 5500 deals with four main subjects: the plan's financial statements, actuarial data, administrative data, and any benefits covered by insurance. The annual report is due at the end of the seventh month following the end of the plan year. A plan that does not seem likely to complete the report in time should file IRS Form 5558, Application for Extension of Time to File Certain Employee Plan Returns, to get an extension of up to two and a half months. [See <http://www.dol.gov/ebsa/5500main.html> for documents and information about the Form 5500]

But, although some compliance requirements have been eased, some have become more stringent. Starting with the 2002 plan year, some small plans (usually those having fewer than 100 participants) will be required to get a report from an independent auditor to accompany their Form 5500-series filing, even though they were excused from the audit requirement in earlier years. However, audit waivers are available for plans with fewer than 100 participants, or those with participants in the 80–120 range if they filed as a small plan the year before, if at least 95% of plan assets are managed by professionals, as long as participants get additional disclosures in the summary annual report. [See <http//www.dol.gov/ebsa/faqs/faq_auditwaiver.html>]

A "large plan" is one with 100 or more participants as of the beginning of the plan year, and a "small plan" has fewer. If the number of participants at the beginning of a plan year was 80 to 120 and a Form 5500 was filed for the previous plan year, the plan has the right to elect to complete the Form 5500 and the schedules using the same category as the previous year.

The DOL, the IRS, and the PBGC collaborated on the development of the EFAST system for electronic filing of the 5500 series of forms. It has been superseded by the EFAST2 system, which took effect starting with the 2009 plan year. (However, plans that cover only the business owner continue to file Form 5500-EZ or 5500-SF on paper.) Form 5500 can be e-filed using the DOL's IFILE Web-based system, a private Web-based system, or a third-party software application that sends data to the DOL. [SunGard Relius, *Getting Ready for EFAST2*, 2009 (benefitslink.com)]

The EBSA announced in early 2013 that migration to the fully electronic EFAST2 system is complete for all filing years, and paper filings will no longer be accepted. [Notice: <http://www.dol.gov/find/20130128>, FAQs at <http://www.dol.gov/ebsa/faqs/faq_dfvc.html>. See Rebecca Moore, *EBSA Updates Delinquent Filer Correction Program*, plansponsor.com (Jan. 28, 2013).]

Under IRS proposed regulations published in mid-2013, the administrators of large (250 or more tax returns filed per year) 401(k) and other plans would have to file Form 5500 and Form 8955-SSA electronically or on specified magnetic media. The proposals do not deal with ERISA reporting requirements. For plan years beginning on or after January 1, 2014, failure to make a required electronic filing will be penalized as failure to file. Waivers are theoretically available for hardship cases, but the preamble to the proposal says that waivers will rarely be granted. In practical terms, the proposal does not greatly change the employers' obligations, because DOL already required e-filing of Form 5500 and 5500-SF, and IRS's FIRE system allows e-filing for Form 8955-SSA. However, the small number of companies that file Form 5500-EZ and also file at least 250 returns a year must e-file the Form 5500-EZ. [*Employee Retirement Benefit Plan Returns Required on Magnetic Media*, 26 C.F.R. Part 301, 78 Fed. Reg. 53704 (Aug. 30, 2013); see EBIA Weekly, *IRS Proposed Regulations Would Require Electronic Filing for Certain Retirement Plan Reporting* (Sept. 5, 2013) (benefitslink.com)]

Form 8955-SSA is the annual registration statement identifying separated participants with deferred vested benefits, reporting the information about such benefits required by Code § 6057(a) for 401(k)s and other retirement plans. The information used to be reported on Schedule SSA, but it was replaced by Form 8955-SSA for plan years beginning on or after January 1, 2009. Unless there is an extension, Form SSA-8955 must be filed by the last day of the seventh month after the last day of the plan year: July 31 for a calendar year plan. There were few changes between the 2012 and 2013 versions. [EBIA Weekly, *IRS Releases 2013 Form 8955-SSA and Instructions* (Jan. 23, 2014) (benefitslink.com)]

Informational copies of the 2013 Form 5500 were released at the end of 2013. A section called Form M-1 compliance information was added to reflect the PPACA rules increasing DOL enforcement authority, and additional filing requirements, for multi-employer welfare plans. Any welfare plan required to file Form M-1 must file Form 5500 no matter the size of the plan or how it is funded. Schedule H has been updated to include a new question about whether defined benefit plans are PBGC-insured. The Schedule SB instructions have been updated to reflect MAP-21 provisions. [Kevin McGuinness, *DOL Releases Updated Form 5500*, plansponsor.com (Dec. 5, 2013)]

The DOL can assess civil penalties of up to $1,100 per day per annual report, running from the date of the failure or refusal to file and until a satisfactory report is filed, against plan administrators who fail or refuse to comply with the annual reporting requirements. A report that is rejected for failure to provide material information has not been "filed."

However, voluntary compliance is usually sought before penalties are imposed. The EBSA sends correspondence asking for additional information if data is omitted, or if the agency thinks corrections are necessary in light of the instructions or to be internally consistent with other data on the form.

The EBSA has discretion to waive all or part of the penalty based on submission of a timely statement showing reasonable cause for failure to file the complete report at the time it was due. Penalties are not assessed during the time when the DOL is considering the statement of reasonable cause.

CHAPTER 12

PLAN DISTRIBUTIONS

§ 12.01 INTRODUCTION

One of the major tasks of plan administration is to distribute benefits from the plan to participants and their designated beneficiaries—although sometimes determining the proper beneficiary is not as easy as it sounds. The plan administrator must communicate with participants and beneficiaries of their distribution options with respect to accrued benefits. The plan administrator has a duty to provide whatever forms are necessary to make an election.

The standard form of distribution is a single-life annuity for single participants and a Qualified Joint and Survivor Annuity (QJSA) for married participants. Before the Pension Protection Act (Pub. L. No. 109-280), plans were required to offer joint and 50% survivor annuities (i.e., the annuity payment is cut in half when one of the annuitants dies). The PPA requires plans to offer joint and 75% survivor annuities as well. The payments under a joint and 75% QJSA will be smaller than under a 50% survivor annuity, or under a single-life annuity covering only one spouse.

The plan must also provide for a Qualified Preretirement Survivor Annuity (QPSA) for married persons who die before their pension enters pay status.

But plans can permit other payment forms: lump sums and annuities offering other provisions (but not extending for a term longer than the life expectancy of the employee or the joint life expectancy of the employee and designated beneficiary). [See I.R.C. § 401(a)(9)(A)(ii)] It's up to the plan whether to offer these alternate forms, or just the standard annuities. [See §§ 12.03, 12.09]

When a corporation is acquired (see § 16.02[A]), one scenario is for the acquired corporation's plan to be terminated, with a distribution to all participants. All benefits become 100% vested when the plan is terminated. Participants must be given distribution election forms. They can take the fund in cash, make an IRA rollover or, if they have been hired by the acquiring corporation and the plan allows, they can make a rollover to the acquiror's plan. When payments are completed, the acquired corporation files a final Form 5500 and the plan is terminated. [Beth Harrington, *Impact Of Merger Or Acquisition On Company Retirement Plans* (Mar. 5, 2014) (benefitslink.com)]

A plan can be disqualified if it makes distributions outside the range of permitted events related to separation from service. A defined benefit or money purchase plan can only make distributions when the participant reaches Normal Retirement Age or separates from service. The rules are different for 401(k) plans: distributions can be made at retirement, death, attainment of age 59, disability, severance from employment, or hardship. Termination of service means ceasing to work for any entity that is treated as the same employer under the Code § 411 rules. However, employers are not prohibited from rehiring a former employee who has received a 401(k) distribution, although the IRS may look to whether there was a true termination or if the so-called termination was merely pretextual. The IRS might also accept distributions made to a person who is rehired for substantially different duties, and on a part-time rather than the previous full-time schedule, but there must have been an intervening period when the person was not employed by the employer.

The Heroes Earnings Assistance and Relief Tax Act (HEART Act; Pub. L. No. 110-245) allows reservists called for at least six months of active duty to take withdrawals from a 401(k) or other defined contribution plan before age 59½ without having to pay the 10% penalty. (The withdrawals are taxable income, however.) This provision was included in the Code; expired; and was revived and made permanent by the HEART Act. Differential pay provided to employees who have been called up (i.e., supplements that the employer provides to make up the difference between military pay and what the servicemember earned while working) must be taken into account when calculating pension benefits. The HEART Act also protects survivor benefits under qualified plans for the survivors of servicemembers killed in the line of duty. [Rebecca Moore, *Reservist Benefits Bill Signed into Law*, plansponsor.com (June 19, 2008)]

ERISA, at 29 U.S.C. § 1053(a), requires pension plans to provide that the right to normal retirement benefit is nonforfeitable at NRA. The Supreme Court denied certiorari in *Fry v. Exelon*, 571 F.3d 644 (7th Cir. 2009), 559 U.S. 936 (Feb. 22, 2010). The Seventh Circuit ruled that, before the PPA, it was lawful to define NRA as five years' service rather than a particular age. [Rebecca Moore, *Supreme Court Lets Stand Alternate Definitions for Retirement Age*, plansponsor.com (Feb. 23, 2010) But see *Laurent v. PriceWaterhouseCooper*, 963 F. Supp. 2d 310 (S.D.N.Y. Aug. 8, 2013), disapproving of using five years of service as an NRA.]

According to the Tenth Circuit, the ERISA ban on forfeitures does not make the plan liable for third-party wrongdoing. It was not a forfeiture when a plan incorrectly paid benefits to a participant's ex-wife instead of to him. It was the participant's fault that he did not give the plan his current address. His ex-wife learned how to access the benefits, got a user ID, changed the account password, filed a change of address form listing her P.O. Box as an address, and withdrew all the money from the account. The participant did not sue his ex-wife; he sued the plan under ERISA § 1132(a)(1)(A) for refusing to distribute the plan funds to him. [*Foster v. PPG Indus. Inc.*, 693 F.3d 1226 (10th Cir. 2012); see Rebecca Moore, *DC Assets Withdrawn Fraudulently Not Forfeited*, plansponsor.com (Dec. 5, 2012)]

In light of the volatility of investments, rising PBGC premiums, and longer lifespans for retirees, defined benefit plan sponsors seek "de-risking" strategies. Traditional strategies include liability-driven investing and annuitizing accrued benefits. Annuitization can be costly, but it transfers all liability risk to a third party. Another option is to cash out pension recipients completely, placing all the risk on them. Two recent IRS Private Letter Rulings (201228045, 201280511), state that this can be done without violating the minimum distribution rules. [Elizabeth Thomas Dold and David N. Levine, *A Look at Retiree Cashouts as the New De-Risking Strategy*, Taxes: The Tax Magazine (November 2012) (benefitslink.com)]

However, there has not been a strong demand for annuitization from plan participants: few young workers are interested in annuitizing. There is a concern about the level of fees and limited portability. A participant who invests in a deferred annuity product, changes jobs, and rolls over the balance may lose expenses already paid. But if the participant leaves the money in the ex-employer's plan, the employee will have to track and manage multiple plans. Another possibility is for a 401(k) account to be used like an annuity as a Social Security bridge strategy: that is, benefits are postponed in order to get a higher amount by delaying the start of Social Security benefits. [Sharon F. Fountain, Bloomberg BNA, *"Annuitizing" a 401(k) – Options for Plan Sponsors and Participants* (Nov. 30, 2012) (benefitslink.com)]

For many years (e.g., DOL Interpretive Bulletin 95-1, Advisory Opinion 2002-14A) the Department of Labor took the position that selecting an annuity provider is a fiduciary decision. In other words, failure to select the safest annuity available could lead to fiduciary liability. Then, in September 2007, to make annuity distributions more attractive, the DOL announced new rules relieving defined contribution plans from the "safest annuity available" rule. PPA § 665 mandated the DOL to issue regulations exempting defined contribution plans from this rule. First the DOL amended Interpretive Bulletin 95-1, effective November 13, 2007, limiting its applicability to defined benefit plans. Under the interim final rules, fiduciaries must select annuity providers with due care and skill, using factors such as the cost of the annuity vis-à-vis the benefits and administrative services offered; the annuity provider's capital, surplus and reserves; its rating; and whether it is covered by a state guarantee program. [Interim final rules, 72 Fed. Reg. 52004 (Sept. 12, 2007); safe harbor for fiduciaries choosing annuity providers, 72 Fed. Reg. 52021 (Sept. 12, 2007), discussed in Guest article, Deloitte Washington Bulletin, *DOL Releases Defined Contribution Plans from "Safest Annuity Available" Standard* (Sept. 17, 2007) (benefitslink.com)]

DOL final regulations on selection of annuity providers for individual account plans (such as 401(k) plans) were published in late 2008, effective December 8, 2008. The PPA limited the application of the Interpretive Bulletin 95-1 "safest available provider" rule to defined benefit plans, raising the question of what standard should be applied to defined contribution plans. To qualify for the safe harbor, the individual account plan fiduciary must perform an objective, thorough, and analytical search to select annuity providers. The selection must reflect a determination that the provider has the ability to make all future payments under the contract, and that the total cost of the annuity contract (including fees and commissions) is reasonable in light of the benefits the contract provides. [DOL Reg. § 2550.404a-4, 73 Fed. Reg. 58447 (Oct. 7, 2008); Amendment to Interpretive Bulletin 95-1, 73 Fed. Reg. 58445 (Oct. 7, 2008); see EBIA Weekly, *DOL Finalizes Annuity Selection Rule and Amendments to Plan Termination Rules for Missing Non-Spouse Beneficiaries* (Oct. 9, 2008) (benefitslink.com); Rebecca Moore, *DOL Issues Final Rules on Missing Benefits and Other PPA Provisions*, plansponsor.com (Oct. 6, 2008)]

Verizon decided to settle about $7.4 billion in liabilities to about 41,000 retirees by purchasing a single-premium group annuity contract from Prudential. The District Court for the Northern District of Texas dismissed a class action by the retirees, who charged a violation of ERISA § 102(b) in that the SPD did not disclose that Verizon retained the right to remove participants from the plan by transferring obligations to an insurance company. The district court held that § 102(b) only requires disclosure of the existing terms of a plan, not possible future changes. The plaintiffs said that the plan amendment and annuity transaction were fiduciary functions and it was a breach of fiduciary duty to avoid the rules that would have applied on termination They pointed out that participants removed from the plan are no longer protected by a PBGC guarantee. The district court held that amending a plan is not a fiduciary function and Verizon was not acting as a fiduciary when it purchased the annuity. The plaintiffs also alleged violation of ERISA § 510 and were discriminated against by being removed from the plan when other participants were allowed to remain. The district court held that the plaintiffs did not prove specific intent to interfere with their rights under the plan and failed to rebut the nondiscriminatory rationale offered by Verizon. The district court held that they did not have a right to continued participation. They could not use ERISA § 409(a), because they did not show a particularized, concrete, actual, or imminent injury, and did not show that the annuity would affect their benefit payments. [*Lee v. Verizon Communications Inc.*, 954 F. Supp. 2d 486 (N.D. Tex. 2013); see Kevin McGuinness, *Court Dismisses Verizon Pension Buy-out Suit,* plansponsor.com (June 25, 2013)]

The normal payment method for a profit-sharing plan or stock bonus plan is a lump sum, not a periodic payment. When a participant in one of these plans dies, the entire vested balance remaining in the account must go to the beneficiary designated by the participant. The spouse's consent is required if a married participant is to designate anyone other than the spouse as beneficiary.

In 2008, the Northern District of Illinois ruled that Verizon was bound by the language in a defined benefit plan document even if there was a drafting error (multiplying the cashout value of an interest in the former plan by a variable transaction factor twice rather than once), but the court ruled in 2009 that Verizon could correct the error and would not be required to provide a $1.67 billion windfall to participants. The 2009 decision treated the error as an honest mistake, and other actions in administering the plan reflected an intent to use the multiplication factor only once. Magistrate Judge Morton Denlow said that employers would be discouraged from adopting plans if they suffered unduly harsh penalties for mistakes. The Seventh Circuit affirmed this decision in August, 2010. [*Young v. Verizon* (N.D. Ill. 2009), *aff'd, Young v. Verizon*, 615 F.3d 808 (7th Cir. 2010). The Supreme Court refused to hear the case (No. 10-765), denying certiorari on May 23, 2011 and rehearing on July 25, 2011.]

A plan participant discovered that, as a result of a change in plan terms, she had been eligible for a full pension for almost eight years. The pension plan refused to pay her, stating that the plan forbids "retroactive payments." The

Fourth Circuit held that it was an abuse of discretion to deny her the payments because the plan explicitly allowed "restorative" benefits to correct administrative errors. [*Helton v. AT&T Inc. Pension Benefit Plan*, 709 F.3d 343 (4th Cir. 2013)]

The First Circuit held that, if a company representative, using an online benefits calculator, tells an employee that his retirement benefits will be greater than they actually are, the employee is only entitled to benefits as properly calculated under the plan, not the greater amount calculated by mistake. [*Livick v. Gillette Co.*, 524 F.3d 24 (1st Cir. 2008)]

However, the Seventh Circuit held that ERISA § 502 does not rule out enforcement of a pension plan's recoupment provisions (by suspending benefits to recover a past overpayment). The CBA said that pension and disability benefits were to be reduced by Social Security benefits payable to the employee, and that a grant of retroactive Social Security benefits would be treated as an overpayment that would trigger an obligation to reimburse the plan. The plaintiffs' argument was that the employer had to sue for equitable relief and could not enforce contract remedies, but the Seventh Circuit said that enforcing a contractual provision, like the CBA reimbursement requirement, is not "judicial relief," and employees can be held to clearly disclosed requirements to repay duplicative payments they have received. [*Northcutt v. GM Hourly Rate Employees Pension Plan*, 467 F.3d 1031 (7th Cir. 2006)]

Under federal law, overpayments must be returned to the pension plan—but the law does not state who must make the payments. Usually, the payor stops or reduces the payments until the overpayments have been recovered. Recoupment is also subject to state trust law, which requires decisions to be made based on equity principles, including "laches" (i.e., if a plan waits too long to recover overpayments, it may be held to have waived the right to repayment). There is no ceiling on the amount a private plan can recoup from later payments, but a multi-employer plan can impose only a 25% reduction, and the PBGC can reduce a pension by only 10% and does not impose interest. [Ellen E. Schultz, *'Overpaid' Pensions Being Seized*, WSJ.com (Aug. 13, 2010)]

The Northern District of New York approved a plan sponsor's order that a retiree pay back close to $730,000 in pension overpayments; the mere fact of payment did not prove that the recipient was entitled to the money. The retiree's breach of contract claim was preempted by ERISA, because his employment contract merely entitled him to payments pursuant to the plan and did not impose a legal duty to pay non-ERISA benefits. The appeals committee interpreted the plan provisions reasonably. The retiree did not work for a covered employer before he was hired by Kaiser in 1997, so he did not have any previous hours of employment. [*Baackes v. Kaiser Foundation Health Plan,* No. 1:12-cv-00583-FJS-RFT, 2014 U.S. Dist. LEXIS 678 (N.D.N.Y. Jan. 3, 2014); see *Benefit Overpayment Refund Request Gets Court Approval,* plansponsor.com (Jan. 8, 2014)]

A surviving spouse applied for benefits when her husband, who was receiving a pension, died. The benefit was much smaller than she expected and she sued to receive what she thought was the correct benefit. The issue was whether the survivor benefit would be offset by Social Security benefits. The Sixth Circuit ruled for the plan, holding that SPD language can control over conflicting plan language—but leaving something out of an SPD does not alter the terms of the plan. [*Lipker v. AK Steel Corp.*, 698 F.3d 923 (6th Cir. 2012); see John Murray and Violet Borowski, *Sixth Circuit Upholds Plan's Interpretation Of Ambiguous Spousal Benefit Provision*, Seyfarth Shaw ERISA & Employee Benefits Litigation Blog (Dec. 13, 2012) (benefitslink.com); Rebecca Moore, *SPD Omission Not a Conflict with Plan Terms*, plansponsor.com (Dec. 21, 2012)]

It was once common for plan sponsors to use the IRS letter forwarding service to locate the payees of benefits. However, effective for requests postmarked on or after August 31, 2012, the IRS no longer treats finding missing participants a "humane purpose." Plan sponsors will, therefore, have to use costlier and more laborious methods. DOL suggests using Internet search, credit reports, and commercial locater services to find missing participants. The Social Security Administration's forwarding service is still available, but at a cost of $25 per forwarded letter; the IRS used to forward up to 50 letters without charge. A terminating pension plan can use the PBGC missing participants program, paying the benefit to the PBGC, which will try to locate the participant. The PPA mandated the extension of this program to terminating 401(k) plans, but the PBGC never issued regulations. The PBGC also helps participants locate missing benefits. [McDermott Will & Emery, *IRS Eliminates Use of Letter Forwarding Service to Find Missing Participants and Beneficiaries* (Sept. 27, 2012) (benefitslink.com)]

[A] Disaster-Related Distributions

The Katrina Emergency Tax Relief Act of 2005 (KETRA), Pub. L. No. 109-73, provided that the 10% penalty on early withdrawals would not be imposed on a "qualified Hurricane Katrina distribution" of up to $100,000 withdrawn by a storm victim from a qualified retirement plan, 403(b) plan, or IRA, although the amounts would be treated as income, recognized over a three-year period. [IRS Publication 4492, *Information for Taxpayers Affected by Hurricanes Katrina, Rita and Wilma*)]

Although qualified hurricane distributions were announced for Hurricanes Katrina, Rita, and Wilma, they were not announced for Hurricane Irene, despite the severe financial impact of that storm. [Keith R. McMurdy, *Employees May Be Eligible for Retirement Funds After Natural Disasters*, Employee Benefit News (Sept. 9, 2011) (benefitslink.com)]

Nor was there a qualified hurricane distribution for Superstorm Sandy. But see IRS Announcement 2012-44, 2012-49 I.R.B. 663, relaxing the requirements for plan loans and hardship distributions for Sandy-related events. See also IR-2012-83 for Code § 7058A relief.

[B] Roth Distributions

The enactment of Roth IRAs and Roth 401(k)s (i.e., accounts that are not tax-advantaged when deposits are made, but permit tax-free withdrawals on appropriate conditions, including retention of the sums within the account for at least five years) created a need for specialized distribution rules.

Proposed regulations on the taxation of Roth 401(k) distributions say that the five-year holding period begins at the beginning of the tax year in which the first Roth 401(k) contribution is made and ends at the end of the fifth tax year. In a direct rollover, the holding period from the sending plan is considered under the receiving plan (this is known as "tacking"—i.e., the earlier holding period is tacked on). However, tacking is not applied if the participant makes an indirect rollover within the 60-day period. Only the taxable part of the distribution can be the subject of an indirect rollover.

Both qualified and nonqualified Roth 401(k) distributions that could otherwise be rolled over can be rolled over directly to another qualified plan that accepts Roth 401(k) contributions. Distributions to a participant can be rolled over to a Roth IRA, and the taxable part of the distribution can be rolled over to another plan that accepts Roth 401(k) funds. Even a person whose AGI is too high to make a Roth IRA contribution can roll funds over into a Roth IRA.

If one Roth plan does a plan-to-plan rollover to another Roth plan, the sending plan must inform the receiving plan that the distribution is a qualified distribution or the amount of the participant's basis and the date the five-year "clock" began to run. Participants are entitled to disclosure of the same information if they receive a distribution.

Partial distributions from a Roth plan allocate taxable income pro rata; that is, if $1,000 in a $10,000 account is income on amounts deposited into the plan, and the account owner receives a nonqualified distribution of $4,000, 10% is attributed to income and therefore is taxable income for the recipient; $3,600 is a nontaxable return of dieferred amounts. Only the amount contributed to the account (not earnings) can become a hardship distribution. [71 Fed. Reg. 4320 (Jan. 26, 2006)]

Final rules were published in April 2007, covering Roth 401(k) distribution issues. As in the proposed regulations, the central question is whether the distribution is a qualified distribution and thus excludable from the recipient's gross income. If the distribution is made to a beneficiary or an alternate payee, the participant's age, death, or disability status is the deciding factor, except for rollovers made by a surviving spouse or alternate payee to his or her own employer's Roth plan. Part of a Roth 401(k) distribution can be rolled over directly to a Roth 401(k) or Roth IRA, but a distribution from a designated Roth account can be rolled over only to a 401(k) plan or a 403(b) plan with a Roth feature. [T.D. 9324, RIN 1545-BF04, 72 Fed. Reg. 21103 (Apr. 30, 2007); see Prudential Retirement

Pension Analyst, *IRS Issues Final Roth 401(k) Distribution Rules* (Apr. 30, 2007) (benefitslink.com)]

See § 12.10 for Roth account rollover issues.

[C] PPA Rules

Although the main focus of the Pension Protection Act (PPA; Pub. L. No. 109-280) is on improving the funding mechanisms, and therefore the stability, of defined-benefit plans (including special rules for at-risk plans), this legislation has an impact on many areas of plan operations.

The Pension Protection Act forbids amendments that increase benefits in certain underfunded defined benefit plans (see § 5.10) unless the plan sponsor makes additional contributions or provides security. (This requirement does not apply to a new plan in its first five years of operation.) The PPA limits benefits that can be paid in a lump sum or other alternate form of distribution when a single-employer defined benefit plan is underfunded. For example, if its AFTAP (percentage of funding) is between 60%–80%, the plan cannot make an accelerated distribution that is greater than 50% of the amount otherwise payable, or that exceeds the present value of the maximum PBGC guarantee for the participant—whichever of the two is lower. See Code § 463(d)(3) and ERISA § 206(g)(3)(C). The PBGC publishes present-value tables every year for this purpose.

When an underfunded plan terminates, additional benefit accruals cease and the PBGC's guarantee covers only amounts earned before termination. If the plan terminates when the employer is bankrupt, only the benefits earned before the bankruptcy filing date are guaranteed. The PBGC pays benefits according to the terms of the plan. Most participants will receive their full benefits, but if the benefits exceed the limit on the PBGC guarantee, the PBGC will make estimated benefit payments while it examines the plan records, reducing any benefits that exceed the guarantee. For 80% of participants, the estimated benefit equals the final benefit, but the PBGC will make a single payment (including interest) to catch up if the final benefit is higher than the estimate. Anyone who retired before the PBGC take-over continues to receive the form of benefit already elected. Those who retire after the take-over choose from among the PBGC's annuity options. A participant who is not yet receiving payments from a terminated plan can begin to collect benefits at the plan's Normal Retirement Age. Someone who has already satisfied all the requirements (such as years of service) for early retirement as of the date of plan termination, or the earlier date on which the sponsor filed for bankruptcy protection, can begin early retirement benefits at early retirement age—but only if he or she is no longer employed by the plan sponsor. [PBGC, *PBGC's Guarantees for Single-Employer Pension Plans Fact Sheet*, <http://www.pbgc.gov/res/factsheets/page/guar-facts.html> (no date, accessed Apr. 14, 2012)]

For annuity dates starting in 2014, the present value of the PBGC's maximum guarantee ranges from $111,472 (at age 25), to $137,179 at 30, $161,327 at 35, $209,553 at 40, $337,939 at 50, $414,487 at 55, $750,830 at 65, and $1,091,293 at 70. [PBGC.gov, *Present Value of PBGC Maximum Guarantee,* <http://www.pbgc.gov/prac/mortality-retirement-and-pv-max-guarantee/present-guarantee.html>, accessed Apr. 7, 2014]

The PPA also changes the interest rate and mortality table for minimum lump sum benefits, by reducing mortality assumptions and by requiring interest rates to be based on corporate bond yields, which will reduce lump sums. Valuation issues, including limitations on distributions made by underfunded plans, are addressed by T.D. 9467, *Measurement of Assets and Liabilities for Pension Funding Purposes, Benefit Restrictions for Underfunded Pension Plans* [T.D. 9467, 2009-50 I.R.B. 760]

An exposure draft of updated mortality tables was released by the Society of Actuaries in mid-2014; if the tables are adopted, employers' liabilities for plan funding will increase significantly, in step with increases in life expectancy. [Meaghan Kilroy, *New Actuary Tables May Be "Nail In The Coffin" For DB Plans*, Pensions & Investments (July 24, 2014) (benefitslink.com)—that is, the increased liabilities may be the final factor leading some sponsors to terminate their defined benefit plans]

In late 2011, the PBGC published a proposed rule for determining benefits in a hybrid plan such as a cash balance plan. When a plan terminates, the variable rate to be used to determine accrued benefits is the average of the interest rates used by the plan in the five years before the date of termination. Variable interest rates create problems for the PBGC when a plan terminates because a participant's exact benefit can only be determined when he or she starts collecting benefits—so it is hard for the PBGC to decide if the benefit is de minimis and can be cashed out in a lump sum. The PBGC will use the present value methodology if the plan uses the § 417(e) present value rules to calculate the value of the lump sum. [76 Fed. Reg. 67105 (Oct. 31, 2011); see Rebecca Moore, *PBGC Issues Proposed Rule on Hybrid Plan Terminations,* plansponsor.com (Oct. 29, 2011); Deloitte's Washington Bulletin, *PBGC Proposes Rules on Determining Benefits in Terminating Hybrid Plans* (Nov. 7, 2011) (benefitslink.com)]

For plan amendments adopted and effective after November 8, 2012, plan sponsors who are bankruptcy debtors are permitted to amend single-employer defined benefit plans to eliminate certain optional forms of benefits without violating the anti-cutback rule. Under IRS regulations finalized in November 2012, optional forms of benefits, such as accelerated benefits that are greater than what the participant would have received as a single-life annuity, can be eliminated when the plan is not fully funded. The proposed regulations require the bankruptcy court rule that eliminating the optional benefit form is necessary to avoid an involuntary or distress termination. The PBGC's consent to terminate is required, based on the agency's conclusion that the plan is unable to provide the benefits guaranteed under ERISA § 404(d)(2). If the sponsor eliminates an optional form of benefit under these regulations and plan does not offer other options with substantial survivor benefits, the sponsor can add other options to provide those benefits as part of the amendment that eliminates the lump sum distribution option. The entire plan amendment is considered together in determining if the amendment can take effect in accordance with § 436(c). [77 Fed. Reg. 66915 (Nov. 8, 2012); see Kristen Heinzinger, *IRS Finalizes Relief for Bankrupt DB Sponsors*, plansponsor.com (Nov. 8, 2012)]

"Banked hours" are hours worked in addition to the minimum number of hours to earn a full year of service credit. They are banked to fill in for years when the participant would otherwise lack a full year's credit, and are cashed in at retirement as additional pension credits. When four union locals merged, they merged their plans, which all had different banked hour rules. Many participants got retrospective increases in their banked hour credits after the merger. The plan trust got into financial trouble and sought to eliminate banked hour benefits. Participants sued, alleging a violation of the anti-cutback provision. The First Circuit ruled that retroactively concurred benefits are benefits attributable to service that are accrued benefits protected by the anti-cutback provision. Even though they were conferred retroactively, the benefits were attributable to prior service. [*Bonneau v. Plumbers and Pipefitters Local Union 51 Pension Trust Fund*, 736 F.3d 33 (1st Cir. 2013)] Proposed regulations published in the fall of 2008 cover the PPA requirement that the notice of a participant's rights to defer an immediate distribution also explain the consequences of taking that distribution. A qualified plan cannot distribute benefits before Normal Retirement Age (NRA) without the consent of the participant, so rules are necessary to determine what constitutes valid and informed consent. There is no official format for the disclosures, but all of the information must be given together (e.g., in a list). However, if the required information is already available in other documents that the plan participant can obtain without charge, it is permissible to give cross-references to the other documents instead of repeating the information.

The regulations also deal with the increased period (rising from 90 to 180 days) for giving notice under Code §§ 402(f) [rollover notices], 411 [notice of the right to defer a distribution], and 417 [notice and election periods for 401(k) plans offering annuity distributions]. Cashouts of over $5,000 from a 401(k) plan require the consent of the plan participant, so the participant must be informed of the consequences of deferring versus receiving the distribution immediately (e.g., tax consequences; investment costs; other plan provisions such as availability of retiree health coverage that affect the decision).

PPA § 829 permits a non-spouse beneficiary to roll over a plan distribution to an IRA. [Prop. Treas. Reg. §§ 1.401(a)-13, 1.401(a)-20, 1.402(f)-1, 1.411(a)-11, 1.417(e)-1, 73 Fed. Reg. 59575 (Oct. 9, 2008); see EBIA Weekly, *IRS Proposes Regulations Addressing Notice of Participant's Right to Defer a Distribution and 180-Day Notice Period* (Oct. 9, 2008) (benefitslink.com)]

In a 2013 decision, the Seventh Circuit noted that a higher discount rate means a higher growth rate over the annuity period and a lower present value for lump sums, whereas a low discount rate means a higher lump sum. In a class action about the discount rates used by pension plans and top hat plans to convert a straight life annuity to lump sum, the Seventh Circuit upheld a grant of summary judgment for the plans. The pension plan used a segment rate of approximately 5.4%. The Seventh Circuit pointed out that the PPA allows retroactive increases in the discount rate, subject to a cap, so the change was not a cutback. While the plan forbade reduction in accrued benefits (the value of the straight-life annuity), it did not prevent a retroactive reduction in the benefits of participants who opted for a lump sum. The top hat plan used a higher discount rate (7.5%) but that was permissible because it was a nonqualified plan and the PPA cap did not apply. The plan also permitted a 7.5% discount rate for any plan that is not tax-preferred, a category that includes top hat plans. [*Dennison v. MONY Life Ret. Income Sec. Plan*, 710 F.3d 741 (7th Cir. 2013); see Brian Stolzenbach, Sam Schwartz-Fenwick and Chris Busey, *Seventh Circuit Reads Plan Language To Discount Plaintiffs' Rate Argument*, Seyfarth Shaw ERISA & Employee Benefits Litigation Blog (Mar. 20, 2013) (benefitslink.com)]

[D] Hardship Distributions

Economic problems increase the number of employees seeking hardship distributions from retirement plans. To prevent disqualifying the plan, the employer and plan administrators must follow both the plan document and legal requirements before allowing hardship distributions. A hardship distribution is permissible only if the plan allows it; if the employee (in some circumstances, the employee's spouse, dependent, or beneficiary) has an immediate and heavy financial need; and the distribution does not exceed the amount required to meet that need. Employees taking distributions should be required to provide verification of hardship was required by the terms of the plan—and that they have exhausted other loans and distributions from other available plans. The plan terms might also impose dollar limits or require distributions to be made only from salary reduction contributions. [<http://www.irs.gov/pub/irs-tege/fall09.pdf>, *Do's and Don'ts of Hardship Distributions* (Aug. 8, 2011)]

PPA § 826 allows a hardship distribution to be made based on the needs of a primary beneficiary who is not the participant's spouse and who has an unconditional right to receive part or all of the account balance when the participant dies. A § 409A plan can consider the needs of a beneficiary in determining if an emergency has occurred.

The recession has also led to more requests for hardship distributions. Participants in 401(k) plans can receive hardship distributions before age 59½ subject to limitations—but only if the plan provides for them. Plans can be disqualified for making improper distributions. Permissible distributions are made for an immediate and heavy financial need of the participant, determined based on all the facts and circumstances.

The regulations say that family funeral expenses count—but buying a boat or television set does not. The distribution must not be greater than the amount required to satisfy needs that cannot be met by other resources reasonably available to the participant (including resources of the participant's spouse), but it is permissible for the distribution to include taxes and penalties reasonably expected to result from the distribution. Unless it has actual knowledge to the contrary, the plan can rely on the participant's written representation that the need cannot be met by insurance; liquidating other assets; ceasing elective contributions; or taking out a commercial loan or a non-taxable loan from the employer's plan.

Hardship distributions cannot be made from accumulated non-elective employer contributions or qualified matching contributions. The plan administrator has discretion to decide if a request qualifies for a distribution, but discretion must be exercised based on the plan's objective, nondiscriminatory standards. The regulations provide a safe harbor set of guidelines that a plan can incorporate (e.g., defining "immediate and heavy financial need"). A distribution can be considered necessary if the employee has already taken all the distributions and non-taxable loans available under all employer-sponsored plans he or she participates in.

An employee who takes a hardship distribution cannot make any elective contribution or after-tax employee contribution to any plan sponsored by the employer for at least six months after the distribution. Administrators should document representations that applicants made about their requests for hardship distributions, and should document why they granted or rejected the application; the source of the distribution; and that it does not exceed the amount needed. [Bruce K. Leigh and Kenneth W. Ruthenberg, Jr., Chang Ruthenberg & Long, *Hardship Distributions and Headaches Down the Road* (2009) (benefitslink.com)]

Rev. Rul. 2010-27, 2010-45 I.R.B. 620 lists examples of expenses that could qualify for an unforeseeable emergency distribution from a 409A plan—e.g., illness or accident affecting participant or spouse, dependents, or beneficiary; family funeral expenses; imminent foreclosure. Emergency distributions can only be made for expenses that cannot otherwise be met by insurance or by liquidating assets. [McGuireWoods LLP Legal Updates, *IRS Issues Guidance on Unforeseeable Emergency Distributions from § 409A and § 457(b) Plans* (Dec. 30, 2010) (benefitslink.com)]

§ 12.02 CASHOUT

Although it is burdensome for a plan to make periodic payments of a very small sum, and it would be convenient to simply close the books by making a one-time payment, participants cannot be forced to "cash out" (take a lump sum instead of a stream of payments) unless their vested balance is very small—$5,000 or less.

EGTRRA provides for automatic rollovers of cashouts from 401(k) plans in amounts between $1,000 and $5,000 to IRAs.

The calculation of the accrued benefit under I.R.C. § 411(a)(7)(B)(i) does not have to include any service with respect to which the employee has already been cashed out at a level below $3,500.

The 2002 technical corrections bill, the Job Creation and Worker Assistance Act of 2002 [Pub. L. No. 107-147] provides that employers can disregard rollovers when they determine whether or not the balance exceeds $5,000 and therefore whether or not it is subject to cashout.

A qualified plan can include a provision cashing out distributions under $5,000; mandatory distributions that exceed $1,000 must be rolled over to an IRA set up by the plan for the participant, unless the recipient makes an affirmative election to roll over the money elsewhere or takes it in cash. Fiduciaries are deemed to have satisfied their duties with respect to rollovers if the plan satisfies the requirements of I.R.C. § 401(a)(31)(B). These rules apply to distributions made without consent of the participant, at normal retirement age or age 62 (whichever is later). An eligible rollover distribution that is a plan loan offset is not subject to the general rules on automatic rollovers. QDROs and distributions to participants' spouses are not covered.

§ 12.03 LUMP SUMS

There is no legal requirement that plans offer lump sum distributions, although it is very common for them to do so for the convenience of retirees who either need a lump sum (to pay the entrance fee to a Continuing Care Retirement Community, for example) or who believe that they can achieve better investment results than a qualified plan, subject to fiduciary requirements, can muster. The interaction between PPA funding requirements and the post-2008 recession made employers less willing to distribute balances, especially large balances, in lump-sum form. Since the stock market decline, the PPA's rules often prevent the 25 highest-compensated employees from taking lump sums, because top earners are forbidden lump sums if the plan assets fall below 110% of liabilities, or if the lump sum represents more than 1% of total plan assets. However, there are loopholes, such as the executive's promise to repay if the plan terminates when it is insufficiently funded, or setting aside funds in an escrow account. [Jilian Mincer, *Execs Finding It Harder to Get Lump Sums*, WSJ.com (May 12, 2009)] The Pension Protection Act says that if any defined benefit plan is severely underfunded, or if the plan is underfunded and the plan sponsor is bankrupt, all payouts must be in annuity form—lump sum distribution is forbidden.

In the fall of 2009, the Supreme Court heard arguments about treatment of lump sums received at the time of the first retirement by rehired employees. The plan had two provisions. The "non-duplication" provision called for offsetting the "floor" amount, based on total years of service with the company. The "phantom account provision" further reduced benefits at retirement. The Second Circuit refused to grant deference to the administrator's determination.

The Supreme Court announced its decision on April 21, 2010, strongly affirming the discretion of plan administrators, and holding that, as long as the plan gives administrators the discretion to interpret the plan, courts must defer to the administrators' decisions as long as they are reasonable. (Of course, this principle does not prevent plan participants from bringing suits that claim that the administrators made an unreasonable decision!) [*Conkright v. Frommert*, 559 U.S. 506 (2010)] The case returned to the Second Circuit, which remanded it for a third time in late 2013. The Second Circuit held that the plaintiffs' suit is meritorious: the proposed offset method was unreasonable, and the SPD was not accurate enough because did not say that the lump sum distribution will reduce the benefit, only that it might. [*Frommert v. Conkright,* 738 F.3d 522 (2d Cir. 2013); see Kevin McGuinness, *Appellate Court Remands Case on Offsetting Pension Benefits*, plansponsor.com (Dec. 31, 2013)]

If a plan offers both lump sums and early retirement subsidies, the plan should specify whether the subsidy can be included in the lump sum, or must be taken in annuity form.

The Seventh Circuit ruled that Cost of Living Increases are accrued benefits required by ERISA (not merely ancillary benefits), and therefore must be included in the calculation of lump sums if annuitants receive COLAs. Failure to do so violates the anti-cutback rule. [*Williams v. Rohm & Haas Pension Plan*, 497 F.3d 710 (7th Cir. 2007); see Rebecca Moore, *COLAs Must Be Included in Lump-Sum Benefits for DB Participants*, plansponsor.com (Aug. 15, 2007); Brian S. King, *Limits on How Plan Benefits Are Provided*, ERISA Law Blog (Aug. 16, 2007) (benefitslink.com)] In March 2008, the Supreme Court refused to hear an appeal of the Seventh Circuit's decision. [Rebecca Moore, *High Court Lets Stand Decision on COLAs in Lump-sum Calculations*, plansponsor.com (Mar. 18, 2008). The case was finally disposed of by a settlement with approximately 18,000 plan participants, with half of the $180 million settlement paid out by September 30, 2010, the other half in September 2011:*Williams v. Rohm & Haas Pension Plan*, No. 4:04-CV-0078-SEB-WGH (S.D. Ind. 2010); see Fred Schneyer, *Rohm and Haas Pension Settlement Gets Final OK*, plansponsor.com (Apr. 14, 2010). The Northern District of Oklahoma followed this reasoning: *Pikas v. Williams Cos. Inc.*, No. 4:08-cv-101-GKF-PJC, 2012 U.S. Dist. LEXIS 150603 (N.D. Okla. Oct. 19, 2012); see Rebecca Moore, *Pension Lump Sums Must Account for COLAs*, plansponsor.com (Jan. 10, 2013)]

§ 12.04 ANTI-ALIENATION RULE

The underlying purpose of pension plans is to provide income to retirees and their families once the individual is no longer able to work. This purpose could not be satisfied if the pension became unavailable for some reason. Therefore, pension, annuity, stock bonus, and profit-sharing plans are subject to anti-alienation requirements under I.R.C. §§ 401(a)(13) and 404(a)(2). The benefits under such plans may not be assigned or alienated in advance. But, just as with any legal rule, there are certain exceptions to what seems to be a blanket prohibition.

Federal tax liens under I.R.C. § 6331 can be enforced; they are not considered to violate this provision. [Treas. Reg. § 1.401(a)-13(b)(2)] The anti-alienation provision does not prevent the IRS from proceeding against an interest in ERISA plan benefits. [*United States v. McIntyre*, 222 F.3d 655 (9th Cir. 2000)]

Once a benefit is in pay status, a participant or beneficiary can make a voluntary revocable assignment of up to 10% of any benefit payment. However, assignments of this type cannot be used to defray the costs of plan administration.

A plan loan is not an improper alienation if:

- The plan includes a specific loan provision;
- Loans are available to all participants on a nondiscriminatory basis;
- The loan is not a prohibited transaction;
- The plan imposes a reasonable interest rate on plan loans;
- The loan is secured by the accrued nonforfeitable benefit. [See I.R.C. § 4975(d)(1) and § 4.18]

The Supreme Court's decision in *Patterson v. Shumate* [504 U.S. 753 (1992)] holds that ERISA's anti-alienation provisions are "applicable non-bankruptcy law" under Bankruptcy Code § 541(c)(1). Therefore, benefits from an ERISA-qualified plan can be excluded from the employee's bankruptcy estate, and will not be available to the employee's creditors.

But because of an earlier Supreme Court decision, *Mackey v. Lanier Collection Agency & Service* [486 U.S. 825 (1988)], pension benefits are protected from creditors, but welfare benefits are not. Creditors are sometimes entitled (within limits) to garnish the wages of debtors, but they cannot garnish future pension benefits. If the plan itself is terminating, creditors cannot garnish employees' interests in the plan, even if one consequence of the termination is that they will receive a lump sum instead of ongoing annuity payments. In 2005, the Supreme Court ruled, in *Rousey v. Jacoway*, 544 U.S. 320, that IRAs are entitled to the same bankruptcy protection as qualified plans. Also in 2005, Congress increased the bankruptcy protection granted to IRAs and qualified plans, via Pub. L. No. 109-8, the Bankruptcy Abuse Prevention and Consumer Protection Act (BAPCA). BAPCA also makes it harder for bankrupt employers to modify their retiree health benefits.

Once the benefits are paid, the anti-alienation provision no longer applies. [See *Robbins v. DeBuono*, 218 F.3d 197 (2d Cir. 2000)] So, unless there is a state law that offers additional protection, the funds can be attached by creditors.

In mid-2003, the Eighth Circuit ruled that a state domestic relations order had higher priority than a prior federal tax lien. Therefore, in a case where the IRS pursued remedies against a divorced airline pilot, the QDRO in the ex-wife's favor prevailed (even though there were technical deficiencies in the order that required it to be reformed twice by the court). The Eighth Circuit read Code § 6323(a) to require the IRS to file a notice of lien to secure its priority in situations like this one, where the ex-wife had the status of a judgment lien creditor. [*United States v. Taylor*, 338 F.3d 947 (8th Cir. 2003)]

§ 12.05 QJSA/QOSA PAYMENTS

The normal method of paying pension plan benefits to married participants is the QJSA, payable for the lives of both the employee and his or her spouse. Once the first spouse dies, the plan can reduce the annuity payable to the survivor—although not more than 50% of the initial payment, for a joint and 50% survivor annuity. Employers can also choose to subsidize the survivor annuity at some level between 50% and 100% of the original payment, and the Pension Protection Act requires a joint and 75% survivor annuity to be offered as an option when a QJSA is required.

In addition to the QJSA/QPSA, a plan can offer term annuities and/or life annuities, and life annuities can include term certain guarantee features.

Why would a couple be willing to waive the standard form and take a payment other than a QJSA? For one thing, the payments might be larger in the short run. The participant might be the first spouse to retire, with additional funds expected in the future from the other spouse's pension. If the spouse who is expected to survive will have ample funds (e.g., from personal assets and insurance on the life of the other spouse), then a reduced or absent survivor annuity may not create problems.

I.R.C. § 417(d) provides that QJSAs are required only if the participant was married for one year or more before plan payments begin, with an exception for participants who marry in the year before payments begin and remain married for one year. To avoid tracking problems, most plans simply offer QJSAs to all married participants whatever the duration of the marriage.

Because of a 1984 federal law, the Retirement Equity Act, the employee spouse cannot waive the QJSA without the written consent of the other spouse. There is a 60-day window for making the waiver, starting 90 days before the annuity start date (the first day of the employee spouse's first benefit period under the plan), ending 30 days before the annuity start date. However, the Small Business Job Protection Act [Pub. L. No. 104-188] amended the Internal Revenue Code to allow QJSA disclosures to be given even after the annuity starting date.

A waiver of the right to receive the pension in QJSA form must be in writing, and must either be notarized or witnessed by a representative of the pension plan. [See Treas. Reg. § 1.417(e)-1(b)(3)] In 2000, when the IRS and DOL were gearing up for implementing electronic filing of notices and disclosures, Proposed Regulations were issued (65 Fed. Reg. 6001) that did not allow a spouse's waiver of the QJSA to be made electronically, because a physical signature and a physical notarization were required. However, the October 20, 2006 Final Rules allow the waiver to be done electronically, as long as there are safeguards for the validity of the signature, and as long as the electronic signature and the verification by the notary can be printed out from the electronic system. [71 Fed. Reg. 61877 (Oct. 20, 2006)]

Furthermore, the waiver must be expressed in a document specifically related to the plan; a prenuptial agreement between the employee and his or her spouse won't work for this purpose. [Treas. Reg. § 1.401(a)-20, Q&A 28] The waiver binds only the spouse who signs it; if the employee and spouse divorce, any subsequent spouse is still entitled to a QJSA unless he or she waives it. [I.R.C. § 417(a)(4)]

An antenuptial agreement did not waive the ex-wife's right to 401(k) funds. The plan participant married the same woman three times and divorced her twice; at the time of his death, a third divorce was in the works. They signed a prenuptial contract before the third wedding waiving all claims in the other's separate property. The agreement defined retirement benefits as separate property. The prenuptial agreement contemplated future execution of a waiver or consent to beneficiary change. Hr consent did not satisfy the requirement if acknowledgment of the effect of the change. ERISA waiver requirements must be strictly complied with. [*MidAmericanPension and Employee Benefits Plan Administrative Committee v. Cox*, 720 F.3d 715 (8th Cir. 2013)]

A business owner was both the sole participant in a plan and the plan representative so the Seventh Circuit held that his spouse's written consent to waive the right to an annuity from the plan was valid, even though her signature was not witnessed. ERISA § 205(C)(2)(A)(iii) requires a spousal waiver of the right to a survivor annuity to be written—and witnessed by a notary or plan representative. After the husband died, the wife sought benefits under the plan. She admitted that she had signed the waiver of joint and survivor annuity, but said the document was invalid because it had not been witnessed. The Seventh Circuit upheld the waiver and awarded benefits to the husband's sons, saying that it would be absurd to invalidate the consent form; the husband obviously knew that his wife had signed the form. [*Burns v. Orthotek, Inc. Employees' Pension Plan and Trust*, 657 F.3d 571 (7th Cir. 2011); see CCH Pensions & Benefits, *Lack Of Witness' Attestation Signature Did Not Invalidate Spouse's Signed Consent to Annuity Waiver* (Nov. 3, 2011) (benefitslink.com)]

In this context, ERISA preempts community property law [*Boggs v. Boggs*, 520 U.S. 833 (1997)], so a spouse who waives the right to a QJSA, can't later assert community property rights in those benefits.

The PPA mandates that plans that have to offer QJSAs must, for plan years beginning after December 31, 2007, offer Qualified Optional Survivor Annuities (QOSAs). A QOSA is a joint and survivor annuity where the survivor receives

75% of the original annuity level (if the QJSA would otherwise provide less) or 50% if the QJSA has a survivor percentage of 75% or more, actuarially equivalent to the single life annuity payable at the same time. If the existing plan terms provide a joint and survivor annuity which satisfies the QOSA percentage requirements, it is not necessary to amend the plan to adopt a QOSA. The requirement is that the QOSA be actuarially equivalent to a single-life annuity; it doesn't have to be equivalent to a QJSA. If the QOSA is actuarially equivalent to the QJSA, the participant's spouse is not required to consent to the participant electing the QOSA. However, spousal consent is required to elect a QOSA which is less valuable than the QJSA. The PPA does not obligate plans to provide an option for the QOSA that works the same way as a qualified pre-retirement survivor annuity does for the QJSA. [Notice 2008-30, 2008-12 I.R.B. 638; see Deloitte Washington Bulletin, *IRS Issues Guidance on PPA Distribution Changes* (Mar. 17, 2008) (benefitslink.com)]

Internal Revenue Code § 417(a)(1)(A)(ii) allows the plan participant to revoke the waiver of QJSA payment at any time before payments begin. The spouse's consent is not required for the revocation, because it has the effect of increasing, not decreasing, the spouse's rights.

[A] Section 415 Regulations

Final Regulations under § 415, reflecting the PPA as well as interim changes since the previous set of Final Regulations issued in 1981, were published in the Federal Register for April 5, 2007, effective for limitation years beginning on or after July 1, 2007. Section 415 governs the limitations on benefits that can be provided under defined benefit plans, as well as the contributions that can be made to 401(k) and other defined benefit plans. For most plans, which are operated on a calendar year, that meant that the new rules would take effect January 1, 2008. Plans can provide that payments in any limitation year will not exceed the § 415(b) limit as of the annuity starting date, and increased pursuant to § 415(d); if this is done, the plan does not require actuarial adjustments for automatic increases unless the benefit is subject to § 417(e)(3).

Under the PPA, compensation used to calculate the "high 3" years does not have to be earned while the employee is an active plan participant. In general, the "high 3" is calculated subject to the annual compensation limit of § 401(a)(17), but the Final Regulations allow grandfathering-in of some additional compensation based on plan provisions that were in effect before April 5, 2007. In general, money received after severance from employment is not considered § 415 compensation, but the Final Regulations allows inclusion of certain payments under bona fide sick or vacation leave plans—even if the payments are made more than 2½ months after severance from employment or the end of the year.

The final regulations allow some payments from non-qualified plans to be treated as § 415 compensation, as well as certain payments to disabled participants. The IRS announced its intentions to revise the rules covering multiple annuity starting dates. Various technical changes are made in the way that defined benefit payouts are adjusted when payment begins between ages 62 and 65. [Final Rule, 72 Fed. Reg. 16878 (Apr. 5, 2007), discussed in Sutherland Asbill & Brennan LLP Legal Alert, *Section 415 Final Regulations Clarify Rules*, (Apr. 10, 2007); Rebecca Moore, *IRS Issues Final, Comprehensive 415 Regulations*, plansponsor.com (Apr. 5, 2007). The final regulations are based on Proposed Regulations, T.D. 7748, 70 Fed. Reg. 31214 (May 31, 2005).]

[B] QLACs

In early 2012, the Treasury proposed a rule, explained in a fact sheet, under which workers would have more options for lifetime income to cope with the potential for living to very old age. The proposal would allow employees who take a lump sum 401(k) distribution to transfer part of the sum to the employer's defined benefit plan (provided that the employer has a defined benefit plan and it accepts such contributions) in exchange for an actuarially fair annuity—perhaps a longevity annuity, a life annuity that begins payments at an advanced age such as 85. This option is referred to as a Qualified Longevity Annuity Contract, or QLAC.

Prior law disfavored longevity annuities by mandating minimum required distribution calculations based on distributing the entire sum over the person's actuarially predicted life expectancy—creating the risk of outliving one's assets.

The proposed regulations make it easier for a plan to offer split options by simplifying the calculation of the benefit. Prior law required the statutory interest rate and mortality assumptions to be used for both the lump sum and the annuity, preventing plans from using their own figures in annuity calculations. The proposal would allow the plan's regular conversion factors to be used for the partial annuity, while the statutory factors apply to the lump sum.

The 2012 proposal identifies certain plan and annuity terms that are deemed to protect spousal rights and for which spousal consent will not be required before the annuity begins. At the annuity start date, the insurer issuing the annuity would be responsible for compliance with the consent requirements. [Proposed Regulations, 77 Fed. Reg. 5443 and 5454 (Feb. 3, 2012); see DOT Retirement Security Fact Sheet, *Helping American Families Achieve Retirement Security by Expanding Lifetime Income Choices* (Feb. 2, 2012); see Retirement Town Hall, *IRS Proposes Rule To Encourage Partial Annuity Distribution Options In Pension Plans* (Feb. 9, 2012) (benefitslink.com)]

When the QLAC rules were finalized in mid-2014, the limit on the amount of the account balance that can be used to purchase the QLAC was changed, to the lesser of $125,000 or 25% of the balance. The QLAC annuity must not be indexed or variable, and must not include a cash surrender provision. Annuity payments must begin no later than the time the participant reaches age 85, but this age limit will be adjusted actuarially to reflect increases in lifespan. [T.D. 9673, 2014-30 I.R.B. 212; see Tara Siegel Bernard, *Longevity Insurance Joins the Menu of Retirement Plan Options*, NYTimes.com (July 1, 2014)]

§ 12.06 POST-DEATH PAYMENTS

The terms of the plan, and the fact situation, determine whether payments must continue after the death of the plan participant. For instance, if the employee was unmarried and received a life annuity, or if the employee was married and the employee and spouse validly waived the QJSA in favor of a life annuity, the plan will have no post-death obligations. Usually, however, the plan will be required to make a single or ongoing distributions to a beneficiary designated by the employee, or named as beneficiary under the terms of the plan.

Internal Revenue Code § 401(a)(9)(B) provides that if an employee dies when an annuity or installment pension with a survivorship feature is in pay status, the plan continues distributions in the same manner, but to the beneficiary rather than the retiree. The general rule is that the plan has five years from the death of the employee to complete distribution of the decedent's entire interest.

The five-year rule does not apply if the decedent's interest is payable to a designated beneficiary in life annuity form, or in installments that do not extend past the beneficiary's life expectancy. In this situation, the plan must begin the distributions no later than December 31 of the year following the date of the employee's death.

Qualified plans are required to provide Qualified Preretirement Survivor Annuities (QPSAs) if a vested plan participant dies before benefits begin. [I.R.C. § 401(a)(11)] The QPSA for a defined benefit plan participant who was eligible to retire at the time of death must be at least as great as what the spouse would have received if the employee had retired with the QJSA on the day before the actual date of death.

In the case of a person who was not yet retirement-eligible on the date of death, the defined benefit plan must calculate the survivor annuity that would have been available if the employee had separated from service on the date he or she died, and survived until the plan's earliest retirement date. The QPSA must be at least equivalent to the QJSA that would have been payable if the employee spouse had died the day after retiring with a QJSA on the plan's earliest retirement date.

In a defined contribution plan, the QPSA must be actuarially equivalent to at least 50% of the nonforfeitable account balance as of the time of death.

The designated beneficiary can also be an irrevocable trust that is valid under state law and has identifiable beneficiaries. It's the responsibility of the employee who wants to take this option to provide the plan with a copy of the trust.

According to I.R.C. § 401(a)(9)(B), if an employee dies once payment of an annuity or installment pension has begun, the plan simply continues the distributions in the same manner—unless, of course, they are supposed to stop at the employee's death.

Plans are allowed to reduce pension benefits to fund the QPSA. Therefore, participants (with the consent of the spouse of a married participant) have the right to waive the QPSA in order to prevent this reduction in the pension amount.

The plan must notify participants of the right to waive the QPSA. The notice must be given in the period that starts on the first day of the plan year in which the participant reaches age 32 and ends with the close of the plan year before the plan year in which the participant reaches age 35. [I.R.C. § 417(a)(3)(B)]

The notice must disclose:

- The terms and conditions of the QPSA;
- The effect of waiving it;
- The spouse's right to invalidate the waiver by withholding consent;
- The participant's right to revoke the waiver and reinstate the QPSA

Rev. Rul. 2012-3, 2012-8 I.R.B. 383 explains how the QJSA and QPSA rules work when a deferred annuity contract is purchased under a profit-sharing plan. Rev. Rul. 2012-4, 2012-8 I.R.B. 386 explains when an annuity provided by a defined benefit plan after a rollover can satisfy §§ 411 and 415. [Rebecca Moore, *IRS Issues Guidance About Annuities in Retirement Plans*, plansponsor.com (Feb. 2, 2012)]

The Tenth Circuit ruled in 2009 that the anti-cutback rule does not apply to a death benefit, or a plan feature that pays a lump sum at retirement that is the actuarial equivalent of a death benefit. The death benefit was not an accrued benefit, because the plan's definition of accrued benefit excluded death benefits. Nor was it a retirement-type subsidy, because that term is limited to benefits that continue after retirement. [*Kerber v. Qwest Pension Plan*, 572 F.3d 1135 (10th Cir. 2009); see Stanley D. Baum, *Tenth Circuit Determines That Elimination of a Pension Plan's Death Benefit Does Not Violate ERISA's Anti-Cutback Rule*, ERISA Lawyer Blog (July 22, 2009) (benefitslink.com). See *In re Lucent*, 541 F.3d 250 (3d Cir. 2008) for the proposition that the death benefit was not an accrued benefit.]

[A] Beneficiary Designation Case Law

Although the broad principle of ERISA preemption is well-settled, there is still tension between federal regulation of pensions and benefits and the traditional state domination of the domestic relations field, so case continue to be decided on issues such as beneficiary designations that have not been updated to reflect the state of the plan participant's family at the time of his or her death.

Federal employees are covered by the Federal Employees' Group Life Insurance Act of 1954 (FEGLIA), which permits employees to name the beneficiary of their life insurance. Death benefits accrue first to the named beneficiary, followed by others in the statutory line of precedence. A Virginia statute revokes the beneficiary designation of a former spouse whenever there is a change in marital status. Another Virginia statutory provision says that, if that provision is preempted by federal law, the ex-spouse will have to compensate the person who would otherwise have received the benefits for the benefits that person lost. Hillman named his first wife Judy Maretta as beneficiary of his FEGLI policy. They divorced and he remarried without changing the beneficiary designation. When Hillman died, Maretta collected the proceeds, and second wife Jacqueline Hillman sued her. The Supreme Court ruled in mid-2013 that state laws are preempted to the extent of any conflict with a federal statute. The relevant federal scheme gives highest priority to the beneficiary by the insured, which must be respected. [*Hillman v. Maretta*, 133 S.Ct. 1943 (2013)]

Boggs and *Egelhoff* hold that the benefits of an ERISA plan pass under the plan's designated terms, and state law cannot be used to divert benefits from the designated beneficiary. *Kennedy* questioned whether "wresting" is allowed; *Hillman v. Maretta* & *Windsor* resolved the issue.

State laws, including trust and estate laws, can govern compensation that is accrued but unpaid at the employee's death that does not consist of ERISA benefits: for example, wages, commissions, and bonuses. But ERISA preempts state court requiring participant to make a beneficiary designation, or a beneficiary to waive or consent to waiver of benefits.

ERISA also preempts laws that revoke beneficiary designation on divorce. Waivers in domestic relations orders that are inconsistent with plan terms are invalid. Best practice is to draft beneficiary designations to explain what happens if a beneficiary dies before the plan participant, and to explain that federal law governs challenges to the effectiveness of the designation (e.g., allegations of fraud or undue influence). The DOL's position is that the plan should bring an interpleader action in QDRO cases if, after the plan makes a determination and its decision has been appealed, there is still conflict about benefit entitlement. But for other disputes, the plan must pay the benefit to the successful claimant, and then defend the denial decision just like any other benefit denial decision.[Albert Feuer, *Determining the Death Beneficiary Under an ERISA Plan and the Rights of Such a Beneficiary*, 54 Tax Management Memorandum 323 Aug. 26, 2013 abstract: benefitslink.com]

The Seventh Circuit held that federal law does not always preempt state law on assignment of plan assets, and Merrill Lynch, as custodian holding assets of an ERISA plan, had to comply with state court order freezing payment of benefits. The Seventh Circuit did not eliminate the plan's obligation to contest the court order; the IRS might try to disqualify the plan for failure to carry out the order. [*Johnson v. Merrill Lynch, Pierce, Fenner & Smith, Inc.*, 719 F.3d 601 (7th Cir. 2013); see Todd B. Castleton, *Court Says ERISA Plan Custodian Had To Comply With State Order Attaching Plan Assets*, Proskauer Rose LLP (Oct. 7, 2013), available at Lexology.com]

IRS Employee Plans News announced in September 2013 that the IRS will no longer allow pre-approved plans to automatically revoke spousal beneficiary designation at legal separation. (Automatic revocation on divorce is still acceptable.) Legal separation only eliminates the requirement that the participant obtain spousal consent to waive spousal death benefit and substitute another beneficiary. The separated spouse will receive the spousal death benefit unless the plan participant waived the death benefit and specifically named a different beneficiary. Automatic revocation language in the plan will not, by itself, satisfy the waiver requirement. The IRS said that an individually designed plan must either eliminate such language or clarify that revocation does not affect the spouse's right to QPSA death benefit. [Rebecca Moore, *Certain Revocations of Spousal Beneficiaries Not Allowed*, plansponsor.com (Sept. 25, 2013); Mazursky Constantine LLC, *IRS: No Automatic Beneficiary Revocation on Legal Separation* (October 9, 2013) (benefitslink.com)]

The Eighth Circuit held that a wife was not properly informed of her waiver of pension rights when she signed a prenuptial agreement. The agreement waived all rights with respect to her husband's separate property, and listed the husband's retirement plan account as an asset. When the husband died, with his parents named as beneficiaries, he had filed for divorce, but the divorce had not yet been finalized. The plan administrator asked the wife to sign a waiver so the benefits could go to the husband's parents. She refused, and the plan asked for court guidance about how to distribute the benefits. The district court awarded the benefits to the parents, but the Eighth Circuit reversed, holding that she prenuptial agreement was not sufficient to satisfy ERISA § 1055(c)(2)(A)(iii)'s requirement for a waiver—leaving the wife as the proper recipient of the benefits. The Eighth Circuit held that the prenuptial agreement did not clearly and expressly inform the wife that she would be entitled to survivor benefits that were waived by the agreement. [*MidAmerican Pension & Emp. Benefits Plan Admin. Comm. v. Cox*, 720 F.3d 715 (8th Cir. 2013); see Kevin McGuinness, *Prenup Not Sufficient Notice of Benefits Waiver*, plansponsor.com (July 22, 2013)]

A divorce court order requiring a plan participant to name his children as retirement plan beneficiaries did not take precedence over his surviving spouse's right to receive a QPSA, because the dissolution agreement in favor of the children did not satisfy the requirements for a QDRO. The agreement did not require action by the plan; did not assign the death benefits to the children; did not specify when the payments began; and did not specifically remove the spouse's right to a QPSA. According to the Ninth Circuit, the QPSA is payable unless the surviving spouse waives it, which was not true in this case. A QDRO can replace the former spouse with the current spouse as payee, but cannot name other beneficiaries without consent of the former spouse. [*Hamilton v. Wash. State Plumbing & Pipefitting Indus. Pension Plan*, 433 F.3d 1091 (9th Cir. 2006), discussed in Rebecca Moore, *Supreme Court Lets Stand QPSA Decision*, plansponsor.com (Oct. 3, 2006)]

Hunter designated his wife as primary beneficiary, and did not designate secondary beneficiaries. When she predeceased him, he did not name a beneficiary. The plan says that in the absence of a valid beneficiary designation, benefits will be distributed to the surviving spouse; if none, the order of distribution is to children, parents, siblings, and the executor of the administrator of the of the estate. The plan distributed the $300,000 benefits to Hunter's six siblings. The stepsons sued to recover the benefits. They said that they were his children as evidenced by Hunter's leaving his estate to his "beloved sons." The Fifth Circuit held that, because the stepson were never adopted, it was reasonable to refuse to treat them as Hunter's children; legal adoption is a reasonable way to determine status as a child of the participant. It cannot be assumed that all stepparents want their stepchildren to inherit from them. The Fifth Circuit said that "equitable adoption" means promises or actions that preclude a person from denying that that person adopted a child. It does not create a parent-child relationship, and is not binding on an ERISA plan. [*Herring v. Campbell*, 690 F.3d 413 (5th Cir. 2012); see Rebecca Moore, *Stepchildren not "Children" for Purposes of Death Benefit*, plansponsor.com (Aug. 20, 2012)]

The widow of a participant in a SERP was not entitled to benefits, because she did not fit the plan's definition of "spouse," and the definition in the plan controls over the language in the SPD. The SERP required the survivor to have been married for at least one year before the participant's retirement, or at least one year before the participant's death, whichever came first; the plan participant married after his retirement. [*Parr v. Diebold Inc.*, No. 5:09 CV 1041, 2010 U.S. Dist. LEXIS 131930 (N.D. Ohio, Nov. 16, 2010); see Plansponsor staff, *Widow Loses SERP Benefits Bid*, plansponsor.com (Nov. 18, 2010)]

According to the Eastern District of Pennsylvania, a participant in a TIAA-CREF annuity plan substantially complied with the plan's requirements to change the beneficiary from his former wife to the man with whom he lived for 27 years, by sending two written notices of intention to change. (The standard for determining the identity of an ERISA plan beneficiary is whether there has been "substantial compliance" with the requirements for changing the beneficiary.) [*Teachers Insurance and Annuity Association of America v. Bernardo*, 683 F. Supp. 2d 344 (E.D. Pa. 2010); see Fred Schneyer, *Court Allows Annuity Contracts Beneficiary Switch*, plansponsor.com (Jan. 29, 2010)]

The Ninth Circuit required a pension trust to recognize a QDRO issued under Washington state law on behalf of a payee who was not married to the plan participant, but had a 30-year quasi-marital relationship with him. The Ninth Circuit gave effect to the court order giving her a 50% interest in the pension benefits, because she was his dependent and therefore an appropriate alternate payee. In this view, ERISA does not define marital property rights, but makes QDROs part of state domestic relations laws; Washington recognizes property divisions between quasi-marital partners. The pension would have been community property if the couple had been married, and a 50-50 division was consistent with state law. [*Owens v. Automotive Machinists Pension Trust*, 551 F.3d 1138 (9th Cir. 2009)]

Early in 2009, the Supreme Court held that DuPont correctly paid retirement benefits to a plan participant's ex-wife, even though she renounced her interest in his retirement benefits when they divorced. The plan participant named his daughter as the new beneficiary—but did not remove his wife's name from the beneficiary designation form. A QDRO was executed at the time of the divorce, but not submitted to the plan. The participant died in 2001, with $402,000 in his pension account. The participant's daughter sued the plan, but the plan followed the beneficiary designation. The Supreme Court ruled that the ex-wife did not attempt to direct her interest in the plan to the estate or another potential beneficiary, so her waiver was not the type of assignment or alienation barred by the Retirement Equity Act. The plan had a procedure for waiving benefits, but the ex-wife did not use it—so in the absence of a QDRO, the plan had to distribute benefits according to the beneficiary designation in its records. [*Kennedy v. DuPont*; 555 U.S. 285 (2009); see Rebecca Moore, *High Court Affirms DuPont's Payment to Ex-wife*, plansponsor.com (Jan. 26, 2009)]

Kennedy requires benefits to be paid to the beneficiary named in the plan, even if there is a state law waiver that purports to exclude that person. Therefore, the Fourth Circuit required payment of retirement plan funds to Erika Byrd's ex-husband Scott Andochick. The couple separated in July 2006, and their settlement agreement waived his interest in her 401(k) plan. They were divorced in December 2008. Byrd died in April 2011 without changing the benefit designation. [*Andochick v. Estate of Byrd*, 709 F.3d 296 (4th Cir. 2013); see Kevin McGuinness, *Plan Must Pay Ex Husband Despite Estate Suit*, plansponsor.com (Mar. 13, 2013)]

Plan participant Dennis Hall named his son as the sole beneficiary of his insurance benefits under an ERISA plan. Subsequently, he filled out and signed—but did not submit—a form naming his wife Jane was sole beneficiary. Hall died in 2011, and his surviving spouse submitted his will as evidence that he intended her to be the beneficiary of the insurance. The Eighth Circuit held that the plan did not abuse its discretion by rejecting this evidence. The will did not expressly dispose of non-estate assets like his life insurance. The terms of the plan required signed beneficiary designation forms to be submitted to the plan within 30 days of the date of the signature, and Hall did not submit the designation form on time (or at all). Plan administrators have discretion to excuse technical errors in a beneficiary designation, but they can also insist on strict conformity to the terms of the plan. The Eighth Circuit held that the plan exercised its discretion reasonably. [*Hall v. Metropolitan Life Ins.*, 750 F.3d 995 (8th Cir. May 8, 2014); see D. Michael Reilly, *ERISA 8th Circuit: Deciding Who Is the Beneficiary-The Abuse of Discretion Standard Trumps the Substantial Compliance Doctrine*, Lane Powell PC (May 14, 2014), available at Lexology.com]

§ 12.07 THE REQUIRED BEGINNING DATE

[A] Theory and Application

Congress' initial reasons for passing ERISA, and for allowing Individual Retirement Accounts (IRAs) revolved around providing current income for workers for the time period between retirement and their death. Not only was estate planning with qualified retirement benefits not considered important, it was not even considered a worthwhile objective—the benefits were supposed to be used up during the individual's lifetime. Therefore, distributions from qualified plans and IRAs were required to start no later than a Required Beginning Date (RBD). The RBD was defined as April 1 of the year after the year in which the individual reached age 70½. An excise tax penalty was imposed on the failure to make at least the Minimum Required Distribution (MRD) each year.

Over the years, theories in Congress and at the IRS have changed. Estate planning for benefits is now treated as a legitimate objective. Furthermore, although the RBD/MRD requirements remain in effect for IRAs, and for qualified plan participants who are corporate officers or directors, or who own 5% or more of the stock in the employer corporation, they have been abolished for rank-and-file employees. If plan participants choose to defer retirement and remain at work past age 70½, they will no longer suffer a tax penalty for doing so.

For plan years beginning on or after January 1, 1997, I.R.C. § 401(a)(9)(C) sets the RBD for a rank-and-file employee at the later of April 1 following the year in which the individual reached age 70½ or that person's actual retirement date. The plan must make actuarial adjustments to the pensions of persons who continue to work after age 70½.

The eventual pension must be at least the actuarial equivalent of the benefits payable as of the date the actuarial increase must begin, plus the actuarial equivalent of any additional benefits that accrue after the starting date, reduced by the actuarial equivalent of whatever retirement benefits are actually distributed after the annuity start date. Employees who stay at work after age 70½ can be given the option of suspending distributions from the plan until they actually retire.

[B] Excise Taxes

The basic tax rule is that amounts received by a plan participant from a plan are taxable income for that year. (Any after-tax contributions made by participants were not deductible when they were made, and will not be taxed again when they are withdrawn. Participants who made after-tax contributions are therefore allowed to calculate an exclusion ratio, so part of each distribution is tax-free to the extent that it can be traced back to past after-tax contributions.)

A 10% excise tax (over and above the normal income tax) is imposed on "premature" distributions. The general rule is that a distribution made before age 59½ is premature. Distributions under a QDRO are not subject to this excise tax. Nor is a distribution considered premature if it is made to a person who has reached age 55 and separated from service. Distributions are not subject to the 10% penalty if they are made after the participant's death, or to employees who are so totally disabled as to be unable to engage in any substantial gainful activity.

The premature distribution excise tax is imposed on lump sums, but not on distributions made over the life, lives, or joint life expectancies of the participant or the participant and one or more beneficiaries. Defined benefit plans are subject to additional rules on this topic. Finally, if a plan participant's unreimbursed medical expenses are high enough to be tax-deductible (over 7.5% of adjusted gross income), plan distributions are not considered premature, even if the participant does not actually use the distributions to pay the medical bills.

Before 1996, plan participants could find themselves between a rock and a hard place. Not only was an excise tax penalty placed on premature withdrawals; a different penalty was imposed on excess lifetime withdrawals from a pension plan but also on excess accumulations of pension benefits within the estate. The SBJPA suspended the tax on excessive distributions for the period 1996–1999, but retained the tax on excessive accumulation in the estate. The Taxpayer Relief Act of 1997 permanently repealed both excise taxes, greatly increasing the financial and estate planning flexibility available to plan participants.

[C] Required Minimum Distributions

An IRS Proposed Regulation [66 Fed. Reg. 3928–3954 (Jan. 17, 2001)] covers required minimum distributions from qualified plans, IRAs, and I.R.C. § 403(b) and § 457 (government and nonprofit-organization) plans, substantially simplifying the 1987 Proposed Rules under Code § 401(a)(8). (The QLAC rules discussed at §12.05[B], above, constitute a partial exception to the RMD requirements.)

The 2001 proposal enacts a single Minimum Distribution Incidental Benefit (MDIB) table, in Treas. Reg. § 1.401(a)(9)-2, to be used to calculate the RMD, with a single table usable whether the beneficiary is a natural person (spouse or non-spouse) or an entity such as a trust or charity. The MDIB table uses the same assumption in all cases: that the beneficiary is 10 years younger than the employee (no matter what their actual ages are). Distributions are made over the predicted life expectancy of a person 10 years younger than the employee. Even greater "stretch-out" is allowed if the beneficiary is the employee's spouse, and is actually more than 10 years younger than the employee, because in that case the calculation of the RMD can be based on the spouse's actual life expectancy. If the employee fails to designate a beneficiary, the RMD is calculated based on the employee's own life expectancy, reduced by one year every year.

The general rule for post-death distributions is that the benefits remaining when the employee dies must be distributed over the life expectancy of the designated beneficiary. The calculation is made in the year the employee dies. If more than one beneficiary is designated (for instance, two or more of the employee's children), then the beneficiary with the shortest life expectancy is treated as the designated beneficiary—whether the employee dies before or after the RBD. If the employee dies without designating a beneficiary, then distribution must be made to his or her intestate distributees, over a period of five years.

The 2002 final rule, Notice 2002-27, 2002-18 I.R.B. 814, makes it easier to distribute benefits to separate accounts with different beneficiaries, slightly simplifies the RMD calculation by eliminating some of the mathematical factors used in the calculation. To clarify that the distribution to beneficiaries must begin in the year of death, Notice 2002-27 requires the beneficiary of a decedent's account to be named by September 30 (rather than December 30) of the year of death. This last change was made to make it clear that distribution to the beneficiaries must start in the year of death.

To prevent abusive planning (e.g., choosing a grandchild as annuitant to stretch out payments), T.D. 9130, 69 Fed. Reg. 33288 (June 15, 2004) forbids use of a joint and survivor annuity with a 100% survivor benefit if the beneficiary is more than 10 years younger than the employee. Additional adjustments are required if the employee starts to receive benefits before age 70 (because the earlier start means that more payments will be made). For annuities with no life contingency, T.D. 9130 lets the recipient change the form that future distributions will take at any time. When a person retires, or when the plan terminates, the form of distribution can be changed prospectively. An employee who marries can change the annuity to a joint and survivor annuity. T.D. 9130 also allows certain payments to children, under Code § 401(a)(9)(F), to receive the same favorable tax treatment as payments to a spouse.

Another Pension Protection Act change allows a non-spouse beneficiary to roll over inherited benefits to an IRA; previously, only a spouse could do this. [See Notice 2007-7, 2007-5 I.R.B. 395]

In October 2008, the Department of Labor published final rules on distributions of 401(k) benefits in terminated plans, when the beneficiary is not the participant's spouse and cannot be located. The rules also cover selection of annuity providers and cross-trading of securities by ERISA plans. Under the PPA, certain retirement benefits of deceased participants can be rolled over into an inherited IRA even if the beneficiary is not the deceased participant's spouse. The new rule, which includes a Prohibited Transaction class exemption, requires rollovers into inherited IRAs when a terminated or abandoned defined contribution plan cannot find the non-spouse beneficiaries of a deceased participant. [73 Fed. Reg. 58445 (Oct. 7, 2008); see Rebecca Moore, *DOL Issues Final Rules on Missing Benefits and Other PPA Provisions*, plansponsor.com (Oct. 6, 2008)]

For 2009 only (and not for other years in which many taxpayers needed relief), the Worker, Retiree, and Employer Recovery Act of 2008 (WRERA) suspended the penalties that would otherwise be imposed for failure to take RMDs from qualified plans or IRAs. [Notice 2009-9, 2009-5 I.R.B. 419]

For 2012 and 2013, Qualified Charitable Distributions (QCDs) are permitted. A QCD is a charitable donation, made by a person who has reached age 70½ and therefore would have to take an RMD from his or her IRA or be penalized. The QCD is transferred directly from the IRA to a qualified charity. The donor can exclude up to $100,000 a year in QCDs from gross income for tax purposes, and QCD amounts are deemed to satisfy the RMD requirement. The distributions are reported on IRS Form 1099-R. QCDs cannot be made from SEP or SIMPLE IRAs. [IRS, *Charitable Donations from IRAs for 2012 and 2013*, <http://www.irs.gov/Retirement-Plans/Charitable-Donations-from-IRAs-for-2012-and-2013> (June 27, 2013)] The provision expired at the end of 2013, although planners hoped that Congress would reinstate it retroactively. [The Slott Report, *IRA Qualified Charitable Distributions Expired for 2014*, <http://www.theslottreport.com/2014/01/ira-qualified-charitable-distributions.html> (Jan. 7, 2014)]

§ 12.08 DIVORCE-RELATED ORDERS

[A] QDROs and QMCSOs

For many couples, one spouse's interest in a retirement plan is a major marital financial asset. In fact, it may be the only significant marital financial asset. Given our society's high divorce rate, plan administrators are often confronted with court orders incident to an employee's separation or divorce—or are faced with conflicting claims after the death of an employee who divorced, remarried, and eventually died without having changed the beneficiary designation from the first to the second spouse.

Although the general rule is that plan benefits cannot be anticipated or alienated, there is an important exception for family law orders that fit the definitions of Qualified Domestic Relations Orders (QDROs) or Qualified Medical Child Support Orders (QMCSOs). [On QMCSOs, see the HHS/DOL Final Rule on National Medical Child Support Notice, 65 Fed. Reg. 82128 (DOL) and 65 Fed.

Reg. 72154 (HHS), and the Compliance Guide for Qualified Medical Child Support Orders (Aug. 13, 2003), <http://www.dol.gov/ebsa/publications/qmcso.html, as discussed at § 18.16.]

Technically speaking, welfare benefit plans are not required to have QDRO procedures, because the QDRO requirements appear in ERISA Title I, Part 2, which does not apply to welfare benefit plans. However, five of the Circuits (the Second, Fourth, Sixth, Seventh, and Tenth) have concluded (in cases about life insurance) that QDRO procedures are required because ERISA doesn't specially say that welfare benefit plans do not have to have QDRO procedures. (The issue for health plans is covered by the QMCSO procedure.)

The Second, Third, Fourth, Seventh, and Tenth Circuits have required top hat plans to enforce QDROs, and the District Court for the District of New Hampshire joined them in late 2009. [*Metropolitan Life v. Drainville*, 2009 U.S. Dist. LEXIS 63613 (D. R.I. July 23, 2009), *MetLife v. Hanson*, 2009 U.S. Dist. LEXIS 92044 (D. N.H. Oct. 1, 2009); see Albert Feuer, *Who Is Entitled to Life Insurance Benefits and Top-Hat Benefits from an ERISA Plan Following a Divorce or a Marital Separation?*, <http://papers.ssrn.com/sol3/papers.cfm?abstract_id=1535733> (Jan. 14, 2010). For cases applying a QDRO-like rationale to divide welfare benefits, see, e.g., *Unicare Life & Health Ins. Co. v. Phanor*, No. 05-11355-JLT (D. Mass. Jan. 30, 2007), as discussed in Fred Schneyer, *Judge Overrides Life Insurance Beneficiary Designation*, plansponsor.com (Feb. 1, 2007); *Deaton v. Cross*, 184 F. Supp. 2d 441 (D. Md. 2002); *Seaman v. Johnson*, 184 F. Supp. 2d 642 (E.D. Mich. 2002)]

Once the administrator determines that a court order has the status of a QDRO, payments can legitimately be made to the alternate payee: i.e., the separated or divorced ex-spouse of an employee.

A QDRO is a court order based on a state domestic relations law (including community property law) dealing with child support, alimony, or marital property rights. No court is allowed to use a QDRO to order a plan to make payments in any type or form not allowed by the plan documents. A QDRO cannot force a plan to pay benefits that have already been assigned to someone else under an earlier QDRO, or to increase the actuarial value of benefits to be paid. The Department of Labor's introduction to the subject of plan administration of QDROs can be found at <http://www.dol.gov/ebsa/faqs/faq_qdro.html.

To be entitled to recognition by the plan, a QDRO must contain at least this much information:

- The recipient's right to plan benefits;
- The names and addresses of the parties;
- The amount or percentage of the plan benefit to be paid to the alternate payee named in the order;
- The time period or number of payments covered by the order;

- The plan(s) it applies to (the same employee might be covered by more than one plan).

Generally, the alternate payee does not receive distributions under the QDRO before the date the employee would be entitled to them. However, distributions can be made from any plan on the earliest date the participant could get the distribution after separation from service, or when the participant reaches age 50—whichever is later. If the plan is drafted to allow it, QDROs can require immediate distribution, or at a time that is not related to the age of the employee spouse.

For QDROs issued when the employee spouse is still working and has not retired, the payments are calculated based on the present value of the normal retirement benefits already accrued as of that time. Early retirement subsidies are not taken into account. The QDRO can provide for recalculation at the time of retirement, in case an early retirement subsidy is actually paid.

The PPA cleared up the question of whether a later, or even posthumous, court order can be a QDRO by holding that an otherwise qualifying court order must be accepted as a QDRO even if it modifies, or is later in time than, another court order: PPA § 1101. The DOL published an Interim Final Rule under PPA § 1001, which says that an order can be a QDRO even if it is later than another order or QDRO, or if it revises the other order. This is true even if the second order involves the same employee but a different alternate payee.

Therefore, a posthumous order, or an order issued after the participant's annuity start date, can be a QDRO. But even after the PPA, a QDRO can only divide benefits as provided by the plan, not require additional forms of benefits. As long as a DRO does not attempt to assign benefits that have already been assigned to a different alternate payee under a different QDRO, an order can be QDRO even if it is issued after, or revises, another DRO. An order can be a QDRO even if it is issued after the participant dies, or after the participant's annuity starting date. However, an order cannot be a QDRO if it orders a plan to provide a type or form of benefit that is not available under the plan. [RIN 1210-AB15, *Final Rule Relating to Time and Order of Issuance of Domestic Relations Orders*, 75 Fed. Reg. 32846 (June 10, 2010); see Rebecca Moore, *EBSA Issues Final Rule on DROs*, plansponsor.com (June 10, 2010)]

[B] QDRO Methodology

Under the "separate interest" method of distribution under a defined benefit plan, the alternate payee gets future payments based on his or her life expectancy, not that of the plan participant. [See, e.g., *In re Marriage of Shelstead*, 66 Cal. App. 4th 893 (1998)] The nonemployee wife was awarded a 50% community property interest in the employee husband's pension plan. The order said that, if the wife died before the husband, she would be able to designate a successor in interest to receive her community-property share. But the California Court of Appeals decided that, although this was a divorce-related order, it was not a QDRO because it did not settle the rights of an alternate payee, and she could leave her share to anyone, not just another acceptable alternate payee.

Under the "shared payment" method, the alternate payee gets a portion of each pension payment made to the plan participant, so both the participant and the alternate payee use the same timing schedule and form of annuity. The alternate payee gets to take advantage of any early retirement incentives elected by the participant. The enhanced benefit under an early retirement plan is actuarially reduced if the alternate payee is younger than the participant (this is often the case, especially if the participant is male and his ex-wife is younger than he is), but is not increased if the alternate payee is older than the participant.

[C] The Administrator's Response

When a plan administrator receives a court order, the first step is to determine whether the order is entitled to QDRO status. However, once ERISA compliance is determined, the administrator must comply with the QDRO, without inquiring as to its acceptability under state law. An employee who opposes the terms of the QDRO has to litigate with the ex-spouse in state court; the plan administrator is not liable for complying with the QDRO. [*Blue v. UAL Corp.*, 160 F.3d 383 (7th Cir. 1998)]

When a plan participant never divorced his first wife, but remarried anyway and the plan documents listed the second wife as his spouse, the Sixth Circuit had to decide which wife was the surviving spouse. This required determining whether Ohio or Michigan law should be followed. The Sixth Circuit opted for Ohio law, where the second marriage occurred and the decedent lived with the second wife until his death. Under Ohio law, the second spouse has the duty of proving that the first marriage ended. She was unable to do so, because there was no record of a divorce. The Sixth Circuit concluded that the first wife was the valid beneficiary. [*Durden v. Daimler Chrysler*, 448 F.3d 918 (6th Cir. 2006)]

If the administrator believes that a document described as a QDRO is a sham, or at least questionable, PWBA Advisory Opinion #99-13A [(Sept. 29, 1999), <http://www.dol.gov/ebsa/regs/AOs/ao1999-13a.html>] provides guidance.

Administrators are "not free to ignore" information casting doubt on the validity of an order. If the administrator finds that evidence credible, the administrator must make a case-by-case determination of the validity of each order, "without inappropriately spending plan assets or inappropriately involving the plan in the state domestic relations proceeding."

Appropriate action could include informing the court of the potential invalidity of the order; intervening in a domestic relations proceeding; or even bringing suit. However, an administrator who can't get a response within a reasonable time from the agency that issued the order "may not independently determine that the order is not valid under state law." [PWBA Advisory Opinion #99-13A (Sept. 29, 1999), <http://www.dol.gov/ebsa/regs/AOs/ao1999-13a.html>] ERISA Opinion Letter 94-32A says that it is improper to charge either the participant or the alternate payee a fee for processing a QDRO.

This determination must be made within a reasonable time. The employee and the proposed alternate payee must be notified promptly that the order was received. The administrator must explain to them how the plan will determine the validity of the alleged QDRO. The funds in question must be segregated, and separately accounted for, until the determination has been made. There is an 18-month limit on keeping the funds in the segregated account. [See EBSA Advisory Opinion 2000-09A (July 12, 2000), <http://www.dol.gov/ebsa/regs/AOs/ao2000-09a.html> for a discussion of what to do when an alternate payee is named under a plan that limits beneficiary designations to spouses, minor children, and parents—but not former spouses.]

[D] QDRO Case Law: *Egelhoff* and After

The Supreme Court decided, in *Egelhoff v. Egelhoff* [532 U.S. 141 (2001)] that ERISA preempts a Washington State law that made all beneficiary designations (in life insurance as well as qualified plans) invalid when the employee or insured person divorced. The Supreme Court decided that the state law "relates to" ERISA plans, and therefore is preempted, because qualified plans can be regulated only by federal, and not state, law.

In 2002, the Seventh Circuit interpreted *Egelhoff* to mean that state laws cannot be used to displace the designation of beneficiaries made under ERISA, because ERISA preempts the state law completely. [*Metropolitan Life Ins. Co. v. Johnson*, 297 F.3d 558 (7th Cir. 2002)] In light of this decision, the Seventh Circuit refused to allow the state-law remedy of imposing a constructive trust to be used to pay the benefits of a deceased, divorced employee's life insurance plan to his 14-year-old daughter (as required by the terms of his divorce agreement) rather than to his ex-wife (who was still named as the beneficiary in the plan documents). Although the divorce agreement included boilerplate waivers of interest in the other spouse's financial assets, the Seventh Circuit did not believe this was specific or explicit enough to disclaim the ex-wife's interest in the ex-husband's benefit plans. [*Melton v. Melton*, 324 F.3d 941 (7th Cir. 2003)]

The message of the Supreme Court's 1997 ruling in *Boggs v. Boggs*, 520 U.S. 833 (1997) is that, although QDROs are saved from ERISA preemption, other domestic relations orders issued by state courts are preempted.

The Second Circuit required a defined contribution plan to distribute assets to a former participant that were wrongly transferred to his wife after they were divorced—even though the plan did not recover the funds from the wife. The plan erroneously transferred half of the plaintiff's pension account to his ex-wife, giving her about $764,000 more than the divorce settlement entitled her to receive. The plaintiff did not discover this for several years. The plan administrator told the ex-wife to return the excess funds; she refused, and the plan sued her. The Second Circuit held that defined contribution plans allocate the risk of investment instability or beneficiary longevity to the employee. In this analysis, plan assets only become benefits when they are distributed at retirement—before that point, no one has a claim to any particular assets in the plan trust. [*Milgram v. Orthopedic Assocs. DC Pension Plan*, 666 F.3d 68 (2d Cir. 2011)]

[E] PBGC QDROs

An extensive document published at PBGC.gov explains how the PBGC handles QDROs in the plans under its trusteeship. The document covers subjects such as how to identify alternate payees, how and when to make payments to the alternate payees, and the rights of alternate payees when the employee spouse dies. The total values of the participant's portion and the alternate payee's portion cannot exceed what the PBGC would have paid to the participant if there had been no QDRO. The document includes two basic model QDROs and special orders for child support and surviving spouse benefits.

Courts often consider the percentage of the benefit earned before, during and after the marriage when they divide pension benefits. The PBGC can use this "marital portion" or "marital fraction" analysis for either a shared payment or a separate interest QDRO.

An original signed order, or a certificated or authenticated copy of the order, should be sent to the PBGC QDRO Coordinator, P.O. Box 151750, Alexandria, VA 22315-1750. (Electronic transmission is not acceptable because of the need for a physical signature.) If the PBGC states that an order is not a valid QDRO, the parties will be given 45 days to appeal, and payments to alternate payees will be suspended, and reinstated if the PBGC later determines that the order was a valid QDRO. The PBGC also informally reviews draft orders to see if they would qualify if submitted in that form. Parties must notify the PBGC Customer Contact Center, (800) 400-7242, if any event occurs that affects a benefit: for example, the death of a participant or alternate payee, or the occurrence of an event named in the order, such as a child's majority or the alternate payee's remarriage.

A valid order should:

- Clearly specify the pension plan to which it applies;
- Clearly identify (including Social Security numbers and mailing addresses) the persons to whom it applies; all alternate and contingent payees;

- Specify the start date and amount to be paid to each alternate payee and the duration of payment, and what amount or percentage of the participant's monthly benefit goes to each alternate payee;
- Mandate payment from the PBGC to the alternate payee, rather than the participant receiving payment and then transmitting it to the alternate payee;
- Explain whether shared payments to the alternate payee survive the participant's death;
- Grant the domestic relations court continuing jurisdiction over the order. [*The Division of Pensions Through Qualified Domestic Relations Orders*, <http://www.dol.gov/ebsa/publications/qdros.html>, or by phone at the EBSA hotline, 1-866-444-EBSA (3272). Forms can be ordered by calling the PBGC at (800) 400-7242]

§ 12.09 REDUCTION OF BENEFIT FORMS

Qualified plans must always offer payments in the form of QJSAs, QOSAs, and QPSAs. What if a plan originally adopts additional, optional forms of benefit payments, then later finds that some of them are unpopular or hard to administer? For years beginning after December 31, 2001, as a result of EGTRRA, I.R.C. § 411(d)(6) and ERISA § 204(g) have been amended to make it easier for defined contribution plans to cut back on the number of benefit options that they offer, especially in connection with plan mergers and other transitions.

A defined contribution plan will not be penalized for reducing participants' accrued benefits if the plan adopts amendments that reduce the number of benefit options—provided that the participant is always entitled to get a single-sum distribution that is based on at least as high a proportion of his or her account as the form of benefit that is being eliminated under the plan amendment. EGTRRA obligates the IRS to issue new regulations no later than December 31, 2003, to this effect, applying to plan years beginning after December 31, 2003 (or earlier, if the IRS so specifies).

Under regulations published at 69 Fed. Reg. 13769 (Mar. 24, 2004), redundant optional forms of benefit can be eliminated, as long as another form in the same "family" remains available (the proposal defines six families of optional benefit forms), and as long as the "core" options remain available. A plan amendment changing the availability of benefit forms cannot be effective for any distribution with an annuity start date within 90 days after adoption of the amendment.

The core options that must be preserved are the straight life annuity, the 75% joint and survivor annuity, life and 10-year certain annuity, and the most valuable option the plan provides for participants with a short life expectancy. As a general rule, lump sum payouts cannot be eliminated by making use of this proposal, and plan amendments eliminating non-core options do not apply to start dates within four years after adoption of the amendment. The proposal imposes additional requirements to protect participants when early retirement benefits and subsidies are altered.

T.D. 9472, 2009-51 I.R.B. 850, is a final rule governing notice requirements under 204(h) for plan amendments that reduce accrued benefits. According to the IRS, reducing or eliminating an early retirement benefit or retirement-type subsidy has the effect of reducing future benefit accruals. Code § 4980F(e)(3) requires notice to be provided within a reasonable time before the plan amendment takes effect. In general, this means 45 days before the effective date (15 days for small or multi-employer plans). Unpredictable contingent event benefits are limited if a plan's AFTAP is, or would be, under 60%, and amendments increasing the plan's liabilities because of a benefits increase are limited if the AFTAP would be under 80%. Certain payments are prohibited when AFTAP is in the 60%–80% range; the sponsor is in Chapter 11; and the plan's actuary cannot certify that AFTAP is at least 100%. Benefit accruals cease when AFTAP falls below 60%. [*IRS Issues Final Rule on Certain Notice Requirements*, plansponsor.com (Nov. 23, 2009). See also proposed regulations, 77 Fed. Reg. 37349 (June 21, 2012) for elimination of some optional benefits from single-employer defined benefit plans sponsored by employers that are bankruptcy debtors.]

Notice 2012-46, 2012-30 I.R.B. 86, effective November 1, 2012, gives the ERISA § 101(j) notice requirements for single-employer plans subject to benefit limitations under § 436. The notice must be understandable by the average participant, containing the plan name, EIN, plan number, and a general description of the payment limitation. The prohibited benefits must be described in detail. The notice must explain when the limitation will cease to apply (e.g., when the AFTAP rises to at least 80%). If the limit is no longer in effect and participants can access distributions that were formerly prohibited, the plan administrator must send a written § 101(j) notice to participants no later than 30 days after the limitations no longer apply. [McGuireWoods LLP, *IRS Provides Guidance on Notices for Funding-Related Pension Plan Benefit Limitations* (Aug. 28, 2012) (benefitslink.com)]

Finkl & Sons Co. contemplated voluntary termination of its pension plan, probably in connection with a planned merger but, after preliminary research, decided the plan was too costly. The plan permitted employees to continue working at Finkl after plan termination while still receiving annuities. The plan also included an anti-cutback clause protecting certain benefits from amendments and the plaintiffs charged that the ability to collect an annuity while continuing to work fell into this category. The Seventh Circuit disagreed: neither ERISA nor the plan's terms guaranteed the right to an immediate annuity while still working. A terminated plan can disburse benefits to active employees—but this plan never terminated. [*Carter v. Pension Plan of A. Finkl & Sons Company for Eligible*

Office Employees, 654 F.3d 719 (7th Cir. 2011), *en banc reh'g denied* (Sept. 21, 2011)]

Although the First Circuit said that the regulation allowing an amendment that reduced a retiree's benefit nearly by half was not fair, the court nevertheless affirmed dismissal of the retiree's case. The plaintiff, Tasker, worked for Airborne Express, which was acquired by DHL close to the time of the plaintiff's retirement. The plan was amended, eliminating the right to transfer balances from the DHL defined contribution to its defined benefit plan. The applicable regulation permitted elimination of the conversion option, so the amendment did not violate the anti-cutback rule. [*Tasker v. DHL Ret. Sav. Plan*, 621 F.3d 34 (1st Cir. 2010). *Andersen v. DHL Ret. Pension Plan*, No. C12-439 MJP, 2012 U.S. Dist. LEXIS 157805 (W.D. Wash. Nov. 2, 2012) dismisses a similar case about the elimination of the transfer option.]

The Third Circuit held that a plan amendment that conditioned receipt of health care benefits from a welfare plan on not getting a lump sum from the pension plan violated the anti-cutback rule. Although in general, welfare benefits are not subject to the anti-cutback rule, the Third Circuit held that the amendment had the effect of decreasing an accrued benefit under the pension plan—because the lump sum became less valuable because health benefits had to be surrendered to get it. [*Battoni v. IBEW Local Union No. 102 Employee Pension Plan*, 594 F.3d 230 (3d Cir. 2010)]

§ 12.10 ROLLOVERS

Because of termination of employment, or termination of a plan itself, a person of working age may become entitled to a plan distribution. If he or she does not need the funds immediately, and would encounter an unwelcome income tax liability, one solution is to "roll over" the funds by placing them into another qualified plan or an IRA within 60 days.

The funds that are rolled over are not available to be spent by the plan participant, and therefore the participant is not taxed.

■ **TIP:** Although employees have a right to roll over these funds, the qualified plan that is the intended recipient does not have an obligation to accept rollovers. So it makes sense for the distributing plan to require employees to submit a statement that the potential recipient is not only qualified to take rollover contributions, but is willing to do so. The recipient plan is allowed to impose conditions, such as the form in which it will accept rollovers and the minimum amount it will accept as a rollover. The recipient plan is also entitled to set its own distribution rules and does not have to follow the rules of the original plan.

A direct rollover is considered a distribution, not a transfer of assets. [Treas. Reg. § 1.401(a)(31)-1] Therefore, the participant and spouse may have to sign a waiver because plan benefits are not being paid in QJSA form.

Rollovers can be carried out either by the plan administrator of the first plan sending a check or wire transfer to the trustee or custodian of the transferee plan, or by giving the participant a check payable to the IRA, plan trustee, or custodian. The IRS has ruled that the 60-day rollover requirement does not apply to a check for a plan distribution that was made payable to the sponsor of a second plan. The check was mailed to the recipient of the distribution, but made payable to her new employer, but she could not have cashed the check; therefore, it was a direct rollover as defined by § 401(a)(31). Her Form 1099-R showed Code G in Box 7, showing a direct rollover with no withholding. The IRS said that the distribution was a direct rollover, so the 60-day rule did not apply, and she could deposit the check in the new employer's plan even after 60 days. [Plansponsor Staff, *60-day Rollover Requirement Doesn't Apply to Check Made to New Plan*, plansponsor.com (Apr. 1, 2010)]

A distribution to a spouse, or a QDRO distribution to an ex-spouse, can also be rolled over, but only to an IRA, not to a qualified plan.

PPA § 829(a) enacts Code § 402(c)(11) that permits non-spouse beneficiaries to roll over a distribution they receive from a qualified plan to an IRA.

IRS Notice 2008-30 explains how to make rollovers to Roth IRAs from other types of plans, pursuant to the expanded options for rollovers under the PPA. Funds can be rolled over directly to a Roth IRA, or the individual can take a plan distribution and roll it over to the Roth IRA within 60 days. Any amount that would be includible in the individual's taxable income if there had been no rollover will also be included in his or her gross income. The rollover is exempt from the 10% penalty on early distribution unless the money is distributed from the Roth IRA within five years. [Notice 2008-30, 2008-12 I.R.B. 638]

The Small Business Jobs and Credit Act of 2010, Pub L. No. 111-240, permits employers to amend a 401(k) plan to allow an eligible rollover distribution (ERD) to be transferred to a designated Roth account within the plan. (The transfer is taxable, not tax-free.) Transfers can be made after September 27, 2010, from a non-designated Roth account in the same plan, and if other requirements are met. However, in-plan conversions can only be made from amounts that could be distributed under the terms of the plan. Participants who rolled over ERD to a designated Roth account could include half of the taxable amount in their 2011 gross income and half for 2012, or could include it all in their 2010 gross income, depending on which provided better tax results. [<http://www.irs.gov>, *New Law Allows In-Plan Rollovers to Designated Roth Accounts*; see Rebecca Moore, *InPlan Roth Conversions Present Challenges*, plansponsor.com (Sept. 28, 2010)]

The American Taxpayer Relief Act of 2012 authorizes in-plant Roth conversions of defined contribution accounts that are not otherwise distributable, with no income limitation. Under prior law, only amounts that were distributable (e.g., to a participant who had reached age 59½) could be converted to Roth form.

Although the provision is effective January 1, 2013, prior account balances can be converted. [Rebecca Moore, *Fiscal Cliff Deal Extends Roth Conversions* plansponsor.com (Jan. 3, 2013)]

The 402(f) notice must be given when a participant gets a distribution that is eligible to be rolled over to an IRA or another qualified plan. A participant can waive the 30-day minimum notice, but not the 180-day maximum notice requirement. The notice must explain the rollover rules, tax consequences of taking a lump sum, the options for direct rollover (e.g., automatic rollover), the mandatory 20% withholding requirement, and tax consequences of options. Notice 2009-68, 2009-39 I.R.B. 423 includes two updated safe harbor notices replacing the ones issued in 2003—one for designated Roth accounts, one for other accounts. (A participant who has both kinds of accounts must receive both notices.)

§ 12.11 WITHHOLDING

A designated distribution is any amount of $200 or more that the participant could roll over, but chooses not to. Under I.R.C. §§ 401(a)(3) and 3405(c), plan administrators have to withhold a mandatory 20% of any designated distribution.

All or part of an employee's balance in a qualified plan is eligible for rollover, except:

- A series of substantially equal periodic payments, made at the rate of at least one payment a year, over the life of the employee or the joint lives of the employee and designated beneficiary;
- Payments made for a term of at least 10 years [See I.R.C. § 402(c)(4)];
- The RMDs under I.R.C. § 401(a)(8) for officers, directors, and 5% stockholders.

In the case of a partial rollover, withholding applies only to the part that the employee withdraws from the plan, not the part that is rolled over.

For amounts that are neither annuities nor eligible rollover distributions, optional withholding can be done at a rate of 10%. The employee can direct the plan not to withhold. During the six months immediately preceding the first payment, and at least once a year once benefits are in pay status, the plan must notify participants of their right to make, renew, or revoke a withholding election. The employer can either include the withheld amounts in each quarterly Form 941 filing, or use Form 941E to report withholding.

Starting January 1, 2010, eligible rollover distributions paid directly to a non-spouse beneficiary are subject to 20% mandatory withholding, not 10% voluntary withholding for non-periodic payments, unless the funds are directly rolled over to an IRA.

The plan administrator is responsible for withholding unless the administrator directs that the insurer or other payer of benefits perform this task. [Treas. Reg. § 31.3405(c)-1]

Whenever designated distributions (i.e., those eligible for withholding) are made, the employer and plan administrator become responsible for making returns and reports to the IRS, participants, and beneficiaries.

A penalty of $50 per day is imposed by I.R.C. § 6704(b), up to a maximum of $50,000, for failure to maintain the required records, although the penalty can be waived if the plan has a good excuse for noncompliance. [See I.R.C. § 6047(b) for the required records reports by employers or plan administrators]

§ 12.12 PLAN LOANS AS DEEMED DISTRIBUTIONS

The federal Website firstgov.gov includes FAQs about plan loans:

- Loans are permitted from qualified plans, but not from IRAs or related plans (SEP, SARSEP, or SIMPLE).
- In fact, taking a loan disqualifies the account from being an IRA, and its entire value must be included in the owner's income for the year of the loan.
- Qualified plans are allowed to, but not required, to offer loans. A plan can limit the size of loans.
- The maximum allowable loan is the smaller of A or B, where A is $50,000 and B is $10,000 or half of the participant's vested valance, whichever is greater.
- A participant can have more than one loan outstanding at a time, as long as the aggregate balance does not exceed the permitted maximum.
- Plans that allow loans must specify application procedures and repayment terms for loans.
- Other than loans for purchase of a principal residence, repayment must be completed within five years, via a series of substantially equal payments made at least quarterly and including both principal and interest.
- Loan repayments are not plan contributions: see Reg. § 1.72(p)-1.
- Loan repayment can be suspended for employees who are on active military duty, or during a leave of absence lasting up to one year. However, an employee returning from leave must make up the missed payments either by making a lump sum repayment or increasing the periodic payments so that the loan does not extend past the original five-year term.

- Plan loans are not dependent on hardship, the employee's reasons for wanting the money, or whether the employee could borrow from other sources.
- It is permissible to make loans to owner-employees as long as all participants have equal access to loans.
- A loan that is not repaid according to the plan's terms is taxed as a plan distribution (and cannot be rolled over to an eligible retirement plan), but there is no plan distribution if the repayment terms are followed.
- After a deemed distribution, a default can be remedied by making the missed payment, but the participant's tax basis in the plan is increased by late repayments.

Code § 72(p) sets out the rules under which plan loans that fail to conform to the requirements will be treated as taxable distributions from the plan, rather than as tax-neutral loans. Regulations on this issue were proposed in 2000 and finalized at the end of 2002. [67 Fed. Reg. 71821 (Dec. 3, 2002)] The Final Regulations apply to loans, assignments, and pledges made on or after January 1, 2004 (although plans can adopt the rules earlier). An exemption is available for loans made under an insurance contract that was in effect on December 31, 2003, that is obligated to offer loans to unsecured contract holders.

A loan will not be treated as a deemed distribution if the plan suspends loan repayment when the borrower is on leave of absence for active military service, even if the leave lasts more than a year, as long as repayments resume when the borrower returns from military service, and repayment is complete by the normal term plus the term of military service. Before these regulations were finalized, the Proposed Regulation imposed a limit of only two loans per plan participant; additional loans would be treated as deemed distributions. The Final Regulations remove the two-loan limit, and allow credit card loans to be secured by amounts in a participant's account. Also see the Servicemembers Civil Relief Act, Pub. L. No. 108-189, which limits the interest on plan loans incurred by employees who later go on active military service.

Also note that, in early 2009, the Federal Reserve Board amended Regulation Z, so that, as of July 1, 2010, most plan loans are exempt under the Truth in Lending Act. The FRB's rationale is that plan loans are different from ordinary loans because there is no third-party creditor, and the principal and interest are reinvested in the participant's account, so participants are less vulnerable than ordinary borrowers. [Rebecca Moore, *Plan Loans Exempt from Truth-in-Lending Disclosure Requirements*, plansponsor.com (Mar. 13, 2009)]

CHAPTER 13

PROCESSING AND REVIEWING CLAIMS AND APPEALS

§ 13.01 INTRODUCTION

All pension and welfare benefit plans that are subject to ERISA Title I are required to maintain a "reasonable claims procedure." An appropriate claims procedure is one that is described in the SPD: does not place undue restrictions or inhibitions on the processing of claims, and satisfies the relevant regulations about filing claims, reviewing submitted claims, and informing participants when a claim is denied. [DOL Reg. § 2560.503]

At the very least, the procedure must give claimants (or their authorized representatives) the right to apply to the plan for review, see the pertinent documents, and submit written comments and issues for resolution.

The plan must give a specific reason if it denies a claim. Claimants must be referred to the relevant plan provision. They must be given information about how to appeal the denial. One of the reasons why the PPACA is so controversial is the extent to which it imposes additional requirements not only for communicating with plan participants about their claims, but also about the timing of claims processing and the addition of a new external claims review step.

In the spring of 2010, the Supreme Court decided *Conkright v. Frommert*, 559 U.S. 506, a suit by a class of Xerox employees who left the company, received lump sums, then were later rehired and eventually retired from Xerox. The Supreme Court granted certiorari on two issues: the amount of deference a district court must give an administrator's interpretation of plan terms outside the context of an actual claim; and whether the Second Circuit applied the correct standard of review (for abuse of discretion or de novo). The court strongly reaffirmed the *Bruch* principle that, if a plan gives administrators the discretion to interpret a plan, then courts must review these decisions deferentially, and a trustee's interpretation of "disputed or doubtful terms" will be upheld if it is reasonable. The case returned to the Second Circuit; in late 2013, the court remanded the case once again. The Second Circuit held that the plaintiffs' suit is meritorious: the proposed offset method was unreasonable, and the SPD was not accurate enough, because it did not say that the lump sum distribution will reduce the benefit, only that it might. [*Frommert v. Conkright*, 738 F.3d 522 (2d Cir. 2013); see Kevin McGuinness, *Appellate Court Remands Case on Offsetting Pension Benefits*, plansponsor.com (Dec. 31, 2013)]

§ 13.02 THIRD-PARTY ADMINISTRATORS (TPAs)

About two-thirds of covered workers in the United States get their benefits from plans that use some degree of third-party administration instead of handling all plan administration in house.

A TPA is an outsourcing firm that handles administrative tasks. It could be a consulting firm or a broad-based benefits administration firm. There are no federal licensing rules for TPAs, although some states impose their own requirements.

If the plan has unexpectedly high claims, TPAs usually provide stop-loss protection with back-up insurance that benefits the plan itself (rather than the employees with high expenses). Having a stop-loss plan doesn't turn a self-insured plan into an insured plan for ERISA purposes.

A TPA can be considered an ERISA fiduciary as long as it satisfies the statutory requirement of holding "any authority or control," even if it does not have discretionary control over the assets of the health plan it administers. The Sixth Circuit held that a TPA's authority to write checks on the plan's account (which continued to be exercised to pay the TPA's fees even after the contract with the plan sponsor ended) provided the necessary degree of authority or control to impose liability after the sponsor company went bankrupt and many employees had unpaid medical bills. [*Briscoe v. Fine*, 444 F.3d 478 (6th Cir. 2006)]

The Sixth Circuit held in 2012 that a TPA becomes a fiduciary when it exercises practical control over the plan's funds. Therefore, a TPA that failed to pay claims under a self-insured ERISA health benefits plan (the TPA misappropriated the funds) violated its fiduciary duty to act solely in the best interests of participants, [*Guyan Int'l Inc. v. Professional Benefits Administrators Inc.*, 689 F.3d 793 (6th Cir. 2012); see EBIA Weekly, *Sixth Circuit Affirms That TPA Breached Fiduciary Duties by Using Plan Assets to Pay Its Expenses Instead of Claims* (Sept. 6, 2012) (benefitslink.com)]

Failure to supervise a TPA can also lead to liability for the sponsor. As a result of a suit brought by the DOL, the president of Clark Graphics was required to restore $505,000 to Clark Graphics' two pension plans, and the plan administrator had to return $567,000 to two plans. The two executives violated their fiduciary duty as trustees when they failed to review or reconcile the participants' trust account statements or ensure that appropriate disclosures were made to participants. [Rebecca Moore, *Employer to Pay $500K for Failing to Monitor TPA*, plansponsor.com (July 18, 2012)]

§ 13.03 HEALTH PLAN CLAIMS

The Department of Labor's Pension and Welfare Benefits Agency (PWBA; later renamed EBSA) published a wide-ranging final rule on claims procedures for health and disability plans, amending 29 C.F.R. § 2560.503-1. [See 65 Fed. Reg. 70246-70271 (Nov. 21, 2000); 66 Fed. Reg. 35887 (July 9, 2001)] The PPACA claims rules (see § 13.03[A], below) build on these rules and add more requirements.

The Final Rule draws a distinction between preservice claims (advance approval of health care services) and postservice claims (where medical care has already been provided). The distinction is made because postservice claims are much less urgent. The employee has already been treated, so the question becomes who will pay the bill, not whether potentially necessary care will be available or not.

Plans are not allowed to impose any fees or costs for appealing a denial. The reviewer cannot be either the person who made the initial denial or someone who works for that person. Whenever there is an issue of medical judgment, such as when treatment is necessary, the plan must consult appropriate health care professionals. The reviewer must examine the claim de novo (from the beginning), not just to see if the initial decision involved an abuse of discretion. The employee is allowed to introduce new facts that they did not provide earlier—even if these facts would not be admissible as evidence in a suit. There can be either a single level of review of denials, or two sequential levels of review, but no additional time is allowed to decide the second level of review.

If a person makes a claim and is denied on the basis of non-eligibility for coverage, the claims procedure will apply because there has been a denial. But if a plan requires preauthorization or otherwise requires submission of pre-service claims, EBSA says that the plan may have to treat an inquiry as a claim that has not been properly filed—and may have to explain how to file the claim.

The EBSA says that the time for making an initial claims decision starts when the claim has been filed in accordance with the plan's reasonable filing procedures—even if the plan does not have all the information needed to decide the claim. Plans are not permitted to extend time limits by asserting that the claim is not a "clean claim" (i.e., that necessary information is missing). Plans must disclose the rules, guidelines, and protocols used to make adverse benefit determinations—even if the rule was developed by a third party that claims that proprietary information is involved. A plan can set a maximum period for filing initial benefit claims—as long as it is a reasonable limit that does not unduly hamper the right to make claims.

In plans where there are two levels of review of adverse benefit determinations, EBSA's position is that the same standards (including time limits) apply to both levels of review. Second-level review is de novo, and must be done by someone other than the first-level decision-maker or his or her subordinate. EBSA says that there cannot be more than two mandatory levels of appeals—but it is legitimate for a plan to offer additional voluntary levels of appeal, such as Alternative Dispute Resolution. Claimants who choose to sue rather than use voluntary remedies have not failed to exhaust administrative remedies. Furthermore, the litigation statute of limitations will be tolled while claimants voluntarily pursue additional levels of appeals. [DOL EBSA, *FAQs About the Benefit Claims Procedure Regulation*, <http://www.dol.gov/ebsa/faqs/faq_claims_proc_reg.html> (undated; last accessed Apr. 7, 2014). See also Technical Release 2011-02, HHS, *Technical Guidance for Non-Federal Governmental Plans*, <http://www.dol.gov/ebsa/newsroom/tr11-02.html? (Aug. 17, 2012), which includes model notices for adverse benefit determinations.]

[See Section [A] below for PPACA's variations on this theme.]

[A] PPACA Requirements

Interim final regulations to implement the claims requirements under PPACA (the health care reform bill) were published in July 2010 by DOL, HHS, and the Treasury. These regulations make insurance companies that provide policies for group health plans subject to the requirements to the same extent as EGHPs are. All plans must have an internal appeals process that grants full and fair review of denials (on an expedited basis, for urgent cases). Plan participants must be given detailed information about why claims were denied, and how to initiate an appeal.

Before these rules were published, most—but not all—states had requirements for independent external review of claims (44 states had such requirements), but there was no uniformity so some states offered much more protection to claimants than others. The new rules set standards for state external review procedures, and establish a federal external review procedure for people who are not covered by a state review process. Participants in self-insured plans are covered by the interim final rules.

PPACA requires all group and individual plans to comply with the ERISA claims/appeals procedure. However, certain plans, such as stand-alone vision plans and welfare benefit plans that are not health-related, are not subject to this requirement. As a result of PPACA, group and individual insured plans and self-insured plans must have both an internal claims/appeal process and an external review process. The Treasury, HHS, and the Department of Labor jointly issued interim final regulations (IFR) on July 22, 2010. The IFR was published in the Federal Register the next day: 75 Fed. Reg. 43330 (July 23, 2010). The IFR supplements, but does not replace, the pre-PPACA claims rules discussed above.

Under PPACA, for covered plans, the appeal and review mandate applies to all adverse benefit determinations. Cancellation or discontinuance of coverage with retroactive effect can be appealed, even if there is no actual benefit denial because of the rescission. Claimants must be notified of the outcome of urgent care claims as soon as possible, considering medical exigencies. The pre-PPACA provision that the time limit is extended if the claimant fails to provide adequate information remains in effect.

Group plans must inform the claimant of any new or additional evidence that the plan used or considered in connection with a claim. Before an appeal can be denied on the basis of a new or additional rationale, the claimant must be informed (without charge) of the evidence supporting the rationale. The information must be provided as soon as possible, definitely early enough for the claimant to respond to it before the final date for submitting information. (The authors of this treatise suggest that a plan that has two levels of appeals might wish to eliminate one to increase the time available for claims processing.)

Under the IFR, the plan must not make the compensation or promotion of people handling claims depend on their denial of a particular claim or a stated percentage of claims, and hiring cannot be based on a propensity to deny claims. If a plan fails to meet all the requirements for internal claims, the claimant is deemed to have exhausted the internal review process—and thus to be entitled to initiate external review or bring suit immediately. In suits under ERISA § 502(a), the case will be reviewed de novo without deference to the claims administrator's decision.

Notices of adverse benefit determinations must include:

- The date of the service
- The name of the health care provider
- Amount of the claim
- The diagnosis and treatment codes, and what they mean
- Other information needed to identify the claim
- The reason(s) for the adverse determination, including the denial code and its meaning, and the standards used by the plan to deny the claim.

In addition to the internal claims process (within the plan), PPACA requires group plans to provide for external review of the plan's claims decisions. If the state has a review process that HHS deems to be acceptable, the state will perform the external review; the federal process is used only in states where there is no adequate state process. PPACA imposes 16 requirements on state external review procedures. The external review decision is binding on the plan and the insurer, but binds the claimant only to the extent that there are no other remedies. In particular, a dissatisfied claimant can still bring a suit under ERISA § 502(a)(1)(B). [Patricia Eschbach-Hall, Jones Day, *Claims and Appeals Procedures: New Internal and External Review Requirements* (August 2010) (benefitslink.com)]

Individuals have four months after a final denial of an internal appeal to request external review. If the claim is urgent, the plan must decide immediately if external review appropriate; for non-urgent claims, the plan has five business days to make the decision. This stage is called "preliminary review." The plan is required to notify the individual of its decision, in writing, within one business day of finishing the preliminary review. The appeal must be referred to an Independent Review Organization (IRO). DOL Technical Release 2010-01 says that, to qualify for the safe harbor, a self-funded plan must rotate claims assignments among three IROs. [Christy Tinnes and Brigen Winters, *External Review: To Delete or Not Delegate?*, plansponsor.com (Oct. 18, 2011)]

Some important amendments to the IFR were published in June, 2011, changing the standard for deciding urgent care claims to making a decision as soon as possible consistent with medical needs, but always within 72 hours—rather than the 24-hour limit mandated by the IFR. The amendments say that, when an external reviewer orders benefits, the plan must provide the benefits without delay—even if it intends to seek judicial review. Under the amendments, the only claims eligible for federal external review are claims involving medical judgment or rescission of coverage—not how the participant's diagnosis is coded, or whether care from an out-of-network specialist should be covered. [*Group Health Plans and Health Insurance Issuers: Rules Relating to Internal Claims and Appeals and External Review Processes*, 76 Fed. Reg. 37208 (June 24, 2011); Technical Release 2011-02, <http://www.dol/gov/ebsa/rewsroom/tr11-02.html> and <http://cciio.cms.gov/resources/files/appeals_srg_06222011.pdf> (June 22, 2011)]

§ 13.04 HIPAA EDI STANDARDS

One reason for high medical costs is that a lot of time and effort is devoted to processing, transmitting, and analyzing information. A number of different standards evolved for storing and displaying health information. To streamline this process, HIPAA requires a uniform set of EDI standards to be placed into effect for health and welfare funds.

HIPAA's EDI standards apply to insured and self-insured EGHPs, health insurers and HMOs, but not to small, self-administered health plans with fewer than 50 participants. Employers are covered only if they administer their own health plans.

The Health Information Technology for Economic and Clinical Health (HITECH) Act, part of the economic stimulus bill (Pub. L. No. 111-5), takes effect February 17, 2010. The HITECH Act expands the privacy and security provisions of HIPAA, and includes a new regulatory structure for electronic medical records. Civil monetary penalties (CMPs) for HIPAA violations have increased; for the most egregious violations, the penalty can reach $1.5 million per year. Persons whose personal health information (PHI) has been disclosed improperly can collect a share of the civil penalties.

Business associates of HIPAA-covered entities are subject to the same privacy rules as the covered entities are, including criminal penalties for violations. HHS' Office of Civil Rights continues to enforce HIPAA compliance, but state Attorneys General have also been given the power to enforce HIPAA by bringing suit in federal district court. [Troutman Sanders LLP, *Keeping Up with Recent Legislation: Numerous Changes to Group Health Plans Required*, plansponsor.com (Feb. 27, 2009)] HHS published extensive proposed regulations (covering more than 50 pages in the Federal Register) in July 2010, implementing the HITECH Act requirements for privacy, data security, compliance, and the imposition of penalties. [RIN 0991-AB57, 75 Fed. Reg. 40868 (July 14, 2010)]

§ 13.05 CASE LAW ON CLAIMS

[A] Generally

Many cases have been litigated over questions of the proper way to handle and process claims within a plan—and especially over the standard of review that courts should apply when reviewing the decisions of plan administrators. If review is *de novo*, the court can consider all aspects of the decision, including its reasonableness and correctness. In most cases, however, the plan sponsor drafted the governing documents to reserve discretion—in which case, the court can only determine if the decision-maker acted arbitrarily and capriciously.

A claims administrator's incorrect statement to a claimant that a plan is not covered by ERISA does not prevent the plan from being an ERISA plan; such misstatements cannot change the plan's status. [*Hill v. Lincoln National Life Ins.*, __ F. Supp. 2d __, No. C -13-00276 EDL, 2013 WL 5863007 (N.D. Cal. Oct. 30, 2013); see D. Michael Reilly, *ERISA: Incorrect Statements During Claims Process Do Not Render ERISA Inapplicable*, Lane Powell PC (Nov. 25, 2013), available at Lexology.com]

The Eleventh Circuit held in early 2014 that plan administrators have an obligation to consider evidence presented by a disability claimant to the SSA in an application for SSDI. Most circuits require administrators to either consider the SSDI award or explain why it is not relevant, but the Eleventh Circuit seems to require the administrator to examine the evidence supporting the award; this might be interpreted to mean that a plan administrator can approve a claim before the SSDI process has been completed, but cannot deny it until then. A plaintiff submitted a disability claim based on tendonitis and degenerative disc disease. The insurer told her to apply for SSDI; she applied that month. The insurer denied the claim in November 2007, with the SSDI determination still unresolved. The plaintiff appealed the insurer's decision. After having her consult two independent doctors, the SSA granted SSDI benefits. The plaintiff informed the defendant of this but did not submit her medical evidence. [*Melech v. Life Ins. Co. of N. Am.*, 739 F.3d 663 (11th Cir. 2014); see Patrick Begos, *Must Disability Claim Administrators Now Obtain The SSDI File In The 11th Circuit?*, Begos Horgan & Brown LLP ERISA Claim Defense Blog (Jan. 20, 2014) (benefitslink.com)]

The Second Circuit required weighing of subjective evidence before rejecting a disability claim. The plaintiff, a lawyer, claimed based on tinnitus, hearing loss, headaches, and vertigo. The insurer said that he did not present objective evidence of significant impairment. The Second Circuit held that subjective evidence is not worthless, and there is no objective test for tinnitus, so the plaintiff could not have submitted such evidence. [*Miles v. Principal Life Ins. Co.*, 720 F.3d 472 (2d Cir. 2013); see Mike Reilly, *Hear This: "Subjective Evidence" is Worth its Weight*, Lane Powell Boom! The ERISA Law Blog (July 3, 2013) (benefitslink.com)]

[B] Experimental Treatment

EGHPs typically refuse to cover experimental treatment, and new forms of treatment are very often more expensive than the ones they replace. There is a long line of cases attempting to distinguish between experimental treatments and those that are novel but are accepted as scientifically valid by the medical community.

In a Wisconsin case involving a clinical trial for specialized chemotherapy for a brain tumor, coverage was denied as experimental. The patient's parents exercised the option of having an independent review organization perform expedited review of the denial. The review organization characterized the proposed treatment as medically necessary and within the standard of care, but still experimental. The state trial court said that Phase II clinical trials were unambiguously excluded from coverage. The state court of appeals reversed, saying that the termination of benefits was arbitrary and capricious; the state supreme court agreed. The denial letter did not provide specific reasons for the denial; the specific plan provision supporting the determination; the review procedures and time limits (including the right to sue); and either an explanation of the scientific or clinical judgment that the treatment was experimental, or a statement that such information will be furnished at no charge on request [*Summers v. Touchpoint Health Plan Inc.*, 2008 WI 45 (Wis. 2008); see Suzanne L. Wynn, *Wisconsin Supreme Court Finds Denial of Health Benefits Arbitrary and Capricious, Lacking Specificity*, Pension Protection Act Blog (May 29, 2008) (benefitslink.com)]

[C] Other Exclusions

When a plan's cosmetic-surgery exclusion specifically mentioned gastric bypass and other procedures used primarily to treat obesity, it was reasonable to deny coverage of a gastric bypass that was medically rather than cosmetically indicated (although the procedure on the 470-pound claimant would probably have been covered if the exclusion had not specifically listed gastric bypass). [*Manny v. Central States Pension & Health & Welfare Funds*, 388 F.3d 241 (7th Cir. 2004) See also *Smith v. Medical Benefit Adm'rs Group Inc.,* No. 09-C-538, 2012 WL 1378097 (E.D. Wis. Apr. 19, 2012): the plan document clearly excluded gastric bypass surgery, so the employee did not make a benefits claim. However, he sued for equitable relief when the claims administrator of his EGHP preauthorized the surgery but denied coverage after the surgery had been performed. The Seventh Circuit held that the plaintiff could not assert a benefit claim because the surgery was clearly excluded. The Seventh Circuit held that ERISA does not permit monetary damages for breach of fiduciary duty—but remanded the case to the district court to see if equitable relief was available.]

Another issue is whether the involvement of alcohol or drugs in an injury will result in claims denial:

- The Sixth Circuit ruled that it was reasonable to conclude that death caused by grossly negligent drunk driving is not accidental, so Personal Accident Insurance benefits could be denied to the beneficiary of a plan participant who died as a result of drunk driving. [*Lennon v. MetLife Ins. Co.*, 504 F.3d 617 (6th Cir. 2007)]
- However, the Fourth Circuit held that a crash caused by driving with a BAC of .289 was still an accident; most drunk drivers are not killed. [*Johnson v. American United Life Ins. Co.*, 716 F.3d 813 (4th Cir. 2013)]

[D] Timing

One of the most significant questions in tort law is when a potential plaintiff can be expected to be aware that an injury has occurred—and, therefore, when the clock starts for determining whether a claim is timely.

The Fourth Circuit ruled that the time starts for determining disability (including elimination periods) based on proof of total disability; it is an abuse of discretion to make a determination based on a particular date where proof is submitted relating to a different date. [*Evans v. Metro. Life Ins. Co.*, 358 F.3d 307 (4th Cir. 2004)]

In a case in which a plaintiff sued for additional benefits more than 10 years after he resigned and received a plan distribution (he said that a break in service should have been included in calculating his benefits), the Ninth Circuit agreed with the employer that the suit was untimely. Even though the plaintiff was not notified of appeal rights or given a full explanation of the reasons behind the benefit denial, he had reason to know that the denial was final, so the six-year statute of limitations expired in 1998. A suit filed in 2003 was untimely. [*Chuck v. Hewlett Packard Co.*, 455 F.3d 1026 (9th Cir. 2006), discussed in *Despite Claims Procedure Violations, Statute of Limitations Began When Employee Had "Reason to Know" of Claim Denial*, EBIA Weekly (Aug. 3, 2006)]

Santaliz-Rios v. Metropolitan Life Ins., 693 F.3d 57 (1st Cir. 2012) applies an insurance policy three-year statute of limitations rather than the Puerto Rico 15-year contract statute of limitations. See EBIA Weekly, *Court Enforces Plan-Imposed Limitations Period for Benefits Claims* (Oct. 25, 2012) (benefitslink.com).]

In late 2013, the Supreme Court ruled that an ERISA plan's three-year contractual statute of limitation was enforceable, even if it elapsed before it was possible for the plaintiff to file her suit. The Supreme Court found the limitation reasonable and not contrary to ERISA. The plaintiff asserted a disability claim in August 2005 but could not sue until exhausting her administrative remedies by pursuing the claims process, which was not completed until November 26, 2007. The plaintiff sued within three years of the final claim denial, but more than five years after her first assertion of the claim. The Supreme Court said that the ERISA regulations about claims generally result in claims being administered within 12–16 months, and it was not unreasonable to allow another 20–24 months to file suit. The Supreme Court said that, in rare cases where the administrative claim process takes so long that the plaintiff cannot file a timely claim, equitable remedies such as tolling, waiver, and estoppel might be available. [*Heimshoff v. Hartford Life*, 134 S. Ct. 604 (2013); see Scott J. Stitt, *U.S. Supreme Court Holds that a Three-Year Contractual Limitations Period for Benefit Claims is Not Unreasonable nor Contrary to ERISA*, Central Ohio Discrimination law firm (Dec. 16, 2013) (benefitslink.com)]

A MetLife employee became unable to work because of chronic pain and depression in 2000. He received STD benefits and worked intermittently for several years. Long-term disability benefits began in March 2005. He believed that his original salary should have been used to calculate benefits, not the lower salary from a non-managerial job he took between periods of collecting benefits. He brought several suits, including two 2012 cases that the district court dismissed for untimeliness, because there was a six-year statute of limitations (borrowed from Massachusetts breach of contract law) and the case involved a determination made in 2005. The plaintiff said that the statute of limitations re-started with each payment, but the First Circuit rejected this theory. Like the Second, Third, and Ninth Circuits, the First Circuit ruled that the cause of action to recover ERISA benefits starts to run as soon as the beneficiary learns that his or her claim has been rejected. Each payment does not start a new limitations period. [*Riley v. Metro. Life Ins. Co.*, 744 F.3d 241 (1st Cir. 2014)]

[E] Other Issues

Health plan fiduciaries have a duty to consider all pertinent available information and to make a decision based on substantial evidence. The Eighth Circuit reversed the lower court's grant of summary judgment to the employer, because the plaintiff should have been permitted to respond to the independent medical examiner's report to offer evidence that her obesity, alone or in conjunction with post-polio syndrome, rendered her totally disabled.

Especially in a situation in which one party has more resources and more power and is able to draft a document which the other party is not in a position to negotiate, courts will often be faced with allegations that a document is ambiguous, and should be construed in favor of the less-powerful party: here, the plan participant rather than the plan, plan administrator, or insurer.

The general rule is that the reviewing court will look only at the documents themselves. However, if a document is ambiguous, "extrinsic" (outside) evidence can be used to aid in its interpretation.

Estoppel is another legal doctrine, one which holds that in certain circumstances, a party will be "estopped" (prevented) from asserting a right that would otherwise apply—e.g., an employer that prevents an employee from filing a timely claim will not be allowed to reject claims on the grounds that they are untimely.

The doctrines of ambiguity and estoppel are often raised in cases involving plan amendments limiting benefits for those who have already retired. See Chapter 9 for retiree health benefits in general, and Chapter 14 for a discussion of the implications of amending a plan.

A litigator started collecting disability benefits for leg and foot pain in 2003. Benefits were discontinued in 2006 because of a functional capacity assessment, two independent medical exams, and a surveillance video. The plaintiff, Truitt, appealed, and her benefits were reinstated. A former boyfriend gave defendant Unum 600 pages of e-mails, documents, and photos showing Truitt working and engaging in recreational activities inconsistent with her claim of disability. Benefits were terminated again, and Truitt sued; Unum counterclaimed to recover $1 million in benefits. The Fifth Circuit held that the burden of generating evidence is not solely on the plan administrator. Unum did not abuse its discretion in using the materials submitted by the ex-boyfriend, because it concluded that the e-mails were authentic and not tampered with. [*Truitt v. Unum Life Ins. Co. of Am.*, 729 F.3d 497 (5th Cir. 2013); see Michael Reilly, *ERISA 5th Circuit: Attorney's Disability Case "Does Not Have A Leg To Stand On" After Scorned Boyfriend Provides Emails*, Lane Powell PC (Sept. 11, 2013), available at Lexology.com]

§ 13.06 *GLENN* AND THE STANDARD OF REVIEW

If and when a plan participant sues in connection with plan benefits, one of the most important questions is the "standard of review" the court will use to assess the plan administrator's decision. The two possibilities are "de novo" review, under which the court considers the question as if it were a new case, or review to see if the administrator abused his or her discretion. Many more plan decisions will be reversed—and many more claimants will win their cases—if the court can look at all the factors underlying the matter, and not just to see if there was an abuse of discretion.

The basic rule, as set by the seminal case of *Bruch v. Firestone Tire & Rubber* [489 U.S. 101 (1989)], is that plan administrators' decisions will be reviewed on a de novo basis, unless the plan itself is drafted to give the fiduciaries discretion over the way the plan operates. If the plan sponsor reserved this discretion, the court's only role is to see whether the administrators abused their discretion.

The mid-2008 Supreme Court decision in *Metropolitan Life Insurance Co. v. Glenn*, 554 U.S. 105 (2008) reaffirms *Bruch.* Wanda Glenn, a Sears employee was diagnosed with heart disease, and received 24 months of disability benefits.

The insurer, Metropolitan Life Insurance Co. (MetLife) encouraged Glenn to apply for Social Security disability benefits. The Social Security Administration concluded that Glenn was unable to work, and granted the benefits. MetLife, however, rejected Glenn's application for long-term disability benefits, because the insurer concluded that Glenn was capable of doing sedentary work.

Glenn challenged the denial of benefits. According to the Sixth Circuit, MetLife should not have denied benefits; it was unduly influenced by its conflict of interest (as both payor of the benefits and decision-maker about qualifications). The *Glenn* decision says that there are four principles that determine what standard of judicial review should be applied in ERISA § 1132(a)(1)(B) cases:

- Trust law principles should be applied, as if the plan administrator were a trustee carrying out fiduciary activities.
- The decision will be reviewed de novo unless the plan specifies review for abuse of discretion only.
- Deferential review is appropriate where the plan gives the plan administrator discretion to determine eligibility.
- If the decision-maker has a conflict of interest—such as a dual role in both granting or denying claims and paying claims that are granted—that is a factor in deciding whether there was an abuse of discretion by the decision-maker.

Glenn extends the conflict of interest analysis to insurers that administer plans, not just to plan sponsors, a step that the Supreme Court felt justified in taking because insurers that administer ERISA plans must act in the best interests of participants. (Furthermore, a sponsor that has a conflict of interest may act according to that conflict when selecting an insurance carrier.)

After *Glenn*, conflict of interest is a factor in the decision, but does not change the standard of review. Courts have devised many different ways to handle the structural conflict of interest when the institution responsible for paying benefits also evaluates claims. One theory is that there is no conflict of interest if the benefits are funded from a trust. [Nancy Pridgen, *Alston & Bird ERISA Litigation Advisory July, The Circuits Are Split: Does MetLife v. Glenn's* "Structural Conflict" *Holding Apply When Employee Benefits Are Funded from a Trust?* (Dec. 23, 2009) (benefitslink.com)]

After *Glenn*, all structural and procedural factors must be considered. In mid-2010, the Second Circuit held that Taft-Hartley plans (administered by a board of trustees including both management and union representatives) are inherently conflicted when they consider whether or not to grant benefits to a plan member. In this case, a worker reported chronic pain and weakness after being injured in an automobile accident. The Second Circuit ruled that the plan did not give enough weight to the testimony of her attending physician, and the independent report should not have concluded that the worker was able to perform three occupations. [*Durakovic v. Building Serv 32 BJ Pension Fund*, 609 F.3d 133 (2d Cir. 2010); see Fred Schneyer, *Appeals Panel Declares Taft Hartley Plans Inherently Conflicted*, plansponsor.com (June 30, 2010)]

[A] Statutes Regulating Discretionary Clauses

"Discretionary clauses" give administrators full authority to interpret the terms of the plan, thereby triggering a more deferential standard of review when a denial is challenged. In mid-2009, the Sixth Circuit and the District Court for the District of Colorado ruled that ERISA does not preempt state laws forbidding discretionary language in insurance policies in ERISA plans. The Sixth Circuit found that a Michigan law banning discretionary language is enforceable because it comes under the insurance savings clause; *Miller* says that a law "regulates insurance" if it directly controls the terms of insurance contracts. The Colorado case says that the state law is valid (because it dictates the conditions under which an insurer will pay for a risk that it has assumed) but it did not apply to the plaintiff's case, because the law was not retroactive. [*American Council of Life Insurers v. Ross*, 558 F.3d 600 (6th Cir. 2009)]

Three court of appeals cases were decided in 2013 on the issue of whether requiring proof to be satisfactory to the insurer is a discretionary clause that will permit review under the "arbitrary and capricious" standard. At first, the consensus was that merely using the words "satisfactory proof" would not confer discretion, because the phrase is ambiguous. Satisfactory proof could either be an objective standard, where the insurer had no discretion, or subjective (i.e., the insurer has discretion).

The Seventh, Eighth, and Tenth Circuits have decided cases saying "proof satisfactory to the insurer" was a discretionary clause because the insurer had the power to make a subjective determination as to whether the proof was satisfactory. The Sixth Circuit held that a requirement of "satisfactory proof" was discretionary. Dictum in a Second Circuit case states that the word "satisfactory" is not enough because no plan would grant benefits on the basis of proof it deemed inadequate. This became the dominant position between 2005 and 2011. The Third and Ninth Circuits said that "proof satisfactory to the insurer" is not clear enough to grant discretion, and the Seventh Circuit reversed itself and joined them. In 2013, *Gross v. Sun Life Assurance. Co. of Canada*, 734 F.3d 1 (1st Cir. 2013) said that "satisfactory to insurer" doesn't grant discretion, so review was de novo, and the Fourth Circuit agrees: *Cosey v. Prudential Ins. Co. of Am.*, 735 F.3d 161 (4th Cir. 2013), but the Sixth Circuit disagreed in mid-2013: *Frazier v. Life Ins. Co. of N. Am.*, 725 F.3d 560 (6th Cir. 2013). [Patrick Begos, *Effect of Requiring "Satisfactory" Proof Is A Popular Issue in the Circuits This Year*, ERISA Claim Defense Blog (Nov. 20, 2013) (benefitslink.com)]

Cigna helped an engineer get SSA disability benefits (which offset his benefits under the CIGNA plan) after multiple foot surgeries left him unable to work.

However, Cigna denied his LTD claim, saying that the definition of disability was different. The Seventh Circuit held that the policy definition was "functionally equivalent" to the SSA's definition, and that the claim denial improperly reflected Cigna's conflict of interest. [*Raybourne v. Cigna Life Ins. Co.*, 700 F.3d 1076 (7th Cir. 2012); see Scott J. Stitt, *The Seventh Circuit Concludes that SSA's Definition of Disability, and Cigna's Definition of Long-Term Disability, Is "Functionally Equivalent."* Arnlaw.com Blog (Apr. 3, 2013) (benefitslink.com)]

§ 13.07 CASE LAW ON CLAIMS PROCEDURAL ISSUES

A fiduciary, including a life insurance company, has a right under ERISA § 502(a) to seek appropriate equitable relief from the courts in order to enforce plan provisions. Therefore, the fiduciary can bring an interpleader action (a suit asking for court guidance on how to dispose of funds whose ownership is disputed) if there are conflicting claims to insurance proceeds—for instance, based on a beneficiary designation and community property law. [*Aetna Life Ins. Co. v. Bayona*, 223 F.3d 1030 (9th Cir. 2000)]

Subrogation (see § 18.17) is another issue that may be involved. It is the right of a party, such as an insurance company or benefit plan that advances money to an injured person to be repaid when the injured person collects damages from the party causing the injury. In a recent Supreme Court case, a plan participant injured in an automobile accident received $100,000 from his own insurer and $10,000 from other sources when he was injured in an automobile accident. After paying his lawyer, he had $66,000 left. His health plan had paid $66,866 of medical expenses for him. He claimed that he was not required to reimburse the health plan, because that would mean that he was not "made whole" for his damages. The Supreme Court held that the SPD for the health plan gave the insurer a right of subrogation, and this right, under contract law, prevailed over McCutchen's equitable arguments about "make-whole" relief. However, the reimbursement provision did not explain how to handle attorneys' fees, so the Supreme Court held that it was possible to apply another equitable doctrine, the "common fund" doctrine to resolve this issue. (This doctrine allows a person who creates a common fund for the benefit of multiple parties to be paid for creating the fund.) [*US Airways, Inc. v. McCutchen*, 133 S. Ct. 1537 (2013); see Sarah Fowles & Angela Marie Hubbell, *Have You Checked Your Plan's Subrogation and Reimbursement Provisions Lately?*, Quarles & Brady LLP Employee Benefits & Executive Compensation Law Blog (April 2013) (benefitslink.com)]

According to the Tenth Circuit, the claims regulation was not violated by failure to disclose documents generated during the administrative appeal process. The point of disclosure is to give claimants enough information to decide whether or not to appeal. At that stage, there was no new factual information or diagnosis to alter the decision process. In the Tenth Circuit analysis, documents have to be produced at only two stages: after the initial claims determination, and after the final decision on appeal (at which point administrative remedies have been exhausted). [*Metzger v. UNUM Life Ins. Co.*, 476 F.3d 1161 (10th Cir. 2007); see *No Deferential Review Where SPD and Certificate, But Not Policy, Grant Discretion to Insurer*, EBIA Weekly (Aug. 24, 2006); *Claimant Has Right to Documents Generated in Administrative Appeal Only After Final Decision*, EBIA Weekly (Mar. 1, 2007)]

[A] HMO and TPA Involvement in Claims

Yet another facet in the complex picture comes from the involvement of HMOs and TPAs in the claims process. The legal questions become much more complex than a simple relationship between employee/plan participant and employer/plan sponsor.

As a general rule, an ERISA plan is the proper defendant if a participant wants to sue for benefits. However, in mid-2013, the Seventh Circuit held that if a health insurer decides all benefit eligibility issues and is the party that legally has an obligation to pay the benefits, an ERISA § 502(a)(1)(B) suit for benefits can be brought against the insurer. In this case, the plaintiffs charged that six insurers violated state law by imposing copayments for chiropractic treatment. [*Larson v. United Healthcare Ins.*, 723 F.3d 905 (7th Cir. 2013); see PLC Legal Update, *Insurers Can Be Sued for Benefits Under ERISA: Seventh Circuit* (July 29, 2013) (benefitslink.com). See also *Cyr v. Reliance Standard Life Ins.*, 642 F.3d 1202 (9th Cir. 2011), also permitting an ERISA § 502(a)(1)(B) suit against an insurer.]

A health plan subject to PPACA has a choice of establishing a direct contractual relationship with an IRO or having the TPA handle the transaction; TPAs frequently have existing IRO relationships. But if the agreement is delegated, the sponsor must ensure that the TPA's contract with the IRO satisfies the requirements of Technical Release 2010-01. The delegation document should spell out the relationship between the plan and the TPA, making it clear what claims are involved. If the TPA that processes medical benefit claims for the plan does not handle prescription drug claims, then the plan must either contract with three more IROs, or delegate the hiring to another party (for example, a pharmacy benefits manager). [Christy Tinnes and Brigen Winters, *External Review: To Delete or Not Delegate?*, plansponsor.com (Oct. 18, 2011)]

In the wake of the Supreme Court's consolidated decision in *Aetna Health Inc. v. Davila*, and *Cigna Healthcare of Texas, Inc. v. Calad*, 542 U.S. 200 (2004), note that plan participants who claim that they were improperly denied necessary health care by a Managed Care Organization will have to bring the cases in federal court. The Supreme Court ruled that ERISA § 502(a) completely preempts state laws purporting to regulate managed care decisions about whether or not to provide treatment.

In the Eleventh Circuit view, whenever an administrator delegates authority to a TPA that is not a fiduciary, the TPA's decisions must be reviewed de novo, but the Tenth Circuit allows the decisions to be reviewed for abuse of discretion. [*Geddes v. United Staffing Alliance Employee Medical Plan*, 469 F.3d 919 (10th Cir. 2006)]

The Southern District of New York ruled in late 2013 that a TPA cannot be sued for violations of the mental health parity requirements because the statute, the Mental Health Parity and Addiction Equity Act (MHPAEA), applies only to insurers and EGHPs. ERISA claims were dismissed because the TPA was not the plan administrator for ERISA purposes. An employee covered by a self-funded group health plan sued claims administrator UnitedHealth Group when claims for psychotherapy were given concurrent and prospective review, when the terms of the plan called for retrospective review and for a second level of appeals. Another plaintiff's son lost coverage for inpatient treatment of his severe mental illness; United said he could be treated as an outpatient. (The plaintiff said that not only was there no available outpatient treatment in the community, but United had also denied coverage for outpatient treatment.) The third plaintiff also had a severely mentally ill child; United rejected coverage of residential treatment, saying that partial hospitalization was appropriate. The district court said that, although this conduct would violate the MHPAEA, United was not subject to the statute; an entity that processes claims and makes coverage determinations when someone else pays the claims is not "offering coverage." The suit could be characterized as one for violation of plan terms, under ERISA § 502(a)(1)(B), but the only proper defendants for such a suit are the plan, the plan trustees, or a plan administrator designated as such under ERISA § 1002(16)(A). [*N.Y. State Psychiatric Ass'n v. UnitedHealth Group*, No. 13 Civ. 1599 CM (S.D.N.Y. Oct. 31, 2013); see David Slaughter, *TPA May Not Be Sued for MHPAEA Violations*, Smart HR (Dec. 9, 2013) (benefitslink.com)]

[B] Exhaustion of Remedies

Exhaustion of remedies is a traditional legal doctrine under which parties will not be permitted to litigate a claim until they have satisfied the applicable administrative requirements—whether that means filing a claim with a state or federal antidiscrimination agency or using the appeals procedures provided by a health or welfare benefit plan. This is an important doctrine for employers, who can eliminate many suits at their earliest stages if the employees had an obligation to access plan remedies but failed or refused to do so. However, a counterbalancing legal doctrine is that employees do not have to exhaust administrative remedies when doing so would be futile.

When the insurer already concluded that a claimant was ineligible for long-term disability benefits (on the grounds that he could perform the duties of his own occupation), it would have been futile for the claimant to ask for a determination that he could not perform the duties of any occupation in order to get a waiver of life insurance premiums. In other words, the insurer could not require a second exhaustion of administrative remedies when the grounds for denying both claims were similar. [*Dozier v. Sun Life Assurance Co. of Canada*, 466 F.3d 532 (6th Cir. 2006), discussed in Roy F. Harmon III, *Sixth Circuit Applies Futility Exception to Enforce Consistency in Claims Review*, <http://www.healthplanlaw.com>. Similarly, *Paese v. Hartford Life & Accident Ins. Co.*, 449 F.3d 435 (2d Cir. 2006) holds that a finding that someone is not totally disabled from his own occupation implies a determination that he is not totally disabled from any occupation]

Chapter 14

AMENDING A PLAN

§ 14.01 INTRODUCTION

It is very likely that, no matter how carefully a plan was drafted, amendments will be required over the course of time. The company's line of business or workforce may change. The business may suffer reverses. And it's more than likely that ERISA and the tax code will change in ways that require corresponding amendments to the plan. Each new tax bill that requires amendments includes a schedule for when plans are required to make their conforming amendments. In recent years, there have been major changes in the law such as the passage of the Genetic Information Nondiscrimination Act (GINA), the Americans with Disabilities Amendments Act (ADAA), and the large-scale revision of the FMLA rules. A legal sea change of this kind requires re-examination of the company's plans to see if once-acceptable provisions now violate a tax or other provision.

Plan amendments can be adopted either prospectively or retroactively. Retroactive amendments can be made until the last day (including extensions) for filing the income tax return for the year the plan was adopted.

The Department of Labor must be notified whenever a plan is materially modified or the information called for by ERISA § 102(b) changes. The DOL must receive an updated SPD when the participants and beneficiaries do. The DOL can reject an incomplete submission, giving the plan administrator 45 days for corrections. The 5500-series form filed with the IRS also requires reporting of the plan amendments and changes in the plan description that occurred during the year.

Plans frequently require amendments to keep up with tax law changes. If a plan obtains a determination letter from the IRS, the plan probably will not be disqualified if the IRS subsequently discovers defects in the plan documents. However, this immunity does not extend to operational defects, only to design defects. See § 14.02, below.

An "operational error" is a failure to comply with the terms of the plan. Often, this can be corrected without IRS involvement and without penalties to the plan. The sponsor must put the plan and its participants in the position they would have been in if there had been no error. However, if correction requires a plan amendment, then it will probably be necessary to use the Employee Plans Compliance Resolution System (EPCRS), as set out most recently in Rev. Proc. 2013-12, and to file under the Voluntary Correction Program (VCP). However, there are five situations under which a sponsor can use the Self-Correction Program (SCP) to adopt a retroactive corrective amendment without making a VCP filing:

- A hardship distribution was made from a plan that did not have a hardship distribution option;
- Making a plan loan where, once again, this option was not included in the plan;

- Letting an employee participate in the plan prematurely—before he or she satisfied the eligibility requirements;
- Allocating a contribution to correct a violation of the § 401(e)(17) compensation limit;
- Correcting an ADP failure by making a Qualified Nonelective Contribution (QNEC) that would not otherwise be available under the plan.

The plan must comply with the requirements of Code §§ 401(a), 410(b), and 411(d)(6). If the correction is a retroactive amendment to allow hardship distributions or loans, the best practice is to make sure that enough non-highly compensated employees (NHCEs) had access to them to satisfy the nondiscrimination rules. Amendments to change eligibility dates should also predominantly benefit NHCEs. The general rule is that correcting operational errors in an individually designed plan by amendment will probably require the sponsor to make an application for a determination letter, reflecting the amendment, the next time the plan's cycle requires a determination letter. If the plan terminates before the next cycle, a determination letter including the amendment will have to be obtained in connection with the termination. But if the plan is an approved prototype or volume submitter plan, a determination letter is not only not required for the amendment, the IRS forbids applying for one. [Sungard Relius, *Self-Correction Program Retroactive Corrective Amendments* (Mar. 29, 2013) (benefitslink.com)]

Rev. Proc. 2013-12, 2013-4 I.R.B. 313 includes a procedure for using Appendix C, Schedule 1 to correct a failure to adopt a mandatory interim amendment that was required to conform to the PPA or HEART Act. The fee for this program is $375. However, the procedure cannot be used to correct failure to adopt an interim amendment required by a pre-EGTRRA restatement—for example, the 401(k) final regulations. Those failures require correction under Appendix C, Schedule 2, which carries a higher fee. [Sungard Relius, *Correcting a Failure to Adopt an Interim Amendment Under the New EPCRS* (Mar. 19, 2013) (benefitslink.com)]

Under Notice 2014-1, 2014-2 I.R.B. 393, plans can be amended to let employees change their cafeteria plan elections mid-year, if they have same-sex spouses and their status has changed either because of the *Windsor* decision or because marriage takes place mid-year. If the employer wishes to adopt changes under Notice 2014-1, the plan must be amended before the end of the first plan year beginning on or after December 16, 2013. The amendment can be effective retroactive to the start of the plan year that includes December 16, 2013. For a calendar-year plan, the amendment must be adopted by December 31, 2014, and can apply retroactive to January 1, 2013 as long as the plan is administered consistently with the provisions of Notice 2014-1. [Stephen A. Riga, *At Year End, IRS Issues Guidance On Cafeteria Plan Transitional Rules For Windsor*, Ogletree Deakins (Dec. 26, 2013), available at Lexology.com]

In most cases, the Internal Revenue Code does not require that employees be notified in advance that the plan will be amended. So they don't have a right to comment on the proposed amendment (although they do have a right to comment on the plan's initial application for a determination letter). The exception is that advance notice is required if the amendment changes the vesting schedules of participants who have three years or more of plan participation, because they have the right to choose between the new and the old schedules. However, ERISA does impose a notice requirement. Once a plan is amended, ERISA §§ 102(a)(1) and 104(b)(1) require participants to get a Summary of Material Modifications (SMM) within 210 days of the end of the plan year in which the change is adopted.

See *Coffin v. Bowater Inc.*, 501 F.3d 80 (1st Cir. 2007): an ERISA plan amendment must be in writing; must be executed by someone authorized to amend the plan; the language must make it clear that the plan is being amended; and any other requirements for amendments set out in the governing documents must be observed. *Halliburton Co. Benefits Comm. v. Graves*, 463 F.3d 360 (5th Cir. 2006) holds that, to amend an ERISA welfare benefit plan, the employer must provide a procedure for amendment, must identify who is authorized to amend, and amendments are effective only if they follow the plan procedure.

The Second Circuit, reversing its own earlier rulings, applied the Supreme Court's *Schoonejongen*, *Jacobson*, and *Spink* decisions to find that employers and plan sponsors are not acting as fiduciaries when they modify, adopt, or amend plans. This is also true of multi-employer plans, so ex-participants and beneficiaries of the Niagara-Gennessee & Vicinity Carpenters Local 280 Pension and Welfare Funds were unable to recover assets that they said were wrongfully depleted by improper plan amendments that, they alleged, violated fiduciary duties. [*Janese v. Fay*, 692 F.3d 221 (2d Cir. 2012); see Rebecca Moore, *Amending a Plan Not a Fiduciary Act*, plansponsor.com (Sept. 18, 2012)]

Verizon chose to purchase a single-premium group annuity contract from Prudential Insurance to settle its liabilities to certain plan beneficiaries. The plaintiffs, about 41,000 retirees, said that the plan amendment and the annuity transaction were fiduciary functions, and there was a breach of fiduciary duty because the termination rules were not applied. However, the District Court for the Northern District of Texas dismissed the suit, holding that amending a plan is not a fiduciary function. [*Lee v. Verizon Commc'ns Inc.*, 954 F. Supp. 2d 486 (N.D. Tex. 2013); see Kevin McGuinness, *Court Dismisses Verizon Pension Buyout Suit*, plansponsor.com (June 25, 2013)]

The Sixth Circuit held that it is permissible for an employer to make reasonable modifications to its retiree health benefits; even if the retiree health benefits have vested, vesting does not mean that the bundle of services becomes fixed for all time. CNH America's 1998 CBA required all retirees to use managed care, reduced their coverage choices, and required them to pay more for out-of-network care. The Sixth Circuit held that it was lawful for the employer to alter the benefits unilaterally, because health care benefits are not like pension benefits, which can be monetized at retirement. The Sixth Circuit remanded the case, defining reasonable changes are those that maintain benefits reasonably commensurate with the old plan; are reasonable when considered in the context of changes in health care; and are roughly consistent with the types of benefits provided to active employees. [*Reese v. CNH America, LLC*, Nos. 11-1359, 11-1857 and 11-1969 (6th Cir. 2012); see Wolters Kluwer Law & Business, *Employer Entitled To Make "Reasonable Modifications" To Retiree Health Care Benefits, Sixth Circuit Rules* (Oct. 5, 2012) (benefitslink.com)]

In mid-2013, the Sixth Circuit once again ruled in favor of employees claiming that a CBA entitled them to lifetime health benefits fully funded by the former employer. The question was whether side letters adopted to cap the employer's health care obligations were part of the CBA. The Sixth Circuit held that the cap agreements did not apply, because they were not ratified by the union. The Sixth Circuit found that there was a vested right to non-contributory health benefits that could not be bargained away without consent of the retirees. However, the Sixth Circuit reinstated the plaintiffs to the plan that was bargained for in 2007, not the more generous earlier plan. The court considered the increased copayments and deductibles under the 2007 plan to be reasonable in light of ever-increasing health care costs. [*Tackett v. M&G Polymers USA*, 733 F.3d 589 (6th Cir. 2013); see Plansponsor Staff, *Court Finds Employer Owes Lifetime Health Benefits*, plansponsor.com (Aug. 21, 2013) *cert. granted* No. 13-1010 (May 5, 2014)]

§ 14.02 FLEXIBILITY THROUGH AMENDMENT

Before 2005, amendments to retirement plans to comply with changes in the law were submitted to the IRS for approval at irregular intervals. The IRS was often confronted with too many submissions at one time. Therefore, in 2005, a cyclical system was implemented, dividing plans into two groups: pre-approved and individually designed.

Most pre-approved plans are either prototype plans or volume submitter plans. A prototype plan has a basic plan document and an adoption agreement. The employer can choose among several plan options offered. A volume submitter plan provides plan language (including some options) that, after approval by the IRS, is used to create plans. Volume submitter plans offer many choices, whereas prototype plans have very few choices and make it difficult to shift the plan to a new provider.

Standardized prototype plans are reviewed on a six-year cycle; the first six-year cycle for preapproved defined contribution plans ended April 30, 2010. The six-year cycle for defined benefit plans ends April 30, 2012. [The ERISA Law Group, *Does Your Company EIN End With a "2" or a "7," or is Your Plan a Multiple Employer Plan?* (February 2012) (benefitslink.com) The IRS maintains a separate six-year submission cycle for pre-approved plans. Individually designed plans are reviewed on a five-year cycle. The cycle that a particular plan belongs to depends on the last digit in its Employer Identification Number (EIN).

On January 31, 2011, the first completed series of determination letter cycles for individually designed plans ended, and a second series began. Letters issued for Cycle A, ending January 31, 2007, expire on January 31, 2012 unless renewed by a timely new application. See Notice 2010-90, 2010-52 I.R.B. 909 for the required changes for Cycle A.

The due date for Cycle B plans (EIN ending in 2 or 7) is January 31, 2013; for Cycle C (3 or 8) it is January 31, 2014, for Cycle D (4 or 9) it is January 31, 2015, and for Cycle E (5 or 10) it is January 31, 2016. [John Anderson, *Does Your Qualified Retirement Plan Need to Be Amended This Year*? Alston & Bird LLP Employee Benefits & Executive Compensation Advisory (Nov. 7, 2011) (benefitslink.com)]

The deadline for Cycle C applications is January 31, 2014, although they could be filed starting in early 2013. (The IRS has pointed out that documents filed early in a cycle get a faster response than those filed later.) Cycle C plans are individually designed plans whose sponsor's EIN ends in 3 or 8. All amendments adopted after the previous restatement must be incorporated into the plan document, and the relevant changes in Notice 2012-76, 2012-52 I.R.B. 775 (2012 Cumulative List of Changes in Plan Qualification Requirements) must be reflected. The sponsor must formally approve and execute the amended plan document. If a private Cycle C plan fails to file its determination letter application on time, its existing determination letter becomes obsolete—and the plan might be audited and found noncompliant. [Spencer Fane, *IRS Now Accepting "Cycle C" Determination Letter Applications* (Feb. 18, 2013) (benefitslink.com)]

In March 2014, the IRS announced that it would issue opinion and advisory letters for pre-approved defined contribution plans that were restated for qualification requirements listed in the 2010 Cumulative List and were filed with the IRS during their second submission period under the Rev. Proc. 2007-44 remedial amendment cycle. In this context, pre-approved plans means master and prototype and volume submitter plans. The letters were expected to issue on March 31, 2014. Employers restating these pre-approved plan documents must adopt the plan document by April 30, 2014. The IRS will accept applications for individual determination letters under the second six-year remedial cycle between May 1, 2014 and April 30, 2016.

The remedial amendment cycle for pre-approved defined contribution plans for changes in the plan qualification requirements on the 2010 Cumulative List ends April 30, 2016. An employer whose defined contribution plan is eligible for the six-year remedial amendment cycle who adopts a Master & Prototype or Volume Submitter plan by April 30, 2016 is considered to have adopted the plan within the six-year remedial amendment cycle. An employer adopting a Master & Prototype plan, whether it is standardized or not, cannot use Form 5307 to apply for the plan's determination letter. An employer adopting a Volume Submitter plan can only use Form 5307 if the employer has modified the terms of the approved plan, but not enough for the plan to become an individually designed plan. Employers permitted to file Form 5307 to get a determination letter can do so between May 1, 2014 and April 30, 2016. [Announcement 2014-16, 2014-17.I.R.B. 983. The 2010 Cumulative List is found at Notice 2010-90, 2010-52 I.R.B. 909.]

The IRS extended the deadline to submit on-cycle applications for opinion and advisory letters for pre-approved defined benefit plans, for the second six-year remedial amendment cycle, until February 2, 2015. The extension applies to defined benefit mass submitter lead and specimen plans, word-for-word identical plans, master and prototype minor modifier placeholder applications, and non-mass-submitter defined benefit plans. The IRS granted the extension based on requests to develop a pre-approved plan program for defined benefit plans with some cash balance features. [Announcement 2014-4, 2014-7 I.R.B. 523; modifies Rev. Proc. 2007-44 and Rev. Proc. 2011-49]

Rev. Proc. 2014-6, 2014-1 I.R.B. 198 gives the procedures (effective February 1, 2014) for issuing determination letters on the qualified status of pension, profit sharing, stock bonus, annuity, and ESOP plans, and explains how to pay user fees at <http://www.pay.gov>. The updated schedule of user fees for requests for letter rulings and determination letters appears in Rev. Proc. 2014-8, 2014-1 I.R.B. 242. [Rebecca Moore, *IRS Updates Procedures for Determination Letters User Fees*, plansponsor.com (Jan. 8, 2014)]

If a sponsor's EIN or controlled group status has changed since its previous determination letter was issued, then the plan's cycle also changes. For example, if the sponsor of a Cycle D plan merges into a company whose EIN begins with 1 or 6, the plan moves to Cycle A. However, if the cycle change occurs during the Cycle A submission window, an automatic extension to January 31, 2013 is granted. [Steptoe & Johnson LLP ERISA Advisory, *The 7th Circuit's Big ERISA Day* (Feb. 15, 2011) (benefitslink.com)]

An employer will be permitted to suspend or reduce safe harbor contributions to a 401(k) plan if it is running at a loss for the plan year—or if the annual safe harbor notice reserves the right to amend the plan to reduce or suspend the contributions. The notice must be given 30 days in advance, explaining the amendment and its consequences for plan participants. The plan must be amended to provide that nondiscrimination testing will be satisfied for the entire year of the suspension or reduction. [T.D. 9641, 78 Fed. Reg. 68735 (Nov. 15, 2013); see Marc D. Bussone et al., *IRS Issues Final Regulations On Suspending Or Reducing Safe Harbor 401(K) Contributions*, Bradley Arant Boult Cummins LLP (Nov. 20, 2013), available at Lexology.com]

Although most plan actions that require communication with the IRS are subject to user fees, Rev. Proc. 2012-8, 2012-1 I.R.B. 235 provides that there is no user fee required if a plan makes an automatic change in its accounting period or accounting method if the change is authorized by a revenue procedure, or if the plan adopts a model amendment word-for-word if the model is published in a revenue procedure that states that the amendment should not be submitted to the

IRS. A user fee applies when the change in funding or account method is discretionary, not mandatory.

In addition to amendments required for tax purposes, amendments for business purposes are common. To preserve flexibility, it's a good idea for the sponsor to draft the plan reserving the right to amend the plan in the future. Plans can be amended to change or eliminate:

- Ancillary life insurance provided in connection with a pension plan;
- Accident or health insurance that is incidental to a pension plan;
- Some Social Security supplements;
- Availability of plan loans;
- Employees' ability to direct investment of their plan accounts or balances;
- The actual investment options available under the plan;
- Employees' ability to make after-tax contributions to the plan, or to make elective salary deferrals to a plan that is not a 401(k) plan;
- Administrative procedures for the plan (although even after the amendments, participants must have a right to fair redress of their grievances);
- Dates used to allocate contributions, forfeitures, earnings, and account balances.

But any amendment must take into account I.R.C. § 411(d)(6), which forbids amendments that reduce accrued benefits, including early retirement benefits and retirement-related subsidies—even if the employees affected by the change consent to it. Furthermore, the general rule is that protected benefits cannot be reduced or eliminated when a plan is merged or its benefits are transferred to another plan.

A current, but not a former, employee can go to court to get a declaratory judgment that a plan has lost its qualification after an amendment. [*Flynn v. C.I.R.*, 269 F.3d 1064 (D.C. Cir. 2001)] The D.C. Circuit considers ex-employees "interested parties" only with respect to termination of a plan.

However, a plan that is subject to the I.R.C. § 412 minimum funding standard can be amended retroactively to reduce accrued benefits—as long as the plan sponsor can prove to the DOL that the sponsor is undergoing substantial business hardship that mandates a cutback in benefits. The amendments must be adopted within 2½ months of the end of the plan year. They must not reduce anyone's accrued benefit for plan years before the beginning of the first plan year that the amendment applies to. IRS approval is required for amendments of this type, and the DOL may have to be notified.

A plan can be amended to change its vesting schedule as long as no participant loses any nonforfeitable accrued benefits.

A defined benefit plan can lose its qualified status if it adopts an amendment that increases plan liabilities, if the result is that the funded current liability falls below 60% for the plan year. The employer can preserve the plan's qualification by posting "adequate" security. Either the corporation must place cash and securities in escrow, or it must obtain a bond from a corporate security company that is acceptable under ERISA § 412. [See I.R.C. § 401(a)(29) and ERISA § 307; poorly funded plans are also subject to requirements under the Pension Protection Act of 2006]

Plan amendments also are required when the law changes to permit novel forms of benefit plans and new types of plans (e.g., the introduction of Roth IRAs and Roth 401(k) plans). Notice 2013-74, 2013-52 I.R.B. 819 provides guidance on "in-plan Roth rollovers": i.e., a rollover within a 401(k) plan to a designated Roth account in the same plan. The deadline for amending a plan to provide for in-plan Roth rollovers is the last day of the first plan year for which the amendment is effective, or December 31, 2014—whichever is later. [Lisa A. Berkowitz Herrnson, *IRS Provides New Guidance On In-Plan Roth Rollovers*, Proskauer Rose (Dec. 17, 2013), available at Lexology.com; Rebecca Moore, *IRS Clarifies Roth In-Plan Rollover Rules*, plansponsor.com (Dec. 12, 2013)]

§ 14.03 CHANGE IN PLAN YEAR

IRS determination letters are not limited to initial qualification of a plan: They can also be obtained for plan amendments. The current employees who are eligible for plan participation are "interested parties" and must be notified of the application for a determination letter. If the proposed amendment changes eligibility for participation, then all employees at the same workplace as the original interested parties must be notified.

The request for change in a retirement plan's plan year is made on Form 5308. IRS approval is automatic as long as:

- No plan year is longer than 12 months. In other words, a year can be broken up into two short years, but two short years can't be consolidated into a long one;
- The change does not have the effect of deferring the time at which the plan becomes subject to changes in the law;
- The plan trust (if any) remains tax-exempt and does not have any Unrelated Business Taxable Income in the short year;
- Legal approval for the change is granted before the end of the short year;
- (Defined benefit plans) The deduction taken for the short year is the appropriate prorated share of the costs for the full year.

§ 14.04 REDUCTION IN FORMS OF DISTRIBUTION

Although it is not permitted to amend a qualified plan in any way that reduces any participant's accrued benefit, it is permissible to amend a plan to eliminate optional forms of benefits (such as periodic payments other than the required QJSA/QPSA). EGTRRA provides that, for plan years beginning after December 31, 2001, defined contribution plans can eliminate certain forms of benefit payout. See § 12.09 for details.

In particular, if funds are transferred from one qualified plan to another (e.g., in connection with a merger or acquisition), the transferee plan will not be required to provide all the payment options that the transferor plan provided. [See I.R.C. § 411(d)(6)(D) and ERISA § 204(g)(4)] However, if payout forms are eliminated, the plan participants must be allowed to take their distributions in lump sum form.

In 2004, the Supreme Court ruled [*Cent. Laborer's Pension Fund v. Heinz*, 541 U.S. 739 (2004)] that a plan amendment increasing the varieties of postretirement employment that would cause a suspension of benefit payments violated the anti-cutback rule.

This decision was reflected in final regulations published in 2005: T.D. 9219, 2005-38 I.R.B. 538. A plan amendment that decreases accrued benefits or places greater restrictions on the right to receive a benefit protected under I.R.C. § 411(d)(6) is in violation of § 411(d)(6) even if the restriction or condition is acceptable under the § 411(a) vesting rules. However, plans can be amended to restrict the availability of benefits accruing after the date of the amendment.

T.D. 9472, 74 Fed. Reg. 61270 (Nov. 24, 2009) is a final rule explaining § 204(h) notice requirements for airlines and certain underfunded single-employer plans. The PPA imposes limits on certain activities if the plan's funding percentage declines below 80%. Amendments that increase the plan's benefit liabilities are forbidden if the AFTAP is below 80%. Some payments are forbidden when AFTAP is in the range of 60%–80%, or the plan sponsor is in Chapter 11. Benefit accruals must cease when AFTAP falls below 60%. The IRS said that reducing or eliminating an early retirement benefit or retirement-type subsidy has the effect of reducing future benefit accruals. Code § 4980F(e)(3) requires the notice to be provided within a reasonable time before the plan amendment takes effect. T.D. 9472 says that, in general, 45 days before the effective date is reasonable—or 15 days for a small or multi-employer plan. For some amendments that took effect before December 31, 2008, notice is acceptable if given at least 30 days before the effective date.

Plans are not required to issue a 204(h) notice if they are amended to adopt the PPA's interest rates and mortality tables, even if the amendment has the effect of reducing the size of lump sum distributions. The First Circuit held that it was permissible for an employer to eliminate the option for participants to move defined contribution plan assets to a defined benefit plan. The rule change did not violate the anti-cutback rule even though it diminished an accrued benefit, because the change conformed to an ERISA exception. [*Tasker v. DHL Ret. Savings Plan*, 621 F.3d 34 (1st Cir. 2010); see Fred Schneyer, *Interplan Asset Transfer Elimination Upheld*, plansponsor.com (Oct. 7, 2010)]

The Tenth Circuit ruled in 2009 that the anti-cutback rule does not apply to a death benefit, or a plan feature that pays a lump sum at retirement that is the actuarial equivalent of a death benefit, because the plan's definition of "accrued benefit" excluded death benefits. [*Kerber v. Qwest Pension Plan*, 572 F.3d 1135 (10th Cir. 2009); See *In re Lucent*, 541 F.3d 25 (3d Cir. 2008) for the proposition that the death benefit was not an accrued benefit]

In contrast, the Tenth Circuit ruled in 2010 that, although welfare benefits are not subject to the anti-cutback rule, a plan amendment that conditioned the receipt of health benefits from a welfare plan on not receiving a lump sum from the pension plan had the effect of amending the pension plan by adding a new condition for receiving an accrued benefit under the pension plan, because a lump sum became less valuable if health benefits had to be surrendered. Therefore, the anti-cutback rule was violated. [*Battoni v. IBEW Local Union No. 102 Employee Pension Plan*, 594 F.3d 230 (3d Cir. 2010)]

§ 14.05 EGTRRA, CHIPRA, AND PPACA CONFORMING AMENDMENTS

It is common for plans to require amendments to conform to changes in tax and labor law (or to take advantage of additional options that have opened up for employers). Because these rules are often complex, difficult, and expensive to administer, it is common for the IRS to publish rules giving plans additional time to comply.

PPA § 1107 says that a timely plan amendment that eliminates or restricts a protected benefit is not be considered a cutback if the benefit reduction was mandated by § 436. [CCH Pensions & Benefits, *IRS Issues Sample Plan Amendment to Satisfy Code Sec. 436 Rules* (Dec. 14, 2011) (benefitslink.com); Rebecca Moore, *IRS Provides Sample Plan Amendment for Underfunded Pension Plan Limitations,* plansponsor.com (Nov. 29, 2011)]

Notice 2012-70, 2012-51 I.R.B. 512 gives defined benefit plans additional time to adopt amendments to comply with Code § 436 (the restrictions on amendments and benefits if a plan's funding falls below certain limits). The previous deadline was the last day of the plan year beginning on or after January 1, 2012. The Notice moves the deadline to the latest of:

- The last day of the plan year beginning on or after January 1, 2013;
- The last day of the first plan year in which the plan is subject to § 436; or
- The due date (with extensions) of the employer's tax return for the year that includes the first day of the plan year when the plan becomes subject to § 436.

Sponsors submitting determination letter applications on or after February 1, 2013 for individually designed plans must adopt the § 436 amendment before submitting the application. (Cycle B plans, filed before February 1, 2013 do not have to comply with § 436.) Notice 2012-70 also extends the relief period under the anti-cutback requirements. [McDermott Will and Emery, *IRS Extends Deadline for Defined Benefit Plans to Adopt Code Section 436 Amendments* (Dec. 13, 2012) (benefitslink.com)]

In late 2007, the IRS issued Rev. Rul. 2007-67, addressing mortality tables and interest rates to be used in calculation of the present value of defined benefit plan lump sums. The ruling permits plan sponsors to incorporate the most current mortality table by reference, so that it will not be necessary to adopt an amendment every time the IRS promulgates new tables. [Fred Schneyer, *Lump Sum Distribution Mortality Table Released*, plansponsor.com (Nov. 6, 2007); Brian M. Pinheiro and Jacquelin M. Gray, *IRS Issues Guidance on Interest Rate and Mortality Table for Calculating Lump Sum Distributions from Defined Benefit Plans in 2008*, Ballard Spahr Andrews & Ingersoll, LLP (Nov. 18, 2007) (benefitslink .com)]

The Society of Actuaries has compiled RP-2014 mortality tables, reflecting increased life expectancies of plan participants. The new tables will increase employer's contributions and lump sum payouts, as well as increasing PBGC variable rate premiums. It was not certain when the new tables would be adopted, but the IRS probably would not approve the new tables for use in 2016. [Kevin McGuinness, *Planning for Mortality Tables Effect on Liabilities*, plansponsor. com (Mar. 14, 2014)]

The year 2009's SCHIP expansion under CHIPRA, the Children's Health Insurance Program Reauthorization Act, Pub. L. No. 111-3, required amendment of EGHPs and cafeteria plans to cope with the additional enrollment rights (e.g., employees and their dependents entitled to state subsidy for health insurance premiums). Coordination of benefit rules may have had to be changed to reflect broader SCHIP coverage. [Norbert F. Kugele, Warner Norcross & Judd LLP, *New Federal SCHIP Law Requires Cafeteria and Health Plan Amendments* (Feb. 10, 2009) (benefitslink.com)]

PPACA compliance requires the adoption of a number of plan amendments:

- Enrollment of persons under 19 without pre-existing condition limitations;
- Coverage of employees' dependent children to age 26, whether or not they are students or married, and whether or not they are tax dependents of the employees; but see <http://www.dol.gov/ebsa/faqs/faq-aca.html> Q&A #14 for some permitted exceptions;
- Elimination of lifetime limits on essential health benefits (guidance has not yet been issued to define "essential," so plans must use a good-faith reasonable interpretation of the term);

- Restrictions on annual limits on essential health benefits; the limit must be at least $750,000 in 2010, rising to $1.25 million in 2012;
- Elimination of retroactive terminations of coverage;
- Amending FSAs, HRAs, and HSAs to eliminate reimbursement of the cost of over-the-counter drugs unless the participant has a prescription.

Non-grandfathered plans must be amended to provide the following:

- Coverage of some preventive services without cost sharing;
- Free choice of primary care provider (who can be a pediatrician for children enrolled in the plan); women can see an OB/GYN without prior authorization or referral;
- Emergency services must be covered without prior authorization, and emergency services must receive the same coverage whether in or out of network;
- The new external claims review process;
- The requirement of not discriminating in favor of highly compensated employees.

[Christy Tinnes and Brigen Winters, *A 2011 Plan Amendment Checklist*, Groom Law Group, plansponsor.com (Oct. 12, 2010)]

In late 2013, the IRS allowed medical flexible spending accounts (FSAs) to offer either a grace period or a carryforward (but not both). Under the grace period, FSA funds, which used to be subject to a "use it or lose it" rule if they were not expended by the end of the plan year, can be used to pay expenses incurred in the first two and a half months of the next plan year. The carryforward is an amount of up to $500 that the employee will now be permitted to retain in the account in the next year. The due date for adopting the plan amendment authorizing carryforward for the 2013 plan year is December 31, 2014. However, if there was a grace period, the amendment to remove it should be signed before the plan year. [Alison M. Stemler, *IRS Allows $500 Carry Forward Of Medical Flexible Spending Accounts*, Frost Brown Todd LLC (Dec. 13, 2013), available at Lexology.com]

§ 14.06 ERISA 204(h) NOTICE

The plan administrator has a duty to notify employees when a defined benefit plan (or any other plan that is subject to the minimum funding requirement) is amended in a way that significantly reduces the rate at which future benefits will accrue. In effect, this is an early warning system that signals to employees that their eventual pensions may be smaller than anticipated.

EGTRRA supplements the rules found at ERISA § 204(h) with a comparable Internal Revenue Code provision, I.R.C. § 4980F, which also imposes an excise tax on failure to make the required notification. See 67 Fed. Reg. 19714 for additional Proposed Regulations on this topic and T.D. 9052, 2003-19 I.R.B. 879 for final regulations.

The notice must be understandable to the average plan participant, and must give enough information for him or her to understand approximately how much his or her benefit entitlement will be reduced by the amendment. See also Proposed Regulations, 69 Fed. Reg. 13769 (Mar. 24, 2004) for eliminating redundant optional forms of benefits within a "family" of defined benefit payment options.

If the plan is significantly underfunded, and therefore is subject to restrictions on benefit accruals, payments, or shutdown benefits, the Pension Protection Act of 2006 (Pub. L. No. 109-280; PPA) requires the plan administrator to give written or electronic notice to plan participants within 30 days of the point at which the restriction takes effect.

In 2012, the Eleventh Circuit held that it did not violate the anti-cutback rule to amend the plan to change the calculation of the Social Security offset for participants who had not yet reached age 52 (the plan's earliest retirement age). The amendment changed the calculation of the Social Security offset by assuming that the individual earned no income after 2003 and by freezing benefit accruals. The Eleventh Circuit said that, because the plaintiff had not reached age 52 when the amendment was adopted, she did not have a vested benefit that could be protected by the anti-cutback rule. The Eleventh Circuit read *Heinz* to mean that a pension plan can be amended with respect to compensation that will be earned in the future for continued future employment. [*Cinotto v. Delta Air Lines Inc.*, 674 F.3d 1285 (11th Cir. 2012)]

§ 14.07 AMENDMENTS TO A BANKRUPT SPONSOR'S PLAN

Under Bankruptcy Code § 522, funds held in a qualified plan are protected from the plan sponsor's creditors—but only if the plan had a favorable determination letter in effect at the time of filing of the bankruptcy petition.

The general rule is that plan benefits may not be increased while the plan sponsor is a bankruptcy debtor. [See I.R.C. § 401(a)(33)] Amendments are forbidden if the plan's liabilities rise because of the benefit increase, or because of a change in the rate of accrual or nonforfeitability of benefits. However, amendments that take effect after the effective date of the plan of reorganization are allowed. So are amendments to plans, whose funded current liability percentage is 100% or more, or amendments approved by the IRS, or amendments required to maintain compliance with tax law changes.

The Bankruptcy Abuse Prevention and Consumer Protection Act (BAPCPA), Pub. L. No. 109-8, the bankruptcy reform legislation adopted in 2005, alters the treatment of retirement plans in bankruptcy. Bankruptcy Code

§ 1114, as amended, prevents a Chapter 11 debtor from terminating or modifying retiree welfare benefits without negotiating with retiree representatives. Benefits must be maintained unless the bankruptcy court approves a change. In addition, the court can set aside amendments to a retiree benefit plan made within 180 days before a bankruptcy filing unless the court finds that it is clearly equitable to modify the plan. The Third Circuit required strict compliance with § 1114, so even though the employer retained the right to amend its plan, it could not terminate retiree health benefits while the company was pursuing a bankruptcy reorganization. [*IUE-CWA v. Visteon Corp.*, 612 F.3d 210 (3d Cir. 2010); see Rebecca Moore, *Visteon Must Follow the Rules Before Terminating Retiree Benefits*, plansponsor.com (July 14, 2010)]

The Third Circuit ruled that a plan amendment, adopted just before a Chapter 11 filing that doubled or even quintupled the pension benefits payable to a group, including many corporate insiders, was void because it was a fraudulent transfer. One factor in the court's decision was the fact that the amendment was described to the board of directors as an "administrative formality," when in fact it was a significant modification to the plan. [*Pension Transfer Corp. v. Beneficiaries Under the Third Amendment to the Fruehauf Trailer Corp. Ret. Plan*, 444 F.3d 203 (3d Cir. 2006)]

Also note that, even if the plan's sponsor is not bankrupt, the Pension Protection Act of 2006 (PPA) restricts amendments that increase benefits at a time when the plan is significantly underfunded.

In March 2011, the PBGC proposed a rule to amend its regulation dealing with benefits payable in terminated single-employer plans. The rule implements PPA § 403, which says that the phase-in period for the guarantee of benefits that are contingent on an "unpredictable contingent event" (the regulation gives the example of a plant shut-down) begins no earlier than the date of the event itself. The rule was necessary because PBGC's guarantee of new pension benefits and benefit increases phases in over a five-year period starting with the later of the date of adoption or the effective date of the change. (This rule was adopted to protect the PBGC against obligations that would be created by plans that knew they were going to terminate adopting new benefits.) The PPA added a new section, ERISA § 4022(b)(8), phasing in the guarantee as if the amendment creating an unpredictable contingent event benefit was adopted on the date of the event, rather than the (usually earlier) date of the plan amendment. The net effect is that the guarantee for benefits that arise from unpredictable contingent events that occur within five years of plan termination is probably lower than the guarantee that would have been available under the pre-PPA law. [PBGC Proposed Rule RIN 1212-AB18, 76 Fed. Reg. 13304 (Mar. 11, 2011)]

Certain single-employer defined benefit plans can be amended, starting August 31, 2012, to eliminate some optional forms of benefits without violating the anti-cutback rule, if the plan sponsor is a bankruptcy debtor; the plan is not fully funded; and the bankruptcy court and the PBGC agree that the amendment is necessary. The benefit form can only be eliminated if the PBGC and bankruptcy court determine that, unless the optional form of benefit is eliminated, the plan will have to go through a distress or involuntary termination. The PBGC must also determine that the plan's assets are insufficient to pay guaranteed benefits. If the sponsor uses these regulations to eliminate an optional form of benefit and the plan does not offer other options that have substantial survivor benefits, the sponsor can add more options to provide survivor benefits, as part of the amendment that eliminates the lump sum distribution option. The entire amendment will be considered in determining if the amendment complies with § 436(c) requirements. [T.D. 9601, 77 Fed. Reg. 66915 (Nov. 8, 2012), finalizing regulations proposed at 77 Fed. Reg. 37349 (June 21, 2012); see Kristen Heinzinger, *IRS Finalizes Relief for Bankrupt DB Sponsors*, plansponsor.com (Nov. 8, 2012)]

§ 14.08 ISSUES HIGHLIGHTED BY THE IRS

IRS' Employee Plans division listed more than a dozen issues that frequently require plan amendments. These issues often prevent the IRS from closing a case until the issues are resolved to the agency's satisfaction:

- Defined benefit plans that do not apply I.R.C. §§ 415(b)(2)(E) and 417(e) properly;
- Defined contribution plans that do not reflect changes in the calculation of the maximum contributions;
- Plans that use the wrong procedure to waive the QJSA;
- Plans that don't meet the effective date requirements of amendments to the Code;
- Plans that can't prove that they complied with earlier tax and pension laws;
- Plans that have not been amended to forbid rollovers of 401(k) plan hardship distributions;
- Plans that do not define "highly compensated employee" properly;
- Top-heavy plans that have not been updated in view of current laws.

[See *Recurring Plan Issues in Determination Case Review*, <http://www.irs.gov/pub/irs-tege/sum01.pdf#page=15> (accessed Apr. 3, 2014)]

Mishandling of forfeitures (which usually occur when a participant leaves the sponsor's employ before becoming fully vested) is a common target of IRS audits. In the first two years, mistakes can be corrected under the EPCRS program. After two years, the VCP must be used unless the failure is considered insignificant. The VCP must be used if the terms of the plan are incorrect and a retroactive plan amendment is required to correct them. [Chadron J. Patton, *Common Plan Mistakes: Failure to Timely Allocate Forfeitures*, Spencer Fane (Nov. 16, 2012) (benefitslink.com)]

CHAPTER 15

ENFORCEMENT AND COMPLIANCE ISSUES FOR QUALIFIED PLANS

§ 15.01 INTRODUCTION

The underlying purpose of ERISA, and of various later pieces of legislation, is to make sure that plan participants and their beneficiaries receive the promised benefits. Therefore, the focus of enforcement is to make sure that plans remain sound, and that participants and beneficiaries do not fall victim to outright fraud, mistake, negligence, poor administration, or declines in the sponsoring company's financial fortunes. Certain types of transactions are prohibited—although "prohibited transaction exemptions" can be obtained in cases where payment of benefits is not placed at real risk. [See § 15.15[C]]

Fiduciary conduct is examined on two levels. Fiduciaries must satisfy their affirmative obligations (to choose proper investments for the plan; to diversify investments unless diversification itself is imprudent; to maintain proper liquidity; to obtain a reasonable yield on plan investments; and to make proper administrative decisions). They are also forbidden to engage in prohibited transactions. In addition to private suits by participants and beneficiaries, the Department of Labor (DOL) and the IRS carry out administrative enforcement efforts and become involved in litigation about plan compliance and participant and beneficiary rights.

The PBGC announced late in 2012 that it would not take action under ERISA § 4062(e) against creditworthy companies or small pension plans (those with fewer than 100 participants). Therefore, about 92% of applicable plan sponsors would not be required to give financial guarantees. The PBGC took this step to concentrate its enforcement resources on companies with a substantial risk of defaulting on their obligations. Regulations were proposed in August 2010, but they were unpopular with the business community and were withdrawn. More favorable proposed regulations were published in March 2012, designating three categories of financial strength; strong, moderately strong and weak. [R. Randall Tracht, Brian J. Dougherty, Lisa H. Barton, and Eric P. Sarabia, *PBGC Changes Enforcement Policy Under ERISA Section 4062(e)*, Morgan, Lewis & Bockius (Nov. 13, 2012) (benefitslink.com)]

In order to work with stakeholders to develop new standards, the PBGC suspended §4062(e) enforcement entirely between July 2014 and the end of the year, although plan sponsors were advised to continue reporting new §4062(e) events as they occurred. [PBGC Press Release No. 14-09, *PBGC Issues Moratorium on 4062(e) Enforcement*, <http://www.pbgc.gov/news/press/releases/pr14-09.html?cid=CPAD01PRJUL0820141> (July 8, 2014)]

In April 2013, the PBGC proposed to modify the reportable event rules under ERISA § 4043, so that plans and sponsors that qualify for a financial soundness safe harbor based on credit reports would be relieved of the obligation to report. [78 Fed. Reg. 20039 (Apr. 3, 2013); see Buck Consultants FYI, *PBGC Reproposes Reportable Event Rules* (Apr. 5, 2013) (benefitslink.com) The PBGC offered further guidance in May, 2013, defining a creditworthy company as one whose unsecured debt is rated at least Baa3 by Moody's or BBB- by Standard & Poor's, or which has a D&B Financial Stress Score of at least 1477 and does not have an excessive amount of secured debt. Certain factors such as lack of ongoing operations or transactions that cause a downgrade prevent a company from being deemed creditworthy. [See PLC Employee Benefits & Employee Compensation, *PBGC Releases Enforcement Guidelines for ERISA Section 4062(e) Financial Assurance Program* (May 3, 2013) (benefitslink.com)]

A pension plan is a legal entity that can sue or be sued under ERISA Title I. [See ERISA § 502(d)] Unless somebody is found liable in an individual capacity, the plan is responsible for paying all money judgments.

Because the management of plan assets for the sole benefit of participants and beneficiaries is so central to plan operation, the identification, duties, and liabilities of fiduciaries are central to plan enforcement.

ERISA § 402(a)(1) requires all plans either to have a named fiduciary, or to explain in the plan document how fiduciaries will be selected. Under ERISA § 411, a convicted felon is not permitted to serve as plan administrator, fiduciary, officer, trustee, custodian, counsel, agent, consultant, or employee with decision-making authority for 13 years after his or her conviction or the end of his or her prison term, whichever comes later.

Asserting that someone has breached fiduciary duties depends on being able to characterize that party as a fiduciary. Furthermore, the party must have been acting in a fiduciary capacity at the time. In 1995, in a welfare benefit plan case, the Supreme Court said that plan sponsors are generally free to amend or terminate welfare plans. In 1999, the Supreme Court extended this principle to pension plans and made it clear that, when they amend a plan, sponsors are acting as the settlers of the plan trust and not as fiduciaries of the plan.

Citing these cases, the Second Circuit abrogated some of its former decisions and held that employers and plan sponsors are not acting as fiduciaries when they modify, adopt, or amend plans—including multi-employer plans. The suit was brought on behalf of ex-participants and beneficiaries of a union pension and welfare fund. The plaintiffs wanted to recover assets that they claimed were wrongfully depleted by improper plan amendments that violated fiduciary duty. [*Janese v. Fay*, 692 F.3d 221 (2d Cir. 2012); see Rebecca Moore, *Amending a Plan Not a Fiduciary Act*, plansponsor.com (Sept. 18, 2012); see *Curtiss-Wright v. Schoonejongen*, 514 U.S. 73 (1995); *Lockheed v. Spink*, 517 U.S. 882 (1999)]

Investors in Bernard L. Madoff Investment Securities LLC could not recover funds when the firm was liquidated. The Securities Investor Protection Act provides benefits to "customers" of failed brokerage firms, who share in the recovery of the cash and securities in the liquidation. But Judge Denise Cote ruled that ERISA claimants are not customers. In an ERISA-regulated plan, the assets are owned by the plan's trustees, rather than by the participants. [*Securities Investor Prot. Corp. v. Jacqueline Green Rollover Account*, No. 12 civ 1039 (DLC), 2012 U.S. Dist. LEXIS 104024 (S.D.N.Y. July 25, 2012); see Jay Polansky, *Participants in ERISA-Regulated Plans Cannot Recover Funds From Madoff*, plansponsor.com (July 27, 2012)]

Breach of fiduciary duty claims is a very active area of litigation. There are many arguments that the employer and other defendants can raise:

- ERISA preemption;
- Plaintiff's lack of standing to sue;
- Suing the wrong defendant(s);
- Bringing suit after the statute of limitations has run;
- Demand for improper relief—e.g., seeking legal relief when only equitable relief is available; seeking individual relief when relief must be sought on behalf of the plan as a whole.

Courts have come up with many different answers to the question of who is the proper defendant in an ERISA case. ERISA § 502(a)(1)(B) says that a civil action may be brought by a participant or beneficiary to collect benefits under the plan—but does not say who the participant or beneficiary can sue. Section 502(d)(2) says that a money judgment against a plan is enforced only against the plan, unless another person is individually liable. In cases of benefit denial, the plan administrator is the proper defendant. ERISA § 3(16) says that the plan sponsor is the plan administrator, unless the terms of the plan say otherwise. If the plan designates an administrator, then it may be necessary to sue the designated administrator and not the employer—unless the employer has actual control over the operations of the plan.

Depending on the court and the fact situation:

- Only the plan as entity can be sued;
- The plan can be sued, but so can other parties;
- The formal administrator of the plan can be sued;
- A "de facto" plan administrator can be sued, even if he, she, or it is not formally designated as plan administrator, on the basis of control over the plan;
- Plan fiduciaries, including administrators, can be sued;
- An insurer can be sued (perhaps only if there is no plan or plan administrator that could be held liable).

[William F. Hanrahan and Lars C. Golumbic, *ERISA Benefits Litigation: Who Can Be Sued?* <http://www.groom.com/_news/ERISABenefitsLitigation.html> (Summer 2006) (benefitslink.com); Terry Price, *Federal Court Rulings Identify Employers as Liable Party in ERISA Benefits Action*, Employee Benefit News (Sept. 15, 2006) (benefitslink.com)]

The Supreme Court ruled in favor of an employer, acting both as plan sponsor and administrator, that terminated pension plans by purchasing annuities for participants. The union representing the company's employees urged that, instead, the company's plans should be merged into the union's multi-employer plan. The Supreme Court ruled that a bankrupt company does not have a fiduciary duty to consider the merger option. It did not violate ERISA for the company to put the plan through a standard termination and then purchase annuities to cover the payment obligations: terminating the plan in that manner ended the applicability of ERISA to the plan's assets and the employer's obligations. [*Beck v. PACE Int'l Union*, 551 U.S. 96 (2007); see Adrien Martin, *Supreme Court: Plan Mergers Considered an Alternative to Termination*, plansponsor.com (June 12, 2007); *(AP) High Court Goes Against Labor in Pension Case* (June 12, 2007) (law.com)]

In 2010, the Supreme Court strongly reaffirmed the principles of *Bruch* and favored administrators' powers by holding that courts should apply a deferential standard of review to the decisions of plan administrators who are empowered under the plan to interpret plan terms. [*Conkright v. Frommert*, 559 U.S. 506 (2010)]

The Second Circuit remanded *Frommert* to the District Court for the Western District of New York, for the third time. The plaintiffs are Xerox plan participants who retired with lump sums, but were later rehired. Their retirement benefits were reduced by prior distributions, using the "phantom account offset" method, which they alleged violated ERISA's notice provision. In December 2013, the Second Circuit held that the suit was meritorious. The proposed offset method was unreasonable, and the SPD was not accurate because it did not clearly disclose that the lump sum distribution would reduce benefits. [*Frommert v. Conkright*, 738 F.3d 522 (2d Cir. 2013); see Kevin McGuinness, *Appellate Court Remands Case on Offsetting Pension Benefits*, plansponsor.com (Dec. 31, 2013)]

See § 15.09[C] for the crucial 2011 decision in *Amara v. Cigna*, discussing the remedies available under ERISA § 502.

The final regulations under Code § 415, published in the Federal Register on April 4, 2007 (72 Fed. Reg. 16878) state that annual additions to the plan, for purposes of computing the § 415 limit, do not include payments made to the plan to restore losses due to a fiduciary's action or failure to act that could have been penalized under ERISA or any other applicable law as breaches of fiduciary duty.

Note that the Pension Protection Act of 2006 imposes a penalty of up to $100,000 and/or 10 years' imprisonment for coercive interference with rights under ERISA.

The Second Circuit ordered a profit-sharing plan to repay a participant approximately $1.5 million in assets from his account when half the balance was wrongfully transferred to the participant's ex-wife. The participant was entitled to recover the money even though the plan was unable to recoup it from the ex-wife even after the Northern District of New York granted the plan a judgment against her. The Second Circuit held that undistributed funds held in trust are not "benefits" as defined by the anti-alienation provision and, in any event, ERISA's anti-alienation provision permits plan assets to be used to satisfy a judgment against the plan itself. Paying the judgment was a ministerial function, not a discretionary fiduciary function that could give rise to liability. The Northern District of New York dismissed charges against the plan's TPA, holding that it was not acting in a fiduciary capacity when the mistaken transfer was made. [*Milgram v. Orthopedic Assocs.*, 666 F.3d 68 (2d Cir. 2011); see Rebecca Moore, *Plan Must Restore Misplaced Assets Although not Recovered,* plansponsor.com (Jan. 17, 2012)]

In 2010, the Supreme Court ruled that ERISA plaintiffs who sue under § 502(g)(1) can be awarded attorneys' fees even if they are not the prevailing party in the suit, because that section of ERISA gives the district court discretion to award attorneys' fees to either party. (This is in contrast to § 502(g)(2), a suit alleging that contributions to a multi-employer plan are delinquent; § 502(g)(2) limits fee awards to plaintiffs who obtain a judgment in favor of the pension plan.) This decision makes it likely that more pension plans will have to pay attorneys' fees to plaintiffs who achieve a degree of success in challenges to the plan. [*Hardt v. Reliance Ins. Co.,* 560 U.S. 242 (2010); see Workplace Prof Blog, *ERISA Supreme Court Attorney Fees Case Goes Way of Plaintiffs* (May 24, 2010) (benefitslink.com)]

Hardt's five-factor test for awarding attorneys' fees to a plan participant who wins an ERISA case focuses on the degree of success on the merits; the extent to which the opponent was culpable or acted in bad faith; the opponent's capacity to pay a fee award; the deterrent effect that the award would have to prevent similar conduct by others; if the plaintiff established an important point of ERISA law or benefited all of the beneficiaries of the plan; and the relative strength of the parties' positions. The Second Circuit held that it was error for the district court to consider only the degree of the insurer's bad faith in denying a claim, rather than all the factors. [*Donachie v. Liberty Life Assur. Co. of Boston,* 745 F.3d 41 (2d Cir. 2014); see PLC, *Second Circuit Clarifies Its Standards for Awarding ERISA Attorneys' Fees* (Mar. 14, 2014) (benefitslink.com)]

§ 15.02 WHO IS A FIDUCIARY?

In general legal terms, a fiduciary is anyone responsible for another party's money or property. Fiduciaries have a legal duty to behave honestly and conscientiously, and to avoid promoting their own self-interest at the expense of the owner of the assets.

Many types of people who deal with pension and benefit plans are considered fiduciaries under ERISA—including some people who do not think of themselves in that way or do not understand their responsibilities and potential liabilities.

Fiduciary liability extends far beyond embezzlement and other criminal acts. It is even possible for one fiduciary's mistake or wrongdoing to get a group of other fiduciaries into trouble.

An individual, business, or institution that deals with a plan becomes a fiduciary whenever, and to the extent that, he or she:

- Exercises any discretionary authority (i.e., is able to make decisions) or control over the management of the plan;
- Exercises any authority (even if it isn't discretionary) over the management and disposition of plan assets. The distinction is made because the greatest potential for abuse exists when money is at stake;
- Receives direct or indirect compensation for giving the plan investment advice about its assets;
- Has any discretionary authority or responsibility for day-to-day plan administration (as distinct from plan management).

In other words, if a plan hires attorneys, accountants, or actuaries to provide advice, those professionals will usually not become fiduciaries of the plan, because they do not control the direction that the plan takes. They merely provide technical information that the administrator and other fiduciaries use to make decisions.

Just having custody of plan assets doesn't necessarily make the custodian a fiduciary, so a law firm did not become a fiduciary by acting as an escrow agent for funds belonging to one of its clients. (The issue arose when a partner in the law firm embezzled some of the money.) [*Burtch v. Ganz* (*In re Mushroom Transport Co. Inc.*), 382 F.3d 325 (3d Cir. 2004)] A custodian that transfers retirement plan assets at the direction of plan trustees is not a fiduciary, and is not liable under ERISA for the plan's losses, merely because it had check-writing authority. The custodian did not exercise authority or control over the assets. [*Erickson v. ING Life Ins. & Annuity Co.*, 731 F. Supp. 2d 1057 (D. Idaho 2010); see Rebecca Moore, *Court Finds Directed Custodian Not a Fiduciary Under ERISA*, plansponsor.com (July 29, 2010)]

A financial consulting firm that appraised the employer's stock is not a fiduciary, and is not liable for an Employee Stock Ownership Plan's losses. [*Keach v. U.S. Trust Co.*, 234 F. Supp. 2d 872 (C.D. Ill. 2002)]

■ **TIP:** If the professional adviser is not a fiduciary, ERISA probably will not preempt state-law malpractice suits brought by the plan.

Similarly, a stockbroker who simply executes the fiduciaries' orders to adjust the plan's investment portfolio is not a fiduciary—but an investment manager who has a role in setting the plan's investment policy is very definitely a fiduciary.

The Ninth Circuit held that being a fiduciary for ERISA purposes does not necessarily entail being a fiduciary as defined by Bankruptcy Code § 523(a)(4), the Bankruptcy Code provision that prevents bankruptcy discharge of debts for fiduciary fraud. [*Hunter v. Philpott*, 373 F.3d 873 (9th Cir. 2004)]

ERISA says that if the employer responsible for maintaining a defined benefit plan is a member of a controlled group, all members of the group are jointly and severally liable for funding the plan. If the sponsor can no longer pay the benefits, the PBGC can terminate the plan and make the sponsor and its controlled group pay the unfunded benefit liabilities. Under ERISA, once the plan is terminated, all parties except the PBGC are limited in relief they can obtain from either the current or former controlled group. The PBGC can get legal or equitable relief against the controlled group for failure to fund the plan; any other party can only get equitable relief.

The Eleventh Circuit ruled that a corporate employer undergoing bankruptcy reorganization cannot pursue an action for the benefit of its bankruptcy estate (and its unsecured creditors) against the employer's former owner for liabilities arising from the termination of a pension plan. The Eleventh Circuit accepted the bankruptcy trustee's contention that the paper company's ex-owner's principal purpose for selling the company was evasion of liability if the PBGC terminated the pension plan. The Eleventh Circuit said that the owner and other members of the controlled group would be treated as members of the controlled group at the time the plan terminated on March 1, 2004.

But ERISA says that a current or former controlled group's duty to pay unfunded benefit liabilities is owed to the plan's beneficiaries. The Eleventh Circuit found that the company's new owner wanted to secure those liabilities for division among the PBGC and other unsecured creditors. The complaint said that if the trustee failed to recover on its $55 million claim against the former controlled group, the bankruptcy estate would be less than $15 million (from sale of the debtor's assets); the PBGC would receive about $8.25 million. (The PBGC was unable to sue the controlled group for termination liability, because the statute of limitations had run.) The court read the complaint to mean that any money recovered by the trustee would enter the bankruptcy estate and be allocated among all general unsecured creditors, including the PBGC. [*Durango-Georgia Paper Co v. H.G. Estate LLC*, 739 F.3d 1263 (11th Cir. 2014); see *11th Circuit Discredits Company's Intent for Pension Claim*, plansponsor.com (Jan. 16, 2014)]

A Third-Party Administrator (TPA) can be considered an ERISA fiduciary even if it does not have discretionary control over the assets of the health plan it administered; the statutory language is "any authority or control." The Sixth Circuit held that a TPA's authority to write checks on the plan's account (which continued to be exercised to pay the TPA's fees even after the contract with the plan sponsor ended) provided the necessary degree of authority or control to impose liability after the sponsor company went bankrupt and many employees had unpaid medical bills. [*Briscoe v. Fine*, 444 F.3d 478 (6th Cir. 2006)]; on remand, the Western District of Kentucky held that the administrative services contract made the employer, not the plan, responsible for paying the TPA's fee, so it was a breach of fiduciary duty for the TPA to pay itself out of plan assets. It was also a breach of fiduciary duty to submit the COBRA premiums and funded claims reserve to the employer, which the TPA knew was in bad financial shape and likely to appropriate the money—which belonged to the plan and the plan participants, not the employer. [*Briscoe v. Preferred Health Plan, Inc.*, CIVIL ACTION NO. 3:02CV-264-S,2008 WL 4146381 (W.D. Ky. Sept. 2, 2008)]

A TPA hired as a health plan claims administrator to pay medical providers misappropriated the money. Many claims were not paid. The TPA had agreements to pay claims under self-insured ERISA health benefit plans funded by both employer contributions and employee payroll deductions. An employer discovered that funds were not accounted for and claims were not paid and sued the TPA. The Sixth Circuit held that a TPA becomes a fiduciary when it exercises practical control over the funds of an ERISA plan, even if its contract disclaims fiduciary status. Misappropriating plan assets violates the duty to act solely in the interests of participants. [*Guyan Int'l Inc. v. Professional Benefits Adm'rs Inc.*, 689 F.3d 793 (6th Cir. 2012)]

A TPA that retained part of the money transferred by self-insured employers to pay benefits was sued by sponsors. At an earlier stage of the case, the District Court for the Eastern District of Michigan ruled that the TPA was a fiduciary to the plan, and violated the ERISA ban on self-dealing. The TPA deceived the plans about its charges and how it operated. Although the ERISA statute of limitations for fiduciary breach is six years from discovery of the breach, the district court allowed additional time to sue because of the TPA's fraud and concealment. For breach of the duty of loyalty and for giving the plans false information for submission in Form 5500, the District Court for the Eastern District of Michigan awarded more $5 million in damages, plus attorneys' fees, costs, and interest. [*Hi-Lex Controls Inc. v. Blue Cross & Blue Shield of Michigan*, No. 11-cv-12557-14, 2013 WL 2285453 (E.D. Mich. 2013); see EBIA Weekly, *Court Awards Over $5 Million for TPA's Breach of Fiduciary Duty* (June 6, 2013) (benefitslink.com)]

Sponsors are required to monitor TPA performance. The DOL sued Clark Graphics for ERISA violations. The company's president was ordered to restore $505,000 to Clark Graphics' two pension plans. The plan administrator had to give back $425,000 to the profit sharing plan and $143,000, minus payments made by others, to the defined benefit plan. The business' owners were charged with dereliction of their fiduciary duty as trustees because they did not monitor the activities of the plan administrator, Pension Retirement Planning, which offered third-party record-keeping services to about 50 plans between 2000 and 2010. The owners did not review or reconcile the trust account statements for the plans or make sure that the administrator issued participant statements. Some plan participants did not get correct benefits because of the TPA's failure to maintain accurate records. [Rebecca Moore, *Employer to Pay $500K for Failing to Monitor TPA*, plansponsor.com (July 18, 2012)]

The District Court for the Southern District of New York dismissed claims against a TPA for violating the Mental Health Parity and Addiction Equity Act (MHPAEA), because that statute applies only to EGHPs and insurers. The plaintiffs challenged denials or terminations of mental health coverage required by family members. In these cases, the self-funded group health plans retained UnitedHealth Group as claims administrator, but the district court held that UnitedHealth was not the plan administrator for ERISA purposes. The district court held that an entity that processes claims and makes coverage determinations about claims that will be paid by another party does not offer coverage. The suits could be characterized as alleging violations of plan terms (ERISA § 502(a)(1)(B))—but the proper defendants in that case would be the plan, the plan trustees, or the plan administrator designated under ERISA § 1002(16)(A). [*N.Y. State Psychiatric Ass'n v. UnitedHealth Group*, No. 13 Civ. 1599 CM (S.D.N.Y. Oct. 31, 2013); see *David Slaughter, TPA May Not Be Sued for MHPAEA Violations*, Smart HR (Dec. 9, 2013) (benefitslink.com)]

In late 2010, DOL proposed the first update to the definition of "fiduciary" since shortly after ERISA was enacted. DOL wants to restore the simple two-part test for fiduciary status, removing the requirements of a mutual understanding; that advice be given on a regular basis; and that it be a primary basis for investment of the plan assets. Under the proposal, a fiduciary is a party that renders investment advice about any plan assets (or has any authority or responsibility to do so) and receives direct or indirect compensation for the advice.

Explicitly claiming ERISA fiduciary status orally or in writing makes a party a fiduciary, if a fee is received, because claiming the status enhances the party's influence and creates the impression that the advice is valuable. However, mere provision of investment education materials is not advice. Making investments or an investment available without regard to individualized needs of plan or participants does not constitute investment advice as long as the provider discloses in writing to plan fiduciary that it is not undertaking to provide impartial investment advice.

The revised definition says that a party is not a fiduciary if it can show that the recipient of advice knows or reasonably should know that the person giving the advice is selling or buying a security, or acts on behalf of someone who is, and is therefore not impartial. So the person isn't providing impartial investment advice. The advice must also be rendered for a fee to be covered. [FR Doc 2010-26236, 75 Fed. Reg. 65263 (Oct. 22, 2010); see Judy Ward, *DOL Broadens Fiduciary Net*, plansponsor.com (Oct. 22, 2010)]

In September 2011, EBSA announced that the 2010 rules would be re-proposed, but it proved to be a lengthy business. The DOL had planned to release an updated version of the rule in August 2014, with a broad definition of fiduciary (including anyone who provides investment services to a plan for a fee). However, in May 2014, the DOL announced that the fiduciary rule would not be issued at least until January 2015 (although the SEC might use its authority under the Dodd-Frank Act to issue its own definition of "fiduciary").

[See ThinkAdvisor, *DOL to Delay Fiduciary Redraft Release Until January*, <http://www.thinkadvisor.com/2014/05/27/dol-to-delay-fiduciary-redraft-release-until-janua> (May 27, 2014); Bloomberg BNA Pension & Benefits Blog, *DOL Continues Work on Fiduciary Rules, Guide for Fee Disclosures, Official Says*, <http://www.bna.com/dol-continues-work-b17179890289/> (May 7, 2014)]

§ 15.03 FIDUCIARY DUTIES

[A] ERISA Requirements

ERISA imposes four major duties on fiduciaries:

- Loyalty;
- Prudence;
- Acting in accordance with the plan documents;
- Monitoring the performance of anyone to whom fiduciary responsibility has been delegated.

The source of the duty of loyalty is the ERISA mandate that plan assets be held for the exclusive benefit of participants and beneficiaries. Once assets have been placed into the plan trust, or used to buy insurance, they can no longer be used for the benefit of the employer.

The duty of prudence requires fiduciaries to behave with the level of care, skill, prudence, and diligence that a hypothetical prudent person would use to handle the same tasks. This hypothetical prudent person is familiar with the plan and its situation—not the "man on the street" who lacks specialized knowledge.

Although trust law requires every asset within a trust to satisfy the prudent person test, DOL Reg. § 2550.404a-1(c)(2) allows the fiduciary to select assets by considering the relevant facts and circumstances, including the role of the individual investment within the portfolio. Relying on expert advice is encouraged, but it does not guarantee that an investment choice will be considered prudent.

In general, it will not be considered a breach of fiduciary duty to make a mistake in calculations. [See, e.g., *Livick v. Gillette Co.*, 492 F. Supp. 2d 1 (D. Mass. 2007), discussed in Rebecca Moore, *Miscalculation of Benefits Not a Fiduciary Breach*, plansponsor.com (June 14, 2007)] The Second Circuit rejected a former employee's argument that it was a breach of fiduciary duty for the administrator of a stock option plan to tell her that she could exercise her options after retirement. Not only were the communications not intentionally false, the Second Circuit said that the advice was not even really wrong. The court ruled that, even if there had been an unintentional misstatement about the consequences for non-ERISA stock option plan, of a retirement decision under an ERISA plan, there would not have been a violation of fiduciary duty. [*Bell v. Pfizer*, 626 F.3d 66

(2d Cir. 2010); see Michael Melbinger, Winston & Strawn LLP, *A $327 Million Stock Option Mistake* (Sept. 2, 2010) (benefitslink.com)]

The Third Circuit ruled that a woman who retired based on alleged misrepresentations about the pension her husband would receive did not make out a case of breach of fiduciary duty. To prove detrimental reliance, there must be both injury and reasonableness. The plaintiff must have engaged in some action; merely expecting continued benefits is not enough. The wife was not a participant in the plan and the couple's retirement decisions did not change their benefits in any way. [*Shook v. Avaya Inc.*, 625 F.3d 69 (3d Cir. 2010); see Stanley D. Baum, *Third Circuit Holds That a Beneficiary's Decision to Retire Is Not the Detrimental Reliance Needed to Establish a Claim for Breach of Fiduciary Duty Under ERISA*, ERISA Lawyer Blog (Nov. 4, 2010) (benefitslink.com)]

[B] Diversification

The general rule is that ERISA requires fiduciaries to diversify unless diversification is imprudent (the fiduciary has to prove this). There is an exception for Employee Stock Option Plans (ESOPs), which are designed to invest in employer stock. Consequently, ESOP fiduciaries do not have a duty to diversify. The non-ESOP fiduciary is supposed to select a balanced portfolio that is responsive to current conditions. The portfolio's liquidity and current return must be considered in light of anticipated needs for cash flow. Fiduciaries are not restricted to a "legal list" of investments, and are permitted to take a certain amount of risk, as long as the risk is reasonable in the context of the entire portfolio.

In early 2002, the failure of Enron Corporation highlighted the entire question of investment in employer securities. The basic ERISA rule is that plans can invest in employer securities only if they are "qualifying employer securities" such as stock and eligible debt instruments. Defined benefit plans are subject to additional limitations on holdings of employer securities. [See § 6.09[C] for additional discussion of this issue in the context of 401(k) plans.]

The Supreme Court delayed deciding a case about the ability of Enron shareholders to sue Wall Street investment banks that failed to detect, or at least warn, them of Enron's impending collapse, but eventually denied certiorari early in 2008. [*Univ. of Cal. Regents v. Merrill Lynch*, 482 F.3d 372 (5th Cir.), *cert. denied*, 128 S. Ct. 1120 (2008); see Rebecca Moore, *Supreme Court Delays Decision on Enron Case*, plansponsor.com (June 25, 2007)]

ERISA § 404(c) offers fiduciaries protection against liability. (It covers qualified defined contribution plans and the portions of defined benefit plans that allow direction of investment of individual accounts.) In general, fiduciaries have a duty to diversify and choose investments prudently, but 404(c) indemnifies them for losses in accounts where the participant exercises independent control over the investment of the account, after choosing from among a broad range of investments.

"Broad range of investments" is defined to mean that the participant has the chance to pick investments that will determine the return on the account, and can diversify to reduce risk. There must be at least three main diversified categories of investment choices offered, with materially different risk and return categories, so that the participant can assemble a portfolio with normal and appropriate risk and return characteristics. Employer stock cannot be made one of the core investments. Participants must be allowed to give investment instructions at least once per quarter—more frequently if market volatility requires.

The participant must have a reasonable opportunity to give instructions to an identified fiduciary, who is required to carry out the instructions as given. (Under limited circumstances, the fiduciary can ignore the instructions—for example, if the instruction would be a prohibited transaction or would subject the plan to taxable income.) Under this safe harbor provision, the fiduciary can hire a third-party service provider to carry out the instructions when it is prudent to do so. The participant is also considered to control the account when the fiduciary makes default investments under the default investment safe harbor—but if the plan does not qualify for the safe harbor, it can be held liable for losses in the value of default investments.

Plans that seek to use the safe harbor must disclose that the plan is using § 404(c) to relieve fiduciaries of liability; must describe the investment options and how to give investment directions; and that additional information is available on request (e.g., the annual operating expenses for each investment option, and how to get copies of prospectuses and financial statements). Item 8a of the Form 5500 asks if the plan or any portion of the plan intends to comply with § 404(c); the form must be signed under penalty of perjury. [Prudential Retirement Pension Analyst, *Department of Labor Requirements for Participant-Directed Investments* (July 2008) (benefitslink.com)]

Enhanced diversification rights are mandated by the PPA. In mid-2007, EBSA issued final regulations concerning penalties for plan administrators who fail to inform participants and beneficiaries of their right to diversify out of investments in employer securities. For plan years beginning after December 31, 2006, a civil penalty of up to $100 per day can be imposed under ERISA § 502(c)(7) for failure to provide the notice. [72 Fed. Reg. 44970 (Aug. 10, 2007), discussed in *EBSA Reg. Provides Penalties for Failure to Notify Participants of Stock Diversification Rights Under PPA*, CCH Pension & Benefits (Aug. 21, 2007) (benefits link.com); *EBSA Publishes Final Diversification Fine Rule*, NU Online News Service (Aug. 10, 2007) (benefitslink.com). The corresponding DOL regulation appears at 72 Fed. Reg. 44991 (Aug. 10, 2007).]

T.D. 9484 provides final regulations under Code § 401(a)(35), explicating the PPA's diversification requirements for defined contribution plans that hold publicly traded employer stock. For plan participants who have at least three years of service, their beneficiaries, and the beneficiaries of deceased participants, the plan must allow divestment of employer securities and re-investment in a reasonable menu of choices At least three varied options other than employer stock, each of them diversified, must be offered. Divestment opportunities must be provided at reasonable intervals, at least quarterly. Unless the restriction is required to comply with securities laws, the plan cannot impose conditions on re-investment of employer securities that are not imposed on other investments within the plan. [T.D. 9484, 75 Fed. Reg. 27927 (May 19, 2010); see Rebecca Moore, *IRS Issues Final Regs on Diversification Requirements for Company Stock*, plansponsor.com (May 18, 2010)]

[C] Stock-Drop Cases and Other Investment Issues

A "stock drop" suit charges a plan's fiduciaries with breach of duty because they retained employer stock as a plan investment without divulging to participants that the stock had declined in value or become risky (e.g., because of the plan sponsor's involvement in derivatives or other risky financial transactions). Another stock drop allegation is that the employer's stock represents too large a part of the plan's investments, and the plan should have been more diversified. Almost all stock drop cases are dismissed. Stock-drop cases frequently are associated with securities law cases, but ERISA cases are easier to bring because securities law requires proof of "scienter" (an enhanced form of intent). Courts of Appeals usually follow three principles:

- The amount of deference fiduciaries receive depends on the amount of discretion the plan design gives them;
- Mere fluctuations in the price of the employer's stock will not show that the fiduciaries were imprudent to keep the stock in the plan; something else has to be present;
- Possible liability factors include breaches of the duty of loyalty (misrepresenting or concealing material facts).

As of mid-2014, the Third, Fifth, Sixth, Ninth, and Eleventh Circuits had all adopted some version of the *Moench* presumption (named after *Moench v. Robertson*, 62 F.3d 553 (3d Cir. 1995): that is, the fiduciaries of a plan were presumed to be prudent when they retained employer stock as a plan investment. A drop in the stock price was not enough to rebut the presumption. The courts differed in the stage of the case at which the presumption was applied, and what plaintiffs had to do to rebut the presumption.

However, in June 2014, the Supreme Court rejected the presumption of prudence. [*Fifth Third Bancorp et al. v. Dudenhoeffer*, No. 12-751 (U.S. June 25, 2014); see Thomas E. Clark Jr., *Supreme Court Rejects the Moench Presumption-Vacates and Remands Fifth Third Case*, Fiduciary Matters Blog (June 25, 2014) (benefitslink.com)]

Although this is an ESOP case, the Supreme Court held that ESOP fiduciaries have the same duties as other fiduciaries, except that ESOP fiduciaries are not obligated to diversify plan investments, because ESOPs are intended to invest in employer securities. The Supreme Court said that the presumption makes it too difficult for plaintiffs to pursue their suits—and also said that the way for courts to determine the merits of a case is to examine the allegations of the complaint rather than presuming that fiduciaries acted prudently. If the complaint says that the fiduciaries had access to inside information that should have led them to divest the employer stock, the Supreme Court held that the plaintiff must allege an action that the fiduciaries could have taken without violating federal securities laws (which forbid trading on inside information). Sometimes it would be imprudent for fiduciaries to divest, if large sales of the employer's securities would disrupt the market and lead to further depression in the stock price.

The Fifth Circuit used this case to revive a suit by four employees of BP who said that they were deceived into continuing to invest in the employer's stock after 2010's catastrophic Deepwater Horizon oil spill. The suit was dismissed in 2012 based on the *Moench* presumption. After the presumption was struck down, the suit could be revived; it was remanded to the district court for the new pleading standard to be applied. [*Whitley v. BP PLC*, No. 12-20670 (5th Cir. July 15, 2014); see Reuters, *U.S. Court Revives BP Retirement-Plan Lawsuit* (July 15, 2014) (benefitslink.com)]

Despite the general lack of success for plaintiffs, there have been some multi-million-dollar settlements in stock drop cases. The *Dudenhoeffer* decision will probably encourage settlements, because it means that fewer cases will be dismissed at early stages, so plans and their fiduciaries may be willing to settle to avoid a prolonged, expensive trial. Wyeth agreed to pay $2 million to settle a case on the prudence of retaining company stock in the 401(k) plan. The plaintiffs alleged that Wyeth was aware that a new drug was ineffective. When investors heard that the FDA gave only conditional approval to sell that drug, Wyeth's stock fell 10% and continued declining. The suit was dismissed in April 2010, but settled pending the plaintiffs' appeal. The settlement obtained preliminary approval on January 3, 2013: <http://www.plansponsor.com/uploadedFiles/Plan_Sponsor/news/Rules,_Regs/HerreraWyethSettlement.pdf>. [Jay Polanski, *Wyeth Settles Stock Drop Suit*, plansponsor.com (Jan. 4, 2013)]

The district court certified a Rule 23(b)(2) class of more than 4,000 current and former participants in a cash balance plan who alleged that they were not credited with correct benefits over a period of 23 years. The claims included whipsaw, cutback, and wearaway claims (see Chapter 7). The Seventh Circuit affirmed class certification, holding that the requirement about relief under a single injunction or declaratory judgment does not apply where each member of the subclass has the same claim. The Seventh Circuit said that perhaps the proceedings could be bifurcated, with sub-classes that obtained declaratory relief under Rule 23(b)(2) following up with a (b)(3) opt-out proceeding to set relief for the individual class members. [*Johnson v. Meriter Health Servs. Emp. Ret. Plan*, 702 F.3d 364 (7th Cir. 2012); see Mark Casciari and Sara Eber, Seyfarth Shaw ERISA & Employee Benefits Litigation Blog, *Rule 23(b)(2) Certification—The*

Seventh Circuit Strikes Again, This Time In The ERISA Defined Benefit Context (Dec. 5, 2012) (benefitslink.com). But see *Nationwide Life Ins. Co. v. Haddock*, 460 Fed. Appx. 26 (2d Cir. 2012), an unpublished case that vacated certification of a class action for breach of fiduciary duty on the grounds that the monetary relief would be more than incidental.]

According to the Seventh Circuit, the fiduciaries of a thrift plan did not have an obligation to disclose to plan participants that they had decided to sell their own positions in the company stock. (The fiduciaries made the required SEC filings.) Furthermore, the plan required employer contributions to be held in employer stock, so divestiture was not an option. [*Nelson and Wycoff v. Hodowal*, 512 F.3d 347 (7th Cir. 2008); see Rebecca Moore, *Plan Fiduciaries Not Required to Announce Own Stock Sale to Participants*, plansponsor.com (Jan. 7, 2008)]

In 2008, the Ninth Circuit joined the First, Third, Fourth, Sixth, Seventh, and Eleventh Circuits in holding that former employees who have received a full distribution of their benefits under a defined contribution plan have standing to sue under ERISA to recover losses that they say were caused by breach of fiduciary duty. [*Vaughn v. Bay Environmental Mgmt.*, 544 F.3d 1008 (9th Cir. 2008); see *Lanfear v. Home Depot, Inc.*, 544 F.3d 1008 (11th Cir. 2008); *Evans v. Akers*, 534 F.3d 65 (1st Cir. 2008); *In re Mutual Funds Inv. Litig.*, 529 F.3d 207 (4th Cir. 2008); *Bridges v. Am. Elec. Power Co.*, 498 F.3d 442 (6th Cir. 2007); *Graden v. Conexant Sys. Inc.*, 496 F.3d 291 (3d Cir. 2007); and *Harzewski v. Guidant Corp.*, 489 F.3d 799 (7th Cir. 2007). For subsequent cases see, e.g., *Harris v. Amgen, Inc.*, 573 F.3d 728 (9th Cir. 2009); But see *Gipson v. Wells Fargo & Co.*, No. 08-4546 (PAM/FLN), 2009 U.S. Dist. LEXIS 20740 (D. Minn. Mar. 13, 2009) holding that a former employee who had her entire account distributed did not have standing to raise a fiduciary breach claim.]

On a related issue, the Sixth Circuit ruled in mid-2012 that a stock-drop plaintiff did not have standing to sue because she could not demonstrate actual injury. She alleged that the company's stock price was artificially inflated because the company failed to disclose its inappropriate tax and lending practices. However, the plaintiff sold over 80% of her company stock holdings at a time when she charged the price was unfairly high—so if there was wrongdoing, she benefited from it rather than being harmed by it. [*Taylor v. KeyCorp.*, 680 F.3d 609 (6th Cir. 2012)]

[D] Fiduciary Duties in Health Plans

ERISA's regulation of pension plans is extremely detailed, whereas its regulation of welfare benefit plans (a category that includes health plans) is limited. Nevertheless, ERISA often preempts state regulation, and the Supreme Court has frequently ruled in favor of plan administrators in health cases.

According to the Supreme Court, an HMO is not acting as a fiduciary when, acting through its doctors, it makes a "mixed" decision about medical treatment and health plan eligibility. [*Pegram v. Herdrich*, 530 U.S. 211 (2000)] Therefore, even if plan participants are right that the plan refused them necessary treatments in order to increase its profits, they have not stated a cause of action for breach of fiduciary duty.

The Supreme Court returned to the question of review of HMO coverage decisions in mid-2004: *Aetna Health Inc. v. Davila* and *Cigna Healthcare of Texas, Inc. v. Calad*, 542 U.S. 200 (2004). One of the plaintiffs alleged harm caused by denial of coverage of an expensive arthritis drug; the other claimed that she was prematurely discharged from the hospital, leading to complications of surgery. They sued under a Texas state law dealing with HMO negligence. The Supreme Court held that ERISA completely preempts the state law, because ERISA covers all cases where someone claims that coverage was denied under a plan that is a welfare benefit plan for ERISA purposes. However, in this case, the Supreme Court clarified its earlier *Pegram v. Herdrich* decision. In that case, HMOs were held not to be fiduciaries to the extent that they act through their physicians to make mixed eligibility and treatment decisions. The 2004 decision says that HMOs are fiduciaries when they make pure eligibility decisions. The consequence is that if patients sue in state court, claiming that they were wrongfully denied health benefits, the case is completely preempted by ERISA and can be removed to federal court.

As long as the employer unambiguously reserved the right to amend the plan in the plan documents, the courts of appeals usually agree that there is no ERISA liability for changing health benefits. However, in 2009, the Third Circuit held Unisys liable for fiduciary breach when it did not remind employees that their retiree benefits could be reduced—even though there was reservation language in the SPD. The Third Circuit ordered the lifetime retiree health benefits at no cost to the retirees restored—an order that remained in effect because the Supreme Court denied certiorari. The Third Circuit found the reservation language in the SPD irrelevant, because it was not distributed until after the participants retired. [*In re Unisys Corp. Retiree Med. Benefits ERISA Litig.*, 579 F.3d 220 (3d Cir. 2009), *cert. denied*, 130 S. Ct. 1546. See John R. Richards and Christopher A. Weals, Law360, *Why the 3rd Circ.'s Unisys Decision Defies ERISA* (Jan. 29, 2010) (benefitslink.com); Rebecca Moore, *Supreme Court Won't Review Whether Unisys Misled Participants*, plansponsor.com (Feb. 23, 2010);]

Until 2006, Menasha Corporation retirees and their spouses continued to receive health insurance from the company. Between ages 62–65, the company paid 80% of the premium; when retirees turned 65, the company paid 100% of the premium. In 2006, however, Menasha informed the plaintiffs that it was adopting a new health plan and premiums would no longer be 100% covered. The plaintiffs sued, alleging violations of the Labor Management Relations Act, 29 U.S.C. § 185 and the Employee Retirement Income Security Act, 29 U.S.C. § 1132. The district court ruled in the plaintiffs' favor as to employee coverage but in favor of defendant as to spouses. The Sixth Circuit reversed in part, ruling for the plaintiffs. Although healthcare is a "welfare benefit," not entitled to the same ERISA protection as pension benefits, certain actions by employers will waive the employers' right to alter welfare benefits. In this case, Menasha waived the right to change the benefits by providing vested healthcare coverage to retired employees and spouses, and by agreeing that CBAs could only be modified with signed, mutual consent of the parties. [*Moore v. Menasha Corp.*, 690 F.3d 444 (6th Cir. 2013)]

See § 9.05[C] for more discussion of fiduciary issues in retiree health benefit plans.

Another emerging issue is the treatment of same-sex married couples in benefit plans. (See §18.06.) Generally, the trend is to require benefits for the same-sex spouses of plan participants. However, in mid-2014 the Southern District of New York ruled that a self-insured health plan's exclusion of same-sex spouses did not violate ERISA. An employee of St. Joseph's Hospital married another woman in 2011 and tried to add her spouse under the plan. When the application was denied, pursuant to the plan provision that denied coverage to domestic partners and same-sex spouses, the employee sued under ERISA §510 (interference with attainment of benefits). The Southern District of New York held that ERISA accords employers broad discretion in drafting plan terms, and does not explicitly forbid discrimination against same-sex couples. There was no adverse employment action, and therefore no violation of §510. The district court said that the *Windsor* decision does not require plans to include same-sex spouses. Although most insurance regulation is done by the states—and New York State recognizes same-sex marriage—the plan in this case was self-insured, so it was not subject to state insurance law. [*Roe v. Empire Blue Cross/Blue Shield*, 2014 WL 1760343 (S.D.N.Y. May 1, 2014); see Roberta Chevlowe and Joseph Clark, *Despite Windsor, Federal Court Rejects Challenge to a Self-Insured ERISA Health Plan's Denial of Coverage for Same-Sex Spouses*, Proskauer's ERISA Practice Center Blog (May 21, 2014) (benefitslink.com)]

Financially troubled companies sometimes fail to carry out their obligations to contribute to health plans, and sometimes they misappropriate employee health plan contributions and use them to pay corporate debts instead. In such situations, the employer's bankruptcy often ensues, and the priority of various claims has to be sorted out. The Ninth Circuit has ruled that an employer automatically becomes a fiduciary by breaching its agreement to make contributions, but the Tenth Circuit disagrees, stating that a delinquent employer contributor is just a debtor that owes money to the plan, not a fiduciary. [*Holdeman v. Devine*, 474 F.3d 770 (10th Cir. 2007). Compare *In re Luna*, 406 F.3d 1992 (10th Cir. 2005) with *Northern Cal. Retail Clerks Unions & Food Employers Joint Pension Trust Fund v. Jumbo Mkts., Inc.*, 906 F.2d 1371, 1372 (9th Cir. 1990). On remand, the District Court for the District of Utah held that the CEO did not breach his fiduciary duties. Decisions about plan funding were treated as business and not fiduciary decisions, so ERISA was not involved. Furthermore, the court held that there was no evidence that plan participants would have been better off if the CEO had resigned and another fiduciary had been appointed: *Holdeman v. Devine*, 474

F.3d 770 (D. Utah 2007); see Rebecca Moore, *CEO Had No Obligation to Resign as Fiduciary of Health Plan*, plansponsor.com (Nov. 7, 2007)]

§ 15.04 DUTIES OF THE TRUSTEE

Usually, pension and welfare benefit plans will be organized in trust form. Every trust must have at least one trustee. ERISA § 403(a) provides that the trustee can be named in the instrument itself, appointed under a procedure set out in the plan, or appointed by a named fiduciary.

The trustee has exclusive authority and discretion to manage and control the plan's assets. If there are multiple trustees, they must jointly manage and control, although ERISA § 403(a) permits them to delegate some duties. Certain fiduciary duties can be delegated—it depends on whether trustee responsibility or other duties are involved.

To implement the requirement that pension plans be operated solely in the interests of participants and beneficiaries, DOL ruled in late 2007 that it is improper for plan fiduciaries to use pension assets for political activities or furtherance of public debates, if the expenditures are not connected to increasing the value of the plan's investments. Fiduciaries who vote proxies must consider only factors that affect the value of plan investments, not general political or ethical factors. [DOL Advisory Opinion 2007-07A, <http://www.dol.gov/ebsa> (Dec. 21, 2007)] In an Interpretive bulletin dated October 17, 2008, the DOL held that pension funds subject to ERISA are not permitted to vote their proxies, and if they do vote, federal prosecution is possible. The DOL's rationale is that exercising fiduciary authority to promote legislative, regulatory, or public policy issues violates the "exclusive purpose" rule. This is a reversal of DOL's 1994 position that shareholders have a duty to vote proxies on the shares held in their portfolios. [John Richardson, *Americans Must Not Vote!* Global Investment Watch (Oct. 27, 2008) (benefitslink.com)]

A plan can be drafted to make its trustee subject to a named fiduciary who is not a trustee—for example, to make the trustee report to an administrative committee. If this is done, the trustee must comply with "proper" directions given by the named fiduciary, if they are in accordance with the plan's procedures and not contrary to law.

If there has been a proper appointment of an investment manager, the trustee does not have to manage or invest the assets placed under the investment manager's control. Crucially, the trustee will not be liable for the acts or omissions of the investment manager. The trustee has a duty to make sure that the manager charges reasonable fees; performance-based fees, rather than flat fees determined in advance, are allowed.

The Supreme Court refused, in early 2007, to hear appeals about the State Street Bank & Trust's performance as directed trustee of United Air Lines' Employee Stock Ownership Plan. Therefore, the Seventh Circuit opinion will not be challenged. The Seventh Circuit ruled that it was not a breach of fiduciary duty to retain the stock, and the participants did not prove when it would have been feasible to sell the stock in order to reduce the risk to participants. [Fred Schneyer, *Supreme Court Refuses United Airlines ESOP Appeals*, plansponsor.com (Feb. 21, 2007)]

Another issue is the extent of liability—including personal liability of individuals who committed the wrongdoing—when there is a failure to remit amounts to a plan on schedule. For example, a company in financial trouble may succumb to the temptation to use insurance premiums or amounts that should be contributed to a pension plan to pay corporate creditors rather than for the specific purpose for which they should have been used.

The Fourth Circuit affirmed the theft convictions of two plan administrators (the company's president and its CFO) who did not deposit the contributions. Once due and payable, contributions become plan assets. An earlier Tenth Circuit ruling is that once an employer has paid wages or salaries to employees, it has a contractual duty to contribute to its ERISA plans; the contractual obligation itself is a plan asset. The defendants fell behind on vendor payments, made false financial statements, and borrowed money when the company was in financial trouble. They indicated on the Form 5500 that the contributions had been made to two pension plans and a health care plan, but in fact they used the money (over $329,000) to pay the company's bills. [*United States v. Jackson*, 524 F.3d 532 (4th Cir. 2008); see Rebecca Moore, *Unpaid Contributions Constitutes ERISA Theft*, plansponsor.com (May 5, 2008)]

§ 15.05 THE EMPLOYER'S ROLE

Although it might be predicted that the heaviest liability for plan misconduct would fall on the company that sponsors the plan, this is not always the case. The corporation might not be a fiduciary, or might not be acting in a fiduciary capacity in a particular case.

To prevent conflicts of interest, ERISA §§ 403, 4042, and 4044 allow fiduciaries to perform certain actions without violating the duty to maintain the plan for the sole benefit of participants and beneficiaries. Employer contributions can be returned if:

- The contributions were made based on a mistake of fact;
- The plan is not qualified under I.R.C. §§ 401(a) or 403(a);
- The income tax deduction for part or all of the contribution is disallowed;
- The contribution could be treated as an excess contribution under I.R.C. § 4975.

Nor is there a conflict of interest if the fiduciary follows PBGC requirements for a distribution incident to a plan termination.

In mid-2008, the Supreme Court decided *Metropolitan Life Insurance Co. v. Glenn*, 554 U.S. 105 (2008), applying trust law principles to determine the standard of judicial review in ERISA § 1132(a)(1)(B) cases. If the plan administrator has the discretion to determine eligibility for benefits, deferential review will be applied, but if the decision-maker (whether an insurer or a plan sponsor) has a conflict of interest, that conflict of interest will be factored into deciding whether the decision was arbitrary and capricious. However, the mere fact that there is a conflict of interest will not prevent the court from applying a deferential standard of review to the administrator's decisions. [Nancy Pridgen, Alston & Bird ERISA Litigation Advisory July, *The Circuits Are Split: Does MetLife v. Glenn's* "Structural Conflict" *Holding Apply When Employee Benefits Are Funded from a Trust?* (Dec. 23, 2009) (benefitslink.com)]

If a plan grants the decisionmaker discretion to interpret the terms of the plan, a court reviewing the benefit denial uses the deferential "abuse of discretion" standard rather than the tougher de novo standard. A 2012 Seventh Circuit case involves a plan document that gave discretionary authority to the benefits committee, which was also the plan administrator. The plan administrator exercised its power to delegate by delegating to the insurer. However, the insurer was exiting the market and the policy was administered by an agent who was not named in the plan documents. The Seventh Circuit upheld the denial of benefits because the designation was not arbitrary or capricious. [*Aschermann v. Aetna Life Ins. Co.*, 689 F.3d 726 (7th Cir. 2012)]

In August 1997, the plan was amended to permit some participants, including Helton, to elect a full benefit at age 55. AT&T sent letters and amended the SPD, but Helton said she didn't get the communications. She was eligible for full pension benefits in October 2001. AT&T said it sent her a pension package with forms to complete (she said she didn't get it) but destroyed her records, pursuant to policy, when the forms were not returned. In 2009, when Helton was close to 65, she asked AT&T how much her pension would be. When she found out about her earlier eligibility, she applied for back payments, which were denied on the grounds that the plan does not provide retroactive payments. The Fourth Circuit did not consider the breach of fiduciary duty claim, finding that it was proper to award relief under ERISA § 1132(a)(1)(B). The plan gave full discretion to the plan committee, so the standard is abuse of discretion. The version of the pension plan in effect when Helton tried to recover lost benefits explicitly allowed "restorative" benefits to correct administrative errors. The Fourth Circuit said that remand to the plan is the appropriate remedy in many cases, but it is not required, especially if there is evidence of abuse of discretion. [*Helton v. AT&T Inc. Pension Benefit Plan*, 709 F.3d 343 (4th Cir. 2013)]

§ 15.06 INVESTMENT MANAGERS

[A] Qualified Managers Under ERISA

If the plan so permits, ERISA allows fiduciaries to delegate their investment duties to a qualified investment manager.

There are four categories of qualified investment managers:

- Investment advisers who are registered under the federal Investment Company Act—whether they are independent consultants or in-house employees of the plan;
- Trust companies;
- Banks;
- Qualified insurance companies.

ERISA requires the manager to acknowledge in writing that he, she, or it has become a fiduciary with respect to the plan.

DOL Reg. § 2510.3-21(c) explains who will be deemed qualified to render investment advice:

- Those who give advice about the value of securities or recommend investing, buying, or selling securities (or other property, such as real estate);
- Those who are given discretion to buy or sell securities for the plan;
- Those who give advice, on a regular basis, under an oral or written agreement, if the advice is intended to serve as a primary basis for investing plan funds.

As long as the fiduciaries were prudent when they chose the manager (and continued to review the manager's performance), the fiduciaries will not be liable for acts and omissions committed by the manager.

A broker-dealer, bank, or reporting dealer does not become a fiduciary if its only role is to take and execute buy and sell orders for the plan. [DOL Reg. § 2510.3-21(d)(1)] The investment manager is a fiduciary only as to whatever percentage of the overall investment he or she can influence (except in situations where ERISA § 405(a) makes the investment manager responsible for breaches by co-fiduciaries).

Investment managers, also known as "§ 3(38) managers," actually choose, remove, and replace investments from a plan. A fiduciary safe harbor is available if a plan sponsor or its plan committee is prudent in selecting an investment manager and then monitoring its performance. The safe harbor requires the manager to be a bank, registered investment adviser, or insurance company that has the power to manage, acquire, or dispose of plan assets—and that acknowledges its fiduciary status in writing. The fiduciary must engage in an objective process to discover the adviser's qualifications and manager's experience. The adviser's compensation must be reasonable and disclosed in the service agreement. (Information about advisers can be found on the Form ADV Part 2 that they file with the SEC, and the SEC can also state whether the manager has been disciplined for securities law violations.) The fiduciary should get a written description of the manager's investment process—e.g., whether generally accepted investment theories are used; whether the manager provides reports that can be used to monitor performance; how services will be tailored for the plan's needs; and whether the manager has enough liability insurance for the amount under management. [Fred Reish, *'Safe' Hows,* plansponsor.com (October 2011)]

In mid-2005, DOL and the SEC released suggestions for fiduciaries to help them choose and monitor investment consultants (complementing earlier DOL guidance about doing the same for employee benefit plan service providers such as recordkeepers). The SEC's concern is that investment consultants can experience conflicts of interest, especially in "pay to play" arrangements whereby the consultants are compensated by brokers or money managers for offering access to the consultant's plan clients.

The two federal agencies released a list of issues that a fiduciary must consider:

- Is the consultant registered as an investment adviser? If so, the fiduciary should review the disclosures on Part II of SEC's Form ADV.
- Get written acknowledgment that the consultant is a fiduciary and will comply with fiduciary obligations.
- Find out if the consultant or a related company has relationships with the money managers recommended and whether the consultant receives payments or trades by the money managers that the consultant recommends.
- Ask about the consultant's policy on conflicts of interest.

DOL suggests including questions on these topics in any request for proposals for a new consultant—and perhaps even seeking written answers from existing consultants. The RFP also can be used to obtain representations and warranties of compliance, collect information about the consultant's insurance coverage and willingness to indemnify the client. Plans should determine when the contract can be terminated either for cause or for the convenience of the parties; the plan's right to continue using materials developed by the service provider for the plan; liquidated damages for failure to satisfy contractual standards; and any pending litigation or complaints outstanding against the service provider. [McDermott Newsletters, *Recent Guidance on Selecting and Monitoring Service Providers* (June 27, 2005) (benefitslink.com)]

[B] The Role of the Insurer

The Supreme Court's decision in *John Hancock Mutual Life Insurance v. Harris Trust* [510 U.S. 86 (1993)] holds that assets held in an insurer's general account and not guaranteed by the insurer are plan assets subject to ERISA's fiduciary requirements.

DOL issued interim regulations covering insurance contracts sold before December 31, 1998; later contracts are all covered by ERISA fiduciary rules. DOL's Interpretive Bulletin 95-1 says that a fiduciary who chooses annuities to distribute plan benefits has a fiduciary duty to choose the safest available contract, based on factors such as the insurer's size and reputation, the insurer's other lines of business, and the size and provisions of the proposed contracts.

§ 15.07 DUTY TO DISCLOSE

Employees have a right to information about their benefit options, and fiduciaries have a corresponding duty to make complete, accurate disclosure. Furthermore, they need information about the way the plan is expected to evolve, so they can make future plans.

The classic test, stemming from *Fischer v. Philadelphia Electric Co.* [96 F.3d 1533 (3d Cir. 1996)] is that plan participants who inquire must not only be informed about the current structure of the plan—they must be informed of proposals that are under "serious consideration" by management. [Some cases say that, although information must be provided to those who ask for it, it need not be volunteered if there is no request, e.g., *Bins v. Exxon Co.*, 220 F.3d 1042 (9th Cir. 2000); *Hudson v. General Dynamics Corp.*, 118 F. Supp. 2d 226 (D. Conn. 2000). But other cases say that there is a fiduciary duty to give information whenever silence could be harmful to beneficiaries' financial interests. See *Krohn v. Huron Mem. Hosp.*, 173 F.3d 542 (6th Cir. 1999)] The Fifth Circuit refused to adopt the "serious consideration" test: *Martinez v. Schlumberger Ltd.*, 338 F.3d 407 (5th Cir. 2003), even though seven Courts of Appeals use this test. The Fifth Circuit assesses whether the information that was not given would have been material to a reasonable person's decision to retire.

The fiduciary must provide complete and accurate information about the tax consequences of options under a plan. [*Farr v. U.S. West Commc'ns Inc.*, 58 F.3d 1361 (9th Cir. 1998)] But it is not a fiduciary breach to distribute benefits in accordance with the participant's own instructions, even if the fiduciary allegedly gave inaccurate tax advice. [*Glencoe v. TIAA*, 69 F. Supp. 2d 849 (S.D.W. Va. 1999)]

The Seventh Circuit ruled in mid-2010 that an HMO violated its fiduciary duty to plan participants by instructing participants to contact the call center for information—without telling them that they were not entitled to rely on statements from customer service representatives as to whether or not a procedure was covered by the plan. The [*Kenseth v. Dean Health Plan Inc.,* 610 F.3d 452 (7th Cir. 2010) In subsequent proceedings, the Seventh Circuit held that compensation in money (the cost of the surgery) is not necessarily considered a legal rather than an equitable remedy, so it may be available under ERISA § 502(a)(3): *Kenseth v. Dean Health Plan, Inc.*, 722 F.3d 869 (7th Cir. 2013); see PLC, *Expanded ERISA Remedies Available in Fiduciary Breach Claims: Seventh Circuit* (June 18, 2013) (benefitslink.com)]

According to the Second Circuit, ERISA § 104(b)(4) requires the plan administrator to provide copies of "plan documents" on request. In 2002, the Sixth Circuit held that affirmatively misleading employees about the continuation of health benefits, inducing them to retire early, is a fiduciary breach, even though not all the plaintiffs asked specific questions about future benefits. The appropriate test is whether the information is materially misleading, whether or not the employer intended to mislead or was negligent in providing the misleading information. [*James v. Pirelli Armstrong Tire Co.*, 305 F.3d 439 (6th Cir. 2002)]

The Fifth Circuit upheld an award of over $243,000 in damages and fees for the employer's failure to provide a copy of the SPD and rollover election forms. The plaintiff, Kujanek orally requested information about rolling over his plan balance (which was about $490,000 when he quit his job in 2007). The plan, relying on SPD language that all requests must be written, ignored his request. He did not receive a distribution until the value of the account had fallen to $306,000. The Fifth Circuit held that his request for a distribution triggered a fiduciary duty to provide the forms. [*Kujanek v. Houston Poly Bag*, 658 F.3d 483 (5th Cir. 2012); see Spencer Fane Britt & Browne LLP Insights, *Federal Appeals Court Upholds $243,000 Damage and Fee Award for Employer's Failure to Provide SPD and Election Forms* (Mar. 1, 2012) (benefitslink.com)]

§ 15.08 PENALTIES FOR FIDUCIARY BREACH

A fiduciary that breaches the required duties can be sued by plan participants, plan beneficiaries, and/or the Department of Labor. Penalty taxes can be imposed for improper transactions involving the plan. Generally speaking, ERISA § 509 grants relief to the plan itself; participants and beneficiaries find their remedies under ERISA § 502(a)(3).

A large, overlapping, and potentially confusing variety of Civil Monetary Penalties (CMPs) can be imposed under various provisions of ERISA. The same action often violates several different sections, with penalties at least potentially assessed for each, such as:

- § 209(b) failure to furnish or maintain records;
- § 502(c)(1)(A) failure to notify participants of their rights to COBRA benefits;
- § 502(c)(1)(B) failure to provide required information on a timely basis;

- § 502(c)(2) failure or refusal to file an annual report;
- § 502(c)(3) failure to notify participants and beneficiaries when the plan fails to satisfy the minimum funding requirements; failure to give notice when excess pension assets are transferred to a 401(h) retiree health benefits account;
- § 503(c)(5) failure or refusal to file information required under ERISA § 101(g);
- § 503(c)(6) failure or refusal to comply with a participant's or beneficiary's request for information subject to disclosure under ERISA § 104(a)(6).

Most penalties are defined as a maximum amount per day—usually $110 or $1100. Courts hearing such cases have the discretion to reduce or even abate the penalty, based on factors such as the employer's inability to pay, its basic good faith, or extenuating factors such as destruction of records in circumstances beyond the employer's control.

The DOL published final regulations, effective March 3, 2009, covering the assessment of penalties under ERISA § 502(c)(4) when plan administrators fail to provide notices as required by the PPA (e.g., limitations on distributions from underfunded plans; employer's potential liability for withdrawal from a multiemployer plan). The amount of the penalty depends on the degree of willfulness, subject to a maximum of $1,000 per violation per day. (Each person entitled to notification is a separate violation.) The DOL sets a tentative penalty level, and notifies the plan administrator. After the notice of assessment is served, the administrator has 30 days to show reasonable cause why the penalty should be reduced. Responsible parties are not only jointly and severally liable, they are also personally liable for the penalties.

Administrators of automatic contribution arrangements must give participants notice of their rights and obligations under the arrangement, including the right not to have elective contributions made on their behalf, and the right to change the percentage contributed. The timing for making the election must be explained, as well as how the contributions will be invested if no election is made. Generally, the due date for the notice is within 30 days of the time a person becomes eligible under the plan. [Final Regs, 74 Fed. Reg. 17 (Jan. 2, 2009); see Deloitte's Washington Bulletin, *Procedures for Assessing Civil Penalties Under ERISA § 502(c)(4) Are Finalized*, <http://benefitslink.com/articles/guests/ wash bull090112a.html> (Jan. 12, 2009)]

A fiduciary who is guilty of a breach of duty is personally liable to the plan and must compensate it for any loss in asset value caused by the violation. The fiduciary must also "disgorge" (surrender) any personal financial advantage improperly obtained: see ERISA § 409. However, there is liability only if there is a causal connection between a breach and the loss or the improper profits. Fiduciaries are not expected to guarantee that the plan will never lose money.

A plan can get a court order removing a faithless fiduciary from office. The removed fiduciary can be ordered to pay the plan's attorneys' fees plus interest on the sum involved. But plan participants cannot get an award of punitive damages, no matter how outrageous the fiduciary's conduct (although some courts will order punitive damages payable to the plan itself). In the most serious cases, a fiduciary can be subject to criminal charges instead of, or in addition to, civil penalties.

Plans can have "bad boy" clauses. For example, under ERISA § 206(d) and I.R.C. § 401(a)(13)(C) fiduciaries who are also plan participants can have their pensions reduced if they breach fiduciary duty, if they are convicted of crimes against the plan, or if they lose or settle a civil suit or enter into a settlement with the Department of Labor or PBGC. For example, the DOL obtained a consent judgment from Barstow Truck Parts and Equipment Co. and its president, James M. Rajacich Senior, requiring $118,249 to be returned to the profit-sharing plan. He forfeited his own benefits for misconduct, and was required to return unpaid loan amounts with interest, plus a civil money penalty of $23,650. [Rebecca Moore, *Company President to Restore Plan for Loan Repayments*, plansponsor.com (Dec. 10, 2010)]

§ 15.09 ERISA § 502

[A] Generally

ERISA § 502 gives participants and beneficiaries, the DOL, and fiduciaries many remedies against abuses and risks to the plan. In fact, an important part of litigation planning is deciding which subsection of ERISA § 502 to invoke—defendants can get a case dismissed if the wrong subsection is charged or if the plaintiff asks for remedies that are unavailable under that subsection.

Under ERISA § 502, "participant" means an employee or ex-employee who is or may become eligible to receive any benefit under the plan. "Beneficiary" either means someone eligible or potentially eligible to receive benefits under the plan terms, or as designated by a participant.

Participants and beneficiaries (but not the DOL, the employer, or the plan itself) can use ERISA § 502(a)(1)(B) to sue for benefits due under the terms of the plan, to enforce rights under the terms of the plan, or to clarify rights to future benefits under the terms of a plan.

Civil actions under ERISA § 502(a)(2) can be brought by participants, beneficiaries, or the DOL when a breach of fiduciary duty is alleged.

The DOL, participants, beneficiaries, or fiduciaries can sue under ERISA §§ 502(a)(3) and (5) to enjoin violations of ERISA Title I, to get equitable relief under Title I, or to impose penalties on PIIs for engaging in prohibited transactions. The remedies under ERISA § 502(a)(3) can include ordering return of misappropriated plan assets, plus the profits improperly earned on them—but this remedy is not available in situations where the defendant did not hold or profit from plan assets.

When plan participants sued John Hancock under ERISA and the Investment Company Act of 1940 (ICA) for charging retirement plans excessive fees on annuity contracts offered to plan participants, the district court granted Hancock's motion to dismiss. The district court ruled that the ICA fee claims were invalid because the participants were no longer investors in the funds and an ownership interest is required to bring a derivative suit. On the ERISA claims, the district court said that participants failed to make a pre-suit demand on the trustees and did not join the trustees as parties. The Third Circuit affirmed on the ICA claim but vacated and remanded on the ERISA counts. An ICA § 36(b) suit is similar to a derivative suit and the recovery goes to the company. FRCP 23.1 requires continuous ownership, and ex-participants no longer have a real interest in getting a recovery. However, ERISA §§ 502(a)(2) and (3) allow a suit by a participant, beneficiary, or fiduciary for injunction, other appropriate equitable relief, to redress violations, or enforce ERISA or the terms of the plan. Pre-suit demand and mandatory joinder of trustees are not required. Unlike some other ERISA sections, § 502(a) does not limit who can be named as a defendant. According to the Third Circuit, mandatory joinder would, in effect, require trustees to sue themselves—which would not further the purposes of ERISA. [*Santomenno v. John Hancock Life Ins. Co.*, 677 F.3d 178 (3d Cir. 2012)]

The question of what constitutes "appropriate equitable relief" is a difficult one, and many cases have been decided on this issue. In particular, the question of whether participants could sue for reduction in value of their own individual accounts—rather than the value of the plan as a whole—was an important litigation issue that was not resolved until 2008, when the Supreme Court ruled that ERISA § 502(a)(2) does not grant a remedy for individual remedies as distinct from injuries to the plan—but it does permit recovery for fiduciary breaches that impair the value of the assets in a particular account, because the goal of ERISA § 409 is to safeguard the benefits that participants are entitled to.

The Third Circuit held that a former employee's signed release of her claims against the employer could interfere with her ability to represent the class of employees in a stock-drop suit, because the defendant might have specific legal defenses against her that did not apply to other participants. The district court had held that the release was void under ERISA § 410 (which says that provisions that purport to relieve a fiduciary from liability are void as against public policy), so she could be the class representative. The Third Circuit, however, said that § 410 deals with agreements that alter the fiduciary's responsibilities, not individual legal releases. But the Third Circuit said that the release did not prevent the plaintiff from bringing a § 502(a)(2) claim on behalf of the plan. [*In re Schering-Plough ERISA Litig.*, 589 F.3d 585 (3d Cir. 2009); see Fred Schneyer, *Employee's Lawsuit Release Could Imperil Class Action Status*, plansponsor.com (Dec. 22, 2009).

Although *Massachusetts Mutual Life Insurance v. Russell* [473 U.S. 134 (1985)] interprets ERISA § 502(a)(3) as limited to remedies for the plan as a whole, the plan in that case was a disability plan providing a fixed benefit, so administrator misconduct could not affect individual accounts unless the whole plan was at risk of default. The plaintiff in that case actually received the full benefit she was entitled to; she sued for damages for delay in claim processing. Furthermore, the Supreme Court read that case as involving a defined benefit plan in a benefits universe dominated by such plans. The *LaRue* case, in contrast, involved a defined contribution plan, for which a participant's entitlement can be reduced by fiduciary misconduct even if the plan as a whole remains solvent. The Supreme Court sent the case back to the district court, giving the plaintiff a chance to prove that the fiduciary was to blame for the decline in value of his account. Section 502(a)(2) carries out the purposes of ERISA § 409, which obligated fiduciaries to manage, administer, and invest plan assets properly so that participants and beneficiaries will eventually receive the benefits they were promised under the plan. In a defined benefit plan, fiduciary misconduct creates or increases the risk that the plan will default, so the previous decisions look at the effect of misconduct on the entire plan. In a defined contribution plan, misconduct can reduce the value of some but not all accounts—but the misconduct is still the type that ERISA § 409 is intended to deter or redress. [*LaRue v. DeWolff, Boberg & Assocs., Inc.*, 552 U.S. 248 (2008)]

Although technically the result was a victory for LaRue, after the Supreme Court remanded his case, James LaRue apparently ran out of money to continue litigating, so he settled with DeWolff, Boberg. The District of South Carolina's October 21, 2008 order approving the settlement said that the statute of limitations had expired on the events LaRue characterized as fiduciary breaches, so he could not refile later. The case was dismissed with prejudice, although he could bring a further suit for post-2002 events for which the statute of limitations had not run. [Fred Schneyer, *LaRue Bows Out of Legal Fight*, plansponsor.com (Oct. 30, 2008)]

The Seventh Circuit allowed a class of defined contribution plan participants to sue for relief under ERISA § 502, taking the position that the shift from defined benefit plans (the predominant plan type when ERISA was enacted) to defined contribution plans requires re-thinking the remedies available under § 502.

A 2008 Supreme Court decision allows individual defined contribution participants to seek relief; the Seventh Circuit extended this to a plaintiff class in a case alleging excessive fees. The Seventh Circuit held that a plan and its individual participants can be injured at the same time, if excessive fees are charged, or if imprudent choices are included in the plan's investment portfolio. However, the Seventh Circuit, while opening up the potential for class actions, said that the classes actually certified were improperly defined, because they did not have enough similarity because some class members were satisfied with their investment results. It would also be improper to certify a class that involved some fees that are fund-specific and other fees that are imposed equally on all plan participants. [*Beesley v. International Paper Co./Spano v. Boeing*, 633 F.3d 574 (7th Cir. 2011); see Rebecca Moore, *Court OKs Class Actions for ERISA Cases*, plan sponsor.com (Jan. 24, 2011); Groom Law Group, *Seventh Circuit Vacates Class Certifications in 401(k) Fee Cases* (Jan. 31, 2011) (benefitslink.com); Fred Schneyer, *7th Circuit Stock-Drop Rulings Seen as Helping Employers*, plansponsor.com (Jan. 31, 2011)] On remand from the Seventh Circuit, the District Court for the Southern District of Illinois certified a class of participants in Boeing's 401(k) plan who alleged breach of fiduciary duty: excessive administration fees; failure to disclose material information about the fees; and imprudent mutual fund investments. The district court approved of plaintiffs' designation of subclasses (one for each mutual fund at issue) and limitation of the class to participants during the time of the alleged breach. The Seventh Circuit had held that the original class of all past and future participants was excessively broad. [*Spano v. Boeing Co.*, 294 F.R.D. 114 (S.D. Ill. 2013); see Todd Mobley, *Seventh Circuit Again Grants Class Certification In Excessive Fee Case*, Proskauer Rose LLP (Oct. 17, 2013), available at Lexology.com]

However, after *Dukes v. Wal-Mart* (see § 42.06 [A]), all types of employment class actions will be more difficult to maintain. *Dukes* creates problems for stock drop plaintiffs because the participants invested in the plan for differing periods of time, with different investment experiences.

The number of stock drop cases filed decreased, in part because of the relative strength of the stock market, meaning that there were fewer declines in value. Many plans phased out employer stock, so there was no risk that decline in its value would lead to suits, and *Dukes* created significant difficulties for would-be class action plaintiffs. [Ian Morrison and Anne Harris, *Where Oh Where Did The Stock Drops Go?*, Seyfarth Shaw ERISA & Employee Benefits Litigation Blog (Dec. 2, 2013) (benefitslink.com)]

In 2010, the Sixth Circuit joined the Second, Third, Fifth, Seventh, and Ninth Circuits in allowing equitable estoppel to be used for relief from harsh pension plan provisions, even if the provisions are not inequitable. (Previously, the Sixth Circuit only applied equitable estoppel in the context of welfare benefits.) This case arose when the plaintiff took early retirement after he was told how large a pension the defined benefit plan would pay him. After he had been receiving benefits for about two years, the plan administrator told him that, as a result of a computer error, he was receiving about $500 a month too much, and he had to repay more than $11,000. He sued, taking the position that the Third-Party Administrator made a contract to pay him the amount of benefits originally stated, and that he took early retirement based on those representations. The Sixth Circuit allowed him to assert estoppel based on gross negligence that was severe enough to be tantamount to fraud. However, the Sixth Circuit rejected his ERISA § 502(a)(1)(B) claim, because the benefit election form was not a plan amendment, plan modification, or separate contract providing additional benefits; it merely stated the amount of the benefit. The Sixth Circuit also dismissed the plaintiff's fiduciary breach claim. [*Bloemker v. Laborers' Local 265 Pension Fund*, 605 F.3d 436 (6th Cir. 2010); see CCH Pension & Benefits, *Court Applies Equitable Estoppel Rules to Pension Cases with Unambiguous Terms* (June 14, 2010) (benefitslink.com)]

An ERISA § 502(a)(3) suit for individual equitable relief can be maintained against a company that deceived its employees about benefit safety if they were transferred to a new division that was spun off by the company. The Supreme Court ruled that the corporation was acting as a fiduciary when it lied about benefit security. [*Varity Corp. v. Howe*, 514 U.S. 1082 (1996)]

The rule of *Varity v. Howe* is that, when a claimant has an adequate claim for benefits available under ERISA § 502(a)(1)(B), a claim for equitable relief under § 502(a)(3) is inappropriate because it is duplicative. See, e.g., *Korotynska v. Met Life*, 474 F.3d 101 (4th Cir. 2006). But after the *Cigna* decision in 2011, suggesting that equitable remedies such as surcharge might be permissible under § 502(a)(3), many plaintiffs added equitable claims to their complaints. District courts in the Fourth and Eleventh Circuits joined other circuits in holding that *Varity* is still good law after *Cigna: Biglands v. Raytheon*, 801 F. Supp. 2d 781 (N.D. Ind. 2011); *Spivey v. Cigna*, No. 2:13cv461-WHA (wo), 2013 U.S. Dist. LEXIS 130219 (M.D. Ala. Sept. 12, 2013); *Harp v. Liberty Mut.*, No. 1:12CV640, 2013 U.S. Dist. LEXIS 140083 (M.D.N.C. Sept. 30, 2013). [Womble Carlyle Sandridge & Rice LLP, *District Courts In 11th And 4th Circuits Re-Affirm Varity Rule In Face Of Amara-Like Claims*, Lexology.com (Oct. 21, 2013)]

A party in interest to a prohibited transaction with a plan can be liable under ERISA § 502(a)(3), even if the defendant is not a fiduciary [*Harris Trust v. Salomon Bros.*, 530 U.S. 238 (2000)]

An employee (in this case, an early retiree) who is misled about the tax consequences of taking a lump sum payout is entitled to rescission as other equitable relief under ERISA § 502(a)(3), but the Fourth Circuit allowed only partial rescission when the employee's unreasonable delay in seeking a remedy was prejudicial to the employer. [*Griggs v. DuPont*, 385 F.3d 440 (4th Cir. 2004)]

ERISA § 502(a)(3) is also used by benefit plans to recover payments made on behalf of plan participants (e.g., when a participant is injured in an accident and later settles or wins a tort case about the accident). See § 18.17 for further discussion of subrogation. [Important recent subrogation cases include *US Airways v. McCutchen*, 133 S. Ct. 1537 (2013), followed in *Quest Diagnostics v. Bomani*, No. 11-CV-00951 (D. Conn. June 19, 2013)]

Certiorari was denied in a case brought by a Supplemental Needs Trust on the issue of whether depositing funds into a trust, on behalf of insured tortfeasors, to benefit a health plan beneficiary who settled a case prevented the plan from exercising ERISA subrogation to recover. Griffin, a participant in FK Industries, Inc's ERISA welfare benefit plan, was seriously injured in a 2006 automobile accident. The welfare benefit plan, administered by ACS Recovery Services, Inc. paid more than $50,000 of medical expenses. Griffin reached a settlement with the other driver. The settlement was first allocated to Griffin's attorney, additional medical expenses, and to Griffin's wife's divorce settlement. The balance, with a present value of $148,000, was paid by the other driver's insurer to an assignee that was authorized to buy a Hartford Life Annuity that made monthly payments to Griffin's Special Needs Trust. The FK welfare benefit plan had a first lien on all recoveries and forbade participants to take any action that would impair the plan's right of recovery. The result of the settlement was that neither ACS Recovery Services nor FK Industries received any funds. ACS and FK sued the trust, the trustee, Griffin, and his wife, seeking to impose a constructive trust of at least $50,000, and asked for an injunction preventing the defendants from interfering with the plan's right to be reimbursed for the funds advanced for Griffin's care. The Fifth Circuit's decision (which stands, because the Supreme Court did not review it) allowed ACS to recover the costs it incurred on Griffin's behalf from the SNT. The trust could be sued under ERISA; and the trust funds were directly traceable to Griffin's tort recovery. The plan had a pre-existing equitable lien on the tort recovery. [*Larry Griffin Special Needs Trust v. ACS Recovery Servs., Inc., cert. denied*, 134 S. Ct. 618 (2013); see Wolters Kluwer Law & Business News Center, *Supreme Court Declines Request By Special Needs Trust To Review ERISA Plan's Right To Reimbursement* (Nov. 22, 2013) (benefitslink.com)]

Section 502(a)(6) authorizes civil actions by the DOL to collect the excise tax on prohibited transactions or the penalty tax on fiduciary violations. State governments (but NOT the DOL) can sue under § 502(a)(7) to enforce compliance with a Qualified Medical Child Support Order (QMCSO). The states have a role to play here because they have traditionally been empowered to deal with family law issues such as child support.

Funds from an insurance contract or annuity purchased in connection with termination of participant status can be secured by a suit under § 502(a)(9). Suit can be brought by the DOL, fiduciaries, or persons who were participants or beneficiaries at the time of the violation—but suit can only be brought if the purchase of the policy or annuity violated the terms of the plan or violated fiduciary obligations.

ERISA § 502(c) allows the Department of Labor to impose a penalty of $110 per day (dating from the date of failure or refusal to furnish the documents) against a plan administrator who doesn't comply with a participant's or beneficiary's request for plan documents within 30 days. Administrators can be penalized even if the failure is not deliberate—but not if it is due to matters beyond their reasonable control.

Both the federal and the state courts have jurisdiction under § 502(e) when participants or beneficiaries bring suit to recover benefits, clarify their rights to future benefits, or enforce rights under any plan that falls under ERISA Title I. Although ERISA does not rule out binding arbitration of claims, any other Title I claim can only be heard in a federal, not a state, court.

ERISA § 502(i) requires the DOL to impose a civil penalty on fiduciaries who violate the fiduciary responsibility provisions of Title I. A nonfiduciary who knowingly participates in a fiduciary violation can also be penalized under this section. The base penalty is 20% of the penalty that the court orders under ERISA § 502(a)(2) or (5). If the fiduciary or person who assisted the fiduciary in the breach settled with the DOL to avoid being taken to court, the base penalty is 20% of the amount of the settlement. The penalty can be reduced or even waived if the person acted reasonably and in good faith. Because the main objective of this section is to safeguard the plan, a reduction or waiver can also be obtained if the fiduciary or helper would not be able to reimburse the plan without severe financial hardship if the full penalty were assessed.

Section 502(k) permits plan administrators, fiduciaries, participants, and beneficiaries to sue the Department of Labor itself in district court in order to compel the agency to undertake an action required by ERISA Title I, to prevent the Department from acting contrary to Title I, or to review a final order of the Secretary of Labor.

Section 502 also permits fiduciaries to ask the court to remove another fiduciary from office, or to issue an injunction against anyone who has violated ERISA Title I or the plan's own terms.

It is mandatory for the DOL to impose civil penalties, under § 502(l), against a fiduciary who knowingly violates the Title I provisions on fiduciary responsibility, and also against anyone who knowingly participates in a violation. The basic penalty is 20% of the court order under §§ 502(a)(2) or (5), or the settlement with DOL in such a case. However, any penalty imposed under § 502(i), or any prohibited transaction excise tax, can be used to offset the § 502(l) penalty. The Secretary of Labor has discretion to reduce or waive the penalty in two circumstances: if the fiduciary acted reasonably and in good faith—or if waiver permits the fiduciary to reimburse the plan for its losses.

[B] Issues Under *Knudson, Sereboff,* and *McVeigh*

In 2002, the Supreme Court decided *Great-West Life & Annuity Insurance Co. v. Knudson* [534 U.S. 204 (2002)]. The Supreme Court ruled that a health plan and its administrator cannot sue under ERISA § 502(a)(3) when they claim that beneficiaries violate the terms of the plan by refusing to reimburse the plan for amounts the plan spent on the beneficiaries' medical care. The Supreme Court reached this conclusion because § 502(a)(3) refers to cases that traditionally came under the heading of "equity." Contract suits traditionally were considered suits at "law," not "equity."

After *Knudson*, plans faced three hurdles in bringing claims for restitution. First, the defendant (in many such cases, the plan participant, because the plan itself is the plaintiff) must have been unjustly enriched. In some cases, the defendant will have to have possession of specific property that really belongs to the plaintiff—and equitable relief must be appropriate.

In mid-2006, the Supreme Court revisited ERISA subrogation issues twice. In *Sereboff v. Mid Atlantic Medical Services Inc.* [547 U.S. 356 (2006)], the petitioners were covered by an ERISA plan that included a subrogation provision. The petitioners settled tort claims related to an automobile accident. Their insurer sued under ERISA § 502(a)(3) to recoup medical expenses paid on their behalf. The petitioners set aside part of the tort recovery, corresponding to the insurer's claim. The Supreme Court ruled that the insurer was entitled to recover the amount expended on the petitioners' medical care. The insurer acted as a fiduciary seeking "appropriate equitable relief" to enforce plan terms, as permitted by ERISA § 502(a)(3). Unlike *Knudson*, the disputed funds in this case were in the petitioners' possession and set aside in a separate account. The Supreme Court treated the insurer's claim as equitable not because it was a claim for subrogation, but because it was the equivalent of an action to enforce an equitable lien created by agreement.

A month later, in *Empire Healthchoice Assurance, Inc. v. McVeigh* [547 U.S. 677 (2006)], ruled that an insurer's attempt to recover health care costs paid on behalf of an injured federal employee had to be litigated in state court rather than federal court: there was no jurisdiction under 28 U.S.C. § 1331. Although the worker was covered under the Federal Employees Health Benefits Act, a statute that includes a provision that the terms of the federal plan's insurance contracts will preempt state or local law about health benefit plans, the Supreme Court held that the case for reimbursement does not "arise under federal law" and therefore there is no federal jurisdiction.

In 2013, the Supreme Court ruled in a case in which a plan participant received $110,000 in settlement funds after an automobile accident. He paid a 40% contingent fee to his lawyer, so he had $66,000 after that. His health plan sought to recover the $66,866 it had paid for his care. The plan participant, McCutchen, said that he was not obligated to reimburse the health plan, because if he did, he would not have received any compensation for the injuries he suffered. The Supreme Court ruled that the health plan's SPD clearly and explicitly gave the insurer a right of subrogation. This right, deriving from contract law, prevailed over McCutchen's equitable arguments about "make-whole" relief. However, the reimbursement provision did not explain how to handle attorneys' fees, so the Supreme Court held that it was possible to apply another equitable doctrine, the "common fund" doctrine to resolve this issue. (This doctrine allows a person who creates a common fund for the benefit of multiple parties to be paid for creating the fund.) [*US Airways, Inc. v. McCutchen*, 133 S. Ct. 1537 (2013); see Sarah Fowles and Angela Marie Hubbell, *Have You Checked Your Plan's Subrogation and Reimbursement Provisions Lately?*, Quarles & Brady LLP Employee Benefits & Executive Compensation Law Blog (April 2013) (benefitslink.com)]

Subrogation issues are also discussed in Chapter 18.

[C] *Amara v. Cigna*

Cigna employees filed a class action after their plan's cash balance conversion. (See Chapter 7 for more discussion of cash balance plans.) At the time of the conversion, Cigna distributed summaries and an SPD stating that the new plan provided an overall improvement in retirement benefits; that participants' opening account balance equaled the full value of their accrued benefits; and the conversion did not save money for the employer. The employees contested these statements, arguing that the opening account balance was less than full value because it did not reflect the previous plan's early retirement subsidy. They also claimed that many participants were subject to wearaway, and that the employer saved $10 million a year by converting the plan. (Cigna later conceded this point, but said that it spent the money on other benefit plans.)

The district court agreed with the plaintiffs that the plan materials were false and misleading. The district court ruled that there was likely harm even without a showing of detrimental reliance by the plaintiffs (i.e., that they were harmed by relying on the employer's statements). The district court ordered Cigna to reform the plan to conform to the descriptions given to the employees. The district court interpreted ERISA § 502(a)(1)(B) to allow plan participants to sue to obtain benefits that were due under the plan, or to clarify their right to future benefits. The district court ordered the plan to give participants their pre-conversion frozen benefits, plus the cash balance benefits earned after the conversion. However, the district court read § 502(a)(3) to provide only the types of "equitable" relief that traditionally were ordered by equity courts before the two court systems (law and equity) were merged. Therefore, the district court did not order any compensatory damages.

In 2011, the Supreme Court held that the terms of an SPD are not part of the plan itself, and the SPD merely communicates about the plan. The plan's settlor determines the terms of the plan; the administrator provides the SPD. In effect, the Supreme Court overruled the line of decisions allowing enforcement of the terms of the SPD where it conflicts with the plan terms.

The Supreme Court also said that errors in an SPD cannot be enforced through a contractual claim for benefits under ERISA § 502(a)(1)(B). Merely showing likely harm to a class is not enough to support relief. The Supreme Court also held that courts do not have authority under § 502(a)(1)(B) to reform the terms of a plan. These parts of the holding are pro-employer.

But, with regard to what constitutes appropriate equitable relief under ERISA § 502(a)(3), the Supreme Court left open the possibility of obtaining reformation, equitable estoppel, and even surcharge (i.e., requiring the trustee to reimburse the plan). The Supreme Court said that a showing of detrimental reliance is usually not required in equitable proceedings for reformation or surcharges. Plaintiffs must show actual harm and causation—but actual reliance on the SPD would not have to be proved. The Supreme Court vacated the Second

Circuit decision, and remanded the case for determination of the availability of equitable remedies. [*Amara v. Cigna*, 131 S. Ct. 1866 (2011)]

On remand, the District Court for the District of Connecticut ordered reformation of CIGNA's cash balance plan, holding that both reformation and surcharge are appropriate equitable remedies. The district court applied the Second Circuit's "likely harm" standard to decide that CIGNA was liable for giving inadequate disclosures of the conversion from the defined benefit to the defined contribution plan. The district court ordered the plan to pay the class members all accrued benefits under both plans. CIGNA argued that the remedies should be based on trust rather than contract principles, but the district court said that the economic reality is that the pension plan stems from the employment contract between employer and employees. The district court held that equity courts have the power to reform contracts that, as a result of mutual mistake or because of one-sided mistake and fraud on the other side, fail to express the parties' intention. The district court ruled that CIGNA engaged in inequitable conduct. The defective notice caused employees to misunderstand the contract. CIGNA not only did not correct their misunderstanding, but also prevented employees from understanding the differences between the old and new plans and misled them into thinking their accrued benefits would be protected. [*Amara v. CIGNA Corp.*, Civil No. 3:01cv2361 (JBA) 2012 U.S. Dist. LEXIS 180355 (D. Conn. Dec. 20, 2012); see Mark Casciari and Sara Eber, *Amara—The Beat Goes On*, Seyfarth Shaw ERISA & Employee Benefits Litigation Blog (Jan. 10, 2013) (benefitslink .com); Rebecca Moore, *Court Makes Repeat Decision in Amara v. CIGNA Corp*, plansponsor.com (Jan. 23, 2013). See also *Helton v. AT&T Inc. Pension Benefit Plan*, 709 F.3d 343 (4th Cir. 2013), holding that a retiree who was not informed of a plan change that would have allowed her to collect a full pension at an earlier age was not barred by *Amara* from recovering the benefits once she became aware of their availability.]

Gearlds alleged that his employer negligently induced him to take early retirement by promising health benefits. The district court dismissed the case, arguing that all he asked for was compensatory damages (past and future medical expenses, attorneys' fees and costs), which are not an available equitable remedy. However, the Fifth Circuit said that *Amara* allows relief that makes a plaintiff whole for losses caused by breach of fiduciary duty. [*Gearlds v. Entergy Servs. Inc.*, 709 F.3d 448 (5th Cir. 2013); see Rebecca Moore, *5th Circuit Revives Suit for Retiree Medical Benefits* (Mar. 8, 2013)]

The Ninth Circuit enforced the less favorable terms of the plan document rather than the more generous terms of the SPD in a case where—unlike *Amara*—there was no evidence of mistake, fraud, duress, undue influence, or intent to deceive. Nor did the plaintiffs show that their position would have been different if they had received accurate SPDs. [*Skinner v. Northrop Grumman Retirement Plan B*, 673 F.3d 1162 (9th Cir. 2012); see Spencer Fane Britt & Brown LLP, *Federal Appeals Court Rejects Equitable Remedies When SPD Promises More Generous Benefits Than Pension Plan Document* (May 18, 2012) (benefitslink.com)]

The Sixth Circuit found disgorgement (in this case, $3.8 million in profits constituting unjust enrichment to the insurer) to be an appropriate equitable remedy in an ERISA case about denial of long-term disability benefits. The calculation was based on the defendant's return on average equity and not its investment income, because the money was not segregated into an investment account, but kept in a general account that could be used for any business purpose. The Sixth Circuit found that denial of benefits was an abuse of discretion, and permitted disgorgement in addition to benefit recovery, joining the Eighth Circuit in holding that this does not provide a double recovery. In the Sixth Circuit view, *Varity* (denying remedies under ERISA § 502(a)(3), a catch-all provision, if the plaintiff has a remedy for benefits under § 502(a)(1)(B)) did not apply in this case, because the plaintiff had two separate claims. [*Rochow v. Life Ins. Co. of N. Am.*, 737 F.3d 415 (6th Cir. 2013); see Haynes and Boone LLP, *Participant Awarded $3.8 Million As Disgorgement Of Profits Made On Unpaid Benefit* (Jan. 13, 2014), available at Lexology.com; Mike Reilly, *6th Circuit: Reversing Decades Of Precedent—Court Orders Disgorgement Of Profits In Long Term Disability Case*, Boom: The ERISA Law Blog (Dec. 10, 2013) (benefitslink.com); Workplace Prof Blog, *6th Cir: ERISA Remedy for Wrongful Denial of Benefits May Include Disgorgement Remedy under Section 502(a)(3)* (Dec. 9, 2013) (benefitslink.com)]

§ 15.10 ERISA § 510

ERISA § 510 makes it unlawful to interfere with ERISA rights, or to discharge or discriminate against a participant for exercising ERISA rights. The typical examples are firing an employee to prevent benefit accrual, or firing someone in retaliation for making a claim for plan benefits. As the number of layoffs increases, companies are at greater risk that laid-off employees will charge that they lost their jobs to cut benefit costs. Sometimes § 510 claims arise in the context of a wrongful discharge, ADEA, or whistleblower case. Section 510 is enforced under § 502, so the possible remedies are a grant of benefits, reinstatement, or injunctions—but not punitive or compensatory damages. Successful plaintiffs often receive attorneys' fees and costs. Back pay can be allowed as a form of restitution, but money damages are not allowed because § 502 offers only equitable relief.

ERISA preempts state-law wrongful termination claims when the former employee claims termination was motivated by interference with ERISA rights. [*Ingersoll-Rand v. McClendon*, 498 U.S. 133 (1990)] Section 510 applies to welfare benefit plans as well as pension plans. [*Inter-Modal Rail Employees v. Atchison, Topeka & Santa Fe R.R.*, 520 U.S. 510 (1997)] However, refusal to rehire laid off workers who have credited service, as part of a policy of reducing pension obligations, does not violate § 510 because the people who seek to be rehired have not yet been hired or promised benefits. [*Becker v. Mack Trucks Inc.*, 281 F.3d 372 (3d Cir. 2002)]

The Tenth Circuit held that a group of terminated employees who were not rehired after the sale of their employer's facility failed to prove a conspiracy between the employer and the purchaser to violate ERISA § 510 by selling the facility, getting rid of older employees, and depriving them of their pensions. The Tenth Circuit concluded that the seller did not consider pension costs until after the sale. Both before and after the sale, most of the workers were over 40, but the percentage of over-40 workers rehired was lower than the pre-acquisition workforce. The Tenth Circuit held that § 510 is not violated if the employer is motivated by legitimate business reasons, even if the result is that some laid-off workers lose pension eligibility. [*Apsley v. Boeing Co.*, 691 F.3d 1184 (10th Cir. 2012)]

Verizon proposed to fund about $7.5 billion in retiree benefits for about 41,000 management retirees by purchasing a single-premium group annuity from Prudential. Verizon said that the annuity payments would be the same as the pension payments. The plaintiffs charged that the transaction violated ERISA § 510 by denying them the protection of ERISA. (29 C.F.R. § 2510.3-3(d)(2)(ii) says that a person is not a plan participant if the entire benefit is fully guaranteed by an insurance company.) The Northern District of Texas denied a TRO and preliminary injunction that would have halted the transaction. The district court said that the annuity provided the same survivor benefits and other rights as the retirees already had. Because the contract terms remained the same, the district court said that they could not show a risk of loss of benefits. Because amending or terminating a pension plan is not a fiduciary act, the fiduciary duty claim was dismissed. Although there is a fiduciary duty to be prudent in selecting an annuity provider, but the annuity purchase itself is not treated as an investment subject to the fiduciary duty to diversify. The plaintiffs argued that all of the transferred assets were invested with Prudential, but the district court said that the duty to diversify did not apply in this context; fiduciary duty meant prudent selection of an insurer. The district court held that an SPD is only required to explain the current terms of a plan, not potential changes. [*Lee v. Verizon*, No. 3:12-cv-04834-D, 2012 U.S. Dist. LEXIS 173559 (N.D. Tex. Dec. 7, 2012); see Kristen Heinzinger, *Court Approves Verizon Pension Buyout*, plansponsor.com (Dec. 7, 2012 The entire case was dismissed in June 2013. [954 F. Supp. 2d 486 (N.D. Tex. 2013)] The district court found that ERISA protects benefits, but does not require that the original source that provides the benefits be maintained: see Maria Wood, *Judge Disconnects Lawsuit Vs. Verizon Pension Transfer*, LifeHealthPro, <http://www.lifehealthpro.com/2013/06/26/judge-disconnects-lawsuit-vs-verizon-pension-trans> (June 26, 2013).]

When employees charge retaliation in violation of ERISA § 510, there is an important question as to whether the employee must have participated in a formal action or proceeding to be protected. The Second, Third, and Fourth Circuits require a formal proceeding; the Fifth and Ninth say that unsolicited informal complaints are also covered. The Seventh Circuit held that, at least if a plan's anti-relation provision is ambiguous, doubts must be resolved in the employee's favor. Therefore, a plaintiff who made internal complaints and contacted the DOL (but did not make a formal complaint) alleging that funds withheld from his pay were not deposited into his retirement and health savings accounts could bring a § 510 retaliation action when he was fired. The Seventh Circuit said that § 510 applies as long as the employee's grievance is within the scope of § 510, even if the employer did not solicit information and if the employee suffered retaliation because of raising the issue. The employee must have a substantial complaint and a plausible grievance (although he or she does not have to be factually correct); and the complaint must be substantial. [*George v. Junior Achievement of Central Indiana, Inc.*, 694 F.3d 812 (7th Cir. 2012) see also *Edwards v. Cornell & Son Inc.*, 610 F.3d 217 (3d Cir. 2010), *cert. denied*, 131 S. Ct. 1604 (2011)]

A single, unsolicited complaint to the employer about alleged violations of ERISA is not enough to support an ERISA §510 claim if the employee is terminated. (The plaintiff was first removed as ESOP trustee, then fired, for e-mailing the chairman of the board threatening to report ERISA violations in the course of the board election.) The Sixth Circuit joined the Second, Third, and Fourth Circuits in holding that unsolicited complaints do not constitute an "inquiry or proceeding" as defined by §510—although the Fifth, Seventh, and Ninth Circuits disagree. The Sixth Circuit said that there are two kinds of anti-retaliation clauses in federal law. One of them is an "opposition" clause that protects people who oppose violations of the law; the Consumer Financial Protection Act, Title VII, and the Fair Labor Standards Act are drafted this way. The other is a "participation" clause that forbids retaliation against people who participate in proceedings or hearings. The Sixth Circuit said that ERISA §510 is a participation provision, so protection is triggered only by a proceeding or hearing. [*Sexton v. Panel Processing*, No. 13-1604 (6th Cir. May 9, 2014); see Matthew Loughran, *Sixth Circuit: ERISA Section 510 Requires Employee Action Within Formal Proceeding*, Bloomberg BNA Daily Labor Report (May 13, 2014) (benefitslink.com)]

§ 15.11 OTHER ENFORCEMENT ISSUES

[A] Generally

Criminal penalties can be imposed under ERISA § 511, making it a crime, punishable by up to one year's imprisonment and/or a fine of $10,000, to use or threaten force, fraud, or violence to restrain, coerce, or intimidate a participant or beneficiary, in order to interfere with or prevent exercise of any right under the terms of the plan or under Title I.

ERISA § 409(a) makes a breaching fiduciary personally liable to the plan to make up for losses caused by the breach (such as the difference between what the plan would have earned given appropriate investments, minus its actual earnings). The breaching fiduciary is also liable for any other legal and equitable remedies the plan chooses to impose.

However, in *Peacock v. Thomas* [516 U.S. 349 (1996)], the plaintiff won an ERISA case against his employer, but could not collect the judgment, allegedly because a corporate officer who was not a fiduciary misappropriated the funds that could have been used to satisfy the judgment. The plaintiff could not "pierce the corporate veil" and make the corporate officer personally liable, for various technical legal reasons. For one thing, the case was not closely enough related to ERISA for the federal courts to get involved. Anyway, a federal court cannot enforce a judgment against someone who was not liable for it in the first place.

The Department of Labor has authority under ERISA § 504(a)(2) to investigate whether a Title I violation has occurred so the employer might be ordered to submit books, papers, and records for DOL examination. This can be done only once per 12-month period unless the DOL has reasonable cause to believe that Title I was violated. The DOL also has subpoena power over books, records, and witnesses under § 504(c), but the subpoena can be enforced only if the agency shows that the investigation has a legitimate purpose, the inquiry is relevant to that purpose, and the government does not already have the information.

For purposes of compliance with a DOL investigative audit under ERISA § 504, the fiduciary exception to attorney-client privilege covers communications about plan administration between an ERISA trustee and the plan's attorney. Therefore, two multi-employer pension funds had to turn over plan administration materials about the decision to invest in entities related to Bernard Madoff. The funds asserted attorney-client and work-product privilege to avoid turning over the materials to the DOL. The fiduciary exception was created under trust law and holds that advice that trustees get about trust administration goes to the trust beneficiaries, not to the trustees. The funds were unsuccessful in asserting privilege because they did not provide privilege logs or say which litigation the documents were prepared for. [*Solis v. The Food Employers Labor Relations Ass'n,* 644 F.3d 221 (4th Cir. 2011)]

ERISA § 515 permits a civil action against an employer for delinquency in making contributions. This section does not have a statute of limitations, so most courts that have considered the issue use a six-year statute of limitations (typical for contract cases). The statute of limitations is clear under a similar provision, ERISA § 4003(e)(1) (which correlates with I.R.C. § 412(n)). If an employer fails to make a required contribution to the plan, at a time when the plan's funded current liability percentage is lower than 100% and the employer owes the plan more than $1 million (including interest), then all of the employer's real and personal property becomes subject to a lien in favor of the plan.

The plan that was supposed to, but didn't, make the payment has an obligation to notify the PBGC within 10 days of the payment due date. The PBGC has six years from the date of the missed payment, or three years from the time it knew or should have known about the missed payment, to sue in federal District Court to enforce the lien. Fraud or concealment by the employer extends the statute of limitations to six years from the PBGC's discovery of the true state of affairs.

Excise taxes are imposed under § 4975 for the employer's failure to make timely payments of elective deferrals into the plan trust. (The excise tax is sent to the IRS with Form 5330.) Small (under 100 participant) plans are entitled to a safe harbor as long as employee contributions are deposited within seven business days of receipt. The safe harbor offers relief from the general rule that employers must deposit contributions as soon as they can be segregated from the employer's assets, but in any case within 15 business days of the end of the month of receipt. [73 Fed. Reg. 11072 (Feb. 29, 2008); see *EBSA Proposes Seven-Day Employee Contrib Safe Harbor*, plansponsor.com (Feb. 28, 2008)]

The Fourth Circuit allowed participants in a defined benefit plan to continue to pursue their fiduciary breach claim even after the plan was turned over to the PBGC. In other words, the right to sue does not end when a plan is terminated, and the PBGC is not the only potential plaintiff. The Fourth Circuit also held that in general, the PBGC cannot make lump sum payments from its own funds, but can do so in its role as statutory trustee. However, state-law claims against the investment manager, such as violation of the Unfair and Deceptive Trade Practices Act, were preempted by ERISA. [*Wilmington Shipping Co. v. New England Life Ins. Co.*, 496 F.3d 326 (4th Cir. 2007)]

[B] Sarbanes-Oxley Act and Dodd-Frank Act

The penalty for willful violation of reporting or disclosure rules [29 U.S.C. § 1311] was increased dramatically by the Sarbanes-Oxley Act [Pub. L. No. 107-204]. The maximum penalty under this provision (whether or not the violator is a publicly traded corporation) is $100,000 rather than $5,000 for an individual; 10 years rather than one year of imprisonment; and $500,000 rather than $100,000 if the violator is a corporation.

See the DOL final rule [68 Fed. Reg. 3729 (Jan. 24, 2003)] for the effects of the Sarbanes-Oxley Act on penalties. Although the main focus of this rule is on the penalties imposed pursuant to ERISA § 502(c)(7) for failure to provide proper notice of a blackout period, the Sarbanes-Oxley Act made several changes in penalty levels that apply to all ERISA violations, not just those involving corporate governance. The maximum penalty under ERISA § 502(c)(2) is $1,000 per day; starting on the date the plan administrator failed or refused to file the annual report. The maximum penalty under ERISA § 502(c)(5) is $1,000 per day (for violations occurring after March 24, 2003, the penalty can be up to $1,100 a day. [See 68 Fed. Reg. 2875 (Jan. 22, 2003)] Failure to furnish documents on request of plan participants, beneficiaries, or their designates can be penalized by up to $110 a day, subject to a maximum of $1,100 per request.

In all these cases, the plan administrator is entitled to notice and hearing before imposition of the penalty, and the administrator will be permitted to introduce evidence of why it would not be equitable to impose a penalty (e.g., the administrator acted in good faith and the non-compliance was due to factors beyond his or her control).

Sarbanes-Oxley also limits the availability of plan loans to the officers and directors of the sponsor corporation. EBSA issued a Field Assistance Bulletin that such limitations do not violate ERISA. [EBSA Advisory Opinion 2003-04A, <http://www.dol.gov/ebsa/regs/aos/ao2003-04a.html>]

The Dodd-Frank Act, Pub. L. No. 111-203, regulating financial services, was passed after the 2008 stock market crash. It includes a bounty program under § 922: whistleblowers can receive 10–30% of fines and settlements garnered by enforcement actions triggered by their claims. The IRS also offers rewards of 15–30% of the proceeds of enforcement actions involving more than $2 million or involving taxpayers whose annual gross income exceeds $200,000. The IRS is not required to pay the whistleblower until the accused has exhausted all legal appeals and paid the IRS. Under the SEC and CFTC whistleblower programs, the minimum reward is $100,000, with no cap, if the tip leads to penalties of more than $1 million. Initially, the Dodd-Frank program was limited to insider trading, but now most kinds of investment fraud are covered. [Jenna Greene, *SEC Proposes New Whistleblower Rules*, The BLT: The Blog of Legal Times (Nov. 3, 2010) (law.com); Jean Eaglesham and Ashby Jones, *Whistleblower Bounties Pose Challenges*, WSJ.com (Dec. 13, 2010). The proposed rules were finalized in 2011: <http://www.sec.gov/rules/final/2011/34-64545.pdf> (May 25, 2011), effective August 12, 2011.] See 79 Fed. Reg. 18630 (Apr. 3, 2014) for OSHA's interim final regulation explaining how whistleblowers can file a complaint of violations of Dodd-Frank Act §1057.

A mid-2013 Fifth Circuit decision holds that a person who makes an internal complaint about wrongdoing (in this case, possible violations of the Foreign Corrupt Practice Act) is not a whistleblower for Dodd-Frank Act purposes, which requires providing the SEC with information about violations of the securities laws. Therefore, retaliation based on an internal complaint is not covered by the Dodd-Frank Act. [*Asadi v. G.E. Energy LLC*, 720 F.3d 620 (5th Cir. 2013)]

In 2014, the Supreme Court extended the definition of "whistleblower" under Sarbanes-Oxley to include employees of companies that are not publicly traded, but that are contractors for publicly traded companies. Mutual funds are generally operated as public companies without employees; advice is rendered and services are performed under contract with private companies. The whistleblowers in this case alleged mutual fund irregularities; they worked for a service provider company. Dodd-Frank's whistleblower provisions are not restricted to public companies, but were unavailable in this case because it arose before Dodd-Frank's effective date. [*Lawson v. FMR Inc.*, 134 S. Ct. 1158 (2014); see Tony Mauro, *Justices Deliver Rare Win For Whistleblowers*, Legal Times (Mar. 4, 2014), available at law.com]

§ 15.12 LIABILITY OF CO-FIDUCIARIES

If a plan's assets are held by more than one trustee, the general rule is that all the trustees are jointly responsible for management, unless the plan's trust instrument either makes a specific allocation of responsibility, or sets up a procedure for allocating responsibility.

ERISA § 405(c)(1) allows a plan to make an explicit allocation of fiduciary responsibility (other than the responsibility of trustees) among the named fiduciaries. The plan can also have procedures for fiduciaries to designate a party other than a named fiduciary to carry out fiduciary responsibilities under the plan. In general, a fiduciary who designates someone else will not be responsible for the acts or omissions of the designee. The two major exceptions occur when making or continuing the designation violates the designor's duties under ERISA § 404(a)(1), or when ERISA § 405(a) makes the designor responsible for the co-fiduciary's breach.

Every trustee has a legal duty to use reasonable care to make sure the other fiduciaries do not breach their duties. Any fiduciary's misconduct implicates all the others. Fiduciaries are liable for the acts and omissions of their fellow fiduciaries if:

- They knowingly participate in, or knowingly conceal, a breach on another party's act;
- They facilitate someone else's breach by failing to perform their own fiduciary duties as stated by § 404(a)(2);
- They know about a breach by another fiduciary, but fail to take reasonable steps to remedy it.

Under a 1993 Supreme Court case, the plan can also get equitable remedies (but not damages) from a nonfiduciary who cooperated with a fiduciary who breached fiduciary duty. [*Mertens v. Hewitt Assocs.*, 508 U.S. 248 (1993)] Some courts have applied *Mertens* to prevent any claims by plans against nonfiduciaries. This only puts more pressure on the fiduciaries, because then they are the only possible defendants if something goes wrong. But fiduciaries cannot be liable for other fiduciaries' conduct occurring before they themselves became fiduciaries. Nor do they have a duty to remedy breaches that occurred before their tenure or after they cease to be fiduciaries.

Investment advisor Barry Stokes stole millions of dollars from employee benefits plans under his management. The fiduciary accounts for those plans were held in Regions Bank. Stokes' bankruptcy trustee and several of Stokes' clients asserted that the bank negligently or knowingly let Stokes steal from fiduciary accounts at the bank. The Sixth Circuit held that ERISA preempted the plaintiffs' state-law claims—but affirmed the district court's dismissal of the ERISA claims. The Sixth Circuit held that the bankruptcy trustee had standing to pursue ERISA claims against Regions Bank, acting as an ERISA fiduciary rather than as the trustee of the debtor's estate. A plaintiff can obtain both equitable relief and damages from fiduciaries who breach their duty, but can only get equitable relief from nonfiduciaries. However, the Sixth Circuit held that Regions was not a fiduciary even though it had custody of plan assets and earned fees for holding the assets. [*McLemore v. Regions Bank*, 682 F.3d 414 (6th Cir. 2012)]

A non-fiduciary who knowingly participates in a fiduciary's violation of the anti-kickback provision, ERISA § 406(b)(3), can be penalized under ERISA § 502(a)(3) even if the non-fiduciary is not a party in interest. The case involved a financial planner who signed up many of his clients in a tax avoidance scheme. [*National Security Systems, Inc. v. Iola*, 700 F.3d 65 (3d Cir. 2012); see ERISA Litigation Update, *Third Circuit Holds Nonfiduciary Who Is Not a "Party in Interest" May Be Liable For Participation in Fiduciary's Violation of ERISA Section 406(b)(3)* (Dec. 13, 2012) (benefitslink.com)]

The Fourth Circuit reversed dismissal of a complaint charging 401(k) plan fiduciaries with breach of the duty of prudence when they liquidated two of the plan's investment funds at a loss. The district court dismissed the complaint because it said that the plan's sponsors had amended the plan to eliminate those two funds, and that the amendment was a "settlor act" that did not trigger fiduciary duty analysis. The Fourth Circuit allowed the plaintiffs to pursue their claim because the amendment did not remove the fiduciaries' discretion to maintain the funds, so the decision to liquidate them could be imprudent. [*Tatum v. RJ Reynolds Tobacco Co.*, 392 F.3d 636 (4th Cir. 2004)] But the "settlor act" argument prevailed in a 2010 Eighth Circuit case, which found that plan trustees acted as settlers rather than fiduciaries when they amended an early retirement plan to allow certain laid-off employees access to benefits not available under the original plan. [*Schultz v. Windstream Commc'ns, Inc.*, 600 F.3d 948 (8th Cir. 2010)]

§ 15.13 BONDING

The basic rule set down by ERISA § 412(a) is that all fiduciaries, and plan officials who are not fiduciaries but who handle plan assets, must be bonded. Generally, the employer will maintain a single bond covering all of its plans that are subject to ERISA Title I. Recovery on behalf of one plan must not be allowed to reduce the amount available to the other plans below the minimum requirement.

The exceptions are some banks and insurance companies with assets over $1 million, and administrators, officers, and employees who deal with unfunded plans. (An unfunded plan is one whose assets come from the general funds of the employer or a union, even if the funds derive in part from employee contributions.) A bond is not required for amounts characterized as general assets of the employer until they are transferred to the insurers that pay the actual benefits.

Various forms of bonds are acceptable:

- Blanket bond (covering all the fiduciaries and everyone who handles the plan's money);
- Individual bond;
- Name schedule bond (covering a group of named individuals);
- Position schedule bond (covering whoever fills certain jobs or stands in certain relationships to the plan).

The bond must be issued by a corporate surety that holds a Department of Treasury Certificate of Authority. To be acceptable, the bond must not have a deductible, and must cover claims discovered after termination or cancellation of the bond. The amount of the bond must be large enough to cover the plan's potential losses caused by plan officials' dishonesty or fraud. Before the PPA, the bond was required to be 10% of the funds handled, with a minimum of $1,000 and a maximum of $500,000, but, for plans that hold employer stock, and for plan years beginning after January 1, 2007, the Pension Protection Act of 2006 (PPA) increases the maximum to $1 million. If the DOL finds out that a plan does not have the required bond, it can order the company to get a bond; permanently bar the fiduciary from ever serving as an ERISA plan fiduciary; remove the plan administrator and appoint an independent trustee; or impose penalties. [Janelle Sotelo, *Fidelity Bond v. Fiduciary Liability Ins.*, <http://www.preceptgroup.com/blog> (Feb. 19, 2009)]

A fidelity bond is not the same thing as fiduciary liability insurance. ERISA § 412(a) requires bonding of all plan officials. The fidelity bond protects the plan against losses caused by an official's fraud or dishonesty. The fidelity bond carrier has a duty to report the amount of its coverage on the plan's Form 5500.

ERISA does not require fiduciary liability insurance. The insurance protects the plan against losses caused by breaches of fiduciary responsibility, but also protects the fiduciaries who are insureds under the policy from personal liability. Generally speaking, the fidelity bond is a plan expense that can be paid from plan assets, but fiduciary liability insurance premiums are not. [Carrie Byrnes and Tim Zehnder, *Fiduciary Bonds and Fiduciary Liability Insurance—Do You Need Both?*, Bryan Cave Benefits and Executive Compensation Blog (Mar. 13, 2014) (benefitslink.com)]

Coverage under a fiduciary liability policy is triggered when the claim is made, not when the alleged wrongdoing occurred. While the fiduciary liability policy is in force, it will cover claims reported during the policy period. But if a policy is cancelled or is not renewed, then future claims will not be covered even if they relate to acts that occurred before cancellation or nonrenewal. Extended reporting period (ERP) coverage is optional: in exchange for an additional premium, ERP coverage applies to claims filed during a specified period (usually 12 months post-policy expiration) relating to events while the policy was in force.

Standard ERP coverage will not provide complete protection in a merger or plan termination situation, because there is a possibility that fiduciary breaches will be alleged until the statute of limitations (which could be as long as six years) has elapsed since the merger or termination.

"Tail coverage" protects the trustees of merged or terminated plans. Insurers do not have to provide tail coverage under a basic policy; the purchaser must negotiate the terms of coverage and the premium. Insurers are often reluctant to offer as much coverage as the trustees want. It is wise to include a provision forbidding cancellation of the policy after the premium has been paid. According to Segal Select Insurance, the premium for a six-year tail policy is likely to be two or three times the premium for the underlying fiduciary liability insurance when the plan was in operation. Tail coverage is usually paid from the assets of the plan that is being merged or is terminating, so it is important to arrange and pay for the coverage before the plan assets have all been distributed.

Instead of tail coverage, the successor plan might obtain a "merged-plan" endorsement, but the merged plan must continue to renew the coverage every year until the statute of limitations has expired, and the insurer may change the available coverage and liability limits. [Segal Select Insurance Fiduciary Shield, *If a Plan Merger or Termination Is on the Horizon, Seek Tail Coverage* (March 2014) (benefitslink.com)]

§ 15.14 INDEMNIFICATION

ERISA § 410 says that language in a plan, or in a side agreement with a fiduciary, is void as against public policy if it limits the fiduciary's liability for breach of fiduciary duty. However, the employer (as distinct from the plan) can permissibly indemnify the fiduciary or buy insurance covering the fiduciary. The fiduciary can also buy his or her own insurance coverage. [See § 43.08 for more discussion of fiduciary liability insurance] The sponsor corporation can also agree to use corporate assets to indemnify the fiduciary. This is allowed by the Department of Labor, and it is not considered a prohibited transaction.

§ 15.15 PROHIBITED TRANSACTIONS

[A] Generally

Objectivity is one of the most important fiduciary characteristics. ERISA bans certain types of transactions between a plan and parties who might lose objectivity because of those transactions. "Parties in interest" and "disqualified persons" are blocked from certain categories of transactions, even if a particular transaction is fair.

Title I of ERISA makes any one of these a prohibited transaction if it occurs between the plan and a party in interest:

- Sale, exchange, or lease of property, including the plan's assumption of a mortgage, or a mortgage placed on the property by a party in interest during the 10 years before the transfer of the property to the plan;
- Extensions of credit;
- Furnishing goods or services;
- Transfers or uses of plan assets for the benefit of a party in interest;
- Acquisition or holding of employer securities that are not qualified, or in excess of the normal limit (usually 10% of the fair market value of the plan assets);
- Use of plan income or assets by a fiduciary in her or her personal interest or for his or her own account;
- Payments to a fiduciary for his or her own account, made by anyone who deals with the plan;
- Conflict of interest: the fiduciary acts on behalf of a party, or representing a party, in any transaction representing the plan—if the interests of the party the fiduciary represents are adverse to the interests of the plan or of its participants and beneficiaries.

[B] Parties in Interest

ERISA § 3(14) defines "party in interest" (PII) very broadly:

- Any fiduciary or relative of a fiduciary;
- Plan employees or persons who provide counsel to the plan—or their relatives;
- The plan's service providers and their relatives;
- Any employer or employee organization (e.g., union) whose members are covered by the plan;
- Anyone who owns 50% or more of the employer corporation, whether ownership is direct or indirect; relatives of the 50% owner;
- A corporation, partnership, trust, or estate that is 50% or more controlled by anyone in one of the categories above (unless they are involved only as relatives of a person involved with the plan);
- Employees, officers, and directors of organizations in the list (or anyone with similar powers and responsibilities without the formal title);
- Employees, officers, and directors (or those with similar rights and duties) of organizations in the list;
- Employees, officers, and directors of the plan;

- Anyone who has a direct or indirect 10% share ownership in the plan or an organization closely related to the plan;
- Anyone with a direct or indirect 10% interest in the capital or profits of a partnership or joint venture with anyone on the list.

Any participant, beneficiary, or plan fiduciary can bring suit for "appropriate equitable relief" under ERISA § 406 when an individual or business that is a "party in interest" (e.g., the employees and service providers of the plan) enters into a prohibited transaction—even if this individual or business is not an ERISA fiduciary. [*Harris Trust & Savings Bank v. Salomon Smith Barney*, 530 U.S. 238 (2000)] Therefore, the party in interest can be enjoined by a court, or required to make restitution to the plan, if the prohibited transaction results in financial losses to the plan.

A disqualified person who engages in a prohibited transaction can be required to pay an excise tax, even if he or she didn't know the transaction was prohibited. The excise tax is 15% of the amount involved per year. An additional tax of 100% of the amount involved is imposed when the IRS notifies the disqualified person that the transaction is prohibited, but the transaction is not rescinded within 90 days of receipt of the notice. The excise tax is payable to the IRS. In addition, the Department of Labor can impose a civil penalty that is more or less equivalent to the excise tax if a plan that is not qualified under Title I engages in a prohibited transaction.

The rules for welfare benefit plans are slightly different: The excise tax, under ERISA § 502(i) and I.R.C. § 4975(f)(5), is 5% of the amount of the prohibited transaction, and this amount is cumulated if the prohibited transaction continues over several years. There is a 100% excise tax for failure to correct a prohibited transaction after receipt of notice from the IRS.

[C] Prohibited Transaction Exemptions

Because the prohibited transaction rules are so broad, the DOL has the power to grant "Prohibited Transaction Exemptions" (PTEs) for technically improper transactions that in fact are advantageous to the plan and benefit the plan's participants.

Exemptions fall into two main categories: the specific exemptions set out in ERISA § 408, and those granted by DOL and the Treasury based on a determination that the proposed exemption is administratively feasible; serves the best interests of participants and beneficiaries; and protects the rights of participants and beneficiaries.

To get an individual exemption, a plan must apply to the relevant agency or agencies, and also give notice to affected parties and publish a notice in the Federal Register, so affected parties can submit comments. Affected parties can place their comments (positive or negative) on the record. In some cases, a hearing will be required before the exemption is granted (e.g., when a fiduciary seeks permission to deal with the plan for his own account or to represent an adverse party).

ERISA includes statutory exemptions for loans to PIIs who are also plan participants or beneficiaries, as long as the loans are made on fair terms; for payment of reasonable compensation to PIIs for services they provide to the plan, rental of real estate to the plan at reasonable rates, and other deals that are the equivalent of arm's length transactions. There is also a statutory exemption for investing more than 10% of the plan's assets in qualifying employer securities and real property, as long as the plan purchases these items at a reasonable price and does not have to pay a commission to acquire them from the employer. Depending on the type of security, the plan will not be permitted to hold more than 25% to 50% of the entire issue.

"Class exemptions" have also been adopted for frequent transactions that are not harmful to the plan or its participants. Class exemptions have been granted, for instances, in connection with interest-free loans; mortgage loans to PIIs; and hiring PIIs to provide investment advice to the plan.

The Pension Protection Act of 2006 (Pub. L. No. 109-280) grants a Prohibited Transaction Exemption when fiduciaries provide investment advice to 401(k) plan participants after December 31, 2006—as long as the investment advice relies on an independently verified computer model, or the advisor's compensation is not dependent on the investments that the adviser suggests. However, the PPA doubles the size of the bond that fiduciaries must provide if the plan holds employer securities: under previous law, $500,000 was required, and now $1 million is required. (The legislative intent was to improve retirement security by enhancing savings rates and participation rates in 401(k) plans by making it easier to have a 401(k) plan.)

EBSA final regulations explain the PTE for fiduciaries who provide investment advice to plan participants, and who receive fees from the provider of the investment (e.g., a mutual fund). The exemption is limited to investment advice that is given by means of an unbiased computer model, or by an adviser who receives level fees that do not vary based on the selection of investments. The fees must be disclosed, and advisers receiving exemptions are subject to annual compliance audits. [76 Fed. Reg. 66637 (Oct. 27, 2011)]

§ 15.16 PAYMENT OF PLAN EXPENSES

One of the EBSA's top enforcement priorities is to make plan sponsors reimburse plans for expenses that were paid out of plan assets but should have been paid by the sponsors themselves. The DOL said that its regional offices would be conducting more plan expense audits than before. If a violation is found, not only must the employer reimburse the plan, but anyone involved in the transaction is subject to a 20% penalty. The Department of Labor can refer the case to the IRS for collection of the excise tax on prohibited transactions.

"Settlor functions" (decisions about establishing a plan or about plan design) are discretionary and not subject to the ERISA fiduciary requirements. Therefore, the expenses of performing settlor functions are not expenses of plan administration, and it is improper to use plan assets to pay them.

Plan-wide basic administrative services can be paid from the assets of an ERISA plan, because they are fiduciary rather than settlor expenses. For example, the plan can pay for record-keeping, accounting, legal services dealing with fiduciary issues, trustee services, custodial services, annual or other periodic compliance audits, completion of legally mandated forms such as Form 5500, processing claims, and communicating with participants. Expenses for investment advice, educational seminars, and providing electronic access to plan information can also be paid out of plan assets. So can management fees and sales charges for plan investments.

However, settlor expenses that cannot be paid out of plan assets include, e.g., legal services for setting up a plan; costs of plan design; legal fees for plan termination; and most actuarial services used for planning.

Certain expenses related to fiduciary implementation of the settlor's decisions can be paid from plan assets: drafting legally required plan amendments, such as those required to maintain qualified status; nondiscrimination testing; applying for IRS determination letters; liability insurance covering plan fiduciaries; PBGC premiums (except for years when the plan is involved in distress or involuntary termination); fiduciary bonding. Sanctions and penalties can be paid out of plan assets if they were imposed on the plan—but not if they were imposed on a plan administrator in his personal capacity. Sanctions for late payment of PBGC premiums can be paid from plan assets (as long as the plan is not involved in a distress or involuntary termination)—but correction costs under the Voluntary Fiduciary Correction Program cannot be. [Andree M. St. Martin and Jennifer E. Eller, *Paying Employee Benefit Plan Expenses Chart*, Practical Law Co. (undated, accessed Mar. 27, 2014) (benefitslink.com) (a chart giving the source for the treatment of various items)]

§ 15.17 SERVICE PROVIDERS

Part of the fiduciary's duty of prudence is intelligent and informed selection of service providers for the plan, followed by monitoring of the job that the service providers do. Although it is understandable that fiduciaries will think first of their friends, colleagues, or relatives in selecting a service provider, the baseline is that they must deal only with people who have at least the minimum qualifications and experience to do the tasks they are hired for. A thorough reference check should be performed.

Compensation must be at least reasonably comparable to market rates for the same work. Selection by competitive bidding is helpful. Before retaining a service provider, it is vital to determine whether the fee that is quoted covers all the necessary services, or whether it is possible or likely that additional fees will be incurred, based on the predicted activities of the plan. The fiduciary doesn't always have to select the low bidder, but must be able to justify the selection as providing the best value on balance.

The Eighth Circuit upheld an award of $14.3 million against a 401(k) plan sponsor for breaching the fiduciary duty to control the costs of recordkeeping. The plaintiffs alleged that the sponsor breached its fiduciary duty by failing to monitor costs; paying above-market costs; and choosing investments that were more expensive than comparable investments. The Eighth Circuit found that it was acceptable to pay for recordkeeping through revenue sharing and bundled service agreements—but the fiduciaries failed to investigate adequately before incurring the costs. However, the Eighth Circuit remanded a separate award of $21.8 million in alleged financial losses that were calculated by comparing the investment results of one of the plan's investments in a mutual fund to the returns of a different mutual fund; the Eighth Circuit held that the hindsight calculation was too speculative. The Eighth Circuit also reversed $1.7 million against Fidelity; the district court found that Fidelity breached its fiduciary duty when it failed to pay "float" income (interest earned before plan assets were transferred from one account to another) to the 401(k) plan. The Eighth Circuit held that these amounts did not constitute plan assets. As a result, Fidelity could not be liable for attorneys' fees or costs in the litigation. [*Tussey et al. v. ABB*, 746 F.3d 327 (8th Cir. 2014); see Goodwin Proctor ERISA Litigation Update, *In Tussey, Eighth Circuit Weighs in On Excessive Fee Claims* (Mar. 20, 2014) (benefitslink.com) Both sides moved for rehearing en banc, but the Eighth Circuit denied both motions on May 20, 2014, without writing an opinion. Both sides were expected to appeal to the Supreme Court. See Thomas E. Clark, *8th Circuit Denies Both Rehearing Pensions in Tussey v. ABB—Next Up is the Supreme Court*, Fiduciary Matters blog (May 22, 2014) (benefitslink.com)]

Seventy thousand individual employees and ex-participants in the International Paper 401(k) plan reached a $30 million settlement with the company in a case about excessive fees and inappropriate investments. This was believed to be the second-highest payment in a fee dispute. (The largest required Cigna Corp. to pay $35 million for naming itself as plan administrator and offering imprudent investment alternatives.) The International Paper plaintiffs alleged excessive retention of employer stock in the plan; fraudulent reporting of performance history for the funds in the plan; and improper delays in the employer's submission of contributions to the plan. [Kelly Greene, *International Paper Pays $30 Million Over 401(k) Claims*, WSJ.com (Oct. 1, 2013)]

The DOL published a final rule February 3, 2012 about the disclosures a plan's service providers must give the fiduciaries, to show that providers' compensation paid out of plan assets does not exceed what is reasonable. For this purpose, providers include registered investment advisors, certain broker-dealers, TPAs, and others receiving $1,000 or more in direct or indirect compensation from plan assets. The final rules extend the deadline three months, making the compliance date July 1, 2012 rather than April 1, 2012, but the rules say this is probably the last extension.

No form is prescribed for the disclosures (known as the "408(b)(2) notice"), although they must be in writing. Failure to comply with these requirements is a prohibited transaction for the fiduciary, whereas compliance entitles the fiduciary to a prohibited transaction exemption.

If the provider fails to respond to the fiduciary's request for information relating to future services within 90 days, the final rule requires the fiduciary to terminate the service arrangement as fast as it can. The final rule also permits providers to furnish a reasonable, good-faith estimate of compensation or costs that are difficult to itemize—as long as they disclose their calculation method. Disclosures of indirect compensation from third parties to service providers must also disclose the calculation method. [DOL Final Rule, 77 Fed. Reg. 5632 (Feb. 3, 2012); see § 6.07[B] for further discussion of fee disclosure.]

An Notice of Proposed Rulemaking was published in the Federal Register for March 12, 2014, proposing to require a guide to be provided to disclosures by covered service providers that appear in multiple or lengthy documents. The guide assists plan fiduciaries in locating specific items of information that relate to their contracts with the service provider—e.g., the services that will be provided, if the provider has fiduciary status, how much the service provider will be paid, plus required investment disclosures for fiduciary, brokerage, and recordkeeping services (e.g., total annual operating expenses). [FR Doc 2014-04868, 79 Fed. Reg. 13949 (Mar. 12, 2014); see DOL Fact Sheet, *Proposed Regulation to Require a Guide to Assist Plan Fiduciaries in Reviewing 408(b)(2) Disclosures* (March 2014), <http://www.dol.gov/ebsa/newsroom/fs408(b)(2)disclosures.html>]

A mid-2012 final rule revises the procedure for mailing or e-filing certain notices with DOL under the ERISA § 408(b)(2) rules for fiduciary-level fee disclosure. Fiduciaries must file these notices to get prohibited transaction relief. Relief is available if, when fiduciaries find out that there has been a discovery failure, they make a written request for the missing information to the service provider. If the service provider does not comply within 90 days, the fiduciary must notify the DOL, either mailing a written notice to DOL, EBSA Office of Enforcement, P.O. Box 75296, Washington, D.C. 20013, or using the link at <www.dol.gov/ebsa/regs/feedisclosurefailurenotice.html>. The advantage of using the Website is that it provides immediate electronic confirmation that notice is received. [Final Rule, DOL EBSA, *Amendment Relating to Reasonable Contract or Arrangement Under Section 408(b)(2)—Fee Disclosure*, 77 Fed. Reg. 41678 (July 16, 2012)]

Fiduciaries must assess the potential risk of loss, and the cost to the plan, if the service provider causes loss to the plan and is indemnified. Furthermore, indemnification or waiver of liability that relates to willful misconduct or fraud is void as against public policy, and it is neither prudent nor reasonable for fiduciaries to agree to such provisions.

ERISA and IRS rules forbid fiduciaries to deal with plan assets in their own interest. Unless a PTE is available, they cannot provide investment advice to participants if the advice increases the fees of the fiduciaries or their affiliates. The PPA created a PTE for advisers who give advice for a fee under an eligible arrangement—one that either has fees that are not affected by the specific advice given, or that are based on a certified, objective computer model. The DOL issued final rules about this PTE on October 24, 2011, effective December 27, 2011. These rules are also referred to as § 408(g) regulations. The DOL's fact sheet on the regulations estimates that 16,000 investment advisory firms will be subject to the exemption, and will offer investment advice to plans with about 17 million participants and beneficiaries, some 3.5 million of whom will access the advice.

The fiduciaries subject to the rule include banks; insurance companies; broker-dealers; registered investment advisers; and their affiliates, employees, representatives, and agents. A party that develops or markets computer programs for financial advice is also deemed to be a fiduciary adviser. The investment advice arrangement must be authorized by a plan fiduciary who is objective, and the fiduciary advisor must obtain an independent audit each year. Arrangements permitted under earlier guidance can still be used.

The final rule says that a fee-leveling arrangement must:

- be based on generally accepted investment theories that consider historic returns of different asset classes over a defined period of time;
- consider the fees and expenses of the recommended investments;
- reflect the adviser's knowledge of the participant or beneficiary's needs—such as age, life expectancy, distance from retirement age, other assets and income sources, and investment preferences; and
- not base the adviser's fees or compensation on the investment options chosen by the participant (although in some circumstances, compensation or bonuses based on the organization's overall profitability will be permitted).

Computer models must employ generally accepted investment theories that consider fees and expenses and historic risks and returns. [76 Fed. Reg. 66637 (Oct. 27, 2011)]

[A] Fees

Nature proverbially abhors a vacuum, and given the general lack of success with stock-drop suits, unhappy plan participants have sought other causes of action. In recent years, they have often alleged that the value of their accounts was impaired by payment of excessive fees.

February 2009 saw the first significant ruling in the wave of ERISA litigation challenging excessive fees. The Seventh Circuit affirmed the dismissal of all claims in *Hecker v. Deere & Co.*, rejecting the plaintiff's theories about excessive fees and improper revenue sharing. In 2006, before the DOL proposals requiring disclosure, fiduciaries had no duty to inform participants about revenue sharing between service providers. As long as a plan offered a sufficient mix of investment options with different fees, it was not a breach of duty to choose one with fees that could be characterized as "excessive"—or to offer multiple choices, some of which might be imprudent. It was also permissible to select all funds from a single management company. The Seventh Circuit treated the DOL safe harbor as an affirmative defense. Certiorari was denied in early 2010 [*Hecker v. Deere & Co.*, 556 F.3d 575 (7th Cir. 2009), *cert. denied*, 130 S. Ct. 1141 (Jan. 19, 2010); see Steve Saxon, Saxon Angle: *Seventh Sojourn*, plansponsor.com (May 2009); Fred Reish and Bruce Ashton, *The New Take on 404(c): Confusion in the Federal Courts* (May 13, 2009) (benefitslink.com).

In mid-2013, the *Nolte v. CIGNA* case settled for $35 million. The case was filed by participants in the Cigna employees' 401(k) plan. The plaintiffs charged that the plan was not operated for the exclusive benefit of participants, but as a profit center for CIGNA, which charged unreasonable fees, did not require competitive bids for plan services, and engaged in prohibited transactions. The retirement division was sold to Prudential Financial in 2004 but plan participants did not share in the profits. The plaintiffs alleged that when Prudential took over the plan, Prudential also derived unreasonable and prohibited fees from the plan. [FRA PlanTools, *Breaking-Cigna and Prudential Settle Excessive Fee Lawsuit for $35 Million* (June 21, 2013) (benefitslink.com)]

In April 2013, the Seventh Circuit upheld American United Life Insurance's revenue-sharing practices in a suit brought by the trustee of a profit-sharing plan to which American United provided recordkeeping and administrative services. The trustee alleged that it was a breach of fiduciary duty for American United to receive revenue sharing payments from mutual fund providers that were not disclosed to clients. The plaintiff (and the Department of Labor) said that American United was a functional fiduciary under ERISA § 3(21)(A)(i) because of its authority to choose the mutual funds in which plan assets were invested. But the Seventh Circuit disagreed, holding that choice of mutual funds does not make a party a fiduciary; it would only be a fiduciary if the claim involved the way assets were handled, not revenue sharing. Certiorari was denied February 24, 2014. [*Leimkuehler v. American United Life Ins. Co.*, 713 F.3d 905 (7th Cir. 2013), *cert. denied*, 134 S. Ct. 1280 (2014); see Bloomberg BNA Pensions & Benefits Daily, *High Court Won't Consider Fiduciary Status Of Profit-Sharing Plan Record-Keeper* (Feb. 24, 2014) (benefitslink.com)]

The plaintiffs alleged that Harris Associates LP charged twice as much for managing a fund family as it charged its independent clients for similar investment services. Harris said that its fees were at or only slightly above the median for comparable mutual funds. In 2010, the U.S. Supreme Court adopted the standard used by most federal courts, and held that the correct legal standard in an excessive fund fee case was whether the fees were so disproportionately large that they could not have been the product of arm's length bargaining. The case was remanded to the Seventh Circuit for reconsideration of its ruling that mutual fund managers can only be held liable if the allegedly excessive fees are fraudulent. [*Jones v. Harris*, 559 U.S. 335 (2010); see Fred Schneyer, *High Court Sides with Investors in Fee Case*, plansponsor.com (Mar. 30, 2010]

The Supreme Court vacated an Eighth Circuit decision about whether mutual fund fees violated § 36(b) of the Investment Company Act. The Eighth Circuit had relied on the marketplace to prevent excessively high fees from being imposed. However, the U.S. Supreme Court remanded the case to comply with *Jones v. Harris*, where the standard is whether a fee is so unreasonably large that obviously there was no arm's length bargaining between the fund and its clients. [*Ameriprise Fin. Inc. v. Gallus*, 130 S. Ct. 2340 (2010)] The Eighth Circuit considered the case twice on remand, in March 2011 and April 2012. The 2012 decision held that the plaintiffs did not prove that the fees were so disproportionately large that they could not have been bargained for and could not be reasonable for the services rendered. [*Gallus v. Ameriprise,* 675 F.3d 1173 (8th Cir. 2012)]

The Seventh Circuit ruled in late 2011 that it is lawful for plan administrators to offer only retail mutual funds as investments, concluding that market competition will keep the fees down to a reasonable level. Exelon's defined contribution plan had 32 investment options, 24 of them retail mutual funds (all no-load, with expense ratios in the range of 0.03%–0.96%). The plaintiffs' theory was that it violated ERISA to require plan participants to pay the same fees as the general public. They also alleged that the plan should have offered institutional-class funds. The Seventh Circuit held that fiduciaries do not have to find the least-expensive funds; their duty is to offer a range of funds. Furthermore, retail funds have greater liquidity than institutional funds, and retail funds do not necessarily charge higher fees. The Seventh Circuit found that ERISA does not impose a duty to make the plan more valuable to participants; it is legitimate for the employer to act in its own interests when deciding how much to contribute. [*Loomis v. Exelon,* 658 F.3d 667 (7th Cir. 2011)]

Since 2006, there have been numerous lawsuits about 401(k) plan fees, but no clear trend has emerged. These suits usually allege that a plan paid excessive fees, as a result of practices such as sharing fees with service providers, stocking the plan with actively managed funds instead of lower-fee index funds, and investing in more expensive share classes. The Ninth Circuit held that the six-year statute of limitations began when the decision was made to include the allegedly improper investment in the plan. Although fiduciaries have an ongoing duty to be prudent, the statute of limitations is six years rather than the three years under the "actual knowledge" standard. The *Moench* presumption was applied.

The Ninth Circuit held that fiduciaries can be liable based on selecting the plan's investment option; the § 404(c) safe harbor does not apply to designating investment options. Revenue sharing is not a prohibited transaction, because a PTE is available. It is not per se imprudent to include retail funds in the portfolio (rather than institutional funds only), and the portfolio can also include short-term funds. However, it was imprudent to include three particular retail funds because the plan failed to consider the differences between the retail funds and their institutional counterparts. Even though they used a consultant, the fiduciaries still had an obligation to consider all the available share classes for the fund. [*Tibble v. Edison*, No. 711 F.3d 1061 (9th Cir. 2013); see Scott J. Stitt, *An Overview of the Tibble v. Edison Decision From the Ninth Circuit Concerning the Fees Charged to Participants in a 401(k) Plan*, James E. Arnold & Associates, LPA arnlaw.com (Mar. 24, 2013) (law.com) The Ninth Circuit denied rehearing in August 2013, amending the opinion but reaffirming the principle that the six-year statute of limitations applies. The amended opinion noted that there are circumstances in which plan administrators will not be entitled to deference, such as failure to look out for the best interests of plan participants, but did not find such circumstances present. [729 F.3d 1110 (9th Cir. 2013); see Thomas E. Clark Jr., *Breaking: 9th Circuit Amends Tibble v. Edison Opinion on Rehearing*, FRA Plan Tools (Aug. 2, 2013) (benefitslink.com)]

The Fourth Circuit held that plaintiffs did not have standing to sue the Bank of America for investing defined benefit plan assets in funds affiliated with the bank. The plaintiffs did not allege any injury in fact because they did not say that they were deprived or benefits or likely to be deprived of them in the future. The Fourth Circuit has read Supreme Court precedents to mean that defined benefit plan participants only have an interest in their own future payments, not the fund's assets. The Supreme Court has not decided whether the possibility that a plan will terminate while it is underfunded and when the PBGC will not pay full benefits constitutes injury in fact, and the Fourth Circuit was unwilling to rule on that issue in this case. The Fourth Circuit also dismissed similar claims about the 401(k) plan. The plaintiffs alleged that each time the plan committee met and failed to remove the funds that were affiliated with the bank was a new fiduciary breach. However, the Fourth Circuit found that this claim was time-barred, because the statute of limitations was six years from the initial selection of the funds in 1999; the suit was not brought until 2006. [*David v. Alphin*, 704 F.3d 327 (4th Cir. 2013); see Plansponsor staff, *Bank of America Wins Suit Over Affiliated Fund Use*, plansponsor.com (Jan. 22, 2013)]

The Third Circuit, joining the Seventh and Eighth Circuits, allowed the district court to dismiss an ERISA breach of fiduciary duty claim premised on including funds in the 401(k) plan that had excessive fee profiles—as long as the fiduciary selected a sufficiently broad range of funds with varying fee characteristics. In this case, the plaintiffs said that including retail mutual funds in the plan breached fiduciary duty because the fees were excessive. However, the Unisys 401(k) plan had 73 different investment options, including 67 individual retail mutual funds of varying characteristics, so the Third Circuit found that there was an appropriate range of options. The Third Circuit held that Fidelity was not a fiduciary for the purpose of selecting plan options; it was merely a directed trustee that could not control the investment options. Although the plan sponsor asserted the § 404(c) safe harbor, the Third Circuit refused to rule on this issue because it had already decided that the complaint was properly dismissed. [*Renfro v. Unisys Corp.*, 671 F.3d 314 (3d Cir. 2011); see Richard Black, *The Latest Word on 401(k) Fee Litigation: Third Circuit Narrows Plaintiffs' Ability to Bring ERISA Breach of Fiduciary Duty Claims*, Littler Mendelson ASAP (August 2011) (benefitslink .com); Rebecca Moore, *Court Upholds Decision for Fidelity Unisys in Excessive Fee Case*, plansponsor.com (Sept. 9, 2011)]

The Eighth Circuit ruled that a participant in an overfunded defined benefit plan did not have standing to sue the plan for fiduciary breach. The plaintiff said that the plan engaged in prohibited transactions when it invested in funds offered by its subsidiaries and affiliates, resulting in abnormally high fees. The plan was always overfunded, and paid all the benefits owed to participants. The existence of the surplus meant that the plan's investment loss did not cause actual injury to the plaintiff's interest in the plan. The court said that a contrary ruling would allow participants to sue on behalf of the plan when they had not experienced injuries. [*McCullough v. Aegon*, 585 F.3d 1082 (8th Cir. 2009); *Court Says Participant in Overfunded DB Plan Has No Standing*, plansponsor.com (Nov. 4, 2009). See *Harley v. Minnesota Mining & Mfg. Co.*, 248 F.3d 901 (8th Cir. 2002)]

After summary judgment was granted for the defendant in an excessive fee class action about a 401(k) plan, the Seventh Circuit reversed in part, on the issue of whether it was prudent to maintain the company stock fund as a unitized fund with no trading limits. The Seventh Circuit also reversed summary judgment for the defendants on the issue of whether it was prudent to pay $43–$65 per participant per year for recordkeeping services, when the plan had not solicited bids for these services since 1995. Relying on an expert can be evidence of prudence, but is not enough, taken by itself, to establish prudence. The company apparently did not take its expert's advice that fees should drop as the size of the plan increased. [*George v. Kraft Foods Global, Inc.*, 641 F.3d 786 (7th Cir. 2011) The suit was settled for $9.5 million in 2012: No. 1:08-cv-3799, 2012 U.S. Dist. LEXIS 26536 (N.D. Ill. Feb. 29, 2012); see Rebecca Moore, *Settlement Entered in Kraft Excessive Fees Case*, plansponsor.com (Mar. 7, 2012)]

§ 15.18 ERISA LITIGATION

[A] Generally

The provisions of ERISA are enforced both by the federal government and by private litigation.

In ERISA litigation, as in many other types of cases involving plans, the basic questions include who can be sued, who is a proper plaintiff (especially in the class action context), the proper court for the case, when the suit must be filed to be timely, and what remedies can be ordered if the case is proved.

Jury trials are usually unavailable in ERISA § 502(a)(1)(B) and (a)(3) cases. Another possibility is that a jury will be empanelled in these cases, but it will only determine the part of the case relating to breach of contract. The judge in the case will decide claims of breach of fiduciary duty. However, *Knudson* treated the payment of a sum of money as a legal rather than an equitable remedy. *Cigna v. Amara* has been followed by cases such as *Smith v. State Farm Group Long Term Disability Plan*, No. 12 C 9210, 2013 U.S. Dist. LEXIS 121572 (N.D. Ill. Aug. 27, 2013), denying jury trial. The Eastern District of Missouri did permit jury trial, but it is an outlier. [*Hellmann v. Cataldo*, No. 12-cv-02177-AGF, 2013 U.S. Dist. LEXIS 117676 (E.D. Mo. Aug. 20, 2013); see Ada W. Dolph and Justin T. Curley, *The Jury Is In: No Jury Trials In ERISA Cases*, Seyfarth Shaw LLP (Dec. 10, 2013), available at Lexology.com]

By and large, ERISA cases are treated like contract cases. Therefore, the damages available to a winning plaintiff basically put the plaintiff in the position he or she would have been in if the contract had been complied with. "Extracontractual" damages (like damages for negligent or intentional infliction of emotional distress) will probably not be available. In most ERISA cases, punitive damages are also ruled out.

Most courts continue to apply ERISA if a claims administrator incorrectly tells a claimant that the plan is not covered by ERISA; in a late 2013 California case, for example, plaintiff Hill claimed LTD benefits. The claim summary and legal referral form incorrectly described the group and claim as exempt from ERISA. The plaintiff argued that, therefore, the disability policy was not an ERISA plan. The district court applied ERISA because employee statements cannot change the status of a plan. There was no evidence that the plaintiff even knew about the claim summary or referral form, much less relied on them. The district court found a triable issue of fact as to whether the disability policy was subject to ERISA. [*Hill v. Lincoln National Life Ins.*, No. C-13-00276-EDL, 2013 WL 5863007 (N.D. Cal. Oct. 30, 2013); see D. Michael Reilly, *ERISA: Incorrect Statements During Claims Process Do Not Render ERISA Inapplicable*, Lane Powell PC (Nov. 25, 2013), available at Lexology.com]

In any ERISA action brought by participants, beneficiaries, or fiduciaries, the winning side (whether plaintiff or defendant) can be awarded reasonable costs and attorneys' fees if the court thinks this is appropriate. Usually the attorneys' fee award starts out with the "lodestar" figure. This is the number of hours the winning lawyer spent on the case, multiplied by an hourly rate the court considers reasonable. In rare cases, the lodestar is reduced: if the court thinks the lawyer wasted time, for instance. Sometimes the fee award is greater than the lodestar amount, if the case was especially difficult, the lawyer broke new ground with innovative legal theories, or took on an unpopular case.

Thanks to a 2010 Supreme Court decision, § 502(g)(1) plaintiffs do not have to be the "prevailing party" to be awarded attorneys' fees, because that section (unlike § 502(g)(2)) gives the district court discretion to award attorneys' fees to either side. [*Hardt v. Reliance Ins. Co.*, 560 U.S. 242 (2010); see Workplace Prof Blog, *ERISA Supreme Court Attorney Fees Case Goes Way of Plaintiffs* (May 24, 2010) (benefitslink.com)] But that ruling left questions open, such as whether remand of a benefits decision to the administrator is enough (because it gives the claimant the possibility of receiving additional benefits), or whether a court finding of ERISA violation is required. The "prevailing party" analysis has been replaced by a more fact-intensive consideration of success on the merits—so defendants may have to pay the plaintiff's fees even if the case is settled or withdrawn. [See Renee DeMoss, *Attorney Fee Awards Under ERISA: How Much Success Is Enough?* GableGotwals Insurance Law Update (Sept. 19, 2011) (benefits link.com)]

As Chapter 40 shows, arbitration assumes an increasingly large role in the resolution of disputes within the U.S. legal system. The Ninth Circuit ruled that the arbitration clause in an investment management agreement between an employer and its investment advisor did not obligate a plan participant to arbitrate fiduciary breach claims. There was no proof that the participant knowingly exploited the agreement that included the arbitration clause. There was no evidence that the agreement, which was not signed by the plan participants, was intended to affect their rights to sue. [*Comer v. Micor Inc.*, 436 F.3d 1098 (9th Cir. 2006)]

A late 2013 article predicts that ERISA class actions may disappear within two decades or so. Although class action lawyers typically receive 20–40% of a common fund recovery, attorneys' fees for individual ERISA fiduciary breach claims are subject to judicial review and are usually based on lodestar factors so they can be much lower. Many employers have arbitration agreements requiring arbitration of ERISA claims; the ERISA statute does not forbid mandatory arbitration (neither does the FLSA) and courts are starting to consider the enforceability of ERISA class action waivers: e.g., *Sutherland v. Ernst & Young LLP*, 726 F.3d 290 (2d Cir. 2013); *Owen v. Bristol Care, Inc.*, 702 F.3d 1050 (8th Cir. 2013); *Quilloin v. Tenet Health System Phila., Inc.*, 673 F.3d 221 (3d Cir. 2012); *Tenet Healthsystem Phila., Inc. v. Rooney*, civil action no. 12-mc-58, 2012 U.S. Dist. LEXIS 116280 (E.D. Pa. Aug. 14, 2012); *Luchini v. Carmax, Inc.*, case no. CV F 12-0417 LJO DLB, 2012 U.S. Dist. LEXIS 102198 (E.D. Cal. July 23, 2012). However, DOL regulations impose certain conditions on enforceable arbitration clauses (see 29 C.F.R. § 2560.503-1): benefit claimants must not be required to pay arbitration costs, and mandatory arbitration clauses cannot prevent claimants from appealing the arbitrator's decision in court.

■ **TIP**: The AAA has a new procedure for recruiting former judges to serve on arbitration appeals panels; the new panels can hear claims that an arbitration award is based on material, prejudicial errors of law and/or fact determinations that are clearly erroneous. Resort to this appeals procedure can be added as an option for an ERISA plan. [James Baker, *A Sea Change for ERISA Litigation,* Baker & McKenzie (December 2013) (benefitslink.com)]

[B] Preemption

In many instances, cases involving benefits will have to be brought in federal rather than state courts, because of ERISA preemption. According to the Seventh Circuit [*Metro. Life Ins. Co. v. Johnson*, 297 F.3d 558 (7th Cir. 2002)], the federal doctrine of "substantial compliance" preempts state law for suits involving alleged changes in the beneficiaries of a plan. In this case, life insurance benefits went to the children of a deceased beneficiary who failed to fully comply with the plan's provisions for beneficiary designation, because the court ruled that the decedent gave proof of his intent and took steps to carry out a change of beneficiary.

In its *Aetna Health Inc. v. Davila*, and *Cigna Healthcare of Texas, Inc. v. Calad*, 542 U.S. 200 (2004), decision, the Supreme Court ruled that ERISA completely preempts HMO participants' claims that they were improperly denied health care.

In general, ERISA will preempt state laws in cases requiring interpretation of plan documents. There is an exception to preemption for "the business of insurance"—so a number of cases deal with the question of whether federal or state courts should handle certain cases in which health or other insurance is involved in a benefit plan.

The preemption issue is very significant in these emotive cases, because if the case can be heard in state court, punitive damages could be available—and a sympathetic jury could impose heavy punitive damages.

In mid-2009, the Sixth Circuit and the District Court for the District of Colorado ruled that ERISA does not preempt state laws forbidding discretionary language in insurance policies in ERISA plans, because of the savings clause (state laws that "regulate insurance" are not preempted). [*American Council of Life Insurers v. Ross*, 558 F.3d 600 (6th Cir. 2009); *McClenahan v. Metro. Life Ins. Co.*, 621 F. Supp. 2d 1135 (D. Colo. 2009); see EBIA Weekly, *ERISA Does Not Preempt State Laws Preventing Insurers From Including Discretionary Language in Insurance Policies* (May 28, 2009) (benefitslink.com)]

But preemption was held not to occur in certain instances:

- A plan brought state claims (e.g., malpractice, breach of contract, promissory estoppel) against its actuary, claiming that the actuary's wrongdoing resulted in the plan being underfunded. However, the actuary was not a fiduciary and the Second Circuit held that ERISA does not preempt state-law negligence claims against nonfiduciaries. But the court also ruled that the remedies under ERISA are the only remedies available—

the plan could not get consequential damages against the actuary. [*Gerosa v. Savasta & Co.*, 329 F.3d 317 (2d Cir. 2003)]

- Claims of malpractice, negligent misrepresentation, and breach of contract were brought by ESOP participants against an investment firm they allege undervalued that plan's stock during the process of terminating the plan. (When the company was sold after the plan was terminated, the per-share price was much higher than the price plan participants received for their ESOP shares.) Resolving the charges against the investment firm did not require interpretation of the plan, so the case could be remanded to state court. ERISA's civil enforcement provisions were not triggered because the plaintiffs did not charge fiduciary breach, nor did they seek to recover plan benefits. [*Clark v. Ameritas Inv. Corp.*, D. Neb., No. 4:05CV3251 (Dec. 27, 2005)]
- The Sixth Circuit held that claims by executives of Metaldyne corporate executives' about cancellation of their SERP plan could be tried in state court. Metaldyne was once partially owned by Heartland Industrial Partners, LP, an investment firm. In mid-2006, Heartland agreed to sell its Metaldyne stake to another investment firm. The SERP included change in control provisions under which Metaldyne would owe the plaintiffs about $13 million. The Metaldyne board canceled the SERP to avoid this obligation. The SERP participants sued in state court for tortious interference with contractual relations. The Sixth Circuit found that these claims were not preempted by ERISA because the state court would not have to interpret the SERPs, just calculate damages if the plaintiffs proved that canceling them violated state law. [*Gardner v. Heartland Industrial Partners*, 715 F.3d 609 (6th Cir. 2013); see Stephen D. Rosenberg, *Cancelling a SERP and the Limits of Preemption*, Boston ERISA Law Blog (June 25, 2013) (benefitslink.com); Stanley D. Baum, *ERISA-Sixth Circuit Holds That State-Law Claim for Tortious Interference With a Contract Is Not Completely Preempted by ERISA*, <http://www.erisalawyerblog.com/2013/05/erisa-sixth-circuit-holds-that-2.html> (May 20, 2013)]

See § 15.09[B] for discussion of developments in the treatment of subrogation and removal of cases to federal court. Also note that, for cases filed after the February 18, 2005, effective date of the Class Action Fairness Act (Pub. L. No. 109-2), the federal system may be the only appropriate venue for certain class actions brought by health plan participants.

[C] Exhaustion of Remedies

The court system is supposed to handle major conflicts, not minor everyday disputes that can and should be addressed in less complex and less socially expensive ways. Therefore, plaintiffs often have a legal duty of "exhaustion of remedies." That is, they will not be permitted to bring court cases until they have pursued all the administrative remedies within the system they are challenging. ERISA requires every plan to have a system for pursuing claims and appealing claims denials. So the general rule is that would-be plaintiffs must go through these steps before filing suit. This is not stated in so many words in ERISA itself, but judges have looked to ERISA's legislative history and other labor laws to determine when this requirement should be implied.

Plaintiffs clearly have to exhaust their remedies within the plan when their case involves benefits. Courts are split as to whether ERISA § 510 plaintiffs (interference with protected rights; see above) are required to exhaust their remedies. Exhaustion of remedies will not be required if:

- Going through channels would be futile;
- It was impossible to pursue plan remedies because the defendant wrongfully denied the plaintiff access to the plan's claims procedures;
- Irreparable harm would ensue if exhaustion of remedies was required;
- Participants and beneficiaries did not know how to enforce their rights, because they were deprived of information about claims procedures.

[D] Statute of Limitations

ERISA § 525 permits a civil action against an employer for delinquency in making contributions. This section does not contain an express statute of limitations; most courts use a six-year statute of limitations, treating the case as the equivalent of an action to enforce a written contract.

The statute of limitations for an ERISA § 409 case (breach of fiduciary duty) derives from ERISA § 413. The suit must be brought within three years of the time the plaintiff discovered the alleged wrongdoing, or six years from the date of the last breach or the last date on which the omission could have been cured—whichever is earlier.

The Third Circuit found that ERISA's six-year statute of limitations for fiduciary breaches barred claims about misrepresentations of pension benefits. The statute began to run when the allegedly misleading statements were made, not when the participants relied on the representations to their detriment. [*Ranke v. Sanofi-Synthelabo Inc.*, 436 F.3d 197 (3d Cir. 2006)]

According to the Ninth Circuit, an ERISA cause of action accrues either at the time the claim is actually denied, or when the claimant has reason to know of the denial. Therefore, a suit was untimely even though the pension plan violated its duties under ERISA to give the employee reasons for the denial and a reasonable opportunity for review. He knew that the employer was going to pay benefits below the level he expected, because of a break in service; he also had actual notice that the decision to accept a lump-sum payout would be irrevocable. [*Chuck v. Hewlett Packard Corp.*, 455 F.3d 1026 (9th Cir. 2006); see Rebecca Moore, *ERISA Claim Is Time-barred in Spite of Disclosure Violation*, plansponsor.com (Aug. 4, 2006)]

Similarly, the Sixth Circuit ruled that a suit was untimely where trustees began to worry about their financial advisor some six to seven years before bringing suit. [*Wright v. Heyne*, 349 F.3d 321 (6th Cir. 2003)] The Third and Fifth Circuits start the statute of limitations running with knowledge that the facts constitute a breach of fiduciary duty; the Sixth, Seventh, Ninth, and Eleventh Circuits use the knowledge of the underlying facts; and the Second Circuit uses a hybrid test—knowledge of all the facts necessary to constitute a claim, including expert opinions and understanding of harmful consequences.

Former employee of SunTrust Banks, Inc. brought a putative class action alleging that adding SunTrust proprietary mutual funds as plan investments for the 401(k) plan breached the fiduciary duties of loyalty and prudence. The plaintiffs charged that these funds had inferior performance and higher fees than other available funds. The defendants said the complaint was untimely. The statute of limitations for an ERISA fiduciary breach claim is the earlier of three years after the plaintiff obtained actual knowledge of the breach, or six years after the breach (date of last action that was part of the violation; or, for an omission, the last date on which the fiduciary could have cured the omission or breach). The Eleventh Circuit held that the motion to dismiss was premature, without evidence about when the plaintiff had actual knowledge. The funds had definitely been in the plan for more than six years, so the question was whether there was a continuing breach. The Eleventh Circuit found the compliant untimely because the accrual date was the date the funds were selected. [*Fuller v. SunTrust Banks, Inc.*, 744 F.3d 685 (11th Cir. 2014); see Katherine Lange, *Southeastern ERISA Watch: Eleventh Circuit Joins Fourth Circuit in Rejecting Continuing Breach Approach to ERISA's Statute of Limitation* (Mar. 11, 2014) (benefitslink.com)]

The Second Circuit held that the district court properly used New York's borrowing statute to determine limitations period for an ERISA § 502 pension benefits claim. Plan participants living in Pennsylvania said that elimination of many participants through layoffs and divestitures was a partial termination entitling them to accrued benefits. They sued in 2009 concerning benefits claims made in 2003. The suit would have been timely if it were filed in New York, where the statute of limitations would be six years, but the Pennsylvania four-year statute of limitations applied, so the suit was untimely. Because § 502(a)(1)(B) does not prescribe an explicit statute of limitations, the courts usually "borrow" the relevant state statute of limitations. The only reason not to bring this suit in Pennsylvania was that the case was untimely; the Second Circuit deterred forum shopping by applying the Pennsylvania rule. [*Muto v. CBS Corp.*,

668 F.3d 53 (2d Cir. 2012); see CCH Pensions & Benefits, *District Court Properly Applied Forum State's Borrowing Statute to Determine Limitations Period for Pension Benefits Claim* (Mar. 30, 2012) (benefitslink.com)]

Because § 510 does not include an explicit statute of limitations, the First Circuit held that the *state* statute of limitation for the most similar type of case should be applied in § 510 cases. Furthermore, the First Circuit used the state's three-year statute of limitations for personal injury cases, not the six-year statute of limitations for contract cases—so the plaintiff's suit was dismissed as time-barred. [*Muldoon v. C.J. Muldoon & Sons Inc.*, 278 F.3d 31 (1st Cir. 2002)]

According to the First, Third, Seventh, Eighth, Ninth, and District of Columbia Circuits, the six-year statute of limitations under ERISA § 413 "in case of fraud or concealment," can be applied only when both fraud and concealment are charged. The Second Circuit disagrees, allowing the six-year statute of limitations for claims of either fraud or concealment. [*Caputo v. Pfizer Inc.*, 267 F.3d 181 (2d Cir. 2001)]

In a case that did not allege separate dishonest concealment, the Sixth Circuit rejected application of a six-year statute of limitations in a suit against a plan administrator and employer whose pension calculations were allegedly inaccurate. The plaintiffs sued for breach of fiduciary duty, for accounting, restitution, and other ERISA equitable relief; fraud; negligence; and promissory estoppel. The district court found all the claims to be time-barred. The plaintiffs obtained actual knowledge of the events in 2003, so their suit would be timely under a six-year but not under a three-year statute of limitations. The plaintiffs also sued their union, but the Sixth Circuit held that the plaintiffs did not prove that the union was an ERISA fiduciary. The Sixth Circuit held that the non-ERISA claims such as fraud and negligence were preempted by ERISA. [*Cataldo v. United States Steel Corp.*, 676 F.3d 542 (6th Cir. 2012); see Sam D'Orazio, *Case Sensitive: Statute of Limitations*, plansponsor (magazine) (November 2012)]

If the source of the suit is a fiduciary's omission rather than a wrongful action, the time limit is six years from the last date the fiduciary could have cured the problem.

The Hartford Life & Accident Insurance Co. insurance policy covering Wal-Mart's group disability plan (an ERISA plan) requires suits to be filed within three years after proof of loss is due. The Supreme Court upheld the contractual three-year limitation, finding that contract limitations are enforceable if the period is reasonable and does not violate a statute. There is no ERISA statute of limitations, so contractual limitations can be imposed on ERISA plans. The limitation was upheld even though it prevented the plaintiff from bringing suit. She asserted a disability claim in August 2005, and could not sue until the administrative claims process was exhausted on November 26, 2007. The suit was brought within three years of the final claim denial but more than five years after the first assertion of the claim. The Supreme Court noted that the ERISA claims regulations usually result in claims being administered within 12–16 months, so it was not unreasonable to allow a further 20–24 months for the claimant to bring suit.

The Supreme Court noted that, in rare cases where the administrative claims process takes so long that the claimant cannot sue, equitable remedies such as tolling or waiver and estoppel might be available. [*Heimeshoff v. Hartford Life & Accident Ins. Co.*, 134 S. Ct. 604 (Dec. 16, 2013); see Scott J. Stitt, *U.S. Supreme Court Holds that a Three-Year Contractual Limitations Period for Benefit Claims is Not Unreasonable nor Contrary to ERISA*, Central Ohio Discrimination law firm (Dec. 16, 2013) (benefitslink.com)]

§ 15.19 CORRECTION PROGRAMS

[A] Plan Deficiency Aids

One of the central tenets of tax and ERISA enforcement for plans is that, wherever possible, plans should be encouraged to determine where they fall short of compliance, and to correct the problems before regulators detect them. The IRS publishes Alert Guidelines, Explanations, & Plan Deficiency Paragraphs [<http: //www.irs.gov/retirement/article/0,,id=97188,00.html>] so businesses can see the standards that IRS reviewers use when they review retirement plans for compliance. Each worksheet comes with explanatory text. The IRS Checksheets, also known as Plan Deficiency Paragraphs, are standardized text that plans can use to draft provisions that will satisfy IRS requirements.

[B] Voluntary Correction

The IRS has engaged in ongoing efforts to allow plans to correct failures without losing qualification. The Department of Labor encourages voluntary return to compliance by plan administrators.

The Employee Plans Compliance Resolution System (EPCRS) provides three levels of corrections of inadvertent errors that do not involve deliberate engagement in abusive tax strategies (e.g., inappropriate tax shelters):

- The Self-Correction Program (SCP) allows the least complex types of plans (403(b), SEPs, and SIMPLE IRAs) to correct minor operational failures. These corrections are performed purely in house, do not generate penalties, and need not involve or even be disclosed to the IRS.
- The Voluntary Correction Program (VCP) permits a plan sponsor who detects mistakes before an audit to correct those mistakes and pay a fee that is smaller than the penalties that would be imposed on deficiencies uncovered in an audit.
- The Correction on Audit Program (Audit CAP) permits correction in response to an audit, with sanctions reflecting the extent and seriousness of the deficiency.

EPCRS procedures are revised frequently. Most recently, Rev. Proc. 2013-12, 2013-6 I.R.B. 478 updates EPCRS, superseding Rev. Proc. 2008-50, revising the VCP submission procedures. There are rules for plans subject to § 436 restrictions and the safe harbor correction methods and fee structures have been changed. Under prior law, corrections for missed matching contributions had to be made as qualified non-elective contributions, which were 100% vested immediately. The new rules allow some corrective matching contributions to be made. A plan that provides elective deferrals and non-elective employer contributions can use the self-correction program if it corrects annual additions greater than permitted by § 415(c) by returning elective deferrals to the employees—but the return of elective deferrals must occur within two and a half months after the end of the plan's limitation year. There is also a limited extension of the self-correction program correction period and the 150-day VCP correction period for some plan sponsors trying to find lost participants and who can n longer rely on the IRS' letter forwarding program. Plans must submit Forms 8950 (VCP application) and 8951 (compliance fee) with their VCP submission. The IRS processes fees by converting checks to electronic funds transfers, which take less time to process. Therefore, plans writing checks for VCP fees must be sure that there are available funds to satisfy the funds transfer.

Appendix C to this Revenue Procedure contains the model VCP submission documents, which must be used as published by the IRS without modification. In addition to the Model Compliance Statement, the Revenue Procedure includes schedules dealing with, for example, SIMPLE IRAs, plan loan failures, and failure to distribute excess elective deferrals. [Rebecca Moore *IRS Updates Compliance Resolution System*, plansponsor.com (Jan. 3, 2013); SunGard Relius, *The New EPCRS, Just Released!* (Jan. 3, 2013) (benefitslink.com); McKay Hochman Company, Inc., *E-mail Alert 2013-13* (Aug. 27, 2013) (benefitslink.com)]

Rev. Proc. 2012-35, 2012-37 I.R.B. 341 states that, for requests postmarked on or after August 31, 2012, the IRS will no longer forward letters on behalf of retirement plan sponsors, administrators, or trustees of abandoned plans. The IRS changed its policy in light of the other options available to find missing participants. The change affects sponsors and administrators who want to use EPCRS to correct failures requiring payment of additional benefits, so future EPCRS guidance will give an extended correction period for those affected by the change. [Plansponsor staff, *IRS Stops Forwarding Letters for Missing Participants*, plansponsor.com (Sept. 4, 2012)]

See <http://www.dol.gov/ebsa/actuarialsearch.html> for EBSA's online tools for employees and employers. When civil penalties are due for delinquent filings of annual reports, the tools permit plan administrators to return to compliance under the Delinquent Filer Voluntary Compliance Program by filing the overdue reports.

Plan administrators can use the Delinquent Filer Voluntary Compliance Program (DFVCP) to reduce the civil penalties they may be subject to—as long as they make the required DFVCP filings before the DOL gives the administrator written notice of failure to file a timely annual report under ERISA Title I. (Form 5500-EZ filers and filers of Form 5500 for one-participant plans for business proprietors are not eligible for DFVCP because they are not covered by Title I.) An IRS late-filer penalty letter won't keep plan from participating in DFVCP, but a DOL Notice of Intent to Assess Penalty always does.

The EFAST2 FAQ explains how to file a delinquent Form 5500 under DFVCP, and the DOL has posted an online penalty calculator for DFVCP.

DFVCP penalties can be paid by check, sending the check and a paper copy of Form 5500, or Form 5500-SF, or the plan (without attachments or schedules) to DFVCP, P.O. Box 71361, Philadelphia, PA 19176-1361. The penalties can also be paid electronically at <https://www.askebsa.dol.gov/dfvcepay/calculator>.

Failure to make a timely Form 5500 filing can be penalized by both the DOL and the IRS. DOL civil penalties are up to $1,100 per day. The IRS penalties, which apply in addition to the DOL penalties, can be as high as $25/day, subject to a cap of $15,000 per return. [Thomas E. Funk et al., *IRS Issues New Relief From Form 5500 Series Late Filer Penalties For Certain Employee Benefit Plans*, Reinhart Boerner Van Deuren SC (June 16, 2014), available at Lexology .com] Plan administrators are personally liable for ERISA § 502(c) civil penalties, and the penalties cannot be paid from the assets of an employee benefit plan.

EBSA announced in early 2013 that migration to the fully electronic EFAST2 system is complete for all filing years and paper filings will no longer be accepted. See the DOL Website for an explanation of which version of the Form 5500/5500SF is required for your plan, and which schedules to use. The announcement, which primarily deals with the DFVC program, says that, although DFVC does not offer relief from late filing penalties under the Code or ERISA Title IV, the PBGC has agreed to provide some ERISA § 4071 penalty relief for delinquent filings of annual reports if the conditions of the DFVC program are satisfied. The IRS announced that it would issue separate guidance on penalty relief for Form 5500/5500-SF delinquencies where both DFVC and IRS requirements are met. [Notice: <http://www.dol.gov/find/20130128>, FAQs at <http://www.dol.gov/ebsa/faqs/faq_dfvc.html>. See Rebecca Moore, *EBSA Updates Delinquent Filer Correction Program*, plansponsor.com (Jan. 28, 2013).]

The guidance was forthcoming in mid-2014. Notice 2014-35, 2014-20 I.R.B. . . . provides that to avoid IRS penalties, even a plan that has gone through DFVC must submit a separate IRS filing. Furthermore, this requirement applies retroactively to all DFVC filings since 2009. Notice 2014-35 offers relief for years in which the plan not only satisfies the DFVC requirements, but also submits a complete Form 8955-SSA for the year within 30 days after the DFVC filing, or before December 1, 2014. Form 5500-EZ and Form 5500-SF filers cannot use this relief, but there is a separate pilot project starting June 2, 2014 and ending June 2, 2015 to grant them relief: Rev. Proc. 2014-32, 2014- . . . I.R.B. . . .]

CHAPTER 16

EFFECT OF CORPORATE TRANSITIONS ON PENSION AND BENEFIT PLANS

§ 16.01 INTRODUCTION

A qualified plan can change its form for several reasons: by amendment, by termination, or as a response to a change in form in the corporation that sponsors the plan. The sponsoring corporation can merge with or be acquired by another company, and some or all of the first plan's employees can become employees of the new or surviving corporation. The transition may be primarily motivated by corporate needs or primarily to change the form or operation of the plan (e.g., combining several existing plans for ease of administration or to cut costs).

Basic fiduciary principles continue to apply during a transition, and plans must still be maintained for the sole benefit of participants and beneficiaries. Therefore, the Supreme Court decided that plan participants and beneficiaries can sue under ERISA § 502(a)(3) to get equitable relief for themselves, when a company spun off its money-losing divisions to a new, financially unstable corporation and then lied to employees about the safety of their benefits if they transferred to the new corporation. [*Varity Corp. v. Howe*, 516 U.S. 489 (1996)]

However, because pension benefits vest but welfare benefits (including retiree health and insurance benefits) generally do not, ERISA fiduciary duty is not violated by transferring the obligation to pay nonpension retiree benefits to a new company spun off from the former employer. Nor will the courts hear an ERISA contract claim.

Code § 6058(b) requires filing of an actuarial statement at least 30 days before a merger, consolidation, or transfer of assets to another plan, even if the transfer is part of a spin-off. IRS Form 5310-A, Notice of Plan Merger or Consolidation, Spinoff, or Transfer of Plan Assets or Liabilities is filed to give notice of the combination of two or more plans into a single plan, splitting a plan into two or more spinoff plans, or a transfer of assets or liabilities to another plan. However, penalties will not be imposed for failure to file Form 5310-A in certain cases, such as when defined contribution plans are merged, but the sum of the account balances in each plan equals the fair market value of the plan assets; or two defined benefit plans are merged when the total liabilities of the smaller plan are less than 3% of the assets of the larger plan. [IRS Publication 794, *Favorable Determination Letter* (January 2013), <http://www.irs.gov/pub/irs-pdf/p794.pdf>]

The Sixth Circuit allowed claims by executives of Metaldyne about cancellation of their SERP plan to be tried in state court. Metaldyne was once partially owned by the investment firm Heartland Industrial Partners, LP. In mid-2006, Heartland agreed to sell its Metaldyne stake to another investment firm. The SERP included change in control provisions under which Metaldyne would owe the plaintiffs about $13 million. To avoid having to make these payments, Metaldyne's board terminated the SERP. The SERP participants sued in state court for tortious interference with contractual relations. The Sixth Circuit found that these claims were not preempted by ERISA because the state court would not have to interpret the SERPs, just calculate damages if the plaintiffs proved that canceling them violated state law. [*Gardner v. Heartland Indus. Partners*, 715 F.3d 609 (6th Cir. 2013); see Stephen D. Rosenberg, *Cancelling a SERP and the Limits of Preemption*, Boston ERISA Law Blog (June 25, 2013) (benefitslink.com); Stanley D. Baum, *ERISA: Sixth Circuit Holds That State-Law Claim for Tortious Interference With a Contract Is Not Completely Preempted by ERISA*, <http://www.erisalawyerblog.com/2013/05/erisa-sixth-circuit-holds-that-2.html> (May 20, 2013)]

See Chapter 43 for discussion of business-related liability insurance in general. Corporate and plan transitions can give rise to liability, with questions about who is responsible for actions at what time, so it is wise to have appropriate insurance coverage. Coverage under a fiduciary liability policy is triggered when the claim is made, not when the alleged wrongdoing occurred. While the fiduciary liability policy is in force, it will cover claims reported during the policy period. But if a policy is cancelled or is not renewed, then future claims will not be covered even if they relate to acts that occurred before cancellation or nonrenewal. Extended reporting period (ERP) coverage is optional: in exchange for an additional premium, ERP coverage applies to claims filed during a specified period (usually 12 months post-policy expiration) relating to events while the policy was in force.

Standard ERP coverage will not provide complete protection in a merger or plan termination situation, because there is a possibility that fiduciary breaches will be alleged until the statute of limitations (which could be as long as six years) has elapsed since the merger or termination.

"Tail coverage" protects the trustees of merged or terminated plans. Insurers do not have to provide tail coverage under a basic policy; the purchaser must negotiate the terms of coverage and the premium. Insurers are often reluctant to offer as much coverage as the trustees want. It is wise to include a provision forbidding cancellation of the policy after the premium has been paid. According to Segal Select Insurance, the premium for a six-year tail policy is likely to be two or three times the premium for the underlying fiduciary liability insurance when the plan was in operation. Tail coverage is usually paid from the assets of the plan that is being merged or is terminating, so it is important to arrange and pay for the coverage before the plan assets have all been distributed.

Instead of tail coverage, the successor plan might obtain a "merged-plan" endorsement, but the merged plan must continue to renew the coverage every year until the statute of limitations has expired, and the insurer may change the available coverage and liability limits. [Segal Select Insurance Fiduciary Shield, *If a Plan Merger or Termination Is on the Horizon, Seek Tail Coverage* (March 2014) (benefitslink.com)]

§ 16.02 CHOICE OF FORM

[A] Generally

Companies considering a merger or acquisition must consider the plan design options that are available for the type of transaction selected. Nondiscrimination testing will probably be required, and there will be compliance requirements for the surviving plan. The presence or absence of golden parachutes, retiree health benefit obligations, and COBRA obligations must be determined. Worker Adjustment and Retraining Notification Act (WARN) [29 U.S.C. § 2101 *et seq.*] notification may also be required if there is a significant reduction in the workforce after the corporate transition. [See § 30.10] Plan discrimination testing must also be repeated after a change of corporate organization. [See § 4.22] Changes in ownership or the form of ownership of a corporation sponsoring a plan may constitute "reportable events" of which the PBGC must be notified (in case the plan is unable to meet its payment obligations and the PBGC has to take over). The test of whether two companies are alter egos (and therefore one must make up for the other's delinquent contributions to a pension plan) comes from basic corporate law. Does one company control the other so closely that the second corporation has no independent existence? Is the second corporation only a sham used for fraudulent purposes?

In a stock sale, the acquiror buys 100% of the target's shares. All assets or liabilities of the target thereby become assets or liabilities of the acquiror. Unless the target plan is terminated before the transaction, the acquiror becomes the sponsor of the target's retirement plans. This could be costly, especially for defined benefit and retiree health plans.

In an asset sale, the acquiror purchases all of the target's assets but the target's corporate existence continues. Usually the sale proceeds are used to satisfy the target's liabilities and then the target is shut down. But as long as the target continues in existence, it is still the plan sponsor. The plan could be continued for the benefit of its remaining employees. Terminated employees would be paid out of the target's plan. If the acquiror becomes the sponsor of the target's plan, it has three options:

- Maintain both plans, especially if the target is considered a separate division. The acquiror becomes the sponsor and administrator of the target's plan. Former employees of the target still have their salary deferrals deposited into the target's plan. However, the employees are now employed by the acquiror, so coverage, participation, and nondiscrimination testing are based on the combined group of employees. However, under this scenario, the acquiror must pay two sets of plan administration costs. There might be problems with the target's plan that are not immediately evident.

- Merge the plans, giving the target's plan participants the same vested benefits after as before the merger. The acquiror will be responsible for historical activities of the target's plan.
- Terminate the target's plan (the most common option). At termination, all benefits become 100% vested. The target must distribute benefits to the participants, who can take the funds in cash, carry out IRA rollovers, or, if they have been hired by the acquiror and the plan allows, roll over the funds to the acquiror's plan. Once payouts are finished, the target's plan files a final Form 5500 and is terminated. If the acquiror chooses, it can amend its plan to provide that service with the target counts toward eligibility and/or vesting for the acquiror's plan. Otherwise, the target's ex-employees will be treated as new hires. [Beth Harrington, *Impact of Merger or Acquisition on Company Retirement Plans* (Mar. 5, 2014) (benefitslink.com)]

[B] T.D. 8928

[1] Generally

T.D. 8928, 66 Fed. Reg. 1843 (Jan. 10, 2001), provides that, when a corporation makes an asset sale (of substantially all the assets of a trade or business, or an asset as substantial as a factory or a corporate division), it is treated as the successor employer if the seller entirely ceases to provide group health plans, and the buyer maintains business operations using the assets. A transfer (e.g., in bankruptcy) is considered an asset sale if it has the same effect as a sale would have.

The plans that the seller maintained before the transaction could be retained, frozen, or terminated. A buyer who adopts an existing plan could agree to assume liability only going forward, with the seller retaining liability for violations of the plan rules that occurred before the sale. As for plans maintained by the buyer before the transaction, the buyer's and seller's plans could merge. [See below for the anticutback rules and the requirement of crediting prior service to the new plan]

Like all rules, this has exceptions. If the transaction is in effect a merger rather than an asset sale, liabilities will be characterized as they would be in a merger. If the buying corporation is a mere continuation of the selling corporation, or if the transaction is a fraud intended to escape liability, the transaction will be disregarded.

If only plan assets, and not the operating terms of the two plans, are merged, then the transaction is not considered a plan amendment that has the effect of reducing plan accruals. However, if the plans merge and one adopts the other's formulas and definitions, the original plan is deemed to have been amended. If benefits are reduced, notice must be given under ERISA § 204.

[2] ERISA Issues

In most instances, duplicative plans are merged, or some of them are eliminated. The seller's plan generally transfers assets (and related liabilities) either to the buyer's existing plans or to a newly created plan. ERISA does not require employees to be represented in the negotiations; but once the deal is consummated, the surviving and new plans must be operated subject to fiduciary standards, and mandatory communications must be made to employees.

A corporation's decision to terminate or amend a plan, or to spin off part of a plan, is a discretionary "settlor" function, and the plan sponsor does not act as a fiduciary. The amount of assets to be assigned to a spun-off plan, or the decision to transfer employer securities to a new plan created as part of a spin-off, is not a fiduciary decision. However, the fiduciaries of the plan making the transfers must comply with the plan merger and asset transfer standards set out in ERISA § 208.

Many transactions are structured so that the buyer assumes the seller's responsibility for providing unfunded benefits, such as retiree health coverage. The seller's decision to transfer the liability, and the buyer's commitment to accept it, are also settlor functions and therefore cannot give rise to a claim for breach of fiduciary duty. However, ERISA § 208 does require that each participant receive at least as good a benefit package if the plan were terminated just after the transaction as he or she would have received if the plan had terminated just before the transaction. It should also be remembered that plan assets must not be used for purposes other than paying benefits.

The Third Circuit rejected a class action brought by 277 plaintiffs who said they were entitled to pensions from Siemens if their employment ended. The plaintiffs worked for Westinghouse before Siemens bought the unit where they worked in late 1997. The Westinghouse plan said that "permanent job separation" benefits would not accrue if employees were hired by the purchaser or their employment ended after 1998. The Third Circuit said that Siemens did not establish or maintain this plan, so it was not responsible for plan benefits. ERISA § 208 says that participants cannot be denied benefits if their plan consolidates with another plan or transfers its assets and liabilities to another plan. However, this section does not create entitlement to benefits that do not exist under the plan and ERISA § 204(g) does not protect cutback of an earlier retirement benefit for persons who do not satisfy the conditions for the benefit. These plaintiffs were offered employment by Siemens, so they did not qualify under the terms of the plan. [*Shaver v. Siemens Corp.*, 670 F.3d 462 (3d Cir. 2012); see Amaris Elliott-Engel, *3rd Circuit Rejects ERISA Benefits for Siemens Plaintiffs*, The Legal Intelligencer (Mar. 1, 2012) (law.com)]

Former Anheuser-Busch employees sought benefits under a plan enhancing the pension benefits of employees involuntarily terminated within three years of a change in control. InBev acquired Anheuser-Busch in a 2008 hostile takeover.

On October 1, 2009, InBev spun off four plants which were sold to Ball Corporation. The plaintiffs were hired by Ball, and ceased to be participants in the Anheuser-Busch plan. The district court dismissed the case, holding that there was no involuntary termination—the plaintiffs were employed by a successor corporation. The Sixth Circuit reversed: the plan referred to employees involuntarily ceasing to be employed by a member of Anheuser-Busch's controlled group. Ball was not a member of the controlled group. [*Adams v. Anheuser-Busch Cos. Inc.*, No. 13-3149 (6th Cir. July 11, 2014); see Rebecca Moore, *Anheuser-Busch Pension Participants Owed Enhanced Benefits*, plansponsor.com (Aug. 7, 2014)]

The Second Circuit held in 2009 that a claim of breach of fiduciary duty cannot be based on oral statements that alter plan terms. Plan participants alleged that they were told that pension accruals after a merger would take pre-merger service into account, but after the merger, accruals reflected only post-merger service. The Second Circuit said that even if those statements had been made, they could not alter the terms of the plan. [*Ladouceur v. Credit Lyonnais*, 584 F.3d 510 (2d Cir. 2009); see Mercer Select US, *Claim for Fiduciary Breach Can't Rest on Oral Statements Altering Plan Terms, Appeals Court Rules* (Oct. 8, 2009) (benefitslink.com)]

On another ERISA issue, the Ninth Circuit ruled in late 2002 that two companies violated ERISA § 510 (the ban on taking adverse employment action against a person to prevent access to plan benefits) when, under an asset purchase agreement, the seller's active employees were hired and given health coverage, but employees who were on extended leave of absence were denied coverage until they returned to work. Selecting employees for termination on the basis of medical or disability leave violates § 510. [*Lessard v. Applied Risk Mgmt.*, 307 F.3d 1020 (9th Cir. 2002)] The Seventh Circuit held that Abbott Laboratories and its spinoff Hospira, did not violate ERISA § 510 when Hospira was spun off. For a two-year period, Abbott and Hospira agreed not to hire each other's employees. Before the transaction, employees were covered by the Abbott pension plan; afterward, some employees were classified as Hospira employees, and Hospira had a 401(k) plan with an employer match but did not have a pension plan. Non-vested pension rights in the Abbott plan were eliminated for these employees. The no-hire agreement prevented them from retiring from Abbott before the spinoff, taking their pensions, and going back to work for Hospira. The Seventh Circuit held that Abbott and Hospira did not act with intent to interfere with pension benefits. The decision to spin off the division and set a no-hire policy was not motivated by employee benefits. The plaintiffs also sued for breach of fiduciary duty, but this claim failed because Abbott was not involved in the Hospira benefits plan and Abbott disclosed that the spinoff might alter employee benefits. [*Nauman v. Abbott Labs. and Hospira, Inc.*, 669 F.3d 854 (7th Cir. 2012)]

A group of terminated employees who were not rehired after their employer's facility was sold sued, alleging a conspiracy by the employer and the purchaser to violate ERISA § 510 by terminating older employees and depriving them of pension benefits. The Tenth Circuit ruled for the employer, holding that pension issues were not even considered until after the sale so they could not have motivated the sale. The Tenth Circuit held that there is no § 510 violation if the employer acted for legitimate business reasons, even if some laid-off employees lost pension eligibility. [*Apsley v. Boeing Co.*, 691 F.3d 1184 (10th Cir. 2012)]

[C] Labor Law Implications of Choice of Form

Labor law follows the basic rule that a merger or sale of stock obligates the acquiring company to assume the liabilities of the acquired or selling company. This includes the Collective Bargaining Agreement (CBA). But in an asset sale, the CBA is not assumed unless the purchaser voluntarily takes it on, or unless there is another reason to view the buyer as a successor or surrogate of the seller.

Yet even if the company is not fully bound by its predecessor's CBA, it could still have a duty to bargain in good faith with the existing union, based on continuity linking the old and new enterprises. If a transaction lacks real substance, the successor could be forced to assume the predecessor's labor-law obligations. The main test is whether there has been a significant practical change or whether operations continue despite a nominal change in ownership.

In addition to situations in which one entity replaces another, two or more enterprises can be treated as a "single employer" for labor-law purposes. One might be treated as an alter ego (surrogate) of the other. If a parent company and its subsidiary engage in the same line of business, the NLRB will probably treat them as a single enterprise, not two. Furthermore, "joint employers" that are separate entities but share decision making about labor issues may be treated together by the NLRB.

Either a purchaser must be prepared to take on the predecessor's union contracts and other labor-law obligations, or must structure the transaction to be free of such obligations. Also note that a change in corporate ownership (even if corporate structure remains the same) can lead the state to revoke the privilege to self-insure against Worker's Compensation claims.

A new company that adopts an existing operation can unilaterally change the wage scale, unless it's "perfectly clear" that the new owner will hire all of the old employees. In a "perfectly clear" case where the new owner does not consult with the union and there is no evidence of what would have emerged if there had been negotiations, the employees are given the benefit of the doubt. It is assumed that the former wage rate would have continued and would not have been diminished. So new ownership in a "perfectly clear" case cannot lead to wage cuts unless the union agrees.

In its 1999 decision in *St. Elizabeth's Manor* [329 N.L.R.B. 341 (1999)], the NLRB created a "successor bar" rule under which an incumbent union would be given a reasonable amount of time, after a corporate takeover, to bargain with the successor employer without challenges to the union's majority status. However, the NLRB overruled this decision in mid-2002. Under the new rule, in a successorship situation the incumbent union is entitled to rebuttable presumption of continuing majority status—but if there is evidence to rebut the presumption, an otherwise valid challenge to majority status will be allowed to proceed. [*MV Transportation*, 337 N.L.R.B. 129 (2002)]

When S&F Market Street Healthcare acquired a nursing home previously owned by Candlewood, it offered temporary employment to Candlewood employees. The NLRB treated S&F as a successor employer bound by Candlewood's CBA, because it did not notify employees that their terms and conditions of employment would change. However, the D.C. Circuit ruled in mid-2009 that S&F was not a successor, and it could implement new terms and conditions. Generally speaking, a successor that has not bargained for the CBA is not bound by the substantive terms of a predecessor's CBA, unless it is perfectly clear that the new employer plans to retain all of the former employees. In this case, it was obvious that significant changes would be made, and employees were warned that they were offered only temporary at-will employment and not all former employees would be retained. [*S&F Market Street Healthcare LLC v. NLRB*, 570 F.3d 354 (D.C. Cir. 2009)]

A construction company was sold to a non-union employer. To preserve jobs, the union entered into an agreement to withdraw its challenge to the transaction in exchange for the buyer continuing to make timely contributions to the ERISA plan, and the other to hire the existing workforce, with a new CBA to be negotiated. However, neither agreement covered successor liability for delinquent contributions. Although ERISA successor liability can be imposed for delinquent plan contributions in the context of a merger, this is not always true in an asset sale. Nevertheless, the Third Circuit held the successor company liable, based on factors such as continuity of operations and workforce, the purchaser's knowledge of the plan, and the employees' inability to obtain relief from the seller corporation. [*Einhorn v. Ruberton Constr. Co.*, 632 F.3d 89 (3d Cir. 2011)]

The Eighth Circuit held in early 2014 that the purchaser of a business has USERRA obligations. The seller corporation's failure to list the plaintiff as an active employee when it sold its assets to another company violated USERRA by failing to treat the plaintiff, who was deployed on active military duty, on parity with other employees on leave. While the plaintiff (Dorris) was serving in Iraq, his employer, TXD Services, LP, sold its assets to an unrelated company, Foxxe Energy, which took over its operations. The purchase agreement obligated Foxxe to make a reasonable effort to employ all the active employees on the list submitted by TXD. Dorris was not hired by Foxxe when he returned from deployment in December 2008, although he was eventually hired in April 2009. He brought a USERRA suit against TXD, which argued that being out of business was a changed circumstance that relieved it of having to rehire the plaintiff. The Ninth Circuit held that an employee on military leave has rights under USERRA to the same rights and benefits as employees not on military leave. Employers have better records than employees, so it was up to TXD to explain whether employees on long-term non-military leave were included in the hire list. [*Dorris v. TXD Servs., LP*, No. 12-3096, 2014 U.S. App. LEXIS 3716, 97 Empl. Prac. Dec. (CCH) P45,028 (8th Cir. Feb. 27, 2014); see *Employers Must Treat Employees on Military Leave like Those on Comparable Leaves, Appeals Court Rules*, Jackson Lewis P.C. (Mar. 3, 2014), available at Lexology.com]

[D] Transitions and Unemployment Insurance

Although it is a comparatively minor cost, the acquirer of a business may wish to take advantage of the amount of FUTA tax already paid by the transferor of the business for the part of the year before the transition. The successor employer can rely on wages paid (and therefore on FUTA payments made) by the predecessor if either one of two circumstances exists. The first is that the transferee acquires substantially all the property used in the transferor's entire trade or business (or in a separate unit of the trade or business). The other is that, whether or not the property was acquired, at least one employee from the old business remains employed immediately after the transfer.

■ **TIP:** A multistate operation will usually be permitted to combine wages paid in the various states for FUTA purposes.

The IRS' view, for FICA and tax withholding as well as FUTA purposes, is that, in a statutory merger or consolidation, the surviving corporation is the same taxpayer and the same corporation as the predecessor corporation(s). Of course, that means that the successor will have to pay any taxes due but unpaid by the predecessor—unless the successor gives the local administrative agency adequate written notice.

However, most state unemployment laws provide that companies remain subject to unemployment insurance laws for at least two years once they have acquired an experience rating—with the result that the transferor may remain liable in a year after it ceases operations, unless it applies to the local administrative agency for a determination that it is no longer an employer.

If the predecessor has acquired a good experience rating, the successor will probably be able to take over the experience rating with the rest of the operation, as long as operations remain more or less the same, at the original business location, and the workforce remains stable. Altering these important factors in effect creates a new enterprise, which will have to acquire its own experience rating.

For example, in 2006 the transferee entity of a nursing home could take advantage of the previous owner's experience rate, even though the transfer occurred by lease agreement rather than sale. [*Jefferson Medical Associates LLC*, Unempl. Ins. Rep. (CCH) ¶ 10,193 (Ohio App. 2006)]

[E] COBRA Issues

Depending on the structure of the transaction, it is likely that some of the employees of one or both of the companies involved in a transition will lose their jobs. Perhaps as a result of the deal, some individuals will remain employed but will cease to be covered by an Employer Group Health Plan (EGHP). If a COBRA event occurs, unless the organization is too small to be covered, it will be necessary to provide COBRA notice. In the context of a corporate transition, that raises the question of who is responsible for providing the notice.

The crucial question is whether there has been a qualifying event. If there has, the structure of the transaction (stock sale versus asset sale) will determine the allocation of the notice burden. COBRA provides that an M&A qualified beneficiary may have a qualifying event if he or she was last employed by the acquired corporation (in a stock sale) or was last employed in connection with the assets being sold in an asset sale. However, a stock sale is not a COBRA qualifying event if the employee continues to be employed by the acquired organization after the transactions, even if the employee is no longer covered by an EGHP.

An asset sale results in a qualifying event for those whose employment is associated with the purchased assets, unless the buying corporation is a successor employer and the employee is employed by the buying corporation immediately after the sale. There is no COBRA event after an asset sale for people who retain their coverage under the selling corporation's EGHP. A successor employer is either a mere continuation of the former employer company; an entity that results from the merger or consolidation of the employer corporation; or a continuation of the business operations associated with the purchased assets.

If a COBRA event does result, and the selling corporation continues to maintain an EGHP, it is responsible for providing continuation coverage (and COBRA notice) to the M&A qualified beneficiaries. If the selling corporation does not continue to maintain an EGHP, in a stock sale the EGHP of the buying corporation has the COBRA duties. In an asset sale, the EGHP of the buyer corporation is responsible for COBRA only if the buyer corporation continues the business operations associated with the assets without interruption and without substantial change. The buyer and seller corporations can re-allocate the burden by contract—but if the party who agrees to undertake the COBRA obligations fails to do so, the originally responsible party still retains its legal liability. [Kenneth W. Ruthenberg Jr., *Don't Pick up COBRA as Part of Your Next Deal—Negotiating COBRA Liability in Business Transactions* (Sept. 10, 2002), <http://www.insurancethoughtleadership.com/articles/dont-pick-up-cobra-as-part-of-your-next-deal#axzz325WWYia4> (Aug. 29, 2011)]

[F] Bankruptcy as a Transition

When a bankrupt company operates as a Debtor in Possession under Chapter 11, the benefit plans will usually remain in operation during the reorganization process, but a Chapter 7 liquidating bankruptcy will probably lead to termination of the plans.

The Supreme Court's 2007 *Beck* decision made it clear that a bankrupt company does not have a fiduciary duty to consider the option of merging its pension plan into a union multi-employer plan rather than adopting the company's preferred alternative of carrying out a standard termination and buying annuities to satisfy payment obligations. The Supreme Court's rationale was that terminating a plan is a business decision made by the plan sponsor in its role as settlor of the trust that administers the plan. In this reading, this is not an administrative decision made by the plan's fiduciaries—even if they are the same people as those who carry out the settlor functions. Furthermore, ERISA's termination section (§ 4041) does not discuss mergers. [*Beck v. PACE Int'l Union*, 551 U.S. 96 (2007)]

In 2011, the Third Circuit became the first court of appeals to rule that a claim against a debtor for post-petition liability for withdrawing from a multi-employer pension plan receives administrative expense priority in the company's Chapter 11 bankruptcy case. The Multi-Employer Pension Plan Amendments of 1980 amended ERISA to make employers who withdraw from multi-employer plans liable for their pro rata share of unfunded, vested benefits as of the time of withdrawal.

The Third Circuit balanced Bankruptcy Code and ERISA objectives by apportioning the withdrawal liability between the pre- and post-petition time periods. The post-petition portion can be an administrative expense; the balance was deemed to be a general unsecured claim. The Third Circuit limited the size of the administrative expense claim to prevent the estate from being swallowed up by the withdrawal liability claim. [*In re Marcal Paper Mills, Inc.*, 650 F.3d 311 (3d Cir. 2011).

The PBGC does not get involved in a standard termination because the plan has adequate assets to satisfy its obligations. If a distress termination occurs, the PBGC is required to pay the guaranteed benefits. The PBGC allows distress terminations in Chapter 11 bankruptcy cases if the bankruptcy court makes a determination, under ERISA § 1341(c), that the employer will not be able to pay all of its debts under a reorganization plan and will not be able to stay in business unless the pension plan is terminated.

The court has to decide whether there is any feasible reorganization plan that would preserve the pension plan; it is not restricted to considering the plan proposed by the debtor. An important question is whether financing could be obtained to continue the business—and if the parties that might provide the financing insist on termination of the pension plan. The company must explore alternatives, such as eliminating only some pension plans and maintaining others; exploring funding waivers; freezing future benefit accruals, but not terminating the plan; and looking for non-pension means of saving money.

The PBGC is entitled to press two types of claims against the bankrupt sponsor of the plan: a plan asset insufficiency claim and a claim for unpaid funding contributions accruing after the petition. A plan insufficiency claim is a general unsecured claim to the extent that it involves plan benefits employees earned before the petition. The unpaid funding contributions get priority as administrative expenses. [Daniel J. Morse, *Practical Results of Rejecting, Terminating Pension Plans Are Significant*, Turnaround Management Association (May 1, 2006), <https://www.turnaround.org/Publications/Articles.aspx?objectID=6146>] The PBGC contended—and the D.C. Circuit agreed—that Thunderbird Mining Co. was still trying to get new orders after production at a plant stopped. Therefore, it was not shut down when the pension plan terminated. Eveleth Mines made a Chapter 11 filing. Its wholly owned subsidiary, Thunderbird, ceased production and laid off all the hourly employees except for four. Eveleth told the employees that the closure would be temporary if it received the orders it anticipated. There had been shut-downs in the past, but this time, unlike past layoffs, the plant was not kept in standby condition. The PBGC concluded that the plan had a funded ratio of only 52% and no realistic prospect of adequate funding. The PBGC concluded that the plan would not be able to pay benefits as they came due, and losses would increase unreasonably unless the plan was terminated quickly. The PBGC sued to terminate the plan, effective July 24, 2003. Participants in the Thunderbird plan applied for shutdown pension benefits, arguing that the shutdown was intended to be permanent. The bankruptcy court approved the sale of Eveleth's assets. However, the purchasers of the assets hired the hourly employees under a new CBA. [*United Steel, Paper & Forestry Workers v. PBGC*, 707 F.3d 319 (D.C. Cir. 2013); see Rebecca Moore, *Court Agrees With PBGC Denial of Shutdown Benefits*, plansponsor.com (Jan. 23, 2013)]

A corporation contemplating bankruptcy will have to determine the future of its plans, including who will serve as administrator and trustee before and after bankruptcy and how benefits will be distributed from a terminated plan.

Severance benefits usually come from the employer's assets, and may have the status of a priority claim in bankruptcy. The Bankruptcy Abuse Prevention and Consumer Protection Act (BAPCA; Pub. L. No. 109-8), 2005's bankruptcy reform legislation, affects the treatment of pensions and employee benefits in several ways.

When an employer files for bankruptcy protection, wage and benefit claims for 180 days (rather than prior law's 90 days) are priority claims, and $10,000 per employee in wages and benefits (raised from the previous level of $4,000) counts as a third-priority claim. The $10,000 figure is indexed for inflation. The bankruptcy trustee can avoid transfers made to or for the benefit of corporate insiders during two years (rather than one) prior to the filing. Transfers made under an employment contract can be avoided by the trustee—whether or not the transfers caused the employer to become insolvent—if they occurred outside the ordinary course of business. BAPCA also places limits on retention bonuses and severance benefits that can be paid to corporate insiders.

The employer's creditors are not permitted to reach amounts contributed by employees, or withheld from their wages for contribution, to a plan when the amounts are in the employer's hands because they have not yet been placed into the plan.

If the employer modified retiree welfare benefits (e.g., retiree health plans) within the 180 days before filing of the bankruptcy petition, any party of interest can apply for a court order. The modification will be enjoined unless the court rules that the balance of equities clearly supports the modification.

Usually conflicts arise when bankruptcy results in a reduction of benefits. The Third Circuit ruled that plan amendments adopted just before a Chapter 11 filing, which resulted in the doubling or even quintupling of pension benefits for certain participants (including corporate insiders), was invalid as a fraudulent conveyance. The court also criticized the introduction of the amendment to the board of directors as an "administrative formality" as evidence of bad faith and the use of a surplus in the union side of the pension accounts to fund the new benefits. [*Pension Transfer Corp. v. Beneficiaries Under Third Amendment to Fruehauf Corp. Ret. Plan*, 444 F.3d 203 (3d Cir. 2006)]

A later Third Circuit case holds that, even if a company has reserved the right to amend or terminate a plan (e.g., a retiree health plan), the company still must comply with the BAPCPA requirements for obtaining court approval for changes to the plan. [*IUE-CWA v. Visteon Corp.*, 612 F.3d 210 (3d Cir. 2010); see Rebecca Moore, *Visteon Must Follow the Rules Before Terminating Retiree Benefits*, plansponsor.com (July 14, 2010)]

See Chapter 19 for a discussion of the obligation to provide continuation coverage under COBRA (as modified by the ARRA subsidy program). Even if a health plan is terminated, outstanding claims will have to be satisfied. Under HIPAA (also discussed in Chapter 19) employees are entitled to certificates of creditable coverage showing their date of enrollment in the plan, so they can establish their entitlement to purchase individual coverage.

§ 16.03 THE ANTICUTBACK RULE

Internal Revenue Code § 411(d)(6) forbids amendments that reduce accrued benefits, including early retirement benefits and the availability of additional forms of payment over and above the required QJSA and QPSA. But according to *Board of Trustees of the Sheet Metal Workers Nat'l Pension Fund v. C.I.R.* [117 T.C. 220 (2001)], only employees, not retirees, can "accrue" benefits. Therefore, eliminating post-retirement Cost of Living Increases doesn't violate the anticutback rule, because the benefits weren't "accrued."

In 2004, the Supreme Court ruled [*Cent. Laborer's Pension Fund v. Heinz*, 541 U.S. 739 (2004)] that an amendment increasing the varieties of postretirement employment that would cause the suspension of benefit payments violated the anti-cutback rule. [See T.D. 9219, 2005-38 I.R.B. 538 and T.D. 9280, 72 Fed. Reg. 45379 (Aug. 9, 2006) for Final Regulations reflecting *Heinz*.]

If a plan is spun off, the spin-off plan is required to maintain the old plan's payment options as to benefits accrued before the spinoff.

In a merger, employees are permitted to retain their premerger pay-out options. In practice, this means that if a merged plan wants to have a single payout structure, it must improve the less-favorable plan to equal the options under the more-favorable plan.

Section 411(a)(10)(B) requires that individuals who had three years of service before the corporate transition will be entitled to keep the old vesting schedule, if it is more favorable to them than the newly adopted one. Employers have an obligation to inform employees of this option.

According to I.R.C. § 414(l), if plans (even plans maintained by the same employer) merge or consolidate, or if a plan's assets and liabilities are transferred to another plan, each participant's benefit immediately after the transition, calculated on a termination basis, must be at least as great as his or her benefit would have been if the plan had terminated immediately before the transition.

The regulations for this section say that a transfer of assets and liabilities from one plan to another will be treated as a spinoff followed by a merger. This usually means that Form 5310-A has to be filed at least 30 days before the merger, spinoff, or asset transfer.

Section 414(l) requires a plan's actuaries to make reasonable assumptions about expected retirement age, mortality, and interest rates before and after the asset transfer. The termination assumptions that the PBGC uses offer a safe harbor because using them is always deemed reasonable, but their use is not mandatory.

The Secretary of the Treasury has the power to enforce ERISA § 208, which is very similar to I.R.C. § 414(l). The Department of Labor has indirect enforcement powers under ERISA § 208, because of its enforcement powers over fiduciary conduct.

Internal Revenue Code § 414 has separate rules for merging two defined contribution plans; two defined benefit plans; and one plan of each type to make sure that participants' entitlement to benefits is not reduced as a result of the transaction. There are further requirements to be observed if one of the plans is fully funded but the other is underfunded. For defined benefit plans, this section serves two policy purposes. It avoids manipulation of funding by means of moving plan assets between the plans of a controlled group of corporations, and it prevents the dilution of benefits within the ERISA § 4044 priority order for categories of assets during a termination.

The priority order is as follows:

- Assets are allocated to benefits coming from participant contributions;
- Benefits going to individuals who were already getting benefits during the three years before the termination;
- Benefits to persons who could have been getting benefits during that three-year period;
- PBGC-guaranteed benefits;
- Other nonforfeitable benefits;
- Everything else.

The First Circuit ruled in 2010 that it was permissible for a plan to eliminate an option for participants to move assets from a defined contribution plan to a defined benefit rule. The First Circuit held that the rule change did not violate the anti-cutback rule, even though it had the effect of diminishing an accrued benefit. Tasker retired from Airborne in 2004; at about the same time, DHL acquired Airborne and merged Airborne's defined contribution and defined benefit plans into its own plans, which eliminated Tasker's right to transfer his balance between plans. Tasker sued, charging that his actual retirement benefit was lower than estimated because the transfer option had been eliminated. But the First Circuit, although decrying the unfairness of the result, held that, although Tasker's actual pension was only about half of what he had expected, DHL did not violate any of ERISA's statutory requirements. [*Tasker v. DHL Ret. Sav. Plan*, 621 F.3d 34 (1st Cir. 2010)]

In a case of first impression, the First Circuit held in 2013 that retroactively conferred benefits are "benefits attributable to service" that are considered accrued benefits under the anti-cutback rules. Banked hours are hours worked in a year over and above the number of hours needed to earn a full year of service credit. They are banked for purposes such as filling in during a year when the participant does not have a full year of credit. They are cashed in at retirement as additional pension credits. Four union locals merged, also merging their pension plans. All of the plans had different banked hour rules, so they were unified at the highest level. The result was that many participants, including the plaintiffs, received retrospective increases in the levels of banked hour credits after the merger. Eventually the merged pension trust got into financial trouble and wanted to reduce the retrospective banked hour benefits to the level each participant would have received under the original plan he belonged to before the merger. The First Circuit held that ERISA does not limit accrued benefits to those that were promised in advance. Although these benefits were conferred retroactively, they were nonetheless attributable to prior service. [*Bonneau v. Plumbers & Pipefitters Local Union 51 Pension Trust Fund*, 736 F.3d 33 (1st Cir. 2013)]

§ 16.04 NOTICE OF REDUCTION OF BENEFITS

ERISA § 204(h) requires notices of reductions in future benefits. to be given before the effective date of any amendment that eliminates or reduces an early retirement benefit or early retirement subsidy. An excise tax is imposed on failure to provide proper notice.

Notice is due a reasonable time before the effective date of the plan amendment. The notice can be given before the formal adoption of the amendment, as long as there is no material change before the amendment is finally adopted. If there is an "egregious" failure to provide notice, then the amendment cannot take effect, and individuals affected by the change get the larger of the pre- or post-amendment form of the benefit.

Under T.D. 9052, [T.D. 9052, RIN 1545-BA08] notice must generally be given 45 days in advance of the event (even if this is earlier than the adoption date of the plan amendment that institutes the cutback). A small plan (one with fewer than 100 participants) is allowed to give less notice: 15 days. The 15-day rule also applies when a § 204(h) amendment is adopted in connection with a corporate acquisition or disposition.

Furthermore, if the amendment is adopted to deal with transfers of liabilities from one plan to another in connection with a transfer, merger, or consolidation of assets or liabilities under Code § 414(l), and the amendment cuts back on early retirement benefits or subsidies but does not significantly reduce the rate of future benefit accrual, the notice can be given after the amendment takes effect—but not more than 30 days afterward. The Final Regulations are in Q&A form, and provide model text that can be used to provide notice.

The IRS modified its position in July 2003, allowing defined contribution plans (including 401(k)s) to reduce alternate benefit forms without 90 days' advance notice—as long as the change was reflected in a timely revised SPD or Summary of Material Modifications. [68 Fed. Reg. 40581 (July 8, 2003)] Similar relief was proposed for defined benefit plans. [69 Fed. Reg. 13769 (Mar. 24, 2004)]

Proposed Regulations [70 Fed. Reg. 47155 (Aug. 12, 2005)] cover the interaction of the anti-cutback rules with the § 411(a) nonforfeitability requirements. There are two ways to reduce or eliminate a benefit: (1) if the benefit is redundant, that is, duplicates another benefit in the same family, 90 days' notice is required; or (2) if the benefit is a core option, such as the straight life annuity and the 10-year certain/life annuity, four years' notice is required. Benefits also can be eliminated when they have been available for a meaningful length of time but no one ever elected them. The IRS returned to this issue with Final Regulations published at 71 Fed. Reg. 45379 (Aug. 9, 2006). This Final Rule also includes a test of utilization to determine whether certain benefit forms (e.g., retirement-type subsidies; optional forms of benefit) are so seldom used that employers are permitted to amend the plan to eliminate them.

T.D. 9472, 2009-51 I.R.B. 850, is a final rule governing notice requirements under § 204(h) for plan amendments that reduce accrued benefits. Code § 4980F(e)(3) requires notice to be provided within a reasonable time before the plan amendment takes effect. In general, that means 45 days before the effective date (15 days for small or multi-employer plans). However, for some amendments that took effect by December 31, 2008, notice is acceptable if given at least 30 days before the effective date. [T.D. 9472, 2009-51 I.R.B. 850]

§ 16.05 THE MINIMUM PARTICIPATION RULE

Initially, minimum participation rules were applied to both defined contribution and defined benefit plans. However, the Small Business Job Protection Act of 1996 [Pub. L. No. 104-188] eliminated this rule for defined contribution plans—now only defined benefit plans are required to have a minimum number or percentage of participants. This is significant in the context of corporate transitions because asset buyers often decline to adopt the seller's plan. If the plan is not adopted, there is a risk that the new plan will fail to cover the mandated number or percentage of employees.

Some relief is available under I.R.C. § 410(b)(6)(C), which allows one year after an acquisition or the disposition of a corporation to satisfy the minimum participation requirement. But after that, the plan is likely to become disqualified—unless it has been terminated in the interim.

A possible strategy is to freeze the plan. However, if too many participants choose to cash out, that creates difficulties. Two or more plans can be merged into a larger plan, offering a benefit structure at least as favorable as the most favorable of the merged plans, no later than the fifteenth day of the tenth month after the end of the plan year.

§ 16.06 IN-SERVICE DISTRIBUTIONS AND REHIRING

The underlying purpose of pension plans is to provide postretirement financial security. Therefore, "in-service distributions" (distributions from the plan while the individual is still working) historically were severely discouraged by the Code. Although many government agency employers had phased retirement plans, few private-sector employers did so. There are some special rules governing taxation of in-service distributions during a transition. Treasury Regulation § 1.401-1(b)(1)(i) provides that defined benefit plans cannot make in-service distributions before the employee's retirement or termination of employment—unless the plan itself is terminated. But a defined contribution plan that is not a 401(k) plan can use the two-year/five-year rule. That is, contributions can be withdrawn from the plan after the contributions have been in the plan for two years, or the participant has five years of plan participation.

■ **TIP:** EGTRRA eliminates the "same desk" rule for 401(k) plans. In other words, when there is a merger consolidation, or liquidation, participants in a 401(k) plan will be entitled to take a distribution from the plan even if the successor company hires them and they have not separated from service. Congress intended to increase the portability of pensions in this situation.

Because of the abolition of the same desk rule, distributions can be made from the seller's plan in either an asset or a stock sale, to employees who go to work for the buyer or stay at the subsidiary that has been sold, as long as that subsidiary drops participation in the plan by the time of the sale. Distributions are not allowed if the subsidiary that is the subject of the sale retains the plan, the buyer takes over as plan sponsor, or assets are transferred to a plan maintained by the buyer corporation. In most cases, a plan amendment will be required. It probably makes sense to permit distributions to any participant who is transferred out of the seller's controlled group as a result of a stock sale, sale of assets, or other corporate transaction. Similarly, employees who took substantially similar jobs with the buyer corporation were not "released" from employment and therefore were not entitled to severance pay. [*Cassidy v. Akzo Nobel Salt Inc.*, 308 F.3d 613 (6th Cir. 2002)] The termination plan defined release as permanent separation initiated by the employer for reasons such as lack of work, RIF, or unsatisfactory performance by the employee.

Under the Pension Protection Act, Pub. L. No. 109-280, employees who have reached age 62 can lawfully receive in-service distributions under a phased retirement plan: see § 9.06. See also T.D. 9235, 2007-24 I.R.B. 1386 (Final Regulations on the definition of Normal Retirement Age).

§ 16.07 TAX ISSUES

If, after a merger, liquidation, or reorganization, the surviving company maintains the predecessor corporation's qualified plan, I.R.C. § 381 generally provides that the original plans' tax attributes are passed on to the successor plan. If two qualified plans consolidate, the deductions taken by each employer before the consolidation will not be retroactively disqualified by the consolidation.

The acquiring corporation can keep up the plan for the benefit of those covered by it under the old ownership—with no obligation to cover the workers who were its own employees before the acquisition.

Asset purchases that result in the liquidation of the seller company or acquisition of its assets by the purchaser company, can create "orphan plans" (plans with no sponsor), which create tax problems. Once a plan loses its sponsor, it can lose tax-qualified status. There may also be ERISA fiduciary liability issues about managing, reporting, and distributing assets from the plan. The IRS' Employee Plans Compliance Resolution System (EPCRS; see § 15.19[B]) has a process for correcting errors of orphan plans. [Keith R. McMurdy, *Don't Let Your Plan*

Become an Orphan, Fox Rothschild LLP Employee Benefits Legal Blog (Jan. 24, 2012) (benefitslink.com)]

The Sixth Circuit applied labor, not corporation, law to determine whether a company is subject to the FMLA, finding that it is irrelevant for this purpose whether there is a transfer of assets or a merger with the seller. The plaintiff was re-hired by the company that underbid his former employer for a Postal Service delivery contract. The second company did not acquire the previous employer or its assets. The Sixth Circuit did not rule that a merger or transfer of assets is always required to impose successor liability: legal obligations, such as those under a CBA, also count. The Sixth Circuit pointed out that the FMLA defines "employer" to include successors in interest, and the Regulations (29 C.F.R. § 825.107) adopt the Title VII standard for successorship in interest. [*Cobb v. Contract Transp., Inc.*, 461 F.3d 632 (6th Cir. 2006)]

The risk of acquisition or merger makes corporate recruitment more difficult, because top candidates have a realistic fear that they will lose their jobs during a shake-up. Employment agreements with prominent candidates often include "golden parachutes" (providing generous compensation if the job is lost because of a corporate transition) and "golden handcuffs" (retention bonuses that are forfeited if the individual quits shortly after being hired). Most of these programs only take effect when employees have involuntary job loss; some plans have a "window period" during which payments will be made even if the employee quits voluntarily. See § 1.01[B] for discussion of limitations on golden parachutes and other severance payments to top management of financial services companies receiving federal bail-out funds.

A "stay bonus" for remaining with the new owner is a fixed benefit (and therefore a fixed incremental cost for the business buyer). The bonus is paid after the employee has remained for a certain period of time. It could also be combined with a golden parachute. For instance, the executive could be offered two months' salary as a bonus for staying a year, or given a severance package of three months' salary and outplacement assistance if terminated without good cause within 18 months of the transition.

Internal Revenue Code § 280G does not allow corporations to deduct "excess parachute payments." Any "disqualified person" who receives an excess parachute payment is subject to a 20% excise tax, under I.R.C. § 4999. A parachute payment is a payment of compensation, contingent on a change in ownership, and equal to three times or more of the base amount (roughly speaking, the base amount is the individual's normal compensation). There are many ways to draft parachute agreements. A safe harbor cutback provides that payments will be reduced to equal the maximum amount that will not trigger the excise tax. A valley provision, also known as a better-off cutback, reduces the payment the same way, unless the executive would be better off financially by receiving the higher amount and paying taxes on it. A full gross-up reimburses the executive for the excise tax; this is very expensive for the payor corporation, especially because the gross-up payment is not deductible. Public companies must also consider the probable reactions of shareholders. A modified gross-up calls for limitation to the maximum amount that will not trigger excise tax. [PLC Employee Benefits & Executive Compensation, *Addressing Sections 280G and 4999 in Executive Employment Agreements* (Apr. 16, 2013) (benefitslink.com)]

Code § 409A is the IRS' attempt to control inappropriate deferral of non-qualified deferred compensation. (See § 8.02[D]) Section 409A potentially applies to many compensation arrangements in change of control situations: severance agreements, stock options, and incentive agreements, for example. Violating § 409A can lead to accelerated inclusion in income for the person receiving the compensation, and a 20% federal tax penalty. California imposes its own 20% penalty as well.

A single-trigger arrangement provides benefits upon change in control, even if the executive is not terminated at the time of the acquisition. Double-trigger arrangements, which require an adverse employment action within a specified time of the change in control, are growing in popularity. Post-change in control severance usually is paid in a lump sum, because after the change, the restrictive covenants are less of a concern to the acquired company. The executive also wants to receive the funds in a lump sum to avoid being at the mercy of the acquiring company's CEO and management team.

One potential risk is that alternative payment methods under a double-trigger severance plan could fall under § 409A. The company might fail to recognize this because the pre- and post-change severance arrangements are specified in different documents—for example, the overall severance plan and an individual executive's change-in-control agreement. A double-trigger arrangement typically becomes subject to § 409A if the "good reason" payment trigger is excessively broad—say, if it allows the executive to resign and collect severance based on a minor reduction in pay or duties; if the installment payments exceed $490,000 (indexed for inflation), or the payments extend more than two years after separation from service. Because of economic uncertainty, "earn-outs" have become more popular in private company acquisitions. The earn-out provides for future payments to the seller of the acquired company if the company reaches certain business milestones—typically, within two to five years, although the period could be 10 years or even longer. A stock option cash-out or management incentive plan can be subject to an earn-out without violating § 409 as long as payments are made at the same time, and generally on the same terms and conditions, to payments to the shareholders as a whole. To qualify for this treatment, the earn-out payments generally must be made within five years of the transaction's closing date, although § 409A permits limited customized alternatives tailored to the situation of an earn-out that exceeds five years.

Earn-outs are speculative and difficult to value. There are risks: if the earn-out is overvalued, there will be penalties for a § 409A violation, but if it is undervalued, the option-holders will suffer economic harm. Some companies value the earn-out at the time of the assumption, whereas others use an "open transaction" approach, adjusting the options to reflect the earn-out only as it is paid. The issue could also be avoided by requiring option holders to exercise their options just before the transaction. [Juliano P. Banuelos, *Recent Compensation Trends in Mergers and Acquisitions and Section 409A*, Orrick Perspectives (October 2011) (benefitslink.com)]

As well as their tax implications, golden parachutes have ramifications for corporate law and securities regulation. Exchange Act § 14A, enacted by the Dodd-Frank Act, requires a non-binding shareholder vote about golden parachute compensation. The vote cannot be used to overrule the Board of Directors' decision, change the board's fiduciary duties, or restrict the ability of shareholders to include their own proposals in the corporation's proxy materials. The proxy or consent solicitation material for a meeting at which shareholders will be asked to approve an acquisition, merger, consolidation, or the sale or disposition of substantially all assets of the company must disclose any agreements between the party soliciting the proxy and the top managers of either the acquired or acquiring company with respect to the executive's present, deferred, or contingent compensation based on the transaction. Proxy statements must include a separate resolution, subject to shareholder vote, to approve any compensation agreements—unless the shareholders have already approved the agreement through a "Say on Pay" vote. This provision is effective for shareholder meetings that occur after January 21, 2011. [Michael S. Melbinger, Winston & Strawn LLP, *Executive Compensation Blog* (Aug. 12, 2010) (benefitslink.com)]

§ 16.08 THE PBGC EARLY WARNING PROGRAM

PBGC's Early Warning Program is supposed to reduce the agency's risk of loss in the context of corporate transitions by giving the PBGC the power to review transactions of below-investment-grade companies with extensive liabilities and other plans with more than $5 million in unfunded current liability. Certain types of transactions have been identified as potential problem areas: the breakup of a controlled group; a leveraged buyout; major divestiture by a company that retains significantly underfunded pension liabilities; or transfer of significantly underfunded pension liabilities in connection with sale of a business. [This program is discussed in Harold J. Ashner, *Dealing with the Pension Benefit Guaranty Corporation*, Tax Management Compensation Planning Journal, <http://www.keightleyashner.com/publications/Dealing_with[. . .]> (January 2006)]

RIN 1212-AB03 is PBGC's final rule for calculating the liability when an employer with an underfunded pension plan closes a facility and lays off a significant percentage of its workforce. The final regulations exclude retirees and former employees who separated from service before cessation of operations from the calculations. If the plan is terminated within five years, the liability amount goes to the plan; if there is no termination, the money is returned to the employer. The PBGC refused to enact a small-plan exception, because small companies usually have only one business location, so shutdown would lead to plan termination in any case. [71 Fed. Reg. 34819 (June 16, 2006), discussed in (no by-line) *PBGC Finalizes Regs on Computing Liability When Employer Substantially Ceases Operations*, Pension & Benefits Week (RIA) (June 26, 2006)]

In 2013, the PBGC proposed regulations under which most (perhaps as many as 90%) of plans would qualify for waivers of reporting requirements, based on plan size (fewer than 100 participants) and/or financial soundness.

As a general rule, there is a reportable event when the number of participants falls below 80% of the number of participants at the end of the previous year, or below 75% of the number at the beginning of the previous year, but the proposal waives reporting of this event for small (fewer than 100 participant) plans. Larger plans would only have to report if the reduction was caused by a single event such as reorganization or mass layoff; if the reduction occurred in a period of 30 days or less; or if the number of participants in the same year falls by more than 20%. Large plans can use the financial soundness safe harbor to avoid reporting based on reduction in the number of participants.

Reporting is not required if there has been a reorganization within a controlled group of corporations leading to one member of the group ceasing to exist because it has been merged into another member of the group. Prior law made it a reportable event when there is a default in payment of over 30 days on a loan of $10 million or more—not only by the plan sponsor, but any member of a controlled group of corporations it belongs to. Written notice of default based on reduced cash reserves or a lender's acceleration of a loan is also a reportable event. The proposed regulations not only retain this requirement but make it stronger: reporting is required when there is a loan acceleration or any kind of default, including a lender's waiver of its right to declare a default. Small plans and plans entitled to the financial soundness safe harbor must still report this event. [78 Fed. Reg. 20039 (Apr. 3, 2013); see Rebecca Moore, *PBGC Proposed Reduced Reporting Obligations*, plansponsor.com (Apr. 2, 2013); Buck Consultants FYI, *PBGC Reproposes Reportable Event Rules* (Apr. 5, 2013) (benefits link.com) In May, 2013 the PBGC gave more guidance about what constitutes a creditworthy company, based on, for example, the rating of the company's debt, its Financial Stress Score, or its debt: asset ratio. See PLC Employee Benefits & Employee Compensation, *PBGC Releases Enforcement Guidelines for ERISA Section 4062(e) Financial Assurance Program* (May 3, 2013) (benefits link.com).]

The PBGC announced a moratorium on §4062(e) enforcement for the second half of 2014, so that the PBGC could continue to develop rules for determining which pension plans are genuinely at risk. However, plans were instructed to continue to report new §4062(e) events as they occur, although the PBGC would not take action on the events. [PBGC Press Release No. 14-09, *PBGC Issues Moratorium on 4062(e) Enforcement*, <http://www.pbgc.gov/news/press/releases/pr14-09.html?cid=CPAD01PRJUL0820141> (July 8, 2014)]

The PBGC filed a complaint in the District Court for the Eastern District of Pennsylvania to involuntarily terminate Saint-Gobain Containers' defined benefit plan before a corporate transaction that would alter the sponsor's controlled group. The PBGC asserted that Saint-Gobain's acquisition (by stock purchase) by Ardagh Group, SA would move the plant to a weaker controlled group. On October 4, 2013, the district court ruled that it would make a de novo determination about whether to terminate the plan: the PBGC's determination would not be granted administrative deference. Therefore, the court would be able to consider evidence not in the PBGC administrative record. The PBGC characterized its decision to terminate the plan as an informal adjudication that operates as an agency action under the Administrative Procedure Act, but the district court rejected this argument: ERISA § 4042(c) requires a court to determine whether to terminate the plan, and the PBGC determination has no legal effect without a court order. [*PBGC v. Saint-Gobain Container Benefits Comm.*, No. 13-02069 (E.D. Pa. 2013); see Justin Alex, *The PBGC Not Entitled to Administrative Deference for Involuntary Plan Termination*, Proskauer's ERISA Practice Center Blog (Oct. 22, 2013) (benefitslink.com)]

§ 16.09 STOCK OPTIONS

During the late lamented Internet boom, stock options were greatly cherished by employees because of the possibility of purchasing stock for a few dollars and being able to resell it at a much higher price—especially if the company was a start-up with the potential for a high-flying Initial Public Offering. Under current depressed stock market conditions, far fewer employees hold options that can be exercised profitably. However, in the hope that conditions will turn around again, the topic is worth discussing.

Mergers raise many questions about stock options, including:

- Do employees of the acquired company forfeit their outstanding options?
- Are their options bought out?
- Do they receive options in the acquirer company in exchange?

One of the factors fueling the economic boom of the late 1990s and early 2000s was the incentive to mergers and acquisitions offered by "pooling of interest" accounting. When pooling of interest was available, it allowed two companies to exchange equity securities and pool their bookkeeping and accounting thereafter. The net result was that the company's reported earnings would be higher, because there was no need to amortize goodwill as an expense. In contrast, if the transaction had to be accounted for under the purchase method, the acquirer would be deemed to purchase the acquired company, and the financial statements of the combined entity must reflect the fair value of the company's assets and liabilities. However, for most transactions initiated after June 30, 2001, pooling of interest accounting is unavailable—the purchase method must be used instead. For most plans, all outstanding stock options will vest upon a change in control; vested options can be exercised within a limited period, such as 30 or 60 days.

[See § 22.02 for further discussion of stock options]

Treatment of outstanding options is an important part of M&A planning. Whether vesting should be accelerated when there is a change in control is a business decision, separate from consideration of the transaction's effect on outstanding options. The board of directors should be allowed maximum flexibility to decide, at the time of a transaction, whether options that have not already been exercised should be canceled; if the options should be taken over or substituted by the acquiring corporation; or cashed out for the difference between the exercise price of the option and the price per share of the stock to be received in the transaction. One possibility is to cancel the out-of-the-money options without consideration, but to pay cash for the in-the-money options. The acquiring company may wish to assume the target company's options instead of substituting them; substitution could deplete the acquiror's equity incentive plan pool—or could have the inadvertent effect of modifying the awards in a way that triggers § 409A or makes the options non-qualified.

If the acquiring company is a public corporation, the stock exchanges allow the remaining shares under the target company's assumed plan pool to be issued without approval by the shareholders. But the acquiror may prefer to substitute rather than assuming the target's options, if the acquiror wants all of its options to have uniform terms and conditions. Shares underlying substituted options do not have to be registered; there is already a registration statement in effect (which is not true of assumed options). The acquiror may prefer not to assume the options if their terms, or the size of the class qualifying for options, is not consistent with the acquiror's corporate culture. An acquiror that does not pay cash for the underlying stock in the transaction may prefer not to cash out the stock options, so the plan must be flexible enough to permit termination of the options instead. If the options are canceled, the optionees can exercise their vested options until the transaction closes. Cashing out options benefits the acquiror because it does not have to administer the options after the closing; it does not incur a compensation expense; its shareholders' equity is not diluted; and employees can get cash for their equity without having to pay out-of-pocket to fund the exercise price. Holders of options in private companies like cash-outs because the optionees can receive liquidity without having to make an investment.

It must be decided (either when the options are granted in the first place, or when a corporate transition occurs) whether vesting should be accelerated if the transaction constitutes a change of control. The acceleration provisions can be embodied in the incentive plan, or in agreements outside the plan, such as the option award, executives' employment contracts, their severance, or retention agreements. In addition to the conventional single- and double-trigger arrangements, hybrid arrangements are possible, such as partial vesting on change of control, with additional vesting if a second triggering event occurs. Or, vesting might depend on the way the options are treated in the transaction. For example, vesting might be accelerated only if the awards are not assumed by the acquiror, which would mean that the optionee would not be able to vest at a later time, even if he or she remains employed. [Pamela B. Greene and Ann Margaret Eames, *Stock Options in Merger & Acquisition Transactions*, Corporate & Securities Advisory (June 6, 2011) (benefitslink.com)]

CHAPTER 17
PLAN TERMINATION

§ 17.01 INTRODUCTION

When companies start a pension plan, they usually do so in good faith, and with the intention of keeping the plan in operation as long as it is necessary to provide benefits. However, ERISA and the Internal Revenue Code recognize that sometimes it will be necessary to terminate a pension plan—usually because the sponsoring corporation is ceasing operations, being absorbed by another company, or has financial difficulties so severe that it cannot continue to meet its obligations. There are even some rare circumstances under which the plan is *over* funded, and the employer is able to terminate the plan, distribute its assets, and retain the plan surplus for its own benefit.

Plan termination is usually voluntary, premised on the employer's decision to shut down the plan. However, courts, based on a determination that the economic security of plan participants is at risk, can order involuntary terminations. The legal system provides structures for winding up pension plans in an orderly way. Usually, the plan's assets are applied to purchase annuities that will pay participants' pensions as they become entitled to receive them.

A Towers Watson study says that, among companies that have frozen their plans, over 70% of companies that still enroll new hires in pension plans expect to keep doing that five years from now, but, almost 40% expect to terminate them and settle liabilities within five years: 58% said they have/expect to make lump sum payouts to eliminate pension risk; 87% of companies expecting to terminate plans think they'll use lump sum offers as part of the process. Half of the respondents said they already have a plan to reduce pension risk by moving to fixed-income investments as their funded status improves; another quarter are planning to do it in 2014 or maybe 2015. About 30% still have open pension plans; 73% of them said it was important for recruiting, 87% for retention. [James Willhite, *Pension Terminations May Spike in the Near-Term*, WSJ.com (Nov. 12, 2013)]

Under the relevant legal and tax rules, a plan termination can be either complete or partial. When a termination occurs, all accrued benefits vest immediately—including benefits that would not vest until later under the plan's normal vesting schedule. This requirement is imposed to reduce the temptation to terminate expensive and inconvenient plans!

Terminating a plan involves both the IRS and the Department of Labor (DOL). Both ERISA and the IRC must be consulted. There are forms to be filed, consents to be secured, and disclosure obligations to the participants and beneficiaries of the plan. Then, the plan's assets are distributed within an "administratively reasonable time" (generally defined as one year or less). But if the process continues for too long, the plan may be treated as if it had not terminated, and reports under I.R.C. §§ 6057–6059 will still be required. Section 6059 applies only to defined benefit plans.

■ **TIP:** Under some circumstances, a Reduction in Force (RIF) is deemed to cause a partial termination (for which vesting will be required). Therefore, before implementing an RIF, the company should determine the pension implications of the program.

A federal agency called the Pension Benefit Guaranty Corporation (PBGC) plays an important role in the termination of defined benefit plans. When a plan termination is contemplated, the plan notifies the PBGC, which has 60 days (or longer, if the plan consents to an extension) to review the proposed termination for any improprieties.

The PBGC also has the power to ask the federal court system to close down a pension plan (even if the employer has not sought to terminate the plan) and supervise the orderly distribution of its assets. The PBGC is not involved in the termination of defined contribution plans, because each participant in such a plan has an individual account that can be distributed to him or her.

There are certain exceptions to these general rules. Benefits are not guaranteed if they become nonforfeitable only because of the termination; nor does the agency guarantee benefits in full if the plan was in effect for less than 60 months before it terminated. If a benefit was scheduled to increase under a plan amendment that was either made or took effect within 60 months prior to the termination, the PBGC will not guarantee the increase.

The PBGC's guarantee applies only to benefits accrued before a plan terminates—and only to benefits accrued before the filing date if the employer is bankrupt when the plan terminates. In general, the PBGC pays benefits according to the terms of the plan, but if an individual's full benefit exceeds the PBGC's limit, the PBGC pays estimated benefits while it examines the plan records, and then reduces benefits to the limit. For about 80% of participants and beneficiaries, the estimated benefit is the same as the final benefit; but if the estimated benefits are lower than the actual benefit, the PBGC will make a single payment (including interest) to catch up. [PBGC, *PBGC's Guarantees for Single-Employer Pension Plans Fact Sheet*, <http://www.pbgc.gov/about/factsheets/page/guar-facts.html> (undated, accessed Apr. 4, 2014)]

Terminating a plan requires bringing it into conformity with all legal and regulatory changes since the last update and there are usually several federal statutes each year requiring conforming amendments.

Coverage under a fiduciary liability policy is triggered when the claim is made. Extended reporting period (ERP) coverage is optional, at extra cost. It covers claims filed during a specified period (typically, one year after the policy expired), relating to events during the policy term. Standard ERP coverage will not provide complete protection when a plan terminates because fiduciary breaches might be alleged for up to six years (the longest statute of limitations likely to be applied) after the plan was terminated. "Tail coverage" protects the trustees of terminated plans. According to Segal Select Insurance, the premium for a six-year tail policy is likely to be two or three times as high as the underlying fiduciary liability insurance for the pre-termination period. Tail coverage is usually paid from the assets of the plan that is being merged or is terminating, so it is important to arrange and pay for the coverage before the plan assets have all been distributed. [Segal Select Insurance Fiduciary Shield, *If a Plan Merger or Termination Is on the Horizon, Seek Tail Coverage* (March 2014) (benefitslink.com)]

[A] New Rules Under the PPA

The Pension Protection Act of 2006, Pub. L. No. 109-280, has affected most areas of pension and benefit law, and plan termination is no exception. The variable rate premium was capped for employers with 25 or fewer employees. To deter manipulation of employee censuses, the same participant count is used for both the flat- and variable-rate premiums. The PPA imposed a new category of premiums, a termination premium of $1,250 per participant per year for three years.

See <http://www.pbgc.gov/prac/prem/premium-rates.html> for the premium rates prevailing in 2013, reflecting subsequent legislation including the Moving Ahead for Progress in the 21st Century (MAP-21) Act, Pub. L. No. 112-140. The flat rate PBGC premium for 2014 is $49/participant for single-employer plans ($7 more than the 2013 level), $12/participant for multi-employer plans (no change). The variable rate premium for single-employer plans rises from $9 to $14 per $1,000 of unfunded vested benefit, reflecting both indexing and the $4 increase provided by MAP-21. The cap on the variable premium rises from $400 (2013) to $412 (2014), although the cap may be lower for plans with fewer than 25 participants. [Sarah Roe Sise and Carrie Elizabeth Byrnes, *PBGC Premium Rates Increase In 2014 For Single-Employer Plans Time To Cash-Out Some Deferred Vested Participants?*, Bryan Cave LLP (Nov. 15, 2013), available at Lexology.com]

Under the Bipartisan Budget Act of 2013, Pub. L. No. 113-67, the proposed flat rate premium is $57/participant, the variable rate is $14/$1,000 UVB, with a cap of at least $412. For 2016, the proposed flat rate is $64, the variable rate at least $29, and the proposed cap $500, with those figures to be indexed in 2017. [Buck Consultants FYI, *PBGC Premium Hikes in Final Budget Deal*, Vol. 36 Issue 105 (Dec. 27, 2013) (benefitslink.com)]

If a plan is at risk (see Chapter 5 for more discussion), it will be limited in its ability to provide shutdown benefits, unless the employer either makes additional contributions to strengthen the plan, or provides security for the benefits. Participants in at-risk plans are entitled to notification about the limits on distributions. Furthermore if a distress or involuntary termination occurs, the plan must inform the participants (within 15 days of the PBGC filing) of the information contained in the notice to the PBGC (new ERISA § 4041(c)(2)(D), 4042(c)(3)).

The D.C. Circuit held that shutdown benefits were not payable when Thunderbird Mining Corporation, a wholly owned subsidiary of Eveleth Mines, terminated its pension plan, because Thunderbird was not "shut down." The company was still trying to get new orders after production was stopped at its plant, although production had ceased and all except four hourly employees had been laid off. The bankruptcy court approved the sale of the Eveleth assets; the purchaser hired the hourly employees under a new CBA. [*United Steel Workers v. PBGC*, 707 F.3d 319 (D.C. Cir. 2013); see Rebecca Moore, *Court Agrees With PBGC Denial of Shutdown Benefits*, plansponsor.com (Jan. 23, 2013)]

In mid-2008, the PBGC proposed a rule under the PPA, to treat the termination date of a plan that ends when its employer is in bankruptcy as of the date of the filing of the bankruptcy petition, not the actual date of termination. The effect of this rule is that the benefits guaranteed by the PBGC will probably be somewhat smaller, because amounts earned by plan participants after the date of the bankruptcy filing will not be guaranteed by the PBGC. The rule was finalized in mid-2011. [Proposed Rule, 73 Fed. Reg. 37390 (July 1, 2008); see *Pension Guarantees Fact Sheet*, <http://www.pbgc.gov/media/key-resources-for-the-press/content/page13542.html> Final Rule, 76 Fed. Reg. 34590 (June 14, 2011).]

Some employers that downsized have been required to settle PBGC claims under ERISA § 4062(c), which allows the PBGC to demand immediate escrow payments or posting of bond when cessation of operations results in separation from service of 20% or more of the participants in a defined benefit plan. PBGC regulations say the amount of liability is the amount by which the plan is underfunded, calculated as if the plan terminated immediately after cessation of operations, multiplied by the percentage reduction in active participants. To satisfy its claim, the PBGC can demand that the amount of liability be placed into escrow, or that the employer purchase a bond of up to 150% of the liability amount, to protect the plan in case there is an involuntary or distress termination. If an involuntary or distress termination occurs, the escrow funds or bond proceeds are considered plan assets. However, if five years passes without an involuntary or distress termination, then the bond is canceled or the escrow money is returned. The PBGC is not required to pay interest on the funds. [Final Rule, RIN 1212-AB03, 71 Fed. Reg. 34819 (June 16, 2006)]

In effect, the sponsor of a single-employer plan is treated as if it were a multi-employer plan. In mid-2010, the PBGC proposed amendments to the rules for termination of single-employer plans to clarify the treatment of substantial cessation of operations as defined by ERISA § 4062(e). The 2006 final rule explains how to compute the employer's liability; the 2011 proposal explains what constitutes a § 4062(e) event. Certain events are treated as predicting that the plan is likely to terminate within five years when it is underfunded—whether or not particular risk factors are present in the case of an individual plan.

The proposal says that § 4062(e) is triggered when "an operation" at a "facility in any location" ceases—even if the employer transfers the operation to another facility. Determining whether "cessation" has occurred depends on whether there has only been a cutback or contraction in the operation—or if the change is so major that the operation can no longer be considered ongoing. The proposal has separate rules for voluntary and involuntary discontinuances of activities. The PBGC must be notified within 60 days after withdrawal from the plan. The employer must maintain a specific amount in escrow or a corresponding bond for five years from the date of withdrawal. If the plan terminates during this five-year period, the bond or escrow is applied toward any underfunding. However, § 4063(e) authorizes the PBGC to waive this liability if the sponsors of the plan have an appropriate indemnity agreement, and the PBGC can make alternative arrangements to satisfy the obligation (see § 4067).

Under the proposal, the "active participant base" means the baseline number of active participants used to determine if a 20% reduction has occurred. If the employer has two or more plans, § 4062(e) applies separately to each, not on an aggregate basis.

Cessation has occurred when the employer no longer conducts the operation at the facility on an ongoing basis, but activity that does not further the purpose of the operation is disregarded, so operations may be considered terminated even if maintenance and security are kept up. Continuance or resumption at another facility or by another employer is disregarded in determining if a cessation occurred.

The § 4062(e) event consists of two parts (cessation and 20% drop in participant count). For discontinuance as a result of employee action (e.g., a strike) the cessation date is delayed until after the employee action ends, plus a week for the employer to resume work. If there is cessation due to a sudden and unanticipated event not caused by employee action, such as a natural disaster, the cessation date is deferred for 30 days.

The 60-day period for notice does not begin until both cessation and reduction in the number of employees have occurred. Only current employees are included in calculating the number of participants just before cessation. However, an employee does not have to accrue benefits to be considered a participant: The PBGC does not want employers to be able to benefit from plan freezes. There is no small plan exemption under this rule. The PBGC says that small plans are adequately protected under the rule, and they have less potential for underfunding and accordingly less exposure. [PBGC, *Liability for Termination of Single-Employer Plans; Treatment of Substantial Cessation of Operations*, FR Doc 2010-19695, RIN 1212-AB20, 75 Fed. Reg. 48283 (Aug. 10, 2010) The forms package for reporting is available at <http://www.pbgc.gov/docs/Package_4062-E_ppsd.d10.pdf> (undated, accessed Apr. 4, 2014)]

A late 2012 PBGC announcement says that about 92% of plan sponsors will not have to provide guarantees under § 4062(e) enforcement because the PBGC declines to take action against creditworthy companies or small pension plans (fewer than 100 participants). This is a policy change: the PBGC used to enforce all § 4062(e) cases. Section 4062(e) requires companies with defined benefit plans to report cessation of operations at a facility where more than 20% of employees have separated from employment so that they can be asked for financial security. The PBGC proposed regulations in August 2010, which were withdrawn after industry protests that many companies are unlikely to default because the plan is small or the plan is strong enough to satisfy its pension obligations. More lenient regulations were proposed in March 2012, dividing companies into three categories of financial strength. [PBGC, *Frequently Asked Questions 4062(e) Pilot Program*, <http://www.pbgc.gov/about/faq/pg/frequently-asked-questions-4062.html> (un dated, accessed Apr. 4, 2014) The policy continued to evolve, and a moratorium on §4062(e) enforcement was called for the second half of 2014. Reporting of § 4062(e) events continued to be required, but the PBGC promised that no enforcement action would be taken with respect to those events before 2015 at the earliest. [PBGC Press Release No. 14-09, *PBGC Issues Moratorium on 4062(e) Enforcement*, <http://www.pbgc.gov/news/press/releases/pr14-09.html?cid=CPAD01PRJUL0820141> (July 8, 2014)]

§ 17.02 TERMINATION TYPES

Once the decision to terminate the plan is made, the date of termination must be chosen. The corporation's Board of Directors will probably have to pass a resolution to this effect. Participants and beneficiaries are entitled to between 60 and 90 days' notice of the impending termination. Benefits will probably be distributed as annuities, lump sums, and/or transfers to IRAs and other qualified plans. If it is determined that the assets are sufficient to satisfy all benefit obligations, then the IRS and PBGC forms are prepared and submitted. The relevant forms include PBGC Form 500 and IRS Forms 5310, 6088, and 8717. Participants and beneficiaries are given an official Notice of Plan Benefits. They are also entitled to 45 days' notice of which insurer will provide the annuities for benefits distributed in this form.

Once the forms are filed, the PBGC has 60 days to raise any concerns it has. The IRS can take as long as 18 months to review filings and issue a determination letter. But once the determination letter has been issued, the funds must be distributed within 120 days.

The three most common funding strategies are:

- Contributing a minimum amount for an ongoing plan each year until termination, with a final contribution when the plan's assets are distributed—typically, 18–24 months after the termination date)
- Contributing a level amount each year until the year of planned termination—e.g., if termination is set for five years in the future, spread the cost evenly over the five-year period

- Fully funding the plan under the PPA rules for ongoing plans, using investment income to make up for the shortfall when the plan is terminated.

The first alternative is probably the most expensive, but it reduces the time frame until termination—and risk increases over time. [*Principal Life Ins Co. Thought Capital: Winding Down Your Hard-Frozen Defined Benefit (DB) Plan* (March 2012) (benefitslink.com)]

[A] Generally

There are two types of voluntary termination: standard and distress. See 29 C.F.R. Part 4041 for Regulations. A standard termination, governed by ERISA § 4041, is used by plans that have at least enough assets to pay the benefits guaranteed by the PBGC. All terminations are handled as standard terminations unless the PBGC permits a "distress termination," which imposes lower obligations on the plan.

Under ERISA § 4044, there are six priority categories of accrued benefits. When the plan's assets are distributed, all Category-1 claims must be paid, then all Category-2 claims, and so on, until the assets are exhausted. Therefore, in many instances some of the classes will go unpaid. The categories, in descending order of priority, are:

- Voluntary employee contributions made to the plan. (NOTE: These amounts are NOT guaranteed by the PBGC, because they fall outside the definition of "basic benefits.");
- Mandatory contributions that employees made to the plan, plus 5% interest;
- Annuity benefits that derive from employer contributions, if the annuity was or could have been in pay status three years or more before termination of the plan. ("Could have been" refers to the situation in which employees continue to work despite their eligibility for early retirement);
- All other PBGC-guaranteed benefits;
- All other nonforfeitable benefits;
- All benefits that are accrued but forfeitable.

Before a plan administrator can actually make any distributions, there is a legal obligation to determine the plan's ability to pay benefits at the level deemed appropriate by the PBGC. The plan administrator must notify the PBGC if the plan is unable to pay the guaranteed benefits. The PBGC makes its own determination and issues notices. If, on the other hand, the administrator determines that the PBGC-guaranteed benefits, but not all the guaranteed liabilities, can be paid, then the plan should distribute the assets but notify the PBGC.

If the PBGC affirms the administrator's characterization, it will issue a Notice of Liability resolving the issue of the plan's sufficiency. The plan administrator is obligated to provide a new valuation of the plan's liabilities and guaranteed benefits. An enrolled actuary must certify the valuation.

Hughes Aircraft Co. v. Jacobson [525 U.S. 432 (1999)], which involved several other pension issues, also affects plan termination. This case involves a plan partially funded by mandatory employee contributions. The employer suspended its own contributions at a time when the plan had a surplus. The employer created a new, noncontributory plan for new plan participants. Participants in the existing plan charged the employer with ERISA violations in connection with the amendment. The Supreme Court held that the employees were not entitled to an order terminating the plan voluntarily because the changes in plan structure did not constitute an ERISA § 4041(a)(1) voluntary termination. As long as a plan continues to provide benefits to participants and to accumulate funds for future payments, termination is not appropriate.

Under the Supreme Court's 2007 *Beck* ruling, it is not a violation of fiduciary duty for a bankrupt company to put the plan through a standard termination (and purchase annuities to satisfy the obligation to pay benefits) in lieu of merging the pension plan into a multi-employer union-run fund. [*Beck v. PACE Int'l Union*, 551 U.S. 96 (2007)]

Also note that the final regulations about nonqualified plans such as top-hat plans provide that terminating and then liquidating a nonqualified plan may be considered a prohibited acceleration of payments that results in the recipient being taxed under Code § 409A. There is an exception to this rule if the employer terminates all the plans of the same type, pays out benefits over a period of one to two years, and refrains from adopting new plans of the same type for three years. [Final Regulations, 73 Fed. Reg. 19234 (Apr. 17, 2007)]

[B] Standard Termination

The steps in a standard termination are:

- Plan sponsor decides to terminate the plan, e.g., because the plan is too expensive, or the amount of contributions is too hard to predict.
- Sponsor ensures that the plan has enough assets to satisfy all of its liabilities. It may be necessary for the plan sponsor to make a "top-up" contribution to ensure the necessary level of assets. Or, the sponsor can "freeze and wait," giving § 204(h) notice and hoping that the funding gap will be eliminated if the plan's economic condition improves. If the plan

is not able to distribute all required benefits in full, a standard termination is unavailable, and only a distress termination or involuntary termination remains possible.

- Standard termination is not permitted if it violates an existing CBA. The PBGC refuses to intervene when a union challenges a proposed standard termination; the challenge has to be resolved as a labor dispute.
- Sponsor decides what replacement benefits participants will receive (e.g., the company could adopt a new 401(k) plan).
- Not only must the legally required notices be issued, plan participants should be kept informed about the rationale for the termination and how it will affect them economically.
- The plan's investment strategy may have to change, e.g., to make sure that there is enough liquidity to distribute benefits. If there are any excess assets remaining after participants receive their benefits, either the remaining funds will revert to the employer (if reversion is allowed) or will be distributed among the participants.
- The plan may have to be amended, e.g., to permit lump sum distributions or to eliminate ancillary benefits such as life insurance that are not protected by ERISA. If the plan is not already frozen, the sponsor will probably want to amend it to freeze benefit accruals as of the planned date of termination, even if the standard termination has not been completed. The PBGC's regulations disregard any amendment adopted after a termination date if it reduces benefits (even optional benefits), unless the amendment was required by the Internal Revenue Code.
- The PBGC requires plans to perform a "diligent search" to locate missing participants. [See, e.g., Harold J. Ashner, *Planning a Standard Termination—A Checklist for Practitioners*, 16 J. of Pension Benefits No. 1 (Winter 2009) (benefitslink.com)]

The appropriate PBGC form for carrying out a standard termination is Form 500 (Standard Termination Notice).

When a plan goes through a standard termination, ERISA § 4050 provides for payment of a designated amount to the PBGC to cover claims from missing participants. The calculation usually depends on the most valuable annuity benefit payable under ERISA assumptions about missing participants, which use the Part 4044 interest assumptions, but with a different mortality table. Until 2007, the PBGC used the table in Rev. Rul. 95-6, but effective February 27, 2007, a blend of mortality rates for healthy males and healthy females (50% each) taken from Part 4044 will be used instead. [RIN 1212-AB08; see (No by-line) *PBGC Revises Mortality Assumptions in Regulations*, CCH Pension and Benefits (Jan. 25, 2007) (benefitslink.com)] See Mortality tables for 2014 valuation dates, <http://www.

pbgc.gov/prac/mortality-retirement-and-pv-max-guarantee/erisa-mortality-tables/erisa-section-4044-mortality-table-for-2014-valuation-dates.html> (accessed Apr. 4, 2014) for the dates in 2014.

To find missing participants, terminating plans can use the PBGC's missing participants program, paying the benefits to the PBGC, which then searches for the participants. Although the PPA mandated that the PBGC extend this program to cover terminating 401(k) plans, the PBGC did not issue implementing regulations. The DOL's suggestions for finding missing participants include commercial locater services, internet searches, and consulting credit reports.

Effective for requests postmarked on or after August 31, 2012, the IRS will no longer forward letters from plan sponsors who need to find the payees of benefits. Rev. Proc. 2012-35, 2012-37 I.R.B. 341 states that the IRS no longer considers finding missing participants a "humane purpose." The IRS service was free for up to 50 participants. The ending of this options means employers will have to use a more difficult and expensive method. The Social Security Administration's forwarding service is still available, but it costs $25 per letter. Sponsors and administrators who want to use EPCRS (see § 15.19[B]) and must find missing participants to pay additional benefits will be affected by the change, so the IRS said that it would publish EPCRS guidance with an extended correction period for employers affected by the change. [McDermott Will & Emery, *IRS Eliminates Use of Letter Forwarding Service to Find Missing Participants and Beneficiaries* (Sept. 27, 2012) (benefitslink.com); Plansponsor staff, *IRS Stops Forwarding Letters for Missing Participants*, plansponsor.com (September 4, 2012)]

In August 2014, the DOL issued Field Assistance Bulletin 2014-01, explaining how to find missing participants and distribute their account balances, given that the IRS letter-forwarding service is no longer available. If notice cannot be given to participants through first-class mail or e-mail, the DOL says that the employer can use certified mail; check its records other than the records of the terminated plan (e.g., EGHP records, which may be more current); ask the beneficiary designated under the plan how to locate the participant; or use no-fee Internet tools like public record databases and Internet search mechanisms. The DOL says that the duties of prudence and loyalty may require a plan fiduciary to take additional steps if the participant still cannot be located; the size of the account should be balanced against the cost of additional search (e.g., by hiring an investigator or purchasing access to credit reports). The DOL says that if a participant cannot be located, or does not give distribution instructions, fiduciaries should consider transferring the benefits into an IRA. As a last resort the funds may have to be deposited into a bank account for the participant, or transferred to the state unclaimed property fund. It may be necessary to withhold income tax on such amounts. [DOL FAB 2014-01, <http://www.dol.gov/ebsa/regs/fab2014-1.html> (Aug. 14, 2014); see Rebecca Moore, *DOL Issues Guidance for Locating Missing Participants*, plansponsor.com (Aug. 14, 2014)]

Within 120 days after the proposed termination date, the plan administrator must submit a Schedule EA-5 of the Form 500, a certificate prepared by a PBGC-enrolled actuary to the PBGC. The certificate estimates the value of the plan assets and the present value of plan liabilities, so that the actuary can certify that assets are adequate to satisfy the liabilities. The administrator must also furnish any other information the PBGC requests. The plan administrator must certify under penalty of perjury that the actuary's certificate is correct, and that the information given to the PBGC has been accurate and complete.

Once all the assets are distributed, the administrator must file PBGC Form 501 within 30 days of the final distribution, to prove that the assets were distributed. The penalty for a late form can be up to $1,100 a day. [See 29 C.F.R. § 4010.13] Late filing can also have the effect of creating a last, short plan year for the plan—thereby reducing the refund of the PBGC premium that the employer would otherwise be entitled to receive.

The ERISA § 204(h) notice of the amendment (including disclosure of its effective date) must be given. [See § 5.07 for further discussion of this issue]

[C] Notification

The DOL's *Reporting and Disclosure Guide for Employee Benefit Plans* [<http://www.dol.gov/ebsa/pdf/rdguide.pdf> (August 2013)] explains that voluntary standard termination of a single-employer plan that is insured by the PBGC and has enough assets to provide all plan benefits is a nine-step process:

- Choose the termination date
- Issue a Notice of Intent to Terminate (NOIT) to the affected parties (other than the PBGC); Appendix B of the Form 500 package includes a model NOIT
- Issue a Notice of Plan Benefits to participants and beneficiaries no later than the time Form 500, the Standard Termination Notice, is filed with the PBGC
- File the PBGC Form 500 no later than 180 days after the proposed termination date. The PBGC has 60 days to review Form 500 for compliance
- File a Notice of Annuity Information if any benefits may be distributed in annuity form. The notice is due no later than 45 days before the distribution date
- Distribute the plan assets needed to satisfy all plan benefits in time for the distribution deadline; the distribution deadline is 180 days after the 60-day PBGC review period ends, or 120 days after receipt of a favorable IRS determination letter, whichever is later (provided that the plan

administrator requested the determination letter no later than the time Form 500 was filed with the PBGC)

- If there are any missing participants, use the procedure described in PBGC Schedule MP
- Give participants who receive their benefits in annuity form a Notice of Annuity Contract within 30 days of final distribution of all benefits
- File Form 501, the Post-Distribution Certificate, with the PBGC within 30 days of distribution of all benefits. The PBGC's policy is that it will not impose penalties for late filing of Form 501 unless it is filed more than 90 days after the distribution deadline, including any extensions.

The reporting and disclosure requirements for a standard termination, as prescribed by ERISA §§ 4041, 4050, and 29 C.F.R. (Parts 4041 and 4050) are:

- Notice of intent to terminate (NOIT);
- Standard Termination Notice (Form 500, including Schedule EA-S);
- Notice of plan benefits (NOPB);
- Notice of annuity information
- Notice of annuity contract
- Post-Distribution Certification (Form 501);
- Schedule MP (Missing Participants).

At least 60 days but not more than 90 days before the proposed date of a voluntary termination, the plan administrator must provide notice of the intended termination. [ERISA § 4041(a)(2)] Notice must be given to plan participants; their beneficiaries; alternate payees under domestic relations orders; and the employees' collective bargaining representative (if the workplace is unionized). Anyone who becomes a beneficiary of a deceased participant or becomes an alternate payee (e.g., as a result of divorce) after the proposed termination date but before the plan's assets have been distributed is also entitled to a NOIT.

■ **TIP:** Selection of the insurer is a fiduciary decision, subject to the normal rules of fiduciary duty. The notice must also identify a contact person who will answer questions about the termination process.

Items to be disclosed on the NOIT include:

- The sponsor's name and EIN
- The plan's name and plan number
- Name, address, and telephone number of a contact person

- The fact that the sponsor intends to carry out a standard termination
- Proposed termination date; this can be a Saturday, Sunday, or federal holiday
- A statement that another notice will be given if the termination does not occur, or the termination date changes
- A statement that the plan assets must be adequate to provide all plan benefits for a standard termination to occur
- The applicable statement about the end of benefit accruals (see below)
- A statement that everyone entitled to benefits will receive a written notification explaining benefits
- How to get a copy of the updated SPD; the plan administration can also include a copy of the SPD with each copy of the NOIT
- Disclosure that the PBGC guarantee ends when all the assets have been distributed
- For people whose benefits are already in pay status on the proposed termination date, either a statement that their benefits will not be affected by the termination, or an explanation of how they will be affected
- Notice of annuity information, unless the participant will be cashed out by receiving a lump sum; e.g., the name and address of all insurers from whom annuity contracts will be purchased, and the facts that the insurer becomes responsible for payment once the annuity is purchased, and that state guaranty associations back up this obligation
- If the transaction is a spin-off/termination, participants and beneficiaries of the original plan must be notified 60–90 days before the proposed termination date, receiving information about annuities furnished by the surviving plan.

There are three possibilities for cessation of benefit accruals: either they cease on the termination date (but continue if the plan does not terminate); a plan amendment is adopted, pursuant to ERISA § 204(h), cutting off benefit accruals as of a specified date; or benefit accruals have already ceased, pursuant to § 204(h), before the NOIT was issued.

The NOPB explains who is the sponsor of the plan, who can be contacted for benefit questions, and the amount of the benefit. If the benefit is only estimated, that must be disclosed. For people already receiving benefits, the NOPB explains the amount and form of benefits payable as of the termination date; any benefits payable on the participant's death, and who they go to; and an explanation of any change in the benefit that has happened or is scheduled to happen after termination of the plan. For participants who will be cashed out involuntarily, the

NOPB explains how much the benefit is; who the beneficiary is; and beneficiary's entitlement to death benefits. For lump sum benefits other than involuntary cashouts, the NOPD explains which mortality table will be used to value the lump sum, how interest rates are used in the calculation, and what the interest rates are. If the benefits will not be paid in a lump sum, the NOPD explains how the payment will differ from the plan's normal retirement benefit. For people whose benefits are not yet in pay status, the NOPB explains the basic form of distribution at normal retirement age, alternative benefit forms, any benefits available before NRA, and information about lump sum calculations.

Once the plan assets have been distributed, Form 501 (Post-Distribution Certification) must be given to the PBGC within 30 days of the end of the distribution processes. The PBGC has announced that it will not impose penalties for late submission of this form if it is provided within 90 days after the deadline, including any extensions. Schedule MP, alerting the PBGC to the existence of participants or beneficiaries whose addresses the plan administrator cannot find, is filed with Form 501.

The PPA enacted new ERISA sections, § 4041(c)(2)(D), 4042(c)(3), requiring plan participants to be given the same information about involuntary and distress terminations as the plan furnishes to the PBGC. The new requirement replaces the participant notice formerly required under ERISA § 4011. See <http://www.pbgc.gov/documents/500_instructions.pdf> for the Form 500 instructions. Information about plan termination must also be provided in the Summary Plan Description (SPD) furnished to plan participants. Form 500 is filed with Schedule EA-S, which specifies that the plan's assets are sufficient to satisfy its obligations.

If the PBGC deems the Form 500 to be incomplete, or the plan fails to submit additional information requested by the PBGC, the PBGC has the power to issue a Notice of Noncompliance, which stops the standard termination process—and restores the plan to status as an ongoing plan. A Notice of Noncompliance can also be issued if the plan administrator fails to properly complete the distribution of all plan assets.

[D] Distress Termination

A plan that does not have enough assets to pay all the benefit liabilities can apply to the PBGC for a "distress" termination, which is available only if the plan's sponsors (and the other corporations that are part of a controlled group of corporations with the sponsor) can prove financial hardship, e.g., involvement in voluntary or involuntary bankruptcy or insolvency proceedings. See 29 C.F.R §§ 4041.41–4041.50.

If a company makes a Chapter 11 filing, seeking bankruptcy reorganization, a distress termination will be permitted only if the bankruptcy court decides that terminating the plan is necessary, or that the company cannot remain in business and pay its debts if it maintains the plan.

The PBGC's *Distress Termination Filing Instructions* are available online at <http://www.pbgc.gov/Documents/600_instructions.pdf> (accessed Apr. 4, 2014).

When the PBGC takes over a plan in a distress termination, the employer is liable to the PBGC for the amount of underfunding, which in most cases will become a general unsecured claim. The PBGC is often one of the debtor's largest unsecured creditors, entitled to a pro rata share of the recovery for the class of general unsecured creditor. It is a basic fact of bankruptcy that the amount of influence a creditor has is proportionate to the size of its claim. The PBGC receives distributions under the debtor's reorganization plan—often in the stock of the reorganized debtor company, which the PBGC sells to recoup some funds. [Ronald Silverman and Scott Seamon, *The Unexpected Guest*, N.Y.L.J. (Dec. 13, 2010) (law.com)]

Distress termination might also be permitted if the sponsor proves to the PBGC that terminating the plan is essential to paying its debts and remaining in operation. A distress termination might also be available if pension costs have become intolerable only because of the decline in the covered workforce—loss of stock market value of the plans' assets would not be considered an acceptable rationale.

The documents required for a distress termination are:

- Form 600 (Distress Termination Notice of Intent to Terminate), given to the PBGC;
- Notice of Intent to Terminate (NOIT; given to all other interested parties, such as participants, beneficiaries, unions, and alternate payees; the plan must also disclose whatever information was submitted to the PBGC within 15 days of a request, or whenever the plan updates the information given to the PBGC that was the subject of a previous request);
- Notice of request to bankruptcy court (given to the PBGC whenever the plan asks the Bankruptcy Court to approve plan termination as part of the bankruptcy process);
- Form 601 (Distress Termination Notice for a single-employer plan);
- Form 602 (post-distribution certification) furnished to the PBGC within 30 days of completion of the distribution process; here, too, the PBGC will not assess penalties if the form is furnished within 90 days of the end of the process;
- Schedule MP (Missing Participants).

To request a distress termination, the plan must file PBGC Form 600 and 601 to notify the PBGC and the plan's participants, respectively. Affected participants must get at least 60 days' notice but not more than 90 days' notice, using a Notice of Intent to Terminate (NOIT). Form 601 must be filed on or before the 120th day after the proposed termination date. The duty to notify participants is more or less the same for standard and distress terminations. A distress termination calls for actuarial certification, using Schedule EA-D of the Form 601. The PBGC must be informed about participants and beneficiaries, within 120 days after the proposed termination date, or 30 days after the PBGC informs the plan that requirements for a distress termination have been satisfied—whichever is later.

For a distress termination to be permitted, the PBGC must make a determination that the plan sponsor and any affiliated corporations all satisfy at least one financial distress test (different corporations can satisfy different tests), such as: a liquidating bankruptcy petition has been filed; a petition for bankruptcy reorganization has been filed, and the court approves plan termination because the reorganization would otherwise be impossible; the sponsor or an affiliate must terminate the plan to stay in business; or the cost of pension coverage has become unreasonably burdensome—but only because of the decline in the number of covered employees.

Starting on the proposed termination date, the plan reduces the benefits of participants who are already receiving benefits to the amount of the maximum PBGC guarantee.

If the plan has enough assets to pay the guaranteed benefits, the PBGC issues a "distribution notice." Within 15 days of receiving this notice, the plan administrator must give each participant and beneficiary a notice of impending distribution. Unless an extension has been granted, the distribution must begin within 60 days and be completed within 240 days. Then PBGC Form 602 (Post-Distribution Certification) must be filed within 30 days of the completion of distribution of the assets. If the plan does not have enough assets to satisfy all benefits liabilities, the plan sponsor and all members of its controlled group are jointly and severally liable to the PBGC for all unfunded benefit liabilities calculated under 29 C.F.R. 4022 Subpart D.

When Metaldyne Corporation went out of business, the District Court for the District of Columbia ruled that Asahi, the Japanese company that bought Metaldyne Corp. was liable for the termination premiums and other obligations resulting from the dissolution of Metaldyne's pension plan. The district court did not set specific damages, but held that the acquisition made Asahi a controlled group member of Metaldyne, making it liable for unfunded benefit liabilities and termination premiums for the plan. Discovery in the suit revealed that Asahi managers were aware of the pension liabilities and were aware of significant underfunded obligations to both union and non-union employees. The PBGC warned Asahi that it was still responsible for pension liabilities after its U.S. based wholly owned subsidiary, created to carry out the acquisition filed as a Chapter 11 debtor in possession in the Southern District of New York bankruptcy court. The PBGC took over as trustee of the plan. [*PBGC v. Asahi Tec [sic] Corp.*, No. 10-1936 (ABJ), 2013 WL 5503191 (D.D.C. Oct. 4, 2013); see John Manganaro, *Japanese Firm Ruled Liable for U.S. Subsidiary Pension Obligations*, plansponsor.com (Oct. 25, 2013)]

The Eleventh Circuit held that the bankruptcy trustee of a bankrupt sponsor cannot sue the former owner of the corporation on behalf of the estate and the unsecured creditors for liabilities from termination of the plan. ERISA provides that, once a plan is terminated, all parties except the PBGC are limited in the relief they can receive from either the current or former controlled group. The PBGC can obtain legal or equitable relief against the controlled group for failure to fund the plan, but all other parties can only obtain equitable relief. The bankruptcy trustee sued on behalf of non-PBGC parties. The district court held that the trustee sought a lump-sum amount, which is a legal remedy. The Eleventh Circuit, however, held in early 2014 that it was irrelevant whether the remedies were legal or equitable: the trustee does not have a cause of action to recover funds for the bankruptcy estate. ERISA does not make the controlled group's duty to pay unfunded benefit liability run to the plan sponsor. It runs to the beneficiaries of the plan, not the bankrupt sponsor's unsecured creditors. Furthermore, the statute of limitations had run, so the PBGC could no longer sue the controlled group for termination liability. [*Durango-Georgia Paper Co v. H.G. Estate LLC*, 739 F.3d 1263 (11th Cir. 2014)]

As soon as possible after receiving an application for a distress termination, the PBGC is supposed to rule on the application. If the agency turns down the application and the plan has enough assets to satisfy its liabilities, a standard termination is carried out. But if the assets are inadequate and the PBGC is not cooperative, the plan cannot go through a voluntary termination at all. The plan will also have to reverse the benefit reductions and return to the previous level of payment. [PBGC, *What Is a Distress Termination?*, <http://www.pbgc.gov/prac/terminations/distress-terminations.html> (undated, accessed Apr. 4, 2014). The distress termination filing instructions are available at <http://www.pbgc.gov/Documents/600_instructions.pdf> (undated, accessed Apr. 4, 2014).]

[E] Partial Termination

Full vesting is required when a plan is terminated or partially terminated, but there is no simple definition of "partial termination." The IRS says that partial termination occurs when there is a substantial reduction in the number or percentage of plan participants—e.g., when there has been a significant layoff. Hence, a company considering layoffs must consider whether the action will have implications on the pension plan. An amendment that excludes a group of employees from the plan could also trigger partial termination. Partial termination also requires allocation of forfeitures and other unallocated amounts held by the plan. Whether partial termination has occurred is determined by all the facts and circumstances, but IRS guidance says that partial termination is presumed when there has been 20% turnover. The presumption can be rebutted by showing that this level of turnover is routine. [Holland & Hart LLP, *Layoffs May Trigger 100% Vesting in Retirement Plans* (Jan. 9, 2009) (benefitslink.com)]

The IRS is pursuing both defined benefit and defined contribution plans that have experienced partial termination events. When a partial termination occurs, all affected participants become 100% vested, although usually they will not receive distributions except to the extent they are eligible because of termination of employment. The IRS Employee Plans Compliance Unit's Partial Termination/ Partial Vesting Project uses data from Form 5500 filings to discover partial termination events (involuntary removal of a group of employees from plan participation when there has been a significant reduction in the participant group). A partial termination could be caused by plant shutdown, layoffs, downsizing, restructuring, or a sale that excludes a group of participants from the plan. The determination that a partial termination has occurred is a fiduciary decision generally made by the plan administrator or administrative committee. Although there are IRS guidelines, the determination must be made based on the facts and circumstances of the case.

The IRS uses a rebuttable presumption that there has been a partial termination if there has been a 20% turnover rate within a short period of time. The turnover rate equals the number of participants whose severance from employment is initiated by the employer during the applicable period divided by the sum of the number of participants at the start of the applicable period and the participants added during the applicable period.

The IRS treats any separation from service other than death, disability, or retirement at normal retirement age as employer-initiated, unless the employer can verify that the employee chose to leave or was terminated for cause. Events outside the employer's control, such as economic conditions, are still considered employer-initiated. The employer's normal turnover rate is also a factor: if this year's rate is 22% but the historical rate is 10%, the IRS might be persuaded that the current turnover rate is really only 12%, so there has not been a partial termination. For 401(k) plans, all employees eligible to make elective deferrals are considered participants, whether or not they actually make deferrals. [Lisa B. Zimmer, *Partial Plan Termination . . . What's That?* Warner Norcross & Judd LLP (Nov. 11, 2011) (benefitslink.com)]

If participation levels drop purely as a result of voluntary employee turnover and the employer's actions did not cause the reduction, there has not been a partial termination. However, in some cases employees allege that they were constructively terminated rather than quitting voluntarily or that they were fraudulently induced to take severance. To defend itself, the employer needs records showing whether departing employees quit or were laid off. Despite the Revenue Ruling using a 20% standard for partial terminations, some courts have found a partial termination based on the number rather than percentage of layoffs if they were motivated by a desire to reduce employer contributions or increase forfeitures. [Jeffrey C. Chang, *A Question of Vesting – Determining If Your Plan Has Suffered A Partial Termination*, Chang Ruthenberg & Long (undated, last accessed Mar. 30, 2013) (benefitslink.com)]

The Seventh Circuit rule is that events from more than one plan year can be used to determine if a partial termination has occurred, when an employee alleges that his balances should vest fully because of the termination. [*Matz v. Household Int'l Tax Reduction Inv. Plan*, 227 F.3d 971 (7th Cir. 2000); see also *Sea Ray v. Robinson*, 164 F.3d 981 (6th Cir. 1999)] The Sixth Circuit's rationale in this situation is that, if review was limited to a single year, employers would be able to escape liability by firing some employees in December, some in January. [*Sea Ray*, 164 F.3d 981]

On a related issue, the *Matz* court required counting of both vested and nonvested participants to determine whether a partial termination occurred. However, the Supreme Court ordered the court to reconsider its opinion because of *United States v. Mead Corp.* [533 U.S. 218 (2001)], a Supreme Court case about the extent to which courts have to abide by the rules of administrative agencies. This time, the Seventh Circuit decided that only nonvested participants should be counted in deciding if there has been a partial termination. [*Matz v. Household Int'l Tax Reduction Inv. Plan*, 265 F.3d 572 (7th Cir. 2001)] Litigation in the case continued, and in 2004 the Seventh Circuit adopted the IRS' formula, on the grounds that at-will employees have no reasonable expectation of receiving benefits before vesting occurs, because the at-will employees can be terminated at any time. The Seventh Circuit set 20% as the dividing line: there is a rebuttable presumption that there is no partial termination when reduction in plan participation is below 20%, and a rebuttable presumption of partial termination when plan participation drops by more than 20%. [*Matz v. Household Int'l Tax Reduction Inv. Plan*, 388 F.3d 570 (7th Cir. 2004). See also 441 F.3d 500 (7th Cir. 2006) for class certification issues in this litigation.]

[F] Orphan Plans

Although in most cases, termination will be performed by the plan sponsor, an "abandoned" or "orphan" plan is one which no longer has a plan sponsor, or whose sponsor has ceased to conduct business.

When an asset purchase results in the liquidation of the seller company, or when corporate assets are acquired by a buyer, some legacy retirement plans can become orphan plans if they are forgotten or abandoned. The lack of a sponsor may lead to the plan losing its tax-qualified status. There are also fiduciary issues about managing the plan's assets, reporting, and distributions. EPCRS (see § 15.19[B]) includes an orphan plan process. [Keith R. McMurdy, *Don't Let Your Plan Become an Orphan*, Fox Rothschild LLP Employee Benefits Legal Blog (Jan. 24, 2012) (benefitslink.com)]

In March 2005, the DOL issued guidance for winding up of orphan plans by Qualified Termination Administrators (QTAs) who have the power to distribute the benefits from individual account plans when they deem the plan to be abandoned (e.g., there have been no contributions to, or distributions from, the plan over a 12-month period or the sponsor corporation has been liquidated in a Chapter 11 bankruptcy proceeding). A QTA must be a person or entity who could serve as an IRA trustee, such as a bank, insurer, or mutual fund.

The QTA must also notify the DOL that the plan is abandoned, that it intends to serve as QTA, the estimated value of the plan assets, and similar items. The DOL has issued a model notice that can be used for this purpose. There is a safe harbor for balances rolled over to IRAs.

The abandoned plan process requires the use of a Qualified Termination Administrator (QTA), a party eligible to serve as trustee or issuer of an individual retirement plan and who holds the abandoned plan's assets. The QTA must make a finding that the sponsor no longer exists, cannot be found, or can no longer maintain the plan. The plan is officially deemed terminated 90 days after EBSA's Office of Enforcement acknowledges receipt of the notice of plan abandonment.

In order to wind up an abandoned 401(k) plan, the QTA:

- Updates the plan records;
- Calculates benefits payable to each participant and beneficiary;
- Reports any delinquent contributions;
- Uses plan assets to pay the reasonable expenses of serving as QTA;
- Notifies the participants and beneficiaries of the upcoming termination. The notice must include the statement that actual benefits may be more or less than the estimate because of investment gains or losses and administrative expenses. The QTA must explain distribution options to the participants and beneficiaries, warning them that if they do not make an election within 30 days, the QTA will deposit the account balance in an IRA, a federally insured interest-bearing bank account, or send it to the unclaimed property fund of the state of the participant's last known address;
- Distributes the benefits;
- Files the Special Terminal Report for Abandoned Plans;
- Circulates a final notice.

In late 2012, the DOL announced its intention to extend the Abandoned Plan Program so that Chapter 7 bankruptcy trustees could use streamlined termination and distribution procedures to distribute the assets of individual account retirement plans of bankrupt companies. The QTA does not have to file a Form 5500 for the abandoned plan, but does have to file a summary terminal report after the plan has been wound up. Under the 2012 proposal, a Chapter 7 plan is deemed abandoned on the date the bankruptcy court enters an order for relief. The trustee, or the trustee's designee using information provided by the trustee, must determine if it makes economic sense to collect the delinquent contributions (in other words, if the cost of collection is less than the amount to be collected). If collection is financially viable, the trustee has a duty to collect the delinquent contributions. [EBSA Fact Sheet, *Proposed Amendments to the Abandoned Plan Program*, <http://www.dol.gov.ebsa/pdf/fsAPPamendment.pdf> (December 2013)]

§ 17.03 THE PBGC'S ROLE

A great deal of work is required to terminate a plan and wind up its affairs. For most participants, it takes the PBGC about three years to process a termination and provide finalized benefits. Most employees are not subject to recoupment. However, the delays and uncertainty make it difficult for participants in a terminating plan to make financial plans.

The PBGC sends a letter to participants informing them that their plan has been terminated and the PBGC has taken over as trustee. Once the PBGC determines the benefit, it sends a "benefit determination letter" explaining the final benefit amount. The PBGC continues making payments to retirees, with any adjustments required to reflect the limits on the PBGC guarantee

In the case of a single-employer plan, the PBGC guarantees payment of all nonforfeitable benefits. However, the PBGC guarantee is subject to a maximum limitation, with the result that some participants will not receive the full benefit they would have received had the plan not terminated.

Persons who were already retired before the PBGC takeover continue to receive the benefit form they elected. Those who retire later choose among the PBGC's retirement options. Most de minimis benefits (under $5,000) will be cashed out in a lump sum. Monthly benefits under $50 will be paid in a single annual check. Other benefits will be paid monthly. If the plan has adequate assets, some participants will receive more than the basic PBGC guarantee, usually if they retired, or could have retired, three years before the guarantees took effect.

A participant who has not yet commenced benefit payments from a terminated plan can begin benefits at the plan's normal retirement date. A person who has satisfied all requirements (such as years of service) for early retirement as of the date of plan termination (or bankruptcy filing date) can commence early retirement payments at early retirement age—but only if he or she no longer works for the employer.

For benefits already in pay status, the guarantee is based on age at the date the guarantee takes effect but for those not already receiving benefits, the guarantee is based on the age at which payments begin (with adjustments for disabled participants). The maximum guarantee is also adjusted for payment forms other than the single-life annuity. [PBGC.gov, *PBGC's Guarantees for Single-Employer Pension Plans Fact Sheet*] In a standard termination, a fully funded plan terminates; the PBGC does not become a trustee. In a distress termination, the sponsors must apply the limits themselves, so benefits are reduced as of the date of termination. The PBGC sometimes needs years to make the calculations for an involuntary termination.

When the benefit is changed, underpaid retirees usually get a lump sum back payment with interest. Overpaid beneficiaries do not have to pay interest; their future monthly payments are reduced to make up the difference. Under PBGC regulations, the most that the monthly benefit can be reduced is 10% of the monthly benefit, or the amount in excess of the maximum guaranteed benefit—whichever is larger. The PBGC reports that most overpayments are less than $3,000, and the usual repayment amount is about $16 per month. [GAO-10-181T, *PBGC, Workers and Retirees Experience Delays and Uncertainty When Underfunded Plans Are Terminated*, testimony of Barbara D. Bovbjerg (Oct. 29, 2009)]

[A] PBGC Guarantee

Defined benefit plans pay premiums to the PBGC annually, providing funds for the federal agency to supervise plan terminations and, if necessary, assume payment of a terminating or terminated plan's obligations to its participants. The Deficit Reduction Act of 2005, Pub. L. No. 109-171, increased the PBGC premium for single-employer plans from its long-held $19 per employee per year to $30. DRA '05 also institutes inflation-indexing of the premium. Amounts determined under DRA 2005 rules are: the 2013 flat-rate premium is $42/participant, rising to $49/participant in 2014 and $50/participant in 2015. The variable-rate premium goes from $9/$1,000 unfunded vested benefits in 2013 to $14 in 2014 and $18 in 2015. However, in all three years, the variable-rate premium is subject to a cap of $400/participant. [PBGC, *Pension Insurance Premiums Fact Sheet*, <http://www.pbgc.gov/res/factsheets/page/premiums.html> (last accessed Aug. 19, 2013)]. The premium has been increased by the Moving Ahead for Progress in the 21st Century Act (MAP-21; Pub. L. No. 112-140) and by the Bipartisan Budget Act of 2013, Pub. L. No. 113-67. The cap on the variable premium rises from $400 (2013) to $412 (2014), although the cap may be lower for plans with fewer than 25 participants. The proposed 2015 premiums are a flat rate of $57/participant, a variable rate of $14/$1,000 unfunded vested benefits, subject to a cap of at least $412. The proposed 2016 rates are $64 flat rate, variable rate of at least $29, and a cap of $500, with those figures to be indexed in 2017. [Sarah Roe Sise and Carrie Elizabeth Byrnes, *PBGC Premium Rates Increase In 2014 For Single-Employer Plans Time To Cash-Out Some Deferred Vested Participants?*, Bryan Cave LLP (Nov. 15, 2013), available at Lexology.com; Buck Consultants FYI, *PBGC Premium Hikes in Final Budget Deal*, Vol. 36 Issue 105 (Dec. 27, 2013) (benefitslink.com)]

Certain terminations are also subject to a one-time payment of $1,250. The PBGC guarantee is intended to protect the employees of the plan, not the sponsor corporation. If the assets of a terminating plan are not large enough to pay the benefits, the PBGC makes the payments and then seeks recoupment from the corporation. However, an employer's liability to the PBGC is capped at 70% of its net worth, or 75% of the unfunded guaranteed benefits.

The due date for a terminating plan's final premium is the filing date for the post-distribution certificate. This rule was adopted because the final premium was sometimes forgotten in standard terminations when the due date was months after the plan closed its books. Furthermore, plans will generally be exempt from the variable rate premium for the year in which a standard termination is completed, and small plans may be exempt from the variable rate premium for the first year of coverage. [79 Fed. Reg. 13547 (Mar. 11, 2014); see Rebecca Moore, *PBGC Finalizes Premium Changes*, plansponsor.com (Mar. 10, 2014)]

In April 2009, the Second Circuit held that PBGC termination premiums are not contingent pre-petition claims that can be discharged under Chapter 11. Therefore, companies that terminate their plans post-filing may still have to pay the premium. The Second Circuit ruled that the PBGC's right to termination premiums does not arise until after the discharge, so there was no valid right before bankruptcy decided by non-bankruptcy law (the test of a dischargeable pre-petition claim). Certiorari was denied in late 2009. [*PBGC v. Oneida Ltd.*, 562 F.3d 154 (2d Cir. 2009); see Felice R. Yudkin, *Second Circuit Finds Termination Premiums Non-Dischargeable in Bankruptcy*, Bankruptcy & Restructuring Law Monitor (May 5, 2009) (benefitslink.com); Rebecca Moore, *High Court Lets Stand Decision on Discharging PBGC Termination Premiums*, plansponsor.com (Dec. 15, 2009)]

Form 500 requires employers to explain why the plan is terminating; if there are multiple reasons, they must be ranked in order of importance. The PBGC said that the most common reason was restructuring of the retirement program, followed by the cost of providing the benefits, adverse business conditions, the expense of administering the plan, sale of the company, and liquidation.

The PBGC guarantees "basic benefits." (The PBGC has legal authority to set up a separate trust fund to guarantee nonbasic benefits, but it has chosen not to do so.) The basic benefit guaranteed by the PBGC is a monthly life annuity that lasts for the participant's life. (This is in contrast to the joint and survivor annuity that is the normal payment form for a married participant to receive under an ongoing plan.) The annuity begins at age 65.

Benefits and increases that were not in effect for five years before the termination date/bankruptcy filing date receive only partial, phased-in protection: the PBGC guarantees 20% or $20 per month of the increase (whichever is larger) of the increase for each full year since the increase took effects. Shut-down benefits are phased in depending on the number of years since the plant closing or other shutdown event. [PBGC.gov, *PBGC's Guarantees for Single-Employer Pension Plans Fact Sheet*]

The amount that the PBGC guarantees depends on the year in which the PBGC takes over the plan; the age of the participant; and whether the benefit is accessed as a single life annuity or as a joint and survivor annuity. The single life benefit will be larger than the joint and survivor annuity because payments must be made for two lives so more payments must be made.

Age	*Annual maximum single life annuity*	*Monthly maximum single life annuity*	*Monthly maximum joint + 50% survivor annuity*
45	$ 14,829	$ 1,235	$ 1,112
50	$ 20,761	$ 1,730	$ 1,557
55	$ 26,693	$ 2,224	$ 2,002
60	$ 38,556	$ 3,213	$ 2,891
65	$ 59,320	$ 4,943.18	$ 4,448.86
70	$ 98,468	$ 8,205	$ 7,385
75	$180,327	$15,027	$13,524

[PBGC press release, *PBGC Maximum Insurance Benefit Increases for 2014*, <http://www.pbgc.gov/news/press/releases/pr13-13.html> (Nov. 6, 2013)]

About 85% of retirees whose pension is paid by the PBGC receive the full amount of benefit they were promised, although a person entitled to a very large pension may find that it exceeds the maximum guarantee. [PBGC press release, *PBGC Maximum Insurance Benefit Increases for 2014*, <pbgc.gov> (Nov. 6, 2013)]

For annuity dates starting in 2014, the present value of the PBGC's maximum guarantee ranges from $111,472 (at age 25), to $137,179 at 30, $161,327 at 35, $209,553 at 40, $337,939 at 50, $414,487 at 55, $750,830 at 65, and $1,091,293 at 70. [PBGC.gov, *Present Value of PBGC Maximum Guarantee*, <http://www.pbgc.gov/prac/mortality-retirement-and-pv-max-guarantee/present-guarantee.html#2014> (accessed Apr. 4, 2014)]

When a plan is to be terminated, the PBGC:

- Determines if the benefit is nonforfeitable and payable in periodic installments; if so, it is a guaranteed basic benefit;
- Performs actuarial calculations to convert benefits in other forms to straight life annuities commencing at age 65.

The PBGC has the power to assess penalties if an employer was late in paying its PBGC premiums, or if the employer failed to provide the required notices to employees.

The PBGC adopted a rule in 2011, implementing PPA § 403. The rule makes the phase-in period for the guarantee of benefits contingent on an "unpredictable contingent event" begin no earlier than the event itself. (The PBGC's example of such an event is a plant shut-down.) The rule was necessary because PBGC's guarantee of new pension benefits and benefit increases phases in over a five-year period starting with the later of the date of adoption or the effective date of the change, and the PBGC wanted to protect itself against plans adopting new benefits when they knew they were going to terminate. The net effect is that the guarantee for benefits that arise from unpredictable contingent events that occur within five years of plan termination is probably lower than the guarantee that would have been available under the pre-PPA law. [76 Fed. Reg. 34590 (June 14, 2011)]

The rule was finalized in May 2014. The PBGC determines the date of an Unpredictable Contingent Event by consideration of all facts and circumstances, including the plan provisions, the level of activity in the facility that is being shut down, and the permanence of the situation. Depending on the terms of the plan, the determination might be made for the facility as a whole, on a participant-by-participant basis, or on another basis. The provisions of the plan determine whether the determination is made for the entire facility; on a participant-by-participant basis; or otherwise. Phasing in of a UCEB guarantee starts on the latest of the adoption date of the UCEB provision, its effective date, or the date of the event. [79 Fed. Reg. 25667 (May 16, 2013); see Robert B. Wynne and James P. McElligott Jr., *Final Rule Issued on Phase-In of PBGC Guarantee for Shut-down Pensions*, McGuire Woods LLP (May 8, 2014), available at Lexology.com]

Variable interest rates create serious problems when the plan is terminated because a participant's exact benefit can only be determined at the time benefits begin—but the PBGC needs to know if the benefit amount is de minimis and, therefore, can be made in a single payment. A PBGC proposed regulation, implementing PPA § 2006, was published in late 2011.

The proposed regulation explains how to determine the benefits payable when a hybrid plan (e.g., cash balance or pension equity) terminates: a variable rate is used that is an average of rates used in the five years before termination. In a distress termination, the proposed termination date determines the benefits under the plan. If the proposed termination date is deferred, the benefits accrued between the proposed and actual termination dates are recalculated with the interest rate that would have applied before the final termination date. [Proposed Regulations, 76 Fed. Reg. 67105 (Oct. 31, 2011; see Deloitte's Washington Bulletin, *PBGC Proposes Rules on Determining Benefits in Terminating Hybrid Plans* (Nov. 7, 2011) (benefitslink.com)]

Mid-2009 PBGC proposed regulations explain USERRA rights in connection with the ERISA requirement that guaranteed benefits be nonforfeitable when a plan terminates. For USERRA re-employment on or after December 12, 1994, the PBGC proposed to amend 29 C.F.R. Part 4022 to deem participants to have satisfied the conditions for reemployment as of the termination date of the plan as long as the veteran returns to his or her prior job within the USERRA time frame, even if re-employment actually occurs after the plan's termination date. If the plan sponsor is bankrupt at the time of plan termination, the bankruptcy filing date is treated as the termination date for various purposes, including USERRA. [PBGC Proposed Rule, FR Doc E9-17623, *USERRA Benefits Under Title IV of ERISA*, 74 Fed. Reg. 37666 (July 29, 2009); see CCH Pension & Benefits, *PBGC Issues Proposed Regs on Interaction of USERRA Rules and ERISA Benefit Guarantee* (Aug. 18, 2009) (benefitslink.com)]

[B] Proposal on Payment Forms

Regulations proposed in 2000 and adopted, more or less intact, in 2002 [PBGC No. 02-14 (Dec. 22, 2000) [65 Fed. Reg. 81456 (Dec. 26, 2000), 67 Fed. Reg. 16949 (Apr. 18, 2002)] discuss payment options when the PBGC takes over a plan. Participants can select alternative annuity benefit forms—straight life, five, 10, or 15 years certain and continuous; joint and survivor annuities with various levels of benefits, and "pop-up" annuities that increase if the beneficiary dies before the participant. (Alternate payment forms require the consent of spouses of married participants.) The regulations also discuss inheritance of payments to a deceased participant.

Some changes were made in the definition of "earliest PBGC Retirement Date." The regulations define the "earliest PBGC Retirement Date" as the earliest date the plan participant could retire for the purposes of ERISA Title IV. Usually, this will mean either age 55 or the first date the participant could retire and collect an immediate annuity, whichever is later.

[C] Penalties and PBGC Enforcement

The PBGC, like the IRS, has the power to assess penalties if required documents are omitted, if documents are filed but are late, if payments are not made, or if payments are made but in an untimely fashion. The PBGC can waive penalties if the failure was due to factors outside the business' control. Penalties can be waived in full or in part, e.g., if there were factors preventing timely full compliance, but the plan was dilatory in getting back into compliance.

Penalties can be waived if payment would impose undue hardship on the business. "Reasonable cause" that might justify a waiver requires a showing that even ordinary business care and prudence would not have permitted full timely payment. Reasonable reliance on incorrect advice from a PBGC employee could give rise to a waiver—but reliance on the plan's own professional advisors will not. [PBGC Final Regulations, 71 Fed. Reg. 66867 (Nov. 17, 2006)]

[D] QDROs in Plans Under PBGC Control

Qualified Domestic Relations Orders (QDROs) are discussed in detail at § 12.08. If the PBGC takes over a plan some of whose benefits must be paid to alternate payees (ex-spouses and separated spouses of participants), it issues two standard QDRO forms (Model Separate Interest; Model Shared Payment) for use by domestic relations courts. PBGC QDROs either specify or give the alternate payee discretion to control the time at which benefits begin, how the benefits are paid, the percentage of the pension payment going to the alternate payee, and how long the alternate payments begin. The Model Separate Interest Form is used when the order is issued before the benefits are in pay status. In effect, the pension account is divided into two, one for the participant, the other for the alternate beneficiary. The Shared Payment Form divides each payment, as it comes due, between participant and alternate beneficiary.

[*The Division of Pensions Through Qualified Domestic Relations Orders*, <http://www.dol.gov/ebsa/publications/qdros.html> (undated, accessed Apr. 4, 2014)]

§ 17.04 INVOLUNTARY TERMINATION

[A] Basic Procedure

ERISA § 4042 governs involuntary termination proceedings brought when the plan assets are less than the total of guaranteed benefits. The PBGC asks the appropriate federal district court to oust the plan administrator and appoint a trustee to wind up the plan. ERISA § 4062(b)(1) makes the employer liable to the PBGC for the total amount of unfounded plan liabilities on the termination date, plus interest starting on the termination date.

The PBGC is empowered to ask for involuntary termination if:

- The plan has failed to meet its minimum funding standards;
- The plan cannot pay current benefits when due;
- The plan has been required to report one or more distributions to a "substantial owner" (10% shareholder);
- The PBGC's losses are expected to increase "unreasonably" unless the plan is terminated.

If the plan does not even have enough assets to pay its current benefits, much less to keep paying benefits as they come due; or the plan has applied for a distress termination but lacks money to fund the guaranteed benefits, the PBGC has an obligation to seek involuntary termination. [PBGC, *Pension Plan Termination Fact Sheet*, <http://www.pbgc.gov/about/factsheets/page/termination.html> (accessed Apr. 4, 2014)]

The PBGC moved for involuntary termination of Saint-Gobain Containers' defined benefit plan, arguing that the planned acquisition (by stock purchase) of Saint-Gobain by Ardagh Group, SA would move the plan from a stronger to a weaker controlled group. The District Court for the Eastern District of Pennsylvania refused to grant administrative deference to the PBGC's decision to terminate the plan. The district court ruled that it would make a de novo determination about the need to terminate the plan, and could consider evidence outside the PBGC's administrative record. The district court noted that ERISA § 4042(c) requires a court to determine whether to terminate the plan. A PBGC determination to close a plan has no legal effect without a court order. [*PBGC v. Saint-Gobain Container Benefits Comm.*, No. 13-02069, 2013 U.S. Dist. LEXIS 144515 (E.D. Pa. Oct. 4, 2013); see Justin Alex, *The PBGC Not Entitled to Administrative Deference for Involuntary Plan Termination*, Proskauer's ERISA Practice Center Blog (Oct. 22, 2013) (benefitslink.com)]

If the PBGC brings an involuntary termination proceeding under ERISA Title IV, it will not be a "core proceeding" for bankruptcy purposes. The practical implication is that the District Court reviews all the issues in the bankruptcy case—it does not have to accept the rulings of the Bankruptcy Court. This, in turn, could make a difference in terms of setting the date of plan termination, which determines the interest rates and other calculations to be used. [*In re United Air Lines Inc.*, 337 B.R. 904 (N.D. Ill. 2006)]

[B] The Role of the Trustee

If the district court appoints a trustee, the plan must be terminated. The PBGC can also force termination of a plan even without such an appointment. If a trustee is appointed, his or her duty is to keep the plan administrator, participants, beneficiaries, unions, and employers with potential ERISA liability informed about the progress of the termination. The trustee has the power to demand turnover of some or all of the plan's records and assets. The trustee has a choice of either continuing the pattern of benefit payments in place before the trustee's appointment, or limiting payment of benefits to the basic benefits.

Under ERISA § 4062(d), the employer is liable for the unpaid contributions to the trustee plan. The employer must provide the trustee with cash, or securities acceptable to the trustee, in an amount equal to:

- The accumulated funding deficiencies under I.R.C. § 412(a);
- Any funding deficiencies that the IRS waived under I.R.C. § 412(c) before the termination date;
- All decreases in the minimum funding standard permitted by I.R.C. § 412(e) before the termination date, plus interest running from the termination date.

Under certain circumstances outlined in ERISA § 4069(b), a successor corporation can become liable for such amounts, if the sponsor reorganizes; the purpose of the reorganization was to evade liability; and reorganization occurred within the five years before a plan termination that would have caused liability. In this context, reorganization means a merger, consolidation, or becoming a division of another company; changing identity, form, or place or organization; or the liquidation of a subsidiary into its parent.

Also note that ERISA § 4062(b) provides that when an employer ceases operations at a facility, leading to separation from service of 20% or more of the total number of plan participants, the employer either has to fund the guaranteed benefits immediately, or make provision for their funding.

[C] Calculations for Involuntary or Distress Terminations

Under 29 C.F.R. Part 4044, benefits under a plan going through an involuntary or distress termination are calculated based on a determination of the likelihood (low/medium/high) that the participant will retire early in various years. Then, once early retirement benefits are computed, the total value of benefits under the plan can be computed. The process uses the Unreduced Retirement Age, which is either the normal retirement age or the earliest age at which a pension can be paid without actuarial reduction—whichever is earlier.

Table I-14, Appendix D, is used to compute the value of early retirement benefits in an involuntary or distress termination whose valuation date is in 2014.

In this table, "year" means the year in which the unreduced benefit becomes payable. The "low" and "high" benefits are dollar amounts; the "medium" benefits are a range between the two figures.

TABLE I-14
RETIREMENT RATE CATEGORY TABLE

Year	*Low*	*Medium*	*High*
2015	<$614	$614-2,594	>$2,594
2016	<$627	$627-$2,651	>$2,651
2017	<$641	$641-$2,710	>$2,710
2018	<$655	$655-$2,769	>$2,769
2019	<$670	$670-$2,830	>$2,830
2020	<$685	$685-$2,893	>$2,893
2021	<$700	$700-$2,956	>$2,956
2022	<$715	$715-$3,021	>$3,021
2023	<$731	$731-$3,088	>$3,088
2024 or later	<$ 747	$747-$3,156	>$3,156

[See 78 Fed. Reg. 72018 (Dec. 2, 2013)]

The PBGC publishes mortality tables, updated annually, to calculate the present value of annuities in involuntary termination situations. See <http://www.pbgc.gov/prac/mortality-retirement-and-pv-max-guarantee/erisa-mortality-tables/erisa-section-4044-mortality-table-for-2014-valuation-dates.html> for the § 4044 mortality table for valuation dates in 2014.

§ 17.05 PLAN REVERSIONS

Before ERISA, it was legal for an employer to simply wind up a plan and take back its assets. But under current law, a plan provision that calls for reversion (or increased reversion) cannot become effective until the end of the fifth calendar year following the year of adoption. In other words, employers have to wait at least five years to take advantage of a reversion opportunity. Furthermore, if the plan called for mandatory contributions, once the benefits are paid off, assets must be allocated to mandatory contributions before the reversion occurs.

An employer that is entitled to a reversion must pay 50% of the reversion amount as an excise tax. However, if the employer establishes a qualified replacement plan or amends the terminating plan to increase benefits, the excise tax is reduced to 20%. IRS Form 5330 is used to pay the excise tax. It is due the last day of the month after the month in which the reversion occurred.

§ 17.06 EFFECT ON BENEFITS

[A] Forfeit of Benefits

Benefits become nonforfeitable when a plan terminates or partially terminates. A defined contribution plan's benefits become nonforfeitable if and when the employer completely ceases its contributions to the plan. If a defined benefit plan terminates within 10 years of its creation, I.R.C. § 411(d)(2) imposes limits on the benefits that can be paid to the 25 highest-compensated individuals covered by the plan. This rule prevails even if it results in the loss of some accrued benefits.

In the Seventh Circuit view, the employees of a bankrupt company raised a sufficient claim of breach of fiduciary duty by alleging that the company's executives failed to provide ongoing funding for a health plan that was terminated as part of the bankruptcy process. The executives were fiduciaries because of their control over the committee that invested the plan's assets. However, the Seventh Circuit dismissed claims of breach of fiduciary duty by not giving notice of the likelihood of plan termination, on the ground that there is no duty to disclose likely future termination unless plan participants are deliberately misled. [*Baker v. Kingsley*, 387 F.3d 649 (7th Cir. 2004)]

[B] The Anticutback Rule

Whether deliberately or inadvertently, employers sometimes make cutbacks in a plan, or scale it down. The effect can be inadvertent if the employer lacks the money to make a required deposit, or simply is ignorant of what the legal requirements are. The consequences are not always those intended by the employer. The worst-case scenario is that the plan will be treated as partially terminated, and then retroactively disqualified, obligating the employer to pay back taxes for prior plan years. Retroactive disqualification also harms employees, who are likely to owe back taxes. Furthermore, distributions from a disqualified plan cannot be rolled over to a qualified plan.

A plan is frozen if it is amended to keep the plan trust in existence, but without further contributions or accrual of benefits. A frozen plan is still subject to the top-heavy plan rules, and still has to provide QJSAs and QPSAs on the same terms as if it had not been frozen.

If it is uncertain whether there has been a partial termination, Form 5300 can be filed to request an IRS determination letter. If the IRS rules that there has been a partial termination, the event must be reported to the PBGC (as must a 20% cut in the workforce, or a plan amendment that reduces the accrual of benefits by 50% or more for 50% or more of the workforce).

See 77 Fed. Reg. 37349 (June 21, 2012) for proposed regulations allowing plan sponsors in bankruptcy to amend their single-employer defined benefit plans to eliminate optional forms of benefit that are not permitted because the plan is underfunded. Under the conditions prescribed in the regulations (e.g., approval of the PBGC and bankruptcy court), eliminating the optional benefit forms will not violate the anti-cutback rule.

§ 17.07 REPORTING AND COMPLIANCE

When a plan is terminated, IRS Form 5310 is used to request an IRS determination letter stating that the associated plan trust did not become disqualified or lose its exempt status. Form 6088 must be filed in conjunction with this form, listing up to 25 owners or 5% shareholders of the employer corporation who received any distribution from the plan during the preceding five years.

The general rule is that Form 5310-A must be filed 30 days or more before a transfer of plan assets to another qualified retirement plan because of a merger, consolidation, or change in ownership of assets or liabilities. When two defined contribution plans merge or a defined contribution plan is spun off, or a defined benefit plan engages in a merger or spinoff that has only minimal effects, the Form 5310-A filing is not required.

In the somewhat unlikely case that the trust of a terminating plan has more assets than are needed to pay all the plan benefits, and therefore the employer recovers those excess assets, Form 5319 must be filed by the last day of the month after the month in which the employer recouped the assets. This is also the form the employer uses to pay the excise tax on the recouped funds.

The Form 5500-series annual report must be filed for the year of the merger, consolidation, division, or termination. If a trust is frozen (the plan maintains its assets, although benefit accruals have stopped), the 5500-series filing is required in every year until all the assets have been distributed. Form 8955-SSA is submitted to the IRS to identify separated plan participants who are entitled to deferred vested benefits. For instructions, see <http://www.irs.gov/pub/irs-pdf/i8955ssa.pdf>. The information used to be reported on Schedule SSA, but it was replaced by Form 8955-SSA for plan years beginning on or after January 1, 2009. Unless there is an extension, Form SSA-8955 must be filed by the last day of the seventh month after the last day of the plan year: July 31 for a calendar year plan. There were few changes between the 2012 and 2013 versions. [EBIA Weekly, *IRS Releases 2013 Form 8955-SSA and Instructions* (Jan. 23, 2014) (benefits link.com)]

A late-2010 proposed rule, RIN 1210-AB 18, effective January 18, 2011, clarifies the ERISA § 101(f) mandate for annual funding notices for defined benefit plans. It also covers reporting requirements for plans taken over by the PBGC. Because ERISA Title IV imposes separate disclosure requirements in this situation, EBSA believes that a funding notice may be unnecessary or even confusing when the PBGC becomes the trustee of a terminated single-employer plan, or where a terminated single-employer plan has already satisfied all its liabilities. [75 Fed. Reg. 70625 (Nov. 18, 2010); see Fred Schneyer, *EBSA Releases DB Funding Notice Proposed Rule*, plansponsor.com (Nov. 17, 2010)]

§ 17.08 PAYMENT OF EXPENSES

It is appropriate for fiduciaries to use plan assets to pay the expenses of an ongoing plan. However, the decision to terminate a plan is a business decision made by the plan's settlor, and not a fiduciary decision. That means that some of the termination expenses relate to settlor functions—and it violates ERISA to use plan assets to pay settlor expenses. These expenses are considered fiduciary expenses that can properly be paid out of plan assets:

- Getting an audit;
- Preparing and filing the final annual report;
- Amending the plan to carry out the termination;
- Calculating benefits;
- Preparing benefit statements;
- Notifying participants and beneficiaries about their rights incident to termination.

However, the cost of maintaining the plan's tax-qualified status—including the cost of getting determination letters—is a settlor expense. Legal fees for plan termination are considered settlor expenses. The general rule is that PBGC premiums can be paid out of plan assets, because they are considered to relate to fiduciary implementation of settlor decisions. However, premiums for years when the plan is involved in a distress or involuntary termination cannot be paid out of plan assets. Similarly, sanctions for late payment of PBGC premiums can be paid from plan assets, except sanctions imposed when the plan was involved in a distress or involuntary termination. Plan assets can be used to pay sanctions and penalties that were imposed on the plan, but not those imposed on a plan administrator in his or her individual capacity. [Andree M. St. Martin and Jennifer E. Eller, *Paying Employee Benefit Plan Expenses Chart*, Practical Law Co. (undated) (benefitslink.com) (chart giving the source for the treatment of various items)]

PART IV
BENEFIT PLANS

CHAPTER 18

EMPLOYEE GROUP HEALTH PLANS (EGHPs)

§ 18.01 INTRODUCTION

Health insurance costs are a major planning factor for business. For many years, health care costs, and therefore insurance costs, rose much faster than inflation, until employers faced a heavy burden. In the 1970s and 1980s, there was a vast shift from indemnity insurance [see § 18.12] to some form of managed care. The promise of managed care was that eliminating waste and keeping employees healthier would reduce costs.

However, by the end of the twentieth century, managed care was a problem in and of itself. Insurers began to charge the kind of double-digit annual premium increases that caused so much pain in the 1970s. Many patients were dissatisfied with managed care, charging that they were often denied access to necessary care. Doctors were dissatisfied, with the restrictions on their freedom to prescribe, with the amount of paperwork they had to do, and with both the size and speed of their reimbursement from managed care organizations (MCOs).

Just as there has been a transition from defined-benefit to defined-contribution or employee-funded retirement plans, health plans have shifted from the once-predominant indemnity plan to a heavy dominance of some form of managed care. Some employers have always chosen to self-insure rather than purchase insurance; others have switched to self-insurance to cut costs. A new form that is emerging is the so-called defined contribution or consumer-driven health plan (CDHP).

The passage of health care reform legislation, the Patient Protection and Affordable Care Act, Pub. L. No. 111-148 (PPACA) is discussed below, in § 18.19. The legislation attracted a great deal of opposition, and implementation was marked by many challenges and many delays.

In mid-2012, the Supreme Court did not find PPACA unconstitutional. However, that did not end challenges to the validity of the statute as a whole or to the mandate that employer plans cover contraceptives: see § 18.19[M].

The Fourth Circuit ruled in 2013 that the employer mandate (that large employers provide insurance) does not violate the Commerce Clause of the Constitution, and also found the individual mandate constitutional. The Supreme Court rejected Liberty University's broad-based challenge to this ruling; the Supreme Court denied certiorari on December 2, 2013. [*Liberty Univ. v. Lew*, 732 F.3d 72 (4th Cir. 2013), *cert. denied*, 134 S. Ct. 683 (Dec. 2, 2013); see Lyle Denniston, *Challenge to ACA Employer Mandate Fails*, SCOTUSblog (Dec. 2, 2013) (benefitslink.com)]

The D.C. Circuit rejected a constitutional challenge to the PPACA individual mandate. The D.C. Circuit ruled that the mandate is a law about a tax but, because it is designed to expand insurance coverage rather than to raise money for the federal treasury, it is not a revenue measure that would have had to be originated in the House of Representatives. (The Origination Clause of the Constitution requires all federal laws to raise revenue to be propounded first by the House of Representatives rather than the Senate.) [*Sissel v. Dep't of Health &*

Human Servs., No. 13-5202 (D.C. Cir. July 28, 2014); see Lyle Denniston, *Appeals Court Rejects New Test of Health Care Mandate*, SCOTUSblog (July 29, 2014) (law.com)]

In March 2014, 86% of private-sector full-time employees had access to employer-sponsored health insurance, but only 23% of part-time employees had health insurance access. In small businesses, 57% of employees had access, but in large businesses (100 or more employees), nearly all employees (84%) had access. [Kevin McGuinness, *BLS Reports on Access to Health and Retirement Benefits*, plansponsor.com (July 28, 2014)]

Of the employer costs for employee compensation in private industry (which average $29.99/hour in March 2014), the average cost of health insurance benefits was $2.36/hour worked, representing 7.9% of total compensation. By comparison, a decade earlier, in March 2004, health benefits cost an average of $1.53 (6.6% of total compensation), so both the absolute amount and the proportion of compensation devoted to health benefits increased. [BLS news release USDL-14-1075, *Employer Costs for Employee Compensation March 2014,* <http://www.bls.gov/news.release/pdf/ecec.pdf>. For more information about health insurance benefits, see National Compensation Survey: Employee Benefits in the United States, March 2013, at <www.bls.gov/ncs/ebs/benefits/2013/benefits.htm>]

Federal law makes the EGHP the primary payor and Medicare only the secondary payor for Medicare beneficiaries who continue to be employed. However, this provision is poorly enforced, and in many instances, Medicare ends up paying for health care for working elderly people, where the EGHP should have been the primary payor. One of the provisions of the Medicare, Medicaid & SCHIP Extension Act of 2007, Pub. L. No. 110-173 § 111, requires EGHPs to report to Medicare Insurers and self-funded EGHPs must report to HHS on situations in which the EGHP had primary responsibility. Failure to make the report is punishable by a civil money penalty of $1,000 per day of noncompliance for each individual for whom reports should have been made—in addition to any other civil money penalty that can be imposed for failure to pay for that individual's care. Reporting is also required for liability insurance (including self-insurance), automobile no-fault insurance, and Worker's Compensation plans, and failure to report is subject to the same penalty [McDermott Newsletters, *Medicare Secondary Payor Reporting Requirements Will Affect Self-Insured Health Care Providers, Captive Insurers* (Jan. 6, 2009) (benefitslink.com); Jessica Forbes Olson & Leslie J. Anderson, Dorsey & Whitney LLP, *New Medicare Secondary Payer Reporting Requirements* (Aug. 14, 2008) (benefitslink.com)]

Reporting to CMS (Centers for Medicare and Medicaid Services) is also required for worker's compensation claims involving Medicare beneficiaries, so Medicare can be reimbursed if it pays medical expenses for a worker who eventually received WC. [Littler, Mendelsohn Press Releases, *New Medicare Secondary Payer Reporting Obligations for Workers' Compensation Plans,*

<http://www.littler.com/PressPublications/Lists/ASAPs/DispAsaps.aspx?id=1359&asapType=National> (April 2009)]

One of the most important differences between ERISA's pension plan provisions and its welfare benefit plan provisions is that, by and large, welfare benefits do not vest, and can be altered or terminated if the plan document retains the sponsor's discretion to do so. However, in some situations, the employer will be deemed to have a contractual obligation to maintain the plan. In a unionized company, the CBA will impose further limitations on the employer's ability to alter the health plans it maintains. [For the requirements for Summary Plan Descriptions (SPDs) for health plans, see § 11.02[B].]

In mid-2013, the Supreme Court ruled that § 2 of the federal Defense of Marriage Act was unconstitutional, with the result that same-sex married couples became eligible for a variety of federal employment-related benefits. See § 18.06.

DOL, HHS, and the IRS jointly proposed rules on December 24, 2013 expanding the definition of "excepted benefits" under the HIPAA portability rules. Excepted benefits include accident insurance, disability insurance, Workers' Compensation, on-site medical clinics, long-term care, and Medigap insurance. Benefits that constitute excepted benefits under HIPAA are exempt from the pre-PPACA portability rules and are also exempt from GINA Title I, the MHPAEA, WHCRAA, and Newborn's and Mother's Act. HIPAA-excepted benefits do not have to comply with the PPACA prohibition on annual limits, offer coverage to age 26, provide mandated preventive care, or satisfy rules for limits on OOP spending. However, ERISA, COBRA, the ADA, and GINA Title II (the employment title) do apply to most excepted benefits. The December 2013 proposal makes three major changes: (1) It permits no-cost dental and vision coverage to be offered under a separate policy, or if there is a separate election/opt out for the coverage; (2) EAPs are excepted if they do not provide significant benefits in the form of medical care. [78 Fed. Reg. 77632 (Dec. 24, 2013); see Christy Tinnes and Brigen Winters, *Second Opinions: Agencies Issue New HIPAA Excepted Benefits Proposed Rules* (Jan. 8, 2014) (benefitslink.com)]

§ 18.02 THE HEALTH CARE LANDSCAPE

Although initially the employer group health plan market was divided only between self-insured and indemnity insurance plans, today managed care is dominant. There are many types of managed care plans. At one time the Health Management Organization (HMO) was the dominant managed care form, but today its predominance is yielding to plans that provide somewhat more flexibility and provider choice for patients. The Consumer-Driven Health Plan (CDHP), such as the high-deductible health plan used in conjunction with a Health Savings Account (HSA) is gaining prominence: see § 18.18, below.

"Mini-meds" are plans that cap benefits, sometimes at levels as low as $3,000 a year. At least 1,200 employers, with a total of almost four million enrollees, offered mini-med plans that did not satisfy PPACA minimum coverage requirements. These plans were most common in low-wage industries such as retailing, restaurants, and agriculture. In response to PPACA requirements, Darden Restaurants, Home Depot, and Trader Joe's, which used to have mini-med plans, announced that they would stop insuring part-time employees. [Scott Thurm, *Firms Drop, Rather Than Upgrade, Cheapest Health Plans*, WSJ.com (Sept. 25, 2013)]

Transgender people often suffer discrimination, disrespect, and hostility from health care providers. The National Transgender Discrimination Survey reports that 20% of transsexuals say they have been denied medical care because of their gender identity and one-quarter have been verbally harassed in a health care setting; 2% have been physically assaulted when seeking health care. Before PPACA, they were also at risk of losing or being unable to obtain employer-based health coverage because of employment discrimination. Starting in 2014, PPACA forbids denials for pre-existing conditions, and Title VII extends to health care. HHS has confirmed that, therefore, gender identity discrimination in health care is unlawful; health care discrimination complaints are handled by the HHS Office of Civil Rights. PPACA also includes funding for cultural competency training for healthcare workers to teach them about transgender issues. [Marisa Carroll, *What the Affordable Care Act Means for Transgender People*, The Nation (Aug. 14, 2012) (benefitslink.com); Michelle Andrews, *HHS Says Health Plans Cannot Discriminate Against Transgender People*, Kaiser Health News (Sept. 3, 2012) (benefitslink.com)]

On July 21, 2014, President Obama signed an executive order forbidding federal contractors to discriminate against transgender (or gay, lesbian, or bisexual) persons. The executive order does not exempt religious organizations. [Peter Baker, *Obama Calls for a Ban on Job Bias Against Gays*, NYTimes.com (July 21, 2014)]

The Fairness for All Marylanders Act, signed May 15, 2014 forbids gender identity discrimination in the workplace. All employers are covered. As of October 1, 2014, it is illegal for an employer to discriminate against an applicant or employee on account of transgender status. [Meredith Campbell, *Maryland Workplace Transgender Bias Ban*, Shulman Rogers Gandal Pordy & Ecker PA (May 28, 2014), available at Lexology.com]

Oregon and California regulators ordered health insurers to stop denying coverage on basis of gender identity. [AP, *Ore., Calif., Require Transgender Health Coverage*, NYTimes.com (Jan. 11, 2013)]

A lawsuit against the state of Oregon was settled with an agreement requiring insurance coverage for gender reassignment surgery for state employees; the state was required to pay $36,000 and change its policies so that medically necessary treatment for gender reassignment is covered. Hysterectomies were covered for other medical reasons, so they had to be covered for gender reassignment as well. [Rebecca Moore, *Ore. Adds Gender Reassignment to Health Care Coverage*, plansponsor.com (Jan. 25, 2013)]

In early 2012, it was reported that one-third of very large employers provide benefits for transgender employees—five times more than the year before. The Human Rights Campaign's Corporate Equality Index raised consciousness on this issue by publicizing five criteria for benefits for transgendered employees: the availability of short-term leave for transition, mental health counseling, hormone therapy, health care coverage to monitor hormone use, and surgical procedures. The average cost for male to female transition is about $17,000, plus $1,000 for therapy, $1,500 for hormones, and $500 for lab tests and medical visits. [Lisa V. Gillespie, *One-Third of Major Employers Now Offer Transgendered Employees Coverage for Gender-Reassignment Surgery*, Employee Benefit News (Feb. 1, 2012) (benefitslink.com)]

"CAM" is an abbreviation for "complementary and alternative medicine," and a number of insurers offer coverage or discounts. For example, Cigna's Healthy Rewards program offers discounts for acupuncture, chiropractic, massage, natural supplements, and other health and wellness products and services. However, because of the lack of scientific proof for most of these interventions, they are not covered as standard benefits. Companies with drug-free workplace policies are especially interested in modalities such as acupuncture and yoga that can be useful back therapy that gets people back to work without using painkillers that are contraindicated in the workplace. [Kathleen Koster, *Alternative Medicine Reduces Pain, Drives Health Costs Down*, Employee Benefit News (Feb. 1, 2011) (benefitslink.com)]

§ 18.03 BENEFITS MANDATES

[A] Generally

One important characteristic of the health care reform legislation is that it phases in a standard package of required health care benefits. But even before the PPACA, there were both federal and state limitations on the principle that employers had complete discretion as to which benefits would be included in their plans.

At the federal level, the Children's Health Insurance Program Reauthorization Act of 2009, Pub. L. No. 111-3 (CHIPRA), requires employers to amend their EGHP and cafeteria plans to allow special enrollment of employees and dependents who either lose their Medicaid or SCHIP eligibility, or have become eligible to participate in the EGHP because the state will provide assistance with the employee's responsibility for health insurance premiums. [Troutman Sanders LLP, *Keeping up with Recent Legislation—Numerous Changes to Group Health Plans Required*, plansponsor.com (Feb. 27, 2009); Norbert F. Kugele, Warner

Norcross & Judd LLP, *New Federal SCHIP Law Requires Cafeteria and Health Plan Amendments* (Feb. 10, 2009) (benefitslink.com)]

A new model notice about CHIPRA eligibility was issued May 2, 2014. [<http://www.dol.gov/ebsa/chipmodelnotice.doc>; see Timothy Jost, *Implementing Health Reform: COBRA/ACA Interaction and Other Developments*, Health Affairs Blog (May 3, 2014) (benefitslink.com)]

The HITECH Act (Health Information Technology for Economic and Clinical Health Act), part of the economic stimulus bill, expands HIPAA's privacy and security provisions. Business associates of covered entities are subject to the same privacy rules as the covered entities themselves, including criminal penalties. Business associates who discover a breach of the confidentiality or security rules by the covered entity are supposed to either take steps to cure the breach, or terminate their business relationship with the covered entity. Business associates must notify covered entities (who must then notify the affected individual participants) when there has been a breach of unsecured PHI. The covered entity is required to notify HHS—and the news media—if more than 500 people were affected by the breach.

Civil monetary penalties (CMPs) have been increased, and part of a CMP can be distributed to individuals whose PHI was improperly disclosed. The Office of Civil Rights retains its role in enforcing HIPAA compliance, but state attorneys general have been given enforcement powers through suits in federal district courts.

The HITECH Act includes many new regulations for electronic medical records; an accounting must be given of how the records were used and disclosed in the previous three years. The new requirements are generally effective February 17, 2010. [Troutman Sanders LLP, *Keeping Up With Recent Legislation—Numerous Changes to Group Health Plans Required*, plansponsor.com (Feb. 27, 2009)]

In April 2013, the Council for Affordable Health Insurance (CAHI) announced that in 2012 there were 2,271 mandates nationwide—far more than the 850 mandates in existence in 1992 when CAHI began collecting the information. CAHI says that mandates can increase the cost of basic health coverage anywhere from 10% to over 50%. CAHI found that the states varied widely in their mandate practice: Rhode Island imposes 69 mandates, Idaho only 13. The most popular mandates were mammography screening and minimum maternity stay, required by all the states, and breast reconstruction and mental health parity, required in 48 states, whereas only one state mandates cardiovascular disease screening and one state requires organ transplant donor coverage. [Council for Affordable Health Insurance, *CAHI Identifies 2,271 State Health Insurance Mandates*, <http://www.cahi.org/cahi_contents/newsroom/article.asp?id=1115> (Apr. 9, 2013, accessed Apr. 5, 2014)]

[B] Maternity Stays

The Newborns' and Mothers' Health Protection Act of 1996 (NMHPA) [Pub. L. No. 104-204] and the Taxpayer Relief Act of 1997 [Pub. L. No. 105-35; Final Regulations, 73 Fed. Reg. 62410 (Oct. 20, 2008)] combine ERISA and tax code provisions to mandate that group health plans (both insured and self-insured, whatever the number of participants) provide at least a minimum hospital stay for childbirth. The minimum is 48 hours after a vaginal delivery, 96 hours after a Caesarian section, although earlier discharge is permitted if the mother wishes and her attending physician consents.

However, the plan is not allowed to offer financial incentives to the physician or the mother to shorten the stay. If the plan does not provide hospitalization benefits for childbirth, it is not required to add those benefits because of this legislation. State laws requiring a longer maternity stay are not preempted. On a related issue, in late 2011, California adopted legislation (SB 299/AB 592 and SB 222/AB 210) to enhance employment and insurance protection for pregnant women, requiring maintenance of at least the same level of insurance benefits during pregnancy-related leave that the employee had before taking leave, and requiring all individual policies to cover maternity services. The law covers all employers of five or more. [Helene Wasserman and Michelle Barrett, *The Stork Has Landed: California Employers Must Maintain and Insurers Must Provide Pregnancy Benefits*, Littler Mendelson (Oct. 19, 2011) (benefitslink.com)]

An early 2013 California Court of Appeal decision holds that an employee disabled by pregnancy complications (including prescribed bed rest) was entitled to additional leave as a reasonable accommodation under Fair Employment and Housing Act (FEHA) even though she had used up her California Pregnancy Disability Leave Law and California Family Rights Act leave. The employer gave her 19 weeks of leave, including accrued vacation time. She was fired when she exhausted her leave entitlement but was still on bed rest and could not perform the essential functions of her job. The court of appeal ruled that the plain language of California's Pregnancy Disability Leave Law is that it supplements other FEHA entitlements. [*Sanchez v. Swissport, Inc.*, 213 Cal. App. 4th 1331 (2013); see Jackson Lewis LLP Workplace Resource Center, *No Statutory Cap on Pregnancy Leave, California Court of Appeal Rules* (Mar. 4, 2013) (benefitslink.com)]

[C] Women's Health and Cancer Rights Act (WHCRA)

The Women's Health and Cancer Rights Act (WHCRA) [Pub. L. No. 105-277], became law on October 21, 1998, effective for plan years beginning on or after that date. The Act provides that if an EGHP covers mastectomies, it must also cover reconstructive breast surgery if the patient wants it and her attending physician prescribes it. This includes reconstruction of the mastectomized breast;

surgery on the other breast to balance the patient's appearance; prostheses; and treatment of physical complications of mastectomy. Deductibles and co-insurance for reconstructive surgery must be comparable to those imposed on other procedures.

EGHPs (and the insurers and HMOs that provide the medical and surgical benefits) have an ongoing obligation to notify new plan participants of their WHCRA rights, and to renew the notice annually. (It is not necessary for both the EGHP and insurer or HMO to furnish the notice, as long as one of them does.)

It did not violate the WHCRA (or ERISA) for a plan to limit reimbursement for bilateral breast reconstruction performed by non-network surgeons to 150% of the cost of unilateral reconstruction. Nor was the plan required to pay for private duty nurses, because the plan specifically excluded that service. Although plans that cover mastectomy must cover reconstruction "in a manner determined in consultation with the attending physician and the patient," deductibles and coinsurance can be imposed, and the plan can negotiate the level and type of reimbursement with the provider. [*Krauss v. Oxford Health Plans, Inc.*, 517 F.3d 614 (2d Cir. 2008)]

A participant in a self-insured health plan sued the plan's claims administrator for refusing to pay the full cost of her breast reconstruction surgery. The benefit denial, a short notation on a check stub, did not satisfy ERISA requirements because it did not explain the denial, refer to the relevant plan provisions, or explain the appeals process. The SPD also called for notice within 30 days, but the plaintiff did not receive it for four months. However, the court held that the SPD adequately explained the WHCRA notice requirement. [*Haag v. MVP Healthcare*, 866 F. Supp. 2d 137 (N.D.N.Y. 2012)]

[D] Contraceptives

A December 14, 2000, EEOC decision [available at <http://www.eeoc.gov/policy/docs/qanda-decision-contraception.html> (accessed Apr. 5, 2014)] agrees with the charging parties, a group of female employees, that it violates Title VII for a plan to fail to cover prescription contraceptive drugs and devices when it covers other types of preventive medical care, and when it covers vasectomy and tubal ligation (permanent surgical methods of contraception). The EEOC treats the distinction as discrimination on the basis of sex (in that only women use birth control pills, diaphragms, and IUDs) and pregnancy. The EEOC ruled that the Pregnancy Discrimination Amendment forbids discrimination on the basis of potential as well as actual pregnancy.

In March 2007, the Eighth Circuit ruled against a class of 1,500 female employees protesting the exclusion of contraceptives (prescription or over-the-counter) from the plan. The Eighth Circuit held that contraception is not related to pregnancy for purposes of the Pregnancy Discrimination Act because contraception prevents, rather than treats, pregnancy, and because contraceptives used by both male and female employees were excluded. (However, in practical terms, the case became moot when the plan agreed to cover contraceptives after the suit was filed.) [*In re Union Pacific Railroad Employment Practices Litigation*, 479 F.3d 936 (8th Cir. 2007); see Fred Schneyer, *Union Pacific Ex-Contraceptives Policy Upheld*, plansponsor.com (Mar. 16, 2007)]

The California Supreme Court required Catholic Charities of Sacramento, Inc., to cover prescription contraceptives under its health and disability insurance plans. This employer brought suit, challenging the validity of the state statute because it required Catholic Charities to reimburse for contraceptives despite its moral opposition to contraception. The statute offers an exemption for religious employers, but the state Supreme Court rejected that characterization of Catholic Charities, which was not organized to inculcate religious tenets, was not a non-profit organization, and did not primarily serve and primarily employ members of a particular religion. Therefore, it was subject to the general mandate to reimburse the cost of prescription contraceptives. [*Catholic Charities of Sacramento, Inc. v. Superior Court of Sacramento County*, 32 Cal. 4th 527 (Cal. 2004), *cert. denied*, 543 U.S. 816 (2004)] In September, 2010, the United States Conference of Catholic Bishops wrote to HHS to oppose mandatory inclusion of contraception and sterilization as preventive services in individual and group health plans. The bishops described fertility as a healthy condition, and argued that such procedures are risky to women's life and health, and do not prevent abortion because abortion is not a disease. [<http://www.usccb.org/news/archived.cfm?release Number=10-162>; see Rebecca Moore, *Catholic Bishops Ask HHS Not to Require Coverage of Birth Control*, plansponsor.com (Sept. 23, 2010)]

In 2007, the New York Court of Appeals upheld the validity of the Women's Health and Wellness Act, which requires contraceptive coverage in all plans that cover prescription drugs. The statute has a religious exemption, but it is a narrow one (covering only organizations dedicated to religious worship and excluding those that provide, e.g., social services under faith-based control). The language of the religious exception, which limits coverage to employers whose main purpose is promotion of theological values and who primarily employ and serve members of their own faith, is drawn from a California law that also has survived challenge. [*Catholic Charities of the Diocese of Albany v. Serio*, 7 N.Y.3d 510 (2006). The U.S. Supreme Court refused to hear an appeal of the Court of Appeals decision: Fred Schneyer, *U.S. Supreme Court Rejects NY Contraceptive Coverage Appeal*, plansponsor.com (Oct. 2, 2007).]

PPACA's rules for preventive care require non-grandfathered health plans to cover all FDA-approved methods of contraception, with no deductible or other cost sharing from the employee. An HHS Interim Final Rule (IFR) gave religious employers an extra year to comply, and gave them the option of buying insurance without contraceptive coverage. A religious employer is defined as a nonprofit organization that primarily serves and employs people of a particular faith, and the organization's purpose is inculcating the religious values of that faith. [76 Fed.

Reg. 46621 (Aug. 3, 2011); List of mandated services: <http://www.hrsa.gov/womensguidelines>]

The United States Conference of Catholic Bishops announced that, despite the extra year given for compliance, it would sue to challenge the preventive health services rule. [Mary Agnes Carey and Shefali S. Kulkarni, *Bishops Will Sue Feds Over Contraception Rule*, Kaiser Health News (Jan. 20, 2012) (benefitslink.com)] In response, the administration said that religious employers opposed to birth control would not have to pay for it directly: insurers would be required to offer contraceptive coverage without explicit charge to either the religious employer or the employee. [77 Fed. Reg. 8725 (Feb. 12, 2012)] The bishops said this compromise was not adequate because it would not work for religious employers who self-insure. [Rebecca Moore, *Catholic Bishops Still Object to Contraception Coverage Rules*, plansponsor.com (May 18, 2012)]

Challenges to the contraceptive mandate were also asserted by closely held businesses, which argued that being required to cover contraceptives (or contraceptives that they believed actually aborted a fertilized egg rather than preventing conception) violated the corporation's rights under the Religious Freedom Restoration Act (RFRA).

In June 2014, the Supreme Court ruled that it violates the RFRA to require closely held corporations to abide by contraception mandate, because corporations are "persons" as defined by the RFRA, and free exercise of religion is not restricted to non-profit organizations. The Supreme Court held that the RFRA was enacted to protect business owners from having to choose between their religious convictions and complying with the law. [*Burwell v. Hobby Lobby*, No. 13-354/*Conestoga Wood Specialties v. Burwell*, No. 13-356 (June 30, 2014); see Adam Liptak, *Justices Rule in Favor of Hobby Lobby*, NYTimes.com (June 30, 2014)] In response the Obama administration announced that employers that refuse to cover contraception because of the business' religious convictions must disclose this fact to their employees. If only some contraceptives are excluded, the extent of exclusion must be disclosed. [Stephanie Armour, *Health Plans Must Disclose Changes to Contraceptive Coverage*, WSJ.com (July 18, 2014)]

It is difficult to estimate how many women will actually be affected by the *Hobby Lobby* decision. Census Bureau figures show that at least 42% of workers are employed by closely held corporations—including the massive Wal-Mart. But comparatively few corporations will seek to assert religious convictions. [Dan Diamond, Advisory Board Daily Briefing, *How Many People Will Be Affected By Supreme Court's Hobby Lobby Decision?* (June 30, 2014) (benefitslink.com)]

The Supreme Court ordered that a Catholic religious order, the Little Sisters of the Poor did not have to file the EBSA Form 700 with its insurer to claim a religious objective to providing contraceptives. The Supreme Court also issued an order allowing Wheaton College, a religious institution, to terminate coverage of contraceptives without filing Form 700, arguing that filing the form would result in the coverage it found objectionable being provided from other sources. [Jess

Bravin, *High Court Female Justices Dissent From Wheaton Contraception Order*, WSJ.com (July 3, 2014)]

[E] Mental Health Parity

A very controversial 1996 federal statute, the Veterans' Affairs, Housing and Urban Development and Independent Agencies Appropriations Act [Pub. L. No. 104-204], imposed a requirement of parity in EGHPs with more than 50 participants. Under the parity provision, plans that did not impose lifetime or annual limits on medical and surgical benefits could not do so on mental health benefits, and plans that imposed limits had to apply the same limits to mental health as to medical/surgical benefits. In 1996, this requirement was made part of ERISA.

The Mental Health Parity Act was permitted to expire, and then was revived several times through short-term extensions, from Pub. L. No. 107-116, Pub. L. No. 107-147, Pub. L. No. 107-313, Pub. L. No. 108-197, Pub. L. No. 108-311, Pub. L. No. 109-151, and Pub. L. No. 109-432.

Mental health parity requirements were made permanent, as the Paul Wellstone and Pete Domenici Mental Health Parity and Addiction Equity Act (MHPAEA) by the Emergency Economic Stabilization Act, Pub. L. No. 110-343. Employers of 50 or more employees are covered. The MHPAEA extends the parity requirement to substance abuse treatment. The financial requirements and treatment limitations for mental health or substance abuse treatment cannot be more restrictive than the predominant requirements or limitations that apply to substantially all of the plan's medical and surgical benefits. It is now unlawful to impose separate treatment limitations on mental health/substance abuse treatment—e.g., frequency of treatment, number of visits, days of coverage. The criteria for determining the medical necessity of mental illness and substance abuse treatment must be disclosed on request to current or potential participants and beneficiaries of the plan, and to contracting providers. Participants and beneficiaries are entitled to request an explanation of denials of mental health and substance abuse benefits. [Interim final regulations: T.D. 9479, 75 Fed. Reg. 5410 (Feb. 2, 2010); EBSA, *FAQs About Affordable Care Act Implementation Part VII*, <http://www.dol.gov/ebsa/faqs/faq-aca7.html> (Nov. 17, 2011)]

Employers are entitled to exemption from the parity requirement if the cost of parity exceeds 2% of total plan costs (in the first year of the requirement) or 1% in later plan years. [Edward I. Leeds and Clifford J. Schoner, Ballard Spahr Andrews & Ingersoll, LLP, *Expansion of Mental Health Parity Requirements* (Oct. 8, 2008) (benefitslink.com); EBIA Weekly, *New Law Expands Mental Health Parity Requirements for Group Health Plans* (Oct. 3, 2008) (benefitslink.com)]

In November 2013, DOL, HHS, and the Treasury published joint final rule on mental health parity to implement the MHPAEA by ensuring that features such as copayments, deductibles, and limits on visits are not more restrictive for mental health/substance abuse treatment than for medical/surgical treatment. The rules extend protection of consumers to intermediate care settings such as residential treatment and intensive outpatient care; clarify the disclosure requirements; and make it clear that parity applies to all plan standards, including geographic limits, facility limits, and network adequacy. The final regulations apply to EGHPs for plan years beginning on or after July 1, 2014; for calendar year plans, that means January 1, 2015. The final regulations exempt employers that had fewer than 50 employees in the previous calendar year—but the PPACA essential health benefit rules require non-grandfathered individual and small group plans to comply with the MHPAEA. [78 Fed. Reg. 68240 (Nov. 13, 2013); fact sheet at <http://cms.hhs.gov/CCIIO/Programs-and-Initiatives/Other-Insurance-Protections/mhpaea_factsheet.html> (undated, accessed Apr. 5, 2014); see EBSA News Release No. 13-2158-NAT, *Administration Issues Final Mental Health And Substance Use Disorder Parity Rule* (Nov. 8, 2013); Proskauer Client Alert, *Final Regulations for the Mental Health Parity and Addiction Equity Act of 2008* (Dec. 2, 2013) (benefitslink.com)]

But even with the rule in place, practical problems remain. Psychiatrists are much less likely than other doctors to accept insurance: 55% of psychiatrists and 89% of other doctors take insurance. Medicare and Medicaid patients find it particularly difficult to locate a participating doctor. The supply of psychiatrists is increasing slower than the demand, so psychiatrists can often count on a steady supply of private-pay patients. There are also many psychiatrists in solo practice and solo practitioners are less likely to take insurance because they lack the clerical staff to handle the paperwork. [Robert Pear, *Fewer Psychiatrists Seen Taking Health Insurance*, NYTimes.com (Dec. 11, 2013)]

The Southern District of New York held that a TPA cannot be sued for violating the MHPAEA (plaintiffs charged that they or their relatives were improperly denied access to psychiatric care), because the statute applies only to EGHPs and insurers. An entity that processes claims and makes coverage determinations when another company will pay the claims is not offering coverage. The suit could be characterized as an ERISA § 502(a)(1)(B) suit for violation of plan terms—but in that case, the proper defendants are the plan itself, the plan trustees, or the plan administrator designated under ERISA § 1002(16)(A). [*N.Y. State Psychiatric Ass'n v. UnitedHealth Group*, No. 13 Civ. 1599 CM, 2013 U.S. Dist. LEXIS 158438 (S.D.N.Y. Oct. 31, 2013); see David Slaughter, *TPA May Not Be Sued for MHPAEA Violations*, Smart HR (Dec. 9, 2013) (benefitslink.com)]

Principal Life Insurance, the insurer and claims administrator, denied many hospital charges for treatment of SW, a minor, for an eating disorder, on the grounds that the policy limits had been exceeded. The plan imposed a 10-day limit on inpatient mental health services, so it paid for 10 days of hospitalization in 2006 and only the first 10 days of a hospitalization in 2007. The Eighth Circuit held that there was insufficient evidence to treat the hospitalization as focused on SW's mental rather than her physical health. [*Wrenn v. Principal Life Ins. Co.*,

636 F.3d 921 (8th Cir. 2011); see Roy F. Harmon, *Eighth Circuit Holds Mental Health Treatment Limitation Inapplicable* (Mar. 4, 2011) (benefitslink.com)]

The Ninth Circuit held that insurance coverage of residential treatment for anorexia nervosa was not required by the Blue Shield policy—but was required by the MHPEA. California's mental health parity law requires coverage of medically necessary treatment of severe mental illness, and anorexia is considered a severe mental illness. It would be irrational to pay for 100 days of treatment in a skilled nursing facility that was not suitable for Harlick's condition while excluding suitable and effective care. [*Harlick v. Blue Shield of California*, 656 F.3d 832 (9th Cir. 2011), later proceedings 686 F.3d 699 (9th Cir. 2012)]

[F] Other Inclusion Issues

The Supreme Court affirmed, without opinion, the Seventh Circuit's decision in *Doe v. Mut. of Omaha.* [179 F.3d 557 (7th Cir. 1999)] The Seventh Circuit ruled that it is not a violation of Title II of the Americans With Disabilities Act for either an insured or a self-insured health plan to impose a lower lifetime cap on AIDS-related conditions than on other conditions (e.g., $25,000 versus $1 million). The rationale is that Mutual of Omaha didn't refuse to sell policies to people with AIDS, although the policy was worth far less to a person with AIDS or an AIDS-related condition than someone with other health problems.

EGHPs are forbidden to discriminate against employees or their dependents who suffer from end-stage renal disease (ESRD). Internal Revenue Code § 5000 imposes a heavy penalty: 25% of the employer's health care expenses (not just the amount that would have been paid for ESRD coverage in the absence of discrimination). Also note that ERISA § 609(d) requires plans to maintain their coverage of pediatric vaccines at least at the May 1, 1993 level.

In January 2003, the Second Circuit ruled that it is not a violation of Title VII for a plan to exclude coverage of surgical procedures to correct infertility that are performed only on women, because infertility affects male and female participants equally. The district court hearing this case applied the "equal access" standard often used in ADA cases, asking whether all employees have equal access to plan benefits. However, the Second Circuit held that this is not an appropriate standard in a Title VII case, in which the relevant standard is whether sex-specific conditions exist. If they do, the next inquiry is whether excluding coverage of those conditions results in a plan that has inferior coverage for one sex. The Second Circuit said that the Pregnancy Discrimination Act's ban on discrimination on the basis of pregnancy or related conditions does not extend to discrimination on the basis of infertility, because both men and women have reproductive capacity and can be infertile. [*Saks v. Franklin Covey Co.*, 316 F.3d 337 (2d Cir. 2003)]

According to Mercer's 2013 study, about two-thirds of businesses with 500 or more employees pay for an initial evaluation by a fertility specialist—but only 27% cover in vitro fertilization; 41% of these large employers cover fertility drugs. Fifteen states have mandates for some kind of infertility coverage, but subject to various conditions. For example, Arkansas, Hawaii, Maryland, and Texas mandate coverage only of fertilization of a married woman's eggs with her husband's sperm. Only eight states (Arkansas, Connecticut, Hawaii, Illinois, Maryland, Massachusetts, New Jersey, and Rhode Island) require coverage of in vitro fertilization. Sometimes the insurer imposes medical restrictions. For example, Aetna requires a woman to try artificial insemination 12 times at her own expense before coverage is available; Cigna requires six tries. [Tara Siegel Bernard, *Insurance Coverage for Fertility Treatments Varies Widely*, NYTimes .com (July 25, 2014)]

PPACA requires coverage of adult children up to age 26; by the time it was passed, more than two-thirds of the states had already expanded the age to which dependent coverage would be available, sometimes extending coverage even more than the PPACA requirement; some states require coverage to age 30. These state laws do not apply to self-insured medical plans, but do apply to EGHPs and possibly to stand-alone insured dental and vision plans. (Extending the parent's policy was usually more affordable than buying a policy for the adult child—especially if the adult child had a pre-existing condition.) [Louise Radnofsky, *Millions of Young Adults Join Parents' Health Plans*, WSJ.com (June 8, 2012)]

EGHPs that cover the daughters of participants who have not reached age 26 do not necessarily have to provide pregnancy coverage. The Pregnancy Discrimination Act (see § 34.06) requires EGHPs that cover 15 or more people to provide maternity benefits for employees and their spouses, but does not require dependent coverage. In 2008, approximately 2.8 million women, or 12% of the 15–25 age cohort, became pregnant. In 2007, the average cost of uncomplicated maternity care/delivery was $10,652. Pregnant teenagers are at especially high risk for premature delivery and babies with low birthweight. [Michelle Andrews, *Some Plans Deny Pregnancy Coverage For Dependent Children*, Kaiser Health News (Aug. 6, 2012) (benefitslink.com)]

[G] State Mandatory Coverage

PPACA takes the approach of requiring both businesses and individuals to purchase health insurance coverage, or pay a fine—an approach that was already pioneered by several of the states, including California and Massachusetts. However, Massachusetts' state budget for 2014 includes repeal of the state's employer mandate. Governor Deval Patrick announced that the repeal would be carried out even though the federal employer mandate was delayed until 2015. [Kaiser Health News, *Mass. Employer Health Insurance Mandate Repeal Moves Forward*, <http://www.kaiserhealthnews.org/daily-reports/2013/july/12/health-reform-state-issues.aspx> (July 12, 2013)]

By mid-2007, Rhode Island, Connecticut, and Missouri had joined Massachusetts in requiring some employers to establish cafeteria plans qualifying under

Code § 125, and Maine adopted a universal health plan, but it attracted few new subscribers, perhaps because many potential insured persons found the premiums unaffordable. [Sibson Consulting, *More States Enact Cafeteria Plan Mandates* (Aug. 10, 2007) (benefitslink.com); Pam Belluck, *Maine Learns Expensive Lesson as Universal Health Plan Stalls*, N.Y. Times, Apr. 30, 2007, at A1]

Mandates have also been adopted at the local level, e.g., by San Francisco. The Ninth Circuit ruled in September 2008 that San Francisco Administrative Code § 14.3(a), the ordinance requiring a minimum level of employer spending on health care, is not preempted by ERISA [*Golden Gate Rest. Assn v. City & County of San Francisco*, 546 F.3d 639 (9th Cir. 2008)]. The Ninth Circuit declined to review that decision en banc and, on March 29, 2009, the Supreme Court denied the restaurant trade association's request for an emergency order enjoining enforcement of the law. [Jerry Geisel, *Supreme Court Refuses to Stay S.F. Health Spending Law*, Business Insurance (Mar. 30, 2009) (benefitslink .com)]

Before PPACA, the general legal principle was that it was entirely up to employers to decide whether or not to offer insurance coverage. However, some attempts were made to require large employers to provide health insurance. Legislation was introduced in about 30 states. Maryland passed a bill, nicknamed the "Wal-Mart law," requiring a minimum level of health care spending by large employers. The governor vetoed it, but the state legislature overrode the veto. Early in 2007, the Fourth Circuit held that the statute was invalid—imposing Maryland-only requirements, contrary to ERISA's mandate of uniform national rules. [*Retail Industry Leaders Assn. v. Fielder*, 475 F.3d 180 (4th Cir. 2007). Although PPACA does not have provisions dealing specifically with the very largest employers, it does impose heavier requirements on "large employers" (those with 50 or more employees) than on smaller employers.

§ 18.04 DENTAL PLANS

Many medium-sized and large companies offer some form of dental coverage. As with most health-related benefits, the prevalence of the benefit increases directly with the size of the company.

Most dental plans offer fee for service coverage, although some plans use HMOs or PPOs. An emerging new form, endorsed by the American Dental Association in 1996, is the direct reimbursement plan: a fee-for-service plan where employees choose their own dentists. The plan sets a limit; up to the limit, the employee is entitled to payment of a percentage of dental expenses, e.g., full coverage of the first $100 in expenses, 50% reimbursement of the next $1,800, phasing out at a plan limit of $1,000 in benefits.

The National Association of Dental Plans Group Purchaser Behavior Study said that separate dental plans are becoming more popular: 59% of respondents had a separate policy, usually purchased from a stand-alone carrier. However, there was a decline in dental policies purchased as a package from the health insurance carrier's dental affiliate or partner. Policy purchasers said that cost was the most important factor in choosing a new dental carrier. Employers said that they offer dental benefits based on requests from employees, the value of dental health in general health, and affordability. However, 21% of employers with fewer than 100 employees in the group (i.e., those who will be eligible to use the Exchanges as soon as they start up) said that they were not likely to continue dental coverage outside the Exchange format. Since 2008, dental policies, like EGHPs in general, have been increasing the amount that employees must contribute toward the cost of their coverage. [Rebecca Moore, *More Employers Offering Dental Benefits,* plansponsor.com (Sept. 15, 2011)]

The basic structure of a dental plan is a schedule of covered procedures and payments for each (which might be defined as dollar amounts or percentages). The dentist who renders the care is paid for each service to covered employees (in a fee-for-service plan) or receives capitated or other prearranged compensation under an HMO or PPO plan. There is an increasing trend to require advance approval of large non-emergency claims.

The general rule is that the percentage of coverage is inversely related to the expected cost of the service. Low-cost procedures like X-rays and examinations get a higher percentage of reimbursement (often, 100%, but limitations to two exams and cleanings per year are also common) than fillings, root canals, and dental surgery (typically reimbursed at an 80% level). Prosthetics and orthodontia are typically reimbursed at a 50% level. Dental plans typically exclude cosmetic dentistry, hospitalization for inpatient dental procedures, and amounts that would be covered by other insurance (including Worker's Compensation). Usually, dental plans impose an annual maximum. [M.P. McQueen, *Health Plans Expand Dental Benefits*, Wall St. J., Sept. 19, 2006, at D1]

§ 18.05 PRESCRIPTION DRUG COVERAGE

Many companies' EGHPs provide at least some coverage of prescription drugs, as a complement to medical treatment. Some employers offer separate prescription drug plans with the objective of saving money by ordering in bulk. Some prescription drug plans also cover employees' dependents—often, with some degree of financial responsibility on the employee's part.

See Chapter 9 for a discussion of the effect of Medicare Part D (prescription drug coverage) on EGHP and retiree health plan operations. Group health plans that cover anyone eligible for Medicare Part D (whether as an active worker, a retiree, a spouse, or a dependent) and that cover prescription drugs must disclose to CMS, within 60 days of the start of each new plan year, whether the prescription drug coverage is creditable or noncreditable, by making an electronic filing at <http://www.cms.hhs.gov/CreditableCoverage>. [Warner Norcross & Judd LLP, *Your*

Medicare Part D Disclosure to CMS May Be Due Soon, <http://www.wnj.com/Publications/Your-Medicare-Part-D-Disclosure-to-CMS-May-Be> (Jan. 29, 2009)]

The typical prescription drug plan covers only outpatient drugs; drugs taken by hospital patients come under the hospital care benefit. The usual plan imposes a copayment on each prescription (e.g., \$5–\$25). Overall dollar limitations on reimbursement per plan year are common. However, many plans are bedeviled by high increases, such as 15%–20% a year, in prescription drug costs.

In an effort to keep costs down, or at least to tamp down the speed of the rate of increase, plan sponsors are altering prescription drug plan design, incorporating features such as imposing higher copayments; imposing a coinsurance percentage instead of a flat amount; requiring doctors to get prior authorization for expensive drugs; requiring a trial of a less expensive drug before a more expensive one is prescribed ("step therapy"); raising the copayment on proprietary drugs when a generic formulation is available ("therapeutic focus"); excluding coverage of drugs prescribed for off-label uses; and having two or even three tiers with a \$100 copayment in the highest tier and lower copayments for generics and less expensive branded drugs. Plans often try to reduce costs by encouraging the use of generic rather than brand-name drugs (e.g., by imposing higher copayments on brand-name drugs; limiting reimbursement to drugs appearing on a formulary set in advance; refusing reimbursement for drugs that are not deemed safe and effective or cost-effective; and requiring prior approval of prescriptions so doctors will test the less expensive drug before prescribing the more expensive alternative). [Bob Kalman, Buck Consultants, *How to Manage Pharmacy Benefits Plans: Part 1: Getting the Plan Design Right* (February 2012) (benefitslink.com)]

The Henry J. Kaiser Family Foundation's report on 2013 health care trends shows that 81% of workers with prescription drug coverage are in plans that have three or even more tiers of cost sharing. The average 2013 copayment in these plans is \$10 for first-tier drugs, \$29 for second-tier drugs, \$52 for third-tier drugs, and \$80 for fourth-tier drugs (if the plan has a fourth tier)—almost identical to the 2012 levels. [Henry J. Kaiser Family Foundation, *2013 Employer Health Benefits Survey*, <http://kff.org/report-section/2013-summary-of-findings> (Aug. 20, 2013, accessed Apr. 5, 2014)]

§ 18.06 DOMESTIC PARTNER BENEFITS, CIVIL UNIONS, AND SAME-SEX MARRIAGE

[A] Current Trends

Not all employees fit neatly into the categories of "married" or "single." Some employees live with a domestic partner, whether in a nonmarital cohabitation relationship or with a same-sex partner. An increasing number of companies are offering health or other benefits to the unmarried domestic partners of employees. The federal Defense of Marriage Act (DOMA) provided that only marriages between a man and a woman are recognized for federal purposes. Some of the states adopted similar legislation or amendments to the state constitution. The California Supreme Court authorized same-sex marriage but the decision was overturned by a voter referendum, Proposition 8. On May 26, the California Supreme Court upheld the validity of the referendum, with the result that same-sex marriage was no longer lawful. However, the approximately 18,000 same-sex marriages performed between the May court decision and the passage of Proposition 8 in November remain valid, on the grounds that the voters rejected the creation of any additional same-sex marriages, but Proposition 8's terms do not make it retroactive. [John Schwartz, *California Supreme Court Upholds Ban on Same-Sex Marriage*, <http://www.nytimes.com> (May 26, 2009). The Supreme Court heard an appeal of this case in 2013.]

In June, 2013, the Supreme Court ruled that § 3 of the federal DOMA was unconstitutional: it violates due process and equal protection, because it does not serve any legitimate state purpose to disparage same-sex marriages in comparison to male/female marriages, and it deprives same-sex married couples of valuable protections. (Section 3 provides that a same-sex partner cannot be treated as a "spouse" under federal law.) The Supreme Court found that DOMA § 3 improperly interferes with the states' regulation of marriage. The Supreme Court upheld the lower court ruling that invalidates California's Proposition 8 (the referendum forbidding same-sex marriage), on the grounds that the plaintiffs did not have standing to sue when the state of California no longer defended the validity of Proposition 8. [*United States v. Windsor*, 133 S. Ct. 2675 (2013); *Hollingsworth v. Perry*, 133 S. Ct. 2652 (2013).]

Supreme Court Justice Kennedy denied request from Prop 8 supporters to stay issuance of same-sex marriage licenses in California. [AP, *Justice Denies Request to Halt Gay Marriages*, NYTimes.com (June 30, 2013)]

At press time in August 2014, there were 19 states in which it was clear that same-sex marriage (SSM) was legal. This occurred in eight states by court decision (California, Connecticut, Iowa, Massachusetts, New Jersey, New Mexico, Oregon, and Pennsylvania), in eight states by act of the state legislature (Delaware, Hawaii, Illinois, Minnesota, New Hampshire, New York, Rhode Island, and Vermont) and in three states by popular vote: Maine, Maryland, and Washington State. (SSM was also legal in Washington, D.C.) The remaining states theoretically banned same-sex marriage. However, these bans were found to be unconstitutional by judges—usually federal District Court judges—in 12 states: Arkansas, Colorado, Florida, Idaho, Indiana, Kentucky, Michigan, Oklahoma, Texas, Utah, Virginia, and Wisconsin. [*Gay Marriage Pros and Cons*, <http://gaymarriage.procon.org/view.resource.php?resourceID=004857> (last updated Aug. 18, 2014)]

The states varied in their responses to court decisions challenging state Defense of Marriage Acts. Some state governors and Attorneys General declined to appeal; others vigorously pursued appeals. As of August 2014, the Fourth and

Tenth Circuits had ruled that bans on SSM are unconstitutional, and the Sixth Circuit had heard arguments but had not rendered a decision. Appellate hearings were scheduled in the Seventh and Ninth Circuits. However, implementation of these decisions was stayed pending motions for rehearing and the strong possibility of the Supreme Court agreeing to hear at least one of the cases. The Sixth Circuit includes Michigan, Ohio, Kentucky, and Tennessee. [The Sixth Circuit cases include *DeBoer v. Snyder,* No. 14-1341; see Eric Eckholm, *One Court, Three Judges and Four States With Gay Marriage Cases*, NYTimes.com (Aug. 6, 2014). The Tenth Circuit case is *Kitchen v. Herbert*, No. 13-4178 (10th Cir. June 25, 2014); see Jack Healy, *Appeals Court Rejects Utah's Ban on Gay Marriage, Prodding Supreme Court*, NYTimes.com (June 25, 2014). The Fourth Circuit case is *Bostic v. Schaefer*, No. 14-1167 (4th Cir. July 28, 2014); see Jess Bravin, *Supreme Court Blocks Start of Same-Sex Marriages in Virginia*, WSJ.com (Aug. 20, 2014).]

[B] Taxation of Same-Sex Spouse and Domestic Partner Benefits

Various retirement issues (such as whether a pension will be paid as a QJSA) are governed by federal law. One reason why the Supreme Court DOMA decisions were so significant is that many employment issues depend on whether another person is the employee's "spouse" or not. Spouses are allowed to file joint income tax returns; unmarried cohabitants are not, so the Supreme Court decision makes it possible for married same-sex couples to file jointly.

The general rule is that a same-sex couple will be treated as spouses if they live in the state where they were married, if the state recognizes same-sex marriages—or perhaps if they live in a different state but that state recognizes (gives legal effect to) out-of-state same-sex marriages. However, there are still many and complex issues to be resolved.

On August 29, 2013, the IRS enunciated the basic principle that same-sex married couples are married for federal tax purposes if they entered into a marriage that was legal where it was celebrated—whether or not they currently live in a state that recognizes same-sex marriage. This principle is set out in Rev. Rul. 2013-17, 2013-38 I.R.B. 201. [IR-2013-72, <http://www.irs.gov/uac/Newsroom/Treasury-and-IRS-Announce-That-All-Legal-Same-Sex-Marriages-Will-Be-Recognized-For-Federal-Tax-Purposes;-Ruling-Provides-Certainty,-Benefits-and-Protections-Under-Federal-Tax-Law-for-Same-Sex-Married-Couples> (Aug. 29, 2013)]

Notice 2013-61, 2013-44 I.R.B. 432, is the IRS's simplified procedure to correct over-withholding of federal income tax and FICA tax on benefits that were provided to same-sex spouses on an after-tax basis. Under Notice 2013-61, employees seeking refunds of previous over-withholding and employers who paid

FICA tax on health coverage for same-sex spouses, can net out the over-withholding for a quarter of a year instead of filing an amended return. Employers can also file a single Form 941-X amended return for the final quarter of each year instead of amending for each quarter. Employers can make a refund to the affected employees by the time the Form 941 for the quarter is due, reducing the amount of taxable wages on the Form 941. The employer should write "Windsor" on the form to indicate what is being done. For years before 2013, the FICA statute of limitations is three years, so refunds may be available for FICA over-withholding in the years 2010–2012. For FICA tax only, the employer can handle pre-2013 years by reimbursing employees for the amount of over-withholding, filing Form W-2C, filing a Form 941-X for each year within the limitations period (labeled WINDSOR on page 1), and obtaining statements from the employees in question that they are not seeking reimbursement and will not seek it in the future. [Durward James Gehring, *IRS Announces Special Procedures For Correcting Overwithholding On Same-Gender Spouse Benefit*, Seyfarth Shaw LLP (Sept. 25, 2013), available at Lexology.com; *IRS Clarifies Same-sex Marriage Rules for Payroll*, Infinisource Newsroom (Sept. 26, 2013) (benefitslink.com)]

Notice 2014-1, 2014-2 I.R.B. 270 covers cafeteria plan elections, FSAs, HSAs, and dependent care assistance program limits for same-sex married couples. Pursuant to *Windsor*, the IRS allows mid-year changes in pre-tax premium elections. Elections can be changed to reflect the legal status of a same-sex couple during the plan year that includes either June 26, 2013, the date of the *Windsor* decision, or December 16, 2013, the date of the IRS notice dealing with same-sex married couples. Elections could also be changed between June 26, 2013 and the end of 2013. The notice says that employers should use the plan's existing rules to determine the date when the new election becomes effective. When an employer is notified that an employee has a same-sex spouse, the employer must permit the employee to pay on a pre-tax basis to cover the spouse, even if the employee previously paid with after-tax dollars. As an alternative, the employee can continue to pay for the spouse's coverage with after-tax dollars for the rest of the plan year, then seek a tax refund. A Health FSAs can reimburse expenses of a same-sex spouse and dependents, incurred from start of plan year that includes June 26, 2013 (or the date of the marriage, if later). Not all of the tax changes are favorable to same-sex couples. Before *Windsor*, it was possible for each spouse to contribute the household maximum limit to an HSA or Dependent Care Assistance Plan (DCAP); this is no longer possible because they are not considered a single household. If they contribute more than the limit, they can either prospectively reduce contributions to an acceptable level or take a distribution of the excess contributions before their filing date for the 2013 return. Failure to correct makes them liable to excise taxes under Code § 4973, and excess contributions to a DCAP are included in taxable income. To permit the election changes prescribed by Notice 2014-1, the plan must be amended before the end of the first plan year beginning on or after December 16, 2013. The amendment can be effective retroactive to the start of the plan year including December 16,

2013. For a calendar year plan, the amendment must be adopted by December 31, 2014. [Stephen A. Riga, *At Year End, IRS Issues Guidance On Cafeteria Plan Transitional Rules For Windsor*, Ogletree Deakins (Dec. 26, 2013), available at Lexology.com]

Marriage has implications for pension and benefit plans: e.g., qualified plans must provide a QJSA and QPSA and spousal consent is required to waive the QJSA or QPSA. Minimum distribution rules and rollover rules give surviving spouses additional options not available to beneficiaries who are not spouses and there are QDRO rules for allocating pensions on divorce. The IRS extended its general principle (that same sex marriages are effective for federal law purposes if they were legal at the place of celebration) to these pension provisions. Plans must adopt these principles as of June 26, 2013. Plans can adopt amendments reflecting the *Windsor* decision as of a date earlier than June 26, 2013 (the date of the decision), and must reflect *Windsor* as of June 26, 2013. A plan amendment may be required if the plan's terms limit "marriage" to male/female couples. The deadline for adopting the *Windsor* amendment is December 31, 2014, or a later date required by Rev. Proc. 2007-44 § 5.05. Although in general plans whose funding percentage falls below the levels specified in § 436(c) cannot adopt amendments that increase benefits, Windsor-conforming amendments are exempt from this requirement. [Notice 2014-19, 2014-17 I.R.B. 979]

The Obama administration announced on June 20, 2014 that a wide range of benefits would be available to same-sex married couples, and most federal agencies would consider them married. However, the statutes governing the Veterans' Administration and the Social Security Administration currently limit certain benefits to persons who are treated as married in the state in which they reside—even if they married in a different state in which SSM is recognized. [Colleen M. Nelson, *Same-Sex Benefits Expansion Comes With Caveats*, WSJ.com (June 20, 2014)]

States vary in their treatment of same-sex married couples. According to the ADP Research Institute, some states, such as Missouri and Oregon, recognize same-sex marriages for state income tax purposes, even though same-sex couples cannot marry in the state. Georgia, Idaho, Kansas, Louisiana, Michigan, Mississippi, Nebraska, North Carolina, North Dakota, Ohio, Oklahoma, Utah, Virginia, and Wisconsin do not recognize SSM for state income tax purposes. Alabama, Arkansas, Colorado, Indiana, Montana, South Carolina, and West Virginia do not have SSM but have not issued a ruling on state taxation of same-sex married couples. The issue does not arise in Arkansas, Florida, Nevada, New Hampshire, South Dakota, Tennessee, Texas, Washington, and Wyoming, which do not have state income tax withholding. [Plansponsor staff, *States Rule on Taxation for Same Gender Couples*, plansponsor.com (Dec. 19, 2013)]

State taxing agencies in Nebraska, North Carolina, Ohio, and Wisconsin issued guidance informing employers that the state does not recognize same-sex marriage, so employers that provide health coverage for employees' same-sex spouses may have to withhold state income tax on the value of the coverage.

[Megal E. Hladilek and Atul Jain, *Same-Sex Spouse Health Coverage-Recent Developments in State Tax*, Faegre Baker Daniels (Apr. 16, 2014) (benefitslink .com)]

Washington State's Referendum 74, passed in November 2012, amends state law to provide that any existing registered domestic partnership is automatically converted to marriage as of June 30, 2014, unless one partner is age 62 or older; the couple has already gone through a marriage ceremony; or the registered domestic partnership has been dissolved. Therefore, the former registered domestic partners are spouses for employment purposes. [Kevin McGuinness, *Same-Gender Partnerships Now Marriages in Washington State*, plansponsor.com (July 2, 2014)]

In some circumstances, domestic partners who are not married can get favorable federal income tax treatment.

Under Treas. Reg. § 1.106-1, employees are not taxed on coverage provided to their spouse or dependents. However, there is no regulatory language about domestic partners. Therefore, unless the relationship is recognized by the state as spousal, or unless the domestic partner qualifies as a dependent under I.R.C. § 152(a)(8) (i.e., the employee domestic partner provides at least half the support for the other domestic partner), the employee will have taxable income equal to the value of the dependent coverage. However, if the cohabitation relationship is illegal under local law, I.R.C. § 152(b)(5) forbids treatment of the non-employee domestic partner as a dependent of the employee domestic partner.

If the non-employee domestic partner can be claimed as a dependent of the employee domestic partner, then the cost of domestic partner benefits is exempt from FICA and FUTA. But if the cost is taxable to the employee, both FICA and FUTA will apply in addition to income tax. Under Treas. Reg. § 1.61-21(b)(1), the gross income for the employee is the fair market value of the taxable fringe benefit, minus any amount the employee paid for it. Because the employee was taxed at the time the coverage was provided, neither the employee nor the domestic partner will be taxed if, for instance, health insurance or other reimbursement is provided later on.

As of March 2013: 72% of civilian workers had access to employment-based health benefits, which were nearly always extended to spouses and children. However, only 32% of civilian workers had benefits that extended to unmarried same-sex domestic partners, and 26% had benefits extended to other-sex domestic partners. This BLS survey deals with access, not the percentage of employees using the benefits. About a quarter (28%) of civilian workers had defined benefit pension benefits that made a survivor benefit available to a spouse, but only 15% had defined benefit pension benefits with a survivor benefit for unmarried same-sex partners, and only 14% had such a benefit for unmarried other-sex partners. Domestic partner benefits were most likely to be available to high-income workers and unionized workers: 51% of workers under a CBA had health benefits that could be extended to same-sex domestic partners versus 28% for workers who did not have a CBA. [Elizabeth Ashack, *Employer-Sponsored*

Benefits Extended to Domestic Partners, BLS Beyond the Number Vol. 3 No. 6, <http://www.bls.gov/opub/btn/volume-3/employer-sponsored-benefits-extended-to-domestic-partners.htm> (March 2014)]

Even before the mid-2013 Supreme Court rulings, the IRS granted some favorable tax treatment to registered domestic partners in California, Nevada, and Washington, because these are community-property states. [IRS Q&As for Registered Domestic Partners in Community Property States & Same-Sex Spouses in California, <http://www.irs.gov/uac/Answers-to-Frequently-Asked-Questions-for-Registered-Domestic-Partners-and-Individuals-in-Civil-Unions> (Sept. 16, 2011)]

[C] Employer Responsibilities

The rule under *Windsor* is that, for purposes of federal benefits (including ERISA, the FMLA, COBRA coverage, and income tax) same-sex marriage is treated on a par with male/female marriage. But family law is usually state law, with the definition of "spouse" left up to the states.

Certain fringe benefits (e.g., employee discounts, group term life insurance) are tax-free to employees and their spouses or dependents. When a same-sex partner is considered a spouse, the employer does not have to impute income on the value of health benefits provided to a same-sex spouse, or withhold income tax and pay FICA tax on this imputed income for same-sex married couples. The payroll system will probably require re-programming accordingly.

One important issue that remains uncertain is treatment of same-sex partners who are civil union or domestic partners but not legally married. Treatment of retirement benefits already being paid, in non-QJSA form, to a person who has a same-sex spouse will also have to be resolved. [Vicki Nielsen, *Supreme Court DOMA Decision—Part I: Fringe Benefits and Other Tax Implications*, Ogletree Deakins, <http://blog.ogletreedeakins.com/supreme-court-doma-decision-part-i-fringe-benefits-and-other-tax-implications/> (July 23, 2013)]

In mid-2014, the District Court for the Southern District of New York held that it did not violate ERISA for a self-insured health plan to exclude coverage of same-sex spouses. As a self-insured plan, it was not subject to state insurance law, because ERISA preempts state law. The plan explicitly excluded same-sex spouses from coverage. An employee who was married to another woman sued under ERISA § 510 (interference with attainment of benefits). However, the district court held that there was no adverse employment action and therefore no ERISA violation, and *Windsor* does not require all plans to exercise their substantial measure of discretion to include same-sex spouses. [*Roe v. Empire Blue Cross Blue Shield*, 2014 WL 1760343 (S.D.N.Y. May 1, 2014); see Roberta Chevlowe and Joseph Clark, *Despite Windsor, Federal Court Rejects Challenge to a Self-Insured ERISA Health Plan's Denial of Coverage for Same-Sex Spouses*, Proskauer's ERISA Practice Center Blog (May 21, 2014) (benefitslink.com)]

§ 18.07 TAX ISSUES IN EGHPs

For both the employer and the employee, the major EGHP tax issues fall under I.R.C. §§ 104–106. It is often in the best interests of both employer and employee for benefits to be provided under a plan of accident and health insurance (A&H). This result is desirable because the employer can deduct its costs of offering such a plan, and the employee does not have taxable income because the plan exists.

See § 18.19[B][6] for PPACA's rules on nondiscrimination in EGHPs. [IRS Notice 2011-1, 2011-2 I.R.B. 259 delays the required compliance date for the PPACA nondiscrimination requirement to insured health plans, until regulations or other official guidance is published, on the theory that employers do not have the necessary compliance information otherwise: Bond Schoeneck & King, PLLC, *Tax Break Extension Legislation Includes Employee Benefits Provisions and IRS Delays Compliance with Nondiscrimination Rules for Insured Group Health Plans* (December 2010) (benefitslink.com)]

Because it had not completed drafting regulations (although they were supposed to be finished by September 2010), the IRS announced that it would not enforce the anti-discrimination requirement in 2014. The IRS continued to struggle with valuing health benefits and conceptualizing discrimination in the health context. [Robert Pear, *Rules for Equal Coverage by Employers Remain Elusive Under Health Law*, NYTimes.com (Jan. 18, 2014)]

Section 104 provides that an employee does not have gross income when he or she receives A&H insurance benefits that the employee paid for, or that derive from employer contributions that have already been taxed to the employee. For years after 1996, amounts paid under other arrangements having the effect of A&H plans will be taxed as if they did, in fact, come from an A&H plan. Section 105 provides that amounts an employee receives from an A&H plan are taxable if they are paid by the employer or stem from employer contributions not already taxed to the employee. If the employer reimburses medical expenses incurred by the employee for him- or herself and family, if the expenses would be deductible under I.R.C. § 213 (medical diagnosis and treatment, rather than cosmetic or experimental procedures), and if they have not already been deducted by the employee, then the employee has no gross income as a result of the medical expense reimbursement.

The employee can rely on I.R.C. § 105 to exclude amounts that were not received from an insurance policy, as long as they were received under a "plan." For this purpose, a plan is a structured arrangement—although it need not be legally enforceable or even written. The purpose of the plan must be to provide benefits to common-law employees (not independent contractors or self-employed persons) in the event of personal injury or sickness. If the plan is not legally enforceable, Treas. Reg. § 1.105-5 imposes the additional requirement that it be communicated to employees before they encounter any covered health expenses.

The third section of the trilogy, I.R.C. § 106, provides that employees do not have gross income if their employers provide them with A&H insurance.

The IRS issued final regulations in May 2014, providing that, under Code § 402(a), starting with the 2015 tax year, amounts paid from a qualified retirement plan to pay accident or health insurance premiums will be taxable to the participants in the plan, unless an exemption is available. Amounts used to pay premiums for disability insurance that replaces retirement contributions when an employee becomes disabled qualify for an exemption. Retirees are not taxed on plan payments of medical benefits. To qualify for an exemption, the aggregate contribution for benefits cannot exceed 25% of total plan contributions. The plan must set up a separate account to fund those benefits. If unallocated contributions or forfeitures are used to pay accident or health premiums, this constitutes a taxable distribution. [T.D. 9665, 79 Fed. Reg. 26838 (May 12, 2014). See The Tax Adviser, *Final Rules Govern Tax Treatment of Distributions to Pay Accident or Health Insurance Premiums*, <http://www.aicpa.org/interestareas/tax/newsandpublications/taxnews/pages/20140509.aspx?action=print> (May 9, 2014); Jane Meacham, *Premiums Paid By Retirement Plans Become Taxable in 2015*, Smart HR (May 9, 2014) (benefitslink.com)]

On July 31, 2006, Final Regulations were published explaining comparability testing for employer contributions to HSAs. An employer who contributes to any employee's HSA has to make comparable contributions for all employees with HSAs. The employer's failure to do so is penalized under Code § 4980G by an excise tax of 35% of the aggregate employer contribution to all employee HSAs for the year. [Watson Wyatt Insider, *IRS Issues Final Regulations on Comparable Contributions to HSAs* (September 2006) (benefitslink.com); Nevin E. Adams, *HSA Comparability Rules Published*, plansponsor.com (July 28, 2006).

These excise taxes are reported on Form 8928. The excise tax, $100 per beneficiary per day, is also imposed for failure to comply with other requirements, such as rules about mental health parity and pre-existing condition limitations. [IRS Instructions for Form 8928 (2012), see Maureen Maly and Natalie Kohner, *IRS Updates Form 8928 for Self-Reporting of Excises Taxes Owed for PPACA Failures*, Beyond Health Care Reform Blog (Feb. 6, 2012) (benefitslink.com)]

Small employers (with up to 25 employees and average wages up to $50,000) may be eligible for a tax credit, for 2010–2013 plus any two years after that: See Code § 45R. For 2010–2013, the maximum credit is 35% of the premium paid by an eligible small business (25% of premiums paid by an eligible tax-exempt organization). The credit is computed on Form 8941 and included on the tax return as a general business credit. [See § 18.19[C]; <http://www.irs.gov/newsroom/article/0,,id=220839,00.html>; Fred Schneyer, *Tax Officials Distribute Small Business Health Credit*, plansponsor.com (Dec. 2, 2010)]

The IRS Website says that, for tax years beginning in 2014 or later, the maximum credit is 50% of the premium, and unused credit amounts can be carried back or forward to other tax years. The credit is refundable. [IRS, *What You*

Need to Know About the Small Business Health Care Tax Credit, <http://www.irs.gov/uac/Small-Business-Health-Care-Tax-Credit-for-Small-Employers> (last updated June 26, 2014)]

The PPACA requires self-insured plans and issuers of health insurance policies to make small payments, reported on IRS Form 720. For plan years ending on or after October 1, 2012 and before October 1, 2019, the fee is $1 per covered person for the first year, $2 per covered person for the second year, with inflation adjustments in subsequent years. The money is used for quality assurance activities. [77 Fed. Reg. 22691 (Apr. 17, 2012); [<http://www.dol.gov/ebsa/healthreform>; see DOL, *FAQs About Affordable Care Act Implementation Part XI* (Jan. 24, 2013) (benefitslink.com)]

§ 18.08 HEALTH-BASED DISCRIMINATION

PPACA's ban on pre-existing condition limitations in health plans builds on a 2001 HHS/IRS interim regulation on discrimination based on health factors. For questions and answers about the rule, see <http://www.dol.gov/ebsa/faqs/faq_hipaa_ND.html>. This rule implements a HIPAA provision, Code § 9802/ERISA § 702, forbidding discrimination in health coverage. EGHPs and insurers are forbidden to discriminate against, or charge higher premiums to, individual participants or beneficiaries on the basis of individual health factors such as health status, claims experience, or medical history. Note that whether a plan provision complies with HIPAA doesn't determine whether or not it violates the Americans with Disabilities Act (ADA).

Certain plans are exempt from the interim final rule, such as benefits that are not covered by HIPAA (e.g., long-term care insurance); single-participant plans; and self-funded plans that elect under 45 C.F.R. § 146.180 to opt out of the nondiscrimination requirements.

The Genetic Information Nondisclosure Act (GINA, Pub. L. No. 110-233) was enacted on May 21, 2008 and took effect November 21, 2009. It forbids employers to require genetic testing or to consider genetic information for hiring, firing, or promotions, and also forbids health insurers to deny coverage or set premium or deductible levels on the basis of genetic test results. GINA restricts the extent to which employers and insurers can ask for family medical histories. It is unlawful for an EGHP to give financial incentives (e.g., rebates or reduced premiums) for completing family medical histories as part of a health risk assessment. However, an EGHP can request family medical history to determine if an employee should be placed in a wellness or disease management program, as long as the employee gives the information voluntarily, and the information is only requested after plan enrollment and is not used in underwriting. Extensive interim final regulations covering GINA Title I § 103 were jointly issued by the IRS, DOL, and CMS in 2009. The HIPAA portability provisions already forbade group health plans and group health insurers from imposing pre-existing condition limitations solely based on genetic information. (Of course, the GINA regulations predate the restrictions on pre-existing condition limitations enacted by the PPACA.)

The 2009 GINA regulations forbid adjusting premiums or contribution rates for an EGHP because of the genetic information of one or more group members. Even genetic information that is legitimately acquired cannot be used to discriminate, although a group premium can be increased based on a manifestation of a disease or disorder. Group rates do not have to be reduced by costs relating to benefits for genetic tests and counseling services that are permitted.

GINA Title II forbids employment discrimination based on genetic information, and limits the employer's use of genetic information. It is under the jurisdiction of the EEOC, which issued a Notice of Proposed Rulemaking at 74 F.R. 9056 (Mar. 20, 2009). There is an exception for wellness programs, but only under GINA Title II, not Title I. [EBSA.gov, *FAQs on the Genetic Information Nondiscrimination Act* (Sept. 15, 2010) (benefitslink.com); see Hewitt Associates, *DOL Updates GINA Information on WebSite* (Sept. 20, 2010) (benefitslink .com)]

The EEOC issued final regulations for GINA Title II, the employment title, effective January 10, 2011. Under the Title II final regulations, an employer is not liable for inadvertent acquisitions of genetic information, or if information is provided voluntarily (e.g., under a wellness program), if family history is obtained to comply with state or local law, as part of an FMLA certification, or some employer leave policies. Nor are employers liable if the information is publicly available, comes from genetic monitoring that is required by law or offered on a voluntary basis, or is acquired by a forensic lab for law enforcement purposes. However, employers must keep exempt genetic information confidential, separate from ordinary personnel records.

GINA Title I and Title II are considered separate, so an employer will not be subject to double liability for Title II claims involving matters enforced under Title I. But it is possible to violate both titles and be penalized, for example, for requiring submission of genetic information to participate in an EGHP. An early 2011 article suggests putting a GINA disclaimer on all forms requesting medical information (such as FMLA forms, WC forms, pre-employment and return-to-work medical forms, ADA forms) so genetic information will not be included on the forms. GINA should be mentioned in the employee handbook, and employees should be informed that genetic information is protected. The required GINA notice should also be posted with the other required notices in the workplace. [GINA recordkeeping requirements: 77 Fed. Reg. 5396 (Feb. 3, 2012)]

On January 17, 2013, HHS published a final rule covering the application of the HIPAA privacy rule to Titles I and II of GINA. Genetic information is considered health information, which cannot be used for underwriting purposes (except for long-term care insurance policies). Effective March 26, 2013, the final rule gives covered entities until September 23, 2013 to comply. [Katherine

Georger, *New HIPAA Final Rule Implements GINA Restriction on Use and Disclosure of Genetic Information for Underwriting Purposes*, Holland & Hart LLP News Update (Jan. 23, 2013) (benefitslink.com)]

§ 18.09 HEALTH SAVINGS ACCOUNTS (HSAs) AND ARCHER MSAs

Current health policy relies heavily on tax-favored accounts that combine a high-deductible health policy (HDHP) with an investment account. Within statutory limits, account holders are entitled to deduct contributions to the investment account and employers' contributions to the accounts are not taxable income for the employee. The intention is that the account, over time, will generate investment returns that, in conjunction with the original deposits, can be applied toward the account holder's medical expenses. There are several kinds of tax-favored health accounts; collectively, they are sometimes referred to as Consumer-Driven Health Plans (CDHPs).

The tax rules governing HDHPs, Medical Savings Accounts (MSAs), as well as the PPACA rules, limit the amount of cost-sharing that plan participants will be responsible for; the out-of-pocket limit for family coverage is usually twice the limit for employee-only coverage. In plan years beginning in 2014, the HDHP limits and the PPACA limits are the same, but the 2015 figures are different. The PPACA limits are determined based on HHs's calculation of the average change in health insurance premiums, whereas the HDHP limits are adjusted based in changes in the Consumer Price Index—which is always lower than health insurance premium inflation. For 2015, the PPACA out-of-pocket limit is $6,600 for a self-only plan, $13,200 for family coverage; the HDHP figures are $150 and $300 lower, respectively. A health plan whose out-of-pocket limit is greater than $6,450 for self-only or $12,900 for family coverage is not an HDHP, and does not provide the required coverage for the plan participant to be eligible for HSA contributions. A health plan that is not grandfathered and is not an HDHP can set out of pocket limits as high was $6,600 for self-only, $13,200 for family coverage. [Jeannie Wilcox, *Beware: Next Year, HSA-Compatible HDHPs Cannot Use ACA Out-of-Pocket Limit*, Lockton Health Reform & Compliance Services Blog (Apr. 30, 2014) (benefitslink.com)]

[A] MSAs

In addition to imposing health insurance portability requirements, HIPAA enacted I.R.C. § 220, which adds a new type of health plan for taxable years that begin after December 31, 1996. The "Medical Savings Account" (MSA), started out as a small-scale pilot project for the years 1997–2000. The MSA account is tax-exempt, but account owners do not get a tax deduction when they withdraw funds from the account to pay medical expenses, because the contributions have already received favorable tax treatment. Funds taken from the account for any other purpose are not only taxable income but subject to an excise tax. The tax, formerly 15%, rose to 20% for distributions after 2010. [IRS Publication 969, *Health Savings Accounts and Other Tax-Favored Health Plans*, <http://www.irs.gov/pub/irs-pdf/p969.pdf> for 2013 returns (accessed Apr. 5, 2014)]

The Community Renewal Tax Relief Bill of 2000 (H.R. 5652), passed on December 15, 2000, renamed the account the Archer MSA (after Representative Bill Archer, Republican of Texas) and extended its lifetime for a further two years. Then the Job Creation and Worker Assistance Act of 2002 [Pub. L. No. 107-147], extended the availability of Archer MSAs until December 31, 2003.

The Archer MSA program was terminated at the end of 2005, but was retroactively reinstated in December 2006. [Announcement 2007-44, 2007-9 I.R.B. 1238]

MSAs are subject to limits. For 2013, the deductible must fall between $2,150 and $3,200 (individual coverage), $4,300–$6,450 (family coverage), and out of pocket expenses are capped at $4,300 (individual), $7,850 (family). See Rev. Proc. 2012-41, 2012-45 I.R.B. 539. For 2014, Rev. Proc. 2014-35, <http://www.irs.gov/pub/irs-drop/rp-14-35.pdf> provides that the annual deductible must be in the range $2,200–$3,500 (self-only), $4,350–$6,550 (family coverage). The individual cap on out-of-pocket expenses is $4,350 (individual), $8,000 (family).

[B] HSAs Under MPDIMA

Division B of the Medicare Prescription Drug Improvement and Modernization Act of 2003 (MPDIMA; Pub. L. No. 108-173) is called the Health Savings and Affordability Act of 2003. MPDIMA provides for two new kinds of accounts: the Health Savings Security Account (HSSA) and the Health Savings Account (HSA). See § 9.10 for a discussion of the effect of MPDIMA's Medicare prescription drug plan on retiree health benefits and corporate accounting.

HSSAs are designed for uninsured persons or those who are covered only under a high deductible plan. This discussion focuses on the employment-related HSA plan structure, which is much easier to understand in the context of Archer MSAs and other plans than when viewed in isolation.

Starting January 1, 2004, individuals under age 65 who have a qualified health plan can contribute to HSAs, with the maximum contribution limited to the HDHP's deductible. The limit is increased for persons aged 55–65, who are allowed to make catch-up contributions (as originally enacted in 2004, this amount was $500 a year; increases phased in until the amount reached $1,000 in 2009, remaining at that level in 2012). If both spouses are 55 or over, a married couple is allowed to make two catch-up contributions. Eligible individuals (persons covered by an HDHP, and not covered by another plan that duplicates the HDHP's coverage) can receive a tax deduction. [Treasury Dept. Office of Public Affairs JS-1045 *Treasury Secretary Snow Statement on Health Savings Accounts* (Dec. 8, 2003) <http://treas.gov/press/releases/js1045.htm> (no www)]

The HSA itself is a trust created exclusively for the purpose of paying the qualified medical expenses of an eligible person. The term "qualified medical expenses" has the same definition as in Code § 220(d)(2). If funds are paid or distributed out of an HSA, and are used to pay the account beneficiary's qualified medical expenses, they do not constitute taxable income for the beneficiary. However, amounts that are distributed but are used for other purposes not only constitute gross income for the employee, but also are subject to a 15% excise tax penalty. The excise tax is waived if the distribution is made after the beneficiary's death; after the beneficiary becomes totally disabled; or after the beneficiary becomes eligible for Medicare.

The Eighth Circuit Bankruptcy Appeals Panel (BAP) held in mid-2013 that a Chapter 7 debtor could not protect his HSA from the claims of creditors. He described it as either exempt under the Bankruptcy Code's protection of health insurance plans regulated by state law or was a right to receive disability benefits or payments because of personal injury. The BAP said that an HSA is merely a trust account that gives the account holder unrestricted access to assets. It is not a health insurance plan merely because tax penalties are imposed for using the funds for non-health purposes. [*In re Leitch*, BAP No. 13-6009, 494 BR 918, 2013 WL 3722091 (B.A.P. 8th Cir. July 16, 2013); see EBIA Weekly, *HSA Denied Bankruptcy Protection* (Aug. 15, 2013) (benefitslink.com)]

For 2014, the limit on the deduction for self-only coverage is $3,300, or $6,550 for family coverage. A high-deductible health plan is one with an annual deductible of at least $1,250 for self-only coverage, $2,500 for family coverage, and the out-of-pocket limit is $6,350 for self-only, $12,700 for family coverage. [Rev. Proc. 2013-25, 2013-21 I.R.B. 1110]

Under Rev. Proc. 2014-30, 2014-20 I.R.B. 1009, the limit on the deduction for self-only coverage is $3,350, the family limit is $6,650, and, to be an HDHP, the deductible must be at least $3,350 for single coverage, $6,650 for family coverage. The out-of-pocket limits are $6,450 and $12,900 respectively.

If an employee and his or her spouse have separate self-only HDHP coverage, each can contribute the single-person maximum to a separate HSA. If one spouse has family HDHP coverage, both spouses are considered to have family coverage, so the couple can contribute up to the family maximum, plus an additional $1,000 if one is over 55, $2,000 if both are over 55. Spouses can either establish separate accounts or share an HSA; contributions are allocated 50-50 to each account unless the spouses agree on a different allocation.

The investment firm Devenir said that as of mid-2013, there were over 9.1 million HSA accounts, with a total of $18.1 billion in assets—a 29% increase in both number of accounts and assets since mid-2012. In 2013, the average HSA balance was $1,891. [Devenir press release, *Health Savings Accounts Reach $18.1 Billion in June*, plansponsor.com (Aug. 6, 2013)]

On the compliance front, MPDIMA adds a new Code § 106(e) that states that an employer's contributions to an HSA are considered to be contributions under an Accident & Health plan. The employer's contributions are not subject to

FICA or FUTA—but they must be shown on the employee's Form 1099. Failure to provide the mandated reports is penalized under Code § 6693(a). An employer that commits to making HSA contributions for employees, but fails to do so, is penalized under Code § 4980G.

PPACA did not eliminate HSAs; in fact, the Insurance Exchanges will offer them. [Ron Lieber, *Health Savings Accounts Survive Medical Overhaul*, NYTimes.com (Mar. 26, 2010)]

[C] IRS Guidance on MSAs and HSAs

Shortly after MPDIMA was passed, the IRS provided guidance in Notice 2004-2, 2004-2 I.R.B. 269 and Notice 2004-50, 2004-33 I.R.B. 196.

A Medicare-eligible person who has not yet enrolled can maintain an HSA, but can no longer contribute to the HSA after enrolling in Medicare.

Another related tax-advantaged form is the Health Flexible Savings Account (Health FSA).

[D] Plan Comparisons

ERISA and the Internal Revenue Code make it possible for employers to offer a (potentially confusing) variety of tax-advantaged health insurance plans. By far the most popular arrangement is the Health Savings Account used in conjunction with a High-Deductible Health Plan, and this is the arrangement that is most favored under current tax law. (See § 18.10 below for Medical Expense Reimbursement Plans, § 18.11 for Flexible Spending Accounts (FSAs), and § 18.18 for Health Reimbursement Arrangement (HRA) plans.)

An HSA is an account established by an individual to pay his or her medical expenses, whereas an HRA is a benefit plan established by an employer. A Health FSA is also a benefit plan created by an employer; it reimburses employees for qualified medical expenses. An HSA must be coordinated with a High Deductible Health Plan (HDHP); health FSAs and HRAs can be coordinated but do not have to be. Only employees can contribute to HRAs, whereas HSAs and Health FSAs can include contributions from the employer and/or employee.

There is no contribution limit for HRAs. The maximum HSA contribution is $3,300 (self-only coverage), $6,550 for family coverage, with an additional $1,000 catch-up contribution allowed for people who are at least 55 years old at the end of the tax year. HSAs and Health FSAs can include pre-tax employee contributions, whereas HRAs are solely funded by the employer. HSAs are not covered by COBRA; HRAs generally are; some Health FSAs are subject to COBRA. HSAs are portable, but the other two types of account are not, because the employee is not the owner of the account.

If there is a balance in an HSA account at the end of the year, it will generally be carried over to the next year; HRA balances can usually be carried over.

A Health FSA can either allow a grace period of up to two and a half months into the next year to use the account to pay health bills, or can allow up to $500 to carry over to the next year. [HR 360 Inc. Employee Benefit Series, *HSA/FSA/HRA Comparison of Key Features for 2014* (benefitslink.com)]

§ 18.10 MEDICAL EXPENSE REIMBURSEMENT PLANS

Medical expense reimbursement plans usually reimburse employees directly for their medical expenses. Payment comes from the employer's resources, not from an insurance policy. Usually, the plan sets a maximum: e.g., only claims of $X per year will be covered. The plan can also be coordinated with insurance, so that the employer pays up to a certain amount, with insurance covering the rest.

The plan must cover employees, although it is not a legal requirement that it cover all employees. The plan can be informal. There is no legal requirement that the plan be in writing, unless it is a "welfare benefit plan" for ERISA purposes. In any case, employees must be given reasonable notice of the plan's existence and of how it operates.

For tax purposes, the most important question is whether the plan shifts risk to a third party (other than the employer and employee). A plan that uses a third-party administrator (TPA) to handle administrative or bookkeeping services does not shift risk to the TPA. The employer's costs of maintaining a self-insured plan will probably be deductible, as ordinary and necessary business expenses.

Internal Revenue Code § 105(h) governs self-insured medical expense reimbursement plans—those whose benefits are not payable exclusively from insurance. Plans of this type must satisfy coverage and nondiscrimination tests to qualify:

- The IRS issues a determination letter stating that the plan is nondiscriminatory;
- The plan covers at least 70% of all employees;
- At least 70% of all employees are eligible for the plan, and 80% or more of the eligible employees are actually covered.

The plan is not discriminatory if the benefits provided for highly compensated employees (HCEs) and their dependents are also provided for other employees. The plan can impose a dollar maximum on the benefits paid on behalf of any individual, but cannot set the maximum at a percentage of compensation, because that would improperly favor HCEs.

If a self-insured medical reimbursement plan is discriminatory, then the HCEs (but not the rank-and-file employees) will have taxable income equal to the employer's plan contributions on their behalf; the taxable income is subject to income tax withholding, but not FICA or FUTA. [See I.R.C. § 3121(a)(2)(B)]

§ 18.11 FLEXIBLE SPENDING ACCOUNTS (FSAs)

A Flexible Spending Account (FSA), also known as a medical flexible spending account or flex account, is an arrangement (either stand-alone or part of a cafeteria plan) under which an employer diverts some cash compensation into a separate account. The funds must be identified for a specific use: either for dependent care expenses, or for medical expenses that are not reimbursed by insurance or directly by the employer. The maximum amount of reimbursement that can be made "reasonably available" to a participant during a period of coverage is limited to 500% of the total premium for the coverage. FSA reimbursement must be made available at least monthly, or when the level of expenses reaches a reasonable minimum amount such as $50.

Funds targeted for medical care cannot be used for dependent care, and vice versa. A medical expense FSA must last at least twelve months, although a short first year, when the plan is initially adopted, is allowed. Premiums for other health coverage cannot be reimbursed by the FSA.

Before 2012, there was no limit on health FSAs, but PPACA imposes a $2,500 maximum. Benefits USA's 2012/2013 survey says 89.7% of respondents offer an FSA, and 23.6% of employees at those companies enroll in them. [Linda Panszczyk, *Big Change In Store For Health FSAs In 2013*, CCH Benefits Talk Blog (Nov. 12, 2012) (benefitslink.com). See Notice 2012-40, 2012-26 I.R.B. 1046 for calculation of cap amounts.]

To receive reimbursement, the FSA participant must submit a written statement from an independent third party (such as the doctor or medical office administrator) to confirm that a medical expense of $X has been incurred, and that this expense was neither reimbursed by nor eligible for reimbursement under any other plan. [Randy Myers, *Flex Abilities (Flexible Spending Accounts)*, plan sponsor.com (April 2006)] Since 2005, FSAs are allowed to carry over unused amounts from one year to the next.

Initially, sums were forfeited to the extent they were not used for medical expenses during the plan year. Then the IRS permitted a grace period for reimbursement of expenses incurred in the two and a half months after the end of the plan year. Notice 2013-71, 2013-47 I.R.B. 532, modifies the cafeteria plan "use it or lose it" rules by allowing a carryover of $500 to the next year. In light of the limit on FSA contributions, the Treasury saw less need to prevent excess sheltering of funds in FSA accounts. The plan must elect between allowing the two and a half month grace period and the carryover; it cannot provide both. Even if there is no grace period, a "run-out" is allowed: using prior-year funds early in the next year to pay expenses incurred in the prior year. This differs from a grace period, which allows use of amounts from Year #1 to be used to pay Year #2 expenses. Notice 2013-71 says that carryforward coverage ends with the termination of employment unless COBRA is elected. Therefore, employees who have carryforward accounts must be offered the chance to make a COBRA election (see Chapter 19). [Fisher & Phillips LLP, *IRS Publishes New Cafeteria Plan Rule*,

Lexology.com (Nov. 1, 2013); Alison M. Stemler, *IRS Allows $500 Carry Forward Of Medical Flexible Spending Accounts*, Frost Brown Todd LLC (Dec. 13, 2013), available at Lexology.com; AP, *Rollovers for Flexible Spending Accounts*, NYTimes.com (Oct. 31, 2013); John D. McKinnon, *U.S. Allows $500 Rollovers in FSA Health Savings Accounts*, WSJ.com (Oct. 31, 2013); Fisher & Phillips LLP, *IRS Publishes New Cafeteria Plan Rule* (Nov. 1, 2013), available at Lexology.com]

The Heroes Earnings Assistance and Relief Tax Act (HEART Act, Pub. L. No. 110-245) allows employers to amend their FSA plans so that reservists called up for six months or more of active duty can take "Qualified Reservist Distributions," withdrawing their FSA balances as a taxable cash distribution. [IRS Notice 2008-82, 2008-41 I.R.B. 853]

Rev. Rul. 2010-23, 2010-39 I.R.B. 388, says that a tax-free arrangement can only reimburse OTC drugs if the drugs are prescribed by a physician.]

§ 18.12 EGHP STRUCTURES

Originally, indemnity plans were the standard; now, that role is held by managed care plans of various types. Within the managed care category, HMOs were once dominant, but now must share the spotlight with other plan forms that offer greater choice of health care providers. Recently, attention has been given to defined contribution and voucher plans.

Usually, indemnity plans are divided into "basic" and "major medical" models. Basic coverage encompasses surgery, hospitalization, and care provided by physicians during a hospital stay. A major medical plan pays when other coverage is exhausted. A comprehensive major medical plan combines basic and major medical features, whereas a supplemental plan offers pure excess insurance.

The standard model for indemnity insurance calls for the patient to be responsible for paying a deductible each year (e.g., $X, or $X per family member) before the plan has any responsibility for payments. Most plans also impose a co-insurance responsibility: In an 80/20 plan, for example, once the deductible is satisfied, the patient is responsible for 20% of the bill—or 20% of the "schedule amount" that the plan pays for the service, plus the full difference between the actual charge and the schedule amount. It is also typical for indemnity plans to include a "stop-loss" provision that represents the maximum out-of-pocket spending an individual or family will incur under the plan. But the plan, in turn, usually limits its exposure by imposing overall limits on each employee's coverage, whether per year or over a lifetime.

Reimbursement to providers under indemnity plans is generally made on the basis of the table of "usual, customary and reasonable charges" promulgated by the insurer. These are either historical figures or a schedule of charges for various items.

§ 18.13 MANAGED CARE

[A] Concepts and Models

Managed care was a response to the climate of the 1970s and 1980s, when employers were faced with explosive increases in insurance premiums. Theoretically, managed care will encourage participants to adopt healthier lifestyles and, by deploying preventive care effectively, will detect disease early when it is more likely to be curable.

A common feature of managed care plans is utilization review. Patients may be required to consult a "gatekeeper" primary care physician before they can be referred to a specialist. Nonemergency procedures may have to be approved in advance by a claims reviewer. Patients' operations and hospital stays will be assessed for medical necessity.

In some managed care models, the employee is required to get all care within a closed network of providers; otherwise, reimbursement will not be available for out-of-network care (except in emergencies or when necessary care is not available within the network). But the trade-off is that the employee either gets care within the network at no additional charge, or pays only a small amount per visit, per prescription, or per service.

Managed care plans typically have their own payment schedules, which may be significantly lower than actual health care costs encountered in the community. The managed care plan's reimbursement to the patient may be defined in terms of this schedule, with the result that the patient has very significant copayment responsibilities. If a patient has satisfied the deductible and is charged $1,000 for a procedure and the health plan's schedule amount is $800; it pays 80% of the schedule amount, or $640, making the patient responsible for the remaining $360.

Generally, employees will be given one open enrollment period a year. During this time, employees who have just become eligible will be able to select one of the options available under the plan. Employees who have already selected a plan option will be able to change their selection. Once made, a decision is usually irrevocable until the next open enrollment period. Most open enrollment periods occur in the autumn, but this is by custom; it is not a legal requirement.

The Kaiser Foundation reported that in 2012, 16% of covered workers were enrolled in an HMO, 56% in a PPO, 9% in a POS plan, and 19% in a high-deductible plan. Less than 1% were enrolled in the now-misnamed "conventional" (i.e., indemnity) plan. In 2013, 14% of workers were enrolled in an HMO, 57% in a PPO plan, 9% in a POS plan, and 20% in a high-deductible plan; again, less than 1% were enrolled in indemnity plans. [Henry J. Kaiser Family Foundation, *2013 Employer Health Benefits Survey*, <http://kff.org/report-section/2013-summary-of-findings> (Aug. 20, 2013)]

In 2003, the Supreme Court upheld state "any willing provider" laws (statutes requiring MCOs to accept all licensed health care providers who apply; about half the states have such laws). The MCOs' argument was that closed networks control costs by imposing lower fees, but the Supreme Court said that extending the freedom of health care providers to offer care, and making more options available to patients, should be accorded higher priority. [*Kentucky Ass'n of Health Plans v. Miller*, 538 U.S. 329 (2003); see also *Prudential Ins. Co. of Am. v. Nat'l Park Med. Ctr., Inc.*, 413 F.3d 897 (8th Cir. 2005): Arkansas' "any willing provider law," requiring MCOs to open the network to any qualified health provider, "regulates insurance" and therefore is not preempted by ERISA]

[B] Health Maintenance Organizations

The Health Maintenance Organization, or HMO, is both a network of providers and a mechanism for financing health care. The theory is that participating providers are paid on a "capitated" basis. That is, they receive a fee "per head" covering all medical services under the plan for a particular employee or dependent of an employee. The theory is that, because providers do not receive more if their patients get additional health services, they will not be motivated to order unnecessary services for purely financial reasons.

In a "staff model" HMO the health professionals are salaried employees of the HMO. In the more prevalent Individual Practice Association (IPA) model HMO, the health professionals enter into contracts with the IPA, and the IPA negotiates with the HMO to set a reimbursement schedule for each service on the schedule.

Under the "group model," the HMO enters into contracts with independent group practices that are responsible for administrative tasks and are usually paid on a capitated basis. The "network model" HMO's doctors practice primarily in fee-for-service mode However, they also agree to provide certain services to HMO patients, once again generally in exchange for a capitation fee.

Federally qualified HMOs must provide an obligatory package of services including both primary and specialty physician services; hospital inpatient and outpatient care; emergency medical treatment; short-term outpatient mental health treatment; referrals and treatment of substance abuse; home health care; and preventive health care. Federally qualified HMOs can also provide additional, optional services such as long-term care, longer-term mental health treatment, dental and vision care; physical therapy; and prescription drugs. Optional services do not have to be provided on a capitated basis, and the HMO can impose fees on such services.

[C] Preferred Provider Organizations (PPOs)

A PPO is an administrative structure under which health care providers become "preferred" by affiliating with the structure. Employers negotiate with the

PPO to set the rate scale for specified health services. In 2007, the PPO was the managed care form with the most enrollees.

There is no set enrollment period for employees to join a PPO. Nor is there a single centralized entity that has complete financial responsibility for the enrollees' care. Sponsorship of PPOs is quite diverse: They might be created by a hospital or other health care provider, a health insurer, entrepreneur, or group of doctors.

[D] Point of Service (POS) Plans

A point of service plan is a hybrid of indemnity and HMO concepts. Participants can select their providers from a network, but they are not obligated to get their care within the network. If they do, their only copayment responsibility is a small amount per visit. Indemnity concepts such as an annual deductible and a co-insurance percentage apply when they choose out-of-network care. POS plans usually impose a high coinsurance percentage, such as 40%, on out-of-network care.

[E] Managed Care Cost Reduction Techniques

Utilization review (UR) is a cornerstone of managed care cost-cutting. In traditional fee-for-service medicine, the health care provider determines which treatments will be used, and the payor reimburses for part or all of the care ordered by the provider.

Managed care adds "gatekeepers"—reviewers who determine whether a claim satisfies the requirements of the plan. In many instances, the plan will require prior approval of claims, and will deny or reduce claims for non-emergency services that did not receive this approval in advance. UR also includes concurrent review (e.g., reviewing the need for continued hospitalization while the patient is still in the hospital) and retrospective review (after treatment is completed).

Procedural controls are common. Most plans will pay for a second opinion prior to surgery, but will not pay for surgery unless the second opinion confirms the recommendation for surgery. Cost-cutting techniques also include adopting a fixed payment schedule, and favoring outpatient and home care over hospitalization.

A carve-out is a discount mechanism under which particular forms of medical expense, or high-cost conditions, are managed separately from the rest of the health plan.

[F] Cost Trends

Managed care became popular because of undesirable increases in the cost of indemnity health plans. However, managed care has not lived up to its promise of reducing health care costs. Managed care premiums have always risen much faster than inflation. In response, employers often shifted much or all of the increase to employees, requiring them to pay premiums for the first time, or increasing their premiums, deductibles, and/or coinsurance.

In addition to shifting more of the premium to employees, employers adopted cost cutting measures such as having only high-deductible health plans; imposing a surcharge on spousal coverage if the spouse could be covered elsewhere; reducing the size of the network; and imposing extra fees for using certain doctors or hospitals. [Anna Wilde Mathews, *Choosing the Right Health-Care Plan*, WSJ.com (Oct. 22, 2011)] Other cost control measures include imposing a formulary for prescription drugs, using a "tiered" system under which reimbursement is higher for generic than for brand-name drugs, restricting or eliminating family benefits, and performing audits to make sure that ineligible persons are not covered under the plan.

According to the 2014 Milliman Medical Index, the average cost of health care for a family of four was $23,215. Of that amount, employers paid $13,520—58%. The growth rate in health costs from 2013–2014 was 5.4%, the lowest annual increase since 2002. Between 2007 and 2014, employer health care costs increased an average of 6% a year. Employee contributions, via payroll deductions and out-of-pocket costs, grew an average of 8% a year. [Christopher S. Girod et al., *2014 Milliman Medical Index*, Milliman Insight (May 20, 2014) (benefitslink.com)]

Usually employees of small businesses have much higher out-of-pocket payment obligations than employees of large businesses—and PPACA probably will not change this situation. KFF reported that employees of companies with fewer than 200 employees paid an average of $1,715 a year for deductibles—about twice as much as employees of larger companies. KFF said that about 58% of insured workers at smaller firms had an annual deductible of $1,000 or more, and for family coverage, a deductible of $3,000–$5,000 is typical. PPACA imposes a maximum deductible of $2,000 for an individual, $4,000 for a family in some small employers' new and non-grandfathered plans. Insurers can seek a waiver of this requirement by claiming that the plan would not be affordable without a waiver. According to KFF, average premiums for coverage of a single worker are $5,884 a year—74% higher than a decade earlier. Usually employees pay $1,000 of that. [Sarah E. Needleman and Angus Loten, *The Perils of Out-of-Pocket Health Costs*, WSJ.com (Sept. 18, 2013)]

In 2013, the Wall Street Journal predicted that PPACA would lead both to higher enrollment and to greater pressure on employers to shift costs (e.g., by raising employees' premiums, shifting toward HDHPs, and charging more for family coverage). About 6% of employers do not cover spouses who can get coverage elsewhere and another 6% impose a surcharge on spousal coverage. KFF reported that in 2013, employees paid 18% of the cost of individual coverage and 29% of the cost of family coverage. PPACA measures affordability for the employer's "pay or play" obligation by individual coverage, so imposing higher premiums for family coverage does not violate the employer's responsibility. For example, Gannett replaced the two family plans it operated with one HDHP with a $3,000 deductible. Slightly over half of its employees have individual coverage with a $1,500 deductible. At one time, Gannett had sliding scale premiums for low-wage workers, but eliminated that feature, so some workers saw their family premiums increase by 60%. [Theo Francis, *Companies Prepare to Pass More Health Costs to Workers*, WSJ.com (Nov. 24, 2013)]

Starting in 2014, UPS, attributing the decision to PPACA cost increases, will cut off health benefits for working spouses of thousands of its workers. About 15,000 out of 33,000 covered spouses would be affected by the change. However, the change does not apply to spouses of unionized workers, who are a majority of the UPS workforce. UPS said that spouses would not be removed from the plan if they cannot get other coverage. Mercer Consulting said that in 2008, 3% of companies with more than 500 employees excluded spouses who could get other coverage, a percentage that doubled by 2012. Mercer Consulting said that 12% of companies with between 500 and 4,999 employees imposed surcharges, e.g., $100/month above the cost of the spouse's coverage if the spouse could obtain other health coverage. [Timothy W. Martin, Betsy Morris, and Scott Thurm, *UPS to End Health Benefits for Some Working Spouses of Employees*, WSJ.com (Aug. 21, 2013)]

A Towers Watson/National Business Group on Health study reports that, in 2013 employees contribute 42% more to coverage than they did five years ago, whereas employer contribution rose 32% in this period. In 2011, employees paid 34% of the cost of health care in the form of premiums and out-of-pocket spending, a proportion that rose to 37% in 2013. Annual salary increases over the last three years averaged less than 2%, so employees are falling behind. Eighty percent of employees surveyed by Towers Watson said that they would continue to raise employee obligations in the next three years. In 2012, the average employee contribution was $2,658, which was expected to increase 9%, to $2,888, in 2013. [Ann Carrns, *Workers' Share of Health Costs Is Likely to Continue Rising*, NYTimes.com (Mar. 7, 2013)]

[G] Choosing a Managed Care Plan

Most employers can choose among several or many managed care plan vendors (although they won't be able to take advantage of this to bargain for low prices!). When an employer chooses a plan, cost considerations are important, but they don't tell the whole story. PPACA's Insurance Exchanges are intended to make the health insurance market more competitive, thus lowering premiums.

Employees may initially be glad to sign up with an HMO that imposes low copayments, but they will be dissatisfied if they have to travel too far to find a network provider, or wait too long for appointments. Other possible sources of discontent are difficulties in getting referrals to specialists, and denial of access to prescriptions, tests, and treatments that the patients and/or doctors think are likely to be beneficial.

When an account representative approaches you, collect as much information as you can about the plan, its history, and its results (including references from other subscribers). You can find out how an HMO, PPO, or POS selects the physicians in its network, and how doctors in the network resolve problems among themselves—and with the managed care plan about preferred treatment methods.

Your state insurance department will probably have information about the plan's operations, loss ratios (percentage of premiums used to pay claims rather than profits or administrative expenses) and how complaints have been resolved in the past.

Factors to consider are:

- Number of health care providers in the network or participating in the plan;
- Qualifications of health care providers (board certification or eligibility; hospital affiliations; any past complaints or suits);
- How the provider pattern fits your employee census (Are there too many obstetricians and not enough cardiologists, or vice versa?);
- Quality of hospitals and other facilities involved with the plan;
- Utilization review and other cost-control measures;
- Availability of primary care physicians at off hours (to cut down on the number of emergency room visits);
- Use of claims management to coordinate treatment of serious illness and injury to promote rehabilitation;
- How premiums compare to those of other MCOs—however, a low premium may simply mean that you will face exceptionally large increases in the future;
- Measures the plan takes to promote consumer satisfaction (telephone help lines, clear explanations of claims procedures, swift resolution of claims disputes, periodic surveys to assess consumers' reactions to the plan).

[H] Self-Insured Plans

As insurance premiums increase, more and more employers adopt, or at least consider adopting, self-insured plans. However, a self-insured plan has a heavy administrative and disclosure burden. Reinsurance is vital, because even a young and healthy group of employees can incur catastrophically high claims if even one employee is in a serious accident or has a child with major health care needs. Furthermore, health care providers tend to shift costs onto self-payors.

The PPACA requires the DOL to report to Congress each year about self-insured employee health benefit plans, based on data from Form 5500s filed by health plans. [Seth Harris (Acting Secretary of Labor) Report to Congress: *Annual Report on Self-Insured Group Health Plans*, <http://www.dol.gov/ebsa/pdf/ACAReporttoCongress033113.pdf> (March 2013)]

One coping mechanism is to use a Blue Cross or other entity as a Third-Party Administrator (TPA), which could give your plan access to the insurer's discount structure.

In a specific stop-loss plan, the insurer agrees to reimburse the employer or other plan sponsor for any claim that exceeds a specified amount (the "retention"). An aggregate stop-loss plan covers all claims above the retention in a particular year. In effect, a stop-loss plan works like an insurance policy with a very high deductible. But from the insurer's viewpoint, a specified stop-loss plan is more favorable, because although the insurer collects premiums in either case, it has no direct liability to the employees covered by a stop-loss plan, and cannot be sued by them for allegedly improper denials of claims or refusals to pre-approve treatment. A stop-loss plan ends on a particular date, and the insurer is not responsible for claims that accrued by that date but have not yet been filed. In contrast, an insured plan is responsible for these "tail" or IBNR (Incurred But Not Reported) claims.

However, the stop-loss premium will be very high if the plan experiences many claims in the early years of self-insurance. Stop-loss insurers have tactics to protect themselves, such as "lasering"–raising the dollar amount the employer is responsible for before stop-loss coverage is available for high-risk employees. Broader self-insurance could create problems for the Exchanges, if companies with a healthy young workforce gamble on remaining self-insured (whereas companies with older, sicker employees join the Exchange). Sometimes stop-loss insurers also avoid state taxes on insurance premiums by creating plans that are self-insured in name only (e.g., with a stop-loss policy that is triggered at only $10,000). For this reason, New York and Oregon forbid the sale of stop-loss coverage to very small groups (under 50 employees). [John Tozzi, *Small Business Makes a Risky Bet on Health Care*, Bloomberg Businessweek (Apr. 5, 2012) (benefitslink.com)]

For the years 2014–2016, PPACA provides a temporary reinsurance program to stabilize premiums after insurers are required to accept all applicants for individual coverage. Insurers and plan sponsors must pay into the stabilization fund; the fee is $63 per person per year. Some of the reinsurance payments will also go to the U.S. Treasury's general funds [77 Fed. Reg. 73118 (Dec. 7, 2012)]

§ 18.14 EMPLOYER LIABILITY FOR HEALTH PLAN ACTIONS

[A] Generally

The managed care relationship has three parts: the managed care organization (MCO) that provides care; the employer that enters into a contract with the MCO; and the employee or dependent that receives health care. When there is a bad result (whether or not malpractice occurred), the employee might want to sue the employer as well as the MCO.

Initially, employers usually avoided liability because the health plan provided the actual treatment (or claims denial). In many cases, plans escaped liability as well, because ERISA preempts state law but says virtually nothing about the plan's obligations. This state of affairs led to many demands for increased regulation (especially state regulation) to protect health care consumers. Many of these explosive issues are beyond the scope of this book, because they involve the employer and the EGHP only indirectly.

The Supreme Court has tackled some of these issues. *Humana Inc. v. Forsyth* [525 U.S. 299 (1999)] permitted EGHP members to bring a RICO suit for insurance fraud when they alleged that they were overbilled as part of a conspiracy to force them to make excessive copayments. The significance of a RICO suit is that treble damages can be ordered. The defendant claimed that the McCarran-Ferguson Act [15 U.S.C. §§ 1011–1015] (which exempts "the business of insurance" from antitrust regulation) preempts the RICO suit. However, the Supreme Court held that RICO does not invalidate or supersede state insurance laws, so the McCarran-Ferguson Act does not bar the RICO suit.

The Supreme Court returned to EGHP ERISA issues in April 1999, finding in *UNUM Life Ins. Co. of Am. v. Ward* [526 U.S. 358 (1999)] that ERISA does not preempt state "notice-prejudice" laws. These laws prevent insurers from denying claims because they were filed late, unless the delay actually prejudiced the insurer's interests. This decision does not harm employers who administer EGHPs, because it says that although the employer is the insurer's "agent," the employer's role "relates to" an ERISA plan and therefore ERISA preempts suits against the employer with respect to this role.

In mid-2000, the Supreme Court decided, in *Pegram v. Herdrich* [530 U.S. 211 (2000)], that when an HMO, acting through its doctors, makes a mixed decision about medical treatment and health plan eligibility (rather than a purely medical decision about what kind of operation is proper for a particular diagnosis, or a purely financial decision), then the HMO is not acting as a fiduciary. Therefore, even if patients are correct that the HMO refused them necessary and medically valid treatment because the HMO wanted to increase its profits by cutting the amount of care available to subscribers, this would not state a cause of action for breach of fiduciary duty.

In mid-2004, the Supreme Court ruled that ERISA completely preempts HMO participants' claims of improper denial of health benefits. Therefore, any such suits that are filed in state court can be removed to federal court. Only the ERISA remedies, and not state tort remedies such as punitive damages, will be available. In the Supreme Court's view, ERISA contains a complete set of remedies, which Congress intended to be exclusive. However, ERISA stands for "Employee Retirement Income Security Act," and although the statute contains lengthy provisions about pension plans and their administration, it has far less to say about welfare benefit plans such as health plans—and nothing at all to say about the activities of health insurers—who are third parties in the employer/employee relationship anyway. [*Aetna Health Inc. v. Davila, Cigna Healthcare of Tex., Inc. v. Calad*, 542 U.S. 200 (2004)]

The Sixth Circuit held in 2012 that a TPA that is authorized to pay medical claims on behalf of employers is an ERISA fiduciary: a party is a fiduciary to the extent of exercising any discretionary authority or control over plan management, or any authority or control over the management or disposition of plan assets. [*Guyan Int'l Inc. v. Professional Benefits Admins, Inc.*, 689 F.3d 793 (6th Cir. 2012); see Rebecca Moore, *TPA Authorized to Pay Claims Is a Fiduciary* plan sponsor.com (Sept. 24, 2012)]

[B] ERISA Preemption Issues

One of the themes of this book is that the balance between state and federal law is critical to the entire subject of employment law. In many cases, plaintiffs who are seeking faster resolution or a greater breadth of remedies will file cases in state court. Often, the employer will then claim that the case can be heard (if at all) in the federal courts, because ERISA preempts the state-law cause of action.

Many older cases became irrelevant in light of the *Davila/Calad* decision, the Supreme Court's ruling that ERISA completely preempts HMO participants' claims of improper denial of health benefits. This ruling rendered invalid the managed care patients' rights laws of eleven states (Arizona, California, Georgia, Maine, New Jersey, North Carolina, Oklahoma, Oregon, Texas, Washington, and West Virginia), and required ERISA plan participants to litigate their claims in federal court (where certain state tort remedies, including punitive damages, are not available). [*Aetna Health Inc. v. Davila*, and *Cigna Healthcare of Tex., Inc. v. Calad*, 542 U.S. 200 (2004)]

The Supreme Court ruled in mid-2006 that certain claims must be litigated in state, not federal, court. [*Empire Healthchoice Assurance, Inc. v. McVeigh*, 547

U.S. 677 (2006)] The injured employee was covered by a plan subject to the Federal Employees Health Benefits Act (FEHBA). FEHBA says that the terms of insurance contracts insuring federal employees preempt state or local law about health benefit plans. Nevertheless, when an insurer sought reimbursement of amounts it spent on the care of a federal employee who received an automobile injury settlement, the Supreme Court required the case to be heard in state court. The Supreme Court ruled that there was no federal jurisdiction under 28 U.S.C. § 1331, because the claim for reimbursement did not arise under federal law, so federal jurisdiction could not be triggered.

§ 18.15 LABOR LAW ISSUES IN THE EGHP

A 1996 NLRB ruling holds that an employer's reservation of the right to "amend or modify" the health plan did not give the employer the power to replace the existing fee-for-service plan with a managed care plan. Such a change is so sweeping that the employer cannot implement it unilaterally without bargaining. [*Loral Defense Systems-Akron,* 320 NLRB No. 54 (Jan. 31, 1996), *aff'd,* 200 F.3d 436 (6th Cir. 1999)]

Although it deducted premiums from an employee's pay, a West Virginia employer failed to remit the premiums to the insurer of the health plan. The employee encountered a very large medical bill, which the insurer refused to pay. The employee sued the employer and its owners (in their role as administrators of the health plan) for breach of fiduciary duty. The Southern District of West Virginia held that the employer and owners were fiduciaries because of their discretionary authority over premium payment. Commingling plan assets (the premiums) with the employer's general assets and using the funds to pay the employer's operating expenses breached the duty of loyalty. Commingling also violated the duty to hold plan assets in trust, and the defendants were also culpable for failing to disclose circumstances that could affect the benefits available under the plan. [*Cook v. Jones & Jordan Eng'g, Inc.*, Civil Action No. 5:06-cv-00627, 2009 WL 37376 (S.D. W. Va. 2009); see EBIA Weekly, *Employee Wins Claims for Breach of Fiduciary Duty Against Employer That Failed to Pay Health Plan Premiums to Insurer* (Feb. 12, 2009) (benefitslink.com)]

§ 18.16 QUALIFIED MEDICAL CHILD SUPPORT ORDERS (QMCSOs)

Divorce courts often issue orders explaining how to divide an employee spouse's retirement benefits with the divorcing non-employee spouse. These orders are called Qualified Domestic Relations Orders, or QDROs. [See § 12.08] The counterpart for the EGHP is the QMCSO, which supplements COBRA continuation coverage as an additional means of protecting children against loss of health care coverage as a result of their parents' divorce. [See § 12.08[A]] A

QMCSO is a court order that requires a parent covered by an EGHP to take whatever steps are necessary to enroll the child ("the alternate recipient") in the health plan—whether that includes notifying the plan or paying insurance premiums.

A valid QMCSO must identify:

- Every plan it applies to;
- The period of time covered by the order;
- The type of coverage the plan must give each alternate recipient (or a method of determining the coverage);
- The name and last known mailing address of the employee parent and each alternate recipient.

When a health plan receives a document described as a QMCSO, the plan has an obligation to review it to see if it is a valid order. Every health plan must have a written document setting out its procedure for reviewing QMCSOs. Courts do not have the power to order benefits that are not provided under the plan—so, for instance, if a plan does not offer dependent coverage, a QMCSO cannot create this coverage.

The plan administrator must notify the participant and the alternate recipients that the order has been received, and how the plan will analyze the order's validity. If, as usually happens, the plan approves the order as valid, then the participant and alternate recipients must be notified. Because the alternate recipients are children, they can designate a parent, stepparent, or attorney to receive copies of the notice on their behalf.

State governments (but NOT the DOL) can sue under I.R.C. § 502(a)(7) to enforce compliance with a Qualified Medical Child Support Order (QMCSO). The states have a role to play here because they have traditionally been empowered to deal with family law issues such as child support.

A 1998 law, the Child Support Performance and Incentives Act [Pub. L. No. 105-200], requires state child-support enforcement agencies to protect children's rights to medical coverage. The DOL and HHS published a Final Rule giving the text for the National Medical Child Support Notice. [See 65 Fed. Reg. 82128 and 82154 (Dec. 27, 2000)] State agencies have been required to use the form to enforce child support orders since October 1, 2001, either by informing the child support enforcement agency that the employee who is the subject of the order does not have health coverage; has been terminated; or by sending Part B of the form to the plan administrator for coverage of the children under the health plan (if they are eligible).

The IRS (which has jurisdiction over COBRA eligibility questions) has ruled that a child enrolled in an EGHP under a QMCSO who loses coverage as a result of a qualifying event is a qualified beneficiary who is entitled to make a COBRA election.

§ 18.17 THE EMPLOYER'S RIGHT OF SUBROGATION

Subrogation is a legal concept under which a party that advances expenses can recover them when the person who received the funds is reimbursed for those expenses. More specifically, if an EGHP covers the medical treatment of an injured employee, or dependent of an employee, the EGHP will have a legal right to part of the verdict or settlement that the employee receives from suing whoever caused the accident or manufactured the dangerous product.

In the typical subrogation case, a plan participant is injured, and the plan provides funds for treatment of his or her injuries. Then the injured person settles a case, or wins a judgment, against the person responsible for the injuries. In practical terms, that usually means a liability insurance company gets involved. The EGHP then attempts to recover the benefits from the injured person's tort recovery.

For the plan to have a right of subrogation, the plan language, or the insurance covering the plan, must provide this right explicitly. State law must also be consulted to see if limitations are imposed on subrogation—but even if they are, the federal courts may conclude that the state limitations are preempted by ERISA, e.g., *Levine v. United Healthcare Corp.* [402 F.3d 156 (3d Cir. 2005)] Some state laws facilitate subrogation: for instance, by requiring the participant to agree to subrogation as a condition of receiving benefits under the plan.

The Supreme Court decided a subrogation case. [*Great-West Life & Annuity Ins. Co. v. Knudson,* 534 U.S. 204 (2002)] In this case, the plan called for recovery from plan beneficiaries if they recovered any payments from third parties. The plan paid most of the $411,157.11 in medical expenses when a car crash rendered an employee quadriplegic. She settled her tort case; the settlement allocated only $13,828.70 to past medical expenses. The Supreme Court refused to allow the plan to sue under ERISA § 503(a)(3) (civil action to enjoin an act or practice violating the terms of the plan), or to obtain equitable relief to collect more of the funds it had advanced. The Supreme Court refused to permit the plan to bring such a suit, ruling that compelling payment of money due under a contract is not an "equitable" remedy.

The Supreme Court held that an insurer's civil action to recover amounts advanced for health care is "appropriate equitable relief" permitted by ERISA § 502(a)(3)(B), because injured plan participants were the equivalent of trustees because they agreed to set aside part of their tort recovery to reimburse the insurer. [*Mid Atl. Med. Servs., LLC v. Sereboff,* 547 U.S. 356 (2006)]

The "make-whole" doctrine also has to be considered in cases where the injured person has received a recovery, but less than an amount necessary to compensate for all injuries received. This doctrine absolves the injured person of having to reimburse the plan until he or she has been "made whole." Yet another factor is the "common fund" doctrine: whether the EGHP's right of recovery is reduced to account for attorneys' fees paid to the injured person's attorney. The rationale for this doctrine is that without the attorney, there would have been no "common fund" for the injured person and the plan to share, and therefore both of them should contribute toward the fees.

In 2013, the Supreme Court held that contract principles govern when a participant receives less than full compensation for injuries. The common fund doctrine is subject to the terms of an ERISA plan. In this case, the plan paid about $67,000 of medical expenses for the participant; he received $110,000 in tort damages. After paying his attorney, he had less than $66,000, and would have received no recovery if he reimbursed the plan. The Third Circuit held that the plan was not entitled to be reimbursed for all the funds advanced, because it would be inequitable to deprive the victim of any recovery. The Supreme Court vacated and remanded the case. However, because the plan did not specifically explain how attorneys' fees would be handled, the Supreme Court allowed the use of the common fund doctrine to prevent the victim from owing more to the plan than he actually received from his tort case. [*US Airways Inc. v. McCutchen*, 133 S. Ct. 1537 (2013). Similar principles were applied to a self-insured medical plan: *Quest Diagnostics v. Bomani*, No. 11-CV-00951 (D. Conn. June 19, 2013); see Anthony Cacace, *Express Plan Terms Allow Self-Insured Plan to Recover Medical Benefits Paid to Employee Post-McCutchen*, Proskauer's ERISA Practice Center Blog (June 25, 2013) (benefitslink.com)]

Certiorari was denied in a case brought by a Supplemental Needs Trust on the issue of whether depositing funds into a trust, on behalf of insured tortfeasors, to benefit a health plan beneficiary who settled a case, prevented the plan from exercising ERISA subrogation to recover. Griffin, a participant in FK Industries, Inc's ERISA welfare benefit plan, was seriously injured in a 2006 automobile accident. The welfare benefit plan, administered by ACS Recovery Services, Inc. paid more than $50,000 of medical expenses. Griffin reached a settlement with the other driver. The settlement was first allocated to Griffin's attorney, additional medical expenses, and to Griffin's wife's divorce settlement. The balance, with a present value of $148,000, was paid by the other driver's insurer to an assignee that was authorized to buy a Hartford Life Annuity that made monthly payments to Griffin's Special Needs Trust. The FK welfare benefit plan had a first lien on all recoveries and forbade participants to take any action that would impair the plan's right of recovery. The result of the settlement was that neither ACS Recovery Services nor FK Industries received any funds. ACS and FK sued the trust, the trustee, Griffin, and his wife, seeking to impose a constructive trust of at least $50,000, and asked for an injunction preventing the defendants from interfering with the plan's right to be reimbursed for the funds advanced for Griffin's care. The Fifth Circuit's decision (which stands, because the Supreme Court did not review it) allowed ACS to recover the costs it incurred on Griffin's behalf from the SNT. The trust could be sued under ERISA; and the trust funds were directly traceable to Griffin's tort recovery. The plan had a pre-existing equitable lien on the tort recovery. [*Larry Griffin Special Needs Trust v. ACS Recovery Servs., Inc.*, 134 S. Ct. 618 (2013); see Wolters Kluwer Law & Business News Center,

Supreme Court Declines Request By Special Needs Trust To Review ERISA Plan's Right To Reimbursement (Nov. 22, 2013) (benefitslink.com)]

The factors to consider in drafting a subrogation provision that will provide the most protection for the plan, and enable full recovery, include:

- Scope of obligation—all covered persons (including dependents) have to reimburse the plan; if only the participant has a duty to reimburse, the plan probably will not be able to look to family members for reimbursement.
- Source of recovery: is reimbursement required from all sources including underinsured/uninsured motorist coverage or only from liability coverage?
- Priority of payment: does the plan disclaim the Make Whole Rule or settle the priority of payment?
- Attorneys' fees and costs: does the subrogation provision explicitly disclaim the common fund doctrine? If not, it's likely that the plan's recovery will be reduced by one-third to account for the insured person's attorneys' fees.
- Allocations: Are all amounts received by the injured person presumed to recover medical expenses, or is recovery limited to the extent settlement agreement earmarks amounts for medical expenses? If the latter, then the plan will not have access to judgment or settlement funds allocated to pain and suffering.
- Cooperation: if the plan does not include a clause requiring the participant to cooperate in recovery efforts, the plan may find out that recovery rights have not been protected.
- What is the "res" (fund or other legal entity) from which insurer can recover?
- Does the subrogation provision appear in the plan document, the SPD, or both? If both, the provisions should be consistent between the two.
- Ruling out the common fund doctrine might discourage the injured employee from seeking recovering from the tortfeasor—which means that the plan itself would have to sue the tortfeasor to get back the funds advanced for the employee's treatment.

[Sarah Fowles and Angela Marie Hubbell, *Have You Checked Your Plan's Subrogation and Reimbursement Provisions Lately?*, Quarles & Brady LLP Employee Benefits & Executive Compensation Law Blog (April 2013) (benefits link.com)]

§ 18.18 DEFINED CONTRIBUTION, CDHP, AND HRA PLANS

A defined contribution health plan, also known as a "consumer-driven" plan, is another way of limiting the employer's exposure to cost increases. The most popular form of CDHP is the Health Savings Account, separately or in tandem with a high-deductible health policy (HDHP).

The employer agrees to give the employee a fixed amount that can be applied to a menu of health care choices. The employer's exposure is limited and is not subject to health care price increases. In effect the voucher works like a defined contribution or 401(k) plan, shifting control to the employees—but also putting them at risk of bad or simply unlucky decisions. The rationale is that greater employee liability for health care costs will lead employees to become better informed and shop for more economical medical care.

In a fixed-dollar contribution plan, the employer offers a choice of health plans and gives each worker a certain amount of compensation to buy insurance. Employees who want a more expensive policy must use their own pretax dollars to pay the difference. In a fixed-percentage contribution plan, the employer's contribution is defined as a percentage of the premium, with the rest paid by the employee.

Employers could also combine a high deductible health plan with a funded or unfunded account for medical expenses. The employer might set up an account in which funds are accumulated on behalf of active employees, to be used for their eventual retiree health expenses.

Defined contribution plans are touted as means of improving employees' consumerism and health care shopping behavior, although that was also an argument used in favor of managed care, which is now failing to control costs.

In 2013, about 15% of eligible persons had an HRA or HSA. These accounts took off in 2007, when the number of accounts rose 101% and assets rose 282% from the previous year. Growth slowed down in 2008–2010, accelerated in 2011, and continued very strong in 2012, when both assets and accounts rose by 40%. [EBRI Fast Facts #267, *Healthy Growth for Health Savings Accounts* (Feb. 6, 2014) (benefitslink.com)]

In 2013, CDHPs continued their growth. They were the second most prevalent plan type (following PPOs) and could surpass PPOs in the next three to five years. The Aon Hewitt 2013 Health Care Survey of 800 large and mid-sized employees said that 56% of respondents offer CDHPs as a plan choice, and 30% are considering offering one in the next three to five years. Ten percent of respondents had a CDHP as their sole health plan; another 44% might do so in three to five years. Employers experienced 4% cost increases in CDHPs versus 6% in PPOs, 7% in HMOs, and 6% in EPOs. To encourage CDHP enrollment, employers are using tactics like subsidizing premiums at a higher level than other plans (44% of respondents did this), making the CDHP the default plan (22%) and covering preventive medications without a deductible (44%). [Aon Hewitt, *Aon Hewitt Research Finds Consumer-Driven Health Plans Continue to Grow in*

Popularity, CDHPs are the Second Most Prevalent Plan Offered by U.S. Employers (Oct. 9, 2013) (benefitslink.com)]

If the arrangement constitutes a Flexible Spending Account, then Internal Revenue Code requirements will have to be satisfied. If the arrangement is trust-funded, it may become an ERISA welfare benefit plan, with additional requirements to meet. Very possibly, the IRS will treat the arrangement as a self-insured medical plan, in which case there may be nondiscrimination, COBRA, and HIPAA compliance obligations. Questions of dependent coverage will have to be worked out.

CDH plans can be combined with HRAs and the plan can be set up so that the employee is required to satisfy a deductible before accessing HRA funds. Another option is for the employer to cover up to 100% of preventive care services, or require employees to use HRA amounts for this purpose. The employer can also impose a cap, such as $3,000 a year, on the amount that can be rolled over from year to year within an HRA.

An HRA is a plan that is 100% funded by employer contributions and provides reimbursement for medical expenses incurred during the 12-month plan year (but not before). In fact, carryover of unused amounts is not only permitted, it is mandatory. The balance in the HRA may be used to provide coverage of medical expenses; and the balance must be used for this purpose if a COBRA event occurs. Distributions for any purpose other than paying medical expenses jeopardizes the exclusion from income of all distributed amounts. Notice 2002-45 says that any expense that qualifies under § 213(d) can be reimbursed from the HRA, including insurance premiums, with one major exception. Because of § 106(c), no amount that constitutes a "qualified long-term care service" under § 7702B(c) can be reimbursed because health FSAs are not allowed to cover long-term care.

The HRA was authorized in 2002 to permit employers to provide employees with pre-tax dollars to pay for medical care and services. The combination of an HRA and an HDHP gives employees both conventional catastrophic coverage after the deductible is met and help with pre-deductible expenses. However, PPACA enacted Public Health Services Act § 2711 which forbids annual dollar limits—and HRAs, by definition, are limited. DOL/HHS/Treasury FAQs posted on the DOL Website on January 24, 2013 says that standalone HRAs are unacceptable because they may violate PPACA's limit of 3:1 for age-related premium disparity. [Timothy Jost, *Implementing Health Reform: Health Reimbursement Arrangements And More*, Health Affairs Blog (Jan. 25, 2013) (benefitslink.com); Alden J. Bianchi and Gary E. Bacher, *Stand-Alone HRAs: DOL, IRS, HHS Put the Brakes On*, Mintz Levin (Feb. 2, 2013) (benefitslink.com)]

For the period ending December 31, 2013, there were 10.7 million HSA accounts, with assets over $19.3 billion. This was 30% more accounts and 25%

more assets than the previous year. At the end of 2013, the average account balance for funded HSA accounts was $2,356, up 3.2% from the previous year average of $2,283. [Devenir, *Year-End 2013 Devenir HSA Research Report* (Feb. 12, 2014) (benefitslink.com)]

Guidance was provided by the IRS in Notice 2013-54, 2013-40 I.R.B. 287 and by the DOL in Technical Release 2013-03 about compliance issues for HRAs and Health FSAs. HRAs and Health FSAs are considered group health plans subject to PPACA requirements—including the ban on annual dollar limits on essential health benefits and the requirement of providing certain preventive services without cost-sharing. Violations are subject to excise taxes of $100 per person per day under Code § 4980D. For plan years beginning on or after January 1, 2014, the plan must either be integrated with an EGHP or be limited to providing excepted benefits (e.g., retiree health care; dental and vision benefits). HRAs and Health FSAs are treated as minimum essential coverage that will prevent covered employees from receiving premium subsidies for Exchange coverage. A traditional standalone HRA generally cannot comply with PPACA and cannot be used by an employer to pay premiums for an employee's individually purchased health insurance. For plan years beginning on or after January 1, 2014, a health FSA must either be limited to excepted benefits, or be offered through a § 125 cafeteria plan. [Taylor Wedge French, James P. McElligott Jr., and Larry R. Goldstein, *New Requirements Affect HRAs, FSAs And Employer Payment Plans Beginning In 2014*, McGuire Woods LLP (Oct. 13, 2013), available at Lexology.com]

A standalone HRA was also known as an "employer payment plan" or "employer health care arrangement," under which employers reimbursed employees for the premiums on health insurance the employees obtained individually. Some employers offered this type of plan instead of maintaining an EGHP. Current IRS thinking is that employer payment plans are subject to the EGHP requirements about minimum essential benefits and preventive care. Employer payment plans have been characterized as "dumping" employees into the Exchanges; IRS FAQs issued in May 2014 say that employers can be penalized $100 per day for every employee who obtains Exchange coverage in connection with an employer payment plan. Notice 2013-54 covers employer payment plans. The DOL issued Technical Release 2013-03, which is substantially similar to Notice 2013-54. [IRS, *Employer Health Care Arrangements*, <http://www.irs.gov/uac/Newsroom/Employer-Health-Care-Arrangements> (May 13, 2014); see Robert Pear, *I.R.S. Bars Employers From Dumping Workers Into Health Exchanges*, NYTimes.com (May 25, 2014); Lindsey Surratt, *IRS Highlights Stiff Penalty for Reimbursing Individual Premiums* (May 21, 2014) (benefitslink.com)]

§ 18.19 HEALTH CARE REFORM UNDER PPACA

[A] Introduction

In March 2010, Congress passed the Patient Protection and Affordable Care Act, Pub. L. No. 111-144. Almost immediately, a package of amendments was passed: the Health Care and Education Affordability Reconciliation Act of 2010, Pub. L. No. 111-152. For convenience, in this book the abbreviation "PPACA" will be used to refer to the main bill, as amended by the reconciliation bill.

The focus of the legislation is on extending insurance coverage to more Americans. This discussion focuses on employers' duties and entitlements under PPACA, although the law naturally has major impact on health care users and providers, on insurers, and on the Medicare and Medicaid programs.

The central goal of PPACA is that, eventually, as many people as possible will be covered by an EGHP or individual policy that provides "minimum essential coverage." The statutory objective is that the subsidies and tax incentives will lead to the creation of many new plans and coverage of a higher percentage of the employee population.

The state insurance exchanges are supposed to help people find coverage. Employers who do not offer compliant health coverage are subject to penalties. The program calls for employers to be taxed if they fail to offer minimum coverage to their employees, or if they offer coverage that does not satisfy federal standards of affordability. At the other end of the scale, there are new taxes on "Cadillac plans" that are deemed to be overly generous. But the program offers carrots as well as sticks for employers: federal subsidies for plans that cover low-income employees, and a special subsidy program for small employers. PPACA has somewhat different rules for "grandfathered plans" (EGHPs (Employer Group Health Plan) already in existence when the law was enacted) and for new plans.

The FPL (federal poverty level) is an important concept for understanding PPACA. Many rights and responsibilities are determined based on whether an employee's household income falls below the FPL, or whether it exceeds 400% of the FPL. For 2014, the FPL for a one-person family is $11,670, for a two-person family, $15,730, and for a three-person family, $19,790. [79 Fed. Reg. 3593 (Jan. 22, 2014)]

As part of its mission of expanding health insurance coverage, PPACA requires that, for plan years beginning on or after January 1, 2014, health insurance issuers must accept all applications from employers, although enrollment can be restricted to open enrollment periods plus special enrollment periods. (There must be special enrollment periods associated with COBRA qualifying events.) Insurers can only deny renewal if the plan fails to pay its premiums; if the plan sponsor engaged in fraud or intentional misrepresentation of material facts; or if, after proper notice, the issuer has discontinued that type of coverage.

Before PPACA, there were important protections against loss of coverage under COBRA (Consolidated Omnibus Budget Reconciliation Act) (see § 19.02), and a 2009 statute, the American Recovery and Reinvestment Act (ARRA), Pub. L. No. 111-5, made it possible for some workers to receive a subsidy to help them afford COBRA coverage (see § 19.02[F]). According to the Employee Benefits Security Administration (EBSA), PPACA essentially had no effect on the availability or duration of COBRA continuation coverage or the ARRA subsidy. The subsidy expired on May 31, 2010, but persons who were already eligible on that date could get up to 15 months of subsidy. [EBSA, *FAQ on Health Care Reform and COBRA*, <http://www.dol.gov/ebsa/faqs/faq-PPACA.html> (accessed Apr. 23, 2010)]

Medicaid also gave states the option of expanding Medicaid coverage, with the federal government paying the full cost of expansion for 2014 to 2016 and at least 90% of the cost afterward. However, for political reasons, some states rejected Medicaid expansion. [Louise Radnofsky, *In Medicaid, a New Health-Care Fight*, WSJ.com (Feb. 10, 2013)]

[B] Employer Mandates

Although there are a number of employer mandates that took effect as soon as PPACA was passed, or six months later, perhaps the most important PPACA provision is the requirement that employers (other than very small employers) offer either affordable coverage of a package of minimum basic benefits to their employees, or pay a penalty to the federal government (see § 18.19[H] below). As discussed below, the employer shared responsibility payments (aka "pay or play") were supposed to take effect January 1, 2014, but the effective date was postponed. See § 18.19[B][3] for discussion of the way in which some rules are relaxed for "grandfathered" plans—those already in existence when PPACA was enacted.

[1] Mandates in General

Starting with the first plan year that begins six months after PPACA's enactment, health plans must cover participants' dependent adult children up to the age of 26 if the adult children are not eligible to enroll in another group plan. CHIP (Children's Health Insurance Program) (see § 18.03[A]) has been reauthorized for an additional two years, until fiscal 2015. Starting January 1, 2014, the option under CHIPRA (Children's Health Insurance Program Reauthorization Act), the legislation authorizing this program, of offering a premium subsidy to help employers cover low-income children, if the subsidy is cost-effective, will be available, and will not be limited to children under age 19.

Plans must eliminate lifetime dollar limits and restrictive annual limitations on the essential health benefits. A group or individual insurer is permitted to rescind a policy if and only if there was fraud or intentional misrepresentation of material fact. The enrollee is entitled to prior notice of cancellation of coverage, which is allowed only for nonpayment of premium, plan termination, moving outside the plan's service area, not being in the association anymore if coverage is limited to association members, or discontinuation of that type of coverage (which requires 90 days' notice).

As of January 1, 2014, waiting periods of more than 90 days before a new hire can participate in the health plan are forbidden, and so are annual dollar limits on benefits a participant can receive under the health plan. [Workforce.com, *Understanding Key Provisions in Federal Health Care Reform Legislation* (Mar. 22, 2010) (benefitslink.com). Final regulations were published in 2014: 79 Fed. Reg. 10295 (Feb. 24, 2014); see Kevin McGuinness, *Final Regs Announced for ACA Waiting Period Limit*, plansponsor.com (Feb. 20, 2014).] Additional regulations were published in mid-2014. An "otherwise eligible individual" cannot be required to wait more than 90 days before coverage takes effect. The February 2014 regulations allowed a bona fide orientation period. The subsequent regulations consider a period of up to one month to be a reasonable and bona fide orientation period. [79 Fed. Reg. 35942 (June 25, 2014); see HighRoads Contributor, *Final ACA Rule Permits One-Month Orientation Period* (June 25, 2014) (benefitslink.com)]

Starting January 1, 2014, pre-existing condition exclusions (PCEs) cannot be imposed on any enrollee in a non-grandfathered plan. That is, group health plans and insurers cannot use a person's pre-existing health condition to deny or limit coverage. Eligibility cannot be conditioned on a participant's, or dependent of a participant's, medical condition, claims experience, receipt of health care, medical history, genetic information, or disability. Premiums cannot be increased based on health factors.

All plans must offer preventive services without requiring any cost-sharing by employees: all the preventive services and immunizations recommended by the U.S. Preventive Services Task Force and the Centers for Disease Control, and the preventive services for children (e.g., immunization) recommended by the Health Resources and Services Administration.

A January 9, 2014 FAQ published by DOL, the Treasury, and HHS says that, for plan years that begin on or after September 24, 2014 (for calendar year plans, this means that the requirement takes effect January 1, 2015), non-grandfathered EGHPs must cover medications like tamoxifen and raloxifene to women who have a high risk of breast cancer at no charge to the employee. [FAQs, <http://www.dol.gov/ebsa/faqs/faq-aca18.html> (Jan. 9, 2014); see Peter K. Bradley et al., *New Guidance Regarding Preventive Services, Cost Sharing, and Wellness*, Hodgson Russ LLP (Mar. 31, 2014), available at Lexology.com]

Health plans must permit enrollees to choose any available participating primary care provider, including a pediatrician for children covered by the plan. Emergency services in a hospital Emergency Room have to be covered without prior authorization, even if the hospital is not part of the plan's network. Women must be allowed to receive obstetric and gynecological services without a referral from a primary care provider. This requirement is effective for plan years beginning on or after six months from PPACA's enactment date. (The enactment date is March 23, 2010, so six months later is September 23, 2010.)

As originally enacted, PPACA required that, as of January 1, 2014, Employers with over 50 employees would have to provide "free choice" vouchers to employees with income below 400% of the FPL, and who would have high financial obligations under the employer's plan. However, this requirement was repealed in April 2011 as part of the negotiations to pass a budget bill. [Deloitte's Washington Bulletin, *Budget Bill Cuts Into PPACA: Free Choice Vouchers to be Eliminated* (Apr. 18, 2011) (benefitslink.com)]

Group health plans and health insurers have to have an effective claims appeals process, including internal claims appeals and notification to employees. At a minimum, the process must include:

- An established internal claims appeal process;
- Notice to participants of internal and external appeals procedures;
- A provision allowing an enrollee to review his or her file, present evidence and testimony in the appeal, and retain coverage during the appeal.

PPACA gives group health plans and insurers two options for external review: either comply with state external review requirements that include the protections of the NAIC (National Association of Insurance Commissioners) Uniform External Review Model Act, or if the state requirements are less protective or the plan is self-funded so those requirements do not apply, the plan must implement an external review process that satisfies the NAIC requirements. [Christine C. Rinn, *Health Insurance Reforms Under PPACA: The Future Is Now*, <http://www.crowell.com/PDF/events/hoops-2010/Health-Insurance-Market-Reforms-Under-PPACA.pdf>]

PPACA adds a new ERISA § 715(a), Code § 9815(a)(1) to apply the requirements of the Public Health Service Act (PHS) Part A, Title XXVII to EGHPs and health insurers. Section 2719 of the PHS provides the standards for internal claims and appeals and external review. In general, § 2719 requires an effective internal claims and appeals process, incorporating the DOL claims regulation (29 C.F.R. § 2560.503-1).

In June 2010, the Treasury, DOL, and HHS issued a joint interim final rule (IFR) detailing the requirements for internal claims and appeals (grandfathered plans are exempt). Plans must disclose new rationales and new evidence considered in appeals. Hiring and compensation of decision-makers must not create incentives to deny benefits. The IFR increases the amount of information that must be provided in denial notices. A plan's failure to satisfy the claims requirements allows the claimant to proceed directly to an internal appeal—or to bring a suit. [Interim Final Rule: 75 Fed. Reg. 43330 (July 23, 2010). See EBSA Technical Release 2010-01 for external review procedures; see 75 Fed. Reg. 52597 (Aug. 26, 2010) for model notices for internal and external review.]

In mid-2011, the IFR was amended. Instead of the IFR's absolute 24-hour deadline for deciding urgent care claims, the old standard (as soon as possible, definitely within 72 hours) was reinstated. Plan materials may have to be translated if over 10% of the population of the county speaks certain non-English languages. Benefits must be provided immediately if ordered by an external reviewer, even if the plan intends to seek judicial review. [*Group Health Plans and Health Insurance Issuers: Rules Relating to Internal Claims and Appeals and External Review Processes*, 76 Fed. Reg. 37208 (June 24, 2011); Technical Release 2011-02, <http://www.dol/gov/ebsa/rewsroom/tr11-02.html> and <http://cciio.cms.gov/resources/files/appeals_srg_06222011.pdf> (June 22, 2011)]

If a company offers health coverage and has over 200 employees, it must maintain the enrollment of its existing employees, and automatically enroll new full-time employees in the plan—but must give them adequate notice and a chance to opt out of coverage (e.g., to purchase coverage through an Exchange). Automatic enrollment is subject to any allowable waiting periods. [Hinda Chaikind and Chris L. Peterson, *Summary of Potential Employer Penalties Under PPACA (P.L. 111-148)*, Congressional Research Service, <http://www.ncsl.org/documents/health/EmployerPenalties.pdf> (Apr. 5, 2010)]

CMS published a final rule to prevent discrimination against persons with pre-existing conditions. Beginning in 2014, coverage cannot be denied based on pre-existing condition exclusions (PCEs) or other health conditions. Policies in the individual market will be guaranteed available and will be offered during open enrollment periods; policies in the group market will be continuously available year round. The only rating factors allowed in the individual/small group market are age (where premiums for the oldest enrollees cannot be more than three times those for the youngest), family size, geography, and tobacco use (1.5 times higher for tobacco users). There must be a single, statewide risk pool for the small group market and one for the individual market, unless insurers want a single pool for both. [CMS Final Rule, 78 Fed. Reg. 13406 (Feb. 27, 2013); CMS, *Overview: Final Rule for Health Insurance Market Reform*, <http://www.cms.gov/CCIIO/Resources/Files/Downloads/market-rules-technical-summary-2-27-2013.pdf> (Feb. 27, 2013)]

The PPACA enacts Public Health Service Act § 2708, imposing a 90-day limit on plan waiting periods. Notice 2012-58, 2012-41 I.R.B. 436 describes the safe harbors employers can use to determine who is a full-time employee; clarifies the existing safe harbor for current employees; and creates a new safe harbor for newly hired employees. Notice 2012-59, 2012-41 I.R.B. 43 says that PPACA does not require offering coverage to particular employees or classes of employees, but no otherwise eligible employee or dependent can be required to wait more than 90 days before coverage becomes effective. [See also DOL Technical Release 2012-01, *Automatic Enrollment, Employer Shared Responsibility and*

Waiting Periods, <http://www.dol.gov/ebsa/newsroom/tr12-01.html> (Feb. 9, 2012, accessed Apr. 5, 2014).]

Starting January 1, 2011, health insurers and the administrators of self-insured plans must report their "loss ratios" (percentage of premiums used to pay medical claims and not used for administrative expenses or profits) to Health and Human Services (HHS). The minimum required loss ratio for large-group plans (with 100 or more enrollees) is 85% loss ratio. Small-group plans must have an 80% loss ratio. State laws that require higher loss ratios are not preempted. However, HHS has discretion to adjust these percentages if an 80% loss ratio would destabilize the individual market. Health insurers that fail to satisfy the loss ratio standards must give each customer a pro rata rebate. This topic is discussed further at § 18.19[O][4], below.

It is illegal to retaliate against an employee who gets a tax credit, or who provides information about a violation of the employer's obligations under the Fair Labor Standards Act (e.g., automatic enrollment for companies with over 200 employees; providing notice about employees' rights to secure coverage under an Exchange): see PPACA § 1558. Retaliation complaints are filed with OSHA; the deadline is 180 days after the retaliatory act.

If the evidence shows retaliation, and settlement is not reached, OSHA orders the employer to reinstate the employee with back pay. OSHA findings become a final order of the DOL unless appealed within 30 days. The employee can seek district court review if a final DOL decision has not been rendered within 210 days of the filing date of the complaint, or 90 days after OSHA issued written findings. [OSHA Fact Sheet, *Filing Whistleblower Complaints under the Affordable Care Act*, <http://www.osha.gov/Publications/whistleblower/OSHAFS-3641.pdf> (February 2013, accessed Apr. 4, 2014)]

PPACA amends the Fair Labor Standards Act to require employers to provide break time and a private place other than a restroom stall for employees who are breast-feeding to express and store milk. This PPACA provision does not preempt state laws that offer more protection to employees.

[2] The Essential Health Benefits Package

The essential health benefits package specifies the benefits, cost-sharing standards, and levels of coverage that must be offered for a plan to be PPACA-compliant. (Self-insured plans are not subject to the PPACA provisions dealing with essential health benefits.) Qualified Health Plans (QFPs) have to provide coverage of essential benefits at Bronze, Silver, Gold, or Platinum levels. The difference among the plans is that the Bronze level provides benefits actuarially equivalent to 60% of the full actuarial value of benefits under the plan (i.e., participants can be required to pay 40% of the cost of care); Silver provides actuarial equivalent of 70% of the full actuarial value; Gold, 80% and Platinum, 90% (i.e., the participant pays only 10% of the cost of care). HHS will issue regulations explaining how to calculate actuarial value.

Individual and small group policies for insured plans must equal the benefits available under a typical employer-sponsored plan. For plan years beginning on or after January 1, 2014, health insurers selling in the individual or small group market must ensure that their coverage includes the essential health benefits package, and that insured persons are not subjected to cost-sharing obligations greater than the permitted levels.

Starting in 2014, the minimum services are:

- Outpatient health care;
- Emergency services;
- Hospitalization;
- Maternity/newborn care;
- Mental health and substance abuse services;
- Prescription drugs;
- Services and devices for physical therapy and rehabilitation;
- Lab tests;
- Preventive and wellness services, including management of chronic disease;
- Pediatric services, including oral and vision care.

This is just a minimum list: plans are permitted to provide additional services. The scope of benefits must be equivalent to a typical employer-sponsored plan; PPACA required the DOL to conduct a survey to define the typical EGHP benefit package.

Essential health benefits must not be denied based on age, life expectancy, disability, degree of medical dependency, or quality of life. Benefit design (coverage, reimbursement rates) must not discriminate on the basis of age, disability, or predicted lifespan. Emergency Room services must be covered even if the facility is not in the insurer's provider network, and the patient's cost-sharing for emergency services cannot be higher than for an in-network facility.

As a general rule, in the small-group market, insured persons cannot be required to pay an annual deductible greater than $2,000 (self-only) or $4,000 (family) coverage. Cost-sharing means deductibles, copayments, and coinsurance, but not premiums or payments for non-covered services. For 2014, total cost-sharing is not permitted to exceed the HSA limitations on out-of-pocket costs (for 2010 and 2011), that means $5,950 for self-only and $11,900 for family coverage: see Rev. Proc. 2009-29, 2009-22 I.R.B. 1050. For 2015 and later years, the amounts will be increased by the same percentage as the change in the average per capita premium for the United States as a whole. [National Conference of State Legislatures, *American Health Benefit Exchanges* (Jan. 26, 2012) (benefits link.com); Robert Pear, *Health Care Law to Allow States to Pick Benefits*, NYTimes.com (Dec. 16, 2011)]

PPACA does not mandate dental or vision coverage for adults, but dental and vision insurance for children and youths under age 19 is generally required for Exchange policies and in the individual and small-employer markets. As of January 1, 2014, PPACA requires non-grandfathered health plans to cover 10 essential health benefit categories, including pediatric services, which include dental/vision care up to age 19. Exchange plans must include pediatric vision and dental, unless there is a stand-alone dental plan with pediatric coverage. Plans covering over 50 employees do not have to offer essential health benefits; they must offer minimum essential coverage, but that does not require dental or vision coverage. [William N. Anspach, Jr., *Dental And Vision Coverage Under The Affordable Care Act*, Much Shelist PC (Dec. 17, 2013), available at Lexology .com]

Catastrophic plans (offering limited coverage for very high expenses, leaving the rest of the financial burden on the insured person) can be offered on the individual market only, not the group market, and only to people who are under age 30 or exempt from the individual requirement of maintaining minimum coverage. Catastrophic plans cover the essential benefit package, but only after the insured person has spent the HSA out-of-pocket limit on care.

HHS proposed regulations on essential health benefits, actuarial value, and accreditation were published on November 26, 2012 then finalized February 20, 2013. Also on February 20, HHS published calculators for determining the actuarial value of individual and small group plans and determining whether large-employer plans satisfy the minimum value requirement. For 2014 only, there is a special transition rule for plans that have different service providers for various benefits, each of which sets a maximum on out of pocket expenses. The group coverage will be deemed compliant as long as the major medical coverage's out-of-pocket maximum does not exceed the PPACA permitted level, and no other separate coverage exceeds the limit. [Timothy Jost, *Implementing Health Reform: The Essential Health Benefits Final Rule,* Health Affairs Blog (Feb. 20, 2013) (benefitslink.com)]

[3] Grandfathered Plans

In order to pass the controversial health care reform package, it was necessary to promise plan participants that they would be able to keep their existing health insurance—which requires granting some additional leeway to plans that were in existence on March 23, 2010, when PPACA was enacted. PPACA applies to both insured and self-insured employer plans. However, there are some differences in the rules applied to grandfathered group health plans and new group health plans, with grandfathered plans exempt from some requirements. Grandfathered plans are deemed to provide minimum essential coverage for purposes of the mandate.

A plan continues to be treated as a grandfathered plan even if new employees and their families are allowed to enroll in the plan. Family members are allowed to join grandfathered plans if, on March 23, 2010, the terms of the plan would have allowed enrollment. New employees and their families can enroll in a grandfathered health plan. It is not clear under the statute whether a plan can be modified (e.g., by changing insurance carriers) and retain grandfathered status, but HHS may issue explanatory regulations.

As of the first plan year beginning on or after September 23, 2010 (i.e., six months after PPACA's enactment), grandfathered plans are not allowed to impose lifetime benefit limits; they cannot revoke coverage except for fraud, cannot impose annual dollar limits on essential health benefits as defined by HHS; they must allow coverage of participants' children up to age 26 if the adult child is not eligible for another EGHP; they cannot impose pre-existing condition limitations (PCEs) on enrollees under age 19; and they must offer certain preventive health care services and immunizations without charge to the participant. For plan years beginning on or after January 1, 2014, grandfathered plans are not allowed to impose excessive waiting periods before a new hire can join the plan.

Grandfathered plans are not required to provide the essential benefits without cost-sharing, so if they required deductibles and coinsurance for these benefits before PPACA, they can continue to do so. Nor do they have to offer preventive care services without cost-sharing. They are not required to allow participants to access emergency services without certification and without restriction to in-network providers. Grandfathered plans are not subject to the requirement that participants have a free choice of primary care physician, and do not have to allow the selection of an OB/gyn or a pediatrician as a primary care physician. [McGuire Woods Healthcare Reform Guide, *Installment No. 2, Grandfathered Health Plans—What They Are and Why They're Important,* <http://www.mcguirewoods.com/news-resources/item.asp?item=4719>]Plans retain their eligibility for the special grandfather rules unless they significantly reduce the employer's financial role or significantly increase participants' financial obligations. [Christy Tinnes and Brigen Winters (Groom Law Group), *What Does Being Grandfathered Really Mean?*, plansponsor.com (Oct. 26, 2010). See 75 Fed. Reg. 34537 (June 17, 2010) for HHS/DOL/IRS regulations about retaining grandfathered status when the plan's insurer is changed.]

[4] Cadillac Plans

Starting January 1, 2018, a 40% excise tax will be imposed on health coverage providers to the extent that the total value of employer-sponsored health coverage for a particular participant is greater than $10,200 (individual) or

$27,500 (family coverage). Higher values (an additional $1,650 individual/ $3,450 family coverage) are allowed, and the excise tax is not imposed if the participant is in a high-risk job (e.g., police or firefighter) or is a retiree who is over 55 but not yet eligible for Medicare. The tax is imposed on the insurer (for an EGHP) or the employer (for an HSA, MSA, or self-insured health plan).

Up to 75% of plans might incur Cadillac plan penalties unless employers can reduce costs; $20 copayments for doctor's office visits and $500 deductibles are likely to be casualties of the move to avert Cadillac plan treatment. The issue is a particular sore point for unionized employees, especially members of public employee unions, who traditionally accepted comparatively low wages in order to secure generous benefit packages. [Reed Abelson, *High-End Health Plans Scale Back to Avoid "Cadillac Tax,"* NYTimes.com (May 27, 2013)]

[5] Self-Insured Plans

Most of the PPACA requirements apply to self-insured as well as insured group health plans:

- Discrimination based on pre-existing conditions or health status is forbidden;
- If the plan already provides dependent coverage, participants' adult children must be covered until age 26;
- Large plans (over 200 full-time employees) must automatically enroll new hires in one of the plans;
- Participants must be given at least 60 days' notice of any material modifications in the plan's coverage or terms if the modifications are not disclosed in the plan's SPD;
- If the plan covers emergency services at all, it must cover out-of-network emergency services;
- Ban on annual and lifetime benefit limits;
- Coverage must not be rescinded unless the participant committed fraud or intentional misrepresentation of material fact;
- Certain preventive services must be covered without cost-sharing obligations for participants;
- Self-insured plans can qualify as grandfathered plans, and family members of participants can be enrolled without forfeiting grandfathered status;
- The plan must allow a pediatric and OB/GYN services to be obtained without a referral from a gatekeeper;

- The plan must distribute the standardized summary of benefits and coverage, as prescribed by DOL—and failure to do so can be penalized by up to $1,000 per offense;
- Participants are entitled to the claims appeal process (internal and external) set out by PPACA, but self-insured plans are not under the jurisdiction of state insurance ombudsmen, nor do they have to comply with state standards for external review.

However, some PPACA requirements do not apply to self-insured plans:

- They are not required to offer the minimum benefits package specified under PPACA;
- They are allowed to provide better coverage to highly compensated employees than to rank-and-file employees;
- They are not subject to the annual limitation on health plan deductibles;
- The reasonableness of the level of the employer's contributions to fund the plan is not subject to review by the DOL, and self-insured plans will not be subject to the standardized operating rules that DOL will prescribe for health and welfare plans;
- State ombudsmen do not have jurisdiction over complaints against self-insured plans.

[6] Nondiscrimination Requirements

PPACA § 2716 makes fully insured group health plans subject to the Code § 105(h) nondiscrimination rules. Previously, only self-insured plans were subject to these rules. To comply, the plan must benefit 70% of all employees, or, if 70% of employees are eligible to participate, 80% of the eligible employees must participate. It is not considered unlawful discrimination to exclude employees with less than three years of service; those under 25; part-time or seasonal employees; employees covered under a CBA (Collective Bargaining Agreement); and non-resident aliens. [Nelson Mullins Riley & Scarborough, LLP, *The Odd Couple: Healthcare Reform and Executive Compensation* (Apr. 15, 2010) (benefitslink.com)]

However, in early 2014 the IRS announced that, because it had been unable to draft regulations, it would not enforce this requirement during 2014. [Robert Pear, *Rules for Equal Coverage by Employers Remain Elusive Under Health Law*, NYTimes.com (Jan. 18, 2014)]

As long as they remain grandfathered, grandfathered plans are exempt from the nondiscrimination requirement. The nondiscrimination rules do not apply to plans that are exempt from Code § 100/ERISA Part 7, such as stand-alone insured dental and vision plans and stand-alone plans that cover only retirees.

The penalties under the nondiscrimination rules are considered excise rather than income taxes, so if an insured plan discriminates, the highly compensated employees are not taxed on their benefits, but the employer is subject to an excise tax penalty of $100 per day per participant (under Code § 4980D). Small employers—those with fewer than 50 employees—are exempt from the excise tax. The excise tax is capped at 10% of the aggregate amount the employer paid or incurred for the plan during the previous tax year, or $500,000, whichever is less. Excise tax liability is reported on Form 8928. The nondiscrimination requirement can be enforced by the Department of Labor, and participants and beneficiaries have the right to sue to enforce it. [Steven Friedman, Terri Solomon, and Stephanie Kastrinsky, *Employers with Insured Health Plans Must Take Care in Providing Healthcare Subsidies to Departing Executives*, Littler Mendelson (Oct. 29, 2012) (benefitslink.com)]

[C] Small Business Tax Credit

For tax years beginning after December 31, 2009, PPACA enacts a new Code § 45R, making a new tax credit available to certain small business employers. A small business, defined as one with 25 or fewer employees, whose average annual wages are under $50,000, is eligible for a tax credit that can be as much as 35% of the non-elective contributions made on behalf of employees for their health insurance premiums. For this purpose, leased employees count in determining the number of employees, but owners of 5% or more of the company's stock and 2% shareholders in S Corporations do not count. To qualify for the credit, the employer must contribute at least half the premium for the coverage, and must make uniform payments on behalf of all employees. However, the credit will be limited if the employer pays an above-average premium for its coverage. A qualifying arrangement is one for which the employer pays health insurance premiums equaling at least 50% of the premium for the coverage. The credit cannot exceed the average premium for the small group market in the relevant state, or area within the state. Multi-state employers apply the average premium limitation separately for each state. [See also FAQs at <http://www.irs.gov/newsroom/article/0,,id=220839,00.html> (Dec. 3, 2013, accessed Apr. 5, 2014)]

The employer receives the maximum amount of credit if it has 10 or fewer employees, with average wages under $20,000 (this amount will be adjusted for inflation beginning in 2013). Average wages are rounded down to the next $1,000—that is, a wage of $32,408 is treated as $32,000.

The credit phases down, but is not eliminated, if the employer has more than 10 but fewer than 25 Full-Time Equivalents (FTEs), and is eliminated once the number of FTEs reaches 25. It also phases down as the average wage increases.

The number of FTEs is calculated by dividing the number of hours worked by 2,080.

For tax years 2010–2013, the credit is 35% of the employer's total non-elective contributions on behalf of employees for qualified health coverage, subject to a limit based on the average premium for coverage for small groups.

For tax years after 2013, the maximum credit rises to 50% of the non-elective contributions for premiums for purchases from a health insurance exchange, once again subject to the average small-group premium as a limitation. For years after 2013, the qualified arrangement must offer insurance through an Exchange; in earlier years, using an Exchange is optional. [CCH Pension & Benefits, *Health Reform 2010: Small Employer Health Insurance Credit* (Apr. 12, 2010) (benefitslink.com)] Unless Congress extends it, the health insurance credit can be claimed for only two tax years that begin after 2013: for calendar year small employers, this means the years 2014 and 2015. [EBIA Weekly, *IRS Releases 2013 Form 8941 and Instructions for Claiming Small Business Health Care Tax Credit* (Jan. 16, 2014) (benefitslink.com)]

This credit is a component of the general business credit under Code § 38(b)(36), claimed on Form 3800. Form 8941 is used to calculate the credit so it can be carried back one tax year and forward 20 tax years. The credit can also be claimed in full against both regular and AMT (Alternative Minimum Tax) liabilities.

As of March 1, 2013, when automatic budget cuts were imposed as a result of the Balanced Budget and Emergency Deficit Control Act of 1985 mandatory "sequester," the refundable portion of the Code § 45R tax credit was reduced by 8.7%. The reduction is imposed until the end of the fiscal year (Sept. 30, 2013). [Cynthia Stamer, *Sequester Will Cut ACA Small Businesses Health Care Tax Credits*, WSJ.com (Mar. 5, 2013)]

Another credit, the Health Coverage Tax Credit (Code § 35), was payable on account of people aged 55 and over who receive their pensions from the PBGC, people who are eligible for Trade Adjustment Assistance (TAA); (see § 19.02[F]), and older workers who receive wage subsidies under the Alternative TAA program or the Reemployment TAA program. The Trade Adjustment Assistance Extension Act of 2011, Pub. L. No. 112-40 modifies the Health Coverage Tax Credit. Before the 2011 amendment, the credit was 65% of qualified health insurance premiums for eligible individuals and families, but the 2011 act retroactively increases the percentage to 72.5%, beginning with coverage months that start after February 2, 2011. (For some months before February 13, 2011, the credit level was 80% of the premium.) Pub. L. No. 112-40 also modified COBRA by extending the maximum COBRA coverage period for TAA and ATAA eligible persons and PBGC payees until the later of their maximum COBRA period or January 1, 2014. But terminated COBRA coverage is not retroactively restored by the statute. The COBRA extension probably does not apply to people whose COBRA coverage lapsed before November 20, 2011. [Allison Ullman, Seth Perretta, and Joel Wood, *Recently Enacted Trade Adjustment Assistance Extension*

Act of 2011 Affects Health Coverage Tax Credit and COBRA Continuation Coverage, Crowell & Moring LLP (Nov. 10, 2011) (benefitslink.com)]

Numerous business tax credits expired at the end of 2013, and the § 35 credit was one of them. [IRS, *HCTC: Latest News and Background*, <http://www.irs.gov/Individuals/HCTC:-Latest-News-and-Background> (Jan. 1, 2014)]

[D] Extended Coverage of Participants' Children

Before PPACA, many plans offered family coverage: coverage not just of the employee participating in the plan, but of the employee's spouse and children. Traditionally, children were eligible for coverage only until they reached the age of majority or married. Then there was a trend toward covering adult "children" of plan participants: see § 18.03[F] for a discussion of state laws requiring extended coverage, e.g., if the child was a full-time student. The federal "Michelle's Law" also required extended coverage of adult offspring with disabilities.

There are two aspects to coverage of adult children under PPACA. PPACA requires group health plans (including self-insured plans) to allow participants to continue coverage of their children until the child turns age 26, even if the child is not a student and even if the child is married. But for plan years beginning after January 1, 2014, grandfathered group health plans do not have to extend adult dependent coverage if the child is eligible to enroll in another EGHP (e.g., because of the child's own employment or spouse's employment).

The Department of Labor (DOL) and HHS joined together to publish Interim Final Regulations on May 10, 2010, dealing with the requirement of covering adult children until age 26—whether or not the child is a dependent for tax purposes, and whether or not he or she is a student. Plans can charge more for family than for single coverage, or for larger families but cannot increase the premium based on the child's age. Married adult children are entitled to coverage, but the parent's EGHP does not have to cover the child's spouse or children. Adult children who "aged out" of the plan under its pre-PPACA terms, but who have not reached 26, must be given notice and at least 30 days to enroll in the plan—even if this is not the normal open enrollment period for the plan. Employers must give notice of the new enrollment right. PPACA does not preempt state laws requiring even greater access to the plan. [Proskauer Client Alert, *Health Coverage for Children: Interim Final Regulations*, <http://www.proskauer.com/publications/client-alert/health-coverage-for-children-to-age-26/> (May 11, 2010)]

The other aspect is tax treatment of this coverage. The reconciliation bill amended the Internal Revenue Code to allow plan participants to exclude from income reimbursements they receive for medical expenses of an adult child who has not reached age 27 at the end of the calendar year. (In other words, the age limit is different for tax purposes than for purposes of regulating health plans.) See Notice 2010-38, 2010-20 I.R.B. 682.

Also note that in 10 states (Connecticut, Florida, Illinois, Nebraska, New Jersey, New York, Ohio, Pennsylvania, South Dakota, and Wisconsin) coverage may have to be extended even past age 26. Such coverage is taxable unless the child is a "qualifying child" or "qualifying relative" for federal tax purposes. [Buck Research FYI, *States Address Tax Consequences of Health Coverage for Adult Children* (Sept. 16, 2011) (benefitslink.com); Cynthia Lee, *Wisconsin Bill Passed to Conform State Tax Treatment of Coverage of Adult Children,* Beyond Health Care Reform Blog (Oct. 28, 2011) (benefitslink.com)]

[E] Retiree Issues

PPACA requires a federal appropriation of $5 billion to reimburse employers for part of the costs that their EGHPs encounter to cover early retirees (aged 55–64) and their dependents for the gap period between retirement and Medicare eligibility. This program is known as Early Retiree Reinsurance Program (ERRP). CMS announced that the Early Retiree Reinsurance Program would stop accepting applications on May 5, 2011, because the money had run out. [CMS report, <http://cciio.cms.gov/resources/files/errp_progress_report_3_31_11.pdf>; see Rebecca Moore, *Early Retiree Reinsurance Program to End* (Apr. 1, 2011) (benefitslink.com)]

The program's termination was announced for January 1, 2014. [78 Fed. Reg. 23936 (Apr. 23, 2013); see Kevin McGuinness, *ERRP Will Sunset at Start of 2014*, plansponsor.com (May 17, 2013)]

PPACA does not eliminate the subsidy that employers receive for furnishing prescription drug coverage to retirees that is actuarially equivalent to Medicare Part D coverage (see § 9.10[B]). However, PPACA reduces the value of the tax break. Qualifying employers continue to receive the subsidy, and the subsidy is not taxable income. However, under pre-PPACA law, the subsidy was deductible to the employer, but starting in 2013 the deduction will no longer be available.

[F] Cafeteria Plans, HSAs, HRAs, and FSAs

A cafeteria plan can provide a plan through the Exchange only if the employer is considered a "qualified" employer for the Exchange: i.e., an employer with fewer than 100 employees, that makes all of its full-time employees eligible to purchase coverage from the Exchange. This rule is effective for tax years beginning after December 31, 2013. Beginning in 2017, states can allow large employers to use the Exchange as well. In states that permit this option, large employers can also offer Exchange plans under a cafeteria plan.

As a counterpart to SIMPLE IRAs (see § 4.06[G]), PPACA allows certain small employers to provide simple cafeteria plans, which are deemed to satisfy the nondiscrimination rules. For years beginning after December 31, 2010, an eligible employer is one who had an average of 100 or fewer employees in either of the two preceding years, if the employer was in existence throughout the year. If it was not, then the employer can be eligible if it reasonably expects to average 100 or fewer employees on business days during the current year. If the employee census later grows, the employer can maintain an existing Simple Cafeteria Plan as long as it has under 200 employees.

The employer contribution must be at least 6% of the employee's compensation for the year, or twice the employee's salary reduction contribution—whichever is less. Employees who worked for at least 1,000 hours in the previous year are eligible to participate, but employees can be excluded if they are covered by a CBA, are under 21, or have not performed at least one year of service for the employer. [Gary B. Kushner, Kushner & Co., *New Simple Cafeteria Plans* (Aug. 14, 2010) (benefitslink.com)]

Starting 2011, reimbursement under FSA, HRA, or HSA is limited to prescription drugs, and is not available for over-the-counter drugs. The additional tax imposed on distributions from an HSA or MSA not used for qualified medical expenses rises, to 20%.

As of January 1, 2013, contributions to an FSA for medical expenses are limited to $2,500 a year (a figure that will be adjusted for inflation).

[G] Wellness Programs

For PPACA purposes, a wellness program is one that is offered by an employer to promote health or prevent disease. All similarly situated individuals must be allowed to participate in the program, and health status factors must not be used in deciding who qualifies for a rebate or premium discount.

Wellness programs must be reasonably targeted at improving health or preventing illness, and are not allowed to operate as a subterfuge to justify health status discrimination. A reasonable alternative standard must be offered for people whose medical condition keeps them from achieving a stated goal. Pre-PPACA law says that premium discounts for achieving objectives cannot be more than 20% of employee's premium. Under PPACA, starting 2014, the discount can be 30% or even as much as 50%, with wellness discounts extended to the individual market with a ten-state demonstration project beginning July 2014. PPACA allows employees who meet health benchmarks to get waivers of co-payments and deductibles and relief from surcharges. [Roni Caryn Rabin, *Will Health Overhaul Incentives also Penalize Some Workers?*, NYTimes.com (Apr. 12, 2010)]

Joint HHS, DOL, and Treasury proposed rules on wellness programs, reflecting PPACA provisions, were released, effective for plan years beginning on or after January 1, 2014. The rules support wellness programs, including participatory programs that are generally available without regard to the individual's health status, such as reimbursement of gym membership or payment for filling out a health risk survey. Programs that are contingent on health (i.e., the reward is triggered by meeting specific health standards such as giving up smoking) must be reasonably designed to promote health or prevent disease, and must not be overly burdensome on participants. Alternative means to qualify must be provided for employees who have a medical reason for being unable to satisfy the health-related standard. The rules were finalized in 2013, via T.D. 9620, 2013-27 I.R.B. 1, effective January 1, 2014. The final rules endorse the value of wellness programs, but they limit potentially discriminatory underwriting practices. [See DOL's report on wellness programs, <http://www.dol.gov/ebsa/pdf/workplace wellnessstudyfinal.pdf>, discussed in Plansponsor staff, *Wellness Program Final Rules Issued*, plansponsor.com (May 29, 2013)]

A January 9, 2014 FAQ published by DOL, the Treasury, and HHS answers some questions about wellness programs. For example, if an employee's doctor says that the outcome-based wellness program is not medically appropriate for the employee, then the plan must provide a reasonable alternative standard such as an activity-only program (e.g., a weight-loss program). [FAQs, <http://www.dol.gov/ebsa/faqs/faq-aca18.html> (Jan. 9, 2014); see Peter K. Bradley et al., *New Guidance Regarding Preventive Services, Cost Sharing, and Wellness*, Hodgson Russ LLP (Mar. 31, 2014), available at Lexology.com]

DOL commissioned a study from the RAND Corporation, which found that about half of employers of 50 or more employees have some kind of wellness program; 90% of employers with more than 50,000 employees have a wellness program. The survey found significant cost savings from programs for management of chronic illness—but no net savings from lifestyle management programs (weight loss, stress reduction). RAND studied over 67,000 people eligible for PepsiCo's Healthy Living program. After seven years of continuous participation, there was an average monthly reduction in health costs of $30 per member. However, this was due to disease management, which reduced health costs by $136/month because of a 29% reduction in hospital admissions; lifestyle programs had no effect on costs. Viewed together, the programs saved $1.46 for every dollar spent, but that broke down to $3.78 per expended dollar for disease management, only 48 cents per dollar for lifestyle. [Ann Carrns, *Study Raises Questions for Employer Wellness Programs*, NYTimes.com (Jan. 6, 2014)]

Fidelity Investments/National Business Group on Health's survey shows that employers plan to spend an average of $594 per employee on wellness-based incentives in their EGHPs in 2014. The most popular programs focus on lifestyle management, such as exercise, weight loss, stress management, chronic illness management, and flu shots. Ninet-five percent of the survey respondents planned to offer health improvement programs for employees. In 2009, 57% of wellness programs offered incentives for employees to participate, rising to 74% in 2014. Incentives may be offered via cash or gift card. [Kevin McGuinness, *Corporate Wellness Incentives Spending to Increase*, plansponsor.com (Feb. 20, 2014)]

The Eleventh Circuit upheld a wellness program, calling for blood tests and an online risk assessment questionnaire, under the ADA safe harbor for insurance plans that engage in good faith in underwriting and classifying risks. [*Seff v. Broward Cnty.*, 691 F.3d 1221 (11th Cir. 2012)]

Penn State University, in response to controversy, amended its wellness program that was criticized as coercive and unduly punitive. The university removed the $100 per month noncompliance fee imposed on employees who refused to fill out an online questionnaire calling for intimate details—including whether women planned to become pregnant over the next year. [Natasha Singer, *Health Plan Penalty Ends at Penn State*, NYTimes.com (Sept. 18, 2013)]

[H] Penalties for Failure to Offer Affordable Coverage

A large employer (one with over 50 employees) is subject to a fine (the "assessable payment") if it fails to offer its full-time employees and their dependents the opportunity to receive minimum essential coverage under a plan sponsored by the employer—but only if at least one full-time employee has enrolled in an Exchange and received a premium tax credit or cost-sharing reduction. Large employers can avoid the assessable payment by providing their employees vouchers for purchasing coverage from an Exchange. The IRS issued proposed regulations and an FAQ on the Code § 4980H "shared responsibility" (aka "pay or play") obligation at the beginning of 2013. [78 Fed. Reg. 217 (Jan. 2, 2013)]

The assessable payment was originally scheduled to begin January 1, 2014. However, on July 2, 2013, the Obama administration announced a one-year delay in the effective date of this requirement. The applicability of the individual mandate to maintain insurance was not delayed. The same announcement also delayed the Code § 6055 reporting requirement for self-insured plans and insurers with respect to minimum essential coverage.

The effective dates were postponed once again in February 2014. For companies with 100 or more employees, the effective date has been postponed until January 1, 2015. In 2015, companies with 100 or more employee will be penalized if they fail to offer affordable coverage to at least 70% of their full-time employees; as of January 1, 2016, they will be required to offer affordable coverage to 95% of their full-time employees. However, medium-sized companies (50–99 employees) have been given an additional year, until January 1, 2016, before they will be subject to the pay or play requirement. As for how many employees will be affected by the postponements, the Department of the Treasury estimates that two-thirds of employees work for companies that have at least 100 employees; a further 7% are employed by companies with between 50 and 99 workers. [Robert Pear, *Further Delays for Employers in Health Law*, NYTimes.com (Feb. 10, 2014)]

Employers with at least 50 full-time employees are subject to the shared responsibility requirements. Companies with common ownership, or that are otherwise related, are combined to meet the 50-employee threshold. A plan provides minimum value if it covers at least 60% of the total allowed cost of benefits expected to be incurred under the plan. HHS and the IRS have published a minimum value calculator, and regulations were proposed May 3, 2013 on other methods for determining minimum value. The employer is not subject to the shared responsibility payment if an employee enrolls in Medicare or Medicaid, or buys a Marketplace policy but does not receive a premium credit, or if an employee purchases Marketplace coverage for spouse or dependents. The shared responsibility payment will be indexed for inflation, and 2014 will be included in the index, even though no shared responsibility payments will be assessed in that year. The IRS will adopt procedures to notify employers that the IRS believes that some employees received a premium tax credit; the employer will be given a chance to respond before the IRS sends a notice and demand for payment. The shared responsibility payment is not included in the employer's income or employment tax forms. [Notice 2013-45, 2013-3 I.R.B. 116]

The penalty imposed on the employer for failure to provide affordable coverage is calculated based on the employer's contribution to self-only coverage, not family coverage. But if an employee buys coverage through an Exchange and receives a premium tax credit, the employer will not be penalized as long as it otherwise satisfies the requirement of affordable coverage. A plan was originally considered affordable for dependents if the employee's contribution for his or her own coverage does not exceed 9.5% of household income. One problem is that the employer is not necessarily aware of the employee's household income level. The proposal says that regulations will be published including a safe harbor based on the employee's W-2. The employer will not have to pay a penalty if the employee's required contribution does not exceed 9.5% of that employee's W-2 wages from that employer. [Christy Tinnes and Brigen Winters, *Proposed Regulation on PPACA Premium Tax Credit* series, plansponsor.com (Sept. 20, Sept. 27, Oct. 11, 2011)]

There was a slight inflation adjustment announced in mid-2014: for 2015, coverage is considered affordable if it does not cost more than 9.56% of the employee's household income for the relevant year. [Rev. Proc. 2014-37, 2014-33 I.R.B. 363; see Benefit Revolution, *IRS Increases Affordability Percentage Under Employer Mandate for 2015*, <http://benefitrevolution.blogspot.com/2014/08/irs-increases-affordability-percentage.html> (Aug. 1, 2014)]

In late 2012, the Obama administration explained that employers are required to offer coverage to employees and their children, but "dependent" means children only; it is not required that coverage be offered to employees' spouses. Employers will not be penalized if family coverage is not affordable. The IRS said that employers would receive a one-time reprieve if they do not offer coverage to the dependents of full-time employees—provided that they take steps in 2014 to come into compliance so that, in 2015 when dependent coverage is required, it will be provided. [Robert Pear, *Employers Must Offer Family Health Care, Affordable or Not, Administration Says*, NYTimes.com (Dec. 31, 2012)]

The proposed regulations treat children up to age 26 as dependents—but spouses are not considered dependents because they are not explicitly named by PPACA. All employers in a controlled group are aggregated to determine if an employer is subject to the penalty. However, the penalty is applied separately to each member of the controlled group, so compliant members will not be penalized. Although dependents must be offered coverage, the employer does not have to subsidize their health coverage the way employee health coverage is subsidized. [Mark Stember, Kilpatrick Townsend Health & Welfare Blog, *Employer Penalty Guidance* (Dec. 31, 2012) (benefitslink.com); Janet Adamy, *Under Health Law, Employers Must Insure Workers' Dependents*, WSJ.com (Dec. 29, 2012)]

A final rule was published in February 2014, dealing with the responsibilities of mid-sized employers under the § 4980H shared responsibility requirement. An "applicable large employer" (ALE) had 50–100 full-time employees in 2014. (Only common-law employees are counted, and full-time means employment of 30 hours/week or 130 hours/month.) ALEs will not be subject to penalties until 2016 if they comply with the final rule, but they cannot obtain relief if they reduce the size of their workforce or overall employee hours to meet the size requirement. Transition relief will also be denied if they eliminate or materially reduce health coverage that was in effect as of February 9, 2014. Companies with common ownership are combined to determine if they constitute a large employer subject to the shared responsibility mandate, but common ownership is disregarded when computing penalties, with the amount determined separately for each of the related companies. Affordability calculations are difficult, because the employer does not know the employee's household income.

The final rule provides three safe harbors that can be applied to any reasonable category of employees, on a uniform and consistent basis for all employees in a category. The employer is not penalized if it satisfies a safe harbor based on 9.5% of W-2 wages, a figure based on the employee's pay rate at the beginning of the coverage period, or (for hourly employees) the lowest rate during a calendar month. The penalty is not charged even if the employee is eligible for a premium tax credit: i.e., if the coverage is not affordable under the different standard used by the Exchange. [T.D. 9655, *Shared Responsibility for Employers Regarding Health Coverage*, 79 Fed. Reg. 8544 (Feb. 12, 2014); see IRS.gov, *Questions and Answers on Employer Shared Responsibility Provisions Under the Affordable Care Act* (Feb. 11, 2014); Timothy J. Stanton and Aimee E. Dreiss, *What Does the ACA Shared Responsibility Final Rule Mean to Large Employers?*, Ogletree Deakins (Feb. 20, 2014) (benefitslink.com); Joanne C. Youn and Brady McDaniel, *Final IRS Regulations On Employer Shared Responsibility*, Caplin & Drysdale (Feb. 12, 2014), available at Lexology.com]

[I] The CLASS Act

The Community Living Assistance Services and Support (CLASS) Act was intended to facilitate saving by employees for the cost of home care. However, the program never took effect.

In October 2011, HHS announced that the CLASS Act program was financially unsustainable and would not be implemented. [Rebecca Moore, *Repeal of Long-Term Care Provision of Health Reform Heads to House*, plansponsor.com (Jan.19, 2012)] At the beginning of 2013, as part of the "fiscal cliff" deal to resolve the budget crisis, the CLASS Act was formally repealed.

[J] PPACA Effects on Employees

The intention of PPACA is to provide most people with at least the minimum benefits package, with limits on employee payments responsibilities, through their employment. The health care reform legislation provides both "carrots" and "sticks"—many employees will be able to receive premium credits or vouchers to help them pay for insurance; temporary high-risk pools followed by Insurance Exchanges will be available to cover workers who do not receive employment-related insurance coverage.

[1] Premium Credits

PPACA allows workers with household income between 100% and 400% of the federal poverty level (FPL) to receive a refundable tax credit if their employer fails to offer creditable coverage and if the employees purchase coverage under an Exchange. The premium credit is defined as 2% of income for taxpayers whose income equals 100% of FPL, increasing to 9.5% of income for employees whose income is in the 300%–400% FPL range.

A taxpayer will not be eligible for the tax credit if he or she is eligible for "minimum essential coverage," including coverage under an eligible employer-sponsored plan that pays at least 60% of the cost of a plan that provides the minimum essential benefits. (A person who could enroll in an employer's plan, but chooses not to, does not qualify for the premium tax credit.)

The Administration announced that tax credits would not be available to employees who receive their health coverage under multi-employer plans, which are common in the construction industry. This was unpopular with unions; the Administration's argument was that multi-employer plan participants receive a substantial tax benefit in the form of employer contributions that are not taxed. [Robert Pear, *Administration Rejects Union Pleas on Health Law*, NYTimes.com (Sept. 13, 2013)]

See proposed regulations, 78 Fed. Reg. 4593 (Jan. 22, 2013) for HHS's procedure for verifying eligibility for the credit.

Opponents of PPACA brought several suits to challenge the legality of the subsidy, arguing that the subsidy could only be paid in states that have established their own Exchange, not in states that declined to set up an Exchange and where the federal Exchange is in operation. For 2014, subsidies are available to individuals with income under $45,960, and the amount increases with family size; the maximum for a four-person family is $94,200. Only 14 states have their own Exchanges; the federal Exchange covers about 4.5 million people, some of whom cannot afford health insurance without a subsidy. They will not be penalized for failure to maintain insurance coverage—but, of course, they will not be insured.

On July 22, 2014, a circuit split was created when the D.C. Circuit accepted this argument and ruled against the subsidy—but the Fourth Circuit held that the subsidy is available to financially qualified people whether they purchase coverage from a state or federal Exchange. At press time in 2014, similar cases were pending in the Seventh and Tenth Circuits. It is possible that either the Fourth or D.C. Circuit will grant en banc review, and an appeal to the Supreme Court is possible—especially after the Seventh and Tenth Circuits have ruled, potentially creating an even wider circuit split. [Compare *Halbig v. Burwell*, No. 14-5018 (D.C. Cir. July 22, 2014) with *King v. Burwell*, No. 14-1158 (4th Cir. July 22, 2014). See Robert Pear, *Courts Issue Conflicting Rulings on Health Care Law*, NYTimes.com (July 22, 2014); Margot Sanger-Katz, *After Health Law Ruling, Here Are Possible Next Steps*, NYTimes.com (July 22, 2014)]

[2] Individual Penalties

Although PPACA provides rights for individuals, including greater access to health insurance because they cannot be turned down for coverage because of PCEs, the law also imposes individual personal responsibility requirements. Starting in 2014, a "shared responsibility payment" is imposed for each month that a person fails to maintain minimum essential health coverage for themselves and their dependents. The penalty is imposed on the taxpayer, so in effect dependent children are exempt from the penalty. The coverage can be obtained either through an EGHP or by purchasing an individual policy; the Exchanges exist to make it easier to obtain individual coverage.

The penalty is the larger of a flat dollar amount per person, or a percentage of household income, starting at 1.09% in 2014, 2.0% in 2015, reaching 2.5% in 2016 and then indexed for inflation. For families, the penalty per child is half the individual penalty, subject to a cap amount no matter how large the family is. Married couples are jointly liable for the penalty. But the federal government will not bring criminal prosecutions or impose liens or levies for failure to pay it. [Congressional Budget Office, *Payments of Penalties for Being Uninsured Under the Patient Protection and Affordable Care Act*, <http://www.cbo.gov/ftpdocs/113xx/doc11355/Individual_Mandate_Penalties-04-22.pdf> (Apr. 22, 2010, accessed Apr. 5, 2014)]

No penalty is imposed on persons with income below $10,150. The penalty is a flat rate of $95 for persons whose annual household income is between $10,150 and $19,650, and otherwise is 1% of annual household income. [Ferdous Al-Faruque, *IRS: Wealthy Facing Max Fine of Nearly $2,500 for Not Having Insurance*, <http://thehill.com/policy/healthcare/213308-uninsured-could-be-fined-almost-2500> (July 24, 2014)]

Rev. Proc. 2014-46, 2014-33 I.R.B. 367, sets the maximum penalty for 2014 at $204 (single individual), $1,020 (family of five), because PPACA limits the penalty to the national average premium for purchasing Bronze coverage from an Exchange.

The *Wall Street Journal* reported that, while about 30 million people in the United States would be uninsured in 2016, only about four million people would be subject to the penalty. Close to 90% of the uninsured would not be subject to penalties, because they would qualify for one of the 14 available hardship exemptions (e.g., people with extensive medical debt, those who had a significant casualty loss that prevents them from buying insurance, people at risk of eviction). Approximately 21 states rejected Medicaid expansion, and there is an exemption for people who would have had Medicaid coverage if their state had not rejected it. [Stephanie Armour, *Fewer Uninsured Face Fines as Health Law's Exemptions Swell*, WSJ.com (Aug. 6, 2014)]

Secretary of HHS Sebelius said that the deadline for signing up for coverage would not be extended, nor would the individual mandate be stayed, so the six-month open enrollment period would end on March 31. [Robert Pear, *Health Mandate Won't Be Delayed, Sebelius Says*, NYTimes.com (Mar. 12, 2014)] Nevertheless, shortly before the open enrollment period ended, the administration announced that extra time would be granted for people who made an attempt to apply but had difficulty completing the application because of technical problems with the Exchange Website. Some of the state exchanges (in Maryland, Minnesota, and Nevada) had already granted an extension for the same reason. In addition, CMS also allowed late sign-ups for people with changes in circumstances (e.g., getting a divorce or becoming unemployed) as long as they signed up within 60 days of the event. People who started the application process before March 31 were given until April 15 to complete it. [Robert Pear, *U.S. to Extend Sign-Up Period for Insurance*, NYTimes.com (Mar. 25, 2014); Louise Radnofsky and Anna Wilde Mathews, *Extension of Health Law Signup Period Worries Insurers*, WSJ.com (Mar. 26, 2014); Louise Radnofsky, *Health Enrollment Extension to End April 15*, WSJ.com (Apr. 2, 2014)]

[3] Taxes on High-Income Participants

Although the focus of this discussion of PPACA is on the employer's point of view, certain provisions affecting individuals are crucial to understanding PPACA. One of the ways that the health care reform program will be funded is through increasing the Medicare tax imposed on plan participants with especially high income.

Before PPACA, the FICA payroll tax was imposed on all earned income up to the FICA limit (for 2012, it is $110,100, for 2013, it is $113,700, and for 2014, it is $117,000), and the Medicare tax was imposed on all income without the limit. (For employees, the employer and employee each pay 1.45%; self-employed persons pay 2.9%.) Starting in 2013, the 1.45% Medicare payroll tax rises to 2.35% for high-income persons. Only the employee's share, not the employer's share, rises. For this purpose, a high-income taxpayer is one with total earned income plus investment income greater than $250,000 (joint return) or $200,000 (other returns). Although in general self-employed persons can deduct half of the regular FICA tax, the additional Medicare tax is not deductible. Elective contributions are generally subject to FICA tax, but the additional Medicare tax does not apply to elective contributions or to earnings on qualified plans, including 401(k) plans. Tax-exempt bond interest and profits on the sale of the taxpayer's principal residence are not included in gross income, so they are not included in the Medicare tax base.

The reconciliation bill imposes an additional Medicare tax equal to 3.8% of certain investment income (the smaller of net investment income, or modified AGI minus $250,000 for joint returns, $125,000 for married persons filing separate returns, and $200,000 for other filing statuses). See T.D. 9645, 2013-51 I.R.B. 738 for final regulations on the additional Medicare tax enacted on high earners, e.g., how to withhold the additional tax and correct overpayments and underpayments. The employer must withhold the additional tax from wages over $200,000 paid to anyone, irrespective of the recipient's filing status or wages paid by other employers. The employer cannot modify its withholding of additional Medicare tax. However, a person who expects to owe more than the amount withheld by the employer can increase withholding on the W-4 (e.g., a joint return where neither spouse earns over $200,000, but the total is over $250,000). [Carrie Elizabeth Byrnes and Timothy Zehnder, *IRS Issues "Additional Medicare Tax" Final Rules*, Bryan Cave LLP (Dec. 10, 2013), available at Lexology.com]

[K] Recordkeeping, Reporting, and Disclosure

PPACA imposes many information requirements on health plans—communication with employees about their health plans and communication with regulators to ensure that employers satisfy their obligations (and also to claim the financial assistance they are entitled to).

Many of the provisions of PPACA require notices to be furnished, either to specific participants, or as a part of the plan's general benefits materials. See <http://www.dol.gov/ebsa/healthreform> (accessed Apr. 5, 2014) for model notices for several of these forms. Many plans include these notices in the annual enrollment package or the plan's SPD.

All plans, including grandfathered plans, must offer a one-time special enrollment period for adult children who were not covered because of age or who aged out of the plan, and for persons who lost coverage because they reached the plan's maximum coverage, and notice must be given of the special enrollment period.

PPACA also requires notices of:

- Grandfathered status;
- Patient Protection Model Notice: If the plan requires participants to designate a primary care provider, how to choose one; notice that female enrollees can see a OB/GYN without prior authorization or referral. (Not required for grandfathered plans);
- Explanation of the external review process; many plans include this in the SPD (Not required for grandfathered plans);
- Notice of internal adverse benefit determination;
- Advance notice that coverage will be cancelled or rescinded. [Christy Tinnes and Brigen Winters, *What Notices Are Required by PPACA?*, plansponsor.com (Sept. 21, 2010)]

As a parallel to the Summary Plan Description for a pension plan (see § 11.02), the employer must give each employee a one- to four-page summary of health care benefits that explains the covered benefits, exclusions, cost sharing, and continuation coverage. For readability, the summary must be in 12-point or larger type. This document is referred to as the Summary of Benefits and Coverage (SBC). PPACA says that this explanation must be "culturally and linguistically appropriate" for the beneficiary who receives it. If the health plan changes, the employer must update the summary to reflect material modifications, at least 60 days before the change. Satisfying this requirement also satisfies the ERISA requirement of providing a Summary of Material Modification (SMM). The summary must be provided to job applicants when they apply, to enrollees before they enroll or re-enroll, and to the policyholder or certificate holder when the policy is issued or the certificate is delivered. The SBC can be furnished either on paper, or electronically as long as the DOL's electronic disclosure safe harbor (see 29 C.F.R. § 2520.104b-1) is satisfied. Willful failure to provide an SBC is subject to a fine of $1,000 per failure (each person affected constituting a separate offense) and is also subject to an excise tax of $100 per day per person affected under Code § 4980D.

The new standards preempt state requirements that are less protective, but states have the power to impose separate additional disclosure requirements on health insurers.

The insurers of insured plans provide the SBC to the plan, and the plan and the insurer are jointly responsible for giving participants the SBC, but only one has to furnish the SBC, not both. The plan administrator is responsible for providing SBCs to participants of self-insured plans. Although grandfathered plans and HRAs are required to furnish the SBC, the requirement does not apply to retiree-only plans or plans such as stand-alone vision and dental plans that are exempt from HIPAA requirements.

The SBC must include:

- A uniform glossary of insurance and medical terms so that consumers may compare health coverage and understand the terms of (or exceptions to) their coverage;
- A description of the coverage, including cost sharing for each category of benefits;
- Exceptions, reductions and limitations on coverage;
- Cost-sharing provisions of coverage, including deductibles, coinsurance and co-payment obligations;
- The renewability and continuation of coverage provisions;
- A "coverage facts label" that includes examples to illustrate common benefits scenarios (including pregnancy and serious or chronic medical conditions);
- For coverage beginning on or after January 1, 2014, a statement of whether the plan provides minimum essential coverage and whether the plan pays at least 60 percent of the total cost of benefits;
- A statement that the SBC is only a summary and that the plan document, policy or certificate of coverage should be consulted to determine the governing contractual provisions of coverage;
- Contact information for questions and for obtaining a copy of the plan document or insurance policy, certificate or contract of insurance;
- For plans that maintain one or more provider networks, an Internet address for obtaining a list of network providers;
- For plans that use a prescription drug formulary, an Internet address for obtaining information on prescription drug coverage;
- An Internet address for obtaining the uniform glossary.

[FAQs, <http://www.dol.gov/ebsa/faqs/faq-aca7.html> (accessed Apr. 5, 2014)]

Starting March 13, 2013, employers must give their employees (and new employees as they are hired) information about how the Insurance Exchanges work and how to contact them. If the employer pays less than 60% of the actuarial value of the total cost of health benefits, the employer also has a duty to inform employees that they may be eligible for a tax credit if they buy insurance through an Exchange—but that they will lose any employer contribution made to provide health coverage for that employee. Employers are not fined if employees in this situation purchase their coverage from the Exchange. [Laura Meckler and Janet Adamy, *Key Part of Health Law to Be Clarified*, WSJ.com (Mar. 25, 2010)]

PPACA § 9002 requires employers to disclose the aggregate cost of employer-sponsored coverage on Form W-2, whether the employee or employer pays. Only the total amount must be reported; an itemized breakdown is not required. Salary reduction contributions to FSAs under a cafeteria plan and contributions to MSAs or HSAs are not considered employer-sponsored coverage, so they do not have to be disclosed on the Form W-2. [Notice 2012-9, 2012-4 I.R.B. 315] Final Regulations on the Code § 6055 requirements for minimum essential health coverage were published on March 10, 2014. The regulations explain the requirements imposed on companies with 50 or more full-time employees to report to the IRS and to employees about health care coverage available to employees. The requirements will be used by the IRS to enforce the pay-or-play mandate once it takes effect and to administer the tax credit that certain individuals will receive for buying health care coverage on an Exchange under Code § 36B. The penalty for not providing coverage will not be imposed on companies with 50–99 employees until 2016, but reporting under § 6056 is nonetheless required for 2015.

Reports, on Form 1095-B, are submitted to the IRS by February 28 of the year after the calendar year of the coverage in question. If the employer is required to file at least 250 returns, the reports must be e-filed; in that case, the deadline is March 31 of the year after the year in which coverage was provided.

Information is reported to employees on Form 1095-C (as of March 2013, the form had not yet been published), then transmitted to the IRS on Form 1094-C. The due date for health coverage provided in calendar 2015, for employers with 50 or more employees is March 1, 2016 for paper filings, and March 31, 2016 for e-filing. E-filing is mandatory for employers who are required to file 250 or more tax returns. The due date for information statements sent to employees is February 1, 2016. Notice to employees can be given electronically if the employees agree.

There are two ways that employers can satisfy their obligations under § 6056: either they can certify with respect to a particular full-time employee that the employee was offered affordable coverage, and minimum essential coverage was offered to the employee's spouse and dependents, or the employer certifies that affordable health coverage satisfying the minimum value requirements was offered to at least 98% of its full-time employees. There is a special transition rule for 2015 only for employers that made a qualifying offer of coverage to at least 95% of its full-time workforce.

Employers that offer a self-funded plan are required by § 6055 to make information reports to the IRS and employees when they provide minimum essential coverage. The reports are used to determine if the individual had the coverage required by the individual mandate. Employers that sponsor self-funded plans can use Form 1094-C to combine reporting for §§ 6055 and 6056.

Failure to satisfy these reporting requirements can be penalized under § 6721 (failure to file required information returns) and § 6722 (failure to provide payees with reports). However, if there is reasonable cause, § 6724 may offer relief by waiving penalties. There is a special transition rule for returns and statements filed in 2016 dealing with 2015 coverage: penalties will not be imposed for incorrect or incomplete information, but relief will not be granted if employers fail to make required reports, or if they do not attempt in good faith to comply.

Code § 6056 requires employers to report both to employees and the IRS. The reporting requirement was supposed to start earlier, but now has been delayed until 2015: see Notice 2013-45, 2013-31 I.R.B. 116. The IRS needs the information to administer the health care reform program; employees need the information to determine if they are entitled to a federal subsidy to help them with their share of health insurance premiums. [Chadron J. Patton, *Final Regulations Streamline ACA Reporting Rules*, Spencer Fane Britt & Browne (Mar. 13, 2014), available at Lexology.com]

The IRS has issued guidance on employer's compliance responsibilities. [See IRS, *Form W-2 Reporting of Employer-Sponsored Health Coverage*, <http://www.irs.gov/uac/Form-W-2-Reporting-of-Employer-Sponsored-Health-Coverage> (last updated May 5, 2014); see Bill O'Malley and Jill Harris, *New Information Reporting Requirements Under the Affordable Care Act*, McGladrey Tax Alert (Aug. 7, 2014) (benefitslink.com)] The IRS posted drafts of the 1094 and 1095 forms series on July 24, 2014. [<http://www.irs.gov/uac/Comment-on-Tax-Forms-and-Publications>; see Todd Leeuwenburgh, *IRS Issues Info on Exchange Eligibility, Penalties and Subsidies*, Smart HR (July 25, 2014) (benefitslink.com)]

Group plans will also have to report to HHS and plan participants about the plan's provisions to improve health outcomes (Public Health Service Act § 2717, which has been incorporated into ERISA § 715), but regulations have not yet been issued on how to report. [79 Fed. Reg. 13220 (Mar. 10, 2014); see Chadron J. Patton, *Final Regulations Streamline ACA Reporting Rules*, Spencer Fane Britt & Browne (Mar. 13, 2014), available at Lexology.com; Norbert F. Kugele, *Affordable Care Act Requires More Reports*, Warner Norcross & Judd LLP (Feb. 7, 2014), available at Lexology.com]

PPACA compliance requires the adoption of a number of plan amendments:

- Enrollment of persons under 19 without pre-existing condition limitations;
- Coverage of employees' dependent children to age 26, whether or not they are students or married, and whether or not they are tax dependents of the employees; but see <http://www.dol.gov/ebsa/faqs/faq-aca.html> Q&A #14 for some permitted exceptions;

- Elimination of lifetime limits on essential health benefits (guidance has not yet been issued to define "essential," so plans must use a good-faith reasonable interpretation of the term);
- Restrictions on annual limits on essential health benefits; the limit must be at least $750,000 in 2010, rising to $1.25 million in 2012;
- Elimination of retroactive terminations of coverage;
- Amending FSAs, HRAs, and HSAs to eliminate reimbursement of the cost of over-the-counter drugs unless the participant has a prescription.

Non-grandfathered plans must be amended to provide:

- Coverage of some preventive services without cost sharing;
- Free choice of primary care provider (who can be a pediatrician for children enrolled in the plan); women can see an OB/GYN without prior authorization or referral;
- Emergency services must be covered without prior authorization, and emergency services must receive the same coverage whether in- or out of network;
- The new external claims review process;
- The requirement of not discriminating in favor of highly compensated employees.

[Christy Tinnes and Brigen Winters, Groom Law Group, *A 2011 Plan Amendment Checklist*, plansponsor.com (Oct. 12, 2010)]

[L] Health Insurance Exchanges and High-Risk Pools

One of the main drivers behind the legislation was the perception that many individuals and small businesses found it difficult to buy and maintain health insurance. PPACA's response to this problem is the creation of health insurance exchanges: the SHOP Exchange (Small Business Health Options Program) and an individual exchange. All policies offered by the exchanges must meet the federal standards for essential health benefits. For this purpose, a small employer is one that has between one and 100 employees, although until 2016, a state has the option to limit the small-group market to employers with fewer than 50 employees. Starting in 2017, states also have the option to allow companies with more than 100 employees to purchase insurance from the SHOP Exchange. Starting in 2016, two or more states can join in a Health Care Choice Compact, offering at least two qualified health plans that are available in more than one state. The intention is that competition across state lines will be more vigorous and will result in lower premiums.

On July 11, 2011, HHS issued proposed regulations on the establishment of exchanges and Qualified Health Plans (QHPs). The proposal explains the general requirements a state exchange must meet to be approved by HHS, the minimum requirements health insurers must satisfy to participate in an Exchange, and how small employers can obtain coverage through the SHOP Exchange. Future guidance will deal with subjects like which benefits are "essential health benefits" and determining the actuarial value of coverage offered by an Exchange.

The SHOP exchanges must allow a qualified employer (i.e., a small employer that makes all of its full-time employees eligible for Exchange coverage) to select the level of coverage for which QHPs will be available to employees. HHS regulations published March 11, 2013 indicated that insurers were not ready to launch the SHOP as scheduled in 2014. The SHOP was supposed to give businesses with up to 100 employees a competitive market where they can purchase coverage for their employees. [Drew Armstrong, *Small-Business Insurance Market Delayed*, Treasury & Risk (Apr. 1, 2013) (benefitslink.com)]

On October 27, 2013, HHS announced that small businesses would not be able to enroll online in the SHOP exchange until November 2014—i.e., the open enrollment period for 2015. The administration conceded that the HealthCare.gov site was not able to handle small business signups. The administration encouraged small businesses to sign up with an agent, broker, or directly with an insurer who could help them complete the small business credit application. [Timothy Jost, *Implementing Health Reform: The Delay Of SHOP Exchange Online Enrollment*, Health Affairs Blog (Nov. 28, 2013) (benefitslink.com); Louise Radnofsky, *Obama Administration Delays Online Health-Insurance Sign-Ups for Small Businesses*, WSJ.com (Nov. 27, 2013)]

As of the beginning of 2013, 18 states were conditionally approved to run their own state-based exchanges: California, Colorado, Connecticut, the District of Columbia, Hawaii, Idaho, Kentucky, Maryland, Massachusetts, Minnesota, Nevada, New Mexico, New York, Oregon, Rhode Island, Utah, Vermont, and Washington. Two states (Arkansas and Delaware) were conditionally approved to operate exchanges in conjunction with the federal government. [Center for Consumer Info & Insurance Oversight (CCIIO) *State Health Insurance Marketplaces* (Jan. 3, 2013) (benefitslink.com)] Montana, New Jersey, Tennessee, North Carolina, Ohio, Virginia, and Missouri refused to set up state exchanges. [Louise Radnofsky, *Six More States Reject Role In Health-Care Exchanges*, WSJ.com (Feb. 15, 2013)]

[M] Timeline

The original PPACA statute included a timetable for various activities. However, for reasons including political challenges and difficulties in setting up the computer system for enrollment, a number of delays and postponements were granted. Provisions taking effect in 2010 include:

- The subsidy program for small employers takes effect;
- The subsidy program for coverage of non-Medicare-eligible retirees begins;
- All individual and group policies must cover employees' adult children up to age 26;
- A temporary nationwide high-risk pool will be set up to cover people with pre-existing conditions; this pool will be replaced by the Exchanges in 2014;
- Lifetime maximums on coverage are forbidden, although, until 2014, annual maximums can be imposed, subject to limits set by HHS;
- EGHPs must provide coverage for preventive care, without imposing cost-sharing on plan beneficiaries: e.g., immunizations, preventive care for children, Pap smears, etc.;
- Insurers can only rescind coverage on the basis of fraud, not because the individual makes expensive claims;
- Health plans must report their loss ratios.

Provisions taking effect in 2011 include:

- If loss ratios are less than 85% (large group plans) or 80% (individual and small group plans), then the insurer must give rebates to consumers;
- HRAs and health FSAs can no longer cover over-the-counter drugs that are not prescribed by a doctor. HSAs and MSAs can still cover them, but not on a tax-free basis;
- New uniform rules on verifying eligibility and claims status will be published.

Provisions taking effect in 2012 include:

- New uniform rules for electronic funds transfers and health care payments take effect.

Provisions taking effect in 2013 include:

- The uniform rules on claims and eligibility verification take effect.

Provisions taking effect in 2014 include:

- The temporary high-risk pool and the temporary reinsurance program for employees over age 55 end; the American Health Benefit Exchanges go into operation;

- Employers can offer financial rewards to employees who participate in wellness programs;
- Companies with over 200 employees can auto-enroll employees into health plans offered by the employer, although employees can opt out of these plans;
- Persons whose income is below 133% of the federal poverty level are eligible for Medicaid (unless they live in a state that refused Medicaid expansion);
- Persons whose income does not exceed 400% of the federal poverty level are protected by a sliding scale of maximum out of pocket payments. See Rev. Proc. 2014-33 I.R.B. 363 for calculation of the premium tax credit. An employee cannot receive the premium tax credit if the employer offered "affordable" coverage; Rev. Proc. 2014-37, 2014-33 I.R.B. 363 defines this as coverage that does not cost more than 8.05% (originally 8.0%, but adjusted for inflation) of household income;
- Limits are imposed on waiting periods for coverage and deductibles for small-group health plans;
- Medicare tax rate increases to 2.35% for high-income taxpayers ($250,000 for joint returns, $200,000 for other returns). High-income taxpayers are also subject to a 3.8% assessment on their unearned income;
- FSA contributions for medical expenses are limited to $2,500 per year (adjusted for inflation);
- Uniform rules about health plan enrollment, disenrollment, and premium payments will be published;

The key elements of the employer mandate for 2015 are the following.

- To avoid the shared responsibility penalty, minimum essential coverage must be offered to at least 70% of full-time employees (a special rule for 2015 only; after 2015, coverage must be offered to 95% of employees).
- Employees are considered "seasonal" employees only if their customary annual employment is six months or less.
- The final regulations include a list of factors for determining if a person is a variable-hour employee.
- The final regulations explain when a staffing firm's offer of coverage satisfies the client-employer's obligation to offer coverage. If a worker is not a common-law employee of the staffing firm, the offer of coverage is treated as made by the client employer, but only if the fee charged to the

client-employer is higher than the fee that would be charged if the employee did not enroll in health coverage.

[T.D. 9655, *Shared Responsibility for Employers Regarding Health Coverage*, 79 Fed. Reg. 8544 (Feb. 12, 2014), also available at 2014-9 I.R.B. 541]

Provision taking effect in 2016 is:

- States can get together to create "health choice compacts" where insurers can sell policies in any state within the compact; the objective is increasing competition and thereby decreasing premiums.

Provision taking effect in 2018 is:

- Insurers have to pay an excise tax on "Cadillac plans" (EGHPs that cost more than $10,200 for individual or $27,500 for family coverage).

There have been enough delays in implementation of various PPACA provisions to earn their own timeline:

- Spring 2013: one-year delay in the option to give workers on the small business marketplace a choice of plans rather than a single plan;
- July 2, 2013: one-year delay in the application of the "pay or play" large-business mandate;
- September 26, 2013: one-month delay in the opening of the small business marketplace, with the new date set at November 1, 2013;
- October 23, 2013: individuals given until March 31, 2014 (rather than February 15, 2014) to sign up in a plan and avoid penalties;
- November 14, 2013: insurers asked to reinstate plans that were canceled for non-compliance with minimum coverage requirements;
- November 22, 2013: deadline extended until December 23, 2013 to sign up for health coverage effective January 1, 2014; 2015 insurance enrollment period extended for a month, until November 15, 2014 (i.e., after the midterm elections);
- November 27, 2013: online enrollment in the small business marketplace delayed again, this time for a year (until November 2014);
- December 19, 2013: one-month extension of the program for covering persons with serious illnesses; announcement that people with canceled policies will not be penalized in 2014 if they have only catastrophic coverage, not PPACA-compliant coverage;

- December 23, 2013: 24-hour extension, due to Website delays, for signing up for coverage to take effect January 1, 2014;
- February 10, 2014: another one-year delay, until 2016, before employers of 50–99 employees will be subject to "pay or play" penalties; temporary reduction in the percentage of employees that companies with 100 or more employees must cover.

[Robert Pear, *Further Delays for Employers in Health Law*, NYTimes.com (Feb. 10, 2014); Louise Radnofsky and Theo Francis, *Obama Delays Health-Insurance Mandate for Firms Again*, WSJ.com (Feb. 10, 2014)]

[N] The Future of PPACA

The PPACA is an extremely controversial statute and its legality became the subject of many challenges. In mid-2012, the Supreme Court decided a case about the legality of the "individual mandate" (i.e., the requirement that individuals either maintain health insurance coverage—under an EGHP or by individual purchase—or pay a monetary penalty). The Supreme Court's majority found that Congress exceeded its power under the Commerce Clause when it imposed the individual mandate. However, the mandate was upheld as a valid tax, so most of the PPACA was not struck down. There was one exception: the provision imposing financial penalties on states that reject Medicaid expansion was found invalid. [*National Federation of Independent Business v. Sebelius*, consolidated with *Dep't of HHS v. Florida*, and *Florida v. Dep't of HHS*, 132. S. Ct. 2566 (2012).]

Many challenges were filed to various aspects of PPACA, raising important questions about whether for-profit businesses can assert rights to religious freedom. The Supreme Court remanded the case of *Liberty University v. Lew* to the Fourth Circuit to consider challenges to PPACA's individual and employer mandates. The Fourth Circuit found PPACA to be constitutionally acceptable, because the Commerce Clause permits Congress to regulate compensation in interstate commerce. The Fourth Circuit rejected religious arguments, finding PPACA to be a neutral law of general applicability that does not substantially burden free exercise of religion. [*Liberty Univ. v. Lew*, 733 F.3d 72 (4th Cir. 2013). Certiorari was denied in December 2013, as No. 13-306. See Lyle Denniston, *Challenge To ACA Employer Mandate Fails*, SCOTUSblog (Dec. 2, 2013), available at law.com]

On July 22, 2014, both the D.C. and Fourth Circuits issued rulings on whether tax credits are available whether the individual signs up with a state or federal Exchange. However, the two courts disagreed. The D.C. Circuit said that the subsidy is only available in states that have a state Exchange. The Fourth Circuit held that the subsidy is available no matter which Exchange is utilized. Cases on this issue were pending in the Seventh and Tenth Circuits as of August 2014. [Compare *Halbig v. Burwell*, No. 14-5018 (D.C. Cir. July 22, 2014) with *King v.*

Burwell, No. 14-1158 (4th Cir. July 22, 2014). See Robert Pear, *Courts Issue Conflicting Rulings on Health Care Law*, NYTimes.com (July 22, 2014); Margot Sanger-Katz, *After Health Law Ruling, Here Are Possible Next Steps*, NYTimes .com (July 22, 2014).]

[O] Implementing Regulations

After the passage of PPACA, HHS and the other agencies involved in health law enforcement issued several major regulations. Several of them took the form of interim final regulations (IFRs). Frequently, HHS, DOL, and the Treasury joined in issuing regulations affecting all of their areas of responsibility. Several states adopted statutes to conform to PPACA: For example, Delaware, Kentucky, Minnesota, and Virginia adopted statutes requiring health plans to cover participants' adult children up to age 26; Hawaii, Indiana, Maryland, and Oklahoma passed protective laws for employees with preexisting conditions; and Connecticut, Georgia, Idaho, and Maine imposed medical loss ratios that insurers must satisfy.

[1] T.D. 9491

T.D. 9491, 75 Fed. Reg. 37188 (June 28, 2010) was issued by HHS, DOL, and the Treasury on June 28, 2010. This rule deals with pre-existing condition exclusions (PCEs), limits on policy benefits, rescission, provider choice, and emergency services. PCEs are now defined to include limitations based on health status information, e.g., information from health examinations or questionnaires. Once a person is covered by a plan, coverage can only be rescinded for fraud or intentional misrepresentation of material fact.

[2] T.D. 9489

T.D. 9489, 2010-29 I.R.B. 55, provides a set of Interim Final Rules for grandfathered plans. Plan materials for such plans must disclose that the plan is grandfathered; plan benefits must be described; and contact information must be provided to ask questions or submit complaints. T.D. 8489 includes a model notice for this purpose.

[3] T.D. 9493

T.D. 9493, 2010-35 I.R.B. 273, 73 Fed. Reg. 41726 (July 19, 2010) deals with the requirement of covering preventive services by non-grandfathered plans. In-network preventive services must be provided without any cost-sharing by the participant, although cost-sharing can be imposed on out-of-network services, and the plan can refuse to cover out-of-network services.

[4] Loss Ratios

A health insurance company's loss ratio is the percentage of the premiums that it collects that it distributes in the form of benefits. The higher the loss ratio, the more of the premium is used to provide health care; the lower the ratio, the more of the premium that goes toward the insurer's operating costs and profits.

Rebates are required if MLR falls below 85% (large group) or 80% (small group). Rebates can take the form of a premium credit, a check for a lump sum, or a lump sum reimbursement to the account the enrollee used to pay the premium. A CMP of $100/day can be imposed for each individual affected by the violation of the reporting and rebate requirements. [75 Fed. Reg. 74864 (Dec. 1, 2010); see CCH Pension & Benefits, *Medical Loss Ratio Rules will Affect 64 Million Covered by Group Plans* (Nov. 29, 2010) (benefitslink.com)]

HHS's determination of whether a premium increase is reasonable includes whether the insurer's loss ratio was at least 80%, and whether the insurer provided substantial evidence that the increase was necessary. Insurers must disclose their spending on medical care, expected future claims costs, and administration (including executive compensation). [PPACA § 1003; Regulations at 75 Fed. Reg. 81009 (Dec. 23, 2010) and 76 Fed. Reg. 29964 (May 23, 2011)]

Since PPACA was passed, the number of states with authority to reject unreasonable increases has risen from 30 to 37. In early 2012, HHS said that independent experts determined that premiums in Alabama, Arizona, Pennsylvania, Virginia, and Wyoming were unreasonable because not enough was spent on medical care and quality improvement. New Mexico rejected a request for a 9.7% premium increase, reducing it to 4.7%; Connecticut limited a proposed 12.9% increase to 3.9%; and New York reduced a 12.7% increase to 8.2%. [<http://companyprofiles.healthcare.gov.> For general rate review information, see <http://www.healthcare.gov/law/features/costs/rate-review/> and Rebecca Moore, *HHS Deems Rate Hikes in Five States Unreasonable*, plansponsor.com (Jan. 13, 2012)]

[5] Waivers

Until 2014, HHS has the power to permit plans to set limits on annual benefits so that coverage can continue with minimal impact on premiums. On June 28, 2010, the Federal Register published an interim final regulation (IFR) allowing EGHPs to impose an annual limit on essential benefits—but the limit must be at least $750,000 (for years beginning between September 30, 2010 and September 23, 2011), at least $1.25 million (years beginning between September 24,

2011 and September 23, 2012) and at least $2 million (years beginning between September 24, 2012 and January 1, 2014).

Waivers are not available with respect to lifetime dollar limits on essential benefits, only on annual limits.

The administration allowed "mini-med" plans (plans with low benefit caps) relief on benefit limits and loss ratios on the theory that without these one-year waivers employees would lose coverage or would have to pay much higher premiums, and at least low-wage earners would have some access to insurance in the interim until the Exchanges begin in 2014. [Janet Adamy and Avery Johnson, *Rules Eased for Some Health Plans*, WSJ.com (Nov. 23, 2010)]

On June 17, 2011, the administration announced that it would stop granting new waivers after September 22, 2011, although existing waivers could be extended through 2013. [Janet Adamy, *Obama Administration to End New Waivers Under Health Law*, WSJ.com (June 18, 2011)]

This position changed in 2014, however. An administration source said that renewal of non-compliant policies would be permitted for two more years, to carry out the president's pledge that people who liked their health plans would be allowed to retain them. [Crain's Chicago Business, *Obama To Allow Two-Year Renewal Of Old Health Plans* (Mar. 5, 2014) (benefitslink.com); Robert Pear, *Further Delays for Employers in Health Law*, NYTimes.com (Feb. 10, 2014); Louise Radnofsky and Theo Francis, *Obama Delays Health-Insurance Mandate for Firms Again*, WSJ.com (Feb. 10, 2014)]

CHAPTER 19

HEALTH INSURANCE CONTINUATION AND PORTABILITY (COBRA AND HIPAA)

§ 19.01 INTRODUCTION

The two dominant mechanisms for providing health insurance coverage in our society are employee group health plans (EGHPs) and the Medicare system for senior citizens and the disabled. However, there are many instances in which a person has lost coverage under one EGHP and is not (or is not yet) covered by another one, and is not eligible for Medicare. Individual health coverage is expensive—and furthermore, the ex-employee or a member of his or her family might have a medical condition that makes insurance harder to obtain or raises its cost even higher.

Two federal statutes, the Comprehensive Omnibus Budget Reconciliation Act (COBRA) and the Health Insurance Portability and Accessibility Act (HIPAA) work together to make the transition between EGHPs, or from EGHP coverage to individual health coverage, at least somewhat smoother. Both statutes impose responsibilities on the employer, so the health plan administrator must be aware of these duties. The health care reform act, PPACA (see § 18.19) creates a new paradigm under which, for the first time, employers have a duty to provide health insurance, and individuals have a duty to purchase health insurance.

Commentators differ as to what will happen to COBRA after PPACA is fully phased in. One view is that the PPACA Marketplace will replace COBRA coverage, because COBRA beneficiaries pay the full health insurance premium and many people qualify for subsidies under PPACA. Those who elect COBRA do so because they think it will be a good financial value—which means they tend to have below-average health and expect to use a lot of health care. The two-month grace period allows them time to consider if they expect high health costs. COBRA elections can be costly to self-insured ex-employers. A 2009 survey by Spencer's Benefits Reports found that the average COBRA user cost the ex-employer $3,000, or 54% more than the average active worker, and 20% of respondents found that COBRA users cost twice as much as the average active employee. [Kaiser Health News, *Swapping COBRA For Obamacare Likely To Be Windfall For Big Business* (Sept. 23, 2013) (benefitslink.com)]

The latest version of the COBRA notice, published in May 2014 includes information comparing COBRA coverage to insurance purchased on an Exchange.

However, some people will continue to make COBRA elections if their policy is not available through an exchange, and they want to keep it—especially if they are already receiving treatment. Finding in-network doctors can be difficult, and the Exchanges do not make it easy to find out which doctors and specialists are available. [Jared Bilski, *3 Reasons COBRA Will Live On After Obamacare*, HR Benefits Alert (Nov. 26, 2013) (benefitslink.com)]

As part of the ongoing attempt to stimulate the economy, Congress passed the ARRA, American Recovery & Reinvestment Act of 2009 [Pub. L. No. 111-5, Title III] early in 2009, providing subsidies for COBRA premiums. See § 19.02[F]. This was a temporary program that expired in 2010.

The Supreme Court refused to review an unpublished Sixth Circuit case about conversion of group to individual life insurance after an employee's termination. The Sixth Circuit held that people who were denied life insurance benefits under policies that were not converted could not sue the plan administrator for breach of ERISA fiduciary duty. In this case, the employee took a leave of absence after a disabling stroke in 2001, and was fired in March 2002 when he could not return to work after the leave of absence. To convert his group policy to individual coverage, he would have had to have made an election within 31 days of receiving conversion notice; apply to the insurer; and take over premium payments. The Sixth Circuit held that COBRA does not require the employer to provide notice of the right to convert group life insurance. The requirement of COBRA notice applies only to health insurance. [*Walker v. Federal Express Corp.*, 133 S. Ct. 851 (2013); see Bloomberg BNA Pension & Benefits Daily, *Supreme Court Declines to Review Individual Relief Ruling Under ERISA* (Jan. 8, 2013) (law.com)]

The New Jersey Star-Ledger reported that a qualified beneficiary who has leukemia lost coverage because his premium payment was 26 cents short. Sergio Branco and his wife contacted the DOL because he was afraid his marrow transplant would be canceled. The DOL got the coverage reinstated retroactively and the transplant was scheduled. The COBRA regulations have a special rule for premium payments that are short by an insignificant amount, defined as the lesser of 10% of the amount due or $50. The plan must either treat the payment as made in full or inform the qualified beneficiary that there is a shortfall and give a reasonable period (e.g., 30 days) to make the payment. A health care provider told Branco that he had "no coverage"; the regulations require plan administrators to give a complete response about the status of coverage during the grace period. [Gwen Cofield, *Bad Press for Ending COBRA Due to 26 Cents Premium Shortfall Shows Need to Know the Rules*, SmartHR (Aug. 27, 2013) (benefitslink.com)]

Not strictly in the COBRA context, but dealing with issues of continued coverage, the Children's Health Insurance Program Reauthorization Act of 2009 (CHIPRA; Pub. L. No. 111-3, signed February 4, 2009) requires employers to amend their plans to permit special enrollment of employees and dependents if they lose their Medicaid or SCHIP coverage—or if they become eligible under Medicaid or SCHIP for the state to assist them with paying EGHP premiums and other financial responsibilities. [CHIPRA, Pub. L. No. 111-3; see EBIA Weekly, *New Law Establishes Additional Special Enrollment Rights, Notice, and Disclosure Obligations for Group Health Plans* (Feb. 4, 2009) (benefitslink.com) EBSA published a new model notice about CHIPRA eligibility on May 2, 2014; it is available at <http://www.dol.gov/ebsa/chipmodelnotice.doc>.]

CHIP has been financed until 2015, and PPACA did not alter this. PPACA essentially leaves the COBRA system intact (although the provision in the House version of the legislation that would have extended COBRA subsidies until 2014 when the exchanges become available was not adopted in the final version).

§ 19.02 COBRA CONTINUATION COVERAGE

Continuation coverage is the right of a "qualified beneficiary" (i.e., a former employee or his or her spouse and dependents) to maintain coverage under the employer's group health plan after a "COBRA event." Some of the important legal questions include which employers are subject to COBRA; which employees, ex-employees, and their family members are permitted to make a COBRA election; and what the employer's responsibilities are to furnish notice of COBRA rights.

[A] Qualifying Events

A COBRA event is either personal or work-related and poses a threat to coverage under the ordinary circumstances:

- The employee is terminated or has hours reduced (unless termination is for gross misconduct);
- The employee divorces or becomes legally separated;
- The employee's dependent child ceases to be covered by the plan (usually because of "aging out");
- The employee's employer files for bankruptcy protection;
- The employee becomes Medicare-eligible (which entitles the employee's spouse to COBRA coverage);
- The employee dies (obviously, this is only a COBRA event for the survivors).

Although COBRA does not define "gross misconduct," the standard is probably the same as "willful misconduct"—substantial and willful disregard of the employer's best interests. [See, e.g., *Chatterjee v. School Dist. of Philadelphia*, 170 F. Supp. 2d 509 (E.D. Pa. 2001); *Lloyd v. Hanover Foods Corp.*, 72 F. Supp. 2d 469 (D. Del. 1999); *Pomales v. Celulares Telefonica, Inc.*, Civ. No. 02-1256 (D.P.R. 2005); see Rebecca Moore, *Termination for Gross Misconduct Not COBRA Qualifying Event*, plansponsor.com (May 19, 2006)]

Two of the most common COBRA events are divorce or legal separation. As long as one spouse notifies the plan or the COBRA administrator within 60 days of the event, the plan will have obligations. For example, if the plan does not terminate spousal coverage based on legal separation, the non-employee spouse will remain covered, and there will be no need for COBRA. If the employee drops the non-employee spouse from coverage during the annual open enrollment period, the plan has no COBRA obligations because the loss of coverage is caused by the employee's election, which not a COBRA qualifying event. The COBRA regulations (although not the statute) include an "anticipation of divorce" rule: the plan must make COBRA coverage available to the non-participant spouse, even if he or she was not enrolled in the plan at the time of the divorce, if the participant eliminated coverage in anticipation of the divorce. The IRS has not issued regulations on this point, and there is no DOL model COBRA notice for it. The firm of Foley & Lardner recommends discussing this rule in the SPD and/or the COBRA election materials. If the plan administrator is uncertain why a spouse has been dropped, the administrator should ask the participant or the spouse. The 36-month COBRA period begins with the date of the divorce, not the date of termination of coverage, so claims do not have to be covered between the date coverage was dropped and the date of divorce or legal separation. [Foley & Lardner LLP, *"We Have To Offer COBRA, When?" The "In Anticipation Of Divorce" Rule date?* (Feb. 14, 2014) (benefitslink.com)]

Whenever a "qualifying event" occurs, anyone who performs services for the employer and is covered by the EGHP must be given COBRA rights—including partners, self-employed people who are allowed to participate in the plan, and eligible independent contractors.

If a cafeteria plan includes health benefits, COBRA applies only to benefits actually elected by a plan participant, not those that he or she declines. COBRA does not apply to Flexible Spending Accounts, Medical Savings Accounts, or to plans that are substantially limited to qualified long-term care services, because these are not deemed to be conventional health plans. The District Court for the District of Kansas ruled that a long-term disability plan does not have to give COBRA notices; although it is a welfare benefit plan, it is not a "group health plan," because a group health plan provides medical care rather than benefits for persons who are unable to work. [*Ernisse v. L.L. & G., Inc.*, Case No. 07-2579-JAR, 2008 WL 4499974 (D. Kan. Sept. 29, 2008); see EBIA Weekly, *Employer Was Not Required to Provide a COBRA Election Notice for Its Long-Term Disability Plan* (Oct. 16, 2008) (benefitslink.com)]

When a person makes a COBRA election, health insurance coverage continues under the EGHP—but the employee, not the employer, pays the premium. (The employer can also agree to subsidize the COBRA premium, e.g., as an early retirement incentive.) The employer can impose an administrative charge of up to 2% of the premium, but no other fees or charges. The COBRA premium is set once a year, in advance.

There are three basic methods of structuring continuing coverage in a severance package. The "choice method" gives a choice between COBRA coverage and an alternative set out in the severance package; consecutive coverage offers a certain number of months of coverage as if the ex-employee were still active, followed by 18 months of COBRA coverage; or concurrent coverage (e.g., 12 months of coverage at the active rate, followed by six months of COBRA coverage, for a total of 18 months of continuation coverage). The plan and paperwork for the severance must make it clear how the coverage is structured.

[B] Covered Businesses

Businesses are subject to COBRA if they have 20 or more employees on a typical workday, and if they maintain a group health plan (either insured or self-insured). Most of the states (all except Alabama, Alaska, Arizona, Delaware, Hawaii, Idaho, Indiana, Michigan, Montana, Virginia, and Washington) have COBRA expansion statutes that require companies with fewer than 20 employees to provide the equivalent of the federal COBRA notice and continuation coverage rights.

The length of the required period of continuation coverage ranges from four months (Arkansas) to 36 months (in California, Minnesota, Nevada, New Hampshire, North Dakota, South Dakota, and Texas). [Kaiser Family Foundation, *Expanded COBRA Continuation Coverage for Small Firm Employees, 2010*, See <http://scorecard.assetsandopportunity.org/2013/measure/expanded-cobra-coverage>

The District Court for the District of Idaho held that an employer violated COBRA by providing only three months of COBRA coverage rather than the required 18 months. Although the employer had fewer than 20 employees, it was part of a controlled group with over 20 employees. The district court rejected the employer's argument that the employee signed a COBRA election form agreeing to three-month coverage and paid only three months of premiums. [*Warnecke v. Nitrocision LLC*, No. 4:10–cv–00334–CWD. 2012 WL 5987429 (D. Idaho Nov. 29, 2012); see Gwen Cofield, Smart HR Blog, *Common Control Means COBRA's Small Employer Exception Does Not Apply* (Dec. 7, 2012) (benefitslink.com)]

The 20-employee figure does not include employees working "under the table." Furthermore, the District Court for the District of Arizona ruled that vacation and holiday pay can be considered in determining whether someone has worked 1,250 hours and therefore is a full-time employee eligible for COBRA, but vacation and holiday pay do not count as hours worked for determining the number of full-time employees and thus whether the employer is subject to COBRA. [*Galati v. D & R Excavating, Inc.*, No. CV 04-1684-PHX-NVW, 2006 U.S. Dist. LEXIS 28723 (D. Ariz. 2006)]

The Sixth Circuit held, in mid-2007, that in rare cases it will be possible for an employer with fewer than 20 employees to be sued under COBRA—for example, if the employer's statements or behavior would lead a reasonable plaintiff to believe that he or she had COBRA coverage. But the actual plaintiff lost her case. She alleged that she overheard corporate managers talking about providing benefits to another employee; but even if this conversation did take place, no one said anything about COBRA coverage for the plaintiff. [*Thomas v. Miller*, 489 F.3d 293 (6th Cir. 2007), discussed in Roy F. Harmon III, *COBRA Requirements May Apply to Employers Having Less Than 20 Employees* (June 28, 2007) (benefitslink.com)]

The Northern District of Ohio found an employer grossly negligent for not knowing that it was not subject to COBRA because it had fewer than 20 employees. The district court refused to dismiss a qualified beneficiary's equitable estoppel claim. A corporate officer was laid off in early 2009. After receiving a COBRA notice, he made the election and paid premiums for 13 months. He filed a complaint with the Department of Labor against his former employer (the court record did not explain what kind of complaint). The DOL informed the company that it was not subject to COBRA, so the insurer retroactively terminated the plaintiff's coverage. He was reimbursed for the premium payments, but had more than $7,000 of medical expenses. The district court held that in general, a mere mistake will not support a claim for equitable estoppel—but the employer knew how many employees it had and the insurance contract made the employer responsible for complying with state and federal law. [*Hanysh v. Buckeye Extrusion Dies, Inc.*, No. 4:11 CV 528, 2012 WL 3852569 (N.D. Ohio Sept. 5, 2012); see Gwen Cofield, *Employer Can't Pin COBRA Compliance on Insurer, Court Points Out*, Smart HR (Sept. 18, 2012) (benefitslink.com)] Self-insured plans are subject to COBRA, too. The "premium" for them is a reasonable estimate, using reasonable actuarial assumptions, of the cost of providing health coverage for employees similarly situated to the qualified beneficiary.

Continuation coverage must be the same as active employees receive, although continuation coverage can change as the underlying plan changes. If the employer terminates or reduces coverage in an EGHP, qualified beneficiaries must be allowed to elect coverage under whatever plan the employer continues to maintain for similarly situated active employees. The employer cannot condition continuation coverage on submission of evidence of insurability. [See I.R.C. § 4980B(f)(2)(D)]

[C] Family Rights

The employee's spouse and children may also have independent rights to maintain coverage: for instance, after a divorce, when the former employee dies, or when the former employee becomes eligible for Medicare. (In this situation, the former employee no longer has COBRA rights—but, because Medicare does not cover spouses or dependents, these family members have COBRA rights.)

The one-time employee can exercise the COBRA election on behalf of his or her spouse and children, and the spouse can exercise the election on behalf of the children. However, only plan participants, not their beneficiaries, are entitled to receive penalties if the plan administrator fails to provide COBRA notice. [*Wright v. Hanna Steel Corp.*, 270 F.3d 1336 (11th Cir. 2001)]

As a result of the Supreme Court's June, 2013 decision striking down part of the federal Defense of Marriage Act (DOMA; see § 18.06), same-sex married couples are entitled to spousal coverage under COBRA. If a state "mini-COBRA" law is in effect, it may also require coverage of registered domestic partners or civil union partners.

[D] Duration of Coverage

COBRA specifies minimum obligations that employers must meet; they always have discretion to provide additional coverage. The basic duration of COBRA continuation coverage for ex-employees is 18 months, starting with the qualifying event. In some instances, ARRA will increase the duration of coverage: see § 19.02[F]. However, if the ex-employee satisfies the Social Security Administration definition of total disability (basically, is incapable of substantial gainful activity), the employee and family members are entitled to 29 months of continuation coverage, not 18. But for the 11 months after the end of the normal 18-month term, the employer can lawfully charge the employee 150% of the premium, not just the normal 102%.

Qualified beneficiaries can get 29 months of continuation coverage with respect to the same qualifying event if they are qualified with respect to a termination of employment or a reduction in hours; they became disabled within the first 60 days of COBRA continuation coverage; and they give the plan administrator a copy of the determination of disability within 60 days of the date it was issued and also within the initial 18-month COBRA period.

Notification is crucial. The District Court for the Northern District of Ohio held in 2013 that COBRA coverage of the participant's spouse would not be extended to 29 months when the notification was not given, even though the plan administrator had actual knowledge that the participant was disabled. The plan explicitly required notice of disability as a condition of the extension. [*Rayle v. Wood Cnty. Hosp.*, No. 3:12-cv-02052-0, 2013 WL 1654898 (N.D. Ohio 2013). See EBIA Weekly, *Actual Notice of Employee's Disability Insufficient to Extend COBRA Coverage When Plan's Notice Procedures Were Not Followed* (May 16, 2013) (benefitslink.com)]

If the qualifying event is the ex-employee's becoming eligible for Medicare, his or her qualified beneficiaries are entitled to 36 months of continuation coverage. See Rev. Rul. 2004-22, 2004-10 I.R.B. 553, providing that Medicare entitlement is not a second qualifying event for a beneficiary who would not have lost coverage under the plan as a result of Medicare entitlement. If the plan does not terminate coverage for the employee's spouse, the spouse is entitled to only 18 months of continuation coverage because there has not been a second qualifying event.

However, COBRA entitlement ends if:

- The employer terminates and does not replace the EGHP for active employees (in effect, there is no longer any plan whose coverage can be continued);

- The qualified beneficiary fails to pay the COBRA premium;
- The qualified beneficiary gains coverage under another EGHP;
- The employee becomes eligible for Medicare (although family members still have COBRA rights).

Utah held that although COBRA eligibility can be terminated based on qualifying for Medicare, it cannot be terminated based on qualifying for Medicaid; public policy is to prevent insurers from transferring responsibility to the Medicaid program, which is publicly funded. [*Mellor v. Wasatch Crest Mut. Ins. Co.*, 2009 Utah 5 (Utah 2009); see EBIA Weekly, *Health Plan Insurer Could Not Terminate COBRA Coverage When Qualified Beneficiary Became Covered Under Medicaid* (Feb. 12, 2009) (benefitslink.com)]

The Supreme Court ruled, in *Geissal v. Moore Med. Group* [524 U.S. 74 (1998); on remand, 158 F. Supp. 2d 957 (E.D. Mo. 2001). In 2003, the Eighth Circuit required Moore to pay the Geissal estate over $200,000 in attorneys' fees and court costs, 338 F.3d 926 (8th Cir. 2003)], that the employer can terminate COBRA coverage if the employee gains access to other coverage AFTER making a COBRA election, but cannot terminate COBRA eligibility on the basis of coverage (for instance, coverage under a spouse's plan) that the employee had access to before the COBRA election.

[E] COBRA Regulations

The IRS published important Proposed Regulations at 63 Fed. Reg. 708 (Jan. 7, 1998), adopted as 26 C.F.R. § 54.4980B-1 to conform COBRA to HIPAA (see below), the Small Business Job Protection Act [Pub. L. No. 104-188], and various other statutes. As a result of these changes, qualified beneficiaries can get 29 months (rather than the basic 18 months) of COBRA coverage with respect to the same qualifying event if:

- They are all qualified with respect to a termination of employment or a reduction in hours;
- They became disabled (as defined by the Social Security Administration) within the first 60 days of COBRA continuation coverage;
- They gave the plan administrator a copy of the determination of disability within the initial 18-month COBRA period and also within 60 days of the date the determination was issued.

During the 11-month extension, the employer can charge a premium that is 150% of the applicable premium, whereas the employer is limited to charging 102% of the premium during the 18-month basic COBRA period. Charging 150% is not considered premium discrimination on the basis of health status, so I.R.C.

§ 9802(b) is not violated. If there is a second qualifying event during a disability extension, then COBRA coverage can last for 36 months, with the 150% premium charged until the end of the 36-month period.

HIPAA entitles children born to, or adopted by, covered employees during a period of COBRA coverage to be covered by COBRA. The child's maximum coverage period runs from the date of the employee's qualifying event, and not from the child's birth or adoption. The effect is that the child's COBRA coverage ends at the same time as the coverage of other family members.

[F] TAAP and ARRA Subsidy Programs

Acknowledging that the high cost of COBRA premiums can be burdensome on people who have lost their jobs, Congress has enacted two subsidy programs to reduce these costs.

The earlier program, the Trade Act of 2002 [Pub. L. No. 107-210] enacted a tax credit under Code § 35: workers who were displaced by factors such as overseas business or imports could qualify for a tax credit equal to 65% of the COBRA premium. The credit was refundable (i.e., persons with no tax liability could receive a refund). The credit could be submitted to the health plan, so the qualifying individuals would have to pay only 35% of the COBRA premium. The Trade Act credit applied only to persons not covered by other government or private insurance programs; aged 55–64 and receiving guarantee payments from the PBGC; or unemployed and entitled to Trade Adjustment Assistance benefits under the Trade Act. [Jerry Geisal, *Congress Extends Health Premium Subsidies*, workforce.com (Oct. 1, 2008) (benefitslink.com)]

The Trade Adjustment Assistance Program (TAAP) was expanded in May 2009. Benefits include unemployment benefits, retraining, and 80% of the cost of medical insurance for workers who lost their jobs because of their employer's overseas move or foreign competition.

The economic stimulus plan enhanced TAAP, so that displaced workers could receive as much as 156 weeks of training and up to 156 weeks of cash payments. The tax credit for health insurance premiums rises from 65% to 80%. A wage subsidy of up to $12,000 (rather than the $10,000 under prior law) is provided for up to two years so workers over 50 can be re-employed at a reduced salary. Unemployment benefits can be paid for two and a half rather than two years. White-collar workers as well as manufacturing workers can qualify for benefits. Late 2010 legislation, H.R. 6517, extended the federal Health Coverage Tax Credit Subsidy for health insurance premiums, but only for six weeks (through February 12, 2011). [Jerry Geisel, *Obama Signs Extension of Health Insurance Tax Credit*, Business Insurance (Dec. 30, 2010) (benefitslink.com)] Congress did not take further action, so the credit reverted to the 65% level on February 13, 2011. [Jerry Geisel, *Health Insurance Subsidy Reverts to 65%*, Business Insurance (Feb. 22, 2011) (benefitslink.com)]

Pub. L. No. 112-40, the Trade Adjustment Assistance Extension Act of 2011 (October 21, 2011), reauthorized the TAA program until December 31, 2013. Coverage for TAA/ATAA eligible individuals and people who receive pensions from the PBGC is extended until the later of their maximum COBRA period or January 1, 2014. However, it does not appear that terminated COBRA coverage is revived by this legislation.

For months beginning after February 12, 2011, this statute also increases the Health Coverage Tax Credit (HCTC); (see Code § 35) to 72.5% of the health insurance premiums of eligible individuals and their families. (The previous level was 65%, although for months before February 13, 2011, it was 80%). In general, the HCTC is available to persons eligible under TAA or the Alternative Trade Adjustment Assistance Program (ATAAP), and to retirees who receive their pensions from the PBGC and who have lost employer coverage. It is not clear, but apparently some people who received the 65% credit will be eligible for the additional 7.5% for certain months. The HCTC is scheduled to expire January 1, 2014, when the Exchanges are expected to be in operation. [See Allison Ullman, Seth Perretta, and Joel Wood, *Recently Enacted Trade Adjustment Assistance Extension Act of 2011 Affects Health Coverage Tax Credit and COBRA Continuation Coverage*, Crowell & Moring LLP (Nov. 10, 2011) (benefitslink.com); EBIA Weekly, *Legislation Amends the Health Coverage Tax Credit* (Oct. 27, 2011) (benefitslink.com)]

However, the § 35 credit was one of many business tax credits that expired at the end of 2013 and was not revived. [IRS, *HCTC: Latest News and Background*, <http://www.irs.gov/Individuals/HCTC:-Latest-News-and-Background> (Jan. 1, 2014)]

Pub. L. No. 111-5, the American Recovery and Reinvestment Act of 2009 (ARRA), created a temporary program to provide up to nine months of federally funded COBRA subsidies (later extended to 15 months by the Department of Defense Appropriations Act of 2010, Pub. L. No. 111-118). Employers advanced 65% of the COBRA premium and later claimed a payroll tax credit; the employees paid the other 35%. After two extensions, under the Temporary Extension Act of 2010 (TEA), Pub. L. No. 111-144 and the Continuing Extension Act of 2010, Pub. L. No. 111-157, the program expired in 2010. [Walecia Konrad, *Patient Money: Health Law Preserves COBRA Plan*, NYTimes.com (Apr. 2, 2010); Bucks Editors, *How the Health Care Bill Affects COBRA*, Bucks Blog NYTimes .com (Mar. 24, 2010)]

§ 19.03 COBRA AND THE FMLA

Taking FMLA leave [see Chapter 38] is not in and of itself a COBRA-qualifying event. But if an employee who was covered by the EGHP before or during the FMLA leave fails to return to work after the FMLA leave, there is a qualifying event for this person (and any dependent at risk of losing health coverage) as of the last day of the FMLA leave. The employer is not allowed to make the ex-employee reimburse the employer for health premiums paid during the leave.

However, there is no qualifying event if, while the employee is on leave, the employer eliminates EGHP coverage for the entire group of workers the person on leave belonged to. The rationale is that the worker would have lost health coverage even if he or she had not taken leave.

The qualifying event for an employee who does not return to work occurs on the last day of the FMLA leave, and the regular COBRA notice must be given. The qualifying event occurs even if the employee had an obligation to pay health insurance premiums during the leave but failed to do so. State laws that require a longer leave than the 12-week FMLA period are disregarded in determining whether a qualifying event has occurred.

§ 19.04 COBRA NOTICE

[A] Generally

One of the most important tasks in COBRA administration is timely issuance of the proper notices, as provided by I.R.C. § 4980B(f)(6)(A) and ERISA § 606. There are three types of COBRA notice: one given to employees as soon as they become eligible for participation in the health plan (informing them of COBRA rights they might have in the future), the one given to a qualified beneficiary in connection with a COBRA event, and the notice of rights under ARRA. The employer has an obligation to notify the plan administrator when employment-related qualifying events occur, such as when an employee is terminated or laid off, or when the company files in Chapter 11 for bankruptcy protection. The responsibility for reporting personal qualifying events, such as divorce or separation, rests on the qualified beneficiary.

There are three timing requirements. The employee must give notice to the plan that a qualifying event has occurred within 60 days of the event. At that point, the employer has 30 days to notify the plan administrator that there has been a qualifying event for which COBRA notice must be provided; and the plan administrator has a further 14 days to actually issue the notice.

A COBRA notice should explain:

- Who can be a qualified beneficiary;
- What events trigger the right to continuation coverage;
- How and when to elect coverage;
- The right to reject the coverage (e.g., for financial reasons);
- Rights of the other qualified beneficiaries if one qualified beneficiary waives the election;
- Obligation to pay the premiums on time;
- How long the coverage will last;

- Events that will allow the employer to terminate continuation coverage;
- If the health plan satisfies PPACA's minimum coverage and affordability standards;
- How to purchase coverage on a health insurance Exchange;
- Eligibility criteria for premium tax credits under PPACA.

Notice must be furnished to covered employees and covered spouses on the earlier of two dates: 90 days from the first date of coverage (or the date on which the plan first becomes subject to COBRA, if that happens later), or the date on which the plan administrator has to provide a COBRA election notice.

The election notice must be furnished within 44 days of the qualifying event—or the date the qualified beneficiary ceases to be covered under the plan, if the plan's terms date the start of COBRA coverage from the loss of plan coverage.

Plans must provide notice when coverage is unavailable. The notice of unavailability must be given within 14 days of receiving notice of a qualifying event when the plan denies coverage—whether or not the notice was given in proper form. Termination notices must be given as soon as practicable after the plan administrator determines that continuation coverage is ending.

In May 2013, the DOL issued Tech Release 2013-02 <http://www.dol.gov/ebsa/newsroom/tr13-02.html> (May 8, 2013), including a model form for informing employees about COBRA rights in a legal environment that includes PPACA. The DOL returned to the subject about a year later, publishing a proposal that includes updated notices intended to bring COBRA and PPACA into better alignment, and to give employees more information about their options. [79 Fed. Reg. 26192 (May 7, 2014); see Timothy Jost, *Implementing Health Reform: COBRA/ACA Interaction and Other Developments*, Health Affairs Blog (May 3, 2014) (benefitslink.com)]

Although the COBRA notice must be written, an oral waiver of the election has been held to be valid and enforceable. [*Hummer v. Sears, Roebuck & Co.*, 1994 U.S. Dist. LEXIS 3659 (E.D. Pa. Mar. 21, 1994)] However, in 2002 the Eighth Circuit ruled that while the initial COBRA notice (given when a person becomes eligible for health plan participation) must be in writing, the notice about the availability of the COBRA election can be given orally to a terminating employee. [*Chesnut v. Montgomery*, 307 F.3d 698 (8th Cir. 2002)]

A recurring issue is what must be done to demonstrate an adequate attempt to furnish notice.

Mailing to the employee's last known address is generally considered sufficient, at least if the Post Office does not return the notice. Even if the employee does not in fact receive the notice, the employer is not liable if a proper attempt to notify was made:

- Notice was not sent to the plaintiff's last known address when it was sent to the P.O. Box he used when he was on active military duty, but the box was no longer active. The district court held that, because letters to the P.O. Box were marked "undeliverable" and the employer sent at least one letter to the correct address before the COBRA notice was mailed, the employer did not act in good faith when it failed to follow up on the returned letters. [*Boddicker v. Esurance Ins. Servs., Inc.*, CIV. 09-4027-KES, 2011 WL 6372863 (D.S.D. Dec. 20, 2011); see EBIA Weekly, *Court Imposes Statutory Penalties for Failure to Send COBRA Election Notice to Employee's Last-Known Address* (Jan. 5, 2012) (benefitslink.com)]

- The Southern District of Illinois required a case to go to trial when there was a factual dispute over the employee's last known address. The employee informed the employer about a change of address, which was entered into the payroll system. (The system for insurance purposes was separate.) Later, however, the employee herself put the wrong address on her health insurance enrollment form. The TPA sent COBRA notice to the address in the insurance records, but the plaintiff had moved. EBIA Weekly suggests asking all employees to confirm their current address in writing and having the employer confirm that the entity that gives the notices has that address. [*Munsamy v. Rittenhouse Senior Living of Indianapolis, LLC*, No. 1:10-cv-294-RLY-TAB, 2012 WL 1035019 (S.D. Ind. Mar. 27, 2012); see EBIA Weekly, *COBRA Claim Continues to Trial to Resolve* "Last-Known Address" *Issues* (May 17, 2012) (benefitslink.com)].
- The Eastern District of Arkansas ruled against a former employee who said that he was not given COBRA notice. The employer created a presumption of receipt of the notice by submitting its log of notices, date-stamped by the Postal Service. The employer stated that whenever its TPA was notified of a COBRA qualifying event, it processed, printed, and mailed the election notice to the beneficiary, then showed the log to a USPS clerk who verified that the mailed items corresponded to the log entries. The employee's testimony that he did not receive the notice could not overcome the presumption of receipt. [*Hearst v. Progressive Foam Techs., Inc.*, 2010 WL 143751 (E.D. Ark. Jan. 12, 2010); see EBIA Weekly, *COBRA Election Notice Presumed Received Based on Date-Stamped Evidence of Mailing by U.S. Postal Service* (Feb. 25, 2010) (benefitslink.com)]
- The District Court for the Middle District of Alabama approved a $1.3 million settlement in a class action against an employer in its role as administrator of the group health plan. The employer ran into unexpected financial difficulties and closed, terminating the class plaintiffs. The plaintiffs said they did not receive COBRA notices or information about ARRA subsidies. They charged that the company withheld health insurance premiums from their last paycheck but did not submit them to the insurer, so they lost insurance and could not elect continuation coverage. [*Hornsby v. Macon Cnty. Greyhound Park, Inc.*,

Case No. 3:10-CV-680-MHT CLASS ACTION (WO), 2013 WL 1747539 (M.D. Ala. Jan. 16, 2013); see EBIA Weekly, *Employer Agrees to Costly Settlement in COBRA Class Action Over ARRA Notices* (May 9, 2013) (benefitslink.com); Gwen Cofield, *$1.3M Settlement in COBRA/ ARRA Class Action Now Final*, SmartHR (Apr. 26, 2013) (benefitslink .com)]

Although an employee received COBRA notice 64 days after termination, it was dated much earlier, suggesting that it was actually sent within the 44-day time frame. The employer continued to pay the premiums for two months, until the end of the month when the notice was received. The Eastern District of Michigan refused to impose penalties because the employee did not lose anything as a result of the arguable untimeliness of the notice. EBIA's comment is that the statute merely requires the employer to furnish the notice within 44 days, even when it received later—but many courts have imposed statutory penalties even without a showing of prejudice. [*Pethers v. Metro Lift Propane*, No. 09-CV-10516, 2010 WL 3023887 (E.D. Mich. July 29, 2010)]

The District Court for the District of Idaho held that the duty to provide COBRA notice falls on the plan administrator; in this case, the employer was not the administrator and, as long as it notified the administrator of a qualifying event, the employer was not liable for the administrator's alleged failure to send the notice to the right address. [*Mirceau v. Idaho*, 2011 WL 3439178 (D. Idaho 2011)]

The District Court for the District of Maryland treated the employer, not the TPA, as the plan administrator responsible for providing COBRA notice. The SPD named the employer as plan administrator, and the TPA's service agreement said that it merely provided administrative and claims processing services. According to the TPA's record, the notice was sent five days after the end of the 44-day election period, but no penalties were assessed because the employee did not show prejudice from the delay. Furthermore, the employee received a new package offering a retroactive election when it was discovered that the first notice had not been received. [*Myers v. Carroll Indep. Fuel Co.*, Civil Action No. RDB 09-1633, 2011 WL 43085 (D. Md. Jan. 6, 2011)]

Department of Labor Advisory Opinion 99-14A allows the health plan to satisfy the notice requirement by sending a single notice to multiple beneficiaries living at the same address: e.g., one first-class letter covering the employee, spouse, and dependent children. But there must either be a separate election notice in the mailing for each qualified beneficiary, or an explanation of their independent rights to elect coverage. [See <http://www.dol.gov/ebsa/regs/AOs/ao1999-14a.html>; see, e.g., *McDermott v. Case Windham Pub. Schs.*, 225 F. Supp. 2d 180 (D. Conn. 2002), *Starr v. Metro Sys. Inc.*, 2004 U.S. Dist. LEXIS 15744 (D. Minn. Aug. 10, 2004)—but an administrator who is on notice of the employee's divorce cannot treat notice to the employee as notice to his or her ex-spouse: *Phillips v. Saratoga Harness Racing Inc.*, 233 F. Supp. 2d 361 (N.D.N.Y. 2002)]

Qualified beneficiaries must be given a period of at least 60 days to either accept or waive continuation coverage. The election period must begin no later than the time EGHP coverage would end if there were no election. In other words, notice must be given early enough to prevent any gap in coverage. The Eleventh Circuit has ruled that if the COBRA notice fails to specify the 60-day period, then the right to make the election extends indefinitely. [*Branch v. G. Bernd Co.*, 955 F.2d 1574 (11th Cir. 1992)] The Fifth Circuit ruled that an employer can have a COBRA election period of any length, as long as the period is at least 60 days. Participants in a plan that failed to set an election deadline could therefore make a COBRA election at any time during the 18 months following the qualifying event. [*Lifecare Hosps. Inc. v. Health Plus of La. Inc.*, 418 F.3d 436 (5th Cir. 2005)]

If an ex-employee needs only a certain number of months of COBRA coverage (usually the waiting period for eligibility in a new plan), COBRA does not permit the ex-employer's plan to require the ex-employee to pay for a full 18 months of retroactive coverage. [*Popovits v. Circuit City Stores Inc.*, 185 F.3d 726 (7th Cir. 1999)]

The first premium payment is not due until 45 days after the election. Qualified beneficiaries get an automatic grace period of at least 30 days, during which coverage cannot be terminated for nonpayment of premiums—even if the underlying EGHP has a shorter grace period. But if the plan provides a longer grace period, the employee must be permitted to take advantage of it.

There is no statute of limitations in the COBRA statute, so a basic issue in these cases is when the cause of action accrued. The Western District of Kentucky wanted to borrow the statute of limitations from the most analogous state statute, the Kentucky Unfair Claims Settlement Practices Act, but that law didn't have a statute of limitations either, so the magistrate judge applied the statutory five-year default, which is used in cases where no other time period is prescribed. [*Gilbert v. Norton Healthcare, Inc.*, CIVIL ACTION NO. 3:10CV-380-S, 2012 U.S. Dist. LEXIS 17553 (W.D. Ky. Feb. 10, 2012); see Roy F. Harmon III, *Five Year Limitations Period For COBRA Notification Lapse* (Feb. 20, 2012) (benefitslink.com)]

[B] Penalties for Notice Failure

The Internal Revenue Code and ERISA § 502(g) impose a penalty of $110 per day per beneficiary for noncompliance, subject to a maximum of $220 per family per day. There is also a limit of the smaller of $500,000 or 10% of the amount the employer paid (or incurred obligations for) its EGHPs in the preceding year. Furthermore, a health plan that does not conform to COBRA does not generate I.R.C. § 162 "ordinary and necessary business expenses." Therefore, the employer is denied a deduction for health plan costs.

The penalty is imposed on the employer. It can also be imposed on the individuals responsible for administering the plan or providing benefits under it, if those individuals have contractual responsibility for running the plan. A third-party administrator (TPA) would fall into this category unless factors beyond the administrator's control prevented the notice from being given.

There is a cap of $2 million for all plans administered, for an administrator who fails to satisfy all the COBRA requirements, but who is not guilty of willful neglect and who did have reasonable support for his or her decisions.

The penalty can be reduced or waived if no one had reason to know that the appropriate notices were not given, or if the failure to notify was corrected within 30 days after a responsible person became aware of the failure.

In addition to the statutory penalties, any person or organization can be sued under ERISA Title I by someone who lost coverage because of the defendant's actions or inaction.

In the Hostess bankruptcy case, the Eighth Circuit held that Hostess did not have to pay penalties for initial and election notice failures because, in effect, the plaintiff received two years of free health coverage. Because of an inefficient clerical system, Hostess could not prove that plaintiff Sean Deckard received an initial COBRA notice or that he received an election notice when he was terminated in September 2006. His termination was not processed for almost two years, so he remained in the health plan (receiving about $19,000 worth of benefits) without having to pay premiums. When Hostess discovered the mistake, his coverage was cancelled retroactive to his termination, and the health insurer tried to recover the benefits from health providers, who moved against Deckard. Hostess reinstated his coverage. CIGNA returned about $2,400 recovered from health providers; Deckard got back approximately $230 of the $693 he had been required to pay. Deckard filed a claim in the Hostess bankruptcy case seeking COBRA penalties for the six months when the coverage was cancelled. The Eighth Circuit held that penalties were inappropriate: Hostess had acted in good faith, Deckard's damages were not related to lack of notice, and he benefited by receiving two years of free health coverage. [*In re Interstate Bakeries Corp.*, 704 F.3d 528 (8th Cir., 2013); see Gwen Cofield, *COBRA Penalties Not Needed Due to 'Free' Coverage*, Smart HR Blog, (Feb. 1, 2013) (benefitslink.com)]

The Southern District of New York held that an employer's mistake in not sending a COBRA notice for four months did not constitute retaliation for the employee's filing a Title VII charge with the EEOC. The employer successfully argued that, when the mistake was discovered, the ex-employee was offered retroactive COBRA coverage, and she did not make a COBRA election after receiving notice. The district court limited Title VII claims to actions that affect current employment or the ability to be employed in the future, and this plaintiff was not seeking employment: she had filed for Social Security Disability benefits. [*Thompson v. Morris Heights Health Ctr.*, No. 09 civ. 7239 (PAE), 2012 WL 1145964 (S.D.N.Y. Apr. 6, 2012); see EBIA Weekly, *No Title VII Retaliation*

Claim for Employee Who Received Late COBRA Notice (Apr. 19, 2012) (benefits link.com)]

IRS Form 8928 must be filed to self-report any failure to satisfy the Code § 4980B requirements to provide COBRA continuation coverage. The form must be filed by any employer, group health plan, plan administrator, or plan sponsor that is subject to the excise tax for failure to provide continuation coverage. Form 8928 is due by the due date for the responsible party's federal income tax return. Interest is charged on taxes not paid by the due date (even if the responsible party obtained an extension of time to file by using Form 7004), and there are also penalties for late filing of returns and late payment of the tax. [Form 8928 instructions, <http://www.irs.gov/instructions/i8928/ch01.html> (December 2009)]

Until 2010, there was little IRS enforcement of compliance with COBRA rules, but now that self-reporting on Form 8928 is required, the IRS has stepped up audits of COBRA compliance. On March 26, 2012, the IRS posted information for IRS examiners to use in assessing COBRA compliance, instructing the examiners that they must request copies of the employer's COBRA manual, COBRA notices, health plan documents, and the company's internal audit procedures. Examiners also have the power to request many other documents, such as data about everyone who has had a qualifying event and how beneficiaries receive COBRA notice. If coverage was denied on the grounds of gross misconduct, the examiner can check with local unemployment benefits administrators to see if those benefits were denied for misconduct as well. Examiners are also allowed to contact COBRA-qualified beneficiaries for information about the plan. [Thompson Media, *15 Things the IRS May Ask Employers in a COBRA Coverage Audit* (Mar. 28, 2012) (benefitslink.com)]

§ 19.05 HEALTH INSURANCE PORTABILITY

[A] Coverage

An important focus of the PPACA is to permit previously uninsured individuals, or individuals who once had insurance coverage but had to drop it, to resume their insured status. The PPACA also restricts the use of pre-existing condition exclusions (PCEs): denials or limitations of coverage based on the applicant's or insured person's health status. However, an earlier statute already tackled some of the same concerns.

The Health Insurance Portability and Accountability Act of 1996 (HIPAA) [I.R.C. Chapter 100, §§ 9801–9806], also known as the Kennedy-Kassebaum Act, copes with the situation in which a person leaves employment with one employer, gets another job, and experiences health care bills before he or she is covered by the new employer's plan, or where the new plan might exclude coverage of the ailment as a pre-existing condition.

For plan years beginning after June 30, 1997, the HIPAA "creditable coverage" requirement in effect allows coverage to carry over from one plan to the other, as long as employees use COBRA (or other means) to make sure that there is never a gap of 63 days or more in coverage.

Although plans can control costs by imposing pre-existing condition limitations, the scope of the limitation is restricted. Under HIPAA, the most stringent definition of "pre-existing condition" that a plan can apply is a mental or physical condition for which medical advice, diagnosis, care, or treatment was sought during the six-month period before the enrollment date. In general, the maximum duration for a pre-existing condition limitation is 12 months from the enrollment date for the current health plan. The enrollment date is the earlier of the first day of the waiting period for enrollment or the date of actual enrollment. Late enrollees (who fail to enroll in the plan during the open enrollment period, or the first period of eligibility) can be subject to an 18-month rather than a 12-month pre-existing condition limitation.

The Genetic Information Nondiscrimination Act (GINA, Pub. L. No. 110-233) requires genetic testing information to be kept separate from other medical data.

"Creditable coverage" means coverage from another EGHP, from individual health insurance, from Medicare Part A or B, or from Medicaid. Health plan coverage ceases to be creditable, and therefore is not portable to a new plan, if there is a break of 63 days or more during which the employee is completely without health insurance. The so-called affiliation period (the waiting period after a new employee enrolls in a new health plan) is not considered a period of being uninsured.

The mental health parity requirement applies to HIPAA.

[B] Nondiscrimination Requirements

HIPAA forbids discrimination in benefits in health plans. (In this context, discrimination is closer to the Title VII sense than the pension plan sense of not favoring highly compensated employees.) Under HIPAA, it is unlawful for a plan to base its rules for eligibility or continued eligibility, or its definition of the waiting period, on an employee's or dependent's:

- Health status;
- Physical or mental health condition;
- Claims experience;
- Past receipt of health care;
- Medical history;
- Genetic information;

- Evidence of insurability;
- Disability.

None of these factors can be used to increase the premium or other contribution that an individual plan participant has to pay, when compared to other similarly situated participants. HIPAA does not limit the premiums or co-payments that employers can require participants to pay. It is also legitimate to offer employees discounts, rebates, or reductions in their co-payment obligations based on their participation in health promotion and disease prevention programs (such as smoking cessation or weight loss programs).

Almost six years after interim and proposed regulations were issued, DOL, HHS, and the IRS teamed up again to issue Final Regulations covering HIPAA's nondiscrimination rules for wellness programs. The Final Regulations, appearing in the Federal Register on December 13, 2006.

The final rule allows health incentives under wellness plans that satisfy certain criteria. (See § 18.19[G]) Wellness programs are acceptable if they are available to all similarly situated individuals, and either the sponsor does not offer rewards, or the rewards are not dependent on health status. Acceptable provisions include reimbursement of gym membership and health risk assessments that are not punitive. Programs that do not fit into one of these safe harbors can still qualify under HIPAA—e.g., as long as the program is reasonable, and the reward does not exceed 20% of the total cost of coverage paid by the employer and employee. [Lockton Compliance Alert, *Feds Finally Finalize HIPAA Nondiscrimination Regulations, Clarify Wellness Programs*, <http://www.?2007_Final%20Nondiscrim%20Regs_Inc@20Wellness_v2.pdf> (Jan. 9, 2007); Rebecca Moore, *Feds Clarify HIPAA Rules for Wellness Rewards*, plansponsor.com (Dec. 13, 2006)]

Further rules were promulgated by HHS, DOL, and the Treasury in mid-2013. These rules increase the maximum reward to 30% of total cost of coverage (50% for smoking cessation programs), but programs must not be overly burdensome on participants and must not discriminate on the basis of health status. [T.D. 9620, 2013-27 I.R.B. 1; FAQs, <http://www.dol.gov/ebsa/faqs/faq-aca18.html> (Jan. 9, 2014); see Peter K. Bradley et al., *New Guidance Regarding Preventive Services, Cost Sharing, and Wellness*, Hodgson Russ LLP (Mar. 31, 2014), available at Lexology.com]

The PPACA statute also forbids discrimination on the basis of health status. Although the IRS was supposed to publish regulations no later than September 2010, it was announced at the beginning of 2014 that the regulations were not finished, so the anti-discrimination requirement would not be enforced in 2014. [Robert Pear, *Rules for Equal Coverage by Employers Remain Elusive Under Health Law*, NYTimes.com (Jan. 18, 2014)]

It is common for executives' employment agreements to specify their entitlement to various kinds of payments on termination. When there is no agreement, the employer often provides severance benefits, including subsidized health care coverage, in exchange for release of employment-related claims. Sometimes the employer will continue to cover the ex-employee as if he or she were still an active employee for a certain number of months or years—often, as long as severance pay continues. When this coverage ends, the ex-employee is eligible to make a COBRA election.

Another approach is to subsidize COBRA coverage, usually by the employer making direct premium payments to the insurer. Before PPACA, self-insured employers had to be careful to avoid discrimination in favor of HCEs. If the company paid 18 months of premiums for HCEs but only one month for rank and file workers (or no payment at all for non-HCEs), the HCE might be taxed not only on the premiums but on all health benefits. To avoid this, employers often made cash severance payments that could, but did not have to be, used to pay COBRA premiums. Some employers "gross up" these amounts (increase the payment to account for the ex-employee's tax obligations). Pre-PPACA, the nondiscrimination rules did not apply to insured plans.

But, as a result of PPACA, all non-grandfathered insured group plans are now subject to anti-discrimination requirements, and once regulations are issued, penalties will be imposed on the employer, not the employee receiving the discriminatory benefits. The penalty can be as much as $100 per day of noncompliance times the number of employees suffering discrimination, with a cap of the lower of $500,000 or 10% of the employer's aggregate cost of EGHPs for the preceding year. The penalty is waived for small employers (fewer than 50 employees) or if the employer acted with reasonable cause and did not neglect the requirements. The nondiscrimination rules were supposed to take effect on the first day of the plan year after the year in which the IRS issued regulations—but, as of late 2012, the regulations had not been issued. [Steven Friedman, Terri Solomon, and Stephanie Kastrinsky, Littler Mendelson, *Employers with Insured Health Plans Must Take Care in Providing Healthcare Subsidies to Departing Executives* (Oct. 29, 2012) (benefitslink.com)]

[C] Insurers' Obligations

One of Congress's rationales in passing HIPAA was that employers, especially small companies, often had difficulty getting insurance—and once they had insurance, they often faced cancellation of coverage or at least excessively high rate increases.

HIPAA imposes obligations on insurers with respect to group health policies. The rules are different for "small employer" coverage (2–50 employees) and "large employer coverage" (groups of more than 50 employees). HIPAA's general requirement is that insurers who sell small employer coverage within a state must sell to all small employers who want to purchase the coverage, although there is no corresponding obligation to sell to would-be large-group buyers.

In either the small- or the large-group market, the insurer has an obligation to renew coverage or continue it in force as long as the purchase chooses, unless the purchaser:

- Stops paying the premiums;
- Commits fraud related to the policy;
- The insurer withdraws from the relevant market within the state;
- Plan enrollees move outside the service area for a network plan;
- (In a plan based on association membership) enrollees cease to be members of the association;
- The purchaser violates the rules on participation or contributions to the plan.

If an insurer discontinues one kind of group coverage but maintains others, all affected plan sponsors, participants, and beneficiaries are entitled to 90 days' notice of the discontinuance. The plan sponsor must be given the option to purchase the other coverage that the insurer offers in that market.

The insurer must act uniformly, without considering the existing or potential health problems of plan participants and beneficiaries, or the claims experience of the plan sponsor. An insurer that chooses to discontinue all of its coverage in the small- or large-group market must give state insurance regulators 180 days' notice of intent to discontinue. An insurer that withdraws will be barred from re-entering the market for five years. This requirement is imposed to prevent insurers from leaving and re-entering the market purely based on their own needs.

The Ninth Circuit held that Montana's "little HIPAA" law, Code § 33-22-526, is preempted by ERISA, but did not decide whether a state statute that provided more protection than HIPAA would be preempted. [*Fossen v. Blue Cross and Blue Shield of Montana, Inc.*, 660 F.3d 1102 (9th Cir. 2011); see Haynes and Boone Blogs, *Ninth Circuit Holds that Federal HIPAA Preempts Montana's* "Little HIPAA" *Law* (Feb. 2, 2012) (benefitslink.com)]

As the various PPACA provisions take effect, HIPAA's insurance provisions will be less significant, although the privacy rules will retain their significance. For example, PPACA's insurance Exchanges (also known as the Marketplace) are designed to make it easier for both individuals and businesses to compare insurance plans and obtain coverage. At first, the business Marketplace will be limited to small business purchasers, but PPACA is drafted so that eventually large businesses will also be able to get Marketplace coverage.

[D] Exceptions to the Portability Rule

Plans of certain types are not subject to the portability rules, because they are not deemed to be health benefit plans:

- Plans that offer accident and/or disability insurance;
- Liability insurance plans;
- Insured plans that provide medical benefits that are secondary or incidental to other benefits;
- Limited scope plans providing, e.g., dental, vision, or long-term care benefits;
- Coverage that is limited to a specified disease or illness;
- Fixed-indemnity plans (e.g., hospitalization insurance);
- Medicare Supplementary (Medigap) insurance.

Plans that cover only a single current employee are not subject to portability requirements.

Flexible Spending Accounts (FSAs) are "excepted benefits" under ERISA §§ 732 and 733(c) and I.R.C. §§ 9831 and 9832(c). Therefore, health insurance portability is not required for these plans. [See the "clarification of regulations" jointly issued by the IRS, the Pension and Welfare Benefit Administration, and the Department of Health and Human Services at 62 Fed. Reg. 67688 (Dec. 29, 1997)] The FSA is excepted from HIPAA if the employee's maximum FSA benefit for the year does not exceed twice the employee's salary reduction election for the year, as long as the employee has other EGHP coverage and as long as the FSA provides at least some benefits that are not "excepted benefits."

At the end of 2013, DOL, HHS, and the IRS published proposed rules expanding the definition of "excepted benefits" under the HIPAA portability rules. Excepted benefits include, e.g., accident insurance; disability insurance; Workers' Compensation; limited vision and dental programs; long-term care; and Medigap (Medicare supplemental coverage). HIPAA excepted benefits are exempt from the pre-PPACA portability rules, as well as from GINA Title I, the MHPAEA, WHCRAA, and the Newborn's and Mother's Act. However, excepted benefits are subject to ERISA, COBRA, the ADA, and GINA Title II (the employment title), and to the HIPAA privacy and security rules.

PPACA adopted the HIPAA excepted benefits rule, with the result that HIPAA excepted benefits do not have to comply with the prohibition on annual limits, cover participants' children to age 26, provide mandated preventive care, or satisfy the limits on out-of-pocket spending.

The 2013 proposal permits plans to offer no-cost dental and vision coverage under a separate policy, or if there is a separate election or opt out. EAPs that do not provide significant medical care are also excepted. [78 Fed. Reg. 77632

(Dec. 24, 2013); see Christy Tinnes and Brigen Winters, *Second Opinions: Agencies Issue New HIPAA Excepted Benefits Proposed Rules* (Jan. 8, 2014) (benefits link.com)]

[E] Penalties and Enforcement

Health plans are subject to a penalty tax, under I.R.C. Chapter 100, for failure to comply with the HIPAA portability rules.

HHS' interim final rule, effective November 30, 2009 for violations occurring on or after February 18, 2009, increases the HIPAA CMP schedule. Penalties range from $100 to $50,000 per violation, with a cap of $1.5 million for all violations of the same requirement in a calendar year. Under prior law, lack of knowledge of the violation was an affirmative defense. The Interim Final Rule allows covered entities and their associates to be penalized up to $50,000 even if they did not know there was a violation. If the entity did not know of the violation, the range is $100 to $1.5 million, but if there was reasonable cause for the violation and there was no willful neglect, the minimum penalty is $1,000. In the presence of willful neglect, where the violation was corrected within 30 days of discovery, the minimum is $10,000; the minimum is $50,000 if willful neglect was not corrected within 30 days. [74 Fed. Reg. 56123 (Oct. 30, 2009).] The 2010 Notice of Proposed Rulemaking, 75 Fed. Reg. 40868 (July 14, 2010) discussed in § 19.05[F], below, also discusses CMPs.

[F] Data Privacy and Security

As discussed in § 26.07, HIPAA also penalizes misuse of Protected Health Information (PHI). "Covered entities"—typically, an insurer or self-insured plan—are not permitted to use or disclose PHI without the consent of the subject of the information. [See 45 C.F.R. Parts 160 and 164 and HHS's FAQ at <http://www.hhs.gov/ocr/hipaa/privacy.html>. Information about privacy enforcement was added in April 2007: see <http://www.hhs.gov/ocr/privacy/enforcement>] The privacy rules are limited to health plans, not other welfare benefit plans (including disability plans), and PHI can lawfully be used for payment, treatment, or health care operations. In an insured EGHP, the insurer rather than the plan is the covered entity. The covered entity must provide privacy notices to plan members explaining their rights to data confidentiality.

A final enforcement rule was published, at 71 Fed. Reg. 8390 (Feb. 16, 2006), effective March 16, 2006, covering the HIPAA privacy, security, and EDI rules and the rules about unique identifiers.

The Health Information Technology for Economic and Clinical Health (HITECH) Act, part of the economic stimulus bill, took effect February 17, 2010, expanding HIPAA's privacy and security provisions and adding a new regulatory structure for electronic medical records. The HITECH Act increases the civil monetary penalties (CMPs) that can be imposed for violations and the individuals whose PHI has been disclosed improperly can collect a share of the civil penalties.

Business associates of HIPAA-covered entities are subject to the same privacy rules as the covered entities are, including criminal penalties for violations. A business associate that discovers that a covered entity with which it has a business relationship has breached the security or confidentiality rules is supposed to take steps to cure the breach—or terminate the contract. Notice must be given to individuals whose PHI was improperly disclosed; and if 500 or more people were affected by the breach, disclosure to HHS and the news media is also required. Covered entities and their business associates who use electronic health records are required to provide an accounting of how the electronic records were used and disclosed in the previous three years. HHS' Office of Civil Rights continues to enforce HIPAA compliance, but state Attorneys General have also been given the power to enforce HIPAA by bringing suit in federal district court. [Troutman Sanders LLP, *Keeping up with Recent Legislation: Numerous Changes to Group Health Plans Required*, plansponsor.com (Feb. 27, 2009)]

Many courts have held that there is no private cause of action for violation of HIPAA's privacy rules: enforcement must come from the government—HHS for civil actions, the Department of Justice for criminal cases. [See, e.g., *Acara v. Banks*, 470 F.3d 569 (5th Cir. 2006); *Lester v. M&M Knopf Auto Parts*, 04-CV-850S, 2006 WL 2806465 99 (W.D.N.Y. Sept. 28, 2006)]

The Northern District of Georgia dismissed a HIPAA claim against a third-party administrator (TPA) that allegedly improperly gave the plaintiff's employer information from her FMLA file, which included medical and therapy records. The employer wanted the information in connection with a separate sex discrimination suit filed by the plaintiff. The contract between the employer and the TPA said that information collected under the FMLA plan would only be used to administer that plan, not for employment-related actions unless authorized by the employee. The Northern District said that the TPA was neither a covered entity nor a business associate of a covered identity because FMLA and STD plans are not covered entities. Other claims against the TPA were also dismissed, although the decision did not address the merits of claims against the employer. [*Floyd v. SunTrust Banks, Inc.*, No. 1:10-CV-2620-RWS, 2011 WL 2441744 (N.D. Ga. June 13, 2011)]

Data confidentiality protects the patient against improper disclosure of PHI by health care providers and insurers. The related subject of "data security" is tackled by a final rule appearing at 68 Fed. Reg. 8333 (Feb. 20, 2003). Covered entities are required to carry out technical, physical, and business procedures to protect PHI from unauthorized access (e.g., by hackers), and to have compliance programs so their employees carry out the program.

After issuing interim final rules in 2009 [RIN 009-AB56, 75 Fed. Reg. 42740 (Aug. 24, 2009) and a 2010 Notice of Proposed Rulemaking dealing with privacy, security, and enforcement [RIN 009-AB56, 75 Fed. Reg. 40868 (July 14,

2010), at the beginning of 2013 HHS' Office of Civil Rights (OCR) published an omnibus restatement of the HIPAA privacy and security rules, reflecting the HITECH Act Amendments. Covered entities and their contractors and subcontractors are subject to civil and criminal penalties for violations of the privacy, security, and breach notification rules. Security breaches must be reported to HHS each year, and large-scale breaches must also be reported to the individuals involved and to the news media. There are requirements for using encryption and destruction of obsolete information to prevent unauthorized persons from accessing protected health information (PHI). Penalties assessed for failure to notify individuals of breach of their PHI and failure to notify the media when required have increased. The penalty ranges between $100 and $50,000 per violation in situations where the covered entity did not know of the violation (and could not have known by exercising reasonable diligence). If there was reasonable cause for the violation, and there was no willful neglect, the penalty range is $1,000 to $50,000. Where willful neglect occurred, the penalty range is $10,000–$50,000 if the violation was corrected on a timely basis—and at least $50,000 for offenses of willful neglect that were not timely corrected. However, in each penalty category, there is a cap of $1.5 million on total penalties for all violations of the same provision. The actual penalty imposed within the penalty range for a particular offense depends on factors such as the nature and extent of the violation and the extent of the harm it caused.

This rule makes some changes to conform HIPAA to the Genetic Information Nondiscrimination Act (GINA) Title I (health coverage) and Title II (employment). For example, GINA treats genetic information as health information and health plans must be informed that it is forbidden to use or disclose genetic information for underwriting purposes. (However, the information can be used for underwriting of long-term care insurance.) The final rule became effective on March 26, 2013 and covered entities must comply by September 23, 2013 [78 Fed. Reg. 5566 (Jan. 25, 2013) Cynthia Marcotte Stamer, Solutions Law Press HR & Benefits Update, *OCR Publishes Long-Anticipated Omnibus Restatement of HIPAA Privacy, Security, Breach Notification & Enforcement Rules* (Jan. 13, 2013) (benefitslink.com); Katherine Georger, Holland & Hart LLP News Update, *New HIPAA Final Rule Implements GINA Restriction on Use and Disclosure of Genetic Information for Underwriting Purposes* (Jan. 23, 2013) (benefitslink.com)]

The District Court for the District of Connecticut entered a protective order in an FMLA retaliation case. The plaintiff said that she was fired for taking leave after her husband's surgery; the employer said that she was fired for leave abuse (claiming FMLA leave while vacationing in Mexico). The employer sought discovery of the husband's medical records, which the plaintiff said were both protected by HIPAA and irrelevant, because he was not a party to the suit. The district court entered the protective order, permitting disclosure of the husband's condition only for the period between the surgery and the plaintiff's termination. The employer was forbidden to use the information for non-litigation purposes and ordered to return or destroy the data after the resolution of the suit. [*Tavares v. Lawrence & Mem'l Hosp.*, No. 3:11-CV-770 (CSH), 2012 U.S. Dist. LEXIS 146614(D. Conn. Oct. 10, 2012); see Wolters Kluwer Law & Business News Center, *Husband's Medical Records Must Be Disclosed To Former Employer In Employee's Lawsuit Based On FMLA* (Nov. 2, 2012) (benefitslink.com)]

In 2012, BlueCross BlueShield (BCBS) of Tennessee agreed to pay HHS $1.5 million to settle HITECH charges about a 2009 data breach. Fifty-nine unencrypted hard drives were stolen from a disused Chattanooga call center. The drives contained PHI (such as Social Security numbers and diagnoses) for more than a million BlueCross customers. [HHS Website for reporting breaches: <http://www.hhs.gov/ocr/privacy/hipaa/administrative/breachnotificationrule/brinstruction.html>; see Beth Moskow-Schnoll, Jean C. Hemphill, Evan W. Krick, and Edward I. Leeds, *Data Breach Leads to First HITECH Enforcement Settlement*, Ballard Spahr (Mar. 19, 2012) (benefitslink.com); Shannon Green, *$1.5M HHS Data Breach Settlement Is First Under HITECH Law*, Corporate Counsel (Mar. 21, 2012) (law.com)]

HHS's Office for Civil Rights settled with a health plan network about violations of the HIPAA privacy and security rule. The plan notified HHS of a breach of PHI after its online application database had a breach of electronic PHI. The settlement said that the plan didn't implement adequate policies and procedures re access to the database, do an adequate technical evaluation in response to the upgrade, or verify identity of people seeking access to the PHI on the database. The settlement was reached before the final HITECH Act regulations took effect on September 23, 2013, when the Office for Civil Rights gained authority to enforce the security rules directly against the business associates of covered entities. [HHS News Release on a Resolution Agreement (July 11, 2013); see EBIA Weekly, *Software Upgrade With Inadequate Safeguards Leads to $1.7 Million HIPAA Security Settlement* (July 18, 2013) (benefitslink.com)]

In late 2102, HHS settled HIPAA charges against the Massachusetts Eye and Ear Infirmary when a personal laptop containing unencrypted PHI of patients and research subjects was stolen. The Infirmary agreed to pay $1.5 million over a three-year period, and to comply with a correction plan to improve security measures and usage of portable devices. HHS news release, <http://www.hhs.gov/ocr/privacy/hipaa/enforcement/examples/meei-agreement.html> (Sept. 17, 2012); see EBIA Weekly, *Unencrypted Laptop Leads to $1.5 Million HIPAA Security Settlement* (Oct. 11, 2012) (benefitslink.com)]

On January 2, 2013, the OCR announced that the Hospice of North Idaho was required to pay a $50,000 penalty for potential violations in connection with theft of a laptop containing unencrypted PHI. This was the first settlement in a case where the breach involved fewer than 500 people. [Cynthia Marcotte Stamer, Solutions Law Press HR & Benefits Update, *OCR Publishes Long-Anticipated Omnibus Restatement of HIPAA Privacy, Security, Breach Notification & Enforcement Rules* (Jan. 13, 2013) (benefitslink.com)]

Two unencrypted laptops were stolen from a conference room at corporate headquarters; the computers contained personal information of about 1.2 million customers. A class action was filed charging the company with inadequate safeguarding of personal information. The district court dismissed the suit for lack of cognizable injury, but it was reinstated by the Eleventh Circuit, including a count of unjust enrichment (on the theory that the part of the premium that should have been used to provide security was misappropriated). There was a $3 million settlement, with class members receiving up to $10 a year, with a maximum of $30, for unjust enrichment, plus reimbursement of monetary losses due to data theft. The agreement obtained preliminary approval from the District Court for the Southern District of Florida, with a final approval hearing scheduled for February 28, 2014. [*Unopposed Motion in Support of Preliminary Approval of Class Action Settlement in Resnick/Curry v. AvMed, Inc.*, No. 1:10-cv-24513-JLK (S.D. Fla.); see Alfred J. Saikali, *$3,000,000 Settlement Reached In Data Breach Lawsuit*, Shook Hardy & Bacon LLP (Oct. 22, 2013), available at Lexology.com]

CHAPTER 20
DISABILITY PLANS

§ 20.01 INTRODUCTION

Because of an acute illness, a chronic illness, or an injury (work-related or otherwise), many working-age individuals will go through brief, extended, or permanent periods during which they are unable to perform their normal jobs. The rate of disability in the United States is increasing for many reasons: the aging of the workforce; greater incidence of obesity and sedentary lifestyles; and medical improvements that make it possible for people to survive for many years despite significant impairments. [M.P. McQueen, *Workplace Disabilities Are on the Rise*, Wall St. J., May 1, 2007, at D1] Many employers either provide disability insurance under an ERISA plan, or give employees the option to purchase disability coverage on their own, at a lower premium than they could find in the ordinary individual market.

There are both public (Social Security Disability Income; Worker's Compensation) and private systems for dealing with disability. The Supreme Court ruled that the Commissioner of Social Security reasonably construed the definition of disability to deny benefits to a claimant who was healthy enough to do her former job (elevator operator) even though that job no longer exists in significant numbers within the national economy. [*Barnhart v. Thomas*, 540 U.S. 20 (2003)] Some states require employers to provide disability benefits; in other states, employers often do this as an employee benefit. Benefits are analyzed as short-term disability (STD) or long-term disability (LTD), with separate standards for each.

Returning to the subject of disability in 2008, the Supreme Court upheld the Kentucky state retirement system's practice of calculating disability retirement benefits by including extra years of service for those who became disabled before normal retirement age, but not for those who were disabled after normal retirement age. The Supreme Court did not consider this to be age discrimination; depending on the age at hire, some younger workers did better than older workers, and some older workers did better than younger workers, under the system. The court held that, in drafting the ADEA, Congress considered it acceptable to consider age when setting disability benefit formulas. [*Kentucky Ret. Systems v. EEOC*, 554 U.S. 135 (2008)]

Because disability claims are administered by the same insurance company that pays claims that are granted, the legal system had to determine the effect of this conflict of interest on the standard of review. Should a court review a claims decision deferentially, or only see if there was an abuse of discretion and sustain the decision if it was not arbitrary and capricious? This is discussed in *Metropolitan Life v. Glenn*, 554 U.S. 105 (2008). See § 20.07 for post-*Glenn* case law, and Chapter 13 for the subject of claims in general.

The Sixth Circuit affirmed an award of improperly denied LTD benefits and awarded $3.8 million in disgorgement of the insurer's profits for breach of fiduciary duty. The Sixth Circuit held that disgorgement was an appropriate equitable remedy to prevent unjust enrichment and did not constitute double recovery when coupled with an award of improperly denied benefits. *Varity v. Howe* 516 U.S. 489 (1996) did not apply, because the plaintiff asserted two different claims. (The Eighth Circuit had already reached this conclusion.) The amount was based on the defendant's return on its average equity, not investment income, because the funds were kept in a general account that could be used for any business purpose, not in a segregated investment account. The Sixth Circuit has agreed to re-hear this case en banc. [*Rochow v. Life Ins. Co. of N. Am.*, 737 F.3d 415 (6th Cir. 2013); see Haynes and Boone LLP, *Participant Awarded $3.8 Million As Disgorgement Of Profits Made On Unpaid Benefit*, Lexology.com (Jan. 13, 2014); Mike Reilly, *6th Circuit: Reversing Decades of Precedent—Court Orders Disgorgement of Profits in Long Term Disability Case*, Boom: The ERISA Law Blog (Dec. 10, 2013) (benefitslink.com); Workplace Prof Blog, *6th Cir: ERISA Remedy for Wrongful Denial of Benefits May Include Disgorgement Remedy under Section 502(a)(3)* (Dec. 9, 2013) (benefitslink.com)]

The Sixth Circuit held that a long-term disability claimant who files for bankruptcy but fails to list the LTD claim in the bankruptcy estate will probably not be estopped from suing for wrongful denial of disability benefits. There was no evidence of intentional concealment, and Ohio exempts disability insurance proceeds from the debtor's estate, so there was no motive to conceal the claim. [*Javery v. Lucent Tech, Inc. Long Term Disability Plan*, 741 F.3d 686 (6th Cir. 2014); see Mike Reilly, *6th Circuit: Failing to Disclose Disability Claim in Bankruptcy Not Fatal to Disability Lawsuit*, Lane Powell Boom! The ERISA Law Blog (Feb. 6, 2014) (benefitslink.com)]

Under the FMLA, although the provisions about substituting paid for unpaid leave do not apply when an employee receives disability benefits during an FMLA leave, the employer and employee can, by agreement, supplement disability benefits by running paid leave concurrently with FMLA leave. (See Chapter 38.)

§ 20.02 EMPLOYMENT-BASED PLANS

Usually, a short-term disability (STD) is defined either as one that lasts less than six months, or one that lasts less than a year. Long-term disability benefits typically terminate after a period of years (e.g., five years) or at age 65, when the employee would presumably be retiring anyway.

A typical arrangement is for the employer to self-insure for short-term disability, but to buy long-term disability (LTD) insurance (possibly with the covered employees contributing part of the cost). It is also typical for STD and LTD plans to use different definitions of disability. The long-term plan has more restrictive definitions, because the employer's possible exposure is greater.

Using an "own occupation" definition (the person is disabled when unable to carry out the duties of the pre-disability occupation) makes it easier to qualify for benefits than using an "any occupation" definition (benefits stop as soon as the person is able to return to any work, or any work suitable to his or her education and training). Another frequent plan design is for the definition to start out as "own-occ" but switch after two years to inability to perform any occupation suitable to the individual's education and training.

Benefits from group disability plans are offset by Social Security Disability Income; benefits from individual policies are not.

Plaintiff Hannington's disability benefits under an ERISA plan were offset by his service-related disability compensation under the Veterans' Benefits Act (VBA). The ERISA plan paid 60% of pre-disability salary, reduced by "other income" as defined by the plan. The "other income" provision covers disability benefits under the Social Security Act, Railroad Retirement Act, or "any other similar act or law." The plan administrator was also the insurer, so there was a conflict of interest. The district court held that the VBA benefits were not "similar to" the Social Security Act or Railroad Retirement Act, so they should not have offset the benefits under the ERISA disability plan. Because of the conflict of interest, the First Circuit reviewed the plan's decision de novo and concluded that the VBA benefits are not "similar" to the SSA or RRA benefits because they are based on military service rather than employment. The VBA benefit is funded by Congressional appropriations; the ERISA benefits are funded by taxes on employers and employees. Congress did not enact a provision requiring offset of VBA benefits against SSA or RRA benefits The First Circuit held that the offset was improper, because the VBA benefits did not constitute "other income" as defined by the ERISA plan. [*Hannington v. Sun Life & Health Ins. Co.*, 711 F.3d 226 (1st Cir. 2013)]

LTD plans usually replace 60%–70% of pre-disability income; 60% is the most common level. The plan may also limit income replacement from all sources, including Worker's Compensation and Social Security, to a percentage such as 75% of pre-disability income. Many group plans offset (reduce) disability benefits to account for government benefits and damages received from tort suits or settlements (e.g., if the employee was injured in an accident or by a defective product), whereas individual policies generally do not require benefit offsets. The Ninth Circuit held that it was not an abuse of discretion for a plan to deduct SSDI (Social Security Disability Income) payments from the benefits paid by two LTD plans. The plain language of the plan explained the plan's right to be reimbursed for overpayments, and defined other sources of income (specifically including Social Security benefits) as overpayments. The Ninth Circuit also allowed a double offset of the SSDI benefit from two separate plans. [*Renfro v. The Funky Door LTD Plan*, 686 F.3d 1044 (9th Cir. 2012)]

Another cost-saving measure for a group plan is to have benefits start after a waiting period, so that the plan covers situations in which work ability is impaired for a long time, but not ordinary illnesses and minor injuries (which are probably covered by sick leave anyway).

A Taft-Hartley plan is a temporary disability plan jointly run by employers and a union. The plan's goal is to assist employees who are in financial need because of a disability, while also helping them return to work as soon as possible (if they can be rehabilitated adequately). A 2010 Second Circuit decision treats Taft-Hartley plan benefit decisions as inherently subject to a conflict of interest when they make benefit decisions. The Second Circuit ruled that the plan did not give enough weight to the testimony of the attending physician of an employee, injured in an automobile accident, who claimed ongoing pain and weakness. The court also said that the independent report should not have concluded that the worker was capable of performing three occupations. [*Durakovic v. Building Serv. 32 BJ Pension Fund*, 609 F.3d 133 (2d Cir. 2010)]

Highly compensated employees, who often experience crushing income loss after disability (because disability benefits are capped at a level far below their pre-disability income) can be good subjects for corporate disability buy-up policies—supplemental group disability plans providing additional income replacement.

The buy-up plan could be either employer paid, in which case the employer can deduct the premiums and the employee does not have taxable income because of the premium payments, but benefits will be taxable when received; or the employer sponsors the plan, allowing insurers to sign up employees who pay for their own coverage but can then receive benefits tax-free. The second approach is more popular. A disability buy-up can also be included in a cafeteria plan, so that premiums are paid with pre-tax dollars but benefits are taxable. In this case, the coverage will be portable, and employees can take it with them when they change jobs. In a hybrid plan, the employer pays the premiums for a select group of employees; other employees can participate by paying premiums.

Buy-up plans are structured with two tiers. The first tier is a guaranteed issue policy issued at standard rates without underwriting. The second tier has limited underwriting, which may lead to higher premiums or some coverage restrictions. [See Assurant Employee Benefits, *Long-Term Disability Glossary of Terms*, <http://www.assurantemployeebenefits.com/816/aebcom/xhtml_clip/disabilityedu/aeb_glossary.pdf> (accessed May 19, 2014)]

As an incentive for rehabilitation, the plan may continue benefits at a low level while the individual engages in a trial period of re-employment, or undertakes part-time or lower-level work in an attempt to re-enter the workforce. [See Chapter 37 for a discussion of the Age Discrimination in Employment Act (ADEA) [29 U.S.C. §§ 621 *et seq.*] implications of disability plans]

§ 20.03 STATE MANDATES

In five states (California, Hawaii, New York, New Jersey, and Rhode Island), employers are required to provide TDI (Temporary Disability Insurance) coverage for between 26 and 52 weeks of non-occupational temporary disability for industrial and commercial workers. Either the state administers a fund from which employer contributions are distributed to disabled employees, or the state maintains a fund but gives employers the choice of self-insuring, buying insurance, or paying into a union-sponsored disability plan.

TDI benefits are offset (that is, reduced) by Worker's Compensation and unemployment benefits.

§ 20.04 COMPLIANCE ISSUES

[A] ERISA Compliance

For ERISA purposes, most disability arrangements are welfare benefit plans, and therefore subject to disclosure, filing, and fiduciary requirements. Some disability plans, however, are top-hat plans that only cover executives, so the employer's disclosure obligations are more limited. If a plan is maintained only to comply with Worker's Compensation or state mandates, then ERISA § 4(b)(3) exempts the plan from ERISA compliance obligations. ERISA compliance is also excused in situations where an employer makes payments out of its general assets to an employee who is out of work for medical reasons. [See 29 C.F.R. § 2510.3-1(b)(2)]

The Middle District of Florida held that Lockheed Martin did not violate the ERISA ban on interference with benefits (ERISA § 510) when it terminated an employee for excessive absence. The plaintiff did not prove that she was terminated because of the cost of her STD benefits; she had been put on a performance improvement plan for excessive absences and poor work even before she applied for STD. She was only terminated after being denied STD (for lack of proof that her condition made it impossible for her to work) and then refusing to either return to work or provide medical documentation of her inability to return. [*Mundale v. Lockheed Martin Corp.*, No. 8:08-CV-217-T-24-TBM (M.D. Fla. Jan. 26, 2009); see Rebecca Moore, *Court Finds No Interference of Benefits in Excessive Absence Termination*, plansponsor.com (Feb. 5, 2009)]

The Eastern District of California ruled in early 2013 that a Worker's Compensation release did not release an ERISA disability claim. The release did not explicitly mention the ERISA plan or ERISA claims. Teresa Duncan made an LTD claim under an ERISA plan and received disability benefits between 2005 and 2010. She settled her Worker's Compensation claim in 2008 and gave a release of all claims, saying she would not "be able to go back to the defendant for additional treatment or disability payments." The district court held that the standard language in Worker's Compensation releases applies only to Worker's Compensation claims, and there was no mention of ERISA. [*Duncan v. Hartford Life and Accident Ins. Co.*, No. 2:11-cv-1536-GEB-CKD, 2013 WL 506465 (E.D. Cal. Feb. 8, 2013); see Mike Reilly, *Releases Should Explicitly Release ERISA*

Claims and ERISA Plan, Lane Powell Boom: The ERISA Law Blog (Feb. 26, 2013) (benefitslink.com)]

If the employee pays all the premiums for LTD insurance, and the employer's only role is to administer the payments (without giving its approval of the policy), then ERISA does not preempt a suit by the employee against the insurer claiming bad faith termination of benefits. There are two tests for deciding whether ERISA preempts litigation about a disability policy:

- Was there a "plan, fund or program"? In this case, a plan was clearly present—but it was not an ERISA plan;
- Does the arrangement qualify for the ERISA safe harbor? The safe harbor is available if the employer does not make any contributions to the plan; the plan is completely voluntary; the employer does not profit from the plan (although it can legitimately receive a reasonable administrative fee); and the employer allows one or more insurers to publicize the availability of the program, but does not endorse or recommend it.

An employer's offering a group supplemental LTD policy with a group discount was enough employer involvement to create an ERISA plan. The plaintiff applied for an individual policy through a hospital plan that gave discounts to medical residents. Several years after leaving the hospital's employ, McCann collected LTD benefits. When the benefits were terminated, McCann sued the insurer for breach of contract, treating it as group insurance exempt from ERISA under the safe harbor regulation, 29 C.F.R. § 2510.3-1(j). Defendant Provident said that it was an ERISA plan. The safe harbor exempts group insurance plans if participation is voluntary and the employer does not make any contributions, confining its involvement to collecting premiums and submitting them to the insurer. The Third Circuit found that there was an ERISA plan even though the policy did not take effect until after McCann left employment. [*McCann v. UNUM Provident*, 3:11-cv-03241-MLC-TJB, 2013 WL 396182 (Jan. 31, 2013); see D. Ward Kallstrom and Michelle M. Scannell, *It's an ERISA Plan? District Court Construes Group Discount as Employer Contribution under DOL Group Insurance Safe Harbor Analysis* Seyfarth Shaw ERISA & Employee Benefits Litigation Blog (Feb. 15, 2013) (benefitslink.com). The definition of ERISA plan comes from *Shaver v. Siemens Corp.*, 670 F.3d 462 (3d Cir. 2012).]

Even arrangements that are exempt from ERISA (and therefore from federal ERISA suits) as payroll practices are vulnerable to state-court suits charging, for example, bad faith. [*Street v. Ingalls Mem'l Hosp.*, Case No. 06 C 2963, 2007 U.S. Dist. LEXIS 18643 (N.D. Ill. Mar. 15, 2007); see EBIA Weekly, *Short-Term Disability Payment Policy Not an ERISA Plan; No Interest on Delayed Payments* (Mar. 29, 2007)]

ERISA does not preempt state "notice-prejudice" laws. Such laws prevent insurers from denying a claim on the basis that the insured person did not give timely notice of the covered event, unless the delay really causes harm to the insurer. [*Daug v. UNUM Life Ins. Co.*, 1999 WL 238236 (10th Cir. 1999); *Cisneros v. UNUM*, 134 F.3d 939 (9th Cir. 1999)]

[B] Tax Issues

Whether an employer can get a tax deduction for the cost of its disability plan depends on satisfying I.R.C. § 162 (ordinary and necessary business expenses). The employer's contributions must also satisfy I.R.C. § 104.

From the employee's viewpoint, the key section is I.R.C. § 106, which excludes employer coverage under an accident and health insurance (A&H) plan from the employee's gross income. This section is usually interpreted to include the premiums that the employer pays to maintain an insured disability plan, as well as the value of coverage under a self-insured disability plan. After a disability occurs, the benefits received by the employee under A&H or disability insurance must be included in income to the extent that they are attributable to previously excluded employer contributions. Amounts paid directly by the employer to the employee are also includible in gross income.

However, benefits paid for permanent loss (or loss of use) of a body part or its function, or for disfigurement, are not included in the employee's income, as long as the benefit is computed without regard to absence from work.

A settlement in a retaliatory discharge case described the proceeds as compensation for emotional distress; in 2014, the Tax Court held that even if there are physical manifestations of emotional distress, that is not sufficient to make the settlement one for "physical injury" as set out in § 104(a)(2). [*Sharp v. Comm'r*, TCM 2013-90 (Dec. 20, 2013); see William Hays Weissman, *U.S. Tax Court Decision Shows Importance Of Carefully Drafting Settlement Agreements*, Littler Mendelson (Jan. 6, 2014), available at Lexology.com]

[C] ADA Compliance

It should also be noted that a disability plan that imposes lower limits for mental health care than for care of physical ailments may violate the Americans with Disabilities Act (ADA). The Mental Health Parity Act [42 U.S.C. § 300gg] makes it unlawful for employee group health plans to set lower limits for mental health care than for treatment of physical illnesses. This statute, however, is not applicable to disability plans.

Early in 2000, the Supreme Court affirmed (without opinion) [528 U.S. 1106 (2000)] the Seventh Circuit's decision in *Doe v. Mutual of Ohio* [179 F.3d 557 (7th Cir. 2000)] It does not violate the ADA's public accommodations title for an insured or self-insured health plan to impose a lower cap on benefits for AIDS-related illnesses or conditions than for other ailments. The Supreme Court would not grant privileged status to diseases that cause ADA disability over other diseases that do not.

ADA Title IV immunizes insurer and benefit plan decisions based on underwriting, classifying, or administering risk, as long as the decisions are not a subterfuge to escape ADA compliance. Decisions that have actuarial support are likely to qualify for this safe harbor.

The Ninth Circuit held that a teacher who applied for medical leave and disability benefits on the basis of total disability when her back condition worsened could sue under the ADA, alleging that she was denied reasonable accommodation. In the Ninth Circuit view, the ADA and disability claims were not necessarily inconsistent. The applications did not consider reasonable accommodation, future ability to work, or ability to perform other jobs. [*Smith v. Clark Cnty. Sch. Dist.*, 727 F.3d 950 (9th Cir. 2013); see Sarah R. Peace, *Employees May Take "Total Disability" And Seek Accommodation Too*, Sherman & Howard LLC (Aug. 22, 2013), available at Lexology.com]

[D] EEOC Compliance Manual

EEOC directives do not have the force of law. Even Regulations promulgated by this agency have often been invalidated by court decisions. However, you should consult Section 3 of the EEOC's Compliance Manual, issued October 3, 2000 [<http://www.eeoc.gov/policy/docs/benefits.html>] for EEOC policy on what constitutes discrimination on the basis of age or handicap, and what "equal" benefits mean in the context of disability benefits.

The revised Compliance Manual permits employers to reduce long-term disability benefits to account for Social Security Disability Income, Worker's Compensation, and other non-age-based government benefits. LTD benefits paid to older workers can also be reduced by pension benefits that come from employer contributions, under two conditions. Either the employee voluntarily opts to receive the pension (at any age) or has reached age 62 of the plan's normal retirement age (whichever is later) and is eligible for a full, unreduced pension. In plans partially funded by employee contributions, the employer is only permitted to reduce benefits that can be traced back to its own contributions, not employee contributions.

The EEOC position is that disability retirement benefits are not equal if they are calculated on the basis of the number of years the employee would have worked until NRA, because that approach favors younger employees. But disability benefits under government programs can legitimately be used to reduce disability benefits paid by the employer.

[E] Other Compliance Issues

Disability benefits are not considered "medical care," so when an employee is terminated, the right to COBRA continuation coverage [see Chapter 19] extends to the employee group health plan but not to the long-term disability plan.

The District Court for the Northern District of Ohio held in 2013 that even the plan administrator's actual knowledge that a former employee was disabled (and received Social Security disability benefits) was not enough to extend her husband's COBRA continuation coverage duration from 18 to 29 months, where the plan explicitly provided that coverage would only be extended if the plan participant provided notice of disability to the plan administrator. [*Rayle v. Wood Cnty. Hosp.*, No. 3:12-cv-02052-0, 2013 WL 1654898 (N.D. Ohio Apr. 16, 2013). See EBIA Weekly, *Actual Notice of Employee's Disability Insufficient to Extend COBRA Coverage When Plan's Notice Procedures Were Not Followed* (May 16, 2013) (benefitslink.com)]

The Eleventh Circuit ruled that SSDI decisions (and information submitted by the claimant in his or her SSDI application) should be taken into account in determining whether a claimant satisfies the policy's definition of disability. If the SSDI decision is not rendered until after the claim denial but during the administrative appeal, the Eleventh Circuit apparently reduced a claimant's burden of proof. Even though the claimant refused to submit the evidence to the insurer that was submitted to the Social Security Administration, the Eleventh Circuit required the insurer to consider that evidence. The decision implies that the insurer might have to defer its determination until the SSDI process is complete or perhaps the administrator can approve a claim before the SSDI process is finished, but cannot deny it until then. [*Melech v. Life Ins. Co. of N. Am.*, 739 F.3d 663 (11th Cir. 2014); see Mike Reilly, *11th Cir.-Social Security Determinations Issued AFTER Initial Claim Denial Must Be Considered?*, Boom! The ERISA Law Blog (Feb. 4, 2014) (benefitslink.com); Patrick Begos, *Must Disability Claim Administrators Now Obtain The SSDI File In The 11th Circuit?*, Begos Horgan & Brown LLP ERISA Claim Defense Blog (Jan. 20, 2014) (benefitslink .com)]

The Family and Medical Leave Act [Pub. L. No. 103-3; see Chapter 38] may entitle the employee to claim unpaid leave for personal medical needs, or the need to care for a sick family member.

The Supreme Court ruled in May 2010 that an employee, who applied for LTD benefits from a plan insured by Reliance Standard, was entitled to attorneys' fees when the trial court found that the benefit denial was an abuse of discretion. The court remanded to give Reliance 30 days to reconsider; if it did not, judgment would be entered for the plaintiff. Reliance granted the benefits, but argued that an attorneys' fee award was inappropriate because the plaintiff received only a remand, not court-ordered benefits. The Supreme Court held that the relevant ERISA section gives the district court discretion to award attorneys' fees to either side—fee awards are not limited to prevailing parties. [*Hardt v. Reliance Standard Life Ins.,* 560 U.S. 242 (2010); See also *Williams v. Metropolitan Life Ins. Co.,* 609 F.3d 622 (4th Cir. 2010), awarding attorneys' fees to a disability claimant who had a degree of success in arguing that she suffered ongoing pain and loss of function in her hands and wrists, and eventually received LTD benefits for carpal tunnel syndrome.]

The District Court for the District of Colorado required forms for obtaining medical information to be focused as narrowly as possible on the doctor's assessment of the employee's ability to perform job duties, and also required a system for controlling access to information about employees. The defendant's medical authorization form, used to determine eligibility for short-term disability benefits, said that the information would only be used to evaluate if the employee's condition satisfies federal, state, or local FMLA laws, disability laws, Workers' Compensation laws, or the employer's welfare benefit plan. The district court held that, although the information might be needed in its role as plan administrator, a jury could conclude that there was a risk that the information would be disseminated in a manner exceeding the job related/business necessity standard. [*Fraser v. Avaya, Inc.*, No. 10-cv-00800-RPM, 2013 U.S. Dist. LEXIS 126034 (D. Colo. Sept. 4, 2013); see William A. Nolan, *Decision Reminds Employers: Minimalist Medical Inquiries Are A Must*, Barnes & Thornburg LLP (Sept. 9, 2013), available at Lexology.com]

The First Circuit held that a disability plan's Functional Capacity Evaluation does not have to be performed by a doctor to be valid. Nor was it an abuse of discretion to deny benefits to a claimant who failed to cooperate with the evaluation performed by a physical therapist. The terms of the plan required claimants to cooperate, and a video showed that the plaintiff did not perform lifting, pushing, pulling, or climbing activities and gave only "sub-maximal" effort to tasks during the evaluation. [*Ortega-Candelaria v. Johnson & Johnson*, No. 13-1564, 2014 WL 2696725 (1st Cir. June 25, 2014); see D. Michael Reilly, *ERISA (1st Cir.): Lack of Cooperation During Functional Capacity Evaluation Bars Disability Claim*, Lane Powell PC (June 20, 2014), available at Lexology.com]

§ 20.05 CASE LAW ON "TOTAL DISABILITY"

In many instances, the question is not how to interpret the plan—the question is whether or not the claimant satisfies the plan's definition of "total disability." It may be inability to perform the applicant's own occupation, or any occupation for which his or her education and training qualifies him or her—or the definition may shift depending on the length of the period of disability.

Even if the question is ability to engage in "any gainful occupation," most courts will require consideration of the individual's earnings history and the availability of jobs in the relevant geographic area. The Utah Supreme Court held that an injured worker's past earnings can be considered in a permanent total disability case. The claimant, a building engineer, had a lower back injury in 2001. The ALJ found him permanently and totally disabled, in part because the only available employment paid less than the state's average weekly wage. The injured worker's former employer and its insurer said that under Utah law, the determination of available work is based only on the employee's age, education, work experience, medical capacity, and residual functional capacity. The Utah Supreme Court held that past work experience also includes consideration of the wages the worker earned prior to becoming disabled. [*LPI Servs. v. McGee*, 215 P.3d 135 (Utah 2009); see Rebecca Moore, *Utah Court Says Wages Can Be Considered in Disability Determination*, plansponsor.com (July 27, 2009)]

The Second Circuit held that the fact that an employee continues to work does not prevent him from showing that he was disabled, if there is evidence that the disability was very severe. In this case, an office administrator who suffered a head injury experienced a decline in work performance and ability to interact with others, and was fired about a year after the accident. She was treated for headaches, mood changes, sleep disorder, and impaired memory. The Second Circuit rejected the insurer's conclusion, that the disability was only partial or temporary, for lack of evidence. [*O'Hara v. National Union Fire Ins.*, 642 F.3d 110 (2d Cir. 2011)]

The First Circuit held that denial of benefits on the basis of an unwritten exclusion was unreasonable. The plaintiff was an anesthesiologist who obtained LTD benefits for part of an inpatient stay to treat her addiction to Fentanyl. At that point, her claim was denied on the grounds that the risk of relapse was not a continuation of disability. The district court awarded benefits for the 36-month maximum term under the plan, and the First Circuit affirmed. The First Circuit held that the plaintiff's risk of relapse was significant, because the plaintiff had a bad back and a stressful job with convenient access to drugs—and the insurer should have written in an exclusion for relapse if that was the intention in designing the policy. However, the Fourth Circuit has reached the opposite conclusion: that no matter how significant the risk of relapse, the risk, without an actual relapse, will not support a disability claim. [*Colby v. Union Sec. Ins. Co. & Mgmt. Co. for Merrimack Anesthesia Assocs. Long-Term Disability Plan*, 705 F.3d 58 (1st Cir. 2013); see Ron Kramer and Jim Goodfellow, *First Circuit: Unwritten Risk of Relapse Exclusion is Unreasonable, Creates Split with Fourth Circuit*, Seyfarth Shaw ERISA & Employee Benefits Litigation Blog (Feb. 4, 2013) (benefitslink.com)]

§ 20.06 EFFECT OF PLAN AMENDMENTS

The Sixth Circuit held that it was not an abuse of discretion to amend a multi-employer pension plan to impose a two-year cap on occupational disability benefits: the plan did not provide vested welfare benefits. The plaintiff was injured at work in 1990, and began to receive disability benefits under the Indiana Laborer's Pension Fund. In 2001, he was informed that benefits under the Total and Permanent Disability Benefit category were canceled, but he would receive Occupational Disability benefits until the plan's early retirement age. The plan gave the trustees authority to determine benefit eligibility and amend the plan—but amendments reducing vested benefits were restricted. In 2004, the occupational disability benefit was amended to cut off benefits at early retirement age or December 31, 2006, whichever came first. The Sixth Circuit ruled that welfare benefits can be terminated at any time as long as termination is consistent with the terms of the plan. [*Price v. Board of Trustees of the Indiana Laborer's Pension Fund*, 707 F.3d 647 (6th Cir. 2013); see Bloomberg BNA, *Sixth Circuit Upholds Plan Amendment Retroactively Limiting Disability Benefits* (Feb. 19, 2013) (benefitslink.com)]

According to a 2006 Second Circuit decision, the standard for judicial review of an administrator's benefit determination is the SPD that was in effect when the plaintiff became disabled—and not the amended SPD in effect when the application was denied. (The later SPD granted discretion to the plan administrator; the earlier one did not.) The right to benefits vested when the plaintiff became disabled, so the second SPD could not apply. [*Gibbs v. Cigna*, 440 F.3d 571 (2d Cir. 2006)]

§ 20.07 CLAIMS PROCEDURES AND THE STANDARD OF REVIEW AFTER *GLENN*

[A] Generally

See Chapter 13 for a discussion of claims procedures, including the additional requirements imposed by PPACA, the health care reform statute. Also see Chapter 11 for discussion of which documents (e.g., guidelines used in analyzing claims) participants are entitled to receive on request.

[B] De Novo or Abuse of Discretion?

When a case gets to court, the question is whether the plan administrator's decisions will be reviewed "de novo" (the court examines all aspects of the case for the first time) or whether the administrator's decisions will be valid.

Before the Supreme Court's 2008 decision in *Metropolitan Life v. Glenn*, 554 U.S. 105 (2008), the courts of appeals developed a number of different standards for reviewing claims decisions. In many cases, benefit claimants asserted that courts should perform de novo review of benefit determinations because the decision was made by an insurer that had a conflict of interest because it both made the claims decision and paid the benefits, so extending more benefits would reduce its profitability. However, in many of these cases, the plan was drafted to give the plan administrator discretion to make decisions—which would make the standard of review whether the decision-maker acted arbitrarily and capriciously.

Glenn involved a claimant who received 24 months of disability benefits for heart disease. The plan administrator, MetLife, had discretionary authority. MetLife encouraged Glenn to apply for SSDI benefits, which she received. Then MetLife concluded that Glenn was capable of working, and terminated her benefits. The Supreme Court found that MetLife's conflict of interest was one factor in reviewing the decision, but all facts and circumstances must be considered. *Glenn* applied the same analysis whether the plan was self-administered by the employer or was administered by an insurance company that had a financial interest in the outcome of its determinations.

After *Glenn*, conflict of interest is a factor in the decision, but decisions are not automatically reviewed de novo if there was a conflict of interest. The Fourth Circuit ruled that before *Glenn*, it used a modified abuse of discretion standard that reduced the amount of deference accorded to decision-makers who had a conflict of interest. After *Glenn*, its new test is whether the decision to terminate disability benefits was reasonable and whether there was an abuse of discretion.

After reconsidering a 2003 ruling, the First Circuit joined the Third, Seventh, and Ninth Circuits and held that a policy provision requiring proof of disability "satisfactory to Sun Life" did not confer enough discretionary authority for the insurer's decisions to be reviewed deferentially. The First Circuit found that the disability plan was an ERISA plan because it was a component of a unified plan that gave employees unified plan communications, with the employer receiving unified billing statements from providers. The program did not qualify for the safe harbor for voluntary plans: it was fully funded by the employer, so the safe harbor for plans without employer contributions was inapplicable. The case was remanded because de novo review found the plaintiff's medical evidence adequate to demonstrate entitlement to disability benefits—but the insurer's surveillance showed her performing activities inconsistent with her claim. [*Gross v. Sun Life Assurance Co. of Canada*, 734 F.3d 1 (1st Cir. 2013); see Jacklyn Wille, *First Circuit Applies De Novo Judicial Review Despite Plan's 'Satisfactory to Us" Language*, Bloomberg BNA Pensions & Benefits Daily (Aug. 20, 2013) (benefitslink.com); the previous precedent is *Brigham v. Sun Life of Canada*, 317 F.3d 72 (1st Cir. 2003); Stephen D. Rosenberg, *A State of the Art ERISA Benefits Decision from the First Circuit*, Boston ERISA Law Blog (Aug. 26, 2013) (benefitslink.com)]

In a Fourth Circuit case, the LTD plan, administered by Prudential permitted benefit payments only if the claimant submitted proof of continuing disability satisfactory to Prudential. Like five other circuits (the First, Second, Third, Seventh, and Ninth), the Fourth Circuit held that this language is not an unambiguous grant of discretionary authority. Therefore, claims decisions were reviewed de novo. The Fourth Circuit found the "satisfactory to us" language inherently ambiguous because it could be construed as meaning only that the decision-maker had to be persuaded to pay the benefits. (Benefits for sleep disorder, fibromyalgia, dizziness, and dysautonomia were terminated when Prudential said that the plaintiff's documentation did not prove ongoing impairment.) [*Cosey v. Prudential Ins. Co. of Am.*, 735 F.3d 161 (4th Cir. 2013); see Jacklyn Wille, *Fourth Circuit: No Deferential Review Despite Plan's 'Satisfactory To Us' Language*, Bloomberg BNA Pension and Benefits Blog (Nov. 21, 2013) (benefitslink.com); D. Michael Reilly, *4th Circuit: Clearer Language Now Needed To Confer Discretion*, Lane Powell PC (Nov. 25, 2013), available at Lexology.com]

Spradley, a 37-year veteran at Owens-Illinois took early retirement at age 55 because of a disability. About nine months before his retirement, he submitted a claim stating that the Social Security Administration found him to be permanently and totally disabled as of March 1, 2008. The plan says that PTD (permanently and totally disabled) life insurance benefits are payable to a person who becomes permanently and totally disabled before age 65, files a claim within 12 months of leaving employment, and is unable to engage in significant gainful activities—or who is under 65 and receives SSDI. Spradley received a denial letter that referred only to health insurance, not the PTD life insurance he applied for. He appealed the denial, which was upheld on the grounds that health insurance is available only to active employees. He brought an ERISA suit. The defendant argued that PTD life insurance is available only for temporary disability. The district court ordered payment of benefits. The Tenth Circuit found that the denial was inappropriate (using the arbitrary and capricious standard), and the district court should have entered judgment for the plaintiff based on the record instead of remanding for further proceedings—which would only give the plan a chance to fabricate more excuses. [*Spradley v. Owens-Illinois Hourly Employees Welfare Benefit Plan*, 686 F.3d 1135 (10th Cir. 2012)]

Cigna helped an engineer apply for SSA disability benefits after he had multiple surgeries on one foot and ongoing, disabling pain. Cigna denied his LTD claim, asserting that the policy used a different definition of "disability" than the federal system. The Seventh Circuit rejected this argument, finding the two definitions functionally equivalent and attributing the claim denial to Cigna's conflict of interest. [*Raybourne v. Cigna,* 700 F.3d 1076 (7th Cir. 2012); see Scott J. Stitt, *The Seventh Circuit Concludes that SSA's Definition of Disability, and Cigna's Definition of Long-Term Disability, Is "Functionally Equivalent."* Arnlaw.com Blog (Apr. 3, 2013) (benefitslink.com)]

[C] The Treating Physician Rule

When the Social Security Administration decides whether an applicant is entitled to receive SSDI benefits, it uses the "treating physician" rule. In other words, the opinion of a physician who actually treats the claimant is given more weight than the opinion of a physician-reviewer who looks at the patient's medical file but doesn't actually examine the patient. There was a Circuit split as to whether this rule should be applied in the context of an ERISA plan.

The Supreme Court resolved the Circuit split through its May 2003 decision in *Black & Decker Disability Plan v. Nord*. [538 U.S. 822 (2003)] The Supreme Court ruled that the Social Security rule does not have to be followed in cases involving private ERISA plans rather than public benefits. According to the Supreme Court, neither the ERISA statute nor the Department of Labor's regulations demand any special deference for the opinion of the treating physician. Furthermore, in January 2005, the Sixth Circuit ruled that not only is the treating physician rule not mandatory, but an ERISA plan administrator is not bound by the Social Security Administration's determination that a person is totally and completely disabled to the extent that payment of SSDI benefits is justified. The court ruled that it was not arbitrary and capricious for the plan to base its conclusion that the plaintiff was not disabled on the opinions of an independent neurologist and psychiatrist who reviewed the plaintiff's medical records. [*Whitaker v. Hartford Life & Accident Ins. Co.*, 404 F.3d 947 (6th Cir. 2005)]

§ 20.08 APPEALS OF CLAIM DENIALS

The Ninth Circuit said that it was "illogical" and "implausible" to refuse to grant LTD payments to a Honda employee who was disabled by Chronic Fatigue Syndrome (CFS) and who qualified for Social Security disability payments. His claim was denied on the grounds that there were no objective physical findings substantiating his illness, although he submitted medical evidence of having an unusually severe case of CFS. The Ninth Circuit found an abuse of discretion: disregarding ample medical evidence and insisting on objective findings where there is no objective medical test available. [*Salomaa v. Honda*, 642 F.3d 666 (9th Cir. 2011); see Tim Hull, *Man with Controversial Illness Can Get Benefits*, Courthouse News Service (Mar. 10, 2011) (benefitslink.com)]

The Second Circuit held that subjective evidence must be weighed before rejecting a disability claim (in this case, based on tinnitus, hearing loss, headaches, and vertigo). The fact that evidence is subjective does not make it worthless. Furthermore, there is no accepted objective test for tinnitus, so the claimant could not have submitted objective evidence. [*Miles v. Principal Life Ins. Co.*, 720 F.3d 472 (2d Cir. 2013); see Mike Reilly, *Hear This: "Subjective Evidence" is Worth its Weight*, Lane Powell Boom! The ERISA Law Blog (July 3, 2013) (benefitslink.com)]

Eligibility determinations for an LTD plan were delegated to Reliance Standard Life Insurance by the employer, which was the plan's sponsor and administrator. The loss of the administrative file for a disability benefits claim is not necessarily fatal to review of decision terminating benefits. The plaintiff, Schorsch was not given plan documents or an SPD. In 1993, Schorsch was totally disabled by an auto accident. In 2006, Reliance requested an independent medical examination. Based in part on surveillance, Reliance determined that Schorsch could work a medium-duty job, and terminated her disability benefits. Schorsch's attorney sent a notice of intent to seek reconsideration, but did not submit a request for review. When Schorsch sued for resumption of the benefits, Reliance admitted that it had lost the administrative record of her claim. However, the Seventh Circuit held that Scorsch failed to exhaust her administrative remedies, and held that the insurer's errors were relevant only if Schorsch had reasonably relied on them when she did not seek review of the termination. The termination letter provided adequate notice of the reasons for the decision and how the review process worked. Because the employer was not the insurer's agent, the Seventh Circuit declined to penalize the employer for the loss of the documents. [*Schorsch v. Reliance Standard Life Ins. Co.*, 693 F.3d 734 (7th Cir. 2012); see Mike Reilly, *Failure to Exhaust Defense Trumps Missing Administrative Record*, Lane Powell BOOM: The ERISA Law Blog (Aug. 30, 2012) (benefitslink.com)]

The Sixth Circuit held that termination of LTD benefits was supported by substantial evidence. Guardian Life Insurance decided that a former CEO who had several operations for a herniated disk was able to return to work; was participating in a new venture; and, although he was not getting paid yet, had an employment agreement promising him a $115,000 salary. (His previous salary was $140,000.) The Sixth Circuit held that, to terminate LTD benefits, it is not necessary that the insured earn as much as before the disability, as long as he or she is able to perform the major duties of a consistent occupation. [*Schwalm v. Guardian Life Ins. Co. of Am.*, 626 F.3d 299 (6th Cir. 2010)]

LTD benefits were wrongfully denied when the claimant's doctors ordered indefinite restrictions forbidding the claimant to pinch with more than five pounds of force, kneel, or squat. The employer said that an indefinite restriction was not a permanent one, so she was not disabled. The Eighth Circuit ruled that the denial was an abuse of discretion, because in context, it was clear that the plaintiff had a permanent disability. It was not an abuse of discretion for the district court to award attorneys' fees to the plaintiff because this was not a close case—the employer obviously refused to give credence to the medical evidence. [*Rote v. Titan Tire Corp.*, 611 F.3d 960 (8th Cir. 2010)]

The Third Circuit ruled in mid-2009 that it was not arbitrary and capricious to consider ALS a pre-existing condition (defined by the policy as one for which medical treatment or advice was rendered within three months before the coverage date) for a policy with an effective date of coverage of July 1, 2006. ALS was not definitively diagnosed until March 27, 2007, the day before Doroshow applied for LTD benefits—but earlier, on May 16, 2006, Doroshow's doctor said that he had a motor neuron disease but the doctor did not think it was ALS. The Third Circuit found it reasonable to say that Doroshow received advice about ALS in the three months before the coverage date. In general, ruling out a condition is not advice or treatment for that condition, in this case an ALS diagnosis was under consideration. Doroshow had a family history of ALS, so he had a suspected condition without a confirmatory diagnosis, which can be considered a pre-existing condition. [*Doroshow v. Hartford Life & Accident Ins. Co.*, 574 F.3d 230 (3d Cir. 2009)]

The Ninth Circuit held that conflict of interest must be considered in determining whether an insurer abused the discretion it was granted under a discretionary clause. The plaintiff was rendered quadriplegic by an accident three months after starting a new job. His salary was $200,000, and he was guaranteed a $300,000 bonus for the first year if he performed as anticipated and had not quit or been terminated for cause. He sued when the employer's LTD plan calculated his benefits based on $200,000 in earnings (i.e., excluding the bonus). The Ninth Circuit, noting that the employer's HR department submitted a claim form describing the plaintiff's compensation as $500,000 (and the premiums were based on that level of compensation) remanded for consideration of whether it was an abuse of discretion to exclude the bonus from the benefit calculation. [*Stephan v. UNUM Life Ins. Co. of Am.*, 697 F.3d 917 (9th Cir. 2012)]

The Seventh Circuit said that it was not arbitrary and capricious to decide that an HIV-positive person could perform sedentary work despite his fatigue, neuropathy, and opportunistic infections. The plaintiff's viral load had decreased and four health professionals said that he could at least attempt sedentary work (although two health professionals disagreed). The plaintiff admitted that there were days when he was healthy enough to do a full day's work. The Seventh Circuit found that it was not irrational for the insurer to consider the effect of AIDS treatment and longer and healthier lifespans for HIV-positive persons. [*Jenkins v. Price Waterhouse LTD Plan*, 564 F.3d 856 (7th Cir. 2009)]

Truitt, a litigator, claimed disability (leg and foot pain) and started getting benefits in 2003. Benefits were discontinued in 2006 because of a surveillance video, two Independent Medical Exams, and a functional capacity assessment. Benefits were reinstated after Truitt appealed. Her ex-boyfriend gave Unum 600 pages of e-mails, documents, and photos showing Truitt working and performing recreational activities inconsistent with her disability claim. Unum used this evidence to terminate benefits again. Truitt sued, saying her computer was hacked and the e-mails should not have been used. Unum counterclaimed for refund of $1 million in benefits. The Fifth Circuit held that the burden of generating evidence is not solely on the plan administrator, and Unum didn't abuse its discretion by using the e-mails sent by the ex-boyfriend because it identified the evidence as supporting the benefit denial. The Fifth Circuit ruled that the e-mails were authentic and not tampered with and remanded for the district court to apply federal common law to reassess the reimbursement claim. [*Truitt v. Unum Life Ins. Co. of Am.*, 729 F.3d 497 (5th Cir. 2013); see Michael Reilly, *5th Circuit: Attorney's Disability Case "Does Not Have A Leg To Stand On" After Scorned Boyfriend Provides Emails*, Lane Powell PC (Sept. 11, 2013), available at Lexology.com]

The Ninth Circuit held that the statute of limitations for filing an ERISA claim for denial of protected benefits is four years (for contract claims) even if the insurance plan or ERISA itself does not have an explicit time limit. Withrow became permanently disabled in 1986 and was approved for disability benefits in 1987. In 1990, she began a series of inquiries about whether her benefit payment was correctly canceled; the insurer never replied. In 2003, Withrow filed an internal appeal with the insurer, seeking an increase. This request was denied early in 2004. Withrow sued the insurer for denial of ERISA benefits in February 2006. An ERISA claim accrues either at the point of benefit denial or when the claimant had reason to know the claim was denied, so Withdrow's claim was held to have accrued in 2004 when her attorney was informed that the claim was denied. [*Withrow v. Bache Halsey Stuart Shield Inc., Protection Plan,* 655 F.3d 1032 (9th Cir. 2011); see Thomas E. Donahue, Michael B. Horrow, Nichole D. Podgurski, Jason A. Cole, *California's 9th Circuit Rules Timing Critical for Filing ERISA Claims*, Donahue & Horrow LLP (undated) (benefitslink.com)]

A MetLife employee became unable to work because of chronic pain and depression in 2000. He received STD benefits and worked intermittently for several years. Long-term disability benefits began in March 2005. He believed that his original salary should have been used to calculate benefits, not the lower salary from a non-managerial job he took between periods of collecting benefits. He brought several suits, including two 2012 cases that the district court dismissed for untimeliness because there was a six-year statute of limitations (borrowed from Massachusetts breach of contract law) and the case involved a determination made in 2005. The plaintiff said that the statute of limitations re-started with each payment, but the First Circuit rejected this theory. Like the Second, Third, and Ninth Circuits, the First Circuit ruled that the cause of action to recover ERISA benefits starts to run as soon as the beneficiary learns that his or her claim has been rejected. Each payment does not start a new limitations period. [*Riley v. Metro. Life Ins. Co.,* 744 F.3d 241 (1st Cir. 2014)]

Heimeshoff, the Supreme Court case upholding a contractual three-year statute of limitations, is a disability case. Because ERISA has no statute of limitations, one must be borrowed; the Supreme Court held that the statute of limitations can be set by contract as long as the period is reasonable and does not conflict with another applicable statute of limitations. [*Heimeshoff v. Hartford Life & Accident Ins. Co.*, 134 S. Ct. 604 (2013)]

CHAPTER 21

INSURANCE FRINGE BENEFITS

§ 21.01 INTRODUCTION

In addition to plans in which insurance operates behind the scenes (health plans; pension plans funded by insurance contracts), some fringe benefit plans exist to provide insurance coverage to employees. This chapter covers life insurance and long-term care insurance (LTCI) fringe benefits.

§ 21.02 LIFE INSURANCE FRINGE BENEFITS

Life insurance is a very popular benefit. Not only do many employers offer it, but when it is available it is almost universally chosen. According to BLS' National Compensation Survey, in March 2013, 57% of workers had access to workplace life insurance benefits, and 55% participated—so the take-up rate was 97%. Higher-paid workers were more likely to have access. Workers in the highest-paid 25% had a 84% access rate and 83% participation rate, whereas workers in the lowest-paid quadrant had an access rate of 22% and a participation rate of 20%. Full-time workers were much more likely to have access to life insurance and to participate than part-time workers, as is true of nearly all benefits. [BLS Economic News Release, *Table 5. Life Insurance Benefits: Access, Participation, and Take-Up Rates*, <http://www.bls.gov/news.release/ebs2.t05.htm> (last accessed Mar. 24, 2014)]

Among workers with basic life insurance entitlement through work, only 5% had to contribute for the coverage. There were differences by region, type of industry, and whether the workers were union or non-union, but the differences were slight. [BLS, *Life Insurance Plans: Employee Contribution Requirements, Private Industry Workers, National Compensation Survey, March* 2013, <http://www.bls.gov/ncs/ebs/benefits/2013/ownership/private/table13a.htm> (last accessed Mar. 24, 2014)]

[A] Favorable Tax Treatment

The Internal Revenue Code authorizes several mechanisms under which employers can provide life insurance to employees at little or no income tax cost to the employees. (These mechanisms are distinct from the "key-person" insurance coverage that pays benefits to the corporation itself when it becomes necessary to replace a top executive or creative person.) The basic rule is that, if the employer pays the premiums and the insurance proceeds go to the beneficiary designated by the employee, the employee will have taxable income and the employer will be able to deduct the cost of providing the insurance. (The employer gets a deduction only for "ordinary and necessary business expenses.") However, the Code also provides certain relief measures that limit or eliminate the tax cost of these fringe benefits.

In mid-2005, the IRS issued T.D. 9223 to forbid abusive transactions involving "springing value" life insurance policies transferred to employees. The transactions are abusive because the purpose is to have an employee who has received a policy from a § 412(i) plan taxed at the cash surrender value of the policy, which is low. T.D. 9223 makes the employee taxable on the full fair market value (FMV) of the transferred life insurance contract. [*Final Regulations: Value of Life Insurance Contracts When Distributed from a Qualified Retirement Plan*, 2005-39 I.R.B. 591 (Aug. 26, 2005); 2004 Proposed Regulations were published at 69 Fed. Reg. 7384; see also Rev. Proc. 2004-16, 2004-10 I.R.B. 559, and Rev. Rul. 2004-20, 2004-10 I.R.B. 546]

An individual insurance contract plan is exempt from the minimum funding requirement of I.R.C. § 412 if it satisfies six requirements:

1. It is funded exclusively by the purchase of individual annuity and/or insurance contracts from a licensed life insurance company, although purchases can be made either directly by the employer or through a trust or custodial account.
2. The contract provides for level premium payments, either annual or more frequent.
3. The benefits under the plan equal benefits provided under each contract at the plan's Normal Retirement Age, guaranteed by the carrier to the extent premiums have been paid.
4. The premiums payable for the current and all previous plan years were paid before lapse (or the contract is reinstated).
5. There has never been a security interest at any time during the plan year affecting rights under the contract (although a security interest created after the distribution of the contract to the participant is permissible).
6. There are no policy loans outstanding at any time during the plan year prior to distribution of the policy.

The employer can deduct contributions used to pay premiums on the insurance contract if the plan holds the contract until the employee's death or until the contract is distributed or sold to the employee (e.g., at retirement).

The IRS targets plans involving specially designed life insurance policies whose cash surrender value is temporarily set far lower than the premiums paid. Such policies are distributed or sold to employees at the artificial cash surrender value; the "springing" feature then returns the value of the policy to something more commercially realistic.

Announcement 2005-80, 2005-46 I.R.B. 967, lists § 412(i) defined benefit plans and 20 other tax-saving devices that are deemed improper by the IRS. The § 412(i) programs targeted by the IRS include plans in which the life insurance death benefits are greater than the benefits specified in the plan documents, or those in which the rights of plan participants to buy life insurance contracts under the plan are extremely unequal.

[B] Employee-Owned, Employer-Paid Insurance

It is common for employers to pay the premiums for life insurance owned by the employees covered by the plan. Treas. Reg. § 1.1035-1 gives the employer an income tax deduction for the cost of the plan, provided that the employer is not the beneficiary, and also limited by the I.R.C. § 162 "ordinary and necessary" rule.

The premiums that the employer pays are taxable income for the employee, but the insurance proceeds are not taxable income for the beneficiary who receives them. [See I.R.C. § 101] If the employee borrows against the policy, interest on the loan (unlike most forms of personal interest) is deductible.

> ■ **TIP:** Employer-pay life insurance plans are not subject to nondiscrimination requirements, so it is perfectly legitimate for the employer to furnish insurance to the employees the employer particularly wants to motivate, without making the plan available to the whole workforce.

Most group life insurance policies include a "portability" (also known as "right of conversion") provision under which employees can convert their employment-related coverage to an individual policy. Employers have a responsibility to tell employees about the right to convert group to individual life insurance at termination of employment, and the right to apply for waiver of premium if the employees become disabled or are absent from work. Failure to give the required information can subject the employer to liability. The employer should inform the departing employee to contact the insurer as soon as possible, because the group plan may impose a deadline for conversion and submission of the first individual premium payment. [Ford & Harrison Practical Insights: *Liability for Termination of Group Life Insurance Coverage* (October 2009) (benefitslink.com)]

The Western District of Wisconsin held that the SPD for a group life insurance plan adequately explained, in plain language, the right to accelerate life insurance benefits (to collect benefits while the insured person is still alive but severely ill). Therefore, the employer did not violate its fiduciary duty even though it did not remind the employee's wife (who became his surviving spouse) of the availability of the accelerated benefits option. [*Pfeil v. Edward Kraemer & Sons Inc.*, No. 09-cv-wmc (W.D. Wis. June 1, 2010); see Rebecca Moore, *Failure to Mention Benefit Option Explained in SPD No Fiduciary Breach*, plansponsor.com (June 8, 2010)]

[C] Company-Owned Life Insurance (COLI)

Under this variation, the policies are owned by the company itself, and can be used to finance death benefits paid under the employer's benefit plans. Cash-value insurance can be used to finance retirement benefits. The beneficiary of the plan, or the estate of the deceased employee, does have income under I.R.C. § 101(a), because the death benefits are deemed to be paid directly by the employer and not by an insurer.

When the employer owns the COLI policy and uses it only to fund the death benefit, the employee does not have taxable income during his or her life from either the policy's cash surrender value or the premium payments that the employer makes—as long as the employee's beneficiary is only an unsecured creditor with respect to the proceeds of the policy.

Usually, the corporation is not entitled to a deduction for the premiums it pays for COLI, because of the employer's interest as a beneficiary. However, there is an exception to this rule for premiums paid for certain annuity contracts used in connection with COLI plans.

For COLI policies issued after August 17, 2006, the PPA enacts a new Code § 101(j). In general, employers will have income if they receive insurance proceeds on the lives of employees and former employees (minus the costs, such as premiums, that the employer paid for the policy). Insurance proceeds are not taxable if the employer satisfied notice and consent requirements:

- Before the policy was issued, the employer gave written notice to the potential insured of the intention to purchase insurance on the employee's life, and the maximum size of policy that could be purchased.
- The potential insured consents in writing to the coverage (including the possibility that it will continue after the person ceases to be employed).
- The employer discloses that the proceeds of the policy will go to the employer, not the employee's family.

If these disclosure and consent requirements are satisfied, then the employer can exclude the policy proceeds from gross income as long as the insured was employed by the company at any time during the 12 months before his or her death, or the insured was a director or HCE when the policy was issued. Nor does the employer have taxable income to the extent that policy proceeds are paid to the insured's family or to the beneficiary (including a trust) designated by the employee. Insurance proceeds used to buy out the interest of the decedent's family in the business are also excluded from the employer company's income. In other words, proceeds of "key-person" policies will generally be excluded. Post-PPA COLI ownership imposes a duty of filing information returns about the policy. [Bond, Schoeneck & King PLLC Tax Law Information Memo, *Tax Law*

Change Affects Taxation of Proceeds from Employer-Owned Life Insurance (October 2006) <http://www.bsk.com>]

See 72 Fed. Reg. 63838 (Nov. 13, 2007) for IRS regulations implementing the PPA's provisions about employer-owned life insurance. For tax years ending on or after November 14, 2007, a policyholder owning employer-owned life insurance contracts issued after August 17, 2006 must attach Form 8925 to the income tax return. The form discloses the number of employees covered by employer-provided life insurance contracts; whether each one consented in writing, in advance, to be insured and for coverage to continue after employment ends. [Sutherland Asbill & Brennan LLP, *Legal Alert: IRS Issues Forms to Report Employer-Owned Life Insurance* (Feb. 7, 2008)]

See also Final Regulations under Code § 6039I (COLI reporting): T.D. 9431, 2008-41 I.R.B. 1235. When an employee dies, the employer can recover tax-free only the portion of the death benefits equal to the premiums paid by the employer. However, for certain highly compensated employees, where the employer notifies the insured and obtains his or her consent, death benefits paid to a family member or trust or used to buy an equity interest in the employer company are tax-free: Notice 2009-48, 2009-24 I.R.B. 1085.

One factor impelling Congress to regulate COLI was the belief that COLI carried the potential for abuse. In 2002 and 2003, a series of articles in the *Wall St. J.* severely criticized COLI (calling it "janitor insurance" or "dead peasant insurance"), because in some instances, a corporation collects significant insurance benefits on the lives of low-paid workers who had little or no personal or company-provided insurance and whose families therefore were left poorly provided for. Insurance benefiting the company when nonkey employees die was criticized as unfair, because the insurance is sometimes maintained on retirees and other ex-employees, so companies benefit by the death of persons who are no longer employees at all, much less key employees. (Initially, corporations were only deemed to have an insurable interest in the lives of key employees, but this rule was changed in the 1980s.)

This type of insurance can also be used by corporations for financial manipulation. Corporations can deduct the insurance premiums they pay for this purpose; and, because they are insurance policies, the buildup of cash value is not taxed, and increase in cash value can be used to improve the financial results on the company's books. The insurance proceeds are not taxable income, so the company can get a windfall if someone dies after a short period of employment. The insurance can also be used as collateral for loans, or policy loans can be taken against the insurance. [Theo Francis, *Workers' Lives: Best Tax Break?*, Wall St. J., Feb. 19, 2003, at C1; Ellen E. Schultz and Theo Francis, *Death Benefit: How Corporations Built Finance Tool Out of Life Insurance*, Wall St. J., Dec. 30, 2002, at A1; Theo Francis and Ellen E. Schultz, *Tax Advantages of Life Insurance Help Lift Income*, Wall St. J., Dec. 30, 2002, at A8]

[D] Section 79 (Group-Term Life)

Internal Revenue Code § 79 allows an employer to establish a written, nondiscriminatory plan to provide term life insurance policies to a group of employees. (Term life insurance is pure insurance, with no cash value.) Employees can receive up to $50,000 worth of coverage under the plan with no tax consequences to them. But if the employer provides coverage over $50,000, the employee does have taxable income. The calculation is based on an official IRS table. The excess coverage is subject to FICA tax but not FUTA tax or income tax withholding. [I.R.C. § 3121(a)(2)]

The table was revised effective July 1, 1999. [See 64 Fed. Reg. 29788 (June 3, 1999)] At press time in 2014, this table was still current, according to the IRS Website.

Employee's Age	*Prior Law*	*Revised Rates*
Up to 25	.08	.05
25–29	.08	.06
30–34	.09	.08
35–39	.11	.09
40–44	.17	.10
45–49	.29	.15
50–54	.48	.23
55–59	.75	.43
60–64	1.17	.66
65–70	2.10	1.27
>70	3.76	2.06

A Section 79 plan must either be available to all employees, or to groups of employees defined in a way that does not allow selection of employees based on individual characteristics. So the plan can condition eligibility on factors related to age or employment, but not on the amount of the corporation's stock that the person owns. Nor can the amount of coverage be based on individual factors (although it can be proportionate to compensation). As a general rule, Section 79 plans must cover at least 10 employees.

To satisfy the nondiscrimination test, the plan must benefit at least 70% of the sponsoring company's employees, and not more than 15% of the participants may be key employees. If the group-term life insurance plan is part of a cafeteria plan, it must also satisfy the I.R.C. § 125 rules. If the plan fails the nondiscrimination test, then highly compensated employees will have to include the full cost of coverage (not just the coverage over and above $50,000) in income.

The IRS' mid-2007 cafeteria plan proposals include a simplified rule for calculating the cost of group-term life insurance. There is a safe harbor for premium-only cafeteria plans that do not discriminate as to eligibility. The proposal also includes a simplified rule for calculating the cost of group-term life insurance: the amount taxable to the employee is based entirely on the cost of any excess coverage under Table I of the § 79 regulations. [72 Fed. Reg. 43938 (Aug. 6, 2007)]

The Moving Ahead for Progress in the 21st Century Act (MAP-21; Pub. L. No. 112-141) allows sponsors of over-funded defined benefit pension plans to use Code § 401(h) to transfer funds from the pension plan to an account to provide retiree benefits: either health benefits or group-term life insurance (generally limited to $50,000 per person). Section 401(h) was scheduled to expire on December 31, 2013, but MAP-21 not only extended its applicability until December 31, 2021 but also added group-term life to health benefits as a possible 401(h) benefit. The life insurance assets must be kept in a separate account within the 401(h) plan, segregated both from the general assets of the defined benefit plan and the retiree health benefit account.

[E] Split Dollar

A split dollar plan is a benefit arrangement that divides ownership, and possibly premium payments, between an employer and an employee. Each year the employer makes a contribution equal to the policy's increase in cash value for the year. Under the "endorsement method," the employer owns the policy. The policy is endorsed to allocate cash value and death benefit between employer and employee. Under the "collateral assignment" method, either the employee or a third party owns the policy and then assigns it to the employer. At the employee's death, the employer receives either the cash value of the policy or an amount representing the premiums paid; the rest of the benefits go to the employee's designated beneficiary. If the plan is an "equity split dollar plan," the employer is entitled to repayment of the premiums it paid, while the rest of the proceeds go to the designated beneficiary.

Split dollar plans became popular as a way to enhance the compensation of top executives without angering the shareholders by disclosing the full value of the compensation package, and while giving executives the security of benefits backed by the insurer's resources. [For historical perspective on split dollar, see, e.g., Theo Francis and Ellen E. Schultz, *Insurers Move to Protect Executive Policy*, Wall St. J., Dec. 30, 2002, at C1]

However, beginning in 2001, the IRS launched an attack on split dollar as a compensation mechanism. Another factor was the Sarbanes-Oxley Act's ban on personal loans to the directors and officers of public corporations, a provision that brought new sales of corporate split dollar policies to a halt because of uncertainties as to whether split dollar arrangements would be treated as interest-free loans to executives.

Notice 2007-34, 2007-17 I.R.B. 996, explains the interface between split-dollar insurance and non-qualified plans. Insurance arrangements that provide nothing but death benefits, or that generate amounts that are included in income, are exempt from taxation under § 409A. The cost of current life insurance protection is excluded from § 409A, even if there are additional economic benefits under the arrangement. But policy cash value that is available to the employee, and is payable in a year after the year of service is likely to be deferred compensation under § 409A. Split-dollar loans generally do not give rise to § 409A deferred compensation—unless, for example, loan amounts are waived, cancelled, or forgiven. Notice 2009-48, 2009-24 I.R.B. includes split-dollar contracts in the definition of employer-owned life insurance subject to Code § 60391. [See Nevin E. Adams, *IRS Sets Out Limits for Employer-Owned Life Insurance Expense*, plansponsor.com (May 26, 2009)]

[F] Case Law on Life Insurance Fringe Benefits

Life insurance plans, like other employee benefit plans, often give rise to disputes about benefit eligibility and whether a survivor beneficiary has been properly designated.

Spradley, a 37-year veteran at Owens-Illinois, took early retirement at age 55 because of a disability. About nine months before his retirement, he submitted a claim stating that the Social Security Administration found him to be permanently and totally disabled as of March 1, 2008. Under the plan, PTD life insurance benefits are payable to persons who are unable to engage in substantial gainful activities because of a permanent and total disability commencing before age 65, and who file a claim within 12 months of leaving employment—or who are under 65 and receive SSDI. Spradley received a denial letter that referred only to health insurance, not the PTD life insurance he applied for. He appealed the denial, which was upheld on the grounds that health insurance is available only to active employees. He brought an ERISA suit. The defendant argued that PTD life insurance is available only for temporary disability. The district court ordered payment of benefits. On appeal, the question was whether the plan administrator's denial was arbitrary and capricious. The Tenth Circuit found that the denial was inappropriate, and the district court should have entered judgment for the plaintiff based on the record instead of remanding for further proceedings—which would only give the plan a chance to fabricate more excuses. [*Spradley v. Owens-Illinois Hourly Emps. Welfare Benefit Plan*, 686 F.3d 1135 (10th Cir. 2012)]

The Northern District of Ohio held that a divorce decree making the employee's child the sole beneficiary of a life insurance policy is a QDRO. The district court noted that welfare benefit plans can have QDROs: see 29 U.S.C. § 1144(b)(7), and life insurance plans are welfare benefit plans. (The employee remarried, then designated his second wife as 100% beneficiary of his life insurance, despite the divorce decree.) [*Metropolitan Life Ins. Co. v. Darkow*, No. 5:09CV02482, 2010 U.S. Dist. LEXIS 77187 (N.D. Ohio July 30, 2010); see Rebecca Moore, *Divorce Decree Naming Child as Life Insurance Beneficiary Is a QDRO*, plansponsor.com (Aug. 4, 2010)]

The Sixth Circuit held that an insurer is not obligated to provide life insurance benefits that are contrary to state law (in this case, portable term insurance, which was illegal in Michigan), so the District Court was correct to dismiss a surviving spouse's claim. When the decedent resigned from his job, he was given the right to convert the life insurance under an employee welfare plan to a group policy—contingent upon whether he lived in a state that approved such a continuation. When the widow's claim for death benefits that would have been payable if the policy had been converted was denied, she sued for the life insurance benefits and statutory penalties for failure to provide plan documents. [*Morrison v. Marsh & McLennan*, 439 F.3d 295 (6th Cir. 2006)]

In a 2012 Fourth Circuit case, a life insurance/accidental death & disability plan was offered, with coverage for employees' children. The plaintiff, McCravy, filed a claim after her daughter died. The claim was denied, on the grounds that the daughter was no longer eligible for coverage after she reached age 19—but the plan continued to accept premiums for the coverage. The Fourth Circuit ruled that McCravy was entitled not only to a return of the premiums but also to a surcharge, as equitable relief under ERISA § 502(a)(3). [*McCravy v. MetLife,* 690 F.3d 176 (4th Cir. 2012); see Rebecca Moore, *4th Circuit Uses High Court Decision to Allow for Surcharge*, plansponsor.com (July 16, 2012)]

§ 21.03 LONG-TERM CARE INSURANCE PLANS

Long-term care insurance (LTCI) is private insurance, sold by life and health insurers, that covers the cost of home and institutional care for the frail elderly and disabled. There is an increasing trend for employers to offer group long-term care insurance plans as an employee benefit—and to permit employees not only to purchase coverage for themselves and their spouses, but for their parents. Individual coverage for senior citizens can be difficult to find, and is often expensive when it is available.

LTCI and benefits services provider EM-Power Services says that reasons for employers to offer workplace LTCI include:

- Reductions in health costs caused by caregiver stress;
- Better productivity, because caregivers miss less work;
- Helping employees avert family financial problems—the high cost of long-term care; depletes the savings even of affluent families;

- An LTCI program can be provided at little or no cost to the employer;
- The providers of LTCI can educate employees about elder care issues.

[Amanda McGrory, *5 Reasons To Offer LTCI In 2012*, Benefits Pro (Jan. 23, 2012) (benefitslink.com)]

The American Association of Long Term Care Insurance reported that in 2013, the industry paid close to $7.5 billion in claims to 273,000 employees. Almost all policies are now individual; although at one time, employer-sponsored plans made up about a third of the LTCI market, it has declined to the point that Genworth is the only company continuing to focus on the employer-sponsored LTCI market. Genworth covers about 270,000 federal employees, as well as employees of CalPERS. Transamerica Life also sells group policies. [Jill Cornfield, *Will Employers Respond to Long-Term Care Concerns?*, plansponsor.com (Feb. 6, 2014)]

Certain kinds of LTCI are tax-favored: for policies that satisfy federally prescribed criteria, LTCI premiums are tax-deductible (within limits), and a certain amount of benefits can be received under the policy even if the insured person has no taxable income. (If the policy is an indemnity policy that pays the full cost of care, then the entire amount is tax-free—but indemnity policies are rare.) The cost figures for this purpose are adjusted every year.

For 2014, the potentially deductible long-term care insurance premium is limited to $370 (person under 40), $700 (ages 40–50), $1,400 (ages 50–60), $3,720 (60–70), and $4,660 (over 70). The periodic payment that can be received under a long-term care insurance policy is $330. [Rev. Proc. 2013-35, 2013-47 I.R.B. 537]

Starting in 2013, fewer taxpayers will be able to claim medical expense deductions, because even qualified medical expenses are deductible only to the extent that they exceed 10% of Adjusted Gross Income (AGI). Previously, qualified expenses over 7.5% of AGI were deductible. Senior citizens, who usually have higher medical expenses than younger people, get a relief provision: the 10% limit does not apply to persons aged 65 or over until 2017.

CHAPTER 22

OTHER FRINGE BENEFITS

§ 22.01 INTRODUCTION

This book has already dealt with issues of setting and administering current compensation (pay planning), deferred compensation (pension planning), and the provision of several of the major types of fringe benefits: health plans, disability coverage, and life insurance plans.

This chapter traces their tax, ERISA, and state-law consequences. The availability of benefits tends to fluctuate based on employers' needs: when employees are hard to recruit, benefits often become more generous—especially if employers can put together a package of benefits that are low or moderate in cost, but highly valued by employees. However, the economic decline beginning in 2008 not only created something of a buyer's market for employment, but also reduced the amount of funds many corporations had available for benefits and other compensation.

For tax purposes, the most relevant sections include I.R.C. § 162 (allowing a deduction for all of the employer's ordinary and necessary business expenses, including the employer's contributions to unfunded welfare benefit plans) and I.R.C. §§ 419 and 419A, which set limits on the deductions.

In general, employers will be able to deduct direct payments of benefits or expenses. Employers can make contributions that bear a reasonable actuarial relationship to the amounts that will be needed to pay benefits in the future. In some circumstances, a statutory safe harbor allows deductible contributions.

If a funded welfare plan earns income (e.g., from investments), that income will probably be taxed to the employer that maintains the plan. Unrelated business taxable income (UBTI) earned by the plan will almost certainly be taxed to the employer. [See Chapter 1, §§ 1.08, 1.12 for a discussion of some of the issues of determining who is an "employee" who is or might be eligible for plan participation]

The American Taxpayer Relief Act, Pub. L. No. 112-40 (ATRA; popularly known as the "fiscal cliff" bill) does not provide guidance about supplemental withholding so employers should continue using the optional 25% supplemental withholding rate on supplemental wages up to $1 million. This legislation extends the exclusion of up to $5,250 per year in education assistance from the recipient's gross income after its scheduled expiration date in 2012. The exclusion has been made permanent. ATRA also makes favorable tax treatment of employer assistance with adoption costs permanent. [Baker McKenzie Executive Compensation & Employee Benefits, *New Tax Rates in Effect for 2013* (Jan. 3, 2013) (benefitslink.com)]

For 2013, the maximum adoption credit and tax exclusion amount is $12,970 per child; eligibility phases down starting at $194,580, ending at $234,580. For 2014, the corresponding amounts are $13,190 credit/tax exclusion and phase-out between $197,880 and $237,880. Form 8839 can now be e-filed;

previously, it had to be filed on paper. Until 2012, the credit was refundable. For 2013, taxpayers can have credit carryforwards from 2012, or to 2014. Married taxpayers who file separate returns can claim an adoption credit carryforward if they filed a joint return in the year the adoption expenses first became allowable. [EBIA Weekly, *IRS Releases 2013 Form 8839 (Qualified Adoption Expenses) and Instructions* (Jan. 2, 2014) (benefitslink.com)]

§ 22.02 STOCK OPTIONS

[A] Generally

Stock options give employees (either a broad base of employees, or top executives only) the right to purchase stock in the employer corporation at a particular price at a stated time. The intention is that the exercise price will be far below the market value of the shares. However, under current conditions, many options are "underwater" (see § 22.02[G])—that is, they are almost certain not to be exercised, because the holder of the option would have to pay far more than the market price to exercise the option.

For tax purposes, stock options are divided into statutory and non-statutory options. Statutory options are granted as part of an employee stock purchase plan or incentive stock option program; all other options are non-statutory. The distinction is significant because the two types of options are taxed differently. The IRS says that options granted under an Employee Stock Ownership Plan (ESOP) or an Incentive Stock Option (ISO) plan will generally be statutory options, whereas other options are non-statutory. A person receiving a grant of statutory options generally does not have income either at the time of the grant or when the option is exercised, although exercise of an ISO may be subject to Alternative Minimum Tax. See the instructions for Form 6251.

But when the stock obtained via the option is sold, the taxpayer's income or loss will be treated as a capital gain or capital loss (depending on whether the stock was sold for more or less than the option price). If the stock is sold before the holding period expires, then the income from the sale will be ordinary income. The employer must issue Form 3921 when an ISO is exercised, to give the employee the information needed to determine if any tax is payable because of an ISO-related transaction. The employer must issue Form 3922 when an employee sells or otherwise transfers stock acquired via an ESOP option.

For non-statutory options, the primary tax question is whether the fair market value of the option can be readily determined (e.g., if it is actively traded on an established market.) The IRS says that most non-statutory options do not have a readily determined fair market value, so granting the option is not a taxable event—but the fair market value of the stock minus the amount paid for it constitutes taxable income when the option is exercised. The employee will have income or loss (generally capital rather than ordinary) on selling the stock obtained under the option. [IRS Topic 427, *Stock Options*, <http://www.irs.gov/taxtopics/tc427.html> (last updated Feb. 27, 2014). See IRS Publication 525, *Taxable and Nontaxable Income*, for guidance on classifying options.]

For practical and tax reasons, the employer will probably want to impose some limitations on the options. A typical restriction is the employee's obligation to put (resell) the stock back to the corporation on termination of employment. An arrangement like this includes a method of calculating the put price (e.g., book value or a set P/E ratio).

A stock bonus plan is very similar to a profit-sharing plan from both the labor law and tax perspectives. However, distributions are generally made in the employer's common stock rather than in cash. Employees must be given put options obligating the employer to repurchase shares of stock that are not readily tradeable on an established market.

An Employee Stock Ownership Plan (ESOP) is a stock bonus plan or a plan combining stock bonus and money-purchase features. ESOPs invest primarily in the employer's common stock. The Internal Revenue Code contains additional rules for leveraged ESOPs that borrow the funds used to purchase the stock. ESOPs are often adopted as a defense against hostile takeovers of the issuing corporation. Furthermore, because ESOPs are designed to invest in employer stock, fiduciaries of such plans are not vulnerable to "stock-drop" suits that are common in 401(k) plans when the value of the employer's stock has declined, and plan participants charge that fiduciaries should have removed the stock from the list of available plan investments, or at least diminished its importance.

Usually, an ESOP works by issuing options allowing participating employees to purchase employer stock. The employee makes an election to have a particular amount or a percentage of after-tax wages deducted from pay and accumulated. After the regular purchase period ends, the option is exercised and the shares are purchased at the option price. If the conditions under the Code are satisfied, the employee does not have income—and the employer does not have a compensation deduction—at the time the shares are acquired. The employee must be employed at the time of the grant, and up to three months before the exercise, and the employee must hold the shares for one year from the transfer of the shares, or two years from the grant of the option, whichever is later. (This is also true of ISOs.)

Under § 423 final regulations effective January 1, 2010, stock acquired under an Employee Stock Purchase Plan (ESPP) option receives favorable treatment if the statutory requirements are satisfied. Section 423 forbids employees to acquire shares at a rate exceeding $25,000 in fair market value of stock for each calendar year in which an option remains outstanding and exercisable, calculated the same way as the $100,000 limitation on ISOs.

The employee is not taxed (but the employer does not receive a deduction) when the option is exercised, if the purchase price is at least 85% of the FMV of the stock when the option was granted or when it is exercised (whichever is less); the plan and the offering satisfy the § 423 requirements; and the employee holds the stock for at least two years from grant and one year from exercise of the option. For nonqualified options, the employee has ordinary income at the time of exercise, equal to any excess of fair market value over the exercise price.

An employer can make multiple, successive, or overlapping offerings, with different option terms. If an offering under an ESPP fails to satisfy the § 423 requirements, stock purchased in that offering does not receive favorable tax treatment, but it does not disqualify other offerings that comply with the rules. Most ESPPs accumulate employees' contributions in an unfunded account that is used to buy the stock at a set price on a set date.

The plan, including the maximum number of shares available, must be approved by stockholders within 12 months before or after the adoption date of the plan. The regulations clarify some questions about which company's shareholders must approve the plan in a mergers and acquisitions context. Other than the four statutory exceptions, options must be granted to all employees of any corporation whose employees receive any options. Up to $25,000 worth of stock can be optioned for each year the option is outstanding, whether or not the option is exercisable. The exercise price must be at least 85% of the FMV at the time of grant or exercise.

An option is considered granted only when the maximum number of shares that can be purchased under the option is determinable. If the plan uses an open formula, where the number of shares depends on the share price and accumulation account at the date of exercise, the option is only considered granted when it is exercised—unless the overall maximum number of shares is stated from the outset. The plan must provide that options can be granted only to employees, not independent contractors, and anyone who owns 5% or more of the company's stock must not receive options under the plan. The plan cannot allow for redemption more than 27 months from the date of the grant (or five years, if the option price is at least 85% of the FMV at the date of exercise).

If the exercise price of options is not determinable on the grant date—for example, if it is based on the fair market value on a later date—then the participant's tax liability when the shares are sold may depend on the exercise price per share, determined as if the option had been exercised on the grant date. Therefore, Form 3922 requires the company to report information for this calculation.

Form 3921 (ISOs) reports:

- Grant and exercise date of the ISO;
- Exercise price per share;
- FMV of a share on the exercise date;
- Number of shares transferred in exercise of the ISO.

Form 3922 (ESOP shares) reports:

- Grant and exercise date of the option;

- FMV of a share on the grant date and exercise date;
- The price paid per share on the exercise date;
- Number of shares to which title was transferred;
- Date of the first transfer of title;
- (If the exercise price was not fixed or determinable on the grant date) Exercise price per share, calculated as if the option had been exercised on the grant date.

An option issuer's failure to make a timely Form 3921 or 3922 filing is penalized by up to $50 per form (capped at $250,000 per year). Failure to give employees forms relating to their options is penalized by $50 per form, up to a maximum of $100,000 per year. Electronic filing is mandatory if the employer files 250 or more forms. [Fred Schneyer, *Employee Stock Reporting Deadlines Approaching*, plansponsor.com (Nov. 19, 2010); Vorys, Sater, Seymour and Pease LLP Client Alert, *Reminder—Reporting Required for Exercise of ISOs, ESPP Options* (Nov. 18, 2010) (benefitslink.com)]

Stock appreciation rights (SARs) are really a form of cash compensation. The grantee of SARs gets money from the corporation, based on the price of the company stock. If, for instance, a corporate Vice President has SARs for 1,000 shares, the corporation will pay him or her the difference between the FMV of those shares at the time of exercise and the FMV at the time of grant. SARs are not usually issued by themselves, but to accompany stock options. A restricted stock plan grants stock outright, although with restrictions that defer taxation until the restrictions lapse. Phantom stock plans entitle the plan participant to receive cash and/or stock equal to the value of a hypothetical award of shares, although the participants do not actually receive ownership of the shares, only compensation equal to their value. [Sverre Roang, *Executive Compensation: Besides Stock Options, What Else Is There?*, Wisconsin Technology News (Apr. 2, 2008), <http://wistechnology.com/articles/4658> (accessed Apr. 8, 2014)]

A public company must satisfy the requirements under Code § 162(m) for restricted stock and restricted stock units (RSUs) to be fully deductible. Under § 162(m), the general rule is that a public company is limited to a $1 million compensation deduction apiece for its CEO and four other highest compensated officers. But there is an exception: the $1 million limit does not apply to qualified performance-based compensation that is only paid if the payee meets at least one objective performance goal that was set in advance. The performance-based compensation must have been ordered either by the company's board or a compensation committee consisting of outside directors and the terms of the plan are disclosed to, and approved by, the shareholders in advance. In mid-2012, the IRS issued guidance on whether dividends on restricted stock and the equivalent on RSUs must satisfy the § 162(m) requirements separately to be treated as fully deductible performance-based compensation: Rev. Rul. 2012-19, 2012-28 I.R.B. 16.

Restricted stock is company stock that is released based on a vesting schedule, whereas RSUs are a right to get vested stock in the future. Usually, restricted stock carries voting rights but RSUs do not. Some companies make "dividend equivalent" payments on RSUs: cash payments equivalent to the dividends on the restricted stock for the period between the grant and the vesting date. Rev. Rul. 2012-19 says that to qualify for exemption from the $1 million exemption, the dividends or dividend equivalents can only be payable if the payee meets performance goals. However, the performance goals for this purpose do not have to be the same ones for granting the underlying restricted stock or RSUs.

Public corporations should not only review their stock compensation plans for compliance, they should check the tax consequences of other documents, such as severance plans and golden parachutes, involving employees who receive grants of restricted stock and/or RSUs. [Buck Consultants FYI, *IRS Clarifies Treatment of Performance-Based Restricted Stock and Restricted Stock Units* (Aug. 8, 2012) (benefitslink.com)]

As long as stock options are issued "at the money" rather than at a discount, they are not subject to Code § 409A (the tax provisions dealing with certain non-qualified plans).

Nor does I.R.C. § 409A apply to stock appreciation rights (SARs) that are issued by a public company if the rights are settled in employer stock; they are not discounted, and therefore do not have the effect of deferring compensation.

A junior stock plan is another motivational device. Executives are given the right to buy junior stock (stock in the employer corporation with reduced dividend rights and voting powers). Owners of junior stock can convert it to ordinary common stock by achieving specified performance goals.

In 2011, the Supreme Court of Texas held that it is lawful for an employer to require an employee to give a covenant not to compete in exchange for letting the employee exercise stock options—as long as the noncompete agreement is reasonable in time, geographic area, and scope of activity, whether or not the employee had access to confidential information. The state Supreme Court said that stock options that are reasonably related to goodwill or other protectable interests such as confidential information and trade secrets create the necessary connection between the noncompete clause and the business interests. In this case, the stock options were ancillary to the protection of goodwill, so the agreement could be legitimate. The case was remanded to the trial court to determine the reasonableness of the agreement. [*Marsh USA Inc. v. Cook*, 354 S.W.3d 764 (Tex. 2011)]

The Idaho Supreme Court ruled that stock options are not wages under state law—so it was not a violation of state law to fire an employee for intending to exercise his stock options. The court defined "wages" under state law to mean compensation for services rendered, determined on the basis of time, task, piecework, or commissions—categories that do not include stock options. Therefore, firing someone for reasons related to stock option exercise did not violate the public policy exception to employment at will, because "wages" meant only monetary compensation paid on a periodic basis, not non-monetary compensation paid in stock. [*Paolini v. Albertson's Inc.*, 143 Idaho 547 (2006); see Adrien Martin, *Idaho Court Rules Stock Options Are Not Wages*, plansponsor.com (Jan. 30, 2007)]

The California Supreme Court held that Citigroup's voluntary employee compensation plan, allowing employees to elect to take some of their compensation in reduced-price shares of restricted stock, did not violate the California Labor Code's requirement of prompt payment of "earned wages" when an employee quits or is fired. Incentive compensation is not like vacation pay (compensation for past services, which vests pro rata as soon as the employee performs substantial services). Incentive compensation is an inducement for the employee to continue working and achieving goals. [*Schachter v. Citigroup, Inc.*, 47 Cal. 4th 610 (Cal. 2009)]

See § 1.01[A] for discussion of advisory "say on pay" votes that public corporations must hold as a result of the Dodd-Frank Act (Pub. L. No. 111-203), the extensive package of financial services regulatory legislation that was enacted in July 2010.

[B] Incentive Stock Options (ISOs)

Internal Revenue Code § 422 creates a specially tax-favored category of Incentive Stock Options (ISOs). An ISO plan is permitted to discriminate in favor of highly compensated employees. However, favorable tax consequences are available to the employee only if he or she retains the shares for at least one year from the exercise of the option and two years from the grant of the option.

Incentive Stock Options (ISOs) can only be granted to company employees and not to directors, consultants, or advisors who are not employees. The exercise price of an ISO must be at least equal to the FMV of the underlying security on the date of the grant. If the grantee owns 10% or more of the company's stock, the exercise price must be at least 110% of FMV at the date of the grant. Employees themselves can only exercise ISOs, during their lifetimes. Employees are only allowed to transfer ISOs by will or in intestacy.

ISOs must be granted under a plan adopted by the issuing company's Board of Directors and approved by stockholders. The grant must be made within 10 years of the date the plan was adopted. ISOs must be exercised within 10 years of the grant (five years, if the grantee is a 10% stockholder), or three months after termination of employment, whichever is earlier. (An extension is available if employment terminates due to death or disability.) The aggregate FMV of underlying securities for any ISO first exercisable in a calendar year cannot exceed

$100,000 determined at the time of the grant. If all these conditions are met, there is no taxable income for the employee at the time of the grant or when the option is exercised. However, the difference between the value of the security at the time of the exercise of the ISO and the exercise price is an adjustment item for alternative minimum tax purposes. If the underlying securities are held for at least one year after exercise, or two years after the grant, any gain or loss from disposition of the securities is considered a long-term capital gain or loss for the employee. But if the holding period requirements are not satisfied, then the options will generally be taxed as nonqualified stock options (NQSOs). [Foley & Lardner LLP, *ISO v. NQSO: The Difference Or Lack Thereof*, Lexology.com (Sept. 6, 2013)]

Section 251 of the American Jobs Creation Act of 2004 (Pub. L. No. 108-357) amends I.R.C. § 3121(a), § 421(b), and § 423(c) to provide that FICA and FUTA "wages" do not include remuneration derived from exercising an Incentive Stock Option or an option to buy stock under an ESOP. (Nor does this remuneration count toward the person's future Social Security benefits.) The spread (the difference between the stock's FMV and the option price) is not income at the time of the exercise. However, if the statutory holding period is satisfied, it does constitute capital gain once the stock is disposed of. This treatment is effective for stock acquired through options exercised after the enactment of the AJCA.

Code § 425 provides that an ISO loses its entitlement to favorable tax treatment if it is modified, unless the modified option meets the ISO requirements as of the date of the modification, or unless changes are made in connection with a corporate transaction. As long as the option itself provides for employer discretion (e.g., to pay a bonus or make a loan when an option is exercised), the exercise of discretion is not a modification of the option.

An out-of-the-money option has no economic value and, therefore, does not operate as an incentive to the option-holder. Therefore, in bad economic times, repricing is common: companies either reduce the exercise price of the employees' outstanding stock options to the current price or raise the exercise price to provide tax benefits for the holders of the options. Section 409A requires an ISO's exercise price to be at least equal to the stock price on the date of the option grant. For a private company, it must be at least equal to the fair market value of the stock, calculated by reasonably applying a reasonable valuation method reflecting the facts and circumstances at the date of valuation. Otherwise, discount stock options—those granted at an exercise price below the stock price on the grant date—are subject to ordinary income tax plus a 20% penalty tax when they vest, measured on the difference between the stock price at the time of vesting and the exercise price.

Notice 2008-113, 2008-51 I.R.B. 1305, provides that outstanding discount stock options that otherwise satisfy § 422 can be turned into ISOs by increasing the exercise price to the stock price at the option grant date. But repriced options satisfy § 409A only if the discount price was erroneously set on the date of the grant; the options are repriced before the employee exercises them; and repricing occurs not later than the last day of the employee's tax year in which the options were granted. However, if the employee is not an "insider" as defined by Securities Exchange Act § 16 at any time during the year of the grant, options can be repriced until the last day of the employee's tax year immediately following the year of the grant.

Employees must be given the choice of whether or not to take the repricing offer; if they refuse, the options continue to be treated as discount options. Accepting the offer provides the tax benefits of an ISO, but does not necessarily maximize the future profit that can be obtained from the option. [Jin Dong Park, *Upward Stock Option Repricing*, J. of Accountancy (September 2011) (benefits link.com)]

[C] Nonqualified Stock Options (NQSOs)

NQSOs can be granted to anyone, not just employees, and there are no prescribed exercise terms or price or transfer restrictions. However, if an NQSO's exercise price is below the FMV of the security at the grant date, it is subject to Code § 409A. The grant of an NQSO is not a taxable event, but the holder has taxable ordinary income at the time of exercise, equal to the difference in the value of the security at the time of exercise and the exercise price. If the holder is an employee of the company, withholding and employment taxes apply. [Foley & Lardner LLP, *ISO v. NQSO: The Difference Or Lack Thereof*, Lexology.com (Sept. 6, 2013)]

There is no tax effect at the time of the grant of an NQSO, as long as the option itself does not have a readily ascertainable market value (i.e., the options are not traded actively). When the option is exercised, the employee has taxable income, equal to the FMV of the stock minus the consideration paid for the option. However, if the stock received by exercising the option is not transferable, and is subject to a substantial risk of forfeiture, then income is not taxed until the condition lapses. At that time, the amount of gain is determined, using the then-current FMV of the stock.

The FMV of the stock at the time of the exercise of the option, minus the price of the option, is a preference item for Alternative Minimum Tax purposes.

The American Jobs Creation Act of 2004, Pub. L. No. 108-357, changed the tax effectiveness of discount stock options (non-qualified stock options with an exercise price lower than the stock's fair market value on the grant date). Under prior law, the question was whether the discount was so deep that the grant should be treated as direct issuance of the stock. For example, if options were granted to buy $10/share stock for a penny a share, that would be treated as a direct grant; but if the exercise price for the same stock were $8, the option feature would be recognized, and there would be a taxable event only at exercise of the option.

The AJCA subjects discount stock options to the I.R.C. § 409A deferred compensation rules (see Chapter 8). Deferred compensation can be paid only on the occurrence of specified events: death, separation from service, disability, change in control, unforeseen financial hardship, or the arrival of the date specified in the plan. The taxable income equals the option spread (the exercise price minus the current FMV of the stock). The spread is also subject to a 20% excise tax penalty.

The First Circuit decided, in 2008, that a stock option plan was not required to permit NQSOs to be exercised a week after the plan's deadline (three years post-retirement). Delaware law requires strict observance of the terms and conditions of stock option plans. There was no cause for estoppel here, because when he retired, the plaintiff was aware of his retirement date and of the three-year requirement, and his employer did not deprive him of information needed to exercise the options. [*Mariasch v. The Gillette Co.*, 521 F.3d 68 (1st Cir. 2008). The strict-observance rule comes from *First Marblehead Corp. v. House*, 473 F.3d 1 (1st Cir. 2006); later proceedings, upholding the jury verdict that the president of a financial services company reasonably relied on misrepresentations that the options had a duration of 10 years, no damages were awarded because he would not in fact have exercised the options during the three months before they expired, because the company was in financial trouble at that time and the president did not have the $80,000 cash that would have been required to exercise the options: 541 F.3d 36 (1st Cir. 2008)]

[D] Option Taxation Under I.R.C. § 83

Internal Revenue Code § 83 governs all transfers of property in exchange for performance of services, so it is important to stock option taxation but also has broader applicability. Under I.R.C. § 83, the person who performs the services has taxable income, at ordinary income (not capital gains) rates at the time that the rights in the property become transferable or are no longer subject to a substantial risk of forfeiture.

The amount of ordinary income to be recognized equals the fair market value (FMV) of the property minus any amount the employee paid for it. The options can be made forfeitable if the employee leaves before a certain number of years of employment. That motivates the employee to stay longer by offering tax incentives: There is no taxable income until the restriction lapses.

The point at which an option becomes subject to I.R.C. § 83 depends on whether it has an ascertainable market value (for instance, if it is traded on an established market). If so, and if the option is vested, it is taxed as soon as it is granted—not at the later point when it is exercised. Options that have no ascertainable FMV do not become subject to I.R.C. § 83 until they are exercised, on the theory that an option with an FMV can be sold as a separate asset.

Therefore, the employee faces taxation at two stages. The first is when the option can be exercised and the stock purchased; the second is when the stock is sold. (Gains from the sale of stock are capital gains; they do not generate ordinary income.)

Stock options are vested when the stock is transferable and there is no longer a substantial risk of forfeiture. (Sometimes stock awarded to employees is endorsed on its face to prevent transfer.) Section 83 holds that property is subject to a substantial risk of forfeiture if the right to receive the property is conditioned on future performance of substantial services ("earn-out restriction").

There's no bright-line test for when services are substantial; it depends on factors such as the regularity with which services are supposed to be performed and the amount of time needed to perform them. A retiree whose consulting agreement allows him or her to keep the stock while failing to perform the services is not performing substantial services.

Under I.R.C. § 83, refraining from performing services (e.g., under a noncompete clause) can also give rise to a substantial risk of forfeiture.

For purposes of the Exchange Act of 1934's ban on "short-swing" profits earned by officers, directors, or 10% shareholders of public companies, Internal Revenue Code § 83(c)(3) provides that rights are not vested at any time that the person receiving stock options cannot sell the stock without violating the short-swing profit rules. That means that the insider who gets a stock option has no income either for six months or until the first day that the stock can be sold.

In early 2014, the IRS finalized regulations to clarify when there is a "substantial risk of forfeiture" on transfer of stock that is treated as employee compensation under § 83. The May 2012 proposals, published as REG-141075-09, were adopted with a few clarifications. Under the final rules, substantial risk of forfeiture can be established only through a service condition or a condition related to the purpose of the transfer (e.g., achieving a performance goal). In other words, substantial risk of forfeiture can only be established if the employee's rights in the property depend on performance or refraining from performance (e.g., under a noncompete agreement). In determining substantial risk based on a condition related to the purpose of the transfer, both the likelihood of the event occurring and the likelihood of the forfeiture being enforced must be considered. In general, transfer restrictions such as lock-ups, bans on insider trading, and blackout periods do not create a substantial risk of forfeiture. But if the stock cannot be sold because of Exchange Act § 16(b)'s short-swing profit rules, unless the taxpayer elects under § 83(b) to be taxed when the stock is issued, the stock is considered subject to a substantial risk of forfeiture. [T.D. 9659, 2014-12 I.R.B. 653; see Sally P. Schreiber, *Final Substantial-Risk-Of-Forfeiture Rules Are Released*, AICPA.com (Feb. 25, 2014) (benefitslink.com); Sharon L, Klingelsmith, Mona Ghude, and Sharde Armstrong, *IRS Issues Final Regulations on Property Transferred for Services Under Section 83*, Drinker Biddle & Reath LLP, Lexology.com (Mar. 27, 2014)]

IRS's § 83 regulations say that a provision calling for forfeiture of stock if the employee is discharged for cause or for committing a crime does not create a substantial risk of forfeiture. Nevertheless, in 2014 the Tax Court held that the discharge for cause provision in the taxpayer's employment agreement did create a substantial risk of forfeiture. The clause permitted termination for cause for several reasons, including failure to perform his duties diligently and adhere to the employment agreement. The Tax Court said that the regulations, as interpreted, focus on termination for committing a crime, which is unusual enough not to constitute a substantial risk. In this case, however, the Tax Court believed that the broader terms in the taxpayer's employment agreement did create a substantial risk of forfeiture. [*Austin v. Comm'r*, 141 T.C. No. 18 (2013); see Michael G. Falk, *Definition of "Substantial Risk of Forfeiture" Gets Murky?*, Winston & Strawn LLP (Apr. 4, 2014) (benefitslink.com)]

The health care reform law, PPACA, imposes additional taxes on high-income earners: AGI over $200,000 on a single return, $250,000 on a joint return. For these high earners, an additional Medicare tax of 0.9% is imposed on wages, self-employment income, and taxable fringe benefits. In addition, there is a 3.8% surtax on net investment income. The investment surtax applies to gains on non-qualified stock options when they are issued, and on restricted stock when it vests. Tax treatment of dividends on restricted stock depends on whether a § 83(b) election to accelerate income tax was made. If it was made, the 3.8% tax applies to the dividends, but if it was not made, then the dividends are subject to the 0.9% tax. [Laura Saunders, *Tax Report: The New Investment Taxes*, WSJ.com (July 7, 2012)]

See T.D. 9645, 2013-51 I.R.B. 738 for final regulations on the additional Medicare tax enacted on high earners by PPACA. The regulations explain how to withhold the additional tax and correct overpayments and underpayments. The employer must withhold the additional tax from wages over $200,000 paid to anyone, irrespective of the recipient's filing status or wages paid by other employers. The employer cannot modify its withholding of additional Medicare tax. However, a person who expects to owe more than the amount withheld by the employer can increase withholding on the W-4 (e.g., a joint return where neither spouse earns over $200,000, but the total is over $250,000). [Carrie Elizabeth Byrnes and Timothy Zehnder, *IRS Issues "Additional Medicare Tax" Final Rules*, Bryan Cave LLP (Dec. 10, 2013), available at Lexology.com]

In the usual stock option situation, until the option vests, the corporation is still considered the owner of the stock. The dividends on the stock are considered additional compensation for the employee. On the other hand, the corporation can deduct these dividends (as employee compensation) even though under ordinary circumstances a corporation cannot deduct the dividends that it pays.

The employee has the right to elect immediate taxation in the year of the transfer of the property, even if I.R.C. § 83 would not otherwise impose tax. This is a reasonable choice where otherwise the appreciation on the stock would be taxed as compensation.

■ **TIP:** If the employee pays the tax right away and later has to forfeit the options (e.g., by quitting his or her job), the tax already paid is not refundable.

The employer can deduct the compensation that the employee includes in income under I.R.C. § 83 (as long as the compensation is reasonable). The deduction is taken in the employer's tax year that includes the year in which the employee includes the sum in his or her income. Nearly all employees pay taxes on a calendar-year basis, whereas most corporations operate on a fiscal year. The employer gets an immediate deduction if the property is vested as soon as it is transferred, or if the employee exercises the election to be taxed immediately.

To sum up the ISO/NQSO distinction, when an individual is granted NQSOs:

- (At time of grant) If there is no readily ascertainable FMV, there is no tax effect;
- (At time of grant) If there is an ascertainable FMV, § 83 governs taxation;
- (At time of exercise) The employee has taxable income equal to the FMV of the stock minus consideration paid for the option. However, if the stock received on exercise of the option is nontransferable and subject to a substantial risk of forfeiture, taxable income is not a factor until the condition lapses. At that point, gain is determined based on the FMV at the time of the lapse. If the employee actually sells the stock purchased under the option, then he or she will have capital gain or loss on the sale;
- The employer gets a deduction equal to the individual's gain.

If the employee gets ISOs instead of NQSOs:

- (At time of grant) The employee has no taxable income;
- (At time of exercise) The employee has no income;
- (At time of disposition of stock) The employee has capital gain or loss, with consequences depending on the length of the holding period;
- The employer does not get a deduction. [I.R.C. § 421(a)(2)]

If an employee disposes of shares obtained under an ISO within two years of the grant of the option or one year of exercising the option, any gain is ordinary income, and the employer is entitled to a tax deduction equal to this amount.

Taxpayers have often raised the argument that there is no taxable transfer of non-statutory options until the sale of the shares, if they financed the purchase with margin debt, because their own capital is not at risk until then. However, this argument has been rejected by the Tax Court and by the Fifth and Ninth Circuits, the Court of Federal Claims, and the Western District of Washington. [*Racine v. Comm'r*, 92 T.C.M. 100, 102 (2006); *Facq v. Comm'r*, 91 T.C.M. 1201 (2006), *Cidale v. United States*, 475 F.3d 685 (5th Cir. 2007); *United States v. Tuff*, 469

F.3d 1249 (9th Cir. 2006); *Facq v. United States*, 363 F. Supp. 2d 1288 (W.D. Wash. 2005); *Palahnuk v. United States*, 70 Fed. Cl. 87 (Fed. Cl. 2006)]

The Eighth Circuit ruled in 2010 that Nestle Purina Petcare could not deduct cash distribution, redemptive dividends paid to ESOP participants. Employees leaving the company had to instruct the ESOP trust to convert the value of the preferred stock allocated to the account into cash and/or shares of employer common stock. When participants chose to take cash, the trust could require that the employer pay the trust a "redemptive dividend" to purchase the stock. The employer wanted to deduct over $9 million in redemptive dividends, but the Tax Court said that the payments were not deductible dividends: § 162(k)(1) rules out a § 404(k) deduction for amounts paid to an ESOP trust to redeem shares of the corporation's stock, and the Eighth Circuit affirmed. [*Nestle Purina Petcare Co. v. Comm'r*, 594 F. 3d 968 (8th Cir. 2010)]

[E] Securities Law Issues for Stock Option Plans

Federal securities laws and state Blue Sky Laws must be consulted before offering stock options (or any other form of securities-based compensation). Public companies have an established obligation to disclose option transactions to their shareholders, and to reflect them in SEC filings and on proxy statements. The Exchange Act also forbids insiders to take short-swing profits.

For fiscal years ending on or after March 15, 2002, and for proxies for shareholder meetings or shareholder actions on or after June 15, 2002, the SEC has imposed additional disclosure requirements on reporting companies that offer stock compensation plans. Disclosure is now required of plans offering equity compensation, whether or not approved by security holders.

For each category, the reporting company must put a table in the Form 10-K (the annual report) and in the proxy statement whenever shareholders are asked to approve a compensation plan that includes securities. The table should have three columns:

Number of securities to be issued on exercise of outstanding options, rights, and warrants;

- The weighted average exercise price for the outstanding options, rights, and warrants;
- Securities not reflected in the first column, still available to be issued in the future under equity compensation plans. [See *New Disclosure Rules for Stock Plans*, Watson Wyatt Insider, <http://www.watsonwyatt.com/us/pubs/insider/showarticle.asp?ArticleID=9588&Component=The+Insider>]

The SEC adopted a final rule in late 2007 exempting certain stock options from registration under Exchange Act § 12(g). The rule provides one exemption for public companies that are required to file reports under the Exchange Act ("reporting companies"), another for non-reporting companies (e.g., smaller or private corporations). The exemption is limited to stock options issued as compensation, and does not extend to the underlying stock. [72 Fed. Reg. 69554 (Dec. 7, 2007)]

The SEC's 2006 final rule on disclosure of executive compensation requires public corporations to discuss stock options in the Compensation Discussion and Analysis disclosed to stockholders. Effective for fiscal years beginning on or after December 15, 2006, annual reports, proxy statements, and registration statements will have to give far more detail about option grants to and exercises by top management. A Summary Compensation Table is required, giving dollar amounts for stock awards and stock option awards (measured as of the grant date, using FAS 123R; see below). If the closing market price on the grant date is higher than the exercise price, the closing price must be disclosed. To prevent abusive backdating of options, the date that the decision to make the grant of options must be disclosed, if it is different than the stated grant date. If the exercise price of an option is different from the closing market price on the grant date, the methodology for calculating the price must be disclosed. [SEC Press Release, *SEC Votes to Adopt Changes to Disclosure Requirements Concerning Executive Compensation and Related Matters*, <http://www.sec.gov/news/press/2006/2006-123.htm> (July 26, 2006, accessed Apr. 8, 2014)]

The 2010 financial services reform package, the Dodd-Frank Act (Pub. L. No. 111-203), extends the availability of "clawback": i.e., funds that the corporation can recoup from executives who received stock options or other incentive compensation during the three years before the company had to restate erroneous financial statements.

[F] Accounting Issues

Traditionally, the Financial Accounting Standards Board (FASB) did not require corporations to expense their stock options; the cost merely had to be reflected in the footnotes to the financial statement. Expensing means that the cost of the options is deducted in the year the option is offered. Although taxpayers usually want to increase their deductions to cut their tax bills, there is a countervailing pressure on corporations to report high earnings, so anything that depresses their earnings is unattractive.

This position has evolved since 2004, when FASB 123(R), *Share-Based Payment*, required expensing of stock options and other forms of share-based compensation beginning in July 1, 2005 (public corporations) and January 1, 2006 (non-public corporations). A February 3, 2006 amendment (FAS 123(R)-4), clarifies that stock options and SARs did not have to be classified as liability awards merely because the plan permits contingent cash settlements based on an event outside the employee's control (e.g., a corporate change in control). [Technical corrections were issued in August 2006: see FAS 123R-f, <http://www.fasb.org/cs/BlobServer?blobkey=id&blobnocache=true&blobwhere=1175820926900&blobheader=application%2Fpdf&blobheadername2=Content-Length&blobheadername1=Content-Disposition&blobheadervalue2=42982&blobheadervalue1=filename%3Dfsp_fas123r-4.pdf&blobcol=urldata&blobtable=MungoBlobs>]

FASB 123(R) did not require any particular model (such as the popular Black-Scholes model) to be used in valuing options, but did mandate that valuation reflect issues such as vesting schedules, employee turnover, and expected time of exercise. [Keith Sellers, Yingping Huang and Brett A. King, *Are Your ESO Values on Target?*, Journal of Accountancy, <http://www.journalofaccountancy.com/Issues/2008/Mar/AreYourESOValuesonTarget.htm> (March 2008)]

In mid-2009, FASB re-organized thousands of documents into a new classification of approximately 90 topics. Seven FASB statements about retirement and health plans (Nos. 35, 87, 88, 106, 112, 123(R), 158 were reorganized into five topics:

- 712, post-employment compensation other than retirement;
- 715, retirement benefits;
- 960, accounting for defined benefit plans;
- 962, accounting for defined contribution plans;
- 965, accounting for health and welfare benefit plans.

[CCH Pension and Benefits, *FASB Announces New Codification Structure, Superseding All Existing Statements* (June 26, 2009) (benefitslink.com). See <http://www.fasb.org> for the full codification.]

Accounting Standards Codification (ASC) Topic 718, *Stock Compensation*, sets out a general rule that equity awards granted to employees must be accounted for at fair value, measured at the time of grant (for awards settled in stock) and at the time of settlement or exercise (for awards settled in cash). Fair value is the same as the underlying value of the stock if it is a "full-value" award (e.g., restricted stock and performance shares). If it is an "appreciation" award, such as a stock option or stock appreciation rights, value is estimated under an option pricing model.

Subtopic 718-40 provides guidance for ESOP transactions; Subtopic 718-50 offers guidance for share-based payment transactions with Employee Stock Purchase Plans (ESPPs). A share-based payment arrangement is considered equity if the terms of the award call for settlement solely in company stock—e.g., stock options, ESPPs, stock-settled SARs, restricted shares, and performance shares. Compensation cost for equity awards is based on award's fair value at grant, minus anything paid by the employee; the corporation makes a corresponding credit to its equity, usually paid-in capital. Topic 718 explains how to choose inputs to the option pricing model; estimates must be reasonable, supportable, and determined consistently between periods. Topic 718 says that non-public companies must use the same principles to value equity awards as public companies, unless it is impossible to calculate a fair value. If it is impossible, the historical volatility of an index for the relevant industry (not a broad index like the S&P 500) should be used. [Frederic W. Cook & Co., *Accounting for Stock Compensation Under FASB ASC Topic 718* (Apr. 5, 2010) (benefitslink.com)]

[G] Backdating; Coping with Underwater Options

An option is said to be "underwater" if the value of the stock on the open market declines below the exercise price given in the option. In that case, of course, the employee will not have any advantage from exercising the option. For example, if an employee is given the right to buy 5,000 shares of the company's stock for $50 a share on a specific date on the future, but on that date, the stock is worth only $30 a share, the option is essentially worthless. The corporation can take various measures to alter the options plan so that the grantee of the options will be able to exercise them at a gain. Generally speaking, the grantees will find this a more satisfying tactic than the corporation's shareholders will.

The conventional method of repricing options is to cancel the options and replace them with new options with a lower strike price—or amend the original options to change the strike price. However, in 2003, the New York Stock Exchange and NASDAQ changed their rules to require shareholder approval to reprice options. A newer tactic is to allow a re-grant of a smaller number of new options intended to have the same current value as the old options. This can be more acceptable to shareholders than one-for-one exchanges, because fewer shares are being reallocated, so the effect of dilution is less. This approach can also fit in better with FASB rules. Another possibility is to cancel options and replace them with restricted stock units or phantom stock. Finally, some companies choose to calculate the current value of the underwater options, cancel them, and pay cash for the canceled vested options. [JP Morgan Compensation & Benefit Strategies, *Our Stock Options Are Underwater, We Might Re-Price Them* (Apr. 14, 2009) (benefitslink.com); see also Eric B. Rubin, *Bringing Underwater Stock Options Back to the Surface*, <http://www.shrm.org/hrdisciplines/compensation/articles/pages/underwaterstockoptions.aspx> (Feb. 16, 2009)]

One coping mechanism for price volatility, of doubtful legitimacy, is "backdating": deliberate alterations of grant dates to take advantage of lower stock prices that put options in the money when they're issued. Backdating is sometimes analyzed as breach of fiduciary duty by management. The Internal Revenue Code requires the FMV of options to be set in good faith. Allegations of backdating have been raised in many securities law cases, and some executives have been indicted—and a few convicted—on criminal charges such as fraud and criminal violations of the securities laws.

[H] Change of Control Issues

One of the numerous issues that has to be resolved in a merger or acquisition (see Chapter 16 for a general discussion) is what will happen to stock options in the transition. The problem is especially acute when only part of a company (for instance, a division or subsidiary) is sold, and there are arguments pro and con as to whether the plan's "change in control" threshold (which would lead to immediate vesting of options) has been reached. A common provision says that unvested options are forfeited when a person terminates employment other than in a change-of-control situation, and employees of the merged or acquired company are given a limited time (such as three months) to exercise their stock options; under the original option plan, they might have had as much as 10 years to exercise the options.

Many kinds of compensation arrangements in a change in control situation (for example, stock options, severance arrangements, and incentive plans) can create problems under Code § 409A, the provision dealing with nonqualified plans. If § 409A is triggered, then the amounts must be included in income in the year they are paid even though the purpose of the arrangement was to defer taxation. Furthermore, there is a 20% federal tax penalty—plus an additional 20% penalty on transactions in California. Double trigger plans often provide severance protection both before and after the change in control. Usually, severance before the change is paid in installments to coordinate with the imposition of restrictive covenants after the employee leaves the company. But after the change, restrictive covenants are of less concern, so severance is usually paid as a lump sum.

There are significant § 409A risks for double trigger severance plans with alternative payment methods. Some companies fail to recognize this because the pre- and post-transaction severance provisions are in different documents—such as a company-wide severance plan and an individual change-in-control agreement with a top executive. This problem can be avoided by drafting both agreements with a consistent definition.

A double trigger arrangement typically comes under § 409A if its "good reason" is excessively broad, allowing the executive to quit and collect severance when there has been only a minor reduction in pay or duties). Section 409A may also be triggered if the installment payments exceed $490,000 (as adjusted for inflation) or extend for more than two years after separation from service, if the definition of change in control falls afoul of the statutory definition in § 409A.

Stock options can be assumed in corporate transactions without § 409A penalties if the assumption satisfies the rules for assuming Incentive Stock Options (ISOs). In general, that means that the economics of the option must be preserved: valuing the consideration paid in the acquisition of the target company's stock, potentially including the earn-out. Because earn-outs are speculative, it's very possible that calculation assumptions will eventually be proved wrong, so there is a risk of future § 409A penalties if the transaction is over-valued. If it is under-valued, on the other hand, the option-holders will suffer economic detriment. Some companies value the earn-out at the time of the assumption, whereas others keep the transaction open and adjust the option to reflect the ongoing earn-out payments. The entire issue can be avoided by requiring option holders to exercise their options immediately before the transaction. [Juliano P. Banuelos, *Recent Compensation Trends in Mergers and Acquisitions and § 409A,* Orrick Perspectives (October 2011) (benefitslink.com)]

If the options are cashed out, the acquiring company benefits by not having to administer them after the closing and employees can get money for their options without having to spend money to exercise options.

It is common for vesting of options to be accelerated if there is a change of control. Vesting provisions can be incorporated in the stock option plan itself or in other agreements, such as employment contracts, severance plans, and retention agreements. A single-trigger arrangement accelerates vesting and allows option awards to be exercised as soon as there is a change in control. A double-trigger arrangement requires something else to happen in addition, such as the optionee being fired without cause or resigning for good reason within a specified time after the transaction. [Pamela B. Greene, Ann Margaret Eames, *Stock Options in Merger & Acquisition Transactions,* Corporate & Securities Advisory (June 6, 2011) (benefitslink.com)]

The Fifth Circuit held that one-time Merrill Lynch trader John Young was not entitled to an award under the long-term incentive compensation plan after he quit his job. Young was granted about 15,000 restricted stock units in 2006 that were not exercised. Young argued that he had left for good cause after a change in control (Merrill's January 1, 2009 merger with Bank of America)—an eventuality contemplated by the plan. According to Merrill, the date the merger was consummated was the date of the "change in control." The Fifth Circuit said that the plan committee had the discretion to interpret the terms of the plan and Young did not prove that his interpretation was obviously the correct one. [*Young v. Merrill Lynch*, 658 F.3d 436 (5th Cir. 2011)]

A 2012 Eighth Circuit case permits several former executives to receive performance share and restricted stock awards. The plan, required employment throughout the full three-year performance period to receive a full award, but pro-rated awards would be made in case of retirement or involuntary termination. The plan did not define these terms. The plan gave the Executive Compensation Committee authority to administer the plan and make final, binding determinations. The company was sold, and the office where the plaintiffs worked was closed, before the three-year period ended. They were offered jobs in another city, but did not want to move. A senior executive who was not part of the Compensation Committee decided that the plaintiffs forfeited their awards because they rejected a transfer. The Compensation Committee did not review this decision. The Eighth Circuit held that the plaintiffs were entitled to the award: they should have been treated as retired (because the plan did not impose any age limit on retirement), and it was improper for someone outside the Compensation Committee to make the determination. [*Schaffart v. ONEOK, Inc.*, 686 F.3d 461 (8th Cir. 2012); see PLC, *Terminated Executives Entitled to Payment Under Equity Awards: Eighth Circuit* (July 9, 2012) (benefitslink.com)]

§ 22.03 CAFETERIA PLANS

[A] Plan Characteristics

A cafeteria plan, as defined by I.R.C. § 125, is a written plan under which the employer offers a "menu" of benefits, permitting employees to choose between cash and a group of benefits. The plan must offer at least one taxable and one nontaxable benefit. Other than a 401(k) plan, the cafeteria plan may not offer any pension or deferred compensation benefits.

The I.R.C. § 125 requirements for a valid cafeteria plan are

- All plan participants are employees (although the Proposed Regulations allow ex-employees to be included in the plan, as long as it is not predominantly for their benefits). Spouses and children of employees can receive benefits under the plan, but cannot actively participate (e.g., by choosing the benefits);
- The participant chooses between cash and one or more benefits, although the amount of cash does not have to be as great as the entire cost of the nontaxable benefit [Prop. Reg. § 1.125-1];
- The plan does not discriminate in favor of highly compensated employees (HCEs);
- The benefits provided to HCEs do not exceed 25% of the total benefits for the year;
- The election to take benefits rather than cash must be made before the beginning of the plan year;
- Changes in the election must conform to the Regulations.

The allowable benefits include:

- Accident and health plans;
- Group-term life insurance;
- Disability coverage, including accidental death and dismemberment (ADD) plans;
- Dependent care assistance;
- Benefits that fail nondiscrimination tests and therefore are not part of a qualified plan;

- Vacation days;
- Group automobile insurance or other taxable benefit purchased by the employee with after-tax dollars.

Cafeteria plans are not permitted to include long-term care insurance. Neither can Flexible Spending Accounts (see § 18.11) because FSAs are not allowed to be used to pay insurance premiums.

For plan years that begin on or after January 1, 2013, employee contributions to health FSAs that are made by salary reductions under a Code § 125 cafeteria plan are limited to $2,500 a year. This limitation does not apply to the employer's contribution to the plan, or to employee salary reduction contributions to a cafeteria plan that are used to pay the employee's share of health insurance premiums. Cafeteria plans that include FSAs can be amended to reflect this statutory limitation at any time until the end of calendar 2014, but operational compliance is required after the 2013 plan year. [Code § 125(i); Notice 2012-40, 2012-26 I.R.B. 1046; see Christy Tinnes and Brigen Winters, *Second Opinions: ACA Cap on Contributions to Health FSAs*, plansponsor.com (July 18, 2012)]

Initially, FSA balances were forfeited to the extent they were not used for medical expenses during the plan year. Recently, the IRS has permitted a grace period for reimbursement of expenses incurred in the two and a half months after the end of the plan year. In late 2013, the IRS allowed employers to choose between offering either this grace period or a $500 carryforward of unused funds at any time during the next plan year—but not both. Even plans that do not have a grace period can permit a "runout," i.e., prior-year funds can be used in the next year to pay expenses that were incurred but not paid in the prior year. This is different from a grace period, which allows prior-year funds to be used to pay current-year expenses. For the 2013 plan year, the deadline for adopting a grace period or carryforward amendment is December 31, 2014. [Notice 2013-71, 2013-47 I.R.B. 532; see Alison M. Stemler, *IRS Allows $500 Carry Forward Of Medical Flexible Spending Accounts*, Frost Brown Todd LLC (Dec. 13, 2013), available at Lexology.com; AP, *Rollovers for Flexible Spending Accounts*, NYTimes.com (Oct. 31, 2013); John D. McKinnon, *U.S. Allows $500 Rollovers in FSA Health Savings Accounts*, WSJ.com (Oct. 31, 2013); Fisher & Phillips LLP, *IRS Publishes New Cafeteria Plan Rule* (Nov. 1, 2013), available at Lexology.com]

The nontaxable benefits that can be included in a cafeteria plan are group-term life insurance, medical expense reimbursement, and accident and disability benefits as defined by I.R.C. § 106, dependent care assistance, and paid vacation days.

In a pretax premium plan, a "mini cafeteria" salary reduction plan is used to provide after-tax dollars for the employees to pay insurance premiums. The most common application is health insurance coverage for dependents, in plans where the employer covers employees but dependent coverage is on an "employee pay all" basis. The employer adopts a plan that allows the employee, before the start of the plan year, to elect a reduction in compensation sufficient to pay the employee's share of the premium. These salary reductions are not subject to the employer share of FICA.

If a cafeteria plan fails nondiscrimination testing, then the HCEs will have taxable income. The test for discrimination in benefits is whether contributions are made for each participant in a uniform relationship to compensation. If contributions for each participant are equal to the cost of coverage that the plan incurs for HCEs, or if contributions for each participant are at least equal to 75% of the cost for the similarly situated plan participant who has the highest cost of benefits, the plan satisfies the nondiscrimination tests.

Nontaxable cafeteria plan benefits are not subject to employer or employee FICA taxes. However, amounts placed into a 401(k) plan are subject to both employer and employee shares of FICA and FUTA.

Generally, participants will be given a 30-day period at the end of every year to make the election for the following year. The period might close a few days, or even a month, before the end of the year to give the plan administrators time to process the election request.

Cafeteria plans must be in writing, describe all benefits under the plan, apply uniformly to all participants, and be adopted on or before the first day of the plan's first plan year. Retroactive adoptions and amendments are forbidden.

The only permissible benefits for cafeteria plans are:

- Up to $50,000 group-term life insurance on the lives of employees;
- Accident and Health plans, including health Flexible Spending Accounts and payment of individual A&H premiums or COBRA premiums under an A&H plan;
- Contributions to a Health Savings Account (HSA distributions can be used to pay for long-term care or premiums of qualified long-term care insurance policies);
- Dependent care assistance;
- Adoption assistance;
- 401(k) contributions;
- Short- and long-term disability coverage

However, cafeteria plans are forbidden to offer:

- Scholarships;
- Tuition reduction;
- Employer-provided meals and lodging;
- Educational assistance;

- Long-term care insurance;
- Athletic facilities;
- Commuting benefits;
- Working condition fringe benefits;
- De minimis benefits;
- Employee discounts;
- Cell phones provided by the employer;
- MSA contributions;
- Group-term life insurance on non-employees (e.g., employees' parents).

The written plan document must explain how employees can make elections, the maximum salary reduction the plan will allow, the employer's contributions, and rules for any FSAs and HSAs included in the plan. The Proposed Regulations incorporate some of the safe harbor testing rules of Code § 410(b), with an objective test to determine when the actual election of benefits is discriminatory: when HCEs have higher benefits, measured as a percentage of compensation, than non-HCEs. [IRS Publication 15-B (2014 edition), <http://www.irs.gov/pub/irs-pdf/p15b.pdf>]

See Notice 2014-1, 2014-2 I.R.B. 270 for rules about cafeteria plan elections, FSAs, HSAs, and dependent care assistance program benefits for same-sex married couples. In order to carry out the IRS's principle that same-sex marriages are recognized for tax purposes if they were legal where they were celebrated, elections can be changed to reflect an employee's same-sex marriage. An employer who is notified of an employee's same-sex marriage must permit the employee to pay on a pre-tax basis to provide benefits for the spouse, even if the employee previously paid with after-tax dollars. The employee can also continue to pay for the spouse's coverage with after-tax dollars, then seek a tax refund. A Health FSA can reimburse expenses of a same-sex spouse and dependents, incurred from start of plan year that includes June 26, 2013, the date of the *Windsor* decision, or the date of the marriage, if later. However, it is no longer permitted for each same-sex spouse to contribute the household maximum to an HSA or Dependent Care Assistance Plan (DCAP) because they are considered a single household. [Stephen A. Riga, *At Year End, IRS Issues Guidance On Cafeteria Plan Transitional Rules For Windsor*, Ogletree Deakins (Dec. 26, 2013), available at Lexology.com]

ERISA § 403 does not require cafeteria plans to be managed by a trust (although the terms of the plan itself can require trust management). However, if the plan allows after-tax contributions for the purchase of benefits, such contributions must be placed into trust unless they are used to buy insurance policies.

[B] Cafeteria Plans After HIPAA

Proposed and Temporary Regulations for bringing cafeteria plans into conformity with HIPAA were published at 62 Fed. Reg. 60165 and 60196 (Nov. 7, 1997). Then, in March 2000, the IRS replaced the 1997 Temporary Regulations with T.D. 8878, 65 Fed. Reg. 15548, 2000-15 I.R.B. 857 (Mar. 23, 2000). These Regulations, which were supposed to be final, clarified the circumstances under which employees participating in cafeteria plans can change their elections in connection with accident, health, or group-term life insurance coverage. For example, a change might be needed when a Qualified Medical Child Support Order (QMCSO) is granted, or when the person gains or loses eligibility for Medicare or Medicaid.

At the beginning of 2001, the IRS revised this Treasury Decision. [See T.D. 8921, 66 Fed. Reg. 1837 (Jan. 10, 2001)] T.D. 8921 modifies the T.D. 8878 Final Regulations by allowing cafeteria plan participants to increase or decrease their coverage whenever they have a change-of-status event.

Changes were always allowed on the basis of marriage or divorce. Thanks to T.D. 8921, changes are also permitted when a dependent is born or adopted. An employee who decreases or cancels coverage under the cafeteria plan because of coverage under a spouse or dependent's plan has to certify that he or she is getting other coverage.

The cafeteria plan election can be changed to conform to a domestic relations order, but only if the spouse or former spouse actually provides coverage for the child; T.D. 8921 also allows elections to be changed when the employee's responsibility for payments under the plan increases or decreases significantly. The plan's payment for dependent care cannot be greater than what the employee earns.

The Simple Cafeteria Plan is a new plan form created by the health care reform statute. Small employers can set up Simple Cafeteria Plans starting in 2011. PPACA (the health care legislation) defines a small employer as one that averaged 100 or fewer employees in each of the previous two years. (For employers that have not been in business for two years, a reasonable estimate is used.) The advantage of the Simple Cafeteria Plan over a conventional cafeteria plan is that the employer is not subject to the requirements of nondiscrimination testing. All qualified employees must be eligible to participate if they had at least 1,000 hours of service in the previous plan year, but employees can be excluded if they are younger than 21 (or an even younger age stipulated by the plan), or if they are covered by a CBA. Highly compensated and key employees can participate in the Simple Cafeteria Plan, but the plan must not discriminate in their favor. All eligible employees must be allowed to elect any benefit in the plan under the same terms and conditions as all other participants. The employer sponsoring the plan must make at least a minimum contribution that the participant can apply toward any benefit within the plan. The minimum contribution for non-HCEs must equal or exceed the lesser of a uniform 2% of compensation (whether or not the employee contributes); a match equal to double the employee's contribution; or 6% of compensation. [Gary B. Kushner, Kushner & Co., *New Simple Cafeteria Plans* (Aug. 17, 2010) (benefitslink.com)]

§ 22.04 EDUCATION ASSISTANCE

Employers offer education assistance both because anything that employees consider a valuable benefit is a good motivator, and because a better-educated workforce promotes efficiency and productivity. However, the tax status of this benefit has fluctuated over the past decades.

There were no Code provisions allowing employees to receive educational assistance tax-free before I.R.C. § 127 was enacted in 1978, as a five-year pilot project. It was extended several times, and finally made permanent by the Economic Growth and Tax Relief Reconciliation Act (EGTRRA), which also removed the earlier limitation of the assistance to undergraduate-level education. Under I.R.C. § 127, employees can exclude from income up to $5,250 in benefits under an educational assistance program. The benefits should not be included in Box 1 on Form W-2, because they do not constitute taxable income. [The version of Publication 970, Tax Benefits for Education, for calculating 2012 returns, is available at <http://www.irs.gov/pub/irs-pdf/p970.pdf>]

Although many EGTRRA provisions were scheduled to expire in 2011, legislation passed at the end of 2010 revived many EGTRRA provisions, including educational assistance. This benefit, at the $5,250 level, can be offered tax-free to employees until the end of 2012. [Tax Relief, Unemployment Insurance Reauthorization, and Job Creation Act of 2010, Pub. L. No. 111-312 (Dec. 17, 2010); see EBIA Weekly, *2010 Tax Relief Act Extends Various Benefits, Including Higher Transit/Vanpool Limit, Adoption, and Education Assistance* (Dec. 23, 2010) (benefitslink.com)]

The "fiscal cliff" legislation, the American Taxpayer Relief Act of 2012, extends the educational assistance provision, at the $5,250 level, indefinitely. See IRS guidance at <http://www.irs.gov/uac/Tax-Benefits-for-Education:-Information-Center> (Jan. 24, 2014).

§ 22.05 EMPLOYEE ASSISTANCE PROGRAMS (EAPs)

The purpose of the Employee Assistance Program (EAP) is to help employees cope with stress and other problems. The theory is that sympathetic listening, and referrals for whatever professional services are needed, will ease employees' anxieties and make them more productive. EAPs can offer any combination of one-on-one counseling, information and referral, hotlines and crisis intervention, and informational seminars.

EAPs typically deal with problems such as substance abuse, dependent care, and problems with spouses and children. Many companies have found that early intervention makes it possible to shorten the damage and amount of time that would otherwise be involved, for instance, when the employee "hits bottom" with a drug or alcohol problem, or when an untreated mental illness requires inpatient hospitalization in a crisis. Each dollar invested in EAP services is estimated to return anywhere from two to eight dollars in health and productivity savings.

EAPs also take a role in coordinating an employee's return to work after recuperating from an accident or illness (which may include a shortened or flexible schedule, intermittent FMLA leave, or other accommodations).

The services can be provided in house by the HR department, or contracted out to outside vendors. The second course is more expensive, but it may make the EAP more credible to employees, or may reassure employees that their confidentiality will be protected.

§ 22.06 MISCELLANEOUS FRINGES

Employees do not have taxable income if they receive certain minor fringe benefits provided by the employer on a nondiscriminatory basis to all employees. Under I.R.C. § 132, the benefits are not taxed to the employees. FICA, FUTA, and federal income tax withholding are not required, and the employer share of these taxes does not have to be paid. Generally, the employer will be able to deduct the cost of the program (which is supposed to be nominal, in any case) as long as it fits the definition of an ordinary and necessary business expense.

The categories of miscellaneous fringe benefits authorized under I.R.C. § 132 are:

- No-additional-cost services of the employer company (e.g., air travel for an airline employee; a simple will prepared by a law firm for a non-attorney staffer). The employee must gain access to services normally sold to customers, but the employer must not incur any substantial cost. In effect, the employees are given access to the business's excess capacity;
- Employee discounts; the discount must not exceed the gross profit percentage for goods, or 20% of the cost of services;
- De minimis fringe benefits, such as free beverages at work or small Christmas presents—anything too trivial to account for separately;
- An on-premises eating facility such as a low-cost cafeteria that prepares meals on premises for the convenience of the employer (because employees can take shorter meal breaks because the subsidized dining facility is available). The facility must be owned or operated by the employer, must generate revenue at least equal to its operating costs, and must provide meals during the workday or right before or right after it. It must also be

in or near the workplace, and must be operated by the employer (possibly through a contract with a third-party management company);

- Working condition fringe benefits—goods or services the employee could deduct if he or she paid for them personally. Typical examples are business travel and the use of company cars;
- An on-premises gym for the exclusive use of employees and their families;
- Reimbursement of employment-related moving expenses that would be deductible if the employee paid them directly (but have not in fact been deducted by the employee).

In some years, the transportation fringe benefit has been set at a different level depending upon whether the benefit covers parking or transit passes and vanpooling. The tax exemption for mass-transit fringe benefits fell to $130 for 2014; the benefit for parking rose slightly, from $245 a month to $250 a month. At first, the mass transit benefit was lower than the parking benefit. The two were temporarily equalized between 2009 and 2013, but the equalization provision expired December 31, 2013. The parking benefit continued to rise because, by statute, it is indexed for inflation. [Andrew Grossman, *Mass-Transit Commuters Face a Tax Hit*, WSJ.com (Dec. 29, 2013)]

The Emergency Economic Stabilization Act, Pub. L. No. 110-343, added a new bicycle commuting benefit under Code § 132. Employers can provide employees with tax-free reimbursement of up to $20 a month for each month in which the employee regularly bicycles to work, starting with December 31, 2008. Reimbursable costs include buying a bicycle that is regularly used for commuting, and repairing and storing it. [Rebecca Moore, *Economic Stabilization Plan Includes Bicyclist Benefit*, plansponsor.com (Oct. 29, 2008); EBIA Weekly, *Bicycle Commuting Fringe Benefit Added to Code Section 132(f)* (Oct. 29, 2008) (benefitslink.com)]

IRS Information Letter 2013-0032 says that bicycle share programs are not qualified transportation fringe benefits as defined by Code § 132, so the employer's expenses for a bicycle share program cannot be excluded from the employee's gross income. A bicycle share program is not considered a transit pass because it does not involve mass transit. It does not qualify as bicycle commuting reimbursement because that is limited to employee costs of buying and repairing a bicycle to be used to travel between home and work. [PLC, *IRS: Bike Share Expenses Do Not Qualify for Favorable Fringe Benefit Tax Treatment* (Oct. 2, 2013) (benefitslink.com)]

Under Reg. § 1.132-6(e)(1), de minimis fringes include items such as:

- Occasional typing of personal letters by employees;

- Occasional meals, picnics, or cocktail parties for employees or their guests;
- Birthday or holiday gifts of low value;
- Theater or sports tickets;
- Coffee or snacks provided in the workplace.

However, these are not de minimis:

- Season tickets;
- Country club membership;
- The use of employer-provided vehicles more than one day per month;
- Weekends at facilities owned or leased by the employer.

Reg. § 1.132-6 says that if a benefit is too valuable or is provided too often to be considered de minimis, then the value of the entire benefit must be included in the recipient's gross income, unless it is excluded for another reason (for example, it qualifies as a no-additional-cost fringe or a working-condition fringe benefit).

Under Code § 132(e)(1), cash and benefits that are equivalent to cash, such as gift certificates, are not de minimis because they have a readily ascertainable value, and it is not impracticable for the employer to account for them. A de minimis fringe benefit must be offered in the form of goods or services and not cash—even if it represents an item that would be de minimis if it were distributed in kind. [Bruce M. Bird and J. Harrison McCraw, *De Minimis Fringe Benefit Rules: Current Guidance and Tax Implications*, CPA Journal (April 2006) (benefitslink .com)]

Another Code section, I.R.C. § 119, governs meals and lodging furnished on premises for the convenience of the employer, e.g., a room for a hotel manager who must be around to handle problems as they arise. Such benefits are not taxable income for the employee.

Decline in the real estate market made it difficult for corporations to relocate employees and has led to changes in relocation benefits. "Loss on sale" benefits used to be common (reimbursement for losses when employees had to sell their homes in order to relocate) but have lost popularity because it has become so difficult for corporations to re-sell such homes. So there has been a move to offering assistance with renting out the old home and renting (instead of buying) a home in the new location. The recruitment process for an out-of-town candidate might include consultation with a relocation manager. A lump sum for the move might be offered, or the company might agree to assume some home-sale losses subject to a cap. Or, instead of relocating, an employee or new hire might be permitted to telecommute or stay in hotels or corporate housing part of the time while remaining in his or her current home. [Heather O'Neil, *Relocation Benefits Are on the Move*, Workforce (Feb. 6, 2012) (benefitslink.com)]

§ 22.07 VOLUNTARY EMPLOYEE BENEFIT ASSOCIATIONS (VEBAs)

A Voluntary Employee Benefit Association (VEBA), as defined by I.R.C. § 501(c)(9), is a trust that is funded by employer contributions (with or without employee contributions) and is used to pay benefits to employees who voluntarily exercise the option to participate in the association. VEBAs provide life, sickness, accident, or similar benefits to employee members and their dependents and designated beneficiaries. Benefits that can be offered by a VEBA safeguard or improve health or protect against a contingency that threatens the employee's earning power. But VEBAs are not allowed to offer reimbursement of commuting expenses, profit sharing, or stock bonuses.

The trust itself is not a taxable entity, but VEBA benefits constitute taxable income to the employee unless they are specifically exempted.

The VEBA must be controlled by its employee membership, by a bank or other independent trustee, or by fiduciaries chosen by or on behalf of the membership. A VEBA is considered a welfare plan under ERISA, and therefore is subject to ERISA Parts 1 (notice and reporting), 4 (trust and fiduciary responsibility), and 5 (enforcement).

The Sixth Circuit ruled that the portion of the VEBA contribution used to fund long-term disability benefits was deductible, but the portion used to fund post-retirement benefits and medical benefits for union members was not deductible, because the employer failed to satisfy the I.R.C. § 419A(c)(2) requirements for accumulating assets to prefund the benefits. [*Parker-Hannifin Corp. v. Comm'r*, 139 F.3d 1090 (6th Cir. 1998)]

The VEBAs are at risk of market volatility, because of their partial funding by employer stock and because they also experience large increases in medical costs. Many VEBAs are running out of money so they have to cut costs, reduce benefits, and seek additional funding from sponsors and beneficiaries. According to DOL filings from October, 2011, the largest VEBA, covering over 820,000 former auto workers and their families, is almost $20 billion short. The United Steel Workers Union's 30 VEBAs have been hard-hit by medical cost inflation. The UAW retirees have above-average benefits, providing some leeway for cuts. In 2009, the UAW VEBA severed its ties to the auto makers and became an independent trust—resulting in higher copayments for retirees and reduced prescription drug benefits. [Sharon Terlep and Matthew Dolan, *VEBA Retirement Trusts Face Funding Shortfalls*, WSJ.com (Nov. 7, 2011)]

§ 22.08 FRINGE BENEFIT PLANS: TAX COMPLIANCE

[A] Reporting Requirements

The reporting requirements for a fringe benefit plan are set out in I.R.C. § 6039D. The plan must report:

- Number of employees at the employer company;
- Number of employees eligible to participate in the plan;
- Number actually participating;
- Number of highly compensated employees in each of the above categories;
- The plan's total cost during the year;
- The employer's name, address, and Employer Identification Number;
- The nature of its business.

If any fringe benefits are taxable, the employer can either add them to the regular wages for a payroll period, or withhold federal income tax at the rate for supplemental wages. [The relevant IRS publication is 15-B, Employer's Tax Guide to Fringe Benefits.]

[B] The Employer's Tax Deduction

When it comes to pensions, the tax rules are devised to make sure that the employer contributes enough to fund the plan. In contrast, when it comes to welfare benefits, the tax focus is preventing excessive prefunding of benefit plans. So the relevant Code sections (I.R.C. §§ 419 and 419A) specify a maximum funding level for welfare benefit trusts. If this level is exceeded, the trust is no longer tax-exempt.

Although the employer receives a tax deduction for maintaining a welfare benefit trust, the deduction is limited to the "qualified cost" of the benefit plans for the year. That means the direct cost of funding benefits, plus whatever amount I.R.C. § 419A permits to be added to the account for the year as a safety cushion.

Reference should also be made to I.R.C. § 4976, which imposes a 100% excise tax on disqualified benefit distributions made from funded welfare benefit plans. For instance, retiree health and life insurance benefits for highly compensated employees are supposed to be kept in a separate account from comparable contributions for rank-and-file employees.

Therefore, benefits paid to HCEs from the general account would be disqualified. VEBA benefits to HCEs that violate nondiscrimination requirements are also disqualified, as are amounts that revert to the employer. (An erroneous contribution which is withdrawn by the employer after a determination that it is not deductible is not considered a reversion.)

§ 22.09 ERISA REGULATION OF WELFARE BENEFIT PLANS

[A] Creation and Administration

Although most of the attention goes to ERISA's regulation of pension plans, ERISA also covers welfare benefit plans—a category roughly equivalent to fringe benefit plans. An ERISA welfare benefit plan is created (generally by a corporate resolution passed by the Board of Directors and managed by the relevant corporate officials) and administered to provide one or more of these benefits to plan participants and their beneficiaries:

- Medical benefits;
- Health care;
- Accident insurance;
- Disability benefits;
- Death benefits;
- Supplemental unemployment benefits;
- Vacation benefits;
- Training (e.g., apprenticeship);
- Day care centers (but not dependent care spending reimbursement accounts);
- Scholarships;
- Prepaid legal services;
- Any benefit described in the Labor-Management Relations Act § 302(c) [29 U.S.C. §§ 141–144, etc.] other than death benefits, pensions, or insurance coverage for pensions or death benefits.

The people receiving the benefits must be common-law employees and not independent contractors. For this purpose, employee status depends on agency principles such as who controls and supervises the person, and whether the person can recognize profit or loss from the work relationship. It does not depend on the "reasonable expectations" of the parties. [*Mut. Ins. Co. v. Darden*, 503 U.S. 318 (1992)]

Welfare benefit plans are subject to ERISA Title I. The Eleventh Circuit has ruled that a Title I plan exists if circumstances lead a reasonable person to ascertain the intended benefits, intended beneficiaries, financing sources, and procedure for receiving benefits under the plan. [*Donovan v. Dillingham*, 688 F.2d 1367 (11th Cir. 1982)] A plan can be deemed to exist even if the ERISA rules are not observed, and in fact, even if there is no written instrument.

Severance pay plans are sometimes treated as pension plans, but are more likely to be characterized as welfare benefit plans. DOL Advisory Opinion 84-12A says that a severance pay plan is not a pension plan if:

- Its benefits are not contingent on the employee's retirement;
- Total payments do not exceed twice the employee's compensation for the year before the termination;
- Payments are completed within 24 months after termination of service for the employer.

Under a similar analysis, bonus programs are not treated as pension plans for ERISA Title I purposes unless the payments are systematically deferred at least until termination of employment. DOL Reg. § 2510.3 says that an employer plan that supplements retirement benefits (e.g., until early retirees can qualify for Social Security benefits) can be either a pension or a welfare benefit plan, depending on its terms and how it is administered.

ERISA Title I does not apply to certain payroll practices:

- Extra pay for nonstandard working hours (overtime, shift premiums, holiday premiums);
- Compensation paid when the employee is on sick leave, taking a sick day, or otherwise medically unable to work;
- Compensation paid for other absences, such as vacation days, sabbaticals, and military leave.

In mid-2004, EBSA issued an advisory opinion as to whether a vacation pay plan was a "welfare benefit plan" as defined by ERISA § 3(1). The plan provided paid vacation to eligible employees, based on average hours worked, length of service, and level of employment. EBSA opined that 29 C.F.R. § 2510.3-1 draws a distinction between a welfare benefit plan and a payroll practice, such as paying vacation benefits out of the employer's general assets. The factors in the determination of a welfare benefit include whether the employee's right is contingent on a future occurrence or whether the employee undertakes some risk other than ordinary employment risk. If there is a VEBA or trust involved, ERISA coverage depends on whether the trust is a bona fide separate fund; whether it has a direct legal obligation to pay plan benefits; if the employer's obligation to make contributions is legally enforceable; and whether the contributions are actuarially determined or established via collective bargaining. EBSA concluded that the trust was just a pass-through vehicle for the distribution of ordinary vacation pay. [EBSA Advisory Opinion 2004-08A, 7/2/04, <http://www.dol.gov/ebsa/regs/aos/ao2004-08a.html>]

[B] ERISA Case Law on Welfare Benefits

Where failure to make complete disclosure could be harmful to benefit participants, a benefit plan administrator had a fiduciary duty to give complete and accurate information about the plan. If it is clear that a participant is unaware of important features of the plan, it is not enough simply to answer questions. [*Krohn v. Huron Mem'l Hosp.*, 173 F.3d 542 (6th Cir. 1999)]

Until 2006, Menasha Corporation retirees and their spouses continued to receive health insurance from the company. Between ages 62–65, the company paid 80% of the premium; when retirees turned 65, the company paid 100% of the premium. In 2006, however, Menasha informed the plaintiffs that it was adopting a new health plan, and premiums would no longer be 100% covered. The plaintiffs sued alleging violations of the Labor Management Relations Act, 29 U.S.C. § 185, and ERISA, 29 U.S.C. § 1132. The district court ruled in the plaintiffs' favor as to employee coverage, but in favor of defendant as to spouses. The Sixth Circuit reversed in part, ruling for the plaintiffs. Although healthcare is a "welfare benefit," not entitled to the same ERISA protection as pension benefits, certain actions by employers will waive the employers' right to alter welfare benefits. In this case, Menasha waived the right to change the benefits by providing vested healthcare coverage to retired employees and spouses, and by agreeing that CBAs could only be modified with signed, mutual consent of the parties. [*Moore v. Menasha Corp.*, 690 F.3d 444 (6th Cir. 2013)]

PART V
THE HR FUNCTION

CHAPTER 23

HIRING AND RECRUITMENT

§ 23.01 INTRODUCTION

Efficient hiring practices benefit the company at all levels. Prompt, economical selection of the best person to do the job (whether from inside the company or brought in from outside) will keep operations running smoothly and encourage innovation that will keep the business competitive.

On the downside, bad hiring practices create many kinds of risks such as employment discrimination charges, or charges of negligent hiring or retention (if an employee commits a crime or sexual harassment). Or, a poorly chosen employee can be inefficient, make costly mistakes and have to be replaced, generating additional costs.

The Hiring Inventives to Restore Employment (HIRE) Act was enacted in March 2010. The law provides a payroll tax incentive to employers who hire previously unemployed workers between February 3, 2010 and January 1, 2011: a federal tax credit equal to the 6.2% employer share of FICA tax. The credit could be claimed by creating a new position, but not by firing one worker and replacing him or her. Qualifying workers must have been unemployed or worked only limited hours in the 60 days before being hired. [Rebecca Moore, *New Law Offers Tax Incentives for Hiring*, plansponsor.com (Mar. 18, 2010)]

This credit was not renewed after it expired. However, the Tax Relief, Unemployment Insurance Reauthorization, and Job Creation Act of 2010 (TRUI; Pub. L. No. 111-312) provided a different kind of payroll tax cut: reduction of the employee (not the employer) share of FICA tax to 4.2%. The Middle Class Tax Relief and Job Creation Act of 2012, Pub. L. No. 112-96, extends the 4.2% payroll tax rate until the end of 2012, but it was not extended further. [Naftali Bendavid and Siobhan Hughes, *Congress Reaches Payroll-Tax Deal*, WSJ.com (Feb. 16, 2012); Josh Mitchell and Naftali Bendavid, *Tax Bill Passed by Congress Broadens Jobless Program*, WSJ.com (Feb. 18, 2012)]

In November 2011, Congress passed the VOW to Hire Heroes Act of 2011, including a new tax credit for hiring veterans: up to $9,600 per veteran for for-profit companies, $6,240 for tax-exempt organizations. The maximum credit was granted for hiring veterans with service-connected disabilities. [Notice 2012-13, 2012-9 I.R.B. 421] This credit expired December 31, 2013.

§ 23.02 PRODUCTIVE HIRING

The recession has increased the number of applicants for most jobs, and gives many hiring managers a choice among many qualified (or overqualified) candidates—but when a company seeks to keep payroll manageable, it is important to select the right candidate.

Current employees can be a great starting point for recruitment (and many companies offer bonuses if a current employee recruits someone who is hired and completes a minimum period satisfactorily), but they should not be the only source of recruitment—especially if you want a diverse workforce.

College and graduate school recruitment should not be restricted to those nearby, or only to a small class of Ivy League schools. If nationwide recruitment is a cost problem, the Internet allows nationwide recruiting and low cost. However, resumes posted on the Internet are no more or less truthful than those delivered by traditional means, so reference checks are still required.

See § 25.02[C] for a discussion of recent cases about the effect of covenants not to compete on hiring. However, the opposite tack could also be problematic.

In 2010, the Department of Justice sued Adobe, Apple, Google, Intel, Intuit, LucasFilm, and Pixar, and private class actions were filed alleging that these companies conspired to avoid bidding wars for high-priced talents. The plaintiffs charged the companies with refraining from recruiting each others' employees, and argued that "non-poaching" agreements are per se illegal under Sherman Act § 1. The cases were consolidated in the District Court for the Northern District of California. There were problems with class certification but eventually two settlement agreements were reached involving three defendants. Lucasfilm and Pixar agreed to pay $9 million and Intuit agreed to pay $11 million. Cases remained pending against the other four defendants, with 92% of the potential class members. [*In re: High-Tech Employee Antitrust Litig.*, No. 11-02509 (N.D. Cal., partially settled 2013); see Nick Grimmer and Joseph F. Winterscheid, *$20 Million Settlement In In Re: High-Tech Employee Antitrust Litigation, A Non-Poaching Agreement Case*, McDermott Will & Emery (Oct. 1, 2013), available at Lexology.com]

Apple, Google, and two other defendants moved to dismiss the case against them in March, but the motion was denied. [Dan Levine, *Apple, Google Lose Bid to Avoid Trial on Tech Worker Lawsuit*, Reuters Business & Financial News, <http://www.reuters.com/article/2014/03/29/us-apple-google-ruling-idUSBREA2R20W20140329> (Mar. 28, 2014)]

A settlement was reached in May 2014, under which 64,000 plaintiffs would receive $324.5 million in damages from Apple, Google, Intel, and Adobe. However, Judge Lucy H. Koh of the Central District of California rejected the settlement in August 2014. She said that there was extensive evidence of conspiracy. After paying their lawyers, plaintiffs would receive only about $4,000 each—not enough for a case this strong. Koh pointed out that if the Pixar/LucasFilm settlement were to be extrapolated to the facts of this case, damages would be at least $380 million. [Thomas M. McInerney, *National Implications From Settlement of High-Profile Employee Raiding Case*, Ogletree Deakins (Apr. 26, 2014), available at Lexology.com; David Streifeld, *Court Rejects Deal on Hiring in Silicon Valley*, NYTimes.com (Aug. 8, 2014)]

§ 23.03 ANALYZING JOB REQUIREMENTS

In many cases, poor hiring decisions are made because of lack of insight into the real demands of the job. A candidate is chosen who matches the formal, written job description, but there's a mismatch, because the real job isn't very much like the job description. Often, people are hired on the basis of technical skills, but those skills are seldom used on a day-to-day basis.

The job should be analyzed to see how much time is spent on various tasks, such as working with machinery, writing and analyzing reports, or supervising other workers.

It is important to understand the physical demands of the job, to see who can meet them without accommodation, and what accommodations can reasonably be made to the needs of individuals with disabilities. [See § 36.05 for a discussion of reasonable accommodation.]

The job must be identified as exempt or nonexempt for wage and hour purposes. Sometimes it makes economic sense to restructure job duties so that the job becomes exempt from overtime requirements. However, the change must be real, not just a meaningless title.

There should be a written job description indicating:

- Job title;
- When it has to be filled;
- Why the organization needs someone for that position at all (perhaps the duties could be delegated to existing employees, outsourced, or assigned to temporary or part-time employees);
- Required educational qualifications;
- Necessary skills;
- Standards for defining inadequate, satisfactory, good, and excellent performance; the educational qualifications, skills, and experience that are really needed to perform the job; and standards (as objective as possible) for defining inadequate, satisfactory, good, and excellent performance.

The job description should indicate reporting relationships (whom the jobholder reports to; who reports to him or her). It should explain the promotion potential for the job, including conditions (such as getting an MBA or meeting performance goals). If your company has a grading system, the job grade should be indicated. The job description should also include the salary range.

§ 23.04 RECRUITMENT

It is probably worthwhile to consider promoting existing employees to fill important positions, although sometimes it is necessary to look outside—or desirable to get new skills and viewpoints. Even a policy of promoting from within requires recruiting, to fill entry- and mid-levels that have been vacated by the promoted employees.

The Web and social media (blogs, MySpace, Facebook, etc.) are gaining in importance as recruiting and hiring sources.

The Associated Press reported in February, 2012 that some job applicants are being pressured to turn over their Facebook and other social media passwords so employers can investigate potential hires. In March 2012, Senators Charles Schumer (D.N.Y.) and Richard Blumenthal (D. Conn.) asked the Department of Justice and EEOC to investigate whether it is illegal for employers to seek this information. [Todd Ruger, *Senators Ask Feds to Investigate Employer Requests for Social Media Passwords*, The BLT: The Blog of Legal Times (Mar. 26, 2012) (law.com)]

[See § 27.05 for more discussion of the HR implications of social networking]

In most companies, job postings literally are posted on a bulletin board, leaving the notice up for five to ten days. More and more companies are using the corporate Intranet for this purpose. The posting should explain the nature of the job (although another advantage of recruiting from within is that the applicants will be fairly familiar with it already); the qualifications required; and whether there are any limitations. For instance, seniority is a very significant factor in promotions in a unionized workplace. Some companies have a policy that employees are not allowed to apply for internal vacancies unless they have held their current job for at least six months with satisfactory or better performance appraisals. The usual policy is to keep the application confidential from the applicant's immediate supervisor, until there is the possibility that the promotion will be offered.

The state employment service can be a good resource for low-level jobs, and even some higher-level technical jobs. Unemployment benefits are not available to workers who have voluntarily quit, or who were fired for wrongdoing, so workers receiving benefits are probably not unstable or a bad risk merely on account of being unemployed. Also, people who are employed but want a new job sometimes register with the state employment office because it has contacts with a wide range of employers and because it does not charge jobseekers a fee. To fill higher-level positions, if a local company has had a major downsizing recently, check with the company that handles their executive outplacement.

The New York City Human Rights Law makes it illegal for employers to discriminate based on unemployment. Over two dozen proposals to adopt similar laws are pending at the federal, state, and local level. The states of New Jersey and Oregon, and the City of Chicago forbid help-wanted advertisements that rule out applications from unemployed persons, and the District of Columbia makes it unlawful for an employment agency or employer to treat being unemployed as a factor in hiring or employment decisions. The New York City statute is the only one with a private right of action. The New Jersey Appellate Division upheld

NJSA § 34:8B-1, the state law that forbids job advertisements that say all applicants must be currently employed. (The law does not require employers to hire unemployed persons, interview them, or even consider their applications, as long as they are allowed to apply.) The court found that the law did not infringe on employers' First Amendment rights. The statute was treated as commercial speech, so legal restraints are viewed more indulgently than restraints on political speech. The court found that the law was narrowly tailored to advance the substantial government interest in promoting opportunity for the unemployed. [*New Jersey Dep't of Labor & Workforce Dev. v. Crest Ultrasonics et al.*, 434 N.J. Super. 34, 82 A.3d 258 (N.J. App. Div. 2014); see David G. Islinger and James M. McDonnell, *New Jersey Ban On "Currently Employed" Requirement In Job Ads Resists Constitutional Challenge*, Jackson Lewis PC (Jan. 14, 2014), available at Lexology.com; Phillip H. Wang, *The Unemployed – A Protected Category Coming To A Jurisdiction Near You*, DLA Piper (Sept. 30, 2013), available at Lexology.com]

If you hire someone who held a senior position at one of your competitors, it is possible that the individual had an employment contract with the company that contained a covenant not to compete. Another possibility is that, when his or her severance package was negotiated, a covenant not to compete was signed at that time. Therefore, it is important to find out if a job applicant is subject to such an agreement, and whether taking the job that is offered would violate it.

Even without a covenant not to compete, a competitor could charge that you hired its ex-employee to misappropriate the competitor's customer lists and trade secrets. If you recruited the ex-employee, you might be charged with interference with contractual relationships. So make it part of the interview process to make a record about the circumstances of the contact.

The Seventh Circuit rule is that it's improper to refuse to hire someone merely because of their union sentiments, membership, or activities [*Bloedorn v. Francisco Foods Inc.*, 276 F.3d 270 (7th Cir. 2001)], or even because they're union "salts" (people "salted" into the workforce to spread pro-union ideas). [*Hartman Bros. Heating & Air Conditioning Inc. v. NLRB*, 280 F.3d 1110 (7th Cir. 2002)] However, the Seventh Circuit found that the company's hiring procedure was not tantamount to a refusal to hire or consider pro-union applicants. As long as an employer is not motivated by anti-union animus, for labor law purposes it can freely exercise its business judgment when deciding whom to hire. [*NLRB v. Louis A. Weiss Mem'l Hosp.*, 172 F.3d 432 (7th Cir. 1999)] Even the NLRB itself takes the position that preferring current employees, ex-employees, and people referred by management cannot be interpreted as anti-union discrimination. [*Custom Topsoil, Inc.*, 328 N.L.R.B. 446 (1999). See Chapter 30 for more about labor law concepts]

§ 23.05 SEARCH FIRMS

Businesses often retain search firms for top executive and professional positions, although this can be a costly option.

There are two main types of firms in the search professional. Contingency firms are usually used to find candidates for mid-level jobs; an executive search firm usually gets involved only with upper-level jobs. A search firm works directly for the company seeking to hire an executive. Usually, its contracts require the company to pay for its services whether or not a candidate is hired. In contrast, a contingency firm's clients include both job seekers and companies looking to hire someone, and the company pays a fee if and only if hiring results.

A search firm's fee can be anywhere from 25% to 100% of the first year salary. Contingency firms usually charge less, perhaps 20% to 33% of the first year's salary. Only cash compensation, not bonuses or stock options, is included in the calculation. Both kinds of firms often give refunds if the new hire leaves or has to be discharged during a probationary period such as 90 days.

Many companies are not familiar with search firms, so they do not know what to expect or how to assess the quality of the firm's performance. John Marra, president of the recruitment firm Marra Peters & Partners, has some suggestions:

- Be clear on the criteria you use to judge the firm's performance;
- Get references from past clients and follow them up;
- Tell the search firm what you expect the successful candidate to accomplish the first six months and the first year after hiring, and how you will assess the new hire's performance;
- Ask the search firm to send only candidates who are a good match with your requirements;
- Get the search firm's promise to keep working with you until the vacancy is satisfactorily filled (if necessary, after someone has been hired, terminated after a probationary period, and a new search performed).

Some of the provisions to look for in a recruitment contract are:

- Clarification that the firm does not have the authority to hire someone on behalf of your company, or to promise terms and conditions of employment—only your company's authorized agent can do that;
- A statement that your company is committed to equal employment opportunity principles;
- The firm's agreement that it will be responsible if it commits discrimination in referring candidates to you—and that it will indemnify your company for any liability resulting from its discriminatory referrals;

- A clear statement of the firm's responsibilities, including screening candidates and checking their references;
- Recruiting expenses that your company agrees to pay;
- Whether you have to pay if you hire a candidate obtained through another channel, or only if the recruiter sends the successful candidate to you;
- The recruiter's promise not to contact or solicit your new hire for a period of at least two years.

§ 23.06 JOB APPLICATIONS

Frequently, the first real contact between the corporation and the potential employee occurs when the applicant submits a formal job application. The application is a legal document that can have serious consequences: both as a source of promises that the employer can be held to, and as a source of information whose correctness the applicant can be held responsible for. For example, false statements on an application can constitute "after-acquired evidence" of wrongdoing that can limit the damages available to a successful employee plaintiff. [See § 42.10[C]]

It often makes sense to have a candidate fill out a job application even if he or she has submitted a resume. The resume only includes the information the candidate wants to disclose. The application form is standard, and resumes are very variable, so it is easier to compare applicants if you have the same information about each. The application might ask for:

- Positions held with the last three or four employers;
- Dates of employment;
- Job title;
- Salary;
- Name of immediate supervisor;
- Why the candidate left that job (unless he or she is still employed);
- Permission to contact the supervisor for a reference.

■ **TIP:** In several states (e.g., California, Delaware, Minnesota, Wisconsin), if you require applicants to sign their applications, the state privacy law also requires you to give them a copy of the completed application, or lets employees copy personnel files including job applications.

The application should make it clear that the form is a legal document that can have serious ramifications. It is important to require the applicant to state that all the information given on the application is complete and accurate—and that it will be grounds for discipline or dismissal if the applicant is hired and the employer later finds out that false information was given on the application.

There should be a separate signature line if the employer wants to get a credit report to indicate release of this information. Applicants should be informed when reference checks will be done. The form should clarify that application is being made for at-will employment. If the job offer is conditional on the applicant's passing a physical examination and/or drug and alcohol testing, this should be indicated on the application.

Check state law about which questions are permissible, and which are ruled out by antidiscrimination laws.

See 70 Fed. Reg. 58,947 (Oct. 7, 2005) for DOL's Office of Federal Contract Compliance Programs' Final Rule covering federal contractors' records maintenance obligations with respect to Internet-based job applications. If possible, contractors should collect data on the gender, race, and ethnicity of applicants (including those who apply online). Contractors are required to maintain records of Internet-based expressions of interest that resulted in the contractor considering an applicant for a particular job. [Tresa Baldas, *New Web Hiring Rules Cause Corporate Consternation*, Nat'l L.J. (Dec. 7, 2005) (law.com)]

See 78 Fed. Reg. 58683 (Sept. 24, 2013) for OFCCP regulations under Rehab Act 503: federal contractors are required to collect information about applicants' disabilities pursuant to the OFCCP's goal of having federal contractors hire 7% persons with disabilities. [DOL Final Rule, *Affirmative Action and Nondiscrimination Obligations of Contractors and Subcontractors Regarding Individuals With Disabilities*, 78 Fed. Reg. 58683 (Sept. 24, 2013)]

§ 23.07 ESTABLISHING TERMS AND CONDITIONS

The interview should stress the at-will nature of employment if your company wants the flexibility to terminate employees without a formal structure. Train interviewers to avoid statements such as "If you do a good job, you'll be set for life here" or "We never lay anybody off, no matter how tough the economy gets." Interviewers should also avoid statements about corporate procedure ("We go through all the channels before anybody gets fired") unless they accurately reflect corporate policy and practice.

Interviewers are agents of the company, and even if the employee handbook says that the company is only obligated if there are written contracts, in fact the company is likely to be held accountable for promises made by the interviewer (for instance, about vacation terms, the availability of leave, and education benefits). Even if the interviewer is not a common-law employee of the company, the agency relationship is likely to create liability for the company if the interviewer is guilty of discrimination. [See, e.g., *Halpert v. Manhattan Apartments Inc.*, 580 F.3d 86 (2d Cir. 2009); see Mark Hamblett, *2nd Circuit: Employer May Be Held Liable for Contractor Age Bias,* N.Y.L.J. (Sept. 14, 2009) (law.com)]

Many companies set a salary range rather than an explicit pay rate for a particular job. Interviewers should understand whether or not they can negotiate a salary with a promising candidate, or if that matter will have to be referred to a higher-up. Interviewees should always be told clearly who else is involved in the interview process, what the powers are of each person, and who has the power to actually make a job offer.

§ 23.08 REFERENCE CHECKS

Reference checks have become much more common, as prices have fallen and employers have become more sensitive to potential problems and liability related to the hiring process.

Reference checks on employees (rather than applicants) can also be useful. A lack of candor can be a valid reason for denying a raise or promotion, and "after-acquired evidence" discovered as late as the preparation for a discrimination suit can be used to reduce the recovery a plaintiff can obtain.

In early 2011, the Supreme Court unanimously upheld the federal government's background check procedure for workers employed by federal contractors. Although the Ninth Circuit granted an injunction against enforcement of the procedure, finding that the questions about counseling and drug treatment were too broad, and persons listed as references were asked open-ended questions that were not detailed enough, the Supreme Court held that the process was reasonably related to security needs, and the Privacy Act controls inappropriate releases of information. [*NASA v. Nelson*, 131 S. Ct. 746 (2011); see Rebecca Moore, *High Court Rejects Federal Contract Workers Challenge to Background Checks*, plansponsor.com (Jan. 20, 2011)]

In March 2014, the EEOC and FTC jointly published guidance about background checks, warning employers that whenever background information (from any source) is used to make employment decisions, compliance with anti-discrimination laws (including Title VII, GINA, the ADEA, and the FCRA) is mandatory. The EEOC warned that it is illegal to check background information only because of a person's race, national origin, color, sex, disability, age, or genetic status. "Special care" should be taken when there are problems that may be more common among members of certain groups (e.g., some ethnic groups have higher arrest rates than others).

The EEOC says that "except in rare circumstances" employers should not seek genetic information from applicants or employees, and medical questions should not be asked before a job offer has been made. The FTC says that the FCRA requires safeguards if an employer obtains a credit or criminal background report from a company that compiles background information. The applicant or employee must be given written notice that this information might be used in employment decisions and his or her written consent must be obtained. If an investigative report (based on personal interviews) is ordered, the applicant or employee must be informed of the right to information about the investigation. If adverse actions are taken based on information from a profiling company, the employer must give the applicant or employee a copy of the FTC's summary of FCRA rights, and must give contact information for the profiling company. [EEOC/FTC, *Background Checks: What Employers Need to Know*, <http://www.eeoc.gov/eeoc/publications/background_checks_employers.cfm> (March 2014)]

The EEOC opposes blanket refusals to hire based on criminal records (or credit reports) if the refusal has a disparate impact on minorities, a principle embodied in April 2012 guidance. [EEOC Enforcement Guidance, *Consideration of Arrest and Conviction Records In Employment Decisions Under Title VII of the Civil Rights Act of 1964*, <http://www.eeoc.gov/laws/guidance/arrest_conviction.cfm> (Apr. 25, 2012); see Steven Greenhouse, *Equal Opportunity Panel Updates Hiring Policy*, NYTimes.com (Apr. 25, 2012)]

The National Employment Law Project says that one-quarter of adults have a criminal record that would show up on a background check, so this issue obviously has an impact on many people. The EEOC encourages employers to use a two-step process: first a targeted screen of criminal records that considers what the record was for and when it occurred; the nature of the job; and then how the individual candidate should be assessed. The EEOC does not believe that this process imposes significant costs on employers. [Ilyse Schuman, *EEOC Clarifies Guidance On Criminal Background Checks*, Littler Mendelson (Sept. 25, 2013), available at Lexology.com]

The EEOC has brought suits in Illinois and South Carolina, charging that the defendants' criminal background check policies violated Title VII because they adversely impacted minorities and were not justified by being job-related and consistent with business necessity. The EEOC was unsuccessful in at least two suits: the District Court for the District of Maryland granted summary judgment for the employer, finding that the EEOC's statistical expert was unreliable; the Sixth Circuit upheld the district court's sanctions of almost $752,000 imposed on the EEOC for continuing to litigate a case after it became evident that the defendant did not maintain an unlawful company-wide ban on hiring persons with felony records. [*EEOC v. Freeman*, 961 F. Supp. 2d 783 (D. Md. 2013); *EEOC v. PeopleMark*, 732 F.3d 584 (6th Cir. 2013); see Brian D. Hall, *EEOC's Campaign Against Criminal Background Checks Takes Recent Hits*, Porter Wright Morris & Arthur LLP (Oct. 10, 2013), available at Lexology.com; Joann Coston-Holloway, *EEOC Provides Clarification On Use Of Criminal History Information In Hiring Decisions*, Baker Donelson Bearman Caldwell & Berkowitz PC (Jan. 16, 2014), available at Lexology.com]

More than 50 cities and local governments have "ban the box" laws, forbidding questions about criminal convictions on initial job applications. However, most of those laws apply only to public employers. Private employers are subject to ban the box laws in Hawaii, Massachusetts, Minnesota, and Rhode Island, as well as San Francisco, Seattle (Washington), Buffalo, Newark, and Philadelphia.

[Susan Gross Sholinsky, *Take 5: Views You Can Use: Labor And Employment*, Epstein Becker Green (Nov. 12, 2013), available at Lexology.com] Subsequently, several other jurisdictions adopted "ban the box" laws, including the states of Delaware (public employers), Illinois, and New Jersey, and the city of Baltimore. [Philip L. Gordon and Zoe M. Argento, *Baltimore Becomes the 10th Jurisdiction to "Ban the Box,"* Littler Mendelson (May 16, 2014), available at Lexology.com; Carolyn A. Pellegrini, *Boxing Out in Delaware*, Montgomery McCracken Walker & Rhoads LLP (May 29, 2014), available at Lexology.com; Nora Kersten Walsh and Alexis M. Dominguez, *Illinois' New "Ban the Box" Law Restricts Criminal History Inquiries of Applicants*, Schiff Hardin LLP (Aug. 6, 2014), available at Lexology.com; Christopher Lowe and Alnisa Bell, *New Jersey Joins "Ban the Box" Movement and Chris Christie Safeguards Employers*, Seyfarth Shaw LLP (Aug. 13, 2014), available at Lexology.com]

The ordinances differ on the timing of permitted versus forbidden inquiries. The San Francisco law does not allow employers to ask about convictions or pending criminal charges on an employment application or at a first live interview. But Massachusetts permits inquiries at any time after the initial application; Seattle, after applicants have received initial screening for basic qualifications; Minnesota, after the person has been selected for a job interview; Rhode Island and Buffalo, at the initial interview; Philadelphia and San Francisco, after the initial interview; Hawaii and Newark, after a conditional offer of employment has been extended. [Philip L. Gordon and Zoe M. Argento, *San Francisco's Board Of Supervisors "Bans The Box" And Further Complicates Criminal History Checks By The City's Employers*, Littler Mendelson (Feb. 10, 2014), available at Lexology.com; Todd M. Torres, *Rhode Island Employers May No Longer Ask About Criminal Convictions On Employment Applications*, Ogletree Deakins (Aug. 28, 2013), available at Lexology.com]

Usually, a criminal-record check starts with a trace on the applicant's Social Security number, which generates a list of previous addresses. (Of course, this implies that the applicant was operating "on the books" and using his or her own name!) A complete search looks for outstanding wants and warrants (misdemeanors as well as felonies), motor vehicle reports, credit reports, academic qualifications, and verification of past employment.

A good criminal record check goes back at least seven years. Because many court systems have automated records going back only one to six years, it is often necessary for the research firm to do a manual search (which often costs extra). It is also common for misdemeanor and felony records to be kept in different places, which could also lead to higher fees for separate searches. [Merry Mayer, *Background Checks in Focus*, HR Magazine, Jan. 2002, at 59] Federal contractors, especially defense contractors, must also be alert to the question of which employees will require a security clearance.

§ 23.09 NONDISCRIMINATORY HIRING

Federal law bans discrimination in employment, which definitely includes hiring. Discrimination on account of age, sex, race, disability, religion, and/or national origin is banned. However, even a company that strives to avoid deliberate prejudice can find it hard to eradicate "disparate impact"—apparently neutral practices that actually disadvantage members of one group more than others. For instance, a minimum height requirement screens out more women and certain ethnic groups than white males. That does not mean that employers cannot impose height requirements, as long as it really is necessary to be taller than a certain height to do the job properly.

Other potential sources of disparate impact include:

- Educational standards;
- Pre-employment testing;
- Requirements of military service;
- Referrals from your current workforce (who tend to know people of their own ethnic group);
- Rules about facial hair (which could disadvantage religious applicants, or black men who have ingrown hairs that make shaving painful);
- Refusing to hire anyone who has ever been arrested, filed for bankruptcy, or had a child out of wedlock.

Your attorney should review hiring practices to make sure that they are not discriminatory and that all requirements can be justified in terms of the practical needs of the business and skills that will actually be used on the job. For each position, you should also determine the physical capacities that are central to the job, those that are sometimes used but are peripheral, and those that are never invoked by the job.

If employees request flextime (for parenting needs, as an accommodation to disability, as a religious accommodation, or simply for convenience), you should either be able to grant the request or demonstrate a legitimate business reason why conventional business hours or standard shifts must be observed.

There are two important criteria for assessing interview questions:

- Do the questions relate to legitimate workplace issues, rather than just satisfying curiosity?
- Are they asked uniformly, rather than only to a group of people chosen on the basis of preconceived notions? For instance, it is discriminatory to ask a woman if her husband "lets" her travel on business, but not discriminatory to discuss the amount of travel required with all applicants,

including the number of overnight or prolonged stays required, and to ask all candidates if they are able to travel that much.

Equal employment opportunity law assumes that many candidates will be interviewed for each opening, and there are many reasons why the successful candidate will be selected. There is no reason to collect a great deal of information about candidates who have no real chance of selection. Therefore, some questions are acceptable when a conditional job offer is made that would not be allowed at a first-stage interview.

For instance, marital status and having children are very relevant to participation in an employee group health plan, but irrelevant if the person is not going to get a job offer. So this information should either be requested only after hiring, or collected on a separate sheet of paper and not consulted until after hiring. [See § 36.09 for a discussion of acceptable and unacceptable pre-employment inquiries and tests in the disability context.]

It is not acceptable to ask an interviewee about his or her history of receiving Worker's Compensation benefits, but anyone who gets a conditional job offer can be asked about past injuries that may require accommodation.

There are also circumstances under which the company's commitment to equal employment opportunity must be put into writing: if the company is a federal contractor, for instance.

§ 23.10 PRE-EMPLOYMENT TESTING

It is legitimate for an employer to test job applicants to see if they have relevant skills. Title VII permits the use of professionally developed ability tests that are not designed or administered with a discriminatory motive. A valid test is one that is neither explicitly nor implicitly discriminatory against protected groups; one that tests skills that are actually used in the job; and one that has been validated by psychologists or other experts so that it really offers insight into the issues needed for effective hiring.

A Supreme Court case, *Albemarle Paper Co. v. Moody* [422 U.S. 405 (1975)], holds that if a test has a disproportionate negative effect on a minority group, the test is permissible only if professionally accepted methods verify the test's ability to predict important elements of work behavior. As *Griggs v. Duke Power Co.* [401 U.S. 424 (1971)] says, the point of pre-employment testing is to measure the applicant's performance in the context of a specific job, not in the abstract. Even if the company's pre-employment test is valid, it is discriminatory to give the test only to minority-group members.

However, in 2009, another Supreme Court case (dealing with a promotional exam for firefighters) endorsed properly validated and professionally drafted tests. New Haven, Connecticut refused to certify the test or use the test results to make up a promotion list, because almost all of the highest scoring candidates were white, and the city was afraid of lawsuits from minority firefighters. However, a suit was filed by white firefighters who said they were improperly denied promotions. The Supreme Court said that refusing to certify the test constituted intentional discrimination against the higher scoring white and Hispanic firefighters. Even if it had been sued by minority firefighters, the city could have defended itself by citing the Title VII provision that allows the use of valid, job-related tests that are implemented as a matter of business necessity. [*Ricci v. DeStefano*, 557 U.S. 557 (2009)]

If your company adopts a pre-employment test and monitors the results, discovering that the test has an adverse impact on women and/or members of minority groups, then you should either get rid of the test, change it to remove the adverse impact, or do a validity study that confirms both that the test is a business necessity and that it accurately predicts the skills needed for successful job performance. The Civil Rights Act of 1991 [Pub. L. No. 102-166] says that it is not acceptable to grade minority applicants' tests on a "curve," or to have a lower passing grade for minorities.

Publications about psychological testing are good for finding out which tests have already been validated. Three types of validation are accepted:

- Criterion-related (the test is an accurate predictor of work behavior or other criteria of employee adequacy);
- Content-related (the test accurately duplicates the tasks that will actually be called for in the workplace);
- Construct-related (the test identifies general mental and psychological traits needed to do the job, such as the ability to remain cool under pressure and respond courteously to angry customers).

Some job applicants challenge online pre-employment tests for bias. The employer can be liable if the effect of the test is to exclude protected groups; the company must be able to prove that the traits that are measured are relevant to job performance. For example, Vicky Sandy, who is hearing-impaired, scored low on a 50-question test about cheerfulness, empathy, and self-confidence that Kroger asks cashier applicants to take. She complained to the EEOC that she was discriminated against by being required to take a test that is biased against the hearing-impaired, even those who can work effectively and the EEOC investigated her claim. The EEOC included pre-employment tests in its draft enforcement plan for 2012–2016 (issued Sept. 4, 2012). In 2011, only 164 out of almost 100,000 EEOC complaints referred to testing—perhaps because employees seldom see the test results, so they blame other factors if they are not hired or promoted. In July 2012, Leprino Foods Inc. (a food processor that is a government contractor) settled DOL hiring discrimination charges by agreeing to pay $550,000 in back pay to black, Hispanic, and Asian applicants who were rejected as laborers because they failed the WorkKeys pre-hire test. The DOL's Office of

Federal Contract Compliance Programs (OFCCP) said that the test, which involves math and observation skills, is not relevant to the entry-level jobs for which it was used. [Joseph Walker, *Debating the Legality of Big Data in Hiring*, WSJ.com (Sept. 19, 2012)]

§ 23.11 IMMIGRATION ISSUES

Immigration cases about employer sanctions, document fraud, and unfair employment practices relating to immigration are heard by ALJs working for the Department of Justice's Executive Office for Immigration Review (EOIR). Under 8 U.S.C. § 1324a, employers can be subject to civil penalties for knowingly hiring or continuing to employ aliens who are not authorized to work in the United States, or for failure to prepare and maintain proper documentation on employees' work authorization. There are also penalties for document fraud (8 U.S.C. § 1324c) and unfair practices (8 U.S.C. § 1324b) and discriminating against persons who do have authorization to work in the United States on the basis of their national origin or citizenship. The Department of Justice's Civil Rights Division, Office of Special Counsel for Immigration-Related Unfair Employment Practices handles cases of immigration-related employment discrimination. [DOJ Fact Sheet, *EOIR's Office of the Chief Administrative Hearing Officer*, <http://www.justice.gov/eoir/press/2012/OCAHOFactSheet05292012.pdf> (Oct. 1, 2013)]

[A] Employment Requirement

If an alien wishes to enter this country on the basis of employment, he or she must not only have a definite job offer from a U.S. employer, but the employer must have "labor certification." [<http://workforcesecurity.doleta.gov/foreign/hiring.asp>] That is, the Department of Labor must certify that the job is "open" because the company cannot recruit a qualified U.S. worker at the prevailing wages. First, the employer must use the State Employment Service and post and advertise the job opportunity. The employer must interview any applicants who come through that route, and must file a recruitment report with the DOL explaining why none of those applicants was suitable for the position.

However, certain occupations are considered "shortage" occupations because of a documented difficulty in filling the jobs: nursing, physical therapy, and people of demonstrated exceptional ability in business, science, or the arts. Multinational executives, outstanding university-level teachers, researchers, and people whose jobs are in the national interest do not displace American workers, so labor certification will not be required for such jobs.

Immigration law is basically a federal area, as the Supreme Court pointed out in June 2012, when it struck down most of Arizona's immigration law. The Arizona law made it a misdemeanor for an illegal alien to apply for work, or to work as either an employee or as an independent contractor. The Supreme Court noted that Congress chose not to make it a crime for illegal immigrants to work in the United States. However, the Supreme Court did uphold the part of the Arizona statute that allows the police to check the immigration status of people who have been detained. [*Arizona v. United States*, 132 S. Ct. 2492 (2012) Alabama enacted a statute, the Beason-Hammond Alabama Taxpayer and Citizen Protection Act, with similar immigration provisions. The Eleventh Circuit held that federal immigration law preempts this statute, which made it a crime for unauthorized aliens to work in the United States: *United States v. Alabama*, 691 F.3d 1269 (11th Cir. 2012), rendering the law unenforceable.]

South Carolina's immigration laws were also held to be preempted by federal immigration law. [*United States v. South Carolina*, 720 F.3d 518 (4th Cir. 2013)]

[B] Immigration Categories

Employment-based immigration is regulated under the Immigration Act of 1990. [Pub. L. No. 101-649] There are various categories of employable immigrants, e.g.:

- Priority workers (individuals of extraordinary ability and/or vocational responsibility);
- Professionals with advanced degrees and/or exceptional ability;
- Other workers (skilled workers, professionals without advanced degrees; unskilled workers who have DOL certification that there is a shortage of U.S. workers with similar skills);
- Special immigrants (e.g., religious workers sent to the U.S. by a religious hierarchy);
- Immigrants who have the financial capacity to invest at least $1 million within the United States, employing at least 10 U.S. workers;
- H-1B "specialty occupation" workers who reside temporarily within the United States, and work here, but do not become citizens;
- H-2 temporary non-agricultural workers.

According to the USCIS Website, employers can use the Petition for Nonimmigrant Worker (I-129) not only for H-1B workers but P-1 athletes and entertainers, H-1C registered nurses, P-2 artistic exchange candidates, H-2 temporary laborers, H-3 alien trainees, Q-1 international cultural exchange program participants, O-1 aliens with extraordinary ability, and L-1 intracompany transferees. The H-1B classification is divided into H-1B1 (specialty occupations requiring theoretical and practical application of professional skills) and H-1B2 (exceptional services in a cooperative research and development project administered by the Department of Defense). [USCIS, Temporary Benefits Employment Categories and Required Documentation, <http://www.uscis.gov/portal/site/uscis/menuitem.5af9bb[. . .]>]

In May 2010, the DOL launched a new Website, the H-1B Advisor, to assist employers and potential H-1B visa holders in understanding the requirements of the program. [<http://www.dol.gov/elaws/h1b.htm>]

Although DOL policy, including 2010 amendments to the regulations, requires employers to reimburse H-2B workers (non-agricultural temporary workers) visa, travel, and recruitment expenses, the Fifth Circuit held in 2010 that this is not required by the FLSA itself. Therefore, the Fifth Circuit dismissed an FLSA collective action brought by a group of hotel workers who said that these costs were "tools of the trade" that should have been reimbursed. [*Castellanos-Contreras v. Decatur Hotels LLC*, 622 F.3d 393 (5th Cir. 2010)]

[C] Employer Responsibilities: No-Match Letters and E-Verify

U.S. labor and immigration law places a burden on the employer (or on an agency that gets a fee for recruitment or making referrals) to determine whether job applicants are legally permitted to work in this country. No later than three business days after hiring, the employer must ascertain if the new hire is a U.S. citizen or a legal immigrant who is not only permitted to reside in this country but to work here. Presidential Executive Order 12989 [61 Fed. Reg. 6091 (Feb. 13, 1996)] debars federal contractors from getting further federal contracts after they have been caught knowingly hiring illegal aliens.

The employer responsibilities stem from the Immigration Reform and Control Act of 1986 (IRCA). [7 U.S.C. § 1324a] The employer is responsible for checking documents presented by potential new employees to demonstrate their identity and authorization to work within the United States. (There are people who are lawfully permitted to enter and reside in this country, but not to work here, so there is more to the matter than distinguishing illegal aliens from lawful immigrants.)

The information must be obtained in a way that is not discriminatory against dark-skinned people, or people whose first language is not English.

Both the U.S. Citizenship and Immigration Services (USCIS) and the DOL are entitled to inspect a company's immigration-related forms, but to enter a workplace they must either have a warrant or give 72 hours' notice.

Employment of immigrants requires the employer to work with both the DOL's Employment and Training Administration and the USCIS, which is part of the Department of Homeland Security. Employers can obtain permission to hire foreign workers on either a temporary (e.g., nurses; seasonal agricultural workers; specialized professional workers) or a permanent basis, depending on the facts of the case and the conditions within the U.S. labor market. The overarching policy is that employment of a foreign worker depends on proof that there is a shortage preventing the hiring of U.S. workers for the job. Furthermore, the law requires lawful immigrant workers to receive at least the prevailing wage for their jobs, so immigrant workers cannot be used to depress wages.

The Department of Labor published a Final Rule, effective March 28, 2005, now found at 20 C.F.R. § 656.10 and 20 C.F.R. § 656.15.

Labor certification is the process of petitioning DOL's Employment and Training Administration; the ETA certifies to the USCIS that permitting the person the employer wishes to hire is appropriate because no U.S. worker is available to fill the job. The application is ETA Form 9089, Alien Employment Certification, describing the job duties, qualifications, and experience required. The employer should submit Form 9089 in duplicate, signed by the alien and by an authorized official of the employer company. If the petition for an alien worker (see below) is approved, then the USCIS will forward one copy of the Form 9089 to the Chief of the Division of Foreign Labor Certification.

The employer must obtain a prevailing wage determination from the state workforce agency (to show that the employer is not hiring immigrants in order to depress the wages paid for the job). If the employer has a collective bargaining unit, the employer must either notify the union or post a notice for at least 10 consecutive calendar days, to disclose that labor certification is being sought. If the employer normally uses in-house media, such as an employee newsletter, to announce job openings, the same means must be used to inform employees that labor certification is being sought. Notice of this type should be given not more than 180 and not less than 30 days before the Form I-140 petition is filed.

After labor certification is obtained, the employer files USCIS Form I-140, Immigrant Petition for an Alien Worker, on behalf of the alien worker. [The DOL's explanation of the process can be found at *Hiring Foreign Workers*, <http://www.workforcesecurity.doleta.gov/foreign/hiring.asp> and *Permanent Labor Certification*; see also USCIS, *Guidance for Schedule A Blanket Labor Certifications Effective February 14, 2006*, <http://www.uscis.gov/graphics/lawsregs/handbook/afm_ch22_021406.pdf> (Feb. 24, 2006)]

It is illegal to knowingly hire an ineligible person. Knowledge includes constructive knowledge (reasonable inferences from facts and circumstances, to the degree that a person acting with reasonable care would have to be aware). According to USCIS regulations [see 8 C.F.R. § 274a], these circumstances create an inference of constructive knowledge:

- The employer actually has some information that the person is not eligible for U.S. employment;
- The applicant refuses to complete the I-9 form, or does it improperly;
- The employer acts with "reckless and wanton disregard" of the consequences of hiring ineligible persons.

However, accent and appearance are not acceptable sources of constructive knowledge. Once the employer knows that the hiree is (or has become, because of a change of status) ineligible to work in the United States, continuing employment is unlawful. [See 8 U.S.C. § 1324a]

The federal crime of "aggravated identity theft" (18 U.S.C. § 1028A(a)(1)) carries a mandatory two-year prison sentence if a person convicted of certain crimes committed the crime by knowingly using someone else's means of identification. In a mid-2009 Supreme Court case, the petitioner was a Mexican citizen who, to establish eligibility to work in the United States, gave his employer false Social Security and alien registration cards with his name and identification numbers that belonged to other people. He was arrested for immigration offenses and aggravated identity theft. His argument was that the numbers were chosen at random, and he did not know that they belonged to other people. The Supreme Court ruled that, to convict, the prosecution must show that the defendant knew the identification numbers belonged to someone else. [*Flores-Figueroa v. United States*, 556 U.S. 646 (2009)]

E-Verify is an electronic program for ascertaining employees' right to work in the United States. It began as a voluntary program, although several states (e.g., Arizona, Georgia, Minnesota, South Carolina) passed laws requiring employers in those states to use E-Verify. [Rebecca Moore, *House Bill Would Extend Use of Federal E-Verify Program*, plansponsor.com (Aug. 5, 2008)]

Because of a suit brought by business groups, the DOJ delayed the effective date of mandatory E-Verify until February 20, 2009 (after the deadline for filing final motions and briefs in the suit). [Rebecca Moore, *Department of Justice Delays Effective Date for E-Verify Requirement*, plansponsor.com (Jan. 9, 2009)]

Mandatory status was delayed yet again, to May 21, 2009, so that the incoming Obama administration could review the rule. [Miriam Jordan, *White House Holds Off on Tightening Immigration Checks*, WSJ.com (Jan. 30, 2009). The suits in question were *Chamber of Commerce of the U.S. v. Napolitano*, No. 08-cv-3444AW (D. Md.) (summary judgment in *Chamber of Commerce* was granted to the federal government on August 28, 2009: 648 F. Supp. 2d 726 (D. Md. 2009), <http://www.mdd.uscourts.gov/Opinions/Opinions/chamber082509.pdf> and *AFL-CIO v. Napolitano*, No. 07-cv-4472CRB (N.D. Cal.), no outcome found). [Pamela A. MacLean, *Controversial "E-Verify" Immigration Program on Hold*, Nat'l L.J. (Feb. 3, 2009) (law.com)]

In mid-2009, Department of Homeland Security Secretary Janet Napolitano announced the administration's support for a regulation requiring federal contractors to enroll in E-Verify within 30 days of getting a federal contract, and to use it to check employees' work authorization. The administration concluded that E-Verify is more effective than the No-Match Rule, and the latter was rescinded. Any business receiving a federal contract or subcontract, including ARRA funds, must use E-Verify, with full implementation beginning September 8, 2009. DHS announced that it had new processes to reduce typographical errors and initial mismatches, and to connect to naturalization databases to verify the status of naturalized citizens. [Homeland Security Press Release, *Secretary Napolitano Strengthens Employment Verification with Administration's Commitment to E-Verify*, <http://www.dhs.gov/ynews/releases/pr_1247063976814.shtm> (July 8, 2009)]

As of July 20, 2013, 467,328 employers were enrolled in E-Verify. USCIS's February 2013 survey showed that 80% of E-Verify users had fewer than 300 employees, and 85% of users said they would continue to use it even if it were not legally required, because they said that it is free, easy to use, quick, and reassures their corporate clients that they do not employ illegal workers. However, some employers criticize E-Verify for increasing their hiring costs, because applicants are reluctant to provide information and employers often find that there have been no qualified applicants, and because they need extra staff to handle administration. At least 16 states (e.g., Arizona, Georgia, Mississippi, South Carolina) require employers (or certain categories of employers) to use E-Verify before hiring anybody, but do not require checks of current employees. [Angus Loten, Sarah E. Needleman, and Adam Janofsky, *Small Businesses Say U.S. Background-Check System Has Drawbacks*, WSJ.com (July 24, 2013)]

The federal government responded to criticism by attempts to improve the accuracy of E-Verify. An enhancement was released on November 18, 2013 to fight identity fraud. USCIS can lock an SSN within the E-Verify system if it appears to have been misused, to deter other people from using it. When an attempt is made to use a locked SSN, E-Verify generates a "Tentative Nonconfirmation," and the person who gets the notice will have to contest the finding at the local SSA field office. (Employers are not allowed to take adverse employment action until the problem is resolved.) If the employee provides a valid SSN, the number will be moved to Employment Authorized status. [Andrew W. Merrills, Justin S. Coffey, and Nicole Brooks, *Will The New E-Verify Security Enhancement Help Or Hurt?*, Ogletree Deakins (Jan. 22, 2014), available at Lexology.com]

The Obama administration adopted a new enforcement strategy: "silent raids" under which federal agents examine employment records to find undocumented workers. [Julia Preston, *Illegal Workers Swept From Jobs in* "Silent Raids," WSJ.com (July 9, 2010); Miriam Jordan, *U.S. Expands Crackdown on Firms Hiring Illegal Immigrants*, WSJ.com (Feb. 17, 2011). [Miriam Jordan, *Immigration Audits Drive Illegal Workers Underground*, WSJ.com (Aug. 15, 2011)]

In 2013, there was additional enforcement attention to hiring illegal workers. About a thousand businesses throughout the United States were required to submit documents for audit, although ICE did not release the names of the businesses. When ICE does a document audit, it generally asks for I-9 forms, rosters of workers, weekly work schedules, and payroll documents. If there are mismatches, a notice of suspect documents is issued. The employer must tell the workers in question to either produce legitimate work authorization documents or resign. ICE imposes fines for any clerical errors on the forms or hiring of unauthorized workers.

In previous "silent audits," the employer was given three to four months to submit documents, but the timetable has been accelerated to 20 days, which can be difficult for the employer to meet. In the past four years, more than $100 million in administrative and criminal fines have been imposed in at least 10,000 audits. For example, two Texas businesses, Atrium Corp. and Advanced Containment Systems, paid $2 million each for hiring illegal aliens. Washington State's HerbCo Int'l paid $1 million for hiring unauthorized immigrants and then re-hiring some of them after the audit. According to the Pew Hispanic Center, there are about 11 million undocumented immigrants in the United States, eight million of whom are in the workforce. [Miriam Jordan and Julie Jargon, *U.S. Starts New Push to Find Illegal Workers*, WSJ.com (Sept. 13, 2013)]

Civil fines for violating federal immigration laws on employment were raised in February 2008. Civil penalties under the INA are adjusted for inflation, and the previous adjustment was in 1999, so the average increase was about 25%. The maximum penalty for knowingly employing an unauthorized alien rose from $275 to $375. The maximum penalty for first violations rose from $2,200 to $3,200, and the civil penalty for multiple violations went from $11,000 to $16,000 (all penalties on a per-worker basis). [Rebecca Moore, *DOJ Announces Higher Civil Fines for Employer Immigration Violations*, plansponsor.com (Mar. 3, 2008)]

[D] Employment Verification Documents

Hired individuals prove their eligibility to work within the United States either by showing that they are U.S. citizens (e.g., showing a U.S. passport or birth certificate evidencing birth within the United States) or by showing that they have a so-called green card. (The document, Form I-551, is no longer actually green.)

Since 1997, the Immigration and Naturalization Service has issued Form I-766, a tamper-resistant card issued to aliens whose immigration status permits work within the United States. The I-766 is a List A Employment Authorization Document (EAD): that is, it establishes both the job applicant's identity and his or her entitlement to work.

There are three categories of documents. List A documents can be used to prove both identity and employability; List B documents prove identity only; List C documents prove employability only.

See OMB No. 1615-0047, <http://www.uscis.gov/sites/default/files/files/form/i-9.pdf>, valid until March 31, 2016, the nine-page I-9 form. The Ninth Circuit held that employers are required by 8 U.S.C. § 1324a(b) to enter verification information in Form I-9 § 2 even if copies of supporting documents are attached. The Ninth Circuit held that it is not arbitrary and capricious to require the employer to actually complete the I-9 form. ICE said that there were 43 employees for whom no I-9 forms were submitted; the employee information and attestation sections were incomplete for 65 employees; and the employer verification was incomplete for 110 employees. The ALJ's civil penalty, of close to $287,000, was upheld. The employer had previously been warned by an INS audit (as the agency was then known) that employees had to be trained to verify I-9 forms. The Ninth Circuit held that fines are imposed automatically for substantive violations of § 1324a(b) if there are errors or omissions in the forms that impair ICE's ability to verify the employment status of new hires. [*Ketchikan Drywall Servs., Inc. v. ICE*, 725 F.3d 1103 (9th Cir. 2013); see Jackson Lewis LLP, *Document Copies Do Not Replace Obligation To Complete Form I-9*, Lexology.com (Sept. 6, 2013); Robert S. Groban, Jr. et al., *Ninth Circuit Upholds Civil Penalties For Form I-9 Violations*, Epstein Becker Green (Oct. 29, 2013), available at Lexology.com]

[E] H-1B, H-2A, and H-2B Visas

The H-1B visa is a non-immigrant visa for temporary workers in "specialty occupations." This means jobs that apply a highly specialized body of knowledge in both a theoretical and a practical way. Most H-1B visa holders work in high-tech businesses, such as software development. The initial duration of the visa is three years, although it can be extended for three more years. The worker must have at least a bachelor's degree in his or her specialty field, or must have equivalent qualifications and expertise. If the job requires a state license, the visa holder must have the license.

H-1B workers must be paid either the salary the employer would otherwise pay for the job, or the prevailing wage in the area. This requirement is designed to prevent employers from hiring foreign workers simply to lower wage costs. Willful violation of this requirement or the layoff requirement can be penalized by a $35,000 fine and three years' debarment from federal contracts.

Employers usually recruit workers from foreign students in the United States on student visas and about to graduate from a program that gives them the necessary specialized skills. Immigration law requires the employer to wait until the student graduates before making a job offer. You can get around this problem by having the student get permission from the Immigration and Naturalization Services to add a year of PGPT (post-graduate practical training) to his or her student visa, so you can apply for the H-1B visa during this extra year. The holders of student visas are required to leave the United States by July of the year in which they graduate, unless they have PGPT authorization.

After a two-year DOJ investigation, Infosys Technologies Ltd. Inc. agreed to a $34 million civil settlement, the largest settlement in an immigration case about hiring and relocation of foreign nationals. A whistleblower employee disclosed improper hiring of Indian workers under B-1 business visitor visas when H-1B visas were required. The B-1 visa covers brief business trips; holders of this visa are not permitted to work in the United States. [Beth E. Carlson et al., *Largest Civil Settlement In Immigration Case: Department Of Justice And Infosys Settle Two-Year Investigation For $34 Million*, Faegre Baker Daniels (Oct. 31, 2013), available at Lexology.com]

H-1B visa holders may not be hired until the employer has first attempted to recruit qualified U.S. workers, although a more qualified H-1B applicant can legitimately be preferred to a less-qualified U.S. citizen. Employers are also forbidden to terminate U.S. workers for the purpose of replacing them with H-1B workers. Temporary agencies and other suppliers of contingent workers are forbidden to make any placements of H-1B workers with any company that has displaced U.S. workers.

The DOL regulation not only protects U.S. jobs, but also it protects the H-1B workers from exploitation. They must be given benefits on the same basis as their U.S. counterparts. Whenever their employer places them in a nonproductive category (e.g., there is a temporary lull in work), they must be kept at full salary. It is unlawful for employers to require H-1B workers to reimburse them for the cost of filing the employment petition, or to penalize workers for terminating their work assignment prematurely.

To encourage reporting of misconduct, protection is extended to applicants, employees, and ex-employees who assist the Departments of Labor and Justice in their investigations. In fact, H-1B whistleblowers can be permitted to remain in the United States for up to six years.

Also see the H-1B Visa Reform Act of 2004, enacted as part of Pub. L. No. 108-447, the appropriations act, adding an additional 20,000 H-1B visa slots for visa holders with a Master's Degree or higher from an institution in the United States, and permitting expedited processing for an additional fee. Interim Final Rules were published in mid-2005. [70 Fed. Reg. 23775 (May 5, 2005). See DOL Wage & Hour Division, *Fact Sheet #62A, Changes Made By the H-1B Visa Reform Act of 2004*, <http://www.dol.gov/whd/regs/compliance/FactSheet62/whdfs62A.pdf> (July 2008)]

On March 19, 2008, USCIS issued an interim final rule that forbids employers to file more than one H-1B petition for a particular employee in a fiscal year. Duplicate petitions will be rejected and the filing fees will not be refunded. The purpose of the rule is to prevent employers gaming the system by making multiple applications in the hope that one of them will be accepted. The interim final rule does not apply to applications made by related employers (e.g., a parent company and a subsidiary) to transfer an alien from one job to another.

Only 65,000 new H-1B visas can be granted per year, but the first 20,000 H-1B petitions filed on behalf of aliens who have earned master's or higher degrees in the United States are exempt from the 65,000 cap and subject to a separate "20,000 cap." H-1B petitions are entirely exempt from the numerical limitations if the alien will work in certain educational institutions, their affiliated nonprofit organizations, or nonprofit or governmental research institutions, so employers can make H-1B applications for exempt workers even if no regular

H-1B visa numbers are available. [USCIS, *Fact Sheet: Changes to the FY2009 H-1B Program,* <http://www.uscis.gov/archive/archive-news/fact-sheet-changes-fy2009-h-1b-program>.USCIS's *Handbook for Employers* (Form M-274, Nov. 1, 2007) was posted to <http://www.uscis.gov/files/nativedocuments/m-274.pdf>]

Most visas are issued for computer fields, generally to people from India or China. Only about 30% of H-1B visa applications survive the preliminary stage. In 2011, about 70,000 companies made H-1B applications; almost half made only one application, and most for fewer than 10 visas, suggesting small companies and startups. Small employers say they are unable to compete with large technology firms, and lack the HR staff to handle the paperwork. Legal fees are also a burden. Small business advocates call for a simplified procedure for small firms. [Angus Loten, *For Small Firms, Visas Are a Big Headache*, WSJ.com (Aug. 21, 2013)]

USCIS started to take H-1B applications for fiscal 2015 on April 1, 2014. The cap was 65,000, plus another 20,000 visas under the advanced degree exemption limit. Citizens of Chile and Singapore are entitled to 6,800 visas under free trade agreements. Since 2008, the USCIS has placed all petitions received in the first five days of the cap period into the lottery, even if there are enough applications on the first day to use the entire quota. [Laleh Sharifi, *FY2015 H-1B Cap Filing Season Is Almost Here*, Smith Gambrell & Russell LLP (Jan. 16, 2014), available at Lexology.com] As expected, it took less than a week for requests to reach the 65,000 limit as well as the 20,000 advanced degree limit, so a lottery will be held. [Miriam Jordan, *Big Demand for Skilled-Worker Visas*, WSJ.com (Apr. 7, 2014)]

Once laid off, H-1B visa holders must leave the United States unless they can find a qualifying new job almost immediately. There is no grace period: aliens who do not have another job must either leave within a few days of losing their jobs, or convert their visas to a B1/B2 tourist visa which does not allow them to work (but gives them a little time to sell their homes and arrange for the return to their home countries [Miriam Jordan, *Slump Sinks Visa Program*, WSJ.com (Oct. 29, 2009); Mona Sarika, *Homeward Bound*, WSJ.com (Nov. 9, 2009)]

H-1B visas are required for current employees who have F-1 student visas and will need a new visa when their F-1 employment authorization ends. H-1B visas may also be needed for J-1 academic visa holders receiving practical training. Current employees who hold TN or E-3 visas and are starting the green card process may need to transfer to H-1B status. A rule dating to 2008 gives some students up to 29 months of employment authorization—i.e., three chances to apply for an H-1B visa—if they studied scientific or technical subjects. [Jason E. Burritt and Gabriel Mozes, *H-1B Work Permit Filings: Will You Beat The Cap?*, Lexology.com (Dec. 10, 2013)]

In 1986, the H-2 visa program for unskilled foreign workers was divided into H-2A and H-2B. H-2B permits temporary recruitment of unskilled non-agricultural workers for jobs no qualified U.S. worker will take. Non-immigrant visa petitions are now determined by CIS, an agency within the Department of

Homeland Security. Homeland Security, in turn, designated DOL as the agency to advise it about whether H-2B petitions should be granted. In 2005, the DOL adopted the same wage calculation method as the H-1B program, where the prevailing wage is determined by a four-tier system based on the skill level for the occupation. In 2011, an NPRM was published eliminating the four-tier skill level method on the grounds that it did not provide an appropriate wage level to prevent adverse effects on U.S. workers. The NPRM defined the prevailing wage as the highest of CBA wages, wages under the DBA or SCA for the occupation, or the OES's mean wage rate for that occupation. [76 Fed. Reg. 3452 (Jan. 19, 2011); *Louisiana Forestry Assn Inc. v. Sec'y of Labor*, 745 F.3d 633 (3d Cir. 2014)]

The Ninth Circuit held that it violates the FLSA for an employer to fail to reimburse H-2A (temporary agricultural) workers for their travel and immigration expenses in the first week of employment. The Ninth Circuit applied the FLSA regulations forbidding employee expenses that reduce their compensation below minimum wage, even though the H-2A program has its own reimbursement regulations. The Ninth Circuit deferred to DOL regulations that provide that FLSA rules apply regardless of the H-2A regulations, which merely require reimbursement on completion of part of the work assignment. The Ninth Circuit deferred to the DOL's conclusion that the travel and immigration expenditures reduce the employees' effective wage because the expenses are undertaken on behalf of the employer. [*Rivera v. Peri & Sons Farms*, 735 F.3d 892 (9th Cir. 2013); see Noel P. Tripp, *Ninth Circuit Requires Reimbursement Of H-2A Expenses*, Jackson Lewis LLP (Nov. 26, 2013), available at Lexology.com]

In 2012, the H-2B program was changed to improve job opportunities for Americans while protecting foreign temporary workers. Most H-2B workers are employed by seasonal small businesses such as seafood fishing and processing, hotels and landscaping, and amusement parks. The extensive new rules took effect April 23, 2012.

A new electronic registry was created for posting jobs that employers want to fill with H-2B workers. The recruitment period for Americans is expanded; the employer must hire any qualified local worker who applies up to three weeks before the start of the H-2B contract. The process of labor-market certification has changed. It used to be sufficient to state that there was a search for U.S. workers. Now formal consultation with the state workforce agency is required to demonstrate that U.S. workers were unavailable. Once a migrant worker completes half the contract period, the employer is obligated to pay the guest worker's transportation costs from the home country to the United States. The employer is responsible for all visa fees and must pay for travel home when the job is completed or if the worker is dismissed early. A provision that is particularly unpopular with employers requires foreign workers to be paid for three-quarters of the period of the contract even if there is no work for them. Foreign recruiters are not allowed to charge fees to workers who come to the United States under the H-2B program. [Julia Preston, *Rules Revised for H-2B Guest Worker Program*, NYTimes.com (Feb. 10, 2012)]

The employer must provide copies of any agreements with international recruiters and must disclose the name and location of subcontractors who recruit H-2B workers. A new recertification rule has been added. If a U.S. worker does not appear, or abandons the job before the job order ends, the employer can ask the ETA for expedited re-certification so an H-2B worker can be hired.

The offered wage is the minimum wage or the prevailing wage (if that is higher) and must be paid for the full employment period certified in the application. The employer must provide, without charge, all tools, supplies, and equipment needed for the job and must guarantee employment for at least three-quarters of the workdays in each 12-week period. The employer is obligated to keep accurate records of hours and pay and give workers an earnings statement on or before every payday.

H-2B workers cannot be used to replace strikers or workers who have been locked out. The employer must not lay off U.S. workers in the same occupation and area of intended employment from 120 days before the first date of need to the end of the assignment. Lawful job-related layoffs, for example at the end of the work season, are permissible as long as the H-2B workers are laid off before their U.S. counterparts. The terms and conditions offered to U.S. workers must not be less favorable than those offered to H-2B workers and employers cannot impose restrictions only on the U.S. workers.

It is unlawful for an employer or an employer's agent or attorney to seek or collect any of the costs of certification, such as application costs, legal fees, or recruitment fees; of course kickbacks are forbidden. The employer must pay, or reimburse the worker for, all visa-related expenses in the first workweek.

The employer must post a worker's rights poster in English and in other appropriate languages. [Note that 20 C.F.R. § 655.20(m) just says that the poster must be provided in any language spoken by a significant portion of workers who are not fluent in English, but doesn't state a procedure for determining this].

The 2012 rules forbid employers to retaliate against workers who file complaints, testify, or vindicate the rights of other workers. Employers are forbidden to hold or confiscate workers' immigration documents. The ETA has the power to revoke labor certification for various reasons, including fraud, willful misrepresentation of material fact, substantial failure of the terms and conditions of employment, and non-cooperation with the DOL or its sanctions. Civil monetary penalties of up to $10,000 per violation can be assessed. [Department of Labor Wage and Hour Division (WHD), *H-2B Side-by-Side Comparison of the 2009 and 2012 Rules*, <http://www.dol.gov/whd/immigration/H2BFinalRule/H2BSideBySide.htm> (February 2012)]

The DOL proposed to delay the 2011 wage rule for H-2B petitions indefinitely, to provide time to review comments on the interim final rule. The 2011 rule revised DOL's methodology for calculating the prevailing wage rates for H-2B workers and U.S. workers recruited with temporary labor certification. The rule was originally scheduled to take effect January 1, 2012, but was extended several times, most recently to October 1, 2013. The 2011 appropriations bill did not prohibit the 2011 rule from taking effect, but did not fund publication of the prevailing wage determination. Subsequent appropriations bills continued this tactic, so DOL plans to wait until enforcement funds are available.

DOL and the Department of Homeland Security promulgated an interim final rule calling for prevailing wage determinations to be based on the mean wage for the occupation in the area of employment, rather than on tiers or skill levels. [Interim final rule, 78 Fed. Reg. 24047 (Apr. 24, 2013); see Jason E. Burritt et al., *DOL Proposes To Delay Effective Date Of H-2B Wage Methodology Final Rule Indefinitely*, Seyfarth Shaw LLP (Aug. 29, 2013), available at Lexology.com]

[F] Case Law on Immigration Issues in Employment

A district court held that it was proper for USCIS to deny an H-1B petition for the job of International Recruiter, because the entry-level wage listed on the Labor Condition Application (LCA) was inconsistent with the complexity of the duties. The LCA must attest that the H-1B worker will receive the required wage rate: the greater of the prevailing wage for the geographic area, or the wage the petitioning employer actually pays at the place of employment. The DOL publishes prevailing wage data for four levels of jobs, ranging from entry-level Level I to Level IV, for experienced, self-sufficient employees who use independent judgment. Employers can get a safe harbor by filing DOL Form ETA-9149 with the National Prevailing Wage Center to obtain a direct determination of the prevailing wage, but recently it takes about 12 weeks to get a response, which is too long a delay for filing an H-1B petition. [*Health Carousel v. Bureau of Citizenship and Immigration Service, California Service Center*, No. 1:13-cv-00023, 2014 U.S. Dist. LEXIS 388 (S.D. Ohio Jan. 3, 2014); see Scott T. Decker, *Recent District Court Case Reaffirms The Importance Of A Securing A Proper Prevailing Wage Determination When Filing For H-1B Positions*, Greenberg Traurig LLP (Jan. 22, 2014), available at Lexology .com. Prevailing wage data can be found in the DOL's Online Wage Library, <http://www.flcdatacenter.com/oeswizardstart.aspx>.]

Undocumented aliens are employees entitled to vote in representation elections, even if their status has been challenged under the IRCA. [*NLRB v. Kolkka*, 170 F.3d 937 (9th Cir. 1999)] But an illegal alien is not an "employee" for Worker's Compensation purposes, and therefore cannot receive Comp benefits for an on-the-job injury. [*Granados v. Windson Dev. Corp.*, 257 Va. 103, 509 S.E.2d 290 (1999)], or back pay in a suit alleging unfair labor practices. [*Hoffman Plastic Prods. Inc. v. NLRB*, 535 U.S. 137 (2002); *Palma v. NLRB*, 723 F.3d 176 (2d Cir. 2013)]

The Second Circuit permitted an award of lost earnings—using United States and not home country rates—to an undocumented worker crippled in a fall, because the injury was caused by the employer's violation of scaffolding requirements, not by the employee's ineligibility to work legally in the United States. [*Madeira v. Affordable Hous. Found. Inc.*, 469 F.3d 219 (2d Cir. 2006). See also *Majlinger v. Cassino Contracting Corp.*, 25 A.D. 3d 4, 802 N.Y.S.2d 56 (2d Dept. 2005) allowing compensation for lost U.S. earnings at U.S. rates, holding that this does not conflict with IRCA; *Flores v. Limehouse*, 2006 U.S. Dist. LEXIS 30433 (D.S.C. May 11, 2006) holding that IRCA does not preempt claims by undocumented workers against their employers under RICO and federal and state labor law—even if the workers obtained employment fraudulently; *Rosa v. Partners in Progress, Inc.*, 868 A.2d 994 (N.H. 2005) (for undocumented worker to be able to make a tort claim, the employer must have known or have a duty to know the worker's employment was illegal)]

California Labor Code § 1171.5 says that immigration status is irrelevant to liability issues under the state's labor and employment laws. IRCA preempts state or local laws that impose criminal penalties for employing ineligible aliens, but does not preempt state Worker's Compensation laws. In this reading, the purpose of the Worker's Compensation law is remedial and humanitarian, not penal, and it does not impose penalties for employing aliens, so it does not conflict with and is not preempted by IRCA. Although WC benefits cannot be paid as a direct result of fraudulent misrepresentation, that principle is not applied where use of fraudulent documentation to obtain employment did not cause the physical injury. [*Farmers Brothers Coffee v. Workers' Comp. Appeals Board and Ruiz*, 133 Cal. App. 4th 533 (Cal. App. 2005)]

In 2011, in a suit alleging overtime violations and failure to pay for all hours worked, the District Court for the District of Massachusetts ordered the restaurant to answer written questions about potential class members, but denied the restaurant's motion for information about plaintiffs' immigration status. The district court ruled that allowing recovery by illegal aliens is compatible with federal immigration policy, and there is a consensus that FLSA recoveries are not discretionary—wages must be paid even if the worker is undocumented. [*Lin v. Chinatown Rest. Corp.*, No. 09-11510-GAO, 2011 U.S. Dist. LEXIS 30626 (D. Mass. Mar. 23, 2011) See also *NLRB v. Domsey Trading Corp.*, 636 F.3d 33 (2d Cir. 2011), holding that, in an NLRB compliance hearing about alleged unlawful termination of strikers, the employer has the right to cross-examine plaintiffs about their immigration status, and expert testimony about immigration is admissible.]

Nor, according to the Ninth Circuit, does IRCA preempt California labor laws that forbid employers to fire employees without good cause because it is possible to comply with both laws—for example, by obtaining an H-1B visa for the plaintiff, or granting his request for unpaid leave to resolve his work status. Although the defendant argued that it would have been a violation to continue to employ the plaintiff once his E-1 visa was terminated, the Ninth Circuit held that a person on suspension is not "employed" because he or she does not get paid for performing services. In the Ninth Circuit view, although *Hoffman* requires immediate termination of workers who have no possible claim to legal status, it does not apply to a person who can obtain work authorization relatively quickly. [*Incalza v. Fendi N. Am. Inc.*, 479 F.3d 1005 (9th Cir. 2007). See also *Zamora v. Elite Logistics, Inc.*, 449 F.3d 1106 (10th Cir. 2006), holding that it is a defense in a TVII suit that the employee was put on leave without pay until his immigration status was resolved]

The California Supreme Court returned to this theme in mid-2014, permitting an employee to pursue a discrimination suit even though he presented false work authorization documents to be hired. California took the position that employees and job applicants are entitled to the same protection against discrimination (in this case, termination allegedly for filing a Worker's Compensation claim) as legal workers, although their wage recovery is limited to wages earned before the employer learned of the misrepresentation. The court reached this result because federal law requires termination once an employer learns of an employee's lack of authorization to work in the United States. Illegal workers cannot be reinstated because federal law forbids it. [*Salas v. Sierra Chem. Co.*, No. S196568 (Cal. June 26, 2014); see Jason A. Geller, *California Supreme Court: "Illegal Immigrant Shouldn't Have Been Hired—But Can't Be Fired Illegally,"* Fisher & Phillips LLP (July 3, 2014), available at Lexology.com]

The Eighth Circuit held in mid-2013 that unauthorized aliens could maintain a FLSA suit for willful violations (denial of minimum wage and overtime), on the grounds that employers cannot be entitled to profit from knowingly hiring people who are not authorized to work in the United States. [*Lucas v. Jerusalem Cafe LLC*, 721 F.3d 927 (8th Cir. 2013)]

Tennessee ruled that the survivors of a deceased worker can be "dependents" who receive Worker's Compensation benefits even if they are foreign nationals, not Tennessee residents, if they were actual dependents on the money sent by their deceased son. [Adrien Martin, *Foreign Nationals Can Be Dependents for TN Workers' Comp* [*sic*] *Benefits*, plansponsor.com (Jan. 23, 2007)]

It was an unfair labor practice to contact the INS right after the union won an election, telling eleven employees that they could not work until they straightened out their immigration status. This was a departure from the employer's normal practice. The NLRB said that, although IRCA compliance is important, it must not be used as a smokescreen for anti-union animus. [*Nortech Waste*, 336 N.L.R.B. 79 (2001)]

In 2004, the Seventh Circuit ruled that employees cannot state a RICO claim by alleging that the employer deliberately hired illegal aliens to keep wages down. In such a situation, the defendant company is the "enterprise," so there is no one for it to conspire with for RICO purposes. [*Baker v. IBP Inc.*, 357 F.3d 685 (7th Cir. 2004)] The Eleventh Circuit, however, disagreed, ruling that both RICO and state law claims were raised by allegations that the employer conspired with temporary agencies to hire illegal workers and use false documentation, with the objective of lowering wages and escaping Worker's Compensation responsibilities. The Supreme Court granted certiorari in December of 2005, but dismissed certiorari as improvidently granted in June 2006 and sent the case back to the Eleventh Circuit to resolve some minor issues. [*Williams v. Mohawk Indus. Inc.*, 411 F.3d 1252 (11th Cir. 2005), *cert. granted but dismissed as improvidently granted*, 547 U.S. 516 (2006)]

In September 2008, the Ninth Circuit upheld the Legal Arizona Workers Act, a 2007 Arizona state law penalizing employers who hire illegal aliens, by revoking their state business licenses. The Supreme Court upheld this law in mid-2011, holding that federal immigration law does not preempt the state law, because it is possible for employers to comply with both. IRCA forbids states to impose any criminal or civil sanctions for hiring illegal immigrants, other than through licensing and similar laws—but the Arizona statute is a licensing law because it is enforced by taking away the licenses of companies that hire undocumented workers. [*Chamber of Commerce v. Whiting*, 131 S. Ct. 1968 (2011); see Tony Mauro, *In Blow to Business Groups, Justices Uphold Arizona Law on Hiring Foreign Workers*, Nat'l L.J. (May 26, 2011) (law.com)]

After almost a decade, Wal-Mart prevailed in an FLSA/RICO suit about the company's relationships with contract janitorial services that hire immigrants, allegedly including illegal immigrants. The Third Circuit held that there were too many differences among the plaintiffs to certify an FLSA class action because in order to certify the class, the district court must make a finding that the members of the collective action are similarly situated, but they worked for 70 contractors and subcontractors, in 180 stores in 33 states, and Wal-Mart did not directly set wages and hours. The Third Circuit held that there was no evidence that Wal-Mart itself trafficked or helped workers to stay in the United States illegally. [*Zavala v. Wal-Mart Stores Inc.*, 691 F.3d 527 (3d Cir. 2012)]

The DOJ settled two immigration discrimination cases in late 2013. A civil fine of $43,092 was imposed on Rhode Island's Vincent Procaro, Inc. for requiring non-citizens to produce employment verification documents that were not required of citizens. The company was also required to create a $30,000 fund for back pay to the workers involved. Stellar Staffing, LLC of Birmingham was fined $2,500 for differential document requirements for citizens and non-citizens. [Robert S. Groban, Jr. et al., *DOJ Settles Employment Discrimination Allegations Under IRCA*, Epstein Becker Green (Oct. 29, 2013), available at Lexology.com]

§ 23.12 ADA COMPLIANCE IN HIRING

In 2012, more than 20 years after passage of the ADA, only 17.9% of persons with disabilities were employed, versus 63.7% of non-disabled persons. Most accommodations are free or cost only a few hundred dollars. [Peggy Klaus, *Disabilities Can Be Workplace Assets*, NYTimes.com (Feb. 4, 2012)]

For ADA purposes, some pre-employment inquiries are simply unacceptable; others are permissible only after a conditional job offer has been made.

The EEOC's Technical Assistance Manual for implementation of the ADA defines these pre-hire questions as improper:

- Have you ever been treated for these diseases?
- Have you ever been hospitalized? Why?
- Are there any health factors that prevent you from doing the job you applied for? (However, if the inquiry is restricted to specific job functions, it is permissible to ask about ability to perform those particular functions, and about potential accommodations.)
- How much sick leave did you take last year?
- Are you taking any prescribed medications?
- Have you ever been treated for substance abuse?

When it comes to pre-employment testing, it is discriminatory to give a test in a form or manner that requires the use of an impaired sensory, speaking, or manual skill, unless the point of the test is the degree to which that skill is present. So an assembly-line job may legitimately require manual dexterity. But if the point is to test keyboarding speed, a hearing-impaired person may have to be given a test that includes nonverbal commands as to when to start and stop. It may be necessary to have a test read aloud to a blind or dyslexic person, or to have a sign language interpreter. Every effort should be made to administer the test in a room that is wheelchair-accessible.

■ **TIP:** Tell applicants if there will be a test as part of the interview process. Then it is up to them to explain the nature of any accommodation they need to take the test.

Pre-employment medical examinations are allowed only if the candidate has already met the other criteria, and a conditional job offer has been extended. The examination must be required of everyone in that job category who gets a conditional offer. Once the offer has been made, it is acceptable to ask about past injuries and Worker's Compensation claims.

To avoid violating the Genetic Information Nondiscrimination Act (GINA), it is important to avoid asking about family medical history, because such inquiries can constitute requests for forbidden genetic information.

On January 17, 2013, HHS published a final rule covering the application of the HIPAA privacy rule to Titles I (health coverage) and II (employment) of the Genetic Information Nondiscrimination Act (GINA). Genetic information is considered health information, which cannot be used for underwriting purposes (except for long-term care insurance policies). Covered entities must comply no later than September 23, 2013. [Katherine Georger, *New HIPAA Final Rule Implements GINA Restriction on Use and Disclosure of Genetic Information for Underwriting Purposes*, Holland & Hart LLP News (Jan. 23, 2013) (benefitslink.com)]

Post-offer medical examinations are considered nondiscriminatory, and therefore it is not necessary to provide proof of business necessity. But if the applicant with a disability is in fact qualified for the job, and the offer is withdrawn subsequent to the examination, the employer must show job-related business necessity for canceling the offer, and must also prove that reasonable accommodation to the disability could not be made without undue hardship.

In late 2005, the EEOC issued an Advisory Letter stating that there is an exception to the ADA's ban on disability-related inquiries before making a job offer if the employer has an affirmative action program for people with disabilities. To qualify, the employer's program must include an interview that gives the person with a disability a real opportunity to compete for a job; the information sought must not be greater than what is needed to determine eligibility for the interview; and the applicant must voluntarily provide the information. [EEOC Advisory Letter, <http://www.eeoc.gov/policy/docs/preemp.html> (Nov. 8, 2005)]

For active employees, medical examinations and inquiries about the nature and severity of disability can be required only if they are job-related and consistent with business necessity: For instance, someone has been ill or injured, and the question is fitness to return to work.

The ADA also requires disability-related information to be kept confidential. In fact, it should be collected and maintained on separate forms, and even stored in files separate from general personnel information, although there are certain exceptions to the general rule of confidentiality: GINA also contains confidentiality requirements for genetic information, which must be kept separate from other health information.

- Supervisors and managers can be informed about work restrictions or accommodations that are needed;
- If emergency treatment might be required for a disabled employee (e.g., an epileptic might have a seizure; a diabetic might go into insulin shock or coma), first aid and safety personnel can be informed, so they will be prepared;
- A special post-September 11 rule allows collection of information about special needs for evacuation in an emergency;
- Government officials investigating ADA compliance are entitled to information about the number of employees with disabilities, and the nature of the disabilities.

The ADA forbids employers to ask about prescription drug use unless the workers have been seen to compromise safety or appear unable to function.

(There is an ADA exception: public safety workers such as police and firefighters, who are required to report prescription drug use that could create a threat to public safety.) Even jobs that are subject to federal drug testing requirements (e.g., bus and truck drivers) are tested for only six categories of drugs, and powerful drugs like Xanax, Vicodin, and OxyContin are not included. Many states have drug-free workplace laws, but their provisions vary widely and tend to focus on illegal drugs.

A 2010 Sixth Circuit case involves seven former employees of Dura Automotive Systems, who said that the company's drug testing policy (which led to terminations for taking prescription drugs) violated the ADA. The Sixth Circuit said that the relevant section of the ADA, 42 U.S.C. § 12112(a)(6), makes it unlawful to discriminate against a Qualified Individual with a Disability (QIWD) by using qualification standards that tend to screen out persons with disabilities—unless the standard is job-related and consistent with business necessity. The Sixth Circuit ruled that only a QIWD can sue under this section, although any employee can bring suit under other ADA sections. In this case, at least six of the seven plaintiffs were not disabled as defined by the ADA (the seventh might have had a record of disability), so they could not sue. The case arose before the ADAAA took effect (see § 36.03) so that law did not apply. [*Bates v. Dura Auto. Systems Inc.*, 625 F.3d 283 (6th Cir. 2010)]

If an employee or a job applicant is a veteran and possibly disabilities may be service-related, then both the ADA and USERRA (see § 1.18) may be involved. In fact, USERRA actually requires more of employers, by imposing a duty to assist veterans in becoming qualified for jobs, whereas the ADA just protects the rights of individuals with disabilities who are qualified for the job they hold or have applied for. Both statutes require employers to provide reasonable accommodation. The EEOC guidance says that an employer seeking to hire someone with a service-connected disability can ask if he or she is a disabled veteran—if the employer has an affirmative action obligation, or voluntarily seeks to benefit individuals with disabilities. It is also acceptable to recruit through organizations for veterans with disabilities. But before asking for applicants to voluntarily describe themselves as disabled veterans, the employer must explain that the information will only be used for affirmative action purposes, and will be kept confidential. Although the ADA does not require affirmative action for disabled veterans, it is acceptable for an employer to give a preference to disabled veterans. Recruiting material can be made handicap-accessible, and advertisements can state explicitly that disabled veterans are welcome to apply. [EEOC, *Veterans with Service-Connected Disabilities and the Americans with Disabilities Act (ADA): A Guide for Employers*, <http://www.eeoc.gov/eeoc/publications/ada_veterans_employers.cfm> (Feb. 29, 2008)]

EARN is the Department of Labor's Employer Assistance Resource Network, [<http://askearn.org>] a resource for putting employers in touch with qualified individuals with disabilities. DOL also maintains a Job Accommodation

Network for information about how to make workplace accommodations affordable. [<http://www.jan.wvu.edu>] The DOL points out that even in the boom times of the 1990s, only about 48% of persons with disabilities were employed. But one in five Americans has a disability, and the BLS projects that there will be only 20 million workers available to fill 55 million new jobs by 2008, so employers will have to become more flexible about finding talent in unconventional places.

The tax code provides various employer incentives, such as the § 44 disabled access credit, available for small businesses that make their premises accessible; and the § 190 barrier removal deduction for removing physical, structural, and transportation barriers on business premises. The § 190 deduction can be taken by any size business, but is not available for construction of new premises, only retrofitting; it is limited to $15,000 a year, but larger amounts can be depreciated.

To carry out the administration policy of promoting employment of veterans and workers with disabilities, the Office of Federal Contract Compliance Programs (OFCCP) issued final rules under Rehabilitation Act § 503 and Vietnam Era Veterans' Readjustment Assistance Act of 1974 (VEVRAA) in mid-2013, calling for affirmative action by federal contractors to hire these groups. The affirmative action requirements for veterans apply to contractors with federal contracts or subcontracts over $100,000; the requirements for persons with disabilities apply to all federal contractors holding federal contracts over $10,000. Federal contractors that already had to develop written affirmative action plans now must also set hiring benchmarks for veterans and persons with disabilities. Federal contractors are required to use a three-stage approach to self-identification, asking applicants to identify themselves if they are disabled or veterans. (The EEOC has informed the OFCCP that this inquiry does not violate the ADA.) Data on hiring and recruitment efforts must be retained for three years.

The final rules call for a hiring goal of 7% of the workforce to consist of persons with disabilities, and 8% veterans, covering all groups and jobs. (A small contractor, with under 100 employees, can set a target of 7% employment of PWDs in its total workforce.) These are goals, not quotas, and there is no penalty for non-attainment—but federal contracts can be revoked if the contractor cannot show a legitimate effort to meet the target. [78 Fed. Reg. 58682 (Sept. 24, 2013); see Patrick W. Spangler, Thomas G. Abram, and J. Kevin Hennessy, *Affirmative Action And OFCCP Compliance Update: OFCCP Issues Highly Anticipated Final Disability And Veteran Regulations*, Vedder Price PC (Aug. 28, 2013), available at Lexology.com; Melanie Trottman, *Hiring Rules Help Veterans, Disabled*, WSJ.com (Aug. 28, 2013); Mike Underwood, *Major Changes To Affirmative Action Requirements Effective March 24, 2014*, Porter Wright Morris & Arthur LLP (Oct. 8, 2013), available at Lexology.com; Winston & Strawn LLP, *OFCCP Announces Final Rule On Veterans And Employees With Disabilities*, Lexology.com (Aug. 29, 2013); Fred W. Alvarez et al., *Expanding Compliance Obligations: What Federal Contractors Need To Know About OFCCP's*

New Disability And Veterans Regulations, Jones Day (Oct. 15, 2013), available at Lexology.com]

§ 23.13 CREDIT REPORTING IN THE HIRING PROCESS

A federal law, the Fair Credit Reporting Act (FCRA) [15 U.S.C. §§ 1681a *et seq.*], as amended by the Consumer Credit Reporting Reform Act of 1996 (CCRRA) [Pub. L. No. 104-208], governs the use of credit reports and investigative credit reports not only for making loans and approving credit card applications, but in the employment context as well.

The FCRA provides that a consumer report is a written or oral communication from a consumer reporting agency, dealing with a consumer's entitlement to credit, "character, general reputation, personal characteristics, or mode of living."

An investigative credit report is different in that it involves personal interviews with people who have personal knowledge of the individual. The CCRRA requires employers to give job applicants a written disclosure statement, and to get their consent in writing, before requesting either a consumer report or an investigative consumer report. Furthermore, if the employer wants an investigative report, it must explain to the applicant (via a written disclosure mailed no later than three days after the report is requested) that this type of report covers matters like character and conduct.

The FCRA [see 15 U.S.C. § 1681b(3)(B)] says that "employment purposes" are legitimate reasons for requesting a credit report or investigative credit report. "Employment purposes" means "evaluating a consumer for employment, promotion, reassignment, or retention as an employee." Because the FCRA specifically authorizes the use of credit reporting information in the hiring process, doing so is not employment discrimination.

An "adverse action" includes "denial of employment or any other decision for employment purposes that adversely affects any current or prospective employee." When the credit report is negative, leading to adverse action, the employer must provide oral, written, or electronic (for instance, fax or e-mail) notice of the adverse action. It must also explain how to review the credit report file, correct errors (the negative report might refer to someone else with a similar name, or someone who has appropriated the job applicant's identity) and contest items that the consumer believes to be untrue. Notice must be given after the employer makes the decision, but before the adverse action is implemented.

The CCRRA also imposes an obligation on the employer. Before it gets any reports from a reporting agency, it must give the agency a statement that the employer complies with the various consumer protection requirements of credit reporting law.

As a result of a later statute, the FACTA (Fair and Accurate Credit Transactions Act of 2003; Pub. L. No. 108-159), 15 U.S.C. § 1681a has been amended to add a new subsection (x). Under the new law, a communication is not treated as a consumer report—and therefore is not subject to the FCRA requirements—if the purpose of the communication is job-related and not related to the person's creditworthiness.

To qualify for the FACTA exemption, the communication must be made to an employer as part of an investigation of suspected employment-related misconduct, or in compliance with laws or regulations (including the rules of a self-regulatory organization such as a stock exchange), or under the employer's pre-existing written policies. Reports of this type must not be disclosed to anyone except the employer or its agents, government officials, or self-regulatory organizations, unless disclosure is mandated by law. Furthermore, once the employer gets the information, if the information is the basis of any adverse action against the person, the employer must provide the person with a summary of the communication—but does not have to disclose the sources furnishing the information.

Effective July 21, 2011, the Dodd-Frank Act (Pub. L. No. 111-203) requires employers to disclose whenever credit scores have had an adverse effect on the employer's assessment of a job applicant.

In late 2010, the Third Circuit ruled that it does not violate the bankruptcy law provision 11 U.S.C. § 525(b) to avoid hiring a person because of his previous bankruptcy. (The situation would be different if someone who was already an employee was fired for filing a bankruptcy petition.) [*Rea v. Federated Investors*, 627 F.3d 937 (3d Cir. 2010)]

However, the EEOC's position is that discrimination on the basis of credit history is illegal, because of the disparate impact that such discrimination has on minorities. Employers who face Title VII disparate impact suits may be able to defend themselves by showing the procedure is job-related and consistent with business necessity. But even then, plaintiffs can still prevail by showing that there is an alternate practice that would achieve the same result without discriminatory impact.

In 2014, the Sixth Circuit upheld a district court grant of summary judgment to employer Kaplan Higher Education Corp. The EEOC sued Kaplan, charging that its use of credit checks had a disparate impact on African-American applicants. Although the credit check vendor did not classify the race of applicants, the EEOC charged that a disproportionate number of African-American candidates were screened out because of their credit history. The Sixth Circuit ruled that the EEOC's expert witness identified African-American applicants by viewing their driver's license photographs—a "homemade methodology" that was not tested or validated, and could not be used to prove the case. Furthermore, the EEOC itself uses a credit check process similar to the challenged Kaplan process. [*EEOC v. Kaplan Higher Educ. Corp.*, 748 F.3d 749 (6th Cir. 2014); semble *EEOC v. Freeman*, 951 F. Supp. 2d 783 (D. Md. 2013). See Katharine H. Parker et al., *Sixth Circuit Affirms Summary Judgment Against EEOC in Credit Check Suit*, Proskauer Rose LLP (Apr. 15, 2014), available at Lexology.com. The article says that the states of California, Colorado, Connecticut, Hawaii, Illinois, Maryland, Nevada, Oregon, Vermont, and Washington, and the cities of Chicago and Madison, Wisconsin impose limits on the use of credit history in employment decision-making, although there may be exceptions for information that is substantially job-related, or when disclosures are made to applicants or employees that credit histories will be consulted.]

CHAPTER 24

RECORDKEEPING

§ 24.01 INTRODUCTION

[A] Employer Responsibility in General

Employee records are important in setting compensation, assuring that it is paid appropriately, and administering benefit plans. Proper records are necessary to handle insurance matters, comply with court orders, fill out tax returns and other government documents, and demonstrate EEO and immigration compliance. For a general introduction to federal requirements, [See the interactive *FirstStep Recordkeeping, Reporting & Notices Advisor*, <http://www.dol.gov/elaws/firststeprrn.htm> (last viewed June 10, 2014).

State law may require employees to be granted access (and perhaps to make copies) of their personnel files. For example, Connecticut defines personnel files as papers, documents, and reports about a particular employee, used to determine eligibility for employment, promotion, or discipline. But third-party references, records of stock option plans, security files, investigation reports about misconduct or crimes, and information required by the government and kept in separate files and documents prepared for litigation, are not considered personnel files. Delaware, Illinois, Maine, Massachusetts, Minnesota, Nevada, Oregon, Pennsylvania, and Washington also have laws regulating access to files. [Dabney D. Ware, *When A "Simple" Personnel File Request Is Not So Simple*, Foley & Lardner LLP (Sept. 9, 2013), available at Lexology.com; Susan Gross Sholinsky, *Take 5: Views You Can Use: Labor And Employment*, Epstein Becker Green (Nov. 12, 2013), available at Lexology.com]

Employers cannot evade their responsibility for remittances to benefit funds by failing to keep required records. The Ray Haluch Gravel Company's 2005 CBA required the company to make payments to benefit funds. In 2007, the union demanded additional remittances on behalf of employees whose work records were incomplete. The First Circuit held that it was certain that one employee's account was underpaid: the evidence showed that 75% of the work he did was covered by the CBA, so 75% of his work should have resulted in earning benefits. Other, unidentified employees were also entitled to benefit contributions. The union argued that the lack of proper records about the work performed by the employees shifted the burden of proof to the employer. The First Circuit agreed that burden-shifting was logical in this case because employers have an incentive to under-report the amount of work completed by employees because less work means lower contributions by the employer. The First Circuit remanded the case for calculation of the amount to be remanded. [*Central Pension Fund of the Int'l Union of Operating Eng'rs & Participating Employers v. Ray Haluch Gravel Co.*, 695 F.3d 1 (1st Cir. 2012); see Meg Hunt, *Burden of Proof* plansponsor.com (Jan. 22, 2013). The Supreme Court decided another phase of this case, dealing with the timeliness of a request for attorneys' fees: *Ray Haluch Gravel Co. v. Cent. Pension Fund of the Int'l Union* 134 S. Ct. 773 (Jan. 15, 2014). The case was remanded; a bench (non-jury) trial awarded $18,000 in attorneys' fees, plus about $17,000 in costs, to the Central Pension Fund. The First Circuit upheld the award: *Central Pension Fund of the Int'l Union of Operating Engineers v. Ray Haluch Gravel Co.*, 745 F.3d 1(1st Cir. 2014).

In addition to determining its internal needs for gathering, processing, and deleting information, the company must be aware of legal requirements for record retention, and limitations on document destruction. Destroying documents that are subject to discovery in a court case is at least a civil offense, and may constitute contempt of court or even a criminal offense, depending on circumstances.

All documents in personnel files should be date-stamped when they are received, because it may be necessary to determine what was in the file at a particular time.

> ■ **TIP:** If it is legal and practical to destroy a document, make sure that all paper copies have been destroyed, as well as all computer files (including back-ups, copies on disks, and data uploaded to an Internet site for safekeeping). Just because someone has deleted a file does not mean that it has even been removed from that computer, much less from the entire network.

Whether the records are on paper or electronic, the goal of the corporate record retention policy should be to store and manage information on- and off-site in a systematic and cost effective manner. When necessary, the system must be able to handle litigation-related requests for documents, and managing risk. The policy must satisfy the statutory and regulatory requirements for record retention, applicable statutes of limitations, and best practices for business. Publicly traded companies are subject to additional requirements imposed by the Sarbanes-Oxley Act (for example, communications with the company's audit firm must be retained). The Public Company Accounting Oversight Board (PCAOB) requires accountants to retain audit work papers for at least seven years. Early in 2003, the SEC covered record retention issues in Exchange Act Release No. 47241.

The District Court for the Northern District of Indiana imposed almost $4,500 in penalties for failure to provide historical plan documents. After a participant's death, his widow contacted his employer about his survivor annuity. She was told that he elected against the annuity in 1979. She asked for copies of the plan documents, the SPD and the election and spousal waiver forms, but the employer was unable to locate the documents. The widow sued for statutory penalties for failure to provide documents, breach of fiduciary duty, and failure to maintain a reasonable claims procedure. Statutory damages were awarded, but the court said that plan-wide injunctive relief was unnecessary. [*Hartman v. Dana Holding Corp*, No. 1:12-cv-00445-RBC,2013 U.S. Dist. LEXIS 14537 (N.D. Ind. Oct. 21, 2013); see John Manganaro, *Case Shows Importance of Keeping Documentation*, plansponsor.com (Nov. 18, 2013)]

A Sarbanes-Oxley provision enacted at 18 U.S.C. § 1519 calls for imprisonment of up to 20 years for knowing alteration, destruction, mutilation, falsification, or cover-up of records or documents with the intent to obstruct investigation of any matter under the jurisdiction of a federal department or agency. Even document destruction that occurred before a proceeding commenced can be prosecuted.

Courts have imposed major—even multi-million-dollar—sanctions on companies that destroyed key evidence in violation of court orders. Litigation parties that destroy evidence have also been precluded from introducing their own evidence as a penalty. It is increasingly clear that once litigation begins, a "litigation hold" should be placed on destruction of paper and electronic documents. Once the company becomes aware of impending litigation, employees should be informed of the possibility. They should receive copies of the relevant court orders, and be informed of the penalties for destruction of evidence.

However, if a company has a reasonable policy for when documents should be retained and when they should be destroyed, and the policy is consistently applied, then courts will probably find that it is unreasonable to expect the company to produce documents destroyed pursuant to the policy.

As Chapters 6 and 15 show, a current major litigation topic is whether defined contribution plans select the correct menu of investment options for plan participants—and whether the plan pays excessive fees for the investments in the plan or services to the plan. Even the cost of recordkeeping can create hazards for fiduciaries. In a Western District of Missouri class action, the plaintiffs were awarded $21.8 million against the plan's fiduciaries for failure to choose funds prudently and in accordance with the plan's published policies—and a further $13.4 million for failure to obtain rebates or monitor the cost of recordkeeping.

In 2014, The Eighth Circuit upheld the $14.3 million award against a 401(k) plan sponsor for breaching the fiduciary duty to control the costs of recordkeeping. The plaintiffs alleged that the sponsor breached its fiduciary duty by failing to monitor costs; paying above-market costs; and choosing investments that were more expensive than comparable investments. The Eighth Circuit found that it was acceptable to pay for recordkeeping through revenue sharing and bundled service agreements—but the fiduciaries failed to investigate adequately before incurring the costs. However, the Eighth Circuit remanded the $21.8 million award for alleged plan losses computed by comparing one of the plan's mutual fund investments to the returns of a fund from a different fund family, because the calculation was too speculative. [*Tussey v. ABB Inc.* No. 2:06-CV-04305-NKL, 2012 U.S. Dist. LEXIS 45240 (W.D. Mo. Mar. 31, 2012), *aff'd in part, rev'd in part*, 746 F.3d 327 (8th Cir. 2014); see Andrew Holley and Britta Loftus, *The Importance of* "A Deliberative Process," Dorsey & Whitney (Apr. 4, 2012) (benefitslink.com); Robert Stever, *U.S. Court of Appeals Splits Rulings on ABB 401(k) Mismanagement, Clears Fidelity*, Pensions & Investments (Mar. 20, 2014) (benefitslink.com); Goodwin Proctor ERISA Litigation Update, *In Tussey, Eighth Circuit Weighs in On Excessive Fee Claims* (Mar. 20, 2014) (benefitslink.com)]

[B] 2002 DOL Final Rule

The Department of Labor published Final Rules Relating to Use of Electronic Communication and Recordkeeping Technologies by Employee Pension and Welfare Benefit Plans, updating 29 C.F.R. Part 2520, at 67 Fed. Reg. 17264 (Apr. 9, 2002). This document provides final rules under ERISA Title I for using electronic media to disclose benefit plan information to participants (a topic discussed in Chapter 27) and enacts a safe harbor for using electronic methods of disclosing and maintaining records. The final rule is effective October 9, 2002.

Under the Final Rule, 29 C.F.R. § 2520.107-1, electronic media can be used for maintenance and retention of records, if:

- The system has reasonable controls to ensure integrity, accuracy, authenticity, and reliability of the records.
- The records are maintained in reasonable order, in a safe and accessible place, so they can reasonably be inspected.
- The records can readily be converted into legible and readable hard copy from electronic form.
- The electronic data is labeled, securely stored, and backed up so it can be recovered if the main data repository is destroyed or corrupted.
- The employer retains paper copies of any data that cannot be seamlessly transferred to the electronic system.

The Final Rule permits destruction of paper records that have been transferred without error to the electronic system, unless there is a requirement (under the terms of the plan or an applicable law) that duplicate or substitute records be maintained in paper form.

In 2013, the GAO recommended that DOL and the Treasury clarify the regulatory requirements for delivering pension disclosures electronically. The GAO also recommended giving participants additional chances to opt out of electronic disclosures, including a chance to request all deliveries in hard copy rather than having to make the request on a document-by-document basis. Electronic delivery eliminates printing and mailing costs, and the notices are always available and can be archived—but there is a risk of loss of access if there is a computer malfunction or loss of Internet connection. Electronic delivery also makes the notices vulnerable to hacking and phishing. [GAO-13-594, *Private Pensions: Revised Electronic Disclosure Rules Could Clarify Use and Better Protect Participant Choice*, (Sept. 2013) <http://www.gao.gov/assets/660/657868.pdf>]

See § 27.06 for more discussion of electronic media in pension and tax contexts.

[C] CHIPRA and ARRA Rules

The Children's Health Insurance Program Reauthorization Act of 2009, Pub. L. No. 111-3, which expands the state children's health insurance program, allows states to subsidize coverage provided by employers through their existing EGHPs. Plan administrators must report to the state the information needed to determine which plan participants are entitled to premium assistance from the SCHIP program. Employers therefore must create and maintain records about employees' eligibility for subsidy, and records for administering the subsidies. Employers must distribute the HHS model notice to inform employees about premium assistance. Failure to give notice is penalized by $100/day/participant. [Norbert F. Kugele, Warner Norcross & Judd LLP, *New Federal SCHIP Law Requires Cafeteria and Health Plan Amendments* (Feb. 10, 2009) (benefitslink.com)]

The federal premium subsidy for COBRA premiums under the American Recovery and Reinvestment Act of 2009, Pub. L. 111-5, now expired, also created requirements for retaining records of employee terminations, employees electing COBRA at termination, and employees not electing COBRA but entitled to a notice of their eligibility for the subsidy, and of employee income (to demonstrate eligibility for the subsidy). [Notice 2009-27, 2009-16 I.R.B. 838; see Edward I. Leeds, Ballard Spahr Andrews & Ingersoll, LLP, *Stimulus Package Modifies COBRA, HIPAA, and Other Welfare Benefit Provisions* (Feb. 17, 2009) (benefitslink.com); Michael S. Melbinger, Winston & Strawn LLP, *All Employers' Severance Plans and Agreements Affected by ARRA* (Feb. 20, 2009) (benefitslink.com)]

[D] PPACA (Health Care Reform) Requirements

One reason that PPACA is unpopular is because of the recordkeeping and notice burden. Participants must be notified of their right to keep their adult children in the plan until they reach age 27. The plan must keep track of the facts supporting its entitlement to grandfathered status—or causing loss of that status. When the health insurance exchanges are in operation, it will be necessary for employers to prove that they offer at least minimum required coverage or that they are exempt from the requirement. Otherwise, penalties will be imposed. [Christy Tinnes and Brigen Winters, *What Notices Are Required by PPACA?*, plansponsor.com (Sept. 21, 2010)]

PPACA will eventually require the cost of providing EGHP coverage to be reported on employees' W-2 forms. The reporting is purely informational because the cost of EGHP coverage is not generally taxable. (The exception is the 40% excise tax imposed on Cadillac plans beginning in 2018.) PPACA § 9006 added a requirement that all corporate businesses must issue a Form 1099 to any individual or corporation from which they purchase more than $600 in goods or services in a tax year. This was an immensely unpopular provision because of the vast amount of paperwork it was expected to generate. In February 2011, the Senate voted not to repeal the entire PPACA statute, but did vote to amend this provision (S. 223). The House had already approved similar legislation (H.R. 4 and H.R. 705), and President Obama signed it as Pub. L. No. 112-9, which eliminates the requirement for payments to corporations and for the acquisition of property. [Janet Adamy, *Senate Votes Down Health-Care Repeal*, WSJ.com (Feb. 3, 2011); Plansponsor staff, *Senate Passes Repeal of HCR 1099 Rule*, plansponsor.com (Feb. 21, 2011)]

Final regulations on the Code § 6055 requirements for minimum essential health coverage were published on March 10, 2014. The regulations explain the requirements imposed on companies with 50 or more full-time employees to report to the IRS and to employees about health care coverage available to them. The requirements will be used by the IRS to enforce the pay-or-play mandate once it takes effect, and to administer the tax credit that certain individuals will receive for buying health care coverage on an Exchange under Code § 36B. The penalty for not providing coverage will not be imposed on companies with 50–99 employees until 2016, but reporting under § 6056 is nonetheless required for 2015. Information is reported to employees on Form 1095-C then transmitted to the IRS on Form 1094-C. The due date for health coverage provided in calendar year 2015, for employers with 50 or more employees is March 1, 2016 for paper filings and March 31, 2016 for e-filing. E-filing is mandatory for employers who are required to file 250 or more tax returns. The due date for information statements sent to employees is February 1, 2016. Notice to employees can be given electronically if the employees agree.

There are two ways that employers can satisfy their obligations under § 6056: either they can certify with respect to a particular full-time employee that the employee was offered affordable coverage, and minimum essential coverage was offered to the employee's spouse and dependents, or the employer certifies that affordable health coverage satisfying the minimum value requirements was offered to at least 98% of its full-time employees. There is a special transition rule for 2015 only for employers that made a qualifying offer of coverage to at least 95% of its full-time workforce.

Employers that offer a self-funded plan are required by § 6055 to make information reports to the IRS and employees when they provide minimum essential coverage. The reports are used to determine if the individual had the coverage required by the individual mandate. Employers that sponsor self-funded plans can use Form 1094-C to combine reporting for §§ 6055 and 6056.

Failure to satisfy these reporting requirements can be penalized under § 6721 (failure to file required information returns) and § 6722 (failure to provide payees with reports). However, if there is reasonable cause, § 6724 may offer relief by waiving penalties. There is a special transition rule for returns and statements filed in 2016 dealing with 2015 coverage: penalties will not be imposed for incorrect or incomplete information, but relief will not be granted if employers fail to make required reports, or if they do not attempt in good faith to comply. [79 Fed. Reg. 13220 (Mar. 10, 2014); see Chadron J. Patton, *Final Regulations Streamline ACA Reporting Rules*, Spencer Fane Britt & Browne (Mar. 13, 2014), available at Lexology.com]

§ 24.02 OSHA RECORDS

[A] Injury and Illness Recordkeeping

Complying with the Occupational Safety and Health Act [see Chapter 31] requires constant accumulation of data on a day-by-day basis, followed by compilation of annual records.

Effective January 1, 2002, OSHA changed the reporting requirements found in 29 C.F.R. Part 1904 ("Recording and Reporting Occupational Injuries and Illnesses"). The new requirements are simplified, streamlined, and work better with computer technology than the old requirements. The new forms can be downloaded from <http://www.osha.gov> or ordered by telephone from the OSHA publication office at (202) 693-1888. The Final Rule appears at 66 Fed. Reg. 5916 (Jan. 19, 2001). Although most of the changes went into effect as scheduled, the effective date of the rules about hearing loss and reporting of musculoskeletal disorders were delayed until January 1, 2003. [See 66 Fed. Reg. 35113 (July 3, 2001)]

Under the prior rules, employers were required to make incident reports on Form 101, Supplementary Record of Occupational Injury and Illnesses. The replacement form is Form 301, the Injury and Illness Incident Report.

The prior rules called for the employer to collate all the 101 forms to create the annual Form 200, Log and Summary of Occupational Injuries and Illnesses. The new forms are 300, Log of Work-Related Injuries and Illnesses, and 300A, Summary of Work-Related Injuries and Illnesses. [See 29 C.F.R. § 1904.4]

The forms are used to report new cases of work-related illness or injury. The OSHA 301 Incident Report must be completed within seven calendar days of receiving information about the incident. The OSHA 300 log requires a short description of each incident. The OSHA 300-A summary is compiled at the end of the year, using this log.

All businesses have to make a report of OSHA if an incident in the workplace results in a death, or if three or more workers are hospitalized. However, it is not necessary for companies in low-hazard businesses such as retail, service, finance, real estate, or insurance to maintain OSHA illness and industry records unless OSHA specifically requests such records. [See <https://www.osha.gov/recordkeeping/ppt1/RK1exempttable.html> for information about the exemption]

In late 2013, OSHA published a Notice of Proposed Rulemaking (NPRM) to improve tracking of workplace injuries. The NPRM does not increase employers' obligations to keep records but requires electronic submission of injury and illness data to OSHA, which will publish the information on its Website and may create a database. Reporting companies with 250 or more employees in the previous year must submit Forms 300 and 301 electronically each quarter. Reporting companies with 20 or more employees in designated high-risk injuries (e.g., constructing and manufacturing) must submit Form 300A information annually (total number of cases in each classification, number of days of work lost, total number and type of injuries and illnesses). Form 300A replaces the annual Data Initiative Survey and the requirements imposed by § 1904.41(a). The list of designated industries can be found in Part 1904, Subpart E, Appendix A. [Nickole C. Winnett, *OSHA's Proposed Electronic Recordkeeping Rule*, Jackson Lewis LLP (Nov. 14, 2013), available at Lexology.com; Heather MacDougall, *OSHA Proposes Major Recordkeeping Change*, Akerman LLP (Nov. 12, 2013), available at Lexology.com]

The Occupational Safety and Health Review Commission (OSHRC) heard oral arguments in November 2010 (the first oral arguments allowed in four years) in a case about the length of time in which a company can be cited for OSH reporting violations. OSHA said that the DOL has six months from the time it discovers, or should have discovered, the facts needed in order to issue a citation. However, the DOL policy is that an inaccurate log entry violates the law until it has been corrected, or until the five-year period for record retention has expired—and the statute of limitations does not begin with the date the entry was or should have been made. OSHRC held that failure to keep proper records can be treated as a continuing violation of OSHA's five-year record retention requirement, and fined the company $13,300 for recordkeeping violations. [*Secretary of Labor v. AKM LLC dba Volks Constructors* OSHRC No. 06-1990, 2011 WL 896347 (OSHRC Mar. 11, 2011)]

Then, however, the D.C. Circuit reversed OSHRC in an unpublished decision, and ruled that the statute of limitations for recordkeeping violations is only six months, not five years. The D.C. Circuit rejected the continuing violation theory, holding that all the violations charged were separate events. Although it enunciated a six-month statute of limitations for pure recordkeeping violations, the D.C. Circuit left the way open for tolling the statute of limitations for a genuine ongoing violation, such as continuing to require employees to use unsafe equipment. [*Sec'y of Labor v. AKM LLC dba Volks Constructors*, No. 11-1106, 2012 WL 1142273 (unpublished) (D.C. Cir. Apr. 6, 2012)]

[B] Asbestos, Lead, and Noise Monitoring Records

If the workplace noise level is high, the employer not only must monitor exposure, but must maintain records for two years. Records of employees' hearing tests must be retained at least as long as they work for the employer. Exposure monitoring records and asbestos and lead medical surveillance records should be retained for at least 30 years after termination of employment of the individual monitored.

Asbestos monitoring records should indicate:

- Each monitored employee's name, Social Security number, extent of exposure;
- If a respirator was worn; if so, what kind;
- Date the asbestos level was monitored;
- The workplace operation or process that was monitored;
- How the samples were taken and evaluated;
- Evidence supporting the scientific validity of the sampling methodology;
- How long the sampling process lasted; number of samples taken; sampling results.

For each employee subject to medical surveillance, the record should give his or her name and Social Security number, the employee reports of asbestos-related medical conditions; and a written report from the doctor who performs the surveillance, indicating whether the employee actually is suffering effects of asbestos exposure.

For testing of lead rather than asbestos, the employer must maintain written records of tests determining whether the ambient lead level exceeds the Permissible Exposure Limit (PEL). The test record should indicate:

- Name and Social Security number of each monitored employee;
- Date of the test;
- Area that was monitored;
- Previous airborne lead readings taken at the same place;
- Employee complaints that might be related to lead exposure;
- Any other evidence suggestive of lead exposure.

[C] OSHA Postings

Employers must post a notice of OSHA rights, as mandated by 29 C.F.R. § 1903.2(a). Failure to post is subject to a civil penalty of up to $7,000 per violation, but normally the penalty will be $1,000.

An employer who receives an OSHA citation must post a copy of the citation near each place where a violation occurred. The copy must be left in place for three working days or until the violation is corrected—whichever comes first. Posting is also required if the employer contests a citation or files a petition for modification of abatement. Failure to make these postings can result in a $1,000 fine.

§ 24.03 TITLE VII RECORDKEEPING AND NOTICE REQUIREMENTS

The Equal Employment Opportunity Commission (EEOC) requires companies with 100 or more employees to file an annual report. The Employer Information Report (EEO-1) is a simple two-page form that tracks the composition of the workforce. The due date is September 30 of each year. A copy of the most recent report must be kept on file at every company required to file (either at the "reporting unit" or the company's or division's headquarters). The EEOC also has the right to require other reports about employment practices if the agency thinks additional reports are necessary to carry out Title VII or the Americans With Disabilities Act.

The federal Website GovDocs has been updated to incorporate the Genetic Information Nondiscrimination Act (GINA; see § 34.01[B]), and the EEOC released its GINA-compliant poster; see <http://www.eeoc.gov/employers/upload/eeoc_self_print_poster.pdf> (accessed Mar. 20, 2014). GovDocs has compliance materials such as electronic posters for all the states, and automatically sends new posters to subscribers when there are changes. [David L. Woodard and Susanna Knutson Gibbons, Poyner Spruill LLP, *Check Your Posters—Passage of the Genetic Information Nondiscrimination Act Imposes New Obligations and Posting Requirements on Employers* (Mar. 1, 2010) (benefitslink.com); Rebecca Moore, *GovDocs Updates Labor Law Materials*, plansponsor.com (Nov. 2, 2009) and *EEOC Updates Notice to Employees*, plansponsor.com (Oct. 27, 2009)]

The EEOC published a final rule on February 3, 2012 extending the Title VII and ADA recordkeeping requirements to entities covered by GINA. As of April 3, 2012, employers with 15 or more employees must retain all personnel and employment records for at least one year, and retain documents about any GINA charges until those charges have been disposed of. Documents include requests for accommodation, application forms, hiring, promotion, demotion, transfer, layoff, and termination data and records of pay, tenure, training, and apprenticeship. Records must be retained for at least a year after any employee's involuntary termination. [77 Fed. Reg. 5396 (Feb. 3, 2012); see PLC Labor & Employment, *EEOC Issues Final Rule Extending Title VII and ADA Recordkeeping Requirements to GINA* (Feb. 2, 2012) (benefitslink.com)]

Records of application forms, requests for accommodation, and other employment-related data must be preserved for one year. The one-year period starts either when the data is collected or the personnel action is taken, whichever is later. Personnel records of fired employees must also be kept for one year after employment ends. [Press Release, *Recordkeeping Guidance Clarifies Definition of* "Job Applicant" *for Internet and Related Technologies* (Mar. 3, 2004),

<http://www.eeoc.gov/eeoc/newsroom/release/3-3-04.cfm>; a notice appeared in the March 4, 2004, Federal Register, 69 Fed. Reg. 10152]

Under a final rule published in late 2005, a person is considered an "Internet applicant" if the federal contractor accepts expressions of interest in a job through the Internet, e-mail, the employer's Website, or a resume databank. The applicant must have used the Internet or related means to submit an expression of interest in the job; the contractor must have considered the person for a particular position; the expression of interest must have demonstrated that the applicant had at least the basic qualifications for the job; and the person must have never removed him- or herself from consideration for the job before receiving a job offer. Contractors are not required to maintain records of electronic expressions of interest unless the contractor actually considered the person for a particular job. Federal contractors are permitted to have rules under which they reject general expressions of interest in working for their company that are not submitted for a particular position. It also is lawful to reject expressions of interest that do not meet the contractor's requirements. [70 Fed. Reg. 58945 (Oct. 7, 2005)]

The EEOC proposed revisions to the EEO-1 form in mid-2003 [68 Fed. Reg. 34965 (June 11, 2003)] and finalized them in late 2005. [70 Fed. Reg. 72194 (Nov. 28, 2005)] Except in cases in which the employer cannot get Internet access, filing must be done electronically; see the instructions at <http://www.eeoc.gov/eeo1survey/howtofile.html> (accessed Mar. 20, 2014). The revised EEO-1 form increases the five racial/ethnic categories to seven: There is a new "two or more races" category, and the "Asian or Pacific Islander" category has been divided into "Asian" and "Native Hawaiian or other Pacific Islander." The category "Black" has been changed to "Black or African American," "Hispanic" is now "Hispanic or Latino," and the job category of "Officials and Managers" has been divided into an Executive/Senior Level category and a First/Mid-Level Officials and Managers group. Business and financial occupations are now to be disclosed as Professionals rather than as Officials and Managers. The EEOC wants racial and ethnic categories to be determined by employees' self-identification, not visual identifications made by the employer.

In September 2006, the Office of Federal Contract Compliance Programs eliminated the federal contractor's EEO survey, because it more or less duplicated the information collected on the EEO-1. [71 Fed. Reg. 53032 (Sept. 8, 2006); see Rebecca Moore, *EO Survey Eliminated for Federal Contractors*, plansponsor.com (Sept. 11, 2006)]

The Office of Federal Contract Compliance Programs (OFCCP) issued two rules in October 2013, effective March 24, 2014, expanding federal contractors' affirmative action obligations toward veterans and Persons With Disabilities (PWDs). The rules implement the Vietnam Era Veterans' Readjustment Assistance Act (VEVRAA) and Rehabilitation Act § 503. Federal contractors are required to collect and retain data about their success in recruiting and hiring PWDs and veterans. The requirements apply to federal contractors with contracts over $10,000 (PWDs) or $100,000 (veterans). Federal contractors must ask job applicants to self-identify if they are veterans or PWDs. Data on hiring and recruiting must be maintained for three years, and federal contractors must perform an annual review of their success in meeting their hiring targets. Records must be kept of the number of applicants who are protected veterans vis a vis the total number of applicants; the number of job openings; and the number of jobs filled. Similar records must be kept for PWDs. The OFCCP, in collaboration with the EEOC, will publish an official form on its Website for collecting the required information. Disability self-identifications must be kept in separate data files that are confidential and not included in the employee's personnel or medical file. The self-identification files should be submitted to the compliance officer during an audit. [Mike Underwood, *Major Changes To Affirmative Action Requirements Effective March 24, 2014*, Porter Wright Morris & Arthur LLP (Oct. 8, 2013), available at Lexology.com; Winston & Strawn LLP, *OFCCP Announces Final Rule On Veterans And Employees With Disabilities* (Aug. 29, 2013), available at Lexology.com; Patrick W. Spangler, Thomas G. Abram, and J. Kevin Hennessy, *Affirmative Action And OFCCP Compliance Update: OFCCP Issues Highly Anticipated Final Disability And Veteran Regulations*, Vedder Price PC (Aug. 28, 2013), available at Lexology.com]

If a discrimination charge is made, all records relating to the employment action involved in the charge must be retained until there has been a final disposition of the charge. According to 29 C.F.R. § 1602.14, this means that either the case is over, or the employee's time to sue has elapsed.

Users of pre-employment tests must maintain records about the validation of the test, including statistical studies to determine if the test has adverse impact on protected classes of applicants and employees.

Employers also have to make records that are relevant to charges of unlawful employment practices and maintain those records. [See 42 U.S.C. § 2000e-8(c)]

A general overview on posting requirements appears in the DOL's "eLaws Power Advisor," <http://www.dol.gov/compliance/topics/posters.htm> (accessed Mar. 20, 2014).

One of the many notices that must be posted in the workplace is the official EEOC notice about equal employment opportunity and how to file a charge. [42 U.S.C. § 2000e-10] If the employer willfully violates this requirement, a fine of up to $100 can be imposed for each separate offense.

Other mandatory posters include:

- Employee Rights Under the Fair Labor Standards Act
- Job Safety and Health: It's the Law
- Employee Rights and Responsibilities under the Family and Medical Leave Act
- Equal Employment Opportunity Is the Law

- Migrant and Seasonal Agricultural Worker Protection Act Notice
- Employee Rights for Workers with Disabilities Paid at Special Minimum Wages
- Employee Polygraph Protection Act Notice
- Your Rights Under USERRA (revised July 2008)
- Genetic Information Nondiscrimination Act information

In late 2012, New Jersey enacted a law requiring companies with 50 or more employees to post a notice about the right to gender equity in pay, benefits, and other terms and conditions of employment. Posting was required as of January 6, 2014. In lieu of posting a printed poster in the workplace, employers can post the information on a Website to which all employees have access. [<http://lwd.dol.state.nj.us/labor/forms_pdfs/EmployerPosterPacket/genderequityposter.pdf>; see McCarter & English LLP, *Attention Employers: New Poster Requirement In New Jersey Regarding Gender Equity In Pay And Compensation*, Lexology.com (Jan. 21, 2014)]

In late 2010, the NLRB announced that companies would be required to post notices on its bulletin boards to inform employees of their rights to unionize. [Notice of Proposed Rulemaking, 75 Fed. Reg. 80410 (Feb. 22, 2010). See also Steven Greenhouse, *U.S. Proposes Posted Notice of the Right to Unionize*, NYTimes.com (Dec. 21, 2010); Fred Schneyer, *NLRB Proposes Workplace Notice Rule*, plansponsor.com (Dec. 23, 2010)]

The posting requirement was supposed to take effect November 14, 2011, but it was delayed, first until January 31, 2012, then until April 30, 2012, in response to business criticisms. [Steven Greenhouse, *N.L.R.B. Tells Companies to Ease Right to Unionize*, NYTimes.com (Aug. 25, 2011); Tara Cantore, *NLRB Postpones Required Date to Post Employee Rights,* plansponsor.com (Dec. 27, 2011) and *NLRB Postpones Implementation Date for Notice Posting Rule*, plansponsor.com (Oct. 5, 2011)]

Two circuit courts (the Fourth and the D.C. Circuits) found the posting requirement inappropriate and unenforceable. The Fourth Circuit said that Congress intended the NLRB's powers to be limited, dealing only with Unfair Labor Practices and representation elections—and that the NLRB's powers are triggered only by a complaint or an election petition. In this analysis, posting requirements imposed by other agencies such as OSHA and the EEOC are based on statutory authorization from Congress, whereas the NLRB has not been given this power. Rather than uphold part of the posting requirement but remove the NLRB's power to treat failure to post as an Unfair Labor Practice, the Fourth Circuit struck down the entire regulation, concluding that the NLRB would not want to have a purely advisory rule that it was unable to enforce. [*Chamber of Commerce v. NLRB*, 721 F.3d 152 (4th Cir. 2013); see Jenna Greene, *Fourth Circuit*

Strikes NLRB Poster Rule, The BLT (Blog of Legal Times (June 14, 2013) (law.com); *Nat'l Ass'n of Mfrs. v. NLRB*, 717 F.3d 947 (D.C. Cir. 2013)]

On September 4, 2013, the D.C. Circuit denied the NLRB's petition for rehearing in *National Association of Manufacturers v. NLRB*. The Fourth Circuit also denied rehearing of its similar decision, on August 13, 2013. The NLRB requested two extensions of time to file certiorari petitions, but the final deadline, January 2, 2014, passed without a petition being filed, and the NLRB announced that it was no longer seeking review of these decisions. [Christine Holst, *The Hits Keep Coming: D.C. Circuit Denies Rehearing For NLRB Notice Posting Case*, Barnes & Thornburg LLP (Sept. 6, 2013), available at Lexology.com; Benjamin P. Glass, *NLRB Throws In The Towel On Notice Posting Rule*, Ogletree Deakins (Jan. 3, 2014), available at Lexology.com; Hunton & Williams LLP, *NLRB Declines To Take Union-Poster Dispute To High Court*, Lexology.com (Jan. 8, 2014)]

§ 24.04 FMLA RECORDS

Federal law does not impose any specific form for keeping FMLA records, so any paper or electronic method can be used to record the necessary information:

- Basic payroll data for each employee, such as hours worked; pay rate; supplemental wages or wage deductions; total compensation paid;
- Dates on which FMLA leave was taken;
- Hours of leave (if less than a day was taken);
- Copies of the employee's notice to the employer of impending leave;
- Copies of the employer's disclosure materials about FMLA rights;
- Documentation of the employer's leave policy;
- Records of payment of premiums for employee benefit plans;
- Records of any dispute about when employees are entitled to leave or reinstatement after a leave.

■ **TIP:** Because employee medical records, including certification of serious medical condition and fitness to return to work, are confidential, they should be kept physically separate from the employee's other records, to prevent unauthorized access to the data. [See § 26.07 about privacy requirements]

The required FMLA poster and forms were revised; the new versions expire February 28, 2015. The new poster must be displayed starting March 8, 2013 in all business locations, even if there are no FMLA-eligible employees at that location. The information can also be given electronically.

The DOL stopped publishing the model forms as appendices to the FMLA regulations. Instead, they appear on the DOL site, making it possible for the agency to amend the forms without going through the Office of Management and Budget. The new regulations instruct employers about their GINA confidentiality obligations: it is permissible to disclose genetic information or family history that is consistent with the FMLA.

Employers are permitted to adapt the forms rather than using them unaltered, provided that the employer's version does not call for disclosure of more information by the employee or health care provider than the FMLA regulations permit.

The new forms added in 2013 are:

- WH-380-E certification of health care provider of serious health condition (employee);
- WH-380-F health care provider certification for family member's serious health condition;
- WH-381 notice of eligibility, rights, and responsibilities;
- WH-382 designation notice;
- WH-383 reserved;
- WH-384 certification of exigency of military family leave;
- WH-385 certification of serious injury or illness of a servicemember for military family leave;
- WH-385-V certification of serious injury or illness of a veteran for military caregiver leave.

[*Airline Flight Crew Technical Corrs. Act*, Pub. L. No. 111-119; see Jackson Lewis LLP, *Workplace Resource Center Labor Department Releases New FMLA Model Forms and Notice Poster* (Feb. 27, 2013) (benefitslink.com); Jeff Nowak, *Employers Must Begin Using Updated FMLA Forms and Poster Starting March 8, 2013*, Franczek Radelet FMLA Insights (Feb. 28, 2013) (benefitslink.com)]

§ 24.05 IMMIGRATION RECORDS

The information collected to verify identity and eligibility to work in the United States [see § 23.11[D]] must be retained for three years after the date of hiring. Records should be retained for three years from the date of recruiting or referral with respect to applicants who were not hired or who did not accept a job offer. Certifications of employment eligibility furnished by state employment services must also be retained for three years. For former employees, the record-retention period is the later of three years after hiring, or one year after termination.

The Ninth Circuit ruled that employers must complete Form I-9 (verification of employee's permission to work in the United States) even if they attach copies of supporting documents. The Ninth Circuit held that copying and retaining the supporting documents does not constitute adequate compliance with the Immigration and Naturalization Act (INA). [*Ketchikan Dry Wall Servs. v. ICE*, 725 F.3d 1103 (9th Cir. 2013); see Jackson Lewis LLP, *Document Copies Do Not Replace Obligation To Complete Form I-9*, Lexology.com (Sept. 6, 2013)]

§ 24.06 EMPLOYMENT TAX RECORDS

Newly hired employees should be asked to provide a W-4 (withholding exemptions) form, so the appropriate number of exemptions can be used to withhold income taxes. An employee about to retire should be asked for Form W-4P to determine whether pension withholding should be done, and if so, in what amount. Note that, in recent years, the FICA and FUTA payroll taxes have been adjusted several times, so it is essential to use the appropriate withholding tables for the pay period. IRS Publication 15, Employer's Tax Guide, requires at least the following information to be collected by the employer and made available for IRS review on request:

- Dates and amounts of all payments of wages and pensions;
- Fair market value of any wages paid other than in cash (e.g., in merchandise or services);
- Each employee's name, address, Social Security number, and job title;
- Dates each employee started and terminated employment;
- Dates and amounts of any payments made by the employer, or by an insurer or other third party, to employees who were out sick or injured;
- Copies of W-4 and W-4P forms;
- W-2 forms sent to employees but returned as undeliverable;
- Copies of all tax returns;
- Records of dates and amounts of tax deposits.

The Pension Protection Act of 2006, Pub. L. No. 109-280, adds a new section to the Internal Revenue Code, § 6039I, requiring the owners of employer-owned life insurance contracts issued after the PPA took effect to report to the IRS each year on the number of employees the company has, how many of them are covered by company-owned life insurance, the amount of insurance in force under those insurance policies, the nature of the company's business, and that all employees covered under the COLI program have consented to being covered (or the number of employees who are covered but did not provide a written consent form). Businesses with COLI programs are required to keep any records necessary for determining if the PPA COLI rules have been complied with.

For tax years ending on or after November 14, 2007, a policyholder owning employer-owned life insurance contracts issued after August 17, 2006 must attach Form 8925 to the income tax return. The form discloses the number of employees covered by employer-provided life insurance contracts; whether each one consented in writing, in advance, to be insured and for coverage to continue after employment ends. [Sutherland Asbill & Brennan LLP, *Legal Alert: IRS Issues Forms to Report Employer-Owned Life Insurance* (Feb. 7, 2008)]

§ 24.07 UNEMPLOYMENT INSURANCE RECORDS

FUTA records must show the total amount of remuneration to employees in the calendar year, the amount of wages subject to tax, and the contributions made to the state unemployment insurance funds of each state in which the company does business. The records must be kept open to inspection by the IRS and state unemployment tax officials.

Records must be organized by pay period (dates the period starts and ends; total remuneration including commissions paid in the period) and by employee. The records to be kept for each worker include:

- Name;
- Social Security number;
- Date of hiring (or rehiring) and termination;
- Place of work;
- Wages for each payroll period;
- Wage rate;
- Date wages were paid;
- Amount of expense reimbursement granted;
- Time lost when worker was unavailable for work.

Although unemployment insurance information can be released to government agencies other than the employment security agency (child support enforcement agencies, for example), in general the information is confidential and should not be disclosed to unauthorized parties.

§ 24.08 RECORD-RETENTION REQUIREMENTS

Various state and federal laws require retention of records (about individual employees and summaries reflecting the entire corporate experience). The enterprise should draft its record-retention policies to comply with statutory requirements:

- Title VII: Personnel and employment records as well as EEO-1 reports must be kept for six months. Records relating to a discrimination charge must be retained until the charge is disposed of;
- Equal Pay Act: Records of a pay differential imposed on the basis of sex must be kept for two years;
- FMLA: Records must be retained for three years;
- FICA/FUTA: Records of withholding and paying these taxes must be retained for four years;
- ERISA: There are two record retention provisions. Section 107 requires the filer or certifier of certain information (for example, Form 5500) to maintain sufficient records to explain, corroborate, substantiate, or clarify the filing or certification. Relevant records might include plan documents, e-mails, work records, or spreadsheets. Such records must be maintained for six years after the date they were filed (including any amendments). But ERISA § 209 requires all such information to be retained for as long as it might be relevant to determining benefit entitlement—which is tantamount to requiring them to be retained indefinitely. Retention is the responsibility of the employer, not its TPA. Section 107 does not impose money penalties for violations and the § 209 civil penalty is small, but failure to retain required information might be deemed a breach of fiduciary duty, or might embroil the employer in a costly suit over benefits. [Jewell Lim Esposito, *How Long to Retain ERISA Plan Records? Forever,* Employee Benefits Unplugged (Aug. 30, 2011) (benefitslink.com)];
- Federal contractors: Information about the employer's contractor status must be retained for three years;
- OSHA: The record-retention requirement for employee exposure to toxic substances is very long: 30 years;
- Tax records: The minimum retention period is four years;
- ADEA: 29 C.F.R. § 1627.3(b)(2) requires a benefit plan that is subject to the ADEA to be kept on file while the plan is in operation, and for at least one year after its termination.

Joint guidance about background checks, published by the EEOC and FTC in March 2014, says that personnel or employment records, including job applications, must be kept for at least one year after the record was made, or the personnel action was taken (whichever is later). For federal contractors that have 150 or more employees, and federal contracts of at least $150,000, the DOL extends this retention requirement to two years. When a discrimination charge is made, employment records must be retained at least until completion of the case. The FTC says that background reports can be discarded after record retention obligations have been satisfied—but they must be disposed of in a manner that preserves privacy (e.g., shredding or burning paper; deleting electronic files so that they cannot be retrieved). [EEOC/FTC, *Background Checks: What Employers Need to Know*, <http://www.eeoc.gov/eeoc/publications/background_checks_employers.cfm> (Mar. 2014)]

CHAPTER 25
CORPORATE COMMUNICATIONS

§ 25.01 INTRODUCTION

Communications within the corporation, and from the corporation to outsiders, have tremendous practical and legal consequences. To avoid trouble, everyone in a position to speak for the corporation should be aware of these potential ramifications and should be very careful about what is communicated (because not only are there things that should not be said, but items that must be accurately disclosed in various contexts) and in what form.

An emerging issue is the extent to which employers can adopt contract provisions that vary the timing rules under state law. In late 2013, the Supreme Court upheld a disability policy's contractual requirement that suits be filed within three years after proof of loss was due. In this case, the plaintiff sued within three years of the final claim denial, but more than five years after she first asserted her claim. The Supreme Court said that the contract provision was reasonable and enforceable. [*Heimeshoff v. Hartford Life & Accident Ins. Co.*, 134 S. Ct. 604 (2013); see Scott J. Stitt, *U.S. Supreme Court Holds that a Three-Year Contractual Limitations Period for Benefit Claims is Not Unreasonable nor Contrary to ERISA*, Central Ohio Discrimination law firm (Dec. 16, 2013) (benefitslink.com)]

The district court dismissed an FLSA/EPA suit against FedEx, brought by an employee who charged that she was paid less than co-workers. The claims were timely under the statutes, but the district court enforced the employment agreement, which required suits to be brought within six months. The Sixth Circuit held that reducing the statute of limitations was an unlawful waiver of the plaintiff's rights under the FLSA and, because the EPA is part of the FLSA, protection under that statute cannot be waived either. [*Boaz v. FedEx Customer Info. Servs., Inc.*, 725 F.3d 603 (6th Cir. 2013); see Matthew J. Thomas, *Employers Cannot Shorten Limitations Periods For FLSA Or Equal Pay Claims*, Jenner & Block (Oct. 31, 2013), available at Lexology.com]

Forum selection and choice of law clauses in employment and noncompete agreements are also significant. The recent Supreme Court *Atlantic Marine* decision holds that contractual forum selection clauses will be enforced except in the more egregious cases. This is beneficial to employers that want to avoid involvement of states like California that disfavor noncompete agreements. [*Atlantic Marine Constr. Co., Inc. v. U.S. Dist. Court for the W. Dist. of Texas*, 134 S. Ct. 568 (2013); see Kenneth Kirschner, Robin J. Samuel, and Caroline H. Cheng, *Supreme Court Decision Allows Employers To More Easily Enforce Forum Selection Clauses*, Hogan Lovells (Jan. 6, 2014), available at Lexology.com]

In a case so perfect that it sounds like an urban legend, the headmaster of a Florida prep school brought an ADEA case after his termination. The case was mediated and an $80,000 settlement agreed to. The settlement agreement included a confidentiality provision forbidding discussion of the settlement. However, the plaintiff's daughter posted to her Facebook page that her parents "won" the suit. The school was able to get the settlement vacated and the suit dismissed.

[Christopher M. Ernst, *Confidentiality Agreements Really Do Mean "Confidential,"* Bricker & Eckler LLP (Mar. 3, 2014), available at Lexology.com]

§ 25.02 EMPLOYMENT CONTRACTS

[A] Basic Considerations

Labor law aspects of Collective Bargaining Agreements between an employer and a union are discussed in Chapter 30. For employees who are not union members, there are both advantages and disadvantages to entering into a written employment contract. The written contract reduces uncertainty, and that is good—but it also limits flexibility, and that can create problems. An individual written employment contract should cover issues such as:

- Duration of employment;
- Renewal provisions (including the amount of notice to be given);
- The duties the employee will perform;
- Promotion possibilities;
- Compensation and benefits, including contingent compensation—contingent on results and/or bonuses and stock options;
- Rights in inventions and other intellectual property developed by the employee during the contract term; treatment of intellectual property developed while the contract is in force but not during working hours, or not of the type the employee was hired to produce;
- Covenant not to compete with the employer, and agreement not to solicit its employees and customers, even after termination of employment. Even in a jurisdiction that is not opposed to these provisions (see § 25.02[C] below), to be enforceable, these agreements must be reasonable in both duration and geographic scope, and must not be so severe that they prevent the individual from earning a living;
- Severability: If any contract provision is invalid, that provision will be removed from the contract, and the rest of the contract will remain valid and enforceable;
- Alternative Dispute Resolution: Whether disputes about the contract will be resolved by an arbitrator, mediator, or other decision maker other than a court. If so, whether class arbitration will be permitted.

[B] Employment Contract Case Law

Individual employment contracts are usually analyzed under the same rules as ordinary commercial contracts, so it is relevant whether there was a meeting of the minds; each side obtained consideration; and there was no mistake about the terms. (Relief for one or both parties may be available if there was a mistake, especially mutual mistake.) The Statute of Frauds is another fundamental contract rule, one that says that a contract that lasts a year or more can only be enforced if it is in writing.

The Fifth Circuit upheld the dismissal of state-law claims relating to William Sullivan's hiring as CEO of Leor Energy. An employment contract was drafted and never signed. Sullivan was fired after a brief time at Leor. The unsigned contract was not enforceable because of the Statute of Frauds. Texas law says that just because it is possible that a contract could be terminated within a year (Sullivan's contract allowed either side to terminate the agreement) does not mean it is not for a fixed term of over one year. Sullivan also asserted that the Statute of Frauds did not apply because he had partially performed the agreement, but the Fifth Circuit held that the "partial performance" exception only applies when not applying it would mean that fraud was tolerated. In this case, Sullivan was paid a salary for his work, so he was not defrauded. [*Sullivan v. Leor Energy LLC*, 600 F.3d 542 (5th Cir. 2010)]

Under New York common law, at-will employees cannot sue for wrongful discharge. In 2012, the New York Court of Appeals refused to make an exception for hedge fund compliance officers. The plaintiff said that he was fired for objecting to improper trading. The Court of Appeals ruled that state common law is not required to take a more active role merely because there are federal law compliance requirements. The plaintiff could not make use of federal whistleblower protection because there was no evidence that he told anyone outside the firm about the alleged misconduct. [*Sullivan v. Harnisch*, 19 N.Y.3d 259; 969 N.E.2d 758; 946 N.Y.S.2d 540 (2012)]

[C] Noncompete Case Law

A restrictive covenant is an employment contract provision imposing a limitation (such as time, scope, and/or geographic area) on the employee's ability to work in that occupation or profession when employment ends. A restraint is reasonable if it is reasonably limited in time and scope, is no greater than needed to protect the employer's legitimate interests, does not impose undue hardship on the employee, and is not harmful to the public. Covenants can be enforced by preliminary injunction based on a showing of risk of irreparable injury. New York will enforce reasonable restrictive covenants but disfavors covenants that prevent the employee from getting a similar job. In New York, a restriction on the ability to work for a competitor is invalid unless the employee's services are unique and extraordinary, or the employee is a member of a learned profession. [Andrew Zwerling, *The Interplay of Restrictive Covenants, Preliminary Injunctions and Arbitration*, N.Y.L.J. (Nov. 25, 2013), available at law.com]

States differ in their approach to covenants not to compete, and some states forbid or disfavor them, whereas others will enforce them—but in any case, a covenant not to compete will be enforced only if it is reasonable in its geographic scope and duration. The California Business and Professions Code makes most noncompetes unenforceable. A 2012 New Hampshire statute says that a noncompete is void if it is not given to job applicants or promotion candidates before the job or promotion offer.

The District Court for the District of Minnesota held that the terms of a noncompete agreement were overbroad and so vague as to be unenforceable. The agreement was 17 years old; the company had been sold twice in the interim; and it referred to a written employment agreement which was never executed or clearly defined. The agreement did not set a geographic limit and the court said that the employee was "left guessing" about the scope of the agreement. The district court refused to reform the agreement to make it enforceable, ruling that it would have had to divine the intent of the parties 17 years later when the corporate identity of the employer had changed. [*Gavaras v. Greenspring Media, LLC, et al.*, Civil No. 13-3566, 2014 U.S. Dist. LEXIS 3812, 164 Lab. Cas. (CCH) ¶ 61,438 (D. Minn. Jan. 13, 2014); see Michael T. Miller, *Minnesota Court Declines To "Blue-Pencil" Noncompete Agreement*, Briggs and Morgan (Jan. 29, 2014), available at Lexology.com]

Multi-state employers must consider the enforceability of noncompete agreements in different states. For example, North Dakota, by statute, forbids enforcement of noncompetes, whereas Oklahoma might enforce them but on very restrictive conditions. A "red pencil" state may find the entire agreement unenforceable if there is one overbroad provision, whereas a "blue pencil" state would strike out the offending provisions but enforce the rest. (Provisions will only be removed, not added.) Most states are "purple pencil" states that might redraft provisions to render the agreement enforceable. New Mexico, Utah, and Vermont have not taken a position on this issue. [Hans Murphy, *Different Strokes for Different Folks (or Red, Blue, and Purple-Pencil America: How the 50 States Differ on Revising Non-Competes)*, Barnes & Thornburg's Employment Law Currents Blog, <http://www.btcurrents.com/different-strokes-for-different-folks-or-red-blue-and-purple-pencil-america-ihow-the-50-states-differ-on-revising-non-competes-01-03-2014> (Jan. 3, 2014) (benefitslink.com); the article includes a map showing which category each state falls into]

Another area of state-to-state difference is when noncompetes can be signed. In early 2014, the District Court for the Southern District of Alabama held that a noncompete agreement can only be signed after employment begins. However, Minnesota and Oregon have held that a restrictive covenant must be signed before employment starts for employment itself to constitute consideration. The Alabama case involves a pharmacist who signed a noncompete March 29, 2011 for an offer to start work on April 11, 2011. The district court would not grant the employer an injunction to enforce the agreement because Alabama holds that contracts that restrain the exercise of a lawful profession are void except as set out in the state statute. The statute permits an employee to agree to refrain from carrying out a similar business or solicit the employer's customers in a specified county, city, or smaller unit. But Alabama requires the employment relationship to exist at the time the agreement is signed. Minnesota does not have a noncompete statute but its case law says that an offer of employment is adequate consideration for a noncompete—yet continued employment is not. Oregon makes a noncompete agreement void unless the employer informs the employee, in a written offer of employment received at least two weeks before the first day of employment, that the noncompete is a required condition of employment—or the employer and employee enter into the agreement when the employee is promoted. This provision does not apply to confidentiality agreements or non-solicit or non-service agreements. [*Dawson v. Ameritox, Ltd.*, No. 13-0614-KD-M, 2014 U.S. Dist. LEXIS 801 (S.D. Ala. Jan. 6, 2014); see V. John Ella and Thomas A. Davis, *Should A Non-Compete Be Signed Before Or After Employment Begins? Answer: It Depends*, Jackson Lewis PC (Jan. 19, 2014), available at Lexology.com]

In restrictive covenant cases, the employer may be able to seek a preliminary injunction if violation of the covenant could cause irreparable injury. If the contract provides for arbitration as a means of dispute resolution, it is common to make an exception for injunctions. If so, there will be a two-step process: first a suit about the availability of an injunction, followed by arbitration of the underlying dispute. The AAA rules that took effect October 1, 2013 give arbitrators the power to award emergency injunctive relief. [Andrew Zwerling, *The Interplay of Restrictive Covenants, Preliminary Injunctions and Arbitration*, N.Y.L.J. (Nov. 25, 2013), available at law.com]

Drafting suggestions for covenants not to compete that will be enforceable include:

- Describe the scope of prohibited activities in a way that will continue to apply if the employee's job responsibilities change.
- Make the covenant applicable to other activities the employee is involved in during his or her tenure.
- In states where the enforceable portions of a covenant will be enforced and the rest will be stricken, describe the restrictions broadly but include alternatives—if a covenant covering the entire state is stricken, the employer will have no protection, but a covenant limited to a certain number of miles or a particular geographic area might be limited by a court but otherwise upheld. The clause could also give a list of prohibited activities, but specify that the covenant applies only to activities the employee actually engages in during the term of the agreement.

- Specify liquidated damages, because, when an employer moves for a TRO and preliminary injunction, it will be difficult to calculate the damages for violation of the covenant. The amount of liquidated damages must reflect reasonable assumptions about potential damages, and must not be punitive. One option is to call for a larger amount in the first month, on the theory that the initial violation may include disclosure of trade secrets or interference with goodwill that cannot be remedied even by a prompt injunction, plus smaller amounts for each month that the violations continue.
- Some employers permit the employee to buy out of the covenant by paying a significant sum before competing, to compensate the employer for lost income.
- A "fail-safe" clause states that both parties intend the covenant to be enforceable, and it was a significant factor in the hiring decision—so the employee agrees to pay a fixed amount to make up for non-enforcement of the covenant, if the employee leaves before the employer receives full consideration for the agreement.
- If state law allows, call for the employee to pay the employer's attorneys' fees for disputes about the covenant. [Lee A. Spinks, *Now That We Know The Basic Rules . . . Drafting Covenants Not To Compete To Maximize The Likelihood Of Enforcement*, Poyner Spruill LLP (Nov. 11, 2013), available at Lexology.com]

The *Wall Street Journal* published two articles about noncompetes in mid-2013, noting that the frequency of employers requiring noncompete agreements has increased—and so has the number of cases challenging these agreements. Top executives may be out of the workforce for prolonged periods to avoid violating a noncompete; or their new employers may have to pay large sums to an ex-employer to avoid claims, or may have to reimburse the employees for extensive severance benefits they gave up to take the new job. Venture capital availability is greater in states that limit noncompetes than in those (e.g., Florida and Massachusetts) that favor enforcement of such clauses. In 2012, there were 760 published court opinions in cases about noncompetes, 61% higher than the number 10 years earlier. The total number of lawsuits is probably much higher, because many of these cases are settled and do not yield a published opinion. Joann S. Lublin, *Companies Loosen the Handcuffs on Non-Competes*, WSJ.com (Aug. 12, 2013); Ruth Simon & Angus Loten, *Litigation Over Noncompete Clauses Is Rising*, WSJ.com (Aug. 14, 2013)]

Late in 2012, the Supreme Court held that the Oklahoma Supreme Court was wrong to hold that the noncompete provisions in two employment contracts were void because they violated public policy. The decision should have been left up to the arbitrator. The clause referred to any "dispute, difference or unresolved question." When two employees quit and went to work for a competitor,

Nitro-Lift demanded arbitration. The ex-employees sued in Oklahoma state court to enjoin enforcement of the noncompete agreement, which they said was null and void. The Oklahoma Supreme Court asked the parties to show why the state law limiting the enforceability of noncompete agreements should not be applied. The Supreme Court held that the FAA applies in both federal and state courts and attacks on the validity of the contract (rather than on the validity of the arbitration clause) must be resolved by the arbitrator. The validity of the arbitration clause is determined by the court. If the arbitration clause is valid, then the validity of the rest of the contract is decided by the arbitrator. [*Nitro-Lift Techs., LLC v. Howard*, 133 S. Ct. 500 (2012)]

A Fifth Circuit case involved the Cantrells' merger of their accounting firm with another firm. They entered into employment agreements with the purchaser. Patrick Cantrell retired; Carol gave notice of retirement two years later. The defendant charged Carol with violating the noncompete provision in the agreement and fired her for cause. The purchaser company did not make deferred compensation payments to either spouse, arguing that Carol's wrongdoing violated the noncompete provision. When they sued to recover the deferred compensation, the defendant said that they could not be sued in state court because the employment agreements were part of an ERISA plan. The Fifth Circuit held that the agreements were subject to state law: a one-time calculation of deferred compensation under a fixed formula does not constitute an ERISA plan. [*Cantrell v. Briggs & Veselka Co.*, 728 F.3d 444 (5th Cir. 2013); see Kevin McGuinness, *Employment Agreement Provisions Not an ERISA Plan*, plansponsor.com (Oct. 7, 2013)]

In 2011, the Supreme Court of Texas held that it is permissible for an employer to require an employee to sign a covenant not to compete in exchange for letting the employee exercise stock options as long as the noncompete agreement is reasonable in time, scope of activity, and geographic area. In Texas, a noncompete agreement is enforceable if it is part of, or ancillary to, an otherwise enforceable agreement. Consideration such as stock options that is reasonably related to goodwill, trade secrets, confidential information, or other protectable interests creates the necessary connection between the noncompete and the business' interests. The stock options were reasonably related to protecting corporate goodwill, so the noncompete was ancillary to an agreement. [*Marsh USA Inc. v. Cook*, 354 S.W.3d 764 (Tex. 2011); see John L. Utz, *Noncompete as Condition for Option Exercise in Texas*, Utz, Miller & Eickmann LLC (Sept. 20, 2011) (benefitslink.com)]

EMC sought a preliminary injunction to prevent Christopher Blotto from competing, soliciting EMC's employees or customers, or using confidential business information. The district court granted a preliminary injunction with respect to the confidential information only, denying it for competition and solicitation, on the grounds that the one-year term of the noncompete had already expired. The First Circuit affirmed, holding that, when a time period has expired, even if the delay was caused by legal proceedings, an injunction is not the proper remedy; damages are. Because the employer drafted the agreement, it could have provided that the one-year term would be suspended during litigation or that it would not start until there was a preliminary finding of impropriety. [*EMC Corp. v. Arturi*, 655 F.3d 75 (1st Cir. 2011)]

The First Circuit upheld the district court's issuance of a preliminary injunction preventing an ex-employee from doing business with his ex-employer's customers—even if the customers initiated the contact. The defendant was an account executive who worked under a non-solicitation/non-disclosure agreement. He went to work with a competitor, and dealt with some customers of his former employer. The employer obtained a preliminary injunction for one year dealing with these customers. The First Circuit held that there is no real distinction between soliciting business and merely "accepting" it. Non-solicitation agreements protect the ex-employer's accrued goodwill, no matter who makes the first contact. [*Corporate Technologies, Inc. v. Harnett*, 731 F.3d 6 (1st Cir. 2013); see Erik Weibust, *First Circuit Holds That Solicitation Is Barred By Non-Compete Agreement Regardless Of Who Initiates Contact*, Seyfarth Shaw LLP (Sept. 24, 2013), available at Lexology.com]

Frequently, employment agreements forbid raiding or soliciting employees from the former workplace. Some New York cases treated these provisions like covenants not to compete—but they are actually quite different. An agreement that forbids a former employee from going to work for a competitor could be challenged as hindering the employee's ability to earn a living but an anti-raiding clause does not, making it inherently more reasonable and less restrictive than a noncompete. However, in late 2012, the Western District of New York applied the test of reasonableness to a no-raid clause. To be reasonable, such a clause might be limited only to personnel with whom the employee worked in the previous year or two, or only if the employees who leave the employer actually go to work for a competitor. [*Renaissance Nutrition v. Jarrett*, No. 08-CV-800S, 2012 WL 42171 (W.D.N.Y. Jan. 9, 2012); see Lloyd B. Chinn and Rebecca L. Berkebile, *Evaluating the Enforceability of Anti-Raiding Provisions*, N.Y.L.J. (Dec. 10, 2012) (law.com)]

Such no-raid agreements may also create antitrust problems. Such an agreement may be acceptable if it is ancillary to legitimate collaborative activities—but otherwise it might be challenged as per se illegal and probably will not be analyzed under the more lenient "rule of reason" standard. [*In re: High-Tech Employee Antitrust Litig.* (N.D. Cal., settled 2013); see Nick Grimmer and Joseph F. Winterscheid, *$20 Million Settlement In In Re: High-Tech Employee Antitrust Litigation, A Non-Poaching Agreement Case*, McDermott Will & Emery (Oct. 1, 2013), available at Lexology.com]

The Eleventh Circuit upheld the grant of an injunction for violation of a covenant not to complete. According to the Eleventh Circuit, if a restrictive covenant is enforceable, it creates a rebuttable presumption of irreparable injury. However, the Eleventh Circuit held that $1,659,000 in damages was excessive because the plaintiff did not establish that the defendant's solicitation of a former client cost the plaintiff the contract. To receive damages, the former employer must show that it sustained a loss, and its lost profits were directly caused by the defendant's breaches of the restrictive covenants. In this case, the former employer tried to recover "ill gotten gains" from the new employer—which wasn't even a party to the suit. [*Proudfoot Consulting Corp. v. Gordon*, 576 F.3d 1223 (11th Cir. 2009) See also *Environmental Servs., Inc. v. Carter*, 9 So.3d 1258 (Fla. Dist. Ct. App. 2009) holding that a noncompete provision that forbade the employee from performing services for any customer of the ex-employer that the employee had business-related contact with during employment was justified by the former employer's business interest in maintaining client relationships]

California law actually forbids noncompete agreements, although, in the right case, California might agree with the 20 states that accept the "inevitable disclosure" doctrine—i.e., that an ex-employee can be enjoined from going to work for a competitor of the former employer, if the inevitable result would be disclosure of the ex-employer's trade secrets, even if the ex-employee does not intend to do so.

In mid-2008, the California Supreme Court found most covenants not to compete invalid under California law, because the state law gives workers freedom to compete and solicit their former clients when they change jobs. Employers can only restrain former employees from engaging in their trade or profession if the agreement falls within one of the statutory exceptions.

However, California has adopted the Uniform Trade Secrets Act, which allows protection of some information, including client lists. The California Supreme Court also dismissed the plaintiff's claim that requiring him to sign the noncompete agreement interfered with his economic advantage, because it did not try to release any statutory claims that could not be waived. (The plaintiff was an accountant who worked for Arthur Andersen until the firm went under; his division was sold to another financial services company that required employees to release all their claims against Arthur Andersen; he refused to sign, was fired without severance, and his job offer was rescinded.) [*Edwards v. Arthur Andersen*, 44 Cal. 4th 937 (Cal. 2008); see Labor Code § 16600.]

Also note that even though California law bars covenants not to compete, a California court does not have the power to issue an injunction forbidding the parties in a California suit from bringing suit in a different state to enforce the covenant not to compete. [*Advanced Bionics Corp. v. Medtronic Inc.*, 29 Cal. 4th 697, 59 P.3d 231, 128 Cal. Rptr. 2d 172 (2002)] The theory is that judges should respect the powers of other judges, especially those in other states.

New York considers noncompete agreements an unreasonable restraint on trade. To enforce one, the employer must show that the covenant is reasonable in duration and scope, does not harm the public interest, does not subject the employee to undue hardship, and is no broader than needed to protect the employer's protectable interests. An employee on "garden leave" (i.e., paid to remain at home and not take another job) is still subject to the duty of loyalty to the employer. The "employee choice" doctrine says that courts will not analyze the reasonableness of a covenant that gives an employee a choice between competing (and forgoing benefits) and not competing (and receiving benefits). It is common for employers to require job applicants to disclose terminations for cause. Failure to disclose could justify firing the new employee. In other words, it is often rational for employees to quit before they can be terminated for cause. [Alexandra Wald and Nathaniel P.T. Read, *To Quit or Not to Quit?* N.Y.L.J. (Nov. 13, 2012) (law.com)]

The Third Circuit upheld an injunction against Chris Botticella, one of the handful of people who knew the trade secrets for making Thomas' English muffins, on the grounds that muffin manufacturer Bimbo proved that, without an injunction, it was likely that its trade secrets would be misappropriated. It is not necessary to show that it would be "virtually impossible" for the ex-employee to perform the new job without using the ex-employer's trade secrets. [*Bimbo Bakeries USA Inc. v. Botticella*, 613 F.3d 102 (3d Cir. 2010); see Shannon P. Duffy, *Court May Block Executive's Start Date at Competitor Due to Muffin Trade Secrets* (July 28, 2010) (law.com)]

The general rule is that employees who are not bound by employment agreements or termination agreements containing noncompete clauses are free to compete with the employer after they leave. A top executive may be considered a fiduciary as to the employer. A principle of corporate law called the "corporate opportunity doctrine" imposes a duty on a current employee to disclose to the employer whenever a business opportunity arises that is appropriate for the corporation, and it is improper for an executive to take personal advantage of the opportunity at the corporation's expense.

Three weeks after quitting as a WEC project director, Mike Miller made a presentation to a potential WEC customer on behalf of a competitor. The customer entered into a contract with the competitor. WEC charged that Miller, on behalf of the competitor, downloaded proprietary WEC info to his own computer and used it in the presentation. WEC sued Miller, his assistant, and ARC under the Computer Fraud and Abuse Act (CFAA). The Fourth Circuit held that the CFAA does not apply to this situation. To maintain a civil suit under the CFAA, at least one of five additional factors must be proved. WEC had policies forbidding unauthorized use of proprietary information, and forbidding downloading proprietary information to a personal computer. However, Miller's authorization to access the information in the first place was not restricted. Like the Ninth Circuit, the Fourth Circuit held that the CFAA does not cover misappropriation of trade secrets or violation of corporate use policy committed by a person who had access to the information. [*WEC Carolina Energy Solutions LLC v. Miller*, 687 F.3d 199 (4th Cir. 2012)]

Merely announcing a new job on LinkedIn will not violate most non-solicitation agreements. For example, the Massachusetts Superior Court held that an updated profile reflecting the new job was not necessarily solicitation that violated the noncompete agreement: the ex-employee was not prohibited from recruiting in fields where her former employer did not operate. [*KNF&T Inc. v.*

Muller, 31 Mass. L. Rptr. 561 (Mass. Super. Ct. 2013); see Sheri Qualters, *LinkedIn Post Likely Didn't Violate Non-Compete Clause*, Nat'l L.J. (Nov. 4, 2013), available at law.com]

§ 25.03 EMPLOYEE HANDBOOKS

[A] Generally

Employee handbooks are traditional in large corporations, as a means of creating a uniform culture and distributing information to what can be a large, diverse, and widely disseminated group of employees. Handbooks are useful in training new hires about the employer's expectations. They provide a ready reference about work rules—and employee discipline often revolves around claimed infractions of these rules, so employees must be informed of the rules.

Not all handbooks are printed; more and more companies are using the Web or an intranet to provide information.

A 2014 article challenges the conventional wisdom by arguing that employee handbooks are no longer useful. In this view, the handbook's social media policies are likely to be obsolete. Employees probably don't care about the company history and mission statement. Few employees will read all the work rules and in an at-will work environment, they can be terminated for work misconduct even if there are no published rules. ERISA requires distribution of non-handbook documents explaining benefits. The author of the article says that the only potentially useful content for a handbook could be a statement that employment is at will; an anti-harassment policy that will satisfy the employer's obligations; the 29 C.F.R. § 541.603 FLSA safe harbor notice; election options under the FMLA; and information about the Sarbanes-Oxley hotline for whistleblowers. [Kevin Connelly, *Employee handbooks (1971 – 2014): R.I.P.* DLA Piper (Feb. 4, 2014), available at Lexology.com; see <http://www.labordish.com/files/2014/02/12-sample-handbook_final.pdf>, a 39-page template for modern employee handbooks]

Even if this is not the employer's intention, statements made in the handbook may be deemed to create a binding contract. Furthermore, once the employer is deemed to have created a contract, some courts will say that the employer can no longer amend that contract whenever it wants to, without providing additional consideration to the employees in return for the change. Although some courts say that the fact that the employee continues to work for the employer provides consideration, others require the employees to get some additional benefit if the employer wants to alter the contract.

Florida's position is that policy documents such as employee handbooks are generally non-binding and do not create enforceable contract rights. A 2013 case involved an employer that induced the plaintiff to continue working at the company by offering a long-term incentive plan. However, the company was being "run down," ceasing operations other than collecting its portfolio of structured settlements. The plaintiff resigned in December 2009. She asked for value of her vested shares and sued for breach of contract when she did not receive the payments. The employer said that the plan was not a contract or offer and it did not contain explicit language forming a binding contract. The Florida Court of Appeals reversed the trial court's grant of summary judgment for the employer, finding that there were questions for the jury as to whether there had been offer and acceptance. To avoid this result, employers should draft incentives to state specifically that the employer has discretion over awards. [*Turton v. Singer Asset Fin. Co., LLC*, 120 So. 3d 635 (Fla. 4th DCA 2013); see Richard D. Tuschman, *Continued Employment In Dead-End Job May Entitle Employee To Incentive Benefits*, Akerman Senterfitt (Sept. 24, 2013), available at Lexology.com]

A "Woolley disclaimer" states that an employee handbook is not a contract. The District Court for the District of New Jersey refused to enforce an arbitration clause that was included in a manual with a Woolley disclaimer, finding that the arbitration clause was unenforceable because the employer could unilaterally modify any provision without notice to employees. The result is that in New Jersey, or a state with similar laws, a stand-alone arbitration agreement protects the employer's interests better. [*Raymours Furniture Co., Inc. v. Rossi*, No. 13-4440, 2014 U.S. Dist. LEXIS 1006 (D.N.J. Jan. 2, 2014); see Joseph C. O'Keefe et al., *A Woolley Situation: District Of New Jersey Refuses To Enforce Arbitration Clause In Employee Handbook*, Proskauer Rose LLP (Feb. 27, 2014), available at Lexology.com]

The California Court of Appeal ruled in 2013 that the updated arbitration agreement in the employee handbook, issued after the plaintiffs' claims accrued and they filed their class action complaint, did not bind the employees in their wage and hour suit. The employer could only enforce the policy in the handbook issued by the prior owner of the company. [*Avery v. Integrated Healthcare Holdings, Inc.*, 159 Cal. Rptr. 3d 444 (Cal. App. 2013); see Howard S. Suskin, *Updated Arbitration Agreement Does Not Bind Employees*, Jenner & Block (Sept. 13, 2013), available at Lexology.com]

Although the Tenth Circuit revived ADA and FMLA claims in a case where an employee's termination may have been caused by his taking extensive leave, the Tenth Circuit upheld dismissal of his claims under Wyoming law for breach of implied employment contract. Wyoming law only recognizes these claims if the terms of the employee handbook have been violated; but the employer's handbook unambiguously permitted termination for a serious offense such as the safety violation the plaintiff was charged with. [*Smothers v. Solvay Chemicals, Inc.*, No. 12-8013 (10th Cir. Jan. 21, 2014); see Wolters Kluwer Law & Business News Center, *Decision By Committee Does Not Insulate Employer From Potential Liability For FMLA, ADA Claims* (Feb. 14, 2014) (benefitslink.com)]

The NLRB said that a car dealership's employee handbook provision forbidding pins, insignia, and other message clothing not provided by the employer is overly restrictive and violates NLRA § 8(a)(1). The NLRB's position is that a rule against union insignia is presumptively invalid. The presumption can be overcome only by a showing of special circumstances (e.g., the rule is needed for safety or to maintain production or discipline). The NLRB accepted the argument that pins can injure employees or damage vehicles but required the handbook to be amended to permit other kinds of message clothing. [*Boch Imports, Inc.*, NLRB, No. 1-CA-83551 (Jan. 13, 2014); see Maria Greco Danaher, *Prohibiting "Message" Clothing Without Business Reason Violates The NLRA*, Ogletree Deakins (Feb. 10, 2014), available at Lexology.com; Joel S. Barras, *NLRB Judge Invalidates Company Dress Code*, Reed Smith LLP (Jan. 17, 2014), available at Lexology.com]

■ **TIP:** Many federal and state statutes limit the policies that employers can adopt. For example, a policy against leaves of less than one day could violate the Family and Medical Leave Act, or might be a refusal to make a reasonable accommodation required by the Americans with Disabilities Act.

Typical subjects for coverage in the handbook include:

- Training;
- Benefits (health plan, dental plan, disability, etc.);
- Access to profit-sharing plans;
- Defined benefit, defined contribution, 401(k), and other pension plans;
- Stock options;
- Vacations, leave (including sick leave, pregnancy, and military leave), holidays, and time off;
- Explanation of employees' statutory rights under, e.g., the Family and Medical Leave Act (FMLA), ADA, USERRA, etc.;
- Employer's policy of checking all references provided;
- Policy of employing only U.S. citizens and noncitizens who can lawfully work within the United States;
- Drug-free workplace policy, including circumstances under which drug testing will be required;
- Policies about e-mail and Internet use in the workplace;
- Policies about employment of both spouses in a couple, or more than one family member;
- Antiharassment policy; commitment to investigate charges; alternative reporting procedures if the supervisor is the alleged harasser;

- Policies about conflict of interests and acceptance of gifts from suppliers;
- Confidentiality of the employer's intellectual property;
- Employees' patent rights (if any) in inventions they develop while they are working for the employer;
- What will be considered a disciplinary offense;
- Discipline procedure (e.g., oral reprimand, followed by a written warning; suspension after two written warnings for the same offense; retention of warnings in the personnel record for at least a year; and termination; immediate termination will be permitted in the case of a serious, dangerous, or criminal act).

[B] At-Will Employment

For employees who are not unionized, and who do not have individual employment contracts, it is often a good idea to put a disclaimer in the handbook:

- Employees are hired at will;
- They can be fired when the employer sees fit; it is not necessary for the employer to demonstrate good cause for the discharge;
- The information in the handbook is for guidance only, and does not bind the employer to a contract.

To be legally effective, a disclaimer must be clear and conspicuous. It cannot be buried in small print somewhere in the back of the book. In fact, the first page is an excellent location. When a disclaimer is issued, it does not apply to people who were already employees and working under the old policy.

The mere fact that the employer has a system of progressive discipline, spelled out in the handbook, does not mean that the employee is no longer an at-will employee. However, it makes sense to include a disclaimer explaining the function of the disciplinary system.

The more specific a provision is, the more likely that courts are to construe it as creating a formal contract. However, in order to win when they charge breach of this implied contract, employees may have to show detrimental reliance (i.e., that they relied on the provision, and this reliance was harmful for them). At the very least, employees will have to prove that they read the handbook, because it is hard to claim reliance on an unread provision.

[C] Orientation Checklists

It is a good idea to provide orientation to train new hires. It is even better to standardize the orientation process, with standard documents for welcoming and instructing new employees. Both the employee and the supervisor handling the orientation should sign the document, so that later on the employee will not be able to claim that lifetime employment was promised if the document clearly states that employment is at will.

The orientation checklist should cover subjects such as:

- The company's equal employment opportunity policies;
- The company's position on unionization and union activity (get legal advice before promulgating a policy!);
- Which unions (if any) that are already recognized as bargaining agents for the employees;
- The terms of the formal probation process (if there is one);
- What a new hire has to do to become a permanent employee, but make sure that no promises are made of indefinite tenure or lifetime employment;
- The new employee's job title, duties, and promotion path;
- The compensation and benefit package for the job (including vacation days, vacation banking, disability benefits, sick leave, options under the group health plan, and severance pay);
- Work rules;
- Circumstances under which the employee can be terminated.

Even if the manual indicates the employees will be on probation for a certain length of time after being hired, they will still be entitled to good faith and fair dealing from the employer. In fact, some courts will allow probationary employees to sue for wrongful termination, if the employer did not offer them long-term employment after the end of the probation period.

[D] Legal Consequences of Handbooks

Early in 2004, the NLRB ruled that it violates federal labor law to promulgate a handbook provision that restricts employee communications with other employees and the press about the terms and conditions of employment (such as wages and grievances). The employer could not forbid discussion of company issues in public areas other than the casino floor. Discussions on the casino floor, however, could be banned by analogy with the retail sales area of a store. It was improper for the handbook to forbid communicating any information about the company to the media without management approval; even a rule that is never enforced can have a chilling effect. [*Double Eagle Hotel & Casino*, 341 NLRB No. 17 (Jan. 30, 2004)]

Denial of unemployment benefits was proper for a claimant who was terminated for absenteeism. When she was hired, she signed an acknowledgment that she received the company handbook, which included the employment policy. Her position was that she was entitled to benefits—that her actions could not be willful or wanton because she misinterpreted the attendance policy. But the employer gave the claimant coaching warning her that she was at risk of termination for noncompliance, and it was therefore just to terminate her when she did not improve, and denial of unemployment benefits was also justified for violation of a known employer policy when the potential consequences were also known. [*Jackson*, Unemp. Ins. Rep. (CCH) ¶ 8317 (Del. Super. Ct. 2008)]

§ 25.04 WORK RULES

Some organizations are small enough, informal enough, or simple enough in operation that they do not need written work rules. But in the larger organization, or even a small operation where the work rules could become an issue, a written list of rules (in the handbook or set out separately) can be very useful.

The work rules document should make it clear that the employer is the only one to make work rules and that the employer has the right to modify them at any time. The rules themselves are not a contract with the employees that has to be negotiated, or that has to be maintained in its original form.

Work rules deal with issues such as:

- Workplace safety and security (not letting in unauthorized persons; wearing protective equipment in construction areas or where hazardous chemicals are present);
- Emergency procedures in case of fires, chemical spills, etc.;
- Where (if anyplace!) smoking is allowed in the workplace; if smoking is banned inside the workplace, limitations on going outside for smoking breaks;
- Requirement of on-time arrival and staying until the end of the work day or shift;
- Dress and grooming rules—are uniforms required for any job titles? Which days are "casual" days, and what is acceptable business casual clothing? Are there any limitations or bans on facial hair, hairstyles, makeup, or jewelry? (Make sure that these rules do not violate employees' rights to reasonable accommodation of their religious practices);

- Availability of paid and unpaid leave; how to request leave. Some companies maintain a no-fault absence policy, under which employees get a certain number of days off no matter what the reason is, but discipline can be imposed for excessive absence. A paid leave bank is similar, but allows unused days to be carried over or cashed out. Get legal advice about harmonizing your leave policy with legal requirements for disability and unpaid family leave;
- Bans on horseplay, substance abuse, possession of alcohol in the workplace, and removing products or materials (even waste or spoiled items) without permission;
- Bans on harassment, fighting, and weapons;
- Control of solicitation within the workplace. A "no-solicitation" rule can be very helpful, not only in restricting union activity, but in improving efficiency and avoiding conflict among employees. It can get pretty expensive to come to work each day if you are asked to contribute to everyone's favorite charity and chip in for presents for people who are getting married, leaving the company, having a baby, in the hospital, etc. An effective no-solicitation rule must be appropriately communicated to employees, it must be nondiscriminatory, and it must be applied uniformly. So if one employee is given permission to sell raffle tickets for the Catholic Church, while another is denied permission to raise money for the NAACP (or vice versa), it will appear that the employer is guilty of discrimination;
- The extent to which employees are permitted to inspect their own personal records or show them to an attorney, union representative, etc. Check your state law: It probably requires employees to have access to their records, and also protects privacy rights by limiting disclosure of personal information to anyone except the employee without the employee's consent. [See § 26.07 for rules on privacy of health records];
- Ethical standards imposed on employees: for example, when they are allowed to accept gifts from a potential supplier; use of inside information; lobbying, political activities, and donations;
- How to find additional work-related information and answers to questions: for instance, through the HR department, the Employee Assistance Program, or the corporate intranet.

■ **TIP:** Even though the work rules are not contractual in nature, it is a good idea to have employees sign a notice stating that they received a copy of the work rules and had a chance to read and become familiar with them. The notice may come in handy later if the employee claims that he or she never saw the rules or didn't understand them.

§ 25.05 SYSTEMS OF PROGRESSIVE DISCIPLINE

One approach to at-will employment is for the employer to take and maintain a consistent position that only the employer determines the quality of the employee's work performance. Employees can therefore be disciplined or fired based on the employer's sole determination that their work is unsatisfactory. In a unionized workplace, it is almost certain that the collective bargaining agreement will require a system of progressive discipline, where all the steps, from a verbal warning through levels of reprimands, must be followed before the employee can be fired.

There are various reasons why even a nonunion workplace might have a progressive discipline system. It could improve efficiency. Sometimes, employees really do not know that their work is below par, so it is better to show them how to improve instead of firing them. Also, if the employer voluntarily adopts a progressive discipline system, this could make employees less interested in unionizing.

The downside is that having specific rules to follow limits the employer's flexibility. Even in a nonunion setting, the disciplinary system may be treated by courts as a contractual obligation, so that once the system is set up, it has to be maintained in the future.

Usually, a system of progressive discipline begins with an oral warning explaining why the supervisor is dissatisfied with the employee's performance. The next step is a written warning. If performance is still unsatisfactory, discipline proceeds to a probationary period or suspension (usually unpaid, lasting three–five days), then demotion or termination.

All the steps, including oral warnings, should be documented in the employee's personnel record. The written warning should include a place for the employee's signature, indicating that the document has been read. The employee should be given a copy for reference. It is often helpful to let the employee include a brief written statement giving his or her side of the story.

It is important to monitor the reasons for an employee's lateness or absence. Discipline or discharge could constitute a violation of a statute if the employee has been injured (and qualified for Worker's Compensation), is disabled as defined by the ADA, or is taking care of a sick family member and therefore is entitled to FMLA leave.

All investigations should be documented, to show that the employer is acting on the basis of facts and not discrimination against members of a protected group.

An objective party should review all termination decisions. The best time is after tempers have had a chance to cool, but promptly enough to demonstrate the employer's efficiency and involvement. Before a termination, review the process to see that the employee received the appropriate warnings; the investigation gave enough weight to the employee's explanation; and the employee was treated fairly, objectively, and on a par with other similarly situated employees.

In general, employees who are discharged for cause are not entitled to severance pay (see Chapter 3). However, the employee handbook may have been written in such general terms that it constitutes a contract to pay severance benefits, even in connection with a discharge for cause. Severance policies that are written and communicated to workers may become welfare benefit plans subject to ERISA. If there is no formal plan, and the employer has not entered into an express or implied contract, then it is completely at the employer's discretion to grant or withhold severance benefits.

§ 25.06 EMPLOYEE EVALUATIONS

Regular evaluations of employee performance can be critical in making sure that the organization meets its goals. Employees who are not performing up to par can be identified and given the training, encouragement, or whatever they need to improve. When it's time to award merit raises and bonuses, the performance appraisal should identify the stars.

A well-done performance appraisal identifies real problems in employee performance and gives insights into solutions. Some of the basic issues for performance reviews include:

- Whether the quantity of work performed by the employee has been satisfactory;
- Quality of the work;
- The employee's knowledge of the job;
- His or her dependability, initiative, and adaptability;
- The extent to which the employee has learned new skills, and seems likely to be able to acquire the skills that will be needed in the future;
- The extent of the employee's cooperation, attendance, and punctuality;
- Areas in which the employee needs to improve.

However, performance appraisals must be carefully done. If they're mishandled, the result is often to subject the employer to liability for wrongful termination or employment discrimination. There are many reasons why the appraisal process itself doesn't work well:

- Managers do not have time to do a thoughtful job of appraising performance, so they decide to err on the side of generosity;
- The appraisals do not seem to actually be used for anything, so managers put down whatever seems uncontroversial—or simply update the previous year's forms without much thought;

- In a large work group, managers may not know very much about what individual employees are doing;
- Managers want to be liked by the employees who report to them; they're afraid that a tough-minded appraisal could create hostility and reduce motivation;
- Ambitious managers want to give themselves an indirect pat on the back, hoping that they will be seen as outstanding leaders if all their subordinates are doing a great job;
- A bad appraisal could be attacked as the product of racism, sexism, sexual harassment, or retaliation. However, the answer is **not** to give everyone good marks because it looks very suspicious if the employer claims that someone who got a long line of excellent appraisals was fired for poor performance.

At a minimum, the employee should be shown a written performance appraisal, be given an opportunity to discuss it, and should be asked to sign a statement that he or she has read the document. Some states make it a legal requirement that the employee must be allowed to add comments; it is a good idea anyway.

The modern form of appraisal is the "360-degree review," which has input from more than one person, including co-workers and customers. However, it can be hard to gather all the necessary information, and not everyone will be candid. An alternative might be to have more frequent but informal reviews: for instance, at the end of every project, or every quarter or twice a year.

§ 25.07 MANDATORY PREDISPUTE ARBITRATION PROVISIONS

Employers, faced with the delay, high costs, and significant risks of employment litigation, often seek to require in advance that employees will raise any discrimination claims using the arbitration process rather than litigation (see Chapter 40).

To have a chance of enforcement, a handbook provision must make it clear which statutes are covered, and clearly and explicitly indicate that arbitration is the sole remedy. It makes sense to have the employee sign a document when he or she receives the handbook—not only stating that the handbook has been received, but that the employee has read its contents and understands them.

In recent years, most cases have come down on the side of arbitration, even if it is compelled by a mandatory predispute arbitration clause (i.e., if employees had to agree to arbitrate their claims as a condition of being hired)—a proposition that was approved by the Supreme Court in *Circuit City v. Adams.* [532 U.S. 105 (2002)] The jurisdiction and the facts of the case will determine whether the fact that the employee continues to work after the arbitration requirement has been imposed constitutes acceptance of the terms of the arbitration provision. [For example, *In Re Dallas Peterbilt Ltd.*, 196 S.W.3d 161 (Tex. 2006); *In re Dillard Dep't Stores, Inc.*, 198 S.W.3d 778 (Tex. 2006); *Hardin v. First Cash Fin. Servs. Inc.*, 465 F.3d 470 (10th Cir. 2006); *Berkley v. Dillard's Inc.*, 450 F.3d 775 (8th Cir. 2006), hold that continued employment constitutes acceptance, but *Leodori v. CIGNA Corp.*, 814 A.2d 1098 (N.J. 2003), says that it does not]

The Supreme Court ruled in 2009 that a labor union could require arbitration of a grievance brought by workers who said they were demoted because of age discrimination—the Supreme Court rejected drawing a distinction between collective bargaining agreements (CBAs) and individual contracts that contain arbitration clauses. [*14 Penn Plaza LLC v. Pyett,* 556 U.S. 247 (2009)] Another Supreme Court decision—in a consumer protection rather than an employment case—has been read to mean that federal law supports arbitration so strongly that state rulings about the unconscionability of arbitration agreements will be preempted. [*AT&T Mobility LLC v. Concepcion,* 131 S. Ct. 1740 (Apr. 27, 2011)]

In a decision covering all employees whose employers are engaged in interstate commerce (whether or not the company is unionized—about 25% of nonunion workers are subject to arbitration clauses), the NLRB ruled in early 2012 that requiring employees to waive collective actions and class arbitration and arbitrate all employment disputes individually violates the NLRA. The NLRB said that it was not bound by *AT&T Mobility* because that case does not apply to rights specifically guaranteed to employees by the NLRA. [*D.R. Horton and Michael Cuda*, 357 NLRB No. 184, Case 12-CA-25764 (Jan. 3, 2012).] In 2013, however, the Fifth Circuit held that it is permissible for an employer to impose a class action arbitration waiver; it is not inconsistent with the employees' legal right under the NLRA to pursue collective action. But the Fifth Circuit held that the arbitration agreement must clarify that employees do not waive the right to file NLRB complaints. [*DR Horton v. NLRB*, 737 F.3d 344 (5th Cir. 2013); see AP, *Court Blocks Labor Board on Lawsuits*, NYTimes.com (Dec. 3, 2013), *reh'g denied*, No. 12-60031 (5th Cir. Apr. 16, 2014)]

The Second Circuit upheld an arbitration agreement's waiver of class and collective actions in a case where the plaintiff alleged that she was wrongfully denied $1,867 in overtime. The plaintiff said that it would cost $200,000 in attorneys' fees, costs, and expert testimony to recover less than $2,000, but the Second Circuit held that it is lawful for an employer to rule out class and collective actions even if the practical effect is that small claims cannot be brought. [*Sutherland v. Ernst & Young*, 726 F.3d 290 (2d Cir. 2013); see Manatt Phelps & Phillips LLP, *Reversing Circuit Precedent, 2nd Circuit Upholds FLSA Collective Action Waiver* (Aug. 28, 2013), available at Lexology.com. The Second Circuit based its decision on *Italian Colors*, a Supreme Court decision that is not an employment case; the Supreme Court permitted contract clauses that forbid class arbitration.]

If your company is a federal contractor, however, its post-2009 ability to enforce mandatory arbitration clauses is severely limited. A provision in the federal spending bill for the Department of Defense for the years 2009–2010

(§ 8116) forbids defense contractors holding contracts or subcontracts over $1 million to enforce mandatory arbitration clauses. The defense contractor cannot be paid by the federal government unless it agrees not to enter into or enforce any employment contract making it a condition of employment for an employee or independent contractor to agree to arbitrate Title VII claims or many other tort claims. The Department of Defense has the power to grant a waiver for national security reasons, although the waiver must be disclosed to the public. [David Ingram, *Obama Signs Into Law Restriction on Arbitration Clauses*, Nat'l L.J. (Dec. 22, 2009) (law.com)]

A mid-2014 presidential Executive Order holds that if a federal contract is for $1 million or more, the contractor will not be permitted to impose a requirement of predispute arbitration for Title VII, sexual harassment, or sexual assault cases. [Fact Sheet, *Fair Play and Safe Workplaces Executive Order*, <http://www.wh.gov/ltpPD> (July 31, 2014)]

The fact that a statute can be enforced through federal lawsuits does not rule out arbitration, so the Fifth Circuit upheld mandatory arbitration of USERRA claims brought by a Marine reservist who said he was harassed and eventually fired because of his military status. [*Garrett v. Circuit City Stores*, 449 F.3d 672 (5th Cir. 2006). See § 1.18 for more discussion of USERRA]

However, an employer seeking to enforce an arbitration agreement must be careful to abide by the agreement itself. In late 2005, for example, the Ninth Circuit ruled that an employer that unilaterally imposed an arbitration policy had to arbitrate an employee's claims of wrongful termination (the employer said that she was fired for falsifying a time sheet). The employee sued in state court; the employer removed the case to federal court and sought to compel arbitration, but the federal courts refused to compel arbitration because the employer had failed to cooperate with the requirements of AAA arbitration required by the arbitration policy. [*Brown v. Dillard's Inc.*, 430 F.3d 1004 (9th Cir. 2005)]

California has decided a number of cases in which arbitration agreements have been found unconscionable—but many of these cases have been reversed by the Supreme Court or the Ninth Circuit, and most other states have not followed California's example. In 2013, The California Supreme Court overturned its 2011 decision (that an employee could not be required to waive his or her right to a "Berman" wage claims hearing before the state Labor Commission). In 2013, the Supreme Court said that the FAA preempts the state law that forbids such a waiver. However, the case was remanded to determine if the arbitration clause itself was unconscionable; the court said that unconscionable arbitration clauses can be invalidated despite *Concepcion* and *Italian Colors*. [*Sonic-Calabasas A, Inc. v. Moreno*, 57 Cal. 4th 1109 (Cal. 2013); see Winston & Strawn LLP, *Reversing Previous Ruling, California Supreme Court Holds Arbitration Agreement That Waives Right To An Administrative Hearing May Be Enforceable*, Lexology.com (Oct. 22, 2013)]

In mid-2014, California ruled that an employee's waiver of class arbitration is enforceable. However, employers cannot require employees to waive the right to bring Private Attorney General (PAGA) wage claims. [*Iskanian v. CLS Transp.*

Los Angeles LLC, No. S204032 (Cal. June 23, 2014); see Mark A. Neubauer and Meredith M. Moss, *California Law on Arbitration Changes . . . Again*, Carlton Fields Jorden Burt (June 23, 2014), available at Lexology.com]

The Washington Supreme Court refused to compel arbitration based on an unconscionable arbitration clause that the court considered overly broad and excessively limiting of employee rights. The clause imposed a statute of limitations of 14 days (state law calls for three years); back pay was limited to either two or four months, whereas state law allows recovery of three years of back pay and employees could find themselves paying an excessive share of costs. Therefore, employees were permitted to maintain a class action. [*Hill et al. v. Garda CL Northwest*, 179 Wash. 2d 47, 308 P.3d 635 (Wash. 2013); see Michael Droke, *Washington Supreme Court Invalidates Overbroad Arbitration Agreement*, Dorsey & Whitney LLP (Sept. 13, 2013), available at Lexology.com; Howard S. Suskin, *Arbitration Agreement Unconscionable Due To Time, Damages And Fee Provisions*, Jenner & Block (Nov. 29, 2013), available at Lexology.com]

Plaintiffs were mortgage loan officers who were not paid overtime because they were classified as independent contractors. They filed a class/collective action under the FLSA and the Ohio Minimum Fair Wage Standards Act. The Sixth Circuit held that the employer could compel individual arbitration even after the expiration of the plaintiffs' employment contracts. The contracts contained an arbitration clause, but did not specify whether class arbitration was available, so the Sixth Circuit held that class-wide arbitration is available only if the agreement specifically permits it. [*Huffman v. The Hilltop Cos.*, 747 F.3d 391 (6th Cir. 2014); see Gregory V. Mersol, *Sixth Circuit Holds That Duty to Arbitrate Survives Expiration of Employment Contract, Requires Individual Arbitration*, Baker & Hostetler LLP (Mar. 28, 2014), available at Lexology.com. It was already clear that CBA disputes must be arbitrated even after the expiration of the CBA: *Litton Financial Printing v. NLRB*, 501 U.S. 190 (1991). See also *Reed Elsevier, Inc. ex rel. LexisNexis Div. v. Crockett*, 734 F.3d 594 (6th Cir. 2013): when the contract is silent on the issue of class arbitration, class arbitration is not available.]

However, another Sixth Circuit case holds that a new arbitration agreement signed by a person who had left the company, brought an FLSA suit, and was rehired did not prevent class arbitration. Russell's first arbitration agreement did not mention class claims. The new arbitration agreement required individual arbitration, but the Sixth Circuit held that the language of the agreement was prospective only and did not preclude litigation of a suit that was already underway when the second agreement was signed. [*Russell v. Citigroup, Inc.*, 748 F.3d 677 (6th Cir. 2014); see Amy Cadle Hocevar, *Agreement to Arbitrate Does Not Apply Retroactively to Bar Pending Case* (Apr. 8, 2014), available at Lexology.com]

§ 25.08 DEFAMATION

A hostile or unflattering statement that a company or one of its agents makes about a job applicant, employee, or former employee could become the focus of charges, or even a lawsuit. However, there are several circumstances under which negative statements are legally protected. For one thing, the statements might have been demonstrably true. They might have been made without malice, or in a privileged context.

Slander is defined as communicating a defamatory statement orally or otherwise informally. Libel means communicating a defamatory statement more broadly ("publishing" it). A defamatory statement is one that attributes serious misconduct to someone else. The victim of slander or libel can sue and obtain tort damages, unless the statement was privileged in some way.

The basic rule is that a plaintiff not only has to prove that defamation occurred, but also that some actual damages were suffered because of the defamation. But there are some statements so negative that they are automatically presumed to damage the reputation of the person about whom they are made. A plaintiff who proves such "defamation per se" can win without proving actual damages (concrete injury attributable to the defamation).

To support a suit, the alleged slander or libel must be a statement of fact, not a mere opinion or a general, imprecise statement ("Marcia is hard to work with"; "Steve seems to be working through some problems in his life."). A pure opinion cannot be defamatory, because it is not a statement of fact, but a statement of fact backing up that opinion can be defamatory. A corporation is liable for the statements of its employees and agents, as long as they were acting within the scope of their employment.

Truth is always a defense to a defamation charge: For instance, it is not defamatory to say that an employee was fired for stealing office supplies if this is what actually happened. If the employer believes a statement is true, and the statement is communicated without malice, then the employer is entitled to a defense. The jury, not the judge, decides whether or not a statement was communicated with malice.

A statement has not been "published" to the extent that a libel charge can be made if it is communicated only to the plaintiff, or to someone who is acting on behalf of the plaintiff (including a friend or an investigator who calls to find out what the employer is saying about the employee). Courts take different positions about communications that stay within the employer corporation. Some courts say that this is so narrow that no publication has occurred, whereas others accept the plaintiff's argument that dissemination was broad enough to constitute libel.

Although employers are hesitant to communicate about employees, technology like e-mail, blogging, and social networking makes it easier to disseminate information—positive or negative—about employees. Not only references, but performance reviews, outplacement interviews, and written or electronic conversations can give rise to defamation suits. Former employees, who may feel that they have little chance of getting another job in the current economy, also have less to lose, may be more likely to file a defamation suit. More and more suits involve "defamation by conduct" such as subjecting an employee to an undeserved investigation of alleged wrongdoing. Attorneys for employers suggest making sure that corporate policies are applied evenly (e.g., requiring all terminated employees to turn in their company laptops immediately) so no one can claim to have been singled out unfairly.

§ 25.09 PRIVILEGED STATEMENTS

[A] Generally

Some kinds of communication are essential to the operation of businesses and the legal system, so they are afforded special treatment. They are referred to as "privileged," and by definition cannot be defamatory.

Restatement of Torts (2d) § 596 permits a privilege when the publisher and the recipient of the information share a common interest, such as making sure that honest, qualified individuals are hired and retain their jobs.

In addition to absolute privilege, "qualified" privilege exists in some circumstances. A qualified privilege is one that can be taken away under some circumstances, whereas an absolute privilege survives all kinds of challenges. If the employer asserts a qualified privilege, it has the burden of proving that it is entitled to the privilege.

If a corporation has an audit committee, discussion of possible embezzlement or securities violations are probably entitled to qualified privilege as long as they remain within the committee, and are not disclosed (other than to law enforcement officials, which is the subject of another privilege). If there has been an investigation about workplace matters, disclosing the results of the investigation to the employees at large would probably also be privileged.

Even though they are not law enforcement officials, the EEOC and unemployment officials are close enough so that communications to them are privileged. There is at least a qualified privilege to make statements in the course of processing a union grievance or issuing dismissal letters required under a collective bargaining agreement. In fact, in some states (Michigan, New Mexico, Louisiana, Missouri) the privilege is absolute, not qualified.

California [Cal. Civ. Code § 47(c)] gives employers a qualified privilege for statements made without malice and on the basis of credible evidence. Alaska presumes [Alaska Stats. § 09.65.160] that employers act in good faith when they discuss their employees with other prospective employers. However, if the employer acts recklessly, maliciously, or contrary to the employee's civil rights, the privilege is no longer available.

In any state, employers are probably entitled to a qualified privilege when they make good-faith comments on employee performance to someone who has a legitimate right to the information. However, some degree of caution must be exercised. Not all co-workers necessarily have a legitimate interest in performance appraisals.

There is a qualified privilege to protect the safety of employees who might hurt themselves, or might be hurt by others. (Communications that are privileged in the context of a defamation suit are probably also privileged if the employee sues for violation of privacy instead of, or in addition to, defamation.)

However, even if a privilege initially exists, it can be sacrificed—most typically, by failure to act in good faith, or by making statements without proof and with reckless disregard as to whether or not they are true.

It was long assumed that employers could instruct employees to keep complaints and investigations confidential. However, the NLRB sometimes challenges confidentiality requirements on the grounds that they can violate NLRA § 8(a)(1) by suppressing discussion of ongoing investigations of employee misconduct.

- Hyundai America Shipping Agency, 357 NLRB No. 80 (2011): it was unlawful for the employer to routinely forbid employees to discuss investigations, without considering whether confidentiality was necessary to protect the integrity of the investigation.
- Banner Estrella Medical Center 358 NLRB No. 93 (2012): it is a violation of NLRA § 8(a)(1) to impose a blanket confidentiality policy for internal workplace investigations. The NLRB said that the employer has the burden of proof that there is a legitimate business need for confidentiality in a particular situation (e.g., witness protection, a risk of destruction of evidence or fabricated testimony).
- Verso Paper (NLRB Division of Advice No. 30-CA_89350 (Jan. 29, 2013) says that an employer policy "directing" employees not to discuss investigations with co-workers is permissible if necessary to protect the integrity of an investigation and to keep witnesses from being harassed; in such cases, employees can be disciplined for breaking confidentiality.
- Design Technology Group LLC (NLRB Apr. 19, 2013): a handbook rule forbidding employees to disclose their wages or compensation to third parties, including co-workers, violates the NLRA; it was unlawful to fire three employees for posting Facebook messages complaining about a supervisor who belittled their fears about working late in a dangerous neighborhood.
- Quicken Loans Inc. (NLRB June 21, 2013): the NLRB found an employment agreement invalid because employees were forbidden to disclose any proprietary or confidential information to anyone. Confidential information was defined to include personnel lists, contact information for workers, and employee handbooks; the ALJ said that it violates NLRA § 7 to forbid discussion of wages or benefits.
- Dish Network Corp. (NLRB 2013): the NLRB found a social media rule unlawful; it forbade disparaging or defamatory comments about the company, its products or services, customers, or employee, and it forbade employees to contact the media, talk to government agencies, or make

public communications without permission. [Baker & McKenzie Labor year in review: *NLRB Targets Non-Unionized Employers And Expands Worker Rights* (Dec. 21, 2013), available at Lexology.com. *Banner Estrella* and *Hyundai America Shipping Agency* are on appeal to the D.C. Circuit.

The Fifth Circuit agreed with the NLRB that the employer's confidentiality policy violated NLRA § 8(a)(1) because it prevented employees from discussing wages. The policy forbade employees to copy or share confidential information, broadly defined to include personnel information and documents. In the Fifth Circuit view, employees have a right to discuss wages with co-workers; there was no evidence that employees used this information outside the company. The Fifth Circuit examined the written terms of the policy, not the way it was implemented, so it rejected the employer's argument that the policy was not used to suppress discussion of wages. [*FlexFrack Logistics v. NLRB*, 746 F.3d 205 (5th Cir. 2014). The employer raised a challenge based on *Noel Canning*, but the Fifth Circuit held that this argument was not raised on a timely basis.]

But employers can probably require confidentiality in appropriate cases if it is necessary to protect witnesses, avoid cover-ups, and prevent destruction of evidence. Employers should protect themselves by having formal policies. The complainant should be asked if he or she wants the investigation to remain confidential (and this is usually the case). The employer should protect itself by getting a written statement of this intent. [Catherine Dunn, *NLRB Rules on Keeping Employees From Discussing HR Investigations*, Corporate Counsel (Aug. 31, 2012) (law.com)]

[B] Attorney-Client Privilege

The term "privilege" is also applied to communications that are privileged in the sense of being protected from disclosure. To do a good job, lawyers must learn all the facts of the situation, not just the facts that put their clients in a favorable light. Certain information is privileged if a client communicates it to a lawyer. The lawyer cannot be required to disclose this information—in fact, in most instances, it is unethical for the lawyer to disclose the information without the client's consent.

The factors that determine the availability of attorney-client privilege include:

- Whether the client approached the lawyer specifically to seek legal advice (as distinct from a casual chat, or when the lawyer played another role, such as giving business advice or serving as a director of a company);

- Whether the lawyer is acting as a lawyer, not a director or business advisor;
- Whether the communication relates to the lawyer-client relationship;
- Whether the client intends the information to be confidential;
- Whether the client did anything (deliberately or inadvertently) to remove the privilege; for instance, material distributed by the corporation will not be privileged.

It can be hard to determine the status of corporate documents.

A report might be confidential only if it were drafted specifically as a confidential document for transmission to the attorney.

If the primary purpose of a communication is to get legal advice, a secondary business motive will not take away the privilege. But the privilege will be waived (that is, surrendered) if the corporation voluntarily distributes the document to non-attorneys, or discloses or allows the disclosure of a significant part of the document. For instance, if a corporation issues a press release about a development, or sends an employee to read a technical paper at an industry conference, it will not be able to argue that the press release or the technical paper is confidential.

However, a statement made by an employee who is not acting as an agent of the employer, but is simply an independent witness to an event probably will not be confidential, no matter why the statement was made.

In addition to the attorney-client privilege, the law of evidence contains a separate "work product" privilege. Work product is material prepared by attorneys and their employees as part of representing a client. Work product is also confidential and cannot become part of the discovery process before litigation.

The New Jersey Supreme Court ruled that the attorney-client privilege outweighs corporate policy about use of workplace computers. Therefore, a plaintiff suing her employer had a reasonable expectation that e-mails to and from her lawyer using her personal, password-protected Yahoo account, would be private even though they were sent on a laptop owned by the company. [*Stengart v. Loving Care Agency Inc.*, 990 A.2d 650 (N.J., 2010); see Michael Booth, *Privilege Trumps Company E-Mail Surveillance*, N.J.L.J. (Apr. 1, 2010) (law.com)]

The District Court for the Eastern District of New York applied the attorney-client and work product privileges narrowly, and required production of documents in an employment discrimination case. The court held that the defendant's outside counsel was business-related (how to respond to employee complaints; whether to conduct an internal investigation) rather than legal. Attorney-client privilege was not available, because of the business purpose for the communications, and it was not work product, because advice about proper HR management would have been given even without the threat of litigation. [*Koumoulis v. Independent Fin. Mktg. Grp., Inc.*, No. 10-CV-0887 (E.D.N.Y Jan. 21, 2014); see A. Sonu Ray, *Privilege Does Not Cover Communications With Outside Counsel*

Relating To Business-Related Advice, E.D.N.Y. Holds, Ogletree Deakins (Feb. 27, 2014), available at Lexology.com]

[C] Self-Critical Analysis

When a company finds out that misconduct may have occurred and launches an investigation, the company has to decide if it should report any misconduct that it discovers to the authorities. If the company's stock is publicly traded, disclosure will probably be required by the securities laws and the company will be liable under the anti-fraud provisions of federal securities laws. Financial institutions are required to file a Suspicious Activities Report with the FinCEN (Financial Crimes Enforcement Network) when they become aware of potential illegalities. Federal regulations make government contractors subject to debarment or suspension for knowing failure to make timely disclosure of credible evidence of fraud, conflict of interest, bribery, or False Claims Act violations in connection with performance of a government contract.

If the corporation itself is clearly a victim (e.g., of embezzlement or theft of trade secrets) then self-reporting can result in help from the authorities. There are more advantages than disadvantages in reporting offenses committed by an employee with little corporate exposure (e.g., a criminal act carried out on company property, but not related to the criminal's employment). The stronger the evidence, the stronger the case for reporting—especially since the likelihood that regulators will discover the wrongdoing also increases. The Department of Justice Principles of Federal Prosecution of Business Organizations permit prosecutors to treat timely, voluntary disclosure of wrongdoing as a mitigating factor, and cooperation with the authorities can affect the decision of what crimes to charge. The DOJ's Antitrust Division offers amnesty to the first corporation to confess to an antitrust violation—and turn in the other co-conspirators. [Michael B. Mukasey and Andrew J. Ceresney, *Should Corporations Self-Report Wrong doing*?, N.Y.L.J. (Oct. 1, 2010) (law.com)]

Companies that want to improve diversity and eliminate discrimination often make studies of their employment and HR practices. Can discrimination plaintiffs require the company to disclose those documents, and use them to prove that the company used discriminatory employment practices?

Several federal courts have recognized a "self-critical analysis privilege": in other words, that these reports are internal documents that should not have to be revealed to plaintiffs, because companies should be encouraged to be candid about their discrimination problems instead of suppressing what they know to avoid embarrassing disclosures in lawsuits.

The opposite view is that the documents were prepared as part of the company's Title VII compliance program, would eventually be reported to the EEOC, and therefore could not reasonably be described as privileged. Even under this argument, a distinction might be drawn between a self-critical analysis that a company originated voluntarily and one that is mandated by the EEOC or by federal contract regulators. Or the court might require the company to produce hard information like statistics about workplace diversity, but permit the analytical part of the report to remain confidential.

It also helps to control dissemination of sensitive documents. The fewer people who have access to the document, and the more they agree that the company needs to analyze its performance in order to improve, the less likely they are to disclose the document in a way that is harmful or embarrassing to the corporation.

§ 25.10 DUTY TO COMMUNICATE

Not only are there situations in which an employer becomes liable for defamation or other disclosures; sometimes the employer can get into trouble for failing to communicate. There might be a duty to disclose dangerousness, so that other employers will not hire someone who puts their other employees or customers at risk. A subsequent employer may sue if the first employer fails to reveal relevant information, such as a job applicant's dismissal for stealing or workplace drug dealing.

Employers have a legal duty to protect customers and co-workers. That makes them negligent if they know that someone is dangerous, but they still retain him or her as an employee. This is true even if the risk is of conduct outside the scope of employment. An employer who knows that an employee has violent tendencies can be liable because of workplace assaults committed by that person, even if the assaults are not only not part of the job, but are contrary to the employer's policy and work rules. However, if the injured person is a fellow employee, it is very likely that the employee's only remedy will be through the Worker's Compensation system. [See § 33.03 for the concept of WC exclusivity]

Employers can be sued for negligent hiring or negligent entrustment if they hire someone for a safety-critical job but fail to check that person's references. In some contexts (such as hiring workers for a nursing home or day care center) there may be a duty to consult a special database maintained by the state or by a licensing organization to list individuals who are ineligible for employment because they have been convicted of a crime.

An employer will probably be exempt from liability for negligent hiring if a thorough investigation is performed before hiring; but if an employer fails to discover information that would have been disclosed by an ordinary background check, liability is a possibility.

Discrimination plaintiffs sometimes add a negligent hiring claim to their complaints. Their theory is that the employer was negligent in hiring and/or retaining a supervisor who was racist, sexist, or otherwise prone to engage in discriminatory conduct. The advantage to the plaintiff is that, although the discrimination claim is subject to the Civil Rights Act of 1991 (CRA '91) cap on damages (see § 42.12[B]), the negligent hiring claim is not. Also, it is hard to introduce evidence into a discrimination case about acts of discrimination or harassment carried out against employees other than the plaintiff, but this is relevant evidence in a negligent hiring case.

The employer might also be liable for negligent supervision, if the court or jury accepts the argument that the supervisor would not have been able to carry out the act of discrimination or harassment if the employer had managed the facility better.

The Federal Trade Adjustment Assistance Extension Act of 2011 required all the states to adopt unemployment insurance integrity provisions dealing with recovery of erroneous benefit payments. The states had to adopt new laws no later than October 21, 2013 penalizing employers and their agents for patterns of failure to make timely, adequate responses to state agencies' requests for information about overpayments. Compliance is especially difficult with respect to employees who have separation or settlement agreements under which the employer agrees not to challenge the ex-employee's unemployment benefit claim. Most states will not consider one non-response a "pattern," but it is probably better to remove such provisions from your agreements, and train your managers not to promise that benefit claims will not be contested. Separation and settlement agreements should be clear about how you will respond to information requests, and what reason you will give for the separation. Make sure that you respond promptly to requests, and instruct your TPAs to do the same. [Eric J. Janson and Marc R. Jacobs, *You (Don't) Have The Right To Remain Silent – How New Unemployment Insurance Integrity Laws May Affect Your Separation And Settlement Agreements With Departing Employees*, Seyfarth Shaw LLP (Nov. 12, 2013), available at Lexology.com]

§ 25.11 RESPONSES TO REFERENCE CHECKS

The employer has to steer between two hazards: neither committing defamation, nor failing to disclose information that must be divulged. One approach that often works is just to confirm the start and end dates of a former employee's employment, and then say that it is against company policy to discuss ex-employees. Another possibility is to disclose only information that is fully documented by HR files.

> ■ **TIP:** If your state gives employees the right to review their files and make their own comments, make sure that any response to an inquiry includes the employee's comments. For instance, "Ms. Jones was dismissed for excessive lateness and poor performance. However, she said that other people were late just as often, and we should have been more sympathetic about her performance because her mother had just died." That way, the questioner gets both sides of the story.

According to employment lawyer Wendy Bliss, it is perfectly legitimate for a former employer to provide information about the candidate's performance as a member of a work team, and the adequacy of his or her work habits. But information should be disseminated only if it is truthful, work-related, and can be supported by documentation. Bliss suggests that employers should have a written policy about what kind of information will be given in references—and who will be allowed to provide this information. Information should not be released without a signed consent and release form (including a liability waiver) from the employee.

If an employee's resignation or termination is being negotiated, one area of negotiation is what will be said in response to reference checks.

It may be easier to get reference check information by asking about a job candidate's strengths and accomplishments as an employee, rather than stating or implying that you want negative information. No one is going to sue for defamation for being described as "hard working," "effective," or "creative"!

The growing trend toward outsourcing functions opens new risks if background checks are omitted, but the law is not clear as to whether the employer or the staffing agency is responsible for performing the checks. Hence, employers who are concerned about liability risks should either perform or make sure that the staffing agency performs background checks on:

- Anyone working in a customer's home;
- Anyone working with children or vulnerable adults (e.g., the elderly or disabled);
- Anyone with access to bank accounts, Social Security numbers, trade secrets, or other confidential information.

The employer's contract with the agency should include a warranty that the agency has performed background checks on all agency workers and certification that the check did not show anything precluding placement of the worker. The agency should warrant that background checks were performed in accordance with the FCRA and state laws. Employers should make sure that the agency maintains adequate liability insurance and should seek indemnification from the agency. [Tresa Baldas, *Outsourced Employees Triggering More Suits*, Nat'l L.J. (Feb. 22, 2006.) (law.com)]

§ 25.12 NEGOTIATED RESIGNATIONS

In some cases, an employee has been guilty of misconduct so serious (securities fraud or embezzlement, for example) that immediate removal is needed to reduce the risk to the corporation. In other cases, it will be less clear that employment must be ended—situations that fall under the Hollywood euphemism "creative differences." In such a situation, both parties benefit if they negotiate a resignation. The employee will leave on a stipulated date, and will release the company from all claims of employment-related discrimination. [See Chapter 37, § 37.07[A] for the specific problems of drafting a release that will satisfy the provisions of the Older Workers Benefit Protection Act (OWBPA). Pub. L. No. 101-433]

A resignation agreement is a contract and therefore is subject to the ordinary rules of contract law. For instance, if the employer deliberately misleads an employee, or subjects him or her to undue influence, the resignation agreement will be void and the employer will not be able to enforce it against the employee. The implications of the agreement are serious enough that first-line supervisors should not be allowed to negotiate. Either a trained HR staffer or an attorney should take on this role.

The agreement covers issues such as:

- The employee represents that he or she has not already filed any charges, or instituted litigation against the employer. If legal action is already in the works, settlement discussions or conciliation from the antidiscrimination agency is in order, but it is too late to negotiate a simple resignation agreement;
- The employee waives all claims against the employer. Drafting the proper, enforceable language is an intricate legal task;
- The employee agrees to treat the resignation as voluntary, and therefore not to apply for unemployment compensation;
- The employer should state that it does not admit liability of any kind, but is only using the agreement to clarify the issues;
- The employer should specify the kind of reference it will give the employee, and how it will handle reference checks from potential future employers;
- The employee should waive any merit-based bonuses that would otherwise be payable in the year of the resignation;
- The employee should agree to return all materials in his or her possession containing trade secrets or other proprietary materials of the employer, and should agree to refrain from using the employer's proprietary/trade secret information in any later employment;
- The employee should agree to keep the terms of the agreement confidential.

§ 25.13 RELEASES

An employee who has already filed discrimination charges may be willing to settle those charges, receiving some consideration in exchange for releasing the employer from further threat of suit by that employee. (However, a suit brought by another employee, or by the EEOC, continues to be a risk.) During the negotiations before a resignation, the employer and employee could agree on a severance package that winds up their relationship, making it clear that the soon-to-be-ex-employee will not bring any discrimination charges.

A release is a contract, a legal agreement for surrendering claims that already exist. A release can be quite general, simply referring to "all claims" or quite specific, spelling out a whole laundry list of claims. A release of liability could be combined with reasonable covenants not to compete and provisions about the employer's intellectual property.

Courts might refuse to enforce a release that is too general, on the grounds that it is not specific enough to inform employees of their rights. But a release that is too detailed can put ideas into the heads of employees who had no real intention of bringing suit—or who didn't know the vast and exotic variety of ways in which they can make trouble for the employer!

Before payments of pensions and benefits begin, the plan might require the potential participant or beneficiary to sign a release stating that the plan has computed the amounts of benefits correctly, or that the participant or beneficiary waives all claims against the plan except the right to receive benefits as specified by the plan.

Courts are split as to whether such mandatory releases are enforceable. If all plan participants and beneficiaries have to sign, the release becomes part of ordinary plan administration, and there is no additional consideration for it. The employer gets something (freedom from suits and other claims) but doesn't give up anything in return (the benefits would be available under the plan anyway).

All contracts require consideration to be enforceable. Each party must receive something under the contract. In a typical release situation, the employer provides additional benefits (e.g., extra severance pay; outplacement assistance; early retirement incentives) over and above normal severance. The employee offers the employer a release of all claims, thus sparing the employer the risk of having to defend against charges. If each party gets something of value, the court probably won't worry about exact equivalence, as long as the parties knew their rights and understood all the implications of the release.

A general release covers all claims in existence at the time of the release; a limited release covers only the types of claims named in the release itself.

■ **TIP:** A release covering an injured worker who is entitled to Worker's Compensation is valid only if it is approved by a Worker's Compensation judge. Special care is required in drafting the release. If the worker releases claims relating to compensable physical injury, he or she will still have the right to bring suit on other grounds, such as claims that the employer acted in bad faith or intentionally inflicted emotional distress on the employee.

A Worker's Compensation release that did not explicitly mention ERISA claims or the ERISA plan did not release the employer from an

ERISA disability claim. Teresa Duncan received disability benefits under an ERISA long-term disability plan from 2005 to 2010. She settled her WC claim in 2008 and released all claims. The release form said she would not "be able to go back to the defendant for additional treatment or disability payments." The Eastern District of California held in early 2013 that the standard language in WC releases applies only to WC claims, not ERISA claims. [*Duncan v. Hartford Life &Accident Ins. Co.*, No. 2:11-cv-01536-GEB-CKD, 2013 WL 506465 (E.D. Cal. Feb. 7, 2013); see Mike Reilly, Lane Powell Boom: The ERISA Law Blog, *Releases Should Explicitly Release ERISA Claims and ERISA Plan* (Feb. 26, 2013) (benefitslink.com)]

The Seventh Circuit ruled in early 2011 that WARN Act claims can be waived in a voluntary general release. The Seventh Circuit upheld the release because the release (and the severance agreements in connection with closing DHL Express shipping facilities) were negotiated by the union; were not ambiguous; and suggested consulting a lawyer before signing. [*Ellis v. DHL Express Inc. USA*, 633 F.3d 522 (7th Cir. 2011)]

However, as the FMLA regulations provide (see Chapter 38), the Department of Labor says that it is invalid for employees to give an advance release of claims that might arise under the FMLA in the future. But with respect to FMLA claims that have already arisen, it is legitimate for employers to offer—and employees to sign—a release of existing claims. Supervision by the Department of Labor, or by a court, is not required.

These issues arose in a 2014 Eleventh Circuit case. An employee who had taken extensive FMLA leave received a poor performance evaluation. The employer gave her a choice between a Performance Improvement Plan (with goals that she would be terminated for failure to meet) and accepting 13 weeks of severance benefits in exchange for a waiver of her FMLA claims. She took the severance, then joined two other employees as plaintiffs in a suit for FMLA interference and retaliation. She claimed that the release was invalid as a prospective waiver. She argued that the rights were prospective because she had an outstanding request for FMLA leave when she signed the waiver. The Eleventh Circuit held that prospective rights in this context are rights to take FMLA leave in the unspecified future; a prospective waiver is a waiver of an event that has not happened yet. In this case, Paylor validly released a claim that had already accrued. She received consideration for the release in the form of severance pay that would not otherwise have been available. [*Paylor v. Hartford Fire Ins.*, 748 F.3d 1117 (11th Cir. 2014); see Liebert Cassidy Whitmore, *Employee Who Waived FMLA Claims by Signing Severance Agreement Could Not Then Bring Lawsuit Alleging FMLA Violations* (May 10, 2014), available at Lexology.com]

The Tax Court agreed with the IRS: a settlement agreement between a university and a former professor who claimed that her colleagues created a hostile work environment that forced her out was taxable income for the professor. The Tax Court rejected the professor's contention that the funds were tax-exempt as an award for personal physical injuries under Code § 104(a)(2). The Tax Court held that settlement agreements are interpreted under their express language, and the agreement contained only one reference to its being conditioned on the plaintiff settling her Workers' Compensation claim. In the Tax Court view, the settlement could have reflected non-Workers' Compensation claims, and the plaintiff failed to prove that the settlement, described as for emotional distress, was for physical injury. Even if emotional distress has physical manifestations, that is not sufficient to exclude settlement proceeds from taxable income. [*Sharp v. Comm'r*, T.C. Memo 2013-290 (2013); see William Hays Weissman, *U.S. Tax Court Decision Shows Importance Of Carefully Drafting Settlement Agreements*, Littler Mendelson (Jan. 6, 2014), available at Lexology.com]

In mid-2009, the EEOC published a guidance document in Question & Answer form covering waivers of discrimination claims in severance agreements. The EEOC noted that older employees are often targeted because they earn more than less experienced, younger co-workers.

The document is intended for employees, and includes sample language and examples of adequate consideration and knowing and voluntary waivers. In general, it re-states existing principles rather than breaking new ground. To be valid, waivers must be knowing and voluntary, written clearly enough for employees to understand them, must not be induced by improper conduct on the employer's part, and the employee must be given access to counsel and given enough time to consider the terms. Employees must receive some additional consideration for signing the waiver that they would not otherwise receive. Waivers must not give up the right to pursue remedies for future acts of discrimination. Waivers should not limit employees' right to testify or participate in EEOC proceedings. [EEOC, *Understanding Waivers of Discrimination Claims in Employee Severance Agreements*, <http://www.eeoc.gov/policy/docs/qanda_severance-agreements.html> (July 15, 2009; Appendix B revised April 2010). See *EEOC v. Watkins Motor Lines, Inc.*, 553 F.3d 593 (7th Cir. 2009): the EEOC can continue to investigate and pursue claims made by a person who signed a waiver. The guidance is discussed in Kevin B. Leblang and Robert N. Holtzman, *Time for Employers to Review Their Severance Agreements*, Metropolitan Corporate Counsel (Feb. 1, 2010) (benefitslink.com)]

States take varying approaches about what can be covered by a general release. Some states say that they can cover all claims, known or unknown, but other states say that a general release is not effective for claims that the employee did not know about or suspect at the time the release was signed. Under this theory, people can only give up claims that they know about and decide are worth less than the benefits under the release.

In 1996, Accenture amended its pension plan to exclude employees in various departments. The plaintiff, Hakim, was eligible to participate when the amendment was adopted, but was promoted in 1999 to an ineligible position. In 2003, he was RIF'd and signed a release of all claims. In 2008, he applied for additional pension benefits, claiming that the notice of the 1996 amendment did not satisfy ERISA requirements. The Seventh Circuit held that pension entitlements (vested benefits the plaintiff is entitled to under the plan terms) are subject to the ERISA anti-alienation provision but contested pension claims are not. A contested pension claim is one that the claimant had actual or constructive knowledge at the time of the release, when the claimant decided not to pursue it. A release cannot bar recovery of the pension as of the time of the relief, but can bar claims based on alleged ERISA violations of which the plaintiff has notice. [*Hakim v. Accenture United States Pension Plan*, 718 F.3d 675 (7th Cir. 2013)]

The California Court of Appeal ruled that USERRA rights (see § 1.18) cannot be eliminated by a contract; 38 U.S.C. § 4302(b) says that USERRA supersedes any state law or contract that reduces, limits, or eliminates any rights under the statute. Therefore, a release of rights in a severance agreement was unenforceable to the extent that it dealt with allegations he was terminated because of his military status. California Civil Code § 1542 provides that a general release does not extend to claims of material importance that the creditor does not know about at the time of the release. The plaintiff said that the release was invalid because it did not include an explicit waiver of § 1542, but the court of appeals held that although it is good practice to include a § 1542 waiver, it is not absolutely necessary: a proper release will be enforced if it is knowing and voluntary. [*Perez v. Uline*, 157 Cal. App. 4th 953 (Cal. App. 2007)]

However, a 2010 Sixth Circuit decision holds that a release under IBM's Individual Separation Allowance Plan prevented an ex-employee from asserting USERRA claims. The court found that the release was enforceable because it was knowing and voluntary; there was no evidence of fraud or overreaching; and the release form was not ambiguous. [*Wysocki v. IBM*, 607 F.3d 1102 (6th Cir. 2010)]

Although it is common for employment, change in control, and severance agreements to condition payment of severance or other compensation on the employee's signing a general release of all claims against the employer, the documents must be carefully drafted in light of Code § 409A. (See § 8.02[D]) In general, § 409A allows a severance agreement to permit payment at any time during the 90 days after the event—but only if the employee does not have a direct or indirect election about when to receive the benefits.

Executives can create problems for their former employers if they do not sign the release until the calendar year after employment ends. Problems can be averted by drafting releases to say that if benefits could be paid in two different tax years, depending on when the employee signs the release, benefits will automatically be paid in the later year, no matter when the release is signed.

A new rule took effect April 1, 2011. If the payment window between an event and the deadline for payment overlaps the end of a calendar year, generally payments cannot begin until the year in which the payment window ends. For most plans, problems did not start until the fourth quarter of 2011, because the payment window for § 409A plans is usually 90 days or less, so payments in the first three quarters will not overlap two calendar years. But some plans do allow payments to be made either in the year of the event or the following two and a half months. Penalties will be imposed if payments that were supposed to be made in 2012 were made in 2011, unless a correction procedure is available. The rule allows the payment window to be shortened from 90 days to a shorter period (e.g., 30 or 45 days), which could be a good tax move although it increases the problems of administration.

A further complication is that ADEA releases generally require 45 days notice, and employees must be given seven days after signing to revoke their consent. Therefore, severance payments are generally reserved until after the revocation period ends. [McGuireWoods LLP, *Employee Release Provisions Present Section 409A Trap for the Unwary* (Aug. 31, 2011); George L. Chimento, *Release Me: 4th Quarter Complication for 409A Plans* (Oct. 14, 2011) (benefitslink.com)]

The Dodd-Frank Act forbids some kinds of waivers, but the authors of a recent article argue that only prospective waivers are banned; it is legitimate for severance or separation agreements to release whistleblower claims that are already in existence. Dodd-Frank's predecessor statute, the Sarbanes-Oxley Act, makes it unlawful for an employer to retaliate against someone who performs certain kinds of whistleblower activity. Dodd-Frank broadens the categories of protected employees and protected conduct. Dodd-Frank amends Sarbanes-Oxley to forbid waiver of whistleblower rights by agreement, including a predispute arbitration agreement. [David E. Schwartz and Madeline Stavis, *Waivers of Whistleblower Claims After Dodd-Frank*, N.Y.L.J. (Oct. 21, 2013), available at law.com]

The SEC said that it has received reports about language in severance agreements that inhibits disclosure of the employer's improper activities. The Dodd-Frank Act gives the SEC the power to prosecute employers for retaliatory actions and conditions in employment or severance agreements that forbid reporting wrongdoing violate public policy. The risk is that employees, who need severance benefits and a good reference, will accept questionable terms such as agreeing to pay over any award to the company, or agreeing to notify the company before contacting the SEC or other enforcement agency. [Ben DiPietro, *Companies Trying to Contain Potential Whistleblowers*, WSJ.com (May 14, 2013)]

§ 25.14 SARBANES-OXLEY AND DODD-FRANK NOTICES

The Sarbanes-Oxley Act of 2002 [Pub. L. No. 107-204] became law in July 2002. It is a wide-ranging piece of legislation; many of the issues it covers are outside the scope of this book because they involve corporate governance and accuracy in accounting. However, the Sarbanes-Oxley Act also deals with "blackout periods" in individual account plans such as 401(k) plans. If a blackout period does occur, the corporation is required, by Sarbanes-Oxley Act § 306(b), to provide advance notice to plan participants that their ability to control their plan accounts will be limited during the blackout period, and a plain English explanation of the effect on their rights. [See 68 Fed. Reg. 3715 (Jan. 24, 2003) for DOL's Final Rule on this subject]

The general rule is that the notice must be given at least 30 days, but not more than 60 days, before the start of the blackout period, although exceptions are recognized if circumstances make it unfeasible to give the notice at the regular time. The notice must disclose the start and end dates of the blackout period and explain the extent to which participants' ability to change their plan investments or get distributions or loans from the plan will be affected. The notice must be written, rather than verbal, but it can be distributed electronically.

Civil money penalties of up to $100 per participant per day can be imposed on the plan administrators as individuals if the required notice is not given (although DOL also has discretion to suspend penalties if the imposition of penalties would be unjust). The Final Rules for Sarbanes-Oxley civil penalties were published by the DOL at 68 Fed. Reg. 3729 (Jan. 24, 2003).

The notice must be in writing—so a speech to the workforce wouldn't count—but it can be handed to participants, mailed, or distributed electronically. [See 68 Fed. Reg. 3729 (Jan. 24, 2003) for the text of a model notice that can be used to comply with the disclosure requirement] The model notice ("Important Notice Concerning Your Rights Under the [Plan Title] Plan") includes:

- The reason why a blackout period is imposed;
- The extent of the restrictions, including the statement "whether or not you are planning retirement in the near future, we encourage you to carefully consider how this blackout period may affect your retirement planning as well as your overall financial plan";
- The expected beginning and ending dates of the period; a toll-free telephone number or URL the participants can access to check to see if the blackout period is still in effect;
- A warning of the need to check and perhaps re-balance the participant's overall investment strategy because of the effect of the trading restrictions
- (If the full 30-day notice is impossible) The reason why the regular notice could not be given;
- Name, address, and telephone number of a contact person who can answer questions about the blackout period and its effects.

Sarbanes-Oxley is one of several statutes giving protection to whistleblowers: persons who disclose corporate wrongdoing to law enforcement authorities. Corporations are forbidden to retaliate against whistleblowers.

The most recent form of whistleblower protection derives from PPACA § 1558, which amends the Fair Labor Standards Act to protect employees against retaliation for disclosing violations of PPACA Title I. [OSHA Fact Sheet, OSHAFS-3641.pdf?, *Filing Whistleblower Complaints under the Affordable Care Act*; see PLC Employee Benefits & Executive Compensation, *OSHA Rules Address Retaliation Complaint Procedures under Health Care Reform* (Feb. 25, 2013) (benefitslink.com)]

Although it is predominantly aimed at preventing future stock market crashes, the Dodd-Frank Wall Street Reform and Consumer Protection Act, Pub. L. No. 111-203, has some implications for corporate governance and corporate communications. The Dodd-Frank Act and the SEC's final whistleblower rules affect three aspects of corporate internal investigations:

- Teaching employees about internal corporate controls;
- Performing the investigation;
- Dealing with regulators.

For almost a decade, internal investigations were based on Sarbanes-Oxley, including its requirement for internal controls such as "up the ladder" reporting requirements and the role of independent directors, especially the audit committee, in ensuring compliance. Both internal and outside investigators need strategies for handling the consequences of reporting violations to regulators before there has been an in-house investigation. Employees must learn to use the internal reporting mechanisms.

The possibility that employees will go straight to regulators in the hope of collecting rewards puts pressure on businesses to report their own violations, to achieve cooperation credit, and to avoid negative response from shareholders. If the whistleblower goes to the company first and the company itself gives the SEC information leading to a successful investigation, the whistleblower gets credit for all of the information provided by the company. But if the whistleblower interferes with the internal investigation, the reward for the whistleblower will be reduced. It is unlawful to penalize whistleblowers whether or not the SEC ever investigates the complaint if the reported conduct actually violated the law or the whistleblower received an award. However, if an employee's knowledge of potential investigations comes from an attorney during an interview in an internal investigation, Rule 21F-4(b)(4)(vi) says that the information is not original and cannot support a whistleblower complaint. [Final Regulations, 76 Fed. Reg. 34,300 (June 13, 2011), effective Aug. 12, 2011; see Steven S. Sparling and Arielle Warshall Katz, *Internal Investigation Strategies in a Post Dodd-Frank World*, N.Y.L.J. (Aug. 11, 2011) (law.com)]

See Chapter 39 for further discussion of whistleblower issues.

CHAPTER 26

PRIVACY ISSUES

§ 26.01 INTRODUCTION

For the employee, a significant part of each working day is spent in the workplace. The employer takes on some of the roles of the government. Do employees have the same civil rights with respect to their employers as citizens have with respect to their governments? In some ways, the answer is "Yes," but in other ways, the legal system balances the employer's need for honesty, sobriety, and efficiency in the workplace against the employees' desire for privacy. Many (if not most) constitutional rights are limitations on government power, not the power of private entities such as employers.

Many of the topics in this book are either completely regulated by federal laws, or federal laws are dominant, but in the privacy arena, state laws are very significant. Most states have laws on access and copying of personnel files, so that employees can view and copy their own files, but access by outsiders is restricted.

Connecticut defines a personnel file as papers, documents, reports, and electronic communications about a particular employee's character, credit, and work habits, used by the employer to determine the employee's eligibility for employment, promotion, or adverse personnel actions. (Massachusetts uses a similar definition.) Connecticut grants employees and former employees the right to review their files, with some exclusions. They can make copies, but are not allowed to remove documents from the place of inspection. If they disagree with an item, they can place a response in the file or ask the company to remove it. However, the Connecticut definition of personnel file excludes third-party references; the records of stock option plans; the employer's planning documents for future business operations; documents prepared for use in suits or grievance proceedings; and documents of investigations or crime and misconduct. [Dabney D. Ware, *When A "Simple" Personnel File Request Is Not So Simple*, Foley & LardnerLLP (Sept. 9, 2013), available at Lexology.com]

The Supreme Court ruled that a corporation does not have a right of "personal privacy," using the ordinary definition of "personal." The Freedom of Information Act (FOIA) mandates that federal agencies make their records and documents publicly available. However, there is an exception for law enforcement records whose disclosure could reasonably be deemed an unwarranted invasion of personal privacy. A competitor of AT&T made a FOIA request for documents that AT&T gave the FCC during an investigation. Although the Third Circuit agreed with AT&T that the corporation had a privacy right that could prevent disclosure of the documents, the Supreme Court reversed in March 2011—although a corporation has the legal status of a "person," the concept of "personal privacy" is limited to human beings, and has traditionally been applied only to individuals. [*FCC v. AT&T*, 131 S. Ct. 1177 (2011); see Marcia Coyle, *Court Adds Claws to Cat's Paw Claims—But Hisses at Case Over Corporate Privacy*, Nat'l L.J. (Mar. 1, 2011) (law.com)]

In a case brought by a pilot who concealed his HIV status (the FAA would not issue medical certificates to HIV-positive people) and who was fired and indicted for making false statements to a government agency when his status was uncovered in a federal investigation of invalid FAA certifications, the Supreme Court held that the suit could not be maintained against the federal Department of Transportation. The Privacy Act sets standards for management of federal records and allows suits for actual damages when an intentional or willful violation affects an individual. The Supreme Court held that the Privacy Act does not unequivocally authorize damages for mental and emotional distress—so there was no clear waiver of sovereign immunity, and the plaintiff could not sue the federal agency. [*FAA v. Cooper,* 132 S. Ct. 1441 (2012)]

An early 2011 Second Circuit ruling holds that it does not violate an employee's right of privacy to disclose that she has fibromyalgia: unlike HIV/AIDS or transexuality, it is not a condition that creates a constitutionally protected privacy right. In the Second Circuit, privacy rights in medical information vary based on the condition. There is no history of discrimination against sufferers from fibromyalgia. Nor did the plaintiff allege that disclosing her condition exposed her to discrimination or intolerance. The issue is not the seriousness of the condition, but the extent of the risk of discrimination. The court also held that the investigators had a right to publicize investigations into potential fraud or misconduct. [*Matson v. Board of Educ. of City Sch. Dist of N.Y.*, 631 F.3d 57 (2d Cir. 2011)]

A 2005 article in the American Journal of Public Health found that workplaces that allow guns are five times as likely to have a workplace death as companies that forbid all weapons. The Law Center to Prevent Gun Violence reports that approximately 20 states have laws allowing employees who have gun licenses to bring firearms to work. So-called "Bring Your Gun to Work" laws allow an employer to ban guns in working areas (although they must do so with a clear, conspicuous sign), but employees must be allowed to keep licensed firearms in their cars in the parking lot. Keeping up with the varying state laws can be difficult for multi-state employers. Some states do not allow employers to search employees' vehicles for weapons; others do not even allow the employer to ask employees or applicants if they own guns. Illinois's Firearm Concealed Carry Act allows licensed gun owners who pass a background check and safety training to get a permit to carry concealed firearms. Concealed carry permits are not necessarily included in background checks, so some commentators advise requiring employees to report all gun permits to the HR department. [James R. Glenn and Thomas G. Hancuch, *Bring Your Guns To Work: How State Gun Laws Are Aiming Directly At The Workplace*, Vedder Price PC (Sept. 5, 2013), available at Lexology.com. The article says the states in question include Florida, Georgia, Minnesota, Oklahoma, Tennessee, Texas, Utah, and Wisconsin, and says Pennsylvania and South Carolina are considering adopting similar laws; Sara Murrah, *Guns In The Parking Lot: A Delicate Workplace Issue*, WSJ.com (Oct. 15, 2013).]

§ 26.02 POLYGRAPH TESTING

There are many problems with using polygraphy ("lie detector tests") in the workplace setting. These tests are expensive and not very reliable. The real test is whether the employee is nervous, and a practiced liar may be far less nervous than a timid but honest employee.

There are outright bans on polygraph testing in the workplace in Massachusetts, Michigan, Minnesota, and Oregon. Alaska, Connecticut, Delaware, Hawaii, Maine, Nebraska, New Jersey, New York, Rhode Island, West Virginia, and Wisconsin forbid employers to require, request, or even suggest testing. In one of these states, it violates public policy to fire someone for refusing to take a polygraph test, because the test cannot be demanded as a condition of employment. In Illinois, Maine, Michigan, Nevada, New Mexico, and Virginia, testing is not forbidden, but polygraph operators have to be licensed.

The Federal Employee Polygraph Protection Act of 1988. [Pub. L. No. 100-347, 29 U.S.C. § 2001; EPPA] forbids most private employers from using polygraph tests for pre-employment screening. In the workplace itself, it is permissible to polygraph employees but only in the course of an ongoing investigation about economic loss or injury to the employer's business. (In this context, drug tests and written or oral "honesty tests" are not considered polygraph examinations.)

Under the federal law, an employee can be asked to submit to polygraph testing only if:

- He or she has access to the property involved in the inquiry;
- The employer has a reasonable suspicion about the employee's involvement;
- Before the examination, the employer provides the employee with a specific written statement about the nature of the investigation and the basis for the employer's suspicion of the employee.

The employer is required to keep these statements on file for three years after they are issued.

The employer must advise the employee of his or her rights:

- To refuse the test or stop it after it has begun;
- To seek representation by a lawyer or other person (such as a union representative);
- To review the questions before the test;
- To review the results before the employer uses them as a premise for adverse employment action.

The employee must be notified that test results may be turned over to prosecutors.

In an EPPA suit, the Fourth Circuit held that the polygraph does not have to be the sole reason for the discharge for EPPA to be violated, but the employer is automatically liable (unless an exception applies) if the polygraph was the sole reason for the discharge. There is an exception for ongoing investigations of economic loss or injury to the employer's business, when the employer reasonably suspects the employee is involved. There is a Department of Labor regulation, 29 C.F.R. § 801.4(c), that says that it violates EPPA for an employer to receive polygraph information from law enforcement, but the Fourth Circuit held that the regulation is invalid, because employers have to participate actively to be held liable. [*Worden v. Suntrust Banks Inc.*, 549 F.3d 334 (4th Cir. 2008)]

An Eleventh Circuit case arose when a bank branch manager was fired after $58,000 disappeared from two ATMs at the bank. Surveillance cameras showed the plaintiff and his four employees repeatedly violated the bank policy requiring two people to be present whenever cash was handled or secure areas were accessed. The ex-manager was fired after refusing to take a polygraph test. The bank said that he was fired for violating the two-person access policy, not for his refusal. The Eleventh Circuit affirmed summary judgment for the defendant on the polygraph claim, holding that an inventory shortage by itself is not enough to justify a polygraph but if there is additional evidence of theft and reasonable suspicion, it is lawful to ask for the test. Mere access or opportunity is not tantamount to reasonable suspicion, but other evidence (such as information from co-workers) can justify a polygraph request. [*Cummings v. Washington Mut.*, 650 F.3d 1387 (11th Cir. 2011)]

In 2006, the Eleventh Circuit ruled that a company did not violate the Employee Polygraph Protection Act by accepting the union's proposal that miners who were fired for theft be allowed to take a polygraph test so they could clear their names and be rehired. The company was not liable because the proposal was for the employee's own good, and there was no evidence that the company exerted pressure on the union to propose the testing. Nor was the union liable, because it acted on behalf of its members. [*Watson v. Drummond Co.*, 436 F.3d 1310 (11th Cir. 2006)]

§ 26.03 DRUG USE IN THE WORKPLACE

[A] A Pervasive Problem

Drug use in the workplace, and the effects of off-premises drug use at work, are significant problems. Many employers, because of the nature of their business (e.g., public transportation and public safety) or because they are federal contractors, are subject to legal mandates to maintain a drug-free workplace.

Drug users (primarily users of illegal drugs, but sometimes of prescription drugs) are likely to be impaired during working hours. They may use or even deal drugs in the workplace. If they can't afford to pay for their drugs, they are very likely to steal, embezzle, or commit industrial espionage to get drug money. Employees who are already breaking the law by illegal drug use may lose their inhibitions against committing other crimes as well.

HHS's 2012 National Survey on Drug Use and Health found that 8.9% of full-time and 12.5% of part-time employees currently use illicit drugs, as do 18.8% of unemployed adults. Out of 21.5 million current users of illegal drugs in 2012, about two-thirds (14.6 million) were employed full- or part-time. Marijuana was the most common illegal drug, with 18.9 million past-month users in 2012. Heroin use increased from 373,000 in 2007 to 669,000 in 2012. The number of methedrine users declined from 731,000 in 2006 to 440,000 in 2012. HHS estimated that there were 1.9 million first-time non-medical users of pain relief drugs. In 2012, approximately 22.2 million people were classified as substance abusers or dependent on substances; 2.8 million used both illicit drugs and alcohol, 4.5 million only used drugs, and 14.9 million only used alcohol. [Roger S. Kaplan and Kathryn J. Russo, *National Drug Abuse Survey: Workplace Abuse Persists; Marijuana, Heroin Use Gain*, Jackson Lewis LLP (Sept. 11, 2013), available at Lexology.com]

Quest Diagnostics's 25th Anniversary Drug Testing Index shows a 75% decline in drug use by American workers since 1998, when Quest started collecting data shortly after passage of the 1988 Drug-Free Workplace Act. In 1988, 13.6% of the workforce tested positive, falling to 3.5% in 2012. Looking at the federally mandated safety sensitive workforce, positive tests fell from 2.6% in 1992 to 1.6% in 2012. However, the rate of positive tests for amphetamines, including methedrine, was at its highest level since 1997, reflecting the presence of prescription drugs such as Adderall. Positive tests for hydrocodone and hydromorphine more than doubled, and rose 71% for oxycodone. According to Quest, in 2012, a majority of Americans misused their prescription drugs, including amphetamines and opioids. [Roger S. Kaplan, *Drug Use Among U.S. Workers Declines 74% Over Past 25 Years, But Amphetamine And Opiate Use Grows*, Jackson Lewis PC (Dec. 2, 2013), available at Lexology.com]

Federal law requires drug testing for some categories of workers, such as truckers and workers in environmental cleanup. These jobs require hard physical labor, with high turnover. Employers find that many applicants fail drug tests, especially tests for abuse of prescription drugs.

Federal Department of Transportation (DOT) rules require mass transit, aviation, rail, and motor carrier workers who fail a drug test (or refuse to take one) to successfully complete drug treatment and pass a series of urine tests before they can return to any safety-sensitive duties. In 2008, the regulations were amended to require the urine testing to be done by direct inspection (by a person of the same sex as the worker). The D.C. Circuit upheld the regulations, finding that they were not arbitrary and capricious. It was rational for the DOT to require direct inspection because cheating on drug tests is so widespread. It was not irrational to impose the direct inspection method for return-to-duty tests but not examinations after an accident, because of the differing likelihood of cheating. There is a compelling public interest in transportation safety, so the procedure falls under the Fourth Amendment exception for warrantless searches that promote a compelling public interest. [*BNSF Railway Co. v. United States Dep't of Transp.*, 566 F.3d 200, 1378 (D.C. Cir. 2009); the DOT regulations were published at 73 Fed. Reg. 62,910 (Oct. 22, 2008)]

The abuse of legal substances, such as alcohol and prescription drugs, also creates problems for employers. A 2010 Sixth Circuit case was brought by seven employees fired for failing drug tests for prescription drugs. The Sixth Circuit ruled that six out of the seven plaintiffs were not disabled for ADA purposes (the seventh one might have had a record of disability). The ADA forbids imposition of qualification standards that tend to screen out individuals with a disability, unless those qualifications are job-related and consistent with business necessity. [*Bates v. Dura Auto Sys. Inc.*, 625 F.3d 283 (6th Cir. 2010)]

Under the Federal Drug-Free Workplace Act, [41 U.S.C. § 701] companies with federal procurement contracts over $25,000 (and many companies are federal contractors) must certify to the contracting agency that they will provide a drug-free workplace. The contract will not be awarded if they do not make the certification.

The contractor-employer's obligations are to:

- Notify employees that using, possessing, and selling drugs is prohibited, and what the penalties will be if these rules are violated;
- Set up a drug-free awareness program;
- Order employees to abide by the program and notify the employer if they are convicted of a drug offense (even one occurring off-premises);
- Notify the contracting agency within 10 days of receiving such a report from an employee;
- Impose penalties on all employees convicted of drug violations that are related to the workplace;
- Continue to make a good-faith effort to keep drugs out of the workplace.

If the employer is a defense contractor, it must do regular drug tests on employees in "sensitive positions," in other words, those with access to classified information.

In an increasing number of states, medical marijuana is either legal or under consideration. In October 2009, the Department of Justice announced that it would not prosecute medical marijuana users, leaving enforcement in the hands of state and local governments. Nevertheless, federal law permits discharge or other adverse job action when an employee tests positive for marijuana, even medical marijuana. A Colorado state law forbids firing employees for lawful off-duty behavior, which might include medical marijuana use.

In addition, if a medical marijuana user has a disability for ADA purposes, adverse employment action on this basis could violate the ADA. In 2003, the U.S. Supreme Court held that even in a state that permits medical marijuana, an employer can penalize an employee who tests positive for drugs, and in 2005 the Supreme Court permitted the federal government to enforce the Controlled Substances Act's prohibition of medical marijuana even if the usage conforms to state law. [See also *Roe v. TeleTech Customer Care Mgmt. (Colorado), LLC*, 171 Wash. 2d 736, 257 P.3d 586 (Wash. 2011) and *Emerald Steel Fabricators Inc. v. Bureau of Labor & Indus.*, No. BOLI 3004, LA A130422 (Or. 2010)]

In August 2013, Illinois became the 20th state in which medical marijuana is legal under a four-year pilot project authorized by the Compassionate Use of Medical Cannabis Pilot Program Act. Registered users are not permitted to possess or use marijuana in vehicles, in public places, or on school grounds. Employers cannot penalize employees merely because they are registered users, but can forbid marijuana use at work and maintain a reasonable drug-free workplace policy. An employer cannot discriminate against an applicant who tests positive for marijuana on a pre-employment drug screen, but can refuse to hire, or discipline an employee who fails a drug test even if he or she is a registered user, if the effect is loss of a federal contract or federal funding. [Ogletree Deakins, *New Medical Marijuana Law Will Impact Illinois Employers*, Lexology.com (Aug. 26, 2013)]

Although medical marijuana is legal in 20 states (and recreational marijuana is legal in Colorado and Washington), courts consistently permit firing employees who test positive for marijuana, even if they are certified for medical marijuana and did not use the drug in the workplace. There are cases of this type from the Sixth and Ninth Circuits and from Colorado, Michigan, Washington, Oregon, Montana, and California.

Some medical marijuana statutes forbid employers to penalize a medical marijuana cardholder or registered qualifying patient for having a positive drug test, while permitting employers to ban use, possession, and impairment by marijuana during working hours.

Other laws permit the employer to conclude that a positive test is proof of workplace impairment, which would justify firing even a cardholder (someone who cannot be arrested for drug possession). Federally regulated employers are required to observe drug-free workplace laws. [Katharine J. Liao, *Reefer Madness: Employees May Use Medical Marijuana Yet Be Fired For Doing So*, DLA Piper (Nov. 11, 2013), available at Lexology.com; see, e.g., *Curry v. MillerCoors, Inc.*, No. 12-cv-02471 JLK, 2013 WL 4494307 (D. Colo. Aug. 21, 2013) (paraplegic treating pain); *Coats v. Dish Network*, 2013 COA 62, 303 P.3d 147 (Colo. App. 2013) (quadriplegic alleging lawful activity discrimination; the court held that marijuana use is not "lawful" in this context because it violates federal law). See also Kathryn J. Russo and Dona Vetrano Pryor, *Demystifying Employer Drug*

Policies In Medical Marijuana States, Jackson Lewis LLP (Oct. 31, 2013), available at Lexology.com; Nathan Koppel, *Legal Pot Use in Colorado Could Still Get You Fired*, WSJ.com (Apr. 25, 2013); Gregory J. Millman, *Medical Marijuana Poses Litigation Risk to Employers*, WSJ.com (Aug. 15, 2013).]

In some cases, medical marijuana users, although not violating the law, will develop problems associated with marijuana use that require referral to the Employee Assistance Program or other mental health/substance abuse resources.

[B] Case Law on Drug Testing

Pre-employment drug testing is more likely to be upheld by the courts than testing of current employees, on the theory that employees have a legitimate right of privacy. (For example, in late 2003 West Virginia ruled that because of the lower expectation of privacy, it is permissible to require job applicants to take a drug test even though state law bars mandatory testing of employees. [*Baughman v. Wal-Mart Stores Inc.*, 215 W. Va. 45 (W. Va. 2003)] A late 2013 article, noting that about 20 million people have paruresis (inability to urinate when observed), suggests that a new hire or employee's claim of a medical condition that makes it impossible to provide a urine sample should be treated as a request for disability accommodation. In 2011, the EEOC announced its position that bladder functions are a major life activity. But a refusal to be tested without an assertion of medical reasons does not require accommodation. It could violate the ADA to ask if a medical condition is involved. It is impossible to ask for medical documentation before a random test, and putting employees on notice allows them time to "clean up" by abstaining from drugs. When medical claims are made, consider whether blood, saliva, or hair could be sampled instead for drug testing. There might also be conditions (such as a private restroom with the water running) that could permit the applicant to give a sample. There are no post-ADAAA cases on this issue, but in 2010, the Second Circuit held that allowing an employee to submit a doctor's note about paruresis is a reasonable accommodation. In 2012, the District Court for the Western District of Virginia held that sporadic inability to urinate is not a substantial limitation. [Sara Eber, *You're In . . . If You've Got Urine. What To Look Out For Before Telling A New Hire, "You Gotta Go,"* Seyfarth Shaw LLP (Oct. 17, 2013), available at Lexology.com. See *Linkous v. CraftMaster Mfg., Inc.*, No. 7:10-CV-00107, 2012 WL 2905598 (W.D. Va. July 16, 2012); *Kinneary v. City of New York*, 601 F.3d 151 (2d Cir. 2010).]

Employers must consult state law to see what types of drug tests are permitted. In late 2013, the District Court for the District of Maryland held that state law forbids private employers to perform breath alcohol tests on employees: the statute allows only testing of blood, urine, hair, and saliva. However, the plaintiffs' claim for invasion of privacy was dismissed, because the district court held that employees had no privacy interest in the information gathered through breath testing. [*Whye, et al. v. Concentra Health Servs., Inc.*, No. 12-cv-3432 (ELH) (D.

Md. Sept. 24, 2013); see Kathryn Barry, *Federal Court Holds Breath Testing for Alcohol Is Illegal in Maryland*, Jackson Lewis LLP (Oct. 25, 2013), available at Lexology.com]

Cases in Arizona and California say that it does not violate public policy to discharge a worker based on his or her refusal to take a drug test. [*AFL-CIO v. Cal. Unemployment Ins. Appeals Bd.*, 23 Cal. App. 4th 51, 28 Cal. Rptr. 2d 210 (1994); *Hart v. Seven Resorts Inc.*, 191 Ariz. 297 (Ariz. App. 1997)] An employee who took prescription painkillers hurt his finger at work. He was sent to the hospital to see if he needed stitches. He refused to take a post-accident drug test at the hospital, even though they explained to him that the test looked for illegal rather than prescription drugs. He was warned he would be fired for refusing to be tested. After his termination, he brought an ADA suit claiming that he was fired on the basis of disability. The trial court ruled in his favor but the Iowa Court of Appeals reversed, holding that the employer had the right to mandate post-accident testing, and there was no evidence that the test requirement was a pretext for terminating him. [*Brown v. Mystique Casino*, 840 N.W.2d 726 (Iowa App. 2013); see Kathryn J. Russo, *Employee Using Prescription Medications Could Not Refuse Drug Test Under Theory That Employer "Knew" He Would Refuse*, Jackson Lewis LLP (Oct. 7, 2013), available at Lexology.com]

An arbitrator's award, requiring reinstatement of an employee who was fired after failing a drug test, could not be enforced, because it violated the well-established public policy against allowing drug users to keep safety-sensitive jobs. [*Exxon Corp. v. Esso Worker's Union*, 118 F.3d 841 (1st Cir. 1997)] However, two years later, the Tenth Circuit upheld an award reinstating a truck driver who admitted to smoking marijuana two days before an accident. The arbitrator read the CBA's requirement of discharge only for "just cause" to require proof of on-the-job drug use, drug dealing, or impairment, not just off-hours drug use. [*Kennecott Utah Copper Corp. v. Becker*, 195 F.3d 1201 (10th Cir. 1999)]

Current substance abuse is not a disability for ADA purposes (although it is unlawful to discriminate against someone who is now clean and sober because of a past history of substance abuse).

The ADA has a safe harbor [42 U.S.C. § 12114(b)] for people who have completed a rehab program. Just entering a program isn't enough; the safe harbor is for people with a history of staying clean.

Courts have come to varying conclusions as to whether or not a person fired for failing a drug test will be entitled to unemployment benefits, or will be deemed to have been terminated for misconduct. For example, an Idaho employee who failed a drug test was held ineligible for benefits: the employer clearly communicated its legitimate business interests in maintaining a drug-free workplace and in employees refraining even from off-premises use of illegal drugs. [*Desilet*, Unempl. Ins. Rep. (CCH) ¶ 8499 (Idaho 2006)]

In *Smith v. Zero Defects Inc.*, [132 Idaho 881 (1999)] the employer's policy called for termination of any employee testing with a detectable level of alcohol or illegal drugs. The plaintiff tested positive for amphetamines during a random test; he was not impaired at that particular time. However, Idaho (like Nebraska, Nevada, Oklahoma, and Utah—but unlike Arizona, Kansas, Oregon, and Washington) considers violation of an employer's zero-tolerance policy to be misconduct that is serious enough to prevent the employee from getting unemployment insurance benefits, even if he or she was not impaired at the time of the test. In other words, off-duty drug use can be serious enough to block unemployment benefit eligibility.

Michigan governor Rick Snyder signed a bill creating a one-year pilot program under which workers who fail drug tests administered by an employer will not be entitled to unemployment benefits. Businesses are not required to notify the state if applicants refuse to be tested, or if they fail a drug test, but if they convey the information, the unsuccessful applicants will lose UI eligibility. [AP, *Michigan: Failing Drug Test Could Imperil Jobless Pay*, NYTimes.com (Oct. 29, 2013)]

But if the drug-free workplace policy is not explicit enough [*Comer*, Unempl. Ins. Rep. (CCH) ¶ 8635 (Mo. App. 2006)], or if the employer fails to demonstrate the validity of the test itself [*Owen County*, Unempl. Ins. Rep. (CCH) ¶ 8607 (Ind. App. 2006)], then benefits might be available.

An unemployment insurance claimants who successfully appealed a denial of benefits could not get damages against his ex-employer under the state drug testing law, because the statute made an exception for drug tests required by federal law, and he had worked for a government contractor with a federal testing mandate. [*Welcher*, Unempl. Ins. Rep. (CCH) ¶ 9085 (Ia. App. 2006)]

[C] Tobacco Issues

Tobacco is a drug, albeit a legal one. Some employers are providing incentives to encourage employees to stop smoking (e.g., paying for smoking cessation classes or offering a bonus); others are imposing penalties on those who smoke (e.g., higher insurance premiums), even outside the workplace, or requiring nicotine testing as part of the pre-employment drug test. Many of the states have "lawful activities" statutes that protect employees who smoke away from the worksite from discrimination. However, some companies refuse to hire smokers; others fire employees who are found to smoke (even off-site), and sometimes employers deliberately refrain from asking job applicants because they assume smokers will lie. [Jeremy Smerd, *Smoker? Can't Work Here, More Firms Say*, workforce.com (Nov. 9, 2007) (benefitslink.com)]

§ 26.04 CRIMINAL RECORD AND CREDIT CHECKS

A federal law, the Fair Credit Reporting Act (FCRA), [15 U.S.C. § 1681] as amended by the Consumer Credit Reporting Reform Act of 1996, [Pub. L. No. 104-208] governs the access of businesses to credit reports. Although credit reports are most commonly used in the context of loans or merchandise sales, it is also fairly common for potential employers to run a credit check before making a job offer.

Under the FCRA, employers must notify applicants before they seek credit information as part of the application process. A civil penalty is imposed for ordering a credit check without the mandatory notification. The employer must also notify applicants and employees before any negative employment-related action is taken on the basis of an investigative credit report.

The FCRA allows credit reporting agencies to disclose the information they have gathered to companies that use the information for "employment purposes," i.e., evaluating the subject of the credit report for employment, promotion, retention as an employee, or reassignment. The reporting agency is allowed to furnish a report discussing the job applicant's or employee's creditworthiness, standing, character, and reputation.

The FTC and EEOC published joint guidance reminding employers that the FCRA requires safeguards if an employer obtains a credit or criminal background report from a company that compiles background information. The applicant or employee must be given written notice that this information might be used in employment decisions and his or her written consent must be obtained. If an investigative report (based on personal interviews) is ordered, the applicant or employee must be informed of the right to information about the investigation. If adverse actions are taken based on information from a profiling company, the employer must give the applicant or employee a copy of the FTC's summary of FCRA rights, and must give contact information for the profiling company. [EEOC/FTC, *Background Checks: What Employers Need to Know*, <http://www.eeoc.gov/eeoc/publications/background_checks_employers.cfm> (March 2014)]

The EEOC lost a case against Kaplan Higher Education Corporation. The EEOC alleged that Kaplan's use of credit checks had a disparate impact on African-American applicants. However, the Sixth Circuit held that the methodology of the EEOC's expert witness for identifying the race of applicants was deficient, and lacked scientific accuracy and verification. Furthermore, the EEOC itself uses a similar credit check process for applicants for jobs with the agency. [*EEOC v. Kaplan Higher Educ. Corp.*, 748 F.3d 749 (6th Cir. 2014); semble *EEOC v. Freeman*, 951 F. Supp. 2d 783 (D. Md. 2013). See Katharine H. Parker et al., *Sixth Circuit Affirms Summary Judgment Against EEOC in Credit Check Suit*, Proskauer Rose LLP (Apr. 15, 2014), available at Lexology.com. The article says that the states of California, Colorado, Connecticut, Hawaii, Illinois, Maryland, Nevada, Oregon, Vermont, and Washington, and the cities of Chicago and Madison, Wisconsin have enacted restrictions on the use of credit history by employers. Some of these statutes permit exceptions for job-related information, or for situations when applicants and employees are informed that their credit histories will be consulted.]

As a result of the Dodd-Frank Act, Pub. L. No. 111-203, starting July 21, 2011, employers have been required to inform job applicants whenever the employer has obtained the applicant's credit scores, and those scores have had an adverse effect on the employer's decision on the application.

2003 legislation, the Fair and Accurate Credit Transactions Act (FACTA; Pub. L. No. 108-159) amends 15 U.S.C § 1681a, enacting a new subsection (x) under which a communication will not be treated as a consumer report (and therefore will not be subject to FCRA requirements) if it is a job-related communication not related to the creditworthiness of the individual. The communication must be made to the employer as part of an investigation of suspected workplace misconduct, or under the employer's pre-existing policies or under any law or regulation. To qualify for the exemption, the information must be disclosed only to the employer or to government officials or self-regulatory officials—unless broader disclosure is mandated by law. If the employer uses the information as the basis of any adverse action against the subject of the investigation, the subject must be furnished a summary of the information. The employer, however, is not obligated to disclose the sources of the information.

Under the Intelligence Reform and Terrorism Prevention Act of 2004, Pub. L. No. 108-458 (Dec. 17, 2004), private employers can access the FBI criminal records database to obtain information about employees or applicants for private security jobs. Section 6403 of the statute provides that, on the written consent of the employee or applicant, the employer can submit fingerprints or other means of identification to the state's investigative agency for a background check. (States can opt out of the background check system by passing a law, or if the state governor issues an order to this effect.) The state investigative agency will notify the employer if the applicant or employee has been convicted of a felony, an offense involving dishonesty, or a false statement in the previous 10 years, and whether there have been any unresolved felony charges in the previous year. The employer has an obligation to disclose the information to the employee. [See also § 23.08]

The Supreme Court unanimously upheld the standard background check procedure that the Department of Commerce requires of government contractors. The standard background check requires employees to answer whether they used, possessed, supplied, or manufactured illegal drugs in the past year. If so, they must provide information about any treatment or counseling received. Employees are also required to sign a release for personal information from schools and employers. The government submits a questionnaire to employees' references, asking about adverse information and reasons to question the employee's honesty or truthfulness. The Supreme Court found these inquiries reasonable, and the Privacy Act limits disclosure of the information to the public. [*NASA v. Nelson*, 131 S. Ct. 746 (2011); see Rebecca Moore, *High Court Rejects Federal Contract Workers Challenge to Background Checks*, plansponsor.com (Jan. 20, 2011)]

The EEOC's position is that a blanket refusal to hire based on the applicant's credit reports or criminal records is illegal if it has a disparate impact on racial minorities: EEOC Enforcement Guidance, *Consideration of Arrest and Conviction Records In Employment Decisions Under Title VII of the Civil Rights*

Act of 1964, <http://www.eeoc.gov/laws/guidance/arrest_conviction.cfm> (Apr. 25, 2012)]

Although a group of state Attorneys General asked the EEOC to reconsider its guidelines, EEOC chair Jacqueline A. Berrien replied that this guidance merely updates and restates the existing EEOC position. The EEOC encourages employers to consider the nature of the record, and the length of time that has elapsed since the offense. [Ilyse Schuman, *EEOC Clarifies Guidance On Criminal Background Checks*, Littler Mendelson (Sept. 25, 2013), available at Lexology.com; Gerald L. Maatman, Jr. and Howard M. Wexler, *EEOC Responds To Attorneys' General Criticism Of EEOC's "Misguided" Position On Criminal Background Screens*, Seyfarth Shaw LLP (Sept. 23, 2013), available at Lexology.com. The Attorneys General signing the letter came from Alabama, Colorado, Georgia, Kansas, Montana, Nebraska, South Carolina, Utah, and West Virginia.]

At least two courts rejected the EEOC's litigating position on this subject. The District Court for the District of Maryland granted summary judgment for the employer, finding that the EEOC's statistical expert was unreliable; the Sixth Circuit upheld the district court's sanctions of almost $752,000 imposed on the EEOC for continuing to litigate a case after it became evident that the defendant did not maintain an unlawful company-wide ban on hiring persons with felony records. [*EEOC v. Freeman*, No. 09-CV-2573 (D. Md. Aug. 9, 2013); *EEOC v. PeopleMark*, 732 F.3d 584 (6th Cir., 2013); see Brian D. Hall, *EEOC's Campaign Against Criminal Background Checks Takes Recent Hits*, Porter Wright Morris & Arthur LLP (Oct. 10, 2013), available at Lexology.com; Joann Coston-Holloway, *EEOC Provides Clarification On Use Of Criminal History Information In Hiring Decisions*, Baker Donelson Bearman Caldwell & Berkowitz PC (Jan. 16, 2014), available at Lexology.com]

Although the Third Circuit was uncomfortable with "bright-line" tests (refusal to hire any person with a criminal conviction), the court accepted the employer's business necessity defense because the plaintiff did not rebut testimony about risk due to hiring convicted persons. [*El v. Se. Penn. Transit Auth.*, 479 F.3d 232 (3d Cir. 2007)]

More than 50 cities and local governments have "ban the box" laws, forbidding questions about criminal convictions on initial job applications. However, most of those laws apply only to public employers. Private employers are subject to ban the box laws in Hawaii, Massachusetts, and Minnesota, as well as Seattle (Washington), Buffalo, Newark, N.J., and Philadelphia. [Susan Gross Sholinsky, *Take 5: Views You Can Use: Labor And Employment*, Epstein Becker Green (Nov. 12, 2013), available at Lexology.com]

Other jurisdictions subsequently adopted ban the box laws, e.g., the states of Illinois and New Jersey; Delaware, for public employees only; and the city of Baltimore. [Philip L. Gordon and Zoe M. Argento, *Baltimore Becomes the 10th Jurisdiction to "Ban the Box,"* Littler Mendelson (May 16, 2014), available at Lexology.com; Carolyn A. Pellegrini, *Boxing Out in Delaware*, Montgomery McCracken Walker & Rhoads LLP (May 29, 2014), available at Lexology.com;

Nora Kersten Walsh and Alexis M. Dominguez, *Illinois' New "Ban the Box" Law Restricts Criminal History Inquiries of Applicants*, Schiff Hardin LLP (Aug. 6, 2014), available at Lexology.com; Christopher Lowe and Alnisa Bell, *New Jersey Joins "Ban the Box" Movement and Chris Christie Safeguards Employers*, Seyfarth Shaw LLP (Aug. 13, 2014), available at Lexology.com]

San Francisco's Fair Chance Ordinance, signed into law February 14, 2014, does not permit employers with 20 or more employees in San Francisco to ask about convictions or pending criminal charges on an employment application or at a first live interview. Other "ban the box" jurisdictions set different timetables for criminal history inquiries. Massachusetts permits inquiries at any time after the initial application; Seattle, after applicants have received initial screening for basic qualifications; Minnesota, after the person has been selected for a job interview; Rhode Island and Buffalo, at the initial interview; Philadelphia and San Francisco, after the initial interview; Hawaii and Newark, after a conditional offer of employment has been extended. [Philip L. Gordon and Zoe M. Argento, *San Francisco's Board Of Supervisors "Bans The Box" And Further Complicates Criminal History Checks By The City's Employers*, Littler Mendelson (Feb. 10, 2014), available at Lexology.com; Todd M. Torres, *Rhode Island Employers May No Longer Ask About Criminal Convictions On Employment Applications*, Ogletree Deakins (Aug. 28, 2013), available at Lexology.com]

§ 26.05 GENETIC TESTING

In addition to a variety of state laws, Congress adopted protection against genetic discrimination in the Genetic Information Nondisclosure Act (GINA; Pub. L. No. 110-233). The statute forbids discrimination on the basis of genetic predisposition to disease, but not disease already manifested. Genetic discrimination cases require use of the Title VII process, including the requirement of a Right to Sue letter. The federal law does not preempt more protective state laws. [Jane Zhang and Shirley S. Wang, *Bill on Genetic Bias Advances*, Wall St. J., Apr. 25, 2008, at A11]

Title I of GINA applies to group health plans maintained by private employers, as well as to unions, government employers, and insurers. Title II applies to entities covered by Title VII. GINA Title II prohibits the use of genetic information in employment and restricts the acquisition and disclosure of genetic information. The EEOC was empowered to issue regulations under Title II of GINA, and to enforce it, effective November 21, 2009, for employers of 15 or more employees.

The EEOC proposed regulations on March 2, 2009, clarifying the definition of "genetic information" and providing guidance on proper use of the information. A party subject to Title II of GINA is permitted to obtain genetic information only if it was:

- Acquired inadvertently (e.g., volunteered by the employee, or overheard);
- Aggregate information, not individually identifiable, stemming from genetic counseling at a wellness program;
- Information given to an employer to certify eligibility for leave;
- Information from genetic monitoring required by law (e.g., by OSHA);
- Voluntarily authorized in writing by the employee.

There is a limited exception for information obtained by law enforcement or the military to assist in genetic identification, and for publicly available information.

In order to prevent genetic markers for a disease being treated as preexisting conditions, the regulations define "manifestation of disease" as a condition that has been or reasonably could be diagnosed by a health care professional. Therefore, the presence of a genetic marker, even one that assures that the individual is certain to develop the disease in the future, is not a manifestation of disease.

However, even if the employer has obtained the information legitimately, the information must be kept confidential and must not be used to discriminate. Genetic information (except publicly available information) must be kept in a separate, confidential file rather than in an ordinary personnel file.

Genetic information can be disclosed only to the person it relates to; to an occupational health researcher carrying out research pursuant to federal regulations; or in response to a court order that specifically calls for information. However, information may not be disclosed in response to a discovery request that is not under a court order (e.g., a party in a lawsuit asks for the information). Disclosure is permitted to government officials assessing the company's GINA compliance, in connection with a request for leave, or to officials investigating contagious disease or an imminent hazard of death or life-threatening illness.

Employers should make sure that doctors avoid questions about family medical history in post-offer, pre-employment medical examinations and fitness for duty exams. Nor may genetic information be obtained in connection with the interactive process of establishing reasonable accommodation to disability.

■ **TIP:** The EEOC says that the best practice for an employer asking for documentation of disability is to state in the request that genetic information, including family medical history, should not be provided.

Employers were required to begin posting the official GINA information no later than November 21, 2009. [RIN 3046-AA84, 74 Fed. Reg. 9056 (Mar. 2, 2009); see Margaret Hart Edwards, *Proposed Regulations Under Federal Genetic Information Nondiscrimination Act (GINA) Suggest Employer Action Now*, LittlerASAPs, <http://www.littler.com/PressPublications/Lists/ASAPs/DispAsaps.aspx?id=1344&asapType=National> (March 2009)]

The EEOC published a final rule on recordkeeping requirements under GINA. As of April 3, 2012, companies with 15 or more employees must retain all personnel and employment records relating to GINA for at least one year. If charges are filed under GINA, relevant documents must be retained until final disposition of the case. If an employee is involuntarily terminated, records must be kept for a year after termination. The relevant documents in this context include requests for accommodation; application forms; records of hiring, promotion, demotion, transfer, layoff, and termination; and records about terms of employment, e.g., pay, training, and tenure. [77 Fed. Reg. 5396 (Feb. 3, 2012), finalizing the Notice of Proposed Rulemaking, 76 Fed. Reg. 31892 (June 2, 2011).]

On January 17, 2013, HHS published a final rule covering the application of the HIPAA privacy rule to GINA Titles I (health coverage) and II (employment). The final rule specifies that genetic information is considered health information, which cannot be used for insurance underwriting purposes other than for long-term care insurance policies. [Katherine Georger, *New HIPAA Final Rule Implements GINA Restriction on Use and Disclosure of Genetic Information for Underwriting Purposes*, Holland & Hart LLP News Update (Jan. 23, 2013) (benefitslink.com)]

The EEOC's first GINA case, against Fabricut, alleging that employees were sent to a particular laboratory for physicals and were required to complete a family history questionnaire, was settled via a $50,000 consent decree.

Genetic discrimination is one of the six priorities listed in the EEOC's Strategic Enforcement Plan. The EEOC filed its first class action GINA suit in May 2013, against a skilled nursing facility in Corning, New York that required post-offer, pre-employment medical examinations, and annual examinations for employees, that included improper questions about family medical history. The District Court for the Western District of New York approved a consent decree on January 9, 2014 settling the case. One hundred thirty-eight people from whom genetic information was sought were awarded $110,000. [*EEOC v. Founders Pavilion*, No. 6-13-cv-06250 (W.D.N.Y., settled 2014); see Elizabeth Tempio Clement, *EEOC Settles First Systemic GINA Lawsuit Against Nursing Home*, Littler Mendelson (Jan. 17, 2014), available at Lexology.com; William A. Wright, *GINA Enforcement Takes Off*, Sherman & Howard LLC (Nov. 12, 2013), available at Lexology.com]

§ 26.06 SEARCHES AND SURVEILLANCE

[A] Constitutional Limits on Employees

Although the Constitution puts limits on unreasonable searches and seizures, the focus is on the activities of public agencies such as the police and the military. Therefore, it is very unlikely that the actions of a private employer would have a constitutional dimension, or that the employee would be able to invoke the Fourth Amendment as protection against searches and seizures.

It is becoming more common for employers to use tracking devices (such as sensors that employees wear around their necks, or placed on furniture) to find out how employees work and what can be done to enhance productivity. Companies that use these devices handle privacy issues by letting employees opt out of tracking or by pointing out that employees' movements can already be tracked with smartphones and ID badges. [*Tracking Sensors Invade the Workplace*, WSJ.com (Mar. 6, 2013)]

However, an employer's surveillance activities might constitute an invasion of privacy, which could furnish grounds for a suit by an employee.

An employer can legitimately order a workplace search if there is a good reason in the first place (such as getting evidence of embezzlement, theft of products, or other work-related misconduct) and the scope of the search is appropriate to satisfying that purpose. But, because the employer controls the workplace but employees control their own personal possessions such as coats and handbags, get legal advice about how to handle a search.

Surveillance programs are most likely to survive legal challenge if:

- They are created in response to a real problem (e.g., inventory shrinkage) or a real threat (e.g., potential employer liability);
- Employees are accurately informed of the purposes and content of the program;
- Surveillance is restricted to the least intrusive method that is still effective.

The Third Circuit ruled that Labor Management Relations Act (LMRA) § 301 does not preempt state laws about wiretaps and privacy, so state tort claims about workplace surveillance are not ruled out. Suit was brought to protest audio and video surveillance of the time clock area that was imposed without notice to the employees. The court held that it is not necessary to interpret the CBA to determine whether surveillance violated employee rights; merely looking at the CBA to see if it has a surveillance clause is not a contract interpretation. Tort claims are preempted by LMRA § 301 only if they involve a duty of care imposed by a CBA. [*Kline v. Sec. Guards Inc.*, 386 F.3d 246 (3d Cir. 2004)]

The First Circuit says that it does not violate the Fourth Amendment for a public employer to use silent video cameras for surveillance of the work area. In this case, the work environment was an open space with no assigned offices, cubicles, workstations, or desks, so the court concluded that it would not be reasonable to assume that privacy would be available in such an environment. [*Vega-Rodriguez v. P.R. Tel. Co.*, 110 F.3d 174 (1st Cir. 1997)]

In a unionized company, surveillance might be a mandatory bargaining subject, not a management prerogative. Early in 2002, the Supreme Court permitted unionized employees to sue in state court for invasion of privacy because of video surveillance of company bathrooms. The employer, a trucking company, said that the cameras were installed to frustrate drug dealing and drug use, and were not aimed at urinals or bathroom stalls. The issue in *Consolidated Freightways v. Cramer* [534 U.S. 1078 (2002)] was whether LMRA § 301 preempts the state law forbidding undisclosed videotaping of employees. The Supreme Court held that it does not, so state-law suits can go forward—even though the case might be interpreted as involving interpretation of a collective bargaining agreement (the usual test for LMRA § 301 preemption).

The NLRB ruled that it was a violation of federal labor law to install hidden surveillance cameras, without bargaining in a room where the employer suspected illegal drugs were sold. The NLRB ordered the company to bargain on the issue. [*Anheuser-Busch Inc.*, 324 NLRB No. 49 (July 22, 2004); see also *Brewers and Maltsters v. NLRB*, 414 F.3d 36 (D.C. Cir. 2005); *Nat'l Steel Corp. v. NLRB*, 324 F.3d 928 (7th Cir. 2003)]

When employees take FMLA leave or make a disability claim, the employer may order video surveillance—e.g., to determine if employees are performing tasks that they claim are impossible because of job-related injuries. Such surveillance is usually upheld by the courts. For example, *Vail v. Raybestos*, 533 F.3d 904 (7th Cir. 2008) upheld surveillance of an employee who took leave for migraines and was found to run a lawn service on the side; the court said that the surveillance provided the employer with an honest suspicion about the validity of the leave request. In *Crouch v. Whirlpool*, 447 F.3d 984 (7th Cir. 2006), the Seventh Circuit upheld the validity of videotaping a suspected leave abuser, who was caught doing yard work and flying to Las Vegas when he was off work due to a knee injury. The pending case *Weimer v. Honda*, No. 2:06-cv-00844, 2008 U.S. Dist. LEXIS 98508 (S.D. Ohio. Dec. 5, 2008), involves an employee who suffered a concussion, then was fired after he was videotaped building a new porch for his house. He sued for FMLA retaliation, claiming that he was waiting for clearance from his doctor to return to work. [Tresa Baldas, *Spying Employers Raise Legal Hackles*, Nat'l L.J. (Aug. 19, 2008) (law.com. The district court ruled for the defendant; the Sixth Circuit affirmed, in an unpublished decision: 356 Fed. Appx. 812 (6th Cir. 2009)]

The Pennsylvania Superior Court ruled in mid-2010 that it was not an invasion of privacy to tape a WC claimant while he was praying at his mosque. The court said that WC claimants have a diminished expectation of privacy and know that they might be investigated. Pennsylvania law is not clear about the amount of privacy required in religious settings; the lower court treated the mosque as a public place. The plaintiff was praying right in front of a plate glass window, and the investigator was lawfully present in the parking lot across from the mosque. [*Tagouma v. Investigative Consultant Servs. Inc.*, 2010 Pa. Super. 147 (Pa. Super. 2010); see Rebecca Moore, *Videotaping Workers Comp Claimant Praying not Invasion of Privacy*, plansponsor.com (Aug. 16, 2010)]

[B] Wiretapping

Wiretapping, and other forms of interception of wire, oral, and electronic communications, including e-mail (or electronic or mechanical interception of conversations) are covered by the federal Omnibus Crime Control and Safe Streets Act of 1968. [18 U.S.C. §§ 2511 *et seq.*] Interceptions by the employer are regulated. Interceptions are prohibited only if the employee had a reasonable expectation that the communication would not be subject to interception.

For instance, if a telephone salesperson has known from the beginning of the job that contact with customers is subject to monitoring, there would be no reasonable expectation of privacy. But even if interception of calls is legitimate, the employer must cease the interception if it is clear that a particular call is personal and not business-related. One of the parties to a communication has a right to intercept it; so does anyone with explicit or implicit consent to intercept.

The federal statute imposes penalties for improper interception that can be as high as $10,000. Punitive damages can be imposed on an employer that acted wantonly, recklessly, or maliciously.

[C] Internet and E-Mail Monitoring

Apart from the fact that employees are not supposed to use the company computer system for personal purposes, employee e-mails can subject the employer to liability (in the context of sexual or racial harassment, for example, or concealment of improprieties). See § 27.06for discussion of the human resources implications of social networking.

State and federal wiretap statutes typically include a "provider exception," under which the provider of communications is allowed to intercept messages on the system. An employer is clearly a provider when it owns the equipment on which the employees communicate.

Most employers have broad policies that warn employees that e-mails can be monitored, usually stated in the employee handbook or displayed on the log-in screen for the e-mail system. Software is now available to mechanize e-mail monitoring, so the IT department will not have to do so manually. E-mail monitoring usually begins only after there has been a problem, such as an allegation of harassment or misuse of proprietary information. Employees should probably be informed that their e-mail has been read, which has the effect of reinforcing the employer's e-mail policy. [Shannon Green, *When Should Employers Be Monitoring Employee Email?* Corporate Counsel (Mar. 13, 2013) (law.com)]

In late 2007, the NLRB voted 3-2 to permit employers to restrict the use of the company e-mail system for union organizing campaigns and distributing union news, on the grounds that personal use of the e-mail system can be restricted. However, to be valid, a ban on personal use must be evenly applied, not limited to union applications. [The Guard Publishing Company d/b/a The

Register-Guard and Eugene Newspaper Guild, CWA Local 37194. Cases 36–CA–8743-1, 36–CA–8849-1, 36–CA–8789-1, and 36–CA–8842-1] The D.C. Circuit upheld the NLRB's Unfair Labor Practice decision when a newspaper disciplined the union president for sending three union-related e-mails to co-workers. Although the newspaper's e-mail policy forbade using the system for commercial ventures, religious or political causes, or outside organizations, the NLRB found that personal e-mails were common and did not result in discipline. The D.C. Circuit said that the policy did not rule out sending union e-mails that merely clarified facts about a union rally and did not call for action. [*Guard Publishing Co. v. NLRB*, 571 F.3d 53 (D.C. Cir. 2009)]

In June 2010, the Supreme Court made its first ruling on privacy issues related to workplace texting. However, the Supreme Court kept its ruling narrow. It decided that it was reasonable, under the Fourth Amendment, for the city of Ontario to perform an audit of employees' messages on pagers owned by the city to determine if the city should upgrade to a plan giving employees more minutes on their pagers. The Supreme Court declined to decide the broader issue of whether the plaintiff, a police sergeant who sent private messages (some of them sexually oriented) on his work-issued pager, had a reasonable expectation of privacy in those text messages. The decision concentrated on whether the search of the pagers was legitimate, work-related, and not excessive in scope; because it was, the Supreme Court ruled in favor of the city. [*Ontario v. Quon*, 560 U.S. 746 (2010); see Tony Mauro, *Supreme Court Allows Search of Employee's City-Owned Pager*, Nat'l L.J. (June 18, 2010) (law.com)]

Some cases hold that employees have a greater expectation of privacy when:

- The employer allows some personal use of the electronic network, but imposes imprecise standards such as "subject to the highest standards of morality" (e.g., *Bowman v. Butler Township Board of Trustees*, 2009 Ohio 6128 (Ohio App. 2009);
- The employer is a multi-national corporation, and reviews electronic communications of employees located in the European Union, even though they are protected by EU law (Directive 2002/58/EC);
- The employee was disciplined for communications not made during work hours, and not made on the employer's system (e.g., N.Y. Lab. Law § 201-d(2)(a); Cal. Lab. Code §§ 1101–1102);
- The company is subject to a collective bargaining agreement that limits electronic monitoring, and the employer fails to comply.

However, in some circumstances there might even be a duty to monitor—for example, if the employer is on notice of unlawful usage of the network that could be harmful to others such as accessing child pornography, or creating a hostile work environment by displaying pornography on the corporate computer system. See, e.g., *Doe v. XYC Corp.*, 887 A.2d 1156 (N.J. Super. 2005). Note also that FTC guidelines at 16 C.F.R. Part 255 that took effect December 1, 2009 make employers liable for failure to create and enforce policies restricting employees from endorsing the employer's products on a blog or social networking site without disclosing the employee's relationship to the employer. [Daniel L. Prywes, *Electronic Privacy and the Supreme Court*, The Corporate Counselor (Feb. 9, 2010) (law.com)]

A number of states (including California, Colorado, and New York) have statutes that forbid employers from disciplining employees for lawful conduct that they engage in off company premises. However, there are exceptions for conduct reasonably related to the employee's job, or when the conduct creates a conflict of interest for the employer (for example, with respect to trade secrets) or impairs the employer's business interests. Several states (Connecticut, Louisiana, New York, South Carolina, Washington, and the District of Columbia) forbid discipline on the basis of engaging in political activities or speech.

New Jersey adopted a law in August, 2013 forbidding employers to require employees or job applicants to turn over their social media user names or passwords. The Commissioner of Labor and Workforce Development can fine violators $1,000 for a first offense and $2,500 for repeat offenses. The law also forbids retaliation for exercising these rights, or for refusal to disclose passwords. Social media accounts used for business purposes are not covered, and employers are permitted to ask employees or applicants if they have private social media accounts, and to access publicly available social media pages. [David K. Reid, *New Jersey Social Media Privacy Bill Signed By Gov. Christie*, Day Pitney LLP (Aug. 30, 2013), available at Lexology.com. The states of Arkansas, California, Illinois, Maryland, New Mexico, Oregon, and Washington also have employment-related social media privacy laws.]

However, in another perspective on social media, the financial regulatory organization FINRA has asked the legislators of about a dozen states to add exemptions to state privacy laws so that financial firms would gain additional power to examine employees' social media accounts to investigate indications of possible fraud. The National Conference of State Legislatures said that 35 states had introduced social media privacy legislation in 2013. California, Illinois, Maryland, Michigan, and Utah adopted privacy laws. [Jean Eaglesham and Michael Rothfeld, *Wall Street Battles States on Social-Media Protections*, WSJ.com (Apr. 22, 2013)]

A hospital nurse who posted to Facebook that she hated her supervisor and had been forced to work on Mother's Day after taking a 17% pay cut could not show that firing her violated her CBA or her free speech rights under the California constitution. She was fired the day after the post after some co-workers and a manager who were Facebook friends reported the post to management. She was denied unemployment benefits. She sued for breach of contract, a claim that was dismissed because she failed to exhaust administrative remedies (the CBA's mandatory grievance procedure). The District Court for the Northern District of California did not permit her to argue that defects in union representation excused her from the obligation of exhausting the grievance procedure. Her free speech claim was dismissed because the authorities she cited related to speech in public places, and she did not allege that she engaged in concerted activities protected by the NLRA. [*Guevarra v. Seton Med. Ctr.*, No. C 13-2267 CW, 2013 U.S. Dist. LEXIS 169849 (N.D. Cal. Dec. 2, 2013); see Keahn N. Morris, *Employer Could Discharge Nurse For Facebook Tirade, Court Finds*, Jackson Lewis PC (Dec. 27, 2013), available at Lexology.com]

The NLRB started coming to grips with social media issues in October 2010. Since then, a consensus has emerged: the NLRB will challenge employer conduct that impairs employees' ability to engage in concerted activity—including discussion of working conditions. However, purely personal communications, especially if malicious, will not be deemed protected.

An NLRB ALJ ordered Hispanics United of Buffalo to reinstate five employees who were fired after posting Facebook complaints about work. The ALJ held that the terminated employees engaged in protected concerted activity because they discussed job performance and staffing levels. It was not required that they make a formal effort to change working conditions or communicate their concerns to the employer. One employee put a co-worker's allegation that the organization didn't do enough to help its clients on Facebook. Other employees replied, saying they did the best they could under adverse conditions. The five respondents were fired for harassing the original poster. [Tara Cantore, *Employer Ordered to Reinstate Employees Fired for Facebook Posts*, plansponsor.com (Oct. 17, 2011). Michael C. Schmidt, *Deciphering the NLRB's Stance on Social Media Issues*, N.Y.L.J. (Oct. 24, 2011) (law.com). The NLRB's *Operations Management Memo* discusses seven social media cases: NLRB, Memorandum OM 12-31, *Acting General Counsel Issues Second Social Media Report* (Jan. 24, 2012) (benefitslink.com). The NLRB issued a social media report on May 30, 2012. [See <http://www.nlrb.gov/news-outreach/news-story/acting-general-counsel-releases-report-employer-social-media-policies>]

In an important opinion, the Fourth Circuit ruled in September 2013 that "liking" something on Facebook (in this case, a deputy sheriff liking the candidate running against the deputy's boss) is free speech protected by the First Amendment. The court said it was the Internet equivalent of putting a sign on the lawn. The NLRB has also decided cases where it found that there was protected collective activity when co-workers liked or commented on a post. [*Bland v. Roberts*, 730 F.3d 368 (4th Cir. 2013); see Sara H. Jodka, *Fourth Circuit Holds "Liking" A Facebook Page Is Protected Speech In The Public Employment Context. What Does This Mean In The Private Employment Context? Well, It Won't Stop Those Annoying Farmville Or Candy Crush Invitations*, Porter Wright Morris & Arthur LLP (Sept. 19, 2013), available at Lexology.com; Joe Palazzolo, *Facebook 'Likes' Are Protected by First Amendment*, WSJ.com (Sept. 18, 2013)]

The District Court for the District of New Jersey ruled in mid-2013 that it can violate the Stored Communications Act to discipline employees based on non-public posts to their Facebook wall (the post is an electronic communication that is archived; friends-only pages are not publicly available). In this case, however, the court found that the employer was not liable, because it was alerted to the post by a co-worker who was friended and therefore authorized to view the post and who voluntarily reported it to the employer. [*Ehling v. Monmouth-Ocean Hosp. Serv. Corp.*, 961 F. Supp. 2d 659 (D.N.J. 2013); see Barnes & Thornburg LLP, *Employers May Inadvertently Break The Law When They Discipline Employees For Facebook "Wall" Posts*, Lexology.com (Aug. 30, 2013); Philip L. Gordon, *New Jersey Court's Decision Provides Roadmap For Access To Employees' Restricted Social Media Content*, Littler Mendelson (Aug. 27, 2013), available at Lexology.com]

Another issue is whether the employer is entitled to access e-mails sent on its system that the employee claims are entitled to attorney-client privilege (for example, when an employee communicates with his or her attorney about a Title VII suit against the employer). See, e.g.,

- E-mails were not privileged because the employee was aware of the employer's policy (that the e-mail system was restricted to use for business only, and the employer retained the right to access and disclose communications on the system) *Scott v. Beth Israel Med. Ctr. Inc.*, 17 Misc. 3d 934 (N.Y. Sup. 2007).
- E-mails sent to the employee's lawyer on a personal, password-protected, Web-based Yahoo account on a laptop issued by the employer were held to be privileged in *Stengart v. Loving Care Agency Inc.*, 973 A.2d 390 (N.J. Super. A.D. July 29, 2009), *aff'd*, 201 N.J. 300 (2010).
- E-mails to the employee's attorney were privileged although sent on the employer's computer, because there was no policy against personal use, and the employee password-protected the e-mails and kept them in a separate folder: *People v. Jiang*, 131 Cal. App. 4th 1027, 33 Cal. Rptr. 184 (2005).
- *Pure Power Boot Camp Inc. v. Warrior Fitness Boot Camp*, LLC, 587 F. Supp. 2d, 548 (S.D.N.Y. 2008) holds that it violated the Stored Communications Act to access a former employee's Hotmail e-mails from the company computer without consent. Although the employee was on notice that company computers could be searched for evidence of personal use, he did not know that his Web-based e-mail accounts like Hotmail could be included. The court held that the company policy did not waive privacy rights in Web-based accounts. [Anthony E. Davis, Attorney-Client Privilege in Work E-Mails N.Y.L.J. (Nov. 5, 2009) (law.com); on the *Stengart* affirmance, see Michael Booth, *Privilege*

Trumps Company E-Mail Surveillance, N.J.L.J. (Apr. 1, 2010) (law.com)]

§ 26.07 HIPAA PRIVACY RULES

Congress passed the Health Insurance Portability and Accessibility Act (HIPAA). [Pub. L. No. 104-191], covering many issues related to health insurance and health care. The statute ordered Congress to issue federal health care privacy standards by August 21, 1999. However, Congress failed to meet this deadline, which gave the Department of Health and Human Services the right to draft regulations.

HHS published a Final Rule on HIPAA enforcement in February 2006. [71 Fed. Reg. 8390 (Feb. 16, 2006), discussed in Segal Capital Checkup, *Final HIPAA Enforcement Rule*, <http://www.segalco.com/publications/capitalcheckup/031509no2.html> (Mar. 15, 2006)] HIPAA enforcement relies largely on HHS investigation of complaints of violations and efforts to obtain voluntary compliance by conciliation. Civil monetary penalties are imposed only if conciliation fails. HHS also carries out compliance reviews independent of complaints.

The HITECH Act (Health Information Technology for Information and Clinical Health Act; part of the American Recovery and Reinvestment Act of 2009, Pub. L. No. 111-5), took effect February 17, 2010, strengthening the privacy and security provisions of HIPAA, and increasing civil monetary penalties for HIPAA violations.

The Eastern District of Michigan granted summary judgment for an employer who fired an employee for FMLA abuse based on vacation pictures posted to Facebook showing her engaging in physical activities. The plaintiff first claimed that she used a wheelchair in the airport to and from the trip, and then admitted this was a lie. Her dishonesty was a legitimate, non-FMLA-related reason to fire her: *Lineberry v. Detroit Med. Ctr.*, No. 11-13752 (E.D. Mich. Feb. 5, 2013).]

After issuing interim final rules in 2009 [RIN 009-AB56, 75 Fed. Reg. 42740 (Aug. 24, 2009)] and a 2010 Notice of Proposed Rulemaking dealing with privacy, security, and enforcement [RIN 009-AB56, 75 Fed. Reg. 40868 (July 14, 2010)], at the beginning of 2013, HHS' Office of Civil Rights (OCR) published an omnibus restatement of the HIPAA privacy and security rules reflecting the HITECH Act Amendments. Covered entities and their contractors and subcontractors are subject to civil and criminal penalties for violations of the privacy, security, and breach notification rules. Security breaches must be reported to HHS each year and large-scale breaches must also be reported to the individuals involved and to the news media. There are requirements for using encryption and destruction of obsolete information to prevent unauthorized persons from accessing protected health information (PHI).

Penalties for failure to notify individuals of breach of their PHI and failure to notify the media when required have increased. The penalty ranges between $100 and $50,000 per violation in situations where the covered entity did not know of the violation (and could not have known by exercising reasonable diligence). If there was reasonable cause for the violation and there was no willful neglect, the penalty range is $1,000 to $50,000. Where willful neglect occurred, the penalty range is $10,000–$50,000 if the violation was corrected on a timely basis—and at least $50,000 for offenses of willful neglect that were not timely corrected.

However, in each penalty category, there is a cap of $1.5 million on total penalties for all violations of the same provision. The actual penalty imposed within the penalty range for a particular offense depends on factors such as the nature and extent of the violation and the extent of the harm it caused. [78 Fed. Reg. 5566 (Jan. 25, 2013); see Cynthia Marcotte Stamer, Solutions Law Press HR & Benefits Update, *OCR Publishes Long-Anticipated Omnibus Restatement of HIPAA Privacy, Security, Breach Notification & Enforcement Rules* (Jan. 13, 2013) (benefitslink.com); Katherine Georger, Holland & Hart LLP News Update, *New HIPAA Final Rule Implements GINA Restriction on Use and Disclosure of Genetic Information for Underwriting Purposes* (Jan. 23, 2013) (benefitslink.com)]

There is no private right of action for violation of the HIPAA privacy rules (i.e., employees cannot sue if they claim their PHI was improperly disclosed or used). Instead, enforcement is the province of government agencies—HHS in the civil context, the Department of Justice in the criminal arena. However, under the HITECH Act, aggrieved individuals can receive a share of civil penalties collected for privacy breaches involving their data. [See, e.g., *Acara v. Banks*, 470 F.3d 569 (5th Cir. 2006)] A HIPAA privacy rule violation could be admissible as evidence in a private civil suit for, e.g., RICO violations or negligent infliction of emotional distress. [See, e.g., *Acosta v. Byrum*, 638 S.E.2d 246 (N.C. App. 2006), discussed in Roy Harmon III, *HIPAA Violations as a Basis for Private Causes of Action* (Feb. 6, 2007) <http://www.healthplanlaw.com>]

If the EGHP is funded by insurance and the employer-plan sponsor has no access to PHI, the insurer has full responsibility for privacy compliance. Such EGHPs are not directly affected by the privacy rules. A plan sponsor that does have access to PHI has an obligation to amend the plan document to institute privacy procedures under which participants can inspect (and, if necessary, correct) their PHI and control disclosure of the PHI to others. The plan sponsor must give the plan a certificate of complying amendments and safeguards. The plan must have a privacy officer, and it must modify contracts with business associates to make sure that PHI is protected.

A self-insured or self-administered plan doesn't have an insurer in the picture to handle privacy concerns, so the plan document must be amended to control dissemination of PHI; privacy safeguards and certification are required; a privacy officer must be appointed; and business associates' access to PHI must be controlled.

■ **TIP:** The privacy rules apply only to health plans, not to other types of welfare benefit plans (for instance, short-term and long-term disability plans, Worker's Compensation, and sick pay) even though administering these plans requires insight into the health status of employees.

The individual who is the subject of the information must give specific authorization before a covered entity can use protected health information for any reason other than payment, treatment, or health care operations. A covered entity is a health plan, health care clearinghouse, or health care provider that ever transmits health information electronically. PHI means all individually identifiable information that is transmitted or maintained in any form by a covered entity. A fully insured group health plan is not required to issue the Notice of Privacy Practices to its plan participants. The HMO or issuer of the plan has this responsibility. However, a self-insured plan does have to provide the Notice. For people already in the group, notice is required as of the plan's compliance date (and within 60 days after a material revision). New participants get the notice at enrollment. The notice must be written in plain English or otherwise effectively communicate how PHI can be used, and explain when the individual must authorize disclosure of information about him- or herself.

Enforcing this Regulation is the responsibility of the Department of Health and Human Services' Office of Civil Rights, which handles a spectrum of tasks from providing technical guidance and doing compliance reviews to complaint investigations, assessing civil penalties, and making referrals for criminal prosecution.

CHAPTER 27

THE ROLE OF THE COMPUTER IN HR

§ 27.01 INTRODUCTION

Corporate human resource functions have always been number-intensive, from calculating a payroll to preparing reports on the nature of the workforce. Therefore, the HR department was an "early adopter" of all kinds of technology, going as far back as tabulating machines, through mainframe computers using punched cards, to the desktop PC, to today's networked systems. (Ironically, computer networks have something in common with the old-style mainframe with "dumb terminals" linked to it.)

Not only are computers used within the business, and not only are functions such as payroll preparation and tax reporting compliance often outsourced by electronic means, computerized communications continue to gain in importance. The Internet provides vast information and calculation resources for the HR department.

In addition to functions performed on the employer's computer system, functions accessing the Internet and using mobile devices are extremely significant, both for their business potential and for the problems they might create— not least of which is the amount of work time that employees spend on personal computing and social networking. In response to the age of social networking, the NLRB maintains its own Facebook page, YouTube channel, and Twitter feed.

A BYOD ("bring your own device") policy calls for employees to use their own electronic devices rather than using devices provided by the employer, with the company offering information storage. The benefit to the company is reduction in hardware costs and, because employees choose the devices, they do not resent being provided with devices they disfavor. But the policy can also create problems. Employees may want to take the phone number—and contact data— when they leave the company. They might apply for overtime compensation for time spent checking e-mails. If the employer remotely wipes devices belonging to a terminated employee, it is likely to cause ill-will, although perhaps it could be lawful if the employee received advance written notice of this possibility. It is unclear how litigation holds affect employees' personal devices.

The company should determine whether the policy is limited to smartphones or whether tablets are included as well. Employers should inform employees that they will not be reimbursed for lost or damaged devices, or for damage to the device or the employee's data. Some companies provide data plans for BYOD equipment. The policy should require all devices used at work to be password-protected with a strong password. Employees should be warned that they do not have privacy rights in employer information on the devices and that the employer has the right to access the device physically or remotely. Employees should be instructed to report the loss or theft of such a device immediately, and not to permit third parties to use the device. If employees are forbidden to access certain sites (e.g., Facebook or shopping sites) they should also be forbidden to do so on the device during work hours. Anti-harassment policies (e.g., not using work computers to access pornography) should be extended to devices as well.

[Ben H. Bodzy, Lawrence S. Eastwood, and Megan Sutton, *PCBYOD – Bring Your Own Device Policies*, Baker Donelson Bearman Caldwell & Berkowitz (Aug. 23, 2013), available at Lexology.com; Tina A. Syring-Petrocchi, *Five Things To Consider When Creating A Bring Your Own Device (BYOD) Policy*, Barnes & Thornburg LLP (Oct. 14, 2013), available at Lexology.com]

On November 7, 2013 OSHA issued a Notice of Proposed Rulemaking to improve tracking of workplace injuries and illnesses. The rule calls for employers with 250 or more workers to make a quarterly electronic report of the illness and injury data already submitted to OSHA; employers with 20 or more employees in high-risk industries such as construction, nursing facilities, and warehouses will have to submit data annually. The high-risk industry data would be posted on the OSHA site with personal identifying information stripped out. [78 Fed. Reg. 67253 (Nov. 8, 2013); see Jennifer Cerven, *OSHA Develops Plan To Publish Injury And Illness Data Online*, Barnes & Thornburg LLP (Nov. 12, 2013), available at Lexology.com; Heather MacDougall, *OSHA Proposes Major Recordkeeping Change*, Akerman LLP (Nov. 12, 2013), available at Lexology.com; Nickole C. Winnett, *OSHA's Proposed Electronic Recordkeeping Rule*, Jackson Lewis LLP (Nov. 14, 2013), available at Lexology.com]

Another aspect of OSHA's online presence is that whistleblowers who are covered by any of the 22 statutes administered by OSHA, including Sarbanes-Oxley Act § 806, can file complaints online in addition to the existing procedures for mailing the complaint or calling or visiting an OSHA office. Tips and applications for SEC and CFTC rewards under the Dodd-Frank Act can also be submitted online. [<http://www.whistleblowers.gov/complaint_page.html>; see James L. Curtis and Craig B. Simonsen, *OSHA "Launches Online Form" For Filing Whistleblower Complaints*, Seyfarth Shaw LLP (Dec. 6, 2013), available at Lexology.com; John F. Fullerton III, *DOL Announces That Whistleblower Complaints Can Be Filed On-Line*, Epstein Becker Green (Dec. 6, 2013), available at Lexology.com; William Walden, *OSHA Online Retaliation Complaint Form is Live and Freely Available*, Quarles & Brady LLP Labor & Employment Law Update (Dec. 2013) (benefitslink.com)]

§ 27.02 INTERNET RESEARCH

Many Websites specialize in providing information about the HR function. The Society for Human Resources Management (SHRM) has a secure commerce server for online book orders, so credit card orders are safe. [See <http://shrmstore.shrm.org> (no www)] HR Magazine's site has a "conference room" for online chat with other HR professionals. The articles archive for HR Magazine appears at <http://www.shrm.org/hrmagazine/articles> (members only).

Law firm Websites are also an excellent source of up-to-date information about court cases, new tax rulings, and compliance matters.

If you need information about outplacement, or need to find an experienced professional in your area, see the Association of Career Firm's site, <http://www.aocfi.org>. The International Foundation of Benefit Plans can be found at <http://www.ifebp.org>.

The best government sites, such as <http://www.irs.ustreas.gov> are full of useful forms, explanations, and news summaries, as well as offering the full text of new regulations. It is worth scheduling time to regularly review the Pension and Welfare Benefit Administration and Occupational Safety and Health Administration sites to monitor ongoing developments; to see if you want to post an official comment on a proposal or testify at a hearing; or if there are new forms and publications available. The IRS launched its Retirement Plan Navigator in September 2009 to help small businesses choose plans, maintain the tax-qualified status of plans, and use correction programs if necessary. The site provides side-by-side comparisons of plan features of IRAs, 401(k)s, profit-sharing plans, defined benefit plans, and tax-exempt plans. [<http://www.retirementplans.irs.gov>; see Fred Schneyer, *IRS Site Helps Employers Navigate Retirement Plan Waters*, plansponsor.com (Sept. 18, 2009)]

The Department of Labor has an immense bank of information online. Their main site is <http://www.dol.gov>. The Bureau of Labor Statistics reports the relative strengths of various employment sectors and employment cost trends. [See <http://www.bls.gov>] It also disseminates statistics on occupational safety and health. [See <http://www.bls.gov/bls/safety.htm>. OSHA's home page is <http://www.osha.gov>] Federal contracting compliance information is available from the Office of Federal Contract Compliance Programs (OFCCP), <http://www.dol.gov/ofccp/ofcpinfo.htm>.

The DOL has revised its Employment Law Guide, explaining the major laws that it enforces, and helping small businesses to develop wage, benefit, health and safety, and anti-discrimination policies. The update covers increases in minimum wages and FMLA expansions. The guide is a companion to the online FirstStep overview advisor, <dol.gov/elaws/firststep> (accessed Apr. 8, 2014); the law guide is <dol.gov/compliance/guide/index.htm> (accessed Apr. 8, 2014). In May 2010, the DOL launched a new Website, the H-1B Advisor, to assist employers and potential H-1B visa holders in understanding the requirements of the program. [<http://www.dol.gov/elaws/h1b.htm> (accessed Apr. 8, 2014), and a Disability Nondiscrimination Law Advisor (part of the eLaws series) for employers to make sure their policies do not discriminate against persons with disabilities. The Disability Advisor contains a series of questions; the employer's answers generate a list of federal anti-discrimination laws that are likely to apply. [<http://www.dol.gov/elaws/odep.htm> (accessed Apr. 8, 2014)]

The Employee Benefits Security Administration, a subagency of DOL, has its site at <http://www.dol.gov/ebsa>. For Worker's Compensation information, see <http://www.dol.gov/owcp/Regs/unifiedagenda/main.htm> (accessed Apr. 8,

2014). The Wage and Hour Division's Web presence is <http://www.dol.gov/WHD/workers.htm> (accessed Apr. 8, 2014). See <http://www.pbgc.gov> for coverage of the expansion of PBGC information technology. See <http://www.dol/gov/elaws/ERISAFiduciary.htm> (accessed Apr. 8, 2014) for information about ERISA compliance, tools for plan officials, and an overview of the most common compliance errors reported by EBSA.

§ 27.03 RECRUITING VIA THE INTERNET

If your corporation has a Website, it's easy and inexpensive to add an area for posting job opportunities. You can include an electronic form so even candidates who do not have an electronic resume can submit their qualifications. The form can be used for initial screening of applicants.

To an ever increasing extent, performing a Web search on candidates' names is becoming a normal part of recruitment and hiring—for example, to see if inconsistent resumes have been posted to help-wanted sites, or to check out the candidate's blog (which might, for instance, include indiscreet material about the candidate's current employer, or negative comments about a competitor or an industry as a whole). Corporations also establish and update their own blogs or encourage employees to do so.

Federal contractors who accept Internet-based job applications are subject to DOL's Office of Federal Contract Compliance Programs' Final Rule on recordkeeping. The final rule covers jobs for which the contractor accepts expressions of interest via the Internet, e-mail, employer Websites, or resume databanks. Federal contractors are required, wherever possible, to obtain data on the sex, race, and ethnicity of their employees and job applicants—including those who apply over the Internet. An Internet applicant is one who uses the Internet or related technology to submit an expression of interest and who demonstrates at least basic qualifications for the position, who the federal contractor has considered for a particular position, and who never took him- or herself out of consideration for the job before an offer was made. The rule requires federal contractors to maintain records of Internet-based expressions of interest that resulted in the contractor considering the applicant for a particular job (the OFCCP decided it would be too burdensome to make them retain records of non-specific applications). It is acceptable for federal contractors to discard expressions of interest that do not relate to a particular position or that do not meet the contractor's standards for submitting applications. [70 Fed. Reg. 58,945 (Oct. 7, 2005)]

§ 27.04 BENEFITS MANAGEMENT ONLINE

There are many reasons to limit the corporate content that is publicly available on the Internet: Premature disclosure of confidential information could result in loss of privacy, premature release of corporate plans, exposure of trade secrets, securities law violations, or the like. Corporations also generate a tremendous amount of information that is not security-sensitive, but is not of interest outside the organization.

The cost of implementing an intranet depends on the scope of the project, and whether the project requires full-scale programming or can be implemented wholly or partially with off-the-shelf commercial software packages. Another important question is whether the in-house information technology staff can handle the job, or whether a consultant will be needed.

Almost all (86%) employers distribute health plan Summaries of Benefits and Coverage (SBC) electronically. Nearly half (41%) also distribute paper versions, 14% only distribute paper versions. The convenience of electronic distribution increases with the number of separate SBCs the employer must furnish: almost half of employers must produce more than 10 SBCs, more than 25% had to provide 25–100 SBCs, and 6% had to provide more than 100 versions. [Kevin McGuinness, *Many Using Electronic Distribution for SBCs*, plansponsor.com (Apr. 29, 2013)]

§ 27.05 LEGAL IMPLICATIONS OF E-MAIL AND SOCIAL NETWORKING

The benefits of e-mail in providing a simple method of communications are obvious. However, unencrypted e-mail is not secure. It is much more like a postcard that can be read by anybody than it is like a sealed letter—much less a coded message. Merely clicking a "delete" icon does not remove a message completely and permanently from the entire computer system, network, or service provider that offers e-mail service. So a message that is embarrassing or worse (e.g., one involving racial epithets, sexual harassment, or evidence of corporate wrongdoing) can be found by hostile parties—including plaintiffs' lawyers.

In mid-2010, the Supreme Court decided a case involving text messaging on an older technology (pagers). However, the court refrained from making a broad ruling about employees' expectation of privacy in personal text messages sent from the workplace. Instead, the Supreme Court held that it did not violate the Fourth Amendment for the city of Ontario to perform an audit of employees' messages on city-owned pagers to determine if the city should upgrade to a plan giving employees more minutes on their pagers. The plaintiff was a police sergeant who alleged that it was an unlawful search for the city to examine personal messages that he sent on his city-owned pager. Finding that the search of the pagers was legitimate, work-related, and not excessive in scope, the Supreme Court ruled in favor of the city. [*Ontario v. Quon*, 560 U.S. 746 (2010); see Tony Mauro, *Supreme Court Allows Search of Employee's City-Owned Pager,* Nat'l L.J. (June 18, 2010) (law.com)]

If a company provides e-mail access at work, it should inform employees of the company's policies with respect to e-mail. A reasonable e-mail policy might involve

- Disclosure that the company has the right to monitor employee e-mail. [See § 26.06[C] for a discussion of privacy issues] It would be illegal to fire, or otherwise take action against, an employee who uses e-mail to engage in protected concerted activity such as complaining about safety risks. Threatening or inflammatory messages are not protected under labor law, but a direct protest to management certainly would be. Employee-to-employee communications are probably protected unless they actually threaten the harmonious and efficient operation of the business enterprise;
- Restriction of e-mail to business use. Inexpensive software is available to uninstall or disable games on office computers or networks, and to track usage (e.g., to see if gambling or pornographic sites are being accessed). However, although such measures may increase productivity, they must be balanced against the resentment employees may experience;
- No forwarding of copyrighted materials (for example, newspaper stories or cartoons);
- No use of obscene or suggestive language or slurs against any group;
- No discussion of matters that might have legal consequences (e.g., price fixing or industrial espionage);
- Asking employees to think before they send a message if there is anything in the message that they would not want publicized, or that could put the employer in a bad light.

Most employers maintain broad policies that warn employees that their e-mails can be monitored. The warning is usually conveyed in the employee handbook or on a screen displayed when employees log into the e-mail system. However, in practical terms, employers usually worry more about Internet use than e-mail. Software is now available for e-mail monitoring, saving the effort of having the IT department review the messages manually, but few employers use it. Many employers only begin to review e-mail after a problem has emerged, such as an alleged violation of the anti-harassment policy; alleged hate speech; or misuse of confidential or proprietary information. [Shannon Green, *When Should Employers Be Monitoring Employee Email?* Corporate Counsel (Mar. 13, 2013) (law.com)]

In some cases, the employee's use of the employer's e-mail system, or a company-supplied laptop, to communicate with his or her attorney will remove attorney-client privilege from the communications—especially if the employer has a policy of forbidding non-work related e-mails; monitors e-mails, and has warned employees that their communications are subject to examination. However, it is less likely that employers will be granted discovery of communications made using a laptop that was supplied by the employer but is not connected to the employer's computer network. [A. Michael Weber, *E-Discovery Keeps an Eye on the Job*, N.Y.L.J. (Apr. 21, 2008) (law.com)]

The New Jersey Supreme Court ruled that the attorney-client privilege outweighs corporate policy about use of workplace computers. Therefore, a plaintiff suing her employer had a reasonable expectation that e-mails to and from her lawyer using her personal, password-protected Yahoo account would be private even though they were sent on a laptop owned by the company. (Marina Stengart was going to quit her job and sue Loving Care Agency for constructive discharge and hostile work environment.) The court said that even if the company's policy manual had been clearly written to ban any personal use of company computers, and that the employer could read employees' e-mails, the policy would not be enforceable. The court said that although companies can monitor use of their computers to protect their assets, and employees can be disciplined or fired for excessive personal use during work time, there is no need to read the specific contents of employees' privileged personal communications. [*Stengart v. Loving Care Agency Inc.*, 201 N.J. 300 (N.J. 2010); see Michael Booth, *Privilege Trumps Company E-Mail Surveillance*, N.J.L.J. (Apr. 1, 2010) (law.com)]

[A] Social Networking

Employers should draft and publicize social networking policies, information employees that, for example, they can be fired for social networking abuse, and warning them not to divulge confidential or trade secret information in their posts. Employees should be told not to go online during work hours for non-work purposes, and informed how to act if they might be perceived as spokespersons for the company. The policy should also explain the risk of charges of defamation, harassment, discrimination, and invasion of privacy if social networking is misused.

Regulators and securities industry groups seek exemptions from state law so financial firms would receive additional power to examine employees' social media accounts to investigate misuses of personal accounts for fraud. FINRA asked legislatures of about 10 states to alter their proposed legislation. Social media privacy legislation has been passed in California, Illinois, Maryland, Michigan, and Utah; the national Conference of State Legislatures said that since early 2013, social media privacy legislation has been introduced in 35 states. [Jean Eaglesham and Michael Rothfeld, *Wall Street Battles States on Social-Media Protections*, WSJ.com (Apr. 22, 2013)]

New Jersey has a law, signed August 29, 2013, forbidding employers to require employees or job candidates to disclose their social media user names and passwords (although they may ask if the applicant or employee has a private social media account). There is a fine of $1,000 for a first, $2,500 for repeat offenses, assessed by the Commissioner of Labor and Workforce Development. The law does not apply to social media accounts used for business purposes, and employers can lawfully access an applicant's or employee's publicly available social media pages. Similar laws have been passed in Arkansas, California, Illinois, Maryland, New Mexico, Oregon, and Washington. [David K. Reid, *New Jersey Social Media Privacy Bill Signed By Gov. Christie*, Day Pitney LLP (Aug. 30, 2013), available at Lexology.com; Steven Greenhouse, *Employers' Social Media Policies Come Under Regulatory Scrutiny*, NYTimes.com (Jan. 21, 2013)]

Employees' social networking sites can provide information about what they did when they were on sick leave, and of the true nature of their qualifications. For example, Facebook postings can show employees engaging in physical activities contrary to their representations when they applied for FMLA leave. Employees should be put on notice that the employer has the right to monitor communications on the corporate network, but will not read communications that deal with concerted activity (e.g., union-related messages). Employees should also be warned that the corporate code of conduct governing off-work conduct (for example, maintaining confidentiality of trade secrets) applies online as well. [Catherine Dunn, *More Employers Creating Social Media Policies for the Workplace*, Corporate Counsel (Nov. 29, 2012) (law.com).]

The Fourth Circuit treated a Facebook "Like," in this case a deputy sheriff Liking his boss's electoral opponent, as free speech protected by the First Amendment. Clicking the button publishes a substantive statement of liking something—what the court called the Internet equivalent of putting a sign in your front lawn. [*Bland v. Roberts*, 730 F.3d 368 (4th Cir. 2013); see Joe Palazzolo, *Facebook 'Likes' Are Protected by First Amendment*, WSJ.com (Sept. 18, 2013); see Sara H. Jodka, *Fourth Circuit Holds "Liking" A Facebook Page Is Protected Speech In The Public Employment Context. What Does This Mean In The Private Employment Context? Well, It Won't Stop Those Annoying Farmville Or Candy Crush Invitations*, Porter Wright Morris & Arthur LLP (Sept. 19, 2013), available at Lexology.com]

The Tenth Circuit ruled that an employee who charged that she was terminated for using Facebook to report that she was sexually harassed by her supervisor did not satisfy the requirement of reporting harassment so that the employer can correct it. A complicating factor was that the plaintiff initially denied making the post and refused to make a harassment complaint to the HR department. After she admitted making the post, she was terminated for dishonesty, inappropriate behavior, and disrupting the workplace. The Tenth Circuit held that her employer could not be liable for sexual harassment because even if the plaintiff had never denied making the post, it did not comply with the employer's procedure for reporting harassment. [*Debord v. Mercy Health System of Kansas, Inc.*, 737 F.3d 642 (10th Cir. 2013); see Heather L. Sherrod, *Facebook Posts May Not Be Sufficient Notice Of Sexual Harassment Complaints*, Norton Rose Fulbright LLP (Jan. 10, 2014), available at Lexology.com]

Protection of employee communications is by no means infinite. A nurse employed by a hospital posted a tirade to Facebook, that she hated her supervisor and was forced to work on Mother's Day despite taking a 17% pay cut. Several co-workers and a manager who had her friended reported the post to management, and she was fired the next day. She was denied unemployment benefits. The District Court for the Northern District of California ruled that firing her did not violate the CBA or her free speech rights under the California constitution. Her breach of contract claim was dismissed for failure to exhaust the mandatory grievance procedure required by the CBA. Although the plaintiff alleged defects in the union's representation, the district court held that, because she did not allege a breach of the duty of fair representation, she could not use the alleged deficiencies to avoid the grievance procedure. The free speech claim was dismissed, because the precedents she cited were irrelevant: they involved speech in public places. She did not allege protected concerted activity, so there was no NLRA violation. [*Guevarra v. Seton Med. Ctr.*, No. C 13-2267 CW, 2013 U.S. Dist. LEXIS 169849 (N.D. Cal. Dec. 2, 2013); see Keahn N. Morris, *Employer Could Discharge Nurse For Facebook Tirade, Court Finds*, Jackson Lewis PC (Dec. 27, 2013), available at Lexology.com]

A hospital paramedic posted to her Facebook wall that paramedics should have let a white supremacist murderer die after he was shot by guards. The hospital fired her for "deliberate disregard for patient safety." (The plaintiff alleged that the real motivation was retaliation for Union activity.) The hospital learned about the post from a co-worker who was the plaintiff's Facebook friend, who reported it to the hospital. The District Court for the District of New Jersey held that it can violate the Stored Communications Act (SCA) to discipline an employee based on the contents of nonpublic posts to a Facebook wall. However, in this case the hospital was not liable because the co-worker was authorized to view the post and voluntarily disclosed it to the hospital. Non-public Facebook posts are protected by the SCA, but it is lawful for authorized users to access them. [*Ehling v. Monmouth-Ocean Hosp. Serv. Corp.*, 961 F. Supp. 2d 659 (D.N.J. 2013); see Barnes & Thornburg LLP, *Employers May Inadvertently Break The Law When They Discipline Employees For Facebook "Wall" Posts* (Aug. 30, 2013), available at Lexology.com; Philip L. Gordon, *New Jersey Court's Decision Provides Roadmap For Access To Employees' Restricted Social Media Content*, Littler Mendelson (Aug. 27, 2013), available at Lexology.com]

A Massachusetts trial judge held that a LinkedIn profile alerting 500 of the defendant's contacts about her new job was not necessarily solicitation that violated her non-compete agreement; only soliciting or accepting business from her former employer's field of business would break the agreement. [*KNF&T Inc. v. Muller* 31 Mass. L. Rptr. 561 (Mass. Super. Ct. 2013); see Sheri Qualters, *LinkedIn Post Likely Didn't Violate Non-Compete Clause*, Nat'l L.J. (Nov. 4, 2013), available at law.com]

[1] NLRB Rulings

With respect to social media, the NLRB's question is whether the employer's social media policy impairs the protected right of engaging in concerted mutual aid activities. Employer policies must be reasonable. The NLRB also assessed whether the social media activity is concerted (multiple employees act together), whether the activity is protected (i.e., involves workplace terms and conditions), and whether the employee has forfeited protection (e.g., by making maliciously untrue statements or lying to customers about product quality). It is a defense for the employer that the action would have been taken even if there had been no protected concerted activity: for example, there was a valid, nondiscriminatory reason to discipline or terminate the employee. [Michael C. Schmidt, *Deciphering the NLRB's Stance on Social Media Issues*, N.Y.L.J. (Oct. 24, 2011) (law.com). See, e.g., Rebecca Moore, *NLRB Supports Car Dealership Facebook Firing*, plansponsor.com (Oct. 4, 2011)]]

In 2013, the NLRB continued to reject social media policies that it defined as overly broad, but also upheld discipline of employees for inappropriate social media conduct:

- It was unlawful to have a social media rule forbidding all disparaging or defamatory comments about the company, its employees, customers, products or services, and it was unlawful to require company permission for employees to contact the media, make public comments about the company, or discuss it with government agencies (Dish Network Corp).
- A non-disparagement provision that forbade public criticism, ridicule, or disparagement of the company or its products, policies, officers, directors, shareholders, or employees unlawfully interfered with employees' rights under NLRA § 7; within limits, employees are entitled to seek mutual support and criticize their employer, although "mere griping" is not protected (Quicken Loans Inc.).
- It was unlawful to fire three employees who posted Facebook messages criticizing their supervisor for dismissing their fears of working late in a dangerous neighborhood (Design Technology Group LLC).
- However, profane comments about the company and a supervisor in a private group message on Facebook were unprotected (Tasker Healthcare Group). [Baker & McKenzie, *Labor Year In Review: NLRB Targets Non-Unionized Employers And Expands Worker Rights* (Dec. 21, 2013), available at Lexology.com]
- An NLRB ALJ found that it was concerted activity for two employees of a youth center to discuss workplace concerns on Facebook. But, when they were not rehired as a result, the ALJ recommended dismissal of their ULP charge, because comments showing intent to be insubordinate or uncooperative to the employer waived protection under the NLRA, and the remarks could jeopardize program funding and the safety of program participants. [*Richmond Dist. Neighborhood Ctr.*, (Nov. 5, 2013); see Michael L. Stevens and Karen S. Vladeck, *There Are Limits On Social*

Media: Facebook Comments Found Concerted But Not Protected, Arent Fox LLP (Nov. 21, 2013), available at Lexology.com]

A March 2012 Advice Memorandum from the NLRB's Office of the General Counsel points out that social media guidelines are a mandatory bargaining subject. It violates NLRA § 8(a)(1) for an employer to adopt a work rule that reasonably tends to discourage employees from exercising their rights to protected collective activity. Under this standard, Giant Food's social media policy constrained protected activity to the extent that it forbade use of the employer's logo, graphics, and trademarks, and forbade photographing or video-recording the facility. Employees' references to the employer's logo and trademarks are noncommercial and do not interfere with the employer's business use of its trademarks. Employees were not allowed to refer to "non-public information" in their postings; the General Counsel said that this term was so vague that employees might be discouraged from permissible discussions of working conditions. However, it was legitimate for the policy to forbid defaming or discrediting the company's products or services, and it was legitimate to encourage employees to report violations of the policy to management. [*Giant Food LLC*, Cases 05-CA-064793, 05-CA-065187, and 05-CA-064795, <http://www.nlrb.gov/case/05-CA-064793> (Mar. 21, 2012)]

Some employers protest that the NLRB is extending union concepts to non-unionized employees. The NLRB's May 30, 2012 report on social media says that the key question is whether the employer's restrictions can reasonably be interpreted as having a chilling effect on employees' exercise of NLRA § 7 rights—for example, if employees are forbidden to discuss working conditions or criticize the employer. [See Jenna Greene, *NLRB Report on Social Media Highlights Overbroad Employer Restrictions*, The BLT (May 30, 2012) (law.com)]

§ 27.06 FEDERAL RULES ON DIGITAL COMMUNICATIONS

Many of the rules affecting HR functions were drafted before the heyday of the personal computer, when plan administration generated mounds and mounds of paper (but nothing but paper). Two trends coalesced in the 1980s: personal computing and the drive to make government more efficient and reduce unnecessary paperwork. Obviously, the often-proclaimed Paperless Office never arrived, but to an increasing extent, documents are not only being created on computers but also distributed and retained electronically.

Department of Labor regulations [29 C.F.R. § 2560.104b-1] create a safe harbor for using electronic methods of satisfying the obligation to give various notices to government agencies, plan participants, and beneficiaries under the plan. The overriding objective is finding a method that is reasonably calculated to make sure that the information actually gets into the hands of those who are entitled to it.

The electronic communication must use content, format, and style consistent with the requirements for paper documents. When documents are furnished electronically, participants and beneficiaries must also receive a notice (whether hard-copy or electronic) explaining the significance of the document if it is not immediately apparent. Recipients must also be advised that they have the right to request a paper copy of the document. Furthermore, electronic distribution is permitted only for plan participants who have effective computer access at work, and for participants and beneficiaries who have expressly consented (whether electronically or on a paper document) to receiving digital documents. Documents can properly be furnished online only to people who have provided an e-mail address, given affirmative consent, or confirmed consent electronically, in a manner that shows they can effectively access the means the plan will use to communicate the information.

A valid consent requires advance provision of a clear and conspicuous statement (digital or hard-copy) of the kind of documents covered by the consent; that consent can be withdrawn at any time without financial penalty; how to withdraw consent; how to get hard copies of electronic documents; and the hardware and software requirements for accessing digital documents.

The Summary of Benefits and Coverage (SBC) required by the PPACA (see § 18.19[K] can be distributed electronically to plan participants and beneficiaries who are already covered by an EGHP. DOL electronic disclosure requirements must be satisfied. For eligible people who are not yet enrolled (e.g., newly hired employees), the SBC can be distributed electronically in a readily accessible format, but the plan must make free hard copies available on request. If the electronic distribution occurs via a Website, then the employer must send written notice or e-mail to give the URL for the site and tell employees that they can request free hard copies. [Tracey Giddings and Birgit Anne Waidmann, *Administration Issues Final Rules on PPACA Summary of Benefits and Coverage,* PricewaterhouseCooper HRS Insight 12/06 (Feb. 14, 2012) (benefitslink.com)]

The PBGC's Web-based MyPAA (My Plan Administration Account Authentication Records) system was launched in February 2004. Plans can set up an account with the PBGC, which can be used, e.g., to make filings, pay premiums, make the reports of events required under 29 U.S.C. § 1343, or ask the PBGC questions. [71 Fed. Reg. 31077 (June 1, 2006), discussed in Harold J. Ashner, *PBGC Issues Final Rule Mandating E-Filing of Premium Information*, BNA Pension & Benefits Reporter (June 13, 2006) [<http://www.bna.com> (E-filing_BNA061306.pdf). Electronic filing of Form 5500 became mandatory starting with the 2009 plan year. [Seyfarth.com, *Mandatory Electronic Filing of 5500s to Begin in 2010* (Sept. 30, 2009) (benefitslink.com)]

The PBGC required MyPAA users to adopt new, stronger passwords, 10-24 characters long, containing at least one each of uppercase, lowercase, special characters, and numerals. The new password had to be adopted no later than August 1, 2012. [What's New For Practitioners, <http://www.pbgc.gov/prac/whatsnew.html> (June 18, 2012)]

As of January 1, 2010, all Form 5500s and 5500-SFs must be filed with EFAST-2 approved third party software, or e-filed. Schedule Schedule SSA, the Annual Registration Statement for Deferred Vested Participants, cannot be submitted on EFAST2, even for delinquent or amended filings for years before 2009: Form 8955-SSA must be filed with the IRS. Consult the EFAST-2 FAQ to see if you qualify for filing Form 5500-SF electronically. [EBSA, *Annual Return/Report 5500 Series Forms and Instructions* (benefitslink.com); <http://www.dol.gov/ebsa/5500main.html> undated; accessed August 9, 2012]

An employer maintaining a one-participant plan can file Form 5500-EZ on paper with the IRS, or file Form 5500-SF electronically with the DOL. The IRS' online Employee Plans Newsletter published December 20, 2011 says that, as of January 1, 2012, filing of Form 5500-SF will not be publicly disclosed on the DOL Website (previously, some one-participant plans that did not want such disclosure refrained from e-filing). The 5500 and 5500-SF must be electronically signed by the plan administrator or by a preparer who was authorized to sign on behalf of the plan administrator. [SunGard Relius, *New Form 5500 Guidance* (Dec. 22, 2011) (benefitslink.com)]

In mid-2009, the IRS released specifications for using the FIRE (Filing Information Returns Electronically) system for electronic filing of Forms 1098, 1099, 5498, and W-2G for 2009. The specifications appear in Publication 1220. Three new forms were published: Form 3921 (exercise of a qualified Incentive Stock Option under § 422(b); Form 3922 (transfer of stock acquired through an ESOP); and Form 8935, an airline payments report. [CCH Pension and Benefits, *IRS Issues Electronic/Magnetic Media Specs for 1099s* (July 14, 2009) (benefitslink.com)]

Under proposed regulations effective for plan years beginning on or after January 1, 2014, administrators of plans such as 401(k)s would have to file Form 5500 and Form 8955-SSA electronically or on specified magnetic media if the employer files at least 250 returns of any type, including income tax returns, W-2 and 1099 forms, and employment tax returns. The proposals deal with the tax requirements, which are separate from the ERISA reporting requirements. Failure to file electronically when this is mandatory is considered a failure to file, so the penalty is $25/day up to a maximum of $15,000 for Form 5500. According to EBIA, the proposals do not impose significant changes because DOL already requires Forms 5500 and 5500-SF to be e-filed and Form 8955-SSA could already be e-filed with IRS's FIRE system. But the e-filing obligation has been extended to the limited number of 5500-EZ filers who are required to file more than 250 returns a year. [IRS, *Employee Retirement Benefit Plan Returns Required on Magnetic Media*, 78 Fed. Reg. 53704 (Aug. 30, 2013); see EBIA Weekly, *IRS Proposed Regulations Would Require Electronic Filing for Certain Retirement Plan Reporting* (Sept. 5, 2013) (benefitslink.com)]

Commentator Stephen M. Saxon described the DOL rules for electronic disclosure as "both completely antiquated and ridiculously complex"; the problems associated with these rules inspire some sponsors to continue to issue mandatory disclosures in paper form. The DOL has several approaches to electronic communication of ERISA information. Two of them are found in the electronic disclosure safe harbor, one in the preamble to the final regulations on default investment alternatives, one in FAB 2006-3, and the fifth in DOL Technical Release 2011-03R. The Technical Release described two approaches, but one was temporary and expired in May 2011. A general safe harbor is available for any ERISA-required document. Information can be sent digitally to any participant or beneficiary who has affirmatively consented to electronic delivery. Under the 2002 safe harbor for electronic delivery of information to employees who have computer access, the employer must determine which employees use a computer as an integral part of their jobs. They can be notified electronically. Other employees must affirmatively consent to electronic disclosure—even if, in practice, the employer knows that the employees use company computers during work hours and the employer knows their personal e-mail addresses. Saxon says that updating the electronic disclosure rules is not included in DOL's published regulatory agenda, so it will probably not happen in the near future. [Stephen M. Saxon, *Saxon Angle, The Electronic Age* (January 2013) (plansponsor.com)]

T.D. 9294 is the IRS' Final Rule, explaining how, effective January 1, 2007, qualified plans should use electronic means to provide notices to participants and obtain their consent and elections. The rule also applies to notices provided under various welfare benefit plans (accident & health plans; cafeteria plans; educational assistance plans; qualified transportation fringe plans; Archer MSAs; and HSAs). However, T.D. 9294, as an IRS rule, does not apply to ERISA Title I or IV notices (dealing with, e.g., SPDs, COBRA notices, and notices of benefit suspension) because those documents are under DOL or PBGC jurisdiction. [T.D. 9294, RIN 1545-BD68, 4830-01-p, 2006-48 I.R.B. 980; see Fred Schneyer, *IRS Puts Out Final Rule for Electronic Benefit Notices, Elections*, plansponsor.com (Oct. 19, 2006)]

DOL's final rules on fee disclosure require disclosure of three types of plan information: general information, administrative expenses, and individual expenses. If the plan's quarterly benefit statements satisfy the timing requirements, they can be used to provide these disclosures. Participants and beneficiaries must also be given certain investment-related information (fees, expenses, and investment alternatives) in comparative format, no later than the first date they can direct investments and at least once a year afterward. Investment-related information that is not contained in a pension benefit statement can be provided using the DOL electronic disclosure safe-harbor method or its alternative e-mail method, but not under the IRS electronic disclosure rules.

The initial notice to participants must be delivered on paper unless the recipient is part of a group that has had an e-mail address on file and used that address for dealing with the plan in the 12 months before the initial notice. Annual notices must be delivered on paper unless there is evidence that the recipient interacted with the plan electronically during that time. [DOL Technical Release 2011-03, <http://www.dol.gov/EBSA/pdf/tr11-03.pdf> (Sept. 13, 2011); see EBSA

News, *US Department of Labor Issues Interim E-Disclosure Policy Under Participant Fee Disclosure Regulations* (Sept. 13, 2011) (benefitslink.com); EBIA Weekly, *DOL Issues Interim Policy on Electronic Distribution of Participant-Level Fee Disclosures* (Sept. 15, 2011) (benefitslink.com); Prudential Pension Analyst, *DOL Issues Interim Guidance on Electronic Disclosures to Participants* (December 2012) (benefitslink.com). See also Technical Release 2011-03R, revising and restating Technical Release 2011-03: <http://www.dol.gov/ebsa/newsroom/tr11-03r.html>.]

The GAO recommended that the DOL and the Treasury clarify the regulatory requirements for providing pension disclosures electronically. The GAO recommended giving participants more chances to opt out. The GAO said that the Labor and Treasury requirements are somewhat unclear and not always consistent with one another. The default provisions may also limit participant's ability to opt for ongoing paper delivery rather than on a document-by-document basis. [GAO-13-594, *Private Pensions: Revised Electronic Disclosure Rules Could Clarify Use and Better Protect Participant Choice*, <http://www.gao.gov/products/GAO-13-594> (Sept. 2013)]

[A] Data Security

The recession increased the problems caused by leaks of sensitive or confidential corporate information—so much so that some companies assume that they should make public announcements at the same time as distributing information internally, because the information will leak almost instantly. The American Management Association surveyed 586 employees, 14% of whom admitted to sending confidential or potentially embarrassing corporate e-mails to someone outside the company. Employers are protecting themselves with technical fixes, such as software that blocks certain e-mail addresses and scans e-mail attachments to see if sensitive information is included. [Dana Mattioli, *Leaks Grow in World of Blogs*, WSJ.com (July 20, 2009)]

After issuing interim final rules in 2009 [RIN 009-AB56, 75 Fed. Reg. 42740 (Aug. 24, 2009)] and a 2010 Notice of Proposed Rulemaking dealing with privacy, security, and enforcement [RIN 009-AB56, 75 Fed. Reg. 40868 (July 14, 2010)], at the beginning of 2013 HHS' Office of Civil Rights (OCR) published an omnibus restatement of the HIPAA privacy and security rules, reflecting the HITECH Act Amendments. Covered entities and their contractors and subcontractors are subject to civil and criminal penalties for violations of the privacy, security, and breach notification rules. Security breaches must be reported to HHS each year and large-scale breaches must also be reported to the individuals involved and to the news media. Penalties for failure to notify individuals of breach of their PHI and failure to notify the media when required have increased. The penalty ranges between $100 and $50,000 per violation in situations where the covered entity did not know of the violation (and could not have known by exercising reasonable diligence). If there was reasonable cause for the violation and there was no willful neglect, the penalty range is $1,000 to $50,000. Where willful neglect occurred, the penalty range is $10,000–$50,000 if the violation was corrected on a timely basis—and at least $50,000 for offenses of willful neglect that were not timely corrected. However, in each penalty category, there is a cap of $1.5 million on total penalties for all violations of the same provision. The actual penalty imposed within the penalty range for a particular offense depends on factors such as the nature and extent of the violation and the extent of the harm it caused.

This rule makes some changes to conform HIPAA to the Genetic Information Nondiscrimination Act (GINA) Title I (health coverage) and Title II (employment). For example, GINA treats genetic information as health information and health plans must be informed that it is forbidden to use or disclose genetic information for underwriting purposes. (However, the information can be used for underwriting of long-term care insurance.) The final rule is effective March 26, 2013 and covered entities are given until September 23, 2013 to comply. [78 Fed. Reg. 5566 (Jan. 25, 2013); see Cynthia Marcotte Stamer, Solutions Law Press HR & Benefits Update, *OCR Publishes Long-Anticipated Omnibus Restatement of HIPAA Privacy, Security, Breach Notification & Enforcement Rules* (Jan. 13, 2013) (benefitslink.com);]

An HHS Website for reporting security breaches was established in February 2010; since then, the HHS has received an average of 17 breach reports a month, many of them leading to audits.

Security breaches can have serious financial consequences for companies that break the rules: BlueCross BlueShield of Tennessee agreed to pay the HHS $1.5 million to settle HITECH charges about a 2009 data breach, even though there was no indication that the data was misused. Fifty-nine unencrypted hard drives were stolen from a disused call center in Chattanooga; the drives contained protected data, including Social Security numbers and diagnoses, of more than a million BlueCross subscribers. [HHS Website for reporting breaches: <http://www.hhs.gov/ocr/privacy/hipaa/administrative/breachnotificationrule/brinstruction.html>; see Beth Moskow-Schnoll, Jean C. Hemphill, Evan W. Krick, and Edward I. Leeds, *Data Breach Leads to First HITECH Enforcement Settlement,* Ballard Spahr (Mar. 19, 2012) (benefitslink.com); Shannon Green, *$1.5M HHS Data Breach Settlement Is First Under HITECH Law*, Corporate Counsel (Mar. 21, 2012) (law.com)] See § 19.05[F] for more discussion of HIPAA security rules.

It can be difficult to safeguard business data when employees are terminated. The Computer Fraud and Abuse Act (CFAA) gives employers a civil claim against former employees who seek competitive advantage through wrongful use of information from the employer's computer system. The former employee is liable for accessing a protected computer without authorization, or in excess of authorized access, if it is done knowingly and with intent to defraud, as long as the access furthers the intended fraud and the person obtains anything of value. If a civil violation of the CFAA is proven, then the court can award compensatory damages and/or equitable relief such as an injunction. The statute of limitations is two years from the date of the access or the date it was discovered. The CFAA does not define "without authorization," but 18 U.S.C. § 103(e)(6) defines "exceed authorized access" as using permission to access a computer to obtain or alter information in a way that the user is not allowed to do.

Courts have interpreted this definition differently. Some decisions (e.g., *LVRS Holdings LLC v. Brekka,* 581 F.3d 1127 (9th Cir. 2009) narrowly interpret the statute and limit its application to situations in which the person accessing was an outsider who had no permission to access the system at all—so an employee who exceeds his or her authorized access would not be covered.

Employers can protect themselves against data misuse by:

- Setting up a security system that flags unauthorized access to, or use of, data;
- Having new hires sign a confidentiality agreement that specifically references data protection;
- Exploring the technical feasibility of preventing transmission of certain crucial data to PCs or electronic devices;
- Including discussion of what kinds of remote access are permitted in your firm's telecommuting policy;
- Enforcing the information security policy, and impose even-handed discipline on all detected violations of the policy;
- As soon as possible after a resignation or termination, revoking the individual's log-in privileges on your computer system.

[Compare *Intl Airport Ctrs. LLC v. Citrin*, 440 F.3d 418 (7th Cir. 2006) with, e.g., *Shamrock Foods Co. v. Gast*, 535 F. Supp. 2d 962 (D. Ariz. 2008); *Lasco Foods Inc. v. Hall*, 600 F. Supp. 2d 1045 (E.D. Mo. 2009). *United States v. Mitra*, 405 F.3d 492 (2005) defined "computers" very broadly, so that wireless networking stations and cell phones might also be subject to the CFAA.]

In 2012, the Ninth Circuit adopted a very narrow construction of the CFAA. The court held that the federal law does not penalize violations of employer computer policies or Website terms of service. The defendant in this case worked at an executive search firm; the firm accused him of allowing accomplices to access the employer's database to get information that could be used to help the defendant set up a business competing with his ex-employers. The Ninth Circuit majority said that the federal statute does not criminalize exaggerating on dating sites or using work time for personal Internet use. However, the two dissenting judges said that this case was about deliberate fraud on an employer and the statute penalizes actions undertaken with "intent to defraud." [*United States v. Nosal*, 676 F.3d 854 (9th Cir. 2012)] Similarly, the Fourth Circuit ruled in mid-2012 that it did not violate the CFAA for an employee to download proprietary information into his own computer then use it in a presentation to a potential customer—on behalf of a competitor of his ex-employer, three weeks after quitting his job. Although the CFAA does include a civil provision, it does not apply to misappropriation of trade secrets or violating an employer's usage policy at a time when the individual was entitled to access the computer. [*WEC Carolina Energy Solutions LLC v. Miller*, 687 F.3d 199 (4th Cir. 2012)]

The Seventh Circuit permitted the application of the federal Computer Fraud and Abuse Act, and civil penalties, in the case of an ex-employee who maliciously erased files from the ex-employer's computer system when he left to set up his own business. The statute, intended to penalize computer hacking, applies to transmission of computer code with the intention of damaging a computer system. [*International Airports Ctrs. v. Citrin*, 440 F.3d 418 (7th Cir. 2006)]

The California Court of Appeal held that applicability of California Penal Code § 502(c)(5) (disrupting or denying computer services to an authorized user) is not limited to unauthorized hackers; the section can be violated by an employee who locks the employer out of its own system. In this case, a network engineer tried to preserve his job by preventing anyone else from gaining administrative access to his employer's network. He was sentenced to four years in prison and $1.4 million in restitution. [*People v. Childs*, 220 Cal. App. 4th 1079, 164 Cal. Rptr. 3d 287 (Cal. App. 2013); see Harold Brody et al., *Former Employee Was Properly Convicted For Disrupting Employer's Computer System*, Proskauer Rose LLP (Nov. 11, 2013), available at Lexology.com]

CHAPTER 28

WORK-FAMILY ISSUES

§ 28.01 INTRODUCTION

Employees who have children or who have care responsibilities for their parents seek to balance their roles at work and at home. Even employees who do not have family responsibilities seek work-life balance. There are new kinds of families developing (single parents, blended families, grandparents raising grandchildren). Greater involvement of fathers in hands-on child care also increases the demand for FMLA leave or flexible hours for fathers; however, paternity leave has never really caught on. [See Chapter 38]

An inexpensive work-family tool adopted by some companies is an "autonomy day," on which employees can pursue any project they want. Other low-cost options are linking employees with a database of volunteer activities, a site with information for expectant parents; speakers who talk about subjects like wellness and family finance; a temporary change in shift schedule so employees can pick up their children at school; or allowing employees to work in a vegetable garden that provides relaxation as well as fresh food for the cafeteria. [Cali Williams Yost, *Real-Life Examples Of Simple, Low-Cost Work/Life Efforts*, Business Management Daily (May 28, 2013) (benefitslink.com)]

Certiorari has been granted to determine the employer's duty to accommodate pregnant employees who have pregnancy-related restrictions that prevent them from performing essential functions of their jobs. In 2013, the Fourth Circuit ruled that an employer satisfies the Pregnancy Discrimination Act as long as it treats pregnant and non-pregnant workers comparably, and held that it was legitimate for an employer to reserve light duty assignments for workers injured on the job and to deny them to pregnant workers. [*Young v. UPS*, 707 F.3d 437 (4th Cir. 2013), *cert. granted* (July 1, 2014), as No. 12-1226. See Laura J. Maechtlen and Julie G. Yap, *SCOTUS Agrees to Consider Whether Pregnant Workers Must Be Able to Perform the Essential Functions of the Job*, Seyfarth Shaw LLP (July 9, 2014), available at Lexology.com.]

California adopted new laws, SB 299/AB 592 and SB 222/AB210 to enhance insurance and employment protection during pregnancy. SB 299 amends FEHA, effective January 1, 2012, to require employers to provide the same level of insurance benefits during pregnancy-related leave as the employee had before taking leave; employers are permitted to increase benefits during pregnancy. Even employees who are not eligible for FMLA leave may be entitled to continue their health benefits. The California law applies to all employers of five or more employees, versus 50 employees required for FMLA coverage. [Helene Wasserman and Michelle Barrett, *The Stork Has Landed: California Employers Must Maintain and Insurers Must Provide Pregnancy Benefits*, Littler Mendelson (Oct. 19, 2011) (benefitslink.com)]

Effective January 30, 2014, the New York City Human Rights Law has been amended to require employers of four or more employees to provide reasonable accommodation to pregnant workers, although accommodations that impose undue hardship on the employer are not required. Employees must be notified of the new requirements and a workplace poster is mandatory. [Patricia J. Hill, Matthew W. Clarke, and Jeffrey P. Watson, *New York City Employers Required To Provide Reasonable Accommodations To Pregnant Employees*, Smith Gambrell & Russell LLP (Oct. 14, 2013), available at Lexology.com]

Pregnancy discrimination is a focus of the EEOC's Strategic Enforcement Plan for fiscal 2013–2016. In 2012, the EEOC received 3,745 complaints of pregnancy discrimination and resolved a record number of cases, recovering more than $14 million in settlements. In 2013, there was a $20,000 settlement with Reed Pierce's Sportsman's Grill (Southern District of Mississippi). Adventures in Learning Aurora Inc. settled a case in the Northern District of Illinois for $31,000 after forcing the plaintiff to quit her job in the fourth month of pregnancy. A Comfort Inn that fired a pregnant housekeeper settled for $2,500 in back pay and $25,000 in compensatory and punitive damages. In the Northern District of Mississippi, Landau Uniforms paid $80,000 to settle charges of unequal treatment culminating in termination of a pregnant employee. [Lily M. Strumwasser, *Not Without Warning: The EEOC Continues To File Barrages Of Pregnancy Discrimination Lawsuits*, Seyfarth Shaw LLP (Sept. 19, 2013), available at Lexology.com]

In mid-2014, the EEOC released enforcement guidance on pregnancy discrimination, with a Q&A about the guidance and a fact sheet for small business. It was the first time that the EEOC comprehensively updated its rules since the original drafting of the Compliance Manual in 1983. The 2014 guidance says that the PDA applies not only to current pregnancy or lactation, but discrimination based on past or potential pregnancy. The EEOC's position is that pregnant workers who are able to perform their jobs must not be forced to take leave. The employer must provide light duty, alternative assignments, disability leave, or unpaid leave if it does so for employees with non-pregnancy-related needs. The EEOC says that light duty assignments cannot be restricted to workers with job-related injuries, but if employer policy limits the number or duration of light duty assignments, pregnant workers can be subject to the same limits as non-pregnant workers. [*Enforcement Guidance: Pregnancy Discrimination and Related Issues*, <http://www.eeoc.gov/laws/guidance/pregnancy_guidance.cfm> (July 14, 2014); see M. Scott Young, *EEOC Issues Guidance on Pregnancy Discrimination, Including Light Duty Policies*, Thompson Hine (July 17, 2014), available at Lexology.com]

An FMLA interference/retaliation putative class action was allowed to go to trial when the defendant created a "maternity projection chart" to track each female employee's potential for childbearing, based on age, marital status, and maternity status. An employee alleged that she was demoted two levels and told to prove herself in the new job after she took maternity leave. The plaintiffs cited the chart as evidence that the employer considered employee pregnancy a problem, and offered testimony that an executive said that mothers' performance declines after pregnancy and their priorities shift. [*Stotler v. Institute for Integrative Nutrition, et al.*, No. 13-civ-1275, 2013 U.S. Dist. LEXIS 163796 (S.D.N.Y.

Nov. 18, 2013); see Hannesson Murphy, *Creating A "Maternity Projection Chart" Probably Isn't A Good Idea*, Barnes & Thornburg LLP (Nov. 25, 2013), available at Lexology.com]

The National Women's Law Center said that the number of EEOC charges filed by pregnant women has risen almost 50% in the past decade. Claims are usually based on denial of reasonable accommodation such as rest and bathroom breaks or light duty. In 2012, the EEOC recovered over $14 million in pregnancy discrimination settlements. New Jersey became the ninth state requiring reasonable accommodation of pregnant workers; the others are Alaska, California, Connecticut, Hawaii, Illinois, Louisiana, Maryland, and Texas; there are city laws requiring reasonable accommodation in New York City and Philadelphia. [S. Jeanine Conley and Laura Scully, *Pregnant Employees Become The Subject Of Heightened Attention And New Legislation*, Baker & Hostetler LLP (Feb. 18, 2014), available at Lexology.com]

The Maryland law, the Reasonable Accommodations for Disabilities Due to Pregnancy Act requires employers with 15 or more employees to offer reasonable accommodation unless it is an undue hardship. Pregnancy-related disabilities must be treated on a par with other temporary disabilities. Possible accommodations include changing the pregnant employee's job duties, work hours, or work area; transferring her to a less dangerous or strenuous job; or providing mechanical aids. Employers are not required to discharge other employees, create new jobs, or promote pregnant employees to positions for which they are not qualified. The employer must post, and include in the employee handbook, information about the right to accommodation. [Anne E. DeSalvo, *New Maryland Law Requiring Accommodations for Pregnant Employees Becomes Effective October 1, 2013*, Saul Ewing LLP (September 2013) (benefitslink.com); Richard J. Hafets, Lynn A. Clements, and Donna M. Glover, *Maryland Employers To Provide Pregnant Workers With Accommodation Under New Law*, Jackson Lewis LLP (Sept. 24, 2013), available at Lexology.com]

The San Francisco Family Friendly Workplace Ordinance forbids caregiver discrimination. Employees are entitled to request flexible work arrangements to help care for children, family members with serious health conditions, or parents 65 and over. The statute took effect January 1, 2014, covering private employers with 20 or more employees. A flexible arrangement involves changes in the start or end time of a job, job sharing, reduced hours, telecommuting, part-year employment, or changes in work duties. Employers must grant or deny requests in writing; allowable reasons for denial include excessive cost, negative impact on customer or client demands, and lack of work when the employee wants to work. [Margaret Hart Edwards and Jessica Rothenberg, *San Francisco Adopts Ordinance That Prohibits Caregiver Discrimination And Provides Flexible Work Arrangements For Caregivers*, Littler Mendelson (Oct. 23, 2013), available at Lexology.com]

There were decades when the percentage of mothers in the workforce increased—a trend that reversed itself in 2012. In 2012, 29% of women who were mothers of minor children did not hold paid jobs. In 1967, about 49% of mothers of minors were stay-at-home mothers, but the percentage fell until 1999. Some stay-at-home mothers wanted to work but could not find jobs: in 2000, 1% of survey respondents said they stayed at home because they could not find jobs, versus 6% in 2012. About half (51%) of mothers who did not finish high school did not hold paid jobs, whereas 21% of college-graduate mothers were not employed outside the home. [D'Vera Cohn, *After Decades of Decline, a Rise in Stay-at-Home Mothers*, Pew Research Social & Demographic Trends, <http://www.pewsocialtrends.org/2014/04/08/after-decades-of-decline-a-rise-in-stay-at-home-mothers/> (Apr. 8, 2014); see Jess Bidgood, *Number of Mothers in U.S. Who Stay at Home Rises*, NYTimes.com (Apr. 8, 2014)]

A March 2013 report published by Pew Research Social & Demographic Trends shows that between 1965 and 2011, there were major changes in the way working parents handled family and work tasks. As of 2011, approximately 60% of two-parent households with minor children had two working parents. In 1965, the average number of hours mothers spent on paid work was six hours, combined with 32 hours of housework and 10 hours of child care (a total of 51 hours a week). In 1965, fathers spent an average of 42 hours a week on paid work, four hours on housework, and 2.5 hours on child care (total of 49). In 2011, the picture was very different. Mothers averaged 21 hours of paid work, 18 hours of housework, and 14 hours of child care (53 hours total). Fathers averaged 37 hours of paid work, 10 hours of housework, and 7 hours of child care (54 hours total). Mothers' preference for work scheduling has changed significantly. Almost one-third of mothers of children under 18 said in 2012 that they wanted to work full time; in 2007, only 20% said so. More than half of working mothers of children under 18 found work/life balance somewhat or fairly difficult (56%) with 43% found it not difficult or not too difficult. Men found it somewhat easier: there was a 50-50 split between those finding it not difficult or not too difficult, and those finding it somewhat or very difficult. Forty percent of working mothers and one-third of working fathers of children under 18 report feeling constantly rushed. Nearly half (46%) of fathers and 23% of mothers felt that they do not spend enough time with their children—perhaps because, on the average, mothers spend twice as much time each week on child care as fathers do. [Kim Parker and Wendy Wang, *Modern Parenthood: Roles of Moms and Dads Converge as They Balance Work and Family*, <http://www.pewsocialtrends.org/2013/03/14/modern-parenthood-roles-of-moms-and-dads-converge-as-they-balance-work-and-family/> (Mar. 14, 2013)]

Aon Hewitt's latest survey found that 13% of respondent companies offered paid paternity leave. Yahoo gives new fathers eight weeks of paid paternity leave (new mothers can get 16 weeks of paid maternity leave). The Bank of America offers 12 weeks of paid paternity leave, and Ernst & Young offers six weeks. Businesses do not find this to be an expensive benefit—because few fathers take advantage of it. About 85% of new fathers take off some time after their child's birth, but it is usually limited to one or two weeks. A study published in 2012 by the Universities of Virginia and Connecticut found that 69% of mothers but only

12% of fathers accessed paid leave when it was offered. [Jen Wieczner, *88% of Dads Pass on Paid Paternity Leave*, WSJ.com (May 9, 2013); Lauren Weber, *Why Dads Don't Take Paternity Leave*, WSJ.com (June 12, 2013)]

SHRM said that only 15% of companies offer any paid paternity leave at all. Time Warner has been sued by a male CNN reporter charging discrimination against biological fathers because Time Warner gives mothers and adoptive parents 10 weeks of paid leave, but only two weeks of paid leave to biological fathers. [Tara Siegel Bernard, *Standing Up for the Rights of New Fathers*, NYTimes.com (Nov. 8, 2013)]

Concerns have been raised that there are many "off-ramps" for mothers to leave the workforce, but fewer "on-ramps" to return. Charlotte Hanna, who worked at Goldman Sachs' orientation program for new analysts and associates, said that after she returned from her first maternity leave in 2005, Goldman demoted her and made her feel unwelcome in an all-male environment. She was fired in February 2009, a week before she was supposed to return from her second maternity leave. The complaint for her suit filed in the Southern District of New York in 2010 says that she was hired in 1998, became a vice president in 2000, and was well-regarded. She used a program allowing part-time work after maternity leave, but she said she hit a glass ceiling and was systematically excluded from operations and social functions. The complaint alleges that 75% of those selected for termination in her group had recently taken maternity leave.

Her suit was dismissed on November 20, 2010, pursuant to a confidential settlement; terms were not disclosed. [*Hanna v. Goldman Sachs & Co.*, No. 10-02637 (S.D.N.Y. settlement 2010); see Bob Van Voris, *Goldman Sachs Settles Lawsuit Over Pregnancy Bias With Former Vice President*, Bloomberg <http://www.bloomberg.com/news/2010-11-05/goldman-settles-lawsuit-over-pregnancy-bias-with-former-vice-president.html> (Nov. 5, 2012); Jonathan Stempel, *Judge Dismisses "Mommy Track" Lawsuit Against Goldman Sachs*, Insurance Journal, <http://www.insurancejournal.com/news/national/2010/11/05/114640.htm> (Nov. 5, 2010)]

The first lawsuit under Family Responsibilities Discrimination (FRD) was brought in 1971. There were only eight such cases in the 1970s. Between 1986 and 1995, the Hastings College of the Law Center for WorkLife Law found that there were 97 lawsuits alleging discrimination on the basis of family responsibilities. The number rose to 481 cases in the decade 1996–2005. About 93% of FRD plaintiffs are women. Most allege that they suffered discrimination because of their care needs as parents, but some are caregivers for their parents. The largest award to a successful FRD plaintiff was $25 million, but the average award is about $100,000; employees get settlements or win at trial in about half of FRD cases. [The Hastings study is called *Litigating the Maternal Wall: U.S. Lawsuits Charging Discrimination Against Workers with Family Responsibilities*; see Lisa Belkin, *Family Needs in the Legal Balance*, N.Y. Times (July 30, 2006, section 1, p.1) and Fred Schneyer, *Strong Rise Seen in Family Responsibilities Discrimination Suits*, plansponsor.com (July 10, 2006). See also Dee McAree,

"*Sex-Plus*" *Gender Bias Lawsuits Are on the Rise*, Nat'l L.J. (Mar. 14, 2005) (law.com); discussing, e.g., the suit filed in the Southern District of New York by 12 woman employees alleging a pattern of disparate pay and promotions and denial of access to the management development program after they took FMLA leave for child birth: *Velez v. Novartis*, No. 04 Civ. 09194 (GEL). The case was settled in 2010 for $175 million. Grant McCool and Jonathan Stempel, *Novartis in $175 Million Gender Bias Settlement*, Reuters, <http://www.reuters.com/article/2010/07/14/us-novartis-settlement-idUSTRE66D57Z20100714> (July 14, 2010).]

The Center for WorkLife Law, in its report, "Family Responsibilities Discrimination: Litigation Update 2010," said that family responsibility discrimination plaintiffs are much more likely to win their cases than other plaintiffs. Although discrimination plaintiffs overall win less than 30% of their cases, family responsibility discrimination plaintiffs won 50.7% of their cases, sometimes receiving high damages. Lawsuits alleging discrimination against caregivers almost quadrupled between 2000 and 2010.

Out of more than 2,100 caregiver discrimination cases tracked by the Center for WorkLifeLaw, there were four verdicts or settlements over $10 million (two of them were class actions). Twenty-one cases had verdicts or settlements over $1 million, usually because of high punitive damages. The average verdict or settlement was $578,316. Nearly all (88%) of caregiver-discrimination plaintiffs were women, and female plaintiffs won 51.6% of their cases whereas only 41.9% of male plaintiffs were successful. The Center for WorkLifeLaw noted that many cases reflect the "new supervisor syndrome" (which also operates in other types of workplace discrimination cases): the plaintiff was doing fine and receiving adequate accommodations, until the new supervisor canceled the accommodations. Some caregiver discrimination plaintiffs say their work situation deteriorated when they became pregnant with twins or triplets, or when they were expecting a second child, and management decided that they were not committed to their jobs. Some plaintiffs have alleged preemptive elder care discrimination, charging that a supervisor tries to get rid of them before they devote too much time to caring for their parents. [Preventing Discrimination Against Employees with Family Responsibilities: A Model Policy for Employers, <http://www.worklifelaw.org/pubs/Model_Policy_for_Employers.pdf> (accessed Apr. 8, 2014)]

In a case settled in 2009, Rachel Robinson applied for FMLA leave when her mother had a brain tumor. She took 18 days of leave, then a further 10 days—but then was told to "draw a line" between work and caregiving. She was fired three days later; her mother died within less than a month.

Hastings said that five states and 67 localities forbid discrimination against caregivers and there is a move to extend the protection already given to parents to workers with family responsibilities of all kinds. [Paula Span, *When Work Makes You Choose*, NYTimes.com (Sept. 14, 2012)]

The Families and Work Institute says that 20% of families have a child with some significant physical or mental health problem. Data from the Archives of Pediatric and Adolescent Medicine shows the incidence of disabling conditions affecting children and teenagers rose from 2% in 1960 to 7% today.

The federal Maternal and Child Health Bureau says that 30% of parents have to quit their jobs or cut back on working hours if they have a child with a disability.

MetLife found that 29% of parents in this group have made no financial plans for their child's future, less than half have designated a guardian for their child to serve after their own deaths, and close to two thirds experience barriers in getting information they need. Employers can furnish valuable information about, e.g., Medicaid planning, creating trusts to manage the assets of persons incapable of self-care, and tax issues. However, parents in this situation may be afraid to raise the issue, in case they suffer discrimination based on prejudice against persons with disabilities or because of a perception that the company's health plan will become too costly to be afforded. [Sue Shellenbarger, *Employers Begin to Provide Assistance for Parents of Children with Disabilities*, Wall St. J. (Oct. 13, 2005, at D1)

Nor is child care the only issue. People in mid-life are sometimes called the "sandwich generation" because they have responsibilities for aging parents as well as growing children. Work-life programs have gained prominence since 2001, as hard-pressed companies looked for ways to motivate employees without burdening themselves with very high capital obligations.

There are several broad categories of work-life programs:

[A] Paid Leave Requirements

The Organization for Economic Cooperation and Development reported that the United States is exceptional among 37 other countries, as the only one that does not require any paid leave for new mothers. Estonia offers close to two years of paid leave; Hungary and Lithuania offer at least one and a half years of full paid leave. The worldwide median amount of time off at full salary for new mothers is five to six months. Usually the payments are made by the government, sometimes including contributions from employers. Mexico, like the United States, offers 12 weeks of job protection but not paid leave. The median amount of protected leave for mothers is 13 months. There are 25 countries that require paternity leave; except for Ireland, they all require at least some of the leave to be paid. However, in Greece, Luxembourg, the Netherlands, South Korea, Austria, and Hungary, paternity leave is very limited, being guaranteed for one week or less. [Gretchen Livingston, *Among 38 Nations, U.S. Is The Outlier When It Comes To Paid Parental Leave: Pew Research Center* (Dec. 12, 2013) (benefitslink.com)]

According to the Bureau of Labor Statistics (BLS), in 1992–93, 2% of workers had access to paid maternity benefits, 1% to paid paternity benefits; in 2012, 11% of private sector workers were entitled to paid family leave, not necessarily related to childbirth, and 61% of private sector employees had paid sick leave (only 50% did in 1992–93). In 1992–93, the average full-time private sector worker got eight days of vacation after one year of service, versus 10 days in 2012, rising to 18 days (1992–93) or 20 days (2012) after 20 years' service. [2012 data from BLS. See Catherine Rampell, *Paid Vacation's Decline*, NYTimes.com (Sept. 3, 2013)]

It has traditionally been the employer's prerogative to decide whether leave will be paid or unpaid. The FMLA requires employers to grant leave, within limits, when an employee has a serious health condition or cares for a family member who does However, there is no requirement that the employer pay employees who have taken FMLA leave.

An increasing trend is for states and cities to pass laws requiring paid leave for certain health or family events. So far, these programs are funded by payroll taxes on employees so they do not impose a direct financial burden on employers but, nevertheless, it is inconvenient to have to replace the work of employees on leave and to do the paperwork associated with the paid leave program.

In Connecticut, New York City, San Francisco, Portland (Oregon), Jersey City, Newark, New Jersey, and Washington, D.C., at least some workers are entitled to paid sick leave. A federal Healthy Families Act requiring paid sick leave has been proposed several times but never passed. (This is a fast-moving area of the law, so it is only possible to list examples of statutes of this type, not to provide a comprehensive list of all of them.)

Some states (Connecticut, Hawaii, Illinois, New York, Oregon, and Rhode Island) have laws protecting victims of domestic violence in the workplace: e.g., forbidding discrimination and/or requiring time off to make court appearances and otherwise deal with domestic violence. California requires reasonable accommodation, such as changing the employee's telephone number or office location to hinder stalking. [Susan Gross Sholinsky, *Take 5: Views You Can Use: Labor And Employment*, Epstein Becker Green (Nov. 12, 2013), available at Lexology.com] 2013 Colorado legislation, the Family Care Act, expands the reasons for which family leave can be taken. Colorado does not have a state FMLA. Effective August 7, 2013, this statute entitles eligible employees to an additional 12 weeks of unpaid leave per 12 months to care for a civil union or domestic partner who has a serious health condition. [Fisher & Phillips LLP, *Solutions at Work: Colorado Family Care Act To Go Into Effect* (June 11, 2013) (benefitslink.com)]

On January 29, 2014, the mayor of Newark signed an ordinance requiring private employers to provide paid sick time (although if the company has fewer than 10 employees, the employees are entitled to only 24 hours per year of paid sick time). The ordinance generally became effective on May 29, 2014 (or when the CBA in effect on that date expires). Paid sick time accrues at the rate of one hour per 30 hours worked. Employers can be fined up to $1,000 or imprisoned up to 90 days for each infraction, and employees can either complain to the Newark Department of Child and Family Well-Being or sue their employers for violations of the law. [Ebonee Hamilton Lewis and Lauren Marcus, *Newark Follows Jersey City to Enact Paid Sick Time Law*, Littler Mendelson (Mar. 4, 2014) (benefitslink.com)]

As of January 1, 2014, Portland employers must provide sick leave to all employees, including temporary and part-time workers. If the employer has more than five employees in any location, it must provide up to 40 hours a year of paid sick leave. Employees can use accrued sick time on their 90th day of employment, if they have worked for 240 hours in Portland in a calendar year. [Jackson Lewis LLP, *Portland, Oregon, Issues Rules On Paid Leave*, Lexology.com (Oct. 11, 2013)]

Seattle, San Francisco, and Washington, D.C. also require paid sick leave. Under Seattle's Sick/Safe Leave Law, employees who work in Seattle for more than 240 hours in a calendar year are covered. Companies with up to 250 employees must provide one hour of leave for every 40 hours worked; larger companies must provide an hour of leave for every 30 hours worked. "Safe leave" can be used when the workplace is closed for safety reasons or when the employee or close family member is a victim of domestic violence or stalking. Noncompliant employers can be sued, and the city's civil rights office can seek reinstatement, two years' back pay, attorneys' fees, and up to $10,000 for emotional distress damages on behalf of covered employees. [Jackson Lewis LLP Workplace Resource Center, *Seattle's New Paid Leave Law* (Aug. 13, 2012) (benefitslink.com)]

[B] Leave for Military Families

Also note that the National Defense Authorization Act, signed on January 28, 2008, extends the requirements of the FMLA for families of military service members. An employee can use up to 12 weeks of unpaid leave when his or her spouse, child, or parent is called up or is on active duty in the armed forces. If the service member is seriously injured, his or her family member can take up to 26 weeks of FMLA leave to care for the injured service member. [Fred Schneyer, *FMLA Expansion for Military Family Headed to White House Again*, plansponsor.com (Jan. 23, 2008)] The 2008 revision of the FMLA final regulations makes it clear that intermittent or reduced leave can be taken for military family leave. See § 38.01[A]. [Jennifer Haskin, Will, Faegre & Benson LLP, *Managing Intermittent Leave Under the FMLA* (June 18, 2009) (benefitslink.com)]

Military-related FMLA leave was further expanded by the Defense Department Fiscal Year 2010 authorization bill, also known as the National Defense Authorization Act, signed October 28, 2009. Under prior law, an employee covered by the FMLA could take up to 12 weeks of leave in a 12-month period because of a qualifying exigency resulting from the employee's spouse, child, or parent being called to, or serving on, active duty. The expanded entitlement allows a worker whose spouse, parent, or child is a reservist to take FMLA leave for a qualifying exigency arising from deployment to a foreign country on active duty. There is also a new leave right when an employee's spouse, parent, or child who serves in the regular armed forces is deployed to a foreign country. A military caregiver can take up to 26 weeks of leave per 12-month period to care for a parent, spouse, child, or relative to whom the employee is next of kin, when the servicemember is under treatment for a serious injury or illness incurred in the course of service (or that began before active duty but was aggravated by active duty). The same categories of relatives can take leave to care for an ill or injured veteran who was on active duty within the five years before the date of treatment. The Secretary of Labor can issue regulations defining qualifying illness or injury. [Kilpatrick Stockton LLP, *President Obama Signs Legislation Expanding Family and Medical Leave Act* (Oct. 30, 2009) (benefitslink.com)]

Notice 2010-15, 2010-6 I.R.B. 390, provides guidance in question and answer form about the HEART Act of 2008. The survivor of a deceased servicemember can make a tax-free rollover of the military death benefit and life insurance to the survivor's Roth IRA or education savings account. All qualified plans must provide that the survivors of a person who dies on active service must receive whatever additional benefits would have been provided if the servicemember had returned to work and died while employed. [Rebecca Moore, *IRS Provides Guidance on HEART Act*, plansponsor.com (Jan. 10, 2010)]

Final regulations under the National Defense Authorization Act permit 15 (rather than the earlier limit of five) days of rest-and-recuperation FMLA leave to be taken by an eligible employee. [Jeff Nowak, *DOL Issues Final Rule Implementing FMLA Amendments Expanding Military Family Leave and Leave for Airline Flight Crew Members*, Franczek Radelet FMLA Insights (Feb. 7, 2013) (benefitslink.com)]

Some states, e.g., California, Illinois, Indiana, Maine, Minnesota, Nebraska, New York, Rhode Island, and Washington have their own states providing leave rights to the families of servicemembers. [Buck Consultants FYI, *Washington State Expands Employee Leave Entitlements* (May 19, 2008) (benefitslink.com); George P. Kostakos, Stephen T. Melnick, *New Rhode Island Law Grants Military Families Unpaid Leave*, Littler Mendelson Press Releases (July 2008) (benefitslink.com)]

[C] EEOC Guidance on Best Practices About Caregivers

The EEOC defines "best practices" as "proactive measures that go beyond federal nondiscrimination requirements" to remove barriers to equal employment opportunity. In May 2007, the EEOC issued Enforcement Guidance on employers' responsibilities toward workers who are caregivers for family members.

Although discrimination against caregivers is not per se forbidden, the EEOC warns that in some situations, placing an employee caregiver in an unfavorable position could constitute unlawful disparate treatment that violates Title VII or the Americans With Disabilities Act's ban on discrimination for associating with a person with a disability. The EEOC said that the Guidance does not create a new protected category; it explains the EEOC's enforcement priorities when caregiving is an additional element in an allegation of discrimination, and warns against making employment decisions based on stereotypes—e.g., that women, but not men, will have caregiving responsibilities.

The document points out that African-American women are particularly likely to combine paid work and family responsibilities, and lower-income workers are likely to encounter times when they have care responsibilities but cannot afford to hire someone to take care of the child or elder. However, the EEOC notes that there will probably be no violation of Title VII if employment decisions reflect poor or declining work performance and not assumptions or stereotypes—even if the employee's work is sub-par because of caregiving responsibilities. [EEOC Enforcement Guidance: *Unlawful Disparate Treatment of Workers with Caregiving Responsibilities* Number 915.002 <http://www.eeoc.gov/policy/docs/caregiving.html> (May 23, 2007)]

In April 2009, the EEOC followed up with a 13-page document to help employers adopt work-life policies that will assist employees who are responsible for the care of vulnerable children, parents, and other dependents. The EEOC's suggestions include:

- Train managers about laws affecting caregivers, e.g., the ADA, the EPA, the FMLA, and the PDA;
- Train managers about the text and application of your company's work-life policies;
- Include caregiving in your equal employment opportunity policy—with a broad definition of the people for whom your employees might provide care;
- Do not be influenced by stereotypes (e.g., that mothers of small children are not committed to their careers; that men should not take parenting leave); ask male and female applicants the same questions about their family obligations;
- Allow flexible schedules, formal or informal, where this does not impair operations;
- Communicate job openings and promotions equally; do not assume that caregivers will not want to apply for a job with long hours or a lot of travel;

- Help employees maintain their skills while on leave, facilitate return to the workforce, and include them in recruiting efforts;
- If your organization has non-exempt employees who work overtime, distribute overtime in a family-friendly way (e.g., optimize the use of volunteers instead of ordering caregivers to work overtime assignments when they may not have child care or elder care available);
- Reassign duties that pregnant or caregiving employees cannot handle;
- Allow the use of sick leave or personal days for caregiving needs—even if your company is not legally subject to the FMLA or related state laws; allow free use of intermittent leave for very short-range caregiving needs (such as taking a parent to a medical appointment);
- Provide information and referral services for caregivers; provide services through the EAP; and/or host workplace support groups for caregivers;
- Have an effective complaint procedure for caregivers who suffer discrimination;
- Enforce an anti-retaliation policy that protects caregivers.

[EEOC, *Employer Best Practices for Workers with Caregiving Responsibilities*, <http://www.eeoc.gov/policy/docs/caregiver-best-practices.html> (Feb. 19, 2011, accessed Apr. 8, 2014)]

§ 28.02 EMPLOYER-PROVIDED DAY CARE

One option, perhaps the most appreciated by employees, is for the employer to maintain an on-site day care center. Calculating the costs and benefits of running a day care center can be difficult. Initial expenses can be high, but this perk is valuable in recruiting good employees and retaining employees who need quality care for their children.

On-site care is only feasible for large companies—and probably is more workable outside big cities because metropolitan rents are often prohibitive. An employer-sponsored day care center has to be licensed. It will be subject to ongoing inspections. The employer company could become liable if, for example, a child was injured on the premises, or several children developed a contagious illness. The standard Worker's Compensation insurance policy also excludes injuries that occur in an employer-operated day care center.

It can be convenient for the employer to contract out daily operations to an experienced provider of high-quality child care, although this adds further expenses. The employer can also co-sponsor a nearby child care center that offers care to employees of several companies.

However, it is much more common for employers to reimburse employees for some of their child care expenses. [See § 28.07 for a discussion of child care fringe benefits and their tax implications. A smaller-scale program gives employees "I&R" (information and referral) to child care resources, but does not actually furnish services or funds.]

The Home Depot corporate headquarters in Atlanta, where 5,000 employees work, has an on-site child care center with capacity for 278 children. Home Depot employees who work at nearby stores can also use the facility. The day care center, plus a dependent care hotline, are operated by contractor Bright Horizons, which specializes in employer-sponsored on-site child care and back-up care. Home Depot's summer camp accommodates 48 school-age children. Home Depot also has a comprehensive system of back-up care outside the Atlanta area. Employees who have worked for Home Depot for a year or more can get up to 10 days of back-up care for any dependent, including a sick parent. There is a copayment obligation, but it is much lower than the cost of paying for the care out of pocket. [Andrea Davis, *Home Depot Goes Big With Child Care Center*, Employee Benefit News (Sept. 15, 2012) (benefitslink.com)]

The Tax Relief, Unemployment Insurance Reauthorization, and Job Creation Act of 2010, Pub. L. No. 111-312 extends until the end of 2012 the federal tax credit available to employers who furnish child care services. This legislation defines the credit as 25% of qualified child care expenditures and 10% of child care information and referral expenditures. The credit is capped at $150,000 per year.

The American Taxpayer Relief Act of 2012, Pub. L. No. 112-240, extended the availability of this credit once again. The credit is claimed on Form 8882.

§ 28.03 BREAST FEEDING IN THE WORKPLACE

Breast feeding for at least the first six months of life, and preferably a year, is the medical recommendation for newborn babies. So either new mothers must choose bottle feeding; delay their return to work until they are ready to stop breast feeding; or participate in a workplace lactation program that either allows them to feed their babies at the workplace or gives them an appropriate private place to pump and store breast milk. Workplace lactation programs are a good value for employers, because they aid employee retention. Furthermore, breast-fed babies are often healthier than formula-fed babies, so their parents need less time off to deal with babies' illnesses. The demands of a lactation program are modest. Participating employees need a private, reasonably quiet and pleasant place to express breast milk and a refrigerator or cooler to keep it cool, plus a sink to wash up. Typically, employees will need two 30-minute, or three 20-minute, breaks to express milk.

A number of states have laws requiring employers (or employers with a minimum number of employees) to provide lactation support, such as:

- Adequate breaks to express milk;

- A private place that is not a toilet stall to express milk;
- Refrigeration for expressed milk.

Some of these laws impose fines for violation of the requirements; some allow employees to bring private suits to enforce these rights.

At the time of passage of the Patient Protection and Affordable Care Act (PPACA) in March 2010, there were workplace lactation laws in 24 states: Arkansas, California, Colorado, Connecticut, Georgia, Hawaii, Illinois, Indiana, Maine, Minnesota, Mississippi, Montana, New Mexico, New York, North Dakota, Oklahoma, Oregon, Rhode Island, Tennessee, Texas, Vermont, Virginia, Washington, and Wyoming, as well as in the District of Columbia and Puerto Rico. [Sarah Andrews and Mike Ossip, Morgan Lewis LawFlash, *Healthcare Reform Law Requires Reasonable Break Times and Locations for Nursing Mothers*, <http://www.morganlewis.com/pubs/WashGRPP_NursingMothers_LF_07apr10.pdf> (Apr. 7, 2010) (benefitslink.com)]

The PPACA enacts new 29 U.S.C. § 207(r)(1), requiring all employers subject to the FLSA to provide reasonable breaks to express breast milk for mother of infants up to a year old. A private space other than a restroom must be provided. [Rebecca Moore, *What to Do if Employee Prefers Bathroom for Expressing Milk*, plansponsor.com (Oct 29, 2010).]

Companies with fewer than 50 employees are exempt if the requirement would create undue hardship (significant difficulty or expense for the employer). Although in general, the FLSA requires pay for breaks of less than 20 minutes, the new federal requirement says the break time can be either paid or unpaid. The new law does not preempt state laws that give greater protection to employees. The PPACA provision on breast-feeding amends the FLSA, with the result that employees who are exempt under the FLSA (as executives, professionals, administrative workers, outside salespersons, or computer professionals) are not covered. [Sarah Andrews and Mike Ossip, Morgan Lewis LawFlash, *Healthcare Reform Law Requires Reasonable Break Times and Locations for Nursing Mothers*, <http://www.morganlewis.com/pubs/WashGRPP_NursingMothers_LF_07apr10.pdf> (Apr. 7, 2010) (benefitslink.com); Jackson Lewis, *Health Care Reform Act Requires Employers to Provide Breaks for Breastfeeding* (Mar. 26, 2010) (benefitslink.com)] DOL's Wage and Hour Division has a Fact Sheet, *Break Time for Nursing Mothers*. [<http://www.dol.gov/whd/nursingmothers/faqBTNM.htm> (accessed Apr. 8, 2014)] The Fact Sheet says that the FLSA does not require pay for breaks taken to express milk—but if the employer already provides paid breaks, nursing mothers must be allowed to use their paid breaks to express milk. The general FLSA requirement—that employees must be paid for break time unless they are completely free from work duties—continues to apply in this context. The reasonableness of break time depends on the duration and frequency of permitted breaks, and the employer's obligation depends on the individual employee's needs. On an average, DOL expects that two to three breaks will be required in an eight-hour shift, including time to get to the lactation area (which must be located conveniently enough that the mother is not deterred from taking breaks), any waiting time if the area is full, time to get the breast pump and set it up. The employer must provide a place to store the pump and an insulated container to store the milk. The lactation area need not be reserved exclusively for use by nursing employees, as long as it is private and suitable for expressing breast milk.

In general, lactation should be analyzed based on reasonable break time. DOL's suggestion is to allow two to three breaks of 15–20 minutes each per eight-hour shift, but more may be required in individual cases. Lactating employees can use regularly scheduled breaks available to all employees. Employees should not be disciplined for returning late from a break that was used to express milk. The employer should take into account the time needed for the lactating employee to reach the private place, set up and clean equipment, and store milk. [Jennifer G. Hall, *Accommodating The Breastfeeding Employee*, Baker Donelson Bearman Caldwell & Berkowitz PC (Sept. 12, 2013), available at Lexology.com]

In May 2013, the Fifth Circuit became the first Court of Appeals to decide a case about lactation discrimination. The Fifth Circuit treated lactation as a medical condition related to pregnancy and childbirth because it was a physiological state caused by childbirth. The plaintiff did not ask for accommodation of lactation; she alleged that she was fired merely for saying that she wanted to express milk at work. The Fifth Circuit treated this as sex discrimination that violated Title VII. [*EEOC v. Houston Funding II*, 717 F.3d 425 (5th Cir. May 30, 2013). See William Metke, *Fifth Circuit Holds that Lactation Discrimination Violates Title VII* (May 31, 2013) (benefitslink.com).]

The district court for the Northern District of Iowa ruled that, although PPACA amended the FLSA to mandate that employers give employees reasonable time to express breast milk, there is no private right of action against employers for violating that rule. (Aggrieved employees can file a complaint with the Department of Labor, but cannot file a suit because there are no unpaid wages to sue for.) The plaintiff said that she was allowed to express milk in the store office but subsequently found that there was a video camera there. She was not allowed to cover the camera while pumping milk. However, employees can sue for FLSA retaliation if they are disciplined for complaining about the employer's policies: 29 U.S.C. § 115(a)(3), the FLSA anti-retaliation provision, covers informal as well as formal complaints. [*Salz v. Casey's Mktg. Co.*, No. 11-cv-3055 (N.D. Ohio July 19, 2012); see Lawrence E. Dube, Human Resources Report, *Court Tosses PPACA Lactation Rights Claim But Agrees FLSA Barred Employer Retaliation* (July 23, 2012) (benefitslink.com); Michael P. Maslanka, *Can An Employee Sue If An Employer Doesn't Provide A Place To Express Milk?* Work Matters (Aug. 31, 2012) (benefitslink.com)]

In 2011, the IRS reversed its previous holding and said that breast pumps and supplies to assist lactation qualify as medical care under Code § 213(d), because they affect a structure or function of the mother's body. Therefore, they can be deductible medical expenses. If an FSA, MSA, HRA, or HSA reimburses the cost of these items, the employee does not have taxable income. [IRS Ann. 2011-14, 2011-9 I.R.B. 532]

Concluding that working mothers are the fastest-growing segment of the workforce, the National Business Group on Health released a 71-page toolkit, "Investing in Workplace Breastfeeding Programs and Policies," in early 2011. The kit was developed in conjunction with HHS's Office on Women's Health and Health Resources Services Administration's Maternal and Child Health Bureau. The kit has 10 major sections, including the business case for workplace lactation programs, the available options, experience of major employers, and resources for communicating with employees. [<http://www.businessgrouphealth.org/index.cfm>; see Fred Schneyer, *NBGH Offers Employers Help on Nursing Mothers Rules*, plansponsor.com (Feb. 3, 2011)]

DOL's Wage and Hour Division published an employee rights card giving the requirements for break time, a list of resources that can be scanned with a smartphone, and an explanation about how to file a complaint if lactation benefits are denied. The nursing mothers section of the Wage and Hour Division Website has an employee rights card that can be posted to other Websites. [Laura Fortman and Latifa Lyles, *Know Your Rights: Breastfeeding in the Workplace*, <http://www.dol.gov/whd/nursingmothers/nursingmotherscard.htm> (Aug. 30, 2013)]

Not many insurers have in-network lactation consultants available, and the insurer may refer new mothers to pediatricians who do not have specialized expertise. PPACA allows insurers to limit their networks to state-licensed providers—but there are no state licenses for lactation consultants. As a result, because breastfeeding problems must be resolved quickly to establish the mother–infant relationship, many new mothers have to pay out of pocket to get the assistance they need with breastfeeding. [Catherine Saint Louis, *Breast-Feeding Services Lag the Law*, NYTimes.com (Sept. 30, 2013)]

§ 28.04 ADOPTION ASSISTANCE

Under I.R.C. § 137, as amended by EGTRRA, employers can establish a written adoption assistance program, providing benefits for employees who adopt children. More than 100,000 Americans adopt children each year, so the question is whether the company will offer adoption assistance, and whether employees will get paid leave for adoption.

The tax code provides for two types of assistance. Within limits, certain employees can receive adoption assistance payments from their employers without those benefits being subject to income taxes. There is also a tax credit for adopting a child. Under prior law, more favorable tax treatment was extended when the adoptee had special needs, but current law offers the same treatment whether or not the adoptee has special needs.

PPACA increases the maximum adoption credit to $13,170 per child, $1,000 more than the 2009 level, whether or not the adoptee has special needs. This amount will be adjusted for inflation for tax years beginning after December 31, 2010. The adoption credit has also been made a refundable credit (i.e., if the credit reduces the taxpayer's tax liability below zero, he or she can receive a tax refund).

The 2013 adoption credit, whether or not the child has special needs, is limited to $12,970. It phases out between modified Adjusted Gross Income of $194,850 and $234,580. These figures also apply to adoption assistance programs. [Rev. Proc. 2013-15, 2013-5 I.R.B. 444] Form 8839, which previously had to be filed on paper, can now be e-filed. For 2013, taxpayers can carry the credit forward from 2012 or to 2014; the credit was a refundable one until 2012. [EBIA Weekly Archives, *IRS Releases 2013 Form 8839 (Qualified Adoption Expenses) and Instructions* (Jan. 2, 2014) (benefitslink.com)]

The 2014 adoption credit is $13,190, phasing out between modified AGI of $197,880–$237,880. [Rev. Proc. 2013-35, 2013-47 I.R.B. 537]

Adoption assistance can be offered under a cafeteria plan—a structure that provides tax benefits for employees with no direct cash outlay by the employer. Adoption assistance programs provided to members of the armed forces are automatically treated as qualified, even if they would not otherwise satisfy the § 137 rules. But illegal adoptions, adoptions involving surrogate mothers, adoption of a stepchild, or adoption of an adult do not qualify under § 137.

§ 28.05 CORPORATE ELDER CARE ACTIVITIES

Everybody knows that the U.S. senior citizen population is growing, and soon the huge Baby Boom generation will reach retirement age. The vast majority of care provided to assist elderly people with their illnesses and limitations imposed by aging is unpaid, informal care from family members and friends.

A survey by Coupon Cabin shows that 26% of older baby boomers support adult children financially or the children live with them. Over one-fifth (21%) have supported aging parents financially, and 18% have elderly parents living with them. Close to half (42%) of baby boomers postponed retirement for financial reasons. [Rebecca Moore, *Family Pressures Thwart Boomers' Retirement Plans*, plansponsor.com (Feb. 20, 2013)]

Bankers Life and Casualty reported in 2013 that nearly all baby boomers who cared for a parent or spouse (88%) found that the experience was more difficult than they expected; 34% said it cost more financially, 33% experienced more relationship impact, 57% needed more emotional strength, and 52% said it took more time than they expected. Forty percent of middle-income ($25,000–$75,000 household income) baby boomers have been caregivers—77% of them caring for a parent, the rest for a spouse with a disability. Forty-four percent of women and 32% of men in this cohort report having been caregivers. [Bankers Life & Casualty Co.

Center for a Secure Retirement, *Retirement Care Planning: The Middle-Income Boomer Perspective*, <http://www.centerforasecureretirement.com/media/139741/retirement-care-study.pdf> (Aug. 2013); see Kevin McGuinness, *How Adult Caregiving Can Impact Retirement*, plansponsor.com (Aug. 27, 2013)]

A recent study in the Journal of Applied Gerontology finds that caregiving has an adverse impact on working women, and female caregivers are less likely to be in the labor force than non-caregivers, but caregiving does not have an impact on men's employment status. For people aged 50–61, the 2004 Health and Retirement Study showed that about one-third were family caregivers: 4% caring for a spouse, 15% for a grandchild, and 20% for a parent (including some who cared for multiple family members). For a parent or grandchild, caregiving was defined as at least 100 hours over a two-year period (with no time limit applied for spousal caregivers). In this sample, 7% of women helped their parents with personal needs, versus 3.6% of men. About 16% of men and 20% of women helped their parents with chores, errands, and transportation. Most respondents were in the labor force (working; unemployed but looking for work; recently went on sick leave or were laid off). But women were significantly less likely to be in the workforce if they provided personal care or were caregivers for more than one person. Men's caregiving did not relate to their employment status. (This is an older study, so post-recession patterns might be different.) A longitudinal study shows that caregiving does cause women to withdraw from the workforce, and their poverty rate was already double that for men. [Paula Span, *Work, Women and Caregiving*, NYTimes.com (Nov. 21, 2013)]

Federal legislation, the National Alzheimer's Project Act, Pub. L. No. 111-375, calls for the creation of a national strategic plan to fight Alzheimer's Disease. The law sets up an advisory council from all federal agencies dealing with health, science, and aging, as well as a coordinated national plan to improve early diagnosis and coordination of care, and to research new treatments. [Pam Belluck, *Caring for the Patient With Alzheimer's*, NYTimes.com (Jan. 2, 2011)]

In early 2012, there were an estimated 43 million caregivers taking care of persons who are aged 50 and older; almost a quarter of the caregivers reported difficulty in coordinating care and combining it with work. The National Alliance for Caregiving's June 2011 analysis of data from the U.S. Health and Retirement Study estimates that caregivers age 50 and over sacrifice a lifetime average of $303,880 in wages, pensions, and Social Security benefits (because quitting a job or reducing hours also affects pensions and Social Security benefits). The National Alliance says that, because caring for a person with Alzheimer's Disease is so stressful, being an Alzheimer's caregiver can increase the caregiver's own health bills by an average of $4,766 a year—which means that these caregivers also lose time at work for their own health needs.

Genworth Financial and AARP introduced a new service for AARP members: families of older adults suffering from dementia and other illnesses can assess needs and develop a care plan online, on the phone, or in person with a registered nurse. The fees for the program depend on which services are used, starting at $12.99 for six months of online access, through $149 for a phone assessment, service plan, plus six months' online access, to $489 for an in-home visit. The "service finder" option, giving local information and quality ratings, negotiating discounts for participants, and coordinating the start of care costs $295 over the telephone, $665 in person.

Employees who do not consider themselves caregivers will not access specialized services, so one important role the HR department can play is helping employees recognize that they are caregivers; the realization often comes only after they have been engaged in caregiving for a while as occasional small tasks increase to a major commitment. [Carol Harnett, Human Resource Executive Online, *Caring for the Caregivers* (Feb. 13, 2012) (benefitslink.com)]

§ 28.06 THE CORPORATE ELDER CARE ROLE

One problem with corporate elder care efforts is that they often use a child-care template that is not very effective—child care doesn't require tangling with the Medicare Part D labyrinth, for example! Another problem is that, in a time of soaring benefit costs, corporations are far more willing to provide low-cost I&R than more costly benefits such as paying for geriatric care management or offering paid leave to employees with elder care problems. The I&R system could be limited in scope and could be poorly edited, so that obsolete listings remain, or poor-quality providers are not eliminated. Even if the I&R system is excellent, employees still face a lot of hard work in creating and managing the elder care plan.

A 2010 article lists 10 tips for helping employees with their eldercare problems:

1. Encourage employees over age 40 to talk to their parents about elder planning, including discussing their parents' medical and financial information;
2. Link employees to community resources, such as the Area Agency on Aging and social service agencies;
3. Have books, tapes, etc. on elder care on hand and available as resources;
4. Inform employees about financial and health care proxies;
5. Remind employees that a child assisting parents with financial matters should know the parents' bank accounts, online banking passwords, insurance, etc.;
6. Plan for long-term care, possibly including long-term care insurance in the plan—especially if the employer offers an LTCI plan (see § 21.03) LTCI;

7. Support caregivers by offering counseling or other resources;
8. Encourage employees to take advantage of respite options;
9. Maintain policies and procedures for dealing with caregiving-based absenteeism;
10. Involve the EAP's care managers or private Geriatric Care Managers—especially for long-distance caregivers. [Carolyn Rosenblatt, *10 Tips for Helping Employees With Aging Parents*, workforce.com (April 2010) (benefitslink.com)]

Under an I&R plan, the HR department, Employee Assistance Program, or other relevant department maintains listings of nursing homes, home health agencies, government agencies for the aging, and other resources.

Other elder care resources that employers can provide include:

- Seminars about relevant topics such as Medicare and Medicaid;
- Support groups for caregivers;
- Hotlines giving elder care information;
- Subsidized phone consultations with resource or elder care experts (including those in other geographic areas, where employees' relatives live);
- Directories and other publications;
- Caregiver fairs, providing exhibits from public agencies as well as voluntary organizations and for-profit service vendors;
- Counseling from a psychologist or clinical social worker;
- Subsidies for adult day care for the parent;
- Respite care;
- Emergency care (including care in the home of the elderly person);
- Paratransit, such as wheelchair-accessible vans, to provide transportation to medical appointments and other trips that would otherwise require the employee's services as driver;
- Subsidizing the cost of pagers that the parent can use to contact the employee in an emergency;
- Case management—services of social workers or geriatric care managers (GCMs), who advise the employee about creating and managing a complete elder care plan (The employer could pay care managers to provide in-home assessments of the care needs of employees' elderly relatives; the care manager produces a written report and research recommendations, saving employees a lot of research time. Ceridian

Lifeworks estimates that employers can save three dollars for every dollar spent on a program like this.);

- "Elder-proofing" services to make a senior citizen's home safer;
- Monthly or other regularly scheduled seminars for caregiver employees;
- Special outreach efforts during May (Older Americans Month) and October (National Caregivers Month);
- Discounts on eldercare-related products such as incontinence supplies and nutritional supplements;
- An in-house elder care coordinator (especially if the company has a large workforce, or a workforce with a preponderance of middle-aged and older people who can be expected to have elder care needs);
- Adding elderly dependent parents to the coverage of dependent care accounts.

For the unionized workplace, see the AFL-CIO's worksheet, "Bargaining for Eldercare," available at <http://www.aflcio.com>.

In March 2012, the National Alliance for Caregiving published a report on *Best Practices in Workplace Eldercare,* <http://www.caregiving.org/pdf/research/BestPracticesEldercareFINAL.pdf>. The authors are Donna L. Wagner, Andrea Lindemer, Kelly Niles Yokum, and Mary DeFreest. This report says that the pioneering model for corporate eldercare was the same "resource and referral" model already in use for child care. In 1997, 23% of the employers surveyed used this model. As the 1990s ended, employers began to innovate, adding interventions tailored to individual needs—for example, providing access to elder law attorneys and geriatric care managers. More caregivers gained access to flexible schedules. There were some experiments with on-site support groups for employees, and even adult day care centers in the workplace, but the experiments were seldom used and were not cost-effective.

This report cites the SHRM for the proposition that corporate eldercare activities have declined significantly: in 2007, 22% of employers surveyed offered eldercare referrals, but only 9% did in 2011. In 2007, one-third of employers offered paid family leave; only one-quarter did in 2011.

Hundreds of companies, including Home Depot, Hewlett-Packard, and Yahoo, with millions of employees, offer backup elder care. The mechanism is for the employer to subscribe to a call center, which sends a qualified aide to the elder. The aides are trained and subject to background checks. Typically, the employee can use the service for 10–20 days, paying about $6 an hour for the service, with the company assuming the rest of the cost. Bright Horizons and Care.com are the two largest suppliers of backup elder care. Care.com also offers care planning by licensed social workers, paid for by employers. [Paula Span, *A Way to Stay on the Job*, NYTimes.com (Dec. 18, 2013)]

The American Association of Long Term Care Insurance reported that in 2013, the industry paid almost $7.5 billion in claims to 273,000 people, up 13%. Almost all policies are individual, although employer-sponsored plans used to have about one-third of the market, a share that has steadily fallen. Genworth is the only company that continues to focus on the employer-sponsored market, covering about 270,000 federal employees as well as the employees of CalPERS. Transamerica Life Ins also sells group policies. [Jill Cornfield, *Will Employers Respond to Long-Term Care Concerns?*, Plansponsor.com (Feb. 6, 2014)]

The Health Insurance Portability and Accountability Act (HIPAA) of 1996 [Pub. L. No. 104–191] cleared up some previously murky tax questions. It enacted Code § 7702B, which provides for tax deductions for some LTCI purchasers. In effect, HIPAA places "qualified" long-term care insurance plans on the same footing as Accident & Health (A&H) plans, so the employer will be entitled to a tax deduction (if it does contribute to the premiums) and employees will not have taxable income on account of employer contributions. But HIPAA also makes it clear that LTCI cannot be provided through either a cafeteria plan or a flexible spending account.

Rev. Proc. 2013-35, 2013-47 I.R.B. 537 defines the qualified long-term care insurance policy premiums that can be deducted for 2014 by individual taxpayers, ranging from $370 a year for people who have not reached age 40 to $4,660 for those who are 70 years or older. Up to $330 a day in benefits from a qualified policy can be received tax-free.

§ 28.07 DEPENDENT CARE ASSISTANCE PLANS

The Internal Revenue Code recognizes, and gives favorable tax treatment to, plans under which the employer makes direct payments to provide dependent care to employees, or the employer reimburses employees for certain dependent care expenses. [I.R.C. § 129] The employer is not obligated to pre-fund the plan. It can pay benefits as they arise, out of current income, with no need to maintain a separate account. However, the employer is required to provide reasonable notice to eligible employees that the program is in existence and how it operates.

Employees do not have taxable income because of participation in an I.R.C. § 129 plan. However, the plan cannot pay more for dependent care than the employee earns. (In other words, the plan can't be set up as a perk for employees who are, in essence, on parenthood leave and earn very little.) Furthermore, in effect the plan only assists employees who are single parents, or who are part of a two-career couple, because the employee will have taxable income if the I.R.C. § 129 benefits exceed the income of the employee's spouse, unless that spouse is a full-time student or disabled.

In addition to these limitations, the maximum employer contribution to an I.R.C. § 129 plan that can be excluded from income is $5,000 per employee. This is further reduced to $2,500 in the case of married employees who file separate returns. The § 129 amounts are not indexed for inflation, so those numbers remain current.

For this purpose, dependent care expenses are household services and other expenses that are incurred to permit the employee to hold a job outside the home. In the I.R.C. § 129 context, "dependents" means dependent children under age 15, or a spouse or other dependent (e.g., an aging parent) who is physically or mentally incapable of self-care.

The Code defines a qualified dependent care assistance plan as a written plan for the exclusive benefit of employees, subject to a classification created by the employer but approved as nondiscriminatory by the IRS. To be considered nondiscriminatory, not more than 25% of the contributions to the plan or benefits received from the plan may relate to shareholders, 5% owners, or their families. The average benefits provided under the plan to employees who are not highly compensated must be 55% or more of those provided to highly compensated employees.

If the plan fails to be qualified for this reason, then HCEs (but not other employees) will have taxable income as a result of plan participation. Every year, by January 31, employees must be given a written report of the amounts paid or expenses incurred by the plan for that employee's dependent care in the previous year. An employer-provided day care center is deemed to be a welfare benefit plan, but a dependent care plan that involves reimbursement of employees' dependent care expenses is not.

Dependent-care plans are linked to the Code provisions for a dependent care credit that taxpayers can take. The credit is a sliding-scale percentage (a higher percentage for lower-income people) of qualifying dependent care expenses up to a maximum. The Child and Dependent Care Tax Credit was extended through December 31, 2012 by the Tax Relief, Unemployment Insurance Reauthorization, and Job Creation Act of 2010 (Pub. L. No. 111-312). It was still listed as available by the IRS Website on December 12, 2013, <http://www.irs.gov/taxtopics/tc602.html> (Dec. 12, 2013).

CHAPTER 29
DIVERSITY IN THE WORKPLACE

§ 29.01 INTRODUCTION

It can no longer be assumed that all employees in an organization will be young, able-bodied, Anglo-Saxon males. Greater diversity within a workplace allows recruitment of the best available talent and the widest variety of viewpoints and inputs—but also creates potential for misunderstanding and conflict among employees.

The HR department's mission is to promote efficiency and cooperation—not to eliminate differences or even prejudices. A company's workforce doesn't have to worship together, enjoy the same sporting events, celebrate the same holidays, or even like each other. They do have to understand the factors shaping other peoples' behavior, strive to avoid offending others, be tolerant of unintended offensive remarks and actions, and work together harmoniously and productively.

The Human Rights Campaign, which published its first Corporate Equality Index in 2002, finds that the corporate world (especially law firms and large banks) has become much more gay-friendly over the course of the decade. In the 2002 edition, 13 businesses out of 319 had a perfect score for equal treatment policies about sexual orientation. Since then, more criteria have been added, resulting in 190 out of 636 businesses (including 55 law firms and 22 financial services companies) earning a perfect score. Most participants scored 80% or more, with policies forbidding sexual-orientation and gender identity discrimination and providing benefits for domestic partners. [Tiffany Hsu, *Study: Workplace Friendlier to Gays*, Los Angeles Times (Dec. 12, 2011) (benefitslink.com)]

Exxon Mobil ranks last in the Human Rights Campaign Corporate Equality Index for the Fortune 1000. For 14 years in a row, including sexual orientation in the company's official EEO statement has been on the agenda at its annual shareholder meeting—and has lost every time, although it has obtained more than one-third of the votes. The Human Rights Campaign says that 88% of the Fortune 500 have written nondiscrimination policies on the basis of sexual orientation. Mobil Oil had anti-discrimination policies and covered same-sex partners, but Exxon rescinded those policies when it acquired Mobil in 1999, and did the same when it acquired XTO Energy in 2009. [James B. Stewart, *Exxon Defies Calls to Add Gays to Anti-Bias Policy*, NYTimes.com (May 24, 2013)]

There are 54 million persons with disabilities—the largest minority group in the United States, but the DOL says that only 22% of working-age persons with a disability are employed, whereas 70% of working-age non-disabled persons are employed. A special advertising section in the N.Y. Times in Spring 2010 profiles New Jersey organizations serving the employment needs of persons with disabilities.

Hire Disability Solutions (West Nyack, New Jersey) offers training, staffing, and recruitment and connecting national employers with appropriate candidates.

EmployME! Is a public-private partnership sponsored by the New Jersey Institute of Technology to train adults with physical disabilities for information technology jobs. Candidates are trained for 18 weeks in classrooms equipped with assistive technology and, after training, get placement assistance and individual job coaching. EmployME! Can be reached at (800) 624-9850.

The Think Beyond the Label campaign, <http://www.thinkbeyondthelabel.com>, (accessed Apr. 8, 2014) is a 38-state collaboration with Medicare Infrastructure Grants to raise awareness of the business case for small- and medium-sized businesses to hire people with disabilities. The Website contains information about hiring people with disabilities.

Rutgers, the state university of New Jersey, maintains several research organizations on disability employment issues, including the John J. Heldrich Center for Workforce Development, <http://www.heldrich.rutgers.edu>, which studies workplace best practices and offers research assistance to industry. The Heldrich Center set up the National Technical Assistance and Research Center to Promote Leadership for Increasing Employment and Economic Independence of Adults With Disabilities, which is working with the states of Connecticut, Maryland, and Massachusetts to create state models for creating jobs for persons with disabilities. [Special advertising section, *Diversity & Disability Hiring*, N.Y. Times, Mar. 21, 2010, Business p. 10]

[A] Federal Agency Diversity Standards

Federal government procurement is a major driver of the economy, so standards for federal contractors, as enforced by the Office of Federal Contract Compliance Programs (OFCCP), are significant for businesses that hold federal contracts or are subcontractors of federal contractors.

The OFCCP published a final rule in mid-2013, implementing the Vietnam Era Veterans' Readjustment Assistance Act (VEVRAA) and Rehabilitation Act, § 503. The rule imposes new requirements for federal contractors' affirmative action plans. It also adds a requirement for self-identification as a veteran or person with a disability, new requirements for job listings, changes in the wording of the EEO clause, and additional recordkeeping requirements. Under the final rule, federal contractors that already had an obligation to develop written affirmative action plans are now required to set hiring benchmarks for protected veterans and a hiring goal for Qualified Individuals With Disabilities (QIWDs). Veteran hiring can be compared to a benchmark of the percentage of veterans in the civilian labor force, as set out in the OFCCP Website's benchmark database. The employer can also set its own benchmark, based on the average percentage of veterans in the state's labor force; the number of veterans participating in the state's employment service delivery system; applicant and hiring ratios for the previous year; and the contractor's conclusion about the effectiveness of its outreach and recruitment efforts. The latest Rehabilitation Act regulations set a goal of 7% of each job group in federal contractors' workforces to be QIWDs. If the actual percentage in a work group is lower, the employer must determine if there are impediments to equal employment, and carry out a corrective program. The employer is required to invite covered veterans and QIWDs to self-identify after they have been hired and before starting work. The final rules add a new opportunity to self-identify before a job offer is made, so the contractor can calculate its percentage of veterans and disabled applicants. The invitation to self-identify can be included in application materials, or with the invitation already used to gather information about gender, ethnicity, and race. The 2013 regulation requires contractors to perform a new disability survey in their workforce every five years. Under VEVRAA, federal contractors must keep records of the number of applicants who are protected veterans; the number of job openings; number of applicants for all jobs; and number of jobs filled. Contractors must also keep records about their outreach and recruitment efforts. The Rehabilitation Act regulations require similar documentation of applications, jobs, and hiring. Job listings posted by federal contractors must indicate that they are federal contractors—e.g., by including "VEVRAA Federal Contractor" in the listing. Subcontracts must include an EEO clause—e.g., by citing 41 C.F.R. § 60-300.5(a) and adding, in bold type, "This contractor and subcontractor shall abide by the requirements of 41 C.F.R. § 60-300.5(a). This regulation prohibits discrimination against qualified individuals on the basis of disability, and requires affirmative action by covered prime contractors and subcontractors to employ and advance in employment qualified individuals with disabilities." [Winston & Strawn LLP, *OFCCP Announces Final Rule On Veterans And Employees With Disabilities*, Lexology.com (Aug. 29, 2013)]

President Obama signed an executive order on July 21, 2014. The order prohibits discrimination by federal contractors on the basis of lesbian, bisexual, or transgender status. There is no exemption for religious employers. [Peter Baker, *Obama Calls for a Ban on Job Bias Against Gays*, N.Y. Times, July 21, 2014, *available at* NYTimes.com]

The OFCCP is not the only federal agency concerned with diversity. On October 23, 2013, the Office of the Comptroller of the Currency, Federal Reserve Board, Federal Deposit Insurance Corporation, National Credit Union Administration, Consumer Finance Protection Board, and SEC jointly proposed standards for diversity policies and practices in the entities that they regulate. Section 342 of the Dodd-Frank Act requires each of these agencies to have an Office of Minority and Women Inclusion and to develop diversity standards. The agencies proposed uniform standards in four areas: 1) organizational commitment to diversity and inclusion; 2) employment practices; 3) diversity in procurement and supplier relations; and 4) transparency about these issues. The standards ask businesses to carry out voluntary self-assessments and make voluntary disclosures of the results to the credit-supervising agencies and the public. Organizations should consider diversity and inclusion in their strategies for recruiting, hiring, and promotion, and the policy should involve senior management. Financial organizations should be proactive about seeking diverse candidates for management and board members such as outreach to women's and minority organizations, conferences, and events. Women- and minority-owned businesses should be given a fair chance to compete, and organizations should review their record of diversity in procurement. [Richard M. Alexander et al., *Financial Regulators Propose Joint Standards For Assessing Diversity Policies And Practices*, Arnold & Porter LLP (Oct. 30, 2013), available at Lexology.com]

§ 29.02 THE GLASS CEILING

Unfortunately, some people are actively and consciously hostile to those different from themselves. They engage in whatever discriminatory actions they think they can get away with. However, overt hatred and resentment are not the only factors that block full advancement for qualified women and members of minority groups. There are other, subtler forces at work, sometimes affecting people who on a conscious level are objective and tolerant.

The prejudices of the past cast a long shadow. If law and business schools used to discriminate against minorities and women, then the supply of members of these groups with professional degrees, and with decades of business experience, will be limited. If a company hardly ever recruits women or members of minority groups for its training program, and if its policy is to promote from within, then it will look to its (overwhelmingly white male) middle managers when it's time to fill senior posts.

These subtler barriers to advancement are sometimes called the "glass ceiling": Advancement up to a point is reasonably easy, but there are invisible barriers to achieving the really top jobs. See the reports of a federal commission convened under the Glass Ceiling Act, a provision of the Civil Rights Act of 1999. [Pub. L. No. 102-166]

According to the main report, "Many judgments on hiring and promotion are made on the basis of a look, the shape of a body, or the color of skin." [*A Solid Investment: Making Full Use of the Nation's Human Capital*, <http://digitalcommons.ilr.cornell.edu/cgi/viewcontent.cgi?article=1117&context=key_workplace>]

Although the Glass Ceiling report acknowledges that some factors (such as educational systems and social attitudes) are beyond corporate control, the report identifies some factors that business can control:

- Whether recruitment is narrow or broad-based;
- Extent of outreach efforts;
- Degree to which new hires are assigned to marginal areas or staff jobs that have less promotion potential than more central, line jobs;
- Presence or absence of mentors;

- Whether good performance is rewarded with access to training and prime assignments;
- Access to social events and informal networks (e.g., social and sporting events);
- Help and support from colleagues, versus hostility and demeaning treatment;
- Whether evaluations are objective or merely reflect prejudices.

Certain characteristics are shared by successful diversity programs:

- The CEO actively supports the program;
- The program is comprehensive and inclusive;
- The program has a genuine goal of advancing the most talented people, whatever their background;
- Results are reviewed, and managers are accountable for results;
- The company has long-range relationships with community organizations, not a single effort that is quickly abandoned;
- Recruitment is genuinely diverse;
- Recruiters consult sources such as <www.diversityee.com>, <www.newsjobs.com>, <www.diversity-services.com>, and <www.HireDiversity> to obtain resumes from people from a wide variety of backgrounds;
- The program makes out a business case for diversity and communicates it to employees.

§ 29.03 DIVERSITY TRAINING

Corporations frequently attempt to defuse hostilities within the workplace by offering (or requiring) diversity training. Usually, it is provided by outside contractors. The training could be a voluntary initiative by management, part of a negotiated settlement with the EEOC or a state antidiscrimination agency, or part of the settlement of a court case. The mission of the training is to make employees examine their assumptions and to relate to other employees in a more professional manner.

The goals of diversity training include:

- Finding areas in which the organization is defective;
- Setting goals for improvement;
- Identifying specific steps for reaching the goals;
- Training employees to carry out those steps.

However, diversity training is not without risks and disadvantages. The program can wind up furnishing evidence for a Title VII or other discrimination suit. A well-intentioned program to promote understanding and harmony can worsen the anger and resentment already simmering below the surface. Employees can feel that discussion of other religions or lifestyles is an insult to their own deeply held beliefs. A 2004 case illustrates this risk. AT&T Broadband maintained a diversity policy requiring all employees to "recognize, respect, and value differences." A fundamentalist Christian employee refused to sign the certificate, because his religion teaches that some differences are sinful and do not deserve to be valued. The District of Colorado found that he put the employer on notice of his religious objection to the policy, requiring the employer to start the interactive process of accommodation; not doing so violated the employee's right to religious accommodation. [*Buonanno v. AT&T Broadband LLC*, 313 F. Supp. 2d 1069 (D. Colo. 2004)] An attempt to reach out to traditionally disfavored groups could be construed as reverse discrimination. And, in any event, a diversity training program (which could be viewed as purely cosmetic) is no substitute for effective hiring or for making sure that no one is subjected to a hostile environment in the workplace.

In 2007, the District Court for the District of Columbia held that the existence of a diversity policy cannot be used as evidence of reverse discrimination. The white male plaintiff alleged unsuccessfully that promoting a woman rather than promoting him was discriminatory, and the diversity policy encouraged promotion of women and thereby discriminated against men. The Seventh Circuit held that it was not discriminatory to forbid an employee to form a religious affinity group when race, national origin, gender, and sexual orientation groups were permitted. The company policy forbade groups engaging in religious or political advocacy, and the Seventh Circuit held that the policy was acceptable because it was applied even-handedly to all religious groups. [David K. Haase, *The Legal Pitfalls of Diversity Policies* (special to law.com) (Jan. 2, 2008). See *Jones v. Barnhanke*, 493 F. Supp. 2d 18 (D.D.C. 2007); *Moranski v. GM*, 433 F.3d 537 (7th Cir. 2005)]

§ 29.04 DIVERSITY AUDITS

The prospect of performing a diversity audit raises a similar mix of questions. A company that has central-office commitment to diversity might have very different conditions at the shop-floor level. Furthermore, a multi-unit company can find it difficult to maintain uniform policies throughout.

A well-designed audit can pinpoint the problems and lead to their resolution. However, a badly designed survey does not generate any useful information, but it does generate data that could be damning if a plaintiff discovers it. Doing a diversity audit shows that management cares about the issue. However, that could backfire, if employees expect real change that doesn't come.

■ **TIP:** If a lawyer performs or supervises the audit, there is at least a possibility that potentially embarrassing material can be protected by attorney-client confidentiality. But don't forget that confidentiality is sacrificed if the information is publicized.

Labor lawyers Christine Amalfe and Heather Akawie Adelman give some suggestions for an effective diversity audit:

- The first step is advice from a qualified employment lawyer;
- Concentrate on facts, not subjective comments, when collecting information;
- Destroy the individual survey responses and interview notes once statistical data has been compiled;
- Mark the finished report "privileged and confidential";
- Keep the reports separate from other HR information;
- Control distribution, and do not disclose the results to anyone who does not have a legitimate need to know.

§ 29.05 ENGLISH-ONLY RULES

In many (if not most) workplace situations, the ability to speak and understand English fluently is a valid job qualification. However, a person can be fluent in English even though it is not his or her first language. He or she may be more comfortable speaking other languages. According to the 2000 U.S. Census, 18% of the residents of the United States (47 million people) spoke a language other than English when they were at home. However, this has not frequently been raised as a legal issue: In 1996, the EEOC received a mere 32 complaints about English-only policies, up to only 155 in 2004. [Miriam Jordan, *Employers Requiring "English Only" at Work May Face Bias Suits* and *Employers Provide Language Aid*, Wall St. J., Nov. 8, 2005, at B1, B13]

If the employer bans languages other than English in the workplace, it is easy for national-origin minority groups to show disparate impact.

In some contexts, it is also required that management communicate with workers in languages other than English: for example, the PPACA requires distribution of health plan communications in other languages based on the county population that is literate only in a non-English language.

Many states have enacted statutes making English the official language of the state. In 2014, Alabama, Alaska, Arizona, Arkansas, California, Colorado, Florida, Georgia, Hawaii, Idaho, Illinois, Indiana, Iowa, Kansas, Kentucky, Louisiana, Massachusetts, Mississippi, Missouri, Montana, Nebraska, New Hampshire, North Carolina, Oklahoma, South Carolina, South Dakota, Tennessee, Utah,

Virginia, and Wyoming had "official-English" laws. [Chart, <http://www.us-english.org/view/13> (accessed Apr. 8, 2014)]

An employer who imposes an English-only rule must be able to demonstrate job-relatedness and business necessity: for instance, that there is no other way to meet customer needs or communicate in an emergency. But it would be hard to establish business necessity for forbidding employees to converse in other languages during meals or breaks, or when they are in the restroom or a locker room.

Where a high percentage of employees or customers speak languages other than English, or where the company does a good deal of business in non-English-speaking countries, bilingual employees (whether native speakers or those who have learned the language) can be invaluable. The question then becomes whether the pay rate should be higher for bilingual employees.

In September 2000, the EEOC arranged a settlement of close to $200,000 with an Illinois company that agreed to provide back pay for seven Hispanic workers who quit or were fired under the company's English-only rule, plus punitive damages. [No by-line, *Employer's English-Only Policy Brings a Settlement of $192,500*, N.Y. Times, Sept. 2, 2000, at A12] Years later, the EEOC obtained a settlement from Skilled Healthcare Group, Inc. (a nursing home chain) calling for payments of up to $450,000 plus other relief for a class of 53 Hispanic employees and former employees who were subjected to disparate treatment and harassment and were discriminated against in work assignments, promotion, and pay because of their national origin and Spanish language. The facilities had an English-only policy that covered breaks as well as on-duty hours and even forbade the employees to speak Spanish to Spanish-speaking facility residents of the chain's facilities. [Rebecca Moore, *Nursing Home Group to Pay $450K for National Origin Discrimination*, plansponsor.com (Apr. 21, 2009)]

The EEOC settled an "English only" national origin discrimination case for $450,000 plus injunctive relief. Under 29 C.F.R. § 1606.7 (Guidelines on Discrimination Because of National Origin), the EEOC treats forbidding employees to speak their native language in the workplace as loss of employment opportunities because of national origin. The EEOC recognizes a business necessity defense for English-only rules in some circumstances: emergencies; communicating with customers, supervisor, or co-workers who only speak English; and when supervision requires giving instructions in English. [*EEOC v. Mesa Systems, Inc.*, No. 2:11-cv-01201 (D. Utah 2013); see Hunton & Williams LLP, *Speak Your Mind: English-Only Policies Remain Hot Button Issue* (Nov. 20, 2013), available at Lexology.com]

§ 29.06 PROMOTING DIVERSITY

A lawyer recently got married in a traditional Indian wedding, including the rite of saptapadi (seven sacred vows) and mangal phere (circling the fire to sanctify the marriage). The couple distributed a program so guests could follow the ritual. Two friends narrated the ceremony during the Sanskrit chants. His late 2013 article says that he and his wife wanted to promote understanding of the events to all the guests, so they could participate comfortably in the traditions. Jain says that diversity without inclusion—just putting people from different backgrounds together—lacks deeper purpose and meaning. For everyone to be truly included, you have to understand their backgrounds, cultures, and world-views. [Manish K. Jain, *Inclusion Is A Choice: How My Hindu Wedding Taught Me How To Promote Diversity*, Ogletree Deakins (Dec. 26, 2013), available at Lexology.com]

Michelle Wimes, the director of professional development and inclusion at Ogletree Deakins law firm, discussed common challenges businesses encounter in creating an effective diversity program: connecting diversity to bottom-line results; making employees think of the diversity department as one that serves organizational needs and goals, not just a "party planner" in charge of events and sponsorships; and cultivating a strong pipeline to have plenty of excellent diverse candidates available when there is a job opening (e.g., by working with colleges on internships, coaching, and mentoring). Many organizations examine their vendors' commitment to diversity, so diversity and inclusion can help market to them. [Jathan Janove, *Overcoming Diversity Challenges—Interview With Director Of Professional Development & Inclusion Michelle Wimes*, Ogletree Deakins (Dec. 26, 2013), available at Lexology.com]

Steps to take to promote equality in the workplace—or simply to avoid getting sued—include:

- Broaden your recruitment efforts. Don't recruit only at the nearest colleges, or only at the Ivy League. Low-cost public colleges attract some excellent students who can't afford private institutions, so don't rule them out as sources of recruitment;
- Reward managers who increase the diversity of their workforces (with raises, bonuses, and promotions);
- Compare your diversity efforts to those of competitors;
- Provide newly hired female and minority candidates with the training, access to information, mentoring, and networking that they need to succeed;
- Remind employees to avoid ethnic slurs and statements that could create a hostile environment in all written documents, e-mail, and voice mail messages—and also remind them that supposedly deleted materials can often be restored!

Some companies are appointing a CDO, a Chief Diversity Officer, to handle matters such as recruitment, ethics, and legal compliance to improve the diversity of the company's workforce. The CDO is also responsible for seeing that mentoring, good assignments, and leadership training are available to employees from groups that have been disadvantaged in the workplace. About a quarter of CDOs report directly to the CEO; the rest report to HR or another department. CDOs who report to the CEO probably have greater power and influence. [Leslie Kwoh, *Firms Hail New Chiefs (of Diversity)*, WSJ.com (Jan. 5, 2012)]

Another area of concern is diversity on the board of directors. In early 2013, institutional investors filed shareholder resolutions with 20 major companies protesting the absence of women from the companies' boards. The Thirty Percent Coalition Institutional Investor Committee approached companies including Hartford Financial, Lowe's Companies, and Urban Outfitters Inc. Calvert Investments analyst Christine DeGroot said that female and minority directors help companies widen their customer base and add new perspectives to the board. Making a commitment to adding women and minority directors shows that a company recognizes the value of diversity. [The Thirty Percent Coalition's Website is <http://www.30percentcoalition.org> (accessed Apr. 8, 2014); see Rebecca Moore, *Institutional Investors Encourage Corporate Board Diversity*, plansponsor.com (Feb. 28, 2013).]

Part VI
EMPLOYEE RELATIONS

CHAPTER 30

LABOR LAW

§ 30.01 INTRODUCTION

In the broadest sense, labor law covers the entire relationship between employers and employees. However, the term is usually used in a much narrower sense: to mean the body of law dealing with whether a union will be allowed to organize a workplace; union elections, challenges to elections, and decertification of a union that is guilty of misconduct or that no longer represents employee interests; negotiating a Collective Bargaining Agreement (CBA); interpretation of the CBA; and strikes. Labor law sets rules for conduct by both management and unions.

In most cases, labor law is a matter of federal law. Congress has preempted this issue, in the interest of creating a single, uniform body of law that prevails throughout the country.

The BLS reported that in both 2012 and 2013, 11.3% of the labor force was unionized, but 2013 was the first time in five years than there were more union members in the private than in the public sector: 6.7% in 2013, 6.6% in 2012, versus a union rate of 35.9% in 2012 and 35.3% in 2013. Unions added about 282,000 new private-sector members, but public sector membership fell by 118,000. [Howard M. Bloom and Philip B. Rosen, *2013 Union Membership Holds Steady As Private Sector Growth Offsets Public Sector Decline*, Jackson Lewis PC (Jan. 28, 2014), available at Lexology.com]

Traditionally, unions concentrated on organizing blue-collar workers in large factories. Recently, however, unions have been concentrating on organizing service workers, whose jobs can't be relocated easily, and putting pressure on employers to recognize unions by consent, rather than having a representation election. (There are still about 3,000 representation elections each year, and the results are pretty evenly divided between union and employer victories.)

A fast food organization drive began in late 2012 in New York City. Forty organizers strove to unionize chains such as McDonald's, Wendy's, Dominos, and Taco Bell, with a goal of a $15 hourly wage. This was the largest-scale initiative to date. The New York Department of Labor said that the median pay for fast food workers in New York City is about $9 an hour, or $18,500 a year for full-time work. [Steven Greenhouse, *Drive to Unionize Fast-Food Workers Opens in N.Y.*, NYTimes.com (Nov. 28, 2012)]

Although the Second Circuit held that employees could not be compelled to arbitrate their ADEA claims, despite the arbitration clause in their CBA, the Supreme Court reversed, holding in the spring of 2009 that federal law mandates the enforcement of CBA clauses that unambiguously require union members to arbitrate their ADEA claims. [*14 Penn Plaza LLC v. Pyett*, 556 U.S. 247 (2009); the Supreme Court already held that ADEA claims are arbitrable, in *Gilmer v. Interstate/Johnson Lane Corp.*, 500 U.S. 20 (1991)] The Supreme Court returned to the question of arbitrability in 2010 on another labor law issue, this time deciding that when a CBA's no-strike clause had to be interpreted, it was up to the district court and not the arbitrator to decide when the CBA had been officially ratified. [*Granite Rock Co. v. Int'l Brotherhood of Teamsters*, 561 U.S. 287 (2010)]

Early in 2014, the Supreme Court ruled that, in a unionized workplace, donning and doffing time (putting on and removing protective clothing in a steel mill) was not compensable work time. The court held that the Fair Labor Standards Act issues could have been resolved via collective bargaining. [*Sandifer v. U.S. Steel Corp.*, 134 S. Ct. 870 (2014). See Tony Mauro, *Justices Deliver Major Rulings in Drug, Workplace Cases*, Nat'l L.J. (Jan. 27, 2014), available at law.com]

Early in 2012, the NLRB held that it violates the NLRA for an employer to require that employees waive class arbitration of grievances because employees always have the right to take collective action about grievances, whether in court or in arbitration. This decision covers all employers operating in interstate commerce, whether or not their employees are unionized. However, the NLRB did not decide whether an employer can require employees to arbitrate instead of litigating collective actions. [*D.R. Horton Inc. and Michael Cuda* (NLRB 2012); see Scott Graham, *AT&T Mobility Doesn't Apply in the Workplace, Says NLRB,* Corporate Counsel (Jan. 9, 2012) (law.com)]

But the NLRB's decision was not popular with the courts. The Fifth Circuit held that it is permissible for an employer to impose a class action arbitration waiver; it is not inconsistent with the employees' legal right under the NLRA to pursue collective action. However, the Fifth Circuit held that the arbitration agreement must clarify that employees do not waive the right to file NLRB complaints. [*D.R. Horton v. NLRB*, 737 F.3d 344 (5th Cir. 2013); see AP, *Court Blocks Labor Board on Lawsuits*, NYTimes.com (Dec. 3, 2013), *en banc reh'g denied.* See Keith J. Brodie, *NLRB DR Horton Rehearing Denied*, Barnes & Thornburg LLP (Apr. 17, 2014), available at Lexology.com.]

A report commissioned by Tom Harkin, chair of the Senate Health, Education, Labor and Pension Committee, found that over the past six years, billions of dollars of federal contracts have been awarded to companies that had been found guilty of violating safety or wage laws and been subjected to penalties. Imperial Sugar had $94.8 million in federal contracts in 2012, despite $6 million in OSHA penalties after 2008 explosion that killed 14 workers. Tyson Foods has been awarded $4.2 billion in contracts since 2000, despite 11 fatalities and over $500,000 in safety penalties since 2007. [Steven Greenhouse, *Study Finds Federal Contracts Given to Flagrant Violators of Labor Laws*, NYTimes.com (Dec. 10, 2013)]

An executive order, the Fair Pay and Safe Workplaces Executive Order, was signed in mid-2014 covering federal contracts over $500,000. To prevent the federal government from repeatedly entering into transactions with known labor law violators, contractors who are subject to the order must report violations, dating back three years, of 14 areas of federal and state law. The areas in question involve wages and hours, safety and health, family leave, civil rights, and collective bargaining. [Fact Sheet, *Fair Pay and Safe Workplaces Executive Order*, <http://www.wh.gov/ltpPD> (July 31, 2014). See Michael D. Shear and Steven Greenhouse, *Obama Plans New Scrutiny for Contractors on Labor Practices*, NYTimes.com (July 30, 2014).]

[A] Challenges to the NLRB Itself

As long as the NLRB has been in operation, businesses and unions that object to NLRB decisions have been challenging the correctness, appropriateness, and validity of those decisions. However, in recent years, the NLRB has confronted significant challenges to the way that the organization is constituted and whether it has had the power to issue valid decisions at certain crucial time periods.

In January 2008, the appointment of two NLRB commissioners expired and no one was appointed to replace them, so the NLRB had two members rather than the statutorily prescribed level of five. More than 400 decisions were issued by the two-member NLRB. In mid-2010, the Supreme Court ruled that the NLRB did not have the authority to issue decisions when it had only two members, so all of these decisions were invalid. As a result, many cases were sent back to the NLRB for reconsideration after it once again had a quorum. [*New Process Steel v. NLRB*, 560 U.S. 674 (2010), discussed in Marcia Coyle, *High Court Finds Hundreds of Labor Cases Were Improperly Decided*, Nat'l L.J. (June 18, 2010) (law.com). For an example of a challenge based on the Supreme Court's decision, see *NLRB v. Talmadge Park*, 608 F.3d 913 (2d Cir. 2010).

At the beginning of 2012, the NLRB swore in three new members: Richard Griffin, Sharon Block, and Terence Flynn. These were all recess appointments. [Melanie Trottman, *Labor Board Swears In New Members*, WSJ.com (Jan. 10, 2012)] Terence Flynn resigned on May 27, 2012 after allegations that he leaked internal NLRB information. Flynn denied wrongdoing. [Steven Greenhouse, *Labor Board Member Resigns Over Leak to G.O.P. Allies*, NYTimes.com <http://www.nytimes.com/2012/05/28/business/gop-labor-board-member-terence-flynn-quits-over-leak.html?_r=1> (May 27, 2012)]

An immensely significant D.C. Circuit decision from early 2013 holds that the recess appointments of Sharon Block, Terence Flynn, and Richard Griffin to the NLRB were unconstitutional.

Certiorari was granted, and the Supreme Court agreed with the D.C. Circuit: the appointments were invalid. They were made at a time when the Senate was not truly in recess, because it re-convened every three days for pro forma sessions. The Supreme Court held that valid recess appointments can be made only when a recess lasts 10 days or longer. [*NLRB v. Noel Canning*, 705 F.3d 490 (D.C. Cir. 2013), *aff'd*, No. 12-1281 (U.S. June 26, 2014). See Adam Liptak, *Supreme Court Curbs President's Power to Make Recess Appointments*, NYTimes.com (June 26, 2014). On August 4, 2014, the NLRB issued a press release announcing that the agency ratified all of the actions taken during the period of time covered by this decision: Tony Mauro, *NLRB Ratifies Actions Affected by Noel Canning*, Nat'l L.J. (Aug. 5, 2014), available at law.com.]

There were 436 NLRB decisions during the 18 months when recess appointees were on the NLRB. Not all of those rulings were controversial, and some have already been implemented (e.g., terminated employees have been reinstated, or a new CBA has been negotiated) and it is not worthwhile for employers to challenge them. However, in over 100 of those cases, the employer appealed to federal court, including potentially significant cases about social media and a ban on employees discussing ongoing investigations, so some NLRB decisions are likely to be invalidated on this ground. [Melanie Trottman, *Supreme Court Ruling Forces NLRB to Scramble to Revisit Cases*, WSJ.com (June 26, 2014)]

Another argument is that at least 10 NLRB regional directors were named by the invalidly appointed NLRB members, so the regional directors' decisions should also be struck down. Approximately 600 NLRB decisions and orders have been issued since January 2012, and another 1,400 cases could be challenged if a 2010 recess appointment is found invalid. [Melanie Trottman and Kris Maher, *Companies Challenge Labor Rulings*, WSJ.com (Mar. 8, 2013)]

For example, the Fourth Circuit ruled in mid-2013 that although the NLRB made out its case of unfair labor practices in two refusal-to-bargain cases, the NLRB lacked the power to enter orders because the recess appointments were invalid, and therefore the NLRB lacked a quorum. [*NLRB v. Enterprise Leasing Co. Se. LLC*, 722 F.3d 608 (4th Cir. 2013). The National Chamber Litigation Center maintains a Recess Appointments Litigation Resource Page tracking the progress of the numerous cases dealing with this issue: <http://www.chamberlitigation.com/recess-appointments-litigation-resource-page> (last accessed Apr. 8, 2014)]

Eventually, in August 2013, the Senate confirmed enough NLRB members to bring the Board up to its full strength of five members—the first time this had been true since August 21, 2003. Chairman Mark Gaston Pierce was confirmed for another five-year NLRB term. Four new members were added: Nancy Schiffer, a senior attorney for unions; Harry I. Johnson, III, formerly a partner in the law firm Arent Fox LLP; Kent Hirozawa, one-time chief counsel to Chairman Pearce; and Philip A. Miscimarra, ex-partner in Morgan Lewis & Bockius LLP. Pearce's term lasts until August 27, 2018. Schiffer's term ends December 16, 2014. Johnson's ends August 27, 2015, Hirozawa's ends August 27, 2016, and Miscimarra's ends December 16, 2017. [NLRB Press Release, *The National Labor Relations Board Has Five Senate-Confirmed Members*, <http://www.nlrb.gov/news-outreach/news-story/national-labor-relations-board-has-five-senate-confirmed-members> (Aug. 12, 2013)]

§ 30.02 SOURCES OF LABOR LAW

[A] Generally

The NLRA was supplemented in 1947 by the Labor-Management Relations Act (LMRA) [29 U.S.C. §§ 141–144, etc.], popularly known as the Taft-Hartley Act. The LMRA extends the powers of the NLRB. It outlaws certain kinds of strikes, including jurisdictional strikes, strikes to enforce unfair labor practices (rather than strikes to protest them), and secondary boycotts. A secondary boycott is an attempt to pressure a neutral company to keep it from dealing with a company that the union has a dispute with.

Two real estate developers wanted to lease space to a non-union supermarket in the shopping center they were building. Unions funded 14 suits at every stage of development to keep the developers from renting to the supermarket. All of the cases except one were withdrawn, dismissed, or found to be moot. The district court dismissed the developers' suit, under LMRA § 303, against two union locals. The district court said that most of the legal challenges were not objectively baseless, so the *Noerr-Pennington* doctrine, which preserves the First Amendment right to petition, protected them. The Fourth Circuit reversed: there is an exception to this doctrine for "sham litigation." The Fourth Circuit joined the Second and Ninth Circuits in analyzing a pattern of multiple lawsuits rather than the individual suits to see if there was abuse of the administrative and judicial processes. [*Waugh Chapel South, LLC v. UFCW Local 27*, 728 F.3d 354 (4th Cir. 2013); see Ronald J. Kramer, *UFCW's Secondary, "Sham Litigation" Not Protected By The First Amendment*, Seyfarth Shaw LLP (Aug. 30, 2013), available at Lexology.com]

The Landrum-Griffin Act, known as the Labor-Management Reporting and Disclosure Act of 1959 [Pub. L. No. 86-257], forbids hot-cargo agreements (agreements not to carry the merchandise of a company involved in a labor dispute). It allows prehire agreements in the building and construction industries, and makes it an unfair labor practice to picket in order to force an employer to recognize or bargain with a union.

The Labor-Management Reporting and Disclosure Act (LMRDA) requires employers to make an annual filing, using the LM-10 form, to disclose payments over $250 per year made to unions and union officials. The LM-10 form is due 90 days after the end of the employer's fiscal year. [DOL, *Form LM-10-Employer Reports—Frequently Asked Questions*, <http://www.nlrb.gov/news-outreach/news-story/national-labor-relations-board-has-five-senate-confirmed-members>, discussed in Dechert On Point, *Department of Labor Issues New LM-10 Guidelines*, <http://www.dechert.com/files/Publication/c0ffb95b-511c-4c0c-b9b2-343a21dd1ce1/Presentation/PublicationAttachment/6c80e2c4-e53e-4896-ad80-35b190c1f947/Labor_and_EB_03-06.pdf> (March 2006)]

Certiorari was granted in *Unite Here Local 355 v. Mulhall*, a case about LMRA § 302(a), which makes it a crime for an employer to give "anything of value" to a labor union that represents or seeks to represent its employees. The question before the Supreme Court was whether it is a violation for the employer a promise that it will stay neutral in the organizing process, will give the union access to non-public areas of the employer's premises; and will provide a list of names and contact information for employees. The Supreme Court originally was also going to consider whether it violates § 302(b) for a union to try to enforce the employer's promises. The Eleventh Circuit treated neutrality agreements as unlawful "things of value," although the Third and Fourth Circuits disagreed. The

Supreme Court dismissed the case as improvidently granted on December 10, 2013. [*Unite Here Local 355 v. Mulhall*, 134 S. Ct. 594 (2013); see Brent Kendall and Melanie Trottman, *Supreme Court Takes Pass on Union-Organizing Case*, WSJ.com (Dec. 10, 2013)]

The Norris-LaGuardia Act severely limits the situations in which an employer can secure an injunction against a union, but does not completely rule out all injunctions. Although federal law usually preempts state law in the labor arena, the states do have a limited role in protecting their own legitimate interests. They can pass certain labor laws that will not be federally preempted: For instance, there is a legitimate state interest in preventing violence, so states can regulate how and when picketing can be done. States can legislate in areas such as minimum wages, child labor, and employment discrimination.

States can also cope with issues that are only peripheral to the main purposes of the LMRA. This category includes defamation suits brought by employers against unions, suits dealing with continuation of welfare benefits during strikes, and internal union affairs. States are also allowed to legislate in the area of union security, for instance by passing right-to-work laws forbidding union shops and agency shops. [See § 30.06]

The National Labor Relations Board's (NLRB) jurisdiction is limited to work performed in the United States; the agency has no jurisdiction over temporary work assignments in Canada. [*Asplundh Tree Expert Co. v. NLRB*, 365 F.3d 168 (3d Cir. 2004)]

Although full discussion of public employee unions is beyond the scope of this book, it should be noted that some states have adopted limitations on collective bargaining by public employees as part of a drive to save money. For example, in 2011, Wisconsin adopted Act 10, a statute that severely limits collective bargaining by most employee unions other than police and firefighters. Public employee unions are only permitted to negotiate wages, not vacation days or sick leave, and unions must be recertified annually. The statute has been challenged many times, but has been upheld by both federal and state courts. Challenges based on the First Amendment have been rejected repeatedly. [*Laborers Local 236 v. Walker*, 749 F.3d 628 (7th Cir. 2014); *Madison Teachers, Inc. v. Walker*, 2014 WI 99 (Wis. July 31, 2014). See Reid Wilson, *Wisconsin Supreme Court Upholds State's Union, Voter ID Laws*, Washington Post (July 31, 2014), <http://www.washingtonpost.com/blogs/govbeat/wp/2014/07/31/wisconsin-supreme-court-upholds-walkers-union-voter-identification-laws>.]

[B] NLRA Section 7

The National Labor Relations Act of 1935 (NLRA), also known as the Wagner Act, is one of the bedrock federal labor statutes. The NLRA establishes the National Labor Relations Board (NLRB) as a kind of referee between management and unionized labor.

Section 7 of the NLRA says that employees have the right to engage in "protected concerted activities." In other words, they can act together to form a union, join a union, present grievances, bargain collectively, go on strike, and picket peacefully.

In 2014, an NLRB regional director held that Northwestern University football players on scholarship were employees of the university with the right to organize and bargain collectively. The controversial decision said that football players spend as much as 50 hours a week on football, and coaches have so much control over whether the players can retain their scholarships that it was inaccurate to describe the players as primarily students. [Ben Strauss and Steve Eder, *College Players Granted Right to Form Union*, NYTimes.com (Mar. 26, 2014)]

There can be legitimate business reasons for asking employees to maintain the confidentiality of internal investigations: e.g., protecting witnesses, victims, and the subjects of investigations; suppressing rumors; and encouraging employees to testify. Sometimes government agencies mandate confidentiality of certain information: the EEOC not only requires protection of harassment complaints, but employees must be informed of the confidentiality requirement. However, an NLRB ALJ applied the NLRB rule that prohibits employers from asking complainants not to discuss the matter. *Hyundai America Shipping Agency*, 357 NLRB No. 80 (2011) said that it was unlawful for an employer to routinely tell employees not to discuss investigations, without considering whether confidentiality was necessary to prevent corruption of the investigation.

Banner Estrella Medical Center, 358 NLRB No. 93 (2012) found it unlawful for an employer even to ask complainants not to discuss an ongoing investigation with their co-workers. Both cases were appealed to the D.C. Circuit. In mid-2013, an unrepresented employee was disciplined for telling employees about a completed HR investigation into the employee's allegations against a supervisor. The employer, Boeing, said that the employee violated the confidentiality notice she signed during the investigation forbidding witnesses to discuss the case. The employee filed a ULP charge of unlawful discipline. The employer rescinded the discipline and changed the confidentiality notice to recommend rather than demand confidentiality. The NLRB ALJ interpreted NLRB precedent to forbid blanket confidentiality orders as an infringement on employees' right to discuss the terms and conditions of employment. Even the revised notice was inadequate because of its potential coercive effect. The case is pending before the full NLRB. [*The Boeing Co.*, JD(SF)-34-13 (July 26, 2013); see Kenneth R. Dolin, *How Far is Too Far in Seeking Confidentiality?*, Nat'l L.J. (Sept. 30, 2013), available at law.com]

An April 2013 NLRB Division of Advice memorandum says a confidentiality rule violates § 8(a)(1) by suppressing discussion of ongoing investigations into employee misconduct [Verso Paper, NLRB Div of Advice No. 30-CA_89350 (Jan. 29, 2013)]

A rule in the employee handbook forbidding employees to disclose wages or compensation to other employees or to any third party violates the NLRA. [Design Technology Group LLC, No. 20-CA-03511 (Apr. 19, 2013)]

An employee agreement forbidding employees to disclose any proprietary or confidential information to anyone, including handbooks, personnel lists, phone numbers, and e-mail addresses, was invalid. It violated NLRA § 7 to forbid all discussion of wages, benefits, phone numbers, or addresses. Within limits, employees have a right to criticize their employer and seek support from other workers [Quicken Loans Inc. No. 28-CA-07587 (June 21, 2013)] [Baker & McKenzie, *Labor Year In Review: NLRB Targets Non-Unionized Employers And Expands Worker Rights* (Dec. 21, 2013), available at Lexology.com]

The Fifth Circuit agreed with the NLRB that the employer's confidentiality policy violated NLRA § 8(a)(1) because it prevented employees from discussing wages. The policy forbade employees to copy or share confidential information, broadly defined to include personnel information and documents. In the Fifth Circuit view, employees have a right to discuss wages with co-workers; there was no evidence that employees used this information outside the company. The Fifth Circuit examined the written terms of the policy, not the way it was implemented, so it rejected the employer's argument that the policy was not used to suppress discussion of wages. [*FlexFrack Logistics v. NLRB*, 746 F.3d 205 (5th Cir. 2014). The employer raised a challenge based on *Noel Canning*, but the Fifth Circuit held that this argument was not raised on a timely basis.]

[C] Unfair Labor Practices

Either a union or an employer can be guilty of an "unfair labor practice" (ULP) as defined by the NLRA and the LMRA. The NLRB has the power to issue a "cease and desist" order if it deems that an unfair practice has occurred. The NLRB also has powers to order positive actions, such as ordering an employer to bargain with a union.

NLRA § 8 defines unfair labor practices to include:

- Refusal to engage in collective bargaining—whether the recalcitrant party is management or union;
- Employer domination of a union;
- Retaliation against employees for filing charges with the NLRB or testifying before the agency;
- Discrimination against employees based on either union activities or refusal to join a union. In this context, discrimination includes firing, refusal to hire, refusal to reinstate, demotion, discrimination in compensation, discrimination in work assignments etc. However, if a union security clause is in place, employees can be required to pay union dues or

the equivalent of dues, but they cannot be required to actually join the union;

- Deliberately inefficient work practices that require the employment of excessive numbers of workers ("featherbedding");
- Certain practices occurring during strikes or picketing.

The LMRA penalizes unfair labor practices by unions, including:

- Restraining or coercing employees when they exercise their right to bargain collectively, choose a representative, or vote against unionization;
- Causing an employer to discriminate against any employee;
- Refusing to participate in collective bargaining, once the union becomes the authorized bargaining representative for the employees;
- Engaging in strikes or concerted activity for the purpose of boycotting one employer, forcing another employer to recognize an uncertified union, forcing any employer to recognize a particular union when a different union is actually the authorized bargaining representative, or when a determination of jurisdiction still has to be made;
- Requiring union members in a union shop to pay excessive initiation fees or excessive dues;
- Featherbedding.

A ULP is an employment decision that interferes with the right to organize or discourages union membership. The test of such a decision is whether or not the action was motivated by anti-union animus.

The NLRB considers it a ULP to promulgate work rules that are likely to chill exercise of § 7 rights—even if the rules are never enforced. A rule that explicitly restricts § 7 activity violates the NLRA, and so does a rule that an employee would reasonably construe to prohibit § 7 activity, if the rule was promulgated in response to union activity, or the rule has been applied to restrict the exercise of § 7 rights. The Seventh Circuit held that a hospital unlawfully interfered with nurses' rights to organize and discriminated against a union activist nurse by forbidding solicitation in "patient care areas"—including the breakroom. The NLRB conceded that bans on solicitation in patient areas are valid, but the Seventh Circuit ruled that it was improper to define the breakroom as a patient care area because it was across the corridor from patient rooms. The facially valid anti-solicitation rule was applied in a discriminatory fashion: union solicitation was forbidden, but charitable solicitations and product sales were permitted. [*St. Margaret Mercy Healthcare Ctrs.*, 519 F.3d 373 (7th Cir. 2008)]

It is not an unfair labor practice for an employer to put work rules in the employee handbook against abusive and threatening language and limiting solicitations and distributions within the workplace; pro-union employees can make their point of view known without threatening their opponents, so the rules do not interfere with protected collective activity. [*Adtranz ABB Daimler-Benz Transp. v. NLRB*, 253 F.3d 19 (D.C. Cir. 2001)]

Schoolteacher Robert Green, who is African-American, was fired. He asked the union to grieve on his behalf. The union refused and also refused to represent him in a suit under the state's teacher tenure law. Green brought the suit without union assistance, won the case, and was reinstated. Green alleged that the union represented comparable white employees and that the union refused to help him in retaliation against his earlier opposition to discrimination. The union said that it would not help Green because of a previous suit against it. The district court granted summary judgment for the union on the grounds that Green did not prove that the union owed him a duty of fair representation or breached the CBA. The Seventh Circuit vacated the holding because Title VII forbids discrimination by labor unions, whether or not the union's action violated the CBA. The Seventh Circuit concluded that the district court improperly applied the standards for an FLSA hybrid action (see below) to a Title VII case. [*Green v. American Fed'n of Teachers*, 740 F.3d 1104 (7th Cir. 2014)]

[D] LMRA Preemption

Many cases turn on whether § 301 of the Labor-Management Relations Act (LMRA) should be applied. This section gives federal District Courts jurisdiction over suits for violations of a collective bargaining agreement, as well as suits by one union against another. This section is often applied to bring labor questions into the federal courts—and keep them out of state courts when issues such as wrongful termination and unfair employee discipline are raised.

The most important issue in deciding whether LMRA preemption exists is the relationship between the controversy and the collective bargaining agreement. State laws are preempted whenever it is necessary to interpret the CBA. However, the Supreme Court decided in 1994 that a mere need to refer to the CBA is not enough to justify preemption. The underlying dispute must really involve searching out the meaning of the terms of the contract. [*Lividas v. Bradshaw*, 512 U.S. 107 (1994)]

If the CBA includes a contractual grievance or arbitration provision (and most do), then potential plaintiffs have to exhaust their remedies (complete the entire process) before bringing suit under § 301.

Preemption has been found in cases such as:

- Failure to rehire, negligent and intentional infliction of emotional distress (because deciding the case required interpretation of the CBA's seniority provisions);

- A claim that a worker was denied reinstatement after a period of disability in retaliation for filing a Worker's Compensation claim, because the issue here was the management's exclusive right to hire and fire under the CBA "management rights" clause;

However, preemption was not found in these situations, on the grounds that the court did not have to interpret the CBA to decide the case:

- Retaliatory discharge;
- Discharge of an employee for reasons violating public policy;
- False imprisonment (unreasonable detention of an employee by a security guard);
- Claims about oral contracts other than the CBA (for instance, a verbal promise of lifetime employment) or implied contracts;
- Claims under state antidiscrimination laws on issues that are not normally bargained away during contract negotiations;

In 2012, the Fifth Circuit held that LMRA preemption should not have been applied in a case where a group of former employees raised tort claims against their ex-employer based on hearing loss that they said was caused by failure to abate workplace noise. The plaintiffs raised only state-law tort claims and the charges could be resolved without interpreting the CBA at all. [*McKnight v. Dresser, Inc.*, 676 F.3d 426 (5th Cir. 2012)]

§ 30.03 EMPLOYEE STATUS

[A] Definition of Employee

The NLRA defines the rights of "employees," so an important basic question is who fits into this category. Independent contractors are not employees, but common-law employees under the employer's control in terms of hiring, firing, work methods and results, provision of tools and materials, and employee discipline, are also employees for NLRA purposes.

Employee status is maintained during a temporary layoff, if the worker reasonably expects to be recalled in the future. A sick or injured worker continues to be an employee either until he or she takes another permanent full-time job, or is permanently unable to return to work for physical reasons.

Sometimes retirees who do not have a right or reasonable expectation of re-hiring will not be considered employees. In other instances, however, retirees will continue to be treated as members of the bargaining unit, on the theory that the union bargained for a compensation package covering both active workers and retirees. This is a particularly significant question in terms of retiree health benefits promised "for life" when the employer later claims that the promise expired with the CBA. See § 9.08.

[B] Part-Time and Temporary Workers

Temporary or casual workers will probably not be considered employees. Part-time workers are considered employees, although sometimes it is inappropriate to put them in a bargaining unit with full-timers, if their interests are adverse. In August 2000, the NLRB ruled that temporary workers can be included in the same collective bargaining unit as permanent employees, as long as the characteristics of the job are similar. [*M.B. Sturgis Inc.*, 331 N.L.R.B. 173 (Aug. 25, 2000)]

This reverses earlier NLRB decisions saying that temporary workers could be organized in a bargaining unit with permanent workers only if neither the "supplier employer" (the temp agency or other company that supplied the workers) nor the "user employer" (the place where the work was actually performed) objected. As you can imagine, one or both usually did object!

The NLRB ruled that the union has the right to show that the two companies are really joint employers of the workers, because they both determine the terms and conditions of employment. However, the user employer can rebut the union's contention by showing that the supplier employer maintains the real control over the workers.

The Seventh Circuit held that seasonal employees at a factory were eligible for inclusion in the bargaining unit with permanent employees, based on shared interests and the seasonal workers' reasonable expectation of future employment. The seasonal workers constituted a large part of the workforce; they came from a definable, static group of workers (the local Hispanic population), and all new permanent hires came from the pool of seasonal workers. The Seventh Circuit reached this conclusion although the seasonal employees did not receive the same benefits as the permanent employees; and the employer did not try to recruit former seasonal workers when new workers had to be hired. [*Winkie Mfg. Co. v. NLRB*, 348 F.3d 254 (7th Cir. 2003)]

[C] Supervisors

The text of the NLRA [29 U.S.C. § 152] says that "supervisors" such as foremen and forewomen are not "employees," for the common-sense reason that supervisors promote management interests and therefore do not fit in well with rank-and-file workers, who have different and often opposing interests.

A supervisor is someone who has a formal job title indicating supervisory status, has been held out as a supervisor by management, or is perceived as a supervisor by rank-and-file workers. A supervisor makes independent, individual judgments, can reward or discipline employees (up to and including firing them) and has authority to adjust employee grievances.

To be a supervisor, someone must have supervisory authority on a consistent basis (whether or not it is exercised). Sporadic or limited authority, such as power to take over in an emergency, doesn't make a rank-and-file worker into a supervisor. Courts have expanded the statutory definition, so that managers are not considered employees either, because of their discretion and ability to set corporate policy.

In mid-2001, the Supreme Court resolved a conflict about the status of Registered Nurses in nursing homes. Because the RNs direct the activities of non-RN staff, they are supervisors and cannot be organized in the same unit as the other staffers. [*NLRB v. Kentucky River Cmty. Care Inc.*, 532 U.S. 706 (2001)]

Late in 2006, the NLRB ruled that employees who have been permanently designated as shift supervisors are not entitled to unionize, but also nurses who work supervisory shifts on a rotating basis are not supervisors. An employee is a supervisor if he or she has subordinates; decides what task will be done next or who does it; and this direction reflects independent judgment. The authority to direct work and correct mistakes must come from the employer, and the supervisor must be at risk of adverse consequences because of his or her direction of subordinates. Therefore, in three 2006 cases, the NLRB found that "lead persons" in a factory did not exercise supervisory authority, and charge nurses did not supervise nursing assistants because they could not control their hours or give them assignments. [*Oakwood Healthcare Inc.*, 348 NLRB 37 (Sept. 29, 2006); *Golden Crest Healthcare Center*, 349 NLRB 39 (Sept. 29, 2006); *Croft Metals Inc.*, 348 NLRB 38 (Sept. 29, 2006)]

In 2013, the Sixth Circuit, reversing the NLRB, held that Registered Nurses (RNs) at a nursing home were supervisors because of their power to use independent judgment to assign, direct, and discipline Certified Nurse Assistants at the facility. The Sixth Circuit held that merely reporting misconduct is not supervisory authority, but it is not necessary for a worker to have the power to hire and fire to be considered a supervisor. [*GGNSC Springfield v. NLRB*, 721 F.3d 403 (6th Cir. 2013)]

[D] Union Organizers

A paid union organizer can qualify as a protected "employee" under the NLRA. The fact that he or she is paid a salary by the union does not deprive him or her of the protection of federal labor law. This concept has been extended to treat a volunteer union organizer who is not paid by the union as an employee. [*NLRB v. Town & Country Elec. Inc.*, 516 U.S. 85 (1995); *NLRB v. Fluor Daniel*, 102 F.3d 818 (6th Cir. 1996)]

In general, the LMRA prevents employers from making payments to any union representative, but this rule is not violated by continuing to provide full pay and benefits to a long-tenure employee who served as shop steward and worked full-time representing employees who had grievances. The Ninth Circuit held that it was in the employer's best interests to have grievances handled expeditiously. The shop steward was an employee of the company and not the union because the company controlled his work week; he reported to the company's HR director; and his workplace was the shop floor, not the union hall. [*International Ass'n of Machinists v. B.F. Goodrich*, 387 F.3d 1046 (9th Cir. 2004)]

In appropriate cases, the employer can assert the defense that the union "salts" who applied for jobs were not entitled to be hired because they had a disabling conflict with the employer's interests. However, according to the D.C. Circuit, the disabling conflict defense can only be asserted if a union organizer seeks work while engaged in an economic strike against the employer, or if what is described as protected union organizing activity is actually a cloak for unlawful conduct aimed at sabotage or driving the employer out of business. [*Casino Ready Mix v. NLRB*, 321 F.3d 1190 (D.C. Cir. 2003)] In this case, the union salts responded to an advertisement, and were clearly qualified for the job, so refusal to assign work to them was unlawful discrimination. However, in 2003 the Seventh Circuit held that a construction company's hiring system, which gave preference to former employees and referrals from trusted sources did not violate the LMRA. The union "salts" were not hired—but that was not because of their union affiliation, but because they were walk-ins, the lowest-priority category in the employer's classification. [*International Union of Operating Eng'rs, Local 150 v. NLRB*, 325 F.3d 818 (7th Cir. 2003)]

§ 30.04 ELECTIONS, CERTIFICATION, AND RECOGNITION

[A] Generally

To gain "certification," and thereby become the bargaining agent for the employees (whom the employer must deal with), a union has to win an election supervised by the NLRB. There is a one-year period after the certification election during which no rival union is allowed to seek certification.

A union organizing campaign begins with a petition for certification. Typically, the petition is filed by the union or by an individual employee who is a union supporter. Most organizing work is done by pro-union employees, because employers can and usually do bar non-employees from soliciting on business premises during working hours. [But see § 30.04[H] for exceptions to this rule] If there are two or more unions trying to organize the same workplace, the employer is allowed to express a preference for one over the other.

A certification petition is valid only if at least 30% of the employees in the bargaining unit indicate their interest. Acceptable indications of interest are:

- Authorization cards;
- Union membership cards;

- Applications for membership;
- Records of union dues;
- Employee signatures on certification petitions.

It is a serious unfair labor practice for employers to retaliate against workers because of their union activism, so it is important to document good business reasons for any disciplinary action taken against less-than-optimal workers who also happen to be union activists.

The employer has the right to request a representation election when a majority of the employees have submitted signed authorization cards designating a particular union as their bargaining agent. However, an employer that engages in serious ULPs forfeits the right to call for an election, and can be compelled to bargain with the union, because an employer loses the right to call for an election if it engages in conduct that is likely to disrupt the election. [*NLRB v. Orland Park Motor Cars*, 309 F.3d 452 (7th Cir. 2002)]

BNA reported that there were 66 fewer representation elections in the first half of 2013 than in the first half of 2012. In both years, about two-thirds of private sector organizing drives were successful: unions won 62.6% of 709 elections in the first half of 2012, and 65.2% of 643 elections in the first half of 2013. There were 131 decertification elections in the first half of 2012, only 93 in the first half of 2013. In 2012, unions won 41.2% of decertification elections, versus 39.8% in 2013. The services sector, including health care, was the site of the largest number of NLRB-conducted elections in the first half of 2013; the union won in 70% of these elections. These statistics do not include workplaces organized with consent of management, or through card check authorization agreements. [Gerald F. Lutkus, *Unions Win About Two Out Of Three Elections In 2013*, Barnes & Thornburg LLP (Nov. 21, 2013), available at Lexology.com]

Several states, Arizona, South Carolina, South Dakota, and Utah, have adopted state constitutional amendments in November 2010 requiring secret ballot elections for unionization. The NLRB said that it would file suit against those states, because the amendments are preempted by the NLRA, which permits card check organization under appropriate circumstances. [Melanie Trottman, *Labor Board Warns on Secret Ballots*, WSJ.com (Jan. 15, 2011); Steven Greenhouse, *Labor Board to Sue 4 States Over 'Card Check' for Unionizing*, NYTimes.com (Jan. 14, 2011)]

On November 30, 2011, the NLRB passed a chairman's resolution that limits appeals of union organizing elections in order to speed up the election process. About 90% of elections are held on consent. The resolution limits pre-election litigation about contested elections to matters directly related to the election. Appeals are deferred until after the election, because many disputes are mooted by the result of the election. [Matthew Huisman, *NLRB Votes to Streamline Union Organizing Elections*, Nat'l L.J. (Nov. 30, 2011) (law.com) The rule was proposed at 76 Fed. Reg. 36812 (June 22, 2011) and finalized at 76 Fed. Reg. 80138 (Dec. 22, 2011).]

The resolution included six procedural amendments intended to reduce unnecessary litigation related to elections, such as a limitation of pre-election hearings to evidence relevant to the question of whether an election should be held and consolidating two levels of appeals into a single post-election procedure. [NRLB press release: <http://www.nlrb.gov/publications/rules-regulations/notice-proposed-rulemaking/proposed-amendments-nlrb-election-rules-an/> (Dec. 1, 2011)]

Then, in May 2012, the District Court for the District of Columbia found that this rule was invalidly promulgated because the NLRB did not have a quorum when the rule was adopted. The NLRB had three members at that time; two members (both Democrats) voted for the rule, the one Republican member did not vote at all. The district court said that without three actual votes being cast, there was no quorum. [*Chamber of Commerce of the United States v. NLRB*, 879 F. Supp. 2d 18 (D.D.C. 2012)] In response, the NLRB suspended implementation of the new rule. [<http://www.nlrb.gov/news/nlrb-suspends-implementation-representation-case-amendments-based-court-ruling> (May 15, 2012)] At the end of 2013, the NLRB announced that it would not appeal this decision. [79 Fed. Reg. 7318 (Feb. 6, 2014). See *Chamber of Commerce of the USA v. NLRB*, 879 F. Supp. 2d 18 (D.D.C. 2012) and No. 12-5250 (stipulation of dismissal Dec. 9, 2013).]

In February 6, 2014, the NLRB re-proposed representation election rules that are essentially the same as the previous "quickie" or "ambush election" rule. The proposal calls for electronic filing and transmission of documents such as election petitions. There would be less time between filing of a petition and the election; management opposed the change, arguing that employers would not have enough time to communicate with employees. Voter lists would have to include telephone numbers and e-mail addresses. The proposal limits pre-election hearings to disputes about union representation. All post-election appeals would be unified into a single appeals process. [NLRB, *Amendments to NLRB Election Rules and Regulations Fact Sheet*, <http://www.nlrb.gov/news-outreach/fact-sheets/amendments-nlrb-election-rules-and-regulations-fact-sheet> (accessed Aug. 25, 2014) includes a table comparing the current rules to the NLRB proposal; Terry L. Potter and Joseph C. Orlet, *The National Labor Relations Board Proposes Amendments To Improve Representation Case Procedures*, Husch Blackwell LLP (Feb. 5, 2014), available at Lexology.com; Michael J. Lotito, *NLRB Dismisses Appeal, Opening Door To Re-Issued Election Rule*, Littler Mendelson (Dec. 10, 2013), available at Lexology.com; Nelson D. Cary and Michael J. Shoenfelt, *NLRB Abandons Its Appeal Of Union Election Rule Decision, May Re-Issue Challenged Rule*, Vorys Sater Seymour and Pease LLP (Dec. 13, 2013), available at Lexology.com]

[B] Consent Elections

The NLRB is responsible for determining the validity of the representation petition. If the employer does not oppose holding the election, the election is a consent election. The employer and union sign a contract permitting an election. The NLRB will probably have to accept the consent agreement's definition of the appropriate bargaining unit, unless it violates the law (for instance, by including guards in a mixed bargaining unit).

Within seven days of the time that the appropriate NLRB Regional Director approves a consent agreement, the employer has a duty to submit the "Excelsior List" to the Regional Director. This is a list of the names and addresses of every worker eligible to vote in the consent election. The Regional Director distributes the list to all interested parties. [The name comes from the NLRB case of *Excelsior Underwear Inc.*, 156 N.L.R.B. 271 (1986)]

[C] NLRB Hearings

If the employer objects, but the NLRB finds that there is reasonable cause to believe that the union might be an appropriate representative for the employees, the NLRB holds a nonadversary hearing to determine if there is a question of representation. (Employers who are dissatisfied with the Regional Director's decision can appeal to the central NLRB for review.) This type of hearing cannot be used to raise claims of unfair labor practices by either side.

In most instances, the hearing will result in setting a date for a secret ballot election under NLRB supervision. The NLRB will then certify the result: whether or not the union has secured a majority vote.

A union will be certified as bargaining representative for the unit if it wins the votes of a majority of the voters (not a majority of those eligible to vote). But the election will not be valid unless a "representative number" of eligible employees actually voted. There is no bright-line test for whether the number of voters was representative. Many factors, such as the voter turnout, adequacy of the employees' notice of the election and opportunity to vote, and the presence or absence of unfair practices by the employer, are considered to see if there was a high enough turnout.

[D] Election Procedure

Usually, the election will be held at the workplace, because that is accessible to all employees. However, if there is good cause shown for holding an election somewhere else, or for allowing voting by mail, the NLRB will supervise the out-of-plant election. Elections are held by secret ballot. The voters enter the voting location, have their employee status checked, and then mark their ballots in a closed booth where their selections are not visible. The ballots are collected for later tallying.

Before a certification or deauthorization election, the employer must post an election notice in a conspicuous place in the workplace. The notice must be up for at least three full working days before 12:01 a.m. of the day scheduled for the election. Failure to post the notice can result in the election results being set aside. The notice must give the date, time, and place of the election, and must show a sample ballot so employees will know how to mark it to indicate their choice.

If there are objections to the eligibility of certain voters, or to the mechanics of the election, either the employer or union can file an objection with the NLRB within seven days of the ballot tally. There is no absolute right to get a hearing on the validity of the election: The NLRB Regional Director decides when one is needed.

If an employer relies on the results of an invalid election to change policies within the workplace, the Ninth Circuit said that the appropriate remedy is to hold a new election. [*Gardner Mech. Servs. v. NLRB*, 89 F.3d 586 (9th Cir. 1996)] A bargaining order is improper unless there is proof that it would be impossible to hold a valid election.

[E] Voter Eligibility

The simple answer is that all "employees" in the "bargaining unit" are entitled to vote in a representation election. However, it can be hard to determine the appropriate bargaining unit, and there are some questions about who retains employee status.

A worker who has taken a voluntary leave of absence is entitled to vote unless the relationship with the employer has been severed. If the employee on leave retains seniority and is still in the employer's pension and benefit plans, he or she is probably an eligible voter. Employees on sick leave, disability leave, or maternity leave are entitled to vote, unless they have been formally or constructively terminated from employment. [*Home Care Network Inc.*, 347 NLRB 80 (Aug. 2, 2006)] In 2008, the D.C. Circuit ruled that a bargaining unit member is presumed to remain a member of the unit while on sick leave, long-term disability, or worker's compensation, unless the employer proves that the person has resigned or been terminated. [*Abbott Ambulance of Illinois v. NLRB*, 522 F.3d 447 (D.C. Cir. 2008)]

For laid-off workers, the question is whether they have a reasonable expectation of recall (determined as of the date of the election, not the date of the NLRB pre-election hearing). A person who was lawfully fired before the date of the election is not eligible to vote, but someone who is unlawfully discharged for union activity retains employee status, and therefore is entitled to vote.

Economic strikers (see § 30.09[B] for characterization of strikes) who have not been replaced as to the date of the election are entitled to vote. During the 12 months after the beginning of an economic strike, economic strikers are still entitled to vote if they have been replaced—even if they are not entitled to immediate reinstatement after the strike ends. Employees who are on the preferential reinstatement list are also entitled to vote. But if the election is held more than 12 months after the beginning of a strike, replaced economic strikers are not entitled to vote, even if they still have a reasonable expectation of recall.

Replacement workers hired during an economic strike are entitled to vote in the election, but only if they were employed before the eligibility cutoff date for the election. Unlike economic strikers, unfair labor practice strikers are always eligible to vote in representation elections, but their replacements are never entitled to vote.

[F] Electioneering and Communications

During a certification campaign, both employer and union are entitled to communicate their viewpoints to employees. The employer is considered a "person" entitled to exercise free speech rights, subject to limitations of accuracy and fairness. If the employer overreaches, the election results will be set aside, and the employer will have to go through the whole process again, perhaps with more employee sympathy for the union. In egregious cases, the employer might have to answer charges of an unfair labor practice.

The "critical period" is the time between the filing of a representation petition and the election itself. (For a runoff or rerun election, the critical period begins at the first election, and even conduct occurring before the certification petition was filed might be considered relevant as to the fairness of the election.) The NLRB will observe the conduct of both sides, and has the power to invalidate elections, even if the misconduct is not serious enough to constitute an unfair labor practice. The employer is held responsible for the conduct of its agents, including its lawyers and labor relations consultants.

> ■ **TIP:** An employer can avoid liability for an inappropriate statement by an agent if it repudiates the statement promptly, admitting that it was out of line, restating it in proper form, and giving at least as much publicity to the retraction as to the original communication.

Certification elections are supposed to provide "laboratory conditions" (i.e., pure and untainted) for workplace democracy. Employers are not allowed to conduct pre-election polls, or even ask employees their opinions about unionization, if the inquiry is too close to the time of the election. However, it is accepted labor law that employers can call a meeting of workers on company time for management to assert its arguments against unionization. If the union is permitted to solicit employees during meals and other breaks, the employer can call a mass meeting without giving the union equal time to reply.

During the 24-hour period just before the election, neither management nor union is allowed to make speeches to massed employees on company time. If the employer does this, it is not an unfair labor practice, but it could lead to invalidation of the election. The employer is allowed to distribute printed materials to workers during this time. The employer can also conduct antiunion meetings away from the workplace during the 24-hour period, as long as attendance is voluntary and employees choose to come in on their own time.

These are examples that have been found to constitute unfair labor practices by the employer:

- Announcing benefits on election day;
- Explicitly promising benefits if the union loses;
- Threatening to withhold benefits if the union wins;
- Announcing new benefits during the critical period to show that the employer offers a better deal than the union—unless the benefits were decided before the representation petition was filed, or there is economic justification for providing them at that time;
- Telling employees that unless they returned to work the next day without a union contract, the business would be closed down, and its equipment would be leased, was a threat (an unfair labor practice) and not just a permissible prediction of future events. It was a threat because it referred to events wholly within the employer's control;

However, these have been held not to be improper practices by the employer:

- Delaying pay raises until after the election, as long as timing is the only issue—raises will be paid no matter who wins the election;
- Distributing fact-based (not coercive or threatening) handbills during an organizing drive, saying that unionization would lead to long, bitter negotiations and possibly an ugly strike
- Announcing two new floating holidays the day before the election. The timing of the announcement was logical within the company's fiscal year; it was just a coincidence that it was right before the election.

[G] Buttons and Insignia

The right to free speech extends to employees in the workplace to the extent that workers must be allowed to wear union buttons. They must be allowed to wear union buttons to the poll, even though blatant electioneering like this would not be allowed in a general election.

Wearing union insignia is protected by NLRA § 7, and interfering with this right violates § 8(a)(1), unless the union materials cause a real safety hazard, or there is a real risk of violence between union supporters and opponents. The mere possibility of violence is not enough.

There is a partial exception. Employees who work with the public, and who are required to wear a uniform, can be forbidden to wear all kinds of jewelry, including union buttons. They can be required to wear the standard uniform, not a union T-shirt. But the employer must be careful to communicate the uniform policy, and to enforce it across the board, not just against union insignia.

A hospital that required employees to wear a uniform, and banned all pins except for professional association pins and hospital service awards could lawfully forbid a carpenter from wearing a union button. The Fifth Circuit held that the hospital's interest in maintaining a tranquil and peaceful atmosphere outweighed the carpenter's First Amendment free speech rights. [*Communications Workers of Am. v. Ector County Hosp. Dist.*, 467 F.3d 427 (5th Cir. 2006)] The NLRB found it permissible for a hospital to forbid nurses to wear "RNs Demand Safe Staffing" buttons in areas where they could be seen by patients or their family members. [*Sacred Heart Medical Center*, 347 NLRB 48 (June 30 2006)] A hotel could forbid room service workers from wearing union buttons in public areas, but not in non-public areas, where management's argument that guests were entitled to a luxurious fantasy atmosphere would not apply. [*Starwood Hotels*, 348 NLRB 24 (Sept. 29, 2006)]

The NLRB said that a car dealership's employee handbook provision forbidding pins, insignia, and other message clothing not provided by the employer is overly restrictive and violates NLRA § 8(a)(1). The NLRB's position is that a rule against union insignia is presumptively invalid. The presumption can be overcome only by a showing of special circumstances (e.g., the rule is needed for safety or to maintain production or discipline). The NLRB accepted the argument that pins can injure employees or damage vehicles, but required the handbook to be amended to permit other kinds of message clothing. [*Boch Imports, Inc.*, NLRB, No. 1-CA-83551 (Jan. 13, 2014); see Maria Greco Danaher, *Prohibiting "Message" Clothing Without Business Reason Violates The NLRA*, Ogletree Deakins (Feb. 10, 2014), available at Lexology.com; Joel S. Barras, *NLRB Judge Invalidates Company Dress Code*, Reed Smith LLP (Jan. 17, 2014), available at Lexology.com]

The Starbucks dress code actually required employees to wear a variety of buttons and badges. Two union activist employees were fired for dress code violations. The Second Circuit vacated one termination and remanded the other. Discharge was upheld for an employee who, in addition to dress code violations, frequently missed work and was not well informed about current products. Discharge was remanded for further proceedings in the case of an employee discharged after a profane outburst in a Starbucks store while the worker was off-duty. It was remanded because the outburst was about union matters, and the NLRB was instructed to consider whether protected collective activity is limited to situations in which employees wear their work uniforms. [*NLRB v. Starbucks Corp.,* 679 F.3d 70 (2d Cir. 2012)]

[H] Access by Non-Employees

In most instances, a workplace is private property, not a public space. Therefore, union organizers do not automatically have a right to leaflet or distribute literature if this is contrary to the wishes of the employer or other owner of the property.

An exception might occur in a "company town" situation, where in effect all property is owned by the employer, so there is no public space where the union can distribute literature. [See, e.g., *Lechmere v. NLRB*, 502 U.S. 527 (1991)] Another exception might be a place that is so remote geographically that the union has no reasonable means of communicating with employees outside the workplace.

California law protects reasonable speech in privately owned shopping centers, but does not require shopping centers to allow expressive activities that interfere with normal business opportunities. The D.C. Circuit couldn't figure out whether forbidding all expressive activities on the premises that did not have a permit violated the NLRA, so it sent the case to the California Supreme Court for a determination of whether a mall can impose a rule against urging customers to boycott any of the tenants of the mall. [*Fashion Valley Mall LLC v. NLRB*, 451 F.3d 241 (D.C. Cir. 2006)]

In late 2012, the California Supreme Court ruled that a supermarket's privately owned entrance area is not a "public forum" as defined by the California constitution. Therefore, union picketing in such an area did not have protection under the state constitution. However, two California labor laws protected picketing. This decision conflicts with the D.C. Circuit's decision in 2004 that one of those statutes, the Moscone Act (which forbids injunctions against peaceful picketing) is unconstitutional because it grants greater protection to labor speech than to other forms of speech. [*Ralphs Grocery Co. v. United Food and Commercial Workers Union Local 8,* 55 Cal. 4th 1083, 290 P.3d 1116, 150 Cal. Rptr. 3d 501 (2012)]

The Sixth Circuit found that it was an Unfair Labor Practice for a non-union nursing home to require employees distributing union literature to leave non-working areas of the premises. The court found that the rights of employees who worked at other sites to receive the information outweighed the employer's property rights. There was no proof that nursing home residents would be any more distressed by the presence of union organizers than any other stranger. [*First Healthcare Corp. v. NLRB*, 344 F.3d 523 (6th Cir. 2003)]

The Third Circuit has found that the NLRA is not violated when an employer denies access to its property to union representatives who want to distribute handbills accusing the employer of using underpaid nonunion labor. In this context, the employer's property rights clearly prevail over the union's free speech right—especially because general information aimed at the public, not an actual certification election, was involved. [*Metropolitan Dist. Council of Phila.*

v. NLRB, 68 F.3d 71 (3d Cir. 1995)] In contrast, where employee interests outweighed the employer's security and property rights concerns, the D.C. Circuit ruled that off-site employees must be allowed to distribute pro-union handbills in the plant parking lot. [*ITT Indus. v. NLRB*, 413 F.3d 64 (D.C. Cir. 2005)]

Can a business located in a shopping mall forbid the distribution of union literature in that mall? The Eighth Circuit says that a business that is just a tenant (and therefore does not have exclusive rights to the corridor outside its business location) cannot forbid union handbilling. But the Sixth Circuit says that a mall owner can ban solicitation by union representatives who are not employed at the mall, even if other kinds of solicitation (e.g., for charity) are allowed. [*O'Neil's Markets v. United Food & Commercial Workers*, 95 F.3d 733 (8th Cir. 1996); *Cleveland Real Estate Partners v. NLRB*, 95 F.3d 457 (6th Cir. 1996); *Riesbeck Food Mkts. Inc. v. NLRB*, 91 F.3d 132 (4th Cir. 1996)] Reasonable restrictions on the time, place, and manner of expressive activities can be imposed. Courts give more scrutiny to content-based restrictions on expressive activities than to those that are content-neutral. [*United Brotherhood of Carpenters & Joiners Local 848 v. NLRB*, 540 F.3d 957 (9th Cir. 2008)]

Picketing is a particularly confrontational practice and has the potential to create conflict and danger, especially when persons who wish to enter the premises are told not to cross the line. The Ninth Circuit ruled that the NLRB was not entitled to a preliminary injunction to prevent a union from putting "Labor Dispute" banners outside stores that hire nonunion contractors because banners do not threaten, coerce, or restrain employees or potential customers. [*Overstreet v. United Bhd. of Carpenters & Joiners of Am.*, 409 F.3d 1199 (9th Cir. 2005)]

§ 30.05 THE APPROPRIATE BARGAINING UNIT

Even after winning an election, a union cannot be certified unless it is organized as the appropriate bargaining unit for the enterprise. NLRA § 9(b) gives the NLRB power to determine the appropriate bargaining unit. The basic standard is whether there is a community of interest among the unit members, not just employees in general (who can be expected to want higher wages and better benefits). Neither employer nor union can tell in advance what will be considered the appropriate unit, or how large the unit will be.

The appropriateness of a bargaining unit depends on the duties, skills, and working conditions of the employees who are supposed to have common interests. If there are competing proposed bargaining units for the same company, their relative popularity with employees is highly significant.

A union can be organized by employer, craft, or plan, or a subdivision of one of these categories. A union decision to organize as a craft unit is legally protected. The NLRB does not have the power to decide that a different unit would be more appropriate.

Employees and supervisors cannot be in the same bargaining unit. In fact, in many instances, supervisors cannot unionize at all, because they are considered a part of management. As a general rule, professionals and nonprofessionals cannot be included in a unit, but this rule can be waived if a majority of the professional employees vote to be included. (The nonprofessionals do not get veto power over inclusion of professionals.)

Determination of professional status does not depend entirely on job title. The factual determination is whether the work is predominantly intellectual, is not routine, requires discretion and independent judgment, mandates specialized knowledge, and cannot be standardized as to time. Professionals can still be unionized, but they must consent to inclusion in a nonprofessional bargaining unit instead of having their own.

If plant guards are unionized, they must have their own bargaining unit. They cannot be organized with other employees, because the employer would not feel very secure during a strike if several guards were union activists—much less if one of them was the shop steward!

In mid-2011, the NLRB sided with unions in several cases about organization and representation. In each case, the three Democrats voted against the one Republican on the board. In the *Specialty Healthcare* case, the NLRB ruled that it was permissible to organize a group consisting only of nursing assistants at a long-term care health facility. Management wanted to include other nonprofessionals in the unit to prevent the creation of "mini-bargaining units" targeting small groups of pro-union workers. The NLRB said that an employer that believes the proposed bargaining unit excludes some workers must prove that the excluded workers have an overwhelming community of interest with the workers in the unit. In the case of *Lamons Gasket Company* the NLRB ruled that employees opposed to the union cannot immediately challenge the employer's recognition of a card-check vote. The NLRB decision in *UGL-Unicco Service Company* says that, when a company is sold, neither the new owner, the employees, nor a rival union can immediately challenge the existing union. The incumbent union must be given a fair chance, over a reasonable time, to prove its mettle in collective bargaining. All three of these cases overturned decisions made earlier, when the NLRB was under Republican control. [*Specialty Healthcare and Rehabilitation Center of Mobile*, 357 NLRB No. 83 (2011); see Melanie Trottman, *Labor Board Rulings Likely to Rile Business*, WSJ.com (Aug. 31, 2011)] The Sixth Circuit upheld this NLRB ruling in 2013 [*Kindred Nursing Ctrs. East, LLC v. NLRB*, 727 F.3d 552 (7th Cir. 2013)] permitting a relatively small bargaining unit of employees with a sufficient community of interest even if the unit excludes employees doing similar work; employers dislike this because mini-bargaining units can be easier to organize.

A bargaining unit of canine welfare technicians and instructors was held to be appropriate given their community of interest, even though management wanted the unit to include workers from five other departments (*Guide Dogs for the Blind*, 2013). [Baker & McKenzie, *Labor Year In Review: NLRB Targets Non-Unionized Employers And Expands Worker Rights* (Dec. 21, 2013), available at Lexology.com]

A micro-unit is a small part of the workforce at a site that a union tries to organize. Previously, unions tended to favor broad "wall to wall" units such as all production and maintenance employees in a facility, but unions have had some success with micro-units. The NLRB and some of its regional directors have approved micro-units (such as single departments in a large retail department store) despite the employer's objections. NLRA § 9 rules out some bargaining units (e.g., one including guards with other workers) but does not say what is appropriate, leaving the determination up to the NLRB. [William Ozier, *Micro-Units – What Are They And Why Should I Care?*, Bass, Berry & Sims PLC (Sept. 9, 2013), available at Lexology.com]

§ 30.06 UNION SECURITY

[A] NLRA Prohibitions

Closed shops (where only union members can be hired) are illegal. The NLRA also forbids "preferential hiring" situations under which the employer is obligated to hire only union members unless the union is unable to fill all vacancies with qualified workers.

However, the LMRA authorizes "union shops," where all current employees must be union members, and new hires can be required to join the union after hiring (within seven days in the construction industry, within 30 days in other industries), and "agency shops," where payment of initiation fees and union dues is mandatory, but actual membership is optional. "Union security" measures are available to a union that is the bona fide bargaining representative of the employees in the bargaining unit and there has not been a deauthorization election certified in the year preceding the effective date of the union security agreement.

It is not a breach of a union's duty of fair representation for it to enter into a CBA that contains a union security clause that echoes the wording of NLRA § 8(3)(a). [*Marquez v. Screen Actors Guild*, 525 U.S. 33 (1998)] The plaintiff claimed that she should have been notified of her right not to join the union and to pay the union only for its representational activities.

If the union wants "automatic dues checkoff" (deduction of dues from the paycheck, so the union doesn't have to bill the member), it must have its members provide a written assignment lasting until the contract expires, or for one year, whichever comes first.

In 2011, the Second Circuit held that the Newspaper Guild's right to dues checkoff survived the expiration of the CBA—but so did the arbitration requirements of the CBA, so a dispute about checkoff had to be arbitrated, not litigated. [*Newspaper Guild CWA of Albany v. Hearst Corp.*, 645 F.3d 527 (2d Cir. 2011)]

Under the NLRA [29 U.S.C. § 169], employees who have a religious objection to unionization cannot be forced to join or support a union—even if the workplace is subject to a union security measure. However, to prevent financial windfalls, the employee can be required to contribute the equivalent of the initiation fee to a nonreligious charity of the employee's choice. *Commc'ns Workers of Am. v. Beck* [487 U.S. 735 (1988)] says that employees who do not want to join a union, but who are subject to a union security clause in the CBA, can be charged fees that can be traced back to collective bargaining, contract administration, and pursuing grievances. But they can prevent the union from using their money for political or other "nonrepresentational purposes."

In June, 2007, the Supreme Court ruled that it is permissible for a state to require unions that represent public employees to get affirmative consent from non-members of the union before using their agency fees for political purposes. (In other words, a state can forbid the union to use the agency fees this way unless the non-member employee opts out.) [*Davenport v. Washington Educ. Assn*, 551 U.S. 177 (2007); see Fred Schneyer, *U.S. Supreme Court Deems WA Union Fee Law Constitutional*, plansponsor.com (June 19, 2007)]

The Supreme Court returned to the subject of agency fees early in 2009. The CBA between the State of Maine and the union representing its employees requires non-member employees who are represented by the union to pay a "service fee" equal to the part of the union dues devoted to representational activities such as collective bargaining and contract administration. These funds cannot be used for politics, lobbying, or public relations. A group of petitioners brought suit to avoid being charged for any part of the service fee that covers nationwide litigation that does not directly benefit the union local. The district court and First Circuit upheld the imposition of this part of the fee. The Supreme Court ruled early in 2009 that the First Amendment permits a local union to charge non-members for the expense of national litigation that they could be required to pay for if it were local: i.e., the suit relates to collective bargaining rather than political issues, and the union local has a reasonable expectation that other locals will contribute. [*Locke v. Karass*, 555 U.S. 207 (2009)]

A "Hudson notice" (the name comes from *Chicago Teachers Union v. Hudson* [475 U.S. 292 (1986)]) informs non-members of a union of the "fair share" fees that they are charged to cover their fair share of the union's cost of negotiating and enforcing the CBA. Courts disagree about what constitutes an adequate Hudson notice, and how the union must present the figures. Executive Order 13202, mandating that federal agencies awarding contracts can neither require nor prohibit the contractors from entering into or adhering to agreements with unions, has been upheld by the D.C. Circuit. The court found this to be proprietary action, not regulation, and therefore to be a constitutional exercise of presidential power that is not preempted by the NLRA. [*Bldg. & Constr. Trades Dep't v. Allbaugh*, 295 F.3d 28 (D.C. Cir. 2002)]

A June 2012 Supreme Court case deals with a special assessment imposed on non-Union employees in a public sector agency shop. The special assessment, a 25% increase in monthly dues and removal of the previous cap on dues to create a "fight-back" fund to oppose legislation disfavored by the Union, was held to violate the non-members' First Amendment rights by forcing them into association and speech they did not endorse. The Supreme Court ruled that a separate Hudson notice should have been given. The Supreme Court said that a compulsory subsidy for private speech is permissible only when the fees are a necessary part of the larger purpose that led to the creation of the association. It is unlawful to charge the fee to non-Union members unless they opt out: the charge can only be imposed on non-members who affirmatively opt in to paying it. [*Knox v. SEIU*, 132 S. Ct. 2277 (2012)]

Yet another Supreme Court agency fee case was decided in mid-2014. The Supreme Court ruled that workers who provided home care to Medicaid recipients in Illinois were partial public employees who had the right to refuse to pay fair share fees. The Supreme Court said that the home care aides primarily worked for the elderly and disabled people who received the care, not for the clients, and requiring them to pay agency fees violated their First Amendment rights. However, the Supreme Court did not expand this holding to a more general rule that conventional public employees are exempt from paying agency fees. [*Harris v. Quinn*, No. 11-681 (U.S. June 30, 2014); see Steven Greenhouse, *Supreme Court Ruling Allows Some Public Workers to Opt Out of Union Fees*, NYTimes.com (June 30, 2014)]

During the Bush administration, Executive Order 13201 required federal contractors to post a "Beck notice" to inform employees that they are not obligated to join a union; that they can object to use of their money for non-representation purposes, and can seek a refund of money used in this manner. [69 Fed. Reg. 16375 (Mar. 29, 2004)]

Shortly after his inauguration, President Obama signed three orders to expand the union rights of employees of federal contractors, and to reverse Bush administration policies. The first order (E.O. 13496) revoked E.O. 13201. E.O. 13201 required posting a notice of the right not to join a union. E.O. 13496 requires posting of a balanced notice of employee rights under the NLRA. E.O. 13496 applies to companies that have more than $100,000 in federal contracts. The second order holds that, when a federal agency changes the contractors who provide services to a federal building, the incoming contractor must offer jobs to the outgoing contractor's non-supervisory employees. The third order denies reimbursement of money spent on supporting or deterring employees' rights to unionize or bargain collectively.

DOL Office of Labor-Management Standards, *Executive Order 13496 Notification of Employee Rights Under Federal Labor Law*, <http://www.dol.gov/olms/regs/compliance/EO13496.htm> (undated, accessed June 11, 2014); see Laura Meckler, *Obama to Reverse Bush Labor Policies*, <http://online.wsj.com/news/articles/SB123324342041128947> (Jan. 30, 2009)

Another Obama administration move was the NLRB's publication of regulations requiring employers to display a poster about the right to unionize, bargain collectively, distribute union literature, and be free of retaliation for collective action to improve wages and working conditions. (In effect, this is the converse of the Beck notice.) Originally, the requirement was supposed to take effect November 14, 2011. [Steven Greenhouse, *N.L.R.B. Tells Companies to Ease Right to Unionize*, NYTimes.com (Aug. 25, 2011). In response to protests by business groups, the NLRB twice postponed the effective date of the notice-posting requirement. Tara Cantore, *NLRB Postpones Implementation Date for Notice Posting Rule*, plansponsor.com (Oct. 5, 2011) and *NLRB Postpones Required Date to Post Employee Rights*, plansponsor.com (Dec. 27, 2011)]

Both the D.C. and the Fourth Circuit ruled in 2013 that the posting requirement was invalid. The D.C. Circuit held that the posting rule violates employers' expressive rights. Instead of severing the provision that failure to post is a ULP, the D.C. Circuit invalidated the entire rule, concluding that the NLRB would not want to have a purely voluntary rule that it could not enforce. The Fourth Circuit stated that the NLRB's powers are limited, not extensive, and the NLRB has power to act only when triggered by a certification petition or an Unfair Labor Practices charge. According to the Fourth Circuit, other agencies such as the EEOC and OSHA derive their authority to require posting from their governing statutes, and the NLRA does not authorize a posting requirement. [*Chamber of Commerce v. NLRB*, 721 F.3d 152 (4th Cir. 2013); see Jenna Greene, *Fourth Circuit Strikes NLRB Poster Rule*, The BLT: The Blog of Legal Times (June 14, 2013) (law.com); *Nat'l Ass'n of Mfrs. v. NLRB*, 717 F.3d 947 (D.C. Cir. 2013)]

The NLRB petitioned both the Fourth and D.C. Circuits for rehearing, but the petitions were denied. The NLRB applied for two extensions of time to file certiorari petitions, but the final deadline of January 2, 2014 passed without a filing, and the NLRB lawyers said they were no longer seeking review of these decisions. [Christine Holst, *The Hits Keep Coming: D.C. Circuit Denies Rehearing For NLRB Notice Posting Case*, Barnes & Thornburg LLP (Sept. 6, 2013), available at Lexology.com; Benjamin P. Glass, *NLRB Throws In The Towel On Notice Posting Rule*, Ogletree Deakins (Jan. 3, 2014), available at Lexology.com; Hunton & Williams LLP, *NLRB Declines To Take Union-Poster Dispute To High Court*, Lexology.com (Jan. 8, 2014)]

The Ninth Circuit upheld California Gov't Code §§ 16645–16649 (forbidding companies that receive state grants over $10,000 from using the money to assist, promote, or deter union organizing). The court found that the statute does not violate the First Amendment, does not undermine federal labor policy, and is not preempted by the NLRA. [*Chamber of Commerce v. Lockyer*, 463 F.3d 1076 (9th Cir. 2006)] Certiorari was granted in late 2007. According to the United States Solicitor General, New York, Florida, Illinois, Maine, Massachusetts, Minnesota, North Dakota, Ohio, and Rhode Island have similar laws, and bills of this type have been introduced in New Jersey and Michigan. [The Supreme Court ruled that the California law was preempted by federal labor law. According to the Supreme Court, federal labor law promotes wide-open debate on labor matters, as long as employers refrain from coercion. [*Chamber of Commerce v. Brown*, 554 U.S. 60 (2008)]

The converse of union security is a state "right to work" law that says that unwilling employees cannot be compelled to join unions or pay dues. Early in 2012, Indiana became the twenty-third "right to work" state (i.e., a state forbidding union contracts that obligate non-members to pay representation fees). It was the first state to adopt such a law in more than a decade and the only Midwestern state in that category; most right to work states are in the South (e.g., Alabama, Arkansas, Florida, Georgia, Louisiana, Mississippi, North Carolina, South Carolina, Tennessee, Texas, Virginia). [Monica Davey, *Indiana Becomes 'Right to Work' State*, NYTimes.com (Feb. 1, 2012). According to a graphic in Kris Maher's article, *Despite Win, Right-to-Work Bills Face Long Slog*,WSJ.com (Dec. 13, 2013), Arizona, Idaho, Iowa, Kansas, Nebraska, Nevada, North Dakota, South Dakota, Oklahoma, Utah, and Wyoming were also right to work states.]

Indiana was the 23rd state to forbid collection of agency fees. Lake County Superior Court Judge John Sedia found that Indiana's right to work law violated the state constitution provision that forbids delivery of services without just compensation. The plaintiffs included the International Union of Operating Engineers. The decision says that federal law requires unions to process grievances for non-members, negotiate contracts that benefit both members and non-members, and provide other services to non-members. The right to work law makes it a criminal offense for a union to be paid for services that federal law requires it to provide.

In mid-2014, Lake County Circuit Court judge George Paras also found the right to work law invalid because he said it violated the state constitution's ban on obtaining services without just compensation. Judge Sedia's decision has been appealed, with arguments before the Indiana Supreme Court scheduled for September 4, 2014. [*United Steelworkers v. Zoeller* (Lake Cou. Circuit Court July 17, 2014). See Brandon Smith, *State Supreme Court to Hear Right to Work Case in September*, Indiana Public Media (May 9, 2014), available at <http://indianapublicmedia.org/news/state-supreme-court-hear-work-case-september-66882/>; Peter T. Tschanz, *Indiana Judge Rules State's Right to Work Law Unconstitutional*, Barnes & Thornburg LLP (Sept. 10, 2013), available at Lexology.com; AP, *Indiana Judge Finds Portion of Right to Work Law Unconstitutional*, Indiana Business Journal (Sept. 9, 2013) (benefitslink.com).]

In late 2012, Michigan became the 24th right to work state, as a result of a statute affecting hundreds of thousands of private and public sector union members. (However, the police and fire unions are not affected by the law.) The right to work law means that non-union workers are not required to pay union representation fees. [Matthew Dolan and Kris Maher, *Michigan Approves Union Curbs*, WSJ.com (Dec. 12, 2012); Kris Maher, Q&A: *How Michigan's 'Right-to-Work' Law Will Work*, WSJ.com (Dec. 11, 2012)].

[B] Hiring Halls

Under a union security option, the employer decides who to hire, but the union may be able to get hirees to join or pay dues. A hiring hall works differently. It is a mechanism under which the union selects workers and sends them to the employer, based on the employer's requisition (for six plasterers and two electricians, for example). The union decides which union or nonunion workers will be referred for the job.

An exclusive hiring hall is a relationship under which the employer gets all its workers through union referrals. This is not considered a union security arrangement, so it is legal in the right-to-work states. A nonexclusive hiring hall makes union referral only one of the ways in which the employer can find new workers.

The NLRA provides that it is unlawful for a union to give preference to union members over equally qualified nonmembers in the operation of a nonexclusive hiring hall. The operation and structure of a hiring hall is a mandatory bargaining subject.

In a situation in which union members testified that they often got work for themselves without union referral, the union was not operating an exclusive hiring hall. Therefore, it was a ULP for the union to pressure management to avoid hiring persons who were not referred by the union, or to fire employees for that reason. Enforcement of a hiring hall arrangement depends on the terms of the CBA. Therefore, once the NLRB shows discriminatory conduct that could have affected employee rights, the burden shifts to the employer or union to show that it acted in compliance with the CBA. [*NLRB v. Local 334, Laborers Int'l Union*, 481 F.3d 875, 1639, 1714 (6th Cir. 2007)]

§ 30.07 THE COLLECTIVE BARGAINING PROCESS

[A] Basic Issues

Under the NLRA, the purpose of certifying a union is to provide an ongoing process of collective bargaining between employer and union on important work-related issues, leading to the adoption of a union contract, or Collective Bargaining Agreement (CBA). Even after a CBA is in place, it is still necessary to bargain on "mandatory" issues, and allowable to bargain on "permissive" issues. [See 29 U.S.C. § 158(a)(5)] There are some subjects on which it is illegal to bargain. For instance, it is illegal to implement a closed shop, even if both employer and union are willing.

Mandatory bargaining subjects include:

- Drug testing;
- Dues checkoff (the employer's practice of deducting union dues from paychecks, then forwarding these amounts to the union);

- Work rules;
- Bans on moonlighting by employees;
- Transfers of work out of the bargaining unit;
- Contracting out work done by employees in the bargaining unit (contracting out work done by nonunionized employees is not a mandatory subject of bargaining);
- Bonuses;
- Medical insurance;
- Clauses that forbid strikes and lockouts.

Mandatory bargaining subjects are those that materially or significantly affect the terms or conditions of employment. Issues that have a remote or incidental effect on the work environment are permissible subjects of bargaining.

Where bargaining is required, the employer has a duty to meet with the union at reasonable times to confer over the terms and conditions of employment (such as wages and hours). Insisting that bargaining sessions be held during regular business hours and making negotiating committee members use paid leave to attend the sessions was a management ULP because it interfered with the right to bargain collectively. [*Ceridian Corp. v. NLRB*, 435 F.3d 352 (D.C. Cir. 2006)]

Refusal to bargain is an unfair labor practice. On the other hand, certain issues are established as managerial prerogatives that can be decided unilaterally, without bargaining:

- Complete termination of operations;
- Sale of an entire business;
- A partial closing that has business motivations, and is not the result of anti-union animus;
- Relocation of bargaining-unit work that is motivated by a basic change in the nature of the employer's operations, where the work at the new location is significantly different from the work at the old one.

The basic rule is that bargaining is required if a decision is undertaken to save labor costs, but not if the employer takes on a program of modernization or environmental compliance that costs more than the potential savings on labor costs. Even if the employer has the right to make a decision without union involvement, it has an obligation to engage in "effects bargaining": that is, it must notify the union that the decision has been made, and must bargain about the effects the change will have on union members.

Changing the methods of production is considered a managerial prerogative, although employees who believe that they are adversely affected by the change can file a grievance or seek effects bargaining about the change.

A Gissel bargaining order (stemming from *NLRB v. Gissel Packing Co.*) [395 U.S. 575 (1969)] is an order compelling management to bargain in good faith with a union. Early in 2003, the D.C. Circuit upheld an NLRB order requiring a movie theater chain to bargain with union locals before making the theaters "manager-operated" and firing the union projectionists. Although technological improvements have greatly reduced the amount (and skill level) of the work done by projectionists, eliminating a job classification does not come under the heading of "new or improved work methods" that can be introduced without bargaining. Transfer of work always requires bargaining if it results in loss of bargaining unit jobs. [*Regal Cinemas Inc. v. NLRB*, 317 F.3d 300 (D.C. Cir. 2003)]

Bargaining must be done in good faith. Neither side is obligated to make concessions or give in where it thinks surrender would be imprudent. If the bargaining process comes to an impasse—i.e., neither side is introducing new proposals or yielding on proposals already on the table—then the employer can lawfully cease negotiating and simply put its own proposals into place.

"Regressive bargaining"—withdrawing an offer if the union is unable to meet the employer's time frame—has been upheld by the NLRB in *White Cap, Inc.* [325 NLRB 220 (1998)], unless it is done specifically for the purpose of avoiding a contract. Where the employer has a legitimate business reason for wanting to resolve the issue quickly, regressive bargaining is permissible.

After a collective bargaining agreement expires, there is nothing left to be enforced under contract law. But labor law [NLRA § 8(a)(5)] obligates the employer to maintain the status quo, at least until an impasse is reached and the employer can start implementing its own proposals unilaterally. The employer cannot take advantage of a bargaining impasse to unilaterally impose new provisions, or any provisions more favorable to its own cause than the provisions that were on the table during negotiations.

The Seventh Circuit has ruled (in a case involving a union's request for information about hidden surveillance cameras in the workplace) that the right to bargain about a mandatory bargaining subject can only be waived by a clear and unmistakeable expression of an intention to waive. [*Nat'l Steel Corp. v. NLRB*, 324 F.3d 928 (7th Cir. 2003)] The cameras are mandatory bargaining subjects because, like drug and alcohol tests, they involve the terms and conditions of employment. Furthermore, the employer was merely ordered to bargain and provide the union with information about the cameras; it was not forbidden to use security cameras or ordered to make public disclosure of the location of the cameras. The deployment of hidden surveillance cameras was also treated as a mandatory bargaining subject by *Brewers & Maltsters v. NLRB*, 414 F.3d 36 (D.C. Cir. 2005), because subjects plainly germane to the work environment are mandatory bargaining subjects, unless they are at the core of entrepreneurial control of the workplace. (See § 26.06 for additional discussion of workplace surveillance.)

A growing issue (see §§ 26.06 and 27.05) is the extent to which employers can monitor employees' social media activities.

The NLRB began to confront social media issues in late 2010. Since then, what has emerged as the major question is whether employees use social media to discuss or protest working conditions (which constitutes protected activity) or whether they merely discuss personal issues (which is probably not protected, especially if there are issues of misuse of the employer's proprietary information.) In general, employer policies are tested for reasonableness: are they too broad or impermissibly vague? Do they prevent employees from exercising their rights under the NLRA? In general, employees will be protected if social media is part of collective activity about working conditions—but will not be protected if they are merely griping about personal issues, or their conduct violates reasonable rules of civility.

Finally, employers are entitled to a defense if they would have taken adverse action against the employee even without the protected concerted activity. The NLRB held that a social media rule was unlawful because its ban on disparaging or defamatory comments about the company, its employees, customers, products, or services, and the requirement of prior permission before contacting the media, communicating with the public about the company, or discussing the company with government agencies was overbroad (*Dish Network Corp.* (2013)). It was unlawful to fire three employees who posted Facebook messages criticizing their supervisor's dismissal of their fears of working late in a dangerous neighborhood (*Design Technology Group LLP*, April 18, 2013). [Baker & McKenzie, *Labor Year In Review: NLRB Targets Non-Unionized Employers And Expands Worker Rights* (Dec. 21, 2013), available at Lexology.com]

An NLRB ALJ found that it was concerted activity for two employees of a youth center to discuss workplace concerns on Facebook. They were not rehired after they did so. However, the ALJ recommended dismissal of the ULP charge, because they said they intended to be uncooperative to the employer, which is not protected activity, and their remarks could have jeopardized program funding and the safety of the children in the program. [*Richmond Dist. Neighborhood Center*, NLRB ALJ, No. 20-CA-91748 (Nov. 5, 2013); see Michael L. Stevens and Karen S. Vladeck, *There Are Limits On Social Media: Facebook Comments Found Concerted But Not Protected*, Arent Fox LLP (Nov. 21, 2013), available at Lexology .com]

[B] Typical CBA Clauses

Although the actual contract that emerges from bargaining will reflect the individual needs of the business, and the comparative strengths of management and union, the following are issues that are often addressed in Collective Bargaining Agreements:

- Description of the bargaining unit;
- Management rights;
- Workday and workweek;
- Overtime;
- Classification of jobs for wage purposes;
- Compensation, bonuses, health, and other benefits;
- Paid time off (who is eligible, scheduling time off, who must be notified, which paid holidays are provided);
- Sick leave (number of days available; waiting period; doctors' notes; discipline for misusing sick leave);
- Seniority (what counts as a break in continuous service; effect of corporate transitions on seniority);
- Subcontracting;
- Plant closing and successorship;
- Severance pay;
- Hiring halls;
- Union security;
- Access to premises by non-employee union staff;
- Progressive discipline (the steps such as reprimands, conferences, and written warnings that will be provided before an employee is discharged);
- Drug testing;
- Grievance procedures (scope of disputes covered; how employees can present grievances; whether binding arbitration is required).

[C] Bargaining on Modification, Termination

The employer has an obligation to notify the union whenever it intends to modify or terminate a CBA. The employer must also notify the Federal Mediation and Conciliation Service of the intended action. Sixty days before the contract is scheduled to expire (or 60 days before the intended modification or termination), the employer must notify the union, inviting it to negotiate a new or amended contract. Notice to the FMCS is due 30 days after the notice to the union. Failure to give the required notice is an unfair labor practice. [29 U.S.C. § 158(d)]

The 60-day notice period is referred to as the cooling-off period. The contract remains in effect during this period, and neither strikes nor lockouts are permitted.

Employers need not volunteer information, but they have a duty to provide the union with whatever information (other than confidential or privileged information) the union requests in order to represent the employees adequately. Information relating to wage rates and job descriptions is presumed relevant. The union has to show a specific need for access to the employer's nonpublic financial information—e.g., if the employer claims inability to afford a wage increase. [*Lakeland Bus Lines Inc. v. NLRB*, 347 F.3d 955 (D.C. Cir. 2003)]

§ 30.08 ELECTIONS AFTER CERTIFICATION

Representation elections are not the only kind that can be ordered and supervised by the NLRB. Federal labor law allows a rerun or runoff election to be held to redress an improper election. Once a union is in place, employees can ask that it be deauthorized or decertified. The employer also has the right to challenge a union's majority status.

A rerun election is held if there were election improprieties, or if two unions competed for representation; the ballot included a "no union" choice, and "no union" got as many votes as the other alternatives. (If there is only one union on the ballot, a tie vote means that the union loses, because it failed to attract a majority of the voters.)

A runoff election is held if no choice gets a majority. Only one runoff election can be held, although there could be both a rerun and a runoff election in the same organizing campaign.

A deauthorization petition is filed by a group of employees who want to remove the union's authority to enter into a union shop contract. Therefore, there are no deauthorization petitions in right-to-work states, because there aren't any union shops either. When a majority of the bargaining unit (not just a majority of the voters) vote for deauthorization, the union remains the authorized bargaining representative for the employees, but the employees no longer have to pay union dues.

The purpose of a decertification petition is to remove the union's bargaining authority. The petition can be filed by an employee, a group of employees, or someone acting on behalf of the employees. The employer does not have the right to file a decertification petition, but it does have a free-speech right to inform employees of their right to remove a union that they feel has not represented them adequately.

A decertification petition requires a showing of interest by 30% of the employees in the bargaining unit. Most petitions that are filed get the necessary vote (a majority of actual voters, not eligible voters) and therefore result in decertification of the union.

Decertification petitions cannot be filed at certain times: one year after certification of a union; a reasonable time after an employer's voluntary recognition of a union; or within 12 months of another decertification petition.

The employer has the right to petition the NLRB to determine that the union has lost its majority status. The employer must offer objective evidence of the change, such as employee turnover so heavy that few of the original pro-union workers remain; the union's failure to process employee grievances; or a strike that yielded no benefits for employees. If an employer has information that leads it to doubt the union's majority status, it is an unfair labor practice to enter into a contract with this union and then try to disavow the contract based on those doubts. The appropriate action is to refuse the contract. [*Auciello Iron Works Inc. v. NLRB*, 517 U.S. 781 (1996)]

The general rule, known as the CBA bar, is that no union election can be held while a collective bargaining agreement is in force. However, if there has been a substantial increase in personnel since the contract was signed, a new election may be proper if the union no longer represents a majority of the current workforce.

There used to be another "bar" in effect, the "successor bar" rule of *St. Elizabeth's Manor* [329 NLRB 341 (1999)], under which an incumbent union would be given a reasonable amount of time after a corporate takeover to bargain with the successor employer without challenges to its majority status. However, in 2002, the NLRB overruled that decision [*MV Transportation*, 337 N.L.R.B. 129 (July 19, 2002)] and now takes the position that the incumbent union gets a rebuttable presumption of continuing majority status, but that will not bar an otherwise valid challenge to majority status. It violates federal labor law for an employer to withdraw recognition of a union prematurely, without engaging in bargaining for a reasonable period of time. (However, pursuing reasonable bargaining will remove the taint of an earlier refusal to bargain.) In this case, there were only five bargaining sessions, and apparently the parties were close to reaching agreement when recognition was withdrawn, so the D.C. Circuit upheld the NLRB's ruling against the employer. [*Lee Lumber & Building Materials Corp. v. NLRB*, 310 F.3d 209 (D.C. Cir. 2002)]

§ 30.09 STRIKES

The DOL reported that 2013 saw the first decline in four years in the number of workers out of work because of major strikes or lockouts. There were 15 work stoppages with 1,000 or more workers, involving about 55,000 people; the comparable figures for 2012 were 19 stoppages and 148,000 workers. Time lost to work stoppages was down 74% (290,000 workdays, less than .0005% of all workdays). There were four strikes each in health care and local government—the largest number of strikes in any industry. [Winston & Strawn LLP, *Strikes & Labor Disputes - February 2014*, Lexology.com (Feb. 28, 2014)]

[A] Right to Strike

The NLRA gives employees the right to engage in "protected concerted activities"—joining together to organize, protest, and otherwise assert their interests in a lawful manner. This includes going on strike if a new contract cannot be negotiated, or based on a union's claim that working conditions are bad enough to justify a strike.

A striking union's gamble is that the employer will need to maintain continuous operations and therefore will grant significant concessions before the employees lose too much income by stopping work. But at other times employers actually benefit from strikes, if they can save payroll for a while, shut down an unproductive location, relocate to a lower-cost area (in another state or even another country) or bringing in "striker replacements."

Violence, sabotage, and threats are not protected activity. If a threatened strike would imperil the national health or safety, the President of the United States can order the U.S. Attorney General to petition the appropriate federal court for an 80-day cooling-off period, during which the strike is enjoined.

Secondary strikes and secondary boycotts—actions taken against one employer to put pressure on another employer that does business with the first employer—are banned by NLRA § 8(b)(4). A company that is the victim of a secondary strike or boycott can sue for damages under LMRA § 303.

[B] Types of Strike

Employees can lawfully engage in a work stoppage in three situations:

- An economic dispute with the employer;
- A claim that the employer has committed unfair labor practices;
- A claim that workplace conditions are so unreasonably dangerous that they should not be required to continue work.

An "unfair labor practices" strike is caused in whole or part by unfair labor practices. There must be a causal connection between the strike and the employer practices. If the practices are simply cost-related (such as shift changes), then the strike should be characterized as an economic strike. But a strike that begins as an economic strike can be converted to an unfair labor practices strike if the employer acts unfairly or refuses to accept legitimate offers for return to work.

The main difference between an economic strike and an unfair labor practices strike is the extent of employees' reinstatement rights after the strike ends and they want to go back to work. Some issues are areas of managerial prerogative, so employees cannot lawfully strike to challenge management's decisions in these areas.

29 U.S.C. § 143 makes it a protected concerted activity for employees to refuse to work if there is measurable, objective evidence of undue hazards (not just a subjective feeling that something is wrong). The employees must also articulate goals that the employer can respond to: replace a defective machine or install guard rails, for instance, not just "make the workplace safer." [See Chapter 31 for information about occupational safety and health]

If the underlying strike is lawful, then a sympathy strike (workers outside the striking bargaining unit refuse to cross the picket line) is probably protected concerted activity as defined by the NLRA. A 2003 decision of the Ninth Circuit says that a no-strike provision in a CBA does not bar a sympathy strike for another bargaining unit within the same local union, because the CBA clause did not clearly and unmistakeably waive the right to call a strike in support of fellow union members. [*Standard Concrete Prods. Inc. v. Gen. Truck Drivers Office, Food & Warehouse Union*, 353 F.3d 668 (9th Cir. 2003)]

In contrast to those protected activities, a sitdown strike (an illegal takeover of the employer's premises) is unlawful. A wildcat strike, called by the rank and file without authorization from the union, is not protected activity if the workers want to usurp the union's role as sole bargaining representative for the workers.

A collective bargaining agreement can lawfully be drafted to include a no-strike clause. It is not protected concerted activity to call an economic strike in violation of a no-strike clause. Therefore, the employer can legitimately fire the strikers and deny them reinstatement after the strike ends.

Because of the special risks involved, NLRA § 8(g) requires unions at health care facilities to give at least 10 days' notice before a strike, picket, or concerted refusal to work. The employer must be notified of the date and time the action will commence. The NLRB ruled that starting the strike four hours later than the time stated in the notice violates the notice requirement. Unions are not permitted to make unilateral extensions of strike notices. Therefore, it was not an unfair labor practice to fire nurses involved in the strike. [*Alexandria Clinic PA*, 339 NLRB No. 162 (Aug. 21, 2003)]

[C] Lockouts and Other Employer Activity

The lockout is the employer's counterpart to the union's strike. In a strike, the employees refuse to come to work. In a lockout, the employer refuses to let them in. An employer that undertakes a lockout for business reasons can hire replacement workers. It can enter into a temporary subcontract for the duration of the lockout. However, the employer is not allowed to use the lockout to permanently contract out work formerly performed by employees. Lockouts are lawful if and only if they have a business motivation, not if they are used to prevent the workers from organizing a union, or to avoid bargaining with an incumbent union. However, a lockout is a justified response to a strike that violates a CBA no-strike clause.

It is an unfair labor practice for an employer to institute a lockout that is inherently destructive of the rights of employees. It is also an unfair labor practice to institute a lockout without having legitimate economic business justification (not just the employer's convenience). The mere possibility of a strike if contract negotiations break down is not a sufficient justification for a lockout during collective bargaining; and it might be treated as an unlawful refusal to bargain. Lockouts are analyzed even more stringently outside the strike context, because the union's power is weaker and there is less need for the employer to counter-balance it.

Employers are allowed to close a business, or shut it down temporarily, with economic motivations. But doing it to harm the union is an unfair labor practice. A "runaway shop" (transferring work between existing locations or opening a new location) is an unfair labor practice if it is based on antiunion motivation rather than a desire to enhance profitability.

During a strike, the employer is not permitted to alter the terms and conditions of employment that affect strikers. However, once a CBA expires, the employer is allowed to change those terms as they affect striker replacements.

[D] Striker Replacements

During a strike, employers are entitled to keep their operations open by hiring replacements. Employers can always hire replacements for jobs that are described as temporary stopgaps until the strike ends. The question is whether the employer can hire permanent replacements, outsource functions formerly performed by employees, or keep the replacements and deny reinstatement to the strikers post-strike.

It is not an unfair labor practice to discharge strikers who have lost their employee status, and therefore their protection under the NLRA. The NLRA protects only lawful strikes that are conducted in a lawful manner, are called for a protected purpose, and are authorized by the bargaining unit representative (if there is one).

A strike is lawful if it occurs after the expiration of a CBA, if it is either an economic or an unfair labor practices strike, or if it demands concessions from the employer. Wildcat strikes, sitdown strikes, and strikes contrary to a CBA no-strike clause are not protected. Excessive violence removes employee status, although a minor instance of violence would not prevent the perpetrator from being considered an employee.

In an economic strike, the employer can permanently replace the strikers and keep the replacement workers after the end of the strike. However, strikers are entitled to reinstatement after the strike if they have not been replaced. Delay in reinstating them counts as an unfair labor practice. Even after being replaced, an economic striker is still considered an employee. If the former economic striker makes an unconditional application for reinstatement, the employer must reinstate him if the replacement worker quits or is terminated. If no jobs are available at the time of the application, the employer must reinstate the ex-striker when a job becomes available.

However, the former striker does not have to be reinstated if:

- He or she gets regular and substantial employment somewhere else;
- The employer has a legitimate business reason (violence or sabotage during the strike, for instance) for denying reinstatement;
- The job itself has been eliminated (e.g., due to new technology).

The NLRB's position, which has been upheld by the Seventh Circuit, is that the main issue is whether the replacement workers have a reasonable expectation of recall after being laid off. Strikers are entitled to reinstatement if the replacements did not have a reasonable expectation of recall—unless the employer can prove that the job is vacant or there is good cause not to rehire the striker. A "Laidlaw vacancy," otherwise known as a "genuine job vacancy," occurs if the replacement worker cannot reasonably expect recall after layoff.

Unless there is a legitimate and substantial business reason to depart from the rule, a reinstated economic striker must be treated equally with nonstrikers and permanent replacements, with the same benefits, including paid vacations and accrual of seniority. Normally, reinstatement should return the worker to status quo, but he or she can be demoted for a legitimate business reason such as a risk of sabotage.

[E] Subcontracting

When a strike is imminent, employers who have a pressing business reason, and who are not acting out of antiunion animus, can legitimately subcontract out work that was performed by the bargaining unit, even though employees are displaced. NLRA § 8(a)(3), which penalizes employer actions that are intended to discourage union membership, can be invoked even if there is no direct proof of the employer's motivation—if the employer's action is inherently destructive of important rights of the employees. Subcontracting is a mandatory bargaining subject, so the employer can act unilaterally if a bargaining impasse has been reached.

§ 30.10 THE WARN ACT

The Worker Adjustment Retraining and Notice Act (WARN Act) [29 U.S.C. § 2101] requires employers of 100 or more full-time employees (or a combination of full- and part-timers adding up to at least 100 people and 4,000 work hours a week) to provide notice of a plant closing or mass layoff. At least 60 days' notice must be given to employees, unions, and the federal government. The Act defines a plant closing as employment loss (termination, prolonged layoff, serious cutback in work hours) affecting 50 or more workers during a 30-day period.

A mass layoff has a lesser effect on the individual workers (e.g., potential for recall) and affects 500 people or one-third of the workforce. Anyone rehired within six months, or anyone who elected early retirement, should not be counted in determining if a mass layoff has occurred.

A reduction in force (RIF) may require compliance with the WARN Act or a related state statute (e.g., in California, Connecticut, Illinois, Maine, New Hampshire, New Jersey, New York, Tennessee, and Wisconsin). Penalties imposed for non-compliance can wipe out the savings associated with reducing payroll.

Even employers who qualify for the faltering company exception or the unforeseen business circumstance exception still must give as much notice to employees as is practicable, and the notice itself must explain why the full 60 days of notice was not given.

The faltering company exception applies if the company proves that it was actively seeking capital or new business 60 days before the shutdown; there was a realistic chance of obtaining it; the financing would have been enough to avert shutdown; and giving the notice would have made it impossible to secure the financing.

The unforeseen business circumstances exception requires events that are beyond the employer's control—for example, sudden, dramatic, and unexpected conditions such as unexpected termination of an important contract, a major supplier goes on strike, or the government orders closing of a site without time to prepare. However, this exception is seldom applied when a company was simply in bad financial condition and its finances continued to deteriorate.

Companies that plan RIFs should consider implementing an ERISA severance plan. If there is a plan in place, employees must exhaust the internal claims procedure before suing, and the employer can reserve the discretion to construe the plan terms as long as the employer does not act arbitrarily and capriciously. ERISA claims can be removed to federal court—thus escaping tougher state laws on severance. Furthermore, claims under an ERISA plan can be removed to federal court, and states tend to have tougher laws on severance.

According to the Ninth Circuit, for WARN Act purposes, the "site of employment" for construction workers is the actual job site and not the company headquarters. Therefore, since the site did not have 50 or more workers, the WARN Act did not apply. (There were 33 employees at headquarters plus three outside administrators, and 162 construction workers at sites in seven states.) [*Bader v. Northern Line Layers*, 503 F.3d 813 (9th Cir. 2007)]

Although the WARN Act refers to a "group" of laid-off employees, employers cannot avoid the application of the act by performing layoffs one at a time. All economically motivated layoffs within a 90-day period are aggregated toward the 50-employee figure. [*Hallowell v. Orleans Reg'l Hosp.*, 217 F.3d 379 (5th Cir. 2000)]

If the employer fails to give the required notice, each affected employee is entitled to up to 60 days' back pay (work days, not calendar days) and benefits. A federal civil penalty of up to $500 can also be imposed for every day that the failure to give notice continued. A union can sue for damages on behalf of its members.

The Eighth Circuit ruled that the seller of a business was protected by the WARN Act's sale-of-business exclusion. The buyer promised to hire a substantial number of the seller's employees (and in fact did so), so the seller believed that fewer than 50 employees would lose their jobs. A seller is responsible for providing WARN Act notice up to and including the sale date, but at that point, the purchaser becomes responsible for giving notice of a plant closing. In the Eighth Circuit view, only the party actually causing employment loss must give notice. When a business is sold as a going concern, the sale-of-business exception creates a presumption that the buyer is the employer if the seller continues to employ its employees on the day of the sale. [*Wilson v. Airtherm Prods. Inc.*, 436 F.3d 906 (8th Cir. 2006)]

The Second Circuit held that there is a material question of fact requiring trial of a WARN Act case as to whether HoldCo and its closely held subsidiary were a single employer for WARN Act purposes. The Second Circuit held that a lender is responsible for giving WARN Act notice if it is so entangled with the borrower that it is responsible for managing the borrower's business. However, the Second Circuit refused to extend this principle beyond lenders. The Second Circuit used the five non-exclusive factors from DOL regulations (20 C.F.R. § 639.3(a)(3)) to determine whether related entities constitute a single employer: e.g., common ownership, shared directors and/or officers, de facto control, unified personnel policies, and interdependent operations. [*Guippone v. BH Holdings LLC*, 737 F.3d 221 (2d Cir. 2013)]

The Eleventh Circuit ruled that a covered employer (in this case, a casino dependent on electronic gaming shut down by a government task force on illegal gambling) must provide WARN Act notice even if the unforeseeable business circumstances exception applies. 29 USC § 2102(b) obligates the employer to provide as much notice as practicable, and the notice must say why the period was reduced. The Eleventh Circuit said that the 60-day period can be reduced if necessary, but the employer cannot entirely avoid the notice requirement. [*Sides v. Macon Cnty. Greyhound Park Inc.*, 725 F.3d 1276 (11th Cir. 2013); see Michael C. Wilhelm, *Are WARN Act Notices Required Even When Mass Layoffs Are Unforeseeable?*, Briggs and Morgan (Sept. 12, 2013), available at Lexology.com]

The Northern District of Illinois allowed a class action WARN Act suit to proceed against both a private equity firm and one of its portfolio companies, holding that it is not necessary for the plaintiff to be able to pierce the corporate veil. It can claim that the owner of a company is liable as a single employer if it has enough control. The factors in whether two entities are separate are common ownership; shared directors and officers; de facto control; unified personnel policies from a common source; and dependency of operations. It is not necessary for a plaintiff to prove all of the factors to have a viable claim. Stock ownership alone is not enough to make a parent corporation liable for the subsidiary's actions, but shared management may suffice, with de facto control as the most important factor. [*Young v. Fortis Plastics LLC*, Case No. 3:12-cv-00364, 2013 U.S. Dist. LEXIS 137075 (N.D. Ind. Sept. 24, 2013); see David A. Posner, *A Warning To Private Equity Regarding Potential Liability For Employment Decisions By Portfolio Companies*, Baker & Hostetler LLP (Oct. 3, 2013), available at Lexology .com]

DHL Express announced in late 2009 that five of its six Chicago-area facilities would close. To get severance benefits, employees had to waive all of their claims against the employer, including WARN Act claims. Two of the laid-off workers sued under the WARN Act. The district court held that the WARN Act was not applicable, ruling that there was no plant closing, because the five facilities were not a single site, and the layoffs did not reach 33% of the workforce. Although the plaintiffs alleged that employer pressure and extreme economic uncertainty negated voluntariness, the Seventh Circuit ruled that the severance package was voluntary. The agreements and release were negotiated by the union; were unambiguous; and suggested that employees consult a lawyer. The Seventh Circuit ruled that WARN Act claims can be waived by a voluntary general release. [*Ellis v. DHL Express Inc. USA*, 633 F.3d 522 (7th Cir. 2011)]

A company that provided payroll management services for other companies was not a WARN Act "employer" and could not be held liable for failure to provide notice, because it did not order the closing. [*Administaff Cos., Inc. v. New York Joint Board, Shirt & Leisurewear Div.*, 337 F.3d 454 (5th Cir. 2003)]

A WARN Act event may result in "substantial cessation of operations" as defined by ERISA § 4062(e), which may require giving notice to the PBGC.

§ 30.11 LABOR LAW ISSUES OF SHARED LIABILITY

[A] Possible Scenarios

There are many situations in which more than one company may be deemed to be a particular person's "employer." Sometimes, both companies will be liable, or the actions of one will be attributed to the other, with respect to unfair labor practices, defining the appropriate bargaining unit, or enforcing a collective bargaining agreement.

Vested benefits under a collective bargaining agreement are transferable when the employer transfers employees to another one of its locations, which is covered by another CBA with another union. [*Anderson v. AT&T Corp.*, 147 F.3d 467 (6th Cir. 1998)]

When one company merges with or takes over another, it is common for many or all of the first company's employees to be retained. Whether the acquirer is now the employer, and whether it is bound by the former employer's CBA and other promises to its workers is a factual question, depending on whether or not real operational changes were made.

In connection with CBAs, a "successor company" is one that continues the same business and hires at least half of the old employees. A successor employer is not bound by the predecessor's contracts, but does have an obligation to recognize and consult with the union. The Supreme Court has ruled that a new company becomes a successor if it is clear that all the former employees will be retained. [*NLRB v. Burns Int'l Sec. Servs. Inc.*, 406 U.S. 272 (1972)] *Canteen Corp. v. NLRB* [103 F.3d 1355 (7th Cir. 1997)] holds that a company can also be treated as a successor employer if it fails to give employees enough information about the new wages and working conditions to make a meaningful choice about accepting a job offer from the new employer.

After a merger or the purchase of a business, a successor has a duty to bargain collectively and can be liable for unfair labor practices committed by the predecessor if there is "continuity of identity" with the ex-employer, such as using the same facility to produce identical products and services, using the same or substantially the same labor force, without changes in job description, working conditions, supervision, equipment, or production methods.

An alternate test is whether there is a new corporate entity to replace the predecessor, whether there is a hiatus in the enterprise's operations, and whether the employment relationship with the prior workforce was terminated. If it is perfectly clear under the *Burns International* standard that the new owner will hire the entire existing workforce, then the incoming employer has a duty to consult with the union about wage scales. It cannot unilaterally impose cuts. If there is no such consultation, it is presumed that the negotiations would have continued the prior wage scale.

Generally speaking, a successor that has not bargained for the CBA is not bound by the substantive terms of a predecessor's CBA, unless it is perfectly clear that the new employer plans to retain all of the former employees. The D.C. Circuit treated this as a narrow exception intended to prevent a new employer from deterring employees from applying for other jobs. In this case, it was obvious that significant changes would be made, and employees were warned that they were offered only temporary at-will employment and not all former employees would be retained. [*S&F Market Street Healthcare LLC v. NLRB*, 570 F.3d 354 (D.C. Cir. 2009)]

Another possibility is that two or more enterprises might be deemed to be "alter egos" (substitutes) for one another, even if they are not formally under common control. Alter egos may be held liable for each other's unfair labor practices. The test is whether transferring business from one alter ego operation to another benefits the transferor by eliminating labor relations obligations. The alter ego theory became part of labor law to prevent "double-breasting": the practice of pairing commonly owned firms, one with a union and one nonunionized. If the double-breasted firms are actually alter egos, a federal district court can require the nonunion firm to abide by the union firm's labor agreements, even if there has been no NLRB determination of a single bargaining unit.

Two or more entities organized as legally separate entities might be treated as a "single employer" if there is an integrated enterprise. The factors that determine integration include common ownership, common management, integrated business operations, and centralized control of labor relations.

These tests are similar to the tests to see if companies are alter egos. The difference is that the two alter ego companies are not considered a single enterprise, so all their employees are not necessarily in the same bargaining unit.

A parent company and its subsidiary would probably be treated as a single employer if they were fundamentally in the same industry or business enterprise. This would be manifested by sharing supervisory, technical, and professional personnel; sharing workforce and equipment; having common officers and directors; and operating under the same labor relations policies.

The NLRB might group separate entities together as "joint employers" if they "codetermine" (i.e., make decisions jointly) about essential terms and conditions of employment. Under this theory, the crucial factor is not whether the companies have overlapping ownership, but whether they make joint decisions about hiring and firing, working conditions, compensation, and supervision of employees.

[B] Agents of the Employer

An employer company will be liable for the actions of any "agent" of the company acting in the employer's interest. For example, a labor consultant is considered the employer's agent, but a Chapter 7 bankruptcy trustee is not. The determination uses factors similar to those used in deciding if someone is a common-law employee. The employer's degree of control is crucial: the right to hire and fire the agent; furnishing tools and materials; prescribing what the agent will do and how to do it.

Someone can become an agent of the company either by actual agency (explicitly granted) or apparent agency (where a principal says that the agent can speak for it, or knowingly lets the agent exercise authority). An employer is responsible for the actions performed by a supervisor in the course of actual or apparent authority. Even if a supervisor acts without authority, the employer can become liable by ratifying the supervisor's action (i.e., offering support for it after the fact). In general, however, the employer will not be responsible for actions for someone who is not an employee, or perhaps not a supervisory employee, unless the employer initiates, promotes, or ratifies the conduct. If the agent's improper conduct was an isolated, unpremeditated act, or if the employer repudiates the conduct, it is possible that the employer will be relieved of liability.

In general, the NLRB will blame the employer for an unfair labor practice only if it was committed directly by the employer, or by the employer's agent. But in a representation proceeding, a finding of agency is not required to set aside an election if the election was unfair enough to prevent employees from exercising a rational, unforced choice.

§ 30.12 EMPLOYER DOMINATION

In Europe, "codetermination," where union representatives collaborate closely with management, and where joint management-labor committees play an important decision-making role, is well accepted. However, under U.S. law, employer domination of a labor organization is an unfair labor practice. [See NLRA § 8(a)(2)] Although this provision was originally enacted to bar "sweetheart unions" (formed or taken over by the employer), it has been applied more broadly.

It was a violation of the NLRA for an employer to unilaterally implement a workplace ethics program (WEP) (after consulting with the employees, but not bargaining with the union). Under the WEP, employees could invoke either the WEP process or the grievance procedure to review management decisions about discharge, discipline, or demotion, although the WEP yielded when arbitration was invoked. Grievance procedures are a mandatory bargaining subject, and the CBA already contained a grievance procedure. The Eleventh Circuit held that the employer would have been required to bargain to eliminate the existing grievance procedure, so they could not use the workplace ethics program to perform an end-run around the CBA's grievance procedure. [*Ga. Power Co. v. NLRB*, 427 F.3d 1354 (11th Cir. 2005)]

To avoid NLRB characterization of a work team or quality circle as an unduly dominated "labor organization," the employer should consider these steps:

- Look for a neutral meeting place away from the workplace, such as a local library, Rotary club, or City Hall;
- Rotate membership of the team, to involve as many people as possible and get new viewpoints;
- Focus the team on productivity and workplace issues, not compensation;
- Don't use the team to avoid contract negotiations;
- Employee representatives, not management, should draft the bylaws under which the team operates.

§ 30.13 NLRB JURISDICTION

The National Labor Relations Board has the power to get involved in a situation if:

- It is a labor dispute—i.e., there is any controversy about conditions of employment or representation of workers. Strikes, walkouts, picketing, and employer refusals to bargain are labor disputes;
- It affects interstate commerce. The threshold is so low that virtually any business will be deemed to affect interstate commerce;
- Employers and employees, rather than independent contractors and their clients, are involved;
- The dispute involves working conditions.

The NLRB cannot initiate proceedings on its own: it only has the power to respond to a representation petition or unfair labor practice (ULP) charge. When it has issued a complaint or filed an unfair labor practices charge, the NLRB can ask a federal District Court to issue a temporary injunction. In fact, the agency has an obligation to seek an injunction if it charges unlawful secondary activity (such as striking one employer to put pressure on another), some forms of improper activity, or certain boycotts. However, permanent injunctions are very rare, because of the Norris-LaGuardia Anti-Injunction Act.

Theoretically, the NLRB has jurisdiction over all unfair labor practice claims that require interpretation of a CBA that is still in effect. In practice, the NLRB often declines to exercise its jurisdiction, allowing the parties to use the contract's grievance arbitration machinery, to proceed with ongoing arbitration, or to enforce an arbitration award. However, it is up to the NLRB to intervene or stay out. The employer and union cannot deprive the NLRB of jurisdiction by agreeing to arbitrate.

Except in extraordinary circumstances, courts do not have jurisdiction over any issues that were not raised before the NLRB [*NLRB v. Saint-Gobain Abrasives, Inc.*, 426 F.3d 455 (1st Cir. 2005)]

Documents such as briefs, motions, and requests for permission to appeal in representation cases can be filed electronically at the NLRB e-filing home page, <https://mynlrb.nlrb.gov/portal/nlrb.pt?open=512&objID=202&mode=2>, by filling out a form, attaching the document to the form, and e-mailing it to the NLRB's Office of the Executive Secretary. The agency prefers files in .pdf format, but .doc and .txt files are also acceptable.

§ 30.14 LABOR LAW IMPLICATIONS OF BANKRUPTCY FILINGS

The general rule is that the "automatic stay" on litigation as soon as a bankruptcy petition is filed will protect the company that files from being sued. However, because the NLRB is considered a unit of the federal government exercising its regulatory powers, NLRB unfair labor practices hearings are exempt from the automatic stay. However, the bankruptcy court has the power to enjoin the NLRB from doing anything that would prevent the reorganization of the bankrupt company.

Part of the bankruptcy process is a decision about which executory contracts (i.e., contracts to be performed in the future) will be carried out by the reorganized company and which can and should be rejected. The company seeking bankruptcy protection can petition the court to allow it to assume or reject a CBA. The court's standard for granting a rejection request is whether it would be fair to reject the contract, or whether the union unreasonably refused to accept contract modifications proposed by the employer. The employer does not have to prove that the proposed plan of reorganization will fail unless the contract can be rejected.

However, if the collective bargaining agreement expires while bankruptcy proceedings are pending, the whole issue becomes moot, because there is nothing for the employer to either accept or reject.

The Bankruptcy Abuse Prevention and Consumer Protection Act of 2005, Pub. L. No. 109-8 (BAPCPA), includes various provisions not only extending the exemption of individual debtor's retirement accounts from the bankruptcy estate, but altering the treatment of retirement plans in corporate bankruptcy. The employer's bankruptcy estate does not include funds that the employer withheld or funds received by the employer from employee wages to be paid to ERISA plans, such as defined contribution plans or benefit plans. [See BAPCPA § 323]

Bankruptcy Code § 1114, as amended by BAPCPA § 1403, permits the bankruptcy court to set aside modifications of retiree health plans that the employer made within the 180 days before filing, unless the court finds that the balance of equities clearly supports the changes. (Section 1114 is the provision that requires Chapter 11 debtors to negotiate with retiree representatives rather than unilaterally modifying or terminating retiree welfare benefits. After a bankruptcy filing, the benefits must be maintained unless the bankruptcy court orders or permits modification.)

BAPCPA raises the amount of wages and benefits earned by an employee before the employer's Chapter 11 bankruptcy filing, but not paid before the filing, that can be treated as a priority claim. The amount is now $10,000, rather than $4,925 in unpaid wages and benefits per employee, earned within 180 days before the filing (rather than only 90 days pre-filing under prior law). The $10,000 amount, as adjusted for inflation, is now $10,950. (The Chapter 7 amount is $12,475 earned within 180 days before filing.) BAPCPA also limits the amount of severance or retention bonuses that can be paid to insiders of a bankrupt company.

CHAPTER 31

OCCUPATIONAL SAFETY AND HEALTH

§ 31.01 INTRODUCTION

The federal Occupational Safety and Health Act and the agency that administers it, the Occupational Safety and Health Administration (both abbreviated OSHA) have as their mission protecting employees against unreasonably hazardous workplaces. All employers must satisfy the "general duty standard" of maintaining a workplace that is reasonably free of recognized dangers. Additional standards are imposed in some circumstances, particularly in the construction industry. BLS's annual Workplace Injury and Illness Summary reports about 3 million nonfatal workplace injuries and illnesses in the private sector in 2012, a rate of 3.4/100 full-time equivalents, lower than the 3.5/100 level in 2011, and the fifth year in a row where the rate declined. Injury incidence was 3.3/100 in 2011, falling to 3.2 in 2012. [Ilyse Schuman, *Workplace Injuries And Illnesses Continue To Decline; OSHA Schedules Hearing On Electronic Reporting Proposal*, Littler Mendelson (Nov. 14, 2013), available at Lexology.com]

In 2014, OSHA had about 2,200 inspectors in 10 regional and 90 local offices, responsible for 130 million workers in more than eight million worksites. OSHA carried out 39,228 inspections in fiscal 2013, and there were 50,436 state inspections in that year. OSHA's budget rose from $535,246,000 in fiscal 2013 to $552,247,000 in fiscal 2014. [OSHA, *Commonly Used Statistics*, <http://www.osha.gov/oshstats/commonstats.html> (last accessed Mar. 19, 2014)]

For FY 2013, the 10 most cited standards were fall protection (8,241 citations), hazard communication (6,156 citations), scaffolding (5,423 citations), respiratory protection (3,879 citations), electrical, wiring methods (3,452 citations), powered industrial trucks (3,340 citations), ladders (3,311 citations), lockout/tagout (3,254 citations), general electrical (2,745 citations), and machine guarding (2,701 citations). The top 10 items have remained the same since 2011, with minor year-to-year differences in number of citations. [Lindsay A. Smith, *OSHA Releases 2013 Top 10 Most Cited Standards*, Epstein Becker Green (Nov. 4, 2013), available at Lexology.com]

The Consolidated Appropriations Act of 2014, H.R. 3547, sets OSHA's 2014 funding level at $552.2 million, and the full amount that the White House requested for OSHA enforcement activities, $207.8 million, has been funded. OSHA's 2014 Budget Justification called for implementing a new weighted inspection system to target the most serious hazards, such as refineries, chemical plants, and industries using lead, hexavalent chromium, and crystalline silica. Inspections will be rated on complexity, to focus efforts on the most complex. [James L. Curtis and Craig B. Simonsen, *Funding For OSHA Enforcement Increases Under Law Signed By President*, Seyfarth Shaw LLP (Jan. 23, 2014), available at Lexology.com]

OSHA also protects whistleblowers under a number of statutes, not just those concerned with conventional safety and health issues; see § 31.09[C] below.

Employees are also entitled to whistleblower protection in the context of securities law, and if they report PPACA violations—or if they experience retaliation because they use the insurance Exchanges to obtain health coverage.

Employers are not held to an impossible standard of a hazard-free workplace, but they must be prepared to deal with known hazards (including disease and chemical toxicity as well as accident). They must use the reasonably available methods and technology to keep the dangers within bounds.

The California Court of Appeal ruled in 2011 that Cal OSHA regulations apply only to employees, so an independent contractor air conditioning servicer could not use those standards to prove negligence per se. (He charged the owner of a condominium complex with negligence per se because the ladder from which he fell did not have the state-mandated safety mechanisms.) [*Iversen v. California Village HOA*, 194 Cal. App. 4th 107 (2011)]

A report submitted to the Senate Health, Education, Labor and Pension Committee shows that, in the past six years, billions of dollars in federal contracts have been awarded to companies that have been penalized for violating safety laws. Eighteen federal contractors were in the list of the 100 largest OSHA penalties between 2007 and 2012. For example, Imperial Sugar got $94.8 million in federal contracts in 2012, although it was assessed $6 million in OSHA penalties after the death of 14 workers in an explosion in 2008. Tyson Foods has received $4.2 billion in federal contracts since 2000, even though there have been 11 worker fatalities, and over $500,000 in safety penalties have been imposed since 2007. Acknowledging that penalties might be imposed improperly, the report does not recommend automatic debarment or suspension of contracts. [Steven Greenhouse, *Study Finds Federal Contracts Given to Flagrant Violators of Labor Laws*, NYTimes.com (Dec. 10, 2013)]

§ 31.02 OSHA POWERS

Under the OSH Act, OSHA has the authority to inspect workplaces, order correction of violations, and impose penalties if correction does not occur as mandated. It has been held that it is not a violation of the OSH Act, or the Fourth Amendment's ban on unreasonable searches and seizures, for an OSHA compliance officer to videotape a construction site from across the street before going to the site and presenting his credentials. The theory is that looking at a site (to determine if fall protection techniques were adequate) is not a "search," so no warrant is required. [*L.R. Willson & Sons Inc. v. OSHRC,* 134 F.3d 1235 (4th Cir. 1998)]

The OSH Act also requires employers to keep records of workplace injuries and to use this information to generate annual reports (which must be disclosed to the workforce as well as being submitted to OSHA).

All employers whose operations affect commerce among the states are subject to OSHA. There is no minimum number of employees. However, small-scale or low-risk enterprises are entitled to relaxation of some reporting requirements.

■ **TIP:** An employer who would be damaged by full compliance with OSHA requirements can petition the Secretary of Labor for a temporary or permanent "variance" that protects the company against noncompliance penalties. Variances are effective only for the company that applies for them. It is no defense against a charge of noncompliance that a variance was granted to a different company in a similar situation.

The OSH Act interacts with various other statutes. It is probably a violation of public policy to discharge a worker because he or she filed a Worker's Compensation claim after suffering an occupational injury; to retaliate against a whistleblower who reported unsafe conditions to OSHA; or to take steps against someone who cooperated in an OSHA investigation.

Federal labor law says that a walkout premised on unsafe working conditions will not be treated as a strike. Furthermore, it is a protected concerted activity for workers to complain about safety conditions in the workplace, and therefore the employer cannot use this as a premise for employee discipline. However, state courts will not necessarily consider an OSHA violation relevant evidence of neglect if the employer is sued.

§ 31.03 OSHA REGULATIONS

The main authority for federal regulation of workplace safety comes from the OSH Act itself. OSHA's agency rules appear in the Code of Federal Regulations. In addition to the General Duty Clause, OSHA enforces more specific guidance in the form of the General Industry Standards that cover most industrial workplaces, and the Construction Standards.

The General Industry Standards deal with topics such as:

- Condition of floors (this is called the "walking/working" standard);
- Number and design of entrances and exits;
- Noise control;
- Radiation safety;
- Proper handling of hazardous materials (known as "hazmats")—toxic chemicals and toxic wastes;
- Personal Protective Equipment (PPE) such as respirators, hard hats, steel-toed shoes, work gloves, etc.;
- Fire prevention and safety;
- On-site first aid and medical treatment;
- Requirements for guards on machinery;
- Proper use of tools and other hand-held equipment;

- Welding and cutting;
- Control of electrical hazards;
- Design and maintenance of lifts and powered platforms;
- Access to employees' health records.

The Construction Industry Standards overlap with the General Industry Standards. The two rules sometimes treat the same topics, but the construction rules tend to be more stringent in this case. The construction standards also cover control of asbestos, welding and cutting, scaffolding, steel construction, and the use of masonry and concrete in construction.

[For current recordkeeping requirements, see <https://www.osha.gov/recordkeeping/index.html> (last accessed Mar. 19, 2014)]

For proposed requirements, see the NPRM to improve tracking of workplace injuries that was published November 8, 2013. The NPRM adds three new requirements for electronic submission of illness and injury reports. OSHA will put the information on its Website and may create a searchable database online. The NPRM does not expand recordkeeping requirements, but already-required injury and illness reports now must be submitted electronically. Companies with 10 or fewer employees, or low-hazard industries like finance and retail, will only be required to submit the information if OSHA makes a written request. For reporting companies that had 250 or more employees in the previous year, Form 300 and Form 301 information must be reported electronically each quarter. Reporting companies in designated industries with 20 or more employees must submit Form 300A information annually (total number of cases in each recordkeeping classification, number of lost workdays or days on restricted duty, total number of injuries and illnesses analyzed by type). The NPRM's requirements replace the annual Data Initiative Survey and the requirements of § 1901.41(a). The NPRM applies to designated industries with DART rates reported by the BLS in 2009 of 2.0 or more—e.g., construction, manufacturing, nursing homes, warehouses. See Part 1904, Subpart E, Appendix A for the list of affected industries. Participating employers register with the Website, receiving a login ID and password. Either they can enter data directly to the site, or upload a batch file. [Nickole C. Winnett, *OSHA's Proposed Electronic Recordkeeping Rule*, Jackson Lewis LLP (Nov. 14, 2013), available at Lexology.com; Jennifer Cerven, *OSHA Develops Plan To Publish Injury And Illness Data Online*, Barnes & Thornburg LLP (Nov. 12, 2013), available at Lexology.com; Heather MacDougall, *OSHA Proposes Major Recordkeeping Change*, Akerman LLP (Nov. 12, 2013), available at Lexology.com]

§ 31.04 CONTROLLING PHYSICAL HAZARDS

OSHA published a fact sheet, Crowd Management Safety Guidelines for Retailers, about eliminating work hazards by managing crowds of holiday shoppers. The fact sheet does not impose any new compliance requirements, but it helps employers identify hazards in areas of planning, pre-event set-up, the event, and emergencies. OSHA advises businesses that expect large crowds to hire extra staff as needed; have police officers or trained security personnel present; create a staffing plan with a location designated for each worker; get any necessary permits; consult fire and police departments about safety requirements; post signs with information such as store hours and locations of entrances, exits, and restrooms; and have a rehearsal before the holiday. Well before the date, set up rope lines or barricades; set up communications between employees and emergency responders; place attractive sale items to avoid bottlenecks; and keep carts and other obstacles away from exits. Have first aid kits and defibrillators available, with trained employees. [John C. Artz, *Avoiding Mistletoe Mishaps, Part III: OSHA Releases Crowd Management Safety Guidelines For Retailers*, Ogletree Deakins (Nov. 26, 2013), available at Lexology.com]

[A] Personal Protective Equipment

An important part of the employer's duty of providing a safe workplace is to furnish protective equipment and to make sure that machinery is guarded and that, where appropriate, moving parts will stop before employees are injured.

The legal system treats PPE (Personal Protective Equipment) as essential to workplace safety. Wherever possible, employers should eliminate hazards directly, by reducing the likelihood of falls, falling objects, burns, chemical exposure, etc. But it is not always possible to remove the hazard, and even when it is physically possible, the cost may be prohibitive.

In such situations, the employer has a duty to provide PPE, and the employee has a complementary duty to use it. The employer must provide suitable equipment, in sizes that fit the workers, and must train them in how to use the equipment. The obligation exists whenever a reasonable person, familiar with workplace conditions and industry practices, would require PPE. The industry standard is not a defense, however, if the employer knew or should have known that dangerous conditions were present—for instance, if injuries had occurred in the past under similar circumstances.

A respiratory protection rule took effect October 5, 1998. The standard, known as 1910.134, covers respirator use in general industry, shipyards, longshore work, and construction, but not in agriculture. For guidance to employers, OSHA issued compliance directive CPL 2-0.120, explaining how to analyze workplace hazards, select respirators, when to change the chemical cartridges in respirators, and how to make sure respirators fit properly. [See <http://www.osha.gov>]

At last, final rules were published in November 2007, taking effect six months after publication. The rules require the employer to pay for almost all mandatory PPE (the exceptions being ordinary clothing, weather gear, logging boots, prescription safety glasses, and ordinary safety-toe boots). The rule does not create obligations for employers to provide PPE in any additional situations. [72 Fed. Reg. 65341 (Nov. 15, 2007); see Fred Schneyer, *Feds Finalize Protective Gear Payment Rule*, plansponsor.com (Nov. 16, 2007)]

OSHA imposed the maximum fine of $140,000 for safety violations that led to the fatal electrocution of a Verizon technician in Brooklyn in 2011. OSHA also issued 10 citations for failure to follow safety rules. Verizon did not provide life-saving equipment and did not require protective helmets and gloves to be used during dangerous tasks. Douglas Lalima's death was not reported as required, and the technicians were not adequately trained for working near high-voltage lines. Verizon denied any wrongdoing and said that it would appeal the finding. [Hannah Miet, *Verizon Fined $140,000 After Electrocution Death*, NYTimes.com (Mar. 19, 2012)]

[B] Lockout/Tagout

OSHA's lockout/tagout rule (29 C.F.R. § 1910.147) applies in nonconstruction workplaces where the machinery has potentially dangerous moving parts. The rule imposes obligations on employers to immobilize machinery while it is being serviced, cleaned, repaired, etc. The rule does not apply to normal operation of the machinery, because in those situations the equipment and work routines are supposed to prevent injuries due to moving parts.

To comply with the lockout/tagout rule, machinery could be equipped with a trip control ("panic button") so it can be shut down quickly in an emergency. Blades and other dangerous parts can be protected with guards that protect workers' bodies from contact and prevent scrap materials from becoming projectiles. If guards are impractical, machinery could be equipped with sensing devices that turn off the machine if a body part goes beyond the safe point. Machinery can also be designed to require two hands to operate, so that it will not work when a hand is within reach of moving parts.

[C] Bathroom Breaks

The OSHA general industry sanitation standard [29 C.F.R. § 1910.141] requires the presence of toilet facilities in the workplace. An April 6, 1998, letter from OSHA forbids employers to impose unreasonable restrictions on bathroom use. OSHA inspectors who receive complaints on this issue are directed to investigate the reasonableness of the employer's policy.

Female workers (especially pregnant women) need more bathroom breaks than male workers, although older male workers may need to use the restroom more often because of prostate enlargement.

§ 31.05 CONTROLLING EXPOSURE TO HAZARDOUS CONDITIONS

[A] Generally

The employer must limit employees' exposure to hazardous materials (e.g., asbestos, lead) and conditions (e.g., potentially damaging noise levels). Hazardous substances must be stored properly. Employees must be warned about their presence and taught how to handle the materials safely.

Other laws, such as environmental laws and laws requiring notification to the community of the presence or accidental release of hazardous substances, are also triggered when dangerous materials are used in a workplace. The company must have an emergency-response plan that involves coordination with fire departments and other community resources.

There is no simple solution to the problems of controlling materials that are dangerous from the environmental or workplace safety points of view—without significantly raising manufacturing costs and perhaps impairing competitiveness. A major investigative article in the New York Times in early 2013 discusses "unintended consequences" in regulation. The chemical n-propyl bromide (nPB) is now used six times as often as it was used 15 years ago, despite more than a decade of warnings that nPB causes neurological damage to workers who inhale it. OSHA performed 15 inspections at two locations of the Royale Comfort Seating factories in North Carolina between 1996 and 2011, finding many times that workers were exposed to dangerous concentrations of nPB, were not give respirators, and did not receive proper ventilation. However, five fines were imposed, the largest of which was only $14,000. Several workers have settled Worker's Compensation cases for neurological damage, and Royale has spent almost half a million dollars in settlements and plant upgrades, but OSHA nevertheless found poor air quality resulting from inadequate maintenance. The nPB based glues were adopted not only because they are inexpensive but to replace another chemical, TCA, that OSHA condemned as unsafe. [Ian Urbina, *As OSHA Emphasizes Safety, Long-Term Health Risks Fester*, NYTimes.com (Mar. 30, 2013)]

In 2012, OSHA modified the Hazard Communication Standard at 29 C.F.R. § 1919.1200 to conform to the United Nations's Globally Harmonized System of Classification and Labeling of Chemicals (GHS). The OSHA Hazard Communication Standard requires manufacturers and importers of chemicals to evaluate the hazards of their chemicals, and to label them and use Material Safety Data Sheets (MSDS) to inform customers of the hazards. Employers that have hazardous chemicals in the workplace must label the chemicals, have MSDSs available to workers who might be exposed, and give training on chemical hazards. OSHA supplemented these requirements with GHS provisions, renaming the MSDS as the "labeling and safety data sheets." GHS makes the definitions of hazards more specific and detailed: e.g., explosives are divided into seven categories. For each chemical, there is a signal word such as "Danger," an image (skull and crossbones) and hazard statement (e.g., "Fatal If Swallowed") offering a standard core of information about each chemical. Though previous standards allowed discretion to use whatever language was considered adequate to communicate the risk, GHS labels must explain the measures needed to protect against hazardous exposures and identify the products and suppliers. Employers were required to train their employees in the new system by December 1, 2013, but full compliance on labels and data safety sheets is not required under June 1, 2015. Distributors can continue distributing containers with manufacturer labels until December 1, 2015, and employers have until June 1, 2016 to update their workplace signage and hazard communication programs. [77 Fed. Reg. 17574 (Mar. 26, 2012); see Patricia A. Poole, *OSHA Modifies Hazardous Communication Standard To Conform To UN GHS*, Baker & Hostetler LLP (Sept. 25, 2013), available at Lexology.com; James L. Curtis and Ilana R. Morady, *OSHA Hazcom Compliance—Are You (And Your Company's Policy Manuals And Training Requirements) Ready?*, Seyfarth Shaw LLP (Sept. 11, 2013), available at Lexology.com]

After OSHA issued a citation when a supervising employee worked on a dangerous ledge without fall protection (violating 29 C.F.R. § 1926.501(b)(1)), the Administrative Law Judge (ALJ) upheld the citation and imposed a $5,000 penalty (plus $4,000 for incorrect usage of fall protection by other employees)—but the Fifth Circuit reversed, finding that the decision was based on an error of law. In the Fifth Circuit view, failure to comply with a specific regulation, even if there is substantial danger, is not enough to constitute a violation of the OSH Act. Employers are not strictly liable; they are liable only if they knew or should have known there was a violation. According to the ALJ, the supervisor knew that working without a harness was dangerous and violated OSHA regulations and company safety policy, so his knowledge would be imputed to the employer. But in the Fifth Circuit view, although a company is usually liable for acts of supervisors performing their duties, making a company liable just because a supervisor was aware the he was violating OSHA regulations would be an improper imposition of strict liability. The Fifth Circuit does not impute the supervisor's knowledge of his own misconduct to the employer if the employer's safety policy, training, and discipline make it unforeseeable that the supervisor would break the rules. The burden is on the DOL to prove that the employer should be held responsible. Employee misconduct is an affirmative defense, requiring proof that the employer not only made, but adequately communicated, work rules designed to prevent violations, and has taken steps to detect and correct violations if they do occur. [*W.G. Yates & Sons Const. Co. Inc. v. OSHRC*, 459 F.3d 604 (5th Cir. 2006). Although the Sixth Circuit imputes a supervisor's knowledge of his own misconduct to the employer, the Third and Tenth Circuits disagree: see the cases cited in *Danis-Shook Joint Venture XXV v. Sec'y of Labor*, 319 F.3d 805 (6th Cir.

2003). The Fifth Circuit's analysis of the employee misconduct affirmative defense derives from *Frank Lill & Son, Inc. v. Sec'y of Labor*, 362 F.3d 840 (D.C. Cir. 2004)]

The First Circuit upheld a $33,700 fine for violations of the excavation safety rules. One of the trench diggers was a foreman, thus ruling out the unpreventable employee misconduct (UEM) defense. An employer can be charged with constructive knowledge of safety violations that supervisors know or should know about and the site superintendent was at the site several times an hour. [*P. Gioioso & Sons Inc. v. OSHRC,* No. 675 F.3d 66 (1st Cir. 2012)]

[B] PELs

A PEL, or Permissible Exposure Limit, is set for certain hazardous substances such as asbestos and lead. A PEL is a level of contact with the substance that employees can encounter without becoming endangered. The employer has an obligation to monitor the plant environment to determine the level of the regulated substance, to provide appropriate safety equipment (e.g., face masks and respirators) and to train employees in safety techniques.

OSHA rules require that employees have access to showers, changing rooms, eye baths, first aid, and other measures for preventing long-term contamination. Where necessary, the employer must provide protective clothing and appropriate containers for collecting contaminated clothing for treatment or disposal. Employees must not be permitted to smoke or eat in any environment where asbestos, lead, etc., are present. Warning signs must be posted in danger areas.

The employer's basic job is to keep employee exposure below the PEL. In some instances, this is impossible. When exposure reaches the "action level" defined by OSHA, the employer must take additional steps, such as periodic medical testing of employees to see if they have suffered environmental injury or illness.

The current PELs are more than 40 years old. NIOSH and American Conference of Government Industrial Hygienists (ACGIH) levels are usually stricter than OSHA requirements. Industry points out that NIOSH and the ACGIH can adopt standards without public notice and comment, and do not have to consider technical feasibility. [Jackson Lewis LLP, *OSHA Recommends New Exposure Limits*, Lexology.com (Nov. 22, 2013)]

OSHA issued new voluntary standards for workplace chemical exposure in late 2013, stating that the existing standards are not protective enough. OSHA asked employers to comply voluntarily with the new standards; only the old PELs are enforceable. However, it is likely that the new standards will be treated by plaintiffs' lawyers as the appropriate threshold in toxic tort cases. [Steven M. Siros, *OSHA Issues New "Recommended" Permissible Exposure Levels For Chemicals In The Workplace*, Jenner & Block (Oct. 25, 2013), available at

Lexology.com. See the OSHA toolkit at <http://www.osha.gov/dsg/safer_chemicals/index.html> and annotated list of PELs at <http://www.osha.gov/dsg/annotated-pels/index.html>, discussed in Jodi D. Taylor, *OSHA Web-Based Resources Provide Updated Guidelines To Hazardous Materials Exposure; Compliance Is Voluntary . . . For Now*, Baker Donelson Bearman Caldwell & Berkowitz PC (Nov. 14, 2013), available at Lexology.com.]

In September 2013, after complaints from a hospitalized worker about effects of styrene on lungs, OSHA inspected Fiberdome, Inc's factory and imposed a $49,500 fine, partly for styrene exposure, even though exposure at the factory did not exceed established limits. Fiberdome Inc. was cited for the more general standard requiring freedom from known hazards. This appears to be one of the few times in recent years that OSHA adopted a general duty approach to chemical safety enforcement. [Alexandra Berzon, *OSHA Uses New Way to Enforce Out-of-Date Rules for a Risky Chemical*, WSJ.com (Nov. 20, 2013)]

[C] Noise Levels

In workplaces where the noise level routinely exceeds 85 decibels per eight-hour shift, the employer has an obligation to create and maintain a comprehensive program for hearing conservation. The environmental noise level must be monitored; employees' hearing must be tested (with a baseline reading within six months of initial exposure to high occupational noise levels, and an annual checkup after that), and they must be trained to protect themselves against hearing loss. If any audiometric test shows that an employee's hearing has deteriorated, the employer's obligation is to notify that worker within 21 days and then make sure that the worker uses hearing protection devices in the future.

In the October 19, 2010 Federal Register, OSHA published a proposed interpretation of "feasible administrative or engineering controls" in the context of workplace noise. However, in January 2011, OSHA withdrew the document because of industry complaints about potential costs, saying that it is studying other approaches to abating noise hazards in the workplace. [Fred Schneyer, *OSHA Takes More Time on Noise Standard*, plansponsor.com (Jan. 19, 2011)]

The Fifth Circuit ruled that hearing-loss claims based on charges that the employer failed to monitor noise exposure or protect employees against excessive noise could be heard in state court. The claims were not subject to LMRA § 301 preemption (i.e., the doctrine that cases about interpretation of a CBA must only be heard in the federal system) because the state (Louisiana) had a body of workplace law about the duty to protect employees from injury. The case could be resolved using these principles without even consulting the CBA. Furthermore, Louisiana forbids CBA provisions that eliminate rights to workplace safety. [*McKnight v. Dresser, Inc.*, 676 F.3d 426 (5th Cir. 2012)]

[D] Workplace Violence

Workplace violence can occur among co-workers or other persons entering the workplace (e.g., a domestic abuser or stalker). Late in 2004, the U.S. Supreme Court applied the intentional infliction of emotional distress cause of action against an employer who failed to provide a safe workplace. The plaintiff sued after she was kidnapped from work and raped by her former lover. She informed her employer that she had an order of protection against him and asked not to be assigned to remote locations where she was vulnerable. Her supervisor ignored her concerns and tried to reconcile the couple. After the attack, the plaintiff complained to the employer about the supervisor's facilitation of the attack. She was required to continue reporting to him. The Supreme Court dismissed her constitutional claims but upheld the intentional infliction of emotional distress element of the case because the employer's actions (granting access to the attacker; refusing to let her work in a safer location) inflicted distress over and above that suffered directly from the incident. Worker's Compensation exclusivity did not apply, because the employer's conduct was intentional rather than negligent. Furthermore, most states do not cap damages for intentional infliction of emotional distress. [*Gantt v. Security USA, Inc.*, 543 U.S. 814 (2004)]

According to the Law Center to Prevent Gun Violence, almost half the states have adopted laws that limit employers' ability to forbid firearms in vehicles in the parking lot. Some companies are revising HR policies, training employees to detect early signs of violence, and providing routine security in tense situations like exit interviews. DOL reported 375 on-the-job shootings in 2012—fewer than pre-recession levels. However, in 2005, the American Journal of Public Health noted that workplaces where guns were allowed were five times as likely to have a workplace death as companies that forbid weapons. [Sara Murrah, *Guns in the Parking Lot: A Delicate Workplace Issue*, WSJ.com (Oct. 15, 2013)]

§ 31.06 ERGONOMICS

Ergonomics is the study of the mutual adaptation between tools and the human body. Ergonomically efficient tools will reduce the number, or at least the degree, of injuries associated with tool use.

OSHA has made several attempts to impose ergonomic requirements on industry. This has been an extremely controversial quest. Congress's appropriation bills for OSHA between 1996 and 1998 actually forbade the agency to adopt ergonomics standards.

The Occupational Safety and Health Review Commission (OSHRC) issued an April 1997 decision that was the first declaration that the Secretary of Labor can properly cite ergonomic hazards under the general duty clause. [*Sec'y of Labor v. Pepperidge Farm Inc.*, 65 L.W. 2725 (OSHRC Apr. 26, 1997). See also *Reich v. Arcadian Corp.*, 110 F.3d 1192 (5th Cir. 1997)]

In March 2001, both Houses of Congress used a little-known federal statute called the Congressional Review Act of 1996 (CRA) to repeal the ergonomics regulations and prevent OSHA from enacting substantially similar regulations in the future. [See Steven Greenhouse, *House Joins Senate in Repealing Rules on Workplace Injuries,* N.Y. Times, Mar. 8, 2001, at A19]

A decade later, in 2011, DOL withdrew a proposal that would have required more logging of workplace musculoskeletal disorders. OSHA also withdrew another proposal re workplace noise that would have required installing noise-abating equipment. [Melanie Trottman, *Labor Department Withdraws Record-keeping Proposal*, WSJ.com (Jan. 25, 2011)]

§ 31.07 VARIANCES

The OSH Act permits employers to petition for variances that will excuse them from having to comply with requirements that are particularly onerous. A variance can only be granted if employees will not be exposed to undue risk or danger.

The C.F.R. includes rules for "national security variances" and "experimental variances," but most of the variances granted are classified as either "temporary" or "permanent."

Grounds for a temporary variance are that the company will eventually comply with a new regulation, but cannot do so by its scheduled effective date because of a shortage of staff, materials, or equipment. (Being unable to afford to comply is not considered good cause for a variance.) A temporary variance lasts up to one year. It can be renewed twice, for up to 180 days at a time. The application must demonstrate that the employer is doing everything it can to comply as soon as possible, and that employees are being protected from undue hazards in the meantime.

A permanent variance is granted to an employer whose work methods are unconventional but still provide at least as much protection for employees as the OSHA regulations do. A company asking for a permanent variance can also apply for an interim variance.

The original plus six copies of the variance application and supporting documents must be filed. The documents must be signed by an authorized representative of the company, such as a corporate officer or the corporation's attorney.

Employees are entitled to notice of the variance application. They can ask that a hearing examiner conduct a hearing on the application.

Variance applications are reviewed, and then granted or denied, by the Assistant Secretary of Labor of Occupational Health and Safety in Washington. Anyone affected by a variance after it is granted can petition for modification or revocation of the order granting the variance. After a temporary variance ends, the employer can petition to have it renewed or extended.

§ 31.08 DIVISION OF RESPONSIBILITY

For OSHA purposes, companies are responsible for the safety of their "employees." A company that has all its work done by leased employees or independent contractors will not be subject to OSHA unless the arrangements are only a subterfuge to avoid liability. What counts is the economic reality of the work relationship, including the degree of control over the work, who signs the paycheck, and whether payment is a regular salary or a per-project amount. The power to change working conditions or fire the employee is considered especially significant. If several employers are involved (e.g., a temporary employment agency and its clients), OSHA responsibilities will be allocated based on actual job performance and working conditions. The basic rule is that the general contractor has primary OSHA responsibility for a construction worksite.

OSHA liability of general contractors can derive from several theories:

- A construction contract provision under which the general contractor agrees to provide safety equipment;
- The general contractor's role of controlling conditions because it is in charge of the site;
- The general contractor is the only party involved with the specialized knowledge to abate the hazards;
- The general contractor's actual knowledge of the hazards (by observation or by notice from a subcontractor), creating a duty to cope with the hazards.

In doubtful cases, OSHA cites all possibly responsible parties and then allows them to make arguments why they are not liable. However, both a company that creates a hazard and the actual employer of the employees exposed to the hazard (and who were not protected by their employer) can be found liable.

OSHA uses a two-step test to see whether the Construction Standard should be applied to nonconstruction companies. The tests are ability to direct or control trade contractors, and a degree of involvement in the multiple activities that are needed to complete a construction project.

The Seventh Circuit vigorously affirmed the dismissal of the indictment charging the defendant with a violation of OSH Act § 17(e) after the electrocution death of two employees of the defendant's wholly owned subsidiary. OSHA asserted that the defendant was culpable because it oversaw its subsidiaries' safety programs and provided safety training to employees of the subsidiaries. However, notwithstanding the corporate affiliation, the Seventh Circuit ruled that unless it would be possible to pierce the corporate veil, the parent corporation should not be deemed culpable for deaths of persons employed by another entity. [*United States v. MYR Group, Inc.*, 361 F.3d 364 (7th Cir. 2004)]

§ 31.09 OSHA ENFORCEMENT

[A] Generally

Unlike ERISA enforcement (where federal jurisdiction preempts the state role), OSHA enforcement is coordinated between the states and the federal government. States have discretion to shape the degree of their occupational safety enforcement involvement. They can draft regulatory plans; if the Department of Labor believes the plan does enough to protect worker safety, it becomes an "approved state plan."

OSHA examined the operation of the OSH programs operated by 25 states and territories (out of the total of 27 that have approved state plans). As of September, 2010, 40% of the workplaces in the United States were subject to state OSH plans; the rest were subject to federal OSHA. OSHA started collecting data after deficiencies were found in Nevada's program when many construction-related fatalities were reported. OSHA identified some states that had requirements that offered workers more protection than the federal standards: e.g., California, Minnesota, Oregon, and Washington. OSHA found that Hawaii had problems related to inadequate staffing and funding cutbacks. A federal takeover was a possibility if the state was unable to work out a strategy acceptable to OSHA for improving its regulation of worker safety. [OSHA news release, *Agency Calls for Corrective Action to Keep Workers Safe*, <http://www.dol.gov/opa/media/press/osha/OSHA20101325.htm> (Sept. 29, 2010). The states and territories in question are Alaska, Arizona, California, Connecticut, Hawaii, Indiana, Iowa, Kentucky, Maryland, Michigan, Minnesota, Nevada, New Jersey, New Mexico, New York, North Carolina, Oregon, Puerto Rico, South Carolina, Tennessee, Utah, Vermont, the Virgin Islands, Virginia, Washington, and Wyoming. However, in Connecticut, Illinois, New Jersey, New York, and the Virgin Islands, the state plans cover only public employees, not those in the private sector. The reports themselves are available at <http://www.osha.gov/dcsp/osp/efame/index.html>. See <http://www.osha.gov/dcsp/osp/index.html> for information about state plans in general]

In states that do not have an approved state plan, OSHA has primary responsibility for safety enforcement. State governments, however, are allowed to regulate issues that the OSH Act does not cover (such as boiler and elevator safety) as well as broader safety issues (such as fire protection in buildings that are open to the public).

One important function of state OSH agencies is offering free on-site consultations about how to maintain a safer workplace. The consultation is a simulated inspection, but the inspector is only authorized to point out problem areas and suggest solutions, not to issue citations or penalize the company. The consultation begins with an opening conference with the employer, proceeds to a walk-through and identification of safety problems, and ends with a closing conference about how to solve those problems.

[B] Inspections

Inspections are a central part of OSHA's enforcement function, because direct evidence about workplace conditions is necessary.

A "programmed inspection" takes place on a routine basis, when workplaces are chosen at random from a list of sites with above-average injury rates.

Inspections can also be made based on written complaints from employees, former employees, or their representatives, such as attorneys and union staff. Complaints are made to OSHA's area director or Compliance Officer (CO). OSHA investigates the complaint and sends a copy of the complaint to the employer. (The complainant can request that his or her name be suppressed on the employer's copy.) Depending on the nature of the complaint, OSHA will either send the employer a letter describing the hazard that has been charged and giving a date for abatement, or schedule an inspection. The inspection probably will be scheduled if the employer ignores a letter from OSHA or if there is evidence of other safety problems.

OSHA is supposed to respond to a complaint of imminent danger within one day, to an allegation of a serious hazard within five working days, or within 30 working days if the complaint is less serious. A serious hazard is one that creates a reasonable expectation that it could cause death or irreversible bodily injury.

Generally speaking, OSHA inspections are made on an unannounced basis. However, the employer is entitled to notice if an imminently dangerous situation is alleged (because abatement is more important than detecting violations), if special arrangements are needed for the inspection, or if the inspection will be made outside normal business hours.

The CO shows credentials at the workplace and asks for permission to inspect. If permission is refused, the CO cannot perform a search without an administrative search warrant granted by a court, based on OSHA's showing that it has reason to believe that violations of the General Duty Clause or a more specific standard have occurred. However, courts need far less proof to authorize an administrative search than a search in a criminal case.

The employer is entitled to exclude non-employee third parties (such as union representatives) and is entitled to an opening conference before the inspection begins. This is the most important part of the inspection because it permits the employer to find out why the inspection has been scheduled and to negotiate to narrow the scope of the inspection and the ground rules for conducting it. Possible rules include submission of documents only on written request, and the inspector's agreement to move through the facility only when accompanied by a management escort.

The employer has the right to take its own photographs of whatever the OSHA Compliance Officer (CO) photographs. After an inspection, plaintiffs' attorneys, unions, and competitors may make FOIA requests for the contents of OSHA inspection files, so the employer should inform OSHA of any materials that are trade secrets or confidential business information entitled to protection.

[Eric J. Conn, *What Are Employers' Rights During OSHA Inspections?*, Epstein Becker Green (Oct. 10, 2013), available at Lexology.com]

Most employers grant permission, so the CO explains the procedure during the opening conference. Next is the "walk-through" (employer and employee representatives are allowed to comment). At this stage, the CO makes notes on any hazardous or noncompliant conditions prevailing in the workplace. At this point, the inspector often points out trivial violations that can be corrected on the spot: mopping up a pool of water that could cause a slip, for instance. At this stage, the CO usually asks to see the business's logs, summary reports, exposure records, training records, and other safety-related paperwork.

If the inspection is based on a complaint, the employer has the right to review the complaint, and can instruct the CO to limit the inspection to the issues raised by the complaint. The last part of the inspection is the "closing conference" when the CO reveals findings about potential OSHA violations.

COs do not have the power to issue citations during an inspection. The CO must return to the OSHA office and confer with the Area Director about the level of citation (if any) that should be issued in response to each perceived deficiency.

The procedure is slightly different in the construction industry. A "targeted inspection" is a short-form inspection that concentrates on the major hazards to construction workers' safety: falls, falling objects, electrical hazards, and vehicle accidents. The CO decides whether to do a focused or a full inspection during the opening conference. At sites where the general or prime contractor has a workable safety plan and designates a representative to work with OSHA, only a focused inspection will be performed. In contrast to a nonconstruction inspection, citations can be issued during a focused inspection if there are serious violations, or nonserious violations that are not abated immediately.

Tips for managing OSHA inspections include:

- Train managers how to respond, and whom to call (such as the company's in-house counsel).
- Draft scenarios for responding to accidents, fatalities, vehicle accidents, workplace violence, and natural disaster.
- Ask the OSHA inspector why he arrived; employers are entitled to be notified of complaints.
- Attempt to limit the inspection to the scope of the complaint (although the inspector has the power to broaden the inspection if employees inform them about hazards, or if the inspectors observe hazards).
- Can the inspector establish that any employees were exposed to the condition or reasonably might be expected to be exposed in the course of business? Can the inspector show that the employer knew or should have known of the hazard by exercising reasonable diligence?

- Employers have a duty to provide OSHA 300 Form and hazardous chemicals documentation promptly, but are entitled to a reasonable amount of time to produce other materials. Identify materials that you believe are privileged or are attorney work product.
- Do not volunteer self-audits, insurance documents, or reports from consultants unless your lawyer says they must be provided.
- Did you offer any training or instruction to employees that could reduce the level of citations?
- OSHA's definition of "supervisor" entitled to bind the company is broader than the NLRB or wage and hour definition; provide counsel or sit in with interviews with supervisors.
- If citations are issued, attend the informal conference, and contest any citation for which there is a reasonable argument. [Howard A. Mavity, *How To Manage An OSHA Inspection*, Fisher & Phillips LLP (Nov. 5, 2013), available at Lexology.com]

■ **TIP:** A labor lawyer wrote that when he audits a facility to prepare its defense in an OSHA case, he looks at housekeeping: dirt and sloppiness imply compliance problems. If an OSHA inspector sees a dirty facility, he will take a closer look at lockout/tagout issues and handling of hazardous chemicals; failure to clean up suggests that exits are not kept clear and trip hazards are not removed either. [Howard A. Mavity, *When I Go Into A Workplace, The First Thing I Consider Is Housekeeping*, Fisher & Phillips LLP (Oct. 2, 2013), available at Lexology.com]

[C] Whistleblowers

OSHA is responsible for receiving and processing whistleblower complaints charging violations of a number of environmental statutes in addition to the OSH Act. [See Final Regulation, 69 Fed. Reg. 52,103 (Aug. 24, 2004)]

Dodd-Frank Act § 1057 spells out OSHA's responsibilities for handling whistleblower complaints, and implementing final regulations were published in early 2014. A person who charges retaliation can file a complaint in the local OSHA office within 180 days of the alleged retaliatory act. OSHA notifies the respondent, and both sides have 20 days to submit written statements and evidence. OSHA will only investigate if the complaint establishes a prima facie case that a protected activity was a contributing factor to an adverse employment action taken against the complainant. Even if there is a prima facie case, OSHA will not investigate if the employer provides clear evidence that it would have taken the same adverse action even if there had been no whistleblower activity (e.g., if the employee violated a last chance agreement). [Interim final text of regulations, 79 Fed. Reg. 18630 (Apr. 3, 2014); see Steven J. Pearlman, Harris

Mufson and Allison Lynn Martin, *OSHA Releases Interim Dodd-Frank Whistleblower Regulations*, Proskauer Rose LLP (Apr. 11, 2014), available at Lexology.com]

The OSHA Fact Sheet, *Your Rights as a Whistleblower*, requires complaints to be filed in writing or by telephone. For most statutes (the OSH Act, Clean Air Act, CERCLA, Federal Water Pollution Control Act, Safe Drinking Water Act, Solid Waste Disposal Act, and Toxic Substances Control Act), the complaint must be filed within 30 days of the incident. However, longer reporting periods are permitted for the International Safe Container Act (60 days), Asbestos Hazard Emergency Response Act and Sarbanes-Oxley Act (90 days) and 180 days under the Surface Transportation Assistance Act, Energy Reorganization Act, and Pipeline Safety Improvement Act. In general, if the state has a state OSH plan, retaliation complaints are supposed to be filed with the state agency, although dual filing with OSHA is acceptable.

In addition to hard-copy filings, OSHA solicited public comments on its proposal for online submission of retaliation complaints, then launched the form without final rulemaking or discussion of comments. The 30-section Notice of Whistleblower Complaint form can be used for electronic submission of complaints. [<https://www.osha.gov/whistleblower/WBComplaint.html>; see James L. Curtis and Craig B. Simonsen, *OSHA "Launches Online Form" For Filing Whistleblower Complaints*, Seyfarth Shaw LLP (Dec. 6, 2013), available at Lexology.com]

OSHA's online complaint form for retaliation cases collects information about the complainant and the complainant's employer; asks the complainant to describe the protected activity, how management learned about it, and what retaliatory action was taken. [William Walden, *OSHA Online Retaliation Complaint Form is Live and Freely Available*, Quarles & Brady LLP Labor & Employment Law Update (December 2013) (benefitslink.com)]

An ADR pilot program was created in the Chicago and San Francisco regions for complaints filed with its Whistleblower Protection Program. The pilot offers two voluntary ADR methods: early resolution and mediation. Early resolution tries to resolve the dispute even before OSHA investigation. Mediation brings in as third party either Federal Mediation and Conciliation Services or an attorney selected by the parties. When a whistleblower complaint is filed in the Chicago or San Francisco regions (where the pilots are) complainant will be notified of ADR options. The pilot runs for 120 days, then will be assessed using outcome measures to see if it should be continued, expanded, or terminated. [OSHA Directive 12-01 (October 2012), <https://www.osha.gov/OshDoc/Directive_pdf/DIR_12-01_CPL_02.pdf> (accessed Apr. 9, 2014); see Edwin G. Foulke Jr., *OSHA Announces Alternative Dispute Resolution Pilot Program*, Fisher & Phillips LLP (Oct. 17, 2013), available at Lexology.com]

The Department of Labor ordered the Union Pacific Railroad Co. to pay $400,000 in punitive damages, $90,315 in compensatory damages, $34,900 in attorney's fees, and more than $90,000 back pay to three employees. OSHA found that the company violated the whistleblower provisions of the Federal Railroad Safety Act by firing two employees and suspending one for reporting a work-related injury and discussing concerns about safety hazards in the workplace. The railroad was also ordered to train managers, supervisors, and employees about whistleblowers' rights. [Tara Cantore, *Union Pacific Fined for Retaliation against Whistleblowers*, plansponsor.com (Aug. 26, 2011)]

An OSHA press release dated November 13, 2013 reports that Gaines Motor Lines was ordered to pay $1,070,123 to four whistleblowers, and to reinstate the three survivors (one died in the interim). The award consists of $215,657 in compensatory and $675,000 in punitive damages. [Steven J. Pearlman and Harris Mufson, *OSHA Issues Another $1 Million+ Whistleblower Award, Along With Reinstatement*, Proskauer Rose LLP (Nov. 19, 2013), available at Lexology.com]

PPACA § 1558 forbids employers to retaliate against employees if they receive a health insurance tax credit or reduced cost sharing because they purchase their health insurance from an Exchange. Retaliation is also forbidden against employees who report violations of PPACA Title I. Complaints must be filed within 180 days of the alleged violation. Complaints can be filed by telephoning or going to the local OSHA office or sending a written complaint (faxed, sent electronically, or delivered by hand, mail, or commercial carrier) to the OSHA regional or area office. There is no official form for the complaint. If the evidence shows retaliation, and settlement is not reached, OSHA orders employer to reinstate the employee with back pay. OSHA findings become a final order of the DOL unless appealed within 30 days. Either side can request an ALJ hearing, which can be appealed to DOL Administrative Review Board. If there is no final agency order within 210 days from filing of complaint, or 90 days of employee receiving OSHA findings, employee can sue in district court. [OSHA Fact Sheet, *Filing Whistleblower Complaints under the Affordable Care Act*, <https://www.osha.gov/Publications/whistleblower/OSHAFS-3641.pdf> (last accessed Aug. 29, 2013)]

OSHA issued interim final rules for handling of retaliation complaints on February 22, 2013. The rule deals with the time limits and procedures for employee complaints, and how the complaints will be investigated and reviewed. PPACA Title I includes the ban on coverage limits, the requirements of preventive services and of furnishing a summary of benefits and coverage, and the mandate of covering adult children up to age 26. Employees are protected against retaliation when they provide information (to the employer, to the federal government, or to the state Attorney General) about acts or omissions the employee reasonably thinks violate PPACA Title I. They are also protected if they testify, assist, or participate in a proceeding about Title I. Starting in 2014, employees are protected against retaliation (such as termination of coverage) committed by insurers. The PPACA retaliation rules do not diminish employee rights under a Collective Bargaining Agreement or federal or state law. For example, these rights are in addition to the rights established by ERISA § 510. [<http://www.dol.gov/

find/20130222/OSHA2013.pdf>; see PLC Employee Benefits & Executive Compensation, *OSHA Rules Address Retaliation Complaint Procedures under Health Care Reform* (Feb. 25, 2013) (benefitslink.com)]

§ 31.10 OSHA CITATIONS

[A] Categories of Violations

The CO's comments during an inspection are not official OSHA pronouncements, and the employer cannot be penalized for failing to respond to them. However, penalties can be imposed for failure to respond to a written citation from the OSHA Area Director that is sent within six months after the date of the alleged violation that is cited. The citation form lists the violations, classified by seriousness, imposes penalties, and sets a date for abating each violation. Usually, the citation will be Form OSHA-2, sent by certified mail, although other forms can be used.

OSHA violations are generally divided into four categories: de minimis (trivial), nonserious, serious, and other. Penalties are heavier on willful violations or repeat violations within a three-year period. Criminal penalties might be imposed in the very worst cases, such as the preventable death of an employee.

In 2000, OSHA announced that it would not issue citations based on an employer's own voluntary safety and health audit (although the agency has the power to request internal audit reports). OSHRC ruled in mid-2013 that OSHA intentionally violated this policy by making heavy use of an employer's audit reports to identify issues on which the employer was cited. OSHA used a voluntary audit commissioned by the employer from a third-party safety consultant. Although OSHA violated its own policy, the OSHA ALJ would not vacate the citation of violations self-identified by the employer in the report. [*Sec'y of Labor v. BP Prods. N. Am. Inc.* (OSHRC 2013); see Mark S. Dreux and Matthew C. Thorne, *OSHA Can And Will Use Employers' Internal Safety Audit Reports As A Roadmap To Cite Them: What Employers Can Do To Protect Themselves*, Arent Fox LLP (Sept. 13, 2013), available at Lexology.com]

[B] Penalties

Penalties are set under OSHA § 17 (29 U.S.C. § 666).

It's hard to predict what penalty will be imposed for any particular OSHA violation, because the penalty is set within a framework provided by the statute and regulations. There are many factors involved, primarily the gravity of the violation. However, the size of the business, the employer's past history of violations, and whether or not the employer acted in good faith are all important considerations. Both aggravating and mitigating factors can be applied to set the final amount of the penalty.

The statute imposes penalties as follows:

- Willful or repeated violations of the OSH Act or regulations: penalty of up to $70,000 per violation, minimum penalty of $5,000 per willful violation;
- Penalty of up to $7,000 per serious violation;
- Penalty of up to $7,000 per day for failure to correct a cited violation, although the period is suspended until any review proceeding instituted in good faith is completed;
- Up to $10,000 and/or six months in prison if a violation caused an employee's death (first offense); up to $20,000 and/or one year in prison for repeated violations resulting in employee deaths;
- A fine of up to $1,000 and/or six months in prison for giving advance notice of an inspection;
- Fine of up to $10,000 and/or six months imprisonment for knowing false statement, representation, or certification;
- Fine of up to $7,000 per violation of the posting requirement.

OSHA continues to enforce its 2010 policy of assessing safety violations on a company-wide basis. The effect is higher penalties for repeat violations when a multi-location employer has similar violations anywhere during a five-year period. There is a mandatory fine of $70,000 for repeat violations. [Howard Sokol, *OSHA Charges Retail: Higher Fines For Repeat Violations Across Multiple Locations*, Holland & Knight LLP (Jan. 21, 2014), available at Lexology.com]

Civil penalties are payable to the Secretary of Labor for deposit into the U.S. Treasury; the United States can bring suit to recover penalties. The proper court is the district court for the district in which the violation is alleged to have happened, or where the employer is headquartered.

Failure-to-abate penalties are applied when a cited violation becomes a final order, and the employer fails to correct the violation. Normally, the maximum failure-to-abate penalty will be limited to 30 times the daily proposed penalty for that violation.

OSHA changed its system for calculating administrative penalties effective October 1, 2010, adopting a matrix based on the severity of the violation, probability it will recur, and the degree of risk that the violation creates. For example, the gravity-based penalty for a low-severity, low-gravity, low-probability violation is $3,000, rising to $7,000 for a high-severity, high-gravity, high-probability violation. However, no penalty can exceed the statutory limit for a serious violation ($7,000). The minimum penalty for a serious violation is $500. The minimum penalty for a posting violation is $250 if the company received posters from OSHA.

OSHA reduces penalties for smaller companies (those with fewer than 251 employees): the reduction is 10% if there are 101–250 employees, 30% if there are 26–100 employees, and 60% if there are 1–25 employees. In addition to the reduction based on company size, penalties can be reduced based on the employer's good-faith effort to implement an effective workplace safety program. The 15% "Quick Fix" reduction of penalties for immediate abatement of hazards found during an inspection remains in effect. The adjustment factors are applied serially: i.e., first an initial penalty is proposed.

OSHA's example starts with a $5,000 penalty. First a 10% history reduction is applied, then a 15% good faith reduction, a 15% Quick Fix reduction, then a 30% size reduction—resulting in a penalty of $2,275—significantly higher than the $1,500 penalty calculated under the previous rule. [OSHA, *Administrative Penalty Information Bulletin Effective October 1, 2010 for Federal OSHA*, <https://www.osha.gov/dep/administrative-penalty.html>]

Additional changes were made effective April 1, 2012. The employer's history of past violations will be considered going back five rather than three years—but a "history" reduction of 10% will be applied if the employer was inspected within the five-year time frame and had no serious, willful, repeat, or failure-to-abate violations. But a 10% history increase (not to exceed the statutory maximum) will be imposed on employers cited for any high gravity serious, willful, repeat, or failure-to-abate violations in the previous five years. The time frame for considering repeat violations is also five years. [OSHA Memorandum to regional administrators, *Annual Review and Scheduled Modification to OSHA's Interim Administrative Penalty Policy* (Mar. 27, 2012), <http://www.osha.gov/dep/enforcement/admin_penalty_mar2012.html>]

The "unit of prosecution" issue is how many charges should be filed for multiple similar violations. The OSHA regulations were amended in 2008 to provide that failure to provide respirators or workplace training is considered a separate violation for every employee who was not trained or who did not receive a respirator [29 C.F.R § 1910.9(a) and (b)]. Thirty-three other standards were also amended the same way. The regulations were amended in response to *Chao v. OSHRC*, 401 F.3d 355 (5th Cir. 2005), which held that failing to train eleven employees, and to provide them with respirators, constituted two violations, not 22 (eleven respirator, eleven training). The amendment was challenged by three trade associations that claimed the Secretary did not have authority to issue the amendments, because OSHRC is the only body that has the jurisdiction to set units of prosecution. In 2010, the D.C. Circuit rejected this argument, because setting the unit of prosecution is up to the legislatures, not the courts, and the Secretary of Labor is Congress' stand-in for these matters. [*National Ass'n of Home Builders v. OSHA*, 602 F.3d 464 (D.C. Cir. 2010). For the 2008 amendments, see 73 Fed. Reg. 75,568 and 75,583 (Dec. 12, 2008)]

In 2011, OSHRC accepted the DOL's argument that failure to keep proper records can be treated as a continuing violation of OSHA's five-year record retention requirement. Therefore, penalties could be imposed for violations that occurred over four years before OSHA issued a citation, whereas the construction company defendant argued that OSHA had only six months to bring charges. In addition to the initial failure to log employees' injuries and illnesses as they occurred, OSHRC ruled that AKM LLC failed to meet its obligations to retain the records for five years. [*Secretary of Labor v. AKM LLC dba Volks Constructors*, OSHRC No. 06-1990, 2011 WL 896347 (OSHRC Mar. 11, 2011); see Joseph P. Curtin, William M. Hill, and Peter McCarthy, Mintz Levin OSHA Advisory, *Decision Drastically Expands OSHA's Power to Punish Recordkeeping Violation*, <http://www.mintz.com/newsletter/2011/Advisories/1010-0311-NAT-LIT/1010-0311-NAT-LIT.pdf> (Mar. 31, 2011)]

The following year, however, the D.C. Circuit reversed. The statute of limitations is six months after the "occurrence of any violation." OSHA treated it as a continuing violation. The D.C. Circuit rejected this theory, pointing out that there were separate violations, although it left open the possibility of tolling for a true ongoing violation such as requiring workers to use unsafe equipment [*Sec'y of Labor v. AKM LLC dba Volks Constructors*, No. 11-1106, 2012 WL 1142273 (D.C. Cir. Apr. 6, 2012); see Jenna Greene, *D.C. Circuit: Limit for OSHA Violations Is Six Months, Not Five Years* Blog of Legal Times (Apr. 6, 2012) (law.com). Rehearing was granted, so the case was "de-published." At press time in 2014, there was no subsequent opinion.]

The Severe Violator Enforcement Program (SVEP) is designed to bring recidivists back into compliance, using serious punitive elements such as issuing press releases describing the company as a severe violator; including it in the Severe Violator Log; re-inspecting the violator's facilities and inspecting other facilities within the same corporate enterprise; and requiring additional terms in settlements with the company. OSHA did not publish exit criteria for being released from SVEP until 2013. The criteria are paying all final civil penalties, completing all abatement required by the citations or settlement, addressing any other settlement terms, and completing three full calendar years after final disposition without any related serious violations. Release from the program is at the discretion of the OSHA regional administrator. [Eric J. Conn, *5 Questions We Would Ask OSHA About The Severe Violator Enforcement Program (SVEP)*, Epstein Becker Green (Oct. 23, 2013), available at Lexology.com]

OSHA concluded that the SVEP met several key goals in its first 18 months, and targets offenders who show indifference to safety. The program began in June 2010, replacing the Enhanced Enforcement Program. As of August 2012, 288 SVEP inspections were designated, based on the employer having had a fatality or catastrophe related to major hazards such as falls, amputations, combustible dust, lead, and dangerous chemicals. In February 2012, there had been 180 SVEP cases, leading to 67 settlements. An employer can be removed from SVEP three years after resolving all of its SVEP inspection citations. But employers that fail to abate all hazards, pay all penalties, and otherwise comply with settlements remain in SVEP for three years and then are re-evaluated. [Henry Chajet and

Mark Savit, *OSHA Says SVEP Is A Success*, Jackson Lewis LLP (Nov. 11, 2013), available at Lexology.com]

OSHA issued a press release reporting a $115,400 fine imposed on Jersey Shore Steel for failure to abate, including $111,000 in penalties for lack of written lockout/tagout program; failure to evaluate fork truck operators' performance at least once every three years; and lack of fire extinguisher training, and $4,400 for one repeat violation of failure to guard equipment. [<http://www.osha.gov/ooc/citations/jersey_shore_steel_insp_900106_sept30.pdf>; see Howard A. Mavity, *Don't Slip Up On OSHA Abatement*, Fisher & Phillips LLP (Oct. 24, 2013), available at Lexology.com]

OSHA publishes regional news releases discussing penalties imposed against particular employers, giving the identity of the employer, the amount of the penalty, and why it was applied: e.g., J.C. Stucco and Stone (Lansdowne, Pennsylvania) was fined $73,150 for four repeat and two serious safety violations including fall hazards. [Region 3 News Release 13-330-PHI (osha 13-020, <http://www.osha.gov/pls/oshaweb/owadisp.show_document?p_table=NEWS_RELEASES&p_id=23760> (Mar. 11, 2013). See <http://www.osha.gov/stopfalls> for English and Spanish resources on fall prevention, including fact sheets, posters, and videos.]

Criminal penalties mandated by courts, not directly by OSHA, can be imposed, under OSHA § 17(f)–(h), for giving advance notice of an inspection that is supposed to be made unannounced, for giving false information, or assaulting or interfering with the work of a CO.

OSHA criminal prosecutions are extremely rare, even in cases of obvious disregard of worker safety. About a hundred companies are cited each year for fatal accidents involving workers, but there are never more than a dozen prosecutions in any year. Between 1982 and 2002, according to the *N.Y. Times*, there were over 170,000 occupational deaths. OSHA investigated 1,242 "horror stories": workplaces where willful violations resulted in preventable deaths. Yet even in these worst-case scenarios, OSHA tried to prosecute only 7% of the cases. Out of 2,197 workplace deaths, 1,798 involved rules violations that could have been prosecuted but only 196 cases were referred to prosecutors, who rejected 92 of them. Out of the 81 convictions in the 104 prosecutions that did occur, only 16 prison sentences were imposed. [David Barstow, *U.S. Rarely Seeks Charges for Deaths in Workplace*, N.Y. Times, Dec. 12, 2003, at A1]

There were some later convictions. David Hughart, a former executive of Massey Energy Company, was sentenced to 42 months in federal prison because of the West Virginia coal mine explosion that caused 29 deaths, the worst coal mining disaster in 40 years. He is the highest ranking official charged in the case. Two other Massey managers were also imprisoned. Hughart admitted that he conspired to warn miners when there would be an inspection, and to conceal violations such as excessive coal dust. Kris Maher, *Guilty Plea in Case Tied to Massey Mine Blast*, WSJ.com (Feb. 28, 2013)]

Matthew Lawrence Bowman, ex-owner of Port Arthur Chemical and Environmental Services, was sentenced to a year in prison and a $5,000 fine after pleading guilty to violating the OSH Act and making a false statement in connection with the death of two employees. Bowman admitted that employees were not properly protected against potentially lethal hydrogen sulfide gas. He admitted to ordering employees to falsify transportation documents to conceal the source of toxic wastewater when a disposal facility refused to take any more shipments from the company because of hydrogen sulfide contamination. [Bradford T. Hammock, Henry Chajet, and Mark Savit, *Prison Term For Violation Of Workplace Safety And Environmental Laws*, Jackson Lewis LLP (Nov. 26, 2013), available at Lexology.com; Meagan Noel Newman and Anne D. Harris, *Former President Of Chemical Company Sentenced To One Year Following Employee Fatality*, Seyfarth Shaw LLP (Oct. 29, 2013), available at Lexology.com]

It does not constitute double jeopardy to impose administrative penalties on an employer after it has been convicted of criminal OSHA violations because the administrative penalties are clearly civil and cannot result in imprisonment. [*S.A. Healy Co. v. OSHRC*, 138 F.3d 686 (7th Cir. 1998)]

§ 31.11 OSHA APPEALS

Employers don't have to agree with an OSHA citation. There are several administrative steps that can be taken to protest—although these administrative remedies do have to be exhausted before filing suit.

If an employer challenges a citation, OSHA has to prove that the employer failed to live up to some applicable standard. The agency also has to prove that feasible corrective measures existed that could have brought the employer into compliance. If the standard has a time element (for example, the noise exposure standard does), then OSHA also has to prove that the condition existed long enough and intensely enough to constitute a violation.

OSHA has to prove that the employer knew about the condition or could have become aware by exercising due diligence. It is not necessary to prove that the employer was aware of the standard and deliberately chose to violate it. A supervisor's or foreman's knowledge will be attributed to the employer, unless the employer maintained work rules that satisfied the OSHA standard, communicated those rules to employees, and enforced the work rules.

OSHA is entitled to prove the employer's knowledge (and therefore does not have to prove actual knowledge) in some situations:

- Another employee has already been injured by the same hazardous conditions;
- Several written employee complaints have already been made to OSHA;
- The employer knows that employees habitually omit safety equipment, or otherwise allow hazardous conditions to be present in the workplace;

- The employer doesn't provide enough training;
- The employer doesn't enforce its own safety rules;
- The hazards would easily have been discovered if the employer had performed an adequate inspection.

An employer that receives an OSHA citation has 15 days to file a Notice of Contest, disputing that there was a violation, demanding a fair period of time to abate the violation, or challenging the size of the penalty. If the employer is not sure whether or not to contest, it can schedule an informal conference with the OSHA area director to discuss OSHA's position on workplace conditions and how to improve them. The 15-day limit is strictly applied: OSHRC does not have jurisdiction to review a notice of contest filed after the 15-day period expires. [*Chao v. Russell P. LeFrois Builder, Inc.*, 291 F.3d 219 (2d Cir. 2002)]

There is no official form for the Notice of Contest; it is simply a letter stating in plain English that the employer disagrees with the citation and wants to contest some or all of the violations, to ask for a smaller penalty, and/or ask for more time to comply. If the Notice of Contest is not filed within the required 15 days, the citation becomes final, and no court has the power to reverse it or even to review it.

■ **TIP:** If an employer appeals in bad faith, knowing that the citation is valid, the whole period of time until the challenge is resolved is treated as a period of noncompliance, with additional penalties for each day.

The potential financial impact of an OSHA citation on a business determines the amount of resources needed to defend it. The effect of OSHA citations on collateral litigation (such as Worker's Compensation and wrongful death cases) and other regulatory inspections (e.g., EPA inspections of chemical plants, which use the OSHA inspection as a road map) must be considered. The company must consider whether there is a risk of repeat OSHA citations. If the violation is described as willful, there is a risk of punitive damages in other litigation. Note that bid documents for competitive bidding often ask if there were any willful, repeat, or serious safety violations in the past three years, so it might be worth contesting the citations to avoid ripple effects. [Mark S. Dreux, *Properly Evaluating An OSHA Citation: Should You Contest The Citation?*, Arent Fox LLP (Sept. 27, 2013), available at Lexology.com]

The Fair Play and Safe Workplaces Order, a presidential Executive Order issued July 31, 2014, requires applicants for federal contracts over $500,000 to disclose any violation of various federal statutes in the three-year period before the bid; OSHA is one of the statutes covered by the order. [Executive Order, *Fair Play and Safe Workplaces*, <http://www.whitehouse.gov/the-press-office/2014/07/31/executive-order-fair-pay-and-safe-workplaces> (July 31, 2014)]

When a notice is filed, an OSHA Administrative Law Judge (ALJ) will set a date for a hearing. Although the hearing is informal, it is still governed by the Federal Rules of Evidence. The ALJ's decision becomes final 30 days after it is rendered, unless it is contested.

All Notices of Contest, and all ALJ decisions, are automatically passed along to the Occupational Safety and Health Review Commission (OSHRC). OSHRC has the power to order review of part or all of an ALJ decision. The employer, or any other party adversely affected by the decision, can file a Petition for Discretionary Review. Although it has the power to raise the level of a violation, OSHRC usually doesn't do so.

The employer can raise many arguments to OSHRC:

- The CO got the facts wrong;
- The employer did not know, and had no duty to know, that the violation had occurred;
- The inspection itself was improper—for example, the inspection was really a search, requiring a warrant that had not been obtained;
- OSHA applied the wrong standard;
- The standard itself was invalid, because it was not properly promulgated, or was so vague that employers could not reasonably be expected to understand and comply with it;
- The real cause of the violation was misconduct by employees, beyond the employer's control; this misconduct is unlikely to recur;
- Complying with the OSHA requirement actually increased the hazards to employees rather than decreasing them, but the employer was unable to get a variance.

OSHRC issues an order after considering the employer's arguments and defenses. The employer has 60 days from the date of the OSHRC order to file a further appeal. The employer can now go to federal court, because administrative remedies have been appealed. In fact, the employer can bypass the District Court (the lowest tier in the federal court system, where federal cases normally begin) and appeal either to the Court of Appeals for the Circuit where the violation is alleged to have occurred, or to the District of Columbia Circuit.

OSHRC's obligation, under the OSH Act, is to impose a penalty of $5,000 to $70,000 for each willful violation. The ALJ found that two related companies committed many willful violations of 29 C.F.R. § 1904.2(a) by refusing to record work-related accidents and illnesses. However, the ALJ grouped the violations so that each company was treated as having committed one willful violation, and was assessed with one penalty of $70,000 rather than the $9,000 each for 82 violations, and $8,000 for each of 52 violations, sought by the DOL. The Fifth Circuit agreed with the DOL: ALJs can select a per-violation penalty from within the statutory range, but are not permitted to manipulate the number of violations. DOL can group willful violations at the charging stage—but OSHRC does not have the authority to group per-instance willful violations at the penalty stage. [*Chao v. OSHRC/Chao v. Jindal United Steel Corp.*, 480 F.3d 320 (5th Cir. 2007); the penalty statute is 29 U.S.C. § 666. The circuit courts review OSHRC penalty determinations for abuse of discretion: *Chao v. OSHRC*, 401 F.3d 355 (5th Cir. 2005)]

The Secretary of Labor and OSHRC, both of which are part of the Department of Labor, came into conflict about interpretation of asbestos regulations. The OSHRC found that nine asbestos violations were "not serious," and reduced the overall penalty from $16,875 to $3,150.The Third Circuit reversed OSHRC, finding that the secretary did not have to show that the work in this case could have exposed employees to harmful amount of asbestos. It is presumed that violating Class II asbestos requirements exposes employees to substantial amounts of asbestos. There was a possibility of actual exposure to harmful levels of asbestos, which is all that is required to impose liability. The test is whether secretary demonstrates that the employees did a particular type of asbestos work; there is a presumption under the regulations that the work generates significant asbestos exposure; the employer had actual or constructive notice of the conditions; and the conditions violated the regulations. [*Sec'y of Labor v. Conoco-Phillips Bayway Refinery*, 654 F.3d 472 (3d Cir. 2011). The standards come from *Sec'y of Labor v. Trinity Indus.*, 504 F.3d 397 (3d Cir. 2007)]

OSHA issued citations to the Loretto-Oswego Residential Healthcare Facility for violating employee safety standards (e.g., with respect to eye protection, hepatitis vaccination, training, and electrical equipment). The citations were settled except for one issue: whether some violations were repeated, which depends on whether Loretto-Oswego and two other entities were a single employer for OSH Act purposes. The penalty would be $54,250 for repeat violations, $11,250 otherwise. The three entities shared a president/CEO and CFO/COO. However, the power to hire, fire, and discipline Loretto-Oswego's employees was delegated to its licensed administrator. Nevertheless, the ALJ found repeat violations based on the three entities operating as a single employer. OSHRC reversed. The Department of Labor petitioned for review of the OSHRC decision. Review was denied by the Second Circuit, which deferred to the OSHRC findings, holding that there was substantial evidence of the independence of the facilities. [*Solis v. Loretto Oswego Residential Heath Care Facility*, 692 F.3d 65 (2d Cir. 2012)]

OSHA sought a multi-million-dollar fine against the Imperial Sugar refinery in Georgia, where 13 workers died and 40 were injured when sugar dust exploded in 2008. OSHA alleged that the company was aware of hazards as early as 2002 (including similar conditions at another plant), but failed to correct them. The proposed $8.7 million fine is the third-largest proposed penalty in OSHA history. The penalties include more than $5 million for 120 violations at the plant where the fire occurred and $3.7 million for 91 violations at the other plant. OSHA cited 118 egregious violations. However, ventilation and dust come under the general duty clause, and OSHA cannot issue per-instance violations without a specific standard. [Shaila Dewan, *OSHA Seeks $8.7 Million Fine Against Sugar Company*, N.Y. Times, July 26, 2008, at p. A11]

On September 3, 2009, laborer Nick Revetta died in an explosion at the U.S. Steel plant in Clairton, Pennsylvania when leaking gas ignited and pushed him into a steel column that crushed his head. A co-worker said that potential ignition sources were not properly insulated and safety practices had been deteriorating for five years in order to save money. Based on the co-worker's complaint, OSHA settled the proposed fine of $32,400 for $19,800. The only penalty imposed related to Revetta's death was $10,763 in unrelated fines imposed on an insulation contractor working near the explosion. Ten months later, another explosion hospitalized 17 workers. According to OSHA, U.S. Steel allowed contractors to use a shortcut that was responsible for the explosion; U.S. Steel denied this. In January 2011, OSHA issued 12 violations, one willful, and proposed a $143,000 fine. U.S. Steel appealed. There was a settlement with OSHA on October 26, 2012, calling for a payment of $78,500: [*Solis v. U.S. Steel*, OSHRC Docket No. 11-0361, <http://www.osha.gov/pls/oshaweb/owadisp.show_document?p_table=CWSA&p_id=2206>]

It is a positive trend that the number of workplace fatalities has declined significantly, but this is partially a result of the smaller number of hours worked rather than improved safety. The U.S. fatality rate is six times that of the United Kingdom, where safety rules are tougher. It would take OSHA 130 years to inspect every workplace in the United States. For fiscal 2012, a target of 42,250 inspections (5.6% higher than the previous year's goal) was set, but only 1,118 inspections were actually performed. [Emma Schwartz, Center for Public Integrity, *In U.S. Steel Town, Fatal Gas Explosion Goes Unpunished By OSHA*, iWatch News (May 21, 2012) (benefitslink.com)]

SHRM editor Roy Maurer provided some advice about reducing fines. One important measure is to request an informal conference, which can result in lower penalties, more time to abate hazards, and reclassification or even deletion of some citations. Fines can be reduced by up to 10% if the employer has not had any willful, serious, repeat, or failure-to-abate citations in the preceding five years.

But employers do not qualify for this "Clean History" relief if they have had any of these major citations at any worksite in the United States. Recently, OSHA updated its Field Operations Manual to make it harder for employers to get penalty reductions. The employer must have had an inspection within the previous five years—with no violations being noted at the inspection. Penalties can be reduced 15% under the "quick fix" program if the employer corrects hazards within 24 hours of the inspection. The violation must not have been worse than "moderate-gravity serious," and the employer must undertake substantial permanent corrective actions to qualify. Sometimes OSHA will reduce penalties further and/or structure an installment payment plan, if the employer can show financial hardship; there is no official definition of hardship, so negotiation may be possible. OSHA sometimes reduces penalties based on "Enhanced Abatement" (improvements are extended throughout the corporation, or an external auditor is consulted). Safety improvements can also trigger penalty reductions, although expensive engineering controls might be required. [Roy Maurer, *How to Contest and Reduce OSHA Fines,* <http://www.shrm.org/hrdisciplines/safetysecurity/articles/Pages/Contest-Reduce-OSHA-Fines.aspx> (undated; last accessed Mar. 18, 2013)]

§ 31.12 ABATEMENT

Abatement—removal of hazardous conditions—is the rationale for the whole OSHA process. An uncontested citation, a citation for which the contest period has expired, and a citation where the employer's challenge was partially or wholly unsuccessful, all give rise to abatement responsibilities.

Employers are required to abate violations within the shortest reasonable interval for correction. The CO orders an abatement date. Ordinarily, this will not be more than 30 days, although the initial abatement date could be more than 30 days from the date of the inspection if structural changes are needed, or if abatement relies on components that take a long time to deliver. [See OSHA Field Inspection Reference Manual CPL 2.103, at <http://www.osha.gov>]

■ **TIP:** If a citation notes several violations, only some of which are contested, the appropriate action is to correct the uncontested violations, notify the OSHA area director that correction has occurred, and pay the penalties for the uncontested violations. With respect to contested citations, abatement and payment of fines will be suspended until there is an OSHRC final order.

OSHA reinspects the premises. If the same conditions are detected, penalties of up to $1,000 a day can be imposed. The employer, however, can contest penalties in the same way as an original citation.

The employer is entitled to file a Petition for Modification of Abatement (PMA) with the OSHA Area Director, no later than the scheduled abatement date, if factors beyond the employer's control prevent abatement. The PMA explains what the employer has done to cure the problem, how much additional time is required and why, and what the employer will do to protect employees until full abatement is achieved. The PMA must be posted and served on the employer's workforce, because they have the right to contest it.

If the PMA is uncontested, the Secretary of Labor has the power to approve it. OSHRC holds a hearing on contested PMAs, to determine if the employer did in fact act in good faith and was really unable to achieve full compliance. The employer does not have to comply with the underlying citation during the time that the PMA is under consideration.

An OSHRC ALJ decided in late 2013 that the OSH Act § 20(c) (authorizing OSHRC to grant "other appropriate relief") does not authorize OSHRC to order enterprise-wide abatement (i.e., an order to abate the same or similar hazards at other worksites that were not part of the citation). OSHRC found there was no precedent for interpreting that provision so broadly. [*Delta Elevator Service Corp., dba Delta Beckwith Elevator Co.*, No. 12-1446 (OSHRC 2013); see Stephen C. Yohay, *Judge Rejects OSHA's "Enterprise-Wide" Relief Theory*, Ogletree Deakins (Oct. 29, 2013), available at Lexology.com]

§ 31.13 OSHA CONSULTATION

State OSH agencies, working under grants from the federal OSHA, offer free on-site consultation services to identify and eliminate potential safety problems before they become real ones. The consultants are also available by telephone for advice and discussion. On-site visits are followed up by a written analysis of workplace hazards and suggestions for correction.

The consultants do not have the authority to impose penalties, but participating employers must agree to take steps to correct whatever problems the program uncovered.

Consultations cannot take place while an OSHA inspection is already underway, but if a consultation is scheduled, there is a good chance that OSHA will cancel a scheduled inspection, unless it is investigating a fatality or serious accident, or it is suspected that employees are in imminent danger.

An employer that has completed a consultation, made corrections based on the recommendations, and who posts a notice of correction where employees can see it, is entitled to request one year's immunity from scheduled OSHA inspections.

OSHA gives priority to scheduling consultation in industries with high hazards. The names of companies engaging in consultation will not be disclosed to state or federal enforcers unless the employer refuses to correct imminent hazards that are discovered during the process. [See 29 C.F.R. § 1908.5; for a map of locations, see <http://www.osha.gov/dcsp/smallbusiness/consult_directory.html>]

§ 31.14 VOLUNTARY PROGRAMS

Under the title of Voluntary Protection Programs (VPP), OSHA has three incentive programs (Star, Merit, and Demonstration) for employers with good safety records, who are supposed to serve as examples for other companies. Participants qualify for participation by proving that they maintain safe workplace and provide ongoing safety training for workers. OSHA and state authorities do not do programmed inspections at participating companies, although inspections will still be made if a complaint is registered.

Employers can apply to OSHA for VPP certification. They must complete applications that demonstrate their qualifications for participation. OSHA sends an inspector to check the company's safety records and site conditions, and expects that participants will show continuous improvement in their safety performance.

VPP began in 1982. The Star Program is for sites that are at or below the national average injury rate for their industry. OSHA reviews accident rates every year, and re-evaluates the participants every three to five years. Merit sites have the potential to reach Star status within three years, but in the meantime, they need help with their safety management. OSHA evaluates the site every 18–24 months. The Star Demonstration program is for sites that have reached Star levels, to test alternative means of promoting safety in the workplace. OSHA evaluates Star Demonstration sites every 12–18 months. [OSHA Fact Sheet, *Voluntary Protection Programs*, <http://www.osha.gov/OshDoc/data_General_Facts/factsheet.vpp.pdf>. (August 2009); see also OSHA, *All About VPP*, <http://www.osha.gov/dcsp/vpp/all_about_vpp.html> (undated; last accessed Mar. 20, 2014)]

CHAPTER 32
UNEMPLOYMENT INSURANCE

§ 32.01 INTRODUCTION

Unemployment compensation (UC also known as Unemployment Insurance, or UI) is a state-administered insurance system. Employers make contributions to a fund. The State Employment Security Agencies (SESAs) that administer the system receive federal funding. In exchange, they must perform investigations and other managerial tasks.

Each state creates an Unemployment Insurance Trust Fund from employer contributions. In a few states, employee contributions are also required. However, FICA tax imposes equal (and substantial) burdens on both employer and employee, but unemployment tax is almost exclusively a responsibility of the employer. The theory is that in good times, unemployment will be low, and the fund will accumulate a surplus that can be used in bad times to pay unemployment insurance claims.

The Department of Labor's unadjusted and seasonally adjusted data on the number of unemployment insurance claims can be found at <http://www.dol.gov/ui/data.pdf>. A map with UI contact and other information is posted to <http://www.servicelocator.org/OWSLinks.asp>.

In 2013–2014, although unemployment was very high, the availability of unemployment benefits declined significantly as a result of several factors. Many states reduced the number of weeks of benefits and/or the amount of the benefit and federal programs were cut back or eliminated. As of February 2014, 10.4 million men aged 25–54, the prime working age, more than one-sixth of the men in that cohort, were unemployed; in the early 1970s, the rate for this group was only 6%; 13% in 2007, and almost 20% in 2009. In December 2013, 17% of all working-age men were not working; two-thirds of them were not officially counted as unemployed because they were not looking for work. Forty percent of male job hunters in early 2014 had been unemployed for six months or more. In 1989, 3% of men aged 25–64 received disability benefits, versus 5.5% in 2013. [Mark Peters and David Wessel, *More Men in Prime Working Ages Don't Have Jobs*, WSJ.com (Feb. 5, 2014)]

The National Employment Law Project reported that state UI benefits were at their highest in FY 2009 when they reached $75 billion, but the fiscal 2014 figure was expected to be only $40.5 billion. The project found that 12 states reduced the basic 26-week UI level: benefits in Illinois and Arkansas were reduced to 25 weeks; in South Carolina, Michigan, and Missouri, the basic level is 20 weeks; there are sliding scale eligibility rules in North Carolina (12–20 weeks), Kansas (16–26 weeks), Georgia (14–20 weeks), and Florida (12–23 weeks). As of July 2013, North Carolina stopped furnishing 47 weeks of EUC. The number of weeks of federal benefits is calculated based on the maximum number of weeks of state benefits, so a state-benefit reduction also cuts federal benefits.

There were also benefit cuts: North Carolina reduced its weekly maximum benefit by one-third, to $350 a week; Arkansas froze the weekly benefits; Rhode Island cut average benefits by $100/week; and Wisconsin and Delaware delayed initial payments until a "waiting week" elapses. Drug testing requirements were added in Arizona, Arkansas, Indiana, Kansas, Michigan, Mississippi, Tennessee, and Texas. [Rebecca Dixon, Rick McHugh, and Alexandra Sirota, *Protecting Your State UI Program in 2014: Responding to Likely Challenges* (Feb. 4, 2014), <http://www.nelp.org/page/-/UI/2014/Protecting-Your-State-UI-Program-in-2014.pdf?nocdn=1>; Annie Lowreyjan, *States Cutting Weeks of Aid to the Jobless*, NYTimes.com (Jan. 21, 2014). Under the Michigan law businesses are not obligated to notify the state if applicants refuse to be tested, or if they fail the test, but if they report the information, people who fail drug tests will lose UI eligibility. [AP, *Michigan - Failing Drug Test Could Imperil Jobless Pay*, NYTimes.com (Oct. 29, 2013)]

The Wall Street Journal reported that the states with the worst unemployment problem were not necessarily those offering the greatest duration of benefits, and vice versa. The longest duration of benefits was 86 weeks in Alaska, but Alaska's unemployment rate was 6.7%, below the national average, whereas Michigan, Florida, Georgia, and South Carolina offer a below-average duration of benefits despite severe unemployment. States are motivated to reduce benefits if they owe money to the federal unemployment system and need to repay it; retaining the same level of benefits would require increases in employer contributions, a politically unpopular move. [Ben Casselman, *Jobless Aid Shrinks Unevenly*, WSJ.com (Mar. 19, 2013)]

Federal spending is subject to limits imposed by the "sequester," as a result of the Budget Control Act of 2011, which mandates that the federal government make $85 billion in budget cuts for the 2013 fiscal year. NELP reported in May 2013 that the sequester does not affect the regular state UI benefits received by approximately 3 million private-sector workers and over 50,000 federal workers and servicemembers. However, the sequester affects almost two million workers receiving Emergency Unemployment Compensation (EUC; see 32.02[B]). As of May 3, 2013, 23 states made sequester cuts in EUC benefits, an average of $155 a month. The sequester also reduces federal funding given to the states to manage both unemployment programs—and funds for helping the unemployed find new jobs. [National Employment Law Project Briefing Paper, *The Sequester's Devastating Impact on Families of Unemployed Workers and the Struggling Unemployment Insurance System*, <http://nelp.3cdn.net/e981ef2022538ced66_bfm6b85we.pdf> (May 3, 2013)]

In early 2013, after the automatic cuts under the budget sequester took effect, about 3.8 million people who were unemployed for more than six months faced a cut of approximately 11%, or $32 a week, in the federal unemployment benefit. Before the cuts, the average benefit was $292. The DOL estimate is that on September 30, 2013, $2.3 billion will be cut from the federal benefits, the 14–47 weeks of aid after the state benefits run out, which usually happens after 26 weeks. In January 2013, more than one-third (38.1%) of the unemployed had been out of work for more than six months; the worst-hit were workers over 45. The Urban Institute's 2012 survey showed that workers in their 50s were 20% less likely to be rehired than workers in the 25–34 age range. [Editorial, *As the Budget Cuts Hit Home*, NYTimes.com (Mar. 1, 2013)]

The result of all the trends reducing UI benefits was that only 26% of unemployed workers received UI benefits in January 2014—the lowest percentage since 1950, when the Department of Labor began collecting UI data. [National Employment Law Project, *Share of Unemployed Receiving Jobless Aid Will Hit Record Low* (December 2013), <http://www.nelp.org/page/-/UI/2013/Issue-Brief-Record-Low-Share-Unemployed-Receiving-Jobless-Aid-Renew-EUC.pdf?nocdn=1]>. This issue brief includes a state-by-state table showing decline in benefits receipt between 2010 and 2013.]

Another problem highlighted by the National Employment Law Project is that state UI systems rely on outdated legacy computer systems; federal funding of state UI administration is inadequate to support technology upgrades. As a result, the increasing number of claimants face serious difficulties in getting through on overburdened phone lines, and in making online claims when confronted by backlogs and system outages. [Rebecca Dixon, National Employment Law Project, *Federal Neglect Leaves State Unemployment Systems in a State of Disrepair* (November 2013), <http://www.nelp.org/page/-/UI/2013/NELP-Report-State-of-Disrepair-Federal-Neglect-Unemployment-Systems.pdf?nocdn=1>]

Although the policy that UI beneficiaries must be able to work and available to work had been in existence for a long time, the Department of Labor formalized it in a Final Rule promulgated early in 2007. The publication did not require any new action by the states. [DOL Final Rule, 72 Fed. Reg. 1890 (Jan. 16, 2007)]

■ **TIP:** The Medicare Prescription Drug Improvement and Modernization Act [Pub. L. No. 108-173] provides that one type of "qualified medical expense" that can be withdrawn from a Health Savings Account (HSA) without tax penalty is a premium paid for health insurance by a person receiving federal or state unemployment benefits.

A SUB plan is a severance plan to supplement the payments from state unemployment compensation. To receive SUB pay, an employee must apply for and receive state unemployment benefits, and must verify each week that he or she is still unemployed but is available to work. (Some employers offer a bonus employment incentive payment to encourage workers to find a new job faster.) SUB pay must be periodic (weekly or with each payroll) rather than providing lump sums. A traditional SUB plan terminates payments when the former employee gets a new job or otherwise loses state unemployment benefits. Offset plans (which some states require) reduce the amount the employer pays by the amount of state unemployment benefits. Unless state law forbids, SUB pay can be made from the employer's general assets. If state law does forbid, payments can be made from a trust, which can be but does not have to be a tax-exempt 501(c)(17) trust or a VEBA. SUB pay from an approved plan is not subject to state unemployment taxes. Termination benefits that are excluded from FICA probably will not affect the recipient's eligibility for state unemployment benefits. SUB plans are subject to requirements of state law, which are not necessarily identical to federal tax rules. Some states reserve the right to approve SUB plans—and, as state unemployment insurance trusts become depleted, approval is more likely to be denied. [Vicki M. Nielsen, *The Advantages Of Offering Supplemental Unemployment Benefits Instead Of Severance, Part I: FICA Taxes And More*, Ogletree Deakins (Aug. 26, 2013), available at Lexology.com]

In March 2014, the Supreme Court held that the severance payments constituted FICA wages. The Supreme Court held that severance payments are made only to employees, and they are made because of service to employers because "service" is defined broadly as the entire relationship between the employer and employee. The court noted that the FICA statute provides a list of exemptions from the general rule that all compensation constitutes FICA wages. One of the exemptions is for severance payments made for disability retirement. The Supreme Court said it would not be necessary to specify this exemption if severance pay in general did not constitute FICA wages. Code § 3401(a), dealing with income tax withholding, also has a broad definition of taxable wages, subject to a list of exemptions. The list says that Supplemental Unemployment Benefits are treated as if they were wages: see § 3402(o). Quality Stores interpreted this to mean that, although SUB payments are treated "as if" they were wages, they are not wages for this purpose or for FICA purposes. However, the Supreme Court traced this provision to the history of tax withholding, when Congress wanted to relieve terminated workers from the burden of year-end tax liability. [*United States v. Quality Stores Inc.*, 134 S. Ct. 1395 (2014)]

Some help-wanted advertisements stipulate that the company will not hire unemployed persons, only those who already have another job. Since December 2009, more than 40% of the unemployed have been looking for work for more than six months. According to the DOL, in January 2012, 5.5 million people had been unemployed for more than six months, more than four million for over a year. [Shelly Banjo, *Measures Aim to End Bias Against Long-Term Jobless*, WSJ .com (Feb. 24, 2012)]

The New York City Human Rights Law makes it illegal for an employer to discriminate against unemployed job applicants. More than two dozen federal, state, and local provisions are pending to adopt similar laws. The states Oregon and New Jersey and the city of Chicago, forbid job advertisements that require applicants to be employed. The District of Columbia makes it unlawful for an employer or employment agency to treat unemployment as a factor in employment and hiring decisions, but the New York City law is the only one that grants a private right of action. [Phillip H. Wang, *The Unemployed – A Protected Category Coming To A Jurisdiction Near You*, DLA Piper (Sept. 30, 2013), available at Lexology.com]

The New Jersey Appellate Division upheld NJSA 34:8B-1, a state law forbidding job ads that require all applicants to be currently employed. The court found that the statute did not infringe on employers' First Amendment rights. The court treated advertisements as a form of commercial speech, where restrictions get less stringent judicial scrutiny than political speech. The Appellate Division found that the law is narrowly tailored to advance the substantial government interest in improving opportunities for the unemployed. Furthermore, the law does not mandate that employers consider applications, interview unemployed job applicants, or hire them—but they cannot publish advertisements that rule out the unemployed. Oregon, the District of Columbia, and New York City also protect unemployed job hunters. [*New Jersey Dep't of Labor & Workforce Dev. v. Crest Ultrasonics et al.*, 434 N.J. Super. 34, 82 A.3d 258 (N.J. App. Div. 2014); see David G. Islinger and James M. McDonnell, *New Jersey Ban On "Currently Employed" Requirement In Job Ads Resists Constitutional Challenge*, Jackson Lewis PC (Jan. 14, 2014), available at Lexology.com]

§ 32.02 ELIGIBILITY FOR BENEFITS

In addition to the main program and the federal extensions, the unemployment system also includes benefits for federal workers and former military servicemembers; both programs are administered by state UI agencies on behalf of the federal government. Unemployment Compensation for Federal Civilian Employees (UCFE) provides unemployment benefits to federal civilian workers under the same conditions and in the same amount as benefits for other workers. Unemployment Compensation for Ex-Servicemembers (UCX), provides benefits for honorably discharged ex-servicemembers who completed their first full term of service (although there are some exceptions permitted). Members of the reserves and National Guard need 90 days of continuous active service and separation under honorable conditions to qualify for UCX benefits. [*Unemployment Compensation: Federal-State Partnership*, <http://www.ows.doleta.gov/unemploy/pdf/partnership.pdf> (April 2013, accessed Mar. 29, 2014)]

[A] Generally

Two of the most important determinants in entitlement are whether the employee worked long enough before termination to qualify for benefits; and the reason for termination. The "base period" is the period of time used to analyze whether the job continued long enough.

In most states, the base period is the first four of the preceding five completed calendar quarters. Some states allow the four most recent quarters of employment to be counted. The difference is whether the most recent months of employment (which might have higher earnings) will be counted. Theoretically, only persons who earned at least a minimum amount during the base period can collect UI benefits. In practice, these limits are so low that nearly all employees meet them.

The rationale for the UI system is to provide benefits for employees who lose their jobs through "no fault of their own." But in this context, an employee will not be considered to be at fault even if the employer was justified in firing him or her—for instance, if an employee is fired for incompetence but there was no crime or wrongdoing. For example, in *Time Warner Cable*, Unempl. Ins. Rep. (CCH) ¶ 8314 (Miss. App. 2006), benefits were held to have been correctly paid to a claimant who was terminated for lack of knowledge and judgment needed in his job. Inefficiency, unsatisfactory conduct, and good-faith errors do not constitute misconduct.

In general, benefits will not be available to anyone who quit voluntarily without good cause. However, states vary as to whether employees who quit will be entirely denied UI benefits, or whether benefit eligibility will merely be delayed. If the employer's conduct has been so abusive as to constitute constructive discharge, then the employee will be deemed to have had good cause to resign. For example, the District of Columbia Court of Appeals ruled that a laundry manager was entitled to benefits when she quit, because she had been subjected to frequent verbal abuse. Decision factors include whether the insults were habitual; if the employee was insulted in front of other people; if the insults were related to job duties; and whether the employee protested the abuse to a supervisor or executive. [*Imperial Valet Servs. Inc. v. Alvarado*, No. 12-CV-1173, 2013 WL 3820947 (D.C. App. 2013); see Zoe Tillman, *Verbal Abuse Is "Good Cause" to Quit, D.C. Court Says*, The BLT (Blog of Legal Times) (July 25, 2013) (law.com)]

However, there are situations where the employee is considered to have acted with good cause, even if the employer was not at fault. Many states interpret quitting a job to follow a spouse who has gotten a job elsewhere to constitute good cause.

Pennsylvania ruled that a claimant quit work without good cause when her husband was relocated to Ohio. The claimant failed to show that the move to Ohio caused insuperable problems for commuting, or that maintaining two residences caused economic hardship. The Pennsylvania Commonwealth Court did not necessarily treat maintaining the family unit as good cause to quit. [*Sturpe*, Unempl. Ins. Rep. (CCH) ¶ 12,433 (Pa. Commw. 2003)]

Yet another issue is the treatment of persons who have accepted severance packages (see Chapter 3 for more discussion of severance benefits). The Massachusetts Court of Appeals ruled in 2006 that benefits should have been awarded to claimants who took a voluntary separation package because they had an objectively reasonable belief that they would have been fired if they had not taken the packages. The employer neither announced that employees would be chosen randomly for RIF nor announced criteria for selecting RIF candidates, thus giving employees good cause to cut their losses by taking the package and leaving. [*State Street Bank & Trust Co.*, Unempl. Ins. Rep. (CCH) ¶ 8487 (Mass. App. 2006); see also *Johnson v. Unemployment Compensation Bd. of Review* (Pa.

Commonwealth 2005), discussed in Asher Hawkins, *Bought-Out Verizon Workers Denied Jobless Aid*, The Legal Intelligencer (Mar. 10, 2005) (law.com)]

Employees who took a voluntary separation plan were eligible for benefits, based on testimony from a company Vice President and e-mails from the HR department stating that the plan was implemented because of lack of work. [*Verizon North*, Unempl. Ins. Rep. (CCH) ¶ 10,203 (Ohio App. 2006)]

In contrast, however, an office manager was given the choice between staying on while she looked for a new job, or leaving immediately and receiving severance pay. When she opted to leave right away, she was ineligible for benefits, because she was the one who made the departure decision. [*Arrow Legal Solutions Group PXC*, Unempl. Ins. Rep. (CCH) ¶ 8354 (Utah App. 2006)]

Benefits are also denied to persons who are guilty of "misconduct detrimental to the best interests of the employer." This is interpreted in an industrial rather than moral light, so improper activities are likely to rule out UI benefit eligibility even if they are not criminal in nature. Poor job performance would not be treated as "misconduct," unless it demonstrated gross negligence or willful disregard of the employer's best interests.

Depending on the state, disqualifying misconduct might also have to be work-related. Excessive absence or insubordination might be treated as misconduct. Benefits were properly denied to a claimant who was terminated for excessive absences. On her first day at work, she signed an acknowledgment of receiving the company handbook, including the attendance policy. The claimant asserted that she misinterpreted the policy, so her actions could not be deemed willful or wanton, but the Delaware Superior Court ruled that denial of benefits was correct because the employer coached her about the policy and warned her that she was at risk of termination for continuing to violate it. [*Jackson*, Unempl. Ins. Rep. (CCH) ¶ 8317 (Del. Super. Ct. 2008)]

Being intoxicated on business premises would almost certainly be considered misconduct. For example, Kansas denied benefits for disqualifying misconduct on the basis of the claimant's repeated insubordination to a supervisor in an open area where other workers could hear the interaction, which also involved an unprovoked barrage of vulgar and abusive language. [*Siler*, Unempl. Ins. Rep. (CCH) ¶ 8265 (Kan. App. 2003)] Denial of benefits for work-related misconduct was proper when the claimant gave a supervisor's personal phone number to a former employee who used it to leave an obscene and threatening message. The claimant was present when the call was made, and lied about it afterward, so even if his only involvement was having bad judgment in distributing the number, lying about it was work-related misconduct that ruled out benefits. [*Schwartz*, Unempl. Ins. Rep. (CCH) ¶ 8427 (Tenn. App. 2008)]

A truck driver whose blood alcohol concentration exceeded the legal limit was guilty of disqualifying misconduct, even though he was not convicted of driving under the influence and did not lose his license; he should have known that duty to his employer precluded driving while impaired. [*Risk*, Unempl. Ins. Rep. (CCH) ¶ 8557 (Minn. App. 2003)] Being stopped for a non-work-related DUI, resulting in surrender of the driver's license when the claimant's job at a tire shop required a valid license, constituted disqualifying misconduct. [*Gummert*, Unempl. Ins. Rep. (CCH) ¶ 9126 (Iowa Dist. Ct. 2008)]

A fired legal secretary could obtain benefits: it was not disqualifying misconduct to fail to complete a project before leaving for vacation because it was merely an isolated incident of bad judgment or ordinary negligence, not intentional disregard of the employer's interests. [*Aspen Ridge Law Offices*, Wyo. Sup. Unempl. Ins. Rep. (CCH) ¶ 8209 (Wyo. 2006)]

New York granted unemployment benefits to a Whole Foods Market employee who violated store policy by taking a sandwich out of the trash at the end of his shift. Employees are required to get their supervisors' consent before taking food; servings are usually sample-sized, and must be logged and accounted for. Initially, unemployment benefits were denied on grounds of misconduct. The employee said that his previous supervisor allowed employees to take damaged food that was going to be thrown out and written off. The ALJ sided with the employee, because he had a good record, did not take the sandwich out of the store, and this was an isolated instance of poor judgment that should not be considered misconduct. [Rebecca Moore, *Reason for Denying Unemployment Benefits Sounded Fishy*, plansponsor.com (Mar. 20, 2009). See also Rebecca Moore, *Dillards Tries to Block Unemployment Benefits for Hot Dog* "Thief", plansponsor .com (July 29, 2011):

The Indiana Court of Appeals reversed disqualification of Nolan Koewler, who was fired for eating two hot dogs that were left over after a company picnic. The Review Board concluded that he had been fired for theft, but the Court of Appeals noted that although employees including Koewler were told to put the leftovers away, they were not aware that it was supposed to be saved for Labor Day. Furthermore, the food had been supplied for consumption by employees, and Koewler was not aware that employees were no longer supposed to consume food items. But see Tara Cantore, *Dumpster Diving Employee Can't Get Unemployment,* plansponsor.com (Aug. 25, 2011): An employee fired for taking soup from a dumpster, a violation of the store policy against employees taking anything from the store without paying for it, was terminated for misconduct and, therefore, did not qualify for unemployment benefits.]

Continued eligibility requires the claimant to make a serious search for work. Benefits will be terminated if the claimant receives but rejects a legitimate job offer for suitable work. Benefits will not be paid in any week in which the claimant receives a pension, annuity, retirement pay, or any other private or government payment based on past work history. But benefits can be paid in a week in which the claimant receives a distribution from a profit-sharing plan, because that is not treated as compensation for work. The general rule is that a claimant who has recovered from an injury must return to the employer and offer to work. However, the Iowa District Court ruled in 2008 that a worker who knew that he was only able to do light work, that his employer had no light duty assignments to offer, and someone else had already been hired to replace him was not required to make a futile offer of his unsuitable services in order to receive benefits. [*Riner*, Unempl. Ins. Rep. (CCH) ¶ 9133 (Iowa Dist. Ct. 2008)]

Benefits can be paid based on job loss due to a material change in working conditions imposed by the employer, if the employee has a valid reason for being unable to work under the new conditions. (This is referred to as "voluntary with good cause attributable to the employer.") A published job description can be evidence of the original nature of the job, and therefore whether material change has occurred. If a job is described as a day-shift position, a change to a night or swing shift might well be considered material.

In mid-2003, the New York Court of Appeals ruled that the employee's physical presence is critical, not the location of the employer on whose behalf the work was done. So a worker who telecommuted from Florida could not collect New York unemployment benefits, even though her employer was located in Long Island and work was directed and controlled from New York. [*Allen v. Comm'r of Labor*, 100 N.Y.2d 282 (N.Y. 2003); see John Caher, *N.Y. Court First to Rule on Telecommuting*, New York Law Journal, July 3, 2003 <http://www.law.com>; Al Baker, *Telecommuter Loses Case for Benefits*, N.Y. Times, July 3, 2003, at B1]

Strikers were held to be entitled to benefits after the date that permanent replacements were hired. (The employment relationship is severed when employees have been notified that they have been replaced, or their positions are permanently filled by someone else.) [*M. Conley Co.*, Unempl. Ins. Rep. (CCH) ¶ 10,186 (Ohio 2006)] School district employees were properly denied benefits during a work stoppage. When CBA negotiations reached an impasse, the employer implemented its best and final offer, which was not so unreasonable that employees would feel constrained to strike. Therefore, the work stoppage was a strike, not a lockout, and benefits were unavailable. [*Tietz*, Unempl. Ins. Rep. (CCH) ¶ 10,178 (Ohio App. 2005)] Union members did not get benefits: their work stoppage was not caused by a lockout, and they had the opportunity to return to work when the employer hired permanent replacement workers. [*Magnode*, Unempl. Ins. Rep. (CCH) ¶ 10,195 (Ohio App. 2006)]

[B] BAA-UC

The Department of Labor created a program called BAA-UC (BAA stands for Birth and Adoption) [20 C.F.R. Part 604], through a Notice of Proposed Rulemaking at 64 Fed. Reg. 67972 (Dec. 3, 1999), finalized, without significant changes, at 65 Fed. Reg. 37209 (June 13, 2000). The program allowed new parents to receive unemployment benefits for a one-year period beginning with the week of birth or adoption, because they would be treated as being "able and available for work" during this time period. The DOL regulations gave states the ability to opt in to the program, but no state elected to do so.

A lawsuit [*LPA, Inc. v. Chao*, 211 F. Supp. 2d 160 (D.D.C. 2002)] challenged the BAA-UC program as inconsistent with federal law. Although the suit was dismissed on procedural grounds, it caused the DOL to re-think the program. After review, the DOL decided that the BAA-UC experiment was a bad decision and an invalid interpretation of the rules about availability for work. It would also put additional strain on already hard-pressed state unemployment insurance funds. Therefore, the DOL decided to terminate the experiment, publishing a Notice of Proposed Rulemaking for this purpose at 67 Fed. Reg. 72122 (Dec. 4, 2002).

[C] Federal Statutes Extending UI

A federal statute, 42 U.S.C. § 177(a), the Robert T. Stafford Disaster Relief and Emergency Assistance Act, establishes the Disaster Unemployment Assistance (DUA) program. Up to 26 weeks of benefits can be furnished after a major disaster declared by the President, for unemployment caused by that disaster for which no other benefits are available. DUA eligibility ceases when the state agency finds that unemployment is no longer directly traceable to the major disaster. The minimum weekly amount of benefit is 50% of the state's average UI benefit. The maximum is set by state law.

The DUA benefit is considered a UC benefit. It cannot exceed the maximum benefit payable under the state's UC law. Qualifications for DUA are that the claimant no longer has a job, cannot reach the place of work, is unable to start a promised job; is the household breadwinner; has become head of the household because the former head of the household died in the disaster; or is unable to work because of an injury caused by the disaster. [DOL, *Disaster Unemployment Assistance* fact sheet, <http://workforcesecurity.doleta.gov/unemploy/disaster.asp> (updated July 23, 2010) (accessed Apr. 9, 2014)]

The November 2001 rule provides a definition of "unemployment as a direct result" of a major disaster [20 C.F.R. § 625.5(c)]—DUA benefits are limited to the immediate result of the disaster itself, not more remote consequences of a chain of events that was started or made worse by the disaster. Examples of direct results are unemployment caused by damage to or destruction of the physical worksite, lack of access to the worksite because the government has ordered it closed, or lack of work and lost revenues caused to a business that got the majority of its income from the premises that were damaged, destroyed, or shut down. But "ripple effects" (for instance, if an office building is closed, workers who can't come in to work don't stop at a coffee shop for snacks) are not covered. Beneficiaries can include, for example, workers at airports closed by government orders.

In addition to this federal law, some states have state "optional trigger" laws that let them provide a 13-week extended benefit period for workers who have used up their regular benefits during a period of high unemployment. The weekly amount of Extended Benefits (EB) is the same as the claimant's regular unemployment compensation. The Basic EB program requires states to provide up to 13 weeks of additional benefits, based on unemployment rates. States have the option to provide the additional 13 weeks of EB if unemployment is high, but not as high as the level where EB is mandatory in states where unemployment is high and rising. In addition, in some states with extremely high unemployment, there is a voluntary program adding seven more weeks of EB after the claimant has exhausted other unemployment benefits (not counting Disaster Unemployment Assistance or Trade Readjustment Allowances). However, not everyone who qualifies for regular benefits qualifies for EB.

Although in general, EB is 50% state and 50% federally funded, ARRA included a provision under which the federal government temporarily took over 100% funding of EB. This provision was renewed by Pub. L. No. 111-312, the 2010 tax bill, until January 4, 2012—so several states could offer EB benefits again. [DOL, *100% Federal Funding of Extended Benefits (EB) Extended to January 4, 2012*, <http://www.ows.doleta.gov/unemploy/supp_act_eb.asp> (accessed Mar. 25, 2011)] Subsequently, the American Taxpayer Relief Act of 2012 (ATRA), Pub. L. No. 112-240, extended 100% federal funding of EB until December 31, 2013. [DOL, *100% Federal Funding of Extended Benefits (EB) Extended to December 31, 2013*, <http://workforcesecurity.doleta.gov/unemploy/supp_act_eb.asp> (Jan. 16, 2013)] In February 2012, Congress chose not to update the EB program criteria. The EB program formerly provided 13 or 20 additional weeks of benefits. Starting in mid-2012, states stopped providing EB benefits. The NELP reported that, as of December 2013, no state qualified for EB. [National Employment Law Project, *Share of Unemployed Receiving Jobless Aid Will Hit Record Low* (December 2013), <http://www.nelp.org/page/-/UI/2013/Issue-Brief-Record-Low-Share-Unemployed-Receiving-Jobless-Aid-Renew-EUC.pdf?nocdn=1]>. This issue brief includes a state-by-state table showing decline in benefits receipt between 2010 and 2013.]

A program of Temporary Extended Unemployment Compensation was established under the Job Creation and Worker Assistance Act of 2002 (JWCAA). [Pub. L. No. 107-147] The program was originally scheduled to end as of January 1, 2003. It was extended to June 1, 2003 by Pub. L. No. 108-1 (which doesn't have a short title), and once again to December 31 by Pub. L. No. 108-26 (The Unemployment Compensation Amendments of 2003 Act). However, that was the final extension, and the program ended December 2003.

Emergency Unemployment Compensation (EUC; also known as EUC08) is a federal temporary extension of benefits for people who have collected all their regular state benefits. Although the basic unemployment programs are jointly funded by federal and state governments, EUC is wholly federally funded.

The program was created by Pub. L. No. 110-252, the Supplemental Appropriations Act of 2008, and has been expanded since then in light of ongoing economic problems. Pub. L. No. 110-449, the Unemployment Compensation

Extension Act of 2008, expanded the reach of the program, as did the Worker, Homeownership, and Business Assistance Act of 2009, Pub. L. No. 111-92. The program was extended (saved from termination) by ARRA, Pub. L. No. 111-5, and then by the Department of Defense Appropriations Act, Pub. L. 111-118, the Temporary Extension Act of 2010, Pub. L. No. 111-144, Continuing Extension Act of 2010, Pub. L. No. 111-157, and the Unemployment Compensation Extension Act of 2010, Pub. L. No. 111-205.

EUC was preserved from elimination by the Middle Class Tax Relief and Job Creation Act of 2012, Pub. L. No. 112-96—but that law not only imposes some limitations on persons receiving UI benefits, it phases down the maximum duration of benefits from 99 weeks to 66 weeks (or 73 weeks, in states with high unemployment).

However, EUC was not reauthorized when it expired at the end of 2013, causing loss of benefits to 1.3 million long-term unemployed workers. Federal legislation (S. 1747/H.R. 3546) was introduced to reauthorize EUC for 2014, but at press time in August 2014, it had not passed. [National Employment Law Project, *Share of Unemployed Receiving Jobless Aid Will Hit Record Low* (December 2013), <http://www.nelp.org/page/-/UI/2013/Issue-Brief-Record-Low-Share-Unemployed-Receiving-Jobless-Aid-Renew-EUC.pdf?nocdn=1]>; DOL, *Expiration of Unemployment Insurance Programs*, <http://www.ows.doleta.gov/unemploy/docs/supp_act_eb-euc-expired.pdf> (accessed Apr. 9, 2014)]

When the program was in effect (it was renewed over 10 times, four times retroactively, between July 2008 and December 31, 2013) EUC paid an average of $300 a week to 1.3 million long-term unemployed persons who exhausted the approximately 26 weeks of UI available in most states. [Brenda Cronin, *As the Politics Play Out, Key Jobless Benefit Lapses,* WSJ.com (Dec. 27, 2013); Annie Lowrey, *Benefits Ending for One Million Unemployed*, NYTimes.com (Dec. 27, 2013); Jeremy W. Peters, *Senate Fails to Pass Three-Month Extension of Jobless Aid*, NYTimes.com (Feb. 6, 2014); Janet Hook, *Legislation to Extend Long-Term Jobless Benefits Fails in Senate*, WSJ.com (Feb. 6, 2014)]

A further 850,000 people lost benefits in the first quarter of 2014, with up to 4.8 million people affected by benefit expirations throughout 2014. As of late 2013, EUC had cost a total of about $250 billion. Extending it through 2014 would cost another $25 billion. [Annie Lowrey, *Extension of Benefits for Jobless Is Set to End*, NYTimes.com (Nov. 17, 2013)]

When it is in effect, EUC is organized into four tiers (a tier is a set of extra weeks of benefits provided after the basic state benefits have been exhausted). The duration of the various Emergency Unemployment Compensation (EUC) tiers has been amended several times. The 2013 tiers were 14 weeks (Tier I); 14 weeks if the state unemployment rate is 6% or more (Tier II); 9 weeks if the rate is 7% or more (Tier III); 10 weeks if the rate is 9% or more (Tier IV), so at that point, the maximum number of weeks of benefits was 73—lower than 2010, when the maximum duration of benefits was 99 weeks. [Alison Doyle, "Unemployment Tiers," <http://jobsearch.about.com/od/extended/a/unemployment-tiers.htm?> (undated; accessed Mar. 22, 2012)]

EUC was extended under the Tax Relief, Unemployment Insurance Reauthorization, and Job Creation Act of 2010, Pub. L. No. 111-312, for the period January 3, 2012–June 9, 2014. [DOL, *Emergency Unemployment Compensation (EUC) Extended to January 3, 2012*, <http://www.ows.doleta.gov/unemploy/supp_act.asp>] The American Taxpayer Relief Act extended the expiration date of this program until Jan. 1, 2014, but it does not provide additional weeks of benefits to claimants who had already used up all their entitlement. [DOL, *Emergency Unemployment Compensation (EUC) Extended to January 1, 2014*, <http://workforcesecurity.doleta.gov/unemploy/supp_act.asp> (last accessed Mar. 10, 2013)] [Christine L. Owens, National Employment Law Project press release, *Statement on Congress's Renewal of Unemployment Insurance*, <http://www.c-spanvideo.org/program/309633-4> (Jan. 2, 2013).

The Middle Class Tax Relief and Job Creation Act of 2012, Pub. L. No. 112-96, includes many provisions dealing with UI:

- § 2101: UI benefits are available only to people who are able to work, available to work, and are actively seeking work;
- § 2102: Up to ten states can work with the DOL on demonstration projects to get the long-term unemployed back into the workforce;
- § 2103: Recovery of state and federal overpayments is now mandatory;
- § 2105: States are allowed to pass laws imposing a drug testing requirement in connection with unemployment—but only if the applicant was fired from his or her most recent job because of drug use, or the only suitable work for the applicant is in an industry that conducts regular drug tests pursuant to DOL regulations;
- §§ 2122, 2123: Reauthorization of EUC until January 2, 2013, but with the maximum duration scaling down from 99 weeks to 73 weeks;
- § 2141: EUC and Extended Benefits use the same standard for work search (able and available to work and actively seeking work);
- § 2142: Eligibility of long-term benefit recipients will be re-assessed;
- § 2144: Eligible states can remain entitled to federal EUC funds through the end of the fiscal year by modifying their UI benefits;
- § 2161-2163: Work-sharing provisions
- § 2181-2183: Grants to allow states to set up self-employment assistance programs for the long-term unemployed. The existing Self-Employment Assistance (SEA) program receives additional funding and DOL technical assistance

[United States Senate Committee on Finance, *Summary of the Middle Class Tax Relief and Job Creation Act of 2012*, <http://www.finance.senate.gov/newsroom/chairman/release/?id=c42a8c8a-52ad-44af-86b2-4695aaff5378> (Feb. 16, 2012); Josh Mitchell and Naftali Bendavid, *Tax Bill Passed by Congress Broadens Jobless Program*, WSJ.com (Feb. 18, 2012); Naftali Bendavid and Siobhan Hughes, *Congress Reaches Payroll-Tax Deal*, WSJ.com (Feb. 16, 2012)]

The STC program (for Short-Time Compensation; also known as work-sharing) provides partial unemployment benefits to persons who are still working at the same job, but whose hours have been reduced from full- to part-time.

The Middle Class Tax Relief and Job Creation Act of 2012 encourages states to have STC programs, but the programs must be consistent with the federal definition. The federal government will reimburse up to 100% of certain state STC costs for up to three years. The Middle Class Tax Relief Act also set up a temporary federal STC program, allowing states without their own STC programs to operate a program under a two-year contract with DOL. [DOL, *Unemployment Compensation: Federal-State Partnership*, <http://www.ows.doleta.gov/unemploy/pdf/partnership.pdf> (April 2013, accessed Mar. 29, 2014). This document says that 26 states had STC programs. Another DOL document says that STC programs were in effect in Arizona, Arkansas, California, Colorado, the District of Columbia, Florida, Iowa, Kansas, Massachusetts, Maryland, Maine, Minnesota, Missouri, New Hampshire, New York, Oklahoma, Oregon, Pennsylvania, Texas, Vermont, and Washington. [DOL, *Short-Term Compensation Information for Federal Employees and Employers*, <http://www.dol.gov/sequestration/Short-Time-Compensation-20130405.pdf> (undated, presumed Apr. 5, 2013, accessed Mar. 29, 2014), including links to state STC programs; see also Hunton & Williams LLP, *DOL Launches Website Promoting Work Sharing Programs* (Nov. 21, 2013), available at Lexology.com]

ARRA allowed about 500,000 part-time and low-income workers to receive benefits for the first time. According to the Department of Labor, only 36% of the unemployed actually receive benefits, because applicants must be involuntarily unemployed, and most states denied benefits to a person who is only looking for part-time work. ARRA provided federal funding for states to offer benefits to seekers of part-time work; those who left the workforce for compelling reasons such as caring for a sick child; applicants who have benefit-eligible dependents; and workers who undertook training after exhausting their benefits. [Catherine Rampell, *Stimulus Bill Would Bestow New Aid to Many Workers*, N.Y. Times, Feb. 14, 2009]

Unemployment benefits, retraining, and health insurance subsidies are available under the Trade Adjustment Assistance Program (TAAP) to workers who lost their jobs when their employer moved outside of the United States, or because of foreign competition. A brochure available on the DOL Website (as updated through February 19, 2013) explains that benefits are triggered by filing a petition with DOL, either online or at an American Job Center. The petition can be filed either by an employer, a union official, a job center operator or partner (such as a state workforce agency), or by three or more workers from the same firm. DOL investigates to determine if the layoff is eligible (i.e., was caused by increased importation, outsourcing of production, loss of business from a customer that is also TAAP-eligible, or a declaration of trade injury made by the International Trade Commission. If the DOL certifies eligibility, the state will notify the eligible workers that they can apply for benefits, such as up to 130 weeks of training, wage subsidies, job search allowance, reimbursement for the cost of relocating for a new job, and a tax credit for 72.5% of the premium the individual pays for health insurance. [DOL brochure, *The Trade Adjustment Assistance Program: Back to Work After a Trade-Related Layoff*, <http://www.doleta.gov/tradeact/pdf/2011_brochure.pdf> (accessed Mar. 29, 2014)]

[D] Case Law on Benefit Eligibility

There are a number of reasons why benefits will be denied: that the individual was not totally unemployed; that he or she voluntarily quit his or her past job rather than being involuntarily employed; that he or she was guilty of misconduct (which generally means something worse than sheer incompetence).

A nurse working under an intermittent employment contract was not entitled to benefits after the contract expired: A person who chooses to work under a fixed-term contract is not involuntarily unemployed when the contract ends. [*Brinkman*, Unempl. Ins. Rep. (CCH) ¶ 10,179 (Ohio App. 2005)]

The Tennessee Supreme Court ruled that a licensed time share salesperson was not entitled to unemployment benefits when her service agreement with the timeshare company ended. She was a "licensed real estate agent" excluded from UI benefits. She was paid on a commission basis and was responsible for her own income and payroll taxes. The Tennesse Supreme Court said that time share salespersons are real estate agents because they must be licensed, and are paid commissions for engaging in real estate activities. [*Westgate Smoky Mountains at Gatlinburg v. Phillips, et al.*, No. E2011-02538-SC-R11-CV, 2013 Tenn. LEXIS 1014, Unemployment Ins. Rep. (CCH) P8438 (Tenn. 2013); see James R. Mulroy, II and Donald E. Hayes, Jr., *Time-Share Salesperson Not Entitled To Unemployment Insurance Benefits, Tennessee Supreme Court Rules*, Jackson Lewis PC (Jan. 13, 2014), available at Lexology.com]

According to Louisiana's District Court, providing a false Social Security number and false information about one's criminal record constitutes material misconduct. The job was coordinator of environmental health and safety, so the employer had the right to expect honesty and integrity, and the employer's work rules spelled out a zero-tolerance policy for document falsification. [*Sheppard*, Unempl. Ins. Rep. (CCH) ¶ 9043 (La. Dist. Ct. 2002)]

The Mississippi Court of Appeals denied benefits, on the grounds of disqualifying misconduct, to two claimants who participated in an unauthorized strike that violated the no-strike provision of their Collective Bargaining Agreement (CBA). [*Berry*, Unempl. Ins. Rep. (CCH) ¶ 8284 (Miss. App. 2001)], but union members are entitled to unemployment benefits during a lockout by the employer. [*Schott Glass Technologies Inc.*, Unempl. Ins. Rep. (CCH) ¶ 12,436 (Pa. Commw. 2003)]

Accepting benefits for total disability without actually having the claimed physical limitations was a falsehood in disregard of the employer's interest and standards, and therefore disqualifying misconduct that precluded receipt of UI benefits. [*Downey*, Unempl. Ins. Rep. (CCH) ¶ 12,505 (Pa. Commw. 2006)]

An individual who has a reasonable expectation of reemployment (absolute certainty is not required) will not be required to make a formal search for other work. [*Thomas*, Unempl. Ins. Rep. (CCH) ¶ 9510 (Wis. Cir. 2000)] The claimant, #2 on the seniority list of a unionized workplace where the Collective Bargaining Agreement stipulated recall on the basis of seniority, could reasonably expect to be called back to work when the workplace re-opened after it was purchased. So he could collect unemployment benefits in the interim, even if he didn't make a job search.

The Minnesota Supreme Court held in early 2014 that it is not a violation of public policy to fire an employee for applying for unemployment benefits. (The plaintiff applied for benefits after a reduction in hours.) The plaintiff did not allege that she was required to commit any illegal acts and the court refused to expand the definition of public policy to include all undesirable actions by employers. However, a commentator noted that the plaintiff was likely to apply for benefits once again, and the benefit application would probably not be deemed to be disqualifying misconduct. Minnesota also makes it a misdemeanor for an employer to impede or obstruct an application for unemployment benefits. [*Dukowitz v. Hannon Sec. Servs.*, 841 N.W.2d 147, 164 Lab. Cas. (CCH) P61,435, 97 Empl. Prac. Dec. (CCH) ¶ 44,984 (Minn. 2014); see Michael C. Wilhelm, *Can You Fire An Employee For Applying For Unemployment Benefits?*, Briggs and Morgan (Jan. 7, 2014), available at Lexology.com]

Ability to work is another important criterion. The claimant in *Daniels* [Unempl. Ins. Rep. (CCH) ¶ 9022 (Iowa Dist. Ct. 2000)] was seven months pregnant when her doctor told her to find a job she could do sitting down. She worked as a blackjack dealer, required to stand for her entire seven-hour shift. Her employer put her on medical leave; unemployment benefits were denied because of her medically based inability to work. A pregnant security guard had good reason—health concerns—to leave her job when accepting reassignment would have required taking three buses to work, and her obstetrician advised her not to take buses during her third trimester. [*Gibson*, Unempl. Ins. Rep. (CCH) ¶ 8979 (Fla. App. 2006)]

A New Jersey claimant received $600 a week in benefits from October 10 to December 11, 2010. On December 15, she went to Jamaica and the Virgin Islands, returning to New Jersey December 31, 2010. She argued that she applied for jobs online, but the New Jersey Appellate Division held that she was not available to start work right away—it is impossible for a person outside the United States to be "ready, willing, and able" to work. The only exceptions to the immediate availability requirement are jury duty, job training programs, and family funerals. [*Vialet v. Board of Review*, DOCKET NO. A-1226-11T2, 2012 N.J. Super. Unpub. LEXIS 2420 (Oct. 26, 2012); see Charles Toutant, *Online Job Seeker Overseas Held Ineligible for Unemployment Pay*, N.J.L.J. (Oct. 29, 2012) (law.com)]

Benefits were available to a worker who discovered, when she returned to work after maternity leave, that her job had been filled by someone else, and the employer violated the FMLA (see Chapter 38) by failing to reinstate her in her former job or offer her an equivalent position. [*Bordon*, Unempl. Ins. Rep. (CCH) ¶ 8634 (Mo. App. 2006)]

The Michigan Circuit Court deemed it good reason to quit after the claimant's request for a raise was turned down after she was given more office duties and an additional day of janitorial work. The employer's alteration of working conditions by increasing her duties constituted good reason to quit. [*Express Plumbing Heating/Mechanical Inc.*, Unempl. Ins. Rep. (CCH) ¶ 10,211 (Mich. Cir. Ct. 2008)]

The District of Columbia Court of Appeals found that a worker had good cause to quit when her boss yelled at her and habitually insulted her while she was working. Good cause is a fact determination based on the reactions of a reasonably prudent person under similar circumstances. Allegations of verbal abuse are assessed on the totality of circumstances: whether insults were habitual; if employees were insulted in front of others; how offensive the language was; and whether the employee tried to protest abusive conduct. [*Imperial Valet Servs., Inc. v. Alvarado*, 72 A.3d 165, Unemployment Ins. Rep. (CCH) ¶ 8371 (D.C. 2013)]

[E] Cases Involving Drugs

Missouri held that an employee was not disqualified from benefits when he was fired after a positive marijuana test. Because the company's drug-free workplace policy did not use the word "misconduct," the Missouri Court of Appeals held that he was not on notice that drug use would preclude receipt of benefits. However, the court remanded the case for determination under the general misconduct standard, and to apply the state law holding that an employer does not have to show a demonstrable impact of drug use on the employee's ability to do his or her job. [*Comer*, Unempl. Ins. Rep. (CCH) ¶ 8635 (Mo. App. 2006)]

The Indiana Court of Appeals reversed the denial of benefits to a claimant who was fired after failing a random drug test. The employer did not show that the claimant knowingly violated a rule. Although the policy of discharging employees who tested positive was reasonable and was uniformly applied, the employer failed to disclose what test was used, what the cutoff levels were, or why the test should be considered valid, so it was impossible to determine if the claimant really used drugs. [*Owen County*, Unempl. Ins. Rep. (CCH) ¶ 8607 (Ind. App. 2006)] The Oregon Court of Appeals said that it was not disqualifying misconduct for an employee to refuse when the employer ordered him to take a drug test on his own time, without compensation, after being written up for insubordination. [*Andrews*, Unempl. Ins. Rep. (CCH) ¶ 8878 (Or. App. 2000)] The court held that the employer's policy of requiring a drug test after all reprimands was not reasonable in cases where there was no evidence of drug use.

The Michigan Court of Appeals held in 2008 that a positive marijuana test was disqualifying misconduct even though the employer did not establish the chain of custody for the specimen. An unemployment benefits board can rely on evidence that is not admissible in court. Because there was no evidence that the test was inaccurate, denial of benefits was supported by substantial evidence. [*Ciaravino*, Unempl. Ins. Rep. (CCH) ¶ 10,213 (Mich. App. 2008)]

A claimant's successful appeal of denial of benefits did not entitle him to a civil remedy against his former employer under the state drug testing law. The state statute ruled out remedies where the drug test was required by federal law, and his ex-employer was a defense contractor. [*Welcher*, Unempl. Ins. Rep. (CCH) ¶ 9085 (Iowa App. 2006)]

§ 32.03 CALCULATION OF BENEFITS

[A] Basic Calculation

The actual benefit depends either on the claimant's average weekly wage, or the wage earned in the quarter of the base period when wages were highest. For partial weeks of unemployment, a reduced benefit is available, although the various states use different calculation methods.

Individual claimants are usually assigned a 52-week "benefit year," beginning when the claim is filed, although some states use the same benefit year for all claimants. Usually, a one-week waiting period is imposed before benefits become payable. Most states limit the payment of basic benefits to 26 weeks, although a few states permit 30 weeks of payments. Once claimants use up the basic benefit, they must wait until the next benefit year before starting another base period and therefore qualifying for unemployment benefits all over again. So someone who receives benefits in a particular benefit year will have to be re-employed and work for at least a second base period before qualifying for a second benefit period.

[B] Benefit Offsets

Benefit offsets may be applied in two situations: if the unemployment benefit is reduced because other income is received, or if the UI benefits offset other amounts that the person would otherwise be entitled to receive.

As noted above, payments (e.g., pension, IRA) reduce entitlement to unemployment compensation if they can be traced to work done by the employee in the past. The offset is applied only to a plan maintained or contributed to by the company that was the employer during the base payment period, or the employer that is chargeable with the unemployment claim. So if the pension was earned at Company A, but the worker became unemployed while working for Company A, pension will not offset the unemployment insurance benefit.

New York reformed its unemployment insurance system to protect employers from having to cover $200 million in interest payments on the loan to fund the state's trust fund. As of January 1, 2014, there is a new severance pay offset for unemployment benefits: an employee who receives severance pay ("dismissal pay") within 30 days of dismissal is ineligible for UI in weeks during which the severance payment exceeds the state's maximum weekly benefit (at that time, $405, rising to $420 in October 2014). Pensions, accrued leave, and SUB benefits are not considered dismissal pay. Severance paid in a lump sum is allocated on a weekly basis. After exhaustion of severance pay, the employee can collect benefits for the remaining weeks that benefits are available. If the initial payment, or a lump sum severance payment, is made more than 30 days after the last day of employment, the employee is immediately eligible for UI benefits. [Barbara E. Hoey and Mark A. Konkel, *Severance Payments Offset NY Unemployment Insurance Benefits As Of January 1, 2014*, Kelley Drye & Warren LLP (Feb. 11, 2014), available at Lexology.com; Christopher J. Collins and Jonathan Sokolowski, *New York Unemployment Benefits No Longer Available To Former Employees Receiving Severance*, Sheppard Mullin Richter & Hampton LLP (Jan. 10, 2014), available at Lexology.com]

States differ in their treatment of rollovers. Some states (e.g., New York and North Carolina) require a reduction of unemployment benefits because of rollovers; the other states do not. The Department of Labor's interpretation is that rollovers should not reduce unemployment benefits, but each state is permitted to set its own unemployment rules; this is not an exclusively federal area of regulation. [See Dori R. Perrucci, *When Pension and Unemployment Checks Don't Mix*, N.Y. Times, Jan. 13, 2001, at Bus. 8] Furthermore, reduction is necessary only for amounts based on the claimant's own past work history, not when a person receiving benefits gets a distribution as a surviving spouse.

A claimant's failure to report part-time income was caused by mistake and bad communications, rather than fraudulent intent, so he was required to repay the overpayment but was not subject to fraud penalties. [*Orzel*, Unempl. Ins. Rep. (CCH) ¶ 8655 (N.J. Super. Ct. 2006)]

About half the states deny unemployment benefits in weeks in which Worker's Compensation benefits are also received, or consider the Comp benefit income that reduces the benefit. (There is also a question of whether someone whose condition is bad enough to justify Comp benefits is "ready and able" to work even if he or she wants to work.)

Vacation pay also generally offsets unemployment benefits although an exception might be made if the claimant is deemed to be on vacation involuntarily rather than choosing to take time off.

Back pay awarded in a Title VII case generally is not reduced by UI. However, some courts, like the Second Circuit, say that courts that hear Title VII cases have discretion to reduce the award to account for UI received. A nurse for the Federal Department of Veterans Affairs was terminated, appealed her termination, and received unemployment benefits in the interim before she was reinstated with back pay. The plain language of the Federal Back Pay Act provides that people who receive a back pay award are deemed to have performed services during that period. Hence, the claimant had remuneration and it was proper to order payback of unemployment benefits received in the interim. [*Braselton*, Unempl. Ins. Rep. (CCH) ¶ 10,221 (Ohio App. 2008)]

§ 32.04 EXPERIENCE RATING

[A] Determination of Rating

The unemployment insurance rate that employers pay to help fund the system is partially based on their "experience" (the number of claims against them). The more claims, the higher the insurance rate. Seasonal businesses in particular often have a regular pattern of laying off workers who rely on UI until they are rehired.

The standard rate is 5.4%, although many employers qualify for a more favorable experience rate because of their record of few discharges and layoffs. The treatment of new employers varies from state to state. Some states impose a higher initial rate, until the employer can demonstrate its compliance with filing and payment requirements and its low experience of unemployment. On the other hand, some states have a special low rate for new employers until and unless they demonstrate bad claims experience. Some states even allow a zero rate (no tax at all) on employers with especially good claims experience. But all employers may become subject to the standard rate, and perhaps even additional "subsidiary contributions" if the state as a whole has a high unemployment rate and consequently has a low balance in its UI fund. A few states (Alaska, New Jersey, Pennsylvania) also require employee contributions to the system.

Employers in over half the states owe billions of dollars to the federal government for UI benefits. Thirty-five of the states borrowed federal money because their UI trust funds were too small to cope with recession-related unemployment.

Seven of them opted to cut benefits to unemployment claimants to repay the federal loan. One problem with the current system is that the wage bases are so low, making it difficult for states to collect significant amounts. In over half of the states, the base is $15,000 or less. Federal law merely requires the state base to be as high as the federal base, which has been unchanged (at $7,000) since 1983. In 1983, that was 40% of the average wage, but it is now less than 20% of the average wage, and a small fraction of the FICA base. States are allowed to make voluntary repayments of federal loans at times when their UI contributions are greater than outgoing benefit payments. Theoretically, states can use general revenues to repay the federal government, but that is difficult when unemployment is rife and states have large and growing deficits. [Jasmine Tucker, *Employers in Many States Face Tax Hike to Help Repay Federal UI Loans*, National Academy of Social Insurance (Feb. 3, 2012) (benefitslink.com); Sara Murray, *Benefits Tax Hits Businesses Twice*, WSJ.com (Sept. 28, 2011)]

There are four basic methods of experience rating:

- Variations in payroll over time (showing whether the workforce has increased or decreased);
- Reserve ratio;
- Benefit ratio;
- Ratio of benefits to wages.

Some states use hybrid methods. States often permit joint filing and risk pooling: joint payment by a group of employers who get a combined experience rate for the group as a whole. A further refinement is a distinction between "charging" and "noncharging" claims. Some claims are not charged against the last employer's experience rating: for instance, claims for very brief periods of unemployment, or cases where the employee spent very little time working for the last employer. In some states, the employer is not charged for benefits paid after a period of disqualification based on voluntary quitting or misconduct, or when benefits are terminated because of the claimant's failure to seek suitable work. The rationale is that employers should not be penalized for circumstances beyond their control.

Another question is whether all employers in the base period, or only the last one in the series, will be charged with the claim. If more than one employer is charged, they might be charged with the most recent employer charged first, or the charge might be divided proportionate to the amount of wages they paid during the base period.

States vary greatly in their UI wage bases. As of July 2013 (the last date for which figures were published by DOL's ETA), the wage base is $7,000 in Arizona and California; $7,700 in Louisiana; $8,000 in Alabama, Florida, Kansas, and Virginia; $8,500 in Maryland, New York, and Pennsylvania; $9,000 in the

District of Columbia, Nebraska, Ohio, Tennessee, and Texas; $9,300 in Kentucky, $9,500 in Georgia, Indiana and Michigan; $10,500 in Delaware; $11, 300 in Colorado; $12,000 in Arkansas, Maine, South Carolina, and West Virginia; $12,900 in Illinois; $13,000 in Missouri and South Dakota; $14,000 in Massachusetts, Mississippi, New Hampshire, and Wisconsin; $15,000 in Connecticut; $16,000 in Vermont; $20,100 in Oklahoma; $20,200 generally, but $21,700 for some employers, in Rhode Island; $20,900 in North Carolina; $22,900 in New Mexico; $23,800 in Wyoming; $26,000 in Iowa; $26,900 in Nevada; $27,900 in Montana; $29,000 in Minnesota; $30,300 in Utah; $30,900 in New Jersey; $31,800 in North Dakota; $34,100 in Oregon; $34,800 in Idaho; $36,900 in Alaska; $39,600 in Hawaii; and $39,800 in Washington State. (In 2012, Hawaii had the highest wage base, but it traded places with Washington State in 2013.) [*Significant Provisions of State Unemployment Insurance Laws Effective July 2013*, <http://www.ows.doleta.gov/unemploy/content/sigpros/2010-2019/January2013.pdf>, <http://www.ows.doleta.gov/unemploy/content/sigpros/2010-2019/July2013.pdf> (accessed Mar. 29, 2014)]

Each edition of *Significant Provisions* also includes state-by-state data about the weekly benefit amount, number of benefit weeks available, and the minimum, maximum, and new employer rates of unemployment tax.

"SUTA dumping," to avoid the federal State Unemployment Tax Act, is the practice of transferring employees from a unit with high turnover (which increases unemployment tax liability) to one with low turnover, then eliminating the first unit and creating a new unit for further transfers. According to Kelly Services, the practice began in the mid-1990s, but was fairly rare then because the economy was booming; it gained attractiveness after the 2001 stock market crash. [Michael Schroeder, *Tax Dodge Faces Extinction*, Wall St. J., Aug. 4, 2004, at A4] Congress considered this practice such a threat to the soundness of the unemployment insurance system that it passed legislation, the SUTA Dumping Prevention Act of 2004, Pub. L. No. 108-295.

[B] Collateral Estoppel

Two related legal doctrines, collateral estoppel and res judicata, may come into play in contesting unemployment claims. An employer's unsuccessful contest of one worker's claim could harm the employer in later lawsuits. Legal advice is required as to the comparative risk of letting a claim go through without opposition (which will increase the employer's experience rating and therefore its rates) or contesting the claim but losing and being at a disadvantage when similar claims are made later.

The doctrine of res judicata refers to a matter that has already been tried. If one court has already dealt with a case, a higher court may handle an appeal of the matter, but a different court, which is not in the same line of authority, will not decide a matter that has already been decided. The doctrine of res judicata applies only to the same legal issues and the same or closely related parties. So if one employee sues his or her employer for race discrimination, the defense of res judicata will not be available if a different employee sues another employer for race discrimination. But Employee A's suit against Company B may have "collateral estoppel" effect on Employee C's suit against Company B, because Employee A's suit involves decisions on some basic issues about Company B's policies.

Either side can use collateral estoppel. In a later court case, the employer says that the administrative decision proves that the employee was guilty of misconduct, so terminating the employee was not wrongful. [See Chapter 39 for wrongful termination suits] The employee might assert that having received unemployment benefits proves that he or she did not quit and was not guilty of misconduct. Usually, administrative decisions in an unemployment matter will be granted collateral estoppel effect—but some states say that only a court decision can have that effect.

According to the Third Circuit, the ALJ's holding of misconduct in his unemployment compensation hearing did not prevent the employee from bringing suit for wrongful discharge. The station agent says that he put $80 for a ticket change fee in a drawer near the boarding gate, but the money was not entered into the computer system. The passenger complained when he was charged again for the fee that he paid in cash. The ticket agent was fired for violating the airline's rules. The unemployment ALJ denied benefits for questionable conduct and violation of procedure. In the Virgin Islands, the rule is that an unemployment insurance finding of misconduct does not preclude a wrongful discharge claim, because the two laws have different objectives. The facts and issues are different, and the wrongful termination statute does not refer to misconduct, so finding that the employee was guilty of misconduct does not resolve the issue of wrongful termination. [*Gonzalez v. AMR*, 548 F.3d 219 (3d Cir. 2008)]

[C] Planning Steps to Reduce Unemployment Tax Liability

The unemployment insurance system is designed to stabilize employment, so it penalizes employers who dislocate workers unnecessarily. Terminated employees often find it much easier to get a new job if their employment record indicates that they quit instead of being fired. Agreeing to treat the termination as a resignation can benefit both employer and employee, if the employer's experience rate stays low. But employees must understand the effect that the characterization of the termination will have on their UI application.

Companies can take various steps to reduce their experience rating and therefore their liability for unemployment tax:

- Understanding the nature and interaction of the federal and state payroll taxes;

- Reducing FUTA payments appropriately to compensate for state tax payments;
- Making sure taxes are paid when due;
- Reviewing state experience records for correctness;
- Understanding the experience rating system and the claims appeal procedure;
- Transferring employees within the organization instead of terminating them, to reduce unemployment claims;
- Analyzing operations to see if they could be made more consistent, less seasonal (thus avoiding layoffs and terminations);
- Firing unsatisfactory employees quickly, before they become eligible for benefits;
- Holding exit interviews with employees who quit, with a view to resolving problems that lead to resignations;
- Scheduling layoffs for Fridays, not earlier in the week wherever possible, because all the states provide benefits for partial weeks of employment;
- Maintaining adequate documentation of misconduct (which will also be useful if the terminated employee makes discrimination or wrongful termination claims);
- Monitoring all benefit claims and appealing claims that the company believes to be unfounded (e.g., employees who quit asserting involuntary termination).

The laws in over half the states (Arkansas, Arizona, Colorado, Georgia, Indiana, Kansas, Kentucky, Louisiana, Maine, Massachusetts, Michigan, Minnesota, Missouri, Nebraska, North Carolina, North Dakota, New Jersey, New Mexico, New York, Ohio, Pennsylvania, South Dakota, Texas, Washington, Wisconsin, West Virginia) allow employers to make intentional overpayments of unemployment insurance taxes resulting in a lower tax rate for the next tax period; sometimes the numbers work out so that a small voluntary contribution produces a large reduction in future liabilities. Equifax also pointed out that two or more legal entities may have the right to create a joint account combining their experience ratings to achieve a single UI tax rate. The organizations do not have to set up a new entity or alter their organizational structures. In Arizona, Arkansas, Connecticut, Hawaii, Missouri, New Jersey, New York, Ohio, South Carolina, and West Virginia, the joint account for rating purposes is locked in for a period of years, ranging from one year in Connecticut, Hawaii, Ohio, and West Virginia, to five years in South Carolina. There are other states (not listed by Equifax) where joint accounts are allowed—but once they are elected, the participating employers are permanently "locked in." [Equifax Workforce Solutions, *Tax Intelligence: State Unemployment Special Rating Strategies*, <http://www.talx.com/News/Tax Intelligence/2013-08-ETS-Tax-Intelligence-2014-State-Unemployment-Savings-Strategies.pdf> (August 2013)]

§ 32.05 ADMINISTRATION AND APPEALS

Traditionally, states required in-person application for unemployment benefits; now virtually all the states permit claims to be filed remotely (e.g., via telephone or the Internet). If and when an ex-employee applies for UI benefits, the employer is asked for the reason for the termination. The employer is given a certain number of days to contest the claim. Once this period elapses, the employer can no longer protest the granting of benefits. If the employer objects to the grant of benefits, the state agency that administers unemployment benefits will assess the matter. The decision can be appealed to an Administrative Law Judge, an administrative board, and finally through the state court system (the federal courts are not appropriate for these questions).

If the employer fails to meet its burden of proof about the employee's disqualification at the administrative hearing, the case will not be remanded to give the employer another chance—and a remand will probably not be granted to submit additional evidence [Holmes, *Unempl. Ins. Rep.* (CCH) ¶ 8664 (La. App. 2001)], so it's important to prepare well for the initial administrative hearing.

According to the Federal Reserve Bank (St. Louis), in 2011, of the $108 billion in UI benefits paid in 2011, $3.3 billion were fraudulent because the claimants had unreported income. The DOL said that in the period 2009–2012, 33 states had error rates of 10% or more. For example, Alabama's average overpayment rate was 16.62%. DOL estimated that less than 3% of overpayments were attributable to employers, 49.25% to claimants, and 15.64% to state UI agencies.

The Unemployment Insurance Integrity Act, part of the Federal Trade Adjustment Assistance Extension Act of 2011, required all the states to adopt changes in their UI laws, including integrity provisions to reduce erroneous payments. Congress wanted to deter employers from failing to respond to claim notices because they considered charges to their reserve accounts as a simple cost of doing business.

The states were given until October 21, 2013 to adopt laws penalizing employers and employers' agents, including TPAs, for failure to give timely and adequate responses to state requests for information about overpaid unemployment claims. By October 1, 2013, all the states but Georgia, Michigan, Missouri, and Vermont had adopted the necessary laws.

Penalties are imposed for a pattern of failure to respond. Many of the state integrity laws include penalties and civil fines. The overpaid claim is charged to the employer's experience rating and cannot receive a refund. Although states probably will not treat a single failure to respond as a pattern, employers should review their separation and settlement agreements to see if the employer agrees not to challenge the separated employee's unemployment claim. Separation agreements should include clear language about what the employer will do when an information request is received. Employers should also make sure that their TPAs respond promptly to state requests. [Eric J. Janson and Marc R. Jacobs, *You (Don't) Have The Right To Remain Silent – How New Unemployment Insurance Integrity Laws May Affect Your Separation And Settlement Agreements With Departing Employees*, Seyfarth Shaw LLP (Nov. 12, 2013), available at Lexology.com; G.J. Stillson MacDonnell and William Hays Weissman, *Federal Unemployment Insurance Integrity Act Creates Tough New Standards For Employers Responding To State Unemployment Insurance Claim Notices*, Littler Mendelson (Oct. 11, 2013), available at Lexology.com]

New Jersey enacted legislation on August 19, 2013, implementing the Trade Adjustment Assistance Extension Act penalties on employers who fail to make a timely response to a state unemployment office's request for information. Similar laws in Minnesota, South Carolina, Wyoming, and Iowa require the employer to reimburse the state unemployment account for the overpayment, but the New Jersey law does not include this requirement. [Stacey D. Adams and Jessica R. Agarwal, *New Jersey Law Penalizes Employers For Failing To Timely Respond To Requests Regarding Unemployment Insurance*, Littler Mendelson (Aug. 29, 2013), available at Lexology.com]

§ 32.06 FUTA COMPLIANCE

Employers (but not employees) have an obligation to make payments under the Federal Unemployment Tax Act (FUTA) to fund the federal program of unemployment insurance. The general rule is that the basic federal FUTA tax rate is 6.2%, but this tax is imposed only on the first $7,000 of wages.

The states set their own taxable wage bases. Starting with calendar 2010, the 6.2% FUTA rate drops to 6.0%. Most employers actually pay a lower rate, because they qualify for a 5.4% credit for state employment taxes they have already paid. This is sometimes referred to as the "normal credit" or "90% credit." Sometimes the company will qualify for an even lower FUTA rate if its experience rating is good. The additional credit equals the difference between the basic state rate of 5.4% and the employer's actual experience rate. However, the full credit can be claimed only in states that the Department of Labor certifies as compliant with federal requirements To qualify for the full credit, the employer must make all state contributions by January 31 (the due date for Form 940). For 2010 and later years, the effective tax rate therefore can be as low as 0.6%. [*Unemployment Insurance Tax Topic: Unemployment Insurance Taxes*, <http://workforcesecurity.doleta.gov/unemploy/uitaxtopic.asp> (Dec. 20, 2012, accessed Apr. 9, 2014)]

If the state has not repaid money borrowed from the federal government, it will be classified as a "credit reduction state." The state will not be entitled to the full credit, so employers in that state will have to pay more FUTA tax when they file Form 940. Schedule A of Form 940 is used to report wages paid in any credit reduction state (including by a multi-state employer that has employees in a credit reduction state).

ADP Research Institute said that there were 13 credit reduction states in 2014: Arkansas, California, Connecticut, Delaware, Georgia, Indiana, Kentucky, Missouri, New York, North Carolina, Ohio, Rhode Island, and Wisconsin, requiring most employers in these states to pay an extra $21 per worker per year. [ADP Research Institute, *Federal Unemployment Tax Act (FUTA) Increases for 2013* (Nov. 15, 2013) (benefitslink.com)]

The employer reports its FUTA liability on IRS Form 940. See IRS Tax Topics, Topic 759 for an explanation of depositing FUTA taxes and filing Form 940. When FUTA tax for the year exceeds $500, the employer must make at least one quarterly payment. FUTA liability under $500 in a quarter is carried forward to the next quarter. But when cumulative liability reaches $500, a deposit must be made by the last day of month after the end of the quarter. [<http://www.irs.gov/taxtopics/tc759.html> (updated Mar. 20, 2014)]

In 2006, the IRS discontinued the short-form Form 940-EZ, but redesigned Form 940 to be more logical and easier to use.

CHAPTER 33

WORKER'S COMPENSATION

§ 33.01 INTRODUCTION

The states administer the Worker's Compensation ("Worker's Compensation" or WC) system to provide income to individuals who are unable to work because of employment-related illnesses and injuries. WC benefits, like unemployment insurance benefits, are funded by insurance maintained by the employer.

The WC system balances the interests of employers and employees: the employees' need for continuing income; the employer's need to have claims resolved quickly, in an administrative system that is not prone to make large sympathy awards the way the jury system is. Employers have a duty to make a prompt report of all accidents to the agency that administers the WC system. If an employee claims job-related injury or illness, the claim is heard by a WC tribunal. Depending on the state, this may be referred to as a board or a commission. The tribunal decides if the claim is valid. If so, benefits are awarded: reimbursement of medical expenses, plus weekly income.

WC benefits do not begin until a waiting period (typically three to seven days) has elapsed. This serves to distinguish genuine temporary disability from minor incidents without lasting consequences. However, most state WC laws also provide that, if a disability continues for a period of time (set by the state at anywhere from five days to over seven weeks), retroactive payments dating back to the original date of the injury will be granted.

The weekly benefit is usually limited to half to two-thirds of the pre-accident wage, subject to fixed minimum and maximum payments (often keyed to the state's average income) and also subject to an overall limitation on payments. In some states, additional payments are available if the worker has dependent children—especially in cases where the work-related incident caused the death of the worker. A burial benefit is also paid in death cases. Depending on the state it ranges between $1,000 and $5,000.

In 1999, the Supreme Court decided a Worker's Compensation case, *American Manufacturers Mut. Ins. Co. v. Sullivan.* [526 U.S. 46 (1999)] Under Pennsylvania's WC Act, once liability is no longer contested, the employer (or its insurer) has an obligation to pay for all reasonable or necessary treatment. However, an insurer or a self-insured employer is permitted to withhold payment for disputed treatment pending utilization review by an independent third party. The Supreme Court ruled that private insurers doing utilization review are not "state actors" subject to the Due Process clause of the Constitution. Employees have no property rights until treatments have been found reasonable and necessary. Therefore, the insurer has no obligation to notify employees, or to hold a hearing, if it withholds benefits until review has been completed and a decision made in the employees' favor.

A 2010 press release issued by the New York State Insurance Department reports that Alexis Muniz was sentenced to restitution and three years' probation when a Facebook posting showed that she stole $8,975 in WC benefits, collected while she was working full time. She boasted on her Facebook page about how much she earned as an apartment manager. [Fred Schneyer, *Facebook Posting Reveals Workers Comp Theft*, plansponsor.com (Sept. 14, 2010)]

§ 33.02 CLASSIFICATION OF BENEFITS

[A] Type and Degree of Disability

If the initial tribunal accepts the contention that the worker is genuinely disabled, and the disability is in fact work-related, benefits are awarded based on the type and degree of disability.

There are four categories:

- Permanent total disability;
- Permanent partial disability;
- Temporary total disability;
- Temporary partial disability.

Permanent disability payments can be based on wage loss, earning capacity, physical impairment, or some combination. A "schedule injury" is loss of a finger, toe, arm, eye, or leg. The schedule determines the number of weeks of benefits payable for such an injury. Death benefits are also available to the survivors of persons killed in work-related incidents. For injuries such as back strains related to lifting, the tribunal must make a case-by-case determination of the number of weeks of disability that can be anticipated, and the seriousness of the disability.

Benefits can be granted for either "disability" or "impairment." The difference is that disability is defined to mean loss of wages, whereas impairment is permanent partial disability that does not cause wage loss.

The concept of Maximum Medical Improvement (MMI) comes into play in the case of a temporary disability. MMI is a doctor's opinion that there is no reasonable medical probability of further improvement in function (as determined based on factors such as current and proposed treatment, history of improvement, and pre-existing conditions). Most states impose an obligation on the employer to notify the employee that MMI has been reached, and the employee is likely to lose benefits within 90 days unless he or she returns to work or finds other employment. Benefits can be extended past the MMI if the claimant makes an honest effort yet cannot find suitable work.

In addition to making wage-based payments, the employer must provide the employee with reasonable and necessary medical treatment, continued as long as the injured employee's medical condition requires. Most states include chiropractic in the definition of medical care. Many include home health attendants as well.

In two 2009 cases, the Utah Supreme Court allowed employers and insurers to reduce Worker's Compensation medical expenses to reflect only the work-related portion of a claimant's injury. One case involved carpal tunnel syndrome, which the ALJ found to be only 10% work-related. The other case involved a lower back injury. The Utah Supreme Court interpreted state law to mean that, because medical benefits compensate the injured worker, only the part of the medical benefit reflecting the work-related part of the injury should be the responsibility of the WC system. [*Ameritech Library Servs. v. Utah Labor Comm'n*, 2009 UT 20 (2009); *Dale T. Smith Sons v. Utah Labor Comm'n*, 2009 UT 19 (2009); see Rebecca Moore, *UT Court Says Employers Can Apportion Worker's Comp*, plansponsor.com (Apr. 10, 2009)]

However, at about the same time, the Utah Supreme Court also held that it is unconstitutional to reduce Workers' Compensation benefits to offset Social Security benefits. The agency argued that coordinating the benefits served the valid purpose of keeping the insurance fund solvent, but the Utah Supreme Court said that reducing Workers' Compensation benefits for disabled persons over 65 does not achieve this objective, and that Social Security benefits and Workers' Compensation benefits serve different purposes and are not substitutes for one another. (The law that was struck down provided that someone who qualified for both benefits, and who had received 312 weeks of Workers' Compensation, the Workers' Compensation benefits would be reduced by 50% of the Social Security benefit.) [*Merrill v. Utah Labor Comm'n,* 2009 UT 74 (2009); Rebecca Moore, *Social Security Offset of Workers' Comp Unconstitutional*, plansponsor.com (Apr. 28, 2009)]

A 2011 Georgia Court of Appeals decision permitted aggravation of an injured employee's condition by light duty work to be treated as a new injury because the job responsibilities changed and the claimant was not performing his normal or ordinary duties. The claimant was an assistant pressman who suffered a work-related neck and arm injury in October 2002. He had carpal tunnel surgery and received WC benefits, including permanent partial disability. He returned to light duty work (including quality control and fulfillment) in mid-2003 with a permanent restriction on lifting, pushing, or pulling over 15 pounds. He said that the work exceeded his medical restrictions 40% of the time but his supervisors refused to modify the assignment. He was laid off in April 2008 and had lumbar fusion surgery in October 2008. He filed a claim for medical and temporary total disability benefits, which was granted because he worked under strenuous new circumstances that exceeded his light duty restriction. [*R.R. Donnelley v. Ogletree,* 312 Ga. App. 475 (2011); see Tara Cantore, *Employee Eligible for New Comp Claim Based on New Injury*, plansponsor.com (Oct. 24, 2011)]

[B] Compensable Injuries

Whether an incident is covered by WC depends on several factors, e.g., employee status and the connection between employment and the injury.

It is significant whether the injured person is a common-law employee rather than an independent contractor. Early in 2002, California ruled that even a hirer of an independent contractor can be liable to the contractor (or employees of the contractor) if, for example, the hirer provides unsafe equipment or makes another affirmative contribution to the injury—merely controlling safety conditions at the site is not enough to impose liability. [*McKown v. Wal-Mart Stores Inc.*, 27 Cal. 4th 219, 38 P.3d 1094, 115 Cal. Rptr. 2d 868 (2002); *Hooker v. DOT*, 27 Cal. 4th 198, 38 P.3d 1081, 115 Cal. Rptr. 2d 853 (2002)]

The California Court of Appeal struck down a state statute that mandates a payment of $250,000 to the estate of employees without dependents if their death is work-related. According to the court, the statute is unconstitutional: making estates automatic beneficiaries would require an amendment to the state Constitution, because California law does not permit expansion of the class of WC beneficiaries past the list provided in the state Constitution. Furthermore, the policy reason for having WC laws is to support workers or their dependents after job-related injury or death, and payments to the estate do not serve this purpose. [*Six Flags, Inc. v. Workers' Comp Appeals Bd.*, 145 Cal. App. 4th 91 (2006); see Rebecca Moore, *CA Court Denies Workers' Comp to Estate*, plansponsor.com (Nov. 29, 2006). The statute is Labor Code § 4702(a)(6)(B)]

Sometimes injuries occurring outside the workplace will be covered—e.g., if the employer sent the employee to make a delivery or perform an errand, and the injury occurred in that place or en route. Injuries occurring during employer-sponsored athletics, or at a company picnic or holiday party, are probably compensable. Injuries on company premises during scheduled breaks are probably compensable, but employees take unscheduled breaks at their own risk because such injuries are considered to occur outside working hours. If employees are engaged in work-related tasks, injuries occurring at home can be compensable. [*A.E. Clevite, Inc. v. Tjas*, 996 P.2d 1072 (Utah App. 2000) (worker who became a paraplegic when he slipped while salting down his driveway so it would be safe for the expected delivery of a work-related package)]

In 2007, Georgia upheld the award of WC benefits to the dependent 11-year-old son of a worker killed in the crash of a company vehicle, even though the decedent was a Florida resident who was delivering his family's furniture to a storage facility while he was on sick leave. Georgia applied the "continuous employment" doctrine: benefits are available whenever an employee is required to live and work within an area accessible to the job site. The decedent had to take a temporary residence in Georgia to supervise a construction job. The Georgia court did not deem his medical leave status to make the continuous employment doctrine inapplicable. [*Ray Bell Constr. Co. v. King*, 281 Ga. 853 (2007); see Adrien Martin, *Workers' Comp Award Upheld on Grounds of "Continuous*

Employment," plansponsor.com (Mar. 29, 2007); Alyson M. Palmer, *Ga. High Court Ruling May Widen Workers' Comp Net for Traveling Employees*, Fulton County Daily Report (Mar. 29, 2007) (law.com)]

The Maine Supreme Judicial Court held that a worker who was injured when returning to work from a lunch break was entitled to benefits, because the staircase where she fell was part of the workplace. The employer said that under the "coming and going principle," the injury was not compensable because an accident off premises when an employee goes to or from work is not in the course of employment. But the Maine court granted benefits because injury occurred during an "insubstantial deviation" from employment; she was not reckless; and she did not violate work rules. [*Fournier v. Aetna, Inc.*, 2006 ME 71, 899 A.2d 787 (2006); see Rebecca Moore, *Worker Who Fell Returning from Lunch Is Entitled to Benefits*, plansponsor.com (June 16, 2006) On the "coming and going principle" in the context of employer liability for an automobile accident, see *Moradi v. Marsh USA*, 219 Cal. App. 4th 886 (Cal. App. Sept. 17, 2013); Gregory C. Cheng, *California Employer Held Liable for Employee's Accident During Commute*, Ogletree Deakins (Oct. 25, 2013), available at Lexology.com]

Early in 2010, the South Carolina Supreme Court ruled that a packing house seasonal worker who broke an ankle in the barracks provided by his employer was entitled to Worker's Compensation, even though he was not working at the time the injury occurred. The court ruled that migrant workers did not earn enough to be able to afford other housing (and there were no short-term rentals available anyway), so in effect they were required to live on the grounds of the packing house. The living arrangement accommodated the employer's work schedule, which varied with weather and crop conditions. The plaintiff was injured in a fall before his first day of work, when he fell on a sidewalk that was wet with water from the outdoor sink used to wash clothes. The court cited decisions in four other states applying the "bunkhouse rule," where WC benefits are available to injured workers who are hurt on the employer's premises when they are required to be there. [*Pierre v. Seaside Farms*, 386 S.C. 534, 689 S.E.2d 615 (S.C. 2010), see Fred Schneyer, *SC High Court Rules for Injured Migrant Worker*, plansponsor.com (Feb. 17, 2010)]

Whether an incident is covered by WC may also depend on whether it results from an "accident" (an unexpected occurrence with a definite time, place, and occasion) and whether there is any reason to remove the incident from coverage (e.g., the employee's substance abuse was a causative factor).

Connecticut allowed benefits for an employee whose shoulders were dislocated when fellow-workers tried to restrain him during a seizure to prevent him from hurting himself. The court attributed the injury to the restraint, not the seizure. The employer's argument was that awarding WC benefits would discourage co-workers from trying to offer aid, but the court said that potential good Samaritans would not distinguish between potential WC and non-WC cases. [*Blakeslee v. Platt Bros. & Co.*, 279 Conn. 239 (Conn. 2006), discussed in Adrien Martin,

Employee Awarded Workers Comp for Injuries from Helpful Coworkers, plansponsor.com (Aug. 1, 2006)]

One of the most vital factors is the employer's degree of control over the employee's activities. A Missouri case [*Leslie v. School Servs. & Leasing Inc.*, 947 S.W.2d 97 (Mo. App. 1997)] holds that a job applicant injured during training had not become an "employee," and therefore was not covered by WC. In this case, the potential employer didn't require her to take the training, didn't control her activities during the training process, and in fact didn't even guarantee her a job if she completed the training successfully.

In 2004, the New Jersey Supreme Court ruled that injuries occurring during a recreational or social activity can come under WC provided that the employee believed that he or she was required to engage in the activity. [*Lozano v. De Luca Constr. Co.*, 178 N.J. 513; 842 A.2d 156 (N.J. Super. Ct. App. Mar. 2004). Note that N.J.S.A. § 34:15-7 allows payment of WC benefits for recreational injuries sustained through activities that are a regular incident of employment and produce benefit for the employer over and above improved employee fitness and morale]

At-work assaults raise difficult questions. The general rule is that injuries caused by assaults are compensable if the job increases the risk of encountering dangerous people (e.g., convenience store clerks are at risk of being robbed). But if the assault occurred for personal reasons, for instance if an abusive spouse commits an assault at the victim's workplace, the fact that the assault occurred at work will not necessarily render the injury a compensable one, if it is not work-related in any way. The WC system is essentially a no-fault system, so it will not be necessary to decide if the employer was at fault in not having a better security system. Virginia refused to apply WC exclusivity in the case of a paramedic who had a seizure and died three days after a co-worker deliberately shocked her with live defibrillator paddles, because an assault or horseplay is purely personal and not attributable to the employer. [*Hilton v. Martin, Va.*, 275 Va. 176 (2008), discussed in Fred Schneyer, *VA Paramedic's Death Ruled Outside Workers' Comp Coverage*, plansponsor.com (Feb. 12, 2008)]

The Delaware Supreme Court allowed an employee injured by horseplay to bring a personal injury suit against the co-workers who injured him. The court used the four-part "Larson Test" (named after the treatise Larson's Workers' Compensation Law): the scope and seriousness of the deviation of the conduct from employment activities; if the conduct was separate from work duties or commingled with them; if the nature of the job typically includes horseplay; and whether the employer tolerated horseplay. In this case, a pipefitter/welder sued three co-workers for wrapping him in duct tape; he had to have back and knee surgery and counseling after the injury. He sued the co-workers for more than $74,000 in medical expenses and $142,000 lost wages and also sought future medical expenses. The Delaware Supreme Court remanded the case for a determination of whether the prank fell outside the scope of employment. [*Grabowski v. Mangler*, 938 A.2d 637 (Del. 2007). See Sheri Qualters, *A New Test for Workplace* "Horseplay," Nat'l L.J. (July 19, 2007)] On remand, the Delaware Supreme Court upheld summary judgment for the defendants. The injuries occurred at a time when there was no work to be done; horseplay was so frequent as to be an accepted part of the workday; and the prank was performed quickly without substantial abandonment of duties. [*Grabowski v. Mangler*, 956 A.2d 1217 (Del. 2008)]

Schmidt v. Smith [155 N.J. 44, 713 A.2d 1014 (1998)] says that bodily injury caused by sexual harassment is covered by the employer liability section of the Worker's Compensation insurance policy, because this section of the policy is designed to make funds available to compensate employees for their work-related injuries, even those for which Worker's Compensation payments are not available.

The Pennsylvania Supreme Court, without really exploring the policy issues, upheld a lower court's determination to uphold an award of Worker's Compensation benefits to an illegal alien, on the grounds that the employer did not show that the injured person failed to satisfy the requirements of a section of the Worker's Compensation Act. However, if the employer applies for suspension of such benefits, the employer does not have to make a showing of job availability. [*Reinforced Earth Co. v. WC Appeals Bd. (Astudillo)*, 810 A.2d 99 (Pa. 2002)] In contrast, *Granados v. Windson Dev. Corp.* [257 Va. 103, 509 S.E.2d 290 (1999)], held that an alien who was hired after submitting forged immigration documents could not become a lawful employee entitled to Worker's Compensation, because no employment contract could be formed.

The Second Circuit approved an award of lost earnings to an undocumented alien worker after he was crippled in a fall attributed to violations of the scaffolding requirements for work sites. New York case law specifically rejects the concept that the damages should be limited on the basis of what the worker would earn in his or her home country. The jury awarded $638,671.63 in compensatory damages, including about $93,000 for incurred expenses, $46,000 for past pain and suffering, $40,000 for lost earnings, $230,000 for future pain and suffering over the plaintiff's predicted life expectancy, and $230,000 for 26 years of future lost earnings. [*Madeira v. Affordable Hous. Found. Inc.*, 469 F.3d 219 (2d Cir. 2006). See also *Majlinger v. Cassino Contracting Corp.*, 25 A.D.3d 4, 802 N.Y.S.2d 56 (2d Dept. 2005) allowing compensation for lost U.S. earnings at U.S. rates, holding that this does not conflict with the federal immigration statute, IRCA; *Flores v. Limehouse*, No. 2:04-1295-CWH 2006 U.S. Dist. LEXIS 30433 (D.S.C. May 11, 2006) holding that IRCA does not preempt claims by undocumented workers against their employers under RICO and federal and state labor law—even if the workers obtained employment fraudulently; *Rosa v. Partners in Progress, Inc.*, 868 A.2d 994 (N.H. 2005) (for undocumented worker to be able to make a tort claim, the employer must have known or have a duty to know the worker's employment was illegal)]

When an illegal alien worker was injured in a fall from a roof, the Louisiana Court of Appeal found three parties, including Vaughan Roofing, liable for providing WC benefits. When Vaughan Roofing appealed, the Supreme Court denied certiorari, refusing to decide whether I.R.C. preempts the state ruling that illegal workers are entitled to WC benefits. [*Vaughan Roofing & Sheet Metal LLC v. Rodriguez, cert. denied*, 131 S. Ct. 1572 (2011); see Plansponsor staff, *U.S. Supreme Court Turns Away Illegal Immigrant Case*, plansponsor.com (Mar. 2, 2011)]

Tennessee awarded survivor benefits to foreign nationals (Mexicans) who were dependents of a worker who died in a work-related accident, although the court found they were not wholly dependent on remittances from their son and therefore the case remanded to determine the correct benefit to be paid. [*Fusner v. Coop Constr. Co.*, 211 S.W.3d 686 (Tenn. Sup. 2007); see Adrien Martin, *Foreign Nationals Can Be Dependents for TN Workers' Comp [sic] Benefits*, plansponsor.com (Jan. 23, 2007)]

Ohio ruled that David Gross, a teenager who suffered severe burns when cleaning the pressure cooker at work, could collect WC even though he was fired for breaking the safety rules. Previously, the Ohio Supreme Court ruled against Gross, on the grounds that termination for misconduct constituted voluntary abandonment of employment. However, the case went to the Tenth Circuit and then was sent back to state court, and this time, the worker received an award based on the no-fault nature of the WC system. [Adrien Martin, *Worker Who Broke Safety Rules Gets Workers' Comp*, plansponsor.com (Sept. 28, 2007)]

If the incident is covered, the next question is whether WC exclusivity applies. [See § 33.03]

[C] Problems of Co-Employment

There are many reasons for employers to use temporary, contingent, part-time, or leased workers. In some cases, employee leasing results in lower WC costs. For employers who do not self-insure, the insurance rate has a lot to do with past experience. The smaller the workplace, the greater the impact that a few claims—especially a few very large claims—will have on its experience rating. That is one of the motivations for using leased workers to replace some or all of a company's common-law employees. [See § 1.09 for more about employee leasing]

Although a large leasing company will not qualify for small business discounted rates, a leasing company can offer the services of a broad range of workers, some in low-risk occupations such as office work.

In its initial years, a leasing company will probably qualify for low rates, because there has not been enough time for many accidents to happen. Abuses of the system are possible, if companies dissolve and re-form to manipulate their experience rates. Just for this reason, some states (e.g., Arizona, California,

Colorado, Florida, Nevada, New Hampshire, New Mexico, Oregon, South Carolina, Texas, and Utah) disregard the presence of leasing companies, and still require the underlying employer to buy WC insurance and maintain its own experience rating.

Furthermore, state courts may decide that the leasing company or temporary agency's client is the actual employer, because it has real control over the worker's activities and therefore is legally responsible for compensation for injuries. Both companies might also be treated as co-employers.

Another possibility is that, if the underlying employer takes the position that the leasing company is the true employer, the underlying employer might be treated as a third party that can be sued for tort claims and cannot assert WC exclusivity. The underlying employer might be sued for negligence or for violating established safety rules, and might be forced to pay damages (including punitive damages). Nor would the employee's WC benefits be used to offset the underlying employer's liability in this situation.

The National Association of Insurance Commissioners (NAIC) has drafted an Employee Leasing Registration Model Act under which leasing firms must register with the state before they purchase WC insurance. At the time of registration, they must disclose their ownership and their past WC history. Registration will not be permitted if the company has had its insurance policies terminated in the past for failure to pay premiums.

The "borrowed servant" doctrine says that if an employer lends an employee to someone else to perform a "special service," the recipient of the special service is considered the employer of the borrowed employee if the recipient can control the details of the work. According to the Eighth Circuit, this requires a contract for hire and the employee's consent to the special employment relationship—and the burden of proof is on the party citing the doctrine. Therefore, an employee of the Truck Crane Service Co., injured on a job site operated by Maguire Tank Inc., and who received WC benefits from Truck Crane, nevertheless could sue Maguire Tank. Maguire Tank did not direct or control the injured person's actions. He merely worked there for a day and was not instructed in how to do his job by Maguire Tank employees. In fact, the injury occurred after the job was finished and part of a crane that was being prepared for shipping fell and injured the plaintiff's arm. [*Lundstrom v. Maguire Tank Inc.*, 509 F.3d 864 (8th Cir. 2007)]

In Delaware, a general contractor does not have a duty to protect the employees of its independent contractors against the hazards of the contract, unless the general contractor actively controls the manner or method of performing the work, voluntarily undertakes responsibility for safety measures, or controls the premises where the work is done. In a case where a worker was seriously injured after a fall from a roof (he was not wearing a safety harness although he owned one and it was at the job site), Delaware held that the general contractor was not liable, even though it made checklists, informed the independent contractor of safety problems, and even finally terminated the contract because of the safety issues. Delaware held that the Restatement (2d) of Torts § 411 does not create a cause of action by employees of an independent contractor, against the general contractor for failure to use due care in selecting an independent contractor. By and large, employees are restricted to the Worker's Compensation system for work-related injuries, and it would be unfair to permit employees of an independent contractor to sue the general contractor when the general contractor's own employees would be limited to WC for their own comparable injuries. [*Urena v. Capano Homes, Inc.*, 930 A.2d 877 (Del. 2007)]

The Texas Supreme Court ruled that if a general contractor provides Worker's Compensation insurance to a subcontractor, the general contractor cannot be sued for negligence by the subcontractor's employees. A premises owner can be deemed a general contractor if it fits under the definition in the WC Act. [*Entergy v. Summers*, 282 S.W.3d 433 (Tex. 2009); see Fred Schneyer, *General Contractor Deserves Workers' Comp Liability Coverage*, plansponsor.com (Apr. 6, 2009)]

[D] How the WC System Handles Disease Claims

WC benefits are also available if an employee develops a work-related disease. However, occupational diseases create some difficult problems of analysis. Disease is covered only if there is a close connection between onset of the disease and the work environment. This is fairly clear for "brown lung" disease and cotton mills, but more difficult if the claim is that nonsmoking employees have been harmed by cigarette smoke exhaled by customers and co-employees who smoke.

Depending on the state, benefits may also be available if workplace conditions aggravate a disease that the individual already had. In California, Florida, Kentucky, Maryland, Mississippi, North Dakota, and South Carolina, WC benefits will be available but will be reduced to compensate for the pre-existing condition. If, for instance, the worker's condition was 25% due to workplace factors, 75% due to the preexisting condition, only 25% of the full benefit will be payable.

Occupational disease creates difficult questions involving "long tail" claims: claims made on the basis that it took years, or even decades, for the symptoms caused by occupational exposure to hazardous substances to manifest themselves. During this long period of time, the employee could have held several jobs (involving exposure to different hazards) and/or engaged in behavior such as smoking that is hazardous or compounds other hazards.

The general rule under the legal system is that claims are timely if they are filed within a reasonable time after the individual first experiences disability or symptoms, and could reasonably be expected to draw a connection between work exposure and illness.

Another question is whether the employee's exposure was extensive enough to trigger the claimed symptoms. The epidemiology (disease pattern) for similar exposures should be studied to see if the employee's alleged experience is typical.

Furthermore, one disease claim by an employee could trigger a wave of related claims from other employees who actually are ill, believe themselves to be ill because they have developed psychosomatic symptoms, or who just hope for easy money.

Asbestos-related disease is "bodily injury by disease" rather than "bodily injury by accident" under WC and employer liability insurance policies. Asbestos exposure is not an accident because it is not violent and because it develops over a latency period rather than right away. [*Riverwood Int'l Corp. v. Employers Ins. of Wausau*, 420 F.3d 378 (5th Cir. 2005)]

An appellate court in New Jersey upheld a $7.5 million jury award to a former Exxon worker and his wife. The court found Exxon liable for Bonnie Anderson's mesothelioma not only because she worked there for 12 years, but because she washed her husband's work clothes for 24 years. The court rejected Exxon's argument that her claim was barred by WC exclusivity, because Exxon took on a separate, independent role with respect to Ms. Anderson's non-occupational exposure to asbestos. (Occupational exposure was ruled out, because her work as an electrician did not involve contact with asbestos.) New Jersey's rule is that employers have a duty to protect the spouses of employees, as well as employees, from asbestos exposure. [*Anderson v. A J Friedman Supply Co. Inc.*, 416 N.J. Super. 46 (2010)]

The Seventh Circuit had to decide whether an employee's common-law negligence claim was a claim to satisfy the insuring agreement of an excess WC policy, under the employer liability laws. A former employee of TKK died of mesothelioma. TKK was named as defendant in a negligence suit. TKK notified its excess WC carrier of the suit. TKK retained primary responsibility for defending, settling, and paying claims of up to $275,000 per occurrence. After incurring about $400,000 in legal fees, TKK settled the suit. Safety National denied coverage, treating the negligence claim as a common-law claim that was not covered by the policy and was not brought under WC or employer liability laws. In Illinois, the Workers' Occupational Disease Act (ODA) is the exclusive remedy for employees who are injured at work or contract occupational disease. The Seventh Circuit held that the ODA does not cover all potential common-law claims, so employer liability should not be defined only as ODA statutory claims. The Seventh Circuit affirmed the district court's finding that the definition of "employer liability law" was broad enough to include common-law claims, even groundless claims for which the employer had an affirmative defense. [*TKK USA, Inc. v. Safety Nat'l Cas. Corp.*, 727 F.3d 782 (7th. Cir. 2013); see Brian Margolies, *Seventh Circuit Addresses Coverage Under Workers' Comp Policy*, Traub Lieberman Straus & Shrewsberry LLP (Jan. 8, 2014), available at Lexology.com]

[E] Psychological Injuries

By and large, the WC system deals with palpable physical injuries and diseases, although in some circumstances mental and emotional illnesses can be compensable. Emotional and mental injuries are analyzed in three categories:

- Mental-physical—physical impact of mental conditions, such as chest pains and high blood pressure;
- Physical-mental—such as suffering a phobia after being involved in an accident or developing "AIDS-phobia" after a needle-stick incident;
- Mental-mental—injuries with no physical component.

In all the states, mental-physical and physical-mental injuries are compensable as long as a causal connection between the two is established. Compensability of mental-mental injuries is less clear-cut. Some states, including Alabama, Florida, Georgia, Kansas, Minnesota, Montana, Nebraska, Ohio, Oklahoma, and South Dakota refuse to compensate cases where there is no demonstrated physical involvement. In the other states, it may be necessary to prove a connection to a severe, unpredictable event, and compensability may depend on whether the onset was gradual or sudden.

Rigoberto Garcia suffered a traumatic head injury after falling from a 24-foot ladder while picking avocados. He filed a WC claim for psychiatric injury. He had been employed for about two months at the time of the injury. California's Labor Code § 3208.3(d) generally bars psychiatric injury claims by people employed for less than six months, with an exception for psychiatric injury caused by a sudden and extraordinary employment condition. The California Court of Appeal denied the claim, ruling that falling off a ladder is an occupational hazard of the job. [*State Comp. Ins. Fund v. Workers' Comp. Appeals Bd.*, 204 Cal. App. 4th 766 (Cal. App. 2012)]

The Nevada Supreme Court permitted survivors to file a WC claim if a suicide is closely enough connected to a workplace injury. To prevail, the survivors must show that the industrial injury caused a psychological ailment severe enough to override rational judgment, and that caused the suicide. In this case, a bartender suffered chronic back pain after a workplace fall, and one of his doctors testified that he committed suicide because of the pain. [*Vredenburg v. Sedgwick CMA*, 188 P.3d 1084 (Nev. Sup. 2008); Fred Schneyer, *Nevada High Court Sanctions Worker's Comp Claims for Suicide*, plansponsor.com (July 28, 2008); suicide can be compensable, even if the worker suffered from pre-existing depression, as long as a work-related injury was at least a contributing cause of the suicide: *Altes v. Petrocelli Elec. Co.*, 270 A.D.2d 767 (N.Y. Sup. 2000)]

§ 33.03 WC EXCLUSIVITY

The WC system gives employers the protection of "worker's compensation exclusivity"; in other words, in the normal work-related injury or illness case, the employee's only remedy against the employer is to collect compensation benefits. Tort lawsuits are not permitted. However, exclusivity applies only against the employer. If the employee is injured by a product manufactured by the employer, the employee can sue the employer in its capacity as manufacturer. Suits against other manufacturers, or non-employer parties responsible for hazardous conditions at the workplace, are also a possibility. The employer itself can sue the third party in order to recover the medical benefits that the employer provided on behalf of the employee.

WC is essentially a no-fault system, so negligence by any party is usually irrelevant. However, in some states, a worker's failure to use safety equipment can reduce (but not eliminate) the benefits that would otherwise be payable after an accident. Sometimes, the employer's wrongdoing will take the case out of WC exclusivity. Some (but not all) courts would allow an ordinary tort suit against an employer that deliberately concealed information about workplace hazards.

Compensation benefits will be granted only if the employee has medical evidence to prove the connection between the job and the disabling condition. Furthermore, the employee must be incapacitated by the condition, so benefits will not be awarded to a person who stoically continues to work despite pain. Courts have reached different conclusions as to whether a person is permanently and totally disabled only if there is absolutely no job he or she can perform, or whether "human factors" such as job availability within a reasonable commuting distance must be considered.

There are three categories of workplace assaults for WC purposes. There is an inherent connection if the assault is related to employment, e.g., occurs in connection with an employee's termination. An assault might occur in the course of an inherently private dispute not related to employment, such as violence committed by the employee's spouse or partner. A "neutral force" random assault is committed on an employee outside the employment relationship. Inherent connection assaults are compensable under WC; private dispute assaults are not; neutral force incidents might be depending on circumstances. The "street risk" doctrine requires proof either that employees were indiscriminately exposed to dangers from the public, or the employee was assaulted because of his or her connection with the employer. The Tennessee Supreme Court ruled that WC benefits were not available for the widow of an employee whose murder at the workplace remained unsolved. The decedent opened the store; when the store owner arrived at 6 am, he found the body. The court treated the death as a "neutral force assault." The "street risk" doctrine did not apply because the premises were not open to the public at the time of the killing; his job did not involve public contact; and there was no evidence that members of the public were more likely to be close to the store in the early morning than at other times. [*Padilla v. Twin City Fire Ins.*

Co., 324 S.W.3d 507 (Tenn. 2010); see Rebecca Moore, *TN High Court Denies Benefits for Widow of Murdered Employee*, plansponsor.com (Oct. 11, 2010)]

WC exclusivity applies, and the victim does not have the right to bring tort claims against the employer in cases of rape or robbery by an unknown assailant. The Florida Court of Appeals ruled that the parents of a 16-year-old store employee who charged that she was raped by her manager cannot pursue a negligence suit against the store. (Their theory was that the store was negligent in hiring the manager.) The court of appeals held that it was possible that the family had a WC claim, but that would preclude a civil suit. [*John and Jane Doe v. Footstar Corp.*, 980 So. 2d 1266 (Fla. App. 2008); Fred Schneyer, *FL Appellate Court Upholds Sexual Assault Civil Claim Dismissal*, plansponsor.com (May 12, 2008)]

A Workers' Compensation carrier can take a credit under New York's Workers' Compensation Law § 29(4) against the settlement proceeds of a civil suit brought by WC recipient against her employer. The carrier is entitled to offset the full amount of settlement proceeds. Beth V, an aide at a juvenile detention center, told her supervisors and employees that she was afraid of a male resident who made sexual overtures to her. After he assaulted, raped, and abducted her, she received WC benefits for permanent partial disability. She sued the agency and three supervisors, whom she said were aware of the threat, and received a $650,000 settlement described as covering personal injuries. She paid attorneys' fees and satisfied a $2,500 lien to the New York State Crime Victims Board. The WC carrier approved the settlement, reserving its right under § 29(4) to take a credit against her future benefits equal to the net recovery. As a result, benefits were stopped. The plaintiff argued that the insurer was not entitled to a credit, because her suit was for deprivation of civil rights and a hostile work environment, distinct from her WC claim. The carrier said that WC exclusivity does not apply to intentional torts, so the employer and co-workers are treated as third parties, with § 29 preventing double recovery. Under § 29(1), an employee can sue for a negligence or wrong not committed by a co-worker; the carrier has a lien on the WC benefits. Section 29(4) permits crediting the proceeds of the lawsuit against the payment obligation. In this case, the carrier waived its lien, so § 29(4) applied. The New York Court of Appeals held that the proceeds here compensated for the physical and mental injuries that resulted in the WC award, no matter how the recovery was structured for tax purposes. [*In re Beth v. NYS Office of Children & Family Servs.*, 22 N.Y.3d 80 (N.Y. 2013)]

In a suit against the parent company of the company that owned and operated a factory where two workers were severely burned when flammable vapors were ignited, the First Circuit held that to sue a parent company, the employee must establish, by specific facts, that the parent company (either expressly or by implication) assumed primary responsibility for workplace safety. The employee has the burden of presenting specific facts to show such an express or implied duty. [*Mendez-Laboy v. Abbott Labs. Inc.*, 424 F.3d 35 (1st Cir. 2005)]

Although, in general, injuries incurred when going to and returning from work are not covered by WC, the District of Columbia has a "traveling employee" exception that makes WC exclusive for injuries of a person for whom travel is integral to the job. However, relocating to accept a new assignment does not make a person a "traveling employee." For example, an employee who was sent to the Philippines for a two-year assignment was kidnapped, imprisoned, and tortured. Although he worked under an employment contract in which job-related injuries were only covered by WC, the D.C. Circuit ruled that his injuries were not work-related, nor were they a reasonable and foreseeable part of the work, so he could sue his employers for negligence and intentional infliction of emotional distress. [*Khan v. Parsons Global Servs. Ltd.*, 428 F.3d 1079 (D.C. Cir. 2005).

The Texas Supreme Court ruled that a drug sales representative was acting in the scope of her employment (and therefore entitled to WC benefits when she was severely injured in an automobile accident) when driving to a storage unit containing drug samples, after a dinner with clients. The representative usually worked out of her home, but kept samples in a storage unit provided by the employer near her home: *Leordeanu v. American Prot. Ins. Co.*, 330 S.W.3d 239 (Tex. 2010); see Fred Schneyer, *TX Drug Rep Wins Workers Comp Appeal*, plansponsor.com (Dec. 9, 2010)]

The New Jersey Appellate Division extended the "coming and going" rule to grant full WC benefits to an off-site employee who was seriously injured during a five-mile trip to the deli for coffee, because a coffee break is a minor deviation from employment that does not prevent payment of full benefits. An alternative argument was that he was on an authorized "mission" for the employer (going to the union hall to discuss plans for a new project) and was required to be away from the workplace on business. It was reasonable for him to take his coffee break instead of interrupting the union official or simply doing nothing, and in a secluded rural location, it was reasonable to drive five miles to find good coffee. [*Cooper v. Barnickel Enters. Inc.*, 411 N.J. Super. 343; (N.J. App. Div. 2010); see Michael Booth, *Employee Injured in Five-Mile Drive for Coffee Is Eligible for Workers' Comp*, N.J.L.J. (Jan. 14, 2010) (law.com). See also *Sager v. O.A. Peterson Constr. Co.,* 182 N.J. 156 (2004): compensation was awarded when carpenter was injured on way to job site after dinner break in an extended work day, on the grounds that an employee who is doing what he is supposed to be doing, whether on or off premises, is acting in the course of employment.]

The Connecticut Court of Appeals said that a slip-and-fall suit against individual corporate officers of the victim's employer should not have been dismissed, because the defendants were not entitled to a Worker's Compensation exemption. The plaintiff fell in Dymax's parking lot in 2005, suffering a fractured hip and other injuries. After receiving Worker's Compensation benefits, she sued the individual corporate officers because they owned the parking lot and leased it to the corporation. The court of appeals held that, in their role as parking lot owners, the defendants were not entitled to assert WC exclusivity. In some other states (but not in Connecticut), there is a "dual-capacity" doctrine, permitting a suit for injuries sustained while the employer or a co-employee was acting in a non-employment capacity. In this case, the plaintiff was employed by Dymax, not by the Bachmanns as individuals, and her suit asserted a premises liability claim rather than a WC claim. [*Roy v. Bachmann*, 121 Conn. App. 220 (2010); see Fred Schneyer, *Corporate Officers Open to CT Injury Lawsuits*, plansponsor .com (May 18, 2010)]

§ 33.04 ALTERNATIVES FOR INSURING WC

[A] Types of Available Insurance

Depending on state law and the employer's own financial status and risk category, there are several ways to cope with the obligation to provide benefits for injured employees.

- Buying insurance from a state-run fund that is the sole source of WC coverage within the state;
- Buying insurance from a commercial carrier. Nearly all privately purchased policies will follow the form of the "standard policy"—the Worker's Compensation and Employers' Liability Policy developed by the national Council on Compensation Insurance (NCCI);
- Buying insurance from a state fund that competes with commercial carriers;
- Self-insurance (most employers who take this option combine it with third-party administration, reinsurance, or both);
- Insurance through a captive insurer owned by the employer;
- Participating in an assigned risk pool (depending on circumstances, this can be either mandatory or voluntary).

The Supreme Court ruled in mid-2006 that in the context of Chapter 11 bankruptcy, premiums owed to a WC insurer are not unpaid contributions to an "employee benefit plan" and therefore are not accorded priority under 11 U.S.C. § 507(a)(5). [*Howard Delivery Serv. Inc. v. Zurich Am. Ins. Co.*, 547 U.S. 651 (2006)]

[B] State Funds

The states of North Dakota, Ohio, Washington, West Virginia, and Wyoming have monopolistic state funds, i.e., all covered employers have to buy their coverage from the fund. Until July 1, 1997, Nevada was in this category, but now it maintains a state fund but allows private coverage.

The states that have competitive state funds (i.e., the employer chooses whether to purchase coverage from the state funds or a private insurer) are Arizona, California, Colorado, Idaho, Louisiana, Maine, Maryland, Michigan, Minnesota, Montana, New Mexico, Nevada, New York, Oklahoma, Oregon, Pennsylvania, Rhode Island, Texas, and Utah. State funds set their own rates, which can be low because the fund has very low marketing expenses.

Texas allows employers to self-insure for WC, but they must be careful to provide benefits at least roughly comparable to the benefits that would be available under an insured plan. In *Reyes v. Storage & Processors Inc.* [995 S.W.2d 722 (Tex. App. 1999)], the court said that employers cannot require arbitration of claims for work-related injuries if the benefits they provide are substantially less generous than Comp benefits.

[C] Assigned Risk Pools

In any situation in which people or organizations have a legal obligation to maintain insurance coverage, some of them will not be insurable under normal underwriting standards. Assigned risk pools are created to issue coverage. In the WC context, the NCCI administers the National Worker's Compensation Reassurance Pool. It covers about 25% of all employers, making it the largest single WC insurer in the United States.

This WC assigned risk pool has some unusual features. Commercial insurers have to support it by paying "residual market assessments" of approximately 14 cents on every premium dollar they receive. But because of this heavy assessment, commercial insurers are less willing to grant discounts to their insurable customers, thus driving more employers to see the assigned risk pool as an attractive alternative.

[D] Self-Insurance and Captive Companies

In all the states except North Dakota and Wyoming, employers who satisfy certain criteria (e.g., being financially capable of paying all WC claims that arise in the course of operations; posting bond or establishing an escrow) can elect to self-insure.

> ■ **TIP:** Self-insurance is considered a privilege. It can be revoked by the state if an employer fails to file the necessary reports, does not maintain the required amount of excess insurance, or otherwise fails to keep up its end of the bargain. A change in corporate ownership might also lead to revocation of the privilege, even if the corporate structure remains the same.

In practice, self-insurance is practical only for very large companies with six- or seven-figure WC premium obligations; about one-third of the WC market is now self-insured because some economic giants have taken this option.

More than half the states impose a requirement that self-insured companies maintain reinsurance (excess coverage). It is prudent for companies to do this even if it is not required. Self-insured employers generally must show that they have arranged for claims administration, employee communications, and safety programs. These functions are usually performed under a Third Party Administration (TPA) arrangement. An effective TPA should have 24-hour-a-day claims service; low turnover (experienced representatives do a much better job than novices); a high proportion of employees who have obtained professional certification in loss control; quick settlement of claims; and a low average final cost per claim.

In a pure self-insurance arrangement, the employer sets up reserves and pays all WC claims from these reserves. In a group arrangement, several companies join forces. Each one is jointly and severally liable for all Comp claims within the group. Most of the states permit group self-insurance; nationwide, there are over 250 group self-insurance pools. In a limited self-insurance arrangement, the employer is responsible for the Self-Insured Retention (SIR), which is roughly equal to a deductible, and excess insurance pays the rest.

Excess coverage can be written on a per-occurrence or per-loss basis, covering an aggregate amount for the year or per accident per payment year. (The payment year is a relevant concept because the consequences of an injury might extend over several years.) Specific excess insurance limits the employer's liability for claims for any occurrence where the exposure exceeds the SIR. Aggregate excess insurance copes with the possibility of a bad year. The employer has to pay the amount in the aggregate retention or loss fund. This is usually expressed as a percentage, such as 125%, of the reinsurance premium for the year. Aggregate excess coverage usually stops at $1 million or $2 million, so the employer will be at risk once again if the exposure is greater. Specific excess insurance is both easier to obtain and less expensive than aggregate insurance.

To self-insure, the company must file an application with the state (this typically costs $100–$1,000). The employer may have to post a letter of credit as security, and the lending bank will impose fees. Excess insurance and TPA fees each costs about 8%–13% of the amount that would otherwise be the WC premium. States also impose taxes on self-insurance arrangements—about 1%–4% of the premium that would have been charged by an insurer, incurred losses, or paid losses.

Working through a captive insurance company (one that does business only with a company that is its sole shareholder, or a small group of cooperating companies) is another option. The advantage of this arrangement to the employer is the ability to keep the underwriting income (deposits that are the equivalent of premiums, plus investment income), but the company will also have to pay the expenses of the captive insurer.

[E] High-Deductible Plans

A high-deductible plan combines features of both insurance and self-insurance. To reduce its premiums, the employer agrees to accept a higher deductible. Usually, it falls between $100,000 and $1 million, but policies are available with deductibles up to $5 million. Any employer can purchase a high-deductible policy. Unlike self-insurance, there are no financial qualifications imposed by the state.

When a claim is made under a high-deductible plan, the insurer pays the full claim, then bills the policyholder for payments made that fell within the deductible. Bills are usually sent on a monthly basis. Employers who buy high-deductible policies are generally required to create an escrow fund equal to about three months' potential loss payments, and must submit a letter of credit in an amount equal to the deductible. At the end of the first year of high deductible coverage, the letter of credit is adjusted upward or downward to reflect experience. Paid losses are billed until all claims have been closed. The high-deductible insurer may require indemnification or a hold-harmless agreement offering remedies against the employer if, for instance, legislation is passed subjecting the insurer to increased losses that fall within the deductible.

§ 33.05 SETTING THE WC PREMIUM

There are 600 industry classifications, each identified by a four-digit number. An employer's basic WC premium is the "manual rate" for its industry classification. The manual rate is the average cost of WC coverage for the classification, based on the number of claims in the past three years for injuries serious enough to cause lost work time. The rate is sometimes expressed as a percentage of total payroll, but is usually defined as a number of dollars per $100 of payroll. Large employers may qualify for premium discounts, because the administrative expenses are fairly similar for policies of all sizes.

The manual rate is only one factor in setting an individual employer's rate. Experience rating (the employer's actual claims experience for the previous two years) can increase or decrease the base premium that will be imposed in the future. States can also adopt retrospective rating, under which past losses are used to adjust the premium already charged for a particular year, so that either the employer is entitled to a refund or will have to make additional payments.

WC policies have both general inclusions, which recur in many industries (for workers in employee cafeterias, and repair and maintenance crews, for instance) and general exclusions that are written out of ordinary industry classifications (for instance, construction activities performed by employees; running an employer-operated day care center).

§ 33.06 BAN ON RETALIATION

Due to a lower reported injury rate, and some state laws making it harder to qualify for WC benefits, the average cost of WC per $100 payroll fell from $2.67 in 1994 to $1.79 in 2012—a rare commodity that cost less in the later year! But, although the number of workplace injuries reported to OSHA dropped by nearly one-third in the decade ending in 2013, one factor in the decline is not better safety practices, but greater fear of retaliation against employees who report their injuries. In 2012, there were approximately 100 state and federal suits charging Worker's Compensation retaliation, about twice as many as 10 years earlier. [James R. Hagerty, *Workplace Injuries Drop, But Claims of Employer Retaliation Rise*, WSJ.com (July 22, 2013)]

Nearly all the states have passed statutes making it illegal to retaliate against an employee, either specifically for filing a Worker's Compensation claim or for filing any "wage claim" or "wage complaint," a broad category that includes WC. The states are Alabama, Arizona, California, Connecticut, Delaware, Florida, Hawaii, Idaho, Illinois, Indiana, Kansas, Kentucky, Louisiana, Maine, Maryland, Mississippi, Michigan, Minnesota, Missouri, Montana, New Hampshire, New Jersey, New Mexico, New York, North Carolina, North Dakota, Ohio, Oklahoma, Rhode Island, South Carolina, South Dakota, Texas, Vermont, Virginia, Washington, West Virginia, Wisconsin, and Wyoming.

Even in the minority of states that do not have a statute, it is very likely that courts will treat retaliatory discharge as an illegal violation of public policy.

The Tenth Circuit found it likely that UPS retaliated against an injured worker by denying him the opportunity to return to work with lifting restrictions. However, because the plaintiff suffered only monetary harm, the Tenth Circuit found the $2 million district court judgment excessive. After a 2003 injury, the company doctor told plaintiff Jones that he could not lift more than 20 pounds over his head, and carriers must be able to lift 70 pounds routinely. In 2004, two doctors cleared Jones to lift 70 pounds, but a UPS occupational health manager told them not to remove the lifting restrictions. Jones said that UPS retaliated against him for filing a WC claim. The Tenth Circuit found the retaliation claim valid (the occupational health manager intentional interfered with the medical evaluations to prevent his return to work) and found punitive damages appropriate, but said that $2 million was excessive because the manager's conduct did not involve disregard for health or safety. The Tenth Circuit affirmed the $630,000 award of actual damages. [*Jones v. United Parcel Serv. Inc.*, 674 F.3d 1187 (10th Cir. 2011); see Tara Cantore, *Appeals Court Says Judgment in Retaliation Suit Excessive*, plansponsor.com (Oct. 26, 2011). Rehearing was granted March 5, 2012.]

Continental Tire fired a 22-year veteran trucker who refused to take a mandatory drug test after being involved in an accident. He brought a suit for retaliatory termination by filing a Worker's Compensation claim. The Seventh Circuit held that there was no evidence that the employer's explanation—that he was fired for refusing to be tested—was not true. Nor could he prove that requiring post-accident drug testing discouraged employees from filing Worker's Compensation claims. [*Phillips v. Continental Tire The Americas LLC*, 743 F.3d 475 (7th Cir. 2014); see Amanda Mattocks, *Seventh Circuit: Employee Failed to Establish Link Between Termination and Filing of Workers' Comp Claim*, Hinshaw & Culbertson (Mar. 25, 2014), available at Lexology.com]

Minnesota law forbids retaliatory discharge for seeking Worker's Compensation, but allows termination for dishonest behavior, including filing a false WC claim. A 2013 Minnesota case involves an employee who said she slipped in the company parking lot during two of her afternoon breaks, although video from the lot did not show her falling. The employee was fired for filing a false claim. She sued for retaliatory discharge. The district court denied summary judgment for the employer, finding that the investigation was incomplete. The video was of poor quality; not all footage was retained; and it was possible that the employee could have fallen outside camera range. Nor did the employer ask her doctor if her injuries were consistent with her account of the falls. [*Schaefer v. BioLife Plasma LLC*, Civil No. 11-3468 (JRT/LIB), 2013 U.S. Dist. LEXIS 133343 (D. Minn. Sept. 18, 2013); Michael T. Miller, *Beware The Danger Of Firing An Employee For An Allegedly False Workers Compensation Claim*, Briggs and Morgan (Oct. 1, 2013), available at Lexology.com]

Discharge is not the only employment action that can give rise to retaliation charges: A retaliatory demotion, that results in a pay cut, is also wrongful, and can give rise to a lawsuit. [*Brigham v. Dillon Cos. Inc.*, 935 P.2d 1054 (Kan. Sup. 1997)]

The Ninth Circuit ruled that it is not retaliation to fire a worker for lying about previous occupational injuries on a questionnaire. Although the state's Right to Privacy in the Workplace Act forbids employers to ask prospective employees if they have ever filed a Worker's Compensation claim, it is permissible to ask about previous occupational injuries, time lost from work because of work-related injuries, or medical treatment for those injuries, even though it wouldn't be difficult to extrapolate from those disclosures that a Comp claim had been filed. [*Carter v. Tennant Co.*, 383 F.3d 673 (9th Cir. 2004)]

§ 33.07 ADMINISTRATION OF WC

[A] Generally

In most states, employers are required to participate in the WC system (although Texas and New Jersey allow private employers to opt out of the system entirely, as long as they notify the Compensation Commission and their employees that they have left the system). The tradeoff is that injured employees have the right to bring tort suits against employers who are outside the WC system, whereas in most cases workers who are injured in a WC-covered workplace will not be allowed to sue the employer.

Some states allow employees to opt out of WC coverage as long as they do so in writing, within a reasonable time after starting a new job, and before any accident or injury has occurred. Corporate officers are often given the option of leaving the WC system.

In about a third of the states, the state itself runs the WC fund. Those states give employers three choices for handling their responsibilities:

- Pay into the state fund;
- Buy insurance from a private carrier;
- Self-insure by maintaining a segregated fund that contains enough money to handle the expected compensation claims.

In states with no state fund, employers can either buy insurance or self-insure.

The insurance premium depends on the level of risk: A coal mine is much more likely to have occupational injury claims than a boutique. The nationwide average premium is about 2.5% of compensation.

The general rule is that employees are obligated to notify the employer within a short time (usually about five days) after an injury or the onset of an illness. Employers should encourage reporting, because such information is needed for WC and other purposes (OSHA reports, improving safety conditions).

In some WC systems, the employer notifies its WC insurer, which then files the report. In other systems, the employer (whether it has insurance or is self-insured) is responsible for notifying the compensation board. If the employer fails to make the necessary report, the employee will probably be given additional time to pursue his or her claim.

If the employer agrees that the injury or disease is work-related and accepts the employee's characterization of its seriousness, the claim is uncontested. Most states follow the "agreement system" under which a settlement is negotiated by the parties, or by the employee and the employer's WC insurer. In some states, the agency that administers WC claims must approve all settlements, even in uncontested cases. Most settlements involve payment of ongoing benefits at a continuing rate: either a percentage of the employee's pre-accident income, or a percentage of the state's average income. However, there is an increasing trend to settle WC cases for a lump sum.

However, some uncontested cases are treated as "direct payment" cases. Either the employer or the insurer initiates the process, by making the statutory initial installment payment to the employee. Under this option, the employee does not have to sign anything or agree to anything—unlike the agreement system, which results in a written agreement.

WC settlements cover only the matters specifically set out in the agreement, so agreements must be drafted carefully. Employers are allowed to settle claims that have already accrued, but not future claims (such as claims for future medical expenses), because employees cannot be required to give up future claims that are hard to quantify in advance.

Generally, any settlement between employer and employee will be final. However, there are grounds for which agreements can be set aside, such as fraud, mutual mistake of fact (both sides believe something about the employee's condition that turns out not to be accurate), or mistake of law (misinterpretation of the legal rules and their consequences). Usually, the mere fact that the employee did not have a lawyer is not enough to invalidate a settlement—unless, perhaps, the employer prevented the employee from seeking legal advice. Just to be on the safe side, employers should inform employees that they have the right to be represented by counsel.

Contested cases are heard and decided by the agency administering the system. However, there are comparatively few contested cases. In most cases, it is quite clear that there has been an injury. Because WC is a no-fault system, it is not necessary to apportion blame.

In some states, mediation is either an option that is available (but only if both sides agree); in other states, it is compulsory. In mediated cases, a neutral mediator has at least one informal meeting with the parties. Sometimes, the meeting is held off the record, so both sides can speak freely, without having to restrict what they say to things that would help their case in formal legal proceedings. If necessary, the mediator arranges more meetings, until the mediator is either able to facilitate a settlement, or it is clear that an impasse has been reached.

In some states, when mediation fails, binding arbitration can be applied; in other states, the case is sent to the Comp board for adjudication.

Appeal rights are granted to dissatisfied employers and employees. Usually, parties get 30 days to file for an appeal, although the requirements of different states range from 10 days to one year. Grounds for appeal include improprieties in the process and changed circumstances (such as unpredictable improvement or deterioration in the employee's condition) that were unknown at the time of the award.

Many state laws entitle the employee to an additional payment of 10%–20% if the employer is late in making a required payment. Civil fines may also be imposed, and the unpaid amounts could operate as a lien on the employer's assets.

[B] Responding to an Accident

Even before there have been any accidents, your workplace should have an effective procedure in place, and should hold regular drills to make sure everyone can handle the procedure. Make sure that employees learn first aid and CPR. Keep plenty of first aid kits around, with fresh supplies, in convenient locations. It's important to provide first aid for all minor incidents, and immediate medical care in more serious cases.

Somebody must be designated to take charge of taking the injured worker to a doctor's office or hospital emergency room, or to call an ambulance. Someone must be in charge of filing the initial accident report (and an OSHA incident report if necessary). [See § 24.02[A]] Some insurers have 24-hour telephone lines that can be used for WC and OSHA reporting, and to assign a case manager to review utilization of care and the injured person's potential for rehabilitation. There is clear evidence that the earlier and more aggressively rehabilitation can be pursued, the more likely it is that the employee will be able to return to work (or at least to limited duties or a less strenuous job) instead of becoming permanently disabled.

In addition to immediate accident reports, some states require a yearly report of all workplace incidents, similar to the OSHA annual report. [See § 24.02[A]] Follow-up status reports may also be required on individual accidents. Employers who fail to make mandatory reports can be subject to fines; there may even be criminal penalties.

As Chapter 18 shows, managed care dominates the U.S. health care system. It also plays a role in WC cases. Some states such as Connecticut, Florida, and Ohio make managed care involvement in WC cases compulsory. Many other states have laws authorizing managed care as an option in WC cases: Arkansas, California, Georgia, Kentucky, Massachusetts, Minnesota, Missouri, Montana, Nebraska, Nevada, New Hampshire, New Jersey, New York, North Carolina, North Dakota, Oregon, Pennsylvania, Rhode Island, South Dakota, Utah, and Washington.

§ 33.08 WC IN RELATION TO OTHER SYSTEMS

Because WC cases involve physical injury, in an employment context, both health care and employment law can be implicated—for example, ERISA and the ADA.

The U.S. Supreme Court rejected an appeal of a decision that allowed employees with WC claims to pursue a RICO case against their employer. Plaintiffs said that the self-insured Cassens Transportation relied on its claims adjuster and poorly qualified doctors to get medical examinations that would deny WC claims. The case was remanded to the trial court for further proceedings. Business groups wanted the decision reversed, because they saw it as opening the door for bringing WC claims (which are usually heard in state courts) into the federal court system. [*Brown v. Cassens Transp. Co.*, 546 F.3d 347 (6th Cir. 2009); see Fred Schneyer, *Workers Comp RICO Claim Gets Second Chance*, plansponsor.com (Dec. 9, 2009)]

Two Coca-Cola employees sued their employer, its WC TPA, and an examining doctor. They charged a RICO mail fraud scheme to avoid paying benefits for injured employees. The plaintiffs alleged that they were sent to a doctor who would lie and say they were not disabled. The Sixth Circuit, sitting en banc, ruled that WC laws are a creation of state law; they do not permit converting a loss in personal injury litigation into a RICO injury. The article suggests that self-insured employers should use multiple vendors and doctors for independent examinations and reviews; should not promise a reviewing doctor a fixed number of cases a year, should not pressure employees to be treated under their individual health plans rather than WC, and of course should not say anything that sounds like an attempt to influence a report. [*Jackson v. Sedgwick Claims Mgmt Servs., Inc.*, 731 F.3d 556 (6th Cir. 2013); see Brian D. Hall, *Sixth Circuit En Banc Decision Rejects RICO Claim For Alleged Workers' Compensation Fraud*, Porter Wright Morris & Arthur LLP (Nov. 25, 2013), available at Lexology.com]

The Longshore and Harbor Workers' Compensation Act (LHWCA) provides a compensation scheme for disability or death caused by injury on the navigable waters of the United States. Benefits for most disabilities are subject to a cap of twice the national average of weekly wage for the fiscal year of the initial award of benefits. In cases where the employer contests liability or the employee contests employer's actions, the dispute goes to the DOL Office of Workers' Compensation Programs (OWCP). The OWCP attempts conciliation; if there is no resolution, there is an ALJ hearing resulting in a compensation order. After Roberts was injured in 2002, his employer, Sea-Land, voluntarily paid benefits until 2005. Roberts filed an LHWCA claim, which was controverted. In FY 2007, the ALJ awarded benefits at the statutory maximum rate—for 2002. Roberts said that it should have been set at the 2007 rate, because that was when he was "newly awarded compensation." In 2012, the Supreme Court ruled that the date that counts is the date worker becomes disabled because this is when entitlement to benefits is triggered, no matter when—or even whether—a compensation order issues. [*Roberts v. Sea-Land Servs., Inc.*, 132 S. Ct. 1350 (2012)]

The Bankruptcy Code (11 U.S.C. § 509(a)(8)(E)(ii)) gives priority to certain non-dischargeable amounts owed by a debtor to the state if the amounts are an excise tax incurred on a transaction that occurred in the three years before filing of the bankruptcy petition. In 2009, the Ninth Circuit ruled that amounts an employer was legally obligated to pay to the California self-insurance security fund, to reimburse the fund for WC benefits paid to the employer's workers, were not excise taxes, so the self-insurance security fund could not claim the priority for these amounts. [*In re Lorber Indus. of California*, 564 F.3d 1098 (9th Cir. May 4, 2009)]

The Medicare system is a secondary payor with respect to Worker's Compensation: that is, if a Medicare beneficiary also receives WC, the WC system is required to pay for the care first, with Medicare responsible only for amounts not covered by WC. Employers and insurers have a duty to report WC claims involving Medicare beneficiaries who have received a settlement, judgment, award, or other reimbursement of medical expenses on or after July 1, 2009 to the Center for Medicare and Medicaid Services. [Littler, Mendelson Press Releases, *New Medicare Secondary Payer Reporting Obligations for Workers' Compensation Plans*, <http://www.littler.com/PressPublications/Lists/ASAPs/DispAsaps.aspx?id=1359&asapType=National> (April 2009)]

A Worker's Compensation release that did not explicitly mention ERISA claims or the ERISA plan did not release the employer from an ERISA disability claim. Teresa Duncan received disability benefits under an ERISA long-term disability plan from 2005 to 2010. She settled her WC claim in 2008 and released all claims. The release form said she would not "be able to go back to the defendant for additional treatment or disability payments." The Eastern District of California held in early 2013 that the standard language in WC releases applies only to WC claims, not ERISA claims. [*Duncan v. Hartford Life & Accident Ins. Co.*, 2:11-cv-01536-GEB-CKD, 2013 WL 506465 (E.D. Cal. Feb. 8, 2013); see Mike Reilly, *Releases Should Explicitly Release ERISA Claims and ERISA Plan*, Lane Powell Boom: The ERISA Law Blog (Feb. 26, 2013) (benefitslink.com)]

[A] Taxation of WC Benefits

Generally speaking, WC insurance premiums paid by employers, or WC benefits received by employees, are not taxable income for the employee. Therefore, the employer does not have to perform tax withholding on these amounts, or withhold or pay FICA or FUTA tax on them. However, in a limited range of situations, WC benefits will be taxable: e.g., if they are paid to a person who has returned to work in a light-duty position; if they reduce Social Security benefits; or if state law calls for payment of non-occupational disability benefits. [See Chapter 20 for the related topic of disability benefits provided under a fringe benefit plan]

The amount that the employer pays in WC premiums is tax deductible. So are loss amounts paid by a self-insured employer. However, reserves maintained in order to satisfy the deductible under a WC policy are not tax-deductible.

The Tax Court held that emotional distress damages were taxable income for the recipient, a professor who said she was demoted to a secretarial position in retaliation for reporting missing equipment. She brought a WC claim and a separate suit for gross negligence, alleging that some colleagues conspired to force her out. The university agreed to pay three installments of $70,000 each for her emotional distress. The Tax Court adopted the IRS position that the plaintiff did not prove that the amounts were paid for settling a WC claim; the agreement had only one reference to the agreement being conditioned on settlement of the WC claim. The Tax Court said that the settlement could have reflected non-WC claims, and the plaintiff failed to prove that the settlement was for physical injury (see Code § 104(a)(2)); it was described as a settlement of emotional distress claims. The Tax Court cited cases to show that even if there are physical manifestations of emotional distress, that is not sufficient to exclude settlement proceeds from the recipient's income. [*Sharp v. Comm'r*, T.C. Memo 2013-290 (2013); see William Hays Weissman, *U.S. Tax Court Decision Shows Importance Of Carefully Drafting Settlement Agreements*, Littler Mendelson (Jan. 6, 2014), available at Lexology.com]

[B] ERISA

The general tenor of court decisions on this subject is that WC benefits can legitimately be used to offset accrued benefits that derive from the employer's contribution to a pension plan—but only if a statute specifically provides this, or if the plan has been drafted to include this specific provision. ERISA preempts state WC laws to the extent that they "relate" to an ERISA plan.

In 1992, the Supreme Court decided that a state law relates to an ERISA plan if it refers to or has a connection with the plan, even if the effect is indirect, and even if the law was not designed to affect the plan. Therefore, a law requiring employers to provide health insurance to employees who received or were eligible for WC was preempted. [*District of Columbia v. Greater Wash. Bd. of Trade*, 506 U.S. 125 (1992)]

[C] The ADA

A person might claim disability discrimination and also claim eligibility for WC benefits, at the same time or at different times.

The right to get WC benefits is considered a privilege of employment for ADA purposes [see, e.g., *Harding v. Winn-Dixie Stores*, 907 F. Supp. 386 (M.D. Fla. 1995)], so a case can be brought premised on alleged discrimination in this area. However, the ADA does not have the strong preemptive power that ERISA does to rule out state-law claims. In 1998, for instance, a case was allowed to proceed even though the ADA's standard of proof is higher for employees with preexisting conditions. [*Baley v. Reynolds Metals*, 153 Or. App. 498, 959 P.2d 84 (1998)]

The EEOC announced late in 2009 that it had settled with Sears for $6.2 million, in what was then the single largest ADA settlement for a single suit. The EEOC charged that Sears violated the ADA by imposing an inflexible policy calling for termination of anyone who took a WC leave that lasted more than 12 months. The EEOC filed a similar complaint against UPS, also involving a policy under which WC leave over 12 months led to termination. [Rebecca Moore, *Sears Settles Disability Discrimination Suit for $6.2M*, plansponsor.com (Oct. 2, 2009); Lynne Marek, *Sears Agrees to Multimillion-Dollar Settlement Over Firing of Disabled Workers*, Nat'l L.J. (Sept. 30, 2009) (law.com)]

[D] Second Injury Funds

Although they predate the ADA, in a way "second injury funds" serve the same purpose as the ADA: promoting the employment of people with disabilities. Second injury funds (which exist in, for example, California, Missouri, New Jersey, and Washington State) deal with the situation in which a permanent disability is compounded by a later injury to become either a permanent partial disability that is more serious than before, or a permanent total disability. In states that do not have these funds, an employer who hires someone whose pre-existing condition deteriorates because of occupational factors, would be responsible for all of the employee's WC benefits, even though the occupational factors may be comparatively less important than the pre-existing condition.

When there is a second injury fund in the picture, the employer is responsible only for the economic consequences of the later injury. The second injury fund, which is publicly funded, takes on the rest of the economic burden.

The first injury must have been serious enough to be compensable, but need not actually have come under the WC system. For instance, the second injury fund could get involved if a work-related injury aggravates an existing condition caused by a non-work-related automobile accident or a birth defect.

■ **TIP:** To collect from the fund, the employer may have to certify that it knew about the pre-existing condition at the time of hiring. This, in turn, requires asking questions in a way that does not violate the ADA.

The Wyoming Supreme Court held that the Medical Commission's denial of benefits for foot injuries, and a second compensable injury to the claimant's wrist and hip when he fell when his injured foot gave out, was arbitrary and capricious and made without substantial evidence. The "odd lot" doctrine allows a finding of permanent total disability for a worker who, although not altogether unable to work, in practice cannot be employed regularly in the existing labor market. The claimant did light duty work for 13 years, but could not carry out any gainful occupation for which he was reasonably suited by experience and training because the condition of his injured leg deteriorated. A subsequent injury is compensable if the initial compensable injury turns into a condition requiring further treatment, and the second injury is causally related to the first. [*Nagle v. State of Wyoming*, 2008 WY 99, 190 P.3d 159 (Wyo. 2008)]

[E] Social Security Disability Income

In many states, the Social Security Disability Income (SSDI) system is considered the primary payer whenever an employee is injured seriously enough to meet the Social Security Administration's stringent definition of total disability. The states in this category are Alaska, Arkansas, California, Colorado, Florida, Louisiana, Maine, Massachusetts, Michigan, Minnesota, Missouri, Montana,

Nevada, New Jersey, New York, North Dakota, Ohio, Oregon, Utah, Washington, and Wisconsin.

When SSDI is involved, the payments from the federal agency reduce the WC benefit dollar-for-dollar, until the combination of SSDI and WC reaches the level of 80% of the worker's pre-accident earnings. However, SSDI reduces only the part of the benefit that represents lost income, not the part that goes to medical care or legal fees.

The Pennsylvania Commonwealth Court ruled that an employer asserting that a worker on disability can get other employment and earn income has the burden of providing evidence of actual available jobs. Kraft employee Leonard Anterola went on disability after a 2004 knee injury. Three years later, Kraft petitioned to change the employee's disability benefits because they claimed that he could get another job. The WC judge modified the benefits; the appeal board overturned the modification; and Kraft brought suit and lost. [Fred Schneyer, *Disability Change Requires Stronger Job Proof*, plansponsor.com (Feb. 2, 2010)]

§ 33.09 TECHNIQUES FOR LOWERING COMP COSTS

Employers can reduce their costs via good planning—sorting valid from invalid claims, and finding more economical ways to handle the valid claims. Companies have had some success by educating workers that everyone is responsible for reducing injuries and maintaining a safer workplace. Focusing on getting injured workers back to work as soon as possible also helps cut costs. Departments can be made responsible for their own injury rates, and be made responsible for keeping their rates at least as low as those for comparable operations.

HR policies that are associated with lower WC rates include:

- Increasing employee involvement (e.g., through the use of quality circles). The more employees get involved, the more careful they will be about identifying potentially dangerous conditions, finding ways to correct them—and the more motivation they will have to return to work quickly after an injury;
- Strengthening grievance and conflict resolution procedures if dangerous conditions are alleged, and to resolve claims;
- Reducing turnover: Experienced workers are less likely to get hurt than novices;
- Training workers better—especially in lifting and safe handling of hazardous materials;
- Using health maintenance and wellness programs.

The National Institute of Occupational Safety and Health (NIOSH) defines three areas in which employers can be proactive to cut Comp costs:

- Using engineering controls, such as workstation layout, choice of tools, work methods, to tailor the job to fit employee capabilities and limitations;
- Reducing risk exposure through administrative controls, such as more rest breaks, better training, task rotation;
- Supplying workers with Personal Protective Equipment (PPE), although scientific consensus has not been reached on which devices are effective.

An article in CCH's Worker's Compensation newsletter gives some useful tips for spotting claims that might be fraudulent:

- Delayed reporting of injury;
- Accidents of a type that might be staged;
- The worker claiming injury was on probation or has been identified as having a poor work record;
- The alleged injury is not consistent with the worker's assigned duties;
- The injury is reported just after a weekend or holiday—showing that the injury might have been incurred away from the workplace, or work might have exacerbated a non-work-based injury.

Sometimes, a WC insurance premium quote will be inaccurate, and the premium can be reduced simply by:

- Checking to see if payroll is stated accurately, because the higher the payroll, the higher the premium;
- Making sure that employees are assigned to the lowest risk classification that accurately reflects their duties;
- Having your insurance agent review the calculations.

Part VII

SUBSTANTIVE LAWS AGAINST DISCRIMINATION

CHAPTER 34

TITLE VII

§ 34.01 INTRODUCTION

Title VII, passed as part of the Civil Rights Act of 1964, is the main federal civil rights statute that bans discrimination in employment. It has been enacted at 42 U.S.C. §§ 2000e *et seq.* (By the time Title VII came around, the United States Code was pretty much "full-up," leading to some very odd section numbers. Title VII starts with just plain § 2000e, which is divided into subsections running from § 2000e(a) to 2000e(n). The next section is § 2000e-1, with additional sections up to § 2000e-17.)

Title VII is supplemented by other civil rights statutes: Sometimes other parts of the United States Code (such as 42 U.S.C. §§ 1981, 1983, and 1985) are invoked in employment discrimination suits. Disability discrimination is barred by the Americans with Disabilities Act. [See Chapter 36] Age discrimination is barred by the Age Discrimination in Employment Act. [See Chapter 37]

In a sense, the Family and Medical Leave Act, [29 U.S.C. §§ 2601 *et seq.*] discussed in detail in Chapter 38, is also an antidiscrimination statute as well as an employee benefits statute, because it prevents discrimination against individuals who are ill or who must cope with illness as part of their family responsibilities. Note that any federal, state, or local law that creates special rights or preferences for veterans continues in force and is not repealed by Title VII [42 U.S.C. § 2000e-11] a provision that is more prominent in the post-9/11 environment.

The areas of discrimination forbidden by Title VII are race, color, religion, sex, and national origin. These are known as "suspect classifications," because employers are not supposed to discriminate for reasons involving these classifications. It is very common for Title VII suits to involve multiple allegations (e.g., that the plaintiff suffered discrimination and/or harassment because of sex and race, or national origin and religion). In many instances, employees who say they have been discriminated against also say that their employer or ex-employer retaliated against them for protesting the violation of Title VII. Many cases also combine Title VII allegations with allegations under other statutes (e.g., sex and age discrimination under the ADEA).

Also see 42 U.S.C. § 2000e-2(h), which says that it is not an unlawful employment practice for an employer to abide by FLSA § 6(d) [29 U.S.C. § 206(d)] which allows certain differences in the minimum wage.

Title VII enforcement has two aspects: public (governmental) and private (suits brought by employees, job applicants, ex-employees, or groups of people in these categories). Section 2000e-5 gives the Equal Employment Opportunities Commission (EEOC) the power "to prevent any person from engaging in any unlawful employment practice" that is banned by 42 U.S.C. § 2000e-2 or 2000e-3.

In fiscal 2013, the total number of charges of discrimination filed with the EEOC was almost 6% lower than in 2012, but recoveries through the administrative procedure reached the record level of $372.1 million. The number of retaliation charges rose to 38,539 for all statutes; there were 31,208 Title VII retaliation charges. Thirty-five percent of charges (33,068) involved race discrimination. Sex discrimination charges were raised in 29.5% of cases (27,687 charges); national origin discrimination was charged in 3,721 cases (4%), religious discrimination in 3.4% of cases (3,146 charges), color discrimination in 3,146 cases (3.4%), and GINA allegations were made in 333 cases (0.4% of the total). [Barry A. Hartstein, *EEOC Releases Charge Statistics For FY 2013*, Littler Mendelson (Feb. 5, 2014), available at Lexology.com; Melanie Trottman, *Private-Sector Workers File Fewer Complaints, Eeoc Says*, WSJ.com (Feb. 5, 2014)]

State laws still remain in force, although state laws are not permitted to require or even allow anything that is treated as an unlawful employment practice under Title VII [42 U.S.C. § 2000e-7]

A number of cases have been decided about employers' power to set appearance standards. Employees can challenge these rules for several reasons: on the grounds of sexism, racism, or religious discrimination, for example (bans on religious garb: see § 34.07[B], [C] below).

Twenty-two cocktail waitresses at the Borgata Hotel and Casino sued under New Jersey discrimination law, protesting that they must wear skimpy costumes and maintain weight standards, whereas male servers were not subject to equally strict appearance standards. The case was dismissed in mid-2013, because they were clearly on notice that the hotel expected women to conform to appearance standards. The court held that employers can lawfully use sexual objectification and gender stereotypes as long as one gender was not punished or subjected to professional disadvantage. [Parker Poe Adams & Bernstein LLP, *Judge Rejects "Borgata Babes" Sex Discrimination Claim*, Lexology.com (Aug. 9, 2013)]

The EEOC said it was racial bias for Catastrophe Management Solutions to rescind a job offer when Chastity Jones was offered work as a customer service rep but was told grooming policy forbids dreadlocks because of its requirement of a "professional and business-like image." EEOC sued, saying the ban was racial discrimination, singling out specific hairstyles that conflict with "normative standards for other races." [Employment Practices Solutions Inc., *No Dreadlock Policy Seen As Race Discrimination By EEOC*, Lexology.com (Oct. 22, 2013)]

A hotel housekeeper fired for wearing cornrows won $25,000 in damages for race discrimination. The hotel's appearance policy allowed braids, and other employees who were not African or Hispanic (Vazquez is both) were not fired for wearing braided styles. The appearance policy required conservative hairstyles that do not fall into the employee's face or obstruct eye contact; the employer retained the right to require hair to be pulled or tied back, with hair coverings for food service workers. It is up to individual managers to decide what constitutes a conservative style. Managers testified that individual braids were permissible, cornrows that showed the scalp were not. Vazquez was disciplined several times for having braids, and was warned that she would be fired if she did not take out the braids. She was fired after refusing to do so. The termination letter referred to braids rather than cornrows, and a white employee was not disciplined for a braided hairstyle. [*Vazquez v. Caesar's Paradise Resort*, No. 3:CV-09-0625, 2013

U.S. Dist. LEXIS 170178 (M.D. Pa. Dec. 3, 2013); see Saranac Hale Spencer, *Worker Fired for Cornrows Wins Discrimination Suit*, The Legal Intelligencer (Dec. 6, 2013), available at law.com]

Like the Seventh and Ninth Circuits, and most district courts that have considered the issue, the Second Circuit held that filing EEOC charges does not toll the statute of limitations for state-law tort claims, even if the tort claims involve the same facts as the EEOC case. The plaintiff charged hostile work environment, offensive physical conduct, and racially and sexually hostile comments tantamount to constructive discharge. She brought a suit in November 2009, combining Title VII and state tort claims (assault, battery, and intentional infliction of emotional distress). The state law claims were dismissed because they were time-barred: the plaintiff filed them more than one year after her last day of work for the defendant. In the future, it is likely that some plaintiffs will file state tort claims as soon as they make an EEOC charge, and request that the state-law proceedings be stayed until completion of the EEOC investigation. [*Castagna v. Luceno*, 744 F.3d 254 (2d Cir. 2014); P. Kramer Rice, *Second Circuit Holds That EEC Charge Does Not Toll State Law Tort Claims*, Ogletree Deakins (Mar. 31, 2014), available at Lexology.com]

[A] The Ledbetter Act

In 2007, the Supreme Court decided the case *Ledbetter v. Goodyear Tire*, 550 U.S. 618 (2007); see § 42.05[A]. The Supreme Court dismissed Ledbetter's charge that she was the victim of sex discrimination in compensation, holding that to be timely it would have to have been filed within 180 days of the employer's adoption of the discriminatory pay practice.

The first legislation signed by President Obama after his inauguration was the Lilly Ledbetter Fair Pay Act of 2009, Pub. L. No. 111-2, legislation designed to reverse the effect of this Supreme Court decision. Congress found that the short time frame impaired the rights that Congress intended to provide for employees. Under the Ledbetter Act, a discrimination charge is timely if it is filed within 180 days (or within 300 days, in a state with a work-sharing agreement with the EEOC) of any of these events:

- Adoption of a discriminatory practice;
- Employee becomes subject to that practice;
- Employee is affected by application of the practice—including every paycheck reflecting discrimination.

The Ledbetter Act applies to Title VII, the ADA, the ADEA, and the Rehabilitation Act. An employee who succeeds in pursuing a pay discrimination claim under Title VII, the ADEA, or the Rehab Act can recover back pay for up to two years before the filing of the charge, if the compensation discrimination was similar or related to discriminatory acts during the charge filing period.

[B] GINA

The Genetic Information Nondiscrimination Act of 2008 (GINA; Pub. L. No. 110-233, signed May 21, 2008, effective November 21, 2009) extends the protective provisions of Title VII to discrimination based on genetic information. Employers are forbidden to deny hiring, discharge anyone, or discriminate in pay or working conditions on the basis of the results of genetic testing. Health insurers are not permitted to deny coverage or set premiums or deductibles based on genetic test results. The EEOC proposed regulations under GINA prohibit hiring, firing, or other personnel decisions based on genetic predisposition to a disease. Employers are forbidden to deliberately acquire genetic information from employees or job applicants. The "water cooler" exception immunizes a supervisor who inadvertently discovers an employee's condition from statements made by other employees, or if a doctor's note contains the information. Genetic information includes tests of an individual and the individual's medical history and family medical history—but does not include information about a current disease or condition. A person's sex, age, or drug or alcohol test results are not considered genetic information. [Neil Roland, *EEOC Proposes Rules to Bar Genetic Discrimination*, workforce.com (Feb. 26, 2009) (benefitslink.com)]

Family health information can be requested if there are no financial consequences, but there must be no financial benefit or penalty associated with family health information. EGHPs are not permitted to provide incentives, such as lower premiums or rebates, for including family medical histories in health risk questionnaires. GINA and its regulations do permit EGHPs to request family medical histories in order to see if an employee should be placed in a wellness program or a program to manage a disease such as hypertension, but the employees must give the information voluntarily, and the group plan must not use the information for underwriting or request the information before enrollment in the plan. [Steven Greenhouse, *Uses of Medical Histories Are Curtailed Under a New Law*, NYTimes.com (Nov. 15, 2009); Watson Wyatt Insider, *EEOC Proposes Procedural and Administrative Regulations on Genetic Information* (July 2009) (benefitslink.com)]

Unlike HIPAA, GINA does not exempt plans that have fewer than two participants who are current employees. The regulations under GINA Title I took effect January 1, 2010 for calendar-year plans.

On January 17, 2013, HHS published a final rule covering the application of the HIPAA privacy rule to Titles I (health coverage) and II (employment) of the Genetic Information Nondiscrimination Act (GINA). The final rule is effective March 26, 2013; covered entities have until September 23, 2013 to comply. The final rule clarifies that genetic information is considered health information, which cannot be used for underwriting purposes (except for long-term care insurance policies). [Katherine Georger, *New HIPAA Final Rule Implements GINA Restriction on Use and Disclosure of Genetic Information for Underwriting Purposes*, Holland & Hart LLP News Update (Jan. 23, 2013) (benefitslink.com)]

Even pre-GINA, HIPAA forbade imposing Pre-Existing Condition Exclusions (PCEs) solely based on genetic information. HIPAA also forbade discrimination in eligibility, benefits, or premiums for individual policies based on health factors (including genetic information). GINA Title I (prohibiting discrimination in EGHP coverage) broadens the underwriting protection, and forbids insurers to demand genetic tests and restricts the collection of genetic information. The premiums for a plan or group of similarly situated individuals within a plan must not be changed based on the genetic information of one or more individuals in the group. However, premiums can be increased for the group based on an actual disease or disorder experienced by a person in the group. A health care provider treating an individual can legitimately request genetic tests. A plan or insurer can request genetic test results to determine if a claim is payable—but only the minimum amount of information needed to process the claim. [*FAQs on the Genetic Information Nondiscrimination Act*, <http://www.dol.gov/ebsa/faqs/faq-GINA.html> (no date)]

GINA Title II is the employment title. The EEOC issued final regulations on GINA Title II, effective January 10, 2011, and published two question and answer documents, one targeted at small business. The regulations state that an employer is not liable for acquiring genetic information if the information was acquired inadvertently; if the information was provided by the employee voluntarily (including information given in connection with a wellness program); family history information obtained to comply with FMLA certification, the employer's leave policy, or state or local law; publicly available information; or information acquired in connection with law enforcement. Employers who receive exempt genetic information must keep it confidential, typically in a file that is separate from the employee's personal records. It is possible for an employer to violate both Title I and II by the same action, but will not be subject to double liability. Employment attorneys Jeffrey Fraser and Sara Tountas suggest including disclosures about GINA on all forms that call for employees to submit medical information (e.g., FMLA requests, disability forms, pre-employment and return to work medical forms), so genetic information will not be provided inadvertently. [<http://eeoc.gov/laws/types/genetic.cfm>; see Plansponsor staff, *EEOC Issues Final Regs on Genetic Info NonDiscrimination*, plansponsor.com (Nov. 9, 2010); Jeffrey Fraser and Sara Tountas, *New GINA Regulations Require Immediate Employer Action*, Miller Johnson newsletter (Jan. 5, 2011) (benefitslink.com)]

The EEOC published a final rule on recordkeeping requirements under GINA. As of April 3, 2012, companies with 15 or more employees must retain all personnel and employment records relating to GINA for at least one year. If charges are filed under GINA, relevant documents must be retained until final disposition of the case. If an employee is involuntarily terminated, records must be kept for a year after termination. The relevant documents in this context include requests for accommodation, application forms, records of hiring, promotion, demotion, transfer, layoff, and termination; and records about terms of employment, e.g., pay, training, and tenure. [77 Fed. Reg. 5396 (Feb. 12, 2012)]

The EEOC's first GINA case, against Fabricut, alleging that employees were sent to a particular laboratory for physicals and were required to complete a family history questionnaire, was settled via a $50,000 consent decree. The EEOC settled a GINA suit against Founders Pavilion, Inc., a skilled nursing facility in Corning, New York. The District Court for the Western District of New York approved the consent decree January 9, 2014. The facility violated GINA by requiring a post-offer, pre-employment medical examination including questions about family history; employees had to repeat the examination each year. The EEOC also alleged Title VII and ADA violations (firing or refusing to hire on the basis of pregnancy or perceived disability). Under the decree, 138 people from whom genetic information was sought were awarded $110,400; five people who were fired or denied hiring contrary to Title VII or the ADA shared $259,600. [*EEOC v. Fabricut Inc.*, No. 13-CV_248-CVE-PJC (N.D. Okla., settled May 7, 2013); Elizabeth Tempio Clement, *EEOC Settles First Systemic GINA Lawsuit Against Nursing Home*, Littler Mendelson (Jan. 17, 2014), available at Lexology.com; William A. Wright, *GINA Enforcement Takes Off*, Sherman & Howard LLC (Nov. 12, 2013), available at Lexology.com]

§ 34.02 TREATMENT/IMPACT

Title VII discrimination claims are divided into two categories, each of which has its own requirements for drafting complaints and proving the case, and its own defenses that the employer can assert to win its case.

The two categories are disparate treatment and disparate impact. A disparate treatment case alleges that persons were singled out for inferior treatment because of the group they belong to. A disparate impact case alleges subtler forms of discrimination.

For instance, an allegation that a police department refused to hire Hispanics would be a disparate treatment claim. A disparate impact claim might challenge the police department's requirement that all newly hired officers be over 5'10" tall, on the grounds that more Hispanics than people from other backgrounds are unable to meet this requirement, and therefore a requirement that seems at first glance to be acceptable actually discriminates against members of a protected group.

Under Title VII's discrimination (but not its retaliation) provisions, a "mixed motive" case can be maintained. That is, if an employer has several motivations for making an employment decision or adopting an employment practice, Title VII forbids practices that are partially motivated by discrimination against a protected group, not just those where discrimination is the sole motivation. [See 42

U.S.C. § 2000e-2(m)] In mid-2013, the Supreme Court ruled that mixed-motive cases are proper for discrimination based on personal characteristics (race, color, religion, sex, or national origin) but not for retaliation. [*University of Tex. Sw. Med. Ctr. v. Nassar*, 133 S. Ct. 2517 (2013)]

Using *Nassar*'s but-for causation standard, the First Circuit affirmed summary judgment for the employer in a sexual harassment/retaliatory termination case. Co-workers said that new employee Ponte had unusually serious problems settling into the job, and was not prepared for meetings. Ponte said that her supervisor sexually propositioned her on two occasions. She did not report this to the employer until much later, and even then, she merely said that she felt uncomfortable with the supervisor, not that sexual harassment had occurred. Her performance review was poor, reflecting lateness, poor communications, and failure to satisfy the regional sales plan. Ponte was fired in mid-2011. The First Circuit held that the *Nassar* test is that protected activity was the but-for cause of the adverse employment action; Nassar's vague complaints did not set out a but-for cause. Her performance problems began before the alleged harassment, and her supervisor was not the only person to criticize her work. The employer had a legitimate, nondiscriminatory reason to fire her. [*Ponte v. Steelcase Inc.*, 741 F.3d 310 (1st Cir. 2014)]

Under the Supreme Court's June 2003 decision [*Desert Palace, Inc. v. Costa*, 539 U.S. 90 (2003)], a Title VII plaintiff can obtain a mixed-motive jury instruction without necessarily showing direct evidence of discrimination, because the statute does not specifically require direct evidence. Therefore, the general rule of civil litigation—allowing proof by direct and/or circumstantial evidence—applies.

In response to *Smith v. City of Jackson*, 544 U.S. 228 (2005), the Supreme Court's ruling that ADEA disparate impact claims can be brought, but the employer is not liable if the disparate impact is the result of a reasonable factor other than age, the EEOC proposed new regulations, holding that an employment practice with disparate impact on older individuals violates the ADEA unless it is justified by an RFOA. The person challenging the practice has the burden of identifying the specific practice that creates the impact; citing a generalized policy is not sufficient. But once the RFOA exception is raised, it is an affirmative defense—that is, the employer must prove it. [73 Fed. Reg. 168087 (Mar. 31, 2008)] The Supreme Court agreed that RFOA is an affirmative defense: see *Meacham v. Knolls Atomic Power Labs*, 554 U.S. 84 (2008).

The Supreme Court pointed out that Title VII and the ADEA have different language and different requirements, deciding, in mid-2009, that mixed-motive ADEA cases require the plaintiff to prove, by a preponderance of the evidence, that age was the "but-for" cause of the unfavorable employment action: in other words, that the action would never have been taken but-for the plaintiff's being over 40. [*Gross v. FBL Fin. Servs., Inc.*, 557 U.S. 167 (2009)]

In a case brought by an African-American contract attorney, the Southern District of New York granted summary judgment for the law firm. The plaintiff's case relied on statistical evidence that black contract lawyers billed fewer hours than other full-time contract attorneys. The court held that individual private plaintiffs must prove that they were individually subjected to intentional discrimination. In this reading, pattern or practice evidence cannot be used outside the context of a class action, because it forces employers to prove that they did not discriminate, whereas it is up to the plaintiff to prove discrimination. [*Simmons-Grant v. Quinn Emanuel*, No. 1:11-cv-07706 (dismissed, S.D.N.Y.); see Christine Simmons, *Quinn Emanuel Wins Dismissal of Bias Suit*, N.Y.L.J. (Jan. 9, 2013) (law.com) See also *Chin v. Port Auth.*, 685 F.3d 135 (2d Cir. 2012) on pattern-or-practice claims.]

The District Court for the District of Massachusetts required arbitration of a gender bias case against CIGNA Healthcare. The plaintiff alleged that CIGNA's evaluation and promotion practices violated Title VII and Massachusetts anti-discrimination law and that her job was downgraded whereas similarly situated male co-workers received a higher classification. CIGNA argued that the charge had to be arbitrated; the plaintiff said that she had never waived the right to litigate class-based or pattern-or-practice claims. However, the court ruled that pattern-or-practice claims are a method of proving discrimination in a class action, not a separate cause of action. [*Karp v. CIGNA Healthcare Inc.*, 882 F. Supp. 2d 199 (D. Mass. 2012); see Sheri Qualters, *Judge Sends Gender Bias Case Against CIGNA To Arbitration*, Nat'l L.J. (Apr. 19, 2012) (law.com). The Second Circuit reached the same conclusion, compelling arbitration of claims by three Goldman Sachs executives who wanted to assert a pattern-or-practice claim in court: *Parisi v. Goldman, Sachs & Co.*, 710 F.3d 483 (2d Cir. 2013).]

§ 34.03 TITLE VII COVERAGE

Title VII bans "unlawful employment practices." Unlawful employment practices discriminate against an employee or job applicant on the basis of the individual's race, color, religion, sex, or national origin. [42 U.S.C. § 2000e-2(a)] Note that Title VII does not ban sexual-orientation discrimination, but some applicable state and local statutes do.

A July, 2014 Executive Order which applies to federal contractors (although not to employers who are not federal contractors) forbids job discrimination against gay, lesbian, bisexual, and transgender persons. [Peter Baker, *Obama Calls for a Ban on Job Bias Against Gays*, NYTimes.com (July 21, 2014)]

The Department of Labor's Office of Federal Contract Compliance Programs (OFCCP) adopted a directive, DIR-2014-02, effective August 19, 2014. It provides that discrimination on the basis of gender identity or transgender status by federal contractors is unlawful sex discrimination. Note, however, that OFCCP directives do not change laws or regulations, and do not create legally enforceable obligations. [DIR 2014-02, <http://www.dol.gov/ofccp/regs/compliance/directives/dir2014_02.html> (undated, last accessed Aug. 22, 2014)]

Maryland enacted the Fairness for All Marylanders Act, which forbids gender identity discrimination by any employer in Maryland, effective October 1, 2014. (The statute also forbids transgender-based discrimination in housing, public accommodations, and credit applications. [Meredith Campbell, *Maryland Workplace Transgender Bias Ban*, Shulman Rogers Gandal Pordy & Ecker PA (May 28, 2014), available at Lexology.com]

Unlawful employment practices on the part of the employer are defined by 42 U.S.C. § 2000e-2(a) as:

- To fail or refuse to hire;
- To discharge;
- To discriminate with respect to compensation, terms, conditions, or privileges of employment;
- To limit, segregate, or classify employees or job applicants in a way that deprives or tends to deprive them of employment opportunities, or otherwise adversely affects their status as employees.

Title VII also bans discriminatory practices by employment agencies and labor unions, but their activities are outside the scope of this book.

In late 1998, the Fourth Circuit joined the Third, Fifth, Seventh, Eighth, Tenth, Eleventh, and D.C. Circuits in ruling that only employer companies, and not individuals, can be held liable under Title VII. [*Lissau v. S. Food Serv.*, 159 F.3d 177 (4th Cir. 1998); see also *Fantini v. Salem State College*, 557 F.3d 22 (1st Cir. 2009)]

An important—and growing—part of the employment discrimination caseload is the "retaliation" case. Section 2000e-3(a) makes it unlawful for an employer to discriminate against anyone who has opposed an unlawful employment practice or who has "made a charge, testified, assisted, or participated in any manner in an investigation, proceeding, or hearing" under Title VII. [See § 34.08 for more about retaliation cases]

It is also an unlawful employment practice to indicate "any preference, limitation, specification, or discrimination" based on race, color, religion, sex, or national origin in a help-wanted ad, unless belonging to a particular group is a Bona Fide Occupational Qualification (BFOQ). [See 42 U.S.C. § 2000e-3(b)]

It might be a BFOQ to be male or female (e.g., because of authenticity, for an actor or actress; for privacy, for a restroom attendant); to be under 40 (in a job where public safety depends on youthful reactions) or even to belong to a particular religion (e.g., to work in a kosher slaughterhouse). Race is never a BFOQ.

In the disability context, it is a BFOQ not to pose a safety risk to oneself or others. Where safety or efficiency is involved, it may be possible to raise a "business necessity" defense for a discriminatory business practice.

In the twenty-first century, BFOQ cases are not very common. A July 2014 Ninth Circuit case is an interesting exception. The case was brought by male sheriff's deputies who alleged that they were discriminated against by not being allowed to supervise female prisoners. The county explained that the policy was adopted to deter sexual abuse of female inmates and protect privacy. The Ninth Circuit held that a BFOQ defense must be proved by a preponderance of the evidence, by showing that the qualification is reasonably necessary to the essence of the defendant's operations, and nearly all men are unqualified or it is impossible or highly impractical to test to see which men are qualified. The employer must show a high correlation between sex and the ability to perform job functions, and must show alternative approaches are not viable. The Ninth Circuit said that there are ways to prevent sexual abuse of prisoners other than by not hiring men. [*Anderson v. City & Cnty. of San Francisco*, No. 11-16746 (9th Cir. July 2, 2014); see Banu K. Ramachandran, *Ninth Circuit Rejects Bona Fide Occupational Qualification Defense for Sex Discrimination*, Barran Liebman LLP (July 9, 2014), available at Lexology.com]

§ 34.04 EXCEPTIONS TO TITLE VII COVERAGE

[A] Definition of Employer

Perhaps the most important exception is found in 42 U.S.C. § 2000e(b), which defines an "employer" as a natural person or business engaged in an industry affecting commerce—and having 15 or more employees for each work day in 20 or more weeks either in the year in question or the preceding calendar year. So a very small business will be exempt from Title VII. Possibly some businesses with even more than 15 employees will escape coverage because their business does not "affect commerce," but most businesses do sell or at least attempt to make interstate sales, so their business will be deemed to "affect commerce."

The 15-employee figure is calculated based on the number of people on the payroll, not the number of full-time employees. [*Walters v. Metro. Educ. Enters., Inc.*, 519 U.S. 202 (1997)]

Whether a company has 15 employees or not is a substantive element of the Title VII claim (in this case, a sexual harassment charge), not a jurisdictional prerequisite. The practical significance of this 2006 Supreme Court ruling is that the number of employees is an issue that can be waived if it is not raised on time, whereas questions of subject matter jurisdiction can be raised at any time. The Supreme Court decided that the 15-employee requirement is not jurisdictional because it is not found within the part of the Title VII statute that grants jurisdiction to the federal courts. [*Arbaugh v. Y&H Corp.*, 546 U.S. 500 (2006)]

Suit could be brought under Title VII against a U.S.-based parent corporation, even though it had only six employees, because its wholly owned Mexican subsidiary had at least 50 employees. Even though the Mexican employees would not be protected by Title VII, the Ninth Circuit ruled in 2002 that they should be included in the count. [*Kang v. U Lim Am. Inc.*, 296 F.3d 810 (9th Cir. 2002)]

As shown below, there is a "ministerial exception" to accommodate First Amendment freedom of religion (see § 34.07). Another exception is allowed under 42 U.S.C. § 2000e-2(e) if religion, sex, or national origin is a bona fide occupational qualification "reasonably necessary to the normal operation" of the business. Educational institutions sponsored by a religious organization (e.g., Notre Dame or Yeshiva University) or institutions "directed toward the propagation of a particular religion" are permitted to base hiring and other employment decisions on religion—parochial schools can, but do not have to, employ staffers of other religions.

According to the Seventh and Eighth Circuits, Congress took a valid action in 1972 when it abrogated sovereign immunity and made the states subject to Title VII, so Title VII disparate impact suits can be brought against a state employer. [*Nanda v. Board of Trustees of the Univ. of Ill.*, 303 F.3d 817 (7th Cir. 2002); *Okruhlik v. Univ. of Ark.*, 255 F.3d 615 (8th Cir. 2001)]

[B] Aliens

Section 2000e-1 provides that Title VII does not apply to the employment of "aliens." In August 1998, the Fourth Circuit reversed its earlier ruling. Now *Egbuna v. Time-Life Libraries, Inc.* [153 F.3d 184 (4th Cir. 1998)] holds that it is necessary to be a U.S. citizen or an alien holding a valid work visa, to be a "qualified" individual. So an alien who does not have legal worker status in the United States cannot make out a Title VII prima facie case.

Furthermore, an employer does not violate Title VII if it (or a corporation it controls) takes an action with respect to an employee in a foreign country that is necessary to avoid violating that country's law—even if the action would be barred by Title VII if it were taken in the United States. The factors in whether an employer controls a corporation include whether there is common management, ownership, or financial control, and whether the two organizations have related operations. See also § 23.11 on immigration and nationality issues in hiring.

42 U.S.C. § 1981 applies only to conduct within the United States, so this provision does not cover allegations of racial discrimination made by a non-U.S. citizen who was transferred to South African by his U.S. employer. However, he could use § 1981 to charge discrimination while he worked in the United States. [*Ofori-Tenkorang v. Am. Int'l Group Inc.*, 460 F.3d 296 (2d Cir. 2006)]

[C] National Security

42 U.S.C. § 2000e-2(g) enacts a national security exception. It does not violate Title VII to fire or refuse to hire someone who has not met, or no longer meets, security clearance requirements "in effect pursuant to or administered under any statute of the United States or any Executive order of the President."

Engineer Hossein Zeinali, who is of Iranian descent, sued Raytheon for terminating him after the Department of Defense denied him a security clearance. The district court dismissed the race/national origin discrimination charges, holding that the federal courts do not have jurisdiction over security clearance cases. The Ninth Circuit reversed and allowed Zeinali's suit to proceed, because he did not dispute the validity of the denial—only whether it was legitimate for Raytheon to require a security clearance. He produced evidence that non-Iranian engineers without security clearances were allowed to work, so he raised a triable issue about whether having a security clearance was a bona fide requirement for engineers. [*Zeinali v. Raytheon Co*, 636 F.3d 544 (9th Cir. 2011); see Rebecca Moore, *9th Circuit Revives Iranians Bias Lawsuit Against Raytheon*, plansponsor.com (Apr. 5, 2011)]

[D] Seniority Systems

Employers are permitted, under 42 U.S.C. § 2000e-2(h), to abide by "bona fide seniority or merit systems," or to base compensation on quantity or quality of production, or to pay different rates at different locations—even if the result is to provide different standards of compensation or different terms, conditions, or privileges of employment. However, employers are not allowed to impose such differences in treatment if they are "the result of an intention to discriminate" on the basis of race, color, religion, sex, or national origin.

Also see 42 U.S.C. § 2000e-5(e)(2), which says that the unlawful unemployment practice occurs, with respect to a seniority system that was adopted "for an intentionally discriminatory purpose," whether or not the purpose can be discerned from the face of the provision, either when the seniority system is adopted, when the potential plaintiff becomes subject to the seniority system, or when the seniority system is applied in a way that injures the potential plaintiff.

The Lilly Ledbetter Act, Pub. L. No. 111-2, was passed to reaffirm these statutory principles and to overturn a Supreme Court decision that restricted the time to file discrimination suits.

A 2009 Supreme Court decision [*AT&T Corp. v. Hulteen*, 556 U.S. 701 (2009)] holds that AT&T abided by the terms of a bona fide seniority system, and therefore was not guilty of sex discrimination even though the pensions of some female workers were reduced because, before the passage of the Pregnancy Discrimination Act (PDA), AT&T treated pregnancy leave less favorably than other forms of temporary disability leave. (Once the PDA took effect, AT&T changed its policies, so the question was the effect of past discrimination.)

Section 2000e-2(h) also allows employers to use validated pre-employment tests of ability, as long as testing is not designed, intended or used to discriminate. The subject of test scores is taken up again in 42 U.S.C. § 2000e-2(l), which states that it is an unlawful employment practice to adjust scores or use different cutoff scores in hiring or promotion tests, based on the race, color, religion, sex or national origin of the test taker.

Also in 2009, the Supreme Court ruled that a city should not have refused to certify a promotional test for firefighters. The city argued that, because certifying the test would make the city vulnerable to lawsuits from minority firefighters who scored poorly, the test should have been discarded. The Supreme Court, however, held that refusing to certify the promotion list discriminated against high-scoring firefighters (mostly white and Hispanic), so the employer should have relied on its properly validated test. [*Ricci v. DeStefano*, 557 U.S. 557 (2009). CNN reported that payouts to 20 firefighters (19 white, one Hispanic) finally began in 2011; the 20 received $2 million for back pay, attorneys' fees, and pension credits. See Rebecca Moore, *Award Finally Decided in Connecticut Firefighters Suit*, plansponsor.com (Aug. 3, 2011)]]

The following year, the Supreme Court heard another challenge to a firefighters' promotional exam, this time brought by black and Hispanic firefighters. The Supreme Court ruled that challenges to the test were not untimely, although they were brought a number of years after the original test—because, when an employer continues to use an employment practice with disparate impact on a protected group, each use of the practice (i.e., each time a class of firefighters is promoted based on the original test results) can be challenged. [*Lewis v. City of Chicago*, 559 U.S. 932 (2010)]

§ 34.05 RACIAL DISCRIMINATION

[A] Basic Protections

The first equal opportunity laws were bans on racial discrimination. The Civil Rights Act of 1866, enacted at 42 U.S.C. § 1981, was passed to give former slaves the same rights as "white citizens." There is no requirement of a minimum number of employees for a § 1981 suit, and the EEOC and state antidiscrimination procedures do not have to be invoked before bringing suit under this provision.

The Civil Rights Act of 1991 generally requires plaintiffs to proceed under § 1981 if they have claims of racial discrimination, before using Title VII. Compensatory and punitive damages are not available under Title VII for any plaintiff who can get such damages under § 1981.

There have been some major recent cases about race discrimination. The quest to have a completely race-neutral workplace is a difficult one, and claims have been raised both by majority and minority groups that their rights have been violated.

Elzie Fuller III, who is African-American, was a tool and die maker who was RIF'd by Edward B. Stimpson Co. (along with 85 other employees) in February 2009, after working there for about 39 years. About two months before the RIF, the company scheduled workers for layoff based on factors such as productivity, flexibility, attendance, and seniority. The company compiled a spreadsheet classifying employees by department, job classification, race, gender, age, and tenure—including the percentage of employees of each race selected for RIF. The company said that Fuller was selected for layoff because of his very poor attendance record. The District Court for the Southern District of Florida denied summary judgment for the employer because the spreadsheet showed that a reasonable jury could consider race a factor in RIF decisions. Fuller was one of the longest-tenured employees—which gave him many years to be late or miss work, so the attendance rationale might have been pretextual. [*Fuller v. Edward B. Stimpson Co., Inc.*, No. 11-61574-CIV, 2013 WL 4710863 (S.D. Fla. Aug. 30, 2013); see Kathryn J. Hinton, *Employer's Use Of Spreadsheet Categorizing Employees By Race Supports Plaintiff's Discrimination Claim*, Baker, Donelson, Bearman, Caldwell & Berkowitz PC (Sept. 12, 2013), available at Lexology.com]

In mid-2013, the Supreme Court used standards similar to those for sexual harassment cases (see § 35.02) in a case of racial harassment of an African-American employee. The Supreme Court held that the employer is strictly liable if harassment is committed by a supervisor and involves a tangible employment action (e.g., hiring, firing, reassignment) against the victim. If the harasser is a supervisor, but there is no tangible employment action, then the employer can assert an affirmative defense under *Faragher/Ellerth*: that the employer took reasonable care to prevent and correct harassment, but the plaintiff unreasonably failed to take advantage of this procedure. A supervisor is a person authorized to take tangible employment actions against the plaintiff. However, in this case, the harasser was a co-worker of the plaintiff's. In cases of co-worker harassment, the Supreme Court held that the employer is liable only if it was negligent in controlling working conditions. [*Vance v. Ball State Univ.*, 133 S. Ct. 2434 (2013); see Marcia Coyle, *Supreme Court Makes It Harder to Prove Job Bias Claims*, Nat'l L.J. (June 24, 2013) (law.com)]

Even a single racial slur by a supervisor in the presence of another supervisor can be severe enough to create a hostile work environment. [*Taylor v. Metzger*, 706 A.2d 685 (N.J. 1998), although a later case, *Jordan v. Alternative Res. Corp.*, 458 F.3d 332 (4th Cir. 2006), holds that a single racial slur uttered by a colleague (it was directed at a TV news report, not at the plaintiff) was not enough to create a hostile work environment. Therefore, the employee could not prove a retaliation case when his job was eliminated several months later: the incident was isolated and did not alter the terms and conditions of employment]

In 2014, the Fourth Circuit found that allegations that a co-worker twice used a racial slur during a confrontation (the plaintiff was fired a week after the incident) did not alter working conditions enough to create a hostile work environment. However, shortly thereafter, en banc rehearing of the case was granted. [*Boyer-Liberto v. Fountainebleau Corp.*, 752 F.3d 350 (4th Cir. 2014), *reh'g granted*, No. 13-1473 (July 1, 2014); see Kevin M. Ceglowski, *Hostile Work Environment Case Gets Additional Fourth Circuit Scrutiny*, Poyner Spruill LP (July 8, 2014), available at Lexology.com]

The Eighth Circuit found that there was a racially hostile work environment when white co-workers refused to work with the plaintiffs (who are black); there were many racist graffiti in the workplace that remained for months without being removed; rail cars were spray-painted with racist threats; and co-workers displayed Confederate flags and even swastikas. The plaintiffs complained, but management did not help them. The plaintiffs also alleged that white co-workers falsely accused them of safety violations that could have gotten them fired, and that they were disciplined for infractions that white workers were not punished for. [*Watson v. CEVA Logistics, Inc.*, 619 F.3d 936 (8th Cir. 2010)]

After Judges Carnes and Pryor decided that calling a black man "boy" could be racist, they were open to the possibility that bananas could be used for racial harassment, but had other questions about a racially hostile work environment case. Plaintiff Reginald Jones cited bananas being left in his truck as one instance of racial harassment; the site manager said that banana peels were probably garbage left by kids—but there were no banana peels or other garbage on any other driver's truck. Jones said that he had seen co-workers wearing Confederate insignia. UPS said that it responded promptly and appropriately and a manager urged Jones not to resign when he said he was considering it. The Northern District of Alabama granted summary judgment for the employer, denying that bananas had racial connotations and finding that the conditions were not severe and pervasive enough to create a hostile environment. The Eleventh Circuit vacated summary judgment and remanded the case, because a reasonable trier of facts could conclude that the work environment was racially hostile. [*Jones v. UPS Ground Freight*, 683 F.3d 1283 (11th Cir. 2012).

The Eighth Circuit dismissed the Title VII portion of a racial harassment claim, because the employer's racial slurs against several groups, amounting to about one outburst per month over a two-year period, were not severe or pervasive enough to create a hostile work environment. However, the § 1981 claim (termination as retaliation for objecting to the slurs) was permitted to go to trial. [*Bainbridge v. Loffredo Gardens Inc.*, 378 F.3d 756 (8th Cir. 2004)]

The often-cited case of *Herrnreiter v. Chicago Hous. Auth.* [315 F.3d 742 (7th Cir. 2002)] was brought by a white auditor who was transferred by his black supervisor from the agency's investigation division to its auditing division. The Seventh Circuit held that there was no actionable racial discrimination (even though the plaintiff preferred the investigator's job) because he was not demoted to an objectively inferior position or prevented from exercising his professional skills.

There have been a number of major settlements of racial discrimination and harassment cases (e.g., nooses or swastikas displayed in the workplace, hate graffiti, display of minority employees' names on a "hit list") and racially hostile work environments. Settlements usually included injunctions, training, posting of information about the settlement, and monitoring by the EEOC to prevent further offenses. In many of these cases, the employer denied wrongdoing, but stated that it wished to settle to avoid prolonged litigation.

- A suit on behalf of hundreds of African-American brokers, charging Merrill Lynch with systematic channeling of business to white brokers, settled in late 2013 after more than eight years. The district court denied class certification three times. The plaintiffs charged two policies with disparate impact on African-Americans: allowing brokers to choose their own teams and allocating the accounts of departed brokers based on past results. The plaintiffs charged that the voluntary teams excluded black brokers, reducing their compensation and access to new accounts. The Seventh Circuit held that the discretion permitted to managers led to class-wide discrimination. The practices complained of by the plaintiffs were held to be Merrill Lynch practices, not practices that local managers could choose to accept or reject. The Seventh Circuit certified a (b)(2) class for the limited purpose of deciding whether Merrill's practices violated federal law. [D. Lucetta Pope, *Distinguishing Dukes: How Decentralized Decision-Making Led To A $160 Million Agreement To Settle Race Discrimination Claims Against Merrill Lynch*, Faegre Baker Daniels (Dec. 23, 2013), available at Lexology.com]
- The City of New York agreed to settle a seven-year suit brought by the Vulcan Society and the DOJ about two Fire Department of New York (FDNY) entrance exams. The Vulcan Society filed an EEOC charge in 2002; the EEOC referred the case to the Department of Justice, which sued in May 2007. A monitor was appointed to draft a new exam, which was approved in October 2012. The settlement is $98 million in back pay and benefits. Approximately 1,500 candidates receive back pay, benefits, and interest, but plaintiffs who were not hired will not be hired as a result of the settlement. The FDNY agreed to implement changes in recruiting to increase diversity and make the department more representative of the NYC population. (The class now in the academy is 16% black and 27% Hispanic.) [Pervaiz Shallwani, *FDNY Discrimination Suit Settled for $98 Million*, WSJ.com (Mar. 18, 2014)]
- After 20 years, a Department of Labor ALJ ordered the Bank of America to pay about $2.2 million in back wages and interest to 1,147 black job

applicants to resolve charges of race discrimination in hiring tellers and entry-level clerical workers at the bank's Charlotte, North Carolina office between the 1990s and the early 2000s. The OFCCP found systemic hiring discrimination in 1993. About $1 million goes to a group of 1,034 applicants rejected in 1993, the rest to 113 people rejected between 2002 and 2005. Ten people must be offered jobs with appropriate seniority. [Julie Steinberg, *BofA Ordered to Pay About $2.2 Million for Alleged Hiring Bias*, WSJ.com (Sept. 23, 2013)]

Although it is generally thought of as a statute that forbids discrimination by employers, Title VII also forbids unions to commit discrimination. In a recent Seventh Circuit case, schoolteacher Robert Green, who is African-American, was fired. He asked the union to grieve on his behalf. The union refused and also refused to represent him in a suit under the state's teacher tenure law. Green brought the suit without union assistance, won the case, and was reinstated. Green alleged that the union represented comparable white employees, and that the union refused to help him in retaliation against his earlier opposition to discrimination. The union said that it would not help Green because of a previous suit against it. The district court granted summary judgment for the union, on the grounds that Green did not prove that the union owed him a duty of fair representation or breached the CBA. The Seventh Circuit vacated the holding, because Title VII forbids discrimination by labor unions, whether or not the union's action violated the CBA. The Seventh Circuit concluded that the district court improperly applied the standards for an FLSA hybrid action to a Title VII case. [*Green v. American Fed'n of Teachers*, 740 F.3d 1104 (7th Cir. 2014)]

[B] Reverse Discrimination

Although most discrimination suits are brought by members of protected groups charging that they were discriminated against by members of the dominant group, a reverse discrimination suit is brought by members of the dominant group charging that they were discriminated against for being, e.g., white, male, or non-disabled. This issue is intimately related to the question of when, if ever, affirmative action is appropriate: see § 34.05[C], below.

The city of New Haven, Connecticut, gave an examination for firefighters to be promoted to the jobs of lieutenant and captain. Far more white than minority firefighters passed the exam. The city, fearing that it would be sued by minority candidates, discarded the exam and did not promote anyone. The city was sued by white and Hispanic firefighters alleging that their superior test scores entitled them to promotion. The Supreme Court held that the city violated Title VII by refusing to certify the test and make promotions based on the test results, intentionally discriminating against the white and Hispanic firefighters without evidence that it would be liable if it did not make up for past disparate impact. If it had been sued by minority firefighters who charged a violation of Title VII, the Supreme Court said the city could have asserted the Title VII provision allowing valid, job-related tests. [*Ricci v. DeStefano*, 557 U.S. 557 (2009)]

The EEOC announced settlement of a sex discrimination suit against Pure Weight Loss ($16.8 million back pay, $3.15 million in punitive damages) brought by men who had been discriminated against since 1997. In 2002, the EEOC sued, charging discrimination against male job applicants and retaliation against a female employee who protested the discriminatory policy. However, because the company is in Chapter 7, the consent decree gives the EEOC a $20 million claim in the bankruptcy. [Rebecca Moore, *L.A. Weight Loss Settles Gender Discrimination Suit for $20M*, plansponsor.com (Dec. 8, 2008)]

[C] Affirmative Action and Quotas

A very important question in employment law is how to balance the rights of current employees and applicants against the desire to have a workplace that is truly representative and does not reflect past discrimination.

According to 42 U.S.C. § 2000e-2(j), Title VII does not require employers to grant preferential treatment to any individual or any group because the workforce is imbalanced in terms of the number or percentage of workers from groups that have been discriminated against in the past. In other words, employers do not have to use quotas in hiring, promotion, etc.

In 1977, the Supreme Court decided that it is unlawful to perpetuate the present effects of past discrimination, although bona fide seniority systems can be left in operation. [*Teamsters v. U.S.*, 431 U.S. 324 (1977)] Under this approach, preferential hiring of women and minorities might be acceptable to correct an imbalance in the workforce that results from past discrimination. It might also be acceptable to set goals to remove past discrimination and to remove the barriers that existed in the past to prevent racially neutral hiring, but the hiring system must not exclude white applicants.

Cases in the late 1990s say that employers should not set up affirmative action programs merely to enhance diversity within the workplace, but an affirmative action program might be an appropriate corrective measure if there is a history of racism in a particular industry. [*Johnson v. Transp. Agency of Santa Clara County*, 480 U.S. 616 (1987); *Eldredge v. Carpenters Joint Apprenticeship and Training Comm.*, 94 F.3d 1366 (9th Cir. 1996); *Schurr v. Resorts Int'l Hotel*, 196 F.3d 486 (3d Cir. 1999)]

The Supreme Court agreed to hear the case of *Piscataway Twp. Bd. of Educ. v. Taxman* [#96-679, *cert. dismissed*, 522 U.S. 1010 (1997)] involving the important issue of whether a well-qualified employee can be laid off to promote the goal of diversity in the workplace. However, the case was settled out of court in late November 1997, so the Supreme Court did not issue a decision.

[D] Rules for Federal Contractors

In the past two decades or so, affirmative action has been most prominent in the context of government contracts. In 1995, the U.S. Supreme Court decided that race-based preferences in government contracting are permissible only if the actual contractor has been the victim of discrimination—not merely that he or she belongs to a group that has historically been economically disadvantaged. [*Adarand Constructors Inc. v. Pena*, 513 U.S. 1108, and 515 U.S. 200 (1995)] The case continued to bounce up and down the court system with various decisions that had more to do with technical legal issues than with the rights and wrongs of affirmative action. The case was supposed to be reheard by the Supreme Court, but in November 2001, the Supreme Court dismissed certiorari as having been improvidently granted. [*Adarand Constructors v. Mineta*, 534 U.S. 103 (2001)]

Executive Order 11246 requires government contractors and contractors on federally assisted construction projects worth over $10,000 to have a policy of furthering equal employment opportunity. If the contractor or subcontractor has more than 50 employees, and the contract is worth over $50,000, the company must have a formal affirmative action program, which must be submitted to the Office of Federal Contract Compliance Programs (OFCCP) within 30 days of the OFCCP's request to see the program.

Contracts over $1 million require a pre-award audit of the affirmative action program. [See 41 C.F.R. Part 60] There are separate, slightly different, rules for construction contractors.

Compensation discrimination is one of the OFCCP's priorities. It settled with Medtronic, Inc. and Medtronic Interventional Vascular, Inc on allegations that Hispanic senior production associates were paid significantly less than their white counterparts. Seventy-eight Hispanic production workers recovered $290,000 in back wages plus interest. However, shortly before this settlement was announced, the OFCCP lost a case against VF Jeanswear; the ALJ held that it was improper to create a "non-Asian" category to compare with Asian workers. [Gretchen W. Ewalt, *OFCCP Settles Pay Discrimination Claims With Medical Products Manufacturer*, Ogletree Deakins (Sept. 25, 2013), available at Lexology.com]

A company charged with reverse discrimination because of its affirmative action program can cite as a defense that it followed the EEOC's Guidelines on Affirmative Action. To qualify for this defense, the employer must have a written plan. It must act reasonably, taking actions based on self-analysis that leads to a reasonable conclusion that there are actual problems of job bias that require correction. The plan of action must be tailored to eliminate inequality. It must last only as long as it takes to eliminate the effects of past discrimination.

The OFCCP adopted two new rules, effective March 24, 2014, which expand affirmative action requirements for veterans and Persons With Disabilities (PWDs). Federal contractors (with federal contracts and subcontractors over $100,000, for veterans; over $10,000 for PWDs) are required to gather and retain data about the results of their efforts to recruit and hire veterans and PWDs. Subcontractors are covered if their products are eventually sold to the federal government. Covered contractors must set numeric hiring targets: at least 8% of new hires should be veterans, at least 7% should be PWDs. Applicants must be invited to self-identify as veterans or PWDs before a job offer is extended, and the invitation must be repeated when a job offer is made. Recruitment and hiring data must be retained for at least three years. Contractors are required to undertake annual review to analyze the results of their good-faith efforts to hire PWDs and veterans. For companies with an annual affirmative action plan in place on March 24, 2014, the new obligations take effect with the new affirmative action plan year. [78 Fed. Reg. 58682 (Sept. 24, 2013); see Mike Underwood, *Major Changes To Affirmative Action Requirements Effective March 24, 2014*, Porter Wright Morris & Arthur LLP (Oct. 8, 2013), available at Lexology.com]

[E] National Origin Discrimination

Since the September 11 attack, there has been an increase in attention to the related problems of national origin discrimination against people of Middle Eastern and South Asian origin and religious discrimination against Muslims. As the EEOC points out, immigrants are now a substantial part of the workforce.

The EEOC responded to the increasing threat of national origin discrimination by issuing guidance on national origin discrimination. National origin discrimination is often intertwined with other types of discrimination: e.g., based on religion and/or having a native language other than English.

According to the guidance document [EEOC, *National Origin Discrimination*, <http://www.eeoc.gov/laws/types/nationalorigin.cfm> (undated, accessed Mar. 27, 2014); the EEOC also issued a new § 13, "National Origin Discrimination," as part of the agency's manual, <www.eeoc.gov/policy/docs/national-origin.html> replacing transmittals 622 on Citizenship, Residency Requirements, Aliens and Undocumented Workers, and 623, Speak-English-Only Rules and Other Language Policies], national origin discrimination means less-favorable treatment imposed because of someone's country of origin, ethnicity, or accent, or belief that someone has a particular ethnic background. Discrimination on the basis of marriage or other association with people of a disfavored nationality is also covered.

The EEOC position is that employers have a responsibility to prevent or at least correct ethnic slurs that create a hostile work environment. Employment decisions may be made on the basis of accent only if a person's accent materially interferes with job performance. Fluency in English can be imposed as a job requirement only if it is required to do the job; English-only rules are permissible only if they are adopted for nondiscriminatory reasons such as promoting the safe or efficient conduct of the business. The agency's stance is that all antidiscrimination laws apply whether or not the discriminatee is a citizen, although remedies are limited for those who do not have authorization to work in this country.

The EEOC settled an "English only" national origin discrimination case for $450,000 plus injunctive relief. Under 29 C.F.R. § 1606.7 (Guidelines on Discrimination Because of national Origin), the EEOC treats forbidding employees to speak their native language in the workplace as loss of employment opportunities because of national origin. The EEOC recognizes a business necessity defense for English-only rules in some circumstances: emergencies; communicating with customers, supervisor, or co-workers who only speak English; and when supervision requires giving instructions in English. [*EEOC v. Mesa Systems, Inc.*, No. 2:11-cv-01201 (D. Utah 2013); see Hunton & Williams LLP, *Speak Your Mind: English-Only Policies Remain Hot Button Issue* (Nov. 20, 2013), available at Lexology.com]

The EEOC has discussed harassment and discrimination against Asians. [EEOC, *Questions and Answers About Employer Responsibilities Concerning the Employment of Muslims, Arabs, South Asians, and Sikhs* (July 16, 2002) <http://www.eeoc.gov/facts/backlash-employer.html> (modified Mar. 21, 2005, available at the EEOC site on Mar. 27, 2014)] The agency position is that it is impermissible to deny employment (e.g., to people who wear turbans, headscarves, or other religious dress) even if the employer believes that customers will be hostile to such workers. A manager or supervisor who learns about ethnic slurs or harassment in the workplace should tell the harassers to stop doing this, and discipline anyone who is found to have committed harassment. If employees ask for the use of space for prayer, the employer can turn down the request only if the space is legitimately required for business needs. (Employers have a duty of reasonable accommodation to religious practice, whereas they merely need to avoid discrimination on the basis of national origin.) Nor can background checks be made more stringent based on an applicant's country of origin.

The relevant factors in determining whether national origin harassment has occurred include whether physical threats were made or workers were intimidated; whether the conduct was hostile and patently offensive; the frequency of the conduct; the context in which it occurred; and whether management acted appropriately after learning of the conduct.

The Supreme Court denied *certiorari* in a First Circuit case brought by an Afghan Muslim immigrant who charged that he was fired for discriminatory reasons, and that he suffered a hostile work environment after 9/11. The jury found that harassment occurred, but the First Circuit denied damages for lack of proof of lost wages or out of pocket payments for medical treatment or therapy. Therefore, the plaintiff's contention, that the jury should have been instructed on the option of awarding punitive damages in the absence of compensatory damages, was not reviewed by the Supreme Court. [*Azimi v. Jordan's Meats, cert. denied*, 549 U.S. 1279 (2007); see Adrien Martin, *Supreme Court Rejects Discrimination Case by Muslim Immigrant*, plansponsor.com (Mar. 19, 2007)]

The Ninth Circuit ruled that a CEO's insistence on calling an employee "Manny" or "Hank" rather than his Arabic name, Mamdouh el-Hakem, constituted intentional hostile work environment discrimination forbidden by 42 U.S.C. § 1981, even in the absence of racial epithets. [*El-Hakem v. BJY Inc.*, 415 F.3d 1068 (9th Cir. 2005)]

The Tenth Circuit permitted Hispanic employees who said that an English-only policy caused them to be taunted by native English speakers to maintain hostile environment discriminatory impact claims. In the court's view, the employer anticipated that this would happen and had no justification for imposing the policy. [*Maldonado v. Altus*, 433 F.3d 1294 (10th Cir. 2006)]

The Sixth Circuit reversed summary judgment for the employer in a case alleging denial of promotion because of speech characteristics and accent. (EEOC regulations say that denial of opportunity on linguistic grounds can be evidence of national origin discrimination.) The plaintiff filed suit as a race discrimination claim, but the Sixth Circuit re-characterized it as a national origin claim. Evidence that managers treated the plaintiff's accent as a bar to promotion was considered direct evidence of discrimination—so the case was remanded to permit the employer to show it would have made the same decision absent discrimination. [*In re Rodriguez*, 487 F.3d 1001 (6th Cir. 2007) However, the Southern District of New York reached the opposite conclusion in *Altman v. New York City Dept. of Educ.*, No. 06 CV 6319, 2007 WL 1290599 (S.D.N.Y. May 1, 2007), where remarks about accent were not facially discriminatory because English fluency was legitimately related to job performance in the job of teaching English as a second language.]

[F] EEOC 2006 Guidance

In April 2006, the EEOC revised § 15 of its compliance manual with respect to race and color discrimination. Studies show that racial prejudice persists in hiring—for example, white people with criminal records were three times as likely to be offered employment as black people with similar records, temporary agencies preferred white to black applicants, and interviews were 50% more likely to be given based on the same resume if it showed a "white" rather than a "black" surname. [In *El-Hakem v. BJY, Inc.*, 415 F.3d 1068, 1073 (9th Cir. 2005), the Ninth Circuit held that names are often a proxy for race and ethnicity.]

Title VII does not define "race," and neither does the EEOC; federal race/ethnicity data is collected using the OMB's categories (American Indian/Alaska native; Asian; Black (African-American); Native Hawaiian or Other Pacific Islander; and White, plus the ethnic category of Hispanic/Latino). This guidance says that Title VII generally covers:

- Racial or ethnic ancestry; the EEOC notes that race and national origin can overlap, but are not the same thing;

- Perceived race, even if the perception is incorrect;
- Association with someone of a particular race;
- Subgroup or "race plus," e.g., treating black women who have pre-school children worse than white women with pre-school children;
- Physical characteristics associated with race, such as skin color, hair, facial features, height and weight;
- Race-linked illnesses (for example, sickle cell anemia and diabetes). An employer who applies facially neutral standards that exclude the treatment of conditions for which certain ethnic groups are disproportionately at risk must show that the standards are based on generally accepted medical criteria;
- Cultural characteristics related to ethnicity, such as name, dress and grooming practices, accent or manner of speech;
- Reverse discrimination. The EEOC does not require a heightened standard of proof when Caucasian employees raise reverse-discrimination claims, but the ultimate burden of persuasion always rests with the plaintiff.

The EEOC notes that color discrimination can be intra-racial, for example, a black manager's favoring lighter-skinned black subordinates over darker-skinned subordinates.

A complaint can involve any combination of race, color, and national origin; EEOC policy is for complaints to list all allegations that can reasonably be made. Discrimination is also forbidden if it is based on the intersection of two or more protected categories (e.g., Latinos with a disability).

The EEOC's position is that disparate impact analysis applies to all objective or subjective criteria for recruitment, hiring, promotion, or layoff, as well as grooming standards and education requirements. Proof of a disparate impact case begins with a statistical showing that the policy or practice causes significant disparate impact to a protected group. Then the employer has the burden of showing the practice is job-related and consistent with business necessity. Finally, the burden shifts to whether the person challenging the policy or practice can show a less discriminatory alternative method for satisfying the business need.

In assessing arrest records, the employer must evaluate not only the relationship between the charge and the job, but whether or not the arrested person was actually guilty. For conviction records, the employer must consider the nature and gravity of the offense(s); the length of time elapsed since the conviction or completion of the sentence; and the nature of the job. The EEOC considers a blanket refusal to hire anyone who has ever had a conviction of any kind to be inappropriate because it is not job-related or consistent with business necessity. For the EEOC's most recent statement of these principles, see EEOC Enforcement

Guidance, *Consideration of Arrest and Conviction Records In Employment Decisions Under Title VII of the Civil Rights Act of 1964* <http://www.eeoc.gov/laws/guidance/arrest_conviction.cfm> (Apr. 25, 2012)]

The EEOC says that appearance and grooming standards must be neutral, consistently applied, and adopted for nondiscriminatory reasons. Racial or ethnic attire that conforms to the dress code must be allowed. Employers can require hairstyles that are neat, clean and well-groomed, as long as racial differences in hair texture are respected, and the standards are equally applied. The EEOC's basic position is that employers may have to make exception to their "usual rules or preferences" to accommodate religious clothing (e.g., head coverings), avoidance of some clothing items (e.g., some denominations forbid women to wear pants), and grooming practices (e.g., wearing a full beard; dreadlocks or side curls). [EEOC, *Religious Garb and Grooming in the Workplace: Rights and Responsibilities*, <http://www.eeoc.gov/eeoc/publications/qa_religious_garb_grooming.cfm> (Aug. 21, 2014)]

EEOC guidance says that Title VII allows diversity outreach. Affirmative action is action to overcome past or present barriers to equal employment opportunity, and can be court-ordered after a discrimination finding, negotiated as a remedy in a consent decree or settlement agreement, or created pursuant to government regulation. Voluntary affirmative action plans are permitted, for example, to eliminate a manifest imbalance in a job category that has traditionally been segregated. Courts ruling on a voluntary affirmative action plan look at whether it involves a quota or inflexible goal; whether the plan is flexible enough to make each candidate compete against all other qualified candidate; if the plan is unnecessarily harmful to interests of third parties, and whether the plan is temporary and will end when the goal has been met.

Race-based conduct by a supervisor, co-worker, or non-employee who is nevertheless under the employer's control (for example, a customer or business partner) can constitute unlawful harassment if unwelcome and severe or pervasive enough to alter terms and conditions of employment as viewed by a reasonable person in the victim's position. The more severe, the less pervasive it has to be, and vice versa, so a single incident would create an abusive environment only if very severe (e.g., physical).

Employers are generally liable for the acts of supervisors. However, in hostile environment cases when there was no tangible action against the victim, the employer can raise the affirmative defense that it used reasonable care to prevent harassing behavior, or that any harassment was promptly corrected—but the employee unreasonably failed to make use of these procedures. If the harasser is high enough in rank to serve as proxy for the employer (e.g., if the harasser is an owner, president, partner, or corporate officer) then the affirmative defense is not available even for a hostile environment claim. For harassment committed by co-workers or customers on the employer's premises, the employer is liable if it knew or should have known about the conduct and did not take prompt corrective steps. [See <http://www.eeoc.gov/policy/docs/race-color.html> (last revised Feb.

8, 2011). See also Section 13: *National Origin Discrimination* (2002), posted to <http://www.eeoc.gov/policy/docs/national-origin.html>, and *Guidelines on Discrimination Because of National Origin*, at 29 C.F.R. § 1606.1.

[G] Association Discrimination

"Association discrimination" is the claim that persons of one group were subjected to workplace discrimination because of their association with persons of another group.

Early in 2011, the Supreme Court held that Title VII forbids retaliation against a discrimination complainant that takes the form of punishing an associate of that person. In this case, Miriam Regalado filed an EEOC sex discrimination charge against North American Stainless in 2002. Three weeks after the charge was filed, Regalado's then-fiance (they subsequently married) was fired. The Supreme Court's majority opinion says that the Title VII anti-retaliation provision covers any action by an employer that would prevent a reasonable worker from making or pursuing a discrimination charge. There are no hard and fast lines, but firing a close family member is almost always covered by Title VII, a mild reprisal against an acquaintance is not covered, and courts must decide the intermediate cases. A suit can be brought by anyone within the "zone of interests" protected by the law. [*Thompson v. North Am. Stainless*, 131 S. Ct. 863 (2011); see Marcia Coyle, *Court Says Third Parties Can Sue in Retaliation Cases* (Dec. 7, 2010) (law.com)]

The Second Circuit allowed such a case to proceed, holding that Title VII can be violated by firing a white man for associating with a person of another race (in this case, his black wife). Taking adverse action because of an interracial relationship reflects discrimination because it embodies stereotypes about how white people should behave. [*Holcomb v. Iona College*, 521 F.3d 130 (2d Cir. 2008)

On a case brought by a white man who charged that he was fired because he lived with, became engaged to, and eventually married a black woman, the Second Circuit held that engagement to marry is intimate association protected by the First Amendment. (The employer said that he was fired for misconduct including blocking a security camera.) However, the Second Circuit reversed the finding of liability under 42 U.S.C. § 1983 against the individual defendants. It also reversed an award of punitive damages because the First Amendment right of intimate association was not clearly established law at the time of the events. [*Matusick v. Erie Cnty. Water Auth.*, 739 F.3d 51 (2d Cir. 2014); see Mark Hamblett, *Circuit Sees 'Intimate Association' Right in Engagement*, N.Y.L.J. (Jan. 7, 2014), available at law.com]

Thompson opened up a new category of retaliation-by-association suits. *Thompson* creates a zone of interests test for who can sue for retaliation. The Supreme Court did not give hard and fast rules, but suggested a sliding scale: firing a close family member is almost certainly a sustainable claim, whereas a lesser degree of action against an acquaintance almost certainly will not be. Courts have at least been willing to consider cases involving close friends. However, a mid-2013 case, involving alleged retaliation against a co-worker of a district manager who charged the company with discrimination, found that the relationship was not close enough to support an association claim. The co-workers were neighbors and occasionally socialized, but only rarely. A 2012 case refuses to extend the zone of interest to a business entity that allegedly lost a contract with the defendant employer because of its association with a sexual harassment plaintiff, on the grounds that such an extension was not contemplated by *Thompson.* [*Williams v. Daiichi Sankyo*, 947 F. Supp. 2d 1234 (N.D. Ala. 2013); *Crawford v. George & Lynch*, No. 10-949-GMS-SRF, 2012 U.S. Dist. LEXIS 93106 (D. Del. July 5, 2012). See Jack Kiley and Shira Forman, *Recent Decisions Clarify Scope of Third-Party Retaliation Doctrine*, N.Y.L.J. (Oct. 21, 2013), available at law.com]

§ 34.06 SEX DISCRIMINATION

[A] Generally

Discrimination on account of sex is unlawful, except if there is a gender-based (bona fide occupational qualification) BFOQ. The Sixth Circuit held that being female is a BFOQ for working as a correctional officer in a women's prison. [*Everson v. Mich. Dep't of Corrs.*, 391 F.3d 737 (6th Cir. 2004)] In 1983, the Supreme Court decided that it constitutes sex discrimination for a health plan to provide less comprehensive benefits to male employees and their wives than to female employees and their husbands. [*Newport News Shipbuilding v. EEOC*, 462 U.S. 669 (1983)] Note, however, that in mid-2009, the Supreme Court ruled that AT&T did not commit sex discrimination by failing to adapt its pension plan to correct pre-Pregnancy Discrimination Act discrimination in treatment of pregnancy leave. [*AT&T Corp. v. Hulteen*, 556 U.S. 701 (2009)]

Shortly before the trial scheduled for October 23, 2013, Booz Allen Hamilton Inc. settled (on confidential terms) a gender discrimination case brought by ex-partner Molly Finn. Two other gender discrimination suits, one by an ex-partner and another by a one-time staff lawyer, remained pending in the District of Columbia Superior Court, charging that women were forced out before they could attain top leadership positions. Finn was fired in September 2010, when she was the highest-ranking female partner. [Zoe Tillman, *Booz Allen Settles Gender Discrimination Lawsuit*, The BLT: The Blog of Legal Times (Oct. 29, 2013), available at law.com]

Karla Gerner said that the county, her employer, offered her a less favorable severance package than comparable male employees. The district court dismissed, holding that there had been no adverse employment action because severance benefits could only create adverse employment action if there was a contract violation and, in any event, severance benefits are paid after termination and after the employment relationship is over. The Fourth Circuit reversed. Any benefit—even one that the employer is not legally obligated to provide—might be discriminatory. Gerner testified that she was fired only after rejecting the discriminatory severance package, so she was an employee at that time. [*Gerner v. County of Chesterfield*, 674 F.3d 264 (4th Cir. 2012). *Hishon v. King & Spalding*, 469 U.S. 69 (1984) stands for the proposition that discrimination must be avoided in all benefits in the employment relationship.]

A female employee received good reviews and a bonus at the end of 2007. In September 2008, she complained to a company executive about sex discrimination, stating that male peers were paid more. Three weeks later, she was fired for leaving work early. The employer's position statement in response to her EEOC complaint said she was terminated because the business had changed and her skill set was no longer required; the employer pointed out that a man was fired at about the same time. The employer also said that Kwan made multiple serious errors and did not work long enough hours. During discovery, the employer changed its explanation to Kwan's poor performance and behavior, attributing the man's firing to the changing business model. In motion practice and litigation, the employer cited three specific incidents of poor performance—only one of which was mentioned in the EEOC position statement. The district court granted summary judgment for the employer but the Second Circuit reversed, finding that the inconsistency between the EEOC position statement and the later explanations for Kwan's termination and the three-week span between her complaint of sex discrimination and her termination would permit a jury to find for the plaintiff. [*Kwan v. Andalex Group, LLC*, 737 F.3d 834 (2d Cir. 2013); see Michael A. Sands and Sheeva J. Ghassemi-Vanni, *EEOC Position Statement Comes Back To Bite Employer In Civil Lawsuit*, Fenwick & West LLP (Jan. 14, 2014), available at Lexology.com]

On a showing of enough circumstantial evidence that women suffer more bullying and harassment than men, female employees can maintain a Title VII gender-based discrimination action, even if the harassment takes the form of shouting, screaming, foul language, and invading employees' personal space rather than a direct solicitation of sexual activity. [*EEOC v. Nat'l Educ. Ass'n Alaska*, 422 F.3d 840 (9th Cir. 2005); the Eleventh Circuit reached a similar conclusion in 2009, and affirmed that holding en banc in 2010: *Reeves v. C.H. Robinson*, 569 F.3d 1290 (11th Cir. 2009), *aff'd en banc*, 594 F.3d 798 (2010); see Alyson M. Palmer, *11th Circuit:* "Sex Specific" *Profanity Could Win Harassment Case*, Fulton County Daily Report (Jan. 22, 2010) (law.com) and *In Code and in Specifics, Judges Debate Lewd Office Talk*, Fulton County Daily Report (Oct. 7, 2009) (law.com)]

The Seventh Circuit upheld the termination of a man (the only male respiratory therapist out of seven) who was fired for accessing hacking sites and pornography on the office computer system. The plaintiff alleged that, as the only male, he was targeted for investigation when inappropriate sites were accessed.

The Seventh Circuit held that it was reasonable to suspect him because he was logged on to the computer when the inappropriate sites were accessed, and he even admitted accessing 17 of the 31 sites. (He denied going to the hacking sites, and said malware must have gotten loaded onto his computer accidentally.) He did not show that women were allowed to violate the hospital's acceptable computer use policy with impunity. [*Farr v. St. Francis Hosp. & Health Ctr.*, 570 F.3d 829 (7th Cir. 2009)]

It violates the Fourteenth Amendment's guarantee of Equal Protection to apply a facially neutral state law in a way that reflects sexual stereotyping. Therefore, a male state trooper should have been granted a 30-day parental leave when his child was born. (Leave was denied on the basis that only women can be primary caregivers for infants.) However, *Knussman v. Md.* [272 F.3d 625 (4th Cir. 2001)] holds that an award of $375,000 in emotional distress damages was disproportionate to the actual damages that the trooper suffered.

According to the Sixth Circuit, a company's anti-nepotism policy (requiring one spouse to resign when two employees marry) was rational. However, firing someone for criticizing the policy could be a violation of the employee's right of freedom of thought. In *Vaughn v. Lawrenceburg Power Sys.* [269 F.3d 703 (6th Cir. 2001)], the bride agreed to resign, then the groom was fired for agreeing with the statement, "I take it you do not fully agree with our policy." The Sixth Circuit said that antinepotism rules get heightened scrutiny under the First Amendment right of freedom of association if, but only if, they place a direct and substantial burden on the right to marry. [See also *Montgomery v. Carr*, 101 F.3d 1117 (6th Cir. 1996)]

In 2010, the Ninth Circuit certified the largest employment discrimination class ever, including over a million plaintiffs. A class of women charging Wal-Mart with sex discrimination was initially certified in 2004. Extensive litigation ensued about the composition of the class. The Ninth Circuit certified one of the larger classes, but a smaller class was remanded for further analysis.

In mid-2011, however, the Supreme Court issued a ruling that will make it far more difficult for employees of large companies to bring class action discrimination suits. The Supreme Court held that the would-be class members failed to prove that there was a common, company-wide policy of discrimination. In the Supreme Court view, although the plaintiffs alleged that the Wal-Mart corporate culture discriminated against women, the official policy of the chain was to give local managers significant discretion. The Supreme Court's majority opinion said that the plaintiffs complained of millions of employment decisions, not a single employment decision that could properly be addressed in a class action. The Supreme Court also criticized the demand for back pay, and ruled that Wal-Mart was entitled to individual determinations of back pay eligibility for class members, rather than extrapolation from a sample of employees. Some commentators suggested that companies could protect themselves against class actions by delegating to managers. [*Wal-Mart Stores Inc. v. Dukes*, 131 S. Ct. 2541 (2011); see Tony Mauro, *Supreme Court Erects Major Barriers to Class Actions in Wal-Mart*

Ruling, Nat'l L.J. (June 20, 2011) (law.com); Brian Zabcik, *In-House and Labor Lawyers Respond to the Supreme Court's Wal-Mart Decision*, Corporate Counsel (June 22, 2011) (law.com)]

After the Supreme Court ruling, the plaintiffs re-filed a narrower suit, with over 90,000 plaintiffs, against Wal-Mart in the Central District of California, limited to California stores; it is expected that there will be many other suits in other places, rather than another attempt to launch a nation-wide suit. [Andrew Martin, *Women File New Class-Action Bias Case Against Wal-Mart,* NYTimes.com (Oct. 27, 2011)]

Seyfarth Shaw's Annual Workplace Class Action Litigation Report, published January 14, 2013, showed that *Dukes* had a major effect on private class actions. The top 10 employment discrimination class action settlements of 2012 aggregated approximately $49 million. This was the lowest figure since 2006, and far below the pre-*Dukes* 2010 total of $346 million. Employers have become much tougher during settlement litigations. The EEOC reacted by increasing its focus on systemic investigations. [Shannon Green, *Workplace Class Action Litigation Report Outlines a Post-Dukes World*, Corporate Counsel (Jan. 14, 2013) (law.com)]

Although a class was certified about alleged sex discrimination in Costco's promotion practices and corporate culture, after *Dukes* was decided, the Ninth Circuit overturned the certification of the class. The Ninth Circuit said that the district court should have considered if the claims for monetary relief require individual determination. If so, a Rule 23(b)(3) class action is required, and a (b)(2) class action is inappropriate. [*Ellis v. Costco Wholesale Corp.*, 657 F.3d 970 (9th Cir. 2011) On remand, however, the district court once again certified a class of 700 women alleging denial of promotion opportunity to assistant manager and general manager positions. The defendant said that each of the named plaintiffs was denied promotion for personal reasons. However, the district court said that concerns about personal and family needs are universal, not specific to each plaintiff, so any defense based on personal or family circumstances is best handled by class treatment. [*Ellis v. Costco*, 285 F.R.D. 492, 96 Empl. Prac. Dec. (CCH) P44,630 (N.D. Cal. 2012)]

Female store managers at Family Dollar persuaded the Fourth Circuit that their case is not controlled by *Dukes* because there were nationwide policies for salary structures, and high-level management discretion follows common patterns that favor men. But they were merely allowed to amend their complaint, and may not succeed in obtaining nationwide class status. [*Scott v. Family Dollar Stores, Inc.*, 733 F.3d 105 (4th Cir. 2013); see Andrew W. Volin, *Avoiding Dukes*, Sherman & Howard LLC (Oct. 22, 2013), available at Lexology.com; Gregory V. Mersol, *Fourth Circuit Argues With Itself Over Dukes' Application*, Baker & Hostetler LLP (Oct. 24, 2013), available at Lexology.com]

A major sex discrimination suit involving about 44,000 female employees of the largest retail specialty jeweler in the United States was dismissed because the EEOC failed to prove that it undertook a nationwide investigation before bringing charges and for attempting to introduce evidence that was not provided during discovery. The suit began about nine years ago with 19 women in eight states, including New York, filing EEOC charges concerning the denial of equal pay and promotion opportunities. The EEOC's Buffalo office investigated and the EEOC sued in 2008, alleging unlawful employment practices nationwide. The defendant moved for summary judgment, saying that there could not be nationwide allegations without a nationwide investigation; the magistrate judge agreed, stating that the EEOC had the burden of proving that it satisfied all conditions for filing a claim, including a full investigation. [*EEOC v. Sterling Jewelers*, No. 09-cv-00706 (W.D.N.Y., dismissed 2014); see John Caher, *Judge Faults EEOC for Probe Into Discrimination Claim*, N.Y.L.J. (Mar. 13, 2014), available at law.com]

In May 2010, a jury in the Southern District of New York found pharmaceutical company Novartis systematically discriminated against a class of 5,600 female sales representatives in terms of pay and promotion, and also practiced pregnancy discrimination. In July 2010, Novartis agreed to settle the case for a payment of $152.5 million (including about $60 million in back pay) to be paid to the plaintiff class, plus $22.5 million that Novartis agreed to spend on programs to avoid discrimination in the future. The settlement replaces both the compensatory and punitive damage awards, and Novartis agreed not to appeal. The settlement, one of the largest ever achieved in an employment class action, received final approval by the Southern District of New York on November 30, 2010. [*Velez et al. v. Novartis Corp.*, No. 04-09194 (S.D.N.Y. 2010); see Gerald L. Maatman, Jr. and Scott Velasquez, Seyfarth Shaw, *Record Gender Discrimination Class Action Settlement and Fee Award Given Final Approval*, <http://www.workplaceclassaction.com/settlement-issues/record-gender-discrimination-class-action-settlement-and-fee-award-given-final-approval> (Nov. 30, 2010)]

EEOC Enforcement Guidance published in May 2007 stresses that, although the EEOC does not consider being a caregiver for family members to be a separate new protected category, sometimes discrimination on the basis of care-giving will violate existing protection under Title VII and/or the Americans With Disabilities Act. The EEOC says that it may take enforcement steps when a caregiver (male or female) is subjected to stereotyping in hiring or in the work environment. [EEOC Enforcement Guidance: *Unlawful Disparate Treatment of Workers With Caregiving Responsibilities* Number 915.002, <http://www.eeoc.gov/policy/docs/caregiving.html> (updated Feb. 8, 2011, accessed Mar. 27, 2014). In April 2009, the EEOC published additional guidance on this topic at <http://www.eeoc.gov/policy/docs/caregiver-best-practices.html> (Jan. 19, 2011, accessed Mar. 27, 2014); see § 28.01[C].]

[B] The Pregnancy Discrimination Act (PDA)

Section 2000e contains vital definitions for understanding federal antidiscrimination law. Sex discrimination includes, but is not limited to, discrimination "because or on the basis of pregnancy, childbirth, or related medical conditions." [42 U.S.C. § 2000e(k)]

This part of Title VII is referred to as the Pregnancy Discrimination Act (PDA). Under the PDA, women "affected by pregnancy, childbirth, or related medical conditions" have to be treated the same way as "other persons" who are not affected by such conditions, but who are comparable in their ability or inability to work. In other words, the PDA does not treat pregnancy itself as a disability, but to the extent that a particular pregnant worker does encounter disability, the employer must treat it the same way as other non-occupationally related disability.

The PDA requires equal treatment for "all employment-related purposes," including fringe benefits—a category that includes the all-important health benefits. However, employers do not have to provide health coverage if they would not otherwise. Employers have the discretion to provide abortion benefits, and are required to cover medical complications of abortion, but do not have to cover elective abortions, only abortions in situations where the mother's life would be endangered by carrying the fetus to term.

The National Women's Law Center reported that the number of EEOC charges filed by pregnant women rose almost 50% in the past decade. Claims are usually based on denial of reasonable accommodation such as light duty, leave, or rest and bathroom breaks. Pregnancy discrimination is a focus of the EEOC's current (2013–2016) Strategic Enforcement Plan. In 2012, the EEOC recovered more than $14 million in pregnancy discrimination settlements. Nine states (Alaska, California, Connecticut, Hawaii, Illinois, Louisiana, Maryland, New Jersey, and Texas) and several cities (such as New York City and Philadelphia) have laws requiring reasonable accommodation of pregnancy. [S. Jeanine Conley and Laura Scully, *Pregnant Employees Become The Subject Of Heightened Attention And New Legislation*, Baker & Hostetler LLP (Feb. 18, 2014), available at Lexology.com]

Maryland's Reasonable Accommodation for Disabilities Due to Pregnancy Law took effect October 1, 2013. Under the federal PDA, most courts require a pregnancy-related temporary inability to perform job duties to be treated equally with similarly situated employees temporarily disabled for other reasons, but there is no special obligation to offer additional accommodations to pregnancy-related disability. Now that the ADAAA is in effect, medical impairments caused by pregnancy (e.g., gestational diabetes) might require reasonable accommodation. The Maryland law requires companies with 15 or more employees to accommodate disability caused or contributed by pregnancy, unless accommodation imposes undue hardship on the employer. Possible accommodations include changes in job duties or work hours, relocating the work area, providing mechanical aids, or transfer to a safer or less strenuous position. If there is a light duty policy, or a light duty CBA requirement, it must be provided for pregnancy on parity with other disabilities. However, the employer is not required to create new jobs, fire someone else, transfer a more senior employee, or promote a pregnant employee to a job she is not qualified for. [Richard J. Hafets, Lynn A. Clements, and Donna M. Glover, *Maryland Employers To Provide Pregnant Workers With Accommodation Under New Law*, Jackson Lewis LLP (Sept. 24, 2013), available at Lexology.com; Anne E. DeSalvo, *New Maryland Law Requiring Accommodations for Pregnant Employees Becomes Effective October 1, 2013*, Saul Ewing LLP (September 2013) (benefitslink.com)]

The New York City Human Rights Law has been amended, effective January 30, 2014. Employers with four or more employees must provide reasonable accommodation to pregnant workers or workers who have given birth. They are entitled to reasonable accommodations to enable them to perform the essential functions of the job, unless accommodation would impose undue hardship on the employer. [Patricia J. Hill, Matthew W. Clarke, and Jeffrey P. Watson, *New York City Employers Required To Provide Reasonable Accommodations To Pregnant Employees*, Smith Gambrell & Russell LLP (Oct. 14, 2013), available at Lexology.com]

As a threshold question, to succeed, the plaintiff must be a common-law employee, not an independent contractor. [See, e.g., *Alberty-Velez v. Corporacion de Puerto Rico Para La Difusion Publica*, 242 F.3d 418 (1st Cir. 2003). The Ninth Circuit ruled in mid-2010 that insurance agents who sell financial products such as annuities are independent contractors for Title VII purposes (and for ERISA and ADEA purposes). The plaintiff in this case decided when and where to work, maintained an office for which she paid rent, scheduled her own time off; did not receive pay for vacations or sick days; was entirely paid on a commission basis; had the right to sell products other than those sold by the alleged employer; and paid taxes as a self-employed person. [*Murray v. Principal Fin. Group, Inc.*, 613 F.3d 943 (9th Cir. 2010)]

The Eighth Circuit rejected a pregnancy discrimination suit brought by a doctor whose contract to provide emergency medical services at a hospital was terminated. The court found that the doctor worked as an independent contractor, not an employee: she decided which shifts to work and which patients to see, did not receive employee benefits, and paid her own license fees and employment taxes. Her contract, which was terminable by either party at any time, was labeled "Independent Contractor Physician Service Agreement." Therefore, as a non-employee, she was not protected by Title VII. [*Glascock v. Linn Cnty. Emergency Medicine PC*, 698 F.3d 695 (8th Cir. 2012)]

On May 18, 2009, The Supreme Court held that it was not a violation of the PDA for AT&T not to revise its plan retroactively. AT&T acted under a valid seniority system, and thereby qualified for an exception to Title VII. The Supreme

Court refused to apply the Ledbetter Act (§ 34.01[A]), because the original system of service credits was not discriminatory, and therefore employees were not "affected by application of a discriminatory compensation decision or other practice," as the Ledbetter Act says, and without such an effect, the Ledbetter Act does not apply. [*AT&T v. Hulteen*, 556 U.S. 701 (2009)]

If pregnant employees are covered by the plan, the pregnant wives of employees must be covered (in a plan with dependent coverage), and vice versa. However, it is permissible to exclude the pregnancy-related conditions of dependents other than the spouses of employees, as long as the exclusion is applied equally for male and female employees and their dependents.

A policy of restricting light-duty assignments to workers injured on the job who took Worker's Compensation leave was held to be neutral and equitably applied. Therefore, the Sixth Circuit dismissed a pregnant trucker's discrimination case when she was denied light duty after her obstetrician imposed a 20-pound lifting limitation. Pre-pregnancy, she had been able to lift 200 pounds, as the job required. There was no evidence of anti-pregnancy animus, or anyone seeking to get her fired to take her job, and a man recovering from non-work-related surgery would also have been denied a light-duty assignment, so the Sixth Circuit found that the PDA was not violated. [*Reeves v. Swift Transp. Co.*, 446 F.3d 637 (6th Cir. 2006); see Fred Schneyer, *Pregnant Trucker Loses Discrimination Suit Battle*, plansponsor.com (Aug. 29, 2006); earlier, the Fifth Circuit reached a similar conclusion in *Urbano v. Cont'l Airlines*, 138 F.3d 204 (5th Cir. 1998)]

Certiorari has been granted in a Fourth Circuit case on this issue; the Fourth Circuit ruled that it is acceptable for the employer to restrict light duty assignments to workers injured on the job, denying them to pregnant workers who are unable to carry out their original job duties. [*Young v. United Parcel Serv., Inc.*, 707 F.3d 437 (4th Cir. 2013), *cert. granted* as No. 12-1226 (July 1, 2014). See Laura J. Maechtlen and Julie G. Yap, *SCOTUS Agrees to Consider Whether Pregnant Workers Must Be Able to Perform the Essential Functions of the Job*, Seyfarth Shaw LLP (July 9, 2014), available at Lexology.com]

Transferring a pregnant employee from traveling to offer computer technical support to the help desk was an adverse employment action because it reduced her pay, the work was less technical, and the job was considered a demotion. The plaintiff was fired, and the Eleventh Circuit found that her pregnancy was a motivating factor. The plaintiff's supervisor admitted that one reason for the transfer was concern about her pregnancy; she had suffered a previous miscarriage. However, the Eleventh Circuit said that even well-intentioned actions can violate the law. [*Holland v. Gee*, 677 F.3d 1047 (11th Cir. 2012)]

An early 2013 California Court of Appeal decision holds that an employee disabled by pregnancy complications was entitled to additional leave as a reasonable accommodation under FEHA even though she had used up her California Pregnancy Disability Leave Law and California Family Rights Act leave. She had a high risk pregnancy and was prescribed bed rest. The employer gave her 19 weeks of leave, including accrued vacation time. She was fired when she was still on bed rest, couldn't perform the essential functions of her job, and had exhausted her leave entitlement. The court of appeal ruled that the plain language of California's Pregnancy Disability Leave Law is that it supplements other FEHA entitlements. [*Sanchez v. Swissport, Inc.*, 213 Cal. App. 4th 1331, 153 Cal. Rptr. 3d 367 (2013); see Jackson Lewis LLP Workplace Resource Center, *No Statutory Cap on Pregnancy Leave, California Court of Appeal Rules* (Mar. 4, 2013) (benefitslink.com)]

The First Circuit ruled that a job application was ambiguous as to whether people who applied but were not hired were subject to the arbitration clause. Therefore, the First Circuit refused to mandate arbitration in a case where a job applicant asserted pregnancy discrimination. The court concluded that there was a valid arbitration agreement—but the conditions under which it would come into play (the plaintiff being hired and having a dispute with her employer) never occurred. [*Gove v. Career Sys. Dev. Corp.*, 689 F.3d 1 (1st Cir. 2012)]

The EEOC lost a high-profile pregnancy discrimination case. The suit was originally filed in 2007, charging the Bloomberg company with pregnancy discrimination against a group of 78 women. In 2011, the District Court for the Southern District of New York dismissed the class charges, finding that the EEOC failed to produce evidence of a practice of altering the terms and conditions of employment of pregnant employees; the EEOC's case was deemed so weak that the defendant should not have to go to trial on these charges. The EEOC tried to continue the action with 35 individual charges. Summary judgment was granted with respect to some of the plaintiffs, on the grounds that the EEOC failed to perform an adequate investigation or attempt conciliation. The EEOC offered to conciliate, but the district court held that this could not be done once the case had been in progress for more than six years. The district court allowed only claims about one plaintiff's demotion and pay cut to proceed to trial. [*EEOC v. Bloomberg, L.P.*, No. 07 Civ. 8383 (S.D.N.Y. Sept. 3 2013); see Gerald L. Mattman, Jr. and Howard M. Wexler, *The EEOC Suffers Another Resounding Defeat Due to "Shoot First, Aim Later" Tactics*, Seyfarth Shaw LLP (Sept. 10, 2013), available at Lexology.com]

In mid-2013, the Fifth Circuit became the first Court of Appeals to rule on lactation discrimination. The Fifth Circuit held that discriminating against an employing for breast-feeding or expressing milk is unlawful sex discrimination. The plaintiff charged that she was fired merely for saying that she wanted to express milk at work. The Fifth Circuit ruled that lactation is a medical condition related to pregnancy and childbirth because it is a physiological state caused by childbirth. [*EEOC v. Houston Funding II*, 717 F.3d 425 (5th Cir. 2013); see William Metke, *Fifth Circuit Holds That Lactation Discrimination Violates Title VII*, Workplace Prof Blog (May 31, 2013) (benefitslink.com)]

The EEOC published enforcement guidance about pregnancy discrimination in mid-2014, in conjunction with a Q&A about the guidance and a fact sheet for small business. This was the EEOC's first comprehensive update of the rules since the Compliance Manual chapter was published in 1983. The guidance says that the PDA covers not merely current pregnancy or lactation, but discrimination based on past or potential pregnancy. The EEOC's position (which has not always prevailed in court) is that light duty assignments cannot be exclusively reserved for people injured at work. The EEOC says that employers must provide light duty, alternative assignments, disability leave, or unpaid leave for pregnancy-related disability on par with other disability. However, if the employer's policy is to limit the number or duration of light duty assignments, the same restrictions can be applied to pregnant workers as to comparable non-pregnant workers. The EEOC says that pregnant workers cannot be forced to take leave when they are able to perform their jobs, and parental leave must be offered on comparable terms to male and female employees. [Enforcement Guidance, <http://www.eeoc.gov/laws/guidance/pregnancy_guidance.cfm> (July 14, 2014); see M. Scott Young, *EEOC Issues Guidance on Pregnancy Discrimination, Including Light Duty Policies*, Thompson Hine LLP (July 17, 2014), available at Lexology.com]

The EEOC's Strategic Enforcement Plan for FY 2013–2016 calls for an increased focus on investigating pregnancy discrimination allegations. In 2012, the EEOC received 3,745 pregnancy discrimination complaints, and resolved a record number of cases, recovering more than $14 million in settlements. Several important district court cases were resolved in 2013.

The EEOC settled a Southern District of Mississippi case against Reed Pierce's Sportman's Grille for $20,000. In the Northern District of Illinois, Adventures in Learning Aurora Inc. paid $31,000 to settle after forcing the plaintiff to quit when she was in her fourth month of pregnancy. Ramin Inc. settled a housekeeper's case (she was fired when she disclosed her pregnancy) for $2,500 in back pay and $25,000 in compensatory and punitive damages. Landau Uniforms settled a Northern District of Mississippi case for unequal treatment and discharge of a pregnant employee for $80,000.

In the District of Nevada, Engineering Documentation Systems paid $70,000 to settle allegations of derogatory remarks about the plaintiff; denying her an office closer to the restroom to accommodate nausea; changing her job description; and terminating her while she was on leave. The law firm of James E. Brown & Associates rescinded a job offer when it discovered that the applicant was six months pregnant; the case was settled for $18,000 in the District Court for the District of Columbia. Platinum PTS Inc. paid $100,000 to settle a case for firing an employee who missed five days of work after a miscarriage. [Lily M. Strumwasser, *Not Without Warning: The EEOC Continues To File Barrages Of Pregnancy Discrimination Lawsuits*, Seyfarth Shaw LLP (Sept. 19, 2013), available at Lexology.com]

[C] The Equal Pay Act (EPA)

The Equal Pay Act [29 U.S.C. § 206] is related to the Title VII provisions that forbid sex discrimination, but it is not a part of Title VII. The EPA covers all employers with *two* or more employees. It forbids discrimination in compensation, including all forms of benefits, on the basis of sex—if the two jobs are of equal skill, effort, and responsibility and are performed under similar working conditions. In other words, the statute does not apply to "comparable worth" claims under which women claim that a typically female job is of greater value to society than a higher-paid but different job typically performed by men (e.g., child care workers and parking lot attendants). See § 34.06[B] for discussion of the Supreme Court's 2009 *Hulteen* decision, finding that it was not illegal for a pension plan to continue to reflect the effect of pre-Pregnancy Discrimination Act pay inequalities.

Cost-based defenses are not allowed under the EPA, [see 29 C.F.R. § 216(b)] which says that even if it costs more to provide benefits to women than to men, the employer must either eliminate the benefit or provide it to everyone.

The EPA imposes civil penalties on employers who violate it; even criminal penalties, as prescribed by Fair Labor Standards Act § 216(a), are a possibility. Punitive damages are not allowed, but double back pay is. A winning plaintiff can get costs and attorney's fees.

A 2006 Tenth Circuit case explores the differences between Title VII and the EPA. The plaintiff, a marketing service consultant with a law degree, charged that she was paid less than male employees doing the same work. The Tenth Circuit ruled that a claim of salary discrimination can be brought either as a Title VII intentional-discrimination case or an EPA wage discrimination case. It is not necessary to prove intent in an EPA case, whereas a woman charging wage discrimination under Title VII must prove that the employer intentionally paid her less than a similarly situated male employee. The Title VII case uses the familiar *McDonnell-Douglas* analysis. In an EPA case, the plaintiff makes out a *prima facie* case by showing that men earned more for substantially equal work. If this is done, the burden of persuasion shifts to the employer to justify its action using a seniority system; a merit system; pay based on quantity or quality of work; or a pay disparity based on any factor other than sex. [*Mickeson v. N.Y. Life Ins. Co.*, 460 F.3d 1304 (10th Cir. 2006)]

The Eighth Circuit rejected an employer's contention that it applied "factors other than sex" to pay a male new hire $62,500 (the salary that he said he "required") while paying $45,000 to a female manager who was promoted one level above the man. In fact, he was hired to replace her when she was promoted. The Eighth Circuit said that the issue was not whether the new hire was entitled to be paid a market rate—but the employer's failure to justify paying the plaintiff much less than the market rate for her job. [*Drum v. Leeson Electric Corp.*, 565 F.3d 1071 (8th Cir. 2009)]

A state agency gave lateral hires a salary at least as high as they had earned in the past, plus a raise if the salary scale under the new job permitted it. The plaintiff alleged that she and a man with a different title did the same work, but he earned more because the process of setting initial salaries favored him, and the agency's practices maintained the salary gap. Seventh Circuit precedent is that past wages are a "factor other than sex" that will justify pay differentials because federal courts are not entitled to set standards for business practices, and men's higher wages reflect the greater amount of time women spend on child-rearing, something that the Seventh Circuit did not interpret as discrimination. [*Wernsing v. DHS, State of Ill.*, 427 F.3d 466 (7th Cir. 2005). Other circuits, however, have held that past wages constitute a "factor other than sex" only if the employer has an acceptable business reason for using past wages to set starting pay for new hires: *Aldrich v. Randolph Cent. Sch. Dist.*, 963 F.2d 520 (2d Cir.), *cert. denied*, 506 U.S. 965 (1992); *EEOC v. J.C. Penney Co.*, 843 F.2d 249 (6th Cir. 1992); *Kouba v. Allstate Ins. Co.*, 691 F.2d 873 (9th Cir. 1982); *Glenn v. Gen. Motors Corp.*, 841 F.2d 1567 (11th Cir. 1988).]

A contrary result was reached in a 2006 Sixth Circuit Case. Nurse practitioners working for the federal Department of Veterans' Affairs (DVA) brought suit under the EPA and Title VII, alleging they (95% of whom are female) are paid less than physician's assistants (most of whom are male) for performing jobs of equal skill, effort, and responsibility under similar working conditions. The District Court granted summary judgment to the agency, accepting the affirmative defense that it was merely following the two separate statutes that set pay for the two types of health practitioners. The nurse practitioners were required to have master's degrees, whereas the physician's assistants didn't even have to have a bachelor's degree. (In fact, one woman who was qualified as both an NP and a PA worked as a PA because it paid more.) The Sixth Circuit reinstated the suit, noting that the DVA advertised for either an NP or a PA for certain jobs, and the two kinds of workers often filled in for one another. Both statutes allowed the DVA to increase salaries to cope with recruitment problems. The DVA chose to do so for PAs but not for NPs, even though recruitment problems were equally severe. [*Beck-Wilson v. Principi*, 441 F.3d 353 (6th Cir. 2006)]

A nurse charged a hospital with paying a man more for substantially equal work performed under substantially equal conditions. The jury ruled for the defendant. The Eighth Circuit denied the plaintiff's motion for a new trial. The EPA is a strict liability statute (the employer's motivation for unequal pay is irrelevant). The employer's exercise of business judgment is a defense in a Title VII case, but not an EPA case. Therefore, business judgment jury instructions are inappropriate in a pure EPA case, although they can be given in a case that combines EPA and Title VII violations. The Eighth Circuit ruled that the jury instructions were questionable because they included wording that might have implied a business judgment defense—but the Eighth Circuit found that the jury instructions correctly defined other important concepts, and were not defective enough to affect the plaintiff's rights. [*Bauer v. Curators of Univ. of Missouri*, 680 F.3d 1043 (8th Cir. 2012)]

In late 2012, New Jersey enacted a law requiring employers with 50 or more employees to post a notice in the workplace about the right to gender equity in pay, benefits, and other terms and conditions of employment. The official poster was released in early 2014 and posting became mandatory on January 6, 2014. Posting can be done online if all employees have access to the site. [<http://lwd.dol.state.nj.us/labor/forms_pdfs/EmployerPosterPacket/genderequity poster.pdf>; see McCarter & English LLP, *Attention Employers: New Poster Requirement In New Jersey Regarding Gender Equity In Pay And Compensation* (Jan. 21, 2014), available at Lexology.com]

[D] Sexual Orientation and Gender Behavior Discrimination

Although there are a number of state and local laws banning discrimination in the workplace on the grounds of sexual orientation, Title VII does not forbid discrimination on the basis of actual or perceived homosexuality or bisexuality. [See also § 18.06 for health plan issues for employees with same-sex spouses or life partners.] A number of state laws, however, do forbid sexual orientation discrimination. The Human Rights Campaign said that 88% of the Fortune 500 maintain written nondiscrimination policies about sexual orientation, and 21 states, the District of Columbia, and more than 160 counties and cities forbid sexual orientation discrimination. [James B. Stewart, *Exxon Defies Calls to Add Gays to Anti-Bias Policy*, NYTimes.com (May 24, 2013)]

Under a mid-2014 federal Executive Order, federal contractors are forbidden to discriminate in employment against gay, lesbian, bisexual, and transgender people, and the Office of Federal Contract Compliance Programs has adopted a directive defining discrimination based on gender identity or transgender status as sex discrimination. [Peter Baker, *Obama Calls for a Ban on Job Bias Against Gays*, NYTimes.com (July 21, 2014); DIR 2014-02, <http://www.dol.gov/ofccp/regs/compliance/directives/dir2014_02.html> (undated, last accessed Aug. 22, 2014)]

Shortly after the Supreme Court decision that found the federal Defense of Marriage Act Amendment unconstitutional, the *New York Times* pointed out that fewer than half the states had laws forbidding employment discrimination on the basis of sexual orientation or gender identity. [Tara Siegel Bernard, *Fired for Being Gay? Protections are Piecemeal*, NYTimes.com (May 31, 2013). According to the Movement Advancement Project, *Percent of LGBT Population Covered by Laws*, <http://www.lgbtmap.org/equality-maps/employment_non_discrimination_laws> (updated Aug. 20, 2014), the states of California, Colorado, Connecticut, Delaware, Hawaii, Illinois, Iowa, Maine, Maryland, Massachusetts, Minnesota, Nevada, New Jersey, New Mexico, Oregon, Rhode Island, Vermont, Washington, and the District of Columbia forbid sexual orientation and gender discrimination. New Hampshire, New York, and Wisconsin forbid sexual orientation discrimination but not gender identity discrimination. Maryland passed a law forbidding discrimination on the basis of gender identity in March 2014 with an expansive definition of gender identity as identity, appearance, expression, or behavior that is sincerely held as part of the person's core identity. [See Richard J. Hafets, Emmett F. McGee, Jr., and Donna M. Glover, *Maryland to Ban Discrimination on Basis of Gender Identity*, Jackson Lewis PC (Mar. 28, 2014), available at Lexology.com]

Kentucky Baptist Homes for Children, Inc. was sued over its policy of refusing to employ lesbian and gay employees. The suit charged violations of Title VII and the Kentucky Civil Rights Act and the establishment clause of the First Amendment. The Sixth Circuit upheld the district court's dismissal of the employment discrimination claim, but reinstated the First Amendment claims. The agency fired one of the plaintiffs when it discovered she is a lesbian, then promulgated a policy against employing gay people. The other plaintiff is a lesbian who said that she was denied the opportunity to apply for a job there. The Sixth Circuit held that sexual-orientation discrimination is not forbidden by Title VII or the corresponding Kentucky law, and rejected the argument that the plaintiffs were discriminated against because of the employer's religious objection to homosexual conduct, treating that aspect of the case as a pure allegation of sexual-orientation discrimination. [*Pedreira v. Kentucky Baptist Homes for Children Inc.*, 579 F.3d 722 (6th Cir. 2009)]

In some instances, the case revolves around whether a person suffered adverse employment action not because of sexual activities or sexual orientation, but because a male employee was perceived to lack masculinity or a female employee to be unfeminine. (As discussed below at § 34.06[E], however, the highly feminine behavior of a woman becoming a mother also gives rise to workplace litigation.)

Employee plaintiffs have asserted theories of gender non-conformity bias that derive from the discussion of sex stereotyping in *Price Waterhouse*. [*Nichols v. Azteca Rest. Enters. Inc.*, 256 F.3d 864 (9th Cir. 2001); *Higgins v. New Balance Athletic Shoe Inc.*, 194 F.3d 252 (1st Cir. 1999)] Although Title VII does not cover transsexuality, transsexual plaintiffs now raise claims that they are discriminated against because they present themselves as the "other" sex and do not conform to gender stereotypes.

The Sixth Circuit dismissed claims by a private police officer who charged that he was harassed by co-workers because of their perception that he was gay, insufficiently masculine, or both, after he helped a gay doctor with an investigation at the hospital where he worked. The Sixth Circuit said that he failed to make a case, because at most he charged harassment on the basis of perceived homosexuality, and even actual homosexuality is not a suspect classification under Title VII. [*Vickers v. Fairfield Med. Ctr.*, 453 F.3d 757 (6th Cir. 2006)]

The Fifth Circuit, sitting en banc, held in late 2013 that harassment based on gender stereotypes can be actionable under Title VII as "because of sex." The plaintiff, an ironworker, suffered constant verbal and physical harassment, including indecent exposure and jokes about rape, because the supervisor didn't think the victim was manly enough. There was no evidence that the harasser wanted to have sex with the victim, and there was no evidence of hostility toward men in general, or that men and women were treated differently. The Fifth Circuit joined the Third, Seventh, Eighth, and Tenth Circuits in holding that those factors (which come from the Supreme Court's *Oncale* ruling on same-sex harassment) are illustrative, not all required to prove harassment. Therefore, the EEOC could make its case based on harassment for perceived lack of conformity with gender stereotypes (whether or not the victim actually was "manly.") [*EEOC v. Boh Bros. Constr. Co.*, 731 F.3d 444 (5th Cir. 2013); see Dennis A. Clifford and Christopher J. DeGroff, *"Macho Man Discrimination": The EEOC Scores Fifth Circuit Win In Gender-Stereotype Suit*, Seyfarth Shaw LLP (Oct. 3, 2013), available at Lexology.com. The case was subsequently settled by a consent judgment under which Boh Brothers agreed to pay compensatory damages of $125,000: see Manatt Phelps & Phillips LLP, *Same-Sex Harassment Suits Yield Sizable Settlement*, Lexology.com (Mar. 19, 2014).]

An increasing number of Fortune 500 companies provide benefits for gender reassignments (e.g., Apple, General Mills). In 2013, about a quarter of the Fortune 500 offered such benefits, versus 19% in 2012 and none in 2002. Over a dozen states protect transgender persons under their discrimination laws. The consulting firm Jamison Green & Associates says that a company with 200,000 employees could expect about two claims in five years for transition. [Matthew Perrone, *More Large Companies Offer Transgender Workers Health Benefits*, San Jose Mercury News (Oct. 24, 2013) (benefitslink.com)]

The Eighth Circuit held that a female-to-male transsexual who was turned down for a part-time job as a package handler did not prove that hiring was denied because of the plaintiff's membership in a protected group. There was no evidence that the interviewer knew that the plaintiff was transsexual. When it is not clear that a person belongs to a protected group, the plaintiff must prove that the defendant was aware of the plaintiff's status or thought that the plaintiff was a member of the protected group. The Eighth Circuit believed UPS' explanation that Hunter was not hired because of his poor work history and unimpressive interview performance. [*Hunter v. UPS Inc.*, 697 F.3d 697 (8th Cir. 2012)]

Although Title VII does not cover sexual orientation discrimination, the Third Circuit permitted an effeminate gay man to pursue a Title VII claim of harassment based on his failure to conform to gender stereotypes. The Third Circuit said that the case should not have been dismissed, but should have gone to a jury, because it was uncertain whether the case involved sexual orientation or gender discrimination (but affirmed dismissal of his charge that he was harassed for not conforming to his co-workers' religious beliefs). [*Prowel v. Wise Business Forms Inc.*, 579 F.3d 285 (3d Cir. 2009)]

The Ninth Circuit upheld the termination of a casino bartender for refusing to wear makeup. She was fired after close to 20 years of working there and garnering excellent ratings. (She objected to makeup as demeaning and personally offensive.) The Ninth Circuit held that the plaintiff did not have a cause of action under Title VII: she failed to show that the grooming policy imposed greater burdens on female than on male bartenders. For example, she failed to prove the amount of time and money women had to invest to comply with the policy. In the Ninth Circuit, the rule is that employers can impose different grooming standards on men and women, as long as one sex is not burdened more than the other. [*Jespersen v. Harrah's Operating Co.*, 392 F.3d 1076 (9th Cir. 2004)] The case was reheard en banc and affirmed: 444 F.3d 1104 (9th Cir. 2006)]

A hotel desk clerk, whose new boss said she did not have the "pretty Midwestern girl look" that was required, was terminated for "thwarting the interview procedure" and hostility to company policy. The plaintiff had short hair, didn't wear makeup, and wore loose, unfeminine clothing. Before the new Director of Operations took over, the plaintiff Brenna Lewis, had good evaluations, and her direct supervisor was forced to resign for sticking up for Lewis. The Eighth Circuit reversed the grant of summary judgment for the defendant, and remanded the case for further proceedings, holding that women bringing Title VII suits do not have to provide evidence of being treated differently from similarly situated males. In this case, the Director of Operations was the primary decision-maker with the authority to hire and fire. She consistently required front-desk workers to be pretty, and not "tom-boyish." However, the Eighth Circuit's opinion does not state whether Lewis either is or was perceived as a lesbian, or as a female-to-male transsexual. [*Lewis v. Heartland Inns of Am.*, LLC, 591 F.3d 1033 (8th Cir. 2010). On the issue of sex stereotyping, see also *Chadwick v. WellPoint, Inc.*, 561 F.3d 38 (1st Cir. 2009)]

The Obama administration changed the federal job Website, usajobs.gov, to forbid discrimination on the basis of gender identity (transsexuality). The federal government had taken this position informally for several years, but this is a written statement. The federal government is the largest employer in the United States, so its HR decisions have a lot of impact. [*U.S. Job Site Bans Bias Over Gender Identity*, NYTimes.com (Jan. 5, 2010)] In mid-2009, Federal Express amended its anti-discrimination policy to include gender identity. The change was adopted voluntarily, before the shareholder meeting at which a resolution to that effect had been submitted. [Fred Schneyer, *FedEx Adds Gender Identity to Discrim Policy*, [sic] plansponsor.com (July 16, 2009). Wal-Mart added gender identity and expression to its nondiscrimination policy in 2011; sexual orientation was already covered under the company's Discrimination and Harassment Prevention Policy: see *WalMart Adds Transgender Protections*, plansponsor.com (Sept. 29, 2011)]

In 2005, the Sixth Circuit upheld a jury award of $320,000 in damages to a transsexual police officer who was denied promotion to sergeant, and the district court added $527,888 in attorneys' fees and $25,837 in costs. The Sixth Circuit ruled that a reasonable jury could conclude that there had been intentional discrimination because, although the plaintiff's scores during probation were not good, they were better than those of another person who became a sergeant; he was the only person not to become a sergeant after the probationary period in seven years; that the other police officers knew that the plaintiff was in the process of transitioning to being a woman; and that he was often criticized for lacking command presence, which could reasonably be interpreted to mean that he was not masculine. [*Barnes v. City of Cincinnati*, 401 F.3d 729 (6th Cir. 2005)] The Supreme Court denied certiorari (546 U.S. 1003). On transsexuals as a protected class, see *Smith v. City of Salem, Ohio*, 378 F.3d 566 (6th Cir. 2004).

The EEOC obtained a $50,000 settlement for Cori McCreery, who told her supervisors at Don's Valley Market in South Dakota of her intention to transition from male to female. She was fired for making co-workers uncomfortable. This is the maximum statutory penalty for a company with fewer than 100 employees. The EEOC said that upholding stereotypes discriminated against transgender workers. EEOC follows its policy that discriminating against a transgender worker violates Title VII. [*Macy v. Department of Justice* (EEOC 2012), <http://www.eeoc.gov/decisions/0120120821%20Macy%20v%20DOJ%20ATF.txt>; see Sharon B. Bauman et al., *Discrimination Against Transgender Employee Results In $50,000 Settlement*, Manatt Phelps & Phillips LLP (Oct. 14, 2013), available at Lexology.com]

In 2007, the Northern District of Indiana held that while there was no Title VII cause of action for discrimination against a transgendered employee, an employee who was transitioning from male to female could proceed on claims that he was terminated for failure to satisfy male gender stereotypes. The plaintiff was fired for wearing makeup in addition to the prescribed uniform. However, the Northern District held that the plaintiff could win only by proving that the employer was motivated by stereotypes about male and female behavior, not the plaintiff's transsexual status. [*Creed v. Family Express Corp.*, No. 3:06-CV-465RM, 2007 WL 2265630 (N.D. Ind. Aug. 3, 2007)]

The Eleventh Circuit ordered the Georgia General Assembly to reinstate Vandiver Elizabeth Glenn, a transgender woman who worked as an editor for the assembly but was fired after telling her supervisor that she would be changing her name and working dressed as a woman. The Eleventh Circuit said that discrimination on the basis of gender nonconformity is sex-based discrimination that is reviewed using heightened scrutiny under the Equal Protection clause of the Constitution. [*Brumby v. Glenn*, 663 F.3d 1312 (11th Cir. 2011)]

It is common for transgender people to suffer discrimination, respect, and hostility from health care providers. Before PPACA, transgender people who suffered employment discrimination were also deprived of employer-based coverage. Individual insurers often refused to cover them or treated transsexual identity as an excludible pre-existing condition. Furthermore, transgender people who had insurance often found that health care claims were rejected as pre-existing conditions because the insurer treated all health care as related to their gender identity. Starting in 2014, PPACA forbids denials for pre-existing conditions. HHS has confirmed that this provision forbids discrimination based on gender identity. PPACA includes funding to train health care workers in cultural competency when dealing with LGBT patients. [Marisa Carroll, *What the Affordable Care Act Means for Transgender People*, The Nation (Aug. 14, 2012) (benefitslink.com)]

A letter from HHS' Office of Civil Rights clarifies that PPACA's ban on sex discrimination in health insurance extends to discrimination against transsexuals: it is unlawful discrimination for an employer to deny health insurance coverage or benefits based on gender identity or failure to conform to gender stereotypes. Discrimination complaints can be submitted to the Office of Civil Rights and violators can lose federal financial assistance and be subjected to other penalties. However, insurers are not always required to cover surgery for transition.

[Michelle Andrews, *HHS Says Health Plans Cannot Discriminate Against Transgender People*, Kaiser Health News (Sept. 3, 2012) (benefitslink.com)]

Regulators in Oregon and California ordered health insurers to stop denying coverage on the basis of gender identity. Insurers were ordered to pay for hormone therapy, breast reduction, cancer screening, and other medically necessary procedures on the same basis whether or not the patient is transsexual. The decision affects about one-third of citizens of Oregon and 7% of Californians. Most Californians are not affected by the decision because they get their health care through HMOs, which are under a different system of supervision. [AP, *Ore., Calif., Require Transgender Health Coverage*, NYTimes.com (Jan. 11, 2013)]

The state of Oregon settled a lawsuit by agreeing to provide insurance coverage for gender reassignment of state employees; the state agreed to pay $36,000 in damages and provide coverage for all types of reassignment surgery. The suit alleged that, because hysterectomies are covered under the plan, denying coverage when a hysterectomy is part of reassignment is discrimination on the basis of gender. [Rebecca Moore, *Ore. Adds Gender Reassignment to Health Care Coverage*, plansponsor.com (Jan. 25, 2013)]

[E] "Sex-Plus" Discrimination

The sex-plus cause of action asserts that the plaintiff suffered discrimination on the ground of sex and other factors—e.g., motherhood. Title VII does not list parenthood as a protected category. The Pregnancy Discrimination Act and Family and Medical Leave Act are limited to pregnancy and childbirth, and do not forbid bias against women who act as primary caregivers of their children. In 2004, the District Court for the District of Connecticut ruled that child care is gender-neutral and hence not protected under Title VII. [*Guglietta v. Meredith Corp.*, 301 F. Supp. 2d 209 (D. Conn. 2004). However, in a failure to hire/failure to promote case, the same district treated interview questions about child care arrangements as evidence of bias: *Senuta v. Groton, Conn.*, 2002 U.S. Dist. LEXIS 10792 (D. Conn. Mar. 5, 2002)]

The first lawsuit for Family Responsibilities Discrimination (FRD) was brought in 1971, with only eight such cases in the 1970s. Between 1986 and 1995, the Hastings College of the Law Center for WorkLife Law found that there were 97 lawsuits alleging discrimination on the basis of family responsibilities. The number rose to 481 cases in the decade 1996–2005. About 93% of FRD plaintiffs are women. Most allege that they suffered discrimination because of their care needs as parents, but some are caregivers for parents. The largest award to a successful FRD plaintiff was $25 million, but the average award is about $100,000; employees get settlements or win at trial in about half of FRD cases. [The Hastings study is called *Litigating the Maternal Wall: U.S. Lawsuits Charging Discrimination Against Workers with Family Responsibilities*; see Lisa Belkin, *Family Needs in the Legal Balance*, N.Y. Times, July 30, 2006, section 1, p. 1 and Fred Schneyer, *Strong Rise* Seen *in Family Responsibilities Discrimination Suits*, plansponsor.com (July 10, 2006). The Center for WorkLife Law's fact sheet on the issue is found at <http://worklifelaw.org/pubs/FRD_Fact_Sheet.pdf> (undated, accessed Mar. 27, 2014).] A 2009 First Circuit decision permits an employee to pursue a sex discrimination claim that she was denied a promotion because she is the mother of four young children. (The district court had ruled in the employer's favor.) Several Circuits, including the First, have ruled that adverse job action on the basis of being a mother is sex discrimination based on stereotyping. In this case, in effect the plaintiff was told that her work was completely satisfactory, but she would not be promoted because she had young children and was going to school part-time. The plaintiff brought suit after the "team leader" job went to a woman with less experience and a lower performance evaluation than the plaintiff (3.84 versus 4.40). [*Chadwick v. WellPoint Inc.*, 561 F.3d 38 (1st Cir. 2009)]

§ 34.07 RELIGIOUS DISCRIMINATION AND REASONABLE ACCOMMODATION

Religious charges are a comparatively small, but fast-growing, portion of the EEOC's caseload, more than doubling in 15 years. The highest number of EEOC charges of religious discrimination was filed in 2011 (4,151 charges); there were 3,811 religion-based charges in 2012. [Melanie Trottman, *Religious-Discrimination Claims on the Rise*, WSJ.com (Oct. 27, 2013)]

The EEOC announced that in FY 2013, it filed 12 religious discrimination suits, three more than in FY 2012. The agency's guidelines were revised in 2008 to say that non-theistic moral and ethical beliefs can qualify as religious. The EEOC sued Bo-Cherry Inc. (dba Bojangles) in the district court for the Western District of North Carolina for discriminating against a bearded Muslim employee, not allowing him to wear a beard net, and firing him. Dynamic Medical Services was sued in the district court for the Southern District of Florida for forcing employees to attend Scientology classes and firing two who refused. The suit against United Cellular in the Northern District of Alabama charges failure to accommodate a Seventh Day Adventist worker's Sabbath. EEOC religious discrimination settlements in 2013 include:

- $95,000 to a Jehovah's Witness who was denied a day off to attend a religious convention (Ozarks Electric);
- $45,000 for failure to accommodate the Sabbath of a Seventh Day Adventist (Landmark Hotel Group);
- $82,500 for failure to hire an applicant who was asked which churches he attended, when and where he was saved, and if he would come to work early for Bible study (Voss Lighting);
- $158,000 to settle charges for harassing and then firing a Seventh Day Adventist (Maita Chevrolet Geo);
- Two settlements totaling $71,000 with employees who wear hijabs, with an obligation to inform job applicants that variations from the dress code may be available for religious reasons (Abercrombie & Fitch). [Gerald L. Maatman, Jr. and Lily M. Strumwasser, *Compliance: Religious Discrimination—It's On The EEOC's Radar*, Seyfarth Shaw LLP (Nov. 13, 2013), available at Lexology.com]

[A] Employer's Duties and Obligations

Religious issues can arise in the workplace in many contexts: employees' need for time off for prayer, or to observe a Sabbath or attend services or religious events; wearing of religious dress; men wearing beards for religious reasons; and religious objections to joining a union.

The EEOC issued a 97-page revised version of the Compliance Manual § 12 (religious discrimination) on July 22, 2008. The EEOC issued accompanying guidance online: Questions and Answers and a Best Practices document for employers.

The Compliance Manual says that Title VII forbids differential treatment of employees on the basis of their religious beliefs or practices, including atheism. Religious beliefs include moral and ethical beliefs, and are not required to reflect the concept of a deity. Religious harassment, including association-based harassment, is also forbidden. Employers must provide reasonable accommodation of needs based on an employee's sincerely held religious belief, unless the cost or burden to the employer would be more than minimal. As examples of required accommodation, the EEOC lists scheduling changes; changing the tasks assigned to a worker; and allowing religious dress and beard or hairstyles. Employers must not favor expressions of some religions over others. Retaliation is also forbidden.

[Revised § 12 of the Compliance Manual, <http://www.eeoc.gov/policy/docs/religion.pdf> (accessed Mar. 27, 2014); Questions and Answers: Religious Discrimination in the Workplace <http://www.eeoc.gov/policy/docs/qanda_religion.html> (updated Jan. 31, 2011, accessed Mar. 27, 2014); Best Practices for Eradicating Religious Discrimination in the Workplace <http://www.eeoc.gov/policy/docs/best_practices_religion.html> (updated July 23, 2008, accessed Mar. 27, 2014)]

The EEOC issued further guidance on religious dress in the workplace in March 2014. The EEOC's examples include wearing religious articles (such as cross or hijab), avoiding certain garments (women who will not wear pants or short skirts) and shaving/hair length requirements. The EEOC's position is that federal law requires employers to make exceptions to their usual rules or preferences to permit employees to observe religious dress and grooming practices. The EEOC reads Title VII to cover all aspects of religious observance, practice, and belief, whether based on theistic beliefs or non-theistic moral or ethical beliefs. Non-belief is also covered in cases in which the employer tries to make an employee wear religious articles or garb to which the employee objects on grounds of non-belief. However, personal preferences are not protected by Title VII. The EEOC says that a newly adopted observance can be sincere, and so can be a periodic observance (e.g., a Muslim employee who only wears a head covering during Ramadan). Customer preference is not a defense to a discrimination claim. The EEOC says that it is unlawful to assign a worker to a non-customer contact position because of actual or feared customer preference. [EEOC.gov, *Religious Garb and Grooming in the Workplace: Rights and Responsibilities*, <http://www.eeoc.gov/eeoc/publications/qa_religious_garb_grooming.cfm> (undated, accessed Mar. 27, 2014)]

In recent years, religious headgear—generally involving Muslims but sometimes Sikhs or orthodox Jews—has been a litigation focus.

Bilan Nur, a Somali sales representative, was awarded $291,000 in damages ($25,000 back pay, $16,000 compensatory damages, $250,000 in punitive damages) by an Arizona federal court when she was unlawfully terminated for refusing to take off her head covering during her holy month of Ramadan. She had previously been permitted to wear the head covering at work; she was willing to wear a scarf with the corporate logo; and wearing a scarf was not even a violation of the company dress code. [Fred Schneyer, *Alamo Hit with $287,000 Jury Award in Muslim Discrimination Case*, plansponsor.com (June 7, 2007)]

In mid-2012, the MTA (New York City's public transportation authority) agreed to a settlement under which Muslim and Sikh employees can wear religious headgear, as long as the headgear's color is navy blue (the MTA's uniform color); they will not be required to attach MTA logos to the headgear. Eight current and former employees were awarded a total of $184,500 in damages for past denial of reasonable accommodation. [Matt Flegenheimer, *MTA Agrees That Workers May Wear Religious Headgear*, NYTimes.com (May 30, 2012); Ted Mann, *MTA Settles Bias Lawsuit*, WSJ.com (May 31, 2012)]

The Abercrombie & Fitch "Look Policy" governing employees' appearance at work, has been the subject of several religious discrimination cases because of its effect on Muslim employees who wear hijabs. The District Court for the Northern District of California granted summary judgment for the EEOC, rejecting several of the defendant's affirmative defenses (that the Look Policy is protected commercial free speech; that there were no grounds for injunction or punitive damages). Abercrombie argued that the EEOC refused to conciliate in good faith. The District Court for the Northern District of California held that the EEOC satisfied the conciliation obligation by months of extensive discussions before filing suit.

There is a circuit split about the EEOC's conciliation obligations; the Sixth Circuit defers to the agency. In contrast, the Second, Fifth, and Eleventh Circuits require the EEOC to explain to the employer why it believes there is reasonable cause to find a violation of the law; to offer the employer a chance to comply voluntarily; and respond reasonably and flexibly to the employer. Certiorari has been granted in *EEOC v. Mach Mining*, No. 13-1019, to explicate the extent of the EEOC's duty to conciliate.

The district court granted summary judgment for the EEOC on liability, because Abercrombie did not show that allowing workers to wear head coverings would impose an undue hardship. The employee worked mostly in the stockroom, out of public view, so the district court rejected Abercrombie's argument that the Look Policy was commercial free speech because employees served as "brand ambassadors." The district court said punitive damages were warranted given the employer's malice or reckless indifference to the employee's religious obligations. [*EEOC v. Abercrombie & Fitch Stores, Inc.*, 966 F. Supp. 2d 949 (N.D. Cal. 2013); see Gerald L. Maatman, Jr. and Howard M. Wexler, *The EEOC Scores Summary Judgment Win In Religious Discrimination Case*, Seyfarth Shaw LLP (Sept. 9, 2013), available at Lexology.com; Rebecca Ballhaus, *Muslim Fired by Abercrombie Over Head Scarf Wins Bias Suit*, WSJ.com (Sept. 10, 2013). Abercrombie & Fitch paid $71,000 to two Muslim women, one of whom was fired and one denied hiring, for wearing hijabs: Melanie Trottman, *Religious-Discrimination Claims on the Rise*, WSJ.com (Oct. 27, 2013).]

However, the Tenth Circuit ruled for Abercrombie, holding that plaintiff Samantha Elauf wore a headscarf to her job interview but did not mention the scarf, say that she wore it for religious reasons, or request accommodation. The Tenth Circuit held that, because religion is an individual, personal matter, the burden is on the job applicant or employee to request accommodation. [*EEOC v. Abercrombie & Fitch*, 731 F.3d 1106 (10th Cir. 2013); see Seyfarth Shaw, *If You Want A Religious Accommodation, You've Got To Ask For It: What Employers Can Learn From The 10th Circuit's Ruling In EEOC v. Abercrombie & Fitch*, Lexology.com (Oct. 8, 2013)]

After the United States' invasion of Afghanistan in 2001, a Muslim salesman (Mohommed Rafiq) charged that his managers, despite repeated protests, called him "Taliban" managers and co-workers told him to go back home and mocked his religious requirements for daily prayers and halal food. A supervisor ordered him to attend a United Way meeting and gave him a written warning for his "militant stance" and "acting like a Muslim extremist." Rafiq complained to the general manager after an argument with a finance manager and was fired. The EEOC brought a hostile work environment suit, which was dismissed by the district court for lack of evidence of severe and persistent harassment and failure to prove deterioration in quality of life caused by the severity of the harassment. The Fifth Circuit reversed, holding that the pattern of harassment alleged was explicitly based on religion and national origin, and was severe enough to impair daily life. [*EEOC v. WC&M*, 496 F.3d 393 (5th Cir. 2007)]

A Jewish police officer alleged repeated workplace harassment, including frequent anti-Semitic remarks. He was not allowed to wear a yarmulke because it violated the uniform policy, but another officer was allowed to wear Christian religious symbols on his uniform. A New Jersey jury found a hostile work environment but did not award damages, and ruled that the delay in the plaintiff's promotion to corporal was not discriminatory. Both sides appealed. The New Jersey Supreme Court applied the same test for a hostile environment based on religion as for one based on sex or race: whether a reasonable person would consider the antagonistic, degrading, or demeaning acts and comments in his or her presence to be severe or pervasive enough to alter the working conditions for the worse. In this case, the plaintiff was repeatedly subjected to humiliating anti-Semitic comments, not the mere "ribbing" that the defense characterized it as. [*Cutler v. Dorn*, 196 N.J. 419 (N.J. July 31, 2008)]

Religion includes belief and all forms of religious observance and practice. The Eastern District of Wisconsin held that a sincerely held belief that takes the place of religion in the employee's worldview could constitute a religion, whether or not it involves concepts of God or an afterlife. Therefore, it was a violation of Title VII to demote a supervisor for expressing his sincere religious views in favor of white supremacy in a non-work-related newspaper article. The concept of reasonable accommodation applies only to religious observance or practice, not religious ideas. [*Peterson v. Wilmur Commc'ns Inc.*, 205 F. Supp. 2d 1014 (E.D. Wis. 2002)]

However, the California Court of Appeal held that it does not constitute religious discrimination to refuse to hire a vegan who refused to be vaccinated with a vaccine grown in chicken embryos, because beliefs about harming animals are secular, not a religious philosophy, because they were deemed to lack a spiritual or otherworldly component. [*Friedman v. S. Cal. Permanente Med. Group*, 125 Cal. Rptr. 2d 663 (Cal. App. 2002) In contrast, a 2011 case brought by a vegan employee of Cincinnati Children's Hospital, fired for refusing to take a flu shot containing animal products, was settled in October 2013. The employer's motion to dismiss was denied because the question was whether the employee's vegan beliefs were held as sincerely as traditional religious views. [George E. O'Brien Jr., *Hospital Settles Religious Bias Claim With Vegan*, Littler Mendelson (Oct. 9, 2013), available at Lexology.com]

Challenges to the sincerity of an employee's religious beliefs almost never succeed, but employers tend to prevail when the issue is what constitutes reasonable accommodation. An IRS employee, who had to pass a metal detector in the federal building, converted to the Sikh religion, which requires its followers to carry a ceremonial knife. Her Title VII claim was dismissed, because the court rejected her proposed accommodation (carrying a 3" dulled blade or working from home): guards cannot be expected to test the sharpness of weapons, and the plaintiff did not prove she could complete her duties from home. However, her RFRA claim was permitted to continue because that statute applies to federal policies, including access to federal buildings. [*Tagore v. United States*, 735 F.3d 324 (5th Cir. 2013); see David J.B. Froiland, *A "De Minimis" Cost Can Be Enough To Defeat A Religious Accommodation Claim*, Foley & Lardner LLP (Nov. 18, 2013), available at Lexology.com]

The Seventh Circuit reversed summary judgment for the employer, and permitted a Nigerian immigrant to pursue his religious discrimination claim when he was denied unpaid leave to return to Nigeria to perform funeral rites for his father. Adeyeye, who believed that his family's spiritual well-being depended on performance of the rites, took time off without authorization and was fired when he returned from the trip. The Seventh Circuit held that there were genuine questions of material fact precluding summary judgment; Adeyeye informed his employer that he sincerely believed in his funerary obligations, even if the beliefs, a mixture of Christian and animist, was not a conventional religion. Furthermore, the employer frequently hired temporary replacements when regular workers were unavailable, so granting the requested leave would not have imposed undue hardship on the employer. [*Adeyeye v. Heartland Sweeteners*, 712 F.3d 444 (7th Cir. 2013); see Sheri Qualters, *Worker Denied Funeral Leave Has Religious Bias Claim*, Nat'l L.J. (Aug. 1, 2013) (law.com)]

Employers do not have an obligation to incur undue hardship to accommodate religious observance or practice: 42 U.S.C. § 2000e(j). In fact, a 1977 Supreme Court case holds that investing more than a minimal amount in accommodation can actually represent an illegal preference in favor of the employee who receives the accommodation. [*TWA v. Hardison*, 432 U.S. 63 (1977)]

Except in very limited cases (being a priest or minister, for example) religious beliefs are irrelevant to employment and cannot be used as a hiring criterion. Employers are not supposed to prefer one religion over another, or even to prefer organized religion over atheism or agnosticism.

Initially, the Third Circuit held in favor of a woman who claimed that she was subjected to sex discrimination and retaliation when she was fired from her job as a university chaplain. In September 2006, however, the Third Circuit reversed itself and upheld the dismissal of her sex discrimination charges. The Third Circuit joined seven other circuits in applying the ministerial exception to any claim whose resolution would limit a religious institution's designation of who will perform spiritual functions. However, the Third Circuit did permit the plaintiff to pursue claims for breach of contract, because contracts are voluntary and Title VII has mandatory application. [*Petruska v. Gannon Univ.*, 462 F.3d 294 (3d Cir. 2006); see Shannon P. Duffy, *3rd Circuit Reverses Itself on Groundbreaking Sex Discrimination Ruling*, The Legal Intelligencer (Sept. 8, 2006) (law.com)]

The Supreme Court unanimously endorsed the ministerial exception (i.e., held that the First Amendment prevents courts from interfering when a church takes employment action against a minister). This was the first Supreme Court case on this issue, although all 12 Circuits have recognized the principle. The Court left open the possibility of suits for breach of contract or tortuous conduct. The Court said that the ministerial exception is not a jurisdictional bar but an affirmative defense: that is, an employer that asserts the defense has the responsibility for proving that it applies. [*Hosanna-Tabor Evangelical Lutheran Church v. EEOC*, 132 S. Ct. 694 (2012);]

AT&T Broadband maintained a diversity policy requiring all employees to "recognize, respect, and value differences." A fundamentalist Christian employee refused to sign the certificate, because his religion teaches that some differences are sinful and do not deserve to be valued. The District of Colorado found that he put the employer on notice of his religious objection to the policy, requiring the employer to start the interactive process of accommodation; not doing so violated the employee's right to religious accommodation. [*Buonanno v. AT&T Broadband LLC*, 313 F. Supp. 2d 1069 (D. Colo. 2004)]

Probably the most common religious accommodation issue involves work assignments when the employee is supposed to observe a Sabbath, attend religious services, study the scriptures, teach in a religious school, or the like. The consensus is that the employer has to accommodate activities (or non-activities, like avoiding work on the Sabbath) that are mandated by an organized religion, but not employee's personal wishes about religious observance.

The EEOC considers it unlawful discrimination to set overtime rates in a way that disadvantages employees who observe a Sabbath other than Sunday. [See Guidelines, 29 C.F.R. Part 1605] The EEOC considers acceptable accommodations to include voluntary substitution of one employee for another, swapping shifts, lateral transfers, changes of job assignment, and flextime (i.e., the employee makes up the time devoted to religious observance).

However, employers are not required to accommodate religious observance by violating the seniority rights of a nonobservant employee. In the view of the EEOC, it would be undue hardship for the employer to have to pay overtime to other employees to cover for the religious employee or to have an untrained or inexperienced person covering for the religious employee.

When it comes to union security, the National Labor Relations Act, at 29 U.S.C. § 169, provides that if an employee belongs to a religion that has traditionally objected to unions, then the employer cannot require the employee to join or support a union, even if the operation is an agency shop or participates in another union security arrangement. However, the employee's religious objection can be accommodated by requiring him or her to contribute an amount equivalent to the union initiation fee and dues to a charitable organization that is neither a union nor religious in nature. That way the employee does not benefit financially from the antiunion belief, but is not required to perform a religiously repugnant act. The Sixth Circuit upheld the dismissal of a suit brought by a worker who had a religious objection to joining a union. The union told him to donate the equivalent of his agency fees (see § 30.06[A]) to one of three charities chosen by the UAW. The arrangement required him to pay $100 more to charity as a religious objector than he paid in agency fees as an objecting non-member. The Sixth Circuit ruled that, in a religious accommodation case, it is necessary to prove discharge or discipline; merely losing some pay did not constitute an adverse employment action. [*Reed v. Int'l Union, United Auto, Aerospace & Agricultural Implement Workers of Am.*, 569 F.3d 576 (6th Cir. 2009)]

The Second Circuit reversed the lower court and ruled that offering a shift change on Sundays is not a reasonable accommodation to an employee's Sabbath observance. The proposed schedule change allowed him to attend church, but did not satisfy his religious mandate to avoid working at all on Sunday. [*Baker v. Home Depot*, 445 F.3d 541 (2d Cir. 2006). See also Fred Schneyer, *Wal-Mart Accused of Religious Bias*, plansponsor.com (Oct. 4, 2010): the EEOC sued Wal-Mart for back pay, compensatory and punitive damages, and injunctive relief because a 2009 change in the store scheduling system deprived a Mormon store manager of the accommodation of his Sunday Sabbath that he had received since 2005.]

States are not allowed to pass laws that give employees an absolute right to get their Sabbath day as a day off—that would be an unconstitutional establishment of religion. [*Estate of Thornton v. Caldor, Inc.*, 472 U.S. 703 (1985)] However, an employee who is fired for refusing to work on the Sabbath is entitled to collect unemployment benefits. [*Hobbie v. Unemployment Appeals Comm'n of Florida*, 480 U.S. 136 (1987)] Some state laws, including New York's Human Rights Law, make it clear that employees who get time off for religious observances must make up the time at another time that is religiously acceptable.

[B] Steps Toward Religious Accommodation

Bulletin board postings or the corporation's online presence can be used to get volunteers to cover for workers taking prayer time or observing religious holidays. A diverse workforce really helps here—Christian employees can cover the holidays of non-Christian religions, and vice versa. Optional or floating personal days can be used for religious observance.

Because Islam requires five daily prayers, several occurring during the normal work day, it can be difficult to accommodate Muslim employees in a production line environment. Part of the prayer obligation is keyed to sundown, so it does not occur at the same time every day, making it harder to schedule prayers.

The need for Muslims to wash their hands and feet before prayer can cause hazardous wet conditions in the washrooms (or hallways, if water is tracked). One simple solution is to install a special self-draining basin, or arrange to have the floors mopped more often. The EEOC charged meat packer JBS with a pattern or practice of violating Title VII by not accommodating Muslim employees by letting them take unscheduled prayer breaks, or moving the meal break to cover the sunset prayer. The district court found that either of those accommodations would be an undue hardship because of more-than-de-minimis cost in terms of food safety, operational efficiency, and employee safety. They would also inconvenience non-Muslim co-workers who had to fill in. [*EEOC v. JBS USA, LLC*, No. 8:10-CV-318 (D. Neb. Oct. 11, 2013). Findings of Fact and Conclusions of Law available here: <http://www.workplaceclassaction.com/files/2013/10/show_temp.pdf>; see Heather F. Vickles, *EEOC Loses 5-Year Battle To Require Muslim Prayer Accommodations*, Sherman & Howard LLC (Oct. 17, 2013), available at Lexology.com.]

Although it is often impossible to arrange the menu in the employee cafeteria to conform to all dietary requirements, it is a reasonable gesture to provide some vegetarian alternatives, and to make sure that people whose religion bans the consumption of pork or beef will have other menu choices available.

A growing concern for many employers is how to balance some employees' desire to evangelize for their faith against the desire of other employees to maintain their existing religion (or lack thereof) and lifestyle. Cases have been brought alleging a religiously hostile environment caused by unwanted attempts at religious conversion.

Employees who are not allowed to preach in the workplace can invite co-workers to a church service, prayer meeting, Bible study group, etc., that meets outside the workplace, so their religious expression can be continued elsewhere. The Ninth Circuit permitted a government agency employer to restrict prayer meetings and displays of religious symbols in the workplace: employees were allowed to discuss religion with one another, but not with clients, and could display religious items but not where they would be visible to clients. Prayer meetings were permitted in the break room or outside the office, but not in the conference room, which could only be used for business purposes. The Ninth Circuit concluded that the employer had found an appropriate balance between employees' religious rights and the agency's duty of religious neutrality. [*Berry v. Dep't of Social Servs., Tehama Cnty.*, 447 F.3d 642 (9th Cir. 2006); see Rebecca Moore, *Employer's Restrictions of Religious Activity Not Discriminatory*, plansponsor.com (May 2, 2006)]

A Catholic salesperson who was a mother of small children was fired for poor sales performance. The CEO of the company favored employees who shared his views, including evangelical Christianity and a belief that women's primary role is homemaking. The District Court for the District of Michigan found fact issues about whether the plaintiff experienced religious discrimination.

■ **TIP:** might create an inference of religious discrimination by insulting certain religions; favoring co-workers who share their religion; having prayer services in the workplace; or including religious statements in the company's handbook, logos, or e-mail signatures. [*Zsenyuk v. Kamps, Inc.*, No. 12-14625, 2013 U.S. Dist. LEXIS 157455, 97 Empl. Prac. Dec. (CCH) ¶ 44,950 (D. Mich. Nov. 4, 2013); see Dawn Reddy Solowey and Lynn A. Kappelman, *Go Tell It On The Mountain, But Proceed With Caution At Work: When Does A Supervisor's Religious Expression At Work Pose A Risk Of Discrimination Claims From Other Employees?*, Seyfarth Shaw LLP (Dec. 5, 2013), available at Lexology.com]

[C] Case Law on Reasonable Accommodation

The Second Circuit ruled in 2003 that an employer's rejection of an employee's proposed accommodation of religious needs is a discrete act. Therefore, the statute of limitations is 300 days from the occurrence of the act; the statute of limitations does not restart with every scheduled prayer time that the employee was forced to work. Once an employer rejects a proposed accommodation, the facts to make the case are in existence; the decision is not re-implemented periodically. [*Elmenayer v. ABF Freight Sys. Inc.*, 318 F.3d 130 (2d Cir. 2003)]

The Fourth Circuit concluded that reasonable accommodation was provided to the religious beliefs of a worker with a Saturday Sabbath who was also forbidden to work on seven religious holidays. In this case, the seniority-based bidding system for work shifts operated as a significant accommodation in and of itself, as a neutral method of reducing the number of days that an employee must work when he or she prefers not to, whether for religious or any other reason. The plaintiff also had access to holidays and unpaid time off that could be used neutrally for any reason including religious observance. The plaintiff also failed to switch shifts with another employee. Employers are not required to violate the CBA or the seniority system to accommodate religious needs. [*EEOC v. Firestone Fibers & Textiles Co.*, 515 F.3d 307 (4th Cir. 2008)]

According to *Weber v. Roadway Express Inc.* [199 F.3d 270 (5th Cir. 2000)], the employer had no obligation to accommodate a Jehovah's Witness truck driver who wanted to be assigned only male driving partners, because his religion forbade him to take overnight trips with any woman other than his wife. The employer would have encountered a serious burden to reconfigure the schedules. Although the employer had accommodated nonreligious requests in the past, it did so only consistent with business needs and did not have an obligation to encounter undue hardship to accommodate the truck driver.

A temporary employment agency did not violate Title VII when it refused to place a Muslim woman who wears a "khimar" head covering at a printing plant that forbids any kind of head covering as a safety risk. The agency offered the worker, Asthma Suliman, seven other potential placements, which she turned down, so the Eighth Circuit concluded that there had been no adverse job action.

Suliman did not have a guarantee or reasonable expectation of being placed with a particular employer, and offering the other jobs was a reasonable accommodation to Suliman's religious practice. [*EEOC v. Kelly Servs., Inc.*, 598 F.3d 1022 (8th Cir. 2010). The Third Circuit upheld dismissal of an EEOC suit on behalf of a class of Muslim women prison employees who wanted to wear khimars; there was at least a small risk that prisoners could use the head coverings as weapons against prison employees, and theoretically khimars could be used to smuggle drugs or could be used by prisoners to impersonate prison employees. [*EEOC v. Geo Group Inc.*, 616 F.3d 265 (3d Cir. 2010)]

A petroleum company reached a $125,000 religious discrimination settlement with the EEOC after the company enforced its dress code and refused to let a Rastafarian employee wear the headwrap required by her religion. [Adrien Martin, *RaceTrac Settles Religious Discrimination Suit for $125,000*, plansponsor.com (Jan. 22, 2007)] The Seventh Circuit held that it did not constitute religious discrimination to fail to hire an applicant as a security guard because he wore dreadlocks, finding that he did not prove that he mentioned his religious beliefs or that the belief was the reason for the refusal to hire him. (The defendant said that it did not know that he wore dreadlocks for religious reasons.) [*Lord Osunfarian Xodus v. Wackenhut Corp.*, 619 F.3d 1109 (7th Cir. 2010)]

§ 34.08 RETALIATION

Section 8 of the EEOC Compliance Manual (used by EEOC offices), EEOC Directives Transmittal 915.003 (May 20, 1998), covers retaliation. There are three essential elements in a retaliation claim that the EEOC will pursue:

- The charging party engaged in protected activity, such as opposing discrimination or participating in the Title VII complaint process;
- The employer took adverse action against the charging party;
- There was a causal connection between the protected activity and the employer's adverse action.

A retaliation complaint might be proper if the charging party had a reasonable good-faith belief that the employer committed discrimination (even if this belief was incorrect), and the charging party used a reasonable means to protest this to the employer.

It is illegal to retaliate against a charging party if he or she, or someone closely associated with him or her, participated in any statutory enforcement proceeding. This includes any investigation, proceeding, hearing, or suit under any of the statutes enforced by the EEOC. It is unlawful for one employer to retaliate on the basis of a complaint against another employer.

The Supreme Court resolved several questions about the retaliation cause of action in its June 22, 2006, decision in *Burlington Northern & Santa Fe Ry. Co.*

v. White, 548 U.S. 53 (2006). The Supreme Court ruled that retaliation against employees who engage in protected concerted activity is unlawful, whether or not the form the retaliation takes is employment-related. The Supreme Court reached this conclusion based on differences in the statutory language covering the substantive ban on discrimination and the anti-retaliation provision. However, to be actionable, the retaliatory measures must be severe enough that a reasonable employee might have been deterred from pursuing discrimination charges. In the case at bar, there was actionable retaliation because even though the petitioner's job classification did not change, she was assigned less attractive work (more arduous, dirtier, more strenuous) to punish her for complaining about workplace sexual harassment.

In 2013, the Supreme Court made it more difficult for employees to assert Title VII retaliation claims. As a result of this decision, to prevail, the plaintiff must prove that retaliation is the "but-for" cause of the adverse employment action that the employee complains about. It is not enough that retaliation is one of the factors supporting the employer's decision. The Supreme Court therefore mandated a higher standard of proof than the one used by the EEOC. It is also the ADEA standard of proof that the Supreme Court mandated in 2009, in its *Gross v. FBL Financial Services* decision.

The Supreme Court's rationale is that Title VII's retaliation provision is separate from the basic provision forbidding discrimination. Mixed-motive cases are acceptable in cases involving discrimination on the basis of the five personal characteristics listed in Title VII: race, color, religion, sex, and national origin. The Supreme Court majority found that the language of the Title VII retaliation provision has more in common with the ADEA than with the rest of Title VII. [*University of Tex. Sw. Med. Ctr. v. Nassar*, No. 12-484 (U.S. June 24, 2013); see Marcia Coyle, *Supreme Court Makes It Harder to Prove Job Bias*, Nat'l L.J. (June 24, 2013) (law.com)]

The district court dismissed a Title VII retaliation claim for failure to exhaust EEOC administrative remedies, but the Sixth Circuit reinstated the case. Adamov charged that an executive made discriminatory comments about his Azerbaijani origin. Adamov also complained about failure to be promoted. The company fired Adamov, stating that he made a loan to a friend contrary to company ethics policy. He sued the bank and individual supervisors for discrimination and retaliation. Adamov submitted a draft EEOC charge, which was unsigned and undated, and asserted only a Title VII national origin discrimination claim. Before the court ruled on the defense motion to dismiss, Adamov filed a second charge, including a retaliation allegation and the defendant moved to dismiss once again. The district court dismissed the retaliation claim for failure to exhaust administrative remedies but the Sixth Circuit reversed: the administrative exhaustion requirement of Title VII is not essential to the court's jurisdiction, and the defendant forfeited the exhaustion defense by not raising it before the district court. [*Adamov v. U.S. Nat'l Bank Assoc.*, 726 F.3d 851 (6th Cir. 2013); see Steven J Pearlman, Harris Mufson, and Noa M. Baddish, *Sixth Circuit: Failure To Exhaust Administrative Remedies Not A*

Jurisdictional Bar For Title VII Retaliation Claim, Proskauer Rose LLP (Aug. 27, 2013), available at Lexology.com]

The Second Circuit ruled that Title VII's retaliation provisions include both an "opposition" and a "participation" clause. It is unlawful for an employer to retaliate against an employee who opposes the employer's unlawful employment practices. But adverse job action imposed for participation in an employer's internal investigation of harassment charges, with no connection to a formal EEOC investigation, does not entitle the employee to maintain a Title VII retaliation suit. [*Townsend v. Benjamin Enters.*, 679 F.3d 41 (2d Cir. 2012)]

The Seventh Circuit held that telling the employer, during EEOC mediation of a sexual harassment charge, to "shove its settlement offer up its ass" does not constitute activity protected by Title VII. After his termination, the employee sued for retaliation. The Seventh Circuit held that his disruptive conduct during mediation was a legitimate, non-retaliatory reason for termination. [*Benes v. A.B. Data Ltd.*, 724 F.3d 752 (7th Cir. 2013); see Michael C. Wilhelm, *Does Telling An Employer To Take A Settlement Offer And "Shove It Up Your @$%&!" Constitute Protected Activity Under Title VII?*, Briggs and Morgan (Sept. 10, 2013), available at Lexology.com]

The Southern District of New York held that it did not constitute Title VII retaliation to fail to give a timely COBRA notice to a plaintiff who was terminated (allegedly because she filed an EEOC charge). The employer acknowledged the lack of timely notice, but said that she was offered retroactive COBRA coverage but did not make a COBRA election when the notice was available. The Southern District of New York held that the plaintiff failed to show that the defective notice was retaliatory. The plaintiff was not looking for another job (she had applied for Social Security Disability benefits), so the court restricted the application of Title VII to actions affecting current employment or the ability to obtain future employment. [*Thompson v. Morris Heights Health Ctr.*, No. 09 Civ. 7239 (PAE) (THK) 2012 WL 1145964 (S.D.N.Y. Apr. 6, 2012); see EBIA Weekly, *No Title VII Retaliation Claim for Employee Who Received Late COBRA* Notice (Apr. 19, 2012) (benefitslink.com)]

The EEOC might seek temporary or preliminary relief such as injunction if the retaliation places the charging party at risk of irreparable injury and there is a substantial likelihood that the retaliation claim will succeed. The compliance manual notes that all of the statutes enforced by the EEOC make both compensatory and punitive damages available to victims of retaliation.

Retaliation complaints under 42 U.S.C. § 1981 are cognizable. A defendant argued that it was not fair to apply § 1981 in the retaliation context, because it has a longer statute of limitations than Title VII and awards are not subject to the CRA '91 damage caps, but the Supreme Court held that this "end run" is allowed for discrimination claims and should also be allowed for retaliation. [*CBOCS West Inc. v. Humphries*, 553 U.S. 442 (2008)]

Although Title VII retaliation damages are subject to the statutory cap, there is no cap on ADEA or EPA damages.

CHAPTER 35

SEXUAL HARASSMENT

§ 35.01 INTRODUCTION

Sexual harassment is the subjection of an employee to unwanted sexual contact, propositions, or innuendoes. Sexual harassment occurs in two forms: either "quid pro quo" harassment, where an employee is threatened with job detriment for not complying with a sexual proposition or offered job benefits for compliance, or "hostile environment" harassment, where the atmosphere in the workplace is offensive.

Sexual harassment is considered a form of sex discrimination and therefore is forbidden by Title VII. The EEOC has adopted a two-part test. Conduct is unwanted if the employee did not solicit or initiate the conduct, and the employee finds it undesirable or offensive.

The Fourth Circuit refused to apply disparate impact analysis in sexual harassment cases, and ruled late in 2002 that the alleged sexual harassment was not actionable because co-workers would have subjected the plaintiff to the same offensive behavior and vulgar language if she had been male. [*Ocheltree v. Scollon Prods. Inc.*, 308 F.3d 351 (4th Cir. 2002), *on reh'g*, 335 F.3d 325 (4th Cir. 2003)] On rehearing, the court found that a reasonable jury could have found the conduct to be sexually discriminatory against the sole female worker, in the context of a pervasively harassing work environment. However, punitive damages were denied because of lack of proof of employer knowledge sufficient to support punitive damages. The Ninth Circuit also permitted a gender-based harassment action to be maintained based on a showing that women were subjected to a greater degree of bullying, shouting, cursing, and invasion of personal space, even though the perpetrator was not attempting to solicit sexual activity from employees. [*EEOC v. Nat'l Educ. Ass'n Alaska*, 422 F.3d 840 (9th Cir. 2005)]

Even if a supervisor/subordinate relationship is consensual, co-workers may say that the supervisor shows favoritism to the subordinate—and might retaliate against the co-workers. The District Court for the District of Minnesota dismissed co-workers' claims against the employer for sexual harassment and retaliation. The court held that a supervisor's isolated instances of favoritism toward a sexual partner do not violate Title VII or the Minnesota Human Rights Act—to make out a case, sexual favoritism must be widespread. The court also dismissed retaliation claims, because the co-workers could not have had a reasonable belief that this conduct violated applicable law. [*Larsen v. Arthur J. Gallagher & Co,* Civil No. 13-1506 (JNE/SER), Civil No. 13-1560 (JNE/SER), 2013 U.S. Dist. LEXIS 125297 (D. Minn. Sept. 3, 2013); see Michael T. Miller, *Does Paramour Favoritism Constitute Discrimination?*, Briggs and Morgan (Sept. 26, 2013), available at Lexology.com]

The sexual harassment cause of action requires that the victim suffer tangible job action, not merely lack of friendliness or exclusions from workplace social activities. In a 2006 sexual harassment retaliation case, *Burlington Northern & Santa Fe Ry. Co. v. White*, the Supreme Court ruled that retaliation liability is broader than liability for workplace discrimination: retaliation can be actionable even if the employee's job classification and compensation do not change, as long as the retaliatory measures are severe enough to be daunting to a reasonable employee. [548 U.S. 53]

There is a circuit split on the issue of whether rejecting a supervisor's sexual advances is a protected activity for labor law purposes. In 2007, the Fifth Circuit held that rejection of a single advance is not protected, but this conflicts with a 2000 Eighth Circuit ruling that being able to reject unwanted propositions is a clear example of protected activity. In 2008, the Seventh Circuit held that a man who claimed that his supervisor threatened to fire him if he ended a consensual affair with her did not show protected conduct. (The supervisor denies that there was ever a sexual relationship). The supervisor said that the plaintiff was fired for his hostile attitude and unwillingness to work his full shift. In the Seventh Circuit reading, protected conduct requires only the plaintiff's reasonable good-faith belief that the practice he opposed violated Title VII. But in this case, he did not show that he believed the supervisor's conduct was illegal—he merely said that he wanted to end the affair. Therefore, the employer was entitled to JMOL. [*Tate v. Executive Mgmt. Servs. Inc.*, 546 F.3d 528 (7th Cir. 2008); also cf. *LeMaire v. L.A Dept of Transp & Dev*, 480 F.3d 383 (5th Cir. 2007) with *Ogden v. Wax Works, Inc.*, 214 F.3d 999 (8th Cir. 2000)]

Although one or more individuals may commit sexual harassment, it is the employer company that has the legal liability. The only way the employer can avoid liability is by carrying out appropriate investigations of allegations of harassment and by taking appropriate steps to deal with harassment accusations that are well founded.

In 2010, the Ninth Circuit held that a recently widowed male employee was entitled to pursue a charge of hostile environment discrimination continued by ongoing, unwelcome sexual advances from a married female co-worker. His co-workers mocked him as being unmanly or homosexual for rejecting these advances and supervisors did not respond to his complaints. He became depressed, and his work deteriorated to the point that he was fired. The Ninth Circuit held that it cannot be assumed that a heterosexual male will welcome sexual propositions from any and all females. The employer was liable in this case because the victim informed management that the overtures were unwelcome. Perhaps the conduct was not very severe, but it was repetitive, and continued and accelerated over a six-month period. [*EEOC v. Prospect Airport Servs. Inc.*, 621 F.3d 991 (9th Cir. 2010)]

§ 35.02 THE EMPLOYER'S BURDEN

In this context, two of the key cases are *Burlington Indus., Inc. v. Ellerth* [524 U.S. 742 (1998)] and *Faragher v. City of Boca Raton.* [524 U.S. 775 (1998)] If the action that the plaintiff complains of had adverse employment effect on the victim, the employer is absolutely liable. The employer is still liable even if no adverse employment effect occurred—unless the employer can assert as a defense that it maintained proper antiharassment and grievance policies.

The *Ellerth* case involved a sales representative who felt threatened by repeated remarks and gestures from a manager (not her immediate supervisor). She was not deprived of job benefits. Although she knew the company had an antiharassment policy, she did not complain about the harassment while it was occurring. She quit her job but did not attribute her resignation to harassment. Three weeks later, she sent a letter to the company explaining why she resigned.

The Supreme Court's decision was that the supervisor's threats of adverse job action created a hostile work environment. In such a situation, the employer becomes vicariously liable for the supervisor's conduct by:

- Failing to stop it after learning about it;
- Giving the supervisor apparent authority over the victim, thus making harassment possible;
- Allowing the supervisor to actually take adverse job action against the victim.

However, the other side of the coin is that the employer can be free of liability by taking reasonable care to maintain a workable complaint procedure, if the plaintiff fails to use the procedure.

In the *Faragher* case, a lifeguard sued her municipal employer and two supervisors for creating a hostile environment (including lewd touching of female employees). The employer did have an antiharassment policy, but it was not publicized to the employees. The employer didn't supervise the conduct of the supervisors themselves, and didn't create a procedure for reporting to someone other than the supervisor who committed the harassment. Therefore, the Supreme Court held that the employer was legally responsible for the hostile environment, because it failed to communicate the antiharassment policy and didn't track the conduct of supervisors.

In 2003, the Third Circuit (contrary to holdings in the Second and Sixth Circuits) held that the *Ellerth/Faragher* affirmative defense would not be available to employers in situations where the employee was able to prove constructive discharge. The Supreme Court reversed the Third Circuit in mid-2004. The Supreme Court settled a contentious point by holding that the test of constructive discharge is objective (whether a reasonable person would feel compelled to resign) rather than subjective (the individual employee's personal reaction to the situation). The Supreme Court also noted that, although firing an employee is always an official act (and therefore the affirmative defense is not available), constructive discharge is not always an official act of the employer company. Therefore, the company should be given the chance to assert and prove the affirmative defense. [*Suders v. Easton*, 325 F.3d 432 (3d Cir. 2003), *rev'd sub nom. Pa. State Police v. Suders*, 542 U.S. 129 (2004)]

The Second Circuit ruled in 2012 that the *Ellerth/Faragher* affirmative defense cannot be used where the alleged harasser is high enough in the corporate hierarchy to be considered a proxy or alter ego of the organization. In this case, the alleged harasser was a corporate executive and the husband of the company president. The president took over the investigation, hiring an outside HR consultant who said that the charges were unfounded. [*Townsend v. Benjamin Enters. Inc.*, 679 F.3d 41 (2d Cir. 2012)]

It is not always simple to determine whether an individual accused of harassing conduct is a supervisor or not. In mid-2013, the Supreme Court decided a case about the definition of "supervisor" and the employer's burden. The case involved racial rather than sexual harassment, but it relied heavily on *Ellerth/Faragher*, so it will certainly be influential in sexual harassment cases. In a case of harassment by a supervisor, where there was tangible employment action taken against the plaintiff (such as firing or reassigning him or her) then the employer is strictly liable. If the harasser is a supervisor (defined as someone who has the authority to take tangible employment actions against subordinates) and there is no tangible employment action, the *Faragher/Ellerth* affirmative defense can be raised. But if, as in this case, the harasser is considered a co-worker rather than a supervisor, the employer is only liable if the hostile work environment can be attributed to the employer's negligence. [*Vance v. Ball State Univ.*, 133 S. Ct. 2434 (2013); see Marcia Coyle, *Supreme Court Makes It Harder to Prove Job Bias Claims*, Nat'l L.J. (June 24, 2013) (law.com)]

The Tenth Circuit ruled that, in a case where the plaintiff was a prison employee who alleged that her supervising sergeant harassed and sexually assaulted her, although the sexual assault changed the terms and conditions of the plaintiff's employment, there was no exercise of employer authority via official action. The employer was not strictly liable, and could assert the affirmative defense that the plaintiff did not make a proper, timely report. [*Kramer v. Wasatch County Sheriff's Office*, 743 F.3d 726 (10th Cir 2014); see Parker Poe Adams & Bernstein LLP, *Tenth Circuit Says Rape Not Tangible Employment Action for Purposes of Employer Strict Liability* (Mar. 28, 2014), available at Lexology.com]

In a case of first impression, the First Circuit held in mid-2014 that if the harasser is not the complainant's supervisor (in this case of female-on-male harassment, the harasser was a non-manager—in the HR office, ironically enough), the employer is liable only if it was negligent in controlling the working conditions. The Supreme Court has not ruled on quid pro quo harassment by a co-worker (as distinct from hostile work environment harassment). The co-worker made advances to the plaintiff; when he rejected her, she complained about the quality of the plaintiff's work until he got fired. [*Velazquez-Perez v. Developers Diversified Realty Corp.*, No. 12-2226 (1st Cir. May 23, 2014). See Gauri P. Punjabi and Michael S. Arnold, *First Circuit Court of Appeals Holds That Employer Can Be Found Liable Under Quid Pro Quo Sexual Harassment Negligence Theory*, Mintz Levin Cohen Ferris Glovsky and Popeo PC (June 16, 2014), available at Lexology.com]

Although many cases involve the conduct of supervisors (because of their ability to affect working conditions), employers have also been held liable, in appropriate cases, for harassment committed by nonsupervisory, fellow employees, and by customers.

Another 2013 Supreme Court case also affects proof requirements. *University of Texas Southwestern Med. Ctr. v. Nassar*, 133 S. Ct. 2517 (2013) is a Title VII retaliation case. The Supreme Court set a higher standard for proof of retaliation claims than for discrimination claims. In a retaliation case, the plaintiff must show that retaliation was the "but-for" cause of the adverse action; it is not enough that it be one of several motivating factors.

The First Circuit applied the *Nassar* but-for causation standard to affirm summary judgment for the employer in a sexual harassment/retaliatory termination case. The plaintiff was fired in mid-2011. She said that her supervisor propositioned her on two occasions but she did not inform the employer until much later; even then, she merely said she felt uncomfortable with the supervisor but did not charge sexual harassment. The employer said that she was fired for poor performance, tardiness, and ineffective communications. The First Circuit found that her vague complaints could not establish a but-for case. The employer had a legitimate nondiscriminatory reason to fire her. Her performance problems began before the alleged harassment and her supervisor was not the only person to criticize her work. [*Ponte v. Steelcase Inc.*, 741 F.3d 310 (1st Cir. 2014)]

The Tenth Circuit ruled that Facebook posts did not constitute notice to the employer of a sexual harassment complaint. The plaintiff alleged that she was terminated for reporting (via those posts) harassment committed by her supervisor. After several colleagues, including the alleged harasser, saw the posts, the plaintiff denied having posted it and refused to make a complaint, so the HR department was unable to substantiate the allegations. Later, the plaintiff admitted to making the posts. The plaintiff was fired for dishonesty and inappropriate and disruptive behavior. The Tenth Circuit held that the employer was not liable for sexual harassment because it did not have actual or constructive notice of the alleged harassment. Even if the plaintiff had not initially denied making the posts, Facebook communications did not satisfy the employer's procedure for reporting harassment. [*Debord v. Mercy Health System of Kansas, Inc.*, 737 F.3d 642 (10th Cir. 2013); see Heather L. Sherrod, *Facebook Posts May Not Be Sufficient Notice Of Sexual Harassment Complaints*, Norton Rose Fulbright LLP (Jan. 10, 2014), available at Lexology.com]

In what could be the first case of its type, the New Jersey Court of Appeals ruled that a business owner who says that a customer insisted that she have sex with him or he would not place an order could use the New Jersey Law Against Discrimination to sue for discriminatory refusal to do business on the basis of gender. The court found that quid pro quo harassment in business unlawfully interferes with women's ability to earn a living. [*J.T.'s Tire Service v. United Rentals North Am., Inc.*, 411 N.J. Super. 236 (N.J. App. Div. 2010); see Mary Pat

Gallagher, *N.J. Court Allows Business-to-Business Sex Harassment Suit*, N.J.L.J. (Jan. 11, 2010) (law.com)]

The EEOC charged restaurant chain Senor Frog with severe and rampant sexual harassment at a now-closed location. The case was settled for $350,000 and injunctive relief. At least nine female employees were subjected to repeated propositions, explicit sexual remarks, and unwanted touching by managers who committed indecent exposure. Employees were ordered to provide sexual favors for corporate officials. The owner of the chain permitted the Honolulu managers to harass employees. Female bartenders and servers were discriminated against in promotions and earnings. The HR service Altres was a joint employer, so EEOC said it was responsible for the hostile environment. Altres made a separate $150,000 settlement. [Sharon B. Bauman et al., *EEOC Settles "Severe, Rampant" Sexual Harassment Allegations For $350,000*, Manatt Phelps & Phillips LLP (Dec. 20, 2013), available at Lexology.com]

A male waiter charged harassment after he terminated his sexual relationship with a female supervisor. (The supervisor conceded that there had been a relationship, but denied that she harassed him in order to get him to resume the relationship.) The Seventh Circuit held that there was a material issue of fact about the hostile work environment, and remanded to see if there was a basis to find the employer liable. The Seventh Circuit held in early 2010 that the same rules apply for males alleging harassment by females as for females alleging harassment by males: if there was a consensual relationship in the past, the question is whether, by both subjective and objective standards, there was a hostile work environment. The Seventh Circuit found that dismissal six months after complaints to Turner's supervisors were not close enough in time to suggest retaliation—especially since Turner received a positive evaluation in the interim. However, he also received at least 10 reprimands for poor workplace behavior. [*Turner v. The Saloon, Ltd.*, 595 F.3d 679 (7th Cir. 2010)]

The employer's burden rests with the employer—harassed employees can't sue their unions for involvement in the employer's failure to redress sexual harassment. If one union member accuses another of harassment, the union has a duty to give both of them fair representation at the disciplinary hearing—but the union does not have an obligation to investigate or remedy discrimination. [*Thorn v. Amalgamated Transit Union*, 305 F.3d 826 (8th Cir. 2002)]

§ 35.03 APPROPRIATE EMPLOYER RESPONSES

[A] Statutory and Case Law

Most companies are aware of the potential risk of sexual harassment litigation. After the landmark *Ellerth* and *Faragher* cases, the employer must prevent severe, pervasive unwelcome physical and verbal conduct to prevent the development of a hostile, intimidating, or offensive environment. Supervisors and managers must be trained to recognize and report harassment. There must be a chain of command that can bypass an alleged harasser. Employees must believe that their complaints will be taken seriously. Top management must be involved, to prove that the company takes these matters seriously.

If customers commit the harassment, the Tenth Circuit analyzes the situation as if the harassers were co-employees (not supervisors). So the employer will not be strictly liable for the actions of customers, but will be liable if its negligence permitted the harassment to continue. [*Lockard v. Pizza Hut Inc.*, 162 F.3d 1062 (10th Cir. 1998)]

The Southwest Virginia Community Health System agreed to pay $30,000 to settle EEOC charges that a male patient harassed a female receptionist at one of the system's clinics, and that her complaints were ignored. [Kevin M. Ceglowski and David L. Woodard, *EEOC Settlement Reminds Employers Of Responsibility To Protect Employees From Harassment By Third Parties*, Poyner Spruill LLP (Oct. 28, 2013), available at Lexology.com]

If the employer is negligent, it can be held liable for harassment by a non-employee. The Second Circuit held that the employer's response (stopping the harassing conduct; dismissing a player from the football team for harassing the plaintiff; ordering anti-harassment training for the entire athletics staff) was adequate. But the plaintiff's retaliation claim survived a defense motion for summary judgment. Temporal proximity between her complaints and her loss of a graduate assistant position and termination of her student employment privileges was enough to get to trial. [*Summa v. Hofstra Univ.*, 708 F.3d 115 (2d Cir. 2013); see Kevin B. Leblang and Robert N. Holtzman, *Second Circuit Confirms Liability Standard For Non-Worker Harassment While Warning Employers Of The Continuing Perils Of Retaliation Claims*, Kramer Levin Naftalis & Frankel LLP (Oct. 3, 2013), available at Lexology.com]

It is important to look behind supervisors' write-ups to make sure that the lateness, poor work habits, etc., actually occurred—and that one subordinate was not singled out for conduct that was not punished in employees who did not become sexual targets.

Sexual harassment charges require conduct that was unwanted, but some courts weaken the employer's defense in consensual cases. A Seventh Circuit case was brought by a teenage store employee who filed an EEOC charge about inappropriate sexual advances from her 25-year-old shift supervisor, who was convicted of aggravated sexual abuse. The trial court rejected the claim, stating that she engaged in a consensual sexual relationship, but the Seventh Circuit permitted her lawsuit to advance because of her status as a minor. [*Jane Doe v. Oberweis Dairy*, 456 F.3d 704 (7th Cir. 2006); see also *Jane Doe v. Haronmar Inc.*, filed in Broward Circuit Court (Fla.) (June 2007); see Jordana Mishory, *Teen Sues McDonald's Franchisee Over Sex with Boss*, Daily Business Review (June 21, 2007) (law.com)]

The district court made a similar ruling in a case in which a teenage fast-food worker was subjected to sexual harassment by a manager who had had sexual relations with several other employees. The manager fired her for missing a shift (after he re-scheduled her without notice), then rehired her and continued the harassment. The young woman complained repeatedly to shift supervisors and to an assistant manager, who repeatedly frustrated her attempts to file a formal complaint. When the worker's mother came to the restaurant to complain, she was fired again, this time permanently. The district court ruled for the employer, on the grounds that the worker did not invoke the company's complaint procedure, and retaliation for her mother's conduct was not actionable.

In this case, however, the Seventh Circuit reversed, ruling that the reasonableness of an employer's complaint mechanism only affects the employer's liability for damages, not a claim of unlawful termination. The age and sophistication of the complainant are very relevant to the determination of whether the complaint mechanism is adequate. Although employers do not have to have a tailored procedure for each individual, if the business plan is to hire teenage part-time workers, the complaint procedure should be comprehensible to them. At a minimum, employees should have been informed of a toll-free telephone number in the HR department to report complaints; the plaintiff here first was told there was no number to call, then given a wrong number. Furthermore, because a minor has to bring suit by means of a representative, retaliation based on the actions of a young worker's representative should be actionable. [*EEOC v. V&J Foods, Inc.*, 507 F.3d 575 (7th Cir. 2007), discussed in Fred Schneyer, *Appellate Panel Restores Teenager's Sex Harassment Suit*, plansponsor.com (Nov. 7, 2007)]

The District Court for the District of New Jersey granted summary judgment for the employer in a case of alleged hostile work environment created by a shift manager who was not the plaintiff's supervisor. Summary judgment was granted because there was an effective anti-harassment policy, including an effective reporting mechanism, and prompt remedial action was taken: within seven business days of the complaint, the employer completed an internal investigation, discussed the findings with top management, and decided to fire the shift manager. [*Barroso v. Lidestri Foods, Inc.*, No. 11-2059 (NLH/AMD), 2013 WL 1314438 (D.N.J. Mar. 28, 2013); see Carmen J. DiMaria, Evan J. Shenkman and Christopher J. Capone, *Effective Anti-Harassment Policy Warrants Summary Judgment On Hostile Work Environment Claim, District Of New Jersey Holds*, Ogletree Deakins (Sept. 18, 2013), available at Lexology.com]

The employer's failure to investigate a claimant's repeated reports of sexual harassment made her resignation a voluntary quit with good cause attributable to the employer, so benefits were available. [*Yaeger*, Unempl. Ins. Rep. (CCH) ¶ 8915 (Fla. Dist. App. 2001)]

[B] EEOC Enforcement Guidance

The EEOC's position about what employers should do is summed up in its 20-page guidance available online. [*Enforcement Guidance: Vicarious Employer*

Liability for Unlawful Harassment by Supervisors, Number 915.002 (June 18, 1999), <http://www.eeoc.gov/policy/docs/harassment.html> (last accessed Mar. 19, 2014); although the 1999 guidance is largely unchanged, it has been updated to discuss *Vance v. Ball State*; see § 35.02 above.]

The Guidance makes employers responsible for preventing harassment of all kinds—harassment based on sex (including derogation of women or men because they are women or men, even if the harasser is not seeking sexual gratification); race, color, religion, national origin, age, disability, or protected activity such as enforcing legal rights.

Under this Guidance, the employer will not be liable if harassment does not subject the employee to tangible disadvantages, as long as the employer uses reasonable care to prevent harassment. The employer is also free of liability if it takes reasonable steps to correct harassment that has already occurred, provided that the employee is also at fault by failing to take advantage of the policies and procedures in place.

Employers are liable for the actions of "supervisors": i.e., those with the authority to direct daily work activities, or with authority to recommend or implement tangible employment decisions.

Merely having a policy isn't enough: It must really be enforced. The EEOC encourages employers to terminate harassment even before it reaches the severe, protracted level that would justify a lawsuit.

Under the EEOC interpretation, the employer is always liable when a harassing supervisor subjects an employee to tangible employment action. A tangible employment action means a significant change in employment status such as firing, denial of a promotion, reassignment, an undesirable work assignment. An unfulfilled threat, a trivial effect, or causing hurt feelings doesn't count.

This is the minimum that the EEOC will accept as a satisfactory corporate anti-harassment policy:

- Clear explanations of what constitutes prohibited harassment;
- Assurances that employees who report harassment will not suffer retaliation;
- A clear explanation of a workable procedure for investigating complaints promptly, fairly, and thoroughly (with alternatives so that no one will be expected to report harassment to the person who committed it);
- A confidentiality procedure for complaints;
- Assurance of fast, appropriate response when the investigation shows that harassment has occurred.

Adequate responses to confirmation of a harassment allegation include:

- A warning or an oral or written reprimand to the harasser;

- Training and counseling the harasser about why the conduct violated the employer's policy;
- Transferring, reassigning, demoting, suspending, or, in appropriate cases, firing the harasser;
- Monitoring to make sure harassment has ended;
- Allowing the victim to take leave to get out of the range of harassment;
- Correcting the victim's file to remove unfair evaluations;
- Having the harasser apologize to the victim;
- Checking to make sure that there is no retaliation for reporting the harassment.

[C] Internal Investigations of Harassment Allegations

A recent article points out that a company's in-house counsel should not take the lead in investigating discrimination complaints—because the lawyer might have to testify at trial about the reasonableness of the employer's response to employee complaints. If the lawyer testifies, documents might become discoverable, including notes taken by in-house counsel when interviewing employees. In an Ohio case, mistrial was declared after the employer failed to produce the attorney's investigative notes from the internal investigation of allegations of discrimination, harassment, and retaliation. The employer was sanctioned by having to pay over $300,000 of the plaintiffs' attorney's fees because the house counsel had an ethical conflict of interest by performing the investigation. The article suggests having the investigation performed by HR personnel (trained to investigate) or outside consultants, although they should keep in-house counsel informed of the progress of the investigation. [*EEOC v. Spitzer*, 866 F. Supp. 2d 851 (N.D. Ohio 2013); see Jennifer A. Harper, *The Risks Of Using In-House Counsel To Conduct Internal Investigations*, Bean Kinney & Korman PC (Nov. 21, 2013), available at Lexology.com]

In a harassment case, the employer said that it did not have to produce all of its documents from its investigation, because some of the documents were covered by work product or attorney-client privilege. The District Court for the District of Massachusetts said that privilege was waived for the investigation report and all of the documents, interviews, and notes that were part of the investigation, because the investigation was directed and controlled by the attorney. This decision does not say that privilege is waived whenever a lawyer's communications with an investigator merely further the investigation without the lawyer becoming part of it. The best practice to preserve privilege is that lawyers should give instructions to investigators, but then remove themselves from the investigation. [*Koss v. Palmer Water Dep't*, 2013 WL 5564474 (D. Mass. Oct. 7, 2013); see David C. Henderson, *An Employer Waives the Attorney-Client Privilege if its*

Attorney Was "Part and Parcel" of the Sexual Harassment Investigation Offered in Defense, Nutter McClennen & Fish LLP News & Insight (Nov. 5, 2013) (benefitslink.com)]

§ 35.04 HOSTILE WORK ENVIRONMENT HARASSMENT

[A] Generally

A hostile work environment is one where actions are taken to make an employee feel unwelcome. Harassment cases have been recognized dealing with race, religion, disability, and age, as well as cases in which women are made uncomfortable by, e.g., unwanted touching, crude propositions, dirty jokes, pin-ups, etc. Hostile work environment sexual harassment cases have been recognized for many years, dating back to the Supreme Court case of *Meritor Sav. Bank v. Vinson.* [477 U.S. 57 (1986)]

A single act of harassment, if it is severe enough, can create a hostile work environment. The Seventh Circuit permitted a claim of co-worker harassment, who alleged unwelcome physical contact with intimate parts of her body, to proceed to trial. But she did not show that the alleged comments by her supervisor were severe or pervasive enough to create a hostile environment: the court said that she did not show that she felt humiliated or physically threatened, and she did not allege that her work performance was affected. [*Berry v. Chicago Transit Auth.*, 618 F.3d 688 (7th Cir. 2010); see Rebecca Moore, *Court Must Consider Uncorroborated Evidence in Hostile Workplace Suit*, plansponsor.com (Aug. 25, 2010)]

It can be difficult to predict what conduct will be considered sufficiently outrageous to create a hostile environment, because different courts have reached very different conclusions. There is often disagreement about the seriousness of conduct that constitutes harassment, how severe and prolonged it must be, and the extent of injuries that the complainant must suffer before having a sustainable case.

The Eleventh Circuit permitted a female sales representative to pursue a hostile work environment suit because of very frequent use of anti-female language ("bitch" "whore") even though it was not specifically directed at the plaintiff herself. The plaintiff also alleged that there was a lot of workplace discussion about sexual topics, and sexually suggestive radio shows were frequently played in the workplace. Ingrid Reeves resigned her job in 2004 and brought suit. The Northern District of Alabama granted summary judgment for the employer, finding that Reeves herself was not the individual target, so the harassment was not "based on" her sex. A three-judge panel of the Eleventh Circuit reversed this decision in 2008, and was upheld by an en banc panel (of all the judges on the court) in 2010. [*Reeves v. C.H. Robinson*, 594 F.3d 798 (11th Cir. 2010);]

The California Court of Appeal reversed a verdict for the defense, holding that the trial court should have admitted "me too" evidence that the defendant, a lawyer, exhibited gender and racial bias by harassing and berating other women working in his office. The court of appeal found exclusion of this evidence prejudicial to the plaintiff. [*Pantoja v. Anton*, 198 Cal. App. 4th 87 (2011); see Kate Moser, *Court OKs 'Me Too' Testimony in Sex Harass Suit Against Lawyer*, The Recorder (Aug. 9, 2011) (law.com)]

[B] Retaliation

As Chapter 34 discusses, allegations of retaliation for filing discrimination claims are in themselves a major litigation area.

The Supreme Court's 2009 *Crawford* decision, which holds that employees are protected against retaliation if they respond to questioning in an employer's internal investigation—not just if they volunteer information about illegalities in the workplace—began as a sexual harassment case. The plaintiff charged her employer with retaliating against her for testifying in an investigation of charges raised by another employee; Crawford said that she had also been harassed by the same supervisor. [*Crawford v. Metropolitan Gov't of Nashville & Davison County, TN*, 555 U.S. 271 (2009); see Rebecca Moore, *Employees Questioned in Workplace Sexual Harassment Investigations Are Protected*, plansponsor.com (Jan. 26, 2009)]

The First Circuit held that a reasonable jury could believe that the drug company manager plaintiff, Collazo, opposed sexual harassment when he helped a co-worker pursue harassment charges. Although the employer's internal inquiry cleared the alleged harasser, a plaintiff does not have to prove that the conditions he or she opposed actually violated Title VII—only that he or she had a good faith reasonable belief that they did. Management argued that Collazo was fired for performance problems, and because his job was eliminated in a reorganization, but the First Circuit refused to allow reorganization to be used as an excuse for discriminatory or retaliatory termination. Nor was he given any counseling or progressive discipline for the supposed performance problems. Although other employees were transferred, Collazo was the only person terminated, and the only person not given a chance to transfer. Collazo did not get any verbal or written warnings or counseling in the months before his termination, supposedly for deficient performance. [*Collazo v. Bristol-Myers Squibb Mfg. Inc.*, 617 F.3d 39 (1st Cir. 2010)]

§ 35.05 SAME-SEX HARASSMENT

For several years, courts were divided about whether sexual harassment of a male employee by a male supervisor, or a female employee by a female supervisor, was barred by Title VII. Perhaps this reflects a stereotype of sexual harassment as only something that is perpetrated by males against females. Questions were raised as to whether same-sex harassment could be described as occurring "on account of sex," because the harasser is of the same sex as the victim.

The uncertainty was resolved by the Supreme Court in *Oncale v. Offshore Servs. Inc.* [523 U.S. 75 (1998)], which brought same-sex harassment into the ambit of Title VII.

In 1997, 12% of harassment charges were filed by men, a proportion that rose to 16% in FY 2011. Sparks Steak House agreed to pay $600,000 to settle EEOC charges of male/male harassment of waiters by managers. The harassment continued despite complaints from the waiters. The primary harasser, the maitre d'hotel, was given a last chance agreement, but was not fired. [Jenna Greene, *NYC Steakhouse Settles with EEOC over Male-on-Male Harassment Charges*, The BLT (Nov. 16, 2012) (law.com)]

On its own motion, the Eleventh Circuit decided to re-hear *Corbitt v. Home Depot*. The district court and the Eleventh Circuit dismissed the sexual harassment claim (in July and December 2009), but both times the retaliation claim was allowed to proceed. Two male plaintiffs alleged ongoing harassment from a male supervisor, who had a reputation for being vindictive. They were fired after complaining about the harassment, which the district court characterized as insufficient to alter the terms and conditions of employment. [The three decisions are 573 F.3d 1223 (July 10, 2009), 589 F.3d 1136 (Dec. 4, 2009) and 598 F.3d 1259 (Mar. 10, 2010). See Tresa Baldas, *Sex Harassment Suit Given Surprise Third Shot at 11th Circuit*, Nat'l L.J. (Mar. 17, 2010) (law.com)] But before the en banc court could render an opinion, the case was settled in July 2010. [*Corbitt v. Home Depot*, 611 F.3d 1379 (11th Cir. 2010); see Alyson M. Palmer, *Male Employees' Sex Harassment Case Settles Before Full 11th Circuit Rules* (special to law.com (July 30, 2010)]

An oil rig worker said that a bisexual male co-worker harassed him by not only insisting on describing his sexual activities with women, but also propositioning the plaintiff and subjecting him to unwanted sexual touching. The Sixth Circuit held that the plaintiff failed to provide proof of the alleged harasser's sexual orientation, which was necessary to create the inference that the plaintiff was harassed "because of his sex." The Sixth Circuit requires proof of at least one of three elements in a same-sex harassment case: (1) credible evidence that the alleged harasser is homosexual; (2) clear evidence that the harasser is generally hostile to the presence of members of the plaintiff's sex in the workplace; or (3) in a mixed-sex workplace, with worse treatment by the harasser of one sex than the other. All of the oil rig workers were male and there was no evidence that the alleged harasser was hostile to males as a group. Therefore, the Sixth Circuit required proof of the alleged harasser's sexual orientation, and held that a suggestion that he was bisexual was not enough to prove the plaintiff's case. [*Wasek v. Arrow Energy Servs., Inc.*, 682 F.3d 463 (6th Cir. 2012)]

On August 12, 2013, California Governor Brown signed SB 292, amending the Fair Employment and Housing Act (FEHA) to provide that sexual harassment plaintiffs do not have to prove that the harassing conduct was motivated by sexual desire. Under SB 292, the sexual orientation of the victim, or the sexual intent of the harasser is no longer relevant. [Susan W. Pangborn, *New California Law Expands The Concept Of Sexual Harassment*, Kilpatrick Townsend & Stockton LLP (Aug. 14, 2013), available at Lexology.com; Winston & Strawn LLP, *California Governor Signs Bill That Expands Sexual Harassment Standards In Same-Sex Cases*, Lexology.com (Aug. 20, 2013). The legislation overrules *Kelley v. The Conco Cos.*, 196 Cal. App. 4th 191 (2011), which was interpreted to require a motivation of sexual desire in same-sex harassment cases.]

The Fifth Circuit, sitting en banc, held in late 2013 that harassment based on gender stereotypes can be actionable under Title VII as "because of sex." The ironworker plaintiff suffered constant verbal and physical harassment, including indecent exposure and jokes about rape, because the supervisor didn't think the victim was manly enough. There was no evidence that the harasser wanted to have sex with the victim and there was no evidence of hostility toward men in general, or that men and women were treated differently. The Fifth Circuit joined the Third, Seventh, Eighth, and Tenth Circuits in holding that those factors (which come from the Supreme Court's *Oncale* ruling on same-sex harassment) are illustrative, not all required to prove harassment. Therefore, the EEOC could make its case based on harassment for perceived lack of conformity with gender stereotypes (whether or not the victim actually was "manly.") [*EEOC v. Boh Bros. Constr. Co.*, 731 F.3d 444 (5th Cir. 2013); see Dennis A. Clifford and Christopher J. DeGroff, *"Macho Man Discrimination": The EEOC Scores Fifth Circuit Win In Gender-Stereotype Suit*, Seyfarth Shaw LLP (Oct. 3, 2013), available at Lexology.com. The case was subsequently settled by a consent judgment under which Boh Brothers agreed to pay compensatory damages of $125,000: see Manatt Phelps & Phillips LLP, *Same-Sex Harassment Suits Yield Sizable Settlement*, Lexology.com (Mar. 19, 2014).]

The Tenth Circuit, reversing the district court, held that it is possible for women to create a work environment that is hostile to other women (e.g., lewd jokes and offensive touching directed by lesbians against the heterosexual female plaintiff). However, the Tenth Circuit dismissed the retaliation claim because, at worst, there was one instance of discipline, in a situation that could be interpreted as management's attempt to prevent future harassment. [*Dick v. Phone Directories Co.*, 397 F.3d 1256 (10th Cir. 2005)] The Eighth Circuit disagreed, affirming summary judgment for the employer in a case in which a heterosexual female employee said that another heterosexual female employee subjected her (and other women) to unwanted rude, vulgar, and sexually charged behavior, such as sexual innuendo and groping. The plaintiff said that co-worker also engaged in similar conduct toward male employees. The plaintiff said that she complained about 100 times to at least 12 managers, but management denied that she had complained and refused to transfer her out of the baking department. Because the co-worker treated males and females in the same vulgar and inappropriate way, the Eighth Circuit said that the plaintiff could not prove that the conduct was motivated by sexual desire, that harassment was motivated by general hostility to the presence of women—or men—in the workplace, or that the harasser targeted only one sex for harassment. [*Smith v. HyVee Inc.*, 622 F.3d 904 (8th Cir. 2010)]

§ 35.06 ORIENTATION AND PERCEIVED ORIENTATION

Although a number of states and cities have their own laws against sexual-orientation discrimination, Title VII itself does not forbid discrimination on the basis of homosexual or bisexual orientation. [*Higgins v. New Balance Athletic Shoes Inc.*, 194 F.3d 252 (1st Cir. 1999); *Bibby v. Philadelphia Coca-Cola Bottling Co.*, 260 F.3d 257 (3d Cir. 2001)] The *Bibby* case says that three kinds of same-sex harassment are illegal: unwanted sexual advances made toward an employee of the same sex; harassment because the harasser believes that women or men do not belong in that type of workplace; or harassment for failure to behave with appropriate masculinity or femininity.

Some transsexual plaintiffs now raise claims that they are discriminated against because they present themselves as the "other" sex and do not conform to gender stereotypes. [See, e.g., *Tronetti v. TLC Healthnet Lakeshore Hosp.*, 03-CV-0375E(Sc), 2003 WL 22757935 (W.D.N.Y. Sept. 26, 2003); *Barnes v. Cincinnati*, 401 F.3d 729 (6th Cir. 2005), *cert. denied*, 546 U.S. 1003 (2005); *Price Waterhouse, Sex Stereotyping, and Gender Non-Conformity Bias*, 73 LW 2211 (Oct. 19, 2004)]

A transgender plaintiff, Maya Perez, sued Burlington Coat Factory, alleging years of physical and verbal abuse and retaliatory discharge. The California statute, FEHA, has covered gender identity since 2004. Perez alleged that co-workers taunted her and engaged in pushing, shoving, groping, and other forms of physical harassment. Perez also says that customers were verbally abusive and threatening, and that co-workers and supervisors observed harassment but did not intervene until it had escalated. [Evan Hill, *Rare Transgender Employment Discrimination Lawsuit Filed Against Burlington Coat Factory*, The Recorder (Feb. 26, 2009) (law.com)]

Although Title VII does not cover sexual orientation discrimination, the Third Circuit permitted an effeminate gay man to pursue a Title VII claim of harassment based on his failure to conform to gender stereotypes. The Third Circuit said that the case should not have been dismissed, but should have gone to a jury, because it was uncertain whether the case involved sexual orientation or gender discrimination (but affirmed dismissal of his charge that he was harassed for not conforming to his co-workers' religious beliefs). [*Prowel v. Wise Business Forms Inc.*, 579 F.3d 285 (3d Cir. 2009); see Shannon P. Duffy, *3rd Circuit Revives Gay Man's Title VII Suit*, The Legal Intelligencer (Aug. 31, 2009) (law.com); on harassment on the basis of perceived effeminacy, see also *EEOC v. Grief Bros. Corp.*, No. 02-CV-468S, 2004 WL 2202641 (W.D.N.Y. Sept. 30,

2004); *Doe v. City of Belleville*, 119 F.3d 563 (7th Cir. 2001); *Nichols v. Azteca Rest. Enters. Inc.* [256 F.3d 864 (9th Cir. 2001)]

Two mid-2002 cases reached opposite conclusions. The Ohio Court of Appeals agreed that a gay male worker stated a cause of action for severe emotional distress and depression affecting his work performance as a result of continuous harassment, graffiti, and unwelcome sexual remarks. [*Tenney v. GE Corp.*, 2002 Ohio 2975 (Ohio App. 2002)] But, in the Florida Court of District Appeals view, a lesbian did not state an emotional distress claim by alleging a severe and pervasive pattern of harassment by supervisors, including derogatory comments about homosexuality and abusive conduct directed to her as a lesbian, because the court did not find the conduct sufficiently outrageous to be actionable. [*DeLaCampa v. Grifola Am. Inc.*, 819 So. 2d 940 (Fla. Dist. App. 2002)]

A male AT&T Mobility worker lost his case alleging that hostile comments by his supervisor created a hostile work environment. The Sixth Circuit held that he did not prove that he was subjected to unwanted sexual conduct or communications on the basis of sex that substantially interfered with the conditions of employment. The Sixth Circuit characterized the supervisor's statements as teasing or name-calling, insufficient to create an actionable hostile work environment. Plaintiff Kalich contended that the supervisor targeted him for homophobic insults because he knew or suspected Kalich was gay—but in Michigan, sexual orientation is not a protected classification. The Sixth Circuit concluded that the supervisor did not have any sexual interest in Kalich, and treated him rudely and unpleasantly but that was how he treated everyone, irrespective of sex. Furthermore, the Sixth Circuit found that AT&T Mobility was entitled to the *Faragher/Ellerth* defense, because it investigated Kalich's allegations promptly, finished the investigation within 10 business days, and it transferred the alleged harasser and gave him anti-discrimination training and a final warning. [*Kalich v. AT&T Mobility*, 679 F.3d 464 (6th Cir. 2012)]

§ 35.07 WRONGFUL DISCHARGE CLAIMS

Employers often fear that they may be caught between two fires. If they do not respond to allegations, they face EEOC charges and/or lawsuits. But if they fire an alleged harasser, he or she may sue for wrongful termination. It is a delicate balance, but the employer can avoid liability by carrying out a thorough investigation in each case and taking proportionate steps against anyone found to have committed harassment. A complete "paper trail" is very important here (as in many other contexts).

When discriminatory discipline is charged, the question is whether different discipline is imposed for the same offense. A black female employee did not have a discrimination claim when she was fired for groping the genitals of male co-workers, when a white female was not fired for exposing her breasts on request, because the black female had engaged in conduct contrary to the wishes of its recipients, justifying a higher level of discipline. [*Wheeler v. Aventis Pharm.*, 360 F.3d 853 (8th Cir. 2004)]

Another implication of wrongful termination law is that in Maryland, an employee discharged for refusing to have sexual intercourse with a harasser can pursue a tort claim for abusive discharge in addition to the sexual harassment charges. The additional tort claim can be pursued because the state has a public policy against prostitution—and having sex to keep a job is, in effect, prostitution. [*Insignia Residential Corp. v. Ashton, Md.*, 755 A.2d 1080 (Md. 2000)]

§ 35.08 DAMAGE ISSUES

The Seventh Circuit allows a sexual harassment plaintiff to get punitive damages in cases in which there were no compensatory damages. [See *Timm v. Progressive Steel Treating Inc.*, 137 F.3d 1008 (7th Cir. 1998)] This might occur, for instance, where a company fails to establish a complaint procedure and then blames the plaintiff for failure to go through channels. In this case, the plaintiff mitigated her damages so effectively that she got a higher-paying job, and therefore could not collect a back pay award.

The Supreme Court has imposed a general rule, for all kinds of cases, that punitive damages should not be more than nine times compensatory damages. Late in 2003, the District of Columbia Court of Appeals struck down an award of $4.8 million in punitive damages in a sexual harassment retaliation case, finding it to be unconstitutionally excessive (26:1 ratio). The award was also improper because it reflected the defendant's nationwide conduct, not just its treatment of the individual plaintiff. Furthermore, the most relevant civil penalty under the local Human Rights Act was only $50,000 for multiple offenses. [*Daka Inc. v. McCrae*, 839 A.2d 682 (D.C. App. Dec. 24, 2003)]

The Seventh Circuit affirmed a jury award of $15,000 in compensatory and $50,000 punitive damages to a nursing home employee who experienced lewd remarks and inappropriate touching from residents. Her supervisor told her to get a security escort before cleaning the rooms of those residents, but the security guards always said they were too busy to accompany her. The Vice President of Operations said that the nursing facility was the residents' home and nothing was going to change, and it was the employee's fault for making residents want to touch her. Pickett, the employee, thought that this conversation meant that she was fired, so she left the building (which violated the work rules). The next day, when she reported for work, she was told that she had been fired. After she filed an EEOC charge, she was offered reinstatement, which she eventually accepted. The Seventh Circuit held that the jury was justified in believing Pickett's contention that a business can be responsible for sexual harassment committed by third parties, such as customers or nursing home residents, so the question was whether Pickett provided enough evidence of harassment; the Seventh Circuit said she did.

The award of compensatory damages was not obviously excessive, was comparable to awards in similar cases, and the $15,000 jury award fell well within the $200,000 cap on damages. It was not unreasonable for the jury to assume that management was aware of federal laws, so punitive damages were justified. [*Pickett v. Sheridan Health Care Ctr.*, 610 F.3d 434 (7th Cir. 2010)]

A jury found Asarco liable for sexual harassment but found no compensatory damages, so it awarded $1 in nominal damages and $858,750 in punitive damages. The trial court reduced the award to $300,000 under the Title VII cap on damages. The Ninth Circuit, noting that an award of 300,000 times compensatory damages is impermissible, reduced the damages to $125,000, with the alternative of a new trial if Asarco would not accept the reduced damages. [*Arizona v. Asarco*, 733 F.3d 882 (9th Cir. 2013); see John Alan Doran, *New Math. Old Math. Any Old Math Will Do*, Sherman & Howard LLC (Oct. 25, 2013), available at Lexology.com. Rehearing en banc was granted on February 28, 2014 (No. 11-17484), so the case was "de-published."]

Normally, the question is whether the defendant will have to pay the plaintiff's legal fees and costs—but, in rare cases, a prevailing defendant will be entitled to a fee award. The EEOC brought a suit on behalf of more than 200 female truck drivers who said that they suffered sexual harassment, including rape in some cases, by male drivers assigned as trainers by their employers, CRST Van Expedited Inc. The District Court for the Northern District of Iowa not only dismissed the EEOC suit but also ruled that the defendant was the prevailing party in the suit—so the EEOC would have to pay almost $5 million of CRST's legal fees and litigation expenses. The district court found that the EEOC completely mishandled the preparation of the case and entirely failed to prove its pattern-or-practice theory. The district court gave the EEOC only three months for discovery, ruling that any woman for whom the EEOC did not get a deposition would be dismissed from the case. The EEOC took only 150 depositions, so 120 potential plaintiffs were excluded from the case. The district court dismissed all of the plaintiffs' claims because the EEOC did not investigate or attempt conciliation in each individual case. The district court also said that the trainers were not supervisors, so CRST was not vicariously liable for any harassment that occurred.

The EEOC appealed to the Eighth Circuit, which upheld most of the district court's findings. However, the Eighth Circuit ruled that claims of two of the plaintiffs should not have been dismissed. Therefore, CRST was no longer a prevailing defendant, and the EEOC did not have to pay its fees and costs right away (although it might have to at a later stage of the case). The Eighth Circuit held that the EEOC had an obligation to investigate thoroughly before filing suit and to attempt conciliation of each claim. [*EEOC v. CRST Van Expedited Inc.*, 679 F.3d 657 (8th Cir. 2012); *en banc reh'g denied* (June 8, 2012). However, the Eighth Circuit remanded the case to the Northern District of Iowa—which once again ordered the EEOC to pay close to $5 million to CRST for attorneys' fees, court costs, and other expenses, reinstating the finding that CRST was a prevailing defendant. The district court criticized the EEOC for the inadequacy of its investigation and its failure to attempt conciliation, and found the EEOC's pattern or practice claim unreasonable because of the lack of statistics or legal citations to back up the charges. The district court found that the EEOC brought 153 individual claims that were frivolous, unreasonable, or groundless. [*EEOC v. CRST Van Expedited, Inc.*, No. 07-CV-95, 2013 U.S. Dist. LEXIS 107822 (N.D. Iowa Aug. 1, 2013); see Gerald L. Maatman, Jr. and Howard M. Wexler, *Time to Pay Up! EEOC Ordered to Pay $4.694 Million in Fees and Costs for Pursuing "Unreasonable" and "Groundless" Claims*, Lexology.com (Aug. 3, 2013)]

See also *EEOC v. Great Steaks, Inc.*, 667 F.3d 510 (4th Cir. 2012): the jury ruled for the defendant in an EEOC suit charging hostile environment sexual harassment. The Fourth Circuit held that the defendant was not entitled to an award of attorneys' fees under Title VII, the Equal Access to Justice Act, or the federal statute against "vexatious litigation." The Fourth Circuit held that, although a prevailing defendant does not have to prove the plaintiff's subjective bad faith to receive a fee award, the plaintiff must either have made a groundless, unreasonable, or frivolous claim, or must have prolonged the litigation after it was clear that the suit was inappropriate. In this case, even though the EEOC's case was not strong enough to win, it was not worthless.]

§ 35.09 LIABILITY OF INDIVIDUALS

Sexual harassment charges are not really very similar to charges of, say, environmental pollution, commercial fraud, or tax evasion. Although a corporation is only an artificial person, so individuals must commit its wrongful acts, in some cases individuals who commit a tort or a crime are doing so on behalf of the corporation. People who commit sexual harassment may be echoing a corporate culture that tolerates such things, but they are not benefiting the corporation!

Nevertheless, the language of Title VII, like most antidiscrimination statutes, refers only to "employers," and with few exceptions, courts have ruled that only the employer corporation, and not the individual, is liable for harassment. [No individual liability: *Carrisales v. Dep't of Corrs.*, 90 Cal. Rptr. 2d 804 (Cal. 1999); *Smith v. Amedisys Inc.*, 298 F.3d 434 (5th Cir. 2002). But see *Speight v. Albano Cleaners*, 21 F. Supp. 2d 560 (E.D. Va. 1998), where the individual supervisor was held liable, but the corporation was not held liable]

Reno v. Baird [957 P.2d 1333 (Cal. 1998)] holds that an individual manager, although potentially liable for harassment, is not an "employer" under California's antidiscrimination statute. Although the state's Fair Employment and Housing Act defines "employer" to include "any person acting as an agent of an employer, directly or indirectly" the *Baird* court interpreted this language to make employers liable for the action of their agents, not to make agents personally liable.

§ 35.10 INTERACTION WITH OTHER STATUTES

It is a familiar theme throughout this book that legal concepts do not exist in isolation, and a single case may trigger many statutes and regulations.

According to the Kentucky Supreme Court, there is an exception to Worker's Compensation exclusivity for injuries occurring through the "deliberate intention" of the employer. Therefore, although a suit against the employer for the physical and psychological consequences of sexual harassment would not necessarily be barred by WC exclusivity, nevertheless plaintiffs must make a choice. Either they can bring a tort suit (for instance, for intentional or negligent infliction of emotional distress; battery) or file for Worker's Compensation benefits. Acceptance of the Comp benefits rules out a suit involving the same injuries. [*Am. Gen. Life & Accident Ins. Co. v. Hall*, 74 S.W.3d 688 (Ky. Sup. 2002)]

The Bankruptcy Abuse Prevention and Consumer Protection Act of 2005 (BAPCA; Pub.L. No. 109-8) denies a discharge in a Chapter 13 case for civil damages awarded against the debtor when the debtor's willful or malicious injury resulted in personal injury or death to a plaintiff.

A "top-hat" (executive benefit) plan called for payment of benefits on termination, with no qualifications. Because the plan did not mandate forfeiture when an employee was fired for cause, someone who was fired for sexually harassing employees was eligible for the benefits. [*Fields v. Thompson Printing Co.*, 363 F.3d 259 (3d Cir. 2004)]

The Second Circuit required a makeup artist to arbitrate her sexual harassment claims against her employer, Atlantic Video, and against ESPN, even though ESPN did not sign the arbitration agreement. The plaintiff alleged that she was harassed by ESPN personnel, and that Atlantic Video and ESPN engaged in concerted action to allow the harassment to continue. [*Ragone v. Atlantic Video*, 595 F.3d 115 (2d Cir. 2010)]

CHAPTER 36

AMERICANS WITH DISABILITIES ACT (ADA)

§ 36.01 INTRODUCTION

Since its passage in 1990, the Americans With Disabilities Act (ADA) has been contentious and controversial. In recent years, the Supreme Court and the lower courts have greatly limited the scope of this Act, especially in the employment arena. Employers nearly always prevail in these cases, for a variety of reasons, such as lack of proof that:

- The plaintiff was a Qualified Individual With a Disability (QIWD). NOTE: 2011 EEOC guidance does not use the term QIWD; see § 36.04[F] below;
- The plaintiff suffered adverse employment action;
- The plaintiff sought reasonable accommodation;
- A reasonable accommodation could have met the plaintiff's needs without unduly burdening the employer.

Perhaps the suit can be dismissed because it was brought against an employer who is not subject to the ADA, or on grounds of untimeliness.

The ADA starts at 42 U.S.C. § 12101 (regulations at 29 C.F.R. § 1630.1). Title I is the employment title; Title II deals with public services (i.e., provided by government; Title III with public accommodations, and Title IV with miscellaneous issues, some of which relate to employment.

Major legislation, the ADA Amendments Act of 2008, or ADAAA, was passed in 2008 to clarify some disputed ADA issues, and reverse some of the harsher effects of recent Supreme Court precedents. See § 36.03, below. A number of decisions hold that the ADAAA is not retroactive [See, e.g., *EEOC v. Agro Distribution, LLC*, 555 F.3d 462 (5th Cir. 2009)], so there will be a period of time when pre-ADAAA cases continue to be decided by the legal system.

The ABA found that in 1999, employers won 85% of ADA administrative claims—and 95% of ADA lawsuits; it is still unclear how that ADAAA will affect those odds. [Hunton & Williams LLP, *Disability Still Matters In ADA Claims* (Nov. 14, 2013), available at Lexology.com]

In fiscal 2013, 25,957 EEOC charges (27.7% of all charges filed) included a disability discrimination claim. [Barry A. Hartstein, *EEOC Releases Charge Statistics For FY 2013*, Littler Mendelson (Feb. 5, 2014), available at Lexology .com]

§ 36.02 REACH AND RANGE OF ADA TITLE I

According to 42 U.S.C. § 12101, Congress went on record that the over 43 million employees with disabilities (a number that is increasing as the population ages) have a history of social alienation and discrimination in important areas such as work, housing, public accommodations, health services, and education.

Congress declared that people with disabilities are a minority group that has suffered discrimination—and that our national goal in dealing with people with disabilities should be "to assure equality of opportunity, full participation, independent living, and economic self sufficiency." The legislative purpose is given as providing "clear, strong, consistent, enforceable standards addressing discrimination against individuals with disabilities."

A "covered entity," as defined by 42 U.S.C. § 12111(2), means an employer, an employment agency, a union, or a joint labor-management committee.

Only employers who have at least 15 employees in each working day in each of 20 or more weeks in the current or preceding year are subject to the ADA. [42 U.S.C. § 12111(5)]

In an April 22, 2003, decision, the Supreme Court ruled that four physicians who were shareholders and directors of a medical PC were probably not "employees," using the economic reality test. The doctors controlled business operations; they were not subject to the control of others. If so, the professional corporation had fewer than 15 "employees," and the PC's bookkeeper could not bring suit under the ADA, whether or not it was true that she was terminated because of disability. [*Clackamas Gastroenterology Assocs., PC v. Wells*, 538 U.S. 440 (2003)]

An employer with fewer than 15 employees, although exempt under the ADA, can be sued under the Rehabilitation Act. [*Schrader v. Fred A. Ray, MD PC*, 296 F.3d 968 (10th Cir. 2002)]

Individuals are nearly always exempt from being sued under antidiscrimination suits (only the employer company is liable). *Alberte v. Anew Health Care Servs.* [588 N.W.2d 298 (Wis. App. 1998)] permits an ADA suit against an individual who was president, administrator, and 47.5% shareholder in a company accused of disability discrimination. In this reading, the president was the company's agent and personally liable for both compensatory and punitive damages. But this ruling is an anomaly. Far more typically, in mid-2007, the Eleventh Circuit held that individuals cannot be sued for violating the ADA's ban on retaliation in employment, nor under the Florida state statute that forbids HIV/AIDS discrimination. (The plaintiff brought suit against his employer company and three of its officers as individuals.) The Eleventh Circuit concluded that the language of the employment provisions of the ADA is similar to that of Title VII and the ADEA, where individual suits have been ruled out, and cited the Southern District of Florida's conclusion that the state anti-discrimination statute also rules out suits against individuals. [*Albra v. Advan, Inc.*, 490 F.3d 826 (11th Cir. 2007)]

A U.S. citizen who works outside the United States can count as an employee entitled to protection under the ADA. [42 U.S.C. § 12111(4)] However, it is not unlawful for a workplace outside the United States to comply with local law, even if the result is discrimination. Foreign operations of a foreign company that is not controlled by an American employer are exempt from the ADA. [42 U.S.C. § 12112(c)]

Section 12115 requires employers to post notices of ADA rights "in an accessible format" in the workplace.

The ADA does not invalidate or limit the remedies, rights, and procedures of any state or federal law that provides additional protection of the rights of individuals with disabilities. [42 U.S.C. § 12201]

"Mixed-motive" cases (where disability discrimination is alleged to be only one factor in the employer's decision) can be brought in some circuits, where it is not necessary for the plaintiff to allege that the employer was solely motivated by disability discrimination. [*McNely v. Ocala Star-Banner Corp.*, 99 F.3d 1068 (11th Cir. 1996)] However, the Sixth Circuit does not allow mixed-motive cases: to sue there, the plaintiff must allege that disability must have been the sole cause for the employment decision. [*Hedrick v. W. Reserve Care Sys.*, 355 F.3d 444 (6th Cir. 2004)] On the other hand, the Ninth Circuit does permit mixed-motive ADA cases. [*Head v. Glacier Nw.*, 413 F.3d 1053 (9th Cir. 2005)]

Most of the circuits allow hostile environment claims in the ADA context, because the ADA uses the same language as Title VII "terms, conditions and privileges of employment" so the concept of the hostile work environment has been extended to cover the ADA as well as Title VII. [*Shaver v. Indep. Stave Co.*, 350 F.3d 716 (8th Cir. 2003); *Flowers v. S. Reg'l Physician Servs. Inc.*, 247 F.3d 229 (5th Cir. 2001); *Fox v. Gen. Motors Corp.*, 247 F.3d 169 (4th Cir. 2001)] To win a hostile environment suit, the plaintiff must show that he or she is a member of the protected group; that unwelcome harassment occurred; that it resulted from membership in the protected class; and it was severe enough to affect the terms, conditions, or privileges of employment. [*Reedy v. Quebecor Printing Eagle, Inc.*, 333 F.3d 906 (8th Cir. 2003)] In the *Shaver* case, the plaintiff had severe epileptic seizures, and at least some of his colleagues treated him as stupid or mentally ill for that reason or because he had had brain surgery resulting in removal of part of his skull. There is evidence that he was taunted, but the Eighth Circuit concluded that the verbal harassment was not severe enough to rise to the level of an objectively hostile work environment. The plaintiff was upset, but not threatened or traumatized.

Although Congress specifically stated in 42 U.S.C. § 12202 that states are NOT immune from ADA suits, the Supreme Court held in 2001 that Congress had no right to abrogate the states' "sovereign immunity" (freedom from being sued) with respect to ADA Title I cases that seek money damages rather than injunctions, because there was no documentation of a past history of disability discrimination perpetrated by the states themselves. [See *Board of Trustees of the Univ. of Ala. v. Garrett*, 531 U.S. 356 (2001)] In 2002, the Supreme Court held that punitive damages are not available in a suit for discrimination against disability discrimination committed by a public body, or by an agency that receives federal funding. [*Barnes v. Gorman*, 536 U.S. 181 (2002)] The Fifth Circuit later ruled that Congress did not properly abrogate the states' sovereign immunity with respect to ADA Title II either [*Reickenbacker v. Foster*, 274 F.3d 974 (5th Cir. 2001)], and the Second Circuit agrees. [*Garcia v. SUNY Health Sciences Ctr.*, 280 F.3d 98 (2d Cir. 2001)] *Gibson v. Ark. Dep't of Corrs.* [265 F.3d 718 (8th Cir.

2001)] says that although the states themselves are immune from suits for damages under the ADA, state officials can be sued to get prospective injunctive relief. It has also been held that states can be held liable for retaliation against employees who exercise ADA rights. [*Roberts v. Pa. Dep't of Pub. Welfare*, 199 F. Supp. 2d 249 (E.D. Pa. 2002). See Shannon P. Duffy, *States Not Immune From ADA Retaliation Suits*, The Legal Intelligencer (Feb. 27, 2002) (law.com)]

However, the Fifth Circuit ruled that the Eleventh Amendment does not give the states immunity against ADA suits brought by the United States itself seeking victim-specific relief for individuals. In this situation, the individuals themselves would not be able to sue—but one consequence of a state ratifying the U.S. Constitution is consent to being sued by the United States itself and by other states. [*United States v. Miss. Dep't of Pub. Safety*, 321 F.3d 495 (5th Cir. 2003)]

§ 36.03 FORBIDDEN DISCRIMINATION

It is unlawful to discriminate against a qualified individual with a disability (QIWD) because of that person's disability, with respect to the terms, conditions, and privileges of employment: e.g., job application, hiring, promotion, discharge, compensation, and training. [See 42 U.S.C. § 12112]

Section 12112 goes on to enumerate seven types of action that constitute disability discrimination:

- Limiting, segregating, or classifying applicants or employees in ways that affect their opportunities, because of disability;
- Entering into a relationship (for instance, with an employment agency) that results in disability discrimination;
- Using standards, criteria, or methods of administration that either discriminate or perpetuate discrimination by another party under the same administrative control (e.g., another division in the same company);
- Denying jobs or benefits to a qualified person who has a relationship or association with someone else who has a disability (e.g., refusing to hire someone merely because he or she is married to a person with a disability who has high medical bills that might result in higher EGHP premiums);
- Failing to make a reasonable accommodation to known physical or mental limitations of an employee or applicant who is a QIWD—unless the accommodation would work undue hardship on the employer; or denying employment opportunities to QIWDs if the denial is based on the need to accommodate;
- Using employment tests or other standards or criteria that screen out people with disabilities—but a defense is available for job-related measures that are consistent with business necessity;

- Using tests that are biased by an applicant's or employee's impairment (speech difficulties, for instance) and therefore fail to reflect the job aptitudes that the test is supposed to assess.

It is also unlawful to retaliate against anyone who opposed any act of disability discrimination, or who made a charge, testified, assisted, or participated in an investigation, administrative proceeding, or court case. It is unlawful to interfere with the ADA investigation process, or to "coerce, intimidate, threaten, or interfere with" anyone because of enforcement of ADA rights. [42 U.S.C. § 12203]

The ADA Amendments Act of 2008, ADAAA (Pub. L. No. 110-325), was signed September 25, 2008 and took effect January 1, 2009. Congress passed the legislation to reverse various Supreme Court decisions that made it very difficult for ADA claims to succeed because they ruled that a variety of impairments were not ADA "disabilities." As a result of the ADAAA, the central question is not whether the plaintiff has a disability, but whether the employer reasonably accommodated disabled applicants and employees.

The ADAAA adds two lists of major life activities, although the statute specifies that these lists are illustrative, not comprehensive. Major activities of daily living include self-care, manual tasks, seeing, hearing, eating, standing, walking, sleeping, breathing, working, concentrating, thinking, learning, and communicating. The second list is of major body systems (e.g., circulatory, digestive, excretory, reproductive) whose impairment can constitute a disability. An impairment is considered a disability even if it is episodic or in remission, as long as it substantially limits a major life activity during a relapse.

The definition of being "regarded as" having a disability is expanded to forbid employers to discriminate based on their perception of a mental or physical impairment—whether or not the plaintiff can establish that the impairment actually limits or is perceived to substantially limit a major life activity. A "regarded as" claim cannot be based on a transitory impairment—one that actually lasts, or is expected to last, six months or less. Employers do not have a duty to provide reasonable accommodation for a perceived disability. Except for ordinary glasses and contact lenses, mitigating measures are not taken into account in determining whether a person has a disability. [EEOC Notice *Concerning the Americans With Disabilities Act (ADA) Amendments Act of 2008*, <http://www.eeoc.gov/ada/amendments_notice.html> (undated, but refers to EEOC regulations taking effect March 25, 2011; accessed Apr. 9, 2014); see Lawrence A. Lorber, Fredric C. Leffler and Samantha Morris, *Get Ready to Re-Learn the ADA*, Legal Times (Oct. 20, 2008) (law.com)] See § 36.04[F] for EEOC guidance about the ADAAA.

[A] Association

The ADA also forbids discrimination in fringe benefits on the basis of an employee's relationship to or association with a person who has a disability.

The EEOC says that the ADA association provisions forbid employers to discriminate based on stereotyping of people who associate with someone who has a disability: e.g., that a person whose child has a disability will take excessive time off work or that a person who worked or lives with HIV-positive people will develop AIDS. The relationship does not have to be familial, as long as the employer used the relationship to take adverse action. The EEOC does not treat the belief that the person's association with a person with a disability will increase the company's health insurance costs as a legitimate business motivation—but does not require employers to enhance their insurance program to make it more disability-friendly. Employees who seek leave to care for family members with a disability must be treated equally with employees who seek leave for other reasons. [EEOC, *Questions and Answers About the Association Provision of the Americans With Disabilities Act*, <http://www.eeoc.gov/facts/association_ada.html> (Feb. 2, 2011, accessed Apr. 9, 2014). Some of these situations can involve the FMLA, but this guidance is limited to ADA implications.]

Trujillo v. PacifiCorp., 524 F.3d 1149 (10th Cir. 2008), allowed an ADA association discrimination suit to proceed where a married couple were terminated, allegedly for falsifying their time records. According to the plaintiffs, they were fired because their son's terminal illness was very costly for the employer's self-insured medical plan.

California's Michelle Maykin Memorial Donation Protection Act requires paid leave for organ donors. A former branch manager of Auto-Chlor sued for violation of the Maykin Act, association discrimination, and wrongful termination in violation of public policy. He was hired in September 2010. He told Auto-Chlor that he was going to donate a kidney to his disabled sister in February 2011 and received unpaid leave to do so. When the Maykin Act passed, he requested extended and paid leave; he was given unspecified unpaid leave but not paid leave. He was fired two days before the Maykin Act took effect. He went ahead with the donation and sued, saying he was fired so that the employer would not have to provide paid leave or accommodate him after his return. The trial court dismissed the case, but the California Court of Appeal said that the Maykin Act applied prospectively only. However, he was permitted to pursue claims for association discrimination, wrongful termination in violation of public policy, and failure to maintain a nondiscriminatory environment. The court of appeal found it reasonable to infer that Auto-Chlor's actions were undertaken to avoid expenses related to Rope's association with a disabled person. [*Rope v. Auto-Chlor System of Washington, Inc.*, 220 Cal. App. 4th 635 (2013); see Daniel J. McCoy and Saundra L.L.M. Riley, *Discrimination Claim—Based On Association To Disabled Relative—Survives Dismissal Request*, Fenwick & West LLP (Dec. 13, 2013), available at Lexology.com]

EEOC Enforcement Guidance published in mid-2007 points out that, although employees who are caregivers for children or elderly or disabled family members are not entitled to separate protection against discrimination, subjecting a caregiver employee to negative employment actions could violate the ADA's ban on discrimination on the basis of association with a person with a disability. [EEOC Enforcement Guidance: *Unlawful Disparate Treatment of Workers with Caregiving Responsibilities* Number 915.002, <http://www.eeoc.gov/policy/docs/caregiving.html> (updated Feb. 8, 2011, accessed Mar. 27, 2014). See also EEOC, *Employer Best Practices for Workers with Caregiving Responsibilities*, <http://www.eeoc.gov/policy/docs/caregiver-best-practices.html> (Jan. 19, 2011, accessed Mar. 27, 2014).]

§ 36.04 DEFINING "DISABILITY"

[A] Generally

According to 42 U.S.C. § 12102, there are three forms of disability:

- A physical or mental impairment that substantially limits one or more of the major life activities of such individual;
- A record of such an impairment;
- Being regarded as having such an impairment (even if the impairment is only perceived and does not exist).

According to the statute, transvestism is not a disability [42 U.S.C. § 12209], nor are homosexuality, bisexuality, transsexualism, pedophilia, exhibitionism, gender identity disorders, compulsive gambling, kleptomania, pyromania, or current use of illegal drugs. [42 U.S.C. § 12211]

A QIWD is defined by 42 U.S.C. § 12111(8) as one who can perform the essential functions of the job (with or without accommodation). The employer's determination about which functions of a job are essential is entitled to consideration. Written job descriptions used in advertising or job interviews are considered evidence of the essential functions of the job. In other words, these descriptions must be drafted with care!

The EEOC's position is that determining which functions are essential to a job is a complex process involving several factors, e.g.:

- Expertise or skill needed to do that task;
- Other employees available to perform that function (as individuals or as a team);
- If that function is the entire rationale of the job;
- Time spent on that particular function;

- Qualifications of people who held the same job in the past;
- What would happen if the individual did not perform the function in question;
- What the Collective Bargaining Agreement (if there is one) says about the function as it relates to the job.

The Fourth Circuit held that even an impairment expected to last less than six months can be severely limiting (in this case, multiple leg fractures and tendon damage that kept the plaintiff from walking for seven months). The district court dismissed the case, on the grounds that the ADA does not cover temporary disabilities and he could have worked with a wheelchair. The Fourth Circuit reversed, stating that the district court should have considered whether the plaintiff was substantially limited before asking whether he could work with or without accommodation. [*Summers v. Altarum Institute*, 730 F.3d 325 (4th Cir. 2014); see Koryn M. McHone, *Fourth Circuit Court Of Appeals Analyzes The History Of The ADAAA And Remands Case Involving "Temporary Disability" To District Court*, Barnes & Thornburg LLP (Jan. 24, 2014), available at Lexology.com]

The First Circuit held that a restaurant assistant manager who did not recover fully after shoulder surgery was not a qualified individual with a disability, so her failure-to-accommodate/wrongful termination ADA case was properly dismissed. She was unable to perform the many manual tasks required of assistant managers. When she reported to work with a medical release imposing permanent lifting restrictions, she was told that she had been fired because she had used up her FMLA leave but was still disabled. The First Circuit ruled that no reasonable jury could believe that Richardson was able to perform the essential functions of the job. The First Circuit found that the job description made physical tasks central to the job, and Richardson's WC claim was based on her suffering injuries due to repetitive manual work. The First Circuit did not require the interactive process, holding that there was no reasonable accommodation that would have permitted Richardson to do the assistant manager's job. [*Richardson v. Friendly Ice Cream Corp.*, 594 F.3d 69 (1st Cir. 2010)]

The district court granted summary judgment for the employer in an ADA termination case. The Sixth Circuit reversed in part, finding an issue of material fact on the plaintiff's ability to perform the essential functions of the job of excavator operator after losing a leg above the knee. The plaintiff was, therefore, unable to haul the excavator to the worksite because it had a manual transmission and he was only cleared for driving automatic transmission vehicles. However, hauling the excavator was not included in the written job description and excavator operators only hauled the excavator to the site about one-third of the time. [*Henschel v. Clare Cnty. Rd. Comm'n*, 737 F.3d 1017 (6th Cir. 2013); see M. Scott Young, *ADA Claim: Job Descriptions Should Define Essential Functions Of Position*, Thompson Hine LLP (Dec. 17, 2013), available at Lexology.com]

The Tenth Circuit ruled that a function that is rarely required in the normal course of the employee's duties can be an essential job function if the consequences of hiring someone who cannot perform that function are serious enough: e.g., a prison physician's assistant who had several physical impairments that prevented her from complying with a newly adopted policy requiring all inmate-contact personnel to take physical safety training. [*Hennagir v. Utah Dep't of Corrs.*, 587 F.3d 1255 (10th Cir. 2009)]

The District Court for the District of Columbia held that an employee who cannot perform an essential function of the job is not a qualified employee, even if the employer previously excused the employee from that function as a temporary accommodation. The plaintiff said that, despite her nerve condition, she could work as a medical assistant if she was not required to do triage or lift more than 15–20 pounds. The employer argued that it reasonably accommodated her by offering a leave of absence. The district court held that employers are not required to reallocate essential functions, and triage was an essential function of the job; the employer did not waive the essential status by granting a temporary accommodation. [*Hancock v. Washington Hosp. Ctr.*, No. 10-CV-487 (RLW), 2014 WL 60288 (D.D.C. Jan. 7, 2014); see Michael L. Stevens and Karen S. Vladeck, *A Temporary Accommodation Does Not Necessarily Make It A Reasonable Accommodation*, Arent Fox LLP (Jan. 13, 2014), available at Lexology.com]

A Central District of Illinois jury awarded $100,000 in compensatory damages, $115,000 in back pay, and $500,000 in punitive damages against AutoZone for failure to provide reasonable accommodation to a sales manager with a disability. Pursuant to the CRA '91 cap, the punitive damages were reduced to $200,000. The manager was required to mop floors and perform other tasks violating the medical restrictions stemming from permanent neck and back injuries. The jury accepted the EEOC's position that these tasks were not an essential function of the sales manager's job and could have been assigned to other people. [Rebecca Moore, *Court Awards $600K in AutoZone EEOC Case*, plansponsor.com (June 6, 2011); earlier proceedings, *EEOC v. AutoZone Inc.*, 630 F.3d 635 (7th Cir. 2010)] Autozone appealed to the Seventh Circuit, seeking to reduce the compensatory and punitive damages to $10,000 each. The Seventh Circuit refused, holding that the district court did not abuse its discretion, because the compensatory damages were not excessive; the punitive damages were reduced because of the cap; and the ratio between compensatory and other damages was not excessive. The Seventh Circuit held that Autozone's conduct was reprehensible enough to justify reasonable punitive damages, because it forced Shepherd to undergo significant, and eventually disabling, pain. However, the Seventh Circuit ordered a remand to reduce the indefinite injunction to what it deemed a more reasonable three-year term. [*EEOC v. Autozone, Inc.*, 707 F.3d 824 (7th Cir. 2013)]

In June 1999, the Supreme Court decided three major employment-related cases, concluding that an individual is not disabled if the condition has been corrected, e.g., through medication or an assistive device. [*Murphy v. United Parcel*

Serv., 527 U.S. 516 (1999); *Sutton v. United Air Lines*, 527 U.S. 471 (1999); *Albertsons v. Kirkingburg*, 527 U.S. 555 (1999)]. The ADAAA, however, says that ordinary eyeglasses and contact lenses are the only ameliorative measure that can be considered in determining whether a person has an ADA disability.

Courts differ in their attitude toward obesity as a disability. The District Court for the Eastern District of Michigan dismissed Multibrand Field Services, a satellite dish installation company that maintained a policy of not hiring anyone weighing over 250 pounds, because employees must carry approximately 50 pounds of equipment, and the ladders are only rated to 300 pounds. Plaintiff Ayers applied but was not hired because he admitted weighing over 250 pounds. He contended that the restriction violates Michigan's Elliott-Larsen Civil Rights Act, which forbids weight discrimination. He amended his complaint to charge that the policy had a disparate impact on overweight people. The district court dismissed the disparate impact claim because the plaintiff failed to allege the necessary facially neutral policy or practice. Further, the district court ruled that sanctions were warranted, because the plaintiff's lawyer should have known that the disparate impact claim was frivolous. [*Ayers, et al. v. Multibrand Field Servs. Inc.*, Case No. 13-10765, 2013 U.S. Dist. LEXIS 133077 (E.D. Mich. Sept. 18, 2013); see Gerald L. Maatman, Jr. and Howard M. Wexler, *"Weight" Of Authority Leads To Dismissal (And Sanctions) Based On "Frivolous" Disparate Impact Claim*, Seyfarth Shaw LLP (Sept. 25, 2013), available at Lexology.com]

EEOC regulations say that body weight that is above or below the normal range, or that is the product of a physiological disorder, can be an impairment. As of September 2013, the EEOC had brought two morbid obesity disability suits.

The District Court for the District of Alabama rejected an ADA "regarded as" claim brought by a woman who was 5'3" tall and weighed 230 pounds. She said that her weight was neither caused by a medical condition nor caused medical conditions, nor did it affect her ability to work or self-care. The district court said that the plaintiff's obesity is not an impairment, merely a physical characteristic that might be viewed as undesirable, giving the example of a neon green Mohawk hairdo. The district court found a lack of evidence that the plaintiff's weight influenced the termination decision; a slender sales representative was fired at the same time, also for poor sales performance. [*Powell v. Gentiva Health Servs., Inc.*, No. 13-0007-WS-C, 2014 U.S. Dist. LEXIS 17709 (S.D. Ala. Feb. 12, 2014); see Michael J. Soltis, *Obesity, Like A Neon Green Mohawk Hairdo, Not An Impairment Under ADA*, Jackson Lewis PC (Feb. 19, 2014), available at Lexology.com]

The state of Michigan and six cities have laws forbidding discrimination on the basis of physical appearance, including obesity. The Kentucky Court of Appeals permitted a discrimination suit to proceed; the plaintiff is 5'4" tall and weighs 425 pounds. On a day off when she was moving to a new home, she stopped by the office to pick up her paycheck. A manager told her supervisor to fire her for being "overweight and dirty." The trial court granted summary judgment for the employer based on its statement that she was fired for low sales. The appeals court reversed, finding that she was qualified to perform her job and morbid obesity is an underlying physical condition that interferes with self-care and the major life activity of breathing. [*Pennington v. Wagner's Pharmacy*, 2013 Ky. App. LEXIS 104, 15 Accom. Disabilities Dec. (CCH) P15-199 (Ky. App. July 12, 2013); see Sharon B. Bauman et al., *Kentucky Court: Morbidly Obese Employee Disabled, Discrimination Suit Can Go Forward*, Manatt Phelps & Phillips LLP (Sept. 12, 2013), available at Lexology.com]

The Second Circuit described the New York City Human Rights Law as broader than federal law. The Second Circuit remanded to the district court the question of whether the New York law treats obesity as a disability. The plaintiff in this case charges that he was fired by a karate school because of his obesity. The Second Circuit also ruled that ADA retaliation plaintiffs can only sue the employer corporation, not individuals, because the ADA uses Title VII remedies. [*Spiegel v. Schulmann*, 604 F.3d 72 (2d Cir. 2010); see Mark Hamblett, *Judge to Determine if Obesity Constitutes a Disability in Karate Teacher's Suit Over Firing*, N.Y.L.J. (May 12, 2010) (law.com)]

Four revised documents in the EEOC's Question and Answer series have been published. The agency's position is that people with cancer, diabetes, epilepsy, or an intellectual disability are very likely to be considered disabled. The publications provide general information about those conditions; how employers can obtain and use employees' medical information; what questions are permissible; how to provide reasonable accommodation; and how to address safety concerns. [Kevin B. Leblang and Robert N. Holtzman, *Americans with Disabilities Act and Family Medical Leave Act Developments*, Kramer Levin Naftalis & Frankel LLP (Nov. 6, 2013), available at Lexology.com]

[B] Attendance

The question is often raised whether predictable, regular attendance is a fundamental job qualification. If it is, then it does not violate the ADA to fire, refuse to hire, etc., a person who cannot satisfy attendance requirements because of disability. [See, e.g., *EEOC v. Yellow Freight Sys., Inc.*, 253 F.3d 943 (7th Cir. 2001) (granting an unlimited number of sick days is not a reasonable accommodation)] A person whose physical or mental condition precludes working more than 40 hours a week has been held not to be ADA disabled, [*Tardie v. Rehabilitation Hosp. of R.I.*, 168 F.3d 538 (1st Cir. 1999)] given that there are many jobs available that do not require a commitment of over 40 hours a week. Also see *Davis v. Fla. Power & Light*, [205 F.3d 1301 (11th Cir. 2000)] finding that mandatory overtime was an essential function of the job, and it would violate the collective bargaining agreement to provide a no-overtime or selective-overtime arrangement for a disabled worker.

The Fourth Circuit held in 2012 that a maintenance engineer who was able to work eight hours a day, but could not work overtime or rotating shifts, was not disabled. He received long-term disability benefits from May to October 2004, then returned to work; his employer and the union negotiated a new day-shift job with base hours of eight hours a day rather than 10. According to the Fourth Circuit, the First, Third, Fifth, and Eighth Circuits have all ruled that an employee who can work 40 hours a week but not overtime is not substantially limited for ADA purposes. This is a pre-ADAAA case, so the issue is whether the plaintiff was significantly restricted in his ability to perform an entire class of jobs, or a broad range of jobs in various classes. [*Boitnott v. Corning Inc.*, 669 F.3d 172 (4th Cir. 2012)]

In the Eighth Circuit view, firing a dialysis technician who suffered from depression for attendance problems did not violate the ADA. For disabilities that are not open and obvious (including many mental disabilities), the initial burden is primarily on the employee to identify the disability, explain his or her limitations, and suggest reasonable accommodation. The Eighth Circuit held that, because she failed to inform her employer (a hospital) of her specific limitations, the duty to accommodate was not triggered. Allowing absences would not be a reasonable accommodation because the patients she treated were very sick and could not postpone treatment. Permission to take sudden unscheduled absences would have been for the employee's personal benefit, not relevant to the duties of the job. [*Rask v. Fresenius Med. Care N. Am.*, 509 F.3d 466 (8th Cir. 2007); see Rebecca Moore, *Employer Did Not Violate ADA by Not Excusing Unannounced Absences*, plansponsor.com (Dec. 31, 2007). See also *Rehrs v. The Iams Co.*, 486 F.3d 353 (8th Cir. 2007): after a change from fixed to rotating shifts, the Eighth Circuit accepted the employer's argument that ability to rotate shifts was an essential function of the job of warehouse technician because it gave all employees additional opportunities for training and career development, and allowing some employees to work straight shifts as an accommodation would undermine the team concept and burden other workers by having to take on more night shifts.]

The Second Circuit ruled in late 2013 that the defendant employer could not treat regular attendance as an essential job function in all ADA cases. Not only did the employer permit one-hour flextime at the beginning of the workday, but also for years the plaintiff had been given additional leeway in her start time, and she was willing to work late to make up for lost time. [*McMillan v. City of New York*, 711 F.3d 120 (2d Cir. 2013); see Mark S. Kittaka, *Timely Attendance Isn't An Essential Job Function?!?*, Barnes & Thornburg LLP (Oct. 18, 2013), available at Lexology.com; Kevin B. Leblang and Robert N. Holtzman, *Americans With Disabilities Act And Family Medical Leave Act Developments*, Kramer Levin Naftalis & Frankel LLP (Nov. 6, 2013), available at Lexology.com]

The New York Court of Appeals reinstated a disability discrimination claim brought by a former bank executive under the New York City Human Rights Law but affirmed dismissal of his claim under state human rights law. The plaintiff was on paid leave for more than four months for major depression and other illnesses, and could not state his return date. After he was fired, he sued under state and city laws. The New York Court of Appeals held that indefinite leave is never a reasonable accommodation under New York State law, but the broader city law places the burden on the employer to prove that the employee cannot perform essential job functions without reasonable accommodation. [*Romanello v. Intesa Sanpaolo, S.p.A.*, 22 N.Y.3d 881, 998 N.E.2d 1050, 976 N.Y.S.2d 426 (N.Y. Oct. 10, 2013); see Allison E. Ianni, *New York's Highest Court Rules Indefinite Leave Is Not A Reasonable Accommodation Under State Human Rights Law, But May Be Under City Human Rights Law*, Ogletree Deakins (Oct. 17, 2013), available at Lexology.com. But see *Basden v. Prof'l Transp. Inc*, 714 F.3d 1034 (7th Cir. 2013) permitting the employer to treat regular attendance as essential and holding that unreliable attendance does not have to be accommodated. Even though the plaintiff had documentation of a potential diagnosis of multiple sclerosis, the Seventh Circuit held that it was permissible to terminate an employee who asked for an indefinite leave of absence with no diagnosis, prescribed treatment plan, or estimated return date.]

The Eastern District of Texas granted summary judgment for the employer when a plaintiff missed more than 40 days in one year due to acute medical conditions; the court deemed regular attendance to be an essential function of the job—and this was set out in the employee handbook. [*Fuentes v. Krypton Solutions LLC*, No. 4:11cv581, 2013 WL 1391113 (E.D. Tex. Apr. 4, 2013)]

[C] Infertility

A 1996 case says that reproduction is not a major life activity, but in 1997, the Northern District of Illinois disagreed, even though reproduction does not directly affect employment. [Compare *Krauel v. Iowa Methodist Med. Ctr.*, 95 F.3d 674 (8th Cir. 1996), with *Erickson v. Bd. of Governors, Nw. Ill. Univ.*, 911 F. Supp. 316 (N.D. Ill. 1997), *later proceedings*, 207 F.3d 945 (7th Cir. 2000)]

The plaintiff in *Saks v. Franklin Covey Co.* [117 F. Supp. 2d 318 (S.D.N.Y. 2000)] was covered by a self-insured health plan that excluded "surgical impregnation procedures." She sued under Title VII, the ADA, and the Pregnancy Discrimination Act. The court ruled that infertility might be a disability, because it interferes with the major life activity of procreation.

However, the ADA claim was dismissed because all employees got the same coverage; infertile employees were not singled out for inferior coverage of reproductive services. The plan also qualified for the safe harbor for bona fide employee benefit plans. The Title VII claim failed because both male and female infertility were excluded. Surgical procedures were excluded for both female employees and wives of male employees. The PDA claim failed because infertility treatments were equally unavailable to pregnant and nonpregnant employees and beneficiaries.

The Second Circuit affirmed the dismissal in 2003 [*Saks v. Franklin Covey Co.*, 316 F.3d 337 (2d Cir. 2003)], although using a slightly different rationale.

The District Court looked at the question of whether all employees have equal access to plan benefits. The Second Circuit said that this standard, often used in ADA cases, was wrong because this was really a Title VII case. Therefore, the correct standard is whether sex-specific conditions exist. If they do, the question becomes whether excluding coverage for those conditions results in a plan with inferior coverage for one sex.

A late 2010 article says that it is possible that refusing to allow an employee to take intermittent FMLA leave for fertility treatment might violate the ADA or the Pregnancy Discrimination Amendment (PDA). Pregnancy itself is not an ADA disability, but under the ADAAA, it might be possible to argue that a pregnant employee was regarded as disabled.

According to the Northern District of Illinois, it did not violate the ADA to refuse to pay for infertility treatment for an employee's spouse, because the law does not extend to dependents of an employee if the dependents do not perform services for the employer. [*Niemeier v. Tri-State Fire Prot. Dist.*, 2000 U.S. Dist. LEXIS 12621 (N.D. Ill. Aug. 24, 2000)] Furthermore, non-employees can't sue the employer under Title VII or the PDA. The employee had standing (the legal right to pursue the PDA claim), but the claim itself was invalid, because the plan did not cover fertility treatment for either sex.

[D] Psychiatric Disability

ADA regulations [29 C.F.R. § 1630.2(h)(2)] define mental impairment to include developmental disability, learning disabilities, organic brain syndrome, and neurological disease, as well as mental or psychological disorders. The examples given by the EEOC are major depression, bipolar disorder, panic disorder, obsessive-compulsive disorder, post-traumatic stress disorder, schizophrenia, and personality disorders.

The psychiatric profession's official compendium, the Diagnostic and Statistical Manual of Mental Disorders (DSM), is the first step in identifying mental disorders. However, certain disorders are included in the DSM but excluded from ADA coverage—for instance, current drug and alcohol abuse, compulsive gambling, certain sexual disorders, and kleptomania.

Furthermore, persons who are troubled but not classically mentally ill may seek treatment such as family therapy. Such individuals are not impaired for ADA purposes. A mental illness impairment may be present yet not covered by the ADA, if it is mild enough not to substantially limit the impaired person's ability to work and carry out other major life activities.

The District Court for the Eastern District of Washington required Cottonwood Financial to pay $56,500 for unlawfully terminating store manager Sean Reilly because it regarded him as unable to work because of his psychiatric condition (bipolar disorder). Reilly was awarded $6,500 in back pay and $50,000 for emotional pain and suffering. [See EEOC press release, *EEOC Wins Disability*

Discrimination Suit Against Payday Lender "The Cash Store," <http://www1.eeoc.gov/eeoc/newsroom/release/3-28-12a.cfm> (Mar. 28, 2012)]

A recent article suggests that when an employee requests accommodation on the basis of a psychiatric claim, especially a hard-to-document stress claim, the employer should require an independent medical examination (IME) by a doctor it selects. The doctor may have useful ideas for accommodation and a plaintiff's refusal to get an IME can furnish a defense against ADA claims. [*Huiner v. Arlington Sch. Dist.*, No. 11-4172-KES (D.S.D. Sept. 26, 2013); see Lawrence P. Postol, *ADA Stress Claims – They Will Drive You Nuts*, Seyfarth Shaw LLP (Oct. 29, 2013), available at Lexology.com]

As the baby boom generation ages, it will become more common for employers to have to cope with employees who have Alzheimer's disease or other dementias. It has been estimated that 500,000 people under age 65 have early onset Alzheimer's disease, and no one knows how many of them are still in the workforce. Early onset Alzheimer's can cause personality changes (such as obsession or apathy) that create problems at work as well as in their families, although similar symptoms could have many other causes, such as depression and thyroid problems. In some cases, an employee with early onset Alzheimer's might be disciplined or fired for poor performance when he or she should be offered reasonable accommodation or perhaps disability retirement.

The Alzheimer's Association of the National Capital Area created a pilot project for corporate assistance to Alzheimer's caregivers, but the organization was not aware of any corporation with an existing policy or program to help these caregivers. [Beth Baker, *When Alzheimer's Strikes Reasonable Accommodations Might Include Flexible Schedule, Reminders, or Help from a Co-worker*, workforce.com (benefitslink.com)]

An epileptic who was fired after several incidents of aggressive and threatening behavior was neither disabled nor regarded as disabled. The Eighth Circuit held that he did not show that epilepsy substantially limited major non-work life activities. Although the plaintiff's former employer told him to get anger-management therapy, the Eighth Circuit did not deem this to mean that the employer regarded him as having an emotional condition that was substantially limiting. [*Brunke v. Goodyear Tire & Rubber Co.*, 344 F.3d 819 (8th Cir. 2003)]

[E] *Williams* and "Impairment"

Early in 2002, the Supreme Court decided *Toyota Motor Manufacturing, Kentucky, Inc. v. Williams.* [534 U.S. 184 (2002)] The court held that the plaintiff, who had carpal tunnel syndrome, was not disabled for ADA purposes. She was able to care for herself and perform ordinary daily tasks. In this view, merely having an impairment does not make a person disabled, nor does being unable to perform the tasks associated with that person's specific job, as long as the person can perform other tasks.

Williams is one of the cases that the ADAAA is designed to reverse.

The Lilly Ledbetter Fair Pay Act, Pub. L. No. 111-2, also applies to the ADA, so a suit can be brought within 180 days (or, if the state has an anti-discrimination agency, 300 days) of each time that an employee is subjected to discriminatory conduct under the ADA—even if the conduct is the result of a policy that was adopted much earlier.

[F] EEOC Guidance

The EEOC proposed regulations in September 2009 to implement the ADAAA.

Under the proposal, actions based on an impairment include actions based on symptoms of an impairment. Reasonable accommodation is not required in "regarded-as" cases. An impairment that substantially limits one life activity does not have to be shown to limit others. For example, a diabetic whose endocrine system is substantially limited does not also have to show substantial limitation in eating; a person whose normal cell growth is limited by cancer doesn't have to show limitation in working. The examples of episodic or remitting impairments include epilepsy, hypertension, multiple sclerosis, asthma, cancer, depression, bipolar syndrome, and post-traumatic syndrome disorder.

The DOL lists certain impairments as consistently meeting the definition of disability: deafness, blindness, intellectual disability, amputations, use of a wheelchair, autism, cancer, cerebral palsy, diabetes, epilepsy, multiple sclerosis, muscular dystrophy, and major mental illness. However, the EEOC's position is that the fact that a condition does not appear on the list does not mean it is not a disability. Some conditions are disabling for some people but not others, depending on their seriousness: for example, asthma, learning disabilities, back injuries.

The fact that a claimant got another job does not rule out that person's having a substantial limitation in working. Under the proposed regulations, a person with a disability can usually establish coverage by showing a limitation in major life activities other than working, so it will generally be unnecessary to consider whether there is a limitation in working. The new definition of "regarded as disabled" is an adverse action taken by an employer because of an actual or perceived impairment. The employee need not prove that the employer perceived him or her as substantially limited in the ability to perform a major life activity.

Previously, in 2006, the EEOC issued FAQs about the ADA implications of deafness and hearing impairment in an aging population. The EEOC warns employers to assess hearing-impaired workers' abilities on a case-by-case basis, and not to assume that hearing impairment always means that the worker compromises workplace safety. Lip-reading and sign language interpretation are not considered mitigating measures, because they do not improve the person's hearing.

The EEOC says that it is inappropriate to ask questions about hearing tests, hearing aids, and occupationally caused hearing loss during pre-job-offer interviews. However, it is legitimate to direct all job applicants to information (e.g., an HR person; part of the company Website) about reasonable accommodations in the application process.

The EEOC lists sign language interpreters; special telephones; telephone headsets; vibrating or flashing emergency notifications; assistive software; writing notes; assistive listening devices; and devices that translate speech into writing as examples of reasonable accommodation for those with hearing loss. Changing the employee's work area (e.g., away from an area with ambient noises that interfere with a hearing aid) can also be a reasonable accommodation. In some instances, allowing an employee to trade an assignment with another employee to avoid a task that is a small part of the job, and that is difficult for a hearing-impaired person to perform, will be considered a reasonable accommodation. But a solution that deprives the hearing-impaired worker of real-time access to events (e.g., furnishing written minutes after a meeting) is not adequate. [EEOC, *Questions and Answers About Deafness and Hearing Impairments in the Workplace and the Americans With Disabilities Act*, <http://www.eeoc.gov/facts/deafness.html> (Feb. 2, 2011, accessed Apr. 9, 2014)]

UPS policy did not provide interpreters for deaf employees at short meetings. A deaf worker sued, charging that it was not a reasonable accommodation to have someone give him written summaries of the meetings instead of having an interpreter. (The employee has limited reading skills; he repeatedly complained that he did not understand various written materials, but was merely told to look up difficult words in a dictionary.) The district court dismissed the suit but the Ninth Circuit reversed, saying that UPS did not provide effective accommodations. The case was settled in late 2011 for $95,000 plus three years of non-monetary relief (appointing an ADA coordinator, investigating disability discrimination complaints promptly, and providing accommodation to deaf and hearing-impaired employees. [*EEOC v. UPS Supply Chain Solutions*, 620 F.3d 1103 (9th Cir. 2010) Settlement: *EEOC v. UPS Supply Chain Solutions*, No. CV 06-06210 ABC (Ex)]

In 2006, the Ninth Circuit ruled that excluding all deaf people from driving UPS package cars violated the ADA [*Bates v. UPS*, 465 F.3d 1069 (9th Cir. 2006)] Then the case returned to the Ninth Circuit. The en banc panel re-heard the case and reversed the earlier panel decision, vacating class certification and the injunction against UPS. The en banc panel held that UPS can show business necessity by relying on a government safety standard—DOT's hearing acuity requirement for drivers of large trucks—even if the standard was not drafted for the conduct at issue. However, the en banc decision still requires UPS to prove business necessity for refusing to let hearing-impaired people drive trucks. In this reading, an employer seeking to raise a business necessity defense must show that the qualification standard is job-related, consistent with business necessity, and cannot be reached by reasonable accommodation. However, the ADA has no equivalent of a BFOQ defense. Job-relatedness requires the employer to show that the standard fairly and accurately measures the individual's actual ability to perform essential functions of the job. [*Bates v. UPS*, 511 F.3d 974 (9th Cir. 2007)]

§ 36.05 REASONABLE ACCOMMODATION

[A] Employer's Obligation

Employers have an obligation to engage in an interactive process of reasonable accommodation, to permit employment or continued employment of qualified individuals with disabilities. However, it is not required that employers undergo undue hardship in making such accommodations.

The Seventh Circuit ruled that termination does not occur until an employee has unequivocal confirmation of the decision to terminate him or her. Once an employer is on notice that an employee has a disability, it has an obligation to engage in the interactive process. Therefore, it was unlawful to fire a narcoleptic employee who submitted medical documentation of her diagnosis (the employer said it was "just the doctor's opinion"). [*Spurling v. C&M Fine Pack, Inc.*, 739 F.3d 1055 (7th Cir. 2014); see Brett A. Strand, *7th Circuit: Employer Had Knowledge Of Employee's Narcolepsy At Time Of Termination*, Hinshaw & Culbertson (Jan. 21, 2014), available at Lexology.com]

The regulations governing the interactive process appear at 26 C.F.R. Part 163. Best practices for the process include:

- Creating a policy, probably as part of the ADA policy, and preferably included in the employee handbook, to explain the process to employees. At a minimum, employees should be informed that if they request accommodation, their job description will be reviewed to consider the effect of disability on the essential functions of the job.
- Making sure that written job descriptions accurately describe the essential functions. Under the ADA regulations, a task is essential if the job exists to do that task; if it absorbs a high percentage of work time; if no or only a few other employees can do it; a worker was hired for specialized expertise; not performing the task would have serious consequences; the duty is required by the CBA; there is a history of people with that job title performance that function.
- Training supervisors to recognize requests for accommodation; an employee's verbal statement that problems at work are caused by medical needs is probably enough to trigger the process, but merely asking for a new piece of equipment without mentioning disability probably does not. However, supervisors should be trained not to ask questions about disability.

- Holding a personal meeting with the employee, supervisors, and a representative of the HR department to identify the problems and possible solutions, especially solutions suggested by the employee.
- Consulting your Worker's Compensation carrier if the employee was injured at work; there may be state-run programs to modify the workplace.
- Keeping the employee's identity confidential, consult experts such as vocational rehabilitation specialists.
- Requesting information from the employee's doctor—or having the employee obtain the information; be sure to include the GINA safe harbor language in the communication, and limit the request to information that is a business necessity.
- Continuing the process by making sure that accommodations are effective.
- Documenting the process [Jean Ohman Back, *ADA Best Practices For Employers Engaging In An Interactive Process Conversation With Employees?*, Schwabe Williamson & Wyatt (Oct. 16, 2013), available at Lexology.com]

Section 12111(9) says that the category of reasonable accommodation may include making existing facilities readily accessible and usable by QIWDs. It can also include job restructuring, part-time or other altered work schedules, reassignment to a *vacant* position (in April 2002, the Supreme Court ruled that it is not in general "reasonable" to reassign an employee if the reassignment violated an established seniority system—but the employee can demonstrate that an exception should be made in his or her individual case: *U.S. Airways v. Barnett*, 535 U.S. 391 (2002)). Other possible reasonable accommodations include acquiring or modifying equipment, providing training, making readers or interpreters available, etc.

The ADA does not set a specific time limit for leaves. The EEOC's position is that leave of absence may be a reasonable accommodation unless the employer shows that keeping the job open is an undue hardship. Most cases say that a leave of absence cannot be indefinite and it is not reasonable to request leave without specifying a return to work date. The Eighth Circuit held that a request for leave until at least a given date, with no return date, requires the employee to provide at least some information about return and demonstrate that he or she will be able to return to work eventually. The employer can ask for the anticipated return date when leave is taken, or during the interactive process of negotiating accommodation. Instead of automatically terminating the employee for missing the return to work date, the better practice is to make a written request for a new date and ask if the employee can return to work now with or without reasonable accommodation. The employee's inability to supply a return date or failure to respond, can justify termination (unless Worker's Compensation law or the FMLA precludes termination). [*Peyton v. Fred's Stores of Ark.*, 561 F.3d 900 (8th Cir. 2009); see Erin McPhail Wetty, *"See You In . . . Well, I Don't Know When": Is An Unlimited Leave Of Absence A Reasonable Accommodation Under The ADA?*, Seyfarth Shaw LLP (Aug. 28, 2013), available at Lexology.com. See also *Munoz v. Seton HealthCare*, No. A-11-CA-151-LY, 2013 WL 1293425 (W.D. Tex. Mar. 26, 2013); *Ousely v. New Beginnings C-Star, Inc.*, No. 4:09-CV-1957 HEA, 2011 WL 4899950 (E.D. Mo. Oct. 14, 2011) (indefinite leave is not a reasonable accommodation).]

The District Court for the District of Minnesota found it lawful for a senior living facility to terminate an licensed practical nurse who was unable to carry out the essential functions of the job after her FMLA leave for knee surgery expired. After the leave ended, she was told not to kneel, squat, or lift more than 50 pounds for six weeks. She was fired. In her ADA discrimination/FMLA interference and retaliation suit, the district court granted summary judgment for the employer on all counts because kneeling, squatting, and lifting 50 pounds were all essential and embodied in the published job description. The plaintiff said she could have been accommodated if she had been allowed to call for help when residents fell, by giving her an aide, or allowing a further six-week leave until she could return without restrictions. The district court held that employees are not obligated to transfer essential functions or hire additional personnel and a six-week leave would be expensive, would cause hardship to other employees, and would compromise quality of care. [*Attiogbe-Tay v. SE Rolling Hills LLC*, No. 12-1109 (DSD/LIB), 2013 U.S. Dist. LEXIS 159598, 15 Accom. Disabilities Dec. (CCH) ¶ 15-242 (D. Minn. Nov. 7, 2013); see Michael R. Bertoncini, *Inability To Perform Essential Job Functions After FMLA Leave Sinks LPN's Disability Discrimination, FMLA Claims*, Health Care Workplace Update (Nov. 14, 2013), at Lexology.com]

"Auxiliary aids and services" is defined by § 12102 to mean interpreters or other effective methods of communicating with hearing-impaired people, readers, taped texts, and other ways to deliver texts to the visually impaired, acquiring or modifying adaptive equipment or devices, or "other similar services and actions."

Asking for a free reserved parking space on site is a request for ADA accommodation even if it does not involve performance of essential job functions. (The plaintiff was a government lawyer who wanted the parking space because knee problems made it hard to walk.) The district court dismissed the case on the grounds that the plaintiff did not show that denial of on-site parking limited her ability to perform the essential functions of the job. However, the Fifth Circuit held that the employer has a duty to make facilities accessible and providing a parking space potentially does this. The case was remanded; the Fifth Circuit did not say whether providing the parking space would constitute a reasonable accommodation. [*Feist v. State of Louisiana*, 730 F.3d 450 (5th Cir. 2013); see Michael J. Soltis, *ADA Accommodation Request Need Not Relate To Essential Job Functions*, Jackson Lewis LLP (Sept. 23, 2013), available at Lexology.com]

A clear path of at least 36" wide is needed to maneuver a wheelchair through a hall or aisle. Turning requires either a 60" circle or a T-shaped area at least 60" long and 36" wide. Ramps should not be steeper than 1:20. Wheelchair-accessible counters should not be higher than 36". Wheelchair users find hard floors more convenient than carpeted floors, and lever-style knobs are easier to operate than round doorknobs or knobs with thumb latches. [Michael C. Wilhelm, *Tips For Making The Workplace Wheelchair Accessible*, Briggs and Morgan (Sept. 24, 2013), available at Lexology.com]

An undue hardship is an action that requires significant difficulty or expense. [42 U.S.C. § 12111(10)] This determination is made based on factors such as the cost of the accommodation and how it compares to the employer's budget.

The employer must retain records about requests for accommodation for one year after the request or personnel action, whichever is later. [29 C.F.R. § 1602.14]

The Ticket To Work and Work Incentives Improvement Act of 1999 [Pub. L. No. 106-170] allows disabled persons to retain Medicare and/or Medicaid coverage for their health needs after they return to the workforce.

[B] EEOC Enforcement Guidance

On October 17, 2002, the EEOC released a major enforcement guidance. [*Enforcement Guidance: Reasonable Accommodation and Undue Hardship Under the Americans With Disabilities Act*, <http://www.eeoc.gov/policy/docs/accommodation.html>] The EEOC has retained this document on its Website, but warns that it should be interpreted in light of the ADAAA (accessed Apr. 9, 2014).

Under the Guidelines, employers need not eliminate essential job functions. Employers do not have to provide items used for both work and nonwork tasks; employees are responsible for furnishing their own prostheses, eyeglasses, and hearing aids.

Employees who want accommodation must make a clear request but need not use the term "reasonable accommodation," as long as it is clear what they mean. Employers must act on reasonable verbal requests but can ask to have them confirmed by a written memorandum.

The employer can demand reasonable documentation of, for instance, the nature, severity, and duration of the impairment, which activities are impaired, and the extent to which the employee's functional ability is limited. But documentation cannot be required if the disability and accommodation are obvious, or if the employee has already furnished adequate information. The employer can choose its preferred (usually the most cost-effective) reasonable accommodation, and need not follow the employee's suggestion.

Using accrued paid leave, or unpaid leave, is a reasonable accommodation, but employers do not have to offer additional paid leave to employees with a disability. Employees should be allowed to exhaust paid leave before taking unpaid leave. Unless it is an undue hardship, the employer must keep the job open during leave. A leave request need not be granted if the employer can keep the employee at work via a reasonable alternative accommodation.

The EEOC position is that employers should consider ADA and FMLA entitlement separately and then determine whether the two statutes overlap. The EEOC's example is an ADA-disabled person who needs 13 weeks of leave. The FMLA requires only 12 weeks of leave, but the EEOC says the ADA requires the employer to provide the 13th week unless that would be an undue hardship.

If there is a vacant position available for transfer, the employer does not have to train the person with a disability as an accommodation, unless training would be offered to a nondisabled employee. The EEOC position is that a transfer is a reasonable accommodation, so it must be offered even if the employer does not normally provide transfers. It is not enough to allow the disabled employee to compete for a vacant position; it should be offered to any QIWD who wants the transfer as an accommodation.

Final regulations about the ADAAA were published in the Federal Register on March 25, 2011. [76 Fed. Reg. 16977] Under these final regulations (which cover the "Appendix," also known as the Interpretive Guide), a disability is a physical or mental impairment substantially limiting one or more major life activities; a record or history of disability; or being regarded as having a disability. (These three potential litigation areas are sometimes referred to as the three "prongs" of the ADAAA.)

The regulations provide principles for determining whether a person has a disability. An impairment does not have to prevent or severely or significantly restrict performance of a major life activity to be considered a disability. The final regulations state that whether an impairment is a disability should be broadly construed to the maximum extent allowed by law. If an impairment is substantially limiting when it is active, then it is a disability even if it is episodic or in remission. Other than ordinary eyeglasses or contact lenses, mitigating measures are not taken into account in making disability determinations.

An important change is that the final regulations make "individual with a disability" and "qualified individual" separate terms, and the term QIWD, which occurs frequently in earlier ADA cases, is no longer used. In order to focus on whether or not there was discrimination, and not whether the charging party fits within the definition of disability, the final regulations now forbid discrimination on the basis of disability, not discrimination against a QIWD.

Under the 2011 final regulations, major life activities include major bodily functions, such as the functions of the immune system; normal cell growth; and brain, neurological, and endocrine functions. Certain conditions, such as diabetes, epilepsy, bipolar disorder, and being HIV+ are considered to be impairments. The final regulations make it easier for employees to make out a case of regarded-as-disabled liability, because the focus has shifted from the employer's beliefs about the nature of impairment and to the way the employer treated the individual. It's also easier to establish regarded-as liability; now the focus is on treatment of the plaintiff and not on the employer's beliefs about the nature of the impairment. [The regulations, fact sheets, and Q&A can be found at <http://www.eeoc.gov/laws/statutes/adaaa_info.cfm> (accessed Apr. 9, 2014); see Rebecca Moore, *EEOC Announces Final ADA Amendments Act Regs*, plansponsor.com (Mar. 24, 2011)]

The Q&A clear up some difficult and/or disputed points:

- Q6: In general, plaintiffs do not have to use a particular "prong" of the definition of disability to challenge an employer's action, and to win, a plaintiff need only prove discrimination under one "prong." Claims of failure to hire, failure to promote, unlawful termination, and harassment can be brought under any one of the three. But, because accommodation is not required in regarded-as cases, plaintiffs alleging denial of reasonable accommodation must allege either actual disability or a record of disability;
- Q9: To be covered under the disability or record-of-disability prong, it is only necessary to be substantially limited (or have a record of substantial limitation) in one major life activity;
- Q10: The effects of impairment lasting less than six months can still be substantially limiting;
- Q12: Psychotherapy, behavioral therapy, physical therapy, have been added to the list of examples of mitigating measures;
- Q15: The positive effects of mitigating measures cannot be considered in determining whether a person has a disability, but negative effects—such as medication side effects—can be;
- Q16: However, either positive or negative effects of mitigating measures can be considered to see if a person is entitled to reasonable accommodation, or poses a direct threat;
- Q25: A covered entity regards a person as having a disability if the covered entity takes an unlawful action based on an impairment, or based on an impairment the entity believes the individual has, unless the impairment is minor and transitory (expected to last less than six months). This is a change from the original ADA definition. Now, the legality of the employer's action is a separate question from the merits of the charging party's or plaintiff's claim to have a disability, so a defense (even a successful defense) does not eliminate the charging party's or plaintiff's chance to get a trial on the claim. Under the final regulations, an

employer can defend against a regarded-as claim by showing that the impairment (actual or perceived) is both transitory and minor. However, this defense cannot be raised when it is objectively untrue—e.g., claiming that a serious condition such as bipolar disorder is transitory and minor;

- Q31: The ADAAA does not change Worker's Compensation laws or federal or state disability programs;
- Q32: A non-disabled person cannot raise a reverse claim of being denied employment opportunity or reasonable accommodation because of not having a disability. [Questions and Answers on the Final Rule Implementing the ADA Amendments Act of 2008, <http://www.eeoc.gov/laws/regulations/ada_qa_final_rule.cfm>] The EEOC also has publications dealing specifically with small business issues.

For general information about ADA and small business, see <http://www.eeoc.gov/eeoc/publications/adahandbook.cfm> (accessed Apr. 9, 2014). To find nearest Small Business Liaison, see <http://www.eeoc.gov/employers/contacts.cfm> (accessed Apr. 9, 2014). There is also a set of Q&A for small business, overlapping with the general Q&A. Q2 of the small business document says that the ADAAA applies to private employers that have 15 or more employees. The ADAAA change in the definition of disability applies to employers who are federal contractors or who get federal financial assistance (i.e., are subject to the Rehab Act), whether or not they have 15 employees. Q26 states that the interactive process for providing reasonable accommodation has not been altered by the final regulations. [EEOC, *Questions and Answers for Small Businesses: The Final Rule Implementing the ADA Amendments Act of 2008*, <http://www.eeoc.gov/laws/regulations/adaaa_qa_small_business.cfm> (accessed Apr. 9, 2014)]

[C] Case Law

It is very common for summary judgment to be granted to the employer in ADA cases—often on the grounds that the plaintiff did not have a disability for ADA purposes, or that he or she was not qualified, but sometimes on the grounds that there was no reasonable accommodation possible, or that the employer either provided reasonable accommodation or attempted to do so, but the interactive process was frustrated by the employee. A number of cases, however, resulted in summary judgment at the district court level, which was then reversed by the court of appeals, and the case sent back to the district court for a full trial.

Some courts say that the employee must take the first step by requesting accommodation. [*Gaston v. Bellingrath Gardens & Home Inc.*, 167 F.3d 1361 (11th Cir. 1999); *Mole v. Buckhorn Rubber Prods. Inc.*, 165 F.3d 1212 (8th Cir. 1999)] Taylor v. Phoenixville Sch. Dis. [174 F.3d 142 (3d Cir. 1999)] adopts the EEOC position that, as soon as an employee asks for reasonable accommodation, the employer has a duty to engage in an interactive process with the employee and must cooperate with the employee to find out if the employee really is ADA-disabled, finding out what accommodations the employee wants, and determining if they are practical. The employer can decide which reasonable accommodation to offer; it is not obligated to accept the employee's suggestions.

The Seventh Circuit decided that it does not violate the ADA to refuse a software engineer's request to work at home as an accommodation to the fatigue and pain caused by treatment for cancer. In fact, in the Seventh Circuit view, most jobs require supervision, teamwork, and interaction with others, so working at home will rarely constitute a reasonable accommodation. [*Rauen v. United States Tobacco Mfg. Ltd.*, 319 F.3d 891 (7th Cir. 2003); working at home was not a reasonable accommodation for an employee traumatized by witnessing a fatal workplace shooting incident: *Mason v. Avaya Commc'ns, Inc.*, 357 F.3d 1114 (10th Cir. 2004)]

Note, however, that the D.C. Circuit found in 2007 that revoking a disabled worker's previously given permission to work at home two days a week was discriminatory, because the telecommuting arrangement constituted a reasonable accommodation. [*Woodruff v. Peters*, 482 F.3d 521 (D.C. Cir. April 6, 2007); see Fred Schneyer, *FAA Telecommuting Setup Could Be Disabled Worker's Accommodation*, plansponsor.com (May 8, 2007)]

According to *Donahue v. Consol. Rail Corp.* [224 F.3d 226 (3d Cir. 2000)], the employer need not engage in the interactive process if the employee failed to show that there were any available jobs he or she could have done with reasonable accommodation.

Furthermore, a person who claims that his or her injury prevents full-time work, and therefore is allowed to work a part-time schedule, is estopped from claiming that the employer refused accommodation, because the person is unable to work full-time even with accommodation. [*DeVito v. Chicago Park Dist.*, 270 F.3d 532 (7th Cir. 2001)]

The EEOC position [29 C.F.R. § 1630.2(o)], echoed by several appellate cases, is that reassignment to a job that the employee can handle constitutes a reasonable accommodation. [*Dalton v. Subaru-Isuzu Auto., Inc.*, 141 F.3d 667 (7th Cir. 1998); *Cravens v. Blue Cross/Blue Shield*, 214 F.3d 1011 (8th Cir. 2000); *Aka v. Wash. Hosp. Ctr.*, 156 F.3d 1284 (D.C. Cir. 1998)] The disabled person in search of accommodation must be able to prove his or her ability to handle the new job. [*DePaoli v. Abbott Labs.*, 140 F.3d 668 (7th Cir. 1998)] The Second Circuit said that as long as a comparable job is available, it is not a reasonable accommodation to offer an ADA plaintiff reassignment to a part-time job (with much lower compensation and benefits) or to another location (resulting in loss of seniority). [*Norville v. Staten Island Univ. Hosp.*, 196 F.3d 89 (2d Cir. 1999)]

§ 36.06 DEFENSES

[A] Primary Defense

The primary defense, under 42 U.S.C. § 12113, is that the employer's criterion, standards, or tests may screen out individuals with a disability, but are nevertheless appropriate because they are job-related and consistent with business necessity, and the employer cannot achieve the same goals via reasonable accommodation. Qualification standards can lawfully rule out employment of anyone who poses a direct threat to the health or safety of others. According to 42 U.S.C. § 12111(3), a "direct threat" is a significant risk to the health or safety of others that cannot be eliminated by reasonable accommodation.

The defense of "direct threat" is still usable now that the ADAAA is in force but the employer must rely on reasonable medical judgment, based on the most current medical knowledge and objective evidence about the employee's ability to work safely. For example, a mid-2013 case finds that the employer's doctor's opinion that an employee with a seizure disorder, who sometimes needed to be taken to the emergency room from work, was invalid because the doctor used improper methodology. [*EEOC v. Rexnord Indus., LLC*, 966 F. Supp. 2d 829 (E.D. Wis. 2013); see Mark S. Kittaka, *Court Finds Employer's ADA Direct Threat Evidence Insufficient*, Barnes & Thornburg LLP (Sept. 6, 2013), available at Lexology.com]

Furthermore, the Secretary of Health and Human Services publishes a list of infectious and communicable diseases that can be transmitted by food handling. If the risk cannot be eliminated by reasonable accommodation, then an employer can legitimately refuse to assign or continue to assign someone who suffers from such a disease to a food handling position. This provision does not preempt state public health laws about food safety. The Supreme Court greatly increased the applicability of this exception in a June 2002 decision [*Chevron USA Inc. v. Echazabal*, 536 U.S. 73 (2002)] by allowing employers to use it in the context of danger to a job applicant or employee whose own physical condition would be endangered by workplace conditions. In 2012, the Supreme Court gave an expansive interpretation to the "ministerial exception" (the principle that courts will not intervene in a congregation's selection of religious ministers). Cheryl Perich, who taught at a religious school, argued that she was fired in retaliation for threatening to file an ADA suit. (Perich suffers from narcolepsy.) The Supreme Court accepted the employer's argument that Perich, as a "called" teacher (who led prayers and religious activities as well as teaching secular subjects) was a religious minister, so the exception applied. [*Hosanna-Tabor Evangelical Lutheran Church v. EEOC*, 132 S. Ct. 694 (2012).]

[B] Drug and Alcohol Exception

Congress must have been concerned about the potential for claims of disability on the basis of substance abuse, because there are several statutory references. According to 42 U.S.C. § 12111(6), a "drug" is a controlled substance as defined by federal law, and "illegal use of drugs" means using controlled substances, but does not include drugs taken under the supervision of a licensed health professional.

Section 12114 says that an employee or job applicant who is currently engaging in the illegal use of drugs is not a qualified individual with a disability. However, a person who is in rehab, has completed a rehab program, or otherwise stopped using drugs can be considered a qualified individual with a disability. So can a person who is not in fact using illegal drugs, but who is incorrectly perceived to be.

However, a 2013 Fifth Circuit ruling permits enforcement of a corporate policy calling for termination of employees who reject treatment for drug or alcohol problems or who start but fail to complete a treatment program. Leave was granted for a factory worker to be treated for Vicodin addiction. He went through detox but left the program before receiving addiction treatment. The employer said he could be reinstated if he completed the program. He returned to the program, but for only one day, when he checked himself out again. The Fifth Circuit agreed with the district court: summary judgment for the employer was proper in the worker's ADA and FMLA suit. The safe harbor does not protect everyone who enters a treatment program—only those who remain drug-free for a significant amount of time. [*Shirley v. Precision Castparts Corp.*, 726 F.3d 675 (5th Cir. 2013); see Kathryn McGovern, *Employee Who Left Drug Rehab Not Entitled to ADA, FMLA Protections*, Thompson SmartHR Blogs (Aug. 23, 2013) (benefitslink.com)]

The plaintiff in the Supreme Court case of *Raytheon v. Hernandez* [540 U.S. 44 (2003)] was forced to resign after he tested positive for cocaine, thus violating a workplace conduct rule. More than two years later, after he said he had stopped using drugs, he applied to be rehired. Rehiring was denied, on the basis of a corporate policy against rehiring anyone who had been terminated for misconduct. The employee who rejected his application said that she did not know he was a former addict when she denied the application.

The Supreme Court held the no-rehire policy was neutral and satisfied the *McDonnell-Douglas* requirements. On remand, the Ninth Circuit found that there was a genuine issue of material fact as to whether the decision to refrain from rehiring him was disability-based, and therefore the Ninth Circuit reversed the grant of summary judgment for the defense. [362 F.3d 564 (9th Cir. 2004)]

Employers are allowed to forbid the use of alcohol or illegal drugs at the workplace, can enforce the requirements of the Drug-Free Workplace Act, can make a rule that employees not be under the influence of alcohol or drugs when they are at work (even if they used the substances outside the workplace), and can adopt reasonable procedures (including drug testing) to make sure employees are not currently abusing substances. Drug testing is not considered a "medical examination" for ADA purposes. Many of these provisions are repeated in 42 U.S.C. § 12210.

A "last chance" agreement, where reinstatement after rehab is conditional on continued good performance (and perhaps on passing periodic drug tests) has been upheld as a reasonable accommodation to the disability of alcoholism. [See, e.g., *Longen v. Waterous Co.*, 347 F.3d 685 (8th Cir. 2003)]. The Seventh Circuit affirmed summary judgment for the employer on ADA (and FMLA) claims brought by an employee who was already on a Last Chance Agreement and who was fired after coming to work drunk and failing a blood alcohol test. (The Last Chance Agreement subjected her to periodic suspicionless drug/alcohol test, and said that refusing to take a required test was grounds for dismissal.) The Seventh Circuit ruled that she did not show that she had an alcoholism disability, because alcohol did not substantially limit her major life activities. She sought help from the EAP for an alcohol problem, but said it had not yet affected her work. She was fired for coming to work drunk, a violation of the employer's legitimate expectations. According to 42 U.S.C. § 12114(c)(4), alcoholic employees can be held to same qualifications standards as other employees, even if the unsatisfactory performance is related to alcoholism. The Seventh Circuit held that the employer did not fail to accommodate—in fact, it gave her time off for AA meetings. [*Ames v. Home Depot USA Inc.*, 629 F.3d 665 (7th Cir. 2011)]

The Ninth Circuit held that the association representing longshoremen did not violate the ADA (or California's anti-discrimination law) by adopting a "one-strike" rule in response to drug-related injuries and fatalities. The rule disqualified from longshore employment anyone who tested positive for drugs or alcohol when tested by the association. The plaintiff, Lopez, applied to be a longshoreman in 1997. At that time, he used drugs and alcohol, and tested positive for marijuana. In 2002, he stopped using drugs and alcohol. In 2004, he re-applied and was disqualified because of the earlier positive drug test. He brought suit under the ADA, charging that he was discriminated against as a former drug addict who was now abstinent. The Ninth Circuit rejected the argument, finding that there was no proof that the association intentionally discriminated against him on this basis, or that the rule had disparate impact on recovered drug addicts. The rule did not target addicts as distinguished from casual drug users; it disqualified anyone who was unable to pass the drug/alcohol test. [*Lopez v. Pacific Maritime Ass'n*, 636 F.3d 1197 (9th Cir. 2011); see Rebecca Moore, *Failed Drug Test Can Haunt Applicants Later*, plansponsor.com (Mar. 4, 2011)]

■ **TIP:** A substance abuser entering a rehab program (at least if it is an inpatient program) may be entitled to FMLA leave. Reasonable ADA accommodation may require providing additional leave after the 12 weeks of FMLA leave have been used up.

§ 36.07 "REGARDED AS" LIABILITY

The ADA covers qualified individuals who actually do not have a disability, but who are discriminated against because of the perception that they do. The ADAAA expands the definition of "regarded as" to forbid discrimination on the basis of the employer's perception of a mental or physical impairment—whether or not the plaintiff can prove that the impairment actually limits or is perceived to limit a major life activity. However, a "regarded as" claim can only be based on a long-lasting impairment, not one that lasts or is expected to last for less than six months. The ADAAA resolved a circuit split by holding that reasonable accommodation is not required in "regarded-as" cases.

The First Circuit ruled that an intermittently disabling condition (in this case, remitting and relapsing multiple sclerosis) can be a handicap, and the plaintiff, Susanna Sensing, was regarded as disabled after she took medical leave after a major flare-up of the disease. She was not allowed to return to work although she had a doctor's note releasing her to work without restrictions. Her supervisor refused to let her work, saying that if she fell down, it would cost the restaurant hundreds of thousands of dollars. Sensing was offered only one-third the number of hours at a half her original pay. She applied for unemployment because she did not think that this would provide a living wage. The First Circuit held that applying for unemployment did not prove job abandonment; she needed to support herself while waiting for the employer to schedule an independent medical exam. The case was remanded to the district court: a reasonable jury could conclude that the restaurant did not need to fire her for safety reasons, and it appeared suspicious that the employer ignored three doctors' notes clearing Sensing to return to work and never scheduled the independent medical examination that the restaurant said was necessary for her to return to work. [*Sensing v. Outback Steak-house of Florida, Inc.*, 575 F.3d 145 (1st Cir. 2009)]

A "100% healed" policy forbids employees to return to work unless they are free from all medical restrictions; employees who have restrictions are terminated. The Seventh Circuit held in 2011 that 100% healed policies are a per se ADA violation. In 2014, the Northern District of Illinois denied UPS's motion to dismiss in a case about its policy requiring termination after 12 months of leave; the court accepted the EEOC's argument that this is the equivalent of a 100% healed requirement. Although regular attendance can be an essential function of a job, the EEOC's claim was based on the 100% healed standard, not on attendance. [*EEOC v. United Parcel Serv., Inc.*, No. 1:09-cv-05291, 2013 U.S. Dist. LEXIS 4462 (N.D. Ill. Jan. 11, 2014), <http://www.workplaceclassaction.com/files/2013/07/https-ecf-ilnd-uscourts-gov-cgi-bin-show_doc-pl-ad.pdf>; see Stephen C. Sutton, *Another Reminder That Inflexible Employment Policies And The ADA Don't Play Well Together – Court Refuses To Dismiss EEOC Action Based On "100% Healed" Policy*, Baker & Hostetler LLP (Feb. 19, 2014), available at Lexology.com. See also *Powers v. USF Holland, Inc.*, 667 F.3d 815 (7th Cir. 2011); *Kotwica v. Rose Packing Co. Inc.*, 637 F.3d 744 (7th Cir. 2011).]

According to the Second Circuit, a trucking company did not violate the ADA by refusing to hire drivers who used prescription drugs with side effects that could impair their driving ability. According to the Second Circuit, the trucking company did not perceive such persons as disabled. Furthermore, the EEOC's regulation, 29 C.F.R. § 1630.2(j)(3)(i) says that inability to perform a particular job is not the equivalent of a substantial limitation in the activity of working; being a truck driver is not a class of job or a broad range of jobs. The fact that the defendant company did not have any less demanding driving jobs to offer (that might have been performed safely by prescription medication users) does not prove that the defendant regarded the applicants as unfit for any driving position at all. [*EEOC v. JB Hunt Transport*, 321 F.3d 69 (2d Cir. 2003)

§ 36.08 DISABILITY AND THE BENEFIT PLAN

[A] Employer's Obligations and Challenges

Under the ADA, employers are permitted to make benefit plan decisions that are consistent with underwriting, reasonable risk classifications, or actual or reasonably anticipated experience. If the employer does not normally provide health benefits, it has no obligation to provide special insurance coverage for the disabled or to adopt a plan that covers both disabled and nondisabled employees.

Three Circuit Courts (the Sixth, Seventh, and Eleventh) have ruled that a totally disabled retiree or ex-employee is not "qualified" (because he or she is unable to perform job functions) and therefore cannot sue for fringe-benefit discrimination. [*Morgan v. Joint Admin. Bd. Ret. Plan*, 268 F.3d 456 (7th Cir. 2001); *EEOC v. CAN Ins. Cos.*, 96 F.3d 1038 (7th Cir. 1997); *Parker v. Metro. Life Ins. Co.*, 99 F.3d 181, *aff'd*, 121 F.3d 1006 (6th Cir. 1997); *Gonzalez v. Garner Food Servs., Inc.*, 89 F.3d 1523 (11th Cir. 1996)]

The Eighth Circuit dismissed ADA claims by an employee with multiple sclerosis who was fired the day after her employer learned that its health premiums were going to increase by about 30%. The Eighth Circuit held that she did not prove that the employer's explanation—her poor job performance—was pretextual. The Eighth Circuit found that there was no evidence that the manager who fired the plaintiff was even aware that the premium had increased, much less that he blamed the plaintiff for the additional costs. [*Libel v. Adventure Lands of Am.*, 482 F.3d 1028 (8th Cir. 2007); see Adrien Martin, *Court: No Proof That Firing Was Discriminatory*, plansponsor.com (Apr. 23, 2007)]

[B] EEOC Compliance Manual

In 2000, the EEOC redrafted its Compliance Manual Section 3, which can be found at <http://www.eeoc.gov/policy/docs/benefits.html>. As of press time in 2014, the EEOC had not issued a new version of this document. The employer must provide "equal" benefits for all employees, irrespective of disability. However, benefits can be "equal" even if there are certain distinctions drawn on the basis of disability. The employer is entitled to employ practices that reflect sound actuarial principles or are related to actual or reasonably anticipated experience.

The employer can rebut charges of disability discrimination by proving that disparate treatment is necessary to maintain the solvency of the plan, because covering the disabilities at issue would cost enough to threaten the fiscal soundness of the plan, and there is no way to change the plan without affecting disabilities.

In the EEOC view, it violates the ADA to:

- Exclude an employee from participation in a service or disability retirement plan because of disabilities;
- Have a different length of participation requirement in the same plan because of disability;
- Provide different levels of types of coverage within a plan (although coverage levels can be lower in disability than in service retirement plans).

Service retirement benefits can legitimately be denied to any employee who voluntarily took disability retirement.

§ 36.09 QUESTIONS AND MEDICAL TESTS

The general ADA rule is that employers are not permitted to ask job applicants or perform medical exams to find out if the applicant has a disability or to discover the nature and severity of the disability. However, it is permissible to tell the applicant what the job entails and ask about ability to perform these tasks. So "have you ever had any back problems?" is not a legitimate question, but "This job involves lifting 25-pound weights several times an hour, and sometimes involves lifting up to 100 pounds—can you handle that?" is acceptable.

Once the company decides to extend a job offer, then it is permissible to require a medical examination, as long as all employees (whether or not they have a disability) are subject to this requirement, and the results of the examination are kept in separate medical files and kept confidential, disclosed only to persons with a genuine work-related need to know.

Furthermore, any medical examination or inquiries must be job-related and consistent with business necessity. Voluntary medical examinations (including taking medical histories) are allowable if they are part of a program available to all employees at a work site, and an employer can ask about an employee's ability to perform job-related functions. [42 U.S.C. § 12112(d)]

The District Court for the District of Colorado required medical information forms to be focused as narrowly as possible on the doctor's assessment of the employee's ability to perform job duties. There must also be a program to determine who has access to medical information. The defendant's medical authorization form was used to determine eligibility for short-term disability benefits. The form included language that the information would be used only to evaluate whether the employee's condition meets federal, state, or local FMLA or disability laws, state Workers' Compensation laws, or the employer's welfare benefit plan. The district court held that, although the employer might need the information for its role as plan administrator, a jury could conclude that there was a risk that the information would be disseminated in a manner exceeding the job related/business necessity standard. [*Fraser v. Avaya, Inc.*, No. 10-cv-00800-RPM (D. Colo. 2013); see William A. Nolan, *Decision Reminds Employers: Minimalist Medical Inquiries Are A Must*, Barnes & Thornburg LLP (Sept. 9, 2013), available at Lexology.com]

The Sixth Circuit held that psychological counseling an employee was required to undergo (her supervisor thought she might be depressed) could be considered a medical examination, so she could maintain a 42 U.S.C. § 12112(d)(4)(A) claim [the ban on requiring a medical examination to see if an employee has a disability]. The factors include whether the examination was performed by a health care professional, and whether it was designed to find mental impairments. [*Kroll v. White Lake Ambulance Auth.*, 691 F.3d 809 (6th Cir. 2012)]

Use of the Minnesota Multiphasic Personality Inventory (MMPI) as part of a battery of tests required for promotion violated the ADA. The test results were not interpreted by psychologists. The company claimed the tests were scored to determine personality traits, but the practical result was that employees with mental health disorders were denied consideration for promotion. The Seventh Circuit ruled that the MMPI is considered a medical examination because it was designated to diagnose mental illness and, as applied in practice, it impaired the job opportunities for persons with mental illnesses. [*Karraker v. Rent-a-Center, Inc.*, 411 F.3d 831 (7th Cir. 2005)]

A related issue is when genetic information reveals disability or the potential to develop a disability. Title I of the Genetic Information Nondiscrimination Act (GINA; Pub. L. No. 110-233) applies to the group health plans of private employers, and to unions, government employers, and insurers. Title II applies to entities covered by Title VII. The EEOC is the agency in charge of enforcing GINA, and it proposed regulations on March 2, 2009 clarifying the rules for acquiring and disseminating genetic information.

See 29 C.F.R. Part 1635 for final regulations, effective January 10, 2011, under GINA Title II.

GINA defines manifestation of disease to mean a condition that has been, or reasonably could be, diagnosed by a health professional. Merely testing positive for a genetic trait is not considered a manifestation, even if the person tested is certain to develop the disease eventually—a requirement that was adopted to prevent positive markers being classified as preexisting conditions. Employers that require a medical examination after a job offer has been made and before the new hire starts work should make sure that the doctors administering the physicals do not ask about family medical history unless the GINA requirements are satisfied. The same is true of fitness for duty examinations. The EEOC says that the best practice is, when an employee is asked to provide documentation of disability, the request should tell the employee not to provide genetic information (including family medical history). [RIN 3046-AA84, 74 Fed. Reg. 9056 (Mar. 2, 2009); see Margaret Hart Edwards, *Proposed Regulations Under Federal Genetic Information Nondiscrimination Act (GINA) Suggest Employer Action Now*, Littler ASAPs, <http://www.littler.com/PressPublications/Lists/ASAPs/DispAsaps.aspx?id=1344&asapType=National> (March 2009)]

The EEOC's first settlement of a suit about genetic information involved an applicant who was not hired for a clerical job because the employer regarded her as likely to develop carpal tunnel syndrome because of family medical history information that she disclosed in response to an improper inquiry. The employer, Fabricut, Inc. agreed to pay $50,000 and provide other relief. [*EEOC v. Fabricut, Inc.*, No. 13-CV-248-CVE-PJC (N.D. Okla., settled May 7, 2013); see EEOC Press Release, *Fabricut to Pay $50,000 to Settle EEOC Disability and Genetic Information Discrimination Lawsuit*, <http://www.eeoc.gov/eeoc/newsroom/release/5-7-13b.cfm> (May 7, 2013). See Sue Reisinger, *EEOC Gets Tough With Companies on Genetic Privacy*, Corporate Counsel (May 23, 2013) (law.com).]

§ 36.10 INTERACTION WITH OTHER STATUTES

In 2003, the Supreme Court held that, in a suit under the Federal Employers Liability Act (FELA), damages for mental anguish (fear of developing cancer after exposure to asbestos) can be recovered if the plaintiff has already suffered another actionable injury (e.g., asbestosis). Pain and suffering associated with physical injury is actionable, even though independent claims for negligent infliction of intentional distress often are not. Here, the plaintiffs did not seek damages for the increased risk of future cancer. Instead, they sought compensation for their current injuries, which include experiencing fear. However, to win a case of this type, the plaintiff must prove that the alleged fear is genuine and serious. Although this case deals specifically with a federal employment statute, it's an important indication of the Court's thinking on these topics. [*Norfolk & Western Railway Co. v. Ayers*, 538 U.S. 135 (2003)]

On February 28, 2012, the EEOC released two guidance documents protecting veterans with disabilities. The unemployment rate for post-911 veterans is about 12%, 3% higher than the overall rate. The ADAAA requires reasonable accommodation to the impairments of veterans, including traumatic brain injuries and PTSD. Revised guidance for employers explains how the ADA treats recruitment, hiring, accommodation of veterans' disabilities, and the differences in coverage between the ADAAA and USERRA. The revised Guide for Wounded Veterans explains to injured veterans the rights and protections they are entitled to. [CCH Employment Law Daily, *Revised EEOC Guidance Clarifies Interplay Between ADA and USERRA for Employers, Explains Rights to Veterans with Service-Related Disabilities* (March 2012) (benefitslink.com)]

Office of Federal Contract Compliance Programs (OFCCP) regulations under Rehab Act § 503 and the Vietnam Era Veterans' Readjustment Assistance Act (VEVRAA) took effect March 24, 2014, expanding affirmative action requirements for persons with disabilities (PWDs) and veterans. Federal contractors with $10,000 or more in contract value are covered. Subcontractors and sub-subcontractors are covered if their products or services are eventually sold to the federal government. Contractors' affirmative action plans must set a target of 7% disabled employees in each job group, although a contractor with fewer than 100 employees can use a target of 7% employment of PWDs in the total workforce. However, this is a goal, not a quota, and no penalties will be imposed for failure to meet it.

Contractors are required to gather data about their recruitment and hiring efforts, with a three-year retention requirement. Federal contractors are not required to amend affirmative action plans already in place, but new plans prepared after that date must reflect the new rules. A new OFCCP compliance manual is available with the rules, and the agency issued Compliance Directive 307 dealing with discrimination in compensation. Commenters questioned whether the invitation to self-identify violates the ADA's limits on disability inquiries before a job offer has been made. The OFCCP said that the ADA's exception for affirmative action permits self-identification before a job offer. Self-identification materials should stay with the HR department and kept in separate files, not furnished to interviewers or hiring officials. Employers are now required to ask employees to voluntarily self-identify every five years, and must inform employees that they can change their disability status at any time. (See the form on the OFCCP Website.) Federal contractors are required to review the results of their diversity efforts annually. [79 Fed. Reg. 58683 (Sept. 24, 2013); see Fred W. Alvarez et al., *Expanding Compliance Obligations: What Federal Contractors Need To Know About OFCCP's New Disability And Veterans Regulations*, Jones Day (Oct. 15, 2013), available at Lexology.com; Mike Underwood, *Major Changes To Affirmative Action Requirements Effective March 24, 2014*, Porter Wright Morris & Arthur LLP (Oct. 8, 2013), available at Lexology.com; Patrick W. Spangler, Thomas G. Abram, and J. Kevin Hennessy, *Affirmative Action And OFCCP Compliance Update: OFCCP Issues Highly Anticipated Final Disability And Veteran Regulations*, Vedder Price PC (Aug. 28, 2013), available at Lexology.com]

[A] The Rehabilitation Act

The ADA is a successor statute to the Rehabilitation Act of 1973 (29 U.S.C. §§ 793 *et seq.*; "Rehab Act"). There are many circumstances in which the HR department will have to apply the ADA in conjunction with other laws—typically, the FMLA and ERISA.

The Rehab Act applies to federal contractors and subcontractors whose government contract involves more than $2,500, and to federal programs and federal grantees. It does not apply to businesses that are not involved in government contracting.

Rehab Act § 503 protects qualified handicapped applicants against discrimination in employment practices. However, one reason that the ADA was passed is that the Rehab Act does not contain a private right of action. In other words, handicapped persons who charge that they were victims of discrimination cannot sue the alleged discriminators. Another section, § 504, does carry a private right of action, but only for discrimination solely on account of handicap in a federally financed program or activity.

Rehab Act § 503 imposes an affirmative action requirement. Federal contractors must have goals for hiring and promotion of qualified handicapped individuals. However, the Department of Labor does not have the power to enforce this requirement by bringing administrative prosecutions against companies that violate it.

The Ninth Circuit held that the Rehab Act protects independent contractors as well as common-law employees. [*Fleming v. Yuma Reg'l Med. Ctr.*, 587 F.3d 938 (9th Cir. 2009)]

A government employer that warns a pregnant employee that she needs to concentrate on her work might be liable for retaliation under the Rehabilitation Act if her request to work from home is denied. The employee suffered from hyperemesis—excessive vomiting. She asked her supervisor if she could work from home on some days or take a leave of absence. Her supervisor refused to examine the discharge documentation from an emergency room visit, and said that she had to work full-time. She quit and sued for disability discrimination (hyperemesis) and retaliation for requesting accommodation. The District Court for the District of Maryland held in late 2013 that hyperemesis was not a disability because she was sent home from the emergency room without restrictions. However, the retaliation claim could proceed, because the supervisor's statement appeared to be a threat that could deter a reasonable employee from pursuing a discrimination charge. [*Wonasue v. University of Maryland Alumni Ass'n, No.* PWG-11-3657 (D. Md. Nov. 22, 2013); see Michael J. Soltis, *Severe Morning Sickness Not A Disability; Nonetheless, Retaliation Claim Proceeds*, Jackson Lewis PC (Dec. 2, 2013), available at Lexology.com]

A Kansas State University assistant professor sued the school, alleging disability discrimination and retaliation when an extension of her six-month leave of absence was denied (Professor Hwang suffered from cancer). She was granted long-term disability benefits, terminating her employment. The Tenth Circuit held that the Rehabilitation Act was not violated. The plaintiff did not show that she was able to perform the essential functions of the job, and extending the leave and keeping the job open was not a reasonable accommodation. Hwang said that having an inflexible policy limiting leave to six months was discriminatory, but the Tenth Circuit said that even the EEOC's policy manual describes a six-month leave as more than a reasonable time. [*Hwang v. Kansas State Univ.*, No. 13-3070 (10th Cir. May 29, 2014). See Judith Biggs, *Disabled Employee Not Entitled to Additional Leave as Reasonable Accommodation*, Holland & Hart LLP (June 2, 2014), available at Lexology.com]

[B] The ADA and Disability Benefits

A February 12, 1997, EEOC Notice No. 915.002, sets out the EEOC's position that employees can legitimately make ADA claims (based on the assertion that they are qualified to perform essential job functions) at the same time that they apply for disability benefits (which are premised on inability to do gainful work).

This position was adopted by the Supreme Court. [*Cleveland v. Policy Mgmt. Sys. Corp.*, 526 U.S. 795 (1999)] According to *King v. Herbert J. Thomas Mem'l Hosp.* [159 F.3d 192 (4th Cir. 1998)], actually receiving disability benefits (as distinct from just applying for them) prevents an age-discrimination plaintiff from claiming she was able to perform the job at the time of her discharge.

Applying for SSDI does not automatically preclude an ADA suit, a plaintiff who has sworn to his or her inability to work will be required to reconcile that with the position taken in the ADA suit that he or she is qualified to work. [*Gilmore v. AT&T*, 319 F.3d 1042 (8th Cir. 2003); *Lane v. BFI Waste Sys. of N. Am.*, 257 F.3d 766 (8th Cir. 2001)]

On a related issue, late in 2003 the Supreme Court decided that it was reasonable for the Commissioner of Social Security to use that agency's definition of "disability" to deny benefits to a claimant who had recovered to the point of being healthy enough to do her former job—as an elevator operator—even though that job no longer exists in significant numbers within the national economy. [*Barnhart v. Thomas*, 540 U.S. 20 (2003)]

The Ninth Circuit held in 2013 that an elementary school employee's FMLA and insurance disability claims (paid based on an application stating she was totally disabled) were not inconsistent with her ADA claim that she was denied the reasonable accommodation of being permitted to transfer to a less demanding job. The Ninth Circuit held that FMLA and insurance disability applications did not consider her future ability to work, the possibility of doing other jobs, or reasonable accommodation. [*Smith v. Clark County Sch. Dist.*, 727 F.3d 950 (9th Cir. 2013); see Sarah R. Peace, *Employees May Take "Total Disability" And Seek Accommodation Too*, Sherman & Howard LLC (Aug. 22, 2013), available at Lexology.com]

[C] The FMLA

A person with a "serious health condition" (as defined by the FMLA) may also be a QIWD. FMLA leave, although unpaid, is easier to obtain than medical leave as a reasonable ADA accommodation, because employers with 50 or more employees have to grant FMLA leave to eligible employees. Reinstatement after FMLA leave is automatic, but ADA reinstatement requires showing of ability to perform essential work tasks (with or without reasonable accommodation).

It is unclear how much leave must be provided, after FMLA leave is exhausted, as a reasonable accommodation under the ADA. Once an employee has exhausted all leave provided by the employer, including FMLA leave, the employer must assess if the employee is covered by the ADA. If so, the employer must engage in the interactive process, and may have to reassign the employee to a vacant job as a reasonable accommodation.

It has been held that it is lawful to terminate an employee who cannot provide a reasonable estimate of when he or she will be able to resume all of the essential functions of the job. In a case brought by a supervisor of released felony offenders, the written job description listed 18 essential functions, including fieldwork at supervisees' homes. The court said that to show that a request for a leave of absence is reasonable, the employee must provide an estimated date for resuming essential duties, with reassurance that the employee can perform all the essential functions in the near future. [*Robert v. Board of Comm'rs of Brown Cnty.*, 691 F.3d 1211 (10th Cir. 2012); see Jeff Nowak, *An* "Indefinite Reprieve" *of Essential Functions of Job Not a Reasonable Accommodation under the ADA*, Franczek Radelet FMLA Insights (Sept. 5, 2012) (benefitslink.com)]

The Tenth Circuit revived ADA (and FMLA) claims in a case where it was possible that the plaintiff was fired for taking a large amount of leave, not for the employer's explanation that he committed a safety violation and argued with a co-worker about it. The employer said that the termination decision was made by a committee, not the same decision-makers who allegedly treated comparator employees more leniently. The Tenth Circuit held that the decision-making teams overlapped, and there is no hard and fast rule about what constitutes a comparator. The Tenth Circuit held that a reasonable jury could find that the plaintiff, who had chronic pain caused by a degenerative neck injury, had an ADA disability because of serious limitations on his ability to sleep, even though he took pain and sleep medications. [*Smothers v. Solvay Chemicals, Inc.*, No. 12-8013 (10th Cir. Jan. 21, 2014); see Wolters Kluwer Law & Business News Center, *Decision By Committee Does Not Insulate Employer From Potential Liability For FMLA, ADA Claims* (Feb. 14, 2014) (benefitslink.com)]

The District Court for the Eastern District of Texas held that an employee fired shortly after giving notice of her need for cancer surgery and recovery time raised a triable ADA claim, but her FMLA claim failed because she had not been employed long enough to be eligible. [*Dunn v. Chattanooga Publ'g Co.*, No.

1:12-cv-00252 (E.D. Tenn. Jan. 8, 2014); see James R. Mulroy, II and Christopher C. Antone, *Disability Discrimination Claims May Proceed Against Former Employer, Federal Court Rules*, Jackson Lewis PC (Jan. 23, 2014), available at Lexology.com. Note, however, that the Eleventh Circuit reached the opposite conclusion about retaliation against non-FMLA-eligible workers.]

The EEOC's position is that it violates the duty of reasonable accommodation to terminate employees who are unable to return to work or unable to return to full duty at the end of the FMLA leave. This is not necessarily the position that the courts will take, but there have been a number of settlements on this issue, and some employers have agreed to drop policies requiring termination after a certain amount of leave. The employer may be able to show undue hardship because of the cost of giving extended leave (although this argument is harder to sustain when leave is unpaid) or the operational difficulties of changing work schedules or hiring temporary employees to fill in. COBRA allows employers to provide COBRA notice to an employee on extended leave after FMLA leave has been used up, shifting the premium payment obligation to the employee.

The EEOC position is that the employer must hold the job open as an accommodation unless this is an undue hardship. It may also be required to hold open a vacant equivalent position the employee is qualified for, or even vacant non-equivalent jobs the employee is qualified for. However, if the employee fails to apply or reapply for extended leave, it may be possible to terminate the employee for job abandonment. There may also be medical information that justifies denial of further leave. If there is a need to replace an employee who is on extended leave, the employer should document the reasons why this is necessary.

A 2011 article recommends that if an employee's mental or physical condition precludes performing the essential functions of the job with or without reasonable accommodation, the employee should be placed on leave. An FMLA notice should be issued to anyone who misses three or more days at work. Before FMLA or other legally guaranteed leave ends, or when an employee who is not eligible for guaranteed leave applies for leave, the employer should engage in the interactive process to determine if reasonable accommodations are available to return the employee to work. The article suggests requiring that employees re-apply for extended leave at intervals (perhaps every three, six, or twelve months, depending on administrative convenience) but employees should not be terminated for failure to return to work unless they have also failed to apply for extended leave. Employers can tell employees that they must either return to work or be considered to have abandoned the job, if the medical evidence shows that the employee is able to perform the job. But extended leave is a reasonable accommodation if the employee cannot currently perform the essential functions of the job but might be able to do so in the future. Extended leave would not be required if the medical evidence shows that the employee will never be able to return to work, or if the employee has applied for LTD benefits on the basis of permanent total disability.

If the employee has applied for SSDI, the employer should document the interactive process and that the employee is unable to return to work because some courts have held that it is not inconsistent to apply for SSDI and also raise an ADA claim, because SSDI focuses on what the employee is unable to do, whereas the ADA focuses on ability to work with reasonable accommodation. [Kerry Notestine & Kelley Edwards, *Recent EEOC Lawsuits Highlight Importance of Adopting Comprehensive Procedures for Managing Employee Leaves*, Littler Mendelson Insights (February 2011) (benefitslink.com)]

The First Circuit ruled that an employee's seven-week trip to the Philippines with her seriously ill husband, for a faith healing pilgrimage, was not covered by the FMLA. The employee also raised a claim of association discrimination under the ADA, which also failed: it did not violate the ADA to demand verification of her husband's condition, and a paperwork requirement is not an adverse employment action for ADA purposes. [*Tayag v. Lahey Clinic Hosp.*, 632 F.3d 788 (1st Cir. Jan. 2011).

[D] HIPAA and Wellness Programs

Under HIPAA, a plan may not discriminate among similarly situated persons based on their health status, so differences in costs or premiums are forbidden. However, "adherence to programs of health promotion and disease prevention" (i.e., wellness programs) can lawfully give rise to premium discounts or reduced payment responsibilities. Wellness programs can include, for example, assessment of the health risks affecting individual employees, health screening, integration with the corporate attendance program, and diet or exercise plans.

DOL, HHS, and the IRS published final HIPAA regulations about wellness programs in the December 13, 2006 Federal Register. Wellness programs are acceptable if they are available to all similarly situated individuals, and either the sponsor does not offer rewards, or the rewards are not dependent on health status.

[JP Morgan Compensation and Benefits Strategies, *DOL Provides Further Guidance on Wellness Programs* (Mar. 10, 2008) (benefitslink.com)]

The three agencies issued a second set of joint final rules for wellness programs in mid-2013, reaffirming the agencies' belief in the value of these programs in alleviating chronic illness and keeping health care costs in check. The 2013 regulations (effective January 1, 2014) limit underwriting practices that might discriminate on the basis of health status. The final rules are effective January 1, 2014. The rules permit participatory wellness programs that are available to employees without regard to health status (e.g., rewards for taking health information seminars or completing a health questionnaire; paying for health club memberships). The program can offer rewards for meeting a health goal (for example, quitting smoking; meeting a target for weight or blood cholesterol) but the rewards must not discriminate against employees with health problems. [T.D. 9620, 2013-27 I.R.B. 1. See Plansponsor staff, *Wellness Program Final Rules*

Issued, plansponsor.com (May 29, 2013).] 2014 FAQs provide additional detail. For example, if an employee's doctor says that the outcome-based wellness program is not medically appropriate for the employee, the plan must provide a reasonable alternative standard such as an activity-only program (e.g., a weight-loss program). [FAQs, <http://www.dol.gov/ebsa/faqs/faq-aca18.html> (Jan. 9, 2014); see Peter K. Bradley et al., *New Guidance Regarding Preventive Services, Cost Sharing, and Wellness*, Hodgson Russ LLP (Mar. 31, 2014), available at Lexology.com]

The Patient Protection and Affordable Care Act (Pub. L. No. 111-148), the health care reform program adopted in 2010, encourages wellness programs, so this will continue to be a significant issue. See § 18.19[G].

§ 36.11 ADA ENFORCEMENT

The EEOC has enforcement power over the ADA. [42 U.S.C. § 12111(1)] The remedies available for disability discrimination are also available in retaliation cases. [42 U.S.C. § 12203(c)] ADA charges must be filed with the EEOC or the state agency. [See § 41.03 for an explanation of the process] The charge must be filed within 180 days of the last discriminatory act (in nondeferral states) or within 300 days of the last act (in deferral states). The Title VII investigation and conciliation procedures will be followed, and the ADA remedies are equivalent to Title VII remedies, with the distinction that reasonable accommodation can be ordered as an ADA remedy.

The EEOC and the federal courts have discretion to make an attorneys' fee award to the prevailing party. If the United States loses a case, it can be required to pay attorneys' fees—but if the United States wins, the other party cannot be required to compensate the government for the costs of the case. [See 42 U.S.C. § 12205]

§ 36.12 THE ADA PRIMA FACIE CASE

Once a disabled employee makes out a prima facie case, the burden then shifts to the employer to prove, by a preponderance of the evidence, that it either offered the plaintiff reasonable accommodation or was unable to do so because of undue hardship. [*Cmty. Hosp. v. Fail*, 969 P.2d 667 (Colo. Sup. 1998)]

The Fifth Circuit ruled that, even after the ADAAA has taken effect, plaintiffs are still required to prove that they have a disability before they prove discrimination, rejecting the plaintiff's argument that the focus is on the existence of discrimination rather than the presence of a disability. [*Neely v. PSEG*, 736 F.3d 242 (5th Cir. 2013); see Clark Smith, *The Fifth Circuit Clarifies A Plaintiff's Burden Under The Americans With Disabilities Act*, Seyfarth Shaw LLP (Nov. 13, 2013), available at Lexology.com]

§ 36.13 DAMAGES

Although, in the vast majority of cases, employers prevail in ADA cases, there is still the risk that high damages will be awarded in the few cases in which plaintiffs win. The Fourth Circuit upheld a jury award of $8,000 in compensatory and $100,000 in punitive damages to a deaf former package handler at FedEx who was denied reasonable accommodation. Despite numerous requests, he was denied sign language interpreters at employee meetings and training sessions. In the court's view, his supervisors' indifference to the need to accommodate his disability meant that his safety, and perhaps the safety of others, was jeopardized. [*EEOC v. Federal Express Corp.*, 513 F.3d 360 (4th Cir. 2008); see Fred Schneyer, *Deaf Former FedEx Package Handler Wins ADA Award Appeal*, plansponsor.com (Jan. 25, 2008); certiorari was denied: see Rebecca Moore, *Supreme Court Declines Review of FedEx ADA Case*, plansponsor.com (Oct. 9, 2008)]

Although the Second, Eighth, and Tenth Circuits have upheld jury verdicts granting compensatory and punitive damages, the Seventh Circuit interpreted the Civil Rights Act of 1991 to allow compensatory and punitive damages for ADA claims only if they fall under §§ 12112 or 12112(b)(5). Retaliation claims are provided for by § 12203—and therefore the remedies are limited to the equitable relief provided by 42 U.S.C. § 2000e-5(g)(1). Because the plaintiff was only entitled to equitable remedies, she had no right to a jury trial. [*Kramer v. Banc of Am. Sec., LLC*, 355 F.3d 961 (7th Cir. 2004)]

§ 36.14 ARBITRATION OF ADA CLAIMS

Wright v. Universal Mar. Serv. Corp. [525 U.S. 70 (1998)] involves an injured stevedore who was denied employment because potential employers deemed him to be permanently disabled. The plaintiff sued under the ADA without first filing a grievance or going through arbitration under the collective bargaining agreement.

The lower federal courts dismissed his case because of his failure to exhaust grievance remedies, but the Supreme Court unanimously reversed. Although ADA claims are subject to compulsory arbitration under the U-4 (securities industry employment agreement), the Supreme Court treated this case differently because Wright's claims arose under a statute, not a contract. Contract claims are presumed to be subject to arbitration, but statutory claims are not.

For a CBA to rule out litigation of a claim under an antidiscrimination statute, *Wright* says that the CBA must be very clear on that point. A generalized arbitration clause that fails to specify the antidiscrimination statutes that it covers will not be enough to keep disgruntled employees out of the court system.

According to *EEOC v. Waffle House Inc.* [534 U.S. 279 (2002)], the EEOC can pursue an ADA case, including victim-specific relief, even though the employee him- or herself was covered by a mandatory predispute arbitration requirement and would not have been able to sue the employer because of this requirement. [See Chapter 40 for fuller discussion of arbitration and ADR]

CHAPTER 37

AGE DISCRIMINATION IN EMPLOYMENT ACT

§ 37.01 INTRODUCTION

The Age Discrimination in Employment Act (ADEA), unlike Title VII and the ADA, is found in Title 29 of the United States Code starting at Section 621. (Title VII and the ADEA are in Title 42). In other words, Congress considered the ADEA to be labor law instead of civil rights law. [See § 41.06[A] for a discussion of EEOC procedure for filing discrimination charges, and § 42.11 for a discussion of procedural issues arising in private ADEA lawsuits filed by an employee or class of employees]

Congress defined its purpose in passing the ADEA as protecting older people who want to stay in the workforce and are still capable of working from discrimination involving "arbitrary age limits." The ADEA's aim is to "promote employment of older persons based on their ability rather than age; to prohibit arbitrary age discrimination in employment; to help employers and workers find ways of meeting problems arising from the impact of age on employment." [29 U.S.C. § 621]

The basic rule is that anyone over age 40 is protected by the ADEA [29 U.S.C. § 631], so the protected group is not restricted to senior citizens. In a limited range of situations, being under 40 is a bona fide occupational qualification (BFOQ). In other cases, adverse employment action against an older person could be legally justified by a Reasonable Factor Other than Age (RFOA). State age discrimination suits have been upheld when young people are deprived of employment opportunities because of their youth because this, too, is discrimination "on account of age." [*Bergen Commercial Bank v. Sisler*, 157 N.J. 188 (N.J. 1999); *Zanni v. Medaphis Physician Servs. Corp.*, 240 Mich. App. 472 (2000)]

In fiscal 2013, the EEOC received 25,957 age discrimination charges—27.7% of the total number of charges. [Barry A. Hartstein, *EEOC Releases Charge Statistics For FY 2013*, Littler Mendelson (Feb. 5, 2014), available at Lexology.com]

See § 7.04 for discussion of cases considering whether cash balance plans are inherently discriminatory against older employees; nearly all cases have held that they are not, for various rationales (e.g., that the asserted favoritism toward younger employees merely reflects the economic principle of the time value of money).

The Supreme Court denied certiorari in *Drutis v. Quebecor World (USA)*, 555 U.S. 816, a Sixth Circuit case on the issue of whether cash balance plans violate the ADEA. The Supreme Court also refused to hear a challenge to the Seventh Circuit's decision on the IBM cash balance plan. [Fred Schneyer, *U.S. Supreme Court Denies Cash Balance Challenge Review*, plansponsor.com (Oct. 7, 2008)]

The Pension Protection Act of 2006, Pub. L. No. 109-280, amends ADEA § 4(i) (29 U.S.C. § 623(i)). For post-PPA time frames, a plan is not guilty of age discrimination if the participant's accrued benefit is at least as great as the benefit of a similarly situated younger individual who is either a plan participant or potential plan participant. Two participants are considered to be similarly situated if they are the same as to date of hire, period of service, position, compensation, work history, etc., and differ only in their age. In making this determination, the subsidized part of any available early retirement benefit is disregarded. The accrued benefit can be expressed as an annuity payable at NRA, the current value of the accumulated percentage of the employee's final average compensation (the measure used by many defined benefit plans) or the balance of a hypothetical account (i.e., a cash balance plan). [The IRS published final regulations about this safe harbor in late 2010: 75 Fed. Reg. 64123 (Oct. 19, 2010)]

The Lilly Ledbetter Fair Pay Act, Pub. L. No. 111-2 (signed Jan. 29, 2009), amends the ADEA (as well as Title VII, the ADA, and the Rehabilitation Act), to reverse the Supreme Court's *Ledbetter v. Goodyear Tire & Rubber*, 550 U.S. 618 (2007) ruling about the timing of discrimination suits. The Ledbetter Act adds a new ADEA § 7(d)(3), providing that an unlawful employment practice is deemed to occur when it is initially adopted; when a person first becomes subject to the practice—or each time the person is affected by the practice, e.g., every time he or she receives a paycheck that is unfairly low because of discrimination. Depending on whether or not the state has a work-sharing agreement with the EEOC, suit must be brought either within 180 days or 300 days of the last act covered by the Act. A successful plaintiff can recover back pay for up to two years before the date the charge was filed. The Act became effective as if it had become law the day before the Supreme Court *Ledbetter* decision—with the result that any cases that were pending on May 28, 2007, or have been filed since then, can take advantage of the statute's timing rules.

The first federal suit filed under the Ledbetter Act was an ADEA suit filed early in February by Wayne Tomlinson to challenge a cash balance conversion. Tomlinson wanted to reverse a January 21, 2009 decision that his age discrimination suit was untimely.

The District Court for the District of Colorado initially decided in 2009 that Tomlinson's ADEA suit was time-barred. However, on August 28, 2009, the district court reversed its earlier decision and reinstated the ADEA claim. Accrual of pension benefits could plausibly be deemed to be affected by application of a discriminatory compensation decision. Although the court did not find a separate violation each time a pension check was paid, the decision to convert, the actual conversion, and subsequent pension accruals could be treated as separate.

The EEOC Compliance Manual § 2-IVC.4, Compensation Discrimination, has been amended to allow suit 180 or 300 days after receipt of compensation affected by a discriminatory practice, and says the time frames apply to "all forms of compensation, including the payment of pension benefits," but the EEOC "strongly encourages" suit within 180 or 300 days of retirement to make sure that the suit is timely.

In mid-2011, the Tenth Circuit held that El Paso Corporation's cash balance plan did not violate the ADEA or ERISA. The Tenth Circuit adopted the argument that the time value of money is not age discrimination. Claims under ADEA

§ 4(i) would have to be based on discrimination in input (cash balance credits) rather than output. The only input that varied with age was the pay credit, which increased as the employee got older. [*Tomlinson v. El Paso Corp.*, 653 F.3d 1281 (10th Cir. 2011); see Rebecca Moore, *Appellate Court Finds Cash Balance Plan not Age-Biased*, plansponsor.com (Aug. 12, 2011) and CCH Pensions & Benefits, *El Paso Wins Cash Balance Case; No Age Discrimination or Backloading Provisions Were Violated* (Sept. 2, 2011) (benefitslink.com).]

Another recent trend is to bring disparate impact ADEA claims, charging that a seemingly age-neutral policy in fact has unfair effects on older workers. It was not clear, until the Supreme Court's *Smith v. City of Jackson* decision in 2005 that disparate-impact ADEA claims were allowable. [Tresa Baldas, *Age Bias Suits on the Rise with Older Employees Working Longer*, Nat'l L.J. (Mar. 16, 2007) (law.com), *discussing, e.g., Mody v. Gen. Elec.*, No. 3:04 CV 358 (D. Conn. 2006); *Hogan v. City of Hollywood*, No. CACE04014128 (Fla. Cir. Ct. 2006)]

§ 37.02 ADEA EXCEPTIONS

The ADEA bars job discrimination, so a discharge for good cause will not violate the ADEA. As is true of many other labor and anti-discrimination laws, the ADEA exempts very small businesses. The definition of "employer" is limited to industries affecting commerce and having 20 or more employees for each workday in each of 20 or more weeks in the current or previous year. [29 U.S.C. § 630(b)]

The ADEA applies to employees of the United States branch of a foreign corporation that has 20 or more employees worldwide; there need not be 20 employees at the U.S. branch. [*Morelli v. Cedel*, 141 F.3d 39 (2d Cir. 1998)] The number of employees at several small affiliates of a larger corporation can be aggregated for the 20-employee test if the parent company directed the discriminatory act or policy; the original larger enterprise was split up to avoid liability; and the corporate veil can be pierced (i.e., the parent can be held liable for the subsidiaries' debts, torts, and breaches of contract). [*Papa v. Katy Indus. Inc.*, 166 F.3d 937 (7th Cir. 1999)]

Although the general rule under the ADEA is that no one can be compelled to retire simply because of that person's age, there is an important exception. Under 29 U.S.C. § 631, a person who has been a "bona fide executive or high policy maker" for two years just before retirement, can lawfully be compelled to retire at 65, as long as he or she is entitled to aggregate retirement benefits that are the equivalent of an annuity of $44,000 a year or more. EEOC Guidelines [29 C.F.R. § 1625.12(d)] define a bona fide policymaker as the manager of an entire enterprise, or at least a customarily recognized department or subdivision. He or she must direct the work of at least two employees, and must hold a job that regularly involves the exercise of discretionary power. At least 80% of work time (or at least 60% in a retail or service business) must be spent on managing the business rather than on routine tasks. The Higher Education Amendments of 1998 [H.R. 6 (Oct. 7, 1998)] reinstate a traditional ADEA exception. Under the Amendments, it is lawful to require tenured faculty members to retire solely on the basis of age. Although this act affects a small group of individuals, it is significant in showing a possible trend toward restricting the scope of the ADEA and other civil rights legislation.

In late 2007, the mandatory retirement age for commercial pilots was raised from 60 to 65, in conformity with other nations' rules, by the Fair Treatment for Experienced Pilots Act, Pub. L. No. 110-135. The law firm of Kelley Drye & Warren, after being sued by the EEOC, changed its policy and stopped requiring partners to change their status at age 70. Instead of being equity partners sharing in the firm's profits, they would become "life partners" who received payments each year, plus a bonus if they continued to practice law for the firm. The case was settled in April 2012: the firm agreed to pay "life partner" Eugene D'Ablemont $574,000, and also agreed not to reduce partners' compensation because of their age. [*EEOC v. Kelley Drye & Warren*, No. 0655 cv-10 (2d Cir. Settled 2012); see Brian Baxter, *Kelley Drye Settles EEOC Age Discrimination Suit Involving Firm Partner*, AmLaw Daily (Apr. 10, 2012) (law.com)]

Note that, in 2007, the law firm of Sidley Austin settled with a group of ousted partners for $27.5 million; the Seventh Circuit held that the former partners were employees entitled to protection under anti-discrimination laws. The settlement is discussed in the EEOC Management's Discussion and Analysis for FY 2008, <http://www.eeoc.gov/eeoc/plan/archives/annualreports/par/2008/managements_discussion.html> (Nov. 26, 2008)].

PriceWaterhouse requires partners to retire at 60. The EEOC has not brought a suit, but informed PriceWaterhouse (as well as Deloitte and KPMG, which have similar policies) that this policy is discriminatory. An informal letter from the EEOC discusses when mandatory retirement of accounting firm partners will be considered an ADEA violation. There are six factors in the determination of when a person described as a partner is a statutory employee: e.g., if the person participates in management or can influence partnership operations; if his or her work activities are controlled by management. [Parker Poe Adams & Bernstein LLP, *EEOC Believes That Partners Can Be Employees For Age Discrimination Purposes* (Oct. 10, 2013), available at Lexology.com; Employment Practices Solutions Inc., *EEOC: Mandatory Retirement Policies Are Discriminatory*, Lexology.com (Sept. 11, 2013)]

§ 37.03 FORBIDDEN PRACTICES

[A] Statutory Prohibitions

Under 29 U.S.C. § 623, employers are forbidden to:

- Discriminate because of age (by firing or failing or refusing to hire, or in any other way) against anyone in connection with "compensation, terms, conditions, or privileges of employment";
- Use age to "limit, segregate, or classify" employees that reduce employment opportunities or "otherwise adversely affect" status as an employee;
- Reduce any employee's wage rate to comply with the ADEA;
- Discriminate against an employee or job applicant because of that person's protests about age discrimination, or in retaliation for that person's bringing an ADEA charge or involvement in someone else's ADEA charge;
- Publish Help Wanted ads that indicate "any preference, limitation, specification, or discrimination, based on age."

Section 623 also forbids age discrimination perpetrated by employment agencies and unions, but those provisions are outside the scope of this book.

The EEOC has ruled that the ADEA applies to apprenticeship programs. Early in 2005, the Fourth Circuit upheld this rule as valid and not contrary to the Congressional intent in passing the ADEA. [*EEOC v. Seafarers Int'l Union*, 394 F.3d 197 (4th Cir. 2005)]

Only significant employment actions will support a suit.

The Eighth Circuit affirmed dismissal of an ADEA suit, finding that a small reduction in hours, negative performance reviews, and allegations of differential treatment as compared to younger employees (e.g., he claimed that younger workers were given advance notice of inspections) were inadequate to constitute adverse employment actions [*Baucom v. Holiday Cos. Inc.*, 428 F.3d 764 (8th Cir. 2005)]

The Post Office implemented a new staffing plan in June 2009, affecting 280 positions. There were no layoffs, but many employees experienced changes in their shifts and scheduled days off. The plaintiff's job was eliminated. He was given a choice between a residual assignment and bidding for jobs on other tours. He bid on another tour, with the same seniority, opportunities for promotion, and responsibilities as his original job. The District Court for the District of New Jersey dismissed his ADEA suit in mid-2013, finding that there had been no adverse job action because his working conditions remained unchanged. [*Spearman v. Donahoe*, No. 11-6666 (JEI/JS), 2013 U.S. Dist. LEXIS 99536 (D.N.J. July 17, 2013); see Jeffrey A. Gruen, *Shift Change Not Adverse Employment Action*, Day Pitney LLP (Aug. 28, 2013), available at Lexology.com]

In a case of first impression for the Circuit, the Fifth Circuit ruled in 2011 that a hostile work environment suit can be brought under the ADEA. The plaintiff, Dediol, established that: he was over 40; subjected to harassment; it was severe enough to create an objectively intimidating, hostile, or offensive work environment; there was a rationale for imposing liability on the employer. He was also permitted to pursue constructive discharge and religiously hostile work environment claims after being denied permission for time off for a church event. [*Dediol vs. Best Chevrolet Inc.*, 655 F.3d 435 (5th Cir. 2011); see Rebecca Moore, *Court Says Worker Can Claim Hostile Work Environment under ADEA*, plansponsor.com (Sept. 15, 2011)]

An Alameda County judge approved age discrimination claims of 130 employees laid off by the Lawrence Livermore National Laboratory, finding that they provided adequate evidence of disproportionate termination of employees older than age 40 and reassignment of their duties to younger workers. The ex-employees had an average age of 54 and an average tenure of 20 years at the laboratory. This decision affects a group of consolidated suits filed in 2009 after the lab was privatized. [Shelley Eades, *Judge OKs Age Bias Claims Against Lawrence Livermore Lab*, The Recorder (Oct. 17, 2012) (law.com)]

But, in the second phase of the trial, an Oakland jury found for the defense, holding that 2008 mass layoffs did not have an adverse impact on older workers. In May 2013, a jury awarded $2.8 million in economic damages on findings that the lab illegally breached the plaintiffs' employment contracts, but the second jury rejected the disparate impact age claims, rejecting the request for $25 million in emotional distress damages. Claims by another 120 workers remained pending. [*Andrews v. Lawrence Livermore*, No. C 11-3930 CS (Cal. Super. 2013): see <http://www.giccb.com/In-the-News/Case-News.shtml> referring to the case; see Max Taves, *Jury Finds No Age Bias in Lab Layoffs*, The Recorder (Dec. 23, 2013), available at law.com; Adams, Nye, Becht LLP, *Mixed-Bag of Verdicts for Lawrence Livermore Lab Employees*, <http://www.calemployeerights.com/2014/01/mixed-bag-of-verdicts-for-lawrence-livermore-lab-employees-alleging-age-discrimination.html> (Jan. 30, 2014)]; The third phase of the trial, a jury trial of the claims of ten plaintiffs, was set for January 26, 2015 in Alameda County Superior Court. [*Andrews v. Lawrence Livermore Nat'l Sec., LLC*, No. RG09453596 (pending); see Gwilliam Ivary Chiosso Cavalli & Brewer, P.C. Case News, *Trial Set in Litigation Over Layoff at Lawrence Livermore Lab*, <http://www.giccb.com/In-the-News/Case-News.shtml> (undated, viewed Aug. 28, 2014)]

[B] Supreme Court Precedents

A Supreme Court case, *Public Employees Ret. System of Ohio v. Betts* [492 U.S. 158 (1989)], held that the ADEA did not apply to employee benefits. In 1990, Congress amended the statute, adding a new § 630(l), extending the ADEA ban on age discrimination in "compensation, terms, conditions, or privileges of employment" to cover "benefits provided pursuant to a bona fide employee benefit plan."

To win, the ADEA plaintiff does not have to show that he or she was replaced by someone under 40; it may even be possible to win by showing age-motivated replacement by another person over 40 (for instance, choosing someone who will retire soon, thus removing two older workers from the workplace). [*O'Connor v. Consol. Coin Caterers Corp.*, 517 U.S. 308 (1997)]

The Tenth Circuit refused to impose a bright-line test (where an age difference of five years or less would rule out age discrimination), and permitted an ADEA action to proceed when a 62-year-old was replaced by a 57-year-old. The small gap in ages would make it harder for the plaintiff to prevail, but it was only one factor for the jury to consider. [*Whittington v. Nordam Group Inc.*, 429 F.3d 986 (10th Cir. 2005)]

In 2004, the Supreme Court ruled that one group of over-40 workers could not use the ADEA to charge they were the victims of discrimination in favor of another group of over-40 workers who were older than they were. (This was a retiree health benefits case about grandfathered benefits.) The Supreme Court concluded that the ADEA permits employers to favor their oldest group of workers, even at the expense of younger workers who are nevertheless over 40 and covered by the ADEA. [*General Dynamics Land Systems, Inc. v. Cline*, 540 U.S. 581 (2004); see also *Lawrence v. Town of Irondequoit*, 246 F. Supp. 2d 150 (W.D.N.Y. 2002), permitting employers to enhance retiree health benefits for persons over 80.

The EEOC adapted its ADEA regulations to conform to *Cline* and provide that it is lawful to favor the oldest employees over younger, but still, ADEA-eligible, employees. The agency revised § 1625.2 so that its caption is "discrimination prohibited by the Act," rather than "Discrimination between individuals protected by the Act." Asking for a date of birth or age on a job application is not a per se violation, but will be closely scrutinized by the EEOC because it could have the effect of discouraging older applicants.

The final rule, published in mid-2007, states that employers are not required to prefer older individuals, and applicable state or local laws forbidding preferences for older individuals remain valid. [72 Fed. Reg. 36873 (July 6, 2007)]

A group of Mississippi police officers objected to a plan that gave higher percentage raises to police officers with *fewer* than five years' service. Because the veteran officers tended to be older than those with shorter tenure, they alleged that the practice had a disparate impact on older officers, even though it did not explicitly categorize them on the basis of age. The U.S. Supreme Court ruled in the spring of 2005 that the plaintiffs did not have a valid claim—but the Court clarified that, under the right circumstances, disparate-impact ADEA cases can be valid, because the ADEA's statutory language is very close to that of Title VII. However, employers who are charged with disparate impact age discrimination can raise a defense that the disputed practice is based on reasonable factors other than age (RFOA), whereas there is no similar defense in race or sex discrimination cases.

The plaintiffs in this case were unsuccessful because they failed to identify the specific aspect of the pay plan that harmed the interests of older workers. The defendant, on the other hand, had a reasonable explanation for its adoption of the practice: to retain the newer officers, their compensation had to be brought closer to market norms. [*Smith v. City of Jackson, Miss.*, 544 U.S. 228 (2005)]

In mid-2009, the Supreme Court decided, in *Gross v. FBL Financial*, that in order to win, a mixed-motive ADEA plaintiff must prove by a preponderance of the evidence that age was the "but-for" cause of the challenged employment action: that it would never have occurred but-for the plaintiff's age. The burden of persuasion is always on the plaintiff, and can be met by either direct or circumstantial evidence. The burden of persuasion never shifts to the defendant. This is not the same standard applied in Title VII, but the Supreme Court stressed the difference in wording and legislative history between the ADEA and Title VII. [*Gross v. FBL Fin. Servs., Inc.*, 557 U.S. 167 (2009); see Russell E. Adler, Law Firm of Pepper Hamilton LLP, *Supreme Court Ruling Increases Burden on Employees in Age Discrimination Cases* (June 19, 2009) (benefitslink.com)] *St. Mary's Honor Ctr. v. Hicks* [509 U.S. 502 (1993)] says that the plaintiff always has the "ultimate burden of persuasion." So if the judge or jury (whichever is responsible for determining the facts of the case) does not believe the employer's explanation of the reasons behind its conduct, the plaintiff could still lose—if he or she fails to provide adequate evidence. The *Hicks* standard is sometimes called "pretext-plus": The plaintiff has to do more than show the defendant's excuses are a mere pretext for discrimination.

The District Court for the Northern District of Oklahoma allowed the EEOC to go to trial in the case of an employee who said she was fired for being "old and ugly," and the CEO wanted "younger and prettier" property managers to meet with potential tenants. The defendant said that this was a mixed motive case of the type precluded by *Gross*. The district court disagreed: the jury could find that the concept "old and ugly" was related to the *plaintiff's* age. The court said that but-for causation is not sole causation, merely a method of proving nexus between a termination decision and a discriminatory motivation. [*Equal Employment Opportunity Commission v. Kanbar Prop. Mgmt., LLC*, No. 12-CV-00422-JED-TLW, 2013 U.S. Dist. LEXIS 12005, 97 Empl. Prac. Dec. (CCH) P44,894 (N.D. Okla. Aug. 23, 2013); see P. Andrew Torrez, *If You Can't Be Fired For Being Old, Can You Be Fired For Being Old And Ugly? Why This Is A Harder Question Than You Might Think*, Zuckerman Spaeder LLP (Sept. 5, 2013), available at Lexology.com] The case was subsequently settled for $140,000. [Kevin McGuinness, *Company Settles EEOC Age Discrimination Suit*, plansponsor.com (Sept. 11, 2013)]

The Supreme Court initially granted certiorari in the Seventh Circuit case of *Madigan v. Levin*—but then dismissed certiorari as improvidently granted. Levin sued for age discrimination after his termination at age 61. The Seventh Circuit held that, as a state employee, he was not limited to ADEA remedies. The Seventh Circuit, unlike four other circuits, permits state employees to bring age discrimination claims directly under the Fourteenth Amendment's Equal Protection Clause. The case was remanded to the district court for trial. [No. 12-872, dismissed Oct. 15, 2013; see Employment Practices Solutions Inc., *U.S. Supreme Court Does Not Decide Age Discrimination Case*, Lexology.com (Oct. 24, 2013)]

Although the ADEA statute explicitly waives sovereign immunity, permitting suits by state employees, the Supreme Court ruled that Congress violated the

Eleventh Amendment by abrogating sovereign immunity without demonstrating a history of violations of this type committed by state employers. [*Kimel v. Florida Bd. of Regents*, 528 U.S. 62 (1999)]

The Supreme Court's June 2000 decision in *Reeves v. Sanderson Plumbing Prods. Inc.* [530 U.S. 133 (2000)] is a narrow procedural one. It holds that an ADEA plaintiff can defeat a motion for judgment as a matter of law (a procedural technique for terminating a lawsuit without a full trial) by establishing a prima facie case plus enough evidence for a reasonable court or jury to find that the employer's defense is merely pretextual. It is not required that the plaintiff introduce any further evidence at this stage, unless a rational finder of fact would not be able to find the defendant's conduct discriminatory. However, *Reeves* had little practical impact on the litigation climate, it certainly didn't issue in a new pro-plaintiff era.

In 2002, certiorari was granted in *Adams v. Fla. Power*, No. 01-584, on the issue of whether ADEA disparate impact claims are cognizable, but later that year, certiorari was dismissed as improvidently granted: 535 U.S. 228 (2002). The Supreme Court finally resolved the issue in 2005, ruling, in *Smith v. Jackson*, 544 U.S. 228, that disparate impact claims are cognizable.

The Supreme Court permitted an ADEA suit to proceed, after the complainant filed a Form 283 intake questionnaire with the EEOC, but did not file the official Form 5 (charge). The EEOC did not carry out informal dispute resolution with the employer. The Supreme Court held that a valid ADEA charge requires only a few items of information (the name of the charging party, the nature of the allegation, and a request that the EEOC settle a dispute or take remedial action). In this case, the employer was aware that the plaintiff and 13 other employees had alleged age discrimination. The Court remanded the case to the district court, holding that the lower court can make up for the deficiency by attempting to reconcile the parties in a settlement. (The EEOC stated that it has improved its procedures to make sure the same problem will not recur.) [*Federal Express Corp. v. Holowecki*, 552 U.S. 389 (2008); see also *Holender v. Mutual Indus. North Inc.*, 527 F.3d 352 (3d Cir. 2008), in which the Third Circuit allowed a suit to proceed based on the filing of a two-page document, including an EEOC Form 5 ("Charge of Discrimination"). The Third Circuit deemed the document to be a valid charge because it contained the information required by the regulations.]

In February 2008, the Supreme Court did not really resolve the question of whether testimony of bias exhibited by a different supervisor is admissible to show a corporate culture of discrimination. The Court did not adopt the district court's outright ban on testimony by employees of other supervisors, but neither did it adopt the Tenth Circuit's position that such testimony should always be admitted. The Supreme Court required a fact-based inquiry based on balancing relevance against prejudice, and stated that, in general, the courts of appeals should defer to the district court's determination (because the district court hears all of the testimony instead of just seeing the record on appeal). Instead of reversing, the Tenth Circuit should have sent the case back to the district court. Because the two statutes use similar language, the ruling also applies to "different-supervisor" testimony in Title VII cases. The likely result of this decision is that employers will have to fully litigate more cases: fewer cases will be disposed of at the summary judgment stage, because plaintiffs will be able to offer a broader range of evidence at the early stages. [*Sprint/United Mgmt. Co. v. Mendelsohn*, 552 U.S. 379 (2008) Before the Supreme Court decision, Sprint settled ADEA charges brought by 1,700 employees laid off between October 2001 and March 2003 for $57 million; the employees were expected to receive between $4,226 and $35,738 each. The company denied wrongdoing but wanted to reduce its legal fees by settling the case. [Rebecca Moore, *Sprint Settles Age Discrimination Suits for $57M*, plansponsor.com (Sept. 18, 2007)]

The Supreme Court also ruled in 2008 that:

- Federal employees can use the counterpart of the ADEA that covers federal workers to assert age-based retaliation claims. [*Gomez-Perez v. Potter*, 553 U.S. 474 (2008)]
- The employer always has the burden of production and the burden of proof when it comes to the affirmative defense of reasonable factors other than age (RFOA). [*Meacham v. Knolls Atomic Power Labs*, 554 U.S. 84 (2008)]

[C] Employee Status

ADEA cases are limited to the employment context, not all aspects of economic life. Therefore, it could not be an ADEA violation to use age to refuse an automobile dealership to an applicant; dealers are contractors, not employees. [*Mangram v. GM Corp.*, 108 F.3d 61 (4th Cir. 1997)]

Salespersons who are independent contractors are not covered by the ADEA. [*Oestman v. Nat'l Farmers Unions Inc.*, 958 F.2d 303 (10th Cir. 1992)] The Eighth Circuit ruled in 2010 that it was not a violation of the ADEA to fire an independent contractor marketing representative and replace her with a younger employee. [*Ernster v. Luxco, Inc.*, 596 F.3d 1000 (8th Cir. 2010); see CCH Pensions and Benefits, *Independent Contractors Are Not Protected by ADEA When Terminated* (Mar. 19, 2010) (benefitslink.com)]

The critical test of employee status is whether the economic realities of that person's situation are more like employment or more like another relationship (such as being a partner in a partnership). [*EEOC v. Sidley Austin Brown & Wood*, 315 F.3d 696 (7th Cir. 2002). The shareholders in a professional corporation are not counted in determining if the PC has 20 "employees" for business purposes. [*Schmidt v. Ottawa Med. Ctr. PC*, 322 F.3d 461 (7th Cir. 2003)]

■ **TIP:** In April 2003, the Supreme Court ruled (although in an ADA rather than an ADEA case, and a case brought by someone who was an ordinary employee rather than by a shareholder-director) that doctors-shareholders in medical PCs are NOT employees, and are not counted in determining if the business has enough employees to be subject to an anti-discrimination statute. [*Clackamas Gastroenterology Assocs., PC v. Wells,* 538 U.S. 440 (2003)]

[D] Occupational Qualifications and RFOAs

Being under 40 can be a bona fide occupational qualification (BFOQ) for a narrow range of jobs, usually involving public safety (e.g., the strength, agility, and quick reaction time required of police officers and firefighters), [see 29 U.S.C. § 623(f)(1)] but most ordinary private sector jobs will not give rise to a BFOQ defense. The First Circuit held that forced retirement of police officers in Puerto Rico did not violate the ADEA, and the older officers were not entitled to keep their jobs by passing a skills test. [*Correa-Ruiz v. Fortuno*, 573 F.3d 1 (1st Cir. 2009)]

Reasonable factors other than age (RFOA) can offer a defense, as long as the employer used objective, job-related criteria to make the employment decision, and applied those criteria uniformly. Courts have often accepted arguments that the employer's decision was not really age-based, but was inspired by factors that merely tend to go along with age: for instance, the tendency of salaries to rise with experience. Employers in search of cost cutting might discharge higher-paid older workers in order to replace them with lower-paid workers.

The RFOA is an affirmative defense—i.e., one that the employer has to prove, not one that the plaintiff must disprove, and the employer has the burden of production and the burden of proof on the RFOA defense. [*Meacham v. Knolls Atomic Power Labs*, 554 U.S. 84 (2008)]

The EEOC Regulations say that, if the RFOA has a disparate impact on over-40 workers, the employer must prove that it has a business necessity for the action. The EEOC issued an NPR on March 31, 2008, in response to the *Smith v. City of Jackson* decision. Based on the comments received, the EEOC decided to issue further guidance, and about two years later, in February 2010, the EEOC published a Notice of Proposed Rulemaking (NPR) to define "reasonable factors other than age" under the ADEA. The determination of whether an employment practice is based on RFOA is made based on the facts and circumstances, and whether the employer responded prudently to the facts of the case.

RFOAs must be objectively reasonable (assessed from the point of view of a reasonable employer acting under similar circumstances), and the employer must manifest prudence and awareness of responsibilities under the ADEA. A reasonable factor is one that an employer that uses reasonable care to avoid limiting the employment opportunities of older persons would use. Reasonableness is affected by the design of the practice, which must be reasonably administered to further a legitimate business purpose. The NPR permits consideration of job performance, skill sets, and flexibility in deciding who will be affected by a RIF—as long as the employer has made reasonable efforts to be accurate and fair, and has taken steps to ameliorate avoidable harm.

The EEOC suggests training managers to avoid age stereotypes; identifying the specific skills the employer wants to retain after the RIF has been completed; and comparing possible preventive and corrective steps (to avoid or redress harm) to the burden of undertaking those steps. However, the NPR says that if harm is severe, reasonableness includes consideration of whether the employer was aware of other, not unduly burdensome, measures that could have been taken to reduce harm. The NPR does not always require employers to adopt the practice that imposes the least harm on the protected group. [75 Fed. Reg. 7212 (Feb. 18, 2010); see Rebecca Moore, *EEOC Defines Reasonable Factors Other Than Age*, plansponsor.com (Mar. 2, 2010)]

In 2012, the EEOC issued a Q&A, explaining what employers must do to use a Reasonable Factors Other Than Age (RFOA) defense when practices that are neutral on their face but might have disparate impact on older workers are challenged. The employer is only required to prove an RFOA after an employee has identified a specific business practice with disparate impact on older workers. An RFOA is reasonably designed when administered to achieve a legitimate business purpose—for example, a physical test for police patrol officers.

Whether the factors are indeed reasonable depends on, e.g.,

- Their relation to the employer's stated business purpose;
- The extent to which the factor is accurately defined and fairly and accurately applied (application includes training managers and supervisors);
- Limits on supervisors' discretion, especially when the criteria are vulnerable to negative age-based stereotypes;
- The extent to which the employer assessed the adverse impact of the practice on older workers;
- The degree of harm to workers over 40—not just the number of people affected and the extent of the injury, but the employer's measures to reduce harm, balanced against the burden of the actual and potential measures

The EEOC stresses that these are not elements that all employers must prove in every case, merely characteristics of reasonable practices.

The EEOC said that, unlike an employment test that has been challenged under Title VII, it is not necessary for the employer to produce a validation study about the RFOA.

The EEOC says it is not unreasonable to use subjective decision-making (e.g., ranking an applicant or employee's qualities such as flexibility and willingness to learn new things), but it is useful to give supervisors evaluation criteria to help them avoid age-based stereotypes. The EEOC said that employers are not obligated to discover and use the least discriminatory method of achieving the purpose—but attempts to limit harm to older persons are not irrelevant. [EEOC, *Questions and Answers on EEOC Final Rule on Disparate Impact and* "Reasonable Factors Other Than Age" *Under the Age Discrimination in Employment Act of 1967*, <http://www.eeoc.gov/laws/regulations/adea_rfoa_qa_final_rule.cfm> (accessed Apr. 9, 2014); see Rebecca Moore, *EEOC Issues Final Rule Under ADEA*, plansponsor.com (Mar. 30, 2012)]

It is a defense to an age discrimination charge if an employer follows the provisions of "a bona fide seniority system that is not intended to evade" the ADEA's purposes. [29 U.S.C. § 623(f); 29 C.F.R. § 1625.8] However, even a valid seniority system cannot be used to impose involuntary retirement on an employee who is capable of working and wants to continue. Furthermore, older seniority systems (and retirement plans) are not "grandfathered in." Section 623(k) requires all seniority systems and benefit plans to comply with the ADEA, no matter when they were adopted.

§ 37.04 IMPLICATIONS FOR BENEFIT PLANS

[A] Generally

At one time, it would have been accurate to say that the ADEA covered only hiring, firing, and salary, but not employee benefits, based on a Supreme Court decision. [*Public Employees Ret. Sys. of Ohio v. Betts*, 492 U.S. 158 (1989)] In 1990, however, Congress passed a statute, the Older Workers Benefit Protection Act (OWBPA) to make it clear that the ADEA covers all of the terms and conditions of employment, including the full compensation package. Therefore, in the current legal environment, it is important to discover how the ADEA interacts with ERISA, insurance laws, and other laws affecting compensation and benefits.

Section 623(i) takes up the question of how the ADEA interacts with employee benefit plans. Employers are forbidden to "establish or maintain" a pension plan that requires or even permits age-based termination or reduction of pension credits. In a defined benefit plan, benefits must continue to accrue at the same rate. In a defined contribution plan, the employer's allocations must be made to all employees' accounts on the same basis, irrespective of their ages. [29 U.S.C. § 623(i)(1)] People who count as "highly compensated employees" for tax purposes are not entitled to this protection. [See 29 U.S.C. § 623(i)(5)]

The ADEA provides various defenses and safe harbors for employers. Voluntary early retirement plans are allowable as long as they are consistent with the ADEA's purpose of protecting employment rights for older workers. [29 U.S.C. § 623(f)(B)(2)]

It is permissible for a plan to put an upper limit on the amount of benefits a plan can provide to anyone, or to limit the number of years of employment that can be taken into account, as long as these provisions are imposed without regard to age. [29 U.S.C. § 623(i)(2)] For instance, if the plan does not permit crediting of more than 30 years of service, this is an allowable age-neutral provision because it applies to employees with more than 30 years' tenure whether they started working for the company at age 18 or age 40.

Once an employee has reached the plan's Normal Retirement Age (NRA) and has started to receive a pension, then the employer's obligation to continue accruing benefits is satisfied by the actuarial equivalent of the pension benefits themselves. [29 U.S.C. § 623(i)(3)(A)]

Section 623(i)(3)(B) says that, for employees who have reached NRA but have not started to draw a pension (typically, employees who defer their retirement and are still working), and whose benefits have not been suspended pursuant to ERISA § 203(a)(3)(B) or I.R.C. § 411(a)(3)(B), the employer's obligation to keep accruing benefits is satisfied by making an actuarial adjustment to the pension that the employee eventually receives, so that he or she gets a larger pension because of deferred retirement.

Because the ADEA covers persons over age 40, the protected group includes many people who will voluntarily elect early retirement. Section 623(l) says that it does not constitute age discrimination for a pension plan to set a minimum retirement age as a condition for being eligible for either early or normal retirement.

A defined benefit plan can lawfully provide early retirement subsidies, or supplement the Social Security benefits of retirees who get a reduced benefit because they retire before the plan's NRA. [29 U.S.C. § 623(l)(1)(B). With respect to retiree health benefits, also see 29 U.S.C. § 623(l)(2)(D)]

There is no ADEA violation if a departing employee's severance pay is reduced to account for the value of retiree health benefits, and/or the value of additional pension benefits that are made available because of a contingency that is not based on age to a person who is already eligible for a full retirement benefit. [29 U.S.C. § 623(l)(2)] For this purpose, severance pay is defined to include certain supplemental unemployment insurance benefits. [See 29 U.S.C. § 613(l)(2)(C) and I.R.C. § 501(c)(17)]

■ **TIP:** If the employer says that retiree health benefits will be provided, and reduces severance pay accordingly, but fails to provide retiree health benefits, 29 U.S.C. § 623(l)(2)(F) lets employees sue for "specific performance" (i.e., to make the employer provide the benefits). This is an additional right, over and above any other remedies the individual has.

In mid-2003, the EEOC reversed its earlier position and proposed Regulations under which employers would be allowed to coordinate retiree health benefits with Medicare: i.e., it would not be considered an ADEA violation to reduce or even eliminate retiree health benefits at the point at which the ex-employees become eligible for Medicare; the rule was finalized in 2004. [68 Fed. Reg. 41542 (July 14, 2003)]. The EEOC's authority to promulgate this rule was upheld by the

Third Circuit (and certiorari was denied) based on a 2005 Supreme Court administrative law decision requiring deference to an agency's reasonable interpretation of statutes within the agency's scope of operations. [*AARP v. EEOC*, 489 F.3d 558 (3d Cir. 2007); see Jerry Geisel, *Review of Retiree Health Care Bias Ruling Denied*, Business Insurance (Aug. 22, 2007) (benefitslink.com); *AARP v. EEOC, appeal dismissed* 128 S. Ct. 1733 (Mar. 24, 2008). The administrative law case is *National Cable & Telecomm. Ass'n v. Brand X Internet Servs.*, 545 U.S. 967 (2005)]

In December 2007, the EEOC issued a Final Rule reflecting the Third Circuit's decision; the EEOC said that it permitted a narrow exemption from the antidiscrimination rule. The Final Rule permits employers to limit retiree health benefits to retirees who are not yet eligible for Medicare, or to supplement Medicare coverage without making that coverage identical to the coverage that non-Medicare-eligible retirees receive. Companies that offer prescription drug coverage do not have to make it identical for Medicare-eligible and non-eligible retirees. However, the rule affects only the ADEA, not other issues (such as the status of Medicare as secondary payor for Medicare beneficiaries who continue to be employed). [72 Fed. Reg. 72938 (Dec. 26, 2007)]

[B] Case Law on Pension and Benefit Issues

Another of 2008's many Supreme Court age discrimination rulings held that it was not age discrimination for a public retirement system to add years to the disability retirement formula (resulting in a higher benefit) only for employees who became disabled before Normal Retirement Age, not for those—like the plaintiff—who continued to work after Normal Retirement Age, and subsequently became disabled. The Supreme Court held that the difference in treatment was not motivated by age, because age and pension status are distinct. [*Kentucky Ret. Sys. v. EEOC*, 554 U.S. 135 (2008)]

The Seventh Circuit ruled in mid-2010 that a cash balance plan provision that cut off interest credits when a participant reached age 55 did not discriminate against older workers. According to the Seventh Circuit, the interest credits, which were designed to reverse the 8.5% annual discount applied to opening account balances, were not benefit accruals, so discontinuing them did not violate ERISA's ban on age-related cuts in accruals. The plan offered a lump sum cash balance, so it was not an "eligible cash balance plan" under the Treasury regulations. [*Walker v. Monsanto Co. Pension Plan*, 614 F.3d 415 (7th Cir. 2010); Fred Schneyer, *Monsanto Cash Balance Plan Cleared of Age Bias Wrongdoing*, plansponsor.com (Aug. 2, 2010)]

The Eighth Circuit used the familiar rationale that correlation is not causation to hold that plan contributions to a frozen plan on behalf of airline pilots were not reduced "on account of age," although the contributions were based on projected final average earnings for the plaintiffs, and the projected earnings could not be calculated without considering the pilot's age. Many factors, not just age, could reduce projected final average earnings: for example, seniority and position, the number of annual pay increases the pilot had received, and benefits under the frozen plan. [*Northwest Airlines, Inc., v. Phillips,* 675 F.3d 1126 (8th Cir. 2012), see Asset International Inc., *Northwest Pilots' Pension Plan Found Non-Discriminatory* (Apr. 10, 2012) (benefitslink.com); CCH Pension & Benefits, *Airline's Post-Bankruptcy Money Purchase Plan Did Not Illegally Reduce Benefits Due To Age* (Aug. 21, 2012) (benefitslink.com)]

§ 37.05 HEALTH BENEFITS

If the employer maintains a group health plan, the plan must cover over-65 employees on equal terms with younger employees. Either the cost per employee must be the same, irrespective of age, or the employer must offer equal benefits.

Under ADEA § 3(f)(2), an employer can abide by the terms of a bona fide employee benefit plan without violating the ADEA or the OWBPA. A bona fide plan is one which:

- Existed before the challenged employment action occurred;
- The terms of the plan are observed;
- The plan is not used to force anyone into involuntary retirement;
- (Except for voluntary early retirement plans) the costs incurred, or the benefits paid, are equivalent for older and younger employees.

For EEOC regulations on this subject, see 29 C.F.R. § 1625.10.

Under ADEA § 4(f)(2), the employer is allowed to compare costs quoted on the basis of five-year age brackets (e.g., employees aged 30–35). Comparisons must be made using adjacent age brackets: not the costs of employees 65–70 versus those of employees aged 20–25, for instance.

ADEA § 4(l)(3)(B) allows long-term disability benefits to be reduced by pension benefits for which the individual is eligible at age 62 or normal retirement age. Also see Regulations at 29 C.F.R. § 1625.10(f)(1)(ii). The EEOC says it will not pursue an ADEA claim in situations where disability benefits stop at 65 for disabilities occurring before 60, or stop five years after a disability that occurred after age 60.

In a staff informal letter released in November, 2011, the EEOC Office of Legal Counsel explained that the ADEA exemption for coordination with Medicare is limited to retiree benefits, and does not apply to benefits for current active employees. Eliminating EGHP eligibility for current employees when they become eligible for Medicare is an age-based action, so it must satisfy the equal benefit or equal cost test. The availability of Medicare benefits for older employees does not justify depriving older employees of any non-Medicare benefit that is available to younger employees. Equal cost can be analyzed either benefit-by-benefit or for the whole benefit package; eliminating health benefits for Medicare-eligible employees will probably make it impossible to prove equal spending. The EEOC's interpretation is that spending more on another benefit for older employees violates 29 C.F.R. § 1625.10(f)(2)(iii).

Medicare law requires employers who are secondary payors to provide to provide same group coverage to workers and dependents with Medicare as to those without Medicare, so the EEOC says that even without ADEA considerations, Medicare law may prohibit eliminating health coverage for Medicare-eligible actives. [EEOC Informal Discussion Letter, <http://www.eeoc.gov/eeoc/foia/letters/2011/adea_coordinating_medicare.html>; see CCH Pension & Benefits, *ADEA Exemption for Coordination of Health Benefits with Medicare Does Not Permit Employer to Terminate Current Employees' Benefits* (Nov. 18, 2011) (benefitslink.com); EBIA Weekly, *EEOC Letter Addresses Coordination of Current Employees' Health Benefits with Medicare* (Nov. 3, 2011) (benefitslink.com)]

§ 37.06 PROVING THE ADEA CASE

The Tenth Circuit ruled that in order to exhaust their administrative remedies, private-sector employees have a duty to cooperate with the EEOC's investigation of their age bias charges before they file suit. [*Shikles v. Sprint/United Mgmt. Co.*, 426 F.3d 1304 (10th Cir. 2005)]

The Eleventh Circuit ruled in early 2013 that the "cat's paw" theory of liability (developed in the context of USERRA: see § 1.18) is not applicable in ADEA cases. "Cat's paw" liability (also known as "subordinate bias theory" is the principle that the employer can be liable if the actual decision-maker was manipulated by someone else who had a discriminatory intent against the plaintiff. The Eleventh Circuit held that this concept is not applicable to ADEA cases because the ADEA requires but-for causation, whereas USERRA plaintiffs can win by showing that discrimination against servicemembers was one of several motivating factors in the adverse employment decision. [*Sims v. MVM, Inc.*, 704 F.3d 1327 (11th Cir. 2013)]

The Ninth Circuit affirmed summary judgment for the employer in an ADEA case brought by a 66-year-old and a 47-year-old laid off by a television station. However, the court ruled that plaintiffs can make out a prima facie case of disparate-treatment age discrimination purely by statistics, by showing a stark pattern that cannot be explained by anything other than discrimination. In this case, the television station had to cut its budget, and persuaded the court that it was necessary to lay off general-assignment reporters based on the dates their contracts expired—and that on-camera news anchors, whatever their age, had to keep their jobs so viewers would not know that the station was financially troubled. The station also benefited by the "same-actor" inference: i.e., the plaintiffs were laid off by the person who hired them, must have known their ages, and presumably would not have hired them if he objected to working with people over 40. [*Schechner v. KPIX TV CBS*, 686 F.3d 1018 (9th Cir. 2012)]

A police lieutenant, who had been a police officer for 29 years, sued the city when he was not hired when the job of police chief became vacant. He was 51. The newly hired police chief was 43. The District Court for the District of Minnesota (which is in the Eighth Circuit) dismissed the case, finding that an eight-year age difference was not substantial enough to support an ADEA case (but not stating how large a difference would have been adequate). However, courts vary in the extent of difference they require: 10 years in the Seventh Circuit, only three years in the Eleventh Circuit. [*Hilde v. City of Eveleth*, No. 12-2794(RHK/LIB) (D. Minn. Dec. 4, 2013); see Daniel M. Best, *Greater Than Eight For The Eighth*, Squire Sanders (Jan. 21, 2014), available at Lexology.com]

The Northern District of Ohio rejected a driver's claim that he was selected for layoff because of age discrimination. His argument was that his supervisor called driving "a young man's game," and younger drivers were retained. The defendant laid off three drivers (aged 55, 54, and 51) but retained drivers aged 54, 49, 47, 43, 40, 38, and 37. The company said that the plaintiff was laid off because he had a bad attitude and was the subject of a customer complaint. The defendant cited the plaintiff's outburst when he was informed of the layoff as an independent justification for the layoff, but the district court said it was irrelevant because the decision had already been made. However, the district court said that age differential is not enough to make out a prima facie case in an ADEA workforce reduction case. The retained drivers were not significantly younger than the laid-off drivers. The "young man's game" remark was isolated and made six months before the layoff. [*McCormick v. AIM Integrated Logistics*, No. 4:11cv01524, 2013 U.S. Dist. LEXIS 153560 (N.D. Ohio Oct. 25, 2013); see Hanneson Murphy, *Informal Layoff Decision Survives Age Discrimination Claim - But You May Not Want To Try This At Home*, Barnes & Thornburg LLP (Oct. 30, 2013), available at Lexology.com]

The District Court for the District of Connecticut denied summary judgment for the employer in a case brought by a shoe salesman who charged violations of the ADEA and Connecticut anti-discrimination law. The plaintiff was replaced by a younger woman. The plaintiff said his manager told him that the CEO wanted a younger, female sales force. The district court held that he made out a prima facie case; he showed that age was the but-for, not merely a motivating, factor in his termination. The court held that he was qualified by extensive experience and the employer must have known his replacement was younger even if it didn't know her exact age. There was a question of fact as to whether the employer should be grouped with its parent company to reach the minimum number of employees required for ADEA coverage. [*Tremalio v. Demand Shoes, LLC*, No. 3:12-CV-00357 (VLB), 2013 U.S. Dist. LEXIS 140983 (D. Conn. Sept. 30, 2013); see Jaclyn K. Leung, *Connecticut Federal Court Permits Age And Gender Discrimination Claims To Proceed To Trial, Declines To Apply More Stringent*

Federal Standard To State Law Age Claim, Day Pitney LLP (Oct. 17, 2013), available at Lexology.com]

The Fifth Circuit ruled that lack of expertise in the particular type of transaction that was central to the job was a legitimate, nondiscriminatory reason justifying hiring a younger candidate as staff counsel rather than the 68-year-old plaintiff. To win the case, the plaintiff would have had to show that no reasonable and impartial person could have chosen the younger candidate—and that was not true here. [*Moss v. BMC Software*, 610 F.3d 917 (5th Cir. 2010); see Mary Alice Robbins, 5th *Circuit Upholds Summary Judgment for Company in Attorney's Age Discrimination Suit*, Texas Lawyer (July 12, 2010) (law.com)]

[A] Damage Issues

A New Jersey jury awarded $10 million in punitive damages to a former executive of Avaya, Inc., but the trial judge remitted the punitive damages to $3.7 million. Then the New Jersey Appellate Division further reduced the punitives by another $1.25 million, corresponding to the emotional damage award, using the argument that emotional damage awards frequently include a punitive element. In this case, the plaintiff did not allege physical harm or a need for treatment. The final award was $2.465 million in punitive damages, $743,000 compensatory damages, $325,500 in back pay, $167,500 front pay, and $250,000 for emotional distress. [*Saffos v. Avaya, Inc.*, No. A-3189-08 (N.J.A.D. 2011); see Mary Pat Gallagher, *Court Further Slashes Punitives Award In Age Discrimination Suit vs. Avaya*, N.J.L.J. (Mar. 8, 2011) (law.com)]

The Tenth Circuit allows a plaintiff in a race/age discrimination case to receive the statutory maximum damages on a Title VII compensatory damage claim (see § 42.12[B] for discussion of the CRA '91 damage cap), plus ADEA back pay and liquidated damages. On the issue of front pay, both Title VII and the ADEA make this available as a remedy. Reinstatement is the preferred remedy, but this is not always practical—particularly since in this case, the defendant corporation's financial condition was deteriorating, so any job might be short-lived. Furthermore, where there is a hostile environment that renders reinstatement inappropriate, even an unconditional offer of reinstatement in a comparable job does not prevent an award of front pay as an alternative to reinstatement. [*Abuan v. Level 3 Commc'ns, Inc.*, 353 F.3d 1158 (10th Cir. 2003)]

The Second Circuit held that a $250,000 settlement of an ADEA suit constituted FICA wages. The agreement permitted the employer to make all legally required deductions and withholding, but did not characterize the $250,000. The Second Circuit held that the remedies under the ADEA are lost wages, liquidated damages, and equitable relief, plus costs, attorneys' fees, and prejudgment interest. ADEA remedies do not include recovery for pain and suffering or emotional distress (which would probably not be treated as wages). [*Gerstenbluth v. Credit Suisse*, 728 F.3d 139 (2d Cir. 2013)]

As Chapter 40 shows, arbitration is involved for an ever-increasing proportion of employment disputes—although the court's caseload continues to be increased by cases examining the question of whether a particular dispute should be litigated or arbitrated.

In April 2009, the Supreme Court extended its line of pro-arbitration decisions by ruling that federal law mandates enforcement of a CBA clause that clearly and unmistakably obligates union members to arbitrate their ADEA claims. [*14 Penn Plaza LLC v. Pyett*, 556 U.S. 247 (2009); the Supreme Court already held that ADEA claims are arbitrable, in *Gilmer v. Interstate/Johnson Lane Corp.*, 500 U.S. 20 (1991)]

§ 37.07 WAIVERS OF ADEA RIGHTS

[A] Requirements for Valid Waiver

It makes sense for employers to make it part of the severance process to request that terminating employees sign a waiver of their rights to bring suit for discrimination allegedly occurring in the course of the employment relationship. However, in order to be valid and enforceable, a waiver of ADEA rights must be strictly tailored to satisfy the requirements of the Older Workers Benefits Protection Act, a 1990 statute that has been enacted as 29 U.S.C. § 626(f)(1). Furthermore, waivers do not prevent the EEOC from carrying out an age discrimination investigation or bringing suit against the employer. It is unlawful for ADEA waivers to prohibit employees from filing charges with the EEOC or participating in EEOC investigations.

A waiver is not valid if it is not "knowing and voluntary" on the part of the employee. No one can surrender legal rights without receiving full disclosure of the implications of the document he or she signs. The ADEA provides a definition of what is required before a waiver will be considered knowing and voluntary:

- The agreement that contains the waiver must be written in understandable terms;
- The waiver specifically mentions ADEA rights or claims;
- Only claims that have already arisen are waived—not claims that might arise in the future;
- The employee receives something in return for the waiver; it is not enough that the employee receives severance or other benefits that would be provided even if there had been no waiver;
- The document includes a written warning that the employee should consult a lawyer before signing the agreement;

- The employee gets at least 21 days to think over the employer's severance offer. If the agreement is offered to an entire group (e.g., in connection with a layoff or incentives for voluntary departure) then the offer must remain open for at least 45 days;
- When incentives are offered to a group, everyone in the group must get an understandable notification of the features of the program: who can participate; eligibility factors; time limits; and the ages and job titles of everyone eligible or chosen for the program, vis-à-vis the ages of workers in the organizational unit or job classification who were not eligible or selected. (This was included in the law to make it easier for potential plaintiffs to decide if age was an improper factor in selecting employees for the program.)

Waivers are also used when charges have been filed, and then the employer and employee agree on a settlement. In this case, the waiver is only considered knowing and voluntary if all the rules noted above have been observed, and the employee has been given a reasonable time to consider the offer.

Getting a waiver does not provide complete protection for the employer. Sometimes the employee will go to court and sue anyway, claiming that the lawsuit is permissible because the waiver was defective in some way. Section 626(f)(3) provides that it is up to the employer to prove that the waiver satisfied the various requirements and therefore was knowing and voluntary. The employee is not required to prove that the waiver was invalid.

[B] EEOC Rules

The EEOC's rule on waivers, can be found at 29 C.F.R. § 1625.22. A valid ADEA waiver must:

- Be embodied in a written document that contains the entire agreement (the agreement cannot be written but supplemented by oral discussion);
- Be written in plain English, appropriate to the signer's educational level;
- Information about exit incentives must also be understandable;
- Be honest and accurate, not misleading;
- Specify that it relates to ADEA claims;
- Advise the employee to consult an attorney before signing.

In general, waivers can release existing claims but not those that might arise in the future. However, the Final Rule allows an otherwise valid waiver to include the signer's agreement to retire, or otherwise terminate employment at a specified future date.

For the waiver to be valid, the signer must receive consideration specific to the waiver, which he or she would not receive otherwise. Therefore, normal severance pay is not adequate to support a waiver. Nor does it constitute valuable consideration if the employer restores a benefit that was wrongfully terminated in the past. However, the Final Rule says that it is not necessary to give greater consideration to over-40 employees who sign waivers than to under-40 employees, even though the older employees waive an additional range of claims (those arising under the ADEA).

Despite the existence of waivers, a certain number of employees will nevertheless bring age discrimination claims against the employer, claiming that the waivers were invalid and therefore did not constitute a knowing and voluntary waiver of the right to sue.

The Supreme Court's decision in *Oubre v. Entergy Operations Inc.* [522 U.S. 422 (1988)] says that such a person can bring suit under the ADEA even without tendering back (returning) the severance pay received under the agreement that included the allegedly invalid waiver. The rationale is that the defective waiver does not qualify for ratification by the ex-employee, so it is not necessary to return the consideration to avoid ratification.

The EEOC published Final Regulations to implement *Oubre*. [See 29 C.F.R. Part 1625 as amended by 65 Fed. Reg. 77438 (Dec. 11, 2000), effective January 1, 2001], and published guidance in mid-2009 in Question and Answer form, *Understanding Waivers of Discrimination Claims in Employee Severance Agreements*, <www.eeoc.gov/policy/docs/qanda_severance-agreements.html> (July 15, 2009) (accessed Apr. 9, 2014). The EEOC's position is that the existence of a valid waiver is an affirmative defense for the employer. That means that the employer has the burden of proving the validity, but the employee can produce evidence that the waiver was not knowing and voluntary. The EEOC analyzes covenants not to sue in the same way as waivers, and in fact believes they may be even more damaging to employee rights because employees might be deterred from bringing suit with respect to wrongdoing occurring after the covenant was signed.

According to the agency, ordinary contract principles about ratification and tender-back do not apply to employment waivers, because ex-employees might not be able to afford to give back the consideration even if they have a valid claim against the former employer.

Tender-back is not required even if the waiver seems to be lawful, and even if the employee does not allege fraud or duress. Once the case is resolved, the trial court may have to determine the employer's entitlement to restitution, recoupment or set-off. However, the employer can only recover the amount of consideration paid for the waiver, or the amount the plaintiff is awarded for winning the case—whichever is lower. Employees who file suit in bad faith can also be required to pay the employers' attorneys' fees.

The guidance points out that waivers cannot be used to limit an employee's right to testify or participate in any EEOC proceedings. It is not acceptable for an employer to cure a defective waiver by subsequently providing the information that was omitted, then re-starting the period of time to sign the waiver. The EEOC did not take a position as to whether employers must disclose the criteria under which employees were selected for RIF, although some lower courts have required this: see § 37.07[C], below. [Kevin B. Leblang and Robert N. Holtzman, *Time for Employers to Review Their Severance Agreements*, Metropolitan Corporate Counsel (Feb. 1, 2010) (benefitslink.com); Seyfarth Shaw, *EEOC Issues Employee-Friendly Guidance on Separation Agreements* (July 24, 2009) (benefitslink.com)]

[C] Case Law on ADEA Waivers

Oubre, and EEOC's regulations issued in response, make it clear that ADEA waivers and releases can be enforceable—but only if they satisfy all of the requirements of the OWBPA. If restrictions are imposed on the employee's right to sue—including challenges to the validity of the release itself—it is possible that the release will be deemed to violate the OWBPA. The release must be understandable.

Cases on these issues include:

- *Syverson v. IBM*, 472 F.3d 1072 (9th Cir. 2006): IBM's standard release was invalid because it was not understandable—the use of terms "release" and "covenant not to sue" was confusing, and so was the statement that the covenant did not apply to actions based solely on the ADEA, and did not rule out filing an EEOC charge. It was not sufficient for the release to suggest consulting a lawyer, because language that requires a lawyer to be understood is not "calculated to be understood" by participants and beneficiaries, as required by the statute.
- *EEOC v. Lockheed Martin Corp.*, 444 F. Supp. 2d 414 (D. Md. 2006): offering severance benefits in exchange for a release from an employee who had filed an EEOC charge was unlawful retaliation, so the agreement was invalid.

CHAPTER 38

THE FAMILY AND MEDICAL LEAVE ACT (FMLA)

§ 38.01 INTRODUCTION

The Family and Medical Leave Act (FMLA) was enacted on February 3, 1993, as 29 U.S.C. §§ 2601–2654. Congress stated an intention to aid families in which both parents, or the single parent, work outside the home, and to minimize sex discrimination by making leave available in a gender-neutral manner.

The FMLA focuses on two subjects: health care (whether for the employee's own serious health condition or for a family member for whom the employee is a caregiver) and parenting a newborn or newly adopted child. 29 U.S.C. § 2601(a)(2) says that "it is important for the development of children and the family unit that fathers and mothers be able to participate in early childrearing and the care of family members who have serious health conditions."

Under appropriate circumstances, qualifying employees can take up to 12 weeks of leave a year, whether the leave is taken all at once, in several blocks, or intermittently in small units. FMLA leave can be important for preserving the job (and benefits) of someone who has used up all of his or her sick days and is too sick to maintain a normal work schedule, but not sick enough to obtain disability benefits or file for disability retirement.

Employers have the option of providing paid leave under these circumstances, but it does not violate the federal statute for the employer to provide only unpaid FMLA leave. [See § 38.06[G] for state-law developments]

■ **TIP:** Providing unpaid leave to an employee who is exempt from the Fair Labor Standards overtime requirements does not convert the employee from exempt to nonexempt. [29 U.S.C. § 2612(c)]

Leave can be taken, under 29 U.S.C. § 2612, for a total of 12 weeks in any 12-month period (not necessarily a calendar year), when the employee has or adopts or fosters a child (but this leave can only be taken during the first year after the child's birth or after the adoption or foster care placement) or for a serious health condition suffered by the employee or his or her spouse, parent, or child. If the employee is the sick person, the serious health condition must prevent the employee from performing the functions of the job. The FMLA also includes provisions for leave for family members of military personnel.

The employer must give employees at least 60 days' notice of changes in the method of calculating the leave year. [29 C.F.R. § 825.200(d)] The 12-week limit applies per year, not per illness. Therefore, an employee who uses up the allowance is not entitled to additional leave based on events later in the same leave year.

As defined by 29 U.S.C. § 2611(9), a reduced leave schedule is a partial leave under which the employee does work, but for less than the usual number of hours per workday or workweek.

It is unlawful for employers to interfere with employees' exercise of FMLA right or to discriminate or retaliate against them for exercising such rights, charging the employer with FMLA violations, or participating in an investigation. [29 U.S.C. § 2615]

The FMLA does not modify federal or state antidiscrimination laws. [See 29 U.S.C. § 2651(a)] Employers always have a legal right to set up their own policies that are *more* generous than the FMLA: § 2653, and the federal statute does not preempt state and local laws that require employees to offer even more leave than the FMLA does. [29 U.S.C. § 2651(b)] In mid-2005, the DOL issued an opinion that says that state family leave laws are not preempted by the FMLA if they offer more generous benefits than the federal law. [DOL Advisory Opinion 2005-13A, <http://www.dol.gov/ebsa/regs/aos/ao2005-13a.html> (May 31, 2005)]

Employers do not have the power to draft their benefit plans or programs to limit FMLA rights, nor can a Collective Bargaining Agreement be used to cut back FMLA rights. [See 29 U.S.C. § 2652(b)]

DOL figures for 2012 (the last year available) show that 21.0% of eligible employees (and 17.8% of all employees) took FMLA leave, whereas in 2000, FMLA leave was taken by only 17.1% of eligible employees (16.5% of all employees). In 2012, more than half (55%) of FMLA leave was taken because of the employee's own illness; 21% for the birth or adoption of a child; 18% to care for a parent, spouse, or child. Leave was taken for other qualifying reasons 2% of the time; and the reason was unknown—or the employee did not actually qualify for leave—in 4% of the cases. (Out of caution, HR departments often grant leave requests that might not qualify, because it is unclear what constitutes a "serious health condition.") According to the Administrative Office for the U.S. Courts, there were 291 FMLA suits in 2012—rising to 877 suits in 2013. [Joe Palazzolo, *More Workers File Family-Leave Lawsuits*, WSJ.com (Aug. 8, 2014)]

In mid-2012, the DOL published a 20-page FMLA guide, "Need Time? The Employee's Guide to the Family and Medical Leave Act," to explain FMLA rights—and obligations—to employees. [<http://www.dol.gov/whd/fmla/employeeguide.pdf> (undated, accessed Apr. 9, 2012)]

FMLA Title I covers private employment. The statute also has a Title II, covering federal employees. Although the Supreme Court has ruled that Congress exceeded its power when it made state government employers subject to the ADA and ADEA, the Supreme Court reached the opposite conclusion with respect to the FMLA provisions permitting leave to care for a sick family member, finding that Congress validly abrogated state sovereign immunity when it comes to family leave. [*Nevada Dep't of Human Resources v. Hibbs*, 538 U.S. 721 (2003)]

In March 2012, a divided (5-4) Supreme Court held that the states have not waived sovereign immunity and cannot be sued under the FMLA "self-care" provision (i.e., leave taken to care for the employee's own serious health condition) for monetary damages. The Supreme Court held that Congress could not remove states' immunity from suit because there was no widespread evidence of sex discrimination or sex stereotyping that prevented women from taking leave to care for their own illnesses. The four dissenting justices (Ginsburg, Breyer, Sotomayor, and Kagan) identified the whole FMLA as legislation directed at sex discrimination. [*Coleman v. Court of Appeals of Maryland*, 132 S. Ct. 1327 (2012); see Adam Liptak, *Supreme Court Rules on Family Leave Act Suits*, NYTimes.com (Mar. 21, 2012)]

[A] 2008–14 Changes

By 2008, it was clear that the FMLA was in need of clarification and amplification.

Additional protection was added to the FMLA for the families of military servicemembers—the first extension of the FMLA's requirements in the 15 years the law had been in effect. The extension provides up to 12 weeks of unpaid leave when an employee's spouse, child, or parent is called up or is on active duty in the armed forces, and up to 26 weeks when a child, parent, or spouse is injured seriously enough during military service to be unable to continue his or her duties. EBSA issued a massive Notice of Proposed Rulemaking in February 2008, making many clarifications and some changes in FMLA rules. [DOL, EBSA, Notice of Proposed Rulemaking to Amend the FMLA (RIN 1215-AB35) (Feb. 11, 2008)] In light of the many comments received in response to the proposal, the FMLA regulations were revised for the first time in 2008, covering more than 200 pages in the Federal Register. The regulations took effect January 16, 2009 (60 days after the November 17, 2008 posting date).

The extensive new rule retains the six definitions of "serious health condition" for which FMLA leave may be available, and provides regulatory guidance. If the leave involves more than three consecutive calendar days of incapacity plus two health care visits, the two visits must occur within 30 days of the period of incapacity. If the employee asserts a chronic serious health condition, at least two visits per provider per year must be made. The right to reinstatement is in abeyance while an employee works on light duty—but voluntarily accepting a light duty assignment is not FMLA leave. An employer is justified in denying a "perfect attendance" award to an employee who was on FMLA leave, but only if FMLA leave is treated on a parity with other types of leave.

Under the new rules, when an employee requests FMLA leave, or the employer knows that a requested leave may qualify under the FMLA, the employer must notify the employees of their eligibility to take FMLA leave within five business days. (This period can be extended if there are extenuating circumstances; the previous rule gave the employer only two days.)

Notice must be provided about the employee's FMLA rights and responsibilities (such as providing medical certification and paying premiums to continue benefits) when an employee's eligibility is determined at the beginning of the first instance of leave for each reason in the 12-month leave period. All FMLA leave taken for the same reason is considered a single leave. The employee remains eligible for leave for that reason throughout the 12-month period. If the employer believes additional information is needed to complete the medical certification, it must give the employee written notice, and must allow seven calendar days for submission of the information. The employer is justified in refusing to grant leave if the employee fails to submit the complete certification within the cure period. If the employer requests certification, the employee must provide it even if the employee substitutes paid leave for FMLA leave. Unless unusual circumstances preclude using the employer's procedure, the employee has a duty to use these procedures to give notice and call in when they take FMLA leave. Merely calling in sick is not enough to trigger FMLA obligations. The employee must give enough detail for the employer to determine if the leave qualifies under the FMLA. If the leave is for an FMLA-qualifying reason for which leave has already been taken, the employee must specifically reference this reason or need for FMLA leave. [Jeff Nowak, *DOL's Model FMLA Forms Now Approved Through 2015*, Franczek Radelet FMLA Insights (Feb. 14, 2012) (benefitslink.com)]

The new military family leave benefit allows relatives of seriously injured or ill members of the military to take up to 26 weeks off work per year. The definition of family members is broader than in the FMLA in general; the military provision includes siblings and cousins. Servicemembers can make a written designation of a blood relative who would not otherwise be covered to take military caregiver leave. An employee can take more than one leave for different servicemembers, or for a subsequent injury or illness of the same servicemember—but the total military FMLA leave in any 12-month period cannot exceed 26 weeks. Family members are also entitled to 12 weeks of FMLA leave when a servicemember, Reservist, or National Guard member is called up or released to civilian life. Entitlement to this leave is certified on Form WH-384.

If the FMLA leave includes more than three consecutive days of incapacity plus two doctor visits, the two visits must be made within 30 days of the period of incapacity. "Periodic visits" to a health care provider means at least two a year. The "serious illness" form asks the health care provider for the frequency and duration of illness. The final rule clarifies that, although the employer cannot force employees to provide a diagnosis, it is legitimate for the employer to ask. However, the employee's direct supervisor is no longer permitted to contact the employee's health care provider to get medical certification.

To make it easier to administer FMLA leave, the new rules allow the employer to require notice within two days of the absence, or within five days of the leave request. The HR department is permitted to contact the health care provider.

The previous rules allowed employers to demand a fitness for duty exam before the employee returned to work; the final rule obligates the employer to notify employees if an exam is required before returning; the notice must list the essential functions of the employee's job (to show that the employee has recuperated enough to perform them).

Employer and employee can mutually agree to retroactively classify qualifying leave as FMLA leave. The updated rules clarify that it does not violate the FMLA for an employer to use its procedures for requesting medical information under the ADA, paid leave, or Worker's Compensation in the FMLA context.

The DOL's news release explaining the new rules says that the rule has been updated to reflect *Ragsdale*, removing the former "categorical" penalties that required employees who had already taken 30 weeks of leave to receive an additional 12 weeks of leave; the *Ragsdale* court said that the law requires only 12 weeks of leave. The final rule eliminates the penalty, but says that employers can be held liable if an employee suffers individual harm as a result of the employer's failure to satisfy the notification rules. The employer's failure to provide the required written notice can be treated as interference with the employee's FMLA rights, and the potential damages include "any other relief tailored to the harm suffered."

The DOL's position is that prospective waivers of FMLA claims are invalid, but employees can voluntarily agree to settle an FMLA claim that has already matured without DOL supervision or court approval.

New hires must be given a written notice of FMLA rights when they are hired, unless there is an employee handbook that covers this subject. The notice can be posted electronically by satisfying the general electronic notice requirements—but paper copies must be posted where employees who do not have computers can see them.

The employer is permitted to require a new medical certification for each new leave year. If the employee asserts a continuing, open-ended condition, the employer can require recertification of the need for leave every six months (the previous rule was that recertification could be required when the minimum duration specified by the employee had elapsed). If circumstances (the seriousness of the condition, or frequency or duration of absences) change, recertification can be required more often.

The previous regulations required employees to try to schedule their intermittent or reduced schedule leave in a way that did not disrupt the employer's operations; now employees are required to "make a reasonable effort" to avoid undue disruption. The employer must account for the intermittent or reduced schedule leave in increments no greater than the shortest period used for other kinds of leaves (sick leave; vacations) and not less than one hour. The general rule is that the employer is not permitted to reduce the employee's leave entitlement by more than the amount of leave actually taken. However, sometime it is impossible to start or stop part-way through a shift, in which case the entire period the employee must be away from work counts against his or her FMLA entitlement. The revised rules permit temporary transfer of employees who need intermittent or reduced schedule leave, if the need for leave is foreseeable (based on planned medical treatment) or if such leave is permitted for the birth or adoption of a child. However, employers are not allowed to impose temporary transfers when employees have frequent and unpredictable absences caused by a chronic condition.

When an employee is ready to return to work after FMLA leave, the employer can ask for more than a simple statement of ability to return to work. If reasonable safety considerations are involved, the employer can ask for a fitness for duty certificate for intermittent leave.

Although the provisions about substituting paid for unpaid leave do not apply when an employee receives disability benefits during an FMLA leave, the employer and employee can, by agreement, supplement disability benefits by running paid leave concurrently with FMLA leave; this is also true for Worker's Compensation benefits. The employer can consider FMLA leave when awarding bonuses for perfect attendance.

On October 28, 2009, President Obama signed the Defense Department Fiscal Year 2010 Authorization Bill, expanding FMLA entitlement for military families. After the expansion, an employee whose spouse, parent, or child is a reservist can take FMLA leave for a qualifying exigency arising from deployment to a foreign country on active duty, with a new right to leave based on the deployment of the employee's spouse, parent, or child who serves in the regular armed forces to a foreign country.

Military caregiver leave has been expanded to 26 weeks per 12-month period in order to care for a parent, spouse, child, or relative to whom the employee is next of kin. Leave can also be taken when the family member is a veteran being treated for a qualifying illness or injury when the veteran was on active duty during the five years before the date of treatment. [Jeff Nowak, *DOL Issues Final Rule Implementing FMLA Amendments Expanding Military Family Leave and Leave for Airline Flight Crew Members*, Franczek Radelet FMLA Insights (Feb. 7, 2013) (benefitslink.com)]

In March, 2013, the DOL released revised FMLA forms and a new poster. The forms expire February 28, 2015. The poster must be displayed, starting March 8, 2013, even in locations where there are no FMLA-eligible employees. [Jackson Lewis LLP Workplace Resource Center, *Labor Department Releases New FMLA Model Forms and Notice Poster* (Feb. 27, 2013) (benefitslink.com)]

As of March 8, 2013, employers are required to use the updated notice/certification forms and post the new FMLA poster. DOL no longer prints model forms in the appendices to the FMLA regulations: they are posted on the DOL Website, so they can be changed without obtaining the approval of the Office of Management and Budget. DOL has developed a new certification form for leave occasioned by the serious injury or illness of an eligible veteran. Employers are permitted to adapt the forms rather than using them as published by DOL—as long as the employer's version does not call for disclosure of more information than the standard forms require. The updated regulations confirm that employers have obligations to keep genetic information confidential. The new forms are:

- WH-380-E, health care provider's certification of an employee's serious health condition;
- WH-380-F, the counterpart for a family member's serious health condition;
- WH-381, notice of eligibility, rights, and responsibilities;
- WH-382, designation notice;
- WH-384, certification of need for military family leave (number WH-383 is reserved);
- WH-385, certification of servicemember's serious injury or illness;
- WH-385-V, the counterpart for a veteran's serious injury or illness.

[Airline Flight Crew Technical Corrections Act, Pub. L. No. 111-119; see Jeff Nowak, *Employers Must Begin Using Updated FMLA Forms and Poster Starting March 8, 2013*, Franczek Radelet FMLA Insights (Feb. 28, 2013) (benefitslink.com)]

The DOL published a Notice of Proposed Rulemaking in mid-2014 to define "spouse" for FMLA purposes to include same-sex married couples as long as their marriage was recognized at the place where it was celebrated—even if they now reside in a state that does not recognize same-sex marriage. [DOL Wage and Hour Division, *Notice of Proposed Rulemaking to Revise the Definition of "Spouse" Under the FMLA*, 79 Fed. Reg. 36445 (June 27, 2014)]

§ 38.02 FMLA ELIGIBILITY ISSUES

Like most federal employment discrimination laws, the FMLA exempts very small employers. The FMLA applies only to employers engaged in interstate commerce or activities affecting commerce (but most employers fit into this category)—and only if, in the current year or the previous calendar year, there were at least 50 employees on each workday of 20 or more workweeks. Furthermore, the FMLA does not apply when there are fewer than 50 people at that worksite and the total number of employees at all of the employer's sites within a 75-mile radius is less than 50. Anyone who acts on behalf of the employer, whether directly or indirectly, also counts as an employer. So does the successor in interest of a past employer. [29 U.S.C. § 2611(4)]

According to the Fifth Circuit, the definition of an eligible employer subject to the FMLA (at least 50 employees within 75 miles of the worksite) is not a jurisdictional requirement of an FMLA case. The Fifth Circuit remanded a case to see if the employer would be forbidden to raise the defense that it was not covered by the FMLA if the employee was told by the company that she was covered by the Act and relied on this statement. [*Minard v. ITC Deltacom Commc'ns Inc.*, 447 F.3d 352 (5th Cir. 2006)]

The 75-mile requirement was interpreted by the Tenth Circuit as surface miles, not linear miles as the crow flies, so in this case, the surface measurement was 75.6 miles so the employer was not subject to the FMLA. [*Hackworth v. Progressive Cas. Ins. Co.*, 468 F.3d 722 (10th Cir. 2006)]

The Sixth Circuit held, in mid-2006, that whether a company is subject to the FMLA is measured under labor rather than corporate law, and it is irrelevant whether a company transfers its assets or merges with another company. [*Cobb v. Contract Transp., Inc.*, 452 F.3d 543 (6th Cir. 2006), discussed in Rosario Vega Lynn, *Interesting Case on Successors-in-Interest Under FMLA*, Workplace Prof Blog (July 11, 2006) (benefitslink.com). The FMLA regulations, at § 825.107, use the Title VII test for liability of successor employers.]

Even after it is established that an employer is covered, not all employees are entitled to take FMLA leave. Eligibility is limited to an employee who not only has worked for the employer for at least 12 months, but put in at least 1,250 hours for that employer in the preceding year. [See 29 U.S.C. § 2611(2)(A)]

The 1,250 hours are counted back from the time the employee went on FMLA leave, not from the time the employer fired the employee or took other adverse action. Therefore, a plaintiff who took three leaves that she claimed satisfied FMLA requirements, and therefore did not work 1,250 hours during the year before her discharge, was still entitled to bring an FMLA suit. [*Butler v. Owens-Brockway Plastic Prods. Inc.*, 199 F.3d 314 (6th Cir. 1999)]

The Eleventh Circuit ruled in 2012 that the FMLA protects a request made before eligibility is achieved for leave to be taken post-eligibility. The plaintiff was fired after requesting FMLA leave for upcoming childbirth. She was fired after taking time off when her doctor ordered bed rest. The Eleventh Circuit cited 29 C.F.R. § 825.110(d)(4), which says that FMLA eligibility is determined when leave begins and the plaintiff would have been FMLA-eligible when the baby was due. The court also pointed out that FMLA policy is for employees to give employers notice of health events that can be announced in advance (e.g., elective surgery, childbirth), and removing FMLA protection would give employees an incentive not to provide notice—leading to additional inconvenience for employers. [*Pereda v. Brookdale Senior Living Communities Inc.*, 666 F.3d 1269 (11th Cir. 2012)]

A Seventh Circuit plaintiff sued under the FMLA after being fired for receiving more than eight points under the no-fault attendance policy. She said that two of the absences were actually FMLA leave, for which she could not be penalized. However, she was not employed for 1,250 hours during the preceding 12 months, unless she was allowed to toll the 12-month period by adding in time worked during 56 days that preceded the time period, when she was on FMLA leave. The Seventh Circuit ruled that she was not entitled to tolling; the 1,250 hour requirement must be applied strictly. Bailey also charged FMLA retaliation, on the grounds that taking FMLA leave is not allowed to result in the loss of any employment benefit accrued before the date on which leave commenced. Although the Seventh Circuit found that removal of absenteeism points under a rolling no-fault policy was an employment benefit, it did not accrue before the leave commenced, and the FMLA statute says (§ 2614(a)(3)(A)) that employment benefits do not accrue during a period of leave. Forgiveness of attendance points, like seniority, accrues only when an employee is at work, not when he or she is on leave. [*Bailey v. Pregis Innovative Packaging, Inc.*, 600 F.3d 748 (7th Cir. 2010)]

A manager took 12 weeks of FMLA leave, six weeks of unpaid leave, and had about four weeks of intermittent absences in the previous year. The next year, he requested more FMLA leave; his employer said that he did not work 1,250 hours the year before. FMLA expert Jeff Nowak said that FMLA regulations (see 29 C.F.R. § 825.110(c)) presume that exempt employees are always eligible for FMLA leave; the employer has the burden of proving otherwise. Many employers find this difficult because they do not keep track of exempt employees' hours. However, the First Circuit ruled in late 2013 that a teacher who worked only about 660 hours in a school year could not show that work at home (e.g., grading papers) reached the 1,250 hour level, so his FMLA claim was dimsissed. Nowak suggested that an employer might be able to meet the burden by showing that the employee normally worked 40 hours a week in the office, with little or no work at home, and that he did not work while on leave. Note that an employee who claims FMLA leave in a second year for the same reason as FMLA leave was taken in the prior year is deemed eligible for leave, but the employer can re-test eligibility if leave is claimed for a new reason in the same or a subsequent leave year: see 29 C.F.R. § 825.300(b). [Jeff Nowak, *FMLA FAQ: My Employee Took a Whole Lot of Leave Last Year. Is He Even Eligible Now for FMLA Leave?*, Franczek Radelet FMLA Insights (Oct. 24, 2013) (benefitslink.com). See *McArdle v. Town of Dracut*, 732 F.3d 29 (1st Cir. 2013).]

In *Ragsdale v. Wolverine Worldwide* [535 U.S. 81 (2002)], the Supreme Court ruled that the DOL regulation [29 C.F.R. § 825.700(a)] is invalid to the extent that it requires employers to disclose the relationship between FMLA leave and the employer's own leave policies. The revised regulations reflect this decision: see § 38.01[A], above.

Another issue is the ambit of relatives for whom FLMA leave may be taken. In an Eleventh Circuit case from 2013, an employee requested FMLA leave to help her father while he dealt with his brother's terminal illness. The request was granted verbally by a supervisor, and Dawkins took the leave. However, FMLA leave is not available to care for a terminally ill uncle. While Dawkins was away, her temporary promotion was rescinded. Dawkins sued for FMLA retaliation, and asserted equitable estoppel when the employer defended by arguing that she was ineligible for leave. The Eleventh Circuit held that it was not reasonable to rely on the supervisor's approval of the leave. Dawkins knew, from past instances of FMLA leave, that paperwork had to be completed. She also asked for FMLA forms to be sent to her uncle's address, indicating that she was going to take time off anyway. [*Dawkins v. Fulton Cnty. Gov't, Case*, 733 F.3d 1084 (11th Cir. 2013); see Richard D. Tuschman, *Can Employer Who Has Granted Employee's FMLA*

Request Dispute Employee's FMLA Eligibility?, Akerman Senterfitt (Oct. 15, 2013), available at Lexology.com]

The District Court for the Western District of Kentucky ruled that a Sudanese immigrant could not sue under the FMLA, Title VII, or the ADA when he was fired for absences to take care of his pregnant cohabitant. He was not entitled to FMLA leave because his partner was not his spouse and the child hadn't been born yet. Lukudu had received a final written warning because he had 6 1/2 attendance points, and 7 was the termination level. Two days later, his partner was hospitalized. He missed work, reached 7½ attendance points, and was fired. He said that he discussed FMLA leave with his supervisor but he did not submit or even pick up FMLA forms. The district court rejected his FMLA interference and retaliation claims because he was not married and children do not require care before their birth. Even if his partner had a disability, employers are not required to provide accommodations to the spouses or partners of persons with disabilities and there was no evidence that he was terminated because of his association with her. [*Lukudu v. JBS USA, LLC*, CIVIL ACTION NO. 3:12-CV-00704-TBR, 2014 U.S. Dist. LEXIS 33351 (W.D. Ky. Mar. 14, 2014); see Brandi O. Brown, *Unmarried Employee Not Entitled To FMLA Leave To Care For Hospitalized Partner Or Unborn Child*, Employment Law Daily (Mar. 14 2014) (benefitslink.com)]

Under most anti-discrimination suits, the suit must be brought against the employer corporation, and not against individual decision-makers. However, in 2010 the Eastern District of Pennsylvania refused to dismiss claims against three HR executives and a manager accused of conspiring to find an excuse to fire a worker soon after discovering that he needed leave to have surgery, finding that the plaintiff provided evidence that the three had the power to hire and fire. Cases in Utah, Minnesota, and Kansas have limited individual liability under the FMLA to corporate officers, but the Eastern District found them inconsistent with Third Circuit precedent and held that an individual who exercises control over FMLA leave is potentially liable. [*Narodetsky v. Cardone Indus.*, No. 09-4734, 2010 U.S. Dist. LEXIS 16133 (E.D. Pa. Feb. 24, 2010)]

§ 38.03 WHEN LEAVE IS AVAILABLE

An eligible employee can take FMLA leave for his or her own serious health condition or the serious health condition of an eligible family member.

The statute itself defines "serious health condition" as an "illness, injury, impairment, or physical or mental condition" that requires either inpatient care (in a hospital, nursing home or hospice) or at least continuing treatment by a health care provider. [29 U.S.C. §§ 2611(6) and (11)]

Qualifying family members are spouse (husband or wife only—not cohabitant), child (including adopted or foster child) who is either under 18 years old or mentally or physically disabled, or parent (biological parent or someone who played a parental role—but NOT a mother- or father-in-law, even though many individuals become caregivers for their in-laws). [See 29 U.S.C. §§ 2611(7) and (12)]

As a result of the Supreme Court's June 2013 decisions invalidating the federal Defense of Marriage Act, a legally married same-sex spouse counts as a husband or wife for this purpose.

A parent might also qualify for FMLA leave under the expanded definition of military caregiver. If the servicemember's disability continues over a span including at least two years, the parent might qualify for 26 weeks of FMLA leave in the first year, and an additional 12 weeks in the second year. The age at which the disability began is irrelevant for FMLA leave purposes. In 2013, DOL reiterated that leave can be taken to care for an adopted or stepchild, foster child, legal ward, or even someone who has the day to day responsibility of caring for the child or has a financial obligation to support the child. [DOL Wage and Hour Division, Administrator's Interpretation No. 2013-1, Fair Labor Standards Act (Jan. 14, 2013). See Administrator's Interpretation 2010-3 for the in loco parentis relationship. See Spencer Fane Britt & Browne LLP, *FMLA Leave for Employees with Adult Disabled Sons and Daughters* (Jan. 22, 2013) (benefitslink.com)]

Travel time to care for an out-of-state family member is an FMLA gray area. If it is clear that an employee will be needed to care for a family member on a certain date, then travel to arrive by that time is probably part of protected leave. The line seems to be drawn between direct care (covered by the FMLA) and indirect care (e.g., fixing up a relative's house; not covered). [Jeff Nowak, *Does Travel Time Count as FMLA Leave?*, Franczek Radelet FMLA FAQ (Feb. 23, 2011) (benefitslink.com)]

The Eleventh Circuit held that it was permissible to fire an employee who was out of work for four weeks (after being given two weeks' leave) to assist her daughter, who was having a baby. The leave request did not mention either the FMLA or pregnancy complications. Pregnancy in and of itself is not a serious health condition, so a valid FMLA request must assert the need for a caregiver as a result of complications. [*Cruz v. Publix Super Mkts. Inc.*, 428 F.3d 1379 (11th Cir. 2005)]

The Seventh Circuit upheld dismissal of FMLA (and ADA) claims brought by an employee who tested positive for alcohol. The employee was on a last chance agreement after ongoing alcohol problems and a drunk driving arrest. She was tested for alcohol because she appeared to be under the influence of alcohol at work. The plaintiff did not prove she was entitled to FMLA leave. Although substance abuse is considered a serious health condition, this is true only if the employee receives inpatient treatment or is under continuing care from a health care provider. The plaintiff's FMLA retaliation claim failed because she did not show a connection between her alleged request for leave and a materially adverse action. The blood alcohol test could not have been retaliatory, because it was permitted by the Last Chance Agreement, and she was terminated for violating that agreement. [*Ames v. Home Depot USA Inc.*, 629 F.3d 665 (7th Cir. 2011)]

If both spouses work for different employers, each one is entitled to 12 weeks of leave when a child is born or adopted, but if they work for the same employer, the employer can legally require them to split a single 12-week leave period, or to share the 12 weeks when they are caring for the same sick child. [See 29 U.S.C. § 2612(f). The FMLA regulations create a loophole: 29 C.F.R. § 825.120(a)(3) says that if both parents are married and work for the same employer, they are entitled to a combined 12 weeks of baby bonding leave per leave year. However, if they work for the same employer but are not married, each of them can get 12 weeks of leave. Some state laws, e.g., California's, limit the leave to a combined 12 weeks for both parents, whether or not married. [Jeff Nowak, *Where FMLA Bonding Leave Is at Issue, Unmarried Parents Have More Generous Leave Rights*, Franczek Radelet FMLA Insights (Mar. 23, 2011) (benefitslink.com)]

The Colorado Family Care Act expands the premises for FMLA leave by granting eligible employees an additional 12 weeks of unpaid leave per 12-month period to care for a civil union or domestic partner who has a serious health condition. It is effective August 7, 2013. Colorado does not have a state FMLA; the statutory language suggests that this is in addition to federal FMLA leave. [Fisher & Phillips LLP Solutions at Work, *Colorado Family Care Act To Go Into Effect* (June 11, 2013) (benefitslink.com)]

§ 38.04 THE EMPLOYER'S OBLIGATION

It is the employer's responsibility to determine if the FMLA applies, so when an employee calls in sick it is necessary to find out if the employee is likely to miss more than three consecutive days of work, if the employee has a chronic condition that manifests intermittently, if he or she is caring for a family member with a serious health condition, or has pregnancy complications.

To avoid discrimination, there should be a standard list of questions that are asked of everyone who calls in sick: for example, the specific reason for the absence, which job duties the person cannot perform, if he or she has already taken leave for the same condition and when; if he or she is seeing a doctor; when he or she discovered the need for time off; and when he or she will return to work. If FMLA leave has already been taken for the same condition, find out if recertification is appropriate; if there seems to be a pattern of abuse (e.g., an excessive number of Monday and Friday absences); 29 C.F.R. § 825.308(e) permits the employer to check with the employee's doctor to see if three-day weekends are consistent with the medical need for leave. [Jeff Nowak, *Suffering from Super Bowl-Induced FMLA Leave?*, Franczek Radelet FMLA Insights (Feb. 7, 2011) (benefitslink.com)]

Nowak counsels, in the situation where a leave request is denied (particularly at holiday time) and then, at the last minute, the employee requests FMLA leave for a flare-up of a chronic condition, that the employer send a cover letter to the employee. The letter should explain that the FMLA request covers time for which leave was denied, so the employer requires confirmation of the medical need for leave in light of the employee's pattern of leave use. If the employee fails to provide certification, or the certification is dubious, it is legitimate for the employer to ask for clarification or a second opinion. If there is already a certification on file, asking for FMLA leave on days when leave was denied could be considered a significant change in circumstances justifying a recertification request. [Jeff Nowak, *An Employee Requests and is Denied Vacation Leave but Later Takes FMLA Leave for the Same Time Period. What Recourse Does an Employer Have?*, Franczek Radelet FMLA Insights (Jan. 8, 2013) (benefitslink.com)]

The FMLA regulations state that if there is a temporary cessation of one week or more (e.g., a school vacation) then those days that employer activity has ceased do not count against the FMLA entitlement—even if the employee would not have been healthy enough to work. With respect to holidays, if an employee observes a holiday that falls on Friday or Monday and takes the whole week off, the whole workweek should be counted as a full week of FMLA leave. However, if the employee works any part of the workweek, then the holiday cannot be counted as FMLA leave: see 29 C.F.R. § 825.200(h). This section also applies to calculation of FMLA leave when the operation is shut down by a natural disaster. If the employer is shut down for a week or more, the lost days do not reduce the employee's FMLA leave entitlement, even if it is obvious that the employee would not have been able to work during the downtime. [Jeff Nowak, *Calculating FMLA Leave for Holidays, Breaks and Plant Shut Downs*, Franczek Radelet FMLA Insights (Nov. 10, 2011) (benefitslink.com) and *Hurricane Sandy and the FMLA (Part II): How Do Employers Calculate FMLA Leave When the Workplace Closes Because of the Storm?*, Franczek Radelet FMLA Insights (Nov. 2, 2012) (benefitslink.com)]

[A] Benefits

The employer must reinstate the employee after leave, and must maintain all employee benefits during leave. [See 29 U.S.C. § 2615(c) for health coverage requirements] However, the employee does not accrue seniority or additional benefits. FMLA leave is not considered a break in service when pension eligibility is determined.

"Benefits" means all of the employer's benefits (not just those offered under ERISA plans), e.g., "group life insurance, health insurance, disability insurance, sick leave, annual leave, educational benefits, and pensions." [29 U.S.C. § 2611(5)]

When employees are on FMLA leave, the EGHP must maintain their coverage at the original level. If employees are required to pay part of the EGHP premium under normal circumstances, the plan can require them to continue contributing during FMLA leave. Furthermore, if the employee is more than 30 days late paying the premium, health insurance coverage can legitimately be terminated. If coverage is terminated in this manner, but the employee returns to work and is reinstated, then he or she is entitled to immediate reinstatement in the EGHP, with no need to satisfy plan requirements a second time.

If the employee quits instead of returning from leave, the employer is entitled to recover the health premiums expended on the employee's behalf during the leave period. But if the employee files a health claim for treatment during the leave period, a claim that would otherwise be allowable cannot be denied because the employee later terminates employment.

Nowak warns that a policy of recovering health insurance premiums only from new mothers who do not return from maternity leave, but not from other non-returning employees, could violate the PDA. [Jeff Nowak, *When Employee on FMLA Leave Indicates They Will Not Return From FMLA Leave, What Should an Employer Do?*, Franczek Radelet FMLA Insights (June 22, 2012) (benefitslink.com)]

[B] Reinstatement

Section 2614 takes up the subject of reinstatement in more detail. It provides that an employee who returns from leave not only must not lose any benefits because of taking leave, but must be reinstated either in the old job or an equivalent new one. The second job is equivalent to the first if it provides equivalent terms and conditions of employment (benefits, pay, etc.) The right to be rehired in one's former position is not absolute; an employee can be fired if his job has been eliminated when a number of positions were consolidated. [*Yashenko v. Harrah's N.C. Casino Co.*, 446 F.3d 541 (4th Cir. 2006)]

The FMLA creates an exception for employees earning in the top 10% of the employer's workforce. It is not necessary to reinstate them after leave if reinstatement would cause "substantial and grievous economic injury" to the employer, and the employer promptly notifies the employee that reinstatement will be denied.

However, taking FMLA leave does not entitle any employee to anything he or she would not have been entitled to by remaining at work without taking leave.

An employee who returns from FMLA leave and is ready to work is entitled, in the Sixth Circuit view, to immediate reinstatement, not reinstatement a month later. The statute does not provide the employer with additional time to adjust to the employee's return. Therefore, insisting that an employee take a longer leave than the employee could certify to be medically necessary could be treated as interference with FMLA rights. [*Hoge v. Honda of Am. Mfg. Inc.*, 384 F.3d 238 (6th Cir. 2004)]

A number of cases hold that if an employee has committed misconduct serious enough to justify termination, the fact that the employee requests or takes

FMLA leave does not make it unlawful for the employer to fire the employee. See, e.g.,

- Engaging in unauthorized employment during leave, contrary to the terms of the employee handbook. [*Pharakhone v. Nissan N. Am. Inc.*, 324 F.3d 405 (6th Cir. 2003)]
- Refusal to sign a performance improvement plan covering issues that had been reported even prior to the FMLA leave. [*Cole v. State of Illinois*, 562 F.3d 812 (7th Cir. 2009)]

The District Court for the District of Minnesota held that it was lawful for a senior living facility to terminate an LPN who was unable to perform all the essential functions of the job after the FMLA leave for knee surgery expired. She was willing to return to work after the leave, but she was not supposed to kneel, squat, or lift more than 50 pounds; but she was the only LPN on the overnight shift, responsible for 160 assisted living residents. She sued for disability discrimination, failure to accommodate, and FMLA interference and retaliation. The court granted summary judgment for the employer on all counts because the published job description required kneeling, squatting, and lifting 50 pounds. The plaintiff said she could have been accommodated if she had been allowed to call for help when a resident fell, providing her with an aide, or extending her leave for six more weeks until she could return without restrictions. But the court held that employers are not required to transfer essential functions or provide helpers and the six-week leave would be expensive, would burden other employees, and would compromise quality of care. The district court dismissed the FMLA interference claim, because the plaintiff was permitted to take the full 12 weeks of leave. There was no obligation to reinstate her when she was unable to perform essential duties. The FMLA retaliation claim failed for lack of evidence of pretext. [*Attiogbe-Tay v. SE Rolling Hills LLC*, No. 12-1109 (DSD/LIB), 2013 U.S. Dist. LEXIS 159598, 15 Accom. Disabilities Dec. (CCH) ¶ 15-242 (D. Minn. Nov. 7, 2013); see Michael R. Bertoncini, *Inability To Perform Essential Job Functions After FMLA Leave Sinks LPN's Disability Discrimination, FMLA Claims*, Jackson Lewis PC (Nov. 7, 2013), available at Lexology.com]

The Tenth Circuit held that it was lawful to discharge an employee who refused to cooperate with the FMLA process, submitting forms more than seven weeks after her employer's initial request and after there had been several reminders. The Tenth Circuit held that she was fired for her lack of cooperation, not to prevent exercise of her FMLA rights. [*Dalpiaz v. Carbon Cnty.*, No. 13-4062 (10th Cir. July 25, 2014). See Nathan Whatley, *Employee Fired for Failing to Cooperate With FMLA Leave Approval Process*, McAfee & Taft EmployerLINC (Aug. 11, 2014) (benefitslink.com)]

The employer can justify termination based on its honest belief (even if it is mistaken) that the employee deliberately misused FMLA leave.

In most states (although California is an exception), employers can defend against FMLA charges by alleging an honest belief that the employee was abusing leave. However, a complete investigation is required. Tools for fighting abuse include medical certification and recertification and requiring second or even third opinions. If the employee will have an ADA disability after FMLA leave ends, the interactive process (see § 36.05) should begin during the leave. Employers who claim that the leave request is an undue hardship must be able to document the hardship—for example, by showing loss of productivity, lower morale because workers are overburdened, lost sales, or deterioration in customer service. [Jeff Nowak, *Best Practices for Employers When Administering FMLA Leave: A Recap of our Webinar*, Franczek Radelet FMLA Insights (Dec. 12, 2012) (benefitslink.com)]

The "honest belief" defense was also allowed in an interference/retaliation case when a company, suspecting FMLA misuse, placed 35 employees under surveillance and fired one whose car remained in his driveway, and who did not leave the front door of his house, on days that he took leave to visit his mother in a nursing home. (He said that his brother picked him up from the back door.) However, Nowak cautions that the employer must do a meaningful investigation before disciplining an employee for leave misuse: *Scruggs v. Carrier Corp.*, 688 F.3d 821 (7th Cir. 2012)]

Summary judgment for the employer was granted in an FMLA interference/retaliation case, where the employer had a reasonable, honest belief that an employee abused FMLA leave, on the basis of the vacation pictures she posted to Facebook, showing her engaging in strenuous physical activities. During an investigation, the plaintiff admitted that she had lied when she claimed to have used wheelchairs in the airports during her trip. She was fired for dishonesty and falsifying or omitting information in employment records, which the district court found to be a legitimate reason for firing her. [*Lineberry v. Detroit Med. Ctr.*, No. 11-13752, 2013 U.S. Dist. LEXIS 15540 (E.D. Mich. Feb. 5, 2013)]

Anyone who is on FMLA leave can be laid off during a RIF, if he or she would have been laid off anyway. [*O'Connor v. PLA Family Health Plan Inc.*, 200 F.3d 1349 (11th Cir. 2000)]

[C] Interference and Retaliation

Many FMLA complaints include both interference (i.e., a charge that the employer limited or impaired the employee's ability to take FMLA leave he or she was entitled to) and retaliation (i.e., adverse job action imposed because the employee took—or requested—FMLA leave). Under the FMLA regulations, discouraging an employee from using FMLA leave can constitute unlawful interference. The Institute for Integrative Nutrition, whose workforce is largely female, created a "maternity projection chart" to track female employees' potential for having children, based on their age and marital status and perceived likelihood of having children. An employee alleged that she was demoted two levels after taking maternity leave, then told she would have to prove herself in the new job. She and the co-workers who joined her in a putative class action for FMLA interference and retliation were fired. She filed a putative class action with similar co-workers, and they were fired, using the projection chart as evidence that the company viewed pregnant women as a problem. The case survived a motion to dismiss. [*Stotler v. Institute for Integrative Nutrition, et al.*, Case No. 13-civ-1275, 2013 U.S. Dist. LEXIS 163796 (S.D.N.Y. Nov. 18, 2013); see Hannesson Murphy, *Creating A "Maternity Projection Chart" Probably Isn't A Good Idea*, Barnes & Thornburg LLP (Nov. 25, 2013), available at Lexology.com]

Employees on FMLA leave cannot be asked to work—a proposition that requires a definition of "work." The District Court for the Northern District of Ohio permitted an FMLA interference case to continue based on allegations that, while respiratory therapist Julie Vess was on leave to recover from surgery, there were frequent work-related telephone calls, because FMLA interference includes denial of any benefits protected by the FMLA, including the right not to work while on leave. The district court said that the only work tasks that can be required are having the person on leave transmit "institutional knowledge" to new staff, disclose computer passwords, close out assignments, and name other employees who can substitute for the worker on leave. [*Vess v. Select Med. Corp.*, No. 3:11 CV 2549 (N.D. Ohio Mar. 15, 2013); see Daniel Cafaro, *Consider Limiting Work Calls to Employees on FMLA Leave*, Smart HR (Apr. 18, 2013) (benefitslink .com)]

The Eighth Circuit permitted a nurse to pursue an FMLA interference claim. She was fired for job abandonment shortly after being sent home by the HR director after she had a severe panic attack when she was ordered to work in a new unit where she was not trained. The Eighth Circuit found that there were factual issues as to whether her employer was aware of her condition. She was threatened with termination and losing her license for patient abandonment if she did not take the assignment. The HR director told her to go home and return the next day to negotiate the assignment. The next day, she saw her doctor, who prescribed medication, suggested therapy, and gave her a note covering an absence for the rest of the week. She submitted the doctor's note and asked for FMLA forms, but was told that she had been fired for walking off the job. The ex-employer's argument was that she had already been fired when she requested leave so she had no FMLA rights. (The opinion did not discuss the implications of the HR director sending the plaintiff home, or whether it could be considered patient abandonment for a nurse to reject an assignment he or she is not qualified to perform.) The employer also argued that it was not aware of the plaintiff's anxiety disorder, but the Eighth Circuit noted that the FMLA has explicit provisions for a need for leave that arises unexpectedly. [*Clinkscale v. St. Therese of New Hope*, 701 F.3d 825 (8th Cir. 2012), *reh'g denied*, No. 12-1223 (Jan. 3, 2013); see Jackson Lewis LLP, *Nurse who Suffered Panic Attack and was Sent Home Can Pursue FMLA Interference Claim* (Nov. 27, 2012) (benefitslink.com)]

The Tenth Circuit revived FMLA (and ADA) claims because a terminated employee was treated more harshly than co-workers who did not take extensive FMLA leave. The employer said that Smothers was fired for a safety violation and arguing with a co-worker about the violation; he charged FMLA retaliation. Smothers had degenerative disc disease resulting from a neck injury. He had three operations but still had chronic pain and frequently took FMLA leave. He was pressured to change shifts but refused, because it would cut his income by $7,000 a year. An HR representative told Smothers's supervisor that forcing him to change shifts would violate the FMLA. [*Smothers v. Solvay Chemicals, Inc.*, 740 F.3d 530 (10th Cir. 2014); see Wolters Kluwer Law & Business News Center, *Decision By Committee Does Not Insulate Employer From Potential Liability For FMLA, ADA Claims* (Feb. 14, 2014) (benefitslink.com)]

The Seventh Circuit held that a former employee's trip to Las Vegas with her terminally ill mother could be considered family care leave. Although the mother did not receive health care during the trip, a "make a wish" organization helped the family arrange a last family excursion. The Seventh Circuit held that the plaintiff provided the same kind of assistance (bathing, dressing, giving medication, etc.) during the trip that she gave her mother at home. The Seventh Circuit held that the FMLA does not say where care for a seriously ill family member has to be provided and said that the risk of abuse was small because the mother was a hospice patient receiving palliative care. However, the First and Ninth Circuits require active participation in a family member's health treatment to justify FMLA leave. [*Ballard v. Chicago Park Dist.*, 741 F.3d 838 (7th Cir. 2014); see Michael G. Congiu and Carly J. Zuba, *Viva [FMLA Family Care Leave in] Las Vegas*, Littler Mendelson (Jan. 31, 2014) (benefitslink.com)]

Although intent is not required for an interference claim, the Tenth Circuit found that termination two days after a request for FMLA leave was justified by the employee's lack of improvement after receiving mixed feedback in his performance review. The retaliation claim required circumstantial evidence of a retaliatory motive, which the plaintiff could not provide. [*Brown v. ScriptPro LLC*, 700 F.3d 1222 (10th Cir. 2012); see Wolters Kluwer Law & Business, *Evidence Of Employer's Dissatisfaction Is Sufficient To Forestall Employee's FMLA Claim* (Jan. 18, 2013) (benefitslink.com)]

The Fifth Circuit held that summary judgment for the employer was inappropriate in a FMLA retaliation case where a laboratory chemist was suspended for insubordination and poor performance. He submitted a doctor's note saying he needed time off for stress (related to having child custody). A co-worker told the employer that the plaintiff was going to fake a breakdown to avoid having to work. He was fired for performance and insubordination issues, faking a breakdown and not returning to work after the suspension. The Fifth Circuit held that the employer did not prove that the plaintiff would have been fired if he had not taken FMLA leave. The "fake breakdown" allegation was simply accepted without investigation. The court used a mixed motive analysis, placing the burden on the employer to show that the plaintiff would have been fired even if he had not requested FMLA leave. The Fifth Circuit found evidence that the plaintiff's manager wanted to prevent him from getting FMLA leave or punish him for taking it. [*Ion v. Chevron USA*, 731 F.3d 379 (5th Cir. 2013); see Karla E. Sanchez, *It's Hard To Prove You "Would Have" When You Didn't*, Sherman & Howard LLC (Oct. 4, 2013), available at Lexology.com; Wolters Kluwer Law & Business News Center, *Employer Failed To Show It Would Have Fired Employee For Work Issues And Faking Need For FMLA Leave* (Oct. 11, 2013) (benefitslink.com)]

§ 38.05 INTERMITTENT LEAVE

Section 2612(b) governs intermittent leave and leave that produces a reduced work schedule. The FMLA provides the equivalent of 12 weeks of work: up to 480 hours a year for full-time workers, and an equivalent prorated amount for part-time workers, such as 240 hours a year for someone who works a half-time schedule. The FMLA regulations [see 29 C.F.R. § 825.205(b)] refer to the actual number of hours the employee usually works in a week; or in an average week, if the schedule varies. Therefore, a person who is exempt from receiving overtime benefits but who typically works longer than 40 hours a week can get additional intermittent leave because of this work history.

Employers are not obligated to grant intermittent leave for cosmetic procedures. The general rule is that leave to care for a newly born or adopted child must be taken in a block of time off, and not on an intermittent or reduced schedule—unless the employer agrees to the special schedule. Intermittent leave for parents can be denied unless the child has a serious health condition, or unless a pregnant employee has severe morning sickness or needs time off for prenatal care. Leave premised on a serious health condition can be taken intermittently or on a reduced schedule when it is medically necessary.

It is permitted for the employer to use health-related intermittent/reduced leave to offset birth or adoption leave taken by the employee in the same year, but only to the actual extent of intermittent or reduced leave that was taken.

When a health-related intermittent leave can be predicted, based on scheduled medical treatment, the employer can lawfully transfer the employee to an available alternative position—as long as:

- The employee is qualified for the position;
- The two jobs are equivalent in pay and benefits;
- The second job provides a better accommodation to the changed work schedule than the first job did;
- Once the need for intermittent leave ends, the transferred employee must be offered reinstatement in the former job or a comparable job. It violates the FMLA for employers to use transfers deliberately to discourage

the use of FMLA leave or to retaliate against employees who take or request leave.

Human Resource Executive Online points out that employees are only entitled to intermittent or reduced schedule FMLA leave if it is medically necessary for their own serious health condition or to care for a family member. Although determination of an employee's eligibility for FMLA leave can be made only once per 12-month period for all related intermittent absences involving the same health condition, the article recommends that employers re-evaluate eligibility at the beginning of each 12-month period. Under the revised FMLA regulations, it is probably permissible to require call-in before the beginning of the shift. If employees fail to comply with the call-in procedure, it is legitimate to impose discipline, as long as the discipline does not discriminate against employees who take FMLA leave. Employers are justified in asking for more information if employees call in sick without providing enough information to determine if the leave qualifies under the FMLA. However, the employer does not have a duty to inquire further if an employee calls in sick—but if an employee mentions the FMLA, the employer can ask why the employee is taking time off, what the symptoms are, if the employee has a medical appointment, and when the employee plans to return to work. [David B. Calzone, *Managing Intermittent Leave*, Human Resource Executive Online (May 24, 2010) (benefitslink.com)]

An employer that is dubious about the authenticity of a certification can ask the health care provider if he or she prepared the certification, and what it means. The employer can also ask for a second opinion—and, if it conflicts with the initial opinion, can ask for a third opinion to resolve the conflict. However, the employer must pay for the second and third opinions, and the third opinion is binding. [Daniel Cafaro, *7 Best Practices in FMLA Intermittent Leave Administration*, Smart HR (Apr. 12, 2013) (benefitslink.com)]

§ 38.06 RELATING FMLA LEAVE TO OTHER LEAVE

[A] Generally

The simplest example is in the case of an employer that does not offer any form of paid leave. If the employer is subject to the FMLA, it must offer unpaid leave to FMLA-eligible employees. More difficult issues arise when the employee is entitled both to FMLA leave and to some form of paid leave (e.g., vacation; sick leave).

In a controversial 2007 decision, the Seventh Circuit ruled that it violates the FMLA to make an employee use paid sick and vacation leave, even if the employee was also receiving disability benefits under a multi-employer plan. (See 29 C.F.R. § 825.207(d)(1).) Therefore, the Seventh Circuit allows an employee who takes FMLA leave to extend the 12 week allotment under the FMLA by any other paid leave offered by the employer. The employer's theory was that the regulation applies only to benefits under the employer's own temporary disability plan, not a third-party plan, but the Seventh Circuit held that the regulation does not distinguish based on the type of disability plan. [*Repa v. Roadway Express*, 477 F.3d 938 (7th Cir. 2007); see Carla J. Rozycki and David K. Haase, *7th Circuit Rules on FMLA Leave with Disability Benefits*, special to law.com (Mar. 7, 2007) and Fred Schneyer, *Employer Can't Force Paid Leave Substitution Under FMLA*, plansponsor.com (Mar. 7, 2007)]

The Ninth Circuit held that it is not mandatory that employees take FMLA leave whenever they qualify for it; they can affirmatively decline to use FMLA leave, perhaps to save it for later. Therefore, it did not violate the FMLA to fire a worker who asked for vacation, rather than FMLA leave, to care for her sick father in Guatemala. Escriba was fired under a work rule calling for termination when an employee misses more than three days of work without calling in. Escriba (who had previously taken FMLA leave on 15 occasions) asked for two weeks' vacation, which was granted; she was asked if she needed more time but said she did not. The employer's policy required unpaid FMLA leave to run concurrently with paid vacation time, creating an incentive for employees to use their paid time first. The Ninth Circuit rejected Escriba's contention that allowing her to decline FMLA leave was an unlawful waiver: the Ninth Circuit drew a distinction between surrendering a right completely and not using it immediately. However, the Ninth Circuit rejected the employer's application for an award of court costs as a prevaling party. The plaintiff had limited financial resources, the case involved important issues and levying costs against her would discourage other low-income workers from pursuing their rights. [*Escriba v. Foster Poultry Farms, Inc.*, 743 F.3d 1236 (9th Cir. 2014); see Jay-Anne B. Casuga, *Ninth Circuit Upholds Verdict Against Worker Who Expressly Declined Use of FMLA Leave*, Bloomberg BNA (Feb. 27, 2014) (benefitslink.com)]

State law may require employers to provide intermittent leave on more generous terms than the FMLA does. If the employee is also a qualified person with a disability as defined by the ADA, then it may be necessary to grant even more than the equivalent of 12 weeks' intermittent leave as a reasonable accommodation.

Sometimes it is hard to distinguish between leave taken because of complications of pregnancy and leave taken to prepare for parenting. Under Wage and Hour Division regulations, FMLA leave is not available after the employee has taken a disability leave for pregnancy-related complications. However, if there is a post-delivery period when the mother is physically unable to work, that period can be counted as a leave for serious illness, even though it also represents parenting leave. This is especially significant if both parents work for the same employer and would otherwise have to split a single 12-week leave period.

If the state has a law obligating employers to provide paid or partially paid maternity leave, employees are entitled to unpaid FMLA law in addition to the paid leave required by state law. Furthermore, if the state has an FMLA-type law that extends coverage in circumstances that the federal law does not provide for (e.g., taking care of a friend or parent-in-law), the state-required leave is treated as if it were taken for non-FMLA purposes and therefore does not reduce the 12-week FMLA allowance.

A late 2010 article says that it is an open question whether intermittent FMLA leave is available for fertility treatment, because the statute and regulations are silent and there is no clear judicial rule. It is possible that denying the leave might be considered to violate the ADA or PDA. If the employee is covered by the FMLA, then taking intermittent leave for fertility treatment cannot be used as a negative factor in hiring, promotion, or discipline. If leave is requested after a miscarriage or the death of a newborn, some decisions hold that bereavement leave is not covered by the FMLA, unless the bereaved employee has a serious health condition as a result of bereavement. [Keisha-Ann G. Gray, *Procreation Problems*, Human Resource Executive Online (Nov. 2, 2010) (benefitslink.com)]

A seven-week trip to the Philippines, accompanying a seriously ill husband who consulted a faith healer, was not covered by the FMLA, so it was lawful to fire the employee for taking unapproved leave. The retaliation claim failed because the plaintiff not merely obtained FMLA leave when her husband received conventional medical care, but also because a pilgrimage to a spiritual healing center (much less tourism) is not protected by the FMLA. [*Tayag v. Lahey Clinic Hosp. Inc*, 632 F.3d 788 (1st Cir. 2011); see Sheri Qualters, *Spiritual Healing Not Covered by Leave Act, 1st Circuit Rules*, Nat'l L.J. (Jan. 28, 2011) (law.com)]

Statutes governing medical leave typically define the amount of medical leave that must be granted. Conditions that require long-term absences are often severe enough to trigger protection against disability discrimination. Worker's Compensation might also be involved if the illness or injury is work-related.

Many companies maintain a formal policy that sets a maximum length of available medical leave (e.g., six months or a year), with termination for employees who are unable to return to work after exhausting their leave allowance. Multi-state companies must make sure that the policy is acceptable under the laws of all the states in which they do business. Calendar-year employers might face situations in which an employee succeeds in taking 12 weeks' leave in each of two calendar years.

The California Court of Appeal held in 2013 that an employee disabled by the complications of a high-risk pregnancy was entitled to additional leave as a reasonable accommodation under the California civil rights law FEHA, even though she had used up her California Pregnancy Disability Leave Law and California Family Rights Act leave. Her employer allowed her 19 weeks of leave, including accrued vacation time. She was fired when, at the end of that time, she was still on bed rest and could not perform the essential functions of her job. According to the court of appeal, the plain language of the Pregnancy Disability Leave Law is that it supplements and does not replace other FEHA entitlement. [*Sanchez v. Swissport, Inc.*, 213 Cal. App. 4th 1331, 153 Cal. Rptr. 3d 36 (2013);

see Jackson Lewis LLP Workplace Resource Center, *No Statutory Cap on Pregnancy Leave, California Court of Appeal Rules* (Mar. 4, 2013) (benefitslink .com)]

Failure to comply with the FMLA, which allows part-time hours (in conjunction with intermittent leave), can be deemed to violate Title VII: *Orr v. City of Albuquerque*, 417 F.3d 1144, 1151 (10th Cir. 2005); see also *Mickeson v. N.Y. Life Ins. Co.*, 460 F.3d 1304 (10th Cir. 2006): refusing to permit an employee to return to work on a part time basis accelerated depletion of her FMLA leave, so the employee was deprived of salary and benefits, and therefore encountered an adverse job action.

[B] ADA Interface

An employer can satisfy both the FMLA and the ADA by offering a reduced work schedule to a disabled employee until he or she has used the 12 weeks of FMLA leave. After FMLA leave, employees are entitled to reinstatement in a job equivalent to the original job. The FMLA permits the employer to demand a physical exam to determine if a worker can be reinstated after a health-related FMLA leave. To satisfy the ADA as well, the examination must be job-related, not a comprehensive inventory of all physical conditions.

Although the two statutes were designed to accomplish different goals, workers sometimes find that FMLA leave is more accessible than taking time off as an ADA reasonable accommodation. Remember, FMLA leave is available when the employee is the sick person—not just when the employee is a caregiver.

Furthermore, if the company employs at least 50 people and the employee has put in the necessary 1,250 hours in the previous 12 months, entitlement to FMLA leave is automatic. The employer's discretion as to what constitutes a reasonable accommodation is not a factor. The right to reinstatement is also automatic. Employers can raise a defense of unreasonable hardship in ADA cases—but not in FMLA cases.

[D.C. Bar Labor &Employment Law Section seminar (June 11, 2013), discussed in Lydell C. Bridgeford, *Attorneys for Both Plaintiffs, Employers Offer Views on Leave Under the ADA, FMLA*, Bloomberg BNA (June 25, 2013) (benefitslink.com)]

Absences that qualify under the FMLA or ADA should not be counted against an employee's record under a no-fault attendance policy.

Evidence that co-workers said that the plaintiff was acting strangely, that his supervisor knew he was diagnosed with bipolar syndrome and took antidepressants, and that he said he needed counseling for stress a few weeks before he was fired for two unauthorized absences raised an issue of fact about whether employer was on notice of his need for FMLA leave. Summary judgment for the employer was denied on the interference claims. The plaintiff, an engineer, engaged in some disruptive behavior, and his disconnected, rambling conversation alarmed his co-workers. He was fired for lack of cooperation when he failed to attend a mandatory training session. The district court accepted the magistrate's finding that he was not a Qualified Individual With a Disability for ADA purposes (see § 36.04[A]). His difficulties in getting along with co-workers were not tantamount to disability. However, the district court found a triable fact issue on the FMLA interference claim. After his termination, he submitted FMLA documentation of a serious health condition for the two days he missed. [*Koszarsky v. A.O. Smith Corp*, No. 4:12-cv-00939-RBH, 2014 U.S. Dist. LEXIS 2614 (D.S.C. Jan. 9, 2014); see Lorene D. Park, *Coworkers Reporting "Strange" Behavior, Employee Seeking Time Off For "Stress" May Show Employer Knew Of Need For FMLA Leave*, Employment Law Daily (Jan. 14, 2014) (benefitslink.com)]

Worker's Compensation defines disability in terms of specific injuries, such as the loss of hands or feet. The Worker's Compensation laws do not make explicit provision for leaves of absence, but denying reasonable time off could be interpreted as illegal retaliation for filing a Comp claim. However, it is lawful to fire someone who receives Worker's Compensation benefits as long as there is a legitimate non-retaliatory reason for the termination. Recipients of Worker's Compensation benefits are not guaranteed reinstatement if they recover from their injuries. If a work-related injury is also a disability, reasonable accommodation may be required under the ADA.

The EEOC's Enforcement Guidance on Reasonable Accommodation and Undue Hardship specifically says that no-fault leave policies that make termination automatic after a certain amount of leave has been taken violate the ADA.

An employee's job protection does not necessarily end once FMLA leave is used up. The employer must then consider if the employee is covered by the ADA. If so, the employer must engage in the interactive process and reassignment to a vacant position for which the employee is qualified may constitute reasonable accommodation. Holding a job open is a reasonable accommodation that may be required if the employee is expected to be able to return to work quickly. [*Maharaj v. California Bank & Trust*, No. 2:11-cv-00315-GEB-EFB, 2012 WL 5828552 (E.D. Cal., Nov. 15, 2012) *Kranson v. Federal Express Corp.*, No. 11-cv-05826-YGR (N.D. Cal. Oct. 1, 2012) says that holding the job open can constitute reasonable accommodation.]

In a case where an employee was fired shortly after giving notice of her need for surgery and recovery time, the District Court for the Eastern District of Tennessee ruled that she raised a triable ADA claim. However, the employer obtained summary judgment on her FMLA claim because she was not eligible for FMLA leave. She was fired on August 18, effective August 26; the surgery was scheduled for September when she would have been employed for a year, but she had not worked a full year at the time of the termination. (Note that the Eleventh Circuit has allowed workers who are not eligible for FMLA leave to assert claims of FMLA retaliation.) [*Dunn v. Chattanooga Publ'g Co.*, No. 1:12-cv-00252, 2014 U.S. Dist. LEXIS 1937 (E.D. Tenn. Jan. 8, 2014); see James R. Mulroy, II and

Christopher C. Antone, *Disability Discrimination Claims May Proceed Against Former Employer, Federal Court Rules*, Jackson Lewis PC (Jan. 23, 2014), available at Lexology.com]

However, some courts have ruled that indefinite leave is not required as a reasonable accommodation. A 2012 case permits terminating an employee who is unable to give a reasonable estimate of when he or she will be able to resume all essential functions of the job. The plaintiff was a supervisor of felony offenders. The written job description included 18 essential functions, including fieldwork at the homes of persons under supervision. The plaintiff's joint problems required her to use a wheelchair. She took a long leave of absence, returned, then required additional leave for surgery. She was granted additional leave after her FMLA entitlement ended on July 5. She was terminated because she was unable to return to work at full capacity. She brought an ADA failure to accommodate/FMLA retaliation suit. The court held that a request for a leave of absence is reasonable only if the employee can estimate when he or she can resume essential duties. The plaintiff's doctor estimated that she could walk with a cane in a few weeks—but that did not mean that she would be able to perform casework. In this case, the employer prevailed largely because of the detailed job description. [*Robert v. Board of Comm'rs of Brown Cnty.*, 691 F.3d 1211 (10th Cir. 2012); see Jeff Nowak, *An* "Indefinite Reprieve" *of Essential Functions of Job Not a Reasonable Accommodation under the ADA*, Franczek Radelet FMLA Insights (Sept. 5, 2012) (benefitslink.com)]

[C] COBRA and HIPAA

An IRS Final Rule, published starting at 64 Fed. Reg. 5160 (Feb. 3, 1999), provides that merely taking FMLA leave is not a COBRA qualifying event. However, a qualifying event does occur with respect to an employee (and any dependents of the employee who are at risk of losing health coverage) who fails to return to work at the end of the FMLA leave. The typical example is a new mother who does not return to work after the end of maternity leave.

Under the Final Rule, the COBRA qualifying event occurs on the last day of the FMLA leave. The employer is not allowed to condition the COBRA election on the employee paying the EGHP back for premiums paid on his or her behalf during the leave. However, if the employer has actually terminated coverage under the group plan for the whole class of employees that the employee belonged to before the FMLA leave, continuation coverage does not have to be offered to employees who do not return from leave. The HIPAA rules jointly released in late 2004 by the Treasury, DOL, and HHS (69 Fed. Reg. 78800, Dec. 30, 2004, amending 26 C.F.R. §§ 54.9801 to .9807, 29 C.F.R. §§ 701–708, and 45 C.F.R. § 146.20) provide important new guidance on the relationship between the FMLA and HIPAA's portability rules. HIPAA's protection ends if the individual goes for 63 days or more without "creditable coverage." The 2004 rule holds that a period of FMLA leave when the person on leave has not continued group health coverage does not count toward the 63-day period for the person on leave or his or her dependents.

A March 2013 case finds a TPA liable. The plaintiff alleged that he submitted certification for leave from November 22–January 15, and the TPA accepted the certification but granted only four weeks of leave (about half of his request) and said he would have to provide additional medical information to extend his leave. He did not provide the information and was fired. The FMLA claim was dismissed because the TPA was not a proper defendant—but the plaintiff argued tortious interference with his employment relationship, causing his employer to fire him even though he submitted proper certification. The court held that the facts were adequate to suggest denial of meritorious leave so that the TPA could reduce FMLA leave and enhance its own profits. [*Arango v. Work & Well Inc.*, No. 11 C 1525, 2013 U.S. Dist. LEXIS 35904 (N.D. Ill. Mar. 15, 2013); see Jeff Nowak, *Court Rules That Third Party Administrators Can Be Held Liable for FMLA-Related Violations*, Franczek Radelet FMLA Insights (Mar. 18, 2013) (benefitslink.com)]

[D] Cafeteria Plans

The IRS published final regulations, effective October 17, 2001, applicable for cafeteria plan years beginning on or after January 1, 2002, explicating the FMLA obligations of cafeteria plans. [See T.D. 8966, R.I.N. 1545-AT47, 66 Fed. Reg. 52676]

The employer must offer coverage under any group health plan as long as the employee is on paid or unpaid leave, on the same conditions as coverage would have been provided if the employee had continued to work during the leave period.

When the employee is on unpaid FMLA leave, the employer must either allow the employee to revoke the coverage or continue coverage but stop contributing premiums to the plan. The employer can then maintain the coverage by taking over both the employer and the employee share of the premium. The employer can recover the employee share of contributions when the employee returns from the leave. If the employee does not return, 29 C.F.R. § 825.213(a) permits the employer to recover both the employer and the employee shares of the premium from the employee. However, an employee who directed that premium payments be discontinued cannot be required to make contributions until after the end of unpaid leave.

[E] Fair Labor Standards Act

A 1998 Opinion Letter from the Department of Labor [Opinion Letter #89 (1998)] says that salaried workers who are exempt from the FLSA (and therefore are not entitled to overtime pay) are not entitled to FLSA protection merely because their employer docks their paychecks to reflect unpaid FMLA leave, even though pay deductions for absence are more characteristic of FLSA-covered wage workers than of "exempts."

[F] USERRA

Under the Uniformed Services Employment and Reemployment Rights Act [38 U.S.C. §§ 4301 *et seq.*] (USERRA), the Department of Labor indicated in mid-2002 that National Guard members and reservists who are called to active duty, and then released from active duty and return to their civilian jobs, are entitled to count their active duty service toward the 1,250 hour "work" requirement for FMLA eligibility. See § 1.18[A]. See § 31.01[A] for discussion of FMLA rights of the families of servicemembers: leave may be available either to assist the servicemember with deployment or return to civilian life, or to care for a sick or injured servicemember.

[G] State and Local Paid Leave Laws

California was the first state to require paid leave, under S.B. 1661 (2002), effective for leave taken on or after July 1, 2004. Eligible employees (caring for a newborn or newly adopted child or a family member—including a domestic partner—with a serious health condition) can access up to six weeks' paid leave per twelve-month period, under the Family Temporary Disability Insurance program. The leave must run concurrently with FMLA leave and its state equivalent—it does not increase leave entitlement, it merely establishes some circumstances under which leave must be paid. The program is completely funded by deductions from employees' salary; employers are not required to contribute. Eligible workers can receive up to 55% of their wages.

New Jersey's Family Leave Insurance Law, also known as the Paid Leave Act, took effect July 1, 2009. Covered employers (there is no minimum number of employees) must provide up to six weeks of paid family leave, or 42 days of intermittent leave in any 12-month period, so covered employees can care for a sick family member (employee's child, spouse, domestic partner, civil union partner, parent with serious health condition, or child born or adopted within the previous year)—but not for the employee's own serious health condition. The employee receives two-thirds of his or her weekly pay, subject to a statutory maximum. [Mintz, Levin, Cohn, Ferris, Glovsky and Popeo, P.C. Labor and Benefits Alert: *Employers Must Provide Paid Leave to New Jersey Employees Effective July 1, 2009* (June 23, 2009) (benefitslink.com)]

A Connecticut statute passed in May 2011 and taking effect January 1, 2012 requires service businesses with 50 or more employees to allow service workers (i.e., hourly non-exempt employees) to accrue paid sick leave. Covered workers can use up to 40 hours of accrued leave in any year for a serious illness, caregiving for a spouse or child, or needs related to family violence or sexual assault. [Connecticut S.B. 913; see Jason Stanevich and Jennai Williams, Littler Mendelsohn ASAP, *Connecticut is First State to Mandate Paid Sick Leave for Service Workers* (June 2011) (benefitslink.com); AP, *Connecticut Becomes First State Requiring Paid Sick Time*, WSJ.com (July 5, 2011)]

The National Conference of State Legislatures reported that in the 2013 legislative session, 148 bills were introduced in 32 states dealing with family or medical leave. Seventeen states passed bills. Rhode Island adopted a requirement of paid family leave, but Washington suspended effectiveness of its paid family leave law indefinitely. Laws passed in 2013 dealt with extending the circle of family members for whom leave can be taken (e.g., domestic partners). For example California's CA S 770 expands family temporary disability insurance to cover caregiving for more relatives. Colorado expanded the relatives for whom FMLA leave can be taken. Connecticut enacted subsidies under the Care 4 Kids program during unpaid leave for childbirth. Indiana, Kansas, and Mississippi passed laws forbidding local laws to impose employer obligations more extensive than those under federal and state law. Maryland enhanced protection of pregnant workers. Minnesota expanded the definition of "child" for sick leave purposes to cover step, adopted, and foster children. New Jersey passed a law about leave for victims of domestic violence and sexual assault. Oregon mandated up to two weeks of bereavement leave. Vermont passed a law forbidding lactation retaliation and established a committee to study paid leave. [National Conference of State Legislatures, *2013 Family Leave Legislation*, <http://www.ncsl.org/research/labor-and-employment/2013-family-leave-legislation.aspx> (Dec. 31, 2013)]

§ 38.07 NOTIFYING THE EMPLOYER

No one schedules an emergency, of course. However, treatment for some serious health conditions is scheduled in advance (e.g., elective surgery). Section 2612(e) requires the employee to give at least 30 days' notice before leave based on the expected due date of a baby, or the expected placement date for adoption or foster care. If the date of birth or placement is less than 30 days from the time the employee decides to apply for FMLA leave, the employee must give as much notice as is practicable.

The FMLA imposes a duty on employees taking leave based on planned medical treatment to make reasonable efforts to schedule the treatment in the way that causes the least disruption to the employer (as long as this does not endanger the sick person's health). The employee should provide at least 30 days' notice before the leave is scheduled to begin—but if the need for the treatment becomes known less than 30 days in advance, the employee must provide as much notice as is practicable.

§ 38.08 CERTIFICATION OF HEALTH CARE LEAVE

Employers have the right, under 29 U.S.C. § 2613, to require employees to prove that their request for medical leave is supported by a health care provider. This process is called certification. Employees have a duty to furnish the employer with a copy of the certification document, in a timely manner.

DOL regulations provide that the employee is solely responsible for getting medical certification of need for FMLA leave, and the employer does not have to pay for it: see 29 C.F.R. § 825.305(d). However, if the employer requires an additional examination by a doctor selected by the employer, the employer must pay for it. Some states have laws requiring the employer to pay for any medical examination required as a condition of employment. [Jeff Nowak, *Can An Employee Insist That The Employer Pay For FMLA Medical Certification?*, Franczek Radelet FMLA Insights (Feb. 11, 2013) (benefitslink.com)]

FMLA regulations require the employee to return the medical certification form to the employer within 15 calendar days of receiving the blank form, unless there are circumstances that prevent the employee from submitting the form despite diligent good faith efforts: see 29 C.F.R. § 825.305(b). Before taking adverse action against the employee based on failure to return the certification, the employer must make sure that it has notified the employee of the need to return the form and has inquired if anything prevented the return. FMLA expert Jeff Nowak recommends sending a letter to the employee as soon as the fifteenth calendar day passes, offering assistance if the employee needs help completing the form and setting a firm seven-day deadline to receive the form. A telephone call (documented by the employer) should follow if the form is not received. If the employee fails to provide the certification, FMLA leave can be denied after the fifteenth day until certification is received, and days after Day 15 can be treated as unexcused absences. 29 C.F.R. § 825.313(b) says that leave is not FMLA leave if the employee never returns the certification; Nowak reads this to mean that the entire absence, from the first day, is not FMLA leave. [Jeff Nowak, *FMLA FAQ: How Do Employers Count Unexcused Absences When FMLA Medical Certification is Not Returned?*, Franczek Radelet FMLA Insights (Oct. 11, 2012) (benefitslink.com)]

The District Court for the District of Oregon ruled in early 2014 that a company policy of requiring a doctor's note for every FMLA intermittent absence is unlawful because it contradicts the statutory recertification procedure. Oak Harbor Freight Lines believed that some employees abused leave by taking time off on Mondays, Fridays, and before holidays, so Oak Harbor required a doctor's note for all intermittent leave. But 29 C.F.R. § 825.308(a)(c) permits an employer to demand recertification only once every 30 days, unless there has been a change in circumstances or the employer doubts the continuing validity of the certification. The District Court for the District of Oregon held that the attendance policy treated each absence as a separate FMLA leave, and required employees to re-establish eligibility each time. [*Oak Harbor Freight Lines, Inc. v.*

Antti, No. 3:12-cv-00488-KI, 2014 U.S. Dist. LEXIS 20203 (D. Ore. Feb. 19, 2014); see Daniel Cafaro, *Requiring Notes for Each Intermittent FMLA Absence Could Be Improper*, Thompson's HR Compliance Expert (Mar. 21, 2014) (benefitslink.com)]

The FMLA regulations say that the requirement of "continuing treatment by a health care provider" can be satisfied with at least three days of incapacitation, but they do not indicate whether medical testimony is required. A 2010 Third Circuit case holds that the employee's own testimony about the length of incapacitation, in conjunction with medical evidence, can be used to prove eligibility. The Third Circuit held that some medical evidence is required; the employee's unsupported testimony is not enough. The plaintiff was fired for violating the employer's policy requiring a call-in on sick days. The employer said that she did not qualify for FMLA leave because of the lack of proper notice, and because she did not prove three days of incapacitation. The Third Circuit remanded the case to the district court for further proceedings. [*Schaar v. Lehigh Valley Health Servs., Inc.*, 598 F.3d 156 (3d Cir. 2010)]

§ 38.09 DISCLOSURE TO EMPLOYEES

Employers have an obligation to post the standard EEOC notice to inform employees of their rights under the FMLA. Failure to do so can result in a civil penalty of up to $100 per offense. [29 U.S.C. § 2619] The notice, which must be at least 8½ × 11", can be obtained from the local office of the DOL Wage and Hour Division, or can be enlarged and copied from 29 C.F.R. Part 825, Appendix C. Employers who employ a significant number of people who are literate in a language other than English must also post a translation of the notice into that language.

In a recent Third Circuit case, the plaintiff was fired four days after calling in before her shift to say that she was in the emergency room accompanying her mother. Her supervisor merely entered "sick mom" in the log without additional explanation. The Third Circuit held that, while the plaintiff did not provide enough information to indicate that leave was required to care for her mother's serious health condition, the employer had an obligation to inquire, and the timing of her termination raised an inference of FMLA interference. [*Lichtenstein v. University of Pittsburgh Med. Ctr.* 691 F.3d 294 (3d Cir. 2012); see Jeff Nowak, *When Has an Employee Provided Sufficient Notice of the Need for FMLA Leave?*, Franczek Radelet PC FMLA Insights (Sept. 13, 2012) (benefitslink .com)]

The Sixth Circuit held that an employer that did not explain how it calculated FMLA benefits could not terminate an employee for violating the policy. Leave was approved from April 27–June 27, 2005 for a non-work-related shoulder injured. The employee's doctor cleared him to return to work on June 13, 2005. The employer asked why he did not return to work. He said he would return on June 27; his shoulder was still painful. He came to work on June 17, submitting a doctor's note supporting an extension of leave until July 18. He was fired, because the company treated all absences since June 13 as unexcused, so he exceeded the firing level of absences. The Sixth Circuit said that he was vulnerable to being fired if the company calculated backwards from the date of using leave, but not if the company allowed 12 weeks of leave per calendar year. But, because the company failed to disclose its calculation method, it was unlawful to fire the plaintiff. The court awarded liquidated damages, more than $312,000 in back pay and attorneys' fees. [*Thom v. American Standard*, 666 F.3d 968 (6th Cir. 2012); Judy Greenwald, *Employer Did Not Communicate FMLA Policy and Cannot Fire Worker: Appeals Court*, Business Insurance (benefitslink.com)]

For many years, the federal courts followed the "mailbox rule"—a presumption that a letter that was sent to the correct address, with appropriate postage attached, would be delivered. The Third Circuit cast doubt on this rule in a mid-2014 case. A college instructor who was suffering from depression filled out a request form for personal leave. Shortly thereafter, the plaintiff gave her employer medical certification that complied with the FMLA requirements. The request for personal leave was converted to FMLA leave. The college mailed her a notice that her absence would be treated as FMLA leave. She was out on leave for 14 weeks, then provided medical certification of her ability to return to work without restrictions. Then she was informed that she had been terminated for failure to return to work after her 12 weeks of FMLA leave ended. The plaintiff brought suit, alleging that she had not known that her absence was treated as FMLA leave—an allegation that made the issue of whether she received the notices central to the case. The Third Circuit held that, although there is a strong presumption that certified mail will be received, there is a weak presumption that first-class mail is received, and the presumption disappears if the addressee denies receiving it. The court suggested using a form of delivery that provides a verifiable receipt. [*Lupyan v. Corinthian Colls.*, No. 13-1843 (3d Cir. Aug. 5, 2014). See Jeffrey S. Nowak, *A Game-Changing Decision? Sending FMLA Notices to Employees by U.S. Mail May Not Cut It Anymore*, Franczek Radelet PC (Aug. 7, 2014), available at Lexology.com]

Companies that have employee handbooks must include FMLA information in the handbook. Even if there is no handbook, employees who actually request leave are entitled to a written explanation of their rights. Employees must be notified, e.g.,

- That the requested leave reduces the employee's "bank" of FMLA leave for the year;
- Whether the employer requires medical certification of the serious health condition; consequences if the certification is not provided;

- The fact that employees who are entitled to paid leave have a right to substitute paid leave for FMLA leave; the conditions under which the employer will substitute paid leave on its own initiative;
- The employee's right to be reinstated in a comparable job after returning from leave;
- The method for the employee to pay health premiums while he or she is on FMLA leave;
- Disclosure of the employee's obligation to reimburse the employer for premiums if the employee does not return to work after the leave;
- Any requirements for proving fitness for duty before returning to work;
- (For key employees) limitations on the right to reinstatement.

§ 38.10 ADMINISTRATIVE REQUIREMENTS

The Department of Labor's investigative authority under the FMLA is the same as its authority under FLSA § 11(a), including subpoena power. Employers have a duty to make and retain records showing FMLA compliance. The general rule is that the DOL can only require employers and employee plans to submit books and records once a year, unless the DOL is investigating a charge made by an employee, or has reason to believe that there has been an FMLA violation. [29 U.S.C. § 2616]

§ 38.11 FMLA ENFORCEMENT

The proposed federal 2014 budget called for $243 million (a $14 million increase) for the DOL Wage and Hour Division, including $3.4 million targeted to increased FMLA enforcement. [Jared Bilski, *DOL Backing Up FMLA Enforcement Promise: Employers Feel the Pinch*, HR Benefits Alert (Aug. 13, 2013), available at law.com]

[A] Litigation and Arbitration

It is very common for employment discrimination plaintiffs to charge retaliation, either as their sole cause of action, or because they say that the employer retaliated against them for making an internal complaint or filing charges with an anti-discrimination agency. The FMLA is no exception.

The Seventh Circuit rejected the possibility of suing under the FMLA on a theory that a supervisor's actions made the employee's existing health condition worse. The Seventh Circuit held that the cause of an injury is irrelevant under the FMLA, and refused to grant front pay. The alleged conduct that caused his condition to worsen occurred after his second unprotected leave (his FMLA entitlement had been used up during his first leave; the second leave was provided voluntarily by his employer, as a courtesy). If retaliation occurred, it happened after he was no longer eligible under the FMLA. The court said that, although in general stress is bad for health, the FMLA does not cover all health-related issues. [*Breneisen v. Motorola,* 656 F.3d 701 (7th Cir. 2011)]

The FMLA ban on retaliation can be invoked by a worker who claims he or she suffered retaliation for asking for FMLA leave; it is not required that leave was actually granted. The Third Circuit said that employers should not be given an incentive to fire employees for exercising their legal rights. The Third Circuit sent the case back to the District Court, for a jury to determine whether the defendant had constructive notice of the hours that the plaintiff worked at home (and which put her over the 1,250 hour mark for eligibility under the FMLA). But the court rejected the plaintiff's argument that she would be entitled to FMLA leave if the employer failed to advise her about the eligibility rules, because that argument was based on a DOL regulation that was rejected by the courts and that the agency had to revise. [*Erdman v. Nationwide Ins. Co.*, 582 F.3d 500 (3d Cir. 2009)]

The Seventh Circuit allowed an FMLA retaliation case to proceed to the jury when the AMA changed its plan to eliminate one job for budgetary reasons and instead eliminated the job of a veteran employee who had applied for FMLA leave. The Seventh Circuit held that referring to FMLA leave in an e-mail recommending the employee's termination could be deemed retaliation and a reasonable jury could conclude that he was fired for requesting leave. [*Shaffer v. AMA*, 662 F.3d 439 (7th Cir. 2011)]

See also *Richardson v. Monitronics Int'l*, 434 F.3d 327 (5th Cir. 2005) holding that although mixed-motive retaliation cases are possible—if the employer's action was at least partially motivated by retaliation for exercise of FMLA rights—the employer can win by showing that there was cause to fire the employee even if FMLA rights had never been used. *Mauder v. Metro. Transit Auth.* [446 F.3d 574 (5th Cir. 2006)] holds that it was not retaliation to terminate an employee who was already on a corrective action plan, and Type II diabetes and medication side effects causing uncontrollable diarrhea did not constitute a "serious health condition."

Not only do employers face FMLA suits from employees or groups of employees; they can also be sued by the Department of Labor, which can sue on behalf of employees to recover the same kind of damages employees would get. If the DOL wins an FMLA case, the damages got to the employee, not to the government agency (unless it is impossible to locate the employees within three years). [See 29 U.S.C. § 2617(b)] The Secretary of Labor has the power to investigate and try to resolve complaints of FMLA violations, to the same degree as investigations and resolutions of violations of FLSA §§ 6 and 7. But employees are no longer allowed to bring FMLA suits once the DOL starts a suit. [29 U.S.C. § 2617(a)(4)]

FMLA claims can become the subject of arbitration as well as litigation. The Seventh Circuit found that where a Collective Bargaining Agreement included broad anti-discrimination language, the arbitrator did not exceed his powers by interpreting the FMLA as well as the CBA. [*Butler Mfg. Co. v. United Steelworkers*, 336 F.3d 629 (7th Cir. 2003)]

[B] Releases

The 2009 revision of the FMLA rules provides that, while employees cannot waive FMLA claims that arise in the future, if a claim has already arisen, a release does not require DOL or court supervision to be valid. Previously, the Fifth Circuit held that public policy favors enforcement of waivers, and an employee who keeps the money paid for a release ratifies the release. [*Faris v. Williams WPC-I, Inc.*, 332 F.3d 316 (5th Cir. 2003)], whereas the Fourth Circuit required DOL supervision of all FMLA releases, whether retrospective or prospective. [*Taylor v. Progress Energy Inc.*, 493 F.3d 454 (4th Cir. 2007)]

An employee who received a poor performance evaluation after taking extensive FMLA leave was given a choice between a Performance Improvement Plan (under which she would be terminated if she failed to meet the plan's goals) and 13 weeks of severance benefits in exchange for a release of FMLA claims. She accepted the severance, and then joined two other plaintiffs in a suit charging FMLA interference and retaliation. She argued that she did not waive her FMLA rights, because 29 CFR § 825.220 forbids prospective waivers of FMLA rights. The Eleventh Circuit, however, held that a prospective right is the right to take FMLA leave in the future, whereas the plaintiff (Paylor) released a claim that had already accrued. The Eleventh Circuit found the release to be valid and enforceable; it was signed voluntarily by an adult with business experience; she was given 21 days to consider the deal; and she received consideration for the release in the form of severance benefits that would not otherwise have been available. [*Paylor v. Hartford Fire Ins.*, 748 F.3d 1117 (11th Cir. 2014); see Liebert Cassidy Whitmore, *Employee Who Waived FMLA Claims by Signing Severance Agreement Could Not Then Bring Lawsuit Alleging FMLA Violations* (May 10, 2014), available at Lexology.com]

[C] Damages

If the employees win, 29 U.S.C. § 2617(a) provides that the court can order damages equal to the wages and benefits that the employee lost as a result of the violation. Even employees who have not lost compensation can receive damages to compensate them for financial losses (such as costs of hiring someone to care for sick relatives), but damages of this type are limited to 12 weeks' salary for the employee-plaintiff.

Furthermore, winning FMLA plaintiffs can receive double damages: their damages (plus interest) and also an equal amount of liquidated damages. However, if the employer can prove that it acted in good faith and reasonably believed that it was in compliance with the FMLA, the court has discretion not to order double damages.

In a case of first impression, the Ninth Circuit ruled that FMLA front pay, which is awarded either in lieu of reinstatement, or to make up for compensation that was lost between the court's judgment and the plaintiff's reinstatement, is an equitable remedy. Therefore, the amount is determined by the judge, not the jury, and the judge also decides if reinstatement is practical. (The Fourth, Fifth, and Tenth Circuits had already ruled that the judge determines if front pay is available and, if so, how much.) Under the FMLA, liquidated damages are mandatory unless the employer proves both its good faith and that it had reasonable grounds for believing it acted lawfully. However, liquidated damages are not automatically payable in every case in which front pay is ordered, because it is possible for an employer to act in good faith, but for reinstatement to be impractical because of the friction caused by the plaintiff's extensive usage of FMLA leave. [*Traxler v. Multnomah County*, 596 F.3d 1007 (9th Cir. 2010)]

A district court jury awarded $1.2 million in damages and attorneys' fees to Pat Hurley, who was fired after informing his employer that he would need time off to deal with depression. However, the Eleventh Circuit reversed the award in 2014, holding that the FMLA only protects leave for incapacity that has already occurred, not conditions that are likely to occur in the future. [*Hurley v. Kent of Naples*, 746 F.3d 1161 (11th Cir. 2014); see Jeff Nowak, *Employees Can't Take FMLA Leave for "Potential" Absences in the Future* (Mar. 25, 2014) (benefitslink.com)]

An employee who has received an FMLA back pay award is not precluded from receiving liquidated damages for retaliation. The Tenth Circuit held that wages that are temporarily lost but restored after a significant delay must be treated as "lost or denied" for purposes of calculating FMLA liquidated damages. [*Jordan v. U.S. Postal Serv.*, 379 F.3d 1196 (10th Cir. 2004)]

A TGIFridays restaurant in LA had to pay $1,455 in back wages and change its leave policy (at all 272 locations) for failure to reinstate an employee who took leave, and making him wait three weeks for reinstatement (losing salary) when the company's leave policy failed to reflect military family leave, intermittent or reduced schedule leave, and required 12 continuous months of employment rather than 12 months employment. In another case showing the DOL's emphasis on FMLA enforcement, the Putnam County Board of Education had to pay $50,000 in back wages for trying to force the resignation, and eventually firing, a worker who requested FMLA leave. [Jared Bilski, *DOL Backing Up FMLA Enforcement Promise: Employers Feel the Pinch*, HR Benefits Alert (Aug. 13, 2013), available at law.com]

Although most of the remedies are equitable ones, the Southern District of Georgia allows jury trials in FMLA cases, because they are allowed in Fair Labor

Standards Act cases, and the two statutes contain many similar provisions. [*Helmly v. Stone Container Corp.*, 957 F. Supp. 1274 (S.D. Ga. 1997)] So does the Sixth Circuit. [*Frizzell v. Southwestern Motor Freight*, 154 F.3d 641 (6th Cir. 1998)]

In addition to money damages, courts in FMLA cases can award the appropriate equitable relief for the case, including hiring, reinstatement, and promotion. FMLA winners are entitled to receive reasonable costs, defined to include attorneys' fees and expert witness fees. Section 2617(a)(3) makes this automatic for plaintiffs who win, not a matter of discretion for the court.

This is not true of all federal statutes. Some of them do not allow attorneys' fee awards at all, others allow a fee award to any prevailing party (plaintiff or defendant) or leave it up to the court whether an award should be made, or limit fee awards to cases in which the losing party's conduct has been outrageous.

PART VIII

PROCEDURE FOR HANDLING DISCRIMINATION CHARGES

Chapter 39

WRONGFUL TERMINATION AND AT-WILL EMPLOYMENT

§ 39.01 INTRODUCTION

Employees always have the right to quit their jobs, no matter how inconvenient their departure may be for the employer (although employment contracts can require a certain amount of notice, can obligate the employee to compensate the employer for economic loss caused by a resignation, and can impose reasonable restrictions on re-employment and use of the employer's proprietary information).

The employer's right to fire an employee is not so simple and clear-cut. Some employees have written contracts that specify the conditions under which they can be terminated. Unionized employees are covered by collective bargaining agreements (CBAs). In CBAs or individual employment contracts, if the agreement sets out a termination procedure (such as a warning, then a chance for the employee to respond to charges, a suspension, and then termination), then it is a breach of contract to terminate the employee without following the procedure.

Employers may also find that they are subject to responsibilities under implied contracts. The employer's written documents that it issues such as the employee handbook or even its oral statements are deemed to constitute a legally enforceable contract, then the employer will have to abide by that contract.

A supervisor is a representative of the employer when he or she is acting in the scope of his or her job, in a situation in which he or she is authorized to act. The supervisor's conduct will then have legal implications for the employer. A supervisor's negligence or outrageous conduct (such as abusive treatment of an employee that results in emotional distress) can be imputed to the employer. In many instances, the supervisor will *not* be personally liable, e.g., under federal and state antidiscrimination statutes or for inducing a breach of contract.

Even if termination is justifiable, however, it must be carried out in a reasonable manner, avoiding intentional infliction of emotional distress. The employer must also avoid both actionable defamation (destructive false statements) and depriving another employer of the accurate information needed to make a rational hiring decision.

There are also several statutes (e.g., the Sarbanes-Oxley and Dodd-Frank Acts) that protect whistleblowers—employees who expose wrongdoing on the part of the employer—from retaliation. See § 39.04[B] below. Workers' Compensation claimants are also protected against retaliation: see § 39.04[C].

"Constructive discharge" is the legal concept that an employee who responds to intolerable conditions by quitting is entitled to be treated as if he or she had been fired, because the employer's conduct was the equivalent of a discharge. To prove constructive discharge, the employee does not have to prove that the employer intended to force a resignation, only that it was reasonably foreseeable that a reasonable employee would quit under the same circumstances. The Supreme Court's mid-2004 decision, *Pennsylvania State Police v. Suders*, 542 U.S. 129 [(2004)] makes it clear that the test of constructive discharge is objective, not subjective, based on the behavior of the hypothetical reasonable employee rather than the personal reactions of the plaintiff. In a pregnancy discrimination/FMLA case, the Sixth Circuit ruled that a threat of demotion coupled with other factors can constitute constructive discharge. [*Saroli v. Automation & Modular Components, Inc.*, 405 F.3d 446 (6th Cir. 2005)]

The fact situation is not one that is likely to be repeated frequently, but it should be noted that at the end of 2004, the U.S. Supreme Court ruled that it did not violate a police officer's First Amendment or Fourteenth Amendment rights to fire him for selling videos (and police paraphernalia) on the Internet. The videos featured the officer in police-related pornographic scenarios. The Supreme Court held that he was not expressing himself on matters of public concern or commenting on police department operations. [*City of San Diego v. John Roe*, 543 U.S. 77 (2004)]

The vast majority of employees do not have a written contract. They are legally defined as "at-will" employees who work "at the will of the employer." However, at-will employers are not permitted to discharge employees for reasons that violate an antidiscrimination statute, or for reasons contrary to public policy.

Employees who want to bring suit under federal antidiscrimination laws (Title VII, the ADA, the ADEA, and the FMLA) have to satisfy elaborate procedural requirements. [See Chapters 40 and 41] Employees who charge the employer with wrongful termination merely have to go to state court and file a complaint. This is much easier to do, so employers may find themselves fighting on two fronts, or may be able to raise the argument that a wrongful termination case should be dismissed because the employee was required—but failed—to use the procedure for a discrimination suit.

§ 39.02 EMPLOYEE TENURE

Some state court cases consider it an implied promise of continuing employment once an employee has worked for the employer for a long time (say, a decade or more), and a number of states impose an implied covenant of good faith and fair dealing in the employment context.

The Connecticut Court of Appeals ruled that it is permissible to terminate an at-will employee even before work begins: either side can terminate the relationship at any time for any reason, not conditioned on work actually beginning. (The plaintiff was hired for a sales job and asked to submit references; when he reported for work, he was told that there were issues about his references.) He sued, claiming a breach of the employment contract and the contract to hire him, charging that the offer letter constituted negligent misrepresentation. [*Petitte v. DSL.net, Inc.*, 102 Conn. App. 363 (Conn. App. 2007); see Rebeca Moore, *Court Upholds Firing Before Work Commenced*, plansponsor.com (Aug. 22, 2007)]

New York's highest court ruled that an at-will employee can be fired at any time unless there is a statutory ban, an express limitation in an individual employment contract, or the firing reflected a constitutionally impermissible rationale.

Therefore, a group of five financial services money managers who claimed fraudulent inducement because they were not informed of the merger that led to their termination could not sustain a fraudulent inducement claim. [*Smalley v. Dreyfus Corp.*, 10 N.Y.3d 55 (2008); see Fred Schneyer, *NY Court: "At-Will" Workers Can Be Fired Anytime*, plansponsor.com (Feb. 14, 2008); Joel Stashenko, *Terminated At-Will Workers Lose Bid to Press Tort Action Against Dreyfus Corp.*, N.Y.L.J. (Feb. 14, 2008) (law.com)]

The New York Court of Appeals held in mid-2012 that a hedge fund compliance officer who was fired after confronting his boss about allegedly improper trades was an at-will employee not entitled to common-law protection against wrongful termination. Compliance was only part of his job, and the court held that his regulatory and ethical obligations as compliance officer were not so intertwined with his employee responsibilities for separation to be impossible. [*Sullivan v. Harnisch*, 19 N.Y.3d 259 (N.Y. 2012); see John Caher, *At-Will Doctrine Denies Protection for Compliance Head*, N.Y.L.J. (May 9, 2012) (law.com)]

Months before Weiss was scheduled to receive a $60,000 bonus, he was terminated, allegedly for failure to supervise an employee who took kickbacks and was guilty of other financial misconduct. Weiss sued in state court to recover the bonus. The case was removed to federal court on diversity grounds. The jury ruled for Weiss on his breach of contract claim. The employer appealed to the First Circuit, which held that the plan gave a management committee the power to decide if an employee was terminated for good cause and thereby forfeited the bonus. [*Weiss v. DHL Express Inc.*, 718 F.3d 39 (1st Cir. 2013)]

§ 39.03 PROMISSORY ESTOPPEL

The theory of "promissory estoppel" is sometimes decisive in employment cases. The theory is that the employer's promise to the employee estops (precludes) the employer from disavowing that promise, often because the employee has "undergone detrimental reliance" (suffered in some way after relying on a statement or implication from the employer).

The classic example is a top executive recruited from another company, who gives up a high salary and stock options, has expenses of relocation, and then is fired shortly after taking up the new job. However, employees who allege oral promises of permanent employment may find that their claims are barred by a legal doctrine, the Statute of Frauds that requires contracts lasting a year or more to be in writing if they are to be enforceable.

§ 39.04 PUBLIC POLICY

[A] Generally

A whole line of cases permits employees to sue when they are fired for a reason contrary to the public policy of the state. In other words, it is unlawful to fire an employee for doing something that is acceptable or even admirable. For instance, no matter how inconvenient the timing is for the employer, it is not permitted to fire an employee for serving jury duty.

The First Circuit ruled that for a safety engineer to inform his supervisors about potential overtime violations with respect to the security guards he supervised was part of his job duties. Doing so was not protected activity under the Fair Labor Standards Act, so firing him for raising the issue could not be retaliation in violation of the FLSA. [*Claudio-Gotay v. Becton Dickinson Caribe Ltd.*, 375 F.3d 99 (1st Cir. 2004)]

It violates ERISA § 510 to fire an employee merely to prevent access to pension or welfare benefits. [See Chapter 15]

Certiorari was denied in a Third Circuit decision holding that it did not violate ERISA § 510 to fire an HR director for her unsolicited comments to management about what she perceived to be ERISA violations (such as misrepresentation) in the company health plan. The Second and Fourth Circuits have ruled similarly—that protection under § 510 is limited to testimony in a formal inquiry such as a federal investigation. However, the Fifth and Ninth Circuits agree with the DOL, that informal, unsolicited comments are protected. [*Edwards v. A.H. Cornell & Son, Inc.*, 610 F.3d 217 (3d Cir. 2010), *cert. denied*, 131 S. Ct. 1604 (2011); see Jewell Lim Esposito, *Companies Can Safely Fire Someone Who Alleges Internal ERISA Violations*, Employee Benefits Unplugged Blog (Mar. 23, 2011) (benefitslink.com)]

In 2014, the Sixth Circuit held that in theory unsolicited complaints can give rise to an ERISA § 510 cause of action, but, in the particular case, held that a single complaint is not enough. The plaintiff e-mailed the corporation's Chairman of the Board, threatening to report ERISA violations in the election for the board. The Sixth Circuit drew a distinction between two kinds of federal anti-retaliation laws: an "opposition clause" protecting people who oppose violations of the law, and "participation clauses" that limit protection to people who have participated in a formal proceeding. According to the Sixth Circuit, ERISA's anti-retaliation provision is a participation clause (as are the ADA, FMLA, and PPACA protective provisions), whereas Title VII and the FLSA have opposition clauses. [*Sexton v. Panel Processing*, No. 13-1604 (6th Cir. May 9, 2014). See Matthew Loughran, *Sixth Circuit: ERISA Section 510 Requires Employee Action Within Formal Proceeding*, Bloomberg BNA Daily Labor Report (May 13, 2014) (benefitslink.com)]

The Eighth Circuit affirmed summary judgment for the employer in a case where the plaintiff signed an employment contract describing him as an at-will employee. He also received an employee manual that covered acceptable conduct and termination. According to the plaintiff, he was harassed by his supervisors; the supervisors said that he did a poor job. He was fired for intentional falsification of delivery records. He said that this was pretextual, and the real reason was that he complained of harassment. He said that his termination violated public policy, because retaliation against those who make harassment complaints violates public policy. The Eighth Circuit disagreed: there was no violation of a substantial public policy expressed in a statute or judicial decision. Alleging that a company violated its own policies is a contract claim. [*Semple v. Federal Express Corp.*, 566 F.3d 788 (8th Cir. 2009)]

A hospital nurse who posted a tirade on Facebook could not demonstrate that firing her violated the CBA or her free speech rights under the California constitution. Her post said that she hated her supervisor and was angry that she had to work on Mother's Day after receiving a 17% pay cut. Her Facebook friends included some co-workers and a manager who reported her post to management. Her breach of contract claim was dismissed for failure to exhaust the contractual remedies under the CBA. The district court said that the plaintiff's allegations of inadequate union representation did not excuse her from exhausting the grievance procedure. The cases she cited to support her free speech claim were irrelevant because they dealt with speech in public places. She did not allege that she engaged in concerted activity protected by the NLRA. [*Guevarra v. Seton Med. Ctr.*, No. C 13-2267 CW, 2013 U.S. Dist. LEXIS 169849 (N.D. Cal. Dec. 2, 2013); see Keahn N. Morris, *Employer Could Discharge Nurse For Facebook Tirade, Court Finds*, Jackson Lewis PC (Dec. 27, 2013), available at Lexology.com]

A 2010 Sixth Circuit case was brought by an employee who charged that he was fired for refusing to participate in a market allocation conspiracy in the packaged ice industry. (His former employer plead guilty to antitrust charges and agreed to pay a $9 million fine, and three executives plead guilty to individual charges.) He said that he was blackballed and was unable to find another job since exposing the conspiracy. The Sixth Circuit ruled that he was not covered by the Crime Victims' Rights Act: although preventing a person from getting a job may be the subject of a civil action, it is neither inherently criminal nor an inherent part of the antitrust conspiracy. The plaintiff filed a separate RICO suit alleging that he was fired for refusing to participate in the scheme, and because he cooperated with federal authorities. [*In re McNulty*, 597 F.3d 344 (6th Cir. 2010); see Tresa Baldas, *6th Circuit: Whistleblower Not a* "Crime Victim" *Even if He's Been Blackballed*, Nat'l L.J. (Mar. 3, 2010) (law.com)]

The Fifth Circuit reversed a grant of summary judgment for the employer, holding that the company did not show that, absent retaliation, an employee who took FMLA leave would have been fired anyway. The plaintiff suffered from stress related to having sole custody of his child. He applied for FMLA leave, but refused to release his medical records because an EAP counselor told him that the records were confidential. A co-worker told the plaintiff's supervisor that he faked a nervous breakdown to get FMLA leave. He was banned from the clinic when clinic workers said that he made them uncomfortable. He was fired for "abuse of management constituting insubordination," and sued for FMLA interference and retaliation. Management said that he was terminated for unexcused absences, poor performance, and rudeness to clinic employees. The Fifth Circuit held that there was evidence that his termination was intended to prevent him from exercising FMLA rights. The Fifth Circuit said that the argument that he would have been fired anyway was invalid because there was no indication of discipline for the alleged performance issues. His termination letter did not mention alleged misconduct at the clinic and the evidence did not show that he misbehaved at the clinic. [*Ion v. Chevron USA Inc.*, 731 F.3d 379 (5th Cir. 2013); see Wolters Kluwer Law & Business News Center, *Employer Failed To Show It Would Have Fired Employee For Work Issues And Faking Need For FMLA Leave* (Oct. 11, 2013) (benefitslink.com)]

Medical marijuana is legal in 20 states (and recreational marijuana is legal in Colorado and Washington) but courts consistently permit firing employees who test positive for marijuana, even if they are certified for medical marijuana and did not use the drug in the workplace. There are cases of this type from the Sixth and Ninth Circuits and from Colorado, Michigan, Washington, Oregon, Montana, and California. [Katharine J. Liao, *Reefer Madness: Employees May Use Medical Marijuana Yet Be Fired For Doing So*, DLA Piper (Nov. 11, 2013), available at Lexology.com; see, e.g., *Casias v. Wal-Mart Stores Inc.*, 695 F.3d 428 (6th Cir. 2012) (termination for testing positive for medical marijuana was not wrongful); *Curry v. MillerCoors, Inc.*, No. 12-cv-02471 JLK, 2013 WL 4494307 (D. Colo. Aug. 21, 2013) (paraplegic treating pain); *Coats v. Dish Network*, 2013 COA 62 (Colo. App. Apr. 25, 2013) (smoking marijuana violates federal law, so it is not a "lawful activity")] Although some medical marijuana statutes forbid employers to penalize a medical marijuana cardholder or registered qualifying patient for having a positive drug test (e.g., Arizona, Connecticut, Delaware, Maine, Nevada, and Rhode Island), they permit employers to ban use, possession, and impairment by marijuana during working hours. Other laws permit the employer to conclude that a positive test is proof of workplace impairment, which would justify firing even a cardholder. Federally regulated employers are required to observe drug-free workplace laws. [Kathryn J. Russo and Dona Vetrano Pryor, *Demystifying Employer Drug Policies In Medical Marijuana States*, Jackson Lewis LLP (Oct. 31, 2013), available at Lexology.com]

In the case of a drug company manager who said that he was fired for helping one of his subordinates fight sexual harassment by another supervisor, the First Circuit held that a reasonable jury could believe that the plaintiff, Collazo, opposed sexual harassment. Although the employer's internal inquiry cleared the alleged harasser, a plaintiff does not have to prove that the conditions he or she opposed actually violated Title VII—only that he or she had a good faith reasonable belief that they did. Management said that he was fired for poor performance and because his job was eliminated in a reorganization, but these arguments were dubious because he was not given any counseling or progressive discipline for the alleged performance problems, and he was the only employee who was terminated and not given a chance to transfer to a new job during the reorganization. [*Collazo v. Bristol-Myers Squibb Mfg. Inc.*, 617 F.3d 39 (1st Cir. 2010)]

[B] Whistleblower Employees

The case of the "whistleblower" employee is more complex. Employees (often those who are dissatisfied for other reasons) go to the press, or file complaints with enforcement agencies, about some aspect of corporate conduct they find unsatisfactory. In some instances, firing (or taking other adverse employment action) against whistleblowers violates public policy, because in appropriate cases, whistleblowers are exposing violations of law or other improprieties.

At the end of 1998, the Supreme Court held that an action under 42 U.S.C. § 1985 (damage to person or property) can be maintained by an at-will employee who alleges that he was fired for assisting a federal criminal investigation of the employer company. [*Haddle v. Garrison*, 525 U.S. 121 (1998)]

The Supreme Court ruled in 2010 that a whistleblower cannot bring a False Claims Act suit based on information that has already been disclosed in county or state reports. (Previous law said that information in congressional, federal administrative, or GAO reports is already known, and therefore cannot form the basis of a "qui tam" whistleblower action.) [*Graham County Soil & Water Conservation Dist. v. U.S. ex rel. Wilson*, 559 U.S. 280 (2010). See *Rockwell Int'l Corp. v. United States*, 549 U.S. 457 (2007) for the principle that the whistleblower must be the original source of the information, having direct and independent knowledge of the facts of the case. The Supreme Court extended this principle in 2011. *Schindler Elevator Corp. v. United States ex rel. Kirk*, 131 S. Ct. 1885 (2011), ruling that releasing documents pursuant to a FOIA request is a "report" that makes the documents public, so the information in the documents will not support a whistleblower award.]

More recently, the Supreme Court has returned to this subject several times. The Supreme Court ruled that government employees cannot be fired for testifying about government corruption. Generally speaking, government employee whistleblowers are only held to have enforceable First Amendment rights when they speak as citizens, on a matter of public interest, not when they speak as employees. In this case, however, the Supreme Court held that the plaintiff, a state community college employee laid off after testifying at a federal trial about a state legislator's no-show job at the institution, was subpoenaed. He had a legal obligation to testify, and therefore was considered a citizen speaking on a matter of public concern entitled to First Amendment protection. [*Lane v. Franks*, 134 S. Ct. 2369 (2014); see Jess Bravin, *Supreme Court Ruling Protects Whistleblowers*, WSJ.com (June 19, 2014)]

Certiorari was granted in May, 2014, on the issue of whether air marshal Robert MacLean qualifies for protection in connection with informing news media in 2003 about what he considered a bad policy decision by his employer, the Transportation Security Administration. He was fired for violating a provision of the Aviation and Transportation Security Act that forbids divulging security information if the Department of Homeland Security considers the disclosure detrimental to public safety. MacLean, however, said he was covered by the Whistleblower Protection Act, which forbids retaliation for disclosing substantial dangers to public health and safety. [*Dep't of Homeland Sec. v. MacLean*, *cert. granted* as No. 13-894, 134 S. Ct. 2290 (May 19, 2014). See Jess Bravin, *Supreme Court to Hear Case on Whistleblower Protection for Air Marshal*, WSJ.com (May 19, 2014)]

The health care reform act, the Patient Protection and Affordable Care Act (PPACA), Pub. L. No. 111-148, deals with the subject of whistleblower protection. It says that only federal, and not state or local disclosures, will rule out a False Claims Act qui tam action. PPACA § 1558 amends the Fair Labor Standards Act to provide that it is unlawful to discharge or discriminate (in compensation or working conditions) against anyone who has given information to the federal government or a state attorney general, testified or is about to testify, or assisted in a proceeding involving an alleged violation of the health care reform law. OSHA interim final rules were published February 22, 2013 covering complaints made by employees who say they suffered retaliation for receiving a subsidy or tax credit in connection with using a health insurance Exchange (rather than being covered by an EGHP). The general OSHA whistleblower procedures apply in this situation. [<http://www.dol.gov/find/20130222/OSHA2013.pdf>; see PLC Employee Benefits & Executive Compensation, *OSHA Rules Address Retaliation Complaint Procedures under Health Care Reform* (Feb. 25, 2013) (benefitslink.com)]

The Department of Labor ordered the Union Pacific Railroad Co. to pay $400,000 in punitive damages, $90,315 in compensatory damages, $34,900 in attorney's fees, and more than $90,000 back pay to three employees. OSHA found that the company violated the whistleblower provisions of the Federal Railroad Safety Act by firing two employees and suspending one for reporting a work-related injury and discussing concerns about safety hazards in the workplace. The railroad was also ordered to train managers, supervisors, and employees about whistleblowers' rights. [Tara Cantore, *Union Pacific Fined for Retaliation against Whistleblowers*, plansponsor.com (Aug. 26, 2011)]

In addition to its workplace safety responsibilities, OSHA is responsible for enforcing several federal whistleblower statutes, although the Sarbanes-Oxley Act is the only one that deals with financial wrongdoing rather than health and safety.

The federal Sarbanes-Oxley Act [Pub. L. No. 107-204] (also discussed in this book in connection with 401(k) plans and corporate communications—notices to employees about "blackout" periods that restrict their abilities to trade their plan accounts) includes two provisions to protect whistleblowers.

In 2013, the Second Circuit clarified the standard for analyzing Sarbanes-Oxley whistleblower retaliation claims (18 U.S.C. § 1514A). J. Scott Bechtel, VP of technology commercialization for Competitive Technologies Inc., said that he was fired for saying the company should make more Sarbanes-Oxley disclosures.

CTI said he was fired as part of a cost-cutting drive. He filed an OSHA whistleblower complaint. In 2005, OSHA found reasonable cause to believe CTI violated OSHA and ordered Bechtel reinstated with back pay and compensatory damages. Eventually, the ALJ dismissed Bechtel's complaint in 2011. The Second Circuit said that Bechtel had to prove by a preponderance of the evidence that he was engaged in protected activity; that CTI knew it; and that the protected activity was a contributing factor in the adverse employment action. The employer can rebut with clear and convincing evidence it would have done the same thing without protected activity. [*Bechtel v. Administrative Review Bd.*, 710 F.3d 443 (2d Cir. 2013); see Mark Hamblett, *Standard for SOX Whistleblower Retaliation Claims is Clarified*, N.Y.L.J. (Mar. 6, 2013) (law.com)]

The economic stimulus bill ARRA (American Recovery and Reinvestment Act), Pub. L. No. 111-5, includes the McCaskill Act, which gives Sarbanes-Oxley whistleblower employees the right to a jury trial. Employers that receive federal stimulus funds are required to notify employees of their rights as whistleblowers. Any employer (other than a federal agency) that receives stimulus funds is forbidden to fire, demote, or otherwise discriminate against an employee who makes disclosures to a supervisor, regulatory agency, law enforcement agency, grand jury, or court, if the information represents the employee's reasonable belief that the information proves gross mismanagement or waste of stimulus funds. [Maribeth L. Minella, *Stimulus Package Provides for Employee Whistleblower Protection* <http://www.delawareemploymentlawblog.com/2009/02/stimulus-package-provides-for.html> (Feb. 27, 2009)]

Under § 806 of the Sarbanes-Oxley Act, 18 U.S.C. § 1514A is amended to provide that publicly traded companies are forbidden to "discharge, demote, suspend, threaten, harass, or in any other manner discriminate against an employee in the terms and conditions of employment" because the employee has engaged in any lawful act to provide information to the government or participate in an investigation of securities fraud or corporate wrongdoing. (The lawful acts condition is important—whistleblowers are not protected if they commit burglaries or hack computer systems to get this information, for example.)

Someone who believes that he or she has been discriminated against for whistleblowing can file a complaint with the Secretary of Labor; if, after 180 days, the Secretary has not issued a final decision, the whistleblower can sue in federal district court (even if the amount in controversy is below the $75,000 usually required to get to federal court). The Sarbanes-Oxley Act provides for whatever relief is necessary to make a successful whistleblower claimant whole—i.e., compensatory damages, reinstatement with whatever seniority the person would have had without discrimination, back pay plus interest, and compensation for special damages such as attorneys' fees, expert witness fees, and costs.

Also see Sarbanes-Oxley Act § 1107, which provides for fines and/or up to 10 years' imprisonment, for knowing harmful actions, taken with intent to retaliate against someone who provided truthful information about Sarbanes-Oxley violations to any law enforcement officer. This provision covers all actions, including interference with any person's lawful employment or livelihood.

Companies can take steps to encourage employees to report internally rather than immediately contacting outside agencies. The company should have a clear reporting chain, and make sure that information is transmitted to the proper decision-maker. The reporting mechanism should be easy to use and should be explained to employees. Reports should be encouraged, because they can be instrumental in saving the company's reputation by solving problems before they become untenable. In some cases, it is worth allowing customers, suppliers, and consultants to report internally because their outsider perspective can be useful—and they might otherwise be encouraged to seek bounties. [Alexandra Wrage, *8 Ways to Encourage Whistleblowers to Report Internally*, Compliance Insider (May 10, 2012) (law.com)]

The Second Circuit held that whistleblower claims under the Sarbanes-Oxley Act are arbitrable, rejecting the plaintiff's arguments that arbitration does not provide adequate accountability or transparency and does not furnish information that would encourage other employees to make meritorious claims of their own. [*Guyden v. Aetna Inc.*, 544 F.3d 376 (2d Cir. 2008); see Mark Hamblett, *Whistleblower Claims Arbitrable Under SOX, 2nd Circuit Determines*, N.Y.L.J. (Oct. 6, 2008) (law.com)]

Mutual funds are usually organized as publicly traded companies that do not have any employees. Instead, they enter into contracts with private (non-publicly traded) companies that do have employees to provide advice and other services to the mutual funds. In early 2014, the Supreme Court held that Sarbanes-Oxley Act protection against retaliation covers employees of private companies that are contractors for public corporations. The 6–3 majority reached this result because the law was passed in response to the Enron scandal, and such coverage would meet the legislative objective. The plaintiffs were employees of a private subcontractor that advised Fidelity mutual funds; Jackie Lawson and Jonathan Zang (the plaintiffs) were terminated for informing bosses and SEC of their suspicions that Fidelity violated securities laws. (They could not use the Dodd-Frank whistleblower provisions because their actions occurred before Dodd-Frank took effect.) [*Lawson v. FMR Inc.*, 134 S. Ct. 1158 (2014); see Tony Mauro, *Justices Deliver Rare Win For Whistleblowers*, Legal Times (Mar. 4, 2014), available at law.com]

The Dodd-Frank Wall Street Reform and Consumer Protection Act of 2010, Pub. L. No. 111-203, includes an incentive provision for whistleblowers, even if the claim involves a privately held corporation not subject to Sarbanes-Oxley. If whistleblowers voluntarily provide information that leads the federal government to recover more than $1 million for a violation of the federal securities laws (including the Foreign Corrupt Practices Act, abbreviated as FCPA), the SEC has discretion to award them between 10% and 30% of the part of the recovery over and above $1 million. Awards are only available for providing original information, not already available through existing investigations or reports—and that the SEC did not already have. Several very large FCPA penalties had been assessed shortly before the Dodd-Frank Act passed, such as $1.6 billion imposed on Siemens AG and $335 million against Snamprogetti Netherlands B.V. [See Bethany Hensbach, *Whistleblower Provision Likely to Increase FCPA Risk*, <http://www.governmentcontractslawblog.com/2010/08/articles/fcpa/whistleblower-provision-likely-to-increase-fcpa-risk> (Aug. 4, 2010)]

The SEC published final rules about the whistleblower program in May 2011. The rules enhance rewards for employees who go through channels within their company before approaching the SEC; those who go directly to the SEC, without giving the employer a chance to correct the problem, get lower rewards. Employees have up to 120 days after making an internal complaint to go to the SEC. Whistleblowers can get credit if they report a minor violation that would not otherwise qualify for a bounty, if their complaint leads to an internal investigation that uncovers additional wrongdoing that the company discloses to the SEC. [Final rules for the program: <http://www.sec.gov/rules/final/2011/34-64545.pdf> (May 25, 2011) and 76 Fed. Reg. 34300 (June 13, 2011)]

In addition to the SEC rules, there are OSHA rules implementing Dodd-Frank § 1057. The OSHA rules, published in April, 2014, deal with the timing and process for filing an OSHA complaint, and explain OSHA's investigation and appeals methodologies. A person who charges retaliation can file a complaint in the local OSHA office, within 180 days of the alleged retaliatory act. OSHA contacts the respondent, and both sides have 20 days to submit their written statements and evidence. OSHA determines whether or not the complainant has made out a prima facie case that protected activity was a contributing factor in the adverse employment action. But even if a prima facie case has been made, OSHA will not investigate if the employer provides clear and convincing evidence that the same adverse action would have been taken even if there had been no protected activity. [79 Fed. Reg. 18630 (Apr. 3, 2014). See Steven J. Pearlman, Harris Mufson and Allison Lynn Martin, *OSHA Releases Interim Dodd-Frank Whistleblower Regulations*, Proskauer Rose LLP (Apr. 11, 2014), available at Lexology.com]

The SEC paid its sixth whistleblower award in late 2013: $150,000, 30% of the amount collected, for helping to halt a scheme to defraud investors. The fifth award, a month earlier, was for $14 million. In June 2013, three awards were made in the case against hedge fund Locus Offshore Management LLC and its CEO, Andrey Hicks. [Jenna Greene, *With Sixth Payout, SEC Whistleblower Program Gains Steam*, The BLT: Blog of Legal Times (Oct. 31, 2013), available at law.com] In April 2014, the SEC announced that the person who received the first whistleblower award, in 2012, would receive at least one more payment from the SEC. The first payment was based on what the SEC had actually collected, not the court award; as the SEC collects more from the wrongdoer, the whistleblower will receive more money. (The names of the tipster and the company involved were not divulged.) There might also be subsequent payments in the Hicks case.

[Rachel Louise Ensign, *SEC Hands Out More to First-Ever Whistleblower*, WSJ .com (Apr. 4, 2014)]

In mid-2014, the SEC resolved its first Dodd-Frank retaliation case (as distinct from making awards to whistleblowers who reported improprieties). The head trader at a hedge fund reported that the fund engaged in transactions that violated the Investment Advisers Act of 1940. The fund took adverse employment action, and the trader eventually resigned. The fund agreed to pay more than $2.1 million to settle the SEC charges, including a $300,000 civil penalty. It was not disclosed what proportion of those amounts reflected the retaliation charge rather than the underlying Investment Advisers Act violations. [Sutherland Asbill & Brennan LLP Legal Alert, *SEC Launches First Whistleblower Retaliation Case Under Dodd-Frank* (June 20, 2014) (benefitslink.com)]

The SEC's whistleblower rules under the Dodd-Frank Act affect three aspects of corporate internal investigations:

- Teaching employees about the corporation's internal controls;
- Performing the investigation;
- Dealing with regulators.

Dodd-Frank protects whistleblowers whether or not the SEC actually investigates the complaint, if it found any violations, or the whistleblower actually received an award. However, if the employee does not learn about the potential violation that he or she reported from a corporate attorney in the course of a corporate investigation, Rule 21F-4(b)(4)(vi) says that the whistleblower is not the source of the information, and therefore cannot receive an award. [Steven S. Sparling and Arielle Warshall Katz, *Internal Investigation Strategies in a Post Dodd-Frank World*, N.Y.L.J. (Aug. 11, 2011) (law.com)]

The District Court for the District of Nebraska ruled that a report to the SEC is not required for protection against retaliation (although it is required to collect a bounty). The district court ruled that disclosing the results of her internal investigation to FINRA was the equivalent of complying with an SEC rule, because the SEC must approve all FINRA rules and is entitled to amend them. [*Bussing v. Legent Clearing LLC*, No. 8:12-cv-002 38 (D. Neb. 2014); see Samuel Rubenfeld, *Judge Rules Whistleblowers Don't Have to Report to SEC to Get Protection*, WSJ.com (May 30, 2014)]

In a Dodd-Frank whistleblower suit, the plaintiff charged that he was unlawfully terminated as compliance manager in retaliation for reporting violations to the SEC and the Public Company Accounting Oversight Board. He asked for punitive damages and a jury trial. Although he acknowledged that punitive damages were not currently available, he asked for his request to be dismissed without prejudice in case judicial interpretation of the statute changes. The District Court for the Northern District of Georgia rejected the request, holding that the plaintiff can appeal based on any later changes in the rules. The whistleblower provisions of the Dodd-Frank Act do not specify whether jury trial is available (although Dodd-Frank made jury trial available in Sarbanes-Oxley Act § 806 whistleblower cases), so the district court's analysis was based on legal history (whether English courts treated similar suits as arising in law or equity) and whether the plaintiff seeks legal or equitable remedies. The district court found some factors suggesting both: the Dodd-Frank whistleblower claim is similar to the common-law tort of wrongful discharge, for which jury trial is available, but reinstatement, hiring, and back pay are usually considered equitable remedies. On balance, the district court decided that jury trial was unavailable. The principal Dodd-Frank remedies are equitable (reinstatement and back pay). Back pay awards are automatically doubled, but because this is automatic, it is not like monetary damages awarded at the discretion of the jury. Unlike ADEA liquidated damages, doubling does not require a finding that the employer acted willfully. [*Pruett v. BlueLinx Holdings, Inc.*, No. 1:13-cv-02607-JOF, 2013 U.S. Dist. LEXIS 185551 (N.D. Ga. Nov. 12, 2013); see Steven J. Pearlman and Harris Mufson, *Georgia Federal Court Rules That Dodd-Frank Whistleblowers Are Not Entitled To A Jury Trial*, Proskauer Rose LLP (Nov. 14, 2013), available at Lexology.com; Steve Quinlivan, *Whistleblower Not Entitled To Jury Trial*, Leonard, Street and Deinard (Nov. 13, 2013), available at Lexology.com]

The Tenth Circuit held that protection is not limited to reporting fraud against shareholders. Retaliation against any SEC rule is covered—in this case, charging a Lockheed Martin executive with ethics violations in operating a pen pal program for soldiers in Iraq. [*Lockheed Martin Corp. v. Admin. Review Board*, 717 F.3d 1121 (10th Cir. 2013); see Kevin B. Leblang and Robert N. Holtzman, *Whistleblower Claims Under SOX And Dodd-Frank: Recent Developments*, Kramer Levin Naftalis & Frankel LLP (Oct. 3, 2013), available at Lexology.com]

The Fifth Circuit held in mid-2013 that it is necessary to contact the SEC with information about securities law violations to be a Dodd-Frank whistleblower. A person who charges retaliation for filing an internal complaint (in this case, alleged violations of the Foreign Corrupt Practice Act) is not a whistleblower and not protected under the Dodd-Frank Act. [*Asadi v. G.E. Energy LLC*, 720 F.3d 620 (5th Cir. 2013)]

The Third Circuit ruled that all a whistleblower needs is a reasonable belief that the employer has violated or will violate a securities law; the complainant does not have to show that he or she identified a specific statute when making an internal complaint. [*Bechtel v. U.S. DOL*, 710 F.3d 443 (2d Cir. 2013) (Sarbanes-Oxley claim requires whistleblower to prove by a preponderance of the evidence that protected activity was a contributing factor in the adverse employment action; the employer can defend itself with clear and convincing evidence it would have taken the same action without the protected activity—a much higher standard than Title VII, which merely requires a legitimate, nondiscriminatory reason); *Wiest v. Lynch*, 719 F.3d 121 (3d Cir. 2013); see Gregory Keating and Stephen Melnick,

When is a Whistleblower Not a Whistleblower?, Littler Mendelson (Oct. 31, 2013) (benefitslink.com)]

At least five district court cases consider a person who makes an internal report a whistleblower. The District Court for the District of Massachusetts held that an investment banker plaintiff could be a Dodd-Frank whistleblower even though he did not report violations to the SEC until after he was fired. Ellington made an internal report in 2010 about what he called misleading investment reports being distributed to clients. Ellington's charges led the SEC to fine his former employer $200,000. The district court also held that employees can be whistleblowers with respect to conduct that occurred before Dodd-Frank took effect, if Dodd-Frank was in effect when the alleged wrongdoing was reported to the SEC. [*Ellington v. Giacoumakis*, 977 F. Supp. 2d 42 (D. Mass., 2013); see Michael K. Lowman and Keith V. Porapaiboon, *District Court Finds Dodd Frank Anti-Retaliation Protections Apply To Whistleblower Who Went To SEC After Being Fired For Reporting Concerns To Chief Compliance Officer*, Jenner & Block (Oct. 31, 2013), available at Lexology.com; Rachel Louise Ensign, *Another Court Rules in Favor of Internal Whistleblower*, WSJ.com (Oct. 18, 2013)]

The Southern District of New York agreed with a district court in Texas: the Dodd-Frank retaliation provision, 15 U.S.C. § 78u-6(h)(1)(a), does not cover conduct outside the United States. The plaintiff was the Taiwanese compliance officer for the Chinese subsidiary of a German parent corporation. The Southern District said that, although non-U.S. citizens working for non-U.S. subsidiaries can qualify for whistleblower bounty awards, that does not mean that they are covered by the retaliation provision. (The similar Sarbanes-Oxley anti-retaliation provision does not apply extraterritorially either.) Furthermore, the report involved violations of the Foreign Corrupt Practices Act, which is not covered by Sarbanes-Oxley § 806. [*Meng-Lin Liu v. Siemens A.G.*, 978 F. Supp. 2d 325 (S.D.N.Y. 2013); see John F. Fullerton III, *New York Court Finds That Dodd-Frank Whistleblower Anti-Retaliation Provision Does Not Apply Extraterritorially*, Epstein Becker Green (Oct. 23, 2013), available at Lexology.com] The Second Circuit affirmed: No. 13-4385 (2d Cir. Aug. 14, 2014).

In addition to federal statutes, employers risk large verdicts under state statutes, which may have idiosyncratic definitions of "whistleblower." For example, Florida and New Jersey have comprehensive laws that protect employees of private companies who object to unlawful activities, report such activities to government agencies, or participate in government investigations. New York's law is narrower, banning only retaliation for disclosure or threatened disclosure of health care fraud or conduct that substantially endangers public health or safety.

A mental health counselor brought suit under Sarbanes-Oxley and the Florida whistleblower act. She alleged that she was fired for reporting child abuse and fraud to management of the company where she worked. The district court not only granted summary judgment for the defendant on all counts, it awarded attorneys' fees and costs to the defendant. Florida law authorizes a fee award to a prevailing defendant, whereas Sarbanes-Oxley does not. The plaintiff argued that the state provision was preempted by the federal law, but the Eleventh Circuit ruled in mid-2014 that it was not: it is possible to comply with both statutes, and Sarbanes-Oxley is merely silent and does not forbid fee awards to prevailing defendants. [*Smith v. Psychiatric Solutions, Inc.*, 750 F.3d 1253 (11th Cir. 2014); see Daniel A. Krawiec II, *Sarbanes-Oxley Does Not Foreclose Fee Award to Prevailing Employer Under State Law*, Hinshaw & Culbertson (June 2, 2014), available at Lexology.com]

Before 2013, the California Labor Code forbade employers to impair employees' right to report what they reasonably believed to be violations of state or federal law, if reports were made to a government or law enforcement agency. As of January 1, 2014, however, the law extends protection to employees who report illegal behavior internally to a supervisor, to another employee with the power to investigate and cure the violation, or externally to any public body engaged in an investigation. The New Jersey Law Against Discrimination has been amended to forbid retaliation for requesting employment information to investigate discrimination or sue for compensation discrimination. (The law does not require the employer actually to provide the information, only to refrain from retaliation.) Minnesota amended its whistleblower law to clarify that the law is a broad one that forbids penalties against employees for good-faith reporting of a violation, suspected violation, or planned violation of law. [*Mooney v. Atlantic City*, No. L00204710 (N.J. Super. Ct. Law Div. Oct. 17, 2013); *Cadwell v. City of Highland Park*, 2013 WL 3971570 (Mich. Cir. Ct. Feb. 25, 2013); see Harris Mufson and Noa Badish, *State Whistleblowing Laws Provide Whopping Verdicts*, Nat'l L.J. (Jan. 23, 2014), available at law.com]

A Minnesota jury awarded $395,000 under state whistleblower law to Heidi Weber, former dean of a for-profit university's medical assistant program. She complained to school officials that they did not train students adequately, lied to them about their career prospects, and paid commissions to staff to boost enrollment. She was fired in 2011, allegedly for poor performance and lack of leadership. The court found that complaining to her supervisor was protected whistleblower activity. She was awarded $205,000 in lost wages and $190,000 in emotional distress damages. [*Weber v. Minnesota Sch. of Business, Inc., d/b/a/ Globe Univ.*, No. 82-cv-12-2797 (Minnesota 2013). See Steven J. Pearlman and Amanda C. Wiley, *Minnesota Jury Awards Whistleblowing Dean Nearly $400,000*, Proskauer Rose LLP (Sept. 3, 2013), available at Lexology.com. Weber was subsequently awarded $500,000 in attorneys' fees and costs, plus $70,000 in pre-judgment interest: see Kevin Mahoney, *Whistleblower Lawsuit Costs Globe University Nearly $1M*, <http://tcbmag.com/News/Recent-News/2014/February/Whistleblower-Lawsuit-Now-Costs-Globe-University-N> (Feb. 20, 2014).]

Employees of Department of Defense (DOD) prime contractors had partial protection under the Defense Contractor Whistleblower Act, 10 U.S.C. § 2409, and under the False Claims Act's anti-retaliation provisions. But protection was limited to disclosure of information about mismanagement of DOD grants or contracts, dangers to public health or safety, or violations of law relating to the DOD contract or grant. Disclosures were only protected if made to a member of Congress, the Inspector General, or certain DOD or DOJ officials. Additional protection is provided by National Defense Authorization Act of 2013, § 827, the Enhancement of Whistleblower Protections for Contractor Employees of the Department of Defense, which took effect January 1, 2013. Protection now extends to employees of DOD subcontractors, not just prime contractors, whatever the size of the contract, and a broader range of reporting is covered. The Department of Defense published regulations on September 30, 2013 implementing this statute. Contracting officers must include notice of the whistleblower clause in all solicitations and contracts issued on or after September 30, 2013. [Mary E. Pivec and Igor M. Babichenko, *DOD Publishes Emergency Interim Final Rule Protecting Whistleblowers Employed Under A DOD Contract Or Subcontract*, Williams Mullen (Oct. 11, 2013), available at Lexology.com]

[C] WC Claimants

Retaliation against employees who have filed Worker's Compensation claims is unlawful, because public policy favors injured employees receiving income to replace the income lost when they are injured.

Minnesota permits termination for dishonest behavior, including filing a false Worker's Compensation (WC) claim. However, WC law forbids retaliatory discharge for applying for WC benefits. The District Court for the District of Minnesota ruled that summary judgment was unavailable in the case of an employee who said that she was injured by slipping in the company parking lot during breaks. The video from the parking lot did not show her falling. Her insurance claim was denied and she was fired for filing a false claim. The district court held that the employer's investigation was incomplete. The video was of poor quality, and some footage had been deleted; the plaintiff could also have been outside camera range when she fell. The employer did not ask the plaintiff's doctor if her injuries were consistent with her account of the fall. [*Schaefer v. BioLife Plasma LLC*, Civil No. 11-3468, 2013 U.S. Dist. LEXIS 133343 (D. Minn. Sept. 18, 2013); see Michael T. Miller, *Beware The Danger Of Firing An Employee For An Allegedly False Workers Compensation Claim*, Briggs and Morgan (Oct. 1, 2013), available at Lexology.com]

Continental Tire fired a 22-year veteran trucker who refused to take a mandatory drug test after being involved in an accident. He brought a suit for retaliatory termination for filing a Worker's Compensation claim. The Seventh Circuit held that there was no evidence that the employer's explanation—that he was fired for refusing to be tested—was not true. Nor could he prove that requiring post-accident drug testing discouraged employees from filing Worker's Compensation claims. [*Phillips v. Continental Tire The Americas LLC*, 743 F.3d 475 (7th

Cir. 2014); see Amanda Mattocks, *Seventh Circuit: Employee Failed to Establish Link Between Termination and Filing of Workers' Comp Claim*, Hinshaw & Culbertson (Mar. 25, 2014), available at Lexology.com]

In mid-2011, the Ohio Supreme Court held that a machine shop worker who was fired within an hour of reporting a workplace injury—but before he could apply for WC benefits—could sue his ex-employer under the state law forbidding retaliation for making WC claims. [*Sutton v. Tomco* (Ohio 2011); see Sara Kelly, *Court Rules on Injured Worker's Wrongful Termination*, plansponsor.com (June 10, 2011)]

In some ways, termination cases about unemployment insurance raise similar issues about applications and qualification for benefits. The Minnesota Supreme Court held that it is not a violation of public policy to fire an employee for applying for unemployment benefits. (The plaintiff applied for benefits after her work hours were reduced.) Minnesota forbids firing employees who refuse in good faith to violate the law, but the plaintiff in this case did not allege that she was required to commit an illegal act. The court refused to expand the cause of action to cover all terminations that violate public policy. However, it is a misdemeanor under state law for an employer to impede or obstruct an unemployment application. [*Dukowitz v. Hannon Security Servs.*, 164 Lab. Cas. (CCH) P61,435, 97 Empl. Prac. Dec. (CCH) P44,984, 841 N.W.2d 147 (Minn. 2014); see Michael C. Wilhelm, *Can You Fire An Employee For Applying For Unemployment Benefits?*, Briggs and Morgan (Jan. 7, 2014), available at Lexology.com]

§ 39.05 PREEMPTION ARGUMENTS

Preemption is the legal doctrine under which passage of a federal law limits or eliminates the state's power to regulate that subject. ERISA preempts state wrongful termination claims based on alleged termination to avoid paying pension benefits. All such claims must be brought in federal court, under ERISA § 510, and not in state court.

The Family and Medical Leave Act preempts common-law claims of retaliatory discharge when an employee says he or she was fired as punishment for taking FMLA leave. [*Hamros v. Bethany Homes*, 894 F. Supp. 1176 (N.D. Ill. 1995)]

The Sixth Circuit upheld the dismissal of a wrongful termination suit brought by a former Whirlpool executive. Lewis charged that he was fired, in violation of public policy, because he refused to commit the Unfair Labor Practice of firing employees for engaging in union activism. The Sixth Circuit held that Lewis' claim was preempted by the NLRA, so he should have raised his claim before the NLRB. (In fact he did, but the NLRB found that his charge was without merit.) Supervisors are generally excluded from coverage under the NLRA, but there is a cause of action for termination or other discipline for refusing to commit Unfair Labor Practices—but the NLRB has exclusive jurisdiction over such claims. [*Lewis v. Whirlpool Corp.*, 630 F.3d 484 (6th Cir. 2011)]

However, National Labor Relations Act §§ 7 and 8 do not so completely preempt state wrongful discharge claims that the state claims can be removed to federal court. In 2005 the Fourth Circuit held that preemption depends on a preexisting federal cause of action, and the wrongful discharge case was not based on the right to bargain collectively or the ban on unfair labor practices. [*Lontz v. Tharp*, 413 F.3d 435 (4th Cir. 2005)]

Preemption arguments can also be used in state court. If the employee is covered by a state antidiscrimination law that is not preempted by federal law, the employer may be able to get a wrongful termination suit dismissed, because the employee should have sued for discrimination. From the employer's viewpoint, the best-case scenario is that the employee waited too long, so the discrimination charges must be dismissed.

CHAPTER 40

ARBITRATION AND ADR

§ 40.01 INTRODUCTION

For many years, arbitration was a minor and somewhat disfavored part of the legal system. Today, after a long series of pro-arbitration Supreme Court decisions, it is a central part of employer-employee relations (as well as business-consumer relations and commercial arbitration, which are beyond the scope of this book). Arbitration is no longer limited to cases involving unions and unionized employees, and it is very common for employers to require employees to arbitrate work-related disputes, including discrimination charges, rather than litigating them.

Alternative Dispute Resolution (ADR) methods are supposed to be informal, governed more by justice and fairness than by strict rules of legal procedure. Depending on the ADR method, either one person or a panel of people will either assist the parties to work out their own solution (mediation) or will make a decision (arbitration). It has been estimated that an employment lawsuit takes an average of a year and a half from the date the case is filed to resolve, versus only one year for arbitration. Once the case gets to the arbitrator, 90% of arbitration hearings are completed in two days or less.

Both unionized and nonunionized companies often find mediation or arbitration a superior alternative to litigation when employees make claims that they have suffered employment discrimination. In fact, employers often use various methods to make sure that all claims will have to go through arbitration. The question is when and how it is legitimate to impose an arbitration requirement on employees. If the employees freely choose arbitration over litigation, this problem does not arise, but nevertheless, the employer will still have to find a way to present its case effectively to the arbitrator.

The "first principles" of arbitration are that arbitration should be independent of the court system and should provide flexibility and respect the rights of the parties.

The federal statute known as the Railway Labor Act was enacted to resolve labor disputes. It requires minor disputes to be arbitrated before two labor and two industry representatives, plus a neutral referee to break tie votes. First, the parties must engage in "on-property proceedings" (going through the full grievance procedure under the CBA), and try to get a settlement "in conference." If they cannot agree, either side can refer the matter to the National Railroad Adjustment Board for arbitration. An arbitrator's order can be reviewed by the courts for failure to comply with the requirements of the Railway Labor Act, for not confining itself to matters within the jurisdiction of the Board, or for fraud or corruption. There was a circuit split over whether NRAB proceedings can also be reviewed for due process violations as well as these statutory grounds for review. In late 2009, the Supreme Court ruled that statutory and not Constitutional analysis should be applied. As long as a respondent does not seek to modify the Board's judgment, it can cite any information that appears in the record to support the Board's judgment. The Supreme Court held that the requirement to "conference" the dispute is not jurisdictional, so it is not necessary to prove that the dispute was conferenced before the Board hears a dispute. [*Union Pac. R.R. Co. v. Brotherhood of Locomotive Eng'rs*, 558 U.S. 67 (2009)]

OSHA receives approximately 2,500 whistleblower complaints a year under the 22 statutes it administers. The agency launched an ADR pilot program for its Whistleblower Protection Program in its Chicago and San Francisco regions, offering voluntary early resolution and mediation. The early resolution program attempts to resolve disputes even before there has been a formal investigation. The mediation program involves either the Federal Mediation and Conciliation Services or an attorney selected by the parties as a trusted third party. [OSHA Directive 12-01 (October 2012); see Edwin G. Foulke Jr., *OSHA Announces Alternative Dispute Resolution Pilot Program*, Fisher & Phillips LLP (Oct. 17, 2013), available at Lexology.com]

§ 40.02 GRIEVANCES AND DISCIPLINE

[A] "Progressive Discipline"

The typical Collective Bargaining Agreement (CBA) for a unionized company spells out a system of "progressive discipline" under which employees whose work performance is unsatisfactory will be warned, offered guidance and training, and given a series of escalating penalties before being fired. Progressive discipline is sometimes used in nonunionized environment, although less frequently.

The system must make it clear to employees what the employer's expectations are and what the employer intends to do if the rules are violated. Once employees have been told what they are doing wrong, they should be given a reasonable amount of time to correct it. There should be a monitoring process to sort out the employees who have made adequate progress from those who have not. The time period should probably be between 30 and 90 days: Too long a period may make the arbitrator believe that the employer is stringing together isolated, unrelated incidents to make a case.

Employees who have been subject to discipline are likely to feel that they were unfairly singled out—and in some cases, this will result in discrimination or wrongful termination charges. An important HR function is creating a legally sustainable system of progressive discipline, and making sure that supervisors understand the system and apply it objectively.

A legally sustainable disciplinary system should be:

- Consistent—not only must discrimination be avoided but employees should not be subjected to supervisors' whims or penalized when the supervisor has a bad day;

- Well documented—an arbitrator or court should be able to see that each step reflects the employer's own rules;
- Clear—employees should know that if they fail to meet X goals in Y days, they will be put on probation, lose wages, or be terminated;
- Appropriate—the degree of the sanction should reflect the severity of the error or misconduct;
- Reciprocal—employees should get a chance to give their side of the story to an objective decision maker who isn't already committed to management's viewpoint.

Arbitrators will examine the "step formula" under the system and see if it was followed. For example, if the first step results in a determination that the employee was at fault, then he or she might be verbally admonished, whereas by the fourth step, dismissal could be appropriate. If the step formula is not followed, the arbitrator is likely to reverse the decision or substitute a lesser penalty, and there's a good chance that the courts will uphold the arbitrator.

Presenting grievances to the employer is one of the clearest cases of concerted activity protected by the NLRA, whether or not the employees are unionized. However, they must in fact act in concert, or one employee must present a shared grievance. One person pressing his or her own agenda is not protected under the NLRA. For NLRA purposes, a grievance must be something that relates directly to the terms and conditions of employment.

Once they have made a complaint, employees are required to return to work within a reasonable time. In fact, one of the bywords of labor arbitration is "obey now, grieve later."

[B] Grievance Records

It makes sense to buy or design standard forms for keeping track of employee grievances, although there is no specific federal requirement for making such records or keeping them for a particular length of time. The grievance form should contain:

- Identification of the CBA that creates the grievance procedure and the specific clause of that contract that has to be interpreted;
- Date the grievance was submitted;
- Grievance case number;
- Name, department, shift, and job title of the employee who submits the grievance;
- What the employee says is wrong;

- Records of statements by witnesses;
- Documentary evidence relevant to the grievance;
- Whether the employee was represented (e.g., by the shop steward or a fellow employee);
- Written decisions by the first-level supervisor or others involved in processing the grievance;
- A signed statement by the union representative as to whether the union considers the grievance to be adequately resolved;
- Signatures of the employee and all decision makers.

It can be very helpful to analyze past grievances to see how patterns change over time.

[C] NLRB Deference

Although the NLRB has the power, under the NLRA § 10(a), to prevent unfair labor practices, the NLRB will defer to grievance arbitration (i.e., will not interfere) if several criteria are satisfied:

- Understanding the meaning of the CBA is central to resolving the dispute;
- The dispute came up during an ongoing collective bargaining relationship;
- The employees do not claim that the employer prevented them from exercising all their rights under labor law;
- The employer has agreed to a broad-based arbitration clause—in fact, one broad enough to cover the existing dispute.

§ 40.03 MEDIATION

A mediator is a neutral third party who listens to both sides and helps the parties themselves work out a solution that is acceptable to both of them. The American Arbitration Association has a set of uniform Employment Mediation Rules. Parties can trigger this procedure by writing a request to the AAA for mediation, or by filing a Submission to Mediation form, also with the AAA.

One reason that the procedure for filing discrimination charges is so elaborate is that part of the EEOC's job is to attempt mediation of the charge. [See Chapter 41]

§ 40.04 ARBITRATION VS. LITIGATION

Opponents of mandatory arbitration state that the process is pro-employer, not only because it restricts discovery and limits the remedies available to a successful plaintiff, but because there is a risk that arbitrators will (consciously or unconsciously) favor employers. Employers are much more likely to need to choose arbitrators in the future than employees, who typically are involved in only one case.

Many cases have arisen in the court system because one party wants to litigate a dispute and the other says that arbitration is required. The court system then has to determine what parts of the dispute—if any—must be resolved by judges, and what parts are to be decided by arbitrators. The Supreme Court rendered two major decisions on this issue in mid-2010.

The first one was brought by an account manager who sued his former employer, charging that he was subjected to racial discrimination and retaliation. The employer cited the mandatory arbitration agreement to show that the case had to be arbitrated. Jackson, the plaintiff, argued that the arbitration agreement was unconscionable under state law and therefore unenforceable.

The arbitration agreement gave the arbitrator sole authority to resolve disputes about the interpretation, applicability, enforceability, or formation of the agreement. The Supreme Court ruled that it is up to the arbitrator, not the court system, to decide the unconscionability of the entire agreement—if the agreement includes a "delegation clause" that gives the arbitrator this power. In this case, however, the Supreme Court said that Jackson used a mistaken strategy. He challenged the validity of the agreement as a whole, and did not challenge the validity of the delegation clause until his case had reached the Supreme Court, by which time it was too late to raise a new argument. [*Rent-a-Center West v. Jackson*, 561 U.S. 63 (2010)]

Shortly thereafter, when the Supreme Court returned to the question of arbitrators' powers, the Supreme Court ruled that it was up to the district court and not the arbitrator to decide when a CBA had been officially ratified. (The dispute was about whether a strike was unlawful because it violated the no-strike clause in the CBA—which, in turn, required determining when the contract took effect.) The Supreme Court ruled that a court can order arbitration only based on a finding that the parties agreed to arbitrate that type of dispute—including resolving any issues about the validity of the arbitration clause. Because the federal system favors arbitration, there is a presumption of arbitrability—but it applies only if there is a valid arbitration agreement and a question about whether the agreement covers the actual dispute between the parties. The Supreme Court said that in that situation, the court should order arbitration only if the presumption of arbitrability has not been rebutted by the party seeking to litigate the dispute. [*Granite Rock Co. v. Int'l Brotherhood of Teamsters*, 561 U.S. 287 (2010).

Although it is not an employment decision (it involves consumers who wanted to bring a class arbitration about sales tax charged on "free" cell phones), the 2011 Supreme Court decision in *AT&T Mobility LLC v. Concepcion*, 131 S. Ct. 1740 (2011) has often been interpreted to mean that the federal policy in favor of arbitration is so strong that state rulings that arbitration agreements are unconscionable will be preempted.

After *Concepcion*, Nordstrom revised its employee handbook to state that most arbitration class actions were forbidden. When an employee nevertheless filed a class action alleging violation of a number of federal and state employment laws, the Ninth Circuit held that the revision constituted a valid arbitration agreement, and remanded to the district court to order individual arbitration. [*Davis v. Nordstrom, Inc.*, No. 12-17403 (9th Cir. June 23, 2014)]

In a late 2012 summary ruling, the Supreme Court held that the Oklahoma Supreme Court was wrong to hold that the noncompete provisions in two employment contracts were void. (The state court said that the provisions violated the state's public policy against noncompete clauses.) The Supreme Court said that the decision should have been made by the arbitrator. The employment contracts included an arbitration clause covering "any dispute, difference or unresolved question." The two plaintiffs quit their jobs and went to work for a competitor. Their former employer Nitro-Lift demanded arbitration. The plaintiffs sued in Oklahoma state court to enjoin enforcement of the noncompete clauses, which they alleged were null and void. The trial court ordered arbitration, but the Oklahoma Supreme Court asked the parties to show why the state law limiting enforceability of noncompete agreements should not apply. The Supreme Court held that federal substantive law under the FAA applies in both state and federal courts. If an arbitration clause is severable, then its validity is determined by the court system. But attacks on the validity of the contract, not just the validity of the arbitration clause, are resolved by an arbitrator. If the arbitration clause is valid, the validity of the rest of the contract is decided by the arbitrator. [*Nitro-Lift Techs., LLC v. Howard*, 133 S. Ct. 500 (2012)]

The NLRB rejected an arbitration agreement that required employees to waive the option of class arbitration on the grounds that filing a class or collective action about wages, hours, or working conditions is protected concerted activity, whether it occurs in court or before an arbitrator. The NLRB held that employees, whether or not they are unionized, cannot be forced to waive class arbitration. The NLRB said that *AT&T Mobility* was not relevant because it is a consumer class action case, whereas here the employees wanted to enforce substantive workplace rights granted by the NLRA. Furthermore, in the NLRB's view, *AT&T Mobility* involved a conflict between the FAA and state law, triggering the Supremacy Clause of the Constitution—whereas here there is a possible conflict between two federal statutes (the FAA and the NLRA). This decision is subject to review by the Eleventh Circuit or D.C. Circuit. [*D.R. Horton Inc. and Michael Cuda* Case No. 12-CA-25764 (N.L.R.B. Jan. 3, 2012); see Scott Graham, *AT&T Mobility Doesn't Apply in the Workplace, Says NLRB*, Corporate Counsel (Jan. 9, 2012) (law.com); Philip M. Berkowitz, *Developments in Arbitration of Employment Claims*, N.Y.L.J. (Jan. 12, 2012) (law.com)].

However, the Fifth Circuit held that the NLRB was wrong: it is permissible for an employer to impose a class action arbitration waiver; it is not inconsistent with the employees' legal right under the NLRA to pursue collective action. But the Fifth Circuit held that the arbitration agreement must clarify that employees do not waive the right to file NLRB complaints. [*D.R.Horton v. NLRB*, 737 F.3d 344 (5th Cir. 2013); see AP, *Court Blocks Labor Board on Lawsuits*, NYTimes.com (Dec. 3, 2013) *reh'g denied* No. 12-60031 (Apr. 16, 2014)]

Shortly before a merger obtained regulatory approval, an employee who had an employment contract was terminated without cause, triggering payment of a lump-sum severance benefit. The employee said that he did not receive all the benefits he was entitled to, and sought arbitration. The employer moved in the District Court for the District of South Dakota to enjoin arbitration, asserting that the employment contract was an ERISA severance plan, so ERISA preempted the demand for arbitration. The Eighth Circuit held that the employment contract was not an ERISA plan because it covered only one person, but remanded the case because parts of the complaint might be subject to ERISA preemption because of its relation to other plans that are ERISA plans. [*Dakota, Minnesota & Eastern Railroad Corp. v. Schieffer*, 648 F.3d 935 (8th Cir. 2011); see PLC, *One-Person Employment Contract Not an ERISA Plan: Eighth Circuit* (Aug. 15, 2011) (benefitslink.com)]

§ 40.05 LABOR ARBITRATION

[A] Grievance Arbitration and Contract or Interest Arbitration

Arbitration and mediation have a long history as means to settle disputes between labor and management without a strike and without litigation. By agreeing to arbitrate an issue, in effect the union agrees not to strike over that issue. The employer agrees not to take unilateral action.

The two main types of labor arbitration are grievance arbitration (also known as rights arbitration), used when there is a disagreement about interpretation of an existing contract, and contract or interest arbitration, invoked when the parties are not sure which provisions should be included in a new, renewed, or reopened CBA. However, this promotes a somewhat different mind-set from the type of arbitration discussed later in this chapter, where the focus is not on avoiding a strike dealing with an entire bargaining unit, but a court case involving one person's discrimination charge.

Nearly all collective bargaining agreements allow for an in-house grievance procedure, but if that does not resolve the problem, then final, binding arbitration, resulting in a decree that can be enforced by the court system, is the last part of the procedure.

Organizations such as the American Arbitration Association and the Federal Mediation and Conciliation Service maintain lists of qualified arbitrators, who are familiar both with the conditions in a particular industry and with arbitration rules and practices. If there will be only one arbitrator, then both sides will have to agree on an acceptable arbitrator. If there are three arbitrators, usually each side selects one arbitrator, and the two arbitrators select the third.

As a preliminary step, the employer and union try to agree on a statement of the issues involved in the grievance. If they cannot even agree on that, the arbitrator may have to draft the statement.

■ **TIP:** If the employer wants to discharge or discipline an employee, it will proceed first in arbitration; in other matters, the union usually proceeds first.

[B] Arbitrability

If it is not clear whether a company has agreed to submit a particular issue to arbitration, then the issue is arbitrable. This principle comes from "The Steelworkers' Trilogy," three cases decided by the Supreme Court in 1960. [*Steelworkers v. American Mfg. Co.*, 363 U.S. 564 (1960); *United Steelworkers of Am. v. Warrior Gulf Navigation Co.*, 363 U.S. 574 (1960); *United Steelworkers of Am. v. Enter. Wheel & Car Corp.*, 363 U.S. 593 (1960)] If a CBA contains both an arbitration clause and a no-strike clause, any dispute that involves the application and interpretation of the CBA is arbitrable unless arbitration is specifically ruled out by the terms of the contract.

Under the Steelworkers' Trilogy, the language of the CBA is the first thing the arbitrators consult, but this is not the only factor in the analysis. The "law of the shop" (practices that have evolved in that particular operation) can be considered. Factors such as the effect of the arbitrator's decision on productivity, morale, and workplace tensions are also legitimate considerations. Courts can't review the merits of an arbitration decision or whether a different resolution would have been more sensible. All the court can do is decide whether the arbitration award "draws its essence" from the arbitration agreement.

However, because of a later Supreme Court case [*First Options of Chicago, Inc. v. Kaplan*, 514 U.S. 938 (1995)], the court system rather than the arbitrator decides whether a party agreed to arbitrate a particular type of dispute, if there is no clear, unmistakable evidence of the parties' intentions. There is no right to re-arbitrate an issue already considered by the NLRB in an unfair labor practice proceeding.

When Cooper Tire & Rubber signed a CBA, it also signed a side letter limiting its contributions to retiree health benefits. When a dispute arose about one of the terms of the side letter, the union went to federal court to compel arbitration of the retiree's grievance about the benefits. Management's position was that the side letter covering retiree health benefits did not have an arbitration clause. The Sixth Circuit analyzed the case using a "scope" test: that is, unless the parties agreed to the contrary, disputes about a side agreement are arbitrable if the subject matter of the side agreement falls within the scope of the arbitration clause in the CBA. Therefore, the union had standing to arbitrate on behalf of retirees and their survivors. However, the Sixth Circuit vacated the order certifying a class action, because the district court should have required the union to get the consent of the class members to being represented by the union. [*United Steelworkers of Am. v. Cooper Tire & Rubber Co.*, 474 F.3d 271 (6th Cir. 2007).

The "scope" test is also used in the Third, Seventh, and Ninth Circuits. Other courts have used different formulas: in the Second, Fourth, and Eighth Circuits, if the side agreement deals with matters that are not similar to the subject matter of the CBA, then the side agreement is merely collateral to the CBA and is not covered by its arbitration clause. But if the subject matter of the side agreement is integral to the CBA, then side-agreement disputes are arbitrable. [See, e.g., *United Steelworkers v. The Duluth Clinic, Ltd.*, 413 F.3d 786, 788 (8th Cir. 2005)]

[C] Potentially Arbitrable Issues

Many issues have been found potentially arbitrable. In fact, because collective bargaining and arbitration are complementary processes, the list is similar to the list of issues that are mandatory bargaining subjects:

- Sale of a business;
- Relocation of operations;
- Contracting out bargaining unit work;
- Temporary shutdowns;
- Discharge of an individual employee;
- Layoffs;
- Recalls after a layoff;
- Disputes about work assignments (including assigning supervisors to bargaining unit work);
- Work schedules;
- Classification of work;
- Compensation, including bonuses, overtime pay, incentive pay, and severance;
- Vacation, sick leave, and holidays;
- Seniority systems;

- Safety disputes;
- No-strike clauses.

[D] The Process of Labor Arbitration

In most instances, when management and union hit a deadlock over a grievance or dispute, resort to arbitration will be automatic. However, depending on needs and comparative bargaining power, the arbitration clause might be drafted to allow only the union to invoke arbitration. Employees might also be given the right to invoke arbitration in situations where the union declines to press an employee grievance.

■ **TIP:** Even if the CBA does not include a formal arbitration clause, management and union can sign a "submission agreement" agreeing to be bound by the arbitration decision on a one-time basis.

Arbitration clauses usually call for the involvement of either the Federal Mediation and Conciliation Service (FMCS) or the American Arbitration Association (AAA). However, the parties can agree on other ways to resolve disputes if they so choose.

Arbitration begins with a "demand": Either side invokes the CBA arbitration clause and notifies the appropriate agency. The FMCS can be called in by either management or union to assist in the negotiating process. The FMCS can also offer its services, but cannot demand to be made part of the process. FMCS will not mediate a dispute that has only minor effect on interstate commerce if there are other conciliation services (e.g., state agencies) available. The FMCS can also refuse to intervene on behalf of parties who have a record of noncooperation with arbitration, including failure to pay arbitration fees.

Once an arbitration award is rendered, it is usually final, binding, and not subject to judicial review by any court. In other words, agreeing to submit to arbitration is a very significant decision that cannot be undertaken casually. It will probably be impossible to get any kind of review or have the decision set aside. However, a serious irregularity in the process, such as proof that the arbitrator was not impartial, may justify setting aside the award.

The mission of the Federal Mediation and Conciliation Service (FMCS) is to assist in contract negotiation disputes between employers and their unionized employees. The FMCS also assists in mediation of discrimination cases and grievances before they reach the arbitration stage. Parties can request an arbitrator online, at <http://www.fmcs.gov> or can download request forms from the site and then fax them or mail them to the FMCS. [The FMCs' FAQ is at <http://www.fmcs.gov/internet/faq.asp?categoryID=336>; the agency's policies and procedures are at <http://www.fmcs.gov/internet/itemDetail.asp?categoryID=197&itemID=16959>]

[E] Case Law on Labor Arbitration

In late 2000, the Supreme Court decided that, in a unionized workplace, an arbitrator's decision is enforceable by the court system as long as the arbitration award draws its essence from the Collective Bargaining Agreement (CBA). So, unless the arbitrator's decision actually violates a statute or regulation, it must be enforced—even if it violates public policy. [*E. Associated Coal Corp. v. UMW*, 531 U.S. 57 (2000)]

Arbitration awards are quite hard to overturn. For example, a court cannot overturn an award merely because it believes the arbitrator made the wrong decision, or misinterpreted the facts of the case. One of the rare cases in which an award was overturned involved a new zero-tolerance drug policy adopted by an oil refining company for all its facilities nationwide. The policy was challenged by the union, which claimed that it was impermissible to adopt such a policy unilaterally, without bargaining. One arbitrator upheld the policy. The other arbitrator upheld most of the policy, but disapproved of the potential for firing employees immediately, without a chance for rehabilitation. The employer sought to have the district court vacate the award, but the district court upheld. The Third Circuit reversed the district court, finding that the arbitrator exceeded his discretion by attempting to substitute his own discretion in an area of legitimate management prerogative. The Third Circuit held that the award did not draw its essence from the collective bargaining agreement. [*Citgo Asphalt Refining Co. v. Paper, Allied-Industrial Chemical, & Energy Workers Int'l Union Local No. 2-991*, 385 F.3d 809 (3d Cir. 2004)]

[F] Just Cause

One of the distinctive features of a collective bargaining agreement is that it means that employees no longer work at the will of the employer. Therefore, they cannot be discharged, or even subjected to lesser forms of discipline, without just cause. So the arbitrator's task becomes to determine whether the employer did, indeed, act with just cause. The arbitrator must determine if the employee really did whatever the employer claims he or she did; whether the employer offered the employee due process before imposing discipline; and whether the discipline was reasonable and not out of proportion to the offense. Usually, arbitrators divide offenses into very serious offenses such as assaulting someone at work, stealing, or creating a safety hazard (which will justify dismissal) and less serious rules, which are appropriate for progressive discipline such as admonition, notations in the permanent record, or suspension with or without pay.

[G] Contract Interpretation

When arbitrators interpret a contract, their job is to find out what the parties meant. If the language of the contract is plain, clear, and unambiguous, the arbitrator has to follow it—even if the arbitrator doesn't think that the contract as written is very sensible or fair. In fact, if the arbitrator doesn't follow this "plain meaning rule," a court is likely to decide that the arbitrator's award is invalid and not entitled to be enforced by the court system.

In fact, if a contract (any kind of contract, not just a CBA) is supposed to represent the whole agreement between the parties, a legal principle called the "parol evidence rule" says that evidence of anything said or written before or during the negotiations cannot be introduced to contradict the written contract or vary its terms. ("Parol" is an archaic term for "word" or "speech.") However, parol evidence can be used to explain terms that are unclear or ambiguous.

§ 40.06 ARBITRATION OF EMPLOYMENT DISCRIMINATION CLAIMS

[A] Employer-Imposed Clauses

The reputation of arbitration has had its ups and downs. A Supreme Court case, *Alexander v. Gardner-Denver* [415 U.S. 36 (1974)] allowed an employee to litigate after pursuing arbitration remedies, on the grounds that the arbitration provision in the plaintiff's CBA did not offer enough protection for statutory claims—i.e., claims that arise under Title VII, the Americans With Disabilities Act, or other antidiscrimination law.

In 1991, however, the Supreme Court took a different tack. The important case of *Gilmer v. Interstate/Johnson Lane Corp.* [500 U.S. 20 (1991)] allowed an employer to impose mandatory arbitration (under the U-4 securities industry employment agreement) for ADEA claims. The Supreme Court said that it wasn't really contradicting the earlier *Gardner-Denver* decision, because that involved a union contract that the plaintiff was subject to along with all the other union members, whereas Gilmer signed the U-4 agreement as an individual.

Under *Gilmer*, an arbitration clause can be valid as long as the process provides a written award rendered by a neutral arbitrator, and as long as discovery and adequate remedies are available under the arbitration process.

In April 2009, the Supreme Court extended its line of pro-arbitration decisions by holding that an arbitration clause in a CBA prevented employees from litigating ADEA claims when building service employees were re-assigned to lower-paid jobs as porters and cleaners. The union withdrew age discrimination charges because it had consented to the new contract under which the reassignments were made. The individual workers affected by the reassignments filed ADEA charges with the EEOC, and received right to sue letters. The Second Circuit refused to compel arbitration, taking the position that a CBA provision cannot be enforced if it prevents ADEA suits. The Supreme Court reversed, finding that federal law favors arbitration, mandating enforcement of a CBA provision that clearly and unmistakably obligates union members to arbitrate claims. Opponents of the decision said that the Supreme Court allowed unions to bargain away their members' rights to pursue discrimination cases in court. However, the Supreme Court held that union and management mutually agreed on the contract's provisions in bargaining, and the clause would have to be upheld unless the ADEA forbids arbitration. In the Supreme Court view, the ADEA does not contradict the general federal policy of supporting arbitration. [*14 Penn Plaza LLC v. Pyett*, 556 U.S. 247 (2009)]

The *Gilmer* case was the "opening bell" for recognition of employers' right to impose predispute arbitration requirements: That is, employees would be covered by employment agreements, job handbooks, or other means of ensuring that they would have to arbitrate discrimination claims instead of litigating them.

The Sixth Circuit held that a valid arbitration agreement was formed even though the employer did not introduce any documents signed by the plaintiff. The employer said that the documents, which said that they were binding unless the employee opted out, had been sent; she denied receiving them, although she admitted to receiving training about the arbitration program. The Sixth Circuit held that the documents could be presumed to be received, and the opt-out structure was acceptable under state law of offer and acceptance. The burden was on the plaintiff to show that she did not knowingly and voluntarily waive the right to jury trial. [*Tillman v. Macy's, Inc.*, 735 F.3d 453 (6th Cir. 2013); see Pierre H. Bergeron Squire Sanders, *Sixth Circuit Flips Arbitration Decision*, Squire Sanders (Nov. 1, 2013), available at Lexology.com; Todd H. Lebowitz, *Employee Accepted Arbitration Offer When She Continued To Work, Sixth Circuit Rules*, Baker & Hostetler LLP (Oct. 31, 2013), available at Lexology.com]

In another case where the employer permitted employees to opt out of the arbitration requirement, a plaintiff who did not opt out filed a class action charging failure to pay required overtime. The plaintiff said that it was an Unfair Labor Practice to offer employees a benefit to persuade them to avoid engaging in protected concerted activity (i.e., suing the employer in a class action). The Ninth Circuit rejected this creative argument, holding that the plaintiff was unable to prove that arbitration gave employees an immediate benefit. [*Johnmohammadi v. Bloomingdales, Inc.*, No. 12-55578 (9th Cir. June 23, 2014); see Todd A. Dawson, *Ninth Circuit Upholds Employment Arbitration Agreement and Class Waiver*, Baker & Hostetler LLP (June 25, 2014), available at Lexology.com]

The Civil Rights Act of 1991 and the Americans with Disabilities Act (ADA) both include language favoring arbitration and other forms of Alternative Dispute Resolution (ADR) as means of handling discrimination charges. For the ADA provision, see 42 U.S.C. § 12212: Wherever it is lawful and appropriate, ADR (including settlement negotiations, conciliation, facilitation, mediation, fact-finding, minitrials, and arbitration) is "encouraged" when ADA charges are asserted. Similarly, in 2004 the Fifth Circuit ruled that there is no reason why arbitration of Fair Labor Standards Act claims cannot be compelled. [*Carter v. Countrywide Credit Indus., Inc.*, 362 F.3d 294 (5th Cir. 2004)] The Fifth Circuit agreed with the District Court that the contract provision requiring the employer and employee to split the costs of arbitration was invalid—but also agreed with the District Court that the proper remedy was to sever this invalid provision and enforce the rest of the agreement.

The two main ADR methods are arbitration (a trusted person or panel renders a decision) and mediation (a trusted person helps the parties reach a mutually acceptable decision).

> ■ **TIP:** If an employer offers to arbitrate, and the employee refuses, this could be treated as evidence of the employer's good faith—preventing the employee from collecting damages for breach of the covenant of good faith and fair dealing.

An updated arbitration agreement in the employee handbook, issued after the plaintiffs' claims accrued and they filed their original class action complaint, did not bind the employees in their wage and hour suit: the employer was subject to the policy in the handbook issued by the prior owner of the company. [*Avery v. Integrated Healthcare Holdings, Inc.*, 159 Cal. Rptr. 3d 444 (Cal. App. 2013); see Howard S. Suskin, *Updated Arbitration Agreement Does Not Bind Employees*, Jenner & Block (Sept. 13, 2013), available at Lexology.com]

A "Woolley disclaimer" states that an employee manual is not a contract. The District Court for the District of New Jersey refused to enforce an arbitration clause because it was included in a manual with the Woolley disclaimer. The court said that the arbitration clause was unenforceable because the non-contract status of the manual meant that the employer could unilaterally modify the provision without notice to employees. [*Raymours Furniture Co., Inc. v. Rossi*, No. 13-4440, 2014 U.S. Dist. LEXIS 1006 (D.N.J. Jan. 2, 2014); see Joseph C. O'Keefe et al., *A Woolley Situation: District Of New Jersey Refuses To Enforce Arbitration Clause In Employee Handbook*, Proskauer Rose LLP (Feb. 27, 2014), available at Lexology.com]

The First Circuit ruled that a job application was ambiguous as to whether people who applied but were not hired were subject to the arbitration clause. Therefore, the First Circuit refused to mandate arbitration in a case where a job applicant asserted pregnancy discrimination. The court concluded that there was a valid arbitration agreement—but the conditions under which it would come into play (the plaintiff being hired and having a dispute with her employer) never occurred. [*Gove v. Career Sys. Dev. Corp.*, 689 F.3d 1 (1st Cir. 2012)]

Employees challenging arbitration requirements frequently argue that the agreement is unenforceable because of substantive and/or procedural defects that render it unconscionable. Until recent years, there were a number of California cases finding unconscionability—but even in California it is very common for arbitration agreements to be upheld despite unconscionability challenges.

In a class action charging violations of the California Labor Code provisions about overtime, meal and rest breaks, payroll records, and itemized wage statements, the California Court of Appeal found in 2012 that an arbitration agreement was not unconscionable, even though the employer opposed class arbitration. Some factors supported procedural unconscionability: it was a preprinted form, required by the employer; the clause was on page 42 of a 43-page employment agreement; and the arbitration language was not highlighted. However, on balance the court found that the agreement was not substantively unconscionable. The plaintiff did not show that requiring individual arbitration violated any state or federal law or public policy. The California Court of Appeal held that the agreement was silent about class arbitration, so the employer could not be forced into class arbitration. The agreement referred to all claims "between myself and the employer," and the court of appeal said that class arbitration is not between the individual employee and the employer. [*Nelsen v. Legacy Partners Residential, Inc.*, 207 Cal. App. 4th 1115 (2012)]

In 2013, The California Supreme Court overturned its 2011 decision (that an employee could not be required to waive his or her right to a "Berman" wage claims hearing before the state Labor Commission). In 2013, the California Supreme Court said that the FAA preempts the state law that forbids such a waiver. However, the case was remanded to determine if the arbitration clause itself was unconscionable; the court said that unconscionable arbitration clauses can be invalidated despite *Concepcion* and *Italian Colors*. [*Sonic-Calabasas A, Inc. v. Moreno*, 57 Cal. 4th 1109 (Cal. 2013); see Winston & Strawn LLP, *Reversing Previous Ruling, California Supreme Court Holds Arbitration Agreement That Waives Right To An Administrative Hearing May Be Enforceable*, Lexology.com (Oct. 22, 2013)]

A few weeks later, the Ninth Circuit found an arbitration clause unconscionable because job applicants had to agree to arbitration when they applied, but did not get a copy of the arbitration agreement for weeks later; the procedure for selecting arbitrators favored the employer; and employees could not recover their share of arbitration costs if they won the case, making it impractical to pursue many small claims. However, on the same day the Ninth Circuit also decided that claims for public injunctive relief from arbitration are no longer allowed because of *Concepcion*. [*Chavarria v. Ralphs Grocery Store*, 733 F.3d 916 (9th Cir. 2013); *Ferguson v. Corinthian Colleges Inc.*, 733 F.3d 928 (9th Cir. 2013). See Scott M. Pearson and Joseph Escarez, *Recent Decisions Reflect Continuing Resistance To Arbitration In California*, Seyfarth Shaw LLP (Oct. 30, 2013), available at Lexology.com; Lori Phillips, *Surprise! Shocker! Court Invalidates Arbitration Agreement*. . . Sherman & Howard LLC (Oct. 30, 2013), available at Lexology.com; Theodore T. Eidukas, *Clean-Up In Aisle 9: Ninth Circuit Finds Ralphs Grocery Company's Arbitration Policy Unconscionable Under State Law*

Not Preempted By The Federal Arbitration Act, Foley & Lardner LLP (Nov. 4, 2013), available at Lexology.com.]

In mid-2014, the California Supreme Court ruled that, although an employee's waiver of the right to arbitrate on a class basis is enforceable, employers cannot require employees to waive the right to bring Private Attorney General Act (PAGA) claims about wage-and-hour claims. [*Iskanian v. CLS Transp. Los Angeles LLC*, No. S204032 (Cal. June 23, 2014). See Mark A. Neubauer and Meredith M. Moss, *California Law on Arbitration Changes . . . Again*, Carlton Fields Jorden Burt (June 23, 2014), available at Lexology.com]

But, despite the almost universal judicial approval of mandatory arbitration, the executive branch took a step in 2009 that, in practical terms, greatly limited the practicality of mandatory arbitration clauses. A provision in the federal spending bill for the Department of Defense for the years 2009–2010 (§ 8116) forbids most defense contractors to enforce mandatory arbitration clauses. The defense contractor cannot be paid by the federal government unless it agrees not to enter into or enforce any employment contract making it a condition of employment for an employee or independent contractor to agree to arbitrate Title VII claims or many other tort claims. The provision took effect for federal subcontractors six months later. However, the holders of contracts and subcontracts under $1 million are exempt. The Department of Defense has the power to grant a waiver for national security reasons, although the waiver must be disclosed to the public. [David Ingram, *Obama Signs Into Law Restriction on Arbitration Clauses*, Nat'l L.J. (Dec. 22, 2009) (law.com)]

A subsequent Executive Order, the Fair Play and Safe Workplaces Executive Order, issued in July, 2014 provides that, for contracts of $1 million or more, contractors will not be permitted to mandate predispute arbitration of Title VII, sexual harassment, or sexual assault cases. Although the order increases the amount of information that contractors must provide about hours worked, overtime hours, gross pay, and net pay, it does not forbid mandatory arbitration of wage and hour claims. [Fact Sheet, *Fair Pay and Safe Workplaces Executive Order*, <http://www.whitehouse.gov/the-press-office/2014/07/31/fact-sheet-fair-pay-and-safe-workplaces-executive-order> (July 31, 2014)]

[B] AAA Arbitration

The American Arbitration Association (AAA) has long been respected for its work in dispute resolution. The AAA's National Rules for the Resolution of Employment Disputes (promulgated in 1993; amended in 1995 to increase due process protection for employees) cover about three million workers.

The due process standards for fair arbitration require that:

- The employee's role in selecting the arbitrator(s) is equal to the employer's role;
- Each side has a right to counsel;

- The arbitrator can order whatever discovery he or she thinks is necessary;
- The parties are entitled to the same remedies in arbitration that they could get from the court system;
- The arbitrator will provide a written opinion explaining the reasons behind his or her decision;
- Attorneys' fees will be awarded in the interests of justice, so the employee does not have to be successful enough to be considered the "prevailing party" to get a fee award.

■ **TIP:** The employer can indicate in employment applications, the employee handbook, and/or employment contracts that employment disputes will be resolved under AAA rules.

Since 1996, AAA arbitrators have had the power to order discovery. Either employers or employees can be ordered to produce documents, answer written lists of questions, or appear and answer questions posed by an attorney. Under the 1996 rules, any party can be represented by an attorney. The arbitrator has a duty to make a decision and render a written award within 30 days of the end of the hearing. The arbitrator has the power to render whatever award he or she thinks is just, including ordering one side to pay the attorneys' fees and costs of the other side.

The arbitrator gets paid a fee for working on the case, and the AAA itself is entitled to an administration fee. The AAA fee depends on the size of the claim or counterclaim, determined at the time it is filed, not by any later amendments.

The AAA's general policy is that it will administer arbitration even if the employer unilaterally imposed the arbitration requirement as a condition of employment. However, the organization reserves the right to refuse to enforce unfair arbitration policies—policies that fail to provide basic due process protection to employees.

The California Court of Appeal ruled in late 2013 that failure to include a copy of the AAA rules did not prevent an employer from enforcing an arbitration agreement. The rules were readily available online, so the omission did not make the agreement procedurally unconscionable. It was not substantively unconscionable because it was not so one-sided as to shock the conscience; the implied covenant of good faith and fair dealing prevented the employer from undermining the plaintiff's rights. [*Peng v. First Republic Bank*, 219 Cal. App. 4th 1462 (2013); see Sharon B. Bauman et al., *In California, Arbitration Agreement Valid Despite Of Lack Of Rules*, Manatt Phelps & Phillips LLP (Oct. 23, 2013), available at Lexology.com; Daniel J. McCoy and Saundra L.M. Riley, *Arbitration Agreement Withstands Challenge For Lack Of Notice Of Arbitration Rules Or Mutuality*, Fenwick & West LLP (Oct. 16, 2013), available at Lexology.com]

The Fourth Circuit refused to vacate an arbitration award that used the opt-out class certification rules under the AAA Supplementary Rules for Class Arbitration, and not the Fair Labor Standards Act opt-in class certification rules. (The case was brought by three former managers charging that the ex-employer violated the FLSA by failing to pay overtime.) The AAA Class Rules permit the arbitrator to decide if a case should proceed as a class. The Fourth Circuit ruled that the arbitrator rendered a reasoned award, and the arbitration agreement gave the arbitrator the power to render any relief that a court could provide. [*Long John Silver's Rests. v. Cole*, 514 F.3d 345 (4th Cir. 2008)]

In restrictive covenant cases, the employer may be able to seek a preliminary injunction if violation of the covenant could cause irreparable injury. If the contract provides for arbitration as a means of dispute resolution, it is common to make an exception for injunctions. If so, there will be a two-step process: first a suit about the availability of an injunction, followed by arbitration of the underlying dispute. The AAA rules that took effect October 1, 2013 give arbitrators the power to award emergency injunctive relief. [Andrew Zwerling, *The Interplay of Restrictive Covenants, Preliminary Injunctions and Arbitration*, N.Y.L.J. (Nov. 25, 2013), available at law.com]

[C] Securities Industry Arbitration

Workers in the securities industry have to sign a standard employment agreement called the U-4 as a condition of working in the industry. It was the only industry to have a uniform mandatory arbitration requirement, so it served as a kind of "test bed" for studying legal issues about arbitration.

As of August 7, 1997, the National Association of Securities Dealers (NASD) voted to eliminate mandatory arbitration of employment discrimination claims brought by registered brokers under federal and state antidiscrimination statutes.

The New York Court of Appeals ruled in early 2007 that a securities industry employer cannot be sued for defamation in connection with the contents of a NASD U-5 statement (reasons for termination of an employee). The forms are as absolutely privileged as ethics complaints against an attorney, because public policy calls for candor. [*Rosenberg v. MetLife*, 8 N.Y.3d 359 (2007); see Joel Stashenko, *N.Y. High Court Affirms Absolute Privilege for Securities Industry's Termination Notices*, N.Y.L.J. (Mar. 30, 2007)]

[D] Getting Ready for Arbitration

To be prepared for arbitration, you should:

- Review how the dispute arose, and what has already been done to resolve it;

- Check all relevant work rules and policies and how they were applied, both to the grievant and the other employees;
- Makes copies of all relevant documents for your own file, for the employee, and for the arbitrator;
- Inform the employee of documents in the employee's possession that you want copies of, and that you want copies sent to the arbitrator;
- If necessary, ask the arbitrator to subpoena necessary documents that you have not been able to get by informal means;
- Make sure all the witnesses sound accurate and articulate, but not mechanical or coached;
- Anticipate questions that will be asked during cross-examination, and prepare the witnesses to answer them;
- Make a list of points that you want each witness's testimony to put into the record;
- Review collections of published arbitration decisions, because even though arbitrators don't absolutely have to follow past precedents, they will often be swayed by interpretations that other arbitrators have reached in similar cases.

The first stage in an arbitration hearing is the opening statement. Usually, in a case where the employer's termination or discipline is being challenged, the employer will present its case first, because the employer has to prove the justification for its actions. In other types of cases, the employee usually gives the first opening statement. Next comes the other opening statement, and then the side that goes first introduces the testimony of its witnesses; the other side has the right to cross-examine. Then, the parties sum up their cases, and it is up to the arbitrator to decide.

[E] Appeals

In general, the court system tries to get involved with arbitration as little as possible, although arbitration awards can be enforced by the court system, and sometimes disputes about arbitrability or arbitration process are litigated.

Early in 2004, the Ninth Circuit tackled the question of whether the federal courts can hear appeals of arbitration awards in the employer's favor—in other words, whether an employee can challenge an award of $0. The Ninth Circuit said no: when it comes to deciding whether the amount in controversy is the $75,000 required for diversity jurisdiction (jurisdiction based on the parties being citizens of different states), the amount in controversy is the amount actually awarded in the arbitration proceeding, not the amount that the employee claimed he or she was entitled to. [*Luong v. Circuit City Stores Inc.*, 356 F.3d 1188 (9th Cir. 2004)]

Later in the year, however, another panel of the Ninth Circuit allowed a $0 arbitration award to be judicially reviewed if the amount at stake in the underlying dispute satisfies the amount in controversy requirement. [*Theis Research Inc. v. Brown & Bain*, 386 F.3d 1180 (9th Cir. 2004, amended Feb. 18, 2005)]

A multi-district suit about Wal-Mart wage and hour matters was settled. The settlement agreement said that all disputes about attorneys' fees are subject to binding arbitration, without appeal. The Ninth Circuit held in late 2013 that courts have taken two approaches to non-appealability clauses. One way, adopted by the Third, Seventh, and Eleventh Circuits, is to construe a requirement of binding, non-appealable arbitration to rule out federal court review of the merits of the decision—but to allow review on the grounds set out in FAA § 10 for vacating an arbitration award (e.g., fraud or the arbitrator's partiality). The other option is that no appellate review will be permitted at all. The Supreme Court's *Hall Street* decision says that the FAA § 10 criteria for vacating an award are the only criteria that can be used to set aside an award, and parties cannot add more grounds by private contract. The Ninth Circuit interpreted this decision to mean that not only is it impossible to add more grounds for vacating arbitration awards, you cannot eliminate the § 10 grounds either, because the purpose of the FAA is to allow limited judicial review of arbitration awards. [*In re Wal-mart Wage and Hour Employment Practices Litig.*, 737 F.3d 1262 (9th Cir. 2013)]

The AAA's Optional Appellate Arbitration Rules took effect November 1, 2013. Arbitration awards can be reviewed by a panel of arbitrators (or by a single arbitrator, if this is what the parties request). Appellate arbitrators consider allegations that an award was based on a clearly erroneous factual determination and/or material, prejudicial errors of law. [Katharine H. Parker et al., *AAA Adopts Optional Appellate Arbitration Process*, Proskauer Rose LLP (Nov. 12, 2013), available at Lexology.com]

§ 40.07 MANDATORY PREDISPUTE ARBITRATION CLAUSES

[A] "Predispute" vs. "Postdispute" Clauses

There are many ways to draft an arbitration provision. Predispute arbitration clauses specify in advance that future disputes, if they occur, will be arbitrable. Such a provision can be either voluntary or mandatory. If voluntary, arbitration is just one option available for resolving disputes. If mandatory, the employee is blocked from suing the employer. Postdispute arbitration clauses are an agreement between employer and employee after a claim has been raised, and the best way to handle it is via arbitration.

In 1998, the Supreme Court resolved some difficult issues in *Wright v. Universal Maritime Serv. Corp.* [525 U.S. 70 (1998)] In this case, an injured stevedore was denied employment because companies that might have employed him considered him permanently disabled. He sued under the ADA without filing a grievance or going through arbitration under the CBA. The district court dismissed his case because he did not exhaust his grievance remedies. The Fourth Circuit upheld the district court.

However, the Supreme Court reversed the Fourth Circuit. The *Gilmer* case permits compulsory arbitration of an ADA claim, but the Supreme Court ruled that a contract claim must be treated differently from a statutory claim. Contract claims are presumed arbitrable, but statutory claims are not. A CBA must be very explicit to prevent litigation of a claim under a civil rights statute. A general arbitration clause that does not list the civil rights statutes that are covered will not prevent litigation under those statutes.

Early in 2002, the Supreme Court returned to the subject of predispute arbitration mandates. The ruling in *EEOC v. Waffle House Inc.* [534 U.S. 279 (2002)] is that the EEOC can pursue employment discrimination litigation (in this case, involving the Americans with Disabilities Act) even if the employees themselves would be required to submit their disputes to arbitration. The decision is very important as an indicator of legal thinking about arbitration, but it will not have much practical effect, because the EEOC doesn't take on many cases a year, and not all of them involve companies with mandatory arbitration requirements.

Accenture account executive Armand Santoro's employment contract required arbitration of all employment-related disputes, including Title VII and ADEA discrimination claims. Santoro was terminated at age 66, during a cost-cutting campaign, and replaced by a younger man. He brought a suit against his ex-employer under the ADEA, FMLA, and ERISA. Santoro cited the Dodd-Frank Act provision that whistleblowers' right to sue their employers can only be altered by mandatory predispute arbitration requirements if the arbitration clause has an explicit "carve-out" of Dodd-Frank claims. The Fourth Circuit held that this provision is limited to whistleblower claims, and does not prevent enforcement of arbitration clauses in other employment contexts. [*Santoro v. Accenture Fed. Servs.*, 748 F.3d 217 (4th Cir. 2014)]

On the grounds that not every employee who makes an EEOC charge proceeds with the case, the Eighth Circuit said that employers should be allowed to participate in the EEOC process without waiving the right to enforce arbitration clauses. Therefore, if an employee who is covered by an arbitration agreement brings a discrimination charge, the employer's participation in the EEOC investigation does not prevent the employer from enforcing the arbitration clause. [*McNamara v. Yellow Transp., Inc.*, 570 F.3d 950 (8th Cir. 2009)]

The two federal Courts of Appeals that have considered the question have both ruled that USERRA claims are subject to arbitration. *Garrett v. Circuit City Stores*, 449 F.3d 672 (5th Cir. 2006) holds that USERRA's preemption provision does not show that Congress intended to rule out arbitration, because arbitration does not waive any of the substantive rights protected by USERRA. *Landis v. Pinnacle Eye Care*, 537 F.3d 559 (6th Cir. 2008) uses a similar analysis; its concurring opinion says that Congress did not use the kind of unambiguous language that would be necessary to rule out arbitration. [Howard S. Suskin and Benjamin

J. Wimmer, *Arbitrability of USERRA Claims: Battle on the Home Front*, special to law.com (Oct. 15, 2008)]

[B] Claims Other Than Discrimination

Mandatory predispute arbitration clauses are not limited to use in connection with discrimination claims. Five of the federal Circuit Courts have ruled that arbitration can be a proper way to handle ERISA claims. [*Bird v. Shearson Lehman/American Express*, 926 F.2d 116 (2d Cir. 1991); *Pritzer v. Merrill Lynch*, 7 F.3d 1110 (3d Cir. 1993); *Kramer v. Smith Barney*, 80 F.3d 1080 (5th Cir. 1996); *Amulfo P. Sulit, Inc. v. Dean Witter Reynolds, Inc.*, 847 F.2d 475 (8th Cir. 1988); *Williams v. Imhoff*, 203 F.3d 758 (10th Cir. 2000)]

Some courts are beginning to enforce clauses that forbid ERISA class actions and require individual arbitration of such claims: e.g., *Tenet Healthsystem Phila., Inc. v. Rooney*, No. 12-mc-58, 2012 U.S. Dist. LEXIS 116280 (E.D. Pa. Aug. 14, 2012); *Luchini v. Carmax, Inc.*, No. CV F 12-0417 LJO DLB, 2012 U.S. Dist. LEXIS 102198 (E.D. Cal. July 23, 2012). DOL regulations (see 29 C.F.R. § 2560.503-1) impose certain conditions for an arbitration clause to be enforceable: benefit claimants cannot be subjected to arbitration costs, a mandatory arbitration provision must not prevent claimants from exercising their statutory remedies or keep them from going to court to appeal an arbitrator's decision. The new AAA appellate panels, staffed by ex-judges, can be used to assert a claim that the arbitration award reflects clearly erroneous fact determinations and/or material, prejudicial errors of law. [James Baker, *A Sea Change for ERISA Litigation*, Baker & McKenzie (December 2013) (benefitslink.com). See *Owen v. Bristol Care, Inc.*, 702 F.3d 1050 (8th Cir. 2013), and *Quilloin v. Tenet Health System Phila., Inc.*, 673 F.3d 221 (3d Cir. 2012).]

The Eleventh Circuit held that the right to bring FLSA collective actions is not a substantive right that can never be waived. Therefore, it upheld an arbitration agreement forbidding FLSA class claims. The Eleventh Circuit did not find any Congressional intention under the FLSA to overrule the FAA's strong support of arbitration. [*Walthour v. Chipio Windshield Repair*, 745 F.3d 1326 (11th Cir. 2014); see Christina Forte Meddin and Louisa Johnson, *Eleventh Circuit Compels Individual Arbitration of FLSA Claims, Finding Plaintiffs Have No Substantive Right to Proceed Collectively*, Seyfarth Shaw LLP (Mar. 25, 2014), available at Lexology.com; Bennet Alsher, *Eleventh Circuit Upholds Enforceability of Class Action Waiver*, Ford & Harrison LLP (Mar. 25, 2014), available at Lexology.com. The Second, Fourth, Fifth, and Eighth Circuits had already taken this position; see also *Walton v. The Rose Group*, No. 13-1674 (E.D. Pa. 2013), discussed in Saranac Hale Spencer, *Applebee's Squelches Class Action Through Arbitration Clause*, The Legal Intelligencer (Dec. 17, 2013), available at law.com, enforcing an arbitration clause forbidding class arbitration; the judge felt constrained by precedent, although he thought the clause was unfair.]

Russell brought a class action against his employer, Citigroup, at a time when the arbitration agreement did not mention class claims. He charged the company with failure to pay call center workers for time spent logging in and out of their computers. He was later rehired, at a time when the arbitration agreement had been updated and did cover class claims. Citigroup moved to compel arbitration, but the Sixth Circuit held that the new arbitration agreement did not cover lawsuits that were already in progress when the arbitration agreement was signed because the language of the agreement was prospective, so the Sixth Circuit refused to compel arbitration of a claim that was embodied in a suit already in progress. [*Russell v. Citigroup, Inc.*, 748 F.3d 677 (6th Cir. 2014); see Amy Cadle Hocevar, *Agreement to Arbitrate Does Not Apply Retroactively to Bar Pending Case* (Apr. 8, 2014), available at Lexology.com]

The Second Circuit ruled in 2008 that Sarbanes-Oxley Act whistleblower claims are arbitrable, because the test is whether the parties agreed to arbitrate; the scope of the agreement; whether Congress meant that type of claim to be subject to arbitration; and, if only some claims in a complaint have to be arbitrated, whether the proceedings should be suspended until the arbitration has been held. [*Guyden v. Aetna*, 544 F.3d 376 (2d Cir. 2008); see Mark Hamblett, *Whistleblower Claims Arbitrable Under SOX, 2nd Circuit Determines*, N.Y.L.J. (Oct. 6, 2008) (law.com)]

Plaintiffs in a 2014 Sixth Circuit case were mortgage loan officers who were not paid overtime because they were classified as independent contractors. They filed a class/collective action under the FLSA and the Ohio Minimum Fair Wage Standards Act. The Sixth Circuit held that the employer could compel individual arbitration, even after the expiration of the plaintiffs' employment contracts. The contracts contained an arbitration clause but did not specify whether class arbitration was available, so the Sixth Circuit held that class-wide arbitration is available only if the agreement specifically permits it. [*Huffman v. The Hilltop Cos.*, 747 F.3d 391 (6th Cir. 2014); see Gregory V. Mersol, *Sixth Circuit Holds That Duty to Arbitrate Survives Expiration of Employment Contract, Requires Individual Arbitration*, Baker & Hostetler LLP (Mar. 28, 2014), available at Lexology.com. It was already clear that CBA disputes must be arbitrated even after the expiration of the CBA: *Litton Financial Printing v. NLRB*, 501 U.S. 190 (1991). See also *Reed Elsevier, Inc. ex rel. LexisNexis Div. v. Crockett*, 734 F.3d 594 (6th Cir. 2013): when the contract is silent on the issue of class arbitration, class arbitration is not available.]

The Eighth Circuit held that ERISA does not apply to executive's employment contracts that are not part of an ERISA plan—even if the amount to be paid is determined by reference to terms of an ERISA plan. Therefore, a terminated CEO was allowed to arbitrate his claims that he was deprived of benefits to which he was entitled when he was terminated in anticipation of a merger. Although usually employers favor arbitration and employees favor litigation, in this case the employer argued that the dispute involved an ERISA plan and, therefore, had to be litigated in federal court. The Eighth Circuit's decision that it was a pure contract dispute over a free-standing agreement meant that the ex-CEO could arbitrate his claims, including state-law claims for double damages. Because his contract was not part of an ERISA plan, his state-law claims were not preempted. [*Dakota, Minn. & E. Railroad Corp. v. Schieffer*, 715 F. 3d 712 (8th Cir. 2013). See Jeffrey Russell, Jonathan Potts, and Carrie Byrnes, *Eighth Circuit Clarifies the Scope of ERISA's Application to Severance Arrangements*, Bryan Cave ERISA & Benefits Litigation Blog (Apr. 11, 2013) (benefitslink.com)]

As a general rule, a biased arbitration panel is not a ground for refusing to arbitrate, because it is possible to use the bias to overturn the arbitrator's decision once it is rendered. However, the Sixth Circuit applied a different analysis to this situation in which the process of selecting the arbitrator was fundamentally unfair, because it prevented the arbitral forum from being an adequate substitute for the court system. In this instance, the fees paid by the defendant were a major source of revenue for the arbitration provider, causing an obvious conflict of interest. [*Walker v. Ryan's Family Steak Houses, Inc.*, 400 F.3d 370 (6th Cir. 2005)]

The Third Circuit asserted an objective theory of contract formation to hold that a Spanish-speaking worker was bound by the arbitration clause in the English contract he signed—although the bilingual employee who translated the contract for him admitted that he did not translate the arbitration clause. The result was that, when the Spanish-speaking worker was fired and tried to sue for wrongful termination, the Third Circuit required the claim to be arbitrated instead. [*Morales v. Sun Constructors Inc.*, 541 F.3d 218 (3d Cir. 2008)]

[C] Arbitration Costs

American Express Co. v. Italian Colors, 133 S. Ct. 2304 (2013) is not an employment case (it is an antitrust case about disputes between American Express and merchants who accept credit cards), but it is immensely significant to arbitration of employment cases. The Supreme Court ruled that the FAA does not permit a court to invalid a contract's waiver of class arbitration on the grounds that the cost of arbitrating small individual claims would outweigh the potential recovery that could be obtained.

[D] Class Arbitration and Waivers

Throughout the legal system, there has been a trend for decades (encompassing both statutes and court decisions) to limit the availability of class actions. A number of compulsory arbitration agreements required by employers also require employees to waive the option of bringing employment-related claims as class arbitrations—so the court system has also had to determine the validity of such clauses. As of the 2015 edition, the clear legal trend favored the validity of waivers of class arbitration.

The Supreme Court reversed the California Court of Appeal, granting certiorari and remanding for reconsideration in light of *Concepcion.* A putative class of CarMax employees alleged violation of California labor laws. After the case had been stayed for two years, CarMax moved to compel individual arbitration as prescribed by the employment agreement. The plaintiffs argued that CarMax had waived right to arbitrate. They also cited California's "Gentry rule" making a class action waiver invalid if class arbitration is likely to be significantly more effective in vindicating rights than individual litigation or arbitration—a rule that the Supreme Court held to be preempted by *Concepcion.* [*CarMax Auto Superstores California, LLC v. Fowler*, 134 S. Ct. 1277 (2014), *Fowler v. CarMax*, No. B238426 (Cal. App. 2013, unpublished); see Liz Kramer, *The Preemption Club*, Stinson Leonard Street LLP (Mar. 3, 2014), available at Lexology.com. The *Gentry* rule comes from *Gentry v. Superior Court of L.A. Cnty.*, 42 Cal. 4th 443 (2007).]

The Second Circuit upheld an arbitration agreement's waiver of class and collective actions in a case where the plaintiff alleged that she was wrongfully denied $1,867 in overtime. The plaintiff said that it would cost $200,000 in attorneys' fees, costs, and expert testimony to recover less than $2,000. The Second Circuit followed *Italian Colors:* arbitration can be compelled even if the cost would greatly outweigh the potential recovery. [*Sutherland v. Ernst & Young*, 726 F.3d 290 (2d Cir. 2013); see Manatt Phelps & Phillips LLP, *Reversing Circuit Precedent, 2nd Circuit Upholds FLSA Collective Action Waiver* (Aug. 28, 2013), available at Lexology.com]

The Washington Supreme Court refused to compel arbitration based on an unconscionable arbitration clause that the court considered overly broad and excessively limiting of employee rights. The clause imposed a statute of limitations of 14 days (state law calls for three years); back pay was limited to either two or four months, whereas state law allows recovery of three years of back pay, and employees could find themselves paying an excessive share of costs. Therefore, employees were permitted to maintain a class action. [*Hill v. Garda CL Northwest*, 308 P.3d 635 (Wash. 2013); see Michael Droke, *Washington Supreme Court Invalidates Overbroad Arbitration Agreement*, Dorsey & Whitney LLP (Sept. 13, 2013), available at Lexology.com; Howard S. Suskin, *Arbitration Agreement Unconscionable Due To Time, Damages And Fee Provisions*, Jenner & Block (Nov. 29, 2013), available at Lexology.com]

The District Court for the District of Columbia authorized class arbitration by employees seeking back pay, on the grounds that the agreement's choice of law clause prevented the employer from rejecting class arbitration after going through class arbitration with another group of employees in a related case. [*Hill v. Wackenhut Servs. Int'l*, 971 F. Supp. 2d 5 (D.D.C. 2013); see Howard S. Suskin, *Arbitrator's Decision To Permit Class Arbitration On Estoppel Grounds Upheld*, Jenner & Block (Nov. 29, 2013), available at Lexology.com]

The issue of waiver also arises when an employee or group of employees brings a suit; the employer answers the complaint and participates in litigation;

and subsequently attempts to terminate the lawsuit by moving to compel arbitration. The plaintiff(s) then argue(s) that the employer's participation in the suit waived its ability to compel arbitration.

The New Jersey Supreme Court held that the employer waived its contractual right to arbitration when it answered the plaintiff's complaint without raising the affirmative defense of mandatory arbitration; engaged in discovery for 21 months; filed a motion for summary judgment in the lawsuit; did not mention the arbitration clause in its pretrial disclosures; and waited until three days before the trial to move to compel arbitration. Factors as to whether waiver has occurred include whether the party filed motions in the case (especially dispositive motions like summary judgment) and how the motions were resolved; how much discovery was carried on; if the delay in asserting the arbitration clause was tactical; how soon the question of arbitration was raised; and whether the other party was prejudiced by the delay. [*Cole v. Jersey City Med. Ctr.*, 215 N.J. 265, 72 A.3d 224 (2013); see Gregory T. Alvarez and James M. McDonnell, *Invoke It Early And Often: New Jersey Supreme Court Establishes Arbitration Waiver Standards*, Jackson Lewis LLP (Aug. 28, 2013), available at Lexology.com]

But it is more common for employers to be permitted to compel arbitration. In a 2013 Ninth Circuit case, the district court held that a wage and hour defendant waived arbitration by not asserting it in two similar cases that were consolidated with the plaintiff's case. The Ninth Circuit reversed, citing *Italian Colors* for the principle that waiver of arbitration is not favored, and the plaintiff did not show prejudice from the employer's delay in seeking arbitration. The Ninth Circuit also upheld the agreement's waiver of class arbitration. [*Richards v. Ernst & Young, LLP*, 734 F.3d 871 (9th Cir. 2013); see Michael T. Brody, *Ninth Circuit Compels Arbitration Of Wage And Hour Claims*, Jenner & Block (Oct. 31, 2013), available at Lexology.com; Laura Reathaford and Charles J. Stiegler, *Right To Compel Arbitration Agreement Not Waived If Plaintiff Suffered No Prejudice From Delay*, Proskauer Rose LLP (Aug. 26, 2013), available at Lexology.com; Loren Gesinksy, *D.R. Horton Who? Ninth Circuit Sends Claims to Individual Arbitration After Class Certification Below*, Seyfarth Shaw LLP (Aug. 27, 2013), available at Lexology.com]

§ 40.08 FACTORS THAT PROMOTE ADR SUCCESS

Most successful ADR systems embody several steps, including in-house procedures for resolving grievances before outside parties get involved. In-house resolutions can be quick and inexpensive. Using a mediator or arbitrator always involves some degree of delay and expense, even if it is far less than the ruinous effort of litigation.

Any ADR system should specify whether the matter will be heard by one mediator or arbitrator or by a panel. Panels usually have three members; it's definitely better to have an odd number to prevent 2–2 or 3–3 splits.

The ADR policy should specify not only the number but the qualifications of the decision makers. It should be clear which employees will be allowed to use ADR to settle disputes—and which ones will be compelled to use it. The policy should clarify which disputes are involved: All employment-related disputes? All federal statutory discrimination claims? Only certain federal claims? Only claims that would otherwise go to state court?

An appropriate policy is fair to employees, providing them with as much due process protection as litigation would offer. They should have an adequate opportunity to assert claims, get evidence about what the employer did, and receive adequate remedies if the mediator or arbitrator decides in their favor.

The American Bar Association's "Due Process Protocol" sets out these standards for fairness in mandatory arbitration matters:

- The employee is aware of the arbitration requirement and accepts it voluntarily;
- The employee can be represented at arbitration (e.g., by a lawyer or union representative);
- The employee has access to a full range of remedies;

The arbitrator has the power to make the employer pay the employee's arbitration-related costs. Some cases about arbitration take the position that, since the employer wanted arbitration in the first place, it should pay the full cost. The system could also be set up so that the employee never has to pay more than 50% of the cost of arbitration, or never has to pay more than one day's fee for the arbitrators.

CHAPTER 41

EEOC AND STATE ENFORCEMENT OF ANTIDISCRIMINATION LAWS

§ 41.01 INTRODUCTION

The Equal Employment Opportunity Commission (EEOC) is in charge of enforcing Title VII and the Americans with Disabilities Act (ADA). It also enforces the Equal Pay Act (EPA) and Age Discrimination in Employment Act (ADEA), although the enforcement provisions for these acts are slightly different because they reflect their derivation from the Fair Labor Standards Act. EPA complainants do not have to file an EEOC charge; the rules for ADEA charges are found in 29 C.F.R. § 1626.4.

The EEOC is a comparatively small agency, with an annual budget less than $400 million. In the past decade, it has lost about 15% of its full-time employees to job freezes and attrition. [Jacob Gershman, *EEOC Sues Less, but Tactics Draw Flak*, WSJ.com (Feb. 9, 2014)]

The basic enforcement scheme is that people who believe they have been discriminated against file charges with the EEOC. The EEOC works with state antidiscrimination agencies, using methods ranging from informal persuasion to litigation to get employers to comply with the law and eliminate any discriminatory practices occurring in the workplace.

The EEOC can intervene in a suit brought by an employee or can bring its own lawsuits against employers. The EEOC has the power to collect data, investigate allegations of discrimination, view conditions in the workplace, and inspect records. It can also advise employers about how to comply with the law. The EEOC has the power to subpoena witnesses and documents, bring suits, and supervise the collection of damages that courts have ordered or that employers have agreed to pay under a settlement.

The EEOC's subpoena power is granted by 29 C.F.R. § 1601.16. The time to raise objections to an EEOC subpoena is very short. A petition to seek revocation or modification of a subpoena must be mailed to the issuing director (or the general counsel, if the subpoena was issued by the commissioner) within five business days after service of the subpoena. The petition must identify every part of the subpoena being challenged and the rationale for the challenge. The EEOC is required to rule on the petition (granting it and revoking or modifying the subpoena, or denying it) within eight calendar days after receipt, or "as soon as practicable." [Michael C. Wilhelm, *Why Employers Need To Respond To EEOC Subpoenas As Soon As Possible*, Briggs and Morgan (Sept. 16, 2013), available at Lexology.com]

Therefore, the EEOC has a dual role. It investigates charges brought by employees, but it can also litigate as a plaintiff. The theory is that the EEOC acts as plaintiff to preserve the rights of all the employees within the workplace. The EEOC always has a right to investigate and, where it believes a cause of action exists, to litigate. So employees' waivers and releases, or their settlement of claims against the employer, can prevent those employees from suing their employers, but will not prevent a suit by the EEOC. Furthermore, waivers and releases are void as against public policy if they try to prevent employees from assisting in an EEOC investigation.

Similarly, the EEOC can pursue an ADA case (including seeking specific relief for an individual) even if the individual employee was covered by a mandatory predispute arbitration agreement (see § 40.07) and therefore could not sue the employer. [*EEOC v. Waffle House*, 534 U.S. 279 (2002)]

EEOC investigators assign cases to classifications of A (the most serious), B, and C. In an A-1 case, the EEOC itself may pursue the case as plaintiff. An A-2 case is likely to result in a finding of good cause, but no litigation by the EEOC itself. It's a bad sign if the EEOC sends out a questionnaire to potential plaintiffs; asks the defendant for a statement of its position; if the EEOC does not ask the employer to mediate; or if it's a deferral state (see below) but the first contact comes from the federal EEOC.

It is often helpful to demonstrate good faith by offering unconditional reinstatement to a charging party. There are many cases indicating that if the charging party rejects such an offer, he or she will not be eligible for various kinds of relief (back pay, front pay, possibly even court-ordered reinstatement).

The Department of Labor also has the right to sue federal contractors for remedies, including punitive damages, if the contractors are guilty of race, sex, or religious discrimination. Employees of federal contractors get a choice of filing their complaints with the EEOC or the DOL. The EEOC and DOL have a work-sharing plan.

It is often predicted that a poor economic climate will increase the number of discrimination charges filed because unemployed workers are willing to bring charges and risk getting reputations as troublemakers.

A Seyfarth Shaw report shows that in 2013 the EEOC focused on systemic discrimination, disability discrimination, and pregnancy discrimination, but its success in court was mixed and remedies were lower than in 2012. EEOC lawyers filed 131 suits in FY 2013—more than the 122 in 2012 but well below the record figure of 261 in 2011. The EEOC resolved 209 suits in FY 2013, for $39 million in penalties; in 2012, there were 254 resolutions and $44.2 million in penalties. In 2013, the EEOC secured $372 million in monetary benefits from resolving administrative charges, slightly more than the previous year. About two-thirds of the EEOC suits (89 suits, 68%) were filed on behalf of individual discriminatees, 21 suits each were filed for systemic discrimination and for class actions not at a systemic level. The report sharply critiqued the EEOC's handling of systemic discrimination cases, including major defeats in *CRST Van Expedited* and *PeopleMark*. [Jenna Greene, *For EEOC, a Mixed Bag in 2013*, The BLT: The Blog of Legal Times (Jan. 3, 2014), available at law.com]

The "red zone," the last two months of the EEOC's fiscal year, typically shows an increase in litigation activity. In August and September of 2013, for example, 48 out of the 134 EEOC suits for the year were filed. Over two dozen suits (14 of them disability discrimination cases) were filed in the last week of the fiscal year. [Gerald L. Mattman, Jr. and Lily M. Strumwasser, *The EEOC's*

Fiscal Year-End Rush To The Red Zone, Seyfarth Shaw LLP (Oct. 30, 2013), available at Lexology.com]

The EEOC's strategic enforcement plan for fiscal 2012–2016 calls for combining investigation, research, litigation, outreach, and education. The plan defines the agency's national priorities as:

- Eliminating class-based recruitment and hiring discrimination on the basis of race, religion, ethnicity, age, sex, or disability;
- Protecting vulnerable immigrant and migrant workers against pay discrimination, job segregation, human trafficking, harassment, or discrimination; protecting workers who are unaware of their rights or frightened to enforce them;
- Enforcing equal pay laws;
- Keeping up with demographic changes;
- Combating policies and practices that discourage exercise of rights under anti-discrimination laws.

The EEOC has identified pregnancy discrimination as an emerging issue, and the Supreme Court has asked the EEOC for input on accommodations for pregnant employees. [Tamar N. Dolcourt, *The EEOC's Strategic Enforcement Plan: Targets For 2013-2016*, Foley & Lardner LLP (Oct. 28, 2013), available at Lexology.com; Jenna Greene, *EEOC Releases New Strategic Plan, Vows to Fight Systemic Discrimination*, Blog of the Legal Times (Jan. 20, 2012) (law.com); Lily M. Strumwasser, *Not Without Warning: The EEOC Continues To File Barrages Of Pregnancy Discrimination Lawsuits*, Seyfarth Shaw LLP (Sept. 19, 2013), available at Lexology.com]

According to the National Women's Law Center, the number of EEOC charges filed by pregnant women increased almost 50% in the decade before 2014. Claims are usually based on denial of reasonable accommodation—e.g., rest and bathroom breaks, leave, light duty. In 2012, the EEOC recovered over $14 million in pregnancy discrimination settlements. Nine states require reasonable accommodation of pregnant workers: Alaska, California, Connecticut, Hawaii, Illinois, Louisiana, Maryland, New Jersey, and Texas. The cities of New York City and Philadelphia also have laws mandating reasonable accommodation. [S. Jeanine Conley and Laura Scully, *Pregnant Employees Become The Subject Of Heightened Attention And New Legislation*, Baker & Hostetler LLP (Feb. 18, 2014), available at Lexology.com]

Certiorari has been granted in *Young v. UPS*, No. 12-1226, as case about the employer's obligations to provide light-duty assignments for employees with pregnancy-related restrictions.

In fiscal 2013, the number of total charges of discrimination dropped almost 6% from 2012 levels, but the EEOC obtained record recoveries (a total of $372.1

million) under the administrative process. The number of retaliation charges rose. There were 38,539 retaliation charges for all statutes, including 31,208 Title VII retaliation charges. About one-third of all charges (35%; 33,068 charges) alleged race discrimination, 29.5% (27,687 charges) alleged sex discrimination, 28.8% (21,396 charges) alleged age discrimination, 27.7% (25,957 charges) alleged disability discrimination. There were 10,642 charges of national origin discrimination (11.4%), 3,721 (4%) religious discrimination charges, 3,146 (3.4%) charges of color discrimination, and a mere 333 (0.4%) GINA charges. [Barry A. Hartstein, *EEOC Releases Charge Statistics For FY 2013*, Littler Mendelson (Feb. 5, 2014), available at Lexology.com]

The EEOC said that over 70,500 people received benefits through litigation, mediation, conciliation, and/or settlement. The EEOC brought 300 systemic investigations, resulting in 63 settlements and conciliation agreements with an aggregate value of about $40 million. In fiscal 2013, 97,252 charges were resolved; since this is larger than the number of new charges, the agency's backlog diminished. [Scott T. Silverman, *EEOC Obtains Record Relief From Companies*, Akerman LLP (Dec. 19, 2013), available at Lexology.com] The EEOC filed 148 suits in 2013, slightly fewer than the 2012 figure of 155 in 2012. Two hundred twenty-two suits were resolved in 2013. [Melanie Trottman, *Private-Sector Workers File Fewer Complaints, EEOC Says*, WSJ.com (Feb. 5, 2014)] In January 2013, the EEOC won two systemic discrimination cases. The Sixth Circuit finalized its decision to remand the EEOC's sex discrimination case about Cintas' hiring of sales representatives. The Sixth Circuit denied Cintas' motion for reconsideration and none of the judges voted in favor of rehearing en banc. Therefore, the EEOC did not have to pay the $2.6 million of the defendant's attorney's fees that the district court ordered, and the Sixth Circuit revived the EEOC's case. The Sixth Circuit held that the EEOC had acted in good faith and should not have to pay attorney's fees. The district court said that the EEOC erred by suing under § 706 of Title VII, not § 707 (which authorizes pattern-or-practice claims). The Sixth Circuit ruled that, even though there is no specific pattern-or-practice language in § 706, it can still be used in such cases. The EEOC applauded this decision, saying that it permitted a focus in the early stages of the case on whether the employer's ordinary practices were discriminatory rather than whether individual acts of discrimination were committed.

The EEOC sued UPS in 2009 for limiting leave of absence for disabled employees to 12 months and denying them reasonable accommodation. UPS protested that the EEOC named only two employees in its complaint and did not provide enough information about the unidentified workers on behalf the agency sought relief. The district court dismissed the first complaint and two amended complaints. However, when the EEOC moved to appeal the dismissal, the district court permitted the EEOC to file the second amended complaint, which includes detailed factual allegations about the effects of UPS' policy and charged that the policy was applied to all employees across the board. [Jenna Greene, *EEOC*

Scores Wins in Pair of Systemic Discrimination Cases, The BLT (Jan. 18, 2013) (law.com)]

[A] Recent Settlements

The EEOC settled a national origin discrimination case involving an English-only rule. Mesa Systems Inc. agreed to pay $450,000 and provide injunctive relief. The EEOC's position on English-only rules, set out in the Guidelines on Discrimination Because of National Origin, 29 C.F.R. § 1606.7, is that forbidding employees to speak their native language constitutes disadvantage in employment opportunities on account of national origin. However, the EEOC recognizes that in some circumstances, there is a business necessity for communicating in English—in emergencies; when speaking to customers, supervisors, or co-workers who only speak English; or when English is required for the efficiency of a task or project. [*EEOC v. Mesa Systems, Inc.*, No. 2:11-cv-01201 (D. Utah 2013); see Hunton & Williams LLP, *Speak Your Mind: English-Only Policies Remain Hot Button Issue*, Lexology.com (Nov. 20, 2013)]

For recent examples of EEOC settlements, see, e.g., the following:

- Pepsi Beverages settled EEOC race discrimination charges, agreeing to pay $3.13 million and provide job offers and training. The EEOC challenged Pepsi's criminal background check policies. [Tara Cantore, *Pepsi to Pay $3.13M to Resolve Race Bias Charge*, plansponsor.com (Jan. 12, 2012)]
- Sparks Steak House agreed to pay $600,000 to settle EEOC charges of male/male harassment. The complaint accused some managers of regularly engaging in inappropriate touching and groping. The waiters complained but the harassment continued. The maitre d'hotel was the most serious harasser. Management imposed a last chance agreement on him but did not fire him. [Jenna Greene, *NYC Steakhouse Settles with EEOC over Male-on-Male Harassment Charges*, BLT (Nov. 16, 2012) (law.com). Greene reports that the percentage of sexual harassment charges filed by men rose from 12% in 1997 to 16% in 2011.]
- The EEOC charged restaurant chain Senor Frog with severe and rampant sexual harassment at a now-closed location. The case was settled for $350,000 and injunctive relief. At least nine female employees were subjected to repeated propositions, explicit sexual remarks, unwanted touching, by managers who exposed themselves, and they were ordered to provide sexual favors for corporate officials. The owner of the chain permitted the Honolulu managers to harass employees. Female bartenders and servers were discriminated against in promotions and earnings. The HR service Altres was a joint employer, so EEOC said it was responsible for the hostile environment. Altres made a separate $150,000 settlement.

[Sharon B. Bauman et al., *EEOC Settles "Severe, Rampant" Sexual Harassment Allegations For $350,000*, Manatt Phelps & Phillips LLP (Dec. 20, 2013), available at Lexology.com]

- In 2013, there were a number of pregnancy discrimination settlements: $20,000 from Reed Pierce's Sportsmans's Grille (Southern District of Mississippi); $31,000 from Adventures in Learning Aururo Inc. (Northern District of Illinois); $2,500 in back pay and $25,000 in compensatory and punitive damages for a housekeeper who was fired when she disclosed her pregnancy; $80,000 from Landau Uniforms for unequal treatment and discharge of a pregnant employee (Northern District of Mississippi). Platinum PTS Inc. settled a Southern District of Texas case for $100,000 after firing an employee who missed five days of work after a miscarriage. [Lily M. Strumwasser, *Not Without Warning: The EEOC Continues To File Barrages Of Pregnancy Discrimination Lawsuits*, Seyfarth Shaw LLP (Sept. 19, 2013), available at Lexology.com]

- More than two dozen Somali Muslims working as Hertz drivers at Seattle-Tacoma International Airport were fired for refusing to clock out for their prayer breaks. Hertz said that the workers violated the CBA and a settlement reached two years earlier; the union said that the CBA did not require clocking out, The union filed a ULP complaint and EEOC charges. Eight of the 34 were re-hired after signing a clock-out agreement. [Rebecca Moore, *Union Suing Hertz After Firing of Two Dozen Muslims*, plansponsor.com (Oct. 21, 2011). Subsequently, however, the EEOC lost a case charging JBS USA with a pattern or practice of violating Title VII by not permitting Muslim employee to take unscheduled prayer breaks or moving the meal break to cover the sunset prayer. The district court held that those were not reasonable accommodations: they would have a more than de minimis cost in terms of food and employee safety and operational activities, and would inconvenience non-Muslim employees who would have to cover for them. [*EEOC v. JBS USA, LLC*, No. 8:10-CV-318 (D. Neb. Oct. 11, 2013); see Heather F. Vickles, *EEOC Loses 5-Year Battle To Require Muslim Prayer Accommodations*, Sherman & Howard LLC (Oct. 17, 2013), available at Lexology.com]

- In March 2013, Ozarks Electric agreed to pay $95,000 on behalf of a Jehovah's Witness ex-employee who was denied a day off to attend a religious convention. In July of that year, the Landmark Hotel Group paid $45,000 to settle a case about Sabbath accommodation for a Seventh Day Adventist. Voss Lighting agreed to pay $82,500 when it refused to hire an applicant who was asked what church he attended, when and where he was saved, and if he could come in early for Bible study. In September, Maita Chevrolet Geo paid $158,000 in settlement of a case about harassing and firing a Seventh Day Adventist. [Gerald L. Maatman, Jr. and Lily M. Strumwasser, *Compliance: Religious Discrimination—It's On The EEOC's Radar*, Seyfarth Shaw LLP (Nov. 13, 2013), available at Lexology.com]

- Ten months after filing suit against Founders Pavilion, Inc., a Skilled Nursing Facility in Corning, New York, the EEOC settled the case for $370,000. The EEOC said that the facility violated GINA by performing a post-offer, pre-employment medical examination that included questions about family history; employees had to repeat the examination each year. The EEOC also charged Title VII and ADA violations (refusal to hire or firing women for pregnancy or perceived disability). The District Court for the Western District of New York approved the consent decree January 9, 2014. The sum of $110,400 goes to 138 people from whom genetic information was sought, and another $259,600 is payable to five people who were fired or denied hiring for Title VII and ADA violations. [Elizabeth Tempio Clement, *EEOC Settles First Systemic GINA Lawsuit Against Nursing Home*, Littler Mendelson (Jan. 17, 2014), available at Lexology.com]

- An age discrimination suit was filed against Bay State Milling Co. and settled for $80,185. [EEOC case, No. 2:12-cv-14439-DLG (S.D. Fla., settled 2013); see Kevin McGuinness, *Flour Producer Settles Age Discrimination Suit for 80K*, plansponsor.com (Dec. 12, 2013)]

- Kanbar Property Mgmt LLC agreed to pay $140,000 to settle the EEOC's suit about firing a 53-year-old because the CEO wanted "younger and prettier" property managers to meet with and entertain potential tenants. The defendant argued that charging discrimination against the "old and ugly" is a mixed motive case of the type ruled out by *Gross,* but the district court allowed the case to go to trial, ruling that the jury could find that the motivation was age-related. But-for causation is not necessarily sole causation, it merely proves nexus between the discriminatory motivation and the termination decision. [*EEOC v. Kanbar Prop. Mgmt. LLC*, No. 12-CV-422-JED-TLW (N.D. Okla., settled 2013); see Kevin McGuinness, *Company Settles EEOC Age Discrimination Suit*, plansponsor.com (Sept. 11, 2013); P. Andrew Torrez, *If You Can't Be Fired For Being Old, Can You Be Fired For Being Old And Ugly? Why This Is A Harder Question Than You Might Think*, Zuckerman Spaeder LLP (Sept. 5, 2013), available at Lexology.com]

- AT&T agreed to pay $250,000 for firing 53-year-old Terry Pierce because of her age when younger, less effective sales coaches were retained or allowed to transfer. [Kevin McGuinness, *AT&T Settles Age Discrimination Lawsuit*, plansponsor.com (Sept. 3, 2013)]

- Ruby Tuesday Inc. paid $575,000 to settle an ADEA pattern-or-practice class action in the Western District of Pennsylvania. The consent decree covering six restaurants in Pennsylvania and Ohio forbids future age discrimination or retaliation; sets numerical goals for recruiting and hiring persons over 40; and sets compensation and bonuses of managers reflecting their degree of compliance. [*EEOC v. Ruby Tuesday Inc*, No. 09-1330 (settled W.D. Pa. 2013); see Kevin McGuinness, *Ruby Tuesday Settles Age Discrimination Lawsuit*, plansponsor.com (Dec. 10, 2013)]

- The Northern District of Illinois gave final approval in February 2010 to the largest ADA settlement in a single EEOC suit: Sears agreed to pay $6.2 million to settle a nationwide class action about firing of disabled workers. The suit began in 2004 with an employee's charge that he was fired for taking leave after being injured on the job, instead of being granted accommodations that would have permitted him to return to work. The EEOC's discovery revealed hundreds of other employees who were similarly treated. The named plaintiff received $122,500; 235 class members received amounts of $2,250 and up. [*EEOC v. Sears*, No. 04-C-7282 (N.D. Ill. Feb. 5, 2010)]

- Imagine Schools, Inc., a nationwide charter school operator that has over 70 schools in 12 states, agreed to pay $570,000 to settle an EEOC suit in the Western District of Missouri. The EEOC alleged that Imagine Schools violated the PDA when it terminated two pregnant employees (an office manager and an administrative assistant) when it closed a charter school and re-opened a private school at the same location. [Rebecca Moore, *Charter School Operator Settles Pregnancy Discrimination Lawsuit*, plansponsor.com (Mar. 22, 2010)]

[B] Recent Litigation

The EEOC's Guidelines were revised in 2008 to include non-theistic moral and ethical beliefs in the definition of religion. The EEOC filed 12 religious discrimination suits in fiscal 2013, three more than in 2012. The EEOC seldom accepts employers' arguments that an employee's beliefs are not sincere; employers are more likely to prevail on an undue hardship argument. The EEOC has sued Bo-Cherry Inc. (*dba* Bojangles) in the Western District of North Carolina for firing a bearded Muslim employee after not permitting him to wear a beard net. Dynamic Medical Services was sued in the Southern District of Florida for firing two employees who refused to attend Scientology classes. United Cellular was sued in the Northern District of Alabama for refusal to accommodate a Seventh Day Adventist worker's Sabbath. In the Middle District of North Carolina, the EEOC filed a suit against Scottish Food Systems because its dress code required a Pentecostal employee to wear trousers when she says her religion requires her to wear skirts. CONSOL Energy Inc. and Consolidated Coal Co. have been sued in the Northern District of West Virginia by an Evangelical Christian who said that the mandatory biometric hand scanner time clock violated her religious beliefs; the employer refused to let her submit manual time records or report verbally to her supervisor. [Gerald L. Maatman, Jr. and Lily M. Strumwasser, *Compliance: Religious Discrimination—It's On The EEOC's Radar*, Seyfarth Shaw LLP (Nov. 13, 2013), available at Lexology.com]

The Abercrombie & Fitch "Looks Policy" for its employees forbids head coverings, leading to several cases brought by Muslim applicants or employees who wear hijab. Samantha Elauf said Abercrombie was denied hiring on this basis. The district court granted summary judgment for the EEOC, but the Tenth Circuit reversed and granted summary judgment for the employer. The Tenth Circuit said that, at her job interview, Elauf did not mention her hijab or say that she wore it for religious reasons, and she did not request accommodation. The Tenth Circuit said that, because religion is an individual personal matter, the burden is on the job applicant or employee to advise the employer of the need for accommodation. [*EEOC v. Abercrombie & Fitch*, 731 F.3d 1106 (10th Cir. 2013); see Seyfarth Shaw, *If You Want A Religious Accommodation, You've Got To Ask For It: What Employers Can Learn From The 10th Circuit's Ruling In EEOC V. Abercrombie & Fitch*, Lexology.com (Oct. 8, 2013)]

However, in another *Abercrombie & Fitch* case, the District Court for the Northern District of California granted summary judgment for the EEOC, rejecting several of the defendant's affirmative defenses (that the Look Policy is protected commercial free speech; that there were no grounds for injunction or punitive damages). The district court held that the EEOC met its conciliation obligation by months of extensive discussions before filing suit. The district court granted summary judgment for the EEOC on liability, because Abercrombie did not show that allowing workers to wear head coverings would impose an undue hardship. The employee worked mostly in the stockroom, out of public view, so the district court rejected Abercrombie's argument that the Look Policy was commercial free speech because employees served as "brand ambassadors." The district court said punitive damages were warranted given the employer's malice or reckless indifference to the employee's religious obligations. [*EEOC v. Abercrombie & Fitch Stores, Inc.*, 966 F. Supp. 2d 949 (N.D. Cal. 2013); see Gerald L. Maatman, Jr. and Howard M. Wexler, *The EEOC Scores Summary Judgment Win In Religious Discrimination Case*, Seyfarth Shaw LLP (Sept. 9, 2013), available at Lexology.com; Rebecca Ballhaus, *Muslim Fired by Abercrombie Over Head Scarf Wins Bias Suit*, WSJ.com (Sept. 10, 2013)]

The Third Circuit upheld summary judgment for the employer in an EEOC Title VII suit on behalf of female Muslim prison employees who wanted to wear khimars, a type of head covering, at work. The Third Circuit found that the khimars present at least a small danger because they could be used as a weapon against employees, or could be used by prisoners to impersonate guards, and it would be impractical to remove the khimars at each checkpoint. [*EEOC v. Geo*

Group Inc., 616 F.3d 265 (3d Cir. 2010); see *EEOC Wins Settlement of Suit on Behalf of Muslim,* plansponsor.com (Nov. 28, 2011) for Imperial Security's $50,000 settlement in favor of a security guard who was ordered to remove her khimar when she reported for work.]

The National Institute of Mental Health says that 5.7 million adults in the United States are affected by bipolar disorder each year, making it one of the top 10 causes of disability. In 2012, the EEOC won a case against Cottonwood Financial Ltd. in the Eastern District of Washington, one of the first cases involving bipolar disorder. Receptionist Kelly Ferris took medical leave to manage a flare-up of her condition. She said that she was fired after five months, whereas company policy permits an 18-month leave. In September 2012, the EEOC sued the supermarket chain King Soopers for firing a bipolar worker. The year before, King Soopers settled another EEOC case for $80,000, for failing to stop the bullying of a mentally challenged worker. [Ashley Casas, *EEOC Sues Food Retailer for Firing Bipolar Worker*, plansponsor.com (Sept. 19, 2012)]

UPS Supply Chain Solutions agreed to pay $95,000 to settle a disability discrimination suit about denial of accommodation to deaf employee Mauricio Centeno. Centeno was refused a sign language interpreter for training and staff meetings, although his employer knew that he had trouble reading written English. The case was settled after the Ninth Circuit held that employers must provide reasonable accommodations for employment conditions, such as staff meetings, even if they are not essential functions of the job. [*EEOC v. UPS Supply Chain Solutions*, No. CV 06-06210 ABC (Ex); see Tara Cantore, *UPS Unit to Pay $95K to Settle Disability Discrimination Lawsuit*, plansponsor.com (Dec. 15, 2011)]

A significant emerging issue is the scope of the EEOC's duty to conciliate—and what will happen to the case if the EEOC's conciliation efforts are deficient.

The EEOC suffered defeat several times in its case against trucking company CRST Van Expedited Inc. The wider significance is that the EEOC may bring fewer cases on behalf of groups of plaintiffs. The EEOC sued CRST, charging serious sexual harassment, including rape in some cases, of more than 200 female truck drivers by male drivers assigned to train them. The District Court for the Northern District of Iowa not only dismissed the EEOC's case, but also ordered the EEOC to pay more than $4.467 million in fees and expenses to CRST as the prevailing party. After a female driver filed EEOC charges, the EEOC approached more than 2,700 female ex-employees, recruiting more than 200 potential class members. The district court criticized the EEOC for an improper attempt at pursuing a pattern or practice case without producing evidence. The district court eliminated many other potential plaintiffs for various reasons (e.g., they did not allege severe and pervasive harassment; they did not list the potential recovery from the suit in their bankruptcy petitions; they did not complain to CRST and give the company a chance to eliminate the harassment). The district court reduced the plaintiff class to 67, then dismissed all those claims for the EEOC's failure to investigate or attempt conciliation of each individual claim.

The district court also held that the trainers were not supervisors, so CRST would not be vicariously liable if harassment occurred. The Eighth Circuit upheld most of the district court's findings, but ruled that two plaintiffs had viable claims. The Eighth Circuit held that, because CRST was no longer a prevailing defendant, the EEOC did not have to pay CRST's attorneys' fees immediately.

The Eighth Circuit agreed with the district court that the EEOC failed to meet its obligation to attempt conciliation of each claim. What the EEOC should have done was to investigate thoroughly before filing suit, and attempt conciliation of each claim uncovered during the investigation. The case was remanded to the district court, which once again held that CRST was the prevailing defendant, and once again ordered the EEOC to pay almost $5 million to CRST. [*EEOC v. CRST Van Expedited Inc.,* 679 F.3d 657 (8th Cir. 2012); *en banc rehearing denied,* June 8, 2012. *EEOC v. CRST Van Expedited, Inc.*, No. 07-CV-95, 2013 U.S. Dist. LEXIS 107822 (N.D. Iowa Aug. 1, 2013); see Gerald L. Maatman, Jr. and Howard M. Wexler, *Time to Pay Up! EEOC Ordered to Pay $4.694 Million in Fees and Costs for Pursuing "Unreasonable" and "Groundless" Claims* (Aug. 3, 2013), available at Lexology.com]

After this decision, the District Court for the Northern District of Illinois allowed an ADA case to proceed even though the EEOC attempted conciliation in two cases but not in the cases of 17 additional employees who were located during the investigation. The Northern District of Illinois focused on the validity of the claims rather than the correctness of the EEOC pre-trial procedure. In contrast, the District Court for the Eastern District of Washington cited the *CRST* case and ordered mediation because the court found that the EEOC's good-faith conciliation efforts were inadequate. [Compare *EEOC v. United Road Towing Inc.,* No. 10 C 6259 (N.D. Ill. May 11, 2012) with *EEOC v. Evans Fruit Co.,* No. CV-10-3033-LRS (E.D. Wash. May 24, 2012)]

The EEOC's position is that courts do not have oversight powers over the conciliation process, but the Southern District of Texas ruled in late 2013 that Fifth Circuit precedent permits judicial review of conciliation attempts. The district court said that the court must evaluate whether the conciliation requirement was adequately fulfilled. The EEOC must explain to the employer why the EEOC believes a violation of Title VII has occurred; the EEOC must offer an opportunity for voluntary compliance; and its response to the employer must be reasonable and flexible. The district court rejected the EEOC's sovereign immunity argument, holding that sovereign immunity does not permit the EEOC to avoid duties imposed by Congress. [*EEOC v. Bass Pro Outdoor World, LLC, et al.*, Case No. 4:11-CV-3425, 2013 U.S. Dist. LEXIS 142796 (S.D. Tex. Oct. 2, 2013); see Christopher J. DeGroff and Julie G. Yap, *It's Not Just A Speed Bump: The EEOC Loses Another Battle In Its War On The Mandatory Conciliation Process*, Seyfarth Shaw LLP (Oct. 9, 2013), available at Lexology.com]

The Seventh Circuit ruled in late 2013 that the EEOC's mishandling of the conciliation process is not an affirmative defense; the Seventh Circuit did not believe that judges can determine the adequacy of conciliation. However, the Second, Fourth, Fifth, Sixth, Eighth, Tenth, and Eleventh Circuits disagree. (The Second, Fifth, and Eleventh Circuits apply a three-part inquiry to determine if conciliation was adequate; the Fourth, Sixth, and Tenth Circuits require the EEOC to satisfy a test of minimal good faith.) In the Seventh Circuit view, Title VII requires the conciliation agreement to be acceptable to the EEOC, placing the EEOC in control of the process, and the statutory language also mandates that things said during the conciliation process be kept confidential. [*EEOC v. Mach Mining*, 738 F.3d 171 (7th Cir. 2013); see Paul Patten and Rick Cohen, *Seventh Circuit Agrees With EEOC There Is No Affirmative Defense For The EEOC's Failure To Conciliate*, Jackson Lewis PC (Dec. 23, 2013), available at Lexology.com; William J. Anthony, *No Implied Failure-To-Conciliate Defense For Employers Against EEOC, says Seventh Circuit*, Jackson Lewis PC (Dec. 24, 2013), available at Lexology.com. Certiorari was granted on June 30, 2014, as No. 13-1019. See Hunton & Williams LLP, *Supreme Court Grants Certiorari in Mach Mining LLC v. EEOC to Consider "Failure to Conciliate" Affirmative Defense* (July 15, 2014), available at Lexology.com.]

The EEOC suffered defeat in a high-profile systemic pattern or practice pregnancy discrimination class action. Most of the claims were dismissed, and Judge Loretta Preska berated the EEOC for its inaction before suit. The employer, Bloomberg L.P., was granted leave to seek an attorneys' fee award as the prevailing party. Between 2002 and 2009, 603 Bloomberg employees were pregnant or took maternity leave. The EEOC characterized 78 of them as victims of discrimination. The Southern District of New York granted summary judgment for Bloomberg on the class allegations, finding that a reasonable fact-finder could not conclude that Bloomberg had a pattern or practice of decreasing pregnant employees' pay or responsibility. After the pattern or practice claim was dismissed, the EEOC attempted to continue the suit by asserting individual pregnancy discrimination claims on behalf of 29 non-intervening claimants and an additional six intervenors. The district court granted summary judgment for the employer with respect to the non-intervening plaintiffs, finding that the EEOC did not meet its obligations of investigation and conciliation, and did not give Bloomberg enough notice of the nature of the charges against it. Conciliation was inadequate because the EEOC focused on its overly broad systemic claims and did not provide specific information about the individual claims. The district court said that class claims cannot be used to make an end run around the pre-litigation efforts needed to pursue individual suits. In a second, 181-page, decision, the district court granted summary judgment for the employer on most of the six intervenors' claims, leaving only one plaintiff's claims about a demotion and pay cut in 2006. [*EEOC v. Bloomberg L.P.*, 967 F. Supp. 2d 802 (S.D.N.Y. 2013); see Gerald L. Maatman, Jr. and Howard M. Wexler, *The EEOC Suffers Another Resounding Defeat Due To "Shoot First, Aim Later" Tactics*, Seyfarth Shaw LLP (Sept. 10, 2013), available at Lexology.com]

[C] EEOC Guidance Documents

The EEOC issued enforcement guidance about arrest and criminal records in April 2012. [EEOC enforcement guidance, *Consideration of Arrest and Conviction Records in Employment Decisions Under Title VII of the Civil Rights Act of 1964* (Apr. 25, 2012), <http://www.eeoc.gov/laws/guidance/arrest_conviction.cfm>]

Using these principles, the agency filed suits in South Carolina and Illinois, charging that criminal background check policies violated Title VII because they had an adverse impact on minorities and were not job-related and consistent with business necessity. The Attorneys General of West Virginia, Alabama, Kansas, Montana, Colorado, Georgia, Nebraska, South Carolina, and Utah wrote to the EEOC asking it to withdraw the suits and rescind the guidance; the EEOC refused. However, the District Court for the District of Maryland granted summary judgment for the employer in a suit challenging a screening program; the district court found that the plaintiff's statistical expert was unworthy of credence. The Sixth Circuit upheld a $750,000 fee award against the EEOC because the EEOC continued to litigate a case that incorrectly charged PeopleMark with maintaining a company-wide ban on hiring felons. [*EEOC v. PeopleMark*, 732 F.3d 584 (6th Cir. 2013); see Pierre H. Bergeron, *Sixth Circuit Upholds $750,000 Fee Award Against EEOC*, Squire Sanders (Oct. 9, 2013), available at Lexology.com]

In March 2014, the EEOC and FTC jointly published guidance about background checks, warning employers that whenever background information (from any source) is used to make employment decisions, compliance with anti-discrimination laws (including Title VII, GINA, the ADEA, and the Fair Credit Reporting Act—FCRA) is mandatory. The EEOC warned that it is illegal to check background information only because of a person's race, national origin, color, sex, disability, age, or genetic status. "Special care" should be taken when there are problems that may be more common among members of certain groups (e.g., some ethnic groups have higher arrest rates than others). The FTC said that the FCRA requires safeguards if an employer obtains a credit or criminal background report from a company that compiles background information. The applicant or employee must be given written notice that this information might be used in employment decisions and his or her written consent must be obtained. If an investigative report (based on personal interviews) is ordered, the applicant or employee must be informed of the right to information about the investigation. If adverse actions are taken based on information from a profiling company, the employer must give the applicant or employee a copy of the FTC's summary of FCRA rights, and must give contact information for the profiling company. [EEOC/FTC, *Background Checks: What Employers Need to Know*, <http://www.eeoc.gov/eeoc/publications/background_checks_employers.cfm> (March 2014)]

In March 2014, the EEOC released guidance on proper handling of religious garb under corporate dress codes. The examples given include wearing religious articles (e.g., cross or hijab), prohibition on certain garments (women not wearing pants or short skirts), and shaving/hair length requirements. The EEOC's position is that federal law requires employers to make exceptions to their usual rules or preferences if required for employees to observe religious dress and grooming practices. The EEOC says that Title VII covers all aspects of religious observance, practice, and belief whether they are based on belief in God or non-theistic moral or ethical beliefs. Nor can employers require employees to wear religious garb or articles if they object on the basis of their non-belief. However, personal preferences that are not religion-based are not protected. An employee's newly adopted practice can be considered sincere even if it is recent, and wearing religious dress only during sacred periods (e.g., a Muslim employee who wears a scarf only during Ramadan) does not mean that the employee does not hold a sincere belief. Customer preference is not a defense to a discrimination claim, and the EEOC says it is unacceptable to assign an employee to a non-customer-contact position because of actual or feared customer preferences. The EEOC position is that, once an employer becomes aware that religious accommodation is needed, it must accommodate sincere religious beliefs, practices, or observances that conflict with work requirements, unless accommodation imposes an undue hardship on the employer. The need for accommodation is triggered when an employee cites a religious reason for not conforming to employer policy. The employer can require a religious item or attire to be covered when at work—but only if the employee can do so without violating his or her religious beliefs. The EEOC's examples include permitting employees to wear beards (although beard covers can be required for sanitary reasons), wearing yarmulkes, and carrying kirpans (Sikh ritual knives) as long as they are not sharp. [EEOC, *Religious Garb and Grooming in the Workplace: Rights and Responsibilities*, <http://www.eeoc.gov/eeoc/publications/qa_religious_garb_grooming.cfm> (Mar. 6, 2014). See also the EEOC's fact sheet, <http://www.eeoc.gov/eeoc/publications/fs_religious_garb_grooming.cfm> (Mar. 6, 2014).]

§ 41.02 EEOC ADR

At times, the EEOC itself will engage in ADR with employers and employees as an alternative to normal charge processing methods. The EEOC issued two policy statements on these subjects in 1997, although formal regulations were not issued at that time.

Under these policy statements, the EEOC said ADR was not appropriate in some cases. The agency did not treat ADR as fair or appropriate in important test cases where the EEOC wishes to establish policy or set a precedent; where the

EEOC would have to maintain an ongoing presence to monitor compliance; or where the case has significant implications for people besides the parties to the individual charge—for instance, other employees and other companies in the same or different industries.

The EEOC took the position that ADR was fair and appropriate if:

- It is voluntarily elected, not compelled;
- The EEOC provides help to employees who are confused about the process;
- The decision maker (mediator or arbitrator) is truly neutral;
- The proceedings are confidential;
- The outcome of the process is an enforceable written agreement.

The EEOC's home page for mediation can be found at <http://www.eeoc.gov/eeoc/mediation/index.cfm>, containing a number of resources, including a video about the advantages of mediation.EEOC mediation was launched in 1991, with a pilot program in the Philadelphia, New Orleans, Houston, and Washington field offices; the pilot was later extended nationwide. An ADR program was in full operation by April 1999.

The agency says that between 1999 and 2010, close to 136,000 matters have been mediated. Close to 70% (more than 94,000 charges) were resolved. EEOC mediation involves not only EEOC personnel trained in-house and outside contract mediators, but volunteers as well. Mediation is offered as an option early in the process of handling a discrimination charge, but mediation is not provided after the EEOC determines that a charge is without merit, unless the parties request it. The EEOC has entered into 1,573 Universal Agreements to Mediate (UAM)s with local employers and 214 UAMs with regional or national employers. These agreements expedite the mediation process by setting up an ongoing relationship between the company and the EEOC. [EEOC, *History of the EEOC Mediation Program*, <http://www1.eeoc.gov//eeoc/mediation/history.cfm> (accessed Mar. 30, 2014)]

In fiscal 2012, the EEOC said that 11,376 mediations were conducted, leading to 8,714 resolutions, a resolution rate of over three-quarters (76.6%). Monetary benefits of $153.25 million were obtained for 7,488 persons (somewhat lower than the 2011 recovery of $170 million for 8,725 people) and 912 people received non-monetary benefits as a result of EEOC mediation. It took an average of 101 days to close a case in 2012. [EEOC, *EEOC Mediation Statistics FY 1999 Through FY 2012*, <http://www.eeoc.gov/eeoc/mediation/mediation_stats.cfm> (undated, accessed Mar. 30, 2014)]

§ 41.03 TITLE VII ENFORCEMENT

Both the EEOC and state antidiscrimination agencies have a role in investigating an employee's allegations of discrimination. Initial charges can be filed with either the EEOC or the state or local agency.

However, if the employee goes to the EEOC first, it generally "defers" to the state or local agency. That is, it sends the paperwork to the state or local agency, and gives it a 60-day deferral period to resolve the complaint. [See 29 C.F.R. § 1601.74 for a list of state and local agencies that are deemed to have enough enforcement power to handle a discrimination charge] Furthermore, some agencies (listed in 29 C.F.R. § 1601.80) are "certified" by the EEOC, based on a track record of at least four years as a deferral agency, during which time the EEOC found its work product to be acceptable.

Title VII and ADA charges must be filed within the EEOC within 180 days of the time of the alleged discrimination (if there is no deferral agency in the picture) or within 300 days of the alleged discrimination, or 30 days of the time the deferral agency terminates processing of the charge (if a deferral agency is involved).

However, these timing requirements are tricky and provide many opportunities for the employer to get cases dismissed. In a case involving a deferral agency, the filing period is really only 240 days, because of the 60-day period when the EEOC steps aside and lets the deferral agency handle the matter. However, most deferral agencies have what is called "work sharing" agreements with the EEOC. In the jurisdiction of those agencies, an employee's complaint is timely if it is made more than 240, but less than 300, days after the alleged discrimination occurred.

Many cases involve statute of limitations issues and call for determining timing issues of when a discriminatory act occurred. The Supreme Court ruled, in May 2007, that a Title VII pay discrimination charge must be filed within 180 days of the time the discriminatory employment decision was made and communicated to the employee. It is not acceptable to treat discriminatory pay as a continuing violation, for which a charge can be filed within 180 days of any paycheck. The Supreme Court said that if an employer engages in a series of intentionally discriminatory acts, each of which could support a separate charge, then each act counts as a new violation. But continuing to pay a female employee less than a comparable male reflects later effects of past discrimination—so the clock does not start again with each paycheck. [*Ledbetter v. Goodyear Tire & Rubber Co.* (550 U.S. 618 (2007)]

The first law signed by President Obama after his inauguration was the Lilly Ledbetter Fair Pay Act to reverse this ruling. The Ledbetter Act covers cases that had been filed or were pending on the day before the Supreme Court decision. As a result of the Ledbetter Act, a claim is timely if it is filed within 180 days (or 300 days, if applicable) of the adoption of a pay practice; when the worker becomes subject to the policy—or each time the policy is applied to an employee.

Therefore, each new paycheck (or payment of benefits) can start the clock running.

The Fifth Circuit, sitting en banc, held that harassment based on gender stereotypes can be actionable under Title VII as "because of sex." An ironworker suffered constant verbal and physical harassment, including indecent exposure and jokes about rape, because his supervisor did not think the victim was manly enough. There was no evidence that the harasser was trying to have sex with the victim, no evidence of hostility toward men in general, or that men and women were treated differently. However, the Fifth Circuit joined the Third, Seventh, Eighth, and Tenth Circuits in describing those *Oncale* factors (see § 35.05) as illustrative, not the exclusive means of proving harassment. Therefore, the EEOC could make its case based on harassment for perceived lack of conformity with gender stereotypes (whether or not the victim actually was "manly"). [*EEOC v. Boh Bros. Constr. Co.*, 731 F.3d 444 (5th Cir. 2013); see Dennis A. Clifford and Christopher J. DeGroff, *"Macho Man Discrimination": The EEOC Scores Fifth Circuit Win In Gender-Stereotype Suit*, Seyfarth Shaw LLP (Oct. 3, 2013), available at Lexology.com. The case was settled after trial via a consent judgment calling for $125,000 in compensatory damages: see Manatt Phelps & Phillips LLP, *Same-Sex Harassment Suits Yield Sizable Settlement*, Lexology.com (Mar. 19, 2014).]

The EEOC is also the agency responsible for enforcement of Title II of the Genetic Information Nondiscrimination Act of 2008 (GINA; Pub. L. No. 110-233, codified at 42 U.S.C. § 2000ff). Proposed Regulations were published at 74 Fed. Reg. 9056 (Mar. 2, 2009). However, OSHA is responsible for enforcing the laws protecting whistleblowers.

§ 41.04 EEOC INVESTIGATION

If the EEOC can't settle a charge informally, its next step is to investigate the facts and determine if there is reasonable cause to believe that the employee's complaint is well-founded. If it makes such a "reasonable cause" determination, it has an obligation to attempt to conciliate: to get the employer to improve its equal opportunity policies, sign a compliance agreement, and compensate the employee for past discrimination. The EEOC can't close its case file until it has evidence of the employer's actual compliance with the conciliation agreement.

The EEOC published a five-year plan for E-RACE for FY 2008–2013, with five main objectives:

1. Better collection and analysis of data, to identify and redress discrimination
2. Better charge processing by the EEOC itself

3. Training based on new strategies and legal theories to address new issues as they arise (e.g., conviction records, exclusion based on names or zip codes)
4. Improved visibility and a higher public profile for EEOC's efforts to combat race and color discrimination
5. Greater participation by members of the public in averting and eliminating discrimination. [EEOC, *E-RACE Goals and Objectives*, <http://www.eeoc.gov/eeoc/initiatives/e-race/> (Jan. 30, 2008) (accessed Mar. 30, 2014)

As a general rule, an EEOC determination letter is admissible evidence in a suit later brought by the charging party. However, the determination letter is not automatically admissible: The court can keep it out, under Federal Rules of Evidence Rule 403, if the court determines that the probative value of the document is significantly outweighed by negative factors such as prejudice and risk of confusion. [*Coleman v. Home Depot Inc.*, 306 F.3d 1333 (3d Cir. 2002)]

Plaintiff Kwan got good reviews and a bonus at end of 2007. In 2008, she complained to an executive that male peers were paid more than she was. She was fired three weeks later for leaving work early. The employer's position statement in response to Kwan's EEOC complaint said that she was terminated because the business had changed and her skill set was no longer required. The employer said that she made multiple serious errors and did not work long enough hours. However, during discovery, the employer changed its explanation to Kwan's poor performance and behavior. During motion practice and litigation, the employer relied on three specific incidents of poor performance, but only one of them was mentioned in the EEOC position statement. The Second Circuit reversed the district court's grant of summary judgment for the employer in Kwan's retaliation case, finding that the inconsistency between the EEOC position statement and the employer's litigating position and the brief span between her pay discrimination complaint and her termination would permit the case to go to trial. [*Kwan v. Andalex Group, LLC*, 737 F.3d 834 (2d Cir. 2013); see Michael A. Sands and Sheeva J. Ghassemi-Vanni, *EEOC Position Statement Comes Back To Bite Employer In Civil Lawsuit*, Fenwick & West LLP (Jan. 14, 2014), available at Lexology.com]

In mid-2013, the EEOC used Case New Holland Inc's own e-mail network to contact thousands of employees to find plaintiffs for an ADEA class action. On August 1, 2013, the company sued the EEOC and one of its investigators in the District Court for the District of Columbia, seeking declaratory and injunctive relief because the e-mails had been sent before there had been any finding of discrimination. The plaintiff charged the EEOC with violations of the Administrative Procedure Act because it did not have an enabling regulation; the EEOC trespassed on the plaintiff's computer network; and the plaintiff said it should have had the right to be present when its employees were questioned. [Whitney

M. Harmon, *You've Got Mail! The EEOC's Latest Investigation Tactic Could Be Coming To Your Corporate Inboxes*, Baker Donelson Bearman Caldwell & Berkowitz PC (Sept. 12, 2013), available at Lexology.com]

If the EEOC believes that the employer is blocking the process, it sends a written notice demanding compliance. Title VII § 706(c) gives the EEOC discretion to sue the employer if an acceptable conciliation agreement cannot be reached within 30 days after the end of the period when the EEOC defers to state agency jurisdiction, or 30 days of the date a charge is filed with the EEOC. There is no statute of limitations for suits brought directly by the EEOC: They can sue even for events in the distant past.

If and when the EEOC concludes that there is no reasonable cause to believe that the facts are as charged by the employee, the EEOC will inform the charging party of this determination. In Title VII and ADA cases (but not Equal Pay Act or ADEA cases), the charging party can still sue the employer in federal court, but must get a "right to sue" letter from the EEOC indicating that the case has been closed. Usually, the EEOC gets 180 days to attempt conciliation, but the employee can ask for earlier termination of the EEOC's involvement, and earlier issuance of the right-to-sue letter. However, the employee can't bypass the conciliation process entirely.

Once the right-to-sue letter is issued, the employee has only 90 days to file the federal suit. If the 90 days pass without commencement of a suit, the EEOC can still bring suit, on the theory that the potential private plaintiff's inaction has reinstated the agency's own powers.

A major sex discrimination suit involving about 44,000 female employees of the largest retail specialty jeweler in the United States was dismissed because the EEOC failed to prove that it undertook a nationwide investigation before bringing charges, and for attempting to introduce evidence that was not provided during discovery. The suit began about nine years ago with 19 women in eight states, including New York, filing EEOC charges of denial of equal pay and promotion opportunities. The EEOC's Buffalo office investigated and the EEOC sued in 2008 alleging unlawful employment practices nationwide. The defendant moved for summary judgment, saying that there could not be nationwide allegations without a nationwide investigation; the magistrate judge agreed, stating that the EEOC had the burden of proving that it satisfied all conditions for filing a claim, including a full investigation. [*EEOC v. Sterling Jewelers*, No. 09-cv-00706 (W.D.N.Y., dismissed 2014); see John Caher, *Judge Faults EEOC for Probe Into Discrimination Claim*, N.Y.L.J. (Mar. 13, 2014), available at law.com]

The EEOC's investigative powers generally end as soon as a right-to-sue letter has been issued. [*EEOC v. Federal Home Loan Mortgage Co.*, 37 F. Supp. 2d 769 (E.D. Va. 1999)] The exception is the case in which the EEOC thinks its investigation goes beyond the litigation, in which case it can intervene in the employee's private suit or file its own charges. However, the EEOC will not intervene in a suit, or bring a suit, if it makes a "no reasonable cause" determination.

Suits with the EEOC as plaintiff are limited to matters investigated as a result of a charge, not matters outside the scope of the matter for which the EEOC attempted to conciliate. In other words, the EEOC's efforts to conciliate one charge won't make the employer vulnerable to a host of other charges. Furthermore, because of the burden of its workload, the EEOC files only a few hundred suits a year.

A defective EEOC investigation led the Fourth Circuit to uphold an award of $193,000 in attorneys' fees to a prevailing defendant in an EEOC suit. The district court held that it was unreasonable to file the complaint, because events during the EEOC investigation prevented the EEOC from getting either injunctive or monetary relief. A Propak supervisor filed an EEOC charge stating that Propak fired him for his American national origin when he complained that only Hispanic workers were hired for certain supervisory positions. The EEOC spent almost six years investigating the allegation. In September 2004, the EEOC designated the matter as a class case, but did not notify Propak of this for almost four years. The complainant, Quintois, got a right to sue letter and sued Propak in March 2008. His suit was dismissed four months later by agreement of the parties. In September 2008, EEOC issued a determination letter stating that Propak violated Title VII by discriminating against non-Hispanic applicants. During conciliation, the EEOC proposed remedial measures for Propak facilities in North and South Carolina—but those locations were already closed. EEOC sued Propak in August 2009 about events between October 2002 and June 2004, asking for injunctive relief benefiting non-Hispanic persons and monetary relief for non-Hispanic applicants. Summary judgment for Propak was granted, on the basis of laches. Propak was prejudiced by the delay, e.g., it did not have some of the records sought by the EEOC because the company routinely destroyed old records. On appeal to the Fourth Circuit, the EEOC argued that the laches defense does not apply in suits brought by federal agencies. The Fourth Circuit held that prevailing defendants receive attorneys' fee awards only if the plaintiff pursued a claim it knew or should have known was groundless, frivolous, or unreasonable. The Fourth Circuit held that the EEOC failed to identify potential victims in time to get relief for them, and before Propak closed some of its facilities. [*EEOC v. Propak Logistics Inc.*, 746 F.3d 145 (4th Cir. 2014)]

§ 41.05 ADEA ENFORCEMENT

The rules for ADEA cases are similar, but not identical, to those for Title VII cases, so you should check to see if ADEA plaintiffs have violated any of the requirements for that type of suit. For example, in 2009, the Supreme Court ruled that the differences between the statutory language and case law of Title VII and the ADEA mean that ADEA plaintiffs who allege mixed motive discrimination (a combination of valid and illicit motivations for the adverse employment action) can win only if they prove, by a preponderance of the evidence, that the adverse action would never have been taken but for the plaintiff's age falling within the ADEA protected group. [*Gross v. FBL Fin. Servs., Inc.*, 557 U.S. 167 (2009)] The Ledbetter Act (see above) also applies to the ADEA.

In addition to suits brought by employees who charge that they have been subjected to age discrimination, the ADEA statute provides for enforcement by the Secretary of Labor; 29 U.S.C. § 26 gives the Secretary the power to investigate ADEA charges, including subpoenaeing witnesses and inspecting employers' business records. (The DOL has delegated this power to the EEOC.)

Even criminal penalties can be imposed against anyone who "shall forcibly resist, oppose, impede, intimidate or interfere with" a DOL representative engaged in enforcing the ADEA. [See 29 U.S.C. § 629] The criminal penalty is a fine of up to $500 and/or up to one year's imprisonment, although imprisonment will be ordered only in the case of someone who has already been convicted of the same offense in the past.

Although the EEOC can become an ADEA plaintiff, it seldom does so. The cases it selects are usually large-scale, involving egregious practices, many employees, or a pattern or practice of discrimination. The EEOC can bring a suit even if no employee of the company has filed timely charges of age discrimination.

If the EEOC files suit after an employee has already sued based on the same conduct on the employer's part, the earlier individual suit can proceed. However, an individual who wants back pay or other monetary relief cannot file suit after the EEOC starts its own suit, because the EEOC litigates on behalf of all affected employees.

However, if the EEOC complaint covers a pattern or practice of discrimination lasting "up to the present time," this means the date when the EEOC filed its complaint, so an individual can file a private suit charging the employer with committing discrimination after the filing of the EEOC complaint.

The EEOC doesn't need written consent from employees to file a suit on their behalf. The EEOC can seek relief for all employees on the basis of a charge filed by one employee who only reported discrimination against him- or herself. The EEOC can also undertake a single conciliation effort for multiple charges, as long as the employer is notified that the charge involves more than one complainant.

No employee who has already sued the employer can get back pay or other individual relief as part of an EEOC suit involving the same facts. However, if an employee tried to sue, but the case was dismissed on the basis of untimely filing, then the EEOC can bring a suit to get an injunction against the employer, even if the EEOC's case is based on the same facts as the suit that was dismissed.

■ **TIP:** The general rule is that a company that files for bankruptcy protection is entitled to an automatic stay—a period of time during which suits against the company cannot proceed. However, a suit by the EEOC is considered an exercise of the government's regulatory, policing function, and therefore can proceed even while the automatic stay is in place.

Certiorari was granted in 2007 in a case about the extent to which other employees will be permitted to "piggyback" their own charges in an ADEA case where another employee answered the EEOC questionnaire and made a statement (Form 283) but did not file a formal charge (Form 5). The Supreme Court held that employees should not be penalized for the EEOC's mistakes. The Court held that a valid ADEA charge requires only certain information (an allegation; the name of the charging party; and a request that the EEOC take remedial action or settle a dispute), and the intake questionnaire contained enough information to be adequate for this purpose. Although the informal dispute resolution procedure never occurred, the Supreme Court remanded the case to the district court to attempt to facilitate a settlement. [*Holowecki v. Federal Express*, 552 U.S. 389 (2008); see, e.g., Mark Sherman (AP), *Supreme Court Says FedEx Employees Can Sue Over Age Discrimination* (Feb. 28, 2008) (law.com); Fred Schneyer, *Supreme Court Clears FedEx Age Discrimination Case for More Hearings*, plansponsor.com (Feb. 28, 2008)]

§ 41.06 THE FEDERAL-STATE RELATIONSHIP

[A] ADEA Interaction

Unlike ERISA, which preempts whole classes of state laws dealing with certain retirement and employee benefit issues, the ADEA specifically provides for a joint working relationship between the federal government and state antidiscrimination agencies; 29 U.S.C. § 625(b) gives the Secretary of Labor the power to cooperate with state and local agencies to carry out the purposes of ADEA.

Section 633(a) provides that state agencies retain their jurisdiction over age-discrimination claims. However, federal ADEA suits supersede state age-discrimination enforcement efforts. A potential age-discrimination plaintiff has to go through enforcement procedures at both the state and the federal level. However, if the federal charge is filed on time, the complainant doesn't have to complete the state enforcement process—only to file a charge within the state system.

The federal ADEA provides that, if a state has a statute against age discrimination and has an enforcement agency, then potential plaintiffs have to file charges within both systems. The federal-state enforcement relationship revolves around the concepts of "referral" and "deferral."

Referral means that a state has a work-sharing arrangement with the EEOC, as provided by 29 C.F.R. § 1616.9. When an age-discrimination complaint is made to the state agency, the state agency refers it to the EEOC. If the state charge is dismissed, the EEOC has the power to conduct an independent investigation. Originally, the EEOC Regulations listed states that were identified as "referral" states because they had age discrimination laws. However, in August 2002, the

EEOC proposed a set of regulations for ADEA litigation procedures: see 67 Fed. Reg. 52431 (Aug. 12, 2002), finalized at 68 Fed. Reg. 70150 (Dec. 17, 2003). The EEOC says that because most of the states now have laws to forbid age discrimination, it is no longer necessary to maintain these lists. The EEOC will simply make referrals to the state agencies as appropriate.

An additional group of states (Arizona, Colorado, Kansas, Maine, Ohio, Rhode Island, South Dakota, and Washington) are "conditional referral" states. They do have antidiscrimination statutes, but the terms of these state laws are quite different from the federal ADEA. This situation creates the possibility that employees will bring claims that are covered by the state law, but not by the federal law. In such instances, the state-only claims will not be referred to the EEOC. Claims that are covered only by federal law must be filed directly with the EEOC, within 180 days of the discriminatory act.

The deferral concept means that the EEOC defers to the state and does not process the charge for a period of 60 days after the referral, so that the state agency can take action.

Except in a deferral state, the charge must be filed no later than 180 days after the discriminatory act, or the latest act that forms part of a pattern. In a deferral state, the last permissible filing date is either 300 days after the discriminatory act (or last discriminatory act in a series) or 30 days after the state agency dismisses its charge and notifies the complainant of the dismissal—whichever comes earlier. Unlike Title VII plaintiffs, ADEA plaintiffs do not have to get a right-to-sue letter.

If a state has a law against age discrimination, 29 U.S.C. § 633(b) provides that employees may not bring ADEA suits in that state until they have waited 60 days for the state to resolve the charges. If state charges have been dismissed in less than 60 days, the employee doesn't have to wait for the full 60-day period to end. The 60-day period is imposed to allow for conciliation of the charge. [See 29 U.S.C. § 626(d)]

During this period, the EEOC's task is to decide if it has a "reasonable basis to conclude that a violation of the Act has occurred or will occur." If the answer is "yes," the EEOC makes a "good cause" or "reasonable cause" finding—i.e., that the employee had good cause to complain. Then the EEOC will probably issue a Letter of Violation. However, the mere fact that no letter is issued does not prove that the EEOC did not detect any violations.

Courts have reached different conclusions about what to do if the plaintiff does not wait 60 days as required. The Sixth Circuit says that the case should be dismissed (but without prejudice, so it can be refiled later). On the other hand, the Eighth Circuit says that the case should not be dismissed, only suspended pending the administrative disposition of the complaint. [Compare *Chapman v. City of Detroit*, 808 F.2d 459 (6th Cir. 1986), with *Wilson v. Westinghouse Elec. Co.*, 838 F.2d 286 (8th Cir. 1988)] The Final Rule calls for the EEOC to issue a

Notice of Dismissal or Termination when the agency finishes processing a charge. A complainant can file suit in federal or state court at any time after 60 days have passed since the filing of the age discrimination charge—whether or not the EEOC has issued its Notice of Dismissal or Termination. But once the Notice is issued, the complainant has only 90 days from the date of the notice to bring suit; otherwise, the suit will be dismissed as untimely.

Next, the EEOC tries to get the company into compliance by informal persuasion. If the company and the EEOC reach an agreement that the agency believes will eliminate the discrimination, then the agreement will be written down and signed by the EEOC representative, a company representative, and the employee who charged the discrimination. If the charging party is not satisfied, he or she can withdraw the charge. The EEOC still has independent authority to settle on behalf of other employees affecting the discrimination.

On the other hand, if conciliation fails and no agreement is reached, possibly because there has been no discrimination, and therefore, the employer is unwilling to admit culpability and "admit" discrimination that never occurred in the first place, the EEOC and/or the charging party can sue. The charging party's suit must be brought no later than 90 days after receipt of notice from the EEOC that conciliation has failed, but it is not necessary to get a right-to-sue letter.

See 67 Fed. Reg. 52431 (Aug. 12, 2002) and 68 Fed. Reg. 70150 (Dec. 17, 2003). The notices inform the charging party that he or she has a right to sue the alleged perpetrator of age discrimination, but the right expires 90 days after the issue date of the NDT. Each aggrieved person will receive an individual NDT, but for multi-person charges, the NDT will not issue until proceedings end as to all of them.

Despite similarities, the NDT does not work in exactly the same way as a Title VII Right to Sue letter. A potential ADEA plaintiff can file suit at any time once 60 days have passed since the filing of the charge with the administrative agency, whether or not the NDT has issued. However, suit is untimely once 90 days have passed since the NDT date. To prevent confusion, the EEOC amended 29 C.F.R. § 1626.12 to clarify the difference between the notice that is issued when an EEOC conciliation attempt fails and this new type of notice.

The EEOC can terminate further processing of a charge if it discovers that a suit has been filed against the respondent of the charge, unless the agency determines that continued charge processing furthers the aims of the ADEA. However, the EEOC has the authority to investigate age discrimination cases and bring suit even if there is no individual charge filed. This is not true in Title VII or ADA Title I cases. When several people are involved in a charge, the EEOC will not issue an NDT until all the charges have been processed. The agency concluded that issuing a separate NDT to each charging party as his or her case was finished would lead to inefficient multiplication of court proceedings.

[B] State Laws Against Age Discrimination

Most of the states have some kind of law prohibiting age discrimination in employment. These laws may differ from the federal laws, in terms of coverage (e.g., they may cover employers too small to be subject to federal anti-discrimination laws).

Although the procedure varies from state to state, usually a person who claims to be a victim of age discrimination begins the state enforcement process by filing a charge with the state human rights/equal employment opportunity agency, within the time frame set out by the statute. Depending on the statute, this could be anywhere from 30 days after the alleged discriminatory practice to one year plus 90 days of the time the complainant discovered the employer acted illegally.

Most of the states, like the federal government, have a dual system of agency enforcement and private litigation. The agency investigates the charge and issues either a finding of good cause or a no-cause finding. If the agency deems that the charge is well-founded, then it tries to conciliate or sues the employer. On the other hand, if it makes a no-cause finding, or cannot resolve the matter promptly, the employee has the right to bring suit in state court, under the state antidiscrimination law. However, in some states, there is no agency enforcement, so employers are only at risk of private suit. Other states, however, give complainants a choice between going straight to state court without making an agency charge or filing an administrative complaint—but they must choose one or the other.

In 2010, the Tenth Circuit tackled timing issues when charges are filed with both the state agency and the EEOC. The district court dismissed a suit charging national origin, ancestry, and sex discrimination and retaliation because it was filed more than 90 days after the plaintiff, Rodriguez, received a right-to-sue notice from the Colorado Civil Rights Division. Three months after being fired, Rodriguez filed separate charges with the EEOC and the Colorado state agency. The Colorado agency decided that Rodriguez' sex discrimination charge was well-founded, but her other charges were unfounded. The sex discrimination charge was referred for mediation, which was unsuccessful. The Colorado agency issued a right to sue notice dated November 25, 2007.

The EEOC declined to pursue the case, but did not issue a right to sue notice until January 29, 2008. Rodriguez sued in district court, alleging only federal claims, on April 25, 2008—a date that was more than 90 days from the state right to sue notice, but within 90 days from the federal notice. The Tenth Circuit said that the Colorado right to sue notice did not start the filing period running within the federal system. Although Colorado has a work-sharing agreement with the EEOC, the agreement does not give the state agency the power to issue notices on the EEOC's behalf. The EEOC has a duty to give substantial weight to the Colorado agency's determinations, but is not bound by them. The Colorado notice did not inform Rodriguez of her rights under federal law; it included only the state charge number and explained Rodriguez' rights to sue in state court; and it did not mention the federal charge or state that the notice was binding on the EEOC. For all these reasons, the Colorado right to sue notice did not start the clock running for a federal suit. [*Rodriguez v. Wet Ink, LLC*, 603 F.3d 810 (10th Cir. 2010)]

CHAPTER 42

DISCRIMINATION SUITS BY EMPLOYEES: PROCEDURAL ISSUES

§ 42.01 INTRODUCTION

When it comes to litigating discrimination claims, it's understandable that both employers and employees feel vulnerable. Employers often feel that, no matter how little substance there is to a charge of discrimination, the employer will still have to fight the charge (which can be time-consuming and expensive) and might be ordered to pay immense damages. Employees feel that they are at the mercy of employers—that the only means of redress is complex and takes many years, by which time memories will have faded.

The Supreme Court held, in March 2011, that the "cat's paw" theory of liability, i.e., the allegation that an unbiased decision-maker acts on biased reports submitted by lower-level managers who are biased against the plaintiff, is viable. This decision reverses the Seventh Circuit, which had limited the employer's cat's paw liability to situations in which the biased supervisor exercised such singular influence over the decision-maker that the decision-maker engaged in blind reliance. This ruling was made in a USERRA case, but this interpretation of cat's paw liability is likely to apply to Title VII cases as well, because USERRA and Title VII use similar language about "motivating factors" for employment discrimination. However, the ADEA is drafted differently so this decision might not apply. [*Staub v. Proctor Hosp.*, 131 S. Ct. 1186 (2011)]

Early in 2010, the Supreme Court ruled that a corporation's principal place of business is its executive office, and not where its products are sold. The case was brought in California state court by Hertz employees who said they were wrongfully denied overtime and vacation pay. Hertz, which is headquartered in New Jersey, wanted the suit tried in federal court as a diversity case. The Ninth Circuit rejected this argument, finding that Hertz does most of its business in California, so the case was not diverse. The Supreme Court reversed and remanded. The effect of this ruling is that more cases will go to federal court—which is more hostile to class actions than state courts. [*Hertz v. Friend*, 559 U.S. 77 (2010); see AP, *In Unanimous Ruling, Supreme Court Says Business HQ Is Where Executives Are* (Feb. 23, 2010) (law.com)]

The Ninth Circuit held that a clause in an arbitration agreement that forbids all federal court review of the award, including review permitted by FAA § 9, is not enforceable. The Ninth Circuit said that non-appealability clauses have been construed in two ways. The Third, Seventh, and Eleventh Circuits have held that binding, non-appealable arbitration precludes federal court review of the merits of the decision, but does not eliminate appeals under the circumstances permitting an award to be vacated under FAA § 10. The other possibility is that a non-appealability clause eliminates court review entirely. The Ninth Circuit concluded that the FAA's concept of due process in arbitration includes limited judicial review. [*In re Wal-Mart Wage and Hour Employment Practices Litig.*, 737 F.3d 1262 (9th Cir. 2013)]

§ 42.02 CAUSES OF ACTION

In legal parlance, a cause of action is something for which someone can be sued. Employees can charge employers with various kinds of wrongdoing, and the same suit can combine discrimination charges with other causes of action, such as:

- Violation of Title VII of the Civil Rights Act of 1964 (discrimination on the grounds of race, sex, nationality, or color—sexual harassment is considered a type of sex discrimination);
- Violation of the Pregnancy Discrimination Act (PDA), an addition to Title VII, which forbids treating a qualified pregnant employee on less favorable terms than a comparably situated, non-pregnant employee;
- Violation of the Age Discrimination Act (discriminating against an individual who is age 40 or over, in any term or condition of employment, including hiring, firing, promotion, and benefits);
- Violation of 42 U.S.C. § 1981, the Civil War-era statute that gives all citizens the same right to make contracts as "white citizens." Four Circuits allow § 1981 suits by at-will employees who claim they were discharged on the basis of racial prejudice—even though they had no written employment contracts. [*Lauture v. IBM,* 216 F.3d 258 (2d Cir. 2000); *Perry v. Woodward,* 199 F.3d 1126 (10th Cir. 1999); *Spriggs v. Diamond Auto Glass,* 165 F.3d 1015 (4th Cir. 1999); *Fadeyi v. Planned Parenthood,* 160 F.3d 1048 (5th Cir. 1998)] In 2009, the Third Circuit joined the First, Seventh, and Eleventh Circuits in applying 42 U.S.C. § 1981 to independent contractors, in a case involving alleged racist insults and cancellation of a black trainee's contract as a sales representative: *Brown v. J. Kaz Inc. d/b/a Craftmatic of Pittsburgh,* 581 F.3d 175 (3d Cir. 2009); see Zack Needles, *3rd Circuit Extends Civil Rights Protection to Independent Contractors,* The Legal Intelligencer (Sept. 17, 2009) (law.com)]
- Wrongful refusal to re-employ a military veteran, violating USERRA;
- Violation of the Equal Pay Act: paying women less than men for the same job. This law does not permit "comparable worth" claims that allege that a typically female job is more valuable than a different and higher-paid job that is typically performed by men;
- Retaliation against an employee who filed a discrimination claim (or exercised other legal rights, e.g., in connection with unemployment benefits or Worker's Compensation) or cooperated in an investigation;
- Any act of wrongful termination for other reasons (e.g., discharging someone who "blew the whistle" on corporate wrongdoing);

- Violation of labor law (e.g., retaliating against someone for protected activity such as supporting the union or asserting a grievance against the employer). Nearly all labor law claims must be brought in federal, not state, court, because the federal statute the Labor Management Relations Act (LMRA) preempts state regulation—in other words, this is considered purely a federal matter;
- Breach of contract (either an explicit, written contract such as an employment contract or a collective bargaining agreement, or an implied contract);
- Defamation (in the context of an unfavorable reference or unfavorable statements in the press, and if the employer cannot assert a defense of truth);
- Interference with contractual relations, e.g., the employer prevents an ex-employee from getting a new job or establishing a business;
- Infliction of emotional distress (either negligent or intentional).

Frequently, employees will engage in several different proceedings, involving different statutes. Then, it becomes important to determine if the results of one proceeding will affect other proceedings (or prevent potential claims from being pursued). Denial of a person's FMLA claim for being fired while on maternity leave is *res judicata* to Title VII, ADEA, and the Florida Civil Rights Act claims. That is, the negative FMLA ruling is considered to have determined the other claims, because all the claims involve the same facts, which have already been litigated. [*O'Connor v. PCA Family Health Plan,* 200 F.3d 1349 (11th Cir. 2000)]

In mid-2013, the Supreme Court ruled on the important question of who is a "supervisor." The actual case involved a racially hostile workplace, although this concept is most often invoked in sexual harassment cases. The Supreme Court held that the employer is strictly liable if harassment is committed by a supervisor and involves a tangible employment action (e.g., hiring, firing, reassignment) against the victim. If the harasser is a supervisor, but there is no tangible employment action, then the employer can assert an affirmative defense under *Faragher/Ellerth*: that the employer took reasonable care to prevent and correct harassment, but the plaintiff unreasonably failed to take advantage of this procedure. The Supreme Court defined a supervisor as a person authorized to undertake tangible employment actions against the plaintiff. Therefore, the Supreme Court rejected the EEOC's broader definition of a supervisor as someone who either can undertake tangible employment actions, or exercises significant direction over the plaintiff's work. The narrower the definition of supervisor, the fewer cases in which the employer will be strictly liable or will be required to raise the *Faragher/Ellerth* affirmative defense. In this case, the alleged harasser was a co-worker of the plaintiff's, so the Supreme Court held that the employer would be liable only if it was negligent in controlling working conditions. [*Vance v. Ball State Univ.*, 133 S. Ct. 2434 (2013); see Marcia Coyle, *Supreme Court Makes It Harder to Prove Job Bias Claims*, Nat'l L.J. (June 24, 2013) (law.com)]

§ 42.03 STATISTICS ABOUT CHARGES AND RESULTS

In fiscal 2013, the number of total charges of discrimination dropped almost 6% from 2012 levels, but the EEOC obtained record recoveries (a total of $372.1 million) under the administrative process. The number of retaliation charges rose. There were 38,539 retaliation charges for all statutes, including 31,208 Title VII retaliation charges. About one-third of all charges (35%; 33,068 charges) alleged race discrimination, 29.5% (27,687 charges) alleged sex discrimination, 28.8% (21,396 charges) alleged age discrimination, 27.7% (25,957 charges) alleged disability discrimination. There were 10,642 charges of national origin discrimination (11.4%), 3,721 (4%) religious discrimination charges, 3,146 (3.4%) charges of color discrimination, and a mere 333 (0.4%) GINA charges. [Barry A. Hartstein, *EEOC Releases Charge Statistics For FY 2013*, Littler Mendelson (Feb. 5, 2014), available at Lexology.com]

The EEOC said that over 70,500 people received benefits through litigation, mediation, conciliation, and/or settlement. The EEOC brought 300 systemic investigations, resulting in 63 settlements and conciliation agreements with an aggregate value of about $40 million. In fiscal 2013, 97,252 charges were resolved; since this is larger than the number of new charges, the agency's backlog diminished. [Scott T. Silverman, *EEOC Obtains Record Relief From Companies*, Akerman LLP (Dec. 19, 2013), available at Lexology.com] The EEOC filed 148 suits in 2013, slightly fewer than the 2012 figure of 155 in 2012. Two hundred twenty-two suits were resolved in 2013. [Melanie Trottman, *Private-Sector Workers File Fewer Complaints, EEOC Says*, WSJ.com (Feb. 5, 2014)]

See Chapter 41 for more discussion of EEOC statistics on case filings and dispositions.

Professor Theodore Eisenberg, after studying federal civil rights litigation, including employment discrimination, concluded in late 2013 that employment discrimination cases remain a substantial portion of the federal docket, but their percentage representation has steadily declined. The rate of settlement has increased. Median jury awards have risen faster than the rate of inflation—but only a small percentage of cases result in a jury victory for the plaintiff. There may also be a shift toward state court. For example, the Ohio Supreme Court has imposed liability on individual supervisors; if they are sued, diversity is often defeated, and the case remains in the state system. [William A. Nolan, *Behind The Numbers: Employment Discrimination Cases At The Federal Level Decline, But Why?*, Barnes & Thornburg LLP (Nov. 26, 2013), available at Lexology.com]

In its annual workplace class action study for 2013, Seyfarth Shaw concluded that employment discrimination settlements have "waned" since *Dukes* was decided (see § 42.06, below). In 2010, before *Dukes*, the top 10 settlements aggregated $346 million; in 2012, the total was only $45 million. Seyfarth Shaw described the case of *McReynolds v. Merrill Lynch*, 672 F.3d 482 (7th Cir. 2012) as "perplexing": class certification was granted even though individual Merrill Lynch managers had discretion over implementation of company policies. A year later, the case was settled for $160 million, one of the half-dozen largest settlements in recent history. Other leading settlements include the $250 million settlement in early 2003 in *Arnett v. Calpers*, a Northern District of California case about age discrimination against public safety officers who took disability retirement; 1988's $240 million *Kraszewski v. State Farm*, also in the Northern District of California; 2010's Southern District of New York $175 million settlement in *Velez v. Novartis*, a case of pay and promotion discrimination against 5,600 female sales representatives. [Gerald L. Maatman Jr. and David B. Ross, *How A Ruling Shapes A $160 Million Class Action Settlement*, Seyfarth Shaw LLP (Aug. 29, 2013), available at Lexology.com]

§ 42.04 TITLE VII PROCEDURE

[A] Complaining Party

Federal antidiscrimination laws include extremely complicated procedures for bringing a complaint, and one of the employer's main lines of defense is that the potential plaintiff has failed to satisfy the procedural requirements.

42 U.S.C. § 2000e(l) defines "complaining party" in a Title VII case as either the private person who brings a case or the EEOC or the U.S. Attorney General.

[B] The Charging Process

Nearly every phrase or term in this section has already been extensively litigated. Individuals who think they have experienced an unlawful employment practice cannot simply go to the relevant federal court and file a complaint. Instead, they must file a written, sworn document called a "charge" with an administrative agency. Would-be plaintiffs cannot go to court until there has been an administrative investigation and attempts to settle the matter without getting the court system involved.

The EEOC notifies the employer of the charge within 10 days, disclosing the date, place, and circumstances of the allegedly unlawful practices, and then starts an investigation to see if there is reasonable cause for the charge. The EEOC's duty is to complete the investigation as soon as possible—and within 120 days of the filing of the charge (or the referral date) "so far as practicable." (The EEOC has a big backlog and often misses the 120-day deadline.)

A major sex discrimination suit involving about 44,000 female employees of the largest retail specialty jeweler in the United States was dismissed because the EEOC failed to prove that it undertook a nationwide investigation before bringing charges and for attempting to introduce evidence that was not provided during discovery. The suit began about nine years ago with 19 women in eight states, including New York, filing EEOC charges alleging denial of equal pay and promotion opportunities. The EEOC's Buffalo office investigated and the EEOC sued in 2008, alleging unlawful employment practices nationwide. The defendant moved for summary judgment, saying that there could not be nationwide allegations without a nationwide investigation; the magistrate judge agreed, stating that the EEOC had the burden of proving that it satisfied all conditions for filing a claim, including a full investigation. [*EEOC v. Sterling Jewelers*, No. 09-cv-00706 (W.D.N.Y., dismissed 2014); see John Caher, *Judge Faults EEOC for Probe Into Discrimination Claim*, N.Y.L.J. (Mar. 13, 2014), available at law.com]

Grievance procedures under a CBA, or company-sponsored grievance procedures in a nonunion company, have no effect on Title VII suits. So the employee doesn't have to use those procedures before filing a charge with an antidiscrimination agency. On the other hand, ongoing grievances under the CBA won't prevent or delay a Title VII suit.

If the EEOC does not believe that the charge is supported by reasonable cause, it dismisses the charge, and the employee then has the right to sue. In fact, it is not even held against the employee that the EEOC made a "no-cause" finding. A no-cause determination does not prevent the employee from suing. It does not limit the suit, what the employee can try to prove, or even the remedies he or she can receive. The judge or jury makes its own independent inquiry into the facts and is not influenced by the EEOC investigation.

But if the EEOC does believe that the charge is supported, then the EEOC's job is to try to use "informal methods of conference, conciliation, and persuasion" to get the employer to change the employment practice. The conciliation process is confidential, and statements made during the process can only be publicized or used as evidence in litigation based on the written consent of the person making the statement. Violating this confidentiality can be punished by as much as $1,000 fine and/or a year in prison.

The Seventh Circuit ruled in late 2013 that the EEOC's mishandling of the conciliation process is not an affirmative defense; the Seventh Circuit did not believe that judges can determine the adequacy of conciliation. However, the Second, Fourth, Fifth, Sixth, Eighth, Tenth, and Eleventh Circuits disagree. (The Second, Fifth, and Eleventh Circuits apply a three-part inquiry to determine if conciliation was adequate; the Fourth, Sixth, and Tenth Circuits require the EEOC to satisfy a test of minimal good faith.) In the Seventh Circuit view, Title VII requires the conciliation agreement to be acceptable to the EEOC, placing the EEOC in control of the process; the statutory language also mandates that things said during the conciliation process be kept confidential. [*EEOC v. Mach Mining*, 738 F.3d 171 (7th Cir. 2013); see Paul Patten and Rick Cohen, *Seventh Circuit Agrees With EEOC There Is No Affirmative Defense For The EEOC's Failure To Conciliate*, Jackson Lewis PC (Dec. 23, 2013), available at Lexology.com;

William J. Anthony, *No Implied Failure-To-Conciliate Defense For Employers Against EEOC, says Seventh Circuit*, Jackson Lewis PC (Dec. 24, 2013), available at Lexology.com. In *EEOC v. Abercrombie & Fitch Stores, Inc.*, 966 F. Supp. 2d 949 (N.D. Cal. 2013), the district court ruled that the EEOC satisfied its obligation to conciliate by holding months of intensive discussions with the employer prior to filing suit.]

Certiorari was granted on June 30, 2014 in *Mach Mining* as No. 13-1019. See Hunton & Williams LLP, *Supreme Court Grants Certiorari in Mach Mining LLC v. EEOC to Consider "Failure to Conciliate" Affirmative Defense* (July 15, 2014), available at Lexology.com]

If the discrimination charges involve multiple employees, it may be necessary for the EEOC to attempt conciliation with respect to each employee. The agency lost a major case, *EEOC v. CRST Van Expedited Inc.,* 679 F.3d 657 (8th Cir. 2012), On remand, No. 07-CV-95, U.S. Dist. LEXIS 107822 (N.D. Iowa Aug. 1, 2013) for failure to attempt conciliation at the individual level. [See § 41.01[B]]

The EEOC's powers to investigate a charge include having access "at all reasonable times" to all evidence that is relevant to the charges, and the EEOC also is entitled to make copies. [42 U.S.C. § 2000e-8(a)]

Exhaustion of remedies is a requirement. The Tenth Circuit ruled that, in order to exhaust their administrative remedies, private sector employees have a duty to cooperate with the EEOC's investigation of their age bias charges before they file suit. (In this case, after filing a charge, the plaintiff and his attorney canceled three phone interviews scheduled with the EEOC investigator; wouldn't return the investigator's calls; and did not provide any information other than what was contained in the original charge.) Exhaustion of administrative remedies is a prerequisite to suing under the ADEA. Failure to exhaust administrative remedies does not justify summary judgment for the defendant but, according to the Tenth Circuit, will justify dismissal of the case for lack of jurisdiction. [*Shikles v. Sprint/United Mgmt. Co.*, 426 F.3d 1304 (10th Cir. 2005); ADEA suits have also been dismissed for non-cooperation: e.g., *Rann v. Chao*, 346 F.3d 192 (D.C. Cir. 2003). It has been held, in the Title VII context, that failure to cooperate with the EEOC is failure to exhaust administrative remedies: *Brown v. Tomlinson*, 383 F. Supp. 2d 26, 29 (D.D.C. 2005); *Smith v. Koplan*, 362 F. Supp. 2d 266, 268 (D.D.C. 2005)]

A Title VII plaintiff has not exhausted administrative remedies if a suit refers to time frames, discriminatory conduct, or perpetrators different from the ones raised in the administrative charges. In this case, the Fourth Circuit held that evidence of derogatory racial epithets that was not raised until the summary judgment stage of trial was inadmissible; furthermore, the EEOC charges related to supervisors, whereas the epithets were allegedly used by co-workers. [*Chacko v. Patuxent Inst.*, 429 F.3d 505 (4th Cir. 2005)]

The district court dismissed a Title VII retaliation claim for failure to exhaust EEOC administrative remedies, but the Sixth Circuit reinstated the case.

Adamov charged that an executive made discriminatory comments about Adamov's Azerbaijani origin; Adamov also complained about failure to be promoted. The company fired Adamov, stating that he made a loan to a friend contrary to company ethics policy. He sued the bank and individual supervisors for discrimination and retaliation. Adamov submitted a draft EEOC charge, which was unsigned and undated, and asserted only a Title VII national origin discrimination claim. Before the court ruled on the defense motion to dismiss, Adamov filed a second charge, including a retaliation allegation and the defendant moved to dismiss once again. The district court dismissed the retaliation claim for failure to exhaust administrative remedies, but the Sixth Circuit reversed: the administrative exhaustion requirement of Title VII is not essential to the court's jurisdiction, and the defendant forfeited the exhaustion defense by not raising it before the district court. [*Adamov v. U.S. Nat'l Bank Assoc.*, 726 F.3d 851 (6th Cir. 2013); see Steven J Pearlman, Harris Mufson, and Noa M. Baddish, *Sixth Circuit: Failure To Exhaust Administrative Remedies Not A Jurisdictional Bar For Title VII Retaliation Claim*, Proskauer Rose LLP (Aug. 27, 2013), available at Lexology .com]

[C] State Agencies

In a Fifth Circuit case, procedural failures required dismissal of an age-discrimination judgment in favor of the plaintiff. He filed a complaint with the EEOC and did not check the box on the form indicating that he wanted the charge filed with both the EEOC and the Texas Commission on Human Rights. Therefore, he failed to go through the mandatory step of filing a state charge—and his federal lawsuit was invalid. [*Jones v. Grinnell Corp.*, 235 F.3d 972 (5th Cir. 2001)] Although Texas has a work-sharing agreement, this merely means that a single filing can cover both state and federal requirements—not that the state procedure can be ignored, even in a case where the charging party asserts only federal claims.

However, a 2010 case (where the plaintiff, Rodriguez, filed charges with both the state agency and the EEOC) held that a federal suit was timely when it was brought within 90 days of the date of the federal right to sue letter, even though it was filed more than 90 days after the state right to sue letter was issued. Colorado has a work-sharing agreement with the EEOC, but the agreement does not give the state agency the power to act on behalf of the EEOC. Furthermore, the state right to sue letter did not inform Rodriguez of her federal rights, and referred only to the state case. Therefore, Rodriguez' federal suit was timely because it was filed within 90 days of the date of the federal right to sue letter. [*Rodriguez v. Wet Ink, LLC,* 603 F.3d 810 (10th Cir. 2010)]

§ 42.05 TIMING REQUIREMENTS

[A] Generally

Section 2000e-5(c) says that if the state where the alleged unlawful employment practice occurred has a state antidiscrimination law, then EEOC charges may not be filed until 60 days have passed since commencement of state antidiscrimination charges. If the EEOC itself files a charge, it has an obligation to notify the appropriate state authority and give it sixty days to enforce the local law and eliminate the unlawful employment practice.

The basic rule is that, to avoid being dismissed as untimely, EEOC charges must be filed within 180 days of the date of the wrongful action. Then papers must be served on the employer within 10 days. However, if the state has an antidiscrimination agency, the employee has 300 days from the date of the wrongful action to file with the EEOC. There is an additional requirement that the employee not wait more than 30 days after the state or local agency has dismissed a state charge to file with the EEOC. [42 U.S.C. § 2000e-5(e)(1)]

The charge has to be verified (the charging party has to state under penalty of perjury that the statements in the charge are true). [42 U.S.C. § 2000e5(b)] In March 2002, the U.S. Supreme Court upheld an EEOC regulation, 29 C.F.R. § 1601.12(b), that allows "relation back." That is, if a charge is made within the 300-day period but verified later, it will still be timely because the verification "relates back" to the timely charge. The Supreme Court ruled in *Edelman v. Lynchburg Coll.* [535 U.S. 106 (2002)] that Title VII requires both filing within 300 days and verification, but the two need not occur at the same time.

Although Title VII requires charging parties to verify their EEOC charges, the requirement is not jurisdictional, so a court can hear a case based on an unverified charge. Furthermore, if the employer responds to the charge without raising the fact that it is unverified, the employer will not be able to raise this issue later in the case. [*Buck v. Hampton Twp. Sch. Dist.*, 452 F.3d 256 (3d Cir. 2006)]

The Supreme Court resolved another timing issue. If the plaintiff's claim is for only one act of discrimination or retaliation, or for several separate acts, then the claim must meet the 180-day or 300-day requirement to be timely. However, if the plaintiff charges a number of acts that he or she claims made up part of the same practice creating a hostile work environment, then the claim is timely as long as there was at least one act in the series that occurred during the 180-day or 300-day period. [*National R.R. Passenger Corp. v. Morgan,* 536 U.S. 101 (2002)]

Five years later, the Supreme Court ruled that a Title VII pay discrimination charge must be filed within 180 days of the time the discriminatory employment decision was made and communicated to the employee. It is not acceptable to treat discriminatory pay as a continuing violation, for which a charge can be filed within 180 days of any paycheck. The Supreme Court said that if an employer engages in a series of intentionally discriminatory acts, each of which could support a separate charge, then each act counts as a new violation. But continuing to pay a female employee less than a comparable male reflects later effects of past discrimination—so the clock does not start again with each paycheck. [*Ledbetter v. Goodyear Tire & Rubber Co.*, 550 U.S. 618 (2007)]

Legislation was passed and signed in 2009 to reverse this result for Title VII, the ADA, the ADEA, and the Rehabilitation Act: The Lilly Ledbetter Fair Pay Act of 2009, Pub. L. No. 111-2. The Ledbetter Act provides that a charge is timely if filed within 180 days (or 300 days, in certain instances) of the adoption of a discriminatory practice; the employee's becoming subject to that practice; or the employee being affected by the application of the practice. Every paycheck that reflects discrimination can start the time running anew. A successful plaintiff can recover back pay for up to two years before the date of filing of the charge, for similar or related discriminatory acts during the filing period. The Ledbetter Act is retroactive for all cases that were pending on the day before the Supreme Court's decision, but not for cases that were already complete at that time. [Erin Kilgore, *Lilly Ledbetter Fair Pay Act Revives Pay Discrimination Claims,* Louisiana Law Blog (Feb. 13, 2009) (law.com); Sheryl Gay Stolberg, *Obama Signs Equal-Pay Legislation,* <http://www.nytimes.com> (Jan. 30, 2009); SCOTUSblog, *Congress Overturns Court on Job Bias,* <http://www.scotusblog.com/wp/court-overturns-court-on-job-bias> (Jan. 28, 2009); Janell Grenier, Benefitsblog, *Lilly Ledbetter Fair Pay Act of 2009 Passes: Benefits Impacted,* <http://www.benefitscounsel.com/archives/002025.html> (Jan. 28, 2009)]

The Eastern District of Pennsylvania ruled that the Ledbetter Act applies only to charges of sex discrimination in compensation—it cannot be used to extend the time limit for a lawsuit alleging discriminatory denial of a promotion. The court said that each promotion that was denied constituted a separate discriminatory act, so the suit had to be filed within 300 days of the denial of promotion. The plaintiff was not allowed to allege that there was an ongoing pattern of discriminatory denials of promotions, so she could bring suit as long as she sued within 300 days of any act in the series. The court also rejected her argument that not being promoted reduced her compensation, so the Ledbetter Act should apply. [*Rowland v. CertainTeed Corp.*, No. 08-3671, 2009 WL 1444413 (E.D. Pa. May 19, 2009); see Shannon P. Duffy, *Judge: Ledbetter Act Doesn't Apply to Lost Promotion Suit*, the Legal Intelligencer (May 27, 2009) (law.com)]

In 2010, the Supreme Court ruled that discrimination charges brought by Chicago firefighters were not untimely. Although the promotion exam that allegedly had a disparate impact on black and Hispanic firefighters was given many years in the past, the Supreme Court ruled that the unlawful practice could be challenged every time it is used—i.e., every time a new promotion list is issued based on the allegedly biased examination. [*Lewis v. City of Chicago*, 559 U.S. 932 (2010)] In 2011, 19 white firefighters and one Hispanic firefighter began receiving payments under this decision; they will receive a total of $2 million in back pay, pension credits, and attorneys' fees. [Rebecca Moore, *Award Finally Decided in Connecticut Firefighters Suit*, plansponsor.com (Aug. 3, 2011)]

In 2008, the Second Circuit said that, for statute of limitations purposes, a claim of discriminatory loss of seniority occurred on the date when an airline clerk learned he had lost seniority, not on the later date when he was fired: discharge was only the delayed, neutral effect of an alleged earlier act of discrimination. [*Alleyne v. American Airlines*, 548 F.3d 219 (2d Cir. 2008)]

The EEOC has 30 days after filing of a charge, or 30 days after the expiration of the period for referring charges from state agencies, to negotiate with the employer to produce a conciliation agreement that ends the unlawful employment practice. If the 30-day period expires without a conciliation agreement, the EEOC has the power to sue the employer in federal court.

On the other hand, if the EEOC makes a "no-cause" finding about the charge, or 180 days have passed since the charge was filed with the EEOC or referred from the state agency, and the EEOC has not filed suit and there has been no conciliation agreement, then the EEOC will notify the charging party. This is known as a "right-to-sue letter," because it enables the charging party to bring a federal suit.

Some employers draft their job applications to include a limitation on the time within which employees can bring employment-related claims (e.g., six months, rather than the state's statute of limitations, which is likely to be longer). Some courts have upheld these limitations, on the theory that signing the application and taking the job obligates the employee to abide by the limitation. [See, e.g., *Thurman v. DaimlerChrysler, Inc.*, 397 F.3d 352 (6th Cir. 2004)] However, the Eastern District of Michigan refused to apply contract limitations to an ADA or Title VII claim, when the employee's right to sue letter was issued after the limited time period expires; the employee was not allowed to sue before obtaining a right to sue letter. The court found that it would be unfair to apply the limitation—but the limitation would apply if the right to sue letter were issued during the limited period. [*Steward v. DaimlerChrysler Corp.*, 533 F. Supp. 2d 717 (E.D. Mich. 2008)]

In an Equal Pay Act/Fair Labor Standards Act case, the district court enforced FedEx's employment agreement, which required actions to be brought within six months. (The suit was timely under federal law.) The Sixth Circuit reversed, finding that the shortened statute of limitations was an unlawful waiver of the plaintiff's rights under the FLSA; because the EPA is part of the FLSA, the Sixth Circuit did not permit waiver of the EPA claim either. [*Boaz v. FedEx Customer Infor. Servs., Inc.*, 725 F.3d 603 (6th Cir. 2013); see Matthew J. Thomas, *Employers Cannot Shorten Limitations Periods For FLSA Or Equal Pay Claims*, Jenner & Block (Oct. 31, 2013), available at Lexology.com]

In late 2013, the Supreme Court upheld a contractual three-year limitation on bringing suits about an ERISA disability plan. Although this was an ERISA case, it is likely to be influential in employment discrimination cases as well. [*Heimeshoff v. Hartford Life & Accident Ins. Co.*, 134 S. Ct. 604 (2013); see Scott J. Stitt, *U.S. Supreme Court Holds that a Three-Year Contractual Limitations*

Period for Benefit Claims is Not Unreasonable nor Contrary to ERISA, Central Ohio Discrimination law firm (Dec. 16, 2013) (benefitslink.com)]

In nearly all cases, the appropriate defendant is the employer company—there are virtually no situations in which Title VII suits can appropriately be brought against an individual person who is alleged to have performed discriminatory acts. For example, in 2007 the Eleventh Circuit held that individuals cannot be sued under either the ADA provision against retaliation in employment, or the Florida statute forbidding HIV/AIDS discrimination. The court held that the language of the employment provisions of the ADA is similar to that of Title VII and the ADEA, where individual suits have been ruled out; the Southern District of Florida has forbidden suits against individuals under the state HIV/AIDS statute. [*Albra v. Advan, Inc.*, 490 F.3d 826 (11th Cir. 2007)]

In rare cases, individual liability may exist under other federal statutes (e.g., the FLSA, EPA, or FMLA). In 2007, the First Circuit ruled that the president of a hotel was personally liable for wage and hour violations, because he had ultimate control over operations, and was instrumental in causing the corporation to violate the Fair Labor Standards Act. [*Chao v. Hotel Oasis Inc.*, 493 F.3d 26, 42 Cal. 4th (1st Cir. 2007)] The Fifth Circuit held that a supervisor can be personally liable for retaliation in an FMLA wrongful discharge case. [*Modica v. Taylor*, 465 F.3d 174 (5th Cir. 2006)] State courts may be more hospitable; even in a state that applies the concept of employment at will, it is possible that a supervisor would be held liable for discriminatory practices. [See, e.g., *Trau-Med of Am. Inc. v. All State Ins. Co.*, 71 S.W.3d 691, 703 (Tenn. 2002). These issues are discussed in Tresa Baldas, *Employment Litigation Gets Personal for Company Managers*, Nat'l L.J (Aug. 16, 2007) (law.com)]

Section 2000e-5(f)(3) provides that the suit can be filed in any federal District Court in the state where the alleged unlawful employment practice occurred. (The number of federal judicial districts in a state ranges from one to four.) The suit can also be brought in the judicial district where the relevant employment records are kept, or in the district where the plaintiff would have worked if there had been no unlawful employment practice. Finally, if the defendant company can't be found in any of those districts, the plaintiff can sue the defendant company in the judicial district where the company's principal office is located.

There is no explicit statute of limitations in 42 U.S.C. § 1981 (the federal law guaranteeing all persons within the jurisdiction of the United States the same rights to make and enforce contracts that "white citizens" have). Therefore, there was a circuit split on the proper statute of limitations to apply in § 1981 wrongful discharge cases. The split was resolved by the Supreme Court's May 2004 ruling: the statute of limitations is four years, because the current version of § 1981 was enacted by the Civil Rights Act of 1991 (CRA '91). Under federal law, the statute of limitations for all federal laws enacted after December 1, 1990, is four years, so that applies to CRA '91. [*Jones v. R.R. Donnelley & Sons Co.*, 541 U.S. 401 (2004)]

When there is no evidence of actual date on which a complainant received a right to sue letter, it will be presumed that delivery occurred three days after mailing—hence a suit, 98 days after issuance of the letter, was untimely, although the presumption can be rebutted by evidence of delayed receipt. Merely calling mail delivery unreliable is not enough. [*Payan v. Aramark Mgmt. Servs.*, 495 F.3d 1119 (9th Cir. 2007)]

[B] Tolling

In a limited group of circumstances, the statute of limitations can be tolled (suspended) when it would be unjust to insist on strict compliance. Tolling may be permitted if:

- The employer was guilty of deception or some other wrongdoing that prevented the employee from asserting Title VII rights;
- The employee tried to file a timely lawsuit, but the pleading was rejected as defective;
- The employee filed in time, but in the wrong court.

Tolling is usually considered a defense, which means that it is up to the plaintiff to prove that it was available, and not up to the defendant to prove that it was not.

The term "tolling" is sometimes used to cover two different but related concepts. "Equitable tolling" allows a delayed case to continue because, even though the plaintiff's excusable ignorance or oversight caused the delay, the defendant is not prejudiced (harmed) by the delay.

"Equitable estoppel" prevents the defendant from complaining about a delay that was caused in whole or part by the defendant's deceit or other conduct prejudicial to the plaintiff's interests, e.g., if the employee is afraid to approach the EEOC and endanger the internal investigation and grievance procedure that was being carried out. [*Currier v. Radio Free Europe*, 159 F.3d 1363 (D.C. Cir. 1998)]

§ 42.06 CLASS ACTIONS

Class actions are governed by Rule 23 of the Federal Rules of Civil Procedure, especially Rule 23(b). The various subsections of Rule 23 create several alternative methods of litigating a class action, but each method has its own procedural requirements that must be satisfied. The requirements relate to what the plaintiffs want (money damages, or just an injunction?) and how people become members of the class (are they automatically included unless they opt out, or do they have to opt in?). It can also be difficult and expensive for the potential plaintiffs to give the required notice to everyone who might want to join the class.

A case where restaurant waiters said they were forced to share their tips with ineligible employees and were also denied overtime pay raised federal claims via an FLSA collective action, which was combined with a putative class action under the New York labor law. The Second Circuit affirmed certification of the class action, even though the FLSA's collective actions are opt-in (i.e., an employee is involved only if he or she affirmatively agrees to be) and the New York class action was opt-out (all employees are involved unless they refuse to be). The restaurant said that Congress' intent in making FLSA collective actions opt-out would be hampered by combining the case with an opt-out class action, but the Second Circuit rejected this argument. Both suits involved the same fact situation—and the FLSA includes a provision that allows states to pass laws that are even more protective of employees' rights. The Seventh, Ninth, and D.C. Circuits have allowed FLSA collective actions to be combined with state-law class actions, but the Third Circuit has refused to do so. [*Shahriar v. Smith Wollensky Rest. Group*, 659 F.3d 234 (2d Cir. 2011)]

Discrimination cases focusing on monetary damages can be hard to certify as class actions. Rule 23(b)(2) requires not only a common injury but uniform remedies for the whole class. Would-be plaintiffs who can't use Rule 23(b)(2) may have to fall back on Rule 23(b)(3), which requires them to prove that class-wide issues are more important in the case than individual issues. They must also prove that a class action is better than other methods of resolving the dispute. In some cases, a "hybrid" class action will be allowed. First a class is certified under Rule 23(b)(2) to decide if the employer is liable. If it is, damages are determined under Rule 23(b)(2). In recent years, many class actions have been denied certification, or have been certified and then de-certified, based on court findings that each claimant's assertions must be handled individually on a case-by-case basis.

Sometimes employees subject to an arbitration clause want to bring a class arbitration against an employer. To an increasing extent, employers are drafting arbitration clauses to require claims to be arbitrated individually—a practice that the NLRB held to be unlawful. However, the Fifth Circuit permitted employers to require waivers of class arbitration, finding that the waiver is not inconsistent with the right to pursue collective action—as long as the arbitration agreement informs employees that the right to file an NLRB complaint is not waived. [*D.R. Horton v. NLRB*, 737 F.3d 344 (5th Cir. 2013); see AP, *Court Blocks Labor Board on Lawsuits*, NYTimes.com (Dec. 3, 2013). En banc rehearing was denied. See Keith J. Brodie, *NLRB DR Horton Rehearing Denied*, Barnes & Thornburg LLP (Apr. 17, 2014), available at Lexology.com. On the question of availability of class arbitration in Fair Labor Standards Act cases, see, e.g., *Walthour v. Chipio Windshield Repair*, 745 F.3d 1326 (11th Cir. 2014) (joining the Second, Fourth, Fifth, and Eighth Circuits, the Eleventh Circuit held that the right to bring an FLSA collective action is not a substantive legal right that can never be waived, so an arbitration agreement forbidding class claims was upheld); *Walton v. The Rose Group*, No. 13-1674 (E.D. Pa. Dec. 11, 2013) (clause forbidding class arbitration was enforced, even though the judge said it was unfair).]

[A] The *Dukes* Case and Its Implications

In mid-2011, the Supreme Court held that the massive sex discrimination class action against Wal-Mart was improperly certified. The plaintiffs alleged that Wal-Mart's broad corporate culture discriminated against women in pay and promotions, creating a company-wide discriminatory policy. In the view of the Supreme Court majority, Wal-Mart gave store managers a significant amount of discretion, so the existence of sex discrimination would have to be assessed at the individual store level.

The Supreme Court majority opinion held that the plaintiffs failed to show a single policy rather than numerous acts of alleged discrimination against individuals, so there was no common employment decision that could be challenged under Rule 23(a)(2).

Nor could the plaintiffs use Rule 23(b)(2) to seek back pay, even if they called the back pay claims incidental to claims for injunctive relief. The Supreme Court held that Wal-Mart would be entitled to individual determinations of back pay eligibility—it would not be appropriate to determine a class-wide back pay award by extrapolating from a small sample.

Some commentators suggested that the lesson large companies can take from this is that if they establish an overall anti-discrimination policy but delegate significant power to regional managers, they will be able to use the *Wal-Mart* decision to defend themselves—possibly in contexts extending beyond discrimination cases. [*Wal-Mart v. Dukes*, 131 S. Ct. 2541 (2011); see, e.g., Tony Mauro, *Supreme Court Erects Major Barriers to Class Actions in Wal-Mart Ruling*, Nat'l L.J. (June 20, 2011) (law.com]

The district court in Miami dismissed a suit by 11 female Wal-Mart employees in seven Southeastern states. The court said that the suit improperly piggybacked on the national *Dukes* class action that was dismissed by the Supreme Court. The plaintiffs' attorney announced that he would ask for a question to be certified to the Eleventh Circuit for reconsideration of the dismissal. The San Francisco *Dukes* case failed in August 2013, because the district court ruled that a class action was inappropriate because the plaintiffs did not have evidence of a general policy of discrimination. [John Pacenti, *Wal-Mart Wins Another Round in Pay Discrimination Litigation*, Daily Business Review (Sept. 24, 2013), available at law.com]

Female store managers employed by Family Dollar Stores persuaded the Fourth Circuit that *Dukes* did not prevent them from pursuing a class action: there were nationwide policies for salary structures and management discretion followed common patterns favoring men. However, although the plaintiffs were allowed to amend their complaint, it was not clear that they would obtain nationwide class status. The case was remanded to the district court for further development of the record. [*Scott v. Family Dollar Stores, Inc.*, 733 F.3d 105 (4th Cir. 2013), *reh'g denied*, 743 F.3d 886 (4th Cir. 2013); see Andrew W. Volin, *Avoiding Dukes*, Sherman & Howard LLC (Oct. 22, 2013), available at

Lexology.com; Gregory V. Mersol, *Fourth Circuit Argues With Itself Over Dukes' Application*, Baker & Hostetler LLP (Oct. 24, 2013), available at Lexology.com]

In September 2011, the Ninth Circuit ruled for Costco in a case that could have expanded a sex discrimination suit to hundreds of women. The Ninth Circuit reversed certification of a Title VII sex discrimination class. The case was remanded to apply the *Dukes* standard of commonality. In 2012, the District Court for the Northern District of California certified classes under (b)(2) and (b)(3): Classes certified under (b)(2) and (b)(3): injunctive relief class of all current and future employees at any US Costco warehouse who have been/will be subject to rules for promotion to Assistant General Manager and/or General Manager; monetary relief class of all women employed in a warehouse store since January 3, 2002 and were subject to the promotion system. The tentative trial plan is Stage One: for the jury to decide if Costco engaged in a pattern or practice of discrimination; if punitive damages are appropriate; if Costco is liable to the named plaintiffs for sex discrimination—and, if so, for how much. The court decides the prima facie case of disparate impact of Costco employment practices; if so, whether the practices were justified by business necessity and the availability of a less discriminatory alternative; if liability is found on either pattern or practice discrimination or disparate impact, appropriate injunctive relief. Stage Two: individual hearings on damages and individual defenses; if Costco is liable for punitive damages, amount of punitive damages owed to the whole class and to each class member. [*Ellis v. Costco Wholesale Corp.*, 657 F.3d 970 (9th Cir. 2011), *on remand*, 285 F.R.D. 492 (N.D. Cal. 2012)]

The case was eventually settled, and the District Court for the Northern District of California granted final approval of the settlement on May 27, 2014. The settlement obligates Costco to take various steps, including posting some jobs and interviewing all qualified candidates for certain jobs. The settlement creates a formal mechanism for employees to register their interest in some management positions. Some plaintiffs will have access to an arbitration procedure for obtaining damages for discrimination, although damages are capped at the amounts given in the settlement agreement. [Workplace Prof blog, *Ellis v. Costco Update*, <http://lawprofessors.typepad.com/laborprof_blog/2014/06/for-those-following-ellis-v-costco-wholesale-corporation-the-settlement-agreement-is-available-here-httpgenderclassacti.html> (June 4, 2014). The settlement agreement is available at <http://genderclassactionagainstcostco.com/wordpress/wp-content/uploads/Exhibit-1.pdf>.]

The EEOC lost a high-profile case in the Southern District of New York. The case began in 2007, when the EEOC filed a systemic pattern or practice pregnancy discrimination suit against Bloomberg L.P. More than 600 Bloomberg employees were pregnant or took maternity leave between 2002 and 2009. The EEOC identified 78 of them as victims of discrimination. The district court granted summary judgment for Bloomberg on the class allegations, holding that a reasonable fact-finder could not conclude that Bloomberg maintained a practice of decreasing the pay or responsibilities of pregnant workers. After the pattern or practice claims were dismissed, the EEOC attempted to continue the suit by asserting individual claims of pregnancy discrimination on behalf of 29 claimants who had not intervened in the suit, plus six more intervenors. The district court granted summary judgment for the employer with respect to the non-intervening plaintiffs, based on deficiencies in the EEOC's handling of investigation and conciliation, including failure to give Bloomberg adequate notice of the nature of the charges. The district court also found that conciliation was inadequate because it focused on the EEOC's excessively broad systemic claims and did not provide specific information about individual claims. The district court held that the EEOC cannot use class claims to avoid the pre-litigation efforts needed to bring individual suits. The EEOC's request for a stay to negotiate a settlement was denied: the case had already been running for six years. In a second, 181-page decision, the district court granted summary judgment for Bloomberg on most of the claims for the six intervenors, leaving only one count of pregnancy discrimination for one plaintiff that could be pursued. [*EEOC v. Bloomberg L.P.*, No. 07 Civ. 8383, 2013 WL 4799161 (S.D.N.Y. Sept. 9, 2013); see Gerald L. Maatman, Jr. and Howard M. Wexler, *The EEOC Suffers Another Resounding Defeat Due To "Shoot First, Aim Later" Tactics*, Seyfarth Shaw LLP (Sept. 10, 2013), available at Lexology.com]

After eight years and two Supreme Court appeals, a suit by a class of 700 black brokers against Merrill Lynch was settled in mid-2013. The class received $160 million, the largest race discrimination settlement to date. It was possible to certify a class in this case because Merrill Lynch imposed a system of uniform operations and strict centralized controls. *Dukes* means that if local supervisors have discretion, class members only have the same injury if the managers exercise discretion the same way, showing the same bias. The plaintiffs said that, even post-*Dukes*, a class should be certified because of two nationwide policies with disparate impact on African-American brokers: a policy allowing brokers to choose their own teams, and an account distribution policy that allocated a departing broker's accounts to other brokers based on their past results. According to the plaintiffs, the teams excluded black brokers, so their compensation and access to new accounts were limited. The Seventh Circuit certified a (b)(2) class for the limited purpose of deciding whether Merrill's practices violated federal law; if so, mini-trials would be held on individual damages. [*McReynolds v. Merrill Lynch*, 672 F.3d 482 (7th Cir. 2012); see D. Lucetta Pope, *Distinguishing Dukes: How Decentralized Decision-Making Led To A $160 Million Agreement To Settle Race Discrimination Claims Against Merrill Lynch*, Faegre Baker Daniels (Dec. 23, 2013), available at Lexology.com; Gerald L. Maatman Jr. and David B. Ross, *How A Ruling Shapes A $160 Million Class Action Settlement*, Seyfarth Shaw LLP (Aug. 29, 2013), available at Lexology.com]

In April, 2014, the Ninth Circuit permitted a class action by San Francisco police officers who charged that they were wrongfully denied promotion on account of age. The class action will proceed under the California Fair Employment and Housing Act (FEHA). (Originally, the plaintiffs asserted an ADEA pattern or practice claim, but they dropped that claim after class certification was denied.) According to the Ninth Circuit, the district court prematurely considered the merits of the case. The Ninth Circuit held that, at the class certification stage, the district court can only consider the merits to the extent needed to determine if the plaintiffs showed commonality in questions of law or fact. At the certification stage, it is not necessary for the plaintiffs to show that they will prevail on those issues. [*Stockwell v. City & Cnty. of San Francisco*, 749 F.3d 1107 (9th Cir. 2014); see Patrick Dorian, *Ninth Circuit Revives Police Officers' Age Bias Class Action Over Scrapped Exam*, Bloomberg BNA Daily Labor Report (Apr. 25, 2014) (benefitslink.com)]

§ 42.07 THE DISCRIMINATION COMPLAINT

Once the case is cleared for litigation in federal court, the plaintiff must draft a complaint to inform the defendant and the court system of the nature of the allegations against the defendant.

Late in 2001, the Eleventh Circuit adopted a position already held by the Third, Seventh, and Eighth Circuits: An EEOC intake questionnaire constitutes a "charge" if it is verified and has the information a charge would contain, and a reasonable person would consider the questionnaire to manifest an intent to seek Title VII remedies. [*Wilkerson v. Grinnell Corp.*, 270 F.3d 1314 (11th Cir. 2001)]

A similar issue went to the Supreme Court in the ADEA context. The Court permitted an ADEA suit to proceed, after the complainant filed a Form 283 intake questionnaire with the EEOC, but did not file the official Form 5 (charge). The EEOC did not carry out informal dispute resolution with the employer. The Court held that a valid ADEA charge requires only a few items of information (the name of the charging party, the nature of the allegation, and a request that the EEOC settle a dispute or take remedial action). In this case, the employer was aware that the plaintiff and thirteen other employees had alleged age discrimination. The Court remanded the case to the district court, holding that the lower court can make up for the deficiency by attempting to reconcile the parties in a settlement. (The EEOC stated that it has improved its procedures to make sure the same problem will not recur.) [*Federal Express Corp v. Holowecki*, 552 U.S. 389 (2008); see Mark Sherman, AP, *Supreme Court Says FedEx Employees Can Sue Over Age Discrimination* (Feb. 28, 2008) (law.com); Fred Schneyer, *Supreme Court Clears FedEx Age Discrimination Case for More Hearings*, plansponsor.com (Feb. 28, 2008)]

A 2008 Third Circuit case finds that a two-page document, including EEOC Form 5, constituted a charge. The first page gave the plaintiff's date of birth and contact information for the charging party and his employer. The complainant checked the box alleging age discrimination and cross-referenced the second sheet. He signed it in two places, but did not check the box for dual filing with the state agency, and did not have the signatures notarized. The second page, described as an affidavit, described improper questions asked at the interview, leading the plaintiff to believe that he was not offered a job because of his age (59). The EEOC regulations provide that a charge should contain:

- The names, address, and phone numbers of the charging party;
- The name, address, and phone number of the defendant;
- A statement of the facts constituting the alleged discrimination;
- The number of employees the employer has (to establish that the employer is large enough to be subject to federal anti-discrimination statutes);
- Whether or not the charging party has already initiated state proceedings.

About two months later, the EEOC wrote to the plaintiff's attorney asking for more information, stating that the plaintiff would have to provide the information within 33 days. But, instead of submitting the information to the EEOC, the plaintiff brought suit 80 days after submitting the document to the EEOC. The defendant moved to dismiss the case for failure to exhaust administrative remedies; the Third Circuit accepted the two-page document as a charge because it gave notice of the nature of the plaintiff's allegations. [*Holender v. Mutual Indus. North Inc.*, 527 F.3d 352 (3d Cir. 2008)]

The Seventh Circuit held that telling the employer to "shove its settlement offer up its ass" is not activity protected by Title VII. The plaintiff filed a sexual harassment charge; EEOC mediation began while the claimant was still employed. The employer made a settlement offer that the plaintiff found unacceptable; he said they could fire him and he would see them in court. The company did fire him. He then sued for Title VII retaliation. The Seventh Circuit found his inappropriate conduct during mediation to be a legitimate non-retaliatory reason to terminate him; non-protected conduct cannot support a retaliation claim. [*Benes v. A.B. Data Ltd.*, 724 F.3d 752 (7th Cir. 2013); see Michael C. Wilhelm, *Does Telling An Employer To Take A Settlement Offer And "Shove It Up Your @$%&!" Constitute Protected Activity Under Title VII?*, Briggs and Morgan (Sept. 10, 2013), available at Lexology.com]

§ 42.08 MEETING BURDENS

In legal parlance, "the burden of production" means having to provide evidence to prove a particular point, and "the burden of proof" is the standard used to determine if adequate evidence has been supplied.

Section 2000e(m) says that "demonstrates" means "meets the burdens of production and persuasion." This covers the extremely important legal issue of who has to provide evidence of what. It is always easier to wait for the other party to produce evidence and then show that this evidence is incorrect, incomplete, not technically satisfactory, or inadequate to prove the case, than to have to submit independent evidence of one's own viewpoint.

Section 2000e-2(k) explains what the plaintiff has to prove in order to win a disparate-impact case. The complaining party must show that the employer's challenged employment practice has a disparate impact on a protected group. At this stage, the employer has a chance to prove that the employment practice is valid because it is job-related and consistent with the needs of the employer's business. However, if the employer demonstrates that the employment practice does not cause disparate impact, it is not necessary to prove business necessity for that practice. On the other hand, business necessity is only a defense against disparate impact claims, not against claims of intentional discrimination.

Another route for proving disparate impact is for the complaining party to demonstrate disparate impact and also show that the employer refused to adopt an alternative employment practice that would eliminate the disparate impact.

According to the Ninth Circuit, the 1991 amendments to Title VII, allowing proof of violation when discrimination was a motivating factor for the employer (rather than the sole motivating factor) does not require proof of the impermissible factor by direct evidence, because the statutory language does not include the phrase "direct evidence." A year later, the Supreme Court affirmed. [*Costa v. Desert Palace Inc.*, 299 F.3d 838 (9th Cir. 2002), *aff'd*, 539 U.S. 90 (2003)]

On a related issue, the Fifth Circuit ruled in late 2013 that, even after the ADAAA has taken effect, plaintiffs are still required to prove disability before they prove discrimination, rejecting the plaintiff's argument that the new focus is whether discrimination occurred, not whether the employee has a disability. The jury still must find the plaintiff to be a qualified individual with a disability (QIWD) as a predicate to finding disability discrimination. [*Neely v. PSEG*, 735 F.3d 242 (5th Cir. 2013); see Clark Smith, *The Fifth Circuit Clarifies A Plaintiff's Burden Under The Americans With Disabilities Act*, Seyfarth Shaw LLP (Nov. 13, 2013), available at Lexology.com; Hunton & Williams LLP, *Disability Still Matters In ADA Claims*, Lexology.com (Nov. 14, 2013)]

§ 42.09 RETALIATION CHARGES

A high percentage of discrimination cases also involve charges of retaliation. Indeed, in some cases, the judge or jury has ruled that the original charge of discrimination was not supported by adequate evidence—but there was enough evidence of retaliation for making the charge to subject the employer to retaliation liability.

Under a 2006 Supreme Court decision, liability for retaliation is broader than liability for underlying workplace discrimination, and a retaliation case can be sustained even if the employee is not demoted and his or her compensation remains the same—as long as the retaliation is severe enough that a reasonable employee would take it into consideration in deciding whether or not to pursue a discrimination complaint. [*Burlington Northern & Santa Fe Ry. Co. v. White*, 548 U.S. 53 (2006)]

However, in 2013, on another issue, the Supreme Court found that retaliation liability is narrower than Title VII liability in general. The 2013 case was brought by a Muslim professor, who alleged that his supervisor harassed him because of his religion and Middle Eastern national origin, and that his employer retaliated against him by interfering with a job opportunity to punish him for making discrimination charges. The Supreme Court required retaliation plaintiffs to prove that retaliation was the "but-for" cause of the adverse employment action taken against them: i.e., that they would not have been fired, demoted, etc. without a retaliatory motive. This is the same standard used in ADEA cases, but is more restrictive than non-retaliation Title VII cases, where the plaintiff can prevail by showing that discrimination was one of several motivations used by the employer. The Supreme Court held that mixed-motive cases are only proper in cases involving the five criteria based on personal characteristics specified in Title VII: race, color, religion, sex, and national origin. The Supreme Court noted that Title VII's retaliation provisions are in a separate section from the basic protection against discrimination, and considered the language of the retaliation section to be more like the ADEA, hence justifying applying the higher ADEA standard in retaliation cases. [*University of Tex. Sw. Med. Ctr. v. Nassar*, 133 S. Ct. 2517 (June 24, 2013); see Marcia Coyle, *Supreme Court Makes It Harder to Prove Job Bias Claims*, Nat'l L.J. (June 24, 2013) (law.com)]

The First Circuit used *Nassar*'s "but-for" causation standard to affirm summary judgment for the employer in a Title VII sexual harassment/retaliatory termination case. The *Nassar* test is that protected activity is the but-for cause of adverse employment action. In this case, the plaintiff's performance problems began before the alleged harassment by her supervisor; she did not make a complaint of sexual harassment to the employer; and co-workers said that her work performance was substandard. Therefore, the employer had a legitimate, nondiscriminatory reason to fire her. [*Ponte v. Steelcase Inc.*, 741 F.3d 310 (1st Cir. 2014)]

The Supreme Court's 2009 *Crawford* decision holds that employees are protected against retaliation based on their answering questions during an internal investigation; it is not necessary for the employee to have volunteered the information or initiated the investigation, because participating in an investigation can constitute the type of active and consistent opposition to an unlawful practice that triggers entitlement to protection against retaliation. [*Crawford v. Metropolitan Gov't of Nashville & Davison County, TN*, 555 U.S. 271 (2009); see Rebecca Moore, *Employees Questioned in Workplace Sexual Harassment Investigations Are Protected*, plansponsor.com (Jan. 26, 2009)]

The Supreme Court ruled in early 2011 that Title VII forbids retaliation against someone who has filed a discrimination complaint if the retaliation takes the form of reprisals against a person who associates with the complainant. (In this case, it was the complainant's then-fiance who eventually became her husband.) The opinion says that Title VII's ban on retaliation extends to any action that would prevent a reasonable worker from making or pursuing a discrimination charge. Although it is difficult to draw firm lines, firing a close family member is very likely to be deemed retaliation; mild reprisal against an acquaintance is very unlikely to be; courts must find the balance in the intermediate areas. On the question of who is allowed to sue for retaliation, the Supreme Court said that as well as the person engaging in the protected activity, a suit can be brought by anyone within the zone of interests protected by Title VII. [*Thompson v. North Am. Stainless*, 131 S. Ct. 863 (2011)]

The Supreme Court did not give hard and fast rules for defining the zone, but suggested a sliding scale: firing a close family member is almost certainly a sustainable claim, whereas a lesser degree of action against an acquaintance almost certainly will not. Courts have at least been willing to consider cases involving close friends. However, a mid-2013 case, involving alleged retaliation against a co-worker of a district manager who charged the company with discrimination, found that the relationship was not close enough to support an association claim. The co-workers were neighbors and occasionally socialized, but only rarely. A 2012 case refuses to extend the zone of interest to a business entity that allegedly lost a contract with the defendant employer because of its association with a sexual harassment plaintiff on the grounds that such an extension was not contemplated by *Thompson*. [*Williams v. Daiichi Sankyo*, 947 F. Supp. 2d 1234 (N.D. Ala. 2013); *Crawford v. George & Lynch*, Civil Action No. 10-949-GMS-SRF, 2012 U.S. Dist. LEXIS 93106 (D. Del. July 5, 2012). See Jack Kiley and Shira Forman, *Recent Decisions Clarify Scope of Third-Party Retaliation Doctrine*, N.Y.L.J. (Oct. 21, 2013), available at law.com.]

The Second Circuit reversed a grant of summary judgment for the employer in a Title VII retaliation case because only three weeks elapsed between the plaintiff's complaint to her supervisor that male peers were paid more than she was and her termination. The employer gave several explanations of why the plaintiff was terminated, and there were inconsistencies between the employer's position statement to the EEOC and the evidence submitted in discovery and litigation. [*Kwan v. Andalex Group, LLC*, 737 F.3d 834 (2d Cir. 2013); see Michael A. Sands and Sheeva J. Ghassemi-Vanni, *EEOC Position Statement Comes Back To Bite Employer In Civil Lawsuit*, Fenwick & West LLP (Jan. 14, 2014), available at Lexology.com]

The Fourth Circuit held that the Fair Labor Standards Act (FLSA's) ban on retaliation applies only to employees, not to potential employees. Therefore, a job applicant cannot use this provision to sue a company that refused to hire her because of the FLSA suit she brought against a different employer. (The plaintiff got a job offer contingent on completing some forms; the offer was withdrawn after she disclosed the lawsuit on one of the forms.) [*Dellinger v. Science Applications Int'l Corp.* 649 F.3d 226 (4th Cir. 2011); see Sheri Qualters, *4th Circuit:*

Anti-Retaliation Provision of Wage Law Does Not Cover Job Applicants, Nat'l L.J. (Aug. 15, 2011) (law.com)]

The Third Circuit ruled early in 2006 that retaliation claims can be premised on a hostile work environment. Most of the circuits allow retaliation claims premised on retaliation that takes the form of severe or pervasive harassment, but the Fifth and Eighth Circuits require an ultimate employment decision to sustain a retaliation claim. [*Jensen v. Potter*, 435 F.3d 444 (3d Cir. 2006)]

The anti-retaliation provisions of Title VII protect a person who is named as a voluntary witness in a Title VII case, even if he or she is not called to testify at the trial. [*Jute v. Hamilton Sundstrand Corp.*, 420 F.3d 166 (2d Cir. 2005)] In mid-2010, the Second Circuit rejected an original theory put forward by a plaintiff. The court ruled that declining to investigate an employee's complaint of workplace discrimination (in this case, race discrimination) does not constitute retaliation for making the charge. [*Fincher v. Depository Trust & Clearing Corp.*, No. 08-5013-cv (2d Cir. May 14, 2010)]

PPACA § 1558 amended the Fair Labor Standards Act to prevent employers from retaliating against employees who receive a subsidy or tax credit for purchasing health care coverage from an insurance Exchange. Employees are protected against retaliation if they provided or were about to provide information about PPACA Title I violations to the employer, the federal government, or a state attorney general. Retaliation is also forbidden for testifying or being about to testify in a proceeding about such a violation, assisting in or participating in a proceeding, or objecting to or refusing to participate in a proceeding. Starting in 2014, employees are also protected against retaliation (such as termination of coverage) by EGHP insurers. However, retaliation complaints are processed by OSHA, not by the EEOC. [OSHA Fact Sheet, *Filing Whistleblower Complaints under the Affordable Care Act*, <http://www.osha.gov/Publications/whistleblower/OSHAFS-3641.pdf > (Feb. 2013); see PLC Employee Benefits & Executive Compensation, *OSHA Rules Address Retaliation Complaint Procedures under Health Care Reform* (Feb. 25, 2013) (benefitslink.com)]

§ 42.10 TITLE VII LITIGATION

[A] Three-Step Process

A Title VII case is very different from other civil cases, because so much revolves around questions of intentions and statistics, not just the proof of simple facts.

The basic Title VII case is a three-step process. The plaintiff establishes a prima facie case: the basic facts that are suggestive of discrimination. This is sometimes referred to as "McDonnell-Douglas burden-shifting analysis" after the Supreme Court case that established this technique.

After the plaintiff submits a prima facie case, the defendant can ask the court to dismiss the case at that stage (summary judgment), if the prima facie case would not be good enough for the plaintiff to win if the defendant did not submit a case of its own.

On the other hand, if the prima facie case is strong enough to keep the case going, the defendant employer gets a chance to rebut the plaintiff's charge of discrimination. The employer can do this by proving a legitimate, nondiscriminatory reason for the job action against the plaintiff. The employer can also prevail by proving that its action was impelled by business necessity. If summary judgment is not granted, then there will have to be a full trial. The jury (or the judge, if there is no jury in the case) will have to decide the facts.

The third step is the plaintiff's again. At this stage, the plaintiff gets to show "pretextuality": that the employer's allegedly nondiscriminatory reasons are fabricated to hide its discriminatory motive.

Whether a company actually has 15 employees is a substantive element of the Title VII case, not a jurisdictional prerequisite. Therefore, if the issue is not raised in a timely fashion, it is waived. The Supreme Court held early in 2006 that the 15-employee requirement is not jurisdictional because it does not appear in the part of the Title VII statute that grants jurisdiction to the federal courts. The court's lack of subject matter jurisdiction can be raised at any point in the case. [*Arbaugh v. Y&H Corp.*, 546 U.S. 500 (2006); similarly, *Minard v. ITC Deltacom Commc'ns Inc.*, 447 F.3d 352 (5th Cir. 2006) for the FMLA]

[B] Elements of the Prima Facie Case

The kind and amount of evidence that the plaintiff has to introduce to make a prima facie case depends on the kind of case (sex discrimination, sexual harassment, age discrimination, racial discrimination, etc.) and whether the plaintiff charges disparate treatment or disparate impact. Disparate treatment is a practice of intentional discrimination against an individual or group, whereas disparate impact is a practice that seems to be neutral and nondiscriminatory, but that has a heavier negative impact on some groups than others.

Furthermore, if the plaintiff charges that an employment practice has a disparate impact, and the employer responds by showing business necessity for that practice, the plaintiff can nevertheless win by proving that there was an alternative practice that would also have satisfied business necessity, but the employer refused to adopt that practice.

If a workplace decision involves many factors (for instance, promotion could be based on educational attainment, objective measures such as sales performance or departmental productivity, written tests, interviews, and assessments from supervisors), and the plaintiff challenges more than one of those criteria, the plaintiff has to be able to prove that each of those factors had harmful disparate impact on the plaintiff. If the various elements can't be separated and analyzed individually, then the whole decision-making practice can be treated as a single employment practice.

The "mixed motive" case works somewhat differently. It arises out of the situation in which several motivations influence the employer's decision. Some of them are lawful, others are discriminatory. The plaintiff can win a mixed motive case by showing that the discriminatory motive was influential. It is not necessary to prove that there were no legitimate motives involved. However, if the employer would have done the same thing even without a discriminatory motive being present, then the remedies available to the plaintiff will be reduced.

To establish the prima facie case, the plaintiff must show the following:

- That he or she belonged to a protected group;
- He or she had the necessary qualifications for the job (allegation of discriminatory failure to hire);
- He or she was doing an adequate job (if the allegation is improper discharge or failure to promote).

While disparate treatment cases usually depend on direct or indirect evidence of explicit discrimination, disparate impact cases usually turn on statistics about matters such as job applications and the composition of the workforce.

In mid-2003, the Supreme Court's *Desert Palace, Inc. v. Costa* decision [539 U.S. 90 (2003)] resolved a Circuit split. The First, Fourth, Eighth, and Eleventh Circuits had ruled that once the defendant meets its burden by articulating a legitimate nondiscriminatory reason for the job action, the plaintiff can get a jury instruction on mixed motive only by showing direct evidence. But the Supreme Court sided with the Ninth Circuit and allowed the instruction to be given on the basis of circumstantial evidence. In this case, the plaintiff, a truck driver, said that the employer's stated reason for firing her (a fight with another employee) was another instance of being treated more harshly than male co-workers for the same conduct. She also alleged that she was discriminated against when overtime work was available, and that supervisors were aware of and tolerated sex-based slurs against her.

The Supreme Court agreed that a mixed-motive jury charge can be given whenever the amount of evidence (whether direct or circumstantial) is adequate. This ruling therefore means that more cases will be submitted to the jury, and more plaintiffs will have a chance of prevailing. [See Shannon P. Duffy, *High Court Paves Easier Road to Jury for Discrimination Plaintiffs,* The Legal Intelligencer (June 11, 2003) (law.com)]

The California Supreme Court required new jury instructions in pregnancy discrimination cases, reflecting the requirement that pregnancy be a substantial motivating reason for the employment action. The California Court of Appeal applied this case to hold that it was error to instruct the jury that the plaintiff only had to prove that her pregnancy-related leave of absence was a motivating reason for her discharge. The court of appeal held that the employer was not entitled to a jury instruction on mixed motive or the "same decision" defense (i.e., that it would have taken the same action without a discriminatory or retaliatory motive) because those are affirmative defenses, and the employer did not plead them. [*Alamo v. Practice Mgmt. Info. Corp.*, 219 Cal. App. 4th 466 (2013); see Harold Brody et al., *Employer Was Entitled To "Substantial Motivating Factor" Jury Instruction*, Proskauer Rose LLP (Nov. 11, 2013), available at Lexology.com. See *Harris v. City of Santa Monica*, 56 Cal. 4th 203 (2013).]

A unanimous Supreme Court endorsed the "ministerial exception" in early 2012, holding that the First Amendment prevents courts from intervening when a minister is fired. All 12 of the circuits have recognized this exception, although this was the first time the Supreme Court dealt with the issue. The Court said that the ministerial exception is not a bar to a court's jurisdiction; it is an affirmative defense that has to be proved by the defendant raising it. The Supreme Court said that ministers can still sue for tortious conduct or breach of contract. The plaintiff, Cheryl Perich, alleged that she was fired in retaliation for threatening to file an ADA suit (she suffers from narcolepsy). The Sixth Circuit ruled for Perich, holding that she spent 45 minutes a day teaching religion and the rest of the time teaching secular subjects. The Supreme Court found this unpersuasive: all ministers have secular duties. [*Hosanna-Tabor Evangelical Lutheran Church v. EEOC* 132 S. Ct. 694 (2012); see Tony Mauro, *Unanimous High Court Finds for Church in EEOC Fight*, Nat'l L.J. (Jan. 11, 2012) (law.com)]

In a gender bias case, the District Court for the District of Massachusetts ruled in 2012 that a pattern-or-practice claim is a method of proving discrimination in a class action, not a free-standing cause of action. The plaintiff charged that CIGNA Healthcare's evaluation and promotion practices discriminated against women, violating Title VII and state law. CIGNA argued that the claims had to be arbitrated. The plaintiff said that the arbitration clause did not waive the right to litigate class-based or pattern-or-practice claims. The district court held that CIGNA's policies and procedures forbid class arbitration, so Karp had to pursue individual arbitration for her claim. [*Karp v. CIGNA Healthcare Inc.*, No. 11-10361-TSH, 2012 WL 1358652 (D. Mass. Sept. 14, 2012); see Sheri Qualters, *Judge Sends Gender Bias Case Against CIGNA To Arbitration*, Nat'l L.J. (Apr. 19, 2012) (law.com). See also *Chin v. Port Auth.*, 685 F.3d 135 (2d Cir. 2011) and *Parisi v. Goldman, Sachs & Co.*, 710 F.3d 483 (2d Cir. 2013): pattern or practice claims are limited to the class action context.]

[C] Evidence

Not only can each side introduce evidence about the course of the plaintiff's employment with the defendant company; in appropriate cases, the employer can introduce evidence about the plaintiff that the employer did not have at the time of the employment action.

The basic case on the use of after-acquired evidence is *McKennon v. Nashville Banner Pub. Co.* [513 U.S. 352 (1995)] In this case, the employer was allowed to introduce, at the trial, negative evidence about the plaintiff that the defendant learned after the employment action. Although the after-acquired evidence couldn't have motivated the employer, it was still relevant to the plaintiff's qualifications and credibility, so it can be introduced at trial.

In many cases, the plaintiff introduces statistics to show a pattern of discrimination by the employer. To prevail, a plaintiff must identify a specific employment practice that discriminates, not just rely on bottom-line numbers about the employer's work-force. The plaintiff must present statistical evidence of a kind and degree adequate to show that the practice has caused denial of promotion because of the applicants' membership in a protected group. When read in conjunction with the other evidence, adequate statistics must be of a kind and degree that reveals a causal relationship between the allegedly discriminatory practice and the disparity between actual promotions of group members, and the promotions that could be expected if there had been no discrimination.

In deciding whether to admit expert evidence at the class certification stage of an employment discrimination case, courts focus on whether the expert opinion meets the test of scientific validity. In employment discrimination cases, the plaintiffs usually want to introduce expert testimony consisting of statistics that show that there has been disparate impact or a pattern or practice of discrimination. [Elise M. Bloom and Amanda D. Haverstick, *Class Actions After 'Dukes,'* N.Y.L.J. (Oct. 24, 2011) (law.com)]

Another potential issue is that if a company's in-house counsel investigates discrimination charges, the attorney might become a witness at trial, testifying to the reasonableness of the employer's response to allegations. With the attorney as witness, documents, including the lawyer's interviews with employees, could become discoverable. The District Court for the Northern District of Ohio declared a mistrial after an employer refused to produce investigative notes made by in-house counsel during an internal investigation of allegations of harassment, discrimination, and retaliation. The employer had to pay more than $300,000 of the plaintiffs' attorneys' fees as a sanction, because there was a conflict of interest caused by the involvement of in-house counsel in the investigation. Therefore, HR staff should be trained to investigate, and report results to in-house counsel, or the investigation should be performed by outside consultants—not in-house counsel. [*EEOC v. Spitzer et al.*, 866 F. Supp. 2d 851 (N.D. Ohio 2012); Jennifer A. Harper, *The Risks Of Using In-House Counsel To Conduct Internal Investigations*, Bean Kinney & Korman PC (Nov. 21, 2013), available at Lexology.com]

In a sexual harassment case, the defendant said that it did not have to produce all the documents from its investigation of the harassment charges because some of them were covered by attorney-client or work-product privilege. The District Court for the District of Massachusetts ruled that privilege was waived for the investigation report and all of its supporting documents because the attorneys directed the investigator and controlled his investigation. However, privilege would not have been waived if the lawyer merely gave directions about how to investigate and did not participate. [*Koss v. Palmer Water Dep't*, 2013 WL 5564474 (D. Mass. Oct. 7, 2013); see David C. Henderson, *An Employer Waives the Attorney-Client Privilege if its Attorney Was "Part and Parcel" of the Sexual Harassment Investigation Offered in Defense*, Nutter McClennen & Fish LLP News & Insight (Nov. 5, 2013) (benefitslink.com)]

[D] Admissible and Inadmissible Evidence

The Second Circuit ruled that racist comments by a white employee can be used to show that the work environment was hostile to black people, even if the remarks were made after the black plaintiff resigned. [*Whidbee v. Garzarelli Food Specialties*, 223 F.3d 62 (2d Cir. 2000)] But testimony by four of the plaintiff's co-workers (that a supervisor's treatment of the demoted black employee was racially motivated) should not have been admitted. [*Hester v. BIC Corp.*, 225 F.3d 178 (2d Cir. 2000)] The witnesses could testify about their observations, but because they didn't know how good or bad the plaintiff's work performance actually was, they couldn't testify about the supervisor's motivation.

In mid-2011, the California Court of Appeal held that the trial court should have admitted "me too" evidence in a sexual harassment hostile work environment case. In other words, evidence that the defendant harassed other women should have been admitted because excluding it was prejudicial to the plaintiff's case. The court of appeal said that the evidence tended to show the defendant's bias against women and tended to disprove the legitimacy of his stated reason for firing the plaintiff. [*Pantoja v. Anton*, 198 Cal. App. 4th 87 (Cal. App. 2011); see Kate Moser, *Court OKs 'Me Too' Testimony in Sex Harass Suit Against Lawyer*, The Recorder (Aug. 9, 2011) (law.com)]

In 2014, the Fourth Circuit dismissed a Title VII case, in which the plaintiff was fired a week after an argument with a co-worker. The co-worker used an offensive racist term about the plaintiff. A three-judge panel of the Fourth Circuit found that this did not alter working conditions enough to create a hostile work environment. However, shortly thereafter, en banc rehearing of the case was granted. [*Boyer-Liberto v. Fountainebleau Corp.*, 752 F.3d 350 (4th Cir. 2014), *reh'g granted*, No. 13-1473 (July 1, 2014); see Kevin M. Ceglowski, *Hostile Work Environment Case Gets Additional Fourth Circuit Scrutiny*, Poyner Spruill LP (July 8, 2014), available at Lexology.com]

[E] Other Litigation Issues

If the plaintiff files suit in state court, the employer often tries to get the case removed to federal court. State courts usually have less crowded calendars, so cases can be decided faster. Sometimes, state law permits the employee to assert additional causes of action, or to get remedies that would not be available in federal court. Sometimes, too, a particular action is subject to state but not federal law. For example, some states ban discrimination in workplaces that are too small to be covered by the federal law. Sexual-orientation discrimination is not covered by Title VII, but is covered by certain state or local laws.

In many cases, federal law preempts state law. In other words, certain matters, such as most of labor law and benefit law, are covered by federal law, and the states cannot interfere. Therefore, if a plaintiff's state-court claims operate in one of these preempted areas, the employer has a strong argument for getting the case removed to federal court, or even dismissed.

Norman Carpenter sued Mohawk Industries for wrongful termination. He alleged that, at a time when he was unaware that the company was the defendant in a pending class action charging the company with conspiring to use undocumented workers to drive down the wages of legal workers, he told Mohawk's HR department about undocumented aliens working at the company. Carpenter said that company lawyers pressured him to recant and he was fired when he would not. As part of his wrongful termination suit, Carpenter tried to get information from Mohawk about his meeting with the lawyer and the decision to fire him. Mohawk said that the information was protected by attorney-client privilege. The Supreme Court held in late 2009 that a court order requiring disclosure of allegedly privileged material is not a collateral order that is entitled to immediate appeal, because there are other measures, such as postjudgment review, that the party seeking to protect the information can use. [*Mohawk Indus., Inc. v. Carpenter*, 558 U.S. 100 (2009)]

As Chapter 40 shows, in many instances, a would-be plaintiff is subject to a mandatory arbitration clause that requires arbitration of all discrimination claims. The general principle is that pre-dispute arbitration requirements (i.e., an agreement to arbitrate disputes that arise in the future) will be enforceable even if the plaintiff charges a violation of rights under federal anti-discrimination laws.

§ 42.11 ADEA SUITS

[A] Generally

It is clear that the ADEA creates a private right of action—i.e., individuals can bring suit if they claim to have been subjected to age discrimination in employment. [See 29 U.S.C. § 626(c)] The statute is not very detailed. It says only that individuals can sue for "such legal or equitable relief as will effectuate the purposes" of the ADEA. However, a suit brought by the Secretary of Labor will terminate the rights of individuals to bring their own lawsuits involving their ADEA claims.

Under 29 U.S.C. § 626(d), would-be ADEA plaintiffs have to file their charges within 180 days of the alleged unlawful practice. In a "referral" state (a state whose antidiscrimination agency has a work-sharing agreement) the charge has to be filed within 300 days of the alleged unlawful practice. If the state-law proceedings are terminated, the potential plaintiff must file the charge within 30 days of the termination of the state proceeding.

When a charge is filed, all potential defendants are notified. In both the Title VII and ADEA contexts, the Secretary's duty is to "promptly seek to eliminate any alleged unlawful practice by informal methods of conciliation, conference, and persuasion."

In the federal system, whether a case can be heard by a jury (instead of just a judge) depends on several factors, including the preferences of the litigants and the nature of the suit itself. The basic rule is that juries are more appropriate for cases seeking money damages than those asking for purely equitable remedies such as injunctions or reinstatement. However, ADEA plaintiffs can demand a jury trial whenever they seek money damages, even if there are also equitable claims in the same suit.

When third parties, including independent contractors, are authorized to make hiring decisions on behalf of an employer, the Second Circuit held that the employer can be liable under the ADEA if the third party commits discrimination. General agency principles are used to assess the third party's authority. This is a fact inquiry, so summary judgment is not appropriate. [*Halpert v. Manhattan Apartments Inc.*, 580 F.3d 86 (2d Cir. 2009)]

[B] Timing Issues for ADEA Suits

The EEOC proposed regulations (67 Fed. Reg. 52431, Aug. 12, 2003) and finalized them at the end of 2003 (68 Fed. Reg. 70150, Dec. 17, 2003; effective January 16, 2004). Under the now-applicable regulations, the EEOC will dismiss (as untimely) charges filed more than 180 days after the discriminatory act—or more than 300 days in a referral jurisdiction. Extra time may be available if the charging party has a valid claim to waiver, estoppel, or equitable tolling.

The EEOC has a statutory obligation to try to eliminate alleged unlawful practices by means of informal conciliation. If the EEOC tries to conciliate but fails, it will give the charging party a notice—but the notice will be clearly labeled to distinguish it from the Notice of Dismissal or Termination, which is issued in ADEA cases as a rough parallel to the Right to Sue letter in other discrimination cases.

An age discrimination charging party does not have to wait until the NDT is issued to sue—as long as he or she waits at least 60 days after the charge was filed. But once the NDT is issued, the complainant has only 90 days to file suit (which can be filed in either federal or state court), or the case will be dismissed as untimely.

Federal employees are subject to some special rules. They can go straight to the District Court to assert ADEA claims without going through the normal administrative process. According to the First Circuit, when they do so, the appropriate statute of limitations is the one found in the Fair Labor Standards Act, not Title VII. [*Rossiter v. Potter,* 357 F.3d 26 (1st Cir. 2004)]

However, under 29 C.F.R. § 1614.407(a), suit must be brought within 90 days of the final agency action. A plaintiff's final agency action occurred on June 15, 2001, making the last day to file September 13, 2001. His attorney filed the complaint on the 12th, expecting it to be delivered the next day. However, it was not actually delivered until the 18th. The Eighth Circuit found the case untimely, and would not grant equitable tolling. The plaintiff was deemed to have had adequate notice of the filing requirements, he had a lawyer, and the delay was not the fault of the clerk's office; it was not reasonable to expect next-day delivery from 450 miles away. [*Hallgren v. U.S. Dep't of Energy,* 331 F.3d 588 (8th Cir. 2003)]

It is in the employer's best interest for the court to rule that the cause of action "accrued" earlier, i.e., that the clock started ticking when the employee had to file suit. The earlier the cause of action accrues, the more likely it is that a claim can be dismissed as untimely.

If the alleged discriminatory act is firing the employee, there is a single act of discrimination. Most cases hold that the discriminatory act occurs on the date the plaintiff is unambiguously informed that he or she will be fired. The important date is the date of this notice, and not the first warning the plaintiff receives of impending termination, and not the last day the employee works for the employer or the last date he or she is on the payroll. The notice does not have to be formal, or even written, but it must be a definite statement that a final decision has been made to terminate the employee.

It is harder to place other discriminatory acts on a time continuum. It has been held that a claim of failure to promote accrues when the employees know or should have known about the facts that support the claim—probably, that a younger individual received the promotion that the plaintiff wanted.

If there is only a single employment decision, there is only a single act that might be discriminatory. However, some courts allow a plaintiff to argue that there was a continuing violation lasting over a period of time—for example, that the plaintiff kept his or her job, but was denied promotions he or she deserved because of age discrimination. In a case where the court accepts the continuing violation theory, the cause of action accrues with the last discriminatory act in the series. A filing that is timely for one act of discrimination will be timely for all acts of discrimination in the same series.

A bad performance appraisal that makes an employee more vulnerable to being laid off or RIFed (but that is not an actual threat of dismissal unless performance improves) is generally not considered an employment action that could give rise to an ADEA claim.

For discriminatory layoff charges, courts reach different conclusions as to when the cause of action accrues. One theory is that accrual occurs on the actual date of layoff. The other is that the cause of action accrues later, when the possibility of reinstatement ends because the employer has filled the last job for which the plaintiff might have been recalled.

[C] Tolling the ADEA Statute of Limitations

The statute of limitations can be tolled (suspended), giving employees additional time to litigate, in various circumstances—usually as a result of deception or other misconduct on the part of the employer. However, certain circumstances have been held not to be wrongful conduct, and will not toll the statute of limitations:

- Putting an employee on "special assignment" until termination takes effect;
- Offering a severance benefits package. However, offering a lavish severance package, but preventing employees from discussing it, was held to discourage employees from vindicating their legal rights, and therefore to toll the statute of limitations.

■ **TIP:** The statute of limitations is not tolled during the employer's in-house grievance procedure. However, a collective bargaining agreement provision is invalid if it terminates the employee's right to pursue a grievance once he or she files age discrimination charges with the EEOC or the local antidiscrimination agency. The clause is void because it punishes employees for exercising their legal rights.

Even if tolling occurs, it probably cannot last beyond the point at which an employee who took reasonable steps to investigate would have been aware of discrimination.

Do not forget that 29 U.S.C. § 627 requires the employer to post a notice of ADEA rights. The EEOC and Department of Labor distribute free copies of the mandatory notice; posters can also be purchased from many publishers. If the notice is duly posted, then the court will presume that the employee could have read the poster and become aware of at least basic ADEA rights.

However, if the information is not posted, the court may conclude that the employer deprived the employee of access to information about ADEA rights, thus tolling the statute of limitations. Yet some courts say that the real test is whether the employee actually was aware of what the ADEA says. Given actual knowledge, the court may decide that the absence of a poster in the workplace does not justify extending the time to bring suit.

[D] The ADEA Plaintiff's Burden of Proof

The *McDonnell-Douglas* pattern applies in ADEA cases. That is, first the plaintiff introduces evidence of a prima facie case of discrimination. If the evidence (taken at face value) is inadequate, the defendant employer can get summary judgment—that is, can have the case dismissed because of this inadequacy.

If, however, the case is good enough to survive a motion for summary judgment, it is the employer's turn at bat. By and large, proof is up to the plaintiff, but a BFOQ is an affirmative defense, which means that the employer has the burden of proving it. [*W. Air Lines Inc. v. Criswell,* 472 U.S. 400 (1985)] In non-BFOQ cases, the employer can rebut the prima facie case by showing a legitimate, nondiscriminatory reason for the conduct challenged by the employee. Then the employee gets another chance, to demonstrate that the employer's justification is actually a pretext for discrimination. *Meacham v. Knolls Atomic Power Labs* [554 U.S. 84 (2008)], similarly holds that the reasonable factors other than age (RFOA) defense is also an affirmative defense.

It is not necessary in all cases for the plaintiff to prove that he or she was replaced by someone under 40 (i.e., outside the protected group). [*O'Connor v. Consol. Coin Caterers Corp.*, 517 U.S. 308 (1997)] It is possible, although difficult, for the plaintiff to win a case in which he or she was replaced by another person over 40, as long as improper age-related motives are shown.

In 1993, the Supreme Court set a new standard for proving ADEA cases based on age-related factors rather than on age itself. For instance, a 30-year-old cannot have 30 years' employment experience, but a 38-year-old employee might have worked for the company for 20 years, and therefore have more seniority than a 50-year-old hired only 10 years earlier. In that example, the allegedly age-related factors of higher salary and benefits would actually make the 38-year-old the more expensive employee.

The key case on this issue is *Hazen Paper Co. v. Biggins* [507 U.S. 604 (1993)] which requires the plaintiff to prove that the employer's decision was influenced by age, not merely by age-related factors.

In 2009, the Supreme Court agreed to hear a mixed motive age discrimination case, to determine the burden of proof. The Supreme Court ruled that, in order to win, a mixed-motive ADEA plaintiff must prove by a preponderance of the evidence that age was the "but-for" cause of the challenged employment action: that it would never have occurred but-for the plaintiff's age. The burden of persuasion is always on the plaintiff, and can be met by either direct or circumstantial evidence. The burden of persuasion never shifts to the defendant. This is not the same standard applied in Title VII, but the Supreme Court stressed the difference in wording and legislative history between the ADEA and Title VII [*Gross v. FBL Fin. Servs., Inc.*, 557 U.S. 167 (2009)]

Early in 2008, the Supreme Court did not fully resolve the question about whether ADEA plaintiffs can prove a corporate culture of discrimination by introducing testimony of employees who did not have the same supervisor as the plaintiff. The Court would not entirely rule out the use of such testimony, requiring instead that in each case, the facts should be examined to see if the probative value of the testimony outweighed the risk of possible prejudice. The Court ruled that, in general, the district court's determination is entitled to a high measure of deference, because the lower court hears testimony rather than merely relying on the record on appeal. The relevant provision of the ADEA is drafted similarly to Title VII, so the same principle should also apply in Title VII cases. [*Sprint/United Mgmt. Co. v. Mendelsohn,* 552 U.S. 379 (2008); see, e.g., Fred Schneyer, *Supreme Court Reverses Age Discrimination Ruling on Procedural Grounds*, plansponsor.com (Feb. 27, 2008)]

Direct evidence of age discrimination is hard to find—especially since even employers who do practice discrimination usually have enough sophistication to conceal it. As a practical matter, then, most ADEA cases will be based on statistical evidence in support of the allegation, with or without evidence about statements made by executives and supervisors. Statistics are especially prominent in disparate impact cases.

However, the legal trend has been to reduce the credence given to statistics. In *St. Mary's Honor Ctr. v. Hicks* [509 U.S. 502 (1993)], the court held that the plaintiff always has the "ultimate burden of persuasion." So if the fact-finder (which will be the jury or the judge in a nonjury case) doesn't believe the employer's explanation of why its conduct was legitimate, the plaintiff can still lose—if the plaintiff simply fails to offer enough evidence. The *Hicks* standard is sometimes called "pretext-plus": The plaintiff has to do more than just show that the defendant's excuses are a mere pretext for discrimination.

[E] The ADEA Prima Facie Case

The basic prima facie (initial) case for an ADEA lawsuit is:

- The plaintiff belongs to the protected group—that is, is over 40;
- The plaintiff was qualified for the position he or she held or applied for;
- The plaintiff was not hired, discharged, demoted, deprived of a raise, or otherwise disfavored because of age;
- (In appropriate cases) The plaintiff was replaced—especially by someone under 40, although it is not absolutely required that the replacement come from outside the protected age group. If the charge is a discriminatory RIF, plaintiffs must show that age was a factor (although not necessarily the only factor) in targeting them for termination, or at least that the employer was not age-neutral in implementing the RIF program.

> Employers can defend against an accusation of a discriminatory RIF by showing good economic reason for cutting back; it isn't necessary to show that the company would be at the brink of bankruptcy without the reductions.

Depending on the type of case, the court where it is heard and the individual facts, the plaintiff may have to prove that his or her own qualifications and/or job performance were satisfactory, or may have to prove that they were superior to those of the person who replaced him or her.

In 2012, the EEOC issued a Q&A explaining what employers must do to use a Reasonable Factors Other Than Age (RFOA) defense when practices that are neutral on their face but might have disparate impact on older workers are challenged. The employer is only required to prove an RFOA after an employee has identified a specific business practice with disparate impact on older workers. An RFOA is reasonably designed and administered to achieve a legitimate business purpose—for example, a physical test for police patrol officers.

Whether the factors are indeed reasonable depends on, e.g.:

- Their relation to the employer's stated business purpose;
- The extent to which the factor is accurately defined and fairly and accurately applied (application includes training managers and supervisors);
- Limits on supervisors' discretion, especially when the criteria are vulnerable to negative age-based stereotypes;
- The extent to which the employer assessed the adverse impact of the practice on older workers;
- The degree of harm to workers over 40—not just the number of people affected and the extent of the injury, but the employer's measures to reduce harm, balanced against the burden of the actual and potential measures.
- The EEOC stresses that these are not elements that all employers must prove in every case, merely characteristics of reasonable practices.

The EEOC said that, unlike an employment test that has been challenged under Title VII, it is not necessary for the employer to produce a validation study about the RFOA.

The EEOC says it is not unreasonable to use subjective decision-making (e.g., ranking an applicant or employee's qualities such as flexibility and willingness to learn new things) but it is useful to give supervisors evaluation criteria to help them avoid age-based stereotypes. The EEOC said that employers are not obligated to discover and use the least discriminatory method of achieving the purpose—but attempts to limit harm to older persons are not irrelevant. [EEOC,

Questions and Answers on EEOC Final Rule on Disparate Impact and "Reasonable Factors Other Than Age" *Under the Age Discrimination in Employment Act of 1967*, <http://www.eeoc.gov/laws/regulations/adea_rfoa_qa_final_rule.cfm> (accessed Apr. 10, 2014); see Rebecca Moore, *EEOC Issues Final Rule Under ADEA*, plansponsor.com (Mar. 30, 2012)]

[F] ADEA Class Actions

Sometimes, an employee contends that he or she is the only person to suffer discrimination. Sometimes, however, it is alleged that the company engages in a pattern or practice of discrimination, affecting many people, and it becomes necessary to determine whether it is appropriate to certify a class action (i.e., to allow employees to combine their claims and present a single body of evidence).

The question of timing in class actions was addressed in *Armstrong v. Martin Marietta Corp.* [138 F.3d 1374 (11th Cir. 1998)] Certain employees were dismissed as plaintiffs from a pending ADEA class action. They brought their own suits. The Eleventh Circuit held that the statute of limitations is tolled (suspended) while a class action is pending, but starts all over again as soon as the district court issues an order denying class certification.

Would-be plaintiffs who are thrown out of a class action because they are not similarly situated to the proper plaintiffs must file their own suits within 90 days of being removed from the class. Equitable tolling (i.e., permitting an action that would otherwise be too late to continue, on the grounds of fairness) can be granted only if the EEOC actually misinformed the plaintiffs about the statute of limitations, not if the plaintiffs simply failed to consider this issue or made an incorrect determination of how long they had to bring suit.

§ 42.12 TITLE VII REMEDIES

[A] Fundamental Remedies

Once the case gets to court and is tried to a conclusion (many cases are either settled along the way, or are dismissed before a full trial has occurred), and if the plaintiff wins (most employment discrimination cases are won by the employer), then the question becomes what remedies the court will order. Remedies are governed by 42 U.S.C. § 2000e-5(g).

The fundamental remedies under this section are equitable: hiring or reinstatement (plus up to two years' back pay for the time the plaintiff would have been working absent discrimination). Furthermore, the amount that the plaintiff earned in the meantime—or could have earned by making reasonable efforts—is offset against the back pay. In other words, plaintiffs have a duty to mitigate their damages. They have an obligation to use their best efforts to earn a living, instead of relying on the hope the defendant employer will eventually be ordered to pay up.

If the plaintiff further succeeds in proving disparate treatment (as distinct from facially neutral practices that have a disparate impact on the group the plaintiff belongs to), then compensatory damages can be awarded to the plaintiff as reimbursement for costs (such as job hunting or therapy) incurred directly as a result of the discrimination.

However, in cases of racial discrimination, the plaintiff must look to the Civil Rights Act of 1866 [42 U.S.C. § 1981], and not to Title VII, for compensatory and punitive damages. If the alleged discrimination consists of failing to accommodate a disability, the employer will not have to pay compensatory damages if it made a good-faith effort at reasonable accommodation, even if the offer of accommodation was later deemed inadequate.

If the court finds that the employer engaged in the unlawful employment practice that the plaintiff charged, it can enjoin the respondent from continuing that abusive practice. The court can order the defendant to take remedial steps, including but not limited to hiring an applicant or reinstating an ex-employee.

Employers cannot be ordered to hire, reinstate, or promote anyone, or pay back pay to him or her, if the employment action was taken "for any reason other than discrimination on account of race, color, religion, sex, or national origin" or unlawful retaliation. [42 U.S.C. § 2000e-5(g)(2)(A)]

In a mixed-motive case where the defendant demonstrates that, although a discriminatory motive was present, it would have taken the same action (e.g., fired or refused to promote the plaintiff) purely on the basis of the other motivations even if there had been no discrimination, then the court can grant a declaratory judgment (a declaration that the employment practice was unlawful), enjoin its continued use, or award attorneys' fees that can be traced directly to the mixed-motive claim. But, because the employer would have taken the same action even without discrimination, the court cannot award damages to the plaintiff or order the defendant to hire, rehire or promote the plaintiff. [42 U.S.C. § 2000e-5(g)(2)(B)]

The court has discretion, under 42 U.S.C. § 2000e-5(k), to order the loser—whether plaintiff or defendant—to pay the winner's attorneys' fees (including fees for expert witnesses, which can be very high) and court costs. However, losing defendants can't be ordered to pay fees to the EEOC. If the EEOC sues a company and loses, it can be ordered to reimburse the defendant for its fees and costs for the suit.

Also note that 42 U.S.C. § 2000e-2(n) provides that employees usually cannot challenge employment practices that were adopted based on a court order or to carry out a consent decree in an employment discrimination case, if the employees knew about the case and either had their interests represented or had a chance to voice their objections. However, employees who actually were parties in the case can enforce their rights under the order or settlement, and judgments and orders can be challenged on the grounds of fraud or the court's lack of jurisdiction over the case.

One important factor in analyzing employment cases is what claim(s) the employee raises. Some employment discrimination claims fit into the "breach of contract" category, but most of them are more like "tort" claims. The importance of the tort/contract distinction is that the remedies are different for the two categories. If a plaintiff proves breach of contract, the court's job is to put the plaintiff back in the position he, she, or it would have been in if the contract had been carried out. In the context of an employment contract, or implied employment contract, that probably means earnings and fringe benefits that were lost because of the breach, possibly plus out-of-pocket expenses for finding a new job. (The doctrine of mitigation of damages requires plaintiffs to do whatever they can to limit the amount of damages they suffer—which definitely includes finding a new job if at all possible, pending resolution of the claims against the former employer.)

Back pay is not limited to simple salary. It includes benefits, overtime, shift differentials, merit raises, and the like. However, if the employer can prove that the employee would have been laid off, or was unavailable for work, back pay will not be available for the time the employee would not have been working anyway.

Fringe benefits are valued at the cost the employee would have to pay to replace them, not the (probably lower) cost the employer incurred to offer them.

Amounts earned in the new job reduce what the ex-employer will have to pay in damages. On the other hand, to the extent that the plaintiff proves that the employer committed one or more torts, the successful plaintiff can be awarded back pay, front pay (moving from the end of the trial forward), lost earnings, medical expenses, and value of pain and anguish, and emotional distress. The plaintiff's spouse might be granted an award for loss of consortium (marital services that were not rendered because of the employer's wrongdoing). In most states, interest on the judgment, running from the time the case is decided, can also be ordered—which mounts up quickly if the award is in six or seven figures.

Sometimes, front pay and reinstatement can be combined, i.e., if the remedies don't overlap, chronologically or economically. Front pay can be awarded to get the plaintiff to the "point of employability," at which point he or she can be reinstated.

The equitable remedy of front pay can be denied to an employee whose conduct after termination renders her ineligible for reinstatement. This case involved a sexual harassment plaintiff who got another job at a bank, who was fired for attempting to process an unauthorized loan application. The case was remanded to determine if her misconduct in the second job would preclude reinstatement in the first job. [*Sellers v. Mineta*, 358 F.3d 1058 (8th Cir. 2004)]

Many discrimination cases can be brought by the plaintiff in federal court, because there is a federal question (alleged violation of a federal statute). If the plaintiff chooses to sue in state court instead, the issue arises of whether the defendant can get the case removed to federal court. Further issues arise when the reason for going to federal court is "diversity" (the plaintiff and defendant are citizens of different states). Federal courts have jurisdiction in diversity cases if, and only if, the amount in controversy is at least $75,000.

[B] CRA '91 Cap on Damages

The Civil Rights Act of 1991 (CRA '91) [Pub. L. No. 102-166] imposes a cap on total damages that can be awarded to a successful Title VII plaintiff: The amount depends on the size of the corporate defendant, not the number or seriousness of the charges. The cap applies to punitive damages and most compensatory damages (but not to medical bills or other monetary losses that the plaintiff incurred before the trial).

Companies with fewer than 15 employees are exempt from Title VII, so the cap calculation begins at the 15-employee level. The damage cap is $50,000 for a company with 15–100 employees. The cap is set at $100,000 for companies with 101–200 employees, $200,000 for 201–500 employees, and $300,000 for companies with over 500 workers.

The First Circuit ruled in mid-2011 that the number of employees for purposes of the CRA '91 damage cap is determined at the time of the discrimination, not at the time the court renders its decision. The District Court for the District of Puerto Rico awarded $300,000 in a sexual harassment case. The trial judge reduced this award to $50,000. On appeal, the First Circuit increased the compensatory damages to $200,000. The size of the employer's workforce had fallen dramatically between 2004 (when the alleged discrimination occurred) and the 2008 verdict. The First Circuit also held that the number of employees is an affirmative defense that has to be proved by the employer. [*Hernandez-Miranda v. Empresas Diaz Masso Inc.*, 651 F.3d 167 (1st Cir. 2011)]

In mid-2011, the Third Circuit reduced a $10 million jury award for racial discrimination received by three former police officers to $900,000. The officers brought only federal claims, so the $300,000 cap on damages applied. (If they had brought and prevailed on claims under Pennsylvania law, damages for those claims would not have been capped.) The plaintiffs, who are white, alleged that they suffered retaliation for protesting mistreatment of black co-workers. One of the plaintiffs was told that if he filed an EEOC charge, his supervisor would make his life "a living nightmare." In a separate opinion, $208,000 in back pay was awarded to one of the plaintiffs. [*McKenna v. Philadelphia,* 649 F.3d 171 (3d Cir. 2011); see Shannon P. Duffy, *3rd Circuit Upholds Slashing $10 Million Verdict to $900,000,* The Legal Intelligencer (Aug. 19, 2011) (law.com)]

[C] Punitive Damages

One of the most controversial questions is the matter of punitive damages. Theoretically, punitive damages are supposed to be quite rare, ordered only in those cases when the defendant's conduct has been worse than merely negligent or improper.

A defendant that has acted maliciously, or at least with reckless indifference to the plaintiff's rights, can be ordered to pay punitive damages. The employer's conduct need not be "egregious" for punitive damages to be available. [*Kolstad v. Am. Dental Ass'n,* 527 U.S. 526 (1999)]

BlueLinx holdings moved to dismiss Pruett's whistleblower suit. The plaintiff, a former compliance manager, alleged that he was terminated in retaliation for reporting violations to the SEC and the Public Company Accounting Oversight Board. He asked for jury trial and punitive damages. He conceded that punitive damages were not currently available, but asked for the request to be dismissed without prejudice in case judges change their interpretation of the statute. The District Court for the Northern District of Georgia dismissed the punitive damage claim with prejudice, holding that if the law changed, the plaintiff could renew his motion. On the question of jury trial, the court concluded that a Dodd-Frank whistleblower claim has some resemblance to the common-law tort of wrongful discharge, for which jury trial is available, but the Dodd-Frank remedies of reinstatement, hiring, and back pay are usually considered equitable remedies. [*Pruett v. BlueLinx Holdings, Inc.*, CIVIL ACTION NO. 1:13-cv-02607-JOF, 2013 U.S. Dist. LEXIS 185551 (N.D. Ga. Nov. 12, 2013)]

In a case of religious discrimination against a Muslim employee who wore a head covering, the District Court for the Northern District of California held that punitive damages were appropriate because of the defendant's malice or reckless indifference to the plaintiff's religious obligations. [*EEOC v. Abercrombie & Fitch Stores, Inc.*, 966 F. Supp. 2d 949 (N.D. Cal. 2013)]

The general rule in the federal system—not just in employment discrimination cases—is that "double digit" punitive damages (i.e., more than 10 times the compensatory damages) are inappropriate, and that it is also inappropriate to impose punitive damages in a particular case because of the defendant's wrongful conduct in other cases or other states. According to the Fourth Circuit, it was permissible to award $100,000 to a wrongfully demoted employee who was not awarded any compensatory damages on her sex discrimination claim. The Fourth Circuit deemed the judge's award of $410,000 in back pay and interest to justify the punitive damage award, because the loss of income she suffered was actionable harm, the lost back pay was roughly equivalent to compensatory damages, and there is no explicit statutory condition under CRA '91 that punitive damages are dependent on compensatory damages. [*Corti v. Storage Tech. Corp.*, 304 F.3d 336 (4th Cir. 2002)]

The jury in a sexual harassment case found Asarco liable, but did not find any compensatory damages, so it awarded $1 in nominal damages and $858,750 in punitive damages. The trial court applied the Title VII cap to reduce the damages to $300,000. The Ninth Circuit found that 300 times compensatory damages was unacceptable, so it ordered either retrial or a further reduction of the damages to $125,000. [*Arizona v. Asarco*, 733 F.3d 882 (9th Cir. 2013); see John Alan Doran, *New Math. Old Math. Any Old Math Will Do*, Sherman & Howard LLC (Oct. 25, 2013), available at Lexology.com]

There are not many instances in which very large punitive damages have actually been paid. Such awards are vulnerable to being reduced on appeal. Or the plaintiff may feel both emotionally vindicated and sick of litigating the case, and may settle the case post-trial for much less than the theoretical award. Nevertheless, even if the order is never carried out, it can be a real public relations disaster for a company to be ordered to pay millions of dollars as a punishment.

The EEOC's Compliance Manual lists appropriate factors for deciding whether the employer acted with malice or reckless indifference:

- Degree of unacceptability of the conduct;
- The nature, severity, and extent of the harm suffered by the complaining employee;
- The duration of the conduct: A practice that persists for years is more serious than one that is terminated after a short period of time;
- Whether there was an extensive pattern of past discrimination, or only a few isolated incidents;
- Whether the employer tried to remedy the situation, or exacerbated it by covering up or retaliating against complainants.

The District Court for the Southern District of California affirmed a jury award of $4,650,000 for a supervisor who was fired in retaliation for identifying possible violations of California requirements for rest periods. The award consisted of $300,000 in economic damages, $850,000 in non-economic damages, and $3.5 million in punitive damages. [*Steffens v. Regus Group, PLC*, No. 09cv1494-LAB (BLM), 2013 U.S. Dist. LEXIS 116536 (S.D. Cal. Aug. 16, 2013); see Michael A, Sands and Dan Ko Obuhanych, *$4.6m Jury Verdict In Retaliation Lawsuit Confirmed*, Fenwick & West LLP (Sept. 17, 2013), available at Lexology.com]

[D] Attorneys' Fees and Costs

Under appropriate circumstances, a court can award attorneys' fees and costs to the "prevailing party"—and there has been a good deal of litigation, inside and outside the employment discrimination context, on the issue of who has been successful enough to receive a fee award.

In 2010, the Supreme Court ruled that a specific section of ERISA (§ 502(g)(1)) gives the district court discretion to award attorneys' fees to either party, not necessarily to the "prevailing" party. (In contrast, ERISA § 502(g)(2), about delinquent contributions to a multi-employer plan, limits fee awards to the prevailing party.) Therefore, it was not an abuse of discretion to grant attorneys' fees to a claimant who went to court after being denied long-term disability benefits. The district court found that the insurer abused its discretion when it denied the benefits, and remanded for the insurer to reconsider; if it did not, the trial court said that it would enter judgment for the plaintiff. The benefits were granted, and the district court awarded attorneys' fees. The Fourth Circuit found that this was an abuse of discretion, because the plaintiff received only a remand, not substantive benefits. The Supreme Court reversed, citing the statutory language that does not require the party seeking fees to have prevailed. [*Hardt v. Reliance Ins. Co.*, 560 U.S. 242 (2010); see Workplace Prof Blog, *ERISA Supreme Court Attorney Fees Case Goes Way of Plaintiffs* (May 24, 2010) (benefitslink.com); Marcia Coyle, *Supreme Court Smooths Path to Plaintiff Fees in Disability Cases,* Nat'l L.J. (May 25, 2010) (law.com).

Shortly thereafter, the Fourth Circuit applied this case to award attorneys' fees to a claimant who was granted summary judgment when the district court found that she was entitled to long-term disability benefits for carpal tunnel syndrome. The Fourth Circuit found that there was no inherent bias in the termination of long-term disability benefits after two years—but the denial was not supported by substantial evidence, because the plaintiff's pain and loss of function continued: *Williams v. Metropolitan Life Ins. Co.*, 609 F.3d 622 (4th Cir. 2010); see Plansponsor Staff, *4th Circuit Upholds Award of Benefits and Attorneys' Fees in LTD Case,* plansponsor.com (July 2, 2010)]

Federal Rules of Civil Procedure Rule 68 provides that when the defendant makes a formal settlement offer before the trial; the plaintiff rejects the offer; and the plaintiff wins the case, but is awarded less than the offer, the defendant is entitled to reimbursement of litigation costs. However, the Third Circuit ruled that the defendant can never recover attorneys' fees under this provision, because the plaintiff's suit was not frivolous—the plaintiff merely made a bad strategic decision in a valid case. [*Tai Van Le v. Univ. of Pa.*, 321 F.3d 403 (3d Cir. 2003)]

It is rare but not unheard-of for an employer to receive a fee award as a prevailing defendant: for example, when the EEOC's investigation lasted more than six years; many remedies were unavailable (plants where discrimination allegedly occurred had closed); and the defendant was prejudiced by the delay (old personnel records had been routinely destroyed), the Fourth Circuit upheld an award of approximately $193,000 against the EEOC. [*EEOC v. Propak Logistics Inc.*, 746 F.3d 145 (4th Cir. 2014)]

§ 42.13 SETTLEMENT OF A DISCRIMINATION SUIT

[A] Generally

Suits can be settled at any time before a verdict or judicial decision is rendered. In fact, they can even be settled after the judge and jury have spoken. As long as there are appeal rights that could be exercised, the case is still open for negotiation. The objective of any settlement is to provide something for both parties: for the defendant employer, the chance to dispose of the case expeditiously and to eliminate the risk of a huge jury verdict; for the plaintiff, the chance to get at least some money quickly instead of many years later. At a very early stage, the matter might be resolved by an agreement to let the employee resign instead of being fired and receive severance pay, and perhaps some other benefits, in exchange for releasing the employer from all liability. Both sides must agree on how the matter will be treated for unemployment insurance purposes (based on counsel from a lawyer).

In a situation where the employer acknowledges that the plaintiff has a valid case, or at least that the claims have some validity, the employer may want to settle early to limit its possible liability exposure and bad publicity.

Even if the employer thinks the plaintiff's claims are fabricated, exaggerated, or legally invalid, it still might be prudent to settle the case because of the sheer cost and effort involved in litigating a major suit, even if the final result is victory for the employer.

Usually, cases are settled somewhere around halfway between the plaintiff's demand and the defendant's counter-offer. Of course, both sides know this, and it influences the amounts they suggest at the negotiating table. No one should ever engage in negotiations without authority actually to settle the case, and without a range of acceptable settlement figures.

Seyfarth Shaw's Annual Workplace Class Action Litigation Report published January 14, 2013 shows that *Dukes* immediately had a tremendous impact on private class action suits. Employers are taking a much harder line during settlement negotiations. The total involved in 2012's top 10 employment discrimination class settlements was approximately $46 million. This was the lowest figure since 2006, and much lower than the $346 million total from 2010. The EEOC has responded by increasing its systemic investigations, although it filed only half as many suits in 2012 as in 2011. The continuing problems of the economy will probably result in more class actions and collective actions alleging wage and hour violations. [Shannon Green, *Workplace Class Action Litigation Report Outlines a Post-Dukes World*, Corporate Counsel (Jan. 14, 2013) (law.com)]

■ **TIP:** Cases that are settled quickly are also often settled within the policy limits of the employer's liability insurance policy. Therefore, the insurer will assume the entire cost of settlement. Moreover, if the employer

> does a prompt investigation of the allegations, negotiates in good faith, and does not unduly delay the settlement, the employer has not acted outrageously and has not violated the norms of public policy. Therefore, there will probably be no grounds for assessing punitive damages against the employer.

When a settlement is reached, there are two major legal documents to be prepared. The first is a court order dismissing the case with prejudice (i.e., in a way that prevents it from being refiled later) and a release containing the terms of the settlement. It is usually prudent to try to provide the text of the release, in order to control the basic form of its terms. The 2009 Family and Medical Leave Act regulations (see Chapter 38) make it explicit that, while prospective waivers are forbidden (i.e., employees cannot give up the right to bring suit for violations that might occur in the future), employees can settle FMLA claims that have already accrued without court approval or the supervision of the Department of Labor.

Mid-2009 EEOC guidance includes a section on Older Workers Benefit Protection Act (OWBPA) waivers. A waiver covering a group or class of employees carries additional disclosure requirements. There are seven factors under the OWBPA for determining whether an ADEA waiver is knowing and voluntary. It must be written in a manner that can be clearly understood; must specifically mention ADEA rights or claims; must inform employees of the right to consult a lawyer; must give the employee at least 21 days to consider the offer and seven days to revoke acceptance; the waiver cannot cover claims to arise in the future; and the employee must receive some consideration for the waiver that would not otherwise be available. A waiver is invalid if obtained by fraud or undue influence, or if there has been a material mistake, omission, or misstatement. [Rebecca Moore, *EEOC Issues Guidance on Waivers for Departing Employees*, plansponsor.com (Aug. 12, 2009)]

A settlement can be offered without admitting culpability. Also, under 29 C.F.R. § 1601.20(a), the EEOC has the power to dismiss an employee's discrimination charge if the employee rejects a written settlement offer from the employer that is a legitimate offer of "full relief" (i.e., adequate compensation for the discrimination suffered by the employee). The EEOC sends the employee a strongly worded form letter that gives him or her only two choices: to accept the settlement offer promptly, or have the EEOC charge dismissed. (This only means that the EEOC will not be involved in the case, not that the employee is prevented from suing.)

Full relief means that the employee gets full back pay, plus any out-of-pocket expenses related to discrimination (such as moving expenses after a wrongful termination, or psychological counseling for a stressed-out employee). Compensation must also be included for nonmonetary losses such as loss of sleep, anxiety, and indigestion.

However, the employer must be aware that settling with one employee is not necessarily the end of the problem. It is against public policy (and a court might issue an injunction forbidding this) to include a provision in a settlement agreement that forbids a current or former employee to cooperate with an EEOC investigation. A settlement can prevent a person from pursuing his or her own claims against the employer, but the EEOC's right to investigate workplace conditions, and pursue claims on its own behalf (and on behalf of other employees) continues.

[B] Tax Factors in Settling Discrimination Cases

The plaintiff's objective is to wind up with the best after-tax result from pursuing or settling a case. In some instances, appropriate structuring of the settlement can produce a better after-tax result for the plaintiff while reducing the cash-flow impact on the defendant.

Damages for breach of contract are taxable income for the plaintiff, because they are treated as delayed payment of compensation that the employee would have received earlier if there had been no breach of contract.

The treatment of tort damages is more complex. Damages are not taxable if they are payable because of the plaintiff's "personal injury." The Supreme Court has ruled that Title VII damages and ADEA damages are not received for personal injury, because they are not similar enough to the damages received in traditional tort cases (car crashes, for instance). [*United States v. Burke,* 504 U.S. 229 (1992); *Commissioner of Internal Revenue v. Schleier,* 515 U.S. 323 (1995)] Nevertheless, in 2006 the D.C. Circuit held that compensatory damages for emotional distress and loss of reputation are not taxable, and it was unconstitutional to apply section 104(a)(2) [the definition of "personal physical injury"] to the plaintiff, because compensation for non-physical personal injury should not have to be included in income if it is unrelated to lost earnings. [*Murphy v. IRS*, 460 F.3d 79 (D.C. Cir. 2006)]

Later, this anomalous result was reversed. The IRS asked for rehearing en banc (i.e., by all of the judges of the D.C. Circuit, not just a panel consisting of some of them). Instead of granting en banc rehearing, the original three-judge panel re-heard the case and reversed its earlier holding. This time around, the D.C. Circuit joined the other Circuits in treating the amount as taxable income. [*Murphy v. CIR*, 493 F.3d 170 (D.C. Cir. 2007); see, e.g. (AP) *D.C. Circuit: Damages for Emotional Distress Part of Gross Income* (July 5, 2007) (law.com). See also *Polone v. CIR*, 479 F.3d 1019 (9th Cir. 2007).]

The Small Business Job Protection Act of 1996 clarified the application of I.R.C. § 104(a)(2), the provision on taxation of damages. Starting August 21, 1996, damages received for "personal physical injuries" and physical illness are received free of tax—for instance, if the employer's wrongful conduct makes the employee physically ill. Damages for emotional distress are taxable except to the extent of medical expenses for their treatment.

Taxable damages that are wage replacements (under the FLSA, NLRA, Title VII, and ADEA, for example) may be FICA wages and may be subject to withholding. But see *Newhouse v. McCormack & Co.* [157 F.3d 582 (8th Cir. 1998)], where front and back pay awarded under the ADEA to a job applicant who was not hired was not considered "wages" subject to tax withholding. The Second Circuit held that settlement proceeds in an ADEA suit were wages subject to FICA. The agreement expressly permitted the employer to deduct and withhold all sums subject to withholding under applicable laws and regulations, but did not state how the $250,000 settlement proceeds would be treated for tax purposes. A court analyzing a settlement payment looks first to the nature of the claim that was settled, then remedies under governing law, then the parties' intention. In ADEA cases, the remedies are lost wages, liquidated damages, and equitable relief—but not pain and suffering or emotional distress damages (which would probably not be treated as wages). [*Gerstenbluth v. Credit Suisse*, 728 F.3d 139 (2d Cir. 2013)]

In a Title VII retaliation case, the Tax Court reaffirmed that emotional distress damages are taxable income for the person who receives them. The plaintiff, Sharp, was a professor who charged that she was demoted to a secretarial position in retaliation for reporting missing equipment. She said that she became depressed and suffered associated physical symptoms as a result of the stressful, hostile work environment. Her suit was settled; the university agreed to make three $70,000 installment payments to compensate her for emotional distress. She did not report the first installment as taxable income, deeming it to be damages for personal physical injury, exempted by Code § 104(a)(2). The IRS assessed tax on the funds. Sharp went to the Tax Court, which ruled in the IRS's favor and held that an accuracy-related penalty was due. The Tax Court said that the settlement agreement had only one reference to being conditioned on settling her Worker's Compensation claim. The settlement was for emotional distress, rendering the proceeds taxable income for the plaintiff. [*Sharp v. Comm'r*, No. 2013-290 (T.C. Dec. 23, 2013); see William Hays Weissman, *U.S. Tax Court Decision Shows Importance Of Carefully Drafting Settlement Agreements*, Littler Mendelson (Jan. 6, 2014), available at Lexology.com]

A longstanding circuit split was resolved by the U.S. Supreme Court's January 2005 decision in *Comm'r v. Banks*, 543 U.S. 426 (2005). A judgment or settlement paid to a winning plaintiff's attorney under a contingent fee agreement must be included in the plaintiff's gross income, irrespective of whether state law gives the attorney special rights (over and above normal contract law rights) over amounts awarded to prevailing plaintiffs.

Section 703 of the American Jobs Creation Act (Pub. L. No. 108-357) makes attorneys' fees in employment discrimination cases an above-the-line deduction, although this is not true of attorneys' fees in other types of cases. *Banks* was decided after the enactment of this legislation, but the law is not retroactive.

The Second Circuit held that a Title VII award of back and front pay was subject to deductions of federal and state taxes, because the judgment replaced wages that the plaintiff lost due to discrimination and he would have had to pay taxes if there had been no discrimination and he had earned his ordinary salary. [*Noel v. New York State Office Of Mental Health Cent. New York Psychiatric Ctr.*, 697 F.3d 209 (2d Cir. 2012)]

The Third Circuit held that prevailing plaintiffs in employment discrimination cases (in this case, the winner of an ADA suit) can receive an additional award to make up for the negative tax consequences of receiving a back pay award in a lump sum. The Third Circuit's rationale was that anti-discrimination statutes seek to make the plaintiff whole for the losses suffered, and the tax problems are a result of the underlying discrimination. The Tenth Circuit has ruled similarly, but the D.C. Circuit has held that plaintiffs are never entitled to a supplemental award to improve their tax position. [*Eshelman v. Agere Systems Inc.*, 554 F.3d 426 (3d Cir. 2009); see Shannon P. Duffy, *Tax Needs May Require Additional Award in Employment Cases*, The Legal Intelligencer (Feb. 4, 2009) (law.com); the earlier cases are *Sears v. Atcheson, Topeka & Santa Fe R.R*, 749 F.3d 1451 (10th Cir. 1984) and *Dashnaw v. Pena*, 12 F.3d 1112 (D.C. Cir. 1994)]

A Recent IRS Chief Counsel Memo (CCM) explains the four-step approach to taxation of settlements of employment discrimination claims. The first step is the origin of the claim; if the payment is based on wages, it must be reported on Form W-2, not Form 1099-MISC. The second step is that severance payments generally constitute gross income for the recipient, unless an exclusion is available. The most common exclusions involve reimbursement of medical costs and damages for physical injury or illness (Code § 104(a)(2)). If any part of a severance payment is taxable to the recipient, the allocable part of the attorney's fee is also gross income. The third step is that severance pay, back pay, and front pay, unless excluded from gross income, are FICA and FUTA wages subject to withholding, even if they are paid after employment ends. If the settlement does not allocate part of the payment to attorneys' fees, or if the settlement was not made under a fee-shifting statute (e.g., Title VII, ADA, ADEA), the entire attorneys' fee award is subject to employment taxes. But if an employment-related claim under a fee-shifting statute is settled, any amount clearly allocated to attorneys' fees by the settlement will not be taxed as wages. Step 4 is reporting the entire payment to settle a wage-based claim on the ex-employee's Form W-2. But if the settlement agreement specifically makes a reasonable allocation for attorneys' fees, the employer reports the fee payments on separate 1099-MISCs, one to the former employee and one to the attorney. [IRS Chief Counsel Memo No. 20133501F (Aug. 20, 2013); see J. Mark Poerio, *Severance Pay And Employment Taxes: Addressed In IRS Chief Counsel Memo*, Paul Hastings LLP (Sept. 16, 2013), available at Lexology.com]

CHAPTER 43

INSURANCE COVERAGE FOR CLAIMS AGAINST THE EMPLOYER

§ 43.01 INTRODUCTION

It is only prudent for a company to maintain insurance against significant risks. However, although the potential risk exposure in a discrimination, harassment, or wrongful termination suit is quite large, it can be difficult to buy insurance that will fully cover these claims—or even cover them at all. In addition, the collapse of the financial markets beginning in 2008 has given rise to a wide variety of securities-related claims, including those brought by employees whose pensions were jeopardized.

A basic principle of insurance law is that you can't buy insurance to protect yourself against the consequences of your own intentional wrongdoing.

The current interpretation of this rule is that it does not violate public policy for companies to buy insurance covering employment-related liability, because this enhances the winning plaintiffs' chances to collect. This benefit is deemed to outweigh the risk that companies will be more willing to engage in improper employment practices if they know they are protected by insurance.

A related policy question is whether insurance can cover punitive damages. About two-thirds of the states that have decided cases about this say yes. However, punitive damages for intentional wrongdoing cannot be covered, and most punitive damages are imposed precisely because of the intentionality of the defendant's wrongful conduct.

One hundred twenty days before current coverage expires, insured companies should analyze their liability insurance portfolio, and confer with an insurance agent, the general counsel, and the risk manager to create a current risk profile for the company and determine what coverage is available at what cost to insure against this risk. Insurers issue Conditional Notice of Non-Renewal Letters about 90 days before a policy expires, indicating that they do not wish to renew a policy but that they might offer terms on receipt of additional information about the insured company. The outcome of the strategy meeting should assist the company in negotiating renewals where non-renewal has been threatened—or in seeking alternative coverage. [DeAndre Salter and Karen Kutger, *As Prices Rise on Executive Liability Coverage, Strategy and Negotiations Enter Tough Terrain*, N.Y.L.J. (Mar. 26, 2009) (law.com)]

The District Court for the Middle District of Georgia ruled in mid-2013 that a professional liability policy did not cover a billing and collection servicer's obligation to indemnify a client for employee embezzlement. The district court applied the exclusion for criminal, fraudulent, dishonest, or knowingly wrongful acts. The embezzler diverted medical insurance checks to her personal bank account. The servicer's client demanded reimbursement of the stolen funds, and the servicer sought coverage from its professional liability insurer. The insurer said that the insured's obligation stemmed from contract, not a duty imposed by law, but the district court rejected this argument. Billing services were covered by the policy because there was an independent duty to exercise reasonable care in supervising employees, so the claim fell within the scope of coverage. However, the embezzler was considered to be an insured, so coverage for negligent supervision was barred by the exclusion for knowing, wrongful acts by an insured. [*Nat'l Reimbursement Grp., Inc. v. Gemini Ins. Co.*, No. 5:13-cv-145 (MTT), 2013 WL 4495846 (M.D. Ga. Aug. 21, 2013); see Wiley Rein LLP, *Claim For Employee Embezzlement Alleges A Wrongful Act But Is Excluded*, Lexology.com (Sept. 3, 2013)]

§ 43.02 COMMERCIAL GENERAL LIABILITY

[A] Use of the CGL Policy

Most businesses get their basic liability coverage under the Commercial General Liability (CGL) policy. In fact, for most companies, this is the only liability insurance.

The CGL has two basic aims. The first is to provide a defense (i.e., supply a lawyer who will investigate, negotiate, and settle or try the case). The second is to pay whatever settlement or judgment the defendant company would otherwise have to pay to a successful plaintiff. The insurer's obligation is subject to the insured's obligation to pay a deductible. The insurer is not required to pay more than the limits of the policy. CGL policies are not really uniform. The Insurance Standards Organization (ISO) has published a very influential model policy, but insurers have the option of tailoring the model as they see fit.

Furthermore, the insurer must only pay for covered claims, not excluded ones. ISO has drafted an "employment-related practices exclusion," and the trend is for recent policies to follow this and simply exclude all claims related to a plaintiff's employment by a defendant. Even this is not as simple as it seems. For instance, a court might rule that the real injury to the plaintiff occurred after he or she was fired and therefore ceased to be an employee.

Even if the policy doesn't exclude all employment-related claims, there may be other factors that prevent the employer from collecting benefits under the policy.

[B] Bodily Injury and Personal Injury

Coverage A of the CGL provides liability insurance when the insured becomes liable to someone who has suffered "bodily injury." It's rare for employment plaintiffs to claim that they suffered physically. Usually, they assert that they lost economic benefits (such as salary and pension) because of the employer's wrongful conduct. CGL Coverage A will *not* apply to charges of breach of contract or other economic consequences.

For this and other reasons, plaintiffs often ask for damages based on their emotional suffering. Their complaints allege pain and suffering, intentional infliction of emotional distress, or negligent infliction of emotional distress. (The availability of these causes of action varies between the federal and state systems, and from state to state.)

Most courts that have dealt with this question say that there is no "bodily injury" in an emotional suffering case unless the plaintiff can prove that there was at least some physical consequence of the emotional injury: an ulcer or high blood pressure, for instance. Even if there are physical consequences, they could be considered basically economic and therefore outside the scope of Coverage A.

The CGL's Coverage B deals with liability that the insured encounters for "personal injury" (such as libel or slander) or advertising injury (such as defaming another company's products in your ads). Coverage B might get involved in an employment-related case if, for instance, the plaintiff claims that the employer not only fired him or her, but blacklisted him or her and used a campaign of lies to prevent the ex-employee from getting another job or establishing business relationships.

[C] CGL Case Law

Under liability insurance and Worker's Compensation insurance policies, asbestos-related disease is "bodily injury by disease" and not "bodily injury by accident." Asbestos exposure is not an accident because of its non-violent nature and because injuries develop over a latency period rather than manifesting immediately. [*Riverwood Int'l Corp. v. Employers Ins. of Wausau*, 420 F.3d 378 (5th Cir. 2005)]

A California court tackled some complex issues of successor liability and insurance in the early 2003 case of *Henkel Corp. v. Hartford Accident & Indem. Co.* [29 Cal. 4th 934, 62 P.3d 69, 129 Cal. Rptr. 2d 828 (2003)] The plaintiff, Henkel, bought Amchem's metallic products line and assumed all related liabilities. The question facing the court was whether Henkel also acquired the benefits of the insurance policies issued by Hartford to Amchem to cover lawsuits alleging injuries from exposure to chemicals during the policy period.

According to the superior court, there are three situations in which the buyer of corporate assets can become liable for the torts of the predecessor company (even without explicitly assuming the liabilities by contract). The buyer of assets can become liable if the transaction is a merger or consolidation, the purchasing corporation is a continuation of the selling corporation, or the transfer is fraudulent or undertaken to escape liability. The second possibility is that the acquirer of a product line can become liable for injuries caused by the predecessor's defective products if the acquisition extinguishes remedies against the predecessor business. There are also some statutes (such as the environmental statute CERCLA) that impose successor liability no matter what the contract says.

In mid-2007, the Indiana Court of Appeals reached a different result, holding that a company that becomes subject to liability as a result of a merger or acquisition can seek coverage under the acquired company's occurrence-based policy. The insurance company does not have to give prior approval to transfer of coverage to the acquirer. The Indiana Court of Appeals ruled that it would be a windfall for insurers if acquirers could not get coverage, and it would deter acquisitions if acquirers could not insure the liabilities incident to the new asset—clearly, insurers will not issue retroactive coverage for past losses. [*Travelers Cas. & Sur. Co. v. United States Filter Corp.*, 870 N.E.2d 529 (Ind. App. 2007); see Rebecca Moore, *Liabilities Acquired with New Firms Covered under Existing Policies*, plansponsor.com (July 27, 2007)] The victory was short-lived, however: In late 2008, the Indiana Supreme Court reversed (895 N.E.2d 1172 (Ind. 2008)), holding that the insurance policies all contained a ban on assignment of the policy without consent of the insurer. The Indiana Supreme Court found that policy rights can only be assigned if the insurer consents—or unless there has already been a loss that triggers the right to payment of a claim, in which case the right to payment can be transferred without the insurer's consent. But here, there was neither consent nor a post-loss assignment, so the Supreme Court ruled in the insurers' favor.

A CGL policy covered "directors," defined as executive officers and directors. The Eighth Circuit ruled in mid-2014 that a supervisor's acts were not covered by the policy—he was not a director. The case arose when an injured worker sued the company and his supervisor, charging that the supervisor was negligent in allowing the worker to drive a truck that the supervisor knew was defective. The Eighth Circuit interpreted "director" to mean "member of the board of directors," rather than "someone who directs the work of other employees." [*United Fire & Cas. v. Thompson*, No. 13-2352 (8th Cir. July 11, 2014). See Amy B. Briggs et al., *Insured Person Under CGL Policy Did Not Include Supervisory Employee*, Manatt Phelps & Phillips LLP (July 30, 2014), available at Lexology.com]

§ 43.03 OCCURRENCES AND THE PROBLEM OF INTENTION

Coverage under Coverage A depends on there being an "occurrence," which is defined as an accident that was neither intended nor expected by the insured. Coverage B does not have an occurrence requirement, but it does exclude coverage of personal injuries that stem from a willful violation of the law, committed by or with the consent of the insured company.

At first glance, it would seem that employment cases could never be covered under the CGL, because the plaintiff accuses someone of deliberately injuring him or her. The picture is far more complex. Some discrimination charges allege "disparate treatment" (roughly speaking, intentional discrimination), while others claim "disparate impact" (subtle negative effects on a protected group of employees). An employer's actions in adopting a policy or publishing an employee manual could have unintended consequences, which could possibly be treated as CGL "occurrences."

However, intentional discrimination would not be. Courts often treat some conduct (e.g., sexual harassment) as being so likely to have bad consequences for their victims that the consequences are presumed to have been intended, or at least expected, by the insured company.

Employment discrimination plaintiffs usually want the insurance company to be involved, because they know that liability insurance is another potential source of payment if they settle or win the case. In this instance, they are on the same side as the employer. They both want the CGL to cover the employee's claim. One simple strategy is for plaintiffs to add claims of negligent supervision by the employer, or negligent infliction of emotional distress, in the hope that these charges of negligence will be classified as covered "occurrences." The CGL exclusion of "intentional" conduct does not apply to conduct that is negligent, or even grossly negligent. However, this tactic usually fails because the negligence charges are treated as purely incidental to more important charges of intentional conduct.

In most instances, termination of an employee, even wrongful termination, does not involve the intention or expectation of harm, so the insurer will probably have a duty to defend. CGL personal injury coverage often excludes damage resulting from the willful violations of a penal statute or ordinance, committed by the insured or with the knowledge of the insured. Civil rights laws are not considered "penal statutes" for this purpose. Even if actions are "willful" for Title VII purposes, the criminal law exclusion will not be triggered.

Some CGL policies offer an endorsement or rider (at additional cost over the basic premium) that covers discrimination and harassment claims, often by broadening the underlying policy's definition of personal injury.

CGL policies typically exclude bodily injury to employees, arising out of and in the course of employment, whether the employer is liable as an employer or in other capacities. But that provision is probably included in the policy simply for coordination with Worker's Compensation. The employee could succeed in arguing that the tort claims they make do not arise out of or in the course of the employment relationship, because supervisors are not employed to commit discrimination or harassment. The insurer may have at least a duty to defend. Furthermore, occupational injuries could be treated as a known risk that employees are aware of, whereas discrimination and harassment are not risks of the same category.

§ 43.04 EMPLOYMENT PRACTICES LIABILITY INSURANCE

Because of the gaps in CGL coverage of employment matters, a separate form of policy, Employment Practices Liability Insurance (EPLI) evolved as of about 1990. The EPLI is designed to cover damages, judgments, settlements, defense costs, and attorneys' fee awards in the employment liability context (suits, proceedings, or written demands seeking to hold the employer civilly liable). Events included under the EPLI are discrimination, sexual harassment, and wrongful termination, but not "golden parachutes" (payments to top managers who lose their jobs because of corporate transitions) or contractual obligations to make payments to terminated employees. The EPLI policy generally excludes criminal charges, fines, punitive damages, retaliation, and any amounts that are uninsurable because of a relevant state law.

The usual coverage limit is $1 million–$5 million, but some insurers offer "jumbo" policies of up to $100 million in coverage.

EPLI owners can benefit even if they are never sued, because insurers require insured parties to audit their HR functions, improve their procedures, and add new procedures to minimize the risk of suit. The policy may offer access to valuable low-cost consulting services, and compliance advice that would otherwise carry a high price tag.

A claims-made policy is one that provides coverage when claims are made while the insured still has coverage, but not for claims made after coverage expires, even if the allegedly wrongful conduct occurred while the policy was still in force. The ISO EPLI form modifies this by covering claims made during the 30 days after policy expiration, unless another insurer is already in the picture. If the same employee makes multiple claims, they are all considered to have arisen on the date of the first claim, so coverage will be continuous, and it will not be necessary to figure out whether the initial or the later insurer is responsible. Sometimes, it is a false economy to replace a liability insurance policy if the new policy has a waiting period, creating a gap in coverage.

An HR blog looks at five main issues in researching and comparing EPLI policies:

Coverage—are only the standard issues (wrongful discharge, employment discrimination, harassment) covered, or are additional issues, such as negligent hiring, defamation, and infliction of emotional distress covered as well? Are claims covered only if asserted by full-time permanent employees, or are claims from independent contractors, part-time, temporary, seasonal, and temporary workers covered too?

Exclusions—all EPLI policies exclude punitive damages, and most of them list the statutes for which coverage will not be available, e.g., FLSA, WARN Act, NLRA, OSHA, or the ADA. The impact of an exclusion depends on the relevance of the topic to the company's business. Multi-state corporations may face a variety of risks under the different state laws, so it may be necessary to pay for coverage in multiple states to be protected against risks generated by individual state laws.

Deductibles, policy limits—these are usually applied on a per-claim as well as an aggregate basis, e.g., $250,000 per claim subject to a cap of $1 million on all claims. Accepting greater risk, by buying a policy with a higher deductible and/or lower cap, can be a cost-saving measure, but it leaves the insured vulnerable to more of the same risks that motivated buying the policy in the first place.

Timing issues—most EPLI policies are written on a "claims made" basis (i.e., to be covered, a claim must relate to conduct within the coverage period) and reported to the insurer during the prescribed reporting period. It is often necessary, even after discontinuing an EPLI policy, to purchase "long tail" coverage to account for claims that developed in earlier years but were not asserted until later. In some instances, long-simmering claims will be barred by statute of limitations and EEOC filing issues—but there are instances in which a claim covering many years of employment practices will be valid and will have to be defended. And, even if the claim itself is valid and requires a defense, if the insured fails to give timely notice to the insurer, the insurer may be relieved of responsibility.

Defense counsel, defense costs, and settlement—Generally, legal costs are included within the policy limit. If the claim is resolved in the employer's favor, this is not a problem, but if the employee prevails, amounts expended on defense are no longer available to pay the settlement or judgment awarded to the plaintiff or plaintiff class. Be aware that it is common for insurers to want to settle cases when the employer wants to fight to the last ditch, perhaps to clear its name and promote its good reputation. The policy might be drafted to give the insurer the right to settle even over the employer's objections. "Hammer clauses" are also common: i.e., the employer retains control over settlement—but if the employer rejects a settlement offer, insurance will not cover any discrepancy between the eventual settlement or judgment and the amount for which the employer could have settled the case. [Michael Moore, *Employment Practices Liability Insurance: Five Things Every HR Generalist Should Know*, <http://www.paemploymentlawblog.com/2008/02/articles/employer-liability/[. . .]> (Feb. 12, 2008)]

Two commentators suggest the following questions for evaluating an EPLI policy:

- Does it cover all employees? What about the liability consequences of actions of leased employees and independent contractors?
- Are former employees covered?
- Are claims for breach of explicit or implied employment contract covered by or excluded from the policy?
- Does the insurer have to provide you with a defense in administrative (e.g., EEOC and local antidiscrimination agencies) proceedings, or only at trial? (Only a small percentage of discrimination charges make it to the trial stage, but the investigative stage can be very unpleasant for the employer.)

- Are retaliation claims (including retaliation for filing Worker's Compensation claims) covered? (This is a large and growing part of the discrimination caseload.)
- Are injunctive and declaratory relief covered, or only money damages?
- Is the deductible imposed on a per-year or per-claimant basis? (If the latter is true, an insured employer might end up having to pay several deductibles a year.)

[Stephanie E. Trudeau and William Edwards, Employment Law Letter, archived at <http://www.ulmer.com>]

§ 43.05 OTHER INSURANCE

The business insurance portfolio could also include other types of insurance, such as excess liability (supplementing the CGL), umbrella coverage (with a broader definition of "personal injury"), Worker's Compensation insurance (see Chapter 33 for more detailed consideration of WC issues) and Directors' and Officers' (D&O) coverage.

[A] Excess Liability and Umbrella Coverage

Every CGL policy has limits: maximum amounts of coverage obtainable under particular circumstances. If your company already has maximum CGL coverage, but feels that more is necessary, there are two ways to supplement it.

The first is "follow-form" excess liability insurance, which increases the dollar amount of coverage available under your CGL, Worker's Compensation, and Business Automobile Liability coverage, but subject to the same terms and exclusions. For many companies, an "umbrella" policy is a better choice, because it is more broadly defined and may cover situations that were excluded by the underlying policy. This kind of "gap" coverage is generally subject to a "retained limit," another term for "deductible."

Umbrella policies offer coverage in more situations because their definition of "personal injury" is broader than Coverage A or Coverage B of the standard CGL. A typical provision includes both bodily injury and mental injury, mental anguish, shock, sickness, disease, discrimination, humiliation, libel, slander, defamation of character, and invasion of property. Therefore, many employment-related claims would be covered.

[B] Worker's Compensation

Specialized Worker's Compensation coverage is available to deal with the employer's obligation to pay benefits to employees who are injured in job-related situations. Of course, because of WC exclusivity, the employer does not have to worry about ordinary liability suits from injured workers, although there may be special situations in which suit can be brought (against the employer or another party, such as the manufacturer of unsafe factory machinery) even though Worker's Compensation is involved. In a WC employment liability policy, Worker's Compensation is Coverage A; the employment liability (e.g., bodily injury that is not subject to WC exclusivity) is Coverage B.

A company had two liability policies (covering bodily injury caused by accident) and a third, Worker's Compensation policy covering bodily injury caused by accident. The company and its president were sued by a former employee for wrongful termination, false imprisonment, interference with FMLA rights, and intentional infliction of emotional distress. The Seventh Circuit held that coverage was not triggered, because the employee alleged only intentional, not accidental, injuries. The plaintiff said that the company's president forced him to sit through a two-hour meeting after he fell at work and ruptured a muscle; the injury required an operation and five days of hospitalization. He claimed that the company president kept trying to get him to return to work before he was ready, and finally fired him. The company (Granite) tried to involve its CGL and WC insurers and its insurer under an Excess and Umbrella policy, characterizing the case as one about an accidental workplace fall. The Seventh Circuit, however, said that the case was about intentional acts (infliction of emotional distress, wrongful termination) so coverage was unavailable. [*Lucterhand v. Granite Microsystems*, 564 F.3d 809 (7th Cir. 2009)]

The Seventh Circuit had to decide whether an employee's common-law negligence claim against his employer was a "claim under employer liability laws" to satisfy the insuring agreement of an excess Worker's Compensation policy. The employee died of mesothelioma, and TKK was sued for negligence. TKK gave timely notice of suit to its excess WC carrier. TKK retained primary responsibility for defending, settling, and paying claims of up to $275,000 per occurrence. TKK settled the suit, incurring more than $400,000 in legal fees. The excess insurer, Safety National, denied coverage, on the grounds that the suit was for common-law negligence and was not brought under WC or employer liability laws. In Illinois, the Workers' Occupational Diseases Act is the exclusive remedy for employees who are injured at work or contract occupational disease. It bars common-law claims, so it offered a defense to the negligence claims, although TKK did not raise it as an affirmative defense. Safety National said that, because the Occupational Diseases Act was the sole means of recovery for the claims but it was not mentioned in the suit, the costs of defense and settlement were not covered by the policy as WC or employer liability claims. TKK said that the policy covered claims that were groundless, or even fraudulent. The Seventh Circuit held that the Occupational Diseases Act did not cover all potential common-law claims, so "employer liability laws" meant more than statutory claims under the Occupational Diseases Act. The Seventh Circuit affirmed the district court, which held that "employer liability law" was broad enough to include groundless common-law claims for which the employer had an affirmative defense. [*TKK USA, Inc., v. Safety Nat'l Cas. Corp.*, 727 F.3d 782 (7th. Cir. 2013); see Brian Margolies, *Seventh Circuit Addresses Coverage Under Workers' Comp Policy*, Traub Lieberman Straus & Shrewsberry LLP (Jan. 8, 2014), available at Lexology.com]

[C] Directors' and Officers' Liability (D&O)

D&O insurance covers the situation in which a corporation' directors and officers get not only themselves but the corporation into trouble. Frequently, executives will not agree to serve as directors or officers unless the corporation first promises them indemnification, i.e., that the corporation will pay the executive whatever amount he or she has to pay because of liability incurred while acting as a director or officer.

D&O insurance, in turn, reimburses the corporation for whatever it spends on indemnification, subject to a deductible and up to the limit of the policy.

In a case of first impression, the Second Circuit ruled in late 2010 that it is unlawful for a company to agree to indemnify its CEO or CFO for compensation or proceeds of stock sales that they are required to disgorge under Sarbanes-Oxley § 304 (the "clawback" provision that requires CEOs and CFOs to reimburse their employers for incentive compensation received or stock sale profits recognized in the 12 months after the filing of a financial statement that had to be restated due to misconduct). In 2006, the corporation's CFO and Chief Operation Officer were charged with civil accounting fraud as well as criminal charges. In 2007, the company restated its financial statements for the years 2003–2005. A derivative and class action suit against the company was settled in 2008; the indemnification occurred at this time. After the federal prosecutor appealed, the Second Circuit overturned the settlement, agreeing that indemnification was inappropriate. Because there is no private right to sue under Sarbanes-Oxley § 304, all enforcement is done by the SEC, so indemnification was an attempt to relieve the CEO and CFO of their burdens under Sarbanes-Oxley. The SEC might make similar arguments against indemnification re Dodd-Frank Act clawbacks—although it is not clear if the Dodd-Frank clawback provision allows private suits. [*Cohen v. Viray*, 622 F.3d 188 (2d Cir. 2010)]

[D] Errors & Omissions (E&O)

Errors and Omissions insurance pays, on behalf of the insured, all loss for which the insured person is not indemnified by the insured organization if the person is liable because of any wrongful act he or she committed or attempted. In general, committing disparate treatment discrimination will be considered a wrongful act that can be covered under the policy, unless the policy definition covers only negligent, and not intentional, acts and omissions.

In many companies, E&O insurance is complemented by D&O insurance that covers the company for losses it incurs when it indemnifies directors and officers acting in that capacity.

An important issue is whether or not administrative actions (such as state agency and EEOC proceedings, subpoenas, and federal grand jury target letters) are considered "claims or suits" for insurance purposes. Businesses also often encounter expenses for their own administrative or internal investigations. The insurer is likely to make the argument that back pay awarded to a prevailing plaintiff is equitable relief and not "damages" that could be covered under the policy.

However, many courts have rejected this argument and required liability insurers to handle back-pay awards against their policyholders. E&O insurers may also resist paying back pay if the policy excludes amounts owed under a "contractual obligation," but here again, the insured will probably prevail if a back pay award is made. D&O or E&O coverage for subpoena or investigation compliance must be negotiated before your company becomes a target. If the policy specifically refers to an indictment, a Grand Jury subpoena would probably not be treated as a "claim." Other decisions say that an investigation in and of itself is not a request for relief, but subpoenas and investigative demands have been found to be claims when the insured was required to produce testimony and documents as part of an ongoing investigation of the corporation. [Joseph D. Jean and Rachel M. Wrightson, *Ensuring Coverage for Actions in Response to Investigations*, N.Y.L.J. (July 10, 2009) (law.com)]

Another insurance form covers plans, administrators, and trustees against allegations of impropriety. Many employment-related claims involve ERISA allegations, so the employer should at least consider adding this coverage to its insurance portfolio.

§ 43.06 DUTY OF THE INSURANCE CONTRACT

[A] Duty to Defend

A lesser-known, but perhaps more important, part of the liability insurance policy is the insurer's duty to defend. That is, whenever a claim is made against the employer, the insurer has to provide a lawyer and take care of the case. However, usually the insurer is in control of the litigation, and decides how vigorously to defend the case and when to settle (although some policies return control of litigation to the insured). Most policies are drafted so that, if the insured company settles the case without consent and participation of the insurer, the insured company will not be able to recover any part of the settlement costs from the insurer.

The insurer's duty to indemnify is the duty to pay on the insured's behalf when the insured settles or loses a lawsuit. The duty to defend is much broader. If the allegations against an insured company are invalid, or can't be proved, then the liability insurer's role is to get the charge dismissed, even though there is no liability to indemnify. In general, if the charges combine claims that are covered by liability insurance with others that are not, the insurer has a duty to defend against all the charges, not just the covered ones.

Usually, the insurer's duty to defend is triggered by a "claim" made against the insured employer. This is usually interpreted as filing a complaint with a court. EEOC or local agency proceedings are not generally considered "claims," so an insured company is on its own for a significant part of the process before the duty to defend begins.

ERISA § 504 gives the DOL broad power to investigate ERISA violations, and responding to the investigation can be expensive in terms of legal fees and other expenses. A mid-2011 article points out that, if a notice of claim is filed relative to expenses of responding to a DOL investigation, the liability insurer can accept the notice as a claim; deny the notice of claim; or accept the notice as a circumstance that may give rise to a claim in the future. But there must be a claim to trigger defense coverage; a circumstance is not enough. Even if the claim is denied, having filed the notice helps the plan because it prevents the insurer from denying later claims on the grounds of late notice (i.e., that the plan did not give the insurer timely notice of a potential claim). The article says that the key is what the DOL tells the plan. If the DOL begins merely by requesting documents without identifying a possible violation that is under investigation, then the insurance carrier will probably state that there has been no claim because there is no allegation of a wrongful act. There might be a claim if the DOL identifies an official enforcement issue after investigation, and issues a Notice Letter, aka voluntary charging letter or 10-day letter, to the plan. However, by that time, the plan probably has incurred extensive legal fees in response to the investigation. The article suggests that plan fiduciaries can improve the odds of the situation being treated as a claim by contacting the insurer as soon as possible after the DOL begins to investigate. The situation is more likely to be treated as a claim if DOL has targeted a specific person of interest or target issue. If DOL issues any subpoenas, the insurer should be informed. [Segal, *Fiduciary Liability Policies May Not Cover Costs Associated with DOL Investigations,* The Fiduciary Shield (July 2011) (benefitslink.com)]

[B] Duties of the Insured

Insurance companies are relieved of their obligation to pay claims if the insured company fails to satisfy its obligations. The most obvious duty is paying premiums. Liability policies also require the insured to notify the insurer as soon as possible whenever a "claim" is made. Therefore, legal advice is necessary to determine which allegations have the legal status of a claim.

As government investigations (e.g., dealing with the Foreign Corrupt Practices Act) become more common, it is important to know when an investigation triggers coverage. The Eastern District of Virginia followed the Second Circuit in holding that search warrants and investigatory subpoenas can trigger insurance coverage. PSI was a NASA contractor; its D&O coverage applied to the company and individuals. NASA issued a warrant and subpoena. A few months later, the U.S. Attorney's Office notified PSI that a civil investigation was underway dealing with its participation in an SBA program. PSI sought defense costs from its insurer, which denied coverage, stating that there was no "claim." The district court disagreed: the policy's definition of "claim" was broad enough to encompass all written demands for relief as well as judicial, administrative, and regulatory proceedings. The insurer had a duty to defend because the warrant was a written demand for non-monetary relief: production of documents.

> ■ **TIP:** Companies that receive investigative letters, warrants, or subpoenas, even without a formal demand or claim, should contact their D&O insurance carrier as soon as possible. [*Protection Strategies, Inc. v. Starr Indem. & Liab. Co.*, Civil Action No. 1:13-CV-00763, 2013 U.S. Dist. LEXIS 187451 (E.D. Va. Sept. 10, 2013); see Amy B. Briggs et al., *Virginia Federal Court Rules Under D&O Policy That Search Warrant And Subpoena Trigger Defense Obligation Even Without A Formal Complaint Or Demand,* Manatt Phelps & Phillips LLP (Oct. 2, 2013), available at Lexology.com. See *MBIA Inc. v. Federal Ins. Co.*, 652 F.3d 152 (2d Cir. 2011)]

The District Court for the Eastern District of Michigan held that a letter from an insured company (a funeral home and cemetery operator) to its insurer, referring to newspaper articles about the company's improper investment activities, did not constitute adequate notice to preserve coverage for an employment claim made after the policy expired. The employment claim did not relate back to any suits during the policy period. The insured had a liability policy from April 20, 2005 to October 20, 2006. The insurer opted not to renew the policy. On October 19, 2006, the company's CEO sent the letter, which said that the CEO believed the policy was not renewed because of the negative articles. Although the letter said that no formal demands had been made against the company, in fact five suits had been filed during the policy period. In 2007, after expiration of the policy, a former employee obtained a judgment in a wrongful termination suit. The successful plaintiff started a garnishment proceeding against the insurer to recover the amount of the judgment. The district court granted summary judgment for the insurer because the claim was not made during the policy period. The CEO's letter was not a notice of a potential claim. The policy required specific notice to preserve future employment claims. [*Lemons v. Mikocem, LLC*, No. 12-11474, 2013 WL 5291513 (E.D. Mich. Sept. 19, 2013); see Wiley Rein LLP, *No Coverage For Employment Action Filed After Policy's Expiration*, Lexology.com (Sept. 25, 2013)]

Interstate Cleaning Corporation (ICC) was sued in Hawaii state court for sexual harassment. ICC deemed it a mere nuisance suit, and did not notify its insurer of the complaint. ICC refused the plaintiff's offer to settle the case for

$25,000. The plaintiff won in state court and agreed to settle for a smaller amount. When ICC finally informed its insurer of the suit, the insurer refused coverage, stating that the CGL policy did not cover sexual harassment. When ICC sued the insurer, the Eighth Circuit held that, in general, insured parties have a duty to give immediate notice of claim to their insurers, although this requirement can be excused when it is not reasonably possible to provide notice. But an insurer that is not prejudiced by failure to give notice cannot use the failure as an excuse to avoid providing a defense or paying benefits. In this case, late notice did prejudice the insurer because it was unable to investigate or participate in settlement negotiations. Therefore, it was not obligated to defend or indemnify the insureds. [*Interstate Cleaning Corp. v. Commercial Underwriters Ins. Co.*, 325 F.3d 1024 (8th Cir. 2003)]

§ 43.07 QUESTIONS OF TIMING

Liability policies are divided into "occurrence" and "claims-made" policies. If there is an "occurrence" covered by the policy (see above), all the occurrence policies in force at that time must make payments. But the insured doesn't get five times the amount of the liability. Coverage is coordinated (divided among them) to prevent windfalls.

A claims-made policy works differently. It covers only claims that are made during the policy term with respect to events that happened during the policy term. Because this can be a difficult standard to meet, claims-made policies are often extended to cover events after the policy's "retroactive date." There may also be an "extended reporting period" after the policy expires, where events are covered if they occurred while the policy was still in force, but were reported later.

Coverage under a fiduciary liability policy is triggered when the claim is made, not when the alleged wrongdoing occurred. While the fiduciary liability policy is in force, it will cover claims reported during the policy period. But if a policy is cancelled or is not renewed, then future claims will not be covered even if they relate to acts that occurred before cancellation or nonrenewal. Extended reporting period (ERP) coverage is optional: in exchange for an additional premium, ERP coverage applies to claims filed during a specified period (usually 12 months post-policy expiration) relating to events while the policy was in force.

Standard ERP coverage will not provide complete protection in a merger or plan termination situation because there is a possibility that fiduciary breaches will be alleged until the statute of limitations (which could be as long as six years) has elapsed since the merger or termination.

"Tail coverage" protects the trustees of merged or terminated plans. Insurers do not have to provide tail coverage under a basic policy; the purchaser must negotiate the terms of coverage and the premium. Insurers are often reluctant to offer as much coverage as the trustees want. It is wise to include a provision forbidding cancellation of the policy after the premium has been paid. According to Segal Select Insurance, the premium for a six-year tail policy is likely to be two or three times the premium for the underlying fiduciary liability insurance when the plan was in operation. Tail coverage is usually paid from the assets of the plan that is being merged or is terminating, so it is important to arrange and pay for the coverage before the plan assets have all been distributed.

Instead of tail coverage, the successor plan might obtain a "merged-plan" endorsement, but the merged plan must continue to renew the coverage every year until the statute of limitations has expired, and the insurer may change the available coverage and liability limits. [Segal Select Insurance Fiduciary Shield, *If a Plan Merger or Termination Is on the Horizon, Seek Tail Coverage* (March 2014) (benefitslink.com)]

§ 43.08 FIDUCIARY LIABILITY INSURANCE

A fidelity bond makes a plan whole when it suffers losses from dishonest or fraudulent acts by employees who handle plan participants' money or securities. All qualified plans must maintain an ERISA fidelity bond in the amount of 10% of the amount handled (see ERISA § 412). "Plan officials" must be bonded; not only plan fiduciaries but also anyone who handles property of the plan is considered an official. The typical duration of a fidelity bond is three years, and the amount must be adjusted each year to make sure the 10% requirement is satisfied. The PPA increases the maximum amount of the fidelity bond required for plans that hold employer stock, for plan years beginning after January 1, 2007, from $500,000 to $1 million. If the DOL discovers that the plan does not have the necessary bond, it can order the company to get a bond; permanently bar the fiduciary from ever serving as an ERISA plan fiduciary; remove the plan administrator and appoint an independent trustee; or impose penalties. The fidelity bond carrier must report the amount of its coverage on the plan's Form 5500.

In contrast, fiduciary liability insurance protects the plan sponsor and its officers, directors, and employees from common-law, ERISA, and other statutory liability. ERISA does not require plans to maintain fiduciary liability insurance. Generally speaking, the fidelity bond is a plan expense that can be paid from plan assets, but fiduciary liability insurance premiums are not. [Carrie Byrnes and Tim Zehnder, *Fiduciary Bonds and Fiduciary Liability Insurance—Do You Need Both?*, Bryan Cave Benefits and Executive Compensation Blog (Mar. 13, 2014) (benefitslink.com)]

Where the policy covers the plan itself, the insurer can sue the fiduciary to recover the amount it had to pay out because of the fiduciary's conduct. Fiduciary liability insurance is usually available only in limited amounts, on a claims-made basis.

Fiduciary insurers do not cover attorneys' fees when the DOL gives notice of an investigation because there is often a gap between the time when fiduciary consults an attorney and the time when the insurer recognizes its duty to defend. The insurer may require a written allegation of wrongdoing to find that a claim has been made. However, the DOL usually waits until after requesting documents or interviews to file written allegations. A VC (voluntary charging) letter sets out findings of violations and says the DOL has finished its investigation. If the insurer refuses to cover legal fees during the investigation, the fiduciary must seek payment of fees from the plan or plan sponsor. But for ESOPs and multi-employer plans, DOL's position is that it is inappropriate for the plan to indemnify the fiduciary or advance fees. One possible solution is to purchase an insurance endorsement for the gap, known as "pre-claim investigation" coverage of defense costs; at least two insurers sell this coverage. [Stephen M. Saxon, *Saxon Angle: How to Close the Gap*, plansponsor.com (Feb. 11, 2014)]

Other than banks, insurance companies, and broker-dealers, ERISA § 412 requires every fiduciary and every person who handles property of an employee benefit plan to be bonded. All plan trustees are fiduciaries; others can become fiduciaries through their relationship to a plan (discretionary authority or control over management of the plan—or any authority or control, discretionary or otherwise, over plan assets). Anyone who provides investment advice to the plan is also a fiduciary. DOL has required bonding of anyone whose duties involve receiving, keeping, or disbursing plan funds, having access to plan funds, or having the capacity to cause losses to the plan through fraud or dishonesty. Section 412 makes it illegal for any plan official to permit another plan official handle the plan's property without being bonded. In other words, anyone who has an obligation to be bonded must enforce this requirement on everyone else who has to be bonded. Several forms of fiduciary bond are available, so the plan must select the right form—and, if necessary, increase the bonding if the existing bond does not cover all the fiduciaries of the plan. [Joe Faucher, Reish & Reacher ERISA Controversy Report, *ERISA Fidelity Bonds—Who Needs Them, and Who is Responsible for Securing Them?* (February 2011) (law.com)]

Fiduciary liability insurance is an asset of the plan, but also protects trustees' personal assets. Furthermore, a fiduciary who breaches his or her duty may not be able to afford to reimburse the plan for its full losses.

For the policy to be truly useful, the definition of the "insured" should include the plan and/or trust, all past, present and future trustees and employees, and their successors. Coverage for the spouse of an insured if named as an additional defendant should also be included. The general rule is that most fiduciary liability policies don't cover third-party administrators or service providers who act as fiduciaries, although it may be possible to add them to the policy under an endorsement.

The definition of "loss" should include defense costs (including costs for investigators and expert witnesses) settlements, judgments, and pre- and post-judgment interest. Although liability insurance typically excludes coverage of fines and penalties, IRS Employee Plans Compliance Resolution System (EPCRS) penalties and amounts paid to the DOL when it wins or settles an ERISA § 502(l) case are usually either included in the basic coverage or added by endorsement.

■ **TIP:** The entire policy has to be examined to see if there are additional limitations—for instance, the definition of "loss" may exclude fines and penalties.

Most fiduciary liability policies are claims-made policies. At each anniversary date, the insured can evaluate and adjust the policy limits and scope of coverage, bearing affordability in mind. Once a policy is purchased, it is hard to change carriers, because the application requires a warranty that there are no known claims or circumstances that would be excluded by the new insurer if they were fully disclosed—and it's very common for companies to face claims of this type!

Attorney Stephen Saxon published some suggestions about obtaining fiduciary liability insurance:

- Buy a "nonrecourse rider" if the plan pays for the insurance. ERISA prohibits fiduciaries from using plan assets to pay for fiduciary liability insurance, unless the plan has recourse against the fiduciary. The rider prevents the insurer from proceeding against the fiduciary in case there is a covered loss.
- Find out if the policy limits include defense costs, because if they do, an expensive defense can exhaust the policy.
- Check to see if the deductible applies to all the claims within a policy period or whether each allegation is subject to a separate deductible. Waiving the deductible for claims against individual fiduciaries is a common provision.
- The policy application will ask the trustees if they are aware of any potential claims (and there will be no coverage for claims that the trustees knew about but did not disclose), so obtain legal advice on how to answer the question completely and accurately.
- If the policy covers attorneys' fees on a "pay on behalf of" basis (i.e., the insured can select counsel rather than having to be represented by the insurer's attorneys) the policy will be much more useful if the fees are reimbursed as they are incurred, instead of only at the end of the case. [Stephen M. Saxon, *Insurance Policies: Tips on Securing Fiduciary Liability Insurance*, plansponsor.com, <http://www.plansponsor.com/magazine_type1_print.jsp?RECORD_ID=31594> (Apr. 2, 2006)]

A mid-2011 article points out some common misconceptions that fiduciaries often have about fiduciary liability insurance:

- That an ERISA fidelity bond protects their personal assets; the purpose of the fidelity bond is to protect the plan and its participants against misconduct by the fiduciary;
- That employee benefit liability policies cover fiduciaries fully; their errors and omissions in administration of the benefit plan itself are covered, but other aspects, such as investment of plan assets, are not necessarily covered;
- That D&O policies cover fiduciaries; this is true only with respect to activities in their capacity as directors and officers, not in their capacity as fiduciaries, and ERISA claims are usually excluded by D&O policies;

Fiduciaries will be entitled to indemnification of all personal liabilities; this is not necessarily true, because ERISA prevents plans from indemnifying fiduciaries for breach of fiduciary duty. [Jerry Kalish, *Four Misconceptions About Fiduciary Liability Insurance*, Retirement Plan Blog (June 7, 2011) (benefitslink.com)

INDEX

References are to section number.

B

C

D

G

H

I

J

M

N

O

P

Q

R

S

T

U

V